LAROUSSE

DICCIONARIO
Pocket

ESPAÑOL
INGLÉS

INGLÉS
ESPAÑOL

LAROUSSE

Dirección de la obra
Project Management

Sharon J. Hunter

Redacción
Editors

Joaquín A. Blasco, Dileri Borunda Johnston, Isabel Ferrer Marrades,
José A. Gálvez, Ana Cristina Llompart Lucas, Julie Muleba,
Victoria Ordóñez Diví, José María Ruiz Vaca, Carol Styles Carvajal,
Eduardo Vallejo

Dirección general
Publishing Manager

Janice McNeillie

Informática
Prepress

David Reid

ISBN 84-8332-474-1
SPES Editorial, S.L. Aribau, 197-199, 3ª, 08021 Barcelona

ISBN 2-03-542051-2
Distribución/Sales: Houghton Mifflin Company, Boston

LAROUSSE

Pocket
DICTIONARY

SPANISH
ENGLISH

ENGLISH
SPANISH

LAROUSSE

Achevé d'imprimer par l'Imprimerie
Maury-Eurolivres à Manchecourt
N° de projet 11000515
Dépôt légal : février 2005 - N° d'imprimeur : 112043

Imprimé en France - (Printed in France)

A NUESTROS LECTORES

El nuevo Diccionario POCKET Larousse es la herramienta de trabajo ideal para todas las situaciones lingüísticas, desde el aprendizaje de idiomas en la escuela y en casa hasta los viajes al extranjero.

Este diccionario está pensado para responder de manera práctica y rápida a los diferentes problemas que plantea la lectura del inglés actual. Con sus más de 55.000 palabras y expresiones y por encima de las 80.000 traducciones, este diccionario permitirá al lector comprender con claridad un amplio espectro de textos y realizar traducciones del inglés de uso corriente con rapidez y corrección.

Esta nueva obra recoge también numerosas siglas y abreviaturas actuales, además de nombres propios y términos comerciales e informáticos.

Gracias al análisis claro y detallado del vocabulario básico, así como de los indicadores de sentido que guían hacia la traducción más adecuada, se ayuda al usuario a escribir en inglés con precisión y seguridad.

Se ha puesto especial cuidado en la presentación de las entradas, tanto desde el punto de vista de su estructura como de la tipografía empleada. Para aquellos lectores que todavía están en un nivel básico o intermedio en su aprendizaje del inglés, el POCKET es el diccionario ideal.

Le invitamos a que se ponga en contacto con nosotros si tiene cualquier observación o crítica que hacer; entre todos podemos hacer del POCKET un diccionario aún mejor.

El Editor

TO OUR READERS

This new edition of the Larousse POCKET dictionary continues to be a reliable and user-friendly tool for all your language needs, from language learning at school and at home to travelling abroad. This handy dictionary is designed to provide fast and practical solutions to the various problems encountered when reading present-day Spanish. With over 55,000 references and 80,000 translations, it enables the user to read and enjoy a wide range of texts and to translate everyday Spanish quickly and accurately. This new dictionary also features up-to-date coverage of common abbreviations and acronyms; proper names, business terms and computing vocabulary.

Writing basic Spanish accurately and confidently is no longer a problem thanks to the POCKET's detailed coverage of essential vocabulary, and helpful sense-markers which guide the user to the most appropriate translation.

Careful thought has gone into the presentation of the entries, both in terms of layout and typography. The POCKET is the ideal reference work for all learners from beginners up to intermediate level.

Send us your comments or queries – you will be helping to make this dictionary an even better book.

The Publisher

Abbreviations

Abreviaturas

abbreviation	*abbr/abrev*	abreviatura
adjective	*adj*	adjetivo
administration	ADMIN	administración
adverb	*adv*	adverbio
aeronautics, aviation	AERON	aeronáutica
agriculture	AGR	agricultura
Latin American Spanish	*Amér*	español latinoamericano
anatomy	ANAT	anatomía
Andean Spanish	*Andes*	español de los Andes
before noun	*antes de s*	antes de sustantivo
archeology	ARCHEOL	arqueología
architecture	ARCHIT/ARQUIT	arquitectura
Argentinian Spanish	*Arg*	español de Argentina
article	*art*	artículo
astrology	ASTROL	astrología
astronomy	ASTRON	astronomía
automobile, cars	AUT(OM)	automóviles
auxiliary	*aux*	auxiliar
biology	BIOL	biología
Bolivian Spanish	*Bol*	español de Bolivia
botany	BOT	botánica
Central American Spanish	*CAm*	español de Centroamérica
Caribbean Spanish	*Carib*	español del Caribe
chemistry	CHEM	química
Chilean Spanish	*Chile*	español de Chile
cinema, film-making	CIN(EMA)	cine
Colombian Spanish	*Col*	español de Colombia
commerce, business	COM(M)	comercio
comparative	*compar*	comparativo
information technology	COMPUT	informática
conjunction	*conj*	conjunción
construction, building	CONSTR	construcción
continuous	*cont*	continuo
Costa Rican Spanish	*CRica*	español de Costa Rica
Cono Sur Spanish	*CSur*	español del Cono Sur
Cuban Spanish	*Cuba*	español de Cuba
culinary, cooking	CULIN	cocina
definite	*def*	determinado
demonstrative	*demos*	demostrativo
sport	DEP	deporte
juridical, legal	DER	derecho
pejorative	*despec*	despectivo
dated	*desus*	desusado
ecology	ECOLOG	ecología
economics	ECON	economía
school, education	EDUC	educación, escuela
electricity, electronics	ELEC(TR)	electricidad, electrónica
especially	*esp*	especialmente
exclamation	*excl*	interjección
feminine noun	*f*	sustantivo femenino
informal	*fam*	familiar
pharmacology, pharmaceuticals	FARM	farmacología, farmacia
figurative	*fig*	figurado
finance, financial	FIN	finanzas

Abbreviations

Abbreviaturas

physics	FÍS	física
formal	*fml*	formal, culto
photography	FOTO	fotografía
soccer	FTBL	fútbol
inseparable	*fus*	inseparable
generally	*gen*	generalmente
geography	GEOGR	geografía
geology, geological	GEOL	geología
geometry	GEOM	geometría
grammar	GRAM(M)	gramática
Guatemalan Spanish	*Guat*	español de Guatemala
history	HIST	historia
humorous	*hum*	humorístico
industry	IND	industria
indefinite	*indef*	indeterminado
informal	*inf*	familiar
information technology	INFORM	informática
exclamation	*interj*	interjección
invariable	*inv*	invariable
ironic	*iro/irón*	irónico
juridical, legal	JUR	juridico, derecho
linguistics	LING	lingüística
literal	*lit*	literal
literature	LITER	literatura
phrase(s)	*loc*	locución, locuciones
masculine noun	*m*	sustantivo masculino
mathematics	MAT(H)	matemáticas
mechanical engineering	MEC	mecánica
medicine	MED	medicina
metallurgy	METAL	metalurgia
weather, meteorology	METEOR	meteorología
Mexican Spanish	*Méx*	español de México
military	MIL	militar
mining	MIN	mineralogía
mythology	MYTH/MITOL	mitología
music	MUS/MÚS	música
noun	*n*	sustantivo
nautical, maritime	NAUT/NÁUT	náutica
Nicaraguan Spanish	*Nic*	español de Nicaragua
numeral	*num/núm*	número
oneself	*o.s*	
Panamanian Spanish	*Pan*	español de Panamá
pejorative	*pej*	despectivo
personal	*pers*	personal
Peruvian Spanish	*Perú*	español de Perú
pharmacology, pharmaceuticals	PHARM	farmacología, farmacia
photography	PHOT	fotografía
phrase(s)	*phr*	locución, locuciones
physics	PHYS	física
plural	*pl*	plural
politics	POL(ÍT)	política
possessive	*poss/poses*	posesivo
past participle	*pp*	participio pasado
press, journalism	PRENS	periodismo

Abbreviations

Abreviaturas

preposition	*prep*	preposición
Porto Rican Spanish	*PRico*	español de Puerto Rico
pronoun	*pron*	pronombre
psychology	PSYCH/PSICOL	psicología
past tense	*pt*	pasado, pretérito
chemistry	QUÍM	química
registered trademark	®	marca registrada
railways	RAIL	ferrocarril
relative	*relat*	relativo
religion	RELIG	religión
River Plate Spanish	*RP*	español del Río de la Plata
noun	*s*	sustantivo
someone, somebody	*sb*	
school, education	SCH	educación, escuela
Scottish English	*Scot*	inglés de Escocia
separable	*sep*	separable
singular	*sg*	singular
slang	*sl*	argot
sociology	SOCIOL	sociología
Stock Exchange	ST EX	bolsa
something	*sthg*	
subject	*subj/suj*	sujeto
superlative	*superl*	superlativo
bullfighting	TAUROM	tauromaquia
theatre	TEATR	teatro
technical, technology	TECH/TECN	técnico, tecnología
telecommunications	TELEC(OM)	telecomunicaciones
television	TV	televisión
printing, typography	TYPO	imprenta
uncountable noun	*U*	sustantivo 'incontable'
British English	*UK*	inglés británico
university	UNI	universidad
Uruguayan Spanish	*Urug*	español de Uruguay
American English	*US*	inglés americano
verb	*vb/v*	verbo
Venezuelan Spanish	*Ven*	español de Venezuela
veterinary science	VETER	veterinaria
intransitive verb	*vi*	verbo intransitivo
impersonal verb	*v impers*	verbo impersonal
pronominal verb	*vpr*	verbo pronominal
transitive verb	*vt*	verbo transitivo
vulgar	*vulg*	vulgar
zoology	ZOOL	zoología
cultural equivalent	≈	equivalente cultural

La ordenación alfabética en español

En este diccionario se ha seguido la ordenación alfabética internacional. Esto significa que las entradas con **ch** aparecerán después de **cg** y no al final de **c**; del mismo modo las entradas con **ll** vendrán después de **lk** y no al final de **l**. Adviértase, sin embargo, que la letra **ñ** sí se considera letra aparte y sigue a la **n**.

Spanish alphabetical order

The dictionary follows international alphabetical order. Thus entries with **ch** appear after **cg** and not at the end of **c**. Similarly, entries with **ll** appear after **lk** and not at the end of **l**. Note, however, that **ñ** is treated as a separate letter and follows **n**.

Los compuestos en inglés

En inglés se llama compuesto a una locución sustantiva de significado único pero formada por más de una palabra; p.ej. **point of view**, **kiss of life** o **virtual reality**. Uno de los rasgos distintivos de este diccionario es la inclusión de estos compuestos con entrada propia y en riguroso orden alfabético. De esta forma **blood test** vendrá después de **bloodshot**, el cual sigue a **blood pressure**.

English compounds

A compound is a word or expression which has a single meaning but is made up of more than one word, e.g. **point of view**, **kiss of life** and **virtual reality**. It is a feature of this dictionary that English compounds appear in the A-Z list in strict alphabetical order. The compound **blood test** will therefore come after **bloodshot** which itself follows **blood pressure**.

Marcas registradas

Los nombres de marca aparecen señalados en este diccionario con el símbolo ®. Sin embargo, ni este símbolo ni su ausencia son representativos de la situación legal de la marca.

Trademarks

Words considered to be trademarks have been designated in this dictionary by the symbol ®. However, neither the presence nor the absence of such designation should be regarded as affecting the legal status of any trademark.

Phonetics

English vowels

[ɪ]	pit, big, rid
[e]	pet, tend
[æ]	pat, bag, mad
[ʌ]	run, cut
[ɒ]	pot, log
[ʊ]	put, full
[ə]	mother, suppose
[i:]	bean, weed
[ɑ:]	barn, car, laugh
[ɔ:]	born, lawn
[u:]	loop, loose
[ɜ:]	burn, learn, bird

English diphthongs

[eɪ]	bay, late, great
[aɪ]	buy, light, aisle
[ɔɪ]	boy, foil
[əʊ]	no, road, blow
[aʊ]	now, shout, town
[ɪə]	peer, fierce, idea
[eə]	pair, bear, share
[ʊə]	poor, sure, tour

English semi-vowels

[j]	you, spaniel
[w]	wet, why, twin

English consonants

[p]	pop, people
[b]	bottle, bib
[t]	train, tip
[d]	dog, did
[k]	come, kitchen
[g]	gag, great
[tʃ]	chain, wretched
[dʒ]	jet, fridge
[f]	fib, physical
[v]	vine, live
[θ]	think, fifth
[ð]	this, with
[s]	seal, peace
[z]	zip, his
[ʃ]	sheep, machine

Fonética

Vocales españolas

[i]	piso, imagen
[e]	tela, eso
[a]	pata, amigo
[o]	bola, otro
[u]	luz, luna

Diptongos españoles

[ei]	ley, peine
[ai]	aire, caiga
[oi]	soy, boina
[au]	causa, aula
[eu]	Europa, deuda

Semivocales españolas

[j]	hierba, miedo
[w]	agua, hueso

Consonantes españolas

[p]	papá, campo
[b]	vaca, bomba
[β]	curvo, caballo
[t]	toro, pato
[d]	donde, caldo
[k]	que, cosa
[g]	grande, guerra
[ɣ]	aguijón, iglesia
[tʃ]	ocho, chusma
[f]	fui, afán
[θ]	cera, paz
[ð]	cada, pardo
[s]	solo, paso
[z]	andinismo
[x]	gemir, jamón

[ʒ]	usual, measure	[m]	madre, cama
[h]	how, perhaps	[n]	no, pena
[m]	metal, comb	[ŋ]	banca, encanto
[n]	night, dinner	[ɲ]	caña
[ŋ]	sung, parking	[l]	ala, luz
[l]	little, help	[ɾ]	atar, paro
[r]	right, carry	[r]	perro, rosa
		[ʎ]	llave, collar

Los símbolos ['] y [ˌ] indican que la sílaba siguiente lleva un acento primario o secundario respectivamente.

The symbol ['] indicates that the following syllable carries primary stress and the symbol [ˌ] that the following syllable carries secondary stress.

El símbolo [ʳ] en fonética inglesa indica que la r al final de palabra se pronuncia sólo cuando precede a una palabra que comienza por vocal. Adviértase que casi siempre se pronuncia en inglés americano.

The symbol [ʳ] in English phonetics indicates that the final r is pronounced only when followed by a word beginning with a vowel. Note that it is nearly always pronounced in American English.

CONJUGACIONES ESPAÑOLAS

ENGLISH VERB TABLES

Conjugaciones españolas

Llave: A = presente indicativo, **B** = imperfecto indicativo, **C** = pretérito perfecto simple, **D** = futuro, **E** = condicional, **F** = presente subjuntivo, **G** = imperfecto subjuntivo, **H** = imperativo, **I** = gerundio, **J** = participio

acertar A acierto, acertamos, etc., **F** acierte, acertemos, etc., **H** acierta, acierte, acertemos, acertad, etc.

adquirir A adquiero, adquirimos, etc., **F** adquiera, adquiramos, etc., **H** adquiere, adquiramos, adquirid, etc.

AMAR A amo, amas, ama, amamos, amáis, aman, **B** amaba, amabas, amaba, amábamos, amabais, amaban, **C** amé, amaste, amó, amamos, amasteis, amaron, **D** amaré, amarás, amará, amaremos, amaréis, amarán, **E** amaría, amarías, amaría, amaríamos, amaríais, amarían, **F** ame, ames, ame, amemos, améis, amen, **G** amara, amaras, amara, amáramos, amarais, amaran, **H** ama, ame, amemos, amad, amen, **I** amando, **J** amado, -da

andar C anduve, anduvimos, etc., **G** anduviera, anduviéramos, etc.

avergonzar A avergüenzo, avergonzamos, etc., **C** avergoncé, avergonzó, avergonzamos, etc., **F** avergüence, avergoncemos, etc., **H** avergüenza, avergüence, avergoncemos, avergonzad, etc.

caber A quepo, cabe, cabemos, etc., **C** cupe, cupimos, etc., **D** cabré, cabremos, etc., **E** cabría, cabríamos, etc., **F** quepa, quepamos, cabed, etc., **G** cupiera, cupiéramos, etc., **H** cabe, quepa, quepamos, etc.

caer A caigo, cae, caemos, etc., **C** cayó, caímos, cayeron, etc., **F** caiga, caigamos, etc., **G** cayera, cayéramos, etc., **H** cae, caiga, caigamos, caed, etc., **I** cayendo

conducir A conduzco, conduce, conducimos, etc., **C** conduje, condujimos, etc., **F** conduzca, conduzcamos, etc., **G** condujera, condujé-ramos, etc., **H** conduce, conduzca, conduzcamos, conducid, etc.

conocer A conozco, conoce, conocemos, etc., **F** conozca, conozcamos, etc. **H** conoce, conozca, conozcamos, etc.

dar A doy, da, damos, etc., **C** di, dio, dimos, etc., **F** dé, demos, etc., **G** diera, diéramos, etc., **H** da, dé, demos, dad, etc.

decir A digo, dice, decimos, etc., **C** dije, dijimos, etc., **D** diré, diremos, etc., **E** diría, diríamos, etc., **F** diga, digamos, etc., **G** dijera, dijéramos, etc., **H** di, diga, digamos, decid, etc., **I** diciendo, **J** dicho, -cha

dormir A duermo, dormimos, etc., **C** durmió, dormimos, durmieron, etc., **F** duerma, durmamos, etc., **G** durmiera, durmiéramos, etc., **H** duerme, duerma, durmamos, dormid, etc., **I** durmiendo

errar A yerro, erramos, etc., **F** yerre, erremos, etc., **H** yerra, yerre, erremos, errad, etc.

estar A estoy, está, estamos, etc., **C** estuve, estuvimos, etc., **F** esté, estemos, etc., **G** estuviera, estuviéramos, etc., **H** está, esté, estemos, estad, etc.

HABER A he, has, ha, hemos, habéis, han, **B** había, habías, había, habíamos, habíais, habían, **C** hube, hubiste, hubo, hubimos, hubisteis, hubieron, **D** habré, habrás, habrá, habremos, habréis, habrán, **E** habría, habrías, habría, habríamos, habríais, habrían, **F** haya, hayas, haya, hayamos, hayáis, hayan, **G** hubiera, hubieras, hubiera, hubiéramos, hubierais, hubieran, **H** he, haya, hayamos, habed, hayan, **I** habiendo, **J** habido, -da

hacer A hago, hace, hacemos, etc., **C** hice, hizo, hicimos, etc., **D** haré, haremos, etc., **E** haría, haríamos, etc., **F** haga, hagamos, etc., **G** hiciera, hiciéramos, etc., **H** haz, haga, hagamos, haced, etc., **J** hecho, -cha

huir A huyo, huimos, etc., **C** huyó, huimos, huyeron, **F** huya, huyamos, etc. **G** huyera, huyéramos, etc. **H** huye, huya, huyamos, huid, etc., **I** huyendo

ir A voy, va, vamos, etc., **C** fui, fue, fuimos, etc., **F** vaya, vayamos, etc., **G** fuera, fuéramos, etc., **H** ve, vaya, vayamos, id, etc., **I** yendo

leer C leyó, leímos, leyeron, etc., **G** leyera, leyéramos, etc., **I** leyendo

lucir A luzco, luce, lucimos, etc., **F** luzca, luzcamos, **H** luce, luzca, luzcamos, lucid, etc.

mover A muevo, movemos, etc., **F** mueva, movamos, etc., **H** mueve, mueva, movamos, moved, etc.

nacer A nazco, nace, nacemos, etc., **F** nazca, nazcamos, etc., **H** nace, nazca, nazcamos, naced, etc.

oír A oigo, oye, oímos, etc., **C** oyó, oímos, oyeron, etc., **F** oiga, oigamos, etc., **G** oyera, oyéramos, etc., **H** oye, oiga, oigamos, oíd, etc., **I** oyendo

oler A huelo, olemos, etc., **F** huela, olamos, etc., **H** huele, huela, olamos, oled, etc.

parecer A parezco, parece, parecemos, etc., **F** parezca, parezcamos, etc., **H** parece, parezca, parezcamos, pareced, etc.

PARTIR A parto, partes, parte, partimos, partís, parten, **B** partía, partías, partía, partíamos, partíais, partían, **C** partí, partiste, partió, partimos, partisteis, partieron, **D** partiré, partirás, partirá, partiremos, partiréis, partirán, **E** partiría, partirías, partiría, partiríamos, partiríais, partirían, **F** parta, partas, parta, partamos, partáis, partan, **G** partiera, partieras, partiera, partiéramos, partierais, partieran, **H** parte, parta, partamos, partid, partan, **I** partiendo, **J** partido, -da.

pedir A pido, pedimos, etc., **C** pidió, pedimos, pidieron, etc., **F** pida, pidamos, etc., **G** pidiera, pidiéramos, etc., **H** pide, pida, pidamos, pedid, etc., **I** pidiendo

poder A puedo, podemos, etc., **C** pude, pudimos, etc., **D** podré, podremos, etc., **E** podría, podríamos, etc., **F** pueda, podamos, etc., **H** puede, pueda, podamos, poded, etc., **I** pudiendo

poner A pongo, pone, ponemos, etc., **C** puse, pusimos, etc., **D** pondré, pondremos, etc., **E** pondría, pondríamos, etc., **F** ponga, pongamos, etc., **G** pusiera, pusiéramos, etc., **H** pon, ponga, pongamos, poned, etc., **J** puesto, -ta

querer A quiero, queremos, etc., **C** quise, quisimos, etc., **D** querré, querremos, etc., **E** querría, querríamos, etc., **F** quiera, queramos, etc., **G** quisiera, quisiéramos, etc., **H** quiere, quiera, queramos, quered, etc.

reír A río, reímos, etc., **C** rió, reímos, rieron, etc., **F** ría, riamos, etc., **G** riera, riéramos, etc., **H** ríe, ría, riamos, reíd, etc., **I** riendo

saber A sé, sabe, sabemos, etc., **C** supe, supimos, etc., **D** sabré, sabremos, etc., **E** sabría, sabríamos, etc., **F** sepa, sepamos, etc., **G** supiera, supiéramos, etc., **H** sabe, sepa, sepamos, sabed, etc.

salir A salgo, sale, salimos, etc., **D** saldré, saldremos, etc., **E** saldría, saldríamos, etc., **F** salga, salgamos, etc., **H** sal, salga, salgamos, salid, etc.

sentir A siento, sentimos, etc., **C** sintió, sentimos, sintieron, etc., **F** sienta, sintamos, etc., **G** sintiera, sintiéramos, etc., **H** siente, sienta, sintamos, sentid, etc., **I** sintiendo

SER A soy, eres, es, somos, sois, son, **B** era, eras, era, éramos, erais, eran, **C** fui, fuiste, fue, fuimos, fuisteis, fueron, **D** seré, serás, será, seremos, seréis, serán, **E** sería, serías, sería, seríamos, seríais, serían, **F** sea, seas, sea, seamos, seáis, sean, **G** fuera, fueras, fuera, fuéramos, fuerais, fueran, **H** sé, sea, seamos, sed, sean, **I** siendo, **J** sido, -da

sonar A sueno, sonamos, etc., **F** suene, sonemos, etc., **H** suena, suene, sonemos, sonad, etc.

TEMER A temo, temes, teme, tememos, teméis, temen, **B** temía, temías, temía, temíamos, temíais, temían, **C** temí, temiste, temió, temimos, temisteis, temieron, **D** temeré, temerás, temerá, temeremos, temeréis, temerán, **E** temería, temerías, temería, temeríamos, temeríais, temerían, **F** tema, temas, tema, temamos, temáis, teman, **G** temiera, temieras, temiera, temiéramos, temierais, temieran, **H** teme, tema, tememos, temed, teman, **I** temiendo, **J** temido, -da

tender A tiendo, tendemos, etc., **F** tienda, tendamos, etc., **H** tiende, tendamos, etc.

tener A tengo, tiene, tenemos, etc., C tuve, tuvimos, etc., D tendré, tendremos, etc., E tendría, tendríamos, etc., F tenga, tengamos, etc., G tuviera, tuviéramos, etc., H ten, tenga, tengamos, tened, etc.

traer A traigo, trae, traemos, etc., C traje, trajimos, etc., F traiga, traigamos, etc., G trajera, trajéramos, etc., H trae, traiga, traigamos, traed, etc., I trayendo

valer A valgo, vale, valemos, etc., D valdré, valdremos, etc., F valga, valga-mos, etc., H vale, valga, valgamos, valed, etc.

venir A vengo, viene, venimos, etc., C vine, vinimos, etc., D vendré, vendremos, etc., E vendría, vendríamos, etc., F venga, vengamos, etc., G viniera, viniéramos, etc., H ven, venga, vengamos, venid, etc., I viniendo

ver A veo, ve, vemos, etc., C vi, vio, vimos, etc., G viera, viéramos, etc., H ve, vea, veamos, ved, etc., I viendo, J visto, -ta.

English Irregular Verbs

Infinitive	Past Tense	Past Participle	Infinitive	Past Tense	Past Participle
arise	arose	arisen	forget	forgot	forgotten
awake	awoke	awoken	freeze	froze	frozen
be	was/were	been	get	got	got (*US* gotten)
bear	bore	born(e)			
beat	beat	beaten	give	gave	given
begin	began	begun	go	went	gone
bend	bent	bent	grind	ground	ground
bet	bet/ betted	bet/ betted	grow	grew	grown
			hang	hung/ hanged	hung/ hanged
bid	bid	bid			
bind	bound	bound	have	had	had
bite	bit	bitten	hear	heard	heard
bleed	bled	bled	hide	hid	hidden
blow	blew	blown	hit	hit	hit
break	broke	broken	hold	held	held
breed	bred	bred	hurt	hurt	hurt
bring	brought	brought	keep	kept	kept
build	built	built	kneel	knelt/ kneeled	knelt/ kneeled
burn	burnt/ burned	burnt/ burned			
			know	knew	known
burst	burst	burst	lay	laid	laid
buy	bought	bought	lead	led	led
can	could	-	lean	leant/ leaned	leant/ leaned
cast	cast	cast			
catch	caught	caught	leap	leapt/ leaped	leapt/ leaped
choose	chose	chosen			
come	came	come	learn	learnt/ learned	learnt/ learned
cost	cost	cost			
creep	crept	crept	leave	left	left
cut	cut	cut	lend	lent	lent
deal	dealt	dealt	let	let	let
dig	dug	dug	lie	lay	lain
do	did	done	light	lit/lighted	lit/lighted
draw	drew	drawn	lose	lost	lost
dream	dreamed/ dreamt	dreamed/ dreamt	make	made	made
			may	might	-
drink	drank	drunk	mean	meant	meant
drive	drove	driven	meet	met	met
eat	ate	eaten	mow	mowed	mown/ mowed
fall	fell	fallen			
feed	fed	fed	pay	paid	paid
feel	felt	felt	put	put	put
fight	fought	fought	quit	quit/ quitted	quit/ quitted
find	found	found			
fling	flung	flung	read	read	read
fly	flew	flown	rid	rid	rid

Infinitive	Past Tense	Past Participle	Infinitive	Past Tense	Past Participle
ride	rode	ridden	spin	spun	spun
ring	rang	rung	spit	spat	spat
rise	rose	risen	split	split	split
run	ran	run	spoil	spoiled/ spoilt	spoiled/ spoilt
saw	sawed	sawn			
say	said	said	spread	spread	spread
see	saw	seen	spring	sprang	sprung
seek	sought	sought	stand	stood	stood
sell	sold	sold	steal	stole	stolen
send	sent	sent	stick	stuck	stuck
set	set	set	sting	stung	stung
shake	shook	shaken	stink	stank	stunk
shall	should	-	strike	struck	struck/ stricken
shed	shed	shed			
shine	shone	shone	swear	swore	sworn
shoot	shot	shot	sweep	swept	swept
show	showed	shown	swell	swelled	swollen/ swelled
shrink	shrank	shrunk			
shut	shut	shut	swim	swam	swum
sing	sang	sung	swing	swung	swung
sink	sank	sunk	take	took	taken
sit	sat	sat	teach	taught	taught
sleep	slept	slept	tear	tore	torn
slide	slid	slid	tell	told	told
sling	slung	slung	think	thought	thought
smell	smelt/ smelled	smelt/ smelled	throw	threw	thrown
			tread	trod	trodden
sow	sowed	sown/ sowed	wake	woke/ waked	woken/ waked
speak	spoke	spoken	wear	wore	worn
speed	sped/ speeded	sped/ speeded	weave	wove/ weaved	woven/ weaved
spell	spelt/ spelled	spelt/ spelled	weep	wept	wept
			win	won	won
spend	spent	spent	wind	wound	wound
spill	spilt/ spilled	spilt/ spilled	wring	wrung	wrung
			write	wrote	written

ESPAÑOL-INGLÉS
SPANISH-ENGLISH

A

a¹ (*pl* aes), **A** (*pl* Aes) *f* [letra] a, A.

a² *prep* (*a* + *el* = *al*) - **1.** [periodo de tiempo]: **a las pocas semanas** a few weeks later; **al día siguiente** the following day - **2.** [momento preciso] at; **a las siete** at seven o'clock; **a los 11 años** at the age of 11; **al caer la noche** at nightfall; **al oír la noticia, se desmayó** on hearing the news, she fainted - **3.** [frecuencia]: **40 horas a la semana** 40 hours per o a week; **tres veces al día** three times a day - **4.** [dirección] to; **voy a Sevilla** I'm going to Seville; **me voy al extranjero** I'm going abroad; **llegó a Barcelona/la fiesta** he arrived in Barcelona/at the party - **5.** [posición]: **a la puerta** at the door; **está a la derecha/izquierda** it's on the right/left - **6.** [distancia]: **está a más de cien km de aquí** it's more than a hundred km from here - **7.** [con complemento indirecto] to; **dáselo a Juan** give it to Juan; **dile a Juan que venga** tell Juan to come - **8.** [con complemento directo]: **quiere a sus hijos/su gato** she loves her children/her cat - **9.** [cantidad, medida, precio]: **a cientos/miles/docenas** by the hundred/thousand/dozen; **a 90 km por hora** (at) 90 km per hour; **¿a cuánto están las peras?** how much are the pears?; **ganaron tres a cero** they won three nil - **10.** [modo]: **lo hace a la antigua** he does it the old way; **a lo Mozart** in Mozart's style; **a cuadros** checked; **a escondidas** secretly; **poco a poco** little by little - **11.** [instrumento]: **escribir a máquina** to use a typewriter; **a lápiz** in pencil; **a mano** by hand - **12.** (*después de verbo y antes de infin*) [finalidad] to; **entró a pagar** he came in to pay; **aprender a nadar** to learn to swim - **13.** (*después de sust y antes de infin*) [complemento de nombre]: **temas a tratar** matters to be discussed - **14.** [en oraciones imperativas]: **¡a la cama!** go to bed!; **¡a bailar!** let's dance!

abad, desa *m,f* abbot (*f* abbess).

abadía *f* abbey.

abajo ◇ *adv* - **1.** [posición - gen] below; [- en edificio] downstairs; **vive (en el piso de) ~** she lives downstairs; **está aquí/allí ~** it's it's

down here/there; **más ~** further down - **2.** [dirección] down; **ve ~** [en edificio] go downstairs; **hacia/para ~** down, downwards; **calle/escaleras ~** down the street/stairs; **río ~** downstream - **3.** [en un texto] below. ◇ *interj*: **¡~ la dictadura!** down with the dictatorship!
➤ **de abajo** *loc adj* bottom.

abalanzarse *vpr*: **~ sobre** to fall upon; **~ hacia** to rush towards.

abalear *vt Andes, CAm, Ven* to shoot at.

abalorio *m* (*gen pl*) [bisutería] trinket.

abanderado *m lit & fig* standard-bearer.

abandonado, da *adj* - **1.** [desierto] deserted - **2.** [desamparado] abandoned - **3.** [descuidado - persona] unkempt; [- jardín, casa] neglected; **dejar ~** to abandon.

abandonar *vt* - **1.** [gen] to abandon; [lugar, profesión, cónyuge] to leave - **2.** [desatender - obligaciones, estudios] to neglect.
➤ **abandonarse** *vpr* [a una emoción]: **~se a** [desesperación, dolor] to succumb to; [bebida, drogas] to give o.s. over to.

abandono *m* - **1.** [acción - gen] abandonment; [- de lugar, profesión, cónyuge] leaving; [- de obligaciones, estudios] neglect - **2.** [estado] state of abandon - **3.** DEP: **ganar por ~** to win by default.

abanicar *vt* to fan.

abanico *m* [para dar aire] fan.

abaratar *vt* to reduce the price of.

abarcar *vt* [incluir] to embrace, to cover.

abarrotado, da *adj*: **~ (de)** [teatro, autobús] packed (with); [desván, baúl] crammed (with).

abarrotar *vt*: **~ algo (de** o **con)** [teatro, autobús] to pack sthg (with); [desván, baúl] to cram sthg full (of).

abarrotería *f CAm, Méx* grocer's (shop) *UK*, grocery store *US*.

abarrotero, ra *m,f CAm, Méx* grocer.

abarrotes *mpl Amér* groceries.

abastecer *vt*: **~ algo/a alguien (de)** to supply sthg/sb (with).

abastecimiento *m* [cantidad] supply; [acción] supplying.

abasto *m*: no dar ∼ para hacer algo to be unable to cope with doing sthg; no doy ∼ con tanto trabajo I can't cope with all this work.

abatible *adj* reclining; de alas ∼s gate-legged.

abatido, da *adj* dejected.

abatir *vt* - 1. [derribar - muro] to knock down; [- avión] to shoot down - 2. [desanimar] to depress.

◆ **abatirse** *vpr*: ∼se (sobre) to swoop (down on).

abdicación *f* abdication.

abdicar *vi* to abdicate.

abdomen *m* abdomen.

abdominal *adj* abdominal.

abecé *m lit & fig* ABC.

abecedario *m* [alfabeto] alphabet.

abedul *m* birch (tree).

abeja *f* bee.

abejorro *m* bumblebee.

aberración *f* aberration; eso es una ∼ that's absurd.

abertura *f* opening.

abertzale [aβerˈtʃale] *adj & mf* Basque nationalist.

abeto *m* fir (tree).

abierto, ta ◇ *pp* ▷ abrir. ◇ *adj* [gen] open; dejar el grifo ∼ to leave the tap on; bien *o* muy ∼ wide open.

abigarrado, da *adj* multi-coloured; *fig* motley.

abismal *adj* vast, colossal.

abismo *m* [profundidad] abyss.

abjurar *vi culto*: ∼ de algo to abjure sthg.

ablandar *vt* [material] to soften.

◆ **ablandarse** *vpr* [material] to soften, to become softer.

abnegación *f* abnegation, self-denial.

abochornar *vt* to embarrass.

◆ **abochornarse** *vpr* to get embarrassed.

abofetear *vt* to slap.

abogacía *f* legal profession.

abogado, da *m,f* lawyer, attorney *US*; ∼ defensor counsel for the defence; ∼ del estado public prosecutor.

abogar *vi fig* [defender]: ∼ por algo to advocate sthg; ∼ por alguien to stand up for sb.

abolengo *m* lineage.

abolición *f* abolition.

abolir *vt* to abolish.

abolladura *f* dent.

abollar *vt* to dent.

abominable *adj* abominable.

abonado, da *m,f* [de teléfono, revista] subscriber; [al fútbol, teatro, transporte] season-ticket holder.

abonar *vt* - 1. [pagar] to pay; ∼ algo en la cuenta de alguien to credit sb's account with sthg - 2. [tierra] to fertilize.

◆ **abonarse** *vpr*: ∼se (a) [revista] to subscribe (to); [fútbol, teatro, transporte] to buy a season ticket (for).

abonero, ra *m,f Méx* hawker, street trader.

abono *m* - 1. [pase] season ticket - 2. [fertilizante] fertilizer - 3. [pago] payment - 4. *Méx* [plazo] instalment.

abordar *vt* - 1. [embarcación] to board - 2. *fig* [tema, tarea] to tackle.

aborigen *adj* [indígena] indigenous; [de Australia] aboriginal.

aborrecer *vt* [actividad] to abhor; [persona] to loathe.

abortar *vi* [MED - espontáneamente] to have a miscarriage, to miscarry; [- intencionadamente] to have an abortion.

aborto *m* [MED - espontáneo] miscarriage; [- intencionado] abortion.

abotonar *vt* to button up.

◆ **abotonarse** *vpr* to do one's buttons up; [abrigo, camisa] to button up.

abovedado, da *adj* arched, vaulted.

abrasar *vt* - 1. [quemar - casa, bosque] to burn down; [- persona, mano, garganta] to burn; murieron abrasados they were burned to death - 2. [desecar - suj: sol, calor, lejía] to scorch; [- suj: sed] to parch.

abrazadera *f* TECN brace, bracket; [en carpintería] clamp.

abrazar *vt* [con los brazos] to hug, to embrace; ∼ fuerte a algn to hold sb tight.

◆ **abrazarse** *vpr* to hug *o* embrace (each other).

abrazo *m* embrace, hug; un (fuerte) ∼ [en cartas] best wishes.

abrebotellas *m inv* bottle opener.

abrecartas *m inv* paper knife, letter opener.

abrelatas *m inv* tin opener *UK*, can opener *US*.

abreviar *vt* [gen] to shorten; [texto] to abridge; [palabra] to abbreviate; [viaje, estancia] to cut short.

abreviatura *f* abbreviation.

abridor *m* - 1. [abrebotellas] (bottle) opener - 2. [abrelatas] (tin) opener *UK*, (can) opener *US*.

abrigar *vt* - 1. [arropar - suj: persona] to wrap up; [- suj: ropa] to keep warm - 2. *fig* [albergar - esperanza] to cherish; [- sospechas, malas intenciones] to harbour.

◆ **abrigarse** *vpr* [arroparse] to wrap up.

abrigo *m* - 1. [prenda] coat, overcoat - 2. [refugio] shelter.

abril *m* April; *ver también* septiembre.

abrillantar *vt* to polish.

abrir ◇ *vt* - 1. [gen] to open; [alas] to

spread; [melón] to cut open - **2**. [puerta] to unlock, to open; [pestillo] to pull back; [grifo] to turn on; [cremallera] to undo - **3**. [túnel] to dig; [canal, camino] to build; [agujero, surco] to make. ◇ *vi* [establecimiento] to open.

◆ **abrirse** *vpr* - **1**. [sincerarse]: ~se a alguien to open up to sb, to confide in sb - **2**. [cielo] to clear.

abrochar *vt* [camisa, botón] to do up; [cinturón] to fasten.

◆ **abrocharse** *vpr* to do up; [cinturón] to fasten.

abrumar *vt* [agobiar] to overwhelm.

abrupto, ta *adj* [escarpado] sheer; [accidentado] rugged.

absceso *m* abscess.

absentismo *m* [de terrateniente] absentee landownership.

ábside *m* apse.

absolución *f* - **1**. DER acquittal - **2**. RELIG absolution.

absoluto, ta *adj* [gen] absolute; [silencio, obediencia] total.

◆ **en absoluto** *loc adv* [en negativas] at all; [tras pregunta] not at all; ¿te gusta? — en ~ do you like it? — not at all; nada en ~ nothing at all.

absolver *vt* : ~ a alguien (de algo) DER to acquit sb (of sthg); RELIG to absolve sb (of sthg).

absorbente *adj* - **1**. [que empapa] absorbent - **2**. [actividad] absorbing.

absorber *vt* - **1**. [gen] to absorb - **2**. [consumir, gastar] to soak up.

absorción *f* absorption.

absorto, ta *adj* : ~ (en) absorbed *o* engrossed (in).

abstemio, mia *adj* teetotal.

abstención *f* abstention.

abstenerse *vpr* : ~ (de algo/de hacer algo) to abstain (from sthg/from doing sthg); le han recomendado que se abstenga del alcohol she has been advised to stay off the alcohol.

abstinencia *f* abstinence.

abstracción *f* [gen] abstraction.

abstracto, ta *adj* abstract.

abstraer *vt* to consider separately, to detach.

abstraído, da *adj* lost in thought, engrossed.

absuelto, ta *pp* ▷ **absolver**.

absurdo, da *adj* absurd.

◆ **absurdo** *m* : decir/hacer un ~ to say/ do something ridiculous.

abuchear *vt* to boo.

abuelo, la *m,f* [familiar] grandfather (*f* grandmother).

◆ **abuelos** *mpl* grandparents.

abulia *f* apathy, lethargy.

abúlico, ca *adj* apathetic, lethargic.

abultado, da *adj* [paquete] bulky; [labios] thick; [cantidad, cifra] inflated.

abultar ◇ *vt* - **1**. [hinchar] to swell - **2**. [exagerar] to blow up. ◇ *vi* [ser muy grande] to be bulky.

abundancia *f* - **1**. [gran cantidad] abundance; en ~ in abundance - **2**. [riqueza] plenty, prosperity.

abundante *adj* abundant.

abundar *vi* [ser abundante] to abound.

aburguesarse *vpr* to adopt middle-class ways.

aburrido, da ◇ *adj* - **1**. [harto, fastidiado] bored; estar ~ de hacer algo to be fed up with doing sthg - **2**. [que aburre] boring. ◇ *m,f* bore.

aburrimiento *m* boredom; ¡qué ~! what a bore!

aburrir *vt* to bore; me aburre I'm bored of it.

◆ **aburrirse** *vpr* to get bored; [estar aburrido] to be bored.

abusado, da *adj Méx* astute, shrewd.

abusar *vi* - **1**. [excederse] to go too far; ~ de algo to abuse sthg; ~ del alcohol to drink too much; ~ de alguien to take advantage of sb - **2**. [forzar sexualmente]: ~ de alguien to sexually abuse sb.

abusivo, va *adj* [trato] very bad, appalling; [precio] extortionate.

abuso *m* [uso excesivo]: ~ (de) abuse (of); ~ de confianza breach of confidence; ~s deshonestos sexual abuse (*U*).

abyecto, ta *adj culto* vile, wretched.

a/c *abrev de* a cuenta.

a. C. (*abrev de* antes de Cristo) BC.

acá *adv* - **1**. [lugar] here; de ~ para allá back and forth - **2**. [tiempo]: de una semana ~ during the last week.

acabado, da *adj* - **1**. [completo] perfect, consummate - **2**. [fracasado] finished, ruined.

◆ **acabado** *m* [de producto] finish; [de piso] décor.

acabar ◇ *vt* - **1**. [concluir] to finish - **2**. [consumir - provisiones, dinero] to use up; [- comida] to finish. ◇ *vi* - **1**. [gen] to finish, to end; ~ de hacer algo to finish doing sthg - **2**. [haber hecho recientemente]: ~ de hacer algo to have just done sthg; acabo de llegar I've just arrived - **3**. [terminar por - persona]: ~ por hacer algo, ~ haciendo algo to end up doing sthg - **4**. [destruir]: ~ con [gen] to destroy; [salud] to ruin; [paciencia] to exhaust; [violencia, crimen] to put an end to.

◆ **acabarse** *vpr* **- 1.** [agotarse] to be used up, to be gone; **se nos ha acabado el petróleo** we're out of petrol; **se ha acabado la comida** there's no more food left, all the food has gone **- 2.** [concluir] to finish, to be over **- 3.** *loc*: **¡se acabó!** [¡basta ya!] that's enough!; [se terminó] that's it, then!

acabóse *m fam*: **¡es el ~!** it really is the limit!

academia *f* **- 1.** [para aprender] school **- 2.** [institución] academy.

◆ **Real Academia Española** *f institution that sets lexical and syntactical standards for Spanish.*

académico, ca *adj* academic.

acaecer *v impers culto* to occur.

acallar *vt* to silence.

acalorado, da *adj* **- 1.** [por calor] hot **- 2.** [apasionado - debate] heated.

acalorar *vt* [enfadar]: **~ a alguien** to make sb hot under the collar.

◆ **acalorarse** *vpr* [enfadarse] to get aroused *o* excited.

acampanado, da *adj* flared.

acampar *vi* to camp.

acanalado, da *adj* [columna] fluted; [tejido] ribbed; [hierro, uralita] corrugated.

acantilado *m* cliff.

acaparar *vt* **- 1.** [monopolizar] to monopolize; [mercado] to corner **- 2.** [guardarse] to hoard.

acápite *m Amér* paragraph.

acaramelado, da *adj fig* [pegajoso] sickly sweet.

acariciar *vt* **- 1.** [persona] to caress; [animal] to stroke **- 2.** *fig* [idea, proyecto] to cherish.

acarrear *vt* **- 1.** [transportar] to carry; [carbón] to haul **- 2.** *fig* [ocasionar] to bring, to give rise to.

acaso *adv* perhaps; **¿~ no lo sabías?** are you trying to tell me you didn't know?; **por si ~** (just) in case; **¿~ es culpa mía?** is it my fault?

◆ **si acaso** *loc adv* [en todo caso] if anything. *loc conj* [en caso de que] if.

acatar *vt* to respect, to comply with.

acatarrarse *vpr* to catch a cold.

acaudalado, da *adj* well-to-do, wealthy.

acaudillar *vt* to lead.

acceder *vi* **- 1.** [consentir]: **~ (a algo/hacer algo)** to agree (to sthg/to do sthg) **- 2.** [tener acceso]: **~ a** to enter **- 3.** [alcanzar]: **~ a** [trono] to accede to; [poder] to come to; [cargo] to obtain.

accesible *adj* [lugar] accessible.

accésit *m inv* consolation prize.

acceso *m* **- 1.** [entrada]: **~ (a)** entrance (to) **- 2.** [paso]: **~ (a)** access (to); **~ a Internet** Internet access **- 3.** [carretera] access road,

ramp *US* **- 4.** *fig* & MED [de tos] **fit**; [de fiebre, gripe] bout.

accesorio, ria *adj* incidental.

◆ **accesorio** *(gen pl)* *m* accessory.

accidentado, da *<> adj* **- 1.** [vida, viaje] eventful **- 2.** [terreno, camino] rough, rugged. *<> m,f* injured person, victim.

accidental *adj* [imprevisto] accidental; [encuentro] chance.

accidentarse *vpr* to be involved in *o* have an accident.

accidente *m* **- 1.** [desgracia] accident; **~ de avión/coche** plane/car crash; **~ de tráfico** road accident **- 2.** *(gen pl)* [del terreno] unevenness *(U)*.

acción *f* **- 1.** [gen] action **- 2.** [hecho] deed, act **- 3.** FIN share; **~ ordinaria/preferente** ordinary/preference share.

accionar *vt* to activate.

accionista *mf* shareholder.

acechar *vt* **- 1.** [vigilar] to observe, to keep under surveillance; [suj: cazador] to stalk **- 2.** [amenazar] to be lying in wait for.

acecho *m* observation, surveillance; **estar al ~ de** to lie in wait for; *fig* to be on the lookout for.

aceite *m* oil; **~ de colza/girasol/oliva** rapeseed/sunflower/olive oil.

aceitera *f* oil can.

◆ **aceiteras** *fpl* cruet *(sg)*.

aceitoso, sa *adj* oily.

aceituna *f* olive.

aceleración *f* acceleration.

acelerador, ra *adj* accelerating.

◆ **acelerador** *m* accelerator.

acelerar *<> vt* [avivar] to speed up; TECN to accelerate. *<> vi* to accelerate.

◆ **acelerarse** *vpr* to hurry up.

acelga *f* chard.

acento *m* **- 1.** [gen] accent **- 2.** [intensidad] stress, accent.

acentuación *f* accentuation.

acentuar *vt* **- 1.** [palabra, letra - al escribir] to accent, to put an accent on; [- al hablar] to stress **- 2.** *fig* [realzar] to accentuate.

◆ **acentuarse** *vpr* [intensificarse] to deepen, to increase.

acepción *f* meaning, sense.

aceptable *adj* acceptable.

aceptación *f* **- 1.** [aprobación] acceptance **- 2.** [éxito] success, popularity.

aceptar *vt* to accept.

acequia *f* irrigation channel.

acera *f* [para peatones] pavement *UK*, sidewalk *US*.

acerbo, ba *adj culto* [mordaz] caustic, cutting.

acerca ◆ **acerca de** *loc adv* about.

acercar *vt* to bring nearer *o* closer; ¡acércame el pan! could you pass me the bread?

◆ **acercarse** *vpr* [arrimarse - viniendo] to come closer; [- yendo] to go over.

acero *m* steel; ~ **inoxidable** stainless steel.

acérrimo, ma *adj* [defensor] diehard *(antes de sust)*; [enemigo] bitter.

acertado, da *adj* **- 1.** [con acierto - respuesta] correct; [- comentario] appropriate **- 2.** [oportuno] good, clever.

acertar ◇ *vt* **- 1.** [adivinar] to guess (correctly) **- 2.** [el blanco] to hit **- 3.** [elegir bien] to choose well. ◇ *vi* **- 1.** [atinar]: ~ **(al hacer algo)** to be right (to do sthg) **- 2.** [conseguir]: ~ **a hacer algo** to manage to do sthg **- 3.** [hallar]: ~ **con** to find.

acertijo *m* riddle.

acervo *m* [patrimonio] heritage.

achacar *vt* : ~ **algo a alguien/algo** to attribute sthg to sb/sthg.

achantar *vt fam* to put the wind up.

◆ **achantarse** *vpr fam* to get the wind up.

achaparrado, da *adj* squat.

achaque *m* ailment.

achatado, da *adj* flattened.

achicar *vt* **- 1.** [tamaño] to make smaller **- 2.** [agua - de barco] to bale out **- 3.** *fig* [acobardar] to intimidate.

achicharrar *vt* [chamuscar] to burn.

◆ **achicharrarse** *vpr* **- 1.** *fig* [de calor] to fry, to roast **- 2.** [chamuscarse] to burn.

achicoria *f* chicory.

achuchado, da *adj fam* hard, tough.

achuchar *vt fam* [abrazar] to hug.

achurar *vt RP* **- 1.** [acuchillar] to stab to death **- 2.** [animal] to disembowel.

aciago, ga *adj culto* black, fateful.

acicalar *vt* [arreglar] to do up.

◆ **acicalarse** *vpr* to do o.s. up.

acicate *m fig* [estímulo] incentive.

acidez *f* **- 1.** [cualidad] acidity **- 2.** MED : ~ **(de estómago)** heartburn.

ácido, da *adj* **- 1.** QUÍM acidic **- 2.** [bebida, sabor, carácter] acid, sour.

◆ **ácido** *m* QUÍM acid.

acierto *m* **- 1.** [a pregunta] correct answer **- 2.** [habilidad, tino] good *o* sound judgment **- 3.** [éxito] success.

aclamación *f* [ovación] acclamation, acclaim; **por** ~ unanimously; **entre aclamaciones** to great acclaim.

aclamar *vt* to acclaim.

aclaración *f* explanation.

aclarar *vt* **- 1.** [ropa] to rinse **- 2.** [explicar] to clarify, to explain **- 3.** : ~ **la voz** [carraspeando] to clear one's throat.

◆ **aclararse** *vpr* **- 1.** [entender] to understand **- 2.** [explicarse] to explain o.s.

aclaratorio, ria *adj* explanatory.

aclimatación *f* acclimatization.

aclimatar *vt* **- 1.** [al clima]: ~ **algo/a alguien (a)** to acclimatize sthg/sb (to) **- 2.** [al ambiente]: ~ **algo/a alguien a algo** to get sthg/sb used to sthg.

◆ **aclimatarse** *vpr* **- 1.** [al clima]: ~**se (a algo)** to acclimatize (to sthg) **- 2.** [al ambiente] to settle in; ~**se a algo** to get used to sthg.

acné *m* acne.

acobardar *vt* to frighten, to scare.

◆ **acobardarse** *vpr* to get frightened *o* scared; ~**se ante** to shrink back from.

acodarse *vpr* : ~ **(en)** to lean (on).

acogedor, ra *adj* [país, persona] friendly, welcoming; [casa, ambiente] cosy.

acoger *vt* **- 1.** [recibir] to welcome **- 2.** [dar refugio] to take in.

◆ **acogerse a** *vpr* [inmunidad parlamentaria etc] to take refuge in; [ley] to have recourse to.

acogida *f* reception; ~ **familiar** fostering.

acolchar *vt* to pad.

acometer ◇ *vt* **- 1.** [atacar] to attack **- 2.** [emprender] to undertake. ◇ *vi* [embestir]: ~ **contra** to hurtle into.

acometida *f* **- 1.** [ataque] attack, charge **- 2.** [de luz, gas etc] (mains) connection.

acomodado, da *adj* [rico] well-off, well-to-do.

acomodador, ra *m,f* usher (*f* usherette).

acomodar *vt* **- 1.** [instalar - persona] to seat, to instal; [- cosa] to place **- 2.** [adaptar] to fit.

◆ **acomodarse** *vpr* [instalarse] to make o.s. comfortable; ~**se en** to settle down in.

acomodaticio, cia *adj* [complaciente] accommodating.

acompañamiento *m* CULIN & MÚS accompaniment.

acompañante *mf* [compañero] companion; MÚS accompanist.

acompañar *vt* **- 1.** [ir con]: ~ **a alguien** [gen] to go with *o* accompany sb; [a la puerta] to show sb out; [a casa] to walk sb home; **te acompaño** I'll come with you **- 2.** [estar con]: ~ **a alguien** to keep sb company **- 3.** [adjuntar] to enclose **- 4.** MÚS to accompany.

acompasar *vt* : ~ **algo (a)** to synchronize sthg (with).

acomplejar *vt* to give a complex.

◆ **acomplejarse** *vpr* to develop a complex.

acondicionado, da *adj* equipped; **aire** ~ air conditioned.

acondicionador *m* **- 1.** [de aire] (air) conditioner **- 2.** [de pelo] conditioner.

acondicionar *vt* **- 1.** [reformar] to condition,

to convert, to upgrade - **2.** [preparar] to prepare, to get ready.

acongojar *vt* to distress, to cause anguish to.

aconsejar *vt* [dar consejos]: ~ **a alguien (que haga algo)** to advise sb (to do sthg); **te aconsejo que vayas al médico** I'd advise you to see a doctor.

acontecer *v impers* to take place, to happen.

acontecimiento *m* event; **adelantarse** o **anticiparse a los** ~ **s** to jump the gun; [prevenir] to take preemptive measures.

acopio *m* stock, store.

acoplar *vt* - **1.** [encajar] to attach, to fit together - **2.** FERROC to couple - **3.** *fig* [adaptar] to adapt, to fit.

acorazado, da *adj* armour-plated.

◆ **acorazado** *m* battleship.

acordar *vt*: ~ **algo/hacer algo** to agree on sthg/to do sthg.

◆ **acordarse** *vpr*: ~**se (de algo/de hacer algo)** to remember (sthg/to do sthg); ~**se de haber hecho algo** to remember doing sthg.

acorde ◇ *adj* [en consonancia]: ~ **con** in keeping with. ◇ *m* MÚS chord.

acordeón *m* accordion.

acordonar *vt* [lugar] to cordon off.

acorralar *vt lit & fig* to corner.

acortar *vt* - **1.** [falda, pantalón etc] to take up; [cable] to shorten - **2.** [plazo,vacaciones] to cut short - **3.** [extensión] to shorten.

◆ **acortarse** *vpr* [días] to get shorter; [reunión] to end early.

acosar *vt* - **1.** [hostigar] to harass - **2.** [perseguir] to pursue relentlessly.

acoso *m* [hostigamiento] harassment; ~ **sexual** sexual harassment.

acostar *vt* [en la cama] to put to bed.

◆ **acostarse** *vpr* - **1.** [irse a la cama] to go to bed - **2.** [tumbarse] to lie down - **3.** *fam* [tener relaciones sexuales]: ~**se con alguien** to sleep with sb.

acostumbrado, da *adj* - **1.** [habitual] usual - **2.** [habituado]: **estar** ~ **a** to be used to.

acostumbrar ◇ *vt* [habituar]: ~ **a alguien a algo/a hacer algo** to get sb used to sthg/to doing sthg. ◇ *vi* [soler]: ~ **a hacer algo** to be in the habit of doing sthg; **acostumbro a levantarme temprano** I usually get up early.

◆ **acostumbrarse** *vpr* [habituarse]: ~**se a algo/a hacer algo** to get used to sthg/to doing sthg.

acotación *f* [nota] note in the margin.

acotar *vt* - **1.** [terreno, campo] to enclose, to demarcate; *fig* [tema etc] to delimit - **2.** [texto] to write notes in the margin of.

acrecentar *vt* to increase.

acreditado, da *adj* - **1.** [médico, abogado etc] distinguished; [marca] reputable - **2.** [embajador, representante] accredited.

acreditar *vt* - **1.** [certificar] to certify; [autorizar] to authorize - **2.** [confirmar] to confirm - **3.** [embajador] to accredit - **4.** FIN to credit.

acreedor, ra ◇ *adj*: **hacerse** ~ **de algo** to earn sthg, to show o.s. to be worthy of sthg. ◇ *m,f* creditor.

acribillar *vt* [herir]: ~ **(a)** to pepper o riddle (with); ~ **a balazos** to riddle with bullets.

acrílico, ca *adj* acrylic.

acritud, acrimonia *f* - **1.** [de olor] acridity, pungency; [de sabor] bitterness - **2.** *fig* [mordacidad] venom - **3.** [desavenencia] acrimony.

acrobacia *f* [en circo] acrobatics *(pl)*.

acróbata *mf* acrobat.

acta *f* (el) - **1.** [de junta, reunión] minutes *(pl)*; **levantar** ~ to take the minutes - **2.** [de defunción etc] certificate; ~ **notarial** affidavit.

◆ **actas** *fpl* minutes.

actitud *f* [disposición de ánimo] attitude.

activar *vt* - **1.** [gen] to activate - **2.** [explosivo] to detonate.

actividad *f* [acción] activity; [trabajo] work.

activo, va *adj* - **1.** [gen & GRAM] active - **2.** [trabajador] hard-working.

◆ **activo** *m* FIN assets *(pl)*; ~ **y pasivo** assets and liabilities.

acto *m* - **1.** [acción] act; **hacer** ~ **de presencia** to show one's face; ~ **de solidaridad** show of solidarity - **2.** [ceremonia] ceremony - **3.** TEATR act.

◆ **en el acto** *loc adv* on the spot, there and then; **murió en el** ~ she died instantly.

actor, triz *m,f* actor (*f* actress).

actuación *f* - **1.** [conducta, proceder] conduct, behaviour - **2.** [interpretación] performance.

actual *adj* - **1.** [existente] present, current - **2.** [de moda] modern, present-day - **3.** [de actualidad] topical.

actualidad *f* - **1.** [momento presente] current situation; **de** ~ [moderno] in fashion; [de interés actual] topical; **en la** ~ at the present time, these days - **2.** [noticia] news *(U)*; **ser** ~ to be making the news.

actualizar *vt* [información] to update; [tecnología, industria] to modernize; INFORM to upgrade.

actualmente *adv* [hoy día] these days, nowadays; [en este momento] at the (present) moment.

actuar *vi* [gen] to act; ~ **de** to act as.

acuarela *f* watercolour.

acuario *m* aquarium.

◆ **Acuario** ◇ *m* [zodiaco] Aquarius. ◇ *mf* [persona] Aquarius.

acuartelar *vt* to confine to barracks.

acuático, ca *adj* aquatic.

acuchillar *vt* - **1.** [apuñalar] to stab - **2.** [mueble, parquet] to grind down.

acuciar *vt culto* [suj: persona] to goad; [suj: necesidad, deseo] to press.

acuclillarse *vpr* to squat (down).

acudir *vi* - **1.** [ir] to go; [venir] to come - **2.** [recurrir]: ~ **a** to go *o* turn to - **3.** [presentarse]: ~ **(a)** [escuela, iglesia] to attend; [cita, examen] to turn up (for); *fig* [memoria, mente] to come (to).

acueducto *m* aqueduct.

acuerdo *m* agreement; **de** ~ all right, O.K.; **de** ~ **con** [conforme a] in accordance with; **estar de** ~ **(con alguien/en hacer algo)** to agree (with sb/to do sthg); **llegar a un** ~, **ponerse de** ~ to reach agreement.

acumular *vt* to accumulate.

acunar *vt* to rock.

acuñar *vt* - **1.** [moneda] to mint - **2.** [palabra] to coin.

acuoso, sa *adj* watery.

acupuntura *f* acupuncture.

acurrucarse *vpr* [por frío] to huddle up; [en sitio agradable] to curl up.

acusación *f* [inculpación] charge.

acusado, da ◇ *adj* [marcado] marked, distinct. ◇ *m,f* [procesado] accused, defendant.

acusar *vt* - **1.** [culpar] to accuse; DFR to charge; ~ **a alguien de algo** [gen] to accuse sb of sthg; DER to charge sb with sthg - **2.** [mostrar] to show.

acusativo *m* accusative.

acuse ◆ **acuse de recibo** *m* acknowledgement of receipt.

acústico, ca *adj* acoustic.

◆ **acústica** *f* [de local] acoustics *(pl)*.

adagio *m* [sentencia breve] adage.

adaptación *f* - **1.** [aclimatación]: ~ **(a)** adjustment (to) - **2.** [modificación] adaptation.

adaptar *vt* - **1.** [acomodar, ajustar] to adjust - **2.** [modificar] to adapt.

◆ **adaptarse** *vpr*: ~**se (a)** to adjust (to).

adecentar *vt* to tidy up.

adecuado, da *adj* appropriate, suitable.

adecuar *vt* to adapt.

◆ **adecuarse a** *vpr* - **1.** [ser adecuado] to be appropriate for - **2.** [adaptarse] to adjust to.

adefesio *m fam* [persona fea] fright, sight.

a. de JC., a.JC. (*abrev de* **antes de Jesucristo**) BC.

adelantado, da *adj* advanced; **llevo el**

reloj ~ my watch is fast; **por** ~ in advance.

adelantamiento *m* AUTOM overtaking.

adelantar ◇ *vt* - **1.** [dejar atrás] to overtake - **2.** [mover hacia adelante] to move forward; [pie, reloj] to put forward - **3.** [en el tiempo - trabajo, viaje] to bring forward; [- dinero] to pay in advance. ◇ *vi* - **1.** [progresar] to make progress - **2.** [reloj] to be fast.

◆ **adelantarse** *vpr* - **1.** [en el tiempo] to be early; [frío, verano] to arrive early; [reloj] to gain; ~**se a alguien** to beat sb to it - **2.** [en el espacio] to go on ahead.

adelante ◇ *adv* forward, ahead; **(de ahora) en** ~ from now on, in future; **más** ~ [en el tiempo] later (on); [en el espacio] further on. ◇ *interj*: **¡** ~ **!** [¡siga!] go ahead!; [¡pase!] come in!

adelanto *m* advance.

adelgazar ◇ *vi* to lose weight, to slim. ◇ *vt* to lose.

ademán *m* [gesto - con manos etc] gesture; [- con cara] face, expression; **en** ~ **de** as if to.

además *adv* [con énfasis] moreover, besides; [también] also; ~ **de** as well as, in addition to.

adentrarse *vpr*: ~ **en** [jungla etc] to enter the heart of; [tema etc] to study in depth.

adentro *adv* inside; **tierra** ~ inland; **mar** ~ out to sea.

adepto, ta *m,f*: ~ **(a)** follower (of).

aderezar *vt* [sazonar - ensalada] to dress; [- comida] to season.

aderezo *m* [aliño - de ensalada] dressing; [- de comida] seasoning.

adeudar *vt* - **1.** [deber] to owe - **2.** COM to debit.

◆ **adeudarse** *vpr* to get into debt.

adherir *vt* to stick.

◆ **adherirse** *vpr* - **1.** [pegarse] to stick - **2.** [mostrarse de acuerdo]: ~**se a** to adhere to.

adhesión *f* [apoyo] support.

adhesivo, va *adj* adhesive.

◆ **adhesivo** *m* [pegatina] sticker.

adicción *f*: ~ **(a)** addiction (to).

adición *f* addition.

adicional *adj* additional.

adicto, ta ◇ *adj*: ~ **(a)** addicted (to). ◇ *m,f*: ~ **(a)** addict (of).

adiestrar *vt* to train; ~ **a alguien en algo/ para hacer algo** to train sb in sthg/to do sthg.

adinerado, da *adj* wealthy.

adiós ◇ *m* goodbye. ◇ *interj*: **¡** ~ **!** goodbye!; [al cruzarse con alguien] hello!

adiposo, sa *adj* adipose.

aditivo *m* additive.

adivinanza *f* riddle.

adivinar *vt* **-1.** [predecir] to foretell; [el futuro] to tell **-2.** [acertar] to guess (correctly).

adivino, na *m,f* fortune-teller.

adjetivo *m* adjective.

adjudicación *f* awarding.

adjudicar *vt* [asignar] to award.

➡ **adjudicarse** *vpr* [apropiarse] to take for o.s.; ~**se un premio** to win a prize.

adjuntar *vt* to enclose.

adjunto, ta ◇ *adj* [incluido] enclosed; ~ **le remito ...** please find enclosed ... ◇ *m,f* [auxiliar] assistant.

administración *f* **-1.** [suministro] supply; [de medicamento, justicia] administering **-2.** [gestión] administration **-3.** [gerentes] management; [oficina] manager's office.

➡ **Administración** *f* [gobierno] administration; **Administración local** local government; **Administración pública** civil service.

administrador, ra *m,f* **-1.** [de empresa] manager **-2.** [de bienes ajenos] administrator.

administrar *vt* **-1.** [gestionar - empresa, finca etc] to manage, to run; [- casa] to run **-2.** [país] to run the affairs of **-3.** [suministrar] to administer.

administrativo, va *adj* administrative.

admirable *adj* admirable.

admiración *f* **-1.** [sentimiento] admiration; **causar** ~ to be admired; **sentir** ~ **por algn** to admire sb **-2.** [signo ortográfico] exclamation mark.

admirar *vt* **-1.** [gen] to admire **-2.** [sorprender] to amaze.

➡ **admirarse** *vpr*: ~**se (de)** to be amazed (by).

admisible *adj* acceptable.

admisión *f* **-1.** [de persona] admission **-2.** [de solicitudes etc] acceptance; **prueba de** ~ entrance exam.

admitir *vt* **-1.** [acoger, reconocer] to admit; ~ **a alguien en** to admit sb to **-2.** [aceptar] to accept.

ADN (*abrev de* **ácido desoxirribonucleico**) *m* DNA.

adobar *vt* to marinate.

adobe *m* adobe.

adobo *m* [salsa] marinade.

adoctrinar *vt* to instruct.

adolecer ➡ **adolecer de** *vi* to suffer from.

adolescencia *f* adolescence.

adolescente *adj & mf* adolescent.

adonde *adv* where; **la ciudad** ~ **vamos** the city we are going to, the city where we are going.

adónde *adv* where.

adopción *f* [de hijo, propuesta] adoption; [de ley] passing.

adoptar *vt* [hijo, propuesta] to adopt; [ley] to pass.

adoptivo, va *adj* [hijo, país] adopted; [padre] adoptive.

adoquín (*pl* **adoquines**) *m* cobblestone.

adorable *adj* [persona] adorable; [ambiente, película] wonderful.

adoración *f* adoration; **sentir** ~ **por alguien** to worship sb.

adorar *vt* **-1.** [reverenciar] to worship **-2.** [pirrarse por] to adore.

adormecer *vt* [producir sueño] to lull to sleep.

➡ **adormecerse** *vpr* to nod off, to drop off.

adormilarse *vpr* to doze.

adornar *vt* to decorate.

adorno *m* decoration.

adosado, da *adj* [casa] semi-detached.

adquirir *vt* **-1.** [comprar] to acquire, to purchase **-2.** [conseguir - conocimientos, hábito, cultura] to acquire; [- éxito, popularidad] to achieve; [- compromiso] to undertake.

adquisición *f* **-1.** [compra, cosa comprada] purchase **-2.** [obtención] acquisition **-3.** [de costumbres] adoption.

adquisitivo, va *adj* purchasing (*antes de sust*).

adrede *adv* on purpose, deliberately.

adrenalina *f* adrenalin.

adscribir *vt* **-1.** [asignar] to assign **-2.** [destinar] to appoint *o* assign to.

➡ **adscribirse** *vpr*: ~**se (a)** [grupo, partido] to become a member (of); [ideología] to subscribe (to).

adscrito, ta ◇ *pp* ▷ **adscribir**. ◇ *adj* assigned.

aduana *f* [administración] customs (*pl*); **pasar por la** ~ to go through customs.

aducir *vt* to adduce.

adueñarse ➡ **adueñarse de** *vpr* **-1.** [apoderarse] to take over, to take control of **-2.** [dominar] to take hold of.

adulación *f* flattery.

adulador, ra *adj* flattering.

adular *vt* to flatter.

adulterar *vt* [alimento] to adulterate.

adulterio *m* adultery.

adúltero, ra ◇ *adj* adulterous. ◇ *m,f* adulterer (*f* adulteress).

adulto, ta *adj & m,f* adult.

adusto, ta *adj* dour.

advenedizo, za *adj & m,f* parvenu (*f* parvenue).

advenimiento *m* [llegada] advent; [al trono] accession.

adverbio *m* adverb.

adversario, ria *m,f* adversary.

adversidad *f* adversity.

adverso, sa *adj* [gen] adverse; [destino] unkind; [suerte] bad; [viento] unfavourable.

advertencia *f* warning; **servir de** ~ **to** serve as a warning; **hacer una** ~ **a alguien** to warn sb.

advertir *vt* - 1. [notar] to notice - 2. [prevenir, avisar] to warn; **te advierto que no deberías hacerlo** I'd advise against you doing it; **te advierto que no me sorprende** mind you, it doesn't surprise me.

adviento *m* Advent.

adyacente *adj* adjacent.

aéreo, a *adj* - 1. [del aire] aerial - 2. AERON air *(antes de sust).*

aerobic [ae'roβik] *m* aerobics *(U).*

aeroclub *(pl* **aeroclubs)** *m* flying club.

aerodeslizador *m* hovercraft.

aerodinámico, ca *adj* - 1. FÍS aerodynamic - 2. [forma, línea] streamlined.

aeródromo *m* airfield, aerodrome.

aeroespacial *adj* aerospace *(antes de sust).*

aerogenerador *m* wind turbine.

aerógrafo *m* airbrush.

aerolínea *f* airline.

aeromozo, za *m,f Amér* air steward *(f* air hostess).

aeronauta *mf* aeronaut.

aeronaval *adj* air and sea *(antes de sust).*

aeronave *f* [gen] aircraft; [dirigible] airship.

aeroplano *m* aeroplane.

aeropuerto *m* airport.

aerosol *m* aerosol.

aerostático, ca *adj* aerostatic.

aeróstato *m* hot-air balloon.

aerotaxi *m* light aircraft *(for hire).*

afabilidad *f* affability.

afable *adj* affable.

afamado, da *adj* famous.

afán *m* - 1. [esfuerzo] hard work *(U)* - 2. [anhelo] urge; **tener** ~ **de algo** to be eager for sth; ~ **de conocimiento** thirst for knowledge.

afanador, ra *m,f Méx* cleaner.

afanar *vt fam* [robar] to pinch, to swipe.

◆ **afanarse** *vpr* [esforzarse]: ~**se (por hacer algo)** to do everything one can (to do sthg).

afanoso, sa *adj* - 1. [trabajoso] hard, demanding - 2. [que se afana] keen, eager.

afear *vt* to make ugly.

afección *f* MED complaint, disease.

afectación *f* affectation.

afectado, da *adj* - 1. [gen] affected - 2. [afligido] upset, badly affected.

afectar *vt* - 1. [gen] to affect - 2. [afligir] to upset, to affect badly.

afectísimo, ma *adj* [en cartas]: **suyo** ~ yours faithfully.

afectivo, va *adj* - 1. [emocional] emotional - 2. [cariñoso] affectionate, loving.

afecto *m* affection, fondness; **sentir** ~ **por alguien, tenerle** ~ **a alguien** to be fond of sb.

afectuoso, sa *adj* affectionate, loving.

afeitar *vt* [pelo, barba] to shave.

◆ **afeitarse** *vpr* to shave.

afeminado, da *adj* effeminate.

aferrarse *vpr*: ~ **a** *lit & fig* to cling to.

Afganistán Afghanistan.

afianzamiento *m* [en cargo, liderazgo] consolidation.

afianzar *vt* [objeto] to secure.

◆ **afianzarse** *vpr* to steady o.s.; ~**se en algo** [opinión etc] to become sure o convinced of sthg; [cargo, liderazgo] to consolidate sthg.

afiche *m Amér* poster.

afición *f* - 1. [inclinación] fondness, liking; **tener** ~ **a algo** to be keen on sthg - 2. [en tiempo libre] hobby; **por** ~ **as a hobby** - 3. [aficionados] fans *(pl).*

aficionado, da ⬦ *adj* - 1. [interesado] keen; **ser** ~ **a algo** to be keen on sthg - 2. [no profesional] amateur. ⬦ *m,f* - 1. [interesado] fan; ~ **al cine** film buff - 2. [amateur] amateur.

aficionar *vt*: ~ **a alguien a algo** to make sb keen on sthg.

◆ **aficionarse** *vpr*: ~**se a algo** to become keen on sthg.

afilado, da *adj* [borde, filo] sharp; [dedos] pointed.

afilar *vt* to sharpen.

afiliado, da *m,f*: ~ **(a)** member (of).

afiliarse *vpr*: ~ **a** to join, to become a member of.

afín *adj* [semejante] similar, like.

afinar *vt* - 1. MÚS [instrumento] to tune; ~ **la voz** to sing in tune - 2. [perfeccionar, mejorar] to fine-tune - 3. [pulir] to refine.

afinidad *f* [gen & QUÍM] affinity.

afirmación *f* statement, assertion.

afirmar *vt* - 1. [confirmar] to confirm - 2. [decir] to say, to declare - 3. [consolidar] to reaffirm - 4. CONSTR to reinforce.

afirmativo, va *adj* affirmative.

aflicción *f* suffering, sorrow.

afligir *vt* [afectar] to afflict; [causar pena] to distress.

aflojar ⬦ *vt* [destensar] to loosen; [cuerda] to slacken. ⬦ *vi* - 1. [disminuir] to abate, to die down - 2. *fig* [ceder] to ease off.

◆ **aflojarse** *vpr* [gen] to come loose; [cuerda] to slacken.

aflorar *vi fig* [surgir] to (come to the) surface, to show.

afluencia *f* stream, volume.

afluente *m* tributary.

afluir ◆ **afluir a** *vi* **- 1.** [gente] to flock to **- 2.** [sangre, fluido] to flow to.

afonía *f* loss of voice.

afónico, ca *adj*: **quedarse** ~ to lose one's voice.

aforo *m* [cabida] seating capacity.

afortunadamente *adv* fortunately.

afortunado, da *adj* **- 1.** [agraciado] lucky, fortunate **- 2.** [oportuno] happy, felicitous.

afrenta *f* [ofensa, agravio] affront.

África Africa.

africano, na *adj* & *m,f* African.

afrontar *vt* [hacer frente a] to face.

afuera *adv* outside; **por (la parte de)** ~ on the outside.

◆ **afueras** *fpl*: **las** ~**s** the outskirts.

afuerita *adv Amér fam* right outside.

afusilar *vt Amér fam* to shoot.

agachar *vt* to lower; [la cabeza] to bow.

◆ **agacharse** *vpr* [acuclillarse] to crouch down; [inclinar la cabeza] to stoop.

agalla *f* ZOOL gill.

◆ **agallas** *fpl fig* guts; **tener** ~**s** to have guts.

agarradero *m* **- 1.** [asa] hold **- 2.** *fam fig* [pretexto] pretext, excuse.

agarrado, da *adj* **- 1.** [asido]: ~ **(de)** gripped (by); ~**s del brazo** arm in arm; ~**s de la mano** hand in hand **- 2.** *fam* [tacaño] tight, stingy.

agarrar *vt* **- 1.** [asir] to grab **- 2.** [pillar - ladrón, resfriado] to catch; *Amér* [tomar] to take.

◆ **agarrarse** *vpr* [sujetarse] to hold on.

agarrón *m* [tirón] pull, tug.

agarrotar *vt* [parte del cuerpo] to cut off the circulation in; [mente] to numb.

◆ **agarrotarse** *vpr* **- 1.** [parte del cuerpo] to go numb **- 2.** [mecanismo] to seize up.

agasajar *vt* to lavish attention on, to treat like a king.

ágata *f (el)* agate.

agazaparse *vpr* **- 1.** [para esconderse] to crouch **- 2.** [agacharse] to bend down.

agencia *f* **- 1.** [empresa] agency; ~ **matrimonial** marriage bureau; ~ **de viajes** travel agency **- 2.** [sucursal] branch.

agenda *f* **- 1.** [de notas, fechas] diary; [de teléfonos, direcciones] book **- 2.** [de trabajo] agenda.

agente ◇ *mf* [persona] agent; ~ **de policía** *o* **de la autoridad** policeman (*f* policewoman); ~ **de aduanas** customs officer; ~ **de cambio (y bolsa)** stockbroker; ~ **secreto** secret agent. ◇ *m* [causa activa] agent.

ágil *adj* [movimiento, persona] agile.

agilidad *f* agility.

agilizar *vt* to speed up.

agitación *f* **- 1.** [intranquilidad] restlessness **- 2.** [jaleo] racket, commotion **- 3.** [conflicto] unrest.

agitar *vt* **- 1.** [mover - botella] to shake; [- líquido] to stir; [- brazos] to wave **- 2.** [inquietar] to perturb, to worry **- 3.** [alterar, perturbar] to stir up.

◆ **agitarse** *vpr* [inquietarse] to get worried.

aglomeración *f* build-up; [de gente] crowd.

aglomerar *vt* to bring together.

◆ **aglomerarse** *vpr* to amass.

agnóstico, ca *adj* & *m,f* agnostic.

agobiado, da *adj*: ~ **(de)** [trabajo] snowed under (with); [problemas] weighed down (with).

agobiar *vt* to overwhelm.

◆ **agobiarse** *vpr* to feel overwhelmed, to let things get one down.

agobio *m* **- 1.** [físico] choking, suffocation **- 2.** [psíquico] pressure.

agolparse *vpr* [gente] to crowd round; [sangre] to rush.

agonía *f* **- 1.** [pena] agony **- 2.** [del moribundo] death throes *(pl)*.

agonizante *adj* dying.

agonizar *vi* [expirar] to be dying.

agosto *m* **- 1.** [mes] August; *ver también* **septiembre - 2.** *loc*: **hacer su** ~ to line one's pockets.

agotado, da *adj* **- 1.** [cansado]: ~ **(de)** exhausted (from) **- 2.** [producto] out of stock, sold out **- 3.** [pila, batería] flat.

agotador, ra *adj* exhausting.

agotamiento *m* [cansancio] exhaustion.

agotar *vt* [gen] to exhaust; [producto] to sell out of; [agua] to drain.

◆ **agotarse** *vpr* **- 1.** [cansarse] to tire o.s. out **- 2.** [acabarse] to run out; [libro, disco, entradas] to be sold out; [pila, batería] to go flat.

agraciado, da *adj* **- 1.** [atractivo] attractive, fetching **- 2.** [afortunado]: ~ **con algo** lucky enough to win sthg.

agraciar *vt* [embellecer] to make more attractive *o* fetching.

agradable *adj* pleasant.

agradar *vt* to please.

agradecer *vt* [suj: persona]: ~ **algo a alguien** [dar las gracias] to thank sb for sthg; [estar agradecido] to be grateful to sb for sthg.

agradecido, da *adj* [ser] grateful; [estar] appreciative.

agradecimiento *m* gratitude.

agrado *m* [gusto] pleasure; **esto no es de mi** ~ this is not to my liking.

agrandar *vt* to make bigger.

agrario, ria *adj* [reforma] agrarian; [producto, política] agricultural.

agravante ◇ *adj* aggravating. ◇ *m o f* - **1.** [problema] additional problem - **2.** DER aggravating circumstance.

agravar *vt* [situación] to aggravate; [impuestos etc] to increase (the burden of).

◆ **agravarse** *vpr* to get worse, to worsen.

agraviar *vt* to offend.

agravio *m* - **1.** [ofensa] offence, insult - **2.** [perjuicio] wrong.

agredir *vt* to attack.

agregado, da *m,f* - **1.** EDUC assistant teacher - **2.** [de embajada] attaché; ~ **cultural** cultural attaché.

◆ **agregado** *m* [añadido] addition.

agregar *vt* : ~ **(algo a algo)** to add (sthg to sthg).

agresión *f* [ataque] act of aggression, attack.

agresividad *f* aggression.

agresivo, va *adj lit & fig* aggressive.

agresor, ra *m,f* attacker, assailant.

agreste *adj* [abrupto, rocoso] rugged.

agriar *vt* [vino, leche] to (turn) sour.

◆ **agriarse** *vpr lit & fig* to turn sour.

agrícola *adj* agricultural; [pueblo] farming *(antes de sust).*

agricultor, ra *m,f* farmer.

agricultura *f* agriculture.

agridulce *adj* bittersweet; CULIN sweet and sour.

agrietar *vt* - **1.** [muro, tierra] to crack - **2.** [labios, manos] to chap.

◆ **agrietarse** *vpr* [la piel] to chap.

agrio, agria *adj* - **1.** [ácido] sour - **2.** *fig* [áspero] acerbic, bitter.

agronomía *f* agronomy.

agropecuario, ria *adj* farming and livestock *(antes de sust).*

agrupación *f* [asociación] group, association.

agrupamiento *m* [concentración] grouping.

agrupar *vt* to group (together).

◆ **agruparse** *vpr* - **1.** [congregarse] to gather (round) - **2.** [unirse] to form a group.

agua *f (el)* water; ~ **mineral sin gas/con gas** still/sparkling mineral water; **venir como** ~ **de mayo** to be a godsend.

◆ **aguas** *fpl* - **1.** [manantial] waters, spring *(sg)* - **2.** [de río, mar] waters; ~**s territoriales** *o* **jurisdiccionales** territorial waters; ~**s internacionales** international waters - **3.** [de diamantes, telas] water *(U).*

◆ **agua de colonia** *f* eau de cologne.

◆ **agua oxigenada** *f* hydrogen peroxide.

◆ **aguas residuales** *fpl* sewage *(U).*

aguacate *m* [fruto] avocado (pear).

aguacero *m* shower.

aguachirle *f* dishwater *(U)*, revolting drink.

aguado, da *adj* [con demasiada agua] watery; [diluido a propósito] watered-down.

aguafiestas *m y f inv* spoilsport.

aguafuerte *m* etching.

aguamarina *f* aquamarine.

aguamiel *f Amér* [bebida] *water mixed with honey or cane syrup*; *Carib, Méx* [jugo] maguey juice.

aguanieve *f* sleet.

aguantar *vt* - **1.** [sostener] to hold - **2.** [resistir - peso] to bear - **3.** [tolerar, soportar] to bear, to stand; **no sé cómo la aguantas** I don't know how you put up with her - **4.** [contener - risa] to contain; [- respiración] to hold.

◆ **aguantarse** *vpr* - **1.** [contenerse] to restrain o.s., to hold o.s. back - **2.** [resignarse]: **no quiere** ~**se** he refuses to put up with it.

aguante *m* - **1.** [paciencia] self-restraint, tolerance - **2.** [resistencia] strength; [de persona] stamina.

aguar *vt* - **1.** [mezclar con agua] to water down - **2.** *fig* [estropear] to spoil, to ruin.

aguardar *vt* to wait for, to await.

aguardiente *m* spirit, liquor.

aguarrás *m* turpentine.

agudeza *f* [gen] sharpness.

agudizar *vt fig* [acentuar] to exacerbate, to make worse.

◆ **agudizarse** *vpr* [crisis] to get worse.

agudo, da *adj* - **1.** [gen] sharp; [crisis, problema, enfermedad] serious, acute - **2.** *fig* [perspicaz] keen, sharp - **3.** *fig* [ingenioso] witty - **4.** MÚS [nota, voz] high, high-pitched.

agüero *m* : **de buen/mal** ~ that bodes well/ ill.

aguijón *m* - **1.** [de insecto] sting - **2.** *fig* [estímulo] spur, stimulus.

aguijonear *vt* - **1.** [espolear]: ~ **a alguien para que haga algo** to goad sb into doing sthg - **2.** *fig* [estimular] to drive on.

águila *f (el)* - **1.** [ave] eagle - **2.** *fig* [vivo, listo] sharp *o* perceptive person; **¿** ~ **o sol?** *Méx* heads or tails?

aguileño, ña *adj* aquiline.

aguilucho *m* eaglet.

aguinaldo *m* Christmas box.

agüita *f Chile* herbal tea.

aguja *f* - **1.** [de coser, jeringuilla] needle; [de hacer punto] knitting needle - **2.** [de reloj] hand; [de brújula] pointer; [de iglesia] spire - **3.** FERROC point - **4.** [de tocadiscos] stylus, needle.

◆ **agujas** *fpl* [de res] ribs.

agujerear *vt* to make a hole o holes in.

agujero *m* hole.

agujetas *fpl*: tener ∼ to feel stiff.

aguzar *vt* - 1. [afilar] to sharpen - 2. *fig* [apetito] to whet; [ingenio] to sharpen.

ah *interj*: ¡∼! [admiración] ooh!; [sorpresa] oh!; [pena] ah!

ahí *adv* there; **vino por** ∼ he came that way; **la solución está** ∼ that's where the solution lies; ¡∼ **tienes!** here you are!, there you go!; **de** ∼ **que** [por eso] and consequently, so; **está por** ∼ [en lugar indefinido] he/she is around (somewhere); [en la calle] he/she is out; **por** ∼, **por** ∼ *fig* something like that; **por** ∼ **va la cosa** you're not too far wrong.

ahijado, da *m,f* [de padrinos] godson (*f* goddaughter).

ahijuna, aijuna *interj Amér fam* wow!

ahínco *m* enthusiasm, devotion.

ahíto, ta *adj culto* [saciado]: **estar** ∼ to be full.

ahogar *vt* - 1. [en el agua] to drown; [asfixiar] to smother, to suffocate - 2. [estrangular] to strangle - 3. [extinguir] to extinguish, to put out - 4. *fig* [controlar - levantamiento] to quell; [- pena] to hold back, to contain - 5. [motor] to flood.

◆ **ahogarse** *vpr* - 1. [en el agua] to drown - 2. [asfixiarse] to suffocate.

ahogo *m* - 1. [asfixia] breathlessness, difficulty in breathing - 2. *fig* [económico] financial difficulty.

ahondar *vi* [profundizar] to go into detail; ∼ **en** [penetrar] to penetrate deep into; [profundizar] to study in depth.

ahora ◇ *adv* - 1. [en el presente] now; ∼ **mismo** right now; **por** ∼ for the time being; **de** ∼ **en adelante** from now on - 2. [pronto] in a second o moment; ¡hasta ∼! see you in a minute! ◇ *conj* [pero] but, however; ∼ **que** but, though; ∼ **bien** but, however.

ahorcar *vt* to hang.

◆ **ahorcarse** *vpr* to hang o.s.

ahorita, ahoritita *adv CAm, Méx fam* right now.

ahorrador, ra ◇ *adj* thrifty, careful with money. ◇ *m,f* thrifty person.

ahorrar *vt* to save.

◆ **ahorrarse** *vpr*: ∼**se algo** to save o spare o.s. sthg.

ahorro *m* - 1. [gen] saving - 2. *(gen pl)* [cantidad ahorrada] savings *(pl)*.

ahuecar *vt* [poner hueco - manos] to cup.

ahuevado, da *adj Andes, CAm fam* [tonto] daft.

ahumado, da *adj* smoked.

ahumar *vt* - 1. [jamón, pescado] to smoke

- 2. [habitación etc] to fill with smoke.

ahuyentar *vt* - 1. [espantar, asustar] to scare away - 2. *fig* [apartar] to drive away.

aijuna = ahijuna.

airado, da *adj* angry.

airar *vt* to anger, to make angry.

◆ **airarse** *vpr* to get angry.

airbag *m* airbag.

aire *m* - 1. [fluido] air; **al** ∼ exposed; **al** ∼ **libre** in the open air; **estar en el** ∼ to be in the air; **tomar el** ∼ to go for a breath of fresh air - 2. [viento] wind; [corriente] draught; **hoy hace (mucho)** ∼ it's (very) windy today - 3. *fig* [aspecto] air, appearance.

◆ **aires** *mpl* [vanidad] airs (and graces).

◆ **aire (acondicionado)** *m* air-conditioning.

airear *vt fig* [contar] to air (publicly).

◆ **airearse** *vpr* to get a breath of fresh air.

airoso, sa *adj* - 1. [garboso] graceful, elegant - 2. [triunfante]: **salir** ∼ **de algo** to come out of sthg with flying colours.

aislado, da *adj* - 1. [gen] isolated - 2. TECN insulated.

aislar *vt* - 1. [gen] to isolate - 2. TECN to insulate.

ajá *interj*: ¡∼! [sorpresa] aha!; *fam* [aprobación] great!

ajar *vt* [flores] to wither, to cause to fade; [piel] to wrinkle; [colores] to make faded; [ropa] to wear out.

◆ **ajarse** *vpr* [flores] to fade, to wither; [piel] to wrinkle, to become wrinkled.

ajardinado, da *adj* landscaped.

ajedrez *m inv* chess.

ajeno, na *adj* - 1. [de otro] of others; **jugar en campo** ∼ to play away from home - 2. [extraño]: ∼ **a** having nothing to do with; ∼ **a nuestra voluntad** beyond our control.

ajetreo *m* - 1. [tarea] running around, hard work - 2. [animación] (hustle and) bustle.

ají *m Andes, RP* chilli (pepper).

ajiaco *m Andes, Carib* chilli-based stew.

ajillo ◆ **al ajillo** *loc adj* CULIN *in a sauce made with oil, garlic and chilli.*

ajo *m* garlic; **andar** o **estar en el** ∼ *fig* to be in on it.

ajustado, da *adj* [ceñido - ropa] tight-fitting; [- tuerca, pieza] tight; [- resultado, final] close.

ajustadores *mpl Col, Cuba* bra *(sg)*.

ajustar *vt* - 1. [arreglar] to adjust - 2. [apretar] to tighten - 3. [encajar - piezas de motor] to fit; [- puerta, ventana] to push to - 4. [pactar - matrimonio] to arrange; [- pleito] to settle; [- paz] to negotiate; [- precio] to fix, to agree.

ajuste *m* [de pieza] fitting; [de mecanismo] adjustment; [de salario] agreement; ~ **de cuentas** *fig* settling of scores.

al ⊳ **a**.

ala *f (el)* - **1.** ZOOL & POLÍT wing - **2.** [parte lateral - de tejado] eaves *(pl)*; [- de sombrero] brim - **3.** DEP winger, wing.
◆ **ala delta** *f* [aparato] hang glider.

alabanza *f* praise.

alabar *vt* to praise.

alabastro *m* alabaster.

alacena *f* kitchen cupboard.

alacrán *m* [animal] scorpion.

alado, da *adj* [con alas] winged.

alambique *m* still.

alambre *m* wire; ~ **de espino** *o* **púas** barbed wire.

alameda *f* - **1.** [sitio con álamos] poplar grove - **2.** [paseo] tree-lined avenue.

álamo *m* poplar.

alano *m* [perro] mastiff.

alarde *m*: ~ **(de)** show *o* display (of); **hacer** ~ **de algo** to show sthg off, to flaunt sthg.

alardear *vi*: ~ **de** to show off about.

alargador *m* extension lead.

alargar *vt* - **1.** [ropa] to lengthen - **2.** [viaje, visita, plazo] to extend; [conversación] to spin out.
◆ **alargarse** *vpr* [hacerse más largo - días] to get longer; [- reunión] to be prolonged.

alarido *m* shriek, howl.

alarma *f* [gen] alarm; **dar la** ~ to raise the alarm; ~ **de coche** car alarm.

alarmante *adj* alarming.

alarmar *vt* - **1.** [avisar] to alert - **2.** *fig* [asustar] to alarm.
◆ **alarmarse** *vpr* [inquietarse] to be alarmed.

alarmista *mf* alarmist.

alazán, ana *adj* chestnut.

alba *f (el)* [amanecer] dawn, daybreak.

albacea *mf* executor (*f* executrix).

albahaca *f* basil.

albanés, esa *adj & m,f* Albanian.
◆ **albanés** *m* [lengua] Albanian.

Albania Albania.

albanokosovar *adj & mf* Kosovar Albanian.

albañil *m* bricklayer.

albañilería *f* [obra] brickwork.

albarán *m* delivery note.

albaricoque *m* apricot.

albedrío *m* [antojo, elección] fancy, whim; **a su** ~ as takes his/her fancy; **libre** ~ free will; **a su libre** ~ of his/her own free will.

alberca *f* - **1.** [depósito] water tank - **2.** *Méx* [piscina] swimming pool.

albergar *vt* - **1.** [personas] to accommodate, to put up - **2.** [odio] to harbour; [esperanzas] to cherish.
◆ **albergarse** *vpr* to stay.

albergue *m* accommodation *(U)*, lodgings *(pl)*; [de montaña] shelter, refuge; ~ **de juventud** *o* **juvenil** youth hostel.

albino, na *adj & m,f* albino.

albis ◆ **in albis** *loc adv* : **estar in** ~ to be in the dark; **quedarse in** ~ not to have a clue *o* the faintest idea.

albóndiga *f* meatball.

alborada *f* [amanecer] dawn, daybreak.

alborear *v impers*: **empezaba a** ~ dawn was breaking.

albornoz *m* bathrobe.

alborotar ◇ *vi* to be noisy *o* rowdy. ◇ *vt* [amotinar] to stir up, to rouse.
◆ **alborotarse** *vpr* [perturbarse] to get worked up.

alboroto *m* - **1.** [ruido] din - **2.** [jaleo] fuss, to-do; **armar un** ~ to cause a commotion.

alborozar *vt* to delight.

alborozo *m* delight, joy.

albufera *f* lagoon.

álbum *(pl* **álbumes***) m* album.

alcachofa *f* BOT artichoke.

alcahuete, ta *m,f* [mediador] go-between.

alcalde, desa *m,f* mayor (*f* mayoress).

alcaldía *f* [cargo] mayoralty.

alcance *m* - **1.** [de arma, misil, emisora] range; **de corto/largo** ~ short-/long-range - **2.** [de persona]: **a mi/a tu** *etc* ~ within my/your *etc* reach; **al** ~ **de la vista** within sight; **fuera del** ~ **de** beyond the reach of - **3.** [de reformas etc] scope, extent.

alcanfor *m* camphor.

alcantarilla *f* sewer; [boca] drain.

alcantarillado *m* sewers *(pl)*.

alcanzar ◇ *vt* - **1.** [llegar a] to reach - **2.** [igualarse con] to catch up with - **3.** [entregar] to pass - **4.** [suj: bala etc] to hit - **5.** [autobús, tren] to manage to catch. ◇ *vi* - **1.** [ser suficiente]: ~ **para algo/hacer algo** to be enough for sthg/to do sthg - **2.** [poder]: ~ **a hacer algo** to be able to do sthg.

alcaparra *f* caper.

alcayata *f* hook.

alcázar *m* fortress.

alce *m* elk, moose.

alcoba *f* bedroom.

alcohol *m* alcohol.

alcohólico, ca *adj & m,f* alcoholic.

alcoholímetro *m* [para la sangre] Breathalyzer® *UK*, drunkometer *US*.

alcoholismo *m* alcoholism.

alcohotest *(pl* **alcohotests***) m* Breathalyzer® *UK*, drunkometer *US*.

alcornoque *m* -1. [árbol] cork oak -2. *fig* [persona] idiot, fool.

aldaba *f* [llamador] doorknocker.

aldea *f* small village.

aldeano, na *m,f* villager.

aleación *f* [producto] alloy; ~ **ligera** light alloy.

aleatorio, ria *adj* [número] random; [suceso] chance *(antes de sust)*.

aleccionar *vt* to instruct, to teach.

alegación *f* allegation.

alegar *vt* [motivos, pruebas] to put forward; ~ **que** to claim (that).

alegato *m* -1. DER & *fig* plea -2. [ataque] diatribe.

alegoría *f* allegory.

alegórico, ca *adj* allegorical.

alegrar *vt* [persona] to cheer up, to make happy; [fiesta] to liven up; **me alegra que me lo preguntes** I'm glad you asked me that.

◆ **alegrarse** *vpr* [sentir alegría]: ~**se (de algo/por alguien)** to be pleased (about sthg/for sb).

alegre *adj* -1. [contento] happy -2. [que da alegría] cheerful, bright -3. *fam* [borracho] tipsy.

alegría *f* -1. [gozo] happiness, joy -2. [motivo de gozo] joy.

alegrón *m fam* pleasant surprise.

alejamiento *m* -1. [distancia] distance -2. [separación - de objetos etc] separation; [- entre personas] estrangement.

alejar *vt* -1. [poner más lejos] to move away -2. *fig* [ahuyentar] to drive out.

◆ **alejarse** *vpr*: ~**se (de)** [ponerse más lejos] to go *o* move away (from); [retirarse] to leave.

aleluya *interj*: ¡~! Hallelujah!

alemán, ana *adj* & *m,f* German.

◆ **alemán** *m* [lengua] German.

Alemania Germany.

alentador, ra *adj* encouraging.

alentar *vt* to encourage.

alergia *f lit* & *fig* allergy; **tener ~ a algo** to be allergic to sthg; ~ **primaveral** hay fever.

alérgico, ca *adj lit* & *fig*: ~ **(a)** allergic (to).

alero *m* -1. [del tejado] eaves *(pl)* -2. DEP winger, wing.

alerta *adj inv* & *adv* alert. ◇ *f* alert.

alertar *vt* to alert.

aleta *f* -1. [de pez] fin; ~ **dorsal** dorsal fin -2. [de buzo, foca] flipper -3. [de coche] wing.

aletargar *vt* to make drowsy, to send to sleep.

◆ **aletargarse** *vpr* to become drowsy *o* sleepy.

aletear *vi* to flap *o* flutter its wings.

alevín *m* -1. [cría de pez] fry, young fish -2. *fig* [persona] novice, beginner.

alevosía *f* -1. [traición] treachery.

alfabetizar *vt* -1. [personas] to teach to read and write -2. [ordenar] to put into alphabetical order.

alfabeto *m* alphabet.

alfalfa *f* alfalfa, lucerne.

alfarería *f* [técnica] pottery.

alféizar *m* window-sill.

alférez *m* ≃ second lieutenant.

alfil *m* bishop.

alfiler *m* -1. [aguja] pin; ~ **de gancho** *Andes*, *RP, Ven* safety pin -2. [joya] brooch, pin.

alfombra *f* [grande] carpet; [pequeña] rug.

alfombrar *vt* to carpet.

alfombrilla *f* -1. [alfombra pequeña] rug -2. [felpudo] doormat -3. [del baño] bathmat -4. INFORM: ~ **(del ratón)** mouse mat.

alforja *f* (*gen pl*) [de caballo] saddlebag.

alga *f* (el) [de mar] seaweed *(U)*; [de río] algae *(pl)*.

algarroba *f* [fruto] carob *o* locust bean.

álgebra *f* (el) algebra.

álgido, da *adj* [culminante] critical.

algo ◇ *pron* -1. [alguna cosa] something; [en interrogativas] anything; **¿te pasa ~?** is anything the matter?; ~ **es** ~ something is better than nothing; **por** ~ **lo habrá dicho** he must have said it for a reason; **o** ~ **así** or something like that -2. [cantidad pequeña] a bit, a little; ~ **de** some, a little -3. *fig* [cosa importante] something; **se cree que es** ~ he thinks he's something (special). ◇ *adv* [un poco] rather, somewhat. ◇ *m*: **tiene un** ~ there's something attractive about him.

algodón *m* cotton; ~ **(hidrófilo)** FARM cotton wool *UK*, absorbent cotton *US*.

algoritmo *m* INFORM algorithm.

alguacil *m* [del juzgado] bailiff.

alguien *pron* -1. [alguna persona] someone, somebody; [en interrogativas] anyone, anybody; **¿hay ~ ahí?** is anyone there? -2. *fig* [persona de importancia] somebody; **se cree** ~ she thinks she's somebody (special).

alguno, na ◇ *adj antes de sust masculino* **algún** -1. [indeterminado] some; [en interrogativas] any; **¿tienes algún libro?** do you have any books?; **algún día** some *o* one day; **ha surgido algún (que otro) problema** the odd problem has come up -2. *(después de sust)* [ninguno] any; **no tengo interés** ~ I have no interest, I haven't any interest. ◇ *pron* -1. [persona] someone, somebody; *(pl)* some people; [en interrogativas] anyone, anybody; **¿conocisteis a** ~**s?** did you get to know any?; ~**s de**, ~**s (de) entre** some *o* a few of -2. [cosa] the odd one, some *(pl)*, a few *(pl)*; [en interrogativas] any; **me salió mal ~** I got the odd one wrong.

alhaja *f* [joya] jewel.

alhelí (*pl* **alhelíes**) *m* wallflower.

aliado, da *adj* allied.

alianza *f* **-1.** [pacto, parentesco] alliance **-2.** [anillo] wedding ring.

aliar *vt* [naciones] to ally.

  ➨ **aliarse** *vpr* to form an alliance.

alias ⬦ *adv* alias. ⬦ *m inv* alias; [entre amigos] nickname.

alicaído, da *adj* [triste] depressed.

alicates *mpl* pliers.

aliciente *m* **-1.** [incentivo] incentive **-2.** [atractivo] attraction.

alienación *f* **-1.** [gen] alienation **-2.** [trastorno psíquico] derangement, madness.

aliento *m* [respiración] breath; **tener mal ~** to have bad breath; **cobrar ~** to catch one's breath; **sin ~** breathless.

aligerar *vt* **-1.** [peso] to lighten **-2.** [ritmo] to speed up; [el paso] to quicken **-3.** *fig* [aliviar] to relieve, to ease.

alijo *m* contraband *(U)*.

alimaña *f* pest *(fox, weasel etc)*.

alimentación *f* **-1.** [acción] feeding **-2.** [comida] food **-3.** [régimen alimenticio] diet.

alimentar *vt* [gen] to feed; [motor, coche] to fuel.

  ➨ **alimentarse** *vpr* [comer]: **~se de** to live on.

alimenticio, cia *adj* nourishing; **productos ~s** foodstuffs; **valor ~** food value.

alimento *m* [gen] food; [valor nutritivo] nourishment; **~s transgénicos** GM foods.

alineación *f* **-1.** [en el espacio] alignment **-2.** DEP line-up.

alinear *vt* **-1.** [en el espacio] to line up **-2.** DEP to select.

  ➨ **alinearse** *vpr* POLÍT to align.

aliñar *vt* [ensalada] to dress; [carne] to season.

aliño *m* [para ensalada] dressing; [para carne] seasoning.

alioli *m* garlic mayonnaise.

alisar *vt* to smooth (down).

aliscafo *m RP* hydrofoil.

alistarse *vpr* to enlist; *Amér* [aprontarse] to get ready.

aliviar *vt* **-1.** [atenuar] to soothe **-2.** [aligerar - persona] to relieve; [- carga] to lighten.

alivio *m* relief; **¡qué ~!** what a relief!

aljibe *m* [de agua] cistern.

allá *adv* **-1.** [espacio] over there; **~ abajo/arriba** down/up there; **más ~** further on; **más ~ de** beyond; **¡~ voy!** I'm coming! **-2.** [tiempo]: **~ por los años cincuenta** back in the 50s; **~ para el mes de agosto** around

August some time **-3.** *loc:* **~ él/ella** *etc* that's his/her *etc* problem.

allanamiento *m* forceful entry; **~ de morada** breaking and entering.

allanar *vt* **-1.** [terreno] to flatten, to level **-2.** [irrumpir en] to break into.

allegado, da *m,f* **-1.** [familiar] relative **-2.** [amigo] close friend.

allí *adv* there; **~ abajo/arriba** down/up there; **~ mismo** right there; **está por ~** it's around there somewhere; **hasta ~** up until then.

alma *f*(el)**-1.** [gen] soul **-2.** [de bastón, ovillo] core.

almacén *m* warehouse.

  ➨ **(grandes) almacenes** *mpl* department store *(sg)*.

almacenar *vt* **-1.** [gen & INFORM] to store **-2.** [reunir] to collect.

almendra *f* almond.

almendro *m* almond (tree).

almíbar *m* syrup.

almidón *m* starch.

almidonar *vt* to starch.

almirantazgo *m* [dignidad] admiralty.

almirante *m* admiral.

almirez *m* mortar.

almizcle *m* musk.

almohada *f* pillow.

almohadilla *f* [gen, TECN & ZOOL] pad; [cojín] small cushion.

almorrana *f* (gen pl) piles *(pl)*.

almorzar ⬦ *vt* [al mediodía] to have for lunch. ⬦ *vi* [al mediodía] to have lunch.

almuerzo *m* [al mediodía] lunch.

aló *interj Andes, Carib* [al teléfono] hello?

alocado, da *m,f* crazy person.

alojamiento *m* accommodation; **buscar ~** to look for accommodation.

alojar *vt* to put up.

  ➨ **alojarse** *vpr* **-1.** [hospedarse] to stay **-2.** [introducirse] to lodge.

alondra *f* lark.

alpargata *f* (gen pl) espadrille.

Alpes *mpl*: **los ~** the Alps.

alpinismo *m* mountaineering.

alpinista *m* mountaineer.

alpiste *m* [semilla] birdseed.

alquilar *vt* [casa, TV, oficina] to rent; [coche] to hire.

  ➨ **alquilarse** *vpr* [casa, TV, oficina] to be for rent; [coche] to be for hire; **'se alquila'** 'to let'.

alquiler *m* **-1.** [acción - de casa, TV, oficina] renting; [- de coche] hiring *UK*, rental *US*; **de ~** [casa] rented; [coche] hire *(antes de sust) UK*, rental *(antes de sust) US*; **tenemos pisos de ~** we have flats to let *UK*, we have apartments to rent *US* **-2.** [precio - de casa, oficina] rent; [- de televisión] rental; [- de coche] hire *UK*, rental *US*.

alquimia *f* alchemy.

alquitrán *m* tar.

alrededor *adv* **- 1.** [en torno] around; **mira a tu ~** look around you; **de ~** surrounding **- 2.** [aproximadamente]: **~ de** around, about.

◆ **alrededores** *mpl* surrounding area *(sg)*; **en los ~es de Londres** in the area around London.

◆ **alrededor de** *loc prep* around.

alta ▷ **alto**.

altanero, ra *adj* haughty.

altar *m* altar.

altavoz *m* [gen] speaker; [para anuncios] loudspeaker.

alteración *f* **- 1.** [cambio] alteration **- 2.** [excitación] agitation **- 3.** [alboroto] disturbance; **~ del orden público** breach of the peace.

alterar *vt* **- 1.** [cambiar] to alter **- 2.** [perturbar - persona] to agitate, to fluster; [- orden público] to disrupt.

◆ **alterarse** *vpr* [perturbarse] to get agitated *o* flustered.

altercado *m* argument, row.

alternar ◇ *vt* to alternate. ◇ *vi* **- 1.** [relacionarse]: **~ (con)** to mix (with), to socialize (with) **- 2.** [sucederse]: **~ con** to alternate with.

◆ **alternarse** *vpr* **- 1.** [en el tiempo] to take turns **- 2.** [en el espacio] to alternate.

alternativa ▷ **alternativo**.

alternativamente *adv* [moverse] alternately.

alternativo, va *adj* **- 1.** [movimiento] alternating **- 2.** [posibilidad] alternative.

◆ **alternativa** *f* [opción] alternative.

alterno, na *adj* alternate; ELECTR alternating.

alteza *f fig* [de sentimientos] loftiness.

◆ **Alteza** *f* [tratamiento] Highness; **Su Alteza Real** His Royal Highness (*f* Her Royal Highness).

altibajos *mpl fig* [de vida etc] ups and downs.

altiplano *m* high plateau.

altisonante *adj* high-sounding.

altitud *f* altitude.

altivez *f* haughtiness.

altivo, va *adj* haughty.

alto, ta *adj* **- 1.** [gen] high; [persona, árbol, edificio] tall; [piso] top, upper; **alta fidelidad** high fidelity; **~s hornos** blast furnace **- 2.** [ruidoso] loud **- 3.** [avanzado] late; **a altas horas de la noche** late at night, in the small hours.

◆ **alto** ◇ *m* **- 1.** [altura] height; **mide dos metros de ~** [cosa] it's two metres high;

[persona] he's two metres tall **- 2.** [interrupción] stop **- 3.** [lugar elevado] height; **en lo ~ de** at the top of **- 4.** MÚS alto **- 5.** *loc*: **pasar por ~ algo** to pass over sthg. ◇ *adv* **- 1.** [arriba] high (up) **- 2.** [hablar etc] loud. ◇ *interj*: **¡~!** halt!, stop!

◆ **alta** *f (el)* [del hospital] discharge; **dar de alta** *o* **el alta a alguien** to discharge sb (from hospital).

altoparlante *m Amér* loudspeaker.

altramuz *m* lupin.

altruismo *m* altruism.

altura *f* **- 1.** [gen] height; [en el mar] depth; **ganar ~** to climb; **tiene dos metros de ~** [gen] it's two metres high; [persona] he's two metres tall **- 2.** [nivel] level; **está a la ~ del ayuntamiento** it's next to the town hall **- 3.** [latitud] latitude.

◆ **alturas** *fpl* [el cielo] Heaven *(sg)*; **a estas ~s** *fig* this far on, this late.

alubia *f* bean.

alucinación *f* hallucination.

alucinado, da *adj* **- 1.** MED hallucinating **- 2.** *fam* [sorprendido] gobsmacked.

alucinante *adj* **- 1.** MED hallucinatory **- 2.** *fam* [extraordinario] amazing.

alucinar ◇ *vi* MED to hallucinate. ◇ *vt fam fig* [seducir] to captivate.

alud *m lit* & *fig* avalanche.

aludido, da *m,f*: **el ~** the aforesaid; **darse por ~** [ofenderse] to take it personally; [reaccionar] to take the hint.

aludir *vi*: **~ a** [sin mencionar] to allude to; [mencionando] to refer to.

alumbrado *m* lighting.

alumbramiento *m* [parto] delivery.

alumbrar *vt* **- 1.** [iluminar] to light up **- 2.** [instruir] to enlighten **- 3.** [dar a luz] to give birth to.

aluminio *m* aluminium.

alumnado *m* [de escuela] pupils *(pl)*; [de universidad] students *(pl)*.

alumno, na *m,f* [de escuela, profesor particular] pupil; [de universidad] student.

alunizar *vi* to land on the moon.

alusión *f* [sin mencionar] allusion; [mencionando] reference.

alusivo, va *adj* allusive.

aluvión *m* **- 1.** [gen] flood **- 2.** GEOL alluvium.

alza *f (el)* rise; **en ~** FIN rising; *fig* gaining in popularity.

alzamiento *m* uprising, revolt.

alzar *vt* **- 1.** [levantar] to lift, to raise; [voz] to raise; [vela] to hoist; [cuello de abrigo] to turn up; [mangas] to pull up **- 2.** [aumentar] to raise.

◆ **alzarse** *vpr* **- 1.** [levantarse] to rise **- 2.** [sublevarse] to rise up, to revolt.

a.m. (*abrev de* **ante meridiem**) a.m.

ama ⊳ **amo**.

amabilidad *f* kindness; ¿tendría la ~ de
...? would you be so kind as to ...?

amable *adj* kind; ¿sería tan ~ de ...? would
you be so kind as to ...?

amaestrado, da *adj* [gen] trained; [en cir-
co] performing.

amaestrar *vt* to train.

amagar ◇ *vt* - **1.** [dar indicios de] to show
signs of - **2.** [mostrar intención] to threaten;
le amagó un golpe he threatened to hit him.
◇ *vi* [tormenta] to be imminent, to
threaten.

amago *m* - **1.** [indicio] sign, hint - **2.** [amena-
za] threat.

amainar *vi lit & fig* to abate, to die down.

amalgama *f* QUÍM & *fig* amalgam.

amalgamar *vt* QUÍM & *fig* to amalgamate.

amamantar *vt* [animal] to suckle; [bebé] to
breastfeed.

amanecer ◇ *m* dawn; **al** ~ at dawn. ◇ *v
impers*: **amaneció a las siete** dawn broke at
seven.

amanerado, da *adj* [afectado] mannered,
affected.

amansar *vt* - **1.** [animal] to tame - **2.** *fig* [per-
sona] to calm down.

amante *mf* - **1.** [querido] lover - **2.** *fig* [aficio-
nado]: **ser** ~ **de algo/hacer algo** to be keen
on sthg/doing sthg; **los** ~s **del arte** art
lovers.

amañar *vt* [falsear] to fix; [elecciones, resulta-
do] to rig; [documento] to doctor.

amaño *m* (*gen pl*) [treta] ruse, trick.

amapola *f* poppy.

amar *vt* to love.

amarar *vi* [hidroavión] to land at sea; [vehí-
culo espacial] to splash down.

amargado, da *adj* [resentido] bitter.

amargar *vt* to make bitter; *fig* to spoil, to
ruin.

amargo, ga *adj lit & fig* bitter.

amargoso, sa *adj Amér* bitter.

amargura *f* [sentimiento] sorrow.

amarillento, ta *adj* yellowish.

amarillo, lla *adj* [color] yellow.
➡ **amarillo** *m* [color] yellow.

amarilloso, sa *adj Amér* yellowish.

amarra *f* mooring rope *o* line.

amarrar *vt* - **1.** NÁUT to moor - **2.** [atar] to tie
(up); ~ **algo/a alguien a algo** to tie sthg/sb
to sthg.

amarre *m* mooring.

amarrete *adj Andes, RP fam pey* mean, tight.

amasar *vt* - **1.** [masa] to knead; [yeso] to mix
- **2.** *fam fig* [riquezas] to amass.

amasia *f CRica, Méx, Perú* mistress.

amasijo *m fam fig* [mezcla] hotchpotch.

amateur [ama'ter] (*pl* **amateurs**) *adj & mf*
amateur.

amatista *f* amethyst.

amazona *f fig* [jinete] horsewoman.

Amazonas *m*: **el** ~ the Amazon.

ambages *mpl*: **sin** ~ without beating
about the bush, in plain English.

ámbar *m* amber.

ambición *f* ambition.

ambicionar *vt* to have as one's ambition.

ambicioso, sa *adj* ambitious.

ambidextro, tra ◇ *adj* ambidextrous.
◇ *m,f* ambidextrous person.

ambientación *f* - **1.** CIN, LITER & TEATR setting
- **2.** RADIO sound effects (*pl*).

ambientador *m* air freshener.

ambiental *adj* - **1.** [físico, atmosférico]
ambient - **2.** ECOLOG environmental.

ambiente *m* - **1.** [aire] air, atmosphere
- **2.** [circunstancias] environment - **3.** [ámbi-
to] world, circles (*pl*) - **4.** [animación] life, atmosphere - **5.** *Andes, RP* [habitación] room.

ambigüedad *f* ambiguity.

ambiguo, gua *adj* [gen] ambiguous.

ámbito *m* - **1.** [espacio, límites] confines (*pl*);
una ley de ~ **provincial** an act which is provincial in its scope - **2.** [ambiente] world,
circles (*pl*).

ambivalente *adj* ambivalent.

ambos, bas ◇ *adj pl* both. ◇ *pron pl* both
(of them).

ambulancia *f* ambulance.

ambulante *adj* travelling; [biblioteca]
mobile.

ambulatorio *m* state-run surgery *o* clinic.

ameba *f* amoeba.

amedrentar *vt* to scare, to frighten.

amén *adv* [en plegaria] amen.
➡ **amén de** *loc prep* - **1.** [además de] in addition to - **2.** [excepto] except for, apart
from.

amenaza *f* threat; ~ **de bomba** bomb
scare; ~ **de muerte** death threat.

amenazar *vt* to threaten; ~ **a alguien con
hacerle algo** to threaten to do sthg to sb;
~ **a alguien con hacer algo** to threaten sb
with doing sthg; **amenaza lluvia** it's
threatening to rain.

amenidad *f* [entretenimiento] entertaining
qualities (*pl*).

ameno, na *adj* [entretenido] entertaining.

América America; ~ **del Sur** South America; ~ **Central** Central America.

americana ⊳ **americano**.

americano, na *adj & m,f* American.
➡ **americana** *f* [chaqueta] jacket.

ameritar *vt Amér* to deserve.

amerizar *vi* [hidroavión] to land at sea;

[vehículo espacial] to splash down.

ametralladora f machine gun.

ametrallar vt [con ametralladora] to machinegun.

amianto m asbestos.

amígdala f tonsil.

amigdalitis f inv tonsillitis.

amigo, ga ⬦ adj - 1. [gen] friendly - 2. [aficionado]: ~ de algo / hacer algo keen on sthg/doing sthg. ⬦ m,f - 1. [persona] friend; hacer ~ de to make friends with; hacerse ~s to become friends; ~ íntimo close friend - 2. fam [compañero, novio] partner; [amante] lover.

amigote, amiguete m fam pal, mate UK.

amiguismo m: hay mucho ~ there are always jobs for the boys.

aminoácido m amino acid.

aminorar vt to reduce.

amistad f friendship; hacer o trabar ~ (con) to make friends (with).
◆ **amistades** fpl friends.

amistoso, sa adj friendly.

amnesia f amnesia.

amnistía f amnesty.

amo, ama m,f - 1. [gen] owner - 2. [de criado, situación etc] master (f mistress).
◆ **ama de casa** f housewife.
◆ **ama de llaves** f housekeeper.

amodorrarse vpr to get drowsy.

amoldar vt [adaptar]: ~ (a) to adapt (to).
◆ **amoldarse** vpr [adaptarse]: ~se (a) to adapt (to).

amonestación f - 1. [reprimenda] reprimand - 2. DEP warning.

amonestar vt - 1. [reprender] to reprimand - 2. DEP to warn.

amoníaco, amoniaco m [gas] ammonia.

amontonar vt - 1. [apilar] to pile up - 2. [reunir] to accumulate.
◆ **amontonarse** vpr - 1. [personas] to form a crowd - 2. [problemas, trabajo] to pile up; [ideas, solicitudes] to come thick and fast.

amor m love; hacer el ~ to make love; por ~ al arte for the love of it.
◆ **amor propio** m pride.

amoral adj amoral.

amoratado, da adj [de frío] blue; [por golpes] black and blue.

amordazar vt [persona] to gag; [perro] to muzzle.

amorfo, fa adj [sin forma] amorphous.

amorío m fam [romance] fling.

amoroso, sa adj [gen] loving; [carta, relación] love (antes de sust).

amortajar vt [difunto] to shroud.

amortiguador, ra adj [de ruido] muffling; [de golpe] softening, cushioning.
◆ **amortiguador** m AUTOM shock absorber.

amortiguar vt [ruido] to muffle; [golpe] to soften, to cushion.

amortización f ECON [de deuda, préstamo] amortization, paying-off; [de inversión, capital] recouping; [de bonos, acciones] redemption; [de bienes de equipo] depreciation.

amortizar vt - 1. [sacar provecho] to get one's money's worth out of - 2. [ECON - deuda, préstamo] to amortize, to pay off; [- inversión, capital] to recoup; [- bonos, acciones] to redeem.

amotinar vt to incite to riot; [a marineros] to incite to mutiny.
◆ **amotinarse** vpr to riot; [marineros] to mutiny.

amparar vt - 1. [proteger] to protect - 2. [dar cobijo a] to give shelter to, to take in.
◆ **ampararse** vpr - 1. fig [apoyarse]: ~se en [ley] to have recourse to; [excusas] to draw on - 2. [cobijarse]: ~se de o contra to (take) shelter from.

amparo m [protección] protection; al ~ de [persona, caridad] with the help of; [ley] under the protection of.

amperio m amp, ampere.

ampliación f - 1. [aumento] expansion; [de edificio, plazo] extension - 2. FOT enlargement.

ampliar vt - 1. [gen] to expand; [local] to add an extension to; [plazo] to extend - 2. FOT to enlarge, to blow up.

amplificación f amplification.

amplificador m ELECTRÓN amplifier.

amplificar vt to amplify.

amplio, plia adj - 1. [sala etc] roomy, spacious; [avenida, gama] wide - 2. [ropa] loose - 3. [explicación etc] comprehensive; en el sentido más ~ de la palabra in the broadest sense of the word.

amplitud f - 1. [espaciosidad] roominess, spaciousness; [de avenida] wideness - 2. [de ropa] looseness - 3. fig [extensión] extent, comprehensiveness.

ampolla f - 1. [en piel] blister - 2. [para inyecciones] ampoule - 3. [frasco] phial.

ampuloso, sa adj pompous.

amputar vt to amputate.

Amsterdam Amsterdam.

amueblar vt to furnish.

amurallar vt to build a wall around.

anacronismo m anachronism.

anagrama m anagram.

anal adj ANAT anal.

anales mpl lit & fig annals.

analfabetismo m illiteracy.

analfabeto, ta adj & m,f illiterate.

analgésico, ca *adj* analgesic.
➡ **analgésico** *m* analgesic.
análisis *m inv* analysis; ~ **de sangre** blood test.
analizar *vt* to analyse.
analogía *f* similarity; **por** ~ by analogy.
analógico, ca *adj* INFORM & TECN analogue, analog.
análogo, ga *adj*: ~ **(a)** analogous *o* similar (to).
ananá, ananás *m RP* pineapple.
anaquel *m* shelf.
anarquía *f* - 1. [falta de gobierno] anarchy - 2. [doctrina política] anarchism.
anárquico, ca *adj* anarchic.
anarquista *adj & mf* anarchist.
anatema *m* [maldición] curse, anathema.
anatomía *f* anatomy.
anca *f* (el) haunch; ~s **de rana** frogs' legs.
ancestral *adj* ancestral; [costumbre] age-old.
ancho, cha *adj* [gen] wide; [prenda] loose-fitting; **te va** *o* **está** ~ it's too big for you; **a mis/tus** *etc* **anchas** *fig* at ease; **quedarse tan** ~ not to care less.
➡ **ancho** *m* width; **a lo** ~ crosswise; **cinco metros de** ~ five metres wide; **a lo** ~ **de** across (the width of); ~ **de vía** gauge.
anchoa *f* anchovy *(salted)*.
anchura *f* - 1. [medida] width - 2. [de ropa] bagginess.
anciano, na ◇ *adj* old. ◇ *m,f* old person, old man *(f* old woman).
➡ **anciano** *m* [de tribu] elder.
ancla *f* (el) anchor.
anclar *vi* to anchor.
andadas *fpl*: **volver a las** ~ *fam fig* to return to one's evil ways.
andadura *f* walking.
ándale *interj CAm, Méx fam* come on!
Andalucía Andalusia.
andaluz, za *adj & m,f* Andalusian.
andamio *m* scaffold.
andanada *f* MIL & *fig* broadside.
andando *interj*: ¡~! come on!, let's get a move on!
andante *adj* [que anda] walking.
andanza *f* (gen pl) [aventura] adventure.
andar ◇ *vi* - 1. [caminar] to walk; [moverse] to move - 2. [funcionar] to work, to go; **las cosas andan mal** things are going badly - 3. [estar] to be; ~ **preocupado** to be worried; ~ **tras algo/alguien** *fig* to be after sthg/sb - 4. *(antes de gerundio)*: ~ **haciendo algo** to be doing sthg; **anda echando broncas a todos** he's going round telling everybody off; **anda buscando algo** he's looking for sthg - 5. [ocuparse]: ~ **en** [asuntos, líos] to be involved in; [papeleos, negocios] to be

busy with - 6. [hurgar]: ~ **en** to rummage around in - 7. [alcanzar, rondar]: **anda por los 60** he's about sixty. ◇ *vt* - 1. [recorrer] to go, to travel - 2. *CAm* [llevar puesto] to wear. ◇ *m* gait, walk.
➡ **andarse** *vpr* [obrar]: ~**se con cuidado/misterios** to be careful/secretive.
➡ **andares** *mpl* [de persona] gait *(sg)*.
➡ **anda** *interj*: ¡~! [sorpresa, desilusión] oh!; [¡vamos!] come on!; [¡por favor!] go on!; ¡~ **ya!** [incredulidad] come off it!
andén *m* FERROC platform.
Andes *mpl*: **los** ~ the Andes.
andinismo *m Amér* mountaineering.
andinista *mf Amér* mountaineer.
Andorra Andorra.
andorrano, na *adj & m,f* Andorran.
andrajo *m* [harapo] rag.
andrajoso, sa *adj* ragged.
andrógino, na *adj* androgynous.
androide *m* [autómata] android.
anduviera *etc* ⊳ **andar**.
anécdota *f* anecdote.
anecdótico, ca *adj* - 1. [con historietas] anecdotal - 2. [no esencial] incidental.
anegar *vt* [inundar] to flood.
➡ **anegarse** *vpr* - 1. [inundarse] to flood; **sus ojos se anegaron de lágrimas** tears welled up in his eyes - 2. [ahogarse] to drown.
anejo, ja *adj*: ~ **(a)** [edificio] connected (to); [documento] attached (to).
➡ **anejo** *m* annexe.
anemia *f* anaemia.
anemómetro *m* anemometer.
anémona *f* anemone.
anestesia *f* anaesthesia.
anestésico, ca *adj* anaesthetic.
➡ **anestésico** *m* anaesthetic.
anexar *vt* [documento] to attach.
anexión *f* annexation.
anexionar *vt* to annex.
anexo, xa *adj* [edificio] connected; [documento] attached.
➡ **anexo** *m* annexe.
anfetamina *f* amphetamine.
anfibio, bia *adj lit & fig* amphibious.
anfiteatro *m* - 1. CIN & TEATR circle - 2. [edificio] amphitheatre.
anfitrión, ona *m,f* host *(f* hostess).
ángel *m lit & fig* angel; ~ **custodio** *o* **de la guarda** guardian angel; **tener** ~ to have something special.
angelical *adj* angelic.
angina *f* (gen pl) [amigdalitis] sore throat; **tener** ~**s** to have a sore throat.
➡ **angina de pecho** *f* angina (pectoris).
anglicano, na *adj & m,f* Anglican.
anglosajón, ona *adj & m,f* Anglo-Saxon.

Angola Angola.

angora f [de conejo] angora; [de cabra] mohair.

angosto, ta adj culto narrow.

angostura f [bebida] angostura.

anguila f eel.

angula f elver.

angular adj angular.

◆ **gran angular** m FOT wide-angle lens.

ángulo m - 1. [gen] angle - 2. [rincón] corner.

anguloso, sa adj angular.

angustia f [aflicción] anxiety.

angustiar vt to distress.

◆ **angustiarse** vpr [agobiarse]: ~se (por) to get worried (about).

angustioso, sa adj [espera, momentos] anxious; [situación, noticia] distressing.

anhelante adj: ~ (por algo/hacer algo) longing (for sthg/to do sthg), desperate (for sthg/to do sthg).

anhelar vt to long o wish for; ~ hacer algo to long to do sthg.

anhelo m longing.

anhídrido m anhydride; ~ carbónico carbon dioxide.

anidar vi [pájaro] to nest.

anilla f ring.

anillo m [gen & ASTRON] ring; ~ de boda wedding ring.

ánima f (el) soul.

animación f - 1. [alegría] liveliness - 2. [bullicio] hustle and bustle, activity - 3. CIN animation.

animado, da adj - 1. [con buen ánimo] cheerful - 2. [divertido] lively - 3. CIN animated.

animador, ra m, f - 1. [en espectáculo] compere - 2. [en fiesta de niños] children's entertainer - 3. [en béisbol etc] cheerleader.

animadversión f animosity.

animal ◇ adj - 1. [reino, funciones] animal (antes de sust) - 2. fam [persona - basto] rough; [- ignorante] ignorant. ◇ mf fam fig [persona] animal, brute. ◇ m animal; ~ doméstico [de granja etc] domestic animal; [de compañía] pet; ~ de tiro draught animal.

animar vt - 1. [estimular] to encourage - 2. [alegrar - persona] to cheer up - 3. [avivar - fuego, diálogo, fiesta] to liven up; [comercio] to stimulate.

◆ **animarse** vpr - 1. [alegrarse - persona] to cheer up; [- fiesta etc] to liven up - 2. [decidir]: ~se (a hacer algo) to finally decide (to do sthg).

ánimo ◇ m - 1. [valor] courage - 2. [aliento] encouragement; dar ~s a alguien to encourage sb - 3. [humor] disposition. ◇ interj [para alentar]: ¡~! come on!

animoso, sa adj [valiente] courageous; [decidido] undaunted.

aniñado, da adj [comportamiento] childish; [voz, rostro] childlike.

aniquilar vt to annihilate, to wipe out.

anís (pl anises) m - 1. [grano] aniseed - 2. [licor] anisette.

aniversario m [gen] anniversary; [cumpleaños] birthday.

ano m anus.

anoche adv last night, yesterday evening; antes de ~ the night before last.

anochecer ◇ m dusk, nightfall; al ~ at dusk. ◇ v impers to get dark.

anodino, na adj [sin gracia] dull, insipid.

anomalía f anomaly.

anómalo, la adj anomalous.

anonadado, da adj [sorprendido] astonished, bewildered.

anonimato m anonymity; permanecer en el ~ to remain nameless.

anónimo, ma adj anonymous.

◆ **anónimo** m anonymous letter.

anorak (pl anoraks) m anorak.

anorexia f anorexia.

anormal adj [anómalo] abnormal.

anotación f [gen] note; [en registro] entry; ~ al margen marginal note.

anotar vt - 1. [apuntar] to note down, to make a note of - 2. [tantear] to notch up.

◆ **anotarse** vpr [matricularse] to enrol.

anquilosamiento m - 1. [estancamiento] stagnation - 2. MED paralysis.

anquilosarse vpr - 1. [estancarse] to stagnate - 2. MED to become paralysed.

ansia f (el) - 1. [afán]: ~ de longing o yearning for - 2. [ansiedad] anxiousness; [angustia] anguish; comer con ~ to eat ravenously.

ansiar vt: ~ hacer algo to long o be desperate to do sthg.

ansiedad f - 1. [inquietud] anxiety; con ~ anxiously - 2. PSICOL nervous tension.

ansioso, sa adj [impaciente] impatient; estar ~ por o de hacer algo to be impatient to do sthg.

antagónico, ca adj antagonistic.

antagonista mf opponent.

antaño adv in days gone by.

antártico, ca adj Antarctic.

◆ **Antártico** m: el Antártico the Antarctic; el océano Glacial Antártico the Antarctic Ocean.

Antártida f: la ~ the Antarctic.

ante[1] m - 1. [piel] suede - 2. [animal] elk, moose.

ante[2] prep - 1. [delante de, en presencia de] before - 2. [frente a - hecho, circunstancia] in the face of.

ante todo *loc adv* - 1. [sobre todo] above all - 2. [en primer lugar] first of all.

anteanoche *adv* the night before last.

anteayer *adv* the day before yesterday.

antebrazo *m* forearm.

antecedente ◇ *adj* preceding, previous. ◇ *m* [precedente] precedent.

antecedentes *mpl* [de persona] record *(sg)*; [de asunto] background *(sg)*; **poner a alguien en ~s de** [informar] to fill sb in on; **una persona sin ~s** a person with a clean record.

anteceder *vt* to come before, to precede.

antecesor, ra *m,f* [predecesor] predecessor.

antedicho, cha *adj* aforementioned.

antelación *f:* **con ~** in advance, beforehand; **con dos horas de ~** two hours in advance.

antemano

de antemano *loc adv* beforehand, in advance.

antena *f* - 1. RADIO & TV aerial *UK*, antenna *US*; **~ parabólica** satellite dish - 2. ZOOL antenna.

anteojos *mpl Amér* glasses.

antepasado, da *m,f* ancestor.

antepenúltimo, ma *adj* & *m,f* last but two.

anteponer *vt:* **~ algo a algo** to put sthg before sthg.

anterior *adj* - 1. [previo]: **~ (a)** previous (to); **el día ~** the day before - 2. [delantero] front *(antes de sust)*.

anterioridad *f:* **con ~** beforehand; **con ~ a** before, prior to.

anteriormente *adv* previously.

antes *adv* - 1. [gen] before; **no importa si venís ~** it doesn't matter if you come earlier; **ya no nado como ~** I can't swim as I used to; **lo ~ posible** as soon as possible; **mi coche de ~** my old car - 2. [primero] first; **esta señora está ~** this lady is first - 3. [expresa preferencia]: **~ ... que** rather ... than; **prefiero la sierra ~ que el mar** I like the mountains better than the sea; **iría a la cárcel ~ que mentir** I'd rather go to prison than lie.

antes de *loc prep* before; **~ de hacer algo** before doing sthg.

antes (de) que *loc conj* before; **~ (de) que llegarais** before you arrived.

antesala *f* anteroom; **estar en la ~ de** *fig* to be on the verge of.

antiadherente *adj* non-stick.

antiaéreo, a *adj* anti-aircraft.

antibala, antibalas *adj inv* bullet-proof.

antibiótico, ca *adj* antibiotic.

antibiótico *m* antibiotic.

anticiclón *m* anticyclone.

anticipación *f* earliness; **con ~** in advance; **con un mes de ~** a month in advance; **con ~ a** prior to.

anticipado, da *adj* [elecciones] early; [pago] advance; **por ~** in advance.

anticipar *vt* - 1. [prever] to anticipate - 2. [adelantar] to bring forward - 3. [dinero] to pay in advance.

anticiparse *vpr* - 1. [suceder antes] to arrive early; **se anticipó a su tiempo** he was ahead of his time - 2. [adelantarse]: **~se a alguien** to beat sb to it.

anticipo *m* [de dinero] advance.

anticonceptivo, va *adj* contraceptive.

anticonceptivo *m* contraceptive.

anticongelante *adj* & *m* antifreeze.

anticonstitucional *adj* unconstitutional.

anticorrosivo, va *adj* anticorrosive.

anticuado, da *adj* old-fashioned.

anticuario, ria *m,f* [comerciante] antique dealer; [experto] antiquarian.

anticucho *m Andes* kebab.

anticuerpo *m* antibody.

antidepresivo, va *adj* antidepressant.

antidepresivo *m* antidepressant (drug).

antidisturbios *mpl* [policía] riot police.

antidopaje *m* doping tests *(pl)*.

antidoping [anti'ðopin] *adj* doping *(antes de sust)*.

antídoto *m* antidote.

antier *adv Amér fam* the day before yesterday.

antiestético, ca *adj* unsightly.

antifaz *m* mask.

antigás *adj inv* gas *(antes de sust)*.

antigualla *f despec* [cosa] museum piece; [persona] old fogey, old fossil.

antiguamente *adv* [hace mucho] long ago; [previamente] formerly.

antigubernamental *adj* anti-government.

antigüedad *f* - 1. [gen] antiquity - 2. [veteranía] seniority.

antigüedades *fpl* [objetos] antiques; **tienda de ~es** antique shop.

antiguo, gua *adj* - 1. [viejo] old; [inmemorial] ancient - 2. [anterior, previo] former.

antihéroe *m* antihero.

antihigiénico, ca *adj* unhygienic.

antihistamínico *m* antihistamine.

antiinflamatorio *m* anti-inflammatory drug.

antílope *m* antelope.

antinatural *adj* unnatural.

antiniebla ▷ **faro.**

antioxidante *m* rustproofing agent.

antipatía *f* dislike; **tener ~ a alguien** to dislike sb.

antipático, ca *adj* unpleasant.

antípodas *fpl*: las ~ the Antipodes.

antiquísimo, ma *adj* ancient.

antirreglamentario, ria *adj* DEP illegal, against the rules.

antirrobo *m* [en coche] antitheft device; [en edificio] burglar alarm.

antisemita *adj* anti-Semitic.

antiséptico, ca *adj* antiseptic.

➡ **antiséptico** *m* antiseptic.

antiterrorista *adj* anti-terrorist.

antítesis *f inv* antithesis.

antitetánico, ca *adj* anti-tetanus *(antes de sust)*.

antivirus *m inv* INFORM antivirus system.

antojarse *vpr* **- 1.** [capricho]: se le antojaron esos zapatos he fancied those shoes; se le ha antojado ir al cine he felt like going to the cinema; cuando se me antoje when I feel like it **- 2.** [posibilidad]: se me antoja que ... I have a feeling that ...

antojitos *mpl Méx* snacks, appetizers.

antojo *m* **- 1.** [capricho] whim; [de embarazada] craving; a mi/tu *etc* ~ my/ your *etc* (own) way **- 2.** [en la piel] birthmark.

antología *f* anthology.

antónimo *m* antonym.

antonomasia *f*: por ~ par excellence.

antorcha *f* torch.

antracita *f* anthracite.

antro *m despec* dive, dump.

antropófago, ga *m,f* cannibal.

antropología *f* anthropology.

anual *adj* annual.

anualidad *f* annuity, yearly payment.

anuario *m* yearbook.

anudar *vt* to knot, to tie in a knot.

anulación *f* [cancelación] cancellation; [de ley] repeal; [de matrimonio, contrato] annulment.

anular *vt* **- 1.** [cancelar - gen] to cancel; [- ley] to repeal; [- matrimonio, contrato] to annul **- 2.** DEP to call off; [- gol] to disallow; [- resultado] to declare void.

anunciación *f* announcement.

➡ **Anunciación** *f* RELIG Annunciation.

anunciante *mf* advertiser.

anunciar *vt* **- 1.** [notificar] to announce **- 2.** [hacer publicidad de] to advertise **- 3.** [presagiar] to herald.

➡ **anunciarse** *vpr*: ~se en to advertise in, to put an advert in.

anuncio *m* **- 1.** [notificación] announcement; [cartel, aviso] notice; [póster] poster **- 2.**: ~ (publicitario) advertisement, advert; ~s por palabras classified adverts **- 3.** [presagio] sign, herald.

anverso *m* [de moneda] head, obverse; [de hoja] front.

anzuelo *m* [para pescar] (fish) hook.

añadido, da *adj*: ~ (a) added (to).

añadidura *f* addition; por ~ in addition, what is more.

añadir *vt* to add.

añejo, ja *adj* **- 1.** [vino, licor] mature; [tocino] cured **- 2.** [costumbre] age-old.

añicos *mpl*: hacer *o* hacerse ~ to shatter.

añil *adj & m* [color] indigo.

año *m* year; en el ~ 1939 in 1939; los ~s 30 the thirties; ~ académico/escolar/fiscal academic/school/tax year; ~ bisiesto/solar leap/solar year; ~ nuevo New Year; ¡Feliz Año Nuevo! Happy New Year!

➡ **años** *mpl* [edad] age *(sg)*; ¿cuántos ~s tienes? — tengo 17 ~s how old are you? — I'm 17 (years old); los de 25 ~s the 25-year-olds; cumplir ~s to have one's birthday; cumplo ~s el 25 it's my birthday on the 25th.

añoranza *f*: ~ (de) [gen] nostalgia (for); [hogar, patria] homesickness (for).

añorar *vt* to miss.

apabullar *vt* to overwhelm.

apacentar *vt* to graze.

apacible *adj* [gen] mild, gentle; [lugar, ambiente] pleasant.

apaciguar *vt* **- 1.** [tranquilizar] to calm down **- 2.** [aplacar - dolor etc] to soothe.

➡ **apaciguarse** *vpr* **- 1.** [tranquilizarse] to calm down **- 2.** [aplacarse - dolor etc] to abate.

apadrinar *vt* **- 1.** [niño] to act as a godparent to **- 2.** [artista] to sponsor.

apagado, da *adj* **- 1.** [luz, fuego] out; [aparato] off **- 2.** [color, persona] subdued **- 3.** [sonido] muffled; [voz] quiet.

apagar *vt* **- 1.** [extinguir - fuego] to put out; [- luz] to put off; [- vela] to extinguish **- 2.** [desconectar] to turn *o* switch off **- 3.** [aplacar - sed] to quench **- 4.** [rebajar] to soften; [- sonido] to muffle.

➡ **apagarse** *vpr* [extinguirse - fuego, vela, luz] to go out; [- dolor, ilusión, rencor] to die down; [- sonido] to die away.

apagón *m* power cut.

apaisado, da *adj* oblong.

apalabrar *vt* [concertar] to make a verbal agreement regarding; [contratar] to engage on the basis of a verbal agreement.

apalancar *vt* [para abrir] to lever open; [para mover] to lever.

apalear *vt* to beat up.

apañado, da *adj fam* [hábil, mañoso] clever, resourceful.

apañar *vt fam* **- 1.** [reparar] to mend **- 2.** [amañar] to fix, to arrange.

➡ **apañarse** *vpr fam* to cope, to manage; **apañárselas (para hacer algo)** to manage (to do sthg).

apaño *m fam* **- 1.** [reparación] patch **- 2.** [chanchullo] fix, shady deal **- 3.** [acuerdo] compromise.

apapachar *vt Méx* [mimar] to cuddle; [consentir] to spoil.

apapacho *m Méx* cuddle.

aparador *m* [mueble] sideboard.

aparato *m* **- 1.** [máquina] machine; [de laboratorio] apparatus *(U)*; [electrodoméstico] appliance; **~ de radio** radio; **~ de televisión** television set **- 2.** [dispositivo] device **- 3.** [teléfono]: **¿quién está al ~?** who's speaking? **- 4.** [MED - prótesis] aid; [- para dientes] brace **- 5.** ANAT system **- 6.** POLÍT machinery **- 7.** [ostentación] pomp, ostentation.

aparatoso, sa *adj* **- 1.** [ostentoso] ostentatious, showy **- 2.** [espectacular] spectacular.

aparcamiento *m* **- 1.** [acción] parking **- 2.** [parking] car park *UK*, parking lot *US*; [hueco] parking place.

aparcar ◇ *vt* [estacionar] to park. ◇ *vi* [estacionar] to park.

aparcero, ra *m,f* sharecropper.

aparear *vt* [animales] to mate.

➡ **aparearse** *vpr* [animales] to mate.

aparecer *vi* **- 1.** [gen] to appear **- 2.** [acudir]: **~ por (un lugar)** to turn up at (a place) **- 3.** [ser encontrado] to turn up.

aparejado, da *adj*: **llevar ~** [acarrear] to entail.

aparejador, ra *m,f* quantity surveyor.

aparejo *m* **- 1.** [de caballerías] harness **- 2.** MEC block and tackle **- 3.** NÁUT rigging.

➡ **aparejos** *mpl* equipment *(U)*; [de pesca] tackle *(U)*.

aparentar ◇ *vt* **- 1.** [fingir] to feign **- 2.** [edad] to look. ◇ *vi* [presumir] to show off.

aparente *adj* [falso, supuesto] apparent.

aparición *f* **- 1.** [gen] appearance **- 2.** [de ser sobrenatural] apparition.

apariencia *f* [aspecto] appearance; **guardar las ~s** to keep up appearances; **las ~s engañan** appearances can be deceptive.

apartado, da *adj* **- 1.** [separado]: **~ de** away from **- 2.** [alejado] remote.

➡ **apartado** *m* [párrafo] paragraph; [sección] section.

➡ **apartado de correos** *m* PO Box.

apartamento *m* apartment, flat *UK*.

apartar *vt* **- 1.** [alejar] to move away; [quitar] to remove **- 2.** [separar] to separate **- 3.** [escoger] to take, to select.

➡ **apartarse** *vpr* **- 1.** [hacerse a un lado] to move to one side, to move out of the way **- 2.** [separarse] to separate; **~se de** [gen] to

move away from; [tema] to get away from; [mundo, sociedad] to cut o.s. off from.

aparte ◇ *adv* **- 1.** [en otro lugar, a un lado] aside, to one side; **bromas ~** joking apart; **dejar algo ~** to leave sthg aside; **poner algo ~** to put sthg aside; **impuestos ~** before tax **- 2.** [además] besides; **~ de fea ...** besides being ugly ... **- 3.** [por separado] separately. ◇ *m* **- 1.** [párrafo] new paragraph **- 2.** TEATR aside.

➡ **aparte de** *loc prep* [excepto] apart from, except from.

apasionado, da ◇ *adj* passionate. ◇ *m,f* lover, enthusiast.

apasionante *adj* fascinating.

apasionar *vt* to fascinate; **le apasiona la música** he's mad about music.

➡ **apasionarse** *vpr* to get excited.

apatía *f* apathy.

apático, ca *adj* apathetic.

apátrida *adj* stateless.

apdo. *abrev de* **apartado**.

apeadero *m* [de tren] halt.

apear *vt* [bajar] to take down.

➡ **apearse** *vpr* [bajarse]: **~se (de)** [tren] to alight (from), to get off; [coche] to get out (of); [caballo] to dismount (from).

apechugar *vi*: **~ con** to put up with, to live with.

apedrear *vt* [persona] to stone; [cosa] to throw stones at.

apegarse *vpr*: **~ a** to become fond of *o* attached to.

apego *m* fondness, attachment; **tener/tomar ~ a** to be/become fond of.

apelación *f* appeal.

apelar *vi* **- 1.** DER to (lodge an) appeal; **~ ante/contra** to appeal to/against **- 2.** [recurrir]: **~ a** [persona] to go to; [sentido común, bondad] to appeal to; [violencia] to resort to.

apelativo *m* name.

apellidarse *vpr*: **se apellida Suárez** her surname is Suárez.

apellido *m* surname.

apelmazar *vt* **- 1.** [jersey] to shrink **- 2.** [arroz, bizcocho] to make stodgy.

➡ **apelmazarse** *vpr* **- 1.** [jersey] to shrink **- 2.** [arroz, bizcocho] to go stodgy.

apelotonar *vt* to bundle up.

➡ **apelotonarse** *vpr* [gente] to crowd together.

apenado, da *adj Andes, CAm, Carib, Méx* [avergonzado] ashamed, embarrassed.

apenar *vt* to sadden.

apenas *adv* **- 1.** [casi no] scarcely, hardly; **~ me puedo mover** I can hardly move **- 2.** [tan sólo] only; **~ hace dos minutos** only two minutes ago **- 3.** [tan pronto como] as soon as; ~ llegó, sonó el teléfono no sooner had he arrived than the phone rang.

apéndice *m* appendix.

apendicitis *f inv* appendicitis.

apercibir *vt* [amonestar] to reprimand, to give a warning to.

➭ **apercibirse de** *vpr* to notice.

aperitivo *m* [bebida] aperitif; [comida] appetizer.

apero *m* (*gen pl*) tool; ~s de labranza farming implements.

apertura *f* - **1.** [gen] opening; [de año académico, temporada] start - **2.** POLÍT [liberalización] liberalization (*especially that introduced in Spain by the Franco regime after 1970*).

aperturista *adj & mf* progressive.

apesadumbrar *vt* to weigh down.

➭ **apesadumbrarse** *vpr* to be weighed down.

apestar *vi:* ~ (a) to stink (of).

apetecer *vi:* ¿te apetece un café? do you fancy a coffee?; me apetece salir I feel like going out.

apetecible *adj* [comida] appetizing, tempting; [vacaciones etc] desirable.

apetito *m* appetite; abrir el ~ to whet one's appetite; perder el ~ to lose one's appetite; tener ~ to be hungry.

apetitoso, sa *adj* [comida] appetizing.

apiadar *vt* to earn the pity of.

➭ **apiadarse** *vpr* to show compassion; ~se de to take pity on.

ápice *m* - **1.** [pizca] iota; no ceder un ~ not to budge an inch - **2.** [punto culminante] peak, height.

apicultura *f* beekeeping.

apilar *vt* to pile up.

➭ **apilarse** *vpr* to pile up.

apiñar *vt* to pack *o* cram together.

➭ **apiñarse** *vpr* to crowd together; [para protegerse, por miedo] to huddle together.

apio *m* celery.

apisonadora *f* steamroller.

aplacar *vt* to placate; [hambre] to satisfy; [sed] to quench.

➭ **aplacarse** *vpr* to calm down; [dolor] to abate.

aplanar *vt* to level.

aplastante *adj fig* [apabullante] overwhelming, devastating.

aplastar *vt* - **1.** [por el peso] to flatten - **2.** [derrotar] to crush.

aplatanar *vt fam* to make listless.

aplaudir *vt & vi* to applaud.

aplauso *m* - **1.** [ovación] round of applause; ~s applause (*U*) - **2.** *fig* [alabanza] applause.

aplazamiento *m* postponement.

aplazar *vt* to postpone.

aplicación *f* [gen & INFORM] application.

aplicado, da *adj* [estudioso] diligent.

aplicar *vt* [gen] to apply; [nombre, calificativo] to give.

➭ **aplicarse** *vpr* [esmerarse]: ~se (en algo) to apply o.s. (to sthg).

aplique *m* wall lamp.

aplomo *m* composure; perder el ~ to lose one's composure.

apocado, da *adj* timid.

apocalipsis *m o f inv* calamity.

➭ **Apocalipsis** *m o f* Apocalypse.

apocarse *vpr* [intimidarse] to be frightened *o* scared; [humillarse] to humble o.s.

apodar *vt* to nickname.

apoderado, da *m, f* - **1.** [representante] (official) representative - **2.** TAUROM agent, manager.

apoderar *vt* [gen] to authorize, to empower; DER to grant power of attorney to.

➭ **apoderarse de** *vpr* - **1.** [adueñarse de] to seize - **2.** *fig* [dominar] to take hold of, to grip.

apodo *m* nickname.

apogeo *m fig* height, apogee; estar en (pleno) ~ to be at its height.

apolillar *vt* to eat holes in.

➭ **apolillarse** *vpr* to get moth-eaten.

apolítico, ca *adj* apolitical.

apología *f* apology, eulogy.

apoltronarse *vpr* - **1.** [apalancarse]: ~ (en) to become lazy *o* idle (in) - **2.** [acomodarse]: ~ en to lounge in.

apoplejía *f* apoplexy.

apoquinar *vt & vi fam* to fork out.

aporrear *vt* to bang.

aportación *f* [contribución] contribution.

aportar *vt* [contribuir con] to contribute.

aposentar *vt* to put up, to lodge.

➭ **aposentarse** *vpr* to take up lodgings.

aposento *m* - **1.** [habitación] room - **2.** [alojamiento] lodgings (*pl*).

apósito *m* dressing.

aposta, apostas *adv* on purpose, intentionally.

apostar ◇ *vt* - **1.** [jugarse] to bet - **2.** [emplazar] to post. ◇ *vi:* ~ (por) to bet (on).

➭ **apostarse** *vpr* [jugarse] to bet; ~se algo con alguien to bet sb sthg.

apostas = aposta.

apostilla *f* note.

apóstol *m lit & fig* apostle.

apóstrofo *m* GRAM apostrophe.

apoteósico, ca *adj* tremendous.

apoyar *vt* - **1.** [inclinar] to lean, to rest - **2.** *fig* [basar, respaldar] to support.

➭ **apoyarse** *vpr* - **1.** [sostenerse]: ~se en to lean on - **2.** *fig* [basarse]: ~se en [suj: tesis, conclusiones] to be based on, to rest on; [suj:

persona] to base one's arguments on - **3.** [respaldarse] to support one another.

apoyo *m lit & fig* support.

apreciable *adj* - **1.** [perceptible] appreciable, significant - **2.** *fig* [estimable] worthy.

apreciación *f* [consideración] appreciation; [estimación] evaluation.

apreciar *vt* - **1.** [valorar] to appreciate; [sopesar] to appraise, to evaluate - **2.** [sentir afecto por] to think highly of - **3.** [percibir] to tell, to make out.

aprecio *m* esteem.

aprehender *vt* [coger - persona] to apprehend; [- alijo, mercancía] to seize.

aprehensión *f* [de persona] arrest, capture; [de alijo, mercancía] seizure.

apremiante *adj* pressing, urgent.

apremiar ⋄ *vt* [meter prisa]: ~ **a alguien para que haga algo** to urge sb to do sthg. ⋄ *vi* [ser urgente] to be pressing.

apremio *m* [urgencia] urgency.

aprender ⋄ *vt* - **1.** [estudiar] to learn - **2.** [memorizar] to memorize. ⋄ *vi*: ~ **(a hacer algo)** to learn (to do sthg).

aprendiz, za *m,f* - **1.** [ayudante] apprentice, trainee - **2.** [novato] beginner.

aprendizaje *m* - **1.** [acción] learning - **2.** [tiempo, situación] apprenticeship.

aprensión *f*: ~ **(por)** [miedo] apprehension (about); [escrúpulo] squeamishness (about).

aprensivo, va *adj* - **1.** [miedoso] apprehensive - **2.** [hipocondríaco] hypochondriac.

apresar *vt* [suj: animal] to catch; [suj: persona] to capture.

aprestar *vt* - **1.** [preparar] to prepare, to get ready - **2.** [tela] to size.

◆ **aprestarse a** *vpr*: ~**se a hacer algo** to get ready to do sthg.

apresto *m* size.

apresurado, da *adj* hasty, hurried.

apresurar *vt* to hurry along, to speed up; ~ **a alguien para que haga algo** to try to make sb do sthg more quickly.

◆ **apresurarse** *vpr* to hurry.

apretado, da *adj* - **1.** [gen] tight; [triunfo] narrow; [esprint] close; [caligrafía] cramped - **2.** [apiñado] packed.

apretar ⋄ *vt* - **1.** [oprimir - botón, tecla] to press; [- gatillo] to pull, to squeeze; [- nudo, tuerca, cinturón] to tighten; **el zapato me aprieta** my shoe is pinching - **2.** [estrechar] to squeeze; [abrazar] to hug - **3.** [comprimir - ropa, objetos] to pack tight - **4.** [juntar - dientes] to grit; [- labios] to press together. ⋄ *vi* [calor, lluvia] to get worse, to intensify.

◆ **apretarse** *vpr* [agolparse] to crowd together; [acercarse] to squeeze up.

apretón *m* [estrechamiento] squeeze; ~ **de manos** handshake.

apretujar *vt* - **1.** [gen] to squash - **2.** [hacer una bola con] to screw up.

◆ **apretujarse** *vpr* [en banco, autobús] to squeeze together; [por frío] to huddle up.

apretujón *m fam* [abrazo] bearhug.

aprieto *m fig* fix, difficult situation; **poner en un** ~ **a alguien** to put sb in a difficult position; **verse** o **estar en un** ~ to be in a fix.

aprisa *adv* quickly.

aprisionar *vt* - **1.** [encarcelar] to imprison - **2.** [inmovilizar - atando, con camisa de fuerza] to strap down; [- suj: viga etc] to trap.

aprobación *f* approval.

aprobado, da *adj* [aceptado] approved.

◆ **aprobado** *m* EDUC pass.

aprobar *vt* - **1.** [proyecto, moción, medida] to approve; [ley] to pass - **2.** [comportamiento etc] to approve of - **3.** [examen, asignatura] to pass.

aprontarse *vpr* RP [prepararse] to get ready; **¡aprontate para cuando llegue tu papá!** just wait till your daddy gets here!

apropiación *f* [robo] theft.

apropiado, da *adj* suitable, appropriate.

apropiar *vt*: ~ **(a)** to adapt (to).

◆ **apropiarse de** *vpr lit & fig* to appropriate.

aprovechable *adj* usable.

aprovechado, da *adj* - **1.** [caradura]: **es muy** ~ he's always sponging off other people - **2.** [bien empleado - tiempo] well-spent; [- espacio] well-planned.

aprovechamiento *m* [utilización] use.

aprovechar ⋄ *vt* - **1.** [gen] to make the most of; [oferta, ocasión] to take advantage of; [conocimientos, experiencia] to use, to make use of - **2.** [lo inservible] to put to good use. ⋄ *vi* [ser provechoso] to be beneficial; **¡que aproveche!** enjoy your meal!

◆ **aprovecharse** *vpr*: ~**se (de)** to take advantage (of).

aprovisionamiento *m* supplying.

aproximación *f* - **1.** [acercamiento] approach - **2.** [en cálculo] approximation.

aproximadamente *adv* approximately.

aproximado, da *adj* approximate.

aproximar *vt* to move closer.

◆ **aproximarse** *vpr* to come closer.

aptitud *f* ability, aptitude; **tener** ~ **para algo** to have an aptitude for sthg.

apto, ta *adj* - **1.** [adecuado, conveniente]: ~ **(para)** suitable (for) - **2.** [capacitado - intelectualmente] capable, able; [- físicamente] fit - **3.** CIN: ~ **/no** ~ **para menores** suitable/unsuitable for children.

apuesta *f* bet.

apuesto, ta *adj* dashing.

apunado, da *adj Andes*: **estar** ~ to have altitude sickness.

apuntador, ra *m,f* prompter.

apuntalar *vt lit & fig* to underpin.

apuntar *vt* - **1.** [anotar] to make a note of, to note down; ~ **a alguien** [en lista] to put sb down - **2.** [dirigir - dedo] to point; [- arma] to aim; ~ **a alguien** [con el dedo] to point at sb; [con un arma] to aim at sb - **3.** TEATR to prompt - **4.** *fig* [indicar] to point out.

◆ **apuntarse** *vpr* - **1.** [en lista] to put one's name down; [en curso] to enrol - **2.** [participar]: ~**se (a hacer algo)** to join in (doing sthg).

apunte *m* [nota] note.

◆ **apuntes** *mpl* EDUC notes.

apuñalar *vt* to stab.

apurado, da *adj* - **1.** [necesitado] in need; ~ **de** short of - **2.** [avergonzado] embarrassed - **3.** [difícil] awkward.

apurar *vt* - **1.** [agotar] to finish off; [existencias, la paciencia] to exhaust - **2.** [meter prisa] to hurry - **3.** [preocupar] to trouble - **4.** [avergonzar] to embarrass.

◆ **apurarse** *vpr* - **1.** [preocuparse]: ~**se (por)** to worry (about) - **2.** [darse prisa] to hurry.

apuro *m* - **1.** [dificultad] fix, difficult situation; **estar en** ~**s** to be in a tight spot - **2.** [penuria] hardship *(U)* - **3.** [vergüenza] embarrassment; **me da** ~ **(decírselo)** I'm embarrassed (to tell her).

aquejado, da *adj*: ~ **de** suffering from.

aquejar *vt* to afflict.

aquel, aquella (*mpl* **aquellos,** *fpl* **aquellas**) *adj demos* that, (*pl*) those.

aquél, aquélla (*mpl* **aquéllos,** *fpl* **aquéllas**) *pron demos* - **1.** [ése] that (one), (*pl*) those (ones); **este cuadro me gusta pero** ~ **del fondo no** I like this picture, but I don't like that one at the back; ~ **fue mi último día en Londres** that was my last day in London - **2.** [nombrado antes] the former - **3.** [con oraciones relativas] whoever, anyone who; ~ **que quiera hablar que levante la mano** whoever wishes 0 anyone wishing to speak should raise their hand; **aquéllos que ...** those who ...

aquella ▷ **aquel.**

aquélla ▷ **aquél.**

aquello *pron demos (neutro)* that; ~ **de su mujer es una mentira** all that about his wife is a lie.

aquellos, aquellas ▷ **aquel.**

aquéllos, aquéllas ▷ **aquél.**

aquí *adv* - **1.** [gen] here; ~ **abajo/arriba** down/up here; ~ **dentro/fuera** in/out here; ~ **mismo** right here; **por** ~ over here - **2.** [ahora] now; **de** ~ **a mañana** between now and tomorrow; **de** ~ **a poco** shortly,

soon; **de** ~ **a un mes** a month from now, in a month.

ara *f(el)* [altar] altar.

◆ **en aras de** *loc prep culto* for the sake of.

árabe ◇ *adj* Arab, Arabian. ◇ *mf* [persona] Arab. ◇ *m* [lengua] Arabic.

Arabia Saudí, Arabia Saudita Saudi Arabia.

arábigo, ga *adj* - **1.** [de Arabia] Arab, Arabian - **2.** [numeración] Arabic.

arado *m* plough.

arancel *m* tariff.

arándano *m* bilberry, blueberry *US*.

arandela *f* TECN washer.

araña *f* - **1.** [animal] spider - **2.** [lámpara] chandelier.

arañar *vt* [gen] to scratch.

arañazo *m* scratch.

arar *vt* to plough.

araucano, na *adj* Araucanian.

arbitraje *m* - **1.** [DEP - en fútbol etc] refereeing; [- en tenis, críquet] umpiring - **2.** DER arbitration.

arbitrar ◇ *vt* - **1.** [DEP - en fútbol etc] to referee; [- en tenis, críquet] to umpire - **2.** DER to arbitrate. ◇ *vi* - **1.** [DEP - en fútbol etc] to referee; [- en tenis, críquet] to umpire - **2.** DER to arbitrate.

arbitrariedad *f* [cualidad] arbitrariness.

arbitrario, ria *adj* arbitrary.

arbitrio *m* [decisión] judgment.

árbitro *m* - **1.** [DEP - en fútbol etc] referee; ~ **asistente** assistant referee; [- en tenis, críquet] umpire - **2.** DER arbitrator.

árbol *m* - **1.** BOT tree - **2.** TECN shaft; ~ **de levas** camshaft - **3.** NÁUT mast.

◆ **árbol genealógico** *m* family tree.

arboleda *f* grove.

arbusto *m* bush, shrub.

arca *f(el)* [arcón] chest.

◆ **arcas** *fpl* coffers; ~**s públicas** Treasury *(sg)*.

arcada *f* - **1.** (*gen pl*) [de estómago] retching *(U)*; **me dieron** ~**s** I retched - **2.** [ARQUIT - arcos] arcade; [- de puente] arch.

arce *m* maple.

arcén *m* [de autopista] hard shoulder *UK*, shoulder *US*; [de carretera] verge.

archiconocido, da *adj fam* very well-known.

archiduque, quesa *m,f* archduke (*f* archduchess).

archipiélago *m* archipelago.

archivador, ra *m,f* archivist.

◆ **archivador** *m* filing cabinet.

archivar *vt* [guardar - documento, fichero etc] to file.

archivo *m* - **1.** [lugar] archive; [documentos] archives (*pl*); **imágenes de** ~ TV library

pictures - 2. [informe, ficha] file **- 3.** INFORM file.

arcilla *f* clay.

arco *m* **- 1.** GEOM arc **- 2.** ARQUIT arch; ~ **de herradura** horseshoe arch; ~ **triunfal** o **de triunfo** triumphal arch **- 3.** DEP, MIL & MÚS bow.

➡ **arco iris** *m* rainbow.

arcón *m* large chest.

arder *vi* to burn; [sin llama] to smoulder; ~ **de** *fig* to burn with; **está que arde** [persona] he's fuming; [reunión] it's getting pretty heated.

ardid *m* ruse, trick.

ardiente *adj* [gen] burning; [líquido] scalding; [admirador, defensor] ardent.

ardilla *f* squirrel.

ardor *m* **- 1.** [quemazón] burning (sensation); ~ **de estómago** heartburn **- 2.** *fig* [entusiasmo] fervour.

arduo, dua *adj* arduous.

área *f (el)* **- 1.** [gen] area; ~ **metropolitana / de servicio** metropolitan/service area **- 2.** DEP : ~ **(de castigo** o **penalti)** (penalty) area.

arena *f* **- 1.** [de playa etc] sand; ~**s movedizas** quicksand *(U)* **- 2.** [para luchar] arena **- 3.** TAUROM bullring.

arenal *m* sandy ground *(U)*.

arenga *f* harangue.

arenilla *f* [polvo] dust.

arenoso, sa *adj* sandy.

arenque *m* herring.

arepa *f Carib, Col pancake made of maize flour.*

aretes *mpl Andes, Méx* earrings.

argamasa *f* mortar.

Argel Algiers.

Argelia Algeria.

Argentina Argentina.

argentino, na *adj & m,f* Argentinian.

argolla *f* **- 1.** [aro] (large) ring **- 2.** *Andes, Méx* [alianza] wedding ring.

argot *m* **- 1.** [popular] slang **- 2.** [técnico] jargon.

argucia *f* sophism.

argüir ◇ *vt culto* **- 1.** [argumentar] to argue **- 2.** [demostrar] to prove, to demonstrate. ◇ *vi* [argumentar] to argue.

argumentación *f* line of argument.

argumentar *vt* **- 1.** [teoría, opinión] to argue **- 2.** [razones, excusas] to allege.

argumento *m* **- 1.** [razonamiento] argument **- 2.** [trama] plot.

aria *f* MÚS aria.

aridez *f* [gen] dryness; [de zona, clima] aridity.

árido, da *adj* [gen] dry; [zona, clima] arid.

➡ **áridos** *mpl* dry goods.

Aries ◇ *m* [zodiaco] Aries. ◇ *mf* [persona] Aries.

ariete *m* HIST & MIL battering ram.

ario, ria *adj & m,f* Aryan.

arisco, ca *adj* surly.

arista *f* edge.

aristocracia *f* aristocracy.

aristócrata *mf* aristocrat.

aritmético, ca *adj* arithmetic.

➡ **aritmética** *f* arithmetic.

arma *f (el)* **- 1.** [instrumento] arm, weapon; ~ **blanca** blade, weapon with a sharp blade; ~ **de fuego** firearm; ~ **homicida** murder weapon **- 2.** *fig* [medio] weapon.

armada ➪ **armado.**

armadillo *m* armadillo.

armado, da *adj* **- 1.** [con armas] armed **- 2.** [con armazón] reinforced.

➡ **armada** *f* [marina] navy; [escuadra] fleet.

armador, ra *m,f* shipowner.

armadura *f* **- 1.** [de barco, tejado] framework; [de gafas] frame **- 2.** [de guerrero] armour.

armamentista, armamentístico, ca *adj* arms *(antes de sust).*

armamento *m* [armas] arms *(pl).*

armar *vt* **- 1.** [montar - mueble etc] to assemble; [- tienda] to pitch **- 2.** [ejército, personas] to arm **- 3.** *fam fig* [provocar] to cause; ~ **la** *fam* to cause trouble.

➡ **armarse** *vpr* **- 1.** [con armas] to arm o.s. **- 2.** [prepararse] : ~**se de** [valor, paciencia] to summon up **- 3.** *loc* : **se armó la gorda** o **la de San Quintín** o **la de Dios es Cristo** *fam* all hell broke loose.

armario *m* [para objetos] cupboard, closet *US*; [para ropa] wardrobe *UK*, closet *US*; ~ **empotrado** fitted cupboard/wardrobe.

armatoste *m* [mueble, objeto] unwieldy object; [máquina] contraption.

armazón *f* [gen] framework, frame; [de avión, coche] chassis; [de edificio] skeleton.

armería *f* **- 1.** [museo] military o war museum **- 2.** [depósito] armoury **- 3.** [tienda] gunsmith's (shop).

armiño *m* [piel] ermine; [animal] stoat.

armisticio *m* armistice.

armonía *f* harmony.

armónico, ca *adj* harmonic.

➡ **armónica** *f* harmonica.

armonioso, sa *adj* harmonious.

armonizar ◇ *vt* **- 1.** [concordar] to match **- 2.** MÚS to harmonize. ◇ *vi* [concordar] : ~ **con** to match.

arnés *m* armour.

➡ **arneses** *mpl* [de animales] harness *(U).*

aro *m* **- 1.** [círculo] hoop; TECN ring; **los** ~**s olímpicos** the Olympic rings **- 2.** *Amér* [pendiente] earring.

aroma *m* [gen] aroma; [de vino] bouquet; CULIN flavouring.

aromático, ca *adj* aromatic.

arpa *f (el)* harp.

arpía *f fig* [mujer] old hag.

arpillera *f* sackcloth, hessian.

arpón *m* harpoon.

arquear *vt* [gen] to bend; [cejas, espalda, lomo] to arch.

✦ **arquearse** *vpr* to bend.

arqueología *f* archeology.

arqueólogo, ga *m,f* archeologist.

arquero *m* - 1. DEP & MIL archer - 2. *Amér* [portero de fútbol] goalkeeper.

arquetipo *m* archetype.

arquitecto, ta *m,f* architect.

arquitectura *f* lit & fig architecture.

arrabal *m* [barrio pobre] slum *(on city outskirts)*; [barrio periférico] outlying district.

arrabalero, ra *adj* - 1. [periférico] outlying - 2. [barriobajero] rough, coarse.

arracimarse *vpr* to cluster together.

arraigado, da *adj* [costumbre, idea] deeply rooted; [persona] established.

arraigar *vi* lit & fig to take root.

✦ **arraigarse** *vpr* [establecerse] to settle down.

arraigo *m* roots *(pl)*; **tener mucho** ~ to be deeply rooted.

arrancar ⬦ *vt* - 1. [desarraigar - árbol] to uproot; [- malas hierbas, flor] to pull up - 2. [quitar, separar] to tear *o* rip off; [cable, página, pelo] to tear out; [cartel, cortinas] to tear down; [muela] to pull out, to extract; [ojos] to gouge out - 3. [arrebatar]: ~ **algo a alguien** to grab *o* snatch sthg from sb - 4. AUTOM & TECN to start; INFORM to start up - 5. *fig* [obtener]: ~ **algo a alguien** [confesión, promesa, secreto] to extract sthg from sb; [sonrisa, dinero, ovación] to get sthg out of sb; [suspiro, carcajada] to bring sthg from sb. ⬦ *vi* - 1. [partir] to set off - 2. [suj: máquina, coche] to start - 3. [provenir]: ~ **de** to stem from.

arranque *m* - 1. [comienzo] start - 2. AUTOM starter motor - 3. *fig* [arrebato] fit.

arrasar *vt* to destroy, to devastate.

arrastrar ⬦ *vt* - 1. [gen] to drag *o* pull along; [pies] to drag; [carro, vagón] to pull; [suj: corriente, aire] to carry away - 2. *fig* [convencer] to win over, to sway; ~ **a alguien a algo/a hacer algo** to lead sb into sthg/to do sthg; **dejarse** ~ **por algo/alguien** to allow o.s. to be swayed by sthg/sb - 3. *fig* [producir] to bring. ⬦ *vi* [rozar el suelo] to drag (along) the ground.

✦ **arrastrarse** *vpr* to crawl; *fig* to grovel.

arrastre *m* - 1. [acarreo] dragging - 2. [pesca] trawling - 3. *Esp fam*: **estar para el** ~ to

have had it - 4. *RP fam*: **tener** ~ to be popular with members of the opposite sex.

arre *interj* ¡ ~ ! gee up!

arrear *vt* - 1. [azuzar] to gee up - 2. *fam* [propinar] to give.

arrebatado, da *adj* - 1. [impetuoso] impulsive, impetuous - 2. [ruborizado] flushed - 3. [iracundo] enraged.

arrebatar *vt* - 1. [arrancar]: ~ **algo a alguien** to snatch sthg from sb - 2. *fig* [cautivar] to captivate.

✦ **arrebatarse** *vpr* [enfurecerse] to get furious.

arrebato *m* - 1. [arranque] fit, outburst; **un** ~ **de amor** a crush - 2. [furia] rage, fury.

arrebujar *vt* [amontonar] to bundle (up).

✦ **arrebujarse** *vpr* [arroparse] to wrap o.s. up.

arreciar *vi* - 1. [temporal etc] to get worse - 2. *fig* [críticas etc] to intensify.

arrecife *m* reef.

arreglado, da *adj* - 1. [reparado] fixed, repaired; [ropa] mended - 2. [ordenado] tidy - 3. [bien vestido] smart - 4. [solucionado] sorted out - 5. *fig* [precio] reasonable.

arreglar *vt* - 1. [reparar] to fix, to repair; [ropa] to mend - 2. [ordenar] to tidy (up) - 3. [solucionar] to sort out - 4. MÚS to arrange - 5. [acicalar] to smarten up; [cabello] to do.

✦ **arreglarse** *vpr* - 1. [apañarse]: ~**se (con algo)** to make do (with sthg); **arreglárselas (para hacer algo)** to manage (to do sthg) - 2. [acicalarse] to smarten up.

arreglo *m* - 1. [reparación] mending, repair; [de ropa] mending - 2. [solución] settlement - 3. MÚS (musical) arrangement - 4. [acuerdo] agreement; **llegar a un** ~ to reach agreement.

arrellanarse *vpr* to settle back.

arremangar, remangar *vt* to roll up.

✦ **arremangarse** *vpr* to roll up one's sleeves.

arremeter ✦ **arremeter contra** *vi* to attack.

arremetida *f* attack.

arremolinarse *vpr* - 1. *fig* [personas]: ~ **alrededor de** to crowd around - 2. [agua, hojas] to swirl (about).

arrendamiento, arriendo *m* - 1. [acción] renting, leasing - 2. [precio] rent, lease.

arrendar *vt* - 1. [dar en arriendo] to let, to lease - 2. [tomar en arriendo] to rent, to lease.

arrendatario, ria *m,f* leaseholder, tenant.

arreos *mpl* harness *(U)*.

arrepentido, da ⬦ *adj* repentant. ⬦ *m,f* POLÍT *person who renounces terrorist activities*.

arrepentimiento *m* regret, repentance.

arrepentirse *vpr* to repent; ~ **de algo/de haber hecho algo** to regret sthg/having done sthg.

arrestar *vt* to arrest.

arresto *m* [detención] arrest.

arriar *vt* to lower.

arriba ◇ *adv* - **1.** [posición - gen] above; *Amér* [encima de] above; [- en edificio] upstairs; **vive (en el piso de)** ~ she lives upstairs; **está aquí/allí** ~ it's up here/there; ~ **del todo** right at the top; **más** ~ further up - **2.** [dirección] up; **ve** ~ [en edificio] go upstairs; **hacia/para** ~ up, upwards; **calle/escaleras** ~ up the street/stairs; **río** ~ upstream - **3.** [en un texto] above; **el** ~ **mencionado** ... the above-mentioned ... - **4.** *loc*: **de** ~ **abajo** [cosa] from top to bottom; [persona] from head to toe o foot; **mirar a alguien de** ~ **abajo** [con desdén] to look sb up and down. ◇ *prep*: ~ **(de)** *Amér* [encima de] on top of. ◇ *interj*: **¡**~ ...**!** up (with) ...**!**; **¡**~ **los mineros!** up (with) the miners!; **¡**~ **las manos!** hands up!

◆ **arriba de** *loc prep* more than.

◆ **de arriba** *loc adj* top; **el estante de** ~ the top shelf.

arribar *vi* to arrive; NÁUT to reach port.

arribeño, ña *m,f Amér fam* highlander.

arribista *adj & m,f* arriviste.

arriendo *m* ⊳ **arrendamiento**.

arriesgado, da *adj* [peligroso] risky.

arriesgar *vt* to risk; [hipótesis] to venture, to suggest.

◆ **arriesgarse** *vpr* to take risks/a risk.

arrimar *vt* [acercar] to move o bring closer; ~ **algo a** [pared, mesa] to move sthg up against.

◆ **arrimarse** *vpr* [acercarse] to come closer o nearer; ~**se a algo** [acercándose] to move closer to sthg; [apoyándose] to lean on sthg.

arrinconar *vt* - **1.** [apartar] to put in a corner - **2.** [abandonar] to discard, to put away - **3.** *fig* [persona - dar de lado] to cold-shoulder; [- acorralar] to corner.

arrodillarse *vpr* to kneel down; *fig* to go down on one's knees, to grovel.

arrogancia *f* arrogance.

arrogante *adj* arrogant.

arrojar *vt* - **1.** [lanzar] to throw; [con violencia] to hurl, to fling - **2.** [despedir - humo] to send out; [- olor] to give off; [- lava] to spew out - **3.** [echar]: ~ **a alguien de** to throw sb out of - **4.** [resultado] to produce, to yield - **5.** [vomitar] to throw up.

◆ **arrojarse** *vpr* to hurl o.s.

arrojo *m* courage, fearlessness.

arrollador, ra *adj* overwhelming; [belleza, personalidad] dazzling.

arrollar *vt* - **1.** [atropellar] to knock down, to run over - **2.** [tirar - suj: agua, viento] to sweep away - **3.** [vencer] to crush.

arropar *vt* [con ropa] to wrap up; [en cama] to tuck up.

◆ **arroparse** *vpr* to wrap o.s. up.

arroyo *m* [riachuelo] stream.

arroz *m* rice; ~ **blanco** white rice; ~ **con leche** rice pudding.

arruga *f* - **1.** [en ropa, papel] crease - **2.** [en piel] wrinkle, line.

arrugar *vt* - **1.** [ropa, papel] to crease, to crumple - **2.** [piel] to wrinkle.

◆ **arrugarse** *vpr* - **1.** [ropa] to get creased - **2.** [piel] to get wrinkled.

arruinar *vt lit & fig* to ruin.

◆ **arruinarse** *vpr* to go bankrupt, to be ruined.

arrullar *vt* to lull to sleep.

◆ **arrullarse** *vpr* [animales] to coo.

arrumar *vt Andes, Ven* to pile up.

arsenal *m* - **1.** [de barcos] shipyard - **2.** [de armas] arsenal - **3.** [de cosas] array.

arsénico *m* arsenic.

art. (*abrev de* **artículo**) art.

arte *m o f (en sg gen m; en pl f)* - **1.** [gen] art; ~ **dramático** drama - **2.** [don] artistry - **3.** [astucia] artfulness, cunning; **malas** ~**s** trickery *(U)*.

◆ **artes** *fpl* arts; **bellas** ~**s** fine arts.

artefacto *m* [aparato] device; [máquina] machine.

arteria *f lit & fig* artery.

artesa *f* trough.

artesanal *adj* [hecho a mano] handmade.

artesanía *f* craftsmanship; **de** ~ [producto] handmade.

artesano, na *m,f* craftsman (*f* craftswoman).

ártico, ca *adj* arctic.

◆ **Ártico** *m*: **el Ártico** the Arctic; **el océano Glacial Ártico** the Arctic Ocean.

articulación *f* - **1.** ANAT & TECN joint - **2.** LING articulation.

articulado, da *adj* articulated.

articular *vt* [palabras, piezas] to articulate.

artículo *m* [gen] article; ~ **de fondo** editorial, leader; ~ **de primera necesidad** basic commodity.

artífice *mf fig* architect.

artificial *adj* artificial.

artificio *m fig* [falsedad] artifice; [artimaña] trick.

artificioso, sa *adj fig* [engañoso] deceptive.

artillería *f* artillery.

artillero *m* artilleryman.

artilugio *m* gadget, contrivance.

artimaña *f (gen pl)* trick, ruse.

artista *mf* - **1.** [gen] artist - **2.** [de espectáculos] artiste; ~ **de cine** movie actor (*f* actress).

artístico, ca *adj* artistic.

artritis *f inv* arthritis.

arzobispo *m* archbishop.

as *m* - 1. [carta, dado] ace - 2. [campeón]: **un ~ del volante** an ace driver.

asa *f (el)* handle.

asado, da ◇ *adj* roasted. ◇ *m* - 1. roast - 2. *Col, CSur* [barbacoa] barbecue.

asador *m* - 1. [aparato] roaster - 2. [varilla] spit.

asaduras *fpl* offal *(U)*; [de pollo, pavo] giblets.

asalariado, da ◇ *adj* wage-earning. ◇ *m,f* wage earner.

asalmonado, da *adj* salmon (pink).

asaltante *mf* [agresor] attacker; [atracador] robber.

asaltar *vt* - 1. [atacar] to attack; [castillo, ciudad etc] to storm - 2. [robar] to rob - 3. *fig* [suj: dudas etc] to assail.

asalto *m* - 1. [ataque] attack; [de castillo, ciudad] storming - 2. [robo] robbery - 3. DEP round.

asamblea *f* assembly; POLÍT mass meeting.

asar *vt* [alimentos - al horno] to bake; [- a la parrilla] to grill; [- en asador] to roast.

ascendencia *f* - 1. [linaje] descent - 2. [extracción social] extraction - 3. *fig* [influencia] ascendancy.

ascender ◇ *vi* - 1. [subir] to go up, to climb - 2. [aumentar, elevarse] to rise, to go up - 3. [en empleo, deportes]: ~ **(a)** to be promoted (to) - 4. [totalizar - precio etc]: ~ **a** to come *o* amount to. ◇ *vt* : ~ **a alguien (a)** to promote sb (to).

ascendiente *mf* [antepasado] ancestor.

ascensión *f* ascent.

◆ **Ascensión** *f* RELIG Ascension.

ascenso *m* - 1. [en empleo, deportes] promotion - 2. [escalada] ascent - 3. [de precios, temperaturas] rise.

ascensor *m* lift *UK*, elevator *US*.

ascético, ca *adj* ascetic.

asco *m* [sensación] revulsion; **siento ~** I feel sick; **¡qué ~ de tiempo!** what foul weather!; **me da ~** I find it disgusting; **¡qué ~!** how disgusting *o* revolting!; **hacer ~s a** to turn one's nose up at; **estar hecho un ~** *fam* [cosa] to be filthy; [persona] to be a real sight.

ascua *f (el)* ember.

aseado, da *adj* [limpio] clean; [arreglado] smart.

asear *vt* to clean.

◆ **asearse** *vpr* to get washed and dressed.

asediar *vt* to lay siege to; *fig* to pester, to badger.

asedio *m* siege; *fig* pestering, badgering.

asegurado, da *m,f* policy-holder.

asegurar *vt* - 1. [fijar] to secure - 2. [garantizar] to assure; **te lo aseguro** I assure you; ~ **a alguien que ...** to assure sb that ... - 3. COM : ~ **(contra)** to insure (against); ~ **algo en** [cantidad] to insure sthg for.

◆ **asegurarse** *vpr* [cerciorarse]: ~ **se de que ...** to make sure that ...

asentamiento *m* [campamento] settlement.

asentar *vt* - 1. [instalar - empresa, campamento] to set up; [- comunidad, pueblo] to settle - 2. [asegurar] to secure; [cimientos] to lay.

◆ **asentarse** *vpr* - 1. [instalarse] to settle down - 2. [sedimentarse] to settle.

asentir *vi* - 1. [estar conforme]: ~ **(a)** to agree (to) - 2. [afirmar con la cabeza] to nod.

aseo *m* [limpieza - acción] cleaning; [- cualidad] cleanliness.

◆ **aseos** *mpl* toilets *UK*, restroom *(sg) US*.

aséptico, ca *adj* MED aseptic.

asequible *adj* - 1. [accesible, comprensible] accessible - 2. [precio, producto] affordable.

aserradero *m* sawmill.

aserrar *vt* to saw.

asesinar *vt* to murder; [rey, jefe de estado] to assassinate.

asesinato *m* murder; [de rey, jefe de estado] assassination.

asesino, na *m,f* murderer (*f* murderess); [de rey, jefe de estado] assassin; ~ **en serie** serial killer.

asesor, ra *m,f* adviser; FIN consultant; ~ **fiscal** tax consultant.

asesorar *vt* to advise; FIN to provide with consultancy services.

◆ **asesorarse** *vpr* to seek advice; ~ **se de** to consult.

asesoría *f* [oficina] consultant's office.

asestar *vt* [golpe] to deal; [tiro] to fire.

aseveración *f* assertion.

asfaltado *m* [acción] asphalting, surfacing; [asfalto] asphalt, (road) surface.

asfalto *m* asphalt.

asfixia *f* asphyxiation, suffocation.

asfixiar *vt* [ahogar] to asphyxiate, to suffocate.

◆ **asfixiarse** *vpr* [ahogarse] to asphyxiate, to suffocate.

así ◇ *adv* [de este modo] in this way, like this; [de ese modo] in that way, like that; **era ~ de largo** it was this/that long; ~ **es/era/fue como ...** that is how ...; ~ ~ [no muy bien] so so; **algo ~** [algo parecido] something like that; ~ **es** [para asentir] that is correct, yes; **y ~ todos los días** and the same thing happens day after day; ~ **como** [también] as well as, and also; [tal como] just as, exactly as; ~ **no más** *Amér fam* [de repente] just like that. ◇ *conj* **-1.** [de modo que]: ~ **(es) que** so **- 2.** [aunque] although **- 3.** [tan pronto como]: ~ **que** as soon as **- 4.** *Amér* [aun si] even if. ◇ *adj inv* [como éste] like this; [como ése] like that.

➔ **así y todo, aun así** *loc adv* even so.

Asia Asia.

asiático, ca *adj & m,f* Asian, Asiatic.

asidero *m* [agarradero] handle.

asiduidad *f* frequency.

asiduo, dua *adj & m,f* regular.

asiento *m* [en casa, teatro] seat; **tomar** ~ to sit down.

asignación *f* **- 1.** [atribución] allocation **- 2.** [sueldo] salary.

asignar *vt* **- 1.** [atribuir]: ~ **algo a alguien** to assign *o* allocate sthg to sb **- 2.** [destinar]: ~ **a alguien** a to send sb to.

asignatura *f* EDUC subject.

asilado, da *m,f* person living in an old people's home, convalescent home etc.

asilo *m* **- 1.** [hospicio] home; ~ **de ancianos** old people's home **- 2.** *fig* [amparo] asylum; ~ **político** political asylum **- 3.** [hospedaje] accommodation.

asimilación *f* [gen & LING] assimilation.

asimilar *vt* [gen] to assimilate.

asimismo *adv* [también] also, as well; *(a principio de frase)* likewise.

asir *vt* to grasp, to take hold of.

asistencia *f* **- 1.** [presencia - acción] attendance; [- hecho] presence **- 2.** [ayuda] assistance; ~ **médica** medical attention; ~ **sanitaria** health care; ~ **técnica** technical assistance **- 3.** [afluencia] audience **- 4.** DEP assist.

asistenta *f* cleaning lady.

asistente *mf* **- 1.** [ayudante] assistant, helper; ~ **personal** INFORM personal digital assistant; ~ **social** social worker **- 2.** [presente] person present; **los** ~**s** the audience *(sg)*.

asistido, da *adj* AUTOM power *(antes de sust)*; INFORM computer-assisted.

asistir ◇ *vt* [ayudar] to attend to. ◇ *vi*: ~ **a** to attend, to go to.

asma *f(el)* asthma.

asno *m* *lit & fig* ass.

asociación *f* association; ~ **de padres de alumnos** parent-teacher association; ~ **de vecinos** residents' association.

asociado, da ◇ *adj* [miembro] associate. ◇ *m,f* [miembro] associate, partner.

asociar *vt* [relacionar] to associate.

➔ **asociarse** *vpr* to form a partnership.

asolar *vt* to devastate.

asomar ◇ *vi* [gen] to peep up; [del interior de algo] to peep out. ◇ *vt* to stick; ~ **la cabeza por la ventana** to stick one's head out of the window.

➔ **asomarse a** *vpr* [ventana] to stick one's head out of; [balcón] to come/go out onto.

asombrar *vt* [causar admiración] to amaze; [causar sorpresa] to surprise.

➔ **asombrarse** *vpr*: ~**se (de)** [sentir admiración] to be amazed (at); [sentir sorpresa] to be surprised (at).

asombro *m* [admiración] amazement; [sorpresa] surprise.

asombroso, sa *adj* [sensacional] amazing; [sorprendente] surprising.

asomo *m* [indicio] trace, hint; [de esperanza] glimmer.

aspa *f(el)* X-shaped cross; [de molino] arms *(pl)*.

aspaviento *m (gen pl)* furious gesticulations *(pl)*.

aspecto *m* **- 1.** [apariencia] appearance; **tener buen/mal** ~ [persona] to look well/awful; [cosa] to look nice/horrible **- 2.** [faceta] aspect; **en todos los** ~**s** in every respect.

aspereza *f* roughness; *fig* sourness.

áspero, ra *adj* **- 1.** [rugoso] rough **- 2.** *fig* [desagradable] sharp, sour.

aspersión *f* [de jardín] sprinkling; [de cultivos] spraying.

aspersor *m* [para jardín] sprinkler; [para cultivos] sprayer.

aspiración *f* **- 1.** [ambición & LING] aspiration **- 2.** [de aire - por una persona] breathing in; [- por una máquina] suction.

aspirador *m*, **aspiradora** *f* vacuum cleaner, hoover®; **pasar la** ~ to vacuum, to hoover.

aspirante *mf*: ~ **(a)** candidate (for); [en deportes, concursos] contender (for).

aspirar ◇ *vt* [aire - suj: persona] to breathe in, to inhale; [suj: máquina] to suck in. ◇ *vi*: ~ **a algo** [ansiar] to aspire to sthg.

aspirina® *f* aspirin.

asquear *vt* to disgust, to make sick.

asqueroso, sa *adj* disgusting, revolting.

asta *f(el)* **- 1.** [de bandera] flagpole, mast **- 2.** [de lanza] shaft; [de brocha] handle **- 3.** [de toro] horn.

asterisco *m* asterisk.

astigmatismo *m* astigmatism.

astilla *f* splinter.

astillero *m* shipyard.

astringente *adj* astringent.

astro *m* ASTRON heavenly body; *fig* star.

astrofísica *f* astrophysics *(U)*.

astrología *f* astrology.

astrólogo, ga *m,f* astrologer.

astronauta *mf* astronaut.

astronomía *f* astronomy.

astrónomo, ma *m,f* astronomer.

astroso, sa adj [andrajoso] shabby, ragged.

astucia f - **1.** [picardía] cunning, astuteness - **2.** (gen pl) [treta] cunning trick.

astuto, ta adj [ladino, tramposo] cunning; [sagaz, listo] astute.

asueto m break, rest; **unos días de** ~ a few days off.

asumir vt - **1.** [gen] to assume - **2.** [aceptar] to accept.

asunción f assumption.

➡ **Asunción** f: **la Asunción** RELIG the Assumption.

Asunción GEOGR Asunción.

asunto m - **1.** [tema - general] subject; [- específico] matter; [- de obra, libro] theme; ~**s a tratar** agenda (sg) - **2.** [cuestión, problema] issue - **3.** [negocio] affair, business (U); **no es** ~ **tuyo** it's none of your business.

➡ **asuntos** mpl POLÍT affairs; ~**s exteriores** foreign affairs.

asustado, da adj frightened, scared.

asustar vt to frighten, to scare.

➡ **asustarse** vpr: ~**se (de)** to be frightened o scared (of).

atacar vt [gen] to attack.

atadura f lit & fig tie.

atajar ◇ vi [acortar]: ~ **(por)** to take a short cut (through). ◇ vt [contener] to put a stop to; [hemorragia, inundación] to stem.

atajo m - **1.** [camino corto, medio rápido] short cut; **coger** o **tomar un** ~ to take a short cut - **2.** despec [panda] bunch.

atalaya f - **1.** [torre] watchtower - **2.** [altura] vantage point.

atañer vi - **1.** [concernir]: ~ **a** to concern - **2.** [corresponder]: ~ **a** to be the responsibility of.

ataque m - **1.** [gen & DEP] attack - **2.** fig [acceso] fit, bout; ~ **cardíaco** o **al corazón** heart attack; ~ **de nervios** nervous breakdown.

atar vt - **1.** [unir] to tie (up) - **2.** fig [constreñir] to tie down.

atardecer ◇ m dusk. ◇ v impers to get dark.

atareado, da adj busy.

atascar vt to block (up).

➡ **atascarse** vpr - **1.** [obstruirse] to get blocked up - **2.** fig [detenerse] to get stuck; [al hablar] to dry up.

atasco m - **1.** [obstrucción] blockage - **2.** AUTOM traffic jam.

ataúd m coffin.

ataviar vt [cosa] to deck out; [persona] to dress up.

➡ **ataviarse** vpr to dress up.

atavío m [indumentaria] attire (U).

atemorizar vt to frighten.

➡ **atemorizarse** vpr to get frightened.

Atenas Athens.

atenazar vt - **1.** [sujetar] to clench - **2.** fig [suj: dudas] to torment, to rack; [suj: miedo, nervios] to grip.

atención ◇ f - **1.** [interés] attention; **llamar la** ~ [atraer] to attract attention; **poner** o **prestar** ~ to pay attention; ~ **al cliente** customer service department; ~ **personalizada** personalized service; ~ **psiquiátrica** psychiatric treatment - **2.** [cortesía] attentiveness (U). ◇ interj: ¡ ~ ! [en aeropuerto, conferencia] your attention please!

➡ **atenciones** fpl attentions, attentiveness (U).

atender ◇ vt - **1.** [satisfacer - petición, ruego] to attend to; [- consejo, instrucciones] to heed; [- propuesta] to agree to - **2.** [cuidar de - necesitados, invitados] to look after; [- enfermo] to care for; [- cliente] to serve; ¿**le atienden?** are you being served? ◇ vi [estar atento]: ~ **(a)** to pay attention (to).

atenerse ➡ **atenerse a** vpr - **1.** [promesa, orden] to stick to; [ley, normas] to abide by - **2.** [consecuencias] to bear in mind.

atentado m: ~ **contra alguien** attempt on sb's life; ~ **contra algo** crime against sthg.

atentamente adv [en cartas] Yours sincerely o faithfully.

atentar vi: ~ **contra (la vida de) alguien** to make an attempt on sb's life; ~ **contra algo** [principio etc] to commit a crime against sthg.

atento, ta adj - **1.** [pendiente] attentive; **estar** ~ **a** [explicación, programa, lección] to pay attention to; [ruido, sonido] to listen out for; [acontecimientos, cambios, avances] to keep up with - **2.** [cortés] considerate, thoughtful.

atenuante m DER extenuating circumstance.

atenuar vt [gen] to diminish; [dolor] to ease; [luz] to filter.

ateo, a ◇ adj atheistic. ◇ m,f atheist.

aterciopelado, da adj velvety.

aterrador, ra adj terrifying.

aterrar vt to terrify.

aterrizaje m landing.

aterrizar vi [avión] to land.

aterrorizar vt to terrify; [suj: agresor] to terrorize.

atesorar vt [riquezas] to amass.

atestado m official report.

atestar vt - **1.** [llenar] to pack, to cram - **2.** DER to testify to.

atestiguar vt to testify to.

atiborrar vt to stuff full.

➡ **atiborrarse** vpr fam fig: ~**se (de)** to stuff one's face (with).

ático m [para vivir] penthouse; [desván] attic.

atinar vi [adivinar] to guess correctly; [dar

en el blanco] to hit the target; ~ **a hacer algo** to succeed in doing sthg; ~ **con** to hit upon.

atingencia f *Amér* [relación] connection.

atípico, ca *adj* atypical.

atisbar vt - **1.** [divisar, prever] to make out - **2.** [acechar] to observe, to spy on.

atisbo m *(gen pl)* trace, hint; [de esperanza] glimmer.

atizar vt - **1.** [fuego] to poke, to stir - **2.** *fam* [puñetazo, patada] to land, to deal.

atlántico, ca *adj* Atlantic.

→ **Atlántico** m: el (océano) Atlántico the Atlantic (Ocean).

atlas m *inv* atlas.

atleta mf athlete.

atlético, ca *adj* athletic.

atletismo m athletics (U).

atmósfera f lit & fig atmosphere.

atole m *CAm, Méx* drink made of corn meal.

atolladero m [apuro] fix, jam; **meter en/sacar de un** ~ **a alguien** to put sb in/get sb out of a tight spot.

atolondrado, da *adj* - **1.** [precipitado] hasty, disorganized - **2.** [aturdido] bewildered.

atómico, ca *adj* atomic; [central, armas] nuclear.

atomizador m atomizer, spray.

átomo m lit & fig atom; **ni un** ~ **de** without a trace of.

atónito, ta *adj* astonished, astounded.

atontado, da *adj* - **1.** [aturdido] dazed - **2.** [tonto] stupid.

atontar vt [aturdir] to daze.

atormentar vt to torture; fig to torment.

atornillar vt to screw.

atorón m *Méx* traffic jam.

atorrante *adj* *RP* [holgazán] lazy.

atosigar vt fig to harass.

atracador, ra m,f [de banco] armed robber; [en la calle] mugger.

atracar ⬦ vi NÁUT: ~ **(en)** to dock (at). ⬦ vt [banco] to rob; [persona] to mug.

→ **atracarse** vpr: ~**se de** to eat one's fill of.

atracción f - **1.** [gen] attraction - **2.** [espectáculo] act - **3.** fig [centro de atención] centre of attention - **4.** *(gen pl)* [atracción de feria] fairground attraction.

atraco m robbery.

atracón m *fam* feast; **darse un** ~ to stuff one's face.

atractivo, va *adj* attractive.

→ **atractivo** m [de persona] attractiveness, charm; [de cosa] attraction.

atraer vt [gen] to attract.

atragantarse vpr: ~ **(con)** to choke (on).

atrancar vt - **1.** [cerrar] to bar - **2.** [obturar] to block.

→ **atrancarse** vpr - **1.** [atascarse] to get

blocked - **2.** fig [al hablar, escribir] to dry up.

atrapar vt [agarrar, alcanzar] to catch.

atrás *adv* - **1.** [detrás - posición] behind, at the back; [- movimiento] backwards; **quedarse** ~ fig to fall behind - **2.** [antes] earlier, before.

atrasado, da *adj* - **1.** [en el tiempo] delayed; [reloj] slow; [pago] overdue, late; [número, copia] back *(antes de sust)* - **2.** [en evolución, capacidad] backward.

atrasar ⬦ vt to put back. ⬦ vi to be slow.

→ **atrasarse** vpr - **1.** [demorarse] to be late - **2.** [quedarse atrás] to fall behind.

atraso m [de evolución] backwardness.

→ **atrasos** mpl *fam* arrears.

atravesar vt - **1.** [interponer] to put across - **2.** [cruzar] to cross - **3.** [perforar] to go through - **4.** fig [vivir] to go through.

→ **atravesarse** vpr [interponerse] to be in the way.

atrayente *adj* attractive.

atreverse vpr: ~ **(a hacer algo)** to dare (to do sthg); **se atreve con todo** he can tackle anything.

atrevido, da *adj* [osado] daring; [caradura] cheeky.

atrevimiento m - **1.** [osadía] daring - **2.** [insolencia] cheek.

atribución f - **1.** [imputación] attribution - **2.** [competencia] responsibility, duty.

atribuir vt [imputar]: ~ **algo a** to attribute sthg to.

→ **atribuirse** vpr [méritos] to claim for o.s.; [poderes] to assume; ~**se la responsibilidad** to claim responsibility.

atributo m attribute.

atril m [para libros] bookrest; MÚS music stand.

atrocidad f [crueldad] atrocity.

atropellado, da *adj* hasty.

atropellar vt - **1.** [suj: vehículo] to run over - **2.** fig [suj: persona] to trample on.

→ **atropellarse** vpr [al hablar] to trip over one's words.

atropello m - **1.** [por vehículo] running over - **2.** fig [moral] abuse.

atroz *adj* atrocious; [dolor] awful.

ATS *(abrev de* **ayudante técnico sanitario)** mf qualified nurse.

atte. *abrev de* **atentamente.**

atuendo m attire.

atún m tuna.

aturdido, da *adj* dazed.

aturdir vt [gen] to stun; [suj: alcohol] to fuddle; [suj: ruido, luz] to confuse, to bewilder.

audacia f [intrepidez] daring.

audaz *adj* [intrépido] daring.

audición f - **1.** [gen] hearing - **2.** MÚS & TEATR audition.

audiencia *f* - **1.** [público, recepción] audience; **índice de** ~ audience ratings - **2.** [DER - juicio] hearing; [- tribunal, edificio] court.

audífono *m* hearing aid.

audiovisual *adj* audiovisual.

auditivo, va *adj* ear *(antes de sust)*.

auditor, ra *m,f* FIN auditor.

auditorio *m* - **1.** [público] audience - **2.** [lugar] auditorium.

auge *m* [gen & ECON] boom.

augurar *vt* [suj: persona] to predict; [suj: suceso] to augur.

augurio *m* omen, sign.

aula *f* (el) [de escuela] classroom; [de universidad] lecture room.

aullar *vi* to howl.

aullido *m* howl.

aumentar ⬦ *vt* - **1.** [gen] to increase; [peso] to put on - **2.** [en óptica] to magnify - **3.** [sonido] to amplify. ⬦ *vi* to increase; [precios] to rise.

aumento *m* - **1.** [incremento] increase; [de sueldo, precios] rise; **ir en** ~ to be on the increase - **2.** [en óptica] magnification.

aun ⬦ *adv* even. ⬦ *conj*: ~ **estando cansado, lo hizo** even though he was tired, he did it; **ni** ~ **puesta de puntillas llega** she can't reach it, even on tiptoe; ~ **cuando** even though; ~ **así** even so.

aún *adv* [todavía] still; *(en negativas)* yet, still; **no ha llegado** ~ he hasn't arrived yet, he still hasn't arrived.

aunar *vt* to join, to pool.

◆ **aunarse** *vpr* [aliarse] to unite.

aunque *conj* - **1.** [a pesar de que] even though, although; [incluso si] even if - **2.** [pero] although.

aúpa *interj*: ¡~! [¡levántate!] get up!; ¡~ **el Atleti!** up the Athletic!

aupar *vt* to help up; *fig* [animar] to cheer on.

◆ **auparse** *vpr* to climb up.

aureola *f* - **1.** ASTRON & RELIG halo - **2.** *fig* [fama] aura.

auricular *m* [de teléfono] receiver.

◆ **auriculares** *mpl* [cascos] headphones.

aurora *f* first light of dawn.

auscultar *vt* to sound *(with a stethoscope)*.

ausencia *f* absence; **brillar por su** ~ to be conspicuous by one's/its absence.

ausentarse *vpr* to go away.

ausente ⬦ *adj* - **1.** [no presente] absent; **estará** ~ **todo el día** he'll be away all day - **2.** [distraído] absent-minded. ⬦ *mf* - **1.** [no presente]: **criticó a los** ~**s** he criticized the people who weren't there - **2.** DER missing person.

auspicio *m* [protección] protection; **bajo los** ~**s de** under the auspices of.

austeridad *f* austerity.

austero, ra *adj* [gen] austere.

austral ⬦ *adj* southern. ⬦ *m* [moneda] austral.

Australia Australia.

australiano, na *adj* & *m,f* Australian.

Austria Austria.

austríaco, ca *adj* & *m,f* Austrian.

autarquía *f* - **1.** POLÍT autarchy - **2.** ECON autarky.

auténtico, ca *adj* [gen] genuine; [piel, joyas] genuine, real; **un** ~ **imbécil** a real idiot; **es un tío** ~ he's a genuine bloke.

auto *m* - **1.** *fam* [coche] car; *CSur* [vehículo] car - **2.** DER judicial decree.

autoadhesivo, va *adj* self-adhesive.

autobiografía *f* autobiography.

autobús *m* bus.

autocar *m* coach.

autoconsumo *m*: **para** ~ for personal use.

autocontrol *m* self-control.

autóctono, na *adj* indigenous, native.

autodefensa *f* self-defence.

autodeterminación *f* self-determination.

autodidacta *adj* self-taught.

autoescuela *f* driving school.

autoestop, autostop *m* hitch-hiking; **hacer** ~ to hitch-hike.

autoestopista, autostopista *mf* hitch-hiker.

autógrafo *m* autograph.

autómata *m* *lit & fig* automaton.

automático, ca *adj* automatic.

◆ **automático** *m* [botón] press-stud.

automatización *f* automation.

automóvil *m* car *UK*, automobile *US*.

automovilismo *m* motoring; DEP motor racing.

automovilista *mf* motorist, driver.

automovilístico, ca *adj* motor *(antes de sust)*; DEP motor-racing *(antes de sust)*.

autonomía *f* [POLÍT - facultad] autonomy; [- territorio] autonomous region.

autonómico, ca *adj* autonomous.

autónomo, ma ⬦ *adj* - **1.** POLÍT autonomous - **2.** [trabajador] self-employed; [traductor, periodista] freelance. ⬦ *m,f* self-employed person; [traductor, periodista] freelance.

autopista *f* motorway *UK*, freeway *US*.

autopsia *f* autopsy, post-mortem.

autor, ra *m,f* - **1.** LITER author - **2.** [de crimen] perpetrator.

autoridad *f* - **1.** [gen] authority - **2.** [ley]: **la** ~ the authorities *(pl)*.

autoritario, ria *adj* & *m,f* authoritarian.

autorización *f* authorization.

autorizado, da *adj* -**1.** [permitido] author-ized -**2.** [digno de crédito] authoritative.

autorizar *vt* -**1.** [dar permiso] to allow; [en situaciones oficiales] to authorize -**2.** [capa-citar] to allow, to entitle.

autorretrato *m* self-portrait.

autoservicio *m* -**1.** [tienda] self-service shop -**2.** [restaurante] self-service restau-rant.

autostop = autoestop.

autostopista = autoestopista.

autosuficiencia *f* self-sufficiency.

autovía *f* dual carriageway *UK*, state high-way *US*.

auxiliar ◇ *adj* [gen & GRAM] auxiliary. ◇ *mf* assistant; ~ **administrativo** office clerk. ◇ *vt* to assist, to help.

auxilio *m* assistance, help; **primeros ~s** first aid (*U*); ¡socorro, ~! help!, help!

auyama *f* Carib, Col pumpkin.

av., avda. (*abrev de* **avenida**) Ave.

aval *m* -**1.** [persona] guarantor -**2.** [docu-mento] guarantee, reference.

avalancha *f* lit & fig avalanche.

avalar *vt* to endorse, to guarantee.

avance *m* -**1.** [gen] advance -**2.** FIN [anticipo] advance payment -**3.** [RADIO & TV - meteoro-lógico etc] summary; [- de futura programa-ción] preview; ~ **informativo** news (*U*) in brief.

avanzar ◇ *vi* to advance. ◇ *vt* -**1.** [ade-lantar] to move forward -**2.** [anticipar] to tell in advance.

avaricia *f* greed, avarice.

avaricioso, sa *adj* avaricious, miserly.

avaro, ra *adj* miserly, mean.

avasallar *vt* [arrollar] to overwhelm.

avatar *m* (*gen pl*) vagary, sudden change.

avda. = av.

ave *f* (el) [gen] bird; ~ **rapaz** o **de rapiña** bird of prey.

AVE (*abrev de* **alta velocidad española**) *m* Spanish high-speed train.

avecinarse *vpr* to be on the way.

avellana *f* hazelnut.

avemaría *f* (el) [oración] Hail Mary.

avena *f* [grano] oats (*pl*).

avenencia *f* [acuerdo] compromise.

avenida *f* avenue.

avenido, da *adj*: **bien/mal ~s** on good/bad terms.

avenirse *vpr* [ponerse de acuerdo] to come to an agreement; ~ **a algo/a hacer algo** to agree on sthg/to do sthg.

aventajado, da *adj* [adelantado] outstan-ding.

aventajar *vt* [rebasar] to overtake; [estar por delante de] to be ahead of; ~ **a alguien en algo** to surpass sb in sthg.

aventón *m* CAm, Méx, Perú: **dar ~ a alguien** to give sb a lift.

aventura *f* -**1.** [gen] adventure -**2.** [relación amorosa] affair.

aventurado, da *adj* risky.

aventurero, ra ◇ *adj* adventurous. ◇ *m,f* adventurer (*f* adventuress).

avergonzar *vt* -**1.** [deshonrar] to shame -**2.** [abochornar] to embarrass.

➤ **avergonzarse** *vpr*: ~**se (de)** [por cul-pa] to be ashamed (of); [por timidez] to be embarrassed (about).

avería *f* [de máquina] fault; AUTOM break-down.

averiado, da *adj* [máquina] out of order; [coche] broken down.

averiar *vt* to damage.

➤ **averiarse** *vpr* [máquina] to be out of or-der; AUTOM to break down.

averiguación *f* investigation.

averiguar *vt* to find out.

aversión *f* aversion.

avestruz *m* ostrich.

aviación *f* -**1.** [navegación] aviation -**2.** [ejército] airforce.

aviador, ra *m,f* aviator.

aviar *vt* [comida] to prepare.

avicultura *f* poultry farming.

avidez *f* eagerness.

ávido, da *adj*: ~ **de** eager for.

avinagrado, da *adj* lit & fig sour.

avío *m* [preparativo] preparation.

➤ **avíos** *mpl* -**1.** *fam* [equipo] things, kit (*U*) -**2.** [víveres] provisions (*pl*).

avión *m* plane, airplane *US*; **en ~** by plane; **por ~** [en un sobre] airmail; ~ **a reacción** jet; ~ **de papel** paper aeroplane.

avioneta *f* light aircraft.

avisar *vt* -**1.** [informar]: ~ **a alguien** to let sb know, to tell sb -**2.** [advertir]: ~ **(de)** to warn (of) -**3.** [llamar] to call, to send for.

aviso *m* -**1.** [advertencia, amenaza] warning -**2.** *Amér* [anuncio] advertisement, advert; ~ **clasificado** classified advertisement -**3.** [notificación] notice; [en teatros, aero-puertos] call; **hasta nuevo ~** until further notice; **sin previo ~** without notice.

avispa *f* wasp.

avispado, da *adj* *fam* sharp, quick-witted.

avispero *m* [nido] wasp's nest.

avituallar *vt* to provide with food.

avivar *vt* -**1.** [sentimiento] to rekindle -**2.** [color] to brighten -**3.** [fuego] to stoke up.

axila *f* armpit.

axioma *m* axiom.

ay (*pl* **ayes**) *interj*: ¡~! [dolor físico] ouch!; [sorpresa, pena] oh!; ¡~ **de ti si te cojo!**

Heaven help you if I catch you!

aya ▷ **ayo.**

ayer ◇ *adv* yesterday; *fig* in the past; ~ **(por la) noche** last night; ~ **por la mañana** yesterday morning; **antes de** ~ the day before yesterday. ◇ *m fig* yesteryear.

ayo, aya *m,f* [tutor] tutor (*f* governess).

ayuda *f* help, assistance; ECON & POLÍT aid; ~ **en carretera** breakdown service; ~ **humanitaria** humanitarian aid.

ayudante *adj* & *mf* assistant.

ayudar *vt* to help; ~ **a alguien a hacer algo** to help sb (to) do sthg; **¿en qué puedo** ~**le?** how can I help you?

◆ **ayudarse** *vpr*: ~**se de** to make use of.

ayunar *vi* to fast.

ayunas *fpl*: **en** ~ [sin comer] without having eaten; *fig* [sin enterarse] in the dark.

ayuno *m* fast; **hacer** ~ to fast.

ayuntamiento *m* - **1.** [corporación] ≃ town council - **2.** [edificio] town hall *UK*, city hall *US*.

azabache *m* jet; **negro como el** ~ jet-black.

azada *f* hoe.

azafata *f*: ~ **(de vuelo)** air hostess *UK*, air stewardess.

azafate *m CAm, Carib, Méx, Perú* [bandeja] tray.

azafrán *m* saffron, crocus.

azahar *m* [del naranjo] orange blossom; [del limonero] lemon blossom.

azalea *f* azalea.

azar *m* chance, fate; **al** ~ at random; **por (puro)** ~ by (pure) chance.

azorar *vt* to embarrass.

◆ **azorarse** *vpr* to be embarrassed.

azotar *vt* [suj: persona] to beat; [en el trasero] to smack, to slap; [con látigo] to whip.

azote *m* - **1.** [golpe] blow; [en el trasero] smack, slap; [latigazo] lash - **2.** *fig* [calamidad] scourge.

azotea *f* [de edificio] terraced roof.

azteca *adj* & *mf* Aztec.

azúcar *m o f* sugar; ~ **blanquilla/moreno** refined/brown sugar.

azucarado, da *adj* sweet, sugary.

azucarero, ra *adj* sugar *(antes de sust).*

◆ **azucarero** *m* sugar bowl.

azucena *f* white lily.

azufre *m* sulphur.

azul *adj* & *m* blue.

azulejo *m* (glazed) tile.

azuzar *vt* [animal] to set on.

B

b, B *f* [letra] b, B.

baba *f* [saliva - de niño] dribble; [- de adulto] spittle, saliva; [- de perro] slobber; **echar** ~**s** to drool.

babear *vi* [niño] to dribble; [adulto, animal] to slobber; *fig* to drool.

babero *m* bib.

babi *m* child's overall.

bable *m* Asturian dialect.

babor *m*: **a** ~ to port.

babosada *f CAm, Méx fam* daft thing.

baboso, sa *adj* [adulto, animal] slobbering.

◆ **babosa** *f* ZOOL slug.

babucha *f* slipper.

baca *f* roof *o* luggage rack.

bacalao *m* [fresco] cod; [salado] dried salted cod; **partir** *o* **cortar el** ~ *fam fig* to be the boss.

bacanal *f* orgy.

bache *m* - **1.** [en carretera] pothole - **2.** *fig* [dificultades] bad patch - **3.** [en un vuelo] air pocket.

bachillerato *m Spanish two-year course of secondary studies for academically orientated 16-18-year-olds.*

bacinica *f Amér* chamber pot.

bacon ['beikon] *m inv* bacon.

bacteria *f* germ; ~**s** bacteria.

badén *m* [de carretera] ditch.

bádminton ['baðminton] *m inv* badminton.

bafle (*pl* **bafles**), **baffle** (*pl* **baffles**) *m* loudspeaker.

bagaje *m fig* background; ~ **cultural** cultural baggage.

bagatela *f* trifle.

Bahamas *fpl*: **las** ~ the Bahamas.

bahía *f* bay.

bailaor, ra *m,f* flamenco dancer.

bailar ◇ *vt* to dance. ◇ *vi* [danzar] to dance.

bailarín, ina *m,f* dancer; [de ballet] ballet dancer; **prima bailarina** prima ballerina.

baile *m* - **1.** [gen] dance; ~ **clásico** ballet; ~ **de salón** ballroom dancing - **2.** [fiesta] ball.

bambolear

baja f ⊳ bajo.

bajada f - **1.** [descenso] descent; ~ **de bandera** [de taxi] minimum fare - **2.** [pendiente] (downward) slope - **3.** [disminución] decrease, drop.

bajamar f low tide.

bajar ◇ vt - **1.** [poner abajo - libro, cuadro etc] to take/bring down; [- telón, ventanilla, mano] to lower - **2.** [descender - montaña, escaleras] to go/come down - **3.** [precios, inflación, hinchazón] to reduce; [música, volumen, radio] to turn down; [fiebre] to bring down - **4.** [ojos, cabeza, voz] to lower. ◇ vi - **1.** [descender] to go/come down; ~ **por algo** to go/come down to get sthg; ~ **corriendo** to run down - **2.** [disminuir] to fall, to drop; [fiebre, hinchazón] to go/come down; [Bolsa] to suffer a fall.

➜ **bajarse** vpr: ~**se (de)** [coche] to get out (of); [moto, tren, avión] to get off; [árbol, escalera, silla] to get/come down (from).

bajativo m Andes, RP [licor] digestive liqueur; [tisana] herbal tea.

bajeza f - **1.** [cualidad] baseness - **2.** [acción] nasty deed.

bajial m Méx, Perú lowland.

bajo, ja adj - **1.** [gen] low; [persona] short; [planta] ground (antes de sust); [sonido] soft, faint; **en voz baja** in a low voice - **2.** [territorio, época] lower; **el ~ Amazonas** the lower Amazon - **3.** [pobre] lower-class - **4.** [vil] base.

➜ **bajo** ◇ m - **1.** (gen pl) [dobladillo] hem - **2.** [piso] ground floor flat - **3.** [MÚS - instrumento, cantante] bass; [- instrumentista] bassist. ◇ adv - **1.** [gen] low - **2.** [hablar] quietly, softly. ◇ prep - **1.** [gen] under - **2.** [con temperaturas] below.

➜ **baja** f - **1.** [descenso] drop, fall - **2.** [cese]: **dar de baja a alguien** [en una empresa] to lay sb off; [en un club, sindicato] to expel sb; **darse de baja (de)** [dimitir] to resign (from); [salirse] to drop out (of) - **3.** [por enfermedad - permiso] sick leave (U); [- documento] sick note, doctor's certificate; **estar/darse de baja** to be on/to take sick leave; **baja por maternidad/paternidad** maternity/paternity leave - **4.** MIL loss, casualty.

bajón m slump; **dar un** ~ to slump; [suj - mercado, producción] to slump; [- persona] to go downhill.

bajura ⊳ pesca.

bala f - **1.** [proyectil] bullet; **como una** ~ fig like a shot - **2.** [fardo] bale.

balacear vt Amér [tirotear] to shoot.

balada f ballad.

balance m - **1.** [COM - operación] balance; [- documento] balance sheet - **2.** [resultado] outcome; **hacer** ~ **(de)** to take stock (of).

balancear vt [cuna] to rock; [columpio] to swing.

➜ **balancearse** vpr [en cuna, mecedora] to rock; [en columpio] to swing; [barco] to roll.

balanceo m - **1.** [gen] swinging; [de cuna, mecedora] rocking; [de barco] roll - **2.** Amér AUTOM wheel balance.

balancín m - **1.** [mecedora] rocking chair; [en jardín] swing hammock - **2.** [columpio] seesaw.

balanza f - **1.** [báscula] scales (pl) - **2.** COM: ~ **comercial/de pagos** balance of trade/payments.

balar vi to bleat.

balaustrada f balustrade.

balazo m [disparo] shot; [herida] bullet wound.

balbucear, balbucir vi & vt to babble.

balbuceo m babbling.

balbucir = balbucear.

Balcanes mpl: **los** ~ the Balkans.

balcón m [terraza] balcony.

balde m pail, bucket.

➜ **en balde** loc adv in vain; **no ha sido en** ~ it wasn't in vain.

baldosa f [en casa, edificio] floor tile; [en la acera] paving stone.

baldosín m tile.

balear ◇ vt Amér to shoot. ◇ adj Balearic.

Baleares fpl: **las (islas)** ~ the Balearic Islands.

baleo m Amér shootout.

balido m bleat, bleating (U).

balín m pellet.

balístico, ca adj ballistic.

baliza f NÁUT marker buoy; AERON beacon.

ballena f [animal] whale.

ballesta f - **1.** HIST crossbow - **2.** AUTOM (suspension) spring.

ballet [ba'le] (pl ballets) m ballet.

balneario m - **1.** [con baños termales] spa - **2.** Amér [con piscinas etc] ≃ lido.

balompié m football.

balón m [pelota] ball; ~ **de reglamento** regulation ball.

baloncesto m basketball.

balonmano m handball.

balonvolea m volleyball.

balsa f - **1.** [embarcación] raft - **2.** [estanque] pond, pool.

bálsamo m - **1.** FARM balsam - **2.** [alivio] balm.

balsero, ra m,f Cuba refugee fleeing Cuba on a raft.

Báltico m: **el (mar)** ~ the Baltic (Sea).

baluarte m - **1.** [fortificación] bulwark - **2.** fig [bastión] bastion, stronghold.

bambolear vi to shake.

◆ **bambolearse** *vpr* [gen] to sway; [mesa, silla] to wobble.

bambú (*pl* **bambúes** *o* **bambús**) *m* bamboo.

banal *adj* banal.

banana *f Amér* banana.

banca *f* - **1.** [actividad] banking; ~ **en línea** online banking; ~ **telefónica** telephone banking - **2.** [institución]: **la** ~ the banks *(pl)* - **3.** [en juegos] bank - **4.** *Andes, RP* [escaño] seat.

bancario, ria *adj* banking *(antes de sust)*.

bancarrota *f* bankruptcy; **en** ~ bankrupt.

banco *m* - **1.** [asiento] bench; [de iglesia] pew - **2.** FIN bank - **3.** [de peces] shoal - **4.** [de ojos, semen etc] bank - **5.** [de carpintero, artesano etc] workbench.

◆ **banco de arena** *m* sandbank.

◆ **Banco Mundial** *m*: **el Banco Mundial** the World Bank.

banda *f* - **1.** [cuadrilla] gang; ~ **terrorista** terrorist organization - **2.** MÚS band - **3.** [faja] sash - **4.** [cinta] ribbon - **5.** [franja] stripe - **6.** RADIO waveband - **7.** [margen] side; [en billar] cushion; [en fútbol] touchline; **fuera de** ~ out of play; **sacar de** ~ to throw the ball in.

◆ **banda ancha** *f* INFORM broadband.

◆ **banda magnética** *f* magnetic strip.

◆ **banda sonora** *f* soundtrack.

bandada *f* [de aves] flock; [de peces] shoal.

bandazo *m* [del barco] lurch; **dar** ~**s** [barco, borracho] to lurch; *fig* [ir sin rumbo] to chop and change.

bandear *vt* to buffet.

bandeja *f* tray; **servir** *o* **dar algo a alguien en** ~ *fig* to hand sthg to sb on a plate; ~ **de entrada** INFORM inbox; ~ **de salida** INFORM outbox.

bandera *f* flag; **jurar** ~ to swear allegiance (to the flag); **estar hasta la** ~ to be packed.

banderilla *f* TAUROM banderilla, *barbed dart thrust into bull's back.*

banderín *m* [bandera] pennant.

bandido, da *m,f* - **1.** [delincuente] bandit - **2.** [granuja] rascal.

bando *m* - **1.** [facción] side; **pasarse al otro** ~ to change sides - **2.** [de alcalde] edict.

bandolero, ra *m,f* bandit.

◆ **bandolera** *f* [correa] bandoleer; **en bandolera** slung across one's chest.

bandurria *f* small 12-stringed guitar.

banjo ['banjo] *m* banjo.

banquero, ra *m,f* banker.

banqueta *f* - **1.** [asiento] stool - **2.** *CAm, Méx* [acera] pavement *UK*, sidewalk *US*.

banquete *m* [comida] banquet.

banquillo *m* - **1.** [asiento] low stool - **2.** DEP bench.

banquina *f* RP verge.

bañada *f* *Amér* [acción de bañarse] bath.

bañadera *f* *Arg* [bañera] bath.

bañado *m* RP marshy area.

bañador *m* [de mujer] swimsuit; [de hombre] swimming trunks *(pl)*.

bañar *vt* - **1.** [asear] to bath; MED to bathe - **2.** [sumergir] to soak, to submerge - **3.** [revestir] to coat.

◆ **bañarse** *vpr* - **1.** [en el baño] to have *o* take a bath, to bathe *US* - **2.** [en playa, piscina] to go swimming.

bañera *f* bathtub, bath.

bañista *mf* bather.

baño *m* - **1.** [acción - en bañera] bath; [- playa, piscina] swim; **darse un** ~ [en bañera] to have *o* take a bath; [en playa, piscina] to go for a swim - **2.** [bañera] bathtub, bath - **3.** [cuarto de aseo] bathroom - **4.** [capa] coat.

baqueta *f* MÚS drumstick.

bar *m* bar.

barahúnda *f* racket, din.

baraja *f* pack (of cards).

barajar *vt* - **1.** [cartas] to shuffle - **2.** [considerar - nombres, posibilidades] to consider; [- datos, cifras] to marshal, to draw on.

baranda, barandilla *f* [de escalera] handrail; [de balcón] rail.

baratija *f* trinket, knick-knack.

baratillo *m* [tienda] junkshop; [mercadillo] flea market.

barato, ta *adj* cheap.

◆ **barato** *adv* cheap, cheaply.

barba *f* beard; ~ **incipiente** stubble; **por** ~ [cada uno] per head.

barbacoa *f* barbecue.

barbaridad *f* - **1.** [cualidad] cruelty; **¡qué** ~**!** how terrible! - **2.** [disparate] nonsense *(U)* - **3.** [montón]: **una** ~ **(de)** tons (of); **se gastó una** ~ she spent a fortune.

barbarie *f* [crueldad - cualidad] cruelty, savagery; [- acción] atrocity.

barbarismo *m* - **1.** [extranjerismo] foreign word - **2.** [incorrección] substandard usage.

bárbaro, ra ◇ *adj* - **1.** HIST barbarian - **2.** [cruel] barbaric, cruel - **3.** [bruto] uncouth, coarse - **4.** *fam* [extraordinario] brilliant, great. ◇ *m,f* HIST barbarian.

◆ **bárbaro** *adv fam* [magníficamente]: **pasarlo** ~ to have a wild time.

barbecho *m* fallow (land); **estar en** ~ to be left fallow.

barbería *f* barber's (shop).

barbero, ra *m,f* barber.

barbilampiño, ña *adj* beardless.

barbilla *f* chin.

barbo *m* barbel; ~ **de mar** red mullet.

barbotar *vi* & *vt* to mutter.

barbudo, da *adj* bearded.

barca *f* dinghy, small boat.

barcaza *f* barge.

barco *m* [gen] boat; [de gran tamaño] ship; **en ~** by boat; **~ cisterna** tanker; **~ de guerra** warship; **~ mercante** cargo ship; **~ de vapor** steamer, steamboat; **~ de vela** sailing boat, sail boat *US*.

baremo *m* [escala] scale.

bario *m* barium.

barítono *m* baritone.

barman (*pl* **barmans**) *m* barman, bartender *US*.

barniz *m* [para madera] varnish; [para loza, cerámica] glaze.

barnizar *vt* [madera] to varnish; [loza, cerámica] to glaze.

barómetro *m* barometer.

barón, onesa *m,f* baron (*f* baroness).

barquero, ra *m,f* boatman (*f* boatwoman).

barquillo *m* CULIN cornet, cone.

barra *f* **-1.** [gen] bar; [de hielo] block; [para cortinas] rod; [en bicicleta] crossbar; **la ~** [de tribunal] the bar; **~ de labios** lipstick; **~ de pan** baguette, French stick **-2.** [de bar, café] bar (*counter*); **~ libre** *unlimited drink for a fixed price* **-3.** [signo gráfico] slash, oblique stroke **-4.** *Andes, RP* [de amigos] gang; **~ brava** *RP* group of violent soccer fans **-5.** INFORM : **~ de estado** status bar; **~ de herramientas** tool bar; **~ de menús** menu bar.

barrabasada *f* fam mischief (*U*).

barraca *f* **-1.** [chabola] shack **-2.** [caseta de feria] stall **-3.** [en Valencia y Murcia] thatched farmhouse.

barranco *m* **-1.** [precipicio] precipice **-2.** [cauce] ravine.

barraquismo *m* shanty towns (*pl*).

barrena *f* drill.

barrenar *vt* [taladrar] to drill.

barrendero, ra *m,f* street sweeper.

barreno *m* **-1.** [instrumento] large drill **-2.** [agujero - para explosiones] blast hole.

barreño *m* washing-up bowl.

barrer *vt* **-1.** [con escoba, reflectores] to sweep **-2.** [suj: viento, olas] to sweep away.

barrera *f* **-1.** [gen] barrier; FERROC crossing gate; [de campo, casa] fence; **~s arancelarias** tariff barriers **-2.** DEP wall.

◆ barrera de seguridad *f* [en carretera] safety barrier.

barriada *f* **-1.** neighbourhood, area **-2.** *Amér* [pobre] shanty town.

barricada *f* barricade.

barrido *m* **-1.** [con escoba] sweep, sweeping (*U*) **-2.** TECN scan, scanning (*U*) **-3.** CIN pan, panning (*U*).

barriga *f* belly.

barrigón, ona *adj* paunchy.

barril *m* barrel; **de ~** [bebida] draught.

barrio *m* [vecindario] area, neighborhood *US*.

barriobajero, ra *adj despec* low-life (*antes de sust*).

barrizal *m* mire.

barro *m* **-1.** [fango] mud **-2.** [arcilla] clay **-3.** [grano] blackhead.

barroco, ca *adj* ARTE baroque.

◆ barroco *m* ARTE baroque.

barrote *m* bar.

bartola ◆ a la bartola *loc adv fam*: **tumbarse a la ~** to lounge around.

bártulos *mpl* things, bits and pieces.

barullo *m* fam **-1.** [ruido] din, racket; **armar ~** to raise hell **-2.** [desorden] mess.

basar *vt* [fundamentar] to base.

◆ basarse en *vpr* [suj: teoría, obra etc] to be based on; [suj: persona] to base one's argument on.

basca *f* [náusea] nausea.

báscula *f* scales (*pl*).

bascular *vi* to tilt.

base *f* **-1.** [gen, MAT & MIL] base; [de edificio] foundations (*pl*); **~ naval** naval base **-2.** [fundamento, origen] basis; **sentar las ~s para** to lay the foundations of **-3.** [de partido, sindicato]: **las ~s** the grass roots (*pl*), the rank and file **-4.** *loc*: **a ~ de** by (means of); **me alimento a ~ de verduras** I live on vegetables; **a ~ de bien** extremely well; **a ~ de trabajar mucho** by working hard.

◆ base de datos *f* INFORM database.

básico, ca *adj* basic; **lo ~ de** the basics of.

basílica *f* basilica.

basta *interj*: **¡~!** that's enough!; **¡~ de chistes/tonterías!** that's enough jokes/of this nonsense !

bastante *◇ adv* **-1.** [suficientemente] enough; **es lo ~ lista para ...** she's smart enough to ... **-2.** [considerablemente - antes de adj o adv] quite, pretty; [- después de verbo] quite a lot; **me gustó ~** I quite enjoyed it, I enjoyed it quite a lot. *◇ adj* **-1.** [suficiente] enough; **no tengo dinero ~** I haven't enough money **-2.** [mucho]: **éramos ~s** there were quite a few of us; **tengo ~ frío** I'm quite *o* pretty cold.

bastar *vi* to be enough; **basta con que se lo digas** it's enough for you to tell her; **con ocho basta** eight is enough; **baste decir que ...** suffice it to say that ...; **con la intención basta** it's the thought that counts.

◆ bastarse *vpr* to be self-sufficient.

bastardo, da *adj* **-1.** [hijo etc] bastard (*antes de sust*) **-2.** *despec* [innoble] mean, base.

bastidor *m* [armazón] frame.
◆ **bastidores** *mpl* TEATR wings; **entre ~es**
fig behind the scenes.

basto, ta *adj* coarse.
◆ **bastos** *mpl* [naipes] ≃ clubs.

bastón *m* -1. [para andar] walking stick
-2. [de mando] baton -3. [para esquiar] ski
stick.

basura *f* lit & fig rubbish *UK*, garbage *US*,
trash *US*; **tirar algo a la ~** to throw sthg
away; **~ radioactiva** radioactive waste.

basurero *m* -1. [persona] dustman *UK*, garbage man *US* -2. [vertedero] rubbish dump.

bata *f* -1. [de casa] housecoat; [para baño, al
levantarse] dressing gown, robe *US* -2. [de
médico] white coat; [de laboratorio] lab
coat.

batacazo *m* bump, bang.

batalla *f* battle; **de ~** [de uso diario] everyday.

batallar *vi* [con armas] to fight.

batallón *m* MIL batallion.

batata *f* sweet potato.

bate *m* DEP bat.

batear ◇ *vt* to hit. ◇ *vi* to bat.

batería *f* -1. ELECTR & MIL battery -2. MÚS
drums *(pl)* -3. [conjunto] set; [de preguntas]
barrage; **~ de cocina** pots *(pl)* and pans.

batido, da *adj* -1. [nata] whipped; [clara]
whisked -2. [senda, camino] well-trodden.
◆ **batido** *m* [bebida] milkshake.
◆ **batida** *f* -1. [de caza] beat -2. [de policía]
combing, search.

batidora *f* [eléctrica] mixer.

batín *m* short dressing gown.

batir *vt* -1. [gen] to beat; [nata] to whip; [ré-
cord] to break -2. [suj: olas, lluvia, viento] to
beat against -3. [derribar] to knock down
-4. [explorar - suj: policía etc] to comb, to
search.
◆ **batirse** *vpr* [luchar] to fight.

batuta *f* baton; **llevar la ~** *fig* to call the
tune.

baúl *m* -1. [cofre] trunk -2. *Arg, Col* [malete-
ro] boot *UK*, trunk *US*.

bautismo *m* baptism.

bautista *mf* RELIG Baptist.

bautizar *vt* -1. RELIG to baptize, to christen
-2. *fam fig* [aguar] to dilute.

bautizo *m* RELIG baptism, christening.

baya *f* berry.

bayeta *f* -1. [tejido] flannel -2. [para fregar]
cloth; [de gamuza] chamois.

bayo, ya *adj* bay.

bayoneta *f* bayonet.

baza *f* -1. [en naipes] trick -2. *loc:* **meter
~ en algo** to butt in on sthg; **no pude
meter ~ (en la conversación)** I couldn't get
a word in edgeways; **no jugó bien su ~** he

didn't play his cards right.

bazar *m* bazaar.

bazo *m* ANAT spleen.

bazofia *f* -1. [comida] pigswill *(U)* -2. *fig* [li-
bro, película etc] rubbish *(U)*.

bazuca, bazooka *m* bazooka.

BCE (*abrev de* **Banco Central Europeo**) *m*
ECB.

be *f Amér:* **~ larga** *o* **grande b**.

beatificar *vt* to beatify.

beato, ta *adj* -1. [beatificado] blessed
-2. [piadoso] devout -3. *fig* [santurrón] sanctimonious.

bebe, ba *m CSur fam* baby.

bebé *m* baby; **~ probeta** test-tube baby.

bebedero *m* [de jaula] water dish.

bebedor, ra *m,f* heavy drinker.

beber ◇ *vt* [líquido] to drink. ◇ *vi* [tomar
líquido] to drink.

bebida *f* drink; **~ alcohólica** alcoholic
drink.

bebido, da *adj* drunk.

beca *f* [del gobierno] grant; [de organización
privada] scholarship.

becar *vt* [suj: gobierno] to award a grant to;
[suj: organización privada] to award a
scholarship to.

becario, ria *m,f* [del gobierno] grant holder;
[de organización privada] scholarship
holder.

becerro, rra *m,f* calf.

bechamel [betʃa'mel], **besamel** *f* bécha-
mel sauce.

bedel *m* janitor.

befa *f* jeer; **hacer ~ de** to jeer at.

begonia *f* begonia.

beige [beis] *adj inv* & *m inv* beige.

béisbol *m* baseball.

belén *m* [de Navidad] crib, Nativity scene.

belfo, fa *adj* thick-lipped.

belga *adj* & *mf* Belgian.

Bélgica Belgium.

Belice Belize.

bélico, ca *adj* [gen] war *(antes de sust)*; [acti-
tud] bellicose, warlike.

belicoso, sa *adj* bellicose; *fig* aggressive.

beligerante *adj* & *m,f* belligerent.

bellaco, ca *m,f* villain, scoundrel.

belleza *f* beauty.

bello, lla *adj* beautiful.

bellota *f* acorn.

bemol ◇ *adj* flat. ◇ *m* MÚS flat; **tener (muchos) ~es** [ser difícil] to be tricky; [tener va-
lor] to have guts; [ser un abuso] to be a bit
rich *o* much.

bencina *f Chile* petrol *UK*, gas *US*.

bencinera *f Chile* petrol station *UK*, gas
station *US*.

bendecir *vt* to bless.

bendición *f* blessing.

bendito, ta *adj* - **1.** [santo] holy; [alma] blessed; ¡~ **sea Dios!** *fam fig* thank goodness! - **2.** [dichoso] lucky - **3.** [para enfatizar] damned.

benefactor, ra *m,f* benefactor (*f* benefactress).

beneficencia *f* charity.

beneficiar *vt* to benefit.

➡ **beneficiarse** *vpr* to benefit; ~**se de algo** to do well out of sthg.

beneficiario, ria *m,f* [de herencia, póliza] beneficiary; [de cheque] payee.

beneficio *m* - **1.** [bien] benefit; **a** ~ **de** [gala, concierto] in aid of; **en** ~ **de** for the good of; **en** ~ **de todos** in everyone's interest; **en** ~ **propio** for one's own good - **2.** [ganancia] profit.

beneficioso, sa *adj*: ~ **(para)** beneficial (to).

benéfico, ca *adj* - **1.** [favorable] beneficial - **2.** [rifa, función] charity (*antes de sust*); [organización] charitable.

beneplácito *m* consent.

benevolencia *f* benevolence.

benevolente, benévolo, la *adj* benevolent.

bengala *f* - **1.** [para pedir ayuda, iluminar etc] flare - **2.** [fuego artificial] sparkler.

benigno, na *adj* - **1.** [gen] benign - **2.** [clima, temperatura] mild.

benjamín, ina *m,f* youngest child.

berberecho *m* cockle.

berenjena *f* aubergine *UK*, eggplant *US*.

Berlín Berlin.

berma *f Andes* hard shoulder *UK*, shoulder *US*.

bermejo, ja *adj* reddish.

bermellón *adj inv* & *m* vermilion.

bermudas *fpl* Bermuda shorts.

Berna Berne.

berrear *vi* - **1.** [animal] to bellow - **2.** [persona] to howl.

berrido *m* - **1.** [del becerro] bellow, bellowing (*U*) - **2.** [de persona] howl, howling (*U*).

berrinche *m fam* tantrum; **coger** *o* **agarrarse un** ~ to throw a tantrum.

berro *m* watercress.

berza *f* cabbage.

besamel = **bechamel**.

besar *vt* to kiss.

➡ **besarse** *vpr* to kiss.

beso *m* kiss; **dar un** ~ **a alguien** to kiss sb, to give sb a kiss.

bestia ◇ *adj* - **1.** [ignorante] thick, stupid - **2.** [torpe] clumsy - **3.** [maleducado] rude. ◇ *mf* [ignorante, torpe] brute. ◇ *f* [animal] beast; ~ **de carga** beast of burden.

bestial *adj* - **1.** [brutal] animal, brutal; [apetito] tremendous - **2.** *fam* [formidable] terrific.

bestialidad *f* - **1.** [brutalidad] brutality - **2.** *fam* [tontería] rubbish (*U*), nonsense (*U*) - **3.** *fam* [montón]: **una** ~ **de** tons (*pl*) *o* stacks (*pl*) of.

best-seller [bes'seler] (*pl* **best-sellers**) *m* best-seller.

besucón, ona *adj fam* kissy.

besugo *m* - **1.** [pez] sea bream - **2.** *fam* [persona] idiot.

besuquear *vt fam* to smother with kisses.

➡ **besuquearse** *vpr fam* to smooch.

betabel *m Méx* beetroot *UK*, beet *US*.

betarraga *f Chile* beetroot *UK*, beet *US*.

bético, ca [andaluz] Andalusian.

betún *m* - **1.** [para calzado] shoe polish - **2.** QUÍM bitumen.

bianual *adj* - **1.** [dos veces al año] twice-yearly - **2.** [cada dos años] biennial.

biberón *m* (baby's) bottle; **dar el** ~ **a** to bottle-feed.

Biblia *f* Bible.

bibliografía *f* bibliography.

bibliorato *m RP* lever arch file.

biblioteca *f* - **1.** [gen] library - **2.** [mueble] bookcase.

bibliotecario, ria *m,f* librarian.

bicarbonato *m* FARM bicarbonate of soda.

bicentenario *m* bicentenary.

bíceps *m inv* biceps.

bicho *m* - **1.** [animal] beast, animal; [insecto] bug - **2.** [pillo] little terror.

bici *f fam* bike.

bicicleta *f* bicycle.

bicicletear *vi RP fam* to speculate using money owed to someone else.

bicolor *adj* two-coloured.

bidé *m* bidet.

bidimensional *adj* two-dimensional.

bidón *m* drum (*for oil etc*); [lata] can, canister; [de plástico] (large) bottle.

biela *f* connecting rod.

bien ◇ *adv* - **1.** [como es debido, adecuado] well; **has hecho** ~ you did the right thing; **habla inglés** ~ she speaks English well; **cierra** ~ **la puerta** shut the door properly; **hiciste** ~ **en decírmelo** you were right to tell me - **2.** [expresa opinión favorable]: **estar** ~ [de aspecto] to be nice; [de salud] to be *o* feel well; [de calidad] to be good; [de comodidad] to be comfortable; **está** ~ **que te vayas, pero antes despídete** it's all right for you to go, but say goodbye first; **oler** ~ to smell nice; **pasarlo** ~ to have a good time; **sentar** ~ **a alguien** [ropa] to suit sb; [comida] to agree with sb; [comentario] to please sb - **3.** [muy, bastante] very; **hoy me he levantado** ~ **temprano** I got up nice and early today; **quiero un vaso de agua ~ fría** I'd like a nice cold glass of water - **4.** [vale, de acuerdo] all right, OK; **¿nos vamos? — ~** shall we go? —all right *o* OK - **5.** [de buena gana, fácilmente] quite happily; **ella ~ que lo haría, pero no la dejan** she'd be happy to do it, but they won't let her - **6.** *loc:* **¡está ~!** [bueno, vale] all right then!; [es suficiente] that's enough!; **¡ya está ~!** that's enough!; **¡muy ~!** very good!, excellent! ⋄ *adj inv* [adinerado] well-to-do. ⋄ *conj:* **~ ...** ~ either ... or; **dáselo ~ a mi hermano, ~ a mi padre** either give it to my brother or my father. ⋄ *m* good; **el ~ y el mal** good and evil; **por el ~ de** for the sake of; **lo hice por tu ~** I did it for your own good.

➡ **bienes** *mpl* - **1.** [patrimonio] property *(U)*; **~es inmuebles** *o* **raíces** real estate *(U)*; **~es gananciales** shared possessions; **~es muebles** personal property *(U)* - **2.** [productos] goods; **~es de consumo** consumer goods.

➡ **más bien** *loc adv* rather; **no estoy contento, más ~ estupefacto** I'm not so much happy as stunned.

➡ **no bien** *loc adv* no sooner, as soon as; **no ~ me había marchado cuando empezaron a ...** no sooner had I gone than they started ...

➡ **si bien** *loc conj* although, even though.

bienal *f* biennial exhibition.

bienaventurado, da *m,f* RELIG blessed person.

bienestar *m* wellbeing.

bienhechor, ra *m,f* benefactor (*f* benefactress).

bienio *m* [periodo] two years (*pl*).

bienvenido, da ⋄ *adj* welcome. ⋄ *interj*: **¡~!** welcome!

➡ **bienvenida** *f* welcome; **dar la bienvenida a alguien** to welcome sb.

bies *m inv* bias binding; **al ~** [costura] on the bias; [sombrero] at an angle.

bife *m Andes, RP* steak.

bífido, da *adj* forked.

biftec = **bistec**.

bifurcación *f* [entre calles] fork; TECN bifurcation.

bifurcarse *vpr* to fork.

bigamia *f* bigamy.

bígamo, ma ⋄ *adj* bigamous. ⋄ *m,f* bigamist.

bigote *m* moustache.

bigotudo, da *adj* with a big moustache.

bikini = **biquini**.

bilateral *adj* bilateral.

biliar *adj* bile (*antes de sust*).

bilingüe *adj* bilingual.

bilis *f inv lit & fig* bile.

billar *m* - **1.** [juego] billiards (*U*) - **2.** [sala] billiard hall.

billete *m* - **1.** [dinero] note *UK*, bill *US* - **2.** [de rifa, transporte, cine etc] ticket; **~ de ida** single (ticket); **~ de ida y vuelta** return (ticket) *UK*, round-trip (ticket) *US*; **~ sencillo** single (ticket) *UK*, one-way (ticket) *US* - **3.** [de lotería] lottery ticket.

billetera *f*, **billetero** *m* wallet.

billón *núm* billion *UK*, trillion *US*; *ver también* **seis**.

bingo *m* - **1.** [juego] bingo - **2.** [sala] bingo hall - **3.** [premio] (full) house.

binóculo *m* pince-nez.

biocombustible *m* biofuel.

biodegradable *adj* biodegradable.

bioética *f* bioethics.

biografía *f* biography.

biográfico, ca *adj* biographical.

biógrafo, fa *m,f* [persona] biographer.

biología *f* biology.

biológico, ca *adj* biological.

biólogo, ga *m,f* biologist.

biombo *m* (folding) screen.

biopsia *f* biopsy.

bioquímico, ca ⋄ *adj* biochemical. ⋄ *m,f* [persona] biochemist.

➡ **bioquímica** *f* [ciencia] biochemistry.

biorritmo *m* biorhythm.

biotecnología *f* biotechnology.

binóculo *m* pince-nez.

biotopo *m* biotope.

bipartidismo *m* two-party system.

bipartito, ta *adj* bipartite.

biplaza *m* two-seater.

biquini, bikini *m* [bañador] bikini.

birlar *vt fam* to pinch, to nick.

Birmania Burma.

birome *f RP* Biro®.

birra *f fam* beer.

birrete *m* - **1.** [de clérigo] biretta - **2.** [de catedrático] mortarboard.

birria *f fam* [fealdad - persona] sight, fright; [- cosa] monstrosity.

bis (*pl* **bises**) ⋄ *adj inv*: **viven en el 150 ~** they live at 150a. ⋄ *m* encore.

bisabuelo, la *m,f* great-grandfather (*f* great-grandmother); **~s** great-grandparents.

bisagra *f* hinge.

bisección *f* bisection.

bisectriz *f* bisector.

biselar *vt* to bevel.

bisexual *adj & mf* bisexual.

bisiesto ⊳ **año**.

bisnieto, ta *m,f* great-grandchild, great-grandson (*f* great-granddaughter).

bisonte *m* bison.

bisoño, ña *m,f* novice.

bistec, biftec *m* steak.

bisturí (*pl* bisturíes) *m* scalpel.

bisutería *f* imitation jewellery.

bit [bit] (*pl* bits) *m* INFORM bit.

bíter, bitter *m* bitters (U).

bizco, ca *adj* cross-eyed.

bizcocho *m* [de repostería] sponge.

bizquear *vi* to squint.

blanco, ca ◇ *adj* white. ◇ *m,f* [persona] white (person).

◆ **blanco** *m* **- 1.** [color] white **- 2.** [diana] target; **dar en el ~** DEP & MIL to hit the target; *fig* to hit the nail on the head **- 3.** *fig* [objetivo] target; [de miradas] object **- 4.** [espacio vacío] blank (space).

◆ **blanca** *f* MÚS minim; **estar** *o* **quedarse sin blanca** *fig* to be flat broke.

◆ **blanco del ojo** *m* white of the eye.

◆ **en blanco** *loc adv* **- 1.** [gen] blank; **se quedó con la mente en ~** his mind went blank **- 2.** [sin dormir]: **una noche en ~** a sleepless night.

blancura *f* whiteness.

blandengue *adj* lit & fig weak.

blandir *vt* to brandish.

blando, da *adj* **- 1.** [gen] soft; [carne] tender **- 2.** *fig* [persona - débil] weak; [- indulgente] lenient, soft.

blandura *f* **- 1.** [gen] softness; [de carne] tenderness **- 2.** *fig* [debilidad] weakness; [indulgencia] leniency.

blanquear *vt* **- 1.** [ropa] to whiten; [con lejía] to bleach **- 2.** [con cal] to whitewash **- 3.** *fig* [dinero] to launder.

blanquecino, na *adj* off-white.

blanqueo *m* **- 1.** [de ropa] whitening; [con lejía] bleaching **- 2.** [encalado] whitewashing **- 3.** *fig* [de dinero] laundering.

blanquillo *m* CAm, Méx [huevo] egg.

blasfemar *vi* RELIG: **~ (contra)** to blaspheme (against).

blasfemia *f* RELIG blasphemy.

blasfemo, ma *adj* blasphemous.

bledo *m*: **me importa un ~ (lo que diga)** *fam* I don't give a damn (about what he says).

blindado, da *adj* armour-plated; [coche] armoured.

bloc [blok] (*pl* blocs) *m* pad; **~ de dibujo** sketchpad; **~ de notas** notepad.

bloque *m* **- 1.** [gen & INFORM] block **- 2.** POLÍT bloc **- 3.** MEC cylinder block.

bloquear *vt* **- 1.** [gen & DEP] to block **- 2.** [aislar - suj: ejército, barcos] to blockade; [- suj: nieve, inundación] to cut off **- 3.** FIN to freeze.

bloqueo *m* **- 1.** [gen & DEP] blocking; **~ mental** mental block **- 2.** ECON & MIL blockade

- 3. FIN freeze, freezing (U).

blues [blus] *m inv* MÚS blues.

blusa *f* blouse.

blusón *m* [camisa] long shirt; [de pintor] smock.

bluyín *m*, **bluyínes** *mpl* Amér, Andes, Ven jeans (*pl*).

boa *f* ZOOL boa.

bobada *f* fam: **decir ~s** to talk nonsense.

bobina *f* **- 1.** [gen] reel; [en máquina de coser] bobbin **- 2.** ELECTR coil.

bobo, ba ◇ *adj* **- 1.** [tonto] stupid, daft **- 2.** [ingenuo] naïve, simple. ◇ *m,f* **- 1.** [tonto] fool, idiot **- 2.** [ingenuo] simpleton.

boca *f* **- 1.** [gen] mouth; **~ arriba/abajo** face up/down; **abrir** *o* **hacer ~** to whet one's appetite; **se me hace la ~ agua** it makes my mouth water **- 2.** [entrada] opening; [de cañón] muzzle; **~ de metro** tube *o* underground entrance UK, subway entrance US.

◆ **boca a boca** *m* mouth-to-mouth (resuscitation).

bocacalle *f* [entrada] entrance (to a street); [calle] side street; **gire en la tercera ~** take the third turning.

bocadillo *m* CULIN sandwich.

bocado *m* **- 1.** [comida] mouthful **- 2.** [mordisco] bite.

bocajarro ◆ **a bocajarro** *loc adv* [disparar] point-blank; **se lo dije a ~** I told him to his face.

bocanada *f* [de líquido] mouthful; [de humo] puff; [de viento] gust.

bocata *m* fam sarnie.

bocazas *m y f inv* fam despec big mouth, blabbermouth.

boceto *m* sketch, rough outline.

bocha *f* [bolo] bowl.

◆ **bochas** *fpl* [juego] bowls (U).

bochorno *m* **- 1.** [calor] stifling *o* muggy heat **- 2.** [vergüenza] embarrassment.

bochornoso, sa *adj* **- 1.** [tiempo] stifling, muggy **- 2.** [vergonzoso] embarrassing.

bocina *f* **- 1.** AUTOM & MÚS horn **- 2.** [megáfono] megaphone, loudhailer.

bocón, cona *m,f* Amér fam bigmouth, blabbermouth.

boda *f* [ceremonia] wedding; [convite] reception.

bodega *f* **- 1.** [cava] wine cellar **- 2.** [tienda] wine shop; [bar] bar **- 3.** [en buque, avión] hold.

bodegón *m* ARTE still life.

bodrio *m* fam despec [gen] rubbish (U); [comida] pigswill (U); **¡qué ~!** what a load of rubbish!

body ['boði] (*pl* bodies) *m* body.

BOE (*abrev de* **Boletín Oficial del Estado**) *m* official Spanish gazette.

bofetada *f* slap (in the face).
bofetón *m* hard slap (in the face).
bofia *f fam*: **la ~** the cops *(pl)*.
boga *f*: **estar en ~** to be in vogue.
bogavante *m* lobster.
Bogotá Bogotá.
bohemio, mia *adj* - **1.** [vida etc] bohemian - **2.** [de Bohemia] Bohemian.
boicot *(pl* boicots) *m* boycott.
boicotear *vt* to boycott.
bóiler *m Méx* boiler.
boina *f* beret.
boîte [bwat] *(pl* boîtes) *f* nightclub.
boj *(pl* bojes) *m* [árbol] box.
bol *(pl* boles) *m* bowl.
bola *f* - **1.** [gen] ball; [canica] marble; **~ del mundo** globe; **~s de naftalina** mothballs - **2.** *fam* [mentira] fib.
bolada *f RP fam* opportunity.
bolea *f* DEP volley.
bolear *vt Méx* [embetunar] to shine, to polish.
bolera *f* bowling alley.
bolero, ra *m,f Méx* shoeshine, bootblack *UK*.
boleta *f Amér* [recibo] receipt; *CAm, CSur* [multa] parking ticket; *Cuba, Méx, RP* [para voto] ballot, voting slip.
boletería *f Amér* [de cine, teatro] box office; [de estación] ticket office.
boletero, ra *m,f Amér* box office attendant.
boletín *m* journal, periodical; **~ de noticias** *o* **informativo** news bulletin; **~ meteorológico** weather forecast; **~ de prensa** press release; **Boletín Oficial del Estado** *official Spanish gazette*.
boleto *m* - **1.** [de lotería, rifa] ticket; [de quinielas] coupon - **2.** *Amér* [para medio de transporte] ticket.
boli *m fam* Biro®.
boliche *m* - **1.** [en la petanca] jack - **2.** [bolos] ten-pin bowling - **3.** [bolera] bowling alley - **4.** *Amér* [tienda] small grocery store - **5.** *CSur fam* [bar] cheap bar or café.
bólido *m* racing car.
bolígrafo *m* ballpoint pen, Biro®.
bolita *f CSur* [pieza] marble; **jugar a las ~s** to play marbles.
bolívar *m* bolivar.
Bolivia Bolivia.
boliviano, na *adj & m,f* Bolivian.
bollo *m* - **1.** [para comer - de pan] (bread) roll; [- dulce] bun - **2.** [abolladura] dent; [abultamiento] bump.
bolo *m* - **1.** DEP [pieza] skittle - **2.** [actuación] show - **3.** *CAm fam* [borracho] boozer.
➤ **bolos** *mpl* [deporte] skittles.
bolsa *f* - **1.** [gen] bag; **~ de aire** air pocket;

~ de basura bin liner; **~ de deportes** holdall, sports bag; **~ de plástico** [en tiendas] carrier *o* plastic bag; **~ de viaje** travel bag; **~ de patatas fritas** packet of crisps - **2.** FIN: **~ (de valores)** stock exchange, stock market; **la ~ ha subido/bajado** share prices have gone up/down; **jugar a la ~** to speculate on the stock market - **3.** MIN pocket - **4.** ANAT sac - **5.** *RP* [saco de dormir] sleeping bag.
bolsillo *m* pocket; **de ~** pocket *(antes de sust)*; **lo pagué de mi ~** I paid for it out of my own pocket.
bolso *m* bag; [de mujer] handbag, purse *US*.
boludear *vi RP fam* [decir tonterías] to talk nonsense; [hacer tonterías, perder el tiempo] to mess about *o* around.
boludo, da *m,f RP fam* [estúpido] prat *UK*, jerk *US*; [perezoso] lazy slob.
bomba ◇ *f* - **1.** [explosivo] bomb; **~ atómica** atom *o* nuclear bomb; **~ de mano** (hand) grenade; **~ de humo** *lit* smoke bomb; *fig* smokescreen - **2.** [máquina] pump - **3.** *fig* [acontecimiento] bombshell - **4.** *Chile, Col, Ecuad, Ven* [surtidor de gasolina] petrol station *US*, gas station *US* - **5.** *loc*: **pasarlo ~** *fam* to have a great time. ◇ *adj inv fam* astounding.
bombacha *f RP* [braga] knickers *UK*, panties *US*; [pantalón] *loose trousers worn by gaucho*.
bombachos *mpl* baggy trousers.
bombardear *vt lit & fig* to bombard.
bombardeo *m* bombardment.
bombardero *m* [avión] bomber.
bombazo *m fig* [noticia] bombshell.
bombear *vt* [gen & DEP] to pump.
bombero, ra *m,f* - **1.** [de incendios] fireman (*f* firewoman) - **2.** *Ven* [de gasolinera] petrol-pump *UK o* gas-pump *US* attendant.
bombilla *f* light bulb.
bombillo *m CAm, Col, Méx* light bulb.
bombín *m* bowler (hat).
bombita *f RP* light bulb.
bombo *m* - **1.** MÚS bass drum - **2.** *fam fig* [elogio] hype; **a ~ y platillo** with a lot of hype - **3.** MEC drum.
bombón *m* [golosina] chocolate.
bombona *f* cylinder; **~ de butano** (butane) gas cylinder.
bonachón, ona *adj fam* kindly.
bonanza *f* - **1.** [de tiempo] fair weather; [de mar] calm at sea - **2.** *fig* [prosperidad] prosperity.
bondad *f* [cualidad] goodness; [inclinación] kindness; **tener la ~ de hacer algo** to be kind enough to do sthg.
bondadoso, sa *adj* kind, good-natured.
boniato *m* sweet potato.

bonificar *vt* **- 1.** [descontar] to give a discount of **- 2.** [mejorar] to improve.

bonito, ta *adj* pretty; [bueno] nice.

➤ **bonito** *m* bonito (tuna).

bono *m* **- 1.** [vale] voucher **- 2.** COM bond.

bonobús *m* ten-journey bus ticket.

bonoloto *m* Spanish state-run lottery.

boñiga *f* cowpat.

boquerón *m* (fresh) anchovy.

boquete *m* hole.

boquiabierto, ta *adj* open-mouthed; *fig* astounded, speechless.

boquilla *f* **- 1.** [para fumar] cigarette holder **- 2.** [de pipa, instrumento musical] mouthpiece **- 3.** [de tubo, aparato] nozzle.

borbotear, borbotar *vi* to bubble.

borbotón *m*: **salir a borbotones** to gush out.

borda *f* NÁUT gunwale.

➤ **fuera borda** *m* [barco] outboard motorboat; [motor] outboard motor.

bordado, da *adj* embroidered.

➤ **bordado** *m* embroidery.

bordar *vt* [al coser] to embroider.

borde ◇ *adj fam* [antipático] stroppy, miserable. ◇ *m* [gen] edge; [de carretera] side; [del mar] shore, seaside; [de río] bank; [de vaso, botella] rim; **al ~ de** *fig* on the verge o brink of.

bordear *vt* [estar alrededor de] to border; [moverse alrededor de] to skirt (round).

bordillo *m* kerb.

bordo ➤ **a bordo** *loc adv* on board.

bordó *RP* ◇ *adj inv* burgundy. ◇ *m inv* burgundy.

borla *f* tassel; [pompón] pompom.

borrachera *f* **- 1.** [embriaguez] drunkenness (U); **agarrar** o *Esp* **coger una ~** to get drunk **- 2.** *fig* [emoción] intoxication.

borracho, cha ◇ *adj* [ebrio] drunk. ◇ *m,f* [persona] drunk.

➤ **borracho** *m* [bizcocho] ≃ rum baba.

borrador *m* **- 1.** [de escrito] rough draft; [de dibujo] sketch **- 2.** [goma de borrar] rubber *UK*, eraser *US*.

borrar *vt* **- 1.** [hacer desaparecer - con goma] to rub out *UK*, to erase *US*; [- en ordenador] to delete; [- en casete] to erase **- 2.** [tachar] to cross out; *fig* [de lista etc] to take off **- 3.** *fig* [olvidar] to erase.

borrasca *f* area of low pressure.

borrego, ga *m,f* [animal] lamb.

borrón *m* blot; *fig* blemish; **hacer ~ y cuenta nueva** to wipe the slate clean.

borroso, sa *adj* [foto, visión] blurred; [escritura, texto] smudgy.

Bosnia Bosnia.

bosnio, nia *adj* & *m,f* Bosnian.

bosque *m* [pequeño] wood; [grande] forest.

bosquejar *vt* [esbozar] to sketch (out).

bosquejo *m* [esbozo] sketch.

bostezar *vi* to yawn.

bostezo *m* yawn.

bota *f* **- 1.** [calzado] boot; **~s de agua** o **de lluvia** wellingtons **- 2.** [de vino] small leather container in which wine is kept.

botana *f* Méx snack, appetizer.

botánico, ca ◇ *adj* botanical. ◇ *m,f* [persona] botanist.

➤ **botánica** *f* [ciencia] botany.

botar ◇ *vt* **- 1.** NÁUT to launch **- 2.** *fam* [despedir] to throw o kick out **- 3.** [pelota] to bounce **- 4.** *Andes, CAm, Carib, Méx* [tirar] to throw away. ◇ *vi* **- 1.** [saltar] to jump **- 2.** [pelota] to bounce.

bote *m* **- 1.** [tarro] jar **- 2.** [lata] can **- 3.** [botella de plástico] bottle **- 4.** [barca] boat; **~ salvavidas** lifeboat **- 5.** [salto] jump; **dar ~s** [gen] to jump up and down; [en tren, coche] to bump up and down **- 6.** [de pelota] bounce; **dar ~s** to bounce.

botella *f* bottle; **de ~** bottled; *Cuba*: **pedir ~** to hitchhike; **dar ~ a alguien** to give sb a ride, to give sb a lift.

botellín *m* small bottle.

boticario, ria *m,f* desus pharmacist, chemist *UK*.

botijo *m* earthenware jug.

botín *m* **- 1.** [de guerra, atraco] plunder, loot **- 2.** [calzado] ankle boot.

botiquín *m* [caja] first-aid kit; [mueble] first-aid cupboard; [enfermería] first-aid post.

botón *m* button; **~ de marcado abreviado** TELEC speed-dial button.

➤ **botones** *m inv* [de hotel] bellboy, bellhop *US*; [de oficinas etc] errand boy.

boutique [bu'tik] *f* boutique.

bóveda *f* ARQUIT vault.

box (*pl* **boxes**) *m* **- 1.** [de coches] pit; **entrar en ~es** to make a pit stop **- 2.** *Amér* boxing.

boxeador, ra *m,f* boxer.

boxear *vi* to box.

boxeo *m* boxing.

bóxer (*pl* **bóxers**) *m* boxer.

boya *f* **- 1.** [en el mar] buoy **- 2.** [de una red] float.

boyante *adj* **- 1.** [feliz] happy **- 2.** [próspero - empresa, negocio] prosperous; [- economía, comercio] buoyant.

bozal *m* [gen] muzzle.

bracear *vi* [nadar] to swim.

braga (*gen pl*) *f* knickers (*pl*).

bragueta *f* flies (*pl*) *UK*, zipper *US*; **tienes la ~ abierta** your flies are undone.

braille ['braile] *m* Braille.

bramar *vi* **- 1.** [animal] to bellow **- 2.** [persona - de dolor] to groan; [- de ira] to roar.

bramido *m* **-1.** [de animal] bellow **- 2.** [de persona - de dolor] groan; [- de ira] roar.

brandy *m* brandy.

branquia *(gen pl)* *f* gill.

brasa *f* ember; **a la ~** CULIN barbecued.

brasero *m* brazier.

brasier, brassier *m* *Carib, Col, Méx* bra.

Brasil: (el) ~ Brazil.

brasileño, ña, brasilero, ra *Andes, CSur, Ven* <> *adj* Brazilian. <> *m,f* Brazilian.

brassier = brasier.

bravata *(gen pl)* *f* **-1.** [amenaza] threat **- 2.** [fanfarronería] bravado *(U)*.

braveza *f* bravery.

bravío, a *adj* [salvaje] wild; [feroz] fierce.

bravo, va *adj* **-1.** [valiente] brave **- 2.** [animal] wild **- 3.** [mar] rough.

◆ **bravo** <> *m* [aplauso] cheer. <> *interj*: ¡~! bravo!

bravuconear *vi despec* to brag.

bravura *f* **-1.** [de persona] bravery **- 2.** [de animal] ferocity.

braza *f* **-1.** DEP breaststroke; **nadar a ~** to swim breaststroke **- 2.** [medida] fathom.

brazada *f* stroke.

brazalete *m* **-1.** [en la muñeca] bracelet **- 2.** [en el brazo] armband.

brazo *m* **-1.** [gen & ANAT] arm; [de animal] foreleg; **cogidos del ~** arm in arm; **en ~s** in one's arms; **luchar a ~ partido** [con empeño] to fight tooth and nail; **quedarse** *o* **estarse con los ~s cruzados** *fig* to sit around doing nothing; **ser el ~ derecho de alguien** to be sb's right-hand man (*f* woman) **- 2.** [de árbol, río, candelabro] branch; [de grúa] boom, jib.

◆ **brazo de gitano** *m* ≃ swiss roll.

brea *f* **-1.** [sustancia] tar **- 2.** [para barco] pitch.

brebaje *m* concoction, foul drink.

brecha *f* **-1.** [abertura] hole, opening **- 2.** MIL breach **- 3.** *fig* [impresión] impression.

bregar *vi* **-1.** [luchar] to struggle **- 2.** [trabajar] to work hard **- 3.** [reñir] to quarrel.

breña *f* scrub.

bretel *m* *CSur* strap; **un vestido sin ~es a** strapless dress.

breve <> *adj* brief; **en ~** [pronto] shortly; [en pocas palabras] in short. <> *f* MÚS breve.

brevedad *f* shortness; **a** *o* **con la mayor ~** as soon as possible.

brevet *m* *Chile* [avión] pilot's licence *UK* *o* license *US*; *Ecuad, Perú* [automóvil] driving licence *UK*, driver's license *US*; *RP* [velero] sailing licence *UK* *o* license *US*.

brezo *m* heather.

bribón, ona *m,f* scoundrel, rogue.

bricolaje *m* D.I.Y., do-it-yourself.

brida *f* [de caballo] bridle.

bridge *m* bridge.

brigada <> *m* MIL ≃ warrant officer. <> *f* **-1.** MIL brigade **- 2.** [equipo] squad, team; **~ antidisturbios/antidroga** riot/drug squad.

brillante <> *adj* **-1.** [reluciente - luz, astro] shining; [- metal, zapatos, pelo] shiny; [- ojos, sonrisa, diamante] sparkling **- 2.** [magnífico] brilliant. <> *m* diamond.

brillantina *f* brilliantine, Brylcreem®.

brillar *vi* lit & *fig* to shine.

brillo *m* **-1.** [resplandor - de luz] brilliance; [- de estrellas] shining; [- de zapatos] shine **- 2.** [lucimiento] splendour, brilliance.

brilloso, sa *adj* *Amér* shining.

brincar *vi* **-1.** [saltar] to skip (about); **~ de alegría** to jump for joy.

brinco *m* jump.

brindar <> *vi* to drink a toast; **~ por algo/ alguien** to drink to sthg/sb. <> *vt* to offer.

◆ **brindarse** *vpr*: **~se a hacer algo** to offer to do sthg.

brindis *m* inv toast.

brío *m* [energía, decisión] spirit, verve.

brisa *f* breeze.

británico, ca <> *adj* British. <> *m,f* British person, Briton; **los ~s** the British.

brizna *f* **-1.** [filamento - de hierba] blade; [- de tabaco] strand **- 2.** *fig* [un poco] trace, bit.

broca *f* (drill) bit.

brocha *f* brush; **~ de afeitar** shaving brush.

brochazo *m* brushstroke.

broche *m* **-1.** [cierre] clasp, fastener **- 2.** [joya] brooch.

broma *f* [ocurrencia, chiste] joke; [jugarreta] prank, practical joke; **en ~** as a joke; **gastar una ~ a alguien** to play a joke *o* prank on sb; **ni en ~** *fig* no way, not on your life.

bromear *vi* to joke.

bromista *mf* joker.

bronca ⊳ bronco.

bronce *m* [aleación] bronze.

bronceado, da *adj* tanned.

◆ **bronceado** *m* tan.

bronceador, ra *adj* tanning *(antes de sust)*, suntan *(antes de sust)*.

◆ **bronceador** *m* [loción] suntan lotion; [leche] suntan cream.

broncear *vt* to tan.

◆ **broncearse** *vpr* to get a tan.

bronco, ca *adj* **-1.** [grave - voz] harsh; [- tos] throaty **- 2.** *fig* [brusco] gruff, surly.

◆ **bronca** *f* **-1.** [jaleo] row **- 2.** [regañina] scolding, telling-off; **echar una bronca a alguien** to give sb a row, to tell sb off **- 3.** *RP* *fam* [rabia]: **me da bronca** it hacks me off; **el jefe le tiene bronca** the boss has got it in for her.

bronquio *m* bronchial tube.

bronquitis *f inv* bronchitis.

brotar *vi* **- 1.** [planta] to sprout, to bud **- 2.** [agua, sangre etc]: ~ **de** to well out up out of **- 3.** *fig* [esperanza, sospechas, pasiones] to stir **- 4.** [en la piel]: **le brotó un sarpullido** he broke out in a rash.

brote *m* **- 1.** [de planta] bud, shoot **- 2.** *fig* [inicios] sign, hint.

broza *f* [maleza] brush, scrub.

bruces ➭ **de bruces** *loc adv* face down; **se cayó de** ~ he fell headlong, he fell flat on his face.

bruja ➭ brujo.

brujería *f* witchcraft, sorcery.

brujo, ja *adj* [hechicero] enchanting, captivating.
➭ **brujo** *m* wizard, sorcerer.
➭ **bruja** ◇ *f* **- 1.** [hechicera] witch, sorceress **- 2.** [mujer fea] hag **- 3.** [mujer mala] (old) witch. ◇ *adj inv* *Méx fam*: **estar bruja** to be broke.

brújula *f* compass.

bruma *f* [niebla] mist; [en el mar] sea mist.

bruñido *m* polishing.

brusco, ca *adj* **- 1.** [repentino, imprevisto] sudden, abrupt **- 2.** [tosco, grosero] brusque.

Bruselas Brussels.

brusquedad *f* **- 1.** [imprevisión] suddenness, abruptness **- 2.** [grosería] brusqueness.

brutal *adj* [violento] brutal.

brutalidad *f* [cualidad] brutality.

bruto, ta ◇ *adj* **- 1.** [torpe] clumsy; [ignorante] thick, stupid; [maleducado] rude **- 2.** [sin tratar]: **en** ~ [diamante] uncut; [petróleo] crude **- 3.** [sueldo, peso etc] gross. ◇ *m,f* brute.

bubónica ➭ peste.

bucal *adj* oral.

Bucarest Bucharest.

bucear *vi* [en agua] to dive, to swim underwater.

buceo *m* (underwater) diving.

bucle *m* [rizo] curl, ringlet.

Budapest Budapest.

budismo *m* Buddhism.

buen ➭ bueno.

buenas ➭ bueno.

buenaventura *f* [adivinación] fortune; **leer la** ~ **a alguien** to tell sb's fortune.

bueno, na *(compar* mejor, *superl m* el mejor, *superl f* la mejor) *adj (antes de sust masculino:* buen*)* **- 1.** [gen] good **- 2.** [bondadoso] kind, good; **ser** ~ **con alguien** to be good to sb **- 3.** [curado, sano] well, all right **- 4.** [apacible - tiempo, clima] nice, fine **- 5.** [aprovechable] all right; [comida] fresh **- 6.** [uso enfático]: **ese buen hombre** that

good man; **un buen día** one fine day **- 7.** *loc*: **de buen ver** good-looking, attractive; **de buenas a primeras** [de repente] all of a sudden; [a simple vista] at first sight, on the face of it; **estar** ~ *fam* [persona] to be a bit of all right, to be tasty; **estar de buenas** to be in a good mood; **lo** ~ **es que ...** the best thing about it is that ...
➭ **bueno** ◇ *m* CIN: **el** ~ the goody. ◇ *adv* **- 1.** [vale, de acuerdo] all right, O.K. **- 2.** [pues] well. ◇ *interj Méx* [al teléfono]: **¡** ~ **!** hello.
➭ **buenas** *interj*: **¡buenas!** hello!; *Col, Méx*: **¿buenas?** [al teléfono] hello.

Buenos Aires Buenos Aires.

buey *(pl* bueyes*)* *m* ox.

búfalo *m* buffalo.

bufanda *f* scarf.

bufar *vi* [toro, caballo] to snort.

bufé *(pl* bufés*)*, **buffet** *(pl* buffets*)* *m* [en restaurante] buffet.

bufete *m* lawyer's practice.

buffet = bufé.

bufido *m* [de toro, caballo] snort.

bufón *m* buffoon, jester.

buhardilla *f* [habitación] attic.

búho *m* owl.

buitre *m* lit & *fig* vulture.

bujía *f* AUTOM spark plug.

bulbo *m* ANAT & BOT bulb.

buldozer *(pl* buldozers*)*, **bulldozer** *(pl* bulldozers*)* [bul'doθer] *m* bulldozer.

bulevar *(pl* bulevares*)* *m* boulevard.

Bulgaria Bulgaria.

búlgaro, ra *adj* & *m,f* Bulgarian.
➭ **búlgaro** *m* [lengua] Bulgarian.

bulín *m* RP bachelor pad.

bulla *f* racket, uproar; **armar** ~ to kick up a racket.

bullanguero, ra ◇ *adj* noisy, rowdy. ◇ *m,f* noisy o boisterous person.

bulldozer = buldozer.

bullicio *m* [de ciudad, mercado] hustle and bustle; [de multitud] hubbub.

bullicioso, sa *adj* **- 1.** [agitado - reunión, multitud] noisy; [- calle, mercado] busy, bustling **- 2.** [inquieto] rowdy, boisterous. ◇ *m,f* rowdy o boisterous person.

bullir ◇ *vi* **- 1.** [hervir] to boil; [burbujear] to bubble **- 2.** *fig* [multitud] to bustle; [ratas, hormigas etc] to swarm; [mar] to boil; ~ **de** to seethe with. ◇ *vpr* to budge, to move.

bulto *m* **- 1.** [volumen] bulk, size; **escurrir el** ~ [trabajo] to shirk; [cuestión] to evade the issue **- 2.** [abombamiento - en rodilla, superficie etc] bump; [- en maleta, bolsillo etc] bulge **- 3.** [forma imprecisa] blurred shape **- 4.** [paquete] package; [maleta] item of luggage; [fardo] bundle; ~ **de mano** piece o item of hand luggage.

bumerán (*pl* **bumeráns**), **bumerang** (*pl* **bumerangs**) *m* boomerang.

bungalow [buŋga'lo] (*pl* **bungalows**) *m* bungalow.

búnquer (*pl* **búnquers**), **bunker** (*pl* **bunkers**) *m* [refugio] bunker.

buñolería *f* stand or shop selling doughnuts.

buñuelo *m* [CULIN - dulce] ≃ doughnut; [- de bacalao etc] ≃ dumpling.

BUP *m* academically oriented secondary-school course formerly taught in Spain for pupils aged 14-17, now known as the bachillerato.

buque *m* ship; ~ **de nodriza** supply ship; ~ **de vapor** steamer, steamship.

burbuja *f* bubble; **con** ~**s** fizzy; **hacer** ~**s** to bubble.

burbujear *vi* to bubble.

burdel *m* brothel.

burdo, da *adj* [gen] crude; [tela] coarse.

burgués, esa *adj* middle-class, bourgeois.

burguesía *f* middle class; HIST & POLÍT bourgeoisie.

burla *f* - **1.** [mofa] taunt; **hacer** ~ **de** to mock - **2.** [broma] joke; ~**s aparte** joking aside - **3.** [engaño] trick.
   ◆ **burlas** *fpl* ridicule (U), mockery (U).

burlar *vt* [esquivar] to evade; [ley] to flout.
   ◆ **burlarse de** *vpr* to make fun of.

burlesco, ca *adj* [tono] jocular; LITER burlesque.

burlón, ona *adj* [sarcástico] mocking.

burocracia *f* bureaucracy.

burócrata *mf* bureaucrat.

burrada *f* [acción, dicho]: **hacer** ~**s** to act stupidly; **decir** ~**s** to talk nonsense.

burrito *m* CAm, Méx burrito.

burro, rra *m,f* - **1.** [animal] donkey; **no ver tres en un** ~ *fam* to be as blind as a bat - **2.** *fam* [necio] dimwit.

bursátil *adj* stock-market (antes de sust).

bus (*pl* **buses**) *m* AUTOM & INFORM bus.

busca ◇ *f* search; **en** ~ **de** in search of; **la** ~ **de** the search for. ◇ *m* ▷ **buscapersonas**.

buscapersonas, busca *m inv* bleeper, pager.

buscar ◇ *vt* - **1.** [gen] to look for; [provecho, beneficio propio] to seek; **voy a** ~ **el periódico** I'm going for the paper o to get the paper; **ir a** ~ **a alguien** to pick sb up; **'se busca camarero'** 'waiter wanted' - **2.** [en diccionario, índice, horario] to look up - **3.** INFORM to search for. ◇ *vi* to look.
   ◆ **buscarse** *vpr*: **buscársela** to be asking for it.

buscón, ona *m,f* [estafador] swindler.

buseca *f* RP tripe stew.

buseta *m* Col, CRica, Ecuad, Ven minibus.

búsqueda *f* search.

busto *m* - **1.** [pecho] chest; [de mujer] bust - **2.** [escultura] bust.

butaca *f* - **1.** [mueble] armchair - **2.** [en cine] seat.

butano *m* butane (gas).

butifarra *f* type of Catalan pork sausage.

buzo *m* - **1.** [persona] diver - **2.** [chándal] tracksuit; Arg, Chile, Perú [lana] sweater, jumper UK.

buzón *m* letter box; **echar algo al** ~ to post sthg; ~ **de sugerencias** suggestion box; ~ **de voz** voice mail.

byte [bait] (*pl* **bytes**) *m* INFORM byte.

C

c, C *f* [letra] c, C.

c., **c/**[1] (abrev de **calle**) St.

c/[2] - **1.** (abrev de **cuenta**) a/c - **2.** = **c**.

cabal *adj* - **1.** [honrado] honest - **2.** [exacto; completo] complete.
   ◆ **cabales** *mpl*: **no estar en sus** ~**es** not to be in one's right mind.

cábala *f* (gen pl) [conjeturas] guess.

cabalgar *vi* to ride.

cabalgata *f* cavalcade, procession.

caballa *f* mackerel.

caballería *f* - **1.** [animal] mount, horse - **2.** [cuerpo militar] cavalry.

caballeriza *f* stable.

caballero ◇ *adj* [cortés] gentlemanly. ◇ *m* - **1.** [gen] gentleman; [al dirigir la palabra] sir; **ser todo un** ~ to be a real gentleman; **'caballeros'** [en aseos] 'gents'; [en grandes almacenes] 'menswear' - **2.** [miembro de una orden] knight.

caballete *m* - **1.** [de lienzo] easel - **2.** [de mesa] trestle - **3.** [de nariz] bridge.

caballito *m* small horse, pony.
   ◆ **caballitos** *mpl* [de feria] merry-go-round (sg).

caballo *m* - **1.** [animal] horse; **montar a** ~ to ride - **2.** [pieza de ajedrez] knight - **3.** [naipe] ≃ queen - **4.** MEC: ~ **(de fuerza** o **de vapor)** horsepower.
   ◆ **caballo de Troya** *m* Trojan horse.

cabaña *f* - **1.** [choza] hut, cabin - **2.** [ganado] livestock (U).

cabaret (*pl* **cabarets**) *m* cabaret.

cabecear *vi* - **1.** [persona - negando] to shake one's head; [- afirmando] to nod one's head - **2.** [caballo] to toss its head - **3.** [dormir] to nod (off).

cabecera *f* - **1.** [gen] head; [de cama] head-board - **2.** [de texto] heading; [de periódico] headline - **3.** [de río] headwaters (*pl*).

cabecilla *mf* ringleader.

cabellera *f* long hair (*U*).

cabello *m* hair (*U*).

caber *vi* - **1.** [gen] to fit; **no cabe nadie más** there's no room for anyone else; **no me cabe en el dedo** it won't fit my finger - **2.** MAT: **nueve entre tres caben a tres** three into nine goes three (times) - **3.** [ser posible] to be possible; **cabe destacar que ...** it's worth pointing out that ...

cabestrillo ➡ **en cabestrillo** *loc adj* in a sling.

cabestro *m* [animal] leading ox.

cabeza *f* - **1.** [gen] head; **por ~** per head; **obrar con ~** to use one's head; **tirarse de ~ (a)** to dive (into); **venir a la ~** to come to mind; **~ (lectora)** [gen] head; [de tocadiscos] pickup - **2.** [pelo] hair - **3.** [posición] front, head; **a la** *o* **en ~** [en competición etc] in front, in the lead; [en lista] at the top *o* head - **4.** *loc:* **andar** *o* **estar mal de la ~** to be funny in the head; **se le ha metido en la ~ que ...** he has got it into his head that ...; **sentar la ~** to settle down.
➡ **cabeza de ajo** *f* head of garlic.
➡ **cabeza rapada** *mf* skinhead.
➡ **cabeza de turco** *f* scapegoat.

cabezada *f* - **1.** [de sueño] nod, nodding (*U*); **dar ~s** to nod off - **2.** [golpe] butt.

cabezal *m* [de aparato] head.

cabezón, ona *adj* [terco] pigheaded, stubborn.

cabida *f* capacity.

cabina *f* - **1.** [locutorio] booth, cabin; **~ de prensa** press box - **2.:** **~ telefónica** phone box *UK*, phone booth - **3.** [de avión] cockpit; [de camión] cab; **~ de mandos** flight deck - **4.** [vestuario - en playa] bathing hut; [- en piscina] changing cubicle.

cabinero, ra *m,f* *Col* air steward (*f* air hostess).

cabizbajo, ja *adj* crestfallen, downcast.

cable *m* cable; **televisión por ~** cable television.

cablegrafiar *vt* to cable.

cabo *m* - **1.** GEOGR cape - **2.** NÁUT cable, rope - **3.** MIL corporal - **4.** [trozo] bit, piece; [trozo final] stub, stump; [de cuerda] end - **5.** *loc:* **llevar algo a ~** to carry sthg out.
➡ **cabo suelto** *m* loose end.
➡ **al cabo de** *loc prep* after.

cabra *f* [animal] goat; **estar como una ~** *fam* to be off one's head.

cabré ➡ **caber**.

cabrear *vt* *mfam*: **~ a alguien** to get sb's goat, to annoy sb.

cabría ➡ **caber**.

cabriola *f* prance; **hacer ~s** to prance about.

cabrita *f* *Amér* popcorn.

cabrito *m* [animal] kid (goat).

cabro, bra *m,f* *Chile fam* kid.

cabrón, ona *vulg* ◇ *adj:* **¡qué ~ eres!** you bastard! ◇ *m,f* bastard (*f* bitch).

cabuya *f* *CAm, Col, Ven* rope.

caca *f* *fam* - **1.** [excremento] pooh - **2.** [cosa sucia] nasty *o* dirty thing.

cacahuate *m* *CAm, Méx* peanut.

cacahuete *m* peanut.

cacao *m* - **1.** [bebida] cocoa - **2.** [árbol] cacao.

cacarear *vi* [gallo] to cluck, to cackle.

cacatúa *f* [ave] cockatoo.

cacería *f* hunt.

cacerola *f* pot, pan.

cachalote *m* sperm whale.

cacharro *m* - **1.** [recipiente] pot; **fregar los ~s** to do the dishes - **2.** *fam* [trasto] junk (*U*), rubbish (*U*) - **3.** [máquina] crock; [coche] banger.

cachear *vt* to frisk.

cachemir *m*, **cachemira** *f* cashmere.

cacheo *m* frisk, frisking (*U*).

cachet [ka'tʃe] *m* - **1.** [distinción] cachet - **2.** [cotización de artista] fee.

cachetada *f* *fam* smack.

cachete *m* - **1.** [moflete] chubby cheek - **2.** [bofetada] slap.

cachirulo *m* [chisme] thingamajig.

cachivache *m* *fam* knick-knack.

cacho *m* - **1.** *fam* [pedazo] piece, bit - **2.** *Andes, Ven* [asta] horn.

cachondearse *vpr* *fam*: **~ (de)** to take the mickey (out of).

cachondeo *m* *fam* - **1.** [diversión] lark - **2.** *despec* [cosa poco seria] joke.

cachondo, da *adj* *fam* - **1.** [divertido] funny - **2.** [salido] randy.

cachorro, rra *m,f* [de perro] puppy; [de león, lobo, oso] cub.

cacique *m* - **1.** [persona influyente] cacique, local political boss - **2.** [jefe indio] chief, cacique.

caco *m* *fam* thief.

cacto, cactus (*pl* **cactus**) *m* cactus.

cada *adj inv* - **1.** [gen] each; [con números, tiempo] every; **~ dos meses** every two months; **~ cosa a su tiempo** one thing at a time; **~ cual** each one, every one; **~ uno de** each of - **2.** [valor progresivo]: **~ vez más**

more and more; ~ **vez más largo** longer and longer; ~ **día más** more and more each day - **3**. [valor enfático] such; **¡se pone ~ sombrero!** she wears such hats!

cadalso *m* scaffold.

cadáver *m* corpse, (dead) body.

cadena *f* - **1**. [gen] chain; **en ~** [accidente] multiple - **2**. TV channel - **3**. [RADIO - emisora] station; [- red de emisoras] network - **4**. [de proceso industrial] line; ~ **de montaje** assembly line - **5**. [aparato de música] sound system - **6**. GEOGR range.
◆ **cadena perpetua** *f* life imprisonment.

cadencia *f* [ritmo] rhythm, cadence.

cadera *f* hip.

cadete *m* - **1**. cadet - **2**. RP [recadero] errand boy, office junior.

caducar *vi* - **1**. [carnet, ley, pasaporte etc] to expire - **2**. [medicamento] to pass its use-by date; [alimento] to pass its sell-by date.

caducidad *f* expiry.

caduco, ca *adj* - **1**. [viejo] decrepit; [idea] outmoded - **2**. [desfasado] no longer valid.

caer *vi* - **1**. [gen] to fall; [diente, pelo] to fall out; **dejar ~ algo** to drop sthg; ~ **bajo** to sink (very) low; **estar al ~** to be about to arrive - **2**. [al perder equilibrio] to fall over *o* down; ~ **de un tejado/caballo** to fall from a roof/horse - **3**. [fig [sentar]: ~ **bien/mal (a alguien)** [comentario, noticia etc] to go down well/badly (with sb) - **4**. *fig* [mostrarse]: **me cae bien/mal** I like/don't like him - **5**. *fig* [estar situado]: **cae cerca de aquí** it's not far from here - **6**. *fig* [recordar]: ~ **(en algo)** to be able to remember (sthg).
◆ **caer en** *vi* - **1**. [entender] to get, to understand; [solución] to hit upon - **2**. [coincidir - fecha] to fall on; **cae en domingo** it falls on a Sunday - **3**. [incurrir] to fall into.
◆ **caerse** *vpr* - **1**. [persona] to fall over *o* down - **2**. [objetos] to drop, to fall - **3**. [desprenderse - diente, pelo etc] to fall out; [- botón] to fall off; [- cuadro] to fall down.

café (*pl* **cafés**) *m* - **1**. [gen] coffee; ~ **solo/con leche** black/white coffee; ~ **instantáneo** *o* **soluble** instant coffee - **2**. [establecimiento] cafe.

cafeína *f* caffeine.

cafetera ▷ **cafetero**.

cafetería *f* cafe.

cafetero, ra *m,f* - **1**. [cultivador] coffee grower - **2**. [comerciante] coffee merchant.
◆ **cafetera** *f* - **1**. [gen] coffee pot - **2**. [en bares] expresso machine; [eléctrica] percolator, coffee machine.

cafiche *m Andes fam* pimp.

cagar *vi vulg* [defecar] to shit, to crap.
◆ **cagarse** *vpr vulg lit & fig* to shit o.s.

caído, da *adj* [árbol, hoja] fallen.

◆ **caída** *f* - **1**. [gen] fall, falling (*U*); [de diente, pelo] loss - **2**. [de paro, precios, terreno]: **caída (de)** drop (in) - **3**. [de falda, vestido etc] drape.
◆ **caídos** *mpl*: **los ~s** the fallen.

caiga *etc* ▷ **caer**.

caimán *m* - **1**. [animal] alligator, cayman - **2**. *fig* [persona] sly fox.

caja *f* - **1**. [gen] box; [para transporte, embalaje] crate; ~ **de zapatos** shoebox; **una ~ de cervezas** a crate of beer; ~ **torácica** thorax - **2**. [de reloj] case; [de engranajes etc] housing; ~ **de cambios** gearbox - **3**. [ataúd] coffin - **4**. [de dinero] cash box; ~ **fuerte** *o* **de caudales** safe, strongbox - **5**. [en tienda, supermercado] till; [en banco] cashier's desk - **6**. [banco]: ~ **(de ahorros)** savings bank, ≃ savings and loan association *US* - **7**. [hueco] well; [- de chimenea, ascensor] shaft - **8**. IMPRENTA case - **9**. [de instrumento musical] body; ~ **de resonancia** sound box; ~ **de ritmos** drum machine.
◆ **caja negra** *f* black box.
◆ **caja registradora** *f* cash register.

cajero, ra *m,f* [en tienda] cashier; [en banco] teller.
◆ **cajero** *m*: ~ **(automático)** cash machine, cash dispenser, ATM *US*.

cajetilla *f* - **1**. [de cigarrillos] packet - **2**. [de cerillas] box.

cajón *m* - **1**. [de mueble] drawer - **2**. [recipiente] crate, case.
◆ **cajón de sastre** *m* muddle, jumble.

cajuela *f Méx* boot *UK*, trunk *US*.

cal *f* lime.

cala *f* - **1**. [bahía pequeña] cove - **2**. [del barco] hold.

calabacín *m* courgette *UK*, zucchini *US*.

calabaza *f* pumpkin, squash *US*, gourd.

calabozo *m* cell.

calada ▷ **calado**.

calado, da *adj* soaked.
◆ **calado** *m* NÁUT draught.
◆ **calada** *f* [de cigarrillo] drag.

calamar *m* squid.

calambre *m* - **1**. [descarga eléctrica] (electric) shock - **2**. [contracción muscular] cramp (*U*).

calamidad *f* calamity; **ser una ~** *fig* to be a dead loss.

calaña *f despec*: **de esa ~** of that ilk.

calar ◇ *vt* - **1**. [empapar] to soak - **2**. *fig* [persona] to see through - **3**. [gorro, sombrero] to jam on - **4**. [sandía, melón] to cut a sample of - **5**. [perforar] to pierce. ◇ *vi* - **1**. NÁUT to draw - **2**. *fig* [penetrar]: ~ **en** to have an impact on.
◆ **calarse** *vpr* - **1**. [empaparse] to get soaked - **2**. [motor] to stall.

calavera *f* [cráneo] skull.

◆ **calaveras** *fpl Méx* [luces] tail lights.
calcar *vt* -**1.** [dibujo] to trace -**2.** [imitar] to copy.
calce *m* -**1.** [cuña] wedge -**2.** *Guat, Méx, PRico* DER footnote.
calceta *f* stocking; **hacer** ~ to knit.
calcetín *m* sock.
calcificarse *vpr* to calcify.
calcinar *vt* [quemar] to burn, to char.
calcio *m* calcium.
calco *m* -**1.** [reproducción] tracing -**2.** *fig* [imitación] carbon copy.
calcomanía *f* transfer.
calculador, ra *adj lit* & *fig* calculating.
◆ **calculadora** *f* calculator.
calcular *vt* -**1.** [cantidades] to calculate -**2.** [suponer] to reckon.
cálculo *m* -**1.** [operación] calculation -**2.** [ciencia] calculus -**3.** [evaluación] esti- mate -**4.** MED stone, calculus.
caldear *vt* -**1.** [calentar] to heat (up) -**2.** *fig* [excitar] to warm up, to liven up.
caldera *f* -**1.** [recipiente] cauldron -**2.** [má- quina] boiler.
calderilla *f* small change, coppers *(pl) UK*.
caldero *m* cauldron.
caldo *m* -**1.** [sopa] broth -**2.** [caldillo] stock -**3.** [vino] wine.
calefacción *f* heating; ~ **central** central heating.
calefactor *m* heater.
calefón *m CSur* water heater.
calendario *m* calendar; ~ **escolar/laboral** school/working year.
calentador *m* -**1.** [aparato] heater -**2.** [pren- da] legwarmer.
calentar ◇ *vt* [subir la temperatura de] to heat (up), to warm (up). ◇ *vi* [entrenarse] to warm up.
◆ **calentarse** *vpr* [por calor - suj: persona] to warm o.s., to get warm; [- suj: cosa] to heat up.
calentura *f* -**1.** [fiebre] fever, temperature -**2.** [herida] cold sore.
calesita *f RP* merry-go-round *UK*, carousel *US*.
calibrar *vt* -**1.** [medir] to calibrate, to gauge -**2.** [dar calibre a - arma] to bore -**3.** *fig* [juz- gar] to gauge.
calibre *m* -**1.** [diámetro - de pistola] calibre; [- de alambre] gauge; [- de tubo] bore -**2.** [instrumento] gauge -**3.** *fig* [tamaño] size.
calidad *f* -**1.** [gen] quality; **de** ~ quality *(an- tes de sust)*; ~ **de vida** quality of life -**2.** [cla- se] class -**3.** [condición]: **en** ~ **de** in one's capacity as.
cálido, da *adj* warm.
caliente *adj* -**1.** [gen] hot; [templado]

warm; **en** ~ *fig* in the heat of the moment -**2.** *fig* [acalorado] heated.
calificación *f* -**1.** [de película] rating -**2.** EDUC mark.
calificar *vt* -**1.** [denominar]: ~ **a alguien de algo** to call sb sthg, to describe sb as sthg -**2.** EDUC to mark -**3.** GRAM to qualify.
calificativo, va *adj* qualifying.
◆ **calificativo** *m* epithet.
caligrafía *f* -**1.** [arte] calligraphy -**2.** [tipo de letra] handwriting.
cáliz *m* RELIG chalice.
calizo, za *adj* chalky.
◆ **caliza** *f* limestone.
callado, da *adj* quiet, silent.
callar ◇ *vi* -**1.** [no hablar] to keep quiet, to be silent -**2.** [dejar de hablar] to be quiet, to stop talking. ◇ *vt* -**1.** [ocultar] to keep quiet about; [secreto] to keep -**2.** [acallar] to si- lence.
◆ **callarse** *vpr* -**1.** [no hablar] to keep quiet, to be silent -**2.** [dejar de hablar] to be quiet, to stop talking; **¡cállate!** shut up! -**3.** [ocultar] to keep quiet about; [secreto] to keep.
calle *f* -**1.** [vía de circulación] street, road; ~ **arriba/abajo** up/down the street; ~ **de dirección única** one-way street; ~ **peatonal** pedestrian precinct; ~ **sin salida** dead end, blind alley -**2.** DEP lane -**3.** *loc*: **dejar a al- guien en la** ~ to put sb out of a job; **echar a alguien a la** ~ [de un trabajo] to sack sb; [de un lugar público] to kick *o* throw sb out.
callejear *vi* to wander the streets.
callejero, ra *adj* [gen] street *(antes de sust)*; [perro] stray.
◆ **callejero** *m* [guía] street map.
callejón *m* alley; ~ **sin salida** cul-de-sac; *fig* blind alley, impasse.
callejuela *f* backstreet, side street.
callista *mf* chiropodist.
callo *m* [dureza] callus; [en el pie] corn.
◆ **callos** *mpl* CULIN tripe *(U)*.
calma *f* -**1.** [sin ruido o movimiento] calm; **en** ~ calm -**2.** [sosiego] tranquility; **tóma- telo con** ~ take it easy -**3.** [apatía] sluggish- ness, indifference.
calmante ◇ *adj* soothing. ◇ *m* sedative.
calmar *vt* -**1.** [mitigar] to relieve -**2.** [tranqui- lizar] to calm, to soothe.
◆ **calmarse** *vpr* to calm down; [dolor, tempestad] to abate.
caló *m* gypsy dialect.
calor *m* [gen] heat; [sin quemar] warmth; **entrar en** ~ [gen] to get warm; [público, de- portista] to warm up; **hacer** ~ to be warm *o* hot; **tener** ~ to be warm *o* hot.
caloría *f* calorie.
calumnia *f* [oral] slander; [escrita] libel.

calumniar *vt* [oralmente] to slander; [por escrito] to libel.

calumnioso, sa *adj* [de palabra] slanderous; [por escrito] libellous.

caluroso, sa *adj* **-1.** [gen] hot; [templado] warm **-2.** *fig* [afectuoso] warm.

calva ⊳ calvo.

calvario *m fig* [sufrimiento] ordeal.

calvicie *f* baldness.

calvo, va *adj* bald.

➡ **calva** *f* [en la cabeza] bald patch.

calza *f* [cuña] wedge, block.

calzado, da *adj* [con zapatos] shod.

➡ **calzado** *m* footwear.

➡ **calzada** *f* road.

calzar *vt* **-1.** [poner calzado] to put on **-2.** [llevar un calzado] to wear; **¿qué número calza?** what size do you take? **-3.** [poner cuña a] to wedge, to block.

➡ **calzarse** *vpr* to put on.

calzo *m* [cuña] wedge.

calzón *m* **-1.** *Esp* [deportivo] shorts **-2.** *Andes, Méx, RP* [braga] knickers *UK*, panties *US*.

calzoncillo *m* (gen pl) underpants (pl), shorts (pl) *US*.

cama *f* bed; **estar en** o **guardar ~** to be in bed; **hacer la ~** to make the bed; **~ individual/de matrimonio** single/double bed.

camada *f* litter.

camafeo *m* cameo.

camaleón *m lit & fig* chameleon.

cámara ⊳ *f* **-1.** [gen & TECN] chamber; **~ alta/baja** upper/lower house; **~ de aire/gas** air/gas chamber **-2.** CIN, FOT & TV camera; **a ~ lenta** *lit & fig* in slow motion; **~ de seguridad** security camera; **~ de vídeo** video camera **-3.** [de balón, neumático] inner tube **-4.** [habitáculo] cabin. ⊳ *mf* [persona] cameraman (*f* camerawoman).

camarada *mf* POLÍT comrade.

camarero, ra *m,f* [de restaurante] waiter (*f* waitress); [de hotel] steward (*f* chambermaid).

camarilla *f* clique; POLÍT lobby, pressure group.

camarón *m* shrimp.

camarote *m* cabin.

cambiante *adj* changeable.

cambiar ⊳ *vt* **-1.** [gen] to change; **~ libras por euros** to change pounds into euros **-2.** [canjear]: **a ~ algo (por)** to exchange sthg (for). ⊳ *vi* **-1.** [gen] to change; **~ de** [gen] to change; **~ de casa** to move house; **~ de trabajo** to move jobs **-2.** AUTOM: **~ de marcha** to change gear.

➡ **cambiarse** *vpr*: **~se (de)** [ropa] to change; [casa] to move; **~se de vestido** to change one's dress.

cambio *m* **-1.** [gen] change; **~ climático** climate change; **~ de domicilio** change of address; **~ de guardia** changing of the guard **-2.** [trueque] exchange; **a ~ (de)** in exchange o return (for) **-3.** [FIN - de acciones] price; [- de divisas] exchange rate; **'cambio' 'bureau de change'** **-4.** AUTOM: **~ de marchas** o **velocidades** gear change; **~ de sentido** U-turn.

➡ **cambio de rasante** *m* brow of a hill.

➡ **libre cambio** *m* **-1.** ECON [librecambismo] free trade **-2.** FIN [de divisas] floating exchange rates (pl).

➡ **en cambio** *loc adv* **-1.** [por otra parte] on the other hand, however **-2.** [en su lugar] instead.

camelar *vt fam* [seducir, engañar] to butter up, to win over.

camelia *f* camellia.

camello, lla *m,f* [animal] camel.

➡ **camello** *m fam* [traficante] drug pusher o dealer.

camellón *m* *Col, Méx* central reservation *UK*, median (strip) *US*.

camerino *m* dressing room.

camilla ⊳ *f* [gen] stretcher; [de psiquiatra, dentista] couch. ⊳ *adj* ⊳ mesa.

caminante *mf* walker.

caminar ⊳ *vi* **-1.** [a pie] to walk **-2.** *fig* [ir]: **~ (hacia)** to head (for). ⊳ *vt* [una distancia] to travel, to cover.

caminata *f* long walk.

camino *m* **-1.** [sendero] path, track; [carretera] road; **~ de montaña** mountain path; **abrir ~ a** to clear the way for; **abrirse ~** to get on o ahead **-2.** [ruta] way; **a medio ~** halfway; **estar a medio ~** to be halfway there; **quedarse a medio ~** to stop halfway through; **~ de** on the way to; **en el** o **de ~** on the way; **ir ~ de** to be heading for **-3.** [viaje] journey; **ponerse en ~** to set off **-4.** *fig* [medio] way.

camión *m* **-1.** [de mercancías] lorry *UK*, truck *US*; **~ articulado** articulated lorry *UK* o truck *US*; **~ cisterna** tanker; **~ de la mudanza** removal van **-2.** *CAm, Méx* [bus] bus.

camionero, ra ⊳ *adj* *CAm, Méx* bus. ⊳ *m,f* lorry driver *UK*, trucker *US*.

camioneta *f* van.

camisa *f* **-1.** [prenda] shirt **-2.** *loc*: **meterse en ~ de once varas** to complicate matters unnecessarily; **mudar** o **cambiar de ~** to change sides.

➡ **camisa de fuerza** *f* straitjacket.

camisería *f* [tienda] shirt shop, outfitter's.

camiseta *f* **-1.** [prenda interior] vest *UK*, undershirt *US* **-2.** [de verano] T-shirt **-3.** [DEP - de tirantes] vest; [- de mangas] shirt.

camisola *f* **-1.** [prenda interior] camisole

- **2.** *Amér* DEP sports shirt.
camisón *m* nightdress.
camorra *f* trouble; **buscar** ~ to look for trouble.
camote *m Andes, CAm, Méx* [batata] sweet potato.
campamento *m* camp.
campana *f* bell; ~ **extractora de humos** extractor hood.
campanada *f* - **1.** [de campana] peal - **2.** [de reloj] stroke - **3.** *fig* [suceso] sensation.
campanario *m* belfry, bell tower.
campanilla *f* - **1.** [de la puerta] (small) bell; [con mango] handbell - **2.** [flor] campanula, bellflower.
campanilleo *m* tinkling *(U).*
campante *adj fam*: **estar** o **quedarse tan** ~ to remain quite unruffled.
campaña *f* - **1.** [gen] campaign; **de** ~ MIL field *(antes de sust)* - **2.** *RP* [campo] countryside.
campechano, na *adj fam* genial, good-natured.
campeón, ona *m,f* champion.
campeonato *m* championship; **de** ~ *fig* terrific, great.
campero, ra *adj* country *(antes de sust)*; [al aire libre] open-air.
   ~ **campera** *f* - **1.** [bota] ≃ cowboy boot - **2.** *RP* [chaqueta] jacket.
campesino, na *m,f* [gen] farmer; [muy pobre] peasant.
campestre *adj* country *(antes de sust)*.
camping ['kampin] *(pl* **campings)** *m* - **1.** [actividad] camping; **ir de** ~ to go camping - **2.** [lugar de acampada] campsite.
campito *m Amér* property, estate.
campo *m* - **1.** [gen & INFORM] field; ~ **de aviación** airfield; ~ **de batalla** battlefield; ~ **de tiro** firing range; **dejar el** ~ **libre** *fig* to leave the field open - **2.** [campiña] country, countryside; **a** ~ **traviesa** cross country - **3.** [DEP - de fútbol] pitch; [- de tenis] court; [- de golf] course - **4.** *CSur* [hacienda] cattle ranch - **5.** *Andes* [lugar] room, space.
   ~ **campo de concentración** *m* concentration camp.
camuflaje *m* camouflage.
cana ⊳ **cano.**
Canadá: **(el)** ~ Canada.
canadiense *adj & m,f* Canadian.
canal *m* - **1.** [cauce artificial] canal; ~ **de riego** irrigation channel - **2.** GEOGR channel, strait - **3.** RADIO & TV channel; ~ **por cable** cable channel - **4.** ANAT canal, duct - **5.** [de agua, gas] conduit, pipe - **6.** *fig* [medio, vía] channel.
canalizar *vt* - **1.** [territorio] to canalize; [agua] to channel - **2.** *fig* [orientar] to channel.

canalla *mf* swine, dog.
canalón *m* [de tejado] gutter; [en la pared] drainpipe.
canapé *m* - **1.** CULIN canapé - **2.** [sofá] sofa, couch.
Canarias *fpl*: **las (islas)** ~ the Canary Islands, the Canaries.
canario, ria ⊳ *adj* of the Canary Islands. ⊳ *m,f* [persona] Canary Islander.
   ~ **canario** *m* [pájaro] canary.
canasta *f* [gen & DEP] basket.
canastilla *f* - **1.** [cesto pequeño] basket - **2.** [de bebé] layette.
canasto *m* large basket.
cancán, cancanes *mf RP* tights *UK*, pantyhose *US*.
cancela *f* wrought-iron gate.
cancelación *f* cancellation.
cancelar *vt* - **1.** [anular] to cancel - **2.** [deuda] to pay, to settle - **3.** *Chile,Ven* [cuenta] to pay.
cáncer *m* MED & *fig* cancer.
   ~ **Cáncer** ⊳ *m* [zodiaco] Cancer. ⊳ *mf* [persona] Cancer, Cancerian.
cancerígeno, na *adj* carcinogenic.
canceroso, sa *adj* [úlcera, tejido] cancerous; [enfermo] suffering from cancer.
canchero, ra *adj RP fam* streetwise, savvy.
canciller *m* - **1.** [de gobierno, embajada] chancellor - **2.** [de asuntos exteriores] foreign minister.
canción *f* song; ~ **de cuna** lullaby.
cancionero *m* songbook.
candado *m* padlock.
candela *f* - **1.** [vela] candle - **2.** *Amér* [fuego] fire.
candelabro *m* candelabra.
candelero *m* candlestick; **estar en el** ~ *fig* to be in the limelight.
candente *adj* - **1.** [incandescente] red-hot - **2.** *fig* [actual] burning *(antes de sust)*.
candidato, ta *m,f* candidate.
candidatura *f* [para un cargo] candidacy.
candidez *f* ingenuousness.
cándido, da *adj* ingenuous, simple.
candil *m* - **1.** [lámpara] oil lamp - **2.** *Méx* [araña] chandelier.
candilejas *fpl* footlights.
canela *f* cinnamon.
canelo, la *adj fam fig* [inocentón] gullible.
canelón *m* CULIN cannelloni *(pl).*
cangrejo *m* crab.
canguro ⊳ *m* [animal] kangaroo. ⊳ *mf fam* [persona] babysitter; **hacer de** ~ to babysit.
caníbal *mf* cannibal.
canica *f* [pieza] marble.
   ~ **canicas** *fpl* [juego] marbles.
caniche *m* poodle.

canijo, ja *adj* sickly.

canilla *f* - **1.** [espinilla] shinbone - **2.** *RP* [grifo] tap *UK*, faucet *US* - **3.** *Amér* [pierna] leg.

canillita *m RP fam* newspaper vendor.

canino, na *adj* canine.
→ **canino** *m* [diente] canine (tooth).

canjear *vt* to exchange.

cano, na *adj* grey.
→ **cana** *f* grey hair.

canoa *f* canoe.

canódromo *m* greyhound track.

canon *m* - **1.** [norma] canon; **como mandan los cánones** according to the rules - **2.** [modelo] ideal - **3.** [impuesto] tax - **4.** MÚS canon.

canónigo *m* canon.

canonizar *vt* to canonize.

canoso, sa *adj* [pelo] grey; [persona] greyhaired.

cansado, da *adj* - **1.** [agotado] tired; ~ **de algo/de hacer algo** tired of sthg/of doing sthg - **2.** [pesado, cargante] tiring.

cansador, ra *adj Andes, RP* [que cansa] tiring; [que aburre] tiresome, boring.

cansancio *m* tiredness.

cansar ⋄ *vt* to tire (out). ⋄ *vi* to be tiring.
→ **cansarse** *vpr:* ~**se (de)** *lit & fig* to get tired (of).

Cantábrico *m:* **el (mar)** ~ the Cantabrian Sea.

cantaleta *f Amér* nagging.

cantante ⋄ *adj* singing. ⋄ *mf* singer.

cantaor, ra *m,f* flamenco singer.

cantar ⋄ *vt* - **1.** [canción] to sing - **2.** [bingo, línea, el gordo] to call (out); ~ **victoria** to claim victory; ~ **a alguien las cuarenta** to give sb a piece of one's mind. ⋄ *vi* - **1.** [persona, ave] to sing; [gallo] to crow; [grillo] to chirp - **2.** *fam fig* [confesar] to talk.

cántaro *m* large pitcher; **llover a** ~**s** to rain cats and dogs.

cante *m:* ~ **(jondo** *o* **hondo)** flamenco singing.

cantera *f* [de piedra] quarry.

cantero *m CSur, Cuba* [de flores] flowerbed.

cantidad *f* - **1.** [medida] quantity - **2.** [abundancia] abundance, large number; **en** ~ in abundance; ~ **de** lots of; **en** ~**s industriales** in industrial quantities - **3.** [número] number - **4.** [suma de dinero] sum (of money).

cantilena, cantinela *f:* **la misma** ~ *fig* the same old story.

cantimplora *f* water bottle.

cantina *f* [de soldados] mess; [en fábrica] canteen; [en estación de tren] buffet; [bar] snack bar.

cantinela = cantilena.

canto *m* - **1.** [acción, arte] singing - **2.** [canción] song - **3.** [lado, borde] edge; **de** ~ edgeways - **4.** [de cuchillo] blunt edge

- **5.** [guijarro] pebble; ~ **rodado** [pequeño] pebble; [grande] boulder.

cantor, ra *m,f* singer.

canturrear *vt & vi fam* to sing softly.

canuto *m* - **1.** [tubo] tube - **2.** *fam* [porro] joint.

caña *f* - **1.** BOT cane; ~ **de azúcar** sugarcane - **2.** *Esp* [de cerveza] half; **una** ~ one beer - **3.** *Andes, Cuba, RP* [aguardiente] *type of rum made using sugar cane spirit.*
→ **caña de pescar** *f* fishing rod.

cañabrava *f Cuba, RP* kind of cane.

cáñamo *m* hemp.

cañería *f* pipe.

cañero, ra *m,f Amér* [trabajador] sugar plantation worker.

caño *m* [de fuente] jet.

cañón *m* - **1.** [arma] gun; HIST cannon; ~ **antiaéreo** anti-aircraft gun; ~ **de nieve** snow cannon - **2.** [de fusil] barrel; [de chimenea] flue; [de órgano] pipe - **3.** GEOGR canyon.

caoba *f* mahogany.

caos *m inv* chaos.

caótico, ca *adj* chaotic.

cap. *(abrev de* **capítulo***)* ch.

capa *f* - **1.** [manto] cloak, cape; **andar de** ~ **caída** to be in a bad way; **de** ~ **y espada** cloak and dagger - **2.** [baño - de barniz, pintura] coat; [- de chocolate etc] coating - **3.** [estrato] layer; GEOL stratum, layer; ~ **de ozono** ozone layer; ~ **de hielo** sheet of ice - **4.** [grupo social] stratum, class - **5.** TAUROM cape.

capacidad *f* - **1.** [gen] capacity; **con** ~ **para 500 personas** with a capacity of 500 - **2.** [aptitud] ability; **no tener** ~ **para algo/para hacer algo** to be no good at sthg/at doing sthg.
→ **capacidad de decisión** *f* decision-making ability.
→ **capacidad de trabajo** *f* capacity for hard work.

capacitación *f* training.

capacitar *vt:* ~ **a alguien para algo** [habilitar] to qualify sb for sthg; [formar] to train sb for sthg.

capar *vt* to castrate.

caparazón *m lit & fig* shell.

capataz *mf* foreman (*f* forewoman).

capaz *adj* - **1.** [gen] capable; ~ **de algo/de hacer algo** capable of sthg/of doing sthg - **2.** [atrevido]: **ser** ~ to dare; **ser** ~ **de hacer algo** to bring oneself to do sthg - **3.** [espacioso]: **muy/poco** ~ with a large/small capacity; ~ **para** with room for.

capazo *m* large wicker basket.

capellán *m* chaplain.

caperuza *f* [gorro] hood.

capicúa *adj inv* reversible.

capilla *f* chapel; **~ ardiente** funeral chapel.

cápita ✦ **per cápita** *loc adj* per capita.

capital ◇ *adj* **-1.** [importante] supreme **-2.** [principal] main. ◇ *m* ECON capital. ◇ *f* [ciudad] capital; **soy de Barcelona ~** I'm from the city of Barcelona.

capitalismo *m* capitalism.

capitalista *adj* & *m,f* capitalist.

capitalizar *vt* **-1.** ECON to capitalize **-2.** *fig* [sacar provecho] to capitalize on.

capitán, ana *m,f* captain.

capitanear *vt* DEP & MIL to captain.

capitel *m* capital.

capitoste *mf despec* big boss.

capitulación *f* capitulation, surrender.

capitular *vi* to capitulate, to surrender.

capítulo *m* **-1.** [sección, división] chapter **-2.** *fig* [tema] subject.

capó, capot [ka'po] *m* bonnet *UK*, hood *US*.

caporal *m* MIL ≃ corporal.

capot = capó.

capota *f* hood *UK*, top *US*.

capote *m* **-1.** [capa] cape with sleeves; [militar] greatcoat **-2.** TAUROM cape.

capricho *m* **-1.** [antojo] whim, caprice; **darse un ~** to treat o.s. **-2.** MÚS & ARTE caprice.

caprichoso, sa *adj* capricious.

Capricornio ◇ *m* [zodiaco] Capricorn. ◇ *mf* [persona] Capricorn.

cápsula *f* **-1.** [gen & ANAT] capsule **-2.** [tapón] cap.
　✦ **cápsula espacial** *f* space capsule.

captar *vt* **-1.** [atraer - simpatía] to win; [- interés] to gain, to capture **-2.** [entender] to grasp **-3.** [sintonizar] to pick up, to receive **-4.** [aguas] to collect.

captura *f* capture.

capturar *vt* to capture.

capucha *f* hood.

capuchón *m* cap, top.

capullo, lla *m,f vulg* [persona] prat.
　✦ **capullo** *m* **-1.** [de flor] bud **-2.** [de gusano] cocoon.

caqui, kaki *adj inv* [color] khaki.

cara *f* **-1.** [rostro, aspecto] face; **~ a** face to face; **de ~** [sol, viento] in one's face **-2.** [lado] side; GEOM face **-3.** [de moneda] heads *(U)*; **~ o cruz** heads or tails; **echar algo a ~ o cruz** to toss (a coin) for sthg **-4.** *fam* [osadía] cheek; **tener (mucha) ~**, **tener la ~ muy dura** to have a cheek **-5.** *loc*: **de ~ a** with a view to; **echar en ~ algo a alguien** to reproach sb for sthg; **romper** *o* **partir la ~ a alguien** to smash sb's face in; **verse las ~s** [pelearse] to have it out; [enfrentarse] to fight it out.

carabina *f* **-1.** [arma] carbine, rifle **-2.** *fam fig* [mujer] chaperone.

Caracas Caracas.

caracol *m* **-1.** [animal] snail **-2.** [concha] shell **-3.** [rizo] curl.
　✦ **escalera de caracol** *f* spiral staircase.

caracola *f* conch.

carácter *(pl* caracteres*)* *m* **-1.** [de persona] character; **tener buen/mal ~** to be good-natured/bad-tempered **-2.** [índole] nature; **con ~ de urgencia** as a matter of urgency; **una reunión de ~ privado/oficial** a private/official meeting **-3.** INFORM character; **~ alfanumérico** alphanumeric character; **caracteres de imprenta** typeface *(sg)* **-4.** BIOL trait.

característico, ca *adj* characteristic.
　✦ **característica** *f* characteristic.

caracterización *f* **-1.** [gen] characterization **-2.** [maquillaje] make-up.

caracterizar *vt* **-1.** [definir] to characterize **-2.** [representar] to portray **-3.** [maquillar] to make up.
　✦ **caracterizarse por** *vpr* to be characterized by.

caradura *adj fam* cheeky.

carajillo *m* coffee with a dash of liqueur.

carajo *interj mfam*: **¡~!** damn it!

caramba *interj*: **¡~!** [sorpresa] good heavens!; [enfado] for heaven's sake!

carambola *f* cannon *(in billiards)*.
　✦ **carambolas** *interj Amér*: **¡~s!** good heavens!

caramelo *m* **-1.** [golosina] sweet **-2.** [azúcar fundido] caramel.

carátula *f* **-1.** [de libro] front cover; [de disco] sleeve **-2.** [máscara] mask.

caravana *f* **-1.** [gen] caravan *UK*, trailer *US* **-2.** [de coches] tailback.
　✦ **caravanas** *fpl Amér* [pendientes] earrings.

caray *interj*: **¡~!** [sorpresa] good heavens!; [enfado] damn it!

carbón *m* [para quemar] coal.

carboncillo *m* charcoal; **al ~** in charcoal.

carbonilla *f* [ceniza] cinder.

carbonizar *vt* to char, to carbonize.

carbono *m* carbon.

carbunclo *m* anthrax.

carburador *m* carburettor.

carburante *m* fuel.

carca *adj fam despec* old-fashioned.

carcajada *f* guffaw; **reír a ~s** to roar with laughter.

carcamal *mf fam despec* old crock.

carcasa *m* [para teléfono móvil] fascia.

cárcel *f* prison; **estar en la ~** to be in prison.

carcelero, ra *m,f* warder, jailer.

carcoma *f* -**1.** [insecto] woodworm - **2.** [polvo] wood dust.

carcomer *vt lit* & *fig* to eat away at.

carcomido, da *adj* [madera] wormeaten.

cardar *vt* -**1.** [lana] to card - **2.** [pelo] to back-comb.

cardenal *m* -**1.** RELIG cardinal - **2.** [hematoma] bruise.

cardiaco, ca, cardíaco, ca *adj* cardiac, heart *(antes de sust)*.

cárdigan, cardigán *m* cardigan.

cardinal *adj* cardinal.

cardiólogo, ga *m,f* cardiologist.

cardo *m* [planta] thistle.

carecer *vi*: ~ de algo to lack sthg.

carencia *f* [ausencia] lack; [defecto] deficiency.

carente *adj*: ~ de lacking (in).

carestía *f* [escasez] scarcity, shortage.

careta *f* -**1.** [máscara] mask; ~ antigás gas mask - **2.** *fig* [engaño] front.

carey *m* [material] tortoiseshell.

carga *f* -**1.** [acción] loading; de ~ frontal front-loading - **2.** [cargamento - de avión, barco] cargo; [- de tren] freight; [- de camión] load - **3.** [peso] load - **4.** *fig* [sufrimiento] burden - **5.** [ataque, explosivo] charge; volver a la ~ *fig* to persist - **6.** [de batería, condensador] charge - **7.** [para mechero, bolígrafo] refill - **8.** [impuesto] tax; ~ fiscal tax burden.

cargado, da *adj* -**1.** [abarrotado]: ~ (de) loaded (with); un árbol ~ de fruta a tree laden with fruit - **2.** [arma] loaded - **3.** [bebida] strong - **4.** [bochornoso - habitación] stuffy; [- tiempo] sultry, close; [- cielo] overcast - **5.**: ~ de hombros round-shouldered *(antes de sust)*.

cargador *m* [de arma] chamber.

cargamento *m* cargo.

cargante *adj fam fig* annoying.

cargar ◇ *vt* -**1.** [gen] to load; [pluma, mechero] to refill - **2.** [peso encima] to throw over one's shoulder - **3.** ELECTR to charge; INFORM to load - **4.** *fig* [responsabilidad, tarea] to give, to lay upon; ~ a alguien de deudas to encumber sb with debts - **5.** [producir pesadez - suj: humo] to make stuffy; [- suj: comida] to bloat - **6.** [gravar]: ~ un impuesto a algo/alguien to tax sthg/sb - **7.** [importe, factura, deuda]: ~ algo (a) to charge sthg (to); cárguelo a mi cuenta charge it to my account. ◇ *ví* [atacar]: ~ (contra) to charge.

◆ **cargar con** *vi* -**1.** [paquete etc] to carry away - **2.** *fig* [coste, responsabilidad] to bear; [consecuencias] to accept; [culpa] to get.

◆ **cargarse** *vpr* -**1.** *fam* [romper] to break - **2.** *fam* [matar - persona] to bump off; [- animal] to kill - **3.** [de humo] to get stuffy

- **4.** ELECTR to become charged; INFORM to load.

cargo *m* -**1.** [gen, ECON & DER] charge; sin ~ free of charge; correr a ~ de to be borne by; las personas a mi ~ the people in my care; hacerse ~ de [asumir el control de] to take charge of; [ocuparse de] to take care of; [comprender] to understand - **2.** [empleo] post, position; es un ~ público he holds public office.

cargosear *vt CSur* to annoy, to pester.

cargoso, sa *adj CSur* annoying.

carguero *m* cargo boat.

Caribe *m*: el (mar) ~ the Caribbean (Sea).

caribeño, ña *adj* Caribbean.

caricatura *f* caricature.

caricia *f* [a persona] caress; [a perro, gato etc] stroke.

caridad *f* charity.

caries *f inv* tooth decay; tengo dos ~ I have two cavities.

cariño *m* -**1.** [afecto] affection; tomar ~ a to grow fond of; con mucho ~ with great affection - **2.** [cuidado] loving care - **3.** [apelativo] love.

cariñoso, sa *adj* affectionate.

carisma *m* charisma.

carismático, ca *adj* charismatic.

Cáritas *f charitable organization run by the Catholic Church.*

caritativo, va *adj* charitable.

cariz *m* look, appearance; tomar mal/buen ~ to take a turn for the worse/better.

carmesí (*pl* carmesíes) *adj* & *m* crimson.

carmín ◇ *adj* [color] carmine. ◇ *m* -**1.** [color] carmine - **2.** [lápiz de labios] lipstick.

carnada *f lit* & *fig* bait.

carnal *adj* -**1.** [de la carne] carnal - **2.** [primo] first *(antes de sust)*.

carnaval *m* carnival.

carnaza *f lit* & *fig* bait.

carne *f* -**1.** [de persona, fruta] flesh; en ~ viva raw; ser de ~ y hueso *fig* to be human - **2.** [alimento] meat; ~ de cerdo pork; ~ de cordero lamb; ~ picada mince; ~ de ternera veal; ~ de vaca beef; ser ~ de cañón to be cannon fodder; poner la ~ de gallina a alguien [de frío] to give sb goose pimples; [de miedo] to give sb the creeps.

◆ **carne de membrillo** *f* quince jelly.

carné (*pl* carnés), **carnet** (*pl* carnets) *m* [documento] card; ~ de conducir driving licence; ~ de identidad identity card; ~ de estudiante student card; ~ de prensa press pass.

carnicería *f* -**1.** [tienda] butcher's - **2.** *fig* [masacre] carnage *(U)*.

carnicero, ra *m,f lit* & *fig* [persona] butcher.

carnitas *fpl Méx* *small pieces of braised pork.*

carnívoro, ra adj carnivorous.
→ **carnívoro** m carnivore.
carnoso, sa adj fleshy; [labios] full.
caro, ra adj [precio] expensive.
→ **caro** adv: **costar** ~ to be expensive; fig to cost dear; **vender** ~ **algo** to sell sthg at a high price; fig not to give sthg up easily; **pagar** ~ **algo** fig to pay dearly for sthg; **salir** ~ to be expensive; fig to cost dear.
carozo m RP stone, pit US.
carpa f - 1. [pez] carp - 2. [de circo] big top; [para fiestas etc] marquee - 3. Amér [tienda de campaña] tent.
carpeta f file, folder.
carpintería f - 1. [arte] carpentry; [de puertas y ventanas] joinery - 2. [taller] carpenter's/joiner's shop.
carpintero, ra m,f carpenter; [de puertas y ventanas] joiner.
carraca f [instrumento] rattle.
carraspear vi [toser] to clear one's throat.
carraspera f hoarseness.
carrera f - 1. [acción de correr] run, running (U) - 2. DEP & fig race; ~ **armamentística** o **de armamentos** arms race; ~ **ciclista** cycle race; ~ **de coches** motor race; ~ **de obstáculos** steeplechase - 3. [trayecto] route - 4. [de taxi] ride - 5. [estudios] university course; **hacer la** ~ **de derecho** to study law (at university) - 6. [profesión] career - 7. [en medias] ladder UK, run US.
carreta f cart.
carrete m - 1. [de hilo] bobbin, reel; [de alambre] coil - 2. FOT roll (of film) - 3. [para pescar] reel - 4. [de máquina de escribir] spool.
carretera f road; **viaje por** ~ road journey; ~ **de circunvalación** ring road; ~ **comarcal** ≃ B road UK; ~ **de cuota** Méx toll road; ~ **nacional** ≃ A road UK, state highway US; Méx: ~ **de cuota** toll road.
carretilla f wheelbarrow.
carril m - 1. [de carretera] lane; ~ **bici** cycle lane; ~ **bus** bus lane - 2. [de vía de tren] rail.
carrillo m cheek; **comer a dos** ~s fig to cram one's face with food.
carrito m trolley UK, cart US.
carro m - 1. [vehículo] cart; ~ **de combate** MIL tank - 2. [de máquina de escribir] carriage - 3. Andes, CAm, Carib, Méx [automóvil] car - 4. Méx: ~ **comedor** [en tren] dining car, restaurant car.
carrocería f bodywork UK, body.
carromato m [carro] wagon.
carroña f carrion.
carroza f [vehículo] carriage.
carruaje m carriage.
carrusel m [tiovivo] carousel, merry-go-round.

carta f - 1. letter; **echar una** ~ to post a letter; ~ **de presentación** letter of introduction; ~ **de recomendación** reference (letter) - 2. [naipe] (playing) card; **echar las** ~s **a alguien** to tell sb's fortune (with cards) - 3. [en restaurante] menu - 4. [mapa] map; NÁUT chart - 5. [documento] charter; ~ **verde** green card - 6. loc: **jugarse todo a una** ~ to put all one's eggs in one basket; **dar** ~ **blanca a algn** to give sb carte blanche.
→ **carta de ajuste** f test card.
→ **Carta de Derechos** f Bill of Rights.
→ **Carta Magna** f Constitution.
cartabón m set square.
cartapacio m [carpeta] folder.
cartearse vpr to correspond.
cartel m - 1. [póster] poster; 'prohibido fijar ~es' 'billposters will be prosecuted' - 2. [letrero] sign.
cártel m cartel.
cartelera f - 1. [tablón] hoarding, billboard - 2. PRENS entertainments page; **estar en** ~ to be showing; **lleva un año en** ~ it's been running for a year.
cárter m AUTOM housing.
cartera f - 1. [para dinero] wallet - 2. [para documentos] briefcase; [sin asa] portfolio; [de colegial] satchel - 3. COM, FIN & POLÍT portfolio - 4. [bolsillo] pocket flap - 5. Andes, CSur [bolso] handbag UK, purse US.
carterista mf pickpocket.
cartero, ra m,f postman (f postwoman).
cartílago m cartilage.
cartilla f - 1. [documento] book; ~ **(de ahorros)** savings book - 2. [para aprender a leer] primer.
cartón m - 1. [material] cardboard; ~ **piedra** papier mâché - 2. [de cigarrillos, leche] carton; [de huevos] box.
cartucho m [de arma] cartridge.
cartujo, ja adj Carthusian.
cartulina f card; ~ **amarilla/roja** FTBL yellow/red card.
casa f - 1. [edificio] house; ~ **adosada** semi-detached house; ~ **de campo** country house; ~ **unifamiliar** house (usually detached) on an estate; **echar** o **tirar la** ~ **por la ventana** to spare no expense; **ser de andar por** ~ [sencillo] to be simple o basic - 2. [hogar] home; **en** ~ at home; **ir a** ~ to go home; **pásate por mi** ~ come round to my place; **jugar en** ~/**fuera de** ~ to play at home/away - 3. [empresa] company; **vino de la** ~ house wine - 4. [organismo]: ~ **Consistorial** town hall; ~ **de huéspedes** guesthouse; ~ **de juego** gambling house; ~ **de putas** brothel; ~ **de socorro** first-aid post.
casaca f frock coat.

casado, da *adj*: ~ **(con)** married (to).

casamiento *m* wedding, marriage.

casar ◇ *vt* **-1.** [en matrimonio] to marry **- 2.** [unir] to fit together. ◇ *vi* to match.

◆ **casarse** *vpr*: ~**se (con)** to get married (to).

cascabel *m* (small) bell.

cascada *f* [de agua] waterfall.

cascado, da *adj* **- 1.** *fam* [estropeado] bust; [persona, ropa] worn-out **- 2.** [ronco] rasping.

cascanueces *m inv* nutcracker.

cascar *vt* **- 1.** [romper] to crack **- 2.** *fam* [pegar] to thump.

◆ **cascarse** *vpr* [romperse] to crack; **cascársela** *vulg* to jerk off.

cáscara *f* **- 1.** [de almendra, huevo etc] shell **- 2.** [de limón, naranja] skin, peel **- 3.** [de plátano] skin.

cascarilla *f* husk.

cascarón *m* eggshell.

cascarrabias *m y f inv* grouch, misery guts *(sg)*.

casco *m* **- 1.** [para la cabeza] helmet; [de motorista] crash helmet **- 2.** [de barco] hull **- 3.** [de ciudad]: ~ **antiguo** old (part of) town; ~ **urbano** city centre **- 4.** [de caballo] hoof **- 5.** [envase] empty bottle.

caserío *m* [casa de campo] country house.

casero, ra ◇ *adj* **-1.** [de casa - comida] home-made; [- trabajos] domestic; [- reunión, velada] at home; [de la familia] family *(antes de sust)* **- 2.** [hogareño] home-loving. ◇ *m,f* [propietario] landlord (*f* landlady).

caserón *m* large, rambling house.

caseta *f* **- 1.** [casa pequeña] hut **- 2.** [en la playa] bathing hut **- 3.** [de feria] stall, booth **- 4.** [para perro] kennel **- 5.** *Méx*: ~ **de cobro** tollbooth; ~ **telefónica** phone box, phone booth *US*.

casete, cassette [ka'sete] ◇ *f* [cinta] cassette. ◇ *m* [aparato] cassette recorder.

casi *adv* almost; ~ **me muero** I almost *o* nearly died; ~ **no dormí** I hardly slept at all; ~, ~ almost, just about; ~ **nunca** hardly ever; ~ **nada** hardly anything.

casilla *f* **- 1.** [de caja, armario] compartment; [para cartas] pigeonhole **- 2.** [en un impreso] box **- 3.** [de ajedrez etc] square.

casillero *m* **- 1.** [mueble] set of pigeonholes **- 2.** [casilla] pigeonhole.

casino *m* [para jugar] casino.

caso *m* **- 1.** [gen, DER & GRAM] case; **el** ~ **es que** the fact is (that); **en el mejor/peor de los** ~**s** at best/worst; **en todo** ~ in any case; ~ **clínico** clinical case **- 2.** [ocasión] occasion; **en** ~ **de** in the event of; **en** ~ **de que** if; **(en)** ~ **de que venga** should she come; **en cualquier** *o* **todo** ~ in any event

o case **- 3.** *loc*: **hacer** ~ **a** to pay attention to; **no hacer** *o* **venir al** ~ to be irrelevant; **tú ni** ~ take no notice.

caspa *f* dandruff.

casquete *m* [gorro] skullcap.

casquillo *m* [de munición] case; ~ **de bala** bullet shell.

cassette = **casete**.

casta *f* **- 1.** [linaje] lineage **- 2.** [especie, calidad] breed **- 3.** [en la India] caste.

castaña *f* ▷ **castaño**.

castañetear *vi* [dientes] to chatter.

castaño, ña *adj* [color] chestnut.

◆ **castaño** *m* **- 1.** [color] chestnut **- 2.** [árbol] chestnut (tree).

◆ **castaña** *f* [fruto] chestnut.

castañuela *f* castanet; **estar como unas** ~**s** to be very happy.

castellano, na *adj* & *m,f* Castilian.

◆ **castellano** *m* [lengua] (Castilian) Spanish.

castidad *f* chastity.

castigador, ra *adj fam* seductive.

castigar *vt* **- 1.** [imponer castigo] to punish **- 2.** DEP to penalize **- 3.** [maltratar] to damage.

castigo *m* **- 1.** [sanción] punishment **- 2.** [sufrimiento] suffering *(U)*; [daño] damage *(U)* **- 3.** DEP penalty.

castillo *m* [edificio] castle; ~ **de naipes** house of cards.

castizo, za *adj* pure; [autor] purist.

casto, ta *adj* chaste.

castor *m* beaver.

castrar *vt* [animal, persona] to castrate; [gato] to doctor.

castrense *adj* military.

casual *adj* chance, accidental.

casualidad *f* coincidence; **fue pura** ~ it was sheer coincidence; **dio la** ~ **de que ...** it so happened that ...; **por** ~ by chance; **¡qué** ~! what a coincidence!

casualmente *adv* by chance.

casulla *f* chasuble.

cataclismo *m* cataclysm.

catacumbas *fpl* catacombs.

catador, ra *m,f* taster.

catalán, ana *adj* & *m,f* Catalan, Catalonian.

◆ **catalán** *m* [lengua] Catalan.

catalejo *m* telescope.

catalizador, ra *adj fig* [impulsor] catalysing *(antes de sust)*.

◆ **catalizador** *m* **- 1.** QUÍM & *fig* catalyst **- 2.** AUTOM catalytic converter.

catalogar *vt* **- 1.** [en catálogo] to catalogue **- 2.** [clasificar]: ~ **a alguien (de)** to class sb (as).

catálogo *m* catalogue.

Cataluña Catalonia.

catamarán *m* catamaran.

cataplasma *f* MED poultice.

catapulta *f* catapult.

catar *vt* to taste.

catarata *f* - 1. [de agua] waterfall - 2. *(gen pl)* MED cataract.

catarro *m* cold.

catastro *m* land registry.

catástrofe *f* catastrophe; [accidente] disaster; ~ **aérea** air disaster; ~ **natural** natural disaster.

catastrófico, ca *adj* catastrophic.

catch [katʃ] *m* DEP all-in wrestling.

catchup ['ketʃup], **ketchup** *m inv* ketchup.

catear *vt fam* - 1. *Esp:* **he cateado las matemáticas** I failed *o* flunked *US* maths - 2. *Amér* [registrar] to search.

catecismo *m* catechism.

cátedra *f* - 1. [cargo - en universidad] chair; [- en instituto] post of head of department - 2. [departamento] department.

catedral *f* cathedral.

catedrático, ca *m,f* [de universidad] professor; [de instituto] head of department.

categoría *f* - 1. [gen] category; ~ **gramatical** part of speech - 2. [posición social] standing; **de** ~ important - 3. [calidad] quality; **de (primera)** ~ first-class.

categórico, ca *adj* categorical.

catequesis *f inv* catechesis.

cateto, ta *m,f despec* country bumpkin.

catolicismo *m* Catholicism.

católico, ca ◇ *adj* Catholic. ◇ *m,f* Catholic.

catorce *núm* fourteen; *ver también* **seis**.

catorceavo, va *núm* fourteenth.

catre *m* [cama] camp bed.

catrín, trina *m,f CAm, Méx fam* toff.

cauce *m* - 1. AGR & *fig* channel - 2. [de río] river-bed.

caucho *m* [sustancia] rubber.

caudaloso, sa *adj* - 1. [río] with a large flow - 2. [persona] wealthy, rich.

caudillo *m* [en la guerra] leader, head.

causa *f* - 1. [origen, ideal] cause; **por una buena** ~ for a good cause - 2. [razón] reason; **a** ~ **de** because of - 3. DER case.

causalidad *f* causality.

causante *adj:* **la razón** ~ the cause.

causar *vt* [gen] to cause; [impresión] to make; [placer] to give; ~ **asombro a alguien** to amaze sb.

cáustico, ca *adj lit* & *fig* caustic.

cautela *f* caution, cautiousness; **con** ~ cautiously.

cauteloso, sa *adj* cautious, careful.

cautivador, ra ◇ *adj* captivating,

enchanting. ◇ *m,f* charmer.

cautivar *vt* - 1. [apresar] to capture - 2. [seducir] to captivate, to enchant.

cautiverio *m*, **cautividad** *f* captivity.

cautivo, va *adj* & *m,f* captive.

cauto, ta *adj* cautious, careful.

cava ◇ *m* [bebida] cava, *Spanish champagne-type wine.* ◇ *f* [bodega] wine cellar.

cavar *vt* & *vi* [gen] to dig; [con azada] to hoe.

caverna *f* cave; [más grande] cavern.

cavernícola *mf* caveman (*f* cavewoman).

caviar (*pl* **caviares**) *m* caviar.

cavidad *f* cavity; [formada con las manos] cup.

cavilar *vi* to think deeply, to ponder.

cayado *m* [de pastor] crook.

cayera *etc* ▷ **caer.**

caza ◇ *f* - 1. [acción de cazar] hunting; **salir** *o* **ir de** ~ to go hunting; ~ **furtiva** poaching - 2. [animales, carne] game. ◇ *m* fighter (plane).

cazabe *m Amér* cassava bread.

cazabombardero *m* fighter-bomber.

cazador, ra *m,f* [persona] hunter.
◆ **cazadora** *f* [prenda] bomber jacket.

cazalla *f* [bebida] aniseed-flavoured spirit.

cazar *vt* - 1. [animales etc] to hunt - 2. *fig* [pillar, atrapar] to catch; [en matrimonio] to trap.

cazo *m* saucepan.

cazoleta *f* - 1. [recipiente] pot - 2. [de pipa] bowl.

cazuela *f* - 1. [recipiente] pot; [de barro] earthenware pot; [para el horno] casserole (dish) - 2. [guiso] casserole, stew; **a la** ~ casseroled.

cazurro, rra *adj* [bruto] stupid.

c/c *(abrev de* **cuenta corriente)** a/c.

CC OO *(abrev de* **Comisiones Obreras)** *fpl Spanish communist-inspired trade union.*

CD *m* - 1. *(abrev de* **club deportivo)** sports club; [en fútbol] FC - 2. *(abrev de* **compact disc)** CD.

CD-R *(abrev de* **compact disc recordable)** *m* CD-R.

CD-RW *(abrev de* **compact disc rewritable)** *m* CD-RW.

CE *f* *(abrev de* **Comunidad Europea)** EC.

cebada *f* barley.

cebar *vt* - 1. [sobrealimentar] to fatten (up) - 2. [máquina, arma] to prime - 3. [anzuelo] to bait - 4. *RP* [mate] to prepare, to brew.
◆ **cebarse en** *vpr* to take it out on.

cebo *m* - 1. [para cazar] bait - 2. *fig* [para atraer] incentive.

cebolla *f* onion.

cebolleta *f* - 1. BOT spring onion - 2. [en vinagre] pickled onion; [muy pequeña] silver-skin onion.

cebollino *m* **-1.** BOT chive; [cebolleta] spring onion **- 2.** *fam* [necio] idiot.

cebra *f* zebra.

cecear *vi* to lisp.

ceceo *m* lisp.

cecina *f* dried, salted meat.

cedazo *m* sieve.

ceder ◇ *vt* **-1.** [traspasar, transferir] to hand over **- 2.** [conceder] to give up; **'ceda el paso'** 'give way'; ~ **la palabra a alguien** to give the floor to sb. ◇ *vi* **-1.** [venirse abajo] to give way **- 2.** [destensarse] to give, to become loose **- 3.** [disminuir] to abate **- 4.** [rendirse] to give up; ~ **a** to give in to; ~ **en** to give up on **- 5.** [ensancharse] to stretch.

cedro *m* cedar.

cédula *f* document; ~ **(de identidad)** *Amér* identity card.

CEE (*abrev de* **Comunidad Económica Europea**) *f* EEC.

cegar *vt* **-1.** [gen] to blind **- 2.** [tapar - ventana] to block off; [- tubo] to block up.
◆ **cegarse** *vpr lit* & *fig* to be blinded.

cegato, ta *fam adj* short-sighted.

ceguera *f* lit & *fig* blindness.

ceja *f* ANAT eyebrow; **se le metió entre** ~ **y** ~ *fam* he got it into his head.

cejar *vi*: ~ **en** to give up on.

celda *f* cell.

celebración *f* **-1.** [festejo] celebration **- 2.** [realización] holding.

celebrar *vt* **-1.** [festejar] to celebrate **- 2.** [llevar a cabo] to hold; [oficio religioso] to celebrate **- 3.** [alegrarse de] to be delighted with **- 4.** [alabar] to praise, to applaud.
◆ **celebrarse** *vpr* **-1.** [festejarse] to be celebrated; **esa fiesta se celebra el 24 de Julio** that festivity falls on 24th July **- 2.** [llevarse a cabo] to take place, to be held.

célebre *adj* famous, celebrated.

celebridad *f* **-1.** [fama] fame **- 2.** [persona famosa] celebrity.

celeridad *f* speed.

celeste *adj* [del cielo] celestial, heavenly.

celestial *adj* celestial, heavenly.

celestina *f* lovers' go-between.

celibato *m* celibacy.

célibe *adj* & *mf* celibate.

celo *m* **-1.** [esmero] zeal, keenness **- 2.** [devoción] devotion **- 3.** [de animal] heat; **en** ~ on heat, in season **- 4.** [cinta adhesiva] Sellotape® UK, Scotch tape® US.
◆ **celos** *mpl* jealousy (U); **dar** ~**s a alguien** to make sb jealous; **tener** ~**s de alguien** to be jealous of sb.

celofán *m* cellophane.

celosía *f* lattice window, jalousie.

celoso, sa *adj* **-1.** [con celos] jealous **- 2.** [cumplidor] keen, eager.

celta ◇ *adj* Celtic. ◇ *mf* [persona] Celt. ◇ *m* [lengua] Celtic.

céltico, ca *adj* Celtic.

célula *f* cell.
◆ **célula fotoeléctrica** *f* photoelectric cell, electric eye.
◆ **célula madre** *f* stem cell.

celulitis *f inv* cellulitis.

celulosa *f* cellulose.

cementerio *m* **-1.** [para personas] cemetery, graveyard **- 2.** [de cosas inutilizables] dump; ~ **de automóviles** *o* **coches** scrapyard.

cemento *m* [gen] cement; [hormigón] concrete; ~ **armado** reinforced concrete.

cena *f* dinner, evening meal; **dar una** ~ to give a dinner party; ~ **de negocios** business dinner.

cenagal *m* bog, marsh.

cenagoso, sa *adj* muddy, boggy.

cenar ◇ *vt* to have for dinner. ◇ *vi* to have dinner.

cencerro *m* cowbell; **estar como un** ~ *fam fig* to be as mad as a hatter.

cenefa *f* border.

cenicero *m* ashtray.

cenit = **zenit**.

cenizo, za *adj* ashen, ash-grey.
◆ **cenizo** *m* **-1.** [mala suerte] bad luck **- 2.** [gafe] jinx.
◆ **ceniza** *f* ash.
◆ **cenizas** *fpl* [de cadáver] ashes.

censar *vt* to take a census of.

censo *m* **-1.** [padrón] census; ~ **de población** population census; ~ **electoral** electoral roll **- 2.** [tributo] tax.

censor, ra *m, f* [funcionario] censor.

censura *f* **-1.** [prohibición] censorship **- 2.** [organismo] censors (*pl*) **- 3.** [reprobación] censure, severe criticism.

censurar *vt* **-1.** [prohibir] to censor **- 2.** [reprobar] to censure.

centavo, va *núm* hundredth.

centella *f* **-1.** [rayo] flash **- 2.** [chispa] spark.

centellear *vi* [luz] to sparkle; [estrella] to twinkle.

centelleo *m* [de luz] sparkle, sparkling (U); [de estrella] twinkle, twinkling (U).

centena *f* hundred; **una** ~ **de** a hundred.

centenar *m* hundred; **un** ~ **de** a hundred.

centenario, ria *adj* [persona] in one's hundreds; [cifra] three-figure (*antes de sust*).
◆ **centenario** *m* centenary; **quinto** ~ five hundredth anniversary.

centeno *m* rye.

centésimo, ma *núm* hundredth.

centígrado, da *adj* centigrade.

centigramo *m* centigram.

centilitro *m* centilitre.

centímetro *m* centimetre.

céntimo *m* [moneda] cent.

centinela *m* sentry.

centollo *m* spider crab.

centrado, da *adj* - **1.** [basado]: ~ **en** based on - **2.** [equilibrado] stable, steady - **3.** [rueda, cuadro etc] centred.

central ◇ *adj* central. ◇ *f* - **1.** [oficina] headquarters, head office; [de correos, comunicaciones] main office; ~ **telefónica** telephone exchange - **2.** [de energía] power station; ~ **nuclear** nuclear power station.

centralista *adj & m,f* centralist.

centralita *f* switchboard.

centralización *f* centralization.

centralizar *vt* to centralize.

centrar *vt* - **1.** [gen & DEP] to centre - **2.** [arma] to aim - **3.** [persona] to steady, to make stable - **4.** [atención, interés] to be the centre of.
◆ **centrarse** *vpr* - **1.** [concentrarse]: ~**se en** to concentrate *o* focus on - **2.** [equilibrarse] to find one's feet.

céntrico, ca *adj* central.

centrifugadora *f* [para secar ropa] spindryer.

centrifugar *vt* [ropa] to spin-dry.

centrista *adj* centre *(antes de sust)*.

centro *m* - **1.** [gen] centre; **ser de** ~ POLÍT to be at the centre of the political spectrum; ~ **de cálculo** computer centre; ~ **de planificación familiar** family planning clinic; ~ **social** community centre - **2.** [de ciudad] town centre; **me voy al** ~ I'm going to town; ~ **urbano** town centre.
◆ **centro comercial** *m* shopping centre.
◆ **centro de mesa** *m* centrepiece.
◆ **centro de salud** *m* health centre.

Centroamérica *f* Central America.

centroamericano, na *adj* Central American.

centrocampista *mf* DEP midfielder.

ceñir *vt* - **1.** [apretar] to be tight on - **2.** [abrazar] to embrace.
◆ **ceñirse** *vpr* - **1.** [apretarse] to tighten - **2.** [limitarse]: ~**se a** to keep *o* stick to.

ceño *m* frown, scowl; **fruncir el** ~ to frown, to knit one's brow.

cepa *f* lit & fig stock.

cepillar *vt* - **1.** [ropa, pelo, dientes] to brush - **2.** [madera] to plane.

cepillo *m* - **1.** [para limpiar] brush; [para pelo] hairbrush; ~ **de dientes** toothbrush - **2.** [de carpintero] plane.

cepo *m* - **1.** [para cazar] trap - **2.** [para vehículos] wheel clamp - **3.** [para sujetar] clamp.

cera *f* [gen] wax; [de abeja] beeswax; **hacerse la** ~ **en las piernas** to wax one's legs; ~ **depilatoria** hair-removing wax.

cerámica *f* - **1.** [arte] ceramics *(U)*, pottery - **2.** [objeto] piece of pottery.

ceramista *mf* potter.

cerca ◇ *f* [valla] fence. ◇ *adv* near, close; **por aquí** ~ nearby; **de** ~ [examinar, ver] closely; [afectar, vivir] deeply.
◆ **cerca de** *loc prep* - **1.** [en el espacio] near, close to - **2.** [aproximadamente] nearly, about.

cercado *m* - **1.** [valla] fence - **2.** [lugar] enclosure.

cercanía *f* [proximidad] nearness, closeness.
◆ **cercanías** *fpl* [de ciudad] outskirts, suburbs.

cercano, na *adj* - **1.** [pueblo, lugar] nearby - **2.** [tiempo] near - **3.** [pariente, fuente de información]: ~ **(a)** close (to).

cercar *vt* - **1.** [vallar] to fence (off) - **2.** [rodear, acorralar] to surround.

cerciorar *vt* to assure; ~**se (de)** to make sure (of).

cerco *m* - **1.** [gen] circle, ring - **2.** [de puerta, ventana] frame - **3.** [asedio] siege.

cerdo, da *m,f* - **1.** [animal] pig *(f* sow*)* - **2.** *fam fig* [persona] pig, swine.
◆ **cerda** *f* [pelo - de cerdo, jabalí] bristle; [- de caballo] horsehair.

cereal *m* cereal; ~**es** (breakfast) cereal *(U)*.

cerebro *m* - **1.** [gen] brain - **2.** *fig* [cabecilla] brains *(sg)* - **3.** *fig* [inteligencia] brains *(pl)*.

ceremonia *f* ceremony.

ceremonial *adj & m* ceremonial.

ceremonioso, sa *adj* ceremonious.

cereza *f* cherry.

cerezo *m* [árbol] cherry tree.

cerilla *f* match.

cerillo *m* *CAm, Ecuad, Méx* match.

cerner, cernir *vt* [cribar] to sieve, to sift.
◆ **cernerse** *vpr* - **1.** [ave, avión] to hover - **2.** *fig* [amenaza, peligro] to loom.

cernícalo *m* - **1.** [ave] kestrel - **2.** *fam* [bruto] brute.

cernir = **cerner**.

cero ◇ *adj inv* zero. ◇ *m* - **1.** [signo] nought, zero; [en fútbol] nil; [en tenis] love; **dos goles a** ~ two goals to nil, two nil - **2.** [cantidad] nothing - **3.** FÍS & METEOR zero; **sobre/bajo** ~ above/below zero - **4.** *loc*: **ser un** ~ **a la izquierda** *fam* [un inútil] to be useless; [un don nadie] to be a nobody; **partir de** ~ to start from scratch; *ver también* **seis**.

cerquillo *m* *Amér* fringe *UK*, bangs *US (pl)*.

cerrado, da *adj* - **1.** [al exterior] closed, shut; [con llave, pestillo etc] locked; ~ **a** closed to - **2.** [tiempo, cielo] overcast; **era noche cerrada** it was completely dark - **3.** [rodeado] surrounded; [por montañas] walled in

- 4. [circuito] closed **- 5.** [curva] sharp, tight **- 6.** [vocal] close **- 7.** [acento, deje] broad, thick.

cerradura *f* lock.

cerrajero, ra *m,f* locksmith.

cerrar ◇ *vt* **- 1.** [gen] to close; [puerta, cajón, boca] to shut, to close; [puños] to clench; [con llave, pestillo etc] to lock **- 2.** [tienda, negocio - definitivamente] to close down **- 3.** [apagar] to turn off **- 4.** [bloquear - suj: accidente, inundación etc] to block; [- suj: policía etc] to close off **- 5.** [tapar - agujero, hueco] to fill, to block (up); [- bote] to put the lid o top on **- 6.** [cercar] to fence (off), to enclose **- 7.** [cicatrizar] to heal, to close up **- 8.** [ir último en] to bring up the rear of **- 9.:** ~ **un trato** to seal a deal. ◇ *vi* to close, to shut; [con llave, pestillo etc] to lock up.

◆ **cerrarse** *vpr* **- 1.** [al exterior] to close, to shut **- 2.** [incomunicarse] to clam up; ~**se a to close one's mind to**; ~**se en banda** to close ranks **- 3.** [herida] to heal, to close up **- 4.** [acto, debate, discusión etc] to (come to a) close.

cerrazón *f* fig stubbornness, obstinacy.

cerro *m* hill.

cerrojo *m* bolt; **echar el** ~ to bolt the door.

certamen *m* competition, contest.

certero, ra *adj* **- 1.** [tiro] accurate **- 2.** [opinión, respuesta etc] correct.

certeza *f* certainty.

certidumbre *f* certainty.

certificación *f* **- 1.** [hecho] certification **- 2.** [documento] certificate.

certificado, da *adj* [gen] certified; [carta, paquete] registered.

◆ **certificado** *m* certificate; ~ **de estudios** school-leaving certificate; ~ **médico** medical certificate.

certificar *vt* **- 1.** [constatar] to certify **- 2.** [en correos] to register.

cerumen *m* earwax.

cervato *m* fawn.

cervecería *f* **- 1.** [fábrica] brewery **- 2.** [bar] bar.

cervecero, ra *m,f* [que hace cerveza] brewer.

cerveza *f* beer; ~ **de barril** draught beer; ~ **negra** stout; ~ **rubia** lager.

cesante *adj* **- 1.** [destituido] sacked; [ministro] removed from office **- 2.** *CSur, Méx* [en paro] unemployed.

cesantear *vt Chile, RP* to make redundant.

cesar ◇ *vt* [destituir] to sack; [ministro] to remove from office. ◇ *vi* [parar]: ~ **(de hacer algo)** to stop o cease (doing sthg); **no cesaba de llorar** he didn't stop crying; **no cesa de intentarlo** she keeps trying; **sin** ~ non-stop, incessantly.

cesárea *f* caesarean (section).

cese *m* **- 1.** [detención, paro] stopping, ceasing **- 2.** [destitución] sacking; [de ministro] removal from office.

cesión *f* cession, transfer.

césped *m* [hierba] lawn, grass *(U)*.

◆ **césped artificial** *m* artificial turf.

cesta *f* basket.

◆ **cesta de la compra** *f* **- 1.** fig cost of living **- 2.** [para compras en Internet] shopping basket.

◆ **cesta de Navidad** *f* Christmas hamper.

cesto *m* [cesta] (large) basket.

cetro *m* **- 1.** [vara] sceptre **- 2.** fig [reinado] reign.

cf., cfr. *(abrev de confróntese)* cf.

cg *(abrev de centigramo)* cg.

chabacano, na *adj* vulgar.

◆ **chabacano** *m Méx* [fruto] apricot.

chabola *f* shack; **barrios de** ~**s** shanty town *(sg)*.

chacal *m* jackal.

chacarero, ra *m,f Andes, RP* [agricultor] farmer.

chacha *f* maid.

chachachá *m* cha-cha.

cháchara *f* fam chatter, nattering; **estar de** ~ to have a natter.

chachi *adj inv* fam cool, neat US.

chacra *f* Andes, RP farm.

chafar *vt* **- 1.** [aplastar] to flatten **- 2.** fig [estropear] to spoil, to ruin.

◆ **chafarse** *vpr* [estropearse] to be ruined.

chaflán *m* [de edificio] corner.

chagra *Amér* ◇ *mf* peasant, person from the country. ◇ *f* farm.

chal *m* shawl.

chalado, da *adj* fam crazy, mad.

chalar *vt* to drive round the bend.

chalé (*pl* **chalés**), **chalet** (*pl* **chalets**) *m* [gen] detached house (with garden); ~ **pareado** semi-detached house; [en el campo] cottage; [de alta montaña] chalet.

chaleco *m* waistcoat, vest *US*; [de punto] tank-top; ~ **salvavidas** life jacket.

chalet = **chalé.**

chamaco, ca *m,f Méx* fam kid.

chamarra *f* sheepskin jacket.

chamba *f CAm, Méx, Perú, Ven* fam odd job.

chambón, bona *m,f Amér* fam sloppy o shoddy worker.

chamiza *f* [hierba] thatch.

chamizo *m* **- 1.** [leña] half-burnt wood *(U)* **- 2.** [casa] thatched hut.

champán, champaña *m* champagne.

champiñón *m* mushroom.

champú (*pl* **champús** *o* **champúes**) *m* shampoo.

chamuscar *vt* to scorch; [cabello, barba, tela] to singe.

◆ **chamuscarse** *vpr* [cabello, barba, tela] to get singed.

chamusquina *f* scorch, scorching (*U*); **me huele a ~** *fam fig* it smells a bit fishy to me.

chance ◇ *f Amér* opportunity, chance. ◇ *adv Méx* maybe.

chanchada *f Amér* [trastada] dirty trick.

chancho *m Amér* pig (*f* sow).

chanchullo *m fam* fiddle, racket.

chancla *f* [chancleta] low sandal; [para la playa] flip-flop.

chancleta *f* low sandal; [para la playa] flip-flop.

chándal (*pl* **chandals**), **chandal** (*pl* **chandals**) *m* tracksuit.

changa *f Bol, RP* odd job.

changador, ra *m,f RP* porter.

changarro *m Méx* small store.

chanquetes *mpl* whitebait (*pl*).

chantaje *m* blackmail; **hacer ~ a** to blackmail; **~ emocional** emotional blackmail.

chantajear *vt* to blackmail.

chanza *f* joke; **estar de ~** to be joking.

chao *interj fam*: **¡ ~ !** bye!, see you!

chapa *f* - **1.** [lámina - de metal] sheet, plate; [- de madera] board; **de tres ~s** three-ply - **2.** [tapón] top, cap - **3.** [insignia] badge - **4.** [ficha de guardarropa] metal token *o* disc - **5.** *Col, Cuba, Méx* [cerradura] lock - **6.** *RP* [de matrícula] number plate *UK*, license plate *US*.

◆ **chapas** *fpl* [juego] *children's game played with bottle tops*.

chapado, da *adj* [con metal] plated; [con madera] veneered; **~ a la antigua** *fig* stuck in the past, old-fashioned.

chaparro, rra ◇ *adj* short and squat. ◇ *m,f* [persona] short, squat person.

chaparrón *m* downpour; *fam fig* [gran cantidad] torrent.

chapopote *m Carib, Méx* bitumen, pitch.

chapotear *vi* to splash about.

chapucear *vt* to botch (up).

chapucero, ra ◇ *adj* [trabajo] shoddy, sloppy; [persona] bungling. ◇ *m,f* bungler.

chapulín *m CAm, Méx* grasshopper.

chapurrear, chapurrar *vt* to speak badly.

chapuza *f* - **1.** [trabajo mal hecho] botch (job) - **2.** [trabajo ocasional] odd job.

chapuzón *m* dip; **darse un ~** to go for a dip.

chaqué (*pl* **chaqués**) *m* morning coat.

chaqueta *f* jacket; [de punto] cardigan.

chaquetón *m* short coat.

charanga *f* [banda] brass band.

charca *f* pool, pond.

charco *m* puddle.

charcutería *f* - **1.** [tienda] *shop selling cold cooked meats and cheeses,* ≃ delicatessen - **2.** [productos] cold cuts (*pl*) and cheese.

charla *f* - **1.** [conversación] chat - **2.** [conferencia] talk.

charlar *vi* to chat.

charlatán, ana ◇ *adj* talkative. ◇ *m,f* - **1.** [hablador] chatterbox - **2.** [mentiroso] trickster, charlatan.

charlotada *f* [payasada] clowning around (*U*).

charlotear *vi* to chat.

charnego, ga *m,f pejorative term referring to immigrant to Catalonia from another part of Spain.*

charol *m* - **1.** [piel] patent leather - **2.** *Andes* [bandeja] tray.

charola *f Bol, CAm, Méx* tray.

charque, charqui *m Andes, RP* jerked *o* salted beef.

chárter *adj inv* charter (*antes de sust*).

chasca *f Andes* [greña] mop of hair.

chascar ◇ *vt* - **1.** [lengua] to click - **2.** [dedos] to snap. ◇ *vi* - **1.** [madera] to crack - **2.** [lengua] to click.

chasco *m* [decepción] disappointment; **llevarse un ~** to be disappointed.

chasis *m inv* AUTOM chassis.

chasquear ◇ *vt* - **1.** [látigo] to crack - **2.** [la lengua] to click. ◇ *vi* [madera] to crack.

chasquido *m* [de látigo, madera, hueso] crack; [de lengua, arma] click; [de dedos] snap.

chatarra *f* - **1.** [metal] scrap (metal) - **2.** [objetos, piezas] junk.

chateo *m* [en bar] pub crawl, pub crawling (*U*); INFORM chatting; **ir de ~** to go out drinking.

chato, ta ◇ *adj* - **1.** [nariz] snub; [persona] snub-nosed - **2.** [aplanado] flat - **3.** *RP* [mediocre] commonplace. ◇ *m,f fam* [apelativo] love, dear.

◆ **chato** *m* [de vino] small glass of wine.

chau, chaucito *interj Bol, CSur, Perú fam* bye!, see you!

chauvinista = chovinista.

chaval, la *m,f fam* kid, lad (*f* lass).

chavo, va *fam* ◇ *m* [dinero]: **no tener un ~** to be penniless. ◇ *m,f Méx* [chico] guy; [chica] girl.

che[1] *interj RP fam*: **¿como andés, ~?** hey, how's it going?; **¡ ~, vení para acá!** hey, over here, you!

che[2]**, ché** *interj* hey!

checo, ca *adj & m,f* Czech.

◆ **checo** *m* [lengua] Czech.

chef [ʃef] (*pl* **chefs**) *m* chef.

chele, la *CAm* ◇ *adj* [rubio] blond (*f* blonde); [de piel blanca] fair-skinned. ◇ *m,f* [rubio] blond(e); [de piel blanca] fair-skinned person.

chelín *m* shilling.

chelo, la ◇ *adj Amér* blond (*f* blonde). ◇ *m* MÚS [instrumento] cello. ◇ *mf* MÚS [instrumentista] cellist.

cheque *m* cheque *UK*, check *US*; **extender un** ∼ to make out a cheque; ∼ **cruzado** *o* **barrado** crossed cheque; ∼ **(de) gasolina** petrol voucher; ∼ **nominativo** cheque in favour of a specific person; ∼ **al portador** cheque payable to the bearer; ∼ **de viaje** *o* **de viajero** traveller's cheque; ∼ **regalo** gift voucher.

chequear *vt* -**1.** MED: ∼ **a alguien** to examine sb, to give sb a checkup -**2.** [comprobar] to check.

chequeo *m* -**1.** MED checkup -**2.** [comprobación] check, checking *(U)*.

chequera *f* chequebook *UK*, checkbook *US*.

chévere *adj Andes, CAm, Carib, Méx fam* great, fantastic.

chic *adj inv* chic.

chica *f* -**1.** [joven] girl -**2.** [tratamiento] darling -**3.** [criada] maid.

chicano, na *adj & m,f* Chicano, Mexican-American.

◆ **chicano** *m* [lengua] Chicano.

chicarrón, ona *m,f* strapping lad (*f* strapping lass).

chícharo *m CAm, Méx* pea.

chicharra *f* ZOOL cicada.

chicharro *m* [pez] horse mackerel.

chicharrón *m* [frito] pork crackling.

◆ **chicharrones** *mpl* [embutido] *cold processed meat made from pork*.

chichón *m* bump.

chicle *m* chewing gum.

chiclé, chicler *m* AUTOM jet.

chico, ca *adj* [pequeño] small; [joven] young; **cuando era** ∼ when I was little.

◆ **chico** *m* -**1.** [joven] boy -**2.** [tratamiento] sonny, mate -**3.** [recadero] messenger, office-boy.

chicote *m Amér* [látigo] whip.

chifla *f* [silbido] whistle.

chiflado, da *adj fam* crazy, mad.

chiflar ◇ *vt fam* [encantar]: **me chiflan las patatas fritas** I'm mad about chips. ◇ *vi* [silbar] to whistle.

◆ **chiflarse** *vpr*: **chiflarse por algo** *o* **alguien** to go crazy about sthg *o* sb.

chiflido *m Amér* whistling.

chigüín, güina *m,f CAm fam* kid.

chilacayote *m Méx* pumpkin, gourd.

chilango, ga *adj Méx* of/from Mexico City.

chile *m* chilli.

Chile Chile.

chileno, na *adj & m,f* Chilean.

chillar ◇ *vi* -**1.** [gritar - personas] to scream, to yell; [- ave, mono] to screech; [- cerdo] to squeal; [- ratón] to squeak -**2.** [- chirriar] to screech; [puerta, madera] to creak; [bisagras] to squeak. ◇ *vt fam* [reñir] to yell at.

chillido *m* [de persona] scream, yell; [de ave, mono] screech; [de cerdo] squeal; [de ratón] squeak.

chillón, ona *adj* -**1.** [voz] piercing -**2.** [persona] noisy, screeching -**3.** [color] gaudy.

chilpayate, ta *m,f Méx* kid.

chilpotle *m Méx smoked or pickled jalapeño chilli*.

chimbo, ba *adj Col, Ven fam* [falso] counterfeit; [de mala calidad] lousy.

chimenea *f* -**1.** [hogar] fireplace -**2.** [en tejado] chimney.

chimpancé *m* chimpanzee.

china ▷ **chino**.

China: **(la)** ∼ China.

chinampa *f Méx man-made island for growing flowers, fruit and vegetables, found in Xochimilco, near Mexico City*.

chinchar *vt fam* to pester, to bug.

◆ **chincharse** *vpr fam*: **ahora te chinchas** now you can lump it.

chinche ◇ *adj fam fig* annoying. ◇ *f* [insecto] bedbug.

chincheta *f* drawing pin *UK*, thumbtack *US*.

chinchín *m* [brindis] toast; **¡**∼**!** cheers!

chinchón *m strong aniseed liquor*.

chinchulín *m Andes, RP piece of sheep or cow intestine, plaited and then roasted*.

chinga *f Méx mfam* [paliza]: **me dieron una** ∼ they kicked the shit out of me; [trabajo duro]: **es una** ∼ it's a bitch of a job.

chingar ◇ *vt* -**1.** *Esp, Méx mfam* [molestar]: ∼ **a alguien** to get up sb's nose, to piss sb off -**2.** *mfam* [estropear] to bust, to knacker *UK* -**3.** *Esp, Méx vulg* [acostarse con] to screw, to fuck. ◇ *vi vulg* [fornicar] to screw, to fuck.

◆ **chingarse** *vpr mfam* [beberse] to knock back.

chino, na *adj & m,f* -**1.** Chinese -**2.** *Andes, RP* [mestizo] person of mixed ancestry.

◆ **chino** *m* -**1.** [lengua] Chinese -**2.** [piedra] pebble.

◆ **china** *f* -**1.** [piedra] pebble -**2.** [porcelana] china.

chip (*pl* **chips**) *m* INFORM chip.

chipirón *m* baby squid.

Chipre Cyprus.

chipriota *adj* & *mf* Cypriot.

chiqueo *m Méx* show of affection.

chiquilín, lina *m,f RP* small boy (*f* small girl).

chiquillo, lla *m,f* kid.

chiquito, ta *adj* tiny.

  ➞ chiquito *m* [de vino] small glass of wine.

chiribita *f* [chispa] spark.

chirimbolo *m fam* thingamajig, whatsit.

chirimoya *f* custard apple.

chiringuito *m fam* [bar] refreshment stall.

chiripa *f fam fig* fluke; **de** o **por ~** by luck.

chirivía *f* BOT parsnip.

chirla *f* small clam.

chirona *f fam* clink, slammer; **en ~** in the clink.

chirriar *vi* [gen] to screech; [puerta, madera] to creak; [bisagra, muelles] to squeak.

chirrido *m* [gen] screech; [de puerta, madera] creak; [de bisagra, muelles] squeak.

chis = chist.

chisme *m* - 1. [cotilleo] rumour, piece of gossip - 2. *fam* [cosa] thingamajig, thingy.

chismorrear *vi* to spread rumours, to gossip.

chismoso, sa ◇ *adj* gossipy. ◇ *m,f* gossip, scandalmonger.

chispa *f* - 1. [de fuego, electricidad] spark; **echar ~s** *fam* to be hopping mad - 2. [de lluvia] spot (of rain) - 3. *fig* [pizca] bit; **una ~ de sal** a pinch of salt - 4. *fig* [agudeza] sparkle.

chispear ◇ *vi* - 1. [chisporrotear] to spark - 2. [relucir] to sparkle. ◇ *v impers* [llover] to spit (with rain).

chisporrotear *vi* [fuego, leña] to crackle; [aceite] to splutter; [comida] to sizzle.

chist, chis *interj* ¡~! ssh!

chistar *vi*: me fui sin ~ I left without a word.

chiste *m* joke; **contar ~s** to tell jokes; **~ verde** dirty joke.

chistera *f* [sombrero] top hat.

chistorra *f type of cured pork sausage typical of Aragon and Navarre.*

chistoso, sa *adj* funny.

chita ➞ a la chita callando *loc adv fam* quietly, on the quiet.

chitón *interj* quiet!

chivar *vt fam* to tell secretly.

  ➞ chivarse *vpr fam*: **~se (de/a)** [niños] to split (on/to); [delincuentes] to grass (on/to).

chivatazo *m fam* tip-off; **dar el ~** to grass.

chivato, ta *m,f fam* [delator] grass, informer; [acusica] telltale.

chivo, va *m,f* kid, young goat; **ser el**

~ expiatorio *fig* to be the scapegoat.

choc (*pl* chocs), **choque, shock** [tʃok] *m* shock.

chocante *adj* startling.

chocar ◇ *vi* - 1. [colisionar]: **~ (contra)** to crash (into), to collide (with) - 2. *fig* [enfrentarse] to clash. ◇ *vt fig* [sorprender] to startle.

chochear *vi* [viejo] to be senile.

chocho, cha *adj* - 1. [viejo] senile - 2. *fam fig* [encariñado] soft, doting.

choclo *m Andes, RP* corncob, ear of maize o corn *US*.

chocolate *m* [para comer, beber] chocolate; **~ (a la taza)** thick drinking chocolate; **~ blanco** white chocolate; **~ con leche** milk chocolate.

chocolatina *f* chocolate bar.

chófer (*pl* chóferes) *m,f* chauffeur.

chollo *m fam* [producto, compra] bargain; [trabajo, situación] cushy number.

cholo, la *m,f Andes sometimes pejorative term for a mestizo who moves to the city from a rural area.*

chomba, chompa *f Andes* sweater.

chompipe *m CAm, Méx* turkey.

chongo *m Méx* [moño] bun.

chopo *m* poplar.

chopp *m CSur* [cerveza] (mug of) beer.

choque *m* - 1. [impacto] impact; [de coche, avión etc] crash; **~ frontal** head-on collision - 2. *fig* [enfrentamiento] clash; **~ cultural** culture shock - 3. = choc.

chorizar *vt fam* to nick, to pinch.

chorizo *m* - 1. [embutido] *highly seasoned pork sausage* - 2. *fam* [ladrón] thief.

choro *m Andes* mussel.

chorrada *f mfam* rubbish (U); **eso es una ~** that's rubbish; **decir ~s** to talk rubbish.

chorrear *vi* - 1. [gotear - gota a gota] to drip; [- en un hilo] to trickle - 2. [brotar] to spurt (out), to gush (out).

chorro *m* - 1. [de líquido - borbotón] jet, spurt; [- hilo] trickle; **salir a ~s** to spurt o gush out; **~ de vapor** steam jet - 2. *fig* [de luz, gente etc] stream; **tiene un ~ de dinero** she has loads of money; **a ~s** in abundance.

  ➞ chorro, rra *m,f RP fam* [ladrón] thief.

choteo *m fam* joking, kidding; **tomar algo a ~** to take sthg as a joke.

choto, ta *m,f* - 1. [cabrito] kid, young goat - 2. [ternero] calf.

chovinista, chauvinista [tʃoβi'nista] ◇ *adj* chauvinistic. ◇ *mf* chauvinist.

choza *f* hut.

christmas = crismas.

chubasco *m* shower.

chubasquero *m* raincoat, mac.

chúcaro, ra *adj Andes, CAm, RP fam* [animal] wild; [persona] unsociable.

chuchería *f* - **1.** [golosina] sweet - **2.** [objeto] trinket.

chucho *m fam* mutt, dog.

chueco, ca *adj Amér* [torcido] twisted; *Méx fam* [proyecto, razonamiento] shady; *Amér* [patizambo] bowlegged.

chufa *f* [tubérculo] tiger nut.

chulear *vi fam* [fanfarronear]: ~ **(de)** to be cocky (about).

chulería *f* [descaro] cockiness.

chuleta *f* - **1.** [de carne] chop; ~ **de cordero** lamb chop - **2.** [en exámenes] crib note.

chullo *m Bol, Perú* woollen cap.

chulo, la ◇ *adj* - **1.** [descarado] cocky; **ponerse** ~ to get cocky - **2.** *fam* [bonito] lovely. ◇ *m,f* [descarado] cocky person.
  ◆ **chulo** *m* [proxeneta] pimp.

chumbera *f* prickly pear.

chumbo ▷ **higo**.

chungo, ga *adj fam* [persona] horrible, nasty; [cosa] lousy.
  ◆ **chunga** *f fam*: **tomarse algo a chunga** to take sth as a joke.

chuño *m Andes, RP* potato starch.

chupa *f fam*: ~ **de cuero** leather jacket.

chupachup® (*pl* **chupachups**) *m* lollipop.

chupado, da *adj* - **1.** [delgado] skinny - **2.** *fam* [fácil]: **estar** ~ to be dead easy o a piece of cake.
  ◆ **chupada** *f* [gen] suck; [fumando] puff, drag.

chupamedias *mf Andes, RP, Ven fam* toady.

chupar *vt* - **1.** [succionar] to suck; [fumando] to puff at - **2.** [absorber] to soak up - **3.** [quitar]: ~ **le algo a alguien** to milk sb for sthg; ~ **le la sangre a alguien** *fig* to bleed sb dry.

chupe *m Andes, Arg* stew.

chupete *m* dummy *UK*, pacifier *US*.

chupi *adj fam* great, brill.

chupón, ona *m,f fam* [gorrón] sponger, cadger.
  ◆ **chupón** *m Méx* [chupete] dummy *UK*, pacifier *US*.

churrería *f* shop selling 'churros'.

churro *m* [para comer] dough formed into sticks or rings and fried in oil.

churrusco *m* piece of burnt toast.

churumbel *m fam* kid.

chusco, ca *adj* funny.
  ◆ **chusco** *m fam* bread bun.

chusma *f* rabble, mob.

chut (*pl* **chuts**) *m* kick.

chutar *vi* [lanzar] to shoot.
  ◆ **chutarse** *vpr mfam* to shoot up.

chute *m mfam* FTBL shot; [de droga] fix.

CIA (*abrev de* **Central Intelligence Agency**) *f* CIA.

cía., Cía. (*abrev de* **compañía**) Co.

cianuro *m* cyanide.

ciático, ca *adj* sciatic.
  ◆ **ciática** *f* sciatica.

cibercafé *m* cybercafe, Internet cafe.

ciberespacio *m* cyberspace.

cicatero, ra *adj* stingy, mean.

cicatriz *f* lit & fig scar.

cicatrizar ◇ *vi* to heal (up). ◇ *vt fig* to heal.

cicerone *mf* guide.

cíclico, ca *adj* cyclical.

ciclismo *m* cycling.

ciclista *mf* cyclist.

ciclo *m* - **1.** [gen] cycle; ~ **vital** life cycle - **2.** [de conferencias, actos] series - **3.** [de enseñanza] stage.

ciclocrós *m* cyclo-cross.

ciclomotor *m* moped.

ciclón *m* cyclone.

cicuta *f* hemlock.

ciego, ga ◇ *adj* - **1.** [invidente] blind; **quedarse** ~ to go blind; **a ciegas** *lit & fig* blindly - **2.** *fig* [enloquecido]: ~ **(de)** blinded (by) - **3.** [pozo, tubería] blocked (up). ◇ *m,f* [invidente] blind person; **los** ~**s** the blind.

cielo *m* - **1.** [gen] sky - **2.** RELIG heaven - **3.** [nombre cariñoso] my love, my dear - **4.** *loc*: **clama al** ~ it's outrageous; **como llovido del** ~ [inesperadamente] out of the blue; [oportunamente] at just the right moment; **ser un** ~ to be an angel.
  ◆ **cielos** *interj*: **¡** ~ **s!** good heavens!

ciempiés *m inv* centipede.

cien - **1.** = **ciento** - **2.**: **poner a alguien a** ~ *fam* [excitar] to make sb feel horny.

ciénaga *f* marsh, bog.

ciencia *f* [gen] science.
  ◆ **ciencias** *fpl* EDUC science (U).
  ◆ **ciencia ficción** *f* science fiction.
  ◆ **a ciencia cierta** *loc adv* for certain.

cieno *m* mud, sludge.

científico, ca ◇ *adj* scientific. ◇ *m,f* scientist.

cientista *mf CSur*: ~ **social** social scientist.

ciento, cien *núm* a o one hundred; ~ **cincuenta** a o one hundred and fifty; **cien mil** a o one hundred thousand; ~**s de** hundreds of; **por** ~ per cent; ~ **por** ~, **cien por cien** a hundred per cent; ~**s de veces** hundreds of times; **a** ~**s** by the hundred; *ver también* **seis**.

cierne ◆ **en ciernes** *loc adv*: **estar en** ~**s** to be in its infancy; **una campeona en** ~**s** a budding champion.

cierre *m* - **1.** [gen] closing, shutting; [con

llave] locking; [de fábrica] shutdown; RADIO & TV closedown; ~ **patronal** lockout - **2**. [mecanismo] fastener; ~ **metálico** [de tienda etc] metal shutter; ~ **relámpago** *Andes, Arg, Méx* [cremallera] zip *UK*, zipper *US*.

cierto, ta *adj* - **1**. [verdadero] true; **estar en lo ~** to be right; **lo ~ es que ...** the fact is that ... - **2**. [seguro] certain, definite - **3**. [algún] certain; ~ **hombre** a certain man; **en cierta ocasión** once, on one occasion; **durante ~ tiempo** for a while.
◆ **cierto** *adv* right, certainly.
◆ **por cierto** *loc adv* by the way.

ciervo, va *m,f* deer, stag (*f* hind).

CIF (*abrev de* **código de identificación fiscal**) *m* tax code.

cifra *f* [gen] figure.

cifrar *vt* - **1**. [codificar] to code - **2**. *fig* [centrar] to concentrate, to centre.
◆ **cifrarse en** *vpr* to amount to.

cigala *f* Dublin Bay prawn.

cigarra *f* cicada.

cigarrillo *m* cigarette.

cigarro *m* - **1**. [habano] cigar - **2**. [cigarrillo] cigarette.

cigüeña *f* stork.

cigüeñal *m* crankshaft.

cilindrada *f* cylinder capacity.

cilíndrico, ca *adj* cylindrical.

cilindro *m* [gen] cylinder; [de imprenta] roller.

cima *f* - **1**. [punta - de montaña] peak, summit; [- de árbol] top - **2**. *fig* [apogeo] peak, high point.

cimbrear *vt* - **1**. [vara] to waggle - **2**. [caderas] to sway.

cimentar *vt* - **1**. [edificio] to lay the foundations of; [ciudad] to found, to build - **2**. *fig* [idea, paz, fama] to cement, to consolidate.

cimiento *m* (*gen pl*) CONSTR foundation; **echar los ~s** *lit & fig* to lay the foundations.

cinc, zinc *m* zinc.

cincel *m* chisel.

cincelar *vt* to chisel.

cincha *f* girth.

cinco *núm* five; **¡choca esos ~!** *fig* put it there!; **estar sin ~** *fig* to be broke; *ver también* **seis.**

cincuenta *núm* fifty; **los (años) ~** the fifties; *ver también* **seis.**

cincuentón, ona *m,f* fifty-year-old.

cine *m* cinema; **hacer ~** to make films; ~ **de terror** horror films.

cineasta *mf* film maker *o* director.

cineclub *m* - **1**. [asociación] film society - **2**. [sala] club cinema.

cinéfilo, la *m,f* film buff.

cinematografía *f* cinematography, film-making.

cinematográfico, ca *adj* film (*antes de sust*).

cinematógrafo *m* [local] cinema.

cínico, ca ◇ *adj* cynical. ◇ *m,f* cynic.

cinismo *m* cynicism.

cinta *f* - **1**. [tira - de plástico, papel] strip, band; [- de tela] ribbon; ~ **adhesiva** *o* **autoadhesiva** adhesive *o* sticky tape; ~ **métrica** tape measure - **2**. [de imagen, sonido, ordenadores] tape; ~ **limpiadora** head-cleaning tape; ~ **magnetofónica** recording tape; ~ **de vídeo** videotape - **3**. [mecanismo] belt; ~ **transportadora** conveyor belt; ~ **de equipajes** baggage carousel - **4**. [película] film.

cintura *f* waist.

cinturilla *f* waistband.

cinturón *m* - **1**. [cinto] belt - **2**. AUTOM ring road - **3**. [cordón] cordon.
◆ **cinturón de castidad** *m* chastity belt.
◆ **cinturón de seguridad** *m* seat *o* safety belt.
◆ **cinturón de miseria** *m* *Amér* slum *or* shanty town area round a large city.

ciprés *m* cypress.

circo *m* [gen] circus.

circuito *m* - **1**. DEP & ELECTRÓN circuit - **2**. [recorrido] tour.

circulación *f* - **1**. [gen] circulation; ~ **de la sangre** circulation of the blood - **2**. [tráfico] traffic.

circular ◇ *adj* & *f* circular. ◇ *vi* - **1**. [pasar]: ~ **(por)** [líquido] to flow *o* circulate (through); [persona] to move *o* walk (around); [vehículos] to drive (along) - **2**. [de mano en mano] to circulate; [moneda] to be in circulation - **3**. [difundirse] to go round.

círculo *m* *lit & fig* circle.
◆ **círculos** *mpl* [medios] circles.
◆ **círculo polar** *m* polar circle; **el ~ polar ártico/antártico** the Arctic/Antarctic Circle.
◆ **círculo vicioso** *m* vicious circle.

circuncisión *f* circumcision.

circundante *adj* surrounding.

circundar *vt* to surround.

circunferencia *f* circumference.

circunloquio *m* circumlocution.

circunscribir *vt* - **1**. [limitar] to restrict, to confine - **2**. GEOM to circumscribe.
◆ **circunscribirse a** *vpr* to confine o.s. to.

circunscripción *f* [distrito] district; MIL division; POLÍT constituency.

circunscrito, ta ◇ *pp* ▷ **circunscribir.**

◇ *adj* restricted, limited.

circunstancia *f* circumstance; **en estas ~s** under the circumstances; **~ atenuante/agravante/eximente** DER extenuating/aggravating/exonerating circumstance.

circunstancial *adj* [accidental] chance *(antes de sust).*

circunvalar *vt* to go round.

cirio *m* (wax) candle; **montar un ~** to make a row.

cirrosis *f inv* cirrhosis.

ciruela *f* plum; **~ pasa** prune.

cirugía *f* surgery; **~ estética** O **plástica** cosmetic O plastic surgery.

cirujano, na *m,f* surgeon.

cisco *m* -1. [carbón] slack; **hecho ~** *fig* shattered - 2. *fam* [alboroto] row, rumpus.

cisma *m* -1. [separación] schism - 2. [discordia] split.

cisne *m* swan.

cisterna *f* [de retrete] cistern.

cistitis *f inv* cystitis.

cita *f* -1. [entrevista] appointment; [de novios] date; **concertar una ~** to make an appointment; **darse ~** to meet; **tener una ~** to have an appointment - 2. [referencia] quotation.

citación *f* DER summons *(sg).*

citar *vt* -1. [convocar] to make an appointment with - 2. [aludir] to mention; [textualmente] to quote - 3. DER to summons.

◆ **citarse** *vpr*: **~se (con alguien)** to arrange to meet (sb).

citología *f* -1. [análisis] smear test - 2. BIOL cytology.

cítrico, ca *adj* citric.

◆ **cítricos** *mpl* citrus fruits.

CiU *(abrev de* **Convergència i Unió**) *f Catalan coalition party to the centre-right of the political spectrum.*

ciudad *f* [localidad] city; [pequeña] town.

◆ **Ciudad del Cabo** *f* Cape Town.

◆ **Ciudad del Vaticano** *f* Vatican City.

◆ **Ciudad de México** *f* Mexico City.

ciudadanía *f* -1. [nacionalidad] citizenship - 2. [población] public, citizens *(pl).*

ciudadano, na *m,f* citizen.

cívico, ca *adj* civic; [conducta] public-spirited.

civil ◇ *adj lit* & *fig* civil. ◇ *m* [no militar] civilian.

civilización *f* civilization.

civilizado, da *adj* civilized.

civilizar *vt* to civilize.

civismo *m* -1. [urbanidad] community spirit - 2. [cortesía] civility, politeness.

cizaña *f* BOT darnel; **meter** O **sembrar ~** to sow discord.

cl *(abrev de* **centilitro**) cl.

clamar ◇ *vt* -1. [expresar] to exclaim - 2. [exigir] to cry out for. ◇ *vi* -1. [implorar] to appeal - 2. [protestar] to cry out.

clamor *m* clamour.

clamoroso, sa *adj* -1. [rotundo] resounding - 2. [vociferante] loud, clamorous.

clan *m* -1. [tribu, familia] clan - 2. [banda] faction.

clandestino, na *adj* clandestine; POLÍT underground.

claqué *m* tap dancing.

claqueta *f* clapperboard.

clara ⊳ **claro.**

claraboya *f* skylight.

clarear *v impers* -1. [amanecer]: **empezaba a ~** dawn was breaking - 2. [despejarse] to clear up, to brighten up.

◆ **clarearse** *vpr* [transparentarse] to be see-through.

claridad *f* -1. [transparencia] clearness, clarity - 2. [luz] light - 3. [franqueza] candidness - 4. [lucidez] clarity; **explicar algo con ~** to explain sthg clearly.

clarificar *vt* -1. [gen] to clarify; [misterio] to clear up - 2. [purificar] to refine.

clarín *m* [instrumento] bugle.

clarinete *m* [instrumento] clarinet.

clarividencia *f* farsightedness, perception.

claro, ra *adj* -1. [gen] clear; **~ está que ...** of course ...; **dejar algo ~** to make sthg clear; **a las claras** clearly; **pasar una noche en ~** to spend a sleepless night; **poner algo en ~** to get sthg clear, to clear sthg up; **sacar algo en ~ (de)** to make sthg out (from); **tener algo ~** to be sure of sthg - 2. [luminoso] bright - 3. [color] light - 4. [diluido - té, café] weak; [- salsa] thin.

◆ **claro** ◇ *m* -1. [en bosque] clearing; [en multitud, texto] space, gap - 2. METEOR bright spell. ◇ *adv* clearly. ◇ *interj*: **¡~!** of course!; **¡~ que no!** of course not!; **¡~ que sí!** yes, of course.

◆ **clara** *f* [de huevo] white.

clase *f* -1. [gen] class; **~ alta/media** upper/middle class; **~ obrera** O **trabajadora** working class; **~ social** social class; **~ preferente/turista** club/tourist O coach US class; **primera ~** first class - 2. [tipo] sort, kind; **toda ~ de** all sorts O kinds of - 3. [EDUC - asignatura, alumnos] class; [- aula] classroom; **dar ~s** [en un colegio] to teach; [en una universidad] to lecture; **~s particulares** private classes O lessons.

clásico, ca ◇ *adj* -1. [de la Antigüedad] classical - 2. [ejemplar, prototípico] classic - 3. [peinado, estilo, música etc] classical - 4. [habitual] customary - 5. [peculiar]: **~ de** typical of. ◇ *m,f* [persona] classic.

clasificación *f* classification; DEP (league) table.

clasificar *vt* to classify.
◆ **clasificarse** *vpr* [ganar acceso]: ~**se (para)** to qualify (for); DEP to get through (to).

clasista *adj* class-conscious; *despec* snobbish.

claudicar *vi* [ceder] to give in.

claustro *m* - 1. ARQUIT & RELIG cloister - 2. [de universidad] senate.

claustrofobia *f* claustrophobia.

cláusula *f* clause.

clausura *f* - 1. [acto solemne] closing ceremony - 2. [cierre] closing down - 3. RELIG religious seclusion.

clausurar *vt* - 1. [acto] to close, to conclude - 2. [local] to close down.

clavadista *mf CAm, Méx* diver.

clavado, da *adj* - 1. [en punto - hora] on the dot - 2. [parecido] almost identical; **ser ~ a alguien** to be the spitting image of sb.

clavar *vt* - 1. [clavo, estaca etc] to drive; [cuchillo] to thrust; [chincheta, alfiler] to stick - 2. [cartel, placa etc] to nail, to fix - 3. *fig* [mirada, atención] to fix, to rivet.

clave ◇ *adj inv* key; **palabra ~** keyword. ◇ *m* MÚS harpsichord. ◇ *f* - 1. [código] code; **en ~** in code - 2. *fig* [solución] key; **la ~ del problema** the key to the problem - 3. MÚS clef; **~ de sol** treble clef - 4. INFORM key.

clavel *m* carnation.

clavicémbalo *m* harpsichord.

clavicordio *m* clavichord.

clavícula *f* collar bone.

clavija *f* - 1. ELECTR & TECN pin; [de auriculares, teléfono] jack - 2. MÚS peg.

clavo *m* - 1. [pieza metálica] nail; **agarrarse a un ~ ardiendo** to clutch at straws; **dar en el ~** to hit the nail on the head; **¡por los ~s de Cristo!** for heaven's sake! - 2. BOT & CULIN clove - 3. MED [para huesos] pin.

claxon (*pl* cláxones) *m* horn; **tocar el ~** to sound the horn.

clemencia *f* mercy, clemency.

clemente *adj* [persona] merciful, clement.

cleptómano, na *m,f* kleptomaniac.

clerical *adj* clerical.

clericó *m RP* drink made of white wine and fruit.

clérigo *m* [católico] priest; [anglicano] clergyman.

clero *m* clergy.

clic *m* INFORM click; **hacer ~ en algo** to click on sthg.

cliché, clisé *m* - 1. FOT negative - 2. IMPRENTA plate - 3. *fig* [tópico] cliché.

cliente, ta *m,f* [de tienda, garaje, bar] customer; [de banco, abogado etc] client; [de hotel] guest; **~ habitual** regular customer.

clientela *f* [de tienda, garaje] customers (*pl*); [de banco, abogado etc] clients (*pl*); [de hotel] guests (*pl*); [de bar, restaurante] clientele.

clima *m* lit & fig climate.

climatizado, da *adj* air-conditioned.

climatizar *vt* to air-condition.

climatología *f* - 1. [tiempo] weather - 2. [ciencia] climatology.

clímax *m inv* climax.

clínico, ca *adj* clinical.
◆ **clínica** *f* clinic.

clip *m* [para papel] paper clip.

clisé = cliché.

clítoris *m inv* clitoris.

cloaca *f* sewer.

cloquear *vi* to cluck.

cloro *m* chlorine.

clorofluorocarbono *m* chlorofluorocarbon.

cloruro *m* chloride.

clóset, clósets *m Amér* fitted cupboard.

clown *m* clown.

club (*pl* clubs *o* clubes) *m* club; **~ de fans** fan club; **~ de fútbol** football club; **~ náutico** yacht club; **~ nocturno** nightclub.

cm (*abrev de* **centímetro**) cm.

CNT (*abrev de* **Confederación Nacional del Trabajo**) *f Spanish anarchist trade union federation created in 1911.*

Co. (*abrev de* **compañía**) Co.

coacción *f* coercion.

coaccionar *vt* to coerce.

coagular *vt* [gen] to coagulate; [sangre] to clot; [leche] to curdle.
◆ **coagularse** *vpr* [gen] to coagulate; [sangre] to clot; [leche] to curdle.

coágulo *m* clot.

coalición *f* coalition; **formar una ~** to form a coalition.

coartada *f* alibi.

coartar *vt* to limit, to restrict.

coba *f fam* [halago] flattery; **dar ~ a alguien** [hacer la pelota] to suck up *o* crawl to sb; [aplacar] to soft-soap sb.

cobalto *m* cobalt.

cobarde ◇ *adj* cowardly. ◇ *mf* coward.

cobardía *f* cowardice.

cobertizo *m* - 1. [tejado adosado] lean-to - 2. [barracón] shed.

cobertura *f* - 1. [gen] cover - 2. [de un edificio] covering - 3. PRENS: **~ informativa** news coverage - 4. TELEC: **no tengo ~** my network doesn't cover this area.

cobija *f Amér* [manta] blanket.

cobijar *vt* - 1. [albergar] to house - 2. [proteger] to shelter.
◆ **cobijarse** *vpr* to take shelter.

cobijo *m* shelter; **dar ~ a alguien** to give

shelter to sb, to take sb in.
cobra *f* cobra.
cobrador, ra *m,f* [del autobús] conductor (*f* conductress); [de deudas, recibos] collector.
cobrar ⬦ *vt* - **1.** [COM - dinero] to charge; [- cheque] to cash; [- deuda] to collect; **cantidades por ~** amounts due; **¿me cobra, por favor?** how much do I owe you? - **2.** [en el trabajo] to earn, to be paid - **3.** [adquirir - importancia] to get, to acquire; **~ fama** to become famous - **4.** [sentir - cariño, afecto] to start to feel. ⬦ *vi* [en el trabajo] to get paid.
cobre *m* copper; **no tener un ~** *Amér* to be flat broke.
cobrizo, za *adj* [color, piel] copper (*antes de sust*).
cobro *m* [de talón] cashing; [de pago] collection; **llamada a ~ revertido** reverse charge call *UK*, collect call *US*; **llamar a ~ revertido** to reverse the charges *UK*, to call collect *US*.
coca *f* - **1.** [planta] coca - **2.** *fam* [cocaína] coke.
Coca-Cola® *f* Coca-Cola®, Coke®.
cocaína *f* cocaine.
cocción *f* [gen] cooking; [en agua] boiling; [en horno] baking.
cóccix, coxis *m inv* coccyx.
cocear *vi* to kick.
cocer *vt* - **1.** [gen] to cook; [hervir] to boil; [en horno] to bake - **2.** [cerámica, ladrillos] to fire.
➦ **cocerse** *vpr fig* [plan] to be afoot.
coche *m* - **1.** [automóvil] car, automobile *US*; **ir en ~** [montado] to go by car; [conduciendo] to drive; **~ de alquiler** hire car; **~ blindado** armoured car; **~ de bomberos** fire engine; **~ de carreras** racing car; **~ celular** police van; **~ familiar** estate car *UK*, station wagon *US* - **2.** [de tren] coach, carriage; **~ cama** sleeping car, sleeper; **~ restaurante** restaurant *o* dining car - **3.** [de caballos] carriage.
➦ **coche bomba** *m* car bomb.
cochera *f* [para coches] garage; [de autobuses, tranvías] depot.
cochinilla *f* - **1.** [crustáceo] woodlouse - **2.** [insecto] cochineal.
cochinillo *m* sucking pig.
cochino, na ⬦ *adj* - **1.** [persona] filthy - **2.** [tiempo, dinero] lousy. ⬦ *m,f* [animal - macho] pig; [- hembra] sow.
cocido *m* stew.
cociente *m* quotient; **~ intelectual** intelligence quotient, I.Q.
cocina *f* - **1.** [habitación] kitchen - **2.** [electrodoméstico] cooker, stove; **~ eléctrica/de gas** electric/gas cooker - **3.** [arte] cooking; **alta ~** haute cuisine; **~ casera** home

cooking; **~ española** Spanish cuisine *o* cooking; **libro/clase de ~** cookery book/class.
cocinar *vt* & *vi* to cook.
cocinero, ra *m,f* cook; **haber sido ~ antes que fraile** to know what one is talking about.
cocker *m* cocker spaniel.
coco *m* [árbol] coconut palm; [fruto] coconut.
cocodrilo *m* crocodile.
cocotero *m* coconut palm.
cóctel, coctel *m* - **1.** [bebida, comida] cocktail; **~ de gambas** prawn cocktail - **2.** [reunión] cocktail party.
➦ **cóctel molotov** *m* Molotov cocktail.
coctelera *f* cocktail shaker.
codazo *m* nudge, jab (*with one's elbow*); **abrirse paso a ~s** to elbow one's way through; **dar un ~ a alguien** [con disimulo] to give sb a nudge, to nudge sb; [con fuerza] to elbow sb.
codearse *vpr*: **~ (con)** to rub shoulders (with).
codera *f* elbow patch.
codicia *f* [avaricia] greed.
codiciar *vt* to covet.
codicioso, sa *adj* greedy.
codificar *vt* - **1.** [ley] to codify - **2.** [un mensaje] to encode - **3.** INFORM to code.
código *m* [gen & INFORM] code; **~ postal** post *UK o* zip *US* code; **~ territorial** area code; **~ de barras/de señales** bar/signal code; **~ de circulación** highway code; **~ civil/penal** civil/penal code.
codillo *m* [de jamón] shoulder.
codo *m* [en brazo, tubería] elbow; **estaba de ~s sobre la mesa** she was leaning (with her elbows) on the table; **dar con el ~** to nudge.
codorniz *f* quail.
coeficiente *m* - **1.** [gen] coefficient - **2.** [indice] rate.
coercer *vt* to restrict, to constrain.
coetáneo, a *adj* & *m,f* contemporary.
coexistir *vi* to coexist.
cofia *f* [de enfermera, camarera] cap; [de monja] coif.
cofradía *f* - **1.** [religiosa] brotherhood (*f* sisterhood) - **2.** [no religiosa] guild.
cofre *m* - **1.** [arca] chest, trunk - **2.** [para joyas] jewel box.
coger ⬦ *vt* - **1.** [asir, agarrar] to take - **2.** [atrapar - ladrón, pez, pájaro] to catch - **3.** [alcanzar - persona, vehículo] to catch up with - **4.** [recoger - frutos, flores] to pick - **5.** [quedarse con - propina, empleo, piso] to take - **6.** [quitar]: **~ algo (a alguien)** to take sthg (from sb) - **7.** [tren, autobús] to take, to catch - **8.** [contraer - gripe, resfriado] to

catch, to get - 9. [sentir - manía, odio, afecto] to start to feel; ~ **cariño/miedo a** to become fond/scared of **- 10.** [oír] to catch; [entender] to get **- 11.** [sorprender, encontrar]: ~ **a alguien haciendo algo** to catch sb doing sthg; **lo cogieron robando** they caught him stealing **- 12.** [sintonizar - canal, emisora] to get, to receive **- 13.** *Méx, RP,Ven vulg* [tener relaciones sexuales con] to screw, to fuck. ◇ *vi* [dirigirse]: ~ **a la derecha/la izquierda** to turn right/left.

◆ **cogerse** *vpr* **- 1.** [agarrarse]: ~**se de** *o* a **algo** to cling to *o* clutch sthg **- 2.** [pillarse]: ~**se los dedos/la falda en la puerta** to catch one's fingers/skirt in the door.

cogida *f* [de torero]: **sufrir una** ~ to be gored.

cognac = **coñá.**

cogollo *m* **- 1.** [de lechuga] heart **- 2.** [brote - de árbol, planta] shoot.

cogorza *f fam*: **agarrarse una** ~ to get smashed, to get blind drunk; **llevar una** ~ to be smashed, to be blind drunk.

cogote *m* nape, back of the neck.

cohabitar *vi* to cohabit, to live together.

cohecho *m* bribery.

coherencia *f* [de razonamiento] coherence.

coherente *adj* coherent.

cohesión *f* cohesion.

cohete *m* rocket.

cohibido, da *adj* inhibited.

cohibir *vt* to inhibit.

◆ **cohibirse** *vpr* to become inhibited.

COI (*abrev de* **Comité Olímpico Internacional**) *m* IOC.

coima *f Andes, RP fam* bribe, backhander *UK*.

coincidencia *f* coincidence; **¡qué** ~**!** what a coincidence!

coincidir *vi* **- 1.** [superficies, versiones, gustos] to coincide **- 2.** [personas - encontrarse] to meet; [- estar de acuerdo] to agree; **coincidimos en una fiesta** we saw each other at a party.

coito *m* (sexual) intercourse.

coja ▷ **coger.**

cojear *vi* **- 1.** [persona] to limp **- 2.** [mueble] to wobble.

cojera *f* [acción] limp; [estado] lameness.

cojín *m* cushion.

cojinete *m* [en eje] bearing; [en un riel de ferrocarril] chair.

cojo, ja ◇ *v* ▷ **coger.** ◇ *adj* **- 1.** [persona] lame **- 2.** [mueble] wobbly. ◇ *m,f* cripple.

cojón *m* (*gen pl*) *vulg* ball.

◆ **cojones** *interj vulg*: **¡cojones!** [enfado] for fuck's sake!

cojonudo, da *adj vulg* bloody brilliant.

cojudez *f Andes mfam*: **¡que** ~ **!** [acto] what

a bloody *UK o* goddamn *US* stupid thing to do!; [dicho] what a bloody *UK o* goddamn *US* stupid thing to say!

cojudo, da *adj Andes mfam* bloody *UK o* goddamn *US* stupid.

col *f* cabbage; ~ **de Bruselas** Brussels sprout; **entre** ~ **y** ~**, lechuga** variety is the spice of life.

cola *f* **- 1.** [de animal, avión] tail **- 2.** [fila] queue *UK*, line *US*; **¡a la** ~**!** get in the queue! *UK*, get in line! *US*; **hacer** ~ to queue (up) *UK*, to stand in line *US*; **ponerse a la** ~ to join the end of the queue *UK o* line *US* **- 3.** [pegamento] glue **- 4.** [de clase, lista] bottom; [de desfile] end **- 5.** [peinado]: ~ **(de caballo)** pony tail **- 6.** *Amér fam* [nalgas] bum *UK*, fanny *US*.

colaboración *f* **- 1.** [gen] collaboration **- 2.** [de prensa] contribution, article.

colaborador, ra *m,f* **- 1.** [gen] collaborator **- 2.** [de prensa] contributor, writer.

colaborar *vi* **- 1.** [ayudar] to collaborate **- 2.** [en prensa]: ~ **en** *o* **con** to write for, to work for **- 3.** [contribuir] to contribute.

colación *f*: **sacar** *o* **traer algo a** ~ [tema] to bring sthg up.

colado, da *adj* **- 1.** [líquido] strained **- 2.** [enamorado]: **estar** ~ **por alguien** *fam* to have a crush on sb.

◆ **colada** *f* [ropa] laundry; **hacer la colada** to do the washing.

colador *m* [para líquidos] strainer, sieve; [para verdura] colander.

colapsar ◇ *vt* to bring to a halt, to stop. ◇ *vi* to come *o* grind to a halt.

colapso *m* **- 1.** MED collapse, breakdown; **sufrir un** ~ to collapse; ~ **nervioso** nervous breakdown **- 2.** [de actividad] stoppage; [de tráfico] traffic jam, hold-up.

colar *vt* [verdura, té] to strain; [café] to filter.

◆ **colarse** *vpr* **- 1.** [líquido]: ~**se por** to seep through **- 2.** [persona] to slip, to sneak; [en una cola] to jump the queue *UK o* line *US*; ~**se en una fiesta** to gatecrash a party.

colateral *adj* [lateral] on either side.

colcha *f* bedspread.

colchón *m* [de cama] mattress; ~ **inflable** air bed.

colchoneta *f* [para playa] beach mat; [en gimnasio] mat.

cole *m fam* school.

colear *vi* [animal] to wag its tail.

colección *f* lit & fig collection.

coleccionable ◇ *adj* collectable. ◇ *m* special supplement in serialized form.

coleccionar *vt* to collect.

coleccionista *mf* collector.

colecta *f* collection.

colectividad *f* community.

colectivo, va ◇ *adj* collective. ◇ *m Andes* [taxi] collective taxi; *Andes, Bol* [autobús] bus.
 ➡ **colectivo** *m* group.
colector *m* - **1**. [sumidero] sewer; ~ **de basuras** chute - **2**. MEC [de motor] manifold.
colega *mf* - **1**. [compañero profesional] colleague - **2**. [homólogo] counterpart, opposite number - **3**. *fam* [amigo] mate.
colegiado, da *adj* who belongs to a professional association.
 ➡ **colegiado** *m* DEP referee.
colegial, la *m,f* schoolboy (*f* schoolgirl).
colegio *m* - **1**. [escuela] school; ~ **concertado** private school with state subsidy; ~ **de curas** school run by priests; ~ **de monjas** convent school - **2**. [de profesionales]: ~ **(profesional)** professional association.
 ➡ **colegio electoral** *m* [lugar] polling station; [votantes] ward.
 ➡ **colegio mayor** *m* hall of residence.
cólera ◇ *m* MED cholera. ◇ *f* [ira] anger, rage; **montar en** ~ to get angry, to lose one's temper.
colérico, ca *adj* [carácter] bad-tempered.
colesterol *m* cholesterol.
coleta *f* pigtail.
coletilla *f* postscript.
colgado, da *adj* - **1**. [cuadro, jamón etc]: ~ **(de)** hanging (from) - **2**. [teléfono] on the hook.
colgador *m* hanger, coathanger.
colgante ◇ *adj* hanging. ◇ *m* pendant.
colgar ◇ *vt* - **1**. [suspender, ahorcar] to hang; ~ **el teléfono** to hang up - **2**. [imputar]: ~ **algo a alguien** to blame sthg on sb. ◇ *vi* - **1**. [pender]: ~ **(de)** to hang (from) - **2**. [hablando por teléfono] to hang up, to put the phone down.
colibrí *m* hummingbird.
cólico *m* stomachache.
coliflor *f* cauliflower.
colilla *f* [cigarette] butt *O* stub.
colimba *f Arg fam* military service.
colina *f* hill.
colindante *adj* neighbouring, adjacent.
colisión *f* [de automóviles] collision, crash; [de ideas, intereses] clash.
colisionar *vi* [coche]: ~ **(contra)** to collide (with), to crash (into).
collar *m* - **1**. [de personas] necklace - **2**. [para animales] collar.
collarín *m* surgical collar.
colmado, da *adj*: ~ **(de)** full to the brim (with).
 ➡ **colmado** *m* grocer's (shop).
colmar *vt* - **1**. [recipiente] to fill (to the brim) - **2**. *fig* [aspiración, deseo] to fulfil.
colmena *f* beehive.

colmillo *m* - **1**. [de persona] eye-tooth - **2**. [de perro] fang; [de elefante] tusk.
colmo *m* height; **para** ~ **de desgracias** to crown it all; **es el** ~ **de la locura** it's sheer madness; **¡eso es el** ~**!** *fam* that's the last straw!
colocación *f* - **1**. [acción] placing, positioning; [situación] place, position - **2**. [empleo] position, job.
colocado, da *adj* - **1**. [gen] placed; **estar muy bien** ~ to have a very good job - **2**. *fam* [borracho] legless; [drogado] high, stoned.
colocar *vt* - **1**. [en su sitio] to place, to put - **2**. [en un empleo] to find a job for - **3**. [invertir] to place, to invest.
 ➡ **colocarse** *vpr* - **1**. [en un trabajo] to get a job - **2**. *fam* [emborracharse] to get legless; [drogarse] to get high *O* stoned.
colocón *m fam*: **llevar un** ~ [de droga] to be high; [de bebida] to be pissed.
colofón *m* [remate, fin] climax, culmination.
Colombia Colombia.
colombiano, na *adj* & *m,f* Colombian.
colon *m* colon.
colonia *f* - **1**. [gen] colony - **2**. [perfume] eau de cologne - **3**. *Méx* [barrio] district; ~ **proletaria** shanty town, slum area.
colonial *adj* colonial.
colonización *f* colonization.
colonizador, ra *m,f* colonist.
colonizar *vt* to colonize.
colono *m* settler, colonist.
coloquial *adj* colloquial.
coloquio *m* - **1**. [conversación] conversation - **2**. [debate] discussion, debate.
color *m* [gen] colour; ~ **rojo** red; ~ **azul** blue; **¿de qué** ~**?** what colour?; **una falda de** ~ **rosa** a pink skirt; **a todo** ~ in full colour; **de** ~ [persona] coloured; **en** ~ [foto, televisor] colour.
colorado, da *adj* [color] red; **ponerse** ~ to blush, to go red.
colorante *m* colouring.
colorear *vt* to colour (in).
colorete *m* rouge, blusher.
colorido *m* colours (*pl*).
colosal *adj* - **1**. [estatura, tamaño] colossal - **2**. [extraordinario] great, enormous.
coloso *m* - **1**. [estatua] colossus - **2**. *fig* [cosa, persona] giant.
columna *f* - **1**. [gen] column - **2**. *fig* [pilar] pillar.
 ➡ **columna vertebral** *f* spinal column.
columnista *mf* columnist.
columpiar *vt* to swing.
 ➡ **columpiarse** *vpr* to swing.
columpio *m* swing.

colza *f* BOT rape.

coma ◇ *m* MED coma; **en ~** in a coma. ◇ *f* **-1.** GRAM comma **-2.** MAT ≃ decimal point.

comadreja *f* weasel.

comadrona *f* midwife.

comal *m* CAm, Méx clay or metal dish used for baking tortillas.

comandancia *f* **-1.** [rango] command **-2.** [edificio] command headquarters.

comandante *m* [MIL - rango] major; [- de un puesto] commander, commandant.

comandar *vt* MIL to command.

comando *m* MIL commando.

comarca *f* region, area.

comba *f* **-1.** [juego] skipping; **jugar** *o* **saltar a la ~** to skip **-2.** [cuerda] skipping rope.

combar *vt* to bend.
◆ **combarse** *vpr* [gen] to bend; [madera] to warp; [pared] to bulge.

combate *m* [gen] fight; [batalla] battle.

combatiente *mf* combatant, fighter.

combatir ◇ *vi*: **~ (contra)** to fight (against). ◇ *vt* to combat, to fight.

combativo, va *adj* combative.

combi *m* [frigorífico] fridge-freezer.

combinación *f* **-1.** [gen] combination **-2.** [de bebidas] cocktail **-3.** [prenda] slip **-4.** [de medios de transporte] connections (*pl*).

combinado *m* **-1.** [bebida] cocktail **-2.** DEP combined team **-3.** Amér [radiograma] radiogram.

combinar *vt* **-1.** [gen] to combine **-2.** [bebidas] to mix **-3.** [colores] to match.

combustible ◇ *adj* combustible. ◇ *m* fuel.

combustión *f* combustion.

comecocos *m inv fam* [para convencer]: **este panfleto es un ~** this pamphlet is designed to brainwash you.

comedia *f* **-1.** [obra, película, género] comedy **-2.** *fig* [engaño] farce; **hacer la ~** to pretend, to make believe.

comediante, ta *m,f* actor (*f* actress); *fig* [farsante] fraud.

comedido, da *adj* moderate, restrained.

comedirse *vpr* to be restrained.

comedor *m* [habitación - de casa] dining room; [- de fábrica] canteen.

comensal *mf* fellow diner.

comentar *vt* [opinar sobre] to comment on; [hablar de] to discuss.

comentario *m* **-1.** [observación] comment, remark **-2.** [crítica] commentary.
◆ **comentarios** *mpl* [murmuraciones] gossip (*U*).

comentarista *mf* commentator.

comenzar ◇ *vt* to start, to begin; **~ a hacer algo** to start doing *o* to do sthg; **~ diciendo que ...** to start *o* begin by

saying that ... ◇ *vi* to start, to begin.

comer ◇ *vi* [ingerir alimentos - gen] to eat; [- al mediodía] to have lunch. ◇ *vt* **-1.** [alimentos] to eat **-2.** [en juegos de tablero] to take, to capture **-3.** *fig* [consumir] to eat up.
◆ **comerse** *vpr* **-1.** [alimentos] to eat **-2.** [desgastar - recursos] to eat up; [- metal] to corrode **-3.** [en los juegos de tablero] to take, to capture **-4.** Amér vulg [fornicar]: **~se a** to fuck.

comercial *adj* commercial.

comercializar *vt* to market.

comerciante *mf* tradesman (*f* tradeswoman); [tendero] shopkeeper.

comerciar *vi* to trade, to do business.

comercio *m* **-1.** [de productos] trade; **~ electrónico** e-business; **~ exterior/interior** foreign/domestic trade; **~ justo** fair trade; **libre ~** free trade **-2.** [actividad] business, commerce **-3.** [tienda] shop.

comestible *adj* edible, eatable.
◆ **comestibles** *mpl* [gen] food (*U*); [en una tienda] groceries.

cometa ◇ *m* ASTRON comet. ◇ *f* kite.

cometer *vt* [crimen] to commit; [error] to make.

cometido *m* **-1.** [objetivo] mission, task **-2.** [deber] duty.

comezón *f* [picor] itch, itching (*U*).

cómic (*pl* cómics), **comic** (*pl* comics) *m* (adult) comic.

comicios *mpl* elections.

cómico, ca ◇ *adj* **-1.** [de la comedia] comedy (antes de sust), comic **-2.** [gracioso] comic, comical. ◇ *m,f* [actor de teatro] actor (*f* actress); [humorista] comedian (*f* comedienne), comic.

comida *f* **-1.** [alimento] food (*U*); **~ basura** junk food; **~ chatarra** Amér junk food; **~ rápida** fast food **-2.** [almuerzo, cena etc] meal **-3.** [al mediodía] lunch; **~ de negocios** business lunch.

comidilla *f fam*: **ser/convertirse en la ~ del pueblo** to be/to become the talk of the town.

comienzo *m* start, beginning; **a ~s de los años 50** in the early 1950s; **dar ~** to start, to begin.

comillas *fpl* inverted commas, quotation marks; **entre ~** in inverted commas.

comilona *f fam* [festín] blow-out.

comino *m* [planta] cumin, cummin; **me importa un ~** I don't give a damn.

comisaría *f* police station, precinct US.

comisario, ria *m,f* **-1.**: **~ (de policía)** police superintendent **-2.** [delegado] commissioner.

comisión *f* **-1.** [de un delito] perpetration **-2.** COM commission; **(trabajar) a ~ (to**

work) on a commission basis - **3**. [delegación] commission, committee; **Comisión Europea** European Comission; ~ **investigadora** committee of inquiry; ~ **permanente** standing commission; **Comisiones Obreras** Spanish Communist-inspired trade union.

comisura *f* corner (of mouth, eyes).

comité *m* committee.

comitiva *f* retinue.

como ⬦ *adv* - **1**. *(comparativo)*: **tan ... ~ ...** as ... as ...; **es (tan) negro ~ el carbón** it's as black as coal; **ser ~ algo** to be like sthg; **vive ~ un rey** he lives like a king; **lo que dijo fue ~ para ruborizarse** his words were enough to make you blush - **2**. [de la manera que] as; **lo he hecho ~ es debido** I did it as o the way it should be done; **me encanta ~ bailas** I love the way you dance - **3**. [según] as; ~ **te decía ayer ... as** I was telling you yesterday ... - **4**. [en calidad de] as; **trabaja ~ bombero** he works as a fireman; **dieron el dinero ~ anticipo** they gave the money as an advance - **5**. [aproximadamente] about; **me quedan ~ cien euros** I've got about a hundred euros left; **tiene un sabor ~ a naranja** it tastes a bit like an orange. ⬦ *conj* - **1**. [ya que] as, since; ~ **no llegabas, nos fuimos** as o since you didn't arrive, we left - **2**. [si] if; ~ **no me hagas caso, lo pasarás mal** if you don't listen to me, there will be trouble.

⬧ **como que** *loc conj* - **1**. [que] that; **le pareció ~ que lloraban** it seemed to him (that) they were crying - **2**. [expresa causa]: **pareces cansado — ~ que he trabajado toda la noche** you seem tired — well, I've been up all night working.

⬧ **como quiera** *loc adv* [de cualquier modo] anyway, anyhow.

⬧ **como quiera que** *loc conj* - **1**. [de cualquier modo que] whichever way, however; ~ **quiera que sea** whatever the case may be - **2**. [dado que] since, given that.

⬧ **como si** *loc conj* as if.

cómo *adv* - **1**. [de qué modo, por qué motivo] how; **¿~ lo has hecho?** how did you do it?; **¿~ son?** what are they like?; **no sé ~ has podido decir eso** I don't know how you could say that; **¿~ que no la has visto nunca?** what do you mean you've never seen her?; **¿a ~ están los tomates?** how much are the tomatoes?; **¿~? ¿~?** *fam* [¿qué dices?] sorry?, what? - **2**. [exclamativo] how; **¡~ pasan los años!** how time flies!; **¡~ no!** of course!; **está lloviendo, ¡y ~!** it isn't half raining!

cómoda *f* chest of drawers.

comodidad *f* comfort, convenience (U); **para su ~** for your convenience.

comodín *m* [naipe] joker.

cómodo, da *adj* - **1**. [confortable] comfortable; **ponte ~** make yourself comfortable, make yourself at home; **sentirse ~ con alguien** to feel comfortable with sb - **2**. [útil] convenient - **3**. [oportuno, fácil] easy.

comoquiera *adv* : ~ **que** [de cualquier manera que] whichever way, however; [dado que] since, seeing as.

compa *mf fam* pal, mate UK, buddy US.

compact *m* compact disc.

compactar *vt* to compress.

compact disk, compact disc *m* compact disc.

compacto, ta *adj* compact.

compadecer *vt* to pity, to feel sorry for.

⬧ **compadecerse de** *vpr* to pity, to feel sorry for.

compadre *m fam* [amigo] friend, mate UK, buddy US.

compadrear *vi RP fam* to brag, to boast.

compaginar *vt* [combinar] to reconcile.

⬧ **compaginarse** *vpr*: ~**se con** to square with, to go together with.

compañerismo *m* comradeship.

compañero, ra *m,f* - **1**. [acompañante] companion - **2**. [pareja] partner; ~ **sentimental** partner - **3**. [colega] colleague; ~ **de clase** classmate; ~ **de piso** flatmate.

compañía *f* company; **le perdieron las malas ~s** he was led astray by the bad company he kept; **en ~ de** accompanied by, in the company of; **hacer ~ a alguien** to keep sb company; ~ **de seguros** insurance company; ~ **teatral** o **de teatro** theatre company.

comparación *f* comparison; **en ~ con** in comparison with, compared to.

comparar *vt* : ~ **algo (con)** to compare sthg (to).

comparativo, va *adj* comparative.

comparecer *vi* to appear.

comparsa ⬦ *f* TEATR extras *(pl)*. ⬦ *mf* - **1**. TEATR extra - **2**. *fig* [en carreras, competiciones] also-ran; [en organizaciones, empresas] nobody.

compartimento, compartimiento *m* compartment; ~ **de fumadores** smoking compartment.

compartir *vt* - **1**. [ganancias] to share (out) - **2**. [piso, ideas] to share.

compás *m* - **1**. [instrumento] pair of compasses - **2**. [MÚS - periodo] bar; [- ritmo] rhythm, beat; **al ~ (de la música)** in time (with the music); **llevar el ~** to keep time; **perder el ~** to lose the beat.

compasión *f* compassion, pity; **¡por ~!** for pity's sake!; **tener ~ de** to feel sorry for.

compasivo, va *adj* compassionate, sympathetic.

compatibilizar *vt* to make compatible.

compatible *adj* [gen & INFORM] compatible.

compatriota *mf* compatriot, fellow countryman (*f*fellow countrywoman).

compendiar *vt* [cualidades, características] to summarize; [libro, historia] to abridge.

compendio *m* -1. [libro] compendium -2. *fig* [síntesis] epitome, essence.

compenetración *f* mutual understanding.

compenetrarse *vpr* to understand each other.

compensación *f* [gen] compensation; **en ~ (por)** in return (for); **~ económica** financial compensation.

compensar *vt* -1. [valer la pena] to make up for; **no me compensa (perder tanto tiempo)** it's not worth my while (wasting all that time) -2. [indemnizar]: **~ a alguien (de *o* por)** to compensate sb (for).

competencia *f* -1. [entre personas, empresas] competition; **hacer la ~ a** to compete with -2. [incumbencia] field, province -3. [aptitud, atribuciones] competence.

competente *adj* competent; **~ en materia de** responsible for.

competer ➔ competer a *vi* [gen] to be up to, to be the responsibility of; [una autoridad] to come under the jurisdiction of.

competición *f* competition.

competidor, ra *m,f* competitor.

competir *vi*: **~ (con/por)** to compete (with/for).

competitividad *f* competitiveness.

competitivo, va *adj* competitive.

compilar *vt* [gen & INFORM] to compile.

compinche *mf fam* crony.

complacencia *f* pleasure, satisfaction.

complacer *vt* to please.

complaciente *adj* -1. [amable] obliging, helpful -2. [indulgente] indulgent.

complejo, ja *adj* complex.

➔ complejo *m* complex; **~ deportivo** sports complex; **~ hotelero** hotel complex; **~ industrial** industrial park; **~ turístico** tourist development; **~ vitamínico** vitamin complex.

complementar *vt* to complement.

➔ complementarse *vpr* to complement each other.

complementario, ria *adj* complementary.

complemento *m* -1. [añadido] complement -2. GRAM object, complement.

completamente *adv* completely, totally.

completar *vt* to complete.

completo, ta *adj* -1. [entero, perfecto] complete; **por ~** completely; **un deportista muy ~** an all-round sportsman -2. [lleno] full.

complexión *f* build; **de ~ atlética** with an athletic build; **de ~ fuerte** well-built, with a strong constitution.

complicación *f* -1. [gen] complication -2. [complejidad] complexity.

complicado, da *adj* -1. [difícil] complicated -2. [implicado]: **~ (en)** involved (in).

complicar *vt* [dificultar] to complicate.

cómplice *mf* accomplice.

complicidad *f* complicity.

complot, compló *m* plot, conspiracy.

componente *m* -1. [gen & ELECTR] component -2. [persona] member.

componer *vt* -1. [constituir, ser parte de] to make up -2. [música, versos] to compose -3. [arreglar - algo roto] to repair.

➔ componerse *vpr* [estar formado]: **~se de** to be made up of, to consist of.

comportamiento *m* behaviour.

comportar *vt* to involve, to entail.

➔ comportarse *vpr* to behave.

composición *f* composition.

compositor, ra *m,f* composer.

compostura *f* -1. [reparación] repair -2. [de persona, rostro] composure -3. [en comportamiento] restraint.

compota *f* CULIN stewed fruit *(U)*.

compra *f* purchase; **ir de ~s** to go shopping; **ir a *o* hacer la ~** to do the shopping; **~ al contado** cash purchase; **~ a plazos** hire purchase.

comprador, ra *m,f* [gen] buyer, purchaser; [en una tienda] shopper, customer.

comprar *vt* -1. [adquirir] to buy, to purchase; **~ algo a alguien** to buy sth from sb -2. [sobornar] to buy (off), to bribe.

compraventa *f* buying and selling, trading.

comprender *vt* -1. [incluir] to include, to comprise -2. [entender] to understand; **hacerse ~** to make o.s. understood.

➔ comprenderse *vpr* [personas] to understand each other.

comprensión *f* understanding.

comprensivo, va *adj* understanding.

compresa *f* [para menstruación] sanitary towel UK, sanitary napkin US.

comprimido, da *adj* compressed.

➔ comprimido *m* pill, tablet.

comprimir *vt* to compress.

comprobante *m* [documento] supporting document, proof; [recibo] receipt.

comprobar *vt* [averiguar] to check; [demostrar] to prove.

comprometer *vt* -1. [poner en peligro - éxito etc] to jeopardize; [- persona] to compromise -2. [avergonzar] to embarrass.

➔ comprometerse *vpr* -1. [hacerse responsable]: **~se (a hacer algo)** to commit o.s. (to doing sthg) **- 2.** [ideológicamente, moralmente]: ~**se (en algo)** to become involved (in sthg).

comprometido, da *adj* **- 1.** [con una idea] committed **- 2.** [difícil] compromising, awkward.

compromiso *m* **- 1.** [obligación] commitment; [acuerdo] agreement **- 2.** [cita] engagement; **sin** ~ without obligation **- 3.** [de matrimonio] engagement; ~ **matrimonial** engagement **- 4.** [dificultad, aprieto] compromising *o* difficult situation; **me pones en un** ~ you're putting me in an awkward position.

compuerta *f* sluice, floodgate.

compuesto, ta ◇ *pp* ▷ **componer.** ◇ *adj* [formado]: ~ **de** composed of, made up of.

◆ **compuesto** *m* GRAM & QUÍM compound.

compungido, da *adj* contrite, remorseful.

computador *m*, **computadora** *f* computer.

computar *vt* [calcular] to calculate.

cómputo *m* calculation.

comulgar *vi* RELIG to take communion.

común *adj* **- 1.** [gen] common; **por lo** ~ generally; **poco** ~ unusual **- 2.** [compartido - amigo, interés] mutual; [- bienes, pastos] communal **- 3.** [ordinario - vino etc] ordinary, average; ~ **y corriente** perfectly ordinary.

comuna *f* **- 1.** commune **- 2.** *Amér* [municipalidad] municipality.

comunicación *f* **- 1.** [gen] communication; **ponerse en** ~ **con alguien** to get in touch with sb **- 2.** [escrito oficial] communiqué; [informe] report.

◆ **comunicaciones** *fpl* communications.

comunicado, da *adj*: **bien** ~ [lugar] well-served, with good connections.

◆ **comunicado** *m* announcement, statement; ~ **oficial** communiqué; ~ **a la prensa** press release.

comunicar ◇ *vt* **- 1.** [transmitir - sentimientos, ideas] to convey; [- movimiento, virus] to transmit **- 2.** [información]: ~ **algo a alguien** to inform sb of sthg, to tell sb sthg. ◇ *vi* **- 1.** [hablar - gen] to communicate; [- al teléfono] to get through; [escribir] to get in touch **- 2.** [dos lugares]: ~ **con algo** to connect with sthg, to join sthg **- 3.** [el teléfono] to be engaged *UK*, to be busy *US*.

◆ **comunicarse** *vpr* **- 1.** [hablarse] to communicate (with each other) **- 2.** [dos lugares] to be connected.

comunicativo, va *adj* communicative, open.

comunidad *f* community; ~ **autónoma**

autonomous region; **Comunidad Económica Europea** European Economic Community.

comunión *f lit* & *fig* communion; **hacer la primera** ~ to take one's First Communion.

comunismo *m* communism.

comunista *adj* & *mf* communist.

comunitario, ria *adj* **- 1.** [de la comunidad] community *(antes de sust)* **- 2.** [de la CEE] Community *(antes de sust)*, of the European Community; **política comunitaria** EU *o* Community policy.

con *prep* **- 1.** [gen] with; **¿** ~ **quién vas?** who are you going with?; **lo ha conseguido** ~ **su esfuerzo** he has achieved it through his own efforts; **una cartera** ~ **varios documentos** a briefcase containing several documents **- 2.** [a pesar de] in spite of; ~ **todo despite everything;** ~ **lo estudioso que es, le suspendieron** for all his hard work, they still failed him **- 3.** [hacia]: **para** ~ **towards; es amable para** ~ **todos** she is friendly towards *o* with everyone **- 4.** *(+ infin)* [para introducir una condición] by *(+ gerund)*; ~ **hacerlo así** by doing it this way; ~ **salir a las diez es suficiente** if we leave at ten, we'll have plenty of time **- 5.** [a condición de que]: ~ **(tal) que** *(+ subjuntivo)* as long as; ~ **que llegue a tiempo me conformo** I don't mind as long as he arrives on time.

conato *m* attempt; ~ **de robo** attempted robbery; **un** ~ **de incendio** the beginnings of a fire.

concatenar, concadenar *vt* to link together.

concavidad *f* [lugar] hollow.

cóncavo, va *adj* concave.

concebir ◇ *vt* [plan, hijo] to conceive; [imaginar] to imagine. ◇ *vi* to conceive.

conceder *vt* **- 1.** [dar] to grant; [premio] to award **- 2.** [asentir] to admit, to concede.

concejal, la *m,f* (town) councillor.

concentración *f* **- 1.** [gen] concentration **- 2.** [de gente] gathering.

concentrado *m* concentrate.

concentrar *vt* **- 1.** [gen] to concentrate **- 2.** [reunir - gente] to bring together; [- tropas] to assemble.

◆ **concentrarse** *vpr* to concentrate.

concéntrico, ca *adj* concentric.

concepción *f* conception.

concepto *m* **- 1.** [idea] concept **- 2.** [opinión] opinion; **te tiene en muy buen** ~ she thinks highly of you **- 3.** [motivo]: **bajo ningún** ~ under no circumstances; **en** ~ **de** by way of, as.

concernir *v impers* to concern; **en lo que concierne a** as regards; **por lo que a mí me**

concierne as far as I'm concerned.

concertado, da *adj* [centro de enseñanza] state-assisted, ≃ grant-maintained *UK*; **hospital** ~ *private hospital that has been contracted to provide free treatment for social security patients.*

concertar ◇ *vt* [precio] to agree on; [cita] to arrange; [pacto] to reach. ◇ *vi* [concordar]: ~ **(con)** to tally (with), to fit in (with).

concertina *f* concertina.

concesión *f* - 1. [de préstamo etc] granting; [de premio] awarding - 2. COM & *fig* concession.

concesionario, ria *m,f* [persona con derecho exclusivo de venta] licensed dealer; [titular de una concesión] concessionaire, licensee.

concha *f* - 1. [de los animales] shell - 2. [material] tortoiseshell - 3. *Ven* [de frutas] peel, rind.

conchabarse *vpr fam*: ~ **(contra)** to gang up (on).

concheto, ta ◇ *adj RP fam* posh. ◇ *m,f* rich kid.

conciencia, consciencia *f* - 1. [conocimiento] consciousness, awareness; **tener/tomar** ~ **de** to be/become aware of; ~ **de clase** class consciousness; ~ **social** social conscience - 2. [moral, integridad] conscience; **a** ~ conscientiously; **me remuerde la** ~ I have a guilty conscience; **tener la** ~ **tranquila** to have a clear conscience.

concienciar *vt* to make aware.

◆ **concienciarse** *vpr* to become aware.

concientizar *vt Amér*: ~ **a alguien de algo** to make sb aware of sthg.

◆ **concientizarse** *vpr*: ~**se (de)** to become aware (of).

concienzudo, da *adj* conscientious.

concierto *m* - 1. [actuación] concert - 2. [composición] concerto.

conciliar *vt* to reconcile; ~ **el sueño** to get to sleep.

concilio *m* council.

concisión *f* conciseness.

conciso, sa *adj* concise.

conciudadano, na *m,f* fellow citizen.

cónclave, conclave *m* conclave.

concluir ◇ *vt* to conclude; ~ **haciendo** *o* **por hacer algo** to end up doing sthg. ◇ *vi* to (come to an) end.

conclusión *f* conclusion; **llegar a una** ~ to come to *o* to reach a conclusion; **en** ~ in conclusion.

concluyente *adj* conclusive.

concordancia *f* [gen & GRAM] agreement.

concordar ◇ *vt* to reconcile. ◇ *vi* - 1. [estar de acuerdo]: ~ **(con)** to agree *o* tally (with) - 2. GRAM: ~ **(con)** to agree (with).

concordia *f* harmony.

concretar *vt* [precisar] to specify, to state exactly.

◆ **concretarse** *vpr* [materializarse] to take shape.

concreto, ta *adj* specific, particular; **en** ~ [en resumen] in short; [específicamente] specifically; **nada en** ~ nothing definite.

◆ **concreto armado** *m Amér* reinforced concrete.

concurrencia *f* - 1. [asistencia] attendance; [espectadores] crowd, audience - 2. [de sucesos] concurrence.

concurrido, da *adj* [bar, calle] crowded, busy; [espectáculo] well-attended.

concurrir *vi* - 1. [reunirse]: ~ **a algo** to go to sthg, to attend sthg - 2. [participar]: ~ **a** [concurso] to take part in, to compete in; [examen] to sit *UK*, to take.

concursante *mf* [en concurso] competitor, contestant; [en oposiciones] candidate.

concursar *vi* [competir] to participate; [en oposiciones] to be a candidate.

concurso *m* - 1. [prueba - literaria, deportiva] competition; [- de televisión] game show; **fuera de** ~ out of the running - 2. [para una obra] tender; **salir a** ~ to be put out to tender - 3. [ayuda] cooperation.

condado *m* [territorio] county.

condal *adj*: **la Ciudad** ~ Barcelona.

conde, desa *m,f* count (*f* countess).

condecoración *f* [insignia] medal.

condecorar *vt* to decorate.

condena *f* sentence.

condenado, da *adj* - 1. [a una pena] convicted, sentenced; [a un sufrimiento] condemned - 2. *fam* [maldito] damned, wretched.

condenar *vt* - 1. [declarar culpable] to convict - 2. [castigar]: ~ **a alguien a algo** to sentence sb to sthg - 3. [recriminar] to condemn.

condensar *vt lit* & *fig* to condense.

condescendencia *f* [benevolencia] graciousness, kindness; [altivez] condescension.

condescender *vi*: ~ **a** [con amabilidad] to consent to, to accede to; [con desprecio] to deign to, to condescend to.

condescendiente *adj* obliging.

condición *f* - 1. [gen] condition; **condiciones de un contrato** terms of a contract; **con una sola** ~ on one condition - 2. [naturaleza] nature - 3. [clase social] social class.

◆ **condiciones** *fpl* - 1. [aptitud] talent (*U*), ability (*U*) - 2. [circunstancias] conditions; **condiciones atmosféricas/de vida** weather/living conditions - 3. [estado] condition (*U*); **estar en condiciones de** *o* **para hacer**

algo [físicamente] to be in a fit state to do sthg; [por la situación] to be in a position to do sthg; **estar en buenas condiciones** [casa, coche] to be in good condition; [carne, pescado] to be fresh; **estar en malas condiciones** [casa, coche] to be in bad condition; [carne, pescado] to be off.

condicional *adj* & *m* conditional.

condicionar *vt* : ∼ **algo a algo** to make sthg dependent on sthg.

condimento *m* seasoning *(U)*.

condolencia *f* condolence.

condolerse *vpr*: ∼ **(de)** to feel pity (for).

condón *m* condom.

cóndor *m* condor.

conducción *f* [de vehículo] driving.

conducir ◇ *vt* - **1.** [vehículo] to drive - **2.** [dirigir - empresa] to manage, to run; [- ejército] to lead; [- asunto] to handle - **3.** [a una persona a un lugar] to lead. ◇ *vi* - **1.** [en vehículo] to drive - **2.** [a sitio, situación]: ∼ **a** to lead to.

conducta *f* behaviour, conduct.

conducto *m* - **1.** [de fluido] pipe - **2.** *fig* [vía] channel - **3.** ANAT duct.

conductor, ra *m, f* - **1.** [de vehículo] driver - **2.** FÍS conductor.

conectar *vt*: ∼ **algo (a** *o* **con)** to connect sthg (to *o* up to).

➤ **conectarse** *vpr*: ∼ **se a Internet** to get connected to the Internet.

conejillo ➤ **conejillo de Indias** *m* guinea pig.

conejo, ja *m, f* rabbit *(f doe)*.

conexión *f* - **1.** [gen] connection - **2.** RADIO & TV link-up; ∼ **a Internet** Internet connection; ∼ **vía satélite** satellite link.

conexo, xa *adj* related, connected.

confabularse *vpr*: ∼ **se (para)** to plot *o* conspire (to).

confección *f* - **1.** [de ropa] tailoring, dressmaking - **2.** [de comida] preparation, making; [de lista] drawing up.

confeccionar *vt* - **1.** [ropa] to make (up); [lista] to draw up - **2.** [plato] to prepare; [bebida] to mix.

confederación *f* confederation.

conferencia *f* - **1.** [charla] lecture; **dar una** ∼ to give a talk *o* lecture - **2.** [reunión] conference - **3.** [por teléfono] (long-distance) call; **poner una** ∼ to make a long-distance call; ∼ **a cobro revertido** reverse-charge call *UK*, collect call *US*.

conferir *vt* - **1.**: ∼ **algo a alguien** [honor, dignidad] to confer *o* bestow sthg upon sb; [responsabilidades] to give sthg to sb - **2.** [cualidad] to give.

confesar *vt* [gen] to confess; [debilidad] to admit.

➤ **confesarse** *vpr* RELIG : ∼ **se (de algo)** to confess (sthg).

confesión *f* - **1.** [gen] confession - **2.** [credo] religion, (religious) persuasion.

confesionario *m* confessional.

confeti *mpl* confetti *(U)*.

confiado, da *adj* [seguro] confident; [crédulo] trusting.

confianza *f* - **1.** [seguridad]: ∼ **(en)** confidence (in); ∼ **en uno mismo** self-confidence - **2.** [fe] trust; **de** ∼ trustworthy; **ser digno de** ∼ to be trustworthy - **3.** [familiaridad] familiarity; **con toda** ∼ in all confidence; **puedes hablar con toda** ∼ you can talk quite freely; **en** ∼ in confidence; **en** ∼, **no creo que apruebe** don't tell anyone I said this, but I doubt she'll pass.

confiar *vt* - **1.** [secreto] to confide - **2.** [responsabilidad, persona, asunto]: ∼ **algo a alguien** to entrust sthg to sb.

➤ **confiar en** *vi* - **1.** [tener fe] to trust in - **2.** [suponer]: ∼ **en que** to be confident that.

➤ **confiarse** *vpr* [despreocuparse] to be too sure (of o.s.), to be overconfident.

confidencia *f* confidence, secret; **hacer** ∼**s a alguien** to confide in sb.

confidencial *adj* confidential.

confidente *mf* - **1.** [amigo] confidant *(f confidante)* - **2.** [soplón] informer.

configurar *vt* [formar] to shape, to form.

confín *(gen pl) m* - **1.** [límite] border, boundary - **2.** [extremo - del reino, universo] outer reaches *(pl)*; **en los confines de** on the very edge of.

confinar *vt* - **1.** [detener]: ∼ **(en)** to confine (to) - **2.** [desterrar]: ∼ **(en)** to banish (to).

confirmación *f* [gen & RELIG] confirmation.

confirmar *vt* to confirm.

confiscar *vt* to confiscate.

confitado, da *adj* candied; **frutas confitadas** crystallized fruit.

confite *m* sweet *UK*, candy *US*.

confitería *f* - **1.** [tienda] sweetshop, confectioner's - **2.** *RP* [café] cafe.

confitura *f* preserve, jam.

conflictivo, va *adj* [asunto] controversial; [situación] troubled; [trabajador] difficult.

conflicto *m* [gen] conflict; [de intereses, opiniones] clash; **estar en** ∼ to be in conflict; ∼ **armado** armed conflict; ∼ **generacional** generation gap; ∼ **laboral** industrial dispute.

confluir *vi* - **1.** [corriente, cauce]: ∼ **(en)** to converge *o* meet (at) - **2.** [personas]: ∼ **(en)** to come together *o* to gather (in).

conformar *vt* [configurar] to shape.

➤ **conformarse con** *vpr* [suerte, destino] to resign o.s. to; [apañárselas con] to make do with; [contentarse con] to settle for.

conforme ◇ *adj* - **1.** [acorde]: ~ **a** in accordance with - **2.** [de acuerdo]: ~ **(con)** in agreement (with) - **3.** [contento]: ~ **(con)** happy (with). ◇ *adv* [gen] as; ~ **envejecía** as he got older.

conformidad *f* [aprobación]: ~ **(con)** approval (of).

conformista *adj* & *mf* conformist.

confort (*pl* **conforts**) *m* comfort; 'todo ~' 'all mod cons'.

confortable *adj* comfortable.

confortar *vt* to console, to comfort.

confrontar *vt* - **1.** [enfrentar] to confront - **2.** [comparar] to compare.

confundir *vt* - **1.** [trastocar]: ~ **una cosa con otra** to mistake one thing for another; ~ **dos cosas** to get two things mixed up - **2.** [liar] to confuse - **3.** [mezclar] to mix up.
◆ **confundirse** *vpr* - **1.** [equivocarse] to make a mistake; ~**se de piso** to get the wrong flat - **2.** [liarse] to get confused - **3.** [mezclarse - colores, siluetas]: ~**se (en)** to merge (into); [- personas]: ~**se entre la gente** to lose o.s. in the crowd.

confusión *f* - **1.** [gen] confusion - **2.** [error] mix-up.

confuso, sa *adj* - **1.** [incomprensible - estilo, explicación] obscure - **2.** [poco claro - rumor] muffled; [- clamor, griterío] confused; [- contorno, forma] blurred - **3.** [turbado] confused, bewildered.

congelación *f* - **1.** [de alimentos] freezing - **2.** ECON [de precios, salarios] freeze.

congelador *m* freezer.

congelados *mpl* frozen foods.

congelar *vt* [gen & ECON] to freeze.
◆ **congelarse** *vpr* to freeze.

congeniar *vi*: ~ **(con)** to get on (with).

congénito, ta *adj* [enfermedad] congenital; [talento] innate.

congestión *f* congestion.

congestionar *vt* to block.
◆ **congestionarse** *vpr* - **1.** AUTOM & MED to become congested - **2.** [cara - de rabia etc] to flush, to turn purple.

congoja *f* anguish.

congraciarse *vpr*: ~ **con alguien** to win sb over.

congratular *vt*: ~ **a alguien (por)** to congratulate sb (on).

congregación *f* congregation.

congregar *vt* to assemble, to bring together.

congresista *mf* - **1.** [en un congreso] delegate - **2.** [político] congressman (*f* congresswoman).

congreso *m* - **1.** [de una especialidad] congress - **2.** [asamblea nacional]: ~ **de diputados** [en España] *lower house of Spanish* Parliament; ≃ House of Commons *UK*; ≃ House of Representatives *US*; **el Congreso** [en Estados Unidos] Congress.

congrio *m* conger eel.

congruente *adj* consistent, congruous.

conjetura *f* conjecture; **hacer** ~**s**, **hacerse una** ~ to conjecture.

conjugación *f* GRAM conjugation.

conjugar *vt* - **1.** GRAM to conjugate - **2.** [opiniones] to bring together, to combine; [esfuerzos, ideas] to pool.

conjunción *f* ASTRON & GRAM conjunction.

conjunto, ta *adj* [gen] joint; [hechos, acontecimientos] combined.
◆ **conjunto** *m* - **1.** [gen] set, collection; **un** ~ **de circunstancias** a number of reasons - **2.** [de ropa] outfit - **3.** [MÚS - de rock] group, band; [- de música clásica] ensemble - **4.** [totalidad] whole; **en** ~ overall, as a whole - **5.** MAT set.

conjurar ◇ *vi* [conspirar] to conspire, to plot. ◇ *vt* - **1.** [exorcizar] to exorcize - **2.** [evitar - un peligro] to ward off, to avert.

conjuro *m* spell, incantation.

conllevar *vt* [implicar] to entail.

conmemoración *f* commemoration.

conmemorar *vt* to commemorate.

conmigo *pron pers* with me; ~ **mismo/ misma** with myself.

conmoción *f* - **1.** [física o psíquica] shock; ~ **cerebral** concussion - **2.** *fig* [trastorno, disturbio] upheaval.

conmocionar *vt* - **1.** [psíquicamente] to shock, to stun - **2.** [físicamente] to concuss.

conmovedor, ra *adj* moving, touching.

conmover *vt* - **1.** [emocionar] to move, to touch - **2.** [sacudir] to shake.

conmutador *m* - **1.** ELECTR switch - **2.** *Amér* [centralita] switchboard.

connotación *f* connotation; **una** ~ **irónica** a hint of irony.

cono *m* cone.

conocedor, ra *m, f*: ~ **(de)** [gen] expert (on); [de vinos] connoisseur (of).

conocer *vt* - **1.** [gen] to know; **darse a** ~ to make o.s. known; ~ **bien un tema** to know a lot about a subject; ~ **alguien de vista** to know sb by sight; ~ **a alguien de oídas** to have heard of sb - **2.** [descubrir - lugar, país] to get to know - **3.** [a una persona - por primera vez] to meet - **4.** [reconocer]: ~ **a alguien (por algo)** to recognize sb (by sthg).
◆ **conocerse** *vpr* - **1.** [a uno mismo] to know o.s. - **2.** [dos o más personas - por primera vez] to meet, to get to know each other; [- desde hace tiempo] to know each other.

conocido, da ◇ *adj* well-known. ◇ *m, f* acquaintance.

conocimiento *m* **- 1.** [gen] knowledge **- 2.** MED [sentido] consciousness.

◆ **conocimientos** *mpl* knowledge *(U)*; **tener muchos ~s** to be very knowledgeable.

conozca *etc* ⊳ **conocer.**

conque *conj* so; **¿~ te has cansado?** so you're tired, are you?

conquista *f* [de tierras, persona] conquest.

conquistador, ra *m,f* **- 1.** [de tierras] conqueror **- 2.** HIST conquistador.

conquistar *vt* [tierras] to conquer.

consabido, da *adj* [conocido] well-known; [habitual] usual.

consagrar *vt* **- 1.** RELIG to consecrate **- 2.** [dedicar]: **~ algo a algo/alguien** [tiempo, espacio] to devote sth to sth/sb; [monumento, lápida] to dedicate sth to sth/sb **- 3.** [acreditar, confirmar] to confirm, to establish.

consciencia = **conciencia.**

consciente *adj* conscious; **ser ~ de** to be aware of; **estar ~** [físicamente] to be conscious.

conscripto *m Andes, Arg* conscript.

consecución *f* [de un deseo] realization; [de un objetivo] attainment; [de un premio] winning.

consecuencia *f* [resultado] consequence; **a** *o* **como ~ de** as a consequence *o* result of; **atenerse a las ~s** to accept the consequences; **traer como ~** to result in.

consecuente *adj* [coherente] consistent.

consecutivo, va *adj* consecutive.

conseguir *vt* [gen] to obtain, to get; [un objetivo] to achieve; **~ hacer algo** to manage to do sth; **~ que alguien haga algo** to get sb to do sth.

consejero, ra *m,f* **- 1.** [en asuntos personales] counsellor; [en asuntos técnicos] adviser, consultant **- 2.** [de un consejo de administración] member; POLÍT [en España] minister (in an autonomous government).

consejo *m* **- 1.** [advertencia] advice *(U)*; **dar un ~** to give some advice **- 2.** [organismo] council; **~ de administración** board of directors **- 3.** [reunión] meeting.

◆ **Consejo de Europa** *m* Council of Europe.

◆ **consejo de guerra** *m* court martial.

◆ **consejo de ministros** *m* cabinet.

consenso *m* [acuerdo] consensus; [consentimiento] consent.

consentimiento *m* consent.

consentir ◇ *vt* **- 1.** [tolerar] to allow, to permit **- 2.** [mimar] to spoil. ◇ *vi*: **~ en algo/en hacer algo** to agree to sth/to do sth.

conserje *mf* [portero] porter; [encargado] caretaker.

conserjería *f* **- 1.** [de un hotel] reception desk **- 2.** [de un edificio público o privado] porter's lodge.

conserva *f* canned food; **~ de carne** tinned meat; **en ~** tinned, canned.

conservación *f* [gen] conservation; [de alimentos] preservation.

conservacionista ◇ *adj* conservation *(antes de sust).* ◇ *mf* conservationist.

conservante *mf* preservative.

conservar *vt* **- 1.** [gen & CULIN] to preserve; [amistad] to keep up; [salud] to look after; [calor] to retain **- 2.** [guardar - libros, cartas, secreto] to keep.

◆ **conservarse** *vpr* to keep; **se conserva bien** he's keeping well.

conservatorio *m* conservatoire.

considerable *adj* [gen] considerable; [importante, eminente] notable.

consideración *f* **- 1.** [valoración] consideration **- 2.** [respeto] respect; **tratar a alguien con ~** to be nice to sb; **tratar a alguien sin ~** to show no consideration to sb; **en ~ a algo** in recognition of sth **- 3.** [importancia]: **de ~** serious.

considerado, da *adj* [atento] considerate, thoughtful; [respetado] respected, highly-regarded.

considerar *vt* **- 1.** [valorar] to consider **- 2.** [juzgar, estimar] to think.

◆ **considerarse** *vpr* to consider o.s.; **me considero feliz** I consider myself happy.

consigna *f* **- 1.** [órdenes] instructions *(pl)* **- 2.** [para el equipaje] left-luggage office *UK*, checkroom *US.*

consignar *vt* **- 1.** [poner por escrito] to record, to write down **- 2.** [enviar - mercancía] to dispatch **- 3.** [equipaje] to deposit in the left-luggage office.

consigo *pron pers* with him/her, *(pl)* with them; [con usted] with you; [con uno mismo] with o.s.; **~ mismo/misma** with himself/herself; **hablar ~ mismo** to talk to o.s.

consiguiente *adj* consequent; **por ~** consequently, therefore.

consistencia *f* lit & fig consistency.

consistente *adj* **- 1.** [sólido - material] solid **- 2.** [coherente - argumento] sound, convincing **- 3.** [compuesto]: **~ en** consisting of.

consistir ◆ **consistir en** *vi* **- 1.** [gen] to consist of **- 2.** [deberse a] to lie in, to be based on.

consola *f* **- 1.** [mesa] console table **- 2.** INFORM & TECN console; **~ de videojuegos** video console.

consolación *f* consolation.

consolar *vt* to console.

consolidar *vt* to consolidate.

consomé *m* consommé.

consonancia f harmony; **en ~ con** in keeping with.

consonante f consonant.

consorcio m consortium.

conspiración f plot, conspiracy.

conspirador, ra m,f conspirator, plotter.

conspirar vi to conspire, to plot.

constancia f -1. [perseverancia - en una empresa] perseverance; [- en las ideas, opiniones] steadfastness - 2. [testimonio] record; **dejar ~ de algo** [registrar] to put sthg on record; [probar] to demonstrate sthg.

constante <> adj -1. [persona - en una empresa] persistent; [en ideas, opiniones] steadfast - 2. [acción] constant. <> f constant.

constar vi -1. [una información]: **~ (en)** to appear (in), to figure (in); **~ le a alguien** to be clear to sb; **me consta que** I am quite sure that; **que conste que ...** let it be clearly understood that ..., let there be no doubt that ...; **hacer ~** to put on record; **hacer ~ por escrito** to confirm in writing - 2. [estar constituido por]: **~ de** to consist of.

constatar vt [observar] to confirm; [comprobar] to check.

constelación f constellation.

consternación f consternation, dismay.

consternar vt to dismay.

constipado, da adj: **estar ~** to have a cold.
  ⭢ **constipado** m cold; **coger un ~** to catch a cold.

constiparse vpr to catch a cold.

constitución f constitution.

constitucional adj constitutional.

constituir vt -1. [componer] to make up - 2. [ser] to be - 3. [crear] to set up, to constitute.

constituyente adj & m constituent.

constreñir vt [oprimir, limitar] to restrict.

construcción f -1. [gen] construction; **en ~** under construction - 2. [edificio] building.

constructivo, va adj constructive.

constructor, ra adj building (antes de sust), construction (antes de sust).
  ⭢ **constructor** m [de edificios] builder.

construir vt [edificio, barco] to build; [aviones, coches] to manufacture; [frase, teoría] to construct.

consuelo m consolation, solace.

cónsul, consulesa m,f consul.

consulado m [oficina] consulate; [cargo] consulship.

consulta f -1. [pregunta] consultation; **hacer una ~ a alguien** to seek sb's advice; **~ popular** referendum, plebiscite - 2. [despacho de médico] consulting room; **horas de ~** surgery hours.

consultar <> vt [dato, fecha] to look up; [libro, persona] to consult. <> vi: **~ con** to consult, to seek advice from.

consultor, ra m,f consultant.

consultorio m -1. [de un médico] consulting room - 2. [en periódico] problem page; [en radio] programme answering listeners' questions - 3. [asesoría] advice bureau.

consumar vt [gen] to complete; [un crimen] to perpetrate; [el matrimonio] to consummate.

consumición f -1. [acción] consumption; **está prohibida la ~ de bebidas alcohólicas** the consumption of alcohol is prohibited - 2. [bebida] drink; [comida] food; **~ mínima** cover charge.

consumidor, ra m,f [gen] consumer; [en un bar, restaurante] patron.

consumir <> vt -1. [gen] to consume; **consumieron los refrescos en el bar** they had their drinks at the bar - 2. [destruir - suj: fuego] to destroy. <> vi to consume.
  ⭢ **consumirse** vpr -1. [persona] to waste away - 2. [fuego] to burn out.

consumismo m consumerism.

consumo m consumption; **no apto para el ~** unfit for human consumption; **bienes/sociedad de ~** consumer goods/society.

contabilidad f -1. [oficio] accountancy - 2. [de persona, empresa] bookkeeping, accounting; **llevar la ~** to do the accounts.

contable mf accountant.

contacto m -1. [gen] contact; **perder el ~** to lose touch - 2. AUTOM ignition.

contado, da adj [raro] rare, infrequent; **contadas veces** very rarely.
  ⭢ **al contado** loc adv: **pagar al ~** to pay (in) cash.

contador, ra m,f Amér [contable] accountant; **~ público** chartered accountant UK, certified public accountant US.
  ⭢ **contador** m [aparato] meter.

contaduría f Amér: **~ general** audit office.

contagiar vt [persona] to infect; [enfermedad] to transmit.
  ⭢ **contagiarse** vpr [enfermedad, risa] to be contagious; [persona] to become infected.

contagio m infection, contagion.

contagioso, sa adj [enfermedad] contagious, infectious; [risa etc] infectious.

container = **contenedor**.

contaminación f [gen] contamination; [del medio ambiente] pollution.

contaminar vt [gen] to contaminate; [el medio ambiente] to pollute.

contar <> vt -1. [enumerar, incluir] to count - 2. [narrar] to tell; **¡a mi me lo vas a ~!**

you're telling me!, tell me about it! ⬦ *vi* to count.

➤ **contar con** *vi* **-1.** [confiar en] to count on **-2.** [tener, poseer] to have **-3.** [tener en cuenta] to take into account; **con esto no contaba** I hadn't reckoned with that.

contemplación *f* contemplation.

contemplar *vt* [mirar, considerar] to contemplate.

contemporáneo, a *adj* & *m,f* contemporary.

contenedor, ra *adj* containing.

➤ **contenedor, container** *m* [gen] container; [para escombros] skip; **~ de basura** large rubbish bin for collecting rubbish from blocks of flats etc; **~ de vidrio reciclable** bottle bank.

contener *vt* **-1.** [encerrar] to contain **-2.** [detener, reprimir] to restrain, to hold back.

➤ **contenerse** *vpr* to restrain o.s., to hold o.s. back.

contenido *m* [gen] contents *(pl)*; [de discurso, redacción] content.

contentar *vt* to please, to keep happy.

➤ **contentarse** *vpr*: **~se con** to make do with.

contento, ta *adj* [alegre] happy; [satisfecho] pleased; **estar ~con alguien/algo** to be pleased with sb/sthg; **tener ~ a alguien** to keep sb happy.

contestación *f* answer.

contestador (automático) *m* answering machine.

contestar ⬦ *vt* to answer; **contestó que vendría** she answered that she'd come. ⬦ *vi* **-1.** [responder] to answer; **no contestan** there's no answer **-2.** [replicar] to answer back; **no contestes a tu madre** don't answer back to your mother.

contestatario, ria *adj* anti-establishment.

contexto *m* context.

contienda *f* [competición, combate] contest; [guerra] conflict, war.

contigo *pron pers* with you; **~ mismo/misma** with yourself.

contiguo, gua *adj* adjacent.

continencia *f* self-restraint.

continental *adj* continental.

continente *m* GEOGR continent.

contingente ⬦ *adj* unforeseeable. ⬦ *m* **-1.** [grupo] contingent **-2.** COM quota.

continuación *f* continuation; **a ~** next, then.

continuar ⬦ *vt* to continue, to carry on with. ⬦ *vi* to continue, to go on; **~ haciendo algo** to continue doing o to do sthg; **continúa lloviendo** it's still raining; **'continuará'** 'to be continued'.

continuidad *f* [en una sucesión] continuity;

[permanencia] continuation.

continuo, nua *adj* **-1.** [ininterrumpido] continuous **-2.** [constante, perseverante] continual.

contonearse *vpr* [hombre] to swagger; [mujer] to swing one's hips.

contorno *m* **-1.** GEOGR contour; [línea] outline **-2.** *(gen pl)* [vecindad] neighbourhood; [de una ciudad] outskirts *(pl)*.

contorsionarse *vpr* [gen] to do contortions; [de dolor] to writhe.

contra ⬦ *prep* against; **un jarabe ~ la tos** a cough syrup; **en ~** against; **estar en ~ de algo** to be opposed to sthg; **en ~ de** [a diferencia de] contrary to. ⬦ *m*: **los pros y los ~s** the pros and cons.

contraataque *m* counterattack.

contrabajo *m* **-1.** [instrumento] double-bass **-2.** [voz, cantante] low bass.

contrabandista *mf* smuggler.

contrabando *m* [acto] smuggling; [mercancías] contraband; **pasar algo de ~** to smuggle sthg in; **~ de armas** gunrunning.

contracción *f* contraction.

contrachapado, da *adj* made of plywood.

➤ **contrachapado** *m* plywood.

contradecir *vt* to contradict.

contradicción *f* contradiction; **estar en ~ con** to be in (direct) contradiction to.

contradicho, cha *pp* ➣ **contradecir.**

contradictorio, ria *adj* contradictory.

contraer *vt* **-1.** [gen] to contract **-2.** [costumbre, acento etc] to acquire **-3.** [enfermedad] to catch.

➤ **contraerse** *vpr* to contract.

contrafuerte *m* ARQUIT buttress.

contraindicación *f*: **'contraindicaciones: ...'** 'not to be taken with ...'.

contralor *m* Chile inspector of public spending.

contralto *m* [voz] contralto.

contraluz *m* back lighting; **a ~** against the light.

contramaestre *m* **-1.** NÁUT boatswain; MIL warrant officer **-2.** [capataz] foreman.

contrapartida *f* compensation; **como ~** to make up for it.

contrapelo ➤ **a contrapelo** *loc adv* **-1.** [acariciar] the wrong way **-2.** [vivir, actuar] against the grain.

contrapesar *vt* [físicamente] to counterbalance.

contrapeso *m* **-1.** [en ascensores, poleas] counterweight **-2.** *fig* [fuerza que iguala] counterbalance.

contraponer *vt* [oponer]: **~ (a)** to set up (against).

➤ **contraponerse** *vpr* to oppose.

contraportada *f* [de periódico, revista]

back page; [de libro, disco] back cover.

contraproducente *adj* counterproductive.

contrariar *vt* -1. [contradecir] to go against -2. [disgustar] to upset.

contrariedad *f* -1. [dificultad] setback -2. [disgusto] annoyance.

contrario, ria *adj* -1. [opuesto - dirección, sentido] opposite; [-parte] opposing; [-opinión] contrary; **ser ~ a algo** to be opposed to sthg -2. [perjudicial]: **~ a** contrary to.
➡ **contrario** *m* -1. [rival] opponent -2. [opuesto] opposite; **al ~, por el ~** on the contrary; **de lo ~** otherwise; **todo lo ~** quite the contrary.

contrarreloj *adj inv*: **etapa ~** time trial.

contrarrestar *vt* [neutralizar] to counteract.

contrasentido *m* nonsense *(U)*; **es un ~ hacer eso** it doesn't make sense to do that.

contraseña *f* password.

contrastar ◇ *vi* to contrast. ◇ *vt* -1. [probar - hechos] to check, to verify -2. [resistir] to resist.

contraste *m* contrast; **hacer ~ con algo** to contrast with sth; **en ~ con** in contrast to; **por ~** in contrast.

contratar *vt* -1. [obreros, personal, detective] to hire; [deportista] to sign -2. [servicio, obra, mercancía]: **~ algo a alguien** to contract for sthg with sb.

contratiempo *m* [accidente] mishap; [dificultad] setback.

contratista *mf* contractor.

contrato *m* contract; **bajo ~** under contract; **~ matrimonial** marriage contract.

contraventana *f* shutter.

contribución *f* -1. [gen] contribution -2. [impuesto] tax.

contribuir *vi* -1. [gen]: **~ (a)** to contribute (to); **~ con algo para** to contribute sthg towards -2. [pagar impuestos] to pay taxes.

contribuyente *mf* taxpayer.

contrincante *mf* rival, opponent.

control *m* -1. [gen] control; **bajo ~** under control; **fuera de ~** out of control; **perder el ~** to lose one's temper; **~ remoto** remote control -2. [verificación] examination, inspection; **(bajo) ~ médico** (under) medical supervision; **~ antidoping** dope test -3. [puesto policial] checkpoint; **~ de pasaportes** passport control.

controlador, ra *m,f* [gen & INFORM] controller; **~ aéreo** air traffic controller.

controlar *vt* -1. [gen] to control; [cuentas] to audit -2. [comprobar] to check.

controversia *f* controversy.

contundente *adj* -1. [arma, objeto] blunt; [golpe] thudding -2. *fig* [razonamiento, argumento] forceful.

contusión *f* bruise.

conuco *m Carib* [casa y terreno] small plot of land.

convalecencia *f* convalescence.

convaleciente *adj* convalescent.

convalidar *vt* [estudios] to recognize; [asignaturas] to validate.

convencer *vt* to convince; **~ a alguien de algo** to convince sb of sthg.
➡ **convencerse** *vpr*: **~se de** to become convinced of.

convencimiento *m* [certeza] conviction; [acción] convincing.

convención *f* convention.

convencional *adj* conventional.

conveniencia *f* -1. [utilidad] usefulness; [oportunidad] suitability -2. [interés] convenience; **sólo mira su ~** he only looks after his own interests.

conveniente *adj* [útil] useful; [oportuno] suitable, appropriate; [lugar, hora] convenient; [aconsejable] advisable; **sería ~ asistir** it would be a good idea to go.

convenio *m* agreement.

convenir *vi* -1. [venir bien] to be suitable; **conviene analizar la situación** it would be a good idea to analyse the situation; **no te conviene hacerlo** you shouldn't do it -2. [acordar]: **~ en** to agree on.

convento *m* [de monjas] convent; [de monjes] monastery.

converger *vi* to converge.

conversación *f* conversation; **cambiar de ~** to change the subject; **trabar ~ con alguien** to strike up a conversation with sb.
➡ **conversaciones** *fpl* [negociaciones] talks.

conversada *f Amér* chat.

conversar *vi* to talk, to converse.

conversión *f* conversion.

converso, sa *adj* converted.

convertir *vt* -1. RELIG to convert -2. [transformar]: **~ algo/a alguien en** to convert sthg/sb into, to turn sthg/sb into.
➡ **convertirse** *vpr* -1. RELIG: **~se (a)** to convert (to) -2. [transformarse]: **~se en** to become, to turn into.

convexo, xa *adj* convex.

convicción *f* conviction; **tener la ~ de que** to be convinced that.

convicto, ta *adj* convicted.

convidar *vt* [invitar] to invite.

convincente *adj* convincing.

convite *m* -1. [invitación] invitation -2. [fiesta] banquet.

convivencia *f* living together.

convivir *vi* to live together; ~ **con** to live with.

convocar *vt* [reunión] to convene; [huelga, elecciones] to call.

convocatoria *f* - **1.** [anuncio, escrito] notice - **2.** [de examen] diet.

convulsión *f* - **1.** [de músculos] convulsion - **2.** [política, social] upheaval (U).

conyugal *adj* conjugal; **vida** ~ married life.

cónyuge *mf* spouse; **los** ~**s** husband and wife.

coñá, coñac (*pl* coñacs), **cognac** (*pl* cognacs) *m* brandy, cognac.

coñazo *m fam* pain, drag.

coño *vulg* ◇ *m* [genital] cunt. ◇ *interj* - **1.** [enfado] for fuck's sake! - **2.** [asombro] fucking hell!

cookie *f* INFORM cookie.

cooperación *f* cooperation.

cooperar *vi:* ~ **(con alguien en algo)** to cooperate (with sb in sthg).

cooperativo, va *adj* cooperative.

 ➡ **cooperativa** *f* cooperative.

coordinador, ra ◇ *adj* coordinating. ◇ *m,f* coordinator.

coordinar *vt* - **1.** [movimientos, gestos] to coordinate - **2.** [esfuerzos, medios] to combine, to pool.

copa *f* - **1.** [vaso] glass; **ir de** ~**s** to go out drinking; **¿quieres (tomar) una** ~**?** would you like (to have) a drink?; **lleva unas** ~**s de más** she's had one too many - **2.** [de árbol] top; **es un profesional como la** ~ **de un pino** *fam* he's a consummate professional; **es una mentira como la** ~ **de un pino** it's a whopper of a lie - **3.** [en deporte] cup.

 ➡ **copas** *fpl* [naipes] *suit with pictures of goblets in Spanish playing cards.*

COPE (*abrev de* **Cadena de Ondas Populares Españolas**) *f private Spanish radio station.*

Copenhague Copenhagen.

copete *m* [de ave] crest.

copetín *m Amér* [bebida] aperitif; [comida] appetizer.

copia *f* [reproducción] copy; **sacar una** ~ to make a copy; ~ **al carbón** carbon copy; ~ **de seguridad** INFORM backup; **hacer una** ~ **de seguridad de algo** to back sthg up, to make a backup of sthg.

copiar ◇ *vt* [gen] to copy; [al dictado] to take down. ◇ *vi* [en examen] to cheat, to copy.

copiloto *mf* copilot.

copión, ona *m,f* [imitador] copycat; [en examen] cheat.

copioso, sa *adj* copious.

copla *f* - **1.** [canción] folksong, popular song - **2.** [estrofa] verse, stanza.

copo *m* [de nieve, cereales] flake; ~**s de avena** rolled oats; ~**s de maíz** cornflakes.

copropietario, ria *m,f* co-owner, joint owner.

copular *vi* to copulate.

copulativo, va *adj* copulative.

coquetear *vi* to flirt.

coqueto, ta *adj* [persona - que flirtea] flirtatious, coquettish; [- que se arregla mucho] concerned with one's appearance.

coraje *m* - **1.** [valor] courage - **2.** [rabia] anger; **me da mucho** ~ it makes me furious.

coral ◇ *adj* choral. ◇ *m* coral. ◇ *f* - **1.** [coro] choir - **2.** [composición] chorale.

Corán *m:* **el** ~ the Koran.

coraza *f* - **1.** [de soldado] cuirasse, armour - **2.** [de tortuga] shell.

corazón *m* - **1.** [órgano] heart - **2.** [centro - de ciudad, alcachofa] heart; [- de manzana] core - **3.** ▷ **dedo.**

corazonada *f* - **1.** [presentimiento] hunch - **2.** [impulso] sudden impulse.

corbata *f* tie.

Córcega Corsica.

corchea *f* quaver.

corchete *m* - **1.** [broche] hook and eye - **2.** [signo ortográfico] square bracket.

corcho *m* cork.

corcholata *f Méx* metal bottle top.

cordel *m* cord.

cordero, ra *m,f lit & fig* lamb.

cordial *adj* cordial.

cordialidad *f* cordiality.

cordillera *f* mountain range; **la** ~ **Cantábrica** the Cantabrian Mountains.

cordón *m* - **1.** [gen & ANAT] cord; [de zapato] lace; ~ **umbilical** umbilical cord - **2.** [cable eléctrico] flex - **3.** *fig* [para protección, vigilancia] cordon; ~ **sanitario** cordon sanitaire - **4.** *CSur* [de la vereda] kerb *UK*, curb *US.*

cordura *f* [juicio] sanity; [sensatez] sense.

Corea: ~ **del Norte/Sur** North/South Korea.

corear *vt* to chorus.

coreógrafo, fa *m,f* choreographer.

corista *mf* [en coro] chorus singer.

cornada *f* goring.

cornamenta *f* [de toro] horns (*pl*); [de ciervo] antlers (*pl*).

córner *m* corner (kick).

corneta *f* [instrumento] bugle.

cornisa *f* ARQUIT cornice.

coro *m* - **1.** [gen] choir; **contestar a** ~ to answer all at once - **2.** [de obra musical] chorus.

corona *f* - **1.** [gen] crown - **2.** [de flores] garland; ~ **fúnebre/de laurel** funeral/laurel wreath - **3.** [de santos] halo.

coronación *f* [de monarca] coronation.

coronar *vt* - **1.** [persona] to crown - **2.** *fig* [terminar] to complete; [culminar] to crown, to cap.

coronel *m* colonel.

coronilla *f* crown (of the head); **estar hasta la ∼ (de)** to be sick and tired (of).

corpiño *m* - **1.** bodice - **2.** *Arg* [sostén] bra.

corporación *f* corporation.

corporal *adj* corporal.

corporativo, va *adj* corporate.

corpulento, ta *adj* corpulent.

corral *m* [gen] yard; [para cerdos, ovejas] pen.

correa *f* - **1.** [de bolso, reloj] strap; [de pantalón] belt; [de perro] lead, leash - **2.** *TECN* belt; **∼ del ventilador** fan belt.

corrección *f* - **1.** [de errores] correction; **∼ de pruebas** proofreading - **2.** [de exámenes] marking - **3.** [de texto] revision - **4.** [de comportamiento] correctness, courtesy.

correctivo, va *adj* corrective.

➡ **correctivo** *m* punishment.

correcto, ta *adj* - **1.** [resultado, texto, respuesta] correct - **2.** [persona] polite; [conducta] proper.

corredor, ra ◇ *adj* running. ◇ *m,f* - **1.** [deportista] runner - **2.** [intermediario]: **∼ de bolsa** stockbroker; **∼ de comercio** COM registered broker; **∼ de fincas** land agent.

➡ **corredor** *m* [pasillo] corridor, passage.

corregir *vt* [gen] to correct; [exámenes] to mark.

➡ **corregirse** *vpr* to change for the better.

correlación *f* correlation.

correo *m* post UK, mail US; **echar al ∼** to post; **a vuelta de ∼** by return (of post); **∼ aéreo** air mail; **∼ basura** INFORM spam; **∼ certificado** registered post *o* mail; **∼ electrónico** e-mail; **∼ urgente** special delivery; **∼ de voz** voice mail.

➡ **Correos** *m* [organismo] the post office.

correr ◇ *vi* - **1.** [andar de prisa] to run; **a todo ∼** at full speed *o* pelt; **(ella) corre que se las pela** she runs like the wind - **2.** [conducir de prisa] to drive fast - **3.** [pasar por - río] to flow; [- camino, agua del grifo] to run; **deja ∼ el agua del grifo** leave the tap running - **4.** [el tiempo, las horas] to pass, to go by - **5.** [propagarse - noticia etc] to spread. ◇ *vt* - **1.** [recorrer - una distancia] to cover; **corrió los 100 metros** he ran the 100 metres - **2.** [deslizar - mesa, silla] to move *o* pull up - **3.** [cortinas] to draw; **∼ el pestillo** to bolt the door - **4.** [experimentar - aventuras, vicisitudes] to have; [- riesgo] to run; **∼ la** *fam* to go out on the town - **5.** *Amér fam* [despedir] to throw out.

➡ **correrse** *vpr* - **1.** [desplazarse - persona] to move over; [- cosa] to slide - **2.** [pintura, colores] to run.

correspondencia *f* - **1.** [gen] correspondence - **2.** [de metro, tren] connection.

corresponder *vi* - **1.** [compensar]: **∼ (con algo) a alguien/algo** to repay sb/sthg (with sthg) - **2.** [pertenecer] to belong - **3.** [coincidir]: **∼ (a/con)** to correspond (to/with) - **4.** [tocar]: **∼ le a alguien hacer algo** to be sb's responsibility to do sthg - **5.** [a un sentimiento] to reciprocate.

➡ **corresponderse** *vpr* - **1.** [escribirse] to correspond - **2.** [amarse] to love each other.

correspondiente *adj* - **1.** [gen]: **∼ (a)** corresponding (to) - **2.** [respectivo] respective.

corresponsal *mf* PRENS correspondent.

corretear *vi* [correr] to run about.

corrido, da *adj* [avergonzado] embarrassed.

➡ **corrida** *f* - **1.** TAUROM bullfight - **2.** [acción de correr] run; **dar una ∼** to make a dash; **en una ∼** in an instant *o* a flash.

➡ **de corrido** *loc prep* by heart; **recitar algo de ∼** to recite sthg parrot-fashion.

corriente ◇ *adj* - **1.** [normal] ordinary, normal - **2.** [agua] running - **3.** [mes, año, cuenta] current. ◇ *f* - **1.** [de río, electricidad] current; **∼ alterna/continua** alternating/direct current - **2.** [de aire] draught - **3.** *fig* [tendencia] trend, current; [de opinión] tide - **4.** *loc*: **ir contra ∼** to go against the tide; **llevarle** *o* **seguirle la ∼ a alguien** to humour sb. ◇ *m*: **estar al ∼ de** to be up to date with; **poner al ∼** to bring up to date; **ponerse al ∼** to bring o.s up to date; **tener a algn al ∼** to keep sb informed.

corro *m* [círculo] circle, ring; **en ∼** in a circle; **hacer ∼** to form a circle.

corroborar *vt* to corroborate.

corroer *vt* [gen] to corrode; GEOL to erode.

corromper *vt* - **1.** [pudrir - madera] to rot; [- alimentos] to turn bad, to spoil - **2.** [pervertir] to corrupt.

corrosivo, va *adj lit & fig* corrosive.

corrupción *f* - **1.** [gen] corruption - **2.** [de una substancia] decay.

corrusco *m* hard crust.

corsario, ria *adj* pirate *(antes de sust)*.

➡ **corsario** *m* corsair, pirate.

corsé *m* corset.

cortacésped (*pl* **cortacéspedes**) *m* lawnmower.

cortacorriente *m* AUTOM immobilizer.

cortado, da *adj* - **1.** [labios, manos] chapped - **2.** [leche] sour, off; [salsa] curdled - **3.** *fam fig* [tímido] inhibited; **quedarse ∼** to be left speechless.

➡ **cortado** *m* [café] *small coffee with just a little milk*.

cortafuego *m* firebreak.

cortante *adj* - **1.** [afilado] **sharp - 2.** *fig* [frase] cutting; [viento] biting; [frío] bitter.

cortapisa *f* limitation, restriction.

cortar ◇ *vt* - **1.** [seccionar - pelo, uñas] to cut; [- papel] to cut up; [- ramas] to cut off; [- árbol] to cut down - **2.** [amputar] to amputate, to cut off - **3.** [tela, figura de papel] to cut out - **4.** [interrumpir - retirada, luz, teléfono] to cut off; [- carretera] to block (off); [- hemorragia] to stop, to staunch; [- discurso, conversación] to interrupt - **5.** [labios, piel] to chap. ◇ *vt* - **1.** *RP* [comunicación] to hang up - **2.** [producir un corte] to cut - **3.** [cesar una relación] to break *o* split up; **he cortado con mi novio** I've split up with my boyfriend.

◆ **cortarse** *vpr* - **1.** [herirse] to cut o.s.; ~**se el pelo** to have a haircut - **2.** [alimento] to curdle - **3.** [turbarse] to become tonguetied.

cortaúñas *m inv* nail clippers *(pl)*.

corte ◇ *m* - **1.** [raja] cut; [en pantalones, camisa etc] tear; ~ **y confección** [para mujeres] dressmaking; [para hombres] tailoring - **2.** [interrupción]: ~ **de luz** power cut - **3.** [sección] section - **4.** [concepción, estilo] style - **5.** *fam* [vergüenza] embarrassment; **dar** ~ **a alguien** to embarrass sb. ◇ *f* [palacio] court.

◆ **Cortes** *fpl* POLÍT *the Spanish parliament.*

cortejar *vt* to court.

cortejo *m* retinue; ~ **fúnebre** funeral cortège *o* procession.

cortés *adj* polite, courteous.

cortesía *f* courtesy; **de** ~ courtesy.

corteza *f* - **1.** [del árbol] bark - **2.** [de pan] crust; [de queso, tocino, limón] rind; [de naranja etc] peel - **3.** [terrestre] crust.

cortina *f* [de tela] curtain; *fig:* ~ **de agua** sheet of water; ~ **de humo** smoke screen.

cortisona *f* cortisone.

corto, ta *adj* - **1.** [gen] short - **2.** [escaso - raciones] meagre; [- disparo] short of the target; ~ **de vista** short-sighted - **3.** *fig* [bobo] dim, simple - **4.** *loc:* **quedarse** ~ [al calcular] to underestimate; **decir que es bueno es quedarse** ~ it's an understatement to call it good.

cortocircuito *m* short circuit.

cortometraje *m* short (film).

cosa *f* - **1.** [gen] thing; ¿**queréis alguna** ~? is there anything you want?; **no es gran** ~ it's not important, it's no big deal; **poca** ~ nothing much - **2.** [asunto] matter; **esto es otra** ~ that's another matter; **no es** ~ **de risa** it's no laughing matter - **3.** [ocurrencia]: ¡**qué** ~**s tienes!** you do say some funny things! - **4.** *loc:* **como si tal** ~ as if nothing had happened; **eso es** ~ **mía** that's my af-

fair *o* business; **hacer algo como quien no quiere la** ~ [disimuladamente] to do sthg as if one wasn't intending to; [sin querer] to do sthg almost without realizing it; **¡lo que son las** ~**s!** it's a funny old world!; **son las** ~**s de la vida** that's life.

◆ **cosa de** *loc adv* about; **es** ~ **de tres semanas** it takes about three weeks.

coscorrón *m* bump on the head.

cosecha *f* - **1.** [gen] harvest; **ser de la (propia)** ~ **de alguien** to be made up *o* invented by sb - **2.** [del vino] vintage.

cosechar ◇ *vt* - **1.** [cultivar] to grow - **2.** [recolectar] to harvest. ◇ *vi* to (bring in the) harvest.

coser ◇ *vt* [con hilo] to sew; ~ **un botón** to sew on a button. ◇ *vi* to sew; **ser cosa de** ~ **y cantar** to be child's play *o* a piece of cake.

cosido *m* stitching.

cosmético, ca *adj* cosmetic *(antes de sust).*

◆ **cosmético** *m* cosmetic.

◆ **cosmética** *f* cosmetics *(U).*

cosmopolita *adj & m,f* cosmopolitan.

cosmos *m* cosmos.

cosquillas *fpl:* **hacer** ~ to tickle; **tener** ~ to be ticklish.

costa *f* GEOGR coast.

◆ **a costa de** *loc prep* at the expense of; **lo hizo a** ~ **de grandes esfuerzos** he did it by dint of much effort; **vive a** ~ **de sus padres** she lives off her parents.

◆ **a toda costa** *loc prep* at all costs.

costado *m* side; **es francés por los cuatro** ~**s** he's French through and through.

costal *m* sack.

costanera *f* CSur promenade.

costar ◇ *vt* - **1.** [dinero] to cost; ¿**cuánto cuesta?** how much is it? - **2.** [tiempo] to take. ◇ *vi* [ser difícil]: ~ **le a alguien hacer algo** to be difficult for sb to do sthg.

Costa Rica Costa Rica.

costarricense, costarriqueño, ña *adj & m,f* Costa Rican.

coste *m* [de producción] cost; [de un objeto] price; ~ **de la vida** cost of living.

costear *vt* [pagar] to pay for.

costilla *f* - **1.** [de persona, barco] rib - **2.** [de animal] cutlet.

costo *m* [de una mercancía] price; [de un producto, de la vida] cost.

costoso, sa *adj* [operación, maquinaria] expensive.

costra *f* [de herida] scab.

costumbre *f* habit, custom; **coger/perder la** ~ **de hacer algo** to get into/out of the habit of doing sthg; **como de** ~ as usual; **por** ~ through force of habit, out of habit.

costura *f* - **1.** [labor] sewing, needlework

- 2. [puntadas] seam **- 3.** [oficio] dressmaking; **alta** ~ haute couture.

costurero *m* [caja] sewing box.

cota *f* **- 1.** [altura] altitude, height above sea level **- 2.** *fig* [nivel] level, height.

cotarro *m* riotous gathering; **alborotar el** ~ to stir up trouble; **dirigir el** ~ to rule the roost, to be the boss.

cotejar *vt* to compare.

cotejo *m* comparison.

cotidiano, na *adj* daily.

cotilla *mf fam* gossip, busybody.

cotillear *vi fam* to gossip.

cotilleo *m fam* gossip, tittle-tattle.

cotillón *m* New Year's Eve party.

cotización *f* **- 1.** [valor] price **- 2.** [en Bolsa] quotation, price.

cotizar ◇ *vt* **- 1.** [valorar] to quote, to price **- 2.** [pagar] to pay. ◇ *vi* to pay contributions.

◆ **cotizarse** *vpr* **- 1.** [estimarse - persona] to be valued *o* prized **- 2.:** ~**se a** [producto] to sell for, to fetch; [bonos, valores] to be quoted at.

coto *m* preserve; ~ **de caza** game preserve; **poner** ~ **a** to put a stop to.

cotorra *f* [ave] parrot.

COU (*abrev de* **Curso de Orientación Universitaria**) *m one-year course which prepared pupils aged 17-18 for Spanish university entrance examinations.*

country *m Arg luxury suburban housing development.*

coxis *m* = cóccix.

coyote *m* coyote.

coyuntura *f* **- 1.** [situación] moment; **la** ~ **económica** the economic situation **- 2.** ANAT joint.

coz *f* kick.

crac (*pl* cracs), **crack** (*pl* cracks) *m* FIN crash.

crack (*pl* cracks) *m* **- 1.** FIN ▷ crac **- 2.** [droga] crack.

cráneo *m* cranium, skull.

crápula *mf* libertine.

cráter *m* crater.

creación *f* creation.

creador, ra ◇ *adj* creative. ◇ *m,f* creator.

crear *vt* **- 1.** [gen] to create **- 2.** [fundar - una academia] to found.

creatividad *f* creativity.

creativo, va *adj* creative.

crecer *vi* **- 1.** [persona, planta] to grow **- 2.** [días, noches] to grow longer **- 3.** [río, marea] to rise **- 4.** [aumentar - animosidad etc] to grow, to increase; [- rumores] to spread.

◆ **crecerse** *vpr* to become more self-confident.

creces ◆ con creces *adv* with interest.

crecido, da *adj* [cantidad] large; [hijo] grown-up.

◆ **crecida** *f* spate, flood.

creciente *adj* [gen] growing; [luna] crescent.

crecimiento *m* [gen] growth; [de precios] rise.

credibilidad *f* credibility.

crédito *m* **- 1.** [préstamo] loan; **a** ~ on credit; ~ **al consumo** ECON consumer credit **- 2.** [plazo de préstamo] credit **- 3.** [confianza] trust, belief; **digno de** ~ trustworthy; **dar** ~ **a algo** to believe sthg **- 4.** [en universidad] credit.

credo *m* [religioso] creed.

crédulo, la *adj* credulous.

creencia *f* belief.

creer *vt* **- 1.** [gen] to believe; **¡ya lo creo!** of course!, I should say so! **- 2.** [suponer] to think; **creo que no** I don't think so; **creo que sí** I think so; **según creo** to the best of my knowledge **- 3.** [estimar] to think; **lo creo muy capaz de hacerlo** I think he's quite capable of doing it.

◆ **creer en** *vi* to believe in.

◆ **creerse** *vpr* [considerarse] to believe o.s. to be; **¿qué se cree?** who does he think he is?

creíble *adj* credible, believable.

creído, da *adj* [presumido] conceited.

crema *f* **- 1.** [gen] cream; ~ **batida** whipped cream **- 2.** [cosmético, betún] cream; ~ **de afeitar** shaving cream; ~ **dental** toothpaste; ~ **depilatoria** hair remover; ~ **facial** face cream; ~ **hidratante** moisturizer **- 3.** [licor] crème **- 4.** [dulce, postre] custard.

cremallera *f* [para cerrar] zip (fastener), zipper.

crematorio, ria *adj:* **horno** ~ cremator.

◆ **crematorio** *m* crematorium.

cremoso, sa *adj* creamy.

crepe [krep] *f* crepe.

crepitar *vi* to crackle.

crepúsculo *m* [al amanecer] first light; [al anochecer] twilight, dusk.

crespo, pa *adj* tightly curled, frizzy.

cresta *f* **- 1.** [gen] crest **- 2.** [del gallo] comb.

cretino, na *m,f* cretin.

creyente *mf* believer.

cría ▷ **crío.**

criadero *m* [de animales] farm *(breeding place)*; [de árboles, plantas] nursery.

criadillas *fpl* bull's testicles.

criado, da *m,f* servant (*f* maid).

criador, ra *m,f* [de animales] breeder; [de vinos] grower.

crianza *f* **- 1.** [de animales] breeding, rearing **- 2.** [del vino] vintage **- 3.** [educación] breeding.

criar *vt* **- 1.** [amamantar - suj: mujer] to breastfeed; [- suj: animal] to suckle **- 2.** [animales]

to breed, to rear; [flores, árboles] to grow
- **3.** [vino] to mature, to make - **4.** [educar]
to bring up.
 ➡ **criarse** *vpr* [crecer] to grow up.
criatura *f* - **1.** [niño] child; [bebé] baby
- **2.** [ser vivo] creature.
criba *f* - **1.** [tamiz] sieve - **2.** [selección]
screening.
cricket = **criquet**.
crimen *m* crime.
criminal *adj* & *mf* criminal.
crin *f* mane.
crío, cría *m,f* [niño] kid.
 ➡ **cría** *f* - **1.** [hijo del animal] young
- **2.** [crianza - de animales] breeding; [- de
plantas] growing.
criollo, lla *adj* - **1.** [persona] native to Latin
America - **2.** [comida, lengua] creole.
cripta *f* crypt.
criquet, cricket ['kriket] *m* cricket.
crisantemo *m* chrysanthemum.
crisis *f inv* [gen] crisis; ~ **cardíaca** cardiac
arrest, heart failure; ~ **de los cuarenta**
midlife crisis; ~ **económica** recession;
~ **nerviosa** nervous breakdown.
crisma *f fam* bonce, nut; **romperse la** ~ to
crack one's head open.
crismas, christmas *m inv* Christmas card.
crispar *vt* [los nervios] to set on edge; [los
músculos] to tense; [las manos] to clench.
cristal *m* - **1.** [material] glass *(U)*; [vidrio fino]
crystal - **2.** [en la ventana] (window) pane
- **3.** MIN crystal.
cristalera *f* [puerta] French window; [te-
cho] glass roof; [armario] glass-fronted cabinet.
cristalino, na *adj* crystalline.
 ➡ **cristalino** *m* crystalline lens.
cristalizar *vt* - **1.** [una sustancia] to crystallize - **2.** *fig* [un asunto] to bring to a head.
 ➡ **cristalizarse** *vpr* to crystallize.
 ➡ **cristalizarse en** *vpr fig* to develop into.
cristiandad *f* Christianity.
cristianismo *m* Christianity.
cristiano, na *adj* & *m,f* Christian.
cristo *m* crucifix.
 ➡ **Cristo** *m* Christ.
criterio *m* - **1.** [norma] criterion; ~**s de convergencia** [en UE] convergence criteria
- **2.** [juicio] taste, discernment - **3.** [opinión]
opinion.
crítica ⊳ **crítico**.
criticar *vt* - **1.** [enjuiciar - literatura, arte] to review - **2.** [censurar] to criticize.
crítico, ca ◇ *adj* critical. ◇ *m,f* [persona]
critic.
 ➡ **crítica** *f* - **1.** [juicio - sobre arte, literatura]
review - **2.** [conjunto de críticos]: **la** ~ the
critics *(pl)* - **3.** [ataque] criticism.

criticón, ona ◇ *adj* nit-picking, over-
critical. ◇ *m,f* nitpicker.
Croacia Croatia.
croar *vi* to croak.
croata ◇ *adj* Croatian. ◇ *mf* Croat, Croatian.
croissant [krwa'san] *(pl* **croissants)** *m*
croissant.
crol *m* DEP crawl.
cromo *m* - **1.** [metal] chrome - **2.** [estampa]
picture card; **ir hecho un** ~ to be dressed
up to the nines.
cromosoma *m* chromosome.
crónico, ca *adj* chronic.
 ➡ **crónica** *f* - **1.** [de la historia] chronicle
- **2.** [de un periódico] column; [de la televi-
sión] feature, programme.
cronista *mf* [historiador] chronicler; [perio-
dista] columnist.
cronología *f* chronology.
cronometrar *vt* to time.
cronómetro *m* DEP stopwatch; TECN chrono-
meter.
croqueta *f* croquette.
croquis *m inv* sketch.
cross *m inv* [carrera] cross-country race; [de-
porte] cross-country (running).
cruce *m* - **1.** [de líneas] crossing, intersection; [de carreteras] crossroads - **2.** [paso]
crossing; ~ **a nivel** level crossing *UK*,
grade crossing *US*; ~ **de peatones** pedestrian crossing - **3.** [de animales] cross, cross-
breeding *(U)*.
crucero *m* - **1.** [viaje] cruise - **2.** [barco] cruiser - **3.** [de iglesias] transept.
crucial *adj* crucial.
crucificar *vt* [en una cruz] to crucify.
crucifijo *m* crucifix.
crucifixión *f* crucifixion.
crucigrama *m* crossword (puzzle).
crudeza *f* - **1.** [gen] harshness; **con** ~ harshly - **2.** [de descripción, imágenes] brutality,
harsh realism.
crudo, da *adj* - **1.** [natural] raw; [petróleo]
crude - **2.** [sin cocer completamente] under-
cooked - **3.** [realidad, clima, tiempo] harsh;
[novela] harshly realistic, hard-hitting
- **4.** [cruel] cruel.
 ➡ **crudo** *m* crude (oil).
cruel *adj* [gen] cruel.
crueldad *f* - **1.** [gen] cruelty - **2.** [acción
cruel] act of cruelty.
crujido *m* [de madera] creak, creaking *(U)*;
[de hojas secas] crackle, crackling *(U)*.
crujiente *adj* [madera] creaky; [hojas secas]
rustling; [patatas fritas] crunchy.
crujir *vi* [madera] to creak; [patatas fritas, nie-
ve] to crunch; [hojas secas] to crackle; [dien-
tes] to grind.

cruz *f* - **1.** [gen] cross; ~ **gamada** swastika - **2.** [de una moneda] tails *(U)* - **3.** *fig* [aflicción] burden, torment.

◆ **Cruz Roja** *f* Red Cross.

cruza *f Amér* cross, crossbreed.

cruzado, da *adj* - **1.** [cheque, piernas, brazos] crossed - **2.** [animal] crossbred - **3.** [abrigo, chaqueta] double-breasted.

◆ **cruzada** *f lit & fig* crusade.

cruzar *vt* - **1.** [gen] to cross; ~ **los dedos** to cross one's fingers - **2.** [unas palabras] to exchange.

◆ **cruzarse** *vpr* - **1.** [gen] to cross; ~**se de brazos** to fold one's arms - **2.** [personas]: ~**se con alguien** to pass sb.

cta. *(abrev de* **cuenta***)* a/c.

cte. *(abrev de* **corriente***)* inst.

cuaderno *m* [gen] notebook; [en el colegio] exercise book.

◆ **cuaderno de bitácora** *m* logbook.

cuadra *f* - **1.** [de caballos] stable - **2.** *Amér* [en calle] block.

cuadrado, da *adj* [gen & MAT] square; **elevar al** ~ to square.

◆ **cuadrado** *m* square.

cuadragésimo, ma *núm* fortieth.

cuadrar ◇ *vi* - **1.** [información, hechos]: ~ **(con)** to square *o* agree (with) - **2.** [números, cuentas] to tally, to add up. ◇ *vt* [gen] to square.

◆ **cuadrarse** *vpr* MIL to stand to attention.

cuadrícula *f* grid.

cuadrilátero *m* - **1.** GEOM quadrilateral - **2.** DEP ring.

cuadrilla *f* [de amigos, trabajadores] group; [de maleantes] gang.

cuadro *m* - **1.** [pintura] painting, picture - **2.** [escena] scene, spectacle - **3.** [descripción] portrait - **4.** [cuadrado] square; **a** ~**s** check *(antes de sust)*; **quedarse a** ~**s** *fam* to be gobsmacked, to be flabbergasted; **quedarse en** ~**s** to be down to a skeleton staff - **5.** [equipo] team; ~**s medios** middle management - **6.** [gráfico] chart, diagram - **7.** [de la bicicleta] frame - **8.** TEATR scene.

cuádruple *m* quadruple.

cuajar ◇ *vt* [solidificar - leche] to curdle; [- huevo] to set; [- sangre] to clot, to coagulate. ◇ *vi* - **1.** [lograrse - acuerdo] to be settled; [- negocio] to take off, to get going - **2.** [ser aceptado - persona] to fit in; [- moda] to catch on - **3.** [nieve] to settle.

◆ **cuajarse** *vpr* [leche] to curdle; [sangre] to clot, to coagulate.

cuajo *m* rennet.

◆ **de cuajo** *loc adv* : **arrancar de** ~ [árbol] to uproot; [brazo etc] to tear right off.

cual *pron relat* : **el/la** ~ *etc* [de persona] (sujeto) who; *(complemento)* whom; [de cosa]

which; **lo** ~ which; **conoció a una española, la** ~ **vivía en Buenos Aires** he met a Spanish girl who lived in Buenos Aires; **está muy enfadada, lo** ~ **es comprensible** she's very angry, which is understandable; **todo lo** ~ all of which; **sea** ~ **sea** *o* **fuere su decisión** whatever his decision (may be).

cuál *pron (interrogativo)* what; [en concreto, especificando] which one; ¿~ **es tu nombre?** what is your name?; ¿~ **es la diferencia?** what's the difference?; **no sé** ~**es son mejores** I don't know which are best; ¿~ **prefieres?** which one do you prefer?

cualesquiera *pl* ▷ **cualquiera**.

cualidad *f* quality.

cualificado, da *adj* skilled.

cualitativo, va *adj* qualitative.

cualquiera (*pl* **cualesquiera**) ◇ *adj (antes de sust: cualquier)* any; **cualquier día vendré a visitarte** I'll drop by one of these days; **en cualquier momento** at any time; **en cualquier lugar** anywhere. ◇ *pron* anyone; ~ **te lo dirá** anyone will tell you; ~ **que** [persona] anyone who; [cosa] whatever; ~ **que sea la razón** whatever the reason (may be). ◇ *mf* [don nadie] nobody.

cuan *adv* [todo lo que]: **se desplomó** ~ **largo era** he fell flat on the ground.

cuán *adv* how.

cuando ◇ *adv* when; **de** ~ **en** ~ from time to time; **de vez en** ~ now and again. ◇ *conj* - **1.** [de tiempo] when; ~ **llegue el verano iremos de viaje** when summer comes we'll go travelling - **2.** [si] if; ~ **tú lo dices será verdad** it must be true if you say so - **3.** *(después de 'aun')* [aunque] : **no mentiría aun** ~ **le fuera en ello la vida** she wouldn't lie even if her life depended on it.

◆ **cuando más** *loc adv* at the most.

◆ **cuando menos** *loc adv* at least.

◆ **cuando quiera que** *loc conj* whenever.

cuándo *adv* when; ¿~ **vas a venir?** when are you coming?; **quisiera saber** ~ **sale el tren** I'd like to know when *o* at what time the train leaves.

cuantía *f* [suma] amount, quantity; [alcance] extent.

cuantificar *vt* to quantify.

cuantioso, sa *adj* large, substantial.

cuantitativo, va *adj* quantitative.

cuanto, ta ◇ *adj* - **1.** [todo]: **despilfarra** ~ **dinero gana** he squanders all the money he earns; **soporté todas cuantas críticas me hizo** I put up with every single criticism he made of me - **2.** *(antes de adv)* [compara cantidades]: **cuantas más mentiras digas, menos te creerán** the more you lie, the less people will believe you. ◇ *pron relat (gen pl)* [de personas] everyone who; [de cosas] every-thing (that); ~**s fueron alabaron el espec-táculo** everyone who went said the show was excellent; **dio las gracias a todos** ~**s le ayudaron** he thanked everyone who helped him.

◆ **cuanto** ◇ *pron relat (neutro)* **- 1.** [todo lo que] everything, as much as; **come** ~ **quie-ras** eat as much as you like; **comprendo** ~ **dice** I understand everything he says; **to-do** ~ everything **- 2.** [compara cantidades]: ~ **más se tiene, más se quiere** the more you have, the more you want. ◇ *adv* [com-para cantidades]: ~ **más come, más gordo está** the more he eats, the fatter he gets.

◆ **cuanto antes** *loc adv* as soon as poss-ible.

◆ **en cuanto** ◇ *loc conj* [tan pronto como] as soon as; **en** ~ **acabe** as soon as I've fin-ished. ◇ *loc prep* [en calidad de] as; **en** ~ **cabeza de familia** as head of the family.

◆ **en cuanto a** *loc prep* as regards.

cuánto, ta ◇ *adj* **- 1.** *(interrogativo)* how much, *(pl)* how many; **¿cuántas manzanas tienes?** how many apples do you have?; **¿** ~ **pan quieres?** how much bread do you want?; **no sé** ~**s hombres había** I don't know how many men were there **- 2.** *(excla-mativo)* what a lot of; **¡cuánta gente (había)!** what a lot of people (were there)! ◇ *pron (gen pl)* **- 1.** *(interrogativo)* how much, *(pl)* how many; **¿** ~**s han venido?** how many came?; **dime cuántas quieres** tell me how many you want **- 2.** *(exclamativo)*: **¡** ~**s quisie-ran conocerte!** there are so many people who would like to meet you!

◆ **cuánto** *pron (neutro)* **- 1.** *(interrogativo)* how much; **¿** ~ **quieres?** how much do you want?; **me gustaría saber** ~ **te costa-rán** I'd like to know how much they'll cost you **- 2.** *(exclamativo)*: **¡** ~ **han cambiado las cosas!** how things have changed!

cuarenta *núm* forty; **los (años)** ~ the for-ties; *ver también* **seis.**

cuarentena *f* [por epidemia] quarantine.

cuaresma *f* Lent.

cuartear *vt* to cut o chop up.

cuartel *m* MIL barracks *(pl)*; ~ **general** head-quarters *(pl)*.

cuartelazo *m* Amér military uprising, re-volt.

cuarteto *m* quartet.

cuarto, ta *núm* fourth; **la cuarta parte** a quarter.

◆ **cuarto** *m* **- 1.** [parte] quarter; **un** ~ **de hora** a quarter of an hour; **son las dos y** ~ it's a quarter past UK o after US two; **son las dos menos** ~ it's a quarter to UK o of US two **- 2.** [habitación] room; ~ **de baño** bath-room; ~ **de estar** living room; ~ **de**

huéspedes guestroom; ~ **oscuro** FOT dark-room; ~ **secreto** RP voting booth.

◆ **cuarta** *f* [palmo] span.

cuarzo *m* quartz.

cuate, ta *m, f* CAm, Ecuad, Méx fam pal, mate UK, buddy US.

cuatro ◇ *núm* four; **más de** ~ quite a few; *ver también* **seis.** ◇ *adj fig* [poco] a few; **hace** ~ **días** a few days ago.

cuatrocientos, tas *núm* four hundred; *ver también* **seis.**

cuba *f* barrel, cask; **beber como una** ~ to drink like a fish; **estar como una** ~ to be legless o blind drunk.

Cuba Cuba.

cubalibre *m* rum and coke.

cubano, na *adj & m, f* Cuban.

cubertería *f* set of cutlery, cutlery *(U)*.

cúbico, ca *adj* cubic.

cubierto, ta ◇ *pp* ▷ **cubrir.** ◇ *adj* **- 1.** [gen]: ~ **(de)** covered (with); **estar a** ~ [protegido] to be under cover; [con saldo acreedor] to be in the black; **ponerse a** ~ to take cover **- 2.** [cielo] overcast.

◆ **cubierto** *m* **- 1.** [pieza de cubertería] piece of cutlery **- 2.** [para cada persona] place setting.

◆ **cubierta** *f* **- 1.** [gen] cover **- 2.** [de neu-mático] tyre **- 3.** [de barco] deck.

cubilete *m* [en juegos] cup.

cubito *m* **- 1.** [de hielo] ice cube **- 2.** [de caldo] stock cube.

cubo *m* **- 1.** [recipiente] bucket; ~ **de la ba-sura** rubbish bin UK, trashcan US, garbage can US **- 2.** GEOM & MAT cube; **elevar al** ~ to cube.

cubrecama *m* bedspread.

cubrir *vt* **- 1.** [gen] to cover **- 2.** [proteger] to protect **- 3.** [disimular] to cover up, to hide **- 4.** [puesto, vacante] to fill.

◆ **cubrir de** *vt* : ~ **de algo a alguien** to heap sthg on sb.

◆ **cubrirse** *vpr* **- 1.** [taparse]: ~**se (de)** to become covered (with) **- 2.** [protegerse]: ~**se (de)** to shelter (from) **- 3.** [con sombre-ro] to put one's hat on **- 4.** [con ropa]: ~**se (con)** to cover o.s. (with) **- 5.** [cielo] to cloud over.

cucaracha *f* cockroach UK, roach US.

cuchara *f* [para comer] spoon; ~ **de palo** wooden spoon; ~ **de postre** dessert spoon; **meter la** ~ *fam* to butt in.

cucharada *f* spoonful.

cucharilla *f* teaspoon.

cucharón *m* ladle.

cuchichear *vi* to whisper.

cuchilla *f* blade; ~ **de afeitar** razor blade.

cuchillo *m* knife; ~ **de cocina** kitchen knife; ~ **de trinchar** carving knife.

cuchitril *m* hovel.

cuclillas ➡ en cuclillas *loc adv* squatting; **ponerse en ~** to squat (down).

cuclillo *m* cuckoo.

cuco, ca *adj fam* - **1.** [bonito] pretty - **2.** [astuto] shrewd, canny.
➡ **cuco** *m* cuckoo.

cucurucho *m* - **1.** [de papel] paper cone - **2.** [para helado] cornet, cone.

cuello *m* - **1.** [gen] neck; **alargar el ~** to stretch o crane one's neck; **~ de botella** bottleneck; **~ uterino** cervix - **2.** [de prendas] collar; **~ de pico** V-neck; **~ alto** o **de cisne** polo neck *UK*, turtleneck *US*; **hablar para el ~** de su camisa *fam* to talk to o.s.

cuenca *f* - **1.** [de río] basin - **2.** [del ojo] (eye) socket - **3.** [región minera] coalfield.

cuenco *m* earthenware bowl.

cuenta *f* - **1.** [acción de contar] count; **echar ~s** to reckon up; **llevar/perder la ~ de** to keep/lose count of; **~ atrás** countdown - **2.** [cálculo] sum - **3.** BANCA & COM account; **abonar algo en ~** a alguien to credit sthg to sb's account; **~ de gastos** expenditure account; **pagar mil euros a ~** to pay a thousand euros down; **~ de ahorros** savings account; **~ corriente** current account *UK*, checking account *US*; **~ de crédito** current account with an overdraft facility; **~ deudora** overdrawn account; **~ a plazo fijo** deposit account - **4.** [factura] bill *UK*, check *US*; **pasar la ~** to send the bill; **~ por cobrar/pagar** account receivable/payable - **5.** [bolita - de collar, rosario] bead - **6.** *loc:* **a fin de ~s** in the end; **ajustarle a alguien las ~s** to settle an account o a score with sb; **caer en la ~ de algo** to realize sthg; **darse ~ de algo** to realize sthg; **más de la ~** too much; **por mi/tu** *etc* **~** on my/your *etc* own; **tener en ~ algo** to bear sthg in mind.

cuentagotas *m inv* dropper; **a** o **con ~** in dribs and drabs.

cuentakilómetros *m inv* [de distancia recorrida] ≃ milometer; [de velocidad] speedometer.

cuentarrevoluciones *m inv* tachometer, rev counter.

cuento *m* - **1.** [fábula] tale; **~ de hadas** fairy tale - **2.** [narración] short story - **3.** [mentira, exageración] story, lie; **¡puro ~!** what nonsense!; **~ chino** tall story - **4.** *loc:* **tener ~** to put it on.

cuerda *f* - **1.** [para atar - fina] string; [- más gruesa] rope; **~ floja** tightrope - **2.** [de instrumento] string - **3.** [de reloj] spring; **dar ~ a** [reloj] to wind up - **4.** GEOM chord.
➡ **cuerdas vocales** *fpl* vocal cords.

cuerdo, da *adj* - **1.** [sano de juicio] sane - **2.** [sensato] sensible.

cueriza *f Andes fam* beating, leathering.

cuerno *m* [gen] horn; [de ciervo] antler; **saber a ~ quemado** *fam* to be fishy; **¡vete al ~!** *fam* go to hell!

cuero *m* - **1.** [piel de animal] skin; [piel curtida] hide; **~ cabelludo** scalp; **en ~s, en ~s vivos** stark naked - **2.** [material] leather.

cuerpo *m* - **1.** [gen] body; **~ celeste** heavenly body; **a ~** without a coat on; **luchar ~ a ~** to fight hand-to-hand; **tomar ~** to take shape; **en ~ y alma** body and soul - **2.** [tronco] trunk - **3.** [corporación consular, militar etc] corps; **~ de bomberos** fire brigade; **~ diplomático** diplomatic corps.

cuervo *m* crow.

cuesta *f* slope; **~ arriba** uphill; **~ abajo** downhill; **a ~s** on one's back, over one's shoulders; **ir ~ abajo** to decline, to go downhill.

cuestión *f* - **1.** [pregunta] question - **2.** [problema] problem - **3.** [asunto] matter, issue; **en ~** in question, at issue; **ser ~ de** to be a question of.

cuestionar *vt* to question.

cuestionario *m* questionnaire.

cueva *f* cave; **~ de ladrones** den of thieves.

cuico *m Méx fam* cop.

cuidado ⬦ *m* care; **con ~** [con esmero] carefully; [con cautela] cautiously; **tener ~ con** to be careful with; **~s intensivos** intensive care *(U)*; **eso me tiene** o **trae sin ~** I couldn't care less about that. ⬦ *interj*: **¡~!** careful!, look out!

cuidadoso, sa *adj* careful.

cuidar *vt* [gen] to look after; [estilo etc] to take care over; [detalles] to pay attention to.
➡ **cuidar de** *vi* to look after; **cuida de que no lo haga** make sure she doesn't do it.
➡ **cuidarse** *vpr* to take care of o to look after o.s.; **~se de** to worry about.

cuitlacoche *m CAm, Méx* corn smut, *edible fungus which grows on maize.*

culata *f* - **1.** [de arma] butt - **2.** [de motor] cylinder head.

culebra *f* snake.

culebrón *m* TV soap opera.

culinario, ria *adj* culinary.

culminación *f* culmination.

culminar ⬦ *vt*: **~ (con)** to crown (with). ⬦ *vi* to finish, to culminate.

culo *m fam* - **1.** [de personas] backside, bum *UK*; **caerse de ~** *fam* to be flabbergasted, to be gobsmacked; **estar en el ~ del mundo** *fam* to be in the back of beyond; **lamer el ~ a alguien** *fam* to lick sb's arse *UK*, to lick sb's ass *US*; **ser un ~ de mal asiento** to be fidgety - **2.** [de objetos] bottom.

culpa *f* [responsabilidad] fault; **tener la ~ de algo** to be to blame for sthg; **echar la ~ a**

alguien (de) to blame sb (for); **por ~ de** because of.

culpabilidad f guilt.

culpable ⬦ adj : **~ (de)** guilty (of); **declararse ~** to plead guilty. ⬦ mf DER guilty party; **tú eres el ~** you're to blame.

culpar vt : **~ a alguien (de)** [atribuir la culpa] to blame sb (for); [acusar] to accuse sb (of).

cultivar vt [tierra] to farm, to cultivate; [plantas] to grow.
➡ **cultivarse** vpr [persona] to improve o.s.

cultivo m - **1.** [de tierra] farming; [de plantas] growing - **2.** [plantación] crop.

culto, ta adj [persona] cultured, educated; [estilo] refined; [palabra] literary, learned.
➡ **culto** m - **1.** [devoción] worship; **libertad de ~** freedom of worship - **2.** [religión] cult.

cultura f - **1.** [de sociedad] culture - **2.** [sabiduría] learning, knowledge; **~ general** general knowledge.

cultural adj cultural.

culturismo m body-building.

cumbre f - **1.** [de montaña] summit - **2.** fig [punto culminante] peak, pinnacle - **3.** POLÍT summit (conference).

cumpleaños m inv birthday.

cumplido, da adj - **1.** [completo, lleno] full, complete - **2.** [cortés] courteous.
➡ **cumplido** m compliment; **andarse con ~s** to stand on ceremony; **visita de ~** courtesy call.

cumplidor, ra adj reliable, dependable.

cumplimentar vt - **1.** [felicitar] to congratulate - **2.** [cumplir - orden] to carry out; [- contrato] to fulfil.

cumplimiento m [de un deber] performance; [de contrato, promesa] fulfilment; [de la ley] observance; [de órdenes] carrying out; [de condena] completion; [de plazo] expiry.

cumplir ⬦ vt - **1.** [orden] to carry out; [promesa] to keep; [ley] to observe; [contrato] to fulfil - **2.** [años] to reach; **mañana cumplo los 20** I'm 20 o it's my 20th birthday tomorrow - **3.** [condena] to serve; [servicio militar] to do. ⬦ vi - **1.** [plazo, garantía] to expire - **2.** [realizar el deber] to do one's duty; **~ con el deber** to do one's duty; **~ con la palabra** to keep one's word.

cúmulo m - **1.** [de objetos] pile, heap - **2.** fig [de asuntos, acontecimientos] series.

cuna f [para dormir] cot, cradle.

cundir vi - **1.** [propagarse] to spread - **2.** [dar de sí - comida, reservas, tiempo] to go a long way; [trabajo, estudio] to go well.

cuneta f [de una carretera] ditch; [de una calle] gutter.

cuña f - **1.** [pieza] wedge - **2.** [de publicidad]

commercial break - **3.** Andes, RP fam: **tener ~** to have friends in high places.

cuñado, da m,f brother-in-law (f sister-in-law).

cuño m - **1.** [troquel] die - **2.** [sello, impresión] stamp.

cuota f - **1.** [contribución - a entidad, club] membership fee, subscription; [a Hacienda] tax (payment); **~ de entrada** admission fee - **2.** [cupo] quota - **3.** Méx [peaje] toll.

cupiera etc ⊳ **caber**.

cupo ⬦ ⊳ **caber**. ⬦ m - **1.** [cantidad máxima] quota - **2.** [cantidad proporcional] share; [de una cosa racionada] ration.

cupón m [gen] coupon; [de lotería, rifa] ticket.

cúpula f - **1.** ARQUIT dome, cupola - **2.** fig [mandos] leaders (pl).

cura ⬦ m priest. ⬦ f - **1.** [curación] recovery; **tener ~** to be curable - **2.** [tratamiento] treatment, cure; **~ de emergencia** first aid; **~ de reposo** rest cure.

curación f - **1.** [de un enfermo - recuperación] recovery; [- tratamiento] treatment; [de una herida] healing - **2.** [de jamón] curing.

curado, da adj [alimento] cured; [pieles] tanned; **~ de espanto** unshockable.

curandero, ra m,f quack.

curar ⬦ vt - **1.** [gen] to cure - **2.** [herida] to dress - **3.** [pieles] to tan. ⬦ vi [enfermo] to recover; [herida] to heal up.
➡ **curarse** vpr - **1.** [sanar] : **~se (de)** to recover (from) - **2.** [alimento] to cure.

curcuncho, cha ⬦ adj Andes fam [jorobado] hunchbacked. ⬦ m [joroba] hump; [jorobado] hunchback.

curiosear ⬦ vi [fisgonear] to nose around; [por una tienda] to browse round. ⬦ vt [libros, revistas] to browse through.

curiosidad f curiosity.

curioso, sa ⬦ adj - **1.** [por saber, averiguar] curious, inquisitive - **2.** [raro] odd, strange. ⬦ m,f onlooker.

curita m Amér sticking plaster, Band-Aid® US.

currante adj fam hard-working.

currar, currelar vi fam to work.

curre = **curro**.

currelar = **currar**.

currículum (vitae) [kuˈrrikulum (ˈbite)] (pl currícula (vitae) o currículums), **currículo** m curriculum vitae UK, résumé US.

curro, curre m fam work.

cursar vt - **1.** [estudiar] to study - **2.** [enviar] to send - **3.** [dar - órdenes etc] to give, to issue - **4.** [tramitar] to submit.

cursi adj fam [vestido, canción etc] naff, tacky; [modales, persona] affected.

cursilería f [cualidad] tackiness, naffness.

cursillo *m* [curso] short course.

cursiva ⊳ **letra**.

curso *m* - **1.** [año académico] year - **2.** [lecciones] course; ~ **intensivo** crash course; ~ **por correspondencia** correspondence course - **3.** [dirección - de río, acontecimientos] course; [- de la economía] trend; **seguir su** ~ to go on, to continue; **el resfriado debe seguir su** ~ you should allow the cold to run its course; **en** ~ [mes, año] current; [trabajo] in progress.

cursor *m* INFORM cursor.

curtido, da *adj* - **1.** [piel, cuero] tanned - **2.** *fig* [experimentado] seasoned.

curtiembre *f Andes, RP* tannery.

curtir *vt* - **1.** [piel] to tan - **2.** *fig* [persona] to harden.

curva ⊳ **curvo**.

curvatura *f* curvature.

curvo, va *adj* [gen] curved; [doblado] bent.
  ➡ **curva** *f* [gen] curve; [en carretera] bend; **curva cerrada** sharp bend; **curva de nivel** contour line.

cúspide *f* - **1.** [de montaña] summit, top - **2.** *fig* [apogeo] peak, height - **3.** GEOM apex.

custodia *f* - **1.** [de cosas] safekeeping - **2.** [de personas] custody; ~ **preventiva** protective custody.

custodiar *vt* - **1.** [vigilar] to guard - **2.** [proteger] to look after.

custodio *m* guard.

cutáneo, a *adj* skin *(antes de sust)*.

cutícula *f* cuticle.

cutis *m inv* skin, complexion.

cutre *adj fam* - **1.** [de bajo precio, calidad] cheap and nasty - **2.** [sórdido] shabby - **3.** [tacaño] tight, stingy.

cutter (*pl* **cutters**) *m* [artist's] scalpel *(with retractable blade)*.

cuyo, ya *adj* [posesión - por parte de personas] whose; [- por parte de cosas] of which, whose; **ésos son los amigos en cuya casa nos hospedamos** those are the friends in whose house we spent the night; **ese señor,** ~ **hijo conociste ayer** that man, whose son you met yesterday; **un equipo cuya principal estrella ...** a team, the star player of which *o* whose star player ...; **en** ~ **caso** in which case.

CV (*abrev de* **curriculum vitae**) *m* CV.

d, D *f* [letra] d, D.

D. *abrev de* **don**.

dactilar ⊳ **huella**.

dádiva *f* [regalo] gift; [donativo] donation.

dado, da *adj* given; **en un momento** ~ at a certain point; **ser** ~ **a** to be fond of.
  ➡ **dado** *m* dice, die; **echar** *o* **tirar los** ~s to throw the dice; **jugar a los** ~s to play dice.
  ➡ **dado que** *loc conj* since, seeing as.

daga *f* dagger.

dale *interj* ¡ ~ ! – ¡otra vez con lo mismo! there you go again!

dalia *f* dahlia.

dálmata *adj* & *mf* [perro] Dalmatian.

daltónico, ca *adj* colour-blind.

daltonismo *m* colour blindness.

dama *f* - **1.** [mujer] lady - **2.** [en damas] king; [en ajedrez, naipes] queen.
  ➡ **damas** *fpl* [juego] draughts *(U) UK*, checkers *(U) US*.

damisela *f desus* damsel.

damnificar *vt* [cosa] to damage; [persona] to harm, to injure.

danés, esa ◇ *adj* Danish. ◇ *m,f* [persona] Dane.
  ➡ **danés** *m* [lengua] Danish.

danza *f* [gen] dancing; [baile] dance.

danzar *vi* - **1.** [bailar] to dance - **2.** *fig* [ir de un sitio a otro] to run about.

dañar *vt* [vista, cosecha] to harm, to damage; [persona] to hurt; [pieza, objeto] to damage.
  ➡ **dañarse** *vpr* [persona] to hurt o.s.; [cosa] to become damaged.

dañino, na *adj* harmful.

daño *m* - **1.** [dolor] pain, hurt; **hacer** ~ **a alguien** to hurt sb; **hacerse** ~ to hurt o.s. - **2.** [perjuicio - a algo] damage; [- a persona] harm; ~**s colaterales** collateral damage; ~**s y perjuicios** damages.

dar ◇ *vt* - **1.** [gen] to give; [baile, fiesta] to hold, to give; [naipes] to deal; ~ **algo a alguien** to give sthg to sb, to give sb sthg - **2.** [producir - gen] to give, to produce; [- frutos, flores] **to bear**; [- beneficios, intereses] to yield - **3.** [suj: reloj] to strike; **el reloj ha**

dado las doce the clock struck twelve - **4.** [suministrar luz etc - por primera vez] to connect; [- tras un corte] to turn back on; [encender] to turn *o* switch on - **5.** CIN, TEATR & TV to show; [concierto, interpretación] to give - **6.** [mostrar - señales etc] to show - **7.** [untar con] to apply; ~ **barniz a una silla** to varnish a chair - **8.** [provocar - gusto, escalofríos etc] to give; **me da vergüenza/pena** it makes me ashamed/sad; **me da risa** it makes me laugh; **me da miedo** it frightens me - **9.** [expresa acción]: ~ **un grito** to give a cry; ~**le un golpe/una puñalada a alguien** to hit/stab sb; **voy a** ~ **un paseo** I'm going (to go) for a walk - **10.** [considerar]: ~ **algo por** to consider sthg as; **eso lo doy por hecho** I take that for granted; ~ **a alguien por muerto** to give sb up for dead. ◇ *vi* - **1.** [repartir - en naipes] to deal - **2.** [horas] to strike; **han dado las tres en el reloj** three o'clock struck - **3.** [golpear]: **le dieron en la cabeza** they hit him on the head; **la piedra dio contra el cristal** the stone hit the window - **4.** [accionar]: ~ **a** [llave de paso] to turn; [botón, timbre] to press - **5.** [estar orientado]: ~ **a** [suj: ventana, balcón] to look out onto, to overlook; [suj: pasillo, puerta] to lead to; [suj: casa, fachada] to face - **6.** [encontrar]: ~ **con algo/alguien** to find sthg/sb; **he dado con la solución** I've hit upon the solution - **7.** [proporcionar]: ~ **de beber a alguien** to give sb sthg to drink; **le da de mamar a su hijo** she breastfeeds her son - **8.** *loc:* ~ **de sí** [ropa, calzado] to give, to stretch.
◆ **darse** *vpr* - **1.** [suceder] to occur, to happen; **se da pocas veces** it rarely happens - **2.** [entregarse]: ~**se a** [droga etc] to take to - **3.** [golpearse]: ~**se contra** to bump into - **4.** [tener aptitud]: **se me da bien/mal el latín** I'm good/bad at Latin - **5.** [considerarse]: ~**se por** to consider o.s. (to be); ~**se por vencido** to give in - **6.** *loc:* **dársela a alguien** [engañar] to take sb in; **se la da de listo** he makes out (that) he is clever.

dardo *m* dart.

dársena *f* dock.

datar *vt* to date.
◆ **datar de** *vi* to date from.

dátil *m* BOT & CULIN date.

dato *m* [gen] piece of information, fact; ~**s** [gen] information; INFORM data; ~**s personales** personal details.

dcha. (*abrev de* **derecha**) rt.

d. de JC., d.JC. (*abrev de* **después de Jesucristo**) AD.

de *prep* (*de + el = del*) - **1.** [posesión, pertenencia] of; **el coche** ~ **mi padre/mis padres** my father's/parents' car; **es** ~ **ella** it's hers; **la pata** ~ **la mesa** the table leg - **2.** [materia]

(made) of; **un vaso** ~ **plástico** a plastic cup; **un reloj** ~ **oro** a gold watch - **3.** [en descripciones]: **un vaso** ~ **agua** a glass of water; ~ **fácil manejo** user-friendly; **la señora** ~ **verde** the lady in green; **el chico** ~ **la coleta** the boy with the ponytail; **he comprado las peras** ~ **dos euros el kilo** I bought the pears that were *o* at two euros a kilo; **un sello** ~ **50 céntimos** a 50 cent stamp - **4.** [asunto] about; **hablábamos** ~ **ti** we were talking about you; **libros** ~ **historia** history books - **5.** [uso]: **una bici** ~ **carreras** a racer; **ropa** ~ **deporte** sportswear - **6.** [en calidad de] as; **trabaja** ~ **bombero** he works as a fireman - **7.** [tiempo - desde] from; [- durante] in; **trabaja** ~ **nueve a cinco** she works from nine to five; ~ **madrugada** early in the morning; **a las cuatro** ~ **la tarde** at four in the afternoon; **trabaja** ~ **noche y duerme** ~ **día** he works at night and sleeps during the day - **8.** [procedencia, distancia] from; **salir** ~ **casa** to leave home; **soy** ~ **Bilbao** I'm from Bilbao - **9.** [causa, modo] with; **morirse** ~ **hambre** to die of hunger; **llorar** ~ **alegría** to cry with joy; ~ **una patada** with a kick; ~ **una sola vez** in one go - **10.** [con superlativos]: **el mejor** ~ **todos** the best of all; **el más importante del mundo** the most important in the world - **11.** [en comparaciones]: **más/menos** ~ ... more/less than ... - **12.** (*antes de infin*) [condición] if; ~ **querer ayudarme, lo haría** if she wanted to help me, she'd do it; ~ **no ser por ti, me hubiese hundido** if it hadn't been for you, I wouldn't have made it - **13.** (*después de adj y antes de sust*) [enfatiza cualidad]: **el idiota** ~ **tu hermano** your stupid brother - **14.** (*después de adj y antes de infin*): **es difícil** ~ **creer** it's hard to believe.

dé ⊳ **dar.**

deambular *vi* to wander (about).

debajo *adv* underneath; ~ **de** underneath, under; **por** ~ **de lo normal** below normal.

debate *m* debate.

debatir *vt* to debate.
◆ **debatirse** *vpr* [luchar] to struggle; **se debate la vida y la muerte** she's fighting for her life.

debe *m* debit (side).

deber ◇ *vt* [adeudar] to owe; ~ **algo a alguien** to owe sb sthg, to owe sthg to sb. ◇ *vi* - **1.** (*antes de infin*) [expresa obligación]: **debo hacerlo** I have to do it, I must do it; **deberían abolir esa ley** they ought to *o* should abolish that law; **debes dominar tus impulsos** you must *o* should control your impulses - **2.** [expresa posibilidad]: ~ **de:** **el tren debe de llegar alrededor de las diez** the train should arrive at about ten; **deben de ser las diez** it must be ten o'clock; **no debe de ser muy mayor** she can't be very old. ◇ *m* duty.

➡ **deberse** a *vpr* - **1.** [ser consecuencia de] to be due to - **2.** [dedicarse a] to have a responsibility towards.

➡ **deberes** *mpl* [trabajo escolar] homework *(U).*

debidamente *adv* properly.

debido, da *adj* [justo, conveniente] due, proper; **a su ~ tiempo** in due course; **como es ~** properly.

➡ **debido a** *loc conj (a principio de frase)* owing to; *(en mitad de frase)* due to.

débil *adj* - **1.** [persona - sin fuerzas] weak; [condescendiente] lax, lenient - **2.** [voz, sonido] faint; [luz] dim.

debilidad *f* [gen] weakness; **tener ~ por** to have a soft spot for.

debilitar *vt* to weaken.

➡ **debilitarse** *vpr* to become *o* grow weak.

debutar *vi* to make one's debut.

década *f* decade; **la ~ de los sesenta** the sixties.

decadencia *f* [gen] decadence.

decadente *adj* decadent.

decaer *vi* [gen] to decline; [enfermo] to get weaker; [salud] to fail; [entusiasmo] to flag; [restaurante etc] to go downhill.

decaído, da *adj* [desalentado] gloomy, downhearted; [débil] frail.

decaimiento *m* [desaliento] gloominess; [decadencia] decline; [falta de fuerzas] weakness.

decano, na *m,f* [de corporación, facultad] dean.

decapitar *vt* to decapitate, to behead.

decena *f* ten; **una ~ de veces** about ten times.

decencia *f* - **1.** [gen] decency; [en el vestir] modesty - **2.** [dignidad] dignity.

decenio *m* decade.

decente *adj* - **1.** [gen] decent - **2.** [en el comportamiento] proper; [en el vestir] modest - **3.** [limpio] clean.

decepción *f* disappointment; **llevarse una ~** to be disappointed.

decepcionar *vt* to disappoint.

decibelio *m* decibel.

decidido, da *adj* determined.

decidir ◇ *vt* - **1.** [gen] to decide; **~ hacer algo** to decide to do sthg - **2.** [determinar] to determine. ◇ *vi* to decide, to choose.

➡ **decidirse** *vpr* to decide, to make up one's mind; **~se a hacer algo** to decide to do sthg; **~se por** to decide on, to choose.

décima ▷ **décimo**.

decimal *adj* [sistema] decimal.

décimo, ma *núm* tenth; **la décima parte** a tenth.

➡ **décimo** *m* - **1.** [fracción] tenth - **2.** [en lotería] *tenth part of a lottery ticket.*

➡ **décima** *f* [en medidas] tenth; **una décima de segundo** a tenth of a second.

decir *vt* - **1.** [gen] to say; **~ que sí/no** to say yes/no; **¿cómo se dice 'estación' en inglés?** how do you say 'estación' in English?; **¿diga?, ¿dígame?** [al teléfono] hello? - **2.** [contar, ordenar] to tell; **~ a alguien que haga algo** to tell sb to do sthg; **se dice que** they *o* people say (that); **~ la verdad** to tell the truth - **3.** *fig* [revelar] to tell, to show; **eso lo dice todo** that says it all - **4.** *loc*: **~ para sí** to say to o.s.; **es ~** that is, that's to say; **(o) mejor dicho** or rather; **querer ~** to mean; **¿qué quieres ~ con eso?** what do you mean by that?

decisión *f* - **1.** [dictamen, resolución] decision; **tomar una ~** to make *o* take a decision - **2.** [empeño, tesón] determination, resolve; [seguridad, resolución] decisiveness.

decisivo, va *adj* decisive.

declamar *vt & vi* to declaim, to recite.

declaración *f* - **1.** [gen] statement; [de amor, guerra] declaration; **prestar ~** to give evidence; **~ de derechos** bill of rights - **2.** [de impuestos] tax return; **tengo que hacer la ~** I have to do my tax return; **~ conjunta** joint tax return; **~ del impuesto sobre la renta** income tax return.

declarar ◇ *vt* [gen] to declare; [afirmar] to state, to say; **~ culpable/inocente a alguien** to find sb guilty/not guilty. ◇ *vi* DER to testify, to give evidence.

➡ **declararse** *vpr* - **1.** [incendio, epidemia] to break out - **2.** [confesar el amor] to declare one's feelings *o* love - **3.** [dar una opinión]: **~se a favor de algo** to say that one supports sthg; **~se en contra de algo** to say one is opposed to sthg; **~se culpable/inocente** to plead guilty/not guilty.

declinar ◇ *vt* [gen & GRAM] to decline; [responsabilidad] to disclaim. ◇ *vi* [día, tarde] to draw to a close; [fiebre] to subside, to abate; [economía] to decline.

declive *m* - **1.** [decadencia] decline, fall; **en ~ in decline** - **2.** [pendiente] slope.

decodificador = **descodificador**.

decoración *f* - **1.** [acción] decoration; [efecto] décor - **2.** [adorno] decorations *(pl).*

decorado *m* CIN & TEATR set.

decorar *vt* to decorate.

decorativo, va *adj* decorative.

decoro *m* [pudor] decency, decorum.

decoroso, sa *adj* [decente] decent; [correcto] seemly, proper.

decrecer *vi* [gen] to decrease, to decline;

[caudal del río] to go down.

decrépito, ta *adj despec* decrepit.

decretar *vt* to decree.

decreto *m* decree; ~ **ley** decree, ≃ order in council *UK*.

dedal *m* thimble.

dedicación *f* dedication.

dedicar *vt* - **1.** [tiempo, dinero, energía] to devote - **2.** [libro, monumento] to dedicate.

➡ **dedicarse a** *vpr* - **1.** [a una profesión]: ¿a qué se dedica usted? what do you do for a living?; **se dedica a la enseñanza** she works as a teacher - **2.** [a una actividad, persona] to spend time on; **los domingos me dedico al estudio** I spend Sundays studying.

dedicatoria *f* dedication.

dedo *m* - **1.** [de la mano] finger; **contar con los ~s** to count on one's fingers; **dos ~s de whisky** two fingers of whisky; **meterse el ~ en la nariz** to pick one's nose; ~ **gordo** *o* **pulgar** thumb; ~ **índice/meñique** index/little finger - **2.** [del pie] toe - **3.** *loc*: **estar a dos ~s de** to be within an inch of; **hacer ~** *fam* to hitchhike; **nombrar a alguien a ~** to handpick sb; **no mover un ~** not to lift a finger; **pillarse** *o* **cogerse los ~s** *fig* to get one's fingers burnt; **poner el ~ en la llaga** to put one's finger on it.

deducción *f* deduction.

deducir *vt* - **1.** [inferir] to guess, to deduce - **2.** [descontar] to deduct.

defecar *vi* to defecate.

defecto *m* [físico] defect; [moral] fault, shortcoming; ~ **de pronunciación** speech defect.

➡ **por defecto** *loc adv* by default.

defectuoso, sa *adj* [mercancía] defective, faulty; [trabajo] inaccurate.

defender *vt* [gen] to defend; [amigo etc] to stand up for.

➡ **defenderse** *vpr* [protegerse]: ~**se (de)** to defend o.s. (against).

defensa ◇ *f* defence; ~ **personal** self-defence. ◇ *mf* DEP defender; ~ **central** centre-back.

➡ **defensas** *fpl* MED defences; **estoy baja de ~s** my body's defences are low.

defensivo, va *adj* defensive.

➡ **defensiva** *f*: **ponerse/estar a la defensiva** to go/be on the defensive.

defensor, ra ◇ *adj* ➤ **abogado**. ◇ *m,f* [gen] defender; [abogado] counsel for the defence; [adalid] champion; ~ **del pueblo** ≃ ombudsman.

deferencia *f* deference.

deficiencia *f* [defecto] deficiency, shortcoming; [insuficiencia] lack.

deficiente *adj* [defectuoso - gen] deficient;

[audición, vista] defective.

➡ **deficiente (mental)** *mf* mentally handicapped person.

déficit (*pl* **déficits**) *m* ECON deficit.

deficitario, ria *adj* [empresa, operación] loss-making; [balance] negative, showing a deficit.

definición *f* - **1.** [gen] definition; **por ~** by definition - **2.** [en televisión] resolution.

definir *vt* [gen] to define.

➡ **definirse** *vpr* to take a clear stance.

definitivamente *adv* - **1.** [sin duda] definitely - **2.** [para siempre] for good.

definitivo, va *adj* [texto etc] definitive; [respuesta] definite; **en definitiva** in short, anyway.

deforestación *f* deforestation.

deformación *f* [de huesos, objetos etc] deformation; [de la verdad etc] distortion; ~ **física** (physical) deformity; **tener ~ profesional** to be always acting as if one were still at work.

deformar *vt* - **1.** [huesos, objetos etc] to deform - **2.** *fig* [la verdad etc] to distort.

➡ **deformarse** *vpr* to go out of shape.

deforme *adj* [cuerpo] deformed, disfigured; [imagen] distorted; [objeto] misshapen.

defraudar *vt* - **1.** [decepcionar] to disappoint - **2.** [estafar] to defraud; ~ **a Hacienda** to practise tax evasion.

defunción *f* decease, death.

degeneración *f* degeneration.

degenerado, da *adj* & *m,f* degenerate.

degenerar *vi*: ~ **(en)** to degenerate (into).

degollar *vt* [cortar la garganta] to cut *o* slit the throat of; [decapitar] to behead.

degradar *vt* - **1.** [moralmente] to degrade, to debase - **2.** [de un cargo] to demote.

➡ **degradarse** *vpr* to degrade *o* lower o.s.

degustación *f* tasting (*of wines etc*).

dehesa *f* meadow.

dejadez *f* neglect; [en aspecto] slovenliness.

dejado, da *adj* careless; [aspecto] slovenly.

dejar ◇ *vt* - **1.** [gen] to leave; **deja esa pera en el plato** put that pear on the plate; **deja el abrigo en la percha** leave your coat on the hanger; ~ **a alguien en algún sitio** [con el coche] to drop sb off somewhere; **deja algo de café para mí** leave some coffee for me; ~ **algo/a alguien a alguien** [encomendar] to leave sth/sb with sb - **2.** [prestar]: ~ **algo a alguien** to lend sb sth, to lend sth to sb - **3.** [abandonar - casa, trabajo, país] to leave; [- tabaco, estudios] to give up; [- familia] to abandon; ~ **algo por imposible** to give sth up as a lost cause; ~ **a alguien atrás** to leave sb behind - **4.** [permitir]: ~ **a alguien hacer**

algo to let sb do sthg, to allow sb to do sthg; **sus gritos no me dejaron dormir** his cries prevented me from sleeping; **deja que tu hijo venga con nosotros** let your son come with us; ~ **correr algo** *fig* to let sthg be - **5.** [omitir] to leave out; ~ **algo por** *o* **sin hacer** to fail to do sthg; **dejó lo más importante por resolver** he left the most important question unsolved - **6.** [esperar]: ~ **que** to wait until; **dejó que acabara de llover para salir** he waited until it had stopped raining before going out. ◇ *vi* - **1.** [parar]: ~ **de hacer algo** to stop doing sthg; **no deja de venir ni un solo día** he never fails to come - **2.** [expresando promesa]: **no** ~ **de** to be sure to; **¡no dejes de escribirme!** be sure to write to me!

◆ **dejarse** *vpr* - **1.** [olvidar]: ~**se algo en algún sitio** to leave sthg somewhere - **2.** [permitir]: ~**se engañar** to allow o.s. to be taken in.

deje *m* [acento] accent.

dejo *m* [acento] accent.

del ▷ **de.**

delantal *m* apron.

delante *adv* - **1.** [en primer lugar, en la parte delantera] in front; **el de** ~ the one in front; **el asiento de** ~ the seat in front - **2.** [enfrente] opposite - **3.** [presente] present.

◆ **delante de** *loc prep* in front of.

delantero, ra ◇ *adj* front. ◇ *m,f* DEP forward; ~ **centro** centre forward.

◆ **delantera** *f* - **1.** DEP forwards *(pl)*, attack - **2.** *loc*: **coger** *o* **tomar la delantera** to take the lead; **coger** *o* **tomar la delantera a alguien** to beat sb to it; **llevar la delantera** to be in the lead.

delatar *vt* to denounce; *fig* [suj: sonrisa, ojos etc] to betray, to give away.

◆ **delatarse** *vpr* to give o.s. away.

delator, ra *m,f* informer.

delegación *f* - **1.** [autorización, embajada] delegation; ~ **de poderes** devolution (of power) - **2.** [sucursal] branch - **3.** [oficina pública] local office - **4.** *Méx* [comisaría] police station, precinct *US*, station house *US*.

delegado, da *m,f* - **1.** [gen] delegate; ~ **de curso** class representative - **2.** COM representative.

delegar *vt* : ~ **algo (en** *o* **a)** to delegate sthg (to).

deleite *m* delight.

deletrear *vt* to spell (out).

deleznable *adj fig* [malo - clima, libro, actuación] appalling; [- excusa, razón] contemptible.

delfín *m* [animal] dolphin.

delgado, da *adj* [gen] thin; [esbelto] slim.

deliberación *f* deliberation.

deliberar *vi* to deliberate.

delicadeza *f* - **1.** [miramiento - con cosas] care; [- con personas] kindness, attentiveness; **tener la** ~ **de** to be thoughtful enough to - **2.** [finura - de perfume, rostro] delicacy; [- de persona] sensitivity - **3.** [de un asunto, situación] delicacy.

delicado, da *adj* - **1.** [gen] delicate; [perfume, gusto] subtle; [paladar] refined - **2.** [persona - sensible] sensitive; [- muy exigente] fussy; [- educado] polite; **estar** ~ **de salud** to be very weak.

delicia *f* delight.

delicioso, sa *adj* [comida] delicious; [persona] lovely, delightful.

delimitar *vt* [finca etc] to set out the boundaries of; [funciones etc] to define.

delincuencia *f* crime; ~ **juvenil** juvenile delinquency.

delincuente *mf* criminal; ~ **habitual** habitual offender; ~ **juvenil** juvenile delinquent.

delineante *mf* draughtsman (*f* draughtswoman).

delinquir *vi* to commit a crime.

delirante *adj* [gen] delirious.

delirar *vi* [un enfermo] to be delirious; [desbarrar] to talk nonsense.

delirio *m* [por la fiebre] delirium; [de un enfermo mental] ravings *(pl)*; ~**s de grandeza** delusions of grandeur; **con** ~ madly.

delito *m* crime, offence; ~ **común** common law offence; ~ **ecológico** ecological crime; ~ **fiscal** tax offence.

delta *m* *o* *f* delta.

demacrado, da *adj* gaunt.

demagogo, ga *m,f* demagogue.

demanda *f* - **1.** [petición] request; [reivindicación] demand; ~ **salarial** wage claim; **en** ~ **de** asking for - **2.** ECON demand - **3.** DER lawsuit; [por daños y perjuicios] claim; **presentar una** ~ **contra** to take legal action against.

demandante *mf* plaintiff.

demandar *vt* - **1.** DER: ~ **a alguien (por)** to sue sb (for) - **2.** [pedir] to ask for, to seek.

demarcación *f* - **1.** [señalización] demarcation - **2.** [territorio demarcado] area; [jurisdicción] district.

demás ◇ *adj* other; **los** ~ **invitados** the other *o* remaining guests. ◇ *pron*: **lo** ~ the rest; **todo lo** ~ everything else; **los/las** ~ the others, the rest; **por lo** ~ apart from that, otherwise; **y** ~ and so on.

demasiado, da ◇ *adj* too much; *(pl)* too many; **demasiada comida** too much food; ~**s niños** too many children. ◇ *adv* [gen] too much; *(antes de adj o adv)* too; **habla** ~ she talks too much; **iba** ~ **rápido** he was going too fast.

demencia f madness, insanity; ~ **senil** senile dementia.

demencial adj [disparatado] chaotic.

demente adj mad.

democracia f democracy.

demócrata ◇ adj democratic. ◇ mf democrat.

democrático, ca adj democratic.

demografía f demography.

demoler vt [edificio] to demolish, to pull down; fig to destroy.

demolición f demolition.

demonio m **- 1.** lit & fig devil; **un pesado de mil ~s** one hell of a bore **- 2.** [para enfatizar]: **¿qué/dónde ~s ...?** what/where the hell ...?

◆ **demonios** interj: **¡~s!** damn (it)!

demora f delay.

demorar ◇ vt **- 1.** to delay **- 2.** Amér [tardar]: **demoraron 3 días en hacerlo** it took them three days to do it; **demora una hora para vestirse** it takes her one hour to get dressed. ◇ vi Amér [tardar]: **¡no demores!** don't be late.

◆ **demorarse** vpr **- 1.** [retrasarse] to be delayed **- 2.** [detenerse] to stop (somewhere).

demostración f **- 1.** [gen] demonstration; ~ **de afecto** show of affection **- 2.** [de un teorema] proof **- 3.** [exhibición] display; [señal] sign; [prueba] proof.

demostrar vt **- 1.** [hipótesis, teoría, verdad] to prove **- 2.** [alegría, impaciencia, dolor] to show **- 3.** [funcionamiento, procedimiento] to demonstrate, to show.

denegar vt to turn down, to reject.

denigrante adj [humillante] degrading; [insultante] insulting.

denigrar vt [humillar] to denigrate, to vilify; [insultar] to insult.

denominación f naming; '~ **de origen'** 'appellation d'origine'.

denominador m denominator.

denotar vt to indicate, to show.

densidad f [gen & INFORM] density; ~ **de población** population density; **alta/doble ~** INFORM high/double density.

denso, sa adj [gen] dense; [líquido] thick.

dentadura f teeth (pl); ~ **postiza** false teeth (pl), dentures (pl).

dentera f: **dar ~ a alguien** to set sb's teeth on edge.

dentífrico, ca adj tooth (antes de sust).

◆ **dentífrico** m toothpaste.

dentista mf dentist.

dentro adv inside; **está ahí ~** it's in there; **hacia/para ~** inwards; **por ~** (on the) inside; fig inside, deep down.

◆ **dentro de** loc prep in; ~ **del coche** in o inside the car; ~ **de poco/un año** in a while/a year; ~ **de un año terminaré los estudios** I'll have finished my studies within a year; ~ **de lo posible** as far as possible.

denuncia f [acusación] accusation; [condena] denunciation; [a la policía] complaint; **presentar una ~ contra** to file a complaint against.

denunciar vt to denounce; [delito] to report.

departamento m **- 1.** [gen] department **- 2.** [división territorial] administrative district; [en Francia] department **- 3.** [de maleta, cajón, tren] compartment **- 4.** Arg [apartamento] flat UK, apartment US.

dependencia f **- 1.** [de una persona] dependence; [de país, drogas, alcohol] dependency **- 2.** [departamento] section; [sucursal] branch.

◆ **dependencias** fpl [habitaciones] rooms; [edificios] outbuildings.

depender vi to depend; **depende ...** it depends ...

◆ **depender de** vi: ~ **de algo** to depend on sthg; ~ **de alguien** to be dependent on sb; **depende de ti** it's up to you.

dependienta f shop assistant, saleswoman.

dependiente ◇ adj dependent; **un organismo ~ del gobierno central** a body which forms part of the central government. ◇ m salesman, shop assistant UK, salesclerk US.

depilar vt [gen] to remove the hair from; [cejas] to pluck; [con cera] to wax.

depilatorio, ria adj hair-removing.

◆ **depilatorio** m hair-remover.

deplorable adj [suceso, comportamiento] deplorable; [aspecto] sorry, pitiful.

deponer vt **- 1.** [abandonar - actitud] to drop, to set aside; [las armas] to lay down **- 2.** [destituir - ministro, secretario] to remove from office; [- líder, rey] to depose.

deportar vt to deport.

deporte m sport; **hacer ~** to do o practise sports; **hacer ~ es bueno para la salud** sport is good for your health; **practicar un ~** to do a sport; ~**s de competición** competitive sports; ~**s extremos** extreme sports; ~**s náuticos** water sports.

deportista mf sportsman (f sportswoman).

deportivo, va adj **- 1.** [revista, evento] sports (antes de sust) **- 2.** [conducta, espíritu] sportsmanlike.

◆ **deportivo** m sports car.

depositar vt **- 1.** [gen] to place; ~ **algo en alguien** [confianza, ilusiones] to place sthg in sb **- 2.** [en el banco etc] to deposit.

◆ **depositarse** vpr [asentarse] to settle.

desabrochar

depositario, ria *m,f* - **1**. [de dinero] trustee - **2**. [de confianza etc] repository - **3**. [de mercancías etc] depositary.

depósito *m* - **1**. [almacén - de mercancías] store, warehouse; [- de armas] dump, arsenal; ~ **de cadáveres** morgue, mortuary; ~ **de equipaje** left luggage office *UK*, baggage room *US* - **2**. [recipiente] tank; ~ **de agua** [cisterna] water tank; [embalse] reservoir; ~ **de gasolina** petrol tank *UK*, gas tank *US* - **3**. [de dinero] deposit.

depravado, da *adj* depraved.

depreciar *vt* to (cause to) depreciate.

◆ depreciarse *vpr* to depreciate.

depredador, ra ◇ *adj* predatory. ◇ *m,f* predator.

depresión *f* [gen] depression; ~ **nerviosa** nervous breakdown; ~ **posparto** postnatal depression.

depresivo, va ◇ *adj* PSICOL depressive; [deprimente] depressing. ◇ *m,f* depressive.

deprimir *vt* to depress.

◆ deprimirse *vpr* to get depressed.

deprisa, de prisa *adv* fast, quickly; ¡~! quick!

depuración *f* - **1**. [de agua, metal, gas] purification - **2**. *fig* [de organismo, sociedad] purge.

depurar *vt* - **1**. [agua, metal, gas] to purify - **2**. *fig* [organismo, sociedad] to purge.

derecha ▷ **derecho.**

derecho, cha ◇ *adj* - **1**. [diestro] right; **el margen** ~ the right-hand margin - **2**. [vertical] upright; **siempre anda muy derecha** she always walks with a very upright posture - **3**. [recto] straight. ◇ *adv* - **1**. [en posición vertical] upright - **2**. [en línea recta] straight; **todo** ~ straight ahead; **siga todo** ~ **y llegará al museo** continue straight ahead and you'll come to the museum - **3**. [directamente] straight; **se fue derecha a casa** she went straight home.

◆ derecho *m* - **1**. [leyes, estudio] law; **un estudiante de** ~ a law student; ~ **civil/penal** civil/criminal law - **2**. [prerrogativa] right; **con** ~ **a** with a right to; **de pleno** ~ fully-fledged; **el** ~ **al voto** the right to vote; **hacer valer sus** ~**s** to exercise one's rights; **¡no hay** ~ **!** it's not fair!; **reservado el** ~ **de admisión** the management reserves the right of admission; ~ **de asilo** right of asylum; ~ **de réplica** right to reply; ~**s civiles/humanos** civil/human rights - **3**. [de una tela, prenda] right side; **del** ~ right side out.

◆ derecha *f* - **1**. [contrario de izquierda] right, right-hand side; **a la derecha** to the right; **girar a la derecha** to turn right - **2**. POLÍT right (wing); **ser de derechas** to be rightwing.

◆ derechos *mpl* [tasas] duties, taxes; [profesionales] fees; ~**s de aduana** customs duty *(U)*; ~**s de inscripción** membership fee *(sg)*; ~**s de autor** [potestad] copyright *(U)*; [dinero] royalties.

deriva *f* drift; **a la** ~ adrift; **ir a la** ~ to drift.

derivado, da *adj* GRAM derived.

◆ derivado *m* - **1**. [producto] by-product; ~**s lácteos** dairy products - **2**. QUÍM derivative.

derivar ◇ *vt* - **1**. [desviar] to divert - **2**. MAT to derive. ◇ *vi* [desviarse] to change direction, to drift.

◆ derivar de *vi* - **1**. [proceder] to derive from - **2**. GRAM to be derived from.

◆ derivar en *vi* to result in, to lead to.

derogación *f* repeal.

derramamiento *m* spilling; ~ **de sangre** bloodshed.

derramar *vt* [por accidente] to spill; [verter] to pour; ~ **lágrimas/sangre** to shed tears/blood.

derrame *m* - **1**. MED discharge - **2**. [de líquido] spilling; [de sangre] shedding.

derrapar *vi* to skid.

derretir *vt* [gen] to melt; [nieve] to thaw.

◆ derretirse *vpr* [metal, mantequilla] to melt; [hielo, nieve] to thaw.

derribar *vt* - **1**. [construcción] to knock down, to demolish - **2**. [hacer caer - árbol] to fell; [- avión] to bring down - **3**. [gobierno, gobernante] to overthrow.

derribo *m* [material] rubble.

derrocar *vt* [gobierno] to bring down, to overthrow; [ministro] to oust.

derrochar *vt* [malgastar] to squander.

derroche *m* [malgaste] waste, squandering.

derrota *f* [fracaso] defeat.

derrotar *vt* to defeat.

derrotero *m* [camino] direction; **tomar diferentes** ~**s** to follow a different course.

derrotista *adj & mf* defeatist.

derruir *vt* to demolish, to knock down.

derrumbamiento *m* - **1**. [de puente, edificio - por accidente] collapse; [- intencionado] demolition - **2**. *fig* [de imperio] fall; [de empresa etc] collapse.

derrumbar *vt* [puente, edificio] to demolish.

◆ derrumbarse *vpr* [puente, edificio] to collapse; [techo] to fall o cave in.

desabotonar *vt* to unbutton.

◆ desabotonarse *vpr* [suj: persona] to undo one's buttons; [suj: ropa] to come undone.

desabrochar *vt* to undo.

◆ desabrocharse *vpr* [suj: persona] to undo one's buttons; [suj: ropa] to come undone.

desacato *m* **-1.** [gen]: ~ **(a)** lack of respect (for), disrespect (for) **-2.** DER contempt of court.

desacierto *m* [error] error.

desaconsejar *vt*: ~ **algo (a alguien)** to advise (sb) against sthg; ~ **a alguien que haga algo** to advise sb not to do sthg.

desacreditar *vt* to discredit.

desactivar *vt* to defuse.

desacuerdo *m* disagreement.

desafiante *adj* defiant.

desafiar *vt* **-1.** [persona] to challenge; ~ **a alguien a algo/a que haga algo** to challenge sb to sthg/to do sthg **-2.** [peligro] to defy.

desafinar *vi* MÚS to be out of tune.

desafío *m* challenge.

desaforado, da *adj* **-1.** [excesivo - apetito] uncontrolled **-2.** [furioso - grito] furious, wild.

desafortunadamente *adv* unfortunately.

desafortunado, da *adj* **-1.** [gen] unfortunate **-2.** [sin suerte] unlucky.

desagradable *adj* unpleasant.

desagradar *vi* to displease; **su actitud le desagradó** he was displeased at her attitude.

desagradecido, da *m,f* ungrateful person.

desagrado *m* displeasure; **con ~** reluctantly.

desagraviar *vt*: ~ **a alguien por algo** [por una ofensa] to make amends to sb for sthg; [por un perjuicio] to compensate sb for sthg.

desagüe *m* [vaciado] drain; [cañería] drainpipe.

desaguisado *m* [destrozo] damage (U).

desahogado, da *adj* **-1.** [de espacio] spacious, roomy **-2.** [de dinero] well-off, comfortable.

desahogar *vt* [ira] to vent; [pena] to relieve, to ease.

◆ **desahogarse** *vpr* **-1.** [contar penas]: ~**se con alguien** to pour out one's woes *o* to tell one's troubles to sb **-2.** [desfogarse] to let off steam.

desahogo *m* **-1.** [moral] relief, release **-2.** [de espacio] space, room **-3.** [económico] ease.

desahuciar *vt* **-1.** [inquilino] to evict **-2.** [enfermo]: ~ **a alguien** to give up all hope of saving sb.

desahucio *m* eviction.

desaire *m* snub, slight; **hacer un ~ a alguien** to snub sb; **sufrir un ~** to receive a rebuff.

desajuste *m* **-1.** [de piezas] misalignment; [de máquina] breakdown **-2.** [de declaraciones] inconsistency; [económico etc] imbalance.

desalentar *vt* to discourage.

desaliento *m* dismay, dejection.

desaliñado, da *adj* scruffy.

desaliño *m* scruffiness.

desalmado, da *adj* heartless.

desalojar *vt* **-1.** [por una emergencia - edificio, personas] to evacuate **-2.** [por la fuerza - suj: policía, ejército] to clear; [- inquilinos etc] to evict **-3.** [por propia voluntad] to abandon, to move out of.

desamor *m* [falta de afecto] indifference, coldness; [odio] dislike.

desamparado, da *adj* [niño] helpless; [lugar] desolate, forsaken.

desamparar *vt* to abandon.

desamparo *m* [abandono] abandonment; [aflicción] helplessness.

desangrar *vt* **-1.** [animal, persona] to bleed **-2.** *fig* [económicamente] to bleed dry.

◆ **desangrarse** *vpr* to lose a lot of blood.

desanimado, da *adj* [persona] downhearted.

desanimar *vt* to discourage.

◆ **desanimarse** *vpr* to get downhearted *o* discouraged.

desánimo *m* [gen] dejection; [depresión] depression.

desapacible *adj* unpleasant.

desaparecer *vi* **-1.** [gen] to disappear **-2.** [en guerra, accidente] to go missing.

desaparecido, da *m,f* missing person.

desaparición *f* disappearance.

desapego *m* indifference.

desapercibido, da *adj*: **pasar ~** to go unnoticed.

desaprensivo, va *m,f* unscrupulous person.

desaprobar *vt* [gen] to disapprove of; [un plan etc] to reject.

desaprovechar *vt* to waste.

desarmador *m* *Méx* screwdriver.

desarmar *vt* **-1.** [gen] to disarm **-2.** [desmontar] to take apart, to dismantle.

desarme *m* MIL disarmament.

desarraigar *vt* **-1.** [vicio, costumbre] to root out **-2.** [persona, pueblo] to banish, to drive (out).

desarraigo *m* [de árbol] uprooting; [de vicio, costumbre] rooting out; [de persona, pueblo] banishment.

desarreglar *vt* [armario, pelo] to mess up; [planes, horario] to upset.

desarreglo *m* [de cuarto, persona] untidiness; [de vida] disorder.

desarrollado, da *adj* developed.

desarrollar *vt* **-1.** [mejorar - crecimiento, país] to develop **-2.** [exponer - teoría, tema, fórmula] to expound, to explain

- **3.** [realizar - actividad, trabajo] to carry out.
◆ **desarrollarse** *vpr* - **1.** [crecer, mejorar] to develop - **2.** [suceder - reunión] to take place; [- película] to be set.
desarrollo *m* - **1.** [mejora] development; países en vías de ~ developing countries - **2.** [crecimiento] growth, development - **3.** [de idea, argumento, acontecimiento] development.
desarticular *vt* - **1.** [huesos] to dislocate - **2.** *fig* [organización, banda] to break up; [plan] to foil.
desasosegar *vt* to make uneasy.
desasosiego *m* - **1.** [mal presentimiento] unease - **2.** [nerviosismo] restlessness.
desastrado, da *adj* [desaseado] scruffy; [sucio] dirty.
desastre *m* disaster; su madre es un ~ her mother is hopeless.
desastroso, sa *adj* disastrous.
desatar *vt* - **1.** [nudo, lazo] to untie; [paquete] to undo; [animal] to unleash - **2.** *fig* [tormenta, iras, pasión] to unleash; [entusiasmo] to arouse; [lengua] to loosen.
◆ **desatarse** *vpr* - **1.** [nudo, lazo] to come undone - **2.** *fig* [desencadenarse - tormenta] to break; [- ira, cólera] to erupt.
desatascar *vt* to unblock.
desatender *vt* - **1.** [obligación, persona] to neglect - **2.** [ruegos, consejos] to ignore.
desatino *m* - **1.** [locura] foolishness - **2.** [desacierto] foolish act.
desautorizar *vt* - **1.** [desmentir - noticia] to deny - **2.** [prohibir - manifestación, huelga] to ban - **3.** [desacreditar] to discredit.
desavenencia *f* [desacuerdo] friction, tension; [riña] quarrel.
desavenirse *vpr* to fall out.
desayunar ◇ *vi* to have breakfast. ◇ *vt* to have for breakfast.
desayuno *m* breakfast; ~ continental continental breakfast; ~ de trabajo working breakfast.
desazón *f* unease, anxiety.
desbancar *vt* *fig* [ocupar el puesto de] to oust, to replace.
desbandada *f* breaking up, scattering; a la ~ in great disorder.
desbarajuste *m* disorder, confusion.
desbaratar *vt* to ruin, to wreck.
desbloquear *vt* [cuenta] to unfreeze; [país] to lift the blockade on; [negociación] to end the deadlock in.
desbocado, da *adj* [caballo] runaway.
desbocarse *vpr* [caballo] to bolt.
desbolado, da *RP fam* ◇ *adj* messy, untidy. ◇ *m,f* untidy person.
desbole *m* *RP fam* mess, chaos.
desbordar *vt* - **1.** [cauce, ribera] to overflow,

to burst - **2.** [límites, previsiones] to exceed; [paciencia] to push beyond the limit.
◆ **desbordarse** *vpr* - **1.** [líquido]: ~se (de) to overflow (from) - **2.** [río] to overflow - **3.** *fig* [sentimiento] to erupt.
descabalgar *vi* to dismount.
descabellado, da *adj* crazy.
descafeinado, da *adj* [sin cafeína] decaffeinated.
◆ **descafeinado** *m* decaffeinated coffee.
descalabro *m* setback, damage *(U)*.
descalificar *vt* - **1.** [en una competición] to disqualify - **2.** [desprestigiar] to discredit.
descalzar *vt* : ~ a alguien to take sb's shoes off.
◆ **descalzarse** *vpr* to take off one's shoes.
descalzo, za *adj* barefoot.
descaminado, da *adj* *fig* [equivocado]: andar *o* ir ~ to be on the wrong track.
descampado *m* open country.
descansar ◇ *vi* - **1.** [reposar] to rest - **2.** [dormir] to sleep; ¡que descanses! sleep well! ◇ *vt* - **1.** to rest; ~ la vista to rest one's eyes; descansa la cabeza en mi hombro rest your head on my shoulder - **2.** [dormir] to sleep.
descansillo *m* landing.
descanso *m* - **1.** [reposo] rest; tomarse un ~ to take a rest; día de ~ day off - **2.** [pausa] break; CIN & TEATR interval; DEP half-time, interval - **3.** *fig* [alivio] relief.
descapotable *adj* & *m* convertible.
descarado, da *adj* - **1.** [desvergonzado - persona] cheeky, impertinent - **2.** [flagrante - intento etc] barefaced, blatant.
descarga *f* - **1.** [de mercancías] unloading - **2.** [de electricidad] shock - **3.** [disparo] firing, shots *(pl)*.
descargar *vt* - **1.** [vaciar - mercancías, pistola] to unload - **2.** [disparar - munición, arma, ráfaga]: ~ (sobre) to fire (at) - **3.** ELECTR to run down.
◆ **descargarse** *vpr* - **1.** [desahogarse]: ~se con alguien to take it out on sb - **2.** ELECTR to go flat.
descargo *m* - **1.** [excusa]: ~ a argument against - **2.** DER defence - **3.** [COM - de deuda] discharge; [- recibo] receipt.
descarnado, da *adj* - **1.** [descripción] brutal - **2.** [persona, animal] scrawny.
descaro *m* cheek, impertinence.
descarriarse *vpr* - **1.** [ovejas, ganado] to stray - **2.** *fig* [pervertirse] to go astray.
descarrilamiento *m* derailment.
descarrilar *vi* to be derailed.
descartar *vt* [ayuda] to refuse, to reject; [posibilidad] to rule out.
descendencia *f* - **1.** [hijos] offspring - **2.** [linaje] lineage, descent.

descender vi -1. [en estimación] to go down; ~ a segunda to be relegated to the second division - 2. [cantidad, valor, temperatura, nivel] to fall, to drop.
◆ **descender de** vi -1. [avión] to get off - 2. [linaje] to be descended from.

descenso m -1. [en el espacio] descent - 2. [de cantidad, valor, temperatura, nivel] drop.

descentralizar vt to decentralize.

descentrar vt -1. [sacar del centro] to knock off-centre - 2. fig [desconcentrar] to distract.

descifrar vt -1. [clave, mensaje] to decipher - 2. [motivos, intenciones] to work out; [misterio] to solve; [problemas] to puzzle out.

descodificador, decodificador m decoder.

descolgar vt -1. [una cosa colgada] to take down - 2. [teléfono] to pick up, to take off the hook.
◆ **descolgarse** vpr [bajar]: ~se (por algo) to let oneself down o to slide down (sthg).

descolocar vt [objeto] to put out of place, to disturb.

descolorido, da adj faded.

descompasado, da adj excessive, uncontrollable.

descomponer vt -1. [pudrir - fruta] to rot; [- cadáver] to decompose - 2. [dividir] to break down; ~ algo en to break sthg down into - 3. [desordenar] to mess up - 4. [estropear] to damage, to break.
◆ **descomponerse** vpr -1. [pudrirse - fruta] to rot; [- cadáver] to decompose - 2. [averiarse] to break down.

descomposición f -1. [de elementos] decomposition - 2. [putrefacción - de fruta] rotting; [- de cadáver] decomposition - 3. [alteración] distortion - 4. [diarrea] diarrhoea.

descompostura f -1. [falta de mesura] lack of respect, rudeness - 2. Méx, RP [avería] breakdown - 3. Amér [malestar] an unpleasant o nasty turn.

descompuesto, ta ◇ pp ▷ descomponer. ◇ adj -1. [putrefacto - fruta] rotten; [- cadáver] decomposed - 2. [alterado - rostro] distorted, twisted.

descomunal adj enormous.

desconcentrar vt to distract.

desconcertante adj disconcerting.

desconcertar vt to disconcert, to throw.
◆ **desconcertarse** vpr to be thrown o bewildered.

desconchado m [de pintura] peeling paint; [de enyesado] peeling plaster.

desconcierto m [desorden] disorder; [desorientación, confusión] confusion.

desconectar vt [aparato] to switch off; [línea] to disconnect; [desenchufar] to unplug.

desconfianza f distrust.

desconfiar ◆ **desconfiar de** vi -1. [sospechar de] to distrust - 2. [no confiar en] to have no faith in.

descongelar vt -1. [producto] to thaw; [nevera] to defrost - 2. fig [precios] to free; [créditos, salarios] to unfreeze.

descongestionar vt -1. MED to clear - 2. fig [calle, centro de ciudad] to make less congested; ~ el tráfico to reduce congestion.

desconocer vt [ignorar] not to know.

desconocido, da ◇ adj [no conocido] unknown. ◇ m,f stranger.

desconocimiento m ignorance, lack of knowledge.

desconsiderado, da adj thoughtless, inconsiderate.

desconsolar vt to distress.

desconsuelo m distress, grief.

descontado, da adj discounted.
◆ **por descontado** loc adv obviously, needless to say; dar algo por ~ to take sthg for granted.

descontar vt -1. [una cantidad] to deduct - 2. COM to discount.

descontentar vt to upset, to make unhappy.

descontento, ta adj unhappy, dissatisfied.
◆ **descontento** m dissatisfaction.

desconvocar vt to cancel, to call off.

descorazonador, ra adj discouraging.

descorazonar vt to discourage.

descorchar vt to uncork.

descorrer vt -1. [cortinas] to draw back, to open - 2. [cerrojo, pestillo] to draw back.

descortés adj rude.

descoser vt to unstitch.
◆ **descoserse** vpr to come unstitched.

descosido, da adj unstitched.

descoyuntar vt to dislocate.

descrédito m discredit; ir en ~ de algo/alguien to count against sthg/sb.

descreído, da m,f disbeliever.

descremado, da adj skimmed.

describir vt to describe.

descripción f description.

descrito, ta pp ▷ describir.

descuartizar vt [persona] to quarter; [res] to carve up.

descubierto, ta ◇ pp ▷ descubrir. ◇ adj -1. [gen] uncovered; [coche] open - 2. [cielo] clear - 3. [sin sombrero] bareheaded.
◆ **descubierto** m [FIN - de empresa] deficit; [- de cuenta bancaria] overdraft.
◆ **al descubierto** loc adv -1. [al raso] in the open - 2. BANCA overdrawn.

descubrimiento *m* - **1.** [de continentes, invenciones] discovery - **2.** [de placa, busto] unveiling - **3.** [de complots] uncovering; [de asesinos] detection.

descubrir *vt* - **1.** [gen] to discover; [petróleo] to strike; [complot] to uncover - **2.** [destapar - estatua, placa] to unveil - **3.** [vislumbrar] to spot, to spy - **4.** [delatar] to give away.

◆ **descubrirse** *vpr* [quitarse el sombrero] to take one's hat off; ~**se ante algo** *fig* to take one's hat off to sthg.

descuento *m* discount; **hacer** ~ to give a discount; **con** ~ at a discount; **un** ~ **del 10%** 10% off.

descuidado, da *adj* - **1.** [desaseado, - persona, aspecto] untidy; [- jardín] neglected - **2.** [negligente] careless - **3.** [distraído] off one's guard.

descuidar ◇ *vt* [desatender] to neglect. ◇ *vi* [no preocuparse] not to worry; **descuida, que yo me encargo** don't worry, I'll take care of it.

◆ **descuidarse** *vpr* - **1.** [abandonarse] to neglect one's appearance - **2.** [despistarse] not to be careful.

descuido *m* - **1.** [falta de aseo] carelessness - **2.** [olvido] oversight; [error] slip; **en un** ~ by mistake.

desde *prep* - **1.** [tiempo] since; **no lo veo** ~ **el mes pasado/** ~ **ayer** I haven't seen him since last month/yesterday; ~ **ahora** from now on; ~ **hace mucho/un mes** for ages/a month; ~ **... hasta ...** from ... until ...; ~ **el lunes hasta el viernes** from Monday till Friday; ~ **entonces** since then; ~ **que** since; ~ **que murió mi madre** since my mother died - **2.** [espacio] from; ~ **... hasta ...** from ... to ...; ~ **aquí hasta el centro** from here to the centre.

◆ **desde luego** *loc adv* - **1.** [por supuesto] of course - **2.** [en tono de reproche] for goodness' sake!

desdecir ◆ **desdecirse** *vpr* to go back on one's word; ~**se de** to go back on.

desdén *m* disdain, scorn.

desdeñar *vt* to scorn.

desdeñoso, sa *adj* disdainful.

desdibujarse *vpr* to become blurred.

desdicha *f* [desgracia - situación] misery; [- suceso] misfortune; **por** ~ unfortunately.

desdichado, da *adj* [decisión, situación] unfortunate; [persona - sin suerte] unlucky; [- sin felicidad] unhappy.

desdicho, cha *pp* ▷ **desdecir**.

desdoblar *vt* [servilleta, carta] to unfold; [alambre] to straighten out.

desear *vt* - **1.** [querer] to want; [anhelar] to wish; **¿qué desea?** [en tienda] what can I do for you?; ~**ía estar allí** I wish I was there - **2.** [sexualmente] to desire.

desecar *vt* to dry out.

◆ **desecarse** *vpr* to dry out.

desechable *adj* disposable.

desechar *vt* - **1.** [tirar - ropa, piezas] to throw out, to discard - **2.** [rechazar - ayuda, oferta] to refuse, to turn down - **3.** [desestimar - idea] to reject; [- plan, proyecto] to drop.

desecho *m* [objeto usado] unwanted object; [ropa] castoff; **material de** ~ [gen] waste products *(pl)*; [metal] scrap.

◆ **desechos** *mpl* [basura] rubbish *(U)*; [residuos] waste products; ~**s radiactivos** radioactive waste *(U)*.

desembalar *vt* to unpack.

desembarazar *vt* to clear.

◆ **desembarazarse** *vpr*: ~**se de** to get rid of.

desembarcar ◇ *vt* [pasajeros] to disembark; [mercancías] to unload. ◇ *vi* - **1.** [de barco, avión] to disembark - **2.** *Amér* [de autobús, tren] to get off.

◆ **desembarcarse** *vpr Amér* to get off.

desembarco *m* - **1.** [de pasajeros] disembarkation - **2.** MIL landing.

desembarque *m* [de mercancías] unloading.

desembocadura *f* [de río] mouth; [de calle] opening.

desembocar ◆ **desembocar en** *vi* - **1.** [río] to flow into - **2.** [asunto] to result in.

desembolso *m* payment; ~ **inicial** down payment.

desempaquetar *vt* [paquete] to unwrap; [caja] to unpack.

desempatar *vi* to decide the contest; **jugar para** ~ to have a play-off.

desempate *m* final result; **partido de** ~ decider.

desempeñar *vt* - **1.** [función, misión] to carry out; [cargo, puesto] to hold - **2.** [papel] to play - **3.** [joyas] to redeem.

desempeño *m* - **1.** [de función] carrying out - **2.** [de papel] performance - **3.** [de objeto] redemption.

desempleado, da *adj* unemployed.

desempleo *m* - **1.** [falta de empleo] unemployment - **2.** [subsidio] unemployment benefit; **cobrar el** ~ to receive unemployment benefit.

desempolvar *vt* - **1.** [mueble, jarrón] to dust - **2.** *fig* [recuerdos] to revive.

desencadenar *vt* - **1.** [preso, perro] to unchain - **2.** *fig* [suceso, polémica] to give rise to, to spark off; [pasión, furia] to unleash.

◆ **desencadenarse** *vpr* - **1.** [pasiones, odios, conflicto] to erupt; [guerra] to break out - **2.** [viento] to blow up; [tormenta] to burst; [terremoto] to strike.

desencajar *vt* - **1.** [mecanismo, piezas - sin

querer] to knock out of place; [- intenciona-
damente] to take apart - **2.** [hueso] to dislocate.

◆ **desencajarse** *vpr* - **1.** [piezas] to come
apart - **2.** [rostro] to distort, to become
distorted.

desencanto *m* disappointment.

desenchufar *vt* to unplug.

desenfadado, da *adj* [persona, conducta]
relaxed, easy-going; [comedia, programa de
TV] light-hearted; [estilo] light; [en el vestir]
casual.

desenfado *m* [seguridad en sí mismo] self-
assurance; [desenvoltura] ease; [desparpajo]
forwardness, uninhibited nature.

desenfocado, da *adj* [imagen] out of
focus; [visión] blurred.

desenfrenado, da *adj* [ritmo, baile] frantic, frenzied; [comportamiento] uncontrolled; [apetito] insatiable.

desenfreno *m* - **1.** [gen] lack of restraint
- **2.** [vicio] debauchery.

desenfundar *vt* [pistola] to draw.

desenganchar *vt* - **1.** [vagón] to uncouple
- **2.** [caballo] to unhitch - **3.** [pelo, jersey] to
free.

desengañar *vt* - **1.** [a persona equivocada]:
~ **a alguien** to reveal the truth to sb - **2.** [a
persona esperanzada] to disillusion.

desengaño *m* disappointment; **llevarse
un ~ con alguien** to be disappointed in
sb.

desenlace *m* denouement, ending.

desenmarañar *vt* - **1.** [ovillo, pelo] to untangle - **2.** *fig* [asunto] to sort out; [problema]
to resolve.

desenmascarar *vt* [descubrir] to unmask.

desenredar *vt* - **1.** [hilos, pelo] to untangle
- **2.** *fig* [asunto] to sort out; [problema] to resolve.

◆ **desenredarse** *vpr*: ~**se (de algo)** to
extricate oneself (from sthg).

desenrollar *vt* [hilo, cinta] to unwind; [per-
siana] to roll down; [pergamino, papel] to
unroll.

desenroscar *vt* to unscrew.

desentenderse *vpr* to pretend not to hear/
know *etc.*

desenterrar *vt* [cadáver] to disinter; [tesoro,
escultura] to dig up.

desentonar *vi* - **1.** [MÚS - cantante] to sing
out of tune; [- instrumento] to be out of tune
- **2.** [color, cortinas, edificio]: ~ **(con)** to clash
(with).

desentumecer *vt* to stretch.

◆ **desentumecerse** *vpr* to loosen up.

desenvoltura *f* [al moverse, comportarse]
ease; [al hablar] fluency.

desenvolver *vt* to unwrap.

◆ **desenvolverse** *vpr* - **1.** [asunto, proce-
so] to progress; [trama] to unfold - **2.** [perso-
na] to cope, to manage.

desenvuelto, ta ◇ *pp* ▷ desenvolver.
◇ *adj* [al moverse, comportarse] natural;
[al hablar] fluent.

deseo *m* - **1.** [anhelo] wish, desire; **su ~ se
hizo realidad** her wish came true; **buenos
~s** good intentions; **pedir un ~** to make a
wish - **2.** [apetito sexual] desire.

deseoso, sa *adj*: **estar ~ de algo/hacer algo** to long for sthg/to do sthg.

desequilibrado, da *adj* - **1.** [persona] unbalanced - **2.** [balanza, eje] off-centre.

desequilibrio *m* [mecánico] lack of balance; [mental] mental instability.

desertar *vi* to desert.

desértico, ca *adj* [del desierto] desert *(antes
de sust)*; [despoblado] deserted.

desertización *f* [del terreno] desertifica-
tion; [de la población] depopulation.

desertor, ra *m, f* deserter.

desesperación *f* [falta de esperanza] despair, desperation; **con ~** in despair.

desesperado, da *adj* [persona, intento]
desperate; [estado, situación] hopeless; [es-
fuerzo] furious.

desesperante *adj* infuriating.

desesperar ◇ *vt* to exasperate, to drive
mad. ◇ *vi* to despair, to give up *o* lose
hope.

◆ **desesperarse** *vpr* - **1.** [perder la espe-
ranza] to be driven to despair - **2.** [irritarse,
enojarse] to get mad *o* exasperated.

desestabilizar *vt* to destabilize.

desestatización *f* Amér privatization.

desestatizar *vt* Amér to privatize, to sell
off.

desestimar *vt* - **1.** [rechazar] to turn down
- **2.** [despreciar] to turn one's nose up at.

desfachatez *f* fam cheek.

desfalco *m* embezzlement.

desfallecer *vi* - **1.** [debilitarse] to be exhausted; ~ **de** to feel faint from - **2.** [desma-
yarse] to faint.

desfasado, da *adj* [persona] out of touch;
[libro, moda] out of date.

desfase *m* [diferencia] gap; ~ **horario** jet
lag.

desfavorable *adj* unfavourable.

desfigurar *vt* - **1.** [rostro, cuerpo] to disfig-
ure- **2.** *fig* [la verdad] to distort.

desfiladero *m* narrow mountain pass.

desfilar *vi* MIL to parade.

desfile *m* MIL parade; [de carrozas] procession.

desfogar *vt* to vent.

◆ **desfogarse** *vpr* to let off steam.

desgajar *vt* [página] to tear out; [rama] to

break off; [libro, periódico] to **rip up**; [naranja] to **split into segments**.

◆ **desgajarse** *vpr* [rama] to break off; [hoja] to fall.

desgana *f* - **1.** [falta de hambre] lack of appetite - **2.** [falta de ánimo] lack of enthusiasm; **con ~** unwillingly, reluctantly.

desganado, da *adj* [sin apetito]: **estar ~** to be off one's food.

desgarbado, da *adj* clumsy, ungainly.

desgarrador, ra *adj* harrowing.

desgarrar *vt* to rip; **~ el corazón** to break one's heart.

desgarro *m* tear.

desgastar *vt* to wear out.

◆ **desgastarse** *vpr* to wear o.s. out.

desgaste *m* - **1.** [de tela, muebles etc] wear and tear; [de roca] **erosion**; [de pilas] **running down**; [de cuerdas] **fraying**; [de metal] **corrosion** - **2.** [de persona] **wear and tear**; **~ político** erosion of voter confidence.

desglosar *vt* to break down.

desglose *m* breakdown.

desgracia *f* - **1.** [mala suerte] misfortune; **por ~** unfortunately; **tener la ~ de** to be unfortunate enough to - **2.** [catástrofe] disaster; **~s personales** casualties; **es una ~ que ...** it's a terrible shame that ... - **3.** *loc:* **caer en ~** to fall into disgrace; **las ~s nunca vienen solas** it never rains but it pours.

desgraciado, da *adj* - **1.** [gen] unfortunate - **2.** [sin suerte] unlucky - **3.** [infeliz] unhappy.

desgravar *vt* to deduct from one's tax bill.

desgreñado, da *adj* dishevelled.

desguace *m* [de coches] scrapping; [de buques] breaking.

deshabitado, da *adj* uninhabited.

deshabituar *vt* : **~ a alguien (de)** to get sb out of the habit (of).

deshacer *vt* - **1.** [costura, nudo, paquete] to undo; [maleta] to unpack; [castillo de arena] to destroy - **2.** [disolver - helado, mantequilla] to melt; [- pastilla, terrón de azúcar] to dissolve - **3.** [poner fin a - contrato, negocio] to cancel; [- pacto, tratado] to break; [- plan, intriga] to foil; [- organización] to dissolve - **4.** [destruir - enemigo] to rout; [- matrimonio] to ruin.

◆ **deshacerse** *vpr* - **1.** [desvanecerse] to disappear - **2.** *fig* [librarse]: **~se de** to get rid of - **3.** *fig:* **~se en algo (con** *o* **hacia alguien)** [cumplidos] to lavish sthg (on sb); [insultos] to heap sthg (on sb).

desharrapado, da *adj* ragged.

deshecho, cha *⬦ pp* ▷ **deshacer**. *⬦ adj* - **1.** [costura, nudo, paquete] undone; [cama] unmade; [maleta] unpacked - **2.** [enemigo] destroyed; [tarta, matrimonio] ruined

- **3.** [derretido - pastilla, terrón de azúcar] dissolved; [- helado, mantequilla] melted - **4.** [afligido] devastated - **5.** [cansado] tired out.

desheredar *vt* to disinherit.

deshidratar *vt* to dehydrate.

deshielo *m* thaw.

deshilachar *vt* to unravel.

◆ **deshilacharse** *vpr* to fray.

deshinchar *vt* - **1.** [globo, rueda] to let down, to deflate - **2.** [hinchazón] to reduce the swelling in.

◆ **deshincharse** *vpr* [globo, hinchazón] to go down; [neumático] to go flat.

deshojar *vt* [árbol] to strip the leaves off; [flor] to pull the petals off; [libro] to pull the pages out of.

◆ **deshojarse** *vpr* [árbol] to shed its leaves; [flor] to drop its petals.

deshonesto, ta *adj* [sin honradez] dishonest; [sin pudor] indecent.

deshonor *m*, **deshonra** *f* dishonour.

deshonrar *vt* to dishonour.

deshora ◆ a deshora, a deshoras *loc adv* [en momento inoportuno] at a bad time; [en horas poco habituales] at an unearthly hour.

deshuesar *vt* [carne] to bone; [fruto] to stone.

desidia *f* [en el trabajo] neglect; [en el aspecto] slovenliness.

desierto, ta *adj* - **1.** [gen] deserted - **2.** [vacante] void; [- premio] deferred.

◆ **desierto** *m* desert.

designar *vt* - **1.** [nombrar] to appoint - **2.** [fijar, determinar] to name, to fix.

designio *m* intention, plan.

desigual *adj* - **1.** [diferente] different; [terreno] uneven - **2.** [tiempo, persona, humor] changeable; [alumno, actuación] inconsistent; [lucha] unevenly matched, unequal; [tratamiento] unfair, unequal.

desilusión *f* disappointment, disillusionment *(U)*; **llevarse una ~** to be disappointed.

desilusionar *vt* [desengañar] to reveal the truth to; [decepcionar] to disappoint, to disillusion.

◆ **desilusionarse** *vpr* [decepcionarse] to be disappointed *o* disillusioned; [desengañarse] to realize the truth.

desinfección *f* disinfection.

desinfectar *vt* to disinfect.

desinflar *vt* [quitar aire a] to deflate.

◆ **desinflarse** *vpr* [perder aire - gen] to go down; [- neumático] to go flat.

desintegración *f* - **1.** [de objetos] disintegration - **2.** [de grupos, organizaciones] breaking up.

desintegrar *vt* - **1.** [objetos] to disintegrate; [átomo] to split - **2.** [grupos, organizaciones] to break up.

desinterés *m* - **1.** [indiferencia] disinterest, lack of interest - **2.** [generosidad] unselfishness.

desinteresado, da *adj* unselfish.

desinteresarse *vpr*: ~ **de** *o* **por algo** to lose interest in sthg.

desistir *vi*: ~ **(de hacer algo)** to give up *o* to stop (doing sthg).

deslave *m Amér* landslide, landslip *UK*.

desleal *adj* [competencia] unfair; ~ **(con)** disloyal (to).

deslealtad *f* disloyalty.

desleír *vt* [sólido] to dissolve; [líquido] to dilute.

desligar - **1.** [desatar] to untie - **2.** *fig* [separar]: ~ **algo (de)** to separate sthg (from).
➡ **desligarse** *vpr* - **1.** [desatarse] to untie oneself - **2.** *fig* [separarse]: ~**se de** to become separated from; ~**se de un grupo** to distance o.s. from a group.

deslindar *vt* - **1.** [limitar] to mark out (the boundaries of) - **2.** *fig* [separar] to define.

desliz *m* slip, error; **tener** *o* **cometer un** ~ to slip up.

deslizar *vt* [mano, objeto]: ~ **algo en** to slip sthg into; ~ **algo por algo** to slide sthg along sthg.
➡ **deslizarse** *vpr* [resbalar]: ~**se por** to slide along.

deslomar *vt* [a golpes] to thrash.

deslucido, da *adj* - **1.** [sin brillo] faded; [plata] tarnished - **2.** [sin gracia - acto, ceremonia] dull; [- actuación] lacklustre, uninspired.

deslumbrar *vt lit* & *fig* to dazzle.

desmadrarse *vpr fam* to go wild.

desmadre *m fam* chaos, utter confusion.

desmán *m* - **1.** [con la bebida, comida etc] excess - **2.** [abuso de poder] abuse (of power).

desmandarse *vpr* - **1.** [desobedecer] to be disobedient - **2.** [insubordinarse] to get out of hand.

desmantelar *vt* [casa, fábrica] to clear out, to strip; [organización] to disband; [arsenal, andamio] to dismantle; [barco] to unrig.

desmaquillador *m* make-up remover.

desmayar *vi* to lose heart.
➡ **desmayarse** *vpr* to faint.

desmayo *m* [físico] fainting fit; **sufrir** ~**s** to have fainting fits.

desmedido, da *adj* excessive, disproportionate.

desmelenado, da *adj* - **1.** [persona] reckless, wild - **2.** [cabello] tousled, dishevelled.

desmembrar *vt* - **1.** [trocear - cuerpo] to dismember; [- miembro, extremidad] to cut off - **2.** [disgregar] to break up.

desmemoriado, da *adj* forgetful.

desmentir *vt* - **1.** [negar] to deny - **2.** [no corresponder] to belie.

desmenuzar *vt* - **1.** [trocear - pan, pastel, roca] to crumble; [- carne] to chop up; [- papel] to tear up into little pieces - **2.** *fig* [examinar, analizar] to scrutinize.

desmerecer ◇ *vt* to be unworthy of. ◇ *vi* to lose value; ~ **(en algo) de alguien** to be inferior to sb (in sthg).

desmesurado, da *adj* [excesivo] excessive, disproportionate; [enorme] enormous.

desmitificar *vt* to demythologize.

desmontar *vt* - **1.** [desarmar - máquina] to take apart *o* to pieces; [- motor] to strip down; [- piezas] to dismantle; [- rueda] to remove, to take off; [- tienda de campaña] to take down; [- arma] to uncock - **2.** [jinete - suj: caballo] to unseat; [- suj: persona] to help down.

desmoralizar *vt* to demoralize.

desmoronar *vt* [edificios, rocas] to cause to crumble.
➡ **desmoronarse** *vpr* [edificio, roca, ideales] to crumble.

desnatado, da *adj* skimmed.

desnaturalizado, da *adj* [sustancia] adulterated; [alcohol] denatured.

desnivel *m* [del terreno] irregularity, unevenness *(U)*.

desnivelar *vt* to make uneven; [balanza] to tip.

desnucar *vt* to break the neck of.

desnudar *vt* to undress.
➡ **desnudarse** *vpr* to undress, to get undressed.

desnudez *f* [de persona] nakedness, nudity; [de cosa] bareness.

desnudo, da *adj* - **1.** [persona, cuerpo] naked - **2.** *fig* [salón, hombro, árbol] bare; [verdad] plain; [paisaje] bare, barren.
➡ **desnudo** *m* nude.

desnutrición *f* malnutrition.

desobedecer *vt* to disobey.

desobediencia *f* disobedience; ~ **civil** civil disobedience.

desobediente *adj* disobedient.

desocupado, da *adj* - **1.** [persona - ocioso] free, unoccupied; [- sin empleo] unemployed - **2.** [lugar] vacant, unoccupied.

desocupar *vt* [edificio] to vacate; [habitación, mesa] to leave.

desodorante *m* deodorant.

desolación *f* - **1.** [destrucción] desolation - **2.** [desconsuelo] distress, grief.

desolar *vt* - **1.** [destruir] to devastate, to lay waste - **2.** [afligir] to cause anguish to.

desorbitado, da *adj* - **1.** [gen] disproportionate; [precio] exorbitant - **2.** *loc*: **con los ojos** ~**s** pop-eyed.

desorden *m* -1. [confusión] disorder, chaos; [falta de orden] mess; **en ~** topsy-turvy; **poner en ~** to upset, to disarrange - 2. [disturbio] disturbance.

desordenado, da *adj* [habitación, persona] untidy, messy; [documentos, fichas] jumbled (up).

desorganización *f* disorganization.

desorganizar *vt* to disrupt, to disorganize.

desorientar *vt* -1. [en el espacio] to disorientate, to mislead - 2. *fig* [aturdir] to confuse.

◆ **desorientarse** *vpr* -1. [en el espacio] to lose one's way *o* bearings - 2. *fig* [aturdirse] to get confused.

despabilado, da *adj* -1. [despierto] wide-awake - 2. [listo] smart, quick.

despabilar *vt* -1. [despertar] to wake up - 2. [hacer más avispado] to make streetwise.

◆ **despabilarse** *vpr* -1. [despertarse] to wake up - 2. [darse prisa] to hurry up.

despachar ◇ *vt* -1. [mercancía] to dispatch - 2. [en tienda - cliente] to serve; [- entradas, bebidas etc] to sell - 3. *fam fig* [terminar - trabajo, discurso] to finish off; [comida] to polish off - 4. [asunto, negocio] to settle - 5. *Amér* [equipaje] to check in. ◇ *vi* [en una tienda] to serve.

despacho *m* -1. [oficina] office; [en casa] study - 2. [comunicación oficial] dispatch - 3. [venta] sale; [lugar de venta]: **~ de billetes/localidades** ticket/box office.

despacio *adv* slowly.

desparpajo *m fam* forwardness, self-assurance.

desparramar *vt* [líquido] to spill; [objetos] to spread, to scatter.

despecho *m* [rencor, venganza] spite; [desengaño] bitterness; **(hacer algo) por ~** (to do sthg) out of spite.

despectivo, va *adj* -1. [despreciativo] scornful, contemptuous - 2. GRAM pejorative.

despedazar *vt* -1. [físicamente] to tear apart - 2. *fig* [moralmente] to shatter.

despedida *f* [adiós] goodbye, farewell.

despedir *vt* -1. [decir adiós a] to say goodbye to; **fuimos a ~ le a la estación** we went to see him off at the station - 2. [echar - de un empleo] to dismiss, to sack; [- de un club] to throw out - 3. [lanzar, arrojar] to fling; **salir despedido de por/hacia algo** to fly out of/through/towards sthg - 4. *fig* [difundir, desprender] to give off.

◆ **despedirse** *vpr*: **~ se (de)** to say goodbye (to).

despegar ◇ *vt* to unstick. ◇ *vi* [avión] to take off.

◆ **despegarse** *vpr* [etiqueta, pegatina,

sello] to come unstuck.

despegue *m* takeoff; **~ vertical** vertical takeoff.

despeinar *vt* [pelo] to ruffle; **~ a alguien** to mess up sb's hair.

◆ **despeinarse** *vpr* to mess up one's hair.

despejado, da *adj* -1. [tiempo, día] clear - 2. *fig* [persona, mente] alert - 3. [espacio - ancho] spacious; [- sin estorbos] clear, uncluttered.

despejar *vt* [gen] to clear.

◆ **despejarse** *vpr* -1. [persona - espabilarse] to clear one's head; [- despertarse] to wake o.s. up - 2. [tiempo] to clear up; [cielo] to clear.

despeje *m* DEP clearance.

despellejar *vt* [animal] to skin.

despensa *f* larder, pantry.

despeñadero *m* precipice.

despeñar *vt* to throw over a cliff.

◆ **despeñarse** *vpr* to fall over a cliff.

desperdiciar *vt* [tiempo, comida] to waste; [dinero] to squander; [ocasión] to throw away.

desperdicio *m* -1. [acción] waste - 2. [residuo]: **~ s** scraps.

desperdigar *vt* to scatter, to disperse.

desperezarse *vpr* to stretch.

desperfecto *m* [deterioro] damage (U); [defecto] flaw, imperfection.

despertador *m* alarm clock.

despertar ◇ *vt* -1. [persona, animal] to wake (up) - 2. *fig* [reacción] to arouse - 3. *fig* [recuerdo] to revive, to awaken. ◇ *vi* to wake up. ◇ *m* awakening.

◆ **despertarse** *vpr* to wake up.

despiadado, da *adj* pitiless, merciless.

despido *m* dismissal, sacking; **~ colectivo** collective dismissal.

despierto, ta *adj* -1. [sin dormir] awake - 2. *fig* [espabilado, listo] bright, sharp.

despilfarrar *vt* [dinero] to squander; [electricidad, agua etc] to waste.

despilfarro *m* [de dinero] squandering; [de energía, agua etc] waste.

despiole *m RP fam* rumpus, shindy.

despistado, da *adj* absent-minded.

despistar *vt* -1. [dar esquinazo a] to throw off the scent - 2. *fig* [confundir] to mislead.

◆ **despistarse** *vpr* -1. [perderse] to lose one's way, to get lost - 2. *fig* [distraerse] to get confused.

despiste *m* [distracción] absent-mindedness; [error] mistake, slip.

desplante *m* rude remark; **hacer un ~ a alguien** to snub sb.

desplazamiento *m* -1. [viaje] journey; [traslado] move - 2. NÁUT displacement.

desplazar *vt* -1. [trasladar] to move - 2. *fig*

[desbancar] to take the place of; ~ **a al-guien/algo de** to remove sb/sthg from.

➥ **desplazarse** *vpr* [viajar] to travel.

desplegar *vt* - **1.** [tela, periódico, mapa] to unfold; [alas] to spread, to open; [bandera] to unfurl - **2.** [cualidad] to display - **3.** MIL to deploy.

despliegue *m* - **1.** [de cualidad] display - **2.** MIL deployment.

desplomarse *vpr* [gen] to collapse; [techo] to fall in.

desplumar *vt* - **1.** [ave] to pluck - **2.** *fig* [estafar] to fleece.

despoblado, da *adj* unpopulated, deserted.

despojar *vt* : ~ **a alguien de algo** to strip sb of sthg.

➥ **despojarse** *vpr* : ~**se de algo** [bienes, alimentos] to give sthg up; [abrigo, chandal] to take sthg off.

despojo *m* [acción] plundering.

➥ **despojos** *mpl* - **1.** [sobras, residuos] leftovers - **2.** [de animales] offal *(U)*.

desposar *vt* to marry.

➥ **desposarse** *vpr* to get married, to marry.

desposeer *vt* : ~ **a alguien de** to dispossess sb of.

déspota *mf* despot.

despotricar *vi* : ~ **(contra)** to rant on (at).

despreciar *vt* - **1.** [desdeñar] to scorn - **2.** [rechazar] to spurn.

desprecio *m* scorn, contempt.

desprender *vt* - **1.** [lo que estaba fijo] to remove, to detach - **2.** [olor, luz] to give off.

➥ **desprenderse** *vpr* - **1.** [caerse, soltarse] to come *o* fall off - **2.** *fig* [deducirse]: **de sus palabras se desprende que ...** from his words it is clear *o* it can be seen that ... - **3.** [librarse]: ~**se de** to get rid of.

desprendimiento *m* [separación] detachment; ~ **de tierras** landslide.

despreocupado, da *adj* [libre de preocupaciones] unworried, unconcerned; [en el vestir] casual.

despreocuparse ➥ **despreocuparse de** *vpr* [asunto] to stop worrying about.

desprestigiar *vt* to discredit.

desprevenido, da *adj* unprepared; **coger** *o* **pillar** ~ **a alguien** to catch sb unawares, to take sb by surprise.

desprogramar *vt* to deprogramme.

desprolijo, ja *adj Amér* [casa, cuaderno] untidy; [persona] unkempt, dishevelled.

desproporcionado, da *adj* disproportionate.

despropósito *m* stupid remark, nonsense *(U)*.

desprovisto, ta *adj*: ~ **de** lacking in, devoid of.

después *adv* - **1.** [en el tiempo - más tarde] afterwards, later; [- entonces] then; [- justo lo siguiente] next; **poco** ~ soon after; **años** ~ years later; **ellos llegaron** ~ they arrived later; **llamé primero y** ~ **entré** I knocked first and then I went in; **yo voy** ~ it's my turn next - **2.** [en el espacio] next, after; **¿qué viene** ~? what comes next *o* after?; **hay una farmacia y** ~ **está mi casa** there's a chemist's and then there's my house - **3.** [en una lista] further down.

➥ **después de** *loc prep* after; **llegó** ~ **de ti** she arrived after you; ~ **de él, nadie lo ha conseguido** since he did it, no one else has; ~ **de hacer algo** after doing sthg.

➥ **después de todo** *loc adv* after all.

despuntar ◇ *vt* [romper] to break the point off; [desgastar] to blunt. ◇ *vi* - **1.** *fig* [persona] to excel, to stand out - **2.** [alba] to break; [día] to dawn.

desquiciar *vt fig* [desequilibrar] to derange, to disturb mentally; [sacar de quicio] to drive mad.

desquite *m* revenge.

destacamento *m* detachment; ~ **de tropas** task force.

destacar ◇ *vt* - **1.** [poner de relieve] to emphasize, to highlight; **cabe** ~ **que ...** it is important to point out that ... - **2.** MIL to detach, to detail. ◇ *vi* [sobresalir] to stand out.

➥ **destacarse** *vpr* : ~**se (de/por)** to stand out (from/because of).

destajo *m* piecework; **trabajar a** ~ [por trabajo hecho] to do piecework; *fig* [afanosamente] to work flat out.

destapador *m Amér* bottle opener.

destapar *vt* - **1.** [abrir - caja, botella] to open; [olla] to take the lid off; [descorchar] to uncork - **2.** [descubrir] to uncover - **3.** *RP* [desobstruir] to unblock.

➥ **destaparse** *vpr* [desabrigarse] to lose the covers.

destartalado, da *adj* [viejo, deteriorado] dilapidated; [desordenado] untidy.

destello *m* - **1.** [de luz, brillo] sparkle; [de estrella] twinkle - **2.** *fig* [manifestación momentánea] glimmer.

destemplado, da *adj* - **1.** [persona] out of sorts, off colour - **2.** [tiempo, clima] unpleasant - **3.** [carácter, actitud] irritable.

desteñir ◇ *vt* to fade, to bleach. ◇ *vi* to run, not to be colour fast.

desternillarse *vpr* : ~ **de risa** to split one's sides laughing *o* with laughter.

desterrar *vt* [persona] to banish, to exile.

destetar *vt* to wean.

destiempo ➥ **a destiempo** *loc adv* at the wrong time.

destierro *m* exile; **en el ~** in exile.

destilar *vt* [agua, petróleo] to distil.

destilería *f* distillery; **~ de petróleo** oil refinery.

destinar *vt* **-1.: ~ algo a** *o* **para** [cantidad, edificio] to set sthg aside for; [empleo, cargo] to assign sthg to; [carta] to address sthg to; [medidas, programa, publicación] to aim sthg at **-2.: ~ a alguien a** [cargo, empleo] to appoint sb to; [plaza, lugar] to post sb to.

destinatario, ria *m,f* addressee.

destino *m* **-1.** [sino] destiny, fate **-2.** [rumbo] destination; **(ir) con ~ a** (to be) bound for *o* going to; **un vuelo con ~ a ...** a flight to ... **-3.** [empleo, plaza] position, post **-4.** [finalidad] use, function.

destitución *f* dismissal.

destituir *vt* to dismiss.

destornillador *m* screwdriver.

destornillar *vt* to unscrew.

destreza *f* skill, dexterity.

destrozar *vt* **-1.** [físicamente - romper] to smash; [- estropear] to ruin **-2.** [moralmente - persona] to shatter, to devastate; [- vida] to ruin.

destrozo *m* damage (U); **ocasionar grandes ~s** to cause a lot of damage.

destrucción *f* destruction.

destruir *vt* **-1.** [gen] to destroy; [casa, argumento] to demolish **-2.** [proyecto] to ruin, to wreck; [ilusión] to dash.

desuso *m* disuse; **caer en ~** to become obsolete, to fall into disuse.

desvaído, da *adj* [color] pale, washed-out; [forma, contorno] blurred; [mirada] vague.

desvalido, da *adj* needy, destitute.

desvalijar *vt* [casa] to burgle, burglarize *US*; [persona] to rob.

desván *m* attic, loft.

desvanecer *vt* **-1.** [humo, nubes] to dissipate **-2.** [sospechas, temores] to dispel.

◆ **desvanecerse** *vpr* **-1.** [desmayarse] to faint **-2.** [disiparse - humo, nubes] to clear, to disappear; [- sonido, sospechas, temores] to fade away.

desvanecimiento *m* [desmayo] fainting fit.

desvariar *vi* [delirar] to be delirious; [decir locuras] to talk nonsense, to rave.

desvarío *m* **-1.** [dicho] raving; [hecho] act of madness **-2.** [delirio] delirium.

desvelar *vt* **-1.** [quitar el sueño a] to keep awake **-2.** [noticia, secreto etc] to reveal, to tell.

◆ **desvelarse** *vpr CAm, Méx* [quedarse despierto] to stay up *o* awake.

◆ **desvelarse por** *vpr*: **~se por hacer algo** to make every effort to do sthg.

desvelo *m* [esfuerzo] effort.

desvencijado, da *adj* [silla, mesa] rickety; [camión, coche] battered.

desventaja *f* disadvantage; **en ~** at a disadvantage.

desventura *f* misfortune.

desvergonzado, da *adj* shameless, insolent.

desvergüenza *f* [atrevimiento, frescura] shamelessness.

desvestir *vt* to undress.

◆ **desvestirse** *vpr* to undress (o.s.).

desviación *f* **-1.** [de dirección, cauce, norma] deviation **-2.** [en la carretera] diversion, detour.

desviar *vt* [río, carretera, tráfico] to divert; [dirección] to change; [golpe] to parry; [pelota, disparo] to deflect; [pregunta] to evade; [conversación] to change the direction of; [mirada, ojos] to avert.

◆ **desviarse** *vpr* [cambiar de dirección - conductor] to take a detour; [- avión, barco] to go off course; **~se de** to turn off.

desvío *m* diversion, detour.

desvirtuar *vt* [gen] to detract from; [estropear] to spoil; [verdadero sentido] to distort.

desvivirse *vpr*: **~ (por alguien/algo)** to do everything one can (for sb/sthg); **~ por hacer algo** to bend over backwards to do sthg.

detallado, da *adj* detailed, thorough.

detallar *vt* [historia, hechos] to detail, to give a rundown of; [cuenta, gastos] to itemize.

detalle *m* **-1.** [gen] detail; **con ~** in detail; **entrar en ~s** to go into detail **-2.** [atención] kind gesture *o* thought; **¡qué ~!** what a kind gesture!, how thoughtful!; **tener un ~ con alguien** to be thoughtful *o* considerate to sb.

◆ **al detalle** *loc adv* COM retail.

detallista *mf* COM retailer.

detectar *vt* to detect.

detective *mf* detective.

detener *vt* **-1.** [arrestar] to arrest **-2.** [parar] to stop; [retrasar] to hold up.

◆ **detenerse** *vpr* **-1.** [pararse] to stop **-2.** [demorarse] to hang about, to linger.

detenidamente *adv* carefully, thoroughly.

detenido, da ◇ *adj* **-1.** [detallado] careful, thorough **-2.** [arrestado]: **(estar) ~** (to be) under arrest. ◇ *m,f* prisoner, person under arrest.

detenimiento ◆ **con detenimiento** *loc adv* carefully, thoroughly.

detergente *m* detergent.

deteriorar *vt* to damage, to spoil.

◆ **deteriorarse** *vpr fig* [empeorar] to deteriorate, to get worse.

deterioro *m* [daño] damage; [empeoramiento] deterioration.

determinación *f* **- 1.** [fijación - de precio etc] settling, fixing **- 2.** [resolución] determination, resolution **- 3.** [decisión]: **tomar una ~** to take a decision.

determinado, da *adj* **- 1.** [concreto] specific; [en particular] particular **- 2.** [resuelto] determined **- 3.** GRAM definite.

determinar *vt* **- 1.** [fijar - fecha, precio] to settle, to fix **- 2.** [averiguar] to determine **- 3.** [motivar] to cause, to bring about **- 4.** [decidir] to decide; **~ hacer algo** to decide to do sthg.
  ➡ **determinarse** *vpr*: **~se a hacer algo** to make up one's mind to do sthg.

detestar *vt* to detest.

detonante *m* [explosivo] explosive.

detractor, ra *m,f* detractor.

detrás *adv* **- 1.** [en el espacio] behind; **tus amigos vienen ~** your friends are coming on behind; **el interruptor está ~** the switch is at the back **- 2.** [en el orden] then, afterwards; **Portugal y ~ Puerto Rico** Portugal and then Puerto Rico.
  ➡ **detrás de** *loc prep* [gen] behind.
  ➡ **por detrás** *loc adv* at the back; **hablar de alguien por ~** to talk about sb behind his/her back.

detrimento *m* damage; **en ~ de** to the detriment of.

detrito *m* BIOL detritus.
  ➡ **detritos** *mpl* [residuos] waste *(U)*.

deuda *f* debt; **~ pública** ECON national debt UK, public debt US.

deudor, ra ◇ *adj* [saldo] debit *(antes de sust)*; [entidad] indebted. ◇ *m,f* debtor.

devaluación *f* devaluation.

devaluar *vt* to devalue.

devaneos *mpl* [amoríos] affairs; [coqueteos] flirting *(U)*.

devastar *vt* to devastate.

devoción *f*: **~ (por)** devotion (to).

devolución *f* [gen] return; [de dinero] refund.

devolver ◇ *vt* **- 1.** [restituir]: **~ algo (a)** [coche, dinero etc] to give sthg back (to); [producto defectuoso, carta] to return sthg (to) **- 2.** [restablecer, colocar en su sitio]: **~ algo a** to return sthg to **- 3.** [favor, agravio] to pay back for; [visita] to return **- 4.** [vomitar] to bring *o* throw up. ◇ *vi* to throw up.
  ➡ **devolverse** *vpr Andes, Amér, Carib, Méx* to come back.

devorar *vt lit & fig* to devour.

devoto, ta ◇ *adj* [piadoso] devout; **ser ~ de** to have a devotion for. ◇ *m,f* [admirador] devotee.

devuelto, ta *pp* ⊳ **devolver**.

dg *(abrev de decigramo)* dg.

di *etc* **- 1.** ⊳ **dar - 2.** ⊳ **decir.**

día *m* **- 1.** [gen] day; **me voy el ~ ocho** I'm going on the eighth; **¿a qué ~ estamos?** what day is it today?; **¿qué tal ~ hace?** what's the weather like today?; **todos los ~s** every day; **~ de la Madre** Mother's Day; **~ de los enamorados** St Valentine's Day; **~ de los inocentes** ≃ *28th December,* ≃ April Fools' Day; **~ de pago** payday; **~ festivo** (public) holiday; **~ hábil** *o* **laborable** *o* **de trabajo** working day; **de ~ en ~** from day to day, day by day; **del ~** fresh; **hoy (en) ~** nowadays; **todo el (santo) ~** all day long; **el ~ de mañana** in the future; **al ~ siguiente** on the following day; **~ sí y otro no** every other day; **menú del ~** today's menu **- 2.** [luz] daytime, day; **es de ~** it's daytime; **hacer algo de ~** to do sthg in the daytime *o* during the day; **~ y noche** day and night; **en pleno ~,** **a plena luz del ~** in broad daylight **- 3.** *loc:* **estar/ponerse al ~ (de)** to be/get up to date (with); **poner algo/a alguien al ~** to update sthg/sb; **vivir al ~** to live from hand to mouth.
  ➡ **buen día** *interj Amér:* **¡buen ~!** good morning!
  ➡ **buenos días** *interj:* **¡buenos ~s!** [gen] hello!; [por la mañana] good morning!

diabético, ca *adj & m,f* diabetic.

diablo *m lit & fig* devil; **pobre ~** poor devil.

diablura *f* prank.

diabólico, ca *adj* **- 1.** [del diablo] diabolic **- 2.** *fig* [muy malo, difícil] diabolical.

diadema *f* [para el pelo] hairband.

diáfano, na *adj* **- 1.** [transparente] transparent, diaphanous **- 2.** *fig* [claro] clear.

diafragma *m* diaphragm.

diagnosticar *vt* to diagnose.

diagnóstico *m* diagnosis; **~ precoz** early diagnosis.

diagonal *adj & f* diagonal.

diagrama *m* diagram; **~ de flujo** INFORM flow chart *o* diagram.

dial *m* dial.

dialecto *m* dialect.

dialogar *vi:* **~ (con)** [hablar] to have a conversation (with), to talk (to); [negociar] to hold a dialogue *o* talks (with).

diálogo *m* [conversación] conversation; LITER & POLÍT dialogue.

diamante *m* [piedra preciosa] diamond; **~ en bruto** uncut diamond; **ser un ~ en bruto** *fig* to have a lot of potential.

diámetro *m* diameter.

diana *f* **- 1.** [en blanco de tiro] bull's-eye, bull **- 2.** [en cuartel] reveille.

diapasón *m* tuning fork.

diapositiva *f* slide, transparency.

diariero, ra *m,f Andes, RP* newspaper seller.

diario, ria *adj* daily; **a ~** every day; **de ~** daily, everyday; **ropa de ~** everyday clothes.

◆ **diario** *m* **-1.** [periódico] newspaper, daily **-2.** [relación día a día] diary; **~ de sesiones** parliamentary report; **~ de vuelo** log, logbook.

diarrea *f* diarrhoea.

dibujante *mf* [gen] sketcher; [de dibujos animados] cartoonist; [de dibujo técnico] draughtsman (*f* draughtswoman).

dibujar *vt* & *vi* to draw, to sketch.

dibujo *m* **-1.** [gen] drawing; **no se le da bien el ~** he's no good at drawing; **~s animados** cartoons; **~ artístico** art; **~ lineal** technical drawing; **~ al natural** drawing from life **-2.** [de tela, prenda etc] pattern.

diccionario *m* dictionary.

dice ⊳ **decir**.

dicha *f* [alegría] joy.

dicho, cha ⊳ *pp* ⊳ **decir**. ⊳ *adj* said, aforementioned; **~s hombres** the said men, these men; **lo ~** what I/we *etc* said; **o mejor ~** or rather; **~ y hecho** no sooner said than done.

◆ **dicho** *m* saying.

dichoso, sa *adj* [feliz] happy; [afortunado] fortunate.

diciembre *m* December; *ver también* **septiembre**.

dictado *m* dictation; **escribir al ~** to take dictation.

dictador, ra *m,f* dictator.

dictadura *f* dictatorship.

dictamen *m* [opinión] opinion, judgment; [informe] report; **~ facultativo** *o* **médico** medical report.

dictar *vt* **-1.** [texto] to dictate **-2.** [emitir - sentencia, fallo] to pronounce, to pass; [- ley] to enact; [- decreto] to issue.

didáctico, ca *adj* didactic.

diecinueve *núm* nineteen; *ver también* **seis**.

dieciocho *núm* eighteen; *ver también* **seis**.

dieciséis *núm* sixteen; *ver también* **seis**.

diecisiete *núm* seventeen; *ver también* **seis**.

diente *m* tooth; **está echando** *o* **le están saliendo los ~s** she's teething; **~ de leche** milk tooth; **~s postizos** false teeth; **armado hasta los ~s** armed to the teeth; **hablar entre ~s** to mumble, to mutter; **reírse entre ~s** to chuckle.

◆ **diente de ajo** *m* clove of garlic.

diera ⊳ **dar**.

diéresis *f inv* diaeresis.

dieron *etc* ⊳ **dar**.

diesel, diésel *adj* diesel.

diestro, tra *adj* [hábil]: **~ (en)** skilful (at); **a ~ y siniestro** *fig* left, right and centre, all over the place.

dieta *f* MED diet; **~ blanda** soft-food diet; **~ equilibrada** balanced diet; **~ mediterránea** Mediterranean diet.

◆ **dietas** *fpl* COM expenses.

dietético, ca *adj* dietetic, dietary.

◆ **dietética** *f* dietetics *(U)*.

dietista *mf* Amér dietician.

diez ⊳ *núm* ten; *ver también* **seis**. ⊳ *m* [en la escuela] A, top marks *(pl)*.

difamar *vt* [verbalmente] to slander; [por escrito] to libel.

diferencia *f* difference; **con ~** by a long chalk, by far; **es, con ~, el más listo** he's the smartest by far; **partir la ~** to split the difference; **~ horaria** time difference.

diferenciar ⊳ *vt*: **~ (de)** to distinguish (from). ⊳ *vi*: **~ (entre)** to distinguish *o* differentiate (between).

◆ **diferenciarse** *vpr* [diferir]: **~se (de/en)** to differ (from/in), to be different (from/in).

diferente ⊳ *adj*: **~ (de** *o* **a)** different (from *o* to). ⊳ *adv* differently.

diferido ◆ **en diferido** *loc adv* TV recorded.

diferir *vi* [diferenciarse] to differ, to be different.

difícil *adj* difficult; **~ de hacer** difficult to do; **es ~ que ganen** they are unlikely to win.

dificultad *f* **-1.** [calidad de difícil] difficulty **-2.** [obstáculo] problem.

dificultar *vt* [estorbar] to hinder; [obstruir] to obstruct.

difuminar *vt* to blur.

difundir *vt* **-1.** [noticia, doctrina, epidemia] to spread **-2.** [luz, calor] to diffuse; [emisión radiofónica] to broadcast.

◆ **difundirse** *vpr* **-1.** [noticia, doctrina, epidemia] to spread **-2.** [luz, calor] to be diffused.

difunto, ta *m,f*: **el ~** the deceased.

difusión *f* **-1.** [de cultura, noticia, doctrina] dissemination **-2.** [de programa] broadcasting.

diga ⊳ **decir**.

digerir *vt* to digest; *fig* [hechos] to assimilate, to take in.

digestión *f* digestion; **hacer la ~** to digest one's food.

digestivo, va *adj* digestive.

digitador, dora *m,f* Amér keyboarder.

digital *adj* INFORM & TECN digital.

dígito *m* digit.

dignarse *vpr*: **~ a** to deign to.

dignidad *f* [cualidad] dignity.

digno, na *adj* **-1.** [noble - actitud, respuesta] dignified; [- persona] honourable, noble **-2.** [merecedor]: **~ de** worthy of; **~ de**

elogio praiseworthy; ~ **de mención/de ver** worth mentioning/seeing - **3.** [adecuado]: ~ **de** appropriate for, fitting for - **4.** [decente - sueldo, actuación etc] decent, good.

digo ⊳ decir.

dijera *etc* ⊳ decir.

dilapidar *vt* to squander, to waste.

dilatar *vt* - **1.** [extender] to expand; [retina, útero] to dilate - **2.** [prolongar] to prolong - **3.** [demorar] to delay.

dilema *m* dilemma.

diligencia *f* - **1.** [esmero, cuidado] diligence - **2.** [trámite, gestión] business *(U)*; **hacer una** ~ to run an errand - **3.** [vehículo] stagecoach.
   ◆ **diligencias** *fpl* DER proceedings; **instruir** ~s to start proceedings.

diligente *adj* diligent.

diluir *vt* to dilute.
   ◆ **diluirse** *vpr* to dissolve.

diluvio *m lit & fig* flood; **el Diluvio Universal** the Flood.

dimensión *f* dimension; **las dimensiones de la tragedia** the extent of the tragedy.

diminutivo *m* diminutive.

diminuto, ta *adj* tiny, minute.

dimisión *f* resignation; **presentar la** ~ to hand in one's resignation.

dimitir *vi*: ~ **(de)** to resign (from).

dimos ⊳ dar.

Dinamarca Denmark.

dinámico, ca *adj* dynamic.

dinamismo *m* dynamism.

dinamita *f* dynamite.

dinamo, dínamo *f* dynamo.

dinastía *f* dynasty.

dineral *m fam* fortune.

dinero *m* money; **andar bien/mal de** ~ to be well off/short of money; **hacer** ~ to make money; **tirar el** ~ to throw money away; ~ **en metálico** cash; ~ **negro** *o* **sucio** illegally obtained money.

dinosaurio *m* dinosaur.

dintel *m* ARQUIT lintel.

dio ⊳ dar.

diócesis *f* diocese.

dios, sa *m,f* god (*f* goddess).
   ◆ **Dios** *m* God; **a la buena de Dios** any old how; **¡Dios me libre!** God *o* heaven forbid!; **¡Dios mío!** good God!, (oh) my God!; **¡que Dios se lo pague!** God bless you!; **¡por Dios!** for God's sake!; **¡vaya por Dios!** for Heaven's sake!, honestly!

diploma *m* diploma.

diplomacia *f* [gen] diplomacy.

diplomado, da *adj* qualified.

diplomático, ca ◇ *adj lit & fig* diplomatic. ◇ *m,f* diplomat.

diptongo *m* diphthong.

diputación *f* [corporación] committee; ~ **provincial** *governing body of each province of an autonomous region in Spain;* ≃ county council *UK*.

diputado, da *m,f* ≃ Member of Parliament, MP *UK*, representative *US*.

dique *m* - **1.** [en río] dike - **2.** [en puerto] dock; **estar en (el)** ~ **seco** *fig* to be out of action.

dirá ⊳ decir.

dirección *f* - **1.** [sentido, rumbo] direction; **calle de** ~ **única** one-way street; **en** ~ **a** towards, in the direction of - **2.** [domicilio] address; ~ **comercial** business address; ~ **electrónica** *o* **de correo electrónico** e-mail address; ~ **particular** home address - **3.** [mando - de empresa, hospital] management; [- de partido] leadership; [- de colegio] headship; [- de periódico] editorship; [- de película] direction; [- de obra de teatro] production; [- de orquesta] conducting - **4.** [junta directiva] management - **5.** [de vehículo] steering; ~ **asistida** power steering.
   ◆ **Dirección** *f*: **Dirección General de Tráfico** *traffic department (part of the Ministry of the Interior).*

directivo, va ◇ *adj* managerial. ◇ *m,f* [jefe] manager.
   ◆ **directiva** *f* [junta] board (of directors).

directo, ta *adj* - **1.** [gen] direct - **2.** [derecho] straight.
   ◆ **directo** *adv* straight; ~ **a** a straight to.
   ◆ **directa** *f* AUTOM top gear.
   ◆ **en directo** *loc adv* live.

director, ra *m,f* - **1.** [gen] director; [de hotel, hospital] manager (*f* manageress); [de periódico] editor; [de cárcel] governor - **2.** [de obra artística]: ~ **de cine** film director; ~ **de orquesta** conductor - **3.** [de colegio] headmaster (*f* headmistress) - **4.** [de tesis, trabajo de investigación] supervisor; ~ **técnico** DEP trainer.

directorio *m* - **1.** [gen & INFORM] directory - **2.**: ~ **telefónico** *Andes, CAm, Carib, Méx* directory.

directriz *f* GEOM directrix.
   ◆ **directrices** *fpl* [normas] guidelines.

diría ⊳ decir.

dirigente *mf* [de partido político] leader; [de empresa] manager.

dirigir *vt* - **1.** [conducir - coche, barco] to steer; [- avión] to pilot; *fig* [mirada] to direct - **2.** [llevar - empresa, hotel, hospital] to manage; [- colegio, cárcel, periódico] to run; [- partido, revuelta] to lead; [- expedición] to head - **3.** [película, obra de teatro] to direct; [orquesta] to conduct - **4.** [carta, paquete] to address - **5.** [guiar - persona] to guide - **6.** [dedicar]: ~ **algo a** to aim sthg at.

dirigirse vpr - **1.** [encaminarse]: ~**se a** o **hacia** to head for - **2.** [hablar]: ~**se a** to address, to speak to - **3.** [escribir]: ~**se a** to write to.

discar vt Andes, RP to dial.

discernir vt to discern, to distinguish.

disciplina f discipline.

discípulo, la m,f disciple.

disco m - **1.** ANAT, ASTRON & GEOM disc - **2.** [de música] record; **parecer un ~ rayado** fam to go on like a cracked record; ~ **compacto** compact disc; ~ **de larga duración** LP, long-playing record - **3.** [semáforo] (traffic) light - **4.** DEP discus - **5.** INFORM disk; ~ **duro/flexible** hard/floppy disk.

discografía f records previously released (by an artist or group).

disconforme adj in disagreement; **estar ~ con** to disagree with.

discontinuo, nua adj [esfuerzo] intermittent; [línea] broken, dotted.

discordante adj [sonidos] discordant; [opiniones] clashing.

discordia f discord.

discoteca f [local] disco, discotheque.

discreción f discretion.

a discreción loc adv as much as one wants, freely.

discrecional adj [gen] optional; [parada] request (antes de sust).

discrepancia f [diferencia] difference, discrepancy; [desacuerdo] disagreement.

discrepar vi: ~ **(de)** [diferenciarse] to differ (from); [disentir] to disagree (with).

discreto, ta adj - **1.** [prudente] discreet - **2.** [cantidad] moderate, modest - **3.** [normal - actuación] fair, reasonable.

discriminación f discrimination.

discriminar vt - **1.** [cosa]: ~ **algo de** to discriminate o distinguish sthg from - **2.** [persona, colectividad] to discriminate against.

disculpa f [pretexto] excuse; [excusa, perdón] apology; **dar ~s** to make excuses; **pedir ~s a alguien (por)** to apologize to sb (for).

disculpar vt to excuse; ~ **a alguien (de** o **por algo)** to forgive sb (for sthg).

disculparse vpr: ~**se (de** o **por algo)** to apologize (for sthg).

discurrir vi - **1.** [pasar - personas] to wander, to walk; [- tiempo, vida, sesión] to go by, to pass; [- río, tráfico] to flow - **2.** [pensar] to think, to reflect.

discurso m speech.

discusión f - **1.** [conversación] discussion - **2.** [pelea] argument.

discutible adj debatable.

discutir ⬦ vi - **1.** [hablar] to discuss - **2.**

[pelear]: ~ **(de)** to argue (about). ⬦ vt [hablar] to discuss; [contradecir] to dispute.

disecar vt [animal] to stuff; [planta] to dry.

diseminar vt [semillas] to scatter; [ideas] to disseminate.

disentir vi: ~ **(de/en)** to disagree (with/on).

diseñar vt to design.

diseño m design; **ropa de ~** designer clothes; ~ **asistido por ordenador** INFORM computer-aided design; ~ **gráfico** graphic design.

disertación f [oral] lecture, discourse; [escrita] dissertation.

disfraz m [gen] disguise; [para baile, fiesta etc] fancy dress (U).

disfrazar vt to disguise.

disfrazarse vpr to disguise o.s.; ~**se de** to dress up as.

disfrutar ⬦ vi - **1.** [sentir placer] to enjoy o.s. - **2.** [disponer de]: ~ **de algo** to enjoy sthg. ⬦ vt to enjoy.

disgregar vt - **1.** [multitud, manifestación] to disperse, to break up - **2.** [roca, imperio, estado] to break up; [átomo] to split.

disgregarse vpr - **1.** [multitud, manifestación] to disperse, to break up - **2.** [roca, imperio, estado] to break up.

disgustar vt [suj: comentario, críticas, noticia] to upset.

disgustarse vpr: ~**se (con alguien/ por algo)** [sentir enfado] to get upset (with sb/about sthg); [enemistarse] to fall out (with sb/over sthg).

disgusto m - **1.** [enfado] annoyance; [pesadumbre] sorrow, grief; **dar un ~ a alguien** to upset sb; **llevarse un ~** to be upset - **2.** [pelea] tener un ~ **con alguien** to have a quarrel with sb.

disidente mf [político] dissident; [religioso] dissenter.

disimular ⬦ vt to hide, to conceal. ⬦ vi to pretend.

disimulo m pretence, concealment.

disipar vt - **1.** [dudas, sospechas] to dispel; [ilusiones] to shatter - **2.** [fortuna, herencia] to squander, to throw away.

disiparse vpr - **1.** [dudas, sospechas] to be dispelled; [ilusiones] to be shattered - **2.** [niebla, humo, vapor] to vanish.

diskette = **disquete**.

dislexia f dyslexia.

dislocar vt to dislocate.

dislocarse vpr to dislocate.

disminución f decrease, drop.

disminuido, da adj handicapped.

disminuir ⬦ vt to reduce, to decrease. ⬦ vi [gen] to decrease; [precios, temperatura] to drop, to fall; [vista, memoria] to fail;

[días] to get shorter; [beneficios] to fall off.

disolución *f* - **1.** [en un líquido] dissolving - **2.** [de matrimonio, sociedad, partido] dissolution - **3.** [mezcla] solution.

disolvente *adj* & *m* solvent.

disolver *vt* - **1.** [gen] to dissolve - **2.** [reunión, manifestación, familia] to break up.

◆ **disolverse** *vpr* - **1.** [gen] to dissolve - **2.** [reunión, manifestación, familia] to break up.

disparar ◇ *vt* to shoot; [pedrada] to throw. ◇ *vi* to shoot, to fire.

disparatado, da *adj* absurd, crazy.

disparate *m* [acción] silly thing; [comentario] foolish remark; [idea] crazy idea; **hacer ~s** to do silly things; **decir ~s** to make foolish remarks, to talk nonsense.

disparo *m* shot; **~ de advertencia** warning shot; **~ de salida** starting shot.

dispensar *vt* - **1.** [disculpar] to excuse, to forgive - **2.** [rendir]: **~ algo (a alguien)** [honores] to confer sthg (upon sb); [bienvenida, ayuda] to give sthg (to sb) - **3.** [eximir]: **~ a alguien de** to excuse *o* exempt sb from.

dispensario *m* dispensary.

dispersar *vt* - **1.** [esparcir - objetos] to scatter - **2.** [disolver - gentío] to disperse; [- manifestación] to break up; [esfuerzos] to dissipate.

◆ **dispersarse** *vpr* to scatter.

dispersión *f* [de objetos] scattering.

disperso, sa *adj* scattered.

disponer ◇ *vt* - **1.** [gen] to arrange - **2.** [cena, comida] to lay on - **3.** [decidir - suj: persona] to decide; [suj: ley] to stipulate. ◇ *vi* - **1.** [poseer]: **~ de** to have - **2.** [usar]: **~ de** to make use of.

◆ **disponerse a** *vpr*: **~se a hacer algo** to prepare *o* get ready to do sthg.

disponibilidad *f* [gen] availability.

disponible *adj* [gen] available; [tiempo] free, spare.

disposición *f* - **1.** [colocación] arrangement, layout - **2.** [orden] order; [de ley] provision - **3.** [uso]: **a ~ de** at the disposal of; **pasar a ~ policial** to be brought before the judge.

dispositivo *m* device; **~ intrauterino** intrauterine device, IUD.

dispuesto, ta ◇ *pp* ▷ **disponer.** ◇ *adj* [preparado] ready; **estar ~ a hacer algo** to be prepared to do sthg; **estar poco ~ a hacer algo** to be reluctant to do sthg.

disputa *f* dispute.

disputar *vt* - **1.** [cuestión, tema] to argue about - **2.** [trofeo, puesto] to compete for, to dispute; [carrera, partido] to compete in.

disquete, diskette [dis'kete] *m* INFORM diskette, floppy disk.

disquetera *f* INFORM disk drive.

distancia *f* - **1.** [gen] distance; **a ~ from a** distance; **mantener a ~** to keep for a distance; **mantener las ~s** to keep one's distance; **recorrer una gran ~** to cover a lot of ground - **2.** [en el tiempo] gap, space.

distanciar *vt* [gen] to drive apart; [rival] to forge ahead of.

◆ **distanciarse** *vpr* [alejarse - afectivamente] to grow apart; [- físicamente] to distance o.s.

distante *adj* - **1.** [en el espacio]: **~ (de)** far away (from) - **2.** [en el trato] distant.

distar *vi* [hallarse a]: **ese sitio dista varios kilómetros de aquí** that place is several kilometres away from here.

diste *etc* ▷ **dar.**

distendido, da *adj* [informal] relaxed, informal.

distensión *f* - **1.** [entre países] détente; [entre personas] easing of tension - **2.** MED strain.

distinción *f* - **1.** [diferencia] distinction; **a ~ de** in contrast to, unlike; **sin ~** alike - **2.** [privilegio] privilege - **3.** [elegancia] refinement.

distinguido, da *adj* - **1.** [notable] distinguished - **2.** [elegante] refined.

distinguir *vt* - **1.** [diferenciar] to distinguish; **~ algo de algo** to tell sthg from sthg - **2.** [separar] to pick out - **3.** [caracterizar] to characterize.

◆ **distinguirse** *vpr* [destacarse] to stand out.

distintivo, va *adj* distinctive; [señal] distinguishing.

◆ **distintivo** *m* badge.

distinto, ta *adj* [diferente] different.

◆ **distintos, tas** *adj pl* [varios] various.

distorsión *f* [de tobillo, rodilla] sprain; [de imágenes, sonidos, palabras] distortion.

distracción *f* - **1.** [entretenimiento] entertainment; [pasatiempo] hobby, pastime - **2.** [despiste] slip; [falta de atención] absentmindedness.

distraer *vt* - **1.** [divertir] to amuse, to entertain - **2.** [despistar] to distract.

◆ **distraerse** *vpr* - **1.** [divertirse] to enjoy o.s.; [pasar el tiempo] to pass the time - **2.** [despistarse] to let one's mind wander.

distraído, da *adj* - **1.** [entretenido] amusing, entertaining - **2.** [despistado] absentminded.

distribución *f* - **1.** [gen] distribution; **~ de premios** prizegiving - **2.** [de correo, mercancías] delivery - **3.** [de casa, habitaciones] layout.

distribuidor, ra ◇ *adj* [entidad] wholesale; [red] supply *(antes de sust).* ◇ *m,f* [persona] deliveryman *(f* deliverywoman).

◆ **distribuidor** *m* [aparato] vending machine.

distribuir *vt* - **1.** [gen] to distribute; [carga, trabajo] to spread; [pastel, ganancias] to divide up - **2.** [correo, mercancías] to deliver - **3.** [casa, habitaciones] to arrange.

distrito *m* district.

disturbio *m* disturbance; [violento] riot; ~s raciales race riots.

disuadir *vt* : ~ (de) to dissuade (from).

disuasión *f* deterrence.

disuasivo, va *adj* deterrent.

disuelto, ta *pp* ⊳ disolver.

DIU (*abrev de* **dispositivo intrauterino**) *m* IUD.

diurno, na *adj* [gen] daytime (*antes de sust*); [planta, animal] diurnal.

diva ⊳ divo.

divagar *vi* to digress.

diván *m* divan; [de psiquiatra] couch.

divergencia *f* - **1.** [de líneas] divergence - **2.** [de opinión] difference of opinion.

divergir *vi* - **1.** [calles, líneas] to diverge - **2.** *fig* [opiniones]: ~ (en) to differ (on).

diversidad *f* diversity.

diversificar *vt* to diversify.

diversión *f* entertainment, amusement.

diverso, sa *adj* [diferente] different.

◆ **diversos, sas** *adj pl* [varios] several, various.

divertido, da *adj* [entretenido - película, libro] entertaining; [- fiesta] enjoyable; [que hace reír] funny.

divertir *vt* to entertain, to amuse.

◆ **divertirse** *vpr* to enjoy o.s.

dividendo *m* FIN & MAT dividend.

dividir *vt* : ~ (en) to divide (into); ~ entre [gen] to divide between; MAT to divide by.

divinidad *f* divinity, god.

divino, na *adj lit* & *fig* divine.

divisa *f* - **1.** (*gen pl*) [moneda] foreign currency - **2.** [distintivo] emblem.

divisar *vt* to spy, to make out.

división *f* [gen] division; [partición] splitting up.

divo, va *m, f* [MÚS - mujer] diva, prima donna; [- hombre] opera singer.

divorciado, da ◇ *adj* divorced. ◇ *m,f* divorcé (*f* divorcée).

divorciar *vt lit* & *fig* to divorce.

◆ **divorciarse** *vpr* to get divorced.

divorcio *m* DER divorce.

divulgar *vt* [noticia, secreto] to reveal; [rumor] to spread; [cultura, ciencia, doctrina] to popularize.

dizque *adv* *Amér* apparently.

DNI (*abrev de* **documento nacional de identidad**) *m* ID card.

Dña *abrev de* **doña**.

do *m* MÚS C; [en solfeo] doh.

dobladillo *m* [de traje, vestido] hem; [de pantalón] turn-up *UK*, cuff *US*; **hacer un** ~ to turn up, to hem.

doblado, da *adj* - **1.** [papel, camisa] folded - **2.** [voz, película] dubbed.

doblar ◇ *vt* - **1.** [duplicar] to double - **2.** [plegar] to fold - **3.** [torcer] to bend - **4.** [esquina] to turn, to go round - **5.** [voz, actor] to dub. ◇ *vi* - **1.** [girar] to turn - **2.** [campanas] to toll.

◆ **doblarse** *vpr* [someterse]: ~se a to give in to.

doble ◇ *adj* double; **tiene** ~ **número de habitantes** it has double 0 twice the number of inhabitants; **es** ~ **de ancho** it's twice as wide; **una frase de** ~ **sentido** a phrase with a double meaning; ~ **clic** INFORM double click. ◇ *mf* [gen & CIN] double. ◇ *m* [duplo]: **el** ~ twice as much; **gana el** ~ **que yo** she earns twice as much as I do, she earns double what I do. ◇ *adv* double; **trabajar** ~ to work twice as hard.

◆ **dobles** *mpl* DEP doubles.

doblegar *vt* [someter] to bend, to cause to give in.

◆ **doblegarse** *vpr*: ~se (ante) to give in 0 yield (to).

doblez *m* [pliegue] fold, crease.

doce *núm* twelve; *ver también* **seis**.

doceavo, va *núm* twelfth.

docena *f* dozen; **a** 0 **por** ~s by the dozen.

docente *adj* teaching; **centro** ~ educational institution.

dócil *adj* obedient.

doctor, ra *m,f*: ~ (en) doctor (of).

doctrina *f* doctrine.

documentación *f* [identificación personal] papers (*pl*).

documentado, da *adj* [informado - película, informe] researched; [- persona] informed.

documental *adj* & *m* documentary.

documentar *vt* - **1.** [evidenciar] to document - **2.** [informar] to brief.

◆ **documentarse** *vpr* to do research.

documento *m* - **1.** [escrito] document; ~ **nacional de identidad** identity card - **2.** [testimonio] record.

dogma *m* dogma.

dogmático, ca *adj* dogmatic.

dólar *m* dollar.

dolencia *f* pain.

doler *vi* to hurt; **me duele la pierna** my leg hurts; **¿te duele?** does it hurt?; **me duele la garganta/la cabeza** I have a sore throat/a headache.

◆ **dolerse** *vpr*: ~se de 0 por algo [quejarse] to complain about sthg; [arrepentirse] to be sorry about sthg.

dolido, da *adj* hurt.

dolor *m* **-1.** [físico] pain; **siento un ~ en el brazo** I have a pain in my arm; **(tener) ~ de cabeza** (to have a) headache; **~ de estómago** stomachache; **~ de muelas** toothache **-2.** [moral] grief, sorrow.

dolorido, da *adj* [físicamente] sore; [moralmente] grieving, sorrowing.

doloroso, sa *adj* [físicamente] painful; [moralmente] distressing.

domador, ra *m,f* [de caballos] breaker; [de leones] tamer.

domar *vt* [gen] to tame; [caballo] to break in; *fig* [personas] to control.

domesticar *vt lit & fig* to tame.

doméstico, ca *adj* domestic.

domiciliación *f*: **~ (bancaria)** standing order, direct debit (*U*).

domiciliar *vt* [pago] to pay by direct debit o standing order.

domicilio *m* **-1.** [vivienda] residence, home; **~ particular** private residence **-2.** [dirección] address; **sin ~ fijo** of no fixed abode; **~ social** head office.

dominante *adj* **-1.** [nación, religión, tendencia] dominant; [vientos] prevailing **-2.** [persona] domineering.

dominar *⋄ vt* **-1.** [controlar - país, territorio] to dominate, to rule (over); [- pasión, nervios, caballo] to control; [- situación] to be in control of; [- incendio] to bring under control; [- rebelión] to put down **-2.** [divisar] to overlook **-3.** [conocer - técnica, tema] to master; [- lengua] to be fluent in. *⋄ vi* [predominar] to predominate.

◆ dominarse *vpr* to control o.s.

domingo *m* Sunday; *ver también* **sábado.**

dominguero, ra *m,f* Sunday tripper/driver *etc.*

dominical *adj* Sunday (*antes de sust*).

dominicano, na *adj & m,f* Dominican.

dominico, ca *adj & m,f* Dominican.

dominio *m* **-1.** [dominación, posesión]: **~ (sobre)** control (over); **~ de o sobre sí mismo** self-control **-2.** [autoridad] authority, power **-3.** *fig* [territorio] domain; [ámbito] realm **-4.** [conocimiento - de arte, técnica] mastery; [- de idiomas] command.

dominó *m* **-1.** [juego] dominoes (*U*) **-2.** [fichas] set of dominoes.

don *m* **-1.** [tratamiento]: **~ Luis García** [gen] Mr Luis García; [en cartas] Luis García Esquire; **~ Luis** *not translated in modern English or translated as 'Mr' + surname, if known* **-2.** [habilidad] gift; **el ~ de la palabra** the gift of the gab.

donaire *m* [al expresarse] wit; [al andar etc] grace.

donante *mf* donor; **~ de sangre** blood donor.

donar *vt* to donate.

donativo *m* donation.

doncella *f* maid.

donde *⋄ adv* where; **el bolso está ~ lo dejaste** the bag is where you left it; **puedes marcharte ~ quieras** you can go wherever you want; **hasta ~** as far as, up to where; **por ~** wherever. *⋄ pron* where; **la casa ~ nací** the house where I was born; **la ciudad de ~ viene** the town (where) she comes from, the town from which she comes.

◆ de donde *loc adv* [de lo cual] from which.

dónde *adv* (*interrogativo*) where; **¿~ está el niño?** where's the child?; **no sé ~ se habrá metido** I don't know where she can be; **¿a ~ vas?** where are you going?; **¿de ~ eres?** where are you from?; **¿hacia ~ vas?** where are you heading?; **¿por ~?** whereabouts?; **¿por ~ se va al teatro?** how do you get to the theatre from here?

dondequiera ◆ dondequiera que *adv* wherever.

doña *f*: **~ Luisa García** Mrs Luisa García; **~ Luisa** *not translated in modern English or translated as 'Mrs' + surname, if known.*

dopado, da *adj* having taken performance-enhancing drugs.

dopar *vt* to dope.

doping ['dopiŋ] *m* doping.

doquier ◆ por doquier *loc adv* everywhere.

dorado, da *adj lit & fig* golden.

◆ dorada *f* [pez] gilthead.

dorar *vt* **-1.** [cubrir con oro] to gild **-2.** [alimento] to brown.

dormilón, ona *m,f fam* [persona] sleepyhead.

dormir *⋄ vt* [niño, animal] to put to bed; **~ la siesta** to have an afternoon nap. *⋄ vi* to sleep.

◆ dormirse *vpr* **-1.** [persona] to fall asleep **-2.** [brazo, mano] to go to sleep.

dormitar *vi* to doze.

dormitorio *m* [de casa] bedroom; [de colegio] dormitory.

dorsal *⋄ adj* dorsal. *⋄ m* number (*on player's back*).

dorso *m* back; **al ~, en el ~** on the back; **'véase al ~'** 'see overleaf'; **~ de la mano** back of one's hand.

dos *núm* two; **cada ~ por tres** every five minutes, continually; *ver también* **seis.**

doscientos, tas *núm* two hundred; *ver también* **seis.**

dosificar *vt fig* [fuerzas, palabras] to use sparingly.

dosis *f inv lit & fig* dose; **en pequeñas ~** in small doses.

dossier [do'sjer] *m inv* dossier, file.

dotación *f* - **1.** [de dinero, armas, medios] amount granted - **2.** [personal] staff, personnel; [tripulantes] crew; [patrulla] squad.

dotado, da *adj* gifted; **~ de** [persona] blessed with; [edificio, instalación, aparato] equipped with.

dotar *vt* - **1.** [proveer]: **~ algo de** to provide sthg with - **2.** *fig* [suj: la naturaleza]: **~ a algo/alguien de** to endow sthg/sb with.

dote *f* [en boda] dowry.

➡ **dotes** *fpl* [dones] qualities; **~s de mando** leadership qualities.

doy ⊳ **dar**.

Dr. (*abrev de* **doctor**) Dr.

Dra. (*abrev de* **doctora**) Dr.

dragar *vt* to dredge.

dragón *m* dragon.

drama *m* [gen] drama; [obra] play.

dramático, ca *adj* dramatic.

dramatizar *vt* to dramatize.

dramaturgo, ga *m,f* playwright, dramatist.

drástico, ca *adj* drastic.

drenar *vt* to drain.

driblar *vt* DEP to dribble.

droga *f* drug; **la ~** drugs *(pl)*; **~ de diseño** designer drug.

drogadicto, ta *m,f* drug addict.

drogar *vt* to drug.

➡ **drogarse** *vpr* to take drugs.

droguería *f shop selling paint, cleaning materials etc*.

dromedario *m* dromedary.

dto. *abrev de* **descuento**.

dual *adj* dual.

Dublín Dublin.

ducha *f* shower; **tomar** *o* **darse una ~** to have *o* take a shower; **~ de teléfono** hand-held shower.

duchar *vt* to shower.

➡ **ducharse** *vpr* to have a shower.

duda *f* doubt; **poner algo en ~** to call sthg into question; **salir de ~s** to set one's mind at rest; **sin ~** doubtless, undoubtedly; **sin la menor ~** without the slightest doubt; **sin sombra de ~** beyond the shadow of a doubt; **no cabe ~** there is no doubt about it.

dudar ◇ *vi* - **1.** [desconfiar]: **~ de algo/alguien** to have one's doubts about sthg/sb - **2.** [no estar seguro]: **~ sobre algo** to be un-

sure about sthg - **3.** [vacilar] to hesitate; **~ entre hacer una cosa u otra** to be unsure whether to do one thing or another. ◇ *vt* to doubt; **dudo que venga** I doubt whether he'll come.

dudoso, sa *adj* - **1.** [improbable]: **ser ~ (que)** to be doubtful (whether), to be unlikely (that) - **2.** [vacilante] hesitant, indecisive - **3.** [sospechoso] questionable, suspect.

duelo *m* - **1.** [combate] duel; **batirse en ~** to fight a duel - **2.** [sentimiento] grief, sorrow.

duende *m* [personaje] imp, goblin.

dueño, ña *m,f* [gen] owner; [de piso etc] landlord (*f* landlady); **cambiar de ~** to change hands.

duerma *etc* ⊳ **dormir**.

dulce ◇ *adj* - **1.** [gen] sweet - **2.** [agua] fresh - **3.** [mirada] tender. ◇ *m* [caramelo, postre] sweet; [pastel] cake, pastry.

dulcificar *vt* [endulzar] to sweeten.

dulzura *f* [gen] sweetness.

duna *f* dune.

dúo *m* - **1.** MÚS duet - **2.** [pareja] duo; **a ~** together.

duodécimo, ma *núm* twelfth.

dúplex, duplex *m inv* [piso] duplex.

duplicado, da *adj* in duplicate.

➡ **duplicado** *m*: **(por) ~** (in) duplicate.

duplicar *vt* - **1.** [cantidad] to double - **2.** [documento] to duplicate.

➡ **duplicarse** *vpr* to double.

duque, sa *m,f* duke (*f* duchess).

duración *f* length; **de larga ~** [pila, bombilla] long-life; [parado] long-term; [disco] long-playing.

duradero, ra *adj* [gen] lasting; [ropa, zapatos] hard-wearing.

durante *prep* during; **le escribí ~ las vacaciones** I wrote to him during the holidays; **estuve escribiendo ~ una hora** I was writing for an hour; **~ toda la semana** all week.

durar *vi* [gen] to last; [permanecer, subsistir] to remain, to stay; [ropa] to wear well; **aún dura la fiesta** the party's still going on.

durazno *m Amér* peach.

dúrex *m Méx* Sellotape®, Scotch® tape *US*.

dureza *f* - **1.** [de objeto, metal etc] hardness - **2.** [de clima, persona] harshness.

durmiera *etc* ⊳ **dormir**.

duro, ra *adj* - **1.** [gen] hard; [carne] tough - **2.** [resistente] tough - **3.** [palabras, clima] harsh.

➡ **duro** *m* [moneda] five-peseta piece.

e¹, E *f* [letra] e, E.

e² *conj* (*en lugar de 'y' ante palabras que empiecen por 'i' o 'hi'*) and.

ebanista *mf* cabinet-maker.

ébano *m* ebony.

ebrio, ebria *adj* [borracho] drunk.

Ebro *m*: **el** ~ the Ebro.

ebullición *f* boiling; **punto de** ~ boiling point.

eccema *m* eczema.

echar <> *vt* - **1.** [tirar] to throw; [red] to cast - **2.** [añadir]: ~ **algo (a** *o* **en algo)** [vino etc] to pour sthg (into sthg); [sal, azúcar etc] to add sthg (to sthg) - **3.** [carta, postal] to post - **4.** [humo, vapor, chispas] to emit - **5.** [hojas, flores] to shoot - **6.** [expulsar]: ~ **a alguien (de)** to throw sb out (of) - **7.** [despedir]: ~ **a alguien (de)** to sack sb (from) - **8.** [accionar]: ~ **la llave/el cerrojo** to lock/bolt the door; ~ **el freno** to brake, to put the brakes on - **9.** [acostar] to lie (down) - **10.** *fam* [en televisión, cine] to show; **¿qué echan esta noche en la tele?** what's on telly tonight? - **11.** *loc:* ~ **abajo** [edificio] to pull down, to demolish; [gobierno] to bring down; [proyecto] to ruin; ~ **a perder** [vestido, alimentos, plan] to ruin; [ocasión] to waste; ~ **de menos** to miss. <> *vi* [empezar]: ~ **a hacer algo** to begin to do sthg, to start doing sthg; ~ **a correr** to break into a run; ~ **a llorar** to burst into tears; ~ **a reír** to burst out laughing.
 ◆ **echarse** *vpr* - **1.** [acostarse] to lie down - **2.** [apartarse]: ~**se (a un lado)** to move (aside); ~**se atrás** *fig* to back out - **3.** *loc:* ~**se a perder** [comida] to go off, to spoil; [plan] to fall through.

echarpe *m* shawl.

eclesiástico, ca *adj* ecclesiastical.

eclipsar *vt lit & fig* to eclipse.

eclipse *m* eclipse; ~ **lunar** *o* **de luna** lunar eclipse, eclipse of the moon; ~ **solar** *o* **de sol** solar eclipse, eclipse of the sun; ~ **total** total eclipse.

eco *m* [gen] echo; **hacerse** ~ **de** to report; **tener** ~ to arouse interest.

ecología *f* ecology.

ecológico, ca *adj* [gen] ecological; [alimentos] organic.

ecologista <> *adj* environmental, ecological. <> *mf* environmentalist, ecologist.

economato *m* company cooperative shop.

economía *f* - **1.** [gen] economy; ~ **sumergida** black economy *o* market - **2.** [estudio] economics (U); ~ **familiar** home economics - **3.** [ahorro] saving.

económico, ca *adj* - **1.** [problema, doctrina etc] economic - **2.** [barato] cheap, low-cost - **3.** [que gasta poco - motor etc] economical; [- persona] thrifty.

economista *mf* economist.

economizar *vt lit & fig* to save.

ecosistema *m* ecosystem.

ecotasa *f* ecotax.

ecoturismo *m* ecotourism.

ecuación *f* equation.

ecuador *m* equator; **pasar el** ~ to pass the halfway mark.

Ecuador Ecuador.

ecuánime *adj* - **1.** [en el ánimo] level-headed, even - **2.** [en el juicio] impartial, fair.

ecuatoriano, na *adj & m,f* Ecuadorian, Ecuadoran.

ecuestre *adj* equestrian.

edad *f* age; **¿qué** ~ **tienes?** how old are you?; **tiene 25 años de** ~ she's 25 (years old); **una persona de** ~ an elderly person; ~ **adulta** adulthood; ~ **avanzada** old age; ~ **escolar** school age; **Edad Media** Middle Ages (*pl*); ~ **mental** mental age; ~ **del pavo** awkward age; **la tercera** ~ [ancianos] senior citizens (*pl*).

edecán *m Méx* assistant, aide.

edén *m* RELIG Eden; *fig* paradise.

edición *f* - **1.** [acción - IMPRENTA] publication; INFORM , RADIO & TV editing - **2.** [ejemplares] edition.

edicto *m* edict.

edificante *adj* [conducta] exemplary; [libro, discurso] edifying.

edificar *vt* [construir] to build.

edificio *m* building.

edil *m* (town) councillor.

Edimburgo Edinburgh.

editar *vt* - **1.** [libro, periódico] to publish; [disco] to release - **2.** INFORM , RADIO & TV to edit.

editor, ra <> *adj* publishing (*antes de sust*). <> *m,f* - **1.** [de libro, periódico] publisher - **2.** RADIO & TV editor.

editorial <> *adj* publishing (*antes de sust*). <> *m* editorial, leader. <> *f* publisher, publishing house.

edredón *m* eiderdown, comforter *US*; ~ **nórdico** duvet.

educación f -1. [enseñanza] education; ~ **primaria/secundaria** primary/secondary education - 2. [modales] good manners (pl); ¡qué poca ~! how rude!; **mala** ~ bad manners (pl).

educado, da adj polite, well-mannered; **mal** ~ rude, ill-mannered.

educador, ra m,f teacher.

educar vt -1. [enseñar] to educate - 2. [criar] to bring up - 3. [cuerpo, voz, oído] to train.

edulcorante m sweetener.

edulcorar vt to sweeten.

EE UU (abrev de **Estados Unidos**) mpl USA.

efectivamente adv [en respuestas] precisely, exactly.

efectividad f effectiveness.

efectivo, va adj -1. [útil] effective - 2. [real] actual, true; **hacer** ~ [gen] to carry out; [promesa] to keep; [dinero, crédito] to pay; [cheque] to cash.

➡ **efectivo** m [dinero] cash; **en** ~ in cash; ~ **en caja** cash in hand.

➡ **efectivos** mpl [personal] forces.

efecto m -1. [gen] effect; **de** ~ **retardado** delayed-action; ~ **2000** INFORM millennium bug; ~ **dominó** domino effect; ~ **invernadero** greenhouse effect; ~ **óptico** optical illusion; ~**s sonoros/visuales** sound/visual effects; ~**s especiales** special effects; ~**s secundarios** side effects - 2. [finalidad] aim, purpose; **a tal** ~ to that end; **a** ~**s** o **para los** ~**s de algo** as far as sthg is concerned - 3. [impresión] impression; **producir buen/mal** ~ to make a good/bad impression - 4. [de balón, bola] spin; **dar** ~ **a** to put spin on - 5. COM [documento] bill.

➡ **efectos personales** mpl personal possessions o effects.

➡ **en efecto** loc adv indeed.

efectuar vt [gen] to carry out; [compra, pago, viaje] to make.

➡ **efectuarse** vpr to take place.

efeméride f [suceso] major event; [conmemoración] anniversary.

efervescencia f [de líquido] effervescence; [de bebida] fizziness.

efervescente adj [bebida] fizzy.

eficacia f [eficiencia] efficiency; [efectividad] effectiveness.

eficaz adj -1. [eficiente] efficient - 2. [efectivo] effective.

eficiencia f efficiency.

eficiente adj efficient.

efímero, ra adj ephemeral.

efusión f [cordialidad] effusiveness, warmth.

efusivo, va adj effusive.

EGB (abrev de **educación general básica**) f former Spanish primary education system.

egipcio, cia adj & m,f Egyptian.

Egipto Egypt.

egocéntrico, ca adj egocentric, self-centred.

egoísmo m selfishness, egoism.

egoísta ⬦ adj egoistic, selfish. ⬦ mf egoist, selfish person.

ególatra ⬦ adj egotistical. ⬦ mf egotist.

egresado, da m,f Amér graduate.

egresar vi Amér to graduate.

egreso m Amér graduation.

eh interj: ¡ ~ ! hey!

ej. abrev de **ejemplar**.

eje m -1. [de rueda] axle; [de máquina] shaft - 2. GEOM axis - 3. fig [idea central] central idea, basis.

ejecución f -1. [realización] carrying out - 2. [de condenado] execution - 3. [de concierto] performance, rendition.

ejecutar vt -1. [realizar] to carry out - 2. [condenado] to execute - 3. [concierto] to perform - 4. INFORM [programa] to run.

ejecutivo, va ⬦ adj executive. ⬦ m,f [persona] executive.

➡ **ejecutivo** m POLÍT: **el** ~ the government.

ejem interj: ¡ ~ ! [expresa duda] um!; [expresa ironía] ahem!

ejemplar ⬦ adj exemplary. ⬦ m [de libro] copy; [de revista] issue; [de moneda] example; [de especie, raza] specimen; ~ **de muestra** specimen copy.

ejemplificar vt to exemplify.

ejemplo m example; **por** ~ for example; **predicar con el** ~ to practise what one preaches.

ejercer ⬦ vt -1. [profesión] to practise; [cargo] to hold - 2. [poder, derecho] to exercise; [influencia, dominio] to exert; ~ **presión sobre** to put pressure on. ⬦ vi to practise (one's profession); ~ **de** to practise o work as.

ejercicio m -1. [gen] exercise; **hacer** ~ to (do) exercise; ~ **escrito** written exercise; ~ **físico** physical exercise; ~**s de calentamiento** warm-up exercises; ~**s de mantenimiento** keep-fit exercises - 2. [de profesión] practising; [de cargo, funciones] carrying out - 3. [de poder, derecho] exercising - 4. MIL drill - 5. ECON : ~ **económico/fiscal** financial/tax year.

ejercitar vt [derecho] to exercise.

➡ **ejercitarse** vpr: ~**se (en)** to train (in).

ejército m MIL & fig army.

ejote m CAm, Méx green bean.

el, la (mpl **los**, fpl **las**) art (**el** antes de sustantivo femenino que empiece por 'a' o 'ha' tónica; a + el = al; de + el = del) - 1. [gen] the; [en sentido genérico] no se traduce; ~ **coche** the car; **la**

casa the house; **los niños** the children; ~ **agua/hacha/águila** the water/axe/eagle; **fui a recoger a los niños** I went to pick up the children; **los niños imitan a los adultos** children copy adults - **2.** [con sustantivo abstracto] *no se traduce*; ~ **amor** love; **la vida** life - **3.** [indica posesión, pertenencia]: **se partió la pierna** he broke his leg; **se quitó los zapatos** she took her shoes off; **tiene** ~ **pelo oscuro** he has dark hair - **4.** [con días de la semana]: **vuelven** ~ **sábado** they're coming back on Saturday - **5.** [con nombres propios geográficos] the; ~ **Sena** the (River) Seine; ~ **Everest** (Mount) Everest; **la España de la postguerra** post-war Spain - **6.** [con complemento de nombre, especificativo]: ~ **de** the one; **he perdido** ~ **tren, cogeré** ~ **de las nueve** I've missed the train, I'll get the nine o'clock one; ~ **de azul** the one in blue - **7.** [con complemento de nombre, posesivo]: **mi hermano y** ~ **de Juan** my brother and Juan's - **8.** [antes de frase]: ~ **que** [cosa] the one, whichever; [persona] whoever; **coge** ~ **que quieras** take whichever you like; ~ **que más corra** whoever runs fastest - **9.** [antes de adjetivo]: **prefiero** ~ **rojo al azul** I prefer the red one to the blue one.

él, ella *pron pers* - **1.** [sujeto, predicado - persona] he (*f* she); [- animal, cosa] it; **mi hermana es ella** she's the one who is my sister - **2.** *(después de prep)* [complemento] him (*f* her); **voy a ir de vacaciones con ella** I'm going on holiday with her; **díselo a ella** tell her it - **3.** [posesivo]: **de** ~ his; **de ella** hers.

elaborar *vt* [producto] to make, to manufacture; [idea] to work out; [plan, informe] to draw up.

elasticidad *f* [gen] elasticity.

elástico, ca *adj* [gen] elastic.
 ◆ **elástico** *m* [cinta] elastic.

elección *f* - **1.** [nombramiento] election - **2.** [opción] choice.
 ◆ **elecciones** *fpl* POLÍT election *(sg).*

electo, ta *adj* elect; **el presidente** ~ the president elect.

elector, ra *m,f* voter, elector.

electorado *m* electorate.

electoral *adj* electoral.

electricidad *f* electricity; ~ **estática** static electricity.

electricista *mf* electrician.

eléctrico, ca *adj* electric.

electrificar *vt* to electrify.

electrizar *vt* *fig* [exaltar] to electrify.

electrocutar *vt* to electrocute.

electrodoméstico *(gen pl)* *m* electrical household appliance.

electromagnético, ca *adj* electromagnetic.

electrón *m* electron.

electrónico, ca *adj* [de la electrónica] electronic.
 ◆ **electrónica** *f* electronics *(U).*

elefante, ta *m,f* elephant.

elegancia *f* elegance.

elegante *adj* - **1.** [persona, traje, estilo] elegant - **2.** [conducta, actitud, respuesta] dignified.

elegantoso, sa *adj* *Amér* elegant.

elegía *f* elegy.

elegir *vt* - **1.** [escoger] to choose, to select - **2.** [por votación] to elect.

elemental *adj* - **1.** [básico] basic - **2.** [obvio] obvious.

elemento ◇ *m* - **1.** [gen] element - **2.** [factor] factor - **3.** [persona - en equipo, colectivo] individual. ◇ *mf*: **un** ~ **de cuidado** a bad lot; **¡menudo** ~ **está hecho tu sobrino!** your nephew is a real tearaway!

elenco *m* [reparto] cast.

elepé *m* LP (record).

elevación *f* - **1.** [de pesos, objetos etc] lifting; [de nivel, altura, precios] rise - **2.** [de terreno] elevation, rise.

elevado, da *adj* [alto] high; *fig* [sublime] lofty.

elevador *m* - **1.** [montacargas] hoist - **2.** *Méx* [ascensor] lift *UK*, elevator *US*.

elevalunas *m inv* window winder.

elevar *vt* - **1.** [gen & MAT] to raise; [peso, objeto] to lift - **2.** [ascender]: ~ **a alguien (a)** to elevate sb (to).
 ◆ **elevarse** *vpr* [gen] to rise; [edificio, montaña] to rise up; ~ **se a** [altura] to reach; [gastos, daños] to amount *o* come to.

elidir *vt* to elide.

eliminar *vt* [gen] to eliminate; [contaminación, enfermedad] to get rid of.

eliminatorio, ria *adj* qualifying *(antes de sust).*
 ◆ **eliminatoria** *f* [gen] qualifying round; [en atletismo] heat.

elipse *f* ellipse.

élite, elite *f* elite.

elitista *adj* & *mf* elitist.

elixir, elíxir *m* - **1.** FARM : ~ **bucal** mouthwash - **2.** *fig* [remedio milagroso] elixir.

ella ▷ **él.**

ellas *fpl* ▷ **ellos.**

ello *pron pers (neutro)* it; **no nos llevamos bien, pero** ~ **no nos impide formar un buen equipo** we don't get on very well, but it *o* that doesn't stop us making a good team; **no quiero hablar de** ~ I don't want to talk about it; **por** ~ for that reason.

ellos, ellas *pron pers* - **1.** [sujeto, predicado] they; **los invitados son** ~ they are the guests, it is they who are the guests

- 2. *(después de prep)* [complemento] them; **me voy al bar con ellas** I'm going with them to the bar; **díselo a ~** tell them it **- 3.** [posesivo]: **de ~ /ellas** theirs.

elocuencia *f* eloquence.

elocuente *adj* eloquent; **se hizo un silencio ~** the silence said it all.

elogiar *vt* to praise.

elogio *m* praise.

elote *m CAm, Méx* corncob, ear of maize *o* corn *US.*

El Salvador El Salvador.

elucidar *vt* to elucidate, to throw light upon.

elucubración *f* **- 1.** [reflexión] reflection, meditation **- 2.** *despec* [divagación] mental meandering.

elucubrar *vt* **- 1.** [reflexionar] to reflect *o* meditate upon **- 2.** *despec* [divagar] to theorize about.

eludir *vt* [gen] to avoid; [perseguidores] to escape.

emanar ◆ **emanar de** *vi* to emanate from.

emancipación *f* [de mujeres, esclavos] emancipation; [de menores de edad] coming of age; [de países] obtaining of independence.

emancipar *vt* [gen] to emancipate, to free; [países] to grant independence (to).

◆ **emanciparse** *vpr* to free o.s., to become independent.

embadurnar *vt*: **~ algo (de)** to smear sthg (with).

embajada *f* [edificio] embassy.

embajador, ra *m,f* ambassador.

embalaje *m* [acción] packing.

embalar *vt* to wrap up, to pack.

◆ **embalarse** *vpr* [acelerar - corredor] to race away; [- vehículo] to pick up speed.

embalsamar *vt* to embalm.

embalse *m* reservoir.

embarazada ◇ *adj f* pregnant; **dejar ~ a alguien** to get sb pregnant; **quedarse ~** to get pregnant. ◇ *f* pregnant woman.

embarazar *vt* **- 1.** [impedir] to restrict **- 2.** [cohibir] to inhibit.

embarazo *m* **- 1.** [preñez] pregnancy; **interrumpir un ~** to terminate a pregnancy; **prueba del ~** pregnancy test; **~ ectópico** *o* **extrauterino** ectopic pregnancy **- 2.** [timidez] embarrassment.

embarazoso, sa *adj* awkward, embarrassing.

embarcación *f* [barco] craft, boat; **~ pesquera** fishing boat; **~ de recreo** pleasure boat.

embarcadero *m* jetty.

embarcar ◇ *vt* [personas] to board;

[mercancías] to ship. ◇ *vi* to board.

◆ **embarcarse** *vpr* [para viajar] to board.

embargar *vt* **- 1.** DER to seize **- 2.** [suj: emoción etc] to overcome.

embargo *m* **- 1.** DER seizure **- 2.** ECON embargo.

◆ **sin embargo** *loc adv* however, nevertheless.

embarque *m* [de personas] boarding; [de mercancías] embarkation.

embarrancar *vi* to run aground.

embarullar *vt fam* to mess up.

◆ **embarullarse** *vpr fam* to get into a muddle.

embaucar *vt* to swindle, to deceive.

embeber *vt* to soak up.

◆ **embeberse** *vpr*: **~se (en algo)** [ensimismarse] to become absorbed (in sthg); *fig* [empaparse] to immerse o.s. (in sthg).

embellecer *vt* to adorn, to embellish.

embestida *f* [gen] attack; [de toro] charge.

embestir *vt* [gen] to attack; [toro] to charge.

emblema *m* **- 1.** [divisa, distintivo] emblem, badge **- 2.** [símbolo] symbol.

embobar *vt* to captivate.

embocadura *f* [de instrumento] mouthpiece.

embolia *f* embolism.

émbolo *m* AUTOM piston.

embolsarse *vpr* [ganar] to earn.

embonar *vt Andes, Cuba, Méx fam* **- 1.** [ajustar] to suit **- 2.** [abonar] to manure **- 3.** [ensamblar] to join.

emborrachar *vt* to make drunk.

◆ **emborracharse** *vpr* to get drunk.

emborronar *vt* [garabatear] to scribble on; [manchar] to smudge.

emboscada *f* lit & fig ambush.

embotellado, da *adj* bottled.

embotellamiento *m* [de tráfico] traffic jam.

embotellar *vt* [líquido] to bottle.

embragar *vi* to engage the clutch.

embrague *m* clutch; **~ automático** automatic clutch.

embriagar *vt* **- 1.** [extasiar] to intoxicate **- 2.** [emborrachar] to make drunk.

◆ **embriagarse** *vpr* [emborracharse]: **~se (con)** to get drunk (on).

embriaguez *f* **- 1.** [borrachera] drunkenness **- 2.** [éxtasis] intoxication.

embrión *m* embryo.

embrionario, ria *adj fig* [inicial] embryonic.

embrollo *m* **- 1.** [de hilos] tangle **- 2.** *fig* [lío] mess; [mentira] lie.

embromado, da *adj Andes, Carib, RP fam* [complicado] tricky.

embrujar *vt lit* & *fig* to bewitch.

embrujo *m* [maleficio] curse, spell; *fig* [de ciudad, ojos] charm, magic.

embrutecer *vt* to brutalize.

➧ **embrutecerse** *vpr* to become brutalized.

embuchado, da *adj*: **carne embuchada** cured cold meat.

embudo *m* funnel.

embuste *m* lie.

embustero, ra ◇ *adj* lying. ◇ *m,f* liar.

embute *m Amér fam* bribe.

embutido *m* [comida] cold cured meat.

embutir *vt lit* & *fig* to stuff.

emergencia *f* - **1.** [urgencia] emergency; **en caso de** ~ in case of emergency - **2.** [brote] emergence.

emerger *vi* [salir del agua] to emerge; [aparecer] to come into view, to appear.

emigración *f* [de personas] emigration; [de aves] migration.

emigrante *adj* & *mf* emigrant.

emigrar *vi* [persona] to emigrate; [ave] to migrate.

eminencia *f* [persona] leading light.

➧ **Eminencia** *f*: **Su Eminencia** His Eminence.

eminente *adj* [distinguido] eminent.

emirato *m* emirate.

Emiratos Árabes Unidos *mpl*: **los** ~ United Arab Emirates.

emisión *f* - **1.** [de energía, rayos etc] emission - **2.** [de bonos, sellos, monedas] issue - **3.** [RADIO & TV - transmisión] broadcasting; [- programa] programme, broadcast.

emisor, ra *adj* transmitting *(antes de sust)*.

➧ **emisora** *f* radio station; ~ **a pirata** pirate radio station.

emitir ◇ *vt* - **1.** [rayos, calor, sonidos] to emit - **2.** [moneda, sellos, bonos] to issue - **3.** [expresar - juicio, opinión] to express; [- fallo] to pronounce - **4.** RADIO & TV to broadcast. ◇ *vi* to broadcast.

emoción *f* - **1.** [conmoción, sentimiento] emotion - **2.** [expectación] excitement; **¡qué** ~**!** how exciting!

emocionante *adj* - **1.** [conmovedor] moving, touching - **2.** [apasionante] exciting, thrilling.

emocionar *vt* - **1.** [conmover] to move - **2.** [excitar, apasionar] to thrill, to excite.

➧ **emocionarse** *vpr* - **1.** [conmoverse] to be moved - **2.** [excitarse, apasionarse] to get excited.

emotivo, va *adj* [persona] emotional; [escena, palabras] moving.

empacar *vi Amér* to pack.

empachar *vt* to give indigestion to.

➧ **empacharse** *vpr* [hartarse] to stuff o.s.; [sufrir indigestión] to get indigestion.

empacho *m* [indigestión] upset stomach, indigestion.

empadronar *vt* ≃ to register on the electoral roll.

➧ **empadronarse** *vpr* ≃ to register on the electoral roll.

empalagoso, sa *adj* sickly, cloying.

empalizada *f* [cerca] fence; MIL stockade.

empalmar ◇ *vt* [tubos, cables] to connect, to join. ◇ *vi* - **1.** [autocares, trenes] to connect - **2.** [carreteras] to link o join (up).

empalme *m* - **1.** [entre cables, tubos] joint, connection - **2.** [de líneas férreas, carreteras] junction.

empanada *f* pasty.

empanadilla *f* small pasty.

empanar *vt* CULIN to coat in breadcrumbs.

empantanar *vt* to flood.

➧ **empantanarse** *vpr* - **1.** [inundarse] to be flooded o waterlogged - **2.** *fig* [atascarse] to get bogged down.

empañar *vt* - **1.** [cristal] to mist o steam up - **2.** *fig* [reputación] to tarnish.

➧ **empañarse** *vpr* to mist o steam up.

empapar *vt* - **1.** [mojar] to soak - **2.** [absorber] to soak up.

➧ **empaparse** *vpr* - **1.** [mojarse] to get soaked - **2.** [enterarse bien]: **se empapó de sociología antes de dar la conferencia** she did a lot of reading up about sociology before giving her speech; **¡para que te empapes!** *fam* so there!

empapelar *vt* [pared] to paper.

empaque *m Méx* [en paquetes, bolsas, cajas] packing; [en latas] canning; [en botellas] bottling.

empaquetar *vt* to pack, to package.

emparedado, da *adj* confined.

➧ **emparedado** *m* sandwich.

emparedar *vt* to lock away.

emparejar *vt* [aparejar - personas] to pair off; [- zapatos etc] to match (up).

emparentar *vi*: ~ **con** to marry into.

empastar *vt* to fill.

empaste *m* filling.

empatar *vi* DEP to draw; [en elecciones etc] to tie; ~ **a cero** to draw nil-nil.

empate *m* [resultado] draw; **un** ~ **a cero/dos** a goalless/two-all draw.

empedernido, da *adj* [bebedor, fumador] heavy; [criminal, jugador] hardened.

empedrado *m* paving.

empedrar *vt* to pave.

empeine *m* [de pie, zapato] instep.

empellón *m* push, shove; **abrirse paso a empellones** to shove o push one's way through.

empeñado, da *adj* - **1.** [en préstamo] in

pawn - **2.** [obstinado] determined; **estar ~ en hacer algo** to be determined to do sthg.

empeñar *vt* [joyas etc] to pawn.

◆ **empeñarse** *vpr* - **1.** [obstinarse] to insist; **~se en hacer algo** [obstinarse] to insist on doing sthg; [persistir] to persist in doing sthg - **2.** [endeudarse] to get into debt.

empeño *m* - **1.** [de joyas etc] pawning; **casa de ~s** pawnshop - **2.** [obstinación] determination; **poner mucho ~ en algo** to put a lot of effort into sth; **tener ~ en hacer algo** to be determined to do sthg.

empeorar *vi* to get worse, to deteriorate.

empequeñecer *vt* [quitar importancia a] to diminish; [en una comparación] to overshadow, to dwarf.

emperador, emperatriz *m,f* emperor (*f* empress).

◆ **emperador** *m* [pez] swordfish.

emperifollar *vt fam* to doll *o* tart up.

emperrarse *vpr*: **~ (en hacer algo)** to insist (on doing sthg).

empezar ◇ *vt* to begin, to start. ◇ *vi*: **~ (a hacer algo)** to begin *o* start (to do sthg); **~ (por hacer algo)** to begin *o* start (by doing sthg); **para ~** to begin *o* start with; **por algo se empieza** you've got to start somewhere.

empinado, da *adj* steep.

empinar *vt* [levantar] to raise.

◆ **empinarse** *vpr* - **1.** [animal] to stand up on its hind legs - **2.** [persona] to stand on tiptoe.

empírico, ca *adj* empirical.

emplasto *m* FARM poultice.

emplazamiento *m* [ubicación] location.

emplazar *vt* - **1.** [situar] to locate; MIL to position - **2.** [citar] to summon; DER to summons.

empleado, da *m,f* [gen] employee; [de banco, administración, oficina] clerk.

emplear *vt* - **1.** [usar - objetos, materiales etc] to use; [- tiempo] to spend; **~ algo en hacer algo** to use sthg to do sthg - **2.** [contratar] to employ.

◆ **emplearse** *vpr* - **1.** [colocarse] to find a job - **2.** [usarse] to be used.

empleo *m* - **1.** [uso] use; **'modo de ~'** 'instructions for use' - **2.** [trabajo] employment; [puesto] job; **estar sin ~** to be out of work.

emplomadura *f RP* [de diente] filling.

empobrecer *vt* to impoverish.

◆ **empobrecerse** *vpr* to get poorer.

empollar ◇ *vt* - **1.** [huevo] to incubate - **2.** *fam* [estudiar] to swot up on. ◇ *vi fam* to swot.

empollón, ona *mf fam* swot.

empolvarse *vpr* to powder one's face.

empotrado, da *adj* fitted, built-in.

empotrar *vt* to fit, to build in.

emprendedor, ra *adj* enterprising.

emprender *vt* - **1.** [trabajo] to start; [viaje, marcha] to set off on; **~ vuelo** to fly off - **2.** *loc*: **la con alguien** to take it out on sb; **~ la a golpes con alguien** to start hitting sb.

empresa *f* - **1.** [sociedad] company; **pequeña y mediana ~** small and medium-sized business; **~ de trabajo temporal** temping agency - **2.** [acción] enterprise, undertaking.

empresarial *adj* management (*antes de sust*).

◆ **empresariales** *fpl* business studies.

empresario, ria *m,f* [patrono] employer; [hombre, mujer de negocios] businessman (*f* businesswoman); [de teatro] impresario.

empréstito *m* debenture loan.

empujar *vt* to push; **~ a alguien a que haga algo** to push sb into doing sthg.

empuje *m* - **1.** [presión] pressure - **2.** [energía] energy, drive.

empujón *m* [empellón] shove, push; **abrirse paso a empujones** to shove *o* push one's way through.

empuñadura *f* handle; [de espada] hilt.

empuñar *vt* to take hold of, to grasp.

emulsión *f* emulsion.

en *prep* - **1.** [lugar - en el interior de] in; [- sobre la superficie de] on; [- en un punto concreto de] at; **viven ~ la capital** they live in the capital; **tiene el dinero ~ el banco** he keeps his money in the bank; **~ la mesa/el plato** on the table/plate; **~ casa/el trabajo** at home/work - **2.** [dirección] into; **el avión cayó ~ el mar** the plane fell into the sea; **entraron ~ la habitación** they came into the room - **3.** [tiempo - mes, año etc] in; [- día] on; **nació ~ 1940/mayo** he was born in 1940/May; **~ aquel día** on that day; **~ Nochebuena** on Christmas Eve; **~ Navidades** at Christmas; **~ aquella época** at that time, in those days; **~ un par de días** in a couple of days - **4.** [medio de transporte] by; **ir ~ tren/coche/avión/barco** to go by train/car/plane/boat - **5.** [modo] in; **~ voz baja** in a low voice; **lo dijo ~ inglés** she said it in English; **pagar ~ libras** to pay in pounds; **la inflación aumentó ~ un 10%** inflation increased by 10%; **todo se lo gasta ~ ropa** he spends everything on clothes - **6.** [precio] in; **las ganancias se calculan ~ millones** profits are calculated in millions; **te lo dejo en 5.000** I'll let you have it for 5,000 - **7.** [tema]: **es un experto ~ la materia** he's an expert on the subject; **es doctor ~ medicina** he's a doctor of medicine - **8.** [causa] from; **lo detecté ~ su forma de**

hablar I could tell from the way he was speaking - **9.** [materia] in, made of; ~ **seda** in silk - **10.** [cualidad] in terms of; **le supera** ~ **inteligencia** she is more intelligent than he is.

enagua *f (gen pl)* petticoat.

enajenación *f,* **enajenamiento** *m* [locura] insanity; [éxtasis] rapture.

enajenar *vt* - **1.** [volver loco] to drive mad; [extasiar] to enrapture - **2.** [propiedad] to alienate.

enaltecer *vt* to praise.

enamoradizo, za *adj* who falls in love easily.

enamorado, da ◇ *adj:* ~ **(de)** in love (with). ◇ *m,f* lover.

enamorar *vt* to win the heart of.

◆ **enamorarse** *vpr:* ~**se (de)** to fall in love (with).

enano, na *adj & m,f* dwarf; **disfrutar como un** ~ *fam* to have a whale of a time.

enarbolar *vt* [bandera] to raise, to hoist; [pancarta] to hold up; [arma] to brandish.

enardecer *vt* [gen] to inflame; [persona, multitud] to fill with enthusiasm.

encabezamiento *m* [de carta, escrito] heading; [de artículo periodístico] headline; [preámbulo] foreword.

encabezar *vt* - **1.** [artículo de periódico] to headline; [libro] to write the foreword for - **2.** [lista, carta] to head - **3.** [marcha, expedición] to lead.

encabritarse *vpr* - **1.** [caballo, moto] to rear up - **2.** *fam* [persona] to get shirty.

encadenar *vt* - **1.** [atar] to chain (up) - **2.** [enlazar] to link (together).

encajar ◇ *vt* - **1.** [meter ajustando]: ~ **(en)** to fit (into) - **2.** [meter con fuerza]: ~ **(en)** to push (into) - **3.** [hueso dislocado] to set - **4.** [recibir - golpe, noticia, críticas] to take. ◇ *vi* - **1.** [piezas, objetos] to fit - **2.** [hechos, declaraciones, datos]: ~ **(con)** to square (with), to match.

encaje *m* [tejido] lace.

encalar *vt* to whitewash.

encallar *vi* [barco] to run aground.

encaminar *vt* - **1.** [persona, pasos] to direct - **2.** [medidas, leyes, actividades] to aim; **encaminada a** aimed at.

◆ **encaminarse** *vpr:* ~**se a/hacia** to set off for/towards.

encamotarse *vpr Andes, CAm fam* to fall in love.

encandilar *vt* to dazzle, to impress greatly.

encantado, da *adj* - **1.** [contento] delighted; **estar** ~ **con algo/alguien** to be delighted with sth/sb; ~ **de conocerle** pleased to meet you - **2.** [hechizado - casa, lugar] haunted; [- persona] bewitched.

encantador, ra *adj* delightful, charming.

encantar *vt* - **1.** [gustar]: ~ **le a alguien algo/hacer algo** to love sthg/doing sthg; **me encanta el chocolate** I love chocolate; **le encanta bailar** she loves dancing - **2.** [embrujar] to bewitch, to cast a spell on.

encanto *m* - **1.** [atractivo] charm; **ser un** ~ to be a treasure *o* a delight - **2.** [hechizo] spell.

encapotado, da *adj* overcast.

encapotarse *vpr* to cloud over.

encapricharse *vpr* [obstinarse]: ~ **con algo/hacer algo** to set one's mind on sthg/ doing sthg.

encapuchado, da *adj* hooded.

encaramar *vt* to lift up.

◆ **encaramarse** *vpr:* ~**se (a** *o* **en)** to climb up (onto).

encarar *vt* [hacer frente a] to confront, to face up to.

◆ **encararse** *vpr* [enfrentarse]: ~**se a** *o* **con** to stand up to.

encarcelar *vt* to imprison.

encarecer *vt* [productos, precios] to make more expensive.

◆ **encarecerse** *vpr* to become more expensive.

encarecidamente *adv* earnestly.

encarecimiento *m* [de producto, coste] increase in price.

encargado, da ◇ *adj:* ~ **(de)** responsible (for), in charge (of). ◇ *m,f* [gen] person in charge; COM manager (*f* manageress); ~ **de negocios** POLÍT chargé d'affaires.

encargar *vt* - **1.** [poner al cargo]: ~ **a alguien de algo** to put sb in charge of sthg; ~ **a alguien que haga algo** to tell sb to do sthg - **2.** [pedir] to order.

◆ **encargarse** *vpr* [ocuparse]: ~**se de** to be in charge of; **yo me encargaré de eso** I'll take care of *o* see to that.

encargo *m* - **1.** [pedido] order; **por** ~ to order - **2.** [recado] errand - **3.** [tarea] task, assignment.

encariñarse *vpr:* ~ **con** to become fond of.

encarnación *f* [personificación - cosa] embodiment; [- persona] personification.

encarnado, da *adj* - **1.** [personificado] incarnate - **2.** [color] red.

encarnizado, da *adj* bloody, bitter.

encarnizarse *vpr:* ~ **con** [presa] to fall upon; [prisionero, enemigo] to treat savagely.

encarrilar *vt fig* [negocio, situación] to put on the right track, to point in the right direction.

encasillar *vt* [clasificar] to pigeonhole; TEATR to typecast.

encasquetar *vt* - **1.** [imponer]: ~ **algo a**

alguien [idea, teoría] to drum sthg into sb; [discurso, lección] to force sb to sit through sthg - **2.** [sombrero] to pull on.

encasquillarse *vpr* to get jammed.

encauzar *vt* - **1.** [corriente] to channel - **2.** [orientar] to direct.

encendedor *m* lighter.

encender *vt* - **1.** [vela, cigarro, chimenea] to light - **2.** [aparato] to switch on - **3.** *fig* [avivar - entusiasmo, ira] to arouse; [- pasión, discusión] to inflame.

➡ **encenderse** *vpr* - **1.** [fuego, gas] to ignite; [luz, estufa] to come on - **2.** *fig* [ojos] to light up; [persona, rostro] to go red, to blush; [de ira] to flare up.

encendido, da *adj* [luz, colilla] burning; **la luz está encendida** the light is on.

➡ **encendido** *m* AUTOM ignition; ~ **electrónico** electronic ignition.

encerado, da *adj* waxed, polished.

➡ **encerado** *m* [pizarra] blackboard.

encerar *vt* to wax, to polish.

encerrar *vt* - **1.** [recluir - gen] to shut (up *o* in); [- con llave] to lock (up *o* in); [- en la cárcel] to lock away *o* up - **2.** [contener] to contain.

➡ **encerrarse** *vpr* [gen] to shut o.s. away; [con llave] to lock o.s. away.

encestar *vt* & *vi* to score *(in basketball)*.

enceste *m* basket.

encharcar *vt* to waterlog.

➡ **encharcarse** *vpr* - **1.** [terreno] to become waterlogged - **2.** [pulmones] to become flooded.

enchastrar *vt RP fam* to make dirty.

enchilada *f Méx* filled tortilla.

enchilarse *vpr Méx fam* [enfadarse] to get angry.

enchufado, da *adj fam*: **estar** ~ to get where one is through connections.

enchufar *vt* - **1.** [aparato] to plug in - **2.** *fam* [a una persona] to pull strings for.

enchufe *m* - **1.** [ELECTR - macho] plug; [- hembra] socket; ~ **múltiple** adapter - **2.** *fam* [recomendación] connections *(pl)*; **obtener algo por** ~ to get sthg by pulling strings *o* through one's connections.

encía *f* gum.

encíclica *f* encyclical.

enciclopedia *f* encyclopedia.

encierro *m* [protesta] sit-in.

encima *adv* - **1.** [arriba] on top; **yo vivo** ~ I live upstairs; **por** ~ [superficialmente] superficially - **2.** [además] on top of that - **3.** [sobre sí]: **lleva un abrigo** ~ she has a coat on; **¿llevas dinero** ~? have you got any money on you?

➡ **encima de** *loc prep* - **1.** [en lugar superior que] above; **vivo** ~ **de tu casa** I live upstairs

from you - **2.** [sobre, en] on (top of); **el pan está** ~ **de la mesa** the bread is on (top of) the table - **3.** [además] on top of.

➡ **por encima de** *loc prep* - **1.** [gen] over; **vive por** ~ **de sus posibilidades** he lives beyond his means - **2.** *fig* [más que] more than; **por** ~ **de todo** more than anything else.

encina *f* holm oak.

encinta *adj f* pregnant.

enclave *m* enclave.

enclenque *adj* sickly, frail.

encoger ◇ *vt* - **1.** [ropa] to shrink - **2.** [miembro, músculo] to contract. ◇ *vi* to shrink.

➡ **encogerse** *vpr* - **1.** [ropa] to shrink; [músculos etc] to contract; ~ **se de hombros** to shrug one's shoulders - **2.** *fig* [apocarse] to cringe.

encolar *vt* [silla etc] to glue; [pared] to size, to paste.

encolerizar *vt* to infuriate, to enrage.

➡ **encolerizarse** *vpr* to get angry.

encomendar *vt* to entrust.

➡ **encomendarse** *vpr*: ~ **se a** [persona] to entrust o.s. to; [Dios, santos] to put one's trust in.

encomienda *f* - **1.** [encargo] assignment, mission - **2.** *Amér* [paquete] parcel.

encontrado, da *adj* conflicting.

encontrar *vt* - **1.** [gen] to find - **2.** [dificultades] to encounter - **3.** [persona] to meet, to come across.

➡ **encontrarse** *vpr* - **1.** [hallarse] to be; **se encuentra en París** she's in Paris - **2.** [coincidir]: ~ **se (con alguien)** to meet (sb); **me encontré con Juan** I ran into *o* met Juan - **3.** [de ánimo] to feel; **¿cómo te encuentras?** how do you feel?, how are you feeling?; ~ **se bien/mal** to feel fine/ill - **4.** [chocar] to collide.

encorvar *vt* to bend.

➡ **encorvarse** *vpr* to bend down *o* over.

encrespar *vt* - **1.** [pelo] to curl; [mar] to make choppy *o* rough - **2.** [irritar] to irritate.

➡ **encresparse** *vpr* - **1.** [mar] to get rough - **2.** [persona] to get irritated.

encrucijada *f* lit & *fig* crossroads *(sg)*.

encuadernación *f* binding; ~ **en cuero** leather binding; ~ **en tela** cloth binding.

encuadernador, ra *m,f* bookbinder.

encuadernar *vt* to bind.

encuadrar *vt* - **1.** [enmarcar - cuadro, tema] to frame - **2.** [encerrar] to contain - **3.** [encajar] to fit.

encubierto, ta ◇ *pp* ▷ **encubrir**. ◇ *adj* [intento] covert; [insulto, significado] hidden.

encubridor, ra *m,f*: ~ **(de)** accessory (to).

encubrir vt [delito] to conceal; [persona] to harbour.

encuentro m -1. [acción] meeting, encounter; un ~ casual o fortuito a chance meeting -2. DEP game, match -3. [hallazgo] find.

encuesta f -1. [de opinión] survey, opinion poll -2. [investigación] investigation, inquiry.

encuestador, ra m,f pollster.

encuestar vt to poll.

endeble adj [persona, argumento] weak, feeble; [objeto] fragile.

endémico, ca adj MED endemic.

endemoniado, da adj -1. fam [molesto - niño] wicked; [- trabajo] very tricky -2. [desagradable] terrible, foul -3. [poseído] possessed (of the devil).

endenantes adv Amér fam before.

enderezar vt -1. [poner derecho] to straighten -2. [poner vertical] to put upright -3. fig [corregir] to set right, to straighten out.

➡ **enderezarse** vpr [sentado] to sit up straight; [de pie] to stand up straight.

endeudamiento m debt.

endeudarse vpr to get into debt.

endiablado, da adj [persona] wicked; [tiempo, genio] foul; [problema, crucigrama] fiendishly difficult.

endibia = endivia.

endiñar vt fam: ~ algo a alguien [golpe] to land o deal sb sthg; [trabajo, tarea] to lumber sb with sthg.

endivia, endibia f endive.

endomingado, da adj fam dressed-up, dolled-up.

endosar vt -1. [tarea, trabajo]: ~ algo a alguien to lumber sb with sthg -2. COM to endorse.

endulzar vt [con azúcar] to sweeten; fig [hacer agradable] to ease, to make more bearable.

endurecer vt -1. [gen] to harden -2. [fortalecer] to strengthen.

enemigo, ga ◇ adj enemy (antes de sust); ser ~ de algo to hate sthg. ◇ m,f enemy; pasarse al ~ to go over to the enemy.

enemistad f enmity.

enemistar vt to make enemies of.

➡ **enemistarse** vpr: ~se (con) to fall out (with).

energético, ca adj energy (antes de sust).

energía f -1. [gen] energy; ~ atómica o nuclear nuclear power; ~ eléctrica/eólica/hidráulica electric/wind/water power; ~ solar solar energy o power -2. [fuerza] strength; hay que empujar con ~ you have to push hard.

enérgico, ca adj [gen] energetic; [carácter] forceful; [gesto, medida] vigorous; [decisión, postura] emphatic.

energúmeno, na m,f madman (f madwoman); gritaba como un ~ he was screaming like one possessed.

enero m January; ver también septiembre.

enervar vt -1. [debilitar] to sap, to weaken -2. [poner nervioso] to exasperate.

enésimo, ma adj -1. MAT nth -2. fig umpteenth; por enésima vez for the umpteenth time.

enfadado, da adj angry.

enfadar vt to anger.

➡ **enfadarse** vpr: ~se (con) to get angry (with).

enfado m anger.

énfasis m inv emphasis; poner ~ en algo to emphasize sthg.

enfático, ca adj emphatic.

enfatizar vt to emphasize, to stress.

enfermar ◇ vt [causar enfermedad a] to make ill. ◇ vi to fall ill; ~ del pecho to develop a chest complaint.

enfermedad f illness; contraer una ~ to catch an illness; ~ contagiosa contagious disease; ~ de Creutzfeldt-Jakob Creutzfeldt-Jakob disease, CJD; ~ infecciosa/venérea infectious/venereal disease; ~ mental mental illness; ~ profesional occupational disease; ~ terminal terminal illness.

enfermera ▷ enfermero.

enfermería f sick bay.

enfermero, ra m, f male nurse (f nurse).

enfermizo, za adj lit & fig unhealthy.

enfermo, ma ◇ adj ill, sick; caer ~ to fall ill. ◇ m,f [gen] invalid, sick person; [en el hospital] patient; ~ terminal terminally ill patient.

enfilar vt -1. [ir por - camino] to go o head straight along -2. [apuntar - arma] to aim.

enflaquecer vi to grow thin, to lose weight.

enfocar vt -1. [imagen, objetivo] to focus -2. [suj: luz, foco] to shine on -3. [tema, asunto] to approach, to look at.

enfoque m -1. [de imagen] focus -2. [de asunto] approach, angle; dar un ~ nuevo a algo to adopt a new approach to sthg.

enfrascar vt to bottle.

➡ **enfrascarse en** vpr [riña] to get embroiled in; [lectura, conversación] to become engrossed in.

enfrentar vt -1. [hacer frente a] to confront, to face -2. [poner frente a frente] to bring face to face.

➡ **enfrentarse** vpr -1. [luchar, encontrarse] to meet, to clash -2. [oponerse]: ~se con alguien to confront sb.

enfrente *adv* - **1.** [delante] opposite; **la tienda de** ~ the shop across the road; ~ **de** opposite - **2.** [en contra]: **tiene a todos** ~ everyone's against her.

enfriamiento *m* - **1.** [catarro] cold - **2.** [acción] cooling.

enfriar *vt lit & fig* to cool.

  ◆ **enfriarse** *vpr* - **1.** [líquido, pasión, amistad] to cool down - **2.** [quedarse demasiado frío] to go cold - **3.** MED to catch a cold.

enfundar *vt* [espada] to sheathe; [pistola] to put away.

enfurecer *vt* to infuriate, to madden.

  ◆ **enfurecerse** *vpr* [gen] to get furious.

enfurruñarse *vpr fam* to sulk.

engalanar *vt* to decorate.

  ◆ **engalanarse** *vpr* to dress up.

enganchar *vt* - **1.** [agarrar - vagones] to couple; [- remolque, caballos] to hitch up; [- pez] to hook - **2.** [colgar de un gancho] to hang up.

  ◆ **engancharse** *vpr* - **1.** [prenderse]: ~**se algo con algo** to catch sthg on sthg - **2.** [alistarse] to enlist, to join up - **3.** [hacerse adicto]: ~**se (a)** to get hooked (on).

enganche *m* - **1.** [de trenes] coupling - **2.** [gancho] hook - **3.** [reclutamiento] enlistment - **4.** *Méx* [depósito] deposit.

engañar *vt* - **1.** [gen] to deceive; **engaña a su marido** she cheats on her husband - **2.** [estafar] to cheat, to swindle.

  ◆ **engañarse** *vpr* - **1.** [hacerse ilusiones] to delude o.s. - **2.** [equivocarse] to be wrong.

engaño *m* [gen] deceit; [estafa] swindle.

engañoso, sa *adj* [persona, palabras] deceitful; [aspecto, apariencia] deceptive; [consejo] misleading.

engarzar *vt* - **1.** [encadenar - abalorios] to thread; [- perlas] to string - **2.** [enlazar - palabras] to string together.

engatusar *vt fam* to get round; ~ **a alguien para que haga algo** to coax *o* cajole sb into doing sthg.

engendrar *vt* - **1.** [procrear] to give birth to, to beget - **2.** [originar] to give rise to.

engendro *m* - **1.** [obra de mala calidad] monstrosity - **2.** [ser deforme] freak, deformed creature; [niño] malformed child.

englobar *vt* to bring together.

engomar *vt* to stick, to glue.

engordar ◇ *vt* - **1.** [cebar] to fatten up - **2.** *fig* [aumentar] to swell. ◇ *vi* to put on weight.

engorroso, sa *adj* bothersome.

engrampadora *f RP* stapler.

engrampar *vt RP* to staple.

engranaje *m* - **1.** [piezas - de reloj, piñón] cogs *(pl)*; [- AUTOM] gears *(pl)* - **2.** [aparato - político, burocrático] machinery.

engrandecer *vt* - **1.** *fig* [enaltecer] to exalt - **2.** [aumentar] to increase, to enlarge.

engrasar *vt* [gen] to lubricate; [bisagra, mecanismo] to oil; [eje, bandeja] to grease.

engreído, da *adj* conceited, full of one's own importance.

engrosar *vt fig* [aumentar] to swell.

engullir *vt* to gobble up, to wolf down.

enhebrar *vt* [gen] to thread; [perlas] to string.

enhorabuena ◇ *f* congratulations *(pl)*; **dar la** ~ **a alguien** to congratulate sb. ◇ *interj*: **¡** ~ **(por ...)!** congratulations (on ...)!

enigma *m* enigma.

enigmático, ca *adj* enigmatic.

enjabonar *vt* [con jabón] to soap.

enjambre *m lit & fig* swarm.

enjaular *vt* [en jaula] to cage; *fam* [en prisión] to jail, to lock up.

enjuagar *vt* to rinse.

enjuague *m* rinse.

enjugar *vt* - **1.** [secar] to dry, to wipe away - **2.** [pagar - deuda] to pay off; [- déficit] to cancel out.

enjuiciar *vt* - **1.** DER to try - **2.** [opinar] to judge.

enjuto, ta *adj* [delgado] lean.

enlace *m* - **1.** [acción] link - **2.** [persona] go-between; ~ **sindical** shop steward - **3.** [casamiento]: ~ **(matrimonial)** marriage - **4.** [de trenes] connection; **estación de** ~ junction; **vía de** ~ crossover - **5.** INFORM : ~ **de datos** data link; ~ **hipertextual** *o* **de hipertexto** hypertext link.

enlatar *vt* to can, to tin.

enlazar ◇ *vt* : ~ **algo a** [atar] to tie sthg up to; [trabar, relacionar] to link *o* connect sthg with. ◇ *vi* : ~ **en** [trenes] to connect at.

enloquecer ◇ *vt* - **1.** [volver loco] to drive mad - **2.** *fig* [gustar mucho] to drive wild *o* crazy. ◇ *vi* to go mad.

enlutado, da *adj* in mourning.

enmarañar *vt* - **1.** [enredar] to tangle (up) - **2.** [complicar] to complicate, to confuse.

  ◆ **enmarañarse** *vpr* - **1.** [enredarse] to become tangled - **2.** [complicarse] to become confused *o* complicated.

enmarcar *vt* to frame.

enmascarado, da *adj* masked.

enmascarar *vt* [rostro] to mask; *fig* [encubrir] to disguise.

enmendar *vt* [error] to correct; [ley, dictamen] to amend; [comportamiento] to mend; [daño, perjuicio] to redress.

  ◆ **enmendarse** *vpr* to mend one's ways.

enmienda *f* - **1.** [en un texto] corrections *(pl)* - **2.** POLÍT amendment.

enmohecer *vt* [gen] to turn mouldy; [metal] to rust.

enmohecerse *vpr* [gen] to grow mouldy; [metal, conocimientos] to go rusty.

enmoquetar *vt* to carpet.

enmudecer ◇ *vt* to silence. ◇ *vi* [callarse] to fall silent, to go quiet; [perder el habla] to be struck dumb.

ennegrecer *vt* [gen] to blacken; [suj: nubes] to darken.

ennegrecerse *vpr* [gen] to become blackened; [nublarse] to darken, to grow dark.

ennoblecer *vt* -1. *fig* [dignificar] to lend distinction to -2. [dar un título a] to ennoble.

enojar *vt* [enfadar] to anger; [molestar] to annoy.

enojarse *vpr*: ~se (con) [enfadarse] to get angry (with); [molestarse] to get annoyed (with).

enojo *m* [enfado] anger; [molestia] annoyance.

enojoso, sa *adj* [molesto] annoying; [delicado, espinoso] awkward.

enorgullecer *vt* to fill with pride.

enorgullecerse de *vpr* to be proud of.

enorme *adj* [en tamaño] enormous, huge; [en gravedad] monstrous.

enormidad *f* [de tamaño] enormity, hugeness.

enrarecer *vt* -1. [contaminar] to pollute -2. [rarificar] to rarefy.

enrarecerse *vpr* -1. [contaminarse] to become polluted -2. [rarificarse] to become rarefied -3. *fig* [situación, ambiente] to become tense.

enredadera *f* creeper.

enredar *vt* -1. [madeja, pelo] to tangle up; [situación, asunto] to complicate, to confuse -2. [implicar]: ~ a alguien (en) to embroil sb (in), to involve sb (in).

enredarse *vpr* [plantas] to climb; [madeja, pelo] to get tangled up; [situación, asunto] to become confused.

enredo *m* -1. [maraña] tangle, knot -2. [lío] mess, complicated affair; [asunto ilícito] shady affair -3. [amoroso] (love) affair.

enrejado *m* -1. [barrotes - de balcón, verja] railings (*pl*); [- de jaula, celda, ventana] bars (*pl*) -2. [de cañas] trellis.

enrevesado, da *adj* complex, complicated.

enriquecer *vt* -1. [hacer rico] to make rich -2. *fig* [engrandecer] to enrich.

enriquecerse *vpr* to get rich.

enrojecer ◇ *vt* [gen] to redden, to turn red; [rostro, mejillas] to cause to blush. ◇ *vi* [por calor] to flush; [por turbación] to blush.

enrojecerse *vpr* [por calor] to flush; [por turbación] to blush.

enrolar *vt* to enlist.

enrolarse en *vpr* [la marina] to enlist in; [un buque] to sign up for.

enrollar *vt* -1. [arrollar] to roll up -2. *fam* [gustar]: me enrolla mucho I love it, I think it's great.

enroscar *vt* -1. [atornillar] to screw in -2. [enrollar] to roll up; [cuerpo, cola] to curl up.

ensaimada *f cake made of sweet coiled pastry.*

ensalada *f* [de lechuga etc] salad; ~ de frutas fruit salad; ~ mixta mixed salad; ~ rusa Russian salad.

ensaladilla *f*: ~ (rusa) Russian salad.

ensalzar *vt* to praise.

ensambladura *f*, **ensamblaje** *m* [acción] assembly; [pieza] joint.

ensanchar *vt* [orificio, calle] to widen; [ropa] to let out; [ciudad] to expand.

ensanche *m* -1. [de calle etc] widening -2. [en la ciudad] new suburb.

ensangrentar *vt* to cover with blood.

ensañarse *vpr*: ~ con to torment, to treat cruelly.

ensartar *vt* -1. [perlas] to string; [aguja] to thread -2. [atravesar - torero] to gore; [puñal] to plunge, to bury.

ensayar *vt* -1. [gen] to test -2. TEATR to rehearse.

ensayista *mf* essayist.

ensayo *m* -1. TEATR rehearsal; ~ general dress rehearsal -2. [prueba] test; ~ nuclear nuclear test -3. LITER essay -4. [en rugby] try.

enseguida *adv* [inmediatamente] immediately, at once; [pronto] very soon; llegará ~ he'll be here any minute now.

ensenada *f* cove, inlet.

enseñanza *f* [gen] education; [instrucción] teaching; ~ primaria/secundaria primary/secondary education.

enseñar *vt* -1. [instruir, aleccionar] to teach; ~ a alguien a hacer algo to teach sb (how) to do sthg -2. [mostrar] to show.

enseres *mpl* -1. [efectos personales] belongings -2. [utensilios] equipment (*U*); ~ domésticos household goods.

ensillar *vt* to saddle up.

ensimismarse *vpr* [enfrascarse] to become absorbed; [abstraerse] to be lost in thought.

ensombrecer *vt lit & fig* to cast a shadow over.

ensombrecerse *vpr* to darken.

ensoñación *f* daydream.

ensopar *vt Andes, RP, Ven* to soak.

ensordecer ◇ *vt* [suj: sonido] to deafen. ◇ *vi* to go deaf.

ensuciar *vt* to (make) dirty; *fig* [desprestigiar] to sully, to tarnish.

ensuciarse *vpr* to get dirty.

ensueño *m lit & fig* dream; **de ~** dream *(antes de sust)*, ideal.

entablado *m* [armazón] wooden platform; [suelo] floorboards *(pl)*.

entablar *vt* **- 1.** [iniciar - conversación, amistad] to strike up; [negocio] to start up **- 2.** [entablillar] to put in a splint.

entallar *vt* **- 1.** [prenda] to cut, to tailor **- 2.** [madera] to carve, to sculpt.

entarimado *m* [plataforma] wooden platform; [suelo] floorboards *(pl)*.

ente *m* **- 1.** [ser] being **- 2.** [corporación] body, organization; **~ público** [gen] state-owned body *o* institution; [televisión] Spanish state broadcasting company.

entender ⬦ *vt* **- 1.** [gen] to understand; **dar algo a ~** to imply sthg **- 2.** [darse cuenta] to realize **- 3.** [oír] to hear **- 4.** [juzgar] to think; **yo no lo entiendo así** I don't see it that way. ⬦ *vi* **- 1.** [comprender] to understand **- 2.** [saber]: **~ de *o* en algo** to be an expert on sthg; **~ poco/algo de** to know very little/a little about. ⬦ *m*: **a mi ~ ...** the way I see it ...
  ◆ **entenderse** *vpr* **- 1.** [comprenderse - uno mismo] to know what one means; [- dos personas] to understand each other **- 2.** [llevarse bien] to get on **- 3.** [ponerse de acuerdo] to reach an agreement **- 4.** [comunicarse] to communicate (with each other).

entendido, da *m,f*: **~ (en)** expert (on).
  ◆ **entendido** *interj*: **¡~!** all right!, okay!

entendimiento *m* **- 1.** [comprensión] understanding; [juicio] judgment; [inteligencia] mind, intellect **- 2.** [acuerdo] understanding; **llegar a un ~** to come to *o* reach an agreement.

enterado, da *adj*: **~ (en)** well-informed (about); **estar ~ de algo** to be aware of sthg; **darse por ~** to get the message; **no darse por ~** to turn a deaf ear.

enterarse *vpr* **- 1.** [descubrir]: **~ (de)** to find out (about) **- 2.** *fam* [comprender] to get it, to understand **- 3.** [darse cuenta]: **~ (de algo)** to realize (sthg).

entereza *f* [serenidad] composure; [honradez] integrity; [firmeza] firmness.

enternecer *vt* to move, to touch.
  ◆ **enternecerse** *vpr* to be moved.

entero, ra *adj* **- 1.** [completo] whole **- 2.** [sereno] composed **- 3.** [honrado] upright, honest.

enterrador, ra *m,f* gravedigger.

enterrar *vt* [gen] to bury.

entibiar *vt* **- 1.** [enfriar] to cool **- 2.** [templar] to warm.
  ◆ **entibiarse** *vpr* [sentimiento] to cool.

entidad *f* **- 1.** [corporación] body; [empresa] firm, company **- 2.** FILOSOFÍA entity **- 3.** [importancia] importance.

entierro *m* [acción] burial; [ceremonia] funeral.

entlo. *abrev de* entresuelo.

entoldado *m* [toldo] awning; [para fiestas, bailes] marquee.

entonación *f* intonation.

entonar ⬦ *vt* **- 1.** [cantar] to sing **- 2.** [tonificar] to pick up. ⬦ *vi* **- 1.** [al cantar] to sing in tune **- 2.** [armonizar]: **~ (con algo)** to match (sthg).

entonces ⬦ *adv* then; **desde ~** since then; **en *o* por aquel ~** at that time. ⬦ *interj*: **¡~!** well, then!

entornar *vt* to half-close.

entorno *m* **- 1.** [ambiente] environment, surroundings *(pl)* **- 2.** INFORM environment; **~ gráfico** graphic environment; **~ de programación** programming environment.

entorpecer *vt* **- 1.** [debilitar - movimientos] to hinder; [miembros] to numb; [mente] to cloud **- 2.** [dificultar] to obstruct, to hinder.

entrada *f* **- 1.** [acción] entry; [llegada] arrival; **'prohibida la ~'** 'no entry' **- 2.** [lugar] entrance; [puerta] doorway; **'~'** 'way in', 'entrance'; **~ principal** main entrance; **~ de servicio** tradesman's entrance **- 3.** TECN inlet, intake; **~ de aire** air intake **- 4.** [en espectáculos - billete] ticket; [- recaudación] receipts *(pl)*, takings *(pl)*; **~ gratuita** admission free; **~ libre** admission free; **sacar una ~** to buy a ticket **- 5.** [público] audience; DEP attendance **- 6.** [pago inicial] down payment **- 7.** [en contabilidad] income **- 8.** [plato] starter **- 9.** [en la frente] **~s** to have a receding hairline **- 10.** [en un diccionario] entry **- 11.** [principio] start; **de ~** right from the beginning *o* the word go.

entrante ⬦ *adj* [año, mes] coming; [presidente, gobierno] incoming. ⬦ *m* **- 1.** [plato] starter **- 2.** [hueco] recess.

entraña *(gen pl)* *f* **- 1.** [víscera] entrails *(pl)*, insides *(pl)* **- 2.** *fig* [centro, esencia] heart.

entrañable *adj* intimate.

entrañar *vt* to involve.

entrar ⬦ *vi* **- 1.** [introducirse - viniendo] to enter, to come in; [- yendo] to enter, to go in; **~ en algo** to enter sthg, to come/go into sthg; **entré por la ventana** I got in through the window **- 2.** [penetrar - clavo etc] to go in; **~ en algo** to go into sthg **- 3.** [caber]: **~ (en)** to fit (in); **este anillo no te entra** this ring won't fit you **- 4.** [incorporarse]: **~ (en algo)** [colegio, empresa] to start (at sthg); [club, partido político] to join (sthg); **~ de** [botones etc] to start off as **- 5.** [estado físico o de ánimo]: **le entraron ganas de hablar** he suddenly felt like talking; **me está entrando frío** I'm getting cold; **me entró mucha pena** I was filled with pity **- 6.** [periodo de tiempo] to start; **~ en** [edad, vejez] to reach;

[año nuevo] to enter - **7.** [cantidad]: **¿cuántos entran en un kilo?** how many do you get to the kilo? - **8.** [concepto, asignatura etc]: **no le entra la geometría** he can't get the hang of geometry - **9.** AUTOM to engage. ⬦ *vt* [introducir] to bring in.

entre *prep* - **1.** [gen] between; ~ **nosotros** [en confianza] between you and me, between ourselves; ~ **una cosa y otra** what with one thing and another - **2.** [en medio de muchos] among, amongst; **estaba ~ los asistentes** she was among those present; ~ **sí** amongst themselves; **discutían ~ sí** they were arguing with each other.

entreabierto, ta *pp* ▷ entreabrir.

entreabrir *vt* to half-open.

entreacto *m* interval.

entrecejo *m* space between the brows; **fruncir el** ~ to frown.

entrecortado, da *adj* [voz, habla] faltering; [respiración] laboured; [señal, sonido] intermittent.

entrecot, entrecote *m* entrecôte.

entredicho *m*: **estar en** ~ to be in doubt; **poner en** ~ to question, to call into question.

entrega *f* - **1.** [gen] handing over; [de pedido, paquete] delivery; [de premios] presentation; ~ **a domicilio** home delivery - **2.** [dedicación]: ~ **(a)** devotion (to) - **3.** [fascículo] instalment; **publicar por** ~**s** to serialize.

entregar *vt* [gen] to hand over; [pedido, paquete] to deliver; [examen, informe] to hand in; [persona] to turn over.
  ◆ **entregarse** *vpr* [rendirse - soldado, ejército] to surrender; [- criminal] to turn o.s. in.
  ◆ **entregarse a** *vpr* - **1.** [persona, trabajo] to devote o.s. to - **2.** [vicio, pasión] to give o.s. over to.

entreguerras ◆ **de entreguerras** *loc adj* between the wars.

entrelazar *vt* to interlace, to interlink.

entremés *m* CULIN *(gen pl)* hors d'œuvres.

entremeter *vt* to insert, to put in.
  ◆ **entremeterse** *vpr* [inmiscuirse]: ~**se (en)** to meddle (in).

entremezclar *vt* to mix up.
  ◆ **entremezclarse** *vpr* to mix.

entrenador, ra *m,f* coach; [seleccionador] manager.

entrenamiento *m* training.

entrenar *vt* & *vi* to train.
  ◆ **entrenarse** *vpr* to train.

entrepierna *f* crotch.

entresacar *vt* to pick out.

entresijos *mpl* ins and outs.

entresuelo *m* mezzanine.

entretanto *adv* meanwhile.

entretención *f Chile* entertainment.

entretener *vt* - **1.** [despistar] to distract - **2.** [retrasar] to hold up, to keep - **3.** [divertir] to entertain.
  ◆ **entretenerse** *vpr* - **1.** [despistarse] to get distracted - **2.** [divertirse] to amuse o.s. - **3.** [retrasarse] to be held up.

entretenido, da *adj* entertaining, enjoyable.

entretenimiento *m* - **1.** [acción] entertainment - **2.** [pasatiempo] pastime.

entrever *vt* [vislumbrar] to barely make out; [por un instante] to glimpse.

entreverar *CSur vt* to mix.
  ◆ **entreverarse** *vpr* to get tangled.

entrevero *m CSur* [lío] tangle, mess; [pelea] brawl.

entrevista *f* - **1.** [periodística, de trabajo] interview; **hacer una** ~ **a alguien** to interview sb - **2.** [reunión] meeting.

entrevistar *vt* to interview.
  ◆ **entrevistarse** *vpr*: ~**se (con)** to have a meeting (with).

entrevisto, ta *pp* ▷ entrever.

entristecer *vt* to make sad.
  ◆ **entristecerse** *vpr* to become sad.

entrometerse *vpr*: ~ **(en)** to interfere (in).

entrometido, da *m,f* meddler.

entroncar *vi* - **1.** [trenes etc] to connect - **2.** *fig* [relacionarse]: ~ **(con)** to be related (to).

entuerto *m* wrong, injustice.

entumecer *vt* to numb.
  ◆ **entumecerse** *vpr* to become numb.

entumecido, da *adj* numb.

enturbiar *vt lit* & *fig* to cloud.
  ◆ **enturbiarse** *vpr lit* & *fig* to become cloudy.

entusiasmar *vt* - **1.** [animar] to fill with enthusiasm - **2.** [gustar]: **le entusiasma la música** he loves music.
  ◆ **entusiasmarse** *vpr*: ~**se (con)** to get excited (about).

entusiasmo *m* enthusiasm; **con** ~ enthusiastically.

entusiasta ⬦ *adj* enthusiastic. ⬦ *mf* enthusiast.

enumeración *f* enumeration, listing.

enumerar *vt* to enumerate, to list.

enunciar *vt* to formulate, to enunciate.

envainar *vt* to sheathe.

envalentonar *vt* to urge on, to fill with courage.
  ◆ **envalentonarse** *vpr* to become daring.

envanecer *vt* to make vain.
  ◆ **envanecerse** *vpr* to become vain.

envasado *m* [en botellas] bottling; [en latas]

canning; [en paquetes] packing.

envasar *vt* [en botellas] to bottle; [en latas] to can; [en paquetes] to pack.

envase *m* -1. [envasado - en botellas] bottling; [- en latas] canning; [- en paquetes] packing -2. [recipiente] container; [botella] bottle; ~ **desechable** disposable container; ~ **retornable** returnable bottle; ~ **sin retorno** non-returnable bottle.

envejecer ⋄ *vi* [hacerse viejo] to grow old; [parecer viejo] to age. ⋄ *vt* to age.

envejecimiento *m* ageing.

envenenamiento *m* poisoning.

envenenar *vt* to poison.

envergadura *f* -1. [importancia] size, extent; [complejidad] complexity; **una reforma de gran** ~ a wide-ranging reform -2. [anchura] span.

envés *m* reverse (side), back; [de tela] wrong side.

enviado, da *m,f* POLÍT envoy; PRENS correspondent.

enviar *vt* to send; ~ **a alguien a hacer algo** to send sb to do sthg.

enviciar *vt* to addict, to get hooked.
  ➤ **enviciarse** *vpr* to become addicted.

envidia *f* envy; **era la** ~ **de todos** it was the envy of everyone; **dar** ~ **a alguien** to make sb jealous *o* envious; **tener** ~ **de alguien/algo** to envy sb/sthg, to be jealous *o* envious of sb/sthg; **morirse de** ~ to be green with envy.

envidiar *vt* to envy.

envidioso, sa *adj* envious.

envilecer *vt* to debase.

envío *m* -1. COM dispatch; [de correo] delivery; [de víveres, mercancías] consignment; **gastos de** ~ postage and packing *UK*, postage and handling *US*; ~ **a domicilio** home delivery; ~ **contra reembolso** cash on delivery -2. [paquete] package.

enviudar *vi* to be widowed.

envoltorio *m*, **envoltura** *f* wrapper, wrapping.

envolver *vt* -1. [embalar] to wrap (up) -2. [enrollar] to wind -3. [implicar]: ~ **a alguien en** to involve sb in.

envuelto, ta *pp* ⊳ **envolver**.

enyesar *vt* -1. MED to put in plaster -2. CONSTR to plaster.

enzarzar *vt* to entangle, to embroil.
  ➤ **enzarzarse** *vpr*: ~**se en** to get entangled *o* embroiled in.

enzima *f* enzyme.

e.p.d. (*abrev de* **en paz descanse**) RIP.

épica ⊳ **épico**.

épico, ca *adj* epic.
  ➤ **épica** *f* epic.

epidemia *f* epidemic.

epígrafe *m* heading.

epilepsia *f* epilepsy.

epílogo *m* epilogue.

episodio *m* [gen] episode.

epístola *f* culto [carta] epistle; RELIG Epistle.

epitafio *m* epitaph.

epíteto *m* epithet.

época *f* period; [estación] season; **de** ~ period (*antes de sust*); **en aquella** ~ at that time; ~ **dorada** golden age.

epopeya *f* -1. [gen] epic -2. *fig* [hazaña] feat.

equidad *f* fairness.

equidistante *adj* equidistant.

equilibrado, da *adj* -1. [gen] balanced -2. [sensato] sensible.

equilibrar *vt* to balance.

equilibrio *m* balance; **mantenerse/perder el** ~ to keep/lose one's balance; **hacer** ~**s** *fig* to perform a balancing act.

equilibrista *mf* [trapecista] trapeze artist; [funambulista] tightrope walker.

equino, na *adj* equine.

equinoccio *m* equinox.

equipaje *m* luggage *UK*, baggage *US*; **hacer el** ~ to pack; ~ **de mano** hand luggage.

equipar *vt*: ~ **(de)** [gen] to equip (with); [ropa] to fit out (with).

equiparar *vt* to compare.
  ➤ **equipararse** *vpr* to be compared.

equipo *m* -1. [equipamiento] equipment; **caerse con todo el** ~ *fam* to get it in the neck -2. [personas, jugadores] team; ~ **de rescate** rescue team -3. [de música] system.

equis *adj* X; **un número** ~ **de personas** x number of people.

equitación *f* [arte] equestrianism; [actividad] horse riding.

equitativo, va *adj* fair, even-handed.

equivalente *adj & m* equivalent.

equivaler ➤ **equivaler a** *vi* to be equivalent to; *fig* [significar] to amount to.

equivocación *f* mistake; **por** ~ by mistake.

equivocado, da *adj* mistaken.

equivocar *vt* to choose wrongly; ~ **algo con algo** to mistake sthg for sthg.
  ➤ **equivocarse** *vpr* to be wrong; ~**se en** to make a mistake in; **se equivocó de nombre** he got the wrong name.

equívoco, ca *adj* -1. [ambiguo] ambiguous, equivocal -2. [sospechoso] suspicious.
  ➤ **equívoco** *m* misunderstanding.

era ⋄ ⊳ **ser**. ⋄ *f* [periodo] era.

erario *m* funds (*pl*).

erección *f* erection.

erecto, ta *adj* erect.

eres ⊳ **ser**.

erguir *vt* to raise.

◆ **erguirse** *vpr* to rise up.

erigir *vt* [construir] to erect, to build.

erizado, da *adj* [de punta] on end; [con púas o espinas] spiky.

erizar *vt* to cause to stand on end.

◆ **erizarse** *vpr* [pelo] to stand on end; [persona] to stiffen.

erizo *m* - 1. [mamífero] hedgehog - 2. [pez] globefish; ~ **de mar** sea urchin.

ermita *f* hermitage.

erogación *f* Chile [donativo] contribution.

erogar *vt* Chile [donar] to contribute.

erosionar *vt* to erode.

◆ **erosionarse** *vpr* to erode.

erótico, ca *adj* erotic.

erotismo *m* eroticism.

erradicación *f* eradication.

erradicar *vt* to eradicate.

errante *adj* wandering.

errar ◇ *vt* [vocación, camino] to choose wrongly; [disparo, golpe] to miss. ◇ *vi* - 1. [vagar] to wander - 2. [equivocarse] to make a mistake - 3. [al disparar] to miss.

errata *f* misprint.

erróneo, a *adj* mistaken.

error *m* mistake, error; **cometer un** ~ to make a mistake; **estar en un** ~ to be mistaken; **salvo** ~ **u omisión** errors and omissions excepted; ~ **de cálculo** miscalculation; ~ **humano** human error; ~ **de imprenta** misprint; ~ **judicial** miscarriage of justice; ~ **tipográfico** typo, typographical error.

ertzaintza [er'tʃaintʃa] *f Basque regional police force.*

eructar *vi* to belch.

eructo *m* belch.

erudito, ta *adj* erudite.

erupción *f* - 1. GEOL eruption; **en** ~ erupting; **entrar en** ~ to erupt - 2. MED rash.

es ⊳ ser.

esa ⊳ ese².

ésa ⊳ ése.

esbelto, ta *adj* slender, slim.

esbozar *vt* to sketch, to outline; [sonrisa] to give a hint of.

esbozo *m* sketch, outline.

escabechado, da *adj* CULIN marinated.

escabeche *m* CULIN marinade.

escabroso, sa *adj* - 1. [abrupto] rough - 2. [obsceno] risqué - 3. [espinoso] awkward, thorny.

escabullirse *vpr* [desaparecer]: ~ **(de)** to slip away (from).

escacharrar *vt fam* to knacker.

escafandra *f* diving suit.

escala *f* - 1. [gen] scale; [de colores] range; **a** ~ [gráfica] to scale; **a** ~ **mundial** *fig* on a worldwide scale; **a gran** ~ on a large scale;

a pequeña ~ small-scale; **en pequeña** ~ on a small scale; ~ **salarial** salary scale - 2. [en un viaje] stopover; **hacer** ~ to stop over; ~ **técnica** refuelling stop UK, refueling stop US.

escalada *f* - 1. [de montaña] climb; ~ **libre** free climbing - 2. [de violencia, precios] escalation, rise.

escalador, ra *m,f* [alpinista] climber.

escalafón *m* scale, ladder.

escalar *vt* to climb.

escaldar *vt* to scald.

escalera *f* - 1. [gen] stairs *(pl)*, staircase; [escala] ladder; ~ **mecánica** *o* **automática** escalator; ~ **de caracol** spiral staircase - 2. [en naipes] run.

escalfar *vt* to poach.

escalinata *f* staircase.

escalofriante *adj* spine-chilling.

escalofrío *(gen pl) m* shiver; **dar** ~s **a alguien** to give sb the shivers; **tener** ~s to have the shivers.

escalón *m* step; *fig* grade.

escalonar *vt* - 1. [gen] to spread out - 2. [terreno] to terrace.

escalope *m* escalope.

escama *f* - 1. [de peces, reptiles] scale - 2. [de jabón, en la piel] flake.

escamar *vt fam fig* [mosquear] to make suspicious.

escamotear *vt*: ~ **algo a alguien** [estafar] to do *o* swindle sb out of sthg; [hurtar] to rob sb of sthg.

escampar *v impers* to stop raining.

escandalizar *vt* to scandalize, to shock.

◆ **escandalizarse** *vpr* to be shocked.

escándalo *m* - 1. [inmoralidad] scandal; [indignación] outrage - 2. [alboroto] uproar, racket; **armar un** ~ to kick up a fuss.

escandaloso, sa *adj* - 1. [inmoral] outrageous, shocking - 2. [ruidoso] very noisy.

Escandinavia Scandinavia.

escandinavo, va *adj & m,f* Scandinavian.

escanear *vt* to scan.

escáner *(pl* **escáners***) m* - 1. [aparato] scanner - 2. [exploración] scan; **hacerse un** ~ to have a scan.

escaño *m* - 1. [cargo] seat *(in parliament)* - 2. [asiento] bench *(in parliament)*.

escapada *f* - 1. [huida] escape, flight; DEP breakaway - 2. [viaje] quick trip.

escapar *vi* [huir]: ~ **(de)** to get away *o* escape (from).

◆ **escaparse** *vpr* - 1. [huir]: ~**se (de)** to get away *o* escape (from); ~**se de casa** to run away from home - 2. [salir - gas, agua etc] to leak.

escaparate *m* (shop) window.

escapatoria *f* [fuga] escape; **no tener** ~

to have no way out.

escape *m* [de gas etc] leak; [de coche] exhaust; **a ~** in a rush, at high speed.

escaquearse *vpr fam* to duck out; **~ de algo/de hacer algo** to worm one's way out of sthg/doing sthg.

escarabajo *m* beetle.

escaramuza *f* MIL & *fig* skirmish.

escarbar *vt* to scratch, to scrape.

escarcha *f* frost.

escarlata *adj* & *m* scarlet.

escarlatina *f* scarlet fever.

escarmentar *vi* to learn (one's lesson); **¡no escarmienta!** he never learns!; **¡para que escarmientes!** that'll teach you!

escarmiento *m* lesson; **servir de ~** to serve as a lesson.

escarnio *m* mockery, ridicule.

escarola *f* endive.

escarpado, da *adj* [inclinado] steep; [abrupto] craggy.

escasear *vi* to be scarce, to be in short supply.

escasez *f* [insuficiencia] shortage; [pobreza] poverty.

escaso, sa *adj* **- 1.** [insuficiente - conocimientos, recursos] limited, scant; [- tiempo] short; [- cantidad, número] low; [- víveres, trabajo] scarce, in short supply; [- visibilidad, luz] poor; **andar ~ de** to be short of **- 2.** [casi completo]: **un metro ~** barely a metre.

escatimar *vt* [gastos, comida] to be sparing with, to skimp on; [esfuerzo, energías] to use as little as possible; **no ~ gastos** to spare no expense.

escay, skai *m* Leatherette®.

escayola *f* CONSTR plaster of Paris; MED plaster.

escena *f* **- 1.** [gen] scene; **hacer una ~** to make a scene; **~ retrospectiva** flashback **- 2.** [escenario] stage; **poner en ~** to stage; **salir a ~** to go on stage.

escenario *m* **- 1.** [tablas, escena] stage; CIN & TEATR [lugar de la acción] setting **- 2.** *fig* [de suceso] scene.

escenificar *vt* [novela] to dramatize; [obra de teatro] to stage.

escenografía *f* set design.

escepticismo *m* scepticism.

escéptico, ca ◇ *adj* [incrédulo] sceptical. ◇ *m,f* sceptic.

escindir *vt* to split.
 ➔ **escindirse** *vpr*: **~se (en)** to split (into).

escisión *f* [del átomo] splitting; [de partido político] split.

esclarecer *vt* to clear up, to shed light on.

esclava ▷ esclavo.

esclavitud *f* lit & *fig* slavery.

esclavizar *vt* lit & *fig* to enslave.

esclavo, va *m,f* lit & *fig* [persona] slave; **es un ~ del trabajo** he's a slave to his work.

esclerosis *f inv* MED sclerosis; **~ múltiple** multiple sclerosis.

esclusa *f* [de canal] lock; [compuerta] floodgate.

escoba *f* broom; **pasar la ~** to sweep (up).

escocedura *f* [sensación] stinging.

escocer *vi* lit & *fig* to sting.

escocés, esa ◇ *adj* [gen] Scottish; [whisky] Scotch; [tejido] tartan, plaid. ◇ *m,f* [persona] Scot, Scotsman (*f* Scotswoman); **los escoceses** the Scottish, the Scots.
 ➔ **escocés** *m* [lengua] Scots (*U*).

Escocia Scotland.

escoger *vt* to choose.

escogido, da *adj* [elegido] selected, chosen; [selecto] choice, select.

escolar ◇ *adj* school (*antes de sust*). ◇ *mf* pupil, schoolboy (*f* schoolgirl).

escolarizar *vt* to provide with schooling.

escollo *m* **- 1.** [en el mar] reef **- 2.** *fig* stumbling block.

escolta *f* escort.

escoltar *vt* to escort.

escombros *mpl* rubble (*U*), debris (*U*).

esconder *vt* to hide, to conceal.
 ➔ **esconderse** *vpr*: **~se (de)** to hide (from).

escondido, da *adj* [lugar] secluded.
 ➔ **a escondidas** *loc adv* in secret; **hacer algo a escondidas de alguien** to do sthg behind sb's back.

escondite *m* **- 1.** [lugar] hiding place **- 2.** [juego] hide-and-seek.

escondrijo *m* hiding place.

escopeta *f* shotgun; **~ de aire comprimido** air gun; **~ de cañones recortados** sawn-off shotgun.

escoria *f* *fig* dregs (*pl*), scum.

Escorpio, Escorpión ◇ *m* [zodiaco] Scorpio. ◇ *mf* [persona] Scorpio.

escorpión *m* scorpion.
 ➔ **Escorpión** = Escorpio.

escotado, da *adj* low-cut, low-necked.

escote *m* [de prendas] neckline; [de persona] neck; **pagar a ~** to go Dutch; **~ en pico** V-neck; **~ redondo** round neck.

escotilla *f* hatch, hatchway.

escozor *m* stinging.

escribanía *f* Andes, CRica, RP [notaría] ≃ notary public's office.

escribano, na *m,f* Andes, CRica, RP [notario] notary (public).

escribir *vt* & *vi* to write; **~ a lápiz** to write in pencil; **~ a mano** to write by hand, to write in longhand; **~ a máquina** to type.
 ➔ **escribirse** *vpr* **- 1.** [personas] to write to

one another - **2.** [palabras]: **se escribe con 'h'** it is spelt with an 'h'.

escrito, ta ⬦ *pp* ⊳ **escribir.** ⬦ *adj* written; **por** ∼ in writing.

◆ **escrito** *m* [gen] text; [documento] document; [obra literaria] writing, work.

escritor, ra *m,f* writer.

escritorio *m* [mueble] desk, bureau.

escritura *f* - **1.** [arte] writing - **2.** [sistema de signos] script - **3.** DER deed.

escrúpulo *m* - **1.** [duda, recelo] scruple - **2.** [minuciosidad] scrupulousness, great care - **3.** [aprensión] qualm; **le da** ∼ he has qualms about it.

escrupuloso, sa *adj* - **1.** [gen] scrupulous - **2.** [aprensivo] particular, fussy.

escrutar *vt* [con la mirada] to scrutinize, to examine; [votos] to count.

escrutinio *m* count *(of votes)*.

escuadra *f* - **1.** GEOM square - **2.** [de buques] squadron - **3.** [de soldados] squad.

escuadrilla *f* squadron.

escuadrón *m* squadron; ∼ **de la muerte** death squad.

escuálido, da *adj culto* emaciated.

escucha *f* listening-in, monitoring; **estar** *o* **permanecer a la** ∼ to listen in; ∼**s telefónicas** telephone tapping *(U)*.

escuchar ⬦ *vt* to listen to. ⬦ *vi* to listen.

escudería *f* team *(in motor racing)*.

escudo *m* - **1.** [arma] shield - **2.** [moneda] escudo - **3.** [emblema] coat of arms.

escudriñar *vt* [examinar] to scrutinize, to examine; [otear] to search.

escuela *f* school; ∼ **normal** teacher training college; ∼ **nocturna** night school; ∼ **parroquial** parish school; ∼ **privada** private school, public school *UK*; ∼ **pública** state school; ∼ **universitaria** *university which awards degrees after three years of study.*

escueto, ta *adj* [sucinto] concise; [sobrio] plain, unadorned.

escuincle, cla *m,f Méx fam* [muchacho] nipper, kid.

esculpir *vt* to sculpt, to carve.

escultor, ra *m,f* sculptor *(f* sculptress*)*.

escultura *f* sculpture.

escupir ⬦ *vi* to spit. ⬦ *vt* [suj: persona, animal] to spit out; [suj: volcán, chimenea etc] to belch out.

escupitajo *m* gob, spit.

escurreplatos *m inv* dish rack.

escurridizo, za *adj lit & fig* slippery.

escurridor *m* colander.

escurrir ⬦ *vt* [gen] to drain; [ropa] to wring out; [en lavadora] to spin-dry. ⬦ *vi* [gotear] to drip.

◆ **escurrirse** *vpr* [resbalarse] to slip.

ese¹ *f* [figura] zigzag; **hacer** ∼**s** [en carretera]

to zigzag; [al andar] to stagger about.

ese² *(pl* **esos)**, **esa** *(pl* **esas)** *adj demos* - **1.** [gen] that, *(pl)* those - **2.** *(después de sust) fam despec* that, *(pl)* those; **el hombre** ∼ **no me inspira confianza** I don't trust that guy.

ése *(pl* **ésos)**, **ésa** *(pl* **ésas)** *pron demos* - **1.** [gen] that one, *(pl)* those ones - **2.** [mencionado antes] the former - **3.** *fam despec*: ∼ **fue el que me pegó** that's the guy who hit me - **4.** *loc*: **¡a** ∼ **!** stop that man!; **ni por ésas** not even then; **no me lo vendió ni por ésas** even then he wouldn't sell it.

esencia *f* essence.

esencial *adj* essential; **lo** ∼ the fundamental thing.

esfera *f* - **1.** [gen] sphere - **2.** [de reloj] face - **3.** [círculo social] circle; ∼ **de influencia** sphere of influence - **4.** INFORM: ∼ **de arrastre** *o* **de desplazamiento** trackball.

esférico, ca *adj* spherical.

esfero *m Col, Ecuad* ballpoint pen.

esfinge *f* sphinx; **parecer una** ∼ to be inscrutable.

esforzar *vt* [voz] to strain.

◆ **esforzarse** *vpr* to make an effort; ∼**se en** *o* **por hacer algo** to try very hard to do sthg, to do one's best to do sthg.

esfuerzo *m* effort; **hacer un** ∼ to make an effort, to try hard; **sin** ∼ effortlessly.

esfumarse *vpr* [esperanzas, posibilidades] to fade away; [persona] to vanish, to disappear.

esgrima *f* fencing.

esgrimir *vt* - **1.** [arma] to brandish, to wield - **2.** [argumento, hecho, idea] to use, to employ.

esguince *m* sprain.

eslabón *m* link.

eslip *(pl* **eslips)** *m* briefs *(pl)*.

eslogan *(pl* **eslóganes)** *m* slogan.

eslora *f* NÁUT length.

eslovaco, ca *adj & m,f* Slovak, Slovakian.

◆ **eslovaco** *m* [lengua] Slovak.

Eslovaquia Slovakia.

esmaltar *vt* to enamel.

esmalte *m* [sustancia - en dientes, cerámica etc] enamel; [- de uñas] (nail) varnish *o* polish.

esmerado, da *adj* [persona] painstaking, careful; [trabajo] polished.

esmeralda *f* emerald.

esmerarse *vpr*: ∼ **(en algo/hacer algo)** [esforzarse] to take great pains (over sthg/doing sthg).

esmerilar *vt* [pulir] to polish with emery.

esmero *m* great care.

esmoquin *(pl* **esmóquines)** *m* dinner jacket *UK*, tuxedo *US*.

esnifar *vt fam* to sniff *(drugs)*.

esnob *(pl* **esnobs)** *mf* person who wants to be trendy.

eso *pron demos (neutro)* that; ~ **es la Torre Eiffel** that's the Eiffel Tower; ~ **es lo que yo pienso** that's just what I think; ~ **que propones es irrealizable** what you're proposing is impossible; ~ **de vivir solo no me gusta** I don't like the idea of living on my own; ¡~, ~! that's right!, yes!; ¡~ es! that's it; **¿cómo es** ~?, **¿y** ~? [¿por qué?] how come?; **para** ~ **es mejor no ir** if that's all it is, you might as well not go; **por** ~ **vine** that's why I came.

◆ **a eso de** *loc prep* (at) about *o* around.

◆ **en eso** *loc adv* at that very moment.

◆ **y eso que** *loc conj* even though.

esófago *m* oesophagus.

esos, esas ⊳ **ese**.

ésos, ésas ⊳ **ése**.

esotérico, ca *adj* esoteric.

espabilar *vt* -**1.** [despertar] to wake up -**2.** [avispar]: ~ **a alguien** to sharpen sb's wits.

◆ **espabilarse** *vpr* -**1.** [despertarse] to wake up, to brighten up -**2.** [darse prisa] to get a move on -**3.** [avisparse] to sharpen one's wits.

espacial *adj* space *(antes de sust)*.

espaciar *vt* to space out.

espacio *m* -**1.** [gen] space; **no tengo mucho** ~ I don't have much room; **a doble** ~ double-spaced; **por** ~ **de** over a period of; ~ **aéreo** air space; ~ **en blanco** blank -**2.** RADIO & TV programme.

espacioso, sa *adj* spacious.

espada *f* [arma] sword; **estar entre la** ~ **y la pared** to be between the devil and the deep blue sea.

◆ **espadas** *fpl* [naipes] ≃ spades.

espagueti *m* spaghetti *(U)*.

espalda *f* -**1.** [gen] back; **de** ~**s a alguien** with one's back turned on sb; **tumbarse de** ~**s** to lie on one's back; **cubrirse las** ~**s** to cover o.s.; **hablar de alguien a sus** ~**s** to talk about sb behind their back; **volver la** ~ **a alguien** to turn one's back on sb -**2.** [en natación] backstroke.

espantadizo, za *adj* nervous, easily frightened.

espantajo *m* [persona fea] fright, sight.

espantapájaros *m inv* scarecrow.

espantar *vt* -**1.** [ahuyentar] to frighten *o* scare away -**2.** [asustar] to frighten, to scare.

◆ **espantarse** *vpr* to get frightened *o* scared.

espanto *m* fright; **¡qué** ~! how terrible!

espantoso, sa *adj* -**1.** [terrorífico] horrific

-**2.** [enorme] terrible -**3.** [feísimo] frightful, horrible.

España Spain.

español, la ◇ *adj* Spanish. ◇ *m,f* [persona] Spaniard.

◆ **español** *m* [lengua] Spanish.

esparadrapo *m* (sticking) plaster, Band-Aid® *US*.

esparcido, da *adj* scattered.

esparcir *vt* [gen] to spread; [semillas, papeles, objetos] to scatter.

◆ **esparcirse** *vpr* to spread (out).

espárrago *m* asparagus *(U)*.

esparto *m* esparto (grass).

espasmo *m* spasm.

espasmódico, ca *adj* spasmodic.

espatarrarse *vpr fam* to sprawl (with one's legs wide open).

espátula *f* CULIN & MED spatula; ARTE palette knife; CONSTR bricklayer's trowel; [de empapelador] stripping knife.

especia *f* spice.

especial *adj* -**1.** [gen] special; ~ **para** specially for; **en** ~ especially, particularly; **¿alguno en** ~? any one in particular? -**2.** [peculiar - carácter, gusto, persona] peculiar, strange.

especialidad *f* speciality, specialty *US*.

especialista *mf* -**1.** [experto]: ~ **(en)** specialist (in) -**2.** CIN stuntman *(f* stuntwoman).

especializado, da *adj:* ~ **en** specialized (in).

especializar *vt* to specialize.

especie *f* -**1.** BIOL species *(sg)* -**2.** [clase] kind, sort; **pagar en** *o* ~**s** to pay in kind.

especificar *vt* to specify.

específico, ca *adj* specific.

espécimen *(pl* **especímenes)** *m* specimen.

espectacular *adj* spectacular.

espectáculo *m* -**1.** [diversión] entertainment -**2.** [función] show, performance -**3.** [suceso, escena] sight.

espectador *mf* TV viewer; CIN & TEATR member of the audience; DEP spectator; [de suceso, discusión] onlooker.

espectro *m* -**1.** [fantasma] spectre, ghost -**2.** FÍS & MED spectrum.

especulación *f* speculation.

especular *vi:* ~ **(sobre)** to speculate (about); ~ **en** COM to speculate on.

espejismo *m* mirage; *fig* illusion.

espejo *m* lit & *fig* mirror.

espeleología *f* potholing.

espeluznante *adj* hair-raising, lurid.

espera *f* [acción] wait; **en** ~ **de, a la** ~ **de** waiting for, awaiting.

esperanza *f* [deseo, ganas] hope; [confianza, expectativas] expectation; **perder la** ~ to lose hope; **tener ~ de hacer algo** to hope to be able to do sthg; **~ de vida** life expectancy.

esperanzar *vt* to give hope to, to encourage.

esperar ⋄ *vt* **-1.** [aguardar] to wait for **- 2.** [tener esperanza de]: **~ que** to hope that; **espero que sí** I hope so; **~ hacer algo** to hope to do sthg **- 3.** [tener confianza en] to expect; **~ que** to expect (that); **~ algo de alguien** to expect sthg from sb, to hope for sthg from sb **- 4.** [ser inminente para] to await, to be in store for. ⋄ *vi* [aguardar] to wait; **espera y verás** wait and see; **como era de ~** as was to be expected; **hacer ~ a alguien** to keep sb waiting, to make sb wait.
➡ **esperarse** *vpr* **-1.** [imaginarse, figurarse] to expect **- 2.** [aguardar] to wait.

esperma ⋄ *m o f* BIOL sperm. ⋄ *f Amér* [vela] candle.

esperpento *m* [persona] grotesque sight; [cosa] piece of nonsense.

espeso, sa *adj* [gen] thick; [bosque, niebla] dense; [nieve] deep.

espesor *m* **-1.** [grosor] thickness; **tiene 2 metros de ~** it's 2 metres thick **- 2.** [densidad - de niebla, bosque] density; [- de nieve] depth.

espesura *f* **-1.** [vegetación] thicket **- 2.** [grosor] thickness; [densidad] density.

espía *mf* spy.

espiar *vt* to spy on.

espiga *f* **-1.** [de trigo etc] ear **- 2.** [en telas] herringbone **- 3.** [pieza - de madera] peg; [- de hierro] pin.

espigado, da *adj* [persona] tall and slim.

espigón *m* breakwater.

espina *f* [de pez] bone; [de planta] thorn; **me da mala ~** it makes me uneasy, there's something fishy about it; **tener una ~ clavada** to bear a great burden; **sacarse la ~** to get even.
➡ **espina dorsal** *f* spine.
➡ **espina bífida** *f* spina bifida.

espinaca *(gen pl) f* spinach *(U)*.

espinazo *m* spine, backbone.

espinilla *f* **-1.** [hueso] shin, shinbone **- 2.** [grano] blackhead.

espinoso, sa *adj lit & fig* thorny.

espionaje *m* espionage.

espiral *f lit & fig* spiral; **en ~** [escalera, forma] spiral.

espirar *vi & vt* to exhale, to breathe out.

espiritista *adj* spiritualist.

espíritu *m* [gen] spirit; RELIG soul; **~ de equipo** team spirit.
➡ **Espíritu Santo** *m* Holy Ghost.

espiritual *adj & m* spiritual.

espléndido, da *adj* **-1.** [magnífico] splendid, magnificent **- 2.** [generoso] generous, lavish.

esplendor *m* **-1.** [magnificencia] splendour **- 2.** [apogeo] greatness.

espliego *m* lavender.

espoleta *f* [de proyectil] fuse.

espolvorear *vt* to dust, to sprinkle.

esponja *f* sponge; **~ vegetal** loofah, vegetable sponge; **beber como una ~** *fam* to drink like a fish; **tirar la ~** to throw in the towel.

esponjoso, sa *adj* spongy.

espontaneidad *f* spontaneity.

espontáneo, a *adj* spontaneous.

esporádico, ca *adj* sporadic.

esport *adj inv*: **(de) ~** sports *(antes de sust)*.

esposa ⊳ esposo.

esposar *vt* to handcuff.

esposo, sa *m,f* [persona] husband *(f* wife).
➡ **esposas** *fpl* [objeto] handcuffs.

espot *(pl espots) m* advertising spot, commercial.

espray *(pl esprays) m* spray.

esprint *(pl esprints) m* sprint.

espuela *f* [gen] spur.

espuma *f* **-1.** [gen] foam; [de cerveza] head; [de jabón] lather; [de olas] surf; [de caldo] scum; **hacer ~** to foam; **crecer como la ~** to mushroom; **~ de afeitar** shaving foam; **~ seca** carpet shampoo **- 2.** [para pelo] (styling) mousse.

espumadera *f* skimmer.

espumoso, sa *adj* [gen] foamy, frothy; [vino] sparkling; [jabón] lathery.

esputo *m* [gen] spittle; MED sputum.

esqueje *m* cutting.

esquela *f* obituary.

esqueleto *m* [de persona] skeleton.

esquema *m* [gráfico] diagram; [resumen] outline; **su respuesta me rompe los ~s** her answer has thrown all my plans up in the air.

esquemático, ca *adj* schematic.

esquí *(pl esquíes o esquís) m* **-1.** [tabla] ski **- 2.** [deporte] skiing; **~ náutico o acuático** water-skiing.

esquiador, ra *m,f* skier.

esquiar *vi* to ski.

esquilar *vt* to shear.

esquimal *adj & mf* Eskimo.

esquina *f* corner; **a la vuelta de la ~** just round the corner; **doblar la ~** to turn the corner.

esquinazo *m* corner; **dar (el) ~ a alguien** to give sb the slip.

esquirol *m fam* blackleg, scab.

esquivar *vt* [gen] to avoid; [golpe] to dodge.

esquivo, va *adj* shy.

esquizofrenia *f* schizophrenia.
esta ⊳ este².
ésta ⊳ éste.
estabilidad *f* stability.
estabilizar *vt* to stabilize.

◆ **estabilizarse** *vpr* to stabilize, to become stable.

estable *adj* - **1**. [firme] stable - **2**. [permanente - huésped] permanent; [- cliente] regular.

establecer *vt* - **1**. [gen] to establish; [récord] to set - **2**. [negocio, campamento] to set up - **3**. [inmigrantes etc] to settle.

◆ **establecerse** *vpr* - **1**. [instalarse] to settle - **2**. [poner un negocio] to set up a business.

establecimiento *m* - **1**. [gen] establishment; [de récord] setting - **2**. [de negocio, colonia] setting up.

establo *m* cowshed.

estaca *f* - **1**. [para clavar, delimitar] stake; [de tienda de campaña] peg - **2**. [garrote] cudgel.

estacada *f* [valla] picket fence; MIL stockade, palisade; **dejar a alguien en la** ~ to leave sb in the lurch.

estación *f* - **1**. [gen & INFORM] station; ~ **de autocares/de tren** coach/railway station; ~ **de esquí** ski resort; ~ **de gasolina** petrol station; ~ **de servicio** service station; ~ **de trabajo** workstation; ~ **meteorológica** weather station - **2**. [del año, temporada] season.

estacionamiento *m* AUTOM parking; ~ **indebido** parking offence.

estacionar *vt* AUTOM to park.

estacionario, ria *adj* [gen] stationary; ECON stagnant.

estadía *f* CSur stay, stop.

estadio *m* - **1**. DEP stadium - **2**. [fase] stage.

estadista *m* statesman (*f* stateswoman).

estadístico, ca *adj* statistical.

◆ **estadística** *f* - **1**. [ciencia] statistics (U) - **2**. [datos] statistics (*pl*).

estado *m* state; **su** ~ **es grave** his condition is serious; **estar en buen/mal** ~ [coche, terreno etc] to be in good/bad condition; [alimento, bebida] to be fresh/off; ~ **de ánimo** state of mind; ~ **civil** marital status; ~ **de bienestar** welfare state; ~ **de excepción** *o* **emergencia** state of emergency; ~ **de salud** (state of) health; **estar en** ~ (**de esperanza** *o* **buena esperanza**) to be expecting.

◆ **Estado** *m* [gobierno] State; **Estado Mayor** MIL general staff.

◆ **Estados Unidos (de América)** United States (of America).

estadounidense ◇ *adj* United States (*antes de sust*). ◇ *mf* United States citizen.

estafa *f* [gen] swindle; COM fraud.

estafador, ra *m,f* swindler.

estafar *vt* [gen] to swindle; COM to defraud.

estafeta *f* sub-post office.

estallar *vi* - **1**. [reventar - bomba] to explode; [- neumático] to burst; [volcán] to erupt; [cristal] to shatter - **2**. [guerra, epidemia etc] to break out.

estallido *m* - **1**. [de bomba] explosion; [de trueno] crash; [de látigo] crack - **2**. [de guerra etc] outbreak.

Estambul Istanbul.

estamento *m* stratum, class.

estampa *f* - **1**. [imagen, tarjeta] print - **2**. [aspecto] appearance.

estampado, da *adj* printed.

◆ **estampado** *m* [dibujo] (cotton) print.

estampar *vt* - **1**. [imprimir - gen] to print; [- metal] to stamp - **2**. [escribir]: ~ **la firma** to sign one's name.

estampida *f* stampede.

estampido *m* report, bang.

estampilla *f* - **1**. [para marcar] rubber stamp - **2**. *Amér* [sello de correos] stamp.

estancado, da *adj* [agua] stagnant; [situación, proyecto] at a standstill.

estancarse *vpr* [líquido] to stagnate, to become stagnant; [situación] to come to a standstill.

estancia *f* - **1**. [tiempo] stay - **2**. [habitación] room - **3**. *CSur* [hacienda] cattle ranch.

estanciero *m* *CSur* ranch owner.

estanco, ca *adj* watertight.

◆ **estanco** *m* tobacconist's.

estándar (*pl* **estándares**) *adj* & *m* standard.

estandarizar *vt* to standardize.

estandarte *m* standard, banner.

estanque *m* - **1**. [alberca] pond; [para riego] reservoir - **2**. *Amér* [depósito] tank (*of petrol*).

estanquero *mf* tobacconist.

estante *m* shelf.

estantería *f* [gen] shelves (*pl*), shelving (U); [para libros] bookcase.

estaño *m* tin.

estar ◇ *vi* - **1**. [hallarse] to be; **¿dónde está la llave?** where is the key?; **¿está María?** is Maria in?; **no está** she's not in - **2**. [con fechas]: **¿a qué estamos hoy?** what's the date today?; **hoy estamos a martes/a 15 de julio** today is Tuesday/the 15th of July; **estábamos en octubre** it was October - **3**. [quedarse] to stay, to be; **estaré un par de horas y me iré** I'll stay a couple of hours and then I'll go - **4**. (*antes de 'a'*) [expresa valores, grados]: **estamos a veinte grados** it's twenty degrees here; **están a dos euros el kilo** they're two euros a kilo - **5**. [hallarse listo] to be ready; **¿aún no está ese trabajo?** is that piece of work still not ready? - **6**. [servir]: ~ **para** to be (there) for; **para eso están**

los amigos that's what friends are for - **7.** *(antes de gerundio)* [expresa duración] to be; **están golpeando la puerta** they're banging on the door - **8.** *(antes de 'sin' + infin)* [expresa negación]: **estoy sin dormir desde ayer** I haven't slept since yesterday; **está sin acabar** it's not finished - **9.** [faltar]: **eso está aún por escribir** that has yet to be written - **10.** [hallarse a punto de]: ~ **por hacer algo** to be on the verge of doing sthg - **11.** [expresa disposición]: ~ **para algo** to be in the mood for sthg. ⟡ *v copulativo* - **1.** *(antes de adj)* [expresa cualidad, estado] to be; **los pasteles están ricos** the cakes are delicious; **esta calle está sucia** this street is dirty - **2.** *(antes de 'con' o 'sin' + sust)* [expresa estado] to be; **estamos sin agua** we have no water, we're without water - **3.** [expresa situación, acción]: ~ **de:** ~ **de camarero** to work as a waiter, to be a waiter; ~ **de vacaciones** to be on holiday; ~ **de viaje** to be on a trip; ~ **de mudanza** to be (in the process of) moving - **4.** [expresa permanencia]: ~ **en uso** to be in use; ~ **en guardia** to be on guard - **5.** [expresa apoyo, predilección]: ~ **por** to be in favour of - **6.** [expresa ocupación]: ~ **como** to be; **está como cajera** she's a checkout girl - **7.** [consistir]: ~ **en** to be, to lie in; **el problema está en la fecha** the problem is the date - **8.** [sentar - ropa]: **este traje te está bien** this suit looks good on you - **9.** *(antes de 'que' + verbo)* [expresa actitud]: **está que muerde porque ha suspendido** he's furious because he failed.

◆ **estarse** *vpr* [permanecer] to stay; **te puedes** ~ **con nosotros unos días** you can stay o spend a few days with us.

estárter (*pl* **estárters**) *m* starter.

estatal *adj* state *(antes de sust).*

estático, ca *adj* [inmóvil] stock-still.

estatización *f Amér* nationalization.

estatizar *vt Amér* to nationalize.

estatua *f* statue.

estatura *f* height; **de** ~ **media** o **mediana** of average o medium height.

estatus *m inv* status.

estatuto *m* [gen] statute; [de empresa] article (of association); [de ciudad] by-law.

este¹ ⟡ *adj* [posición, parte] east, eastern; [dirección, viento] easterly. ⟡ *m* east; **los países del** ~ the Eastern bloc countries.

este² (*pl* **estos**), **esta** (*pl* **estas**) *adj demos* - **1.** [gen] this, *(pl)* these; **esta camisa** this shirt; ~ **año** this year - **2.** *fam despec* that, *(pl)* those; **no soporto a la niña esta** I can't stand that girl.

éste (*pl* **éstos**), **ésta** (*pl* **éstas**) *pron demos* - **1.** [gen] this one, *(pl)* these (ones); **dame otro boli;** ~ **no funciona** give me another pen; this one doesn't work; **aquellos**

cuadros no están mal, aunque éstos me gustan más those paintings aren't bad, but I like these (ones) better; **ésta ha sido la semana más feliz de mi vida** this has been the happiest week of my life - **2.** [recién mencionado] the latter; **entraron Juan y Pedro,** ~ **con un abrigo verde** Juan and Pedro came in, the latter wearing a green coat - **3.** *fam despec:* ~ **es el que me pegó** this is the guy who hit me.

◆ **en éstas** *loc adv fam* just then, at that very moment.

estela *f* - **1.** [de barco] wake; [de avión, estrella fugaz] trail - **2.** *fig* [rastro] trail.

estelar *adj* - **1.** ASTRON stellar - **2.** CIN & TEATR star *(antes de sust).*

estepa *f* steppe.

estera *f* [tejido] matting; [alfombrilla] mat.

estéreo *adj inv* & *m* stereo.

estereofónico, ca *adj* stereo.

estereotipo *m* stereotype.

estéril *adj* - **1.** [persona, terreno, imaginación] sterile - **2.** [inútil] futile, fruitless.

esterilizar *vt* to sterilize.

esterlina ▷ **libra.**

esternón *m* breastbone, sternum.

esteroides *mpl* steroids.

estética ▷ **estético.**

esteticista, esthéticienne [esteti'θjen] *f* beautician.

estético, ca *adj* aesthetic.

◆ **estética** *f* FILOSOFÍA aesthetics *(U).*

esthéticienne = esteticista.

estiércol *m* [excrementos] dung; [abono] manure.

estigma *m fig* [deshonor] stigma.

estilarse *vpr fam* to be in (fashion).

estilo *m* - **1.** [gen] style; **al** ~ **de** in the style of; ~ **de vida** lifestyle - **2.** [en natación] stroke - **3.** GRAM speech; ~ **directo/indirecto** direct/indirect speech - **4.** *loc:* **algo por el** ~ something of the sort.

estilográfica *f* fountain pen.

estima *f* esteem, respect.

estimación *f* - **1.** [aprecio] esteem, respect - **2.** [valoración] valuation - **3.** [en impuestos] assessment.

estimado, da *adj* [querido] esteemed, respected; **Estimado señor** Dear Sir.

estimar *vt* - **1.** [valorar - gen] to value; [- valor] to estimate - **2.** [apreciar] to think highly of - **3.** [creer] to consider, to think.

estimulante ⟡ *adj* [que excita] stimulating. ⟡ *m* stimulant.

estimular *vt* - **1.** [animar] to encourage - **2.** [excitar] to stimulate.

estímulo *m* - **1.** [aliciente] incentive; [ánimo] encouragement - **2.** [de un órgano] stimulus.

estío *m culto* summer.

estipulación *f* **-1.** [acuerdo] agreement **-2.** DER stipulation.

estipular *vt* to stipulate.

estirado, da *adj* [persona - altanero] haughty; [- adusto] uptight.

estirar ⬦ *vt* **-1.** [alargar - gen] to stretch; [- cuello] to crane **-2.** [desarrugar] to straighten **-3.** *fig* [dinero etc] to make last; [discurso, tema] to spin out. ⬦ *vi:* ~ **(de)** to pull.

➡️ **estirarse** *vpr* **-1.** [desperezarse] to stretch **-2.** [tumbarse] to stretch out.

estirón *m* [acción] tug, pull.

estirpe *f* stock, lineage.

estival *adj* summer *(antes de sust).*

esto *pron demos (neutro)* this thing; ~ **es tu regalo de cumpleaños** this is your birthday present; ~ **que acabas de decir no tiene sentido** what you just said doesn't make sense; ~ **de trabajar de noche no me gusta** I don't like this business of working at night; ~ **es** that is (to say).

➡️ **a todo esto** *loc adv* meanwhile, in the meantime.

➡️ **en esto** *loc adv* just then, at that very moment.

estoc (*pl* estocs) *m* stock.

Estocolmo Stockholm.

estofa *f*: **de baja** ~ [gente] low-class; [cosas] poor-quality.

estofado *m* stew.

estofar *vt* CULIN to stew.

estoicismo *m* stoicism.

estoico, ca *adj* stoic, stoical.

estomacal *adj* [dolencia] stomach *(antes de sust)*; [bebida] digestive.

estómago *m* stomach; **revolver el** ~ **a alguien** to turn sb's stomach; **tener buen** ~ to be tough, to be able to stand a lot.

Estonia Estonia.

estop = stop.

estorbar ⬦ *vt* [obstaculizar] to hinder; [molestar] to bother. ⬦ *vi* [estar en medio] to be in the way.

estorbo *m* [obstáculo] hindrance; [molestia] nuisance.

estornudar *vi* to sneeze.

estos, tas ⊳ este².

éstos, tas ⊳ éste.

estoy ⊳ estar.

estrabismo *m* squint.

estrado *m* platform.

estrafalario, ria *adj* outlandish, eccentric.

estragón *m* tarragon.

estragos *mpl*: **causar** *o* **hacer** ~ **en** [físicos] to wreak havoc with; [morales] to destroy, to ruin.

estrambótico, ca *adj* outlandish.

estrangulador, ra *m,f* strangler.

estrangular *vt* [ahogar] to strangle; MED to strangulate.

estraperlo *m* black market; **de** ~ black market *(antes de sust).*

estratagema *f* MIL stratagem; *fig* [astucia] artifice, trick.

estrategia *f* strategy.

estratégico, ca *adj* strategic.

estrato *m* GEOL & *fig* stratum.

estrechar *vt* **-1.** [hacer estrecho - gen] to narrow; [- ropa] to take in **-2.** *fig* [relaciones] to make closer **-3.** [apretar] to squeeze, to hug; ~ **la mano a alguien** to shake sb's hand.

➡️ **estrecharse** *vpr* [hacerse estrecho] to narrow.

estrechez *f* **-1.** [falta de anchura] narrowness; [falta de espacio] lack of space; [de ropa] tightness; ~ **de miras** narrow-mindedness **-2.** *fig* [falta de dinero] hardship; **pasar estrecheces** to be hard up **-3.** [intimidad] closeness.

estrecho, cha *adj* **-1.** [no ancho - gen] narrow; [- ropa] tight; [- habitación] cramped; ~ **de miras** narrow-minded **-2.** *fig* [íntimo] close.

➡️ **estrecho** *m* GEOGR strait.

estrella *f* [gen] star; *fig* [destino] fate; ~ **de cine** film star *UK*, movie star *US*; ~ **fugaz** shooting star.

➡️ **estrella de mar** *f* starfish.

estrellado, da *adj* **-1.** [con estrellas] starry **-2.** [por la forma] star-shaped.

estrellar *vt* [arrojar] to smash.

➡️ **estrellarse** *vpr* [chocar]: ~**se (contra)** [gen] to smash (against); [avión, coche] to crash (into).

estrellón *m Amér* crash.

estremecer *vt* to shake.

➡️ **estremecerse** *vpr*: ~**se (de)** [horror, miedo] to tremble *o* shudder (with); [frío] to shiver (with).

estremecimiento *m* [de miedo] shudder; [de frío] shiver.

estrenar *vt* **-1.** [gen] to use for the first time; [ropa] to wear for the first time; [piso] to move into **-2.** CIN to release, to show for the first time; TEATR to premiere.

➡️ **estrenarse** *vpr* [persona] to make one's debut, to start.

estreno *m* [de espectáculo] premiere, first night; [de cosa] first use; [en un empleo] debut.

estreñido, da *adj* constipated.

estreñimiento *m* constipation.

estrépito *m* [ruido] racket, din; *fig* [ostentación] fanfare.

estrepitoso, sa *adj* **-1.** [gen] noisy; [aplausos] deafening **-2.** [derrota] resounding; [fracaso] spectacular.

estrés *m inv* stress.

estría *f* [gen] groove; [en la piel] stretch mark.

estribación *f (gen pl)* foothills *(pl)*.

estribar ► estribar en *vi* to be based on, to lie in.

estribillo *m* MÚS chorus; LITER refrain.

estribo *m* -1. [de montura] stirrup - 2. [de coche, tren] step - 3. *loc:* **estar con un pie en el ~** to be ready to leave; **perder los ~s** to fly off the handle.

estribor *m* starboard.

estricto, ta *adj* strict.

estridente *adj* -1. [ruido] strident, shrill - 2. [color] garish, loud.

estrofa *f* stanza, verse.

estropajo *m* scourer.

estropear *vt* -1. [averiar] to break - 2. [dañar] to damage - 3. [echar a perder] to ruin, to spoil.

► estropearse *vpr* -1. [máquina] to break down - 2. [comida] to go off, to spoil; [piel] to get damaged - 3. [plan] to fall through.

estropicio *m:* **hacer** *o* **causar un ~** to wreak havoc.

estructura *f* structure.

estruendo *m* -1. [estrépito] din, roar; [de trueno] crash - 2. [alboroto] uproar, tumult.

estrujar *vt* -1. [limón] to squeeze; [trapo, ropa] to wring (out); [papel] to screw up; [caja] to crush - 2. [abrazar - persona, mano] to squeeze - 3. *fig* [sacar partido de] to bleed dry.

estuario *m* estuary.

estuche *m* -1. [caja] case; [de joyas] jewellery box - 2. [utensilios] set.

estuco *m* stucco.

estudiante *mf* student.

estudiantil *adj* student *(antes de sust)*.

estudiar *◇ vt* to study. *◇ vi* to study; **~ para médico** to be studying to be a doctor.

estudio *m* -1. [gen] study; **estar en ~** to be under consideration; **~ de mercado** [técnica] market research; [investigación] market survey - 2. [oficina] study; [de fotógrafo, pintor] studio - 3. [apartamento] studio apartment - 4. *(gen pl)* CIN, RADIO & TV studio.

► estudios *mpl* [serie de cursos] studies; [educación] education *(U)*; **dar ~s a alguien** to pay for sb's education; **tener ~s** to be well-educated; **~s primarios/secundarios** primary/secondary education.

estudioso, sa *adj* studious.

estufa *f* heater, fire; **~ de gas** gas heater; **~ eléctrica** electric heater.

estupefaciente *m* narcotic, drug.

estupefacto, ta *adj* astonished.

estupendamente *adv* wonderfully;

estoy ~ I feel wonderful.

estupendo, da *adj* great, fantastic.

► estupendo *interj:* **¡~!** great!

estupidez *f* stupidity; **decir/hacer una ~** to say/do sthg stupid.

estúpido, da *adj* stupid.

estupor *m* astonishment.

esturión *m* sturgeon.

estuviera *etc* ⊳ **estar.**

esvástica *f* swastika.

ETA *(abrev de* **Euskadi ta Askatasuna)** *f* ETA, *terrorist Basque separatist organization.*

etapa *f* stage; **por ~s** in stages.

etarra *mf* member of ETA.

etc. *(abrev de* **etcétera)** etc.

etcétera *adv* etcetera.

etéreo, a *adj fig* ethereal.

eternidad *f* eternity; **hace una ~ que no la veo** *fam* it's ages since I last saw her.

eterno, na *adj* eternal; *fam* [larguísimo] never-ending, interminable.

ético, ca *adj* ethical.

► ética *f* [moralidad] ethics *(pl)*.

etílico, ca *adj* QUÍM ethyl *(antes de sust)*; **intoxicación etílica** alcohol poisoning.

etimología *f* etymology.

Etiopía Ethiopia.

etiqueta *f* -1. [gen & INFORM] label; **~ autoadhesiva** sticky label; **~ del precio** price tag - 2. [ceremonial] etiquette; **de ~** formal; **vestir de ~** to wear formal dress.

etiquetar *vt lit & fig* to label; **~ a alguien de algo** to label sb sthg.

etnia *f* ethnic group.

étnico, ca *adj* ethnic.

EUA *(abrev de* **Estados Unidos de América)** *mpl* USA.

eucalipto *m* eucalyptus.

eucaristía *f:* **la ~** the Eucharist.

eufemismo *m* euphemism.

euforia *f* euphoria, elation.

eufórico, ca *adj* euphoric, elated.

eunuco *m* eunuch.

euro *m* [unidad monetaria] euro.

Eurocámara *f* European Parliament.

eurocheque *m* eurocheque *UK*, eurocheck *US*.

eurócrata *adj & mf* Eurocrat.

eurodiputado, da *m,f* Euro-M.P., M.E.P.

Europa Europe.

euroescéptico, ca *m,f* Eurosceptic.

europeo, a *adj & m,f* European.

Euskadi the Basque Country.

euskara, euskera *m* Basque.

eutanasia *f* euthanasia.

evacuación *f* evacuation.

evacuar *vt* [gen] to evacuate; [vientre] to empty, to void.

evadir *vt* to evade; [respuesta, peligro] to avoid.

➤ **evadirse** *vpr*: ~**se (de)** to escape (from).

evaluación *f* **-1.** [gen] evaluation **- 2.** [EDUC - examen] assessment; [periodo] *period of continuous assessment*.

evaluar *vt* to evaluate, to assess.

evangélico, ca *adj* & *m,f* evangelical.

evangelio *m* gospel.

evaporar *vt* to evaporate.

➤ **evaporarse** *vpr* [líquido etc] to evaporate.

evasión *f* **-1.** [huida] escape **- 2.** [de dinero]: ~ **de capitales** *o* **divisas** capital flight; ~ **fiscal** tax evasion **- 3.** [entretenimiento] amusement, recreation; [escapismo] escapism; **de** ~ escapist.

evasivo, va *adj* evasive.

➤ **evasiva** *f* evasive answer.

evento *m* event.

eventual *adj* **-1.** [no fijo - trabajador] temporary, casual; [- gastos] incidental **- 2.** [posible] possible.

eventualidad *f* **-1.** [temporalidad] temporariness **- 2.** [hecho incierto] eventuality; [posibilidad] possibility.

evidencia *f* **-1.** [prueba] evidence, proof; **negar la** ~ to refuse to accept the obvious; **rendirse ante la** ~ to bow to the evidence **- 2.** [claridad] obviousness; **poner algo en** ~ to demonstrate sthg; **poner a alguien en** ~ to show sb up.

evidenciar *vt* to show, to demonstrate.

➤ **evidenciarse** *vpr* to be obvious *o* evident.

evidente *adj* evident, obvious.

evitar *vt* [gen] to avoid; [desastre, accidente] to avert; ~ **hacer algo** to avoid doing sthg; ~ **que alguien haga algo** to prevent sb from doing sthg.

evocación *f* recollection, evocation.

evocar *vt* [recordar] to evoke.

evolución *f* **-1.** [gen] evolution; [de enfermedad] development, progress **- 2.** MIL manoeuvre.

evolucionar *vi* **-1.** [gen] to evolve; [enfermedad] to develop, to progress; [cambiar] to change **- 2.** MIL to carry out manoeuvres.

ex *prep* ex; **el** ~ **presidente** the ex-president, the former president.

exacerbar *vt* **-1.** [agudizar] to exacerbate, to aggravate **- 2.** [irritar] to irritate, to infuriate.

exactitud *f* accuracy, precision.

exacto, ta *adj* **-1.** [justo - cálculo, medida] exact; **tres metros** ~**s** exactly three metres **- 2.** [preciso] accurate, precise; [correcto] correct, right **- 3.** [idéntico]: ~ **(a)** identical (to), exactly the same (as).

➤ **exacto** *interj*: ¡~! exactly!, precisely!

exageración *f* exaggeration; **este precio es una** ~ this price is over the top.

exagerado, da *adj* [gen] exaggerated; [persona] overly dramatic; [precio] exorbitant; [gesto] flamboyant.

exagerar *vt* & *vi* to exaggerate.

exaltado, da *adj* [jubiloso] elated; [acalorado - persona] worked up; [- discusión] heated; [excitable] hotheaded.

exaltar *vt* **-1.** [elevar] to promote, to raise **- 2.** [glorificar] to exalt.

➤ **exaltarse** *vpr* to get excited *o* worked up.

examen *m* **-1.** [ejercicio] exam, examination; **presentarse a un** ~ to sit an exam; ~ **de conducir** driving test; ~ **final/oral** final/oral (exam); ~ **parcial** ≃ end-of-term exam **- 2.** [indagación] consideration, examination; **someter algo a** ~ to examine sthg, to subject sthg to examination.

examinar *vt* to examine.

➤ **examinarse** *vpr* to sit *o* take an exam.

exánime *adj* **-1.** [muerto] dead **- 2.** [desmayado] lifeless.

exasperar *vt* to exasperate, to infuriate.

➤ **exasperarse** *vpr* to get exasperated.

excavación *f* [lugar] dig, excavation.

excavar *vt* [gen] to dig; [en arqueología] to excavate.

excedencia *f* leave (of absence); EDUC sabbatical; ~ **por maternidad** maternity leave.

excedente ⟨⟩ *adj* [producción etc] surplus. ⟨⟩ *m* COM surplus.

exceder *vt* to exceed, to surpass.

➤ **excederse** *vpr* **-1.** [pasarse de la raya]: ~**se (en)** to go too far *o* overstep the mark (in) **- 2.** [rebasar el límite]: **se excede en el peso** it's too heavy.

excelencia *f* [cualidad] excellence; **por** ~ par excellence.

➤ **Su Excelencia** *mf* His Excellency (*f* Her Excellency).

excelente *adj* excellent.

excelentísimo, ma *adj* most excellent.

excentricidad *f* eccentricity.

excéntrico, ca *adj* & *m,f* eccentric.

excepción *f* exception; **a** *o* **con** ~ **de** with the exception of, except for.

➤ **de excepción** *loc adj* exceptional.

excepcional *adj* exceptional.

excepto *adv* except (for).

exceptuar *vt*: ~ **(de)** [excluir] to exclude (from); [eximir] to exempt (from); **exceptuando a ...** excluding ...

excesivo, va *adj* excessive.

exceso *m* [demasía] excess; ~ **de equipaje** excess baggage; ~ **de peso** [obesidad] excess weight.

◆ **excesos** *mpl* [abusos] excesses.

excitación *f* [nerviosismo] agitation; [por enfado, sexo] arousal.

excitado, da *adj* [nervioso] agitated; [por enfado, sexo] aroused.

excitante *m* stimulant.

excitar *vt* - **1.** [inquietar] to upset, to agitate - **2.** [estimular - sentidos] to stimulate; [- apetito] to whet; [- pasión, curiosidad, persona] to arouse.

◆ **excitarse** *vpr* [alterarse] to get worked up o excited.

exclamación *f* [interjección] exclamation; [grito] cry.

exclamar *vt* & *vi* to exclaim, to shout out.

excluir *vt* to exclude; [hipótesis, opción] to rule out; [hacer imposible] to preclude; ~ **a alguien de algo** to exclude sb from sthg.

exclusión *f* exclusion.

exclusivo, va *adj* exclusive.

◆ **exclusiva** *f* - **1.** PRENS exclusive - **2.** COM exclusive o sole right.

Excma. *abrev de* **Excelentísima.**

Excmo. *abrev de* **Excelentísimo.**

excombatiente *mf* ex-serviceman (*f* ex-servicewoman) *UK*, war veteran *US*.

excomulgar *vt* to excommunicate.

excomunión *f* excommunication.

excremento (*gen pl*) *m* excrement (*U*).

exculpar *vt* to exonerate; DER to acquit.

excursión *f* [viaje] excursion, trip; **ir de** ~ to go on an outing o a trip.

excursionista *mf* [en la ciudad] sightseer, tripper; [en el campo] rambler; [en la montaña] hiker.

excusa *f* - **1.** [gen] excuse; **¡nada de** ~**s!** no excuses!; **buscar una** ~ to look for an excuse; **dar** ~**s** to make excuses - **2.** [petición de perdón] apology; **presentar uno sus** ~**s** to apologize, to make one's excuses.

excusar *vt* [disculpar a] to excuse; [disculparse por] to apologize for.

◆ **excusarse** *vpr* to apologize, to excuse o.s.

exento, ta *adj* exempt; ~ **de** [sin] free from, without; [eximido de] exempt from; ~ **de impuestos** tax free.

exequias *fpl* funeral (*sg*), funeral rites.

exhalación *f* [emanación] exhalation, vapour; [suspiro] breath.

exhalar *vt* - **1.** [aire] to exhale, to breathe out; [suspiros] to heave - **2.** [olor] to give off - **3.** [quejas] to utter.

exhaustivo, va *adj* exhaustive.

exhausto, ta *adj* exhausted.

exhibición *f* - **1.** [demostración] show, display - **2.** [deportiva, artística etc] exhibition - **3.** [de películas] showing.

exhibir *vt* - **1.** [exponer - cuadros, fotografías] to exhibit; [- modelos] to show; [- productos] to display - **2.** [lucir - joyas, cualidades etc] to show off - **3.** [película] to show, to screen.

exhortación *f* exhortation.

exhortar *vt*: ~ **a alguien a** to exhort sb to.

exigencia *f* - **1.** [obligación] demand, requirement - **2.** [capricho] fussiness (*U*).

exigente *adj* demanding.

exigir *vt* - **1.** [gen] to demand; ~ **algo de** o **a alguien** to demand sthg from sb - **2.** [requerir, necesitar] to require.

exiguo, gua *adj* [escaso] meagre, paltry; [pequeño] minute.

exiliado, da ◇ *adj* exiled, in exile. ◇ *m,f* exile.

exiliar *vt* to exile.

◆ **exiliarse** *vpr* to go into exile.

exilio *m* exile.

eximir *vt*: ~ **(de)** to exempt (from).

existencia *f* existence.

◆ **existencias** *fpl* COM stock (*U*); **reponer las** ~**s** to restock.

existir *vi* to exist; **existe mucha pobreza** there is a lot of poverty.

éxito *m* - **1.** [gen] success; **con** ~ successfully; **tener** ~ to be successful - **2.** [libro] bestseller; [canción] hit.

exitoso, sa *adj* successful.

éxodo *m* exodus.

exorbitante *adj* exorbitant.

exorcizar *vt* to exorcize.

exótico, ca *adj* exotic.

expandir *vt* to spread; FÍS to expand.

◆ **expandirse** *vpr* to spread; FÍS to expand.

expansión *f* - **1.** FÍS expansion - **2.** ECON growth; **en** ~ expanding - **3.** [recreo] relaxation, amusement.

expansionarse *vpr* - **1.** [desahogarse]: ~ **(con)** to open one's heart (to) - **2.** [divertirse] to relax, to let off steam - **3.** [desarrollarse] to expand.

expansivo, va *adj* - **1.** [gen] expansive - **2.** [persona] open, frank.

expatriar *vt* to expatriate; [exiliar] to exile.

◆ **expatriarse** *vpr* to emigrate; [exiliarse] to go into exile.

expectación *f* expectancy, anticipation.

expectativa *f* [espera] expectation; [esperanza] hope; [perspectiva] prospect; **estar a la** ~ to wait and see; **estar a la** ~ **de** [atento] to be on the lookout for; [a la espera] to be hoping for; ~ **de vida** life expectancy.

expedición *f* [viaje, grupo] expedition; ~ **militar** military expedition; ~ **de salvamento** rescue mission.

expediente *m* - **1.** [documentación] documents (*pl*); [ficha] file - **2.** [historial] record;

~ **académico** academic record *UK*, transcript *US* **- 3.** [investigación] inquiry; **abrir ~ a alguien** [castigar] to take disciplinary action against sb; [investigar] to start proceedings against sb.

expedir *vt* [carta, pedido] to send, to dispatch; [pasaporte, decreto] to issue; [contrato, documento] to draw up.

expedito, ta *adj* clear, free.

expeler *vt* [humo - suj: persona] to blow out; [- suj: chimenea, tubo de escape] to emit; [- suj: extractor, volcán] to expel.

expendedor, ra *m,f* dealer, retailer; [de lotería] seller, vendor.

expendeduría *f* [de tabaco] tobacconist's *UK*, cigar store *US*.

expensas *fpl* [gastos] expenses, costs.

➥ **a expensas de** *loc prep* at the expense of.

experiencia *f* [gen] experience; **por (propia) ~** from (one's own) experience.

experimentado, da *adj* [persona] experienced; [método] tried and tested.

experimentar *vt* **- 1.** [gen] to experience; [derrota, pérdidas] to suffer **- 2.** [probar] to test; [hacer experimentos con] to experiment with *o* on.

experimento *m* experiment.

experto, ta *adj & m,f* expert; **ser ~ en la materia** to be a specialist in the subject; **ser ~ en hacer algo** to be an expert at doing sthg.

expiar *vt* to atone for, to expiate.

expirar *vi* to expire.

explanada *f* [llanura] flat *o* level ground (U).

explayar *vt* to extend.

➥ **explayarse** *vpr* **- 1.** [divertirse] to amuse o.s., to enjoy o.s. **- 2.** [hablar mucho] to talk at length **- 3.** [desahogarse]: **~se (con)** to pour out one's heart (to).

explicación *f* explanation.

explicar *vt* [gen] to explain; [teoría] to expound.

➥ **explicarse** *vpr* **- 1.** [comprender] to understand; **no me lo explico** I can't understand it **- 2.** [dar explicaciones] to explain o.s. **- 3.** [expresarse] to make o.s. understood.

explícito, ta *adj* explicit.

exploración *f* [gen & MED] exploration.

explorador, ra *m,f* explorer; [scout] boy scout (*f* girl guide).

explorar *vt* **- 1.** [gen] to explore; MIL to scout **- 2.** MED to examine; [internamente] to explore, to probe.

explosión *f* lit & fig explosion; **hacer ~** to explode.

explosivo, va *adj* [gen] explosive.

➥ **explosivo** *m* explosive.

explotación *f* **- 1.** [acción] exploitation; [de fábrica etc] running; [de yacimiento minero] mining; [agrícola] farming; [de petróleo] drilling **- 2.** [instalaciones]: **~ agrícola** farm.

explotar ⬦ *vt* **- 1.** [gen] to exploit **- 2.** [fábrica] to run, to operate; [terreno] to farm; [mina] to work. ⬦ *vi* to explode.

expoliar *vt* to pillage, to plunder.

exponer *vt* **- 1.** [gen] to expose **- 2.** [teoría] to expound; [ideas, propuesta] to set out, to explain **- 3.** [cuadro, obra] to exhibit; [objetos en vitrinas] to display **- 4.** [vida, prestigio] to risk.

➥ **exponerse** *vpr* [arriesgarse]: **~se (a)** [gen] to run the risk (of); [a la muerte] to expose o.s. (to).

exportación *f* **- 1.** [acción] export **- 2.** [mercancías] exports (*pl*).

exportar *vt* COM & INFORM to export.

exposición *f* **- 1.** [gen & FOT] exposure **- 2.** [de arte etc] exhibition; [de objetos en vitrina] display; **~ universal** world fair **- 3.** [de teoría] exposition; [de ideas, propuesta] setting out, explanation.

expositor, ra *m,f* [de arte] exhibitor; [de teoría] exponent.

exprés ⬦ *adj* **- 1.** [tren] express **- 2.** [café] espresso. ⬦ *m* = **expreso.**

expresado, da *adj* [mencionado] abovementioned.

expresamente *adv* [a propósito] expressly; [explícitamente] explicitly, specifically.

expresar *vt* to express; [suj: rostro] to show.

expresión *f* expression.

expresivo, va *adj* expressive; [cariñoso] affectionate.

expreso, sa *adj* [explícito] specific; [deliberado] express; [claro] clear.

➥ **expreso** ⬦ *m* **- 1.** [tren] express train **- 2.** [café] expresso. ⬦ *adv* on purpose, expressly.

exprimidor *m* squeezer.

exprimir *vt* [fruta] to squeeze; [zumo] to squeeze out.

expropiar *vt* to expropriate.

expuesto, ta ⬦ *pp* ▷ **exponer.** ⬦ *adj* **- 1.** [dicho] stated, expressed **- 2.** [desprotegido]: **~ (a)** exposed (to) **- 3.** [arriesgado] dangerous, risky **- 4.** [exhibido] on display.

expulsar *vt* **- 1.** [persona - de clase, local, asociación] to throw out; [- de colegio] to expel **- 2.** DEP to send off **- 3.** [humo] to emit, to give off.

expulsión *f* [gen] expulsion; [de clase, local, asociación] throwing-out; DEP sending-off.

exquisitez *f* [cualidad] exquisiteness.

exquisito, ta *adj* exquisite; [comida] delicious, sublime.

extasiarse *vpr*: ~ (ante o con) to go into ecstasies (over).

éxtasis *m inv* ecstasy.

extender *vt* **- 1.** [desplegar - tela, plano, alas] to spread (out); [- brazos, piernas] to stretch out **- 2.** [esparcir - mantequilla] to spread; [- pintura] to smear; [- objetos etc] to spread out **- 3.** [ampliar - castigo, influencia etc] to extend, to widen **- 4.** [documento] to draw up; [cheque] to make out; [pasaporte, certificado] to issue.
➡ **extenderse** *vpr* **- 1.** [ocupar]: ~se (por) to stretch o extend across **- 2.** [hablar mucho]: ~se (en) to enlarge o expand (on) **- 3.** [durar] to extend, to last **- 4.** [difundirse]: ~se (por) to spread (across) **- 5.** [tenderse] to stretch out.

extensión *f* **- 1.** [superficie - de terreno etc] area, expanse **- 2.** [amplitud - de país etc] size; [- de conocimientos] extent **- 3.** [duración] duration, length **- 4.** [sentido - de concepto, palabra] range of meaning; **en toda la ~ de la palabra** in every sense of the word **- 5.** INFORM & TELECOM extension.

extensivo, va *adj* extensive.

extenso, sa *adj* extensive; [país] vast; [libro, película] long.

extenuar *vt* to exhaust completely, to drain.

exterior <> *adj* **- 1.** [de fuera] outside; [capa] outer, exterior **- 2.** [visible] outward **- 3.** [extranjero] foreign. <> *m* **- 1.** [superficie] outside; **en el ~** outside **- 2.** [extranjero] foreign countries *(pl)*; **en el ~ abroad - 3.** [aspecto] appearance.
➡ **exteriores** *mpl* CIN outside shots; **rodar en ~es** to film on location.

exteriorizar *vt* to show, to reveal.

exterminar *vt* [aniquilar] to exterminate.

exterminio *m* extermination.

externalización *f* outsourcing.

externalizar *vt* to outsource.

externo, na *adj* **- 1.** [gen] external; [parte, capa] outer; [influencia] outside; [signo, aspecto] outward **- 2.** [alumno] day *(antes de sust)*.

extinción *f* [gen] extinction; [de esperanzas] loss.

extinguir *vt* [incendio] to put out, to extinguish; [raza] to wipe out; [afecto, entusiasmo] to put an end to.
➡ **extinguirse** *vpr* [fuego, luz] to go out; [animal, raza] to become extinct, to die out; [ruido] to die out; [afecto] to die.

extinto, ta *adj* extinguished; [animal, volcán] extinct.

extintor *m* fire extinguisher.

extirpar *vt* [tumor] to remove; [muela] to extract; *fig* to eradicate, to stamp out.

extorsión *f* **- 1.** [molestia] trouble, bother **- 2.** DER extortion.

extorsionista *mf* extortionist.

extra <> *adj* **- 1.** [adicional] extra **- 2.** [de gran calidad] top quality, superior. <> *mf* CIN extra. <> *m* [gasto etc] extra. <> *f* ⊳ **paga**.

extracción *f* **- 1.** [gen] extraction **- 2.** [en sorteos] draw **- 3.** [de carbón] mining.

extracto *m* **- 1.** [resumen] summary, résumé; ~ **de cuentas** statement (of account) **- 2.** [concentrado] extract.

extraditar *vt* to extradite.

extraer *vt* : ~ (de) [gen] to extract (from); [sangre] to draw (from); [carbón] to mine (from); [conclusiones] to come to o draw (from).

extralimitarse *vpr fig* to go too far.

extranjero, ra <> *adj* foreign. <> *m,f* [persona] foreigner.
➡ **extranjero** *m* [territorio] foreign countries *(pl)*; **estar en el/ir al ~** to be/go abroad.

extrañar *vt* **- 1.** [sorprender] to surprise; **me extraña (que digas esto)** I'm surprised (that you should say that) **- 2.** [echar de menos] to miss.
➡ **extrañarse de** *vpr* [sorprenderse de] to be surprised at.

extrañeza *f* [sorpresa] surprise.

extraño, ña <> *adj* **- 1.** [raro] strange; **¡qué ~!** how odd o strange! **- 2.** [ajeno] detached, uninvolved **- 3.** MED foreign. <> *m,f* stranger.

extraoficial *adj* unofficial.

extraordinario, ria *adj* **- 1.** [gen] extraordinary; **no tiene nada de ~** there's nothing extraordinary about that **- 2.** [gastos] additional; [edición, suplemento] special.
➡ **extraordinario** *m* **- 1.** PRENS special edition **- 3.** ⊳ **paga**.

extraparlamentario, ria *adj* non-parliamentary.

extrapolar *vt* to generalize about, to jump to conclusions about.

extrarradio *m* outskirts *(pl)*, suburbs *(pl)*.

extraterrestre *adj* & *mf* extraterrestrial.

extravagancia *f* eccentricity.

extravagante *adj* eccentric, outlandish.

extravertido, da = extrovertido.

extraviado, da *adj* [perdido] lost; [animal] stray.

extraviar *vt* **- 1.** [objeto] to lose, to mislay **- 2.** [excursionista] to mislead, to cause to lose one's way.
➡ **extraviarse** *vpr* **- 1.** [persona] to get lost **- 2.** [objeto] to go missing.

extravío *m* [pérdida] loss, mislaying.

extremado, da *adj* extreme.

extremar *vt* to maximize.

◆ **extremarse** *vpr* to take great pains o care.

extremaunción *f* extreme unction.

extremidad *f* [extremo] end.

◆ **extremidades** *fpl* ANAT extremities.

extremista *adj* & *mf* extremist.

extremo, ma *adj* [gen] extreme; [en el espacio] far, furthest.

◆ **extremo** *m* - 1. [punta] end - 2. [límite] extreme; **en último** ~ as a last resort; **ser el ~ opuesto** to be the complete opposite - 3. DEP: ~ **derecho/izquierdo** outside right/left.

extrovertido, da, **extravertido, da** *adj* & *m,f* extrovert.

exuberancia *f* exuberance.

exuberante *adj* exuberant.

exudar *vt* to exude, to ooze.

exultante *adj* exultant.

eyaculación *f* ejaculation.

eyacular *vi* to ejaculate.

f, F *f* [letra] f, F.
◆ **23 F** *m* 23rd February, day of the failed coup d'état in Spain in 1981.

f. - 1. (*abrev de* **factura**) inv. - 2. (*abrev de* **folio**) f.

fa *m* MÚS F; [en solfeo] fa.

fabada *f* Asturian stew made of beans, pork sausage and bacon.

fábrica *f* [establecimiento] factory; ~ **de cerveza** brewery; ~ **de conservas** canning plant, cannery; ~ **de papel** paper mill.

fabricación *f* manufacture; **de** ~ **casera** home-made; ~ **en serie** mass production.

fabricante *mf* manufacturer.

fabricar *vt* - 1. [producir] to manufacture, to make - 2. [construir] to build, to construct - 3. *fig* [inventar] to fabricate, to make up.

fábula *f* LITER fable; [leyenda] legend, myth.

fabuloso, sa *adj* - 1. [ficticio] mythical, fantastic - 2. [muy bueno] fabulous, fantastic.

facción *f* POLÍT faction.
◆ **facciones** *fpl* [rasgos] features.

faceta *f* facet.

facha *f* - 1. [aspecto] appearance, look - 2. [mamarracho] mess; **vas hecho una** ~ you look a mess.

fachada *f* ARQUIT façade.

facial *adj* facial.

fácil *adj* - 1. [gen] easy; ~ **de hacer** easy to do - 2. [probable] likely.

facilidad *f* - 1. [simplicidad] ease, easiness; **con** ~ easily; **con la mayor** ~ with the greatest of ease - 2. [aptitud] aptitude; **tener** ~ **para algo** to have a gift for sthg.
◆ **facilidades** *fpl* [comodidades] facilities; **dar** ~**es a alguien para algo** to make sthg easy for sb; ~**es de pago** easy (payment) terms.

facilitar *vt* - 1. [simplificar] to facilitate, to make easy; [posibilitar] to make possible - 2. [proporcionar] to provide; ~ **algo a alguien** to provide o supply sb with sthg.

facsímil, facsímile *m* facsimile.

factible *adj* feasible.

fáctico, ca ▷ **poder**.

factor *m* [gen] factor; ~ **humano** human factor; ~ **de riesgo** risk factor.

factoría *f* [fábrica] factory.

factura *f* - 1. [por mercancías, trabajo realizado] invoice; **pasar** o **presentar una** ~ to send an invoice - 2. [de gas, teléfono] bill; [en tienda, hotel] bill - 3. *Arg* [repostería] cakes and pastries.

facturación *f* - 1. [ventas] turnover *UK*, net revenue *US* - 3. [de equipaje - en aeropuerto] checking-in; [- en estación] registration; **mostrador de** ~ check-in desk.

facturar *vt* - 1. [cobrar]: ~ **le a alguien algo** to invoice o bill sb for sthg - 2. [vender] to turn over - 3. [equipaje - en aeropuerto] to check in; [- en estación] to register.

facultad *f* - 1. [capacidad & UNIV] faculty; ~**es mentales** mental faculties - 2. [poder] power, right.

facultativo, va ◇ *adj* - 1. [voluntario] optional - 2. [médico] medical. ◇ *m,f* doctor.

faena *f* [tarea] task, work *(U)*; **estar en plena** ~ to be hard at work.

faenar *vi* to fish.

fagot *m* [instrumento] bassoon.

fainá *f* RP baked dough made from chickpea flour, served with pizza.

faisán *m* pheasant.

faja *f* - 1. [prenda de mujer, terapéutica] corset; [banda] sash, cummerbund - 2. [de terreno - pequeña] strip; [- grande] belt.

fajo *m* [de billetes, papel] wad; [de leña, cañas] bundle.

falacia *f* deceit, trick.

falda *f* - 1. [prenda] skirt; **estar pegado** o **cosido a las** ~**s de su madre** to be tied to one's mother's apron strings; ~ **escocesa** kilt; ~ **pantalón** culottes *(pl)*; ~ **plisada** o **tableada** pleated skirt - 2. [de montaña] slope, mountainside.

faldón *m* [de ropa] tail; [de cortina, mesa camilla] folds *(pl)*.

falencia *f CSur* shortcoming.

falla *f* [gen & GEOL] fault.

→ **fallas** *fpl* [fiesta] *celebrations in Valencia during which cardboard figures are burnt.*

fallar ◇ *vt* **- 1.** [sentenciar] to pass sentence on; [premio] to award **- 2.** [equivocar - respuesta] to get wrong; [-tiro] to miss. ◇ *vi* **- 1.** [equivocarse] to get it wrong; [no acertar] to miss **- 2.** [fracasar, flaquear] to fail; [plan] to go wrong **- 3.** [decepcionar]: ~ **le a alguien** to let sb down **- 4.** [sentenciar]: ~ **a favor/en contra de** to find in favour of/against.

fallecer *vi* to pass away, to die.

fallecimiento *m* decease, death.

fallo *m* **- 1.** [error] mistake; **¡qué ~!** what a stupid mistake!; ~ **humano** human error **- 2.** [sentencia - de juez, jurado] verdict.

fallutería *f RP fam* hypocrisy.

falo *m* phallus.

falsear *vt* [hechos, historia] to falsify, to distort; [moneda, firma] to forge.

falsedad *f* **- 1.** [falta de verdad, autenticidad] falseness **- 2.** [mentira] falsehood, lie.

falsete *m* falsetto.

falsificar *vt* to forge.

falso, sa *adj* **- 1.** [rumor, excusa etc] false, untrue **- 2.** [dinero, firma, cuadro] forged; [joyas] fake; **jurar en ~** to commit perjury **- 3.** [hipócrita] deceitful.

falta *f* **- 1.** [carencia] lack; **hacer ~** to be necessary; **me hace ~ suerte** I need some luck; **por ~ de** for want o lack of **- 2.** [escasez] shortage **- 3.** [ausencia] absence; **echar en ~ algo/a alguien** [notar la ausencia de] to notice that sthg/sb is missing; [echar de menos] to miss sthg/sb **- 4.** [imperfección] fault; [error] mistake; ~ **de educación** bad manners *(pl)*; ~ **de ortografía** spelling mistake; ~ **de respeto** disrespect, lack of respect **- 5.** [en tenis] foul; [en tenis] fault; **doble ~** double fault **- 6.** DER offence.

→ **a falta de** *loc prep* in the absence of; **a ~ de pan, buenas son tortas** *proverb* half a loaf is better than none.

→ **sin falta** *loc adv* without fail.

faltante *m Amér* deficit.

faltar *vi* **- 1.** [no haber] to be lacking, to be needed; **falta aire** there's not enough air; **falta sal** it needs a bit of salt **- 2.** [estar ausente] to be absent o missing; **falta Elena** Elena is missing **- 3.** [carecer]: **le faltan las fuerzas** he lacks o doesn't have the strength **- 4.** [hacer falta] to be necessary; **me falta tiempo** I need time **- 5.** [quedar]: **falta un mes para las vacaciones** there's a month to go till the holidays; **sólo te falta firmar** all you have to do is sign; **¿cuánto falta para Leeds?** how much further is it to Leeds?; **falta**

mucho por hacer there is still a lot to be done; **falta poco para que llegue** it won't be long till he arrives **- 6.** *loc:* **¡no faltaba o faltaría más!** [asentimiento] of course!; [rechazo] that tops it all!, that's a bit much!

→ **faltar a** *vi* **- 1.** [palabra, promesa] to break, not to keep; [deber, obligación] to neglect **- 2.** [cita, trabajo] not to turn up at; **¡no faltes (a la cita)!** don't miss it!, be there! **- 3.** [no respetar] to be disrespectful towards; ~ **a alguien en algo** to offend sb in sthg.

falto, ta *adj:* ~ **de** lacking in, short of.

fama *f* **- 1.** [renombre] fame; **tener ~** to be famous **- 2.** [reputación] reputation; **tener buena/mala ~** to have a good/bad reputation.

famélico, ca *adj* starving, famished.

familia *f* family; **en ~** in private; **ser de buena ~** to come from a good family; **ser como de la ~** to be like one of the family; ~ **monoparental** one-parent family; ~ **política** in-laws *(pl)*; ~ **real** royal family.

familiar ◇ *adj* **- 1.** [de familia] family *(antes de sust)* **- 2.** [en el trato - agradable] friendly; [- en demasía] overly familiar **- 3.** [lenguaje, estilo] informal, colloquial **- 4.** [conocido] familiar. ◇ *mf* relative, relation.

familiaridad *f* familiarity.

familiarizar *vt:* ~ **(con)** to familiarize (with).

→ **familiarizarse** *vpr:* ~ **se con** [estudiar] to familiarize o.s. with; [acostumbrarse a] to get used to.

famoso, sa *adj* famous.

fanático, ca ◇ *adj* fanatical. ◇ *m,f* [gen] fanatic; DEP fan.

fanatismo *m* fanaticism.

fanfarria *f* **- 1.** *fam* [jactancia] bragging **- 2.** [pieza musical] fanfare; [banda] brass band.

fanfarrón, ona *adj* boastful.

fango *m* mud.

fantasear *vi* to fantasize.

fantasía *f* [imaginación] imagination; [cosa imaginada] fantasy; **de ~** [ropa] fancy; [bisutería] imitation, costume *(antes de sust)*.

fantasma ◇ *m* [espectro] ghost, phantom. ◇ *mf fam* [fanfarrón] show-off.

fantástico, ca *adj* fantastic.

fantoche *m* **- 1.** [títere] puppet **- 2.** [mamarracho] (ridiculous) sight.

fardo *m* bundle.

farfullar *vt* & *vi* to gabble, to splutter.

faringitis *f inv* sore throat.

farmacéutico, ca ◇ *adj* pharmaceutical. ◇ *m,f* chemist, pharmacist.

farmacia *f* [establecimiento] chemist's (shop) *UK*, pharmacy, drugstore *US*; ~ **de**

turno o **de guardia** duty chemist's.

fármaco m medicine, drug.

faro m -1. [para barcos] lighthouse - 2. [de coche] headlight, headlamp; ~ **antiniebla** foglamp.

farol m [farola] street lamp o light; [linterna] lantern, lamp.

farola f [farol] street lamp o light; [poste] lamppost.

farsa f lit & fig farce.

farsante adj deceitful.

fascículo m part, instalment (of serialization).

fascinante adj fascinating.

fascinar vt to fascinate.

fascismo m fascism.

fascista adj & mf fascist.

fase f phase; **en** ~ **terminal** in terminal phase.

fastidiado, da adj [de salud] ill; **ando** ~ **del estómago** I've got a bad stomach.

fastidiar vt -1. [estropear - fiesta etc] to spoil, to ruin; [- máquina, objeto etc] to break - 2. [molestar] to annoy, to bother.
◆ **fastidiarse** vpr -1. [estropearse - fiesta etc] to be ruined; [- máquina] to break down - 2. [aguantarse] to put up with it.

fastidio m -1. [molestia] nuisance, bother; **¡qué** ~ **!** what a nuisance! - 2. [enfado] annoyance.

fastidioso, sa adj [molesto] annoying.

fastuoso, sa adj lavish, sumptuous.

fatal ◇ adj -1. [mortal] fatal - 2. [muy malo] terrible, awful - 3. [inevitable] inevitable. ◇ adv terribly; **pasarlo** ~ to have an awful time; **sentirse** ~ to feel terrible.

fatalidad f -1. [destino] fate, destiny - 2. [desgracia] misfortune.

fatalismo m fatalism.

fatídico, ca adj fateful, ominous.

fatiga f [cansancio] tiredness, fatigue.
◆ **fatigas** fpl [penas] hardships.

fatigar vt to tire, to weary.
◆ **fatigarse** vpr to get tired.

fatigoso, sa adj tiring, fatiguing.

fatuo, tua adj -1. [necio] fatuous, foolish - 2. [engreído] conceited.

fauna f fauna.

favor m favour; **a** ~ **de** in favour of; **hacerle un** ~ **a alguien** [ayudar a] to do sb a favour; fam fig [acostarse con] to go to bed with sb; **pedir un** ~ **a alguien** to ask sb a favour; **tener a** o **en su** ~ **a alguien** to enjoy sb's support.
◆ **por favor** loc adv please.

favorable adj favourable; **ser** ~ **a algo** to be in favour of sthg.

favorecer vt -1. [gen] to favour; [ayudar] to help, to assist - 2. [sentar bien] to suit.

favoritismo m favouritism.

favorito, ta adj & m,f favourite.

fax m inv -1. [aparato] fax (machine); **mandar algo por** ~ to fax sthg - 2. [documento] fax.

fayuquero, ra m,f Méx fam smuggler.

faz f culto -1. [cara] countenance, face - 2. [del mundo, de la tierra] face.

fe f -1. [gen] faith; **hacer algo de buena** ~ to do sthg in good faith; **tener** ~ **en** to have faith in, to believe in - 2. [documento] certificate; ~ **de bautismo** certificate of baptism; ~ **de erratas** errata (pl) - 3. loc: **dar** ~ **de que** to testify that.

fealdad f [de rostro etc] ugliness.

febrero m February; ver también **septiembre**.

febril adj feverish; fig [actividad] hectic.

fecha f [gen] date; [momento actual] current date; **a partir de esta** ~ from today; **hasta la** ~ to date, so far; ~ **de caducidad** [de alimentos] sell-by date; [de carné, pasaporte] expiry date; [de medicamento] 'use before' date; ~ **de nacimiento** date of birth; ~ **tope** o **límite** deadline.

fechar vt to date.

fechoría f bad deed, misdemeanour.

fécula f starch (in food).

fecundación f fertilization; ~ **artificial** artificial insemination; ~ **asistida** assisted fertilization; ~ **in vitro** in vitro fertilization.

fecundar vt -1. [fertilizar] to fertilize - 2. [hacer productivo] to make fertile.

fecundo, da adj [gen] fertile; [artista] prolific.

federación f federation.

federal adj & mf federal.

federar vt to federate.
◆ **federarse** vpr -1. [formar federación] to become o form a federation - 2. [ingresar en federación] to join a federation.

felicidad f happiness.
◆ **felicidades** interj: **¡** ~ **es!** [gen] congratulations!; [en cumpleaños] happy birthday!

felicitación f -1. [acción]: **felicitaciones** congratulations - 2. [postal] greetings card; ~ **de Navidad** Christmas card.

felicitar vt to congratulate; **¡te felicito!** congratulations!; ~ **a alguien por algo** to congratulate sb on sthg.

feligrés, esa m,f parishioner.

felino, na adj feline.

feliz adj -1. [dichoso] happy; **hacer** ~ **a alguien** to make sb happy - 2. [afortunado] lucky - 3. [oportuno] timely.

felpa f [de seda] plush; [de algodón] towelling.

felpudo *m* doormat.

femenino, na *adj* [gen] feminine; BOT & ZOOL female.
➤ **femenino** *m* GRAM feminine.

fémina *f* woman, female.

feminismo *m* feminism.

feminista *adj* & *mf* feminist.

fémur (*pl* **fémures**) *m* femur, thighbone.

fénix *m inv* [ave] phoenix.

fenomenal *adj* [magnífico] wonderful, fantastic.

fenómeno ◇ *m* [gen] phenomenon. ◇ *adv fam* brilliantly, fantastically; **pasarlo ~ to** have a great time. ◇ *interj*: ¡~! great!, terrific!

feo, a *adj* **-1.** [persona] ugly; **le tocó bailar con la más fea** he drew the short straw; **ser más ~ que Picio** to be as ugly as sin **-2.** [aspecto, herida, conducta] nasty; **es ~ escupir** it's rude to spit.

féretro *m* coffin.

feria *f* **-1.** [gen] fair; **~ (de muestras)** trade fair **-2.** [fiesta popular] festival.

feriado *m Amér* (public) holiday.

fermentación *f* fermentation.

fermentar *vt* & *vi* to ferment.

ferocidad *f* ferocity, fierceness.

feroz *adj* **-1.** [animal, bestia] fierce, ferocious **-2.** [fig] [criminal, asesino] cruel, savage **-3.** *fig* [dolor, angustia] terrible.

férreo, a *adj lit* & *fig* iron *(antes de sust)*.

ferretería *f* ironmonger's (shop) *UK*, hardware store.

ferrocarril *m* [sistema, medio] railway, railroad *US*; [tren] train; **por ~** by train.

ferroviario, ria *adj* railway *(antes de sust) UK*, rail *(antes de sust)*, railroad *(antes de sust) US*.

ferry *m* ferry.

fértil *adj lit* & *fig* fertile.

fertilidad *f* lit & fig fertility.

fertilizante *m* fertilizer.

fertilizar *vt* to fertilize.

ferviente *adj* fervent.

fervor *m* fervour.

festejar *vt* [celebrar] to celebrate.

festejo *m* [fiesta] party.
➤ **festejos** *mpl* [fiestas] public festivities.

festín *m* banquet, feast.

festival *m* festival.

festividad *f* festivity.

festivo, va *adj* **-1.** [de fiesta] festive; **día ~** (public) holiday **-2.** [alegre] cheerful, jolly; [chistoso] funny, witty.

feta *f RP* slice.

fetiche *m* fetish.

fétido, da *adj* fetid, foul-smelling.

feto *m* foetus.

feudal *adj* feudal.

FF AA (*abrev de* **Fuerzas Armadas**) *fpl* Spanish armed forces.

fiable *adj* [máquina] reliable; [persona] trustworthy.

fiaca *m RP*: **levantarme esta mañana, me dio una ~** I had to prise myself out of bed this morning.

fiador, ra *m,f* guarantor, surety; **salir ~ por** to vouch for.

fiambre *m* [comida] cold meat *UK*, cold cuts *US*.

fiambrera *f* lunch o sandwich box.

fianza *f* **-1.** [depósito] deposit **-2.** DER bail; **bajo ~** on bail **-3.** [garantía] security, bond.

fiar ◇ *vt* COM to sell on credit. ◇ *vi* COM to sell on credit; **ser de ~** to be trustworthy.
➤ **fiarse** *vpr*: ¡**no te fíes!** don't be too sure (about it)!; **~se de algo/alguien** to trust sthg/sb.

fibra *f* [gen] fibre; [de madera] grain; **~ de vidrio** fibreglass.

ficción *f* [gen] fiction.

ficha *f* **-1.** [tarjeta] (index) card; [con detalles personales] file, record card **-2.** [de guardarropa, aparcamiento] ticket **-3.** [de teléfono] token **-4.** [de juego - gen] counter; [en ajedrez] piece; [en casino] chip; **mover ~** to act **-5.** INFORM card.

fichaje *m* DEP [contratación] signing (up); [importe] transfer fee.

fichar ◇ *vt* **-1.** [archivar] to note down on an index card, to file **-2.** [suj: policía] to put on police files o records **-3.** DEP to sign up. ◇ *vi* **-1.** [suj: trabajador - al entrar] to clock in; [- al salir] to clock out **-2.** DEP: **~ (por)** to sign up (for).

fichero *m* **-1.** [mueble] filing cabinet **-2.** INFORM file.

ficticio, cia *adj* [imaginario] fictitious.

ficus *m inv* rubber plant.

fidedigno, na *adj* reliable.

fidelidad *f* **-1.** [lealtad] loyalty; [de cónyuge, perro] faithfulness **-2.** [precisión] accuracy; **alta ~** high fidelity.

fideo *m* noodle.

fiebre *f* fever; **tener ~** to have a temperature; **~ aftosa** foot-and-mouth disease; **~ del heno** hay fever; **~ reumática/tifoidea** rheumatic/typhoid fever.

fiel *adj* **-1.** [leal - amigo, seguidor] loyal; [- cónyuge, perro] faithful **-2.** [preciso] accurate.
➤ **fieles** *mpl* RELIG: **los ~es** the faithful.

fieltro *m* felt.

fiero, ra *adj* savage, ferocious.
➤ **fiera** *f* [animal] wild animal.

fierro *m Amér* **-1.** [hierro] iron **-2.** [navaja] penknife.

fiesta *f* - 1. [reunión] party; [de pueblo etc] (local) festivities *(pl)*; ~ **benéfica** fête; ~ **de disfraces** fancy-dress party; ~ **mayor** *local celebrations for the festival of a town's patron saint*; **no estar para** ~**s** to be in no mood for joking - 2. [día] public holiday; **ser** ~ to be a public holiday; **hacer** ~ to be on holiday.
➡ **fiestas** *fpl* [vacaciones] holidays.

figura *f* - 1. [gen] figure; [forma] shape; **tener buena** ~ to have a good figure - 2. [en naipes] picture card.

figuraciones *fpl* imaginings.

figurado, da *adj* figurative.

figurar ⬦ *vi* - 1. [aparecer]: ~ **(en)** to appear (in), to figure (in) - 2. [ser importante] to be prominent o important. ⬦ *vt* - 1. [representar] to represent - 2. [simular] to feign, to simulate.
➡ **figurarse** *vpr* [imaginarse] to imagine; **ya me lo figuraba yo** I thought as much.

fijación *f* - 1. [gen & FOT] fixing - 2. [obsesión] fixation.

fijador *m* [líquido] fixative; ~ **de pelo** [crema] hair gel; [espray] hair spray.

fijar *vt* - 1. [gen] to fix; [asegurar] to fasten; [cartel] to stick up; [sello] to stick on - 2. [significado] to establish; ~ **el domicilio** to take up residence; ~ **la mirada/la atención en** to fix one's gaze/attention on.
➡ **fijarse** *vpr* to pay attention; ~**se en algo** [darse cuenta] to notice sthg; [prestar atención] to pay attention to sthg.

fijo, ja *adj* - 1. [gen] fixed; [sujeto] secure - 2. [cliente] regular - 3. [fecha] definite - 4. [empleado, trabajo] permanent.

fila *f* [hilera - gen] line; [- de asientos] row; **en** ~, **en** ~ **india** in line, in single file; **ponerse en** ~ to line up.
➡ **filas** *fpl* MIL ranks; **cerrar** ~**s** *fig* to close ranks.

filántropo, pa *m,f* philanthropist.

filarmónico, ca *adj* philharmonic.

filatelia *f* philately.

filete *m* [CULIN - grueso] (fillet) steak; [- delgado] fillet; [solomillo] sirloin.

filiación *f* POLÍT affiliation.

filial ⬦ *adj* - 1. [de hijo] filial - 2. [de empresa] subsidiary. ⬦ *f* subsidiary.

filigrana *f* [en orfebrería] filigree.

Filipinas *fpl*: **(las)** ~ the Philippines *(sg)*.

filipino, na *adj* & *m,f* Filipino.
➡ **filipino** *m* [lengua] Filipino.

film = **filme**.

filmar *vt* to film, to shoot.

filme *(pl* filmes*)*, **film** *(pl* films*)* *m* film *UK*, movie *US*.

filmoteca *f* [archivo] film library; [sala de cine] film institute.

filo *m* (cutting) edge; **de doble** ~, **de dos** ~**s** *lit* & *fig* double-edged.
➡ **al filo de** *loc prep* just before.

filología *f* - 1. [ciencia] philology - 2. [carrera] language and literature.

filón *m* - 1. [de carbón etc] seam - 2. *fig* [mina] gold mine.

filoso, sa, filudo, da *adj* *Amér* sharp.

filosofía *f* [ciencia] philosophy.

filósofo, fa *m,f* philosopher.

filtración *f* - 1. [de agua] filtration - 2. *fig* [de noticia etc] leak.

filtrar *vt* - 1. [tamizar] to filter - 2. *fig* [datos, noticia] to leak.
➡ **filtrarse** *vpr* - 1. [penetrar]: ~**se (por)** to filter o seep (through) - 2. *fig* [datos, noticia] to be leaked.

filtro *m* [gen] filter; [de cigarrillo] filter, filter tip; ~ **del aceite** oil filter.

filudo, da = filoso.

fin *m* - 1. [final] end; **dar** o **poner** ~ **a algo** to put an end to sthg; **tocar a su** ~ to come to a close; ~ **de semana** weekend; **a** ~**es de** at the end of; **al** o **por** ~ at last, finally; **a** ~ **de cuentas** after all; **al** ~ **y al cabo** after all - 2. [objetivo] aim, goal.
➡ **a fin de** *loc conj* in order to.
➡ **a fin de que** *loc conj* so that.
➡ **en fin** *loc adv* anyway.

final ⬦ *adj* final, end *(antes de sust)*. ⬦ *m* end; ~ **feliz** happy ending; **a** ~**es de** at the end of; **al** ~ [en conclusión] in the end. ⬦ *f* final.

finalidad *f* aim, purpose.

finalista *mf* finalist.

finalizar ⬦ *vt* to finish, to complete. ⬦ *vi*: ~ **(con)** to end o finish (in).

financiación *f* financing.

financiar *vt* to finance.

financiero, ra ⬦ *adj* financial. ⬦ *m,f* [persona] financier.
➡ **financiera** *f* [firma] finance company.

financista *mf* *Amér* financier.

finanzas *fpl* finance *(U)*.

finca *f* [gen] property; [casa de campo] country residence.

fingir ⬦ *vt* to feign. ⬦ *vi* to pretend.

finiquito *m* settlement.

finito, ta *adj* finite.

finlandés, esa ⬦ *adj* Finnish. ⬦ *m,f* [persona] Finn.
➡ **finlandés** *m* [lengua] Finnish.

Finlandia Finland.

fino, na *adj* - 1. [gen] fine; [delgado] thin; [cintura] slim - 2. [cortés] refined - 3. [agudo - oído, olfato] sharp, keen; [- gusto, humor, ironía] refined.
➡ **fino** *m* dry sherry.

finura *f* [gen] fineness; [delgadez] thinness;

[cortesía] refinement; [de oído, olfato] sharpness, keenness; [de gusto, humor, ironía] refinement.

firma *f* **-1.** [rúbrica] signature; [acción] signing **- 2.** [empresa] firm.

firmamento *m* firmament.

firmar *vt* to sign.

firme *adj* **-1.** [gen] firm; [mueble, andamio, edificio] stable **- 2.** [argumento, base] solid **- 3.** [carácter, actitud, paso] resolute.

firmeza *f* **-1.** [gen] firmness; [de mueble, edificio] stability **- 2.** [de argumento] solidity **- 3.** [de carácter, actitud] resolution.

fiscal <> *adj* tax *(antes de sust)*, fiscal. <> *mf* public prosecutor *UK*, district attorney *US*.

fisco *m* treasury, exchequer.

fisgar, fisgonear *vi* [gen] to pry; [escuchando] to eavesdrop.

fisgón, ona *m,f* nosy parker.

fisgonear = fisgar.

físico, ca <> *adj* physical. <> *m,f* [persona] physicist.
 ◆ **físico** *m* [complexión] physique.
 ◆ **física** *f* [ciencia] physics *(U)*.

fisiológico, ca *adj* physiological.

fisionomía, fisonomía *f* features *(pl)*, appearance.

fisioterapeuta *mf* physiotherapist.

fisonomía = fisionomía.

fisura *f* [grieta] fissure.

flacidez, fláccidez *f* flabbiness.

flácido, da, fláccido, da *adj* flaccid, flabby.

flaco, ca <> *adj* thin, skinny. <> *m,f* Amér [como apelativo]: ¿cómo estas, flaca? hey, how are you doing?

flagelar *vt* to flagellate.

flagrante *adj* flagrant.

flamante *adj* [vistoso] resplendent; [nuevo] brand-new.

flambear *vt* to flambé.

flamenco, ca <> *adj* **-1.** MÚS flamenco *(antes de sust)* **- 2.** [de Flandes] Flemish **- 3.** [achulado] cocky; **ponerse** ~ to get cocky. <> *m,f* [de Flandes] Fleming.
 ◆ **flamenco** *m* **-1.** [ave] flamingo **- 2.** [lengua] Flemish **- 3.** MÚS flamenco.

flan *m* crème caramel; **estar hecho** o **como un** ~ to shake like a jelly, to be a bundle of nerves.

flanco *m* flank.

flanquear *vt* to flank.

flaquear *vi* to weaken; *fig* to flag.

flaqueza *f* weakness.

flash [flaʃ] *(pl* flashes) *m* **-1.** FOT flash **- 2.** [informativo] newsflash.

flato *m*: tener ~ to have a stitch.

flatulento, ta *adj* flatulent.

flauta <> *f* flute; ~ **dulce** recorder; **de la gran** ~ *Chile, RP fig* tremendous. <> *interj*: ¡(la gran) ~! *Chile, RP* good grief!, good heavens!

flecha *f* [gen] arrow; ARQUIT spire; **salir como una** ~ to shoot out, to fly out.

flechazo *m fam fig* [amoroso]: **fue un** ~ it was love at first sight.

fleco *m* [adorno] fringe.

flema *f* phlegm.

flemático, ca *adj* [tranquilo] phlegmatic.

flemón *m* gumboil.

flequillo *m* fringe, bangs *(pl) US*.

flete *m* **-1.** [precio] freightage **- 2.** [carga] cargo, freight.

flexible *adj* flexible.

flexo *m* adjustable table lamp o light.

flipar *vi fam* **-1.** [disfrutar] to have a wild time **- 2.** [asombrarse] to be gobsmacked **- 3.** [con una droga] to be stoned o high.

flirtear *vi* to flirt.

flojear *vi* **-1.** [decaer - piernas, fuerzas etc] to weaken; [- memoria] to be failing; [- película, libro] to flag; [- calor, trabajo] to ease off; [- ventas] to fall off **- 2.** *Andes* [holgazanear] to laze about o around.

flojera *f* lethargy, feeling of weakness.

flojo, ja *adj* **-1.** [suelto] loose **- 2.** [débil - persona, bebida] weak; [- sonido] faint; [- tela] thin; [- salud] poor; [- viento] light **- 3.** [inactivo - mercado, negocio] slack.

flor *f* **-1.** BOT flower; **de** ~**es** flowered; **echar** ~**es a alguien** to pay sb compliments; **no tener ni** ~**es (de)** *fam* not to have a clue (about) **- 2.** [lo mejor]: **la** ~ **(y nata)** the crème de la crème, the cream.
 ◆ **a flor de** *loc adv*: **a** ~ **de agua/tierra** at water/ground level.

flora *f* flora.

florecer *vi* to flower; *fig* to flourish.

floreciente *adj fig* flourishing.

florero *m* vase.

florido, da *adj* [con flores] flowery; [estilo, lenguaje] florid.

florista *mf* florist.

floristería *f* florist's (shop).

flota *f* fleet.

flotación *f* [gen & ECON] flotation.

flotador *m* **-1.** [para nadar] rubber ring **- 2.** [de caña de pescar] float.

flotar *vi* [gen & ECON] to float; [banderas] to flutter.

flote ◆ **a flote** *loc adv* afloat; **salir a** ~ *fig* to get back on one's feet.

flotilla *f* flotilla.

fluctuar *vi* [variar] to fluctuate.

fluidez *f* **-1.** [gen] fluidity; [del tráfico] free flow; [de relaciones] smoothness **- 2.** *fig* [en el lenguaje] fluency.

fluido, da *adj* - **1.** [gen] fluid; [tráfico] free-flowing - **2.** [relaciones] smooth - **3.** *fig* [lenguaje] fluent.
 ◆ **fluido** *m* fluid; ~ **eléctrico** electric current *o* power.

fluir *vi* to flow.

flujo *m* flow; ~ **de caja** cash flow.

flúor *m* fluorine.

fluorescente *m* strip light.

fluvial *adj* river *(antes de sust)*.

FM *(abrev de* **frecuencia modulada)** *f* FM.

FMI *(abrev de* **Fondo Monetario Internacional)** *m* IMF.

fobia *f* phobia.

foca *f* seal.

foco *m* - **1.** *fig* [centro] centre, focal point - **2.** [lámpara - para un punto] spotlight; [- para una zona] floodlight - **3.** FÍS & GEOM focus - **4.** *Col, Ecuad, Méx, Perú* [bombilla] light bulb.

fofo, fa *adj* flabby.

fogata *f* bonfire, fire.

fogón *m* [para cocinar] stove.

fogoso, sa *adj* passionate.

fogueo *m*: **de** ~ blank.

foie-gras [fwa'γras] *m* (pâté de) foie-gras.

foja *m Amér* DER [folio] folio.

folclore, folclor, folklor *m* folklore.

fólder *m Andes, CAm, Méx* [carpeta] folder.

folio *m* [hoja] leaf, sheet; [tamaño] folio.

folklor = folclore.

follaje *m* foliage.

folletín *m* [dramón] melodrama.

folleto *m* [turístico, publicitario] brochure; [explicativo, de instrucciones] leaflet.

follón *m fam* - **1.** [discusión] row; **se armó** ~ there was an almighty row - **2.** [lío] mess; **¡vaya** ~ **!** what a mess!

fomentar *vt* to encourage, to foster.

fomento *m* encouragement, fostering.

fonda *f* boarding house.

fondear ◇ *vi* to anchor. ◇ *vt* [sondear] to sound; [registrar - barco] to search.

fondo *m* - **1.** [de recipiente, mar, piscina] bottom; **tocar** ~ [embarcación] to scrape along the sea/river bed; *fig* to hit rock bottom; **doble** ~ false bottom - **2.** [de habitación etc] back; **al** ~ **de** [calle, pasillo] at the end of; [sala] at the back of - **3.** [dimensión] depth - **4.** [de tela, cuadro, foto] background; **al** ~ in the background - **5.** *RP* [patio] back patio - **6.** [de asunto, tema] heart, bottom - **7.** ECON fund; **a** ~ **perdido** non-returnable; ~ **común** kitty; ~ **de amortización/de inversión/de pensiones** ECON sinking/investment/pension fund - **8.** [de biblioteca, archivo] catalogue, collection - **9.** DEP stamina - **10.** *Méx* [combinación] petticoat.
 ◆ **fondos** *mpl* ECON [capital] funds; **recaudar** ~**s** to raise funds.
 ◆ **a fondo** ◇ *loc adv* thoroughly. ◇ *loc adj* thorough.
 ◆ **en el fondo** *loc adv* - **1.** [en lo más íntimo] deep down - **2.** [en lo esencial] basically.

fonético, ca *adj* phonetic.
 ◆ **fonética** *f* [ciencia] phonetics *(U)*.

fono *m Amér fam* phone.

fontanería *f* plumbing.

fontanero, ra *m,f* plumber.

football = fútbol.

footing ['futin] *m* jogging; **hacer** ~ to go jogging.

forajido, da *m,f* outlaw.

foráneo, a *adj* foreign.

forastero, ra *m,f* stranger.

forcejear *vi* to struggle.

fórceps *m inv* forceps.

forense ◇ *adj* forensic. ◇ *mf* pathologist.

forestal *adj* forest *(antes de sust)*.

forja *f* [fragua] forge; [forjadura] forging.

forjar *vt* - **1.** [metal] to forge - **2.** *fig* [inventarse] to invent; [crear] to build up.
 ◆ **forjarse** *vpr fig* [labrarse] to carve out for o.s.

forma *f* - **1.** [gen] shape, form; **dar** ~ **a** to shape, to form; **en** ~ **de** in the shape of; **tomar** ~ to take shape; **guardar las** ~**s** to keep up appearances - **2.** [manera] way, manner; **de cualquier** ~, **de todas** ~**s** anyway, in any case; **de esta** ~ in this way; **de** ~ **que** in such a way that, so that - **3.** ARTE & LITER form - **4.** [condición física] fitness; **estar en** ~ to be fit.
 ◆ **formas** *fpl* - **1.** [silueta] figure *(sg)*, curves - **2.** [modales] social conventions.

formación *f* - **1.** [gen & MIL] formation - **2.** [educación] training; ~ **profesional** vocational training - **3.** [conjunto] grouping.

formal *adj* - **1.** [gen] formal - **2.** [que se porta bien] well-behaved, good - **3.** [de confianza] reliable - **4.** [serio] serious.

formalidad *f* - **1.** [gen] formality - **2.** [educación] (good) manners *(pl)* - **3.** [fiabilidad] reliability - **4.** [seriedad] seriousness.

formalizar *vt* to formalize.

formar ◇ *vt* - **1.** [gen] to form - **2.** [educar] to train, to educate. ◇ *vi* MIL to fall in.
 ◆ **formarse** *vpr* - **1.** [gen] to form - **2.** [educarse] to be trained *o* educated.

formatear *vt* INFORM to format.

formato *m* [gen & INFORM] format.

formica® *f* Formica®.

formidable *adj* [enorme] tremendous; [extraordinario] amazing, fantastic.

fórmula *f* formula; ~ **uno** formula one; **por pura** ~ purely as a matter of form.

formular *vt* to formulate.

formulario *m* form.

fornido, da *adj* well-built.

foro *m* **- 1.** [tribunal] court (of law) **- 2.** TEATR back of the stage; **desaparecer por el ~** to slip away unnoticed **- 3.** [debate] forum; **~ de discusión** INFORM forum.

forofo, fa *m,f fam* fan, supporter.

forraje *m* fodder.

forrar *vt* : **~ (de)** [libro] to cover (with); [ropa] to line (with); [asiento] to upholster (with).

forro *m* **- 1.** [de libro] cover; [de ropa] lining; [de asiento] upholstery **- 2.** *RP fam* [preservativo] rubber, johnny *UK*.

fortalecer *vt* to strengthen.

fortaleza *f* **- 1.** [gen] strength **- 2.** [recinto] fortress.

fortificación *f* fortification.

fortuito, ta *adj* chance *(antes de sust)*.

fortuna *f* **- 1.** [suerte] (good) luck; **por ~** fortunately, luckily **- 2.** [destino] fortune, fate **- 3.** [riqueza] fortune.

forúnculo, furúnculo *m* boil.

forzado, da *adj* forced.

forzar *vt* **- 1.** [gen] to force; **~ la vista** to strain one's eyes **- 2.** [violar] to rape.

forzoso, sa *adj* [obligatorio] obligatory, compulsory; [inevitable] inevitable; [necesario] necessary.

forzudo, da *adj* strong.

fosa *f* **- 1.** [sepultura] grave **- 2.** ANAT cavity; **~s nasales** nostrils **- 3.** [hoyo] pit; **~ marina** ocean trough.

fosfato *m* phosphate.

fosforescente *adj* phosphorescent.

fósforo *m* **- 1.** QUÍM phosphorus **- 2.** [cerilla] match.

fósil *m* CIENCIA fossil.

foso *m* [hoyo] ditch; [de fortaleza] moat; [de garaje] pit; DEP & TEATR pit.

foto *f* photo, picture.

fotocomponer *vt* IMPRENTA to typeset.

fotocopia *f* [objeto] photocopy.

fotocopiadora *f* photocopier.

fotocopiar *vt* to photocopy.

fotoeléctrico, ca *adj* photoelectric.

fotogénico, ca *adj* photogenic.

fotografía *f* **- 1.** [arte] photography **- 2.** [imagen] photograph.

fotografiar *vt* to photograph, to take a photograph of.

fotógrafo, fa *m,f* photographer.

fotomatón *m* passport photo machine.

fotonovela *f* photo story.

fotorrobot *(pl* **fotorrobots)** *f* Identikit® picture.

fotosíntesis *f inv* photosynthesis.

FP *(abrev de* **formación profesional)** *f* vocational training.

frac *(pl* **fracs)** *m* tails *(pl)*, dress coat.

fracasar *vi* : **~ (en/como)** to fail (at/as).

fracaso *m* failure; **todo fue un ~** the whole thing was a disaster.

fracción *f* **- 1.** [gen] fraction; **en una ~ de segundo** in a split second **- 2.** POLÍT faction.

fraccionario, ria *adj* fractional; **moneda fraccionaria** small change.

fractura *f* fracture.

fragancia *f* fragrance.

fraganti → in fraganti *loc adv* : **coger a alguien in ~** to catch sb red-handed *o* in the act.

fragata *f* frigate.

frágil *adj* [objeto] fragile; [persona] frail.

fragilidad *f* [de objeto] fragility; [de persona] frailty.

fragmentar *vt* [romper] to fragment; [dividir] to divide.

fragmento *m* fragment, piece; [de obra] excerpt.

fragor *m* [de batalla] clamour; [de trueno] crash.

fragua *f* forge.

fraguar **◇** *vt* **- 1.** [forjar] to forge **- 2.** *fig* [idear] to think up. **◇** *vi* to set, to harden.

→ fraguarse *vpr* to be in the offing.

fraile *m* friar.

frambuesa *f* raspberry.

francés, esa **◇** *adj* French. **◇** *m,f* Frenchman *(f* Frenchwoman*)*; **los franceses** the French.

→ francés *m* [lengua] French.

Francia France.

franco, ca *adj* **- 1.** [sincero] frank, open; [directo] frank **- 2.** [sin obstáculos, gastos] free **- 3.** *CSur* [de permiso] : **me dieron el día ~** they gave me the day off.

→ franco *m* [moneda] franc.

francotirador, ra *m,f* MIL sniper.

franela *f* flannel.

franja *f* strip; [en bandera, uniforme] stripe; **~ horaria** time zone.

franquear *vt* **- 1.** [paso, camino] to clear **- 2.** [río, montaña etc] to negotiate, to cross **- 3.** [correo] to frank.

franqueo *m* postage.

franqueza *f* [sinceridad] frankness, openness.

franquicia *f* exemption.

franquismo *m* : **el ~** [régimen] the Franco regime; [doctrina] Franco's doctrine.

frasco *m* small bottle.

frase *f* **- 1.** [oración] sentence **- 2.** [locución] expression; **~ hecha** [modismo] set phrase; [tópico] cliché.

fraternidad, fraternización *f* brotherhood, fraternity.

fraterno, na *adj* brotherly, fraternal.

fraude *m* fraud; ~ **electoral** election *o* electoral fraud; ~ **fiscal** tax evasion.

fraudulento, ta *adj* fraudulent.

frazada *f Amér* blanket; ~ **eléctrica** electric blanket.

frecuencia *f* frequency; **con** ~ often; ~ **modulada, modulación de** ~ frequency modulation.

frecuentar *vt* [lugar] to frequent; [persona] to see, to visit.

frecuente *adj* [reiterado] frequent; [habitual] common.

fregadero *m* (kitchen) sink.

fregado, da *adj Andes, Méx, Ven fam* - **1.** [persona - ser] annoying; [- estar]: **perdí las llaves, ¡estoy fregada!** I've lost my keys, I've had it! - **2.** [roto] bust.

fregar *vt* - **1.** [limpiar] to wash; ~ **los platos** to do the washing-up - **2.** [frotar] to scrub - **3.** *Amér fam* [molestar] to bother, to pester - **4.** *Andes, Méx, Ven* [estropear]: **vas a** ~ **el televisión** you're going to bust the television.

fregona *f* - **1.** *despec* [criada] skivvy - **2.** [utensilio] mop; **pasar la** ~ to mop.

freidora *f* [gen] deep fat fryer; [para patatas fritas] chip pan.

freír *vt* CULIN to fry.

frenar ◇ *vt* - **1.** AUTOM to brake - **2.** [contener] to check. ◇ *vi* to stop; AUTOM to brake.

frenazo *m* - **1.** AUTOM: **dar un** ~ to brake hard - **2.** *fig* [parón] sudden stop.

frenesí (*pl* **frenesíes**) *m* frenzy.

frenético, ca *adj* - **1.** [colérico] furious, mad - **2.** [enloquecido] frenzied, frantic.

freno *m* - **1.** AUTOM brake; ~ **de mano** handbrake - **2.** [de caballerías] bit - **3.** *fig* [contención] check; **poner** ~ **a** to put a stop to.

frente ◇ *f* forehead; **arrugar la** ~ to knit one's brow, to frown; ~ **a** ~ face to face; **con la** ~ **muy alta** with one's head held high. ◇ *m* front; **estar al** ~ **(de)** to be at the head (of); **hacer** ~ **a** to face up to; ~ **cálido/frío** warm/cold front.

◆ **de frente** *loc adv* - **1.** [hacia delante] forwards - **2.** [uno contra otro] head on.

◆ **en frente** *loc adv* opposite.

◆ **en frente de** *loc adv* opposite.

◆ **frente a** *loc prep* - **1.** [enfrente de] opposite - **2.** [con relación a] towards.

fresa *f* [planta, fruto] strawberry.

fresco, ca ◇ *adj* - **1.** [gen] fresh; [temperatura] cool; [pintura, tinta] wet - **2.** [caradura] cheeky; **¡qué** ~ **!** what a nerve! ◇ *m,f* [caradura] cheeky person.

◆ **fresco** *m* - **1.** ARTE fresco; **al** ~ in fresco - **2.** [frescor] coolness; **hace** ~ it's chilly;

tomar el ~ to get a breath of fresh air.

frescor *m* coolness, freshness.

frescura *f* - **1.** [gen] freshness - **2.** [descaro] cheek, nerve.

fresno *m* ash (tree).

fresón *m* large strawberry.

frialdad *f* lit & fig coldness.

fricción *f* [gen] friction; [friega] rub, massage.

friega *f* rub, massage.

frigidez *f* frigidity.

frigorífico, ca *adj* [camión] refrigerator *(antes de sust)*; [cámara] cold.

◆ **frigorífico** *m* refrigerator, fridge *UK*, icebox *US*.

frijol, fríjol *m Andes, CAm, Carib, Méx* bean.

frío, a *adj* [gen] cold; [inmutable] cool; **dejar a alguien** ~ to leave sb cold.

◆ **frío** *m* cold; **coger** ~ to catch a chill; **hace** ~ it's cold; **hacer un** ~ **que pela** to be freezing cold; **tener** ~ to be cold; **coger a alguien en** ~ *fig* to catch sb on the hop.

friolento, ta *Amér* ◇ *adj* sensitive to the cold. ◇ *m,f*: **es un** ~ he really feels the cold.

friolero, ra *adj* sensitive to the cold.

frito, ta ◇ *pp* ▷ **freír**. ◇ *adj* - **1.** [alimento] fried - **2.** *fam fig* [persona - harta] fed up (to the back teeth); [- dormida] flaked out, asleep.

◆ **frito** *(gen pl) m* fried food *(U)*.

frívolo, la *adj* frivolous.

frondoso, sa *adj* leafy.

frontal *adj* frontal.

frontera *f* border; *fig* [límite] bounds *(pl)*.

fronterizo, za *adj* border *(antes de sust)*.

frontispicio *m* - **1.** [de edificio] façade; [- remate] pediment - **2.** [de libro] frontispiece.

frontón *m* [deporte] pelota; [cancha] pelota court.

frotar *vt* to rub.

◆ **frotarse** *vpr*: ~ **se las manos** to rub one's hands.

fructífero, ra *adj* fruitful.

frugal *adj* frugal.

fruncir *vt* - **1.** [labios] to purse; ~ **el ceño** to frown - **2.** [tela] to gather.

fruslería *f* triviality, trifle.

frustración *f* frustration.

frustrar *vt* [persona] to frustrate.

◆ **frustrarse** *vpr* - **1.** [persona] to get frustrated - **2.** [ilusiones] to be thwarted; [proyecto] to fail.

fruta *f* fruit; ~ **confitada** candied fruit; ~ **de la pasión** passion fruit; ~ **del tiempo** seasonal fruit.

frutal *m* fruit tree.

frutería *f* fruit shop.

frutero, ra *m,f* [persona] fruiterer.

◆ **frutero** *m* [recipiente] fruit bowl.

frutilla *f* Bol, CSur, Ecuad strawberry.

fruto *m* - **1.** [naranja, plátano etc] fruit; [nuez, avellana etc] nut; ~**s secos** dried fruit and nuts - **2.** [resultado] fruit; **dar** ~ to bear fruit; **sacar** ~ **a** o **de algo** to profit from sthg.

fucsia *f* [planta] fuchsia.

fue - **1.** ▷ **ir** - **2.** ▷ **ser**.

fuego *m* - **1.** [gen & MIL] fire; [de cocina, fogón] ring, burner; **a** ~ **lento/vivo** CULIN over a low/high heat; **pegar** ~ **a algo** to set sthg on fire, to set fire to sthg; **pedir/dar** ~ to ask for/give a light; **¿tiene** ~? have you got a light?; ~**s artificiales** fireworks - **2.** [apasionamiento] passion, ardour.

fuelle *m* [gen] bellows *(pl)*.

fuente *f* - **1.** [manantial] spring - **2.** [construcción] fountain - **3.** [bandeja] (serving) dish - **4.** [origen] source; ~**s oficiales** official sources; ~ **de información/ingresos** source of information/income - **5.**: ~ **de soda** Carib, Chile, Col, Méx cafe.

fuera ◇ - **1.** ▷ **ir** - **2.** ▷ **ser**. ◇ *adv* - **1.** [en el exterior] outside; **le echó** ~ she threw him out; **hacia** ~ outwards; **por** ~ (on the) outside - **2.** [en otro lugar] away; [en el extranjero] abroad; **de** ~ [extranjero] from abroad - **3.** *fig* [alejado]: ~ **de** [alcance, peligro] out of; [cálculos, competencia] aside from; **estar** ~ **de sí** to be beside o.s. (with rage) - **4.** DEP: ~ **de juego** offside. ◇ *interj* ¡~! [gen] (get) out!; [en el teatro] (get) off!

◆ **fuera de** *loc prep* [excepto] except for, apart from.

◆ **fuera de serie** *adj* exceptional, out of the ordinary.

fueraborda *m inv* outboard motor o engine.

fuero *m* - **1.** [ley local] *(gen pl)* ancient regional law still existing in some parts of Spain - **2.** [jurisdicción] code of laws.

fuerte ◇ *adj* - **1.** [gen] strong - **2.** [carácter] strong - **3.** [frío, dolor, color] intense; [lluvia] heavy; [ruido] loud; [golpe, pelea] hard - **4.** [comida, salsa] rich - **5.** [nudo] tight. ◇ *adv* - **1.** [intensamente - gen] hard; [- abrazar, agarrar] tight - **2.** [abundantemente] a lot - **3.** [en voz alta] loudly. ◇ *m* - **1.** [fortificación] fort - **2.** [punto fuerte] strong point, forte.

fuerza *f* - **1.** [gen] strength; [violencia] force; [de sonido] loudness; [de dolor] intensity; **cobrar** ~ to gather strength; **por** ~ of necessity; **tener** ~ to be strong; **tener** ~**s para** to have the strength to; ~ **mayor** DER force majeure; [en seguros] act of God; **no llegué por un caso de** ~ **mayor** I didn't make it due to circumstances beyond my control; **a** ~ **de** by dint of; **a la** ~ [contra la voluntad] by force; [por necesidad] of necessity; **por la** ~ by force; **írsele a alguien la** ~ **por la boca** to be all talk and no action, to be all mouth; ~ **bruta** brute force; ~ **de voluntad** willpower - **2.** FÍS & MIL force; ~ **aérea** airforce; ~ **disuasoria** deterrent; ~ **de la gravedad** force of gravity; ~ **motriz** *lit* motive power; *fig* driving force; ~**s armadas** armed forces; ~**s del orden público** police *(pl)*; ~**s de seguridad** security forces - **3.** ELECTR power; ~ **hidráulica** water power.

◆ **fuerzas** *fpl* [grupo] forces.

fuese - **1.** ▷ **ir** - **2.** ▷ **ser**.

fuga *f* - **1.** [huida] escape; ~ **de capitales** flight of capital - **2.** [escape] leak - **3.** MÚS fugue.

fugarse *vpr* to escape; ~ **de casa** to run away from home; ~ **con alguien** to run off with sb.

fugaz *adj* fleeting.

fugitivo, va *m,f* fugitive.

fui ▷ **ir**.

fulano, na *m,f* what's his/her name, so-and-so.

◆ **fulana** *f* [prostituta] tart, whore.

fulgor *m* shining; [de disparo] flash.

fulminante *adj fig* [despido, muerte] sudden; [enfermedad] devastating; [mirada] withering.

fulminar *vt* [suj: enfermedad] to strike down; ~ **a alguien con la mirada** to look daggers at sb.

fumador, ra *m,f* smoker; ~ **empedernido** chain-smoker; ~ **pasivo** passive smoker; **no** ~ nonsmoker.

fumar *vt* & *vi* to smoke.

fumigar *vt* to fumigate.

función *f* - **1.** [gen] function; [trabajo] duty; **director en funciones** acting director; **entrar en funciones** to take up one's duties - **2.** CIN & TEATR show.

◆ **en función de** *loc prep* depending on.

funcional *adj* functional.

funcionamiento *m* operation, functioning.

funcionar *vi* to work; ~ **con gasolina** to run on petrol; **'no funciona'** 'out of order'.

funcionario, ria *m,f* civil servant.

funda *f* [de sofá, máquina de escribir] cover; [de almohada] case; [de disco] sleeve; [de pistola] sheath.

fundación *f* foundation.

fundador, ra *m,f* founder.

fundamental *adj* fundamental.

fundamentar *vt* - **1.** *fig* [basar] to base - **2.** CONSTR to lay the foundations of.

◆ **fundamentarse en** *vpr fig* [basarse] to be based o founded on.

fundamento *m* **-1.** [base] foundation, basis **- 2.** [razón] reason, grounds *(pl)*; **sin** ~ unfounded, groundless.

fundar *vt* **-1.** [crear] to found **- 2.** [basar]: ~ **(en)** to base (on).

◆ **fundarse** *vpr* [basarse]: ~**se (en)** to be based (on).

fundición *f* **-1.** [fusión - de vidrio] melting; [- de metal] smelting **- 2.** [taller] foundry.

fundir *vt* **-1.** [METAL - plomo] to melt; [- hierro] to smelt **- 2.** ELECTR to fuse; [bombilla, fusible] to blow **- 3.** COM & *fig* to merge.

◆ **fundirse** *vpr* **-1.** ELECTR to blow **- 2.** [derretirse] to melt **- 3.** COM & *fig* to merge **- 4.** *Amér* [arruinarse] to go bust.

fúnebre *adj* funeral *(antes de sust)*.

funeral *(gen pl)* *m* funeral.

funerario, ria *adj* funeral *(antes de sust)*.

◆ **funeraria** *f* undertaker's *UK*, mortician's *US*.

funesto, ta *adj* fateful, disastrous.

fungir *vi Méx, Perú*: ~ **(de** o **como)** to act (as), to serve (as).

funicular *m* **-1.** [por tierra] funicular **- 2.** [por aire] cable car.

furgón *m* AUTOM van; FERROC wagon, van; ~ **celular** o **policial** police van; ~ **de cola** guard's van *UK*, caboose *US*.

furgoneta *f* van.

furia *f* fury; **estar hecho una** ~ to be furious.

furioso, sa *adj* furious.

furor *m* **-1.** [enfado] fury, rage **- 2.** *loc*: **hacer** ~ to be all the rage.

furtivo, va *adj* [mirada, sonrisa] furtive.

furúnculo = **forúnculo**.

fusible *m* fuse.

fusil *m* rifle.

fusilar *vt* [ejecutar] to execute by firing squad, to shoot.

fusión *f* **-1.** [agrupación] merging **- 2.** [de empresas, bancos] merger **- 3.** [derretimiento] melting **- 4.** FÍS fusion.

fusionar *vt* **-1.** [gen & ECON] to merge **- 2.** FÍS to fuse.

◆ **fusionarse** *vpr* ECON to merge.

fusta *f* riding crop.

fustán *m Amér* petticoat.

fuste *m* shaft.

fútbol, football ['fudbol] *m* football, soccer *US*; ~ **sala** indoor five-a-side.

futbolín *m* table football.

futbolista *mf* footballer.

fútil *adj* trivial.

futilidad *f* triviality.

futón *m* futon.

futuro, ra ◇ *adj* future. ◇ *adv*: **a** ~ *CSur, Méx* in the future.

◆ **futuro** *m* [gen & GRAM] future; **en un** ~ **próximo** in the near future.

◆ **futuros** *mpl* ECON futures.

futurología *f* futurology.

g¹, G *f* [letra] g, G.

g² *(abrev de* **gramo)** g.

gabacho, cha *m, f fam despec* Frog, *pejorative term referring to a French person.*

gabán *m* overcoat.

gabardina *f* [prenda] raincoat, mac.

gabinete *m* **-1.** [gobierno] cabinet **- 2.** [despacho] office; ~ **de prensa** press office **- 3.** [sala] study.

gacela *f* gazelle.

gaceta *f* gazette.

gachas *fpl* CULIN (corn) porridge *(U)*.

gacho, cha *adj* drooping.

gafas *fpl* glasses; ~ **bifocales** bifocals; ~ **graduadas** prescription glasses; ~ **de sol** sunglasses.

gafe ◇ *adj* jinxed. ◇ *mf* jinxed person.

gaita *f* [instrumento] bagpipes *(pl)*.

gajes *mpl*: ~ **del oficio** occupational hazards.

gajo *m* [trozo de fruta] segment.

gala *f* **-1.** [fiesta] gala; **ropa/uniforme de** ~ [ropa] full dress/uniform; **cena de** ~ black tie dinner, formal dinner **- 2.** [ropa]: ~**s** finery *(U)*, best clothes **- 3.** [actuación] show **- 4.** *loc*: **hacer** ~ **de algo** [preciarse] to be proud of sthg; [exhibir] to demonstrate sthg.

galán *m* TEATR leading man, lead.

galante *adj* gallant.

galantear *vt* to court, to woo.

galantería *f* **-1.** [cualidad] politeness **- 2.** [acción] gallantry, compliment.

galápago *m* turtle.

galardón *m* award, prize.

galaxia *f* galaxy.

galera *f* galley.

galería *f* **-1.** [gen] gallery; [corredor descubierto] veranda **- 2.** *fig* [vulgo] masses *(pl)*.

◆ **galerías (comerciales)** *fpl* shopping arcade *(sg)*.

Gales: **(el país de)** ~ Wales.

galés, esa ◇ *adj* Welsh. ◇ *m, f* Welshman

m (*f* Welshwoman); **los galeses** the Welsh.

➥ **galés** *m* [lengua] Welsh.

galgo *m* greyhound; **¡échale un ~!** you can forget it!

galimatías *m inv* [lenguaje] gibberish *(U)*; [lío] jumble.

gallardía *f* - **1**. [valentía] bravery - **2**. [elegancia] elegance.

gallego, ga *adj* & *m,f* - **1**. Galician - **2**. *CSur fam* [español] *sometimes pejorative term used to refer to someone or something Spanish*.

➥ **gallego** *m* [lengua] Galician.

galleta *f* CULIN biscuit *UK*, cookie *US*; **~ salada** cracker.

gallina ◇ *f* [ave] hen; **la ~ ciega** blind man's buff; **acostarse con las ~s** to go to bed early; **estar como ~ en corral ajeno** to be like a fish out of water. ◇ *mf fam* [persona] chicken, coward.

gallinero *m* - **1**. [corral] henhouse - **2**. *fam* TEATR gods *(sg)*.

gallo *m* - **1**. [ave] cock *UK*, rooster *US*, cockerel; **en menos que canta un ~** *fam* in no time at all; **otro ~ cantaría** things would be very different - **2**. [al cantar] false note; [al hablar] squeak - **3**. [pez] John Dory.

galo, la ◇ *adj* HIST Gallic; [francés] French. ◇ *m,f* [persona] Gaul.

galón *m* - **1**. [adorno] braid; MIL stripe - **2**. [medida] gallon.

galopar *vi* to gallop.

galope *m* gallop; **al ~** at a gallop; **a ~ tendido** at full gallop.

galpón *m Andes, Carib, RP* shed.

gama *f* [gen] range; MÚS scale.

gamba *f* prawn.

gamberro, rra ◇ *adj* loutish. ◇ *m,f* vandal; [en fútbol etc] hooligan; **hacer el ~** to behave loutishly.

gamo *m* fallow deer.

gamonal *m Andes, CAm, Ven* [cacique] village chief; [caudillo] cacique, local political boss.

gamuza *f* - **1**. [tejido] chamois (leather); [trapo] duster - **2**. [animal] chamois.

gana *f* - **1**. [afán]: **~ (de)** desire *o* wish (to); **de buena ~** willingly; **de mala ~** unwillingly; **me da/no me da la ~ hacerlo** I damn well feel like/don't damn well feel like doing it - **2**. [apetito] appetite.

➥ **ganas** *fpl* [deseo]: **tener ~s de algo/hacer algo**, **sentir ~s de algo/hacer algo** to feel like sthg/doing sthg; **no tengo ~s de que me pongan una multa** I don't fancy getting a fine; **morirse de ~s de hacer algo** to be dying to do sthg; **quedarse con ~s de hacer algo** not to manage to do sthg; **tenerle ~s a alguien** to have it in for sb.

ganadería *f* - **1**. [actividad] livestock

farming - **2**. [ganado] livestock.

ganado *m* livestock, stock; **~ porcino** pigs *(pl)*; **~ vacuno** cattle *(pl)*.

ganador, ra ◇ *adj* winning. ◇ *m,f* winner.

ganancia *f* [rendimiento] profit; [ingreso] earnings *(pl)*; **~s y pérdidas** profit and loss; **~ líquida** net profit.

ganancial ➪ **bien**.

ganar ◇ *vt* - **1**. [gen] to win; [sueldo, dinero] to earn; [peso, tiempo, terreno] to gain - **2**. [derrotar] to beat; **~ a alguien a algo** to beat sb at sthg - **3**. [aventajar]: **~ a alguien en algo** to be better than sb as regards sthg. ◇ *vi* - **1**. [vencer] to win - **2**. [lograr dinero] to earn money - **3**. [mejorar]: **~ en algo** to gain in sthg.

➥ **ganarse** *vpr* - **1**. [conquistar - simpatía, respeto] to earn; [- persona] to win over - **2**. [merecer] to deserve.

ganchillo *m* [aguja] crochet hook; [labor] crochet; **hacer ~** to crochet.

gancho *m* - **1**. [gen] hook; [de percha] peg - **2**. *Andes, CAm, Méx, Ven* [percha] hanger - **3**. [cómplice - de timador] decoy; [- de vendedor] person who attracts buyers - **4**. *fam* [atractivo] sex appeal.

gandul, la *fam* ◇ *adj* lazy. ◇ *m,f* lazybones, layabout.

ganga *f fam* snip, bargain.

gangrena *f* gangrene.

gángster *(pl* **gángsters***) m* gangster.

ganso, sa *m,f* - **1**. [ave - hembra] goose; [- macho] gander - **2**. *fam* [persona] idiot, fool.

garabatear *vi* & *vt* to scribble.

garabato *m* scribble.

garaje *m* garage.

garante *mf* guarantor; **salir ~** to act as guarantor.

garantía *f* - **1**. [gen] guarantee; **de ~** reliable, dependable; **ser ~ de algo** to guarantee sthg; **~s constitucionales** constitutional rights - **2**. [fianza] surety.

garantizar *vt* - **1**. [gen] to guarantee; **~ algo a alguien** to assure sb of sthg - **2**. [avalar] to vouch for.

garbanzo *m* chickpea; **ser el ~ negro de la familia** to be the black sheep of the family.

garbeo *m fam* stroll; **dar un ~** to go for *o* take a stroll.

garbo *m* [de persona] grace; [de escritura] stylishness, style.

garete *m*: **ir** *o* **irse al ~** *fam* to come adrift.

garfio *m* hook.

gargajo *m* phlegm.

garganta *f* - **1**. ANAT throat - **2**. [desfiladero] gorge.

gargantilla *f* choker, necklace.

gárgara *(gen pl) f* gargle, gargling *(U)*; **hacer**

~s to gargle; **mandar a alguien a hacer** ~s *fam* to send sb packing; **¡vete a hacer** ~s! *fam* get lost!

gárgola *f* gargoyle.

garita *f* [gen] cabin; [de conserje] porter's lodge; MIL sentry box.

garito *m despec* [casa de juego] gambling den; [establecimiento] dive.

garra *f* [de animal] claw; [de ave de rapiña] talon; *despec* [de persona] paw, hand; **caer en las** ~s **de alguien** to fall into sb's clutches; **tener** ~ [persona] to have charisma; [novela, canción etc] to be gripping.

garrafa *f* carafe.

garrafal *adj* monumental, enormous.

garrapata *f* tick.

garrapiñar *vt* [fruta] to candy; [almendras etc] to coat with sugar.

garrote *m* - 1. [palo] club, stick - 2. [instrumento] garrotte.

garúa *f* *Andes, RP, Ven* drizzle.

garza *f* heron; ~ **real** grey heron.

gas *m* gas; **con** ~ [agua] sparkling, carbonated; [refresco] fizzy, carbonated; ~ **ciudad/natural** town/natural gas; ~ **butano** butane (gas); ~ **lacrimógeno** tear gas.

➤ **gases** *mpl* [en el estómago] wind *(U)*.

➤ **a todo gas** *loc adv* flat out, at top speed.

gasa *f* gauze.

gaseoducto *m* gas pipeline.

gaseoso, sa *adj* gaseous; [bebida] fizzy.

➤ **gaseosa** *f* lemonade UK, soda US.

gasfitería *f* *Chile, Ecuad, Perú* plumber's (shop).

gasfitero, ra *m,f* *Chile, Ecuad, Perú* plumber.

gasóleo *m* diesel oil.

gasolina *f* petrol UK, gas US; **poner** ~ to fill up (with petrol).

gasolinera *f* petrol station UK, gas station US.

gastado, da *adj* [ropa, pieza etc] worn out; [frase, tema] hackneyed; [persona] broken, burnt out.

gastar ◇ *vt* - 1. [consumir - dinero, tiempo] to spend; [- gasolina, electricidad] to use (up); [- ropa, zapatos] to wear out - 2. *fig* [usar - gen] to use; [- ropa] to wear; [- número de zapatos] to take; ~ **una broma (a alguien)** to play a joke (on sb) - 3. [malgastar] to waste. ◇ *vi* [despilfarrar] to spend (money).

➤ **gastarse** *vpr* - 1. [deteriorarse] to wear out - 2. [terminarse] to run out.

gasto *m* [acción de gastar] outlay, expenditure; [cosa que pagar] expense; [de energía, gasolina] consumption; [despilfarro] waste; **cubrir** ~s to cover costs, to break even; ~ **público** public expenditure; ~s **de envío** postage and packing; ~s **fijos** COM fixed charges *o* costs; [en una casa] overheads; ~s **generales** overheads; ~s **de mantenimiento** maintenance costs; ~s **de representación** entertainment allowance *(sg)*.

gastritis *f inv* gastritis.

gastronomía *f* gastronomy.

gastrónomo, ma *m,f* gourmet, gastronome.

gatas ➤ **a gatas** *loc adv* on all fours.

gatear *vi* to crawl.

gatillo *m* trigger; **apretar el** ~ to press *o* pull the trigger.

gato, ta *m,f* cat; **dar** ~ **por liebre a alguien** to swindle *o* cheat sb; **buscar tres pies al** ~ to overcomplicate matters; **jugar al** ~ **y al ratón** to play cat and mouse; **llevarse el** ~ **al agua** to pull it off; **aquí hay** ~ **encerrado** there's something fishy going on here; **el** ~ **escaldado del agua fría huye** *proverb* once bitten twice shy.

➤ **gato** *m* AUTOM jack.

gauchada *f* *CSur* favour; **hacerle una** ~ **a alguien** to do sb a favour.

gaucho, cha *adj* *RP* helpful, obliging.

➤ **gaucho** *m* gaucho.

gavilán *m* sparrowhawk.

gavilla *f* sheaf.

gaviota *f* seagull.

gay *adj inv & mf* gay *(homosexual)*.

gazmoño, ña *adj* sanctimonious.

gazpacho *m* gazpacho, *Andalusian soup made from tomatoes, peppers, cucumbers and bread, served chilled.*

géiser, géyser *(pl géyseres) m* geyser.

gel *m* gel.

gelatina *f* [de carne] gelatine; [de fruta] jelly.

gema *f* gem.

gemelo, la ◇ *adj* twin *(antes de sust)*. ◇ *m,f* [persona] twin.

➤ **gemelo** *m* [músculo] calf.

➤ **gemelos** *mpl* - 1. [de camisa] cufflinks - 2. [prismáticos] binoculars; [para teatro] opera glasses.

gemido *m* [de persona] moan, groan; [de animal] whine.

Géminis ◇ *m* [zodiaco] Gemini. ◇ *mf* [persona] Gemini.

gemir *vi* - 1. [persona] to moan, to groan; [animal] to whine - 2. [viento] to howl.

gene, gen *m* gene.

genealogía *f* genealogy.

generación *f* generation.

generador, ra *adj* generating.

➤ **generador** *m* generator.

general ◇ *adj* - 1. [gen] general; **por lo** ~, **en** ~ in general, generally - 2. [usual] usual. ◇ *m* MIL general; ~ **de brigada** brigadier

UK, brigadier general *US*; ~ **de división** major general.

generalidad *f* - **1.** [mayoría] majority - **2.** [vaguedad] generalization.

generalísimo *m* supreme commander, generalissimo.

Generalitat [ʒenerali'tat] *f* Generalitat, *autonomous government of Catalonia or Valencia*.

generalizar ⬦ *vt* to spread, to make widespread. ⬦ *vi* to generalize.

◆ **generalizarse** *vpr* to become widespread.

generalmente *adv* generally.

generar *vt* [gen] to generate; [engendrar] to create.

genérico, ca *adj* [común] generic.

género *m* - **1.** [clase] kind, type - **2.** GRAM gender - **3.** LITER genre - **4.** BIOL genus; **el ~ humano** the human race - **5.** [productos] merchandise, goods *(pl)* - **6.** [tejido] cloth, material; ~**s de punto** knitwear *(U)*.

generosidad *f* generosity.

generoso, sa *adj* generous.

genético, ca *adj* genetic.

◆ **genética** *f* genetics *(U)*.

genial *adj* - **1.** [autor, compositor etc] of genius - **2.** [estupendo] brilliant, great.

genio *m* - **1.** [talento] genius - **2.** [carácter] nature, disposition - **3.** [mal carácter] bad temper; **estar de/tener mal ~** to be in a mood/bad-tempered - **4.** [ser sobrenatural] genie.

genital *adj* genital.

◆ **genitales** *mpl* genitals.

genocidio *m* genocide.

genoma *m* genome; ~ **humano** human genome.

gente *f* - **1.** [gen] people *(pl)*; ~ **bien** well-to-do people; ~ **menuda** kids *(pl)* - **2.** *fam* [familia] folks *(pl)*.

gentileza *f* courtesy, kindness.

gentío *m* crowd.

gentuza *f* riffraff.

genuflexión *f* genuflection.

genuino, na *adj* genuine.

GEO (*abrev de* **Grupo Especial de Operaciones**) *m specially trained police force*, ≃ SAS *UK*, ≃ SWAT *US*.

geografía *f* geography; *fig*: **varios puntos de la ~ nacional** several parts of the country; ~ **física** physical geography; ~ **política** political geography.

geógrafo, fa *m,f* geographer.

geología *f* geology.

geólogo, ga *m,f* geologist.

geometría *f* geometry; ~ **del espacio** solid geometry.

geranio *m* geranium.

gerencia *f* [gen] management.

gerente *mf* manager, director.

geriatría *f* geriatrics *(U)*.

germen *m lit* & *fig* germ; ~ **de trigo** wheatgerm.

germinar *vi lit* & *fig* to germinate.

gerundio *m* gerund.

gestar *vi* to gestate.

◆ **gestarse** *vpr*: **se estaba gestando un cambio sin precedentes** the seeds of an unprecedented change had been sown.

gesticulación *f* gesticulation; [de cara] face-pulling.

gesticular *vi* to gesticulate; [con la cara] to pull faces.

gestión *f* - **1.** [diligencia] step, thing that has to be done; **tengo que hacer unas gestiones** I have a few things to do - **2.** [administración] management; ~ **de datos** INFORM data management; ~ **de ficheros** INFORM file management.

gestionar *vt* - **1.** [tramitar] to negotiate - **2.** [administrar] to manage.

gesto *m* - **1.** [gen] gesture; **hacer ~s** to gesture, to gesticulate - **2.** [mueca] face, grimace; **torcer el ~** to pull a face.

gestor, ra ⬦ *adj* managing (*antes de sust*). ⬦ *m,f person who carries out dealings with public bodies on behalf of private customers or companies, combining the role of solicitor and accountant.*

géyser = **géiser**.

ghetto = **gueto**.

giba *f* [de camello] hump.

Gibraltar Gibraltar.

gibraltareño, ña *adj* & *m,f* Gibraltarian.

gigabyte [xiɣa'βait] *m* INFORM gigabyte.

gigante, ta *m,f* giant.

◆ **gigante** *adj* gigantic.

gigantesco, ca *adj* gigantic.

gil, gila *CSur fam* ⬦ *adj* stupid. ⬦ *m* jerk, twit *UK*.

gilipollada, jilipollada *f fam*: **hacer/decir una ~** to do/say sthg bloody stupid.

gilipollas, jilipollas *fam* ⬦ *adj inv* daft, dumb *US*. ⬦ *mf inv* prat.

gimnasia *f* [deporte] gymnastics *(U)*; [ejercicio] gymnastics *(pl)*.

gimnasio *m* gymnasium.

gimnasta *mf* gymnast.

gimotear *vi* to whine, to whimper.

gin [jin] ◆ **gin tonic** *m* gin and tonic.

ginebra *f* gin.

Ginebra Geneva.

ginecología *f* gynaecology.

ginecólogo, ga *m,f* gynaecologist.

gira *f* tour.

girar ⬦ *vi* - **1.** [dar vueltas, torcer] to turn; [rápidamente] to spin - **2.** *fig* [centrarse]:

~ **en torno a** o **alrededor de** to be centred around, to centre on. ◇ *vt* **-1.** [hacer dar vueltas a] to turn; [rápidamente] to spin **-2.** COM to draw **-3.** [dinero - por correo, telégrafo] to transfer, to remit.

girasol *m* sunflower.

giratorio, ria *adj* revolving; [silla] swivel *(antes de sust)*.

giro *m* **-1.** [gen] turn; ~ **de 180 grados** *lit* & *fig* U-turn **-2.** [postal, telegráfico] money order; ~ **postal** postal order **-3.** [de letras, órdenes de pago] draft; ~ **en descubierto** overdraft **-4.** [expresión] turn of phrase.

gis *m Méx* chalk.

gitano, na *m,f* gypsy.

glacial *adj* glacial; [viento, acogida] icy.

glaciar ◇ *adj* glacial. ◇ *m* glacier.

gladiola, gladíolo *m* gladiolus.

glándula *f* gland; ~ **endocrina** endocrine gland; ~ **sebácea** sebaceous gland.

glicerina *f* glycerine.

global *adj* global, overall.

globalización *f* globalization.

globo *m* **-1.** [Tierra] globe, earth **-2.** [aeróstato, juguete] balloon **-3.** [esfera] sphere.

glóbulo *m* MED corpuscle; ~ **blanco/rojo** white/red corpuscle.

gloria *f* **-1.** [gen] glory **-2.** [placer] delight.

glorieta *f* **-1.** [de casa, jardín] arbour **-2.** [plaza - gen] square; [- redonda] circus, roundabout *UK*, traffic circle *US*.

glorificar *vt* to glorify.

glorioso, sa *adj* [importante] glorious.

glosa *f* marginal note.

glosar *vt* **-1.** [anotar] to annotate **-2.** [comentar] to comment on.

glosario *m* glossary.

glotón, ona ◇ *adj* gluttonous, greedy. ◇ *m,f* glutton.

glúcido *m* carbohydrate.

glucosa *f* glucose.

gluten *m* gluten.

gnomo, nomo *m* gnome.

gobernador, ra *m,f* governor.

gobernanta *f* cleaning and laundry staff manageress.

gobernante ◇ *adj* ruling *(antes de sust)*. ◇ *mf* ruler, leader.

gobernar *vt* **-1.** [gen] to govern, to rule; [casa, negocio] to run, to manage **-2.** [barco] to steer; [avión] to fly.

gobiernista ◇ *adj Andes, Méx* pro-government. ◇ *mf* government supporter.

gobierno *m* **-1.** [gen] government **-2.** [administración, gestión] running, management **-3.** [control] control.

goce *m* pleasure.

godo, da ◇ *adj* Gothic. ◇ *m,f* HIST Goth.

gol *(pl* **goles)** *m* goal; **marcar** o **meter un** ~ to score a goal; ~ **del empate** equalizer; ~ **de penalti** penalty goal; ~ **en propia meta** own goal; **meter un** ~ **a alguien** to put one over on sb.

goleador, ra *m,f* goalscorer.

golear *vt* to score a lot of goals against, to thrash.

golf *m* golf.

golfear *vi fam* [vaguear] to loaf around.

golfista *mf* golfer.

golfo, fa *m,f* [gamberro] lout; [vago] layabout.

◆ **golfo** *m* GEOGR gulf, bay.

◆ **Golfo Pérsico** *m*: **el Golfo Pérsico** the Persian Gulf.

golondrina *f* [ave] swallow.

golosina *f* [dulce] sweet; [exquisitez] titbit, delicacy.

goloso, sa *adj* sweet-toothed.

golpe *m* **-1.** [gen] blow; [bofetada] smack; [con puño] punch; [en puerta etc] knock; [en tenis, golf] shot; [entre coches] bump, collision; **a** ~**s** by force; *fig* in fits and starts; **un** ~ **bajo** DEP & *fig* a blow below the belt; ~ **de castigo** [en rugby] penalty (kick); ~ **franco** free kick; ~ **de tos** coughing fit; ~ **de viento** gust of wind **-2.** [disgusto] blow **-3.** [atraco] raid, job, heist *US* **-4.** POLÍT: ~ **(de Estado)** coup (d'état) **-5.** *loc*: **dar el** ~ *fam* to cause a sensation, to be a hit; **no dar** o **pegar** ~ not to lift a finger, not to do a stroke of work.

◆ **de golpe** *loc adv* suddenly.

◆ **de un golpe** *loc adv* at one fell swoop, all at once.

◆ **golpe de gracia** *m* coup de grâce.

◆ **golpe maestro** *m* masterstroke.

◆ **golpe de suerte** *m* stroke of luck.

◆ **golpe de vista** *m* glance; **al primer** ~ **de vista** at a glance.

golpear *vt* & *vi* [gen] to hit; [puerta] to bang; [con puño] to punch.

golpista *mf* person involved in a military coup.

golpiza *f Amér* beating.

goma *f* **-1.** [sustancia viscosa, pegajosa] gum; ~ **arábiga** gum arabic; ~ **de mascar** chewing gum; ~ **de pegar** glue, gum **-2.** [tira elástica] rubber band, elastic band *UK*; ~ **elástica** elastic **-3.** [caucho] rubber; ~ **espuma** foam rubber; ~ **de borrar** rubber *UK*, eraser *US* **-4.** *Cuba, CSur* [neumático] tyre *UK*, tire *US*.

◆ **Goma 2** *f* plastic explosive.

gomería *f CSur* tyre centre.

gomina *f* hair gel.

gong *m inv* gong.

gordinflón, ona *m,f* fatty.

gordo, da ◇ *adj* **- 1.** [persona] fat; **me cae ~ I** can't stand him **- 2.** [grueso] thick **- 3.** [grande] big **- 4.** [grave] big, serious. ◇ *m,f* **- 1.** [persona obesa] fat man (*f* fat woman); **armar la gorda** *fig* to kick up a row *o* stink **- 2.** *Amér* [querido] sweetheart, darling **- 3.** *Amér* [como apelativo]: **¿cómo estás, ~?** hey, how's it going?

➡ **gordo** *m* [en lotería] first prize, jackpot; **el ~** *first prize in the Spanish national lottery.*

gordura *f* fatness.

gorgorito *m* warble.

gorila *m* **- 1.** ZOOL gorilla **- 2.** [guardaespaldas] bodyguard **- 3.** [en discoteca etc] bouncer.

gorjear *vi* to chirp, to twitter.

gorra *f* (peaked) cap; **de ~** for free; **vivir de ~** to scrounge.

gorrear = **gorronear**.

gorrinada *f* [guarrada - acción] disgusting behaviour (*U*); [- lugar] pigsty.

gorrión *m* sparrow.

gorro *m* [gen] cap; [de niño] bonnet; **~ de baño** [para ducha] shower cap; [para piscina] swimming cap.

gorrón, ona *m,f fam* sponger, scrounger.

gorronear, gorrear *vt & vi fam* to sponge, to scrounge.

gota *f* **- 1.** [de agua, leche, sangre] drop; [de sudor] bead; **caer cuatro ~s** to spit (with rain); **la ~ que colma el vaso** the last straw, the straw that breaks the camel's back; **sudar la ~ gorda** to sweat blood, to work very hard **- 2.** [cantidad pequeña]: **una ~ de** a (tiny) drop of; **ni ~:** **no se veía ni ~** you couldn't see a thing; **no tienes ni ~ de sentido común** you haven't got an ounce of common sense **- 3.** [enfermedad] gout.

➡ **gotas** *fpl* [medicamento] drops.

➡ **gota a gota** *m* MED intravenous drip.

➡ **gota fría** *f* METEOR *cold front that remains in one place for some time, causing continuous heavy rain.*

gotear ◇ *vi* [líquido] to drip; [techo, depósito etc] to leak; *fig* to trickle through. ◇ *v impers* [chispear] to spit, to drizzle.

gotera *f* [filtración] leak.

gótico, ca *adj* Gothic.

gourmet = **gurmet**.

gozada *f fam*: **es una ~** it's wonderful.

gozar *vi* to enjoy o.s.; **~ de algo** to enjoy sthg; **~ con** to take delight in.

gozne *m* hinge.

gozo *m* joy, pleasure.

grabación *f* recording; **~ digital** digital recording; **~ en vídeo** video recording.

grabado *m* **- 1.** [gen] engraving; [en madera] carving **- 2.** [en papel - acción] printing; [- lámina] print.

grabar *vt* **- 1.** [gen] to engrave; [en madera]

to carve; [en papel] to print **- 2.** [sonido, cinta] to record, to tape.

➡ **grabarse en** *vpr fig*: **grabársele a alguien en la memoria** to become engraved on sb's mind.

gracia *f* **- 1.** [humor, comicidad] humour; **hacer ~ a alguien** to amuse sb; **no me hizo ~** I didn't find it funny; **¡maldita la ~!** it's not a bit funny!; **¡qué ~!** how funny!; **tener ~** [ser divertido] to be funny; **tiene ~** [es curioso] it's funny; **caer en ~** to be liked **- 2.** [arte, habilidad] skill, natural ability **- 3.** [encanto] grace, elegance **- 4.** [chiste] joke; **hacer una ~ a alguien** to play a prank on sb; **no le rías las ~s** don't laugh when he says something silly.

➡ **gracias** *fpl* thank you, thanks; **~s a Dios** thank God; **dar las ~s a alguien (por)** to thank sb (for); **muchas ~s** thank you, thanks very much.

gracioso, sa ◇ *adj* [divertido] funny, amusing; **¡qué ~!** how funny!; **es ~ que ... it's funny how ...** ◇ *m,f*: **hacerse el ~** to try to be funny.

grada *f* **- 1.** [peldaño] step **- 2.** TEATR row.

➡ **gradas** *fpl* DEP terraces.

gradación *f* [escalonamiento] scale.

gradería *f*, **graderío** *m* TEATR rows (*pl*); DEP terraces (*pl*).

grado *m* **- 1.** [gen] degree **- 2.** [fase] stage, level; [índice, nivel] extent, level; **en ~ sumo** greatly **- 3.** [rango - gen] grade; [- MIL] rank **- 4.** EDUC year, class, grade *US* **- 5.** [voluntad]: **hacer algo de buen/mal ~** to do sthg willingly/unwillingly.

graduación *f* **- 1.** [acción] grading; [de la vista] eye-test **- 2.** EDUC graduation **- 3.** [de bebidas] strength, ≃ proof **- 4.** MIL rank.

graduado, da *m,f* [persona] graduate.

➡ **graduado** *m* [título - gen] certificate; [universitario] degree; **~ escolar** *qualification received on completing primary school.*

gradual *adj* gradual.

graduar *vt* **- 1.** [medir] to gauge, to measure; [regular] to regulate; [vista] to test **- 2.** [escalonar] to stagger **- 3.** EDUC to confer a degree on **- 4.** MIL to commission.

➡ **graduarse** *vpr*: **~se (en)** to graduate (in).

grafía *f* written symbol.

gráfico, ca *adj* graphic.

➡ **gráfico** *m* [gráfica] graph, chart; [dibujo] diagram; **~ de barras** bar chart.

➡ **gráfica** *f* graph, chart.

gragea *f* MED pill, tablet.

grajo *m* rook.

gral. (*abrev de* **general**) gen.

gramática ▷ **gramático**.

gramatical *adj* grammatical.

gramático, ca *adj* grammatical.
➡ **gramática** *f* [disciplina, libro] grammar.

gramo *m* gram.

gramófono *m* gramophone.

gramola *f* gramophone.

gran = grande.

granada *f* - 1. [fruta] pomegranate - 2. [proyectil] grenade.

granate ◇ *m* garnet. ◇ *adj inv* garnet-coloured.

Gran Bretaña *f* Great Britain.

grande ◇ *adj (antes de sust:* **gran***)* - 1. [de tamaño] big, large; [de altura] tall; [de intensidad, importancia] great; **un hombre** ~ a big man; **un gran hombre** a great man; **este traje me está** ~ this suit is too big for me - 2. *loc:* **hacer algo a lo** ~ to do sthg in style; **pasarlo en** ~ *fam* to have a great time; **vivir a lo** ~ to live in style. ◇ *m* [noble] grandee.
➡ **grandes** *mpl* [adultos] grown-ups, adults.
➡ **a lo grande** *loc adv* in style.

grandeza *f* - 1. [de tamaño] (great) size - 2. [de sentimientos] generosity, graciousness.

grandioso, sa *adj* grand, splendid.

grandullón, ona *m,f* big boy (*f* big girl).

granel ➡ **a granel** *loc adv* [sin envase - gen] loose; [- en gran cantidad] in bulk.

granero *m* granary.

granito *m* granite.

granizada *f* METEOR hailstorm.

granizado *m* iced drink.

granizar *v impers* to hail.

granizo *m* hail.

granja *f* farm; ~ **avícola** chicken *o* poultry farm.

granjearse *vpr* to gain, to earn.

granjero, ra *m,f* farmer.

grano *m* - 1. [semilla - de cereales] grain; ~ **de café** coffee bean; ~ **de pimienta** peppercorn - 2. [partícula] grain - 3. [en la piel] spot, pimple - 4. *loc:* **apartar el** ~ **de la paja** to separate the wheat from the chaff; **ir al** ~ to get to the point.

granuja *mf* [pillo] rogue, scoundrel; [canalla] trickster, swindler.

granulado, da *adj* granulated.

grapa *f* - 1. [para papeles etc] staple; [para heridas] stitch, (wire) suture - 2. *CSur* [bebida] grappa.

grapadora *f* stapler.

grapar *vt* to staple.

grasa ▷ **graso**.

grasiento, ta *adj* greasy.

graso, sa *adj* [gen] greasy; [con alto contenido en grasas] fatty.
➡ **grasa** *f* - 1. [en comestibles] fat; [de cerdo] lard; **grasa animal** animal fat; **grasa saturada** saturated fat - 2. [lubricante] grease, oil - 3. [suciedad] grease.

gratén *m* gratin; **al** ~ au gratin.

gratificación *f* - 1. [moral] reward - 2. [monetaria] bonus.

gratificante *adj* rewarding.

gratificar *vt* [complacer] to reward; [retribuir] to give a bonus to; [dar propina a] to tip.

gratinado, da *adj* au gratin.

gratis *adv* [sin dinero] free, for nothing; [sin esfuerzo] for nothing.

gratitud *f* gratitude.

grato, ta *adj* pleasant; **nos es** ~ **comunicarle que ...** we are pleased to inform you that ...

gratuito, ta *adj* - 1. [sin dinero] free - 2. [arbitrario] gratuitous; [infundado] unfair, uncalled for.

grava *f* gravel.

gravamen *m* - 1. [impuesto] tax - 2. [obligación moral] burden.

gravar *vt* [con impuestos] to tax.

grave *adj* - 1. [gen] serious; [estilo] formal; **estar** ~ to be seriously ill - 2. [sonido, voz] low, deep.

gravedad *f* - 1. [cualidad] seriousness - 2. FÍS gravity.

gravilla *f* gravel.

gravitar *vi* to gravitate; *fig* [pender]: ~ **sobre** to hang *o* loom over.

graznar *vi* [cuervo] to caw; [ganso] to honk; [pato] to quack; [persona] to squawk.

graznido *m* [de cuervo] caw, cawing *(U)*; [de ganso] honk, honking *(U)*; [de pato] quack, quacking *(U)*; [de personas] squawk, squawking *(U)*.

Grecia Greece.

gremio *m* [sindicato] (trade) union; [profesión] profession, trade; HIST guild; **ser del** ~ to be in the trade.

greña *(gen pl)* *f* tangle of hair; **andar a la** ~ **(con alguien)** to be at daggers drawn (with sb).

gres *m* stoneware.

gresca *f* row.

griego, ga *adj* & *m,f* Greek.
➡ **griego** *m* [lengua] Greek.

grieta *f* crack; [entre montañas] crevice; [que deja pasar luz] chink.

grifería *f* taps *(pl)*, plumbing.

grifo *m* [llave] tap *UK*, faucet *US*; ~ **monomando** mixer tap.

grillado, da *adj fam* crazy, loopy.

grillete *m* shackle.

grillo *m* cricket.

grima *f* [dentera]: **dar** ~ to set one's teeth on edge.

gringo, ga ◇ *adj pey Esp* [estadounidense] gringo, Yankee; *Amér* [extranjero] gringo, foreign. ◇ *m,f Esp* [estadounidense] gringo, Yank; *Amér* [extranjero] gringo, foreigner.

gripa *f Col, Méx* flu.

gripe *f* flu.

gris ◇ *adj* [color] grey; [triste] gloomy, miserable. ◇ *m* grey.

gritar ◇ *vi* [hablar alto] to shout; [chillar] to scream, to yell. ◇ *vt* : ~ **(algo) a alguien** to shout (sthg) at sb.

griterío *m* screaming, shouting.

grito *m* [gen] shout; [de dolor, miedo] cry, scream; [de sorpresa, de animal] cry; **dar** o **pegar un** ~ to shout o scream (out); **a** ~ **limpio** o **pelado** at the top of one's voice; **pedir algo a** ~s *fig* to be crying out for sthg; **poner el** ~ **en el cielo** to hit the roof; **ser el último** ~ to be the latest fashion o craze, to be the in thing.

Groenlandia Greenland.

grogui *adj lit* & *fig* groggy.

grosella *f* redcurrant; ~ **negra** blackcurrant; ~ **silvestre** gooseberry.

grosería *f* [cualidad] rudeness; [acción] rude thing; [palabrota] swear word.

grosero, ra *adj* **- 1.** [maleducado] rude, crude **- 2.** [tosco] coarse, rough.

grosor *m* thickness.

grotesco, ca *adj* grotesque.

grúa *f* **- 1.** CONSTR crane **- 2.** AUTOM breakdown truck **- 3.** [de la policía] tow truck.

grueso, sa *adj* **- 1.** [espeso] thick **- 2.** [corpulento] thickset; [obeso] fat **- 3.** [grande] large, big **- 4.** [mar] stormy.
  ◆ **grueso** *m* [grosor] thickness.

grulla *f* crane.

grumete *m* cabin boy.

grumo *m* [gen] lump; [de sangre] clot.

gruñido *m* **- 1.** [gen] growl; [de cerdo] grunt; **dar** ~s to growl, to grunt **- 2.** [de persona] grumble.

gruñir *vi* **- 1.** [gen] to growl; [cerdo] to grunt **- 2.** [persona] to grumble.

gruñón, ona *adj fam* grumpy.

grupa *f* hindquarters.

grupo *m* [gen] group; [de árboles] cluster; TECN unit, set; **en** ~ in a group; ~ **de discusión** INFORM forum; ~ **electrógeno** generator; ~ **de noticias** INFORM newsgroup.
  ◆ **grupo sanguíneo** *m* blood group.

gruta *f* grotto.

guacal *m CAm, Méx* [calabaza] gourd; *Col, Méx, Carib* [jaula] cage.

guachada *f RP fam* mean trick.

guachimán *m Amér* night watchman.

guacho, cha *m,f Andes, RP fam* bastard.

guaco *m Amér* *pottery object found in pre-Columbian Indian tomb.*

guadaña *f* scythe.

guagua *f Carib* [autobús] bus; *Andes* [niño] baby.

guajolote *m CAm, Méx* [pavo] turkey; *fig* [tonto] fool, idiot.

guampa *f Bol, CSur* horn.

guanajo *m Carib* turkey.

guantazo *m fam* slap.

guante *m* glove; **echar el** ~ **a algo** *fam* to get hold of sthg, to get one's hands on sthg; **echar el** ~ **a alguien** *fam* to nab sb.

guantera *f* glove compartment.

guapo, pa *adj* **- 1.** [gen] good-looking; [hombre] handsome; [mujer] pretty **- 2.** *fam* [bonito] cool.

guarache *m Méx* **- 1.** [sandalia] *crude sandal with a sole made from a tyre* **- 2.** [parche] patch *(on tyre)*.

guarangada *f Bol, CSur* rude remark.

guarango, ga *adj Bol, CSur* coarse, vulgar.

guarda ◇ *mf* [vigilante] guard, keeper; ~ **jurado** security guard. ◇ *f* **- 1.** [tutela] guardianship **- 2.** [de libros] flyleaf.

guardabarros *m inv* mudguard *UK*, fender *US*.

guardabosque *mf* forest ranger.

guardacoches *mf inv* parking attendant.

guardacostas *m inv* [barco] coastguard boat.

guardaespaldas *mf inv* bodyguard.

guardameta *mf* goalkeeper.

guardapolvo *m* overalls *(pl)*.

guardar *vt* **- 1.** [gen] to keep; [en su sitio] to put away **- 2.** [vigilar] to keep watch over; [proteger] to guard **- 3.** [reservar, ahorrar]: ~ **algo (a** o **para alguien)** to save sthg (for sb) **- 4.** [cumplir - ley] to observe; [- secreto, promesa] to keep.
  ◆ **guardarse de** *vpr* : ~**se de hacer algo** [evitar] to avoid doing sthg; [abstenerse de] to be careful not to do sthg.

guardarropa *m* [gen] wardrobe; [de cine, discoteca etc] cloakroom.

guardarropía *f* TEATR wardrobe.

guardería *f* nursery; [en el lugar de trabajo] crèche.

guardia ◇ *f* **- 1.** [gen] guard; [vigilancia] watch, guard; **montar (la)** ~ to mount guard; ~ **municipal** urban police **- 2.** [turno] duty; **estar de** ~ to be on duty. ◇ *mf* [policía] policeman (*f* policewoman); ~ **de tráfico** traffic warden.
  ◆ **Guardia Civil** *f* : **la Guardia Civil** the Civil Guard, *military-style Spanish security force who police rural areas, highways and borders.*

guardián, ana *m,f* [de persona] guardian; [de cosa] watchman, keeper.

guarecer *vt* : ~ **(de)** to protect o shelter (from).

◆ **guarecerse** *vpr*: ~**se (de)** to shelter (from).

guarida *f* lair; *fig* hideout.

guarnición *f* -1. CULIN garnish -2. MIL garrison.

guarrería *f* -1. [suciedad] filth, muck -2. [acción] filthy thing.

guarro, rra ◇ *adj* filthy. ◇ *m,f* -1. [animal] pig -2. *fam* [persona] filthy *o* dirty pig.

guarura *m Méx fam* bodyguard.

guasa *f fam* [gracia] humour; [ironía] irony; **estar de ~** to be joking.

guasearse *vpr fam*: ~ **(de)** to take the mickey (out of).

guasón, ona *m,f* joker, tease.

Guatemala -1. [país] Guatemala -2. [ciudad] Guatemala City.

guatemalteco, ca, guatemaltés, esa *adj & m,f* Guatemalan.

guau *m* woof.

guay *adj fam* cool, neat.

guayín *m Méx* van.

gubernativo, va *adj* government *(antes de sust)*.

guepardo *m* cheetah.

güero, ra *adj Méx fam* blond (*f* blonde), fairhaired.

guerra *f* war; [referido al tipo de conflicto] warfare; [pugna] struggle, conflict; [de intereses, ideas] conflict; **declarar la ~** to declare war; **en ~** at war; **hacer la ~** to wage war; **~ civil/mundial** civil/world war; **~ fría** cold war; **~ de guerrillas** guerrilla warfare; **~ a muerte** fight to the death; **~ psicológica** psychological warfare; **dar ~** to be a pain, to be annoying.

guerrear *vi* to (wage) war.

guerrero, ra ◇ *adj* warlike. ◇ *m,f* [luchador] warrior.

guerrilla *f* [grupo] guerrilla group.

guerrillero, ra *m,f* guerrilla.

gueto, ghetto ['geto] *m* ghetto.

güevón *m Andes, Arg, Ven vulg* prat *UK*, pillock *UK*, jerk *US*.

guía ◇ *mf* [persona] guide; **~ turístico** tourist guide. ◇ *f* -1. [indicación] guidance -2. [libro] guide (book); **~ de carreteras** road atlas; **~ de ferrocarriles** train timetable; **~ telefónica** telephone book *o* directory.

guiar *vt* -1. [indicar dirección a] to guide, to lead; [aconsejar] to guide, to direct -2. AUTOM to drive; NÁUT to steer.

◆ **guiarse** *vpr*: ~**se por algo** to be guided by *o* to follow sthg.

guijarro *m* pebble.

guillotina *f* guillotine.

guinda *f* morello cherry.

guindilla *f* chilli (pepper).

guineo *m Andes, CAm* banana.

guiñapo *m* [persona] (physical) wreck.

guiño *m* wink.

guiñol *m* puppet theatre.

guión *m* -1. CIN & TV script -2. GRAM [signo] hyphen.

guionista *mf* scriptwriter.

guiri *mf fam despec* foreigner.

guirigay *m fam* [jaleo] racket.

guirlache *m brittle sweet made of roasted almonds or hazelnuts and toffee.*

guirnalda *f* garland.

guisa *f* way, manner; **a ~ de** by way of, as.

guisado *m* stew.

guisante *m* pea.

guisar *vt & vi* to cook.

◆ **guisarse** *vpr fig* to be cooking, to be going on.

guiso *m* dish.

güisqui, whisky *m* whisky.

guitarra *f* guitar; **~ acústica** acoustic guitar.

guitarreada *f CSur* singalong *(to guitars)*.

guitarrista *mf* guitarist.

gula *f* gluttony.

gurí, risa *m,f RP fam* [niño] kid, child; [chico] lad, boy; [chica] lass, girl.

gurmet, gourmet [gur'met] *mf* gourmet.

guru, gurú *m* guru.

gusanillo *m fam*: **el ~ de la conciencia** conscience; **entrarle a uno el ~ de los videojuegos** to be bitten by the videogame bug; **matar el ~** [bebiendo] to have a drink on an empty stomach; [comiendo] to have a snack between meals; **sentir un ~ en el estómago** to have butterflies (in one's stomach).

gusano *m lit & fig* worm.

gustar ◇ *vi* [agradar] to be pleasing; **me gusta esa chica/ir al cine** I like that girl/going to the cinema; **me gustan las novelas** I like novels; **como guste** as you wish. ◇ *vt* to taste, to try.

gustazo *m fam* great pleasure.

gusto *m* -1. [gen] taste; [sabor] taste, flavour; **de buen/mal ~** in good/bad taste; **tener buen/mal ~** to have good/bad taste -2. [placer] pleasure; **con mucho ~** gladly, with pleasure; **da ~ estar aquí** it's a real pleasure to be here; **dar ~ a alguien** to please sb; **mucho ~** pleased to meet you; **tener el ~ de** to have the pleasure of; **tengo el ~ de invitarle** I have the pleasure of inviting you; **tomar ~ a algo** to take a liking to sthg -3. [capricho] whim.

◆ **a gusto** *loc adv*: **hacer algo a ~** [de buena gana] to do sthg willingly *o* gladly; [cómodamente] to do sthg comfortably; **estar a ~** to be comfortable *o* at ease.

gustoso, sa *adj* **- 1.** [sabroso] tasty **- 2.** [con placer]: **hacer algo** ~ to do sthg gladly *o* willingly.

gutural *adj* guttural.

h¹, H *f* [letra] h, H; **por h o por b** *fig* for one reason or another.

h², h. *(abrev de* **hora)** hr, h.

ha ⬦ ⊳ **haber.** ⬦ *(abrev de* **hectárea)** ha.

haba *f* broad bean.

habano, na *adj* Havanan.

➤ **habano** *m* Havana cigar.

haber ⬦ *v aux* **- 1.** [en tiempos compuestos] to have; **lo he/había hecho** I have/had done it; **los niños ya han comido** the children have already eaten; **en el estreno ha habido mucha gente** there were a lot of people at the premiere **- 2.** [expresa reproche]: ~ **venido antes** you could have come a bit earlier; **¡** ~ **lo dicho!** why didn't you say so? **- 3.** [expresa obligación]: ~ **de hacer algo** to have to do sthg; **has de estudiar más** you have to study more. ⬦ *v impers* **- 1.** [existir, estar] **hay** there is/are; **hay mucha gente en la calle** there are a lot of people in the street; **había/hubo muchos problemas** there were many problems; **habrá dos mil** [expresa futuro] there will be two thousand; [expresa hipótesis] there must be two thousand **- 2.** [expresa obligación]: ~ **que hacer algo** to have to do sthg; **hay que hacer más ejercicio one** *o* you should do more exercise; **habrá que soportar su mal humor** we'll have to put up with his bad mood **- 3.** *loc*: **algo habrá** there must be something in it; **allá se las haya** that's his/her/your *etc* problem; **habérselas con alguien** to face *o* confront sb; **¡hay que ver!** well I never!; **no hay de qué** don't mention it; **¿qué hay?** [saludo] how are you doing? ⬦ *m* **- 1.** [bienes] assets *(pl)* **- 2.** [en cuentas, contabilidad] credit (side).

➤ **haberes** *mpl* [sueldo] remuneration *(U).*

habichuela *f* bean.

hábil *adj* **- 1.** [diestro] skilful; [inteligente] clever **- 2.** [utilizable - lugar] suitable, fit **- 3.** DER: **días** ~**es** working days.

habilidad *f* [destreza] skill; [inteligencia] cleverness; **tener** ~ **para algo** to be good at sthg.

habilitar *vt* **- 1.** [acondicionar] to fit out, to equip **- 2.** [autorizar] to authorize.

habiloso, sa *adj Chile fam* shrewd, astute.

habitación *f* [gen] room; [dormitorio] bedroom; ~ **doble** [con cama de matrimonio] double room; [con dos camas] twin room; ~ **individual** *o* **simple** single room; ~ **para invitados** guest room.

habitante *m* [de ciudad, país] inhabitant; [de barrio] resident.

habitar ⬦ *vi* to live. ⬦ *vt* to live in, to inhabit.

hábitat *(pl* **hábitats)** *m* [gen] habitat.

hábito *m* habit; **tener el** ~ **de hacer algo** to be in the habit of doing sthg.

habitual *adj* habitual; [cliente, lector] regular.

habituar *vt*: ~ **a alguien a** to accustom sb to.

➤ **habituarse** *vpr*: ~**se a** [gen] to get used *o* accustomed to; [drogas etc] to become addicted to.

habla *f (el)* **- 1.** [idioma] language; [dialecto] dialect; **de** ~ **española** Spanish-speaking **- 2.** [facultad] speech; **dejar a alguien sin** ~ to leave sb speechless; **quedarse sin** ~ to be left speechless **- 3.** LING discourse **- 4.** [al teléfono]: **estar al** ~ **con alguien** to be on the line to sb.

hablador, ra *adj* talkative.

habladurías *fpl* [rumores] rumours; [chismes] gossip *(U).*

hablante ⬦ *adj* speaking. ⬦ *mf* speaker.

hablar ⬦ *vi*: ~ **(con)** to talk (to), to speak (to); ~ **de** to talk about; ~ **bien/mal de** to speak well/badly of; ~ **en español/inglés** to speak Spanish/English; ~ **en voz alta/baja** to speak loudly/softly; **¡mira quién habla!, ¡mira quién fue a** ~ **!** look who's talking!; **¡ni** ~ **!** no way! ⬦ *vt* **- 1.** [idioma] to speak **- 2.** [asunto]: ~ **algo (con)** to discuss sthg (with).

➤ **hablarse** *vpr* to speak (to each other); **no** ~**se** not to be speaking, not to be on speaking terms; **'se habla inglés'** 'English spoken'.

habrá *etc* ⊳ **haber.**

hacendado, da *m,f* landowner.

hacer ⬦ *vt* **- 1.** [elaborar, crear, cocinar] to make; ~ **un vestido/planes** to make a dress/plans; ~ **un poema/una sinfonía** to write a poem/symphony; **para** ~ **la carne ... - 2.** [construir] to build; **han hecho un edificio nuevo** they've put up a new building **- 3.** [generar] to produce; **el árbol hace sombra** the tree gives shade; **la carretera hace una curva** there's a bend in the road **- 4.** [movimientos, sonidos, gestos] to make; **le hice señas** I signalled to her; **el reloj hace tic-tac** the clock goes tick-tock; ~ **ruido** to make a noise - **5.** [obtener-fotocopia] to make; [- retrato] to paint; [- fotografía] to take - **6.** [realizar - trabajo, estudios] to do; [- viaje] to make; [- comunión] to take; **hoy hace guardia** she's on duty today; **estoy haciendo segundo** I'm in my second year - **7.** [practicar - gen] to do; [- tenis, fútbol] to play; **debes ~ deporte** you should start doing some sport - **8.** [arreglar - casa, colada] to do; [- cama] to make - **9.** [transformar en]: **~ a alguien feliz** to make sb happy; **la guerra no le hizo un hombre** the war didn't make him (into) a man; **hizo pedazos el papel** he tore the paper to pieces; **~ de algo/alguien algo** to make sth/sb into sth; **hizo de ella una buena cantante** he made a good singer of her - **10.** [comportarse como]: **~ el tonto** to act the fool; **~ el vándalo** to act like a hooligan - **11.** [causar]: **~ daño a alguien** to hurt sb; **me hizo gracia** I thought it was funny - **12.** CIN & TEATR to play; **hace el papel de la hija del rey** she plays (the part of) the king's daughter - **13.** [ser causa de]: **~ que alguien haga algo** to make sb do sth; **me hizo reír** it made me laugh; **has hecho que se enfadara** you've made him angry - **14.** [mandar]: **~ que se haga algo** to have sthg done; **voy a ~ teñir este traje** I'm going to have the dress dyed. **◇ vi - 1.** [actuar]: **~ de** CIN & TEATR to play; [trabajar] to act as - **2.** [aparentar]: **~ como si** to act as if; **haz como que no te importa** act as if you don't care - **3.** [procurar, intentar]: **~ por ~ algo** to try to do sthg; **haré por verle esta noche** I'll try to see him tonight - **4.** loc: **¿hace?** all right? **◇ v impers - 1.** [tiempo meteorológico]: **hace frío/sol/viento** it's cold/sunny/windy; **hace un día precioso** it's a beautiful day - **2.** [tiempo transcurrido]: **hace diez años** ten years ago; **hace mucho/poco** a long time/not long ago; **hace un mes que llegué** it's a month since I arrived; **no la veo desde hace un año** I haven't seen her for a year.

◆ hacerse vpr - **1.** [formarse] to form - **2.** [desarrollarse, crecer] to grow - **3.** [guisarse, cocerse] to cook - **4.** [convertirse] to become; **~se musulmán** to become a Moslem - **5.** [crearse en la mente]: **~se ilusiones** to get one's hopes up; **~se una idea de algo** to imagine what sthg is like - **6.** [mostrarse]: **se hace el gracioso/el simpático** he tries to act the comedian/the nice guy; **~se el distraído** to pretend to be miles away.

hacha f (el) axe; **enterrar el ~ de guerra** to bury the hatchet.

hachís, hash [xaʃ] m hashish.

hacia prep - **1.** [dirección, tendencia, sentimiento] towards; **~ aquí/allí** this/that way; **~ abajo** downwards; **~ arriba**
upwards; **~ atrás** backwards; **~ adelante** forwards - **2.** [tiempo] around, about; **~ las diez** around o about ten o'clock.

hacienda f - **1.** [finca] country estate o property - **2.** [bienes] property; **~ pública** public purse.

◆ Hacienda f: **Ministerio de Hacienda** the Treasury.

hada f (el) fairy; **~ madrina** fairy godmother.

haga etc ▷ hacer.

Haití Haiti.

hala interj: **¡~!** [para dar ánimo, prisa] come on!; [para expresar incredulidad] no!, you're joking!; [para expresar admiración, sorpresa] wow!

halagador, ra adj flattering.

halagar vt to flatter.

halago m flattery.

halagüeño, ña adj [prometedor] promising, encouraging.

halcón m - **1.** ZOOL falcon, hawk - **2.** Amér fam [matón] government-paid killer.

hálito m [aliento] breath.

halitosis f inv bad breath.

hall [xol] (pl halls) m entrance hall, foyer.

hallar vt [gen] to find; [averiguar] to find out.

◆ hallarse vpr - **1.** [en un lugar - persona] to be, to find o.s.; [- casa etc] to be (situated) - **2.** [en una situación] to be; **~se enfermo** to be ill.

hallazgo m - **1.** [descubrimiento] discovery - **2.** [objeto] find.

halo m [de astros, santos] halo; [de objetos, personas] aura.

halógeno, na adj QUÍM halogenous; [faro] halogen (antes de sust).

halterofilia f weightlifting.

hamaca f - **1.** [para colgar] hammock - **2.** [tumbona - silla] deckchair; [- canapé] sunlounger.

hambre f - **1.** [apetito] hunger; [inanición] starvation; **tener ~** to be hungry; **matar de ~ a alguien** to starve sb to death; **matar el ~** to satisfy one's hunger; **morirse de ~** to be starving, to be dying of hunger; **pasar ~** to starve - **2.** [epidemia] famine - **3.** fig [deseo]: **~ de** hunger o thirst for.

hambriento, ta adj starving.

hamburguesa f hamburger.

hampa f (el) underworld.

hámster ['xamster] (pl hámsters) m hamster.

hándicap ['xandikap] (pl hándicaps) m handicap.

hará etc ▷ hacer.

haraganear vi to laze about, to lounge around.

harapiento, ta *adj* ragged, tattered.

harapo *m* rag, tatter.

hardware ['xarwar] *m* INFORM hardware.

harén *m* harem.

harina *f* flour; **estar metido en** ~ to be right in the middle of sthg.

harinoso, sa *adj* floury; [manzana] mealy.

hartar *vt* **- 1.** [atiborrar] to stuff (full) **- 2.** [fastidiar]: ~ **a alguien** to annoy sb, to get on sb's nerves.

➡ **hartarse** *vpr* **- 1.** [atiborrarse] to stuff o gorge o.s. **- 2.** [cansarse]: ~**se (de)** to get fed up (with) **- 3.** [no parar]: ~**se de algo** to do sthg non-stop.

hartazgo, hartón *m* fill; **darse un** ~ **(de)** to have one's fill (of).

harto, ta *adj* **- 1.** [de comida] full **- 2.** [cansado]: ~ **(de)** tired (of), fed up (with) **- 3.** *Andes, CAm, Carib, Méx* [mucho] a lot of, lots of; **tiene** ~ **dinero** she has a lot of o lots of money; **de este aeropuerto salen hartos aviones** a lot of o lots of planes fly from this airport.

➡ **harto** *adv* **- 1.** somewhat, rather **- 2.** *Andes, CAm, Carib, Méx fam* [mucho] a lot, very much; [muy] very, really.

hartón = hartazgo.

hash = hachís.

hasta ⬦ *prep* **- 1.** [en el espacio] as far as, up to; **desde aquí** ~ **allí** from here to there; ¿~ **dónde va este tren?** where does this train go? **- 2.** [en el tiempo] until, till; ~ **ahora** (up) until now, so far; ~ **el final** right up until the end; ~ **luego** o **pronto** o **la vista** see you (later) **- 3.** [con cantidades] up to. ⬦ *adv* **- 1.** [incluso] even **- 2.** *CAm, Col, Ecuad, Méx* [no antes de]: **pinteremos la casa** ~ **fin de mes** we won't start painting the house until the end of the month.

➡ **hasta que** *loc conj* until, till.

hastiar *vt* [aburrir] to bore; [asquear] to sicken, to disgust.

➡ **hastiarse de** *vpr* to tire of, to get fed up with.

hastío *m* [tedio] boredom (U); [repugnancia] disgust.

hatillo *m* bundle of clothes.

haya ⬦ *v* ➣ haber. ⬦ *f* [árbol] beech (tree); [madera] beech (wood).

haz ⬦ *v* ➣ hacer. ⬦ *m* **- 1.** [de leña] bundle; [de cereales] sheaf **- 2.** [de luz] beam.

hazaña *f* feat, exploit.

hazmerreír *m* laughing stock.

he ➣ haber.

hebilla *f* buckle.

hebra *f* **- 1.** [de hilo] thread; [de judías, puerros] string; [de tabaco] strand (of tobacco) **- 2.** *loc:* **pegar la** ~ *fam* to strike up a conversation; **perder la** ~ to lose the thread.

hebreo, a *adj* & *m, f* Hebrew.

➡ **hebreo** *m* [lengua] Hebrew.

hechicero, ra *m, f* wizard (*f* witch), sorcerer (*f* sorceress).

hechizar *vt* to cast a spell on; *fig* to bewitch, to captivate.

hechizo *m* **- 1.** [maleficio] spell **- 2.** *fig* [encanto] magic, charm.

hecho, cha ⬦ *pp* ➣ hacer. ⬦ *adj* **- 1.** [acabado, realizado] done; **bien/mal** ~ well/badly done **- 2.** [manufacturado] made; ~ **a mano** handmade; ~ **a máquina** machine-made **- 3.** [convertido en]: **estás** ~ **un artista** you've become quite an artist **- 4.** [formado]: **una mujer hecha y derecha** a fully-grown woman **- 5.** [carne] done; **quiero el filete muy/poco** ~ I'd like the steak well done/rare.

➡ **hecho** *m* **- 1.** [obra] action, deed **- 2.** [suceso] event **- 3.** [realidad, dato] fact.

➡ **de hecho** *loc adv* in fact, actually.

hechura *f* **- 1.** [de traje] cut **- 2.** [forma] shape.

hectárea *f* hectare.

heder *vi* [apestar] to stink, to reek.

hediondo, da *adj* [pestilente] stinking, foul-smelling.

hedor *m* stink, stench.

hegemonía *f* [gen] dominance; POLÍT hegemony.

helada ➣ helado.

heladera *f* *RP* fudge.

heladería *f* [tienda] ice-cream parlour; [puesto] ice-cream stall.

helado, da *adj* **- 1.** [hecho hielo - agua] frozen; [- lago] frozen over **- 2.** [muy frío - manos, agua] freezing.

➡ **helado** *m* ice-cream.

➡ **helada** *f* frost.

helar ⬦ *vt* [líquido] to freeze. ⬦ *v impers:* **ayer heló** there was a frost last night.

➡ **helarse** *vpr* to freeze; [plantas] to be frostbitten.

helecho *m* fern, bracken.

hélice *f* **- 1.** TECN propeller **- 2.** [espiral] spiral.

helicóptero *m* helicopter.

helio *m* helium.

hematoma *m* bruise; MED haematoma.

hembra *f* **- 1.** BIOL female; [mujer] woman; [niña] girl **- 2.** [del enchufe] socket.

hemiciclo *m* [en el parlamento] floor.

hemisferio *m* hemisphere.

hemofilia *f* haemophilia.

hemorragia *f* haemorrhage; ~ **nasal** nosebleed.

hemorroides *fpl* haemorrhoids, piles.

hender, hendir *vt* [carne, piel] to carve open, to cleave; [piedra, madera] to crack open; [aire, agua] to cut o slice through.

hendidura *f* [en carne, piel] cut, split; [en piedra, madera] crack.

hendir = hender.

heno *m* hay.

hepatitis *f inv* hepatitis.

herbicida *m* weedkiller.

herbolario, ria *m,f* [persona] herbalist.

hercio, hertz *m* hertz.

heredar *vt* : ~ (de) to inherit (from).

heredero, ra *m,f* heir (*f* heiress); ~ **forzoso** heir apparent; ~ **universal** residuary legatee.

hereditario, ria *adj* hereditary.

hereje *mf* heretic.

herejía *f* heresy.

herencia *f* [de bienes] inheritance; [de características] legacy; BIOL heredity.

herido, da ◇ *adj* [gen] injured; [en lucha, atentado] wounded; [sentimentalmente] hurt, wounded. ◇ *m,f* [gen] injured person; [en lucha, atentado] wounded person; **no hubo** ~**s** there were no casualties; **los** ~**s** the wounded.

➡ **herida** *f* [lesión] injury; [en lucha, atentado] wound; **herida superficial** flesh wound; **heridas múltiples** multiple injuries.

herir *vt* - **1.** [físicamente] to injure; [en lucha, atentado] to wound; [vista] to hurt; [oído] to pierce - **2.** [sentimentalmente] to hurt.

hermanado, da *adj* [gen] united, joined; [ciudades] twinned.

hermanar *vt* [ciudades] to twin.

hermanastro, tra *m,f* stepbrother (*f* stepsister).

hermandad *f* [asociación] association; [RELIG - de hombres] brotherhood; [- de mujeres] sisterhood.

hermano, na *m,f* brother (*f* sister); ~ **gemelo** twin brother; ~ **mayor** older brother, big brother; ~ **menor** younger brother, little brother; ~ **de sangre** blood brother.

hermético, ca *adj* - **1.** [al aire] airtight, hermetic; [al agua] watertight, hermetic - **2.** *fig* [persona] inscrutable.

hermoso, sa *adj* [gen] beautiful, lovely; [hombre] handsome; [excelente] wonderful.

hermosura *f* [gen] beauty; [de hombre] handsomeness.

hernia *f* hernia, rupture; ~ **discal** slipped disc.

herniarse *vpr* MED to rupture o.s.

héroe *m* hero.

heroico, ca *adj* heroic.

heroína *f* - **1.** [mujer] heroine - **2.** [droga] heroin.

heroinómano, na *m,f* heroin addict.

heroísmo *m* heroism.

herpes *m inv* herpes (*U*).

herradura *f* horseshoe.

herramienta *f* tool.

herrería *f* [taller] smithy, forge.

herrero *m* blacksmith, smith.

herrumbre *f* [óxido] rust.

hertz = hercio.

hervidero *m* - **1.** [de pasiones, intrigas] hotbed - **2.** [de gente - muchedumbre] swarm, throng; [- sitio] place throbbing *o* swarming with people.

hervir ◇ *vt* to boil. ◇ *vi* - **1.** [líquido] to boil - **2.** *fig* [lugar]: ~ **de** to swarm with.

hervor *m* boiling; **dar un** ~ **a algo** to blanch sthg.

heterodoxo, xa *adj* unorthodox.

heterogéneo, a *adj* heterogeneous.

heterosexual *adj* & *mf* heterosexual.

hexágono *m* hexagon.

hez *f* lit & fig dregs (*pl*).

➡ **heces** *fpl* [excrementos] faeces, excrement (*sg*).

hibernar *vi* to hibernate.

híbrido, da *adj* lit & fig hybrid.

➡ **híbrido** *m* [animal, planta] hybrid.

hice *etc* ➡ hacer.

hidalgo *mf* nobleman (*f* noblewoman).

hidratante *m* moisturizing cream.

hidratar *vt* [piel] to moisturize; QUÍM to hydrate.

hidrato *m* : ~ **de carbono** carbohydrate.

hidráulico, ca *adj* hydraulic.

hidroavión *m* seaplane.

hidroeléctrico, ca *adj* hydroelectric.

hidrógeno *m* hydrogen.

hidroplano *m* [barco] hydrofoil.

hiedra *f* ivy.

hiel *f* - **1.** [bilis] bile; **echar la** ~ to sweat blood - **2.** [mala intención] spleen, bitterness.

hielo *m* ice; **con** ~ [whisky] with ice, on the rocks; **romper el** ~ *fig* to break the ice; **ser más frío que el** ~ to be as cold as ice.

hiena *f* hyena.

hierático, ca *adj* solemn.

hierba, yerba *f* - **1.** [planta] herb; **mala** ~ weed - **2.** [césped] grass - **3.** *fam* [droga] grass.

hierbabuena *f* mint.

hierro *m* [metal] iron; **de** ~ [severo] iron (*antes de sust*); ~ **forjado** wrought iron; ~ **fundido** cast iron; ~ **laminado** sheet metal.

hígado *m* liver.

higiene *f* hygiene; ~ **personal** personal hygiene.

higiénico, ca *adj* hygienic; **papel** ~ toilet paper.

higienizar *vt* to sterilize.

higo *m* fig; ~ **chumbo** prickly pear; **de** ~**s a brevas** once in a blue moon; **me importa un**

~ *fam* I couldn't care less.

higuera *f* fig tree.

hijastro, tra *m,f* stepson (*f* stepdaughter).

hijo, ja *m,f* [descendiente] son (*f* daughter); ~ **adoptivo** adopted child; ~ **de papá** *fam* daddy's boy; ~ **no deseado** unwanted child; ~ **único** only child.
◆ **hijo** *m* [hijo o hija] child.
◆ **hijos** *mpl* children.

hilacha *f* loose thread.

hilada *f* row.

hilar *vt* [hilo, tela] to spin; [ideas, planes] to think up.

hilaridad *f* hilarity.

hilera *f* row.

hilo *m* - 1. [fibra, hebra] thread; **colgar** o **pender de un** ~ to be hanging by a thread; **mover los** ~**s** to pull some strings - 2. [tejido] linen - 3. [de metal, teléfono] wire; **sin** ~**s** wireless - 4. [de agua, sangre] trickle - 5. [de pensamiento] thread; [de discurso, conversación] thread; **perder el** ~ to lose the thread; **seguir el** ~ to follow (the thread).

hilvanar *vt* - 1. [ropa] to tack *UK*, to baste *US* - 2. [coordinar - ideas] to piece together.

himno *m* hymn; ~ **nacional** national anthem.

hincapié *m*: **hacer** ~ **en** [insistir] to insist on; [subrayar] to emphasize, to stress.

hincar *vt*: ~ **algo en** to stick sthg into.
◆ **hincarse** *vpr*: ~**se de rodillas** to fall to one's knees.

hincha *mf* [seguidor] fan.

hinchado, da *adj* - 1. [rueda, globo] inflated; [cara, tobillo] swollen - 2. *fig* [persona] bigheaded, conceited; [lenguaje, estilo] bombastic.

hinchar *vt lit & fig* to blow up.
◆ **hincharse** *vpr* - 1. [pierna, mano] to swell (up) - 2. *fig* [de comida]: ~**se (a)** to stuff o.s. (with).
◆ **hincharse a** *vpr* [no parar de]: ~**se a hacer algo** to do sthg a lot.

hinchazón *f* swelling.

hindú (*pl* **hindúes**) *adj & mf* - 1. [de la India] Indian - 2. RELIG Hindu.

hinduismo *m* Hinduism.

hinojo *m* fennel.

hipar *vi* to hiccup, to have hiccups.

hiper *m fam* hypermarket.

hiperactivo, va *adj* hyperactive.

hipérbola *f* hyperbola.

hiperenlace *m* INFORM hyperlink.

hipermercado *m* hypermarket.

hipertensión *f* high blood pressure.

hipertexto *m* INFORM hypertext.

hípico, ca *adj* [de las carreras] horse racing (*antes de sust*); [de la equitación] showjumping (*antes de sust*).

◆ **hípica** *f* [carreras de caballos] horse racing; [equitación] showjumping.

hipnosis *f inv* hypnosis.

hipnótico, ca *adj* hypnotic.

hipnotismo *m* hypnotism.

hipnotizador, ra *adj* hypnotic; *fig* spellbinding, mesmerizing.

hipnotizar *vt* to hypnotize; *fig* to mesmerize.

hipo *m* hiccups (*pl*); **tener** ~ to have (the) hiccups; **quitar el** ~ **a uno** *fig* to take one's breath away.

hipocondriaco, ca *adj & m,f* hypochondriac.

hipocresía *f* hypocrisy.

hipócrita ◇ *adj* hypocritical. ◇ *mf* hypocrite.

hipodérmico, ca *adj* hypodermic.

hipódromo *m* racecourse, racetrack.

hipopótamo *m* hippopotamus.

hipoteca *f* mortgage.

hipotecar *vt* [bienes] to mortgage.

hipotecario, ria *adj* mortgage (*antes de sust*).

hipotenusa *f* hypotenuse.

hipótesis *f inv* hypothesis.

hipotético, ca *adj* hypothetical.

hippy, hippie ['xipi] (*pl* **hippies**) *adj & mf* hippy.

hiriente *adj* [palabras] hurtful, cutting.

hirsuto, ta *adj* [cabello] wiry; [brazo, pecho] hairy.

hispánico, ca *adj & m,f* Hispanic, Spanish-speaking.

hispanidad *f* [cultura] Spanishness; [pueblos] Spanish-speaking world.

hispano, na ◇ *adj* [español] Spanish; [hispanoamericano] Spanish-American; [en Estados Unidos] Hispanic. ◇ *m,f* [español] Spaniard; [estadounidense] Hispanic.

hispanoamericano, na ◇ *adj* Spanish-American. ◇ *m,f* Spanish American.

hispanohablante ◇ *adj* Spanish-speaking. ◇ *mf* Spanish speaker.

histeria *f* MED & *fig* hysteria.

histérico, ca *adj* MED & *fig* hysterical; **ponerse** ~ to get hysterical.

histerismo *m* MED & *fig* hysteria.

historia *f* - 1. [gen] history; ~ **del arte** art history; **hacer** ~ to make history; **pasar a la** ~ to go down in history - 2. [narración, chisme] story; **dejarse de** ~**s** to stop beating about the bush.

historiador, ra *m,f* historian.

historial *m* [gen] record; [profesional] curriculum vitae, résumé *US*; ~ **médico** o **clínico** medical o case history.

histórico, ca *adj* - 1. [de la historia] historical - 2. [verídico] factual - 3. [importante] historic.

historieta f - 1. [chiste] funny story, anecdote - 2. [tira cómica] comic strip.

hito m lit & fig milestone.

hizo ⊳ **hacer**.

hobby ['xoβi] (pl **hobbies**) m hobby.

hocico m [de perro] muzzle; [de gato] nose; [de cerdo] snout.

hockey ['xokei] m hockey; ~ **sobre hielo/patines** ice/roller hockey; ~ **sobre hierba** (field) hockey.

hogar m - 1. [de chimenea] fireplace; [de horno, cocina] grate - 2. [domicilio] home; **artículos para el** ~ household goods; **labores del** ~ housework; ~, **dulce** ~ home, sweet home; ~ **de ancianos** old people's home.

hogareño, ña adj [gen] family (antes de sust); [amante del hogar] home-loving, homely.

hogaza f large loaf.

hoguera f bonfire; **morir en la** ~ to be burned at the stake.

hoja f - 1. [de plantas] leaf; **de** ~ **caduca** deciduous; **de** ~ **perenne** evergreen; [de flor] petal; [de hierba] blade - 2. [de papel] sheet (of paper); [de libro] page - 3. [de cuchillo] blade; ~ **de afeitar** razor blade - 4. [de puertas, ventanas] leaf.
   ◆ **hoja de cálculo** f INFORM spreadsheet.

hojalata f tinplate.

hojaldre m puff pastry.

hojarasca f - 1. [hojas secas] (dead) leaves (pl); [frondosidad] tangle of leaves - 2. fig [paja] rubbish.

hojear vt to leaf through.

hola interj: **¡** ~ **!** hello!

Holanda Holland.

holandés, esa ⬦ adj Dutch. ⬦ m,f [persona] Dutchman (f Dutchwoman).
   ◆ **holandés** m [lengua] Dutch.
   ◆ **holandesa** f [papel] piece of paper measuring 22 × 28 cm.

holding ['xoldin] (pl **holdings**) m holding company.

holgado, da adj - 1. [ropa] baggy, loose-fitting; [habitación, espacio] roomy - 2. [victoria, situación económica] comfortable.

holgar vi [sobrar] to be unnecessary; **huelga decir que ...** needless to say...

holgazán, ana ⬦ adj idle, good-for-nothing. ⬦ m,f good-for-nothing.

holgazanear vi to laze about.

holgura f - 1. [anchura - de espacio] room; [- de ropa] bagginess, looseness; [- entre piezas] play, give - 2. [bienestar] comfort, affluence.

hollar vt to tread (on).

hollín m soot.

holocausto m holocaust.

hombre ⬦ m man; **el** ~ [la humanidad] man, mankind; **el** ~ **de la calle** o **de a pie** the man in the street; ~ **de las cavernas** caveman; ~ **de negocios** businessman; ~ **de palabra** man of his word; **un pobre** ~ a nobody; **¡pobre** ~ **!** poor chap UK o guy!; **de** ~ **a** ~ man to man; **ser un** ~ **hecho y derecho** to be a grown man; **el** ~ **propone y Dios dispone** proverb Man proposes, God disposes ⬦ interj: **¡** ~ **!** **¡qué alegría verte!** (hey,) how nice to see you!
   ◆ **hombre orquesta** (pl **hombres orquesta**) m one-man band.
   ◆ **hombre rana** (pl **hombres rana**) m frogman.

hombrera f [de traje, vestido] shoulder pad; [de uniforme] epaulette.

hombría f manliness.

hombro m shoulder; **a** ~**s** over one's shoulders; ~ **con** ~ shoulder to shoulder; **encogerse de** ~**s** to shrug one's shoulders; **arrimar el** ~ fig to lend a hand; **echarse algo al** ~ fig to shoulder sthg, to take sthg on.

hombruno, na adj mannish.

homenaje m [gen] tribute; [al soberano] homage; **partido (de)** ~ testimonial (match); **en** ~ **de** o **a** in honour of, as a tribute to; **rendir** ~ **a** to pay tribute to.

homenajeado, da m,f guest of honour.

homenajear vt to pay tribute to, to honour.

homeopatía f homeopathy.

homicida ⬦ adj [mirada etc] murderous; **arma** ~ murder weapon. ⬦ mf murderer.

homicidio m homicide, murder; ~ **frustrado** attempted murder.

homilía f homily, sermon.

homogeneizar vt to homogenize.

homogéneo, a adj homogenous.

homologar vt - 1. [equiparar]: ~ **(con)** to bring into line (with), to make comparable (with) - 2. [dar por válido - producto] to authorize officially; [- récord] to confirm officially.

homólogo, ga ⬦ adj [semejante] equivalent. ⬦ m,f counterpart.

homosexual adj & mf homosexual.

hondo, da adj - 1. lit & fig [gen] deep; **tiene tres metros de** ~ it's three metres deep; **lo** ~ the depths (pl); **calar** ~ **en** to strike a chord with; **en lo más** ~ **de** in the depths of - 2. ⊳ **cante**.
   ◆ **honda** f sling.

hondonada f hollow.

hondura f depth.

Honduras Honduras.

hondureño, ña adj & m,f Honduran.

honestidad f [honradez] honesty; [decencia] modesty, decency; [justicia] fairness.

honesto, ta adj [honrado] honest; [decente]

modest, decent; [justo] fair.

hongo m -1. [planta - comestible] mushroom; [- no comestible] toadstool - 2. [enfermedad] fungus.

honor m honour; **hacer ~ a** to live up to; **en ~ a la verdad** to be (quite) honest.

◆ **honores** mpl [ceremonial] honours.

honorable adj honourable.

honorario, ria adj honorary.

◆ **honorarios** mpl fees.

honorífico, ca adj honorific.

honra f honour; **¡y a mucha ~!** and proud of it!

◆ **honras fúnebres** fpl funeral (sg).

honradez f honesty.

honrado, da adj honest.

honrar vt to honour.

◆ **honrarse** vpr: **~se (con algo/de hacer algo)** to be honoured (by sthg/to do sthg).

honroso, sa adj -1. [que da honra] honorary - 2. [respetable] honourable, respectable.

hora f -1. [del día] hour; **a primera ~** first thing in the morning; **a última ~** [al final del día] at the end of the day; [en el último momento] at the last moment; **dar la ~** to strike the hour; **de última ~** [noticia] latest, up-to-the-minute; [preparativos] last-minute; **'última ~'** 'stop press'; **(pagar) por ~s** (to pay) by the hour; **~ de dormir** bedtime; **~s de oficina/trabajo** office/working hours; **~ local/oficial** local/official time; **~ punta** o **pico** Amér rush hour; **~s extraordinarias** overtime (U); **~s libres** free time (U); **~s de visita** visiting times; **~s de vuelo** flying time (sg); **media ~** half an hour - 2. [momento determinado] time; **¿a qué ~ sale?** what time o when does it leave?; **es ~ de irse** it's time to go; **es ~ de cenar** it's time for supper; **a la ~** on time; **cada ~** hourly; **en su ~** when the time comes, at the appropriate time; **¿qué ~ es?** what time is it?; **~ de cerrar** closing time - 3. [cita] appointment; **pedir/dar ~** to ask for/give an appointment; **tener ~ en/con** to have an appointment at/with - 4. loc: **a altas ~s de la noche** in the small hours; **en mala ~** unluckily; **la ~ de la verdad** the moment of truth; **¡ya era ~!** and about time too!

horadar vt to pierce; [con máquina] to bore through.

horario, ria adj time (antes de sust).

◆ **horario** m timetable; **~ comercial/laboral** opening/working hours (pl); **~ intensivo** working day without a long break for lunch; **~ de visitas** visiting hours (pl).

horca f -1. [patíbulo] gallows (pl) - 2. AGR pitchfork.

horcajadas ◆ **a horcajadas** loc adv astride.

horchata f cold drink made from ground tiger nuts or almonds, milk and sugar.

horizontal adj horizontal.

horizonte m horizon.

horma f [gen] mould, pattern; [para arreglar zapatos] last; [para conservar zapatos] shoe tree; [de sombrero] hat block.

hormiga f ant.

hormigón m concrete; **~ armado** reinforced concrete.

hormigueo m pins and needles (pl).

hormiguero ◇ v ◇ **oso**. ◇ m ants' nest.

hormona f hormone.

hornada f lit & fig batch.

hornear vt to bake.

hornillo m [para cocinar] camping o portable stove; [de laboratorio] small furnace.

horno m CULIN oven; TECN furnace; [de cerámica, ladrillos] kiln; **alto ~** blast furnace; **altos ~s** [factoría] iron and steelworks; **~ eléctrico** electric oven; **~ de gas** gas oven; **~ microondas** microwave (oven).

horóscopo m -1. [signo zodiacal] star sign - 2. [predicción] horoscope.

horquilla f [para el pelo] hairpin, bobby pin US.

horrendo, da adj [gen] horrendous; [muy malo] terrible, awful.

horrible adj [gen] horrible; [muy malo] terrible, awful.

horripilante adj [terrorífico] horrifying, spine-chilling.

horripilar vt to terrify, to scare to death.

horror m -1. [miedo] terror, horror; **¡qué ~!** how awful! - 2. (gen pl) [atrocidad] atrocity.

horrorizado, da adj terrified, horrified.

horrorizar vt to terrify, to horrify.

◆ **horrorizarse** vpr to be terrified o horrified.

horroroso, sa adj -1. [gen] awful, dreadful - 2. [muy feo] horrible, hideous.

hortaliza f (garden) vegetable.

hortelano, na m,f market gardener.

hortensia f hydrangea.

hortera adj fam tasteless, tacky.

horticultura f horticulture.

hosco, ca adj [persona] sullen, gruff; [lugar] grim, gloomy.

hospedar vt to put up.

◆ **hospedarse** vpr to stay.

hospicio m [para niños] children's home; [para pobres] poorhouse.

hospital m hospital.

hospitalario, ria adj [acogedor] hospitable.

hospitalidad f hospitality.

hospitalizar vt to hospitalize, to take o send to hospital.

hostal *m* guesthouse.

hostelería *f* catering.

hostia *f* - **1.** RELIG host - **2.** *vulg* [bofetada] bash, punch - **3.** *vulg* [accidente] smash-up.
➥ **hostias** *interj vulg*: ¡~s! bloody hell!, damn it!

hostiar *vt vulg* to bash.

hostigar *vt* - **1.** [acosar] to pester, to bother - **2.** MIL to harass.

hostil *adj* hostile.

hostilidad *f* [sentimiento] hostility.
➥ **hostilidades** *fpl* MIL hostilities.

hotel *m* hotel.

hotelero, ra *adj* hotel *(antes de sust)*.

hoy *adv* - **1.** [en este día] today; **de ~ en adelante** from now on; **~ mismo** this very day; **por ~** for now, for the time being - **2.** [en la actualidad] nowadays, today; **~ día, ~ en día, ~ por ~** these days, nowadays.

hoyo *m* [gen] hole, pit; [de golf] hole.

hoyuelo *m* dimple.

hoz *f* sickle; **la ~ y el martillo** the hammer and sickle.

HTML *(abrev de* **hypertext markup language)** *m* INFORM HTML.

huacal *m* *Méx* - **1.** [jaula] cage - **2.** [cajón] drawer.

hubiera *etc* ⊳ **haber**.

hucha *f* moneybox.

hueco, ca *adj* - **1.** [vacío] hollow - **2.** [sonido] resonant, hollow - **3.** [sin ideas] empty.
➥ **hueco** *m* - **1.** [cavidad - gen] hole; [- en pared] recess - **2.** [tiempo libre] spare moment - **3.** [espacio libre] space, gap; [de escalera] well; [de ascensor] shaft; **hacer un ~ a alguien** to make space for sb.

huela *etc* ⊳ **oler**.

huelga *f* strike; **estar/declararse en ~** to be/to go on strike; **~ de brazos caídos** *o* **cruzados** sit-down (strike); **~ de celo** work-to-rule; **~ de hambre** hunger strike; **~ general** general strike; **~ salvaje** wildcat strike.

huelguista *mf* striker.

huella *f* - **1.** [de persona] footprint; [de animal, rueda] track; **~ digital** *o* **dactilar** fingerprint - **2.** *fig* [vestigio] trace; **sin dejar ~** without (a) trace - **3.** *fig* [impresión profunda] mark; **dejar ~** to leave one's mark.

huérfano, na *adj & m,f* orphan; **es ~ de madre** his mother is dead, he's lost his mother.

huerta *f* [huerto] market garden UK, truck farm US.

huerto *m* [de hortalizas] vegetable garden; [de frutales] orchard.

hueso *m* - **1.** [del cuerpo] bone; **estar calado hasta los ~s** to be soaked to the skin; **ser un ~ duro de roer** to be a hard nut to crack - **2.** [de fruto] stone UK, pit US - **3.** *Amér, Méx fam* [enchufe] contacts *(pl)*, influence - **4.** *Méx fam* [trabajo fácil] cushy job.

huésped, da *m,f* guest.

huesudo, da *adj* bony.

hueva *f* roe.

huevo *m* - **1.** [de animales] egg; **~ a la copa** *o* **tibio** *Andes* soft-boiled egg; **~ escalfado/frito** poached/fried egg; **~ pasado por agua/duro** soft-boiled/hard-boiled egg; **~ de Pascua** Easter egg; **~s revueltos** scrambled eggs; **parecerse como un ~ a una castaña** to be like chalk and cheese - **2.** *(gen pl) vulg* [testículos] balls *(pl)*; **costar un ~** [ser caro] to cost a packet *o* bomb; [ser difícil] to be bloody hard.

huevón, huevona *m,f Andes, Arg, Ven vulg* prat UK, pillock UK, jerk US.

huida *f* escape, flight.

huidizo, za *adj* shy, elusive.

huipil *m CAm, Méx* colourful embroidered dress or blouse traditionally worn by Indian women.

huir *vi* - **1.** [escapar]: **~ (de)** [gen] to flee (from); [de cárcel etc] to escape (from); **~ del país** to flee the country - **2.** [evitar]: **~ de algo** to avoid sthg, to keep away from sthg.

hule *m* oilskin.

humanidad *f* humanity.
➥ **humanidades** *fpl* [letras] humanities.

humanitario, ria *adj* humanitarian.

humanizar *vt* to humanize, to make more human.

humano, na *adj* - **1.** [del hombre] human - **2.** [compasivo] humane.
➥ **humano** *m* human being; **los ~s** mankind *(U)*.

humareda *f* cloud of smoke.

humear *vi* [salir humo] to (give off) smoke; [salir vapor] to steam.

humedad *f* - **1.** [gen] dampness; [en pared, techo] damp; [de algo chorreando] wetness; [de piel, ojos etc] moistness - **2.** [de atmósfera etc] humidity; **~ absoluta/relativa** absolute/relative humidity.

humedecer *vt* to moisten.
➥ **humedecerse** *vpr* to become moist; **~se los labios** to moisten one's lips.

húmedo, da *adj* - **1.** [gen] damp; [chorreando] wet; [piel, ojos etc] moist - **2.** [aire, clima, atmósfera] humid.

humidificar *vt* to humidify.

humildad *f* humility.

humilde *adj* humble.

humillación *f* humiliation.

humillado, da *adj* humiliated.

humillante *adj* humiliating.

humillar *vt* to humiliate.

humillarse *vpr* to humble o.s.

humita *f Andes, Arg paste made of mashed maize UK o corn US kernels mixed with cheese, chilli and onion, wrapped in a maize UK o corn US husk and steamed.*

humo *m* [gen] smoke; [vapor] steam; [de coches etc] fumes *(pl)*; **echar** ~ *lit* to smoke; *fig* to be fuming; **tragarse el** ~ [al fumar] to inhale.

humos *mpl fig* [aires] airs; **bajarle a alguien los** ~**s** to take sb down a peg or two; **tener muchos** ~**s** to put on airs.

humor *m* - **1.** [estado de ánimo] mood; [carácter] temperament; **estar de buen/mal** ~ to be in a good/bad mood - **2.** [gracia] humour; **un programa de** ~ a comedy programme; ~ **negro** black humour - **3.** [ganas] mood; **no estoy de** ~ I'm not in the mood.

humorismo *m* humour; TEATR & TV comedy.

humorista *mf* humorist; TEATR & TV comedian *(f comediana)*.

humorístico, ca *adj* humorous.

hundimiento *m* - **1.** [naufragio] sinking - **2.** [ruina] collapse.

hundir *vt* - **1.** [gen] to sink; ~ **algo en el agua** to put sthg underwater - **2.** [afligir] to devastate, to destroy - **3.** [hacer fracasar] to ruin.

hundirse *vpr* - **1.** [sumergirse] to sink; [intencionadamente] to dive - **2.** [derrumbarse] to collapse; [techo] to cave in - **3.** [fracasar] to be ruined.

húngaro, ra *adj & m,f* Hungarian.

húngaro *m* [lengua] Hungarian.

Hungría Hungary.

huracán *m* hurricane.

huraño, ña *adj* unsociable.

hurgar *vi*: ~ **(en)** [gen] to rummage around (in); [con el dedo, un palo] to poke around (in).

hurgarse *vpr*: ~**se la nariz** to pick one's nose; ~**se los bolsillos** to rummage around in one's pockets.

hurón *m* ZOOL ferret.

hurra *interj* ¡ ~ ! hurray!

hurtadillas **a hurtadillas** *loc adv* on the sly, stealthily.

hurtar *vt* to steal.

hurto *m* theft.

husmear ◇ *vt* [olfatear] to sniff out, to scent. ◇ *vi* [curiosear] to nose around.

huso *m* spindle; [en máquina] bobbin.

huy *interj* ¡ ~ ! [dolor] ouch!; [sorpresa] gosh!

i, I *f* [letra] i, I.

IAE (*abrev de* **Impuesto sobre Actividades Económicas**) *m Spanish tax paid by professionals and shop owners.*

iba ⊳ **ir.**

ibérico, ca *adj* Iberian.

íbero, ra *adj & m,f* Iberian.

íbero, íbero *m* [lengua] Iberian.

iberoamericano, na *adj & m,f* Latin American.

iceberg (*pl* **icebergs**) *m* iceberg.

icono *m* icon.

iconoclasta *mf* iconoclast.

id ⊳ **ir.**

ida *f* outward journey; **(billete de)** ~ **y vuelta** return (ticket).

idea *f* - **1.** [gen] idea; [propósito] intention; **con la** ~ **de** with the idea o intention of; **hacerse a la** ~ **de que ...** to get used to the idea that ...; **hacerse una** ~ **de algo** to get an idea of sthg; ~ **fija** obsession; ~ **preconcebida** preconception; **cuando se le mete una** ~ **en la cabeza ...** when he gets an idea into his head ...; **¡ni** ~ **!** *fam* search me!, I haven't got a clue!; **no tener ni** ~ **(de)** not to have a clue (about) - **2.** [opinión] impression; **cambiar de** ~ to change one's mind.

ideal *adj & m* ideal; **lo** ~ **sería hacerlo mañana** ideally, we would do it tomorrow.

idealista ◇ *adj* idealistic. ◇ *mf* idealist.

idealizar *vt* to idealize.

idear *vt* - **1.** [planear] to think up, to devise - **2.** [inventar] to invent.

ideario *m* ideology.

ídem *pron* ditto.

idéntico, ca *adj*: ~ **(a)** identical (to).

identidad *f* [gen] identity.

identificación *f* identification.

identificar *vt* to identify.

identificarse *vpr*: ~**se (con)** to identify (with).

ideología *f* ideology.

idílico, ca *adj* idyllic.

idilio *m* love affair.

idioma *m* language.

idiosincrasia *f* individual character.

idiota ◇ *adj despec* [tonto] stupid. ◇ *mf* idiot.

idiotez *f* [tontería] stupid thing, stupidity (U).

ido, ida *adj* - 1. [loco] mad, touched - 2. [distraído]: **estar** ~ to be miles away.

idolatrar *vt* to worship; *fig* to idolize.

ídolo *m* idol.

idóneo, a *adj*: ~ **(para)** suitable (for).

iglesia *f* church.

iglú (*pl* **iglúes**) *m* igloo.

ignorancia *f* ignorance.

ignorante ◇ *adj* ignorant. ◇ *mf* ignoramus.

ignorar *vt* - 1. [desconocer] not to know, to be ignorant of - 2. [no tener en cuenta] to ignore.

igual ◇ *adj* - 1. [idéntico]: ~ **(que)** the same (as); **llevan jerseys** ~**es** they're wearing the same jumper; **son** ~**es** they're the same - 2. [parecido]: ~ **(que)** similar (to) - 3. [equivalente]: ~ **(a)** equal (to) - 4. [liso] even - 5. [constante - velocidad] constant; [- clima, temperatura] even - 6. MAT: **A más B es** ~ **a C** A plus B equals C. ◇ *mf* equal; **sin** ~ without equal, unrivalled. ◇ *adv* - 1. [de la misma manera] the same; **yo pienso** ~ I think the same, I think so too; **al** ~ **que** just like; **por** ~ equally - 2. [posiblemente] perhaps; ~ **llueve** it could well rain - 3. DEP: **van** ~**es** the scores are level - 4. *loc*: **dar** *o* **ser** ~ **a alguien** to be all the same to sb; **es** *o* **da** ~ it doesn't matter, it doesn't make any difference.

igualado, da *adj* level.

igualar *vt* - 1. [gen] to make equal, to equalize; DEP to equalize; ~ **algo a** *o* **con** to equate sthg with - 2. [persona] to be equal to; **nadie le iguala en generosidad** nobody is as generous as he is - 3. [terreno] to level; [superficie] to smooth.

→ **igualarse** *vpr* - 1. [gen] to be equal, to equal one another - 2. [a otra persona]: ~**se a** *o* **con alguien** to treat sb as an equal.

igualdad *f* - 1. [equivalencia] equality; **en** ~ **de condiciones** on equal terms; ~ **de oportunidades** equal opportunities (*pl*) - 2. [identidad] sameness.

igualitario, ria *adj* egalitarian.

igualmente *adv* - 1. [también] also, likewise - 2. [fórmula de cortesía] the same to you, likewise.

ikurriña *f* Basque national flag.

ilegal *adj* illegal.

ilegible *adj* illegible.

ilegítimo, ma *adj* illegitimate.

ileso, sa *adj* unhurt, unharmed; **salir** *o* **resultar** ~ to escape unharmed.

ilícito, ta *adj* illicit.

ilimitado, da *adj* unlimited, limitless.

iluminación *f* - 1. [gen] lighting; [acción] illumination - 2. RELIG enlightenment.

iluminar *vt* [gen] to illuminate, to light up.

→ **iluminarse** *vpr* to light up.

ilusión *f* - 1. [esperanza - gen] hope; [- infundada] delusion, illusion; **hacerse** *o* **forjarse ilusiones** to build up one's hopes; **hacerse la** ~ **de** to imagine that; **tener** ~ **por** to look forward to - 2. [emoción] thrill, excitement (U); **¡qué** ~**!** how exciting!; **me hace mucha** ~ I'm really looking forward to it - 3. [espejismo] illusion; ~ **óptica** optical illusion.

ilusionar *vt* - 1. [esperanzar]: ~ **a alguien (con algo)** to build up sb's hopes (about sthg) - 2. [emocionar] to excite, to thrill.

→ **ilusionarse** *vpr* [emocionarse]: ~**se (con)** to get excited (about).

ilusionista *mf* conjurer.

iluso, sa *adj* gullible.

ilusorio, ria *adj* illusory; [promesa] empty.

ilustración *f* - 1. [estampa] illustration - 2. [cultura] learning.

→ **Ilustración** *f* HIST: **la Ilustración** the Enlightenment.

ilustrado, da *adj* - 1. [publicación] illustrated - 2. [persona] learned - 3. HIST enlightened.

ilustrar *vt* - 1. [explicar] to illustrate, to explain - 2. [publicación] to illustrate.

ilustre *adj* [gen] illustrious, distinguished.

imagen *f* [gen] image; TV picture; **ser la viva** ~ **de alguien** to be the spitting image of sb; ~ **borrosa** blur; ~ **congelada** freeze frame; ~ **corporativa** corporate identity.

imaginación *f* - 1. [facultad] imagination; **se deja llevar por la** ~ he lets his imagination run away with him; **pasar por la** ~ **de alguien** to occur to sb, to cross sb's mind - 2. (*gen pl*) [idea falsa] delusion, imagining.

imaginar *vt* - 1. [gen] to imagine - 2. [idear] to think up, to invent.

→ **imaginarse** *vpr* to imagine; **¡imagínate!** just think *o* imagine!; **me imagino que sí** I suppose so.

imaginario, ria *adj* imaginary.

imaginativo, va *adj* imaginative.

imán *m* [para atraer] magnet.

imbécil ◇ *adj* stupid. ◇ *mf* idiot.

imbecilidad *f* stupidity; **decir/hacer una** ~ to say/do sthg stupid.

imborrable *adj fig* indelible; [recuerdo] unforgettable.

imbuir *vt*: ~ **(de)** to imbue (with).

imitación *f* imitation; [de humorista] impersonation; **a** ~ **de** in imitation of; **piel**

de ~ imitation leather.

imitador, ra *m,f* imitator; [humorista] impersonator.

imitar *vt* [gen] to imitate, to copy; [a personajes famosos] to impersonate; [producto, material] to simulate.

impaciencia *f* impatience.

impacientar *vt* to make impatient, to exasperate.

◆ **impacientarse** *vpr* to grow impatient.

impaciente *adj* impatient; ~ **por hacer algo** impatient *o* anxious to do sthg.

impactante *adj* [imagen] hard-hitting; [belleza] striking.

impactar ◇ *vt* [suj: noticia] to have an impact on. ◇ *vi* [bala] to hit.

impacto *m* - **1.** [gen] impact; [de bala] hit - **2.** [señal] (impact) mark; ~**s de bala** bullethole.

impagado, da *adj* unpaid.

impar *adj* MAT odd.

imparable *adj* unstoppable.

imparcial *adj* impartial.

impartir *vt* to give.

impase, impasse [im'pas] *m* impasse.

impasible *adj* impassive.

impávido, da *adj* [valeroso] fearless, courageous; [impasible] impassive.

impecable *adj* impeccable.

impedido, da *adj* disabled; **estar** ~ **de un brazo** to have the use of only one arm.

impedimento *m* [gen] obstacle; [contra un matrimonio] impediment.

impedir *vt* - **1.** [imposibilitar] to prevent; ~ **a alguien hacer algo** to prevent sb from doing sthg - **2.** [dificultar] to hinder, to obstruct.

impenetrable *adj* lit & fig impenetrable.

impensable *adj* unthinkable.

imperante *adj* prevailing.

imperar *vi* to prevail.

imperativo, va *adj* - **1.** [gen & GRAM] imperative - **2.** [autoritario] imperious.

◆ **imperativo** *m* [gen & GRAM] imperative.

imperceptible *adj* imperceptible.

imperdible *m* safety pin.

imperdonable *adj* unforgivable.

imperfección *f* - **1.** [cualidad] imperfection - **2.** [defecto] flaw, defect.

imperfecto, ta *adj* [gen] imperfect; [defectuoso] faulty, defective.

◆ **imperfecto** *m* GRAM imperfect.

imperial *adj* imperial.

imperialismo *m* imperialism.

impericia *f* lack of skill; [inexperiencia] inexperience.

imperio *m* - **1.** [territorio] empire - **2.** [dominio] rule.

imperioso, sa *adj* - **1.** [autoritario] imperious - **2.** [apremiante] urgent, pressing.

impermeable ◇ *adj* waterproof. ◇ *m* raincoat, mac *UK*.

impersonal *adj* impersonal.

impertinencia *f* - **1.** [gen] impertinence - **2.** [comentario] impertinent remark.

impertinente *adj* impertinent.

imperturbable *adj* imperturbable.

ímpetu *m* - **1.** [brusquedad] force - **2.** [energía] energy - **3.** FÍS impetus.

impetuoso, sa *adj* - **1.** [olas, viento, ataque] violent - **2.** [persona] impulsive, impetuous.

impío, a *adj* godless, impious.

implacable *adj* implacable, relentless.

implantar *vt* - **1.** [establecer] to introduce - **2.** MED to insert.

◆ **implantarse** *vpr* [establecerse] to be introduced.

implicación *f* - **1.** [participación] involvement - **2.** (gen pl) [consecuencia] implication.

implicar *vt* - **1.** [involucrar] ~ **(en)** to involve (in); DER to implicate (in) - **2.** [significar] to mean.

◆ **implicarse** *vpr* DER to incriminate o.s.; ~**se en** to become involved in.

implícito, ta *adj* implicit.

implorar *vt* to implore.

imponente *adj* - **1.** [impresionante] imposing, impressive - **2.** [estupendo] sensational, terrific.

imponer ◇ *vt* - **1.**: ~ **algo (a alguien)** [gen] to impose sthg (on sb); [respeto] to command sthg (from sb) - **2.** [moda] to set; [costumbre] to introduce. ◇ *vi* to be imposing.

◆ **imponerse** *vpr* - **1.** [hacerse respetar] to command respect, to show authority - **2.** [prevalecer] to prevail - **3.** [ser necesario] to be necessary - **4.** DEP to win, to prevail.

impopular *adj* unpopular.

importación *f* [acción] importing; [artículo] import.

importador, ra *m,f* importer.

importancia *f* importance; **dar** ~ **a algo** to attach importance to sthg; **quitar** ~ **a algo** to play sthg down.

importante *adj* - **1.** [gen] important; [lesión] serious - **2.** [cantidad] considerable.

importar ◇ *vt* - **1.** [gen & INFORM] to import - **2.** [suj: factura, coste] to amount to, to come to. ◇ *vi* - **1.** [preocupar] to matter; **no me importa** I don't care, it doesn't matter to me; **¿y a ti qué te importa?** what's it got to do with you? - **2.** [en preguntas] to mind; **¿le importa que me siente?** do you mind if I sit down?; **¿te importaría acompañarme?** would you mind coming with me? ◇ *v impers* to matter; **no importa** it doesn't matter.

importe *m* [gen] price, cost; [de factura] total.

importunar *vt* to bother, to pester.

importuno, na = **inoportuno**.

imposibilidad *f* impossibility; **su ~ para contestar la pregunta** his inability to answer the question.

imposibilitado, da *adj* disabled; **estar ~ para hacer algo** to be unable to do sthg.

imposibilitar *vt* : **~ a alguien para hacer algo** to make it impossible for sb to do sthg, to prevent sb from doing sthg.

imposible *adj* - **1.** [irrealizable] impossible - **2.** [insoportable] unbearable, impossible.

imposición *f* - **1.** [obligación] imposition - **2.** [impuesto] tax - **3.** BANCA deposit.

impostor, ra *m,f* [suplantador] impostor.

impotencia *f* impotence.

impotente *adj* impotent.

impracticable *adj* - **1.** [irrealizable] impracticable - **2.** [intransitable] impassable.

imprecisión *f* imprecision, vagueness *(U).*

impreciso, sa *adj* imprecise, vague.

impredecible *adj* unforeseeable; [variable] unpredictable.

impregnar *vt* : **~ (de)** to impregnate (with).

◆ **impregnarse** *vpr* : **~se (de)** to become impregnated (with).

imprenta *f* - **1.** [arte] printing - **2.** [máquina] (printing) press - **3.** [establecimiento] printing house.

imprescindible *adj* indispensable, essential.

impresentable *adj* unpresentable.

impresión *f* - **1.** [gen] impression; [sensación física] feeling; **causar (una) buena/mala ~** to make a good/bad impression; **dar la ~ de** to give the impression of; **tener la ~ de que** to have the impression that - **2.** [huella] imprint; **~ digital** o **dactilar** fingerprint - **3.** [IMPRENTA - acción] printing; [- edición] edition.

impresionable *adj* impressionable.

impresionante *adj* impressive; [error] enormous.

impresionar *vt* - **1.** [maravillar] to impress - **2.** [conmocionar] to move - **3.** [horrorizar] to shock - **4.** FOT to expose. *vi* [maravillar] to make an impression.

◆ **impresionarse** *vpr* - **1.** [maravillarse] to be impressed - **2.** [conmocionarse] to be moved - **3.** [horrorizarse] to be shocked.

impreso, sa *pp* **imprimir**. *adj* printed.

◆ **impreso** *m* - **1.** [texto] printed matter *(U)* - **2.** [formulario] form.

impresor, ra *m,f* [persona] printer.

◆ **impresora** *f* INFORM printer; **impresora**

láser/térmica laser/thermal printer; **impresora de matriz** o **de agujas** dot-matrix printer; **impresora de chorro de tinta** inkjet printer.

imprevisible *adj* unforeseeable; [variable] unpredictable.

imprevisto, ta *adj* unexpected.

◆ **imprevisto** *m* [hecho]: **salvo ~s** barring accidents.

imprimir *vt* - **1.** [gen] to print; [huella, paso] to leave, to make - **2.** *fig* [transmitir]: **~ algo a** to impart o bring sthg to.

improbable *adj* improbable, unlikely.

improcedente *adj* - **1.** [inoportuno] inappropriate - **2.** DER inadmissible.

improperio *m* insult.

impropio, pia *adj* : **~ (de)** improper (for), unbecoming (to).

improvisado, da *adj* [gen] improvised; [discurso, truco] impromptu; [comentario] ad-lib; [cama etc] makeshift.

improvisar *vt* [gen] to improvise; [comida] to rustle up; **~ una cama** to make (up) a makeshift bed. *vi* [gen] to improvise; MÚS to extemporize.

improviso ◆ **de improviso** *loc adv* unexpectedly, suddenly; **coger a alguien de ~** to catch sb unawares.

imprudencia *f* [en los actos] carelessness *(U)*; [en los comentarios] indiscretion.

imprudente *adj* [en los actos] careless, rash; [en los comentarios] indiscreet.

impúdico, ca *adj* immodest, indecent.

impuesto, ta *pp* **imponer**.

◆ **impuesto** *m* tax; **~ de circulación** road tax; **~ sobre el valor añadido** value added tax; **~ sobre la renta** ≃ income tax.

impugnar *vt* to contest, to challenge.

impulsar *vt* - **1.** [empujar] to propel, to drive - **2.** [incitar]: **~ a alguien (a algo/a hacer algo)** to drive sb (to sthg/to do sthg) - **3.** [promocionar] to stimulate.

impulsivo, va *adj* impulsive.

impulso *m* - **1.** [progreso] stimulus, boost - **2.** [fuerza] momentum - **3.** [motivación] impulse, urge.

impulsor, ra *m,f* dynamic force.

impune *adj* unpunished.

impunidad *f* impunity.

impureza *(gen pl)* *f* impurity.

impuro, ra *adj lit* & *fig* impure.

imputación *f* accusation.

imputar *vt* [atribuir]: **~ algo a alguien** [delito] to accuse sb of sthg; [fracaso, error] to attribute sthg to sb.

in **fraganti, vitro.**

inabarcable *adj* unmanageable.

inacabable *adj* interminable, endless.

inaccesible *adj* inaccessible.

inaceptable *adj* unacceptable.

inactividad *f* inactivity.

inactivo, va *adj* inactive.

inadaptado, da *adj* maladjusted.

inadecuado, da *adj* [inapropiado] unsuitable, inappropriate.

inadmisible *adj* inadmissible.

inadvertido, da *adj* unnoticed; **pasar ~ to** go unnoticed.

inagotable *adj* inexhaustible.

inaguantable *adj* unbearable.

inalámbrico, ca *adj* cordless.

➡ **inalámbrico** *m* cordless telephone.

inalcanzable *adj* unattainable.

inalterable *adj* **-1.** [gen] unalterable; [salud] stable; [amistad] undying **- 2.** [color] fast **- 3.** [rostro, carácter] impassive **- 4.** [resultado, marcador] unchanged.

inamovible *adj* immovable, fixed.

inanición *f* starvation.

inanimado, da *adj* inanimate.

inánime *adj* lifeless.

inapreciable *adj* **-1.** [incalculable] invaluable, inestimable **- 2.** [insignificante] imperceptible.

inapropiado, da *adj* inappropriate.

inaudito, ta *adj* unheard-of.

inauguración *f* inauguration, opening.

inaugurar *vt* to inaugurate, to open.

inca *adj* & *mf* Inca.

incalculable *adj* incalculable.

incalificable *adj* unspeakable, indescribable.

incandescente *adj* incandescent.

incansable *adj* untiring, tireless.

incapacidad *f* **-1.** [imposibilidad] inability **- 2.** [inaptitud] incompetence **- 3.** DER incapacity.

incapacitado, da *adj* [DER - gen] disqualified; [- para testar] incapacitated; [- para trabajar] unfit.

incapacitar *vt* : **~ (para)** [gen] to disqualify (from); [para trabajar etc] to render unfit (for).

incapaz *adj* **-1.** [gen]: **~ de** incapable of **- 2.** [sin talento]: **~ para** incompetent at, no good at **- 3.** DER incompetent.

incautación *f* seizure, confiscation.

incautarse ➡ **incautarse de** *vpr* DER to seize, to confiscate.

incauto, ta *adj* gullible.

incendiar *vt* to set fire to.

➡ **incendiarse** *vpr* to catch fire.

incendiario, ria ◇ *adj* **-1.** [bomba etc] incendiary **- 2.** [artículo, libro etc] inflammatory. ◇ *m, f* arsonist, fire-raiser.

incendio *m* fire; **~ forestal** forest fire; **~ provocado** arson.

incentivo *m* incentive; **~ fiscal** tax incentive.

incertidumbre *f* uncertainty.

incesto *m* incest.

incidencia *f* **-1.** [repercusión] impact, effect **- 2.** [suceso] event.

incidente *m* incident; **~ diplomático** diplomatic incident.

incidir ➡ **incidir en** *vi* **-1.** [incurrir en] to fall into, to lapse into **- 2.** [insistir en] to focus on **- 3.** [influir en] to have an impact on, to affect.

incienso *m* incense.

incierto, ta *adj* **-1.** [dudoso] uncertain **- 2.** [falso] untrue.

incineración *f* [de cadáver] cremation; [de basura] incineration.

incinerar *vt* [cadáver] to cremate; [basura] to incinerate.

incipiente *adj* incipient; [estado, etapa] early.

incisión *f* incision.

incisivo, va *adj* **-1.** [instrumento] sharp, cutting **- 2.** *fig* [mordaz] incisive.

inciso, sa *adj* cut.

➡ **inciso** *m* passing remark.

incitante *adj* [instigador] inciting; [provocativo] provocative.

incitar *vt* : **~ a alguien a algo** [violencia, rebelión etc] to incite sb to sthg; **~ a alguien a la fuga/venganza** to urge sb to flee/avenge himself; **~ a alguien a hacer algo** [rebelarse etc] to incite sb to do sthg; [fugarse, vengarse] to urge sb to do sthg.

inclemencia *f* harshness, inclemency.

inclinación *f* **-1.** [desviación] slant, inclination; [de terreno] slope **- 2.** *fig* [afición]: **~ (a o por)** penchant o propensity (for) **- 3.** [cariño]: **~ hacia alguien** fondness towards sb **- 4.** [saludo] bow.

inclinar *vt* **-1.** [doblar] to bend; [ladear] to tilt **- 2.** [cabeza] to bow.

➡ **inclinarse** *vpr* **-1.** [doblarse] to lean **- 2.** [para saludar]: **~se (ante)** to bow (before).

➡ **inclinarse a** *vi* [tender a] to be o feel inclined to.

➡ **inclinarse por** *vi* [preferir] to favour, to lean towards.

incluir *vt* [gen] to include; [adjuntar - en cartas] to enclose.

inclusive *adv* inclusive.

incluso, sa *adj* enclosed.

➡ **incluso** *adv* & *prep* even.

incógnito, ta *adj* unknown.

➡ **incógnita** *f* **-1.** MAT unknown quantity **- 2.** [misterio] mystery.

➡ **de incógnito** *loc adv* incognito.

incoherencia *f* **-1.** [cualidad] incoherence

- 2. [comentario] nonsensical remark.

incoherente *adj* **- 1.** [inconexo] incoherent **- 2.** [inconsecuente] inconsistent.

incoloro, ra *adj lit & fig* colourless.

incomodar *vt* **- 1.** [causar molestia] to bother, to inconvenience **- 2.** [enfadar] to annoy.

◆ **incomodarse** *vpr* [enfadarse]: ~se (por) to get annoyed (about).

incomodidad *f* **- 1.** [de silla etc] uncomfortableness **- 2.** [de situación, persona] awkwardness, discomfort.

incómodo, da *adj* **- 1.** [silla etc] uncomfortable **- 2.** [situación, persona] awkward, uncomfortable.

incomparable *adj* incomparable.

incompatible *adj*: ~ (con) incompatible (with).

incompetencia *f* incompetence.

incompetente *adj* incompetent.

incompleto, ta *adj* **- 1.** [gen] incomplete **- 2.** [inacabado] unfinished.

incomprendido, da *adj* misunderstood.

incomprensible *adj* incomprehensible.

incomprensión *f* lack of understanding.

incomunicado, da *adj* **- 1.** [gen] isolated **- 2.** [por la nieve etc] cut off **- 3.** [preso] in solitary confinement.

inconcebible *adj* inconceivable.

inconcluso, sa *adj* unfinished.

incondicional <> *adj* unconditional; [ayuda] wholehearted; [seguidor] staunch. <> *mf* staunch supporter.

inconexo, xa *adj* [gen] unconnected; [pensamiento, texto] disjointed.

inconformista *adj & mf* nonconformist.

inconfundible *adj* unmistakable; [prueba] irrefutable.

incongruente *adj* incongruous.

inconsciencia *f* **- 1.** [gen] unconsciousness **- 2.** *fig* [falta de juicio] thoughtlessness.

inconsciente *adj* **- 1.** [gen] unconscious **- 2.** *fig* [irreflexivo] thoughtless.

inconsecuente *adj* inconsistent.

inconsistente *adj* [tela, pared etc] flimsy; [salsa] runny; [argumento, discurso etc] lacking in substance.

inconstancia *f* **- 1.** [en el trabajo, la conducta] unreliability **- 2.** [de opinión, ideas] changeability.

inconstante *adj* **- 1.** [en el trabajo, la conducta] unreliable **- 2.** [de opinión, ideas] changeable.

inconstitucional *adj* unconstitutional.

incontable *adj* [innumerable] countless.

incontestable *adj* indisputable, undeniable.

incontinencia *f* incontinence.

incontrolable *adj* uncontrollable.

inconveniencia *f* **- 1.** [inoportunidad]

inappropriateness **- 2.** [comentario] tactless remark; [acto] mistake.

inconveniente <> *adj* **- 1.** [inoportuno] inappropriate **- 2.** [descortés] rude. <> *m* **- 1.** [dificultad] obstacle, problem **- 2.** [desventaja] drawback.

incordiar *vt fam* to bother, to pester.

incorporación *f*: ~ (a) [gen] incorporation (into); [a un puesto] induction (into).

incorporar *vt* **- 1.** [añadir] : ~ (a) [gen] to incorporate (into); CULIN to mix (into) **- 2.** [levantar] to sit up.

◆ **incorporarse** *vpr* **- 1.** [empezar]: ~se (a) [equipo] to join; [trabajo] to start **- 2.** [levantarse] to sit up.

incorrección *f* **- 1.** [inexactitud] incorrectness; [error gramatical] mistake **- 2.** [descortesía] lack of courtesy, rudeness *(U)*.

incorrecto, ta *adj* **- 1.** [equivocado] incorrect, wrong **- 2.** [descortés] rude, impolite.

incorregible *adj* incorrigible.

incredulidad *f* incredulity.

incrédulo, la *adj* sceptical, incredulous; RELIG unbelieving.

increíble *adj* **- 1.** [difícil de creer] unconvincing, lacking credibility **- 2.** *fig* [extraordinario] incredible **- 3.** *fig* [inconcebible] unbelievable.

incrementar *vt* to increase.

◆ **incrementarse** *vpr* to increase.

incremento *m* increase; [de temperatura] rise; ~ **salarial** pay increase.

increpar *vt* **- 1.** [reprender] to reprimand **- 2.** [insultar] to abuse, insult.

incriminar *vt* to accuse.

incrustar *vt* **- 1.** TECN to inlay; [en joyería] to set **- 2.** *fam fig* [empotrar]: ~ **algo en algo** to sink sthg into sthg.

◆ **incrustarse** *vpr* [cal etc] to become encrusted.

incubar *vt* **- 1.** [huevo] to incubate **- 2.** [enfermedad] to be sickening for.

inculcar *vt*: ~ **algo a alguien** to instil sthg into sb.

inculpar *vt*: ~ **a alguien (de)** [gen] to accuse sb (of); DER to charge sb (with).

inculto, ta <> *adj* [persona] uneducated. <> *m,f* ignoramus.

incumbencia *f*: **es/no es de nuestra** ~ it is/isn't a matter for us, it falls/doesn't fall within our area of responsibility.

incumbir ◆ **incumbir a** *vi*: ~ **a alguien** to be a matter for sb, to be within sb's area of responsibility; **esto no te incumbe** this is none of your business.

incumplimiento *m* [de deber] failure to fulfil; [de orden, ley] non-compliance; [de promesa] failure to keep; ~ **de contrato** breach of contract.

incumplir vt [deber] to fail to fulfil, to neglect; [orden, ley] to fail to comply with; [promesa] to break; [contrato] to breach.

incurable adj incurable.

incurrir ➡ incurrir en vi **- 1.** [delito, falta] to commit; [error] to make **- 2.** [desprecio etc] to incur.

incursión f incursion; ~ **aérea** air raid.

indagación f investigation, inquiry.

indagar ◇ vt to investigate, to inquire into. ◇ vi to investigate, to inquire.

indecencia f **- 1.** [cualidad] indecency **- 2.** [acción] outrage, crime.

indecente adj **- 1.** [impúdico] indecent **- 2.** [indigno] miserable, wretched.

indecible adj [alegría] indescribable; [dolor] unspeakable.

indecisión f indecisiveness.

indeciso, sa ◇ adj **- 1.** [persona - inseguro] indecisive; [- que está dudoso] undecided, unsure **- 2.** [pregunta, respuesta] hesitant; [resultado] undecided. ◇ m,f undecided voter.

indefenso, sa adj defenceless.

indefinido, da adj **- 1.** [ilimitado] indefinite; [contrato] open-ended **- 2.** [impreciso] vague **- 3.** GRAM indefinite.

indeleble adj culto indelible.

indemne adj unhurt, unharmed.

indemnización f [gen] compensation; [por despido] severance pay.

indemnizar vt : ~ **a alguien (por)** to compensate sb (for).

independencia f independence; **con ~ de** independently of.

independiente adj **- 1.** [gen] independent **- 2.** [aparte] separate.

independizar vt to grant independence to. **➡ independizarse** vpr: ~**se (de)** to become independent (of).

indeseable adj undesirable.

indeterminación f indecisiveness.

indeterminado, da adj **- 1.** [sin determinar] indeterminate; **por tiempo ~** indefinitely **- 2.** [impreciso] vague.

indexar vt INFORM to index.

India : (la) ~ India.

indiano, na m,f **- 1.** [indígena] (Latin American) Indian **- 2.** [emigrante] *Spanish emigrant to Latin America who returned to Spain having made his fortune.*

indicación f **- 1.** [señal, gesto] sign, signal **- 2.** *(gen pl)* [instrucción] instruction; [para llegar a un sitio] directions *(pl)* **- 3.** [nota, corrección] note.

indicado, da adj suitable, appropriate.

indicador, ra adj indicating *(antes de sust).* **➡ indicador** m [gen] indicator; TECN gauge, meter; ~ **de carretera** road sign;

~ **de velocidad** speedometer.

indicar vt [señalar] to indicate; [suj: aguja etc] to read.

indicativo, va adj indicative. **➡ indicativo** m GRAM indicative.

índice m **- 1.** [gen] index; [proporción] level, rate; ~ **alfabético** alphabetical index; ~ **de audiencia** ratings; ~ **de materias** o **temático** table of contents; ~ **de natalidad** birth rate; ~ **de precios al consumo** retail price index **- 2.** [señal] sign, indicator **- 3.** [catálogo] catalogue **- 4.** [dedo] index finger.

indicio m sign; [pista] clue; [cantidad pequeña] trace.

Índico m: **el (océano)** ~ the Indian Ocean.

indiferencia f indifference.

indiferente adj indifferent; **me es ~** [me da igual] I don't mind, it's all the same to me; [no me interesa] I'm not interested in it.

indígena ◇ adj indigenous, native. ◇ mf native.

indigencia f culto destitution, poverty.

indigente adj destitute, poor.

indigestarse vpr to get indigestion.

indigestión f indigestion.

indigesto, ta adj indigestible; *fam fig* [pesado] stodgy, heavy.

indignación f indignation.

indignar vt to anger. **➡ indignarse** vpr: ~**se (por)** to get angry o indignant (about).

indigno, na adj **- 1.** [gen]: ~ **(de)** unworthy (of) **- 2.** [impropio] not fitting, wrong **- 3.** [vergonzoso] contemptible, shameful.

indio, dia ◇ adj Indian. ◇ m,f Indian; ~ **americano** Native American; **hacer el ~** to play the fool.

indirecto, ta adj indirect. **➡ indirecta** f hint; **lanzar una indirecta a alguien** to drop a hint to sb.

indisciplina f indiscipline.

indiscreción f **- 1.** [cualidad] indiscretion **- 2.** [comentario] indiscreet remark.

indiscreto, ta adj indiscreet.

indiscriminado, da adj indiscriminate.

indiscutible adj [gen] indisputable; [poder] undisputed.

indispensable adj indispensable, essential.

indisponer vt **- 1.** [enfermar] to make ill, to upset **- 2.** [enemistar] to set at odds.

indisposición f [malestar] indisposition.

indispuesto, ta ◇ pp ➡ **indisponer.** ◇ adj indisposed, unwell.

indistinto, ta adj **- 1.** [indiferente]: **es ~** it doesn't matter, it makes no difference **- 2.** [cuenta, cartilla] joint **- 3.** [perfil, figura] indistinct, blurred.

individual *adj* **- 1.** [gen] individual; [habitación, cama] **single**; [despacho] **personal - 2.** [prueba, competición] singles *(antes de sust)*.
  ◆ **individuales** *mpl* DEP singles.

individualizar *vi* to single people out.

individuo, dua *m,f* person; *despec* individual.

indocumentado, da *adj* **- 1.** [sin documentación] without identity papers **- 2.** [ignorante] ignorant.

índole *f* [naturaleza] nature; [tipo] type, kind.

indolencia *f* indolence, laziness.

indoloro, ra *adj* painless.

indómito, ta *adj* **- 1.** [animal] untameable **- 2.** [carácter] rebellious; [pueblo] unruly.

Indonesia Indonesia.

inducir *vt* [incitar]: ~ **a alguien a algo/a hacer algo** to lead sb into sthg/into doing sthg; ~ **a error** to mislead.

inductor, ra *adj* instigating.

indudable *adj* undoubted; **es ~ que ...** there is no doubt that ...

indulgencia *f* indulgence.

indultar *vt* to pardon.

indulto *m* pardon.

indumentaria *f* attire.

industria *f* [gen] industry.

industrial *adj* industrial. ◇ *mf* industrialist.

industrializar *vt* to industrialize.

inédito, ta *adj* **- 1.** [no publicado] unpublished **- 2.** [sorprendente] unprecedented.

inefable *adj* ineffable, inexpressible.

ineficaz *adj* **- 1.** [de bajo rendimiento] inefficient **- 2.** [de baja efectividad] ineffective.

ineficiente *adj* **- 1.** [de bajo rendimiento] inefficient **- 2.** [de baja efectividad] ineffective.

ineludible *adj* unavoidable.

INEM *(abrev de* **Instituto Nacional de Empleo)** *m Spanish department of employment.*

inenarrable *adj* spectacular.

ineptitud *f* ineptitude.

inepto, ta *adj* inept.

inequívoco, ca *adj* [apoyo, resultado] unequivocal; [señal, voz] unmistakeable.

inercia *f* lit & fig inertia.

inerme *adj* [sin armas] unarmed; [sin defensa] defenceless.

inerte *adj* **- 1.** [materia] inert **- 2.** [cuerpo, cadáver] lifeless.

inesperado, da *adj* unexpected.

inestable *adj* lit & fig unstable.

inevitable *adj* inevitable.

inexacto, ta *adj* **- 1.** [impreciso] inaccurate **- 2.** [erróneo] incorrect, wrong.

inexistente *adj* nonexistent.

inexperiencia *f* inexperience.

inexperto, ta *adj* **- 1.** [falto de experiencia] inexperienced **- 2.** [falto de habilidad] unskilful, inexpert.

inexpresivo, va *adj* expressionless.

infalible *adj* infallible.

infame *adj* vile, base.

infamia *f* [deshonra] infamy, disgrace.

infancia *f* [periodo] childhood.

infante, ta *m,f* **- 1.** [niño] infant **- 2.** [hijo del rey] infante (*f* infanta), prince (*f* princess).

infantería *f* infantry.

infantil *adj* **- 1.** [para niños] children's; [de niños] child *(antes de sust)* **- 2.** *fig* [inmaduro] infantile, childish.

infarto *m*: ~ **(de miocardio)** heart attack.

infatigable *adj* indefatigable, tireless.

infección *f* infection.

infeccioso, sa *adj* infectious.

infectar *vt* to infect.
  ◆ **infectarse** *vpr* to become infected.

infecundo, da *adj* [tierra] infertile.

infeliz *adj* **- 1.** [desgraciado] unhappy **- 2.** *fig* [ingenuo] gullible.

inferior ◇ *adj*: ~ **(a)** [en espacio, cantidad] lower (than); [en calidad] inferior (to); **una cifra ~ a 100** a figure under *o* below 100. ◇ *mf* inferior.

inferioridad *f* inferiority.

inferir *vt* **- 1.** [deducir]: ~ **(de)** to deduce (from), to infer (from) **- 2.** [ocasionar - herida] to inflict; [- mal] to cause.

infernal *adj* lit & fig infernal.

infestar *vt* to infest; [suj: carteles, propaganda etc] to be plastered across.

infidelidad *f* [conyugal] infidelity; [a la patria, un amigo] disloyalty.

infiel ◇ *adj* **- 1.** [desleal - cónyuge] unfaithful; [- amigo] disloyal **- 2.** [inexacto] inaccurate, unfaithful. ◇ *mf* RELIG infidel.

infiernillo *m* portable stove.

infierno *m* lit & fig hell; **¡vete al ~!** go to hell!

infiltrado, da *m,f* infiltrator.

infiltrar *vt* [inyectar] to inject.
  ◆ **infiltrarse en** *vpr* to infiltrate.

ínfimo, ma *adj* [calidad, categoría] extremely low; [precio] giveaway; [importancia] minimal.

infinidad *f*: **una ~ de** an infinite number of; *fig* masses of; **en ~ de ocasiones** on countless occasions.

infinitivo *m* infinitive.

infinito, ta *adj* lit & fig infinite.
  ◆ **infinito** *m* infinity.

inflación *f* ECON inflation; ~ **subyacente** underlying inflation.

inflamable *adj* inflammable, flammable.
inflamación *f* MED inflammation.
inflamar *vt* MED & *fig* to inflame.
➡ **inflamarse** *vpr* [hincharse] to become inflamed.
inflamatorio, ria *adj* inflammatory.
inflar *vt* - **1.** [soplando] to blow up, to inflate; [con bomba] to pump up - **2.** *fig* [exagerar] to blow up, to exaggerate.
➡ **inflarse** *vpr*: ~ **se (de)** [hartarse] to stuff o.s. (with).
inflexible *adj* lit & *fig* inflexible.
inflexión *f* inflection.
infligir *vt* to inflict; [castigo] to impose.
influencia *f* influence; **bajo la** ~ **del alcohol** under the influence of alcohol.
influenciable *adj* easily influenced.
influenciar *vt* to influence, to have an influence on.
influir ◇ *vt* to influence. ◇ *vi* to have influence; ~ **en** to influence, to have an influence on.
influjo *m* influence.
influyente *adj* influential.
infografía *f* computer graphics.
información *f* - **1.** [conocimiento] information - **2.** [PRENS - noticias] **news** *(U)*; [- noticia] report, piece of news; [- sección] section, news *(U)*; ~ **meteorológica** weather report o forecast - **3.** [oficina] information office; [mostrador] information desk - **4.** TELECOM directory enquiries *(pl)* UK, directory assistance US.
informal *adj* - **1.** [desenfadado] informal - **2.** [irresponsable] unreliable.
informante *mf* informant, informer.
informar ◇ *vt*: ~ **a alguien (de)** to inform o tell sb (about). ◇ *vi* to inform; PRENS to report.
➡ **informarse** *vpr* to find out (details); ~ **se de** to find out about.
informático, ca ◇ *adj* computer *(antes de sust)*. ◇ *m,f* [persona] computer expert.
➡ **informática** *f* [ciencia] information technology, computing.
informativo, va *adj* - **1.** [instructivo, esclarecedor] informative - **2.** [que da noticias] news *(antes de sust)*; [que da información] information *(antes de sust)*.
➡ **informativo** *m* news (bulletin).
informatizar *vt* to computerize.
informe ◇ *adj* shapeless. ◇ *m* - **1.** [gen] report - **2.** DER plea.
➡ **informes** *mpl* [gen] information *(U)*; [sobre comportamiento] report *(sg)*; [para un empleo] references.
infortunio *m* misfortune, bad luck *(U)*.
infracción *f* infringement; [de circulación] offence.

infraestructura *f* [de organización] infrastructure.
in fraganti *loc adv* red-handed, in the act; **coger a alguien** ~ to catch sb red-handed o in the act.
infrahumano, na *adj* subhuman.
infranqueable *adj* impassable; *fig* insurmountable.
infrarrojo, ja *adj* infrared.
infravalorar *vt* to undervalue, to underestimate.
infringir *vt* [quebrantar] to infringe, to break.
infundado, da *adj* unfounded.
infundir *vt*: ~ **algo a alguien** to fill sb with sthg, to inspire sthg in sb; ~ **miedo** to inspire fear.
infusión *f* infusion; ~ **de manzanilla** camomile tea.
ingeniar *vt* to invent, to devise.
➡ **ingeniarse** *vpr*: **ingeniárselas** to manage, to engineer it; **ingeniárselas para hacer algo** to manage o contrive to do sthg.
ingeniería *f* engineering.
ingeniero, ra *m,f* engineer; ~ **de caminos, canales y puertos** civil engineer.
ingenio *m* - **1.** [inteligencia] ingenuity - **2.** [agudeza] wit, wittiness - **3.** [máquina] device; ~ **nuclear** nuclear device.
ingenioso, sa *adj* [inteligente] ingenious, clever; [agudo] witty.
ingenuidad *f* ingenuousness, naivety.
ingenuo, nua *adj* ingenuous, naive.
ingerencia = **injerencia**.
ingerir *vt* to consume, to ingest.
Inglaterra England.
ingle *f* groin.
inglés, esa ◇ *adj* English. ◇ *m,f* [persona] Englishman *(f* Englishwoman); **los ingleses** the English.
➡ **inglés** *m* [lengua] English.
ingratitud *f* ingratitude, ungratefulness.
ingrato, ta *adj* ungrateful; [trabajo] thankless.
ingrávido, da *adj* weightless.
ingrediente *m* ingredient.
ingresar ◇ *vt* BANCA to deposit, to pay in. ◇ *vi*: ~ **(en)** [asociación, ejército] to join; [hospital] to be admitted (to); [convento, universidad] to enter; ~ **cadáver** to be dead on arrival.
ingreso *m* - **1.** [gen] entry; [en asociación, ejército] joining; [en hospital, universidad] admission - **2.** BANCA deposit; **hacer un** ~ to make a deposit.
➡ **ingresos** *mpl* - **1.** [sueldo etc] income *(U)* - **2.** [recaudación] revenue *(U)*.
inhabilitar *vt* to disqualify.
inhabitable *adj* uninhabitable.

inhabitado, da *adj* uninhabited.
inhalador *m* inhaler.
inhalar *vt* to inhale.
inherente *adj*: ~ **(a)** inherent (in).
inhibir *vt* to inhibit.
◆ **inhibirse de** *vpr* [gen] to keep out of, to stay away from; [responsabilidades] to shirk.
inhóspito, ta *adj* inhospitable.
inhumano, na *adj* [despiadado] inhuman; [desconsiderado] inhumane.
iniciación *f* **-1.** [gen] initiation **- 2.** [de suceso, curso] start, beginning.
inicial *adj* & *f* initial.
inicializar *vt* INFORM to initialize.
iniciar *vt* [gen] to start, to initiate; [debate, discusión] to start off.
iniciativa *f* initiative; **no tener** ~ to lack initiative; **por** ~ **propia** on one's own initiative; ~ **de paz** peace initiative.
inicio *m* start, beginning.
inigualable *adj* unrivalled.
ininteligible *adj* unintelligible.
ininterrumpido, da *adj* uninterrupted, continuous.
injerencia, ingerencia *f* interference, meddling.
injerir *vt* to introduce, to insert.
◆ **injerirse** *vpr* [entrometerse]: ~**se (en)** to interfere (in), to meddle (in).
injertar *vt* to graft.
injerto *m* graft.
injuria *f* [insulto] insult, abuse *(U)*; [agravio] offence; DER slander.
injuriar *vt* [insultar] to insult, to abuse; [agraviar] to offend; DER to slander.
injurioso, sa *adj* insulting, abusive; DER slanderous.
injusticia *f* injustice; ¡**es una** ~! that's unfair!; **cometer una** ~ **con alguien** to do sb an injustice.
injustificado, da *adj* unjustified.
injusto, ta *adj* unfair, unjust.
inmadurez *f* immaturity.
inmaduro, ra *adj* [persona] immature.
inmediaciones *fpl* [de localidad] surrounding area *(sg)*; [de lugar, casa] vicinity *(sg)*.
inmediatamente *adv* immediately, at once.
inmediato, ta *adj* **- 1.** [gen] immediate; **de** ~ immediately, at once **- 2.** [contiguo] next, adjoining.
inmejorable *adj* unbeatable, that cannot be bettered.
inmensidad *f* [grandeza] immensity.
inmenso, sa *adj* [gen] immense.
inmersión *f* immersion; [de submarinista] dive; ~ **lingüística** language immersion.

inmerso, sa *adj*: ~ **(en)** immersed (in).
inmigración *f* immigration.
inmigrante *mf* immigrant.
inmigrar *vi* to immigrate.
inminente *adj* imminent, impending.
inmiscuirse *vpr*: ~ **(en)** to interfere o meddle (in).
inmobiliario, ria *adj* property *(antes de sust)*, real estate US *(antes de sust)*.
◆ **inmobiliaria** *f* [agencia] estate agency UK, real estate agent US.
inmoral *adj* immoral.
inmortal *adj* immortal.
inmortalizar *vt* to immortalize.
inmóvil *adj* motionless, still; [coche, tren] stationary.
inmovilizar *vt* to immobilize.
inmueble ◇ *adj*: **bienes** ~**s** real estate *(U)*. ◇ *m* [edificio] building.
inmundicia *f* [suciedad] filth, filthiness; [basura] rubbish.
inmundo, da *adj* filthy, dirty.
inmune *adj* MED immune.
inmunidad *f* immunity.
inmunizar *vt* to immunize.
inmutar *vt* to upset, to perturb.
◆ **inmutarse** *vpr* to get upset, to be perturbed; **ni se inmutó** he didn't bat an eyelid.
innato, ta *adj* innate.
innecesario, ria *adj* unnecessary.
innoble *adj* ignoble.
innovación *f* innovation.
innovador, ra ◇ *adj* innovative, innovatory. ◇ *m,f* innovator.
innovar *vt* [método, técnica] to improve on.
innumerable *adj* countless, innumerable.
inocencia *f* innocence.
inocentada *f* practical joke, trick.
inocente *adj* **- 1.** [gen & DER] innocent; **declarar** ~ **a alguien** to find sb innocent o not guilty **- 2.** [ingenuo - persona] naive, innocent **- 3.** [sin maldad - persona] harmless.
inodoro, ra *adj* odourless.
◆ **inodoro** *m* toilet UK, washroom US.
inofensivo, va *adj* inoffensive, harmless.
inolvidable *adj* unforgettable.
inoperante *adj* ineffective.
inoportuno, na, importuno, na *adj* **- 1.** [en mal momento] inopportune, untimely **- 2.** [molesto] inconvenient **- 3.** [inadecuado] inappropriate.
inoxidable *adj* rustproof; [acero] stainless.
inquebrantable *adj* unshakeable; [lealtad] unswerving.
inquietar *vt* to worry, to trouble.
◆ **inquietarse** *vpr* to worry, to get anxious.
inquieto, ta *adj* **- 1.** [preocupado]: ~ **(por)**

worried o anxious (about) - **2.** [agitado, emprendedor] restless.

inquietud f [preocupación] worry, anxiety.

inquilino, na m,f tenant.

inquirir vt culto to inquire into, to investigate.

inquisición f [indagación] inquiry, investigation.

➡ **Inquisición** f [tribunal] Inquisition.

inquisidor, ra adj inquisitive, inquiring.

➡ **inquisidor** m inquisitor.

insaciable adj insatiable.

insalubre adj culto insalubrious, unhealthy.

Insalud (abrev de **Instituto Nacional de la Salud**) m ≃ NHS UK, ≃ Medicaid US.

insatisfecho, cha adj - **1.** [descontento] dissatisfied - **2.** [no saciado] not full, unsatisfied.

inscribir vt - **1.** [grabar]: ~ algo (en) to engrave o inscribe sthg (on) - **2.** [apuntar]: ~ algo/a alguien (en) to register sthg/sb (on).

➡ **inscribirse** vpr: ~se (en) [gen] to enrol (on); [asociación] to enrol (with); [concurso] to enter.

inscripción f - **1.** EDUC registration, enrolment; [en censo, registro] registration; [en partido etc] enrolment; [en concursos etc] entry - **2.** [escrito] inscription.

inscrito, ta pp ▷ inscribir.

insecticida m insecticide.

insecto m insect.

inseguridad f - **1.** [falta de confianza] insecurity - **2.** [duda] uncertainty - **3.** [peligro] lack of safety.

inseguro, ra adj - **1.** [sin confianza] insecure - **2.** [dudoso] uncertain - **3.** [peligroso] unsafe.

inseminación f insemination; ~ artificial artificial insemination.

insensatez f foolishness, senselessness; hacer/decir una ~ to do/say sthg foolish.

insensato, ta ◇ adj foolish, senseless. ◇ m,f fool.

insensibilidad f [emocional] insensitivity; [física] numbness.

insensible adj - **1.** [indiferente]: ~ (a) insensitive (to) - **2.** [entumecido] numb - **3.** [imperceptible] imperceptible.

insertar vt [gen & COMPUT]: ~ (en) to insert (into).

inservible adj useless, unserviceable.

insidioso, sa adj malicious.

insigne adj distinguished, illustrious.

insignia f - **1.** [distintivo] badge; MIL insignia - **2.** [bandera] flag, banner.

insignificante adj insignificant.

insinuar vt: ~ algo (a) to hint at o insinuate sthg (to).

➡ **insinuarse** vpr - **1.** [amorosamente]: ~se (a) to make advances (to) - **2.** [asomar]: ~se detrás de algo to peep out from behind sthg.

insípido, da adj lit & fig insipid.

insistencia f insistence.

insistir vi: ~ (en) to insist (on).

insociable adj unsociable.

insolación f MED sunstroke (U); coger una ~ to get sunstroke.

insolencia f insolence; hacer/decir una ~ to do/say sthg insolent.

insolente adj [descarado] insolent; [orgulloso] haughty.

insolidario, ria adj lacking in solidarity.

insólito, ta adj very unusual.

insoluble adj insoluble.

insolvencia f insolvency.

insolvente adj insolvent.

insomnio m insomnia, sleeplessness.

insondable adj lit & fig unfathomable.

insonorizar vt to soundproof.

insoportable adj unbearable, intolerable.

insostenible adj untenable.

inspección f inspection; [policial] search; ~ ocular visual inspection.

inspeccionar vt to inspect; [suj: policía] to search.

inspector, ra m,f inspector; ~ de aduanas customs official; ~ de Hacienda tax inspector.

inspiración f - **1.** [gen] inspiration - **2.** [respiración] inhalation, breath.

inspirar vt - **1.** [gen] to inspire - **2.** [respirar] to inhale, to breathe in.

➡ **inspirarse** vpr: ~se (en) to be inspired (by).

instalación f - **1.** [gen] installation; ~ eléctrica wiring - **2.** [de gente] settling.

➡ **instalaciones** fpl [deportivas etc] facilities.

instalar vt - **1.** [montar - antena etc] to instal, to fit; [- local, puesto etc] to set up - **2.** [situar - objeto] to place; [- gente] to settle.

➡ **instalarse** vpr [establecerse]: ~se en to settle (down) in; [nueva casa] to move into.

instancia f - **1.** [solicitud] application (form) - **2.** [ruego] request; a ~s de at the request o bidding of; en última ~ as a last resort.

instantáneo, a adj - **1.** [momentáneo] momentary - **2.** [rápido] instantaneous.

➡ **instantánea** f snapshot, snap.

instante m moment; a cada ~ all the time, constantly; al ~ instantly, immediately; en un ~ in a second.

instar vt: ~ a alguien a que haga algo to urge o press sb to do sthg.

instaurar vt to establish, to set up.

instigar vt: ~ a alguien (a que haga algo)

to instigate sb (to do sthg); ~ a algo to incite to sthg.

instintivo, va *adj* instinctive.

instinto *m* instinct; **por** ~ instinctively; ~ **maternal** maternal instinct; ~ **de supervivencia** survival instinct.

institución *f* - 1. [gen] institution; **ser una** ~ *fig* to be an institution - 2. [de ley, sistema] introduction; [de organismo] establishment; [de premio] foundation.

instituir *vt* [fundar - gobierno] to establish; [- premio, sociedad] to found; [- sistema, reglas] to introduce.

instituto *m* - 1. [corporación] institute - 2. EDUC : ~ **(de Enseñanza Secundaria)** state secondary school; ~ **de Formación Profesional** ≃ technical college.

➤ **instituto de belleza** *m* beauty salon.

institutriz *f* governess.

instrucción *f* - 1. [conocimientos] education; [docencia] instruction - 2. [DER - investigación] preliminary investigation; [- curso del proceso] proceedings *(pl)*.

➤ **instrucciones** *fpl* [de uso] instructions.

instructivo, va *adj* [gen] instructive; [juguete, película] educational.

instructor, ra ◇ *adj* training, instructing. ◇ *m,f* [gen] instructor, teacher; DEP coach.

instruido, da *adj* educated.

instruir *vt* [enseñar] to instruct.

instrumental *m* instruments *(pl)*.

instrumentista *mf* - 1. MÚS instrumentalist - 2. MED surgeon's assistant.

instrumento *m* - 1. MÚS & *fig* instrument - 2. [herramienta] tool, instrument.

insubordinado, da *adj* insubordinate.

insubordinar *vt* to incite to rebellion.

➤ **insubordinarse** *vpr* to rebel.

insubstancial = insustancial.

insuficiencia *f* - 1. [escasez] lack, shortage - 2. MED failure, insufficiency.

insuficiente ◇ *adj* insufficient. ◇ *m* [nota] fail.

insufrible *adj* intolerable, insufferable.

insular *adj* insular, island *(antes de sust)*.

insulina *f* insulin.

insulso, sa *adj* lit & *fig* bland, insipid.

insultar *vt* to insult.

insulto *m* insult.

insumiso, sa ◇ *adj* rebellious. ◇ *m,f* [gen] rebel; MIL *person who refuses to do military or community service*.

insuperable *adj* - 1. [inmejorable] unsurpassable - 2. [sin solución] insurmountable, insuperable.

insurgente *adj* insurgent.

insurrección *f* insurrection, revolt.

insustancial, insubstancial *adj* insubstantial.

intachable *adj* irreproachable.

intacto, ta *adj* untouched; *fig* intact.

integral *adj* - 1. [total] total, complete - 2. [sin refinar - pan, harina, pasta] wholemeal; [- arroz] brown.

integrante ◇ *adj* integral, constituent; **estado** ~ **de la CE** member state of the EC. ◇ *mf* member.

integrar *vt* - 1. [gen & MAT] to integrate - 2. [componer] to make up.

➤ **integrarse** *vpr* to integrate.

integridad *f* [gen] integrity; [totalidad] wholeness.

íntegro, gra *adj* - 1. [completo] whole, entire; [versión etc] unabridged - 2. [honrado] honourable.

intelecto *m* intellect.

intelectual *adj* & *mf* intellectual.

inteligencia *f* intelligence; ~ **artificial** INFORM artificial intelligence; ~ **emocional** emotional intelligence.

inteligente *adj* [gen & INFORM] intelligent.

inteligible *adj* intelligible.

intemperie *f*: **a la** ~ in the open air.

intempestivo, va *adj* [clima, comentario] harsh; [hora] ungodly, unearthly; [proposición, visita] inopportune.

intención *f* intention; **con** ~ intentionally; **sin** ~ without meaning to; **tener la** ~ **de** to intend to; **tener malas intenciones** to be up to no good; **buena/mala** ~ good/bad intentions *(pl)*; **segunda** ~ underhandedness, duplicity; ~ **de voto** voting intention; **de buenas intenciones está el infierno lleno** *proverb* the road to hell is paved with good intentions.

intencionado, da *adj* intentional, deliberate; **bien** ~ [acción] well-meant; [persona] well-meaning; **mal** ~ [acción] ill-meant, ill-intentioned; [persona] malevolent.

intensidad *f* [gen] intensity; [de lluvia] heaviness; [de luz, color] brightness; [de amor] passion, strength.

intensificar *vt* to intensify.

➤ **intensificarse** *vpr* to intensify.

intensivo, va *adj* intensive.

intenso, sa *adj* [gen] intense; [lluvia] heavy; [luz, color] bright; [amor] passionate, strong.

intentar *vt* : ~ **(hacer algo)** to try (to do sthg).

intento *m* [tentativa] attempt; [intención] intention; ~ **de golpe/robo** attempted coup/robbery; ~ **de suicidio** suicide attempt.

interactivo, va *adj* INFORM interactive.

intercalar *vt* to insert, to put in.

intercambiable *adj* interchangeable.

intercambio *m* exchange; **hacer un ~** to go on an exchange programme; **~ comercial** trade.

interceder *vi*: **~ (por alguien)** to intercede (on sb's behalf).

interceptar *vt* **-1.** [detener] to intercept **-2.** [obstruir] to block.

intercesión *f* intercession.

interés *m* **-1.** [gen & FIN] interest; **de ~** interesting; **esperar algo con ~** to await sthg with interest; **tener ~ en** *o* **por** to be interested in; **tengo ~ en que venga pronto** it's in my interest that he should come soon; **~ acumulado** accrued interest; **~ compuesto** compound interest; **~ simple** simple interest; **intereses creados** vested interests **-2.** [egoísmo] self-interest, selfishness; **por ~ out** of selfishness.

interesado, da ◇ *adj* **-1.** [gen]: **~ (en** *o* **por)** interested (in) **-2.** [egoísta] selfish, self-interested. ◇ *m,f* [deseoso] interested person; **los ~s** those interested.

interesante *adj* interesting; **hacerse el/la ~** to try to draw attention to oneself.

interesar *vi* to interest; **le interesa el arte** she's interested in art.

◆ **interesarse** *vpr*: **~se (en** *o* **por)** to take an interest (in), to be interested (in); **se interesó por tu salud** she asked after your health.

interfaz *f* INFORM interface.

interferencia *f* interference.

interferir ◇ *vt* **-1.** RADIO, TELECOM & TV to jam **-2.** [interponerse] to interfere with. ◇ *vi*: **~ (en)** to interfere (in).

interfono *m* intercom.

interino, na ◇ *adj* [gen] temporary; [presidente, director etc] acting; [gobierno] interim. ◇ *m,f* [gen] stand-in; [médico, juez] locum; [profesor] supply teacher.

◆ **interina** *f* [asistenta] cleaning lady.

interior ◇ *adj* **-1.** [gen] inside, inner; [patio, jardín etc] interior, inside; [habitación, vida] inner **-2.** POLÍT domestic **-3.** GEOGR inland. ◇ *m* **-1.** [parte de dentro] inside, interior **-2.** GEOGR interior, inland area **-3.** [de una persona] inner self, heart; **en mi ~** deep down.

◆ **interiores** *fpl* CIN interiors.

interiorismo *m* interior design.

interiorizar *vt* to internalize; [sentimientos] to bottle up.

interjección *f* interjection.

interlocutor, ra *m,f* interlocutor, speaker; **su ~** the person she was speaking to.

intermediario, ria *m,f* [gen] intermediary; COM middleman; [en disputas] mediator.

intermedio, dia *adj* **-1.** [etapa] intermediate, halfway; [calidad] average; [tamaño] medium **-2.** [tiempo] intervening; [espacio] in between.

◆ **intermedio** *m* [gen & TEATR] interval; CIN intermission.

interminable *adj* endless, interminable.

intermitente ◇ *adj* intermittent. ◇ *m* indicator.

internacional *adj* international.

internado, da *adj* [en manicomio] confined; [en colegio] boarding; POLÍT interned.

◆ **internado** *m* [colegio] boarding school.

internar *vt*: **~ (en)** [internado] to send to boarding school (at); [manicomio] to commit (to); [campo de concentración] to intern (in).

◆ **internarse** *vpr*: **~se (en)** [un lugar] to go *o* penetrate deep (into); [un tema] to become deeply involved (in).

internauta *mf* Internet user.

Internet *f*: **(la) ~** the Internet; **en ~** on the Internet.

interno, na ◇ *adj* **-1.** [gen] internal; POLÍT domestic **-2.** [alumno] boarding. ◇ *m,f* **-1.** [alumno] boarder **-2.** ▷ **médico -3.** [preso] prisoner, inmate.

interpelación *f* formal question.

interpolar *vt* to interpolate, to put in.

interponer *vt* **-1.** [gen] to interpose, to put in **-2.** DER to lodge, to make.

◆ **interponerse** *vpr* to intervene.

interpretación *f* **-1.** [explicación] interpretation; **mala ~** misinterpretation **-2.** [artística] performance **-3.** [traducción] interpreting.

interpretar *vt* **-1.** [gen] to interpret **-2.** [artísticamente] to perform.

intérprete *mf* **-1.** [traductor & INFORM] interpreter **-2.** [artista] performer.

interpuesto, ta *pp* ▷ **interponer**.

interrogación *f* **-1.** [acción] questioning **-2.** [signo] question mark.

interrogante *m o f* [incógnita] question mark.

interrogar *vt* [gen] to question; [con amenazas etc] to interrogate.

interrogatorio *m* [gen] questioning; [con amenazas] interrogation.

interrumpir *vt* **-1.** [gen] to interrupt **-2.** [discurso, trabajo] to break off; [viaje, vacaciones] to cut short.

interrupción *f* **-1.** [gen] interruption; **~ (voluntaria) del embarazo** termination of pregnancy **-2.** [de discurso, trabajo] breaking-off; [de viaje, vacaciones] cutting-short.

interruptor *m* switch.

intersección *f* intersection.

interurbano, na *adj* inter-city; TELECOM long-distance.

intervalo *m* **-1.** [gen & MÚS] interval; [de espacio] space, gap; **a ~s** at intervals **-2.** [duración]: **en el ~ de un mes** in the space of a month.

intervención *f* **-1.** [gen] intervention **-2.** [discurso] speech; [interpelación] contribution **-3.** COM auditing **-4.** MED operation **-5.** TELECOM tapping.

intervenir ⋄ *vi* **-1.** [participar]: **~ (en)** [gen] to take part (in); [pelea] to get involved (in); [discusión etc] to make a contribution (to) **-2.** [dar un discurso] to make a speech **-3.** [interferir]: **~ (en)** to intervene (in) **-4.** MED to operate. ⋄ *vt* **-1.** MED to operate on **-2.** TELECOM to tap **-3.** [incautar] to seize **-4.** COM to audit.

interventor, ra *m,f* COM auditor.

interviú *(pl* **interviús)** *f* interview.

intestino, na *adj* internecine.

➡ **intestino** *m* intestine.

intimar *vi*: **~ (con)** to become intimate *o* very friendly (with).

intimidad *f* **-1.** [vida privada] private life; [privacidad] privacy; **en la ~** in private **-2.** [amistad] intimacy.

íntimo, ma ⋄ *adj* **-1.** [vida, fiesta] private; [ambiente, restaurante] intimate **-2.** [relación, amistad] close **-3.** [sentimiento etc] innermost. ⋄ *m,f* close friend.

intolerable *adj* intolerable, unacceptable; [dolor, ruido] unbearable.

intolerancia *f* [actitud] intolerance.

intoxicación *f* poisoning *(U)*; **~ alimenticia** food poisoning; **~ etílica** alcohol poisoning.

intoxicar *vt* to poison.

intranquilizar *vt* to worry, to make uneasy.

➡ **intranquilizarse** *vpr* to get worried.

intranquilo, la *adj* [preocupado] worried, uneasy; [nervioso] restless.

intranscendente = **intrascendente**.

intransferible *adj* non-transferable, untransferable.

intransigente *adj* intransigent.

intransitable *adj* impassable.

intrascendente, intranscendente *adj* insignificant, unimportant.

intrépido, da *adj* intrepid.

intriga *f* **-1.** [curiosidad] curiosity; **de ~** suspense *(antes de sust)* **-2.** [maquinación] intrigue **-3.** [trama] plot.

intrigar *vt & vi* to intrigue.

intrincado, da *adj* [problema etc] intricate.

intríngulis *m inv fam*: **tiene su ~** it is quite tricky.

intrínseco, ca *adj* intrinsic.

introducción *f*: **~ (a)** introduction (to).

introducir *vt* **-1.** [meter - llave, carta etc] to put in, to insert **-2.** [mercancías etc] to bring in, to introduce **-3.** [dar a conocer]: **~ a alguien en** to introduce sb to; **~ algo en** to introduce *o* bring sthg to.

➡ **introducirse** *vpr*: **~se en** to get into.

introductorio, ria *adj* introductory.

intromisión *f* meddling, interfering.

introspectivo, va *adj* introspective.

introvertido, da *adj & m,f* introvert.

intruso, sa *m,f* intruder; **~ informático** hacker.

intuición *f* intuition.

intuir *vt* to know by intuition, to sense.

intuitivo, va *adj* intuitive.

inundación *f* flood, flooding *(U)*.

inundar *vt* to flood; *fig* to inundate, to swamp.

➡ **inundarse** *vpr* to flood; **~se de** *fig* to be inundated *o* swamped with.

inusitado, da *adj* uncommon, rare.

inútil *adj* **-1.** [gen] useless; [intento, esfuerzo] unsuccessful, vain **-2.** [inválido] disabled.

inutilidad *f* [gen] uselessness; [falta de sentido] pointlessness.

inutilizar *vt* [gen] to make unusable; [máquinas, dispositivos] to disable, to put out of action.

invadir *vt* to invade; **la invade la tristeza** she's overcome by sadness.

invalidez *f* **-1.** MED disablement, disability; **~ permanente/temporal** permanent/temporary disability **-2.** DER invalidity.

inválido, da ⋄ *adj* **-1.** MED disabled **-2.** DER invalid. ⋄ *m,f* invalid, disabled person; **los ~s** the disabled.

invariable *adj* invariable.

invasión *f* invasion.

invasor, ra ⋄ *adj* invading. ⋄ *m,f* invader.

invención *f* invention.

inventar *vt* [gen] to invent; [narración, falsedades] to make up.

➡ **inventarse** *vpr* to make up.

inventario *m* inventory; **hacer el ~** COM to do the stocktaking.

inventiva *f* inventiveness.

invento *m* invention.

inventor, ra *m,f* inventor.

invernadero, invernáculo *m* greenhouse.

invernar *vi* [pasar el invierno] to (spend the) winter; [hibernar] to hibernate.

inverosímil *adj* unlikely, improbable.

inversión *f* **-1.** [del orden] inversion **-2.** [de dinero, tiempo] investment.

inverso, sa *adj* opposite, inverse; **a la inversa** the other way round; **en orden ~** in reverse order.

inversor, ra *m,f* COM & FIN investor.
invertebrado, da *adj* invertebrate.
◆ **invertebrado** *m* invertebrate.
invertido, da *adj* **- 1.** [al revés] reversed, inverted; [sentido, dirección] opposite **- 2.** [homosexual] homosexual.
invertir *vt* **- 1.** [gen] to reverse; [poner boca abajo] to turn upside down, to invert **- 2.** [dinero, tiempo, esfuerzo] to invest **- 3.** [tardar - tiempo] to spend.
investidura *f* investiture.
investigación *f* **- 1.** [estudio] research; ~ **y desarrollo** research and development **- 2.** [indagación] investigation, inquiry; ~ **judicial** judicial inquiry.
investigador, ra *m,f* **- 1.** [estudioso] researcher **- 2.** [detective] investigator.
investigar <> *vt* **- 1.** [estudiar] to research **- 2.** [indagar] to investigate. <> *vi* **- 1.** [estudiar] to do research **- 2.** [indagar] to investigate.
investir *vt*: ~ **a alguien con algo** to invest sb with sthg.
inveterado, da *adj* deep-rooted.
inviable *adj* impractical, unviable.
invidente *mf* blind *o* sightless person; **los** ~**s** the blind.
invierno *m* winter; ~ **nuclear** nuclear winter.
invisible *adj* invisible.
invitación *f* invitation.
invitado, da *m,f* guest.
invitar <> *vt* **- 1.** [convidar]: ~ **a alguien (a algo/a hacer algo)** to invite sb (to sthg/to do sthg) **- 2.** [pagar]: **os invito** it's my treat, this one's on me; **te invito a cenar fuera** I'll take you out for dinner. <> *vi* to pay; **invita la casa** it's on the house.
◆ **invitar a** *vi fig* [incitar]: ~ **a algo** to encourage sthg; **la lluvia invita a quedarse en casa** the rain makes you want to stay at home.
in vitro *loc adv* **- 1.** [de probeta] in vitro **- 2.** ➭ **fecundación**.
invocar *vt* to invoke.
involucrar *vt*: ~ **a alguien (en)** to involve sb (in).
◆ **involucrarse** *vpr*: ~**se (en)** to get involved (in).
involuntario, ria *adj* [espontáneo] involuntary; [sin querer] unintentional.
inyección *f* injection.
inyectar *vt* to inject.
◆ **inyectarse** *vpr* [drogas] to take drugs intravenously; ~**se algo** to inject o.s. with sthg.
iodo = **yodo**.
ion *m* ion.
IPC (*abrev de* **índice de precios al consumo**)

m Spanish cost of living index, ≃ RPI *UK*.
ir *vi* **- 1.** [gen] to go; ~ **hacia el sur/al cine** to go south/to the cinema; ~ **en autobús/coche** to go by bus/car; ~ **en avión** to fly; ~ **en bicicleta** to ride; ~ **andando** to go on foot, to walk; **¡vamos!** let's go! **- 2.** [expresa duración gradual]: ~ **haciendo algo** to be (gradually) doing sthg; **va anocheciendo** it's getting dark; **voy mejorando mi estilo** I'm working on improving my style **- 3.** [expresa intención, opinión]: ~ **a hacer algo** to be going to do sthg; **voy a decírselo a tu padre** I'm going to tell your father **- 4.** [cambiar]: ~ **a mejor/peor** *etc* to get better/worse *etc* **- 5.** [funcionar] to work; **la manivela va floja** the crank is loose; **la televisión no va** the television isn't working **- 6.** [desenvolverse] to go; **le va bien en su nuevo trabajo** things are going well for him in his new job; **su negocio va mal** his business is going badly; **¿cómo te va?** how are you doing? **- 7.** [vestir]: ~ **en/con** to wear; **iba en camisa y con corbata** he was wearing a shirt and tie; ~ **de azul/de uniforme** to be dressed in blue/in uniform **- 8.** [tener aspecto físico] to look like; **iba hecho un pordiosero** he looked like a beggar **- 9.** [vacaciones, tratamiento]: ~ **le bien a alguien** to do sb good **- 10.** [ropa]: ~ **le (bien) a alguien** to suit sb; ~ **con algo** to go with sthg **- 11.** [comentario, indirecta]: ~ **con** *o* **por alguien** to be meant for sb, to be aimed at sb **- 12.** *loc*: **fue y dijo que ...** he went and said that ...; **ni me va ni me viene** *fam* I don't care; **¡qué va!** you must be joking!; **ser el no va más** to be the ultimate.
◆ **ir de** *vi* **- 1.** [película, novela] to be about **- 2.** *fig* [persona] to think o.s.; **va de listo** he thinks he's clever.
◆ **ir por** *vi* **- 1.** [buscar]: ~ **por algo/alguien** to go and get sthg/sb, to go and fetch sthg/sb **- 2.** [alcanzar]: **va por el cuarto vaso de vino** he's already on his fourth glass of wine; **vamos por la mitad de la asignatura** we covered about half the subject.
◆ **irse** *vpr* **- 1.** [marcharse] to go, to leave; ~**se a** to go to; **¡vete!** go away! **- 2.** [gastarse, desaparecer] to go **- 3.** *loc*: ~**se abajo** [edificio] to fall down; [negocio] to collapse; [planes] to fall through.
ira *f* anger, rage.
iracundo, da *adj* angry, irate; [irascible] irascible.
Irán: (el) ~ Iran.
iraní (*pl* **iraníes**) *adj & mf* Iranian.
Iraq: (el) ~ Iraq.
iraquí (*pl* **iraquíes**) *adj & mf* Iraqi.
irascible *adj* irascible.
iris *m inv* iris.
Irlanda Ireland.

irlandés, esa ◇ *adj* Irish. ◇ *m,f* [persona] Irishman (*f* Irishwoman); **los irlandeses** the Irish.
  ● **irlandés** *m* [lengua] Irish.
ironía *f* irony.
irónico, ca *adj* ironic, ironical.
ironizar ◇ *vt* to ridicule. ◇ *vi*: ~ **(sobre)** to be ironical (about).
IRPF (*abrev de* **Impuesto sobre la Renta de las Personas Físicas**) *m* Spanish personal income tax.
irracional *adj* irrational.
irradiar *vt lit & fig* to radiate.
irreal *adj* unreal.
irreconciliable *adj* irreconcilable.
irreconocible *adj* unrecognizable.
irrecuperable *adj* irretrievable.
irreflexión *f* rashness.
irreflexivo, va *adj* rash.
irrefutable *adj* irrefutable.
irregular *adj* [gen] irregular; [terreno, superficie] uneven.
irrelevante *adj* irrelevant.
irremediable *adj* irremediable.
irreparable *adj* irreparable.
irresistible *adj* irresistible.
irresoluto, ta *adj culto* irresolute.
irrespetuoso, sa *adj* disrespectful.
irrespirable *adj* unbreathable.
irresponsable *adj* irresponsible.
irreverente *adj* irreverent.
irreversible *adj* irreversible.
irrevocable *adj* irrevocable.
irrigar *vt* to irrigate.
irrisorio, ria *adj* - **1.** [excusa etc] laughable, derisory - **2.** [precio etc] ridiculously low.
irritable *adj* irritable.
irritar *vt* to irritate.
  ● **irritarse** *vpr* - **1.** [enfadarse] to get angry *o* annoyed - **2.** [suj: piel etc] to become irritated.
irrompible *adj* unbreakable.
irrupción *f* bursting in.
isla *f* island.
islam *m* Islam.
islamismo *m* Islam.
islandés, esa ◇ *adj* Icelandic. ◇ *m,f* [persona] Icelander.
  ● **islandés** *m* [lengua] Icelandic.
Islandia Iceland.
isleño, ña ◇ *adj* island (*antes de sust*). ◇ *m,f* islander.
islote *m* small, rocky island.
Israel Israel.
israelí (*pl* **israelíes**) *adj & mf* Israeli.
istmo *m* isthmus.
Italia Italy.
italiano, na *adj & m,f* Italian.

● **italiano** *m* [lengua] Italian.
itálico, ca *adj* ▷ **letra**.
itinerante *adj* itinerant; [embajador] roving.
itinerario *m* route, itinerary.
ITV (*abrev de* **inspección técnica de vehículos**) *f* annual technical inspection for motor vehicles of ten years or more, ≃ MOT *UK*.
IVA (*abrev de* **impuesto sobre el valor añadido**) *m* VAT.
izar *vt* to raise, to hoist.
izda (*abrev de* **izquierda**) L, l.
izquierda *f* ▷ **izquierdo**.
izquierdo, da *adj* left.
  ● **izquierda** *f* - **1.** [lado] left; **a la izquierda (de)** on *o* to the left (of); **girar a la izquierda** to turn left - **2.** [mano] left hand - **3.** POLÍT left (wing); **de izquierdas** left-wing.

J

j, J *f* [letra] j, J.
ja *interj* ha!
jabalí (*pl* **jabalíes**) *mf* wild boar.
jabalina *f* DEP javelin.
jabón *m* soap; ~ **de afeitar/tocador** shaving/toilet soap.
jabonar *vt* to soap.
jabonera *f* soap dish.
jaca *f* [caballo pequeño] pony; [yegua] mare.
jacal *m Méx* hut.
jacinto *m* hyacinth.
jactarse *vpr*: ~ **(de)** to boast (about *o* of).
jadear *vi* to pant.
jadeo *m* panting.
jaguar (*pl* **jaguars**) *m* jaguar.
jaiba *f Andes, CAm, Carib, Méx* crayfish.
jalea *f* jelly; ~ **real** royal jelly.
jalear *vt* to cheer on.
jaleo *m* - **1.** *fam* [alboroto] row, rumpus - **2.** *fam* [lío] mess, confusion.
jalonar *vt* to stake *o* mark out; *fig* to mark.
Jamaica Jamaica.
jamás *adv* never; **no le he visto** ~ I've never seen him; **la mejor película que** ~ **se haya hecho** the best film ever made; ~ **de los jamases** never ever.
jamón *m* ham; ~ **(de) York** *o* **(en) dulce** boiled ham; ~ **serrano** cured ham, ≃ Parma ham.

Japón: (el) ~ Japan.
japonés, esa *adj* & *m*,*f* Japanese.
➡ **japonés** *m* [lengua] Japanese.
jaque *m*: ~ **mate** checkmate.
jaqueca *f* migraine.
jarabe *m* syrup; ~ **para la tos** cough mixture o syrup.
jarana *f* [juerga]: **estar/irse de** ~ to be/go out on the town.
jaranero, ra *adj* fond of partying.
jardín *m* garden, yard *US*; ~ **botánico** botanical garden; ~ **zoológico** zoological garden, zoo.
➡ **jardín de infancia** *m* kindergarten, nursery school.
jardinera ➪ **jardinero**.
jardinería *f* gardening.
jardinero, ra *m*,*f* gardener.
➡ **jardinera** *f* flowerpot stand.
jarra *f* **-1.** [para servir] jug **-2.** [para beber] tankard.
➡ **en jarras** *loc adv* [postura] hands on hips.
jarro *m* jug.
jarrón *m* vase.
jaspeado, da *adj* mottled, speckled.
jauja *f* *fam* paradise, heaven on earth.
jaula *f* cage.
jauría *f* pack of dogs.
jazmín *m* jasmine.
jazz [jas] *m* jazz.
JC (*abrev de* **Jesucristo**) JC.
je *interj* ha!
jeep [jip] (*pl* **jeeps**) *m* jeep.
jefa ➪ **jefe**.
jefatura *f* **-1.** [cargo] leadership **-2.** [organismo] headquarters, head office.
jefe, fa *m*,*f* [gen] boss; COM manager (*f* manageress); [líder] leader; [de tribu, ejército] chief; [de departamento etc] head; **en** ~ MIL in-chief; ~ **de cocina** chef; ~ **de estación** stationmaster; ~ **de Estado** head of state; ~ **de estudios** deputy head; ~ **de producción/ventas** production/sales manager; ~ **de redacción** editor-in-chief.
jengibre *m* ginger.
jeque *m* sheikh.
jerarquía *f* **-1.** [organización] hierarchy **-2.** [persona] high-ranking person, leader.
jerárquico, ca *adj* hierarchical.
jerez *m* sherry.
jerga *f* jargon; [argot] slang.
jeringuilla *f* syringe.
jeroglífico, ca *adj* hieroglyphic.
➡ **jeroglífico** *m* **-1.** [inscripción] hieroglyphic **-2.** [pasatiempo] rebus.
jerséi (*pl* **jerséis**), **jersey** (*pl* **jerseys**) *m* jumper, pullover.

Jerusalén Jerusalem.
jesuita *adj* & *m* Jesuit.
jesús *interj* [sorpresa] gosh!, good heavens!; [tras estornudo] bless you!
jet [jet] (*pl* **jets**) ⬦ *m* jet. ⬦ *f* ➪ **jet-set**.
jeta *f* *mfam* [cara] mug, face; **tener (mucha)** ~ to be a cheeky bugger.
jet-set ['jetset] *f* jet set.
Jibuti Djibuti.
jícara *f* *CAm, Méx, Ven* calabash cup.
jilguero *m* goldfinch.
jilipollada = **gilipollada**.
jilipollas = **gilipollas**.
jinete *mf* rider; [yóquey] jockey.
jinetera *f* *Cuba fam* prostitute.
jirafa *f* ZOOL giraffe.
jirón *m* [andrajo] shred, rag; **hecho jirones** in tatters.
jitomate *m* *CAm, Méx* tomato.
JJ OO (*abrev de* **juegos olímpicos**) *mpl* Olympic Games.
jockey ['jokei] = **yóquey**.
jocoso, sa *adj* jocular.
joda *f* *RP, Ven fam* [fastidio] pain in the arse *UK* o ass *US*; [juerga]: **irse de** ~ pissing about.
joder *vi* *vulg* **-1.** [copular] to fuck **-2.** [fastidiar] to be a pain in the arse; **¡no jodas!** [incredulidad] bollocks!, pull the other one!
jofaina *f* wash basin.
jolgorio *m* merrymaking.
jolín, jolines *interj* *fam*: **¡** ~ **!** hell!, Christ!
jondo ➪ **cante**.
jornada *f* **-1.** [de trabajo] working day; ~ **intensiva** working day from 8 to 3 with only a short lunch break; **media** ~ half day; ~ **partida** typical Spanish working day from 9 to 1 and 4 to 7 **-2.** [de viaje] day's journey **-3.** DEP round of matches, programme.
➡ **jornadas** *fpl* [conferencia] conference (*sg*).
jornal *m* day's wage.
jornalero, ra *m*,*f* day labourer.
joroba *f* hump.
jorobado, da ⬦ *adj* [con joroba] hunchbacked. ⬦ *m*,*f* hunchback.
jorongo *m* *Méx* **-1.** [manta] blanket **-2.** [poncho] poncho.
jota *f* **-1.** [baile] Aragonese folk song and dance **-2.** [loc]: **no entender** o **saber ni** ~ *fam* not to understand o know a thing.
joto *mf* *Méx fam despec* queer *UK*, faggot *US*.
joven ⬦ *adj* young. ⬦ *mf* young man (*f* young woman); **los jóvenes** young people.
jovial *adj* jovial, cheerful.
joya *f* jewel; *fig* gem.
joyería *f* **-1.** [tienda] jeweller's (shop) **-2.** [arte, comercio] jewellery.

joyero, ra *m,f* [persona] jeweller.
➤ **joyero** *m* [estuche] jewellery box.

juanete *m* bunion.

jubilación *f* [retiro] retirement; ~ **anticipada** early retirement; ~ **forzosa** compulsory retirement; ~ **voluntaria** voluntary retirement.

jubilado, da ◇ *adj* retired. ◇ *m,f* pensioner *UK*, senior citizen.

jubilar *vt*: ~ **a alguien (de)** to pension sb off *o* retire sb (from).
➤ **jubilarse** *vpr* to retire.

jubileo *m* RELIG jubilee.

júbilo *m* jubilation, joy.

judía *f* bean; ~ **blanca/verde** haricot/green bean.

judicial *adj* judicial.

judío, a ◇ *adj* Jewish. ◇ *m,f* Jew (*f* Jewess).

judo = **yudo**.

juega ⊳ **jugar**.

juego *m* - 1. [gen & DEP] game; [acción] play, playing; [con dinero] gambling; **estar/poner en** ~ to be/put at stake; ~ **de azar** game of chance; ~ **de manos** conjuring trick; ~ **de palabras** play on words, pun; ~ **sucio/limpio** foul/clean play; **descubrirle el** ~ **a alguien** to see through sb; **hacerle** *o* **seguirle el** ~ **a alguien** to play along with sb; **estar (en) fuera de** ~ DEP to be offside; *fig* not to know what's going on - 2. [conjunto de objetos] set; ~ **de herramientas** tool kit; ~ **de té/café** tea/coffee service; **hacer** ~ **(con)** to match.
➤ **Juegos Olímpicos** *mpl* Olympic Games.

juerga *f* fam rave-up, binge; **irse/estar de** ~ to go/be out on the town.

juerguista *mf* fam reveller.

jueves *m* inv Thursday; **Jueves Santo** Maundy Thursday; *ver también* **sábado**.

juez *mf* - 1. DER judge; ~ **de paz** Justice of the Peace - 2. [DEP - gen] judge; [- en atletismo] official; ~ **de línea** [fútbol] linesman; [rugby] touch judge; ~ **de salida** starter; ~ **de silla** umpire.

jugada *f* - 1. DEP period of play; [en tenis, ping-pong] rally; [en fútbol, rugby etc] move; [en ajedrez etc] move; [en billar] shot - 2. [treta] dirty trick; **hacer una mala** ~ **a alguien** to play a dirty trick on sb.

jugador, ra *m,f* [gen] player; [de juego de azar] gambler.

jugar ◇ *vi* - 1. [gen] to play; ~ **al ajedrez** to play chess; ~ **en un equipo** to play for a team; **te toca** ~ it's your turn *o* go; ~ **con algo** to play with sthg; ~ **contra alguien** to play (against) sb - 2. [con dinero]: ~ **(a)** to gamble (on); ~ **(a la Bolsa)** to speculate (on the Stock Exchange). ◇ *vt* - 1. [gen] to

play; [ficha, pieza] to move - 2. [dinero]: ~ **algo (a algo)** to gamble sthg (on sthg).
➤ **jugarse** *vpr* - 1. [apostarse] to bet - 2. [arriesgar] to risk - 3. *loc*: **jugársela a alguien** to play a dirty trick on sb.

jugarreta *f* fam dirty trick.

juglar *m* minstrel.

jugo *m* - 1. [gen & ANAT] juice; BOT sap; ~**s gástricos** gastric juices - 2. [interés] meat, substance; **sacar** ~ **a algo/alguien** to get the most out of sthg/sb.

jugoso, sa *adj* - 1. [con jugo] juicy - 2. *fig* [picante] juicy; [sustancioso] meaty, substantial.

juguete *m* lit & *fig* toy; **de** ~ toy *(antes de sust)*; ~ **educativo** educational toy.

juguetear *vi* to play (around); ~ **con algo** to toy with sthg.

juguetería *f* toy shop.

juguetón, ona *adj* playful.

juicio *m* - 1. DER trial; ~ **civil** civil action; ~ **criminal** criminal trial - 2. [sensatez] (sound) judgement; [cordura] sanity, reason; **estar/no estar en su (sano)** ~ to be/not to be in one's right mind; **perder el** ~ to lose one's reason, to go mad - 3. [opinión] opinion; **a mi** ~ in my opinion.
➤ **Juicio Final** *m*: **el Juicio Final** the Last Judgement.

juicioso, sa *adj* sensible, wise.

julepe *m* RP fam scare, fright.

julio *m* - 1. [mes] July; *ver también* **septiembre** - 2. FÍS joule.

junco *m* - 1. [planta] rush, reed - 2. [embarcación] junk.

jungla *f* jungle.

junio *m* June; *ver también* **septiembre**.

júnior (*pl* **júniors**) *adj* - 1. DEP under-21 - 2. [hijo] junior.

junta *f* - 1. [gen] committee; [de empresa, examinadores] board; ~ **directiva** board of directors; ~ **militar** military junta - 2. [reunión] meeting - 3. [juntura] joint; ~ **de culata** gasket.

juntar *vt* [gen] to put together; [fondos] to raise; [personas] to bring together.
➤ **juntarse** *vpr* - 1. [reunirse - personas] to get together; [- ríos, caminos] to meet - 2. [arrimarse] to draw *o* move closer - 3. [convivir] to live together.

junto, ta ◇ *adj* - 1. [gen] together - 2. [próximo] close together. ◇ *adv*: **todo** ~ [ocurrir etc] all at the same time; [escribirse] as one word.
➤ **junto a** *loc prep* - 1. [al lado de] next to - 2. [cerca de] right by, near.
➤ **junto con** *loc prep* together with.

juntura *f* joint.

Júpiter *m* Jupiter.

jurado, da *adj* -**1.** [declaración etc] sworn
-**2.** ⊳ **guarda**.
◆ **jurado** *m* -**1.** [tribunal] jury -**2.** [miembro] member of the jury.
juramento *m* -**1.** [promesa] oath -**2.** [blasfemia] oath, curse.
jurar ◇ *vt* to swear; [constitución etc] to
pledge allegiance to; **te lo juro** I promise, I
swear it; ~ **por ... que** to swear by ... that.
◇ *vi* [blasfemar] to swear; **tenérsela jurada
a alguien** to have it in for sb.
jurel *m* scad, horse mackerel.
jurídico, ca *adj* legal.
jurisdicción *f* jurisdiction.
jurisdiccional *adj* jurisdictional; [aguas]
territorial.
jurisprudencia *f* [ciencia] jurisprudence;
[casos previos] case law.
jurista *mf* jurist.
justa *f* HIST joust.
justamente *adv* -**1.** [con justicia] justly
-**2.** [exactamente] exactly.
justicia *f* -**1.** [gen] justice; [equidad] fairness, justice; **hacer** ~ to do justice; **ser de**
~ to be only fair -**2.** [organización]: **la** ~
the law.
justiciero, ra *adj* righteous.
justificación *f* [gen & IMPRENTA] justification.
justificante *m* documentary evidence *(U)*.
justificar *vt* -**1.** [gen & IMPRENTA] to justify
-**2.** [excusar]: ~ **a alguien** to make excuses
for sb.
◆ **justificarse** *vpr* [suj: persona] to justify
o excuse o.s.
justo, ta *adj* -**1.** [equitativo] fair -**2.** [merecido - recompensa, victoria] **deserved**; [- castigo] **just** -**3.** [exacto - medida, hora] **exact**
-**4.** [idóneo] right -**5.** [apretado] tight; **estar**
o **venir** ~ to be a tight fit.
◆ **justo** *adv* just; ~ **ahora iba a llamarte** I
was just about to ring you; ~ **en medio**
right in the middle.
juvenil *adj* youthful; DEP youth *(antes de
sust)*.
juventud *f* -**1.** [edad] youth; **¡** ~**, divino tesoro!** what it is to be young! -**2.** [conjunto]
young people *(pl)*.
juzgado *m* [tribunal] court; ~ **de guardia**
*court open during the night or at other times when
ordinary courts are shut.*
juzgar *vt* -**1.** [enjuiciar] to judge; DER to try;
~ **mal a alguien** to misjudge sb; **a** ~ **por
(como)** judging by (how) -**2.** [estimar] to
consider, to judge.

k, K *f* [letra] k, K.
kaki = **caqui**.
kárate, cárate *m* karate.
kart *(pl* **karts)** *m* go-kart.
Kazajstán Kazakhstan.
Kenia Kenya.
ketchup ['ketʃup] *m* ketchup.
kg *(abrev de* **kilogramo)** kg.
kibutz [kiβuθ] *(pl* **kibutzim)** *m* kibbutz.
kilo, quilo *m* [peso] kilo.
kilogramo, quilogramo *m* kilogram.
kilometraje, quilometraje *m* ≃ mileage
distance in kilometres.
kilométrico, ca, quilométrico, ca *adj*
[distancia] kilometric.
kilómetro, quilómetro *m* kilometre;
~ **cuadrado** square kilometre; ~**s por hora**
kilometres per hour.
kilovatio, quilovatio *m* kilowatt.
kínder *m Andes, Méx* nursery school *UK*,
kindergarten *US*.
kiosco = **quiosco**.
kiwi *(pl* **kiwis)** *m* [fruto] kiwi (fruit).
km *(abrev de* **kilómetro)** km.
km/h *(abrev de* **kilómetro por hora)** km/h.
KO *(abrev de* **knockout)** *m* KO.
kurdo, da ◇ *adj* Kurdish. ◇ *m,f* Kurd.
Kuwait [ku'βait] Kuwait.

l¹, L *f* [letra] l, L.
l² *(abrev de* **litro)** l.
la¹ *m* MÚS A; [en solfeo] lah.
la² ◇ *art* ⊳ **el**. ◇ *pron* ⊳ **lo**.
laberinto *m lit* & *fig* labyrinth.
labia *f fam* smooth talk; **tener mucha** ~ to

have the gift of the gab.

labio *m* -**1**. ANAT lip; ~ **inferior/superior** lower/upper lip; **leer los** ~**s** to lip-read - **2**. [borde] edge.

labor *f* -**1**. [trabajo] work; [tarea] task; ~**es domésticas** household chores; **ser de profesión sus** ~**es** to be a housewife - **2**. [de costura] needlework; ~**es de punto** knitting.

laborable ▷ **día.**

laboral *adj* labour; [semana, condiciones] working *(antes de sust).*

laboratorio *m* laboratory; ~ **espacial** space laboratory; ~ **fotográfico** photographic laboratory; ~ **de idiomas** *o* **lenguas** language laboratory.

laborioso, sa *adj* [difícil] laborious, arduous.

laborista ◇ *adj* Labour. ◇ *mf* Labour Party supporter *o* member; **los** ~**s** Labour.

labrador, ra *m,f* [agricultor] farmer; [trabajador] farm worker.

labranza *f* farming.

labrar *vt* -**1**. [campo - cultivar] to cultivate; [- arar] to plough - **2**. [piedra, metal etc] to work - **3**. *fig* [desgracia etc] to bring about; [porvenir, fortuna] to carve out.

◆ **labrarse** *vpr* [porvenir etc] to carve out for o.s.

labriego, ga *m,f* farmworker.

laburar *vi RP fam* [trabajar] to work.

laburo *m RP fam* [trabajo] job.

laca *f* -**1**. [gen] lacquer; [para cuadros] lake - **2**. [para el pelo] hairspray.

lacar *vt* to lacquer.

lacayo *m* footman; *fig* lackey.

lacerar *vt* to lacerate; *fig* to wound.

lacio, cia *adj* -**1**. [cabello - liso] straight; [- sin fuerza] lank - **2**. [planta] wilted - **3**. *fig* [sin fuerza] limp.

lacón *m* shoulder of pork.

lacónico, ca *adj* laconic.

lacra *f* scourge.

lacrar *vt* to seal with sealing wax.

lacre *m* sealing wax.

lacrimógeno, na *adj* -**1**. [novela etc] weepy, tear-jerking - **2**. ▷ **gas.**

lacrimoso, sa *adj* -**1**. [ojos etc] tearful - **2**. [historia etc] weepy, tear-jerking.

lactancia *f* lactation; ~ **artificial** bottle-feeding; ~ **materna** breastfeeding.

lactante *mf* breast-fed baby.

lácteo, a *adj* [gen] milk *(antes de sust)*; [industria, productos] dairy.

ladear *vt* to tilt.

ladera *f* slope, mountainside.

ladino, na ◇ *adj* crafty. ◇ *m,f CAm, Méx, Ven* [mestizo hispanohablante] *non-white Spanish-speaking person.*

◆ **ladino** *m* [dialecto] Ladino.

lado *m* -**1**. [gen] side; **en el** ~ **de arriba/abajo** on the top/bottom; **a ambos** ~**s** on both sides; **al otro** ~ **de** on the other side of; **estoy de su** ~ I'm on her side; **de** ~ [torcido] crooked; **dormir de** ~ to sleep on one's side; **de** ~ **a** ~ from side to side; **echar a un** ~ to push aside; **ponerse del** ~ **de alguien** to side with sb; **por un** ~ on the one hand; **por otro** ~ on the other hand - **2**. [lugar] place; **debe estar en otro** ~ it must be somewhere else; **por todos** ~**s** on all sides, all round - **3**. *loc*: **dar de** ~ **a alguien** to cold-shoulder sb; **dejar algo de** ~ *o* **a un** ~ [prescindir] to leave sthg to one side.

◆ **al lado** *loc adv* [cerca] nearby.

◆ **al lado de** *loc prep* [junto a] beside.

◆ **de al lado** *loc adj* next door; **la casa de al** ~ the house next door.

ladrar *vi lit & fig* to bark.

ladrido *m lit & fig* bark, barking *(U).*

ladrillo *m* CONSTR brick.

ladrón, ona *m,f* [persona] thief, robber.

◆ **ladrón** *m* [para varios enchufes] adapter.

lagartija *f* (small) lizard.

lagarto, ta *m,f* ZOOL lizard.

lago *m* lake.

lágrima *f* tear; **deshacerse en** ~**s** to dissolve into tears; **llorar a** ~ **viva** to cry buckets.

lagrimal *m* corner of the eye.

laguna *f* -**1**. [lago] lagoon - **2**. *fig* [en colección, memoria] gap; [en leyes, reglamento] loophole.

La Habana Havana.

La Haya The Hague.

laico, ca *adj* lay, secular.

lama *m* lama.

lamber *vt Amér fam* to lick.

La Meca Mecca.

lamentable *adj* -**1**. [triste] terribly sad - **2**. [malo] lamentable, deplorable.

lamentar *vt* to regret, to be sorry about; **lo lamento** I'm very sorry.

lamento *m* moan, cry of pain.

lamer *vt* to lick.

◆ **lamerse** *vpr* to lick o.s.

lamido, da *adj* skinny.

◆ **lamido** *m* lick.

lámina *f* -**1**. [plancha] sheet; [placa] plate - **2**. [rodaja] slice - **3**. [plancha grabada] engraving - **4**. [dibujo] plate.

laminar *vt* to laminate, to roll.

lámpara *f* -**1**. [aparato] lamp; ~ **de pie** standard lamp; ~ **de soldar** blowtorch; ~ **de techo** ceiling lamp - **2**. [bombilla] bulb - **3**. TECN valve.

lamparón *m* grease stain.

lampiño, ña *adj* [sin barba] beardless, smooth-cheeked; [sin vello] hairless.

lamprea *f* lamprey.

lana f - **1.** wool; **de ~** woollen; **pura ~ virgen** pure new wool; **unos cardan la ~ y otros llevan la fama** *proverb* some do all the work and others get all the credit - **2.** f *Andes, Méx fam* [dinero] dough, cash.

lance m - **1.** [en juegos, deportes] incident; [acontecimiento] event - **2.** [riña] dispute.

lanceta f *Andes, Méx* sting.

lancha f [embarcación - grande] launch; [- pequeña] boat; **~ motora** motorboat, motor launch; **~ salvavidas** lifeboat.

lanero, ra *adj* wool *(antes de sust)*.

langosta f - **1.** [crustáceo] lobster - **2.** [insecto] locust.

langostino m king prawn.

languidecer vi to languish; [conversación, entusiasmo] to flag.

languidez f [debilidad] listlessness; [falta de ánimo] disinterest.

lánguido, da *adj* [débil] listless; [falto de ánimo] disinterested.

lanilla f - **1.** [pelillo] nap - **2.** [tejido] flannel.

lanolina f lanolin.

lanza f [arma - arrojadiza] spear; [- en justas, torneos] lance; **estar ~ en ristre** to be ready for action; **romper una ~ por alguien** to fight for sb.

lanzado, da *adj* [atrevido] forward; [valeroso] fearless.

lanzagranadas m inv grenade launcher.

lanzamiento m - **1.** [de objeto] throwing; [de cohete] launching - **2.** [DEP - con la mano] throw; [- con el pie] kick; [- en béisbol] pitch; **~ de peso** shot put - **3.** [de producto, artista] launch; [de disco] release.

lanzamisiles m inv rocket launcher.

lanzar vt - **1.** [gen] to throw; [con fuerza] to hurl, to fling; [de una patada] to kick; [bomba] to drop; [flecha, misil] to fire; [cohete] to launch - **2.** [proferir] to let out; [acusación, insulto] to hurl; [suspiro] to heave - **3.** [COM - producto, artista, periódico] to launch; [- disco] to release.

◆ lanzarse vpr - **1.** [tirarse] to throw o.s. - **2.** [abalanzarse]: **~se (sobre)** to throw o.s. (upon).

lapa f ZOOL limpet.

La Paz La Paz.

lapicera f CSur ballpoint (pen), Biro®.

lapicero m - **1.** pencil - **2.** CAm, Perú [bolígrafo] ballpoint pen, Biro®.

lápida f memorial stone; **~ mortuoria** tombstone.

lapidar vt to stone.

lapidario, ria *adj* solemn.

lápiz (*pl* **lápices**) m pencil; **escribir algo a ~** to write sthg in pencil; **~ de cejas** eyebrow pencil; **~ de labios** lipstick; **~ de ojos** eyeliner; **~ óptico** INFORM light pen.

lapón, ona *adj* & m, f Lapp.

◆ lapón m [lengua] Lapp.

lapso m space, interval; **~ de tiempo** space o interval of time.

lapsus m inv lapse, slip.

larga ▷ **largo**.

largar vt - **1.** [aflojar] to pay out - **2.** fam [dar, decir] to give; **le largué un bofetón** I gave him a smack.

◆ largarse vpr fam to clear off.

largavistas m inv Bol, CSur binoculars (pl).

largo, ga *adj* - **1.** [en espacio, tiempo] long - **2.** [alto] tall - **3.** [sobrado]: **media hora larga** a good half hour.

◆ largo ◇ m length; **a lo ~** lengthways; **tiene dos metros de ~** it's two metres long; **pasar de ~** to pass by; **a lo ~ de** [en espacio] along; [en el tiempo] throughout; **¡~ de aquí!** go away!, get out of here! ◇ *adv* at length; **~ y tendido** at great length.

◆ larga f: **a la larga** in the long run; **dar largas a algo** to put sthg off.

largometraje m feature film.

larguero m - **1.** CONSTR main beam - **2.** DEP crossbar.

largura f length.

laringe f larynx.

laringitis f inv laryngitis.

larva f larva.

las ◇ *art* ▷ **el.** ◇ *pron* ▷ **lo.**

lasaña f lasagne, lasagna.

lascivo, va *adj* lascivious, lewd.

láser ◇ *adj inv* ▷ **rayo.** ◇ m inv laser.

lástima f - **1.** [compasión] pity - **2.** [pena] shame, pity; **da ~ ver gente así** it's sad to see people in that state; **es una ~ que** it's a shame o pity that; **¡qué ~!** what a shame o pity!; **tener** o **sentir ~ de** to feel sorry for; **quedarse hecho una ~** to be a sorry o pitiful sight.

lastimar vt to hurt.

◆ lastimarse vpr to hurt o.s.

lastimoso, sa *adj* pitiful, woeful.

lastre m - **1.** [peso] ballast - **2.** fig [estorbo] burden.

lata f - **1.** [envase] can, tin; [de bebidas] can; **en ~** tinned, canned - **2.** fam [fastidio] pain; **¡qué ~!** what a pain!; **dar la ~ a alguien** to pester sb.

latente *adj* latent.

lateral ◇ *adj* [del lado - gen] lateral; [- puerta, pared] side. ◇ m - **1.** [lado] side - **2.** DEP: **~ derecho/izquierdo** right/left back.

latido m [del corazón] beat; [en dedo etc] throb, throbbing (U).

latifundio m large rural estate.

latigazo m - **1.** [golpe] lash - **2.** [chasquido] crack (of the whip).

látigo m whip.

latín *m* Latin; **saber (mucho)** ~ *fig* to be sharp, to be on the ball.

latinajo *m fam despec* Latin word used in an attempt to sound academic.

latino, na *adj* & *m,f* Latin.

latinoamericano, na *adj* & *m,f* Latin American.

latir *vi* [suj: corazón] to beat.

latitud *f* GEOGR latitude.

➡ **latitudes** *fpl* [parajes] region *(sg)*, area *(sg)*.

latón *m* brass.

latoso, sa *adj fam* tiresome.

laúd *m* lute.

laureado, da *adj* prize-winning.

laurel *m* BOT laurel; CULIN bay leaf.

➡ **laureles** *mpl* [honores] laurels; **dormirse en los** ~**es** *fig* to rest on one's laurels.

lava *f* lava.

lavabo *m* **-1.** [objeto] washbasin **- 2.** [habitación] lavatory *UK*, washroom *US*; **ir al** ~ to go to the toilet.

lavadero *m* [en casa] laundry room; [público] washing place.

lavado *m* wash, washing *(U)*; ~ **a mano** hand-wash; ~ **de cerebro** brainwashing; ~ **de dinero** money-laundering; ~ **en seco** dry cleaning.

lavadora *f* washing machine; ~ **secadora** washer-drier.

lavamanos *m inv* washbasin.

lavanda *f* lavender.

lavandería *f* laundry; [automática] launderette.

lavaplatos *m inv* [aparato] dishwasher.

lavar *vt* [limpiar] to wash; ~ **a mano** to wash by hand; ~ **en seco** to dry-clean; ~ **y marcar** shampoo and set.

➡ **lavarse** *vpr* [gen] to wash o.s.; [cara, manos, pelo] to wash; [dientes] to clean.

lavativa *f* enema.

lavatorio *m Andes, RP* washbasin *UK*, washbowl *US*.

lavavajillas *m inv* dishwasher.

laxante *m* laxative.

laxar *vt* [vientre] to loosen.

lazada *f* bow.

lazarillo *m* **-1.** [persona] blind person's guide **- 2.** ⊳ **perro**.

lazo *m* **-1.** [atadura] bow; **hacer un** ~ to tie a bow **- 2.** [trampa] snare; [de vaquero] lasso **- 3.** *(gen pl) fig* [vínculo] tie, bond.

Lda. *abrev de* **licenciada**.

Ldo. *abrev de* **licenciado**.

le *pron pers* **-1.** *(complemento indirecto)* [hombre] (to) him; [mujer] (to) her; [cosa] (to) it; [usted] (to) you; ~ **expliqué el motivo** I explained the reason to him/her; ~ **tengo miedo** I'm afraid of him/her; **ya** ~ **dije lo**

que pasaría [a usted] I told you what would happen **- 2.** *(complemento directo)* him; [usted] you **- 3.** ⊳ **se**.

leal *adj*: ~ **(a)** loyal (to).

lealtad *f*: ~ **(a)** loyalty (to).

leasing ['lisin] *(pl* **leasings)** *m system of leasing whereby the lessee has the option of purchasing the property after a certain time.*

lección *f* lesson; **aprenderse la** ~ to learn one's lesson; **dar a alguien una** ~ [como advertencia] to teach sb a lesson; [como ejemplo] to give sb a lesson.

lechal *m* sucking lamb.

leche *f* **-1.** [gen] milk; ~ **condensada/en polvo** condensed/powdered milk; ~ **descremada** *o* **desnatada** skimmed *UK o* skim *US* milk; ~ **merengada** *drink made from milk, egg whites, sugar and cinnamon* **- 2.** *mfam* [bofetada]: **pegar una** ~ **a alguien** to belt *o* clobber sb **- 3.** *mfam* [malhumor] bloody awful mood; **estar de mala** ~ to be in a bloody awful mood; **tener mala** ~ to be a miserable git.

lechera ⊳ **lechero**.

lechería *f* dairy.

lechero, ra ◇ *adj* milk *(antes de sust)*, dairy. ◇ *m,f* [persona] milkman (*f* milkwoman).

➡ **lechera** *f* [para transportar] milk churn; [para beber] milk jug.

lecho *m* [gen] bed; ~ **de muerte** deathbed.

lechón *m* sucking pig.

lechosa *f Carib* papaya.

lechuga *f* lettuce; ~ **iceberg/romana** iceberg/cos lettuce; **ser más fresco que una** ~ to be a cheeky devil.

lechuza *f* (barn) owl.

lectivo, va *adj* school *(antes de sust)*.

lector, ra *m,f* **-1.** [gen] reader **- 2.** EDUC language assistant.

➡ **lector** *m* [de microfilms etc] reader, scanner; ~ **óptico** optical scanner.

lectura *f* **-1.** [gen] reading; **dar** ~ **a algo** to read sthg out loud **- 2.** [de tesis] viva voce **- 3.** [escrito] reading (matter) *(U)* **- 4.** [de datos] scanning; ~ **óptica** optical scanning.

leer ◇ *vt* [gen & INFORM] to read. ◇ *vi* to read; ~ **de corrido** to read fluently; ~ **en voz alta/baja** to read aloud/quietly.

legado *m* **-1.** [herencia] legacy **- 2.** [representante] legation; [-persona] legate.

legajo *m* file.

legal *adj* **-1.** [gen] legal; [hora] standard **- 2.** *fam* [persona] honest, decent.

legalidad *f* legality.

legalizar *vt* [gen] to legalize.

legañas *fpl* sleep *(U) (in the eyes)*.

legañoso, sa *adj* full of sleep.

legar *vt* **-1.** [gen] to bequeath **- 2.** [delegar] to delegate.

legendario, ria *adj* legendary.

legible *adj* legible.

legión *f lit* & *fig* legion.

legionario, ria *adj* legionary.

◆ **legionario** *m* HIST legionary; MIL legionnaire.

legislación *f* [leyes] legislation.

legislar *vi* to legislate.

legislatura *f* [periodo] period of office.

legitimar *vt* - **1.** [legalizar] to legitimize - **2.** [certificar] to authenticate.

legítimo, ma *adj* [gen] legitimate; [auténtico] real, genuine; [oro] pure.

lego, ga ◇ *adj* - **1.** [gen] lay - **2.** [ignorante] ignorant. ◇ *m,f* [gen] layman (*f* laywoman).

legua *f* league; ~ **marina** marine league.

legumbre *(gen pl) f* pulse, pod vegetable.

lehendakari, lendakari [lenda'kari] *m* president of the autonomous Basque government.

leído, da *adj* [persona] well-read.

◆ **leída** *f* reading.

lejanía *f* distance.

lejano, na *adj* distant; **no está** ~ it's not far (away).

lejía *f* bleach.

lejos *adv* - **1.** [en el espacio] far (away); **¿está** ~ **?** is it far?; **a lo** ~ in the distance; **de** *o* **desde** ~ from a distance - **2.** [en el pasado] long ago; [en el futuro] far in the future; **eso queda ya** ~ that happened a long time ago - **3.** *loc:* **ir demasiado** ~ to go too far; **llegar** ~ to go far; **sin ir más** ~ indeed.

◆ **lejos de** ◇ *loc conj* far from; ~ **de mejorar ...** far from getting better ... ◇ *loc prep* far (away) from.

lelo, la ◇ *adj* stupid, slow; **quedarse** ~ to be stunned. ◇ *m,f* idiot.

lema *m* - **1.** [norma] motto; [político, publicitario] slogan - **2.** LING & MAT lemma.

lencería *f* - **1.** [ropa] linen - **2.** [tienda] draper's.

lendakari = lehendakari.

lengua *f* - **1.** [gen] tongue; **sacarle la** ~ **a alguien** to stick one's tongue out at sb; **con la** ~ **fuera** out of breath; ~ **de fuego/tierra** tongue of flame/land; ~ **de víbora** *o* viperina malicious tongue; **darle a la** ~ *fam* to chatter; **irse de la** ~ to let the cat out of the bag; **las malas** ~**s dicen que ...** according to the gossip ...; **morderse la** ~ to bite one's tongue; **¿te ha comido la** ~ **el gato?** has the cat got your tongue?, have you lost your tongue?; **tirar a alguien de la** ~ to draw sb out - **2.** [idioma, lenguaje] language; ~ **materna** mother tongue; ~ **oficial** official language.

lenguado *m* sole.

lenguaje *m* [gen & INFORM] language;
~ **cifrado** code; ~ **corporal** body language; ~ **gestual** gestures *(pl)*; ~ **máquina** machine language; ~ **de programación** programming language; ~ **de los sordomudos** sign language.

lengüeta *f* [gen & MÚS] tongue.

lengüetazo *m*, **lengüetada** *f* lick.

lente *f* lens; ~ **de aumento** magnifying glass; ~**s de contacto** contact lenses.

◆ **lentes** *mpl* [gafas] glasses.

lenteja *f* lentil; **ganarse las** ~**s** to earn one's daily bread.

lentejuela *f* sequin.

lentilla *(gen pl) f* contact lens.

lentitud *f* slowness; **con** ~ slowly.

lento, ta *adj* slow; [veneno] slow-working; [agonía, enfermedad] lingering, long drawn out.

leña *f* [madera] firewood; **echar** ~ **al fuego** to add fuel to the flames *o* fire; **llevar** ~ **al monte** to carry coals to Newcastle.

leñador, ra *m,f* woodcutter.

leño *m* [de madera] log; **dormir como un** ~ to sleep like a log.

Leo ◇ *m* [zodiaco] Leo. ◇ *mf* [persona] Leo.

león, ona *m,f* lion (*f* lioness); *fig* fierce person; **no es tan fiero el** ~ **como lo pintan** *proverb* he/it *etc* is not as bad as he/it *etc* is made out to be.

◆ **león marino** *m* sea lion.

leonera *f fam fig* [cuarto sucio] pigsty.

leonino, na *adj* [contrato, condiciones] one-sided, unfair.

leopardo *m* leopard.

leotardo *m* - **1.** *(gen pl)* [medias] stockings *(pl)*, thick tights *(pl)* - **2.** [de gimnasta etc] leotard.

lépero, ra *adj CAm, Méx fam* [vulgar] coarse, vulgar; *Cuba fam* [astuto] smart, crafty.

lepra *f* leprosy.

leproso, sa *m,f* leper.

lerdo, da *adj* [idiota] dim, slow-witted; [torpe] useless, hopeless.

les *pron pers pl* - **1.** *(complemento indirecto)* (to) them; [ustedes] (to) you; ~ **expliqué el motivo** I explained the reason to them; ~ **tengo miedo** I'm afraid of them; **ya** ~ **dije lo que pasaría** [a ustedes] I told you what would happen - **2.** *(complemento directo)* them; [ustedes] you - **3.** ⊳ **se**.

lesbiano, na *adj* lesbian.

◆ **lesbiana** *f* lesbian.

leseras *fpl Chile fam* nonsense, rubbish *UK*.

lesión *f* - **1.** [herida] injury; ~ **cerebral** brain damage - **2.** DER: ~ **grave** grievous bodily harm.

lesionado, da ◇ *adj* injured. ◇ *m,f* injured person.

lesionar *vt* to injure; *fig* to damage, to harm.

◆ **lesionarse** *vpr* to injure o.s.

letal *adj* lethal.

letanía *(gen pl)* *f lit* & *fig* litany.

letargo *m* ZOOL hibernation.

Letonia Latvia.

letra *f* - 1. [signo] letter - 2. [caligrafía] handwriting - 3. [estilo] script; IMPRENTA typeface; ~ **de imprenta** O **molde** IMPRENTA print; [en formularios etc] block capitals *(pl)*; ~ **mayúscula/minúscula** capital/small letter; ~ **negrita** O **negrilla** bold (face); ~ **versalita** small capital; **la** ~ **con sangre entra** *proverb* spare the rod and spoil the child; **leer la** ~ **pequeña** to read the small print; **mandar cuatro** ~**s a alguien** to drop sb a line - 4. [de canción] lyrics *(pl)* - 5. COM : ~ **(de cambio)** bill of exchange.

◆ **letras** *fpl* EDUC arts.

letrado, da ◇ *adj* learned. ◇ *m,f* lawyer.

letrero *m* sign; ~ **luminoso** neon sign.

letrina *f* latrine.

leucemia *f* leukaemia.

leva *f* MIL levy.

levadura *f* yeast, leaven; ~ **de cerveza** brewer's yeast; ~ **en polvo** baking powder.

levantamiento *m* - 1. [sublevación] uprising - 2. [elevación] raising; ~ **de pesas** DEP weightlifting - 3. [supresión] lifting, removal.

levantar *vt* - 1. [gen] to raise; [peso, capó, trampilla] to lift; ~ **el ánimo** to cheer up; ~ **la vista** O **mirada** to look up - 2. [separar - pintura, venda, tapa] to remove - 3. [recoger - campamento] to strike; [- tienda de campaña, puesto] to take down; [- mesa] to clear - 4. [encender - protestas, polémica] to stir up; ~ **a alguien contra** to stir sb up against - 5. [suspender - embargo, prohibición] to lift; [- pena, castigo] to suspend; [- sesión] to adjourn - 6. [redactar - acta, atestado] to draw up.

◆ **levantarse** *vpr* - 1. [ponerse de pie] to stand up - 2. [de la cama] to get up; ~ **se tarde** to sleep in - 3. [elevarse - avión etc] to take off; [- niebla] to lift - 4. [sublevarse] to rise up - 5. [empezar - viento, oleaje] to get up, to rise; [- tormenta] to gather.

levante *m* - 1. [este] east; [región] east coast - 2. [viento] east wind.

levar *vt* to weigh.

leve *adj* - 1. [gen] light; [olor, sabor, temblor] slight - 2. [pecado, falta, herida] minor - 3. [enfermedad] mild, slight.

levedad *f* lightness; [de temblor etc] slightness; [de pecado, falto, herida] minor nature; [de enfermedad] mildness.

levita *f* frock coat.

levitar *vi* to levitate.

léxico, ca *adj* lexical.

◆ **léxico** *m* [vocabulario] vocabulary.

lexicografía *f* lexicography.

lexicón *m* lexicon.

ley *f* - 1. [gen] law; [parlamentaria] act; **aprobar una** ~ to pass a law; ~ **de incompatibilidades** *act regulating which other positions may be held by people holding public office*; ~ **marcial** martial law; **con todas las de la** ~ in due form, properly - 2. [regla] rule; ~ **del embudo** one law for o.s. and another for everyone else; ~ **de la oferta y de la demanda** law of supply and demand - 3. [de un metal]: **de** ~ [oro] pure; [plata] sterling.

◆ **leyes** *fpl* [derecho] law *(sg)*.

leyenda *f* [narración] legend.

liar *vt* - 1. [atar] to tie up - 2. [envolver - cigarrillo] to roll; ~ **algo en** [papel] to wrap sthg up in; [toalla etc] to roll sthg up in - 3. [involucrar]: ~ **a alguien (en)** to get sb mixed up (in) - 4. [complicar - asunto etc] to confuse; **¡ya me has liado!** now you've really got me confused!

◆ **liarse** *vpr* - 1. [enredarse] to get muddled up - 2. [empezar] to begin, to start.

Líbano *m*: **el** ~ the Lebanon.

libélula *f* dragonfly.

liberación *f* [gen] liberation; [de preso] release.

liberado, da *adj* [gen] liberated; [preso] freed.

liberal *adj* & *mf* liberal.

liberar *vt* [gen] to liberate; [preso] to free; ~ **de algo a alguien** to free sb from sthg.

◆ **liberarse** *vpr* to liberate o.s.; ~ **se de algo** to free O liberate o.s. from sthg.

Liberia Liberia.

libertad *f* freedom, liberty; **dejar** O **poner a alguien en** ~ to set sb free, to release sb; **tener** ~ **para hacer algo** to be free to do sthg; **tomarse la** ~ **de hacer algo** to take the liberty of doing sthg; ~ **de conciencia** freedom of conscience; ~ **condicional** probation; ~ **de expresión** freedom of speech; ~ **de imprenta** O **prensa** freedom of the press.

libertar *vt* [gen] to liberate; [preso] to set free.

libertino, na ◇ *adj* licentious. ◇ *m,f* libertine.

Libia Libya.

libido *f* libido.

libra *f* [peso, moneda] pound; ~ **esterlina** pound sterling.

◆ **Libra** ◇ *m* [zodiaco] Libra. ◇ *mf* [persona] Libran.

librador, ra *m,f* drawer.

libramiento *m*, **libranza** *f* order of payment.

librar ⬦ *vt* **- 1.** [eximir]: ~ **a alguien (de algo/de hacer algo)** [gen] to free sb (from sthg/from doing sthg); [pagos, impuestos] to exempt sb (from sthg/from doing sthg) **- 2.** [entablar - pelea, lucha] to engage in; [- batalla, combate] to join, to wage **- 3.** COM to draw. ⬦ *vi* [no trabajar] to be off work.

➤ **librarse** *vpr* **- 1.** [salvarse]: ~**se (de hacer algo)** to escape (from doing sthg); **de buena te libraste** you had a narrow escape **- 2.** [deshacerse]: ~**se de algo/alguien** to get rid of sthg/sb.

libre *adj* **- 1.** [gen] free; [rato, tiempo] spare; [camino, vía] clear; [espacio, piso, lavabo] empty, vacant; **200 metros** ~**s** 200 metres freestyle; ~ **de** [gen] free from; [exento] exempt from; ~ **de franqueo** post-free; ~ **de impuestos** tax-free; **ir por** ~ to go it alone **- 2.** [alumno] external; **estudiar por** ~ to be an external student.

librecambio *m* free trade.

librería *f* **- 1.** [tienda] bookshop; ~ **de ocasión** second-hand bookshop **- 2.** [mueble] bookcase.

librero, ra *m,f* [persona] bookseller. ⬦ *m* CAm, Col, Méx [mueble] bookcase.

libreta *f* **- 1.** [para escribir] notebook; ~ **de direcciones** address book **- 2.** [del banco]: ~ **(de ahorros)** savings book.

libretista *mf* Amér [guionista] screenwriter, scriptwriter.

libreto *m* **- 1.** MÚS libretto **- 2.** Amér [guión] script.

libro *m* [gen & COM] book; **llevar los** ~**s** to keep the books; ~ **de bolsillo** paperback; ~ **de consulta/cuentos** reference/story book; ~ **de ejercicios** workbook; ~ **de escolaridad** school report; ~ **de familia** *document containing personal details of the members of a family*; ~ **de reclamaciones** complaints book; ~ **de registro (de entradas)** register; ~ **de texto** textbook; ~ **de visitas** visitor's book; **colgar los** ~**s** to give up one's studies; **ser como un** ~ **abierto** to be an open book.

Lic. *abrev de* **licenciado.**

liceal *adj* CSur, Ven secondary school UK, high school US.

licencia *f* **- 1.** [documento] licence, permit; [autorización] permission; ~ **de armas/caza** gun/hunting licence; ~ **de obras** planning permission; ~ **poética** poetic licence **- 2.** MIL discharge **- 3.** [confianza] licence, freedom.

licenciado, da *m,f* **- 1.** EDUC graduate; ~ **en económicas** economics graduate **- 2.** MIL discharged soldier.

licenciar *vt* MIL to discharge.

➤ **licenciarse** *vpr* **- 1.** EDUC : ~**se (en)** to graduate (in) **- 2.** MIL to be discharged.

licenciatura *f* degree.

licencioso, sa *adj* licentious.

liceo *m* **- 1.** EDUC lycée **- 2.** CSur,Ven [instituto] secondary school UK, high school US.

lícito, ta *adj* **- 1.** [legal] lawful **- 2.** [correcto] right **- 3.** [justo] fair.

licor *m* liquor.

licuadora *f* liquidizer, blender.

licuar *vt* CULIN to liquidize.

líder ⬦ *adj* leading. ⬦ *mf* leader.

liderato, liderazgo *m* **- 1.** [primer puesto] lead; [en liga] first place **- 2.** [dirección] leadership.

lidia *f* **- 1.** [arte] bullfighting **- 2.** [corrida] bullfight.

lidiar ⬦ *vi* [luchar]: ~ **(con)** to struggle (with). ⬦ *vt* TAUROM to fight.

liebre *f* ZOOL hare.

lienzo *m* **- 1.** [para pintar] canvas **- 2.** [cuadro] painting.

lifting ['liftin] (*pl* **liftings**) *m* facelift.

liga *f* **- 1.** [gen] league **- 2.** [de medias] suspender.

ligadura *f* **- 1.** MED & MÚS ligature **- 2.** [atadura] bond, tie.

ligamento *m* ANAT ligament.

ligar ⬦ *vt* [gen & CULIN] to bind; [atar] to tie (up). ⬦ *vi* **- 1.** [coincidir]: ~ **(con)** to tally (with) **- 2.** *fam* [conquistar]: ~ **(con)** to get off (with).

ligazón *f* link, connection.

ligereza *f* **- 1.** [levedad] lightness **- 2.** [agilidad] agility **- 3.** [irreflexión - cualidad] rashness; [- acto] rash act; **con** ~ in a superficial manner.

ligero, ra *adj* **- 1.** [gen] light; [dolor, rumor, descenso] slight; [traje, tela] thin **- 2.** [ágil] agile, nimble **- 3.** [rápido] quick, swift **- 4.** [irreflexivo] flippant; **hacer algo a la ligera** to do sthg without much thought; **juzgar a alguien a la ligera** to be quick to judge sb; **tomarse algo a la ligera** not to take sthg seriously.

light [lait] *adj inv* [comida] low-calorie; [refresco] diet (*antes de sust*); [cigarrillos] light.

ligón, ona *adj fam*: **es muy** ~ he's always getting off with sb or other.

liguero, ra *adj* DEP league (*antes de sust*).

➤ **liguero** *m* suspender belt UK, garter belt US.

lija *f* [papel] sandpaper.

lila ⬦ *f* [flor] lilac. ⬦ *adj inv & m* [color] lilac.

lima *f* **- 1.** [utensilio] file; ~ **de uñas** nail file **- 2.** BOT lime.

Lima Lima.

limar *vt* **- 1.** [pulir] to file down **- 2.** [perfeccionar] to polish, to add the finishing touches to.

limitación f **- 1.** [restricción] limitation, limit **- 2.** [distrito] boundaries *(pl)*.

limitado, da *adj* **- 1.** [gen] limited **- 2.** [poco inteligente] dim-witted.

limitar ◇ *vt* **- 1.** [gen] to limit **- 2.** [terreno] to mark out **- 3.** [atribuciones, derechos etc] to set out, to define. ◇ *vi:* ~ **(con)** to border (on).

  ◆ **limitarse a** *vpr* to limit o.s. to.

límite ◇ *adj inv* **- 1.** [precio, velocidad, edad] maximum **- 2.** [situación] extreme; [caso] borderline. ◇ *m* **- 1.** [tope] limit; **dentro de un** ~ within limits; **su pasión no tiene** ~ her passion knows no bounds; ~ **de velocidad** speed limit **- 2.** [confín] boundary.

limítrofe *adj* [país, territorio] bordering; [terreno, finca] neighbouring.

limón m lemon.

limonada f lemonade.

limonero, ra *adj* lemon *(antes de sust)*.

  ◆ **limonero** m lemon tree.

limosna f alms *(pl)*; **pedir** ~ to beg.

limpia f *Amér* cleaning.

limpiabotas mf *inv* shoeshine, bootblack *UK*.

limpiacristales m *inv* window-cleaning fluid.

limpiamente *adv* **- 1.** [con destreza] cleanly **- 2.** [honradamente] honestly.

limpiaparabrisas m *inv* windscreen wiper *UK*, windshield wiper *US*.

limpiar *vt* **- 1.** [gen] to clean; [con trapo] to wipe; [mancha] to wipe away; [zapatos] to polish **- 2.** *fig* [desembarazar]: ~ **algo de algo** to clear sthg of sthg.

limpieza f **- 1.** [cualidad] cleanliness **- 2.** [acción] cleaning; ~ **en seco** dry cleaning **- 3.** [destreza] skill, cleanness **- 4.** [honradez] honesty.

limpio, pia *adj* **- 1.** [gen] clean; [pulcro] neat; [cielo, imagen] clear **- 2.** [neto - sueldo etc] net **- 3.** [honrado] honest; [intenciones] honourable; [juego] clean **- 4.** [sin culpa]: **estar** ~ to be in the clear.

  ◆ **limpio** *adv* cleanly, fair; **pasar** o **poner en** ~ to make a fair copy of, to write out neatly; **sacar algo en** ~ **de** to make sthg out from.

linaje m lineage.

linaza f linseed.

lince m lynx; **ser un** ~ **para algo** to be very sharp at sthg.

linchar *vt* to lynch.

lindar ◆ lindar con *vi* **- 1.** [terreno] to adjoin, to be next to **- 2.** [conceptos, ideas] to border on.

linde m o f boundary.

lindero, ra *adj* [terreno] adjoining, bordering.

◆ **lindero** m boundary.

lindo, da *adj* pretty, lovely; **de lo** ~ a great deal.

línea f **- 1.** [gen, DEP & TELECOM] line; **cortar la** ~ (telefónica) to cut off the phone; ~ **aérea** airline; ~ **de conducta** course of action; ~ **continua** AUTOM solid white line; ~ **de puntos** dotted line **- 2.** [de un coche etc] lines *(pl)*, shape **- 3.** [silueta] figure; **guardar la** ~ to watch one's figure **- 4.** [estilo] style; **de** ~ **clásica** classical **- 5.** [categoría] class, category; **de primera** ~ first-rate **- 6.** INFORM: **en** ~ on-line; **fuera de** ~ off-line **- 7.** *loc:* **en** ~s **generales** in broad terms; **leer entre** ~s to read between the lines.

lineamientos mpl *Amér* [generalidades] outline; [directrices] guidelines.

lingote m ingot.

lingüista mf linguist.

lingüístico, ca *adj* linguistic.

  ◆ **lingüística** f linguistics.

linier [linjer] *(pl* liniers*)* m linesman.

linimento m liniment.

lino m **- 1.** [planta] flax **- 2.** [tejido] linen.

linterna f **- 1.** [farol] lantern, lamp **- 2.** [de pilas] torch *UK*, flashlight *US*.

linyera mf *RP fam* tramp, bum *US*.

lío m **- 1.** [paquete] bundle **- 2.** *fam* [enredo] mess; **hacerse un** ~ to get muddled up; **meterse en** ~s to get into trouble **- 3.** *fam* [jaleo] racket, row **- 4.** *fam* [amorío] affair.

liposucción f liposuction.

liquen m lichen.

liquidación f **- 1.** [pago] settlement, payment **- 2.** [rebaja] clearance sale **- 3.** [fin] liquidation.

liquidar *vt* **- 1.** [pagar - deuda] to pay; [- cuenta] to settle **- 2.** [rebajar] to sell off **- 3.** [malgastar] to throw away **- 4.** [acabar - asunto] to settle; [- negocio, sociedad] to wind up.

líquido, da *adj* **- 1.** [gen] liquid **- 2.** ECON [neto] net.

  ◆ **líquido** m **- 1.** [gen] liquid **- 2.** ECON liquid assets *(pl)* **- 3.** MED fluid.

lira f **- 1.** MÚS lyre **- 2.** [moneda] lira.

lírico, ca *adj* LITER lyrical.

  ◆ **lírica** f lyric poetry.

lirio m iris.

lirón m ZOOL dormouse; **dormir como un** ~ to sleep like a log.

Lisboa Lisbon.

lisiado, da ◇ *adj* crippled. ◇ *m,f* cripple.

lisiar *vt* to maim, to cripple.

liso, sa ◇ *adj* **- 1.** [llano] flat; [sin asperezas] smooth; [pelo] straight; **los 400 metros** ~s the 400 metres; **lisa y llanamente** quite simply; **hablando lisa y llanamente** to put it plainly **- 2.** [no estampado] plain. ◇ *m,f Andes, CAm, Ven* [insolente] cheeky person.

lisonja f flattering remark.

lisonjear vt to flatter.

lista f - **1.** [enumeración] list; **pasar** ~ **to call the register**; ~ **de boda/de espera/de precios** wedding/waiting/price list - **2.** [de tela, madera] strip; [de papel] slip; [de color] stripe.
➤ **lista de correos** f poste restante.

listado, da adj striped.

listín ➤ **listín (de teléfonos)** m (telephone) directory.

listo, ta adj - **1.** [inteligente, hábil] clever, smart; **dárselas de** ~ **to make o.s. out to be clever; pasarse de** ~ **to be too clever by half; ser más** ~ **que el hambre to be nobody's fool** - **2.** [preparado] ready; **¿estáis** ~s? **are you ready?; estás** o **vas** ~ **(si crees que ...) you've got another think coming (if you think that ...).**

listón m lath; DEP bar.

litera f - **1.** [cama] bunk (bed); [de barco] berth; [de tren] couchette - **2.** [vehículo] litter.

literal adj literal.

literario, ria adj literary.

literato, ta m,f writer.

literatura f literature.

litigar vi to go to law.

litigio m DER litigation (U); fig dispute; **en** ~ **in dispute.**

litografía f - **1.** [arte] lithography - **2.** [grabado] lithograph.

litoral ◇ adj coastal. ◇ m coast.

litro m litre.

Lituania Lithuania.

liturgia f liturgy.

liviano, na adj - **1.** [ligero - blusa] thin; [- carga] light - **2.** [sin importancia] slight.

lívido, da adj - **1.** [pálido] very pale, white as a sheet - **2.** [amoratado] livid.

living ['liβin] m CSur living room.

ll, Ll f [letra] ll, Ll.

llaga f lit & fig wound.

llagar vt to wound.

llama f - **1.** [de fuego, pasión] flame; **en** ~s **ablaze** - **2.** ZOOL llama.

llamada f - **1.** [gen] call; [a la puerta] knock; [con timbre] ring - **2.** TELECOM telephone call; **devolver una** ~ **to phone back; hacer una** ~ **to make a phone call;** ~ **urbana/interurbana/a cobro revertido** local/long-distance/reverse-charge call.

llamado, da adj so-called.
➤ **llamado** m Amér [de teléfono] call.

llamamiento m [apelación] appeal, call.

llamar ◇ vt - **1.** [gen] to call; [con gestos] to beckon - **2.** [por teléfono] to phone, to call - **3.** [convocar] to summon, to call; ~ **(a filas)** MIL to call up - **4.** [atraer] to attract, to

call. ◇ vi - **1.** [a la puerta etc - con golpes] to knock; [- con timbre] to ring; **están llamando** there's somebody at the door - **2.** [por teléfono] to phone.
➤ **llamarse** vpr [tener por nombre] to be called; **¿cómo te llamas?** what's your name?; **me llamo Pepe** my name's Pepe.

llamarada f [de fuego, ira etc] blaze.

llamativo, va adj [color] bright, gaudy; [ropa] showy.

llamear vi to burn, to blaze.

llano, na adj - **1.** [campo, superficie] flat - **2.** [trato, persona] natural, straightforward - **3.** [pueblo, clase] ordinary - **4.** [lenguaje, expresión] simple, plain.
➤ **llano** m [llanura] plain.

llanta f - **1.** rim - **2.** Amér [cubierta] tyre UK, tire US.

llanto m tears (pl), crying.

llanura f plain.

llave f - **1.** [gen] key; **bajo** ~ **under lock and key; cerrar con** ~ **to lock; echarla** ~ **to lock up;** ~ **en mano** [vivienda] ready for immediate occupation; ~ **de contacto** ignition key; ~ **maestra** master key - **2.** [del agua, gas] tap UK, faucet US; [de la electricidad] switch; **cerrar la** ~ **de paso to turn the water/gas off at the mains** - **3.** [herramienta] spanner; ~ **inglesa** monkey wrench - **4.** [de judo etc] hold, lock - **5.** [signo ortográfico] curly bracket.

llavero m keyring.

llavín m latchkey.

llegada f - **1.** [gen] arrival - **2.** DEP finish.

llegar vi - **1.** [a un sitio]: ~ **(de) to arrive (from);** ~ **a un hotel/una ciudad** to arrive at a hotel/in a city; **llegaré pronto** I'll be there early - **2.** [un tiempo, la noche etc] to come - **3.** [durar]: ~ **a** o **hasta to last until** - **4.** [alcanzar]: ~ **a to reach; no llego al techo I can't reach the ceiling;** ~ **hasta to reach up to** - **5.** [ser suficiente]: ~ **(para) to be enough (for)** - **6.** [lograr]: ~ **a (ser) algo** to get to be sthg, to become sthg; **si llego a saberlo** if I get to know of it.
➤ **llegarse a** vpr to go round to.

llenar vt - **1.** [ocupar]: ~ **algo (de)** [vaso, hoyo, habitación] to fill sthg (with); [pared, suelo] to cover sthg (with) - **2.** [satisfacer] to satisfy - **3.** [rellenar - impreso] to fill in o out - **4.** [colmar]: ~ **a alguien de** to fill sb with.
➤ **llenarse** vpr - **1.** [ocuparse] to fill up - **2.** [saciarse] to be full - **3.** [cubrirse]: ~se **de** to become covered in.

lleno, na adj - **1.** [gen] full; [cubierto] covered; ~ **de** [gen] full of; [manchas, pósters] covered in; ~ **hasta los topes** full to bursting, packed out - **2.** fam [regordete] chubby.
➤ **de lleno** loc adv full in the face; **acertó**

de ∼ he was bang on target.

llevadero, ra *adj* bearable.

llevar ◇ *vt* -1. [gen] to carry -2. [acompañar, coger y depositar] to take; ∼ **algo/a alguien a** to take sthg/sb to; **me llevó en coche** he drove me there -3. [prenda, objeto personal] to wear; **llevo gafas** I wear glasses; **no llevo dinero** I haven't got any money on me -4. [caballo, coche etc] to handle -5. [conducir]: ∼ **a alguien a algo** to lead sb to sthg; ∼ **a alguien a hacer algo** to lead *o* cause sb to do sthg -6. [ocuparse de, dirigir] to be in charge of; [casa, negocio] to run; **lleva la contabilidad** she keeps the books -7. [hacer - de alguna manera]: **lleva muy bien sus estudios** he's doing very well in his studies -8. [tener - de alguna manera] to have; ∼ **el pelo largo** to have long hair; **llevas las manos sucias** your hands are dirty -9. [soportar] to deal *o* cope with -10. [mantener] to keep; ∼ **el paso** to keep in step -11. [pasarse - tiempo]: **lleva tres semanas sin venir** she hasn't come for three weeks now, it's three weeks since she came last -12. [ocupar - tiempo] to take; **me llevó un día hacer este guiso** it took me a day to make this dish -13. [sobrepasar en]: **te llevo seis puntos** I'm six points ahead of you; **me lleva dos centímetros** he's two centimetres taller than me -14. *loc*: ∼ **consigo** [implicar] to lead to, to bring about; ∼ **las de perder** to be heading for defeat. ◇ *vi* -1. [conducir]: ∼ **a** to lead to; **esta carretera lleva al norte** this road leads north -2. *(antes de participio)* [haber]: **llevo leída media novela** I'm halfway through the novel, **llevo dicho esto mismo docenas de veces** I've said the same thing time and again -3. *(antes de gerundio)* [estar]: ∼ **mucho tiempo haciendo algo** to have been doing sthg for a long time.

◆ **llevarse** *vpr* -1. [coger] to take, to steal -2. [conseguir] to get; **se ha llevado el premio** she has carried off the prize; **yo me llevo siempre las culpas** I always get the blame -3. [recibir - susto, sorpresa etc] to get, to receive; **me llevé un disgusto** I was upset -4. [entenderse]: ∼ **se bien/mal (con alguien)** to get on well/badly (with sb) -5. [estar de moda] to be in (fashion); **este año se lleva el verde** green is in this year -6. MAT: **me llevo una** carry (the) one.

llorar *vi* [con lágrimas] to cry.

lloriquear *vi* to whine, to snivel.

lloro *m* crying *(U)*, tears *(pl)*.

llorón, ona *m,f* crybaby.

lloroso, sa *adj* tearful.

llover *v impers* to rain; **está lloviendo** it's raining.

llovizna *f* drizzle.

lloviznar *v impers* to drizzle.

lluvia *f* METEOR rain; **bajo la** ∼ in the rain; ∼ **ácida** acid rain; ∼ **radiactiva** (nuclear) fallout; ∼ **torrencial** torrential rain.

lluvioso, sa *adj* rainy.

lo, la *(mpl* **los**, *fpl* **las**) *pron pers (complemento directo)* [cosa] it; *(pl)* them; [persona] him *(f* her); *(pl)* them; [usted] you.

◆ **lo** ◇ *pron pers (neutro) (predicado)* it; **su hermana es muy guapa pero él no** ∼ **es** his sister is very good-looking, but he isn't; **es muy bueno aunque no** ∼ **parezca** it's very good, even if it doesn't look it. ◇ *art det (neutro)*: ∼ **antiguo me gusta más que** ∼ **moderno** I like old things better than modern things; ∼ **mejor/peor** the best/ worst part; **no te imaginas** ∼ **grande que era** you can't imagine how big it was.

◆ **lo de** *loc prep*: **¿y** ∼ **de la fiesta?** what about the party, then?; **siento** ∼ **de ayer** I'm sorry about yesterday.

◆ **lo que** *loc conj* what; **acepté** ∼ **que me ofrecieron** I accepted what they offered me.

loa *f* -1. [gen] praise -2. LITER eulogy.

loable *adj* praiseworthy.

loar *vt* to praise.

lobato = **lobezno**.

lobby ['loβi] *(pl* **lobbies**) *m* lobby, pressure group.

lobezno, lobato *m* wolf cub.

lobo, ba *m,f* wolf.

◆ **lobo de mar** *m* [marinero] sea dog.

lóbrego, ga *adj* gloomy, murky.

lóbulo *m* lobe.

local ◇ *adj* local. ◇ *m* -1. [edificio] premises *(pl)* -2. [sede] headquarters *(pl)*.

localidad *f* -1. [población] place, town -2. [asiento] seat -3. [entrada] ticket; **'no hay** ∼ **es'** 'sold out'.

localizar *vt* -1. [encontrar] to locate, to track down -2. [circunscribir] to localize.

loción *f* lotion.

loco, ca ◇ *adj* -1. [gen] mad; **estar** ∼ **de/ por** to be mad with/about; **volverse** ∼ **por** to be mad about; ∼ **de atar** *o* **remate** stark raving mad; **a lo** ∼ [sin pensar] hastily; [temerariamente] wildly -2. [extraordinario - interés, ilusión] tremendous; [- amor, alegría] wild. ◇ *m,f* -1. *lit* & *fig* madman *(f* madwoman), lunatic; **conduce como un** ∼ he drives like a madman -2. *Chile* [molusco] false abalone.

locomoción *f* transport; [de tren] locomotion.

locomotor, ra *o* **triz** *adj* locomotive.

◆ **locomotora** *f* engine, locomotive.

locuaz *adj* loquacious, talkative.

locución *f* phrase.

locura *f* -1. [demencia] madness -2. [imprudencia] folly; **hacer** ∼ **s** to do crazy things;

ser una ~ to be madness.

locutor, ra *m,f* [de radio] announcer; [de televisión] presenter.

locutorio *m* **- 1.** TELECOM phone box *o* booth **- 2.** RADIO studio.

lodo *m lit* & *fig* mud.

logaritmo *m* logarithm.

lógico, ca *adj* logical; **es** ~ **que se enfade** it stands to reason that he should get angry.
  ➡ **lógica** *f* [ciencia] logic.

logístico, ca *adj* logistic.
  ➡ **logística** *f* logistics *(pl)*.

logopeda *mf* speech therapist.

logotipo *m* logo.

logrado, da *adj* [bien hecho] accomplished.

lograr *vt* [gen] to achieve; [puesto, beca, divorcio] to get, to obtain; [resultado] to obtain, to achieve; [perfección] to attain; [victoria, premio] to win; [deseo, aspiración] to fulfil; ~ **hacer algo** to manage to do sthg; ~ **que alguien haga algo** to manage to get sb to do sthg.

logro *m* achievement.

LOGSE *(abrev de* **Ley Orgánica de Ordenación General del Sistema Educativo)** *f Spanish Education Act.*

loma *f* hillock.

lombarda *f* red cabbage.

lombriz *f* earthworm, worm.

lomo *m* **- 1.** [espalda] back **- 2.** [carne] loin **- 3.** [de libro] spine.

lona *f* canvas.

loncha *f* slice; [de beicon] rasher.

lonche *m Perú, Ven* [merienda] *snack eaten during break time.*

lonchería *f Méx, Ven fast-food joint selling tacos etc.*

londinense ◇ *adj* London *(antes de sust).* ◇ *mf* Londoner.

Londres London.

longaniza *f type of spicy, cold pork sausage.*

longitud *f* **- 1.** [dimensión] length; **tiene medio metro de** ~ it's half a metre long; ~ **de onda** wavelength **- 2.** ASTRON & GEOGR longitude.

lonja *f* **- 1.** [loncha] slice **- 2.** [edificio] exchange; ~ **de pescado** fish market.

loro *m* **- 1.** [animal] parrot **- 2.** *loc:* **estar al** ~ *vulg* to have one's finger on the pulse.

los ◇ *art* ▷ **el.** ◇ *pron* ▷ **lo.**

losa *f* **- 1.** [gen] paving stone, flagstone; [de tumba] tombstone **- 2.:** ~ **radiante** *RP* underfloor heating.

loseta *f* floor tile.

lote *m* **- 1.** [parte] share **- 2.** [conjunto] batch, lot **- 3.** *Amér* [de tierra] plot (of land).

loteamiento *m Bol, Urug* parcelling out, division into plots.

loteo *m Andes, Méx, RP* parcelling out, division into plots.

lotería *f* **- 1.** [gen] lottery; **jugar a la** ~ to play the lottery; **le tocó la** ~ she won the lottery; ~ **primitiva** *twice-weekly state-run lottery* **- 2.** [juego de mesa] lotto.

lotización *f Ecuad, Perú* parcelling out, division into plots.

loza *f* **- 1.** [material] earthenware; [porcelana] china **- 2.** [objetos] crockery.

lozanía *f* [de persona] youthful vigour.

lozano, na *adj* **- 1.** [planta] lush, luxuriant **- 2.** [persona] youthfully vigorous.

lubina *f* sea bass.

lubricante, lubrificante ◇ *adj* lubricating. ◇ *m* lubricant.

lubricar, lubrificar *vt* to lubricate.

lucero *m* bright star.

lucha *f* fight; *fig* struggle; **abandonar la** ~ to give up the struggle; ~ **armada** armed struggle; ~ **libre** all-in wrestling.

luchar *vi* to fight; *fig* to struggle; ~ **contra/por** to fight against/for.

lucidez *f* lucidity, clarity.

lúcido, da *adj* lucid.

luciérnaga *f* glow-worm.

lucimiento *m* [de ceremonia etc] sparkle; [de actriz etc] brilliant performance.

lucir ◇ *vi* **- 1.** [gen] to shine **- 2.** [llevar puesto] to wear **- 3.** *Amér* [parecer] to look. ◇ *vt* [gen] to show off; [ropa] to sport.
  ➡ **lucirse** *vpr* **- 1.** [destacar]: ~**se (en)** to shine (at) **- 2.** *fam fig* & *irón* [quedar mal] to mess things up.

lucrativo, va *adj* lucrative; **no** ~ non profit-making.

lucro *m* profit, gain.

lucubrar *vt* to rack one's brains over.

lúdico, ca *adj* [del juego] game *(antes de sust);* [ocioso] of enjoyment, of pleasure.

ludopatía *f* pathological addiction to gambling.

luego ◇ *adv* **- 1.** [justo después] then, next; **primero aquí y** ~ **allí** first here and then there **- 2.** [más tarde] later; **¡hasta** ~**!** see you!, bye!; **hazlo** ~ do it later **- 3.** *Chile, Méx, Ven* [pronto] soon. ◇ *conj* **- 1.** [así que] so, therefore **- 2.:** ~ ~ *Méx fam* [inmediatamente] immediately, straight away; [de vez en cuando] from time to time.

lugar *m* **- 1.** [gen] place; [localidad] place, town; [del crimen, accidente etc] scene; [para acampar, merendar etc] spot; **en primer** ~ in the first place, firstly; **en último** ~ lastly, last; **fuera de** ~ out of place; **no hay** ~ **a duda** there's no room for doubt; **ponte en mi** ~ put yourself in my place; **sin** ~ **a dudas** without a doubt, undoubtedly; **yo en tu** ~ if I were you; **dejar a alguien en**

buen/mal ~ to make sb look good/bad; **poner las cosas en su** ~ to set things straight; **tener** ~ to take place; ~ **de nacimiento** birthplace; ~ **de trabajo** workplace **- 2.** [motivo] cause, reason; **dar** ~ **a** to bring about, to cause **- 3.** [puesto] position.
➡ **en lugar de** *loc prep* instead of.
➡ **lugar común** *m* platitude, commonplace.

lugareño, ña *m,f* villager.

lúgubre *adj* gloomy, mournful.

lujo *m* luxury; *fig* profusion; **permitirse el** ~ **de algo/de hacer algo** to be able to afford sthg/to do sthg.

lujoso, sa *adj* luxurious.

lujuria *f* lust.

lumbago *m* lumbago.

lumbre *f* [fuego] fire; **dar** ~ **a alguien** to give sb a light.

lumbrera *f fam* leading light.

luminoso, sa *adj* [gen] bright; [fuente, energía] light *(antes de sust)*.

luna *f* **- 1.** [astro] moon; ~ **llena/nueva** full/new moon **- 2.** [cristal] window (pane) **- 3.** *loc:* **estar de mala** ~ to be in a bad mood; **estar en la** ~ to be miles away.
➡ **luna de miel** *f* honeymoon.

lunar ◇ *adj* lunar. ◇ *m* **- 1.** [en la piel] mole, beauty spot **- 2.** [en telas] spot; **a** ~**es** spotted.

lunático, ca *m,f* lunatic.

lunes *m inv* Monday; *ver también* **sábado**.

luneta *f* [de coche] windscreen; ~ **térmica** demister.

lupa *f* magnifying glass.

lustrabotas *m inv Andes, RP* shoeshine, bootblack *UK*.

lustrador *m Andes, RP* shoeshine, bootblack *UK*.

lustradora *f Andes, RP* floor polisher.

lustrar *vt* to polish.

lustre *m* [brillo] shine.

lustro *m* five-year period.

lustroso, sa *adj* shiny.

luto *m* mourning; **de** ~ in mourning.

luxación *f* dislocation.

Luxemburgo Luxembourg.

luxemburgués, esa ◇ *adj* Luxembourg *(antes de sust)*. ◇ *m,f* Luxembourger.

luz *f* [gen] light; [electricidad] electricity; [destello] flash (of light); **apagar la** ~ to switch off the light; **a plena** ~ **del día** in broad daylight; **cortar la** ~ to cut off the electricity supply; **dar** *o* **encender la** ~ to switch on the light; **pagar (el recibo de) la** ~ to pay the electricity (bill); **se ha ido la** ~ the lights have gone out; ~ **eléctrica** electric light; ~ **solar** sunlight; **a la** ~ **de** [una vela, la luna etc] by the light of; [los

acontecimientos etc] in the light of; **arrojar** ~ **sobre** to shed light on; **dar a** ~ **(un niño)** to give birth (to a child); **sacar algo a la** ~ [secreto] to bring to light; [obra] to bring out, to publish; **salir a la** ~ [descubrirse] to come to light; [publicarse] to come out; **ver la** ~ to see the light.
➡ **luces** *fpl* AUTOM lights; **poner las luces de carretera** *o* **largas** to put (one's) headlights on full beam; **luces de cruce** *o* **cortas** dipped headlights; **luces de posición** *o* **situación** sidelights.

lycra® *f* Lycra®.

M

m¹, M *f* [letra] m, M.

m² *(abrev de* **metro***)* m.

macabro, bra *adj* macabre.

macana *f CSur, Perú, Ven fam* [disparate] stupid thing; [fastidio] pain, drag; [pena] shame.

macanear *vi CSur fam* [decir tonterías] to talk nonsense; [hacer tonterías] to be stupid.

macarra *m fam* [de prostitutas] pimp; [rufián] thug.

macarrón *m* [tubo] sheath *(of cable)*.
➡ **macarrones** *mpl* [pasta] macaroni *(U)*.

macedonia *f* salad; ~ **de frutas** fruit salad.

macerar *vt* CULIN to soak, to macerate.

maceta *f* [tiesto] flowerpot.

macetero *m* flowerpot holder.

machaca *mf* [trabajador] dogsbody.

machacar ◇ *vt* **- 1.** [triturar] to crush **- 2.** *fig* [insistir] to keep going on about. ◇ *vi fig:* ~ **(sobre)** to go on (about).

machete *m* machete.

machista *adj & mf* male chauvinist.

macho ◇ *adj* **- 1.** BIOL male **- 2.** *fig* [hombre] macho. ◇ *m* **- 1.** BIOL male **- 2.** *fig* [hombre] he-man **- 3.** TECN male part; [de enchufe] pin. ◇ *interj fam:* **¡oye,** ~**!** oy, mate!

macizo, za *adj* solid; **estar** ~ *fam* [hombre] to be hunky; [mujer] to be gorgeous.
➡ **macizo** *m* **- 1.** GEOGR massif **- 2.** BOT: ~ **de flores** flowerbed.

macro *f* INFORM macro.

macrobiótico, ca *adj* macrobiotic.

mácula *f* spot; *fig* blemish.

macuto *m* backpack, knapsack.

madeja f hank, skein; **enredar la ~** to complicate matters.

madera f -1. [gen] wood; CONSTR timber; [tabla] piece of wood; **de ~** wooden; **~ contrachapada** plywood; **tocar ~** to touch wood UK, to knock on wood US -2. [disposición]: **tener ~ de algo** to have the makings of sthg.

madero m [tabla] log.

madrastra f stepmother.

madrazo m Méx hard blow.

madre f -1. [gen] mother; **es ~ de tres niños** she's a mother of three; **~ adoptiva/de alquiler** foster/surrogate mother; **~ biológica** biological mother; **~ de familia** mother; **~ política** mother-in-law; **~ soltera** single mother; **~ superiora** mother superior; **me vale ~** Méx mfam I couldn't give a damn o UK a toss -2. [poso] dregs (pl).
◆ **madre mía** interj: **¡~ mía!** Jesus!, Christ!

Madrid Madrid.

madriguera f [gen & fig] den; [de conejo] burrow.

madrileño, ña m,f native/inhabitant of Madrid.

madrina f [gen] patroness; [de boda] bridesmaid; [de bautizo] godmother.

madroño m -1. [árbol] strawberry tree -2. [fruto] strawberry-tree berry.

madrugada f -1. [amanecer] dawn; **de ~** at daybreak -2. [noche] early morning; **las tres de la ~** three in the morning.

madrugador, ra adj early-rising.

madrugar vi to get up early; fig to be quick off the mark; **a quien madruga Dios le ayuda** proverb the early bird catches the worm.

madurar ◇ vt -1. [gen] to mature; [fruta, mies] to ripen -2. [idea, proyecto etc] to think through. ◇ vi [gen] to mature; [fruta] to ripen.

madurez f -1. [cualidad - gen] maturity; [- de fruta, mies] ripeness -2. [edad adulta] adulthood.

maduro, ra adj [gen] mature; [fruta, mies] ripe; **de edad madura** middle-aged.

maestra ▷ **maestro**.

maestría f [habilidad] mastery, skill.

maestro, tra ◇ adj -1. [perfecto] masterly -2. [principal] main; [llave] master (antes de sust). ◇ m,f -1. [profesor] teacher -2. [sabio] master -3. MÚS maestro -4. Méx [de universidad] lecturer UK, professor US -5. [director]: **~ de ceremonias** master of ceremonies; **~ de cocina** chef; **~ de obras** foreman; **~ de orquesta** conductor.

mafia f mafia.

mafioso, sa m,f mafioso.

magdalena f fairy cake.

magia f magic.

mágico, ca adj -1. [con magia] magic -2. [atractivo] magical.

magisterio m -1. [enseñanza] teaching -2. [profesión] teaching profession.

magistrado, da m,f [juez] judge.

magistral adj -1. [de maestro] magisterial -2. [genial] masterly.

magistratura f -1. [jueces] magistrature -2. [tribunal] tribunal; **~ de trabajo** industrial tribunal.

magnánimo, ma adj magnanimous.

magnate m magnate; **~ del petróleo/de la prensa** oil/press baron.

magnesia f magnesia.

magnesio m magnesium.

magnético, ca adj lit & fig magnetic.

magnetizar vt to magnetize; fig to mesmerize.

magnetofónico, ca adj [cinta] magnetic.

magnetófono m tape recorder.

magnicidio m assassination (of somebody important).

magnificencia f magnificence.

magnífico, ca adj wonderful, magnificent.

magnitud f magnitude.

magnolia f magnolia.

mago, ga m,f -1. [prestidigitador] magician -2. [en cuentos etc] wizard.

magro, gra adj -1. [sin grasa] lean -2. [pobre] poor.
◆ **magro** m lean meat.

magulladura f bruise.

magullar vt to bruise.

mahometano, na adj & m,f Muslim.

mahonesa = **mayonesa**.

maicena f cornflour UK, cornstarch US.

maíz m maize UK, corn US; **~ dulce** sweetcorn.

maja ▷ **majo**.

majadero, ra m,f idiot.

majareta fam ◇ adj nutty. ◇ mf nutcase.

majestad f majesty.
◆ **Su Majestad** f His/Her Majesty.

majestuoso, sa adj majestic.

majo, ja adj -1. [simpático] nice -2. [bonito] pretty.

mal ◇ adj ▷ **malo**. ◇ m -1. [perversión]: **el ~** evil -2. [daño] harm, damage -3. [enfermedad] illness; **~ de montaña** altitude o mountain sickness; **~ de ojo** evil eye -4. [inconveniente] bad thing; **un ~ necesario** a necessary evil. ◇ adv -1. [incorrectamente] wrong; **esto está ~ hecho** this has been done wrong; **has escrito ~ esta palabra** you've spelt that word wrong -2. [inadecuadamente] badly; **la fiesta salió ~** the party went off badly; **oigo/veo ~** I can't

hear/see very well; **encontrarse** ~ [enfermo] to feel ill; [incómodo] to feel uncomfortable; **oler** ~ [tener mal olor] to smell bad; *fam* [tener mal cariz] to smell fishy; **saber** ~ [tener mal sabor] to taste bad; **sentar** ~ **a alguien** [ropa] not to suit sb; [comida] to disagree with sb; [comentario, actitud] to upset sb; **tomar algo a** ~ to take sthg the wrong way **- 3.** [difícilmente] hardly; ~ **puede saberlo si no se lo cuentas** he's hardly going to know it if you don't tell him **- 4.** *loc*: **estar a** ~ **con alguien** to have fallen out with sb; **ir de** ~ **en peor** to go from bad to worse; **no estaría** ~ **que ...** it would be nice if ...
◆ **mal que** *loc conj* although, even though.
◆ **mal que bien** *loc adv* somehow or other.

malabarismo *m lit & fig* juggling (U).

malabarista *mf* juggler.

malacostumbrado, da *adj* spoiled.

malaria *f* malaria.

Malasia Malaysia.

malcriado, da *adj* spoiled.

maldad *f* **- 1.** [cualidad] evil **- 2.** [acción] evil thing.

maldecir <> *vt* to curse. <> *vi* to curse.

maldición *f* curse.

maldito, ta *adj* **- 1.** [embrujado] cursed, damned **- 2.** *fam* [para enfatizar] damned; **¡maldita sea!** damn it!

maleable *adj lit & fig* malleable.

maleante *mf* crook.

malecón *m* [atracadero] jetty

maleducado, da *adj* rude.

maleficio *m* curse.

malentendido *m* misunderstanding.

malestar *m* **- 1.** [dolor] upset, discomfort; **siento un** ~ **en el estómago** I've got an upset stomach; **sentir** ~ **general** to feel unwell **- 2.** [inquietud] uneasiness, unrest.

maleta *f* suitcase; **hacer** *o* **preparar la** ~ to pack (one's bags).

maletero *m* boot *UK*, trunk *US*.

maletín *m* briefcase.

malévolo, la *adj* malevolent, wicked.

maleza *f* [arbustos] undergrowth; [malas hierbas] weeds *(pl)*.

malformación *f* malformation; ~ **congénita** congenital malformation.

malgastar *vt* [dinero, tiempo] to waste; [salud] to ruin.

malhablado, da *adj* foul-mouthed.

malhechor, ra *adj m,f* criminal.

malhumorado, da *adj* bad-tempered; [enfadado] in a bad mood.

malicia *f* [maldad] wickedness, evil; [mala intención] malice.

malicioso, sa *adj* [malo] wicked, evil; [malintencionado] malicious.

maligno, na *adj* malignant.

malla *f* **- 1.** [tejido] mesh; ~ **de alambre** wire mesh **- 2.** [red] net **- 3.** *RP* [traje de baño] swimsuit.
◆ **mallas** *fpl* **- 1.** [de gimnasia] leotard *(sg)*; [de ballet] tights **- 2.** [de portería] net *(sg)*.

Mallorca Majorca.

malo, la, mal (*compar* **peor**, *superl* **el peor**) *adj* (*antes de sust masc sg:* **mal**) **- 1.** [gen] bad; [calidad] poor, bad; **lo** ~ **fue que ...** the problem was (that) ...; **más vale** ~ **conocido que bueno por conocer** *proverb* better the devil you know (than the devil you don't) **- 2.** [malicioso] wicked **- 3.** [enfermo] ill, sick; **estar/ponerse** ~ to be/fall ill **- 4.** [travieso] naughty.
◆ **malo, la** *m,f* [de película etc] villain, baddie.
◆ **malas** *fpl*: **estar de malas** to be in a bad mood; **por las malas** by force.

malograr *vt* **- 1.** to waste **- 2.** *Andes* [estropear] to make a mess of, to ruin.
◆ **malograrse** *vpr* **- 1.** [fracasar] to fail **- 2.** [morir] to die before one's time **- 3.** *Andes* [estropearse - máquina] to break down; [- alimento] to go off, to spoil.

malparado, da *adj*: **salir** ~ **de algo** to come out of sthg badly.

malpensado, da *adj* malicious, evil-minded.

malsano, na *adj* unhealthy.

malsonante *adj* rude.

malta *m* malt.

maltés, esa *adj & m,f* Maltese.

maltratar *vt* **- 1.** [pegar, insultar] to ill-treat **- 2.** [estropear] to damage.

maltrecho, cha *adj* battered; **dejar** ~ **a alguien** to leave sb in a bad way.

malva <> *f* BOT mallow. <> *adj inv* mauve. <> *m* [color] mauve.

malvado, da *adj* evil, wicked.

malversación *f*: ~ **(de fondos)** embezzlement (of funds).

malversar *vt* to embezzle.

Malvinas *fpl*: **las (islas)** ~ the Falkland Islands, the Falklands.

malviviente *mf* *CSur* criminal.

malvivir *vi* to scrape together an existence.

mama *f* **- 1.** [órgano - de mujer] breast; [- ZOOL] udder **- 2.** *fam* [madre] mum, mummy.

mamá (*pl* **mamás**) *f* **- 1.** *fam* mum, mummy **- 2.**: ~ **grande** *Col, Méx fam* grandma.

mamadera *f* *CSur, Perú* [biberón] (baby's) bottle.

mamar <> *vt* **- 1.** [suj: bebé] to suckle **- 2.** [aprender]: **lo mamó desde pequeño** he was immersed in it as a child. <> *vi* to suckle.

mamarracho *m* [fantoche] mess.

mambo *m* mambo.

mamífero, ra *adj* mammal.

◆ **mamífero** *m* mammal.

mamografía *f* MED - **1.** [técnica] breast scanning, mammography - **2.** [resultado] breast scan.

mamotreto *m* - **1.** *despec* [libro] hefty tome - **2.** [objeto grande] monstrosity.

mampara *f* screen.

manada *f* [ZOOL - gen] herd; [- de lobos] pack; [- de ovejas] flock; [- de leones] pride.

manager (*pl* **managers**) *m* manager.

Managua Managua.

manantial *m* spring; *fig* source.

manar *vi* *lit* & *fig*: ~ **(de)** to flow (from).

manazas *adj* *inv* clumsy.

mancha *f* - **1.** [gen] stain, spot; [de tinta] blot; [de color] spot, mark; **extenderse como una ~ de aceite** to spread like wildfire - **2.** ASTRON spot - **3.** [deshonra] blemish; **sin ~** unblemished.

manchar *vt* - **1.** [ensuciar]: ~ **algo (de** *o* **con)** [gen] to make sthg dirty (with); [con manchas] to stain sthg (with); [emborronar] to smudge sthg (with) - **2.** [deshonrar] to tarnish.

manchego, ga *adj* of/relating to La Mancha.

◆ **manchego** ▷ **queso**.

manco, ca *adj* [sin una mano] one-handed; [sin manos] handless; [sin un brazo] one-armed; [sin brazos] armless; **no ser ~ para** *o* **en** to be a dab hand at.

mancomunidad *f* association.

mancorna, mancuerna *f* *Andes, CAm, Méx, Ven* cufflink.

mandado, da *m,f* [subordinado] underling.

◆ **mandado** *m* [recado] errand.

mandamás (*pl* **mandamases**) *mf* bigwig, boss.

mandamiento *m* - **1.** [orden - militar] order, command; [- judicial] writ - **2.** RELIG commandment; **los diez ~s** the Ten Commandments.

mandar ▷ *vt* - **1.** [dar órdenes a] to order; ~ **a alguien hacer algo** to order sb to do sthg; ~ **hacer algo** to have sthg done - **2.** [enviar] to send - **3.** [dirigir, gobernar] to lead, to be in charge of; [país] to rule. ▷ *vi* - **1.** [gen] to be in charge; [jefe de estado] to rule; **aquí mando yo** I'm in charge here; ~ **en algo** to be in charge of sthg - **2.** *despec* [dar órdenes] to order people around - **3.** *loc*: **¿mande?** *fam* eh?, you what?

mandarina *f* mandarin.

mandatario, ria *m,f* representative, agent.

mandato *m* - **1.** [gen] order, command - **2.** [poderes de representación, disposición]

mandate; ~ **judicial** warrant - **3.** POLÍT term of office; [reinado] period of rule.

mandíbula *f* jaw.

mandil *m* [delantal] apron.

Mandinga *m* *Amér* the devil.

mando *m* - **1.** [poder] command, authority; **al ~ de** in charge of; **entregar el ~** to hand over command - **2.** [periodo en poder] term of office - **3.** (*gen pl*) [autoridades] leadership (*U*); MIL command (*U*); ~**s intermedios** middle management (*sg*) - **4.** [dispositivo] control; ~ **automático/a distancia** automatic/remote control.

mandolina *f* mandolin.

mandón, ona ▷ *adj* bossy. ▷ *m,f* bossy-boots.

manecilla *f* [del reloj] hand.

manejable *adj* [gen] manageable; [herramienta] easy to use.

manejar ▷ *vt* - **1.** [conocimientos, datos] to use, to marshal - **2.** [máquina, mandos] to operate; [caballo, bicicleta] to handle; [arma] to wield - **3.** [negocio etc] to manage, to run; [gente] to handle - **4.** *Amér* [vehículo] to drive. ▷ *vi* *Amér* [conducir] to drive.

◆ **manejarse** *vpr* - **1.** [moverse] to move *o* get about - **2.** [desenvolverse] to manage, to get by.

manejo *m* - **1.** [de máquina, mandos] operation; [de armas, herramientas] use; **de fácil ~** user-friendly - **2.** [de conocimientos, datos] marshalling; [de idiomas] command - **3.** [de caballo, bicicleta] handling - **4.** [de negocio etc] management, running - **5.** (*gen pl*) *fig* [intriga] intrigue.

manera *f* way, manner; **lo haremos a mi ~** we'll do it my way; **a mi ~ de ver** the way I see it; **de cualquier ~** [sin cuidado] any old how; [de todos modos] anyway, in any case; **de esta ~** in this way; **de la misma ~** similarly, in the same way; **de mala ~** badly; **de ninguna ~, en ~ alguna** [refuerza negación] by no means, under no circumstances; [respuesta exclamativa] no way!, certainly not!; **de todas ~s** anyway; **en cierta ~** in a way; ~ **de ser** way of being, nature; **de ~ que** [para] so (that); **no hay ~** there is no way, it's impossible; **¡qué ~ de ...!** what a way to ...!

◆ **maneras** *fpl* [modales] manners; **buenas/malas ~** good/bad manners.

manga *f* - **1.** [de prenda] sleeve; **en ~s de camisa** in shirt sleeves; **sin ~s** sleeveless; **andar ~ por hombro** to be a mess - **2.** [manguera] hosepipe - **3.** [de pastelería] forcing *o* piping bag - **4.** DEP stage, round.

mangante *mf* *fam* thief.

mango *m* - **1.** [asa] handle - **2.** [árbol] mango tree; [fruta] mango - **3.**: **no tiene un ~** *RP* *fam* I haven't got a bean, I'm broke.

mangonear *vi fam* - **1.** [entrometerse] to meddle - **2.** [mandar] to be bossy - **3.** [manipular] to fiddle about.

manguera *f* hosepipe; [de bombero] fire hose.

maní, maníes *m Andes, Carib, RP* peanut.

manía *f* - **1.** [idea fija] obsession - **2.** [peculiaridad] idiosyncracy - **3.** [mala costumbre] bad habit - **4.** [afición exagerada] mania, craze - **5.** *fam* [ojeriza] dislike - **6.** PSICOL mania.

maniaco, ca, maníaco, ca ◇ *adj* manic. ◇ *m,f* maniac.

maniatar *vt* to tie the hands of.

maniático, ca ◇ *adj* fussy. ◇ *m,f* fussy person; **es un ~ del fútbol** he's football-crazy.

manicomio *m* mental *o* psychiatric hospital *UK*, insane asylum *US*.

manicuro, ra *m,f* [persona] manicurist.
  ◆ **manicura** *f* [técnica] manicure.

manido, da *adj* [tema etc] hackneyed.

manifestación *f* - **1.** [de alegría, dolor etc] show, display; [de opinión] declaration, expression; [indicio] sign - **2.** [por la calle] demonstration; **hacer una ~** to hold a demonstration.

manifestar *vt* - **1.** [alegría, dolor etc] to show - **2.** [opinión etc] to express.
  ◆ **manifestarse** *vpr* - **1.** [por la calle] to demonstrate - **2.** [hacerse evidente] to become clear *o* apparent.

manifiesto, ta *adj* clear, evident; **poner de ~ algo** [revelar] to reveal sthg; [hacer patente] to make sthg clear.
  ◆ **manifiesto** *m* manifesto.

manillar *m* handlebars *(pl)*.

maniobra *f* - **1.** [gen] manoeuvre; **estar de ~s** MIL to be on manoeuvres; **hacer ~s** AUTOM to manoeuvre - **2.** [treta] trick.

maniobrar *vi* to manoeuvre.

manipulación *f* - **1.** [gen] handling - **2.** [engaño] manipulation.

manipular *vt* - **1.** [manejar] to handle - **2.** [mangonear - información, resultados] to manipulate; [- negocios, asuntos] to interfere in.

maniquí *(pl* **maniquíes)** ◇ *m* dummy. ◇ *mf* [modelo] model.

manirroto, ta ◇ *adj* extravagant. ◇ *m,f* spendthrift.

manitas *mf inv* handy person.

manito *m Méx fam* pal, mate *UK*, buddy *US*.

manivela *f* crank.

manjar *m* delicious food *(U)*.

mano ◇ *f* - **1.** [gen] hand; **a ~** [cerca] to hand, handy; [sin máquina] by hand; **a ~ armada** armed; **dar** *o* **estrechar la ~ a** alguien to shake hands with sb; **darse** *o* **estrecharse la ~** to shake hands; **echar/tender una ~** to give/offer a hand; **¡~s arriba!, ¡arriba las ~s!** hands up!; **~ de obra** [capacidad de trabajo] labour; [trabajadores] workforce - **2.** [ZOOL - gen] forefoot; [- de perro, gato] (front) paw; [- de cerdo] (front) trotter - **3.** [lado]: **a ~ derecha/izquierda** on the right/left - **4.**: **calle de una sola ~** *RP* one-way street; **calle de doble ~** *RP* two-way street - **5.** [de pintura etc] coat - **6.** [influencia] influence - **7.** [partida de naipes] game - **8.** [serie, tanda] series - **9.** *loc*: **bajo ~** secretly; **caer en ~s de alguien** to fall into sb's hands; **con las ~s cruzadas, ~ sobre ~** [sitting around doing nothing; **coger a alguien con las ~s en la masa** to catch sb red-handed *o* in the act; **de primera ~** [coche etc] brand new; [noticias etc] first-hand; **de segunda ~** second-hand; **~ a ~** tête-à-tête; **¡~s a la obra!** let's get down to it!; **tener buena ~ para algo** to have a knack for sthg.

manojo *m* bunch.

manoletina *f* [zapato] *type of open, low-heeled shoe, often with a bow.*

manómetro *m* pressure gauge.

manopla *f* mitten.

manosear *vt* - **1.** [gen] to handle roughly; [papel, tela] to rumple - **2.** [persona] to fondle.

manotazo *m* slap.

mansalva ◆ **a mansalva** *loc adv* [en abundancia] in abundance.

mansedumbre *f* [gen] calmness, gentleness; [de animal] tameness.

mansión *f* mansion.

manso, sa *adj* - **1.** [apacible] calm, gentle - **2.** [domesticado] tame - **3.** *Chile* [extraordinario] tremendous.

manta *f* [para abrigarse] blanket; **~ eléctrica** electric blanket; **~ de viaje** travelling rug; **liarse la ~ a la cabeza** to take the plunge.

manteca *f* fat; [mantequilla] butter; **~ de cacao** cocoa butter; **~ de cerdo** lard.

mantecado *m* - **1.** [pastel] shortcake - **2.** [helado] *ice-cream made of milk, eggs and sugar.*

mantel *m* tablecloth.

mantener *vt* - **1.** [sustentar, aguantar] to support - **2.** [conservar] to keep; [en buen estado] to maintain, to service - **3.** [tener - relaciones, conversación] to have - **4.** [defender - opinión] to stick to, to maintain; [- candidatura] to refuse to withdraw.
  ◆ **mantenerse** *vpr* - **1.** [sustentarse] to subsist, to support o.s. - **2.** [permanecer, continuar] to remain; [edificio] to remain standing; **~se aparte** [en discusión] to stay out of it.

mantenimiento *m* **-1.** [sustento] sustenance **-2.** [conservación] upkeep, maintenance.

mantequilla *f* butter.

mantilla *f* **-1.** [de mujer] mantilla **-2.** [de bebé] shawl.

manto *m* [gen] cloak.

mantón *m* shawl.

manual ◇ *adj* [con las manos] manual. ◇ *m* manual.

manubrio *m* **-1.** crank **-2.** *Amér* [manillar] handlebars *(pl)*.

manufacturar *vt* to manufacture.

manuscrito, ta *adj* handwritten.
➤ **manuscrito** *m* manuscript.

manutención *f* **-1.** [sustento] support, maintenance **-2.** [alimento] food.

manzana *f* **-1.** [fruta] apple **-2.** [grupo de casas] block (of houses).

manzanilla *f* **-1.** [planta] camomile **-2.** [infusión] camomile tea.

manzano *m* apple tree.

maña *f* **-1.** [destreza] skill; **tener ~ para** to have a knack for **-2.** [astucia] wits *(pl)*, guile *(U)*.

mañana ◇ *f* morning; **a la ~ siguiente** the next morning; **a las dos de la ~** at two in the morning; **por la ~** in the morning. ◇ *m*: **el ~** tomorrow, the future. ◇ *adv* tomorrow; **a partir de ~** starting tomorrow, as of tomorrow; **¡hasta ~!** see you tomorrow!; **~ por la ~** tomorrow morning; **pasado ~** the day after tomorrow.

mañanitas *fpl Méx* birthday song *(sg)*.

mañoco *m Ven* tapioca.

mañoso, sa *adj* skilful.

mapa *m* map; **~ de carreteras** road map.

mapamundi *m* world map.

maqueta *f* **-1.** [reproducción a escala] (scale) model **-2.** [de libro] dummy.

maquila *f Amér* [de máquinas] assembly; [de ropas] making-up.

maquiladora *f Amér* assembly plant.

maquillaje *m* **-1.** [producto] make-up **-2.** [acción] making-up.

maquillar *vt* [pintar] to make up.
➤ **maquillarse** *vpr* to make o.s. up.

máquina *f* **-1.** [gen] machine; **a toda ~** at full pelt; **coser a ~** to machine-sew; **escribir a ~** to type; **hecho a ~** machine-made; **~ de afeitar** electric razor; **~ de coser** sewing machine; **~ de escribir** typewriter; **~ fotográfica** camera; **~ tragaperras** o **tragamonedas** *Amér* slot machine, fruit machine *UK* **-2.** [locomotora] engine; **~ de vapor** steam engine **-3.** [mecanismo] mechanism **-4.** *Cuba* [vehículo] car **-5.** [de estado, partido etc] machinery *(U)*.

maquinación *f* machination.

maquinal *adj* mechanical.

maquinar *vt* to machinate, to plot.

maquinaria *f* **-1.** [gen] machinery **-2.** [de reloj etc] mechanism.

maquinilla *f*: **~ de afeitar** razor; **~ eléctrica** electric razor.

maquinista *mf* [de tren] engine driver *UK*, engineer *US*; [de barco] engineer.

mar *m* o *f lit* & *fig* sea; **alta ~** high seas *(pl)*; **~ gruesa** heavy sea; **el ~ del Norte** the North Sea; **llover a ~es** to rain buckets; **la ~ de** [un montón de] loads of, lots of; [muy] really, very.

marabunta *f* [muchedumbre] crowd.

maraca *f* maraca.

maracujá *f Amér* passion fruit.

maraña *f* **-1.** [maleza] thicket **-2.** *fig* [enredo] tangle.

maratón *m lit* & *fig* marathon.

maravilla *f* **-1.** [gen] marvel, wonder; **es una ~** it's wonderful; **hacer ~s** to do o work wonders; **a las mil ~s, de ~** wonderfully; **venir de ~** to be just the thing o ticket **-2.** BOT marigold.

maravillar *vt* to amaze.
➤ **maravillarse** *vpr*: **~se (con)** to be amazed (by).

maravilloso, sa *adj* marvellous, wonderful.

marca *f* **-1.** [señal] mark; [de rueda, animal] track; [en ganado] brand; [en papel] watermark; **~ de nacimiento** birthmark **-2.** [COM - de tabaco, café etc] brand; [- de coche, ordenador etc] make; **de ~** designer *(antes de sust)*; **~ de fábrica** trademark; **~ registrada** registered trademark **-3.** [etiqueta] label **-4.** [DEP - gen] performance; [en carreras] time; [- plusmarca] record.

marcado, da *adj* [gen] marked.
➤ **marcado** *m* **-1.** [señalado] marking **-2.** [peinado] set.

marcador, ra *adj* marking.
➤ **marcador** *m* **-1.** [tablero] scoreboard **-2.** [DEP - defensor] marker; [- goleador] scorer **-3.** *Amér* [rotulador] felt-tip pen; *Méx* [fluorescente] highlighter pen.

marcapasos *m inv* pacemaker.

marcar ◇ *vt* **-1.** [gen] to mark **-2.** [poner precio a] to price **-3.** [indicar] to indicate **-4.** [resaltar] to emphasize **-5.** [número de teléfono] to dial **-6.** [suj: termómetro, contador etc] to read; [suj: reloj] to say **-7.** [DEP - tanto] to score; [- a un jugador] to mark **-8.** [cabello] to set. ◇ *vi* **-1.** [dejar secuelas] to leave a mark **-2.** DEP [anotar un tanto] to score.

marcha *f* **-1.** [partida] departure **-2.** [ritmo] speed; en **~** [motor] running; [plan] under way; **poner en ~** [gen] to start; [dispositivo, alarma] to activate; **ponerse en ~** [persona]

to start off; [máquina] to start; **hacer algo sobre la** ~ to do sthg as one goes along - **3.** AUTOM gear; ~ **atrás** reverse; **dar** ~ **atrás** AUTOM to reverse; *fig* to back out - **4.** MIL & PO-LÍT march - **5.** MÚS march - **6.** [transcurso] course; [progreso] progress - **7.** DEP walk - **8.** *fam* [animación] liveliness, life; **hay mucha** ~ there's a great atmosphere.

marchar *vi* - **1.** [andar] to walk - **2.** [partir] to leave, to go - **3.** [funcionar] to work - **4.** [desarrollarse] to progress; **el negocio marcha** business is going well.

➡ marcharse *vpr* to leave, to go.

marchitar *vt lit* & *fig* to wither.

➡ marchitarse *vpr* - **1.** [planta] to fade, to wither - **2.** *fig* [persona] to languish, to fade away.

marchito, ta *adj* [planta] faded.

marcial *adj* martial.

marco *m* - **1.** [cerco] frame - **2.** *fig* [ambiente, paisaje] setting - **3.** [ámbito] framework - **4.** [moneda] mark - **5.** [portería] goalmouth.

marea *f* [del mar] tide; ~ **alta/baja** high/low tide; ~ **negra** oil slick.

marear *vt* - **1.** [provocar náuseas a] to make sick; [en coche, avión etc] to make travelsick; [en barco] to make seasick - **2.** [aturdir] to make dizzy - **3.** *fam* [fastidiar] to annoy.

➡ marearse *vpr* - **1.** [tener náuseas] to feel sick; [en coche, avión etc] to feel travelsick; [en barco] to get seasick - **2.** [estar aturdido] to get dizzy - **3.** [emborracharse] to get drunk.

marejada *f* [mar rizada] heavy sea.

maremoto *m* tidal wave.

mareo *m* - **1.** [náuseas] sickness; [en coche, avión etc] travelsickness; [en barco] seasickness - **2.** [aturdimiento] dizziness, giddiness - **3.** *fam fig* [fastidio] drag, pain.

marfil *m* ivory.

margarina *f* margarine.

margarita *f* - **1.** BOT daisy; **echar** ~**s a los cerdos** to cast pearls before swine - **2.** IMPRENTA daisy wheel.

margen *m o f* - **1.** *(gen f)* [de río] bank; [de camino] side - **2.** *(gen m)* [de página] margin - **3.** *(gen m)* COM margin - **4.** *(gen m)* [límites] leeway; **dejar al** ~ to exclude; **estar al** ~ **de** to have nothing to do with; **mantenerse al** ~ **de** to keep out of; ~ **de error** margin of error - **5.** *(gen m)* [ocasión]: **dar** ~ **a alguien para hacer algo** to give sb the chance to do sthg.

marginación *f* exclusion.

marginado, da ◇ *adj* excluded. ◇ *m,f* outcast.

maría *f Méx fam* migrant from country to urban areas.

marica *m mfam despec* queer, poof.

Maricastaña ➪ **tiempo**.

maricón *m mfam despec* queer, poof.

marido *m* husband.

marihuana *f* marijuana.

marimacho *m fam* mannish woman; *despec* butch woman.

marina ➪ **marino**.

marinero, ra *adj* [gen] sea *(antes de sust)*; [buque] seaworthy; [pueblo] seafaring.

➡ marinero *m* sailor.

marino, na *adj* sea *(antes de sust)*, marine.

➡ marino *m* sailor.

➡ marina *f* MIL: ~ **(de guerra)** navy.

marioneta *f* [muñeco] marionette, puppet.

➡ marionetas *fpl* [teatro] puppet show *(sg)*.

mariposa *f* - **1.** [insecto] butterfly - **2.** [en natación] butterfly.

mariquita *f* [insecto] ladybird *UK*, ladybug *US*.

marisco *m* seafood *(U)*, shellfish *(U)*.

marisma *f* salt marsh.

marisquería *f* seafood restaurant.

marítimo, ma *adj* [del mar] maritime; [cercano al mar] seaside *(antes de sust)*.

marketing ['marketin] *m* marketing.

mármol *m* marble.

marmota *f* marmot.

mar Muerto *m*: **el** ~ the Dead Sea.

mar Negro *m*: **el** ~ the Black Sea.

marqués, esa *m* marquis *(f* marchioness).

marquesina *f* glass canopy; [parada de autobús] bus shelter.

marrano, na *m,f* - **1.** [animal] pig - **2.** *fam fig* [sucio] (filthy) pig.

mar Rojo *m*: **el** ~ the Red Sea.

marrón *adj* & *m* brown.

marroquí *(pl* **marroquíes)** *adj* & *mf* Moroccan.

Marruecos Morocco.

Marte *m* Mars.

martes *m inv* Tuesday; ~ **de Carnaval** Shrove Tuesday; ~ **y trece** ≃ Friday 13th; *ver también* **sábado**.

martillear, martillar *vt* to hammer.

martillero, ra *m,f CSur* auctioneer.

martillo *m* - **1.** hammer - **2.** *Col* [subasta] auction.

mártir *mf lit* & *fig* martyr.

martirio *m* - **1.** RELIG martyrdom - **2.** *fig* [sufrimiento] trial, torment; **ser un** ~ **chino** to be torture.

martirizar *vt* - **1.** [torturar] to martyr - **2.** *fig* [hacer sufrir] to torment, to torture.

marxismo *m* Marxism.

marxista *adj* & *mf* Marxist.

marzo *m* March; *ver también* **septiembre**.

mas *conj* but.

más ⟨⟩ *adv* -**1.** *(comparativo)* more; **Pepe es ~ alto/ambicioso** Pepe is taller/more ambitious; **tener ~ hambre** to be hungrier *o* more hungry; **~ de/que** more than; **~ ... que ...** more ... than ...; **Juan es ~ alto que tú** Juan is taller than you; **de ~** [de sobra] left over; **hay diez euros de ~** there are ten euros left over; **eso está de ~** that's not necessary -**2.** *(superlativo)*: **el/la/lo ~** the most; **el ~ listo/ambicioso** the cleverest/most ambitious -**3.** *(en frases negativas)* any more; **no necesito ~ (trabajo)** I don't need any more (work) -**4.** *(con pron interrogativos e indefinidos)* else; **¿qué/quién ~?** what/who else?; **nadie ~ vino** nobody else came -**5.** [indica suma] plus; **dos ~ dos igual a cuatro** two plus two is four -**6.** [indica intensidad]: **no le aguanto, ¡es ~ tonto!** I can't stand him, he's so stupid!; **¡qué día ~ bonito!** what a lovely day! -**7.** [indica preferencia]: **~ vale que nos vayamos a casa** it would be better for us to go home -**8.** *loc*: **el que ~ y el que menos** everyone; **es ~** indeed, what is more; **~ bien** rather; **~ o menos** more or less; **¿qué ~ da?** what difference does it make?; **sin ~ (ni ~)** just like that. ⟨⟩ *m inv* MAT plus (sign); **tiene sus ~ y sus menos** it has its good points and its bad points.

◆ **por más que** *loc conj* however much; **por ~ que lo intente no lo conseguirá** however much *o* hard she tries, she'll never manage it.

masa *f* -**1.** [gen] mass -**2.** CULIN dough -**3.** *RP* [pastelillo] cake.

◆ **masas** *fpl*: **las ~s** the masses.

masacre *f* massacre.

masaje *m* massage.

masajista *m* masseur (*f* masseuse).

mascar *vt* & *vi* to chew.

máscara *f* [gen] mask; **~ antigás** gas mask; **~ de oxígeno** oxygen mask.

mascarilla *f* -**1.** MED mask -**2.** [cosmética] face pack.

mascota *f* mascot.

masculino, na *adj* -**1.** BIOL male -**2.** [varonil] manly -**3.** GRAM masculine.

mascullar *vt* to mutter.

masificación *f* overcrowding.

masilla *f* putty.

masivo, va *adj* mass *(antes de sust)*.

masón, ona ⟨⟩ *adj* masonic. ⟨⟩ *m,f* mason, freemason.

masoquista ⟨⟩ *adj* masochistic. ⟨⟩ *mf* masochist.

máster *(pl* **masters)** *m* Master's (degree).

masticar *vt* [mascar] to chew.

mástil *m* -**1.** NÁUT mast -**2.** [palo] pole -**3.** MÚS neck.

mastín *m* mastiff.

masturbación *f* masturbation.

masturbar *vt* to masturbate.

◆ **masturbarse** *vpr* to masturbate.

mata *f* [arbusto] bush, shrub; [matojo] tuft; **~s** scrub.

◆ **mata de pelo** *f* mop of hair.

matadero *m* abattoir, slaughterhouse.

matador, ra *adj fam* [cansado] killing, exhausting.

◆ **matador** *m* matador.

matambre *m* *Andes, Ven* [carne] flank *o* *UK* skirt steak; [plato] *flank steak rolled with boiled egg, olives and red pepper, which is cooked and then sliced and served cold.*

matamoscas *m inv* [pala] flyswat; [esprai] flyspray.

matanza *f* [masacre] slaughter.

matar *vt* -**1.** [gen] to kill; **~ las callando** to be up to sthg on the quiet -**2.** [apagar] to tone down; [- sed] to quench; [- hambre] to stay.

◆ **matarse** *vpr* -**1.** [morir] to die -**2.** [suicidarse, esforzarse] to kill o.s.

matasellos *m inv* postmark.

mate ⟨⟩ *adj* matt. ⟨⟩ *m* -**1.** [en ajedrez] mate, checkmate -**2.** [en baloncesto] dunk; [en tenis] smash -**3.** BOT [bebida] maté.

matemático, ca ⟨⟩ *adj* mathematical. ⟨⟩ *m,f* [científico] mathematician.

◆ **matemáticas** *fpl* [ciencia] mathematics *(U)*.

materia *f* -**1.** [sustancia] matter -**2.** [material] material; **~ prima, primera ~** raw material -**3.** [tema, asignatura] subject; **en ~ de** on the subject of, concerning.

material ⟨⟩ *adj* -**1.** [gen] physical; [daños, consecuencias] material -**2.** [real] real, actual. ⟨⟩ *m* -**1.** [gen] material -**2.** [instrumentos] equipment; **~ de oficina** office stationery.

materialismo *m* materialism.

materialista ⟨⟩ *adj* materialistic. ⟨⟩ *mf* materialist.

materializar *vt* -**1.** [idea, proyecto] to realize -**2.** [hacer tangible] to produce.

◆ **materializarse** *vpr* to materialize.

maternal *adj* motherly, maternal.

maternidad *f* -**1.** [cualidad] motherhood -**2.** [hospital] maternity hospital.

materno, na *adj* maternal; [lengua] mother *(antes de sust)*.

matinal *adj* morning *(antes de sust)*.

matiz *m* -**1.** [variedad - de color, opinión] shade; [- de sentido] nuance, shade of meaning -**2.** [atisbo] trace, hint.

matizar *vt* -**1.** [teñir]: **~ (de)** to tinge (with)

- **2.** *fig* [distinguir - rasgos, aspectos] to distinguish; [- tema] to explain in detail - **3.** *fig* [dar tono especial] to tinge, to colour - **4.** ARTE to blend.

matojo *m* [mata] tuft; [arbusto] bush, shrub.

matón, ona *m,f fam* bully.

matorral *m* thicket.

matraca *f* [instrumento] rattle.

matriarcado *m* matriarchy.

matrícula *f* - **1.** [inscripción] registration - **2.** [documento] registration document - **3.** AUTOM number plate.

  ◆ **matrícula de honor** *f* top marks *(pl)*.

matricular *vt* to register.

  ◆ **matricularse** *vpr* to register.

matrimonial *adj* marital; [vida] married.

matrimonio *m* - **1.** [gen] marriage; **fuera del** ~ out of wedlock; ~ **de conveniencia** marriage of convenience; ~ **religioso** church wedding - **2.** [pareja] married couple.

matriz ◇ *f* - **1.** ANAT womb - **2.** [de talonario] (cheque) stub - **3.** [molde] mould - **4.** MAT matrix. ◇ *adj* [empresa] parent *(antes de sust)*; [casa] head *(antes de sust)*; [iglesia] mother *(antes de sust)*.

matrona *f* - **1.** [madre] matron - **2.** [comadrona] midwife.

matutino, na *adj* morning *(antes de sust)*.

maullar *vi* to miaow.

maxilar *m* jaw.

máxima ▷ máximo.

máxime *adv* especially.

máximo, ma ◇ *superl* ▷ grande. ◇ *adj* maximum, [galardón, puntuación] highest.

  ◆ **máximo** *m* maximum; **al** ~ to the utmost; **llegar al** ~ to reach the limit; **como** ~ [a más tardar] at the latest; [como mucho] at the most.

  ◆ **máxima** *f* - **1.** [sentencia, principio] maxim - **2.** [temperatura] high, highest temperature.

mayo *m* May; *ver también* **septiembre**.

mayonesa, mahonesa *f* mayonnaise.

mayor ◇ *adj* - **1.** *(comparativo)*: ~ **(que)** [de tamaño] bigger (than); [de importancia etc] greater (than); [de edad] older (than); [de número] higher (than) - **2.** *(superlativo)*: **el/la** ~ ... [de tamaño] the biggest ...; [de importancia etc] the greatest ...; [de edad] the oldest ...; [de número] the highest ... - **3.** [adulto] grown-up; **hacerse** ~ to grow up - **4.** [anciano] elderly - **5.** MÚS : **en do** ~ in C major - **6.** *loc*: **al por** ~ COM wholesale. ◇ *mf*: **el/la** ~ [hijo, hermano] the eldest. ◇ *m* MIL major.

  ◆ **mayores** *mpl* - **1.** [adultos] grown-ups - **2.** [antepasados] ancestors, forefathers.

mayoral *m* [capataz] foreman, overseer.

mayordomo *m* butler.

mayoreo *m* *Amér* wholesale; **al** ~ wholesale.

mayoría *f* majority; **la** ~ **de** most of; **la** ~ **de los españoles** most Spaniards; **la** ~ **de las veces** usually, most often; **en su** ~ in the main; ~ **simple** simple majority.

  ◆ **mayoría de edad** *f*: **llegar a la** ~ **de edad** to come of age.

mayorista *mf* wholesaler.

mayoritario, ria *adj* majority *(antes de sust)*.

mayúscula ▷ letra.

mayúsculo, la *adj* tremendous, enormous.

maza *f* mace; [del bombo] drumstick.

mazapán *m* marzipan.

mazmorra *f* dungeon.

mazo *m* - **1.** [martillo] mallet - **2.** [de mortero] pestle - **3.** [conjunto] bundle; [- de naipes] balance (of the deck).

me *pron pers* - **1.** *(complemento directo)* me; **le gustaría verme** she'd like to see me - **2.** *(complemento indirecto)* (to) me; ~ **lo dio** he gave it to me; ~ **tiene miedo** he's afraid of me - **3.** *(reflexivo)* myself.

mear *vi vulg* to piss.

mecachis *interj fam eufemismo*: **¡** ~ **!** sugar! *UK*, shoot! *US*.

mecánico, ca ◇ *adj* mechanical. ◇ *m,f* [persona] mechanic.

  ◆ **mecánica** *f* - **1.** [ciencia] mechanics *(U)* - **2.** [funcionamiento] mechanics *(pl)*.

mecanismo *m* [estructura] mechanism.

mecanografía *f* typing.

mecanógrafo, fa *m,f* typist.

mecapal *m* *CAm, Méx* porter's leather harness.

mecedora *f* rocking chair.

mecenas *mf inv* patron.

mecer *vt* to rock.

  ◆ **mecerse** *vpr* to rock back and forth; [en columpio] to swing.

mecha *f* - **1.** [de vela] wick - **2.** [de explosivos] fuse - **3.** [de pelo] streak.

mechero *m* (cigarette) lighter.

mechón *m* [de pelo] lock; [de lana] tuft.

medalla *f* medal.

medallón *m* - **1.** [joya] medallion - **2.** [rodaja] médaillon; ~ **de pescado** [empanado] fishcake.

media *f* - **1.** ▷ medio - **2.** *Amér* [calcetín] sock.

mediación *f* mediation; **por** ~ **de** through.

mediado, da *adj* [medio lleno] half-full; **mediada la película** halfway through the film.

  ◆ **a mediados de** *loc prep* in the middle of, halfway through.

medialuna *f Amér* croissant.

mediana ⊳ mediano.

mediano, na *adj* **- 1.** [intermedio - de tamaño] medium; [- de calidad] average; **de mediana edad** middle-aged; **de mediana estatura** of medium *o* average height **- 2.** [mediocre] average, ordinary.
 ◆ **mediana** *f* **- 1.** GEOM median **- 2.** [de carretera] central reservation.

medianoche (*pl* **medianoches**) *f* [hora] midnight; **a ~** at midnight.

mediante *prep* by means of.

mediar *vi* **- 1.** [llegar a la mitad] to be halfway through; **mediaba julio** it was mid-July **- 2.** [estar en medio - tiempo, distancia, espacio]: **~ entre** to be between; **media un jardín/un kilómetro entre las dos casas** there is a garden/one kilometre between the two houses; **medió una semana** a week passed by **- 3.** [intervenir]: **~ (en/entre)** to mediate (in/between) **- 4.** [interceder]: **~ (en favor de *o* por)** to intercede (on behalf of *o* for).

mediatizar *vt* to determine.

medicación *f* medication.

medicamento *m* medicine.

medicar *vt* to give medicine to.
 ◆ **medicarse** *vpr* to take medicine.

medicina *f* medicine.

medicinal *adj* medicinal.

medición *f* measurement.

médico, ca ⟨⟩ *adj* medical. ⟨⟩ *m,f* doctor; **~ de cabecera** *o* **familia** family doctor, general practitioner; **~ de guardia** duty doctor; **~ interno** houseman *UK*, intern *US*.

medida *f* **- 1.** [gen] measure; [medición] measurement; **a (la) ~** [gen] custom-built; [ropa] made-to-measure **- 2.** [disposición] measure, step; **tomar ~s** to take measures *o* steps; **~ cautelar** precautionary measure; **~s de seguridad** security measures **- 3.** [moderación] moderation **- 4.** [grado] extent, degree; **en cierta/gran ~** to some/a large extent; **en la ~ de lo posible** as far as possible; **en mayor/menor ~** to a greater/lesser extent; **a ~ que entraban** as they were coming in.
 ◆ **medidas** *fpl* [del cuerpo] measurements.

medidor *m Amér* meter.

medieval *adj* medieval.

medievo, medioevo *m* Middle Ages (*pl*).

medio, dia *adj* **- 1.** [gen] half; **a ~ camino** [en viaje] halfway there; [en trabajo etc] halfway through; **media docena/hora** half a dozen/an hour; **~ pueblo estaba allí** half the town was there; **a media luz** in the half-light; **hacer algo a medias** to half-do sthg; **pagar a medias** to go halves, to share the cost; **un kilo y ~** one and a half kilos; **son (las dos) y media** it's half past (two) **- 2.** [intermedio - estatura, tamaño] medium;

[- posición, punto] middle **- 3.** [de promedio - temperatura, velocidad] average.
 ◆ **medio** ⟨⟩ *adv* half; **~ borracho** half drunk; **a ~ hacer** half done. ⟨⟩ *m* **- 1.** [mitad] half **- 2.** [centro] middle, centre; **en ~ (de)** in the middle (of); **estar por (en) ~** to be in the way; **quitar de en ~ a alguien** to get rid of sb, to get sb out of the way **- 3.** [sistema, manera] means, method; **por ~ de** by means of, through **- 4.** [elemento físico] environment; **~ ambiente** environment **- 5.** [ambiente social] circle; **en ~s bien informados** in well-informed circles **- 6.** DEP midfielder.
 ◆ **medios** *mpl* [recursos] means, resources; **los ~s de comunicación *o* información** the media.
 ◆ **media** *f* **- 1.** [promedio] average **- 2.** [hora]: **al dar la media** on the half-hour **- 3.** (*gen pl*) [prenda] tights (*pl*), stockings (*pl*) **- 4.** DEP midfielders (*pl*).

medioambiental *adj* environmental.

mediocre *adj* mediocre, average.

mediodía (*pl* **mediodías**) *m* [hora] midday, noon; **al ~** at noon *o* midday.

medioevo = medievo.

medir *vt* **- 1.** [gen] to measure; **¿cuánto mides?** how tall are you?; **mido 1,80** ≈ I'm 6 foot (tall); **mide diez metros** it's ten metres long **- 2.** [pros, contras etc] to weigh up **- 3.** [palabras] to weigh carefully.

meditar ⟨⟩ *vi*: **~ (sobre)** to meditate (on). ⟨⟩ *vt* **- 1.** [gen] to meditate, to ponder **- 2.** [planear] to plan, to think through.

mediterráneo, a *adj* Mediterranean.
 ◆ **Mediterráneo** *m*: **el (mar) Mediterráneo** the Mediterranean (Sea).

médium *mf inv* medium.

médula *f* **- 1.** ANAT (bone) marrow; **~ espinal** spinal cord; **~ ósea** bone marrow **- 2.** [esencia] core; **hasta la ~** to the core.

medusa *f* jellyfish.

megafonía *f* public-address system; **llamar por ~ a alguien** to page sb.

megáfono *m* megaphone.

mejicano = mexicano.

Méjico = México.

mejilla *f* cheek.

mejillón *m* mussel.

mejor ⟨⟩ *adj* **- 1.** (*comparativo*) better; **~ (que)** better (than) **- 2.** (*superlativo*): **el/la ~ ... the best ...** ⟨⟩ *mf*: **el/la ~ (de)** the best (in); **el ~ de todos** the best of all; **lo ~ fue que ...** the best thing was that ... ⟨⟩ *adv* **- 1.** (*comparativo*): **~ (que)** better (than); **ahora veo ~** I can see better now; **es ~ que no vengas** it would be better if you didn't come; **estar ~** [no tan malo] to feel better; [recuperado] to be better

- 2. *(superlativo)* best; **el que la conoce** ~ the one who knows her best.
➨ **a lo mejor** *loc adv* maybe, perhaps.
➨ **mejor dicho** *loc adv* (or) rather.
mejora *f* [progreso] improvement.
mejorar ◇ *vt* [gen] to improve; [enfermo] to make better. ◇ *vi* to improve, to get better.
➨ **mejorarse** *vpr* to improve, to get better; **¡que te mejores!** get well soon!
mejoría *f* improvement.
mejunje *m* lit & fig concoction.
melancolía *f* melancholy.
melancólico, ca *adj* melancholic.
melaza *f* molasses *(pl)*.
melena *f* **- 1.** [de persona] long hair *(U)*; **soltarse la** ~ to let one's hair down **- 2.** [de león] mane.
melenudo, da *despec adj* with a mop of hair.
mellado, da *adj* **- 1.** [con hendiduras] nicked **- 2.** [sin dientes] gap-toothed.
mellizo, za *adj* & *m,f* twin.
melocotón *m* peach.
melodía *f* **- 1.** MÚS melody, tune **- 2.** [de teléfono móvil] ring tone.
melódico, ca *adj* melodic.
melodioso, sa *adj* melodious.
melodrama *m* melodrama.
melómano, na *m,f* music lover.
melón *m* [fruta] melon.
meloso, sa *adj* **- 1.** [como la miel] honey; fig sweet **- 2.** [empalagoso] sickly.
membrana *f* membrane.
membresía *f* Amér membership.
membrete *m* letterhead.
membrillo *m* **- 1.** [fruto] quince **- 2.** [dulce] quince jelly.
memela *f* Méx thick corn tortilla, oval in shape.
memorable *adj* memorable.
memorándum (*pl* **memorándums** *o* **memorandos**) *m* **- 1.** [cuaderno] notebook **- 2.** [nota diplomática] memorandum.
memoria *f* **- 1.** [gen & INFORM] memory; **si la** ~ **no me falla** if my memory serves me right; **¡qué** ~ **la mía!** what a memory I have!; **de** ~ by heart; **falta de** ~ forgetfulness; **hacer** ~ to try to remember; **tener buena/mala** ~ to have a good/bad memory; **traer a la** ~ to call to mind; **venir a la** ~ to come to mind **- 2.** [recuerdo] remembrance, remembering **- 3.** [disertación] (academic) paper **- 4.** [informe]: ~ **(anual)** (annual) report.
➨ **memorias** *fpl* [biografía] memoirs.
memorizar *vt* to memorize.
menaje *m* household goods and furnishings *(pl)*; ~ **de cocina** kitchenware.
mención *f* mention; ~ **honorífica** honourable mention.

mencionar *vt* to mention.
menda ◇ *pron fam* [el que habla] yours truly. ◇ *mf* [uno cualquiera]: **vino un** ~ **y ...** this bloke came along and ...
mendigar ◇ *vt* to beg for. ◇ *vi* to beg.
mendigo, ga *m,f* beggar.
mendrugo *m* crust (of bread).
menear *vt* [mover - gen] to move; [- cabeza] to shake; [- cola] to wag; [- caderas] to wiggle.
➨ **menearse** *vpr* **- 1.** [moverse] to move (about); [agitarse] to shake; [oscilar] to sway **- 2.** [darse prisa, espabilarse] to get a move on.
menester *m* necessity.
➨ **menesteres** *mpl* [asuntos] business *(U)*, matters *(pl)*.
menestra *f* vegetable stew.
mengano, na *m,f* so-and-so.
menguante *adj* [luna] waning.
menguar ◇ *vi* [disminuir] to decrease, to diminish; [luna] to wane. ◇ *vt* [disminuir] to lessen, to diminish.
menopausia *f* menopause.
menor ◇ *adj* **- 1.** *(comparativo)*: ~ **(que)** [de tamaño] smaller (than); [de edad] younger (than); [de importancia etc] less *o* lesser (than); [de número] lower (than) **- 2.** *(superlativo)*: **el/la** ~ ... [de tamaño] the smallest ...; [de edad] the youngest ...; [de importancia] the slightest ...; [de número] the lowest ... **- 3.** [de poca importancia] minor; **un problema** ~ a minor problem **- 4.** [joven]: **ser** ~ **de edad** [para votar, conducir etc] to be under age; DER to be a minor **- 5.** MÚS: **en do** ~ in C minor **- 6.** *loc*: **al por** ~ COM retail. ◇ *mf* **- 1.** *(superlativo)*: **el/la** ~ [hijo, hermano] the youngest **- 2.** DER [niño] minor.
Menorca Minorca.
menos ◇ *adj inv* **- 1.** *(comparativo)* [cantidad] less; [número] fewer; ~ **aire** less air; ~ **manzanas** fewer apples; ~ ... **que** ... less/fewer ... than ...; **tiene** ~ **experiencia que tú** she has less experience than you; **hace** ~ **calor que ayer** it's not as hot as it was yesterday **- 2.** *(superlativo)* [cantidad] the least; [número] the fewest; **el que compró** ~ **acciones** the one who bought the fewest shares; **lo que** ~ **tiempo llevó** the thing that took the least time **- 3.** *fam* [peor]: **éste es** ~ **coche que el mío** that car isn't as good as mine. ◇ *adv* **- 1.** *(comparativo)* less; ~ **de/que** less than; **estás** ~ **gordo** you're not as fat **- 2.** *(superlativo)*: **el/la/lo** ~ the least; **él es el** ~ **indicado para criticar** he's the last person who should be criticizing; **ella es la** ~ **adecuada para el cargo** she's the least suitable person for the job; **es lo** ~ **que puedo hacer** it's the least I can do **- 3.** [expresa resta] minus; **tres** ~ **dos igual**

a uno three minus two is one - 4. [con las horas] to; son (las dos) ~ diez it's ten to (two) - 5. loc: es lo de ~ that's the least of it, that's of no importance; hacer de ~ a alguien to snub sb; ¡ ~ mal! just as well!, thank God!; no es para ~ not without (good) reason; venir a ~ to go down in the world. ◇ m inv MAT minus (sign). ◇ prep [excepto] except (for); todo ~ eso anything but that.

● al menos, por lo menos loc adv at least.

● a menos que loc conj unless; no iré a ~ que me acompañes I won't go unless you come with me.

● de menos loc adj [que falta] missing; hay dos euros de ~ there's two euros missing.

menoscabar vt [fama, honra etc] to damage; [derechos, intereses, salud] to harm; [belleza, perfección] to diminish.

menospreciar vt [despreciar] to scorn, to despise; [infravalorar] to undervalue.

mensaje m [gen & INFORM] message; ~ de texto [en teléfono móvil] text message.

mensajero, ra ◇ adj fig announcing, presaging. ◇ m,f [gen] messenger; [de mensajería] courier.

menso, sa adj Méx foolish, stupid.

menstruación f menstruation.

menstruar vi to menstruate, to have a period.

mensual adj monthly; 1.000 euros ~es 1,000 euros a month.

mensualidad f - 1. [sueldo] monthly salary - 2. [pago] monthly payment o instalment.

menta f mint.

mental adj mental.

mentalidad f mentality; ~ abierta/cerrada open/closed mind.

mentalizar vt to put into a frame of mind.

● mentalizarse vpr to get into a frame of mind.

mentar vt to mention.

mente f [gen] mind; traer a la ~ to bring to mind.

mentecato, ta m,f idiot.

mentir vi to lie.

mentira f lie; [acción] lying; aunque parezca ~ strange as it may seem; de ~ pretend, false; parece ~ (que ...) it hardly seems possible (that ...), it's scarcely credible (that ...); ~ piadosa white lie.

mentirijillas ● de mentirijillas fam ◇ loc adv [en broma] as a joke, in fun. ◇ loc adj [falso] pretend, make-believe.

mentiroso, sa ◇ adj lying; [engañoso] deceptive. ◇ m,f liar.

mentón m chin.

menú (pl menús) m - 1. [lista] menu; [comida] food; ~ del día set meal - 2. INFORM menu.

menudencia f trifle, insignificant thing.

menudeo m Amér COM retailing.

menudillos mpl giblets.

menudo, da adj - 1. [pequeño] small - 2. [insignificante] trifling, insignificant - 3. (antes de sust) [para enfatizar] what!; ¡ ~ lío/gol! what a mess/goal!

● a menudo loc adv often.

meñique ▷ dedo.

meollo m core, heart; llegar al ~ de la cuestión to come to the heart of the matter.

mercader mf trader.

mercadería f merchandise, goods (pl).

mercadillo m flea market.

mercado m market; ~ común Common Market.

mercancía f merchandise (U), goods (pl).

● mercancías m inv FERROC goods train, freight train US.

mercante adj merchant.

mercantil adj mercantile, commercial.

mercenario, ria adj & m,f mercenary.

mercería f [tienda] haberdasher's (shop) UK, notions store US.

mercurio m mercury.

Mercurio m Mercury.

merecedor, ra adj: ~ de worthy of.

merecer ◇ vt to deserve, to be worthy of; la isla merece una visita the island is worth a visit; no merece la pena it's not worth it. ◇ vi to be worthy.

merecido m: recibir su ~ to get one's just desserts.

merendar ◇ vi to have tea (as a light afternoon meal). ◇ vt to have for tea.

merendero m open-air café or bar (in the country or on the beach).

merengue m - 1. CULIN meringue - 2. [baile] merengue.

meridiano, na adj - 1. [hora etc] midday - 2. fig [claro] crystal-clear.

● meridiano m meridian.

merienda f tea (as a light afternoon meal); [en el campo] picnic.

mérito m - 1. [cualidad] merit - 2. [valor] value, worth; tiene mucho ~ it's no mean achievement; de ~ worthy, deserving.

merluza f [pez, pescado] hake.

merma f decrease, reduction.

mermar ◇ vi to diminish, to lessen. ◇ vt to reduce, to diminish.

mermelada f jam; ~ de naranja marmalade.

mero, ra adj (antes de sust) mere.

● mero m grouper.

merodear vi: ~ (por) to snoop o prowl (about).

mes *m* -**1.** [del año] month - **2.** [salario] monthly salary.

mesa *f* -**1.** [gen] table; [de oficina, despacho] desk; **bendecir la** ~ to say grace; **poner/quitar la** ~ to set/clear the table; ~ **camilla** *small round table under which a heater is placed*; ~ **de billar** billiard table; ~ **de mezclas** mixing desk; ~ **plegable** folding table - **2.** [comité] board, committee; [en un debate etc] panel; ~ **directiva** executive board o committee.

◆ **mesa redonda** *f* [coloquio] round table.

mesada *f* -**1.** *Amér* [mensualidad] monthly payment, monthly instalment - **2.** *RP* [encimera] worktop.

mesero, ra *m,f CAm, Col, Méx* waiter (*f* waitress).

meseta *f* plateau, tableland.

mesías *m fig* Messiah.

mesilla *f* small table; ~ **de noche** bedside table.

mesón *m* -**1.** HIST inn - **2.** [bar-restaurante] *old, country-style restaurant and bar*.

mestizo, za ◇ *adj.* [persona] half-caste; [animal, planta] cross-bred. ◇ *m,f* half-caste.

mesura *f* -**1.** [moderación] moderation, restraint; **con** ~ [moderadamente] in moderation - **2.** [cortesía] courtesy, politeness.

meta *f* -**1.** [DEP - llegada] finishing line; [- portería] goal - **2.** [objetivo] aim, goal.

metabolismo *m* metabolism.

metáfora *f* metaphor.

metal *m* -**1.** [material] metal - **2.** MÚS brass.

metálico, ca ◇ *adj* [sonido, color] metallic; [objeto] metal. ◇ *m*: **pagar en** ~ to pay (in) cash.

metalizado, da *adj* [pintura] metallic.

metalurgia *f* metallurgy.

metamorfosis *f inv lit* & *fig* metamorphosis.

metate *m Guat, Méx* grinding stone.

metedura ◆ **metedura de pata** *f* clanger.

meteorito *m* meteorite.

meteoro *m* meteor.

meteorología *f* meteorology.

meteorológico, ca *adj* meteorological.

meteorólogo, ga *m,f* meteorologist; RADIO & TV weatherman (*f* weatherwoman).

meter *vt* -**1.** [gen] to put in; ~ **algo/a alguien en algo** to put sthg/sb in sthg; ~ **la llave en la cerradura** to get the key into the lock; **lo metieron en la cárcel** they put him in prison; ~ **dinero en el banco** to put money in the bank - **2.** [hacer participar]: ~ **a alguien en algo** to get sb into sthg - **3.** [obligar a]: ~ **a alguien a hacer algo** to make sb

start doing sthg - **4.** [causar]: ~ **prisa/miedo a alguien** to rush/scare sb; ~ **ruido** to make a noise - **5.** *fam* [asestar] to give; **le metió un puñetazo** he gave him a punch - **6.** [estrechar - prenda] to take in; ~ **el bajo de una falda** to take up a skirt.

◆ **meterse** *vpr* -**1.** [entrar] to get in; ~**se en** to get into - **2.** (*en frase interrogativa*) [estar] to get to; **¿dónde se ha metido ese chico?** where has that boy got to? - **3.** [dedicarse]: ~**se a** to become; ~**se a torero** to become a bullfighter - **4.** [involucrarse]: ~**se (en)** to get involved (in) - **5.** [entrometerse] to meddle, to interfere; **se mete en todo** he never minds his own business; ~**se por medio** to interfere - **6.** [empezar]: ~**se a hacer algo** to get started on doing sthg.

◆ **meterse con** *vpr* -**1.** [incordiar] to hassle - **2.** [atacar] to go for.

meterete *mf CSur fam* busybody, nosey-parker *UK*.

metete *mf Andes, CAm fam* busybody, nosey-parker *UK*.

metiche *mf Méx, Ven fam* busybody, nosey-parker *UK*.

meticuloso, sa *adj* meticulous.

metido, da *adj* -**1.** [envuelto]: **andar** o **estar** ~ **en** to be involved in - **2.** [abundante]: ~ **en años** elderly; ~ **en carnes** plump.

metódico, ca *adj* methodical.

método *m* -**1.** [sistema] method - **2.** EDUC course.

metodología *f* methodology.

metomentodo *fam mf* busybody.

metralla *f* shrapnel.

metralleta *f* submachine gun.

métrico, ca *adj* [del metro] metric.

metro *m* -**1.** [gen] metre - **2.** [transporte] underground *UK*, tube *UK*, subway *US* - **3.** [cinta métrica] tape measure.

metrópoli *f*, **metrópolis** *f inv* [ciudad] metropolis.

metropolitano, na *adj* metropolitan.

mexicanismo, mejicanismo *m* Mexicanism.

mexicano, na, mejicano, na *adj* & *m,f* Mexican.

México, Méjico Mexico.

mezcla *f* -**1.** [gen] mixture; [tejido] blend; [de grabación] mix - **2.** [acción] mixing.

mezclar *vt* -**1.** [gen] to mix; [combinar, armonizar] to blend - **2.** [confundir, desordenar] to mix up - **3.** [implicar]: ~ **a alguien en** to get sb mixed up in.

◆ **mezclarse** *vpr* -**1.** [gen]: ~**se (con)** to mix (with) - **2.** [esfumarse]: ~**se entre** to disappear o blend into - **3.** [implicarse]: ~**se en** to get mixed up in.

mezquino, na *adj* mean, cheap *US*.

mezquita *f* mosque.

mg (*abrev de* **miligramo**) mg.

mi¹ *m* MÚS E; [en solfeo] mi.

mi² (*pl* **mis**) *adj poses* my; ~ **casa** my house; ~**s libros** my books.

mí *pron pers* (*después de prep*) - **1.** [gen] me; **este trabajo no es para** ~ this job isn't for me; **no se fía de** ~ he doesn't trust me - **2.** (*reflexivo*) myself - **3.** *loc*: **¡a** ~ **qué!** so what?, why should I care?; **para** ~ [yo creo] as far as I'm concerned, in my opinion; **por** ~ as far as I'm concerned; **por** ~, **no hay inconveniente** it's fine by me.

mía ▷ **mío**.

miaja *f* crumb; *fig* tiny bit.

miau *m* miaow.

michelines *mpl fam* spare tyre (*sg*).

mico *m fam* [persona] ugly devil; **se volvió** ~ **para abrir la puerta** he had a hell of a job opening the door.

micro ◇ *m fam* (*abrev de* **micrófono**) mike. ◇ *m o f Chile* [microbús] bus, coach *UK*.

microbio *m* germ, microbe.

microbús *m* - **1.** minibus - **2.** *Méx* [taxi] (collective) taxi.

microfilm (*pl* **microfilms**), **microfilme** *m* microfilm.

micrófono *m* microphone.

microondas *m inv* microwave (oven).

microordenador *m* INFORM microcomputer.

microprocesador *m* INFORM microprocessor.

microscópico, ca *adj* microscopic.

microscopio *m* microscope; ~ **electrónico** electron microscope.

miedo *m* fear; **coger** ~ **a algo** to develop a fear of sthg; **dar** ~ to be frightening; **me da** ~ **conducir** I'm afraid o frightened of driving; **por** ~ **de que ...** for fear that ...; **temblar de** ~ to tremble with fear; **tener** ~ to be frightened o scared; **tener** ~ **a** o **de (hacer algo)** to be afraid of (doing sthg); **de** ~ *fam*: **esta película está de** ~ this film is brilliant; **lo pasamos de** ~ we had a whale of a time.

miedoso, sa *adj* fearful.

miel *f* honey.

miembro *m* - **1.** [gen] member - **2.** [extremidad] limb, member; ~ **(viril)** penis.

mientras ◇ *conj* - **1.** [al tiempo que] while; **leía** ~ **comía** she was reading while eating; ~ **más ando más sudo** the more I walk, the more I sweat - **2.** [hasta que]: ~ **no se pruebe lo contrario** until proved otherwise - **3.** [por el contrario]: ~ **(que)** whereas, whilst. ◇ *adv*: ~ **(tanto)** meanwhile, in the meantime.

miércoles *m* Wednesday; ~ **de ceniza** Ash Wednesday; *ver también* **sábado**.

mierda *vulg f* - **1.** [excremento] shit - **2.** [suciedad] filth, shit - **3.** [cosa sin valor]: **es una** ~ it's (a load of) crap - **4.** *loc*: **¡vete a la** ~**!** go to hell!, piss off!

mies *f* [cereal] ripe corn.

◆ **mieses** *fpl* [campo] cornfields.

miga *f* [de pan] crumb.

◆ **migas** *fpl* CULIN fried breadcrumbs; **hacer buenas/malas** ~**s** *fam* to get on well/badly.

migra *f Méx fam pey*: **la** ~ US police border patrol.

migración *f* migration.

migraña *f* migraine.

migrar *vi* to migrate.

migratorio, ria *adj* migratory.

mijo *m* millet.

mil *núm* thousand; **dos** ~ two thousand; ~ **euros** a thousand euros; *ver también* **seis**.

milagro *m* miracle; **de** ~ miraculously, by a miracle.

milagroso, sa *adj* miraculous; *fig* amazing.

milanesa *f RP* Wiener schnitzel, breaded veal escalope.

milenario, ria *adj* ancient.

◆ **milenario** *m* millennium.

milenio *m* millennium.

milésimo, ma *núm* thousandth.

mili *f fam* military service; **hacer la** ~ to do one's military service.

milicia *f* - **1.** [profesión] military (profession) - **2.** [grupo armado] militia.

miliciano, na *m,f* militiaman (*f* female soldier).

milico *m Andes, RP fam pey* [soldado] soldier; [policía] pig.

miligramo *m* milligram.

milímetro *m* millimetre.

militante *adj* & *m,f* militant.

militar ◇ *adj* military. ◇ *mf* soldier; **los** ~**es** the military. ◇ *vi*: ~ **(en)** to be active (in).

milla *f* mile; ~ **(marina)** nautical mile.

millar *m* thousand; **un** ~ **de personas** a thousand people.

millón *núm* million; **dos millones** two million; **un** ~ **de personas** a million people; **un** ~ **de cosas que hacer** a million things to do; **un** ~ **de gracias** thanks a million.

◆ **millones** *mpl* [dineral] millions, a fortune (*sg*).

millonario, ria *m,f* millionaire (*f* millionairess).

millonésimo, ma *núm* millionth.

milpa *f CAm, Méx* cornfield.

mimado, da *adj* spoilt.

mimar *vt* to spoil, to pamper.

mimbre *m* wicker; **de** ~ wickerwork.

mímica *f* - **1.** [mimo] mime - **2.** [lenguaje] sign language.

mimo *m* - **1.** [zalamería] mollycoddling - **2.** [cariño] show of affection - **3.** TEATR mime.

mimosa *f* BOT mimosa.

min (*abrev de* **minuto**) min.

mina *f* GEOL & MIL mine; ~ **de carbón** coalmine.

minar *vt* - **1.** MIL to mine - **2.** *fig* [aminorar] to undermine.

mineral ◇ *adj* mineral. ◇ *m* - **1.** GEOL mineral - **2.** MIN ore.

minería *f* - **1.** [técnica] mining - **2.** [sector] mining industry.

minero, ra ◇ *adj* mining *(antes de sust)*; [producción, riqueza] mineral. ◇ *m,f* miner.

miniatura *f* miniature.

minicadena *f* midi system.

minifalda *f* mini skirt.

minigolf (*pl* **minigolfs**) *m* [juego] crazy golf.

mínimo, ma ◇ *superl* ⊳ **pequeño**. ◇ *adj* - **1.** [lo más bajo posible o necesario] minimum - **2.** [lo más bajo temporalmente] lowest - **3.** [muy pequeño - efecto, importancia etc] minimal, very small; [- protesta, ruido etc] slightest; **no tengo la más mínima idea** I haven't the slightest idea; **como** ~ at the very least; **en lo más** ~ in the slightest.
◆ **mínimo** *m* [límite] minimum.
◆ **mínima** *f* METEOR low, lowest temperature.

ministerio *m* - **1.** POLÍT ministry *UK*, department *US* - **2.** RELIG ministry.
◆ **Ministerio de Asuntos Exteriores** *m* ≃ Foreign Office *UK*, ≃ State Department *US*.
◆ **Ministerio de Economía y Hacienda** *m* ≃ Treasury *UK*, ≃ Treasury Department *US*.
◆ **Ministerio del Interior** *m* ≃ Home Office *UK*, ≃ Department of the Interior *US*.

ministro, tra *m,f* POLÍT minister *UK*, secretary *US*; **primer** ~ prime minister.

minoría *f* minority; **estar en** ~ to be in a *o* the minority; ~**s étnicas** ethnic minorities.

minorista ◇ *adj* retail. ◇ *mf* retailer.

minoritario, ria *adj* minority *(antes de sust)*.

minucia *f* trifle, insignificant thing.

minucioso, sa *adj* - **1.** [meticuloso] meticulous - **2.** [detallado] highly detailed.

minúsculo, la *adj* - **1.** [tamaño] tiny, minute - **2.** [letra] small; IMPRENTA lower-case.
◆ **minúscula** *f* small letter; IMPRENTA lower-case letter.

minusvalía *f* [física] handicap, disability.

minusválido, da ◇ *adj* disabled, handicapped. ◇ *m,f* disabled *o* handicapped person.

minuta *f* - **1.** [factura] fee - **2.** [menú] menu - **3.** *RP* [comida] quick meal.

minutero *m* minute hand.

minuto *m* minute; **guardar un** ~ **de silencio** to observe a minute's silence.

mío, mía ◇ *adj poses* mine; **este libro es** ~ this book is mine; **un amigo** ~ a friend of mine; **no es asunto** ~ it's none of my business. ◇ *pron poses*: **el** ~ mine; **el** ~ **es rojo** mine is red; **esta es la mía** *fam* this is the chance I've been waiting for; **lo** ~ **es el teatro** [lo que me va] theatre is what I should be doing; **los** ~**s** *fam* [mi familia] my folks; [mi bando] my lot, my side.

miope *adj* shortsighted, myopic.

miopía *f* shortsightedness, myopia.

mira ◇ *f* sight; *fig* intention; **con** ~**s a** with a view to, with the intention of. ◇ *interj*: ¡~! look!

mirado, da *adj* [prudente] careful; **bien** ~ [bien pensado] if you look at it closely.
◆ **mirada** *f* [gen] look; [rápida] glance; [de cariño, placer, admiración] gaze; **apartar la mirada** to look away; **dirigir** *o* **lanzar la mirada a** to glance at; **echar una mirada (a algo)** to glance *o* to have a quick look (at sthg); **fulminar con la mirada a alguien** to look daggers at sb; **hay miradas que matan** if looks could kill ...; **levantar la mirada** to look up.

mirador *m* - **1.** [balcón] enclosed balcony - **2.** [para ver un paisaje] viewpoint.

miramiento *m* consideration, circumspection; **andarse con** ~**s** to stand on ceremony; **sin** ~**s** just like that, without the least consideration.

mirar ◇ *vt* - **1.** [gen] to look at; [observar] to watch; [fijamente] to stare at; ~ **algo de cerca/lejos** to look at sthg closely/from a distance; ~ **algo por encima** to glance over sthg, to have a quick look at sthg; ~ **a alguien bien/mal** to think highly/poorly of sb - **2.** [fijarse en] to keep an eye on, to watch - **3.** [examinar, averiguar] to check, to look through; **le miraron todas las maletas** they searched all her luggage; **mira si ha llegado la carta** go and see if the letter has arrived - **4.** [considerar] to consider, to take a look at. ◇ *vi* - **1.** [gen] to look; [observar] to watch; [fijamente] to stare; **mira, yo creo que ...** look, I think that ... - **2.** [buscar] to check, to look; **he mirado en todas partes** I've looked everywhere - **3.** [orientarse]: ~ **a** to face - **4.** [cuidar]: ~ **por alguien/algo** to look after sb/sthg.
◆ **mirarse** *vpr* [uno mismo] to look at o.s.; **si bien se mira** *fig* if you really think about it.

mirilla f spyhole.

mirlo m blackbird.

mirón, ona fam m,f -**1.** [espectador] on-looker -**2.** [curioso] busybody, nosey-parker UK -**3.** [voyeur] peeping Tom.

misa f mass; **ir a** ~ lit to go to mass o church; fam fig to be gospel.

misal m missal.

misántropo, pa m,f misanthrope, mis-anthropist.

miscelánea f -**1.** [miscellany] -**2.** Méx [tien-da] small general store.

miserable ◇ adj -**1.** [pobre] poor; [vivien-da] wretched, squalid -**2.** [penoso, insufi-ciente] miserable -**3.** [vil] contemptible, base -**4.** [tacaño] mean. ◇ mf [ruin] wretch, vile person.

miseria f -**1.** [pobreza] poverty; **vivir en la** ~ to live in poverty -**2.** [cantidad muy pe-queña] pittance -**3.** [desgracia] misfortune -**4.** [tacañería] meanness.

misericordia f compassion; **pedir** ~ to beg for mercy.

mísero, ra adj [pobre] wretched; **ni un** ~ ... not even a measly o miserable ...

misil (pl **misiles**) m missile; ~ **de crucero** cruise missile.

misión f -**1.** [gen] mission; [cometido] task -**2.** [expedición científica] expedition.

misionero, ra adj & m,f missionary.

misiva f culto missive.

mismo, ma ◇ adj -**1.** [igual] same; **el** ~ **pi-so** the same flat; **del** ~ **color que** the same colour as -**2.** [para enfatizar]: **yo** ~ I myself; **en este** ~ **cuarto** in this very room; **en su misma calle** right in the street where he lives; **por mí/ti** ~ by myself/yourself; **¡tú** ~! it's up to you. ◇ pron: **el** ~ the same; **el** ~ **que vi ayer** the same one I saw yester-day; **lo** ~ the same (thing); **lo** ~ **que** the same as; **da** o **es lo** ~ it doesn't matter, it doesn't make any difference; **me da lo** ~ I don't care.

   ◆ **mismo** (después de sust) adv -**1.** [para en-fatizar]: **lo vi desde mi casa** ~ I saw it from my own house; **ahora/aquí** ~ right now/here; **ayer** ~ only yesterday; **por eso** ~ precisely for that reason -**2.** [por ejemplo]: **escoge uno cualquiera — este** ~ choose any — this one, for instance.

misógino, na adj misogynistic.

misterio m mystery.

misterioso, sa adj mysterious.

mística ▷ místico.

místico, ca adj mystical.

   ◆ **mística** f [práctica] mysticism.

mitad f -**1.** [gen] half; **a** ~ **de precio** at half price; **a** ~ **de camino** halfway there; **a** ~ **de película** halfway through the film; **la** ~ **de**

half (of); **la** ~ **del tiempo no está** half the time she's not in; ~ **y** ~ half and half -**2.** [centro] middle; **en** ~ **de** in the middle of; **(cortar algo) por la** ~ (to cut sthg) in half.

mítico, ca adj mythical.

mitigar vt -**1.** [gen] to alleviate, to reduce; [ánimos] to calm; [sed] to slake; [hambre] to take the edge off; [choque, golpe] to sof-ten; [dudas, sospechas] to allay -**2.** [justifi-car] to mitigate.

mitin (pl **mítines**) m rally, meeting.

mito m [gen] myth.

mitología f mythology.

mitote m Méx fam [bulla] racket.

mixto, ta adj mixed; [comisión] joint.

ml (abrev de **mililitro**) ml.

mm (abrev de **milímetro**) mm.

mobiliario m furniture; ~ **urbano** street furniture.

mocasín m moccasin.

mochila f backpack.

mochuelo m little owl.

moción f motion.

moco m fam snot (U); MED mucus (U); **lim-piarse los** ~**s** to wipe one's nose; **sorberse los** ~**s** to sniffle, to snuffle.

mocoso, sa m,f fam despec brat.

moda f [gen] fashion; [furor pasajero] craze; **estar de** ~ to be fashionable o in fashion; **estar pasado de** ~ to be unfashionable o out of fashion; **ponerse de** ~ to come into fashion; ~ **pasajera** fad.

modal adj modal.

   ◆ **modales** mpl manners.

modalidad f form, type; DEP discipline.

modelar vt to model; fig to form, to shape.

modelo ◇ adj model. ◇ mf model. ◇ m -**1.** [gen] model -**2.** [prenda de vestir] num-ber.

módem ['moðem] (pl **módems**) m INFORM modem; ~ **fax** fax modem.

moderación f moderation.

moderado, da adj & m,f moderate.

moderador, ra m,f chair, chairperson.

moderar vt -**1.** [gen] to moderate; [veloci-dad] to reduce -**2.** [debate] to chair.

   ◆ **moderarse** vpr to restrain o.s.

modernizar vt to modernize.

moderno, na adj modern.

modestia f modesty.

modesto, ta adj modest.

módico, ca adj modest.

modificado, da adj modified; ~ **genética-mente** genetically modified.

modificar vt -**1.** [variar] to alter -**2.** GRAM to modify.

modista mf -**1.** [diseñador] fashion designer

- **2.** [que cose] tailor (*f* dressmaker).

modisto *m* - **1.** [diseñador] fashion designer - **2.** [sastre] tailor.

modo *m* [manera, forma] way; **a ~ de** as, by way of; **a mi ~** (in) my own way; **de ese ~** in that way; **de ningún ~** in no way; **de todos ~s** in any case, anyway; **de un ~ u otro** one way or another; **en cierto ~** in some ways; **~ de empleo** instructions *(pl)* for use; **~ de pensar/ser** way of thinking/being; **~ de vida** way of life; **de ~ que** [de manera que] in such a way that; [así que] so.

◆ **modos** *mpl* [modales] manners; **buenos/malos ~s** good/bad manners.

modorra *f fam* drowsiness.

modoso, sa *adj* [recatado] modest; [formal] well-behaved.

modular *vt* to modulate.

módulo *m* - **1.** [gen] module; **~ lunar** lunar module - **2.** [de muebles] unit.

mofa *f* mockery.

mofarse *vpr* to scoff; **~ de** to mock.

moflete *m* chubby cheek.

mogollón *m mfam* - **1.** [muchos]: **~ de** tons *(pl)* of, loads *(pl)* of - **2.** [lío] row, commotion.

moho *m* - **1.** [hongo] mould; **criar ~** to go mouldy - **2.** [herrumbre] rust.

mohoso, sa *adj* - **1.** [con hongo] mouldy - **2.** [oxidado] rusty.

moisés *m inv* Moses basket.

mojado, da *adj* wet; [húmedo] damp.

mojar *vt* [sin querer] to get wet; [a propósito] to wet; [humedecer] to dampen; [comida] to dunk; **moja el pan en la salsa** dip your bread in the sauce.

◆ **mojarse** *vpr* [con agua] to get wet.

mojigato, ta *adj* - **1.** [beato] prudish - **2.** [con falsa humildad] sanctimonious.

mojón *m* [piedra] milestone; [poste] milepost.

molar *m fam vi* to be bloody gorgeous.

molcajete *m Méx* mortar.

molde *m* mould.

moldeado *m* - **1.** [del pelo] soft perm, bodywave - **2.** [de figura, cerámica] moulding.

moldear *vt* - **1.** [gen] to mould - **2.** [modelar] to cast - **3.** [cabello] to give a soft perm to.

mole ◇ *f* hulk. ◇ *m Méx* [salsa] *thick, cooked chilli sauce*; [guiso] *dish served in 'mole' sauce.*

molécula *f* molecule.

moler *vt* - **1.** [gen] to grind; [aceitunas] to press; [trigo] to mill - **2.** *fam* [cansar] to wear out.

molestar *vt* - **1.** [perturbar] to annoy; **¿le molesta que fume?** do you mind if I smoke?; **perdone que le moleste ...** I'm sorry to bother you ... - **2.** [doler] to hurt

- **3.** [ofender] to offend.

◆ **molestarse** *vpr* - **1.** [incomodarse] to bother; **~se en hacer algo** to bother to do sthg; **~se por alguien/algo** to put o.s. out for sb/sthg - **2.** [ofenderse]: **~se (por algo)** to take offence (at sthg).

molestia *f* - **1.** [incomodidad] nuisance; **disculpe las ~s** we apologize for any inconvenience; **si no es demasiada ~** if it's not too much trouble - **2.** [malestar] discomfort; **siento una ~ en el estómago** my stomach doesn't feel too good.

molesto, ta *adj* - **1.** [incordiante] annoying; [visita] inconvenient - **2.** [irritado]: **~ (con)** annoyed (with) - **3.** [con malestar] in discomfort.

molido, da *adj fam* [cansado] worn out; **estar ~ de** to be worn out from.

molinero, ra *m,f* miller.

molinillo *m* grinder; **~ de café** coffee mill *o* grinder.

molino *m* mill; **~ de viento** windmill.

molla *f* [parte blanda] flesh.

molleja *f* gizzard.

mollera *f fam* [juicio] brains *(pl)*.

molusco *m* mollusc.

momentáneo, a *adj* [de un momento] momentary; [pasajero] temporary.

momento *m* [gen] moment; [periodo] time; **llegó un ~ en que ...** there came a time when ...; **a cada ~** all the time; **al ~** straightaway; **a partir de este ~** from this moment (on); **de ~, por el ~** for the time being *o* moment; **del ~** [actual] of the day; **de un ~ a otro** any minute now; **dentro de un ~** in a moment; **desde el ~ (en) que ...** [tiempo] from the moment that ...; [causa] seeing as ...; **en algún ~** sometime; **~s después** moments later; **~ decisivo** turning point.

momia *f* mummy.

monada *f* - **1.** [persona]: **su novia es una ~** his girlfriend is gorgeous; **¡qué ~ de bebé!** what a cute baby! - **2.** [cosa] lovely thing; **¡qué ~ de falda!** what a lovely skirt!

◆ **monadas** *fpl* [gracias] antics; **hacer ~s** to monkey *o* clown around.

monaguillo *m* altar boy.

monarca *m* monarch.

monarquía *f* monarchy.

monárquico, ca *adj* monarchic.

monasterio *m* [de monjes] monastery; [de monjas] convent.

Moncloa *f*: **la ~** *residence of the Spanish premier.*

monda *f* [acción] peeling; [piel] peel; **ser la ~** *mfam* [extraordinario] to be amazing; [gracioso] to be a scream.

mondadientes *m inv* toothpick.

mondadura f [piel] peel.

mondar vt to peel.

mondarse vpr: ~se (de risa) fam to laugh one's head off.

moneda f - 1. [pieza] coin; ser ~ corriente to be commonplace - 2. [divisa] currency.

monedero m - 1. [gen] purse - 2. [tarjeta]: ~ electrónico electronic purse.

monegasco, ca adj & m,f Monacan, Monegasque.

monetario, ria adj monetary.

mongólico, ca MED m,f Down's syndrome person.

mongolismo m Down's syndrome.

monigote m - 1. [muñeco] rag o paper doll - 2. [dibujo] doodle - 3. fig [persona] puppet.

monitor, ra m,f [persona] instructor.

monitor m INFORM & TECN monitor.

monja f nun.

monje m monk.

mono, na <> adj lovely. <> m,f [animal] monkey; mandar a alguien a freír monas fam to tell sb to get lost; ser el último ~ to be bottom of the heap.

mono m - 1. [prenda - con peto] dungarees (pl); [- con mangas] overalls (pl) - 2. fam [abstinencia] cold turkey.

monobloque m Arg tower block.

monóculo m monocle.

monogamia f monogamy.

monografía f monograph.

monolingüe adj monolingual.

monólogo m monologue; TEATR soliloquy.

monopatín m skateboard.

monopolio m monopoly.

monopolizar vt lit & fig to monopolize.

monosílabo, ba adj monosyllabic.

monosílabo m monosyllable.

monotonía f [uniformidad] monotony.

monótono, na adj monotonous.

monovolumen m people carrier.

monseñor m Monsignor.

monserga f fam drivel (U); déjate de ~s, no me vengas con ~s don't give me that rubbish.

monstruo <> adj inv [grande] enormous, monster (antes de sust). <> m - 1. [gen] monster - 2. [prodigio] giant, marvel.

monstruosidad f - 1. [crueldad] monstrosity, atrocity - 2. [fealdad] hideousness - 3. [anomalía] freak.

monstruoso, sa adj - 1. [cruel] monstrous - 2. [feo] hideous - 3. [enorme] huge, enormous - 4. [deforme] terribly deformed.

monta f [importancia] importance; de poca ~ of little importance.

montacargas m inv goods lift UK, freight elevator US.

montaje m - 1. [de máquina] assembly - 2. TEATR staging - 3. FOT montage - 4. CIN editing - 5. [farsa] put-up job.

montante m - 1. [ventanuco] fanlight - 2. [importe] total; ~s compensatorios COM compensating duties - 3. loc: coger el ~ to go away, to leave.

montaña f lit & fig mountain; ir de excursión a la ~ to go on a trip to the mountains; ~ rusa roller coaster, big dipper; hacer una ~ de un grano de arena to make a mountain out of a molehill.

montañero, ra m,f mountaineer.

montañismo m mountaineering.

montañoso, sa adj mountainous.

montar <> vt - 1. [ensamblar - máquina, estantería] to assemble; [- tienda de campaña, tenderete] to put up - 2. [encajar]: ~ algo en algo to fit sthg into sthg - 3. [organizar - negocio, piso] to set up - 4. [cabalgar] to ride - 5. [poner encima]: ~ a alguien en to lift sb onto - 6. [CULIN - nata] to whip; [- claras, yemas] to beat - 7. TEATR to stage - 8. CIN to cut, to edit. <> vi - 1. [subir] to get on; [en coche] to get in; ~ en [gen] to get onto; [coche] to get into; [animal] to mount - 2. [ir montado] to ride; ~ en bicicleta/a caballo to ride a bicycle/a horse.

montarse vpr [gen] to get on; [en coche] to get in; [en animal] to mount; ~se en [gen] to get onto; [coche] to get into; [animal] to mount.

monte m [elevación] mountain; [terreno] woodland; ~ bajo scrub.

monte de piedad m state pawnbroker's.

montepío m mutual aid society.

montés adj wild.

montículo m hillock.

monto m total.

montón m - 1. [pila] heap, pile; a o en ~ everything together o at once; del ~ ordinary, run-of-the-mill - 2. [muchos] loads; un ~ de loads of.

montuno, na adj Andes unsociable.

montura f - 1. [cabalgadura] mount - 2. [arreos] harness; [silla] saddle - 3. [soporte - de gafas] frame; [- de joyas] mounting.

monumental adj - 1. [ciudad, lugar] famous for its monuments - 2. [fracaso etc] monumental.

monumento m monument.

monzón m monsoon.

moña f - 1. fam [borrachera]: coger una ~ to get smashed.

moño m - 1. bun (of hair); estar hasta el ~ (de) to be sick to death (of) - 2. Amér [lazo] bow.

moquear vi to have a runny nose.

moqueta f fitted carpet.

mora *f* - **1.** [de la zarzamora] blackberry - **2.** [del moral] mulberry.

morada *f culto* dwelling.

morado, da *adj* purple.

➡ **morado** *m* [color] purple.

moral ◇ *adj* moral. ◇ *f* - **1.** [ética] morality - **2.** [ánimo] morale.

moraleja *f* moral.

moralizar *vi* to moralize.

morbo *m fam* [placer malsano] morbid pleasure.

morboso, sa *adj* morbid.

morcilla *f* CULIN ≃ black pudding UK, ≃ blood sausage US.

mordaz *adj* caustic, biting.

mordaza *f* gag.

mordedura *f* bite.

morder ◇ *vt* - **1.** [con los dientes] to bite - **2.** [gastar] to eat into. ◇ *vi* to bite; **estar que muerde** to be hopping mad.

➡ **morderse** *vpr*: ~se la lengua/las uñas to bite one's tongue/nails.

mordida *f* CAm & Méx fam [soborno] bribe.

mordisco *m* bite.

mordisquear *vt* to nibble (at).

moreno, na ◇ *adj* - **1.** [pelo, piel] dark; [por el sol] tanned; **ponerse** ~ to get a tan - **2.** [pan, azúcar] brown. ◇ *m,f* [de pelo] dark-haired person; [de piel] dark-skinned person.

morera *f* white mulberry.

moretón *m* bruise.

morfina *f* morphine.

moribundo, da *adj* dying.

morir *vi* - **1.** [gen] to die; ~ **de algo** to die of sthg - **2.** [río, calle] to come out - **3.** [fuego] to die down; [luz] to go out; [día] to come to a close.

➡ **morirse** *vpr* - **1.** [fallecer]: ~se **(de)** to die (of) - **2.** [sentir con fuerza]: ~se **de envidia/ira** to be burning with envy/rage; **me muero de ganas de ir a bailar** I'm dying to go dancing; **me muero de hambre/frío** I'm starving/freezing; ~se **por algo** to be dying for sthg; ~se **por alguien** to be crazy about sb.

mormón, ona *adj* & *m,f* Mormon.

moro, ra ◇ *adj* HIST Moorish. ◇ *m,f* - **1.** HIST Moor; ~**s y cristianos** *traditional Spanish festival involving mock battle between Moors and Christians* - **2.** [árabe] Arab *(N.B.: the term 'moro' is considered to be racist).*

morocho, cha ◇ *adj* Andes, RP [persona] dark-haired; Ven [mellizo] twin. ◇ *m,f* Andes, RP [moreno] dark-haired person; Ven [mellizo] twin.

moronga *f* CAm, Méx black pudding UK, blood sausage US.

moroso, sa COM ◇ *adj* defaulting. ◇ *m,f* defaulter, bad debtor.

morral *m* MIL haversack; [de cazador] game-bag.

morrear *mfam vt* & *vi* to snog.

morriña *f* [por el país de uno] homesickness; [por el pasado] nostalgia.

morro *m* - **1.** [hocico] snout - **2.** *fam* [de coche, avión] nose.

morsa *f* walrus.

morse *m (en aposición inv)* Morse (code).

mortadela *f* Mortadella.

mortaja *f* shroud.

mortal ◇ *adj* mortal; [caída, enfermedad] fatal; [aburrimiento, susto, enemigo] deadly. ◇ *mf* mortal.

mortalidad *f* mortality.

mortandad *f* mortality.

mortero *m* mortar.

mortífero, ra *adj* deadly.

mortificar *vt* to mortify.

mosaico, ca *adj* Mosaic.

➡ **mosaico** *m* mosaic.

mosca *f* fly; **por si las** ~**s** just in case; **¿qué** ~ **te ha picado?** what's up with you?

➡ **mosca muerta** *mf* slyboots, hypocrite.

moscardón *m* ZOOL blowfly.

moscón *m* ZOOL meatfly, bluebottle.

moscovita *adj* & *m,f* Muscovite.

Moscú Moscow.

mosquearse *vpr fam* [enfadarse] to get cross; [sospechar] to smell a rat.

mosquete *m* musket.

mosquetero *m* musketeer.

mosquitero *m* mosquito net.

mosquito *m* mosquito.

mosso d'Esquadra *m member of the Catalan police force.*

mostacho *m* moustache.

mostaza *f* mustard.

mosto *m* [residuo] must; [zumo de uva] grape juice.

mostrador *m* [en tienda] counter; [en bar] bar.

mostrar *vt* to show.

➡ **mostrarse** *vpr* to appear, to show o.s.; **se mostró muy interesado** he expressed great interest.

mota *f* [de polvo] speck; [en tela] dot.

mote *m* - **1.** nickname; **poner un** ~ **a alguien** to nickname sb - **2.** Andes [maíz] stewed maize UK o corn US.

moteado, da *adj* speckled; [vestido] dotted.

motel *m* motel.

motín *m* [del pueblo] uprising, riot; [de las tropas] mutiny.

motivación *f* motive, motivation *(U)*.

motivar vt - **1**. [causar] to cause; [impulsar] to motivate - **2**. [razonar] to explain, to justify.

motivo m - **1**. [causa] reason, cause; [de crimen] motive; **bajo ningún** ~ under no circumstances; **con** ~ **de** [por causa de] because of; [para celebrar] on the occasion of; [con el fin de] in order to; **sin** ~ for no reason - **2**. ARTE , LITER & MÚS motif.

moto f motorbike UK, motorcycle; **ponerse como una** ~ fam [por nervios] to get worked up; [sexualmente] to get horny; [por drogas] to get high.

motocicleta f motorbike, motorcycle.

motociclismo m motorcycling.

motociclista mf motorcyclist.

motoneta f Amér (motor) scooter.

motonetista mf Amér scooter rider.

motor (f motora o motriz) adj motor.

• **motor** m - **1**. [aparato] motor, engine - **2**. [fuerza] dynamic force.

• **motora** f motorboat.

motorismo m motorcycling.

motorista mf motorcyclist.

motriz ⇨ motor.

mousse [mus] m inv CULIN mousse.

movedizo, za adj [movible] movable, easily moved.

mover vt - **1**. [gen & INFORM] to move; [mecánicamente] to drive - **2**. [cabeza - afirmativamente] to nod; [- negativamente] to shake - **3**. [suscitar] to arouse, to provoke - **4**. fig [empujar]: ~ **a alguien a algo/a hacer algo** to drive sb to sthg/to do sthg.

• **mover a** vi - **1**. [incitar] to incite to - **2**. [causar] to provoke, to cause.

• **moverse** vpr - **1**. [gen] to move; [en la cama] to toss and turn - **2**. [darse prisa] to get a move on.

movido, da adj - **1**. [debate, torneo] lively; [persona] active, restless; [jornada, viaje] hectic - **2**. FOT blurred, fuzzy.

• **movida** f fam [ambiente] scene; **la movida madrileña** the Madrid scene of the late 1970s.

móvil ⇨ adj mobile, movable. ⇨ m - **1**. [motivo] motive - **2**. [juguete] mobile.

movilidad f mobility.

movilizar vt to mobilize.

movimiento m - **1**. [gen & POLÍT] movement - **2**. FÍS & TECN motion; **poner en** ~ to put in motion; ~ **sísmico** earth tremor - **3**. [circulación - gen] activity; [- de personal, mercancías] turnover; [- de vehículos] traffic; ~ **de capital** cash flow - **4**. [MÚS - parte de la obra] movement.

moviola f editing projector.

moza ⇨ mozo.

mozárabe ⇨ adj Mozarabic, Christian in the time of Moorish Spain. ⇨ m [lengua] Mozarabic.

mozo, za ⇨ adj [joven] young; [soltero] single, unmarried. ⇨ m,f - **1**. young boy (f young girl), young lad (f young lass) - **2**. Andes, RP [camarero] waiter (f waitress).

• **mozo** m - **1**. [trabajador] assistant (worker); ~ **de estación** (station) porter - **2**. [recluta] conscript.

MP3 (abrev de **MPEG-1 Audio Layer-3**) m [inform] MP3.

mu m [mugido] moo; **no decir ni** ~ not to say a word.

mucamo, ma m,f Andes, RP [en casa] maid; [en hotel] chamberperson (f chambermaid).

muchacho, cha m,f boy (f girl).

• **muchacha** f [sirvienta] maid.

muchedumbre f [de gente] crowd, throng; [de cosas] great number, masses (pl).

mucho, cha ⇨ adj - **1**. [gran cantidad] (en sg) a lot of; (en pl) many, a lot of; (en interrogativas y negativas) much, a lot of; **tengo** ~ **sueño** I'm very sleepy; ~**s días** several days; **no tengo** ~ **tiempo** I haven't got much time - **2**. (en sg) [demasiado]: **hay** ~ **niño aquí** there are too many kids here. ⇨ pron (en sg) a lot; (en pl) many, a lot; **tengo** ~ **que contarte** I have a lot to tell you; **¿queda dinero? - no** ~ is there any money left? - not much o not a lot; ~**s piensan igual** a lot of o many people think the same.

• **mucho** adv - **1**. [gen] a lot; **habla** ~ he talks a lot; **me canso** ~ I get really o very tired; **me gusta** ~ I like it a lot o very much; **no me gusta** ~ I don't like it much; **(no)** ~ **más tarde** (not) much later - **2**. [largo tiempo]: **hace** ~ **que no vienes** I haven't seen you for a long time; **¿dura** ~ **la obra?** is the play long?; ~ **antes/después** long before/after - **3**. [frecuentemente]: **¿vienes** ~ **por aquí?** do you come here often? - **4**. loc: **como** ~ at the most; **con** ~ by far, easily; **ni con** ~ not by a long chalk; **ni** ~ **menos** far from it, by no means; **no está ni** ~ **menos decidido** it is by no means decided.

• **por mucho que** loc conj no matter how much, however much; **por** ~ **que insistas** no matter how much o however much you insist.

mucosidad f mucus.

muda f [ropa interior] change of underwear.

mudanza f move; **estar de** ~ to be moving.

mudar ⇨ vt - **1**. [gen] to change; [casa] to move; **cuando mude la voz** when his voice breaks - **2**. [piel, plumas] to moult. ⇨ vi [cambiar]: ~ **de** [opinión, color] to change; [domicilio] to move.

◆ **mudarse** *vpr:* ~**se (de casa)** to move (house); ~**se (de ropa)** to change.

mudéjar *adj* & *m,f* Mudejar.

mudo, da *adj* **- 1.** [sin habla] dumb **- 2.** [callado] silent, mute; **se quedó** ~ he was left speechless **- 3.** [sin sonido] silent.

mueble ◇ *m* piece of furniture; **los** ~**s** the furniture *(U);* ~ **bar** cocktail cabinet. ◇ *adj* ▷ **bien**.

mueca *f* [gen] face, expression; [de dolor] grimace; **hacer** ~**s** to make faces.

muela *f* [diente - gen] tooth; [- molar] molar.

muelle *m* **- 1.** [de colchón, reloj] spring **- 2.** [en el puerto] **dock, quay;** [en el río] wharf.

muera ▷ **morir**.

muérdago *m* mistletoe.

muermo *m fam* bore, drag; **tener** ~ to be bored.

muerte *f* **- 1.** [gen] death; **hasta la** ~ until death; ~ **cerebral** brain death; ~ **súbita** [de bebé] cot death; FTBL sudden death; [en tenis] tiebreak, tiebreaker; **de mala** ~ third-rate, lousy **- 2.** [homicidio] murder.

muerto, ta ◇ *pp* ▷ **morir**. ◇ *adj* [gen] dead; **caer** ~ to drop dead; **estar** ~ **(de cansancio)** to be dead tired; **estar** ~ **de miedo/frío** to be scared/freezing to death; **estar** ~ **de hambre** to be starving. ◇ *m,f* dead person; [cadáver] corpse; **hubo dos** ~**s** two people died; **el** ~ **al hoyo y el vivo al bollo** *proverb* dead men have no friends *proverb*; **hacer el** ~ to float on one's back.

muesca *f* **- 1.** [concavidad] notch, groove **- 2.** [corte] nick.

muestra *f* **- 1.** [pequeña cantidad] sample **- 2.** [señal] sign, show; [prueba] proof; [de cariño, aprecio] token; **dar** ~**s de** to show signs of **- 3.** [modelo] model, pattern **- 4.** [exposición] show, exhibition.

muestrario *m* collection of samples.

muestreo *m* sample; [acción] sampling.

mugido *m* [de vaca] moo, mooing *(U);* [de toro] bellow, bellowing *(U).*

mugir *vi* [vaca] to moo; [toro] to bellow.

mugre *f* filth, muck.

mugriento, ta *adj* filthy.

mujer *f* woman; [cónyuge] wife; ~ **de la limpieza** cleaning lady; ~ **de negocios** businesswoman.

mujeriego, ga *adj* fond of the ladies.

◆ **mujeriego** *m* womanizer, lady's man.

mujerzuela *f despec* loose woman.

mulato, ta *adj* & *m,f* mulatto.

muleta *f* **- 1.** [para andar] crutch; *fig* prop, support **- 2.** TAUROM muleta, *red cape hanging from a stick used to tease the bull.*

mullido, da *adj* soft, springy.

mulo, la *m,f* ZOOL mule.

multa *f* fine; **poner una** ~ **a alguien** to fine sb.

multar *vt* to fine.

multicopista *f* duplicator, duplicating machine.

multiestación *f:* ~ **(de musculación)** multigym.

multimedia *adj inv* INFORM multimedia.

multimillonario, ria *m,f* multimillionaire.

multinacional *adj* & *f* multinational.

múltiple *adj* [variado] multiple.

◆ **múltiples** *adj pl* [numerosos] many, numerous.

multiplicación *f* multiplication.

multiplicar *vt* & *vi* to multiply.

◆ **multiplicarse** *vpr* **- 1.** [persona] to do lots of things at the same time **- 2.** BIOL to multiply.

múltiplo, pla *adj* multiple.

◆ **múltiplo** *m* multiple; **mínimo común** ~ lowest common multiple.

multitud *f* [de personas] crowd; **una** ~ **de cosas** loads of 0 countless things.

multitudinario, ria *adj* extremely crowded; [manifestación] mass *(antes de sust).*

multiuso *adj inv* multipurpose.

mundanal *adj* worldly.

mundano, na *adj* **- 1.** [del mundo] worldly, of the world **- 2.** [de la vida social] **(high)** society.

mundial ◇ *adj* [política, economía, guerra] world *(antes de sust);* [tratado, organización, fama] worldwide. ◇ *m* World Championships *(pl);* [en fútbol] World Cup.

mundo *m* **- 1.** [gen] world; **irse al otro** ~ to pass away; **el tercer** ~ the Third World; **se le cayó el** ~ **encima** his world fell apart; **todo el** ~ everyone, everybody; **venir al** ~ to come into the world, to be born **- 2.** [experiencia]: **hombre/mujer de** ~ man/woman of the world.

munición *f* ammunition.

municipal ◇ *adj* town *(antes de sust),* municipal; [elecciones] local; [instalaciones] public. ◇ *mf* ▷ **guardia**.

municipio *m* **- 1.** [corporación] town council **- 2.** [territorio] town, municipality.

muñeco, ca *m,f* [juguete] doll; [marioneta] puppet; ~ **de peluche** cuddly 0 soft toy; ~ **de trapo** rag doll.

◆ **muñeco** *m fig* puppet.

◆ **muñeca** *f* **- 1.** ANAT wrist **- 2.** *Andes* & *RP fam* [enchufe]: **tener** ~ to have friends in high places.

◆ **muñeco de nieve** *m* snowman.

muñequera *f* wristband.

muñón *m* stump.

mural ◇ *adj* [pintura] mural; [mapa] wall. ◇ *m* mural.

muralla *f* wall.

murciélago *m* bat.

murmullo *m* [gen] murmur, murmuring *(U)*; [de hojas] rustle, rustling *(U)*; [de insectos] buzz, buzzing *(U)*.

murmuración *f* backbiting *(U)*, gossip *(U)*.

murmurar ◇ *vt* to murmur. ◇ *vi* **- 1.** [susurrar - persona] to murmur, to whisper; [- agua, viento] to murmur, to gurgle **- 2.** [criticar]: **~ (de)** to gossip o backbite (about) **- 3.** [rezongar, quejarse] to grumble.

muro *m lit* & *fig* wall.

mus *m inv* card game played in pairs with bidding and in which players communicate by signs.

musa *f* [inspiración] muse.

musaraña *f* ZOOL shrew; **mirar a las ~s** to stare into space o thin air.

muscular *adj* muscular.

musculatura *f* muscles *(pl)*.

músculo *m* muscle.

musculoso, sa *adj* muscular.

museo *m* museum; **~ de arte** art gallery.

musgo *m* moss.

música ⊳ **músico**.

músico, ca ◇ *adj* musical. ◇ *m,f* [persona] musician.

➡ **música** *f* music; **poner música a algo** to set sthg to music; **música ambiental** background music.

musitar *vt* to mutter, to mumble.

muslo *m* thigh; [de pollo] drumstick.

mustio, tia *adj* **- 1.** [flor, planta] withered, wilted **- 2.** [persona] down, gloomy.

musulmán, ana *adj* & *m,f* Muslim, Moslem.

mutación *f* [cambio] sudden change; BIOL mutation.

mutante *adj* & *m,f* mutant.

mutar *vt* to mutate.

mutilado, da *adj* mutilated.

mutilar *vt* [gen] to mutilate; [estatua] to deface, to spoil.

mutismo *m* [silencio] silence.

mutua ⊳ **mutuo**.

mutual *m CSur, Perú* friendly society, mutual benefit society *US*.

mutualidad *f* [asociación] mutual benefit society.

mutuo, tua *adj* mutual.

➡ **mutua** *f* mutual benefit society.

muy *adv* **- 1.** [mucho] very; **~ bueno/cerca** very good/near; **~ de mañana** very early in the morning; **¡~ bien!** [vale] OK!, all right!; [qué bien] very good!, well done!; **es ~ hombre** he's a real man; **eso es ~ de ella** that's just like her; **eso es ~ de los americanos** that's typically American; **¡el ~ idiota!** what an idiot! **- 2.** [demasiado] too; **es ~ joven para votar** she's too young to vote.

n, N *f* [letra] n, N.

➡ **N** *m*: **el 20 N** *20th November, the date of Franco's death.*

nabo *m* turnip.

nácar *m* mother-of-pearl.

nacer *vi* **- 1.** [venir al mundo - niño, animal] to be born; [- planta] to sprout, to begin to grow; [- pájaro] to hatch (out); **~ de/en** to be born of/in; **~ para algo** to be born to be sthg; **ha nacido cantante** she's a born singer **- 2.** [surgir - pelo] to grow; [- río] to rise, to have its source; [- costumbre, actitud, duda] to have its roots.

nacido, da ◇ *adj* born. ◇ *m,f*: **los ~s hoy** those born today; **recién ~** new-born baby; **ser un mal ~** to be a wicked o vile person.

naciente *adj* **- 1.** [día] dawning; [sol] rising **- 2.** [gobierno, estado] new, fledgling; [interés] growing.

nacimiento *m* **- 1.** [gen] birth; [de planta] sprouting; **de ~** from birth **- 2.** [de río] source **- 3.** [origen] origin, beginning **- 4.** [belén] Nativity scene.

nación *f* [gen] nation; [territorio] country.

➡ **Naciones Unidas** *fpl* United Nations.

nacional *adj* national; [mercado, vuelo] domestic; [asuntos] home *(antes de sust)*.

nacionalidad *f* nationality.

nacionalismo *m* nationalism.

nacionalista *adj* & *m,f* nationalist.

nacionalizar *vt* **- 1.** [banca, bienes] to nationalize **- 2.** [persona] to naturalize.

➡ **nacionalizarse** *vpr* to become naturalized.

nada ◇ *pron* nothing; *(en negativas)* anything; **no he leído ~ de este autor** I haven't read anything by this author; **no hay ~ como un buen libro** there is nothing like a good book; **~ más** nothing else, nothing more; **no quiero ~ más** I don't want anything else; **no dijo ~ de ~** he didn't say anything at all; **de ~** [respuesta a 'gracias'] not at all, you're welcome; **como si ~** as if nothing had happened. ◇ *adv* **- 1.** [en absoluto] at all; **la película no me ha gustado ~** I didn't like the film at all; **no es ~ extraño**

it's not at all strange - **2.** [poco] a little, a bit; **no hace ~ que salió** he left just a minute ago; **~ menos que** [cosa] no less than; [persona] none other than. ◇ *f*: **la ~ nothingness**, the void; **salir de la ~** to appear out of *o* from nowhere.

◆ **nada más** *loc conj* no sooner, as soon as; **~ más salir de casa se puso a llover** no sooner had I left the house than it started to rain, as soon as I left the house, it started to rain.

nadador, ra *m,f* swimmer.

nadar *vi* [gen] to swim; [flotar] to float.

nadería *f* trifle, little thing.

nadie *pron* nobody, no one; **~ lo sabe** nobody knows; **no se lo dije a ~** I didn't tell anybody; **no ha llamado ~** nobody phoned.

nado ◆ **a nado** *loc adv* swimming.

nahua ◇ *adj* Nahuatl, *relating to Nahuatl language, culture or people.* ◇ *mf* Nahuatl (indian), *member of one of a group of Mexican indian peoples.*

naïf [na'if] *adj* naïve, primitivistic.

nailon, nilón, nylon® *m* nylon.

naipe *m* (playing) card.

◆ **naipes** *mpl* cards.

nalga *f* buttock.

nana *f* - **1.** [canción] lullaby - **2.** *Col, Méx* [niñera] nanny.

naranja ◇ *adj inv* orange. ◇ *m* [color] orange. ◇ *f* [fruto] orange.

◆ **media naranja** *f fam* other *o* better half.

naranjo *m* [árbol] orange tree.

narciso *m* BOT narcissus.

narcótico, ca *adj* narcotic.

◆ **narcótico** *m* narcotic; [droga] drug.

narcotizar *vt* to drug.

narcotraficante *mf* drug trafficker.

narcotráfico *m* drug trafficking.

nardo *m* nard, spikenard.

narigudo, da *adj* big-nosed.

nariz *f* - **1.** [órgano] nose; **hablar por la ~** to talk through one's nose; **tener la ~ tapada** to have a stuffed up *o* blocked nose - **2.** [orificio] nostril - **3.** [olfato] sense of smell - **4.** *loc*: **estar hasta las narices (de algo)** *fam* to be fed up to the back teeth (with sthg); **meter las narices en algo** *fam* to poke *o* stick one's nose into sthg.

narración *f* - **1.** [cuento, relato] narrative, story - **2.** [acción] narration.

narrador, ra *m,f* narrator.

narrar *vt* [contar] to recount, to tell.

narrativo, va *adj* narrative.

◆ **narrativa** *f* narrative.

nasal *adj* nasal.

nata *f* - **1.** [gen] *fig* cream; **~ batida** *o* **montada** whipped cream - **2.** [de leche hervida] skin.

natación *f* swimming.

natal *adj* [país] native; [ciudad, pueblo] home *(antes de sust).*

natalidad *f* birth rate.

natillas *fpl* custard *(U).*

nativo, va *adj & m,f* native.

nato, ta *adj* [gen] born; [cargo, título] ex officio.

natural ◇ *adj* - **1.** [gen] natural; [flores, fruta, leche] fresh; **soy rubia ~** I'm a natural blonde; **al ~** [persona] in one's natural state; [fruta] in its own juice; **ser ~ en alguien** to be natural *o* normal for sb - **2.** [nativo] native; **ser ~ de** to come from. ◇ *mf* [nativo] native. ◇ *m* [talante] nature, disposition.

naturaleza *f* - **1.** [gen] nature; **por ~** by nature - **2.** [complexión] constitution.

naturalidad *f* naturalness; **con ~** naturally.

naturalizar *vt* to naturalize.

◆ **naturalizarse** *vpr* to become naturalized.

naturista *mf* person favouring return to nature.

naufragar *vi* [barco] to sink, to be wrecked; [persona] to be shipwrecked.

naufragio *m* [de barco] shipwreck.

náufrago, ga *m,f* shipwrecked person, castaway.

náusea *(gen pl) f* nausea *(U),* sickness *(U);* **me da ~s** it makes me sick; **tener ~s** to feel nauseated, to feel sick.

nauseabundo, da *adj* nauseating, sickening.

náutico, ca *adj* [gen] nautical; DEP water *(antes de sust).*

◆ **náutica** *f* navigation, seamanship.

navaja *f* - **1.** [cuchillo - pequeño] penknife; [- más grande] jackknife - **2.** [molusco] razorshell, razor clam.

navajero, ra *m,f* thug who carries a knife.

naval *adj* naval.

Navarra Navarre.

navarro, rra *adj & m,f* Navarrese.

nave *f* - **1.** [barco] ship; **quemar las ~s** to burn one's boats *o* bridges - **2.** [vehículo] craft; **~ espacial** spaceship, spacecraft - **3.** [de fábrica] shop, plant; [almacén] warehouse - **4.** [de iglesia] nave.

navegación *f* navigation.

navegador *m* INFORM browser.

navegante *mf* navigator.

navegar ◇ *vi* [barco] to sail; [avión] to fly; **~ por Internet** INFORM to surf the Net. ◇ *vt* [barco] to sail; [avión] to fly.

Navidad *f* - **1.** [día] Christmas (Day) - **2.** *(gen* *pl*) [periodo] Christmas (time); **felices ~es** Merry Christmas.

navideño, ña *adj* Christmas *(antes de sust).*

naviero, ra *adj* shipping.

◆ **naviero** *m* [armador] shipowner.

◆ **naviera** *f* [compañía] shipping company.

navío *m* large ship.

nazi *adj & m,f* Nazi.

nazismo *m* Nazism.

neblina *f* mist.

nebuloso, sa *adj* -1. [con nubes] cloudy; [de niebla] foggy -2. [idea, mirada] vague.

◆ **nebulosa** *f* ASTRON nebula.

necedad *f* -1. [estupidez] stupidity, foolishness -2. [dicho, hecho] stupid *o* foolish thing; **decir ~es** to talk nonsense.

necesario, ria *adj* necessary; **un mal ~** a necessary evil; **es ~ hacerlo** it needs to be done; **no es ~ que lo hagas** you don't need to do it; **si fuera ~** if need be.

neceser *m* toilet bag *o* case.

necesidad *f* -1. [gen] need; **tener ~ de algo** to need sthg; **hacer de la ~ virtud** to make a virtue of necessity; **la ~ aguza el ingenio** *proverb* necessity is the mother of invention *proverb* -2. [obligación] necessity; **por ~** out of necessity -3. [hambre] hunger.

◆ **necesidades** *fpl*: **hacer (uno) sus necesidades** *eufemismo* to answer the call of nature.

necesitado, da ◇ *adj* needy. ◇ *m,f* needy *o* poor person; **los ~s** the poor.

necesitar *vt* to need; **necesito que me lo digas** I need you to tell me; **'se necesita piso'** 'flat wanted'.

◆ **necesitar de** *vi* to have need of.

necio, cia *adj* stupid, foolish; *Méx* [fastidioso] boring.

necrología *f* obituary; [lista de esquelas] obituaries *(pl)*, obituary column.

néctar *m* nectar.

nectarina *f* nectarine.

nefasto, ta *adj* [funesto] ill-fated; [dañino] bad, harmful; [pésimo] terrible, awful.

negación *f* -1. [desmentido] denial -2. [negativa] refusal -3. [lo contrario] antithesis, negation -4. GRAM negation.

negado, da *adj* useless, inept.

negar *vt* -1. [rechazar] to deny -2. [denegar] to refuse, to deny; **~ le algo a alguien** to refuse *o* deny sb sthg.

◆ **negarse** *vpr*: **~se (a)** to refuse (to).

negativo, va *adj* [gen] negative.

◆ **negativo** *m* FOT negative.

◆ **negativa** *f* -1. [rechazo] refusal; **una negativa rotunda** a flat refusal -2. [mentís] denial.

negligencia *f* negligence.

negligente *adj* negligent.

negociable *adj* negotiable.

negociación *f* negotiation.

negociante *mf* [comerciante] businessman *(f* businesswoman).

negociar ◇ *vi* -1. [comerciar] to do business; **~ con** to deal *o* trade with -2. [discutir] to negotiate. ◇ *vt* to negotiate.

negocio *m* -1. [gen] business; **el mundo de los ~s** the business world -2. [transacción] deal, (business) transaction; **~ sucio** shady deal, dirty business *(U)* -3. [operación ventajosa] good deal, bargain; **hacer ~** to do well -4. [comercio] trade.

negra ▷ **negro.**

negrero, ra *m,f* -1. HIST slave trader -2. [explotador] slave driver.

negrita, negrilla ▷ **letra.**

negro, gra ◇ *adj* -1. [gen] black -2. [furioso] furious, fuming; **ponerse ~** to get mad *o* angry -3. CIN: **cine ~** film noir. ◇ *m,f* black man *(f* black woman).

◆ **negro** *m* [color] black.

◆ **negra** *f* -1. MÚS crotchet -2. *loc*: **tener la negra** *fam* to have bad luck.

negrura *f* blackness.

nene, na *m,f fam* [niño] baby.

nenúfar *m* water lily.

neocelandés, esa,   neozelandés, esa *m,f* New Zealander.

neologismo *m* neologism.

neón *m* QUÍM neon.

neoyorquino, na ◇ *adj* New York *(antes de sust),* of/relating to New York. ◇ *m,f* New Yorker.

neozelandés, esa = neocelandés.

Nepal: **el ~** Nepal.

Neptuno Neptune.

nervio *m* -1. ANAT nerve; **~ óptico** optic nerve -2. [de carne] sinew -3. [vigor] energy, vigour; **sus niños son puro ~** her kids never sit still for five minutes.

◆ **nervios** *mpl* [estado mental] nerves; **tener ~s** to be nervous; **poner los ~s de punta a alguien** to get on sb's nerves; **tener los ~s de punta** to be on edge.

nerviosismo *m* nervousness, nerves *(pl).*

nervioso, sa *adj* -1. ANAT [sistema, enfermedad] nervous; [- tejido, célula, centro] nerve *(antes de sust)* -2. [inquieto] nervous; **ponerse ~** to get nervous -3. [irritado] worked-up, uptight; **ponerse ~** to get uptight *o* worked up.

nervudo, da *adj* sinewy.

netiqueta *f* INFORM netiquette.

neto, ta *adj* -1. [claro] clear, clean; [verdad] simple, plain -2. [peso, sueldo] net.

neumático, ca *adj* pneumatic.

◆ **neumático** *m* tyre; **~ de repuesto** spare tyre.

neumonía *f* pneumonia.

neurálgico, ca *adj* **- 1.** MED neuralgic **- 2.** [importante] critical.

neurastenia *f* nervous exhaustion.

neurología *f* neurology.

neurólogo, ga *m,f* neurologist.

neurona *f* neuron, nerve cell.

neurosis *f inv* neurosis.

neurótico, ca *adj* & *m,f* neurotic.

neutral *adj* & *m,f* neutral.

neutralidad *f* neutrality.

neutralizar *vt* to neutralize.

neutro, tra *adj* **- 1.** [gen] neutral **- 2.** BIOL & GRAM neuter.

neutrón *m* neutron.

nevado, da *adj* snowy.
  ➥ **nevada** *f* snowfall.

nevar *v impers* to snow.

nevera *f* fridge *UK*, icebox *US*.

nevisca *f* snow flurry.

nexo *m* link, connection; [relación] relation, connection.

ni ◇ *conj:* ~ ... ~ ... neither ... nor ...; ~ mañana ~ pasado neither tomorrow nor the day after; no ... ~ ... neither ... nor ..., not ... or ... (either); no es alto ~ bajo he's neither tall nor short, he's not tall or short (either); no es rojo ~ verde ~ azul it's neither red nor green nor blue; ~ un/ una ... not a single ...; no me quedaré ~ un minuto más I'm not staying for a minute longer; ~ uno/una not a single one; no he aprobado ~ una I haven't passed a single one; ~ que as if; ¡~ que yo fuera tonto! as if I were that stupid! ◇ *adv* not even; anda tan atareado que ~ tiene tiempo para comer he's so busy he doesn't even have time to eat.

Nicaragua Nicaragua.

nicaragüense *adj* & *m,f* Nicaraguan.

nicho *m* niche; ~ **ecológico** ecological niche.

nicotina *f* nicotine.

nido *m* [gen] nest.

niebla *f* [densa] fog; [neblina] mist; **hay ~** it's foggy.

nieto, ta *m,f* grandson (*f* granddaughter).

nieve *f* **- 1.** METEOR snow **- 2.** CULIN : **a punto de ~** beaten stiff **- 3.** *Carib, Méx* [granizado] *drink of flavoured crushed ice.*
  ➥ **nieves** *fpl* [nevada] snows, snowfall *(sg)*.

NIF (*abrev de* **número de identificación fiscal**) *m* ≃ National Insurance number *UK*, *identification number for tax purposes.*

Nilo *m*: **el ~** the (river) Nile.

nilón = **nailon**.

nimiedad *f* **- 1.** [cualidad] insignificance, triviality **- 2.** [dicho, hecho] trifle.

nimio, mia *adj* insignificant, trivial.

ninfa *f* nymph.

ninfómana *f* nymphomaniac.

ninguno, na ◇ *adj (antes de sust masculino:* **ningún***)* no; **no dieron ninguna respuesta** no answer was given; **no tengo ningún interés en hacerlo** I've no interest in doing it, I'm not at all interested in doing it; **no tengo ningún hijo/ninguna buena idea** I don't have any children/good ideas; **no tiene ninguna gracia** it's not funny. ◇ *pron* [cosa] none, not any; [persona] nobody, no one; ~ **funciona** none of them works; **no hay ~** there aren't any, there are none; ~ **lo sabrá** no one *o* nobody will know; ~ **de** none of; ~ **de ellos** none of them; ~ **de los dos** neither of them.

niña ➥ **niño**.

niñería *f* **- 1.** [cualidad] childishness *(U)* **- 2.** [tontería] silly *o* childish thing.

niñero, ra *adj* fond of children.
  ➥ **niñera** *f* nanny.

niñez *f* childhood.

niño, ña ◇ *adj* young. ◇ *m,f* [crío] child, boy (*f* girl); [bebé] baby; **los ~s** the children; ~ **bien** *despec* spoilt brat; ~ **prodigio** child prodigy; **ser el ~ bonito de alguien** to be sb's pet *o* blue-eyed boy.
  ➥ **niña** *f* [del ojo] pupil; **la niña de los ojos** *fig* the apple of one's eye.

nipón, ona *adj* & *m,f* Japanese.

níquel *m* nickel.

niquelar *vt* to nickel-plate.

niqui *m* T-shirt.

níspero *m* medlar.

nitidez *f* clarity; [de imágenes, colores] sharpness.

nítido, da *adj* clear; [imágenes, colores] sharp.

nitrato *m* nitrate.

nitrógeno *m* nitrogen.

nivel *m* **- 1.** [gen] level; [altura] height; **al ~ de** level with; **al ~ del mar** at sea level; ~ **del agua** water level **- 2.** [grado] level, standard; **al mismo ~ (que)** on a level *o* par (with); **a ~ europeo** at a European level; ~ **de vida** standard of living; ~**es de audiencia** ratings.

nivelador, ra *adj* levelling.
  ➥ **niveladora** *f* bulldozer.

nivelar *vt* **- 1.** [allanar] to level **- 2.** [equilibrar] to even out; FIN to balance.

no ◇ *adv* **- 1.** [expresa negación - gen] not; [- en respuestas] no; [- con sustantivos] non-; ~ **sé** I don't know; ~ **veo nada** I can't see anything; ~ **es fácil** it's not easy, it isn't easy; ~ **tiene dinero** he has no money, he hasn't got any money; **todavía ~** not yet; ¿~ **vienes? - ~**, ~ **creo** aren't you coming?

- no, I don't think so; **~ fumadores** non-smokers; **~ bien** as soon as; **~ ya ... sino que ...** not only... but (also) ...; **¡a que ~ lo haces!** I bet you don't do it!; **¿cómo ~?** of course; **pues ~, eso sí que ~** certainly not; **¡que ~!** I said no! **- 2.** [expresa duda, extrañeza]: **¿ ~ irás a venir?** you're not coming, are you?; **estamos de acuerdo, ¿ ~?** we're agreed then, are we?; **es español, ¿ ~?** he's Spanish, isn't he? ◇ *m* no.

n.° *(abrev de número)* no.

nobiliario, ria *adj* noble, nobiliary.

noble *adj & m,f* noble; **los ~s** the nobility.

nobleza *f* nobility.

noche *f* night; [atardecer] evening; **al caer la ~** at nightfall; **ayer por la ~** last night; **esta ~** tonight; **hacer ~ en** to stay the night in; **hacerse de ~** to get dark; **por la ~, de ~** at night; **buenas ~s** [despedida] good night; [saludo] good evening; **~ cerrada** dark night; **~ de bodas** wedding night; **~ del estreno** first *o* opening night; **~ toledana** sleepless night; **de la ~ a la mañana** overnight.

Nochebuena *f* Christmas Eve.

nochero *m* **- 1.** *CSur* night watchman **- 2.** *Amér* [mesita] bedside table.

Nochevieja *f* New Year's Eve.

noción *f* [concepto] notion; **tener ~ (de)** to have an idea (of).

➡ **nociones** *fpl* [conocimiento básico]: **tener nociones de** to have a smattering of.

nocivo, va *adj* [gen] harmful; [gas] noxious.

noctámbulo, la *m,f* night owl.

nocturno, na *adj* **- 1.** [club, tren, vuelo] night *(antes de sust)*; [clase] evening *(antes de sust)* **- 2.** [animales, plantas] nocturnal.

nodriza *f* wet nurse.

Noel ▷ **papá**.

nogal *m* walnut.

nómada ◇ *adj* nomadic. ◇ *mf* nomad.

nombramiento *m* appointment.

nombrar *vt* **- 1.** [citar] to mention **- 2.** [designar] to appoint.

nombre *m* **- 1.** [gen] name; **conocer a alguien de ~** to know somebody by name; **poner ~ a** to name; **sin ~** nameless; **~ y apellidos** full name; **~ compuesto** compound name; **~ de dominio** [inform] domain name; **~ de pila** first *o* Christian name; **~ de soltera** maiden name; **en ~ de** on behalf of; **lo que hizo no tiene ~** what he did is outrageous **- 2.** [fama] reputation; **hacerse un ~** to make a name for o.s.; **tener mucho ~** to be renowned *o* famous **- 3.** GRAM noun; **~ común/propio** common/proper noun.

nomenclatura *f* nomenclature.

nómina *f* **- 1.** [lista de empleados] payroll

- 2. [hoja de salario] payslip.

nominal *adj* nominal.

nominar *vt* to nominate.

nomo, gnomo *m* gnome.

non *m* odd number.

➡ **nones** *adv* [no] no way, absolutely not.

nonagésimo, ma *núm* ninetieth.

nordeste = **noreste**.

nórdico, ca *adj* **- 1.** [del norte] northern, northerly **- 2.** [escandinavo] Nordic.

noreste, nordeste ◇ *adj* [posición, parte] northeast, northeastern; [dirección, viento] northeasterly. ◇ *m* north-east.

noria *f* **- 1.** [para agua] water wheel **- 2.** [de feria] big wheel *UK*, Ferris wheel.

norma *f* standard; [regla] rule; **es la ~ hacerlo así** it's usual to do it this way; **tener por ~ hacer algo** to make it a rule to do sthg; **~s de seguridad** safety regulations.

normal *adj* normal; **~ y corriente** run-of-the-mill; **es una persona ~ y corriente** he's a perfectly ordinary person.

normalidad *f* normality.

normalizar *vt* **- 1.** [volver normal] to return to normal **- 2.** [estandarizar] to standardize.

➡ **normalizarse** *vpr* to return to normal.

normativo, va *adj* normative.

➡ **normativa** *f* regulations *(pl)*.

noroeste ◇ *adj* [posición, parte] northwest, northwestern; [dirección, viento] northwesterly. ◇ *m* northwest.

norte ◇ *adj* [posición, parte] north, northern; [dirección, viento] northerly. ◇ *m* GEOGR north.

norteamericano, na *adj & m,f* North American, American.

Noruega Norway.

noruego, ga *adj & m,f* Norwegian.

➡ **noruego** *m* [lengua] Norwegian.

nos *pron pers* **- 1.** *(complemento directo)* us; **le gustaría vernos** she'd like to see us **- 2.** *(complemento indirecto)* (to) us; **~ lo dio** he gave it to us; **~ tiene miedo** he's afraid of us **- 3.** *(reflexivo)* ourselves **- 4.** *(recíproco)* each other; **~ enamoramos** we fell in love (with each other).

nosocomio *m* *Amér* hospital.

nosotros, tras *pron pers* **- 1.** *(sujeto)* we **- 2.** *(predicado)*: **somos ~** it's us **- 3.** *(después de prep)* *(complemento)*: **ven a comer con ~** come and eat with us **- 4.** *loc*: **entre ~** between you and me, just between the two of us.

nostalgia *f* [del pasado] nostalgia; [de país, amigos] homesickness.

nota *f* **- 1.** [gen & MÚS] note; **tomar ~ de algo** [apuntar] to note sthg down; [fijarse] to take note of sthg; **tomar ~s** to take notes; **~ al**

margen marginal note; ~ **dominante** prevailing mood - **2.** EDUC mark; **sacar** o **tener buenas** ~s to get good marks - **3.** [cuenta] bill - **4.** *loc:* **dar la** ~ to make o.s. conspicuous.

notable ◇ *adj* remarkable, outstanding. ◇ *m* EDUC merit, second class.

notar *vt* - **1.** [advertir] to notice; **te noto cansado** you look tired to me; **hacer** ~ **algo** to point sthg out - **2.** [sentir] to feel; **noto un dolor raro** I can feel a strange pain.

➥ **notarse** *vpr* to be apparent; **se nota que le gusta** you can tell she likes it.

notaría *f* [oficina] notary's office.

notario, ria *m,f* notary (public).

noticia *f* news (U); **una** ~ a piece of news; **¿tienes** ~s **suyas?** have you heard from him?; ~ **bomba** *fam* bombshell.

➥ **noticias** *fpl:* **las** ~s RADIO & TV the news.

notificación *f* notification.

notificar *vt* to notify, to inform.

notoriedad *f* [fama] fame.

notorio, ria *adj* - **1.** [evidente] obvious - **2.** [conocido] widely-known.

novato, ta ◇ *adj* inexperienced. ◇ *m,f* novice, beginner.

novecientos, tas *núm* nine hundred; *ver también* **seis.**

novedad *f* - **1.** [cualidad - de nuevo] newness; [- de novedoso] novelty - **2.** [cambio] change - **3.** [noticia] news (U); **sin** ~ without incident; MIL all quiet.

➥ **novedades** *fpl* [libros, discos] new releases; [moda] latest fashion (sg).

novedoso, sa *adj* new, new.

novel *adj* new, first-time.

novela *f* novel; ~ **policíaca** detective story.

novelesco, ca *adj* - **1.** [de la novela] fictional - **2.** [fantástico] fantastic, extraordinary.

novelista *mf* novelist.

noveno, na *núm* ninth.

noventa *núm* ninety; **los (años)** ~ the nineties; *ver también* **seis.**

noviar *vi CSur, Méx:* ~ **con alguien** to go out with sb, to date sb *US;* **están noviando** they are going out together, they are dating *US.*

noviazgo *m* engagement.

noviembre *m* November; *ver también* **septiembre.**

novillada *f* TAUROM bullfight with young bulls.

novillo, lla *m,f* young bull or cow; **hacer** ~s *fam* to play truant *UK,* to play hooky *US.*

novio, via *m,f* - **1.** [compañero] boyfriend (*f* girlfriend) - **2.** [prometido] fiancé (*f* fiancée) - **3.** [recién casado] bridegroom (*f* bride); **los** ~s the newly-weds.

nubarrón *m* storm cloud.

nube *f* - **1.** [gen] *fig* cloud; ~ **atómica** mushroom cloud; ~ **de tormenta** thundercloud

- **2.** [de personas, moscas] swarm - **3.** *loc:* **poner algo/a alguien por las** ~s to praise sthg/sb to the skies; **por las** ~s [caro] sky-high, terribly expensive.

nublado, da *adj* - **1.** [encapotado] cloudy, overcast - **2.** *fig* [turbado] clouded, darkened.

nublar *vt lit & fig* to cloud.

➥ **nublarse** *vpr* to cloud over.

nubosidad *f* cloudiness, clouds (pl).

nuca *f* nape, back of the neck.

nuclear *adj* nuclear.

núcleo *m* - **1.** [centro] nucleus; *fig* centre *UK,* center *US;* ~ **de población** population centre *UK,* population center *US* - **2.** [grupo] core.

nudillo *m* knuckle.

nudismo *m* nudism.

nudo *m* - **1.** [gen] knot; **se le hizo un** ~ **en la garganta** she got a lump in her throat - **2.** [cruce] junction - **3.** [vínculo] tie, bond - **4.** [punto principal] crux, nub.

nudoso, sa *adj* knotty, gnarled.

nuera *f* daughter-in-law.

nuestro, tra ◇ *adj poses* our; ~ **coche** our car; **este libro es** ~ this book is ours, this is our book; **un amigo** ~ a friend of ours; **no es asunto** ~ it's none of our business. ◇ *pron poses:* **el** ~ ours; **el** ~ **es rojo** ours is red; **ésta es la nuestra** *fam* this is the chance we have been waiting for; **lo** ~ **es el teatro** [lo que nos va] theatre is what we should be doing; **los** ~s *fam* [nuestra familia] our folks; [nuestro bando] our lot, our side.

nueva ➤ **nuevo.**

Nueva York New York.

Nueva Zelanda New Zealand.

nueve *núm* nine; *ver también* **seis.**

nuevo, va ◇ *adj* [gen] new; [patatas, legumbres] new, fresh; [vino] young; **esto es** ~ **para mí, no lo sabía** that's news to me, I didn't know it; **ser** ~ **en** to be new to. ◇ *m,f* newcomer.

➥ **buena nueva** *f* good news (U).

➥ **de nuevo** *loc adv* again.

nuez *f* - **1.** BOT [gen] nut; [de nogal] walnut - **2.** ANAT Adam's apple.

➥ **nuez moscada** *f* nutmeg.

nulidad *f* - **1.** [no validez] nullity - **2.** [ineptitud] incompetence.

nulo, la *adj* - **1.** [sin validez] null and void, invalid - **2.** *fam* [incapacitado]: ~ **(para)** useless (at).

núm. (*abrev de* **número**) No.

numeración *f* - **1.** [acción] numbering - **2.** [sistema] numerals (pl), numbers (pl).

numeral *adj* numeral.

numerar *vt* to number.

numérico, ca *adj* numerical.

número *m* - **1.** [gen] number; ~ **de matrícula** AUTOM registration number; ~ **de serie** serial number; ~ **de teléfono** telephone number; ~ **redondo** round number; **en ~s rojos** in the red; **hacer ~s** to reckon up - **2.** [tamaño, talla] size - **3.** [de publicación] issue, number; ~ **atrasado** back number - **4.** [de lotería] ticket - **5.** [de un espectáculo] turn, number; **montar el ~** *fam* to make o cause a scene.

numeroso, sa *adj* numerous; **un grupo ~** a large group.

nunca *adv (en frases afirmativas)* never; *(en frases negativas)* ever; **casi ~ viene** he almost never comes, he hardly ever comes; **¿~ le has visto?** have you never seen her?, haven't you ever seen her?; **más que ~** more than ever; ~ **jamás** o **más** never more o again.

nuncio *m* nuncio.

nupcial *adj* wedding *(antes de sust)*.

nupcias *fpl* wedding *(sg)*, nuptials; **casarse en segundas ~** to remarry, to marry again.

nutria *f* otter.

nutrición *f* nutrition.

nutricionista *mf Amér* dietician.

nutrido, da *adj* - **1.** [alimentado] nourished, fed; **mal ~** undernourished - **2.** [numeroso] large.

nutrir *vt* - **1.** [alimentar]: ~ **(con** o **de)** to nourish o feed (with) - **2.** [fomentar] to feed, to nurture - **3.** [suministrar]: ~ **(de)** to supply (with).
➡ **nutrirse** *vpr* - **1.** [gen]: ~**se de** o **con** to feed on - **2.** [proveerse]: ~**se de** o **con** to supply o provide o.s. with.

nutritivo, va *adj* nutritious.

nylon® ['nailon] = **nailon**.

ñ, Ñ *f* [letra] ñ, Ñ, *15th letter of the Spanish alphabet.*

ñapa *f Ven fam* bonus, extra.

ñato, ta *adj Andes, RP* snub-nosed.

ñoñería, ñoñez *f* inanity, insipidness *(U)*.

ñoño, ña *adj* - **1.** [remilgado] squeamish; [quejica] whining - **2.** [soso] dull, insipid.

ñudo *Amér*
➡ **al ñudo** *loc adv* in vain.

o¹, O *f* [letra] o, O.

o² *conj ('u' en vez de 'o' antes de palabras que empiezan por 'o' u 'ho')* or; ~ **...** ~ either ... or; ~ **sea (que)** in other words.

o/ *abrev de* **orden.**

oasis *m inv lit* & *fig* oasis.

obcecar *vt* to blind.
➡ **obcecarse** *vpr* to become stubborn; ~**se en hacer algo** to insist on doing sthg.

obedecer ◇ *vt*: ~ **(a alguien)** to obey (sb). ◇ *vi* - **1.** [acatar] to obey, to do as one is told; **hacerse ~** to command obedience - **2.** [someterse]: ~ **a** to respond to - **3.** [estar motivado]: ~ **a** to be due to.

obediencia *f* obedience.

obediente *adj* obedient.

obertura *f* overture.

obesidad *f* obesity.

obeso, sa *adj* obese.

óbice *m*: **no ser ~ para** not to be an obstacle to.

obispo *m* bishop.

objeción *f* objection; **poner objeciones a** to raise objections to; **tener objeciones** to have objections; ~ **de conciencia** conscientious objection.

objetar *vt* to object to; **no tengo nada que ~** I have no objection.

objetivo, va *adj* objective.
➡ **objetivo** *m* - **1.** [finalidad] objective, aim - **2.** MIL target - **3.** FOT lens.

objeto *m* - **1.** [gen] object; **ser ~ de** to be the object of; ~ **volante no identificado** unidentified flying object; ~**s de valor** valuables; ~**s perdidos** lost property *(U)* - **2.** [propósito] purpose, object; **sin ~** [inútilmente] to no purpose, pointlessly; **al** o **con ~ de** [para] in order to, with the aim of.

objetor, ra *m,f* objector; ~ **de conciencia** conscientious objector.

oblicuo, cua *adj* [inclinado] oblique, slanting; [mirada] sidelong.

obligación *f* - **1.** [gen] obligation, duty; **por ~** out of a sense of duty; **antes es la ~ que la devoción** *proverb* business before pleasure - **2.** FIN *(gen pl)* bond, security.

obligar *vt* : ~ **a alguien (a hacer algo)** to oblige *o* force sb (to do sthg).
➤ **obligarse** *vpr* : ~**se a hacer algo** to undertake to do sthg.

obligatorio, ria *adj* obligatory, compulsory.

oboe *m* [instrumento] oboe.

obra *f* **-1.** [gen] work *(U)*; **es** ~ **suya** it's his doing; **poner en** ~ to put into effect; ~ **de caridad** [institución] charity; ~**s sociales** community work *(U)*; **por** ~ **(y gracia) de** thanks to; ~**s son amores y no buenas razones** *proverb* actions speak louder than words *proverb* **- 2.** ARTE work (of art); TEATR play; LITER book; MÚS opus; ~ **maestra** masterpiece; ~**s completas** complete works **- 3.** CONSTR [lugar] building site; [reforma] alteration; '~**s**' [en carretera] 'roadworks'; ~**s públicas** public works.

obrar ⋄ *vi* **-1.** [actuar] to act **- 2.** [causar efecto] to work, to take effect **- 3.** [estar en poder]: ~ **en manos de** to be in the possession of. ⋄ *vt* to work.

obrero, ra ⋄ *adj* [clase] working; [movimiento] labour *(antes de sust).* ⋄ *m,f* [en fábrica] worker; [en obra] workman, labourer; ~ **cualificado** skilled worker.

obscenidad *f* obscenity.

obsceno, na *adj* obscene.

obscurecer = oscurecer.

obscuridad = oscuridad.

obscuro, ra = oscuro.

obsequiar *vt* : ~ **a alguien con algo** to present sb with sthg.

obsequio *m* gift, present.

observación *f* **-1.** [gen] observation; **en** *o* **bajo** ~ under observation **- 2.** [comentario] remark, observation; **hacer una** ~ to make a remark **- 3.** [nota] note **- 4.** [cumplimiento] observance.

observador, ra ⋄ *adj* observant. ⋄ *m,f* observer.

observar *vt* **-1.** [contemplar] to observe, to watch **- 2.** [advertir] to notice, to observe **- 3.** [acatar - ley, normas] to observe, to respect; [- conducta, costumbre] to follow.
➤ **observarse** *vpr* to be noticed.

observatorio *m* observatory.

obsesión *f* obsession.

obsesionar *vt* to obsess.
➤ **obsesionarse** *vpr* to be obsessed.

obsesivo, va *adj* obsessive.

obseso, sa ⋄ *adj* obsessed. ⋄ *m,f* obsessed *o* obsessive person.

obstaculizar *vt* to hinder, to hamper.

obstáculo *m* obstacle; **un** ~ **para** an obstacle to; **poner** ~**s a algo/alguien** to hinder sthg/sb.

obstante ➤ **no obstante** *loc adv* nevertheless, however.

obstetricia *f* obstetrics *(U).*

obstinado, da *adj* [persistente] persistent; [terco] obstinate, stubborn.

obstinarse *vpr* to refuse to give way; ~ **en** to persist in.

obstrucción *f* lit & fig obstruction.

obstruir *vt* **-1.** [bloquear] to block, to obstruct **- 2.** [obstaculizar] to obstruct, to impede.
➤ **obstruirse** *vpr* to get blocked (up).

obtener *vt* [beca, cargo, puntos] to get; [premio, victoria] to win; [ganancias] to make; [satisfacción] to gain.

obturar *vt* to block.

obtuso, sa *adj* **-1.** [sin punta] blunt **- 2.** [tonto] obtuse, stupid.

obús *(pl* **obuses)** *m* [proyectil] shell.

obviar *vt* to avoid, to get round.

obvio, via *adj* obvious.

oca *f* [ave] goose.

ocasión *f* **-1.** [oportunidad] opportunity, chance **- 2.** [momento] moment, time; [vez] occasion; **en dos ocasiones** on two occasions; **en alguna** ~ sometimes; **en cierta** ~ once; **en otra** ~ some other time **- 3.** [motivo]: **con** ~ **de** on the occasion of **- 4.** [ganga] bargain; **de** ~ [precio, artículos etc] bargain *(antes de sust).*

ocasional *adj* **-1.** [accidental] accidental **- 2.** [irregular] occasional.

ocasionar *vt* to cause.

ocaso *m* **-1.** [puesta del sol] sunset **- 2.** [decadencia] decline.

occidental *adj* western.

occidente *m* west.
➤ **Occidente** *m* [bloque de países] the West.

OCDE *(abrev de* **Organización para la Cooperación y el Desarrollo Económico)** *f* OECD.

Oceanía Oceania.

océano *m* ocean; [inmensidad] sea, host.

ochenta *núm* eighty; **los (años)** ~ the eighties; *ver también* **seis.**

ocho *núm* eight; **de aquí en** ~ **días** [en una semana] a week today; *ver también* **seis.**

ochocientos, tas *núm* eight hundred; *ver también* **seis.**

ocio *m* [tiempo libre] leisure; [inactividad] idleness.

ocioso, sa *adj* **-1.** [inactivo] idle **- 2.** [innecesario] unnecessary; [inútil] pointless.

ocre ⋄ *m* ochre. ⋄ *adj inv* ochre.

octágono, na *adj* octagonal.
➤ **octágono** *m* octagon.

octano *m* octane.

octava ⊳ octavo.

octavilla *f* -1. [de propaganda política] pamphlet, leaflet - 2. [tamaño] octavo.

octavo, va *núm* eighth.
➡ **octavo** *m* [parte] eighth.
➡ **octava** *f* MÚS octave.

octeto *m* INFORM byte.

octogenario, ria *adj* & *m,f* octogenarian.

octogésimo, ma *núm* eightieth.

octubre *m* October; *ver también* **septiembre**.

ocular *adj* eye *(antes de sust)*.

oculista *mf* ophthalmologist.

ocultar *vt* -1. [gen] to hide - 2. [delito] to cover up.
➡ **ocultarse** *vpr* to hide.

oculto, ta *adj* hidden.

ocupación *f* -1. [gen] occupation; ~ ilegal de viviendas squatting - 2. [empleo] job.

ocupado, da *adj* -1. [persona] busy - 2. [teléfono, lavabo etc] engaged - 3. [lugar - gen, por ejército] occupied; [plaza] taken.

ocupante *mf* occupant; ~ ilegal de viviendas squatter.

ocupar *vt* -1. [gen] to occupy - 2. [superficie, espacio] to take up; [habitación, piso] to live in; [mesa] to sit at; [sillón] to sit in - 3. [suj: actividad] to take up - 4. [cargo] to hold - 5. [dar trabajo a] to find o provide work for - 6. CAm, Méx [usar] to use.
➡ **ocuparse** *vpr* [encargarse]: ~se de [gen] to deal with; [niños, enfermos, finanzas] to look after.

ocurrencia *f* -1. [idea] bright idea - 2. [dicho gracioso] witty remark.

ocurrir *vi* -1. [acontecer] to happen - 2. [pasar, preocupar]: **¿qué le ocurre a Juan?** what's up with Juan?
➡ **ocurrirse** *vpr* [venir a la cabeza]: **no se me ocurre ninguna solución** I can't think of a solution; **¡ni se te ocurra!** don't even think about it!; **se me ocurre que ...** it occurs to me that ...

odiar *vt* & *vi* to hate.

odio *m* hatred; **tener ~ a algo/alguien** to hate sthg/sb.

odioso, sa *adj* hateful, horrible.

odontólogo, ga *m,f* dentist, dental surgeon.

OEA *(abrev de* **Organización de Estados Americanos)** *f* OAS.

oeste ⬦ *adj* [posición, parte] west, western; [dirección, viento] westerly. ⬦ *m* west.

ofender *vt* [injuriar] to insult; [suj: palabras] to offend, to hurt.
➡ **ofenderse** *vpr*: ~se (por) to take offence (at).

ofensa *f* -1. [acción]: ~ (a) offence (against) - 2. [injuria] slight, insult.

ofensivo, va *adj* offensive.
➡ **ofensiva** *f* offensive.

oferta *f* -1. [gen] offer; '~s de trabajo' 'situations vacant' - 2. ECON [suministro] supply; **la ~ y la demanda** supply and demand; ~ **monetaria** money supply - 3. [rebaja] bargain, special offer; **de ~** bargain *(antes de sust)*, on offer - 4. FIN [proposición] bid, tender; ~ **pública de adquisición** COM takeover bid.

ofertar *vt* to offer.

oficial, la *m,f* [obrero] journeyman; [aprendiz] trainee.
➡ **oficial** ⬦ *adj* official. ⬦ *m* -1. MIL officer - 2. [funcionario] clerk.

oficialismo *m* Amér: **el ~** [gobierno] the Government; [partidarios del gobierno] government supporters.

oficialista *adj* Amér pro-government.

oficiar *vt* to officiate at.

oficina *f* office; ~ **de empleo** job centre; ~ **de turismo** tourist office.

oficinista *mf* office worker.

oficio *m* -1. [profesión manual] trade; **de ~** by trade - 2. [trabajo] job - 3. [experiencia]: **tener mucho ~** to be very experienced - 4. RELIG service.

oficioso, sa *adj* unofficial.

ofimática *f* office automation.

ofrecer *vt* -1. [gen] to offer; [fiesta] to give, to throw; ~ **algo a alguien** to offer sb sthg - 2. [aspecto] to present.
➡ **ofrecerse** *vpr* [presentarse] to offer, to volunteer; ~se a o **para hacer algo** to offer to do sthg.

ofrecimiento *m* offer.

ofrenda *f* RELIG offering; [por gratitud, amor] gift.

ofrendar *vt* to offer up.

oftalmología *f* ophthalmology.

ofuscar *vt* -1. [deslumbrar] to dazzle - 2. [turbar] to blind.
➡ **ofuscarse** *vpr*: ~se (con) to be blinded (by).

ogro *m* ogre.

oh *interj*: **¡~!** oh!

oídas
➡ **de oídas** *loc adv* by hearsay.

oído *m* -1. [órgano] ear; **de ~** by ear; **hacer ~s sordos** to turn a deaf ear - 2. [sentido] (sense of) hearing; **ser duro de ~** to be hard of hearing; **tener ~, tener buen ~** to have a good ear.

oír ⬦ *vt* -1. [gen] to hear - 2. [atender] to listen to ⬦ *vi* to hear; **¡oiga, por favor!** excuse me!; **¡oye!** *fam* hey!

ojal *m* buttonhole.

ojalá *interj*: **¡~!** if only (that were so)!; **¡~ lo haga!** I hope she does it!; **¡~ fuera**

ya domingo! I wish it were Sunday!

ojeada f glance, look; **echar una ~ a algo/alguien** to take a quick glance at sthg/sb, to take a quick look at sthg/sb.

ojear vt to have a look at.

ojera (gen pl) f bags (pl) under the eyes.

ojeriza f fam dislike; **tener ~ a alguien** to have it in for sb.

ojeroso, sa adj with bags under the eyes, haggard.

ojo ◇ m - 1. ANAT eye; **~s saltones** popping eyes - 2. [agujero - de aguja] eye; [- de puente] span; **~ de la cerradura** keyhole - 3. loc: **a ~ (de buen cubero)** roughly, approximately; **andar con (mucho) ~** to be (very) careful; **comerse con los ~s a alguien** fam to drool over sb; **echar el ~ a algo** to have one's eye on sthg; **en un abrir y cerrar de ~s** in the twinkling of an eye; **mirar algo con buenos/malos ~s** to look favourably/unfavourably on sthg; **no pegar ~** not to get a wink of sleep; **tener (buen) ~** to have a good eye. ◇ interj: **¡~!** be careful!, watch out!

ojota f RP [chancletas] flip-flop UK, thong US, Austr.

OK, okey [o'kei] (abrev de **all correct**) interj OK.

okupa m y f mfam squatter.

ola f wave; **~ de calor** heatwave; **~ de frío** cold spell.

ole, olé interj: **¡~!** bravo!

oleada f - 1. [del mar] swell - 2. fig [avalancha] wave.

oleaje m swell.

óleo m oil (painting).

oleoducto m oil pipeline.

oler ◇ vt to smell. ◇ vi - 1. [despedir olor]: **~ (a)** to smell (of) - 2. fam [indicando sospecha]: **~ a** to smack of.

◆ olerse vpr: **~se algo** fam to sense sthg.

olfatear vt - 1. [olisquear] to sniff - 2. [barruntar] to smell, to sense.

◆ olfatear en vi [indagar] to pry into.

olfato m - 1. [sentido] sense of smell - 2. fig [sagacidad] nose, instinct; **tener ~ para algo** to be a good judge of sthg.

oligarquía f oligarchy.

olimpiada, olimpíada f Olympiad, Olympic Games (pl); **las ~s** the Olympics.

olisquear vt to sniff (at).

oliva f olive.

olivar m olive grove.

olivera f olive tree.

olivo m olive tree.

olla f pot; **~ exprés** o **a presión** pressure cooker; **~ podrida** CULIN stew.

olmo m elm (tree).

olor m smell; **~ a** smell of.

oloroso, sa adj fragrant.

◆ oloroso m oloroso (sherry).

OLP (abrev de **Organización para la Liberación de Palestina**) f PLO.

olvidadizo, za adj forgetful.

olvidar vt - 1. [gen] to forget - 2. [dejarse] to leave; **olvidé las llaves en la oficina** I left my keys at the office.

◆ olvidarse vpr - 1. [gen] to forget; **~se de algo/hacer algo** to forget sthg/to do sthg - 2. [dejarse] to leave.

olvido m - 1. [de un nombre, hecho etc] forgetting; **caer en el ~** to fall into oblivion - 2. [descuido] oversight.

ombligo m ANAT navel.

omisión f omission.

omitir vt to omit.

ómnibus m inv - 1. omnibus; FERROC local train - 2. Cuba, Urug [urbano] bus; Andes, Cuba, Urug [interurbano, internacional] intercity bus.

omnipotente adj omnipotent.

omnívoro, ra adj omnivorous.

omoplato, omóplato m shoulder-blade.

OMS (abrev de **Organización Mundial de la Salud**) f WHO.

once núm eleven; ver también **seis**.

ONCE (abrev de **Organización Nacional de Ciegos Españoles**) f Spanish association for the blind, famous for its national lottery.

onceavo, va núm eleventh.

onda f wave; **~ corta/larga/media** short/long/medium wave; **~ expansiva** shock wave; **estar en la ~** fam to be on the ball; **¿qué ~?** Méx, RP fam how's it going?, how are things?

ondear vi to ripple.

ondulación f [acción] rippling.

ondulado, da adj wavy.

ondular ◇ vi [agua] to ripple; [terreno] to undulate. ◇ vt to wave.

ONG (abrev de **organización no gubernamental**) f NGO.

ónice, ónix m o f onyx.

onomástico, ca adj culto onomastic.

◆ onomástica f culto name day.

ONU (abrev de **Organización de las Naciones Unidas**) f UN.

onza f [unidad de peso] ounce.

OPA (abrev de **oferta pública de adquisición**) f takeover bid.

opaco, ca adj opaque.

ópalo m opal.

opción f - 1. [elección] option; **no hay ~** there is no alternative - 2. [derecho] right; **dar ~ a** to give the right to; **tener ~ a** [empleo, cargo] to be eligible for.

opcional adj optional.

OPEP (*abrev de* **Organización de Países Exportadores de Petróleo**) *f* OPEC.

ópera *f* opera; ~ **bufa** comic opera, opera buffa.

operación *f* - **1.** [gen] operation; ~ **quirúrgica** (surgical) operation; ~ **retorno** *police operation to assist return of holidaymakers to their city homes, minimizing traffic congestion and maximizing road safety* - **2.** COM transaction.

operador, ra *m,f* - **1.** INFORM & TELECOM operator - **2.** [de la cámara] cameraman; [del proyector] projectionist.

◆ **operador** *m* MAT operator.

◆ **operador turístico** *m* tour operator.

operar ◇ *vt* - **1.** [enfermo]: ~ **a alguien (de algo)** [enfermedad] to operate on sb (for sthg); **lo operaron del hígado** they've operated on his liver - **2.** [cambio etc] to bring about, to produce. ◇ *vi* - **1.** [gen] to operate - **2.** [actuar] to act - **3.** COM & FIN to deal.

◆ **operarse** *vpr* - **1.** [enfermo] to be operated on, to have an operation; **me voy a ~ del hígado** I'm going to have an operation on my liver - **2.** [cambio etc] to occur, to come about.

operario, ria *m,f* worker.

operativo, va *adj* operative.

◆ **operativo** *m* *Amér* operation.

opereta *f* operetta.

opinar ◇ *vt* to believe, to think. ◇ *vi* to give one's opinion; ~ **de algo/alguien,** ~ **sobre algo/alguien** to think about sthg/sb.

opinión *f* [parecer] opinion; **expresar** *o* **dar una** ~ to give an opinion; **la** ~ **pública** public opinion.

opio *m* opium.

opíparo, ra *adj* sumptuous.

oponente *mf* opponent.

oponer *vt* - **1.** [resistencia] to put up - **2.** [argumento, razón] to put forward, to give.

◆ **oponerse** *vpr* - **1.** [no estar de acuerdo] to be opposed; ~**se a algo** [desaprobar] to be opposed to sthg, to oppose sthg; [contradecir] to contradict sthg; **me opongo a creerlo** I refuse to believe it - **2.** [obstaculizar]: ~**se a** to stand in the way of, to impede.

oporto *m* port (wine).

oportunidad *f* [ocasión] opportunity, chance.

oportunismo *m* opportunism.

oportunista *mf* opportunist.

oportuno, na *adj* - **1.** [pertinente] appropriate - **2.** [propicio] timely; **el momento** ~ the right time.

oposición *f* - **1.** [gen] opposition - **2.** [resistencia] resistance - **3.** (*gen pl*) [examen] public entrance examination; ~ **a profesor** public examination to be a teacher; **preparar oposiciones** to be studying for a public entrance examination.

opositar *vi*: ~ **(a)** to sit a public entrance examination (for).

opositor, ra *m,f* - **1.** [a un cargo] *candidate in a public entrance examination* - **2.** [oponente] opponent.

opresión *f* fig [represión] oppression.

opresivo, va *adj* oppressive.

opresor, ra *m,f* oppressor.

oprimir *vt* - **1.** [apretar - botón etc] to press; [- garganta, brazo etc] to squeeze - **2.** [suj: zapatos, cinturón] to pinch, to be too tight for - **3.** fig [reprimir] to oppress - **4.** fig [angustiar] to weigh down on, to burden.

optar *vi* [escoger]: ~ **(por algo)** to choose (sthg); ~ **por hacer algo** to choose to do sthg; ~ **entre** to choose between.

optativo, va *adj* optional.

óptico, ca ◇ *adj* optic. ◇ *m,f* [persona] optician.

◆ **óptica** *f* - **1.** FÍS optics (*U*) - **2.** [tienda] optician's (shop) - **3.** fig [punto de vista] point of view.

optimismo *m* optimism.

optimista ◇ *adj* optimistic. ◇ *mf* optimist.

óptimo, ma ◇ *superl* ▷ **bueno.** ◇ *adj* optimum.

opuesto, ta ◇ *pp* ▷ **oponer.** ◇ *adj* - **1.** [contrario] conflicting; ~ **a** opposed *o* contrary to - **2.** [de enfrente] opposite.

opulencia *f* [riqueza] opulence; [abundancia] abundance.

opulento, ta *adj* [rico] opulent.

opus *m* MÚS opus.

◆ **Opus Dei** *m*: **el Opus Dei** the Opus Dei, *traditionalist religious organization, the members of which are usually professional people or public figures.*

oración *f* - **1.** [rezo] prayer - **2.** GRAM sentence; ~ **principal/subordinada** main/subordinate clause.

orador, ra *m,f* speaker.

oral ◇ *adj* oral. ◇ *m* ▷ **examen.**

órale *interj* *Méx* fam [de acuerdo] right!, sure!; [¡venga!] come on!

orangután *m* orangutang.

orar *vi* to pray.

órbita *f* - **1.** ASTRON orbit - **2.** [de ojo] eye socket.

orca *f* killer whale.

orden ◇ *m* - **1.** [gen] order; **en** ~ [bien colocado] tidy, in its place; [como debe ser] in order; **por** ~ in order; **las fuerzas del** ~ the forces of law and order; ~ **público** law and order - **2.** [tipo] type, order; **problemas de** ~ **económico** economic problems. ◇ *f* **or-**der; **por** ~ **de** by order of; **estar a la** ~ **del**

· **día** to be the order of the day.
  ◆ **del orden de** *loc prep* around, approximately.
  ◆ **orden del día** *m* agenda.
ordenado, da *adj* [lugar, persona] tidy.
ordenador *m* INFORM computer; ~ **personal** personal computer; ~ **portátil** laptop computer.
ordenanza ◇ *m* [de oficina] messenger. ◇ *f (gen pl)* ordinance, law; ~**s municipales** by-laws.
ordenar *vt* **- 1.** [poner en orden - gen] to arrange, to put in order; [- habitación, armario etc] to tidy (up) **- 2.** [mandar] to order **- 3.** RELIG to ordain **- 4.** *Amér* [solicitar] to order.
  ◆ **ordenarse** *vpr* RELIG to be ordained.
ordeñar *vt* to milk.
ordinariez *f* commonness, coarseness; decir/hacer una ~ to say/do sthg rude.
ordinario, ria *adj* **- 1.** [común] ordinary, usual **- 2.** [vulgar] common, coarse **- 3.** [no selecto] unexceptional **- 4.** [no especial - presupuesto, correo] daily; [- tribunal] of first instance.
orégano *m* oregano.
oreja *f* ANAT ear.
orfanato, orfelinato *m* orphanage.
orfandad *f* orphanhood; *fig* abandonment, neglect.
orfebre *mf* [de plata] silversmith; [de oro] goldsmith.
orfebrería *f* [obra - de plata] silver work; [- de oro] gold work.
orfelinato = orfanato.
orgánico, ca *adj* organic.
organigrama *m* [gen & INFORM] flowchart.
organillo *m* barrel organ.
organismo *m* **- 1.** BIOL organism **- 2.** ANAT body **- 3.** *fig* [entidad] organization, body.
organización *f* organization.
organizar *vt* to organize.
órgano *m* organ.
orgasmo *m* orgasm.
orgía *f* orgy.
orgullo *m* pride.
orgulloso, sa *adj* proud.
orientación *f* **- 1.** [dirección - acción] guiding; [- rumbo] direction **- 2.** [posicionamiento - acción] positioning; [- lugar] position **- 3.** *fig* [información] guidance; ~ **profesional** careers advice *o* guidance.
oriental ◇ *adj* **- 1.** [gen] eastern; [del Lejano Oriente] oriental **- 2.** *Amér* [de Uruguay] Uruguayan. ◇ *mf* **- 1.** oriental **- 2.** *Amér* [de Uruguay] Uruguayan.
orientar *vt* **- 1.** [dirigir] to direct; [casa] to build facing **- 2.** *fig* [medidas etc]: ~ **hacia** to direct towards *o* at **- 3.** *fig* [aconsejar] to give advice *o* guidance to.

  ◆ **orientarse** *vpr* **- 1.** [dirigirse - foco etc]: ~**se a** to point towards *o* at **- 2.** [encontrar el camino] to get one's bearings, to find one's way around **- 3.** *fig* [encaminarse]: ~**se hacia** to be aiming at.
oriente *m* east.
  ◆ **Oriente** *m*: **el Oriente** the East, the Orient; **Oriente Medio/Próximo** Middle/Near East; **Lejano** *o* **Extremo Oriente** Far East.
orificio *m* hole; TECN opening.
origen *m* **- 1.** [gen] origin; [ascendencia] origins *(pl)*, birth; **de** ~ **español** of Spanish origin **- 2.** [causa] cause; **dar** ~ **a** to give rise to.
original ◇ *adj* **- 1.** [gen] original **- 2.** [raro] eccentric, different. ◇ *m* original.
originalidad *f* **- 1.** [gen] originality **- 2.** [extravagancia] eccentricity.
originar *vt* to cause.
  ◆ **originarse** *vpr* to be caused.
originario, ria *adj* **- 1.** [inicial, primitivo] original **- 2.** [procedente]: **ser** ~ **de** [costumbres etc] to come from (originally); [persona] to be a native of.
orilla *f* **- 1.** [ribera - de río] bank; [- de mar] shore; **a** ~**s del mar** by the sea **- 2.** [borde] edge **- 3.** [acera] pavement.
orillar *vt* [dificultad, obstáculo] to skirt around.
orín *m* [herrumbre] rust.
  ◆ **orines** *mpl* [orina] urine *(U)*.
orina *f* urine.
orinal *m* chamberpot.
orinar *vi* & *vt* to urinate.
  ◆ **orinarse** *vpr* to wet o.s.
oriundo, da *adj*: ~ **de** native of.
ornamentación *f* ornamentation.
ornamento *m* [objeto] ornament.
ornar *vt* to decorate, to adorn.
ornitología *f* ornithology.
oro *m* gold; *fig* money, riches *(pl)*; **hacerse de** ~ to make one's fortune; **pedir el** ~ **y el moro** to ask the earth.
  ◆ **oros** *mpl* [naipes] *suit of Spanish cards bearing gold coins.*
  ◆ **oro negro** *m* oil.
orografía *f* [relieve] terrain.
orquesta *f* **- 1.** [músicos] orchestra **- 2.** [lugar] orchestra pit.
orquestar *vt* to orchestrate.
orquestina *f* dance band.
orquídea *f* orchid.
ortiga *f* [stinging] nettle.
ortodoxia *f* orthodoxy.
ortodoxo, xa *adj* orthodox.
ortografía *f* spelling.
ortográfico, ca *adj* spelling *(antes de sust)*.
ortopedia *f* orthopaedics *(U)*.

ortopédico, ca *adj* orthopaedic.

ortopedista *mf* orthopaedist.

oruga *f* caterpillar.

orujo *m* *strong spirit made from grape pressings*.

orzuelo *m* stye.

os *pron pers* - **1.** *(complemento directo)* you; **me gustaría veros** I'd like to see you - **2.** *(complemento indirecto)* (to) you; **~ lo dio** he gave it to you; **~ tengo miedo** I'm afraid of you - **3.** *(reflexivo)* yourselves - **4.** *(recíproco)* each other; **~ enamorasteis** you fell in love (with each other).

osadía *f* - **1.** [valor] boldness, daring - **2.** [descaro] audacity, cheek.

osado, da *adj* - **1.** [valeroso] daring, bold - **2.** [descaro] impudent, cheeky.

osamenta *f* skeleton.

osar *vi* to dare.

oscilación *f* - **1.** [movimiento] swinging; FíS oscillation - **2.** *fig* [variación] fluctuation.

oscilar *vi* - **1.** [moverse] to swing; FíS to oscillate - **2.** *fig* [variar] to fluctuate.

oscurecer ◇ *vt* - **1.** [privar de luz] to darken - **2.** *fig* [mente] to confuse, to cloud. ◇ *v impers* [anochecer] to get dark.

➡ **oscurecerse** *vpr* to grow dark.

oscuridad *f* - **1.** [falta de luz] darkness - **2.** [zona oscura]: **en la ~** in the dark - **3.** *fig* [falta de claridad] obscurity.

oscuro, ra *adj* - **1.** [gen] dark; **a oscuras** in the dark - **2.** [nublado] overcast - **3.** *fig* [inusual] obscure - **4.** *fig* [intenciones, asunto] shady.

óseo, a *adj* bone *(antes de sust)*.

Oslo Oslo.

oso, osa *m,f* bear *(f* she-bear*)*; **~ de felpa** *o* **peluche** teddy bear; **~ hormiguero** anteater; **~ panda** panda; **~ polar** polar bear.

ostensible *adj* evident, clear.

ostentación *f* ostentation, show.

ostentar *vt* [poseer] to hold, to have.

ostentoso, sa *adj* ostentatious.

osteópata *mf* osteopath.

ostión *m* *Chile* [vieira] scallop.

ostra *f* oyster; **aburrirse como una ~** *fam* to be bored to death.

➡ **ostras** *interj* *fam*: **¡~s!** blimey!

OTAN (*abrev de* **Organización del Tratado del Atlántico Norte**) *f* NATO.

OTI (*abrev de* **Organización de Televisiones Iberoamericanas**) *f* *association of all Spanish-speaking television networks*.

otitis *f inv* inflammation of the ear.

otoñal *adj* autumn *UK (antes de sust)*, autumnal *UK*, fall *US (antes de sust)*.

otoño *m lit* & *fig* autumn *UK*, fall *US*.

otorgar *vt* to grant; [premio] to award, to present; DER to execute.

otorrino, na *m,f fam* ear, nose and throat specialist.

otorrinolaringología *f* ear, nose and throat medicine.

otro, tra ◇ *adj* - **1.** [distinto] *(sg)* another, *(pl)* other; **~ chico** another boy; **el ~ chico** the other boy; **(los) ~s chicos** (the) other boys; **no hacer otra cosa que llorar** to do nothing but cry; **el ~ día** [pasado] the other day - **2.** [nuevo] another; **estamos ante ~ Dalí** this is another Dali; **~s tres goles** another three goals. ◇ *pron (sg)* another (one), *(pl)* others; **dame ~** give me another (one); **el ~** the other one; **(los) ~s** (the) others; **yo no lo hice, fue ~** it wasn't me, it was somebody else; **~ habría abandonado, pero no él** anyone else would have given up, but not him; **¡otra!** [en conciertos] encore!, more!

output ['autput] (*pl* **outputs**) *m* INFORM output *(U)*.

ovación *f* ovation.

ovacionar *vt* to give an ovation to, to applaud.

oval *adj* oval.

ovalado, da *adj* oval.

ovario *m* ovary.

oveja *f* sheep, ewe.

➡ **oveja negra** *f* black sheep.

overol, overoles *m* *Amér* [ropa - con peto] dungarees *(pl) UK*, overalls *(pl) US*; [- para bebé] rompers *(pl)*.

ovillo *m* ball *(of wool etc)*; **hacerse un ~** to curl up into a ball.

ovino, na *adj* ovine, sheep *(antes de sust)*.

ovni ['ofni] *m* (*abrev de* **objeto volador no identificado**) UFO.

ovulación *f* ovulation.

ovular ◇ *adj* ovular. ◇ *vi* to ovulate.

oxidación *f* rusting.

oxidar *vt* to rust; QUíM to oxidize.

➡ **oxidarse** *vpr* to get rusty.

óxido *m* - **1.** QUíM oxide - **2.** [herrumbre] rust.

oxigenado, da *adj* - **1.** QUíM oxygenated - **2.** [cabello] peroxide *(antes de sust)*, bleached.

oxigenar *vt* QUíM to oxygenate.

➡ **oxigenarse** *vpr* [airearse] to get a breath of fresh air.

oxígeno *m* oxygen.

oye ⊳ **oír**.

oyente *mf* - **1.** RADIO listener - **2.** [alumno] unregistered student.

ozono *m* ozone.

P

p, P *f* [letra] p, P.

p. - **1.** = **pág** - **2.** *abrev de* **paseo**.

pabellón *m* - **1.** [edifitio] pavilion - **2.** [parte de un edificio] block, section - **3.** [en parques, jardines] summerhouse - **4.** [tienda de campaña] bell tent - **5.** [bandera] flag.

pábilo *m* wick.

PAC (*abrev de* **política agrícola común**) *f* CAP.

pacer *vi* to graze.

pachá (*pl* **pachaes**) *m* pasha; **vivir como un ~** *fam* to live like a lord.

Pachamama *f Andes* Mother Earth.

pachanga *f fam* rowdy celebration.

pacharán *m* liqueur made from anis and sloes.

pachorra *f fam* calmness.

pachucho, cha *adj fam* under the weather.

paciencia *f* patience; **perder la ~** to lose one's patience; **tener ~** to be patient.

paciente *adj & m,f* patient.

pacificación *f* pacification.

pacificar *vt* - **1.** [país] to pacify - **2.** [ánimos] to calm.

pacífico, ca *adj* [gen] peaceful; [persona] peaceable.

Pacífico *m*: **el (océano) ~** the Pacific (Ocean).

pacifismo *m* pacifism.

pacifista *adj & m,f* pacifist.

paco, ca *m,f Andes, Pan fam* cop.

pacotilla *f*: **de ~** trashy, third-rate.

pactar ◇ *vt* to agree to. ◇ *vi*: **~ (con)** to strike a deal (with).

pacto *m* [gen] agreement, pact; [entre países] treaty.

padecer ◇ *vt* to suffer, to endure; [enfermedad] to suffer from. ◇ *vi* to suffer; [enfermedad]: **~ de** to suffer from.

padecimiento *m* suffering.

pádel [pael] *m* ball game for two or four players, played with a small rubber bat on a two-walled court.

padrastro *m* - **1.** [pariente] stepfather - **2.** [pellejo] hangnail.

padre ◇ *m* [gen & RELIG] father. ◇ *adj inv* - **1.** *Esp fam* [enorme] incredible, tremendous - **2.** *Méx fam* [estupendo] fantastic, great.

➤ padres *mpl* [padre y madre] parents.

padrenuestro (*pl* **padrenuestros**) *m* Lord's Prayer.

padrino *m* - **1.** [de bautismo] godfather; [de boda] best man - **2.** [en duelos, torneos etc] second - **3.** *fig* [protector] patron.

➤ padrinos *mpl* [padrino y madrina] godparents.

padrísimo *adj Méx fam* great.

padrón *m* [censo] census; [para votar] electoral roll o register.

padrote *m Méx fam* pimp.

paella *f* paella.

paellera *f* large frying-pan or earthenware dish for cooking paella.

pág., p. (*abrev de* **página**) p.

paga *f* payment; [salario] salary, wages (*pl*); [de niño] pocket money; **~ extra** o **extraordinaria** bonus paid twice a year to Spanish workers.

pagadero, ra *adj* payable; **~ a 90 días/a la entrega** payable within 90 days/on delivery.

pagano, na *adj & m,f* pagan, heathen.

pagar ◇ *vt* [gen] to pay; [deuda] to pay off, to settle; [ronda, gastos, delito] to pay for; [ayuda, favor] to repay; **me las pagarás** *fam* you'll pay for this; **~ el pato/los platos rotos** *fam* to carry the can. ◇ *vi* to pay; **~ en efectivo** o **metálico** to pay (in) cash.

pagaré (*pl* **pagarés**) *m* COM promissory note, IOU; **~ del Tesoro** Treasury note.

página *f* page; **~ inicial** o **de inicio** INFORM home page; **~ Web** Web page; **las ~s amarillas** the Yellow Pages.

pago *m* payment; *fig* reward, payment; **en ~ de** [en recompensa por] as a reward for; [a cambio de] in return for; **~ anticipado/inicial** advance/down payment; **~ por visión** pay-per-view.

➤ pagos *mpl* [lugar]: **por estos ~s** around here.

pai *m CAm & Méx* pie.

paila *f* - **1.** *Andes, CAm & Carib* [sartén] frying pan - **2.** *Chile* [huevos fritos] fried eggs (*pl*).

país *m* country; **los ~es bálticos** the Baltic States.

paisaje *m* [gen] landscape; [vista panorámica] scenery (*U*), view.

paisano, na *m,f* [del mismo país] compatriot, fellow countryman (*f* fellow countrywoman).

➤ paisano *m* [civil] civilian; **de ~** MIL in civilian clothes; **de ~** [policía] in plain clothes.

Países Bajos *mpl*: **los ~** the Netherlands.
País Vasco *m*: **el ~** the Basque Country.
paja *f* **-1.** [gen] straw **-2.** *fig* [relleno] waffle **-3.** *vulg* [masturbación] **wank.**
pajar *m* straw loft.
pájara *f fig* crafty *o* sly woman.
pajarería *f* pet shop.
pajarita *f Esp* [corbata] bow tie.
pájaro *m* ZOOL bird; **~ bobo** penguin; **~ carpintero** woodpecker; **~ de mal agüero** bird of ill omen; **más vale ~ en mano que ciento volando** *proverb* a bird in the hand is worth two in the bush; **matar dos ~s de un tiro** to kill two birds with one stone; **tener ~s en la cabeza** to be scatter-brained *o* empty-headed.
paje *m* page.
pajilla, pajita *f* (drinking) straw.
pajuerano, na *RP* ◇ *adj* [de pueblo] countrified. ◇ *m,f* [palurdo] bumpkin, hick *US*.
Pakistán, Paquistán Pakistan.
pala *f* **-1.** [herramienta] spade; [para recoger] shovel; CULIN slice; **~ mecánica** *o* **excavadora** excavator, digger **-2.** [de frontón, pingpong] bat **-3.** [de remo, hélice] blade.
palabra *f* **-1.** [gen] word; **de ~** by word of mouth, verbally; **no tener ~** to go back on one's word; **tomar** *o* **coger la ~ a alguien** to hold sb to their word; **~ de honor** word of honour **-2.** [habla] speech **-3.** [derecho de hablar] right to speak; **dar la ~ a alguien** to give the floor to sb.
➡ **palabras** *fpl* [discurso] words.
palabrería *f fam* hot air.
palabrota *f* swearword, rude word; **decir ~s** to swear.
palacete *m* mansion, small palace.
palacio *m* palace; **~ de congresos** conference centre.
palada *f* **-1.** [al cavar] spadeful, shovelful **-2.** [de remo] stroke.
paladar *m* palate.
paladear *vt* to savour.
palanca *f* [barra, mando] lever; **~ de cambio** gear lever *o* stick, gearshift *US*; **~ de mando** joystick.
palangana *f* [para fregar] washing-up bowl; [para lavarse] wash bowl.
palco *m* box (at theatre); **~ de autoridades** VIP box.
Palestina Palestine.
palestino, na *adj & m,f* Palestinian.
paleta *f* [gen] small shovel, small spade; [llana] trowel; CULIN slice; ARTE palette; [de ping-pong] bat; *Méx* [helado] ice lolly *UK*, Popsicle® *US*.
paletilla *f* shoulder blade.
paleto, ta *Esp* ◇ *adj* coarse, uncouth. ◇ *m,f* country bumpkin, yokel, hick *US*.

paliar *vt* [atenuar] to ease, to relieve.
palidecer *vi* [ponerse pálido] to go *o* turn pale.
palidez *f* paleness.
pálido, da *adj* pale; *fig* dull.
palillero *m* toothpick holder.
palillo *m* **-1.** [mondadientes] toothpick **-2.** [baqueta] drumstick **-3.** [para comida china] chopstick.
palique *m Esp fam* chat, natter; **estar de ~** to chat, to natter.
paliza *f* **-1.** [golpes, derrota] beating **-2.** [esfuerzo] hard grind.
palma *f* **-1.** [de mano] palm **-2.** [palmera] palm (tree); [hoja de palmera] palm leaf.
➡ **palmas** *fpl* [aplausos] clapping (U), applause (U); **batir ~s** to clap (one's hands).
palmada *f* **-1.** [golpe] pat; [más fuerte] slap **-2.** [aplauso] clap; **~s** clapping (U).
palmar¹ *m* palm grove.
palmar² *fam vi* to kick the bucket, to snuff it.
palmarés *m* **-1.** [historial] record **-2.** [lista] list of winners.
palmear *vi* to clap, to applaud.
palmera *f* [árbol] palm (tree); [datilera] date palm.
palmito *m* **-1.** [árbol] palmetto, fan palm **-2.** CULIN palm heart.
palmo *m* handspan; *fig* small amount; **~ a ~** bit by bit; **dejar a alguien con un ~ de narices** to let sb down.
palmotear *vi* to clap.
palo *m* **-1.** [gen] stick; [de golf] club; [de portería] post; [de la escoba] handle **-2.** [mástil] mast **-3.** [golpe] blow (with a stick) **-4.** [de baraja] suit **-5.** *fig* [pesadez] bind, drag **-6.** *loc*: **a ~ seco** [gen] without anything else; [bebida] neat.
paloma ▷ **palomo.**
palomar *m* dovecote; [grande] pigeon shed.
palomilla *f* **-1.** [insecto] grain moth **-2.** [tornillo] butterfly nut, wing nut **-3.** [soporte] bracket.
palomita *f*: **~s** popcorn (U).
palomo, ma *m,f* dove, pigeon; **paloma mensajera** carrier *o* homing pigeon.
palpable *adj* touchable, palpable; *fig* obvious, clear.
palpar ◇ *vt* **-1.** [tocar] to feel, to touch; MED to palpate **-2.** *fig* [percibir] to feel. ◇ *vi* to feel around.
palpitación *f* beat, beating (U); [con fuerza] throb, throbbing (U).
➡ **palpitaciones** *fpl* MED palpitations.
palpitante *adj* **-1.** [que palpita] beating; [con fuerza] throbbing **-2.** *fig* [interesante - discusión, competición] lively; [- interés, deseo, cuestión] burning.

palpitar *vi* [latir] to beat; [con fuerza] to throb.

palta *f Andes & RP* avocado.

paludismo *m* malaria.

palurdo, da *m,f* country bumpkin, yokel, hick *US*.

pamela *f* sun hat.

pampa *f*: **la** ~ the pampas *(pl)*.

pamplina *(gen pl) f fam* trifle, unimportant thing.

pan *m* - **1.** [alimento] bread; ~ **de molde** *o* **inglés** sliced bread; ~ **integral** wholemeal bread; *Arg* ~ **lactal** sliced bread; ~ **moreno** *o* **negro** [integral] wholemeal *UK o* wholewheat *US* bread; [con centeno] black *o* rye bread; ~ **rallado** breadcrumbs *(pl)* - **2.** [hogaza] loaf - **3.** *loc*: **contigo** ~ **y cebolla** I'll go through thick and thin with you; **llamar al** ~ ~ **y al vino vino** to call a spade a spade; **ser** ~ **comido** to be a piece of cake, to be as easy as pie; **ser el** ~ **nuestro de cada día** to be a regular occurrence, to be commonplace; **ser más bueno que el** ~ to be kindness itself; **no sólo de** ~ **vive el hombre** man cannot live on bread alone.

pana *f* corduroy.

panacea *f lit & fig* panacea.

panadería *f* bakery, baker's.

panadero, ra *m,f* baker.

panal *m* honeycomb.

Panamá Panama.

panameño, ña *adj & m,f* Panamanian.

pancarta *f* placard, banner.

panceta *f* bacon.

pancho, cha *adj fam* calm, unruffled; **estar/quedarse tan** ~ to be/remain perfectly calm.
  ➤ **pancho** *m RP* [comida] hot dog.

páncreas *m inv* pancreas.

panda ◇ *m* ▷ **oso.** ◇ *f Esp* gang.

pandemónium *(pl* **pandemóniums)** *m* pandemonium.

pandereta *f* tambourine.

pandero *m* MÚS tambourine.

pandilla *f* gang.

panecillo *m Esp* bread roll.

panecito *m Amér* bread roll.

panegírico, ca *adj* panegyrical, eulogistic.
  ➤ **panegírico** *m* panegyric, eulogy.

panel *m* - **1.** [gen] panel - **2.** [pared, biombo] screen - **3.** [tablero] board; ~ **solar** solar panel.

panera *f* [para servir] bread basket; [para guardar] bread bin.

pánfilo, la *adj* simple, foolish.

panfleto *m* pamphlet.

pánico *m* panic.

panificadora *f* (large) bakery.

panocha *f* ear, cob.

panorama *m* - **1.** [vista] panorama - **2.** *fig* [situación] overall state; [perspectiva] outlook.

panorámico, ca *adj* panoramic.
  ➤ **panorámica** *f* panorama.

panqueque *m Csur* pancake.

pantaletas *fpl CAm, Carib, Méx* [bragas] panties, knickers *UK*.

pantalla *f* - **1.** [gen & INFORM] screen; ~ **de cristal líquido** liquid crystal display; **la pequeña** ~ the small screen, television - **2.** [de lámpara] lampshade.

pantalón *(gen pl) m* trousers *(pl)*, pants *(pl) US*; ~ **tejano** *o* **vaquero** jeans *(pl)*; ~ **pitillo** drainpipe trousers *(pl)*.

pantano *m* - **1.** [ciénaga] marsh; [laguna] swamp - **2.** [embalse] reservoir.

pantanoso, sa *adj* - **1.** [cenagoso] marshy, boggy - **2.** *fig* [difícil] tricky.

panteón *m* pantheon; [familiar] mausoleum, vault.

pantera *f* panther.

pantimedias *fpl Méx* tights *UK*, pantyhose *US*.

pantorrilla *f* calf.

pantufla *(gen pl) f* slipper.

panty *(pl* **pantys)** *m* tights *(pl)*.

panza *f* belly.

pañal *m* nappy *UK*, diaper *US*; **estar en** ~**es** [en sus inicios] to be in its infancy; [sin conocimientos] not to have a clue.

pañería *f* [producto] drapery; [tienda] draper's (shop), dry-goods store *US*.

paño *m* - **1.** [tela] cloth, material - **2.** [trapo] cloth; [para polvo] duster; [de cocina] tea towel - **3.** [lienzo] panel, length.
  ➤ **paños** *mpl* [vestiduras] drapes; **en**~**s menores** in one's underwear.

pañoleta *f* shawl, wrap.

pañuelo *m* [de nariz] handkerchief; [para el cuello] scarf; [para la cabeza] headscarf; ~ **de papel** paper handkerchief, tissue.

papa *f* potato; **no saber ni** ~ *fam* not to have a clue.
  ➤ **Papa** *m* Pope.

papá *m fam* dad, daddy, pop *US*.
  ➤ **Papá Noel** *m* Father Christmas.

papachador, ra *adj Méx* comforting.

papachar *vt Méx* to spoil.

papada *f* [de persona] double chin; [de animal] dewlap.

papagayo *m* - **1.** [pájaro] parrot - **2.** *Ven* [cometa] kite.

papalote *m CAm, Carib, Méx* kite.

papamoscas *m inv* flycatcher.

papamóvil *m inv* popemobile.

papanatas *m y f inv fam* sucker.

Papanicolau *m* smear test.

papaya *f* [fruta] papaya, pawpaw.

papel *m* **- 1.** [gen] paper; [hoja] sheet of paper; ∼ **celofán** Cellophane; ∼ **confort** *Chile* toilet paper; ∼ **continuo** INFORM continuous paper; ∼ **de embalar** *o* **de embalaje** wrapping paper; ∼ **de estaño** *o* **de aluminio** *o* **de plata** tin *o* aluminium foil; ∼ **de fumar** cigarette paper; ∼ **de lija** sandpaper; ∼ **higiénico** toilet paper; ∼ **madera** *RP* cardboard; ∼ **milimetrado** graph paper; ∼ **pintado** wallpaper; ∼ **reciclado** recycled paper; *Cuba* & *Méx* ∼ **sanitario** toilet paper **- 2.** CIN & TEATR & *fig* role, part; ∼ **principal/secundario** main/minor part; **hacer buen/mal** ∼ to do well/badly **- 3.** FIN stocks and shares *(pl)*; ∼ **moneda** paper money, banknotes *(pl)*.
➤ **papeles** *mpl* [documentos] papers.

papeleo *m* paperwork, red tape.

papelera ▷ **papelero**.

papelería *f* stationer's (shop).

papelero, ra *adj* paper *(antes de sust)*.
➤ **papelera** *f* [cesto - en oficina etc] wastepaper basket *o* bin; [- en la calle] litter bin.

papeleta *f* **- 1.** [boleto] ticket, slip (of paper); [de votación] ballot paper **- 2.** EDUC *slip of paper with university exam results*.

paperas *fpl* mumps.

papi *m* *fam* daddy, dad.

papilla *f* [para niños] baby food; **hecho** ∼ *fam* [cansado] shattered, exhausted; [cosa] smashed to bits, ruined.

papiro *m* papyrus.

paquete *m* **- 1.** [de libros, regalos etc] parcel; ∼ **bomba** parcel bomb; ∼ **postal** parcel **- 2.** [de cigarrillos, klínex, folios etc] pack, packet; [de azúcar, arroz] bag **- 3.** [de medidas] package; ∼ **turístico** package tour **- 4.** INFORM package.

Paquistán = **Pakistán**.

par ◇ *adj* **- 1.** MAT even **- 2.** [igual] equal. ◇ *m* **- 1.** [pareja - de zapatos etc] pair **- 2.** [dos - veces etc] couple **- 3.** [número indeterminado] few, couple; **un** ∼ **de copas** a couple of *o* a few drinks **- 4.** [en golf] par **- 5.** [noble] peer.
➤ **a la par** *loc adv* **- 1.** [simultáneamente] at the same time **- 2.** [a igual nivel] at the same level.
➤ **de par en par** *loc adj*: **abierto de** ∼ **en** ∼ wide open.
➤ **sin par** *loc adj* without equal, matchless.

para *prep* **- 1.** [finalidad] for; **es** ∼ **ti** it's for you; **una mesa** ∼ **el salón** a table for the living room; **esta agua no es buena** ∼ **beber** this water isn't fit for drinking *o* to drink; **te lo repetiré** ∼ **que te enteres** I'll repeat it so you understand; **¿** ∼ **qué?** what for? **- 2.** [motivación] (in order) to; ∼ **conseguir** sus propósitos in order to achieve his aims; **lo he hecho** ∼ **agradarte** I did it to please you **- 3.** [dirección] towards; **ir** ∼ **casa** to head (for) home; **salir** ∼ **el aeropuerto** to leave for the airport **- 4.** [tiempo] for; **tiene que estar acabado** ∼ **mañana** it has to be finished by *o* for tomorrow **- 5.** [comparación]: **está muy delgado** ∼ **lo que come** he's very thin considering how much he eats; ∼ **ser verano hace mucho frío** considering it's summer, it's very cold **- 6.** *(después de adj y antes de infin)* [inminencia, propósito] to; **la comida está lista** ∼ **servir** the meal is ready to be served; **el atleta está preparado** ∼ **ganar** the athlete is ready to win.
➤ **para con** *loc prep* towards; **es buena** ∼ **con los demás** she is kind towards other people.

parabién *(pl* **parabienes)** *m* congratulations *(pl)*.

parábola *f* **- 1.** [alegoría] parable **- 2.** GEOM parabola.

parabólico, ca *adj* parabolic.

parabrisas *m inv* windscreen, windshield *US*.

paracaídas *m inv* parachute.

paracaidista *mf* parachutist; MIL paratrooper.

parachoques *m inv* AUTOM bumper, fender *US*; FERROC buffer.

parada ▷ **parado**.

paradero *m* **- 1.** [de persona] whereabouts *(pl)* **- 2.** *Chile, Col, Méx, Perú* [parada de autobús] bus stop.

paradisiaco, ca, paradisíaco, ca *adj* heavenly.

parado, da ◇ *adj* **- 1.** [inmóvil - coche] stationary, standing; [- persona] still, motionless; [- fábrica, proyecto] at a standstill **- 2.** *Esp* [sin empleo] unemployed, out of work **- 3.** *loc*: **salir bien/mal** ∼ **de algo** to come off well/badly out of sthg. ◇ *m,f Esp* [desempleado] unemployed person; **los** ∼**s** the unemployed.
➤ **parada** *f* **- 1.** [detención] stop, stopping *(U)* **- 2.** DEP save **- 3.** [de autobús] (bus) stop; [de taxis] taxi rank *UK o* stand *US*; [de metro] (underground) station; **parada discrecional** request stop **- 4.** MIL parade.

paradoja *f* paradox.

paradójico, ca *adj* paradoxical, ironical.

parador *m* [hotel]: ∼ **(nacional)** *Esp state-owned luxury hotel, usually a building of historic or artistic importance*.

parafernalia *f* paraphernalia.

parafrasear *vt* to paraphrase.

paráfrasis *f inv* paraphrase.

paragolpes *mpl RP* AUTOM bumper, fender *US*.

paraguas *m inv* umbrella.

Paraguay: **(el)** ~ Paraguay.
paraguayo, ya *adj* & *m,f* Paraguayan.
paragüero *m* umbrella stand.
paraíso *m* RELIG Paradise; *fig* paradise.
paraje *m* spot, place.
paralelismo *m* - 1. GEOM parallelism - 2. [semejanza] similarity, parallels *(pl)*.
paralelo, la *adj*: ~ **(a)** parallel (to).
➡ **paralelo** *m* GEOGR parallel.
➡ **paralela** *f* GEOM parallel (line).
parálisis *f inv* paralysis; ~ **cerebral** cerebral palsy.
paralítico, ca *adj* & *m,f* paralytic.
paralizar *vt* to paralyse.
➡ **paralizarse** *vpr* to become paralysed; [producción etc] to come to a standstill.
parámetro *m* parameter.
páramo *m* moor, moorland *(U)*; *fig* wilderness.
parangón *m* paragon; **sin** ~ unparalleled.
paranoia *f* paranoia.
paranormal *adj* paranormal.
parapente *m* [deporte] parapenting, paragliding; [paracaídas] parapente.
parapentista *m,f* paraglider.
parapetarse *vpr lit* & *fig*: ~ **(tras)** to take refuge (behind).
parapeto *m* [antepecho] parapet; [barandilla] bannister; [barricada] barricade.
parapléjico, ca *adj* & *m,f* paraplegic.
parapsicología *f* parapsychology.
parar ◇ *vi* - 1. [gen] to stop; ~ **de hacer algo** to stop doing sthg; **sin** ~ non-stop - 2. [alojarse] to stay - 3. [recaer]: ~ **en manos de alguien** to come into the possession of sb - 4. [acabar] to end up; **¿en qué parará este lío?** where will it all end? ◇ *vt* - 1. [gen] to stop; [golpe] to parry - 2. [preparar] to prepare, to lay - 3. *Amér* [levantar] to raise.
➡ **pararse** *vpr* - 1. [detenerse] to stop - 2. *Amér* [ponerse de pie] to stand up - 3. *Méx,Ven* [salir de la cama] to get up.
pararrayos *m inv* lightning conductor.
parásito, ta *adj* BIOL parasitic.
➡ **parásito** *m* BIOL & *fig* parasite.
➡ **parásitos** *mpl* [interferencias] statics *(pl)*.
parasol *m* parasol.
parcela *f* - 1. [de tierra] plot (of land) - 2. [de saber] area.
parche *m* - 1. [gen] patch - 2. [chapuza - mal hecha] botch job; [- para salir del paso] makeshift solution.
parchís *m inv* ludo.
parcial ◇ *adj* - 1. [no total] partial - 2. [no ecuánime] biased. ◇ *m* [examen] *end-of-term exam at university.*
parcialidad *f* [tendenciosidad] bias, partiality.

parco, ca *adj* [escaso] meagre; [cena] frugal; [explicación] brief, concise.
pardillo, lla *Esp* ◇ *adj* - 1. [ingenuo] naive - 2. [palurdo] countrified. ◇ *m,f* - 1. [ingenuo] naive person - 2. [palurdo] bumpkin, hick *US*.
pardo, da *adj* greyish-brown, dull brown.
parecer ◇ *m* - 1. [opinión] opinion - 2. [apariencia]: **de buen** ~ good-looking. ◇ *vi (antes de sust)* to look like; **parece un palacio** it looks like a palace. ◇ *v copulativo* to look, to seem; **pareces cansado** you look *o* seem tired. ◇ *v impers* - 1. [opinar]: **me parece que ...** I think *o* it seems to me that ...; **me parece que sí/no** I think/don't think so; **¿qué te parece?** what do you think (of it)? - 2. [tener aspecto de]: **parece que va a llover** it looks like it's going to rain; **parece que le gusta** it looks as if *o* it seems that she likes it; **eso parece** so it seems; **al** ~ apparently.
➡ **parecerse** *vpr*: ~**se (en)** to be alike (in); ~**se a alguien** [físicamente] to look like sb; [en carácter] to be like sb.
parecido, da *adj* similar; **bien** ~ [atractivo] good-looking.
➡ **parecido** *m*: ~ **(con/entre)** resemblance (to/between).
pared *f* - 1. [gen] wall; **las** ~**es oyen** walls have ears; **subirse por las** ~**es** to hit the roof, to go up the wall - 2. [de montaña] side.
paredón *m* (thick) wall; [de fusilamiento] (execution) wall.
parejo, ja *adj*: ~ **(a)** similar (to).
➡ **pareja** *f* - 1. [gen] pair; [de novios] couple; **pareja de hecho** *common-law heterosexual or homosexual relationship*; **son una pareja de hecho** they live together as man and wife; **por parejas** in pairs - 2. [miembro del par - persona] partner; **la pareja de este calcetín** the other sock of this pair.
parentela *f fam* relations *(pl)*, family.
parentesco *m* relationship.
paréntesis *m inv* - 1. [signo] bracket; **entre** ~ in brackets, in parentheses - 2. [intercalación] digression - 3. [interrupción] break.
paria *mf* pariah.
parida *f fam*: **eso es una** ~ that's a load of nonsense; **decir** ~**s** to talk nonsense.
pariente, ta *m,f* [familiar] relation, relative.
parir ◇ *vi* to give birth. ◇ *vt* to give birth to.
París Paris.
parking ['parkin] *(pl* **parkings)** *m* car park *UK*, parking lot *US*.
parlamentar *vi* to negotiate.
parlamentario, ria ◇ *adj* parliamentary. ◇ *m,f* member of parliament.

parlamento *m* POLÍT parliament.

parlanchín, ina *fam* ⬦ *adj* chatty. ⬦ *m,f* chatterbox.

parlante *adj* talking.
  ◆ **parlante** *m Amér* speaker.

parlotear *vi fam* to chatter.

paro *m* -1. *Esp* [desempleo] unemployment - 2. *Esp* [subsidio] unemployment benefit - 3. [cesación - acción] shutdown; [- estado] stoppage; ~ **cardiaco** cardiac arrest.

parodia *f* parody.

parodiar *vt* to parody.

parpadear *vi* -1. [pestañear] to blink - 2. [centellear] to flicker.

párpado *m* eyelid.

parque *m* -1. [gen] park; ~ **acuático** water-park; ~ **de atracciones** amusement park; ~ **eólico** wind farm; ~ **nacional** national park; ~ **tecnológico** science park; ~ **temático** theme park; (~) **zoológico** zoo - 2. [vehículos] fleet; ~ **de bomberos** fire station - 3. [para niños] playpen.

parqué (*pl* **parqués**), **parquet** [par'ke] (*pl* **parquets**) *m* parquet (floor).

parqueadero *m Amér* car park, parking lot US.

parquear *vt Amér* to park.

parquet = **parqué**.

parquímetro *m* parking meter.

parra *f* grapevine.

parrafada *f* earful, dull monologue.

párrafo *m* paragraph.

parranda *f* *fam* [juerga]: **irse de** ~ to go out on the town.

parrilla *f* [utensilio] grill; **a la** ~ grilled, broiled US.

parrillada *f* mixed grill.

párroco *m* parish priest.

parronal *m Chile* vineyard.

parroquia *f* -1. [iglesia] parish church - 2. [jurisdicción] parish - 3. [clientela] clientele.

parroquiano, na *m,f* -1. [feligrés] parishioner - 2. [cliente] customer.

parsimonia *f* deliberation, calmness; **con** ~ unhurriedly.

parte ⬦ *m* report; **dar** ~ (**a alguien de algo**) to report (sthg to sb); ~ **facultativo** *o* **médico** medical report; ~ **meteorológico** weather forecast. ⬦ *f* [gen] part; [bando] side; DER party; **la mayor** ~ **de la gente** most people; **la tercera** ~ **de** a third of; **en alguna** ~ somewhere; **no lo veo por ninguna** ~ I can't find it anywhere; **en** ~ to a certain extent, partly; **estar/ponerse de** ~ **de alguien** to be on/to take sb's side; **por mi** ~ for my part; **por** ~**s** bit by bit; **por una** ~ ... **por la otra** ... on the one hand ... on the other (hand) ...; **tomar** ~ **en algo** to take part in sthg.
  ◆ **de parte de** *loc prep* on behalf of, for; **¿de** ~ **de (quién)?** TELECOM who is calling, please?
  ◆ **por otra parte** *loc adv* [además] what is more, besides.

partera *f* midwife.

parterre *m Esp* flowerbed.

partición *f* [reparto] sharing out; [de territorio] partitioning.

participación *f* -1. [colaboración] participation - 2. [de lotería] share of a lottery ticket - 3. [comunicación] notice.

participante *mf* participant.

participar ⬦ *vi* [colaborar]: ~ (**en**) to take part *o* participate (in); FIN to have a share (in). ⬦ *vt*: ~ **algo a alguien** to notify sb of sthg.

partícipe ⬦ *adj*: ~ (**de**) involved (in); **hacer** ~ **de algo a alguien** [notificar] to notify sb of sthg; [compartir] to share sthg with sb. ⬦ *mf* participant.

partícula *f* particle.

particular ⬦ *adj* -1. [gen] particular; **tiene su sabor** ~ it has its own particular taste; **en** ~ in particular - 2. [no público - domicilio, clases etc] private - 3. [no corriente - habilidad etc] uncommon. ⬦ *mf* [persona] member of the public. ⬦ *m* [asunto] matter.

particularizar ⬦ *vt* [caracterizar] to characterize. ⬦ *vi* -1. [detallar] to go into details - 2. [personalizar]: ~ **en alguien** to single sb out.

partida *f* -1. [marcha] departure - 2. [en juego] game - 3. [documento] certificate; ~ **de defunción/matrimonio/nacimiento** death/marriage/birth certificate - 4. [COM - mercancía] consignment; [- entrada] item, entry.

partidario, ria ⬦ *adj*: ~ **de** in favour of, for. ⬦ *m,f* supporter.

partidista *adj* partisan, biased.

partido *m* -1. POLÍT party - 2. DEP match; ~ **amistoso** friendly (match) - 3. *loc*: **sacar** ~ **de** to make the most of; **tomar** ~ **por** to side with.

partir ⬦ *vt* -1. [dividir] to divide, to split - 2. [repartir] to share out - 3. [romper] to break open; [cascar] to crack; [tronco, loncha etc] to cut. ⬦ *vi* -1. [marchar] to leave, to set off - 2. [basarse]: ~ **de** to start from.
  ◆ **partirse** *vpr* -1. [romperse] to split - 2. [rajarse] to crack.
  ◆ **a partir de** *loc prep* starting from; **a** ~ **de aquí** from here on.

partitura *f* score.

parto *m* birth; **estar de** ~ to be in labour.

parvulario *m* nursery school, kindergarten.

pasa *f* [fruta] raisin; ~ **de Corinto** currant; ~ **de Esmirna** sultana.

pasable *adj* passable.

pasada ⊳ **pasado**.

pasadizo *m* passage.

pasado, da *adj* - **1.** [gen] past; ~ **un año a** year later; **lo** ~, ~ **está** let bygones be bygones - **2.** [último] last; **el año** ~ last year - **3.** [podrido] off, bad - **4.** [hecho - filete, carne] well done.

◆ **pasado** *m* [gen] past; GRAM past (tense).

◆ **pasada** *f* [con el trapo] wipe; [con la brocha] coat.

◆ **de pasada** *loc adv* in passing.

◆ **mala pasada** *f* dirty trick.

pasador *m* - **1.** [cerrojo] bolt - **2.** [para el pelo] slide.

pasaje *m* - **1.** [billete] ticket - **2.** [pasajeros] passengers *(pl)* - **3.** [calle] passage - **4.** [fragmento] passage.

pasajero, ra ◇ *adj* passing. ◇ *m,f* passenger.

pasamanos *m inv* [de escalera interior] bannister; [de escalera exterior] handrail.

pasamontañas *m inv* balaclava (helmet).

pasapalos *mpl Méx,Ven* snacks, appetizers.

pasaporte *m* passport.

pasapuré *m*, **pasapurés** *m inv* food mill.

pasar ◇ *vt* - **1.** [gen] to pass; [noticia, aviso] to pass on; **¿me pasas la sal?** would you pass me the salt?; ~ **algo por** [filtrar] to pass sthg through - **2.** [cruzar] to cross; ~ **la calle** to cross the road; **pasé el río a nado** I swam across the river - **3.** [traspasar] to pass through - **4.** [trasladar]: ~ **algo a** to move sthg to - **5.** [llevar adentro] to show in; **el criado nos pasó al salón** the butler showed us into the living room - **6.** [contagiar]: ~ **algo a alguien** to give sthg to sb, to infect sb with sthg; **me has pasado la tos** you've given me your cough - **7.** [admitir - instancia etc] to accept - **8.** [consentir]: ~ **algo a alguien** to let sb get away with sthg - **9.** [rebasar - en el espacio] to go through; [- en el tiempo] to have been through; ~ **un semáforo en rojo** to go through a red light - **10.** [emplear - tiempo] to spend; **pasó dos años en Roma** he spent two years in Rome - **11.** [padecer] to go through, to suffer; **pasarlo mal** to have a hard time of it - **12.** [sobrepasar]: **ya ha pasado los veinticinco** he's over twenty-five now; **mi hijo me pasa ya dos centímetros** my son is already two centimetres taller than me - **13.** [adelantar - coche, contrincante etc] to overtake - **14.** CIN to show. ◇ *vi* - **1.** [gen] to pass, to go; **pasó por mi lado** he passed by my side; **el autobús pasa por mi casa** the bus goes past *o* passes in front of my house; **el Manzanares pasa**

por **Madrid** the Manzanares goes *o* passes through Madrid; **he pasado por tu calle** I went down your street; ~ **de ... a ...** to go *o* pass from ... to ...; ~ **de largo** to go by - **2.** [entrar] to go/come in; **¡pase!** come in! - **3.** [poder entrar]: ~ **(por)** to go (through); **por ahí no pasa** it won't go through there - **4.** [ir un momento] to pop in; **pasaré por mi oficina/por tu casa** I'll pop into my office/round to your place - **5.** [suceder] to happen; **¿qué pasa aquí?** what's going on here?; **¿qué pasa?** what's the matter?; **pase lo que pase** whatever happens, come what may - **6.** [terminarse] to be over; **pasó la Navidad** Christmas is over - **7.** [transcurrir] to go by - **8.** [cambiar - acción]: ~ **a** to move on to; **pasemos a otra cosa** let's move on to something else - **9.** [conformarse]: ~ **(con/sin algo)** to make do (with/without sthg); **tendrá que** ~ **sin coche** she'll have to make do without a car - **10.** [servir] to be all right, to be usable; **puede** ~ it'll do - **11.** *fam* [prescindir]: ~ **de algo/alguien** to want nothing to do with sthg/sb; **paso de política** I'm not into politics - **12.** [tolerar]: ~ **por algo** to put up with sthg.

◆ **pasarse** *vpr* - **1.** [acabarse] to pass; **siéntate hasta que se te pase** sit down until you feel better - **2.** [emplear - tiempo] to spend, to pass; **se pasaron el día hablando** they spent all day talking - **3.** [desaprovecharse] to slip by; **se me pasó la oportunidad** I missed my chance - **4.** [estropearse - comida] to go off; [- flores] to fade - **5.** [cambiar de bando]: ~ **se a** to go over to - **6.** [omitir] to miss out; **te has pasado una página** you've missed a page out - **7.** [olvidarse]: **pasársele a alguien** to slip sb's mind; **se me pasó decírtelo** I forgot to mention it to you - **8.** [no fijarse]: **pasársele a alguien** to escape sb's attention; **no se le pasa nada** he never misses a thing - **9.** [excederse]: ~ **se de generoso/bueno** to be far too generous/kind - **10.** *fam* [propasarse] to go too far, to go over the top; **te has pasado diciéndole eso** what you said went too far *o* was over the top - **11.** [divertirse]: **¿qué tal te lo estás pasando?** how are you enjoying yourself?; **pasárselo bien/mal** to have a good/bad time.

pasarela *f* - **1.** [puente] footbridge; [para desembarcar] gangway - **2.** [en un desfile] catwalk.

pasatiempo *m* [hobby] pastime, hobby.

Pascua *f* - **1.** [de los judíos] Passover - **2.** [de los cristianos] Easter.

◆ **Pascuas** *fpl* [Navidad] Christmas *(sg)*; **¡felices Pascuas!** Merry Christmas!; **de Pascuas a Ramos** *fam* once in a blue moon.

pase *m* - **1.** [gen, DEP & TAUROM] pass; *ver tam-*

bién **tauromaquia** - **2.** *Esp* [proyección] showing, screening - **3.** [desfile] parade; ~ **de modelos** fashion parade.

pasear ⬥ *vi* to go for a walk. ⬥ *vt* to take for a walk; [perro] to walk; *fig* to show off, to parade.

paseo *m* - **1.** [acción - a pie] walk; [- en coche] drive; [- a caballo] ride; [- en barca] row; **dar un** ~ [a pie] to go for a walk - **2.** [lugar] avenue; ~ **marítimo** promenade - **3.** *loc*: **mandar** *o* **enviar a alguien a** ~ *fam* to send sb packing.

pasillo *m* corridor.

pasión *f* passion.
➤ **Pasión** *f* RELIG: **la Pasión** the Passion.

pasivo, va *adj* - **1.** [gen & GRAM] passive - **2.** [población etc] inactive.
➤ **pasivo** *m* COM liabilities *(pl)*.

pasmado, da *adj* - **1.** [asombrado] astonished, astounded - **2.** [atontado] stunned.

pasmar *vt* to astound.
➤ **pasmarse** *vpr* to be astounded.

pasmo *m* astonishment.

pasmoso, sa *adj* astonishing.

paso *m* - **1.** [gen] step; [huella] footprint - **2.** [acción] passing; [cruce] crossing; [camino de acceso] way through, thoroughfare; **abrir** ~ **a alguien** *lit* & *fig* to make way for sb; **ceder el** ~ **(a alguien)** to let sb past; AUTOM to give way (to sb); **'ceda el** ~' 'give way'; **'prohibido el** ~' 'no entry'; ~ **elevado** flyover; ~ **a nivel** level crossing; ~ **peatonal** *o* **de peatones** pedestrian crossing; ~ **de cebra** zebra crossing - **3.** [forma de andar] walk; [ritmo] pace - **4.** [GEOGR - en montaña] pass; [- en el mar] strait - **5.** *(gen pl)* [gestión] step; [progreso] step forward, advance; **dar los** ~**s necesarios** to take the necessary steps - **6.** *loc*: **a cada** ~ every other minute; **está a dos** *o* **cuatro** ~**s** it's just down the road; **¡a este** ~ **...!** *fig* at that rate **...!**; **estar de** ~ to be passing through; ~ **a** ~ step by step; **salir del** ~ to get out of trouble.
➤ **de paso** *loc adv* in passing.

pasodoble *m* paso doble.

pasota *Esp fam* ⬥ *adj* apathetic. ⬥ *mf* dropout.

pasta *f* - **1.** [masa] paste; [de papel] pulp; ~ **dentífrica** toothpaste - **2.** [CULIN - espagueti etc] pasta; [- de pasteles] pastry; [- de pan] dough - **3.** [pastelillo] pastry - **4.** *Esp fam* [dinero] dough - **5.** [encuadernación]: **en** ~ hardback.

pastar *vi* to graze.

pastel *m* - **1.** [CULIN - dulce] cake; [- salado] pie - **2.** ARTE pastel.

pastelería *f* - **1.** [establecimiento] cake shop, patisserie - **2.** [repostería] pastries *(pl)*.

pasteurizado, da [pasteuri'θaðo, ða] *adj* pasteurized.

pastiche *m* pastiche.

pastilla *f* - **1.** MED pill, tablet - **2.** [de jabón, chocolate] bar - **3.** [de caldo] cube.

pasto *m* - **1.** [sitio] pasture - **2.** [hierba] fodder - **3.** *Amér* [hierba] lawn, grass - **4.** *loc*: **ser** ~ **de las llamas** to go up in flames.

pastón *m fam*: **vale un** ~ it costs a bomb.

pastor, ra *m,f* [de ganado] shepherd (*f* shepherdess).
➤ **pastor** *m* - **1.** [sacerdote] minister - **2.** ▷ **perro.**

pastoso, sa *adj* - **1.** [blando] pasty; [arroz] sticky - **2.** [seco] dry.

pata ⬥ *f* - **1.** [pierna] leg - **2.** [pie - gen] foot; [- de perro, gato] paw; [- de vaca, caballo] hoof - **3.** *fam* [de persona] leg; **a cuatro** ~**s** on all fours; **ir a la** ~ **coja** to hop - **4.** [de mueble] leg; [de gafas] arm - **5.** *loc*: **meter la** ~ to put one's foot in it; **poner/estar** ~**s arriba** to turn/be upside down; **tener mala** ~ to be unlucky. ⬥ *m Perú* [amigo] pal, mate *UK*, buddy *US*.
➤ **patas** *fpl Chile fam* [poca vergüenza] cheek *(U)*.
➤ **pata de gallo** *f* [en la cara] crow's feet *(pl)*.

patada *f* kick; [en el suelo] stamp; **dar una** ~ **a** to kick; **tratar a alguien a** ~**s** to treat sb like dirt.

patalear *vi* to kick about; [en el suelo] to stamp one's feet.

pataleo *m* kicking *(U)*; [en el suelo] stamping *(U)*.

pataleta *f* tantrum.

patán *m* bumpkin.

patata *f* potato; ~**s fritas** [de sartén] chips *UK*, french fries *US*; [de bolsa] crisps *UK*, chips *US*.

paté *m* paté.

patear ⬥ *vt* [dar un puntapié] to kick; [pisotear] to stamp on. ⬥ *vi* [patalear] to stamp one's feet.

patentado, da *adj* patent, patented.

patente ⬥ *adj* obvious; [demostración, prueba] clear. ⬥ *f* - **1.** [de invento] patent - **2.** *CSur* [matrícula] number plate *UK*, license plate *US*.

paternal *adj* fatherly, paternal.

paternidad *f* fatherhood; DER paternity.

paterno, na *adj* paternal.

patético, ca *adj* pathetic, moving.

patetismo *m* pathos *(U)*.

patidifuso, sa *adj fam* stunned, floored.

patilla *f* - **1.** [de pelo] sideboard, sideburn - **2.** [de gafas] arm.

patín *m* - **1.** [calzado - de cuchilla] ice skate; [- de ruedas] roller skate; [- en línea] roller

blade - 2. [patinete] **scooter - 3.** [embarcación] **pedal boat.**

pátina f patina.

patinaje m skating.

patinar vi **- 1.** [sobre hielo] to skate; [sobre ruedas] to roller-skate **- 2.** [resbalar - coche] to skid; [- persona] to slip **- 3.** fam [meter la pata] to put one's foot in it.

patinazo m **- 1.** [de coche] skid; [de persona] slip **- 2.** fam [planchazo] blunder.

patinete m scooter.

patio m [gen] patio, courtyard; [de escuela] playground; [de cuartel] parade ground.

patitieso, sa adj fam **- 1.** [de frío] frozen stiff **- 2.** [de sorpresa] aghast, amazed.

pato, ta m,f duck; **pagar el ~** to carry the can.

patológico, ca adj pathological.

patoso, sa adj fam clumsy.

patota f Perú, RP street gang.

patria ⊳ patrio.

patriarca m patriarch.

patrimonio m **- 1.** [bienes - heredados] inheritance; [- propios] wealth **- 2.** fig [de una colectividad] exclusive birthright.

patrio, tria adj native.
　◆ patria f native country, fatherland.

patriota mf patriot.

patriotismo m patriotism.

patrocinador, ra m,f sponsor.

patrocinar vt to sponsor.

patrocinio m sponsorship.

patrón, ona m,f **- 1.** [de obreros] boss; [de criados] master (f mistress) **- 2.** [de pensión etc] landlord (f landlady) **- 3.** [santo] patron saint.
　◆ patrón m **- 1.** [de barco] skipper **- 2.** [en costura] pattern.

patronal ⟨⟩ adj [empresarial] management (antes de sust). ⟨⟩ f **- 1.** [de empresa] management **- 2.** [de país] employers' organisation.

patronato m [gen] board; [con fines benéficos] trust.

patrono, na m,f **- 1.** [de empresa - encargado] boss; [- empresario] employer **- 2.** [santo] patron saint.

patrulla f patrol; **~ urbana** vigilante group.

patrullar vt & vi to patrol.

paulatino, na adj gradual.

pausa f pause, break; MÚS rest; **con ~** unhurriedly; **hacer una ~** to pause; **~ publicitaria** commercial break.

pausado, da adj deliberate, slow.

pauta f **- 1.** [gen] standard, model; **marcar la ~** to set the standard **- 2.** [en un papel] guideline.

pava ⊳ pavo.

pavada f RP [cosa sin importancia] trifle.

pavimentación f [de carretera] road surfacing; [de acera] paving; [de suelo] flooring.

pavimento m [de carretera] road surface; [de acera] paving; [de suelo] flooring.

pavo, va m,f [ave] turkey; **~ real** peacock (f peahen); **se le subió el ~** she turned as red as a beetroot.

pavonearse vpr despec: **~ (de)** to boast o brag (about).

pavor m terror.

pay m Chile, Méx, Ven pie.

paya f Amér improvised poem accompanied by guitar.

payasada f clowning (U); **hacer ~s** to clown around.

payaso, sa m,f clown.

payo, ya m,f non-gipsy.

paz f peace; [tranquilidad] peacefulness; **dejar a alguien en ~** to leave sb alone o in peace; **estar** o **quedar en ~** to be quits; **hacer las paces** to make (it) up; **poner ~ entre** to reconcile, to make peace between; **que en ~ descanse, que descanse en ~** may he/she rest in peace.

PC m (abrev de **personal computer**) PC.

PD, PS (abrev de **posdata**) PS.

PDF (abrev de **portable document format**) m INFORM PDF.

pdo. abrev de **pasado.**

peaje m toll.

peana f pedestal.

peatón m pedestrian.

peca f freckle.

pecado m sin; **estar en ~** to be in sin; **morir en ~** to die unrepentant; **~ mortal** mortal sin; **sería un ~ tirar este vestido** it would be a crime to throw out this dress.

pecador, ra m,f sinner.

pecaminoso, sa adj sinful.

pecar vi **- 1.** RELIG to sin **- 2.** [pasarse]: **~ de confiado/generoso** to be overconfident/too generous.

pecera f fish tank; [redonda] fish bowl.

pecho m **- 1.** [tórax] chest; [de mujer] bosom **- 2.** [mama] breast; **dar el ~ a** to breastfeed **- 3.** loc: **a lo hecho, ~** it's no use crying over spilt milk; **tomarse algo a ~** to take sthg to heart.

pechuga f [de ave] breast (meat).

pecoso, sa adj freckly.

pectoral adj **- 1.** ANAT pectoral, chest (antes de sust).

peculiar adj **- 1.** [característico] typical, characteristic **- 2.** [curioso] peculiar.

peculiaridad f **- 1.** [cualidad] uniqueness **- 2.** [detalle] particular feature o characteristic.

pedagogía f education, pedagogy.

pedagogo, ga *m,f* educator; [profesor] teacher.

pedal *m* pedal; ~ **de embrague** clutch (pedal); ~ **de freno** brake pedal.

pedalear *vi* to pedal.

pedante *adj* pompous.

pedantería *f* pomposity (U).

pedazo *m* piece, bit; **a ~s** in pieces o bits; **caerse a ~s** to fall to pieces; **hacer ~s** *lit* to break to bits; *fig* to destroy.

pedernal *m* flint.

pedestal *m* pedestal, stand.

pedestre *adj* on foot.

pediatra *mf* pediatrician.

pedicuro, ra *m,f* chiropodist *UK*, podiatrist *US*.

pedido *m* COM order; **hacer un ~** to place an order.

pedigrí, pedigree *m* pedigree.

pedir ◇ *vt* -1. [gen] to ask for; [en comercios, restaurantes] to order; ~ **a alguien haga algo** to ask sb to do sthg; ~ **a alguien (en matrimonio)** to ask for sb's hand (in marriage); ~ **prestado algo a alguien** to borrow sthg from sb -2. [exigir] to demand -3. [requerir] to call for, to need -4. [poner precio]: ~ **(por)** to ask (for); **pide un millón por la moto** he's asking a million for the motorbike. ◇ *vi* [mendigar] to beg.

pedo *m fam* [ventosidad] fart; **tirarse un ~** to fart.

pedrada *f* [golpe] blow o hit with a stone; **a ~s** by stoning; **matar a alguien a ~s** to stone sb to death.

pedregullo *m RP* gravel.

pedrería *f* precious stones (pl).

pedrusco *m* rough stone.

pega *f* [obstáculo] difficulty, hitch; **poner ~s (a)** to find problems (with).

pegadizo, za *adj* -1. [música] catchy -2. [contagioso] catching.

pegajoso, sa *adj* sticky; *despec* clinging.

pegamento *m* glue.

pegar ◇ *vt* -1. [adherir] to stick; [con pegamento] to glue; [póster, cartel] to fix, to put up; [botón] to sew on -2. [arrimar]: ~ **algo a** to put o place sthg against; **pega la silla a la pared** put the chair against the wall -3. [golpear] to hit -4. [propinar - bofetada, paliza etc] to give; [- golpe] to deal -5. [contagiar]: ~ **algo a alguien** to give sb sthg, to pass sthg on to sb. ◇ *vi* -1. [adherir] to stick -2. [golpear] to hit -3. [armonizar] to go together, to match; ~ **con** to go with -4. [sol] to beat down.

◆ **pegarse** *vpr* -1. [adherirse] to stick -2. [agredirse] to fight, to hit one another -3. [golpearse]: ~**se (un golpe) con algo** to hit o.s. against sthg -4. [contagiarse -

enfermedad] to be transmitted, to be passed on; **se me pegó su acento** I picked up his accent.

pegatina *f* sticker.

pegote *m fam* -1. [masa pegajosa] sticky mess -2. [chapucería] botch.

peinado *m* hairdo; [estilo, tipo] hairstyle.

peinar *vt lit* & *fig* to comb.

◆ **peinarse** *vpr* to comb one's hair.

peine *m* comb; **pasarse el ~** to comb one's hair.

peineta *f* comb worn in the back of the hair.

p.ej. (abrev de **por ejemplo**) e.g.

Pekín Peking, Beijing.

pela *f fam* peseta; **no tengo ~s** I'm skint.

peladilla *f* sugared almond.

pelado, da ◇ *adj* -1. [cabeza] shorn -2. [piel, cara etc] peeling; [fruta] peeled -3. [habitación, monte, árbol] bare -4. [número] exact, round; **saqué un aprobado ~** I passed, but only just -5. *fam* [sin dinero] broke, skint. ◇ *m,f* *Andes fam* [niño] kid.

◆ **pelado** *m Esp* haircut.

pelaje *m* [de gato, oso, conejo] fur; [de perro, caballo] coat.

pelar *vt* -1. [persona] to cut the hair of -2. [fruta, patatas] to peel; [guisantes, marisco] to shell -3. [aves] to pluck; [conejos etc] to skin.

◆ **pelarse** *vpr* -1. [cortarse el pelo] to have one's hair cut -2. [piel, espalda etc] to peel.

peldaño *m* step; [de escalera de mano] rung.

pelea *f* -1. [a golpes] fight -2. [riña] row, quarrel.

pelear *vi* -1. [a golpes] to fight -2. [a gritos] to have a row o quarrel -3. [esforzarse] to struggle.

◆ **pelearse** *vpr* -1. [a golpes] to fight -2. [a gritos] to have a row o quarrel.

pelele *m fam despec* [persona] puppet.

peletería *f* [tienda] fur shop, furrier's.

peliagudo, da *adj* tricky.

pelícano, pelicano *m* pelican.

película *f* [gen] film; ~ **muda/de terror** silent/horror film; ~ **del Oeste** western; **de ~** amazing.

peligro *m* danger; **correr ~ (de)** to be in danger (of); **estar/poner en ~** to be/put at risk; **en ~ de extinción** [especie, animal] endangered; **fuera de ~** out of danger; ~ **de incendio** fire hazard; **¡~ de muerte!** danger!

peligroso, sa *adj* dangerous.

pelín *m fam* mite, tiny bit.

pelirrojo, ja ◇ *adj* ginger, red-headed. ◇ *m,f* redhead.

pellejo *m* [piel, vida] skin.

pellizcar *vt* [gen] to pinch.

pellizco *m* pinch; **dar un ~ a alguien** to give sb a pinch.

pelma, pelmazo, za *fam despec* ◇ *adj* annoying, tiresome. ◇ *m,f* bore, pain.

pelo *m* - **1.** [gen] hair - **2.** [de oso, conejo, gato] fur; [de perro, caballo] coat - **3.** [de una tela] nap - **4.** *loc*: **con ~s y señales** with all the details; **no tener ~s en la lengua** *fam* not to mince one's words; **poner a alguien los ~s de punta** *fam* to make sb's hair stand on end; **por los ~s, por un ~** by the skin of one's teeth, only just; **tomar el ~ a alguien** *fam* to pull sb's leg.
◆ **a contra pelo** *loc adv lit & fig* against the grain.

pelota ◇ *f* - **1.** [gen & DEP] ball; **jugar a la ~** to play ball; **~ vasca** pelota; **hacer la ~ (a alguien)** *fam* to suck up (to sb) - **2.** *fam* [cabeza] nut. ◇ *mf* [persona] crawler, creep.

pelotera *f fam* scrap, fight.

pelotón *m* [de soldados] squad; [de gente] crowd; DEP pack.

pelotudo, da *RP fam* ◇ *adj* stupid. ◇ *m,f* jerk.

peluca *f* wig.

peluche *m* plush.

peludo, da *adj* hairy.

peluquería *f* - **1.** [establecimiento] hairdresser's (shop) - **2.** [oficio] hairdressing.

peluquero, ra *m,f* hairdresser.

peluquín *m* toupee; **¡ni hablar del ~!** *fam* it's out of the question!

pelusa *f* - **1.** [de tela] fluff - **2.** [vello] down.

pelvis *f inv* pelvis.

pena *f* - **1.** [lástima] shame, pity; **¡qué ~!** what a shame *o* pity!; **dar ~** to inspire pity; **el pobre me da ~** I feel sorry for the poor chap - **2.** [tristeza] sadness, sorrow - **3.** *(gen pl)* [desgracia] problem, trouble - **4.** *(gen pl)* [dificultad] struggle *(U)*; **a duras ~s** with great difficulty - **5.** [castigo] punishment; **~ capital** *o* **de muerte** death penalty - **6.** *Amér* [vergüenza] shame, embarrassment; **me da ~** I'm ashamed of it - **7.** *loc*: **(no) valer** *o* **merecer la ~** (not) to be worthwhile *o* worth it.

penacho *m* - **1.** [de pájaro] crest - **2.** [adorno] plume.

penal ◇ *adj* criminal. ◇ *m* prison.

penalidad *(gen pl)* *f* suffering *(U)*, hardship.

penalización *f* - **1.** [acción] penalization - **2.** [sanción] penalty.

penalti, penalty *m* DEP penalty.

penar ◇ *vt* [castigar] to punish. ◇ *vi* [sufrir] to suffer.

pender *vi* - **1.** [colgar]: **~ (de)** to hang (from) - **2.** [amenaza etc]: **~ sobre** to hang over.

pendiente ◇ *adj* - **1.** [por resolver] pending; [deuda] outstanding; **estar ~ de**

[atento a] to keep an eye on; [a la espera de] to be waiting for - **2.** [asignatura] failed. ◇ *m* earring. ◇ *f* slope.

pendón, ona *m,f fam* libertine.

péndulo *m* pendulum.

pene *m* penis.

penene *mf* untenured teacher or lecturer.

penetración *f* - **1.** [gen] penetration - **2.** [sagacidad] astuteness, sharpness.

penetrante *adj* - **1.** [intenso - dolor] acute; [- olor] sharp; [- frío] biting; [- mirada] penetrating; [- voz, sonido etc] piercing - **2.** [sagaz] sharp, penetrating.

penetrar ◇ *vi*: **~ en** [internarse en] to enter; [filtrarse por] to get into, to penetrate; [perforar] to pierce; [llegar a conocer] to get to the bottom of. ◇ *vt* - **1.** [introducirse en - suj: arma, sonido etc] to pierce, to penetrate; [- suj: humedad, líquido] to permeate; [- suj: emoción, sentimiento] to pierce - **2.** [llegar a conocer - secreto etc] to get to the bottom of - **3.** [sexualmente] to penetrate.

penicilina *f* penicillin.

península *f* peninsula.

peninsular *adj* peninsular.

penitencia *f* penance.

penitenciaría *f* penitentiary.

penoso, sa *adj* - **1.** [trabajoso] laborious - **2.** [lamentable] distressing; [aspecto, espectáculo] sorry - **3.** *CAm, Carib, Col, Méx* [vergonzoso] shy.

pensador, ra *m,f* thinker.

pensamiento *m* - **1.** [gen] thought; [mente] mind; [idea] idea - **2.** BOT pansy.

pensar ◇ *vi* to think; **~ en algo/en alguien/en hacer algo** to think about sthg/about sb/about doing sthg; **~ sobre algo** to think about sthg; **piensa en un número/buen regalo** think of a number/good present; **dar que ~ a alguien** to give sb food for thought. ◇ *vt* - **1.** [reflexionar] to think about *o* over - **2.** [opinar, creer] to think; **~ algo de alguien/algo** to think sthg of sb/sthg; **pienso que no vendrá** I don't think she'll come - **3.** [idear] to think up - **4.** [tener la intención de]: **~ hacer algo** to intend to do sthg.
◆ **pensarse** *vpr*: **~se algo** to think about sthg, to think sthg over.

pensativo, va *adj* pensive, thoughtful.

pensión *f* - **1.** [dinero] pension - **2.** [de huéspedes] ≃ guest house; **media ~** [en hotel] half board; **estar a media ~** [en colegio] to have school dinners; **~ completa** full board.

pensionista *mf* [jubilado] pensioner.

pentágono *m* pentagon.

pentagrama *m* MÚS stave.

penúltimo, ma *adj & m,f* penultimate, last but one.

penumbra *f* semi-darkness, half-light.

penuria *f* -1. [pobreza] penury, poverty - 2. [escasez] paucity, dearth.

peña *f* [grupo de amigos] circle, group; [club] club; [quinielística] pool.

peñasco *m* large crag o rock.

peñón *m* rock:
- **Peñón** *m*: **el Peñón (de Gibraltar)** the Rock (of Gibraltar).

peón *m* -1. [obrero] unskilled labourer - 2. [en ajedrez] pawn.

peonza *f* (spinning) top.

peor ⬦ *adj* -1. *(comparativo)*: ~ **(que)** worse (than); ~ **para él** that's his problem - 2. *(superlativo)*: **el/la** ~ ... the worst ... ⬦ *pron*: **el/la** ~ **(de)** the worst (in); **el** ~ **de todos** the worst of all; **lo** ~ **fue que** ... the worst thing was that ... ⬦ *adv* -1. *(comparativo)*: ~ **(que)** worse (than); **ahora veo** ~ I see worse now; **estar** ~ [enfermo] to get worse; **estoy** ~ [de salud] I feel worse - 2. *(superlativo)* worst; **el que lo hizo** ~ the one who did it (the) worst.

pepa *f Andes, CAm, Carib, Méx* [pepita] pip; [hueso] stone, pit.

pepinillo *m* gherkin.

pepino *m* BOT cucumber; **me importa un** ~ I couldn't care less.

pepita *f* -1. [de fruta] pip - 2. [de oro] nugget.

peppermint = pipermín.

pequeñez *f* -1. [gen] smallness - 2. *fig* [insignificancia] trifle; **discutir por pequeñeces** to argue over silly little things.

pequeño, ña *adj* small; [hermano] little; [posibilidad] slight; [ingresos, cifras etc] low; **me queda** ~ it's too small for me.

pequinés *m* [perro] Pekinese.

pera *f* -1. [fruta] pear - 2. [para ducha etc] (rubber) bulb - 3. *CSur* [barbilla] chin - 4. *loc*: **pedir** ~**s al olmo** to ask (for) the impossible; **ser la** ~ *fam* to be the limit; **ser una** ~ **en dulce** *fam* to be a gem.

peral *m* pear-tree.

percance *m* mishap.

percatarse *vpr*: ~ **(de algo)** to notice (sthg).

percebe *m* [pez] barnacle.

percepción *f* [de los sentidos] perception; ~ **extrasensorial** extrasensory perception.

perceptible *adj* [por los sentidos] noticeable, perceptible.

percha *f* -1. [de armario] (coat) hanger - 2. [de pared] coat rack - 3. [para pájaros] perch.

perchero *m* [de pared] coat rack; [de pie] coat stand.

percibir *vt* -1. [con los sentidos] to perceive,

to notice; [por los oídos] to hear; [ver] to see - 2. [cobrar] to receive, to get.

percusión *f* percussion.

perdedor, ra *m,f* loser.

perder ⬦ *vt* -1. [gen] to lose; **llevas las de** ~ you can't hope to win; **salir perdiendo** to come off worst - 2. [desperdiciar] to waste - 3. [tren, oportunidad] to miss. ⬦ *vi* -1. [salir derrotado] to lose - 2. *loc*: **echar algo a** ~ to spoil sthg; **echarse a** ~ [alimento] to go off, to spoil.
- **perderse** *vpr* -1. [gen] to get lost; **¡piérdete!** *mfam* get lost! - 2. [desaparecer] to disappear - 3. [desperdiciarse] to be wasted - 4. [desaprovechar]: **¡no te lo pierdas!** don't miss it! - 5. *fig* [por los vicios] to be beyond salvation.

perdición *f* ruin, undoing.

pérdida *f* -1. [gen] loss; **no tiene** ~ you can't miss it - 2. [de tiempo, dinero] waste - 3. [escape] leak.
- **pérdidas** *fpl* -1. FIN & MIL losses; ~**s humanas** loss of life - 2. [daños] damage.

perdidamente *adv* hopelessly.

perdido, da *adj* -1. [extraviado] lost; [animal, bala] stray - 2. [sucio] filthy - 3. *fam* [de remate] complete, utter - 4. *loc*: **dar algo por** ~ to give sthg up for lost; **estar** ~ to be done for o lost.

perdigón *m* pellet.

perdiz *f* partridge.

perdón *m* pardon, forgiveness; **no tener** ~ to be unforgivable; **¡perdón!** sorry!; ~, **¿me deja pasar?** excuse me, could you let me through?

perdonar ⬦ *vt* -1. [gen] to forgive; ~ **le algo a alguien** to forgive sb for sthg; **perdone que le moleste** sorry to bother you - 2. [eximir de - deuda, condena]: ~ **algo a alguien** to let sb off sthg; ~ **le la vida a alguien** to spare sb their life. ⬦ *vi*: **perdone, ¿cómo ha dicho?** excuse me, what did you say?

perdonavidas *m y f inv fam* bully.

perdurar *vi* -1. [durar mucho] to endure, to last - 2. [persistir] to persist.

perecedero, ra *adj* -1. [productos] perishable - 2. [naturaleza] transitory.

perecer *vi* to perish, to die.

peregrinación *f* RELIG pilgrimage.

peregrinaje *m* RELIG pilgrimage.

peregrino, na ⬦ *adj* -1. [ave] migratory - 2. *fig* [extraño] strange. ⬦ *m,f* [persona] pilgrim.

perejil *m* parsley.

perenne *adj* BOT perennial.

pereza *f* idleness.

perezoso, sa *adj* [vago] lazy.

perfección *f* perfection; **es de una gran** ~ it's exceptionally good.

perfeccionar *vt* - **1.** [redondear] to perfect - **2.** [mejorar] to improve.

perfeccionista *adj* & *m,f* perfectionist.

perfecto, ta *adj* perfect.

perfidia *f* perfidy, treachery.

perfil *m* - **1.** [contorno] outline, shape - **2.** [de cara, cuerpo] profile; **de ~** in profile - **3.** *fig* [característica] characteristic - **4.** *fig* [retrato moral] profile - **5.** GEOM cross section.

perfilar *vt* to outline.

◆ **perfilarse** *vpr* - **1.** [destacarse] to be outlined - **2.** [concretarse] to shape up.

perforación *f* - **1.** [gen & MED] perforation - **2.** [taladro] bore-hole.

perforar *vt* [horadar] to perforate; [agujero] to drill; INFORM to punch.

perfume *m* perfume.

perfumería *f* - **1.** [tienda, arte] perfumery - **2.** [productos] perfumes (pl).

pergamino *m* parchment.

pericia *f* skill.

periferia *f* periphery; [alrededores] outskirts (pl).

periférico, ca *adj* peripheral; [barrio] outlying.

perifollos *mpl fam* frills (and fripperies).

perífrasis *f inv*: ~ **(verbal)** compound verb.

perilla *f* goatee; **venir de ~(s)** to be just the right thing.

perímetro *m* perimeter.

periódico, ca *adj* [gen] periodic.

◆ **periódico** *m* newspaper; ~ **dominical** Sunday paper.

periodismo *m* journalism.

periodista *mf* journalist.

periodo, período *m* period; DEP half.

peripecia *f* incident, adventure.

peripuesto, ta *adj fam* dolled-up, tarted-up.

periquete *m*: **en un ~** *fam* in a jiffy.

periquito *m* parakeet.

periscopio *m* periscope.

peritar *vt* [casa] to value; [coche] to assess the value of, to assess the damage to.

perito *m* - **1.** [experto] expert; ~ **agrónomo** agronomist - **2.** [ingeniero técnico] technician.

perjudicar *vt* to damage, to harm.

perjudicial *adj*: ~ **(para)** harmful (to).

perjuicio *m* harm (U), damage (U); **causar ~ a algo/alguien** to do damage to sb/sthg.

perjurar *vi* [jurar en falso] to commit perjury.

perla *f* pearl; ~ **de cultivo** cultured pearl; *fig* [maravilla] gem, treasure; **de ~s** great, fine; **me viene de ~s** it's just the right thing.

perlé *m* beading.

permanecer *vi* - **1.** [en un lugar] to stay - **2.** [en un estado] to remain, to stay.

permanencia *f* - **1.** [en un lugar] staying, continued stay - **2.** [en un estado] continuation.

permanente ◇ *adj* permanent; [comisión] standing. ◇ *f* perm; **hacerse la ~** to have a perm.

permeable *adj* permeable.

permisible *adj* permissible, acceptable.

permisivo, va *adj* permissive.

permiso *m* - **1.** [autorización] permission; **con ~** if I may, if you'll excuse me; **dar ~ para hacer algo** to give permission to do sthg - **2.** [documento] licence, permit; ~ **de armas** gun licence; ~ **de conducir** driving licence *UK*, driver's license *US*; ~ **de residencia** residence permit - **3.** [vacaciones] leave.

permitir *vt* to allow; ~ **a alguien hacer algo** to allow sb to do sthg; **¿me permite?** may I?

◆ **permitirse** *vpr* to allow o.s. (the luxury of); **no puedo permitírmelo** I can't afford it.

permuta, permutación *f* exchange.

permutación = **permuta**.

pernicioso, sa *adj* damaging, harmful.

pero ◇ *conj* but; **la casa es vieja ~ céntrica** the house may be old, but it's central; ~ **¿qué es tanto ruido?** what on earth is all this noise about? ◇ *m* snag, fault; **poner ~s a todo** to find fault with everything.

perol *m* casserole (dish).

perorata *f* long-winded speech.

perpendicular *adj* perpendicular; **ser ~ a algo** to be at right angles to sthg.

perpetrar *vt* to perpetrate, to commit.

perpetuar *vt* to perpetuate.

◆ **perpetuarse** *vpr* to last, to endure.

perpetuo, tua *adj* - **1.** [gen] perpetual - **2.** [para toda la vida] lifelong; DER life (antes de sust).

perplejo, ja *adj* perplexed, bewildered.

perra *f* - **1.** [rabieta] tantrum; **coger una ~** to throw a tantrum - **2.** [dinero] penny; **estoy sin una ~** I'm flat broke - **3.** ⊳ **perro**.

perrera ⊳ **perro**.

perrería *f fam*: **hacer ~s a alguien** to play dirty tricks on sb.

perrero, ra *m,f* [persona] dogcatcher.

◆ **perrera** *f* - **1.** [lugar] kennels (pl) - **2.** [vehículo] dogcatcher's van.

perro, rra *m,f* [animal] dog (f bitch); ~ **callejero** stray dog; ~ **de caza** hunting dog; ~ **de compañía** pet dog; ~ **faldero** lapdog; ~ **lazarillo** guide dog; ~ **lobo** alsatian; ~ **pastor** sheepdog; ~ **policía** police dog; **echar los ~s a alguien** to have a go at sb; **ser ~ viejo** to be an old hand.

◆ **perro caliente** *m* hot dog.
persecución *f* - **1.** [seguimiento] pursuit - **2.** [acoso] persecution.
perseguir *vt* - **1.** [seguir, tratar de obtener] to pursue - **2.** [acosar] to persecute - **3.** [suj: mala suerte, problema etc] to dog.
perseverante *adj* persistent.
perseverar *vi*: ~ **(en)** to persevere (with), to persist (in).
persiana *f* blind, shade *US*; **enrollarse como una** ~ *fam* to go on and on.
persistente *adj* persistent.
persistir *vi*: ~ **(en)** to persist (in).
persona *f* - **1.** [individuo] person; **cien** ~**s** a hundred people; **de** ~ **a** ~ person to person; **en** ~ in person; **por** ~ per head; **ser buena** ~ to be nice; ~ **mayor** adult, grown-up - **2.** DER party - **3.** GRAM person.
personaje *m* - **1.** [persona importante] important person, celebrity; **ser todo un** ~ *fam* to be a real big shot - **2.** [de obra] character.
personal ◇ *adj* [gen] personal; [teléfono, dirección] private, home *(antes de sust)*. ◇ *m* [trabajadores] staff, personnel.
personalidad *f* - **1.** [características] personality - **2.** [persona importante] important person, celebrity.
personalizar *vi* [nombrar] to name names.
personarse *vpr* to turn up.
personero, ra *m,f Amér* spokesperson.
personificar *vt* to personify.
perspectiva *f* - **1.** [gen] perspective - **2.** [paisaje] view - **3.** [futuro] prospect; **en** ~ in prospect.
perspicacia *f* insight, perceptiveness.
perspicaz *adj* sharp, perceptive.
persuadir *vt* to persuade; ~ **a alguien para que haga algo** to persuade sb to do sthg.
◆ **persuadirse** *vpr* to convince o.s.; ~**se de algo** to become convinced of sthg.
persuasión *f* persuasion.
persuasivo, va *adj* persuasive.
pertenecer *vi* - **1.** [gen]: ~ **a** to belong to - **2.** [corresponder] to be up to, to be a matter for.
perteneciente *adj*: **ser** ~ **a** to belong to.
pertenencia *f* - **1.** [propiedad] ownership - **2.** [afiliación] membership.
◆ **pertenencias** *fpl* [enseres] belongings.
pértiga *f* - **1.** [vara] pole - **2.** DEP pole-vault.
pertinaz *adj* - **1.** [terco] stubborn - **2.** [persistente] persistent.
pertinente *adj* - **1.** [adecuado] appropriate - **2.** [relativo] relevant, pertinent.
pertrechos *mpl* - **1.** MIL supplies and ammunition - **2.** *fig* [utensilios] gear *(U)*.
perturbación *f* - **1.** [desconcierto] disquiet, unease - **2.** [disturbio] disturbance; ~ **del**

orden público breach of the peace - **3.** MED mental imbalance.
perturbado, da *adj* - **1.** MED disturbed, mentally unbalanced - **2.** [desconcertado] perturbed.
perturbador, ra ◇ *adj* unsettling. ◇ *m,f* troublemaker.
perturbar *vt* - **1.** [trastornar] to disrupt - **2.** [inquietar] to disturb, to unsettle - **3.** [enloquecer] to perturb.
Perú: **(el)** ~ Peru.
peruano, na *adj* & *m,f* Peruvian.
perversión *f* perversion.
perverso, sa *adj* depraved.
pervertido, da *m,f* pervert.
pervertir *vt* to corrupt.
◆ **pervertirse** *vpr* to become corrupt, to be corrupted.
pesa *f* - **1.** [gen] weight - **2.** *(gen pl)* DEP weights *(pl)*; **alzar** ~**s** to lift weights.
pesadez *f* - **1.** [peso] weight - **2.** [sensación] heaviness - **3.** [molestia, fastidio] drag, pain - **4.** [aburrimiento] ponderousness.
pesadilla *f* nightmare.
pesado, da ◇ *adj* - **1.** [gen] heavy - **2.** [caluroso] sultry - **3.** [lento] ponderous, sluggish - **4.** [duro] difficult, tough - **5.** [aburrido] boring - **6.** [molesto] annoying, tiresome; **¡qué** ~ **eres!** you're so annoying. ◇ *m,f* bore, pain.
pesadumbre *f* grief, sorrow.
pésame *m* sympathy, condolences *(pl)*; **dar el** ~ to offer one's condolences; **mi más sentido** ~ my deepest sympathies.
pesar ◇ *m* - **1.** [tristeza] grief - **2.** [arrepentimiento] remorse - **3.** *loc*: **a** ~ **mío** against my will. ◇ *vt* - **1.** [determinar el peso de] to weigh - **2.** [examinar] to weigh up. ◇ *vi* - **1.** [tener peso] to weigh - **2.** [ser pesado] to be heavy - **3.** [importar] to play an important part - **4.** [entristecer]: **me pesa tener que decirte esto** I'm sorry to have to tell you this.
◆ **a pesar de** *loc prep* despite; **a** ~ **de todo** in spite of everything.
◆ **a pesar de que** *loc conj* in spite of the fact that.
pesca *f* - **1.** [acción] fishing; **ir de** ~ to go fishing; ~ **con caña** angling; ~ **con red** net fishing; ~ **de bajura/altura** coastal/deep-sea fishing - **2.** [lo pescado] catch.
pescadería *f* fishmonger's (shop).
pescadilla *f* whiting.
pescado *m* fish; ~ **azul/blanco** blue/white fish.
pescador, ra *m,f* fisherman *(f* fisherwoman)*.
pescar ◇ *vt* - **1.** [peces] to catch - **2.** *fig* [enfermedad] to catch - **3.** *fam fig* [conseguir] to

get o.s., to land - **4.** *fam fig* [atrapar] to catch.
◇ *vi* to fish, to go fishing.

pescuezo *m* neck.

pese ◆ **pese a** *loc prep* despite; ~ **a que** even though.

pesebre *m* - **1.** [para los animales] manger - **2.** [belén] crib, Nativity scene.

pesero *m CAm* & *Méx* fixed-rate taxi service.

peseta *f* [unidad] peseta.
◆ **pesetas** *fpl fig* [dinero] money (*U*).

pesetero, ra *adj* money-grubbing.

pesimismo *m* pessimism.

pesimista ◇ *adj* pessimistic. ◇ *mf* pessimist.

pésimo, ma ◇ *superl* ⊳ **malo.** ◇ *adj* terrible, awful.

peso *m* - **1.** [gen] weight; **perder** *o* **ganar** ~ to lose/gain weight; **tiene un kilo de** ~ it weighs a kilo; **de** ~ [razones] weighty, sound; [persona] influential; ~ **bruto/neto** gross/net weight; ~ **muerto** dead weight - **2.** [moneda] peso - **3.** [de atletismo] shot - **4.** [balanza] scales (*pl*).

pesquero, ra *adj* fishing.
◆ **pesquero** *m* fishing boat.

pesquisa *f* investigation, inquiry.

pestaña *f* [de párpado] eyelash; ~**s postizas** false eyelashes; **quemarse las** ~**s** *fig* to burn the midnight oil.

pestañear *vi* to blink; **sin** ~ without batting an eyelid.

peste *f* - **1.** [enfermedad, plaga] plague; ~ **bubónica** bubonic plague - **2.** *fam* [mal olor] stink, stench - **3.** *loc*: **decir** ~**s de alguien** to heap abuse on sb.

pesticida *m* pesticide.

pestilencia *f* stench.

pestillo *m* [cerrojo] bolt; [mecanismo, en verjas] latch; **correr** *o* **echar el** ~ to shoot the bolt.

petaca *f* - **1.** [para cigarrillos] cigarette case; [para tabaco] tobacco pouch - **2.** [para bebidas] flask - **3.** *Méx* [maleta] suitcase.
◆ **petacas** *fpl Méx fam* buttocks.

pétalo *m* petal.

petanca *f* game similar to bowls played in parks, on beach etc.

petardo *m* [cohete] banger, firecracker.

petate *m* kit bag.

petición *f* - **1.** [acción] request; **a** ~ **de** at the request of - **2.** DER [escrito] petition.

petiso, sa, petizo, za ◇ *adj Andes* & *RP fam* [person] short. ◇ *m Andes* & *RP* [caballo] small horse.

peto *m* [de prenda] bib; **pantalón con** ~ overalls.

petrificar *vt lit* & *fig* to petrify.

petrodólar *m* petrodollar.

petróleo *m* oil, petroleum.

petrolero, ra *adj* oil (*antes de sust*).
◆ **petrolero** *m* oil tanker.

petrolífero, ra *adj* oil (*antes de sust*).

petulante *adj* opinionated, arrogant.

peúco (*gen pl*) *m* bootee.

peyorativo, va *adj* pejorative.

pez *m* fish; ~ **de colores** goldfish; ~ **de río** freshwater fish; ~ **espada** swordfish; **estar** ~ **(en algo)** to have no idea (about sthg).
◆ **pez gordo** *m fam fig* big shot.

pezón *m* [de pecho] nipple.

pezuña *f* hoof.

piadoso, sa *adj* - **1.** [compasivo] kindhearted - **2.** [religioso] pious.

pianista *mf* pianist.

piano *m* piano.

pianola *f* pianola.

piar *vi* to cheep, to tweet.

PIB (*abrev de* **producto interior bruto**) *m* GDP.

pibe, ba *m,f RP fam* kid.

pica *f* - **1.** [naipe] spade - **2.** [lanza] pike; **poner una** ~ **en Flandes** to do the impossible.
◆ **picas** *fpl* [palo de baraja] spades.

picadero *m* [de caballos] riding school.

picadillo *m* - **1.** [de carne] mince; [de verdura] chopped vegetables (*pl*); **hacer** ~ **a alguien** *fam* to beat sb to a pulp - **2.** *Chile* [tapas] snacks, appetizers.

picado, da *adj* - **1.** [marcado - piel] pockmarked; [- fruta] bruised - **2.** [agujereado] perforated; ~ **de polilla** moth-eaten - **3.** [triturado - alimento] chopped; [- carne] minced; [- tabaco] cut - **4.** [vino] sour - **5.** [diente] decayed - **6.** [mar] choppy - **7.** *fig* [enfadado] annoyed.

picador, ra *m,f* TAUROM picador.

picadora *f* mincer.

picadura *f* - **1.** [de mosquito, serpiente] bite; [de avispa, ortiga, escorpión] sting - **2.** [tabaco] (cut) tobacco (*U*).

picante ◇ *adj* - **1.** [comida etc] spicy, hot - **2.** *fig* [obsceno] saucy. ◇ *m* [comida] spicy food; [sabor] spiciness.

picantería *f Andes* cheap restaurant.

picaporte *m* [aldaba] doorknocker; [barrita] latch.

picar ◇ *vt* - **1.** [suj: mosquito, serpiente] to bite; [suj: avispa, escorpión, ortiga] to sting - **2.** [escocer] to itch; **me pican los ojos** my eyes are stinging - **3.** [triturar - verdura] to chop; [- carne] to mince - **4.** [suj: ave] to peck - **5.** [aperitivo] to pick at - **6.** [tierra, piedra, hielo] to hack at - **7.** *fig* [enojar] to irritate - **8.** *fig* [estimular - persona, caballo] to spur on; [- curiosidad] to prick - **9.** [perforar - billete, ficha] to punch. ◇ *vi* - **1.** [alimento] to be spicy *o* hot - **2.** [pez] to bite - **3.** [escocer] to itch - **4.** [ave] to peck - **5.** [tomar un aperitivo] to nibble - **6.** [sol] to burn - **7.** [dejarse engañar] to take the bait.

◆ **picarse** *vpr* - **1.** [vino] to turn sour - **2.** [mar] to get choppy - **3.** [diente] to get a cavity - **4.** [oxidarse] to go rusty - **5.** *fig* [enfadarse] to get annoyed *o* cross.

picardía *f* - **1.** [astucia] sharpness, craftiness - **2.** [travesura] naughty trick, mischief *(U)*.

picaresco, ca *adj* mischievous, roguish.

◆ **picaresca** *f* - **1.** LITER picaresque literature - **2.** [modo de vida] roguery.

pícaro, ra *m,f* - **1.** [astuto] sly person, rogue - **2.** [travieso] rascal.

picatoste *m* crouton.

pichi *m* pinafore (dress).

pichichi *m* DEP top scorer.

pichincha *f Bol, RP fam* bargain.

pichón *m* - **1.** ZOOL young pigeon.

pickles *mpl RP* pickles.

picnic (*pl* picnics) *m* picnic.

pico *m* - **1.** [de ave] beak - **2.** [punta, saliente] corner - **3.** [herramienta] pick, pickaxe - **4.** [cumbre] peak - **5.** [cantidad indeterminada]: **cincuenta y ∼** fifty-odd, fifty-something; **llegó a las cinco y ∼** he got there just after five - **6.** *fam* [boca] gob, mouth; **cerrar el ∼** to shut up.

picor *m* [del calor] burning; [que irrita] itch.

picoso, sa *adj Méx* spicy, hot.

picotear *vt* [suj: ave] to peck.

pida, pidiera *etc* ⊳ **pedir**.

pie *m* - **1.** [gen & ANAT] foot; **a ∼** on foot; **estar de** *o* **en ∼** to be on one's feet *o* standing; **ponerse de** *o* **en ∼** to stand up; **de ∼s a cabeza** *fig* from head to toe; **seguir en ∼** [vigente] to be still valid; **en ∼ de igualdad** on an equal footing; **en ∼ de guerra** at war; **∼ de foto** caption - **2.** [de micrófono, lámpara etc] stand; [de copa] stem - **3.** *loc*: **al ∼ de la letra** to the letter, word for word; **andar con ∼s de plomo** to tread carefully; **buscarle (los) tres ∼s al gato** to split hairs; **dar ∼ a alguien para que haga algo** to give sb cause to do sthg; **no tener ni ∼s ni cabeza** to make no sense at all; **pararle los ∼s a alguien** to put sb in their place; **tener un ∼ en la tumba** to have one foot in the grave.

piedad *f* - **1.** [compasión] pity; **por ∼** for pity's sake; **tener ∼ de** to take pity on - **2.** [religiosidad] piety.

piedra *f* - **1.** [gen] stone; **∼ angular** *lit & fig* cornerstone; **∼ pómez** pumice stone; **∼ preciosa** precious stone; **∼ de toque** touchstone - **2.** [de mechero] flint.

piel *f* - **1.** ANAT skin; **∼ roja** redskin *(N.B.: the term 'piel roja' is considered to be racist)*; **∼ de gallina** goose bumps; **dejar** *o* **jugarse la ∼** to risk one's neck - **2.** [cuero] leather - **3.** [pelo] fur - **4.** [cáscara] skin, peel.

piensa *etc* ⊳ **pensar**.

pierda *etc* ⊳ **perder**.

pierna *f* leg; **estirar las ∼s** to stretch one's legs.

pieza *f* - **1.** [gen] piece; [de mecanismo] part; **∼ de recambio** *o* **repuesto** spare part, extra *US*; **dejar/quedarse de una ∼** to leave/be thunderstruck - **2.** [obra dramática] play - **3.** [habitación] room.

pifiar *vt* : **∼ la** *fam* to put one's foot in it.

pigmento *m* pigment.

pijama *m* pyjamas *(pl)*.

pila *f* - **1.** [generador] battery - **2.** [montón] pile; **tiene una ∼ de deudas** he's up to his neck in debt - **3.** [fregadero] sink.

pilar *m* lit & fig pillar.

píldora *f* pill; [anticonceptivo]: **la ∼** the pill; **∼ del día siguiente** morning-after pill; **dorar la ∼** to sugar the pill.

pileta *f RP* [piscina] swimming pool; [en baño] washbasin; [en cocina] sink.

pillaje *m* pillage.

pillar ◇ *vt* - **1.** [gen] to catch - **2.** [chiste, explicación] to get - **3.** [atropellar] to knock down. ◇ *vi fam* [hallarse]: **me pilla lejos** it's out of the way for me; **me pilla de camino** it's on my way; **no me pilla de nuevas** it doesn't surprise me.

◆ **pillarse** *vpr* [dedos etc] to catch.

pillo, lla *fam* ◇ *adj* - **1.** [travieso] mischievous - **2.** [astuto] crafty. ◇ *m,f* [pícaro] rascal.

pilotar *vt* [avión] to fly, to pilot; [coche] to drive; [barco] to steer.

piloto ◇ *mf* [gen] pilot; [de coche] driver; **∼ automático** automatic pilot. ◇ *m* - **1.** [luz - de coche] tail light; [- de aparato] pilot lamp - **2.** *CSur* [impermeable] raincoat. ◇ *adj inv* pilot *(antes de sust)*.

piltrafa *(gen pl)* *f* scrap; *fam* [persona débil] wreck.

pimentón *m* - **1.** [dulce] paprika - **2.** [picante] cayenne pepper.

pimienta *f* pepper.

pimiento *m* [fruto] pepper, capsicum; [planta] pimiento, pepper plant; **∼ morrón** sweet pepper; **me importa un ∼** *fam* I couldn't care less.

pimpollo *m* - **1.** [de rama, planta] shoot; [de flor] bud - **2.** *fam fig* [persona atractiva] gorgeous person.

pinacoteca *f* art gallery.

pinar *m* pine wood *o* grove.

pinaza *f* pine needles *(pl)*.

pincel *m* [para pintar] paintbrush; [para maquillar etc] brush.

pinchadiscos *m y f inv* disc jockey.

pinchar ◇ *vt* - **1.** [punzar - gen] to prick; [- rueda] to puncture; [- globo, balón] to burst

- 2. [penetrar] to pierce **- 3.** *fam* [teléfono] to tap **- 4.** *fig* [irritar] to torment **- 5.** *fig* [incitar]: ~ **a alguien para que haga algo** to urge sb to do sthg. ◇ *vi* **- 1.** [rueda] to get a puncture **- 2.** [barba] to be prickly.

◆ **pincharse** *vpr* **- 1.** [punzarse - persona] to prick o.s.; [- rueda] to get a puncture **- 2.** [inyectarse]: ~**se (algo)** [medicamento] to inject o.s. (with sthg); *fam* [droga] to shoot up (with sthg).

pinchazo *m* **- 1.** [punzada] prick **- 2.** [marca] needle mark **- 3.** [de neumático, balón etc] puncture, flat *US*.

pinche ◇ *mf* kitchen boy (*f* kitchen maid). ◇ *adj Méx fam* lousy, damn.

pinchito *m* CULIN **- 1.** [tapa] aperitif on a stick **- 2.** [pincho moruno] shish kebab.

pincho *m* **- 1.** [punta] (sharp) point **- 2.** [espina - de planta] prickle, thorn **- 3.** CULIN aperitif on a stick; ~ **moruno** shish kebab.

pinga *f Andes & Méx vulg* prick, cock.

pingajo *m fam despec* rag.

ping-pong [pin'pon] *m* ping-pong, table-tennis.

pingüino *m* penguin.

pinitos *mpl*: **hacer** ~ *lit & fig* to take one's first steps.

pino *m* pine; **en el quinto** ~ in the middle of nowhere.

pinta ▷ **pinto**.

pintado, da *adj* **- 1.** [coloreado] coloured; 'recién ~' 'wet paint' **- 2.** [maquillado] made-up **- 3.** [moteado] speckled.

◆ **pintada** *f* [escrito] graffiti.

pintalabios *m inv* lipstick.

pintar ◇ *vt* **- 1.** to paint; ~ **algo de negro** to paint sthg black **- 2.** [significar, importar] to count; **aquí no pinto nada** there's no place for me here; **¿qué pinto yo en este asunto?** where do I come in? ◇ *vi* [con pintura] to paint.

◆ **pintarse** *vpr* [maquillarse] to make o.s. up.

pinto, ta *adj* speckled, spotted.

◆ **pinta** ◇ *f* **- 1.** [lunar] spot **- 2.** *fig* [aspecto] appearance; **tener pinta de algo** to look *o* seem sthg; **tiene buena pinta** it looks good **- 3.** [unidad de medida] pint **- 4.** *Méx* [pintada] graffiti (*U*).

pintor, ra *m,f* painter.

pintoresco, ca *adj* picturesque; *fig* [extravagante] colourful.

pintura *f* **- 1.** ARTE painting; ~ **a la acuarela** watercolour; ~ **al óleo** oil painting; **no poder ver a alguien ni en** ~ *fig* not to be able to stand the sight of sb **- 2.** [materia] paint.

pinza (*gen pl*) *f* **- 1.** [gen] tweezers (*pl*); [de tender ropa] peg, clothespin *US* **- 2.** [de animal] pincer, claw **- 3.** [pliegue] fold.

piña *f* **- 1.** [del pino] pine cone **- 2.** [ananás] pineapple **- 3.** *fig* [conjunto de gente] close-knit group.

piñata *f* pot full of sweets which blindfolded children try to break open with sticks at parties.

piñón *m* **- 1.** [fruto] pine nut **- 2.** [rueda dentada] pinion.

pío, a *adj* pious.

◆ **pío** *m* cheep, cheeping (*U*); [de gallina] cluck, clucking (*U*); **no decir ni** ~ *fig* not to make a peep.

piojo *m* louse; ~**s** lice.

piola ◇ *adj Arg fam* **- 1.** [astuto] shrewd **- 2.** [estupendo] fabulous. ◇ *f Amér* [cuerda] cord.

pionero, ra *m,f* pioneer.

pipa *f* **- 1.** [para fumar] pipe **- 2.** [pepita] seed, pip; ~**s (de girasol)** *sunflower seeds coated in salt* **- 3.** *loc*: **pasarlo** *o* **pasárselo** ~ to have a whale of a time.

pipermín, peppermint [piper'min] *m* peppermint liqueur.

pipí *m fam* wee-wee; **hacer** ~ to have a wee-wee.

pique *m* **- 1.** [enfado] grudge **- 2.** [rivalidad] rivalry **- 3.** *loc*: **irse a** ~ [barco] to sink; [negocio] to go under; [plan] to fail.

piquete *m* [grupo]: ~ **de ejecución** firing squad; ~ **(de huelga)** picket.

pirado, da *adj fam* crazy.

piragua *f* canoe.

piragüismo *m* canoeing.

pirámide *f* pyramid.

piraña *f* piranha.

pirarse *vpr fam* to clear off.

pirata ◇ *adj* pirate (*antes de sust*); [disco] bootleg. ◇ *mf lit & fig* pirate; ~ **informático** hacker.

piratear ◇ *vi* **- 1.** [gen] to be involved in piracy **- 2.** INFORM to hack. ◇ *vt* INFORM to hack into.

pirenaico, ca *adj* Pyrenean.

pírex, pyrex® *m* Pyrex®.

Pirineos *mpl*: **los** ~ the Pyrenees.

piripi *adj fam* tipsy.

pirómano, na *m,f* pyromaniac.

piropo *m fam* flirtatious remark, ≃ wolf whistle.

pirotecnia *f* pyrotechnics (*U*).

pirrarse *vpr fam*: ~ **por algo/alguien** to be dead keen on sthg/sb.

pirueta *f* pirouette; **hacer** ~**s** *fig* [esfuerzo] to perform miracles.

piruleta *f* lollipop.

pirulí (*pl* pirulís) *m* lollipop.

pis (*pl* pises) *m fam* pee.

pisada *f* **- 1.** [acción] footstep; **seguir las** ~**s de alguien** to follow in sb's footsteps **- 2.** [huella] footprint.

pisapapeles *m inv* paperweight.

pisar ◇ *vt* - **1.** [con el pie] to tread on - **2.** [uvas] to tread - **3.** *fig* [llegar a] to set foot in - **4.** *fig* [despreciar] to trample on - **5.** *fig* [anticiparse]: ~ **un contrato a alguien** to beat sb to a contract; ~ **una idea a alguien** to think of something before sb; ~ **fuerte** *fig* to be firing on all cylinders. ◇ *vi*: ~ **fuerte** *fig* to be firing on all cylinders.

piscina *f* swimming pool; ~ **al aire libre** open air swimming pool; ~ **climatizada** heated swimming pool.

Piscis ◇ *m* [zodiaco] Pisces. ◇ *mf* [persona] Pisces.

pisco *m Chile, Perú* pisco, *Andean grape brandy.*

piscolabis *m inv fam* snack.

piso *m* - **1.** [vivienda] flat - **2.** [planta] floor - **3.** [suelo - de carretera] surface; [- de edificio] floor - **4.** [capa] layer.

pisotear *vt* - **1.** [con el pie] to trample on - **2.** [humillar] to scorn.

pista *f* - **1.** [gen] track; ~ **de aterrizaje** runway; ~ **de baile** dance floor; ~ **cubierta** indoor track; ~ **de esquí** ski slope; ~ **de hielo** ice rink; ~ **de tenis** tennis court - **2.** *fig* [indicio] clue.

pistacho *m* pistachio.

pisto *m* ≃ ratatouille.

pistola *f* - **1.** [arma - con cilindro] gun; [- sin cilindro] pistol - **2.** [pulverizador] spraygun; **pintar a** ~ to spray-paint.

pistolero, ra *m,f* [persona] gunman.
➡ **pistolera** *f* [funda] holster.

pistón *m* - **1.** MEC piston - **2.** [MÚS - corneta] cornet; [- llave] key.

pitada *f Amér fam* drag, puff.

pitar ◇ *vt* - **1.** [arbitrar - partido] to referee; [- falta] to blow for - **2.** [abuchear]: ~ **a alguien** to whistle at sb in disapproval - **3.** *Amér fam* [fumar] to puff (on). ◇ *vi* - **1.** [tocar el pito] to blow a whistle; [del coche] to toot one's horn - **3.** *loc*: **salir/irse pitando** to rush out/off.

pitido *m* whistle.

pitillera *f* cigarette case.

pitillo *m* [cigarrillo] cigarette.

pito *m* - **1.** [silbato] whistle - **2.** [claxon] horn.

pitón *m* [cuerno] horn.

pitonisa *f* fortune-teller.

pitorrearse *vpr fam*: ~ **(de)** to take the mickey (out of).

pitorro *m* spout.

pivote (*pl* pivotes), **pívot** (*pl* pivots) *m,f* DEP pivot.

pizarra *f* - **1.** [roca, material] slate - **2.** [encerado] blackboard, chalkboard *US*.

pizarrón *m Amér* blackboard.

pizca *f fam* - **1.** [gen] tiny bit; [de sal] pinch - **2.** *Méx* [cosecha] harvest, crop.

pizza ['pitsa] *f* pizza.

pizzería [pitse'ria] *f* pizzeria.

placa *f* - **1.** [lámina] plate; [de madera] sheet; ~ **solar** solar panel - **2.** [inscripción] plaque; [de policía] badge - **3.** [matrícula] number plate - **4.** [de cocina] ring - **5.** ELECTRÓN board - **6.**: ~ **dental** dental plaque.

placaje *m* tackle.

placenta *f* placenta.

placentero, ra *adj* pleasant.

placer *m* pleasure; **ha sido un** ~ **(conocerle)** it has been a pleasure meeting you.

plácido, da *adj* [persona] placid; [día, vida, conversación] peaceful.

plafón *m* ELEC ceiling rose.

plaga *f* - **1.** [gen] plague; AGR blight; [animal] pest - **2.** [epidemia] epidemic.

plagado, da *adj*: ~ **(de)** infested (with).

plagar *vt* : ~ **de** [propaganda etc] to swamp with; [moscas etc] to infest with.

plagiar *vt* [copiar] to plagiarize.

plagio *m* [copia] plagiarism.

plan *m* - **1.** [proyecto, programa] plan - **2.** *fam* [ligue] date - **3.** *fam* [modo, forma]: **lo dijo en** ~ **serio** he was serious about it; **¡vaya** ~ **de vida!** what a life!; **si te pones en ese** ~ ... if you're going to be like that about it ...

plana ⊳ **plano.**

plancha *f* - **1.** [para planchar] iron; ~ **de vapor** steam iron - **2.** [para cocinar] grill; **a la** ~ grilled - **3.** [placa] plate; [de madera] sheet - **4.** IMPRENTA plate.

planchado *m* ironing.

planchar *vt* to iron.

planeador *m* glider.

planear ◇ *vt* to plan. ◇ *vi* - **1.** [hacer planes] to plan - **2.** [en el aire] to glide.

planeta *m* planet.

planicie *f* plain.

planificación *f* planning; ~ **familiar** family planning.

planificar *vt* to plan.

planilla *f Amér* [formulario] form.

plano, na *adj* flat.
➡ **plano** *m* - **1.** [diseño, mapa] plan - **2.** [nivel, aspecto] level - **3.** CIN shot; **primer** ~ close-up - **4.** GEOM plane - **5.** *loc*: **de** ~ [golpear] right, directly; [negar] flatly.
➡ **plana** *f* - **1.** [página] page; **en primera plana** on the front page - **2.** [loc]: **enmendarle la plana a alguien** to find fault with sb.

planta *f* - **1.** BOT & IND plant; ~ **depuradora** purification plant - **2.** [piso] floor; ~ **baja** ground floor - **3.** [del pie] sole.

plantación *f* - **1.** [terreno] plantation - **2.** [acción] planting.

plantado, da *adj* standing, planted; **dejar ~ a alguien** *fam* [cortar la relación] to walk out on sb; [no acudir] to stand sb up; **ser bien ~** to be good-looking.

plantar *vt* - **1.** [sembrar]: **~ algo (de)** to plant sthg (with) - **2.** [fijar - tienda de campaña] to pitch; [- poste] to put in - **3.** *fam* [asestar] to deal, to land.
➦ **plantarse** *vpr* - **1.** [gen] to plant o.s. - **2.** [en un sitio con rapidez]: **~se en** to get to, to reach.

planteamiento *m* - **1.** [exposición] raising, posing - **2.** [enfoque] approach.

plantear *vt* - **1.** [exponer - problema] to pose; [- posibilidad, dificultad, duda] to raise - **2.** [enfocar] to approach.
➦ **plantearse** *vpr*: **~se algo** to consider sthg, to think about sthg.

plantel *m* *fig* [conjunto] group.

plantilla *f* - **1.** [de empresa] staff - **2.** [suela interior] insole - **3.** [patrón] pattern, template.

plantón *m*: dar un **~ a alguien** *fam* to stand sb up.

plañidero, ra *adj* plaintive, whining.

plañir *vi* to moan, to wail.

plasmar *vt* - **1.** *fig* [reflejar] to give shape to - **2.** [modelar] to shape, to mould.
➦ **plasmarse** *vpr* to emerge, to take shape.

plasta ◇ *adj* *mfam*: ser **~** to be a pain. ◇ *mf* *mfam* [pesado] pain, drag.

plástico, ca *adj* [gen] plastic.
➦ **plástico** *m* [gen] plastic.

plastificar *vt* to plasticize.

plastilina® *f* ≃ Plasticine®.

plata *f* - **1.** [metal] silver; **~ de ley** sterling silver; **hablar en ~** *fam* to speak bluntly - **2.** [objetos de plata] silverware - **3.** *Amér* [dinero] money.

plataforma *f* - **1.** [gen] platform; **~ espacial** space station; **~ petrolífera** oil rig - **2.** *fig* [punto de partida] launching pad - **3.** GEOL shelf.

platal *m* *Amér* *fam*: un **~** a fortune, loads of money.

plátano *m* - **1.** [fruta] banana - **2.** [banano] banana tree; [árbol platanáceo] plane tree.

platea *f* stalls (*pl*).

plateado, da *adj* - **1.** [con plata] silver-plated - **2.** *fig* [color] silvery.

plática *f* *CAm, Méx* talk, chat.

platicar *vi* *CAm, Méx* to talk, to chat.

platillo *m* - **1.** [plato pequeño] small plate; [de taza] saucer - **2.** [de una balanza] pan - **3.** (*gen pl*) MÚS cymbal.
➦ **platillo volante** *m* flying saucer.

platina *f* [de microscopio] slide.

platino *m* [metal] platinum.
➦ **platinos** *mpl* AUTOM & MEC contact points.

plato *m* - **1.** [recipiente] plate, dish; **lavar los ~s** to do the washing-up; **pagar los ~s rotos** to carry the can - **2.** [parte de una comida] course; **primer ~** first course, starter; **de primer ~** for starters; **segundo ~** second course, main course - **3.** [comida] dish; **~ combinado** *single-course meal which usually consists of meat or fish accompanied by chips and vegetables*; **~ principal** main course - **4.** [de tocadiscos, microondas] turntable.

plató *m* set.

platónico, ca *adj* Platonic.

platudo, da *adj* *Amér* *fam* loaded, rolling in it.

plausible *adj* - **1.** [admisible] acceptable - **2.** [posible] plausible.

playa *f* - **1.** [en el mar] beach; **ir a la ~ de vacaciones** to go on holiday to the seaside - **2.**: **~ de estacionamiento** *Amér* car park *UK*, parking lot *US*.

play-back ['pleiβak] (*pl* **play-backs**) *m*: hacer **~** to mime (the lyrics).

playero, ra *adj* beach (*antes de sust*).
➦ **playera** *f* *CAm, Méx* [camiseta] T-shirt.
➦ **playeras** *fpl* - **1.** [de deporte] tennis shoes - **2.** [para la playa] canvas shoes.

plaza *f* - **1.** [en una población] square; **~ mayor** main square - **2.** [sitio] place - **3.** [asiento] seat; **de dos ~s** two-seater (*antes de sust*) - **4.** [puesto de trabajo] position, job; **~ vacante** vacancy - **5.** [mercado] market, marketplace - **6.** TAUROM: **~ (de toros)** bull-ring.

plazo *m* - **1.** [de tiempo] period (of time); **en un ~ de un mes** within a month; **mañana termina el ~ de inscripción** the deadline for registration is tomorrow; **a corto/largo ~** [gen] in the short/long term; ECON short/long term; **a ~ fijo** ECON fixed term - **2.** [de dinero] instalment; **a ~s** in instalments, on hire purchase.

plazoleta *f* small square.

plebe *f*: la **~** *lit* & *fig* the plebs.

plebeyo, ya *adj* - **1.** HIST plebeian - **2.** [vulgar] common.

plebiscito *m* plebiscite.

plegable *adj* collapsible, foldaway; [chair] folding.

plegar *vt* to fold; [mesita, hamaca] to fold away.

plegaria *f* prayer.

pleito *m* - **1.** DER [litigio] legal action (*U*), lawsuit; [disputa] dispute - **2.** *Amér* [discusión] argument.

plenario, ria *adj* plenary.

plenilunio *m* full moon.

plenitud *f* [totalidad] completeness, fullness.

pleno, na *adj* full, complete; **en ~ día** in

broad daylight; **en plena guerra** in the middle of the war; **le dio en plena cara** she hit him right in the face; **en ~ uso de sus facultades** in full command of his faculties; **en plena forma** on top form.
➡ **pleno** *m* [reunión] plenary meeting.

pletina *f* cassette deck.

pletórico, ca *adj*: ~ **de** full of.

pliego *m* - **1.** [hoja] sheet (of paper) - **2.** [carta, documento] sealed document o letter; ~ **de condiciones** specifications *(pl)*.

pliegue *m* - **1.** [gen & GEOL] fold - **2.** [en un plisado] pleat.

plisado *m* pleating.

plomería *f* Méx, RP, Ven plumber's.

plomero *m* CAm, Carib, Méx, RP plumber.

plomizo, za *adj* [color] leaden.

plomo *m* - **1.** [metal] lead; **caer a ~** to fall o drop like a stone - **2.** [pieza de metal] lead weight - **3.** [fusible] fuse.

pluma ◇ *f* - **1.** [de ave] feather - **2.** [para escribir] (fountain) pen; HIST quill; ~ **estilográfica** fountain pen - **3.** Carib, Méx [bolígrafo] ballpoint pen. ◇ *adj inv* DEP featherweight.

plum-cake [pluŋ'keik] *(pl* **plum-cakes)** *m* fruit cake.

plumero *m* feather duster; **vérsele a alguien el ~** fam to see through sb.

plumier *(pl* **plumiers)** *m* pencil box.

plumilla *f* nib.

plumón *m* [de ave] down.

plural *adj* & *m* plural.

pluralidad *f* diversity.

pluralismo *m* pluralism.

pluralizar *vi* to generalize.

pluriempleo *m*: **hacer ~** to have more than one job.

plus *(pl* **pluses)** *m* bonus.

pluscuamperfecto *adj* & *m* pluperfect.

plusmarca *f* record.

plusvalía *f* ECON appreciation, added value.

Plutón Pluto.

pluvial *adj* rain *(antes de sust)*.

p.m. *(abrev de* **post meridiem)** p.m.

PNB *(abrev de* **producto nacional bruto)** *m* GNP.

PNV *(abrev de* **Partido Nacionalista Vasco)** *m* Basque nationalist party.

población *f* - **1.** [ciudad] town, city; [pueblo] village - **2.** Chile [chabola] shanty town - **3.** [habitantes] population.

poblado, da *adj* - **1.** [habitado] inhabited; **una zona muy poblada** a densely populated area - **2.** *fig* [lleno] full; [barba, cejas] bushy; ~ **de algo** full of sthg.
➡ **poblado** *m* settlement.

poblador, ra *m, f* settler.

poblar *vt* - **1.** [establecerse en] to settle, to colonize - **2.** *fig* [llenar]: ~ **(de)** [plantas, árboles] to plant (with); [peces etc] to stock (with) - **3.** [habitar] to inhabit.
➡ **poblarse** *vpr* - **1.** [colonizarse] to be settled with - **2.** *fig* [llenarse] to fill up; ~**se (de)** to fill up (with).

pobre ◇ *adj* poor; **¡~ hombre!** poor man!; **¡~ de mí!** poor me! ◇ *mf* [gen] poor person; **los ~s** the poor, poor people; **¡el ~!** poor thing!

pobreza *f* [escasez] poverty; ~ **de** lack o scarcity of.

pochismo *m* Amér fam language mistake caused by English influence.

pocho, cha *adj* - **1.** [persona] off-colour - **2.** [fruta] over-ripe - **3.** Méx fam [americanizado] Americanized.

pochoclo *m* Arg popcorn.

pocilga *f* lit & fig pigsty.

pocillo *m* Amér small cup.

pócima *f* [poción] potion.

poción *f* potion.

poco, ca ◇ *adj* little, not much, *(pl)* few, not many; **poca agua** not much water; **de poca importancia** of little importance; **hay ~s árboles** there aren't many trees; **pocas personas lo saben** few o not many people know it; **tenemos ~ tiempo** we don't have much time; **hace ~ tiempo** not long ago; **dame unos ~s días** give me a few days. ◇ *pron* little, not much, *(pl)* few, not many; **queda ~** there's not much left; **tengo muy ~s** I don't have very many, I have very few; **~s hay que sepan tanto** not many people know so much; **un ~ a bit; ¿me dejas un ~?** can I have a bit?; **un ~ de** a bit of; **un ~ de sentido común** a bit of common sense; **unos ~s** a few.
➡ **poco** *adv* - **1.** [escasamente] not much; **este niño come ~** this boy doesn't eat much; **es ~ común** it's not very common; **es un ~ triste** it's rather sad; **por ~** almost, nearly; - **2.** [brevemente]: **tardaré muy ~** I won't be long; **al ~ de ...** shortly after ...; **dentro de ~** soon, in a short time; **hace ~** a little while ago, not long ago; **~ a ~** [progresivamente] little by little, bit by bit; **¡~ a ~!** [despacio] steady on!, slow down!

podadora *f* Amér garden shears.

podar *vt* to prune.

podenco *m* hound.

poder ◇ *m* - **1.** [gen] power; **estar en/hacerse con el ~** to be in/to seize power; ~ **adquisitivo** purchasing power; **tener ~ de convocatoria** to be a crowd-puller; ~**es fácticos** the church, military and press - **2.** [posesión]: **estar en ~ de alguien** to be in sb's hands - **3.** *(gen pl)* [autorización] power, authorization; **dar ~es a alguien para que haga algo** to authorize sb to do sthg; **por ~es** by proxy. ◇ *vi* **- 1.** [tener facultad] can, to be able to; **no puedo decírtelo** I can't tell you, I'm unable to tell you **- 2.** [tener permiso] can, may; **no puedo salir por la noche** I'm not allowed to *o* I can't go out at night; **¿se puede fumar aquí?** may I smoke here? **- 3.** [ser capaz moralmente] can; **no podemos portarnos así con él** we can't treat him like that **- 4.** [tener posibilidad, ser posible] may, can; **podías haber cogido el tren** you could have caught the train; **puede estallar la guerra** war could *o* may break out; **¡hubiera podido invitarnos!** [expresa enfado] she could *o* might have invited us! **- 5.** *loc:* **a** *o* **hasta más no ~** as much as can be; **es avaro a más no ~** he's as miserly as can be; **no ~ más** [estar cansado] to be too tired to carry on; [estar harto de comer] to be full (up); [estar enfadado] to have had enough; **¿se puede?** may I come in? ◇ *v impers* [ser posible] may; **puede que llueva** it may *o* might rain; **¿vendrás mañana? - puede** will you come tomorrow? - I may do; **puede ser** perhaps, maybe. ◇ *vt* [ser más fuerte que] to be stronger than.

◆ **poder con** *vi + prep* **- 1.** [enfermedad, rival] to be able to overcome **- 2.** [tarea, problema] to be able to cope with **- 3.** [soportar]: **no ~ con algo/alguien** not to be able to stand sthg/sb; **no puedo con la hipocresía** I can't stand hypocrisy.

poderío *m* [poder] power.

poderoso, sa *adj* powerful.

podio, podium *m* podium.

podólogo, ga *m,f* chiropodist.

podrá ⊳ poder.

podrido, da ◇ *pp* ⊳ **pudrir.** ◇ *adj* **- 1.** rotten **- 2.** *RP* [persona]: **estoy ~** I'm fed up.

poema *m* poem.

poesía *f* **- 1.** [género literario] poetry **- 2.** [poema] poem.

poeta *mf* poet.

poético, ca *adj* poetic.

poetisa *f* female poet.

póker = póquer.

polaco, ca *adj* & *m,f* Polish.

◆ **polaco** *m* [lengua] Polish.

polar *adj* polar.

polarizar *vt fig* [miradas, atención, esfuerzo] to concentrate.

◆ **polarizarse** *vpr* [vida política, opinión pública] to become polarized.

polaroid® *f inv* Polaroid®.

polca *f* polka.

polea *f* pulley.

polémico, ca *adj* controversial.

◆ **polémica** *f* controversy.

polemizar *vi* to argue, to debate.

polen *m* pollen.

poleo *m* pennyroyal.

polera *f Arg, Chile, Perú* polo shirt.

poli *fam* ◇ *mf* cop. ◇ *f* cops *(pl)*.

polichinela *m* **- 1.** [personaje] Punchinello **- 2.** [títere] puppet, marionette.

policía ◇ *mf* policeman (*f* policewoman). ◇ *f*: **la ~** the police.

policiaco, ca, policíaco, ca *adj* police *(antes de sust)*; [novela, película] detective *(antes de sust)*.

policial *adj* police *(antes de sust)*.

polideportivo, va *adj* multi-sport; [gimnasio] multi-use.

◆ **polideportivo** *m* sports centre.

poliéster *m inv* polyester.

polietileno *m* polythene *UK*, polyethylene *US*.

polifacético, ca *adj* multifaceted, versatile.

poligamia *f* polygamy.

polígamo, ma *adj* polygamous.

poligloto, ta, polígloto, ta *adj* & *m,f* polyglot.

polígono *m* **- 1.** GEOM polygon **- 2.** [terreno]: **~ industrial/residencial** industrial/housing estate; **~ de tiro** firing range.

polilla *f* moth.

poliomelitis, polio *f inv* polio.

polipiel *f* artificial skin.

Polisario (*abrev de* **Frente Popular para la Liberación de Sakiet el Hamra y Río de Oro**) *m*: **el (Frente) ~** the Polisario Front.

politécnico, ca *adj* polytechnic.

◆ **politécnica** *f* polytechnic.

político, ca *adj* **- 1.** [de gobierno] political **- 2.** [pariente]: **hermano ~** brother-in-law; **familia política** in-laws *(pl)*.

◆ **político** *m* politician.

◆ **política** *f* **- 1.** [arte de gobernar] politics *(U)* **- 2.** [modo de gobernar, táctica] policy.

politizar *vt* to politicize.

◆ **politizarse** *vpr* to become politicized.

polivalente *adj* [vacuna, suero] polyvalent.

póliza *f* **- 1.** [de seguro] (insurance) policy **- 2.** [sello] *stamp on a document showing that a certain tax has been paid.*

polizón *m* stowaway.

polla ⊳ pollo.

pollera *f CSur* skirt.

pollería *f* poultry shop.

pollito *m* chick.

pollo, lla *m,f* ZOOL chick.

◆ **pollo** *m* CULIN chicken.

◆ **polla** *f vulg* cock, prick.

polo *m* **- 1.** [gen] pole; **ser ~s opuestos** *fig* to be poles apart - **2.** ELECTR terminal - **3.** [helado] ice lolly - **4.** [jersey] polo shirt - **5.** DEP polo.

pololo, la *m,f Chile fam* boyfriend (*f* girlfriend).

Polonia Poland.

poltrón, ona *adj* lazy.

● **poltrona** *f* easy chair.

polución *f* [contaminación] pollution.

polvareda *f* dust cloud.

polvera *f* powder compact.

polvo *m* - **1.** [en el aire] dust; **limpiar** *o* **quitar el ~** to do the dusting - **2.** [de un producto] powder; **en ~** powdered; **~s de talco** talcum powder; **~s picapica** itching powder; **estar hecho ~** *fam* to be knackered; **hacer ~ algo** to smash sthg; **limpio de ~y paja** including all charges.

● **polvos** *mpl* [maquillaje] powder (U); **ponerse ~s** to powder one's face.

pólvora *f* [sustancia explosiva] gunpowder; **correr como la ~** to spread like wildfire.

polvoriento, ta *adj* [superficie] dusty; [sustancia] powdery.

polvorín *m* munitions dump.

polvorón *m crumbly sweet made from flour, butter and sugar.*

pomada *f* ointment.

pomelo *m* [fruto] grapefruit.

pómez ➭ **piedra.**

pomo *m* knob.

pompa *f* - **1.** [suntuosidad] pomp - **2.** [ostentación] show, ostentation - **3.:** **~ (de jabón)** (soap) bubble.

● **pompas** *fpl Méx fam* behind, bottom.

● **pompas fúnebres** *fpl* [servicio] undertaker's (*sg*).

pompis *m inv fam* bottom, backside.

pompón *m* pompom.

pomposo, sa *adj* - **1.** [suntuoso] sumptuous; [ostentoso] magnificent, showy - **2.** [lenguaje] pompous.

pómulo *m* [hueso] cheekbone.

ponchar *vt CAm & Méx* to puncture.

ponche *m* punch.

poncho *m* poncho.

ponderar *vt* - **1.** [alabar] to praise - **2.** [considerar] to consider, to weigh up.

ponencia *f* [conferencia] lecture, paper; [informe] report.

poner ➭ *vt* - **1.** [gen] to put; [colocar] to place, to put - **2.** [vestir]: **~ algo a alguien** to put sthg on sb - **3.** [contribuir, invertir] to put in; **~ dinero en el negocio** to put money into the business; **~ algo de mi/tu** *etc* **parte** to do my/your *etc* bit - **4.** [hacer estar de cierta manera]: **~ a alguien en un aprieto/de mal humor** to put sb in a difficult position/in a bad mood; **le has puesto**

colorado you've made him blush - **5.** [calificar]: **~ a alguien de algo** to call sb sthg - **6.** [oponer]: **~ obstáculos a algo** to hinder sthg; **~ pegas a algo** to raise objections to sthg - **7.** [asignar - precio, medida] to fix, to settle; [- multa, tarea] to give; **le pusieron Mario** they called him Mario - **8.** [TELECOM - telegrama, fax] to send; [- conferencia] to make; **¿me pones con él?** can you put me through to him? - **9.** [conectar - televisión etc] to switch *o* put on; [- despertador] to set; [- instalación, gas] to put in - **10.** CIN, TEATR & TV to show; **¿qué ponen en la tele?** what's on the telly? - **11.** [montar - negocio] to set up; **ha puesto una tienda** she has opened a shop - **12.** [decorar] to do up; **han puesto su casa con mucho lujo** they've done up their house in real style - **13.** [suponer] to suppose; **pongamos que sucedió así** (let's) suppose that's what happened; **pon que necesitemos cinco días** suppose we need five days; **poniendo que todo salga bien** assuming everything is going to plan - **14.** [decir] to say; **¿qué pone ahí?** what does it say? - **15.** [huevo] to lay. ➭ *vi* [ave] to lay (eggs).

● **ponerse** ➭ *vpr* - **1.** [colocarse] to put o.s.; **~se de pie** to stand up; **ponte en la ventana** stand by the window - **2.** [ropa, gafas, maquillaje] to put on - **3.** [estar de cierta manera] to go, to become; **se puso rojo de ira** he went red with anger; **se puso colorado** he blushed; **se puso muy guapa** she made herself attractive - **4.** [iniciar]: **~se a hacer algo** to start doing sthg - **5.** [de salud]: **~se malo** *o* **enfermo** to fall ill; **~se bien** to get better - **6.** [llenarse]: **~se de algo** to get covered in sthg; **se puso de barro hasta las rodillas** he got covered in mud up to the knees - **7.** [suj: astro] to set - **8.** [llegar]: **~se en** to get to. ➭ *v impers Amér fam* [parecer]: **se me pone que ...** it seems to me that ...

poney = poni.

pongo *etc* ➭ **poner.**

poni, poney ['poni] *m* pony.

poniente *m* [occidente] West; [viento] west wind.

pontífice *m* Pope, Pontiff.

pop *adj* pop.

popa *f* stern.

pope *m fam fig* [pez gordo] big shot.

popote *m Méx* drinking straw.

populacho *m despec* mob, masses (*pl*).

popular *adj* - **1.** [del pueblo] of the people; [arte, música] folk - **2.** [famoso] popular.

popularidad *f* popularity; **gozar de ~** to be popular.

popularizar *vt* to popularize.

● **popularizarse** *vpr* to become popular.

popurrí *m* potpourri.

póquer, póker *m* [juego] poker.

por *prep* - **1.** [causa] because of; **se enfadó ~ tu comportamiento** she got angry because of your behaviour - **2.** [finalidad] *(antes de infin)* (in order) to; *(antes de sust, pron)* for; **lo hizo ~ complacerte** he did it to please you; **lo hice ~ ella** I did it for her - **3.** [medio, modo, agente] by; **~ mensajero/fax** by courier/fax; **~ escrito** in writing; **lo cogieron ~ el brazo** they took him by the arm; **el récord fue batido ~ el atleta** the record was broken by the athlete - **4.** [tiempo aproximado]: **creo que la boda será ~ abril** I think the wedding will be some time in April - **5.** [tiempo concreto]: **~ la mañana/tarde** in the morning/afternoon; **~ la noche** at night; **ayer salimos ~ la noche** we went out last night; **~ unos días** for a few days - **6.** [lugar - aproximadamente en]: **¿~ dónde vive?** whereabouts does he live?; **vive ~ las afueras** he lives somewhere on the outskirts; **había papeles ~ el suelo** there were papers all over the floor - **7.** [lugar - a través de] through; **iba paseando ~ el bosque/la calle** she was walking through the forest/along the street; **pasar ~ la aduana** to go through customs - **8.** [a cambio de, en lugar de] for; **lo ha comprado ~ poco dinero** she bought it for very little; **cambió el coche ~ la moto** he exchanged his car for a motorbike; **él lo hará ~ mí** he'll do it for me - **9.** [distribución] per; **dos euros ~ unidad** 2 euros each; **20 kms ~ hora** 20 km an *o* per hour - **10.** MAT : **dos ~ dos igual a cuatro** two times two is four - **11.** [en busca del] for; **baja ~ tabaco** go down to the shops for some cigarettes, go down to get some cigarettes; **a ~ for; vino a ~ las entradas** she came for the tickets - **12.** [concesión]: **~ más o mucho que lo intentes no lo conseguirás** however hard you try *o* try as you might, you'll never manage it; **no me cae bien, ~ (muy) simpático que te parezca** you may think he's nice, but I don't like him.

➤ **por qué** *pron* why; **¿~ qué lo dijo?** why did she say it?; **¿~ qué no vienes?** why don't you come?

porcelana *f* [material] porcelain, china.

porcentaje *m* percentage; **trabaja a ~** he works on a commission basis.

porche *m* [soportal] arcade; [entrada] porch.

porción *f* portion, piece.

pordiosero, ra *m,f* beggar.

porfía *f* [insistencia] persistence; [tozudez] stubbornness.

porfiar *vi* [empeñarse]: **~ en** to be insistent on.

pormenor *(gen pl) m* detail; **entrar en ~es** to go into detail.

porno *adj fam* porno.

pornografía *f* pornography.

pornográfico, ca *adj* pornographic.

poro *m* pore.

poroso, sa *adj* porous.

poroto *m Andes, RP* kidney bean.

porque *conj* - **1.** [debido a que] because; **¿por qué lo hiciste? – ~ sí** why did you do it? – just because - **2.** [para que] so that, in order that.

porqué *m* reason; **el ~ de** the reason for.

porquería *f* - **1.** [suciedad] filth - **2.** [cosa de mala calidad] rubbish *(U)*.

porra *f* - **1.** [palo] club; [de policía] truncheon - **2.** *loc:* **mandar a alguien a la ~** *fam* to tell sb to go to hell; **¡y una ~!** like hell!

porrazo *m* [golpe] bang, blow; [caída] bump.

porro *m fam* [de droga] joint.

porrón *m glass wine jar used for drinking wine from its long spout.*

portaaviones = **portaviones**.

portada *f* - **1.** [de libro] title page; [de revista] (front) cover; [de periódico] front page - **2.** [de disco] sleeve.

portador, ra *m,f* carrier, bearer; **al ~** COM to the bearer.

portaequipajes *m inv* - **1.** [maletero] boot *UK*, trunk *US* - **2.** [baca] roofrack.

portafolios *m inv*, **portafolio** *m* [carpeta] file; [maletín] attaché case.

portal *m* [entrada] entrance hall; [puerta] main door.

portalámparas *m inv* socket.

portamonedas *m inv* purse.

portar *vt* to carry.

➤ **portarse** *vpr* to behave; **se ha portado bien conmigo** she has treated me well; **~se mal** to misbehave.

portátil *adj* portable.

portaviones, portaaviones *m inv* aircraft carrier.

portavoz *mf* [persona] spokesman *(f* spokeswoman).

portazo *m:* **dar un ~** to slam the door.

porte *m* - **1.** *(gen pl)* [gasto de transporte] carriage, transport costs *(pl)*; **~ debido/pagado** COM carriage due/paid - **2.** [transporte] carriage, transport - **3.** [aspecto] bearing, demeanour.

portento *m* wonder, marvel.

portentoso, sa *adj* wonderful, amazing.

porteño, ña *adj* from the city of Buenos Aires.

portería *f* - **1.** [de casa, colegio] caretaker's office *o* lodge; [de hotel, ministerio] porter's office *o* lodge - **2.** DEP goal, goalmouth.

portero, ra *m,f* - **1.** [de casa, colegio] caretaker *UK*, super(intendant) *US*; [de hotel, ministerio] porter; ~ **automático** *o* **electrónico** *o* **eléctrico** entry-phone - **2.** DEP goal-keeper.

pórtico *m* - **1.** [fachada] portico - **2.** [arcada] arcade.

portuario, ria *adj* port *(antes de sust)*; [de los muelles] dock *(antes de sust)*; **trabajador** ~ docker.

Portugal Portugal.

portugués, esa *adj* & *m,f* Portuguese.
➡ **portugués** *m* [lengua] Portuguese.

porvenir *m* future.

pos
➡ **en pos de** *loc prep* - **1.** [detrás de] behind - **2.** [en busca de] after; **correr en ~ de alguien** to run after sb.

posada *f* - **1.** [fonda] inn, guest house - **2.** [hospedaje] lodging, accommodation.

posaderas *fpl fam* backside *(sg)*, bottom *(sg)*.

posar ◇ *vt* to put *o* lay down; [mano, mirada] to rest. ◇ *vi* to pose.
➡ **posarse** *vpr* - **1.** [gen] to settle - **2.** [pájaro] to perch; [nave, helicóptero] to come down.

posavasos *m inv* coaster; [de cartón] beer mat.

posdata, postdata *f* postscript.

pose *f* pose; **adoptar una ~** to strike a pose.

poseedor, ra *m,f* owner; [de cargo, acciones, récord] holder.

poseer *vt* [ser dueño de] to own; [estar en poder de] to have, to possess.

poseído, da *adj*: ~ **por** possessed by.

posesión *f* possession.

posesivo, va *adj* possessive.

poseso, sa *m,f* possessed person.

posgraduado, da, postgraduado, da *adj* & *m,f* postgraduate.

posguerra, postguerra *f* post-war period.

posibilidad *f* possibility, chance; **cabe la ~ de que ...** there is a chance that ...

posibilitar *vt* to make possible.

posible *adj* possible; **es ~ que llueva** it could rain; **dentro de lo ~, en lo ~** as far as possible; **de ser ~** if possible; **hacer (todo) lo ~** to do everything possible; **lo antes ~** as soon as possible; **¡no es ~!** surely not!

posición *f* - **1.** [gen] position; **en ~ de descanso** standing at ease - **2.** [categoría - social] status *(U)*; **de buena ~** of high social status; [- económica] situation - **3.** DEP position.

posicionarse *vpr* to take a position *o* stance.

positivo, va *adj* [gen & ELECTR] positive.

poso *m* sediment; *fig* trace.

posponer *vt* - **1.** [relegar] to put behind, to relegate - **2.** [aplazar] to postpone.

pospuesto, ta *pp* ▷ **posponer**.

posta
➡ **a posta** *loc adv* on purpose.

postal ◇ *adj* postal. ◇ *f* postcard.

postdata = **posdata**.

poste *m* post, pole; ~ **de alta tensión** electricity pylon; DEP post.

póster (*pl* **posters**) *m* poster.

postergar *vt* - **1.** [retrasar] to postpone - **2.** [relegar] to put behind, to relegate.

posteridad *f* - **1.** [generación futura] posterity - **2.** [futuro] future.

posterior *adj* - **1.** [en el espacio] rear, back - **2.** [en el tiempo] subsequent, later; ~ **a** subsequent to, after.

posteriori
➡ **a posteriori** *loc adv* later, afterwards.

posterioridad *f*: **con ~** later, subsequently.

postgraduado = **posgraduado**.

postguerra = **posguerra**.

postigo *m* [contraventana] shutter.

postín *m* showiness, boastfulness; **darse ~** to show off; **de ~** posh.

postizo, za *adj* [falso] false.
➡ **postizo** *m* hairpiece.

postor, ra *m,f* bidder.

postre *m* dessert, pudding; **a la ~** *fig* in the end.

postrero, ra *adj (antes de sust masculino sg:* **postrer***) culto* last.

postrimerías *fpl* final stages.

postulado *m* postulate.

postular ◇ *vt* [exigir] to call for. ◇ *vi* [para colectas] to collect.

póstumo, ma *adj* posthumous.

postura *f* - **1.** [posición] position, posture - **2.** [actitud] attitude, stance; **tomar ~** to adopt an attitude.

potable *adj* - **1.** [bebible] drinkable; **agua ~** drinking water.

potaje *m* [CULIN - guiso] vegetable stew; [- sopa] vegetable soup.

potasio *m* potassium.

pote *m* pot.

potencia *f* [gen, MAT & POLÍT] power; **tiene mucha ~** it's very powerful.

potencial ◇ *adj* [gen & FÍS] potential. ◇ *m* - **1.** [fuerza] power - **2.** [posibilidades] potential - **3.** GRAM conditional.

potenciar *vt* - **1.** [fomentar] to encourage, to promote - **2.** [reforzar] to boost, to strengthen.

potente *adj* powerful.

potra ▷ **potro**.

potrero *m Amér* [prado] field, pasture.

potro, tra *m, f* ZOOL colt (*f* filly).

→ **potro** *m* DEP vaulting horse.

pozo *m* well; [de mina] shaft.

PP (*abrev de* **Partido Popular**) *m Spanish political party to the right of the political spectrum.*

práctica ▷ **práctico**.

practicante ◇ *adj* practising. ◇ *mf* -**1.** [de deporte] practitioner; [de religión] practising member of a Church -**2.** MED medical assistant.

practicar ◇ *vt* -**1.** [gen] to practise; [deporte] to play -**2.** [realizar] to carry out, to perform. ◇ *vi* to practise.

práctico, ca *adj* practical.

→ **práctica** *f* -**1.** [gen] practice; [de un deporte] playing; **en la práctica** in practice; **prácticas de tiro** target practice -**2.** [clase no teórica] practical.

pradera *f* large meadow, prairie.

prado *m* meadow.

→ **Prado** *m*: **el (Museo del) Prado** the Prado (Museum).

Praga Prague.

pragmático, ca ◇ *adj* pragmatic. ◇ *m, f* [persona] pragmatist.

pral. *abrev de* **principal**.

praliné *m* praline.

preacuerdo *m* draft agreement.

preámbulo *m* [introducción - de libro] foreword, preface; [- de congreso, conferencia] introduction, preamble.

precalentar *vt* -**1.** CULIN to pre-heat -**2.** DEP to warm up.

precario, ria *adj* precarious.

precaución *f* -**1.** [prudencia] caution, care -**2.** [medida] precaution; **tomar precauciones** to take precautions.

precaver *vt* to guard against.

→ **precaverse** *vpr* to take precautions.

precavido, da *adj* [prevenido] prudent; **es muy ~** he always comes prepared.

precedente ◇ *adj* previous, preceding. ◇ *m* precedent.

preceder *vt* to go before, to precede.

preceptivo, va *adj* obligatory, compulsory.

→ **preceptiva** *f* rules (*pl*).

precepto *m* precept.

preciado, da *adj* valuable, prized.

preciarse *vpr* to have self-respect; **~ de** to be proud of.

precintar *vt* to seal.

precinto *m* seal.

precio *m* lit & fig price; **a cualquier ~** at any price; **poner ~ a la cabeza de alguien** to put a price on sb's head; **¿qué ~ tiene esto?** how much is this?; **subir/bajar los ~s** to raise/lower prices; **al ~ de** fig at the cost of; **~ de fábrica/de coste** factory/cost

price; **~ de salida** starting price; **~ de venta (al público)** retail price.

preciosidad *f* [cosa bonita]: **¡es una ~!** it's lovely o beautiful!

precioso, sa *adj* -**1.** [valioso] precious -**2.** [bonito] lovely, beautiful.

precipicio *m* precipice.

precipitación *f* -**1.** [apresuramiento] haste -**2.** [lluvia] rainfall (*U*).

precipitado, da *adj* hasty.

precipitar *vt* -**1.** [arrojar] to throw o hurl down -**2.** [acelerar] to hasten, to speed up.

→ **precipitarse** *vpr* -**1.** [caer] to plunge (down) -**2.** [acelerarse - acontecimientos etc] to speed up -**3.** [apresurarse]: **~se (hacia)** to rush (towards) -**4.** [obrar irreflexivamente] to act rashly.

precisamente *adv* [justamente]: **¡precisamente!** exactly!, precisely!; **~ por eso** for that very reason; **~ tú lo sugeriste** in fact it was you who suggested it.

precisar *vt* -**1.** [determinar] to fix, to set; [aclarar] to specify exactly -**2.** [necesitar] to need, to require.

precisión *f* accuracy, precision.

preciso, sa *adj* -**1.** [determinado, conciso] precise -**2.** [necesario]: **ser ~ para (algo/ hacer algo)** to be necessary (for sthg/to do sthg); **es ~ que vengas** you must come -**3.** [justo] just; **en este ~ momento** at this very moment.

precocinado, da *adj* pre-cooked.

→ **precocinado** *m* precooked dish.

preconcebido, da *adj* [idea] preconceived; [plan] drawn up in advance.

preconcebir *vt* to draw up in advance.

preconizar *vt* to recommend, to advise.

precoz *adj* [persona] precocious.

precursor, ra *m, f* precursor.

predecesor, ra *m, f* predecessor.

predecir *vt* to predict.

predestinado, da *adj*: **~ (a)** predestined (to).

predestinar *vt* to predestine.

predeterminar *vt* to predetermine.

predicado *m* GRAM predicate.

predicador, ra *m, f* preacher.

predicar *vt* & *vi* to preach.

predicción *f* prediction; [del tiempo] forecast.

predicho, cha *pp* ▷ **predecir**.

predilección *f*: **~ (por)** preference (for).

predilecto, ta *adj* favourite.

predisponer *vt*: **~ (a)** to predispose (to).

predisposición *f* -**1.** [aptitud]: **~ para** aptitude for -**2.** [tendencia]: **~ a** predisposition to.

predispuesto, ta ◇ *pp* ▷ **predisponer**. ◇ *adj*: **~ (a)** predisposed (to).

predominante *adj* predominant; [viento, actitudes] prevailing.

predominar *vi*: ~ **(sobre)** to predominate *o* prevail (over).

predominio *m* preponderance, predominance *(U)*.

preelectoral *adj* pre-election *(antes de sust)*.

preeminente *adj* preeminent.

preescolar *adj* nursery *(antes de sust)*, pre-school.

prefabricado, da *adj* prefabricated.

prefabricar *vt* to prefabricate.

prefacio *m* preface.

preferencia *f* preference; **con** *o* **de** ~ preferably; **dar preferencia** ~ **(a)** to give priority (to); **tener** ~ AUTOM to have right of way; **tener** ~ **por** to have a preference for.

preferente *adj* preferential.

preferentemente *adv* preferably.

preferible *adj*: ~ **(a)** preferable (to).

preferido, da *adj* favourite.

preferir *vt*: ~ **algo (a algo)** to prefer sthg (to sthg); **prefiero que vengas** I'd rather you came.

prefijo *m* - **1.** GRAM prefix - **2.** TELECOM (telephone) dialling code.

pregón *m* [discurso] speech; [bando] proclamation, announcement.

pregonar *vt* - **1.** [bando etc] to proclaim, to announce - **2.** *fig* [secreto] to spread about.

pregunta *f* question; **hacer una** ~ to ask a question.

preguntar ◇ *vt* to ask; ~ **algo a alguien** to ask sb sthg. ◇ *vi*: ~ **por** to ask about *o* after.

◆ **preguntarse** *vpr*: ~**se (si)** to wonder (whether).

prehistoria *f* prehistory.

prehistórico, ca *adj* prehistoric.

prejuicio *m* prejudice.

preliminar ◇ *adj* preliminary. ◇ *m (gen pl)* preliminary.

preludio *m* [gen & MÚS] prelude.

premamá *adj inv* maternity.

prematrimonial *adj* premarital.

prematuro, ra *adj* premature.

premeditación *f* premeditation.

premeditar *vt* to think out in advance.

premiar *vt* - **1.** [recompensar] to reward - **2.** [dar un premio a] to give a prize to.

premier *(pl* **premiers)** *m* British prime minister.

premio *m* [en competición] prize; [recompensa] reward; ~ **gordo** first prize.

premisa *f* premise.

premonición *f* premonition.

premura *f* [urgencia] haste.

prenatal *adj* prenatal, antenatal.

prenda *f* - **1.** [vestido] garment, article of clothing - **2.** [garantía] pledge; **dejar algo en** ~ to leave sthg as a pledge - **3.** [de un juego] forfeit; **jugar a las** ~**s** to play forfeits - **4.** *loc*: **no soltar** ~ not to say a word.

prendarse *vpr* to fall in love with.

prender ◇ *vt* - **1.** [arrestar] to arrest, to apprehend - **2.** [sujetar] to fasten - **3.** [encender] to light - **4.** [agarrar] to grip. ◇ *vi* [arder] to catch (fire).

◆ **prenderse** *vpr* [arder] to catch fire.

prendido, da *adj* caught.

prensa *f* - **1.** [gen] press; ~ **del corazón** romantic magazines *(pl)* - **2.** [imprenta] printing press.

prensar *vt* to press.

preñada, da *adj* - **1.** [mujer] pregnant; **quedarse preñada** to get pregnant - **2.** *fig* [lleno]: ~ **de** full of.

preocupación *f* concern, worry.

preocupado, da *adj*: ~ **(por)** worried *o* concerned (about).

preocupar *vt* - **1.** [inquietar] to worry - **2.** [importar] to bother.

◆ **preocuparse** *vpr* - **1.** [inquietarse]: ~**se (por)** to worry (about), to be worried (about) - **2.** [encargarse]: ~**se de algo** to take care of sthg; ~**se de hacer algo** to see to it that sthg is done; ~**se de que ...** to make sure that ...

preparación *f* - **1.** [gen] preparation - **2.** [conocimientos] training.

preparado, da *adj* - **1.** [dispuesto] ready; [de antemano] prepared - **2.** CULIN ready-cooked.

◆ **preparado** *m* FARM preparation.

preparar *vt* - **1.** [gen] to prepare; [trampa] to set, to lay; [maletas] to pack - **2.** [examen] to prepare for - **3.** DEP to train.

◆ **prepararse** *vpr*: ~**se (para algo)** to prepare o.s. *o* get ready (for sthg); ~**se para hacer algo** to prepare *o* get ready to do sthg.

preparativo, va *adj* preparatory, preliminary.

◆ **preparativos** *mpl* preparations.

preposición *f* preposition.

prepotente *adj* [arrogante] domineering, overbearing.

prerrogativa *f* prerogative.

presa *f* - **1.** [captura - de cazador] catch; [- de animal] prey; **hacer** ~ **en alguien** to seize *o* grip sb; **ser** ~ **de** to be prey to; **ser** ~ **del pánico** to be panic-stricken - **2.** [dique] dam.

presagiar *vt* [felicidad, futuro] to foretell; [tormenta, problemas] to warn of.

presagio *m* - **1.** [premonición] premonition - **2.** [señal] omen; **buen/mal** ~ good/bad omen.

prescindir ◆ **prescindir de** *vi* - **1.** [renunciar a] to do without - **2.** [omitir] to dispense with - **3**. [no tener en cuenta] to disregard.

prescribir ◇ *vt* to prescribe. ◇ *vi* - **1**. [ordenar] to prescribe - **2**. DER to expire, to lapse.

prescripción *f* prescription.

prescrito, ta *pp* ▷ **prescribir**.

presencia *f* [asistencia, aspecto] presence; **en ∼ de** in the presence of.

➤ **presencia de ánimo** *f* presence of mind.

presencial ▷ **testigo**.

presenciar *vt* [asistir] to be present at; [ser testigo de] to witness.

presentación *f* - **1**. [gen] presentation - **2**. [entre personas] introduction.

presentador, ra *m,f* presenter.

presentar *vt* - **1**. [gen] to present; [dimisión] to tender; [tesis, pruebas, propuesta] to hand in, to submit; [solicitud, recurso, denuncia] to lodge; [moción] to propose; [libro, disco] to launch - **2**. [ofrecer - ventajas, novedades] to offer; [- disculpas, excusas] to make; [- respetos] to pay - **3**. [persona, amigos etc] to introduce - **4**. [enseñar] to show - **5**. [tener - aspecto etc] to have, to show; **presenta difícil solución** it's going to be difficult to solve - **6**. [proponer]: **∼ a alguien para** to propose sb for, to put sb forward for.

➤ **presentarse** *vpr* - **1**. [aparecer] to turn up, to appear - **2**. [en juzgado, comisaría]: **∼se (en)** to report (to); **∼se a un examen** to sit an exam - **3**. [darse a conocer] to introduce o.s. - **4**. [para un cargo]: **∼se (a)** to stand O run (for) - **5**. [futuro] to appear, to look - **6**. [problema etc] to arise, to come up.

presente ◇ *adj* - **1**. [gen] present; **aquí ∼** here present; **tener ∼** [recordar] to remember; [tener en cuenta] to bear in mind - **2**. [en curso]: **del ∼ mes** of this month. ◇ *mf* [escrito]: **por la ∼ le informo ...** I hereby inform you ... ◇ *m* - **1**. [gen & GRAM] present - **2**. [regalo] gift, present - **3**. [corriente]: **el ∼** [mes] the current month; [año] the current year.

presentimiento *m* presentiment, feeling.

presentir *vt* to foresee; **∼ que algo va a pasar** to have a feeling that sthg is going to happen; **∼ lo peor** to fear the worst.

preservar *vt* to protect; **∼ algo/alguien de algo** to protect sthg/sb from sthg.

preservativo *m* condom.

presidencia *f* [de nación] presidency; [de asamblea, empresa] chairmanship.

presidenciable *mf Amér* potential presidential candidate.

presidente, ta *m,f* [de nación] president; [de asamblea, empresa] chairman (*f* chairwoman); **∼ (del gobierno)** ≃ prime minister; **∼ de mesa** chief scrutineer.

presidiario, ria *m,f* convict.

presidio *m* prison.

presidir *vt* - **1**. [ser presidente de] to preside over; [reunión] to chair - **2**. [predominar] to dominate.

presión *f* pressure; **altas/bajas presiones** areas of high/low pressure.

presionar *vt* - **1**. [apretar] to press - **2**. *fig* [coaccionar] to pressurize, to put pressure on.

preso, sa *m,f* prisoner.

prestación *f* [de servicio - acción] provision; [- resultado] service.

➤ **prestaciones** *fpl* - **1**. [servicio social] benefits - **2**. [de coche etc] performance features.

prestado, da *adj* on loan; **dar ∼ algo** to lend sthg; **pedir/tomar ∼ algo** to borrow sthg; **vivir de ∼** to live off other people.

prestamista *mf* moneylender.

préstamo *m* - **1**. [acción - de prestar] lending; [- de pedir prestado] borrowing - **2**. [cantidad] loan.

prestar *vt* - **1**. [dejar - dinero etc] to lend, to loan - **2**. [dar - ayuda etc] to give, to offer; [- servicio] to offer, to provide; [- atención] to pay; [- declaración, juramento] to make.

➤ **prestarse a** *vpr* - **1**. [ofrecerse a] to offer to - **2**. [acceder a] to consent to - **3**. [dar motivo a] to be open to.

presteza *f* promptness, speed.

prestidigitador, ra *m,f* conjuror.

prestigio *m* prestige.

prestigioso, sa *adj* prestigious.

presto, ta *adj* [dispuesto]: **∼ (a)** ready (to).

presumible *adj* probable, likely.

presumido, da *adj* conceited, vain.

presumir ◇ *vt* [suponer] to presume, to assume; **es de ∼ que irán** presumably they'll go. ◇ *vi* - **1**. [jactarse] to show off - **2**. [ser vanidoso] to be conceited O vain.

presunción *f* - **1**. [suposición] presumption - **2**. [vanidad] conceit, vanity.

presunto, ta *adj* presumed, supposed; [criminal, robo etc] alleged, suspected.

presuntuoso, sa *adj* [vanidoso] conceited; [pretencioso] pretentious.

presuponer *vt* to presuppose.

presupuesto, ta *pp* ▷ **presuponer**.

➤ **presupuesto** *m* - **1**. [cálculo] budget; [de costo] estimate - **2**. [suposición] assumption.

prêt-à-porter [pretapor'te] (*pl* prêts-à-porter) *m* off-the-peg clothing.

pretencioso, sa *adj* [persona] pretentious; [cosa] showy.

pretender *vt* - **1**. [intentar]: **∼ hacer algo** to try to do sthg - **2**. [aspirar a]: **∼ hacer algo** to aspire O want to do sthg; **∼ que alguien**

haga algo to want sb to do sthg; ¿qué pretendes decir? what do you mean? - 3. [afirmar] to claim - 4. [cortejar] to court.

pretendido, da *adj* supposed.

pretendiente ⬦ *mf* - 1. [aspirante]: ~ (a) candidate (for) - 2. [a un trono]: ~ (a) pretender (to). ⬦ *m* [a una mujer] suitor.

pretensión *f* - 1. [intención] aim, intention - 2. [aspiración] aspiration - 3. [supuesto derecho]: ~ (a *o* sobre) claim (to) - 4. [afirmación] claim - 5. *(gen pl)* [exigencia] demand - 6. *(gen pl)* [presuntuosidad] pretentiousness; **sin pretensiones** unpretentious.

pretérito, ta *adj* past.
➥ **pretérito** *m* GRAM preterite, past.

pretexto *m* pretext, excuse.

prevalecer *vi*: ~ (sobre) to prevail (over).

prevaler *vi*: ~ (sobre) to prevail (over).

prevención *f* [acción] prevention; [medida] precaution.

prevenido, da *adj* - 1. [previsor]: ser ~ to be cautious - 2. [avisado, dispuesto]: estar ~ to be prepared.

prevenir *vt* - 1. [evitar] to prevent; más vale ~ que curar *proverb* prevention is better than cure *proverb* - 2. [avisar] to warn - 3. [prever] to foresee, to anticipate - 4. [predisponer]: ~ a alguien contra algo/alguien to prejudice sb against sthg/sb.

preventivo, va *adj* [medicina, prisión] preventive; [medida] precautionary.

prever ⬦ *vt* - 1. [conjeturar] to foresee, to anticipate - 2. [planear] to plan - 3. [predecir] to forecast. ⬦ *vi*: como era de ~ as was to be expected.

previniera *etc* ⬦ **prevenir**.

previo, via *adj* prior; ~ pago de multa on payment of a fine.

previó *etc* ⬦ **prever**.

previsible *adj* foreseeable.

previsión *f* - 1. [predicción] forecast - 2. [visión de futuro] foresight - 3. *Andes, RP* [social] social security.

previsor, ra *adj* prudent, farsighted.

previsto, ta ⬦ *pp* ⬦ **prever**. ⬦ *adj* [conjeturado] predicted; [planeado] forecast, expected, planned.

prieto, ta *adj* - 1. [ceñido] tight - 2. *Méx fam* [moreno] dark-haired.

prima ⬦ **primo**.

primacía *f* primacy; **tener** ~ **sobre algo** to take priority over sthg.

primar *vi*: ~ (sobre) to have priority (over).

primario, ria *adj* primary; *fig* primitive.

primavera *f* [estación] spring.

primaveral *adj* spring *(antes de sust).*

primer, primera ⬦ **primero**.

primerizo, za *m,f* [principiante] beginner.

primero, ra ⬦ *núm adj antes de sust masculino sg: primer* - 1. [para ordenar] first; **el** ~ **de mayo** the first of May - 2. [en importancia] main, basic; **lo** ~ the most important *o* main thing. ⬦ *núm m y f* - 1. [en orden]: **el** ~ the first one; **llegó el** ~ he came first; **es el** ~ **de la clase** he's top of the class; **a** ~**s de mes** at the beginning of the month - 2. [mencionado antes]: **vinieron Pedro y Juan, el** ~ **con ...** Pedro and Juan arrived, the former with ...
➥ **primero** ⬦ *adv* - 1. [en primer lugar] first - 2. [antes, todo menos]: ~ **morir que traicionarle** I'd rather die than betray him. ⬦ *m* - 1. [piso] first floor - 2. [curso] first year.
➥ **primera** *f* - 1. AUTOM first (gear) - 2. AERON & FERROC first class - 3. DEP first division - 4. *loc*: **de primera** first-class, excellent.

primicia *f* scoop, exclusive.

primitivo, va *adj* - 1. [gen] primitive - 2. [original] original.

primo, ma *m,f* - 1. [pariente] cousin; ~ **hermano** first cousin - 2. *fam* [tonto] sucker; **hacer el** ~ to be taken for a ride.
➥ **prima** *f* - 1. [paga extra] bonus - 2. [de un seguro] premium.
➥ **prima dona** *f* prima donna.

primogénito, ta *adj* & *m,f* first-born.

primor *m* fine thing.

primordial *adj* fundamental.

primoroso, sa *adj* - 1. [delicado] exquisite, fine - 2. [hábil] skilful.

princesa *f* princess.

principado *m* principality.

principal ⬦ *adj* main, principal; [puerta] front.

príncipe *m* prince.

principiante ⬦ *adj* novice, inexperienced. ⬦ *mf* novice, beginner.

principio *m* - 1. [comienzo] beginning, start; **a** ~**s de** at the beginning of; **a** ~**s de siglo** at the turn of the century; **en un** ~ at first - 2. [fundamento, ley] principle; **en** ~ in principle; **por** ~ on principle - 3. [origen] origin, source - 4. [elemento] element.
➥ **principios** *mpl* - 1. [reglas de conducta] principles - 2. [nociones] rudiments, first principles.

pringar ⬦ *vt* - 1. [ensuciar] to make greasy - 2. [mojar] to dip.

pringoso, sa *adj* [grasiento] greasy; [pegajoso] sticky.

pringue *m* [suciedad] muck, dirt; [grasa] grease.

priori ➥ **a priori** *loc adv* in advance, a priori.

prioridad *f* priority; AUTOM right of way.

prioritario, ria *adj* priority *(antes de sust).*

prisa *f* haste, hurry; **a** *o* **de** ~ quickly; **correr** ~ to be urgent; **darse** ~ to hurry (up); **meter** ~ **a alguien** to hurry *o* rush sb; **tener** ~ to be in a hurry.

prisión *f* - **1.** [cárcel] prison - **2.** [encarcelamiento] imprisonment.

prisionero, ra *m,f* prisoner; **hacer** ~ **a alguien** to take sb prisoner.

prisma *m* - **1.** FÍS & GEOM prism - **2.** *fig* [perspectiva] viewpoint, perspective.

prismáticos *mpl* binoculars.

privación *f* [gen] deprivation; [de libertad] loss.

privado, da *adj* private; **en** ~ in private.

privar *vt* [quitar]: ~ **a alguien/algo de** to deprive sb/sthg of.

◆ **privarse de** *vpr* to go without.

privativo, va *adj* exclusive.

privilegiado, da *adj* - **1.** [favorecido] privileged - **2.** [excepcional] exceptional.

privilegiar *vt* [persona] to favour.

privilegio *m* privilege.

pro ◇ *prep* for, supporting; **una asociación** ~ **derechos humanos** a human rights organization. ◇ *m* advantage; **los** ~**s y los contras** the pros and cons.

◆ **en pro de** *loc prep* for, in support of.

proa *f* NÁUT prow, bows *(pl)*; AERON nose.

probabilidad *f* probability; **con toda** ~ in all probability; [oportunidad] likelihood, chance.

probable *adj* probable, likely; **es** ~ **que lluevа** it'll probably rain.

probador *m* fitting room.

probar ◇ *vt* - **1.** [demostrar, indicar] to prove - **2.** [comprobar] to test, to check - **3.** [experimentar] to try - **4.** [degustar] to taste, to try. ◇ *vi*: ~ **a hacer algo** to try to do sthg.

◆ **probarse** *vpr* [ropa] to try on.

probeta *f* test tube.

problema *m* problem.

problemático, ca *adj* problematic.

◆ **problemática** *f* problems *(pl)*.

procedencia *f* - **1.** [origen] origin - **2.** [punto de partida] point of departure; **con** ~ **de** (arriving) from.

procedente *adj* - **1.** [originario]: ~ **de** [gen] originating in; AERON & FERROC (arriving) from - **2.** [oportuno] appropriate; DER fitting, right and proper.

proceder ◇ *m* conduct, behaviour. ◇ *vi* - **1.** [originarse]: ~ **de** to come from - **2.** [actuar]: ~ **(con)** to act (with) - **3.** [empezar]: ~ **(a algo/a hacer algo)** to proceed (with sthg/to do sthg) - **4.** [ser oportuno] to be appropriate.

procedimiento *m* - **1.** [método] procedure, method - **2.** DER proceedings *(pl)*.

procesado, da *m,f* accused, defendant.

procesador *m* INFORM processor; ~ **Pentium**® Pentium® processor; ~ **de textos** word processor.

procesar *vt* - **1.** DER to prosecute - **2.** INFORM to process.

procesión *f* RELIG & *fig* procession.

proceso *m* - **1.** [gen] process - **2.** [desarrollo, intervalo] course - **3.** [DER - juicio] trial; [- causa] lawsuit.

proclama *f* proclamation.

proclamar *vt* - **1.** [nombrar] to proclaim - **2.** [anunciar] to declare.

◆ **proclamarse** *vpr* - **1.** [nombrarse] to proclaim o.s. - **2.** [conseguir un título]: ~**se campeón** to become champion.

proclive *adj*: ~ **a** prone to.

procreación *f* procreation.

procrear *vi* to procreate.

procurador, ra *m,f* DER attorney.

procuraduría *f Méx* ministry of justice.

procurar *vt* - **1.** [intentar]: ~ **hacer algo** to try to do sthg; ~ **que ...** to make sure that ... - **2.** [proporcionar] to get, to secure.

◆ **procurarse** *vpr* to get, to obtain (for o.s.).

prodigar *vt*: ~ **algo a alguien** to lavish sthg on sb.

prodigio *m* [suceso] miracle; [persona] wonder, prodigy.

prodigioso, sa *adj* - **1.** [sobrenatural] miraculous - **2.** [extraordinario] wonderful, marvellous.

pródigo, ga *adj* [generoso] generous, lavish.

producción *f* - **1.** [gen & CIN] production; ~ **en serie** ECON mass production - **2.** [productos] products *(pl)*.

producir *vt* - **1.** [gen & CIN] to produce - **2.** [causar] to cause, to give rise to - **3.** [interés, fruto] to yield, to bear.

◆ **producirse** *vpr* [ocurrir] to take place, to come about.

productividad *f* productivity.

productivo, va *adj* productive; [que da beneficio] profitable.

producto *m* - **1.** [gen & MAT] product; AGR produce *(U)*; ~ **de belleza** beauty product; ~ **interior/nacional bruto** gross domestic/national product; ~ **químico** chemical - **2.** [ganancia] profit - **3.** *fig* [resultado] result.

productor, ra ◇ *adj* producing. ◇ *m,f* CIN [persona] producer.

◆ **productora** *f* CIN [firma] production company.

proeza *f* exploit, deed.

profanar *vt* to desecrate.

profano, na ◇ *adj* - **1.** [no sagrado] profane, secular - **2.** [ignorante] ignorant, uninitiated. ◇ *m,f* layman (*f* laywoman), lay person.

profecía *f* [predicción] prophecy.

proferir *vt* to utter; [insultos] to hurl.

profesar *vt* - 1. [una religión] to follow; [una profesión] to practise - 2. [admiración etc] to profess.

profesión *f* profession.

profesional *adj* & *m,f* professional.

profesionista *mf Méx* professional.

profesor, ra *m,f* [gen] teacher; [de universidad] lecturer; [de autoescuela, esquí etc] instructor.

profesorado *m* [plantilla] teaching staff, faculty *US*; [profesión] teachers *(pl)*, teaching profession.

profeta *m* prophet.

profetisa *f* prophetess.

profetizar *vt* to prophesy.

profiera *etc* ⊳ **proferir**.

prófugo, ga *adj* & *m,f* fugitive.

profundidad *f lit* & *fig* depth; **en ~** in depth; **tiene dos metros de ~** it's two metres deep.

profundizar ◇ *vt fig* to study in depth. ◇ *vi* to go into detail; **~ en** to study in depth.

profundo, da *adj* - 1. [gen] deep - 2. *fig* [respeto, libro, pensamiento] profound, deep; [dolor] intense.

profusión *f* profusion.

progenitor, ra *m,f* father (*f* mother).

◆ **progenitores** *mpl* parents.

programa *m* - 1. [gen] programme - 2. [de actividades] schedule, programme; [de estudios] syllabus - 3. INFORM program.

programación *f* - 1. INFORM programming - 2. TV scheduling; **la ~ del lunes** Monday's programmes.

programador, ra *m,f* [persona] programmer.

programar *vt* - 1. [vacaciones, reforma etc] to plan - 2. CIN & TV to put on, to show - 3. TECN to programme; INFORM to program.

progre *fam mf* progressive.

progresar *vi* to progress, to make progress.

progresión *f* [gen & MAT] progression; [mejora] progress, advance.

progresista *adj* & *m,f* progressive.

progresivo, va *adj* progressive.

progreso *m* progress; **hacer ~s** to make progress.

prohibición *f* ban, banning *(U)*.

prohibido, da *adj* prohibited, banned; **'~ aparcar/fumar'** 'no parking/smoking', 'parking/smoking prohibited'; **'prohibida la entrada'** 'no entry'; **'dirección prohibida'** AUTOM 'no entry'.

prohibir *vt* - 1. [gen] to forbid; **~ a alguien**

hacer algo to forbid sb to do sthg; **'se prohíbe el paso'** 'no entry' - 2. [por ley - de antemano] to prohibit; [- a posteriori] to ban.

prohibitivo, va *adj* prohibitive.

prójimo *m* fellow human being, neighbour.

prole *f* offspring.

proletariado *m* proletariat.

proletario, ria *adj* & *m,f* proletarian.

proliferación *f* proliferation.

proliferar *vi* to proliferate.

prolífico, ca *adj* prolific.

prolijo, ja *adj* [extenso] long-winded.

prólogo *m* [de libro] preface, foreword; *fig* prelude.

prolongación *f* extension.

prolongado, da *adj* long; *fig* [dilatado] lengthy.

prolongar *vt* [gen] to extend; [espera, visita, conversación] to prolong; [cuerda, tubo] to lengthen.

promedio *m* average; **como ~** on average.

promesa *f* [compromiso] promise; **hacer una ~** to make a promise; **romper una ~** to break a promise.

prometer ◇ *vt* to promise. ◇ *vi* [tener futuro] to show promise.

◆ **prometerse** *vpr* to get engaged.

prometido, da ◇ *m,f* fiancé (*f* fiancée). ◇ *adj* [para casarse] engaged.

prominente *adj* - 1. [abultado] protruding - 2. [elevado, ilustre] prominent.

promiscuo, cua *adj* promiscuous.

promoción *f* - 1. [gen & DEP] promotion - 2. [curso] class, year.

promocionar *vt* to promote.

promotor, ra *m,f* promoter; [de una rebelión] instigator.

promover *vt* - 1. [iniciar - fundación etc] to set up; [- rebelión] to stir up - 2. [impulsar] to stimulate - 3. [ocasionar] to cause - 4. [ascender]: **~ a alguien a** to promote sb to.

promulgar *vt* [ley] to enact.

pronombre *m* pronoun.

pronosticar *vt* to predict, to forecast.

pronóstico *m* - 1. [predicción] forecast; **~ del tiempo** weather forecast - 2. MED prognosis; **de ~ grave** serious, in a serious condition.

pronto, ta *adj* quick, fast; [respuesta] prompt, early; [curación, tramitación] speedy.

◆ **pronto** ◇ *adv* - 1. [rápidamente] quickly; **tan ~ como** as soon as - 2. [temprano] early; **salimos ~** we left early - 3. [dentro de poco] soon; **¡hasta ~!** see you soon! ◇ *m fam* sudden impulse.

◆ **al pronto** *loc adv* at first.

◆ **de pronto** *loc adv* suddenly.

◆ **por lo pronto** *loc adv* - 1. [de momento]

for the time being - **2.** [para empezar] to start with.

pronunciación *f* pronunciation.

pronunciado, da *adj* [facciones] pronounced; [curva] sharp; [pendiente, cuesta] steep; [nariz] prominent.

pronunciamiento *m* - **1.** [sublevación] uprising - **2.** DER pronouncement.

pronunciar *vt* - **1.** [decir - palabra] to pronounce; [- discurso] to deliver, to make - **2.** DER to pronounce, to pass.

◆ **pronunciarse** *vpr* - **1.** [definirse]: ~se (sobre) to state an opinion (on) - **2.** [sublevarse] to rise up, to revolt.

propagación *f* - **1.** [gen] spreading *(U)* - **2.** BIOL & FÍS propagation.

propaganda *f* - **1.** [publicidad] advertising *(U)* - **2.** [política, religiosa] propaganda.

propagar *vt* [gen] to spread; [razas, especies] to propagate.

◆ **propagarse** *vpr* - **1.** [gen] to spread - **2.** BIOL & FÍS to propagate.

propasarse *vpr*: ~ (con algo) to go too far (with sthg); ~ con alguien [sexualmente] to take liberties with sb.

propensión *f* propensity, tendency.

propenso, sa *adj*: ~ a algo/a hacer algo prone to sthg/doing sthg.

propicio, cia *adj* - **1.** [favorable] propitious, favourable - **2.** [adecuado] suitable, appropriate.

propiedad *f* - **1.** [derecho] ownership; [bienes] property; ~ privada private property; ~ pública public ownership - **2.** [facultad] property - **3.** [exactitud] accuracy; usar una palabra con ~ to use a word properly.

propietario, ria *m,f* [de bienes] owner.

propina *f* tip; dar de ~ to tip.

propinar *vt* [paliza] to give; [golpe] to deal.

propio, pia *adj* - **1.** [gen] own; tiene coche ~ she has a car of her own, she has her own car; por tu ~ bien for your own good - **2.** [peculiar]: ~ de typical *o* characteristic of; no es ~ de él it's not like him - **3.** [apropiado]: ~ (para) suitable *o* right (for) - **4.** [en persona] himself (*f* herself); el ~ compositor the composer himself.

proponer *vt* to propose; [candidato] to put forward.

◆ **proponerse** *vpr*: ~se hacer algo to plan *o* intend to do sthg.

proporción *f* - **1.** [gen & MAT] proportion; en ~ in proportion to - **2.** *(gen pl)* [importancia] extent, size.

◆ **proporciones** *fpl* [tamaño] size *(sg)*.

proporcionado, da *adj*: ~ (a) [estatura, sueldo] commensurate (with); [medidas] proportionate (to); bien ~ well-proportioned.

proporcionar *vt* - **1.** [facilitar]: ~ algo a alguien to provide sb with sthg - **2.** *fig* [conferir] to lend, to add.

proposición *f* [propuesta] proposal.

propósito *m* - **1.** [intención] intention - **2.** [objetivo] purpose.

◆ **a propósito** ◇ *loc adj* [adecuado] suitable. ◇ *loc adv* - **1.** [adrede] on purpose - **2.** [por cierto] by the way.

◆ **a propósito de** *loc prep* with regard to, concerning.

propuesta *f* proposal; a ~ de at the suggestion of; [de empleo] offer.

propuesto, ta *pp* ▷ **proponer.**

propugnar *vt* to advocate, to support.

propulsar *vt* - **1.** [impeler] to propel - **2.** *fig* [promover] to promote.

propulsión *f* propulsion; ~ a chorro jet propulsion.

propulsor, ra *m,f* [persona] promoter.

◆ **propulsor** *m* - **1.** [dispositivo] engine - **2.** [combustible] propellent.

propusiera *etc* ▷ **proponer.**

prórroga *f* - **1.** [gen] extension; [de estudios, servicio militar] deferment - **2.** DEP extra time.

prorrogar *vt* [alargar] to extend; [aplazar] to defer, to postpone.

prorrumpir *vi*: ~ en to burst into.

prosa *f* LITER prose.

proscrito, ta ◇ *adj* [prohibido] banned. ◇ *m,f* [desterrado] exile.

proseguir ◇ *vt* to continue. ◇ *vi* to go on, to continue.

prosiga *etc* ▷ **proseguir.**

prosiguiera *etc* ▷ **proseguir.**

prospección *f* [gen] exploration; [petrolífera, minera] prospecting.

prospecto *m* leaflet; COM & EDUC prospectus.

prosperar *vi* [mejorar] to prosper, to thrive.

prosperidad *f* - **1.** [mejora] prosperity - **2.** [éxito] success.

próspero, ra *adj* prosperous, flourishing.

prostíbulo *m* brothel.

prostitución *f* [gen] prostitution.

prostituir *vt lit & fig* to prostitute.

◆ **prostituirse** *vpr* to become a prostitute.

prostituta *f* prostitute.

protagonista *mf* [gen] main character, hero (*f* heroine); TEATR lead, leading role.

protagonizar *vt* - **1.** [obra, película] to play the lead in, to star in - **2.** *fig* [crimen] to be one of the main people responsible for; *fig* [hazaña] to play a leading part in.

protección *f* protection; bajo la ~ de alguien under the protection of sb.

proteccionismo *m* protectionism.

protector, ra ◇ *adj* protective. ◇ *m,f* [persona] protector.

proteger *vt* [gen] to protect; ~ **algo de algo** to protect sthg from sthg.

◆ **protegerse** *vpr* to take cover *o* refuge.

protege-slips *m inv* panty pad *o* liner.

protegido, da *m,f* protégé (*f* protégée).

proteína *f* protein; **rico en proteínas** rich in protein.

prótesis *f inv* MED prosthesis; [miembro] artificial limb.

protesta *f* protest; DER objection.

protestante *adj* & *m,f* Protestant.

protestar *vi* - 1. [quejarse]: ~ **(por/contra)** to protest (about/against); **¡protesto!** DER objection! - 2. [refunfuñar] to grumble.

protocolo *m* - 1. [gen & INFORM] protocol - 2. [ceremonial] etiquette.

prototipo *m* - 1. [modelo] archetype - 2. [primer ejemplar] prototype.

protuberancia *f* protuberance, bulge.

provecho *m* - 1. [gen] benefit; **buen** ~ enjoy your meal!; **de** ~ [persona] worthy; **sacar** ~ **de** to make the most of, to take advantage of - 2. [rendimiento] good effect.

provechoso, sa *adj* - 1. [ventajoso] beneficial, advantageous - 2. [lucrativo] profitable.

proveedor, ra *m,f* supplier; ~ **de acceso a Internet** Internet access provider.

proveer *vt* - 1. [abastecer] to supply, to provide - 2. [puesto, cargo] to fill.

◆ **proveerse de** *vpr* - 1. [ropa, víveres] to stock up on - 2. [medios, recursos] to arm o.s. with.

provenir *vi*: ~ **de** to come from.

proverbial *adj* proverbial.

proverbio *m* proverb.

providencia *f* [medida] measure, step.

providencial *adj lit* & *fig* providential.

proviene *etc* ▷ **provenir**.

provincia *f* [división administrativa] province.

◆ **provincias** *fpl* [no la capital] the provinces.

provinciano, na *adj* & *m,f despec* provincial.

proviniera *etc* ▷ **provenir**.

provisión *f* - 1. *(gen pl)* [suministro] supply, provision; [de una plaza] filling *(U)* - 2. [disposición] measure.

provisional *adj* provisional.

provisorio, ria *adj Amér* provisional.

provisto, ta *pp* ▷ **proveer**.

provocación *f* [hostigamiento] provocation.

provocar *vt* - 1. [incitar] to incite - 2. [irritar] to provoke - 3. [ocasionar - gen] to cause - 4. [excitar sexualmente] to arouse - 5. : **¿te provoca hacerlo?** *Carib, Col, Méx* [te apetece]

would you like to do it?

provocativo, va *adj* provocative.

próximamente *adv* soon, shortly; CIN coming soon.

proximidad *f* [cercanía] closeness, proximity.

◆ **proximidades** *fpl* - 1. [de ciudad] surrounding area *(sg)* - 2. [de lugar] vicinity *(sg)*.

próximo, ma *adj* - 1. [cercano] near, close; ~ **a algo** close to sthg; [casa, ciudad] nearby, neighbouring; **en fecha próxima** shortly - 2. [siguiente] next; **el** ~ **año** next year.

proyección *f* - 1. [gen & GEOM] projection - 2. CIN screening, showing - 3. *fig* [trascendencia] importance.

proyectar *vt* - 1. [dirigir - focos etc] to shine, to direct - 2. [mostrar - película] to project, to screen; [- sombra] to cast; [- diapositivas] to show - 3. [planear - viaje, operación, edificio] to plan; [- puente, obra] to design - 4. [arrojar] to throw forwards.

proyectil *m* projectile, missile.

proyecto *m* - 1. [intención] project - 2. [plan] plan - 3. [diseño - ARQUIT] design; IND & TECN plan - 4. [borrador] draft; ~ **de ley** bill - 5. EDUC : ~ **fin de carrera** *design project forming part of doctoral thesis for architecture students etc*; ~ **de investigación** [de un grupo] research project; [de una persona] dissertation.

proyector, ra *adj* projecting.

◆ **proyector** *m* [de cine, diapositivas] projector.

prudencia *f* [cuidado] caution, care; [previsión, sensatez] prudence; [moderación] moderation; **con** ~ in moderation.

prudente *adj* - 1. [cuidadoso] careful, cautious; [previsor, sensato] sensible - 2. [razonable] reasonable.

prueba ◇ *v* ▷ **probar**. ◇ *f* - 1. [demostración] proof; DER evidence, proof; **no tengo** ~ **s** I have no proof - 2. [manifestación] sign, token - 3. EDUC & MED test; ~ **de alcoholemia** Breathalyser® test; ~ **de acceso** entrance examination; ~ **de aptitud** aptitude test; ~ **del embarazo** pregnancy test - 4. [comprobación] test; **a** *o* **de** ~ [trabajador] on trial; [producto comprado] on approval; **es a** ~ **de agua/balas** it's waterproof/bulletproof; **poner a** ~ to (put to the) test - 5. DEP event - 6. IMPRENTA proof.

PS = **PD**.

pseudónimo *m* pseudonym.

psicoanálisis *m inv* psychoanalysis.

psicoanalista *mf* psychoanalyst.

psicodélico, ca *adj* psychedelic.

psicología *f lit* & *fig* psychology.

psicológico, ca *adj* psychological.

psicólogo, ga *m,f* psychologist.

psicópata *mf* psychopath.

psicosis *f inv* psychosis.

psicosomático, ca *adj* psychosomatic.

psiquiatra *mf* psychiatrist.

psiquiátrico, ca *adj* psychiatric.

psíquico, ca *adj* psychic.

PSOE [pe'soe, soe] (*abrev de* **Partido Socialista Obrero Español**) *m major Spanish political party to the centre-left of the political spectrum.*

pta. (*abrev de* **peseta**) pta.

púa *f* - 1. [de planta] thorn; [de erizo] barb, quill; [de peine] spine, tooth; [de tenedor] prong - 2. MÚS plectrum.

pub [pap] (*pl* **pubs**) *m bar (open till late, usually with music).*

pubertad *f* puberty.

pubis *m inv* pubes (*pl*).

publicación *f* publication; ~ **periódica** periodical.

publicar *vt* - 1. [editar] to publish - 2. [difundir] to publicize; [ley] to make public, to pass; [aviso] to issue.

publicidad *f* - 1. [difusión] publicity; **dar ~ a algo** to publicize sthg - 2. COM advertising; TV adverts (*pl*), commercials (*pl*).

publicitario, ria *adj* advertising (*antes de sust*).

público, ca *adj* public; **ser ~** [conocido] to be common knowledge; **en ~** in public.
   ◆ **público** *m* - 1. CIN, TEATR & TV audience; DEP crowd - 2. [comunidad] public; **el gran ~** the (general) public.

publirreportaje *m* [anuncio de televisión] promotional film; [en revista] advertising spread.

pucha *interj Andes, RP fam*: **¡~(s)!** sugar! *UK*, shoot! *US*.

puchero *m* - 1. [perola] cooking pot - 2. [comida] stew.
   ◆ **pucheros** *mpl* [gesto] pout (*sg*); **hacer ~s** to pout.

pucho *m CSur fam* [colilla] cigarette butt; [cigarrillo] cigarette.

pudding = pudin.

púdico, ca *adj* - 1. [recatado] modest - 2. [tímido] bashful.

pudiente *adj* wealthy, well-off.

pudiera *etc* ▷ **poder**.

pudin (*pl* **púdines**), **pudding** ['puðin] (*pl* **puddings**) *m* (plum) pudding.

pudor *m* - 1. [recato] (sense of) shame - 2. [timidez] bashfulness.

pudoroso, sa *adj* - 1. [recatado] modest - 2. [tímido] bashful.

pudrir *vt* - 1. [descomponerse] to rot - 2. [fastidiar] to be fed up.
   ◆ **pudrirse** *vpr* to rot.

puebla *etc* ▷ **poblar**.

pueblerino, na *adj* village (*antes de sust*); *despec* rustic, provincial.

pueblo *m* - 1. [población - pequeña] village; [- grande] town - 2. [nación] people.

pueda *etc* ▷ **poder**.

puente *m* - 1. [gen] bridge; ~ **peatonal** footbridge; **tender un ~** to build bridges - 2. [días festivos]: **hacer ~** *to take an extra day off between two public holidays.*
   ◆ **puente aéreo** *m* [civil] air shuttle; [militar] airlift.

puenting *m* bungee-jumping.

puerco, ca ◇ *adj* dirty, filthy. ◇ *m,f* [animal] pig (*f* sow).

puercoespín *m* porcupine.

puericultor, ra *m,f* nursery nurse.

pueril *adj fig* childish.

puerro *m* leek.

puerta *f* - 1. [de casa] door; [de jardín, ciudad etc] gate; **de ~ en ~** from door to door; **llamar a la ~** to knock on the door; ~ **de embarque** boarding gate; ~ **principal/trasera** front/back door - 2. *fig* [posibilidad] gateway, opening - 3. DEP goal, goalmouth - 4. *loc*: **a las ~s de** on the verge of; **a ~ cerrada** [gen] behind closed doors; [juicio] in camera.

puerto *m* - 1. [de mar] port; ~ **deportivo** marina; ~ **pesquero** fishing port - 2. [de montaña] pass - 3. INFORM port - 4. *fig* [refugio] haven.

Puerto Rico Puerto Rico.

pues *conj* - 1. [dado que] since, as - 2. [por lo tanto] therefore, so; **creo, ~, que ...** so, I think that ... - 3. [así que] so; **querías verlo, ~ ahí está** you wanted to see it, so here it is - 4. [enfático]: **¡~ ya está!** well, that's it!; **¡~ claro!** but of course!

puesto, ta ◇ *pp* ▷ **poner**. ◇ *adj*: **ir muy ~** to be all dressed up.
   ◆ **puesto** *m* - 1. [lugar] place - 2. [empleo] post, position; ~ **de trabajo** job - 3. [en fila, clasificación etc] place - 4. [tenderete] stall, stand - 5. MIL post; ~ **de policía** police station; ~ **de socorro** first-aid post.
   ◆ **puesta** *f* - 1. [acción]: **puesta a punto** [de una técnica] perfecting; [de un motor] tuning; **puesta al día** updating; **puesta en escena** staging, production; **puesta en marcha** [de máquina] starting, start-up; [de acuerdo, proyecto] implementation; **puesta en práctica** implementation.
   ◆ **puesta de sol** *f* sunset.
   ◆ **puesto que** *loc conj* since, as.

puf (*pl* **pufs**) *m* pouf, pouffe.

púgil *m* boxer.

pugna *f* fight, battle.

pugnar *vi fig* [esforzarse]: ~ **por** to struggle *o* fight (for).

puja *f* [en subasta - acción] bidding; [- cantidad] bid.

pujar ◇ *vi* [en subasta] to bid higher. ◇ *vt* to bid.

pulcro, cra *adj* neat, tidy.

pulga *f* flea.

pulgada *f* inch.

pulgar ▷ **dedo**.

pulgón *m* plant louse, aphid.

pulimentar *vt* to polish.

pulir *vt* to polish.
◆ **pulirse** *vpr* [gastarse] to blow, to throw away.

pulmón *m* lung; **tener buenos pulmones** to have a powerful voice.

pulmonía *f* pneumonia.

pulóver *m* *RP* pullover.

pulpa *f* pulp.

púlpito *m* pulpit.

pulpo *m* [animal] octopus.

pulque *m* *CAm, Méx* pulque, *fermented maguey juice*.

pulquería *f* *CAm, Méx* 'pulque' bar.

pulsación *f* - 1. [del corazón] beat, beating *(U)* - 2. [en máquina de escribir] keystroke, tap.

pulsador *m* button, push button.

pulsar *vt* [botón, timbre etc] to press; [teclas de ordenador] to hit, to strike; [teclas de piano] to play; [cuerdas de guitarra] to pluck.

pulsera *f* bracelet; ~ **de tobillo** ankle bracelet.

pulso *m* - 1. [latido] pulse; **tomar el ~ a algo/alguien** *fig* to sound sthg/sb out - 2. [firmeza]: **tener buen** ~ to have a steady hand; **a** ~ unaided; **ganarse algo a** ~ to deserve sthg.

pulular *vi* to swarm.

pulverizador, ra *adj* spray *(antes de sust)*.
◆ **pulverizador** *m* spray.

pulverizar *vt* - 1. [líquido] to spray - 2. [sólido] to reduce to dust; TECN to pulverize - 3. *fig* [aniquilar] to pulverize.

puma *m* puma.

puna *f* *Andes, Arg* altitude sickness.

punción *f* puncture.

punk [paŋk] *(pl* **punks**), **punki** *adj & m,f* punk.

punta *f* - 1. [extremo - gen] point; [- de pan, pelo] end; [- de dedo, cuerno] tip; **de ~ a ~** from one end to the other; **en ~** pointed; **en la otra ~ de algo** at the other end of sthg; **sacar ~ a (un lápiz)** to sharpen (a pencil); **a ~ (de) pala** by the dozen *o* bucket - 2. [pizca] touch, bit; [de sal] pinch.

puntada *f* [pespunte] stitch.

puntaje *m* *CSur* mark *UK*, grade *US*.

puntal *m* [madero] prop; *fig* [apoyo] mainstay.

puntapié *m* kick; **dar un ~ a alguien** to kick sb.

puntear *vt* to pluck.

punteo *m* guitar solo.

puntera ▷ **puntero**.

puntería *f* - 1. [destreza] marksmanship; **hacer** ~ to take aim - 2. [orientación] aim.

puntero, ra ◇ *adj* leading. ◇ *m,f* [líder] leader.
◆ **puntera** *f* [de zapato] toecap.

puntiagudo, da *adj* pointed.

puntilla *f* point lace.
◆ **de puntillas** *loc adv* on tiptoe.

puntilloso, sa *adj* - 1. [susceptible] touchy - 2. [meticuloso] punctilious.

punto *m* - 1. [gen] point; ~ **débil/fuerte** weak/strong point; ~ **de ebullición/fusión** boiling/melting point; ~ **culminante** high point; ~**s a tratar** matters to be discussed; **poner** ~ **final a algo** to bring sthg to a close - 2. [signo ortográfico] dot; ~ **y coma** semicolon; ~**s suspensivos** dots, suspension points; **dos ~s** colon - 3. [marca] spot, dot - 4. [lugar] spot, place; ~ **de venta** COM point of sale - 5. [momento] point, moment; **estar a** ~ to be ready; **estar a** ~ **de hacer algo** to be on the point of doing sthg - 6. [estado] state, condition; **llegar a un** ~ **en que ...** to reach the stage where ...; **poner a** ~ [gen] to fine-tune; [motor] to tune - 7. [cláusula] clause - 8. [puntada - en costura, cirugía] stitch; ~ **de cruz** cross-stitch; **hacer** ~ to knit; **un jersey de** ~ a knitted jumper - 9. [estilo de tejer] knitting; ~ **de ganchillo** crochet - 10. [objetivo] end, target.
◆ **en punto** *loc adv* exactly, on the dot.
◆ **hasta cierto punto** *loc adv* to some extent, up to a point.
◆ **punto de partida** *m* starting point.
◆ **punto de vista** *m* point of view, viewpoint.
◆ **punto muerto** *m* - 1. AUTOM neutral - 2. [en un proceso] deadlock; **estar en un** ~ **muerto** to be deadlocked.

puntuación *f* - 1. [calificación] mark; [en concursos, competiciones] score - 2. [ortográfica] punctuation.

puntual *adj* - 1. [en el tiempo] punctual; **ser** ~ to be on time - 2. [exacto, detallado] detailed - 3. [aislado] isolated, one-off.

puntualidad *f* [en el tiempo] punctuality.

puntualizar *vt* to specify, to clarify.

puntuar ◇ *vt* - 1. [calificar] to mark; DEP to award marks to - 2. [escrito] to punctuate. ◇ *vi* - 1. [calificar] to mark - 2. [entrar en el cómputo]: ~ **(para)** to count (towards).

punzada *f* [dolor intenso] stabbing pain *(U)*; *fig* pang, twinge.

punzante *adj* - 1. [que pincha] sharp - 2. [intenso] sharp, stabbing - 3. [mordaz] caustic.

punzón *m* punch.

puñado *m* handful.

puñal *m* dagger.

puñalada *f* stab; [herida] stab wound.

puñeta ◇ *f fam* [tontería]: **mandar a al-guien a hacer ~s** to tell sb to get lost; **en la quinta ~** in the back of beyond. ◇ *interj fam*: **¡ ~s!** damn it!

puñetazo *m* punch; **lo derribó de un ~** he knocked him to the ground.

puñetero, ra *fam* ◇ *adj* **-1.** [persona] damn; **a ver si arranca el coche de una ~ vez** let's see if this damn car will finally start **-2.** [cosa] tricky, awkward. ◇ *m,f* pain.

puño *m* **-1.** [mano cerrada] fist; **de su ~ y le-tra** in his/her own handwriting **-2.** [de manga] cuff **-3.** [empuñadura - de espada] hilt; [- de paraguas] handle.

pupila *f* pupil.

pupilo, la *m,f* [discípulo] pupil.

pupitre *m* desk.

puré *m* CULIN purée; [sopa] thick soup; **~ de patatas** mashed potatoes *(pl)*; **hacer ~ a al-guien** to beat sb to a pulp.

pureza *f* purity.

purga *f fig* [depuración] purge.

purgante *adj* & *m* purgative.

purgar *vt lit* & *fig* to purge.

purgatorio *m* purgatory.

purificar *vt* to purify; [mineral, metal] to re-fine.

puritano, na *adj* & *m,f* puritan.

puro, ra *adj* **-1.** [gen] pure; [oro] solid **-2.** [conducta, persona] chaste, innocent **-3.** [mero] sheer; [verdad] plain; **por pura casualidad** by pure chance.

➤ **puro** *m* cigar.

púrpura ◇ *adj inv* purple. ◇ *m* purple.

pus *m* pus.

pusilánime *adj* cowardly.

puso *etc* ⊳ **poner**.

puta ◇ *adj* ⊳ **puto**. ◇ *f vulg* whore; **ir de ~s** to go whoring; **de ~ madre** fucking brilliant.

puteada *f CSur fam* swear word.

puto, ta *adj vulg* [maldito] bloody.

➤ **puto** *m vulg* male prostitute.

putrefacción *f* rotting, putrefaction.

puzzle ['puθle], **puzle** *m* jigsaw puzzle.

PVP *(abrev de* **precio de venta al público)** *m* ≃ RRP.

PYME *(abrev de* **Pequeña y Mediana Em-presa)** *f* SME.

pyrex® = **pírex**.

pza. *(abrev de* **plaza)** Sq.

q, Q *f* [letra] q, Q.

q.e.p.d. *(abrev de* **que en paz descanse)** RIP.

que ◇ *pron relat* **-1.** *(sujeto)* [persona] who, that; [cosa] that, which; **la mujer ~ me sa-luda** the woman (who o that is) waving to me; **el ~ me lo compró** the one who bought it from me; **la moto ~ me gusta** the motor-bike (that) I like **-2.** *(complemento directo)* [persona] whom, that; [cosa] that, which; **el hombre ~ conociste ayer** the man (whom o that) you met yesterday; **ese co-che es el ~ me quiero comprar** that car is the one (that o which) I want to buy **-3.** *(complemento indirecto)*: **al/a la ~** (to) whom; **ese es el chico al ~ presté dinero** that's the boy to whom I lent some money **-4.** *(complemento circunstancial)*: **la playa a la ~ fui** the beach where o to which I went; **la mujer con la ~ hablas** the woman to whom you are talking; **la mesa sobre la ~ escribes** the table on which you are writ-ing **-5.** *(complemento de tiempo)*: **(en) ~** when; **el día (en) ~ me fui** the day (when) I left. ◇ *conj* **-1.** *(con oraciones de sujeto)* that; **es importante ~ me escuches** it's impor-tant that you listen to me **-2.** *(con oraciones de complemento directo)* that; **me ha confesa-do ~ me quiere** he has told me that he loves me **-3.** *(comparativo)* than; **es más rápido ~ tú** he's quicker than you; **antes morir ~ vivir la guerra** I'd rather die than live through a war **-4.** [expresa causa]: **hemos de esperar, ~ todavía no es la hora** we'll have to wait, as it isn't time yet **-5.** [expresa consecuencia] that; **tanto me lo pidió ~ se lo di** he asked me for it so insistently that I gave it to him **-6.** [expresa finalidad] so (that); **ven aquí ~ te vea** come over here so (that) I can see you **-7.** (+ *subjuntivo*) [ex-presa deseo] that; **quiero ~ lo hagas** I want you to do it; **espero ~ te diviertas** I hope (that) you have fun **-8.** *(en oraciones exclama-tivas)*: **¡ ~ te diviertas!** have fun!; **¡ ~ te doy un bofetón!** do that again and I'll slap you! **-9.** *(en oraciones interrogativas)*: **¿ ~ quiere ve-nir? pues que venga** so she wants to come?

then let her - **10.** [expresa disyunción] or; **quieras ~ no, harás lo que yo mando** you'll do what I tell you, whether you like it or not - **11.** [expresa hipótesis] if; **~ no quieres hacerlo, pues no pasa nada** it doesn't matter if you don't want to do it - **12.** [expresa reiteración] and; **estaban charla ~ charla** they were talking and talking.

qué ◇ adj [gen] what; [al elegir, al concretar] which; ¿**~ hora es?** what's the time?; ¿**~ coche prefieres?** which car do you prefer?; ¿**a ~ distancia?** how far away? ◇ pron (interrogativo) what; ¿**~ te dijo?** what did he tell you?; **no sé ~ hacer** I don't know what to do; ¿**~?** [¿cómo?] sorry?, pardon? ◇ adv - **1.** [exclamativo] how; ¡**~ horror!** how awful!; ¡**~ tonto eres!** how stupid you are!, you're so stupid!; ¡**~ casa más bonita!** what a lovely house!; ¡**y ~!** so what? - **2.** [expresa gran cantidad]: ¡**~ de ...!** what a lot of ...! ; ¡**~ de gente hay aquí!** what a lot of people there are here!, there are so many people here!

quebradero
◆ **quebradero de cabeza** m headache, problem.

quebradizo, za adj - **1.** [frágil] fragile, brittle - **2.** [débil] frail - **3.** [voz] weak.

quebrado, da adj [terreno] rough, uneven; [perfil] rugged.

quebrantar vt - **1.** [incumplir - promesa, ley] to break; [- obligación] to fail in - **2.** [debilitar] to weaken; [moral, resistencia] to break.
◆ **quebrantarse** vpr [debilitarse] to decline, to deteriorate.

quebranto m [debilitamiento] weakening, debilitation.

quebrar ◇ vt [romper] to break. ◇ vi FIN to go bankrupt.
◆ **quebrarse** vpr - **1.** [romperse] to break - **2.** [voz] to break, to falter.

quechua m [idioma] Quechua.

quedar ◇ vi - **1.** [permanecer] to remain, to stay - **2.** [haber aún, faltar] to be left, to remain; ¿**queda azúcar?** is there any sugar left?; **nos quedan 10 euros** we have 10 euros left; ¿**cuánto queda para León?** how much further is it to León?; ~ **por hacer** to remain to be done; **queda por fregar el suelo** the floor has still to be cleaned - **3.** [mostrarse]: ~ **como** to come across as; ~ **bien/mal (con alguien)** to make a good/bad impression (on sb) - **4.** [llegar a ser, resultar]: **el trabajo ha quedado perfecto** the job turned out perfectly; **el cuadro queda muy bien ahí** the picture looks great there - **5.** [acabar]: ~ **en** to end in; ~ **en nada** to come to nothing - **6.** [sentar] to look; **te queda un poco corto el traje** your suit is a bit too

short; ~ **bien/mal a alguien** to look good/ bad on sb; ~ **bien/mal con algo** to go well/ badly with sthg - **7.** [citarse]: ~ **(con alguien)** to arrange to meet (sb); **hemos quedado el lunes** we've arranged to meet on Monday - **8.** [acordar]: ~ **en algo/en hacer algo** to agree on sthg/to do sthg; ~ **en que ... to** agree that ...; ¿**en qué quedamos?** what's it to be, then? - **9.** fam [estar situado] to be; ¿**por dónde queda?** whereabouts is it?
◆ **quedarse** vpr - **1.** [permanecer - en un lugar] to stay, to remain - **2.** [terminar - en un estado]: ~**se ciego/sordo** to go blind/deaf; ~**se triste** to o feel sad; ~**se sin dinero** to be left penniless; **la pared se ha quedado limpia** the wall is clean now - **3.** [comprar] to take; **me quedo éste** I'll take this one.
◆ **quedarse con** vpr - **1.** [retener, guardarse] to keep - **2.** [preferir] to go for, to prefer.

quedo, da adj quiet, soft.
◆ **quedo** adv quietly, softly.

quehacer (gen pl) m task; ~**es domésticos** housework (U).

queja f - **1.** [lamento] moan, groan - **2.** [protesta] complaint; **presentar una ~** to lodge o make a complaint.

quejarse vpr - **1.** [lamentar] to groan, to cry out - **2.** [protestar] to complain; ~ **de** to complain about.

quejica despec adj whining, whingeing.

quejido m cry, moan.

quejoso, sa adj: ~ **(de)** annoyed o upset (with).

quemado, da adj - **1.** [gen] burnt; **oler a ~** to smell burning; [por agua hirviendo] scalded; [por electricidad] burnt-out; [fusible] blown - **2.** [por sol] sunburnt - **3.** loc: **estar ~** [agotado] to be burnt-out; [harto] to be fed up.

quemador m burner.

quemadura f [por fuego] burn; ~ **en tercer grado** third-degree burning; [por agua hirviendo] scald.

quemar ◇ vt - **1.** [gen] to burn; [suj: agua hirviendo] to scald; [suj: electricidad] to blow - **2.** fig [malgastar] to go through, to fritter away - **3.** fig [desgastar] to burn out - **4.** fig [hartar] to make fed up. ◇ vi [estar caliente] to be (scalding) hot.
◆ **quemarse** vpr - **1.** [por fuego] to burn down; [por agua hirviendo] to get scalded; [por calor] to burn; [por electricidad] to blow - **2.** [por el sol] to get burned - **3.** fig [desgastarse] to burn out - **4.** fig [hartarse] to get fed up.

quemarropa ◆ **a quemarropa** loc adv point-blank.

quemazón f burning; [picor] itch.

quepa etc ▷ **caber**.

queque *m Andes, CAm, Méx* sponge (cake).

querella *f* - **1.** DER [acusación] charge; **presentar una ~ contra alguien** to bring an action against sb - **2.** [discordia] dispute.

querer ⬦ *vt* - **1.** [gen] to want; **quiero una bicicleta** I want a bicycle; **¿quieren ustedes algo más?** would you like anything else?; **~ que alguien haga algo** to want sb to do sthg; **quiero que lo hagas tú** I want you to do it; **~ que pase algo** to want sthg to happen; **queremos que las cosas te vayan bien** we want things to go well for you; **quisiera hacerlo, pero ...** I'd like to do it, but ... - **2.** [amar] to love - **3.** [en preguntas - con amabilidad]: **¿quiere decirle a su amigo que pase?** could you tell your friend to come in, please? - **4.** [pedir - precio]: **~ algo (por)** to want sthg (for); **¿cuánto quieres por el coche?** how much do you want for the car? - **5.** *fig & irón* [dar motivos para]: **tú lo que quieres es que te pegue** you're asking for a smack - **6.** *loc*: **como quien no quiere la cosa** as if it were nothing; **quien bien te quiere te hará llorar** *proverb* you have to be cruel to be kind *proverb*. ⬦ *vi* to want; **ven cuando quieras** come whenever you like *o* want; **no me voy porque no quiero** I'm not going because I don't want to; **queriendo** on purpose; **sin ~** accidentally; **~ decir** to mean; **¿qué quieres decir con eso?** what do you mean by that?; **~ es poder** where there's a will there's a way. ⬦ *v impers* [haber atisbos]: **parece que quiere llover** it looks like rain. ⬦ *m* love.

➤ **quererse** *vpr* to love each other.

querido, da ⬦ *adj* dear. ⬦ *m,f* lover; [apelativo afectuoso] darling.

quesadilla *f CAm, Méx filled fried tortilla.*

queso *m* cheese; **~ de bola** Dutch cheese; **~ manchego** *hard mild yellow cheese made in La Mancha*; **~ para untar** cheese spread; **~ rallado** grated cheese; **dárselas con ~ a alguien** to fool sb.

quibutz [ki'βuθ] (*pl* **quibutzs**), **kibutz** (*pl* **kibutzim**) *m* kibbutz.

quicio *m* jamb; **estar fuera de ~** *fig* to be out of kilter; **sacar de ~ a alguien** *fig* to drive sb mad.

quiebra *f* - **1.** [ruina] bankruptcy; **ir a la ~** to go bankrupt; [en bolsa] crash - **2.** *fig* [pérdida] collapse.

quiebro *m* [ademán] swerve.

quien *pron* - **1.** *(relativo)* [sujeto] who; [complemento] whom; **fue mi hermano ~ me lo explicó** it was my brother who explained it to me; **era Pepe a ~ vi/de ~ no me fiaba** it was Pepe (whom) I saw/didn't trust - **2.** *(indefinido)*: **~es quieran verlo que se acerquen** whoever wants to see it will have to come closer; **hay ~ lo niega** there are those who deny it - **3.** *loc*: **~ más ~ menos** everyone.

quién *pron (interrogativo)* [sujeto] who; [complemento] who, whom; **¿~ es ese hombre?** who's that man?; **no sé ~ viene** I don't know who is coming; **¿a ~es has invitado?** who *o* whom have you invited?; **¿de ~ es?** whose is it?; **¿~ es?** [en la puerta] who is it?; [al teléfono] who's calling?

quienquiera (*pl* **quienesquiera**) *pron* whoever; **~ que venga** whoever comes.

quiera *etc* ⊳ **querer**.

quieto, ta *adj* - **1.** [parado] still; **¡estáte ~!** keep still!; **¡~ ahí!** don't move!

quietud *f* - **1.** [inmovilidad] stillness - **2.** [tranquilidad] quietness.

quijada *f* jaw.

quijotesco, ca *adj* quixotic.

quilate *m* carat.

quilla *f* NÁUT keel.

quilo *etc* = **kilo**.

quilombo *m CSur mfam* [burdel] whorehouse; [lío, desorden] mess.

quimera *f* fantasy.

quimérico, ca *adj* fanciful, unrealistic.

químico, ca ⬦ *adj* chemical. ⬦ *m,f* [científico] chemist.

➤ **química** *f* [ciencia] chemistry.

quina *f* [bebida] quinine.

quincalla *f* trinket.

quince *núm* fifteen; **~ días** a fortnight; *ver también* **seis**.

quinceañero, ra *m,f* teenager.

quinceavo, va *núm* fifteenth.

quincena *f* fortnight.

quincenal *adj* fortnightly.

quincho *m RP* [techo] thatched roof; [en jardín, playa] thatched shelter.

quincuagésimo, ma *núm* fiftieth.

quiniela *f* [boleto] pools coupon.

➤ **quinielas** *fpl* [apuestas] (football) pools; **jugar a las ~s** to play the pools.

➤ **quiniela hípica** *f* sweepstake.

quinientos, tas *núm* five hundred; *ver también* **seis**.

quinina *f* quinine.

quinqué *m* oil lamp.

quinquenio *m* [periodo] five-year period.

quinqui *mf fam* delinquent.

quinta ⊳ **quinto**.

quinteto *m* quintet.

quinto, ta *núm* fifth.

➤ **quinto** *m* - **1.** [parte] fifth - **2.** MIL recruit, conscript.

➤ **quinta** *f* - **1.** [finca] country house - **2.** MIL call-up year.

quintuplicar *vt* to increase fivefold.

➡ **quintuplicarse** *vpr* to increase five-fold.

quiosco, kiosco *m* kiosk; [de periódicos] newspaper stand; ~ **de música** bandstand.

quiosquero, ra *m,f* owner of a newspaper stand.

quipus *mpl Andes* quipus, *knotted cords used for record-keeping by the Incas.*

quirófano *m* operating theatre.

quiromancia *f* palmistry, chiromancy.

quiromasaje *m* (manual) massage.

quirúrgico, ca *adj* surgical.

quisiera *etc* ⊳ **querer.**

quisque *m*: **cada** *o* **todo** ~ every man Jack, everyone.

quisquilloso, sa *adj* **- 1.** [detallista] pernick-ety **- 2.** [susceptible] touchy, over-sensitive.

quiste *m* cyst.

quitaesmalte *m* nail-polish remover.

quitaipón ➡ **de quitaipón** *loc adj* remov-able; [capucha] detachable.

quitamanchas *m inv* stain remover.

quitanieves *m inv* snow plough.

quitar *vt* **- 1.** [gen] to remove; [ropa, zapatos etc] to take off; ~ **le algo a alguien** to take sthg away from sb; **de quita y pon** remov-able; [capucha] detachable **- 2.** [dolor, ansie-dad] to take away, to relieve; [sed] to quench **- 3.** [tiempo] to take up **- 4.** [robar] to take, to steal **- 5.** [impedir]: **esto no quita que sea un vago** that doesn't change the fact that he's a layabout **- 6.** [exceptuar]: **qui-tando el queso, me gusta todo** apart from cheese, I'll eat anything **- 7.** [desconectar] to switch off.

➡ **quitarse** *vpr* **- 1.** [apartarse] to get out of the way **- 2.** [ropa] to take off **- 3.** [suj: man-cha] to come out **- 4.** *loc*: ~ **se a alguien de encima** *o* **de en medio** to get rid of sb.

quitasol *m* sunshade *UK*, parasol.

quite *m* DEP parry; **estar al** ~ to be on hand to help.

Quito Quito.

quizá, quizás *adv* perhaps; ~ **llueva ma-ñana** it might rain tomorrow; ~ **no lo creas** you may not believe it; ~ **sí** maybe; ~ **no** maybe not.

r, R *f* [letra] r, R.

rábano *m* radish; **coger el** ~ **por las hojas** to get the wrong end of the stick; **me impor-ta un** ~ I couldn't care less, I don't give a damn.

rabí *m* rabbi.

rabia *f* **- 1.** [ira] rage; **me da** ~ it makes me mad; **tenerle** ~ **a alguien** *fig* not to be able to stand sb **- 2.** [enfermedad] rabies.

rabiar *vi* **- 1.** [sufrir] to writhe in pain **- 2.** [en-fadarse] to be furious **- 3.** [desear]: ~ **por al-go/hacer algo** to be dying for sthg/to do sthg.

rabieta *f fam* tantrum; **tener una** ~ to throw a tantrum.

rabillo *m* corner; **mirar algo con el** ~ **del ojo** to look at sthg out of the corner of one's eye.

rabioso, sa *adj* **- 1.** [furioso] furious **- 2.** [ex-cesivo] terrible **- 3.** [enfermo de rabia] rabid **- 4.** [chillón] loud, gaudy.

rabo *m* **- 1.** [de animal] tail; ~ **de buey** ox-tail; **irse** *o* **salir con el** ~ **entre las piernas** to go off with one's tail between one's legs **- 2.** [de hoja, fruto] stem.

rácano, na *fam adj* [tacaño] mean, stingy.

RACE (*abrev de* **Real Automóvil Club de España**) *m Spanish automobile association,* ≃ AA *UK*, ≃ AAA *US*.

racha *f* **- 1.** [ráfaga] gust (of wind) **- 2.** [época] spell; [serie] string; **buena/mala** ~ good/ bad patch; **a** ~**s** in fits and starts.

racial *adj* racial.

racimo *m* **- 1.** [de frutos] bunch **- 2.** [de flores] raceme.

raciocinio *m* [razón] (power of) reason.

ración *f* **- 1.** [porción] portion **- 2.** [en bar, res-taurante] *large portion of a dish served as a snack.*

racional *adj* rational.

racionalizar *vt* to rationalize.

racionar *vt* to ration.

racismo *m* racism.

racista *adj & m,f* racist.

radar (*pl* **radares**) *m* radar.

radiación *f* radiation.

radiactivo, va, radioactivo, va *adj* radioactive.
radiador *m* radiator.
radiante *adj* radiant; **lucía un sol ~** it was brilliantly sunny.
radiar *vt* **-1.** [irradiar] to radiate **-2.** [por radio] to broadcast.
radical *adj* & *m,f* radical.
radicar *vi*: **~ en** [suj: problema etc] to lie in; [suj: población] to be (situated) in.
◆ **radicarse** *vpr* [establecerse]: **~se (en)** to settle (in).
radio ◇ *m* **-1.** ANAT & GEOM radius **-2.** [de rueda] spoke **-3.** QUÍM radium. ◇ *f* radio; **oír algo por la ~** to hear sthg on the radio; **oír algo por ~ macuto** *fam* to hear sthg on the bush telegraph; **~ pirata** pirate radio station.
radioactivo = radiactivo.
radioaficionado, da *m,f* radio ham.
radiocasete *m* radio cassette (player).
radiocontrol *m* remote control.
radiodespertador *m* clock radio.
radiodifusión *f* broadcasting.
radioescucha *m y f inv* listener.
radiofónico, ca *adj* radio *(antes de sust)*.
radiograbador *m CSur* radio cassette.
radiografía *f* [fotografía] X-ray; **hacerse una ~** to be X-rayed; [ciencia] radiography.
radionovela *f* radio soap opera.
radiorreloj *m* clock radio.
radiotaxi *m* taxi (with radio link).
radioteléfono *m* radiotelephone.
radioterapia *f* radiotherapy.
radioyente *mf* listener.
RAE *abrev de* **Real Academia Española.**
raer *vt* to scrape (off).
ráfaga *f* [de aire, viento] gust; [de disparos] burst; [de luces] flash.
raído, da *adj* threadbare; [por los bordes] frayed.
raigambre *f* [tradición] tradition.
raíl, rail *m* rail.
raíz (*pl* **raíces**) *f* [gen & MAT] root; **~ cuadrada/cúbica** square/cube root; **a ~ de** as a result of, following; **echar raíces** to put down roots.
raja *f* **-1.** [porción] slice **-2.** [grieta] crack.
rajar *vt* **-1.** [partir] to crack; [melón] to slice **-2.** *mfam* [apuñalar] to slash, to cut up.
◆ **rajarse** *vpr* **-1.** [partirse] to crack **-2.** *fam* [echarse atrás] to chicken out.
rajatabla ◆ **a rajatabla** *loc adv* to the letter, strictly.
ralentí *m* neutral.
rallado, da *adj* grated.
rallador *m* grater.
ralladura *(gen pl) f* grating.
rallar *vt* to grate.
rally ['rali] (*pl* **rallys**) *m* rally.
RAM (*abrev de* **random access memory**) *f* RAM.
rama *f* branch; **andarse por las ~s** *fam* to beat about the bush; **irse por las ~s** *fam* to go off at a tangent.
ramaje *m* branches *(pl)*.
ramal *m* [de carretera, ferrocarril] branch.
ramalazo *m* **-1.** *fam* [hecho que delata] give-away sign; **tener un ~** *fam* to be effeminate **-2.** [ataque] fit.
rambla *f* [avenida] avenue, boulevard.
ramera *f* whore, hooker *US*.
ramificación *f* **-1.** [gen] ramification **-2.** [de carretera, ferrocarril, ciencia] branch.
ramificarse *vpr* **-1.** [bifurcarse] to branch out **-2.** [subdividirse]: **~ (en)** to subdivide (into).
ramillete *m* bunch, bouquet.
ramo *m* **-1.** [de flores] bunch, bouquet **-2.** [rama] branch; **el ~ de la construcción** the building industry.
rampa *f* **-1.** [para subir y bajar] ramp **-2.** [cuesta] steep incline.
rana *f* frog.
ranchero, ra *m,f* rancher.
◆ **ranchera** *f* **-1.** MÚS *popular Mexican song* **-2.** AUTOM estate car.
rancho *m* **-1.** [comida] mess **-2.** [granja] ranch **-3.** [loc]: **hacer ~ aparte** to keep to o.s. **-4.** *CSur, Ven* [choza] shack, shanty; *Ven* [chabola] shanty town.
rancio, cia *adj* **-1.** [pasado] rancid **-2.** [antiguo] ancient **-3.** [añejo - vino] mellow.
rango *m* **-1.** [social] standing **-2.** [jerárquico] rank.
ranking ['raŋkin] (*pl* **rankings**) *m* ranking.
ranura *f* groove; [de máquina tragaperras, cabina telefónica] slot.
rapaces ▻ **rapaz.**
rapapolvo *m fam* ticking-off.
rapar *vt* [barba, bigote] to shave off; [cabeza] to shave; [persona] to shave the hair of.
rapaz, za *m,f fam* lad (*f* lass).
◆ **rapaz** *adj* **-1.** [que roba] rapacious, greedy **-2.** ZOOL ▻ **ave.**
◆ **rapaces** *fpl* ZOOL birds of prey.
rape *m* monkfish; **cortar el pelo al ~ a alguien** to crop sb's hair.
rapé *m (en aposición inv)* snuff.
rapero, ra *m,f* rapper.
rápidamente *adv* quickly.
rapidez *f* speed.
rápido, da *adj* quick, fast; [coche] fast; [beneficio, decisión] quick.
◆ **rápido** ◇ *adv* quickly; **más ~** quicker; **¡ven, ~!** come, quick! ◇ *m* [tren] express train.

◆ **rápidos** *mpl* [de río] rapids.

rapiña *f* -**1.** [robo] robbery with violence -**2.** ▷ **ave.**

rappel ['rapel] (*pl* **rappels**) *m* DEP abseiling; **hacer** ∼ to abseil.

rapsodia *f* rhapsody.

raptar *vt* to abduct, to kidnap.

rapto *m* -**1.** [secuestro] abduction, kidnapping -**2.** [ataque] fit.

raqueta *f* [para jugar - al tenis] racquet; [- al ping pong] bat.

raquítico, ca *adj* -**1.** MED rachitic -**2.** [insuficiente] miserable.

rareza *f* -**1.** [poco común, extraño] rarity -**2.** [extravagancia] idiosyncracy, eccentricity.

raro, ra *adj* -**1.** [extraño] strange; **¡qué** ∼**!** how odd *o* strange! -**2.** [excepcional] unusual, rare; [visita] infrequent -**3.** [extravagante] odd, eccentric -**4.** [escaso] rare; **rara vez** rarely.

ras *m*: **a** ∼ **de** level with; **a** ∼ **de tierra** at ground level; **volar a** ∼ **de tierra** to fly low.

rasante *f* [de carretera] gradient.

rascacielos *m inv* skyscraper.

rascar ⬦ *vt* -**1.** [con uñas, clavo] to scratch -**2.** [con espátula] to scrape (off); [con cepillo] to scrub. ⬦ *vi* to be rough.

◆ **rascarse** *vpr* to scratch o.s.

rasgar *vt* to tear; [sobre] to tear open.

rasgo *m* -**1.** [característica] trait, characteristic -**2.** [trazo] flourish, stroke.

◆ **rasgos** *mpl* -**1.** [del rostro] features -**2.** [letra] handwriting (*U*).

◆ **a grandes rasgos** *loc adv* in general terms.

rasguear *vt* to strum.

rasguñar *vt* to scratch.

rasguño *m* scratch.

raso, sa *adj* -**1.** [cucharada etc] level -**2.** [a poca altura] low -**3.** MIL: **soldado** ∼ private.

◆ **raso** *m* -**1.** [tela] satin.

raspa *f* backbone (of fish).

raspadura *f* (*gen pl*) scraping; [señal] scratch.

raspar *vt* -**1.** [rascar] to scrape (off) -**2.** [rasar] to graze, to shave.

◆ **rasparse** *vpr* to scratch o.s.

rasposo, sa *adj* rough.

rastras ◆ **a rastras** *loc adv*: **llevar algo/a alguien a** ∼ *lit & fig* to drag sthg/sb along.

rastreador, ra *m,f* tracker.

rastrear *vt* [seguir las huellas de] to track.

rastrero, ra *adj* despicable.

rastrillo *m* -**1.** [en jardinería] rake -**2.** [mercado] flea market; [benéfico] jumble sale.

rastro *m* -**1.** [pista] trail; **perder el** ∼ **de**

alguien to lose track of sb; **sin dejar** ∼ without trace -**2.** [vestigio] trace -**3.** [mercado] flea market.

rastrojo *m* stubble.

rasurar *vt* to shave.

◆ **rasurarse** *vpr* to shave.

rata *f* rat.

ratero, ra *m,f* petty thief.

ratificar *vt* to ratify.

◆ **ratificarse en** *vpr* to stand by, to stick to.

rato *m* while; **estuvimos hablando mucho** ∼ we were talking for quite a while; **al poco** ∼ **(de)** shortly after; **pasar el** ∼ to kill time, to pass the time; **pasar un mal** ∼ to have a hard time of it; ∼**s libres** spare time (*U*); **a** ∼**s** at times.

ratón *m* [gen & INFORM] mouse.

ratonera *f* -**1.** [para ratas] mousetrap -**2.** *fig* [trampa] trap.

raudal *m* -**1.** [de agua] torrent -**2.** *fig* [montón] abundance; [de lágrimas] flood; [de desgracias] string; **a** ∼**es** in abundance, by the bucket.

ravioli (*gen pl*) *m* ravioli (*U*).

raya *f* -**1.** [línea] line; [en tejido] stripe; **a** ∼**s** striped -**2.** [del pelo] parting; **hacerse la** ∼ to part one's hair -**3.** [de pantalón] crease -**4.** *fig* [límite] limit; **pasarse de la** ∼ to overstep the mark -**5.** [señal - en disco, pintura etc] scratch -**6.** [pez] ray -**7.** [guión] dash.

rayado, da *adj* -**1.** [a rayas - tela] striped; [- papel] ruled -**2.** [estropeado] scratched.

◆ **rayado** *m* [rayas] stripes (*pl*).

rayar ⬦ *vt* -**1.** [marcar] to scratch -**2.** [trazar rayas] to rule lines on. ⬦ *vi* -**1.** [aproximarse]: ∼ **en algo** to border on sthg; **raya en los cuarenta** he's pushing forty -**2.** [alba] to break.

◆ **rayarse** *vpr* to get scratched.

rayo *m* -**1.** [de luz] ray; ∼ **solar** sunbeam -**2.** FÍS beam, ray; ∼ **láser** laser beam; ∼**s infrarrojos/ultravioleta/uva** infrared/ultraviolet/UVA rays; ∼**s X** X-rays; **caer como un** ∼ *fig* to be a bombshell -**3.** METEOR bolt of lightning; ∼**s** lightning (*U*).

rayón *m* rayon.

rayuela *f* hopscotch.

raza *f* -**1.** [humana] race; ∼ **humana** human race -**2.** [animal] breed; **de** ∼ [caballo] thoroughbred; [perro] pedigree -**3.** *Perú fam* [cara] cheek, nerve.

razón *f* -**1.** [gen] reason; **con** ∼ no vino no wonder he didn't come; **dar la** ∼ **a alguien** to say that sb is right; **en** ∼ **de** *o* **a** in view of; ∼ **de ser** raison d'être; **tener** ∼ **(en hacer algo)** to be right (to do sthg); **no tener** ∼ to be wrong; ∼ **de más para hacer algo** all the more reason to do sthg; **y con** ∼

and quite rightly so - **2**. [información]: **se vende piso**; ~ **aquí** flat for sale: enquire within; **dar** ~ **de** to give an account of - **3**. MAT ratio.
➤ **a razón de** *loc adv* at a rate of.
razonable *adj* reasonable.
razonamiento *m* reasoning *(U)*.
razonar <> *vt* [argumentar] to reason out. <> *vi* [pensar] to reason.
RDSI (*abrev de* **Red Digital de Servicios Integrados**) *f* COMPUT ISDN.
re *m* MÚS D; [en solfeo] re.
reacción *f* reaction; ~ **en cadena** chain reaction.
reaccionar *vi* to react; ~ **a algo** to react to sthg.
reaccionario, ria *adj* & *m,f* reactionary.
reacio, cia *adj* stubborn; **ser** ~ **a** *o* **en hacer algo** to be reluctant to do sthg.
reactivación *f* revival.
reactor *m* - **1**. [propulsor] reactor - **2**. [avión] jet (plane).
readmitir *vt* to accept *o* take back.
reafirmar *vt* to confirm.
➤ **reafirmarse** *vpr* to assert o.s.; ~**se en algo** to become confirmed in sthg.
reajuste *m* - **1**. [cambio] readjustment; ~ **ministerial** cabinet reshuffle - **2**. [ECON - de precios, impuestos] increase; [- de sector] streamlining; [- de salarios] reduction; ~ **de plantilla** redundancies *(pl)*.
real *adj* - **1**. [verdadero] real - **2**. [de monarquía] royal.
realce *m* - **1**. [esplendor] glamour; **dar** ~ **a algo/alguien** to enhance sthg/sb - **2**. [en pintura] highlight.
realeza *f* - **1**. [monarcas] royalty.
realidad *f* - **1**. [mundo real] reality; ~ **virtual** INFORM virtual reality - **2**. [verdad] truth; **en** ~ actually, in fact.
realista <> *adj* realistic. <> *mf* ARTE realist.
realización *f* - **1**. [ejecución] carrying-out; [de proyecto, medidas] implementation; [de sueños, deseos] fulfilment - **2**. [obra] achievement - **3**. CIN production.
realizador, ra *m,f* CIN & TV director.
realizar *vt* - **1**. [ejecutar - esfuerzo, viaje, inversión] to make; [- operación, experimento, trabajo] to perform; [- encargo] to carry out; [- plan, reformas] to implement - **2**. [hacer real] to fulfil, to realize - **3**. CIN to produce.
➤ **realizarse** *vpr* - **1**. [en un trabajo] to find fulfilment - **2**. [hacerse real - sueño, predicción, deseo] to come true; [- esperanza, ambición] to be fulfilled - **3**. [ejecutarse] to be carried out.
realmente *adv* - **1**. [en verdad] in fact, actually - **2**. [muy] really, very.
realquilado, da *m, f* sub-tenant.

realquilar *vt* to sublet.
realzar *vt* - **1**. [resaltar] to enhance - **2**. [en pintura] to highlight.
reanimar *vt* - **1**. [físicamente] to revive - **2**. [moralmente] to cheer up - **3**. MED to resuscitate.
reanudar *vt* [conversación, trabajo] to resume; [amistad] to renew.
reaparición *f* reappearance.
rearme *m* rearmament.
reavivar *vt* to revive.
rebaja *f* - **1**. [acción] reduction - **2**. [descuento] discount; **hacer una** ~ to give a discount.
➤ **rebajas** *fpl* COM sales; **'grandes** ~**s'** 'massive reductions'; **estar de** ~**s** to have a sale on.
rebajado, da *adj* - **1**. [precio] reduced - **2**. [humillado] humiliated.
rebajar *vt* - **1**. [precio] to reduce; **te rebajo 2 euros** I'll knock 2 euros off for you - **2**. [persona] to humiliate - **3**. [intensidad] to tone down - **4**. [altura] to lower.
➤ **rebajarse** *vpr* [persona] to humble o.s.; ~**se a hacer algo** to lower o.s. *o* stoop to do sthg; ~**se ante alguien** to humble o.s. before sb.
rebanada *f* slice.
rebañar *vt* to scrape clean.
rebaño *m* flock; [de vacas] herd.
rebasar *vt* to exceed, to surpass; [agua] to overflow; AUTOM to overtake.
rebatir *vt* to refute.
rebeca *f* cardigan.
rebelarse *vpr* to rebel; ~ **contra alguien/algo** to rebel against sb/sthg.
rebelde <> *adj* - **1**. [sublevado] rebel *(antes de sust)* - **2**. [desobediente] rebellious. <> *mf* [sublevado, desobediente] rebel.
rebeldía *f* - **1**. [cualidad] rebelliousness - **2**. [acción] (act of) rebellion.
rebelión *f* rebellion; ~ **militar** military uprising.
rebenque *m* CSur riding crop.
reblandecer *vt* to soften.
rebobinar *vt* to rewind.
rebosante *adj*: ~ **(de)** brimming *o* overflowing (with).
rebosar <> *vt* to overflow with, to brim with. <> *vi* to overflow; ~ **de** to be overflowing with; *fig* [persona] to brim with.
rebotar *vi*: ~ **(en)** to bounce (off), to rebound (off).
rebote *m* - **1**. [bote] bounce, bouncing *(U)* - **2**. DEP rebound; **de** ~ on the rebound.
rebozado, da *adj* CULIN coated in batter *o* breadcrumbs.
rebozar *vt* CULIN to coat in batter *o* breadcrumbs.

rebuscado, da *adj* recherché, pretentious.

rebuznar *vi* to bray.

recabar *vt* [pedir] to ask for; [conseguir] to obtain.

recadero, ra *m,f* messenger.

recado *m* - 1. [mensaje] message; **mandar ~ de que ...** to send word that ... - 2. [encargo] errand; **hacer ~s** to run errands.

recaer *vi* - 1. [enfermo] to have a relapse - 2. [ir a parar]: ~ **sobre** to fall on - 3. [reincidir]: ~ **en** to relapse into.

recaída *f* relapse.

recalcar *vt* to stress, to emphasize.

recalcitrante *adj* recalcitrant.

recalentar *vt* - 1. [volver a calentar] to warm up - 2. [calentar demasiado] to overheat.

recámara *f* - 1. [de arma de fuego] chamber - 2. *CAm, Col* & *Méx* [dormitorio] bedroom.

recamarera *f CAm, Col, Méx* chambermaid.

recambio *m* spare (part); [para pluma] refill; **de ~** spare.

recapacitar *vi* to reflect, to think; ~ **sobre** to think about.

recapitulación *f* recap, recapitulation.

recargado, da *adj* [estilo etc] overelaborate, affected.

recargar *vt* - 1. [volver a cargar - encendedor, recipiente] to refill; [- batería, pila] to recharge; [- fusil, camión] to reload - 2. [cargar demasiado] to overload - 3. [adornar en exceso] to overelaborate - 4. [cantidad]: ~ **20 euros a alguien** to charge sb 20 euros extra - 5. [poner en exceso]: ~ **algo de algo** to put too much of sthg in sthg.

◆ recargarse *vpr Méx* [apoyarse] to lean.

recargo *m* extra charge, surcharge.

◆ recargarse de *vpr*: recargarse de responsabilidades to take on too much responsibility.

recatado, da *adj* [pudoroso] modest, demure.

recato *m* [pudor] modesty, demureness.

recaudación *f* - 1. [acción] collection, collecting - 2. [cantidad] takings *(pl)*; DEP gate; [de un cine] box office takings.

recaudador, ra *m,f*: ~ **(de impuestos)** tax collector.

recaudar *vt* to collect.

recelar *vi* to be mistrustful; ~ **de** to mistrust.

recelo *m* mistrust, suspicion.

receloso, sa *adj* mistrustful, suspicious.

recepción *f* [gen] reception.

recepcionista *mf* receptionist.

receptáculo *m* receptacle.

receptivo, va *adj* receptive.

receptor, ra *m,f* [persona] recipient.

◆ receptor *m* [aparato] receiver.

recesión *f* recession.

receta *f* - 1. CULIN & *fig* recipe - 2. MED prescription.

rechazar *vt* - 1. [gen & MED] to reject; [oferta] to turn down - 2. [repeler - a una persona] to push away; [- MIL] to drive back, to repel.

rechazo *m* - 1. [gen & MED] rejection; [hacia una ley, un político] disapproval; ~ **a hacer algo** refusal to do sthg - 2. [negación] denial.

rechinar *vi* - 1. [puerta] to creak; [dientes] to grind; [frenos, ruedas] to screech; [metal] to clank - 2. [dando dentera] to grate.

rechistar *vi* to answer back.

rechoncho, cha *adj fam* tubby, chubby.

rechupete ◆ de rechupete *loc adv fam* [gen] brilliant, great; [comida] delicious, scrumptious.

recibidor *m* entrance hall.

recibimiento *m* reception, welcome.

recibir ◇ *vt* - 1. [gen] to receive; [clase, instrucción] to have - 2. [dar la bienvenida a] to welcome - 3. [ir a buscar] to meet. ◇ *vi* [atender visitas] to receive visitors.

◆ recibirse *vpr Amér*: ~se **(de)** to graduate, to qualify (as).

recibo *m* receipt; **acusar ~ de** to acknowledge receipt of; **no ser de ~** to be unacceptable.

reciclaje *m* - 1. [de residuos] recycling - 2. [de personas] retraining.

reciclar *vt* [residuos] to recycle.

recién *adv* - 1. recently, newly; **el ~ casado** the newly-wed; **los ~ llegados** the newcomers; **el ~ nacido** the newborn baby - 2. [hace poco] *Amér* just; ~ **llegó** he has just arrived.

reciente *adj* - 1. [acontecimiento etc] recent - 2. [pintura, pan etc] fresh.

recientemente *adv* recently.

recinto *m* [zona cercada] enclosure; [área] place, area; [alrededor de edificios] grounds *(pl)*; ~ **ferial** fairground *(of trade fair)*.

recio, cia *adj* - 1. [persona] robust - 2. [voz] gravelly - 3. [objeto] solid - 4. [material, tela] tough, strong.

recipiente *m* container, receptacle.

reciprocidad *f* reciprocity.

recíproco, ca *adj* mutual, reciprocal.

recital *m* - 1. [de música clásica] recital; [de rock] concert - 2. [de lectura] reading.

recitar *vt* to recite.

reclamación *f* - 1. [petición] claim, demand - 2. [queja] complaint; **hacer una ~** to lodge a complaint.

reclamar ◇ *vt* [pedir, exigir] to demand, to ask for. ◇ *vi* [protestar]: ~ **(contra)** to protest (against), to complain (about).

reclamo *m* - 1. [para atraer] inducement

- **2.** [para cazar] decoy, lure - **3.** *Amér* [queja] complaint; *Amér* [reivindicación] claim.

reclinar *vt*: ~ **algo (sobre)** to lean sthg (on).

   reclinarse *vpr* to lean back; ~**se contra algo** to lean against sthg.

recluir *vt* to shut *o* lock away, to imprison.

   recluirse *vpr* to shut o.s. away.

reclusión *f* - **1.** [encarcelamiento] imprisonment - **2.** *fig* [encierro] seclusion.

recluso, sa *m,f* [preso] prisoner.

recluta *m* [obligatorio] conscript; [voluntario] recruit.

reclutamiento *m* [de soldados - obligatorio] conscription; [- voluntario] recruitment.

recobrar *vt* [gen] to recover; [conocimiento] to regain; [tiempo perdido] to make up for.

   recobrarse *vpr*: ~**se (de)** to recover (from).

recodo *m* bend.

recogedor *m* dustpan.

recoger *vt* - **1.** [coger] to pick up - **2.** [ordenar, limpiar - mesa] to clear; [- habitación, cosas] to tidy *o* clear up - **3.** [ir a buscar] to pick up, to fetch - **4.** [albergar] to take in - **5.** [cosechar] to gather, to harvest; [fruta] to pick.

   recogerse *vpr* - **1.** [a dormir, meditar] to retire - **2.** [cabello] to put up.

recogido, da *adj* - **1.** [lugar] withdrawn, secluded - **2.** [cabello] tied back.

   recogida *f* - **1.** [gen] collection - **2.** [cosecha] harvest, gathering; [de fruta] picking.

recolección *f* - **1.** [cosecha] harvest, gathering - **2.** [recogida] collection.

recolector, ra *m,f* - **1.** [gen] collector - **2.** [de cosecha] harvester; [de fruta] picker.

recomendación *f (gen pl)* - **1.** [gen] recommendation - **2.** [referencia] reference.

recomendado, da <> *m,f* protégé (*f* protégée). <> *adj Amér* [correspondencia] registered.

recomendar *vt* to recommend; ~ **a alguien que haga algo** to recommend that sb do sthg.

recompensa *f* reward; **en ~ por** in return for.

recompensar *vt* [premiar] to reward.

recomponer *vt* to repair, to mend.

recompuesto, ta *pp* ⊳ **recomponer.**

reconciliación *f* reconciliation.

reconciliar *vt* to reconcile.

   reconciliarse *vpr* to be reconciled.

recóndito, ta *adj* hidden, secret.

reconfortar *vt* - **1.** [anímicamente] to comfort - **2.** [físicamente] to revitalize.

reconocer *vt* - **1.** [gen] to recognize - **2.** MED to examine - **3.** [terreno] to survey.

   reconocerse *vpr* - **1.** [identificarse] to recognize each other - **2.** [confesarse]: ~**se**

culpable to admit one's guilt.

reconocido, da *adj* - **1.** [admitido] recognized, acknowledged - **2.** [agradecido] grateful; **quedo muy** ~ I am very much obliged to you.

reconocimiento *m* - **1.** [gen] recognition - **2.** [agradecimiento] gratitude - **3.** MED examination - **4.** MIL reconnaissance.

reconquista *f* reconquest, recapture.

   Reconquista *f*: **la Reconquista** HIST *the Reconquest of Spain, when the Christian Kings retook the country from the Muslims.*

reconstruir *vt* - **1.** [edificio, país etc] to rebuild - **2.** [suceso] to reconstruct.

reconversión *f* restructuring; ~ **industrial** rationalization of industry.

recopilación *f* [texto - de poemas, artículos] compilation, collection; [- de leyes] code.

recopilar *vt* - **1.** [recoger] to collect, to gather - **2.** [escritos, leyes] to compile.

récord (*pl* **récords**) <> *m* record; **batir un** ~ to break a record. <> *adj inv* record.

recordar <> *vt* - **1.** [acordarse de] to remember; ~ **a alguien algo/que haga algo** to remind sb sthg/to do sthg - **2.** [traer a la memoria] to remind; **me recuerda a un amigo mío** he reminds me of a friend of mine. <> *vi* to remember; **si mal no recuerdo** as far as I can remember.

recordatorio *m* [aviso] reminder.

recordman [reˈkorðman] (*pl* **recordmen** *o* **recordmans**) *m* record holder.

recorrer *vt* - **1.** [atravesar - lugar, país] to travel through *o* across, to cross; [- ciudad] to go round - **2.** [distancia] to cover - **3.** *fig* [con la mirada] to look over.

recorrida *f Amér* [ruta, itinerario] route; [viaje] journey.

recorrido *m* - **1.** [trayecto] route, path - **2.** [viaje] journey.

recortado, da *adj* - **1.** [cortado] cut - **2.** [borde] jagged.

recortar *vt* - **1.** [cortar - lo que sobra] to cut off *o* away; [- figuras de un papel] to cut out - **2.** [pelo, flequillo] to trim - **3.** *fig* [reducir] to cut.

   recortarse *vpr* [figura etc] to stand out, to be outlined; ~**se sobre algo** to stand out against sthg.

recorte *m* - **1.** [pieza cortada] cut, trimming; [de periódico, revista] cutting, clipping - **2.** [reducción] cut, cutback; ~**s presupuestarios** budget cuts.

recostar *vt* to lean (back).

   recostarse *vpr* to lie down.

recoveco *m* - **1.** [rincón] nook, hidden corner - **2.** [curva] bend - **3.** *fig* [lo más oculto]: **los** ~**s del alma** the innermost recesses of the mind.

...eación *f* re-creation.

...crear *vt* - **1.** [volver a crear] to recreate - **2.** [entretener] to amuse, to entertain.

◆ **recrearse** *vpr* - **1.** [entretenerse] to amuse o.s., to entertain o.s. - **2.** [regodearse] to take delight *o* pleasure.

recreativo, va *adj* recreational.

recreo *m* - **1.** [entretenimiento] recreation, amusement - **2.** [EDUC - en primaria] playtime *UK*, recess *US*; [- en secundaria] break *UK*, recess *US*.

recriminar *vt* to reproach.

recrudecerse *vpr* to get worse.

recta ⊳ **recto**.

rectángulo *m* rectangle.

rectificar *vt* - **1.** [error] to rectify, to correct - **2.** [conducta, actitud etc] to improve - **3.** [ajustar] to put right.

rectitud *f* straightness; *fig* rectitude, uprightness.

recto, ta *adj* - **1.** [sin curvas, vertical] straight - **2.** *fig* [íntegro] upright, honourable.

◆ **recto** ⊳ *m* ANAT rectum. ⊳ *adv* straight on *o* ahead.

◆ **recta** *f* straight line; **la recta final** *lit & fig* the home straight.

rector, ra ⊳ *adj* governing, guiding. ⊳ *m,f* - **1.** [de universidad] vice-chancellor *UK*, president *US*.

◆ **rector** *m* RELIG rector.

recuadro *m* box.

recubrir *vt* [gen] to cover; [con pintura, barniz] to coat.

recuento *m* recount.

recuerdo *m* - **1.** [rememoración] memory - **2.** [objeto - de viaje] souvenir; [- de persona] keepsake; **de** ~ as a souvenir.

◆ **recuerdos** *mpl* [saludos] regards; **dale** ~**s de mi parte** give her my regards.

recular *vi* [retroceder] to go *o* move back

recuperable *adj* [gen] recoverable; [fiestas, horas de trabajo] that can be made up later.

recuperación *f* - **1.** [de lo perdido, la salud, la economía] recovery; ~ **de datos** INFORM data recovery - **2.** [fisioterapia] physiotherapy.

recuperar *vt* [lo perdido] to recover; [horas de trabajo] to catch up; [conocimiento] to regain.

◆ **recuperarse** *vpr* - **1.** [enfermo] to recuperate, to recover - **2.** [de una crisis] to recover; [negocio] to pick up; ~**se de algo** to get over sthg.

recurrir *vi* - **1.** [buscar ayuda]: ~ **a alguien** to turn to sb; ~ **a algo** to resort to sthg - **2.** DER to appeal; ~ **contra algo** to appeal against sthg.

recurso *m* - **1.** [medio] resort; **como último** ~ as a last resort - **2.** DER appeal.

◆ **recursos** *mpl* [fondos] resources; **es**

una mujer llena de ~**s** she's a resourceful woman; [financieros] means; **sin** ~**s** with no means of support; ~**s propios** ECON equities.

red *f* - **1.** [malla] net; [para cabello] hairnet - **2.** [sistema] network, system; [de electricidad, agua] mains *(sg)*; ~ **viaria** road network *o* system - **3.** [organización - de espionaje] ring; [- de tiendas] chain - **4.** INFORM network.

◆ **Red** *f*: **la Red** the Net; **navegar por la** ~ to surf the Net.

redacción *f* - **1.** [acción - gen] writing; [- de periódico etc] editing - **2.** [estilo] wording - **3.** [equipo de redactores] editorial team *o* staff - **4.** [oficina] editorial office - **5.** EDUC essay, composition.

redactar *vt* to write (up); [carta] to draft.

redactor, ra *m,f* [PRENS - escritor] writer; [- editor] editor; ~ **jefe** editor-in-chief.

redada *f* [de policía - en un solo lugar] raid; [- en varios lugares] round-up.

redención *f* redemption.

redil *m* fold, pen.

redimir *vt* - **1.** [gen] to redeem - **2.** [librar] to free, to exempt.

◆ **redimirse** *vpr* to redeem o.s.

rédito *m* interest *(U)*, yield *(U)*.

redoblar ⊳ *vt* to redouble. ⊳ *vi* to roll.

redomado, da *adj* out-and-out.

redondear *vt* - **1.** [hacer redondo] to round, to make round - **2.** [negocio, acuerdo] to round off - **3.** [cifra, precio] to round up/down.

redondel *m* - **1.** [gen] circle, ring - **2.** TAUROM bullring.

redondo, da *adj* - **1.** [circular, esférico] round; **a la redonda** around; **caerse** ~ *fig* to collapse in a heap; **girar en** ~ to turn around - **2.** [perfecto] excellent.

reducción *f* - **1.** [gen] reduction; ~ **de gastos** reduction in costs - **2.** [sometimiento] suppression.

reducido, da *adj* - **1.** [pequeño] small - **2.** [limitado] limited - **3.** [estrecho] narrow.

reducir *vt* - **1.** [gen] to reduce - **2.** [someter - país, ciudad] to suppress, to subdue; [- sublevados, atracadores] to bring under control - **3.** MAT [convertir] to convert.

◆ **reducirse a** *vpr* - **1.** [limitarse a] to be reduced to - **2.** [equivaler a] to boil *o* come down to.

reducto *m* - **1.** [fortificación] redoubt - **2.** *fig* [refugio] stronghold, bastion.

redundancia *f* redundancy; **y valga la** ~ if you'll excuse the repetition.

redundante *adj* redundant, superfluous.

redundar *vi*: ~ **en algo** to have an effect on sthg; **redunda en beneficio nuestro** it is to our advantage.

reeditar *vt* to bring out a new edition of; [reimprimir] to reprint.

reelección *f* re-election.

reembolsar, rembolsar *vt* [gastos] to reimburse; [fianza, dinero] to refund; [deuda] to repay.

reembolso, rembolso *m* [de gastos] reimbursement; [de fianza, dinero] refund; [de deuda] repayment; **contra ~** cash on delivery.

reemplazar, remplazar *vt* [gen & INFORM] to replace; **~ algo/alguien por algo/alguien** to replace sthg/sb with sthg/sb.

reemplazo, remplazo *m* -**1.** [gen & INFORM] replacement - **2.** MIL call-up, draft.

reemprender *vt* to start again.

reencarnación *f* reincarnation.

reencuentro *m* reunion.

reestructurar *vt* to restructure.

refacción *f* Andes, CAm, RP, Ven repair; Méx [recambio] spare part.

refaccionar *vt* Andes, CAm, Ven to repair.

refaccionaria *f* Amér repair workshop.

referencia *f* reference; **con ~ a** with reference to.

➤ **referencias** *fpl* [informes] references; **tener buenas ~s** to have good references.

referéndum (*pl* **referéndums**) *m* referendum; **convocar un ~** to call a referendum.

referente *adj*: **~ a** concerning, relating to; **en lo ~ a** regarding.

referir *vt* -**1.** [narrar] to tell, to recount - **2.** [remitir]: **~ a alguien a** to refer sb to - **3.** [relacionar]: **~ algo a** to relate sthg to.

➤ **referirse a** *vpr* to refer to; **¿a qué te refieres?** what do you mean?; **por lo que se refiere a ...** as far as ... is concerned.

refilón

➤ **de refilón** *loc adv* -**1.** [de lado] sideways; **mirar algo de ~** to look at sthg out of the corner of one's eye - **2.** *fig* [de pasada] briefly.

refinado, da *adj* refined.

refinamiento *m* refinement.

refinar *vt* to refine.

refinería *f* refinery.

reflector *m* ELECTR spotlight; MIL searchlight.

reflejar *vt* lit & fig to reflect.

➤ **reflejarse** *vpr* lit & fig: **~se (en)** to be reflected (in).

reflejo, ja *adj* [movimiento, dolor] reflex (antes de sust).

➤ **reflejo** *m* -**1.** [gen] reflection - **2.** [destello] glint, gleam - **3.** ANAT reflex.

➤ **reflejos** *mpl* [de peluquería] highlights.

reflexión *f* reflection; **con ~** on reflection; **sin previa ~** without thinking.

reflexionar *vi* to reflect, to think; **~ sobre algo** to think about sthg.

reflexivo, va *adj* -**1.** [que piensa] reflective, thoughtful - **2.** GRAM reflexive.

reflujo *m* ebb (tide).

reforma *f* -**1.** [modificación] reform; **~ agraria** agrarian reform - **2.** [en local, casa etc] alterations (*pl*); **hacer ~s** to renovate.

➤ **Reforma** *f*: **la Reforma** RELIG the Reformation.

reformar *vt* -**1.** [gen & RELIG] to reform - **2.** [local, casa etc] to renovate, to do up.

➤ **reformarse** *vpr* to mend one's ways.

reformatorio *m* ≃ youth custody centre UK, ≃ borstal UK, reformatory US; [de menores de 15 años] ≃ remand home.

reforzar *vt* to reinforce.

refractario, ria *adj* -**1.** [material] refractory, heat-resistant - **2.** [opuesto]: **~ a** averse to.

refrán *m* proverb, saying.

refregar *vt* -**1.** [frotar] to scrub - **2.** *fig* [reprochar]: **~ algo a alguien** to reproach sb for sthg.

refrenar *vt* to curb, to restrain.

refrendar *vt* [aprobar] to approve.

refrescante *adj* refreshing.

refrescar ◇ *vt* -**1.** [gen] to refresh; [bebidas] to chill - **2.** *fig* [conocimientos] to brush up. ◇ *vi* -**1.** [tiempo] to cool down - **2.** [bebida] to be refreshing.

➤ **refrescarse** *vpr* -**1.** [tomar aire fresco] to get a breath of fresh air - **2.** [beber algo] to have a drink - **3.** [mojarse con agua fría] to splash o.s. down.

refresco *m* -**1.** [bebida] soft drink; **~s** refreshments - **2.** [relevo]: **de ~** new, fresh.

refriega *f* scuffle; MIL fracas, skirmish.

refrigeración *f* -**1.** [aire acondicionado] air-conditioning - **2.** [de alimentos] refrigeration - **3.** [de máquinas] cooling.

refrigerador, ra *adj* cooling.

➤ **refrigerador** *m* [de alimentos] refrigerator, fridge UK, icebox US.

refrigerar *vt* -**1.** [alimentos] to refrigerate - **2.** [local] to air-condition - **3.** [máquina] to cool.

refrigerio *m* snack.

refrito, ta *adj* [demasiado frito] over-fried; [frito de nuevo] re-fried.

➤ **refrito** *m* *fig* [cosa rehecha] rehash.

refuerzo *m* reinforcement, strengthening (U).

refugiado, da *m,f* refugee.

refugiar *vt* to give refuge to.

➤ **refugiarse** *vpr* to take refuge; **~se de algo** to shelter from sthg.

refugio *m* -**1.** [lugar] shelter, refuge; **~ atómico** nuclear bunker - **2.** *fig* [amparo, consuelo] refuge, comfort.

refulgir *vi* to shine brightly.

refunfuñar *vi* to grumble.

refutar *vt* to refute.

regadera *f* - **1.** [para regar] watering can - **2.** *Col, Méx, Ven* [ducha] shower.

regadío *m* irrigated land.

regalado, da *adj* - **1.** [muy barato] dirt cheap - **2.** [agradable] comfortable, easy.

regalar *vt* - **1.** [dar - de regalo] to give (as a present); [- gratis] to give away - **2.** [agasajar]: ~ **a alguien con algo** to shower sb with sthg.

regaliz *m* liquorice.

regalo *m* - **1.** [obsequio] present, gift; **un** ~ **del cielo** a godsend - **2.** [placer] joy, delight.

regalón, ona *adj RP* & *Chile fam* spoilt.

regañadientes ➡ **a regañadientes** *loc adv fam* unwillingly, reluctantly.

regañar ◇ *vt* [reprender] to tell off. ◇ *vi* [pelearse] to fall out, to argue.

regañina *f* [reprimenda] ticking off.

regar *vt* - **1.** [con agua - planta] to water; [- calle] to hose down - **2.** [suj: río] to flow through.

regata *f* NÁUT regatta, boat race.

regatear ◇ *vt* - **1.** [escatimar] to be sparing with; **no ha regateado esfuerzos** he has spared no effort - **2.** DEP to beat, to dribble past - **3.** [precio] to haggle over. ◇ *vi* - **1.** [negociar el precio] to barter, to haggle - **2.** NÁUT to race.

regateo *m* bartering, haggling.

regazo *m* lap.

regeneración *f* regeneration; [moral] reform.

regenerar *vt* to regenerate; [moralmente] to reform.

regentar *vt* [país] to run, to govern; [negocio] to run, to manage; [puesto] to hold.

regente ◇ *adj* regent. ◇ *mf* - **1.** [de un país] regent - **2.** [administrador - de tienda] manager; [- de colegio] governor - **3.** *Méx* [alcalde] mayor (*f* mayoress).

regidor, ra *m, f* TEATR stage manager; CIN & TV assistant director.

régimen (*pl* **regímenes**) *m* - **1.** [sistema político] regime; **Antiguo** ~ ancien régime - **2.** [normativa] rules (*pl*) - **3.** [dieta] diet - **4.** [de vida, lluvias etc] pattern, usual routine; ~ **de vida** lifestyle.

regimiento *m* MIL & *fig* regiment.

regio, gia *adj* - **1.** *lit* & *fig* royal - **2.** *Amér fig fam* fantastic.

región *f* region; MIL district.

regir ◇ *vt* - **1.** [reinar en] to rule, to govern - **2.** [administrar] to run, to manage - **3.** *fig* [determinar] to govern, to determine. ◇ *vi* [ley] to be in force, to apply.

➡ **regirse por** *vpr* to trust in, to be guided by.

registradora *f Amér* cash register.

registrar *vt* - **1.** [inspeccionar - zona, piso] to search; [- persona] to frisk - **2.** [nacimiento, temperatura etc] to register, to record.

➡ **registrarse** *vpr* - **1.** [suceder] to occur, to happen - **2.** [observarse] to be recorded.

registro *m* - **1.** [oficina] registry (office); ~ **civil** registry (office) - **2.** [libro] register - **3.** [inspección] search, searching (*U*) - **4.** INFORM record - **5.** LING & MÚS register.

regla *f* - **1.** [para medir] ruler, rule - **2.** [norma] rule; **en** ~ in order; **por** ~ **general** as a rule, generally - **3.** MAT operation - **4.** *fam* [menstruación] period.

reglamentación *f* [acción] regulation; [reglas] rules (*pl*), regulations (*pl*).

reglamentar *vt* to regulate.

reglamentario, ria *adj* lawful; [arma, balón] within the rules, regulation (*antes de sust*); DER statutory.

reglamento *m* regulations (*pl*), rules (*pl*); ~ **de tráfico** traffic regulations (*pl*).

regocijar

➡ **regocijarse** *vpr*: ~**se (de** *o* **con)** to rejoice (in).

regocijo *m* joy, delight.

regodeo *m* delight, pleasure; [malicioso] (cruel) delight *o* pleasure.

regordete *adj* chubby, tubby.

regresar ◇ *vi* [yendo] to go back, to return; [viniendo] to come back, to return. ◇ *vt Andes, CAm, Carib, Méx* [devolver] to give back.

regresión *f* - **1.** [de epidemia] regression - **2.** [de exportaciones] drop, decline.

regresivo, va *adj* regressive.

regreso *m* return; **estar de** ~ to be back.

reguero *m* [de sangre, agua] trickle; [de harina etc] dribble, trail; **correr como un** ~ **de pólvora** to spread like wildfire.

regulación *f* [gen] regulation; [de nacimientos, tráfico] control; [de mecanismo] adjustment.

regulador, ra *adj* regulating, regulatory.

regular ◇ *adj* - **1.** [gen] regular; [de tamaño] medium; **de un modo** ~ regularly - **2.** [mediocre] average, fair - **3.** [normal] normal, usual. ◇ *adv* all right; [de salud] so-so. ◇ *vt* [gen] to control, to regulate; [mecanismo] to adjust.

➡ **por lo regular** *loc adv* as a rule, generally.

regularidad *f* regularity; **con** ~ regularly.

regularizar *vt* [legalizar] to regularize.

regusto *m* aftertaste; [semejanza, aire] flavour, hint.

rehabilitación *f* - **1.** [de personas] rehabilitation; [en un puesto] reinstatement - **2.** [de local] restoration.

rehabilitar *vt* - 1. [personas] to rehabilitate; [en un puesto] to reinstate - 2. [local] to restore.

rehacer *vt* - 1. [volver a hacer] to redo, to do again - 2. [reconstruir] to rebuild.

◆ **rehacerse** *vpr* [recuperarse] to recuperate, to recover.

rehecho, cha *pp* ▷ rehacer.

rehén (*pl* rehenes) *m* hostage; **tomar como** ~ to take hostage.

rehogar *vt* to fry over a low heat.

rehuir *vt* to avoid.

rehusar *vt* & *vi* to refuse.

Reikiavik Reykjavik.

reimpresión *f* [tirada] reprint; [acción] reprinting.

reina *f* [monarca] queen; ~ **de belleza** beauty queen; ~ **madre** queen mother.

reinado *m* lit & fig reign.

reinante *adj* - 1. [monarquía, persona] reigning, ruling - 2. [viento] prevailing; [frío, calor] current.

reinar *vi* lit & fig to reign.

reincidir *vi*: ~ **en** [falta, error] to relapse into, to fall back into; [delito] to repeat.

reincorporar *vt* to reincorporate.

◆ **reincorporarse** *vpr*: ~**se (a)** to rejoin, to go back to.

reino *m* CIENCIA & POLÍT kingdom; fig realm.

Reino Unido: el ~ the United Kingdom.

reintegrar *vt* - 1. [a un puesto] to reinstate - 2. [dinero] to repay, to reimburse.

◆ **reintegrarse** *vpr*: ~**se (a)** to return (to).

reintegro *m* - 1. [de dinero] repayment, reimbursement; BANCA withdrawal - 2. [en lotería] return of one's stake *(in lottery)*.

reír ◇ *vi* to laugh. ◇ *vt* to laugh at.

◆ **reírse** *vpr*: ~**se (de)** to laugh (at).

reiterar *vt* to reiterate, to repeat.

reiterativo, va *adj* repetitive, repetitious.

reivindicación *f* - 1. [de derechos] claim, demand - 2. [de atentado] claiming of responsibility.

reivindicar *vt* - 1. [derechos, salario etc] to claim, to demand - 2. [atentado] to claim responsibility for.

reivindicativo, va *adj*: plataforma reivindicativa (set of) demands; jornada reivindicativa day of protest.

reja *f* [gen] bars *(pl)*; [en el suelo] grating; [celosía] grille.

rejego, ga *adj Amér fam* [terco] stubborn.

rejilla *f* - 1. [enrejado] grid, grating; [de ventana] grille; [de cocina] grill *(on stove)*; [de horno] gridiron - 2. [para sillas, muebles] wickerwork - 3. [para equipaje] luggage rack.

rejón *m* TAUROM *type of 'banderilla' used by mounted bullfighter.*

rejoneador, ra *m,f* TAUROM *bullfighter on horseback who uses the 'rejón'.*

rejuntarse *vpr fam* to live together.

rejuvenecer *vt* & *vi* to rejuvenate.

relación *f* - 1. [nexo] relation, connection; **con** ~ **a, en** ~ **con** in relation to, with regard to; **tener** ~ **con algo** to bear a relation to sthg; ~ **precio-calidad** value for money - 2. [comunicación, trato] relations *(pl)*, relationship; **relaciones diplomáticas/públicas** diplomatic/public relations - 3. [lista] list - 4. [descripción] account - 5. [informe] report - 6. *(gen pl)* [noviazgo] relationship - 7. MAT ratio; **en una** ~ **de tres a uno** in a ratio of three to one.

◆ **relaciones** *fpl* [contactos] contacts, connections.

relacionar *vt* [vincular] to relate, to connect.

◆ **relacionarse** *vpr*: ~**se (con)** [alternar] to mix (with).

relajación *f* relaxation.

relajar *vt* to relax.

◆ **relajarse** *vpr* to relax.

relajo *m Amér fam* [alboroto] racket, din.

relamer *vt* to lick repeatedly.

◆ **relamerse** *vpr* - 1. [persona] to lick one's lips - 2. [animal] to lick its chops.

relamido, da *adj* prim and proper.

relámpago *m* [descarga] flash of lightning, lightning *(U)*; [destello] flash.

relampaguear *vi* fig to flash.

relatar *vt* [suceso] to relate, to recount; [historia] to tell.

relatividad *f* relativity.

relativo, va *adj* - 1. [gen] relative - 2. [escaso] limited.

relato *m* [exposición] account, report; [cuento] tale, story.

relax *m inv* - 1. [relajación] relaxation - 2. [sección de periódico] personal column.

relegar *vt*: ~ **(a)** to relegate (to); ~ **algo al olvido** to banish sthg from one's mind.

relevante *adj* outstanding, important.

relevar *vt* - 1. [sustituir] to relieve, to take over from - 2. [destituir]: ~ **(de)** to dismiss (from), to relieve (of) - 3. [eximir]: ~ **(de)** to free (from) - 4. [DEP - en partidos] to substitute; [- en relevos] to take over from.

◆ **relevarse** *vpr* to take turns.

relevo *m* - 1. MIL relief, changing - 2. DEP [acción] relay - 3. *loc*: **tomar el** ~ to take over.

◆ **relevos** *mpl* DEP [carrera] relay (race) *(sg)*.

relieve *m* - 1. [gen, ARTE & GEOGR] relief - 2. [importancia] importance; **poner de** ~ to underline (the importance of), to highlight.

religión *f* religion.

religioso, sa ◇ *adj* religious. ◇ *m,f* [monje] monk (*f* nun).

relinchar *vi* to neigh, to whinny.

reliquia *f* relic; [familiar] heirloom.

rellano *m* [de escalera] landing.

rellenar *vt* **-1.** [volver a llenar] to refill **- 2.** [documento, formulario] to fill in *o* out **- 3.** [pollo, cojín etc] to stuff; [tarta, pastel] to fill.

relleno, na *adj* [gen] stuffed; [tarta, pastel] filled.

◆ **relleno** *m* [de pollo] stuffing; [de pastel] filling.

reloj *m* [de pared] clock; [de pulsera] watch; ~ **de arena** hourglass; ~ **de pulsera** watch, wristwatch; **hacer algo contra** ~ to do sthg against the clock.

relojero, ra *m,f* watchmaker.

reluciente *adj* shining, gleaming.

relucir *vi lit* & *fig* to shine; **sacar algo a** ~ to bring sthg up, to mention sthg; **salir a** ~ to come to the surface.

remachar *vt* **-1.** [machacar] to rivet **- 2.** *fig* [recalcar] to drive home, to stress.

remache *m* [clavo] rivet.

remanente *m* **-1.** [de géneros] surplus stock; [de productos agrícolas] surplus **- 2.** [en cuenta bancaria] balance.

remangar = **arremangar**.

remanso *m* still pool.

remar *vi* to row.

rematado, da *adj* utter, complete.

rematar ◇ *vt* **-1.** [acabar] to finish; **y para** ~ **la** *fam* to cap it all **- 2.** [matar - persona] to finish off; [- animal] to put out of its misery **- 3.** DEP to shoot **- 4.** [liquidar, vender] to sell off cheaply. ◇ *vi* [en fútbol] to shoot; [de cabeza] to head at goal.

remate *m* **-1.** [fin, colofón] end **- 2.** [en fútbol] shot; [de cabeza] header at goal.

◆ **de remate** *loc adv* totally, completely.

rembolsar = **reembolsar**.

rembolso = **reembolso**.

remedar *vt* to imitate; [por burla] to ape, to mimic.

remediar *vt* [daño] to remedy, to put right; [problema] to solve; [peligro] to avoid, to prevent.

remedio *m* **-1.** [solución] solution, remedy; **como último** ~ as a last resort; **no hay** *o* **queda más** ~ **que** ... there's nothing for it but ...; **no tener más** ~ to have no alternative *o* choice; **sin** ~ [sin cura, solución] hopeless; [ineludiblemente] inevitably **- 2.** [consuelo] comfort, consolation **- 3.** [medicamento] remedy, cure.

rememorar *vt* to remember, to recall.

remendar *vt* to mend, to darn.

remero, ra *m,f* [persona] rower.

◆ **remera** *f RP* [prenda] T-shirt.

remesa *f* [de productos] consignment; [de dinero] shipment, remittance.

remeter *vt* to tuck in.

remezón *m Andes* & *RP* earth tremor.

remiendo *m* [parche] mend, darn.

remilgado, da *adj* **-1.** [afectado] affected **- 2.** [escrupuloso] squeamish; [con comida] fussy, finicky.

remilgo *m* **-1.** [afectación] affectation **- 2.** [escrupulosidad] squeamishness; [con comida] fussiness.

reminiscencia *f* reminiscence; **tener** ~**s de** to be reminiscent of.

remise *m RP* taxi (*in private car without a meter*).

remisero, ra *m,f RP* taxi driver (*of private car without a meter*).

remiso, sa *adj*: **ser** ~ **a hacer algo** to be reluctant to do sthg.

remite *m* sender's name and address.

remitente *mf* sender.

remitir ◇ *vt* **-1.** [enviar] to send **- 2.** [traspasar]: ~ **algo a** to refer sthg to. ◇ *vi* **-1.** [en texto]: ~ **a** to refer to **- 2.** [disminuir] to subside.

◆ **remitirse** *vpr* **-1.** [atenerse a] to comply with, to abide by **- 2.** [referirse a] to refer to.

remo *m* **-1.** [pala] oar **- 2.** [deporte] rowing.

remoción *f Amér* [de heridos] transport.

remodelar *vt* [gen] to redesign; [gobierno] to reshuffle.

remojar *vt* [humedecer] to soak.

remojo *m*: **poner en** ~ to leave to soak; **estar en** ~ to be soaking.

remolacha *f* beetroot *UK*, beet *US*; [azucarera] (sugar) beet.

remolcador, ra *adj* [coche] tow (*antes de sust*); [barco] tug (*antes de sust*).

◆ **remolcador** *m* [camión] breakdown lorry; [barco] tug, tugboat.

remolcar *vt* [coche] to tow; [barco] to tug.

remolino *m* **-1.** [de agua] eddy, whirlpool; [de viento] whirlwind; [de humo] cloud, swirl **- 2.** [de gente] throng, mass **- 3.** [de pelo] cowlick.

remolón, ona *adj* lazy.

remolque *m* **-1.** [acción] towing **- 2.** [vehículo] trailer.

remontar *vt* [pendiente, río] to go up; [obstáculo] to get over, to overcome.

◆ **remontarse** *vpr* **-1.** [ave, avión] to soar, to climb high **- 2.** [gastos]: ~**se a** to amount *o* come to **- 3.** *fig* [datar]: ~**se a** to go *o* date back to.

remorder *vt fig*: ~ **le a alguien** to fill sb with remorse.

remordimiento *m* remorse; **tener** ~**s de**

conciencia to suffer pangs of conscience.

remoto, ta *adj* remote; **no tengo ni la más remota idea** I haven't got the faintest idea.

remover *vt* - **1.** [agitar - sopa, café] to stir; [- ensalada] to toss; [- bote, frasco] to shake; [- tierra] to turn over, to dig up - **2.** [reavivar - caso policial] to re-open; [- recuerdos, pasado] to stir up, to rake up - **3.** *Amér* [despedir] to dismiss, to sack.

➡ **removerse** *vpr* to move about.

remplazar = reemplazar.

remplazo = reemplazo.

remuneración *f* remuneration.

remunerar *vt* [pagar] to remunerate.

renacer *vi* - **1.** [gen] to be reborn; [flores, hojas] to grow again - **2.** [alegría, esperanza] to return, to revive.

renacimiento *m* [gen] rebirth; [de flores, hojas] budding.

➡ **Renacimiento** *m*: **el Renacimiento** the Renaissance.

renacuajo *m* tadpole; *fam fig* tiddler.

renal *adj* renal, kidney *(antes de sust)*.

rencilla *f* quarrel.

rencor *m* resentment, bitterness.

rencoroso, sa *adj* resentful, bitter.

rendición *f* surrender.

rendido, da *adj* - **1.** [agotado] exhausted, worn-out; **caer** ~ to collapse - **2.** [sumiso] submissive; [admirador] servile, devoted.

rendija *f* crack, gap.

rendimiento *m* - **1.** [de inversión, negocio] yield, return; [de trabajador, fábrica] productivity; [de tierra, cosecha] performance, yield; **a pleno** ~ at full capacity - **2.** [de motor] performance.

rendir ◇ *vt* - **1.** [cansar] to wear out, to tire out - **2.** [rentar] to yield - **3.** [vencer] to defeat, to subdue - **4.** [ofrecer] to give, to present; [pleitesía] to pay. ◇ *vi* [máquina] to perform well; [negocio] to be profitable; [fábrica, trabajador] to be productive.

➡ **rendirse** *vpr* - **1.** [entregarse] to give o.s. up, to surrender - **2.** [ceder]: ~**se a** to submit to, to give in to - **3.** [desanimarse] to give in *o* up.

renegado, da *adj* & *m,f* renegade.

renegar *vi* - **1.** [repudiar]: ~ **de** [ideas] to renounce; [familia] to disown - **2.** *fam* [gruñir] to grumble.

Renfe (*abrev de* **Red Nacional de los Ferrocarriles Españoles**) *f Spanish state railway network*.

renglón *m* line; COM item.

rengo, ga *adj Andes, RP* lame.

renguear *vi Andes, RP* to limp, to hobble.

reno *m* reindeer.

renombrar *vt* INFORM to rename.

renombre *m* renown, fame; **de** ~ famous.

renovación *f* [de carné, contrato] renewal; [de mobiliario, local] renovation.

renovar *vt* - **1.** [cambiar - mobiliario, local] to renovate; [- vestuario] to clear out; [- personal, plantilla] to make changes to, to shake out - **2.** [rehacer - carné, contrato, ataques] to renew - **3.** [restaurar] to restore - **4.** [innovar] to rethink, to revolutionize; POLÍT to reform.

renquear *vi* to limp, to hobble.

renta *f* - **1.** [ingresos] income; ~ **fija** fixed income; ~ **per cápita** *o* **por habitante** per capita income - **2.** [alquiler] rent - **3.** [beneficios] return - **4.** [intereses] interest.

rentable *adj* profitable.

rentar ◇ *vt* - **1.** [rendir] to produce, to yield - **2.** *Méx* [alquilar] to rent. ◇ *vi* to be profitable.

rentista *mf* person of independent means.

renuncia *f* [abandono] giving up; [dimisión] resignation; **presentar la** ~ to resign.

renunciar *vi* - **1.** [abandonar] to give up - **2.** [dimitir] to resign.

➡ **renunciar a** *vi* - **1.** [prescindir de] to give up; [plan, proyecto] to drop; ~ **al tabaco** to give up *o* stop smoking - **2.** [rechazar]: ~ **(a hacer algo)** to refuse (to do sthg).

reñido, da *adj* - **1.** [enfadado]: ~ **(con)** on bad terms *o* at odds (with); **están** ~**s** they've fallen out - **2.** [disputado] fierce, hard-fought - **3.** [incompatible]: **estar** ~ **con** to be at odds with, to be incompatible with.

reñir ◇ *vt* - **1.** [regañar] to tell off - **2.** [disputar] to fight. ◇ *vi* [enfadarse] to argue, to fall out.

reo, a *m,f* [culpado] offender, culprit; [acusado] accused, defendant.

reojo *m*: **mirar algo de** ~ to look at sthg out of the corner of one's eye.

repantigarse *vpr* to sprawl out.

reparación *f* - **1.** [arreglo] repair, repairing *(U)*; **en** ~ under repair - **2.** [compensación] reparation, redress.

reparador, ra *adj* [descanso, sueño] refreshing.

reparar ◇ *vt* [coche etc] to repair, to fix; [error, daño etc] to make amends for; [fuerzas] to make up for, to restore. ◇ *vi* [advertir]: ~ **en algo** to notice sthg; **no** ~ **en gastos** to spare no expense.

reparo *m* - **1.** [objeción] objection - **2.** [apuro]: **no tener** ~**s en** not to be afraid to.

repartición *f* [reparto] sharing out.

repartidor, ra *mf* [gen] distributor; [de butano, carbón] deliveryman *(f* deliverywoman); [de leche] milkman *(f* milklady); [de periódicos] paperboy *(f* papergirl).

repartir *vt* - **1.** [dividir - gen] to share out, to divide; [- territorio, nación] to partition

- 2. [distribuir - leche, periódicos, correo] to deliver; [- naipes] to deal (out) **- 3.** [asignar - trabajo, órdenes] to give out, to allocate; [- papeles] to assign.

reparto *m* **- 1.** [división] division, distribution; ~ **de beneficios** ECON profit sharing; ~ **de premios** prizegiving **- 2.** [distribución - de leche, periódicos, correo] delivery **- 3.** [asignación] giving out, allocation; ~ **a domicilio** home delivery **- 4.** CIN & TEATR cast.

repasador *m RP* tea towel.

repasar *vt* **- 1.** [revisar] to go over; [lección] to revise *UK*, to review *US* **- 2.** [zurcir] to darn, to mend.

repaso *m* [revisión] revision; [de ropa] darning, mending; **dar un** ~ **a algo** to look over sthg; **dar un último** ~ **a algo** to give sthg a final check; **curso de** ~ refresher course.

repatriar *vt* to repatriate.

repecho *m* steep slope.

repelente *adj* **- 1.** [desagradable, repugnante] repulsive **- 2.** [ahuyentador] repellent.

repeler *vt* **- 1.** [rechazar] to repel **- 2.** [repugnar] to repulse, to disgust.

repelús *m*: **me da** ~ it gives me the shivers.

repente *m* [arrebato] fit.

◆ de repente *loc adv* suddenly.

repentino, na *adj* sudden.

repercusión *f* **- 1.** *fig* [consecuencia] repercussion **- 2.** [resonancia] echoes *(pl)*.

repercutir *vi fig* [afectar]: ~ **en** to have repercussions on.

repertorio *m* **- 1.** [obras] repertoire **- 2.** *fig* [serie] selection.

repesca *f* **- 1.** EDUC resit **- 2.** DEP repêchage.

repetición *f* repetition; [de una jugada] action replay.

repetidor, ra *m,f* EDUC student repeating a year.

◆ repetidor *m* ELECTR repeater.

repetir ◇ *vt* to repeat; [ataque] to renew; [en comida] to have seconds of. ◇ *vi* **- 1.** [alumno] to repeat a year **- 2.** [sabor, alimento]: ~ **(a alguien)** to repeat (on sb) **- 3.** [comensal] to have seconds.

◆ repetirse *vpr* **- 1.** [fenómeno] to recur **- 2.** [persona] to repeat o.s.

repicar *vi* [campanas] to ring.

repique *m* peal, ringing *(U)*.

repiqueteo *m* [de campanas] pealing; [de tambor] beating; [de timbre] ringing; [de lluvia, dedos] drumming.

repisa *f* [estante] shelf; [sobre chimenea] mantelpiece.

replantear *vt* **- 1.** [reenfocar] to reconsider, to restate **- 2.** [volver a mencionar] to bring up again.

replegar *vt* [ocultar] to retract.

◆ replegarse *vpr* [retirarse] to withdraw, to retreat.

repleto, ta *adj*: ~ **(de)** packed (with).

réplica *f* **- 1.** [respuesta] reply **- 2.** [copia] replica.

replicar ◇ *vt* [responder] to answer; [objetar] to answer back, to retort. ◇ *vi* [objetar] to answer back.

repliegue *m* **- 1.** [retirada] withdrawal, retreat **- 2.** [pliegue] fold.

repoblación *f* [con gente] repopulation; [con peces] restocking; ~ **forestal** reafforestation.

repoblar *vt* [con gente] to repopulate; [con peces] to restock; [con árboles] to replant, to reafforest.

repollo *m* cabbage.

reponer *vt* **- 1.** [gen] to replace **- 2.** CIN & TEATR to re-run; TV to repeat **- 3.** [replicar]: ~ **que** to reply that.

reportaje *m* RADIO & TV report; PRENS article.

reportar *vt* **- 1.** [traer] to bring **- 2.** *Méx* [denunciar] to report; *Andes, CAm, Méx, Ven* [informar] to report.

◆ reportarse *vpr CAm, Méx, Ven*: ~ **se (a)** to report (to).

reporte *m CAm, Méx* [informe] report; [noticia] news item *o* report.

reportero, ra, repórter *m,f* reporter.

reposado, da *adj* relaxed, calm.

reposar *vi* **- 1.** [descansar] to (have a) rest **- 2.** [sedimentarse] to stand.

reposera *f RP* sun-lounger *UK*, beach recliner *US*.

reposición *f* **- 1.** CIN rerun; TEATR revival; TV repeat **- 2.** [de existencias, pieza etc] replacement.

reposo *m* [descanso] rest.

repostar ◇ *vi* [coche] to fill up; [avión] to refuel. ◇ *vt* **- 1.** [gasolina] to fill up with **- 2.** [provisiones] to stock up on.

repostería *f* [oficio, productos] confectionery.

reprender *vt* [a niños] to tell off; [a empleados] to reprimand.

reprensión *f* [a niños] telling-off; [a empleados] reprimand.

represalia *(gen pl)* *f* reprisal; **tomar** ~**s** to retaliate, to take reprisals.

representación *f* **- 1.** [gen & COM] representation; **en** ~ **de** on behalf of **- 2.** TEATR performance.

representante ◇ *adj* representative. ◇ *mf* **- 1.** [gen & COM] representative; ~ **de la ley** officer of the law **- 2.** [de artista] agent.

representar *vt* **- 1.** [gen & COM] to represent **- 2.** [aparentar] to look; **representa unos 40 años** she looks about 40 **- 3.** [significar] to mean - **4.** [en teatro] to perform; [- papel] to play.

representativo, va *adj* - **1.** [simbolizador]: **ser ~ de** to represent - **2.** [característico, relevante]: **~ (de)** representative (of).

represión *f* repression.

reprimenda *f* reprimand.

reprimir *vt* [gen] to suppress; [minorías, disidentes] to repress.

◆ **reprimirse** *vpr*: **~se (de hacer algo)** to restrain o.s. (from doing sthg).

reprobar *vt* - **1.** to censure, to condemn - **2.** *Amér* [suspender] to fail.

reprochar *vt*: **~ algo a alguien** to reproach sb for sthg.

◆ **reprocharse** *vpr*: **~se algo (uno mismo)** to reproach o.s. for sthg.

reproche *m* reproach.

reproducción *f* reproduction.

reproducir *vt* [gen & ARTE] to reproduce; [gestos] to copy, to imitate.

◆ **reproducirse** *vpr* - **1.** [volver a suceder] to recur - **2.** [procrear] to reproduce.

reptil *m* reptile.

república *f* republic.

República Checa *f* Czech Republic.

República Dominicana *f* Dominican Republic.

republicano, na *adj* & *m,f* republican.

repudiar *vt* - **1.** [condenar] to repudiate - **2.** [rechazar] to disown.

repuesto, ta ◇ *pp* ▷ **reponer**. ◇ *adj*: **~ (de)** recovered (from).

◆ **repuesto** *m* [gen] reserve; AUTOM spare part; **la rueda de ~** the spare wheel.

repugnancia *f* disgust.

repugnante *adj* disgusting.

repugnar *vi*: **me repugna ese olor/su actitud** I find that smell/her attitude disgusting; **me repugna hacerlo** I'm loath to do it.

repujar *vt* to emboss.

repulsa *f* [censura] condemnation.

repulsión *f* repulsion.

repulsivo, va *adj* repulsive.

repuntar *vi* *Amér* [mejorar] to improve.

repunte *m* *Amér* [recuperación] improvement.

reputación *f* reputation; **tener mucha ~** to be very famous.

requerimiento *m* - **1.** [demanda] entreaty; **a ~ de alguien** at sb's request - **2.** [DER - intimación] writ, injunction; [- aviso] summons *(sg)*.

requerir *vt* - **1.** [necesitar] to require - **2.** [ordenar] to demand - **3.** [pedir]: **~ a alguien (para) que haga algo** to ask sb to do sthg - **4.** DER to order.

◆ **requerirse** *vpr* [ser necesario] to be required *o* necessary.

requesón *m* cottage cheese.

requisa *f* [requisición - MIL] requisition; [- en aduana] seizure.

requisito *m* requirement; **~ previo** prerequisite.

res *f* beast, animal.

resabio *m* - **1.** [sabor] nasty aftertaste - **2.** [vicio] persistent bad habit.

resaca *f* - **1.** *fam* [de borrachera] hangover - **2.** [de las olas] undertow.

resalado, da *adj fam* charming.

resaltar ◇ *vi* - **1.** [destacar] to stand out - **2.** [en edificios - balcón] to stick out; [- decoración] to stand out. ◇ *vt* [destacar] to highlight.

resarcir *vt*: **~ a alguien (de)** to compensate sb (for).

◆ **resarcirse** *vpr* to be compensated; **~se de** [daño, pérdida] to be compensated for; [desengaño, derrota] to make up for.

resbalada *f Amér fam* slip.

resbaladizo, za *adj lit* & *fig* slippery.

resbalar *vi* - **1.** [caer]: **~ (con** *o* **sobre)** to slip (on) - **2.** [deslizarse] to slide - **3.** [estar resbaladizo] to be slippery.

◆ **resbalarse** *vpr* to slip (over).

resbalón *m* slip.

rescatar *vt* - **1.** [liberar, salvar] to rescue; [pagando rescate] to ransom - **2.** [recuperar - herencia etc] to recover.

rescate *m* - **1.** [liberación, salvación] rescue - **2.** [dinero] ransom - **3.** [recuperación] recovery.

rescindir *vt* to rescind.

rescisión *f* cancellation.

rescoldo *m* ember; *fig* lingering feeling, flicker.

resecar *vt* [piel] to dry out.

◆ **resecarse** *vpr* - **1.** [piel] to dry out - **2.** [tierra] to become parched.

reseco, ca *adj* - **1.** [piel, garganta, pan] very dry - **2.** [tierra] parched - **3.** [flaco] emaciated.

resentido, da *adj* bitter, resentful; **estar ~ con alguien** to be really upset with sb.

resentimiento *m* resentment, bitterness.

resentirse *vpr* - **1.** [debilitarse] to be weakened; [salud] to deteriorate - **2.** [sentir molestias]: **~ de** to be suffering from - **3.** [ofenderse] to be offended.

reseña *f* [de libro, concierto] review; [de partido, conferencia] report.

reseñar *vt* - **1.** [criticar - libro, concierto] to review; [- partido, conferencia] to report on - **2.** [describir] to describe.

reserva *f* - **1.** [de hotel, avión etc] reservation - **2.** [provisión] reserves *(pl)*; **tener algo de ~** to keep sthg in reserve - **3.** [objeción] reservation - **4.** [de indígenas] reservation - **5.** [de animales] reserve; ~ **natural** nature reserve - **6**. MIL reserve.

◆ **reservas** *fpl* - **1**. [energía acumulada] energy reserves - **2**. [recursos] resources.

reservado, da *adj* - **1**. [gen] reserved - **2**. [tema, asunto] confidential.

◆ **reservado** *m* [en restaurante] private room; FERROC reserved compartment.

reservar *vt* - **1**. [habitación, asiento etc] to reserve, to book - **2**. [guardar - dinero, pasteles etc] to set aside; [- sorpresa] to keep - **3**. [callar - opinión, comentarios] to reserve.

◆ **reservarse** *vpr* - **1**. [esperar]: ~**se para** to save o.s. for - **2**. [guardar para sí - secreto] to keep to o.s.; [- dinero, derecho] to retain (for o.s.).

resfriado, da *adj*: estar ~ to have a cold.

◆ **resfriado** *m* cold; **pescar un** ~ to catch a cold.

resfriar

◆ **resfriarse** *vpr* [constiparse] to catch a cold.

resfrío *m Andes, RP* cold.

resguardar *vt* & *vi*: ~ **de** to protect against.

◆ **resguardarse** *vpr*: ~**se de** [en un portal] to shelter from; [con abrigo, paraguas] to protect o.s. against.

resguardo *m* - **1**. [documento] receipt - **2**. [protección] protection.

residencia *f* - **1**. [estancia] stay - **2**. [localidad, domicilio] residence; **segunda** ~ second home; ~ **canina** kennels - **3**. [establecimiento de estudiantes] hall of residence; [- de ancianos] old people's home; [- de oficiales] residence - **4**. [hospital] hospital - **5**. [permiso para extranjeros] residence permit.

residencial *adj* residential.

residente *adj* & *m,f* resident.

residir *vi* - **1**. [vivir] to reside - **2**. [radicar]: ~ **en** to lie in, to reside in.

residuo *m* *(gen pl)* [material inservible] waste; QUÍM residue; ~**s nucleares** nuclear waste *(U)*; ~**s tóxicos** toxic waste *(U)*.

resignación *f* resignation.

resignarse *vpr*: ~ **(a hacer algo)** to resign o.s. (to doing sthg).

resina *f* resin.

resistencia *f* - **1**. [gen, ELECTR & POLÍT] resistance; **ofrecer** ~ to put up resistance - **2**. [de puente, cimientos] strength - **3**. [física - para correr etc] stamina.

resistente *adj* [gen] tough, strong; ~ **al calor** heat-resistant.

resistir ◇ *vt* - **1**. [dolor, peso, críticas] to withstand - **2**. [tentación, impulso, deseo] to resist - **3**. [tolerar] to tolerate, to stand - **4**. [ataque] to resist, to withstand. ◇ *vi*

- **1**. [ejército, ciudad etc]: ~ **(a algo/a alguien)** to resist (sthg/sb) - **2**. [corredor etc] to keep going; ~ **a algo** to stand up to sthg, to withstand sthg - **3**. [mesa, dique etc] to take the strain; ~ **a algo** to withstand sthg - **4**. [mostrarse firme - ante tentaciones etc] to resist (it); ~ **a algo** to resist sthg.

◆ **resistirse** *vpr*: ~**se (a algo)** to resist (sthg); **me resisto a creerlo** I refuse to believe it; **se le resisten las matemáticas** she just can't get the hang of maths.

resollar *vi* to gasp (for breath); [jadear] to pant.

resolución *f* - **1**. [solución - de una crisis] resolution; [- de un crimen] solution - **2**. [firmeza] determination - **3**. [decisión] decision; DER ruling - **4**. [de Naciones Unidas etc] resolution.

resolver *vt* - **1**. [solucionar - duda, crisis] to resolve; [- problema, caso] to solve - **2**. [decidir]: ~ **hacer algo** to decide to do sthg - **3**. [partido, disputa, conflicto] to settle.

◆ **resolverse** *vpr* - **1**. [solucionarse - duda, crisis] to be resolved; [- problema, caso] to be solved - **2**. [decidirse]: ~**se a hacer algo** to decide to do sthg.

resonancia *f* - **1**. [gen & FÍS] resonance *(U)* - **2**. *fig* [importancia] repercussions *(pl)*.

resonante *adj* resounding; FÍS resonant; *fig* important.

resonar *vi* to resound, to echo.

resoplar *vi* [de cansancio] to pant; [de enfado] to snort.

resoplido *m* [por cansancio] pant; [por enfado] snort.

resorte *m* spring; **saltar como movido por un** ~ to spring up; *fig* means *(pl)*; **tocar todos los** ~**s** to pull out all the stops.

respaldar *vt* to back, to support.

◆ **respaldarse** *vpr* *fig* [apoyarse]: ~**se en** to fall back on.

respaldo *m* - **1**. [de asiento] back - **2**. *fig* [apoyo] backing, support.

respectar *v impers*: **por lo que respecta a alguien/a algo, en lo que respecta a alguien/a algo** as far as sb/sthg is concerned.

respectivo, va *adj* respective; **en lo** ~ **a** with regard to.

respecto *m*: **al** ~, **a este** ~ in this respect; **no sé nada al** ~ I don't know anything about it; **(con)** ~ **a**, ~ **de** regarding.

respetable *adj* - **1**. [venerable] respectable - **2**. [bastante] considerable.

respetar *vt* [gen] to respect; [la palabra] to honour.

respeto *m*: ~ **(a o por)** respect (for); **es una falta de** ~ it shows a lack of respect; **por** ~ **a** out of consideration for.

respetuoso, sa adj: ~ **(con)** respectful (of).

respingo m [movimiento] start, jump.

respingón, ona adj snub.

respiración f breathing; MED respiration.

respirar ◇ vt [aire] to breathe. ◇ vi to breathe; fig [sentir alivio] to breathe again; **sin** ~ [sin descanso] without a break; [atentamente] with great attention.

respiratorio, ria adj respiratory.

respiro m - **1.** [descanso] rest - **2.** [alivio] relief, respite; **dar un** ~ **a alguien** fam to give sb a break.

resplandecer vi - **1.** [brillar] to shine - **2.** fig [destacar] to shine, to stand out.

resplandeciente adj shining; [sonrisa] beaming; [época] glittering; [vestimenta, color] resplendent.

resplandor m - **1.** [luz] brightness; [de fuego] glow - **2.** [brillo] gleam.

responder ◇ vt to answer. ◇ vi - **1.** [contestar]: ~ **(a algo)** to answer (sthg) - **2.** [reaccionar]: ~ **(a)** to respond (to) - **3.** [responsabilizarse]: ~ **de algo/por alguien** to answer for sthg/for sb - **4.** [replicar] to answer back.

respondón, ona adj insolent.

responsabilidad f responsibility; DER liability; **exigir** ~**es a alguien** to hold sb accountable; **tener la** ~ **de algo** to be responsible for sthg; ~ **limitada** limited liability.

responsabilizar vt: ~ **a alguien (de algo)** to hold sb responsible (for sthg).

    ◆ **responsabilizarse** vpr: ~**se (de)** to accept responsibility (for).

responsable ◇ adj responsible; ~ **de** responsible for. ◇ mf - **1.** [culpable] person responsible - **2.** [encargado] person in charge.

respuesta f - **1.** [gen] answer, reply; [en exámenes] answer; **en** ~ **a** in reply to - **2.** fig [reacción] response.

resquebrajar vt to crack.

    ◆ **resquebrajarse** vpr to crack.

resquicio m - **1.** [abertura] chink; [grieta] crack - **2.** fig [pizca] glimmer.

resta f MAT subtraction.

restablecer vt to reestablish, to restore.

    ◆ **restablecerse** vpr [curarse]: ~**se (de)** to recover (from).

restallar vt & vi [látigo] to crack; [lengua] to click.

restante adj remaining; **lo** ~ the rest.

restar ◇ vt - **1.** MAT to subtract - **2.** [disminuir]: ~ **importancia a algo/méritos a alguien** to play down the importance of sthg/sb's qualities. ◇ vi [faltar] to be left.

restauración f restoration.

restaurante m restaurant.

restaurar vt to restore.

restitución f return.

restituir vt [devolver - objeto] to return; [- salud] to restore.

resto m: **el** ~ [gen] the rest; MAT the remainder.

    ◆ **restos** mpl - **1.** [sobras] leftovers - **2.** [cadáver] remains - **3.** [ruinas] ruins.

restregar vt to rub hard; [para limpiar] to scrub.

    ◆ **restregarse** vpr [frotarse] to rub.

restricción f restriction.

restrictivo, va adj restrictive.

restringir vt to limit, to restrict.

resucitar ◇ vt [person] to bring back to life; [costumbre] to resurrect, to revive. ◇ vi [persona] to rise from the dead.

resuello m gasp, gasping (U); [jadeo] pant, panting (U).

resuelto, ta ◇ pp ▷ **resolver.** ◇ adj [decidido] determined.

resulta f: **de** ~**s de** as a result of.

resultado m result.

resultante adj & f resultant.

resultar ◇ vi - **1.** [acabar siendo]: ~ **(ser)** to turn out (to be); **resultó ileso** he was uninjured; **nuestro equipo resultó vencedor** our team came out on top - **2.** [salir bien] to work (out), to be a success - **3.** [originarse]: ~ **de** to come of, to result from - **4.** [ser] to be; **resulta sorprendente** it's surprising; **me resultó imposible terminar antes** I was unable to finish earlier - **5.** [venir a costar]: ~ **a** to come to, to cost. ◇ v impers [suceder]: ~ **que** to turn out that; **ahora resulta que no quiere alquilarlo** now it seems that she doesn't want to rent it.

resumen m summary; **en** ~ in short.

resumir vt to summarize; [discurso] to sum up.

    ◆ **resumirse en** vpr - **1.** [sintetizarse en] to be able to be summed up in - **2.** [reducirse a] to boil down to.

resurgir vi to undergo a resurgence, to be revived.

resurrección f resurrection.

retablo m altarpiece.

retaguardia f [tropa] rearguard; [territorio] rear.

retahíla f string, series.

retal m remnant.

retardar vt [retrasar] to delay; [frenar] to hold up, to slow down.

retazo m remnant; fig fragment.

rete adv Amér fam very.

retén m - **1.** reserve - **2.** Amér [de menores] reformatory, reform school.

retención f - **1.** [en el sueldo] deduction - **2.** (gen pl) [de tráfico] hold-up.

retener vt - **1.** [detener] to hold back; [en comisaría] to detain - **2.** [hacer permanecer] to keep - **3.** [contener - impulso, ira] to hold back, to restrain - **4.** [conservar] to retain - **5.** [quedarse con] to hold on to, to keep - **6.** [memorizar] to remember - **7.** [deducir del sueldo] to deduct.

reticente adj [reacio] unwilling, reluctant.

retina f retina.

retintín m [ironía] sarcastic tone.

retirado, da adj - **1.** [jubilado] retired - **2.** [solitario, alejado] isolated, secluded.

➡ **retirada** f - **1.** MIL retreat; **batirse en retirada** to beat a retreat - **2.** [de fondos, moneda, carné] withdrawal - **3.** [de competición, actividad] withdrawal.

retirar vt - **1.** [quitar - gen] to remove; [- dinero, moneda, carné] to withdraw; [- nieve] to clear - **2.** [jubilar - a deportista] to force to retire; [- a empleado] to retire - **3.** [retractarse de] to take back.

➡ **retirarse** vpr - **1.** [gen] to retire - **2.** [de competición, elecciones] to withdraw; [de reunión] to leave - **3.** [de campo de batalla] to retreat - **4.** [apartarse] to move away.

retiro m - **1.** [jubilación] retirement; [pensión] pension - **2.** [refugio, ejercicio] retreat.

reto m challenge.

retocar vt to touch up.

retoño m BOT sprout, shoot; fig offspring (U).

retoque m touching-up (U); [de prenda de vestir] alteration; **dar los últimos ~s a** to put the finishing touches to.

retorcer vt [torcer - brazo, alambre] to twist; [- ropa, cuello] to wring.

➡ **retorcerse** vpr [contraerse]: **~se (de)** [risa] to double up (with); [dolor] to writhe about (in).

retorcido, da adj - **1.** [torcido - brazo, alambre] twisted - **2.** fig [rebuscado] complicated, involved.

retornable adj returnable; **no ~** non-returnable.

retornar vt & vi to return.

retorno m [gen & INFORM] return; **~ de carro** carriage return.

retortijón (gen pl) m stomach cramp.

retozar vi to gambol, to frolic; [amantes] to romp about.

retractarse vpr [de una promesa] to go back on one's word; [de una opinión] to take back what one has said; **~ de** [lo dicho] to retract, to take back.

retraer vt [encoger] to retract.

➡ **retraerse** vpr - **1.** [encogerse] to retract - **2.** [retroceder] to withdraw, to retreat.

retraído, da adj withdrawn, retiring.

retransmisión f broadcast; **~ en directo/**diferido live/recorded broadcast.

retransmitir vt to broadcast.

retrasado, da <> adj - **1.** [país, industria] backward; [reloj] slow; [tren] late, delayed - **2.** [en el pago, los estudios] behind - **3.** MED retarded, backward. <> m,f: **~ (mental)** mentally retarded person.

retrasar vt - **1.** [aplazar] to postpone - **2.** [demorar] to delay, to hold up - **3.** [hacer más lento] to slow down, to hold up - **4.** [en el pago, los estudios] to set back - **5.** [reloj] to put back.

➡ **retrasarse** vpr - **1.** [llegar tarde] to be late - **2.** [quedarse atrás] to fall behind - **3.** [aplazarse] to be put off - **4.** [reloj] to lose time.

retraso m - **1.** [por llegar tarde] delay; **llegar con (15 minutos de) ~** to be (15 minutes) late - **2.** [por sobrepasar una fecha] time behind schedule; **llevo en mi trabajo un ~ de 20 páginas** I'm 20 pages behind with my work - **3.** [subdesarrollo] backwardness - **4.** MED mental deficiency.

retratar vt - **1.** [fotografiar] to photograph - **2.** [dibujar] to do a portrait of - **3.** fig [describir] to portray.

retrato m - **1.** [dibujo] portrait; [fotografía] photograph; **~ robot** photofit picture; **ser el vivo ~ de alguien** to be the spitting image of sb - **2.** fig [reflejo] portrayal.

retrete m toilet.

retribución f [pago] payment; [recompensa] reward.

retribuir vt [pagar] to pay; [recompensar] to reward.

retro adj old-fashioned.

retroactivo, va adj [ley] retrospective, retroactive; [pago] backdated.

retroceder vi to go back; fig to back down.

retroceso m [regresión - gen] backward movement; [- en negociaciones] setback; [- en la economía] recession.

retrógrado, da adj & m,f reactionary.

retroproyector m overhead projector.

retrospectivo, va adj retrospective.

retrovisor m rear-view mirror.

retumbar vi [resonar] to resound.

reuma, reúma m o f rheumatism.

reumatismo m rheumatism.

reunión f meeting.

reunir vt - **1.** [público, accionistas etc] to bring together - **2.** [objetos, textos etc] to collect, to bring together; [fondos] to raise - **3.** [requisitos] to meet; [cualidades] to possess, to combine.

➡ **reunirse** vpr [congregarse] to meet.

revalidar vt to confirm.

revalorizar, revalorar vt - **1.** [aumentar el valor] to increase the value of; [moneda] to revalue - **2.** [restituir el valor] to reassess in a favourable light.

➡ **revalorizarse, revalorarse** *vpr* [aumentar de valor] to appreciate; [moneda] to be revalued.

revancha *f* - **1.** [venganza] revenge - **2.** DEP return match.

revelación *f* revelation.

revelado *m* FOT developing.

revelador, ra *adj* [aclarador] revealing.

revelar *vt* - **1.** [declarar] to reveal - **2.** [evidenciar] to show - **3.** FOT to develop.

➡ **revelarse** *vpr*: ~se como to show o.s. to be.

revendedor, ra *m,f* ticket tout.

reventa *f* resale; [de entradas] touting.

reventar ◇ *vt* - **1.** [explotar] to burst - **2.** [echar abajo] to break down; [con explosivos] to blow up. ◇ *vi* [explotar] to burst.

➡ **reventarse** *vpr* [explotar] to explode; [rueda] to burst.

reventón *m* [pinchazo] blowout, flat *US*, puncture *UK*.

reverberación *f* [de sonido] reverberation; [de luz, calor] reflection.

reverberar *vi* [sonido] to reverberate; [luz, calor] to reflect.

reverdecer *vi* fig [amor] to revive.

reverencia *f* - **1.** [respeto] reverence - **2.** [saludo - inclinación] bow; [- flexión de piernas] curtsy.

reverenciar *vt* to revere.

reverendo, da *adj* reverend.

➡ **reverendo** *m* reverend.

reverente *adj* reverent.

reversa *f Méx* reverse.

reversible *adj* reversible.

reverso *m* back, other side.

revertir *vi* - **1.** [volver, devolver] to revert - **2.** [resultar]: ~ en to result in; ~ en beneficio/perjuicio de to be to the advantage/detriment of.

revés *m* - **1.** [parte opuesta - de papel, mano] back; [- de tela] other o wrong side; al ~ [en sentido contrario] the wrong way round; [en forma opuesta] the other way round; del ~ [lo de detrás, delante] the wrong way round, back to front; [lo de dentro, fuera] inside out; [lo de arriba, abajo] upside down - **2.** [bofetada] slap - **3.** DEP backhand - **4.** [contratiempo] setback, blow.

revestimiento *m* covering.

revestir *vt* - **1.** [recubrir]: ~ (de) [gen] to cover (with); [pintura] to coat (with); [forro] to line (with) - **2.** [poseer - solemnidad, gravedad etc] to take on, to have.

revisar *vt* - **1.** [repasar] to go over again - **2.** [inspeccionar] to inspect; [cuentas] to audit - **3.** [modificar] to revise.

revisión *f* - **1.** [repaso] revision - **2.** [inspección] inspection; ~ de cuentas audit; ~ médica check-up - **3.** [modificación] amendment - **4.** [AUTOM - puesta a punto] service; [- anual] ≃ MOT (test).

revisor, ra *m,f* [en tren] ticket inspector, conductor *US*; [en autobús] (bus) conductor.

revista *f* - **1.** [publicación] magazine; ~ del corazón gossip magazine; ~ de modas fashion magazine - **2.** [sección de periódico] section, review - **3.** [espectáculo teatral] revue - **4.** [inspección] inspection; pasar ~ a MIL to inspect, to review; [examinar] to examine.

revistero *m* [mueble] magazine rack.

revivir ◇ *vi* to revive. ◇ *vt* [recordar] to revive memories of.

revocar *vt* [gen] to revoke.

revolcar *vt* to throw to the ground, to upend.

➡ **revolcarse** *vpr* to roll about.

revolotear *vi* to flutter (about).

revoltijo, revoltillo *m* jumble.

revoltoso, sa *adj* - **1.** [travieso] mischievous - **2.** [sedicioso] rebellious.

revolución *f* revolution.

revolucionar *vt* [transformar] to revolutionize.

revolucionario, ria *adj & m,f* revolutionary.

revolver *vt* - **1.** [dar vueltas] to turn around; [líquido] to stir - **2.** [mezclar] to mix; [ensalada] to toss - **3.** [desorganizar] to turn upside down, to mess up; [cajones] to turn out - **4.** [irritar] to upset; me revuelve el estómago ó las tripas it makes my stomach turn.

➡ **revolver en** *vi* [cajones etc] to rummage around in.

➡ **revolverse** *vpr* [volverse] to turn around.

revólver *m* revolver.

revuelo *m* [agitación] commotion; armar un gran ~ to cause a great stir.

revuelto, ta ◇ *pp* ▷ revolver. ◇ *adj* - **1.** [desordenado] upside down, in a mess - **2.** [alborotado - época etc] troubled, turbulent - **3.** [clima] unsettled - **4.** [aguas] choppy, rough.

➡ **revuelto** *m* CULIN scrambled eggs *(pl)*.

➡ **revuelta** *f* [disturbio] riot, revolt.

revulsivo, va *adj* fig stimulating, revitalizing.

➡ **revulsivo** *m* fig kick-start, stimulus.

rey *m* king.

➡ **Reyes** *mpl*: los Reyes the King and Queen; (Día de) Reyes Twelfth Night.

reyerta *f* fight, brawl.

rezagado, da *adj*: ir ~ to lag behind.

rezar *vi* - 1. [orar]: ~ **(a)** to pray (to); ~ **por algo/alguien** to pray for sthg/sb - 2. [decir] to read, to say - 3. [corresponderse]: ~ **con** to have to do with.

rezo *m* [oración] prayer.

rezumar ◇ *vt* - 1. [transpirar] to ooze - 2. *fig* [manifestar] to be overflowing with. ◇ *vi* to ooze *o* seep out.

ría *f* estuary.

riachuelo *m* brook, stream.

riada *f* *lit & fig* flood.

ribera *f* [del río] bank; [del mar] shore.

ribete *m* edging *(U)*, trimming *(U)*; *fig* touch, nuance.

ricino *m* [planta] castor oil plant.

rico, ca ◇ *adj* - 1. [gen] rich - 2. [abundante]: ~ **(en)** rich (in) - 3. [sabroso] delicious - 4. [simpático] cute. ◇ *m,f* rich person; los ~s the rich.

rictus *m inv* - 1. [de ironía] smirk - 2. [de desprecio] sneer - 3. [de dolor] wince.

ridiculez *f* - 1. [payasada] silly thing, nonsense *(U)* - 2. [nimiedad] trifle; **cuesta una** ~ it costs next to nothing.

ridiculizar *vt* to ridicule.

ridículo, la *adj* ridiculous; [precio, suma] laughable, derisory.

➤ **ridículo** *m* ridicule; **hacer el** ~ to make a fool of o.s.; **poner** *o* **dejar en** ~ **a alguien** to make sb look stupid; **quedar en** ~ to look like a fool.

riego *m* [de campo] irrigation; [de jardín] watering.

riel *m* - 1. [de vía] rail - 2. [de cortina] (curtain) rail.

rienda *f* [de caballería] rein; **dar** ~ **suelta a** *fig* to give free rein to; **tener a alguien con la** ~ **corta** *fig* to keep sb on a tight rein.

➤ **riendas** *fpl* *fig* [dirección] reins.

riesgo *m* risk; **a todo** ~ [seguro, póliza] comprehensive.

riesgoso, sa *adj Amér* risky.

rifa *f* raffle.

rifar *vt* to raffle.

➤ **rifarse** *vpr* *fig* to fight over, to contest.

rifle *m* rifle.

rigidez *f* - 1. [de un cuerpo, objeto etc] rigidity - 2. [del rostro] stoniness - 3. *fig* [severidad] strictness, harshness.

rígido, da *adj* - 1. [cuerpo, objeto etc] rigid - 2. [rostro] stony - 3. [severo - normas etc] harsh; [- carácter] inflexible.

rigor *m* - 1. [severidad] strictness - 2. [exactitud] accuracy, rigour - 3. [inclemencia] harshness.

➤ **de rigor** *loc adj* usual.

riguroso, sa *adj* - 1. [severo] strict - 2. [exacto] rigorous, disciplined - 3. [inclemente] harsh.

rimar *vt & vi* to rhyme; ~ **con algo** to rhyme with sthg.

rimbombante *adj* [estilo, frases] pompous.

rímel, rimmel *m* mascara.

rincón *m* corner *(inside)*.

rinconera *f* corner piece.

ring *(pl* **rings)** *m* (boxing) ring.

rinoceronte *m* rhinoceros.

riña *f* [disputa] quarrel; [pelea] fight.

riñón *m* kidney.

riñonera *f* [pequeño bolso] bum bag *UK*, fanny pack *US*.

río *m* *lit & fig* river; **ir** ~ **arriba/abajo** to go upstream/downstream; **cuando el** ~ **suena, agua lleva** *proverb* there's no smoke without fire *proverb*.

rioja *m* Rioja (wine).

riojano, na *adj & m,f* Riojan.

riqueza *f* - 1. [fortuna] wealth - 2. [abundancia] richness.

risa *f* laugh, laughter *(U)*; **me da** ~ I find it funny; **¡qué** ~ **!** how funny!; **de** ~ funny.

risotada *f* guffaw; **soltar una** ~ to laugh loudly.

ristra *f* *lit & fig* string.

ristre ➤ **en ristre** *loc adv* at the ready.

risueño, ña *adj* [alegre] smiling.

ritmo *m* - 1. [gen] rhythm; **al** ~ **de** to the rhythm of; **llevar el** ~ to keep time; **perder el** ~ to get out of time; [cardíaco] beat - 2. [velocidad] pace.

rito *m* - 1. RELIG rite - 2. [costumbre] ritual.

ritual *adj & m* ritual.

rival *adj & m,f* rival; **sin** ~ unrivalled.

rivalidad *f* rivalry.

rivalizar *vi*: ~ **(con)** to compete (with).

rizado, da *adj* - 1. [pelo] curly - 2. [mar] choppy.

➤ **rizado** *m* [en peluquería]: **hacerse un** ~ to have one's hair curled.

rizar *vt* [pelo] to curl.

➤ **rizarse** *vpr* [pelo] to curl.

rizo *m* - 1. [de pelo] curl - 2. [del agua] ripple - 3. [de avión] loop - 4. *loc*: **rizar el** ~ to split hairs.

RNE *(abrev de* **Radio Nacional de España)** *f* Spanish national radio station.

roast-beef *(pl* **roast-beefs)**, **rosbif** *(pl* **rosbifs)** [ros'βif] *m* roast beef.

robar *vt* - 1. [gen] to steal; [casa] to burgle, burglarize *US*; ~ **a alguien** to rob sb - 2. [en naipes] to draw - 3. [cobrar caro] to rob.

roble *m* - 1. BOT oak - 2. *fig* [persona] strong person; **más fuerte que un** ~ as strong as an ox.

robo *m* [delito] robbery, theft; [en casa] burglary.

robot (*pl* **robots**) *m* [gen & INFORM] robot.

robótica *f* robotics (U).

robustecer *vt* to strengthen.
➤ **robustecerse** *vpr* to get stronger.

robusto, ta *adj* robust.

roca *f* rock; **firme como una ~** solid as a rock.

rocalla *f* rubble.

roce *m* - 1. [rozamiento - gen] rub, rubbing (U); [- suave] brush, brushing (U); [- FÍS] friction - 2. [desgaste] wear - 3. [rasguño - en piel] graze; [- en zapato, puerta] scuffmark; [- en metal] scratch - 4. [trato] close contact - 5. [desavenencia] brush; **tener un ~ con alguien** to have a brush with sb.

rociar *vt* - 1. [arrojar gotas] to sprinkle; [con espray] to spray - 2. [con vino] to wash down.

rocío *m* dew.

rock, rock and roll *m inv* rock and roll.

rockero, ra, roquero, ra *m,f* - 1. [músico] rock musician - 2. [fan] rock fan.

rocoso, sa *adj* rocky.

rodaballo *m* turbot.

rodado, da *adj* - 1. [piedra] rounded - 2. [tráfico] road (antes de sust) - 3. loc: **estar muy ~** [persona] to be very experienced; **venir ~ para** to be the perfect opportunity to.

rodaja *f* slice.

rodaje *m* - 1. [filmación] shooting - 2. [de motor] running-in - 3. [experiencia] experience.

Ródano *m*: **el ~** the (River) Rhône.

rodapié *m* skirting board.

rodar ⟨⟩ *vi* - 1. [deslizar] to roll; **echar algo a ~** fig to set sthg in motion - 2. [circular] to travel, to go - 3. [caer]: **~ (por)** to tumble (down) - 4. [ir de un lado a otro] to go around - 5. CIN to shoot. ⟨⟩ *vt* - 1. CIN to shoot - 2. [automóvil] to run in.

rodear *vt* - 1. [gen] to surround; **le rodeó el cuello con los brazos** she put her arms around his neck; **~ algo de algo** to surround sthg with sthg - 2. [dar la vuelta a] to go around - 3. [eludir] to skirt around.
➤ **rodearse** *vpr*: **~se de** to surround o.s. with.

rodeo *m* - 1. [camino largo] detour; **dar un ~** to make a detour - 2. (gen pl) [evasiva] evasiveness (U); **andar o ir con ~s** to beat about the bush - 3. [espectáculo] rodeo.

rodilla *f* knee; **de ~s** on one's knees.

rodillera *f* [protección] knee pad.

rodillo *m* [gen] roller; [para repostería] rolling pin.

rodríguez *m inv* grass widower.

roedor, ra *adj* ZOOL rodent (antes de sust).
➤ **roedor** *m* rodent.

roer *vt* - 1. [con dientes] to gnaw (at) - 2. fig

[gastar] to eat away (at).

rogar *vt* [implorar] to beg; [pedir] to ask; **~ a alguien que haga algo** to ask o beg sb to do sthg; **le ruego me perdone** I beg your pardon; **'se ruega silencio'** 'silence, please'.

rogativa (gen pl) *f* rogation.

rojizo, za *adj* reddish.

rojo, ja ⟨⟩ *adj* red; **ponerse ~** [gen] to turn red; [ruborizarse] to blush. ⟨⟩ *m,f* POLÍT red.
➤ **rojo** *m* [color] red; **al ~ vivo** [en incandescencia] red hot; fig heated.

rol (*pl* **roles**) *m* [papel] role.

rollizo, za *adj* chubby, plump.

rollo *m* - 1. [cilindro] roll; **~ de primavera** CULIN spring roll - 2. CIN roll - 3. fam [discurso]: **el ~ de costumbre** the same old story; **tener mucho ~** to witter on - 4. fam [embuste] tall story - 5. fam [pelmazo, pesadez] bore, drag.

ROM (abrev de **read-only memory**) *f* ROM.

Roma Rome.

romance *m* - 1. LING Romance language - 2. [idilio] romance.

románico, ca *adj* - 1. ARQUIT & ARTE Romanesque - 2. LING Romance.

romano, na *adj & m,f* Roman.

romanticismo *m* - 1. ARTE & LITER Romanticism - 2. [sentimentalismo] romanticism.

romántico, ca *adj & m,f* - 1. ARTE & LITER Romantic - 2. [sentimental] romantic.

rombo *m* GEOM rhombus.

romería *f* [peregrinación] pilgrimage.

romero, ra *m,f* [peregrino] pilgrim.
➤ **romero** *m* BOT rosemary.

romo, ma *adj* [sin filo] blunt.

rompecabezas *m inv* - 1. [juego] jigsaw - 2. fam [problema] puzzle.

rompeolas *m inv* breakwater.

romper ⟨⟩ *vt* - 1. [gen] to break; [hacer añicos] to smash; [rasgar] to tear - 2. [interrumpir - monotonía, silencio, hábito] to break; [- hilo del discurso] to break off; [- tradición] to put an end to, to stop - 3. [terminar - relaciones etc] to break off. ⟨⟩ *vi* - 1. [terminar una relación]: **~ (con alguien)** to break o split up (with sb) - 2. [olas, el día] to break; [hostilidades] to break out; **al ~ el alba o día** at daybreak - 3. [empezar]: **~ a hacer algo** to suddenly start doing sthg; **~ a llorar** to burst into tears; **~ a reír** to burst out laughing.
➤ **romperse** *vpr* [partirse] to break; [rasgarse] to tear; **se ha roto una pierna** he has broken a leg.

rompevientos *m Amér* [anorak] anorak; *RP* [suéter] polo-neck jersey.

rompimiento *m* - 1. breaking; [de relaciones] breaking-off - 2. Amér [de relaciones, conversaciones] breaking-off; [de pareja] break-up; [de contrato] breach.

ron *m* rum.

roncar *vi* to snore.

roncha *f* red blotch.

ronco, ca *adj* **-1.** [afónico] hoarse; **se quedó ~ de tanto gritar** he shouted himself hoarse **-2.** [bronco] harsh.

ronda *f* **-1.** [de vigilancia, visitas] rounds *(pl)*; **hacer la ~** to do one's rounds **-2.** *fam* [de bebidas, en el juego etc] round.

rondar ◇ *vt* **-1.** [vigilar] to patrol **-2.** [rayar - edad] to be around. ◇ *vi* [merodear]: **~ (por)** to wander *o* hang around.

ronquera *f* hoarseness.

ronquido *m* snore, snoring *(U)*.

ronronear *vi* to purr.

ronroneo *m* purr, purring *(U)*.

roña ◇ *adj fam* [tacaño] stingy, tight. ◇ *f* **-1.** [suciedad] filth, dirt **-2.** VETER mange.

roñoso, sa ◇ *adj* **-1.** [sucio] dirty **-2.** [tacaño] mean. ◇ *m,f* miser, mean person.

ropa *f* clothes *(pl)*; **~ blanca** linen; **~ de abrigo** warm clothes *(pl)*; **~ de cama** bed linen; **~ hecha** ready-to-wear clothes; **~ interior** underwear; **~ sucia** laundry.

ropaje *m* robes *(pl)*.

ropero *m* **-1.** [armario] wardrobe **-2.** [habitación] walk-in wardrobe; TEATR cloakroom.

roquero = rockero.

rosa ◇ *f* [flor] rose; **estar (fresco) como una ~** to be as fresh as a daisy; **no hay ~ sin espinas** there's no rose without a thorn. ◇ *m* [color] pink. ◇ *adj inv* [color] pink.

◆ **rosa de los vientos** *f* NÁUT compass.

rosado, da *adj* pink.

◆ **rosado** ▻ **vino.**

rosal *m* [arbusto] rose bush.

rosario *m* **-1.** RELIG rosary; **rezar el ~** to say one's rosary **-2.** [sarta] string.

rosbif [ros'βif] **= roast-beef.**

rosca *f* **-1.** [de tornillo] thread **-2.** [forma - de anillo] ring; [- espiral] coil **-3.** CULIN ring doughnut **-4.** *loc*: **pasarse de ~** [persona] to go over the top.

rosco *m* ring-shaped bread roll.

roscón *m* ring-shaped cake; **~ de reyes** *cake eaten on 6th January.*

rosetón *m* [ventana] rose window.

rosquilla *f* ring doughnut.

rosticería *f Chile shop selling roast chicken.*

rostro *m* face.

rotación *f* **-1.** [giro] rotation; **~ de cultivos** crop rotation **-2.** [alternancia] rota; **por ~** in turn.

rotativo, va *adj* rotary, revolving.

◆ **rotativo** *m* newspaper.

◆ **rotativa** *f* rotary press.

rotisería *f CSur* deli.

roto, ta ◇ *pp* ▻ **romper.** ◇ *adj* **-1.** [gen] broken; [tela, papel] torn **-2.** *fig* [deshecho - vida etc] destroyed; [- corazón] broken **-3.** *fig* [exhausto] shattered. ◇ *m,f Chile fam pey* [trabajador] worker.

◆ **roto** *m* [en tela] tear, rip.

rotonda *f* **-1.** [glorieta] roundabout *UK*, traffic circle *US* **-2.** [plaza] circus.

rotoso, sa *adj Andes & RP fam* ragged, in tatters.

rótula *f* kneecap.

rotulador *m* felt-tip pen; [fluorescente] marker pen.

rótulo *m* **-1.** [letrero] sign **-2.** [encabezamiento] headline, title.

rotundo, da *adj* **-1.** [categórico - negativa, persona] categorical; [- lenguaje, estilo] emphatic, forceful **-2.** [completo] total.

rotura *f* [gen] break, breaking *(U)*; [de hueso] fracture; [en tela] rip, hole.

roturar *vt* to plough.

roulotte [ru'lot], **rulot** *f* caravan *UK*, trailer *US*.

rozadura *f* **-1.** [señal] scratch, scrape **-2.** [herida] graze.

rozamiento *m* [fricción] rub, rubbing *(U)*; FÍS friction *(U)*.

rozar *vt* **-1.** [gen] to rub; [suavemente] to brush; [suj: zapato] to graze **-2.** [pasar cerca de] to skim, to shave.

◆ **rozar con** *vi* **-1.** [tocar] to brush against **-2.** *fig* [acercarse a] to verge on.

◆ **rozarse** *vpr* **-1.** [tocarse] to touch **-2.** [pasar cerca] to brush past each other **-3.** [herirse - rodilla etc] to graze **-4.** *fig* [tener trato]: **~se con** to rub shoulders with.

Rte. *abrev de* **remitente.**

RTVE (*abrev de* **Radiotelevisión Española**) *f Spanish state broadcasting company.*

rubeola, rubéola *f* German measles *(U)*.

rubí (*pl* **rubís** *o* **rubíes**) *m* ruby.

rubio, bia ◇ *adj* **-1.** [pelo, persona] blond (*f* blonde), fair; **teñirse de ~** to dye one's hair blond; **rubia platino** platinum blonde **-2.** [tabaco] Virginia *(antes de sust)* **-3.** [cerveza] lager *(antes de sust)*. ◇ *m,f* [persona] blond (*f* blonde), fair-haired person.

rubor *m* **-1.** [vergüenza] embarrassment; **causar ~** to embarrass **-2.** [sonrojo] blush.

ruborizar *vt* [avergonzar] to embarrass.

◆ **ruborizarse** *vpr* to blush.

rúbrica *f* **-1.** [de firma] flourish **-2.** [conclusión] final flourish; **poner ~ a algo** to complete sthg.

rubricar *vt* **-1.** *fig* [confirmar] to confirm **-2.** *fig* [concluir] to complete.

rucio, cia *adj* [gris] grey.

rudeza *f* **-1.** [tosquedad] roughness **-2.** [grosería] coarseness.

rudimentario, ria *adj* rudimentary.

rudimentos *mpl* rudiments.

rudo, da *adj* - **1.** [tosco] rough - **2.** [brusco] sharp, brusque - **3.** [grosero] rude, coarse.

rueda *f* - **1.** [pieza] wheel; ~ **delantera/trasera** front/rear wheel; ~ **de repuesto** spare wheel; **ir sobre** ~**s** *fig* to go smoothly - **2.** [corro] circle.

➤ **rueda de prensa** *f* press conference.

ruedo *m* TAUROM bullring.

ruega *etc* ⊳ **rogar**.

ruego *m* request; ~**s y preguntas** any other business.

rufián *m* villain.

rugby *m* rugby.

rugido *m* [gen] roar; [de persona] bellow.

rugir *vi* [gen] to roar; [persona] to bellow.

rugoso, sa *adj* - **1.** [áspero - material, terreno] rough - **2.** [con arrugas - rostro etc] wrinkled; [- tejido] crinkled.

ruido *m* - **1.** [gen] noise; [sonido] sound; **mucho** ~ **y pocas nueces** much ado about nothing - **2.** *fig* [escándalo] row.

ruidoso, sa *adj* [que hace ruido] noisy.

ruin *adj* - **1.** [vil] low, contemptible - **2.** [avaro] mean.

ruina *f* - **1.** [gen] ruin; **amenazar** ~ [edificio] to be about to collapse; **estar en la** ~ to be ruined; **ser una** ~ to cost a fortune - **2.** [destrucción] destruction - **3.** [fracaso - persona] wreck; **estar hecho una** ~ to be a wreck.

➤ **ruinas** *fpl* [históricas] ruins; **en** ~**s** in ruins.

ruindad *f* - **1.** [cualidad] meanness, baseness - **2.** [acto] vile deed.

ruinoso, sa *adj* - **1.** [poco rentable] ruinous - **2.** [edificio] ramshackle.

ruiseñor *m* nightingale.

ruleta *f* roulette.

ruletear *vi* CAm, Méx fam to drive a taxi.

ruletero *m* CAm, Méx fam taxi driver.

rulo *m* [para el pelo] roller.

rulot = **roulotte**.

ruma *f* Andes, Ven heap, pile.

Rumanía Romania.

rumano, na *adj* & *m,f* Romanian.

➤ **rumano** *m* [lengua] Romanian.

rumba *f* rumba.

rumbo *m* - **1.** [dirección] direction, course; **caminar sin** ~ **fijo** to walk aimlessly; **ir con** ~ **a** to be heading for; **perder el** ~ [barco] to go off course; *fig* [persona] to lose one's way; **tomar otro** ~ to take a different tack - **2.** *fig* [camino] path, direction.

rumiante *adj* & *m* ruminant.

rumiar ⟨⟩ *vt* [suj: rumiante] to chew; *fig* to ruminate, to chew over. ⟨⟩ *vi* [masticar] to ruminate, to chew the cud.

rumor *m* - **1.** [ruido sordo] murmur - **2.** [chisme] rumour; **corre el** ~ **de que** there's a rumour going around that.

rumorearse *v impers*: ~ **que** ... to be rumoured that ...

runrún *m* [ruido confuso] hum, humming *(U)*.

rupestre *adj* cave *(antes de sust)*.

ruptura *f* [gen] break; [de relaciones, conversaciones] breaking-off; [de contrato] breach.

rural *adj* rural.

Rusia Russia.

ruso, sa *adj* & *m,f* Russian.

➤ **ruso** *m* [lengua] Russian.

rústico, ca *adj* - **1.** [del campo] country *(antes de sust)* - **2.** [tosco] rough, coarse.

➤ **en rústica** *loc adj* paperback.

ruta *f* route; *fig* way, course.

rutina *f* [gen & INFORM] routine; **por** ~ as a matter of course.

rutinario, ria *adj* routine.

s, S *f* [letra] s, S.

➤ **S** *(abrev de* **san)** St.

SA *(abrev de* **sociedad anónima)** *f* ≃ Ltd, ≃ PLC.

sábado *m* Saturday; **¿qué día es hoy?** - **(es)** ~ what day is it (today)? - (it's) Saturday; **cada** ~, **todos los** ~**s** every Saturday; **cada dos** ~**s**, **un** ~ **sí y otro no** every other Saturday; **caer en** ~ to be on a Saturday; **te llamo el** ~ I'll call you on Saturday; **el próximo** ~, **el** ~ **que viene** next Saturday; **el** ~ **pasado** last Saturday; **el** ~ **por la mañana/tarde/noche** Saturday morning/afternoon/night; **en** ~ on Saturdays; **nací en** ~ I was born on a Saturday; **este** ~ [pasado] last Saturday; [próximo] this (coming) Saturday; **¿trabajas los** ~**s?** do you work (on) Saturdays?; **un** ~ **cualquiera** on any Saturday.

sábana *f* sheet.

sabandija *f* *fig* [persona] worm.

sabañón *m* chilblain.

sabático, ca *adj* [del sábado] Saturday *(antes de sust)*.

saber ⟨⟩ *m* knowledge. ⟨⟩ *vt* - **1.** [conocer] to know; **ya lo sé** I know; **hacer** ~ **algo a alguien** to inform sb of sthg, to tell sb sthg;

¿se puede ~ qué haces? would you mind telling me what you are doing? - **2.** [ser capaz de]: ~ **hacer algo** to know how to do sthg, to be able to do sthg; **sabe hablar inglés/montar en bici** she can speak English/ride a bike - **3.** [enterarse] to learn, to find out; **lo supe ayer** I only found out yesterday - **4.** [entender de] to know about; **sabe mucha física** he knows a lot about physics. <> *vi* - **1.** [tener sabor]: ~ **(a)** to taste (of); ~ **bien/mal** to taste good/bad; ~ **mal a alguien** *fig* to upset *o* annoy sb - **2.** [entender]: ~ **de algo** to know about sthg - **3.** [tener noticia]: ~ **de alguien** to hear from sb; ~ **de algo** to learn of sthg - **4.** [parecer]: **eso me sabe a disculpa** that sounds like an excuse to me - **5.** *Andes, Arg & Chile fam* [soler]: ~ **hacer algo** to be wont to do sthg.
➡ **saberse** *vpr*: ~**se algo** to know sthg.
➡ **a saber** *loc adv* [es decir] namely.

sabido, da *adj*: **como es (bien)** ~ as everyone knows.

sabiduría *f* - **1.** [conocimientos] knowledge, learning - **2.** [prudencia] wisdom; ~ **popular** popular wisdom.

sabiendas ➡ **a sabiendas** *loc adv* knowingly.

sabihondo, da, sabiondo, da *adj & m,f* know-all, know-it-all.

sabio, bia *adj* - **1.** [sensato, inteligente] wise - **2.** [docto] learned.

sabiondo = **sabihondo**.

sablazo *m fam fig* [de dinero] scrounging *(U)*; **dar un** ~ **a alguien** to scrounge money off sb.

sable *m* sabre.

sablear *vi fam* to scrounge money.

sabor *m* - **1.** [gusto] taste, flavour; **tener** ~ **a algo** to taste of sthg; **dejar mal/buen** ~ **(de boca)** *fig* to leave a nasty taste in one's mouth/a warm feeling - **2.** *fig* [estilo] flavour.

saborear *vt lit & fig* to savour.

sabotaje *m* sabotage.

sabotear *vt* to sabotage.

sabrá *etc* ➡ **saber.**

sabroso, sa *adj* - **1.** [gustoso] tasty - **2.** *fig* [substancioso] tidy, considerable.

sabueso *m* - **1.** [perro] bloodhound - **2.** *fig* [policía] sleuth, detective.

saca *f* sack.

sacacorchos *m inv* corkscrew.

sacapuntas *m inv* pencil sharpener.

sacar <> *vt* - **1.** [poner fuera, hacer salir] to take out; [lengua] to stick out; ~ **algo de** to take sthg out of; **nos sacaron algo de comer** they gave us something to eat; ~ **a alguien a bailar** to ask sb to dance - **2.** [quitar]:

~ **algo (de)** to remove sthg (from) - **3.** [librar, salvar]: ~ **a alguien de** to get sb out of - **4.** [conseguir]: **no sacas nada mintiéndole** you don't gain anything by lying to him - **5.** [obtener - carné, buenas notas] to get, to obtain; [- premio] to win; [- foto] to take; [- fotocopia] to make; [- dinero del banco] to withdraw - **6.** [sonsacar]: ~ **algo a alguien** to get sthg out of sb - **7.** [extraer - producto]: ~ **algo de** to extract sthg from - **8.** [fabricar] to produce - **9.** [crear - modelo, disco etc] to bring out - **10.** [exteriorizar] to show - **11.** [resolver - crucigrama etc] to do, to finish - **12.** [deducir] to gather, to understand; [conclusión] to come to - **13.** [mostrar] to show; **lo sacaron en televisión** he was on television - **14.** [comprar - entradas etc] to get, to buy - **15.** [prenda - de ancho] to let out; [- de largo] to let down - **16.** [aventajar]: **sacó tres minutos a su rival** he was three minutes ahead of his rival - **17.** [DEP - con la mano] to throw in; [- con la raqueta] to serve. <> *vi* DEP to put the ball into play; [con la raqueta] to serve.
➡ **sacarse** *vpr* [carné etc] to get.
➡ **sacar adelante** *vt* - **1.** [hijos] to bring up - **2.** [negocio] to make a go of.

sacarina *f* saccharine.

sacerdote, tisa *m,f* [pagano] priest (*f* priestess).
➡ **sacerdote** *m* [cristiano] priest.

saciar *vt* [satisfacer - sed] to quench; [- hambre] to satisfy, to sate.

saco *m* - **1.** [bolsa] sack, bag; ~ **de dormir** sleeping bag - **2.** *Amér* [chaqueta] coat - **3.** *loc*: **dar por** ~ **a alguien** *mfam* to screw sb; **entrar a** ~ **en** to sack, to pillage; **mandar a alguien a tomar por** ~ *mfam* to tell sb to get stuffed; **no echar algo en** ~ **roto** to take good note of sthg.

sacramento *m* sacrament.

sacrificar *vt* - **1.** [gen] to sacrifice - **2.** [animal - para consumo] to slaughter.

sacrificio *m lit & fig* sacrifice.

sacrilegio *m lit & fig* sacrilege.

sacristán, ana *m,f* sacristan, sexton.

sacristía *f* sacristy.

sacro, cra *adj* [sagrado] holy, sacred.

sacudida *f* - **1.** [gen] shake; [de la cabeza] toss; [de tren, coche] jolt; **dar**~**s** to jolt; ~ **eléctrica** electric shock - **2.** [terremoto] tremor.

sacudir *vt* - **1.** [agitar] to shake - **2.** [golpear - alfombra etc] to beat - **3.** [hacer temblar] to shake - **4.** *fig* [conmover] to shake, to shock - **5.** *fam fig* [pegar] to smack, to give a hiding.

sádico, ca <> *adj* sadistic. <> *m,f* sadist.

sadismo *m* sadism.

saeta *f* - **1.** [flecha] arrow - **2.** MÚS *flamenco-style song sung on religious occasions.*

safari *m* [expedición] safari; **ir de** ~ to go on safari.

saga *f* saga.

sagacidad *f* astuteness.

sagaz *adj* astute, shrewd.

Sagitario ◇ *m* [zodiaco] Sagittarius. ◇ *mf* [persona] Sagittarian.

sagrado, da *adj* holy, sacred; *fig* sacred.

Sahara *m*: **el (desierto del)** ~ the Sahara (Desert).

sal *f* CULIN & QUÍM salt; **la** ~ **de la vida** *fig* the spark of life.
　◆ **sales** *fpl* **- 1.** [para reanimar] smelling salts **- 2.** [para baño] bath salts.

sala *f* **- 1.** [habitación - gen] room; [- de una casa] lounge, living room; [- de hospital] ward; ~ **de embarque** departure lounge; ~ **de espera** waiting room; ~ **de estar** lounge, living room; ~ **de partos** delivery room **- 2.** [local - de conferencias, conciertos] hall; [- de cine, teatro] auditorium; ~ **de fiestas** discotheque **- 4.** [DER - lugar] court (room); [- magistrados] bench.

saladito *m* RP savoury snack o appetizer.

salado, da *adj* **- 1.** [con sal] salted; [agua] salt *(antes de sust)*; [con demasiada sal] salty **- 2.** *fig* [gracioso] witty **- 3.** *CAm, Carib, Méx* [desgraciado] unfortunate.

salamandra *f* **- 1.** [animal] salamander **- 2.** [estufa] salamander stove.

salami, salame *CSur m* salami.

salar *vt* **- 1.** [para conservar] to salt **- 2.** [para cocinar] to add salt to.

salarial *adj* wage *(antes de sust)*.

salario *m* salary, wages *(pl)*; [semanal] wage.

salchicha *f* sausage.

salchichón *m* ≃ salami.

salchichonería *f Méx* delicatessen.

saldar *vt* **- 1.** [pagar - cuenta] to close; [- deuda] to settle **- 2.** *fig* [poner fin a] to settle **- 3.** COM to sell off.
　◆ **saldarse** *vpr* [acabar]: ~**se con** to produce; **la pelea se saldó con 11 heridos** 11 people were injured in the brawl.

saldo *m* **- 1.** [de cuenta] balance; ~ **acreedor/deudor** credit/debit balance **- 2.** [de deudas] settlement **- 3.** *(gen pl)* [restos de mercancías] remnant; [rebajas] sale; **de** ~ bargain **- 4.** *fig* [resultado] balance.

saldrá *etc* ▷ **salir**.

saledizo, za *adj* projecting.

salero *m* **- 1.** [recipiente] salt cellar *UK*, salt shaker *US* **- 2.** *fig* [gracia] wit; [donaire] charm.

salga *etc* ▷ **salir**.

salida *f* **- 1.** [acción de partir - gen] leaving; [- de tren, avión] departure; ~**s nacionales/internacionales** domestic/international departures **- 2.** DEP start; **dar la** ~ to start the race **- 3.** [lugar] exit, way out **- 4.** [momento]: **quedamos a la** ~ **del trabajo** we agreed to meet after work **- 5.** [viaje] trip **- 6.** [aparición - de sol, luna] rise; [- de revista, nuevo modelo] appearance **- 7.** [COM - posibilidades] market; [- producción] output **- 8.** *fig* [solución] way out; **si no hay otra** ~ if there's no alternative **- 9.** *fig* [futuro - de carreras etc] opening, opportunity.

salido, da *adj* **- 1.** [saliente] projecting, sticking out; [ojos] bulging **- 2.** [animal] on heat **- 3.** *mfam* [persona] horny.

saliente ◇ *adj* POLÍT outgoing. ◇ *m* projection.

salino, na *adj* saline.

salir *vi* **- 1.** [ir fuera] to go out; [venir fuera] to come out; ~ **de** to go/come out of; **¿salimos al jardín?** shall we go out into the garden?; **¡sal aquí fuera!** come out here! **- 2.** [ser novios]: ~ **(con alguien)** to go out (with sb) **- 3.** [marcharse]: ~ **(de/para)** to leave (from/for); ~ **corriendo** to go off like a shot **- 4.** [desembocar - calle]: ~ **a** to open out onto **- 5.** [resultar] to turn out; **ha salido muy estudioso** he has turned out to be very studious; **¿qué salió en la votación?** what was the result of the vote?; ~ **elegida actriz del año** to be voted actress of the year; ~ **bien/mal** to turn out well/badly; ~ **ganando/perdiendo** to come off well/badly **- 6.** [proceder]: ~ **de** to come from; **el vino sale de la uva** wine comes from grapes **- 7.** [surgir - luna, estrellas, planta] to come out; [- sol] to rise; [- dientes] to come through; **le ha salido un sarpullido en la espalda** her back has come out in a rash **- 8.** [aparecer - publicación, producto, traumas] to come out; [- moda, ley] to come in; [- en imagen, prensa, televisión] to appear; **¡qué bien sales en la foto!** you look great in the photo!; **ha salido en los periódicos** it's in the papers; **hoy salió por la televisión** he was on television today; ~ **de** CIN & TEATR to appear as **- 9.** [costar]: ~ **(a** o **por)** to work out (at); ~ **caro** [de dinero] to be expensive; [por las consecuencias] to be costly **- 10.** [parecerse]: ~ **a alguien** to turn out like sb, to take after sb **- 11.** [en juegos] to lead; **te toca** ~ **a ti** it's your lead **- 12.** [quitarse - manchas] to come out **- 13.** [librarse]: ~ **de** [gen] to get out of; [problema] to get round **- 14.** INFORM: ~ to quit, to exit.
　◆ **salirse** *vpr* **- 1.** [marcharse - de lugar, asociación etc]: ~**se (de)** to leave **- 2.** [filtrarse]: ~**se (por)** [líquido, gas] to leak o escape (through); [humo, aroma] to come out (through) **- 3.** [rebosar] to overflow; [leche] to boil over; **el río se salió del cauce** the river broke its banks **- 4.** [desviarse]: ~**se (de)**

to come off; **el coche se salió de la carretera** the car came off o left the road - **5.** *fig* [escaparse]: ~**se de** [gen] to deviate from; [límites] to go beyond; ~**se del tema** to digress - **6.** *loc*: ~**se con la suya** to get one's own way.

◆ **salir adelante** *vi* - **1.** [persona, empresa] to get by - **2.** [proyecto, propuesta, ley] to be successful.

salitre *m* saltpetre.

saliva *f* saliva.

salmo *m* psalm.

salmón ◇ *m* [pez] salmon. ◇ *adj & m inv* [color] salmon (pink).

salmonete *m* red mullet.

salmuera *f* brine.

salobre *adj* salty.

salón *m* - **1.** [habitación - en casa] lounge, sitting room; ~ **comedor** living room-dining room; [- en residencia, edificio público] reception hall - **2.** [local - de sesiones etc] hall; ~ **de actos** assembly hall - **3.** [feria] show, exhibition; ~ **de exposiciones** exhibition hall - **4.** [establecimiento] shop; ~ **de belleza/masaje** beauty/massage parlour; ~ **de té** tea-room.

salpicadera *f Méx* mudguard *UK*, fender *US*.

salpicadero *m* dashboard.

salpicar *vt* [rociar] to splash, to spatter.

salpimentar *vt* to season with salt and pepper.

salpullido = **sarpullido**.

salsa *f* - **1.** [CULIN - gen] sauce; [- de carne] gravy; ~ **bechamel** o **besamel** bechamel o white sauce; ~ **rosa** thousand island dressing; ~ **de tomate** tomato sauce; **en su propia** ~ *fig* in one's element - **2.** *fig* [interés] spice - **3.** MÚS salsa.

salsera *f* gravy boat.

saltamontes *m inv* grasshopper.

saltar ◇ *vt* - **1.** [obstáculo] to jump (over) - **2.** [omitir] to skip, to miss out. ◇ *vi* - **1.** [gen] to jump; ~ **de alegría** to jump for joy; [a la comba] to skip; [al agua] to dive; ~ **sobre alguien** [abalanzarse] to set upon sb; ~ **de un tema a otro** to jump (around) from one subject to another - **2.** [levantarse] to jump up; ~ **de la silla** to jump out of one's seat - **3.** [salir para arriba - objeto] to jump (up); [- champán, aceite] to spurt (out); [- corcho, válvula] to pop out - **4.** [explotar] to explode, to blow up - **5.** [romperse] to break - **6.** [reaccionar violentamente] to explode.

◆ **saltarse** *vpr* - **1.** [omitir] to skip, to miss out - **2.** [salir despedido] to pop off - **3.** [no respetar - cola, semáforo] to jump; [- ley, normas] to break.

salteado, da *adj* - **1.** CULIN sautéed - **2.** [espaciado] unevenly spaced.

salteador, ra *m,f*: ~ **de caminos** highwayman.

saltear *vt* CULIN to sauté.

saltimbanqui *mf* acrobat.

salto *m* - **1.** [gen & DEP] jump; **levantarse de un** ~ to leap to sb's feet; [grande] leap; [al agua] dive; ~ **de altura/longitud** high/long jump - **2.** *fig* [diferencia, omisión] gap - **3.** *fig* [progreso] leap forward.

◆ **salto de agua** *m* waterfall.

◆ **salto de cama** *m* negligée.

saltón, ona *adj* [ojos] bulging; [dientes] sticking out.

salubre *adj* healthy.

salud ◇ *f* [lit & fig] health; **estar bien/mal de** ~ to be well/unwell; **beber** o **brindar a la** ~ **de alguien** to drink to sb's health. ◇ *interj*: **¡**~**!** [para brindar] cheers!; **¡a su**~**!** your health!; [después de estornudar] bless you!

saludable *adj* - **1.** [sano] healthy - **2.** *fig* [provechoso] beneficial.

saludar *vt* to greet; ~ **con la mano a alguien** to wave to sb; MIL to salute; **saluda a Ana de mi parte** give my regards to Ana; **le saluda atentamente** yours faithfully.

◆ **saludarse** *vpr* to greet one another.

saludo *m* greeting; **retirarle el** ~ **a alguien** to stop speaking to sb; MIL salute; **Ana te manda** ~**s** [en cartas] Ana sends you her regards; [al teléfono] Ana says hello; **un** ~ **afectuoso** [en cartas] yours sincerely; ~**s** best regards.

salva *f* MIL salvo; **una** ~ **de aplausos** *fig* a round of applause.

salvación *f* - **1.** [remedio]: **no tener** ~ to be beyond hope - **2.** [rescate] rescue - **3.** RELIG salvation.

salvado *m* bran.

salvador, ra *m,f* [persona] saviour.

◆ **Salvador** *m* GEOGR: **El Salvador** El Salvador.

salvadoreño, ña *adj & m,f* Salvadoran.

salvaguardar *vt* to safeguard.

salvaje ◇ *adj* - **1.** [gen] wild - **2.** [pueblo, tribu] savage. ◇ *mf* - **1.** [primitivo] savage - **2.** [bruto] maniac.

salvamanteles *m inv* [llano] table mat; [con pies] trivet.

salvamento *m* rescue, saving; **equipo de** ~ rescue team.

salvar *vt* - **1.** [gen & INFORM] to save; ~ **algo/a alguien de algo** to save sthg/sb from sthg - **2.** [rescatar] to rescue - **3.** [superar - moralmente] to overcome; [- físicamente] to go over o around - **4.** [recorrer] to cover - **5.** [exceptuar]: **salvando algunos detalles** except for a few details.

salvarse *vpr* - **1.** [librarse] to escape - **2.** RELIG to be saved.

salvavidas ◇ *adj inv* life *(antes de sust)*. ◇ *m* [chaleco] lifejacket; [flotador] lifebelt.

salvedad *f* exception.

salvia *f* sage.

salvo, va *adj* safe; **estar a ∼** to be safe; **poner algo a ∼** to put sthg in a safe place.

♦ **salvo** *adv* except; **∼ que** unless.

salvoconducto *m* safe-conduct, pass.

san *adj* Saint; **∼ José** Saint Joseph.

sanar ◇ *vt* [persona] to cure; [herida] to heal. ◇ *vi* [persona] to get better; [herida] to heal.

sanatorio *m* sanatorium, nursing home.

sanción *f* [castigo] punishment; ECON sanction.

sancionar *vt* [castigar] to punish.

sancocho *m* *Andes* stew of beef, chicken or fish, vegetables and green bananas.

sandalia *f* sandal.

sandez *f* silly thing, nonsense *(U)*; **decir sandeces** to talk nonsense.

sandía *f* watermelon.

sándwich ['sanwitʃ] *(pl* **sándwiches)** *m* toasted sandwich.

saneamiento *m* - **1.** [higienización - de tierras] drainage; [- de edificio] disinfection - **2.** *fig* & FIN - de bienes] write-off, write-down; [- de moneda etc] stabilization; [- de economía] putting back on a sound footing.

sanear *vt* - **1.** [higienizar - tierras] to drain; [- un edificio] to disinfect - **2.** *fig* & FIN - bienes] to write off o down; [- moneda] to stabilize; [- economía] to put back on a sound footing.

sanfermines *mpl* festival held in Pamplona when bulls are run through the streets of the town.

sangrar ◇ *vi* to bleed. ◇ *vt* - **1.** [sacar sangre] to bleed - **2.** IMPRENTA to indent.

sangre *f* blood; **no llegó la ∼ al río** it didn't get too nasty.

♦ **sangre fría** *f* sangfroid; **a ∼ fría** in cold blood.

sangría *f* - **1.** [bebida] sangria - **2.** MED bloodletting - **3.** *fig* [ruina] drain.

sangriento, ta *adj* [ensangrentado, cruento] bloody.

sanguijuela *f* lit & *fig* leech.

sanguinario, ria *adj* bloodthirsty.

sanguíneo, a *adj* blood *(antes de sust)*.

sanidad *f* - **1.** [salubridad] health, healthiness - **2.** [servicio] public health; [ministerio] health department.

sanitario, ria *adj* health *(antes de sust)*.

♦ **sanitarios** *mpl* [instalación] bathroom fittings *(pl)*.

San José San José.

sano, na *adj* - **1.** [saludable] healthy; **∼ y salvo** safe and sound - **2.** [positivo - principios, persona etc] sound; [- ambiente, educación] wholesome - **3.** [entero] intact, undamaged.

San Salvador San Salvador.

santería *f* *Amér* [tienda] shop selling religious mementoes such as statues of saints.

santero, ra *adj* pious.

Santiago (de Chile) Santiago.

santiamén

♦ **en un santiamén** *loc adv fam* in a flash.

santidad *f* saintliness, holiness.

santiguar *vt* to make the sign of the cross over.

♦ **santiguarse** *vpr* [persignarse] to cross o.s.

santo, ta ◇ *adj* - **1.** [sagrado] holy - **2.** [virtuoso] saintly - **3.** *fam fig* [dichoso] damn; **todo el ∼ día** all day long. ◇ *m, f* RELIG saint.

♦ **santo** *m* - **1.** [onomástica] saint's day - **2.** *loc*: **¿a ∼ de qué?** why on earth?

♦ **santo y seña** *m* MIL password.

Santo Domingo Santo Domingo.

santuario *m* shrine; *fig* sanctuary.

saña *f* viciousness, malice.

sapo *m* toad.

saque *m* - **1.** [en fútbol]: **∼ de banda** throw-in; **∼ inicial** o **de centro** kick-off; **∼ de esquina/meta** corner/goal kick - **2.** [en tenis etc] serve.

saquear *vt* - **1.** [rapiñar - ciudad] to sack; [- tienda etc] to loot - **2.** *fam* [vaciar] to ransack.

saqueo *m* [de ciudad] sacking; [de tienda etc] looting.

sarampión *m* measles *(U)*.

sarao *m* [fiesta] party.

sarcasmo *m* sarcasm.

sarcástico, ca *adj* sarcastic.

sarcófago *m* sarcophagus.

sardana *f* traditional Catalan dance and music.

sardina *f* sardine; **como ∼s en canasta** o **en lata** like sardines.

sardónico, ca *adj* sardonic.

sargento *mf* - **1.** MIL ≃ sergeant.

sarpullido, salpullido *m* rash.

sarro *m* [de dientes] tartar.

sarta *f* lit & *fig* string; **una ∼ de mentiras** a pack of lies.

sartén *f* frying pan; **tener la ∼ por el mango** to be in control.

sastre, tra *m, f* tailor.

sastrería *f* [oficio] tailoring; [taller] tailor's (shop).

Satanás *m* Satan.

satélite ◇ *m* satellite. ◇ *adj fig* satellite *(antes de sust)*.

satén *m* satin; [de algodón] sateen.

satinado, da *adj* glossy.

sátira *f* satire.

satírico, ca ◇ *adj* satirical. ◇ *m,f* satirist.

satirizar *vt* to satirize.

satisfacción *f* satisfaction.

satisfacer *vt* **- 1.** [gen] to satisfy; [sed] to quench **- 2.** [deuda, pago] to pay, to settle **- 3.** [ofensa, daño] to redress **- 4.** [duda, pregunta] to answer **- 5.** [cumplir - requisitos, exigencias] to meet.

satisfactorio, ria *adj* satisfactory.

satisfecho, cha ◇ *pp* ▷ **satisfacer**. ◇ *adj* satisfied; **~ de sí mismo** self-satisfied; **darse por ~** to be satisfied.

saturar *vt* to saturate.

◆ saturarse *vpr*: **~se (de)** to become saturated (with).

saturnismo *m* lead poisoning.

Saturno Saturn.

sauce *m* willow; **~ llorón** weeping willow.

sauna *f* sauna.

savia *f* sap; *fig* vitality; **~ nueva** *fig* new blood.

saxo *m* [instrumento] sax.

saxofón, saxófono *m* [instrumento] saxophone.

sazón *f* **- 1.** [madurez] ripeness; **en ~** ripe **- 2.** [sabor] seasoning, flavouring.

◆ a la sazón *loc adv* then, at that time.

sazonado, da *adj* seasoned.

sazonar *vt* to season.

scanner [es'kaner] = **escáner**.

schilling = **chelín**.

scout [es'kaut] (*pl* **scouts**) *m* scout.

se *pron pers* **- 1.** (*reflexivo*) [de personas] himself (*f* herself), (*pl*) themselves; [usted mismo] yourself, (*pl*) yourselves; [de cosas, animales] itself, (*pl*) themselves; **~ está lavando, está lavándo~** she is washing (herself); **~ lavó los dientes** she cleaned her teeth; **espero que ~ diviertan** I hope you enjoy yourselves; **el perro ~ lame** the dog is licking itself; **~ lame la herida** it's licking its wound; **~ levantaron y ~ fueron** they got up and left **- 2.** (*reflexivo impersonal*) oneself; **hay que afeitar ~ todos los días** one has to shave every day, you have to shave every day **- 3.** (*recíproco*) each other, one another; **~ aman** they love each other; **~ escriben cartas** they write to each other **- 4.** [en construcción pasiva]: **~ ha suspendido la reunión** the meeting has been cancelled; **'~ prohíbe fumar'** 'no smoking'; **'~ habla inglés'** 'English spoken' **- 5.** (*impersonal*): **en esta sociedad ya no ~ respeta a los ancianos** in our society old people are no longer respected; **~ dice que ...** it is said that ..., people say that ... **- 6.** (*en vez de 'le' o 'les' antes de 'lo', 'la', 'los' o 'las'*) (*complemento indirecto*)

[gen] to him (*f* to her), (*pl*) to them; [de cosa, animal] to it, (*pl*) to them; [usted, ustedes] to you; **~ lo dio** he gave it to him/her *etc*; **~ lo dije, pero no me hizo caso** I told her, but she didn't listen; **si usted quiere, yo ~ lo arreglo en un minuto** if you like, I'll sort it out for you in a minute.

sé ▷ **saber**; **ser**.

sebo *m* fat; [para jabón, velas] tallow.

secador *m* dryer; **~ de pelo** hair-dryer.

secadora *f* clothes *o* tumble dryer.

secar *vt* **- 1.** [desecar] to dry **- 2.** [enjugar] to wipe away; [con fregona] to mop up.

◆ secarse *vpr* [gen] to dry up; [ropa, vajilla, suelo] to dry.

sección *f* **- 1.** [gen & GEOM] section **- 2.** [departamento] department.

seccionar *vt* **- 1.** [cortar] to cut; TECN to section **- 2.** [dividir] to divide (up).

secesión *f* secession.

seco, ca *adj* **- 1.** [gen] dry; [plantas, flores] withered; [higos, pasas] dried; **lavar en ~** to dry-clean **- 2.** [tajante] brusque **- 3.** *loc*: **parar en ~** to stop dead.

◆ a secas *loc adv* simply, just; **llámame Juan a secas** just call me Juan.

secretaría *f* [oficina, lugar] secretary's office **- 3.** [organismo] secretariat; **~ general** general secretariat.

secretariado *m* EDUC secretarial skills (*pl*); **curso de ~** secretarial course.

secretario, ria *m,f* secretary.

secreto, ta *adj* [gen] secret; [tono] confidential; **en ~** in secret.

◆ secreto *m* **- 1.** [gen] secret; **guardar un ~** to keep a secret; **~ bancario** banking confidentiality; **declarar el ~ de sumario** to deny access to information regarding a judicial enquiry **- 2.** [sigilo] secrecy.

secta *f* sect.

sector *m* **- 1.** [gen] sector; [grupo] group **- 2.** [zona] area.

secuaz *mf despec* minion.

secuela *f* consequence.

secuencia *f* sequence.

secuestrador, ra *m,f* **- 1.** [de persona] kidnapper **- 2.** [de avión] hijacker.

secuestrar *vt* **- 1.** [raptar] to kidnap **- 2.** [avión] to hijack **- 3.** [embargar] to seize.

secuestro *m* **- 1.** [rapto] kidnapping **- 2.** [de avión, barco] hijack **- 3.** [de bienes etc] seizure, confiscation.

secular *adj* **- 1.** [seglar] secular, lay **- 2.** [centenario] age-old.

secundar *vt* to support, to back (up); [propuesta] to second.

secundario, ria *adj* secondary.

◆ secundaria *f* secondary education.

secuoya *f* sequoia.

sed ◇ *v* ▷ **ser**. ◇ *f* thirst; **el calor da** ∼ heat makes you thirsty; **tener** ∼ to be thirsty; ∼ **de** *fig* thirst for.

seda *f* silk.

sedal *m* fishing line.

sedante ◇ *adj* MED sedative; [música] soothing. ◇ *m* sedative.

sede *f* **-1.** [emplazamiento] headquarters *(pl)*; [de gobierno] seat; ∼ **social** head office **-2.** [de campeonato] host **-3.** RELIG see.

➡ **Santa Sede** *f*: **la Santa Sede** the Holy See.

sedentario, ria *adj* sedentary.

sedición *f* sedition.

sediento, ta *adj* **-1.** [de agua] thirsty **-2.** *fig* [deseoso]: ∼ **de** hungry for.

sedimentar *vt* to deposit.

➡ **sedimentarse** *vpr* [líquido] to settle.

sedimento *m* **-1.** [poso] sediment **-2.** GEOL deposit.

sedoso, sa *adj* silky.

seducción *f* **-1.** [cualidad] seductiveness **-2.** [acción - gen] attraction, charm; [- sexual] seduction.

seducir *vt* **-1.** [atraer] to attract, to charm; [sexualmente] to seduce **-2.** [persuadir]: ∼ **a alguien para que haga algo** to tempt sb to do sthg.

seductor, ra ◇ *adj* [gen] attractive, charming; [sexualmente] seductive; [persuasivo] tempting. ◇ *m,f* seducer.

segador, ra *m,f* [agricultor] reaper.

segar *vt* **-1.** AGR to reap **-2.** [cortar] to cut off **-3.** *fig* [truncar] to put an end to.

seglar *m* lay person.

segmento *m* **-1.** GEOM & ZOOL segment **-2.** [trozo] piece **-3.** [sector] sector.

segregación *f* **-1.** [separación, discriminación] segregation; ∼ **racial** racial segregation **-2.** [secreción] secretion.

segregar *vt* **-1.** [separar, discriminar] to segregate **-2.** [secretar] to secrete.

seguidilla *f* **-1.** *(gen pl)* [baile] *traditional Spanish dance* **-2.** [cante] *mournful flamenco song.*

seguido, da *adj* **-1.** [consecutivo] consecutive; **diez años** ∼**s** ten years in a row **-2.** [sin interrupción - gen] one after the other; [- línea, pitido etc] continuous.

➡ **seguido** *adv* **-1.** [inmediatamente después] straight after **-2.** [en línea recta] straight on **-3.** *Amér* [frecuentemente] often.

➡ **en seguida** *loc adv* straight away, at once; **en seguida nos vamos** we're going in a minute.

seguidor, ra *m,f* follower.

seguimiento *m* [de noticia] following; [de clientes] follow-up.

seguir ◇ *vt* **-1.** [gen] to follow; ∼ **de cerca**

algo to follow sthg closely; ∼ **de cerca a alguien** to tail sb **-2.** [perseguir] to chase **-3.** [reanudar] to continue, to resume. ◇ *vi* **-1.** [sucederse]: ∼ **a algo** to follow sthg; **a la tormenta siguió la lluvia** the storm was followed by rain **-2.** [continuar] to continue, to go on; ∼ **adelante** to carry on; **¡sigue! ¡no te pares!** go *o* carry on, don't stop!; **sigo trabajando en la fábrica** I'm still working at the factory; **debes** ∼ **haciéndolo** you should keep on *o* carry on doing it; **sigo pensando que está mal** I still think it's wrong; **sigue enferma/en el hospital** she's still ill/at the hospital.

➡ **seguirse** *vpr* to follow; ∼ **se de algo** to follow *o* be deduced from sthg; **de esto se sigue que estás equivocado** it therefore follows that you are wrong.

según ◇ *prep* **-1.** [de acuerdo con] according to; ∼ **su opinión, ha sido un éxito** in his opinion *o* according to him, it was a success; ∼ **yo/tú** *etc* in my/your *etc* opinion **-2.** [dependiendo de] depending on; ∼ **la hora que sea** depending on the time. ◇ *adv* **-1.** [como] (just) as; **todo permanecía** ∼ **lo recordaba** everything was just as she remembered it; **actuó** ∼ **se le recomendó** he did as he had been advised **-2.** [a medida que] as; **entrarás en forma** ∼ **vayas entrenando** you'll get fit as you train **-3.** [dependiendo]: **¿te gusta la música?** - ∼ do you like music? - it depends; **lo intentaré** ∼ **esté de tiempo** I'll try to do it, depending on how much time I have.

➡ **según que** *loc adv* depending on whether.

➡ **según qué** *loc adj* certain; ∼ **qué días la clase es muy aburrida** some days the class is really boring.

segunda ▷ **segundo**.

segundero *m* second hand.

segundo, da ◇ *núm adj* second. ◇ *núm m y f* **-1.** [en orden]: **el** ∼ the second one; **llegó el** ∼ he came second **-2.** [mencionado antes]: **vinieron Pedro y Juan, el** ∼ **con ...** Pedro and Juan arrived, the latter with ... **-3.** [ayudante] number two; ∼ **de abordo** NÁUT first mate.

➡ **segundo** *m* **-1.** [gen] second **-2.** [piso] second floor.

➡ **segunda** *f* **-1.** AUTOM second (gear); **meter la segunda** to go into second (gear) **-2.** AERON & FERROC second class; **viajar en segunda** to travel second class **-3.** DEP second division.

➡ **con segundas** *loc adv* with an ulterior motive.

seguramente *adv* probably; ∼ **iré, pero aún no lo sé** the chances are I'll go, but I'm not sure yet.

seguridad f - 1. [fiabilidad, ausencia de peligro] safety; [protección, estabilidad] security; de ~ [cinturón, cierre] safety (antes de sust); [puerta, guardia] security (antes de sust); ~ ciudadana public safety; ~ vial road safety - 2. [certidumbre] certainty; con ~ for sure, definitely - 3. [confianza] confidence; ~ en sí mismo self-confidence.

◆ **Seguridad Social** f Social Security.

seguro, ra adj - 1. [fiable, sin peligro] safe; [protegido, estable] secure - 2. [infalible - prueba, negocio etc] reliable - 3. [confiado] sure; estar ~ de algo to be sure about sthg - 4. [indudable - nombramiento, fecha etc] definite, certain; tener por ~ que to be sure that - 5. [con aplomo] self-confident; estar ~ de sí mismo to be self-confident.

◆ **seguro** ◇ m - 1. [contrato] insurance (U); ~ a todo riesgo/a terceros comprehensive/third party insurance; ~ de incendios/de vida fire/life insurance; ~ de paro o de desempleo unemployment benefit; ~ del coche car insurance; ~ mutuo joint insurance; ~ de vida life insurance - 2. [dispositivo] safety device; [de armas] safety catch - 3. CAm, Méx [imperdible] safety pin. ◇ adv for sure, definitely; ~ que vendrá she's bound to come.

seis ◇ núm adj inv - 1. [para contar] six; tiene ~ años she's six (years old) - 2. [para ordenar] (number) six; la página ~ page six. ◇ núm m - 1. [número] six; el ~ number six; doscientos ~ two hundred and six; treinta y ~ thirty-six - 2. [en fechas] sixth; el ~ de agosto the sixth of August - 3. [en direcciones]: calle Mayor (número) ~ number six calle Mayor - 4. [en naipes] six; el ~ de diamantes the six of diamonds; echar o tirar un ~ to play a six. ◇ núm mpl - 1. [referido a grupos]: invité a diez y sólo vinieron ~ I invited ten and only six came along; somos ~ there are six of us; de ~ en ~ in sixes; los ~ the six of them - 2. [en temperaturas]: estamos a ~ bajo cero the temperature is six below zero - 3. [en puntuaciones]: empatar a ~ to draw six all; ~ a cero seis-nil. ◇ núm fpl [hora]: las ~ six o'clock; son las ~ it's six o'clock.

seiscientos, tas núm six hundred; ver también **seis**.

seísmo m earthquake.

selección f - 1. [gen] selection; [de personal] recruitment - 2. [equipo] team; ~ nacional national team.

seleccionador, ra m,f - 1. DEP selector, ≃ manager - 2. [de personal] recruiter.

seleccionar vt to pick, to select.

selectividad f [examen] university entrance examination.

selectivo, va adj selective.

selecto, ta adj - 1. [excelente] fine, excellent - 2. [escogido] exclusive, select.

self-service m inv self-service restaurant.

sellar vt - 1. [timbrar] to stamp - 2. [lacrar] to seal.

sello m - 1. [gen] stamp - 2. [tampón] rubber stamp - 3. [lacre] seal - 4. fig [carácter] hallmark.

selva f [gen] jungle; [bosque] forest.

semáforo m traffic lights (pl).

semana f week; entre ~ during the week; la ~ próxima/que viene next week; ~ laboral working week.

◆ **Semana Santa** f Easter; RELIG Holy Week.

semanada f Amér (weekly) pocket money.

semanal adj weekly.

semanario, ria adj weekly.

◆ **semanario** m [publicación semanal] weekly.

semántico, ca adj semantic.

◆ **semántica** f semantics (U).

semblante m countenance, face.

semblanza f portrait, profile.

sembrado, da adj fig [lleno]: ~ de scattered o plagued with.

sembrar vt - 1. [plantar] to sow; ~ algo de algo to sow sthg with sthg - 2. fig [llenar] to scatter, to strew - 3. fig [confusión, pánico etc] to sow.

semejante ◇ adj - 1. [parecido]: ~ (a) similar (to) - 2. [tal] such; jamás aceptaría ~ invitación I would never accept such an invitation. ◇ m (gen pl) fellow (human) being.

semejanza f similarity; a ~ de similar to.

semejar vt to resemble.

◆ **semejarse** vpr to be alike, to resemble each other.

semen m semen.

semental m stud; [caballo] stallion.

semestral adj half-yearly, six-monthly.

semestre m period of six months, semester US; cada ~ every six months.

semidirecto adj express.

semifinal f semifinal.

semilla f seed.

seminario m - 1. [escuela para sacerdotes] seminary - 2. [EDUC - curso, conferencia] seminar; [- departamento] department, school.

sémola f semolina.

Sena m: el ~ the (river) Seine.

senado m senate.

senador, ra m,f senator.

sencillez f - 1. [facilidad] simplicity - 2. [modestia] unaffectedness, naturalness - 3. [discreción] plainness.

sencillo, lla adj - 1. [fácil, sin lujo, llano]

simple - **2.** [campechano] natural, unaffected - **3.** [billete, unidad etc] single.

➡ **sencillo** m - **1.** [disco] single - **2.** *Andes, CAm, Méx fam* [cambio] loose change.

senda f, **sendero** m path.

sendos, das adj pl each, respective; llegaron los dos con ~ paquetes they arrived each carrying a parcel, they both arrived with their respective parcels.

Senegal: (el) ~ Senegal.

senil adj senile.

senior (pl seniors) adj & m senior.

seno m - **1.** [pecho] breast - **2.** [pechera] bosom; **en el** ~ **de** fig within - **3.** [útero]: ~ (materno) womb - **4.** fig [amparo, cobijo] refuge, shelter - **5.** ANAT [de la nariz] sinus.

sensación f - **1.** [percepción] feeling, sensation - **2.** [efecto] sensation - **3.** [premonición] feeling.

sensacional adj sensational.

sensacionalista adj sensationalist.

sensatez f wisdom, common sense.

sensato, ta adj sensible.

sensibilidad f - **1.** [perceptibilidad] feeling - **2.** [sentimentalismo] sensitivity; **tener la** ~ **a flor de piel** to be very sensitive - **3.** [don especial] feel - **4.** [de emulsión fotográfica, balanza etc] sensitivity.

sensibilizar vt - **1.** [concienciar] to raise the awareness of - **2.** FOT to sensitize.

sensible adj - **1.** [gen] sensitive - **2.** [evidente] perceptible; [pérdida] significant.

sensiblero, ra adj despec mushy, sloppy.

sensitivo, va adj - **1.** [de los sentidos] sensory - **2.** [receptible] sensitive.

sensor m sensor; ~ **de humo** smoke detector.

sensorial adj sensory.

sensual adj sensual.

sentado, da adj - **1.** [en asiento] seated; **estar** ~ to be sitting down - **2.** [establecido]: **dar algo por** ~ to take sthg for granted; **dejar** ~ **que ...** to make it clear that ...

sentar ⬦ vt - **1.** [en asiento] to seat, to sit - **2.** [establecer] to establish. ⬦ vi - **1.** [ropa, color] to suit - **2.** [comida]: ~ **bien/mal a alguien** to agree/disagree with sb - **3.** [vacaciones, medicamento]: ~ **bien a alguien** to do sb good - **4.** [comentario, consejo]: **le sentó mal** it upset her; **le sentó bien** she appreciated it.

➡ **sentarse** vpr to sit down.

sentencia f - **1.** DER sentence - **2.** [proverbio, máxima] maxim.

sentenciar vt DER: ~ **(a alguien a algo)** to sentence (sb to sthg).

sentido, da adj [profundo] heartfelt.

➡ **sentido** m - **1.** [gen] sense; **en cierto** ~ in a sense; **en** ~ **literal** in a literal sense;

tener ~ to make sense; ~ **común** common sense; ~ **del humor** sense of humour; **sexto** ~ sixth sense - **2.** [conocimiento] consciousness; **perder/recobrar el** ~ to lose/regain consciousness - **3.** [significado] meaning, sense; **sin** ~ [ilógico] meaningless; [inútil, irrelevante] pointless; **doble** ~ double meaning - **4.** [dirección] direction; **de** ~ **único** one-way.

sentimental adj sentimental.

sentimentaloide adj mushy, sloppy.

sentimiento m - **1.** [gen] feeling - **2.** [pena, aflicción]: **le acompaño en el** ~ my deepest sympathy.

sentir ⬦ vt - **1.** [gen] to feel - **2.** [lamentar] to regret, to be sorry about; **siento que no puedas venir** I'm sorry you can't come; **lo siento (mucho)** I'm (really) sorry - **3.** [oír] to hear. ⬦ m feelings (pl), sentiments (pl).

➡ **sentirse** vpr to feel; **me siento mareada** I feel sick.

seña f [gesto, indicio, contraseña] sign, signal.

➡ **señas** fpl - **1.** [dirección] address (sg); ~**s personales** (personal) description (sg) - **2.** [gesto, indicio] signs; **dar** ~**s de algo** to show signs of sthg; **(hablar) por** ~**s** (to talk) in sign language; **hacer** ~**s (a alguien)** to signal (to sb) - **3.** [detalle] details; **para** o **por más** ~**s** to be precise.

señal f - **1.** [gen & TELECOM] signal; ~ **de alarma/salida** alarm/starting signal; [de teléfono] tone; ~ **de ocupado** engaged tone, busy signal *US* - **2.** [indicio, símbolo] sign; **dar** ~**es de vida** to show signs of life; ~ **de la Cruz** sign of the Cross; ~ **de tráfico** road sign; **en** ~ **de** as a mark o sign of - **3.** [marca, huella] mark; **no dejó ni** ~ she didn't leave a trace - **4.** [cicatriz] scar, mark - **5.** [fianza] deposit.

señalado, da adj [importante - fecha] special; [- personaje] distinguished.

señalar vt - **1.** [marcar, denotar] to mark; [hora, temperatura etc] to indicate, to say - **2.** [indicar - con el dedo, con un comentario] to point out - **3.** [fijar] to set, to fix.

señalización f - **1.** [conjunto de señales] signs (pl); ~ **vial** roadsigns (pl) - **2.** [colocación de señales] signposting.

señalizar vt to signpost.

señor, ra adj [refinado] noble, refined.

➡ **señor** m - **1.** [tratamiento - antes de nombre, cargo] Mr; [- al dirigir la palabra] Sir; **el** ~ **López** Mr López; **¡** ~ **presidente!** Mr President!; **¿qué desea el** ~? what would you like, Sir?; **Muy** ~ **mío** [en cartas] Dear Sir - **2.** [hombre] man - **3.** [caballero] gentleman - **4.** [dueño] owner - **5.** [amo - de criado] master.

señora *f* - **1.** [tratamiento - antes de nombre, cargo] Mrs; [- al dirigir la palabra] Madam; **la señora López** Mrs López; **¡señora presidenta!** Madam President!; **¿qué desea la señora?** what would you like, Madam?; **¡señoras y ~es!** ... Ladies and Gentlemen! ...; **Estimada señora** [en cartas] Dear Madam - **2.** [mujer] lady; **señora de la limpieza** cleaning woman - **3.** [dama] lady - **4.** [dueña] owner - **5.** [ama- de criado] mistress - **6.** [esposa] wife.

◆ **señores** *mpl* [matrimonio]: **los ~es Ruiz** Mr & Mrs Ruiz.

señoría *f* lordship (*f* ladyship).

señorial *adj* [majestuoso] stately.

señorío *m* - **1.** [dominio] dominion, rule - **2.** [distinción] nobility.

señorito, ta *adj fam despec* [refinado] lordly.

◆ **señorito** *m* - **1.** *desus* [hijo del amo] master - **2.** *fam despec* [niñato] rich kid.

◆ **señorita** *f* - **1.** [soltera, tratamiento] Miss - **2.** [joven] young lady - **3.** [maestra]: **la ~** miss, the teacher - **4.** *desus* [hija del amo] mistress.

señuelo *m* - **1.** [reclamo] decoy - **2.** *fig* [trampa] bait, lure.

sepa *etc* ▷ **saber**.

separación *f* - **1.** [gen] separation - **2.** [espacio] space, distance.

separado, da *adj* - **1.** [gen] separate; **está muy ~ de la pared** it's too far away from the wall; **por ~** separately - **2.** [del cónyuge] separated.

separar *vt* - **1.** [gen] to separate; **~ algo de** to separate sthg from - **2.** [desunir] to take off, to remove - **3.** [apartar - silla etc] to move away - **4.** [reservar] to put aside - **5.** [destituir]: **~ de** to remove o dismiss from.

◆ **separarse** *vpr* - **1.** [apartarse] to move apart - **2.** [ir por distinto lugar] to separate, to part company - **3.** [matrimonio]: **~se (de alguien)** to separate (from sb) - **4.** [desprenderse] to come away o off.

separatismo *m* separatism.

separo *m Méx* (prison) cell.

sepia *f* [molusco] cuttlefish.

septentrional *adj* northern.

septiembre, setiembre *m* September; **el 1 de ~** the 1st of September; **uno de los ~s más lluviosos de la última década** one of the rainiest Septembers in the last decade; **a principios/mediados/finales de ~** at the beginning/in the middle/at the end of September; **el pasado/próximo (mes de) ~** last/next September; **en ~** in September; **en pleno ~** in mid-September; **este (mes de) ~** [pasado] (this) last September; [próximo] next September, this coming September; **para ~** by September.

séptimo, ma, **sétimo, ma** *núm* seventh.

septuagésimo, ma *núm* seventieth.

sepulcral *adj fig* [profundo - voz, silencio] lugubrious, gloomy.

sepulcro *m* tomb.

sepultar *vt* to bury.

sepultura *f* - **1.** [enterramiento] burial; **dar ~ a alguien** to bury sb - **2.** [fosa] grave.

sepulturero, ra *m y f* gravedigger.

sequedad *f* - **1.** [falta de humedad] dryness - **2.** *fig* [antipatía] abruptness, brusqueness.

sequía *f* drought.

séquito *m* [comitiva] retinue, entourage.

ser ◇ *v aux (antes de participio forma la voz pasiva)* to be; **fue visto por un testigo** he was seen by a witness. ◇ *v copulativo* - **1.** [gen] to be; **es alto/gracioso** he is tall/funny; **es azul/difícil** it's blue/difficult; **es un amigo/el dueño** he is a friend/the owner - **2.** [empleo, dedicación] to be; **soy abogado/actriz** I'm a lawyer/an actress; **son estudiantes** they're students. ◇ *vi* - **1.** [gen] to be; **fue aquí** it was here; **lo importante es decidirse** the important thing is to reach a decision; **~ de** [estar hecho de] to be made of; [provenir de] to be from; [ser propiedad de] to belong to; [formar parte de] to be a member of; **¿de dónde eres?** where are you from?; **los juguetes son de mi hijo** the toys are my son's - **2.** [con precios, horas, números] to be; **¿cuánto es?** how much is it?; **son 30 euros** that'll be 30 euros; **¿qué (día) es hoy?** what day is it today?, what's today?; **mañana será 15 de julio** tomorrow (it) will be the 15th of July; **¿qué hora es?** what time is it?, what's the time?; **son las tres (de la tarde)** it's three o'clock (in the afternoon), it's three (pm) - **3.** [servir, ser adecuado]: **~ para** to be for; **este trapo es para (limpiar) las ventanas** this cloth is for (cleaning) the windows; **este libro es para niños** this book is (meant) for children - **4.** *(uso partitivo)*: **~ de los que ...** to be one of those (people) who ...; **ése es de los que están en huelga** he is one of those on strike. ◇ *v impers* - **1.** [expresa tiempo] to be; **es muy tarde** it's rather late; **era de noche/de día** it was night/day - **2.** [expresa necesidad, posibilidad]: **es de desear que ...** it is to be hoped that ...; **es de suponer que aparecerá** presumably, he'll turn up - **3.** [expresa motivo]: **es que no vine porque estaba enfermo** the reason I didn't come is that I was ill - **4.** *loc*: **a no ~ que** unless; **como sea** one way or another, somehow or other; **de no ~** por had it not been for; **érase una vez, érase que se era** once upon a time; **no es para menos** not without reason; **o sea** that is (to say), I mean; **por si fuera poco** as if that wasn't enough. ◇ *m* [ente] being;

~ **humano/vivo** human/living being.

SER (*abrev de* **Sociedad Española de Radio-difusión**) *f Spanish independent radio company.*

Serbia Serbia.

serenar *vt* [calmar] to calm.

◆ **serenarse** *vpr* [calmarse] to calm down.

serenata *f* MÚS serenade.

serenidad *f* **- 1.** [tranquilidad] calm **- 2.** [quietud] tranquility.

sereno, na *adj* calm.

◆ **sereno** *m* [vigilante] night watchman.

serial *m* serial.

serie *f* **- 1.** [gen & TV] series *(sg)*; [de hechos, sucesos] chain; [de mentiras] string **- 2.** [de sellos, monedas] set **- 3.** *loc:* **ser un fuera de** ~ to be unique.

◆ **de serie** *loc adj* [equipamiento] (fitted) as standard.

◆ **en serie** *loc adv* [fabricación]: **fabricar en** ~ to mass-produce.

seriedad *f* **- 1.** [gravedad] seriousness **- 2.** [responsabilidad] sense of responsibility **- 3.** [formalidad - de persona] reliability.

serio, ria *adj* **- 1.** [gen] serious; **estar** ~ **to look serious - 2.** [responsable, formal] responsible **- 3.** [sobrio] sober.

◆ **en serio** *loc adv* seriously; **lo digo en** ~ I'm serious; **tomar(se) algo/a alguien en** ~ to take sthg/a alguien seriously.

sermón *m lit* & *fig* sermon; **echar un** ~ **por algo** to give a lecture for sthg.

seropositivo, va MED ◇ *adj* HIV-positive. ◇ *m, f* HIV-positive person.

serpentear *vi* **- 1.** [río, camino] to wind, to snake **- 2.** [culebra] to wriggle.

serpentina *f* streamer.

serpiente *f* [culebra] snake; LITER serpent.

serranía *f* mountainous region.

serrano, na *adj* **- 1.** [de la sierra] mountain *(antes de sust)*, highland *(antes de sust)* **- 2.** [jamón] cured.

serrar *vt* to saw (up).

serrín *m* sawdust.

serrucho *m* handsaw.

servicial *adj* attentive, helpful.

servicio *m* **- 1.** [gen] service; **fuera de** ~ out of order; ~ **de prensa/de urgencias** press/casualty department; ~ **de mesa** dinner service; ~ **militar** military service; ~ **de té** tea set **- 2.** [servidumbre] servants *(pl)* **- 3.** [turno] duty **- 4.** *(gen pl)* [WC] toilet, lavatory, bathroom *US* **- 5.** DEP serve, service.

servidor, ra *m,f* **- 1.** [en cartas]: **su seguro** ~ yours faithfully **- 3.** [yo] yours truly, me.

◆ **servidor** *m* INFORM server.

servidumbre *f* **- 1.** [criados] servants *(pl)* **- 2.** [dependencia] servitude.

servil *adj* servile.

servilleta *f* serviette, napkin.

servilletero *m* serviette o napkin ring.

servir ◇ *vt* to serve; **sírvanos dos cervezas** bring us two beers; **¿te sirvo más patatas?** would you like some more potatoes?; **¿en qué puedo** ~ **le?** what can I do for you? ◇ *vi* **- 1.** [gen] to serve; ~ **en el gobierno** to be a government minister **- 2.** [valer, ser útil] to serve, to be useful; **no sirve para estudiar** he's no good at studying; **de nada sirve que se lo digas** it's no use telling him; ~ **de algo** to serve as sthg.

◆ **servirse** *vpr* **- 1.** [aprovecharse]: ~**se de** to make use of; **sírvase llamar cuando quiera** please call whenever you want **- 2.** [comida, bebida] to help o.s.

sésamo *m* sesame.

sesenta *núm* sixty; **los (años)** ~ the sixties; *ver también* **seis**.

sesgo *m* **- 1.** [oblicuidad] slant **- 2.** *fig* [rumbo] course, path **- 3.** [enfoque] bias.

sesión *f* **- 1.** [reunión] meeting, session; DER sitting, session **- 2.** [proyección, representación] show, performance; ~ **continua** continuous showing; ~ **matinal** matinée; ~ **de tarde** afternoon matinée; ~ **de noche** evening showing **- 3.** [periodo] session.

seso *(gen pl)* *m* **- 1.** [cerebro] brain **- 2.** [sensatez] brains *(pl)*, sense; **sorber el** ~ o **los** ~**s a alguien** to brainwash sb.

sesudo, da *adj* [inteligente] brainy.

set *(pl sets)* *m* DEP set.

seta *f* mushroom; ~ **venenosa** toadstool.

setecientos, tas *núm* seven hundred; *ver también* **seis**.

setenta *núm* seventy; **los (años)** ~ the seventies; *ver también* **seis**.

setiembre = **septiembre**.

sétimo = **séptimo**.

seto *m* fence; ~ **vivo** hedge.

seudónimo = **pseudónimo**.

severidad *f* **- 1.** [rigor] severity **- 2.** [intransigencia] strictness.

severo, ra *adj* **- 1.** [castigo] severe, harsh **- 2.** [persona] strict.

Sevilla Seville.

sevillano, na *adj* & *m,f* Sevillian.

◆ **sevillanas** *fpl* Andalusian dance and song.

sexagésimo, ma *núm* sixtieth.

sexi, sexy *(pl sexys)* *adj* sexy.

sexista *adj* & *m,f* sexist.

sexo *m* [gen] sex.

sexteto *m* MÚS sextet.

sexto, ta *núm* sixth.

sexual *adj* [gen] sexual; [educación, vida] sex *(antes de sust)*.

sexualidad *f* sexuality.

sexy = sexi.

sha [sa, ʃa] *m* shah.

shock = choc.

shorts [ʃor] *mpl* shorts.

show [ʃou] (*pl* shows) *m* show.

si¹ (*pl* sis) *m* MÚS B; [en solfeo] ti.

si² *conj* - 1. *(condicional)* if; ~ viene él yo me voy if he comes, then I'm going; ~ hubieses venido te habrías divertido if you had come, you would have enjoyed yourself - 2. *(en oraciones interrogativas indirectas)* if, whether; **ignoro ~ lo sabe** I don't know if *o* whether she knows - 3. [expresa protesta] but; **¡~ te dije que no lo hicieras!** but I told you not to do it!

sí (*pl* síes) ⬦ *adv* - 1. [afirmación] yes; **¿vendrás? - ~, iré** will you come? - yes, I will; **claro que ~** of course; **creo que ~** I think so; **¿están de acuerdo? - algunos ~** do they agree? - some do - 2. [uso enfático]: **~ que** really, certainly; **~ que me gusta** I really *o* certainly like it - 3. *loc*: **no creo que puedas hacerlo - ¡a que ~!** I don't think you can do it - I bet I can!; **porque ~** [sin razón] because (I/you etc felt like it); **¿~?** [incredulidad] really? ⬦ *pron pers* - 1. *(reflexivo)* [de personas] himself (*f* herself), (*pl*) themselves; [usted] yourself, (*pl*) yourselves; [de cosas, animales] itself, (*pl*) themselves; **lo quiere todo para ~ (misma)** she wants everything for herself; **se acercó la silla hacia ~** he drew the chair nearer (himself); **de (por) ~** [cosa] in itself - 2. *(reflexivo impersonal)* oneself; **cuando uno piensa en ~ mismo** when one thinks about oneself, when you think about yourself. ⬦ *m* consent; **dar el ~** to give one's consent.

siamés, esa *adj* Siamese.

➡ **siamés** *m* [gato] Siamese.

Siberia: (la) ~ Siberia.

Sicilia Sicily.

sicoanálisis = psicoanálisis.

sicodélico = psicodélico.

sicología = psicología.

sicópata = psicópata.

sicosis = psicosis.

sicosomático = psicosomático.

sida *(abrev de síndrome de inmunodeficiencia adquirida)* *m* AIDS.

siderurgia *f* iron and steel industry.

siderúrgico, ca *adj* IND iron and steel *(antes de sust)*.

sidra *f* cider.

siega *f* - 1. [acción] reaping, harvesting - 2. [época] harvest (time).

siembra *f* - 1. [acción] sowing - 2. [época] sowing time.

siempre *adv* [gen] always; **como ~** as usual; **de ~** usual; **lo de ~** the usual; **somos amigos de ~** we've always been friends; **es así desde ~** it has always been that way; **para ~, para ~ jamás** for ever and ever; **¿~ nos vemos mañana?** *Amér* we're still getting together tomorrow, aren't we?

➡ **siempre que** *loc conj* - 1. [cada vez que] whenever - 2. [con tal de que] provided that, as long as.

➡ **siempre y cuando** *loc conj* provided that, as long as.

sien *f* temple.

sienta *etc* ⊳ sentar; sentir.

sierra *f* - 1. [herramienta] saw - 2. [cordillera] mountain range - 3. [región montañosa] mountains (*pl*).

siervo, va *m,f* - 1. [esclavo] serf - 2. RELIG servant.

siesta *f* siesta, nap; **dormir** *o* **echarse la ~** to have an afternoon nap.

siete ⬦ *núm* seven; *ver también* seis. ⬦ *f* RP *fig*: **de la gran ~** amazing, incredible; **¡la gran ~!** *fam* sugar! *UK*, shoot! *US*.

sífilis *f inv* syphilis.

sifón *m* - 1. [agua carbónica] soda (water) - 2. [tubo] siphon.

sigilo *m* [gen] secrecy; [al robar, escapar] stealth.

sigiloso, sa *adj* [discreto] secretive; [al robar, escapar] stealthy.

siglas *fpl* acronym.

siglo *m* - 1. [cien años] century; **el ~ XX** the 20th century; **el ~ III antes de Cristo** the third century before Christ - 2. *fig* [mucho tiempo]: **hace ~s que no la veo** I haven't seen her for ages.

signatura *f* - 1. [en biblioteca] catalogue number - 2. [firma] signature.

significación *f* - 1. [importancia] significance - 2. [significado] meaning.

significado, da *adj* important.

➡ **significado** *m* [sentido] meaning.

significar ⬦ *vt* - 1. [gen] to mean - 2. [expresar] to express. ⬦ *vi* [tener importancia]: **no significa nada para mí** it means nothing to me.

significativo, va *adj* significant.

signo *m* - 1. [gen] sign; **~ de multiplicar/dividir** multiplication/division sign; **~ del zodiaco** sign of the zodiac - 2. [en la escritura] mark; **~ de admiración/interrogación** exclamation/question mark - 3. [símbolo] symbol.

sigo *etc* ⊳ seguir.

siguiente ⬦ *adj* - 1. [en el tiempo, espacio] next - 2. [a continuación] following. ⬦ *mf* - 1. [el que sigue]: **el ~** the next one; **¡el ~!** next, please! - 2. [lo que sigue]: **lo ~** the following.

sílaba *f* syllable.

silbar ◇ *vt* -**1.** [gen] to whistle -**2.** [abuchear] to hiss, to catcall. ◇ *vi* -**1.** [gen] to whistle -**2.** [abuchear] to hiss, to catcall -**3.** *fig* [oídos] to ring.

silbato *m* whistle.

silbido, silbo *m* -**1.** [gen] whistle -**2.** [para abuchear, de serpiente] hiss, hissing *(U)*.

silenciador *m* silencer.

silenciar *vt* to hush up, to keep quiet.

silencio *m* -**1.** [gen] silence; **guardar** ~ **(sobre algo)** to keep silent (about sthg); **reinaba el** ~ **más absoluto** there was complete silence; **romper el** ~ to break the silence -**2.** MÚS rest.

silencioso, sa *adj* silent, quiet.

silicona *f* silicone.

silla *f* -**1.** [gen] chair; ~ **de ruedas** wheelchair; ~ **eléctrica** electric chair; ~ **de tijera** folding chair -**2.** [de caballo]: ~ **(de montar)** saddle.

sillín *m* saddle, seat.

sillón *m* armchair.

silueta *f* -**1.** [cuerpo] figure -**2.** [contorno] outline -**3.** [dibujo] silhouette.

silvestre *adj* wild.

simbólico, ca *adj* symbolic.

simbolizar *vt* to symbolize.

símbolo *m* symbol.

simetría *f* symmetry.

simiente *f culto* seed.

símil *m* -**1.** [paralelismo] similarity, resemblance -**2.** LITER simile.

similar *adj*: ~ **(a)** similar (to).

similitud *f* similarity.

simio, mia *m, f* simian, ape.

simpatía *f* -**1.** [cordialidad] friendliness -**2.** [cariño] affection; **coger** ~ **a alguien** to take a liking to sb; **tener** ~ **a, sentir** ~ **por** to like -**3.** MED sympathy.

simpático, ca *adj* -**1.** [gen] nice, likeable; [abierto, cordial] friendly; **Juan me cae** ~ I like Juan -**2.** [anécdota, comedia etc] amusing, entertaining -**3.** [reunión, velada etc] pleasant, agreeable.

simpatizante *mf* sympathizer.

simpatizar *vi*: ~ **(con)** [persona] to hit it off (with), to get on (with); [cosa] to sympathize (with).

simple ◇ *adj* -**1.** [gen] simple -**2.** [fácil] easy, simple -**3.** [único, sin componentes] single; **dame una** ~ **razón** give me one single reason -**4.** [mero] mere; **por** ~ **estupidez** through sheer stupidity. ◇ *mf* [persona] simpleton.

simplemente *adv* simply.

simpleza *f* -**1.** [de persona] simple-mindedness -**2.** [tontería] trifle.

simplicidad *f* simplicity.

simplificar *vt* to simplify.

simplista *adj* simplistic.

simposio, simposium *m* symposium.

simulacro *m* simulation; ~ **de combate** mock battle; ~ **de incendio** fire drill.

simular *vt* -**1.** [sentimiento, desmayo etc] to feign; **simuló que no me había visto** he pretended not to have seen me -**2.** [enfermedad] to fake -**3.** [combate, salvamento] to simulate.

simultáneo, nea *adj* simultaneous.

sin *prep* without; ~ **alcohol** alcohol-free; **estoy** ~ **una peseta** I'm penniless; **ha escrito cinco libros** ~ **(contar) las novelas** he has written five books, not counting his novels; **está** ~ **hacer** it hasn't been done yet; **estamos** ~ **vino** we're out of wine; ~ **que** *(+ subjuntivo)* without *(+ gerund)*; ~ **que nadie se enterara** without anyone noticing.
◆ **sin embargo** *conj* however.

sinagoga *f* synagogue.

sincerarse *vpr*: ~ **(con alguien)** to open one's heart (to sb).

sinceridad *f* sincerity; [llaneza, franqueza] frankness; **con toda** ~ in all honesty.

sincero, ra *adj* sincere; [abierto, directo] frank; **para ser** ~ to be honest.

síncope *m* blackout; **le dio un** ~ she blacked out.

sincronizar *vt* [regular] to synchronize.

sindical *adj* (trade) union *(antes de sust)*.

sindicalista *mf* trade unionist.

sindicato *m* trade union, labor union *US*.

síndrome *m* syndrome; ~ **de abstinencia** withdrawal symptoms *(pl)*; ~ **de Down** Down's syndrome; ~ **de inmunodeficiencia adquirida** acquired immune deficiency syndrome; ~ **premenstrual** premenstrual syndrome; ~ **tóxico** *toxic syndrome caused by ingestion of adulterated rapeseed oil.*

sinfín *m* vast number; **un** ~ **de problemas** no end of problems.

sinfonía *f* symphony.

sinfónico, ca *adj* symphonic.
◆ **sinfónica** *f* symphony orchestra.

singani *m Bol* grape brandy.

Singapur Singapore.

single ['single] *m* -**1.** single -**2.** *CSur* [habitación] single room.

singular ◇ *adj* -**1.** [raro] peculiar, odd -**2.** [único] unique -**3.** GRAM singular. ◇ *m* GRAM singular; **en** ~ in the singular.

singularidad *f* -**1.** [rareza, peculiaridad] peculiarity -**2.** [exclusividad] uniqueness.

singularizar *vt* to distinguish, to single out.
◆ **singularizarse** *vpr* to stand out, to be conspicuous; ~ **se por algo** to stand out because of sthg.

siniestro, tra *adj* -**1.** [perverso] sinister -**2.** [desgraciado] disastrous.
● **siniestro** *m* disaster; [accidente de coche] accident, crash; [incendio] fire.
sinnúmero *m*: un ~ de countless.
sino *conj* -**1.** [para contraponer] but; **no lo hizo él,** ~ **ella** he didn't do it, she did; **no sólo es listo,** ~ **también trabajador** he's not only clever but also hardworking -**2.** [para exceptuar] except, but; **¿quién** ~ **tú lo haría?** who else but you would do it?; **no quiero** ~ **que se haga justicia** I only want justice to be done.
sinónimo, ma *adj* synonymous; **ser** ~ **de algo** to be synonymous with sthg.
● **sinónimo** *m* synonym.
sinopsis *f inv* synopsis.
síntesis *f inv* synthesis; **en** ~ in short.
sintético, ca *adj* [artificial] synthetic.
sintetizador, ra *adj* synthesizing.
● **sintetizador** *m* synthesizer.
sintetizar *vt* -**1.** [resumir] to summarize -**2.** [fabricar artificialmente] to synthesize.
sintiera *etc* ▷ **sentir**.
síntoma *m* symptom.
sintonía *f* -**1.** [música] signature tune -**2.** [conexión] tuning -**3.** *fig* [compenetración] harmony; **en** ~ **con** in tune with.
sintonizar ◇ *vt* [conectar] to tune in to. ◇ *vi* -**1.** [conectar]: ~ **(con)** to tune in (to) -**2.** *fig* [compenetrarse]: ~ **en algo (con alguien)** to be on the same wavelength (as sb) about sthg.
sinuoso, sa *adj* -**1.** [camino] winding -**2.** [movimiento] sinuous.
sinvergüenza *mf* -**1.** [canalla] rogue -**2.** [fresco, descarado] cheeky person.
sionismo *m* Zionism.
siquiatra = **psiquiatra**.
siquiátrico = **psiquiátrico**.
síquico = **psíquico**.
siquiera ◇ *conj* [aunque] even if; **ven** ~ **por pocos días** do come, even if it's only for a few days. ◇ *adv* [por lo menos] at least; **dime** ~ **tu nombre** (you could) at least tell me your name.
● **ni (tan) siquiera** *loc conj* not even; **ni (tan)** ~ **me hablaron** they didn't even speak to me.
sirena *f* -**1.** MITOL mermaid, siren -**2.** [señal] siren.
Siria Syria.
sirimiri *m* drizzle.
sirviente, ta *m, f* servant.
sisa *f* [en costura] dart; [de manga] armhole.
sisear *vt & vi* to hiss.
sísmico, ca *adj* seismic.
sistema *m* -**1.** [gen & INFORM] system; ~

monetario/nervioso/solar monetary/nervous/solar system; ~ **experto/operativo** INFORM expert/operating system; ~ **dual** TV *system enabling dubbed TV programmes to be heard in the original language*; ~ **métrico (decimal)** metric (decimal) system; ~ **monetario europeo** European Monetary System; ~ **montañoso** mountain chain ○ range; ~ **periódico de los elementos** periodic table of elements -**2.** [método, orden] method.
● **por sistema** *loc adv* systematically.
Sistema Ibérico *m*: **el** ~ the Iberian mountain chain.
sistemático, ca *adj* systematic.
sistematizar *vt* to systematize.
sitiar *vt* [cercar] to besiege.
sitio *m* -**1.** [lugar] place; **cambiar de** ~ **(con alguien)** to change places (with sb); **en otro** ~ elsewhere; **poner a alguien en su** ~ to put sb in his/her place -**2.** [espacio] room, space; **hacer** ~ **a alguien** to make room for sb; **ocupar** ~ to take up space -**3.** [cerco] siege -**4.** INFORM: ~ **Web** Web site -**5.** *Méx* [de taxi] taxi rank *UK* ○ stand *US*.
situación *f* -**1.** [circunstancias] situation; [legal, social] status -**2.** [condición, estado] state, condition -**3.** [ubicación] location.
situado, da *adj* -**1.** [acomodado] comfortably off; **estar bien** ~ to be well off -**2.** [ubicado] located.
situar *vt* -**1.** [colocar] to place, to put; [edificio, ciudad] to site, to locate -**2.** [en clasificación] to place, to rank -**3.** [localizar] to locate, to find.
● **situarse** *vpr* -**1.** [colocarse] to take up position -**2.** [ubicarse] to be located -**3.** [acomodarse, establecerse] to get o.s. established -**4.** [en clasificación] to be placed; **se sitúa entre los mejores** he's (ranked) amongst the best.
skai [es'kai] = **escay**.
ski [es'ki] = **esquí**.
SL (*abrev de* **sociedad limitada**) *f* ≃ Ltd.
slip [es'lip] = **eslip**.
slogan [es'loyan] = **eslogan**.
SME (*abrev de* **sistema monetario europeo**) *m* EMS.
smoking [es'mokin] = **esmoquin**.
s/n *abrev de* **sin número**.
snob = **esnob**.
snowboard *m* snowboard; **hacer** ~ to go snowboarding.
so ◇ *prep* under; ~ **pretexto de** under; ~ **pena de** under penalty of. ◇ *adv*: **¡** ~ **tonto!** you idiot! ◇ *interj* whoa!
sobaco *m* armpit.
sobado, da *adj* -**1.** [cuello, puños etc] worn, shabby; [libro] dog-eared -**2.** *fig* [argumento,

excusa] well-worn, hackneyed.

◆ **sobado** *m* CULIN shortcrust pastry.

sobar *vt* - 1. [tocar] to finger, to paw - 2. *despec* [acariciar, besar] to touch up, to fondle.

soberanía *f* sovereignty.

soberano, na ◇ *adj* - 1. [independiente] sovereign - 2. *fig* [grande] massive; [paliza] thorough; [belleza, calidad] supreme, unrivalled. ◇ *m,f* sovereign.

soberbio, bia *adj* - 1. [arrogante] proud, arrogant - 2. [magnífico] superb.

◆ **soberbia** *f* - 1. [arrogancia] pride, arrogance - 2. [magnificencia] grandeur, splendour.

sobornar *vt* to bribe.

soborno *m* - 1. [acción] bribery - 2. [dinero, regalo] bribe.

sobra *f* excess, surplus; **de** ~ [en exceso] more than enough; [de más] superfluous; **lo sabemos de** ~ we know it only too well.

◆ **sobras** *fpl* [de comida] leftovers.

sobrado, da *adj* - 1. [de sobra] more than enough, plenty of - 2. [de dinero] well off.

sobrante *adj* remaining.

sobrar *vi* - 1. [quedar, restar] to be left over, to be spare; **nos sobró comida** we had some food left over - 2. [haber de más] to be more than enough; **parece que van a** ~ **bocadillos** it looks like there are going to be too many sandwiches - 3. [estar de más] to be superfluous; **lo que dices sobra** that goes without saying.

sobrasada *f Mallorcan spiced sausage.*

sobre¹ *m* - 1. [para cartas] envelope - 2. [para alimentos] sachet, packet.

sobre² *prep* - 1. [encima de] on (top of); **el libro está** ~ **la mesa** the book is on (top of) the table - 2. [por encima de] over, above; **el pato vuela** ~ **el lago** the duck is flying over the lake - 3. [acerca de] about, on; **un libro** ~ **el amor** a book about *o* on love; **una conferencia** ~ **el desarme** a conference on disarmament - 4. [alrededor de] about; **llegarán** ~ **las diez** they'll arrive at about ten o'clock - 5. [acumulación] upon; **nos contó mentira** ~ **mentira** he told us lie upon lie *o* one lie after another - 6. [cerca de] upon; **la desgracia estaba ya** ~ **nosotros** the disaster was already upon us.

sobrecarga *f* - 1. [exceso de carga] excess weight - 2. [saturación] overload.

sobrecargo *m* [de avión] purser.

sobrecoger *vt* - 1. [asustar] to frighten, to startle - 2. [impresionar] to move.

◆ **sobrecogerse** *vpr* - 1. [asustarse] to be frightened, to be startled - 2. [impresionarse] to be moved.

sobredosis *f inv* overdose.

sobreentender = sobrentender.

sobregiro *m* COM overdraft.

sobremesa *f* after-dinner period.

sobrenatural *adj* [extraordinario] supernatural.

sobrenombre *m* nickname.

sobrentender, sobreentender *vt* to understand, to deduce.

◆ **sobrentenderse** *vpr* to be inferred *o* implied.

sobrepasar *vt* - 1. [exceder] to exceed - 2. [aventajar]: ~ **a alguien** to overtake sb.

◆ **sobrepasarse** *vpr* to go too far.

sobrepeso *m* excess weight.

sobreponer, superponer *vt fig* [anteponer]: ~ **algo a algo** to put sthg before sthg.

◆ **sobreponerse** *vpr*: ~ **se a algo** to overcome sthg.

sobreproducción, superproducción *f* ECON overproduction *(U)*.

sobrepuesto, ta, superpuesto, ta *adj* superimposed; ⊳ **sobreponer**.

sobresaliente ◇ *adj* [destacado] outstanding. ◇ *m* [en escuela] excellent, ≃ A; [en universidad] ≃ first class.

sobresalir *vi* - 1. [en tamaño] to jut out - 2. [en importancia] to stand out.

sobresaltar *vt* to startle.

◆ **sobresaltarse** *vpr* to be startled, to start.

sobresalto *m* start, fright.

sobrestimar *vt* to overestimate.

sobretiempo *m Andes* [trabajo] overtime; [en deporte] extra time *UK*, overtime *US*.

sobretodo *m Amér* overcoat.

sobrevenir *vi* to happen, to ensue; **sobrevino la guerra** the war intervened.

sobreviviente = superviviente.

sobrevivir *vi* to survive.

sobrevolar *vt* to fly over.

sobriedad *f* - 1. [moderación] restraint, moderation - 2. [no embriaguez] soberness.

sobrino, na *m,f* nephew (*f* niece).

sobrio, bria *adj* - 1. [moderado] restrained - 2. [no excesivo] simple - 3. [austero, no borracho] sober.

socarrón, ona *adj* sarcastic.

socavar *vt* [excavar por debajo] to dig under; *fig* [debilitar] to undermine.

socavón *m* [hoyo] hollow; [en la carretera] pothole.

sociable *adj* sociable.

social *adj* - 1. [gen] social - 2. COM company *(antes de sust)*.

socialdemócrata *mf* social democrat.

socialismo *m* socialism.

socialista *adj & m,f* socialist.

sociedad *f* - 1. [gen] society; ~ **de consumo** consumer society; ~ **deportiva** sports club; ~ **literaria** literary society - 2. COM [empresa] company; ~ **anónima** public (limited) company UK, incorporated company US; ~ **(de responsabilidad) limitada** private limited company.

socio, cia m,f - **1.** COM partner - **2.** [miembro] member.

sociología f sociology.

sociólogo, ga m,f sociologist.

socorrer vt to help.

socorrismo m first aid; [en la playa] lifesaving.

socorrista mf first aid worker; [en la playa] lifeguard.

socorro <> m help, aid. <> interj help!

soda f [bebida] soda water, club soda US.

sodio m sodium.

soez adj vulgar, dirty.

sofá (pl **sofás**) m sofa; ~ **cama** o **nido** sofa bed.

Sofía Sofia.

sofisticación f sophistication.

sofisticado, da adj sophisticated.

sofocar vt - **1.** [ahogar] to suffocate, to stifle - **2.** [incendio] to put out, to smother - **3.** fig [rebelión] to suppress, to quell - **4.** fig [avergonzar] to mortify.

◆ **sofocarse** vpr - **1.** [ahogarse] to suffocate - **2.** fig [irritarse]: ~**se (por)** to get hot under the collar (about).

sofoco m - **1.** [ahogo] breathlessness (U); [sonrojo, bochorno] hot flush - **2.** fig [vergüenza] mortification - **3.** fig [disgusto]: **llevarse un** ~ to have a fit.

sofreír vt to fry lightly over a low heat.

sofrito, ta pp ▷ **sofreír**.

◆ **sofrito** m fried tomato and onion sauce.

software ['sofwer] m INFORM software.

soga f rope; [para ahorcar] noose.

sois ▷ **ser**.

soja f soya.

sol m - **1.** [astro] sun; **a pleno** ~ in the sun; **al salir/ponerse el** ~ at sunrise/sunset; **hace** ~ it's sunny; **no dejar a alguien ni a** ~ **ni a sombra** not to give sb a moment's peace - **2.** [rayos, luz] sunshine, sun; **tomar el** ~ to sunbathe - **3.** MÚS G; [en solfeo] so - **4.** [moneda] sol.

solamente adv only, just; **vino** ~ **él** only he came.

solapa f - **1.** [de prenda] lapel - **2.** [de libro, sobre] flap.

solapado, da adj underhand, devious.

solar <> adj solar. <> m undeveloped plot (of land).

solario, solárium (pl **solariums**) m solarium.

solazar vt - **1.** to amuse, to entertain - **2.** [aliviar] to solace, to entertain.

soldada f pay.

soldado m soldier; ~ **raso** private.

soldador, ra m,f [persona] welder.

◆ **soldador** m [aparato] soldering iron.

soldar vt to solder, to weld.

soleado, da adj sunny.

soledad f loneliness; **en** ~ alone; culto solitude.

solemne adj - **1.** [con pompa] formal - **2.** [grave] solemn - **3.** fig [enorme] utter, complete.

solemnidad f [suntuosidad] pomp, solemnity; **de** ~ extremely.

soler vi: ~ **hacer algo** to do sthg usually; **aquí suele llover mucho** it usually rains a lot here; **solíamos ir a la playa cada día** we used to go to the beach every day.

solera f - **1.** [tradición] tradition - **2.** [del vino] sediment; **de** ~ vintage.

solfeo m MÚS solfeggio, singing of scales.

solicitar vt - **1.** [pedir] to request; [un empleo] to apply for; ~ **algo a** o **de alguien** to request sthg of sb - **2.** [persona] to pursue; **estar muy solicitado** to be very popular, to be much sought after.

solícito, ta adj solicitous, obliging.

solicitud f - **1.** [petición] request; **presentar una** ~ to submit a request - **2.** [documento] application - **3.** [atención] care.

solidaridad f solidarity; **en** ~ **con** in solidarity with.

solidario, ria adj - **1.** [adherido]: ~ **(con)** sympathetic (to), supporting (of) - **2.** [obligación, compromiso] mutually binding.

solidez f [física] solidity.

solidificar vt to solidify.

◆ **solidificarse** vpr to solidify.

sólido, da adj - **1.** [gen] solid; [cimientos, fundamento] firm - **2.** [argumento, conocimiento, idea] sound.

◆ **sólido** m solid.

soliloquio m soliloquy.

solista <> adj solo. <> mf soloist.

solitario, ria <> adj - **1.** [sin compañía] solitary - **2.** [lugar] lonely, deserted. <> m,f [persona] loner.

◆ **solitario** m [juego] patience.

sollozar vi to sob.

sollozo m sob.

solo, la adj - **1.** [sin nadie] alone; **dejar** ~ **a alguien** to leave sb alone; **se quedó** ~ **a temprana edad** he was on his own from an early age; **a solas** alone, by oneself - **2.** [sin nada] on its own; [café] black; [whisky] neat - **3.** [único] single, sole; **ni una sola gota** not a (single) drop; **dame una sola cosa** give me just one thing - **4.** [solitario] lonely.

◆ **solo** m MÚS solo.

sólo adv only, just; **no** ~ ... **sino (también)** ... not only... but (also) ...; ~ **que** ... only...

solomillo *m* sirloin.

soltar *vt* -**1**. [desasir] to let go of -**2**. [desatar-gen] to unfasten; [-nudo] to untie; [-hebilla, cordones] to undo -**3**. [dejar libre] to release -**4**. [desenrollar-cable etc] to let *o* pay out -**5**. [patada, grito, suspiro etc] to give; **no suelta ni un duro** you can't get a penny out of her -**6**. [decir bruscamente] to come out with.
 ◆ **soltarse** *vpr* -**1**. [desasirse] to break free -**2**. [desatarse] to come undone -**3**. [desprenderse] to come off -**4**. [perder timidez] to let go.

soltero, ra ◇ *adj* single, unmarried. ◇ *m,f* bachelor (*f* single woman).

solterón, ona ◇ *adj* unmarried. ◇ *m,f* old bachelor (*f* spinster, old maid).

soltura *f* -**1**. [gen] fluency -**2**. [seguridad de sí mismo] assurance.

soluble *adj* -**1**. [que se disuelve] soluble -**2**. [que se soluciona] solvable.

solución *f* solution.

solucionar *vt* to solve; [disputa] to resolve.

solventar *vt* -**1**. [pagar] to settle -**2**. [resolver] to resolve.

solvente *adj* -**1**. [económicamente] solvent -**2**. *fig* [fuentes etc] reliable.

Somalia Somalia.

sombra *f* -**1**. [proyección-fenómeno] shadow; [-zona] shade; **dar** ~ **a** to cast a shadow over; **tener mala** ~ to be a nasty swine -**2**. [en pintura] shade -**3**. *fig* [anonimato] background; **permanecer en la** ~ to stay out of the limelight -**4**. [suerte] **buena/mala** ~ good/bad luck.
 ◆ **sombra de ojos** *f* eyeshadow.

sombrero *m* [prenda] hat.

sombrilla *f* sunshade, parasol; **me vale** ~ *Méx fig* I couldn't care less.

sombrío, bría *adj* -**1**. [oscuro] gloomy, dark -**2**. *fig* [triste] sombre, gloomy.

somero, ra *adj* superficial.

someter *vt* -**1**. [a rebeldes] to subdue -**2**. [presentar]: ~ **algo a la aprobación de alguien** to submit sthg for sb's approval; ~ **algo a votación** to put sthg to the vote -**3**. [subordinar] to subordinate -**4**. [a operación, interrogatorio etc]: ~ **a alguien a algo** to subject sb to sthg.
 ◆ **someterse** *vpr* -**1**. [rendirse] to surrender -**2**. [conformarse]: ~**se a algo** to yield *o* bow to sthg -**3**. [a operación, interrogatorio etc]: ~**se a algo** to undergo sthg.

somier (*pl* **somieres**) *m* [de muelles] bed springs (*pl*); [de tablas] slats (*pl*) (*of bed*).

somnífero, ra *adj* somniferous.
 ◆ **somnífero** *m* sleeping pill.

somos ⊳ ser.

son ◇ ⊳ ser. ◇ *m* -**1**. [sonido] sound

-**2**. [estilo] way; **en** ~ **de** in the manner of; **en** ~ **de paz** in peace.

sonajero *m* rattle.

sonambulismo *m* sleepwalking.

sonámbulo, la *m,f* sleepwalker.

sonar[1] *m* sonar.

sonar[2] *vi* -**1**. [gen] to sound; **(así** *o* **tal) como suena** literally, in so many words -**2**. [timbre] to ring -**3**. [hora]: **sonaron las doce** the clock struck twelve -**4**. [ser conocido, familiar] to be familiar; **me suena** it rings a bell; **no me suena su nombre** I don't remember hearing her name before -**5**. [pronunciarse-letra] to be pronounced -**6**. [rumorearse] to be rumoured.
 ◆ **sonarse** *vpr* to blow one's nose.

sonda *f* -**1**. MED & TECN probe -**2**. NÁUT sounding line -**3**. MIN drill, bore.

sondear *vt* -**1**. [indagar] to sound out -**2**. [MIN-terreno] to test; [-roca] to drill.

sondeo *m* -**1**. [encuesta] (opinion) poll -**2**. MIN drilling (*U*), boring (*U*) -**3**. NÁUT sounding.

sonido *m* sound.

sonoro, ra *adj* -**1**. [gen] sound (*antes de sust*); [película] talking -**2**. [ruidoso, resonante, vibrante] resonant.

sonreír *vi* [reír levemente] to smile.
 ◆ **sonreírse** *vpr* to smile.

sonriente *adj* smiling.

sonrisa *f* smile.

sonrojar *vt* to cause to blush.
 ◆ **sonrojarse** *vpr* to blush.

sonrojo *m* blush, blushing (*U*).

sonrosado, da *adj* rosy.

sonsacar *vt* : ~ **algo a alguien** [conseguir] to wheedle sthg out of sb; [hacer decir] to extract sthg from sb; ~ **a alguien** to pump sb for information.

sonso, sa *Amér Fam* ◇ *adj* foolish, silly. ◇ *m,f* fool, idiot.

soñador, ra *m,f* dreamer.

soñar ◇ *vt lit* & *fig* to dream; **¡ni** ~**lo!** not on your life! ◇ *vi lit* & *fig*: ~ **(con)** to dream (of *o* about).

soñoliento, ta *adj* sleepy, drowsy.

sopa *f* -**1**. [guiso] soup -**2**. [de pan] sop, *piece of soaked bread*.

sopapo *m fam* slap.

sope *m Méx* *fried corn tortilla, with beans and cheese or other toppings*.

sopero, ra *adj* soup (*antes de sust*).
 ◆ **sopera** *f* [recipiente] soup tureen.

sopesar *vt* to try the weight of; *fig* to weigh up.

sopetón
 ◆ **de sopetón** *loc adv* suddenly, abruptly.

soplar ◇ *vt* -**1**. [vela, fuego] to blow out -**2**. [ceniza, polvo] to blow off -**3**. [globo etc] to blow up - **4.** [vidrio] to blow - **5.** *fig* [pregunta, examen] to prompt. $\diamond$ *vi* [gen] to blow.

soplete *m* blowlamp.

soplido *m* blow, puff.

soplo *m* - **1.** [soplido] blow, puff - **2.** MED murmur - **3.** *fam* [chivatazo] tip-off.

soplón, ona *m,f fam* grass.

soponcio *m fam* fainting fit; **le dio un ~** [desmayo] she passed out; [ataque] she had a fit.

sopor *m* drowsiness.

soporífero, ra *adj lit* & *fig* soporific.

soportar *vt* - **1.** [sostener] to support - **2.** [resistir, tolerar] to stand; **¡no le soporto!** I can't stand him! - **3.** [sobrellevar] to endure, to bear.

soporte *m* - **1.** [apoyo] support - **2.** INFORM medium; **~ físico** hardware; **~ lógico** software.

soprano *mf* soprano.

sor *f* RELIG sister.

sorber *vt* - **1.** [beber] to sip; [haciendo ruido] to slurp - **2.** [absorber] to soak up, to absorb - **3.** [atraer] to draw *o* suck in.

sorbete *m* sorbet.

sorbo *m* [acción] gulp, swallow; **beber algo de un ~** to drink sthg in one gulp; [pequeño] sip; **beber a ~s** to sip.

sordera *f* deafness.

sórdido, da *adj* - **1.** [miserable] squalid - **2.** [obsceno, perverso] sordid.

sordo, da $\diamond$ *adj* - **1.** [que no oye] deaf - **2.** [ruido, dolor] dull. $\diamond$ *m,f* [persona] deaf person; **los ~s** the deaf.

sordomudo, da $\diamond$ *adj* deaf and dumb. $\diamond$ *m,f* deaf-mute.

sorna *f* sarcasm.

soroche *m Andes, Arg* altitude sickness.

sorprendente *adj* surprising.

sorprender *vt* - **1.** [asombrar] to surprise - **2.** [atrapar]: **~ a alguien (haciendo algo)** to catch sb (doing sthg) - **3.** [coger desprevenido] to catch unawares.

$\blacklozenge$ **sorprenderse** *vpr* to be surprised.

sorprendido, da *adj* surprised; **quedarse ~** to be surprised.

sorpresa *f* surprise; **de** *o* **por ~** by surprise.

sorpresivo, va *adj Amér* unexpected.

sortear *vt* - **1.** [rifar] to raffle - **2.** [echar a suertes] to draw lots for - **3.** *fig* [esquivar] to dodge.

sorteo *m* - **1.** [lotería] draw - **2.** [rifa] raffle.

sortija *f* ring.

sortilegio *m* [hechizo] spell.

SOS *m* SOS.

sosa *f* soda.

sosegado, da *adj* calm.

sosegar *vt* to calm.

$\blacklozenge$ **sosegarse** *vpr* to calm down.

soseras *m y f inv fam* dull person, bore.

sosias *m inv* double, lookalike.

sosiego *m* calm.

soslayo

$\blacklozenge$ **de soslayo** *loc adv* [oblicuamente] sideways, obliquely; **mirar a alguien de ~** to look at sb out of the corner of one's eye.

soso, sa *adj* - **1.** [sin sal] bland, tasteless - **2.** [sin gracia] dull, insipid.

sospecha *f* suspicion; **despertar ~s** to arouse suspicion.

sospechar $\diamond$ *vt* [creer, suponer] to suspect; **sospecho que no la terminará** I doubt whether she'll finish it. $\diamond$ *vi*: **~ de** to suspect.

sospechoso, sa $\diamond$ *adj* suspicious. $\diamond$ *m,f* suspect.

sostén *m* - **1.** [apoyo] support - **2.** [sustento] main support; [alimento] sustenance - **3.** [sujetador] bra, brassiere.

sostener *vt* - **1.** [sujetar] to support, to hold up - **2.** [defender - idea, opinión, tesis] to defend; [- promesa, palabra] to stand by, to keep; **~ que ...** to maintain that ... - **3.** [tener - conversación] to hold, to have; [- correspondencia] to keep up.

$\blacklozenge$ **sostenerse** *vpr* to hold o.s. up; [en pie] to stand up; [en el aire] to hang.

sostenido, da *adj* - **1.** [persistente] sustained - **2.** MÚS sharp.

sota *f* $\simeq$ jack.

sotana *f* cassock.

sótano *m* basement.

soterrar *vt* [enterrar] to bury; *fig* to hide.

soufflé [su'fle] (*pl* **soufflés**) *m* soufflé.

soul *m* MÚS soul (music).

soviético, ca $\diamond$ *adj* - **1.** [del soviet] soviet - **2.** [de la URSS] Soviet. $\diamond$ *m,f* Soviet.

soy $\rhd$ ser.

spaghetti [espa'yeti] = espagueti.

sport [es'port] = esport.

spot [es'pot] = espot.

spray [es'prai] = espray.

sprint [es'prin] = esprint.

squash [es'kwaʃ] *m inv* squash.

Sr. (*abrev de* **señor**) Mr.

Sra. (*abrev de* **señora**) Mrs.

Sres. (*abrev de* **señores**) Messrs.

Srta. (*abrev de* **señorita**) Miss.

Sta. (*abrev de* **santa**) St.

standard [es'tandar] = estándar.

standarizar [estandari'θar] = estandarizar.

starter [es'tarter] = estárter.

status [es'tatus] = estatus.

stereo [es'tereo] = estéreo.

sterling [es'terlin] = **esterlina**.

Sto. (*abrev de* **santo**) St.

stock [es'tok] = **estoc**.

stop, estop [es'top] *m* **-1.** AUTOM stop sign **- 2.** [en telegrama] stop.

stress [es'tres] = **estrés**.

strip-tease [es'triptis] *m inv* striptease.

su (*pl* **sus**) *adj poses* [de él] his; [de ella] her; [de cosa, animal] its; [de uno] one's; [de ellos, ellas] their; [de usted, ustedes] your.

suave *adj* **-1.** [gen] soft **- 2.** [liso] smooth **- 3.** [sabor, olor, color] delicate **- 4.** [apacible - persona, carácter] gentle; [- clima] mild **- 5.** [fácil - cuesta, tarea, ritmo] gentle; [- dirección de un coche] smooth.

suavidad *f* **-1.** [gen] softness **- 2.** [lisura] smoothness **- 3.** [de sabor, olor, color] delicacy **- 4.** [de carácter] gentleness **- 5.** [de clima] mildness **- 6.** [de cuesta, tarea, ritmo] gentleness; [de la dirección de un coche] smoothness.

suavizante *m* conditioner; ~ **para la ropa** fabric conditioner.

suavizar *vt* **-1.** [gen] to soften; [ropa, cabello] to condition **- 2.** [ascensión, conducción, tarea] to ease; [clima] to make milder **- 3.** [sabor, olor, color] to tone down **- 4.** [alisar] to smooth.

subacuático, ca *adj* subaquatic.

subalquilar *vt* to sublet.

subalterno, na *m,f* [empleado] subordinate.

subasta *f* **-1.** [venta pública] auction; **sacar algo a** ~ to put sthg up for auction **- 2.** [contrata pública] tender; **sacar algo a** ~ to put sthg out to tender.

subastar *vt* to auction.

subcampeón, ona *m,f* runner-up.

subconsciente *adj & m* subconscious.

subdesarrollado, da *adj* underdeveloped.

subdesarrollo *m* underdevelopment.

subdirector, ra *m,f* assistant manager.

subdirectorio *m* INFORM subdirectory.

súbdito, ta *m,f* **-1.** [subordinado] subject **- 2.** [ciudadano] citizen, national.

subdivisión *f* subdivision.

subestimar *vt* to underestimate; [infravalorar] to underrate.

  ◆ **subestimarse** *vpr* to underrate o.s.

subido, da *adj* **-1.** [intenso] strong, intense **- 2.** *fam* [atrevido] risqué.

  ◆ **subida** *f* **-1.** [cuesta] hill **- 2.** [ascensión] ascent, climb **- 3.** [aumento] increase, rise.

subir ◇ *vi* **-1.** [a piso, azotea] to go/come up; [a montaña, cima] to climb **- 2.** [aumentar - precio, temperatura] to go up, to rise; [- cauce, marea] to rise **- 3.** [montar - en avión, barco] to get on; [- en coche] to get in; **sube al coche** get into the car **- 4.** [cuenta,

importe]: ~ **a** to come o amount to **- 5.** [de categoría] to be promoted. ◇ *vt* **-1.** [ascender - calle, escaleras] to go/come up; [- pendiente, montaña] to climb **- 2.** [poner arriba] to lift up; [llevar arriba] to take/bring up **- 3.** [aumentar - precio, peso] to put up, to increase; [- volumen de radio etc] to turn up **- 4.** [montar]: ~ **algo/a alguien a** to lift sthg/sb onto **- 5.** [alzar - mano, bandera, voz] to raise; [- persiana] to roll up; [- ventanilla] to wind up.

  ◆ **subirse** *vpr* **-1.** [ascender]: ~**se a** [árbol] to climb up; [mesa] to climb onto; [piso] to go/come up to **- 2.** [montarse]: ~**se a** [tren, avión] to get on, to board; [caballo, bicicleta] to mount; [coche] to get into; **el taxi paró y me subí** the taxi stopped and I got in **- 3.** [alzarse - pernera, mangas] to roll up; [- cremallera] to do up; [- pantalones, calcetines] to pull up.

súbito, ta *adj* sudden; **de** ~ suddenly.

subjetivo, va *adj* subjective.

sub júdice [suβ'djuðiθe] *adj* DER sub judice.

subjuntivo, va *adj* subjunctive.

  ◆ **subjuntivo** *m* subjunctive.

sublevación *f*, **sublevamiento** *m* uprising.

sublevar *vt* **-1.** [amotinar] to stir up **- 2.** [indignar] to infuriate.

  ◆ **sublevarse** *vpr* [amotinarse] to rise up, to rebel.

sublime *adj* sublime.

submarinismo *m* skin-diving.

submarinista *mf* skin-diver.

submarino, na *adj* underwater.

  ◆ **submarino** *m* submarine.

subnormal ◇ *adj* **-1.** *ofensivo* [minusválido] subnormal **- 2.** *fig & despec* [imbécil] moronic. ◇ *mf fig & despec* [imbécil] moron, cretin.

suboficial *m* MIL non-commissioned officer.

subordinado, da *adj & m,f* subordinate.

subordinar *vt* [gen & GRAM] to subordinate; ~ **algo a algo** to subordinate sthg to sthg.

subproducto *m* by-product.

subrayar *vt lit & fig* to underline.

subsanar *vt* **-1.** [solucionar] to resolve **- 2.** [corregir] to correct.

subscribir = **suscribir**.

subscripción = **suscripción**.

subscriptor = **suscriptor**.

subsecretario, ria *m,f* **-1.** [de secretario] assistant secretary **- 2.** [de ministro] undersecretary.

subsidiario, ria *adj* DER ancillary.

subsidio *m* benefit, allowance; ~ **de invalidez** disability allowance; ~ **de paro** unemployment benefit.

subsiguiente *adj* subsequent.

subsistencia f [vida] subsistence.

→ **subsistencias** fpl [provisiones] provisions.

subsistir vi - **1.** [vivir] to live, to exist - **2.** [sobrevivir] to survive.

substancia = sustancia.

substancial = sustancial.

substancioso = sustancioso.

substantivo = sustantivo.

substitución = sustitución.

substituir = sustituir.

substituto = sustituto.

substracción = sustracción.

substraer = sustraer.

subsuelo m subsoil.

subte m RP metro, underground UK, subway US.

subterráneo, a adj subterranean, underground.

→ **subterráneo** m - **1.** underground tunnel - **2.** Arg [metro] underground.

subtítulo m [gen & CIN] subtitle.

suburbio m poor suburb.

subvención f subsidy.

subvencionar vt to subsidize.

subversión f subversion.

subversivo, va adj subversive.

subyacer vi [ocultarse]: ~ **bajo algo** to underlie sthg.

subyugar vt - **1.** [someter] to subjugate - **2.** fig [dominar] to quell, to master - **3.** fig [atraer] to captivate.

succionar vt [suj: raíces] to suck up; [suj: bebé] to suck.

sucedáneo, a adj ersatz, substitute.

→ **sucedáneo** m substitute.

suceder ◇ v impers [ocurrir] to happen; **suceda lo que suceda** whatever happens. ◇ vi [venir después]: ~ **a** to come after, to follow; **a la guerra sucedieron años muy tristes** the war was followed by years of misery.

sucesión f [gen] succession.

sucesivamente adv successively; **y así** ~ and so on.

sucesivo, va adj - **1.** [consecutivo] successive, consecutive - **2.** [siguiente]: **en días** ~**s les informaremos** we'll let you know over the next few days; **en lo** ~ in future.

suceso m - **1.** [acontecimiento] event - **2.** (gen pl) [hecho delictivo] crime; [incidente] incident; **sección de** ~**s** accident and crime reports.

sucesor, ra m,f successor.

suciedad f - **1.** [cualidad] dirtiness (U) - **2.** [porquería] dirt, filth (U).

sucinto, ta adj [conciso] succinct.

sucio, cia adj - **1.** [gen] dirty; [al comer, trabajar] messy; **en** ~ in rough - **2.** [juego] dirty.

suculento, ta adj tasty.

sucumbir vi - **1.** [rendirse, ceder]: ~ **(a)** to succumb (to) - **2.** [fallecer] to die - **3.** [desaparecer] to fall.

sucursal f branch.

sudadera f [prenda] sweatshirt.

Sudáfrica South Africa.

sudafricano, na adj & m,f South African.

Sudán Sudan.

sudar vi [gen] to sweat.

sudeste, sureste ◇ adj [posición, parte] southeast, southeastern; [dirección, viento] southeasterly. ◇ m southeast.

sudoeste, suroeste ◇ adj [posición, parte] southwest, southwestern; [dirección, viento] southwesterly. ◇ m southwest.

sudor m [gen] sweat (U); ~ **frío** cold sweat.

sudoroso, sa adj sweaty.

Suecia Sweden.

sueco, ca ◇ adj Swedish. ◇ m,f [persona] Swede.

→ **sueco** m [lengua] Swedish.

suegro, gra m,f father-in-law (f mother-in-law).

suela f sole.

sueldo m salary, wages (pl); [semanal] wage; **a** ~ [asesino] hired; [empleado] salaried.

suelo ◇ ▷ **soler**. ◇ m - **1.** [pavimento - en interiores] floor; [- en el exterior] ground; **caerse al** ~ to fall over; **besar el** ~ to fall flat on one's face - **2.** [terreno, territorio] soil; [para edificar] land - **3.** [base] bottom - **4.** loc: **echar por el** ~ **un plan** to ruin a project; **estar por los** ~**s** [persona, precio] to be at rock bottom; [productos] to be dirt cheap; **poner** o **tirar por los** ~**s** to run down, to criticize.

suelto, ta adj - **1.** [gen] loose; [cordones] undone; **¿tienes cinco euros** ~**s?** have you got five euros in loose change?; **andar** ~ [en libertad] to be free; [en fuga] to be at large; [con diarrea] to have diarrhoea - **2.** [separado] separate; [desparejado] odd; **no los vendemos** ~**s** we don't sell them separately - **3.** [arroz] fluffy - **4.** [lenguaje, estilo] fluent, fluid - **5.** [desenvuelto] comfortable, at ease.

→ **suelto** m [calderilla] loose change.

suena etc ▷ **sonar²**.

sueño m - **1.** [ganas de dormir] sleepiness; [por medicamento etc] drowsiness; **¡qué** ~**!** I'm really sleepy!; **tener** ~ to be sleepy - **2.** [estado] sleep; **coger el** ~ to get to sleep - **3.** [imagen mental, objetivo, quimera] dream; **en** ~**s** in a dream.

suero m - **1.** MED serum; ~ **artificial** saline solution - **2.** [de la leche] whey.

suerte *f* - **1.** [azar] chance; **la ~ está echada** the die is cast - **2.** [fortuna] luck; **desear ~ a alguien** to wish sb luck; **estar de ~** to be in luck; **por ~** luckily; **¡qué ~!** that was lucky!; **tener (buena) ~** to be lucky; **tener mala ~** to be unlucky - **3.** [destino] fate; **traer mala ~** to bring bad luck - **4.** [situación] situation, lot - **5.** *culto* [clase]: **toda ~ de** all manner of - **6.** *culto* [manera] manner, fashion; **de ~ que** in such a way that.

suéter (*pl* **suéteres**) *m* sweater.

suficiencia *f* - **1.** [capacidad] proficiency - **2.** [presunción] smugness, self-importance.

suficiente ◇ *adj* - **1.** [bastante] enough; [medidas, esfuerzos] adequate; **no llevo (dinero) ~** I don't have enough (money) on me; **no tienes la estatura ~** you're not tall enough - **2.** [presuntuoso] smug, full of o.s. ◇ *m* [nota] pass.

sufragar *vt* to defray.

sufragio *m* suffrage.

sufragista *mf* suffragette.

sufrido, da *adj* - **1.** [resignado] patient, uncomplaining; [durante mucho tiempo] long-suffering - **2.** [resistente - tela] hardwearing; [- color] that does not show the dirt.

sufrimiento *m* suffering.

sufrir ◇ *vt* - **1.** [gen] to suffer; [accidente] to have - **2.** [soportar] to bear, to stand; **tengo que ~ sus manías** I have to put up with his idiosyncrasies - **3.** [experimentar - cambios etc] to undergo. ◇ *vi* [padecer] to suffer; **~ del estómago** *etc* to have a stomach *etc* complaint.

sugerencia *f* suggestion; **hacer una ~** to make a suggestion.

sugerente *adj* evocative.

sugerir *vt* - **1.** [proponer] to suggest; **~ a alguien que haga algo** to suggest that sb should do sthg - **2.** [evocar] to evoke.

sugestión *f* suggestion.

sugestionar *vt* to influence.

sugestivo, va *adj* - **1.** [atrayente] attractive - **2.** [que sugiere] stimulating, suggesting.

suich *m* *Amér* switch.

suiche *m* *Col,Ven* switch.

suicida ◇ *adj* suicidal. ◇ *mf* [por naturaleza] suicidal person; [suicidado] person who has committed suicide.

suicidarse *vpr* to commit suicide.

suicidio *m* suicide.

Suiza Switzerland.

suizo, za *adj* & *m,f* Swiss.

sujeción *f* - **1.** [atadura] fastening - **2.** [sometimiento] subjection.

sujetador *m* bra, brassiere.

sujetar *vt* - **1.** [agarrar] to hold down

- **2.** [aguantar] to fasten; [papeles] to fasten together - **3.** [someter] to subdue; [a niños] to control.

➡ **sujetarse** *vpr* - **1.** [agarrarse]: **~se a** to hold on to, to cling to - **2.** [aguantarse] to keep in place - **3.** [someterse]: **~se a** to keep o stick to.

sujeto, ta *adj* - **1.** [agarrado - objeto] fastened - **2.** [expuesto]: **~ a** subject to.

➡ **sujeto** *m* - **1.** [gen & GRAM] subject - **2.** [individuo] individual.

sulfato *m* sulphate.

sulfurar *vt* [encolerizar] to infuriate.

➡ **sulfurarse** *vpr* [encolerizarse] to get mad.

sultán *m* sultan.

sultana *f* sultana.

suma *f* - **1.** [MAT - acción] addition; [- resultado] total - **2.** [conjunto - de conocimientos, datos] total, sum; [- de dinero] sum - **3.** [resumen]: **en ~** in short.

sumamente *adv* extremely.

sumar *vt* - **1.** MAT to add together; **~ algo a algo** to add sthg to sthg; **tres y cinco suman ocho** three and five are o make eight - **2.** [costar] to come to.

➡ **sumarse** *vpr* - **1.**: **~se (a)** [unirse] to join (in) - **2.** [agregarse] to be in addition to.

sumario, ria *adj* - **1.** [conciso] brief - **2.** DER summary.

➡ **sumario** *m* - **1.** DER indictment - **2.** [resumen] summary.

sumergible *adj* waterproof.

sumergir *vt* [hundir] to submerge; [con fuerza] to plunge; [bañar] to dip.

➡ **sumergirse** *vpr* [hundirse] to submerge; [con fuerza] to plunge.

sumidero *m* drain.

suministrador, ra *m,f* supplier.

suministrar *vt* to supply; **~ algo a alguien** to supply sb with sthg.

suministro *m* [gen] supply; [acto] supplying.

sumir *vt*: **~ a alguien en** to plunge sb into.

➡ **sumirse en** *vpr* - **1.** [depresión, sueño etc] to sink into - **2.** [estudio, tema] to immerse o.s. in.

sumisión *f* - **1.** [obediencia - acción] submission; [- cualidad] submissiveness - **2.** [rendición] surrender.

sumiso, sa *adj* submissive.

sumo, ma *adj* - **1.** [supremo] highest, supreme - **2.** [gran] extreme, great.

sunnita ◇ *adj* Sunni. ◇ *mf* Sunnite, Sunni Moslem.

suntuoso, sa *adj* sumptuous, magnificent.

supeditar *vt*: **~ (a)** to subordinate (to); **estar supeditado a** to be dependent on.

➡ **supeditarse** *vpr*: **~se a** to submit to.

súper ◇ *m fam* supermarket. ◇ *f*: **(gasolina)** ~ ≃ four-star (petrol).

superable *adj* surmountable.

superar *vt* - **1.** [mejorar] to beat; [récord] to break; ~ **algo/a alguien en algo** to beat sthg/sb in sthg - **2.** [ser superior] to exceed, to surpass - **3.** [adelantar - corredor] to overtake, to pass - **4.** [época, técnica]: **estar superado** to have been superseded - **5.** [vencer - dificultad etc] to overcome.
◆ **superarse** *vpr* - **1.** [mejorar] to better o.s. - **2.** [lucirse] to excel o.s.

superávit *m inv* surplus.

superdotado, da *m,f* extremely gifted person.

superficial *adj lit* & *fig* superficial.

superficie *f* - **1.** [gen] surface; **salir a la** ~ to surface - **2.** [área] area.

superfluo, flua *adj* superfluous; [gasto] unnecessary.

superior, ra RELIG *m,f* superior (*f* mother superior).
◆ **superior** ◇ *adj* - **1.** [de arriba] top - **2.** [mayor]: ~ **(a)** higher (than) - **3.** [mejor]: ~ **(a)** superior (to) - **4.** [excelente] excellent - **5.** ANAT & GEOGR upper - **6.** EDUC higher. ◇ *m (gen pl)* [jefe] superior.

superioridad *f lit* & *fig* superiority; ~ **sobre algo/alguien** superiority over sthg/sb.

superlativo, va *adj* - **1.** [belleza etc] exceptional - **2.** GRAM superlative.

supermercado *m* supermarket.

superpoblación *f* overpopulation.

superponer = **sobreponer**.

superpotencia *f* superpower.

superpuesto, ta ◇ *adj* = **sobrepuesto**. ◇ *pp* ▷ **superponer**.

supersónico, ca *adj* supersonic.

superstición *f* superstition.

supersticioso, sa *adj* superstitious.

supervisar *vt* to supervise.

supervisor, ra *m,f* supervisor.

supervivencia *f* survival.

superviviente, sobreviviente ◇ *adj* surviving. ◇ *mf* survivor.

supiera *etc* ▷ **saber**.

suplementario, ria *adj* supplementary, extra.

suplemento *m* - **1.** [gen & PRENS] supplement - **2.** [complemento] attachment.

suplente *mf* - **1.** [gen] stand-in - **2.** TEATR understudy - **3.** DEP substitute.

supletorio, ria *adj* additional, extra.
◆ **supletorio** *m* TELECOM extension.

súplica *f* - **1.** [ruego] plea, entreaty - **2.** DER petition.

suplicar *vt* - **1.** [rogar]: ~ **algo (a alguien)** to plead for sthg (with sb); ~ **a alguien que haga algo** to beg sb to do sthg.

suplicio *m lit* & *fig* torture.

suplir *vt* - **1.** [sustituir]: ~ **algo/a alguien (con)** to replace sthg/sb (with) - **2.** [compensar]: ~ **algo (con)** to compensate for sthg (with).

supo ▷ **saber**.

suponer ◇ *vt* - **1.** [creer, presuponer] to suppose - **2.** [implicar] to involve, to entail - **3.** [significar] to mean - **4.** [conjeturar] to imagine; **lo suponía** I guessed as much; **te suponía mayor** I thought you were older. ◇ *m*: **ser un** ~ to be conjecture.
◆ **suponerse** *vpr* to suppose; **se supone que es el mejor** he's supposed to be the best.

suposición *f* assumption.

supositorio *m* suppository.

supremacía *f* supremacy.

supremo, ma *adj lit* & *fig* supreme.

supresión *f* - **1.** [de ley, impuesto, derecho] abolition; [de sanciones, restricciones] lifting - **2.** [de palabras, texto] deletion - **3.** [de puestos de trabajo, proyectos] axing.

suprimir *vt* - **1.** [ley, impuesto, derecho] to abolish; [sanciones, restricciones] to lift - **2.** [palabras, texto] to delete - **3.** [puestos de trabajo, proyectos] to axe.

supuesto, ta ◇ *pp* ▷ **suponer**. ◇ *adj* supposed; [culpable, asesino] alleged; [nombre] falso; **por** ~ of course.
◆ **supuesto** *m* assumption; **en el** ~ **de que ...** assuming ...; **partimos del** ~ **de que ...** we work on the assumption that ...

supurar *vi* to suppurate, to fester.

sur ◇ *adj* [posición, parte] south, southern; [dirección, viento] southerly. ◇ *m* south.

surcar *vt* [tierra] to plough; [aire, agua] to cut *o* slice through.

surco *m* - **1.** [zanja] furrow - **2.** [señal - de disco] groove; [- de rueda] rut - **3.** [arruga] line, wrinkle.

sureño, ña ◇ *adj* southern; [viento] southerly. ◇ *m,f* southerner.

sureste = **sudeste**.

surf, surfing *m* surfing.

surgir *vi* - **1.** [brotar] to spring forth - **2.** [aparecer] to appear - **3.** *fig* [producirse] to arise.

suroeste = **sudoeste**.

surrealista *adj* & *m,f* surrealist.

surtido, da *adj* [variado] assorted.
◆ **surtido** *m* - **1.** [gama] range - **2.** [caja surtida] assortment.

surtidor *m* [de gasolina] pump; [de un chorro] spout.

surtir *vt* [proveer]: ~ **a alguien (de)** to supply sb (with).
◆ **surtirse de** *vpr* [proveerse de] to stock up on.

susceptible *adj* - **1.** [sensible] sensitive

- 2. [propenso a ofenderse] **touchy - 3.** [posible]: ~ **de** liable to.

suscitar *vt* to provoke; [interés, dudas, sospechas] to arouse.

suscribir *vt* **- 1.** [firmar] to sign **- 2.** [ratificar] to endorse **- 3.** COM [acciones] to subscribe for.

➤ **suscribirse** *vpr* **- 1.** PRENS: ~**se (a)** to subscribe (to) **- 2.** COM : ~**se a** to take out an option on.

suscripción *f* subscription.

suscriptor, ra *m,f* subscriber.

susodicho, cha *adj* above-mentioned.

suspender *vt* **- 1.** [colgar] to hang (up); ~ **algo de algo** to hang sthg from sthg **- 2.** EDUC to fail **- 3.** [interrumpir] to suspend; [sesión] to adjourn **- 4.** [aplazar] to postpone **- 5.** [de un cargo] to suspend.

suspense *m* suspense.

suspensión *f* **- 1.** [gen & AUTOM] suspension **- 2.** [aplazamiento] postponement; [de reunión, sesión] adjournment.

suspenso, sa *adj* **- 1.** [colgado]: ~ **de** hanging from **- 2.** [no aprobado]: **estar ~** to have failed **- 3.** *fig* [interrumpido]: **en ~** pending.

➤ **suspenso** *m* failure.

suspensores *mpl Andes & Arg* braces *UK*, suspenders *US*.

suspicacia *f* suspicion.

suspicaz *adj* suspicious.

suspirar *vi* [dar suspiros] to sigh.

suspiro *m* [aspiración] sigh.

sustancia *f* **- 1.** [gen] substance; **sin ~** lacking in substance **- 2.** [esencia] essence **- 3.** [de alimento] nutritional value.

sustancial *adj* substantial, significant.

sustancioso, sa *adj* substantial.

sustantivo, va *adj* GRAM noun *(antes de sust).*

➤ **sustantivo** *m* GRAM noun.

sustentar *vt* **- 1.** [gen] to support **- 2.** *fig* [mantener - la moral] to keep up; [- argumento, teoría] to defend.

sustento *m* **- 1.** [alimento] sustenance; [mantenimiento] livelihood **- 2.** [apoyo] support.

sustitución *f* [cambio] replacement; **la ~ de Elena por Luis** the substitution of Luis for Elena.

sustituir *vt* : ~ **(por)** to replace (with); **sustituir a Elena por Luis** to replace Elena with Luis, to substitute Luis for Elena.

sustituto, ta *m,f* substitute, replacement.

susto *m* fright.

sustracción *f* **- 1.** [robo] theft **- 2.** MAT subtraction.

sustraer *vt* **- 1.** [robar] to steal **- 2.** MAT to subtract.

➤ **sustraerse** *vpr* : ~**se a** *o* **de** [obligación, problema] to avoid.

susurrar *vt* & *vi* to whisper.

susurro *m* whisper; *fig* murmur.

sutil *adj* [gen] subtle; [velo, tejido] delicate, thin; [brisa] gentle; [hilo, línea] fine.

sutileza *f* subtlety; [de velo, tejido] delicacy, thinness; [de brisa] gentleness; [de hilo, línea] fineness.

sutura *f* suture.

suyo, ya ⬦ *adj poses* [de él] his; [de ella] hers; [de uno] one's (own); [de ellos, ellas] theirs; [de usted, ustedes] yours; **este libro es ~** this book is his/hers *etc*; **un amigo ~** a friend of his/hers *etc*; **no es asunto ~** it's none of his/her *etc* business; **es muy ~** *fam* *fig* he/she is really selfish. ⬦ *pron poses* **- 1.**: **el ~** [de él] his; [de ella] hers; [de cosa, animal] its (own); [de uno] one's own; [de ellos, ellas] theirs; [de usted, ustedes] yours **- 2.** *loc*: **de ~** in itself; **hacer de las suyas** to be up to his/her *etc* usual tricks; **hacer ~** to make one's own; **lo ~ es el teatro** he/she *etc* should be on the stage; **lo ~ sería volver** the proper thing to do would be to go back; **los ~s** *fam* [su familia] his/her *etc* folks; [su bando] his/her *etc* lot.

svástica = **esvástica**.

t¹, T *f* [letra] t, T.

t² *(abrev de* **tonelada***)* t.

tabacalero, ra *adj* tobacco *(antes de sust).*

➤ **Tabacalera** *f state tobacco monopoly in Spain.*

tabaco *m* **- 1.** [planta] tobacco plant **- 2.** [picadura] tobacco **- 3.** [cigarrillos] cigarettes *(pl).*

tábano *m* horsefly.

tabarra *f fam*: **dar la ~** to be a pest.

taberna *f country-style bar, usually cheap.*

tabernero, ra *m,f* [propietario] landlord *(f* landlady); [encargado] bartender *US*, barman *(f* barmaid).

tabique *m* [pared] partition (wall).

tabla *f* - **1.** [plancha] plank; ~ **de planchar** ironing board - **2.** [pliegue] pleat - **3.** [lista, gráfico] table; ~ **periódica** *o* **de los elementos** periodic table - **4.** NÁUT [de surf, vela etc] board - **5.** ARTE panel.

➤ **tablas** *fpl* - **1.** [en ajedrez]: **quedar en** *o* **hacer** ~**s** to end in stalemate - **2.** TEATR stage *(sg)*, boards.

tablado *m* [de teatro] stage; [de baile] dance-floor; [plataforma] platform.

tablao *m* flamenco show.

tablero *m* - **1.** [gen] board - **2.** [en baloncesto] backboard - **3.**: ~ **(de mandos)** [de avión] instrument panel; [de coche] dashboard.

tableta *f* - **1.** MED tablet - **2.** [de chocolate] bar.

tablón *m* plank; [en el techo] beam; ~ **de anuncios** notice board.

tabú *(pl* **tabúes** *o* **tabús)** *adj* & *m* taboo.

tabular *vt* & *vi* to tabulate.

taburete *m* stool.

tacaño, ña *adj* mean, miserly.

tacha *f* - **1.** [defecto] flaw, fault; **sin** ~ faultless - **2.** [clavo] tack.

tachar *vt* - **1.** [lo escrito] to cross out - **2.** *fig* [acusar]: ~ **a alguien de mentiroso** *etc* to accuse sb of being a liar *etc*.

tacho *m* *Andes, RP* waste bin.

tachón *m* - **1.** [tachadura] correction, crossing out - **2.** [clavo] stud.

tachuela *f* tack.

tácito, ta *adj* tacit; [norma, regla] unwritten.

taciturno, na *adj* taciturn.

taco *m* - **1.** [tarugo] plug - **2.** [cuña] wedge - **3.** *fam* *fig* [palabrota] swearword; **soltar un** ~ to swear - **4.** [de billar] cue - **5.** [de hojas, billetes de banco] wad; [de billetes de autobús, metro] book - **6.** [de jamón, queso] hunk - **7.** *Andes, RP* [tacón] heel - **8.** [tortilla de maíz] taco.

tacón *m* heel.

táctico, ca *adj* tactical.

➤ **táctica** *f* *lit* & *fig* tactics *(pl)*.

tacto *m* - **1.** [sentido] sense of touch - **2.** [textura] feel - **3.** *fig* [delicadeza] tact.

tafetán *m* taffeta.

Tailandia Thailand.

taimado, da *adj* crafty.

Taiwán [tai'wan] Taiwan.

tajada *f* - **1.** [rodaja] slice - **2.** *fig* [parte] share; **sacar** ~ **de algo** to get sthg out of sthg.

tajante *adj* [categórico] categorical.

tajo *m* - **1.** [corte] deep cut - **2.** [acantilado] precipice.

Tajo *m*: **el (río)** ~ the (River) Tagus.

tal ◇ *adj* - **1.** [semejante, tan grande] such; **¡jamás se vio cosa** ~**!** you've never seen such a thing!; **lo dijo con** ~ **seguridad que** ... he said it with such conviction that ...; **dijo cosas** ~**es como** ... he said such things as ... - **2.** [sin especificar] such and such; **a** ~ **hora** at such and such a time - **3.** [desconocido]: **un** ~ **Pérez** a (certain) Mr Pérez. ◇ *pron* - **1.** [alguna cosa] such a thing - **2.** *loc*: **que si** ~ **que si cual** this, that and the other; **ser** ~ **para cual** to be two of a kind; ~ **y cual,** ~ **y** ~ this and that; **y** ~ [etcétera] and so on. ◇ *adv*: **¿qué** ~**?** how's it going?, how are you doing?; **¿qué** ~ **fue el viaje?** how was the trip?; **déjalo** ~ **cual** leave it just as it is.

➤ **con tal de** *loc prep* as long as, provided; **con** ~ **de volver pronto** ... as long as we're back early...

➤ **con tal (de) que** *loc conj* as long as, provided.

➤ **tal (y) como** *loc conj* just as *o* like.

➤ **tal que** *loc prep* *fam* [como por ejemplo] like.

taladrador, ra *adj* drilling.

➤ **taladradora** *f* drill.

taladrar *vt* to drill; *fig* [suj: sonido] to pierce.

taladro *m* - **1.** [taladradora] drill - **2.** [agujero] drill hole.

talante *m* - **1.** [humor] mood; **estar de buen** ~ to be in good humour - **2.** [carácter] character, disposition.

talar *vt* to fell.

talco *m* talc, talcum powder.

talego *m* - **1.** [talega] sack - **2.** *mfam* [mil pesetas] 1000 peseta note.

talento *m* - **1.** [don natural] talent; **de** ~ talented - **2.** [inteligencia] intelligence.

talgo *(abrev de* **tren articulado ligero de Goicoechea Oriol)** *m* *Spanish intercity high-speed train.*

talibán ◇ *adj* Taliban. ◇ *m* Taliban.

talismán *m* talisman.

talla *f* - **1.** [medida] size; **¿qué** ~ **usas?** what size are you? - **2.** [estatura] height - **3.** *fig* [capacidad] stature; **dar la** ~ to be up to it - **4.** [ARTE - en madera] carving; [- en piedra] sculpture.

tallado, da *adj* [madera] carved; [piedras preciosas] cut.

tallar *vt* [esculpir - madera, piedra] to carve; [- piedra preciosa] to cut.

tallarín *(gen pl)* *m* noodle.

talle *m* - **1.** [cintura] waist - **2.** [figura, cuerpo] figure.

taller *m* - **1.** [gen] workshop - **2.** AUTOM garage - **3.** ARTE studio.

tallo *m* stem; [brote] sprout, shoot.

talón *m* - **1.** [gen & ANAT] heel; ~ **de Aquiles** *fig* Achilles' heel; **pisarle a alguien los talones** to be hot on sb's heels - **2.** [cheque] cheque; [matriz] stub; ~ **cruzado/devuelto/en blanco** crossed/bounced/blank cheque; ~ **bancario** cashier's cheque *UK*, cashier's check *US*.

talonario *m* [de cheques] cheque book; [de recibos] receipt book.

tamaño, ña *adj* such; **¡cómo pudo decir tamaña estupidez!** how could he say such a stupid thing!
➡ **tamaño** *m* size; **de gran** ~ large; **de** ~ **familiar** family-size; **de** ~ **natural** life-size.

tambalearse *vpr* - **1.** [bambolearse - persona] to stagger, to totter; [- mueble] to wobble, to be unsteady; [- tren] to sway - **2.** *fig* [gobierno, sistema] to totter.

también *adv* also, too; **yo** ~ me too; **Juan está enfermo – Elena** ~ Juan is sick – so is Elena; ~ **a mí me gusta** I like it too, I also like it.

tambo *m RP* dairy farm.

tambor *m* - **1.** MÚS & TECN drum; [de pistola] cylinder - **2.** ANAT eardrum - **3.** AUTOM brake drum.

Támesis *m*: **el (río)** ~ the (River) Thames.

tamiz *m* [cedazo] sieve; **pasar algo por el** ~ to sift sthg.

tamizar *vt* - **1.** [cribar] to sieve - **2.** *fig* [seleccionar] to screen.

tampoco *adv* neither, not ... either; **ella no va y tú** ~ she's not going and neither are you, she's not going and you aren't either; **¿no lo sabías? – yo** ~ didn't you know? – me neither *o* neither did I.

tampón *m* - **1.** [sello] stamp; [almohadilla] inkpad - **2.** [para la menstruación] tampon.

tan *adv* - **1.** [mucho] so; ~ **grande/deprisa** so big/quickly; **¡qué película** ~ **larga!** what a long film!; ~ ... **que** ... so ... that ...; ~ **es así que** ... so much so that ... - **2.** [en comparaciones]: ~ ... **como** ... as ... as ...
➡ **tan sólo** *loc adv* only.

tanda *f* - **1.** [grupo, lote] group, batch - **2.** [serie] series; [de inyecciones] course - **3.** [turno de trabajo] shift.

tándem (*pl* **tándemes**) *m* - **1.** [bicicleta] tandem - **2.** [pareja] duo, pair.

tangente *f* tangent.

tangible *adj* tangible.

tango *m* tango.

tanguero, ra *m,f RP* tango enthusiast.

tanque *m* - **1.** MIL tank - **2.** [vehículo cisterna] tanker - **3.** [depósito] tank.

tantear ◇ *vt* - **1.** [sopesar - peso, precio, cantidad] to try to guess; [- problema, posibilidades, ventajas] to weigh up - **2.** [probar,

sondear] to test (out) - **3.** [toro, contrincante etc] to size up. ◇ *vi* - **1.** [andar a tientas] to feel one's way - **2.** [apuntar los tantos] to (keep) score.

tanteo *m* - **1.** [prueba, sondeo] testing out; [de posibilidades, ventajas] weighing up; [de contrincante, puntos débiles] sizing up - **2.** [puntuación] score.

tanto, ta ◇ *adj* - **1.** [gran cantidad] so much, *(pl)* so many; ~ **dinero** so much money, such a lot of money; **tanta gente** so many people; **tiene** ~ **entusiasmo/~s amigos que** ... she has so much enthusiasm/so many friends that ... - **2.** [cantidad indeterminada] so much, *(pl)* so many; **nos daban** ~**s euros al día** they used to give us so many euros per day; **cuarenta y** ~**s** forty-something, forty-odd; **nos conocimos en el sesenta y** ~**s** we met sometime in the Sixties - **3.** [en comparaciones]: ~ ... **como** as much ... as, *(pl)* as many ... as. ◇ *pron* - **1.** [gran cantidad] so much, *(pl)* so many; **¿cómo puedes tener** ~**s?** how can you have so many? - **2.** [cantidad indeterminada] so much, *(pl)* so many; **a** ~**s de agosto** on such and such a date in August - **3.** [igual cantidad] as much *(pl)*, as many; **había mucha gente aquí, allí no había tanta** there were a lot of people here, but not as many there; **otro** ~ as much again, the same again; **otro** ~ **le ocurrió a los demás** the same thing happened to the rest of them - **4.** *loc*: **ser uno de** ~**s** to be nothing special.
➡ **tanto** ◇ *m* - **1.** [punto] point; [gol] goal; **marcar un** ~ to score - **2.** *fig* [ventaja] point; **apuntarse un** ~ to earn o.s. a point - **3.** [cantidad indeterminada]: **un** ~ so much, a certain amount; ~ **por ciento** percentage - **4.** *loc*: **estar al** ~ **(de)** to be on the ball (about). ◇ *adv* - **1.** [mucho]: ~ **(que** ...) [cantidad] so much (that ...); [tiempo] so long (that ...); **no bebas** ~ don't drink so much; ~ **mejor/peor** so much the better/worse; ~ **más cuanto que** ... all the more so because ... - **2.** [en comparaciones]: ~ **como** as much as; ~ **hombres como mujeres** both men and women; ~ **si estoy como si no** whether I'm there or not - **3.** *loc*: **¡y** ~**!** most certainly!, you bet!
➡ **tantas** *fpl fam*: **eran las tantas** it was very late.
➡ **en tanto (que)** *loc conj* while.
➡ **entre tanto** *loc adv* meanwhile.
➡ **por (lo) tanto** *loc conj* therefore, so.
➡ **tanto (es así) que** *loc conj* so much so that.
➡ **un tanto** *loc adv* [un poco] a bit, rather.

tanzano, na *adj* & *m,f* Tanzanian.

tañido *m* [de campana] ringing.

taoísta *adj* & *m,f* Taoist.

tapa f - **1.** [de caja, baúl, recipiente] lid - **2.** [aperitivo] snack, tapa; **irse de ~s** to go for some tapas - **3.** [de libro] cover - **4.** [de zapato] heel plate - **5.** *Andes & RP* [de botella] top; [de frasco] stopper.

tapadera f - **1.** [tapa] lid - **2.** [para encubrir] front.

tapar vt - **1.** [cerrar - ataúd, cofre] to close (the lid of); [- olla, caja] to put the lid on; [- botella] to put the top on - **2.** [ocultar, cubrir] to cover; [no dejar ver] to block out; [obstruir] to block - **3.** [abrigar - con ropa] to wrap up; [- en la cama] to tuck in - **4.** [encubrir] to cover up.
  ◆ **taparse** vpr - **1.** [cubrirse] to cover (up) - **2.** [abrigarse - con ropa] to wrap up; [- en la cama] to tuck o.s. in.

taparrabos m inv - **1.** [de hombre primitivo] loincloth - **2.** fam [tanga] tanga briefs (pl).

tapete m [paño] runner; [de billar, para cartas] baize.

tapia f (stone) wall.

tapiar vt - **1.** [cercar] to wall in - **2.** [enladrillar] to brick up.

tapicería f - **1.** [tela] upholstery - **2.** [tienda - para muebles] upholsterer's - **3.** [oficio - de muebles] upholstery - **4.** [tapices] tapestries (pl).

tapiz m [para la pared] tapestry; fig [de nieve, flores] carpet.

tapizado m - **1.** [de mueble] upholstery - **2.** [de pared] tapestries (pl).

tapizar vt [mueble] to upholster; fig [campos, calles] to carpet, to cover.

tapón m - **1.** [para tapar - botellas, frascos] stopper; [- de corcho] cork; [- de metal, plástico] cap, top; [- de bañera, lavabo] plug - **2.** [en el oído - de cerumen] wax (U) in the ear; [- de algodón] earplug - **3.** [atasco] traffic jam - **4.** [en baloncesto] block - **5.** *Amér* [fusible] fuse.

taponar vt [cerrar - lavadero] to put the plug in; [- salida] to block; [- tubería] to stop up.

tapujo m: **andarse con ~s** [rodeos] to beat about the bush; **hacer algo sin ~s** to do sthg openly.

taquería f *Méx* [quiosco] taco stall; [restaurante] taco restaurant.

taquigrafía f shorthand, stenography.

taquilla f - **1.** [ventanilla - gen] ticket office, booking office; CIN & TEATR box office; **en ~** at the/ticket/box office - **2.** [recaudación] takings (pl) - **3.** [armario] locker.

taquillero, ra ◇ adj: **es un espectáculo ~** the show is a box-office hit. ◇ m,f ticket clerk.

taquimecanógrafo, fa m,f shorthand typist.

tara f - **1.** [defecto] defect - **2.** [peso] tare.

taracea f inlay.

tarambana adj & m,f fam ne'er-do-well.

tarántula f tarantula.

tararear vt to hum.

tardanza f lateness.

tardar vi - **1.** [llevar tiempo] to take; **esto va a ~ this** will take time; **tardó un año en hacerlo** she took a year to do it; **¿cuánto tardarás (en hacerlo)?** how long will you be (doing it)?, how long will it take you (to do it)? - **2.** [retrasarse] to be late; [ser lento] to be slow; **¡no tardéis!** don't be long!; **~ en hacer algo** to take a long time to do sthg; **no tardaron en hacerlo** they were quick to do it; **a más ~** at the latest.

tarde ◇ f [hasta las cinco] afternoon; [después de las cinco] evening; **por la ~** [hasta las cinco] in the afternoon; [después de las cinco] in the evening; **buenas ~s** [hasta las cinco] good afternoon; [después de las cinco] good evening; **de ~ en ~** from time to time; **muy de ~ en ~** very occasionally. ◇ adv [gen] late; [en exceso] too late; **ya es ~ para eso** it's too late for that now; **~ o temprano** sooner or later.

tardío, a adj [gen] late; [intento, decisión] belated.

tarea f [gen] task; EDUC homework; **~s de la casa** housework (U).

tarifa f - **1.** [precio] charge; COM tariff; [en transportes] fare; **~ plana** flat rate - **2.** (gen pl) [lista] price list.

tarima f - **1.** [estrado] platform - **2.** [suelo] floorboards (pl).

tarjeta f [gen & INFORM] card; **~ de cliente** store card; **~ de crédito/débito** credit/debit card; **~ de embarque** boarding pass; **~ de felicitación** greetings card; **~ postal** postcard; **~ de recarga** top-up card; **~ de sonido/vídeo** sound/video card; **~ telefónica** postcard; **~ de visita** visiting o calling card.

tarot m tarot.

tarrina f tub.

tarro m [recipiente] jar.

tarta f [gen] cake; [plana, con base de pasta dura] tart; [plana, con base de bizcocho] flan.

tartaja ◇ adj fam stammering, stuttering. ◇ mf fam stammerer, stutterer.

tartaleta f tartlet.

tartamudear vi to stammer, to stutter.

tartamudo, da ◇ adj stammering, stuttering. ◇ m,f stammerer, stutterer.

tartana f fam [coche viejo] banger.

tártaro, ra ◇ adj [pueblo] Tartar. ◇ m,f Tartar.

tartera f [fiambrera] lunch box.

tarugo m - **1.** [de madera] block of wood;

[de pan] chunk (of stale bread) - **2.** *fam* [necio] blockhead.

tasa *f* - **1.** [índice] rate; ~ **de mortalidad/natalidad** death/birth rate - **2.** [impuesto] tax; ~**s de aeropuerto** airport tax - **3.** EDUC : ~**s** fees - **4.** [tasación] valuation.

tasación *f* valuation.

tasar *vt* - **1.** [valorar] to value - **2.** [fijar precio] to fix a price for.

tasca *f* ≃ pub.

tatarabuelo, la *m,f* great-great-grandfather (*f* great-great-grandmother).

tatuaje *m* - **1.** [dibujo] tattoo - **2.** [acción] tattooing.

tatuar *vt* to tattoo.

taurino, na *adj* bullfighting (*antes de sust*).

tauro ⬦ *m* [zodiaco] Taurus. ⬦ *mf* [persona] Taurean.

tauromaquia *f* bullfighting.

taxativo, va *adj* precise, exact.

taxi *m* taxi.

taxidermista *mf* taxidermist.

taxímetro *m* taximeter.

taxista *mf* taxi driver.

taza *f* - **1.** [para beber] cup; **una ~ de té** [recipiente] a teacup; [contenido] a cup of tea - **2.** [de retrete] bowl.

tazón *m* bowl.

te *pron pers* - **1.** (*complemento directo*) you; **le gustaría verte** she'd like to see you - **2.** (*complemento indirecto*) (to) you; ~ **lo dio** he gave it to you; ~ **tiene miedo** he's afraid of you - **3.** (*reflexivo*) yourself - **4.** *fam* (*valor impersonal*): **si ~ dejas pisar, estás perdido** if you let people walk all over you, you've had it.

té (*pl* **tés**) *m* tea.

tea *f* [antorcha] torch.

teatral *adj* - **1.** [de teatro - gen] theatre (*antes de sust*); [- grupo] drama (*antes de sust*) - **2.** [exagerado] theatrical.

teatrero, ra *adj fam* theatrical.

teatro *m* - **1.** [gen] theatre; ~ **de la ópera** opera house - **2.** *fig* [fingimiento] playacting.

tebeo® *m* (children's) comic.

techo *m* - **1.** [gen] roof; [dentro de casa] ceiling; ~ **solar** AUTOM sun roof; **bajo ~** under cover - **2.** *fig* [límite] ceiling.
   ◆ **sin techo** *mf*: **los sin ~** the homeless.

techumbre *f* roof.

tecla *f* [gen, INFORM & MÚS] key.

teclado *m* [gen & MÚS] keyboard.

teclear *vt* & *vi* [en ordenador etc] to type; [en piano] to play.

técnico, ca ⬦ *adj* technical. ⬦ *m,f* - **1.** [mecánico] technician - **2.** [experto] expert - **3.** DEP [entrenador] coach, manager UK.
   ◆ **técnica** *f* - **1.** [gen] technique - **2.** [tecnología] technology.

tecnicolor® *m* Technicolor®.

tecnócrata *mf* technocrat.

tecnología *f* technology; ~**s de la información** information technology; ~ **punta** state-of-the-art technology.

tecnológico, ca *adj* technological.

tecolote *m* CAm, Méx [búho] owl; [policía] cop (*on night patrol*).

tedio *m* boredom, tedium.

tedioso, sa *adj* tedious.

Tegucigalpa Tegucigalpa.

teja *f* [de tejado] tile; **color** ~ brick red.

tejado *m* roof.

tejano, na ⬦ *adj* - **1.** [de Texas] Texan - **2.** [tela] denim. ⬦ *m,f* [persona] Texan.
   ◆ **tejanos** *mpl* [pantalones] jeans.

tejemaneje *m fam* - **1.** [maquinación] intrigue - **2.** [ajetreo] to-do, fuss.

tejer ⬦ *vt* - **1.** [gen] to weave; [labor de punto] to knit - **2.** [telaraña] to spin. ⬦ *vi* [hacer ganchillo] to crochet; [hacer punto] to knit.

tejido *m* - **1.** [tela] fabric, material; IND textile - **2.** ANAT tissue.

tejo *m* - **1.** [juego] hopscotch - **2.** BOT yew.

tejón *m* badger.

tel., teléf. (*abrev de* **teléfono**) tel.

tela *f* - **1.** [tejido] fabric, material; [retal] piece of material; ~ **de araña** cobweb; ~ **metálica** wire netting - **2.** ARTE [lienzo] canvas - **3.** *fam* [dinero] dough - **4.** *fam* [cosa complicada]: **tener (mucha)** ~ [ser difícil] to be (very) tricky - **5.** *loc*: **poner en** ~ **de juicio** to call into question.

telar *m* - **1.** [máquina] loom - **2.** (*gen pl*) [fábrica] textiles mill.

telaraña *f* spider's web, cobweb; **la ~ mundial** INFORM the (World Wide) Web.

tele *f fam* telly.

telearrastre *m* ski-tow.

telecomedia *f* television comedy programme.

telecomunicación *f* [medio] telecommunication.
   ◆ **telecomunicaciones** *fpl* [red] telecommunications.

telediario *m* television news (*U*).

teledirigido, da *adj* remote-controlled.

teléf. = **tel.**

telefax *m inv* telefax, fax.

teleférico *m* cable-car.

telefilme, telefilm (*pl* **telefilms**) *m* TV film.

telefonear *vt* & *vi* to phone.

telefónico, ca *adj* telephone (*antes de sust*).

telefonista *mf* telephonist.

teléfono *m* - **1.** [gen] telephone, phone; **coger el** ~ to answer the phone; **hablar por** ~ to be on the phone; **llamar por** ~ to phone;

~ **inalámbrico/móvil** cordless/mobile *UK*
o cell *US* phone; ~ **público** public phone;
~ **WAP** WAP phone **- 2.: (número de)** ~
telephone number.

telegrafía *f* telegraphy.

telegráfico, ca *adj lit* & *fig* telegraphic.

telégrafo *m* [medio, aparato] telegraph.

telegrama *m* telegram.

telele *m*: **le dio un** ~ [desmayo] he had a
fainting fit; [enfado] he had a fit.

telemando *m* remote control.

telemática *f* telematics *(U)*.

telenovela *f* television soap opera.

telepatía *f* telepathy.

telescópico, ca *adj* telescopic.

telescopio *m* telescope.

telesilla *m* chair lift.

telespectador, ra *m,f* viewer.

telesquí *m* ski lift.

teletexto *m* Teletext®.

teletienda *f* home shopping programme.

teletipo *m* **- 1.** [aparato] teleprinter **- 2.** [tex-
to] Teletype®.

teletrabajo *m* teleworking.

televenta *f* **- 1.** [por teléfono] telesales *(pl)*
- 2. [por televisión] *TV advertising in which a
phone number is given for clients to contact.*

televidente *mf* viewer.

televisar *vt* to televise.

televisión *f* **- 1.** [sistema, empresa] television; **salir en** o **por (la)** ~ to be on television; ~ **digital** digital television
- 2. [televisor] television (set).

televisor *m* television (set); ~ **de pantalla
plana** flatscreen television; ~ **panorámico**
o **de pantalla ancha** widescreen television.

télex *m inv* telex.

telón *m* [de escenario - delante] curtain; [-
detrás] backcloth; **el** ~ **de acero** [- HIST] the
Iron Curtain; ~ **de fondo** *fig* backdrop.

telonero, ra *m,f* [cantante] support artist;
[grupo] support band.

tema *m* **- 1.** [asunto] subject **- 2.** MÚS [de composición, película] theme; [canción] song
- 3. EDUC [de asignatura, oposiciones] topic;
[en libro de texto] unit.

temario *m* [de asignatura] curriculum; [de
oposiciones] list of topics.

temático, ca *adj* thematic.
◆ **temática** *f* subject matter.

temblar *vi* **- 1.** [tiritar]: ~ **(de)** [gen] to tremble (with); [de frío] to shiver (with); **tiem-
blo por lo que pueda pasarle** I shudder to
think what could happen to him **- 2.** [vi-
brar - suelo, edificio, vehículo] to shudder, to
shake; [- voz] to tremble, to shake; **dejar algo temblando** *fam fig* [nevera, botella] to
leave sthg almost empty.

temblor *m* shaking *(U)*, trembling *(U)*.

tembloroso, sa *adj* trembling, shaky.

temer ◇ *vt* **- 1.** [tener miedo de] to fear, to
be afraid of **- 2.** [sospechar] to fear. ◇ *vi* to
be afraid; **no temas** don't worry; ~ **por** to
fear for.
◆ **temerse** *vpr*: ~**se que** to be afraid that,
to fear that; **me temo que no vendrá** I'm
afraid she won't come; **me temo que sí/no**
I'm afraid so/not.

temerario, ria *adj* rash; [conducción] reckless.

temeridad *f* **- 1.** [cualidad] recklessness
- 2. [acción] folly *(U)*, reckless act.

temeroso, sa *adj* [receloso] fearful.

temible *adj* fearsome.

temor *m*: ~ **(a** o **de)** fear (of).

temperamental *adj* **- 1.** [cambiante] temperamental **- 2.** [impulsivo] impulsive.

temperamento *m* temperament.

temperatura *f* temperature.

tempestad *f* storm.

tempestuoso, sa *adj lit* & *fig* stormy.

templado, da *adj* **- 1.** [tibio - agua, bebida,
comida] lukewarm **- 2.** GEOGR [clima, zona]
temperate **- 3.** [nervios] steady; [persona, ca-
rácter] calm, composed.

templanza *f* **- 1.** [serenidad] composure
- 2. [moderación] moderation.

templar *vt* **- 1.** [entibiar - lo frío] to warm
(up); [- lo caliente] to cool down **- 2.** [cal-
mar - nervios, ánimos] to calm; [- ira] to restrain **- 3.** TECN [metal etc] to temper **- 4.** MÚS
to tune.
◆ **templarse** *vpr* [lo frío] to warm up; [lo
caliente] to cool down.

temple *m* **- 1.** [serenidad] composure
- 2. TECN tempering **- 3.** ARTE tempera.

templete *m* pavilion.

templo *m lit* & *fig* temple; **como un** ~ *fig*
huge.

temporada *f* **- 1.** [periodo concreto] season;
[de exámenes] period; **de** ~ [fruta, trabajo]
seasonal; ~ **alta/baja** high/low season;
~ **media** mid-season **- 2.** [periodo indefini-
do] (period of) time; **pasé una** ~ **en el extranjero** I spent some time abroad.

temporal ◇ *adj* **- 1.** [provisional] temporary **- 2.** [del tiempo] time *(antes de sust)*
- 3. ANAT & RELIG temporal. ◇ *m* [tormenta]
storm.

temporario, ria *adj Amér* temporary.

temporero, ra *m,f* casual labourer.

temporizador *m* timing device.

temprano, na *adj* early.
◆ **temprano** *adv* early.

ten ▷ tener.
◆ **ten con ten** *m* tact.

tenacidad *f* tenacity.

tenacillas *fpl* [para vello] tweezers; [para rizar el pelo] curling tongs.

tenaz *adj* [perseverante] tenacious.

tenaza *(gen pl)* *f* - **1.** [herramienta] pliers *(pl)* - **2.** [pinzas] tongs *(pl)* - **3.** ZOOL pincer.

tendedero *m* - **1.** [cuerda] clothes line; [armazón] clothes horse - **2.** [lugar] drying place.

tendencia *f* tendency; ~ **a hacer algo** tendency to do sthg.

tendenciosidad *f* tendentiousness.

tendencioso, sa *adj* tendentious.

tender *vt* - **1.** [colgar - ropa] to hang out - **2.** [tumbar] to lay (out) - **3.** [extender] to stretch (out); [mantel] to spread - **4.** [dar - cosa] to hand; [- mano] to hold out, to offer - **5.** [entre dos puntos - cable, vía] to lay; [- puente] to build - **6.** *fig* [preparar - trampa etc] to lay - **7.** *Amér* [cama] to make; [mesa] to set, to lay.

  ➡ tender a *vi* - **1.** [propender]: ~ **a hacer algo** to tend to do something; ~ **a la depresión** to have a tendency to get depressed - **2.** MAT to approach.

  ➡ tenderse *vpr* to stretch out, to lie down.

tenderete *m* [puesto] stall.

tendero, ra *m,f* shopkeeper.

tendido, da *adj* - **1.** [extendido, tumbado] stretched out - **2.** [colgado - ropa] hung out, on the line.

  ➡ tendido *m* - **1.** [instalación - de puente] construction; [- de cable, vía] laying; ~ **eléctrico** electrical installation - **2.** TAUROM front rows *(pl)*.

tendinitis *f inv* tendinitis.

tendón *m* tendon.

tendrá *etc v* ⊳ tener.

tenebroso, sa *adj* dark, gloomy; *fig* shady, sinister.

tenedor¹ *m* [utensilio] fork.

tenedor², ra *m,f* [poseedor] holder; ~ **de libros** COM bookkeeper.

teneduría *f* COM bookkeeping.

tenencia *f* possession; ~ **ilícita de armas** illegal possession of arms.

  ➡ tenencia de alcaldía *f* deputy mayor's office.

tener <> *v aux* - **1.** *(antes de participio)* [haber]: **teníamos pensado ir al teatro** we had thought of going to the theatre; **te lo tengo dicho** I've told you many times - **2.** *(antes de adj)* [hacer estar]: **me tuvo despierto** it kept me awake; **eso la tiene despistada** that has confused her - **3.** [expresa obligación]: ~ **que hacer algo** to have to do sthg; **tiene que ser así** it has to be this way - **4.** [expresa propósito]: **tenemos que ir a cenar un día** we ought to *o* should go for dinner some

time. <> *vt* - **1.** [gen] to have; **tengo un hermano** I have *o* I've got a brother; ~ **fiebre** to have a temperature; **tuvieron una pelea** they had a fight; ~ **un niño** to have a baby; **¡que tengan buen viaje!** have a good journey!; **hoy tengo clase** I have to go to school today - **2.** [medida, edad, sensación, cualidad] to be; **tiene 3 metros de ancho** it's 3 metres wide; **¿cuántos años tienes?** how old are you?; **tiene diez años** she's ten (years old); ~ **hambre/miedo** to be hungry/afraid; ~ **mal humor** to be bad-tempered; **le tiene lástima** he feels sorry for her - **3.** [sujetar] to hold; **¿puedes** ~ **me esto?** could you hold this for me, please?; **tenlo por el asa** hold it by the handle - **4.** [tomar]: **ten el libro que me pediste** here's the book you asked me for; **¡aquí tienes!** here you are! - **5.** [recibir] to get; **tuve un verdadero desengaño** I was really disappointed; **tendrá una sorpresa** he'll get a surprise - **6.** [valorar]: **me tienen por tonto** they think I'm stupid; ~ **a alguien en mucho** to think the world of sb - **7.** [guardar, contener] to keep - **8.** *Amér* [llevar]: **tengo tres años aquí** I've been here for three years - **9.** *loc*: **no las tiene todas consigo** he is not too sure about it; ~ **a bien hacer algo** to be kind enough to do sthg; ~ **que ver con alguien/algo** [estar relacionado] to have something to do with sthg/sb; [ser equiparable] to be in the same league as sthg/sb.

  ➡ tenerse *vpr* - **1.** [sostenerse]: ~**se de pie** to stand upright - **2.** [considerarse]: **se tiene por listo** he thinks he's clever.

tengo ⊳ tener.

tenia *f* tapeworm.

teniente <> *m* lieutenant. <> *adj fam* [sordo] deaf (as a post).

tenis *m inv* tennis; ~ **de mesa** table tennis.

tenista *mf* tennis player.

tenor *m* - **1.** MÚS tenor - **2.** [estilo] tone.

  ➡ a tenor de *loc prep* in view of.

tensar *vt* [cable, cuerda] to tauten; [arco] to draw.

tensión *f* - **1.** [gen] tension; ~ **nerviosa** nervous tension - **2.** TECN [estiramiento] stress - **3.** MED : ~ **(arterial)** blood pressure; **tener la** ~ **alta/baja** to have high/low blood pressure; **tomar la** ~ **a alguien** to take sb's blood pressure - **4.** ELECTR voltage; **alta** ~ high voltage.

tenso, sa *adj* taut; *fig* tense.

tentación *f* temptation; **caer en la** ~ to give in to temptation; **tener la** ~ **de** to be tempted to; **estos bombones son una** ~ these chocolates are really tempting.

tentáculo *m* tentacle.

tentador, ra *adj* tempting.

tentar *vt* - **1.** [palpar] to feel - **2.** [atraer, incitar] to tempt.

tentativa *f* attempt; ~ **de asesinato** attempted murder; ~ **de suicidio** suicide attempt.

tentempié (*pl* **tentempiés**) *m* snack.

tenue *adj* - **1.** [tela, hilo, lluvia] fine - **2.** [luz, sonido, dolor] faint - **3.** [relación] tenuous.

teñir *vt* - **1.** [ropa, pelo]: ~ **algo (de rojo** *etc*) to dye sth (red *etc*) - **2.** *fig* [matizar]: ~ **algo (de)** to tinge sth (with).

● **teñirse** *vpr*: ~**se (el pelo)** to dye one's hair.

teología *f* theology; ~ **de la liberación** liberation theology.

teólogo, ga *m,f* theologian.

teorema *m* theorem.

teoría *f* theory; **en** ~ in theory.

teórico, ca ◇ *adj* theoretical; **clase teórica** theory class. ◇ *m,f* [persona] theorist.

teorizar *vi* to theorize.

tepache *m Méx* *mildly alcoholic drink made from fermented pineapple peelings and unrefined sugar.*

tequila *m,f* tequila.

terapéutico, ca *adj* therapeutic.

terapia *f* therapy; ~ **ocupacional/de grupo** occupational/group therapy.

tercer ⇒ **tercero**.

tercera ⇒ **tercero**.

tercermundismo *m* underdevelopment.

tercermundista *adj* third-world *(antes de sust)*.

tercero, ra *núm (antes de sust masculino sg:* **tercer***)* third.

● **tercero** *m* - **1.** [piso] third floor - **2.** [curso] third year - **3.** [mediador, parte interesada] third party.

● **tercera** *f* AUTOM third (gear).

terceto *m* MÚS trio.

terciar ◇ *vt* [poner en diagonal - gen] to place diagonally; [- sombrero] to tilt. ◇ *vi* - **1.** [mediar]: ~ **(en)** to mediate (in) - **2.** [participar] to intervene, to take part.

● **terciarse** *vpr* to arise; **si se tercia** if the opportunity arises.

tercio *m* - **1.** [tercera parte] third - **2.** TAUROM stage *(of bullfight)*.

terciopelo *m* velvet.

terco, ca *adj* stubborn.

tereré *m Arg, Par* *refreshing maté drink made with lemon juice.*

tergal® *m* Tergal®.

tergiversar *vt* to distort, to twist.

termal *adj* thermal.

termas *fpl* [baños] hot baths, spa *(sg)*.

térmico, ca *adj* thermal.

terminación *f* - **1.** [finalización] completion - **2.** [parte final] end - **3.** GRAM ending.

terminal ◇ *adj* [gen] final; [enfermo] terminal. ◇ *m* ELECTR & INFORM terminal. ◇ *f* [de aeropuerto] terminal; [de autobuses] terminus.

terminante *adj* categorical; [prueba] conclusive.

terminar ◇ *vt* to finish. ◇ *vi* - **1.** [acabar] to end; [tren] to stop, to terminate; ~ **en** [objeto] to end in - **2.** [ir a parar]: ~ **(de/en)** to end up (as/in); ~ **por hacer algo** to end up doing sthg.

● **terminarse** *vpr* - **1.** [finalizar] to finish - **2.** [agotarse] to run out; **se nos ha terminado la sal** we have run out of salt.

término *m* - **1.** [fin, extremo] end; **poner** ~ **a algo** to put a stop to sthg - **2.** [territorio]: ~ **(municipal)** district - **3.** [plazo] period; **en el** ~ **de un mes** within (the space of) a month - **4.** [lugar, posición] place; **en primer** ~ ARTE & FOT in the foreground; **en último** ~ ARTE & FOT in the background; *fig* [si es necesario] as last resort; [en resumidas cuentas] in the final analysis - **5.** [situación, punto] point; ~ **medio** [media] average; [compromiso] compromise, happy medium; **por** ~ **medio** on average - **6.** LING & MAT term; **a mí no me hables en esos** ~**s** don't talk to me like that; **los** ~**s del contrato** the terms of the contract; **en** ~**s generales** generally speaking.

terminología *f* terminology.

termo *m* Thermos® (flask).

termómetro *m* thermometer; **poner el** ~ **a alguien** to take sb's temperature.

termostato *m* thermostat.

terna *f* POLÍT shortlist of three candidates.

ternasco *f* suckling lamb.

ternero, ra *m,f* [animal] calf.

● **ternera** *f* [carne] veal.

ternilla *f* - **1.** CULIN gristle - **2.** ANAT cartilage.

ternura *f* tenderness.

terquedad *f* stubbornness.

terracota *f* terracotta.

terral, tierral *m Amér* dust cloud.

terraplén *m* embankment.

terráqueo, a *adj* Earth *(antes de sust)*, terrestrial.

terrateniente *mf* landowner.

terraza *f* - **1.** [balcón] balcony - **2.** [de café] terrace, patio - **3.** [azotea] terrace roof - **4.** [bancal] terrace.

terremoto *m* earthquake.

terrenal *adj* earthly.

terreno, na *adj* earthly.

● **terreno** *m* - **1.** [suelo - gen] land; [- GEOL] terrain; [- AGR] soil - **2.** [solar] plot (of land) - **3.** DEP: ~ **(de juego)** field, pitch - **4.** *fig* [ámbito] field.

terrestre *adj* - **1.** [del planeta] terrestrial

- 2. [de la tierra] land *(antes de sust)*.

terrible *adj* **-1.** [enorme, insoportable] terrible **- 2.** [aterrador] terrifying.

terrícola *mf* earthling.

territorial *adj* territorial.

territorio *m* territory; **por todo el ~ nacional** across the country, nationwide.

terrón *m* **-1.** [de tierra] clod of earth **- 2.** [de harina etc] lump.

terror *m* [miedo, persona terrible] terror; CIN horror; **película de ~** horror movie; **dar ~** to terrify.

terrorífico, ca *adj* **-1.** [enorme, insoportable] terrible **- 2.** [aterrador] terrifying.

terrorismo *m* terrorism.

terrorista *adj* & *m,f* terrorist.

terroso, sa *adj* **-1.** [parecido a la tierra] earthy **- 2.** [con tierra] muddy.

terso, sa *adj* **-1.** [piel, superficie] smooth **- 2.** [aguas, mar] clear **-3.** [estilo, lenguaje] polished.

tersura *f* **-1.** [de piel, superficie] smoothness **- 2.** [de aguas, mar] clarity.

tertulia *f regular meeting of people for informal discussion of a particular issue of common interest;* **~ literaria** literary circle.

tesela *f* tessera.

tesina *f* (undergraduate) dissertation.

tesis *f inv* [gen & UNIV] thesis.

tesitura *f* [circunstancia] circumstances *(pl)*.

tesón *m* **-1.** [tenacidad] tenacity, perseverance **- 2.** [firmeza] firmness.

tesorero, ra *m,f* treasurer.

tesoro *m* **-1.** [botín] treasure **- 2.** [hacienda pública] treasury, exchequer.

◆ **Tesoro** *m* ECON: **el Tesoro (Público)** the Treasury.

test *(pl* tests*) m* test.

testamentario, ria ◇ *adj* testamentary. ◇ *m,f* executor.

testamento *m* will; *fig* [artístico, intelectual] legacy; **hacer ~** to write one's will.

◆ **Antiguo Testamento** *m* Old Testament.

◆ **Nuevo Testamento** *m* New Testament.

testar ◇ *vi* [hacer testamento] to make a will. ◇ *vt* [probar] to test.

testarudo, da *adj* stubborn.

testear *vt CSur* to test.

testículo *m* testicle.

testificar ◇ *vt* to testify; *fig* to testify to. ◇ *vi* to testify, to give evidence.

testigo ◇ *mf* [persona] witness; **~ de cargo/descargo** witness for the prosecution/ defence; **~ ocular** *o* **presencial** eyewitness. ◇ *m* DEP baton.

◆ **testigo de Jehová** *mf* Jehovah's Witness.

testimonial *adj* [documento, prueba etc] testimonial.

testimoniar *vt* to testify; *fig* to testify to.

testimonio *m* **-1.** [relato] account; DER testimony; **prestar ~** to give evidence **- 2.** [prueba] proof; **como ~ de** as proof of; **dar ~ de** to prove.

teta *f* **-1.** *fam* [de mujer] tit **- 2.** [de animal] teat.

tétanos *m inv* tetanus.

tetera *f* teapot.

tetero *m Col,Ven* baby's bottle.

tetilla *f* **-1.** [de hombre, animal] nipple **- 2.** [de biberón] teat.

tetina *f* teat.

tetona *adj fam* busty.

tetrapléjico, ca *adj* & *m,f* quadriplegic.

tétrico, ca *adj* gloomy.

tetuda *adj fam* busty.

textil *adj* & *m* textile.

texto *m* **-1.** [gen] text; **el Sagrado Texto** the Holy Scripture, the Bible **- 2.** [pasaje] passage.

textual *adj* **-1.** [del texto] textual **- 2.** [exacto] exact.

textura *f* texture.

tez *f* complexion.

ti *pron pers (después de prep)* **-1.** [gen] you; **siempre pienso en ~** I'm always thinking about you; **me acordaré de ~** I'll remember you **- 2.** [reflexivo] yourself; **sólo piensas en ~ (mismo)** you only think about yourself.

tía ⊳ **tío**.

tianguis *m inv CAm* & *Méx* open-air market.

Tíbet *m:* **el ~** Tibet.

tibia *f* shinbone, tibia.

tibieza *f* [calidez] warmth; [falta de calor] lukewarmness.

tibio, bia *adj* **-1.** [cálido] warm; [falto de calor] tepid, lukewarm **- 2.** *fig* [frío] lukewarm.

tiburón *m* [gen] shark.

tic *m* tic.

ticket = **tíquet**.

tictac *m* tick tock.

tiempo *m* **-1.** [gen] time; **al poco ~** soon afterwards; **a ~ (de hacer algo)** in time (to do sthg); **al mismo ~, a un ~** at the same time; **con el ~** in time; **no me dio ~ a terminarlo** I didn't have (enough) time to finish it; **del ~** [fruta] of the season; [bebida] at room temperature; **estar a** *o* **tener ~ de** to have time to; **fuera de ~** at the wrong moment; **ganar ~** to save time; **perder el ~** to waste time; **~ libre** *o* **de ocio** spare time; **a ~ parcial** part-time; **en ~s de Maricastaña** donkey's years ago; **matar el ~** to kill time **- 2.** [periodo largo] long time; **con ~** in good time; **hace ~ que** it is a long time since; **ha-**

ce ~ **que no vive aquí** he hasn't lived here for some time; **tomarse uno su ~** to take one's time - **3.** [edad] age; **¿qué ~ tiene?** how old is he? - **4.** [movimiento] movement; **motor de cuatro ~s** four-stroke engine - **5.** METEOR weather; **hizo buen/mal ~** the weather was good/bad; **si el ~ lo permite** o **no lo impide** weather permitting; **hace un ~ de perros** it's a foul day - **6.** DEP half - **7.** GRAM tense - **8.** [MÚS - compás] time; [- ritmo] tempo.

tienda f - **1.** [establecimiento] shop; **ir de ~s** to go shopping - **2.** [para acampar]: **~ (de campaña)** tent.

tiene ▷ tener.

tienta ➡ **a tientas** loc adv blindly; **andar a ~s** to grope along.

tierno, na adj - **1.** [blando, cariñoso] tender - **2.** [del día] fresh.

tierra f - **1.** [gen] land; **~ adentro** inland; **~ firme** terra firma, dry land - **2.** [materia inorgánica] earth, soil; **un camino de ~ a** dirt track; **pista de ~ batida** clay court - **3.** [suelo] ground; **caer a ~** to fall to the ground; **quedarse en ~** [pasajero] to miss the plane/boat/train; **tomar ~** to touch down - **4.** [patria] homeland, native land; **de la ~** [vino, queso] local - **5.** ELECTR earth UK, ground US; **conectado a ~** earthed UK, grounded US

➡ **Tierra** f: **la Tierra** the Earth.

tierral = terral.

tieso, sa adj - **1.** [rígido] stiff - **2.** [erguido] erect - **3.** fam [muerto] stone dead - **4.** fam [sin dinero] broke - **5.** fig [engreído] haughty.

tiesto m flowerpot.

tifoideo, a adj typhoid (antes de sust).

tifón m typhoon.

tifus m inv typhus.

tigre m tiger.

tigresa f tigress.

tijera (gen pl) f scissors (pl); [de jardinero, esquilador] shears (pl); **unas ~s** a pair of scissors/shears; **meter la ~** lit & fig to cut.

tijereta f [insecto] earwig.

tila f [infusión] lime blossom tea.

tildar vt: **~ a alguien de algo** to brand o call sb sthg.

tilde f - **1.** [signo ortográfico] tilde - **2.** [acento gráfico] accent.

tiliches mpl CAm & Méx bits and pieces.

tilín m tinkle, tinkling (U); **me hace ~** fam I fancy him.

tilma f Méx woollen blanket.

tilo m [árbol] linden o lime tree.

timar vt [estafar]: **~ a alguien** to swindle sb; **~ algo a alguien** to swindle sb out of sthg.

timbal m [MÚS - de orquesta] kettledrum, timbal.

timbre m - **1.** [aparato] bell; **tocar el ~** to ring the bell - **2.** [de voz, sonido] tone; TECN timbre - **3.** [sello - de documentos] stamp; [- de impuestos] seal.

timidez f shyness.

tímido, da adj shy.

timo m [estafa] swindle.

timón m - **1.** AERON & NÁUT rudder - **2.** fig [gobierno] helm; **llevar el ~ de** to be at the helm of - **3.** Andes, Cuba [volante] steering wheel.

timonel, timonero m NÁUT helmsman.

timorato, ta adj [mojigato] prudish.

tímpano m ANAT eardrum.

tina f - **1.** [tinaja] pitcher - **2.** [gran cuba] vat - **3.** CAm, Col, Méx [bañera] bathtub.

tinaja f (large) pitcher.

tinerfeño, ña adj native of/from Tenerife.

tinglado m - **1.** [cobertizo] shed - **2.** [armazón] platform - **3.** fig [lío] fuss - **4.** fig [maquinación] plot.

tinieblas fpl darkness (U); fig confusion (U), uncertainty (U).

tino m - **1.** [puntería] good aim - **2.** fig [habilidad] skill - **3.** fig [juicio] sense, good judgment.

tinta f ink; **~ china** Indian ink; **cargar** o **recargar las ~s** to exaggerate; **saberlo de buena ~** to have it on good authority; **sudar ~** to sweat blood.

➡ **medias tintas** fpl: **andarse con medias ~s** to be wishy-washy.

tinte m - **1.** [sustancia] dye - **2.** [operación] dyeing - **3.** [tintorería] dry cleaner's - **4.** fig [tono] shade, tinge.

tintero m [frasco] ink pot; [en la mesa] inkwell.

tintinear vi to jingle, to tinkle.

tinto, ta adj - **1.** [manchado] stained; **~ en sangre** bloodstained - **2.** [vino] red.

➡ **tinto** m - **1.** [vino] red wine - **2.** Col, Ven [café] black coffee.

tintorera f ZOOL blue shark.

tintorería f dry cleaner's.

tiña f MED ringworm.

tío, a m, f - **1.** [familiar] uncle (f aunt) - **2.** fam [individuo] guy (f bird) - **3.** fam [como apelativo] mate (f darling).

tiovivo m merry-go-round UK, carousel US.

tipear ◇ vt Amér to type. ◇ vi to type.

típico, ca adj typical; [traje, restaurante etc] traditional; **~ de** typical of.

tipificar vt - **1.** [gen & DER] to classify - **2.** [simbolizar] to typify.

tiple mf [cantante] soprano.

tipo, pa *m, f fam* guy (*f* woman).

◆ **tipo** *m* - **1.** [clase] type, sort; **todo ~ de** all sorts of - **2.** [cuerpo - de mujer] figure; [- de hombre] build - **3.** ECON rate; **~ de interés/cambio** interest/exchange rate - **4.** IMPRENTA & ZOOL type.

tipografía *f* [procedimiento] printing.

tipográfico, ca *adj* typographical, printing *(antes de sust)*.

tipógrafo, fa *m, f* printer.

tiquet (*pl* tíquets), **ticket** ['tiket] (*pl* tickets) *m* ticket.

tiquismiquis ◇ *adj inv fam* [maniático] pernickety. ◇ *m y f inv fam* [maniático] fusspot. ◇ *mpl* - **1.** [riñas] squabbles - **2.** [bagatelas] trifles.

TIR *(abrev de* **transport international routier)** *m International Road Transport,* ≃ HGV *UK.*

tira *f* - **1.** [banda cortada] strip - **2.** [de viñetas] comic strip - **3.** *loc:* **la ~ de** *fam* loads *(pl)* of; **la ~** *Méx fam* [la policía] the cops, the fuzz *UK.*

◆ **tira y afloja** *m* give and take.

tirabuzón *m* [rizo] curl.

tirachinas *m inv* catapult.

tiradero *m Amér* rubbish dump.

tirado, da *adj* - **1.** *fam* [barato] dirt cheap - **2.** *fam* [fácil] simple, dead easy; **estar ~** to be a cinch - **3.** *loc:* **dejar ~ a alguien** *fam* to leave sb in the lurch.

◆ **tirada** *f* - **1.** [lanzamiento] throw - **2.** [IMPRENTA - número de ejemplares] print run; [- reimpresión] reprint; [- número de lectores] circulation - **3.** [sucesión] series - **4.** [distancia]: **de 0 en una tirada** in one go.

tirador *m, f* [con arma] marksman.

◆ **tirador** *m* [mango] handle.

◆ **tiradores** *mpl Bol & RP* [tirantes] braces *UK,* suspenders *US.*

tirafondo *m* long screw.

tiraje *m Amér* print run.

tiralíneas *m inv* ruling pen.

tiramisú *m* tiramisu.

tiranía *f* tyranny.

tirano, na ◇ *adj* tyrannical. ◇ *m, f* tyrant.

tirante ◇ *adj* - **1.** [estirado] taut - **2.** *fig* [violento, tenso] tense. ◇ *m* - **1.** [de tela] strap - **2.** ARQUIT brace.

◆ **tirantes** *mpl* [para pantalones] braces *UK,* suspenders *US.*

tirantez *f fig* tension.

tirar ◇ *vt* - **1.** [lanzar] to throw; **~ algo a alguien/algo** [para hacer daño] to throw sthg at sb/sthg; **tírame una manzana** throw me an apple; **tírale un beso** blow him a kiss - **2.** [dejar caer] to drop; [derramar] to spill; [volcar] to knock over - **3.** [desechar, malgastar] to throw away - **4.** [disparar] to fire;

[bomba] to drop; [petardo, cohete] to let off; [foto] to take - **5.** [derribar] to knock down - **6.** [jugar - carta] to play; [- dado] to throw - **7.** [DEP - falta, penalti etc] to take; [- balón] to pass - **8.** [imprimir] to print - **9.** *fam* [suspender] to fail. ◇ *vi* - **1.** [estirar, arrastrar]: **~ (de algo)** to pull (sthg); **tira y afloja** give and take - **2.** [suj: prenda, pernera, manga] to be too tight - **3.** [disparar] to shoot - **4.** *fam* [atraer] to have a pull; **me tira la vida del campo** I feel drawn towards life in the country - **5.** [cigarrillo, chimenea etc] to draw - **6.** [dirigirse] to go, to head - **7.** *fam* [apañárselas] to get by; **ir tirando** to get by; **voy tirando** I'm O.K., I've been worse - **8.** [parecerse]: **tira a gris** it's greyish; **tira a su abuela** she takes after her grandmother; **tirando a** approaching, not far from - **9.** [tender]: **~ para algo** [persona] to have the makings of sthg; **este programa tira a (ser) hortera** this programme is a bit on the tacky side; **el tiempo tira a mejorar** the weather looks as if it's getting better - **10.** [DEP - con el pie] to kick; [- con la mano] to throw; [- a meta, canasta etc] to shoot.

◆ **tirarse** *vpr* - **1.** [lanzarse]: **~se (a)** [al agua] to dive (into); [al vacío] to jump (into); **~se sobre alguien** to jump on top of sb - **2.** [tumbarse] to stretch out - **3.** [pasar tiempo] to spend.

tirita® *f* (sticking) plaster *UK,* ≃ Bandaid® *US.*

tirilla® *f* ≃ neckband.

tiritar *vi*: **~ (de)** to shiver (with).

tiro *m* - **1.** [gen] shot; **pegar un ~ a alguien** to shoot sb; **pegarse un ~** to shoot o.s.; **ni a ~s** never in a million years - **2.** [acción] shooting; **~ al blanco** [deporte] target shooting; [lugar] shooting range; **~ con arco** archery - **3.** [huella, marca] bullet mark; [herida] gunshot wound - **4.** [alcance] range; **a ~ de** within the range of; **a ~ de piedra** a stone's throw away - **5.** [de chimenea, horno] draw - **6.** [de caballos] team - **7.** *fam* [de cocaína] line.

tiroides *m o f inv* thyroid (gland).

tirón *m* - **1.** [estirón] pull - **2.** [robo] bagsnatching - **3.** MED: **~ (muscular)** strained muscle - **4.** *fam* [popularidad] pull.

◆ **de un tirón** *loc adv* in one go.

tironero, ra *m, f* bagsnatcher.

tirotear ◇ *vt* to fire at. ◇ *vi* to shoot.

tiroteo *m* [tiros] shooting; [intercambio de disparos] shootout.

tisana *f* herbal tea.

tisis *f inv* MED (pulmonary) tuberculosis.

titánico, ca *adj* titanic.

títere *m lit & fig* puppet; **no dejar ~ con cabeza** [destrozar] to destroy everything in sight; [criticar] to spare nobody.

◆ **títeres** *mpl* [guiñol] puppet show *(sg)*.

titilar *vi* [estrella, luz] to flicker.

titiritero, ra *m,f* **- 1.** [de títeres] puppeteer **- 2.** [acróbata] acrobat.

tito, ta *m,f fam* uncle (*f* auntie).

titubeante *adj* **- 1.** [actitud] hesitant; [voz] stuttering **- 2.** [al andar] tottering.

titubear *vi* [dudar] to hesitate; [al hablar] to stutter.

titubeo *(gen pl) m* **- 1.** [duda] hesitation; [al hablar] stutter, stuttering *(U)* **- 2.** [al andar] tottering.

titulado, da *m,f* [diplomado] holder of a qualification; [licenciado] graduate.

titular ⬦ *adj* [profesor, médico] official. ⬦ *mf* [poseedor] holder. ⬦ *m (gen pl)* PRENS headline. ⬦ *vt* [llamar] to title, to call.

◆ **titularse** *vpr* **- 1.** [llamarse] to be titled *o* called **- 2.** [licenciarse] ~se (en) to graduate (in) **- 3.** [diplomarse] ~se (en) to obtain a qualification (in).

título *m* **- 1.** [gen] title; ~ de propiedad title deed; ~s de crédito CIN credits **- 2.** [licenciatura] degree; [diploma] diploma; tiene muchos ~s she has a lot of qualifications **- 3.** *fig* [derecho] right; a ~ de as.

tiza *f* chalk; una ~ a piece of chalk.

tiznar *vt* to blacken.

tizne *m o f* soot.

tizón *m* burning stick *o* log.

tlapalería *f Méx* ironmonger's (shop).

toalla *f* [para secarse] towel; ~ de ducha/manos bath/hand towel; arrojar *o* tirar la ~ to throw in the towel.

toallero *m* towel rail.

tobillo *m* ankle.

tobogán *m* [rampa] slide; [en parque de atracciones] helter-skelter; [en piscina] chute, flume.

toca *f* wimple.

tocadiscos *m inv* record player.

tocado, da *adj fam* [chiflado] soft in the head.

◆ **tocado** *m* [prenda] headgear *(U)*.

tocador *m* **- 1.** [mueble] dressing table **- 2.** [habitación - en lugar público] powder room; [- en casa] boudoir.

tocar ⬦ *vt* **- 1.** [gen] to touch; [palpar] to feel **- 2.** [instrumento, canción] to play; [bombo] to bang; [sirena, alarma] to sound; [campana, timbre] to ring; el reloj tocó las doce the clock struck twelve **- 3.** [abordar - tema etc] to touch on **- 4.** *fig* [conmover] to touch **- 5.** *fig* [concernir]: por lo que a mí me toca/a eso le toca as far as I'm/that's concerned. ⬦ *vi* **- 1.** [entrar en contacto] to touch **- 2.** [estar próximo]: ~ (con) [gen] to be touching; [país, jardín] to border (on)

- 3. [llamar - a la puerta, ventana] to knock **- 4.** [corresponder en reparto]: ~ a alguien to be due to sb; tocamos a mil cada uno we're due a thousand each; le tocó la mitad he got half of it; te toca a ti hacerlo [turno] it's your turn to do it; [responsabilidad] it's up to you to do it **- 5.** [caer en suerte]: me ha tocado la lotería I've won the lottery; le ha tocado sufrir mucho he has had to suffer a lot **- 6.** [llegar el momento]: nos toca pagar ahora it's time (for us) to pay now.

◆ **tocarse** *vpr* to touch.

tocayo, ya *m,f* namesake.

tocinería *f* pork butcher's (shop).

tocino *m* [para cocinar] lard; [para comer] fat *(of bacon)*.

◆ **tocino de cielo** *m* CULIN *dessert made of syrup and eggs*.

todavía *adv* **- 1.** [aún] still; [con negativo] yet, still; ~ no lo he recibido I still haven't got it, I haven't got it yet; ~ ayer as late as yesterday; ~ no not yet **- 2.** [sin embargo] still **- 3.** [incluso] even; ~ mejor even better.

todo, da ⬦ *adj* **- 1.** [gen] all; ~ el mundo everybody; ~ el libro the whole book, all (of) the book; ~ el día all day **- 2.** [cada, cualquier]: ~s los días/lunes every day/Monday; ~ español every Spaniard, all Spaniards **- 3.** [para enfatizar]: es ~ un hombre he's every bit a man; ya es toda una mujer she's a big girl now; fue ~ un éxito it was a great success. ⬦ *pron* **- 1.** [todas las cosas] everything, *(pl)* all of them; lo vendió ~ he sold everything, he sold it all; ~s están rotos they're all broken, all of them are broken; ante ~ [principalmente] above all; [en primer lugar] first of all; con ~ despite everything; sobre ~ above all; está en ~ he/she always makes sure everything is just so; ~ lo más at (the) most **- 2.** [todas las personas]: ~s everybody; todas vinieron everybody *o* they all came.

◆ **todo** ⬦ *m* whole. ⬦ *adv* completely, all.

◆ **del todo** *loc adv*: no estoy del ~ contento I'm not entirely happy; no lo hace mal del ~ she doesn't do it at all badly.

todopoderoso, sa *adj* almighty.

todoterreno *m* all-terrain vehicle.

tofe *m* coffee-flavoured toffee.

toga *f* **- 1.** [manto] toga **- 2.** [traje] gown.

toldo *m* [de tienda] awning; [de playa] sunshade.

tolerancia *f* tolerance.

tolerante *adj* tolerant.

tolerar *vt* **- 1.** [consentir, aceptar] to tolerate; ~ que alguien haga algo to tolerate sb doing sthg **- 2.** [aguantar] to stand.

toma *f* **- 1.** [de biberón, papilla] feed; [de medicamento] dose **- 2.** [de sangre] sample

- 3. [de ciudad etc] **capture - 4.** [de agua, aire] inlet; ~ **de corriente** ELECTR socket **- 5.** CIN [de escena] **take.**

◆ **toma de posesión** f **-1.** [de gobierno, presidente] **investiture - 2.** [de cargo] **undertaking.**

tomar ◇ vt **-1.** [gen] to take; [actitud, costumbre] to adopt **- 2.** [datos, información] to take down **- 3.** [medicina, drogas] to take; [comida, bebida] to have; **¿qué quieres ~?** what would you like (to drink/eat)? **- 4.** [autobús, tren etc] to catch; [taxi] to take **- 5.** [considerar, confundir]: **~ a alguien por algo/alguien** to take sb for sthg/sb **- 6.** loc: **~ la con alguien** fam to have it in for sb; **¡toma!** [al dar algo] here you are!; [expresando sorpresa] well I never! ◇ vi **-1.** [encaminarse] to go, to head **- 2.** Amér [beber alcohol] to drink.

◆ **tomarse** vpr **-1.** [comida, bebida] to have; [medicina, drogas] to take **- 2.** [interpretar] to take; **~se algo mal/bien** to take sthg badly/well.

tomate m [fruto] tomato.

tómbola f tombola.

tomillo m thyme.

tomo m [volumen] volume.

ton ◆ **sin ton ni son** loc adv for no apparent reason.

tonada f tune.

tonadilla f ditty.

tonalidad f [de color] tone.

tonel m [recipiente] barrel.

tonelada f tonne.

tonelaje m tonnage.

tónico, ca adj **-1.** [reconstituyente] revitalizing **- 2.** GRAM & MÚS tonic.

◆ **tónico** m [reconstituyente] tonic.

◆ **tónica** f **-1.** [bebida] tonic water **- 2.** [tendencia] trend **- 3.** MÚS tonic.

tonificar vt to invigorate.

tono m **-1.** [gen] tone; **fuera de ~** out of place **- 2.** [MÚS - tonalidad] key; [- altura] pitch **- 3.** [de color] shade; **~ de piel** complexion.

tonsura f tonsure.

tontear vi [hacer el tonto] to fool about.

tontería f **-1.** [estupidez] stupid thing; **decir una ~** to talk nonsense; **hacer una ~** to do sthg foolish **- 2.** [cosa sin importancia o valor] trifle.

tonto, ta ◇ adj stupid. ◇ m,f idiot; **hacer el ~** to play the fool; **hacerse el ~** to act innocent.

◆ **a tontas y a locas** loc adv haphazardly.

toña f **-1.** fam [patada] kick **- 2.** fam [borrachera]: **agarrarse una ~** to get plastered.

top (pl tops) m [prenda] short top.

topacio m topaz.

topadora f RP bulldozer.

topar vi [encontrarse]: **~ con alguien** to bump into sb; **~ con algo** to come across sthg.

tope ◇ adj inv [máximo] top, maximum; [fecha] last. ◇ m **-1.** [pieza] block; [para puerta] doorstop **- 2.** FERROC buffer **- 3.** [límite máximo] limit; [de plazo] deadline **- 4.** [freno]: **poner ~ a** to rein in, to curtail **- 5.** loc: **estar hasta los ~s** to be bursting at the seams.

◆ **a tope** ◇ loc adv [de velocidad, intensidad] flat out. ◇ loc adj fam [lleno - lugar] packed.

topetazo m bump.

tópico, ca adj **-1.** [manido] clichéd **- 2.** MED topical.

◆ **tópico** m cliché.

topo m **-1.** ZOOL & fig mole **- 2.** [lunar] polka dot.

topógrafo, fa m,f topographer.

topónimo m place name.

toque m **-1.** [gen] touch; **dar los últimos ~s a algo** to put the finishing touches to sthg **- 2.** [aviso] warning; **dar un ~ a alguien** [llamar] to call sb; [amonestar] to prod sb, to warn sb **- 3.** [sonido - de campana] chime, chiming (U); [- de tambor] beat, beating (U); [- de sirena etc] blast; **~ de diana** reveille; **~ de difuntos** death knell; **~ de queda** curfew.

toquetear vt [manosear - cosa] to fiddle with; [- persona] to fondle.

toquilla f shawl.

tórax m inv thorax.

torbellino m **-1.** [remolino - de aire] whirlwind; [- de agua] whirlpool; [- de polvo] dustcloud **- 2.** fig [mezcla confusa] spate.

torcedura f [esguince] sprain.

torcer ◇ vt **-1.** [gen] to twist; [doblar] to bend **- 2.** [girar] to turn. ◇ vi [girar] to turn.

◆ **torcerse** vpr **-1.** [retorcerse] to twist; [doblarse] to bend; **me tuerzo al andar/escribir** I can't walk/write in a straight line **- 2.** [dislocarse] to sprain **- 3.** [ir mal - negocios, día] to go wrong; [- persona] to go astray.

torcido, da adj [enroscado] twisted; [doblado] bent; [cuadro, corbata] crooked.

tordo, da adj dappled.

◆ **tordo** m [pájaro] thrush.

torear ◇ vt **-1.** [lidiar] to fight (bulls) **- 2.** fig [eludir] to dodge **- 3.** fig [burlarse de]: **~ a alguien** to mess sb about. ◇ vi [lidiar] to fight bulls.

toreo m bullfighting.

torero, ra m,f [persona] bullfighter.

◆ **torera** f [prenda] bolero (jacket).

tormenta f lit & fig storm.

tormento m torment.

tormentoso, sa adj stormy; [sueño] troubled.

tornado m tornado.

tornar culto ◇ vt - **1.** [convertir]: ~ algo en (algo) to turn sthg into (sthg). ◇ vi - **1.** [regresar] to return - **2.** [volver a hacer]: ~ a hacer algo to do sthg again.

◆ **tornarse** vpr [convertirse]: ~se (en) to turn (into), to become.

torneado, da adj [cerámica] turned.

torneo m tournament.

tornillo m screw; [con tuerca] bolt; le falta un ~ fam he has a screw loose.

torniquete m MED tourniquet.

torno m - **1.** [de alfarero] (potter's) wheel - **2.** [para pesos] winch.

◆ **en torno a** loc prep - **1.** [alrededor de] around - **2.** [acerca de] about; girar en ~ a to be about.

toro m bull.

◆ **toros** mpl [lidia] bullfight (sg), bullfighting (U).

toronja f grapefruit.

torpe adj - **1.** [gen] clumsy - **2.** [necio] slow, dim-witted.

torpedear vt to torpedo.

torpedero m torpedo boat.

torpedo m [proyectil] torpedo.

torpeza f - **1.** [gen] clumsiness; fue una ~ hacerlo/decirlo it was a clumsy thing to do/say - **2.** [falta de inteligencia] slowness.

torre f - **1.** [construcción] tower; ELECTR pylon; ~ (de apartamentos) tower block; ~ de control control tower; ~ de perforación oil derrick - **2.** [en ajedrez] rook, castle - **3.** MIL turret.

torrefacto, ta adj high-roast (antes de sust).

torrencial adj torrential.

torrente m torrent; un ~ de fig [gente, palabras etc] a stream o flood of; [dinero, energía] masses of; un ~ de voz a powerful voice.

torreta f - **1.** MIL turret - **2.** ELECTR pylon.

torrezno m chunk of fried bacon.

tórrido, da adj lit & fig torrid.

torrija f French toast (U) (dipped in milk or wine).

torsión f - **1.** [del cuerpo, brazo] twist, twisting (U) - **2.** MEC torsion.

torso m culto torso.

torta f - **1.** CULIN cake - **2.** Andes, Col, RP, Ven [tarta] cake - **3.** fam [bofetada] thump; dar o pegar una ~ a alguien to thump sb - **4.** fam [accidente] crash.

◆ **ni torta** loc adv fam not a thing.

tortazo m - **1.** fam [bofetada] thump - **2.** fam [accidente] crash.

tortícolis f inv crick in the neck.

tortilla f - **1.** [de huevo] omelette; ~ (a la) española Spanish o potato omelette; ~ (a la) francesa French o plain omelette - **2.** [de maíz] tortilla.

tórtola f turtledove.

tortolito, ta m,f (gen pl) fam [enamorado] lovebird.

tortuga f - **1.** [terrestre] tortoise; [marina] turtle; [fluvial] terrapin - **2.** fam [persona o cosa lenta] snail.

tortuoso, sa adj - **1.** [sinuoso] tortuous, winding - **2.** fig [perverso] devious.

tortura f torture.

torturar vt to torture.

torunda f swab.

tos f cough; ~ ferina = tosferina.

tosco, ca adj - **1.** [basto] crude - **2.** fig [ignorante] coarse.

toser vi to cough.

tosferina, tos ferina f whooping cough.

tostado, da adj - **1.** [pan, almendras] toasted - **2.** [color] brownish - **3.** [piel] tanned.

◆ **tostada** f piece of toast; café con ~s coffee and toast.

tostador m, **tostadora** f toaster.

tostar vt - **1.** [dorar, calentar - pan, almendras] to toast; [- carne] to brown - **2.** [broncear] to tan.

◆ **tostarse** vpr to get brown; ~se (al sol) to sunbathe.

tostón m fam [rollo, aburrimiento] bore, drag.

total ◇ adj - **1.** [absoluto, completo] total - **2.** mfam [estupendo] brill, ace. ◇ m - **1.** [suma] total - **2.** [totalidad, conjunto] whole; el ~ del grupo the whole group; en ~ in all. ◇ adv anyway; ~ que me marché so anyway, I left.

totalidad f whole; en su ~ as a whole.

totalitario, ria adj totalitarian.

totalizar vt to add up to, to amount to.

tóxico, ca adj toxic, poisonous.

◆ **tóxico** m poison.

toxicómano, na m,f drug addict.

toxina f toxin.

tozudo, da adj stubborn.

traba f fig [obstáculo] obstacle; poner ~s (a alguien) to put obstacles in the way (of sb).

trabajador, ra ◇ adj hard-working. ◇ m,f worker.

trabajar ◇ vi - **1.** [gen] to work; ~ de/en to work as/in; ~ en una empresa to work for a firm - **2.** CIN & TEATR to act. ◇ vt - **1.** [hierro, barro, tierra] to work; [masa] to knead - **2.** [mejorar] to work on o at.

trampa

trabajo *m* -**1.** [gen] work; **hacer un buen ~** to do a good job; **~ intelectual/físico** mental/physical effort; **~ manual** manual labour; **~s manuales** [en el colegio] arts and crafts - **2.** [empleo] job; **no tener ~** to be out of work - **3.** [estudio escrito] piece of work, essay - **4.** ECON & POLÍT labour - **5.** *fig* [esfuerzo] effort.

trabajoso, sa *adj* -**1.** [difícil] hard, difficult - **2.** [molesto] tiresome.

trabalenguas *m inv* tongue-twister.

trabar *vt* -**1.** [sujetar] to fasten; [con grilletes] to shackle - **2.** [unir] to join - **3.** [iniciar - conversación, amistad] to strike up - **4.** [obstaculizar] to obstruct, to hinder - **5.** CULIN to thicken.
 ◆ **trabarse** *vpr* -**1.** [enredarse] to get tangled - **2.** *loc*: **se le trabó la lengua** he got tongue-tied.

trabazón *f* [de ideas, episodios] connection; [de discurso, novela] consistency.

trabucar *vt* to mix up.
 ◆ **trabucarse** *vpr* [al hablar] to get tongue-tied.

tracción *f* traction; **~ a las cuatro ruedas** four-wheel drive; **~ delantera/trasera** front-wheel/rear-wheel drive.

tractor *m* tractor.

tradición *f* tradition.

tradicional *adj* traditional.

tradicionalismo *m* traditionalism; POLÍT conservatism.

traducción *f* translation.

traducir ◇ *vt* [a otro idioma] to translate. ◇ *vi*: **~ (de/a)** to translate (from/into).
 ◆ **traducirse** *vpr* [a otro idioma]: **~se (por)** to be translated (by *o* as).

traductor, ra *m, f* translator.

traer *vt* -**1.** [trasladar, provocar] to bring; [consecuencias] to carry, to have; **~ consigo** [implicar] to mean, to lead to - **2.** [llevar] to carry; **¿qué traes ahí?** what have you got there? - **3.** [llevar adjunto, dentro] to have; **trae un artículo interesante** it has an interesting article in it - **4.** [llevar puesto] to wear.
 ◆ **traerse** *vpr*: **traérselas** *fam fig* to be a real handful.

traficante *mf* [de drogas, armas etc] trafficker.

traficar *vi*: **~ (en/con algo)** to traffic (in sthg).

tráfico *m* [de vehículos] traffic; [de drogas, armas] trafficking, dealing.

tragaldabas *m, f* & *inv fam* greedy guts.

tragaluz *m* skylight.

tragaperras *f inv* slot machine.

tragar ◇ *vt* -**1.** [ingerir, creer] to swallow - **2.** [absorber] to swallow up - **3.** *fig* [soportar] to put up with. ◇ *vi* -**1.** [ingerir] to swallow - **2.** [aguantar] to grin and bear it; [acceder, ceder] to give in.
 ◆ **tragarse** *vpr fig* [soportarse]: **no se tragan** they can't stand each other.

tragedia *f* tragedy.

trágico, ca *adj* tragic.

trago *m* -**1.** [de líquido] mouthful; **dar un ~ de algo** to take a swig of sthg; **de un ~** in one gulp - **2.** *fam* [copa] drink - **3.** *fam* [disgusto]: **ser un ~ para alguien** to be tough on sb.

tragón, ona *fam* ◇ *adj* greedy. ◇ *m, f* pig, glutton.

traición *f* -**1.** [infidelidad] betrayal - **2.** DER treason.

traicionar *vt* [persona, país, ideales] to betray.

traicionero, ra *adj* [desleal] treacherous; DER treasonous.

traidor, ra ◇ *adj* treacherous; DER treasonous. ◇ *m, f* traitor.

traiga *etc* ▷ traer.

tráiler ['trailer] (*pl* trailers) *m* -**1.** CIN trailer - **2.** AUTOM articulated lorry - **3.** *Méx* [caravana] caravan *UK*, trailer *US*.

traje *m* -**1.** [con chaqueta] suit; [de una pieza] dress; **ir de ~** to wear a suit; **~ de baño** swimsuit; **~ de chaqueta** woman's two-piece suit - **2.** [regional, de época etc] costume; **~ de luces** matador's outfit - **3.** [ropa] clothes (*pl*); **~ de paisano** [de militar] civilian clothes; [de policía] plain clothes.

trajeado, da *adj fam* [arreglado] spruced up.

trajín *m fam* [ajetreo] bustle.

trajinar *vi fam* to bustle about.

trajo ▷ traer.

tralla *f* [látigo] whip.

trallazo *m fam* DEP powerful shot.

trama *f* -**1.** [de hilos] weft - **2.** [argumento] plot - **3.** [conspiración] intrigue.

tramar *vt* [planear] to plot; [complot] to hatch; **estar tramando algo** to be up to something.

tramitar *vt* -**1.** [suj: autoridades - pasaporte, permiso] to take the necessary steps to obtain; [- solicitud, dimisión] to process - **2.** [suj: solicitante]: **~ un permiso/visado** to be in the process of applying for a licence/visa.

trámite *m* [gestión] formal step; **de ~** routine, formal.
 ◆ **trámites** *mpl* -**1.** [proceso] procedure *(sg)* - **2.** [papeleo] paperwork *(U)*.

tramo *m* [espacio] section, stretch; [de escalera] flight (of stairs).

tramoya *f* TEATR stage machinery *(U)*.

trampa *f* -**1.** [para cazar] trap; *fig* [engaño] trick; **tender una ~ (a alguien)** to set *o* lay a trap (for sb); **hacer ~s** to cheat - **2.** *fam* [deuda] debt.

trampear *vi fam* [estafar] to swindle money.

trampero, ra *m,f* trapper.

trampilla *f* [en el suelo] trapdoor.

trampolín *m* [de piscina] diving board; [de esquí] ski jump; [en gimnasia] springboard.

tramposo, sa ◇ *adj* [fullero] cheating. ◇ *m,f* [fullero] cheat.

tranca *f* - 1. [en puerta, ventana] bar - 2. [arma] cudgel, stick - 3. *loc*: **a ~s y barrancas** with great difficulty.

trancarse *vpr Amér* [atorarse] to get blocked, to get clogged up.

trance *m* - 1. [apuro] difficult situation; **estar en ~ de hacer algo** to be about to do sthg; **pasar por un mal ~** to go through a bad patch - 2. [estado hipnótico] trance.

tranquilidad *f* peacefulness, calmness; **para mayor ~** to be on the safe side.

tranquilizante *m* FARM tranquilizer.

tranquilizar *vt* - 1. [calmar] to calm (down) - 2. [dar confianza] to reassure.
  ◆ **tranquilizarse** *vpr* - 1. [calmarse] to calm down - 2. [ganar confianza] to feel reassured.

tranquillo *m Esp fam*: **coger el ~ a algo** to get the knack of sthg.

tranquilo, la *adj* - 1. [sosegado - lugar, música] peaceful; [- persona, tono de voz, mar] calm; **¡(tú) ~!** *fam* don't you worry! - 2. [velada, charla, negocio] **quiet** - 3. [mente] untroubled; [conciencia] clear - 4. [despreocupado] casual, laid-back.

transacción *f* COM transaction.

transaminasa *f* QUÍM transaminase.

transar *vi Amér* [negociar] to come to an arrangement, to reach a compromise; [transigir] to compromise, to give in.

transatlántico, ca *adj* transatlantic.
  ◆ **transatlántico** *m* NÁUT (ocean) liner.

transbordador *m* - 1. NÁUT ferry - 2. AERON : **~ (espacial)** space shuttle.

transbordar *vi* to change *(trains etc)*.

transbordo *m*: **hacer ~** to change *(trains etc)*.

transcendencia *f* importance; **tener una gran ~** to be deeply significant.

transcendental *adj* - 1. [importante] momentous - 2. [meditación] transcendental.

transcendente *adj* momentous.

transcender *vi* - 1. [extenderse]: **~ (a algo)** to spread (across sthg) - 2. [filtrarse] to be leaked - 3. [sobrepasar]: **~ de** to transcend, to go beyond.

transcribir *vt* [escribir] to transcribe.

transcurrir *vi* - 1. [tiempo] to pass, to go by - 2. [ocurrir] to take place, to go off.

transcurso *m* - 1. [paso de tiempo] passing - 2. [periodo de tiempo]: **en el ~ de** in the course of.

transeúnte *mf* [viandante] passer-by.

transexual *adj* & *m,f* transsexual.

transferencia *f* transfer.

transferir *vt* to transfer.

transfigurarse *vpr* to become transfigured.

transformación *f* - 1. [cambio, conversión] transformation - 2. [en rugby] conversion.

transformador *m* ELECTRÓN transformer.

transformar *vt* - 1. [cambiar radicalmente]: **~ algo/a alguien (en)** to transform sthg/sb (into) - 2. [convertir]: **~ algo (en)** to convert sthg (into) - 3. [en rugby] to convert.
  ◆ **transformarse** *vpr* - 1. [cambiar radicalmente] to be transformed - 2. [convertirse]: **~se en algo** to be converted into sthg.

tránsfuga *mf* POLÍT defector.

transfuguismo *m* POLÍT defection.

transfusión *f* transfusion.

transgredir *vt* to transgress.

transgresor, ra *m,f* transgressor.

transición *f* transition; **periodo de ~** transition period; **~ democrática** transition to democracy.

transido, da *adj*: **~ (de)** stricken (with); **~ de pena** grief-stricken.

transigir *vi* - 1. [ceder] to compromise - 2. [ser tolerante] to be tolerant.

transistor *m* transistor.

transitar *vi* to go (along).

tránsito *m* - 1. [circulación - gen] movement; [- de vehículos] traffic; **pasajeros en ~ a ...** passengers with connecting flights to ... - 2. [transporte] transit.

transitorio, ria *adj* [gen] transitory; [residencia] temporary; [régimen, medida] transitional, interim.

translúcido, da *adj* translucent.

transmisión *f* - 1. [gen & AUTOM] transmission - 2. RADIO & TV broadcast, broadcasting *(U)* - 3. [de herencia, poderes etc] transference.

transmisor, ra *adj* transmission *(antes de sust)*.
  ◆ **transmisor** *m* transmitter.

transmitir *vt* - 1. [gen] to transmit; [saludos, noticias] to pass on - 2. RADIO & TV to broadcast - 3. [ceder] to transfer.

transparencia *f* transparency.

transparentarse *vpr* [tela] to be see-through; [vidrio, líquido] to be transparent.

transparente *adj* [gen] transparent; [tela] see-through.

transpiración *f* perspiration.

transpirar *vi* to perspire.

transplantar *vt* to transplant.

transplante *m* transplant, transplanting *(U)*.

transponer *vt* [cambiar] to switch.

◆ **transponerse** *vpr* [adormecerse] to doze off.

transportador *m* [para medir ángulos] protractor.

transportar *vt* - **1.** [trasladar] to transport - **2.** [embelesar] to captivate.

◆ **transportarse** *vpr* [embelesarse] to go into raptures.

transporte *m* transport *UK*, transportation *US*; ~ **público** *o* **colectivo** public transport *UK o* transportation *US*.

transportista *mf* carrier.

transvase *m* - **1.** [de líquido] decanting - **2.** [de río] transfer.

transversal *adj* transverse.

tranvía *m* tram, streetcar *US*.

trapecio *m* [de gimnasia] trapeze.

trapecista *mf* trapeze artist.

trapero, ra *m,f* rag-and-bone man (*f* rag-and-bone woman).

trapío *m* TAUROM good bearing.

trapisonda *f fam* [enredo] scheme.

trapo *m* - **1.** [trozo de tela] rag - **2.** [gamuza, bayeta] cloth; **pasar el ~ a algo** to wipe sthg with a cloth; **poner a alguien como un ~** to tear sb to pieces.

◆ **trapos** *mpl fam* [ropa] clothes.

tráquea *f* windpipe; MED trachea.

traquetear *vi* [hacer ruido] to rattle.

traqueteo *m* [ruido] rattling.

tras *prep* - **1.** [detrás de] behind - **2.** [después de, en pos de] after; **uno ~ otro** one after the other; **andar ~ algo** to be after sthg.

trasatlántico, ca = transatlántico.

trasbordador, ra = transbordador.

trasbordar = transbordar.

trasbordo = transbordo.

trascendencia = transcendencia.

trascendental = transcendental.

trascendente = transcendente.

trascender = transcender.

trascribir = transcribir.

trascurrir = transcurrir.

trascurso = transcurso.

trasegar *vt* [desordenar] to rummage about amongst.

trasero, ra *adj* back (*antes de sust*), rear (*antes de sust*).

◆ **trasero** *m fam* backside, butt *US*.

trasferencia = transferencia.

trasferir = transferir.

trasfigurarse = transfigurarse.

trasfondo *m* background; [de palabras, intenciones] undertone.

trasformación = transformación.

trasformador = transformador.

trasformar = transformar.

trásfuga = tránsfuga.

trasfusión = transfusión.

trasgredir = transgredir.

trasgresor, ra = transgresor.

trashumante *adj* seasonally migratory.

trasiego *m* [movimiento] comings and goings (*pl*).

traslación *f* ASTRON passage.

trasladar *vt* - **1.** [desplazar] to move - **2.** [a empleado, funcionario] to transfer - **3.** [reunión, fecha] to postpone, to move back.

◆ **trasladarse** *vpr* - **1.** [desplazarse] to go - **2.** [mudarse] to move; **me traslado de piso** I'm moving flat.

traslado *m* - **1.** [de casa, empresa, muebles] move, moving (*U*) - **2.** [de trabajo] transfer - **3.** [de personas] movement.

traslúcido, da = translúcido.

trasluz *m* reflected light; **al ~** against the light.

trasmisión = transmisión.

trasmisor, ra = transmisor.

trasmitir = transmitir.

trasnochar *vi* to stay up late, to go to bed late.

traspapelar *vt* to mislay, to misplace.

trasparencia = transparencia.

trasparentarse = transparentarse.

trasparente = transparente.

traspasar *vt* - **1.** [perforar, atravesar] to go through, to pierce; [suj: líquido] to soak through - **2.** [cruzar] to cross (over); [puerta] to pass through - **3.** [cambiar de sitio] to move - **4.** [vender - jugador] to transfer; [- negocio] to sell (as a going concern) - **5.** *fig* [exceder] to go beyond.

traspaso *m* [venta - de jugador] transfer; [- de negocio] sale (as a going concern).

traspié (*pl* **traspiés**) *m* - **1.** [resbalón] trip, stumble; **dar un ~** to trip up - **2.** *fig* [error] blunder, slip.

traspiración = transpiración.

traspirar = transpirar.

trasplantar = transplantar.

trasplante = transplante.

trasponer = transponer.

trasportar *etc* = transportar.

trasquilar *vt* [esquilar] to shear.

trastabillar *vi* [tambalearse] to stagger; [tropezar] to stumble; [tartamudear] to stutter.

trastada *f fam* dirty trick; **hacer una ~ a alguien** to play a dirty trick on sb.

traste *m* - **1.** MÚS fret - **2.** *CSur fam* [trasero] bottom. *Andes, CAm, Carib, Méx*: ~**s** utensils - **4.** *loc*: **dar al ~ con algo** to ruin sthg; **irse al ~** to fall through.

trastero *m* junk room.

trastienda *f* backroom.

trasto *m* - **1.** [utensilio inútil] piece of junk,

junk (U) - **2.** *fam* [persona traviesa] menace, nuisance.

◆ **trastos** *mpl fam* [pertenencias, equipo] things, stuff (U); **tirarse los ~s a la cabeza** to have a flaming row.

trastocar *vt* [cambiar] to turn upside down.

◆ **trastocarse** *vpr* [enloquecer] to go mad.

trastornado, da *adj* disturbed, unbalanced.

trastornar *vt* - **1.** [volver loco] to drive mad - **2.** [inquietar] to worry, to trouble - **3.** [alterar] to turn upside down; [planes] to disrupt, to upset.

◆ **trastornarse** *vpr* [volverse loco] to go mad.

trastorno *m* - **1.** [mental] disorder; [digestivo] upset - **2.** [alteración - por huelga, nevada] trouble (U), disruption (U); [- por guerra etc] upheaval.

trasvase = transvase.

tratable *adj* easy-going, friendly.

tratado *m* - **1.** [convenio] treaty - **2.** [escrito] treatise.

tratamiento *m* - **1.** [gen & MED] treatment - **2.** [título] title, form of address - **3.** INFORM processing; ~ **de datos/textos** data/word processing; ~ **por lotes** batch processing.

tratar ⬦ *vt* - **1.** [gen & MED] to treat - **2.** [discutir] to discuss - **3.** INFORM to process - **4.** [dirigirse a]: ~ **a alguien de** [usted, tú etc] to address sb as. ⬦ *vi* - **1.** [intentar]: ~ **de hacer algo** to try to do sthg - **2.** [versar]: ~ **de/sobre** to be about - **3.** [tener relación]: ~ **con alguien** to mix with sb, to have dealings with sb - **4.** [comerciar]: ~ **en** to deal in.

◆ **tratarse** *vpr* - **1.** [relacionarse]: ~**se con** to mix with, to have dealings with - **2.** [versar]: ~**se de** to be about; **¿de qué se trata?** what's it about?

tratativas *fpl CSur* negotiation (sg).

trato *m* - **1.** [comportamiento] treatment; **de ~ agradable** pleasant; **malos ~s** battering (U) (of child, wife) - **2.** [relación] dealings (pl) - **3.** [acuerdo] deal; **cerrar** o **hacer un ~** to do o make a deal; **¡~ hecho!** it's a deal! - **4.** [tratamiento] title, term of address.

trauma *m* trauma.

traumatólogo, ga *m,f* traumatologist.

través

◆ **a través de** *loc prep* - **1.** [de un lado a otro de] across, over - **2.** [por, por medio de] through.

◆ **de través** *loc adv* [transversalmente] crossways; [de lado] crosswise, sideways.

travesaño *m* - **1.** ARQUIT crosspiece - **2.** DEP crossbar - **3.** [de escalera] rung.

travesía *f* - **1.** [viaje - por mar] voyage, crossing - **2.** [calle] cross-street.

travestido, da, travestí (*pl* travestís) *m,f* transvestite.

travesura *f* [acción] prank, mischief (U); **hacer ~s** to play pranks, to get up to mischief.

traviesa *f* - **1.** FERROC sleeper (on track) - **2.** CONSTR crossbeam, tie beam.

travieso, sa *adj* mischievous.

trayecto *m* - **1.** [distancia] distance - **2.** [viaje] journey, trip - **3.** [ruta] route; **final de ~** end of the line.

trayectoria *f* - **1.** [recorrido] trajectory - **2.** *fig* [evolución] path.

traza *f* [aspecto] appearance (U), looks (pl); **tener ~s de hacer algo** to show signs of doing sthg; **esto no tiene ~s de acabar pronto** this doesn't look as if it's going to finish soon.

trazado *m* - **1.** [trazo] outline, sketching - **2.** [diseño] plan, design - **3.** [recorrido] route.

trazar *vt* - **1.** [dibujar] to draw, to trace; [ruta] to plot - **2.** [indicar, describir] to outline - **3.** [idear] to draw up.

trazo *m* - **1.** [de dibujo, rostro] line - **2.** [de letra] stroke.

trébol *m* [planta] clover.

◆ **tréboles** *mpl* [naipes] clubs.

trece *núm* thirteen; *ver también* **seis**.

treceavo, va *núm* thirteenth.

trecho *m* [espacio] distance; [tiempo] time, while.

tregua *f* truce; *fig* respite.

treinta *núm* thirty; **los (años) ~** the Thirties; *ver también* **seis**.

treintena *f* thirty.

tremendo, da *adj* [enorme] tremendous, enormous.

trémulo, la *adj* [voz] trembling; [luz] flickering.

tren *m* - **1.** [ferrocarril] train; **ir en ~** to go by train; ~ **de alta velocidad/largo recorrido** high-speed/long-distance train; **estar como (para parar) un ~** to be really gorgeous; **perder el ~** *fig* to miss the boat; **subirse al ~** *fig* to climb on the bandwagon - **2.** TECN line; ~ **de aterrizaje** undercarriage, landing gear; ~ **de lavado** car wash.

trenza *f* - **1.** [de pelo] plait - **2.** [de fibras] braid.

trenzar *vt* - **1.** [pelo] to plait - **2.** [fibras] to braid.

trepa *mf fam* social climber.

trepador, ra ⬦ *adj*: **planta trepadora** climber, creeper. ⬦ *m,f fam* social climber.

trepar ⬦ *vt* to climb. ⬦ *vi* - **1.** [subir] to climb - **2.** *fam* [medrar] to be a social climber.

trepidar *vi* to shake, to vibrate.

tres *núm* three; **ni a la de** ~ not for anything in the world, no way; *ver también* **seis**.

➡ **tres cuartos** *m inv* [abrigo] three-quarter-length coat.

➡ **tres en raya** *m* noughts and crosses *(U) UK*, tick-tack-toe *US*.

trescientos, tas *núm* three hundred; *ver también* **seis**.

tresillo *m* [sofá] three-piece suite.

treta *f* trick.

triangular *adj* triangular.

triángulo *m* GEOM & MÚS triangle.

triates *mpl Amér* triplets.

tribu *f* tribe.

tribulación *f* tribulation.

tribuna *f* - **1**. [estrado] rostrum, platform; [del jurado] jury box - **2**. [DEP - localidad] stand; [- graderío] grandstand - **3**. PRENS : ~ **de prensa** press box; ~ **libre** open forum.

tribunal *m* - **1**. [gen] court; **llevar a alguien/acudir a los** ~es to take sb/go to court - **2**. [de examen] board of examiners; [de concurso] panel.

tributable *adj* taxable.

tributar *vt* [homenaje] to pay; [respeto, admiración] to have.

tributo *m* - **1**. [impuesto] tax - **2**. *fig* [precio] price - **3**. [homenaje] tribute.

triciclo *m* tricycle.

tricornio *m* three-cornered hat.

tricotar *vt & vi* to knit.

tricotosa *f* knitting machine.

tridimensional *adj* three-dimensional.

trifulca *f* *fam* row, squabble.

trigésimo, ma *núm* thirtieth.

trigo *m* wheat.

trigonometría *f* trigonometry.

trilita *f* TNT.

trillado, da *adj fig* well-worn, trite.

trilladora *f* [máquina] threshing machine.

trillar *vt* to thresh.

trillizo, za *m,f* triplet.

trillo *m* thresher.

trillón *m* trillion *UK*, quintillion *US*.

trilogía *f* trilogy.

trimestral *adj* three-monthly, quarterly; [exámenes, notas] end-of-term *(antes de sust)*.

trimestre *m* three months *(pl)*, quarter; [en escuela, universidad] term.

trinar *vi* to chirp, to warble; **está que trina** *fig* she's fuming.

trincar *fam* ◇ *vt* - **1**. [agarrar] to grab - **2**. [detener] to nick, to arrest. ◇ *vi* [beber] to guzzle.

trinchar *vt* to carve.

trinchera *f* - **1**. MIL trench - **2**. [abrigo] trench coat.

trineo *m* [pequeño] sledge; [grande] sleigh.

Trinidad *f*: **la (Santísima)** ~ the (Holy) Trinity.

Trinidad y Tobago Trinidad and Tobago.

trinitrotolueno *m* trinitrotoluene.

trino *m* [de pájaros] chirp, chirping *(U)*; MÚS trill.

trío *m* [gen] trio.

tripa *f* - **1**. [intestino] gut, intestine - **2**. *fam* [barriga] gut, belly.

➡ **tripas** *fpl fig* [interior] insides.

triple ◇ *adj* triple. ◇ *m* - **1**. [tres veces]: **el** ~ three times as much; **el** ~ **de gente** three times as many people - **2**. [en baloncesto] three-pointer.

triplicado *m* second copy, triplicate.

triplicar *vt* to triple, to treble.

➡ **triplicarse** *vpr* to triple, to treble.

trípode *m* tripod.

tripulación *f* crew.

tripulante *mf* crew member.

tripular *vt* to man.

tris *m*: **estar en un** ~ **de (hacer algo)** to be within a whisker of (doing sthg).

triste *adj* - **1**. [gen] sad; [día, tiempo, paisaje] gloomy, dreary; **es** ~ **que** it's a shame o pity that - **2**. *fig* [color, vestido, luz] pale, faded - **3**. *(antes de sust)* [humilde] poor; [sueldo] sorry, miserable; **ni un** ~ *fig* not a single.

tristeza *f* [gen] sadness; [de paisaje, día] gloominess, dreariness.

triturador *m* [de basura] waste-disposal unit; [de papeles] shredder.

triturar *vt* - **1**. [moler, desmenuzar] to crush, to grind; [papel] to shred - **2**. [masticar] to chew.

triunfador, ra *m,f* winner.

triunfal *adj* triumphant.

triunfar *vi* - **1**. [vencer] to win, to triumph - **2**. [tener éxito] to succeed, to be successful.

triunfo *m* [gen] triumph; [en encuentro, elecciones] victory, win.

trivial *adj* trivial.

trivializar *vt* to trivialize.

trizas *fpl*: **hacer** ~ **algo** [hacer añicos] to smash sthg to pieces; [desgarrar] to tear sthg to shreds; **estar hecho** ~ [persona] to be shattered.

trocar *vt* - **1**. [transformar]: ~ **algo (en algo)** to change sthg (into sthg) - **2**. [intercambiar] to swap, to exchange.

trocear *vt* to cut up (into pieces).

trocha *f* [senda] path; [atajo] shortcut.

troche ➡ **a troche y moche** *loc adv* haphazardly.

trofeo *m* trophy.

troglodita *mf* - **1**. [cavernícola] cave dweller,

troglodyte - 2. *fam* [bárbaro, tosco] **rough-neck, brute.**

trola *f fam* fib, lie.

trolebús *m* trolleybus.

trombón *m* [instrumento] trombone; [músico] trombonist.

trombosis *f inv* thrombosis.

trompa *f* **- 1.** [de elefante] trunk; [de oso hormiguero] **snout;** [de insecto] **proboscis - 2.** MÚS horn **- 3.** *fam* [borrachera]: **coger** *o* **pillar una** ~ to get plastered.

trompazo *m fam* bang.

trompear *vt Amér fam* to punch.

◆ **trompearse** *vpr Amér fam* to have a fight.

trompeta *f* trumpet.

trompetista *mf* trumpeter.

trompicar *vi* to stumble.

trompicón *m* [tropezón] stumble; **a trompicones** in fits and starts.

trompo *m* **- 1.** [juguete] spinning top **- 2.** [giro] spin.

trona *f* [para niño] high chair.

tronado, da *adj fam* [loco] nuts, crazy.

tronar ◇ *v impers* & *vi* to thunder. ◇ *vt Méx fam* [fracasar] to fail.

◆ **tronarse** *vpr Amér fam* to shoot o.s.

troncal *adj*: **asignatura** ~ core subject.

tronchar *vt* [partir] to snap.

◆ **troncharse** *vpr fam*: ~**se (de risa)** to split one's sides laughing.

troncho *m* [de lechuga] heart.

tronco, ca *m,f mfam* [tipo] guy, *(f)* bird; [como apelativo] pal, mate.

◆ **tronco** *m* ANAT & BOT trunk; [talado y sin ramas] log; **dormir como un** ~, **estar hecho un** ~ to sleep like a log.

tronera *f* **- 1.** ARQUIT & HIST embrasure **- 2.** [en billar] pocket.

trono *m* throne; **subir al** ~ to ascend the throne.

tropa *f* (*gen pl*) MIL troops *(pl).*

tropecientos, tas *adj fam* loads of.

tropel *m* [de personas] mob, crowd.

tropero *m RP* cowboy.

tropezar *vi* [con el pie]: ~ **(con)** to trip *o* stumble (on).

◆ **tropezarse** *vpr* [encontrarse] to bump into each other, to come across one another; ~**se con alguien** to bump into sb.

◆ **tropezar con** *vi* [problema, persona] to run into, to come across.

tropezón *m* **- 1.** [con el pie] trip, stumble; **dar un** ~ to trip up, to stumble **- 2.** *fig* [desacierto] slip-up, blunder.

◆ **tropezones** *mpl* CULIN small chunks.

tropical *adj* tropical.

trópico *m* tropic.

tropiezo *m* **- 1.** [con el pie] trip, stumble; **dar un** ~ to trip up, to stumble **- 2.** *fig* [equivocación] blunder, slip-up; [revés] setback.

troquel *m* [molde] mould, die.

trotamundos *m y f inv* globe-trotter.

trotar *vi* to trot; *fam fig* [de aquí para allá] to dash *o* run around.

trote *m* [de caballo] trot; **al** ~ at a trot.

troupe [trup, 'trupe] (*pl* **troupes**) *f* troupe.

trovador *m* troubadour.

trozar *vt Amér* [carne] to cut up; [res, tronco] to butcher, to cut up.

trozo *m* [gen] piece; [de sendero, camino] stretch; [de obra, película] extract; **cortar algo en** ~**s** to cut sthg into pieces; **hacer algo a** ~**s** to do sthg in bits.

trucar *vt* to doctor; [motor] to soup up.

trucha *f* [pez] trout.

truco *m* **- 1.** [trampa, engaño] trick; ~ **de magia** magic trick **- 2.** [habilidad, técnica] knack; **coger el** ~ to get the knack; ~ **publicitario** advertising gimmick.

truculento, ta *adj* horrifying, terrifying.

trueno *m* METEOR clap of thunder, thunder *(U).*

trueque *m* **- 1.** COM & HIST barter **- 2.** [intercambio] exchange, swap.

trufa *f* [hongo, bombón] truffle.

truhán, ana *m,f* rogue, crook.

truncar *vt* [frustrar - vida, carrera] to cut short; [- planes, ilusiones] to spoil, to ruin.

trusa *f Carib* [traje de baño] swimsuit; *RP* [faja] girdle.

tu (*pl* **tus**) *adj poses (antes de sust)* your.

tú *pron pers* you; **es más alta que** ~ she's taller than you; **de** ~ **a** ~ [lucha] evenly matched; **hablar** *o* **tratar de** ~ **a alguien** to address sb as 'tú'.

tubérculo *m* tuber, root vegetable.

tuberculosis *f inv* tuberculosis.

tubería *f* **- 1.** [cañerías] pipes *(pl)*, pipework **- 2.** [tubo] pipe.

tubo *m* **- 1.** [tubería] pipe; ~ **de escape** AUTOM exhaust (pipe); ~ **del desagüe** drainpipe **- 2.** [recipiente] tube; ~ **de ensayo** test tube **- 3.** ANAT tract; ~ **digestivo** digestive tract, alimentary canal.

tuerca *f* nut.

tuerto, ta *adj* [sin un ojo] one-eyed; [ciego de un ojo] blind in one eye.

tuétano *m* ANAT (bone) marrow.

tufillo *m* whiff.

tufo *m* [mal olor] stench, foul smell.

tugurio *m* hovel.

tul *m* tulle.

tulipa *f* [de lámpara] tulip-shaped lampshade.

tulipán *m* tulip.

tullido, da ◇ *adj* paralyzed, crippled. ◇ *m,f* cripple, disabled person.

tumba *f* grave, tomb; **ser (como) una ~** to be as silent as the grave.

tumbar *vt* [derribar] to knock over o down.

➡ **tumbarse** *vpr* [acostarse] to lie down.

tumbo *m* jolt, jerk.

tumbona *f* [en la playa] deck chair; [en el jardín] (sun) lounger.

tumor *m* tumour.

tumulto *m* - **1.** [disturbio] riot, disturbance - **2.** [alboroto] uproar, tumult; **un ~ de gente** a crowd of people.

tumultuoso, sa *adj* - **1.** [conflictivo] tumultuous, riotous - **2.** [turbulento] rough, stormy.

tuna *f* - **1.** ➪ **tuno** - **2.** *CAm, Méx* [fruta] prickly pear.

tunante, ta *m,f* crook, scoundrel.

tunda *f fam* [paliza] beating, thrashing.

túnel *m* tunnel.

➡ **túnel de lavado** *m* AUTOM car wash.

Túnez - **1.** [capital] Tunis - **2.** [país] Tunisia.

túnica *f* tunic.

Tunicia Tunisia.

tuno, na *m,f* rogue, scoundrel.

➡ **tuna** *f* group of student minstrels.

tuntún ➡ **al tuntún** *loc adv* without thinking.

tupé *m* [cabello] quiff.

tupido, da *adj* thick, dense.

turba *f* - **1.** [combustible] peat, turf - **2.** [muchedumbre] mob.

turbación *f* - **1.** [desconcierto] upset, disturbance - **2.** [azoramiento] embarrassment.

turbante *m* turban.

turbar *vt* - **1.** [alterar] to disturb - **2.** [emocionar] to upset - **3.** [desconcertar] to trouble, to disconcert.

➡ **turbarse** *vpr* - **1.** [alterarse] to get upset - **2.** [aturdirse] to get embarrassed.

turbina *f* turbine.

turbio, bia *adj* - **1.** [agua etc] cloudy - **2.** [vista] blurred - **3.** *fig* [negocio etc] shady - **4.** *fig* [época etc] turbulent, troubled.

turbulencia *f* - **1.** [de fluido] turbulence - **2.** [alboroto] uproar, clamour.

turbulento, ta *adj* - **1.** [gen] turbulent - **2.** [revoltoso] unruly, rebellious.

turco, ca ◇ *adj* Turkish. ◇ *m,f* [persona] Turk.

➡ **turco** *m* [lengua] Turkish.

turismo *m* - **1.** [gen] tourism; **hacer ~ (por)** to go touring (round); **~ rural** rural tourism - **2.** AUTOM private car.

turista *mf* tourist.

turístico, ca *adj* tourist *(antes de sust)*.

turnarse *vpr*: **~ (con alguien)** to take turns (with sb).

turno *m* - **1.** [tanda] turn, go; **le ha llegado el ~ de hacerlo** it's his turn to do it - **2.** [de trabajo] shift; **trabajar por ~s** to work shifts; **~ de día/noche** day/night shift.

turquesa ◇ *f* [mineral] turquoise. ◇ *adj inv* [color] turquoise. ◇ *m* [color] turquoise.

Turquía Turkey.

turrón *m Christmas sweet similar to marzipan or nougat, made with almonds and honey.*

tute *m* [juego] *card game similar to whist.*

tutear *vt* to address as 'tú'.

➡ **tutearse** *vpr* to address each other as 'tú'.

tutela *f* - **1.** DER guardianship - **2.** [cargo]: **~ (de)** responsibility (for); **bajo la ~ de** under the protection of.

tutelar ◇ *adj* DER tutelary. ◇ *vt* to act as guardian to.

tutor, ra *m,f* - **1.** DER guardian - **2.** [profesor privado] tutor; [- de un curso] form teacher.

tutoría *f* DER guardianship.

tutú *(pl* tutús*) m* tutu.

tuviera *etc* ➪ tener.

tuyo, ya ◇ *adj poses* yours; **este libro es ~** this book is yours; **un amigo ~** a friend of yours; **no es asunto ~** it's none of your business. ◇ *pron poses*: **el ~** yours; **el ~ es rojo** yours is red; **ésta es la tuya** *fam* this is the chance you've been waiting for; **lo ~ es el teatro** [lo que haces bien] you should be on the stage; **los ~s** *fam* [tu familia] your folks; [tu bando] your lot, your side.

TV *(abrev de* **televisión**) *f* TV.

TVE *(abrev de* **Televisión Española**) *f Spanish state television network.*

u[1], U *f* [letra] u, U.

u[2] *conj* or; *ver también* **o[2]**.

ubicación *f* position, location.

ubicar *vt* to place, to position; [edificio etc] to locate.

➡ **ubicarse** *vpr* [edificio etc] to be situated, to be located.

ubre *f* udder.

Ucrania the Ukraine.

Ud., Vd. *abrev de* **usted**.

Uds., Vds. *abrev de* **ustedes**.

UE (*abrev de* **Unión Europea**) *f* EU.

UEFA (*abrev de* **Unión de Asociaciones Europeas de Fútbol**) *f* UEFA.

ufanarse *vpr*: ~ **de** to boast about.

ufano, na *adj* - **1.** [satisfecho] proud, pleased - **2.** [engreído] boastful, conceited.

Uganda Uganda.

UGT (*abrev de* **Unión General de los Trabajadores**) *f major socialist Spanish trade union.*

UHF (*abrev de* **ultra high frequency**) *f* UHF.

ujier (*pl* **ujieres**) *m* usher.

újule *interj Amér* wow!

úlcera *f* MED ulcer.

ulcerar *vt* to ulcerate.

  ◆ **ulcerarse** *vpr* MED to ulcerate.

ulterior *adj culto* [en el tiempo] subsequent, ulterior.

ulteriormente *adv culto* subsequently.

ultimador, ra *m,f Amér* killer.

ultimar *vt* - **1.** [gen] to conclude, to complete - **2.** *Amér* [matar] to kill.

ultimátum (*pl* **ultimátums** *o* **ultimatos**) *m* ultimatum.

último, ma ◇ *adj* - **1.** [gen] last; **por ~** lastly, finally - **2.** [más reciente] latest, most recent - **3.** [más remoto] furthest, most remote - **4.** [más bajo] bottom - **5.** [más alto] top - **6.** [de más atrás] back. ◇ *m,f* - **1.** [en fila, carrera etc]: **el ~** the last (one); **llegar el ~** to come last - **2.** *(en comparaciones, enumeraciones)*: **éste ~ ...** the latter ...

ultra *mf* POLÍT right-wing extremist.

ultraderecha *f* extreme right (wing).

ultraizquierda *f* extreme left (wing).

ultrajar *vt* to insult, to offend.

ultraje *m* insult.

ultramar *m* overseas *(pl)*; **de ~** overseas *(antes de sust)*.

ultramarino, na *adj* overseas *(antes de sust)*.

  ◆ **ultramarinos** ◇ *mpl* [comestibles] groceries. ◇ *m inv* [tienda] grocer's (shop) *(sg)*.

ultranza ◆ **a ultranza** *loc adv* - **1.** [con decisión] to the death - **2.** [acérrimamente] out-and-out.

ultrasonido *m* ultrasound.

ultratumba *f*: **de ~** from beyond the grave.

ultravioleta *adj inv* ultraviolet.

ulular *vi* - **1.** [viento, lobo] to howl - **2.** [búho] to hoot.

umbilical ▷ **cordón**.

umbral *m* - **1.** [gen] threshold - **2.** *fig* [límite] bounds *(pl)*, realms *(pl)*.

un, una ◇ *art antes de sust femenino que empiece por 'a' o 'ha' tónica: un a*, an *(ante sonido vocálico)*; ~ **hombre/coche** a man/car; **una mujer/mesa** a woman/table; ~ **águila/**

hacha an eagle/axe; **una hora** an hour. ◇ *adj* ▷ **uno**.

unánime *adj* unanimous.

unanimidad *f* unanimity; **por ~** unanimously.

unción *f* function.

undécimo, ma *núm* eleventh.

UNED (*abrev de* **Universidad Nacional de Educación a Distancia**) *f Spanish open university.*

ungüento *m* ointment.

únicamente *adv* only, solely.

único, ca *adj* - **1.** [sólo] only; **es lo ~ que quiero** it's all I want - **2.** [excepcional] unique - **3.** [precio, función, razón] single.

unicornio *m* unicorn.

unidad *f* - **1.** [gen, MAT & MIL] unit; **25 euros la ~** 25 euros each; ~ **central de proceso** INFORM central processing unit; ~ **de disco** INFORM disk drive; ~ **monetaria** monetary unit - **2.** [cohesión, acuerdo] unity.

unido, da *adj* united; [familia, amigo] close.

unifamiliar *adj* detached; **vivienda ~ house** *(detached or terraced)*.

unificar *vt* - **1.** [unir] to unite, to join; [países] to unify - **2.** [uniformar] to standardize.

uniformar *vt* - **1.** [igualar] to standardize - **2.** [poner uniforme] to put into uniform.

uniforme ◇ *adj* uniform; [superficie] even. ◇ *m* uniform.

uniformidad *f* uniformity; [de superficie] evenness.

unión *f* - **1.** [gen] union; **en ~ de** together with - **2.** [suma, adherimiento] joining together - **3.** TECN join, joint.

Unión Económica y Monetaria *f* Economic and Monetary Union.

Unión Europea *f*: **la ~** the European Union.

unir *vt* - **1.** [pedazos, habitaciones etc] to join - **2.** [empresas, estados, facciones] to unite - **3.** [comunicar - ciudades etc] to link - **4.** [suj: amistad, circunstancias etc] to bind - **5.** [casar] to join, to marry - **6.** [combinar] to combine; ~ **algo a algo** to combine sthg with sthg - **7.** [mezclar] to mix *o* blend in.

  ◆ **unirse** *vpr* - **1.** [gen] to join together; ~**se a algo** to join sthg - **2.** [casarse]: ~**se en matrimonio** to be joined in wedlock.

unisexo, unisex *adj inv* unisex.

unísono ◆ **al unísono** *loc adv* in unison.

unitario, ria *adj* - **1.** [de una unidad - estado, nación] single; [- precio] unit' *(antes de sust)* - **2.** POLÍT unitarian.

universal *adj* - **1.** [gen] universal - **2.** [mundial] world *(antes de sust)*.

universidad *f* university, college *US*, school *US*.

universitario, ria ◇ *adj* university *(antes de sust)*. ◇ *m,f* [estudiante] university student.

universo *m* - **1.** ASTRON universe - **2.** *fig* [mundo] world.

unívoco, ca *adj* univocal, unambiguous.

uno, una ◇ *adj antes de sust masculino sg: un* - **1.** [indefinido] one; **un día volveré** one o some day I'll return; **había ~s coches mal aparcados** there were some badly parked cars; **había ~s 12 muchachos** there were about o some 12 boys there - **2.** [numeral] one; **un hombre, un voto** one man, one vote; **la fila ~** row one. ◇ *pron* - **1.** [indefinido] one; **coge ~** take one; **~ de vosotros** one of you; **~s ... otros ...** some ... others ...; **~ a otro, ~s a otros** each other, one another; **~ y otro** both; **~s y otros** all of them - **2.** *fam* [cierta persona] someone, somebody; **hablé con ~ que te conoce** I spoke to someone who knows you; **me lo han contado ~s** certain people told me so - **3.** [yo] one; **~ ya no está para estos trotes** one isn't really up to this sort of thing any more - **4.** *loc:* **a una** [en armonía, a la vez] together; **de ~ en ~, ~ a ~, ~ por ~** one by one; **juntar varias cosas en una** to combine several things into one; **lo ~ por lo otro** it all evens out in the end; **más de ~** many people; **una de dos** it's either one thing or the other; **~s cuantos a few; una y no más** once was enough, once bitten, twice shy.

 ◆ **uno** *m* [número] (number) one; **el ~** number one; *ver también* **seis**.

 ◆ **una** *f* [hora]: **la una** one o'clock.

untar *vt* - **1.** [pan, tostada]: **~ (con)** to spread (with); [piel, cara etc] to smear (with) - **2.** [máquina, bisagra etc] to grease, to oil.

untuoso, sa *adj* [graso] greasy, oily.

uña *f* - **1.** [de mano] fingernail, nail; **ser ~ y carne** to be as thick as thieves - **2.** [de pie] toenail - **3.** [garra] claw.

uralita® *f* CONSTR *material made of asbestos and cement, usually corrugated and used mainly for roofing.*

uranio *m* uranium.

Urano *m* Uranus.

urbanidad *f* politeness, courtesy.

urbanismo *m* town planning.

urbanización *f* - **1.** [acción] urbanization - **2.** [zona residencial] (housing) estate.

urbanizar *vt* to develop, to urbanize.

urbano, na *adj* urban, city *(antes de sust)*.

urbe *f* large city.

urdir *vt* - **1.** [planear] to plot, to forge - **2.** [hilos] to warp.

urgencia *f* - **1.** [cualidad] urgency - **2.** MED emergency; **de ~** emergency - **3.** [necesidad] urgent need; **en caso de ~** in case of emergency.

 ◆ **urgencias** *fpl* MED casualty (department) *(sg)*; **ingresar por ~s** to be admitted as an emergency.

urgente *adj* - **1.** [apremiante] urgent - **2.** MED emergency *(antes de sust)* - **3.** [correo] express.

urgir *vi* to be urgently necessary; **me urge hacerlo** I urgently need to do it; **~ a alguien a que haga algo** to urge sb to do sthg.

urinario, ria *adj* urinary.

 ◆ **urinario** *m* urinal, comfort station *US*.

URL *(abrev de uniform resource locator) f* INFORM URL.

urna *f* - **1.** [vasija] urn - **2.** [caja de cristal] glass case - **3.** [para votar] ballot box.

urraca *f* magpie.

URSS *(abrev de Unión de Repúblicas Socialistas Soviéticas) f* USSR.

urticaria *f* nettle rash.

Uruguay: **(el) ~** Uruguay.

uruguayo, ya *adj & m,f* Uruguayan.

usado, da *adj* - **1.** [utilizado] used; **muy ~** widely-used - **2.** [de segunda mano] second-hand - **3.** [gastado] worn-out, worn.

usanza *f* custom, usage; **a la vieja ~** in the old way o style.

usar *vt* - **1.** [gen] to use; **~ algo/a alguien de** o **como algo** to use sthg/sb as sthg - **2.** [prenda] to wear.

 ◆ **usarse** *vpr* - **1.** [emplearse] to be used - **2.** [estar de moda] to be worn.

USB *(abrev de Universal Serial Bus) m* INFORM USB.

usina *f Amér:* **~ eléctrica** power station; **~ nuclear** nuclear power station.

uso *m* - **1.** [gen] use; **al ~** fashionable; **al ~ andaluz** in the Andalusian style; **'de ~ externo'** FARM 'for external use only' - **2.** *(gen pl)* [costumbre] custom - **3.** LING usage - **4.** [desgaste] wear and tear.

usted *pron pers* - **1.** [tratamiento de respeto - sg] you; [- pl]: **~es** you *(pl)*; **contesten ~es a las preguntas** please answer the questions; **me gustaría hablar con ~** I'd like to talk to you; **¡oiga, ~!** hey, you!; **tratar a alguien de ~** *to address sb using the 'usted' form* - **2.** [tratamiento de respeto - posesivo]: **de ~/~es** yours.

usual *adj* usual.

usuario, ria *m,f* user.

usufructo *m* DER usufruct, use.

usura *f* usury.

usurero, ra *m,f* usurer.

usurpar *vt* to usurp.

utensilio *m* [gen] tool, implement; CULIN utensil; **~s de pesca** fishing tackle.

útero *m* womb, uterus.

útil ◇ *adj* [beneficioso, aprovechable] useful. ◇ *m (gen pl)* [herramienta] tool; **~es de**

jardinería gardening tools; AGR implement; ~es de labranza agricultural implements.

utilidad f - **1.** [cualidad] usefulness - **2.** [beneficio] profit.

utilitario, ria adj AUTOM run-around, utility.
◆ **utilitario** m AUTOM run-around car, utility car, compact US.

utilización f use.

utilizar vt [gen] to use.

utopía f utopia.

utópico, ca adj utopian.

uva f grape; ~ **de mesa** dessert grape; ~ **moscatel** muscatel grape; ~ **pasa** raisin; **estar de mala** ~ to be in a bad mood; **tener mala** ~ to be a bad sort, to be a nasty piece of work; ~**s de la suerte** grapes eaten for good luck as midnight chimes on New Year's Eve.

UVI (abrev de **unidad de vigilancia intensiva**) f ICU.

uy interj ahh!, oh!

v, V ['uβe] f [letra] v, V.
◆ **v doble** f W.

v. = vid.

va ⊳ **ir.**

vaca f - **1.** [animal] cow; **ponerse como una** ~ to put on a lot of weight - **2.** [carne] beef.

vacaciones fpl holiday (sg), holidays UK, vacation (sg) US; **estar/irse de** ~ to be/go on holiday.

vacacionista mf Méx tourist.

vacante ⟨⟩ adj vacant. ⟨⟩ f vacancy.

vaciar vt - **1.** [gen]: ~ **algo (de)** to empty sthg (of) - **2.** [dejar hueco] to hollow (out) - **3.** ARTE to cast, to mould.

vacilación f - **1.** [duda] hesitation; [al elegir] indecision - **2.** [oscilación] swaying; [de la luz] flickering.

vacilante adj - **1.** [gen] hesitant; [al elegir] indecisive - **2.** [luz] flickering; [pulso] irregular; [paso] swaying, unsteady.

vacilar vi - **1.** [dudar] to hesitate; [al elegir] to be indecisive - **2.** [voz, principios, régimen] to falter - **3.** [fluctuar - luz] to flicker; [- pulso] to be irregular - **4.** [tambalearse] to wobble, to sway - **5.** fam [chulear] to swank, to show off - **6.** fam [bromear] to take the mickey.

vacilón, ona fam m, f - **1.** [chulo] show-off - **2.** [bromista] tease.
◆ **vacilón** m CAm, Carib, Méx [fiesta] party.

vacío, a adj empty.
◆ **vacío** m - **1.** FÍS vacuum; **envasar al** ~ to vacuum-pack; ~ **de poder** power vacuum - **2.** [abismo, carencia] void - **3.** [hueco] space, gap.

vacuna f vaccine; **poner una** ~ **a alguien** to vaccinate sb.

vacunar vt to vaccinate; ~ **contra algo** to vaccinate against sthg.

vacuno, na adj bovine.

vadear vt to ford; fig to overcome.

vado m - **1.** [en acera] lowered kerb; '~ **permanente**' 'keep clear' - **2.** [de río] ford.

vagabundear vi [vagar]: ~ **(por)** to wander, to roam.

vagabundo, da ⟨⟩ adj [persona] vagrant; [perro] stray. ⟨⟩ m, f tramp, vagrant, bum US.

vagancia f - **1.** [holgazanería] laziness, idleness - **2.** [vagabundeo] vagrancy.

vagar vi: ~ **(por)** to wander, to roam.

vagina f vagina.

vago, ga adj - **1.** [perezoso] lazy, idle - **2.** [impreciso] vague.

vagón m [de pasajeros] carriage, car US; [de mercancías] wagon.

vagoneta f wagon.

vaguedad f - **1.** [cualidad] vagueness - **2.** [dicho] vague remark.

vahído m blackout, fainting fit.

vaho m - **1.** [vapor] steam - **2.** [aliento] breath.

vaina f - **1.** [gen] sheath - **2.** [BOT - envoltura] pod - **3.** Amér fam [engreído] pain in the neck; **¡qué** ~ **!** Col, Perú, Ven fam what a pain! - **4.** Col, Perú & Ven [problema] pain - **5.** Col, Perú & Ven [cosa] thing.

vainilla f vanilla.

vaivén m - **1.** [balanceo - de barco] swaying, rocking; [- de péndulo, columpio] swinging - **2.** [altibajo] ups-and-downs (pl).

vajilla f crockery; **una** ~ a dinner service.

vale ⟨⟩ m - **1.** [bono] coupon, voucher - **2.** [comprobante] receipt - **3.** [pagaré] I.O.U. - **4.** Méx, Ven fam [amigo] pal, mate UK, buddy US. ⟨⟩ interj ⊳ **valer.**

valedero, ra adj valid.

valenciano, na adj & m, f [de Valencia] Valencian.

valentía f [valor] bravery.

valer vt - **1.** [costar - precio] to cost; [tener un valor de] to be worth; **¿cuánto vale?** [de precio] how much does it cost?, how much is it? - **2.** [ocasionar] to earn - **3.** [merecer] to deserve, to be worth - **4.** [equivaler] to be equivalent *o* equal to. ◇ *vi* - **1.** [merecer aprecio] to be worthy; **hacerse** ~ to show one's worth - **2.** [servir]: ~ **para algo** to be for sthg; **eso aún vale** you can still use that; **¿para qué vale?** what's it for? - **3.** [ser válido] to be valid; [en juegos] to be allowed - **4.** [ayudar] to help, to be of use - **5.** [tener calidad] to be of worth; **no** ~ **nada** to be worthless *o* useless - **6.** [equivaler]: ~ **por** to be worth - **7.** *loc*: **más vale tarde que nunca** better late than never; **más vale que te calles/vayas** it would be better if you shut up/left; **¿vale?** okay?, all right?; **¡vale!** okay!, all right!

◆ **valerse** *vpr* - **1.** [servirse]: ~**se de algo/ alguien** to use sthg/sb - **2.** [desenvolverse]: ~**se (por sí mismo)** to manage on one's own - **3.** *loc Méx*: **¡no se vale!** that's not fair!

valeroso, sa *adj* brave, courageous.

valía *f* value, worth.

validar *vt* to validate.

validez *f* validity; **dar** ~ **a** to validate.

válido, da *adj* valid.

valiente *adj* [valeroso] brave.

valija *f* - **1.** [maleta] case, suitcase; ~ **diplo- mática** diplomatic bag - **2.** [de correos] mail- bag.

valioso, sa *adj* - **1.** [gen] valuable - **2.** [inten- to, esfuerzo] worthy.

valla *f* - **1.** [cerca] fence - **2.** DEP hurdle.

◆ **valla publicitaria** *f* billboard, hoard- ing.

vallar *vt* to put a fence round.

valle *m* valley.

valor *m* - **1.** [gen, MAT & MÚS] value; **joyas por** ~ **de ...** jewels worth ...; **sin** ~ worthless - **2.** [importancia] importance; **dar** ~ **a** to give *o* attach importance to; **quitar** ~ **a al- go** to take away from sthg, to diminish the importance of sthg - **3.** [valentía] bravery.

◆ **valores** *mpl* - **1.** [principios] values - **2.** FIN securities, bonds; ~**es en cartera** in- vestments.

valoración *f* - **1.** [de precio, pérdidas] valua- tion - **2.** [de mérito, cualidad, ventajas] eval- uation, assessment.

valorar *vt* - **1.** [tasar, apreciar] to value - **2.** [evaluar] to evaluate, to assess.

vals (*pl* **valses**) *m* waltz.

válvula *f* valve.

◆ **válvula de escape** *f fig* means of let- ting off steam.

vampiresa *f fam* vamp, femme fatale.

vampiro *m* [personaje] vampire.

vanagloriarse *vpr*: ~ **(de)** to boast (about), to show off (about).

vandalismo *m* vandalism.

vanguardia *f* - **1.** MIL vanguard; **ir a la** ~ **de** *fig* to be at the forefront of - **2.** [cultural]

avant-garde, vanguard; **de** ~ avant- garde.

vanidad *f* - **1.** [orgullo] vanity - **2.** [inutilidad] futility.

vanidoso, sa *adj* vain, conceited.

vano, na *adj* - **1.** [gen] vain; **en** ~ in vain - **2.** [vacío, superficial] shallow, superficial.

vapor *m* - **1.** [emanación] vapour; [de agua] steam; **al** ~ CULIN steamed; **de** ~ [máquina etc] steam *(antes de sust)*; **a todo** ~ at full speed; ~ **de agua** FÍS & QUÍM water vapour - **2.** [barco] steamer, steamship.

vaporizador *m* - **1.** [pulverizador] spray - **2.** [para evaporar] vaporizer.

vaporoso, sa *adj* [fino - tela etc] diapha- nous, sheer.

vapulear *vt* to beat, to thrash; *fig* to slate, to tear apart.

vaquero, ra ◇ *adj* cowboy *(antes de sust)*. ◇ *m,f* [persona] cowboy (*f* cowgirl), cow- herd.

◆ **vaqueros** *mpl* [pantalón] jeans.

vara *f* - **1.** [rama, palo] stick - **2.** [de metal etc] rod - **3.** [insignia] staff.

variable *adj* changeable, variable.

variación *f* variation; [del tiempo] change.

variado, da *adj* varied; [galletas, bombones] assorted.

variante ◇ *adj* variant. ◇ *f* - **1.** [variación] variation; [versión] version - **2.** AUTOM by- pass.

variar ◇ *vt* - **1.** [modificar] to alter, to change - **2.** [dar variedad] to vary. ◇ *vi* [cam- biar]: **para** ~ *irón* (just) for a change.

varicela *f* chickenpox.

varicoso, sa *adj* varicose.

variedad *f* variety.

◆ **variedades** *fpl* TEATR variety (*U*), music hall (*U*).

varilla *f* - **1.** [barra larga] rod, stick - **2.** [tira larga - de abanico, paraguas] spoke, rib; [- de gafas] arm; [- de corsé] bone, stay.

vario, ria *adj* [variado] varied, different; *(pl)* various, several.

◆ **varios, rias** *pron pl* several.

variopinto, ta *adj* diverse.

varita *f* wand; ~ **mágica** magic wand.

variz *(gen pl)* *f* varicose vein.

varón *m* [hombre] male, man; [chico] boy.

varonil *adj* masculine, male.

Varsovia Warsaw.

vasallo, lla *m,f* [siervo] vassal.

vasco, ca *adj* & *m,f* Basque.

◆ **vasco** *m* [lengua] Basque.

vascuence *m* [lengua] Basque.

vasectomía *f* vasectomy.

vaselina® *f* Vaseline®.

vasija *f* vessel.

vaso *m* - **1.** [recipiente, contenido] glass; **un**

~ **de plástico** a plastic cup - **2.** ANAT vessel; ~**s sanguíneos** blood vessels.

vástago *m* - **1.** [descendiente] offspring *(U)* - **2.** [brote] shoot - **3.** [varilla] rod.

vasto, ta *adj* vast.

váter = **wáter.**

vaticinar *vt* to prophesy, to predict.

vatio, watio ['batio] *m* watt.

vaya ◇ ▷ **ir.** ◇ *interj* - **1.** [sorpresa] well! - **2.** [énfasis]: ¡~ **moto!** what a motorbike!

VB *abrev de* **visto bueno.**

Vd. = **Ud.**

Vda. *abrev de* **viuda.**

Vds. = **Uds.**

ve ▷ **ir.**

véase ▷ **ver.**

vecinal *adj* [camino, impuestos] local.

vecindad *f* - **1.** [vecindario] neighbourhood - **2.** [alrededores] vicinity - **3.** *Méx* [vivienda] tenement house.

vecindario *m* [de barrio] neighbourhood; [de población] community, inhabitants *(pl).*

vecino, na ◇ *adj* [cercano] neighbouring. ◇ *m,f* - **1.** [de la misma casa, calle] neighbour; [de un barrio] resident - **2.** [de una localidad] inhabitant.

vector *m* vector.

veda *f* - **1.** [prohibición] ban *(on hunting and fishing)*; **levantar la** ~ to open the season - **2.** [periodo] close season.

vedado, da *adj* prohibited.

➡ **vedado** *m* reserve.

vedar *vt* to prohibit.

vedette [be'ðet] *(pl* **vedettes)** *f* star.

vegetación *f* vegetation.

vegetal ◇ *adj* - **1.** BIOL vegetable, plant *(antes de sust)* - **2.** [sandwich] salad *(antes de sust).* ◇ *m* vegetable.

vegetar *vi* to vegetate.

vegetariano, na *adj & m,f* vegetarian.

vehemencia *f* [pasión, entusiasmo] vehemence.

vehemente *adj* [apasionado, entusiasta] vehement.

vehículo *m* [gen] vehicle; [de infección] carrier.

veinte *núm* twenty; **los (años)** ~ the twenties; *ver también* **seis.**

veinteavo, va *núm* twentieth.

veintena *f* - **1.** [veinte] twenty - **2.** [aproximadamente]: **una** ~ **(de)** about twenty.

vejación *f*, **vejamen** *m* humiliation.

vejestorio *m despec* old fogey.

vejez *f* old age.

vejiga *f* bladder.

vela *f* - **1.** [para dar luz] candle; **¿quién le ha dado** ~ **en este entierro?** who asked you to stick your oar in?; **estar a dos** ~**s** not to

have two halfpennies to rub together - **2.** [de barco] sail - **3.** DEP sailing; **hacer** ~ to go sailing - **4.** [vigilia] vigil; **pasar la noche en** ~ [adrede] to stay awake all night; [desvelado] to have a sleepless night.

velada *f* evening.

velado, da *adj* - **1.** [oculto] veiled, hidden - **2.** FOT fogged.

velar ◇ *vi* - **1.** [cuidar]: ~ **por** to look after, to watch over - **2.** [no dormir] to stay awake. ◇ *vt* - **1.** [de noche - muerto] to keep a vigil over - **2.** [ocultar] to mask, to veil.

➡ **velarse** *vpr* FOT to get fogged.

veleidad *f* - **1.** [inconstancia] fickleness, capriciousness - **2.** [antojo, capricho] whim, caprice.

velero *m* sailing boat/ship.

veleta *f* weather vane.

vello *m* - **1.** [pelusilla] down - **2.** [pelo] hair; ~ **púbico** pubic hair.

velloso, sa *adj* hairy.

velo *m lit & fig* veil.

velocidad *f* - **1.** [gen] speed; TECN velocity; **cobrar** ~ to pick up speed; **perder** ~ to lose speed; ~ **máxima** top speed; **a toda** ~ at full speed; **de alta** ~ high-speed; ~ **punta** top speed - **2.** AUTOM [marcha] gear; **cambiar de** ~ to change gear.

velocímetro *m* speedometer.

velódromo *m* cycle track, velodrome.

veloz *adj* fast, quick.

ven ▷ **venir.**

vena *f* - **1.** [gen, ANAT & MIN] vein - **2.** [inspiración] inspiration - **3.** [don] vein, streak; **tener** ~ **de algo** to have a gift for doing sthg.

venado *m* ZOOL deer; CULIN venison.

vencedor, ra ◇ *adj* winning, victorious. ◇ *m,f* winner.

vencer ◇ *vt* - **1.** [ganar] to beat, to defeat - **2.** [derrotar - suj: sueño, cansancio, emoción] to overcome - **3.** [aventajar]: ~ **a alguien** **a** o **en algo** to outdo sb at sthg - **4.** [superar - miedo, obstáculos] to overcome; [- tentación] to resist. ◇ *vi* - **1.** [ganar] to win, to be victorious - **2.** [caducar - garantía, contrato, plazo] to expire; [- deuda, pago] to fall due, to be payable; [- bono] to mature - **3.** [prevalecer] to prevail.

➡ **vencerse** *vpr* [estante etc] to give way, to collapse.

vencido, da *adj* - **1.** [derrotado] defeated; **darse por** ~ to give up - **2.** [caducado - garantía, contrato, plazo] expired; [- pago, deuda] due, payable.

vencimiento *m* [término - de garantía, contrato, plazo] expiry; [- de pago, deuda] falling due.

venda *f* bandage; ~ **de gasa** gauze bandage.

vendaje *m* bandaging; **poner un** ~ to put on a dressing.

vendar *vt* to bandage; ~ **los ojos a alguien** to blindfold sb.

vendaval *m* gale.

vendedor, ra *m,f* [gen] seller; [en tienda] shop O sales assistant; [de coches, seguros] salesman (*f* saleswoman).

vender *vt lit* & *fig* to sell; ~ **algo a** O **por** to sell sthg for.

◆ **venderse** *vpr* - **1.** [ser vendido] to be sold O on sale; **'se vende'** 'for sale' - **2.** [dejarse sobornar] to sell o.s., to be bribed.

vendimia *f* grape harvest.

vendrá *etc* ⊳ **venir**.

veneno *m* [gen] poison; [de serpiente, insecto] venom.

venenoso, sa *adj* - **1.** [gen] poisonous - **2.** *fig* [malintencionado] venomous.

venerable *adj* venerable.

venerar *vt* to venerate, to worship.

venéreo, a *adj* venereal.

venezolano, na *adj* & *m,f* Venezuelan.

Venezuela Venezuela.

venga *interj* come on!

venganza *f* vengeance, revenge.

vengar *vt* to avenge.

◆ **vengarse** *vpr*: ~**se (de)** to take revenge (on), to avenge o.s. (on).

vengativo, va *adj* vengeful, vindictive.

vengo ⊳ **venir**.

venia *f* - **1.** [permiso] permission - **2.** DER [perdón] pardon.

venial *adj* petty, venial.

venida *f* [llegada] arrival.

venidero, ra *adj* coming, future.

venir ◇ *vi* - **1.** [gen] to come; ~ **a/de hacer algo** to come to do sthg/from doing sthg; ~ **de algo** [proceder, derivarse] to come from sthg; **no me vengas con exigencias** don't come to me making demands; ~ **a por algo** to come to pick up sthg; **el año que viene** next year - **2.** [llegar] to arrive; **vino a las doce** he arrived at twelve o'clock - **3.** [hallarse] to be; **su foto viene en primera página** his photo is O appears on the front page; **el texto viene en inglés** the text is in English - **4.** [acometer, sobrevenir]: **me viene sueño** I'm getting sleepy; **le vinieron ganas de reír** he was seized by a desire to laugh; **le vino una tremenda desgracia** he suffered a great misfortune - **5.** [ropa, calzado]: ~ **a alguien** to fit sb; **¿qué tal te viene?** does it fit all right?; **el abrigo le viene pequeño** the coat is too small for her - **6.** [convenir]: ~ **bien/mal a alguien** to suit/not to suit sb - **7.** [aproximarse]: **viene a costar un millón** it costs almost a million - **8.** *loc*: **¿a qué viene esto?** what do you mean by that?, what's

that in aid of?; ~ **a menos** [negocio] to go downhill; [persona] to go down in the world; ~ **a parar en** to end in; ~ **a ser** to amount to. ◇ *v aux* - **1.** *(antes de gerundio)* [haber estado]: ~ **haciendo algo** to have been doing sthg - **2.** *(antes de participio)* [estar]: **los cambios vienen motivados por la presión de la oposición** the changes have resulted from pressure on the part of the opposition - **3.** *(antes de infinitivo)* [estar]: **esto viene a costar unos veinte euros** it costs almost twenty euros.

◆ **venirse** *vpr* - **1.** [volver]: ~**se (de)** to come back O return (from) - **2.** *loc*: ~**se abajo** [techo, estante etc] to collapse; [ilusiones] to be dashed.

venta *f* - **1.** [acción] sale, selling; **estar en** ~ to be for sale; ~ **al contado** cash sale; ~ **a plazos** sale by instalments - **2.** *(gen pl)* [cantidad] sales *(pl)*.

ventaja *f* - **1.** [hecho favorable] advantage - **2.** [en competición] lead; **llevar** ~ **a alguien** to have a lead over sb. ▱

ventajoso, sa *adj* advantageous.

ventana *f* [gen & INFORM] window.

ventanilla *f* - **1.** [de vehículo, sobre] window - **2.** [taquilla] counter.

ventilación *f* ventilation.

ventilador *m* ventilator, fan.

ventilar *vt* - **1.** [airear] to air - **2.** [resolver] to clear up - **3.** [discutir] to air.

◆ **ventilarse** *vpr* [airearse] to air.

ventiscar, ventisquear *v impers* to blow a blizzard.

ventisquero *m* [nieve amontonada] snowdrift.

ventolera *f* [viento] gust of wind.

ventosa *f* [gen & ZOOL] sucker.

ventosidad *f* wind, flatulence.

ventoso, sa *adj* windy.

ventrílocuo, cua *m,f* ventriloquist.

ventura *f* - **1.** [suerte] luck; **a la (buena)** ~ [al azar] at random, haphazardly; [sin nada previsto] without planning O a fixed plan; **por** ~ *fml* luckily - **2.** [casualidad] fate, fortune.

Venus Venus.

ver ◇ *vi* - **1.** [gen] to see - **2.** *loc*: **a** ~ [veamos] let's see; **¿a** ~? [mirando con interés] let me see, let's have a look; **¡a** ~! [¡pues claro!] what do you expect?; [al empezar algo] right!; **dejarse** ~ **(por un sitio)** to show one's face (somewhere); **eso está por** ~ that remains to be seen; **verás, iba a ir pero ...** listen, I was thinking of coming but ...; **ya veremos** we'll see. ◇ *vt* - **1.** [gen] to see; [mirar] to look at; [televisión, partido de fútbol] to watch; **¿ves algo?** can you see anything?; **he estado viendo tu trabajo** I've been looking at your work; **ya veo que**

estás de mal humor I can see you're in a bad mood; **¿ves lo que quiero decir?** do you see what I mean?; **ir a ~ lo que pasa** to go and see what's going on; **es una manera de ~ las cosas** that's one way of looking at it; **yo no lo veo tan mal** I don't think it's that bad - **2.** *loc:* **eso habrá que ~lo** that remains to be seen; **¡hay que ~ qué lista es!** you wouldn't believe how clever she is!; **no puedo ~le (ni en pintura)** *fam* I can't stand him; **si no lo veo, no lo creo** you'll never believe it; **~ venir a alguien** to see what sb is up to. ◇ *m:* **estar de buen ~** to be good-looking.

◆ **verse** *vpr* - **1.** [mirarse, imaginarse] to see o.s.; **~se en el espejo** to see o.s. in the mirror - **2.** [percibirse]: **desde aquí se ve el mar** you can see the sea from here - **3.** [encontrarse] to meet, to see each other; **~se con alguien** to see sb; **hace mucho que no nos vemos** we haven't seen each other for a long time - **4.** [darse, suceder] to be seen - **5.** *loc:* **vérselas venir** *fam* to see it coming; **vérselas y deseárselas para hacer algo** to have a real struggle doing sthg.

◆ **véase** *vpr* [en textos] see.

◆ **por lo visto, por lo que se ve** *loc adv* apparently.

vera *f* - **1.** [orilla - de río, lago] bank; [- de camino] edge, side - **2.** *fig* [lado] side; **a la ~ de** next to.

veracidad *f* truthfulness.

veraneante *mf* holidaymaker, (summer) vacationer *US*.

veranear *vi*: **~ en** to spend one's summer holidays in.

veraneo *m* summer holidays *(pl)*; **de ~** holiday *(antes de sust)*.

veraniego, ga *adj* summer *(antes de sust)*.

verano *m* summer.

veras *fpl* truth *(U)*; **de ~** [verdaderamente] really; [en serio] seriously.

veraz *adj* truthful.

verbal *adj* verbal.

verbena *f* [fiesta] street party *(on the eve of certain saints' days)*.

verbo *m* GRAM verb.

verdad *f* - **1.** [gen] truth; **a decir ~** to tell the truth - **2.** [principio aceptado] fact - **3.** *loc:* **no te gusta, ¿~?** you don't like it, do you?; **está bueno, ¿~?** it's good, isn't it?

◆ **verdades** *fpl* [opinión sincera] true thoughts; **cantarle o decirle a alguien cuatro ~es** *fig* to tell sb a few home truths.

◆ **de verdad** ◇ *loc adv* - **1.** [en serio] seriously - **2.** [realmente] really. ◇ *loc adj* [auténtico] real.

verdadero, ra *adj* - **1.** [cierto, real] true, real; **fue un ~ lío** it was a real mess - **2.** [sin falsificar] real - **3.** [enfático] real.

verde ◇ *adj* - **1.** [gen] green; **estar ~ de envidia** to be green with envy; **poner ~ a alguien** to criticize sb - **2.** [fruta] unripe, green - **3.** *fig* [obsceno] blue, dirty - **4.** *fig* [inmaduro - proyecto etc] in its early stages. ◇ *m* [color] green.

◆ **Verdes** *mpl* [partido]: **los Verdes** the Greens.

verdor *m* [color] greenness.

verdugo *m* - **1.** [de preso] executioner; [que ahorca] hangman - **2.** [pasamontañas] balaclava helmet.

verdulería *f* greengrocer's (shop).

verdulero, ra *m,f* [tendero] greengrocer.

verdura *f* vegetables *(pl)*, greens *(pl)*.

vereda *f* - **1.** [senda] path - **2.** *CSur, Perú* [acera] pavement *UK*, sidewalk *US*.

veredicto *m* verdict.

vergonzoso, sa *adj* - **1.** [deshonroso] shameful - **2.** [tímido] bashful.

vergüenza *f* - **1.** [turbación] embarrassment; **dar ~** to embarrass; **¡qué ~!** how embarrassing!; **sentir ~** to feel embarrassed - **2.** [timidez] bashfulness - **3.** [remordimiento] shame; **sentir ~** to feel ashamed - **4.** [deshonra, escándalo] disgrace; **¡es una ~!** it's disgraceful!

verídico, ca *adj* [cierto] true, truthful.

verificar *vt* - **1.** [comprobar - verdad, autenticidad] to check, to verify - **2.** [examinar - funcionamiento, buen estado] to check, to test - **3.** [confirmar - fecha, cita] to confirm - **4.** [llevar a cabo] to carry out.

◆ **verificarse** *vpr* [tener lugar] to take place.

verja *f* - **1.** [puerta] iron gate; **la ~ de Gibraltar** *the border between Spain and Gibraltar* - **2.** [valla] railings *(pl)* - **3.** [enrejado] grille.

vermú *(pl* **vermús)**, **vermut** *(pl* **vermuts)** *m* - **1.** [bebida] vermouth - **2.** *Andes, RP* [en cine] early-evening showing; *Andes, RP* [en teatro] early-evening performance.

vernáculo, la *adj* vernacular.

verosímil *adj* - **1.** [creíble] believable, credible - **2.** [probable] likely, probable.

verruga *f* wart.

versado, da *adj*: **~ (en)** versed (in).

versar *vi*: **~ sobre** to be about, to deal with.

versátil *adj* - **1.** [voluble] changeable, fickle - **2.** *(considerado incorrecto)* [polifacético] versatile.

versículo *m* verse.

versión *f* [gen] version; [en música pop] cover version; **~ original** CIN original (version).

verso *m* - **1.** [género] verse - **2.** [unidad rítmica] line *(of poetry)* - **3.** [poema] poem.

vértebra *f* vertebra.

vertebrado, da *adj* vertebrate.

◆ **vertebrados** *mpl* ZOOL vertebrates.

vertedero *m* [de basuras] rubbish tip o dump; [de agua] overflow.

verter *vt* - **1.** [derramar] to spill - **2.** [vaciar - líquido] to pour (out); [- recipiente] to empty - **3.** [tirar - basura, residuos] to dump - **4.** *fig* [decir] to tell.
→ **verterse** *vpr* [derramarse] to spill.

vertical ◇ *adj* GEOM vertical; [derecho] upright. ◇ *f* GEOM vertical.

vértice *m* [gen] vertex; [de cono] apex.

vertido *m* - **1.** *(gen pl)* [residuo] waste *(U)* - **2.** [acción] dumping.

vertiente *f* - **1.** [pendiente] slope - **2.** *fig* [aspecto] side, aspect.

vertiginoso, sa *adj* - **1.** [mareante] dizzy - **2.** *fig* [raudo] giddy.

vértigo *m* [enfermedad] vertigo; [mareo] dizziness; **trepar me da** ~ climbing makes me dizzy.

vesícula *f*: ~ **biliar** gall bladder.

vespertino, na *adj* evening *(antes de sust)*.

vestíbulo *m* [de casa] (entrance) hall; [de hotel, oficina] lobby, foyer.

vestido, da *adj* dressed; **ir** ~ to be dressed; **iba** ~ **de negro** he was dressed in black.
→ **vestido** *m* - **1.** [indumentaria] clothes *(pl)* - **2.** [prenda femenina] dress; ~ **de noche** evening dress.

vestidura *(gen pl)* *f* clothes *(pl)*; RELIG vestments *(pl)*; **rasgarse las** ~**s** to make a fuss.

vestigio *m* vestige; *fig* sign, trace.

vestimenta *f* clothes *(pl)*, wardrobe.

vestir ◇ *vt* - **1.** [gen] to dress - **2.** [llevar puesto] to wear - **3.** [cubrir] to cover - **4.** *fig* [encubrir]: ~ **algo de** to invest sth with. ◇ *vi* - **1.** [llevar ropa] to dress - **2.** *fig* [estar bien visto] to be the done thing.
→ **vestirse** *vpr* - **1.** [ponerse ropa] to get dressed, to dress; ~**se de** to wear - **2.** [adquirir ropa]: ~**se en** to buy one's clothes at.

vestuario *m* - **1.** [vestimenta] clothes *(pl)*, wardrobe; TEATR costumes *(pl)* - **2.** [para cambiarse] changing room; [de actores] dressing room.

veta *f* - **1.** [filón] vein, seam - **2.** [faja, lista] grain.

vetar *vt* to veto.

veterano, na *adj & m,f* veteran.

veterinario, ria ◇ *adj* veterinary. ◇ *m,f* [persona] vet, veterinary surgeon.
→ **veterinaria** *f* [ciencia] veterinary science o medicine.

veto *m* veto; **poner** ~ **a algo** to veto sth.

vetusto, ta *adj culto* ancient, very old.

vez *f* - **1.** [gen] time; **una** ~ once; **dos veces** twice; **tres veces** three times; **¿has estado allí alguna** ~? have you ever been there?; **a la** ~ **(que)** at the same time (as); **cada** ~ **(que)** every time; **cada** ~ **más** more and more; **cada** ~ **menos** less and less; **cada** ~ **la veo más feliz** she seems happier and happier; **de una** ~ in one go; **de una** ~ **para siempre** o **por todas** once and for all; **muchas veces** often, a lot; **otra** ~ again; **pocas veces, rara** ~ rarely, seldom; **por última** ~ for the last time; **una** ~ **más** once again; **una y otra** ~ time and again; **érase una** ~ once upon a time - **2.** [turno] turn; **pedir la** ~ to ask who is last.
→ **a veces, algunas ·· ·es** *loc adv* sometimes, at times.
→ **de vez en cuando** *loc a.· ·m* time to time, now and again.
→ **en vez de** *loc prep* instead of.
→ **tal vez** *loc adv* perhaps, maybe.
→ **una vez que** *loc conj* once, after.

VHF *(abrev de* **very high frequency***)* *f* VHF.

VHS *(abrev de* **vídeo home system***)* *m* VHS.

vía ◇ *f* - **1.** [medio de transporte] route; **por** ~ **aérea** [gen] by air; [correo] (by) airmail; **por** ~ **marítima** by sea; **por** ~ **terrestre** overland, by land; ~ **fluvial** waterway - **2.** [calzada, calle] road; ~ **pública** public thoroughfare - **3.** [FERROC - raíl] rails *(pl)*, track; [- andén] platform - **4.** [proceso]: **estar en** ~**s de** to be in the process of; **país en** ~**s de desarrollo** developing country; **una especie en** ~**s de extinción** an endangered species - **5.** ANAT tract - **6.** [opción] channel, path; **por** ~ **oficial/judicial** through official channels/the courts - **7.** [camino] way; **dar** ~ **libre** [dejar paso] to give way; [dar libertad de acción] to give a free rein - **8.** DER procedure. ◇ *prep* via.
→ **Vía Láctea** *f* Milky Way.

viabilidad *f* viability.

viable *adj fig* [posible] viable.

viaducto *m* viaduct.

viajante *mf* travelling salesperson.

viajar *vi* - **1.** [trasladarse, irse]: ~ **(en)** to travel (by) - **2.** [circular] to run.

viaje *m* - **1.** [gen] journey, trip; [en barco] voyage; **¡buen** ~! have a good journey o trip!; **estar/ir de** ~ to be/go away (on a trip); **hay 11 días de** ~ it's an 11-day journey; ~ **de ida/de vuelta** outward/return journey; ~ **de ida y vuelta** return journey o trip; ~ **de negocios** business trip; ~ **de novios** honeymoon; ~ **organizado** package tour - **2.** *fig* [recorrido] trip.
→ **viajes** *mpl* [singladuras] travels.

viajero, ra ◇ *adj* [persona] travelling; [ave] migratory. ◇ *m,f* [gen] traveller; [en transporte público] passenger.

vial *adj* road *(antes de sust)*.

viandante *mf* - **1.** [peatón] pedestrian - **2.** [transeúnte] passer-by.

viario, ria *adj* road *(antes de sust)*.

víbora *f* viper.

vibración *f* vibration.

vibrante *adj* - **1.** [oscilante] vibrating - **2.** *fig* [emocionante] vibrant - **3.** [trémulo] quivering.

vibrar *vi* - **1.** [oscilar] to vibrate - **2.** *fig* [voz, rodillas etc] to shake - **3.** *fig* [público] to get excited.

vicaría *f* [residencia] vicarage.

vicario *m* vicar.

vicepresidente, ta *m,f* [de país, asociación] vice-president; [de comité, empresa] vice-chairman.

viceversa *adv* vice versa.

viciado, da *adj* [aire] stuffy; [estilo] marred.

viciar *vt* [pervertir] to corrupt.

➜ **viciarse** *vpr* [enviciarse] to take to vice.

vicio *m* - **1.** [mala costumbre] bad habit, vice - **2.** [libertinaje] vice - **3.** [defecto físico, de dicción etc] defect.

vicioso, sa ◇ *adj* dissolute, depraved. ◇ *m,f* dissolute person, depraved person.

vicisitud *f* [avatar] *(gen en pl)* vicissitude; **las ~ de la vida** life's ups and downs.

víctima *f* victim; [en accidente, guerra] casualty; **ser ~ de** to be the victim of.

victimar *vt* *Amér* to kill, to murder.

victimario, ria *m,f* *Amér* killer, murderer.

victoria *f* victory; **cantar ~** to claim victory.

victorioso, sa *adj* victorious.

vid *f* vine.

vid., v. *(abrev de* **véase**) v., vid.

vida *f* life; **de por ~** for life; **en ~ de** during the life *o* lifetime of; **en mi/tu** *etc* **~** never (in my/your *etc* life); **estar con ~** to be alive; **ganarse la ~** to earn a living; **pasar a mejor ~** to pass away; **pasarse la ~ haciendo algo** to spend one's life doing sthg; **perder la ~** to lose one's life; **quitar la ~ a alguien** to kill sb; **¡así es la ~!** that's life!, such is life!; **darse** *o* **pegarse la gran ~**, **darse** *o* **pegarse la ~ padre** to live the life of Riley.

vidente *mf* clairvoyant.

vídeo, video *m* - **1.** [gen] video; **grabar en ~** to videotape, to record on video - **2.** [aparato reproductor] video, VCR *US*.

videocámara *f* camcorder.

videocasete *m* video, videocassette.

videoclip *m* (pop) video.

videoclub *(pl* **videoclubes**) *m* video club.

videojuego *m* video game.

videotexto, videotex *m inv* [por señal de televisión] teletext; [por línea telefónica] videotext, viewdata.

vidriera *f* [puerta] glass door; [ventana]

glass window; [en catedrales] stained glass window.

vidrio *m* [material] glass.

vidrioso, sa *adj* - **1.** *fig* [tema, asunto] thorny, delicate - **2.** *fig* [ojos] glazed.

vieira *f* scallop.

viejo, ja ◇ *adj* old; **hacerse ~** to get *o* grow old. ◇ *m,f* - **1.** [anciano] old man (*f* old lady); **los ~s** the elderly; **~ verde** dirty old man (*f* dirty old woman) - **2.** *fam* [padres] old man (*f* old girl); **mis ~s** my folks - **3.** *Amér fam* [amigo] pal, mate.

➜ **Viejo de Pascua** *m Chile*: **Viejo de Pascua** *o* **Pascuero** Father Christmas.

Viena Vienna.

viene ▷ **venir**.

vienés, esa *adj & m,f* Viennese.

viento *m* - **1.** [aire] wind; **hace ~** it's windy; **~ de costado** *o* **de lado** crosswind - **2.** MÚS wind - **3.** *loc*: **contra ~ y marea** in spite of everything; **mis esperanzas se las llevó el ~** my hopes flew out of the window; **~ en popa** splendidly, very nicely.

vientre *m* ANAT stomach.

viera ▷ **ver**.

viernes *m inv* Friday; *ver también* **sábado**.

➜ **Viernes Santo** *m* RELIG Good Friday.

Vietnam Vietnam.

vietnamita *adj & m,f* Vietnamese.

viga *f* [de madera] beam, rafter; [de metal] girder.

vigencia *f* [de ley etc] validity; [de costumbre] use.

vigente *adj* [ley etc] in force; [costumbre] in use.

vigésimo, ma *núm* twentieth.

vigía *mf* lookout.

vigilancia *f* - **1.** [cuidado] vigilance, care; **estar bajo ~** to be under surveillance - **2.** [vigilantes] guards (*pl*).

vigilante ◇ *adj* vigilant. ◇ *mf* guard; **~ nocturno** night watchman.

vigilar ◇ *vt* [enfermo] to watch over; [presos, banco] to guard; [niños, bolso] to keep an eye on; [proceso] to oversee. ◇ *vi* to keep watch.

vigilia *f* [vela] wakefulness; **estar de ~** to be awake.

vigor *m* - **1.** [gen] vigour - **2.** [vigencia]: **entrar en ~** to come into force, to take effect.

vigorizar *vt* [fortalecer] to fortify.

vigoroso, sa *adj* [gen] vigorous, energetic.

vikingo, ga *adj & m,f* Viking.

vil *adj* vile, despicable; [metal] base.

vileza *f* - **1.** [acción] vile *o* despicable act - **2.** [cualidad] vileness.

villa *f* - **1.** [población] small town - **2.** [casa] villa, country house - **3.**: **~ miseria** *Arg, Bol* shanty town.

villancico *m* [navideño] Christmas carol.
villano, na *m,f* villain.
vilo ➡ **en vilo** *loc adv* - **1.** [suspendido] in the air, suspended - **2.** [inquieto] on tenterhooks; **tener a alguien en ~** to keep sb in suspense.
vinagre *m* vinegar.
vinagrera *f* [vasija] vinegar bottle.
➡ **vinagreras** *fpl* CULIN [convoy] cruet *(sg)*.
vinagreta *f* vinaigrette, French dressing.
vinculación *f* link, linking *(U)*.
vincular *vt* - **1.** [enlazar] to link; **~ algo con algo** to link sthg with 0 to sthg; [por obligación] to tie, to bind - **2.** DER to entail.
vínculo *m* [lazo - entre hechos, países] link; [- personal, familiar] tie, bond.
vinícola *adj* [país, región] wine-producing *(antes de sust)*; [industria] wine *(antes de sust)*.
vinicultura *f* wine producing.
vino <> ⊳ **venir.** <> *m* wine; **~ blanco/tinto** white/red wine; **~ dulce/seco** sweet/dry wine; **~ rosado** rosé.
viña *f* vineyard.
viñedo *m* (large) vineyard.
viñeta *f* - **1.** [de tebeo] (individual) cartoon - **2.** [de libro] vignette.
vio ⊳ **ver.**
viola *f* viola.
violación *f* - **1.** [de ley, derechos] violation, infringement - **2.** [de persona] rape.
violador, ra *adj & m,f* rapist.
violar *vt* - **1.** [ley, derechos, domicilio] to violate, to infringe - **2.** [persona] to rape.
violencia *f* - **1.** [agresividad] violence - **2.** [fuerza - de viento, pasiones] force - **3.** [incomodidad] embarrassment, awkwardness.
violentar *vt* - **1.** [incomodar] to embarrass, to cause to feel awkward - **2.** [forzar - cerradura] to force; [- domicilio] to break into.
➡ **violentarse** *vpr* [incomodarse] to get embarrassed, to feel awkward.
violento, ta *adj* - **1.** [gen] violent; [goce] intense - **2.** [incómodo] awkward.
violeta <> *f* [flor] violet. <> *adj inv & m* [color] violet.
violín *m* violin.
violón *m* double bass.
violonchelo, violoncelo *m* cello.
VIP *(abrev de* **very important person)** *mf* VIP.
viperino, na *adj fig* venomous.
viraje *m* - **1.** [giro - AUTOM] turn; [- NÁUT] tack - **2.** *fig* [cambio] change of direction.
virar <> *vt* [girar] to turn (round); NÁUT to tack, to put about. <> *vi* [girar] to turn (round).
virgen <> *adj* [gen] virgin; [cinta] blank;

[película] unused. <> *mf* [persona] virgin. <> *f* ARTE Madonna.
➡ **Virgen** *f*: **la Virgen** RELIG the (Blessed) Virgin; **¡Virgen santa!** good heavens!
virgo *m* [virginidad] virginity.
➡ **Virgo** <> *m* [zodiaco] Virgo. <> *mf* [persona] Virgo.
virguería *f fam* gem.
viril *adj* virile, manly.
virilidad *f* virility.
virtual *adj* - **1.** [posible] possible, potential - **2.** [casi real] virtual.
virtud *f* - **1.** [cualidad] virtue - **2.** [poder] power; **tener la ~ de** to have the power 0 ability to.
➡ **en virtud de** *loc prep* by virtue of.
virtuoso, sa <> *adj* [honrado] virtuous. <> *m,f* [genio] virtuoso.
viruela *f* - **1.** [enfermedad] smallpox - **2.** [pústula] pockmark; **picado de ~s** pockmarked.
virulé
➡ **a la virulé** *loc adj* - **1.** [torcido] crooked - **2.** [hinchado]: **un ojo a la ~** a black eye.
virulencia *f* MED & *fig* virulence.
virus *m inv* [gen & INFORM] virus.
viruta *f* shaving.
visa *f* Amér visa.
visado *m* visa.
víscera *f* internal organ; **~s** entrails.
visceral *adj* ANAT & *fig* visceral; **un sentimiento/una reacción ~** a gut feeling/reaction.
viscoso, sa *adj* [gen] viscous; [baboso] slimy.
➡ **viscosa** *f* [tejido] viscose.
visera *f* - **1.** [de gorra] peak - **2.** [de casco, suelta] visor - **3.** [de automóvil] sun visor.
visibilidad *f* visibility.
visible *adj* visible.
visigodo, da *m,f* Visigoth.
visillo *(gen pl) m* net/lace curtain.
visión *f* - **1.** [sentido, lo que se ve] sight - **2.** [alucinación, lucidez] vision; **ver visiones** to be seeing things - **3.** [punto de vista] (point of) view.
visionar *vt* to view privately.
visionario, ria *adj & m,f* visionary.
visita *f* - **1.** [gen] visit; [breve] call; **hacer una ~ a alguien** to visit sb, to pay sb a visit; **pasar ~** MED to see one's patients - **2.** [visitante] visitor; **tener 0 ~s** to have visitors - **3.** [a página web] hit.
visitante *mf* visitor.
visitar *vt* [gen] to visit; [suj: médico] to call on.
vislumbrar *vt* - **1.** [entrever] to make out, to discern - **2.** [adivinar] to have an inkling of.

➡ **vislumbrarse** *vpr* - **1.** [entreverse] to be barely visible - **2.** [adivinarse] to become a little clearer.

vislumbre *m o f lit* & *fig* glimmer.

viso *m* - **1.** [aspecto]: **tener ~s de** to seem; **tiene ~s de hacerse realidad** it could become a reality - **2.** [reflejo - de tejido] sheen; [- de metal] glint.

visón *m* mink.

víspera *f* [día antes] day before, eve; **en ~s de** on the eve of; **~ de festivo** day prior to a public holiday.

vista ⊳ **visto.**

vistazo *m* glance, quick look; **echar** *o* **dar un ~ a** to have a quick look at.

visto, ta ◇ *pp* ⊳ **ver.** ◇ *adj*: **estar bien/mal ~** to be considered good/frowned upon.

➡ **vista** ◇ *v* ⊳ **vestir.** ◇ *f* - **1.** [sentido] sight, eyesight; [ojos] **eyes** *(pl)* - **2.** [observación] watching - **3.** [mirada] gaze; **alzar/bajar la vista** to look up/down; **fijar la vista en** to fix one's eyes on, to stare at; **a primera** *o* **simple vista** [aparentemente] at first sight, on the face of it; **estar a la vista** [visible] to be visible; [muy cerca] to be staring one in the face - **4.** [panorama] view - **5.** DER hearing; **vista oral** hearing - **6.** *loc*: **conocer a alguien de vista** to know sb by sight; **hacer la vista gorda** to turn a blind eye; **¡hasta la vista!** see you!; **no perder de vista a alguien/algo** [vigilar] not to let sb/sthg out of one's sight; [tener en cuenta] not to lose sight of sb/sthg, not to forget about sb/sthg; **perder de vista** [dejar de ver] to lose sight of; [perder contacto] to lose touch with; **saltar a la vista** to be blindingly obvious.

➡ **vistas** *fpl* [panorama] view *(sg)*; **con vistas al mar** with a sea view.

➡ **visto bueno** *m*: **el ~ bueno** the go-ahead; '**~ bueno**' 'approved'.

➡ **a la vista** *loc adv* BANCA at sight.

➡ **con vistas a** *loc prep* with a view to.

➡ **en vista de** *loc prep* in view of, considering.

➡ **en vista de que** *loc conj* since, seeing as.

➡ **por lo visto** *loc adv* apparently.

➡ **visto que** *loc conj* seeing *o* given that.

vistoso, sa *adj* eye-catching.

visual ◇ *adj* visual. ◇ *f* line of sight.

visualizar *vt* - **1.** [gen] to visualize - **2.** INFORM to display.

vital *adj* [gen] vital; [ciclo] life *(antes de sust)*; [persona] full of life, vivacious.

vitalicio, cia *adj* for life, life *(antes de sust)*.

vitalidad *f* vitality.

vitamina *f* vitamin.

vitaminado, da *adj* with added vitamins, vitamin-enriched.

vitamínico, ca *adj* vitamin *(antes de sust)*.

viticultor, ra *m,f* wine grower, viticulturist.

viticultura *f* wine growing, viticulture.

vitorear *vt* to cheer.

vítreo, a *adj* vitreous.

vitrina *f* - **1.** [en casa] display cabinet; [en tienda] showcase, glass case - **2.** *Andes, Ven* [escaparate] (shop) window.

vitro ➡ **in vitro** *loc adv* in vitro.

vituperar *vt* to criticize harshly, to condemn.

viudedad *f* - **1.** [viudez - de mujer] widowhood; [- de hombre] widowerhood - **2.**: (**pensión de**) **~** widow's/widower's pension.

viudo, da *m,f* widower (*f* widow).

viva ◇ *m* cheer; **dar ~s** to cheer. ◇ *interj* hurrah!; **¡ ~ el rey!** long live the King!

vivac = **vivaque.**

vivacidad *f* liveliness.

vivales *m y f inv* crafty person.

vivamente *adv* - **1.** [relatar, describir] vividly - **2.** [afectar, emocionar] deeply.

vivaque, vivac *m* bivouac.

vivaz *adj* - **1.** [color, descripción] vivid - **2.** [persona, discusión, ojos] lively - **3.** [ingenio, inteligencia] alert, sharp.

vivencia *(gen pl) f* experience.

víveres *mpl* provisions, supplies.

vivero *m* - **1.** [de plantas] nursery - **2.** [de peces] fish farm; [de moluscos] bed.

viveza *f* - **1.** [de colorido, descripción] vividness - **2.** [de persona, discusión, ojos] liveliness; [de ingenio, inteligencia] sharpness.

vívido, da *adj* vivid.

vividor, ra *m,f despec* parasite, scrounger.

vivienda *f* - **1.** [alojamiento] housing - **2.** [morada] dwelling.

viviente *adj* living.

vivir ◇ *vt* [experimentar] to experience, to live through. ◇ *vi* [gen] to live; [estar vivo] to be alive; **~ para ver** who'd have thought it?

vivito *adj*: **~ y coleando** *fam* alive and kicking.

vivo, va *adj* - **1.** [existente - ser, lengua etc] living; **estar ~** [persona, costumbre, recuerdo] to be alive - **2.** [dolor, deseo, olor] intense; [luz, color, tono] bright - **3.** [gestos, ojos, descripción] lively, vivid - **4.** [activo - ingenio, niño] quick, sharp; [- ciudad] lively - **5.** [genio] quick, hot.

➡ **vivos** *mpl*: **los ~s** the living.

➡ **en vivo** *loc adv* [en directo] live.

Vizcaya Vizcaya; **Golfo de ~** Bay of Biscay.

vizconde, desa *m,f* viscount (*f* viscountess).

vocablo *m* word, term.

vocabulario *m* [riqueza léxica] vocabulary.

vocación *f* vocation, calling.

vocacional *adj* vocational.

vocal ⬦ *adj* vocal. ⬦ *f* vowel.

vocalizar *vi* to vocalize.

vocear ⬦ *vt* **-1.** [gritar] to shout *o* call out **-2.** [llamar] to shout *o* call to **-3.** [pregonar mercancía] to hawk. ⬦ *vi* [gritar] to shout.

vociferar *vi* to shout.

vodka ['boθka] *m o f* vodka.

vol. (*abrev de* **volumen**) vol.

volador, ra *adj* flying.

volandas ➡ **en volandas** *loc adv* in the air, off the ground.

volante ⬦ *adj* flying. ⬦ *m* **-1.** [para conducir] (steering) wheel **-2.** [de tela] frill, flounce **-3.** [del médico] (referral) note **-4.** [en bádminton] shuttlecock.

volar ⬦ *vt* [en guerras, atentados] to blow up; [caja fuerte, puerta] to blow open; [edificio en ruinas] to demolish *(with explosives)*; MIN to blast. ⬦ *vi* **-1.** [gen] to fly; [papeles etc] to blow away; ~ a [una altura] to fly at; [un lugar] to fly to; echar(se) a ~ to fly away *o* off **-2.** *fam* [desaparecer] to disappear, to vanish.

volátil *adj* QUÍM & *fig* volatile.

vol-au-vent = **volován**.

volcán *m* volcano.

volcánico, ca *adj* volcanic.

volcar ⬦ *vt* **-1.** [tirar] to knock over; [carretilla] to tip up **-2.** [vaciar] to empty out. ⬦ *vi* [coche, camión] to overturn; [barco] to capsize.

➡ **volcarse** *vpr* [esforzarse]: ~se (con/en) to bend over backwards (for/in).

volea *f* volley.

voleibol *m* volleyball.

voleo *m* volley; a *o* al ~ [arbitrariamente] randomly, any old how.

volován (*pl* **volovanes**), **vol-au-vent** [bolo'βan] (*pl* **vol-au-vents**) *m* vol-au-vent.

volquete *m* dumper truck, dump truck *US.*

voltaje *m* voltage.

voltear ⬦ *vt* **-1.** [heno, crepe, torero] to toss; [tortilla - con plato] to turn over; [mesa, silla] to turn upside-down **-2.** *Amér* [derribar] to knock over; *Andes, CAm, Carib, Méx* [volver] to turn. ⬦ *vi Méx* [torcer] to turn, to go round.

➡ **voltearse** *vpr Andes, CAm, Carib, Méx* [volverse] to turn around.

voltereta *f* [en el suelo] handspring; [en el aire] somersault; ~ lateral cartwheel.

voltio *m* volt.

voluble *adj* changeable, fickle.

volumen *m* **-1.** [gen & COM] volume; a todo

~ at full blast; ~ **de negocio** *o* **ventas** turnover **-2.** [espacio ocupado] size, bulk.

voluminoso, sa *adj* bulky.

voluntad *f* **-1.** [determinación] will, willpower; ~ **de hierro** iron will **-2.** [intención] intention; **buena** ~ goodwill; **mala** ~ ill will **-3.** [deseo] wishes *(pl)*, will; **contra la** ~ **de alguien** against sb's will **-4.** [albedrío] free will; **a** ~ [cuanto se quiere] as much as one likes; **por** ~ **propia** of one's own free will.

voluntariado *m* voluntary enlistment.

voluntario, ria ⬦ *adj* voluntary. ⬦ *m,f* volunteer.

voluntarioso, sa *adj* [esforzado] willing.

voluptuoso, sa *adj* voluptuous.

volver ⬦ *vt* **-1.** [dar la vuelta a] to turn round; [lo de arriba abajo] to turn over **-2.** [poner del revés - boca abajo] to turn upside down; [- lo de dentro fuera] to turn inside out; [- lo de detrás delante] to turn back to front **-3.** [cabeza, ojos etc] to turn **-4.** [convertir en]: eso le volvió un delincuente that made him a criminal, that turned him into a criminal. ⬦ *vi* [ir de vuelta] to go back, to return; [venir de vuelta] to come back from; ~ **atrás** to turn back; **yo allí no vuelvo** I'm not going back there; **vuelve, no te vayas** come back, don't go; ~ **en sí** to come to, to regain consciousness.

➡ **volver a** *vi* [reanudar] to return to; ~ **a hacer algo** [hacer otra vez] to do sthg again.

➡ **volverse** *vpr* **-1.** [darse la vuelta, girar la cabeza] to turn round **-2.** [ir de vuelta] to go back, to return; [venir de vuelta] to come back, to return **-3.** [convertirse en] to become; ~se **loco/pálido** to go mad/pale **-4.** *loc*: ~se **atrás** [de una afirmación, promesa] to go back on one's word; [de una decisión] to change one's mind, to back out; ~se (en) contra (de) alguien to turn against sb.

vomitar ⬦ *vt* [devolver] to vomit, to bring up. ⬦ *vi* to vomit, to be sick.

vómito *m* [substancia] vomit *(U).*

voraz *adj* **-1.** [persona, apetito] voracious **-2.** *fig* [fuego, enfermedad] raging.

vos *pron personal Amér* [tú - sujeto] you; [- objeto] you.

vosotros, tras *pron pers* you *(pl).*

votación *f* vote, voting *(U)*; **decidir algo por** ~ to put sthg to the vote; ~ **a mano alzada** show of hands.

votante *mf* voter.

votar ⬦ *vt* **-1.** [partido, candidato] to vote for; [ley] to vote on **-2.** [aprobar] to pass, to approve *(by vote).* ⬦ *vi* to vote; ~ **por** [emitir un voto por] to vote for; *fig* [estar a favor de] to be in favour of; **~ por que ...** to vote (that) ...; **~ en blanco** to return a blank ballot paper.

voto *m* -**1.** [gen] vote; **~ de confianza/censura** vote of confidence/no confidence -**2.** RELIG vow.

voy ▷ ir.

vóytelas *interj Amér fam* good grief!

voz *f* -**1.** [gen & GRAM] voice; **a media ~** in a low voice, under one's breath; **a ~ en cuello** o **grito** at the top of one's voice; **alzar** o **levantar la ~ a alguien** to raise one's voice to sb; **en ~ alta** aloud; **en ~ baja** softly, in a low voice; **~ en off** CIN voice-over; TEATR voice offstage -**2.** [grito] shout; **a voces** shouting; **dar voces** to shout -**3.** [vocablo] word -**4.** [derecho a expresarse] say, voice; **no tener ni ~ ni voto** to have no say in the matter.

VPO (*abrev de* **vivienda de protección oficial**) *f* ≃ council house/flat *UK*, ≃ public housing unit *US*.

vudú (*en aposición inv*) *m* voodoo.

vuelco *m* upset; **dar un ~** [coche] to overturn; [relaciones] to change completely; [empresa] to go to ruin; **me dio un ~ el corazón** my heart missed o skipped a beat.

vuelo *m* -**1.** [gen & AERON] flight; **alzar** o **emprender** o **levantar el ~** [despegar] to take flight, to fly off; *fig* [irse de casa] to fly the nest; **coger algo al ~** [en el aire] to catch sthg in flight; *fig* [rápido] to catch on to sthg very quickly; **remontar el ~** to soar; **~ chárter/regular** charter/scheduled flight; **~ libre** hang gliding; **~ sin motor** gliding -**2.** [de vestido] fullness; **una falda de ~** a full skirt.

vuelta *f* -**1.** [gen] turn; [acción] turning; **dar la ~ al mundo** to go around the world; **darse la ~** to turn round; **dar ~s (a algo)** [girándolo] to turn (sthg) round; **media ~** MIL about-turn; AUTOM U-turn -**2.** DEP lap; **~ (ciclista)** tour -**3.** [regreso, devolución] return; **billete de ida y ~** return ticket; **a la ~** [volviendo] on the way back; [al llegar] on one's return; **estar de ~** to be back -**4.** [paseo]: **dar una ~** to go for a walk -**5.** [dinero sobrante] change -**6.** [ronda, turno] round -**7.** [parte opuesta] back, other side; **a la ~ de la página** over the page -**8.** [cambio, avatar] change -**9.** *loc*: **a ~ de correo** by return of post; **dar la ~ a la tortilla** *fam* to turn the tables; **dar una ~/dos** *etc* **~s de campana** [coche] to turn over once/ twice *etc*; **darle ~s a algo** to turn sthg over in one's mind; **estar de ~ de algo** to be blasé about sthg; **no tiene ~ de hoja** there are no two ways about it.

vuelto, ta ◇ *pp* ▷ volver. ◇ *adj* turned.

◆ **vuelto** *m Amér* change.

vuestro, tra ◇ *adj* poses your; **~ libro/ amigo** your book/friend; **este libro es ~** this book is yours; **un amigo ~** a friend of yours; **no es asunto ~** it's none of your business. ◇ *pron poses*: **el ~** yours; **los ~s están en la mesa** yours are on the table; **lo ~ es el teatro** [lo que hacéis bien] you should be on the stage; **los ~s** *fam* [vuestra familia] your folks; [vuestro bando] your lot, your side.

vulgar *adj* -**1.** [no refinado] vulgar -**2.** [corriente, ordinario] ordinary, common; **~ y corriente** ordinary.

vulgaridad *f* -**1.** [grosería] vulgarity; **hacer/ decir una ~** to do/say sthg vulgar -**2.** [banalidad] banality.

vulgarizar *vt* to popularize.

vulgo *m despec*: **el ~** [plebe] the masses *(pl)*, the common people *(pl)*; [no expertos] the lay public *(U)*.

vulnerable *adj* vulnerable.

vulnerar *vt* -**1.** [prestigio etc] to harm, to damage -**2.** [ley, pacto etc] to violate, to break.

vulva *f* vulva.

w, W *f* [letra] w, W.

walkie-talkie ['walki'talki] (*pl* **walkie-talkies**) *m* walkie-talkie.

walkman® ['walkman] (*pl* **walkmans**) *m* Walkman®.

WAP (*abrev de* **wireless application protocol**) *m* WAP.

Washington ['waʃiŋton] Washington.

wáter ['bater] (*pl* **wáteres**), **váter** (*pl* **váteres**) *m* toilet.

waterpolo [water'polo] *m* water polo.

watio = vatio.

WC (*abrev de* **water closet**) *m* WC.

Web [web] *f*: **la (World Wide) ~** the (World Wide) Web.

whisky ['wiski] = güisqui.

windsurf ['winsurf], **windsurfing** ['winsurfin] *m* windsurfing.

WWW (*abrev de* **World Wide Web**) *f* WWW.

x, X *f* [letra] x, X.
➤ **X** *mf*: la señora X Mrs X.
xenofobia *f* xenophobia.
xilofón, xilófono *m* xylophone.

y¹, Y *f* [letra] y, Y.
y² *conj* **- 1.** [gen] and; **un ordenador** ∼ **una impresora** a computer and a printer; **horas** ∼ **horas de espera** hours and hours of waiting **- 2.** [pero] and yet; **sabía que no lo conseguiría** ∼ **seguía intentándolo** she knew she wouldn't manage it and yet she kept on trying **- 3.** [en preguntas] what about; **¿** ∼ **tu mujer?** what about your wife?
ya ◇ *adv* **- 1.** [en el pasado] already; ∼ **me lo habías contado** you had already told me; ∼ **en 1926** as long ago as 1926 **- 2.** [ahora] now; [inmediatamente] at once; **hay que hacer algo** ∼ something has to be done now/at once; **bueno, yo** ∼ **me voy** right, I'm off now; ∼ **no es así** it's no longer like that **- 3.** [en el futuro]: ∼ **te llamaré** I'll give you a ring some time; ∼ **hablaremos** we'll talk later; ∼ **nos habremos ido** we'll already have gone; ∼ **verás** you'll (soon) see **- 4.** [refuerza al verbo]: ∼ **entiendo/lo sé** I understand/know. ◇ *conj* [distributiva]: ∼ **(sea) por ...** ∼ **(sea) por ...** whether for ... or ... ◇ *interj* [expresa asentimiento] right!; [expresa comprensión] yes!; **¡** ∼ **,** ∼ **!** *irón* sure!, yes, of course!
➤ **ya no** *loc adv* : ∼ **no ... sino** not only ...,

but.
➤ **ya que** *loc conj* since; ∼ **que has venido, ayúdame con esto** since you're here, give me a hand with this.
yacer *vi* to lie.
yacimiento *m* **- 1.** [minero] bed, deposit; ∼ **de petróleo** oilfield **- 2.** [arqueológico] site.
yanqui *mf* **- 1.** HIST Yankee **- 2.** *fam* [estadounidense] *pejorative term referring to a person from the US,* yank.
yate *m* yacht.
yegua *f* mare.
yema *f* **- 1.** [de huevo] yolk **- 2.** [de planta] bud, shoot **- 3.** [de dedo] fingertip.
Yemen: (el) ∼ Yemen.
yen (*pl* **yenes**) *m* yen.
yerba ▷ **hierba**; ∼ **mate** *RP* yerba maté.
yerbatero *m Andes, Carib* [curandero] healer; [vendedor de hierbas] herbalist.
yermo, ma *adj* [estéril] barren.
yerno *m* son-in-law.
yeso *m* **- 1.** GEOL gypsum **- 2.** CONSTR plaster **- 3.** ARTE gesso.
yeyé (*pl* **yeyés**) *adj* sixties.
yo *pron pers* **- 1.** *(sujeto)* I; ∼ **me llamo Luis** I'm called Luis **- 2.** *(predicado)*: **soy** ∼ it's me **- 3.** *loc*: ∼ **que tú/él** *etc* if I were you/him *etc*.
yodo, iodo *m* iodine.
yoga *m* yoga.
yogur (*pl* **yogures**), **yogurt** (*pl* **yogurts**) *m* yoghurt.
yonqui *mf fam* junkie.
yóquey (*pl* **yóqueys**), **jockey** (*pl* **jockeys**) *m* jockey.
yoyó *m* yoyo.
yuca *f* **- 1.** BOT yucca **- 2.** CULIN cassava, manioc.
yudo, judo ['juðo] *m* judo.
yugo *m lit & fig* yoke.
Yugoslavia Yugoslavia.
yugoslavo, va ◇ *adj* Yugoslavian. ◇ *m,f* Yugoslav.
yugular *adj & f* jugular.
yunque *m* anvil.
yuppie (*pl* **yuppies**), **yuppi** *m y f* yuppie.
yuxtaponer *vt* to juxtapose.
yuxtaposición *f* juxtaposition.
yuxtapuesto, ta *pp* ▷ **yuxtaponer**.
yuyo *m CSur* [hierba medicinal] medicinal herb; [hierba mala] **weed**; [hierba silvestre] wild herb.

Z

z, Z f [letra] z, Z.

zacate m *CAm, Méx* fodder.

zafio, fia adj rough, uncouth.

zafiro m sapphire.

zaga f DEP defence; **a la ∼** behind, at the back; **no irle a la ∼ a alguien** to be every bit o just as good as sb.

zaguán m (entrance) hall.

Zaire Zaire.

zalamería *(gen pl)* f flattery *(U)*; **hacerle ∼s a alguien** to sweet talk sb.

zalamero, ra m,f flatterer; *despec* smooth talker.

zamarra f sheepskin jacket.

zambo, ba m,f knock-kneed person.

zambullir vt to dip, to submerge.

 ◆ **zambullirse** vpr: **∼se (en)** [agua] to dive (into); [actividad] to immerse o.s. (in).

zampar *fam* vi to gobble.

 ◆ **zamparse** vpr to scoff, to wolf down.

zanahoria f carrot.

zanca f [de ave] leg, shank.

zancada f stride.

zancadilla f trip; **poner una** o **la ∼ a alguien** [hacer tropezar] to trip sb up; [engañar] to trick sb.

zancadillear vt [hacer tropezar] to trip up.

zanco m stilt.

zancudo, da adj long-legged.

 ◆ **zancudo** m *Amér* mosquito.

zángano, na m,f *fam* [persona] lazy oaf, idler.

 ◆ **zángano** m [abeja] drone.

zanja f ditch.

zanjar vt [poner fin a] to put an end to; [resolver] to settle, to resolve.

zapallito m *CSur* [calabacín] courgette *UK*, zucchini *US*.

zapallo m *Andes, RP* [calabaza] pumpkin.

zapata f [de freno] shoe.

zapateado m *type of flamenco music and dance*.

zapatear vi to stamp one's feet.

zapatería f - **1.** [oficio] shoemaking - **2.** [taller] shoemaker's - **3.** [tienda] shoe shop.

zapatero, ra m,f - **1.** [fabricante] shoemaker

- **2.** [reparador]: **∼ (de viejo** o **remendón)** cobbler - **3.** [vendedor] shoe seller.

zapatilla f - **1.** [de baile] shoe, pump; [de estar en casa] slipper; [de deporte] sports shoe, trainer - **2.** [de grifo] washer.

zapato m shoe; **∼ de salón** court shoe; **∼ de tacón** high heeled shoe.

zapping ['θapin] m *inv* channel-hopping; **hacer ∼** to channel-hop.

zar, zarina m,f tsar (f tsarina), czar (f czarina).

zarandear vt - **1.** [cosa] to shake - **2.** [persona] to jostle, to knock about.

zarpa f [de animal - uña] claw; [- mano] paw.

zarpar vi to weigh anchor, to set sail; **∼ rumbo a** to set sail for.

zarpazo m clawing *(U)*.

zarza f bramble, blackberry bush.

zarzal m bramble patch.

zarzamora f blackberry.

zarzaparrilla f sarsaparilla.

zarzuela f MÚS zarzuela, *Spanish light opera*.

zas *interj* wham!, bang!

zenit, cenit m *lit & fig* zenith.

zepelín *(pl zepelines)* m zeppelin.

zigzag *(pl zigzags* o **zigzags)** m zigzag; **caminar en ∼** to walk in a zigzag.

zigzaguear vi to zigzag.

zinc = **cinc**.

zíper m *CAm, Méx, Ven* zip *UK*, zipper *US*.

zócalo m - **1.** [de pared] skirting board - **2.** [de edificio, pedestal] plinth.

zoco m souk, Arabian market.

zodiaco, zodíaco m zodiac.

zombi, zombie m,f *lit & fig* zombie.

zona f zone, area; **∼ azul** AUTOM restricted parking zone; **∼ de exclusión** exclusion zone; **∼ verde** [grande] park; [pequeño] lawn.

zoo m zoo.

zoología f zoology.

zoológico, ca adj zoological.

 ◆ **zoológico** m zoo.

zoólogo, ga m,f zoologist.

zopenco, ca *fam* m,f idiot, nitwit.

zoquete ◇ m *CSur* [calcetín] ankle sock. ◇ m,f [tonto] blockhead, idiot.

zorro, rra m,f *lit & fig* fox.

 ◆ **zorro** m [piel] fox (fur).

zozobra f anxiety, worry.

zozobrar vi - **1.** [naufragar] to be shipwrecked - **2.** *fig* [fracasar] to fall through.

zueco m clog.

zulo m hideout.

zulú *(pl zulúes)* adj m & m,f Zulu.

zumbar vi [gen] to buzz; [máquinas] to whirr, to hum; **me zumban los oídos** my ears are buzzing.

zumbido *m* [gen] buzz, buzzing *(U)*; [de máquinas] whirr, whirring *(U)*.

zumo *m* juice.

zurcido *m* **- 1.** [acción] darning **- 2.** [remiendo] darn.

zurcir *vt* to darn.

zurdo, da *adj* [mano etc] left; [persona] left-handed.

➡ **zurda** *f* [mano] left hand.

zurrar *vt* [pegar] to beat, to thrash.

zutano, na *m,f* so-and-so, what's-his-name (*f* what's-her-name).

ENGLISH-SPANISH
INGLÉS-ESPAÑOL

a¹ (*pl* **as** OR **a's**), **A** (*pl* **As** OR **A's**) [eɪ] *n* [letter] a *f*, A *f*.
➤ **A** *n* **- 1.** MUS la *m* **- 2.** SCH [mark] ≃ sobresaliente *m*.

a² [stressed eɪ, unstressed ə (*before vowel or silent 'h'* **an** [stressed æn, unstressed ən])] *indef art* **- 1.** [gen] un (una); **a boy** un chico; **a table** una mesa; **an orange** una naranja; **an eagle** un águila; **a hundred/thousand pounds** cien/mil libras **- 2.** [referring to occupation]: **to be a dentist/teacher** ser dentista/maestra **- 3.** [to express prices, ratios etc] por; **£10 a person** 10 libras por persona; **50 kilometres an hour** 50 kilómetros por hora; **20p a kilo** 20 peniques el kilo; **twice a week/month** dos veces a la semana/al mes.

AA *n* **- 1.** (*abbr of* **Automobile Association**) *asociación británica del automóvil*, ≃ RACE *m* **- 2.** (*abbr of* **Alcoholics Anonymous**) AA *mpl*.

AAA *n* (*abbr of* **American Automobile Association**) *asociación automovilística estadounidense*, ≃ RACE *m*.

aback [əˈbæk] *adv*: **to be taken ~** quedarse desconcertado(da).

abandon [əˈbændən] ◇ *vt* [gen] abandonar; [soccer, rugby match] suspender. ◇ *n*: **with ~** con desenfreno.

abashed [əˈbæʃt] *adj* avergonzado(da).

abate [əˈbeɪt] *vi* [storm] amainar; [noise] disminuir; [fear] apaciguarse.

abattoir [ˈæbətwɑːʳ] *n* matadero *m*.

abbey [ˈæbɪ] *n* abadía *f*.

abbot [ˈæbət] *n* abad *m*.

abbreviate [əˈbriːvɪeɪt] *vt* abreviar.

abbreviation [ə,briːvɪˈeɪʃn] *n* abreviatura *f*.

ABC *n lit & fig* abecé *m*.

abdicate [ˈæbdɪkeɪt] ◇ *vi* abdicar. ◇ *vt* [responsibility] abdicar de.

abdomen [ˈæbdəmen] *n* abdomen *m*.

abduct [əbˈdʌkt] *vt* raptar.

aberration [,æbəˈreɪʃn] *n* aberración *f*, anomalía *f*.

abet [əˈbet] (*pt & pp* **-ted**, *cont* **-ting**) *vt* ⊳ aid.

abeyance [əˈbeɪəns] *n*: **in ~** [custom] en desuso; [law] en suspenso.

abhor [əbˈhɔːʳ] (*pt & pp* **-red**, *cont* **-ring**) *vt* aborrecer.

abide [əˈbaɪd] *vt* soportar, aguantar.
➤ **abide by** *vt fus* [law, ruling] acatar; [principles, own decision] atenerse a.

ability [əˈbɪlətɪ] (*pl* **-ies**) *n* [capability] capacidad *f*, facultad *f*.

abject [ˈæbdʒekt] *adj* **- 1.** [poverty] vil, indigente **- 2.** [person] sumiso(sa); [apology] humillante.

ablaze [əˈbleɪz] *adj* [on fire] en llamas.

able [ˈeɪbl] *adj* **- 1.** [capable]: **to be ~ to do sthg** poder hacer algo; **to feel ~ to do sthg** sentirse capaz de hacer algo **- 2.** [skilful] capaz, competente.

ably [ˈeɪblɪ] *adv* competentemente.

abnormal [æbˈnɔːml] *adj* anormal.

aboard [əˈbɔːd] ◇ *adv* a bordo. ◇ *prep* [ship, plane] a bordo de; [bus, train] en.

abode [əˈbəʊd] *n fml*: **of no fixed ~** sin domicilio fijo.

abolish [əˈbɒlɪʃ] *vt* abolir.

abolition [,æbəˈlɪʃn] *n* abolición *f*.

abominable [əˈbɒmɪnəbl] *adj* abominable, deplorable.

aborigine [,æbəˈrɪdʒənɪ] *n* aborigen *m* OR *f* de Australia.

abort [əˈbɔːt] *vt* **- 1.** [pregnancy, plan, project] abortar; [pregnant woman] provocar el aborto a **- 2.** COMPUT abortar.

abortion [əˈbɔːʃn] *n* aborto *m*; **to have an ~** abortar.

abortive [əˈbɔːtɪv] *adj* frustrado(da), fracasado(da).

abound [əˈbaʊnd] *vi* **- 1.** [be plentiful] abundar **- 2.** [be full]: **to ~ with** OR **in** abundar en.

about [əˈbaʊt] ◇ *adv* **- 1.** [approximately] más o menos, como; **there were ~ fifty/a hundred** había (como) unos cincuenta/cien o así; **at ~ five o'clock** a eso de las cinco **- 2.** [referring to place] por ahí; **to leave things lying ~** dejar las cosas por ahí; **to walk ~** ir andando por ahí; **to jump ~** dar saltos **- 3.** [on the point of]: **to be ~ to do sthg** estar a punto de hacer algo. ◇ *prep*

- **1.** [relating to, concerning] sobre, acerca de; **a film** ~ **Paris** una película sobre París; **what is it** ~ ? ¿de qué trata?; **there's something odd** ~ **that man** hay algo raro en ese hombre - **2.** [referring to place] por; **to wander** ~ **the streets** vagar por las calles.

about-turn *esp UK*, **about-face** *esp US n* MIL media vuelta *f*; *fig* cambio *m* radical, giro *m* de 180 grados.

above [ə'bʌv] <> *adv* - **1.** [on top, higher up] arriba; **the flat** ~ el piso de arriba; **see** ~ [in text] véase más arriba - **2.** [more, over]: **children aged five and** ~ niños de cinco años en adelante. <> *prep* - **1.** [on top of] encima de - **2.** [higher up than, over] por encima de - **3.** [more than, superior to] por encima de; **children** ~ **the age of 15** niños mayores de 15 años.

◆ **above all** *adv* sobre todo, por encima de todo.

aboveboard [ə,bʌv'bɔːd] *adj* limpio(pia).

above-mentioned *adj* arriba mencionado(da).

abrasive [ə'breɪsɪv] *adj* - **1.** [substance] abrasivo(va) - **2.** [person] mordaz.

abreast [ə'brest] <> *adv* : **they were walking four** ~ caminaban en fila de a cuatro. <> *prep*: **to keep** ~ **of** mantenerse al día de.

abridged [ə'brɪdʒd] *adj* abreviado(da).

abroad [ə'brɔːd] *adv* en el extranjero; **to go** ~ ir al extranjero.

abrupt [ə'brʌpt] *adj* - **1.** [sudden] repentino(na), súbito(ta) - **2.** [brusque] brusco(ca), seco(ca).

abscess ['æbsɪs] *n* absceso *m*.

abscond [əb'skɒnd] *vi*: **to** ~ **(with/from)** escaparse OR fugarse (con/de).

abseil ['æbseɪl] *vi*: **to** ~ **(down sthg)** descolgarse OR descender haciendo rappel (por algo).

abseiling ['æbseɪlɪŋ] *n* rappel *m*.

absence ['æbsəns] *n* - **1.** [of person] ausencia *f* - **2.** [of thing] falta *f*.

absent ['æbsənt] *adj* [not present] ausente; **to be** ~ **from** faltar a.

absentee [,æbsən'tiː] *n* ausente *m* OR *f*; *US* ~ **ballot** voto *m* por correo.

absent-minded [-'maɪndɪd] *adj* [person] despistado(da); [behaviour] distraído(da).

absolute ['æbsəluːt] *adj* absoluto(ta); **that's** ~ **rubbish!** ¡menuda tontería es eso!

absolutely ['æbsəluːtlɪ] <> *adv* [completely] absolutamente, completamente; **it was** ~ **delicious** estuvo riquísimo. <> *excl* ¡desde luego!, ¡por supuesto!

absolve [əb'zɒlv] *vt*: **to** ~ **sb (from)** absolver a alguien (de).

absorb [əb'sɔːb] *vt* [gen] absorber; **to be** ~**ed in sthg** *fig* estar absorto OR embebido en algo.

absorbent [əb'sɔːbənt] *adj* absorbente; ~ **cotton** *US* algodón *m* hidrófilo.

absorption [əb'sɔːpʃn] *n* [of liquid] absorción *f*.

abstain [əb'steɪn] *vi* [refrain, not vote]: **to** ~ **(from)** abstenerse (de).

abstemious [æb'stiːmjəs] *adj fml* sobrio(bria), moderado(da).

abstention [əb'stenʃn] *n* abstención *f*.

abstract ['æbstrækt] <> *adj* abstracto(ta). <> *n* [summary] resumen *m*, sinopsis *f*.

absurd [əb'sɜːd] *adj* absurdo(da).

ABTA ['æbtə] (*abbr of* **Association of British Travel Agents**) *n* asociación británica de agencias de viajes.

abundant [ə'bʌndənt] *adj* abundante.

abuse [*n* ə'bjuːs, *vb* ə'bjuːz] <> *n (U)* - **1.** [offensive remarks] insultos *mpl* - **2.** [misuse, maltreatment] abuso *m*. <> *vt* - **1.** [insult] insultar - **2.** [maltreat, misuse] abusar de.

abusive [ə'bjuːsɪv] *adj* [person] grosero(ra); [behaviour, language] insultante, ofensivo(va).

abysmal [ə'bɪzml] *adj* pésimo(ma), nefasto(ta).

abyss [ə'bɪs] *n* abismo *m*.

a/c (*abbr of* **account (current)**) c/c.

AC (*abbr of* **alternating current**) CA *f*.

academic [,ækə'demɪk] <> *adj* - **1.** [of college, university] académico(ca) - **2.** [studious] estudioso(sa) - **3.** [hypothetical]: **that's completely** ~ **now** eso carece por completo de relevancia. <> *n* - **1.** [university lecturer] profesor *m* universitario, profesora *f* universitaria - **2.** [intellectual] académico *m*, -ca *f*.

academy [ə'kædəmɪ] (*pl* -**ies**) *n* academia *f*.

ACAS ['eɪkæs] (*abbr of* **Advisory, Conciliation and Arbitration Service**) *n* organización británica para el arbitraje en conflictos laborales, ≃ IMAC *m*.

accede [æk'siːd] *vi* - **1.** [agree]: **to** ~ **to** acceder a - **2.** [monarch]: **to** ~ **to the throne** subir al trono.

accelerate [ək'seləreɪt] *vi* - **1.** [car, driver] acelerar - **2.** [inflation, growth] acelerarse.

acceleration [ək,selə'reɪʃn] *n* aceleración *f*.

accelerator [ək'seləreɪtə[r]] *n* acelerador *m*.

accent ['æksent] *n lit & fig* acento *m*.

accept [ək'sept] *vt* - **1.** [gen] aceptar - **2.** [difficult situation, problem] asimilar - **3.** [defeat, blame, responsibility] asumir, admitir - **4.** [agree]: **to** ~ **that** admitir que - **5.** [subj: machine - coins, tokens] admitir.

acceptable [ək'septəbl] *adj* aceptable.

acceptance [ək'septəns] *n* - **1.** [gen] aceptación *f* - **2.** [of piece of work, article] aprobación *f* - **3.** [of defeat, blame, responsibility] reconocimiento *m* - **4.** [of person - as part of group etc] admisión *f*.

access ['ækses] *n* - **1.** [entry] acceso *m*

- **2.** [opportunity to use or see] libre acceso *m*; **to have ~ to** tener acceso a.

accessible [ək'sesəbl] *adj* - **1.** [place] accesible - **2.** [service, book, film] asequible - **3.** [for the disabled] para discapacitados.

accessory [ək'sesərɪ] (*pl* -**ies**) *n* - **1.** [of car, vacuum cleaner] accesorio *m* - **2.** JUR cómplice *m* OR *f*.
 ◆ **accessories** *npl* complementos *mpl*.

accident ['æksɪdənt] *n* accidente *m*; **it was an ~** fue sin querer; **by ~** [by chance] por casualidad.

accidental [ˌæksɪ'dentl] *adj* accidental.

accidentally [ˌæksɪ'dentəlɪ] *adv* - **1.** [by chance] por casualidad - **2.** [unintentionally] sin querer.

accident-prone *adj* propenso(sa) a los accidentes.

acclaim [ə'kleɪm] ◇ *n* (U) elogios *mpl*, alabanza *f*. ◇ *vt* elogiar, alabar.

acclimatize, -ise [ə'klaɪmətaɪz], **acclimate** *US* ['æklɪmeɪt] *vi*: **to ~ (to)** aclimatarse (a).

accolade ['ækəleɪd] *n* [praise] elogio *m*, halago *m*; [award] galardón *m*.

accommodate [ə'kɒmədeɪt] *vt* - **1.** [provide room for people - subj: person] alojar; [- subj: building, place] albergar - **2.** [oblige] complacer.

accommodating [ə'kɒmədeɪtɪŋ] *adj* complaciente, servicial.

accommodation *UK* [əˌkɒmə'deɪʃn] *n*, **accommodations** *US* [əˌkɒmə'deɪʃnz] *npl* [lodging] alojamiento *m*.

accompany [ə'kʌmpənɪ] (*pt* & *pp* -**ied**) *vt* acompañar.

accomplice [ə'kʌmplɪs] *n* cómplice *m* OR *f*.

accomplish [ə'kʌmplɪʃ] *vt* [aim, goal] conseguir, alcanzar; [task] realizar.

accomplished [ə'kʌmplɪʃt] *adj* [person] competente, experto(ta); [performance] logrado(da).

accomplishment [ə'kʌmplɪʃmənt] *n* - **1.** [action] realización *f* - **2.** [achievement] logro *m*.

accord [ə'kɔːd] ◇ *n*: **to do sth of one's own ~** hacer algo por propia voluntad; **the situation improved of its own ~** la situación mejoró por sí sola. ◇ *vt*: **to ~ sb sthg, to ~ sthg to sb** conceder algo a alguien.

accordance [ə'kɔːdəns] *n*: **in ~ with** de acuerdo con, conforme a.

according [ə'kɔːdɪŋ] ◆ **according to** *prep* - **1.** [as stated or shown by] según; **to go ~ to plan** ir según lo planeado - **2.** [with regard to] de acuerdo con, conforme a.

accordingly [ə'kɔːdɪŋlɪ] *adv* - **1.** [appropriately] como corresponde - **2.** [consequently] por lo tanto, en consecuencia.

accordion [ə'kɔːdjən] *n* acordeón *m*.

accost [ə'kɒst] *vt* abordar.

account [ə'kaʊnt] *n* - **1.** [with bank, shop etc] cuenta *f* - **2.** [report - spoken] relato *m*; [- written] informe *m* - **3.** [client] cuenta *f*, cliente *m* - **4.** *phr*: **to take ~ of sthg, to take sthg into ~** tener en cuenta algo; **of no ~** sin importancia; **it is of no ~ to me** me es indiferente; **on no ~** bajo ningún pretexto OR concepto.
 ◆ **accounts** *npl* [of business] cuentas *fpl*.
 ◆ **by all accounts** *adv* a decir de todos, según todo el mundo.
 ◆ **on account of** *prep* debido a, a causa de.
 ◆ **account for** *vt fus* - **1.** [explain] justificar, dar razón de - **2.** [represent] representar.

accountable [ə'kaʊntəbl] *adj* [responsible]: **~ (for)** responsable (de).

accountancy [ə'kaʊntənsɪ] *n* contabilidad *f*.

accountant [ə'kaʊntənt] *n* contable *m* OR *f*, contador *m*, -ra *f Amér*.

accrue [ə'kruː] *vi* acumularse.

accumulate [ə'kjuːmjʊleɪt] ◇ *vt* acumular. ◇ *vi* [money, things] acumularse; [problems] amontonarse.

accuracy ['ækjʊrəsɪ] *n* - **1.** [of description, report] veracidad *f* - **2.** [of weapon, marksman] precisión *f*; [of typing, figures] exactitud *f*, corrección *f*.

accurate ['ækjʊrət] *adj* - **1.** [description, report] veraz - **2.** [weapon, marksman, typist] preciso(sa); [figures, estimate] exacto(ta), correcto(ta).

accurately ['ækjʊrətlɪ] *adv* - **1.** [truthfully] verazmente - **2.** [precisely] con precisión.

accusation [ˌækjuː'zeɪʃn] *n* - **1.** [charge] acusación *f* - **2.** JUR denuncia *f*.

accuse [ə'kjuːz] *vt*: **to ~ sb of sthg/of doing sthg** acusar a alguien de algo/de hacer algo.

accused [ə'kjuːzd] (*pl inv*) *n* JUR: **the ~** el acusado, la acusada.

accustomed [ə'kʌstəmd] *adj*: **~ to** acostumbrado(da) a; **to grow ~ to** acostumbrarse a.

ace [eɪs] ◇ *n* - **1.** [playing card] as *m* - **2.** [in tennis] ace *m*. ◇ *vt US*: **to ~ an exam** bordar un examen.

ache [eɪk] ◇ *n* [pain] dolor *m*. ◇ *vi* [hurt] doler; **my back ~s** me duele la espalda.

achieve [ə'tʃiːv] *vt* [success, goal, fame] alcanzar, lograr; [ambition] realizar.

achievement [ə'tʃiːvmənt] *n* - **1.** [accomplishment] logro *m*, éxito *m* - **2.** [act of achieving] consecución *f*, realización *f*.

achiever [ə'tʃiːvər] *n*: **low ~** [at school] estudiante *m* OR *f* de bajo rendimiento escolar.

Achilles' tendon [ə'kɪliːz-] *n* tendón *m* de Aquiles.

acid ['æsɪd] <> adj -1. CHEM ácido(da) -2. [sharp-tasting] agrio (agria) -3. fig [person, remark] mordaz, corrosivo(va). <> n [chemical, drug] ácido m.

acid house n acid house m.

acid rain n lluvia f ácida.

acknowledge [ək'nɒlɪdʒ] vt -1. [accept] reconocer -2. [greet] saludar -3. [letter etc]: to ~ receipt of acusar recibo de -4. [recognize]: to ~ sb as reconocer OR considerar a alguien como.

acknowledg(e)ment [ək'nɒlɪdʒmənt] n -1. [acceptance] reconocimiento m -2. [confirmation of receipt] acuse m de recibo.
  ◆ **acknowledg(e)ments** npl agradecimientos mpl.

acne ['ækni] n acné m.

acorn ['eɪkɔːn] n bellota f.

acoustic [ə'kuːstɪk] adj acústico(ca).
  ◆ **acoustics** npl acústica f.

acquaint [ə'kweɪnt] vt -1. [make familiar]: to ~ sb with sthg [information] poner a alguien al corriente de algo; [method, technique] familiarizar a alguien con algo -2. [make known]: to be ~ed with sb conocer a alguien.

acquaintance [ə'kweɪntəns] n [person] conocido m, -da f.

acquire [ə'kwaɪə'] vt -1. [buy, adopt] adquirir -2. [obtain - information, document] procurarse.

acquisitive [ə'kwɪzɪtɪv] adj consumista.

acquit [ə'kwɪt] (pt & pp -ted, cont -ting) vt -1. JUR: to ~ sb of sthg absolver a alguien de algo -2. [perform]: to ~ o.s. well/badly hacer un buen/mal papel.

acquittal [ə'kwɪtl] n JUR absolución f.

acre ['eɪkə'] n acre m.

acrid ['ækrɪd] adj lit & fig acre.

acrimonious [,ækrɪ'məʊnjəs] adj [words] áspero(ra); [dispute] enconado(da).

acrobat ['ækrəbæt] n acróbata m OR f.

acronym ['ækrənɪm] n siglas fpl.

across [ə'krɒs] <> adv -1. [from one side to the other] de un lado a otro; to walk/run ~ cruzar andando/corriendo -2. [in measurements]: **the river is 2 km ~** el río tiene 2 kms de ancho. <> prep -1. [from one side to the other of] a través de, de un lado a otro de; to walk/run ~ the road cruzar la carretera andando/corriendo -2. [on the other side of] al otro lado de.
  ◆ **across from** prep enfrente de.

acrylic [ə'krɪlɪk] <> adj acrílico(ca). <> n acrílico m.

act [ækt] <> n -1. [action, deed] acto m, acción f; to be in the ~ of doing sthg estar haciendo algo -2. [pretence] farsa f, fachada f -3. [in parliament] ley f -4. [THEATRE - part of play] acto m; [- routine, turn] número m. <> vi -1. [gen] actuar; to ~ as [person]

hacer de, fungir de Méx; [thing] actuar como -2. [behave]: to ~ (as if/like) comportarse (como si/como) -3. fig [pretend] fingir. <> vt [part - in play, film] interpretar.

acting ['æktɪŋ] <> adj [interim] en funciones. <> n actuación f; I like ~ me gusta actuar.

action ['ækʃn] n -1. [gen & MIL] acción f; to take ~ tomar medidas; in ~ [person] en acción; [machine] en funcionamiento; out of ~ [person] fuera de combate; [machine] averiado(da) -2. [deed] acto m, acción f -3. JUR demanda f.

activate ['æktɪveɪt] vt [device] activar; [machine] poner en funcionamiento.

active ['æktɪv] adj -1. [person, campaigner, encouragement, etc] activo(va) -2. [volcano] en actividad; [bomb] activado(da); MIL on ~ duty US en servicio activo.

actively ['æktɪvlɪ] adv [encourage, discourage] activamente.

activity [æk'tɪvətɪ] (pl -ies) n -1. [movement, action] actividad f -2. [pastime, hobby] afición f.

actor ['æktə'] n actor m.

actress ['æktrɪs] n actriz f.

actual ['æktʃʊəl] adj [emphatic]: **the ~ cost is £10** el coste real es de 10 libras; **the ~ spot where it happened** el sitio mismo en que ocurrió.

actually ['æktʃʊəlɪ] adv -1. [really, in truth]: do you ~ like him? ¿de verdad que te gusta?; no one ~ saw her en realidad, nadie la vio -2. [by the way]: ~, I was there yesterday pues yo estuve ayer por allí.

acumen ['ækjʊmen] n: business ~ vista f para los negocios.

acute [ə'kjuːt] adj -1. [illness, pain] agudo(da); [danger] extremo(ma) -2. [perceptive - person] perspicaz -3. [hearing, smell] muy fino(na).

ad [æd] (abbr of advertisement) n anuncio m.

AD (abbr of Anno Domini) d. C.

adamant ['ædəmənt] adj: to be ~ (that) insistir (en que).

Adam's apple ['ædəmz-] n bocado m OR nuez f de Adán.

adapt [ə'dæpt] <> vt adaptar. <> vi: to ~ (to) adaptarse (a).

adaptable [ə'dæptəbl] adj [person] adaptable.

adapter, adaptor [ə'dæptə'] n [ELEC - for several devices] ladrón m; [- for different socket] adaptador m.

add [æd] vt -1. [gen]: to ~ sthg (to sthg) añadir algo (a algo) -2. [numbers] sumar.
  ◆ **add on** vt sep [to bill, total]: to ~ sthg on (to sthg) añadir OR incluir algo (en algo).

◆ **add to** *vt fus* aumentar, acrecentar.

◆ **add up** ◇ *vt sep* [numbers] sumar. ◇ *vi inf* [make sense]: **it doesn't ~ up** no tiene sentido.

added ['ædəd] *adj* [additional] adicional; **with ~ protein** con proteínas añadidas.

adder ['ædə'] *n* víbora *f*.

addict ['ædɪkt] *n* **- 1.** [taking drugs] adicto *m*, -ta *f*; **drug ~** drogadicto *m*, -ta *f*, toxicómano *m*, -na *f* **- 2.** *fig* [fan] fanático *m*, -ca *f*.

addicted [ə'dɪktɪd] *adj* **- 1.** [to drug]: **~ (to)** adicto(ta) (a) **- 2.** *fig* [to food, TV]: **to be ~ (to)** ser un fanático (de).

addiction [ə'dɪkʃn] *n* **- 1.** [to drug]: **~ (to)** adicción *f* (a) **- 2.** *fig* [to food, TV]: **~ (to)** vicio *m* (por).

addictive [ə'dɪktɪv] *adj lit & fig* adictivo(va).

addition [ə'dɪʃn] *n* **- 1.** MATH suma *f* **- 2.** [extra thing] adición *f*, añadido *m* **- 3.** [act of adding] incorporación *f*; **in ~** además; **in ~ to** además de.

additional [ə'dɪʃənl] *adj* adicional.

additive ['ædɪtɪv] *n* aditivo *m*.

address [ə'dres] ◇ *n* **- 1.** [of person, organization] dirección *f*, domicilio *m* **- 2.** COMPUT dirección *f* **- 3.** [speech] discurso *m*, conferencia *f*. ◇ *vt* **- 1.** [letter, parcel, remark]: **to ~ sthg to** dirigir algo a **- 2.** [meeting, conference] dirigirse a, hablar ante **- 3.** [issue] abordar; **to ~ o.s. to sthg** enfrentarse OR abordar algo.

address book *n* agenda *f* de direcciones.

adenoids ['ædɪnɔɪdz] *npl* vegetaciones *fpl* (adenoideas).

adept ['ædept] *adj*: **to be ~ (at sthg/at doing sthg)** ser experto(ta) (en algo/en hacer algo).

adequate ['ædɪkwət] *adj* **- 1.** [sufficient] suficiente **- 2.** [good enough] aceptable, satisfactorio(ria).

adhere [əd'hɪə'] *vi* **- 1.** [to surface, principle]: **to ~ (to)** adherirse (a) **- 2.** [to rule, decision]: **to ~ to** respetar, observar.

adhesive [əd'hi:sɪv] ◇ *adj* adhesivo(va), adherente. ◇ *n* adhesivo *m*.

adhesive tape *n* cinta *f* adhesiva.

adjacent [ə'dʒeɪsənt] *adj*: **~ (to)** adyacente OR contiguo(gua) (a).

adjective ['ædʒɪktɪv] *n* adjetivo *m*.

adjoining [ə'dʒɔɪnɪŋ] ◇ *adj* [table] adyacente; [room] contiguo(gua). ◇ *prep* junto a.

adjourn [ə'dʒɜ:n] *vt* [session] levantar; [meeting] interrumpir.

adjudge [ə'dʒʌdʒ] *vt* declarar.

adjudicate [ə'dʒu:dɪkeɪt] *vi* actuar como juez; **to ~ on** OR **upon sthg** emitir un fallo OR un veredicto sobre algo.

adjust [ə'dʒʌst] ◇ *vt* [machine, setting] ajustar; [clothing] arreglarse. ◇ *vi*: **to ~ (to)** adaptarse OR amoldarse (a).

adjustable [ə'dʒʌstəbl] *adj* [machine, chair] regulable.

adjustment [ə'dʒʌstmənt] *n* **- 1.** [modification] modificación *f*, reajuste *m* **- 2.** *(U)* [change in attitude]: **~ (to)** adaptación *f* OR amoldamiento *m* (a).

ad lib [,æd'lɪb] ◇ *(pt & pp* **-bed**, *cont* **-bing)** ◇ *adj* [improvised] improvisado(da). ◇ *adv* [without preparation] improvisando; [without limit] a voluntad.

◆ **ad-lib** *vi* improvisar.

administer [əd'mɪnɪstə'] *vt* [gen] administrar; [punishment] aplicar.

administration [əd,mɪnɪ'streɪʃn] *n* [gen] administración *f*; [of punishment] aplicación *f*.

administrative [əd'mɪnɪstrətɪv] *adj* administrativo(va).

admirable ['ædmərəbl] *adj* admirable.

admiral ['ædmərəl] *n* almirante *m*.

admiration [,ædmə'reɪʃn] *n* admiración *f*.

admire [əd'maɪə'] *vt*: **to ~ sb (for)** admirar a alguien (por).

admirer [əd'maɪərə'] *n* admirador *m*, -ra *f*.

admission [əd'mɪʃn] *n* **- 1.** [permission to enter] admisión *f*, ingreso *m* **- 2.** [cost of entrance] entrada *f* **- 3.** [of guilt, mistake] reconocimiento *m*.

admit [əd'mɪt] *(pt & pp* **-ted**, *cont* **-ting)** ◇ *vt* **- 1.** [acknowledge, confess]: **to ~ (that)** admitir OR reconocer (que); **to ~ doing sthg** reconocer haber hecho algo; **to ~ defeat** *fig* darse por vencido **- 2.** [allow to enter or join] admitir; **to be admitted to hospital** *UK* OR **to the hospital** *US* ser ingresado en el hospital. ◇ *vi*: **to ~ to sthg** [crime] confesar algo.

admittance [əd'mɪtəns] *n*: **to gain ~ to** conseguir entrar en; **'no ~'** 'prohibido el paso'.

admittedly [əd'mɪtɪdlɪ] *adv* sin duda, indudablemente.

admonish [əd'mɒnɪʃ] *vt* amonestar, apercibir.

ad nauseam [,æd'nɔ:zɪæm] *adv* hasta la saciedad.

ado [ə'du:] *n*: **without further** OR **more ~** sin más preámbulos, sin mayor dilación.

adolescence [,ædə'lesns] *n* adolescencia *f*.

adolescent [,ædə'lesnt] ◇ *adj* **- 1.** [teenage] adolescente **- 2.** *pej* [immature] pueril, infantil. ◇ *n* [teenager] adolescente *m* OR *f*.

adopt [ə'dɒpt] *vt & vi* adoptar.

adoption [ə'dɒpʃn] *n* adopción *f*.

adore [ə'dɔ:'] *vt* **- 1.** [love deeply] adorar, querer con locura **- 2.** [like very much]: **I ~ chocolate** me encanta el chocolate.

adorn [ə'dɔ:n] *vt* adornar.

adrenalin [ə'drenəlın] *n* adrenalina *f*.

Adriatic [,eıdrı'ætık] *n*: the ∼ (Sea) el (mar) Adriático.

adrift [ə'drıft] *<> adj* [boat] a la deriva. *<> adv*: to go ∼ *fig* irse a la deriva.

adult ['ædʌlt] *<> adj* - 1. [fully grown] adulto(ta) - 2. [mature] maduro(ra) - 3. [suitable for adults only] para adultos OR mayores. *<> n* adulto *m*, -ta *f*.

adultery [ə'dʌltərı] *n* adulterio *m*.

advance [əd'vɑːns] *<> n* - 1. [gen] avance *m* - 2. [money] anticipo *m*. *<> comp*: ∼ notice OR warning previo aviso *m*; ∼ booking reserva *f* anticipada. *<> vt* - 1. [improve] promover, favorecer - 2. [bring forward in time] adelantar - 3. [give in advance]: to ∼ sb sthg adelantarle algo a alguien. *<> vi* avanzar.

➤ advances *npl*: to make ∼s to sb [sexual] hacerle proposiciones a alguien, insinuarse a alguien; [business] hacerle una propuesta a alguien.

➤ in advance *adv* [pay] por adelantado; [book] con antelación; [know, thank] de antemano.

advanced [əd'vɑːnst] *adj* - 1. [developed] avanzado(da) - 2. [student, pupil] adelantado(da); [studies] superior.

advantage [əd'vɑːntıdʒ] *n*: ∼ (over) ventaja *f* (sobre); to be to one's ∼ ir en beneficio de uno; to take ∼ of sthg aprovechar algo; to take ∼ of sb aprovecharse de alguien; ∼ Hewitt [in tennis] ventaja de Hewitt.

advent ['ædvənt] *n* [arrival] advenimiento *m*.

➤ Advent *n* RELIG Adviento *m*.

adventure [əd'ventʃəʳ] *n* aventura *f*.

adventure playground *n* UK parque *m* infantil.

adventurous [əd'ventʃərəs] *adj* - 1. [daring] aventurero(ra) - 2. [dangerous] arriesgado(da).

adverb ['ædvɜːb] *n* adverbio *m*.

adverse ['ædvɜːs] *adj* adverso(sa).

advert ['ædvɜːt] *n* anuncio *m*.

advertise ['ædvətaız] *<> vt* anunciar. *<> vi* anunciarse, poner un anuncio; to ∼ for buscar *(mediante anuncio)*.

advertisement [əd'vɜːtısmənt] *n* anuncio *m*.

advertiser ['ædvətaızəʳ] *n* anunciante *m* OR *f*.

advertising ['ædvətaızıŋ] *n* publicidad *f*.

advice [əd'vaıs] *n* (U) consejos *mpl*; to take sb's ∼ seguir el consejo de alguien; a piece of ∼ un consejo; to give sb ∼ aconsejar a alguien.

advisable [əd'vaızəbl] *adj* aconsejable.

advise [əd'vaız] *<> vt* - 1. [give advice to]: to ∼ sb to do sthg aconsejar a alguien que haga algo; to ∼ sb against sthg/against doing sthg desaconsejar a alguien algo/que haga algo - 2. [professionally]: to ∼ sb on sthg asesorar a alguien en algo - 3. [recommend] [caution] recomendar - 4. *fml* [inform]: to ∼ sb (of sthg) informar a alguien (de algo). *<> vi* - 1. [give advice]: to ∼ against sthg desaconsejar algo; to ∼ against doing sthg aconsejar no hacer algo - 2. [professionally]: to ∼ on asesorar en (materia de).

advisedly [əd'vaızıdlı] *adv* [deliberately] deliberadamente; [after careful consideration] con conocimiento de causa.

adviser UK, **advisor** US [əd'vaızəʳ] *n* [of politician, etc] consejero *m*, -ra *f*; [financial, professional] asesor *m*, -ra *f*.

advisory [əd'vaızərı] *adj* [body] consultivo(va), asesor(ra).

advocate [*n* 'ædvəkət, *vb* 'ædvəkeıt] *<> n* - 1. JUR abogado *m* defensor, abogada *f* defensora - 2. [supporter] defensor *m*, -ra *f*, partidario *m*, -ria *f*. *<> vt* abogar por.

Aegean [iː'dʒiːən] *n*: the ∼ (Sea) el mar Egeo.

aerial ['eərıəl] *<> adj* aéreo(a). *<> n* UK [antenna] antena *f*.

aerobics [eə'rəubıks] *n* (U) aerobic *m*.

aerodynamic [,eərəudaı'næmık] *adj* aerodinámico(ca).

aeroplane ['eərəpleın] *n* UK avión *m*.

aerosol ['eərəsɒl] *n* aerosol *m*.

aesthetic, esthetic US [iːs'θetık] *adj* estético(ca).

afar [ə'fɑːʳ] *adv*: from ∼ desde lejos.

affable ['æfəbl] *adj* afable.

affair [ə'feəʳ] *n* - 1. [concern, matter] asunto *m* - 2. [extra-marital relationship] aventura *f* (amorosa) - 3. [event, do] acontecimiento *m*.

affect [ə'fekt] *vt* - 1. [influence, move emotionally] afectar - 2. [put on] fingir, simular.

affected [ə'fektıd] *adj* [insincere] afectado(da).

affection [ə'fekʃn] *n* cariño *m*, afecto *m*.

affectionate [ə'fekʃnət] *adj* cariñoso(sa), afectuoso(sa).

affirm [ə'fɜːm] *vt* afirmar.

affix [ə'fıks] *vt* fijar, pegar.

afflict [ə'flıkt] *vt* aquejar, afligir.

affluence ['æfluəns] *n* prosperidad *f*.

affluent ['æfluənt] *adj* pudiente, adinerado(da).

afford [ə'fɔːd] *vt* - 1. [gen]: to be able to ∼ poder permitirse (el lujo de); we can't ∼ to let this happen no podemos permitirnos el lujo de dejar que esto ocurra - 2. *fml* [provide, give] brindar.

affront [ə'frʌnt] *n* afrenta *f*.

Afghanistan [æf'gænıstæn] *n* Afganistán.

afield [ə'fiːld] *adv*: further ∼ más lejos.

afloat [ə'fləut] *adj lit* & *fig* a flote.

afoot [ə'fut] *adj* [plan] en marcha; there is a

rumour ~ **that** corre el rumor de que.

afraid [əˈfreɪd] *adj* - 1. [gen] asustado(da); **to be ~ of sb** tenerle miedo a alguien; **I'm ~ of them** me dan miedo; **to be ~ of sthg** tener miedo de algo; **to be ~ of doing** OR **to do sthg** tener miedo de hacer algo - 2. [in apologies]: **to be ~ that** temerse que; **I'm ~ so/not** me temo que sí/no.

afresh [əˈfreʃ] *adv* de nuevo.

Africa [ˈæfrɪkə] *n* África.

African [ˈæfrɪkən] ◇ *adj* africano(na). ◇ *n* africano *m*, -na *f*.

African American *n* afroamericano *m*, -na *f*.

aft [ɑːft] *adv* en popa.

after [ˈɑːftər] ◇ *prep* - 1. [gen] después de; **~ all my efforts** después de todos mis esfuerzos; **~ you!** ¡usted primero!; **day ~ day** día tras día; **the day ~ tomorrow** pasado mañana; **the week ~ next** no la semana que viene sino la otra - 2. *inf* [in search of]: **to be ~ sthg** buscar algo; **to be ~ sb** andar detrás de alguien - 3. [with the name of]: **to be named ~ sb/sthg** llamarse así por alguien/algo - 4. [towards retreating person]: **to run ~ sb** correr tras alguien - 5. US [telling the time]: **it's twenty ~ three** son las tres y veinte. ◇ *adv* más tarde, después. ◇ *conj* después (de) que; **~ you had done it** después de que lo hubieras hecho.

◆ **afters** *npl* UK *inf* postre *m*.

◆ **after all** *adv* - 1. [in spite of everything] después de todo - 2. [it should be remembered] al fin y al cabo.

aftereffects [ˈɑːftərɪˌfekts] *npl* - 1. [consequences] secuelas *fpl* - 2. [of drug] efectos *mpl* secundarios.

afterlife [ˈɑːftəlaɪf] (*pl* -**lives** [-laɪvz]) *n* más allá *m*, vida *f* de ultratumba.

aftermath [ˈɑːftəmæθ] *n* [time] periodo *m* posterior; [situation] situación *f* posterior.

afternoon [ˌɑːftəˈnuːn] *n* tarde *f*; **in the ~** por la tarde; **at three in the ~** a las tres de la tarde; **good ~** buenas tardes.

aftershave [ˈɑːftəʃeɪv] *n* loción *f* para después del afeitado.

aftertaste [ˈɑːftəteɪst] *n* - 1. [of food, drink] resabio *m* - 2. *fig* [of unpleasant experience] mal sabor *m* de boca.

afterthought [ˈɑːftəθɔːt] *n* idea *f* a posteriori.

afterward(s) [ˈɑːftəwəd(z)] *adv* después, más tarde.

again [əˈgen] *adv* - 1. [gen] otra vez, de nuevo; **never ~** nunca jamás; **he's well ~ now** ya está bien; **to do sthg ~** volver a hacer algo; **to say sthg ~** repetir algo; **~ and ~** una y otra vez; **all over ~** otra vez desde el principio; **time and ~** una y otra vez - 2. *phr*: **half as much ~** la mitad otra vez;

twice as much ~ dos veces lo mismo otra vez; **then** OR **there ~** por otro lado, por otra parte.

against [əˈgenst] ◇ *prep* contra; **I'm ~ it** estoy (en) contra (de) ello; **to lean ~ sthg** apoyarse en algo; **(as) ~** a diferencia de, en contraste con. ◇ *adv* en contra.

age [eɪdʒ] (*cont* **ageing** OR **aging**) ◇ *n* - 1. [gen] edad *f*; **to come of ~** alcanzar la mayoría de edad; **to be under ~** ser menor (de edad); **what ~ are you?** ¿qué edad tienes?; **to be forty years of ~** tener cuarenta años (de edad); **at the ~ of thirty** a los treinta años - 2. [state of being old] vejez *f*. ◇ *vt* & *vi* envejecer.

◆ **ages** *npl* [long time] siglos *mpl*; **~s ago** hace siglos; **I haven't seen her for ~s** hace siglos que no la veo.

aged [ˈeɪdʒɪd] *npl*: **the ~** los ancianos.

age group *n* (grupo *m* de) edad *f*.

agency [ˈeɪdʒənsɪ] (*pl* -**ies**) *n* - 1. [business] agencia *f* - 2. [organization, body] organismo *m*, instituto *m*.

agenda [əˈdʒendə] *n* - 1. [of meeting] orden *m* del día - 2. [intentions] intenciones *fpl*.

agent [ˈeɪdʒənt] *n* - 1. COMM [of company] representante *m* OR *f*, delegado *m*, -da *f*; [of actor] agente *m* OR *f* - 2. [substance] agente *m* - 3. [secret agent] agente *m* (secreto).

aggravate [ˈægrəveɪt] *vt* - 1. [make worse] agravar, empeorar - 2. [annoy] irritar.

aggregate [ˈægrɪgət] ◇ *adj* total. ◇ *n* [total] total *m*.

aggressive [əˈgresɪv] *adj* - 1. [belligerent - person] agresivo(va) - 2. [forceful - person, campaign] audaz, emprendedor(ra).

aggrieved [əˈgriːvd] *adj* ofendido(da), herido(da).

aghast [əˈgɑːst] *adj*: **~ (at)** horrorizado(da) (ante).

agile [UK ˈædʒaɪl, US ˈædʒəl] *adj* ágil.

agitate [ˈædʒɪteɪt] ◇ *vt* - 1. [disturb, worry] inquietar, perturbar - 2. [shake about] agitar. ◇ *vi* [campaign]: **to ~ for/against** hacer campaña a favor de/en contra de.

AGM *n abbr of* **annual general meeting**.

agnostic [ægˈnɒstɪk] ◇ *adj* agnóstico(ca). ◇ *n* agnóstico *m*, -ca *f*.

ago [əˈgəʊ] *adv*: **a long time/three days/three years ~** hace mucho tiempo/tres días/tres años.

agog [əˈgɒg] *adj* ansioso(sa), expectante.

agonizing [ˈægənaɪzɪŋ] *adj* angustioso(sa).

agony [ˈægənɪ] (*pl* -**ies**) *n* - 1. [physical pain] dolor *m* muy intenso; **to be in ~** morirse de dolor - 2. [mental pain] angustia *f*; **to be in ~** estar angustiado.

agony aunt *n* UK *inf* consejera *f* sentimental.

agree [əˈgriː] ◇ *vi* - 1. [be of same opinion]:

to ~ (with sb about sthg) estar de acuerdo (con alguien acerca de algo); to ~ on sthg [reach agreement] ponerse de acuerdo en algo; to ~ on sthg [be in agreement] estar de acuerdo en algo - 2. [consent]: to ~ (to sthg) acceder a (algo) - 3. [approve]: to ~ with sthg estar de acuerdo con algo - 4. [be consistent] concordar - 5. [food]: to ~ with sb sentarle bien a alguien - 6. GRAMM: to ~ (with) concordar (con). ⬦ vt - 1. [fix] [date, time] acordar, convenir - 2. [be of same opinion]: to ~ that estar de acuerdo en que - 3. [agree, consent]: to ~ to do sthg acordar hacer algo - 4. [concede]: to ~ (that) reconocer que.

agreeable [ə'gri:əbl] adj - 1. [pleasant] agradable - 2. [willing]: to be ~ to sthg/doing sthg estar conforme con algo/hacer algo.

agreed [ə'gri:d] ⬦ adj: to be ~ on sthg estar de acuerdo sobre algo; at the ~ time a la hora acordada OR convenida. ⬦ adv [admittedly] de acuerdo que.

agreement [ə'gri:mənt] n - 1. [accord, settlement, contract] acuerdo m; to be in ~ with estar de acuerdo con - 2. [consent] aceptación f - 3. [consistency] correspondencia f - 4. GRAMM concordancia f.

agricultural [,ægri'kʌltʃərəl] adj agrícola.

agriculture ['ægrikʌltʃəʳ] n agricultura f.

aground [ə'graund] adv: to run ~ encallar.

ahead [ə'hed] adv - 1. [in front] delante - 2. [forwards] adelante, hacia delante; go ~! ¡por supuesto!; right OR straight ~ todo recto OR de frente - 3. [winning] ir en cabeza; [in race] ir en cabeza; [in football, rugby etc] ir ganando - 4. [in better position] por delante; to get ~ [be successful] abrirse camino - 5. [in time]: to look OR think ~ mirar hacia el futuro.

◆ **ahead of** prep - 1. [in front of] frente a - 2. [beating]: to be two points ~ of llevar dos puntos de ventaja a - 3. [in better position than] por delante de - 4. [in time] con anterioridad a; ~ of schedule por delante de lo previsto.

aid [eid] ⬦ n ayuda f; medical ~ asistencia f médica; in ~ of a beneficio de. ⬦ vt - 1. [help] ayudar - 2. JUR: to ~ and abet sb ser cómplice de alguien.

aide [eid] n POL ayudante m OR f.

AIDS, Aids [eidz] (abbr of acquired immune deficiency syndrome) comp: ~ patient sidoso m, -sa f.

ailing ['eiliŋ] adj - 1. [ill] achacoso(sa) - 2. fig [economy] renqueante.

ailment ['eilmənt] n achaque m, molestia f.

aim [eim] ⬦ n - 1. [objective] objetivo m - 2. [in firing gun] puntería f; to take ~ at apuntar a. ⬦ vt - 1. [weapon]: to ~ sthg at apuntar algo a - 2. [plan, action]: to be ~ed

at doing sthg ir dirigido OR encaminado a hacer algo - 3. [campaign, publicity, criticism]: to ~ sthg at sb dirigir algo a alguien. ⬦ vi - 1. [point weapon]: to ~ (at sthg) apuntar (a algo) - 2. [intend]: to ~ at OR for sthg apuntar a OR pretender algo; to ~ to do sthg pretender hacer algo.

aimless ['eimlis] adj sin un objetivo claro.

ain't [eint] inf = am not, are not, is not, have not, has not.

air [eəʳ] ⬦ n - 1. [gen] aire m; into the ~ al aire; by ~ en avión; (up) in the ~ fig en el aire - 2. RADIO & TV: on the ~ en el aire. ⬦ comp aéreo(a). ⬦ vt - 1. [clothes, sheets] airear; [cupboard, room] ventilar - 2. [views, opinions] expresar - 3. US [broadcast] emitir. ⬦ vi [clothes, sheets] airearse; [cupboard, room] ventilarse.

airbag ['eəbæg] n AUT airbag m.

airbase ['eəbeis] n base f aérea.

airbed ['eəbed] n UK colchón m inflable.

airborne ['eəbɔ:n] adj - 1. [troops] aerotransportado(da); [attack] aéreo(a) - 2. [plane] en el aire, en vuelo.

air-conditioned [-kən'diʃnd] adj climatizado(da), con aire acondicionado.

air-conditioning [-kən'diʃniŋ] n aire m acondicionado.

aircraft ['eəkrɑ:ft] (pl inv) n [plane] avión m; [any flying machine] aeronave f.

aircraft carrier n portaaviones m inv.

airdrop ['eədrop] n lanzamiento m con paracaídas.

airfield ['eəfi:ld] n campo m de aviación.

airforce ['eəfɔ:s] n: the ~ las fuerzas aéreas.

air freshener [-'freʃnəʳ] n ambientador m.

airgun ['eəgʌn] n pistola f de aire comprimido.

airhead ['eəhed] n inf cabeza m OR f de chorlito.

airhostess ['eə,həustis] n azafata f, aeromoza f Amér.

airlift ['eəlift] ⬦ n puente m aéreo. ⬦ vt transportar por avión.

airline ['eəlain] n línea f aérea.

airliner ['eəlainəʳ] n avión m (grande) de pasajeros.

airlock ['eəlok] n - 1. [in tube, pipe] bolsa f de aire - 2. [airtight chamber] cámara f OR esclusa f de aire.

airmail ['eəmeil] n: by ~ por correo aéreo.

airplane ['eəplein] n US avión m.

airport ['eəpɔ:t] n aeropuerto m.

airport tax n tasas fpl de aeropuerto.

air raid n ataque m aéreo.

airsick ['eəsik] adj: to be ~ marearse (en el avión).

airspace ['eəspeis] n espacio m aéreo.

air steward *n* auxiliar *m* de vuelo, aeromozo *m Amér.*

airstrip ['eəstrɪp] *n* pista *f* de aterrizaje.

air terminal *n* terminal *f* aérea.

airtight ['eətaɪt] *adj* hermético(ca).

air-traffic controller *n* controlador aéreo *m*, controladora aérea *f*.

airy ['eərɪ] (*compar* **-ier**, *superl* **-iest**) *adj* **-1.** [room] espacioso(sa) y bien ventilado(-da) **-2.** [fanciful] ilusorio(ria) **-3.** [nonchalant] despreocupado(da).

aisle [aɪl] *n* **-1.** [in church] nave *f* lateral **-2.** [in plane, theatre, supermarket] pasillo *m*.

ajar [ə'dʒɑ:'] *adj* entreabierto(ta).

aka (*abbr of* **also known as**) alias.

akin [ə'kɪn] *adj*: ~ **to** sthg/**to doing** sthg semejante a algo/a hacer algo.

alacrity [ə'lækrətɪ] *n* presteza *f*, prontitud *f*.

à la mode [ˌɑ:lɑ:'məʊd] *adj US* [dessert] con helado.

alarm [ə'lɑ:m] ◇ *n* alarma *f*; **to raise** OR **sound the** ~ dar la (voz de) alarma. ◇ *vt* alarmar, asustar.

alarm clock *n* despertador *m*.

alarming [ə'lɑ:mɪŋ] *adj* alarmante.

alas [ə'læs] ◇ *adv* desgraciadamente. ◇ *excl literary* ¡ay!

Albania [æl'beɪnjə] *n* Albania.

Albanian [æl'beɪnjən] ◇ *adj* albanés(esa). ◇ *n* **-1.** [person] albanés *m*, -esa *f* **-2.** [language] albanés *m*.

albeit [ɔ:l'bi:ɪt] *conj fml* aunque, si bien.

album ['ælbəm] *n* **-1.** [of stamps, photos] álbum *m* **-2.** [record] elepé *m*.

alcohol ['ælkəhɒl] *n* alcohol *m*.

alcoholic [ˌælkə'hɒlɪk] ◇ *adj* alcohólico(-ca). ◇ *n* alcohólico *m*, -ca *f*.

alcopop ['ælkəʊpɒp] *n* refresco gaseoso que contiene un cierto porcentaje de alcohol.

alcove ['ælkəʊv] *n* hueco *m*.

alderman ['ɔ:ldəmən] (*pl* **-men** [-mən]) *n* ≃ concejal *m*, -la *f*.

ale [eɪl] *n* tipo de cerveza.

alert [ə'lɜ:t] ◇ *adj* **-1.** [vigilant] atento(ta) **-2.** [perceptive] despierto(ta) **-3.** [aware]: **to be** ~ **to** ser consciente de. ◇ *n* [gen & MIL] alerta *f*; **to be on the** ~ estar alerta. ◇ *vt* alertar; **to** ~ **sb to** sthg alertar a alguien de algo.

A level (*abbr of* **Advanced level**) *n UK* SCH *nivel escolar necesario para acceder a la universidad.*

alfresco [æl'freskəʊ] *adj* & *adv* al aire libre.

algae ['ældʒi:] *npl* algas *fpl*.

algebra ['ældʒɪbrə] *n* álgebra *f*.

Algeria [æl'dʒɪərɪə] *n* Argelia.

alias ['eɪlɪəs] (*pl* **-es**) ◇ *adv* alias. ◇ *n* alias *m inv*.

alibi ['ælɪbaɪ] *n* coartada *f*.

alien ['eɪlɪən] ◇ *adj* **-1.** [from outer space] extraterrestre **-2.** [unfamiliar] extraño(ña), ajeno(na). ◇ *n* **-1.** [from outer space] extraterrestre *m* OR *f* **-2.** JUR [foreigner] extranjero *m*, -ra *f*.

alienate ['eɪljəneɪt] *vt* [make unsympathetic] ganarse la antipatía de.

alight [ə'laɪt] (*pt* & *pp* **-ed**) ◇ *adj* [on fire] ardiendo; **to set sthg** ~ prender fuego a algo. ◇ *vi fml* **-1.** [land] posarse **-2.** [get off]: **to** ~ **from** apearse de.

align [ə'laɪn] *vt* [line up] alinear, poner en línea.

alike [ə'laɪk] ◇ *adj* parecido(da). ◇ *adv* [treat] de la misma forma, por igual; **to look** ~ parecerse.

alimony ['ælɪmənɪ] *n* pensión *f* alimenticia.

alive [ə'laɪv] *adj* **-1.** [living] vivo(va) **-2.** [active, lively] lleno(na) de vida; **to come** ~ [story, description] cobrar vida; [person, place] animarse.

alkali ['ælkəlaɪ] (*pl* **-s** OR **-ies**) *n* álcali *m*.

all [ɔ:l] ◇ *adj* **-1.** (*with sg noun*) todo(da); ~ **the drink** toda la bebida; ~ **day** todo el día; ~ **night** toda la noche; ~ **the time** todo el tiempo OR el rato **-2.** (*with pl noun*) todos(das); ~ **the boxes** todas las cajas; ~ **men** todos los hombres; ~ **three died** los tres murieron. ◇ *pron* **-1.** (*sg*) [the whole amount] todo *m*, -da *f*; **she drank it** ~, **she drank** ~ **of it** se lo bebió todo **-2.** (*pl*) [everybody, everything] todos *mpl*, -das *fpl*; ~ **of them came, they** ~ **came** vinieron todos **-3.** (*with superl*): **he's the cleverest of** ~ es el más listo de todos; **the most amazing thing of** ~ lo más impresionante de todo; **best/worst of** ~ ... lo mejor/peor de todo es que ...; **above** ~ ⊳ **above**; **after** ~ ⊳ **after**; **at** ~ ⊳ **at**. ◇ *adv* **-1.** [entirely] completamente; **I'd forgotten** ~ **about that** me había olvidado completamente de eso; ~ **alone** completamente solo(la) **-2.** [in sport, competitions]: **the score is two** ~ el resultado es de empate a dos; **thirty** ~ [in tennis] treinta iguales **-3.** (*with compar*): **to run** ~ **the faster** correr aun más rápido.

◆ **all but** *adv* casi.

◆ **all in all** *adv* en conjunto.

◆ **all that** *adv*: **she's not** ~ **that pretty** no es tan guapa.

◆ **in all** *adv* en total.

Allah ['ælə] *n* Alá *m*.

all-around *US* = **all-round**.

allay [ə'leɪ] *vt fml* [suspicions, doubts] despejar; [fears] apaciguar.

all clear *n* **-1.** [signal] señal *f* de cese de peligro **-2.** *fig* [go-ahead] luz *f* verde.

allegation [ˌælɪ'geɪʃn] *n* acusación *f*.

allege [ə'ledʒ] *vt* alegar; **to be** ~**d to have done/said** ser acusado de haber hecho/dicho.

allegedly [ə'ledʒɪdlɪ] *adv* presuntamente.

allegiance [ə'li:dʒəns] *n* lealtad *f*.

allergic [ə'lɜ:dʒɪk] *adj lit* & *fig*: ~ **(to sthg)** alérgico(ca) (a algo).

allergy ['ælədʒɪ] *(pl* **-ies)** *n* alergia *f*.

alleviate [ə'li:vɪeɪt] *vt* aliviar.

alley(way) ['ælɪ(weɪ)] *n* callejuela *f*.

alliance [ə'laɪəns] *n* alianza *f*.

allied [ə'laɪd] *adj* - **1.** [powers, troops] aliado(da) - **2.** [subjects] afín.

alligator ['ælɪgeɪtə'] *(pl inv or* **-s)** *n* caimán *m*.

all-important *adj* crucial.

all-in *adj UK* [inclusive] todo incluido.
 ◆ **all in** ◇ *adj inf* [tired] hecho(cha) polvo. ◇ *adv* [inclusive] todo incluido.

all-night *adj* [party etc] que dura toda la noche; [chemist, bar] abierto(ta) toda la noche.

allocate ['æləkeɪt] *vt* : **to** ~ **sthg to sb** [money, resources] destinar algo a alguien; [task, tickets, seats] asignar algo a alguien.

allot [ə'lɒt] *(pt* & *pp* **-ted,** *cont* **-ting)** *vt* [job, time] asignar; [money, resources] destinar.

allotment [ə'lɒtmənt] *n* - **1.** *UK* [garden] *parcela municipal arrendada para su cultivo* - **2.** [share - of money, resources] asignación *f*; [- of time] espacio *m* (de tiempo) concedido.

all-out *adj* [effort] supremo(ma); [war] sin cuartel.

allow [ə'laʊ] *vt* - **1.** [permit] permitir, dejar; **to** ~ **sb to do sthg** permitir *or* dejar a alguien hacer algo - **2.** [set aside - money] destinar; [- time] dejar - **3.** [officially accept - subj: person] conceder; [- subj: law] admitir, permitir - **4.** [concede]: **to** ~ **that** admitir *or* reconocer que.
 ◆ **allow for** *vt fus* contar con.

allowance [ə'laʊəns] *n* - **1.** [money received - from government] subsidio *m*; [- from employer] dietas *fpl* - **2.** *US* [pocket money] paga *f*, asignación *f* semanal - **3.** FIN desgravación *f* - **4.**: **to make** ~**s for sthg/ sb** [forgive] disculpar algo/a alguien; [take into account] tener en cuenta algo/a alguien.

alloy ['ælɔɪ] *n* aleación *f*.

all right ◇ *adv* - **1.** [gen] bien - **2.** [only just acceptably] (más o menos) bien - **3.** [in answer - yes] vale, bueno. ◇ *adj* - **1.** [gen] bien - **2.** [not bad]: **it's** ~**, but ...** no está mal, pero ... - **3.** [OK]: **sorry – that's** ~ lo siento – no importa.

all-round *UK,* **all-around** *US adj* [multiskilled] polifacético(ca).

all-star *adj* [cast] estelar.

all-terrain vehicle *n* todoterreno *m*.

all-time *adj* [favourite] de todos los tiempos; [high, low] histórico(ca).

allude [ə'lu:d] *vi*: **to** ~ **to** aludir a.

alluring [ə'ljʊərɪŋ] *adj* [person] atrayente; [thing] tentador(ra).

allusion [ə'lu:ʒn] *n* alusión *f*.

ally ['ælaɪ] *(pl* **-ies)** *n* aliado *m*, -da *f*.

almighty [ɔ:l'maɪtɪ] *adj inf* [very big] descomunal.

almond ['ɑ:mənd] *n* [nut] almendra *f*.

almost ['ɔ:lməʊst] *adv* casi.

alms [ɑ:mz] *npl dated* limosna *f*.

aloe ['æləʊ] *n* áloe *m*.

aloft [ə'lɒft] *adv* [in the air] en lo alto.

alone [ə'ləʊn] ◇ *adj* solo(la); **to be** ~ **with** estar a solas con. ◇ *adv* - **1.** [without others] solo(la) - **2.** [only] sólo - **3.** *phr*: **to leave sthg/sb** ~ dejar algo/a alguien en paz.
 ◆ **let alone** *conj* no digamos, y mucho menos.

along [ə'lɒŋ] ◇ *adv* - **1.** [forward] hacia delante; **to go** *or* **walk** ~ avanzar; **she was walking** ~ iba andando - **2.** [to this or that place]: **to come** ~ venir; **to go** ~ ir. ◇ *prep* [towards one end of, beside] por, a lo largo de.
 ◆ **all along** *adv* todo el rato; **she knew all** ~ lo sabía desde el principio.
 ◆ **along with** *prep* junto con.

alongside [ə,lɒŋ'saɪd] ◇ *prep* - **1.** [next to] junto a - **2.** [together with] junto con. ◇ *adv* : **to come** ~ ponerse a la misma altura.

aloof [ə'lu:f] ◇ *adj* frío(a), distante. ◇ *adv* distante, a distancia; **to remain** ~ **(from)** mantenerse a distancia (de).

aloud [ə'laʊd] *adv* en alto, en voz alta.

alphabet ['ælfəbet] *n* alfabeto *m*.

alphabetical [,ælfə'betɪkl] *adj* alfabético(ca); **in** ~ **order** en *or* por orden alfabético.

Alps [ælps] *npl*: **the** ~ los Alpes.

already [ɔ:l'redɪ] *adv* ya.

alright [,ɔ:l'raɪt] = **all right**.

Alsatian [æl'seɪʃn] *n* [dog] pastor *m* alemán.

also ['ɔ:lsəʊ] *adv* también.

altar ['ɔ:ltə'] *n* altar *m*.

alt code [ɔ:lt-] *n* COMPUT código *m* alt.

alter ['ɔ:ltə'] ◇ *vt* [modify] alterar, modificar. ◇ *vi* cambiar.

alteration [,ɔ:ltə'reɪʃn] *n* - **1.** [gen] alteración *f* - **2.** [to dress] arreglo *m*.

alternate [*adj* ɔ:l'tɜ:nət, *US* 'ɔ:ltərnət, *vb* 'ɔ:ltərneɪt] ◇ *adj* - **1.** [by turns] alterno(na) - **2.** [every other]: **on** ~ **days/ weeks** cada dos días/semanas. ◇ *n US* sustituto(ta). ◇ *vi*: **to** ~ **(with/between)** alternar (con/entre).

alternating current ['ɔ:ltəneɪtɪŋ-] *n* ELEC corriente *f* alterna.

alternative [ɔ:l'tɜ:nətɪv] ◇ *adj* alternativo(va). ◇ *n* alternativa *f*, opción *f*; **to have no** ~ **(but to do sthg)** no tener más remedio (que hacer algo).

alternatively [ɔ:l'tɜ:nətɪvlɪ] *adv* o bien.

alternator ['ɔ:ltəneɪtə'] *n* ELEC alternador *m*.

although [ɔ:l'ðəʊ] *conj* aunque.

altitude ['æltɪtju:d] *n* altitud *f*.

alto ['æltəʊ] (*pl* -**s**) *n* [female singer] contralto *f*; [male singer] contralto *m*.

altogether [,ɔ:ltə'geðə'] *adv* - **1**. [completely] completamente, totalmente; **not** ~ no del todo - **2**. [considering all things] en conjunto, en general - **3**. [in total] en total.

aluminium UK [,ælju'mɪnɪəm], **aluminum** US [ə'lu:mɪnəm] *n* aluminio *m*.

always ['ɔ:lweɪz] *adv* siempre.

am [æm] *v* ⊳ **be**.

a.m. (*abbr of* **ante meridiem**): **at 3** ~ a las tres de la mañana.

AM (*abbr of* **amplitude modulation**) *n* AM *f*.

amalgamate [ə'mælgəmeɪt] ◇ *vt* [ideas] amalgamar; [companies, organizations] fusionar. ◇ *vi* [of ideas] amalgamarse; [of companies, organizations] fusionarse.

amass [ə'mæs] *vt* [fortune, wealth] amasar.

amateur ['æmətə'] ◇ *adj* aficionado(da); *pej* chapucero(ra), poco profesional. ◇ *n* aficionado *m*, -da *f*; *pej* chapucero *m*, -ra *f*.

amateurish [,æmə'tɜ:rɪʃ] *adj* chapucero(-ra), poco profesional.

amaze [ə'meɪz] *vt* asombrar.

amazed [ə'meɪzd] *adj* asombrado(da).

amazement [ə'meɪzmənt] *n* asombro *m*.

amazing [ə'meɪzɪŋ] *adj* - **1**. [surprising] asombroso(sa) - **2**. [excellent] genial.

Amazon ['æməzn] *n* - **1**. [river]: **the** ~ **el** Amazonas - **2**. [region]: **the** ~ (**Basin**) la cuenca amazónica; **the** ~ **rainforest** la selva amazónica.

ambassador [æm'bæsədə'] *n* embajador *m*, -ra *f*.

amber ['æmbə'] ◇ *adj* - **1**. [amber-coloured] de color ámbar, ambarino(na) - **2**. UK [traffic light] ámbar. ◇ *n* ámbar *m*.

ambiguous [æm'bɪgjʊəs] *adj* ambiguo(-gua).

ambition [æm'bɪʃn] *n* ambición *f*.

ambitious [æm'bɪʃəs] *adj* ambicioso(sa).

amble ['æmbl] *vi* [walk] deambular.

ambulance ['æmbjʊləns] *n* ambulancia *f*.

ambush ['æmbʊʃ] ◇ *n* emboscada *f*. ◇ *vt* emboscar.

amenable [ə'mi:nəbl] *adj* receptivo(va); ~ **to** favorable a.

amend [ə'mend] *vt* [law] enmendar; [text] corregir; [schedule] modificar.
  ◆ **amends** *npl*: **to make** ~**s for sthg** reparar algo.

amendment [ə'mendmənt] *n* [change - to law] enmienda *f*; [- to text] corrección *f*; [- to schedule] modificación *f*.

amenities [ə'mi:nətɪz] *npl* [of town] facilidades *fpl*; [of building] comodidades *fpl*.

America [ə'merɪkə] *n* América.

American [ə'merɪkn] ◇ *adj* americano(-na). ◇ *n* [person] americano *m*, -na *f*.

American football *n* fútbol *m* americano.

American Indian *n* amerindio *m*, -dia *f*.

amiable ['eɪmjəbl] *adj* amable, agradable.

amicable ['æmɪkəbl] *adj* amigable, amistoso(sa).

amid(st) [ə'mɪd(st)] *prep fml* entre, en medio de.

amiss [ə'mɪs] ◇ *adj*: **something's** ~ algo va mal. ◇ *adv*: **to take sthg** ~ tomarse algo a mal.

ammonia [ə'məʊnjə] *n* amoniaco *m*.

ammunition [,æmjʊ'nɪʃn] *n (U)* MIL municiones *fpl*.

amnesia [æm'ni:zjə] *n* amnesia *f*.

amnesty ['æmnəstɪ] (*pl* -**ies**) *n* amnistía *f*.

amok [ə'mɒk] *adv*: **to run** ~ enloquecer atacando a gente de forma indiscriminada.

among(st) [ə'mʌŋ(st)] *prep* entre.

amoral [,eɪ'mɒrəl] *adj* amoral.

amorous ['æmərəs] *adj* apasionado(da).

amount [ə'maʊnt] *n* cantidad *f*.
  ◆ **amount to** *vt fus* - **1**. [total] ascender a - **2**. [be equivalent to] venir a ser.

amp [æmp] *n abbr of* **ampere**.

ampere ['æmpeə'] *n* amperio *m*.

amphibian [æm'fɪbɪən] *n* anfibio *m*.

ample ['æmpl] *adj* - **1**. [enough] suficiente; [more than enough] sobrado(da); **to have** ~ **time** tener tiempo de sobra - **2**. [garment, room] amplio(plia); [stomach, bosom] abundante.

amplifier ['æmplɪfaɪə'] *n* amplificador *m*.

amputate ['æmpjʊteɪt] *vt* & *vi* amputar.

Amsterdam [,æmstə'dæm] *n* Amsterdam.

Amtrak ['æmtræk] *n* organismo que regula y coordina las líneas férreas en Estados Unidos.

amuck [ə'mʌk] = **amok**.

amuse [ə'mju:z] *vt* - **1**. [make laugh, smile] divertir - **2**. [entertain] distraer.

amused [ə'mju:zd] *adj* - **1**. [person, look] divertido(da); **I was not** ~ at OR by that no me hizo gracia eso - **2**. [entertained]: **to keep o.s.** ~ entretenerse, distraerse.

amusement [ə'mju:zmənt] *n* - **1**. [enjoyment] regocijo *m*, diversión *f* - **2**. [diversion, game] atracción *f*.

amusement arcade *n* salón *m* de juegos.

amusement park *n* parque *m* de atracciones.

amusing [ə'mju:zɪŋ] *adj* divertido(da), gracioso(sa).

an [stressed æn, unstressed ən] ⊳ **a²**.

anabolic steroid [,ænə'bɒlɪk-] *n* esteroide *m* anabolizante.

anaemic UK, **anemic** US [ə'ni:mɪk]

adj [ill] anémico(ca).

anaesthetic *UK*, **anesthetic** *US* [ˌænɪs-ˈθetɪk] *n* anestesia *f*; **local/general** ~ anestesia local/general.

analogue, analog *US* [ˈænəlɒg] ⬦ *adj* [watch, clock] analógico(ca). ⬦ *n fml* equivalente *m*.

analogy [əˈnælədʒɪ] (*pl* -ies) *n* analogía *f*.

analyse *UK*, **analyze** *US* [ˈænəlaɪz] *vt* analizar.

analysis [əˈnæləsɪs] (*pl* **analyses** [əˈnæləsiːz]) *n* - **1.** [examination] análisis *m inv* - **2.** [psychoanalysis] psicoanálisis *m inv*.

analyst [ˈænəlɪst] *n* - **1.** [gen] analista *m or f* - **2.** [psychoanalyst] psicoanalista *m or f*.

analytic(al) [ˌænəˈlɪtɪk(l)] *adj* analítico(ca).

analyze *US* = **analyse**.

anarchist [ˈænəkɪst] *n* anarquista *m or f*.

anarchy [ˈænəkɪ] *n* anarquía *f*.

anathema [əˈnæθəmə] *n*: **the idea is** ~ **to me** la idea me parece aberrante.

anatomy [əˈnætəmɪ] (*pl* -ies) *n* anatomía *f*.

ANC (*abbr of* **African National Congress**) *n* ANC *m*.

ancestor [ˈænsestəʳ] *n lit* & *fig* antepasado *m*.

anchor [ˈæŋkəʳ] ⬦ *n* NAUT ancla *f*; **to drop** ~ echar el ancla; **to weigh** ~ levar anclas. ⬦ *vt* - **1.** [secure] sujetar - **2.** *esp US* TV presentar. ⬦ *vi* NAUT anclar.

anchovy [ˈæntʃəvɪ] (*pl inv or* -ies) *n* [salted] anchoa *f*; [fresh, in vinegar] boquerón *m*.

ancient [ˈeɪnʃənt] *adj* - **1.** [gen] antiguo(gua) - **2.** *hum* [very old] vetusto(ta).

ancillary [ænˈsɪlərɪ] *adj* auxiliar.

and [strong form ænd, weak form ənd, ən] *conj* - **1.** [gen] y; (*before 'i' or 'hi'*) e; **fish** ~ **chips** pescado con patatas fritas; **faster** ~ **faster** cada vez más rápido; **it's nice** ~ **easy** es sencillito - **2.** [in numbers]: **one hundred** ~ **eighty** ciento ochenta; **one** ~ **a half** uno y medio; **2** ~ **2 is 4** 2 y 2 son 4 - **3.** [to]: **try** ~ **come** intenta venir; **come** ~ **see the kids** ven a ver a los niños; **wait** ~ **see** espera a ver.

➡ **and so on, and so forth** *adv* etcétera, y cosas así.

Andalusia [ˌændəˈluːzɪə] *n* Andalucía.

Andes [ˈændiːz] *npl*: **the** ~ los Andes.

Andorra [ænˈdɔːrə] *n* Andorra.

anecdote [ˈænɪkdəʊt] *n* anécdota *f*.

anemic *US* = **anaemic**.

anesthetic *etc US* = **anaesthetic**.

anew [əˈnjuː] *adv* de nuevo, nuevamente.

angel [ˈeɪndʒəl] *n* RELIG ángel *m*.

anger [ˈæŋɡəʳ] ⬦ *n* ira *f*, furia *f*. ⬦ *vt* enfadar.

angina [ænˈdʒaɪnə] *n* angina *f* de pecho.

angle [ˈæŋɡl] *n* - **1.** [gen] ángulo *m*; **the picture was hanging at an** ~ [aslant] el cuadro

estaba colgado torcido - **2.** [point of view] enfoque *m*.

Anglepoise lamp® [ˈæŋɡlpɔɪz-] *n* flexo *m*.

angler [ˈæŋɡləʳ] *n* pescador *m*, -ra *f* (*con caña*).

Anglican [ˈæŋɡlɪkən] ⬦ *adj* anglicano(na). ⬦ *n* anglicano *m*, -na *f*.

angling [ˈæŋɡlɪŋ] *n* pesca *f* con caña.

Anglo-Saxon [ˌæŋɡləʊˈsæksn] ⬦ *adj* anglosajón(ona). ⬦ *n* - **1.** [person] anglosajón *m*, -ona *f* - **2.** [language] anglosajón *m*.

angry [ˈæŋɡrɪ] (*compar* -ier, *superl* -iest) *adj* [person] enfadado(da); [letter, look, face] furioso(sa), airado(da); **to be** ~ **at or with sb** estar enfadado con alguien; **to get** ~ **with sb** enfadarse con alguien.

anguish [ˈæŋɡwɪʃ] *n* angustia *f*.

angular [ˈæŋɡjʊləʳ] *adj* [face, body] anguloso(sa).

animal [ˈænɪml] ⬦ *adj* [instincts, kingdom] animal; [rights] de los animales. ⬦ *n* [creature] animal *m*; *pej* [person] animal *m or f*.

animate [ˈænɪmət] *adj* animado(da).

animated [ˈænɪmeɪtɪd] *adj* animado(da).

aniseed [ˈænɪsiːd] *n* anís *m*.

ankle [ˈæŋkl] ⬦ *n* tobillo *m*. ⬦ *comp*: ~ **boots** botines *mpl*; ~ **socks** calcetines *mpl* cortos.

anklet [ˈæŋklɪt] *n US* [ankle sock] calcetín *m* corto.

annex [ˈæneks] ⬦ *n* edificio *m* anejo. ⬦ *vt* anexionar.

annexe [ˈæneks] = **annex**.

annihilate [əˈnaɪəleɪt] *vt* [destroy] aniquilar.

anniversary [ˌænɪˈvɜːsərɪ] (*pl* -ies) *n* aniversario *m*.

announce [əˈnaʊns] *vt* anunciar.

announcement [əˈnaʊnsmənt] *n* anuncio *m*.

announcer [əˈnaʊnsəʳ] *n*: **radio/television** ~ presentador *m*, -ra *f or* locutor *m*, -ra *f* de radio/televisión.

annoy [əˈnɔɪ] *vt* fastidiar, molestar.

annoyance [əˈnɔɪəns] *n* molestia *f*.

annoyed [əˈnɔɪd] *adj*: **to be** ~ **at sthg/with sb** estar molesto(ta) por algo/con alguien; **to get** ~ **at sthg/with sb** molestarse por algo/con alguien.

annoying [əˈnɔɪɪŋ] *adj* fastidioso(sa), irritante.

annual [ˈænjʊəl] ⬦ *adj* anual. ⬦ *n* - **1.** [plant] planta *f* anual - **2.** [book] anuario *m*.

annual general meeting *n* asamblea *f* general anual.

annul [əˈnʌl] (*pt* & *pp* -led, *cont* -ling) *vt* anular.

annum [ˈænəm] *n*: **per** ~ al año.

anomaly [əˈnɒməlɪ] (*pl* -ies) *n* anomalía *f*.

anonymous [ə'nɒnɪməs] *adj* anónimo(-ma).

anorak ['ænəræk] *n* -1. *esp UK* [garment] chubasquero *m*, anorak *m* -2. *UK inf* [boring person] petardo *m*, -da *f*.

anorexia (nervosa) [,ænə'reksɪə (nɜː'vəʊsə)] *n* anorexia *f*.

anorexic [,ænə'reksɪk] ◇ *adj* anoréxico(-ca). ◇ *n* anoréxico *m*, -ca *f*.

another [ə'nʌðəʳ] ◇ *adj* otro(tra); ~ **one** otro(tra); **in ~ few minutes** en unos minutos más. ◇ *pron* otro *m*, -tra *f*; **one after ~** uno tras otro, una tras otra; **one ~** el uno al otro, la una a la otra; **we love one ~** nos queremos.

answer ['ɑːnsəʳ] ◇ *n* -1. [gen] respuesta *f*; **in ~ to** en respuesta a -2. [to problem] solución *f*. ◇ *vt* -1. [reply to] responder a, contestar a -2. [respond to]: **to ~ the door** abrir la puerta; **to ~ the phone** coger OR contestar el teléfono. ◇ *vi* responder, contestar.
◆ **answer back** *vt sep* & *vi* replicar.
◆ **answer for** *vt fus* -1. [accept responsibility for] responder por; **they have a lot to ~ for** tienen mucho que explicar -2. [suffer consequences of] responder de.

answerable ['ɑːnsərəbl] *adj*: ~ **(to sb/for sthg)** responsable (ante alguien/de algo).

answering machine ['ɑːnsərɪŋ-], **answerphone** ['ɑːnsəfəʊn] *n* contestador *m* automático.

ant [ænt] *n* hormiga *f*.

antagonism [æn'tægənɪzm] *n* antagonismo *m*.

antagonize, -ise [æn'tægənaɪz] *vt* provocar la hostilidad de.

Antarctic [æn'tɑːktɪk] ◇ *adj* antártico(-ca). ◇ *n*: **the ~** el Antártico.

Antarctica [æn'tɑːktɪkə] *n* (la) Antártida.

antelope ['æntɪləʊp] (*pl inv OR* -s) *n* antílope *m*.

antenatal [,æntɪ'neɪtl] *adj* prenatal.

antenatal clinic *n* clínica *f* de preparación al parto.

antenna [æn'tenə] (*pl sense 1* -nae [-niː], *pl sense 2* -s) *n* -1. [of insect] antena *f* -2. *US* [aerial] antena *f*.

anthem ['ænθəm] *n* himno *m*.

anthology [æn'θɒlədʒɪ] (*pl* -ies) *n* antología *f*.

antibiotic [,æntɪbaɪ'ɒtɪk] *n* antibiótico *m*.

antibody ['æntɪ,bɒdɪ] (*pl* -ies) *n* anticuerpo *m*.

anticipate [æn'tɪsɪpeɪt] *vt* -1. [expect] prever -2. [look forward to] esperar ansiosamente -3. [preempt] adelantarse a.

anticipation [æn,tɪsɪ'peɪʃn] *n* [excitement] expectación *f*; **in ~ of** en previsión de.

anticlimax [,æntɪ'klaɪmæks] *n* decepción *f*.

anticlockwise [,æntɪ'klɒkwaɪz] *UK adv* en

sentido contrario al de las agujas del reloj.

antics ['æntɪks] *npl* payasadas *fpl*.

anticyclone [,æntɪ'saɪkləʊn] *n* anticiclón *m*.

antidepressant [,æntɪdɪ'presnt] *n* antidepresivo *m*.

antidote ['æntɪdəʊt] *n lit* & *fig* : ~ **(to)** antídoto *m* (contra).

antifreeze ['æntɪfriːz] *n* anticongelante *m*.

antihistamine [,æntɪ'hɪstəmɪn] *n* antihistamínico *m*.

antiperspirant [,æntɪ'pɜːspərənt] *n* antitranspirante *m*.

antiquated ['æntɪkweɪtɪd] *adj* anticuado(-da).

antique [æn'tiːk] ◇ *adj* [furniture, object] antiguo(gua). ◇ *n* antigüedad *f*.

antique shop *n* tienda *f* de antigüedades.

anti-Semitism [,æntɪ'semɪtɪzm] *n* antisemitismo *m*.

antiseptic [,æntɪ'septɪk] ◇ *adj* antiséptico(ca). ◇ *n* antiséptico *m*.

antisocial [,æntɪ'səʊʃl] *adj* -1. [against society] antisocial -2. [unsociable] poco sociable.

antlers ['æntləz] *npl* cornamenta *f*.

anus ['eɪnəs] *n* ano *m*.

anvil ['ænvɪl] *n* yunque *m*.

anxiety [æŋ'zaɪətɪ] (*pl* -ies) *n* -1. [worry] ansiedad *f*, inquietud *f* -2. [cause of worry] preocupación *f* -3. [keenness] afán *m*, ansia *f*.

anxious ['æŋkʃəs] *adj* -1. [worried] preocupado(da); **to be ~ about** estar preocupado por -2. [keen]: **to be ~ that/to do sthg** estar ansioso(sa) por que/por hacer algo.

any ['enɪ] ◇ *adj* -1. *(with negative)* ninguno(na); **I haven't read ~ books** no he leído ningún libro; **I haven't got ~ money** no tengo nada de dinero -2. [some] algún(u-na); **are there ~ cakes left?** ¿queda algún pastel?; **is there ~ milk left?** ¿queda algo de leche?; **have you got ~ money?** ¿tienes dinero? -3. [no matter which] cualquier; ~ **box will do** cualquier caja vale; *see also* **case, day, moment, rate.** ◇ *pron* -1. *(with negative)* ninguno *m*, -na *f*; **I didn't get ~** a mí no me tocó ninguno -2. [some] alguno *m*, -na *f*; **can ~ of you do it?** ¿sabe alguno de vosotros hacerlo?; **I need some matches, do you have ~?** necesito cerillas, ¿tienes? -3. [no matter which] cualquiera; **take ~ you like** coge cualquiera que te guste. ◇ *adv* -1. *(with negative)*: **I can't see it ~ more** ya no lo veo; **he's not feeling ~ better** no se siente nada mejor; **I can't stand it ~ longer** no lo aguanto más -2. [some, a little]: **do you want ~ more potatoes?** ¿quieres más patatas?; **is that ~ better/different?** ¿es así mejor/diferente?

anybody ['enɪˌbɒdɪ] = anyone.

anyhow ['enɪhaʊ] *adv* - 1. [in spite of that] de todos modos - 2. [carelessly] de cualquier manera - 3. [in any case] en cualquier caso.

anyone ['enɪwʌn] *pron* - 1. *(in negative sentences)* nadie; **I don't know** ~ no conozco a nadie - 2. *(in questions)* alguien - 3. [any person] cualquiera.

anyplace *US* = anywhere.

anything ['enɪθɪŋ] *pron* - 1. *(in negative sentences)* nada; **I don't want** ~ no quiero nada - 2. *(in questions)* algo; **would you like** ~ **else?** ¿quiere algo más? - 3. [any object, event] cualquier cosa.

anyway ['enɪweɪ] *adv* - 1. [in any case] de todas formas *OR* maneras - 2. [in conversation] en cualquier caso.

anywhere ['enɪweəʳ], **anyplace** *US* ['enɪpleɪs] *adv* - 1. *(in negative sentences)* en ningún sitio; **I didn't go** ~ no fui a ninguna parte - 2. *(in questions)* en algún sitio; **did you go** ~**?** ¿fuiste a algún sitio? - 3. [wherever] cualquier sitio; ~ **you like** donde quieras.

apart [ə'pɑːt] *adv* - 1. [separated]: **we're living** ~ vivimos separados - 2. [aside] aparte; **joking** ~ bromas aparte.

◆ **apart from** *prep* - 1. [except for] aparte de, salvo - 2. [as well as] aparte de.

apartheid [ə'pɑːtheɪt] *n* apartheid *m*.

apartment [ə'pɑːtmənt] *n esp US* piso *m*, apartamento *m*, departamento *m Amér*.

apartment building *n US* bloque *m* de pisos, bloque *m* de departamentos *Amér*.

apathy ['æpəθɪ] *n* apatía *f*.

ape [eɪp] ◇ *n* simio *m*. ◇ *vt pej* imitar.

aperitif [əperə'tiːf] *n* aperitivo *m*.

aperture ['æpə,tjʊəʳ] *n* abertura *f*.

apex ['eɪpeks] *(pl* -es *OR* apices*)* *n* [top] vértice *m*.

APEX ['eɪpeks] *(abbr of* advance purchase excursion*)* *n UK* (tarifa *f*) APEX *f*.

apices ['eɪpɪsiːz] *pl* ▷ apex.

apiece [ə'piːs] *adv* cada uno(na).

apocalypse [ə'pɒkəlɪps] *n* apocalipsis *m inv.*

●**apologetic** [əˌpɒlə'dʒetɪk] *adj* [tone, look] lleno(na) de disculpas; **to be very** ~ **(about)** no hacer más que disculparse (por).

apologize, -ise [ə'pɒlədʒaɪz] *vi*: **to** ~ **(to sb for sthg)** disculparse (ante alguien por algo); **I** ~**d to her** le pedí perdón.

apology [ə'pɒlədʒɪ] *(pl* -ies*)* *n* disculpa *f*; **Tom sends his apologies** [can't come] Tom se excusa por no poder asistir.

apostle [ə'pɒsl] *n RELIG* apóstol *m*.

apostrophe [ə'pɒstrəfɪ] *n* apóstrofo *m*.

appal *(UK pt & pp* -led, *cont* -ling*)*, **appall** *US* [ə'pɔːl] *vt* horrorizar.

appalling [ə'pɔːlɪŋ] *adj* [shocking] horroroso(sa).

apparatus [ˌæpə'reɪtəs] *(pl inv OR* -es*)* *n* - 1. [equipment] aparatos *mpl*; **a piece of** ~ un aparato - 2. *POL* aparato *m*.

apparel [ə'pærəl] *n US* ropa *f*.

apparent [ə'pærənt] *adj* - 1. [evident] evidente, patente - 2. [seeming] aparente.

apparently [ə'pærəntlɪ] *adv* - 1. [it seems] por lo visto, diz que *Amér* - 2. [seemingly] aparentemente.

appeal [ə'piːl] ◇ *vi* - 1. [request]: **to** ~ **(to sb for sthg)** solicitar (de alguien algo) - 2. [to sb's honour, common sense]: **to** ~ **to** apelar a - 3. *JUR*: **to** ~ **(against)** apelar (contra) - 4. [attract, interest]: **to** ~ **(to)** atraer (a). ◇ *n* - 1. [request] llamamiento *m*, súplica *f*; [fundraising campaign] campaña *f* para recaudar fondos - 2. *JUR* apelación *f* - 3. [charm, interest] atractivo *m*.

appealing [ə'piːlɪŋ] *adj* [attractive] atractivo(va).

appear [ə'pɪəʳ] *vi* - 1. [gen] aparecer - 2. [seem]: **to** ~ **(to be/to do sthg)** parecer (ser/hacer algo); **it would** ~ **that** ... parece que ... - 3. [in play, film, on TV]: **to** ~ **on TV/ in a film** salir en televisión/en una película - 4. *JUR*: **to** ~ **(before)** comparecer (ante).

appearance [ə'pɪərəns] *n* - 1. [gen] aparición *f*; **to make an** ~ aparecer - 2. [of sportsman] actuación *f* - 3. [look - of person, place, object] aspecto *m*.

appease [ə'piːz] *vt* aplacar, apaciguar.

append [ə'pend] *vt fml* - 1. [add]: **to** ~ **sthg (to sthg)** agregar algo (a algo) - 2. [attach] [document]: **to** ~ **sthg (to sthg)** adjuntar algo (a algo).

appendices [ə'pendɪsiːz] *pl* ▷ appendix.

appendicitis [ə,pendɪ'saɪtɪs] *n (U)* apendicitis *f inv.*

appendix [ə'pendɪks] *(pl* -dixes *OR* -dices*)* *n* [gen & *ANAT*] apéndice *m*.

appetite ['æpɪtaɪt] *n* - 1. [for food] apetito *m*; **I no longer have any** ~ **for my food** ya no tengo ganas de comer - 2. *fig* [enthusiasm]: ~ **for** entusiasmo *m* por.

appetizer, -iser ['æpɪtaɪzəʳ] *n* aperitivo *m*, pasapalos *m inv Amér*.

appetizing, -ising ['æpɪtaɪzɪŋ] *adj* [food] apetitoso(sa).

applaud [ə'plɔːd] *vt & vi lit & fig* aplaudir.

applause [ə'plɔːz] *n (U)* aplausos *mpl*.

apple ['æpl] *n* manzana *f*.

applet ['æplɪt] *n COMPUT* applet *m*.

apple tree *n* manzano *m*.

appliance [ə'plaɪəns] *n* aparato *m*.

applicable [ə'plɪkəbl] *adj*: **to be** ~ **(to)** aplicarse (a).

applicant ['æplɪkənt] *n*: ~ **(for)** solicitante *m OR f*(de).

application [ˌæplɪ'keɪʃn] *n* - 1. [gen] aplicación *f* - 2. [for job, college, club]: ~ **(for)**

solicitud *f* (para) - **3.** COMPUT aplicación *f*.

application form *n* impreso *m* de solicitud.

applied [ə'plaɪd] *adj* [science] aplicado(da).

apply [ə'plaɪ] (*pt* & *pp* **-ied**) ⬦ *vt* [gen] aplicar; [brakes] echar. ⬦ *vi* - **1.** [for work, grant] presentar una solicitud; **to ~ to sb for sthg** solicitar a alguien algo - **2.** [be relevant] aplicarse; **to ~ to** concernir a.

appoint [ə'pɔɪnt] *vt* [to job, position]: **to ~ sb (to sthg)** nombrar a alguien (para algo); **to ~ sb as sthg** nombrar a alguien algo.

appointment [ə'pɔɪntmənt] *n* - **1.** [to job, position] nombramiento *m* - **2.** [job, position] puesto *m*, cargo *m* - **3.** [with businessman, lawyer] cita *f*; [with doctor, hairdresser] hora *f*; **to have an ~** [with businessman] tener una cita; [with doctor] tener hora; **to make an ~** concertar una cita.

apportion [ə'pɔːʃn] *vt* [money] repartir; [blame] adjudicar.

appraisal [ə'preɪzl] *n* evaluación *f*, valoración *f*.

appreciable [ə'priːʃəbl] *adj* [difference] apreciable, sensible.

appreciate [ə'priːʃɪeɪt] ⬦ *vt* - **1.** [value, like] apreciar - **2.** [recognize, understand] darse cuenta de - **3.** [be grateful for] agradecer. ⬦ *vi* FIN revalorizarse.

appreciation [ə,priːʃɪ'eɪʃn] *n* - **1.** [liking] aprecio *m* - **2.** [recognition, understanding] entendimiento *m* - **3.** [gratitude] agradecimiento *m* - **4.** FIN revalorización *f*, plusvalía *f*.

appreciative [ə'priːʃjətɪv] *adj* [person, remark] agradecido(da); [audience] entendido(da).

apprehensive [,æprɪ'hensɪv] *adj* aprensivo(va).

apprentice [ə'prentɪs] *n* aprendiz *m*, -za *f*.

apprenticeship [ə'prentɪʃɪp] *n* aprendizaje *m*.

approach [ə'prəʊtʃ] ⬦ *n* - **1.** [arrival] llegada *f* - **2.** [way in] acceso *m* - **3.** [method] enfoque *m*, planteamiento *m* - **4.** [to person]: **to make ~es to sb** hacerle propuestas a alguien. ⬦ *vt* - **1.** [come near to] acercarse a - **2.** [ask]: **to ~ sb about sthg** dirigirse a alguien acerca de algo - **3.** [problem, situation] abordar - **4.** [level, speed] aproximarse a. ⬦ *vi* acercarse.

approachable [ə'prəʊtʃəbl] *adj* accesible.

appropriate [*adj* ə'prəʊprɪət, *vb* ə'prəʊprɪeɪt] ⬦ *adj* apropiado(da), adecuado(da). ⬦ *vt* JUR [take] apropiarse de.

approval [ə'pruːvl] *n* - **1.** [admiration] aprobación *f* - **2.** [official sanctioning] visto *m* bueno - **3.** COMM: **on ~** a prueba.

approve [ə'pruːv] ⬦ *vi* estar de acuerdo; **to ~ of sthg/sb** ver con buenos ojos algo/a alguien. ⬦ *vt* aprobar.

approx. [ə'prɒks] (*abbr of* **approximately**) aprox.

approximate [ə'prɒksɪmət] *adj* aproximado(da).

approximately [ə'prɒksɪmətlɪ] *adv* aproximadamente.

apricot ['eɪprɪkɒt] *n* [fruit] albaricoque *m*, chabacano *m Méx*, damasco *m Andes, CSur*.

April ['eɪprəl] *n* abril *m*; *see also* **September**.

April Fools' Day *n* primero *m* de abril, ≃ Día *m* de los Santos Inocentes.

apron ['eɪprən] *n* [clothing] delantal *m*, mandil *m*.

apt [æpt] *adj* - **1.** [pertinent] acertado(da) - **2.** [likely]: **~ to do sthg** propenso(sa) a hacer algo.

aptitude ['æptɪtjuːd] *n* aptitud *f*.

aptly ['æptlɪ] *adv* apropiadamente.

aqualung ['ækwəlʌŋ] *n* escafandra *f* autónoma.

aquarium [ə'kweərɪəm] (*pl* **-riums** OR **-ria** [-rɪə]) *n* acuario *m*.

Aquarius [ə'kweərɪəs] *n* Acuario *m*.

aquatic [ə'kwætɪk] *adj* acuático(ca).

aqueduct ['ækwɪdʌkt] *n* acueducto *m*.

Arab ['ærəb] ⬦ *adj* árabe. ⬦ *n* [person] árabe *m* OR *f*.

Arabic ['ærəbɪk] ⬦ *adj* árabe. ⬦ *n* [language] árabe *m*.

Arabic numeral *n* número *m* arábigo.

arable ['ærəbl] *adj* cultivable.

arbitrary ['ɑːbɪtrərɪ] *adj* [random] arbitrario(ria).

arbitration [,ɑːbɪ'treɪʃn] *n* arbitraje *m*.

arcade [ɑː'keɪd] *n* - **1.** [shopping arcade] galería *f* comercial - **2.** [covered passage] arcada *f*, galería *f*.

arcade game *n* videojuego *m*.

arch [ɑːtʃ] ⬦ *n* - **1.** ARCHIT arco *m* - **2.** [of foot] puente *m*. ⬦ *vt* arquear.

archaeologist [,ɑːkɪ'ɒlədʒɪst] *n* arqueólogo *m*, -ga *f*.

archaeology [,ɑːkɪ'ɒlədʒɪ] *n* arqueología *f*.

archaic [ɑː'keɪɪk] *adj* arcaico(ca).

archbishop [,ɑːtʃ'bɪʃəp] *n* arzobispo *m*.

archenemy [,ɑːtʃ'enɪmɪ] (*pl* **-ies**) *n* peor enemigo *m*, enemigo acérrimo.

archeology *etc* [,ɑːkɪ'ɒlədʒɪ] = **archaeology** *etc*.

archer ['ɑːtʃər] *n* arquero *m*.

archery ['ɑːtʃərɪ] *n* tiro *m* con arco.

archetypal [,ɑːkɪ'taɪpl] *adj* arquetípico(-ca).

architect ['ɑːkɪtekt] *n* - **1.** [of buildings] arquitecto *m*, -ta *f* - **2.** *fig* [of plan, event] artífice *m* OR *f*.

architecture ['ɑːkɪtektʃər] *n* [gen & COMPUT] arquitectura *f*.

archives ['ɑːkaɪvz] *npl* [of documents] archivos *mpl*.

archway ['ɑ:tʃweɪ] *n* [passage] arcada *f*; [entrance] entrada *f* en forma de arco.

Arctic ['ɑ:ktɪk] ⬦ *adj* GEOGR ártico(ca). ⬦ *n*: the ~ el Ártico.

ardent ['ɑ:dənt] *adj* [supporter, admirer, desire] ardiente, ferviente.

arduous ['ɑ:djʊəs] *adj* arduo(dua).

are [*weak form* əʳ, *strong form* ɑ:ʳ] ⬦ be.

area ['eərɪə] *n* - 1. [region, designated space] zona *f*, área *f*; **in the** ~ en la zona - 2. [of town] zona *f*, barrio *m* - 3. *fig* [approximate size, number]: **in the** ~ **of** del orden de, alrededor de - 4. [surface size] superficie *f*, área *f* - 5. [of knowledge, interest] campo *m*.

area code *n* US prefijo *m* (telefónico).

arena [ə'ri:nə] *n* - 1. SPORT pabellón *m* - 2. *fig* [area of activity]: **she entered the political** ~ saltó al ruedo político.

aren't [ɑ:nt] = are not.

Argentina [,ɑ:dʒən'ti:nə] *n* (la) Argentina.

Argentine ['ɑ:dʒəntaɪn] *adj* argentino(na).

Argentinian [,ɑ:dʒən'tɪnɪən] ⬦ *adj* argentino(na). ⬦ *n* argentino *m*, -na *f*.

arguably ['ɑ:gjʊəblɪ] *adv* probablemente.

argue ['ɑ:gju:] ⬦ *vi* - 1. [quarrel]: **to** ~ **(with sb about sthg)** discutir (con alguien de algo) - 2. [reason]: **to** ~ **(for)** abogar (por); **to** ~ **(against)** oponerse (a). ⬦ *vt*: **to** ~ **that** argumentar que.

argument ['ɑ:gjʊmənt] *n* - 1. [gen] discusión *f*; **to have an** ~ **(with)** tener una discusión (con) - 2. [reason] argumento *m*.

argumentative [,ɑ:gjʊ'mentətɪv] *adj* propenso(sa) a discutir.

arid ['ærɪd] *adj lit & fig* árido(da).

Aries ['eəri:z] *n* Aries *m*.

arise [ə'raɪz] (*pt* arose, *pp* arisen [ə'rɪzn]) *vi* [appear]: **to** ~ **(from)** surgir (de).

aristocrat [UK 'ærɪstəkræt, US ə'rɪstəkræt] *n* aristócrata *m* OR *f*.

arithmetic [ə'rɪθmətɪk] *n* aritmética *f*.

ark [ɑ:k] *n* arca *f*.

arm [ɑ:m] ⬦ *n* - 1. [of person, chair, record player] brazo *m*; ~ **in** ~ del brazo; **to twist sb's** ~ *fig* persuadir a alguien - 2. [of garment] manga *f*. ⬦ *vt* armar. ⬦ *vi* armarse.
  ➔ **arms** *npl* [weapons] armas *fpl*.

armaments ['ɑ:məmənts] *npl* armamento *m*.

armband ['ɑ:mbænd] *n* - 1. [indicating mourning, rank] brazalete *m* - 2. [for swimming] flotador *m* (en los brazos).

armchair ['ɑ:mtʃeəʳ] *n* sillón *m*.

armed [ɑ:md] *adj* - 1. [police, thieves] armado(da) - 2. *fig* [with information]: ~ **with** provisto(ta) de.

armed forces *npl* fuerzas *fpl* armadas.

armed robbery *n* atraco *m* a mano armada.

armhole ['ɑ:mhəʊl] *n* sobaquera *f*, sisa *f*.

armour UK, **armor** US ['ɑ:məʳ] *n* - 1. [for person] armadura *f* - 2. [for military vehicle] blindaje *m*.

armoured car [ɑ:məd-] *n* MIL carro *m* blindado.

armoury UK (*pl* -ies), **armory** US (*pl* -ies) ['ɑ:mərɪ] *n* arsenal *m*.

armpit ['ɑ:mpɪt] *n* sobaco *m*, axila *f*.

armrest ['ɑ:mrest] *n* brazo *m*.

arms control ['ɑ:mz-] *n* control *m* armamentístico.

arms dealer ['ɑ:mz-] *n* traficante *m* OR *f* de armas.

arms race ['ɑ:mz-] *n* carrera *f* armamentística.

army ['ɑ:mɪ] (*pl* -ies) ⬦ *n lit & fig* ejército *m*. ⬦ *comp* del ejército, militar.

A road *n* UK ≃ carretera *f* nacional.

aroma [ə'rəʊmə] *n* aroma *m*.

arose [ə'rəʊz] *pt* ⬦ arise.

around [ə'raʊnd] ⬦ *adv* - 1. [about, round] por ahí; **to walk/look** ~ andar/mirar por ahí - 2. [on all sides] alrededor - 3. [present, available]: **is John** ~? [there] ¿está John por ahí?; [here] ¿está John por aquí? - 4. [turn, look]: **to turn** ~ volverse; **to look** ~ volver la cabeza. ⬦ *prep* - 1. [on all sides of] alrededor de - 2. [about, round - place] por - 3. [in the area of] cerca de - 4. [approximately] alrededor de.

arouse [ə'raʊz] *vt* [excite - feeling] despertar; [- person] excitar.

arrange [ə'reɪndʒ] *vt* - 1. [books, furniture] colocar; [flowers] arreglar - 2. [event, meeting, party] organizar; **to** ~ **to do sthg** acordar hacer algo; **we've** ~ **ed to meet at nine** hemos quedado a las nueve; **to** ~ **sthg for sb** organizarle algo a alguien - 3. MUS arreglar.

arrangement [ə'reɪndʒmənt] *n* - 1. [agreement] acuerdo *m*; **to come to an** ~ llegar a un acuerdo - 2. [of furniture] disposición *f*, colocación *f*; [of flowers] arreglo *m* - 3. MUS arreglo *m*.
  ➔ **arrangements** *npl* preparativos *mpl*.

array [ə'reɪ] *n* [of objects] surtido *m*.

arrears [ə'rɪəz] *npl* [money owed] atrasos *mpl*; **in** ~ [retrospectively] con retraso; [late] atrasado en el pago.

arrest [ə'rest] ⬦ *n* detención *f*, arresto *m*; **under** ~ detenido(da), bajo arresto. ⬦ *vt* - 1. [subj: police] detener, arrestar - 2. [sb's attention] captar, atraer - 3. *fml* [stop] poner freno a.

arrival [ə'raɪvl] *n* llegada *f*; **late** ~ [of train, bus, mail] retraso *m*; **new** ~ [person] recién llegado *m*, recién llegada *f*; [baby] recién nacido *m*, recién nacida *f*.

arrive [ə'raɪv] *vi* - 1. [gen] llegar; **to** ~ **at** [conclusion, decision] llegar a - 2. [baby] nacer.

arrogant ['ærəgənt] *adj* arrogante.

arrow ['ærəʊ] *n* flecha *f*.

arrow key *n* COMPUT tecla *f* de movimiento del cursor.

arse *UK* [ɑːs], **ass** *US* [æs] *n v inf* [bottom] culo *m*.

arsehole *UK* ['ɑːsheʊl], **asshole** *US* ['æsheʊl] *n vulg* **- 1.** [anus] ojete *m* **- 2.** [person] cabrón *m*, -ona *f*.

arsenic ['ɑːsnɪk] *n* arsénico *m*.

arson ['ɑːsn] *n* incendio *m* premeditado.

art [ɑːt] *n* arte *m*.

➡ **arts** *npl* **- 1.** SCH & UNIV [humanities] letras *fpl* **- 2.** [fine arts]: the ~s las bellas artes.

➡ **arts and crafts** *npl* artesanía *f*.

artefact ['ɑːtɪfækt] = **artifact**.

artery ['ɑːtərɪ] (*pl* -**ies**) *n* arteria *f*.

art gallery *n* [public] museo *m* (de arte); [commercial] galería *f* (de arte).

arthritis [ɑːˈθraɪtɪs] *n* artritis *f inv*.

artichoke ['ɑːtɪtʃəʊk] *n* alcachofa *f*.

article ['ɑːtɪkl] *n* artículo *m*; ~ of clothing prenda *f* de vestir.

articulate [*adj* ɑːˈtɪkjʊlət, *vb* ɑːˈtɪkjʊleɪt] ⟨⟩ *adj* [person] elocuente; [speech] claro(-ra), bien articulado(da). ⟨⟩ *vt* [express clearly] expresar.

articulated lorry [ɑːˈtɪkjʊleɪtɪd-] *n UK* camión *m* articulado.

artifact ['ɑːtɪfækt] *n* artefacto *m*.

artificial [ˌɑːtɪˈfɪʃl] *adj* artificial.

artillery [ɑːˈtɪlərɪ] *n* [guns] artillería *f*.

artist ['ɑːtɪst] *n* artista *m* OR *f*.

artiste [ɑːˈtiːst] *n* artista *m* OR *f*.

artistic [ɑːˈtɪstɪk] *adj* **- 1.** [gen] artístico(ca) **- 2.** [good at art]: **to be** ~ tener sensibilidad artística.

artistry ['ɑːtɪstrɪ] *n* maestría *f*.

artless ['ɑːtlɪs] *adj* ingenuo(nua), cándido(da).

as [*unstressed* əz, *stressed* æz] ⟨⟩ *conj* **- 1.** [referring to time - while] mientras; [- when] cuando; **she told it to me** ~ **we walked along** me lo contó mientras paseábamos; ~ **time goes by** a medida que pasa el tiempo; **she rang (just)** ~ **I was leaving** llamó justo cuando iba a salir **- 2.** [referring to manner, way] como; **do** ~ **I say** haz lo que te digo **- 3.** [introducing a statement] como; ~ **you know, ...** como (ya) sabes, ... **- 4.** [because] como, ya que **- 5.** *phr*: ~ **it is** (ya) de por sí. ⟨⟩ *prep* como; **I'm speaking** ~ **a friend** te hablo como amigo; **she works** ~ **a nurse** trabaja de OR como enfermera; ~ **a boy, I lived in Spain** de niño vivía en España; **it came** ~ **a shock** fue una gran sorpresa. ⟨⟩ *adv* (*in comparisons*): ~ **...** ~ tan ... como; ~ **tall** ~ **I am** tan alto como yo; **I've lived** ~ **long** ~ **she has** he vivido durante tanto tiempo como ella; **twice**

~ **big** el doble de grande; **it's just** ~ **fast** es igual de rápido; ~ **much** ~ tanto como; ~ **many** ~ tantos(tas) como; ~ **much wine** ~ **you like** tanto vino como quieras.

➡ **as for, as to** *prep* en cuanto a, por lo que se refiere a.

➡ **as from, as of** *prep* a partir de.

➡ **as if, as though** *conj* como si.

➡ **as to** *prep UK* con respecto a.

a.s.a.p. (*abbr of* **as soon as possible**) a la mayor brevedad posible.

asbestos [æsˈbestəs] *n* amianto *m*, asbesto *m*.

ascend [əˈsend] ⟨⟩ *vt* subir. ⟨⟩ *vi* ascender.

ascendant [əˈsendənt] *n*: **in the** ~ en auge.

ascent [əˈsent] *n* **- 1.** [climb] ascensión *f* **- 2.** [upward slope] subida *f*, cuesta *f* **- 3.** *fig* [progress] ascenso *m*.

ascertain [ˌæsəˈteɪn] *vt* determinar.

ASCII ['æskɪ] (*abbr of* **American Standard Code for Information Interchange**) *n* ASCII *m*.

ascribe [əˈskraɪb] *vt*: **to** ~ **sthg to** atribuir algo a.

ash [æʃ] *n* **- 1.** [from cigarette, fire] ceniza *f* **- 2.** [tree] fresno *m*.

ashamed [əˈʃeɪmd] *adj* avergonzado(da), apenado(da) *Andes, CAm, Méx*; **I'm** ~ **to do it** me da vergüenza hacerlo; **I'm** ~ **of ...** me da vergüenza ...

ashen-faced ['æʃnˌfeɪst] *adj*: **to be** ~ tener la cara pálida.

ashore [əˈʃɔːʳ] *adv* [swim] hasta la orilla; **to go** ~ desembarcar.

ashtray ['æʃtreɪ] *n* cenicero *m*.

Ash Wednesday *n* miércoles *m inv* de ceniza.

Asia [*UK* 'eɪʃə, *US* 'eɪʒə] *n* Asia.

Asian [*UK* 'eɪʃn, *US* 'eɪʒn] ⟨⟩ *adj* asiático(ca); ~ **American** americano(na) de origen asiático. ⟨⟩ *n* asiático *m*, -ca *f*.

aside [əˈsaɪd] ⟨⟩ *adv* **- 1.** [to one side] a un lado; **to move** ~ apartarse; **to take sb** ~ llevar a alguien aparte **- 2.** [apart] aparte; ~ **from** aparte de. ⟨⟩ *n* **- 1.** [in play] aparte *m* **- 2.** [remark] inciso *m*, comentario *m* al margen.

ask [ɑːsk] ⟨⟩ *vt* **- 1.** [question - person]: **to** ~ **(sb sthg)** preguntar (a alguien algo) **- 2.** [put - question]: **to** ~ **a question** hacer una pregunta **- 3.** [request, demand] pedir; **to** ~ **sb (to do sthg)** pedir a alguien (que haga algo); **to** ~ **sb for sthg** pedirle algo a alguien **- 4.** [invite] invitar. ⟨⟩ *vi* **- 1.** [question] preguntar **- 2.** [request] pedir.

➡ **ask after** *vt fus* preguntar por.

➡ **ask for** *vt fus* **- 1.** [person] preguntar por **- 2.** [thing] pedir.

➡ **ask out** *vt sep* [ask to be boyfriend, girlfriend] pedir salir.

askance [ə'skæns] *adv* : **to look ~ at sb** mirar a alguien con recelo.

askew [ə'skju:] *adj* torcido(da).

asking price ['ɑ:skɪŋ-] *n* precio *m* inicial.

asleep [ə'sli:p] *adj* dormido(da); **she's ~** está dormida OR durmiendo; **to fall ~** quedarse dormido.

asparagus [ə'spærəgəs] *n (U)* [plant] espárrago *m*; [shoots] espárragos *mpl*.

aspect ['æspekt] *n* **-1.** [of subject, plan] aspecto *m* **-2.** [appearance] cariz *m*, aspecto *m* **-3.** [of building] orientación *f*.

aspersions [ə'spɜ:ʃnz] *npl* : **to cast ~ on sthg** poner en duda algo.

asphalt ['æsfælt] *n* asfalto *m*.

asphyxiate [əs'fɪksɪeɪt] *vt* asfixiar.

aspiration [,æspə'reɪʃn] *n* aspiración *f*.

aspire [ə'spaɪə'] *vi* : **to ~ to** aspirar a.

aspirin ['æsprɪn] *n* aspirina *f*.

ass [æs] *n* **-1.** [donkey] asno *m*, -na *f* **-2.** *UK inf* [idiot] burro *m*, -rra *f* **-3.** *US v inf* = **arse**.

assailant [ə'seɪlənt] *n* agresor *m*, -ra *f*.

assassin [ə'sæsɪn] *n* asesino *m*, -na *f*.

assassinate [ə'sæsɪneɪt] *vt* asesinar.

assassination [ə,sæsɪ'neɪʃn] *n* asesinato *m*.

assault [ə'sɔ:lt] *n* **-1.** MIL : **~ (on)** ataque *m* (contra) **-2.** [physical attack] : **~ (on sb)** agresión *f* (contra alguien). *vt* [physically] asaltar, agredir; [sexually] abusar de.

assemble [ə'sembl] *vt* **-1.** [gather] juntar, reunir **-2.** [fit together] montar. *vi* reunirse.

assembly [ə'semblɪ] *(pl* -ies) *n* **-1.** [meeting, law-making body] asamblea *f* **-2.** [gathering together] reunión *f* **-3.** *UK* [at school] *reunión de todos los profesores y alumnos de un centro al comienzo de cada día escolar* **-4.** [fitting together] montaje *m*.

assembly hall *n UK* salón *m* de actos.

assembly line *n* cadena *f* de montaje.

assent [ə'sent] *n* consentimiento *m*. *vi* : **to ~ (to)** asentir (a).

assert [ə'sɜ:t] *vt* **-1.** [fact, belief] afirmar **-2.** [authority] imponer.

assertive [ə'sɜ:tɪv] *adj* enérgico(ca).

assess [ə'ses] *vt* evaluar.

assessment [ə'sesmənt] *n* **-1.** [evaluation] evaluación *f* **-2.** [calculation] cálculo *m*.

assessor [ə'sesə'] *n* tasador *m*, -ra *f*.

asset ['æset] *n* **-1.** [valuable quality - of person] cualidad *f* positiva; [- of thing] ventaja *f* **-2.** [valuable person] elemento *m* importante.
 ◆ **assets** *npl* COMM activo *m*.

assign [ə'saɪn] *vt* **-1.** [gen] : **to ~ sthg (to sb)** asignar algo (a alguien); **to ~ sb to sthg** asignar a alguien algo; **to ~ sb to do sthg** asignar a alguien que haga algo **-2.** [designate for specific use, purpose] : **to ~ sthg (to)** destinar algo (a).

assignment [ə'saɪnmənt] *n* **-1.** [task] misión *f*; SCH trabajo *m* **-2.** [act of assigning] asignación *f*.

assimilate [ə'sɪmɪleɪt] *vt* **-1.** [learn] asimilar **-2.** [absorb] : **to ~ sb (into)** integrar a alguien (en).

assist [ə'sɪst] *vt* : **to ~ sb (with sthg/in doing sthg)** ayudar a alguien (con algo/a hacer algo). *vi* ayudar.

assistance [ə'sɪstəns] *n* ayuda *f*, asistencia *f*; **to be of ~ (to)** ayudar (a).

assistant [ə'sɪstənt] *n* ayudante *m* OR *f*; **(shop) ~** dependiente *m*, -ta *f*. *comp* adjunto(ta); **~ manager** director adjunto *m*, directora adjunta *f*; **~ referee** árbitro *m*, asistente *f*.

associate [adj & n ə'səʊʃɪət, vb ə'səʊʃɪeɪt] *adj* asociado(da). *n* socio *m*, -cia *f*. *vt* asociar; **to ~ sthg/sb with** asociar algo/a alguien con; **to be ~ d with** [organization, plan, opinion] estar relacionado con; [people] estar asociado con. *vi* : **to ~ with sb** relacionarse con alguien.

association [ə,səʊsɪ'eɪʃn] *n* **-1.** [organization, act of associating] asociación *f*; **in ~ with** en colaboración con **-2.** [in mind] connotación *f*.

assorted [ə'sɔ:tɪd] *adj* **-1.** [of various types] variado(da) **-2.** [biscuits, sweets] surtido(da).

assortment [ə'sɔ:tmənt] *n* surtido *m*.

assume [ə'sju:m] *vt* **-1.** [suppose] suponer **-2.** [power, responsibility] asumir **-3.** [appearance, attitude] adoptar.

assumed name [ə'sju:md-] *n* nombre *m* falso.

assuming [ə'sju:mɪŋ] *conj* suponiendo que.

assumption [ə'sʌmpʃn] *n* **-1.** [supposition] suposición *f* **-2.** [of power] asunción *f*.

assurance [ə'ʃʊərəns] *n* **-1.** [promise] garantía *f* **-2.** [confidence] seguridad *f* de sí mismo **-3.** [insurance] seguro *m*.

assure [ə'ʃʊə'] *vt* asegurar, garantizar; **to ~ sb of sthg** garantizar a alguien algo; **to be ~ d of sthg** tener algo garantizado; **rest ~ d that ...** ten por seguro que ...

assured [ə'ʃʊəd] *adj* [confident] seguro(ra).

asterisk ['æstərɪsk] *n* asterisco *m*.

astern [ə'stɜ:n] *adv* NAUT a popa.

asthma ['æsmə] *n* asma *f*.

astonish [ə'stɒnɪʃ] *vt* asombrar.

astonishment [ə'stɒnɪʃmənt] *n* asombro *m*.

astound [ə'staʊnd] *vt* asombrar, pasmar.

astray [ə'streɪ] *adv* : **to go ~** [become lost] extraviarse; **to lead sb ~** [into bad ways] llevar a alguien por el mal camino.

astride [ə'straɪd] *adv* a horcajadas. *prep* a horcajadas en.

astrology [ə'strɒlədʒɪ] *n* astrología *f*.

astronaut ['æstrənɔ:t] *n* astronauta *m* OR *f*.

astronomical [,æstrə'nɒmɪkl] *adj lit* & *fig* astronómico(ca).

astronomy [ə'strɒnəmɪ] *n* astronomía *f*.

astute [ə'stju:t] *adj* astuto(ta), abusado(da) *Méx*.

asylum [ə'saɪləm] *n* - 1. [mental hospital] manicomio *m* - 2. [protection] asilo *m*.

asylum seeker [ə'saɪləm'si:kəʳ] *n* peticionario *m*, -ria *f* de asilo.

at [*unstressed* ət, *stressed* æt] *prep* - 1. [indicating place] en; ~ **my father's** en casa de mi padre; **standing** ~ **the window** de pie junto a la ventana; ~ **the bottom of the hill** al pie de la colina; ~ **school/work/home** en la escuela/el trabajo/casa - 2. [indicating direction] a; **to look** ~ **sthg/sb** mirar algo/a alguien - 3. [indicating a particular time]: ~ **a more suitable time** en un momento más oportuno; ~ **midnight/noon/eleven o'clock** a medianoche/mediodía/las once; ~ **night** por la noche; ~ **Christmas/Easter** en Navidades/Semana Santa - 4. [indicating speed, rate, price] a; ~ **100 mph/high speed** a 100 millas por hora/gran velocidad; ~ **£50 (a pair)** a 50 libras (el par) - 5. [indicating particular state, condition]: ~ **peace/war** en paz/guerra; **she's** ~ **lunch** está comiendo - 6. [indicating a particular age] a; ~ **52/your age** a los 52/tu edad - 7. (*after adjectives*): **delighted** ~ encantado con; **experienced** ~ experimentado en; **puzzled/horrified** ~ perplejo/horrorizado ante; **he's good/bad** ~ **sport** se le dan bien/mal los deportes.

◆ **at all** *adv* - 1. (*with negative*): **not** ~ **all** [when thanked] de nada; [when answering a question] en absoluto; **she's not** ~ **all happy** no está nada contenta - 2. [in the slightest]: **anything** ~ **all will do** cualquier cosa valdrá; **do you know her** ~ **all?** ¿la conoces (de algo)?

ate [*UK* et, *US* eɪt] *pt* ⊳ **eat**.

atheist ['eɪθɪɪst] *n* ateo *m*, -a *f*.

Athens ['æθɪnz] *n* Atenas.

athlete ['æθli:t] *n* atleta *m* OR *f*.

athletic [æθ'letɪk] *adj* atlético(ca).

◆ **athletics** *npl* atletismo *m*.

Atlantic [ət'læntɪk] ⋄ *adj* atlántico(ca). ⋄ *n*: **the** ~ **(Ocean)** el (océano) Atlántico.

atlas ['ætləs] *n* atlas *m inv*.

ATM (*abbr of* **automatic teller machine**) *n* cajero automático.

atmosphere ['ætmə,sfɪəʳ] *n* - 1. [of planet] atmósfera *f* - 2. [air in room, mood of place] ambiente *m*.

atmospheric [,ætməs'ferɪk] *adj* - 1. [pressure, pollution] atmosférico(ca) - 2. [attractive, mysterious] sugerente.

atom ['ætəm] *n* PHYS átomo *m*.

atom bomb *n* bomba *f* atómica.

atomic [ə'tɒmɪk] *adj* atómico(ca).

atomic bomb = **atom bomb**.

atomizer, -iser ['ætəmaɪzəʳ] *n* atomizador *m*.

atone [ə'təʊn] *vi*: **to** ~ **for** reparar.

A to Z *n* guía *f* alfabética; [map] callejero *m*.

atrocious [ə'trəʊʃəs] *adj* [very bad] atroz.

atrocity [ə'trɒsətɪ] (*pl* -**ies**) *n* [terrible act] atrocidad *f*.

attach [ə'tætʃ] *vt* - 1. [with pin, clip]: **to** ~ **sthg (to)** sujetar algo (a); [with string] atar algo (a) - 2. [document & COMPUT] adjuntar - 3. [importance, blame]: **to** ~ **sthg (to sthg)** atribuir algo (a algo).

attaché case [ə'tæʃeɪ-] *n* maletín *m*.

attached [ə'tætʃt] *adj* - 1. [fastened on]: ~ **(to)** adjunto(ta) (a) - 2. [fond]: **to be** ~ **to** tener cariño a.

attachment [ə'tætʃmənt] *n* - 1. [device] accesorio *m* - 2. [COMPUT] archivo *m* adjunto - 3. [fondness]: ~ **(to)** cariño *m* (por).

attack [ə'tæk] ⋄ *n*: ~ **(on)** ataque *m* (contra); **terrorist** ~ atentado *m* terrorista; **to be under** ~ estar siendo atacado. ⋄ *vt* - 1. [gen] atacar - 2. [job, problem] acometer. ⋄ *vi* atacar.

attacker [ə'tækəʳ] *n* atacante *m* OR *f*.

attain [ə'teɪn] *vt* lograr, alcanzar.

attainment [ə'teɪnmənt] *n* logro *m*.

attempt [ə'tempt] ⋄ *n*: ~ **(at doing sthg)** intento *m* (de hacer algo); ~ **on sb's life** atentado *m* contra la vida de alguien. ⋄ *vt*: **to** ~ **sthg/to do sthg** intentar algo/hacer algo.

attempted coup [ə'temptɪd'ku:] *n* intentona *f* golpista.

attempted murder [ə'temptɪd-] *n* intento *m* de asesinato.

attend [ə'tend] ⋄ *vt* [go to] asistir a. ⋄ *vi* - 1. [be present] asistir - 2. [pay attention]: **to** ~ **(to)** atender (a).

◆ **attend to** *vt fus* - 1. [matter] ocuparse de - 2. [customer] atender a; [patient] asistir a.

attendance [ə'tendəns] *n* asistencia *f*; **the** ~ **for the match was over 10,000** más de 10.000 personas asistieron al partido.

attendant [ə'tendənt] ⋄ *adj* concomitante. ⋄ *n* [at museum] vigilante *m* OR *f*; [at petrol station, in swimming pool] encargado *m*, -da *f*.

attention [ə'tenʃn] ⋄ *n* (*U*) - 1. [gen] atención *f*; **to bring sthg to sb's** ~, **to draw sb's** ~ **to sthg** llamar la atención de alguien sobre algo; **to attract** OR **catch sb's** ~ atraer OR captar la atención de alguien; **to pay/pay no** ~ **(to)** prestar/no prestar atención (a); **for the** ~ **of** COMM a la atención de; **your** ~ **please!** ¡atención! - 2. [care] asistencia *f*.

◇ *excl* MIL ¡firmes!

attentive [ə'tentɪv] *adj* atento(ta).

Att. Gen. *n* (*abbr of* **Attorney General**) ministro *m*, -ra *f* de Justicia.

attic ['ætɪk] *n* desván *m*, entretecho *m* *Amér*.

attitude ['ætɪtjuːd] *n* - **1.** [way of thinking, acting]: ~ **(to** OR **towards)** actitud *f* (hacia) - **2.** [posture] postura *f*.

attn. (*abbr of* **for the attention of**) a/a.

attorney [ə'tɜːnɪ] *n* US abogado *m*, -da *f*.

attorney general (*pl* **attorneys general**) *n* fiscal *m* general del estado.

attract [ə'trækt] *vt* - **1.** [gen] atraer - **2.** [support, criticism] suscitar.

attraction [ə'trækʃn] *n* - **1.** [gen]: ~ **(to sb)** atracción *f* (hacia OR por alguien) - **2.** [attractiveness - of thing] atractivo *m*.

attractive [ə'træktɪv] *adj* atractivo(va).

attribute [*vb* ə'trɪbjuːt, *n* 'ætrɪbjuːt] ◇ *vt* : to ~ sthg to atribuir algo a. ◇ *n* atributo *m*.

attrition [ə'trɪʃn] *n* desgaste *m*; **war of ~** guerra de desgaste.

aubergine ['əʊbəʒiːn] *n* UK berenjena *f*.

auburn ['ɔːbən] *adj* castaño rojizo.

auction ['ɔːkʃn] ◇ *n* subasta *f*. ◇ *vt* subastar.

auctioneer [ˌɔːkʃə'nɪə'] *n* subastador *m*, -ra *f*.

audacious [ɔː'deɪʃəs] *adj* [daring] audaz; [cheeky] atrevido(da).

audible ['ɔːdəbl] *adj* audible.

audience ['ɔːdjəns] *n* - **1.** [of play, film] público *m* - **2.** [formal meeting, TV viewers] audiencia *f*.

audiotypist ['ɔːdɪəʊˌtaɪpɪst] *n* mecanógrafo *m*, -fa *f* por dictáfono.

audio-visual ['ɔːdɪəʊ-] *adj* audiovisual.

audit ['ɔːdɪt] ◇ *n* auditoría *f*. ◇ *vt* auditar.

audition [ɔː'dɪʃn] *n* prueba *f* (a un artista).

auditor ['ɔːdɪtə'] *n* auditor *m*, -ra *f*.

auditorium [ˌɔːdɪ'tɔːrɪəm] (*pl* **-riums** OR **-ria** [-rɪə]) *n* auditorio *m*.

augment [ɔːg'ment] *vt* acrecentar, aumentar.

augur ['ɔːgə'] *vi* : to ~ **well/badly** ser un buen/mal augurio.

August ['ɔːgəst] *n* agosto *m*; *see also* **September**.

Auld Lang Syne [ˌɔːldlæŋ'saɪn] *n* canción escocesa en alabanza de los viejos tiempos que se canta tradicionalmente en Nochevieja.

aunt [ɑːnt] *n* tía *f*.

auntie, aunty ['ɑːntɪ] (*pl* **-ies**) *n* inf tita *f*.

au pair [ˌəʊ'peə'] *n* au pair *f*.

aura ['ɔːrə] *n* aura *f*, halo *m*.

aural ['ɔːrəl] *adj* auditivo(va).

auspices ['ɔːspɪsɪz] *npl*: **under the ~** bajo los auspicios de.

auspicious [ɔː'spɪʃəs] *adj* prometedor(ra).

Aussie ['ɒzɪ] *n* inf australiano *m*, -na *f*.

austere [ɒ'stɪə'] *adj* austero(ra).

austerity [ɒ'sterətɪ] *n* austeridad *f*.

Australia [ɒ'streɪljə] *n* Australia.

Australian [ɒ'streɪljən] ◇ *adj* australiano(na). ◇ *n* australiano *m*, -na *f*.

Austria ['ɒstrɪə] *n* Austria.

Austrian ['ɒstrɪən] ◇ *adj* austriaco(ca). ◇ *n* austriaco *m*, -ca *f*.

authentic [ɔː'θentɪk] *adj* auténtico(ca).

author ['ɔːθə'] *n* [by profession] escritor *m*, -ra *f*; [of particular book, text] autor *m*, -ra *f*.

authoritarian [ɔːˌθɒrɪ'teərɪən] *adj* autoritario(ria).

authoritative [ɔː'θɒrɪtətɪv] *adj* - **1.** [person, voice] autoritario(ria) - **2.** [study] autorizado(da).

authority [ɔː'θɒrətɪ] (*pl* **-ies**) *n* - **1.** [gen] autoridad *f*; **to be an ~ on** ser una autoridad en - **2.** [permission] autorización *f*.

➜ **authorities** *npl*: **the authorities** las autoridades *fpl*.

authorize, -ise ['ɔːθəraɪz] *vt* : to ~ **(sb to do sthg)** autorizar (a alguien a hacer algo).

autism ['ɔːtɪzm] *n* autismo *m*.

autistic [ɔː'tɪstɪk] *adj* autista.

auto ['ɔːtəʊ] (*pl* **-s**) *n* US coche *m*.

autobiography [ˌɔːtəbaɪ'ɒgrəfɪ] (*pl* **-ies**) *n* autobiografía *f*.

autocratic [ˌɔːtə'krætɪk] *adj* autocrático(ca).

autodisconnect ['ɔːtəʊdɪskə'nekt] ◇ *vi* COMPUT desconectarse automáticamente. ◇ *vt* autografiar.

autograph ['ɔːtəgrɑːf] ◇ *n* autógrafo *m*. ◇ *vt* autografiar.

autoimmune disease [ˌɔːtəʊɪ'mjuːn-] *n* enfermedad *f* autoinmune.

automate ['ɔːtəmeɪt] *vt* automatizar.

automatic [ˌɔːtə'mætɪk] ◇ *adj* automático(ca). ◇ *n* - **1.** [car] coche *m* automático - **2.** [gun] arma *f* automática - **3.** [washing machine] lavadora *f* automática.

automatically [ˌɔːtə'mætɪklɪ] *adv* automáticamente.

automation [ˌɔːtə'meɪʃn] *n* automatización *f*.

automobile ['ɔːtəməbiːl] *n* US coche *m*, automóvil *m*.

autonomous [ɔː'tɒnəməs] *adj* autónomo(ma).

autonomy [ɔː'tɒnəmɪ] *n* autonomía *f*.

autopsy ['ɔːtɒpsɪ] (*pl* **-ies**) *n* autopsia *f*.

autumn ['ɔːtəm] *n* otoño *m*.

auxiliary [ɔːg'zɪljərɪ] (*pl* **-ies**) ◇ *adj* auxiliar. ◇ *n* [medical worker] auxiliar sanitario *m*, auxiliar sanitaria *f*.

Av. (*abbr of* **avenue**) Av.

avail [ə'veɪl] ◇ *n*: **to no ~** en vano. ◇ *vt* : to ~ **o.s. of sthg** aprovechar algo.

available [ə'veɪləbl] *adj* **-1.** [product, service] disponible; **this product is no longer ~** ya no comercializamos este producto **-2.** [person] libre, disponible.

avalanche ['ævəlɑːnʃ] *n lit & fig* avalancha *f*, alud *m*.

avant-garde [ˌævɒŋ'gɑːd] *adj* de vanguardia, vanguardista.

avarice ['ævərɪs] *n* avaricia *f*.

Ave. (*abbr of* **avenue**) Avda.

avenge [ə'vendʒ] *vt* vengar.

avenue ['ævənjuː] *n* **-1.** [wide road] avenida *f* **-2.** *fig* [method, means] vía *f*.

average ['ævərɪdʒ] ◇ *adj* **-1.** [mean, typical] medio(dia) **-2.** [mediocre] regular. ◇ *n* media *f*, promedio *m*; **on ~** de media, por término medio. ◇ *vt* alcanzar un promedio de.

◆ **average out** *vi*: **to ~ out at** salir a una media de.

aversion [ə'vɜːʃn] *n* [dislike]: **~ (to)** aversión *f* (a).

avert [ə'vɜːt] *vt* **-1.** [problem, accident] evitar, prevenir **-2.** [eyes, glance] apartar, desviar.

aviary ['eɪvjərɪ] (*pl* **-ies**) *n* pajarera *f*.

avid ['ævɪd] *adj*: **~ (for)** ávido(da) (de).

avocado [ˌævə'kɑːdəʊ] (*pl* **-s** OR **-es**) *n*: **~ (pear)** aguacate *m*, palta *f Andes, RP*.

avoid [ə'vɔɪd] *vt*: **to ~ (sthg/doing sthg)** evitar (algo/hacer algo); **she's been ~ing** me ha estado esquivándome.

avoidance [ə'vɔɪdəns] ⊳ **tax avoidance**.

await [ə'weɪt] *vt* esperar, aguardar.

awake [ə'weɪk] (*pt* **awoke** OR **awaked**, *pp* **awoken**) ◇ *adj* [not sleeping] despierto(ta). ◇ *vt lit & fig* despertar. ◇ *vi lit & fig* despertarse.

awakening [ə'weɪknɪŋ] *n lit & fig* despertar *m*.

award [ə'wɔːd] ◇ *n* **-1.** [prize] premio *m*, galardón *m* **-2.** [compensation] indemnización *f*. ◇ *vt*: **to ~ sb sthg, to ~ sthg to sb** [prize] conceder OR otorgar algo a alguien; [compensation] adjudicar algo a alguien.

aware [ə'weə'] *adj* **-1.** [conscious]: **~ of** consciente de; **to become ~ of** darse cuenta de **-2.** [informed, sensitive] informado(da), al día; **~ of sthg** al día de algo; **to be ~ that** estar informado de que.

awareness [ə'weənɪs] *n* conciencia *f*.

awash [ə'wɒʃ] *adj lit & fig*: **~ (with)** inundado(da) (de).

away [ə'weɪ] ◇ *adv* **-1.** [move, walk, drive]: **to walk ~ (from)** marcharse (de); **to drive ~ (from)** alejarse (de) (*en coche*); **to turn** OR **look ~** apartar la vista **-2.** [at a distance - in space, time]: **~ from** a distancia de; **4 miles ~** a 4 millas de distancia; **a long way ~** muy lejos; **the exam is two days ~** faltan

dos días para el examen **-3.** [not at home or office] fuera **-4.** [in safe place]: **to put sthg ~** poner algo en su sitio **-5.** [indicating removal or disappearance]: **to fade ~** desvanecerse; **to give sthg ~** regalar algo; **to take sthg ~ from sb** quitarle algo a alguien **-6.** [continuously]: **he was working ~ when** ... estaba muy concentrado trabajando cuando ... ◇ *adj* SPORT [team, supporters] visitante; **~ game** partido *m* fuera de casa.

awe [ɔː] *n* sobrecogimiento *m*; **to be in ~ of sb** sentirse intimidado por alguien.

awesome ['ɔːsəm] *adj* alucinante *Esp*, macanudo(da) *Andes, RP*, padrísimo(ma) *Méx*.

awful ['ɔːfʊl] *adj* **-1.** [terrible] terrible, espantoso(sa); **I feel ~** me siento fatal **-2.** *inf* [very great] tremendo(da); **I like it an ~ lot** me gusta muchísimo.

awfully ['ɔːflɪ] *adv inf* [very] tremendamente.

awhile [ə'waɪl] *adv literary* un rato.

awkward ['ɔːkwəd] *adj* **-1.** [clumsy - movement] torpe; [- person] desgarbado(da) **-2.** [embarrassed, embarrassing] incómodo(da) **-3.** [unreasonable] difícil **-4.** [inconvenient - shape, size] poco manejable; [- moment] inoportuno(na).

awning ['ɔːnɪŋ] *n* toldo *m*.

awoke [ə'wəʊk] *pt* ⊳ **awake**.

awoken [ə'wəʊkn] *pp* ⊳ **awake**.

awry [ə'raɪ] ◇ *adj* torcido(da), ladeado(da). ◇ *adv*: **to go ~** salir mal.

axe UK, **ax** US [æks] ◇ *n* hacha *f*. ◇ *vt* [project, jobs] suprimir.

axes ['æksiːz] *pl* ⊳ **axis**.

axis ['æksɪs] (*pl* **axes**) *n* eje *m*.

axle ['æksl] *n* eje *m*.

aye [aɪ] ◇ *adv* sí. ◇ *n* sí *m*.

azalea [ə'zeɪljə] *n* azalea *f*.

Aztec ['æztek] ◇ *adj* azteca. ◇ *n* [person] azteca *m* OR *f*.

b (*pl* **b's** OR **bs**), **B** (*pl* **B's** OR **Bs**) [biː] *n* [letter] b *f*, B *f*.

◆ **B** *n* **-1.** MUS si *m* **-2.** SCH [mark] ≃ bien *m*.

BA *n* (*abbr of* **Bachelor of Arts**) (*titular de una*) licenciatura de letras.

babble ['bæbl] *vi* [person] farfullar.

baboon [bə'buːn] *n* babuino *m*, papión *m*.

baby ['beɪbɪ] (*pl* **-ies**) ◇ *n* **-1.** [newborn

child] bebé *m*; [infant] niño *m* - **2.** *inf* [term of affection] cariño *m*. ◇ *comp*: ~ **brother** hermanito *m*; ~ **sister** hermanita *f*.

baby buggy *n* - **1.** *UK* [foldable pushchair] sillita *f* de niño (con ruedas) - **2.** *US* = **baby carriage**.

baby carriage *n US* cochecito *m* de niños.

baby food *n* papilla *f*.

baby-sit *vi* cuidar a niños.

baby-sitter [-'sɪtə'] *n* canguro *m OR f*.

bachelor ['bætʃələ'] *n* soltero *m*; ~ **party** *US* despedida *f* de soltero.

Bachelor of Arts *n* ≃ licenciado *m*, -da *f* en Letras.

Bachelor of Science *n* ≃ licenciado *m*, -da *f* en Ciencias.

back [bæk] ◇ *adv* - **1.** [in position] atrás; **stand** ~! ¡échense para atrás!; **to push** ~ empujar hacia atrás - **2.** [to former position or state] de vuelta; **to come** ~ volver; **to go** ~ volver; **to look** ~ volver la mirada; **to walk** ~ volver andando; **to give sthg** ~ devolver algo; **to be** ~ (in fashion) estar de vuelta; **he has been there and** ~ ha estado allí y ha vuelto; **I spent all day going** ~ **and forth** pasé todo el día yendo y viniendo - **3.** [in time]: **two weeks** ~ hace dos semanas; **it dates** ~ **to 1960** data de 1960; ~ **in March** allá en marzo - **4.** [phone, write] de vuelta. ◇ *n* - **1.** [of person] espalda *f*; [of animal] lomo *m*; **lying on one's** ~ tumbado de espaldas; **behind sb's** ~ a espaldas de alguien - **2.** [of hand, cheque] dorso *m*; [of coin, page] reverso *m*; [of car, book, head] parte *f* trasera; [of chair] respaldo *m*; [of queue] final *m*; [of room, cupboard] fondo *m* - **3.** SPORT [player] defensa *m*. ◇ *adj* (*in compounds*) - **1.** [at the back - door, legs, seat] trasero(ra); [-page] último(ma) - **2.** [overdue - pay, rent] atrasado(da). ◇ *vt* - **1.** [support] respaldar - **2.** [bet on] apostar por - **3.** [strengthen with material] reforzar. ◇ *vi* [drive backwards] ir marcha atrás; [walk backwards] ir hacia atrás.

◆ **back to back** *adv* [with backs facing] espalda con espalda.

◆ **back to front** *adv* al revés.

◆ **back down** *vi* echarse *OR* volverse atrás.

◆ **back out** *vi* echarse *OR* volverse atrás.

◆ **back up** ◇ *vt sep* - **1.** [support] apoyar - **2.** COMPUT hacer una copia de seguridad de. ◇ *vi* - **1.** [reverse] ir marcha atrás - **2.** COMPUT hacer copias de seguridad.

backache ['bækeɪk] *n* dolor *m* de espalda.

backbencher [,bæk'bentʃə'] *n UK diputado sin cargo en el gabinete del gobierno o la oposición.*

backbone ['bækbəʊn] *n lit & fig* columna *f* vertebral.

backcloth ['bækklɒθ] *UK* = **backdrop**.

backdate [,bæk'deɪt] *vt* : **a pay rise** ~**d to** **March** un aumento de sueldo con efecto retroactivo desde marzo.

back door *n* puerta *f* trasera.

backdrop ['bækdrɒp] *n lit & fig* telón *m* de fondo.

backfire [,bæk'faɪə'] *vi* - **1.** [motor vehicle] petardear - **2.** [go wrong]: **it** ~ **d on him** le salió el tiro por la culata.

backgammon ['bæk,gæmən] *n* backgammon *m*.

background ['bækgraʊnd] *n* - **1.** [in picture, view] fondo *m*; **in the** ~ [of painting etc] al fondo; [out of the limelight] en la sombra - **2.** [of event, situation] trasfondo *m* - **3.** [upbringing] origen *m*; **family** ~ antecedentes *mpl* familiares - **4.** [knowledge, experience]: **a** ~ **in** conocimientos *mpl* de.

backhand ['bækhænd] *n* revés *m*.

backhanded ['bækhændɪd] *adj fig* equívoco(ca).

backhander ['bækhændə'] *n UK inf*: **to give sb a** ~ untarle la mano a alguien, coimear a alguien *Andes, RP*, morder a alguien *CAm, Méx.*

backing ['bækɪŋ] *n* - **1.** [support] apoyo *m*, respaldo *m* - **2.** [lining] refuerzo *m* - **3.** MUS acompañamiento *m*.

backlash ['bæklæʃ] *n* reacción *f* violenta.

backlit ['bæklɪt] *adj* [display] retroiluminado(da).

backlog ['bæklɒg] *n* acumulación *f*.

back number *n* número *m* atrasado.

backpack ['bækpæk] *n* mochila *f*, macuto *m*.

back pay *n* (*U*) atrasos *mpl*.

back seat *n* asiento *m* trasero *OR* de atrás.

backside [,bæk'saɪd] *n inf* trasero *m*.

backstage [,bæk'steɪdʒ] *adv* entre bastidores.

back street *n UK* callejuela *f* de barrio.

backstroke ['bækstrəʊk] *n* espalda *f* (*en natación*); **to do the** ~ nadar a espalda.

backup ['bækʌp] ◇ *adj* - **1.** [plan] de emergencia, alternativo(va); [team] de apoyo - **2.** COMPUT de seguridad. ◇ *n* - **1.** [support] apoyo *m* - **2.** COMPUT copia *f* de seguridad.

backward ['bækwəd] ◇ *adj* - **1.** [movement, look] hacia atrás - **2.** [country, person] atrasado(da). ◇ *adv US* = **backwards**.

backwards ['bækwədz], **backward** *US* *adv* - **1.** [move, go] hacia atrás; ~ **and forwards** [movement] de un lado a otro - **2.** [back to front] al *OR* del revés.

backwater ['bæk,wɔːtə'] *n fig* páramo *m*, lugar *m* atrasado.

backyard [,bæk'jɑːd] *n* - **1.** *UK* [yard] patio *m* - **2.** *US* [garden] jardín *m* (trasero).

bacon ['beɪkən] *n* bacon *m*, tocino *m*.

bacteria [bæk'tɪərɪə] *npl* bacterias *fpl*.

bad [bæd] (*compar* **worse**, *superl* **worst**)

◇ *adj* **- 1.** [gen] malo(la); **he's ~ at French** se le da mal el francés; **to have a ~ back** estar mal de la espalda; **to go ~** [food] echarse a perder; **too ~!** ¡mala suerte!; **it's not ~ (at all)** no está nada mal; **how are you? — not ~** ¿qué tal? — bien **- 2.** [illness] grave **- 3.** [guilty]: **to feel ~ about sthg** sentirse mal por algo. ◇ *adv US* = **badly**.

badge [bædʒ] *n* **- 1.** [for decoration - metal, plastic] chapa *f*; [- sewn-on] insignia *f* **- 2.** [for identification] distintivo *m*.

badger ['bædʒə^r] ◇ *n* tejón *m*. ◇ *vt*: **to ~ sb (to do sthg)** ponerse pesado(da) con alguien (para que haga algo).

badly ['bædlɪ] (*compar* **worse,** *superl* **worst**) *adv* **- 1.** [not well] mal **- 2.** [seriously] gravemente; **I'm ~ in need of help** necesito ayuda urgentemente.

badly-off *adj* **- 1.** [poor] apurado(da) de dinero **- 2.** [lacking]: **to be ~ for sthg** estar OR andar mal de algo.

bad-mannered [-'mænəd] *adj* maleducado(da).

badminton ['bædmɪntən] *n* bádminton *m*.

bad-tempered [-'tempəd] *adj* **- 1.** [by nature]: **to be ~** tener mal genio **- 2.** [in a bad mood]: **to be ~** estar malhumorado(da).

baffle ['bæfl] *vt* desconcertar.

bag [bæg] (*pt* & *pp* **-ged,** *cont* **-ging**) ◇ *n* **- 1.** [container, bagful] bolsa *f*; **to pack one's ~s** *fig* hacer las maletas **- 2.** [handbag] bolso *m*, cartera *f Andes, RP.* ◇ *vt UK inf* [reserve] pedirse, reservarse.

➤ **bags** *npl* **- 1.** [under eyes]: **to have ~s under one's eyes** *inf* tener ojeras **- 2.** [lots]: **~s of** *inf* un montón de.

bagel ['beɪgl] *n* bollo de pan en forma de rosca.

baggage ['bægɪdʒ] *n esp US* (U) equipaje *m*.

baggage reclaim *n* recogida *f* de equipajes.

baggy ['bægɪ] (*compar* **-ier,** *superl* **-iest**) *adj* holgado(da).

bagpipes ['bægpaɪps] *npl* gaita *f*.

baguette [bə'get] *n* barra *f* de pan.

Bahamas [bə'hɑːməz] *npl*: **the ~** (las) Bahamas.

bail [beɪl] *n* (U) fianza *f*; **on ~** bajo fianza.

➤ **bail out** ◇ *vt sep* **- 1.** [pay bail for] obtener la libertad bajo fianza de **- 2.** [rescue] sacar de apuros. ◇ *vi* [from plane] tirarse en paracaídas *(antes de que se estrelle el avión).*

bailiff ['beɪlɪf] *n* alguacil *m*.

bait [beɪt] ◇ *n lit* & *fig* cebo *m*. ◇ *vt* **- 1.** [put bait on] cebar **- 2.** [tease, torment] hacer sufrir, cebarse con.

bake [beɪk] ◇ *vt* [food] cocer al horno. ◇ *vi* [food] cocerse al horno.

baked beans [beɪkt-] *npl* alubias *fpl* cocidas en salsa de tomate.

baked potato [beɪkt-] *n* patata *f* asada OR al horno.

baker ['beɪkə^r] *n* panadero *m*; **~'s (shop)** panadería *f*.

bakery ['beɪkərɪ] (*pl* **-ies**) *n* panadería *f*, tahona *f*.

baking ['beɪkɪŋ] *n* cocción *f*.

balaclava (helmet) [bælə'klɑːvə-] *n* pasamontañas *m inv*, verdugo *m*.

balance ['bæləns] ◇ *n* **- 1.** [equilibrium] equilibrio *m*; **to keep/lose one's ~** mantener/perder el equilibrio; **it caught me off ~** me pilló desprevenido(da) **- 2.** *fig* [counterweight] contrapunto *m* **- 3.** [of evidence etc] peso *m* **- 4.** [scales] balanza *f* **- 5.** [of account] saldo *m*. ◇ *vt* **- 1.** [keep in balance] poner en equilibrio **- 2.** [compare] sopesar **- 3.** [in accounting]: **to ~ the books/a budget** hacer que cuadren las cuentas/cuadre un presupuesto. ◇ *vi* **- 1.** [maintain equilibrium] sostenerse en equilibrio **- 2.** [in accounting] cuadrar.

➤ **on balance** *adv* tras pensarlo detenidamente.

balanced diet ['bælənst-] *n* dieta *f* equilibrada.

balance of payments *n* balanza *f* de pagos.

balance of trade *n* balanza *f* comercial.

balance sheet *n* balance *m*.

balcony ['bælkənɪ] (*pl* **-ies**) *n* **- 1.** [on building - big] terraza *f*; [- small] balcón *m* **- 2.** [in theatre] anfiteatro *m*, galería *f*.

bald [bɔːld] *adj* **- 1.** [without hair] calvo(va) **- 2.** [tyre] desgastado(da) **- 3.** *fig* [blunt] escueto(ta).

bale [beɪl] *n* bala *f*.

➤ **bale out** *vi UK* **- 1.** [remove water] achicar agua **- 2.** [from plane] tirarse en paracaídas *(antes de que se estrelle el avión).*

Balearic Islands [ˌbælɪ'ærɪk-], **Balearics** [ˌbælɪ'ærɪks] *npl*: **the ~** las Baleares.

baleful ['beɪlfʊl] *adj* maligno(na).

balk [bɔːk] *vi*: **to ~ (at doing sthg)** resistirse (a hacer algo).

Balkans ['bɔːlkənz], **Balkan States** *npl*: **the ~** los Balcanes.

ball [bɔːl] *n* **- 1.** [for tennis, cricket] pelota *f*; [for golf, billiards] bola *f*; [for football, basketball, rugby] balón *m*; **to be on the ~** *fig* estar al tanto de todo **- 2.** [round shape] bola *f* **- 3.** [of foot] pulpejo *m* **- 4.** [dance] baile *m*.

➤ **balls** *v inf* ◇ *npl* [testicles] pelotas *fpl*. ◇ *n* (U) [nonsense] gilipolleces *fpl*.

ballad ['bæləd] *n* balada *f*.

ballast ['bæləst] *n* lastre *m*.

ball bearing *n* cojinete *m* de bolas.

ball boy *n* recogepelotas *m inv*.

ballerina [ˌbælə'riːnə] *n* bailarina *f*.

ballet ['bæleɪ] *n* ballet *m*.

ballet dancer *n* bailarín *m*, -ina *f*.

ball game *n US* [baseball match] partido *m* de béisbol.

ball gown *n* traje *m* de fiesta.
balloon [bə'lu:n] *n* **-1.** [toy] globo *m*
- 2. [hot-air balloon] globo *m* (aerostático)
- 3. [in cartoon] bocadillo *m*.
ballot ['bælət] ◇ *n* [voting process] votación *f.* ◇ *vt* : **to ~ the members on an issue**
someter un asunto a votación entre los afiliados.
ballot box *n* [container] urna *f*; **to decide**
sthg at the ~ decidir algo en las urnas.
ballot paper *n* voto *m*, papeleta *f*, balota *f*
Perú, boleta *f* electoral *Méx, RP*.
ball park *n US* estadio *m* de béisbol.
ballpoint (pen) ['bɔ:lpɔɪnt-] *n* bolígrafo *m*,
pluma *f* atómica *Méx*, esfero *m Col*, birome *f*
RP, lápiz *m* de pasta *Chile*.
ballroom ['bɔ:lrom] *n* salón *m* de baile.
ballroom dancing *n (U)* baile *m* de salón.
balm [bɑ:m] *n* bálsamo *m*.
balmy ['bɑ:mɪ] (*compar* **-ier**, *superl* **-iest**) *adj*
apacible.
balsa ['bɒlsə], **balsawood** ['bɒlsəwʊd] *n*
balsa *f*.
balti ['bɔ:ltɪ] *n* [pan] *cacerola utilizada en la co-*
cina india; [food] *plato indio sazonado con espe-*
cias y preparado en un 'balti'.
Baltic ['bɔ:ltɪk] ◇ *adj* báltico(ca). ◇ *n*: **the**
~ (Sea) el (mar) Báltico.
Baltic Republic *n*: **the ~s** las repúblicas
bálticas.
bamboo [bæm'bu:] *n* bambú *m*.
bamboozle [bæm'bu:zl] *vt inf* camelar, engatusar.
ban [bæn] (*pt & pp* **-ned**, *cont* **-ning**) ◇ *n*:
~ (on) prohibición *f* (de). ◇ *vt* : **to ~ (sb**
from doing sthg) prohibir (a alguien hacer
algo).
banal [bə'nɑ:l] *adj pej* banal, ordinario(ria).
banana [bə'nɑ:nə] *n* plátano *m*, banana *f*
Amér.
band [bænd] *n* **- 1.** [musical group - pop] grupo *m*; [- jazz, military] banda *f* **- 2.** [of thieves
etc] banda *f* **- 3.** [strip] cinta *f*, tira *f* **- 4.**
[stripe, range] franja *f.*
◆ **band together** *vi* juntarse, agruparse.
bandage ['bændɪdʒ] ◇ *n* venda *f.* ◇ *vt*
vendar.
Band-Aid® *n US* ≃ tirita® *f Esp*, ≃ curita *f*
Amér.
b and b, B and B *n abbr of* **bed and break-**
fast.
bandit ['bændɪt] *n* bandido *m*, -da *f*, bandolero *m*, -ra *f*.
bandstand ['bændstænd] *n* quiosco *m* de
música.
bandwagon ['bændwægən] *n*: **to jump on**
the ~ subirse OR apuntarse al carro.
bandwidth ['bændwɪdθ] *n* COMPUT ancho *m*
de banda.
bandy ['bændɪ] (*compar* **-ier**, *superl* **-iest**, *pt*

& pp **-ied**) *adj* [legs] arqueado(da).
◆ **bandy about, bandy around** *vt sep*
sacar a relucir.
bandy-legged [-,legd] *adj* de piernas arqueadas.
bang [bæŋ] ◇ *n* **- 1.** [blow] golpe *m*
- 2. [loud noise] estampido *m*, estruendo *m*.
◇ *vt* **- 1.** [hit - drum, desk] golpear; [- knee,
head] golpearse **- 2.** [door] cerrar de golpe.
◇ *vi* golpear, dar golpes. ◇ *adv* [exactly]:
~ in the middle of justo en mitad de; **~ on**
[correct] muy acertado(da).
◆ **bangs** *npl US* flequillo *m*.
banger ['bæŋəʳ] *n UK* **- 1.** *inf* [sausage] salchicha *f* **- 2.** *inf* [old car] carraca *f*, cacharro
m **- 3.** [firework] petardo *m*.
Bangladesh [,bæŋglə'deʃ] *n* Bangladesh.
bangle ['bæŋgl] *n* brazalete *m*.
banish ['bænɪʃ] *vt lit & fig* desterrar.
banister ['bænɪstəʳ] *n*, **banisters**
['bænɪstəz] *npl* barandilla *f*, pasamanos *m*
inv.
bank [bæŋk] ◇ *n* **- 1.** [gen & FIN] banco *m*
- 2. [by river, lake] ribera *f*, orilla *f* **- 3.** [slope]
loma *f* **- 4.** [of clouds etc] masa *f.* ◇ *vi* **- 1.** FIN :
to ~ with tener una cuenta en **- 2.** [plane] ladearse.
◆ **bank on** *vt fus* contar con.
bank account *n* cuenta *f* bancaria.
bank balance *n* saldo *m* bancario.
bank card = **banker's card**.
bank charges *npl* comisiones *fpl* banca-
rias.
bank draft *n* giro *m* bancario.
banker ['bæŋkəʳ] *n* banquero *m*, -ra *f*.
banker's card *n UK* tarjeta *f* de identificación bancaria.
bank holiday *n UK* día *m* festivo, fiesta *f*
nacional.
banking ['bæŋkɪŋ] *n* banca *f*.
bank manager *n* director *m*, -ra *f* de banco.
bank note *n* billete *m* de banco.
bank rate *n* tipo *m* de interés bancario.
bankrupt ['bæŋkrʌpt] ◇ *adj* [financially]
quebrado(da), en quiebra; **to go ~** quebrar. ◇ *vt* llevar a la quiebra.
bankruptcy ['bæŋkrəptsɪ] (*pl* **-ies**) *n* quiebra *f*, bancarrota *f*; *fig* [of ideas] falta *f* total.
bank statement *n* extracto *m* de cuenta.
banner ['bænəʳ] *n* **- 1.** [carrying slogan] pancarta *f* **- 2.** COMPUT banner *m*, pancarta *f* publicitaria.
bannister ['bænɪstəʳ] *n*, **bannisters**
['bænɪstəz] *npl* = **banister(s)**.
banquet ['bæŋkwɪt] *n* banquete *m*.
banter ['bæntəʳ] *n (U)* bromas *fpl*.
bap [bæp] *n UK* bollo *m* de pan, panecillo *m*.
baptism ['bæptɪzm] *n* bautismo *m*.
baptize, -ise [UK bæp'taɪz, US 'bæptaɪz] *vt*
bautizar.

bar [bɑːʳ] (*pt* & *pp* **-red**, *cont* **-ring**) ◇ *n* **- 1.** [of soap] pastilla *f*; [of gold] lingote *m*; [of wood] barrote *m*; [of metal] barra *f*; **a ~ of chocolate** una chocolatina; **to be behind ~s** estar entre rejas **- 2.** [drinking place] bar *m* **- 3.** [counter] barra *f* **- 4.** *fig* [obstacle] barrera *f*; [ban] prohibición *f* **- 5.** MUS compás *m*. ◇ *vt* **- 1.** [close with a bar] atrancar **- 2.** [block]: **to ~ sb's way** impedir el paso a alguien **- 3.** [ban]: **to ~ sb (from doing sthg)** prohibir a alguien (hacer algo); **to ~ sb from somewhere** prohibir a alguien la entrada en un sitio. ◇ *prep* [except] menos, salvo; **~ none** sin excepción.
◆ **Bar** *n* JUR : **the Bar** *UK conjunto de los abogados que ejercen en tribunales superiores*; *US* la abogacía.

barbaric [bɑːˈbærɪk] *adj* salvaje.

barbecue [ˈbɑːbɪkjuː] *n* barbacoa *f*.

barbed wire [bɑːbd-] *n* alambre *m* de espino.

barber [ˈbɑːbəʳ] *n* barbero *m*; **~'s** peluquería *f*.

barbershop [ˈbɑːbəʃɒp] *n US* barbería *f*.

barbiturate [bɑːˈbɪtjʊrət] *n* barbitúrico *m*.

bar code *n* código *m* de barras.

bare [beəʳ] ◇ *adj* **- 1.** [without covering - legs, trees, hills] desnudo(da); [- feet] descalzo(za) **- 2.** [absolute, minimum] esencial **- 3.** [empty] vacío(a). ◇ *vt* descubrir; **to ~ one's teeth** enseñar los dientes.

bareback [ˈbeəbæk] *adj* & *adv* a pelo.

barefaced [ˈbeəfeɪst] *adj* descarado(da).

barefoot(ed) [ˌbeəˈfʊt(ɪd)] *adj* & *adv* descalzo(za).

barely [ˈbeəlɪ] *adv* [scarcely] apenas.

bargain [ˈbɑːgɪn] ◇ *n* **- 1.** [agreement] trato *m*, acuerdo *m*; **into the ~** además **- 2.** [good buy] ganga *f*, pichincha *f RP*. ◇ *vi*: **to ~ (with sb for sthg)** negociar (con alguien para obtener algo).
◆ **bargain for, bargain on** *vt fus* contar con.

barge [bɑːdʒ] ◇ *n* barcaza *f*. ◇ *vi inf*: **to ~ into** [person] chocarse con; [room] irrumpir en.
◆ **barge in** *vi inf*: **to ~ in (on)** [conversation etc] entrometerse (en).

baritone [ˈbærɪtəʊn] *n* barítono *m*.

bark [bɑːk] ◇ *n* **- 1.** [of dog] ladrido *m* **- 2.** [on tree] corteza *f*. ◇ *vi*: **to ~ (at)** ladrar (a).

barley [ˈbɑːlɪ] *n* cebada *f*.

barley sugar *n UK* azúcar *m* OR *f* cande.

barley water *n UK* hordiate *m*.

barmaid [ˈbɑːmeɪd] *n* camarera *f*.

barman [ˈbɑːmən] (*pl* **-men** [-mən]) *n* camarero *m*, barman *m*.

barn [bɑːn] *n* granero *m*.

barometer [bəˈrɒmɪtəʳ] *n* barómetro *m*; *fig*

[of public opinion etc] piedra *f* de toque.

baron [ˈbærən] *n* barón *m*.

baroness [ˈbærənɪs] *n* baronesa *f*.

barrack [ˈbærək] *vt UK* abroncar, abuchear.
◆ **barracks** *npl* cuartel *m*.

barrage [ˈbærɑːʒ] *n* **- 1.** [of firing] descarga *f*, fuego *m* intenso de artillería **- 2.** [of questions] aluvión *m*, alud *m* **- 3.** *UK* [dam] presa *f*, dique *m*.

barrel [ˈbærəl] *n* **- 1.** [for beer, wine, oil] barril *m* **- 2.** [of gun] cañón *m*.

barren [ˈbærən] *adj* estéril.

barricade [ˌbærɪˈkeɪd] ◇ *n* barricada *f*. ◇ *vt* levantar barricadas en.

barrier [ˈbærɪəʳ] *n lit* & *fig* barrera *f*.

barring [ˈbɑːrɪŋ] *prep* salvo; **~ a miracle** a menos que ocurra un milagro.

barrister [ˈbærɪstəʳ] *n UK* abogado *m*, -da *f* (*de tribunales superiores*).

barrow [ˈbærəʊ] *n* carrito *m*.

bartender [ˈbɑːtendəʳ] *n esp US* camarero *m*, -ra *f*.

barter [ˈbɑːtəʳ] ◇ *n* trueque *m*. ◇ *vt*: **to ~ (sthg for sthg)** trocar (algo por algo).

base [beɪs] ◇ *n* base *f*. ◇ *vt* **- 1.** [place, establish] emplazar; **he's ~d in Paris** vive en París **- 2.** [use as starting point]: **to ~ sthg on** OR **upon** basar algo en. ◇ *adj pej* bajo(ja), vil.

baseball [ˈbeɪsbɔːl] *n* béisbol *m*.

baseball cap *n* gorra *f* de visera.

basement [ˈbeɪsmənt] *n* sótano *m*.

base rate *n* tipo *m* de interés base.

bases [ˈbeɪsiːz] *pl* ▷ **basis**.

bash [bæʃ] *inf* ◇ *n* **- 1.** [attempt]: **to have a ~ at sthg** intentar algo **- 2.** [party] juerga *f*. ◇ *vt* [hit - person, thing] darle un porrazo a; [- one's head, knee] darse un porrazo en.

bashful [ˈbæʃfʊl] *adj* [person] vergonzoso(sa); [smile] tímido(da).

basic [ˈbeɪsɪk] *adj* básico(ca).
◆ **basics** *npl* **- 1.** [rudiments] principios *mpl* básicos **- 2.** [essentials] lo imprescindible.

basically [ˈbeɪsɪklɪ] *adv* **- 1.** [essentially] esencialmente **- 2.** [really] en resumen.

basil [ˈbæzl] *n* albahaca *f*.

basin [ˈbeɪsn] *n* **- 1.** *UK* [bowl] balde *m*, barreño *m* **- 2.** [wash basin] lavabo *m* **- 3.** GEOGR cuenca *f*.

basis [ˈbeɪsɪs] (*pl* **bases**) *n* base *f*; **on the ~ of** de acuerdo con, a partir de; **on a weekly ~** semanalmente; **on a monthly ~** mensualmente.

bask [bɑːsk] *vi* [sunbathe]: **to ~ in the sun** tostarse al sol.

basket [ˈbɑːskɪt] *n* **- 1.** [container] cesta *f* **- 2.** [in basketball] canasta *f*.

basketball [ˈbɑːskɪtbɔːl] *n* baloncesto *m*.

Basque [bɑːsk] ◇ *adj* vasco(ca). ◇ *n*

- 1. [person] vasco *m*, -ca *f* **- 2.** [language] vascuence *m*, euskera *m*.

Basque Country [bɑːsk-] *n*: the ~ el País Vasco, Euskadi.

bass [beɪs] ◇ *adj* bajo(ja). ◇ *n* **- 1.** [singer, bass guitar] bajo *m* **- 2.** [double bass] contrabajo *m* **- 3.** [on hi-fi, amplifier] graves *mpl*.

bass drum [beɪs-] *n* bombo *m*.

bass guitar [beɪs-] *n* bajo *m*.

bassoon [bəˈsuːn] *n* fagot *m*.

bass player [beɪs-] *n* bajista *m* OR *f*.

bastard [ˈbɑːstəd] *n* **- 1.** [illegitimate child] bastardo *m*, -da *f* **- 2.** *v inf pej* cabrón *m*, -ona *f*, concha *f* de su madre *RP*.

bastion [ˈbæstɪən] *n* bastión *m*.

bat [bæt] (*pt* & *pp* **-ted**, *cont* **-ting**) ◇ *n* **- 1.** [animal] murciélago *m* **- 2.** [for cricket, baseball] bate *m* **- 3.** [for table-tennis] pala *f*, paleta *f*. ◇ *vi* batear.

batch [bætʃ] *n* **- 1.** [of bread] hornada *f* **- 2.** [of letters etc] remesa *f* **- 3.** [of work] montón *m* **- 4.** [of products] lote *m*, partida *f*.

bated [ˈbeɪtɪd] *adj*: with ~ breath con el aliento contenido.

bath [bɑːθ] ◇ *n* **- 1.** [bathtub] bañera *f*, bañadera *f Arg*, tina *f Amér* **- 2.** [act of washing] baño *m*, bañada *f Amér*; to have OR take a ~ darse un baño, bañarse. ◇ *vt* bañar.

◆ **baths** *npl UK* [public swimming pool] piscina *f* municipal, alberca *f* municipal *Méx*, pileta *f* municipal *RP*.

bathe [beɪð] ◇ *vt* [wound] lavar. ◇ *vi* bañarse.

bathing [ˈbeɪðɪŋ] *n* (*U*) baños *mpl*.

bathing cap *n* gorro *m* de baño.

bathing costume, bathing suit *n* traje *m* de baño, bañador *m*, malla *f Amér*.

bathrobe [ˈbɑːθrəʊb] *n* **- 1.** [made of towelling] albornoz *m* **- 2.** [dressing gown] batín *m*, bata *f*.

bathroom [ˈbɑːθrʊm] *n* **- 1.** *UK* [room with bath] (cuarto *m* de) baño *m* **- 2.** [toilet] servicio *m*.

bath towel *n* toalla *f* de baño.

bathtub [ˈbɑːθtʌb] *n* bañera *f*.

baton [ˈbætən] *n* **- 1.** [of conductor] batuta *f* **- 2.** [in relay race] testigo *m* **- 3.** *UK* [of policeman] porra *f*.

batsman [ˈbætsmən] (*pl* **-men** [-mən]) *n* bateador *m*.

battalion [bəˈtæljən] *n* batallón *m*.

batten [ˈbætn] *n* listón *m* (de madera).

batter [ˈbætəʳ] ◇ *n* pasta *f* para rebozar; *US* [for cakes] mezcla *f* pastelera. ◇ *vt* **- 1.** [child, woman] pegar **- 2.** [door, ship] golpear.

◆ **batter down** *vt sep* echar abajo.

battered [ˈbætəd] *adj* **- 1.** [child, woman] maltratado(da) **- 2.** [car, hat] abollado(da) **- 3.** [fish, vegetables, etc] rebozado(da).

battery [ˈbætərɪ] (*pl* **-ies**) *n* [of radio, toy] pila *f*; [of car, guns] batería *f*.

battle [ˈbætl] ◇ *n* **- 1.** [in war] batalla *f* **- 2.** [struggle]: ~ (for/against/with) lucha *f* (por/contra/con). ◇ *vi*: to ~ (for/against/with) luchar (por/contra/con).

battlefield [ˈbætlfiːld], **battleground** [ˈbætlgraʊnd] *n lit* & *fig* campo *m* de batalla.

battlements [ˈbætlmənts] *npl* almenas *fpl*.

battleship [ˈbætlʃɪp] *n* acorazado *m*.

bauble [ˈbɔːbl] *n* **- 1.** [ornament] baratija *f* **- 2.** [for Christmas tree] bola *f* de Navidad.

baulk [bɔːk] = **balk**.

bawdy [ˈbɔːdɪ] (*compar* **-ier**, *superl* **-iest**) *adj* verde, picante.

bawl [bɔːl] *vi* **- 1.** [shout] vociferar **- 2.** [cry] berrear.

bay [beɪ] ◇ *n* **- 1.** [of coast] bahía *f* **- 2.** [for loading] zona *f* de carga y descarga **- 3.** [for parking] plaza *f*, estacionamiento *m* **- 4.** *phr*: to keep sthg/sb at ~ mantener algo/a alguien a raya. ◇ *vi* aullar.

bay leaf *n* (hoja *f* de) laurel *m*.

bay window *n* ventana *f* salediza.

bazaar [bəˈzɑːʳ] *n* **- 1.** [market] bazar *m*, zoco *m* **- 2.** *UK* [charity sale] mercadillo *m* benéfico.

B & B *abbr of* **bed and breakfast**.

BBC (*abbr of* **British Broadcasting Corporation**) *n* BBC *f*, compañía estatal británica de radiotelevisión.

BC (*abbr of* **before Christ**) a.C.

be [biː] (*pt* **was** OR **were**, *pp* **been**) ◇ *aux vb* **- 1.** (*in combination with present participle: to form cont tense*) estar; **what is he doing?** ¿qué hace OR está haciendo?; **it's snowing** está nevando; **I'm leaving tomorrow** me voy mañana; **they've been promising it for years** han estado prometiéndolo durante años **- 2.** (*in combination with pp: to form passive*) ser; **to ~ loved** ser amado; **there was no one to ~ seen** no se veía a nadie; **ten people were killed** murieron diez personas **- 3.** (*in question tags*): **you're not going now, are you?** no irás a marcharte ya ¿no?; **the meal was delicious, wasn't it?** la comida fue deliciosa ¿verdad? **- 4.** (*followed by 'to'* + *infin*): **I'm to be promoted** me van a ascender; **you're not to tell anyone** no debes decírselo a nadie. ◇ *copulative vb* **- 1.** (*with adj, n*) [indicating innate quality, permanent condition] ser; [indicating state, temporary condition] estar; **snow is white** la nieve es blanca; **she's intelligent/tall** es inteligente/alta; **to ~ a doctor/plumber** ser médico/fontanero; **I'm Welsh** soy galés; **1 and 1 are 2** 1 y 1 son 2; **your hands are cold** tus manos están frías; **I'm tired/angry** estoy cansado/enfadado; **he's in a difficult position** está en una situación difícil **- 2.** (*referring to health*) estar; **she's ill/better** está enferma/mejor;

how are you? ¿cómo estás?, ¿qué tal?
- **3.** [referring to age]: **how old are you?** ¿qué edad OR cuántos años tienes?; **I'm 20 (years old)** tengo 20 años - **4.** [cost] ser, costar; **how much is it?** ¿cuánto es?; **that will ~ £10, please** son 10 libras; **apples are only 40p a kilo today** hoy las manzanas están a tan sólo 40 peniques el kilo. ◇ *vi* - **1.** [exist] ser, existir; **the worst prime minister that ever was** el peor primer ministro de todos los tiempos; **~ that as it may** aunque así sea; **there is/are** hay; **is there life on Mars?** ¿hay vida en Marte? - **2.** [referring to place] estar; **Valencia is in Spain** Valencia está en España; **he will ~ here tomorrow** estará aquí mañana - **3.** [referring to movement] estar; **where have you been?** ¿dónde has estado? ◇ *impersonal vb* - **1.** [referring to time, dates] ser; **it's two o'clock** son las dos; **it's the 17th of February** estamos a 17 de febrero - **2.** [referring to distance]: **it's 3 km to the next town** hay 3 kms hasta el próximo pueblo - **3.** [referring to the weather]: **it's hot/cold/windy** hace calor/frío/viento - **4.** [for emphasis] ser; **it's me** soy yo.

beach [biːtʃ] ◇ *n* playa *f*. ◇ *vt* varar.

beacon ['biːkən] *n* - **1.** [warning fire] almenara *f* - **2.** [lighthouse] faro *m* - **3.** [radio beacon] radiofaro *m*.

bead [biːd] *n* - **1.** [of wood, glass] cuenta *f*, abalorio *m* - **2.** [of sweat] gota *f*.

beagle ['biːgl] *n* beagle *m*.

beak [biːk] *n* pico *m*.

beaker ['biːkə[r]] *n* taza *f (sin asa)*.

beam [biːm] ◇ *n* - **1.** [of wood, concrete] viga *f* - **2.** [of light] rayo *m*. ◇ *vt* transmitir. ◇ *vi* - **1.** [smile] sonreír resplandeciente - **2.** [shine] resplandecer, brillar.

bean [biːn] *n* CULIN [haricot] judía *f*, habichuela *f*, frijol *m Amér*, poroto *m Andes, CSur*, caraota *f Ven*; [of coffee] grano *m*.

beanbag ['biːnbæg] *n* cojín grande relleno de bolitas de polietileno.

beanshoot ['biːnʃuːt], **beansprout** ['biːnspraʊt] *n* brote *m* de soja.

bear [beə[r]] (*pt* bore, *pp* borne) ◇ *n* [animal] oso *m*, -sa *f*. ◇ *vt* - **1.** [carry] llevar - **2.** [support] soportar - **3.** [responsibility] cargar con - **4.** [marks, signs] llevar - **5.** [endure] aguantar - **6.** [fruit, crop] dar - **7.** [feeling] guardar, albergar. ◇ *vi*: **to ~ left** torcer OR doblar a la izquierda; **to bring pressure/influence to ~ on** ejercer presión/influencia sobre.

➡ **bear down** *vi*: **to ~ down on** echarse encima de.

➡ **bear out** *vt sep* corroborar.

➡ **bear up** *vi* resistir.

➡ **bear with** *vt fus* tener paciencia con; **if you could just ~ with me a moment ...** si no le importa esperar un momento ...

beard [biəd] *n* barba *f*.

bearer ['beərə[r]] *n* - **1.** [of stretcher, news, cheque] portador *m*, -ra *f* - **2.** [of passport] titular *m* OR *f*.

bearing ['beəriŋ] *n* - **1.** [connection]: **~ (on)** relación *f* (con) - **2.** [deportment] porte *m* - **3.** [for shaft] cojinete *m* - **4.** [on compass] rumbo *m*, orientación *f*; **to get one's ~s** orientarse; **to lose one's ~s** desorientarse.

beast [biːst] *n lit & fig* bestia *f*.

beastly ['biːstlɪ] (*compar* -ier, *superl* -iest) *adj dated* atroz.

beat [biːt] (*pt* beat, *pp* beaten) ◇ *n* - **1.** [of drum] golpe *m* - **2.** [of heart, pulse] latido *m* - **3.** MUS [rhythm] ritmo *m*; [individual unit of time] golpe *m (de compás)* - **4.** [of policeman] ronda *f*. ◇ *vt* - **1.** [hit - person] pegar; [- thing] golpear; [- carpet] sacudir - **2.** [wings, eggs, butter] batir - **3.** [defeat]: **it ~s me** *inf* no me lo explico - **4.** [be better than] ser mucho mejor que - **5.** *phr*: **~ it!** *inf* ¡largo! ◇ *vi* - **1.** [rain] golpear - **2.** [heart, pulse] latir; [drums] redoblar.

➡ **beat off** *vt sep* [attackers] repeler.

➡ **beat up** *vt sep inf* dar una paliza a.

➡ **beat up on** *vt sep US inf* dar una paliza a.

beating ['biːtiŋ] *n* - **1.** [hitting] paliza *f*, golpiza *f Amér* - **2.** [defeat] derrota *f*.

beautiful ['bjuːtɪfʊl] *adj* - **1.** [person] guapo(pa) - **2.** [thing, animal] precioso(sa) - **3.** *inf* [very good - shot, weather] espléndido(da).

beautifully ['bjuːtəflɪ] *adv* - **1.** [attractively] bellamente - **2.** *inf* [very well] espléndidamente.

beauty ['bjuːtɪ] (*pl* -ies) *n* belleza *f*.

beauty parlour *n* salón *m* de belleza.

beauty salon *n* = **beauty parlour**.

beauty spot *n* - **1.** [picturesque place] bello paraje *m* - **2.** [on skin] lunar *m*.

beaver ['biːvə[r]] *n* castor *m*.

became [bɪ'keɪm] *pt* ▷ **become**.

because [bɪ'kɒz] *conj* porque.

➡ **because of** *prep* por, a causa de.

beck [bek] *n*: **to be at sb's ~ and call** estar siempre a disposición de alguien.

beckon ['bekən] ◇ *vt* [signal to] llamar (con un gesto). ◇ *vi* [signal]: **to ~ to sb** llamar (con un gesto) a alguien.

become [bɪ'kʌm] (*pt* became, *pp* become) *vi* hacerse; **to ~ happy** ponerse contento; **to ~ suspicious** volverse receloso; **to ~ angry** enfadarse; **he became Prime Minister in 1991** en 1991 se convirtió en primer ministro.

becoming [bɪ'kʌmɪŋ] *adj* - **1.** [attractive] favorecedor(ra) - **2.** [appropriate] apropiado(da).

bed [bed] (*pt & pp* -ded, *cont* -ding) *n* - **1.** [to sleep on] cama *f*; **to go to** ~ irse a la cama; **to make the** ~ hacer la cama; **to put sb to** ~ acostar a alguien; **to go to** ~ **with** *euphemism* acostarse con - **2.** [flowerbed] macizo *m* - **3.** [of sea] fondo *m*; [of river] lecho *m*, cauce *m*.

bed and breakfast *n* [service] cama *f* y desayuno; [hotel] ≈ pensión *f*.

bedclothes ['bedkləʊðz] *npl* ropa *f* de cama.

bedlam ['bedləm] *n* jaleo *m*, alboroto *m*.

bed linen *n* ropa *f* de cama.

bedraggled [bɪ'drægld] *adj* mojado y sucio (mojada y sucia).

bedridden ['bed,rɪdn] *adj* postrado(da) en cama.

bedroom ['bedrom] *n* - **1.** [at home] dormitorio *m*, recámara *f Cam, Méx* - **2.** [in hotel] habitación *f*, recámara *f Cam, Méx*.

bedside ['bedsaɪd] *n* [side of bed] lado *m* de la cama; [of ill person] lecho *m*; ~ **table** mesita *f* de noche, nochero *m Amér*, buró *m Méx*.

bed-sit(ter) *n* UK *habitación alquilada con cama*.

bedsore ['bedsɔːʳ] *n* úlcera *f* por decúbito.

bedspread ['bedspred] *n* colcha *f*.

bedtime ['bedtaɪm] *n* hora *f* de irse a la cama.

bee [biː] *n* abeja *f*.

beech [biːtʃ] *n* haya *f*.

beef [biːf] *n* carne *f* de vaca, carne *f* de res *Amér*.

◆ **beef up** *vt sep inf* reforzar.

beefburger ['biːf,bɜːgəʳ] *n* hamburguesa *f*.

Beefeater ['biːf,iːtəʳ] *n guardián de la Torre de Londres*.

beef jerky *n* US tasajo *m*, cecina *f*.

beefsteak ['biːf,steɪk] *n* bistec *m*, bife *m RP*.

beehive ['biːhaɪv] *n* [for bees] colmena *f*.

beeline ['biːlaɪn] *n*: **to make a** ~ **for** *inf* irse derechito(ta) hacia.

been [biːn] *pp* ⊳ **be**.

beeper ['biːpəʳ] *n* buscapersonas *m inv*.

beer [bɪəʳ] *n* cerveza *f*.

beet [biːt] *n* - **1.** [sugar beet] remolacha *f* azucarera - **2.** US [beetroot] remolacha *f*, betabel *m Méx*, betarraga *f Chile*.

beetle ['biːtl] *n* escarabajo *m*.

beetroot ['biːtruːt] *n* remolacha *f*, betabel *m Méx*, betarraga *f Chile*.

before [bɪ'fɔːʳ] ◇ *adv* antes, endenantes *Amér*; **we went the year** ~ fuimos el año anterior. ◇ *prep* - **1.** [in time] antes de; **they arrived** ~ **us** llegaron antes que nosotros - **2.** [in space - facing] ante, delante de. ◇ *conj* antes de; ~ **it's too late** antes de que sea demasiado tarde.

beforehand [bɪ'fɔːhænd] *adv* con antelación, de antemano.

befriend [bɪ'frend] *vt* hacer OR entablar amistad con.

beg [beg] (*pt* & *pp* **-ged**, *cont* **-ging**) ◇ *vt* - **1.** [money, food] mendigar, pedir - **2.** [favour, forgiveness] suplicar; **to** ~ **sb to do sthg** rogar a alguien que haga algo; **to** ~ **sb for sthg** rogar algo a alguien. ◇ *vi* - **1.** [for money, food]: **to** ~ **(for sthg)** pedir OR mendigar (algo) - **2.** [for favour, forgiveness]: **to** ~ **(for sthg)** suplicar OR rogar (algo).

began [bɪ'gæn] *pt* ⊳ **begin**.

beggar ['begəʳ] *n* [poor person] mendigo *m*, -ga *f*.

begin [bɪ'gɪn] (*pt* **began**, *pp* **begun**, *cont* **-ning**) ◇ *vt*: **to** ~ **(doing** OR **to do sthg)** empezar OR comenzar (a hacer algo). ◇ *vi* empezar, comenzar; **to** ~ **with** para empezar, de entrada.

beginner [bɪ'gɪnəʳ] *n* principiante *m* OR *f*.

beginning [bɪ'gɪnɪŋ] *n* comienzo *m*, principio *m*; **at the** ~ **of the month** a principios de mes.

begrudge [bɪ'grʌdʒ] *vt* - **1.** [envy]: **to** ~ **sb sthg** envidiar a alguien algo - **2.** [give, do unwillingly]: **to** ~ **doing sthg** hacer algo de mala gana OR a regañadientes.

begun [bɪ'gʌn] *pp* ⊳ **begin**.

behalf [bɪ'hɑːf] *n*: **on** ~ **of** UK, **in** ~ **of** US en nombre OR en representación de.

behave [bɪ'heɪv] ◇ *vt*: **to** ~ **o.s.** portarse bien. ◇ *vi* - **1.** [in a particular way] comportarse, portarse - **2.** [in an acceptable way] comportarse OR portarse bien.

behaviour UK, **behavior** US [bɪ'heɪvjəʳ] *n* comportamiento *m*, conducta *f*.

behead [bɪ'hed] *vt* decapitar.

beheld [bɪ'held] *pt* & *pp* ⊳ **behold**.

behind [bɪ'haɪnd] ◇ *prep* - **1.** [in space] detrás de - **2.** [causing, responsible for] detrás de - **3.** [in support of]: **we're** ~ **you** nosotros te apoyamos - **4.** [in time]: **to be** ~ **schedule** ir retrasado(da) - **5.** [less successful than] por detrás de. ◇ *adv* - **1.** [in space] detrás - **2.** [in time]: **to be** ~ **(with)** ir atrasado(da) (con) - **3.** [less successful] por detrás. ◇ *n inf* trasero *m*.

behold [bɪ'həʊld] (*pt* & *pp* **beheld**) *vt* *literary* contemplar.

beige [beɪʒ] *adj* beige.

being ['biːɪŋ] *n* - **1.** [creature] ser *m* - **2.** [state of existing]: **it is no longer in** ~ ya no existe; **to come into** ~ ver la luz, nacer.

belated [bɪ'leɪtɪd] *adj* tardío(a).

belch [beltʃ] ◇ *vt* arrojar. ◇ *vi* - **1.** [person] eructar - **2.** [smoke, fire] brotar.

beleaguered [bɪ'liːgəd] *adj* - **1.** MIL asediado(da) - **2.** *fig* [harassed] acosado(da).

Belgian ['beldʒən] ◇ *adj* belga. ◇ *n* belga *m* OR *f*.

beside

Belgium ['beldʒəm] *n* Bélgica.

Belgrade [ˌbelˈgreɪd] *n* Belgrado.

belie [bɪˈlaɪ] (*cont* **belying**) *vt* **-1.** [disprove] desmentir **-2.** [give false idea of] encubrir.

belief [bɪˈliːf] *n* **-1.** [faith, principle]: ~ **(in)** creencia *f* (en) **-2.** [opinion] opinión *f*.

believe [bɪˈliːv] <> *vt* creer; ~ **it or not** lo creas o no. <> *vi* [know to exist, be good]: **to** ~ **in** creer en.

believer [bɪˈliːvə^r] *n* **-1.** [religious person] creyente *m OR f* **-2.** [in idea, action]: ~ **in sthg** partidario *m*, -ria *f* de algo.

belittle [bɪˈlɪtl] *vt* menospreciar.

bell [bel] *n* [of church] campana *f*; [handbell] campanilla *f*; [handbell, on door, bike] timbre *m*.

belligerent [bɪˈlɪdʒərənt] *adj* **-1.** [at war] beligerante **-2.** [aggressive] belicoso(sa).

bellow ['beləʊ] *vi* **-1.** [person] rugir **-2.** [bull] bramar.

bellows ['beləʊz] *npl* fuelle *m*.

belly ['belɪ] (*pl* **-ies**) *n* **-1.** [of person] barriga *f*, guata *f* *Chile* **-2.** [of animal] vientre *m*.

bellyache ['belɪeɪk] *inf* <> *n* dolor *m* de barriga. <> *vi* gruñir.

belly button *n inf* ombligo *m*.

belong [bɪˈlɒŋ] *vi* **-1.** [be property]: **to** ~ **to** pertenecer a **-2.** [be member]: **to** ~ **to** ser miembro de **-3.** [be situated in right place]: **where does this book** ~? ¿dónde va este libro?; **he felt he didn't** ~ **there** sintió que no encajaba allí.

belongings [bɪˈlɒŋɪŋz] *npl* pertenencias *fpl*.

beloved [bɪˈlʌvd] <> *adj* querido(da). <> *n* amado *m*, -da *f*.

below [bɪˈləʊ] <> *adv* **-1.** [gen] abajo; **the flat** ~ el piso de abajo **-2.** [in text] más abajo; **see** ~ véase más abajo **-3.** [with temperatures]: **thirty degrees** ~ treinta grados bajo cero. <> *prep* **-1.** [lower than in position] (por) debajo de, bajo **-2.** [lower than in rank, number] **por debajo de -3.** [with temperatures]: **thirty degrees** ~ **zero** treinta grados bajo cero.

belt [belt] <> *n* **-1.** [for clothing] cinturón *m*, correa *f* **-2.** TECH [wide] cinta *f*; [narrow] correa *f* **-3.** [of land, sea] franja *f*. <> *vt inf* arrear. <> *vi UK inf* ir a toda mecha.

beltway ['belt,weɪ] *n US* carretera *f* de circunvalación.

bemused [bɪˈmjuːzd] *adj* perplejo(ja).

bench [bentʃ] <> *n* **-1.** [seat] banco *m* **-2.** [in lab, workshop] mesa *f* de trabajo **-3.** [in sport] banquillo *m*. <> *vt SPORT* mandar al banquillo.

bend [bend] (*pt & pp* **bent**) <> *n* curva *f*; **round the** ~ *inf* majareta, majara. <> *vt* doblar. <> *vi* [person] agacharse; [tree] doblarse; **to** ~ **over backwards for** hacer todo lo

humanamente posible por.

beneath [bɪˈniːθ] <> *adv* debajo. <> *prep* **-1.** [under] debajo de, bajo **-2.** [unworthy of] indigno(na) de.

benefactor ['benɪfæktə^r] *n* benefactor *m*.

beneficial [ˌbenɪˈfɪʃl] *adj*: ~ **(to)** beneficioso(sa) (para).

beneficiary [ˌbenɪˈfɪʃərɪ] (*pl* **-ies**) *n* **-1.** JUR [of will] beneficiario *m*, -ria *f* **-2.** [of change in law, new rule] beneficiado *m*, -da *f*.

benefit ['benɪfɪt] <> *n* **-1.** [advantage] ventaja *f*; **for the** ~ **of** en atención a; **to be to sb's** ~, **to be of** ~ **to sb** ir en beneficio de alguien **-2.** ADMIN [allowance of money] subsidio *m*; **to be on** ~ *UK* estar cobrando un subsidio estatal. <> *vt* beneficiar. <> *vi*: **to** ~ **from** beneficiarse de.

Benelux ['benɪlʌks] *n* (el) Benelux; **the** ~ **countries** los países del Benelux.

benevolent [bɪˈnevələnt] *adj* benevolente.

benign [bɪˈnaɪn] *adj* **-1.** [person] bondadoso(sa) **-2.** MED benigno(na).

bent [bent] <> *pt & pp* > **bend.** <> *adj* **-1.** [wire, bar] torcido(da) **-2.** [person, body] encorvado(da) **-3.** *UK inf* [dishonest] corrupto(ta) **-4.** [determined]: **to be** ~ **on sthg/on doing sthg** estar empeñado(da) en algo/en hacer algo. <> *n* [natural tendency] inclinación *f*; ~ **for** don *m OR* talento *m* para.

bequeath [bɪˈkwiːð] *vt lit & fig*: **to** ~ **sb sthg, to** ~ **sthg to sb** legar algo a alguien.

bequest [bɪˈkwest] *n* legado *m*.

berate [bɪˈreɪt] *vt* regañar.

bereaved [bɪˈriːvd] (*pl inv*) *n*: **the** ~ la familia del difunto.

beret ['bereɪ] *n* boina *f*.

berk [bɜːk] *n UK inf* imbécil *m OR f*.

Berlin [bɜːˈlɪn] *n* Berlín.

berm [bɜːm] *n US* arcén *m*.

Bermuda [bəˈmjuːdə] *n* las Bermudas.

Bern [bɜːn] *n* Berna.

berry ['berɪ] (*pl* **-ies**) *n* baya *f*.

berserk [bəˈzɜːk] *adj*: **to go** ~ ponerse hecho(cha) una fiera.

berth [bɜːθ] <> *n* **-1.** [in harbour] amarradero *m*, atracadero *m* **-2.** [in ship, train] litera *f*. <> *vt & vi* atracar.

beseech [bɪˈsiːtʃ] (*pt & pp* **besought** *OR* **beseeched**) *vt literary*: **to** ~ **(sb to do sthg)** suplicar (a alguien que haga algo).

beset [bɪˈset] *adj*: ~ **with** *OR* **by** [subj: person] acosado(da) por; [subj: plan] plagado(da) de.

beside [bɪˈsaɪd] *prep* **-1.** [next to] al lado de, junto a **-2.** [compared with] comparado(da) con **-3.** *phr*: **that's** ~ **the point** eso no viene al caso; **to be** ~ **o.s. with rage** estar fuera de sí; **to be** ~ **o.s. with joy** estar loco(ca) de alegría.

besides [bɪ'saɪdz] ◇ adv además. ◇ prep aparte de.

besiege [bɪ'si:dʒ] vt lit & fig asediar.

besotted [bɪ'sɒtɪd] adj: ~ with embobado(da) con.

besought [bɪ'sɔ:t] pt & pp ⊏ beseech.

best [best] ◇ adj mejor; ~ before ... [on packaging] consumir preferentemente antes de ... ◇ adv mejor; which did you like ~? ¿cuál te gustó más? ◇ n: she's the ~ es la mejor; we're the ~ somos los mejores; to do one's ~ hacerlo mejor que uno puede; to make the ~ of sthg sacarle el mayor partido posible a algo; for the ~ para bien; all the ~ [ending letter] un abrazo; [saying goodbye] que te vaya bien.
◆ at best adv en el mejor de los casos.

best man n ≃ padrino m de boda.

bestow [bɪ'stəʊ] vt fml: to ~ sthg on sb [gift] otorgar OR conceder algo a alguien; [praise] dirigir algo a alguien; [title] conferir algo a alguien.

best-seller n [book] best seller m, éxito m editorial.

bet [bet] (pt & pp bet OR -ted, cont -ting) ◇ n -1. [gen]: ~ (on) apuesta f (a) -2. fig [prediction] predicción f. ◇ vt apostar. ◇ vi -1. [gamble]: to ~ (on) apostar (a) -2. [predict]: to ~ on sthg contar con (que pase) algo.

betray [bɪ'treɪ] vt -1. [person, trust, principles] traicionar -2. [secret] revelar -3. [feeling] delatar.

betrayal [bɪ'treɪəl] n -1. [of person, trust, principles] traición f -2. [of secret] revelación f.

better ['betə'] ◇ adj (compar of good) mejor; to get ~ mejorar. ◇ adv (compar of well) -1. [in quality] mejor -2. [more]: I like it ~ me gusta más -3. [preferably]: we had ~ be going más vale que nos vayamos ya. ◇ n [best one] mejor m OR f; to get the ~ of sb poder con alguien. ◇ vt mejorar; to ~ o.s. mejorarse.

better off adj -1. [financially] mejor de dinero -2. [in better situation]: you'd be ~ going by bus sería mejor si vas en autobús.

betting ['betɪŋ] n (U) apuestas fpl.

betting shop n UK casa f de apuestas.

between [bɪ'twi:n] ◇ prep entre; closed ~ 1 and 2 cerrado de 1 a 2. ◇ adv: (in) ~ en medio, entremedio.

beverage ['bevərɪdʒ] n fml bebida f.

beware [bɪ'weə'] vi: to ~ (of) tener cuidado (con).

bewildered [bɪ'wɪldəd] adj desconcertado(da).

bewitching [bɪ'wɪtʃɪŋ] adj hechizante.

beyond [bɪ'jɒnd] ◇ prep más allá de; ~ midnight pasada la medianoche; ~ my

reach/responsibility fuera de mi alcance/competencia. ◇ adv más allá.

bias ['baɪəs] n -1. [prejudice] prejuicio m -2. [tendency] tendencia f, inclinación f.

biased ['baɪəst] adj parcial; to be ~ towards/against tener prejuicios en favor/en contra de.

bib [bɪb] n [for baby] babero m.

Bible ['baɪbl] n: the ~ la Biblia.

bicarbonate of soda [baɪ'kɑ:bənət-] n bicarbonato m sódico.

biceps ['baɪseps] (pl inv) n bíceps m inv.

bicker ['bɪkə'] vi reñir.

bicycle ['baɪsɪkl] ◇ n bicicleta f. ◇ comp de bicicleta.

bicycle path n camino m para bicicletas.

bicycle pump n bomba f de bicicleta.

bid [bɪd] (pt & pp bid, cont bidding) ◇ n -1. [attempt]: ~ (for) intento m (de hacerse con) -2. [at auction] puja f -3. [financial offer]: ~ (for sthg) oferta f (para adquirir algo). ◇ vt [money] ofrecer; [at auction] pujar. ◇ vi: to ~ (for) [at auction] pujar (por); [contract] hacer una oferta (por).

bidder ['bɪdə'] n postor m, -ra f.

bidding ['bɪdɪŋ] n (U) [at auction] puja f.

bide [baɪd] vt: to ~ one's time esperar el momento oportuno.

bifocals [,baɪ'fəʊklz] npl gafas fpl bifocales.

big [bɪg] (compar -ger, superl -gest) adj -1. [large, important] grande, gran (de hacerse gular nouns); a ~ problem un gran problema; ~ problems grandes problemas -2. [older] mayor -3. [successful] popular.

bigamy ['bɪgəmɪ] n bigamia f.

big deal inf ◇ n: it's no ~ no tiene (la menor) importancia. ◇ excl ¡y a mí qué!

Big Dipper [-'dɪpə'] n UK [rollercoaster] montaña f rusa.

bigheaded [,bɪg'hedɪd] adj inf pej creído(-da).

bigot ['bɪgət] n intolerante m OR f.

bigoted ['bɪgətɪd] adj intolerante.

bigotry ['bɪgətrɪ] n intolerancia f.

big time n inf: the ~ el éxito, la fama.

big toe n dedo m gordo (del pie).

big top n carpa f.

big wheel n UK [at fairground] noria f.

bike [baɪk] n inf [bicycle] bici f; [motorcycle] moto f.

bikeway ['baɪkweɪ] n US [lane] carril-bici m.

bikini [bɪ'ki:nɪ] n biquini m, bikini m.

bile [baɪl] n [fluid] bilis f inv.

bilingual [baɪ'lɪŋgwəl] adj bilingüe.

bill [bɪl] ◇ n -1. [statement of cost]: ~ (for) [meal] cuenta f (de); [electricity, phone] factura f (de) -2. [in parliament] proyecto m de ley -3. [of show, concert] programa m -4. US [banknote] billete m -5. [poster]: 'post OR stick no ~s' 'prohibido fijar carteles'

- 6. [beak] pico m. ◇ vt [send a bill]: **to ~ sb for** mandar la factura a alguien por.

◆ **Bill** n UK inf [police]: **the Bill** la pasma.

billet ['bɪlɪt] n acantonamiento m, alojamiento m.

billfold ['bɪlfəʊld] n US billetera f.

billiards ['bɪljədz] n billar m.

billion ['bɪljən] num **- 1.** [thousand million] millar m de millones; **three ~** tres mil millones **- 2.** UK dated [million million] billón m.

Bill of Rights n: **the ~** las diez primeras enmiendas de la Constitución estadounidense.

bimbo ['bɪmbəʊ] (pl -s OR -es) n inf pej niña f mona, mujer joven, guapa y poco inteligente.

bin [bɪn] n **- 1.** UK [for rubbish] cubo m de la basura; [for paper] papelera f **- 2.** [for grain, coal] depósito m.

bind [baɪnd] (pt & pp bound) vt **- 1.** [tie up] atar **- 2.** [unite - people] unir **- 3.** [bandage] vendar **- 4.** [book] encuadernar **- 5.** [constrain] obligar, comprometer.

binder ['baɪndər] n [cover] carpeta f.

binding ['baɪndɪŋ] ◇ adj obligatorio(ria), vinculante. ◇ n [on book] cubierta f, tapa f.

binge [bɪndʒ] n inf: **to go on a ~** irse de juerga.

bingo ['bɪŋgəʊ] n bingo m.

binoculars [bɪ'nɒkjʊləz] npl prismáticos mpl, gemelos mpl.

biochemistry [ˌbaɪəʊ'kemɪstrɪ] n bioquímica f.

biodegradable [ˌbaɪəʊdɪ'greɪdəbl] adj biodegradable.

bioethics [ˌbaɪəʊ'eθɪks] n (U) bioética f.

biofuel ['baɪəfjʊəl] n biocombustible m.

biography [baɪ'ɒgrəfɪ] (pl -ies) n biografía f.

biological [ˌbaɪə'lɒdʒɪkl] adj biológico(ca).

biology [baɪ'ɒlədʒɪ] n biología f.

biomass ['baɪəʊˌmæs] n biomasa f.

biosphere ['baɪəʊˌsfɪə] n biosfera f.

biotech company ['baɪəʊtek-] n empresa f de biotecnología.

bioterrorism [ˌbaɪəʊ'terərɪzm] n bioterrorismo m.

birch [bɜːtʃ] n [tree] abedul m.

bird [bɜːd] n **- 1.** [animal - large] ave f; [- small] pájaro m **- 2.** UK inf [woman] tía f.

birdie ['bɜːdɪ] n [in golf] birdie m.

bird's-eye view n vista f panorámica.

bird-watcher [-ˌwɒtʃər] n observador m, -ra f de pájaros.

Biro® ['baɪərəʊ] n bolígrafo m, birome f RP, lápiz m de pasta Chile, esfero m Col, pluma f atómica Méx.

birth [bɜːθ] n [gen] nacimiento m; [delivery] parto m; **by ~** de nacimiento; **to give ~ (to)** dar a luz (a).

birth certificate n partida f de nacimiento.

birth control n control m de natalidad.

birthday ['bɜːθdeɪ] n cumpleaños m inv.

birthmark ['bɜːθmɑːk] n antojo m.

birthrate ['bɜːθreɪt] n índice m de natalidad.

Biscay ['bɪskɪ] n: **the Bay of ~** el golfo de Vizcaya.

biscuit ['bɪskɪt] n [in UK] galleta f; US [scone] masa cocida al horno que se suele comer con salsa de carne, bísquet m Méx.

bisect [baɪ'sekt] vt [gen] dividir en dos; MATH bisecar.

bishop ['bɪʃəp] n **- 1.** [in church] obispo m **- 2.** [in chess] alfil m.

bison ['baɪsn] (pl inv OR -s) n bisonte m.

bit [bɪt] ◇ pt ▷ **bite.** ◇ n **- 1.** [piece] trozo m; a ~ of una copia de; a ~ of advice un consejo; a ~ of news una noticia; ~s and pieces UK [objects] cosillas fpl, tiliches mpl Cam, Méx; [possessions] bártulos mpl; **to take sthg to ~s** desmontar algo **-2.** [amount]: **a ~ of** un poco de; **a ~ of shopping** algunas compras; **quite a ~ of** bastante **-3.** [short time]: **(for) a ~** un rato **-4.** [of drill] broca f **-5.** [of bridle] bocado m, freno m **-6.** COMPUT bit m.

◆ **a bit** adv un poco; **a ~ easier** un poco más fácil.

◆ **bit by bit** adv poco a poco.

bitch [bɪtʃ] ◇ n **- 1.** [female dog] perra f **- 2.** v inf pej [unpleasant woman] bruja f. ◇ vi inf [talk unpleasantly]: **to ~ about** poner a parir a.

bitchy ['bɪtʃɪ] (compar -ier, superl -iest) adj inf malicioso(sa).

bite [baɪt] (pt bit, pp bitten) ◇ n **- 1.** [by dog, person] mordisco m; [by insect, snake] picotazo m **-2.** inf [food]: **to have a ~ (to eat)** comer algo **-3.** [wound - from dog] mordedura f; [- from insect, snake] picadura f. ◇ vt **- 1.** [subj: person, animal] morder **- 2.** [subj: insect, snake] picar. ◇ vi **- 1.** [animal, person]: **to ~ (into sthg)** morder (algo); **to ~ off sthg** arrancar algo de un mordisco **-2.** [insect, snake] picar **-3.** [grip] agarrar.

biting ['baɪtɪŋ] adj **- 1.** [very cold] gélido(-da), cortante **- 2.** [caustic] mordaz.

bitten ['bɪtn] pp ▷ **bite.**

bitter ['bɪtər] ◇ adj **- 1.** [coffee, chocolate] amargo(ga) **- 2.** [icy] gélido(da) **- 3.** [causing pain] amargo(ga) **- 4.** [acrimonious] encona-do(da) **- 5.** [resentful] amargado(da), resentido(da). ◇ n UK [beer] tipo de cerveza amarga.

bitter lemon n bíter m de limón.

bitterness ['bɪtənɪs] n **- 1.** [of taste] amargor m **- 2.** [of wind, weather] gelidez f **- 3.** [resentment] amargura f.

bizarre [bɪ'zɑːr] adj [behaviour, appearance]

extravagante; [machine, remark] singular,
extraordinario(ria).

blab [blæb] (*pt* & *pp* **-bed**, *cont* **-bing**) *vi inf* irse de la lengua.

black [blæk] <> *adj* **-1.** [gen] negro(gra); ~ **and blue** amoratado(da); ~ **and white** [films, photos] en blanco y negro; [clear-cut] extremadamente nítido(da) **- 2.** [coffee] solo; [without milk] sin leche **- 3.** [angry] furioso(sa). <> *n* **-1.** [colour] negro *m* **- 2.** [person] negro *m*, -gra *f* **- 3.** *phr*: **in** ~ **and white** [in writing] por escrito; **to be in the** ~ tener saldo positivo. <> *vt UK* [boycott] boicotear.
◆ **black out** *vi* desmayarse, perder el conocimiento.

blackberry ['blækbərɪ] (*pl* **-ies**) *n* **- 1.** [fruit] mora *f* **- 2.** [bush] zarzamora *f*.

blackbird ['blækbɜːd] *n* mirlo *m*.

blackboard ['blækbɔːd] *n* pizarra *f*, encerado *m*, pizarrón *m Amér*.

blackcurrant [ˌblækˈkʌrənt] *n* grosella *f* negra, casis *m*.

blacken ['blækn] *vt* **- 1.** [make dark] ennegrecer **- 2.** [tarnish] manchar.

black eye *n* ojo *m* morado.

blackhead ['blækhed] *n* barrillo *m*.

black ice *n* hielo transparente en las carreteras.

blackleg ['blækleg] *n pej* esquirol *m*.

blacklist ['blæklɪst] *n* lista *f* negra.

blackmail ['blækmeɪl] <> *n lit* & *fig* chantaje *m*. <> *vt lit* & *fig* chantajear.

black market *n* mercado *m* negro.

blackout ['blækaʊt] *n* **- 1.** [in wartime, power cut] apagón *m* **- 2.** [of news] censura *f* **- 3.** [fainting fit] desmayo *m*.

black pudding *n UK* morcilla *f*.

Black Sea *n*: **the** ~ el mar Negro.

black sheep *n* oveja *f* negra.

blacksmith ['blæksmɪθ] *n* herrero *m*.

black spot *n* punto *m* negro.

bladder ['blædə^r] *n* ANAT vejiga *f*.

blade [bleɪd] *n* **- 1.** [of knife, saw] hoja *f* **- 2.** [of propeller] aleta *f*, paleta *f* **- 3.** [of grass] brizna *f*, hoja *f*.

blame [bleɪm] <> *n* culpa *f*; **to take the** ~ **for** hacerse responsable de; **to be to** ~ **for** ser el culpable de. <> *vt* echar la culpa a, culpar; **to** ~ **sthg on sthg/sb, to** ~ **sthg/ sb for sthg** culpar algo/a alguien de algo.

bland [blænd] *adj* soso(sa).

blank [blæŋk] <> *adj* **-1.** [sheet of paper] en blanco; [wall] liso(sa) **- 2.** [cassette] virgen **- 3.** *fig* [look] vacío(a). <> *n* **-1.** [empty space] espacio *m* en blanco **- 2.** MIL [cartridge] cartucho *m* de fogueo.

blank cheque *n* cheque *m* en blanco; *fig* carta *f* blanca.

blanket ['blæŋkɪt] *n* **- 1.** [bed cover] manta *f*, frazada *f Amér* **- 2.** [layer] manto *m*.

blare [bleə^r] *vi* resonar, sonar.

blasé [*UK* 'blɑːzeɪ, *US* ˌblɑːˈzeɪ] *adj*: **to be** ~ **about** estar de vuelta de.

blasphemy ['blæsfəmɪ] (*pl* **-ies**) *n* blasfemia *f*.

blast [blɑːst] <> *n* **- 1.** [of bomb] explosión *f* **- 2.** [of wind] ráfaga *f*; **we had a** ~ *US* lo pasamos genial. <> *vt* [hole, tunnel] perforar *(con explosivos)*. <> *excl UK inf* ¡maldita sea!
◆ **(at) full blast** *adv* a todo trapo.

blasted ['blɑːstɪd] *adj inf* maldito(ta), puñetero(ra).

blast-off *n* despegue *m*.

blatant ['bleɪtənt] *adj* descarado(da).

blaze [bleɪz] <> *n* **- 1.** [fire] incendio *m* **- 2.** *fig* [of colour] explosión *f*; [of light] resplandor *m*; **a** ~ **of publicity** una ola de publicidad. <> *vi lit* & *fig* arder.

blazer ['bleɪzə^r] *n chaqueta de sport generalmente con la insignia de un equipo, colegio etc*.

bleach [bliːtʃ] <> *n* lejía *f*. <> *vt* [hair] blanquear; [clothes] desteñir.

bleached [bliːtʃt] *adj* [hair] teñido(da) de rubio; [jeans] desteñido(da).

bleachers ['bliːtʃəz] *npl US* SPORT graderío *m* descubierto.

bleak [bliːk] *adj* **- 1.** [future] negro(gra) **- 2.** [place, person, face] sombrío(a) **- 3.** [weather] desapacible.

bleary-eyed [ˌblɪərɪˈaɪd] *adj* con los ojos nublados.

bleat [bliːt] *vi* **- 1.** [sheep] balar **- 2.** *fig* [person] quejarse.

bleed [bliːd] (*pt* & *pp* **bled**) <> *vt* [radiator etc] purgar. <> *vi* sangrar.

bleeper ['bliːpə^r] *n* busca *m*, buscapersonas *m inv*.

blemish ['blemɪʃ] *n* [mark] señal *f*, marca *f*; *fig* mancha *f*.

blend [blend] <> *n* **- 1.** [mix] mezcla *f* **- 2.** COMPUT degradado *m*. <> *vt*: **to** ~ **(sthg with sthg)** mezclar (algo con algo). <> *vi*: **to** ~ **(with)** combinarse (con).

blender ['blendə^r] *n* licuadora *f*, túrmix® *f*.

bless [bles] (*pt* & *pp* **-ed** *OR* **blest**) *vt* **- 1.** RELIG bendecir **- 2.** *phr*: ~ **you!** [after sneezing] ¡jesús!; [thank you] ¡gracias!

blessing ['blesɪŋ] *n* **- 1.** RELIG bendición *f* **- 2.** *fig* [good wishes] aprobación *f*.

blest [blest] *pt* & *pp* ▷ **bless.**

blew [bluː] *pt* ▷ **blow.**

blight [blaɪt] *vt* [hopes, prospects] malograr, arruinar.

blimey ['blaɪmɪ] *excl UK inf* ¡ostias!

blind [blaɪnd] <> *adj* **- 1.** [unsighted, irrational] ciego(ga); **a** ~ **man** un ciego; **to go** ~ quedarse ciego **- 2.** *fig* [unaware]: **to be** ~ **to sthg** no ver algo. <> *n* [for window] persiana *f*. <> *npl*: **the** ~ los ciegos. <> *vt* [permanently] dejar ciego(ga); [temporarily] cegar; **to ~ sb to sthg** *fig* no dejar a alguien ver algo.

blind alley *n lit & fig* callejón *m* sin salida.

blind corner *n* curva *f* sin visibilidad.

blind date *n* cita *f* a ciegas.

blinders ['blaɪndəz] *npl US* anteojeras *fpl*.

blindfold ['blaɪndfəʊld] ⬦ *adv* con los ojos vendados. ⬦ *n* venda *f*. ⬦ *vt* vendar los ojos a.

blindly ['blaɪndlɪ] *adv* - 1. [unable to see] a ciegas - 2. *fig* [guess] a boleo; [accept] ciegamente.

blindness ['blaɪndnɪs] *n lit & fig*: **~ (to)** ceguera *f* (ante).

blind spot *n* - 1. [when driving] ángulo *m* muerto - 2. *fig* [inability to understand] punto *m* débil.

blink [blɪŋk] ⬦ *vt* - 1. [eyes]: **to ~ one's eyes** parpadear - 2. *US* AUT: **to ~ one's lights** dar las luces (intermitentemente). ⬦ *vi* parpadear.

blinkers ['blɪŋkəz] *npl UK* anteojeras *fpl*.

bliss [blɪs] *n* gloria *f*, dicha *f*.

blissful ['blɪsful] *adj* dichoso(sa), feliz.

blister ['blɪstə'] ⬦ *n* ampolla *f*. ⬦ *vi* ampollarse.

blithely ['blaɪðlɪ] *adv* alegremente.

blitz [blɪts] *n* MIL bombardeo *m* aéreo.

blizzard ['blɪzəd] *n* ventisca *f* (de nieve).

bloated ['bləʊtɪd] *adj* hinchado(da).

blob [blɒb] *n* - 1. [drop] gota *f* - 2. [indistinct shape] bulto *m* borroso.

bloc [blɒk] *n* bloque *m*.

block [blɒk] ⬦ *n* - 1. [gen] bloque *m* - 2. *US* [of buildings] manzana *f* - 3. [obstruction - physical or mental] bloqueo *m*. ⬦ *vt* - 1. [road] cortar; [pipe] obstruir; [sink, toilet] atascar; **my nose is ~ d** tengo la nariz tapada - 2. [view] tapar - 3. [prevent] bloquear, obstaculizar - 4. COMPUT: **to ~ a stretch of text** seleccionar un bloque de texto.

blockade [blɒ'keɪd] ⬦ *n* bloqueo *m*. ⬦ *vt* bloquear.

blockage ['blɒkɪdʒ] *n* obstrucción *f*.

blockbuster ['blɒkbʌstə'] *n inf* [book] (gran) éxito *m* editorial; [film] (gran) éxito de taquilla.

block capitals *npl* mayúsculas *fpl (de imprenta)*.

block letters *npl* mayúsculas *fpl (de imprenta)*.

bloke [bləʊk] *n UK inf* tío *m*, tipo *m*, chavo *m Méx*.

blond [blɒnd] *adj* rubio(bia), catire(ra) *Carib, Col, Ven*.

blonde [blɒnd] ⬦ *adj* rubia, catira *Carib, Col, Ven*. ⬦ *n* [woman] rubia *f*.

blood [blʌd] *n* sangre *f*; **in cold ~** a sangre fría.

bloodbath ['blʌdbɑːθ, *pl* -bɑːðz] *n* matanza *f*, carnicería *f*.

blood cell *n* glóbulo *m*.

blood donor *n* donante *m* OR *f* de sangre.

blood group *n* grupo *m* sanguíneo.

bloodhound ['blʌdhaʊnd] *n* sabueso *m*.

blood poisoning *n* septicemia *f*.

blood pressure *n* tensión *f* arterial; **to have high/low ~** tener la tensión alta/baja.

blood pudding *n US* morcilla *f*.

bloodshed ['blʌdʃed] *n* derramamiento *m* de sangre.

bloodshot ['blʌdʃɒt] *adj* inyectado(da) (de sangre).

bloodstream ['blʌdstriːm] *n* flujo *m* sanguíneo.

blood test *n* análisis *m inv* de sangre.

bloodthirsty ['blʌd,θɜːstɪ] *adj* sanguinario(ria).

blood transfusion *n* transfusión *f* de sangre.

bloody ['blʌdɪ] ⬦ *adj* - 1. [war, conflict] sangriento(ta) - 2. [face, hands] ensangrentado(da) - 3. *UK v inf* maldito(ta), puñetero(ra), pinche *Méx*; **~ hell!** ¡hostia! ⬦ *adv UK v inf*: **he's ~ useless** es un puto inútil; **it's ~ brilliant** es de puta madre.

bloody-minded [-'maɪndɪd] *adj UK inf* puñetero(ra).

bloom [bluːm] ⬦ *n* flor *f*; **in ~** en flor. ⬦ *vi* florecer.

blooming ['bluːmɪŋ] ⬦ *adj UK inf* [to show annoyance] condenado(da). ⬦ *adv UK inf*: **he's ~ useless** es un inútil del copón.

blossom ['blɒsəm] ⬦ *n* flor *f*; **in ~** en flor. ⬦ *vi lit & fig* florecer.

blot [blɒt] (*pt & pp* -**ted**, *cont* -**ting**) ⬦ *n* [of ink] borrón *m*; *fig* mancha *f*. ⬦ *vt* - 1. [paper] emborronar - 2. [ink] secar.

◆ **blot out** *vt sep* [gen] cubrir, ocultar; [memories] borrar.

blotchy ['blɒtʃɪ] (*compar* -**ier**, *superl* -**iest**) *adj* lleno(na) de manchas.

blotting paper ['blɒtɪŋ-] *n (U)* papel *m* secante.

blouse [blaʊz] *n* blusa *f*.

blow [bləʊ] (*pt* **blew**, *pp* **blown**) ⬦ *vi* - 1. [gen] soplar - 2. [in wind] salir volando, volar - 3. [fuse] fundirse. ⬦ *vt* - 1. [subj: wind] hacer volar - 2. [whistle, horn] tocar, hacer sonar - 3. [bubbles] hacer - 4. [kiss] mandar - 5. [fuse] fundir - 6. [clear]: **to ~ one's nose** sonarse la nariz - 7. *inf* [money] ventilarse; *inf* [chance] echar a perder. ⬦ *n* [hit, shock] golpe *m*.

◆ **blow out** ⬦ *vt sep* apagar. ⬦ *vi* - 1. [candle] apagarse - 2. [tyre] reventar.

◆ **blow over** *vi* - 1. [storm] amainar - 2. [scandal] calmarse.

blow up ◇ vt sep -**1.** [inflate] inflar -**2.** [destroy] volar -**3.** [photograph] ampliar. ◇ vi saltar por los aires.

blow-dry n secado m (con secador).

blowlamp UK ['bləʊlæmp], **blowtorch** esp US ['bləʊtɔːtʃ] n soplete m.

blown [bləʊn] pp ⊳ blow.

blowout ['bləʊaʊt] n [of tyre] pinchazo m, reventón m.

blowtorch esp US = blowlamp.

blubber ['blʌbəʳ] vi pej lloriquear.

bludgeon ['blʌdʒən] vt apalear.

blue [bluː] ◇ adj -**1.** [colour] azul -**2.** inf [sad] triste -**3.** [pornographic - film] equis (inv), porno; [- joke] verde. ◇ n azul m; **out of the** ~ en el momento menos pensado.

blues npl inf [sad feeling] la depre.

bluebell ['bluːbel] n campanilla f.

blueberry ['bluːbəri] n arándano m.

bluebottle ['bluː,bɒtl] n moscardón m, moscón m.

blue cheese n queso m azul.

blue-collar adj: ~ worker obrero m, -ra f.

blue jeans npl US vaqueros mpl, tejanos mpl.

blueprint ['bluːprɪnt] n -**1.** CONSTR cianotipo m -**2.** fig [description] proyecto m.

bluff [blʌf] ◇ adj brusco(ca). ◇ n [deception] farol m; **to call sb's** ~ desafiar a alguien a que haga lo que dice. ◇ vi tirarse un farol.

blunder ['blʌndəʳ] ◇ n metedura f de pata. ◇ vi -**1.** [make mistake] meter la pata -**2.** [move clumsily] ir tropezando.

blunt [blʌnt] adj -**1.** [knife, pencil] desafilado(da) -**2.** [point, edge] romo(ma) -**3.** [forthright] directo(ta), franco(ca).

blur [blɜːʳ] (pt & pp -red, cont -ring) ◇ n imagen f borrosa. ◇ vt -**1.** [vision] nublar -**2.** [distinction] desdibujar, oscurecer.

blurb [blɜːb] n inf texto publicitario en la cubierta o solapa de un libro.

blurt [blɜːt] **blurt out** vt sep espetar, decir de repente.

blush [blʌʃ] ◇ n rubor m. ◇ vi ruborizarse.

blusher ['blʌʃəʳ] n colorete m.

blustery ['blʌstəri] adj borrascoso(sa).

BMX (abbr of bicycle motorcross) n ciclocross m.

BO n (abbr of body odour) olor a sudor.

boar [bɔːʳ] n -**1.** [male pig] verraco m -**2.** [wild pig] jabalí m.

board [bɔːd] ◇ n -**1.** [plank] tabla f -**2.** [for notices] tablón m -**3.** [for games] tablero m -**4.** [blackboard] pizarra f -**5.** COMPUT placa f -**6.** [of company]: ~ (of directors) consejo m de administración -**7.** [committee] comité m, junta f -**8.** UK [at hotel, guesthouse]:

~ **and lodging** comida y habitación; **full** ~ pensión completa; **half** ~ media pensión -**9.**: **on** ~ [ship, plane] a bordo; [bus, train] dentro -**10.** phr: **above** ~ en regla. ◇ vt -**1.** [ship, plane] embarcar en; [train, bus] subirse a, embarcarse en Amér -**2.** [in naval battle] abordar.

boarder ['bɔːdəʳ] n -**1.** [lodger] huésped m OR f -**2.** [at school] interno m, -na f.

boarding card ['bɔːdɪŋ-] n tarjeta f de embarque.

boardinghouse ['bɔːdɪŋhaʊs, pl -haʊzɪz] n casa f de huéspedes.

boarding school ['bɔːdɪŋ-] n internado m.

Board of Trade n UK: **the** ~ ≃ el Ministerio de Comercio.

boardroom ['bɔːdrʊm] n sala f de juntas.

boast [bəʊst] ◇ vt disfrutar de, presumir de tener. ◇ vi: **to** ~ **(about)** alardear OR jactarse (de), compadrear (de) Amér.

boastful ['bəʊstfʊl] adj fanfarrón(ona).

boat [bəʊt] n [large] barco m; [small] barca f; **by** ~ en barco.

boater ['bəʊtəʳ] n [hat] canotié m, sombrero m de paja.

boatswain ['bəʊsn] n NAUT contramaestre m.

bob [bɒb] (pt & pp -bed, cont -bing) ◇ n -**1.** [hairstyle] corte m de chico -**2.** UK inf dated [shilling] chelín m -**3.** = bobsleigh. ◇ vi [boat] balancearse.

bobbin ['bɒbɪn] n bobina f.

bobby ['bɒbi] (pl -ies) n UK inf poli m.

bobsleigh ['bɒbslei] n bobsleigh m.

bode [bəʊd] vi literary: **to** ~ **ill/well for** traer malos/buenos presagios para.

bodily ['bɒdɪli] ◇ adj corporal, físico(ca). ◇ adv: **to lift/move sb** ~ levantar/mover a alguien por la fuerza.

body ['bɒdi] (pl -ies) n -**1.** [gen] cuerpo m -**2.** [corpse] cadáver m -**3.** [organization] entidad f; **a** ~ **of thought/opinion** una corriente de pensamiento/opinión -**4.** [of car] carrocería f; [of plane] fuselaje m -**5.** [item of clothing] body m.

body building n culturismo m.

bodyguard ['bɒdɪɡɑːd] n guardaespaldas m inv, guarura m Méx.

body language n lenguaje m corporal.

body odour n olor m corporal.

body piercing n piercing m.

bodywork ['bɒdɪwɜːk] n carrocería f.

bog [bɒɡ] n -**1.** [marsh] cenagal m, lodazal m -**2.** UK v inf [toilet] baño m.

bogged down [,bɒɡd-] adj -**1.** [in details, work]: ~ **(in)** empantanado(da) (en) -**2.** [in mud, snow]: ~ **in** atascado(da).

boggle ['bɒɡl] vi: **the mind** ~**s!** ¡es increíble!

bogus ['bəʊɡəs] adj falso(sa).

boil [bɔɪl] <> *n* -**1**. MED pústula *f* - **2**. [boiling point]: **to bring sthg to the ~** hacer que algo hierva; **to come to the ~** romper a hervir. <> *vt* -**1**. [water] hervir; **to ~ the kettle** poner el agua a hervir - **2**. [food] cocer. <> *vi* hervir.

● **boil down to** *vt fus* reducirse a.

● **boil over** *vi fig* [feelings] desbordarse.

boiled [bɔɪld] *adj* cocido(da); **~ egg** [hard-boiled] huevo *m* duro; [soft-boiled] huevo *m* pasado por agua; **~ sweets** UK caramelos *mpl* (duros).

boiler ['bɔɪlə'] *n* caldera *f*.

boiler suit *n* UK mono *m*.

boiling ['bɔɪlɪŋ] *adj inf* [hot]: **I'm ~** estoy asado(da) de calor; **it's ~** hace un calor de muerte.

boiling point *n* punto *m* de ebullición.

boisterous ['bɔɪstərəs] *adj* ruidoso(sa), alborotador(ra).

bold [bəʊld] *adj* -**1**. [brave, daring] audaz - **2**. [lines, design] marcado(da) - **3**. [colour] vivo(va) - **4**. TYPO: **~ type** OR **print** negrita *f*.

Bolivia [bə'lɪvɪə] *n* Bolivia.

Bolivian [bə'lɪvɪən] <> *adj* boliviano(na). <> *n* boliviano *m*, -na *f*.

bollard ['bɒlɑːd] *n* [on road] poste *m*.

bollocks ['bɒləks] *npl* UK *v inf* cojones *mpl*.

bologna [bə'ləʊnjə] *n* US [sausage] *embutido ahumado elaborado con distintos tipos de carne.*

bolster ['bəʊlstə'] *vt* reforzar.

● **bolster up** *vt fus* reforzar.

bolt [bəʊlt] <> *n* -**1**. [on door, window] cerrojo *m* - **2**. [type of screw] perno *m*. <> *adv* : **~ upright** muy derecho(cha). <> *vt* -**1**. [fasten together] atornillar - **2**. [door, window] echar el cerrojo a - **3**. [food] tragarse. <> *vi* salir disparado(da).

bomb [bɒm] <> *n* -**1**. bomba *f* - **2**. US *inf* [failure] desastre *m*. <> *vt* bombardear. <> *vi* US *inf* [fail] fracasar estrepitosamente.

bombard [bɒm'bɑːd] *vt* MIL & *fig* : **~ (with)** bombardear (a).

bombastic [bɒm'bæstɪk] *adj* grandilocuente, rimbombante.

bomb disposal squad *n* equipo *m* de artificieros.

bomber ['bɒmə'] *n* -**1**. [plane] bombardero *m* - **2**. [person] terrorista *m* OR *f* que pone bombas.

bombing ['bɒmɪŋ] *n* bombardeo *m*.

bombshell ['bɒmʃel] *n fig* bombazo *m*; **a blonde ~** *inf* una rubia explosiva.

bona fide ['bəʊnə'faɪdɪ] *adj* auténtico(ca).

bond [bɒnd] <> *n* -**1**. [between people] lazo *m*, vínculo *m* - **2**. [binding promise] compromiso *m* - **3**. FIN bono *m*. <> *vt* [glue] adherir; *fig* [people] unir.

bone [bəʊn] <> *n* [gen] hueso *m*; [of fish] raspa *f*, espina *f*. <> *vt* [fish] quitar las espinas a; [meat] deshuesar.

bone-dry *adj* completamente seco(ca).

bone-idle *adj* haragán(ana), gandul(la).

bonfire ['bɒnˌfaɪə'] *n* hoguera *f*.

bonfire night *n* UK noche del 5 de noviembre *en que se encienden hogueras y fuegos artificiales.*

bonk [bɒŋk] UK *v inf* <> *vt* echar un casquete con. <> *vi* echar un casquete.

bonkers ['bɒŋkəz] *adj* UK *inf* chiflado(da).

Bonn [bɒn] *n* Bonn.

bonnet ['bɒnɪt] *n* -**1**. UK [of car] capó *m* - **2**. [hat] toca *f*.

bonny ['bɒnɪ] (*compar* -**ier**, *superl* -**iest**) *adj* *Scot* majo(ja).

bonus ['bəʊnəs] (*pl* -**es**) *n* [extra money] prima *f*; [for increased productivity] plus *m*; *fig* beneficio *m* adicional.

bony ['bəʊnɪ] (*compar* -**ier**, *superl* -**iest**) *adj* -**1**. [person, hand] huesudo(da) - **2**. [meat] lleno(na) de huesos; [fish] espinoso(sa).

boo [buː] (*pl* -**s**) <> *excl* ¡bu! <> *n* abucheo *m*. <> *vt* & *vi* abuchear.

boob [buːb] *n inf* [mistake] metedura *f* de pata.

● **boobs** *npl* UK *v inf* [woman's breasts] tetas *fpl*.

booby trap ['buːbɪ-] *n* [bomb] bomba *f* camuflada.

book [bʊk] <> *n* -**1**. [for reading] libro *m* - **2**. [of stamps] librillo *m*; [of tickets, cheques] talonario *m*; [of matches] caja *f* (*de solapa*). <> *vt* -**1**. [reserve] reservar; **to be fully ~ed** estar completo - **2**. *inf* [subj: police] multar - **3**. UK FTBL mostrar una tarjeta amarilla a. <> *vi* hacer reserva.

● **books** *npl* COMM libros *mpl*.

● **book up** *vt sep*: **to be ~ed up** estar completo.

bookcase ['bʊkkeɪs] *n* estantería *f*.

bookie ['bʊkɪ] *n inf* corredor *m*, -ra *f* de apuestas.

booking ['bʊkɪŋ] *n* -**1**. *esp* UK [reservation] reserva *f* - **2**. UK FTBL tarjeta *f* amarilla.

booking office *n esp* UK taquilla *f*.

bookkeeping ['bʊkˌkiːpɪŋ] *n* contabilidad *f*.

booklet ['bʊklɪt] *n* folleto *m*.

bookmaker ['bʊkˌmeɪkə'] *n* corredor *m*, -ra *f* de apuestas.

bookmark ['bʊkmɑːk] *n* -**1**. separador *m* - **2**. COMPUT marcador *m*.

bookseller ['bʊkˌselə'] *n* librero *m*, -ra *f*.

bookshelf ['bʊkʃelf] (*pl* -**shelves** [-ʃelvz]) *n* [shelf] estante *m*; [bookcase] estantería *f*, librero *m* *Chile, Méx*.

bookshop UK ['bʊkʃɒp], **bookstore** US ['bʊkstɔː'] *n* librería *f*.

book token *n esp* UK vale *m* para comprar libros.

boom [bu:m] ◇ *n* -**1.** [loud noise] estampido *m*, estruendo *m* -**2.** [increase] auge *m*, boom *m* -**3.** [for TV camera, microphone] jirafa *f.* ◇ *vi* -**1.** [make noise] tronar -**2.** ECON estar en auge.

boon [bu:n] *n* gran ayuda *f.*

boost [bu:st] ◇ *n* -**1.** [in profits, production] incremento *m* -**2.** [to popularity, spirits] empujón *m*, estímulo *m.* ◇ *vt* -**1.** [increase] incrementar -**2.** [improve] levantar.

booster ['bu:stə'] *n* MED inyección *f* de revacunación.

boot [bu:t] ◇ *n* -**1.** [item of footwear] bota *f*; [ankle boot] botín *m* -**2.** UK [of car] maletero *m*, cajuela *f Méx*, baúl *m Col, RP*, maletera *f Perú.* ◇ *vt* -**1.** *inf* [kick] dar una patada a -**2.** COMPUT arrancar.
  ◆ **to boot** *adv* además.
  ◆ **boot out** *vt sep inf* echar, poner (de patitas) en la calle.
  ◆ **boot up** *vt sep* COMPUT arrancar.

booth [bu:ð] *n* -**1.** [at fair] puesto *m* -**2.** [for phoning, voting] cabina *f.*

booty ['bu:ti] *n* -**1.** botín *m* -**2.** US *inf* [sexual intercourse]: **to get some ~** mojar el churro *Esp* OR bizcocho *RP*, echarse un caldito *Méx.*

booze [bu:z] *inf* ◇ *n* (U) priva *f.* ◇ *vi* privar, empinar el codo.

bop [bɒp] (*pt* & *pp* -**ped**, *cont* -**ping**) *inf* ◇ *n* -**1.** [disco] disco *f* -**2.** [dance] baile *m.* ◇ *vi* bailar.

border ['bɔ:də'] ◇ *n* -**1.** [between countries] frontera *f* -**2.** [edge] borde *m* -**3.** [in garden] arriate *m.* ◇ *vt* -**1.** [country] limitar con -**2.** [edge] bordear.
  ◆ **border on** *vt fus* rayar en.

borderline ['bɔ:dəlaɪn] ◇ *adj*: **a ~ case** un caso dudoso. ◇ *n fig* límite *m.*

bore [bɔ:'] ◇ *pt* ⊳ **bear.** ◇ *n* -**1.** *pej* [person] pelmazo *m*, -za *f*, pesado *m*, -da *f*; [situation, event] rollo *m*, lata *f* -**2.** [of gun] calibre *m.* ◇ *vt* -**1.** [not interest] aburrir; **to ~ sb stiff** OR **to tears** OR **to death** aburrir a alguien un montón -**2.** [drill] horadar.

bored [bɔ:d] *adj* aburrido(da); **to be ~ with sthg** estar harto de algo.

boredom ['bɔ:dəm] *n* aburrimiento *m.*

boring ['bɔ:rɪŋ] *adj* aburrido(da), cansador(ra) *RP.*

born [bɔ:n] *adj* -**1.** [given life] nacido(da); **to be ~** nacer -**2.** [natural] nato(ta).

borne [bɔ:n] *pp* ⊳ **bear.**

borough ['bʌrə] *n* [area of town] distrito *m*; [town] municipio *m.*

borrow ['bɒrəʊ] *vt*: **to ~ sthg from sb** coger OR tomar algo prestado a alguien; **can I ~ your bike?** ¿me prestas tu bici?

Bosnia ['bɒznɪə] *n* Bosnia.

Bosnia-Herzegovina [-ˌhɜ:tsəgə'vi:nə] *n* Bosnia-Hercegovina.

Bosnian ['bɒznɪən] ◇ *adj* bosnio(nia). ◇ *n* bosnio *m*, -nia *f.*

bosom ['bʊzəm] *n* [of woman] busto *m*, pecho *m.*

boss [bɒs] ◇ *n* jefe *m*, -fa *f.* ◇ *vt pej* mangonear, dar órdenes a.
  ◆ **boss about, boss around** *vt sep pej* mangonear, dar órdenes a.

bossy ['bɒsɪ] (*compar* -**ier**, *superl* -**iest**) *adj* mandón(ona).

bosun ['bəʊsn] = **boatswain.**

botany ['bɒtənɪ] *n* botánica *f.*

botch [bɒtʃ] ◆ **botch up** *vt sep inf* estropear, hacer chapuceramente.

both [bəʊθ] ◇ *adj* los dos, las dos, ambos(bas). ◇ *pron*: **~ (of them)** los dos (las dos), ambos *mpl*, -bas *fpl*; **~ of us are coming** vamos los dos. ◇ *adv*: **she is ~ pretty and intelligent** es guapa e inteligente.

bother ['bɒðə'] ◇ *vt* -**1.** [worry] preocupar; [irritate] fastidiar, fregar *Amér*; **I/she can't be ~ed to do it** no tengo/tiene ganas de hacerlo -**2.** [pester] molestar. ◇ *vi*: **to ~ (doing** OR **to do sthg)** molestarse (en hacer algo); **to ~ about** preocuparse por. ◇ *n* (U) -**1.** [inconvenience] problemas *mpl* -**2.** [pest, nuisance] molestia *f.*

bottle ['bɒtl] ◇ *n* -**1.** [gen] botella *f* -**2.** [of shampoo, medicine - plastic] bote *m*; [- glass] frasco *m* -**3.** [for baby] biberón *m* -**4.** (U) UK *inf* [courage] agallas *fpl.* ◇ *vt* [wine] embotellar.
  ◆ **bottle up** *vt sep* reprimir.

bottle bank *n* contenedor *m* de vidrio.

bottleneck ['bɒtlnek] *n* -**1.** [in traffic] embotellamiento *m* -**2.** [in production] atasco *m.*

bottle-opener *n* abrebotellas *m inv.*

bottom ['bɒtəm] ◇ *adj* -**1.** [lowest] más bajo(ja), de abajo del todo -**2.** [least successful] peor. ◇ *n* -**1.** [lowest part - of glass, bottle] culo *m*; [- of bag, mine, sea] fondo *m*; [- of ladder, hill] pie *m*; [- of page, list] final *m* -**2.** [farthest point] final *m*, fondo *m* -**3.** [of class etc] parte *f* más baja -**4.** [buttocks] trasero *m*, traste *m Amér* -**5.** [root]: **to get to the ~ of** llegar al fondo de.
  ◆ **bottom out** *vi* tocar fondo.

bottom line *n fig*: **the ~ is ...** a fin de cuentas ...

bough [baʊ] *n* rama *f.*

bought [bɔ:t] *pt* & *pp* ⊳ **buy.**

boulder ['bəʊldə'] *n* roca *f* grande y de forma redonda.

bounce [baʊns] ◇ *vi* -**1.** [gen] rebotar -**2.** [person]: **to ~ (on sthg)** dar botes (en algo) -**3.** [cheque] ser rechazado(da) por el banco. ◇ *vt* botar. ◇ *n* bote *m.*

bouncer ['baʊnsə'] *n inf* matón *m*, gorila *m* (de un local).

bound [baʊnd] ◇ *pt & pp* ⊳ **bind**. ◇ *adj* - **1.** [certain]: **it's** ~ **to happen** seguro que va a pasar - **2.** [obliged]: ~ **(by sthg/to do sthg)** obligado(da) (por algo/a hacer algo); **I'm** ~ **to say** OR **admit** tengo que decir OR admitir - **3.** [for place]: **to be** ~ **for** ir rumbo a. ◇ *n* salto *m*. ◇ *vi* ir dando saltos.
◆ **bounds** *npl* [limits] límites *mpl*; **out of** ~**s** (en) zona prohibida.

boundary ['baʊndəri] (*pl* **-ies**) *n* [gen] límite *m*; [between countries] frontera *f*.

bouquet [bəʊ'keɪ] *n* [of flowers] ramo *m*.

bourbon ['bɜːbən] *n* bourbon *m*, whisky *m* americano.

bourgeois ['bɔːʒwɑː] *adj* burgués(esa).

bout [baʊt] *n* - **1.** [attack] ataque *m*, acceso *m* - **2.** [session] racha *f* - **3.** [boxing match] combate *m*.

bow¹ [baʊ] ◇ *n* - **1.** [act of bowing] reverencia *f* - **2.** [of ship] proa *f*. ◇ *vt* inclinar. ◇ *vi* - **1.** [make a bow] inclinarse - **2.** [defer]: **to** ~ **to sthg** ceder OR doblegarse ante algo.

bow² [bəʊ] *n* - **1.** [weapon, for musical instrument] arco *m* - **2.** [knot] lazo *m*.

bowels ['baʊəlz] *npl lit & fig* entrañas *fpl*.

bowl [bəʊl] ◇ *n* [gen] cuenco *m*, bol *m*; [for soup] plato *m*; [for washing clothes] barreño *m*, balde *m*. ◇ *vi* lanzar la bola.
◆ **bowls** *n* (*U*) *juego similar a la petanca que se juega sobre césped.*
◆ **bowl over** *vt sep* - **1.** [knock over] atropellar - **2.** *fig* [surprise, impress] dejar atónito(ta).

bow-legged [,bəʊ'legɪd] *adj* de piernas arqueadas, estevado(da).

bowler ['bəʊlə'] *n* - **1.** CRICKET lanzador *m* - **2.**: ~ **(hat)** bombín *m*, sombrero *m* hongo, tongo *m Chile*.

bowling ['bəʊlɪŋ] *n* (*U*) bolos *mpl*.

bowling alley *n* - **1.** [building] bolera *f* - **2.** [alley] calle *f*.

bowling green *n campo de césped para jugar a los 'bowls'.*

bow tie [bəʊ-] *n* pajarita *f*.

box [bɒks] ◇ *n* - **1.** [container, boxful] caja *f*; [for jewels] estuche *m* - **2.** THEATRE palco *m* - **3.** *UK inf* [television]: **the** ~ la tele - **4.** [in printed questionnaire, etc] casilla *f*. ◇ *vt* [put in boxes] encajonar. ◇ *vi* boxear.

boxer ['bɒksə'] *n* - **1.** [fighter] boxeador *m*, púgil *m* - **2.** [dog] bóxer *m*.

boxer shorts *npl* calzoncillos *mpl*, boxers *mpl*.

boxing ['bɒksɪŋ] *n* boxeo *m*, box *m CAm, CSur, Méx*.

Boxing Day *n fiesta nacional en Inglaterra y Gales el 26 de diciembre (salvo domingos) en que tradicionalmente se da el aguinaldo.*

boxing glove *n* guante *m* de boxeo, guante *m* de box *CAm, CSur, Méx*.

box office *n* taquilla *f*, boletería *f Amér*.

boxroom ['bɒksrʊm] *n UK* trastero *m*.

boy [bɔɪ] ◇ *n* - **1.** [male child] chico *m*, niño *m*, pibe *m RP* - **2.** *inf* [young man] chaval *m*. ◇ *excl*: **(oh)** ~! *US inf* ¡jolín!, ¡vaya, vaya!

boycott ['bɔɪkɒt] ◇ *n* boicot *m*. ◇ *vt* boicotear.

boyfriend ['bɔɪfrend] *n* novio *m*, pololo *m Chile*.

boyish ['bɔɪʃ] *adj* [man] juvenil.

BR (*abbr of* **British Rail**) *n antigua compañía ferroviaria británica*, ≃ Renfe *f*.

bra [brɑː] *n* sujetador *m*, sostén *m*, ajustadores *mpl Cuba*, brasier *m Carib, Col, Méx*, corpiño *m Arg*.

brace [breɪs] ◇ *n* - **1.** [on teeth] aparato *m* corrector - **2.** [pair] par *m*. ◇ *vt* [steady] tensar; **to** ~ **o.s. (for)** *lit & fig* prepararse (para).
◆ **braces** *npl UK* tirantes *mpl*, tiradores *mpl Bol, RP*.

bracelet ['breɪslɪt] *n* brazalete *m*, pulsera *f*.

bracing ['breɪsɪŋ] *adj* tonificante.

bracken ['brækn] *n* helechos *mpl*.

bracket ['brækɪt] ◇ *n* - **1.** [support] soporte *m*, palomilla *f* - **2.** [parenthesis - round] paréntesis *m inv*; [- square] corchete *m*; **in** ~**s** entre paréntesis - **3.** [group] sector *m*, banda *f*. ◇ *vt* [enclose in brackets] poner entre paréntesis.

brag [bræg] (*pt & pp* **-ged**, *cont* **-ging**) *vi* fanfarronear, jactarse, compadrear *Amér*.

braid [breɪd] ◇ *n* - **1.** [on uniform] galón *m* - **2.** [hairstyle] trenza *f*. ◇ *vt* trenzar.

brain [breɪn] *n lit & fig* cerebro *m*.
◆ **brains** *npl* cerebro *m*, seso *m*.

brainchild ['breɪntʃaɪld] *n* invención *f*, idea *f*.

brain surgeon *n* neurocirujano *m*, -na *f*.

brainwash ['breɪnwɒʃ] *vt* lavar el cerebro a.

brainwave ['breɪnweɪv] *n* idea *f* genial.

brainy ['breɪnɪ] (*compar* **-ier**, *superl* **-iest**) *adj inf* listo(ta).

brake [breɪk] ◇ *n lit & fig* freno *m*. ◇ *vi* frenar.

brake light *n* luz *f* de freno.

bramble ['bræmbl] *n* [bush] zarza *f*, zarzamora *f*; [fruit] mora *f*.

bran [bræn] *n* salvado *m*.

branch [brɑːntʃ] ◇ *n* - **1.** [of tree, subject] rama *f* - **2.** [of river] afluente *m*; [of railway] ramal *m* - **3.** [of company, bank] sucursal *f*. ◇ *vi* bifurcarse.
◆ **branch out** *vi* [person] ampliar horizontes; [firm] expandirse, diversificarse.

brand [brænd] ◇ *n* - **1.** [of product] marca *f* - **2.** *fig* [type] tipo *m*, estilo *m* - **3.** [mark] hierro *m*. ◇ *vt* - **1.** [cattle] marcar (con hierro) - **2.** *fig* [classify]: **to** ~ **sb (as sthg)** tildar a alguien (de algo).

brandish ['brændɪʃ] *vt* [weapon] blandir; [letter etc] agitar.

brand name *n* marca *f*.

brand-new *adj* flamante.

brandy ['brændɪ] (*pl* -ies) *n* coñac *m*, brandy *m*.

brash [bræʃ] *adj pej* enérgico e insolente.

brass [brɑːs] *n* - **1.** [metal] latón *m* - **2.** MUS : the ~ el metal.

brass band *n* banda *f* de metal.

brassiere [UK 'bræsɪər, US brə'zɪr] *n* sostén *m*, sujetador *m*.

brat [bræt] *n inf pej* mocoso *m*, -sa *f*.

bravado [brə'vɑːdəʊ] *n* bravuconería *f*.

brave [breɪv] ⟨⟩ *adj* valiente. ⟨⟩ *vt* [weather, storm] desafiar; [sb's anger] hacer frente a.

bravery ['breɪvərɪ] *n* valentía *f*.

brawl [brɔːl] *n* gresca *f*, reyerta *f*.

brawn [brɔːn] *n* (*U*) - **1.** [muscle] musculatura *f*, fuerza *f* física - **2.** *UK* [meat] *carne de cerdo en gelatina.*

bray [breɪ] *vi* [donkey] rebuznar.

brazen ['breɪzn] *adj* [person] descarado(-da); [lie] burdo(da).

brazier ['breɪzjə'] *n* brasero *m*.

Brazil [brə'zɪl] *n* (el) Brasil.

Brazilian [brə'zɪljən] ⟨⟩ *adj* brasileño(ña), brasilero(ra) *Amér.* ⟨⟩ *n* brasileño *m*, -ña *f*, brasilero *m*, -ra *f Amér.*

brazil nut *n* nuez *f* de Pará.

breach [briːtʃ] ⟨⟩ *n* - **1.** [act of disobedience] incumplimiento *m*; ~ **of confidence** abuso *m* de confianza; **to be in** ~ **of sthg** incumplir algo; ~ **of contract** incumplimiento de contrato - **2.** [opening, gap] brecha *f* - **3.** *fig* [in friendship, marriage] ruptura *f*. ⟨⟩ *vt* - **1.** [disobey] incumplir - **2.** [make hole in] abrir (una) brecha en.

breach of the peace *n* alteración *f* del orden público.

bread [bred] *n* - **1.** [food] pan *m*; ~ **and butter** [buttered bread] pan con mantequilla; *fig* [main income] sustento *m* diario - **2.** *inf* [money] pasta *f*.

bread bin *UK*, **bread box** *US n* panera *f*.

breadcrumbs ['bredkrʌmz] *npl* migas *fpl* (de pan); CULIN pan *m* rallado.

breadline ['bredlaɪn] *n*: **to be on the** ~ vivir en la miseria.

breadth [bretθ] *n* - **1.** [in measurements] anchura *f* - **2.** *fig* [scope] amplitud *f*.

breadwinner ['bred,wɪnə'] *n*: **he's the** ~ **es** el que mantiene a la familia.

break [breɪk] (*pt* **broke**, *pp* **broken**) ⟨⟩ *n* - **1.** [gap - in clouds] claro *m*; [- in transmission] corte *m* - **2.** [fracture] fractura *f* - **3.** [pause]: ~ **(from)** descanso *m* (de); **to have** OR **take a** ~ tomarse un descanso - **4.** [playtime] recreo *m* - **5.** *inf* [chance] oportunidad *f*; **a lucky** ~ un golpe de suerte.

⟨⟩ *vt* - **1.** [gen] romper; [arm, leg etc] romperse; **to** ~ **sb's hold** escaparse OR liberarse de alguien - **2.** [machine] estropear - **3.** [journey, contact] interrumpir - **4.** [habit, health] acabar con; [strike] reventar - **5.** [law, rule] violar; [appointment, word] faltar a - **6.** [record] batir - **7.** [tell]: **to** ~ **the news (of sthg to sb)** dar la noticia (de algo a alguien). ⟨⟩ *vi* - **1.** [come to pieces] romperse - **2.** [stop working] estropearse - **3.** [pause] parar; [weather] cambiar - **4.** [start - day] romper; [- storm] estallar, desencadenarse - **5.** [escape]: **to** ~ **loose** OR **free** escaparse - **6.** [voice] cambiar - **7.** [news] divulgarse - **8.** *phr*: **to** ~ **even** salir sin pérdidas ni beneficios.

◆ **break away** *vi* escaparse; **to** ~ **away (from)** [end connection] separarse (de); POL escindirse (de).

◆ **break down** ⟨⟩ *vt sep* - **1.** [destroy gen] derribar, echar abajo; [- resistance] vencer - **2.** [analyse] descomponer. ⟨⟩ *vi* - **1.** [collapse, disintegrate, fail] venirse abajo - **2.** [stop working] estropearse - **3.** [lose emotional control] perder el control - **4.** [decompose] descomponerse.

◆ **break in** ⟨⟩ *vi* - **1.** [enter by force] entrar por la fuerza - **2.** [interrupt]: **to** ~ **in (on sthg/sb)** interrumpir (algo/a alguien). ⟨⟩ *vt sep* - **1.** [horse, shoes] domar - **2.** [person] amoldar.

◆ **break into** *vt fus* - **1.** [house, shop] entrar (por la fuerza) en, allanar; [box, safe] forzar - **2.** [begin suddenly]: **to** ~ **into song/a run** echarse a cantar/correr.

◆ **break off** ⟨⟩ *vt sep* - **1.** [detach] partir - **2.** [end] romper; [holiday] interrumpir. ⟨⟩ *vi* - **1.** [become detached] partirse - **2.** [stop talking] interrumpirse.

◆ **break out** *vi* - **1.** [fire, fighting, panic] desencadenarse; [war] estallar - **2.** [escape]: **to** ~ **out (of)** escapar (de).

◆ **break up** ⟨⟩ *vt sep* - **1.** [ice] hacer pedazos; [car] desguazar - **2.** [relationship] romper; [talks] poner fin a; [fight] poner fin a; [crowd] disolver. ⟨⟩ *vi* - **1.** [into smaller pieces] hacerse pedazos - **2.** [relationship] deshacerse; [conference] concluir; [school, pupils] terminar; **to** ~ **up with sb** romper con alguien - **3.** [crowd] disolverse.

breakage ['breɪkɪdʒ] *n* rotura *f*.

breakdown ['breɪkdaʊn] *n* - **1.** [of car, train] avería *f*; [of talks, in communications] ruptura *f*; [of law and order] colapso *m* - **2.** [analysis] desglose *m*.

breakfast ['brekfəst] *n* desayuno *m*; **to have** ~ desayunar.

breakfast television *n UK* programación *f* matinal de televisión.

break-in *n* robo *m* (*con allanamiento de morada*).

breaking ['breɪkɪŋ] *n*: ~ **and entering** JUR allanamiento *m* de morada.

breakneck ['breɪknek] *adj*: **at** ~ **speed** a (una) velocidad de vértigo.

breakthrough ['breɪkθru:] *n* avance *m*.

breakup ['breɪkʌp] *n* ruptura *f*.

breast [brest] *n* **- 1.** [of woman] pecho *m*, seno *m*; [of man] pecho **- 2.** [meat of bird] pechuga *f*.

breast-feed *vt* & *vi* amamantar, dar de mamar.

breaststroke ['breststrəʊk] *n* braza *f*.

breath [breθ] *n* **- 1.** [act of breathing] respiración *f*; **to take a deep** ~ respirar hondo; **to get one's** ~ **back** recuperar el aliento; **to say sthg under one's** ~ decir algo en voz baja **- 2.** [air from mouth] aliento *m*; **out of** ~ sin aliento.

breathalyse UK, **-yze** US ['breθəlaɪz] *vt* hacer la prueba del alcohol a.

breathe [bri:ð] ⬦ *vi* respirar. ⬦ *vt* **- 1.** [inhale] aspirar **- 2.** [exhale] despedir.

➡ **breathe in** *vt sep* & *vi* aspirar.

➡ **breathe out** *vi* espirar.

breather ['bri:ðə'] *n inf* respiro *m*, descanso *m*.

breathing ['bri:ðɪŋ] *n* respiración *f*.

breathless ['breθlɪs] *adj* **- 1.** [out of breath] jadeante **- 2.** [with excitement] sin aliento (por la emoción).

breathtaking ['breθ,teɪkɪŋ] *adj* sobrecogedor(ra), impresionante.

breed [bri:d] (*pt* & *pp* **bred** [bred]) ⬦ *n* **- 1.** [of animal] raza *f* **- 2.** *fig* [sort] especie *f*. ⬦ *vt* [animals] criar; [plants] cultivar. ⬦ *vi* procrear, reproducirse.

breeding ['bri:dɪŋ] *n* **- 1.** [of animals] cría *f*; [of plants] cultivo *m* **- 2.** [manners] educación *f*.

breeze [bri:z] ⬦ *n* brisa *f*. ⬦ *vi*: **to** ~ **in/ out** entrar/salir como si tal cosa.

breezy ['bri:zɪ] (*compar* **-ier**, *superl* **-iest**) *adj* **- 1.** [windy]: **it's** ~ hace aire **- 2.** [cheerful] jovial, despreocupado(da).

brevity ['brevɪtɪ] *n* brevedad *f*.

brew [bru:] ⬦ *vt* [beer] elaborar; [tea, coffee] preparar. ⬦ *vi* **- 1.** [tea] reposar **- 2.** [trouble] fraguarse.

brewer ['bru:ə'] *n* cervecero *m*, -ra *f*.

brewery ['broərɪ] (*pl* **-ies**) *n* fábrica *f* de cerveza.

bribe [braɪb] ⬦ *n* soborno *m*, coima *f* *Andes, RP*, mordida *f* *Méx*. ⬦ *vt*: **to** ~ **(sb to do sthg)** sobornar (a alguien para que haga algo), coimear (a alguien para que haga algo) *Andes, RP*, mordar (a alguien para que haga algo) *Méx*.

bribery ['braɪbərɪ] *n* soborno *m*.

bric-a-brac ['brɪkəbræk] *n* baratijas *fpl*.

brick [brɪk] *n* ladrillo *m*.

bricklayer ['brɪk,leɪə'] *n* albañil *m*.

bridal ['braɪdl] *adj* nupcial; ~ **dress** traje *m* de novia.

bride [braɪd] *n* novia *f*.

bridegroom ['braɪdgrʊm] *n* novio *m*.

bridesmaid ['braɪdzmeɪd] *n* dama *f* de honor.

bridge [brɪdʒ] ⬦ *n* **- 1.** [gen] puente *m* **- 2.** [on ship] puente *m* de mando **- 3.** [of nose] caballete *m* **- 4.** [card game] bridge *m*. ⬦ *vt fig* [gap] llenar.

bridle ['braɪdl] *n* brida *f*.

bridle path *n* camino *m* de herradura.

brief [bri:f] ⬦ *adj* **- 1.** [short, to the point] breve; **in** ~ en resumen **- 2.** [clothes] corto(-ta). ⬦ *n* **- 1.** JUR [statement] sumario *m*, resumen *m* **- 2.** UK [instructions] instrucciones *fpl*. ⬦ *vt*: **to** ~ **sb (on)** informar a alguien (acerca de).

➡ **briefs** *npl* [underpants] calzoncillos *mpl*; [knickers] bragas *fpl*.

briefcase ['bri:fkeɪs] *n* maletín *m*, portafolios *m inv*.

briefing ['bri:fɪŋ] *n* [meeting] reunión *f* informativa; [instructions] instrucciones *fpl*.

briefly ['bri:flɪ] *adv* **- 1.** [for a short time] brevemente **- 2.** [concisely] en pocas palabras.

brigade [brɪ'geɪd] *n* brigada *f*.

brigadier [,brɪgə'dɪə'] *n* brigadier *m*, general *m* de brigada.

bright [braɪt] *adj* **- 1.** [light] brillante; [day, room] luminoso(sa); [weather] despejado(da) **- 2.** [colour] vivo(va) **- 3.** [lively- eyes] brillante; [- smile] radiante **- 4.** [intelligent- person] listo(ta); [- idea] genial **- 5.** [hopeful] prometedor(ra).

brighten ['braɪtn] *vi* **- 1.** [become lighter] despejarse **- 2.** [become more cheerful] alegrarse.

➡ **brighten up** ⬦ *vt sep* animar, alegrar. ⬦ *vi* **- 1.** [become more cheerful] animarse **- 2.** [weather] despejarse.

brilliance ['brɪljəns] *n* **- 1.** [cleverness] brillantez *f* **- 2.** [of colour, light] brillo *m*.

brilliant ['brɪljənt] *adj* **- 1.** [clever] genial **- 2.** [colour] vivo(va) **- 3.** [light, career, future] brillante **- 4.** *inf* [wonderful] fenomenal, genial.

Brillo pad® ['brɪləʊ-] *n* estropajo *m* (jabonoso) de aluminio.

brim [brɪm] (*pt* & *pp* **-med**, *cont* **-ming**) ⬦ *n* **- 1.** [edge] borde *m* **- 2.** [of hat] ala *f*. ⬦ *vi lit* & *fig*: **to** ~ **with** rebosar de.

brine [braɪn] *n* **- 1.** [for food] salmuera *f* **- 2.** [sea water] agua *f* de mar.

bring [brɪŋ] (*pt* & *pp* **brought**) *vt* [gen] traer; **to** ~ **sthg to an end** poner fin a algo.

➡ **bring about** *vt sep* producir.

➡ **bring around** *vt sep* [make conscious] reanimar, hacer recuperar el conocimiento.

bring back vt sep - 1. [books etc] devolver; [person] traer de vuelta - 2. [memories] traer (a la memoria) - 3. [practice, hanging] volver a introducir; [fashion] recuperar.

bring down vt sep - 1. [from upstairs] bajar - 2. [plane, bird] derribar; [government, tyrant] derrocar - 3. [prices] reducir.

bring forward vt sep - 1. [meeting, elections etc] adelantar - 2. [in bookkeeping] sumar a la siguiente columna.

bring in vt sep - 1. [introduce - law] implantar; [- bill] presentar - 2. [earn] ganar, ingresar.

bring off vt sep [plan] sacar adelante; [deal] cerrar.

bring out vt sep - 1. [new product, book] sacar - 2. [the worst etc in sb] revelar, despertar.

bring round, bring to = bring around.

bring up vt sep - 1. [raise - children] criar - 2. [mention] sacar a relucir - 3. [vomit] devolver.

brink [brɪŋk] n: on the ~ of al borde de.

brisk [brɪsk] adj - 1. [quick] rápido(da) - 2. [trade, business] boyante, activo(va) - 3. [efficient, confident - manner] enérgico(-ca); [- person] eficaz.

bristle ['brɪsl] <> n [gen] cerda f; [of person] pelillo m. <> vi - 1. [stand up] erizarse, ponerse de punta - 2. [react angrily]: to ~ (at) enfadarse (por).

Brit [brɪt] n inf británico m, -ca f.

Britain ['brɪtn] n Gran Bretaña.

British ['brɪtɪʃ] <> adj británico(ca). <> npl: the ~ los británicos.

British Isles npl: the ~ las Islas Británicas.

British Rail n antigua compañía ferroviaria británica, ≃ Renfe f.

Briton ['brɪtn] n británico m, -ca f.

brittle ['brɪtl] adj quebradizo(za), frágil.

broach [brəʊtʃ] vt abordar, sacar a colación.

B road n UK ≃ carretera f comarcal.

broad [brɔːd] <> adj - 1. [shoulders, river, street] ancho(cha); [grin] amplio(plia) - 2. [range, interests] amplio(plia) - 3. [description, outline] general, a grandes rasgos - 4. [hint] claro(ra) - 5. [accent] cerrado(da), marcado(da) - 6. phr: in ~ daylight a plena luz del día. <> n US inf tía f, tipa f.

broad bean n haba f.

broadcast ['brɔːdkɑːst] (pt & pp broadcast) <> n emisión f. <> vt emitir.

broaden ['brɔːdn] <> vt - 1. [road, pavement] ensanchar - 2. [scope, appeal] ampliar. <> vi [river, road] ensancharse; [smile] hacerse más amplia.

broadly ['brɔːdlɪ] adv - 1. [generally] en general - 2. [smile] abiertamente.

broadminded [ˌbrɔːd'maɪndɪd] adj abierto(ta), liberal.

broadsheet ['brɔːdʃiːt] n periódico de calidad (con hojas de gran tamaño).

broccoli ['brɒkəlɪ] n brécol m.

brochure ['brəʊʃəʳ] n folleto m.

broil [brɔɪl] vt US asar a la parrilla.

broke [brəʊk] <> pt ⊳ break. <> adj inf sin blanca, sin un duro, bruja Carib, Méx.

broken ['brəʊkn] <> pp ⊳ break. <> adj - 1. [gen] roto(ta) - 2. [not working] estropeado(da) - 3. [interrupted - sleep] entrecortado(da); [- journey] discontinuo(nua).

broker ['brəʊkəʳ] n [of stock] corredor m; [of insurance] agente m or f.

brolly ['brɒlɪ] (pl -ies) n UK inf paraguas m inv.

bronchitis [brɒŋ'kaɪtɪs] n (U) bronquitis f inv.

bronze [brɒnz] n [metal, sculpture] bronce m.

brooch [brəʊtʃ] n broche m, alfiler m.

brood [bruːd] <> n - 1. [of birds] nidada f - 2. inf [of children] prole f. <> vi: to ~ (over OR about) dar vueltas (a).

brook [brʊk] n arroyo m.

broom [bruːm] n - 1. [brush] escoba f - 2. [plant] retama f.

broomstick ['bruːmstɪk] n palo m de escoba.

Bros., bros. (abbr of brothers) Hnos.

broth [brɒθ] n caldo m.

brothel ['brɒθl] n burdel m.

brother ['brʌðəʳ] n [relative, monk] hermano m.

brother-in-law (pl brothers-in-law) n cuñado m.

brought [brɔːt] pt & pp ⊳ bring.

brow [braʊ] n - 1. [forehead] frente f - 2. [eyebrow] ceja f - 3. [of hill] cima f, cresta f.

brown [braʊn] <> adj - 1. [gen] marrón; [hair, eyes] castaño(ña) - 2. [tanned] moreno(na). <> n marrón m. <> vt [food] dorar.

brown bread n pan m integral.

brownie ['braʊnɪ-] n US bizcocho de chocolate y nueces.

Brownie (Guide) n guía f (7-10 años).

brown paper n (U) papel m de embalar.

brown rice n arroz m integral.

brown sugar n azúcar m moreno, azúcar f morena.

browse [braʊz] <> vi - 1. [person] echar un ojo, mirar; to ~ through hojear - 2. COMPUT navegar. <> vt COMPUT navegar por.

browser ['braʊzəʳ] n COMPUT navegador m.

bruise [bruːz] <> n cardenal m. <> vt - 1. [person, arm] magullar, contusionar; [fruit] magullar - 2. fig [feelings] herir.

brunch [brʌntʃ] n brunch m, combinación de desayuno y almuerzo que se toma por la mañana tarde.

brunette [bruː'net] n morena f.

brunt [brʌnt] *n*: **to bear** OR **take the ~ of** aguantar lo peor de.

brush [brʌʃ] ◇ *n* **-1.** [for hair, teeth] cepillo *m*; [for shaving, decorating] brocha *f*; [of artist] pincel *m*; [broom] escoba *f* **-2.** [encounter] roce *m*. ◇ *vt* **-1.** [clean with brush] cepillar; **to ~ one's hair** cepillarse el pelo **-2.** [move with hand] quitar, apartar **-3.** [touch lightly] rozar.

◆ **brush aside** *vt sep* [dismiss] hacer caso omiso de.

◆ **brush off** *vt sep* [dismiss] hacer caso omiso de.

◆ **brush up** ◇ *vt sep fig* [revise] repasar. ◇ *vi*: **to ~ up on** repasar.

brushwood ['brʌʃwʊd] *n* leña *f*, ramojo *m*.

brusque [bruːsk] *adj* brusco(ca).

Brussels ['brʌslz] *n* Bruselas.

brussels sprout *n* col *f* de Bruselas.

brutal ['bruːtl] *adj* brutal.

brute [bruːt] ◇ *adj* bruto(ta). ◇ *n* **-1.** [large animal] bestia *f*, bruto *m* **-2.** [bully] bestia *m* OR *f*.

BS US (*abbr of* **Bachelor of Science**) *n* (*titular de una*) licenciatura de ciencias.

BSc (*abbr of* **Bachelor of Science**) *n* (*titular de una*) licenciatura de ciencias.

bubble ['bʌbl] ◇ *n* [gen] burbuja *f*; [of soap] pompa *f*. ◇ *vi* **-1.** [produce bubbles] burbujear **-2.** [make a bubbling sound] borbotar.

bubble bath *n* espuma *f* de baño.

bubble gum *n* chicle *m* (de globo).

bubblejet printer ['bʌbldʒet-] *n* COMPUT impresora *f* de inyección.

Bucharest [ˌbuːkəˈrest] *n* Bucarest.

buck [bʌk] (*pl inv* OR **-s**) ◇ *n* **-1.** [male animal] macho *m* **-2.** *esp* US *inf* [dollar] dólar *m* **-3.** *inf* [responsibility]: **to pass the ~ to sb** echarle el muerto a alguien. ◇ *vi* corcovear, encabritarse.

◆ **buck up** *inf* ◇ *vt sep* [improve] mejorar; **~ your ideas up** más vale que espabiles. ◇ *vi* **-1.** [hurry up] darse prisa **-2.** [cheer up] animarse.

bucket ['bʌkɪt] *n* [container, bucketful] cubo *m*.

Buckingham Palace ['bʌkɪŋəm-] *n* el palacio de Buckingham.

buckle ['bʌkl] ◇ *n* hebilla *f*. ◇ *vt* **-1.** [fasten] abrochar con hebilla **-2.** [bend] combar. ◇ *vi* [wheel] combarse; [knees] doblarse.

bud [bʌd] (*pt & pp* **-ded**, *cont* **-ding**) ◇ *n* [shoot] brote *m*; [flower] capullo *m*. ◇ *vi* brotar, echar brotes.

Budapest [ˌbjuːdəˈpest] *n* Budapest.

Buddha ['bʊdə] *n* Buda *m*.

Buddhism ['bʊdɪzm] *n* budismo *m*.

budding ['bʌdɪŋ] *adj* en ciernes.

buddy ['bʌdɪ] (*pl* **-ies**) *n* esp US *inf* [friend] amiguete *m*, -ta *f*, colega *m* OR *f*, compa *m* Amér.

budge [bʌdʒ] ◇ *vt* mover. ◇ *vi* [move] moverse; [give in] ceder.

budgerigar ['bʌdʒərɪgɑː^r] *n* periquito *m*.

budget ['bʌdʒɪt] ◇ *adj* económico(ca). ◇ *n* presupuesto *m*.

◆ **budget for** *vt fus* contar con.

budgie ['bʌdʒɪ] *n inf* periquito *m*.

buff [bʌf] ◇ *adj* color de ante. ◇ *n inf* [expert] aficionado *m*, -da *f*.

buffalo ['bʌfələʊ] (*pl inv* OR **-s** OR **-es**) *n* búfalo *m*.

buffer ['bʌfə^r] *n* **-1.** UK [for trains] tope *m* **-2.** US [of car] parachoques *m inv* **-3.** [protection] defensa *f*, salvaguarda *f* **-4.** COMPUT búfer *m*.

buffet¹ [UK 'bʊfeɪ, US bə'feɪ] *n* **-1.** [meal] bufé *m* **-2.** [cafeteria] cafetería *f*.

buffet² ['bʌfɪt] *vt* [physically] golpear.

buffet car ['bʊfeɪ-] *n* coche *m* restaurante.

bug [bʌg] (*pt & pp* **-ged**, *cont* **-ging**) ◇ *n* **-1.** *esp* US [small insect] bicho *m* **-2.** *inf* [illness] virus *m* **-3.** *inf* [listening device] micrófono *m* oculto **-4.** COMPUT error *m* **-5.** [enthusiasm] manía *f*. ◇ *vt* **-1.** *inf* [spy on - room] poner un micrófono oculto en; [- phone] pinchar, intervenir **-2.** *esp* US *inf* [annoy] fastidiar, jorobar.

bugger ['bʌgə^r] *n* UK *v inf* [unpleasant person] cabrón *m*, -ona *f*; [difficult, annoying task] coñazo *m*.

◆ **bugger off** *vi v inf*: **~ off!** ¡vete a tomar por culo!

buggy ['bʌgɪ] (*pl* **-ies**) *n* **-1.** [carriage] calesa *f* **-2.** [pushchair] sillita *f* de ruedas; US [pram] cochecito *m* de niño.

bugle ['bjuːgl] *n* corneta *f*, clarín *m*.

build [bɪld] (*pt & pp* **built**) ◇ *vt* **-1.** [construct] construir **-2.** *fig* [form, create] crear. ◇ *n* complexión *f*, constitución *f*.

◆ **build (up)on** ◇ *vt fus* [further] desarrollar. ◇ *vt sep* [base on] fundar en.

◆ **build up** ◇ *vt sep* **-1.** [business - establish] poner en pie; [- promote] fomentar **-2.** [person] fortalecer. ◇ *vi* acumularse.

builder ['bɪldə^r] *n* constructor *m*, -ra *f*.

building ['bɪldɪŋ] *n* **-1.** [structure] edificio *m* **-2.** [profession] construcción *f*.

building and loan association *n* US ≃ caja *f* de ahorros.

building site *n* obra *f*.

building society *n* UK ≃ caja *f* de ahorros.

buildup ['bɪldʌp] *n* [increase] acumulación *f*, incremento *m* gradual; [of troops] concentración *f*.

built [bɪlt] *pt & pp* ⊳ **build**.

built-in *adj* **-1.** [physically integrated] empotrado(da) **-2.** [inherent] incorporado(da).

built-up *adj* urbanizado(da).

bulb [bʌlb] n -1. [for lamp] bombilla f - 2. [of plant] bulbo m - 3. [bulb-shaped part] parte f redondeada.

Bulgaria [bʌl'geərɪə] n Bulgaria.

Bulgarian [bʌl'geərɪən] ◇ adj búlgaro(ra). ◇ n -1. [person] búlgaro m, -ra f - 2. [language] búlgaro m.

bulge [bʌldʒ] ◇ n [lump] protuberancia f, bulto m . ◇ vi: to ~ (with) rebosar (de), estar atestado(da) (de).

bulk [bʌlk] ◇ n -1. [mass] bulto m, volumen m - 2. [large quantity]: in ~ a granel - 3. [majority, most of]: the ~ of la mayor parte de. ◇ adj a granel.

bulky ['bʌlkɪ] (compar -ier, superl -iest) adj voluminoso(sa).

bull [bʊl] n -1. [male cow] toro m - 2. [male animal] macho m.

bulldog ['bʊldɒg] n buldog m.

bulldozer ['bʊldəʊzə'] n bulldozer m.

bullet ['bʊlɪt] n -1. [of gun] bala f - 2. [typo] topo m.

bulletin ['bʊlətɪn] n -1. [news] boletín m; [medical report] parte m - 2. [regular publication] boletín m, gaceta f.

bullet-proof adj a prueba de balas.

bullfight ['bʊlfaɪt] n corrida f (de toros).

bullfighter ['bʊl,faɪtə'] n torero m, -ra f.

bullfighting ['bʊl,faɪtɪŋ] n toreo m.

bullion ['bʊljən] n (U) lingotes mpl.

bullock ['bʊlək] n buey m, toro m castrado.

bullring ['bʊlrɪŋ] n -1. [stadium] plaza f (de toros) - 2. [arena] ruedo m.

bull's-eye n diana f.

bully ['bʊlɪ] (pl -ies, pt & pp -ied) ◇ n abusón m, matón m. ◇ vt intimidar.

bum [bʌm] n -1. esp UK inf [bottom] cola f Amér, poto m Chile, Perú, traste m CSur - 2. US inf pej [tramp] vagabundo m, -da f.

bumblebee ['bʌmblbiː] n abejorro m.

bump [bʌmp] ◇ n -1. [lump - on head] chichón m; [- on road] bache m - 2. [knock, blow, noise] golpe m. ◇ vt [car] chocar con OR contra; [head, knee] golpearse en; I ~ed my head on the door me di con la cabeza en la puerta.

◆ **bump into** vt fus [meet by chance] toparse con, encontrarse con.

bumper ['bʌmpə'] ◇ adj abundante; ~ edition edición especial. ◇ n -1. AUT parachoques m inv - 2. US RAIL tope m.

bumptious ['bʌmpʃəs] adj pej engreído(da).

bumpy ['bʌmpɪ] (compar -ier, superl -iest) adj -1. [road] lleno(na) de baches - 2. [ride, journey] con muchas sacudidas.

bun [bʌn] n -1. [cake, bread roll] bollo m - 2. [hairstyle] moño m, chongo m Amér.

◆ **buns** npl US inf trasero m, culo m.

bunch [bʌntʃ] ◇ n [of people] grupo m; [of flowers] ramo m; [of fruit] racimo m; [of keys] manojo m. ◇ vi agruparse.

◆ **bunches** npl [hairstyle] coletas fpl.

bundle ['bʌndl] ◇ n -1. [of clothes] lío m, bulto m; [of notes, papers] fajo m; [of wood] haz m; to be a ~ of nerves fig ser un manojo de nervios - 2. COMPUT paquete m. ◇ vt [clothes] empaquetar de cualquier manera; [person] empujar.

◆ **bundle up** vt sep [put into bundles] liar.

bung [bʌŋ] ◇ n tapón m. ◇ vt UK inf -1. [throw] tirar - 2. [pass] alcanzar.

bungalow ['bʌŋgələʊ] n bungalow m.

bungle ['bʌŋgl] vt chapucear.

bunion ['bʌnjən] n juanete m.

bunk [bʌŋk] n [bed] litera f.

bunk bed n litera f.

bunker ['bʌŋkə'] n -1. [shelter, in golf] bunker m - 2. [for coal] carbonera f.

bunny ['bʌnɪ] (pl -ies) n: ~ (rabbit) conejito m, -ta f.

bunting ['bʌntɪŋ] n (U) [flags] banderitas fpl.

buoy [UK bɔɪ, US 'buːɪ] n boya f.

◆ **buoy up** vt sep [encourage] alentar, animar.

buoyant ['bɔɪənt] adj -1. [able to float] boyante, capaz de flotar - 2. [optimistic gen] optimista; [- market] con tendencia alcista.

burden ['bɜːdn] ◇ n -1. [heavy load] carga f - 2. fig [heavy responsibility]: ~ on carga f para. ◇ vt: to ~ sb with cargar a alguien con.

bureau ['bjʊərəʊ] (pl -x) n -1. [government department] departamento m, oficina f - 2. [office] oficina f - 3. UK [desk] secreter m; US [chest of drawers] cómoda f.

bureaucracy [bjʊə'rɒkrəsɪ] (pl -ies) n burocracia f.

bureaux ['bjʊərəʊz] pl ▷ bureau.

burger ['bɜːgə'] n hamburguesa f.

burglar ['bɜːglə'] n ladrón m, -ona f.

burglar alarm n alarma f antirrobo.

burglarize US = burgle.

burglary ['bɜːglərɪ] (pl -ies) n robo m (de una casa).

burgle ['bɜːgl], **burglarize** US ['bɜːgləraɪz] vt robar, desvalijar (una casa).

burial ['berɪəl] n entierro m.

burly ['bɜːlɪ] (compar -ier, superl -iest) adj fornido(da).

Burma ['bɜːmə] n Birmania.

burn [bɜːn] (pt & pp burnt OR -ed) ◇ vt -1. [gen] quemar - 2. [injure by heat, fire] quemarse - 3. COMPUT estampar. ◇ vi -1. [gen] arder - 2. [be alight] estar encendido(da) - 3. [food] quemarse - 4. [cause burning sensation] escocer - 5. [become sunburnt] quemarse. ◇ n quemadura f.

◆ **burn down** ◇ *vt sep* incendiar. ◇ *vi* [be destroyed by fire] incendiarse.

burner ['bɜːnəʳ] *n* quemador *m*.

Burns' Night *n fiesta celebrada en Escocia el 25 de enero en honor del poeta escocés Robert Burns.*

burnt [bɜːnt] *pt & pp* ▷ **burn**.

burp [bɜːp] *vi inf* eructar.

burrow ['bʌrəʊ] ◇ *n* madriguera *f.* ◇ *vi* - 1. [dig] escarbar (un agujero) - 2. *fig* [in order to search] hurgar.

bursar ['bɜːsəʳ] *n* tesorero *m*, -ra *f*, administrador *m*, -ra *f*.

bursary ['bɜːsərɪ] (*pl* -ies) *n UK* beca *f*.

burst [bɜːst] (*pt & pp* **burst**) ◇ *vi* - 1. [gen] reventarse; [bag] romperse; [tyre] pinchar-se - 2. [explode] estallar. ◇ *vt* [gen] reventar; [tyre] pinchar. ◇ *n* [of gunfire, enthusiasm] estallido *m*.

◆ **burst into** *vt fus* - 1. [tears, song]: to ~ into tears/song romper a llorar/cantar - 2. [flames] estallar en.

◆ **burst out** *vi* [begin suddenly]: to ~ out laughing/crying echarse a reír/llorar.

bursting ['bɜːstɪŋ] *adj* - 1. [full] lleno(na) a estallar - 2. [with emotion]: ~ with rebo-sando de - 3. [eager]: to be ~ to do sthg estar deseando hacer algo.

bury ['berɪ] (*pt & pp* -ied) *vt* - 1. [in ground] enterrar - 2. [hide - face, memory] ocultar.

bus [bʌs] ◇ *n* autobús *m*, micro *m Chile*, ca-mión *m CAm, Méx*, colectivo *m Arg, Bol*, ca-rrito *m por puesto Ven*, ómnibus *m Perú, Urug*, guagua *f Cuba*: by ~ en autobús. ◇ *vt US*: to ~ **tables** [in restaurant] recoger mesas.

bush [bʊʃ] *n* - 1. [plant] arbusto *m* - 2. [open country]: **the** ~ el campo abierto, el monte - 3. *phr*: to beat about the ~ andarse por las ramas.

bushy ['bʊʃɪ] (*compar* -ier, *superl* -iest) *adj* poblado(da), espeso(sa).

business ['bɪznɪs] *n* - 1. (U) [commerce, amount of trade] negocios *mpl*; to be away on ~ estar en viaje de negocios; to mean ~ *inf* ir en serio; to go out of ~ quebrar - 2. [company] negocio *m*, empresa *f* - 3. [concern, duty] oficio *m*, ocupación *f*; mind your own ~! *inf* ¡no te metas donde no te llaman!; that's none of your ~ eso no es asunto tuyo - 4. (U) [affair, matter] asunto *m*.

business class *n* clase *f* preferente.

businesslike ['bɪznɪslaɪk] *adj* formal y efi-ciente.

business lunch *n* comida *f* de trabajo.

businessman ['bɪznɪsmæn] (*pl* -men [-men]) *n* empresario *m*, hombre *m* de nego-cios.

business studies *npl* empresariales *mpl*.

business trip *n* viaje *m* de negocios.

businesswoman ['bɪznɪsˌwʊmən] (*pl* -women [-ˌwɪmɪn]) *n* empresaria *f*, mujer *f* de negocios.

busker ['bʌskəʳ] *n UK* músico *m* ambulante OR callejero.

bus-shelter *n* marquesina *f* (de parada de autobús).

bus station *n* estación *f* OR terminal *f* de autobuses.

bus stop *n* parada *f* de autobús, paradero *m CAm, Andes, Méx*.

bust [bʌst] (*pt & pp* -ed OR **bust**) ◇ *adj inf* - 1. [broken] fastidiado(da), roto(ta) - 2. [bankrupt]: to go ~ quebrar. ◇ *n* [bosom, statue] busto *m*. ◇ *vt inf* [break] fas-tidiar, estropear.

bustle ['bʌsl] ◇ *n* bullicio *m*. ◇ *vi* apresu-rarse.

busy ['bɪzɪ] (*compar* -ier, *superl* -iest) ◇ *adj* - 1. [occupied] ocupado(da); to be ~ doing sthg estar ocupado haciendo algo - 2. [hec-tic - life, week] ajetreado(da); [- town, office] concurrido(da), animado(da); [- road] con mucho tráfico - 3. [active] activo(va). ◇ *vt*: to ~ o.s. (doing sthg) ocuparse (ha-ciendo algo).

busybody ['bɪzɪˌbɒdɪ] (*pl* -ies) *n pej* entro-metido *m*, -da *f*.

busy signal *n US* TELEC señal *f* de comuni-cando.

but [bʌt] ◇ *conj* pero; we were poor ~ happy éramos pobres pero felices; she owns not one ~ two houses tiene no una sino dos casas. ◇ *prep* menos, excepto; everyone ~ Jane was there todos estaban allí, menos Jane; we've had nothing ~ bad weather no hemos tenido más que mal tiempo; he has no one ~ himself to blame la culpa no es de otro más que él OR sino de él. ◇ *adv fml*: had I ~ known de haberlo sa-bido; we can ~ try por intentarlo que no quede.

◆ **but for** *conj* de no ser por.

butcher ['bʊtʃəʳ] ◇ *n* - 1. [occupation] car-nicero *m*, -ra *f*; ~'s (shop) carnicería *f* - 2. [indiscriminate killer] carnicero *m*, -ra *f*, asesino *m*, -na *f.* ◇ *vt* [animal - for meat] ma-tar; *fig* [kill indiscriminately] hacer una car-nicería con.

butler ['bʌtləʳ] *n* mayordomo *m*.

butt [bʌt] ◇ *n* - 1. [of cigarette, cigar] colilla *f* - 2. [of rifle] culata *f* - 3. [for water] tina *f* - 4. [of joke, remark] blanco *m* - 5. *US inf* [bot-tom] trasero *m*, culo *m.* ◇ *vt* topetar.

◆ **butt in** *vi* [interrupt]: to ~ in on sb cor-tar a alguien; to ~ in on sthg entrometerse en algo.

◆ **butt out** *vi US* dejar de entrometerse.

butter ['bʌtəʳ] ◇ *n* mantequilla *f.* ◇ *vt* un-tar con mantequilla.

buttercup ['bʌtəkʌp] *n* ranúnculo *m*.

butter dish *n* mantequera *f*.

butterfly ['bʌtəflaɪ] (*pl* **-ies**) *n* **- 1.** [insect] mariposa *f* **- 2.** [swimming style] (estilo *m*) mariposa *f*.

buttocks ['bʌtəks] *npl* nalgas *fpl*.

button ['bʌtn] ⬦ *n* **- 1.** [gen & COMPUT] botón *m* **- 2.** *US* [badge] chapa *f*. ⬦ *vt* = **button up.**

⬥ **button up** *vt sep* abotonar, abrochar.

button mushroom *n* champiñón *m* pequeño.

buttress ['bʌtrɪs] *n* contrafuerte *m*.

buxom ['bʌksəm] *adj* [woman] maciza, pechugona.

buy [baɪ] (*pt* & *pp* **bought**) ⬦ *vt lit* & *fig* comprar; **to ~ sthg from sb** comprar algo a alguien; **to ~ sb sthg** comprar algo a alguien, comprar algo para alguien. ⬦ *n* compra *f*.

⬥ **buy up** *vt sep* acaparar.

buyer ['baɪə'] *n* [purchaser] comprador *m*, -ra *f*.

buyout ['baɪaʊt] *n adquisición de la mayoría de las acciones de una empresa.*

buzz [bʌz] ⬦ *n* [of insect, machinery] zumbido *m*; [of conversation] rumor *m*; **to give sb a ~** *inf* [on phone] dar un toque *OR* llamar a alguien. ⬦ *vi* **- 1.** [make noise] zumbar **- 2.** *fig* [be active]: **to ~ (with)** bullir (de).

buzzer ['bʌzə'] *n* timbre *m*.

buzzword ['bʌzwɜːd] *n inf* palabra *f* de moda.

by [baɪ] *prep* **- 1.** [indicating cause, agent] por; **caused/written ~** causado/escrito por; **a book ~ Joyce** un libro de Joyce **- 2.** [indicating means, method, manner]: **to travel ~ bus/train/plane/ship** viajar en autobús/tren/avión/barco; **to pay ~ cheque** pagar con cheque; **he got rich ~ buying land** se hizo rico comprando terrenos; **~ profession/trade** de profesión/oficio **- 3.** [beside, close to] junto a; **~ the sea** junto al mar **- 4.** [past] por delante de; **to walk ~ sb/sthg** pasear por delante de alguien/algo; **we drove ~ the castle** pasamos por el castillo (conduciendo) **- 5.** [via, through] por; **we entered ~ the back door** entramos por la puerta trasera **- 6.** [with time - at or before, during] para; **I'll be there ~ eight** estaré allí para las ocho; **~ now** ya; **~ day/night** de día/noche **- 7.** [according to] según; **~ law/my standards** según la ley/mis criterios **- 8.** [in division] entre; **to divide 20 ~ 2** dividir 20 entre 2; **to multiply 20 ~ 2** multiplicar 20 por 2; **twelve feet ~ ten** doce pies por diez **- 9.** [in quantities, amounts] por; **~ the thousand** *OR* **thousands** por miles; **~ the day/hour** por día/horas; **prices were cut ~ 50%** los precios fueron rebajados (en) un 50% **-10.** [indicating gradual change]: **day ~ day** día a día; **one ~ one** uno a uno **- 11.** [to explain a word or expression] por; **what do you mean ~ 'all right'?**; **what do you understand ~ the word 'subsidiary'?** ¿qué entiendes por 'subsidiariedad'? **- 12.** *phr*: **(all) ~ oneself** solo(la); **did you do it all ~ yourself?** ¿lo hiciste tú solo?

bye(-bye) [baɪ(baɪ)] *excl inf* ¡hasta luego!

bye-election = **by-election**.

byelaw ['baɪlɔː] = **bylaw**.

by-election *n* elección *f* parcial.

bygone ['baɪgɒn] *adj* pasado(da).

⬥ **bygones** *npl*: **let ~s be ~s** lo pasado, pasado está.

bylaw ['baɪlɔː] *n* reglamento *m* *OR* estatuto *m* local.

bypass ['baɪpɑːs] ⬦ *n* **- 1.** [road] carretera *f* de circunvalación **- 2.** MED: **~ (operation)** (operación *f* de) by-pass *m*. ⬦ *vt* evitar.

by-product *n* **- 1.** [product] subproducto *m* **- 2.** [consequence] consecuencia *f*.

bystander ['baɪˌstændə'] *n* espectador *m*, -ra *f*.

byte [baɪt] *n* COMPUT byte *m*.

byword ['baɪwɜːd] *n*: **to be a ~ (for)** ser sinónimo de.

c¹ (*pl* **c's** *OR* **cs**), **C** (*pl* **C's** *OR* **Cs**) [siː] *n* [letter] c *f*, C *f*.

⬥ **C** *n* **- 1.** MUS do *m* **- 2.** (*abbr of* **celsius, centigrade**) C.

c² (*abbr of* **cent(s)**) cént.

c. (*abbr of* **circa**) h.

c/a (*abbr of* **current account**) c/c.

cab [kæb] *n* **- 1.** [taxi] taxi *m* **- 2.** [of lorry] cabina *f*.

cabaret ['kæbəreɪ] *n* cabaret *m*.

cabbage ['kæbɪdʒ] *n* col *f*, repollo *m*.

cabin ['kæbɪn] *n* **- 1.** [on ship] camarote *m* **- 2.** [in aircraft] cabina *f* **- 3.** [house] cabaña *f*.

cabin crew *n* personal *m* de a bordo.

cabinet ['kæbɪnɪt] *n* **- 1.** [cupboard] armario *m*; [with glass pane] vitrina *f* **- 2.** POL consejo *m* de ministros, gabinete *m*.

cable ['keɪbl] ⬦ *n* **- 1.** [rope, wire] cable *m* **- 2.** [telegram] cablegrama *m*. ⬦ *vt* cablegrafiar.

cable car *n* teleférico *m*.

cable television, cable TV *n* televisión *f* por cable.

cache [kæʃ] *n* - **1**. [store] alijo *m* - **2**. COMPUT caché *f*.

cache memory *n* COMPUT memoria *f* caché.

cackle ['kækl] *vi* - **1**. [hen] cacarear - **2**. [person] reírse.

cactus ['kæktəs] (*pl* -**tuses** OR -**ti** [-taɪ]) *n* cactus *m inv.*

cadet [kə'det] *n* cadete *m*.

cadge [kædʒ] *vt UK inf* : **to** ~ **sthg** (**off** OR **from sb**) gorronear algo (a alguien).

caesarean (section) [sɪ'zeərɪən-] *UK*, **cesarean (section)** *US n* cesárea *f*.

cafe, café ['kæfeɪ] *n* café *m*, cafetería *f*.

cafeteria [ˌkæfɪ'tɪərɪə] *n* (restaurante *m*) autoservicio *m*, cantina *f*.

cafetiere [ˌkæfə'tjɛə] *n* cafetera *f* de émbolo.

caffeine ['kæfi:n] *n* cafeína *f*.

cage [keɪdʒ] *n* jaula *f*.

cagey ['keɪdʒɪ] (*compar* -**ier**, *superl* -**iest**) *adj inf* reservado(da).

cagoule [kə'gu:l] *n UK* chubasquero *m*, canguro *m*.

cajole [kə'dʒəʊl] *vt* : **to** ~ **sb** (**into doing sthg**) engatusar a alguien (para que haga algo).

cake [keɪk] *n* - **1**. [sweet food] pastel *m*, tarta *f*, torta *f Amér* - **2**. [of fish, potato] medallón *m* empanado - **3**. [of soap] pastilla *f*.

caked [keɪkt] *adj*: ~ **with mud** cubierto(ta) de barro seco.

calcium ['kælsɪəm] *n* calcio *m*.

calculate ['kælkjʊleɪt] *vt* - **1**. [work out] calcular - **2**. [plan]: **to be** ~**d to do sthg** estar pensado(da) para hacer algo.

calculating ['kælkjʊleɪtɪŋ] *adj pej* calculador(ra).

calculation [ˌkælkjʊ'leɪʃn] *n* cálculo *m*.

calculator ['kælkjʊleɪtə'] *n* calculadora *f*.

calendar ['kælɪndə'] *n* calendario *m*.

calendar month *n* mes *m* civil.

calendar year *n* año *m* civil.

calf [kɑ:f] (*pl* **calves**) *n* - **1**. [young animal - of cow] ternero *m*, -ra *f*, becerro *m*, -rra *f*; [- of other animals] cría *f* - **2**. [leather] piel *f* de becerro - **3**. [of leg] pantorrilla *f*.

calibre, caliber *US* ['kælɪbə'] *n* - **1**. [quality] nivel *m* - **2**. [size] calibre *m*.

California [ˌkælɪ'fɔ:njə] *n* California *f*.

calipers *US* = **callipers**.

call [kɔ:l] ◇ *n* - **1**. [cry, attraction, vocation] llamada *f*, llamado *m Amér*; [cry of bird] reclamo *m* - **2**. TELEC llamada *f*, llamado *m Amér*; **to give sb a** ~ llamar a alguien - **3**. [visit] visita *f*; **to pay a** ~ **on sb** hacerle una visita a alguien - **4**. [demand]: ~ **for** llamamiento *m* a - **5**. [summons]: **on** ~ de guardia. ◇ *vt* - **1**. [gen & TELEC] llamar; **I'm** ~**ed Joan** me llamo Joan; **what is it** ~**ed?** ¿cómo se llama?; **he** ~**ed my name** me llamó por el nombre; **we'll** ~ **it £10** dejémoslo en 10 libras - **2**. [announce - flight] anunciar; [- strike, meeting, election] convocar. ◇ *vi* - **1**. [gen & TELEC] llamar; **who's** ~**ing?** ¿quién es? - **2**. [visit] pasar.

➡ **call at** *vt fus* [subj: train] efectuar parada en.

➡ **call back** ◇ *vt sep* - **1**. [on phone] volver a llamar - **2**. [ask to return] hacer volver. ◇ *vi* - **1**. [on phone] volver a llamar - **2**. [visit again] volver a pasarse.

➡ **call for** *vt fus* - **1**. [collect] ir a buscar - **2**. [demand] pedir.

➡ **call in** *vt sep* - **1**. [send for] llamar - **2**. [recall - product, banknotes] retirar; [- loan] exigir pago de.

➡ **call off** *vt sep* - **1**. [meeting, party] suspender; [strike] desconvocar - **2**. [dog etc] llamar *(para deje de atacar)*.

➡ **call on** *vt fus* - **1**. [visit] visitar - **2**. [ask]: **to** ~ **on sb to do sthg** pedir a alguien que haga algo.

➡ **call out** ◇ *vt sep* - **1**. [order to help - troops] movilizar; [- police, firemen] hacer intervenir - **2**. [cry out] gritar. ◇ *vi* gritar.

➡ **call round** *vi* pasarse.

➡ **call up** *vt sep* - **1**. MIL llamar a filas - **2**. *esp US* [on telephone] llamar (por teléfono).

call box *n UK* cabina *f* telefónica.

call centre *n* centro *m* de atención telefónica.

caller ['kɔ:lə'] *n* - **1**. [visitor] visita *f* - **2**. [on telephone] persona *f* que llama.

caller (ID) display *n* [on telephone] identificador *m* de llamada.

call-in *n US* RADIO & TV programa *m* a micrófono abierto.

calling ['kɔ:lɪŋ] *n* - **1**. [profession] profesión *f* - **2**. [vocation] vocación *f*.

calling card *n US* tarjeta *f* de visita.

callipers *UK*, **calipers** *US* ['kælɪpəz] *npl* - **1**. MED aparato *m* ortopédico - **2**. [for measuring] calibrador *m*.

callisthenics [ˌkælɪs'θenɪks] *n UK* calistenia *f*.

callous ['kæləs] *adj* despiadado(da), cruel.

calm [kɑ:m] ◇ *adj* - **1**. [not worried or excited] tranquilo(la) - **2**. [evening, weather] apacible - **3**. [sea] en calma. ◇ *n* calma *f*. ◇ *vt* calmar.

➡ **calm down** ◇ *vt sep* calmar. ◇ *vi* calmarse.

Calor gas® ['kælə'-] *n UK* (gas *m*) butano *m*.

calorie ['kælərɪ] *n* caloría *f*.

calves [kɑ:vz] *pl* ⊳ **calf**.

camber ['kæmbə'] *n* [of road] peralte *m*.

Cambodia [kæm'bəʊdjə] *n* Camboya *f*.

camcorder [ˈkæmˌkɔːdəʳ] *n* camcorder *m*, videocámara *f*.

came [keɪm] *pt* ⊳ **come**.

camel [ˈkæml] *n* camello *m*.

cameo [ˈkæmɪəʊ] (*pl* **-s**) *n* - **1.** [jewellery] camafeo *m* - **2.** [in acting] actuación *f* breve y memorable; [in writing] excelente descripción *f*.

camera [ˈkæmərə] *n* cámara *f*.

➡ **in camera** *adv fml* a puerta cerrada.

cameraman [ˈkæmərəmæn] (*pl* **-men** [-men]) *n* cámara *m*.

camouflage [ˈkæməflɑːʒ] ◇ *n* camuflaje *m*. ◇ *vt* camuflar.

camp [kæmp] ◇ *n* - **1.** [gen & MIL] campamento *m* - **2.** [temporary mass accommodation] campo *m* - **3.** [faction] bando *m*. ◇ *vi* acampar. ◇ *adj inf* amanerado(da).

➡ **camp out** *vi* acampar (al aire libre).

campaign [kæmˈpeɪn] ◇ *n* campaña *f*. ◇ *vi*: **to ~ (for/against)** hacer campaña (a favor de/en contra de).

camp bed *n* cama *f* plegable.

camper [ˈkæmpəʳ] *n* - **1.** [person] campista *m* or *f* - **2.**: **~ (van)** autocaravana *f*.

campground [ˈkæmpgraʊnd] *n* US camping *m*.

camping [ˈkæmpɪŋ] *n* camping *m*, acampada *f*.

camping site, campsite [ˈkæmpsaɪt] *n* camping *m*.

campus [ˈkæmpəs] (*pl* **-es**) *n* campus *m inv*, ciudad *f* universitaria.

can¹ [kæn] (*pt & pp* **-ned**, *cont* **-ning**) ◇ *n* [for drink, food] lata *f*, bote *m*; [for oil, paint] lata; US [for garbage] cubo *m*. ◇ *vt* enlatar.

can² [*weak form* kən, *strong form* kæn] (*pt & conditional* **could**, *negative* **cannot** OR **can't**) *modal vb* - **1.** [be able to] poder; **~ you come to lunch?** ¿puedes venir a comer?; **~ you see/hear something?** ¿ves/oyes algo? - **2.** [know how to] saber; **I ~ speak French** hablo francés, sé hablar francés; **I ~ play the piano** sé tocar el piano - **3.** [indicating permission, in polite requests] poder; **you ~ use my car if you like** puedes utilizar mi coche si quieres; **~ I speak to John, please?** ¿puedo hablar con John, por favor? - **4.** [indicating disbelief, puzzlement]: **you ~'t be serious** estás de broma ¿no?; **what ~ she have done with it?** ¿qué puede haber hecho con ello? - **5.** [indicating possibility] poder; **you could have done it** podrías haberlo hecho; **I could see you tomorrow** podríamos vernos mañana.

Canada [ˈkænədə] *n* (el) Canadá.

Canadian [kəˈneɪdjən] ◇ *adj* canadiense. ◇ *n* [person] canadiense *m* or *f*.

canal [kəˈnæl] *n* canal *m*.

canary [kəˈneərɪ] (*pl* **-ies**) *n* canario *m*.

Canary Islands, Canaries [kəˈneərɪz] *npl*: **the ~** las (islas) Canarias.

cancel [ˈkænsl] (*UK pt & pp* **-led**, *cont* **-ling**, *US pt & pp* **-ed**, *cont* **-ing**) *vt* - **1.** [call off] cancelar, suspender - **2.** [invalidate - cheque, debt] cancelar; [- order] anular.

➡ **cancel out** *vt sep* anular.

cancellation [ˌkænsəˈleɪʃn] *n* suspensión *f*.

cancellation fee *n* tarifa *f* de cancelación.

cancer [ˈkænsəʳ] *n* [disease] cáncer *m*.

➡ **Cancer** *n* Cáncer *m*.

candelabra [ˌkændɪˈlɑːbrə] *n* candelabro *m*.

candid [ˈkændɪd] *adj* franco(ca), sincero(ra).

candidate [ˈkændɪdət] *n*: **~ (for)** candidato *m*, -ta *f* (a).

candle [ˈkændl] *n* vela *f*, esperma *f Amér*.

candlelight [ˈkændllaɪt] *n*: **by ~** a la luz de una vela.

candlelit [ˈkændllɪt] *adj* [dinner] a la luz de las velas.

candlestick [ˈkændlstɪk] *n* candelero *m*.

candour UK, **candor** US [ˈkændəʳ] *n* franqueza *f*, sinceridad *f*.

candy [ˈkændɪ] (*pl* **-ies**) *n esp* US - **1.** (U) [confectionery] golosinas *fpl*; **~ bar** chocolatina *f* - **2.** [sweet] caramelo *m*.

candyfloss UK [ˈkændɪflɒs], **cotton candy** US *n* azúcar *m* hilado, algodón *m*.

cane [keɪn] *n* - **1.** (U) [for making furniture, supporting plant] caña *f*, mimbre *m* - **2.** [walking stick] bastón *m* - **3.** [for punishment]: **the ~** la vara.

canine [ˈkeɪnaɪn] ◇ *adj* canino(na). ◇ *n*: **~ (tooth)** [diente *m*] canino *m*, colmillo *m*.

canister [ˈkænɪstəʳ] *n* [for tea] bote *m*; [for film] lata *f*; [for gas] bombona *f*; **smoke ~** bote de humo.

cannabis [ˈkænəbɪs] *n* cannabis *m*.

canned [kænd] *adj* [food, drink] enlatado(da), en lata.

cannibal [ˈkænɪbl] *n* caníbal *m* or *f*.

cannon [ˈkænən] (*pl inv* OR **-s**) *n* cañón *m*.

cannonball [ˈkænənbɔːl] *n* bala *f* de cañón.

cannot [ˈkænɒt] *fml* ⊳ **can²**.

canny [ˈkænɪ] (*compar* **-ier**, *superl* **-iest**) *adj* [shrewd] astuto(ta).

canoe [kəˈnuː] (*cont* **canoeing**) *n* [gen] canoa *f*, SPORT piragua *f*.

canoeing [kəˈnuːɪŋ] *n* piragüismo *m*.

canon [ˈkænən] *n* - **1.** [clergyman] canónigo *m* - **2.** [general principle] canon *m*.

can opener *n esp* US abrelatas *m inv*.

canopy [ˈkænəpɪ] (*pl* **-ies**) *n* [over bed, seat] dosel *m*.

can't [kɑːnt] = **cannot**.

cantankerous [kænˈtæŋkərəs] *adj* [person] refunfuñón(ona), cascarrabias (*inv*).

canteen [kænˈtiːn] *n* - **1.** [restaurant] cantina *f* - **2.** [set of cutlery] (juego *m* de) cubertería *f*.

canter ['kæntə'] ⟨⟩ *n* medio galope *m*. ⟨⟩ *vi* ir a medio galope.

cantilever ['kæntɪliːvə'] *n* voladizo *m*.

Cantonese [ˌkæntə'niːz] ⟨⟩ *adj* cantonés(esa). ⟨⟩ *n* - 1. [person] cantonés *m*, -esa *f* - 2. [language] cantonés *m*.

canvas ['kænvəs] *n* - 1. [cloth] lona *f* - 2. [for painting on, finished painting] lienzo *m*.

canvass ['kænvəs] ⟨⟩ *vt* - 1. POL [person] solicitar el voto a - 2. [opinion] pulsar. ⟨⟩ *vi* solicitar votos yendo de puerta en puerta.

canyon ['kænjən] *n* cañón *m*.

cap [kæp] (*pt* & *pp* **-ped**, *cont* **-ping**) ⟨⟩ *n* - 1. [hat - peaked] gorra *f*; [- with no peak] gorro *m* - 2. [on bottle] tapón *m*; [on jar] tapa *f*; [on pen] capuchón *m* - 3. [limit] tope *m* - 4. *UK* [contraceptive device] diafragma *m*. ⟨⟩ *vt* - 1. [top]: **to be capped with** estar coronado(da) de - 2. [outdo]: **to ~ it all** para colmo.

capability [ˌkeɪpə'bɪlətɪ] (*pl* **-ies**) *n* capacidad *f*.

capable ['keɪpəbl] *adj* - 1. [able]: **to be ~ of sthg/of doing sthg** ser capaz de algo/de hacer algo - 2. [competent] competente.

capacity [kə'pæsɪtɪ] (*pl* **-ies**) *n* - 1. [gen]: **~ (for)** capacidad *f* (de); **seating ~** aforo *m*; **~ for doing** OR **to do sthg** capacidad de hacer algo - 2. [position] calidad *f*.

cape [keɪp] *n* - 1. GEOGR cabo *m* - 2. [cloak] capa *f*.

caper ['keɪpə'] *n* - 1. [food] alcaparra *f* - 2. *inf* [escapade] treta *f*.

capita ▷ **per capita**.

capital ['kæpɪtl] ⟨⟩ *adj* - 1. [letter] mayúscula - 2. [punishable by death] capital. ⟨⟩ *n* - 1. [of country, main centre] capital *f* - 2.: **~ (letter)** mayúscula *f* - 3. [money] capital *m*; **to make ~ (out) of** *fig* sacar partido de.

capital expenditure *n (U)* inversión *f* de capital.

capital gains tax *n* impuesto *m* sobre plusvalías.

capital goods *npl* bienes *mpl* de capital.

capital investment *n* inversiones *fpl* de capital.

capitalism ['kæpɪtəlɪzm] *n* capitalismo *m*.

capitalist ['kæpɪtəlɪst] ⟨⟩ *adj* capitalista. ⟨⟩ *n* capitalista *m* OR *f*.

capitalize, -ise ['kæpɪtəlaɪz] *vi*: **to ~ on sthg** aprovechar algo, capitalizar algo.

capital punishment *n (U)* pena *f* capital.

Capitol Hill ['kæpɪtl-] *n* el Capitolio, *ubicación del Congreso estadounidense, en Washington*.

capitulate [kə'pɪtjʊleɪt] *vi*: **to ~ (to)** capitular (ante).

Capricorn ['kæprɪkɔːn] *n* Capricornio *m*.

capsize [kæp'saɪz] ⟨⟩ *vt* hacer volcar OR zozobrar. ⟨⟩ *vi* volcar, zozobrar.

capsule ['kæpsjuːl] *n* cápsula *f*.

captain ['kæptɪn] *n* [gen] capitán *m*, -ana *f*; [of aircraft] comandante *m* OR *f*.

caption ['kæpʃn] *n* [under picture etc] leyenda *f*; [heading] encabezamiento *m*.

captivate ['kæptɪveɪt] *vt* cautivar.

captive ['kæptɪv] ⟨⟩ *adj* - 1. [imprisoned] en cautividad, en cautiverio - 2. *fig* [market] asegurado(da). ⟨⟩ *n* cautivo *m*, -va *f*.

captivity [kæp'tɪvətɪ] *n*: **in ~** en cautividad, en cautiverio.

captor ['kæptə'] *n* apresador *m*, -ra *f*.

capture ['kæptʃə'] ⟨⟩ *vt* - 1. [gen] capturar - 2. [audience, share of market] hacerse con; [city] tomar - 3. [scene, mood, attention] captar - 4. COMPUT introducir. ⟨⟩ *n* [of person] captura *f*; [of city] toma *f*.

car [kɑː'] ⟨⟩ *n* - 1. [motorcar] coche *m*, automóvil *m*, carro *m* *Amér*, auto *m* *CSur* - 2. [on train] vagón *m*, coche *m*. ⟨⟩ *comp* [door, tyre etc] del coche; IND del automóvil; [accident] de automóvil.

carafe [kə'ræf] *n* garrafa *f*.

car alarm *n* alarma *f* de coche.

caramel ['kærəmel] *n* - 1. [burnt sugar] caramelo *m* (líquido), azúcar *m* quemado - 2. [sweet] toñe *m*.

carat ['kærət] *n* *UK* quilate *m*.

caravan ['kærəvæn] *n* caravana *f*, roulotte *f*.

caravan site *n* *UK* camping *m* para caravanas OR roulottes.

carbohydrate [ˌkɑːbəʊ'haɪdreɪt] *n* CHEM hidrato *m* de carbono.

◆ **carbohydrates** *npl* [in food] féculas *fpl*.

carbon ['kɑːbən] *n* [element] carbono *m*.

carbonated ['kɑːbəneɪtɪd] *adj* con gas, carbónico(ca).

carbon copy *n* [document] copia *f* en papel carbón; *fig* [exact copy] calco *m*.

carbon dioxide [-daɪ'ɒksaɪd] *n* bióxido *m* OR dióxido *m* de carbono.

carbon monoxide [-mɒ'nɒksaɪd] *n* monóxido *m* de carbono.

carbon paper *n (U)* papel *m* carbón.

car-boot sale *n* venta *f* de objetos usados colocados en el portaequipajes del coche.

carburettor *UK*, **carburetor** *US* [ˌkɑːbə'retə'] *n* carburador *m*.

carcass ['kɑːkəs] *n* [gen] cadáver *m* (de animal); [of bird] carcasa *f*; [at butcher's] canal *m*.

card [kɑːd] ⟨⟩ *n* - 1. [playing card] carta *f*, naipe *m* - 2. [for information, greetings, computers] tarjeta *f*; [for identification] carné *m* - 3. [postcard] postal *f* - 4. [cardboard] cartulina *f*. ⟨⟩ *vt* *US* [ask for ID] pedir el carné a.

◆ **cards** *npl* las cartas, los naipes.

◆ **on the cards** *UK*, **in the cards** *US* *adv* *inf* más que probable.

cardboard ['kɑːdbɔːd] <> n (U) cartón m. <> comp de cartón.

cardboard box n caja f de cartón.

cardholder ['kɑːdˌhəʊldə'] n titular m OR f (de tarjeta de crédito).

cardiac ['kɑːdɪæk] adj cardíaco(ca).

cardigan ['kɑːdɪɡən] n rebeca f, cárdigan m.

cardinal ['kɑːdɪnl] <> adj capital. <> n RELIG cardenal m.

card index n UK fichero m.

cardphone ['kɑːdfəʊn] n tarjeta f telefónica.

card table n mesita f plegable (para jugar a cartas).

care [keə'] <> n - 1. [gen] cuidado m; **medical ~** asistencia f médica; **in sb's ~** al cargo OR cuidado de alguien; **to be in/be taken into ~** estar/ser internado en un centro de protección de menores; **to take ~ of** [person] cuidar de; [animal, machine] cuidar; [deal with] encargarse de; **take ~!** [goodbye] ¡nos vemos!, ¡cuídate!; **to take ~ (to do sthg)** tener cuidado (de hacer algo) - 2. [cause of worry] preocupación f, problema m. <> vi - 1. [be concerned]: **to ~ (about)** preocuparse (de OR por) - 2. [mind]: **I don't ~** no me importa.
◆ **care of** prep al cuidado de, en casa de.
◆ **care for** vt fus dated [like]: **I don't ~ for cheese** no me gusta el queso.

career [kə'rɪə'] <> n carrera f. <> vi ir a toda velocidad.

careers adviser n asesor m, -ra f de orientación profesional.

carefree ['keəfriː] adj despreocupado(da).

careful ['keəfʊl] adj [gen] cuidadoso(sa); [driver] prudente; [work] esmerado(da); **be ~!** ¡ten cuidado!; **to be ~ with money** ser mirado OR cuidadoso con el dinero; **to be ~ to do sthg** tener cuidado de hacer algo.

carefully ['keəflɪ] adv - 1. [cautiously] cuidadosamente, con cuidado; [drive] con cuidado - 2. [thoroughly] detenidamente.

careless ['keəlɪs] adj - 1. [inattentive] descuidado(da) - 2. [unconcerned] despreocupado(da).

caress [kə'res] <> n caricia f, apapacho m Méx. <> vt acariciar.

caretaker ['keəˌteɪkə'] n UK conserje m OR f.

car ferry n transbordador m OR ferry m de coches.

cargo ['kɑːɡəʊ] (pl -es OR -s) n carga f, cargamento m.

car hire n UK alquiler m OR renta f Méx de coches, arrendamiento m de autos CSur.

Caribbean [UK kærɪ'bɪən, US kə'rɪbɪən] n: **the ~ (Sea)** el (mar) Caribe.

caring ['keərɪŋ] adj solícito(ta), dedicado(da).

carnage ['kɑːnɪdʒ] n carnicería f, matanza f.

carnal ['kɑːnl] adj literary carnal.

carnation [kɑː'neɪʃn] n clavel m.

carnival ['kɑːnɪvl] n carnaval m.

carnivorous [kɑː'nɪvərəs] adj carnívoro(ra).

carol ['kærəl] n villancico m.

carousel [ˌkærə'sel] n - 1. esp US [at fair] tiovivo m - 2. [at airport] cinta f transportadora.

carp [kɑːp] (pl inv OR -s) <> n carpa f. <> vi: **to ~ (about)** refunfuñar OR renegar (de).

car park n UK aparcamiento m, parqueadero m Col, Pan, estacionamiento m Amér.

carpenter ['kɑːpəntə'] n carpintero m, -ra f.

carpentry ['kɑːpəntrɪ] n carpintería f.

carpet ['kɑːpɪt] <> n lit & fig alfombra f; **fitted ~** moqueta f. <> vt [fit with carpet] enmoquetar.

carpetbagger ['kɑːpɪtˌbæɡə'] n [politician] candidato m, -ta f cunero(ra).

carpet slipper n zapatilla f.

carpet sweeper [-'swiːpə'] n cepillo m mecánico (de alfombras).

car phone n teléfono m de coche.

car radio n radio f de coche.

car rental n US alquiler m OR renta f Méx de coches, arrendamiento m de autos.

carriage ['kærɪdʒ] n - 1. [horsedrawn vehicle] carruaje m - 2. UK [railway coach] vagón m - 3. [transport of goods] transporte m; **~ paid** OR **free** UK porte pagado - 4. [on typewriter] carro m.

carriage return n retorno m de carro.

carriageway ['kærɪdʒweɪ] n UK calzada f.

carrier ['kærɪə'] n - 1. COMM transportista m OR f - 2. [airline] aerolínea f - 3. [of disease] portador m, -ra f - 4. = carrier bag.

carrier bag n bolsa f (de papel o plástico).

carrot ['kærət] n - 1. [vegetable] zanahoria f - 2. inf [incentive] aliciente m.

carry ['kærɪ] (pt & pp -ied) <> vt - 1. [transport] llevar - 2. [have about one's person] llevar encima - 3. [disease] ser portador de - 4. [involve] acarrear, conllevar - 5. [motion, proposal] aprobar - 6. [be pregnant with] estar embarazada de - 7. MATH llevarse. <> vi [sound] oírse.
◆ **carry away** vt fus: **to get carried away** exaltarse.
◆ **carry forward** vt sep llevar a la página siguiente.
◆ **carry off** vt sep - 1. [make a success of] llevar a cabo - 2. [win] llevarse.
◆ **carry on** <> vt fus - 1. [continue] continuar, seguir; **to ~ on doing sthg** continuar OR seguir haciendo algo - 2. [conversation] mantener. <> vi - 1. [continue]: **to ~ on (with)** continuar OR seguir (con) - 2. inf [make a fuss] exagerar la nota.
◆ **carry out** vt fus - 1. [perform] llevar a cabo - 2. [fulfil] cumplir.

◆ **carry through** vt sep [accomplish] llevar a cabo.

carryall ['kærɔ:l] n US bolsa f de viaje.

carrycot ['kærɪkɒt] n esp UK moisés m, capazo m.

carry-out n US & Scot comida f para llevar.

carsick ['kɑːˌsɪk] adj mareado(da) (al ir en coche).

cart [kɑːt] ◇ n -1. [for horse] carro m, carreta f -2. US [trolley] carrito m. ◇ vt inf acarrear.

carton ['kɑːtn] n -1. [strong cardboard box] caja f de cartón -2. [for liquids] cartón m, envase m.

cartoon [kɑːˈtuːn] n -1. [satirical drawing] chiste m (en viñeta) -2. [comic strip] tira f cómica -3. [film] dibujos mpl animados.

cartridge ['kɑːtrɪdʒ] n -1. [for gun, camera & COMPUT] cartucho m -2. [for pen] recambio m.

cartwheel ['kɑːtwiːl] n voltereta f lateral.

carve [kɑːv] ◇ vt -1. [wood] tallar; [stone] esculpir -2. [meat] trinchar -3. [name, message] grabar. ◇ vi trinchar.

◆ **carve out** vt sep [niche, place] conquistar.

◆ **carve up** vt sep repartir.

carving ['kɑːvɪŋ] n -1. [art, work - wooden] tallado m; [- stone] labrado m, cincelado m -2. [object - wooden, stone] talla f.

carving knife n cuchillo m de trinchar.

car wash n lavado m de coches.

case [keɪs] n -1. [gen & GRAMM] caso m; to be the ~ ser el caso; in that/which ~ en ese/cuyo caso; as OR whatever the ~ may be según sea el caso; in ~ of en caso de -2. [argument] argumentos mpl; the ~ for/against (sthg) los argumentos a favor/en contra (de algo) -3. JUR [trial, inquiry] pleito m, causa f -4. [container - of leather] funda f; [- of hard material] estuche m -5. UK [suitcase] maleta f, petaca f Méx, valija f RP.

◆ **in any case** adv en cualquier caso, de todas formas.

◆ **in case** conj & adv por si acaso; in ~ she doesn't come por si no viene.

cash [kæʃ] ◇ n -1. [notes and coins] (dinero m) efectivo m, metálico m; to pay (in) ~ pagar al contado OR en efectivo -2. inf [money] dinero m, plata f Amér -3. [payment]: ~ in advance pago m al contado por adelantado; ~ on delivery entrega f contra reembolso. ◇ vt cobrar, hacer efectivo.

◆ **cash in** vi: to ~ in on inf sacar partido de.

cash and carry n almacén de venta al por mayor.

cashbook ['kæʃbʊk] n libro m de caja.

cash box n caja f con cerradura (para el dinero).

cash card n esp US tarjeta f de cajero automático.

cash desk n UK caja f.

cash dispenser [-dɪˈspensəʳ] n esp US cajero m automático.

cashew (nut) ['kæʃuː-] n (nuez f de) anacardo m.

cashier [kæˈʃɪəʳ] n cajero m, -ra f.

cash machine = cash dispenser.

cashmere [kæʃˈmɪəʳ] n cachemira f.

cashpoint ['kæʃpɔɪnt] = cash dispenser.

cash register n caja f (registradora).

casing ['keɪsɪŋ] n [of electric cable] revestimiento m.

casino [kəˈsiːnəʊ] (pl -s) n casino m.

cask [kɑːsk] n tonel m, barril m.

casket ['kɑːskɪt] n -1. [for jewels] estuche m -2. US [coffin] ataúd m.

casserole ['kæsərəʊl] n -1. [stew] guiso m -2. [pan] cazuela f, cacerola f.

cassette [kæˈset] n cinta f, casete f.

cassette player n casete m, magnetófono m.

cassette recorder n casete m, magnetófono m.

cast [kɑːst] (pt & pp cast) ◇ n [of play, film] reparto m. ◇ vt -1. [look] echar, lanzar; to ~ doubt on sthg poner algo en duda -2. [light] irradiar; [shadow] proyectar -3. [throw] arrojar, lanzar -4. [choose for play]: to ~ sb as asignar a alguien el papel de -5. [vote] emitir -6. [metal, statue] fundir.

◆ **cast off** vi NAUT soltar amarras.

castanets [ˌkæstəˈnets] npl castañuelas fpl.

castaway ['kɑːstəweɪ] n náufrago m, -ga f.

caste [kɑːst] n casta f.

caster ['kɑːstəʳ] n [wheel] ruedecilla f.

caster sugar n UK azúcar m extrafino.

Castile [kæsˈtiːl] n Castilla.

casting vote ['kɑːstɪŋ-] n voto m de calidad.

cast iron n hierro m fundido.

castle ['kɑːsl] n -1. [building] castillo m -2. [in chess] torre f.

castor ['kɑːstəʳ] = caster.

castor oil n aceite m de ricino.

castor sugar = caster sugar.

castrate [kæˈstreɪt] vt castrar.

casual ['kæʒʊəl] adj -1. [relaxed, indifferent] despreocupado(da) -2. pej [offhand] descuidado(da), informal -3. [chance - visitor] ocasional; [- remark] casual -4. [informal - clothes] de sport, informal -5. [irregular - labourer etc] eventual.

casually ['kæʒʊəlɪ] adv -1. [in a relaxed manner, indifferently] con aire despreocupado -2. [informally] informalmente.

casual sex n relaciones fpl sexuales ocasionales.

casualty

casualty ['kæʒjʊəltɪ] (*pl* **-ies**) *n* **-1.** [gen] víctima *f*; MIL baja *f* **- 2.** (*U*) [ward] urgencias *fpl*.

casualty department *n* unidad *f* de urgencias.

cat [kæt] *n* **-1.** [domestic] gato *m*, -ta *f* **- 2.** [wild] felino *m*.

Catalan ['kætə,læn] ◇ *adj* catalán(ana). ◇ *n* **-1.** [person] catalán *m*, -ana *f* **- 2.** [language] catalán *m*.

catalogue UK, **catalog** US ['kætəlɒg] ◇ *n* **-1.** [of items] catálogo *m* **- 2.** *fig* [series] serie *f.* ◇ *vt* **-1.** [make official list of] catalogar **- 2.** *fig* [list] enumerar.

Catalonia [,kætə'ləʊnɪə] *n* Cataluña.

Catalonian [,kætə'ləʊnɪən] ◇ *adj* catalán(ana). ◇ *n* [person] catalán *m*, -ana *f*.

catalyst ['kætəlɪst] *n lit* & *fig* catalizador *m*.

catalytic convertor [,kætə'lɪtɪk kən'vɜːtə'] *n* catalizador *m*.

catapult ['kætəpʊlt] *n* UK **-1.** HIST [handheld] tirachinas *m inv* **- 2.** HIST [machine] catapulta *f.*

cataract ['kætərækt] *n* [waterfall, in eye] catarata *f.*

catarrh [kə'tɑː'] *n* (*U*) catarro *m*.

catastrophe [kə'tæstrəfɪ] *n* catástrofe *f.*

catch [kætʃ] (*pt* & *pp* **caught**) ◇ *vt* **-1.** [gen]. coger, agarrar *Amér*; [ball] atrapar **- 2.** [fish] pescar; [stop - person] parar **- 3.** [be in time for]: **I've got a train to** ~ tengo que coger un tren; **to** ~ **the (last) post** UK llegar a la (última) recogida del correo **- 4.** [hear clearly] entender, llegar a oír **- 5.** [interest, imagination] despertar **- 6.** [see]: **to** ~ **sight** OR **a glimpse of** alcanzar a ver **- 7.** [hook - shirt etc] engancharse; [shut in door - finger] pillarse **- 8.** [strike] golpear. ◇ *vi* **-1.** [become hooked, get stuck] engancharse **- 2.** [start to burn] prenderse, encenderse. ◇ *n* **-1.** [of ball etc] parada *f* **- 2.** [of fish] pesca *f*, captura *f* **- 3.** [fastener - on door] pestillo *m*; [- on necklace] cierre *m* **- 4.** [snag] trampa *f.*

  ◆ catch on *vi* **-1.** [become popular] hacerse popular **- 2.** *inf* [understand]: **to** ~ **on (to)** caer en la cuenta (de).

  ◆ catch out *vt sep* [trick] pillar.

  ◆ catch up ◇ *vt sep* alcanzar. ◇ *vi*: **we'll soon** ~ **up** pronto nos pondremos a la misma altura; **to** ~ **up on** [sleep] recuperar; [work, reading] ponerse al día con.

  ◆ catch up with *vt fus* **-1.** [group etc] alcanzar **- 2.** [criminal] pillar, descubrir.

catching ['kætʃɪŋ] *adj* contagioso(sa).

catchment area ['kætʃmənt-] *n* UK zona *f* de captación.

catchphrase ['kætʃfreɪz] *n* muletilla *f.*

catchy ['kætʃɪ] (*compar* **-ier**, *superl* **-iest**) *adj* pegadizo(za).

categorically [,kætɪ'gɒrɪklɪ] *adv* [state]

categóricamente; [deny] rotundamente.

category ['kætəgərɪ] (*pl* **-ies**) *n* categoría *f.*

cater ['keɪtə'] ◇ *vi* proveer comida. ◇ *vt* US [party, event] dar el servicio de comida y bebida de.

  ◆ cater for *vt fus* UK [tastes, needs] atender a; [social group] estar destinado(da) a; **I hadn't** ~ **ed for that** no había contado con eso.

  ◆ cater to *vt fus* complacer.

caterer ['keɪtərə'] *n* [firm] empresa *f* de hostelería.

catering ['keɪtərɪŋ] *n* [at wedding etc] servicio *m* de banquetes; [trade] hostelería *f.*

caterpillar ['kætəpɪlə'] *n* oruga *f.*

caterpillar tracks *npl* (rodado *m* de) oruga *f.*

cathedral [kə'θiːdrəl] *n* catedral *f.*

Catholic ['kæθlɪk] ◇ *adj* católico(ca). ◇ *n* católico *m*, -ca *f.*

  ◆ catholic *adj* diverso(sa), variado(da).

Catseyes® ['kætsaɪz] *npl* UK cataforas *mpl*.

cattle ['kætl] *npl* ganado *m* (vacuno).

catty ['kætɪ] (*compar* **-ier**, *superl* **-iest**) *adj inf pej* [spiteful] malintencionado(da).

catwalk ['kætwɔːk] *n* pasarela *f.*

caucus ['kɔːkəs] *n* [political group] comité *m*.

  ◆ Caucus *n* US *congreso de los principales partidos estadounidenses.*

caught [kɔːt] *pt* & *pp* ▷ **catch**.

cauliflower ['kɒlɪˌflaʊə'] *n* coliflor *f.*

cause [kɔːz] ◇ *n* **-1.** [gen] causa *f* **- 2.** [grounds]: ~ **(for)** motivo *m* (para); ~ **for complaint** motivo de queja; ~ **to do** sthg motivo para hacer algo. ◇ *vt* causar; **to** ~ **sb to do sthg** hacer que alguien haga algo.

caustic ['kɔːstɪk] *adj* **-1.** CHEM cáustico(ca) **- 2.** [comment] mordaz, hiriente.

caution ['kɔːʃn] ◇ *n* **-1.** (*U*) [care] precaución *f*, cautela *f* **- 2.** [warning] advertencia *f*, amonestación *f.* ◇ *vt* **-1.** [warn - against danger] prevenir; [- against behaving rudely etc] advertir, avisar **- 2.** UK [subj: policeman]: **to** ~ **sb (for)** amonestar a alguien (por).

cautious ['kɔːʃəs] *adj* prudente, cauto(ta).

cavalier [,kævə'lɪə'] *adj* arrogante, desdeñoso(sa).

cavalry ['kævlrɪ] *n* caballería *f.*

cave [keɪv] *n* cueva *f.*

  ◆ cave in *vi* [roof, ceiling] hundirse, derrumbarse.

caveman ['keɪvmæn] (*pl* **-men** [-men]) *n* cavernícola *m* OR *f*, hombre *m* de las cavernas.

caviar(e) ['kævɪɑː'] *n* caviar *m*.

cavity ['kævətɪ] (*pl* **-ies**) *n* **-1.** [in object, structure] cavidad *f* **- 2.** [in tooth] caries *f inv*.

cavort [kə'vɔːt] *vi* retozar, brincar.

CB *n abbr of* **citizens' band.**

CBI *abbr of* **Confederation of British Industry.**

cc ⋄ *n* (*abbr of* **cubic centimetre**) cc. ⋄ (*abbr of* **carbon copy**) cc.

CD *n* (*abbr of* **compact disc**) CD *m*.

CD burner *n* grabadora *f* de CD.

CD player *n* reproductor *m* de CD.

CD-R (*abbr of* **compact disc recordable**) *n* CD-R *m*.

CD-R drive *n* grabadora *f* de CD-R.

CD rewriter ['si:di:'ri:ˌraɪtə] = **CD-RW drive.**

CD-ROM [ˌsiːdiːˈrɒm] (*abbr of* **compact disc read only memory**) *n* CD-ROM *m*.

CD-ROM burner *n* estampadora *f* de CD.

CD-ROM drive *n* unidad *f* de CD-ROM.

CD-RW (*abbr of* **compact disc rewritable**) *n* CD-RW *m*.

CD-RW drive *n* grabadora *f* de CD-RW.

CD single *n* CD *m* sencillo.

CD tower *n* torre *f* de almacenamiento de CDs.

cease [siːs] *fml* ⋄ *vt* cesar; **to ~ doing** OR **to do sthg** dejar de hacer algo. ⋄ *vi* cesar.

cease-fire *n* alto *m* el fuego.

ceaseless ['siːslɪs] *adj fml* incesante.

cedar (tree) ['siːdə˚] *n* cedro *m*.

ceiling ['siːlɪŋ] *n* - **1.** [of room] techo *m* - **2.** [limit] tope *m*, límite *m*.

celebrate ['selɪbreɪt] ⋄ *vt* celebrar. ⋄ *vi* celebrarlo.

celebrated ['selɪbreɪtɪd] *adj* célebre, famoso(sa).

celebration [ˌselɪˈbreɪʃn] *n* - **1.** (*U*) [activity, feeling] celebración *f* - **2.** [event] fiesta *f*, festejo *m*.

celebrity [sɪ'lebrətɪ] (*pl* -**ies**) *n* celebridad *f*.

celery ['selərɪ] *n* apio *m*.

celibate ['selɪbət] *adj* célibe.

cell [sel] *n* - **1.** BIOL & POL célula *f* - **2.** COMPUT celda *f* - **3.** [prisoner's, nun's or monk's room] celda *f*, separo *m* *Amér.* - **4.** ELEC pila *f*.

cellar ['selə˚] *n* - **1.** [basement] sótano *m* - **2.** [stock of wine] bodega *f*.

cello ['tʃeləʊ] (*pl* -**s**) *n* violoncelo *m*.

Cellophane® ['seləfeɪn] *n* celofán® *m*.

Celsius ['selsɪəs] *adj* centígrado(da); **20 degrees ~** 20 grados centígrados.

Celt [kelt] *n* celta *m* OR *f*.

Celtic ['keltɪk] ⋄ *adj* celta, céltico(ca). ⋄ *n* celta *m*.

cement [sɪ'ment] ⋄ *n* - **1.** [for concrete] cemento *m* - **2.** [glue] cola *f*, pegamento *m*. ⋄ *vt* - **1.** [glue] encolar - **2.** [agreement, relationship] cimentar, fortalecer.

cement mixer *n* hormigonera *f*.

cemetery ['semɪtrɪ] (*pl* -**ies**) *n* cementerio *m*.

censor ['sensə˚] ⋄ *n* censor *m*, -ra *f*. ⋄ *vt* censurar.

censorship ['sensəʃɪp] *n* censura *f*.

censure ['senʃə˚] *vt* censurar.

census ['sensəs] (*pl* -**uses**) *n* censo *m*.

cent [sent] *n* centavo *m*.

centenary *UK* [sen'tiːnərɪ] (*pl* -**ies**), **centennial** *US* [sen'tenjəl] *n* centenario *m*.

center *US* = **centre.**

centigrade ['sentɪgreɪd] *adj* centígrado(da); **20 degrees ~** 20 grados centígrados.

centilitre *UK*, **centiliter** *US* ['sentɪˌliːtə˚] *n* centilitro *m*.

centimetre *UK*, **centimeter** *US* ['sentɪˌmiːtə˚] *n* centímetro *m*.

centipede ['sentɪpiːd] *n* ciempiés *m inv.*

central ['sentrəl] *adj* - **1.** [gen] central; **in ~ Spain** en el centro de España - **2.** [easily reached] céntrico(ca).

Central America *n* Centroamérica.

Central Europe *n* Europa Central.

central heating *n* calefacción *f* central.

centralize, -ise ['sentrəlaɪz] *vt* centralizar.

central locking [-'lɒkɪŋ] *n* cierre *m* centralizado.

central reservation *n UK* mediana *f*.

centre *UK*, **center** *US* ['sentə˚] ⋄ *n* centro *m*; **the ~** POL el centro. ⋄ *adj* - **1.** [middle] central - **2.** POL centrista. ⋄ *vt* centrar.

centre back *n* defensa *m* OR *f* central.

centre forward *n* delantero *m*, -ra *f* centro (*inv*).

centre half = **centre back.**

century ['sentʃʊrɪ] (*pl* -**ies**) *n* siglo *m*.

ceramic [sɪ'ræmɪk] *adj* de cerámica, cerámico(ca).

➜ **ceramics** *n* cerámica *f*.

cereal ['sɪərɪəl] *n* - **1.** [crop] cereal *m* - **2.** [breakfast food] cereales *mpl*.

ceremonial [ˌserɪ'məʊnjəl] *adj* ceremonial.

ceremony ['serɪmənɪ] (*pl* -**ies**) *n* ceremonia *f*; **to stand on ~** andarse con cumplidos OR ceremonias.

certain ['sɜːtn] *adj* - **1.** [gen] seguro(ra); **he's ~ to be late** (es) seguro que llega tarde; **to be ~ (of)** estar seguro (de); **to make ~ (of)** asegurarse (de); **for ~** con toda seguridad - **2.** [particular, some] cierto(ta); **to a ~ extent** hasta cierto punto - **3.** [named person]: **a ~ ...** un (una) tal ...

certainly ['sɜːtnlɪ] *adv* desde luego; **~ not!** ¡claro que no!

certainty ['sɜːtntɪ] (*pl* -**ies**) *n* seguridad *f*.

certificate [sə'tɪfɪkət] *n* [gen] certificado *m*; SCH & UNIV diploma *m*, título *m*; [of birth, death] partida *f*.

certified ['sɜːtɪfaɪd] *adj* [document] certificado(da); [person] diplomado(da).

certified mail *n US* correo *m* certificado.

certified public accountant *n US* contable diplomado *m*, contable diplomada *f*, contador público *m*, contadora pública *f Amér.*

certify ['sɜːtɪfaɪ] (*pt & pp* **-ied**) *vt* **- 1.** [declare true] certificar **- 2.** [declare insane] declarar demente.

cervical [sə'vaɪkl] *adj* cervical.

cervical smear *n* citología *f*, frotis *f* cervical.

cervix ['sɜːvɪks] (*pl* **-ices** [-ɪsiːz]) *n* [of womb] cuello *m* del útero.

cesarean (section) *US* = caesarean (section).

cesspit ['sespɪt], **cesspool** ['sespuːl] *n* pozo *m* negro.

cf. (*abbr of* **confer**) cf., cfr.

CFC (*abbr of* **chlorofluorocarbon**) *n* CFC *m*.

CGI (*abbr of* **computer-generated images**) *n* imágenes *fpl* generadas por ordenador.

Chad [tʃæd] *n* el Chad.

chafe [tʃeɪf] *vt* [rub] rozar.

chaffinch ['tʃæfɪntʃ] *n* pinzón *m*.

chain [tʃeɪn] ◇ *n* cadena *f*; ~ **of mountains** cordillera *f*, cadena *f* montañosa; ~ **of events** serie *f* OR cadena *f* de acontecimientos. ◇ *vt* [person, object] encadenar.

chain reaction *n* reacción *f* en cadena.

chain saw *n* motosierra *f*, sierra *f* mecánica.

chain-smoke *vi* fumar un cigarrillo tras otro.

chain store *n* tienda *f* (*de una cadena*).

chair [tʃeə'] ◇ *n* **- 1.** [gen] silla *f*; [armchair] sillón *m* **- 2.** [university post] cátedra *f* **- 3.** [of meeting] presidencia *f*. ◇ *vt* presidir.

chair lift *n* telesilla *m*.

chairman ['tʃeəmən] (*pl* **-men** [-mən]) *n* presidente *m*.

chairperson ['tʃeə,pɜːsn] (*pl* **-s**) *n* presidente *m*, -ta *f*.

chalet ['ʃæleɪ] *n* chalé *m*, chalet *m*.

chalk [tʃɔːk] *n* **- 1.** [for drawing] tiza *f*, gis *m* *Méx* **- 2.** [type of rock] creta *f*.

chalkboard ['tʃɔːkbɔːd] *n* *US* pizarra *f*, encerado *m*.

challenge ['tʃælɪndʒ] ◇ *n* desafío *m*, reto *m*. ◇ *vt* **- 1.** [to fight, competition]: **to** ~ **sb (to sthg/to do sthg)** desafiar a alguien (a algo/a que haga algo) **- 2.** [question] poner en tela de juicio.

challenging ['tʃælɪndʒɪŋ] *adj* **- 1.** [task, job] estimulante, que supone un reto **- 2.** [look, tone of voice] desafiante.

chamber ['tʃeɪmbə'] *n* [room] cámara *f*.

chambermaid ['tʃeɪmbəmeɪd] *n* [at hotel] camarera *f*.

chamber music *n* música *f* de cámara.

chamber of commerce *n* cámara *f* de comercio.

chameleon [kə'miːljən] *n* camaleón *m*.

champagne [,ʃæm'peɪn] *n* champán *m*.

champion ['tʃæmpjən] ◇ *n* **- 1.** [of competition] campeón *m*, -ona *f* **- 2.** [of cause] defensor *m*, -ra *f*. ◇ *vt* defender.

championship ['tʃæmpjənʃɪp] *n* campeonato *m*.

chance [tʃɑːns] ◇ *n* **- 1.** [luck] azar *m*, suerte *f*; **by** ~ por casualidad **- 2.** [likelihood] posibilidad *f*; **not to stand a** ~ **(of)** no tener ninguna posibilidad (de); **by any** ~ por casualidad, acaso **- 3.** [opportunity] oportunidad *f* **- 4.** [risk] riesgo *m*; **to take a** ~ **(on)** correr un riesgo OR arriesgarse (con). ◇ *adj* fortuito(ta), casual. ◇ *vt* arriesgar; **to** ~ **it** arriesgarse.

chancellor ['tʃɑːnsələ'] *n* **- 1.** [chief minister] canciller *m* **- 2.** *US UNIV* ≃ rector *m*, -ra *f*.

Chancellor of the Exchequer *n* *UK* Ministro *m*, -tra *f* de Economía y Hacienda.

chandelier [,ʃændə'lɪə'] *n* (lámpara *f* de) araña *f*, candil *m* *Méx*.

change [tʃeɪndʒ] ◇ *n* **- 1.** [gen] cambio *m*; ~ **of clothes** muda *f*; **for a** ~ para variar **- 2.** [from payment] vuelta *f*, cambio *m*, vuelto *m* *Amér* **- 3.** [coins] suelto *m*, calderilla *f*, sencillo *m* *Andes*, feria *f* *Méx*, menudo *m* *Col* **- 4.** [money in exchange]: **have you got** ~ **for £5?** ¿tienes cambio de 5 libras? ◇ *vt* **- 1.** [gen] cambiar; **to** ~ **sthg into** transformar algo en; **to** ~ **pounds into euros** cambiar libras en *Esp* OR a euros; **to** ~ **direction** cambiar de rumbo; **to** ~ **one's mind** cambiar de idea OR opinión **- 2.** [goods in shop] cambiar **- 3.** [switch - job, gear, train] cambiar de; **to** ~ **one's shirt** cambiarse de camisa; **to get** ~**d** cambiarse de ropa. ◇ *vi* **- 1.** [alter] cambiar; **to** ~ **into sthg** transformarse en algo **- 2.** [change clothes] cambiarse **- 3.** [change trains, buses] hacer transbordo.

➡ **change over** *vi* [convert]: **to** ~ **over to** cambiar a.

changeable ['tʃeɪndʒəbl] *adj* variable.

change machine *n* máquina *f* de cambio.

changeover ['tʃeɪndʒ,əʊvə'] *n*: ~ **(to)** cambio *m* (a).

changing ['tʃeɪndʒɪŋ] *adj* cambiante.

changing room *n* **- 1.** SPORT vestuario *m* **- 2.** [in clothes shop] probador *m*.

channel ['tʃænl] (*UK pt & pp* **-led**, *cont* **-ling**, *US pt & pp* **-ed**, *cont* **-ing**) ◇ *n* canal *m*. ◇ *vt lit & fig* canalizar.

➡ **Channel** *n*: **the (English) Channel** el Canal de la Mancha.

➡ **channels** *npl* [procedure] conductos *mpl*, medios *mpl*.

Channel Islands *npl*: **the** ~ las islas del canal de la Mancha.

Channel tunnel *n*: **the** ~ el túnel del Canal de la Mancha.

chant [tʃɑːnt] ◇ *n* **- 1.** RELIG canto *m* **- 2.** [of demonstrators] consigna *f*; [at sports match] cántico *m*. ◇ *vt* **- 1.** RELIG cantar **- 2.** [words] corear.

chaos ['keɪɒs] *n* caos *m inv.*

chaotic [keɪˈɒtɪk] *adj* caótico(ca).

chap [tʃæp] *n UK inf* tipo *m*, tío *m*.

chapel ['tʃæpl] *n* capilla *f*.

chaperon(e) ['ʃæpərəʊn] ⬦ *n* carabina *f*, acompañanta *f*. ⬦ *vt* acompañar.

chaplain ['tʃæplɪn] *n* capellán *m*.

chapped [tʃæpt] *adj* agrietado(da).

chapter ['tʃæptəʳ] *n lit & fig* capítulo *m*.

char [tʃɑːʳ] (*pt & pp* -**red**, *cont* -**ring**) ⬦ *n UK* [cleaner] mujer *f* de la limpieza. ⬦ *vt* [burn] carbonizar, calcinar.

character ['kærəktəʳ] *n* -**1.** [nature, quality, letter] carácter *m* -**2.** [in film, book, play] personaje *m* -**3.** *inf* [person of stated kind] tipo *m* -**4.** *inf* [person with strong personality]: **to be a ~** ser todo un carácter.

characteristic [ˌkærəktəˈrɪstɪk] ⬦ *adj* característico(ca). ⬦ *n* característica *f*.

characterize, -ise ['kærəktəraɪz] *vt* -**1.** [typify] caracterizar -**2.** [portray]: **to ~ sthg as** definir algo como.

charade [ʃəˈrɑːd] *n* farsa *f*.
  ➡ **charades** *n* (U) charadas *fpl*.

charcoal ['tʃɑːkəʊl] *n* [for barbecue etc] carbón *m* (vegetal); [for drawing] carboncillo *m*.

charge [tʃɑːdʒ] ⬦ *n* -**1.** [cost] precio *m*; **free of ~** gratis; **will that be cash or ~?** *US* ¿pagará en efectivo o con tarjeta? -**2.** JUR cargo *m*, acusación *f* -**3.** [responsibility]: **to have ~ of sthg** tener algo al cargo de uno; **to take ~ (of)** hacerse cargo (de); **to be in ~** ser el encargado (la encargada); **in ~ of** encargado(da) de -**4.** ELEC carga *f* -**5.** MIL [of cavalry] carga *f*. ⬦ *vt* -**1.** [customer, sum] cobrar; **to ~ sthg to sb** cargar algo en la cuenta de alguien -**2.** [suspect, criminal]: **to ~ sb (with)** acusar a alguien (de) -**3.** [attack] cargar contra -**4.** [battery] cargar. ⬦ *vi* [rush] cargar; **to ~ in/out** entrar/salir en tromba.

charge card *n* tarjeta *f* de compra.

charger ['tʃɑːdʒəʳ] *n* [for batteries] cargador *m*.

chariot ['tʃærɪət] *n* carro *m*, cuadriga *f*.

charisma [kəˈrɪzmə] *n* carisma *m*.

charitable ['tʃærɪtəbl] *adj* -**1.** [person, remark] caritativo(va) -**2.** [organization] benéfico(ca).

charity ['tʃærɪtɪ] (*pl* -**ies**) *n* -**1.** [kindness, money] caridad *f* -**2.** [organization] institución *f* benéfica.

charity shop *n UK* tienda de una entidad benéfica en la que se venden productos de segunda mano donados por simpatizantes.

charm [tʃɑːm] ⬦ *n* -**1.** [appeal, attractiveness] encanto *m* -**2.** [spell] hechizo *m* -**3.** [on bracelet] dije *m*, amuleto *m*. ⬦ *vt* dejar encantado(da).

charming ['tʃɑːmɪŋ] *adj* encantador(ra).

chart [tʃɑːt] ⬦ *n* -**1.** [diagram] gráfico *m* -**2.** [map] carta *f*. ⬦ *vt* -**1.** [plot, map] representar en un mapa -**2.** *fig* [describe] trazar.
  ➡ **charts** *npl*: **the ~s** la lista de éxitos.

charter ['tʃɑːtəʳ] ⬦ *n* [document] carta *f*. ⬦ *comp* chárter *(inv)*, alquilado(da). ⬦ *vt* [plane, boat] fletar.

chartered accountant ['tʃɑːtəd-] *n UK* contable colegiado *m*, contable colegiada *f*, contador colegiado *m*, contadora colegiada *f Amér.*

charter flight *n* vuelo *m* chárter.

chase [tʃeɪs] ⬦ *n* [pursuit] persecución *f*. ⬦ *vt* -**1.** [pursue] perseguir -**2.** [drive away] ahuyentar -**3.** [money, jobs] ir detrás de, ir a la caza de.

chasm ['kæzm] *n* [deep crack] sima *f*; *fig* [divide] abismo *m*.

chassis ['ʃæsɪ] (*pl inv*) *n* [of vehicle] chasis *m inv.*

chaste [tʃeɪst] *adj* casto(ta).

chat [tʃæt] (*pt & pp* -**ted**, *cont* -**ting**) ⬦ *n* [gen & COMPUT] charla *f*, conversación *f Amér*, plática *f CAm, Méx.* ⬦ *vi* [gen & COMPUT] charlar.
  ➡ **chat up** *vt sep UK inf* intentar ligar con, tirarse un lance con *CSur.*

chatiquette ['tʃætɪket] *n* COMPUT etiqueta *f* en los chats.

chat line *n* línea *f* compartida.

chat room *n* COMPUT sala *f* de conversación.

chatter ['tʃætəʳ] ⬦ *n* -**1.** [of person] cháchara *f*, parloteo *m* -**2.** [of bird] gorjeo *m*; [of monkey] chillidos *mpl*. ⬦ *vi* -**1.** [person] parlotear -**2.** [teeth] castañetear.

chatterbox ['tʃætəbɒks] *n inf* parlanchín *m*, -ina *f*.

chatty ['tʃætɪ] (*compar* -**ier**, *superl* -**iest**) *adj* -**1.** [person] dicharachero(ra) -**2.** [letter] informal.

chauffeur ['ʃəʊfəʳ] *n* chófer *m OR f*.

chauvinist ['ʃəʊvɪnɪst] *n* -**1.** [sexist] sexista *m OR f*; **male ~** machista *m* -**2.** [nationalist] chovinista *m OR f*.

cheap [tʃiːp] ⬦ *adj* -**1.** [inexpensive] barato(ta) -**2.** [low-quality] de mala calidad -**3.** [vulgar-joke etc] de mal gusto -**4.** *US* [stingy] mezquino(na). ⬦ *adv* barato.

cheapen ['tʃiːpn] *vt* [degrade] rebajar, degradar.

cheaply ['tʃiːplɪ] *adv* barato.

cheat [tʃiːt] ⬦ *n* tramposo *m*, -sa *f*. ⬦ *vt* engañar, estafar; **to ~ sb out of sthg** estafar algo a alguien. ⬦ *vi* [in exam] copiar; [at cards] hacer trampas.

check [tʃek] ⬦ *n* -**1.** [inspection, test]: **~ (on)** inspección *f OR* control *m* (de); **to keep a ~ on** controlar -**2.** [restraint]: **~ (on)** restricción *f* (en) -**3.** *US* [cheque] cheque *m* -**4.** *US* [bill] cuenta *f*, nota *f*

- 5. *US* [tick] señal *f* de visto bueno **- 6.** [pattern] cuadros *mpl* **- 7.** [in chess] jaque *m*. ◇ *vt* **-1.** [test, verify] comprobar **- 2.** [inspect - machine, product] inspeccionar; [- ticket, passport] revisar, controlar **- 3.** [restrain, stop] refrenar, contener. ◇ *vi* comprobar; **to ~ (for/on sthg)** comprobar (algo).

◆ **check in** ◇ *vt sep* [luggage, coat] facturar, despachar *Amér*. ◇ *vi* **- 1.** [at hotel] inscribirse, registrarse **- 2.** [at airport] facturar.

◆ **check out** ◇ *vt sep* **- 1.** [luggage, coat] recoger **- 2.** [investigate] comprobar **- 3.** *inf* [look at] mirar. ◇ *vi* [from hotel] dejar el hotel.

◆ **check up** *vi*: **to ~ up (on sthg)** informarse (acerca de algo); **to ~ up on sb** hacer averiguaciones sobre alguien.

checkbook *US* = **chequebook**.

checked [tʃekt] *adj* a cuadros.

checkered *US* = **chequered**.

checkers [ˈtʃekəz] *n US (U)* damas *fpl*.

check-in *n* facturación *f*.

check-in desk *n* mostrador *m* de facturación.

checking account [ˈtʃekɪŋ-] *n US* cuenta *f* corriente.

checkmate [ˈtʃekmeɪt] *n* jaque *m* mate.

checkout [ˈtʃekaʊt] *n* caja *f*.

checkpoint [ˈtʃekpɔɪnt] *n* control *m*.

checkroom [ˈtʃekrʊm] *n US* consigna *f*.

checkup [ˈtʃekʌp] *n* chequeo *m*, revisión *f*.

Cheddar (cheese) [ˈtʃedə^r-] *n* (queso *m*) cheddar *m*.

cheek [tʃiːk] *n* **- 1.** [of face] mejilla *f* **- 2.** *inf* [impudence] cara *f*, descaro *m*.

cheekbone [ˈtʃiːkbəʊn] *n* pómulo *m*.

cheeky [ˈtʃiːkɪ] *(compar* **-ier**, *superl* **-iest)** *adj* descarado(da).

cheer [tʃɪə^r] ◇ *n* [shout] aclamación *f*, grito *m* de entusiasmo; **~s** vítores *mpl*. ◇ *vt* **- 1.** [shout approval, encouragement at] aclamar, vitorear **- 2.** [gladden] animar. ◇ *vi* gritar con entusiasmo.

◆ **cheers** *excl* [when drinking] ¡salud!; *UK inf* [thank you] ¡gracias!; *inf* [goodbye] ¡hasta luego!

◆ **cheer up** ◇ *vt sep* animar. ◇ *vi* animarse.

cheerful [ˈtʃɪəfʊl] *adj* [gen] alegre.

cheerio [ˌtʃɪərɪˈəʊ] *excl UK inf* ¡hasta luego!

cheese [tʃiːz] *n* queso *m*.

cheeseboard [ˈtʃiːzbɔːd] *n* tabla *f* de quesos.

cheeseburger [ˈtʃiːzˌbɜːgə^r] *n* hamburguesa *f* con queso.

cheesecake [ˈtʃiːzkeɪk] *n* pastel *m* OR tarta *f* de queso.

cheetah [ˈtʃiːtə] *n* guepardo *m*, onza *f*.

chef [ʃef] *n* chef *m*, jefe *m* de cocina.

chemical [ˈkemɪkl] ◇ *adj* químico(ca). ◇ *n* sustancia *f* química.

chemist [ˈkemɪst] *n* **- 1.** *UK* [pharmacist] farmacéutico *m*, -ca *f*; **~'s (shop)** farmacia *f* **- 2.** [scientist] químico *m*, -ca *f*.

chemistry [ˈkemɪstrɪ] *n* [science] química *f*.

cheque *UK*, **check** *US* [tʃek] *n* cheque *m*, talón *m*.

chequebook *UK*, **checkbook** *US* [ˈtʃekbʊk] *n* talonario *m* de cheques, chequera *f Amér*.

cheque card *n UK* tarjeta *f* de identificación bancaria.

chequered *UK* [ˈtʃekəd], **checkered** *US* [ˈtʃekərd] *adj* **- 1.** [patterned] a cuadros **- 2.** [varied] lleno(na) de altibajos.

cherish [ˈtʃerɪʃ] *vt* **- 1.** [hope, memory] abrigar, albergar **- 2.** [privilege, right] apreciar **- 3.** [person, thing] tener mucho cariño a.

cherry [ˈtʃerɪ] *(pl* **-ies)** *n* [fruit] cereza *f*; **~ (tree)** cerezo *m*.

chess [tʃes] *n* ajedrez *m*.

chessboard [ˈtʃesbɔːd] *n* tablero *m* de ajedrez.

chessman [ˈtʃesmæn] *(pl* **-men** [-men]), **chess piece** *n* pieza *f (de ajedrez)*.

chest [tʃest] *n* **- 1.** ANAT pecho *m* **- 2.** [box, trunk - gen] arca *f*, cofre *m*; [- for tools] caja *f*.

chestnut [ˈtʃesnʌt] ◇ *adj* [colour] castaño(ña). ◇ *n* [nut] castaña *f*; **~ (tree)** castaño *m*.

chest of drawers *(pl* chests of drawers) *n* cómoda *f*.

chew [tʃuː] *vt* **- 1.** [food] masticar **- 2.** [nails] morderse; [carpet] morder.

◆ **chew up** *vt sep* [food] masticar; [slippers] mordisquear; [tape] destrozar.

chewing gum [ˈtʃuːɪŋ-] *n* chicle *m*, goma *f* de mascar.

chic [ʃiːk] *adj* chic *(inv)*, elegante.

chick [tʃɪk] *n* **- 1.** [baby bird] polluelo *m* **- 2.** *inf* [woman] nena *f*.

chicken [ˈtʃɪkɪn] *n* **- 1.** [bird] gallina *f* **- 2.** [food] pollo *m* **- 3.** *inf* [coward] gallina *m* OR *f*.

◆ **chicken out** *vi inf*: **to ~ out (of sthg/of doing sthg)** rajarse (a la hora de algo/de hacer algo).

chickenpox [ˈtʃɪkɪnpɒks] *n* varicela *f*.

chickpea [ˈtʃɪkpiː] *n* garbanzo *m*.

chicory [ˈtʃɪkərɪ] *n* achicoria *f*.

chief [tʃiːf] ◇ *adj* principal. ◇ *n* jefe *m*, -fa *f*.

Chief Executive *n US* [US president] presidente *m*, -ta *f*.

chief executive officer *n US* [head of company] director *m*, -ra *f* general.

chiefly [ˈtʃiːflɪ] *adv* **- 1.** [mainly] principalmente **- 2.** [especially, above all] por encima de todo.

chiffon ['ʃɪfɒn] *n* gasa *f*.

chilblain ['tʃɪlbleɪn] *n* sabañón *m*.

child [tʃaɪld] (*pl* **children**) *n* **-1.** [boy, girl] niño *m*, -ña *f* **-2.** [son, daughter] hijo *m*, -ja *f*.

child abuse *n* (U) malos tratos o abusos deshonestos a menores.

child benefit *n* (U) UK subsidio pagado a todas las familias por cada hijo.

childbirth ['tʃaɪldbɜːθ] *n* (U) parto *m*.

childcare ['tʃaɪldkeəʳ] *n* cuidado *m* de los niños.

childhood ['tʃaɪldhʊd] *n* infancia *f*, niñez *f*.

childish ['tʃaɪldɪʃ] *adj pej* infantil.

childlike ['tʃaɪldlaɪk] *adj* [person] como un niño; [smile, trust] de niño.

childminder ['tʃaɪld,maɪndəʳ] *n* UK niñera *f* (durante el día).

childproof ['tʃaɪldpruːf] *adj* a prueba de niños.

children ['tʃɪldrən] *pl* ▷ **child**.

children's home *n* hogar *m* infantil.

Chile ['tʃɪlɪ] *n* Chile.

Chilean ['tʃɪlɪən] ◇ *adj* chileno(na). ◇ *n* chileno *m*, -na *f*.

chili ['tʃɪlɪ] = **chilli**.

chill [tʃɪl] ◇ *n* **-1.** [illness] resfriado *m* **-2.** [in temperature]: **there's a ~ in the air** hace un poco de fresco. ◇ *vt* **-1.** [drink, food] (dejar) enfriar **-2.** [person - with cold] enfriar; [- with fear] hacer sentir escalofríos.

➤ **chill out** *vi inf* relajarse.

chilli ['tʃɪlɪ] (*pl* -ies) *n* guindilla *f*, chile *m*, ají *m* Andes, RP.

chilling ['tʃɪlɪŋ] *adj* [frightening] escalofriante.

chilly ['tʃɪlɪ] (*compar* -ier, *superl* -iest) *adj* frío(a).

chime [tʃaɪm] ◇ *n* [of clock] campanada *f*; [of bells] repique *m*. ◇ *vi* [bell] repicar; [clock] sonar.

chimney ['tʃɪmnɪ] *n* chimenea *f*.

chimneypot ['tʃɪmnɪpɒt] *n* cañón *m* de chimenea.

chimneysweep ['tʃɪmnɪswiːp] *n* deshollinador *m*, -ra *f*.

chimp [tʃɪmp], **chimpanzee** [,tʃɪmpən'ziː] *n* chimpancé *m* OR *f*.

chin [tʃɪn] *n* barbilla *f*.

china ['tʃaɪnə] *n* porcelana *f*.

China ['tʃaɪnə] *n* la China.

Chinese [,tʃaɪ'niːz] ◇ *adj* chino(na). ◇ *n* **-1.** [person] chino *m*, -na *f* **-2.** [language] chino *m*. ◇ *npl*: **the ~** los chinos.

Chinese leaves *npl* UK (hojas *fpl* de) col *f* china.

chink [tʃɪŋk] ◇ *n* **-1.** [narrow opening] grieta *f*; [of light] resquicio *m* **-2.** [sound] tintineo *m*. ◇ *vi* tintinear.

chip [tʃɪp] (*pt & pp* **-ped**, *cont* **-ping**) ◇ *n*

-1. UK [fried potato chip] patata *f* frita; US [potato crisp] **patata** *f* **frita** (de bolsa o de churrería) **-2.** [fragment - gen] pedacito *m*; [- of wood] viruta *f*; [- of stone] lasca *f* **-3.** [flaw - in cup, glass] desportilladura *f* **-4.** COMPUT chip *m* **-5.** [token] ficha *f*. ◇ *vt* [damage] desportillar.

➤ **chip in** *vi* **-1.** [pay money] poner dinero **-2.** [in conversation] intervenir.

➤ **chip off** *vt sep* desconchar.

chipboard ['tʃɪpbɔːd] *n* aglomerado *m*.

chip shop *n* UK tienda en la que se vende pescado y patatas fritas.

chiropodist [kɪ'rɒpədɪst] *n* podólogo *m*, -ga *f*, pedicuro *m*, -ra *f*.

chirp [tʃɜːp] *vi* [bird] piar; [insect] chirriar.

chirpy ['tʃɜːpɪ] (*compar* -ier, *superl* -iest) *adj esp* UK *inf* alegre.

chisel ['tʃɪzl] *n* [for wood] formón *m*, escoplo *m*; [for stone] cincel *m*.

chit [tʃɪt] *n* [note] nota *f*.

chitchat ['tʃɪttʃæt] *n* (U) *inf* cháchara *f*.

chivalry ['ʃɪvlrɪ] *n* **-1.** *literary* [of knights] caballería *f* **-2.** [good manners] caballerosidad *f*.

chlorine ['klɔːriːn] *n* cloro *m*.

choc-ice ['tʃɒkaɪs] *n* UK bombón *m* helado.

chock [tʃɒk] *n* cuña *f*, calzo *m*.

chock-a-block, chock-full *adj inf*: **~ (with)** hasta los topes (de).

chocolate ['tʃɒkələt] ◇ *n* **-1.** [food, drink] chocolate *m* **-2.** [sweet] bombón *m*. ◇ *comp* de chocolate.

choice [tʃɔɪs] ◇ *n* **-1.** [gen] elección *f*; **to have no ~ but to do sthg** no tener más remedio que hacer algo **-2.** [person chosen] preferido *m*, -da *f*; [thing chosen] alternativa *f* preferida **-3.** [variety, selection] surtido *m*. ◇ *adj* de primera calidad.

choir ['kwaɪəʳ] *n* coro *m*.

choirboy ['kwaɪəbɔɪ] *n* niño *m* de coro.

choke [tʃəʊk] ◇ *n* AUT estárter *m*. ◇ *vt* **-1.** [subj: person] estrangular, ahogar **-2.** [subj: fumes] asfixiar, ahogar; [subj: fishbone etc] hacer atragantarse **-3.** [block - pipes, gutter] atascar. ◇ *vi* [on fishbone etc] atragantarse; [to death] asfixiarse.

cholera ['kɒlərə] *n* cólera *m*.

choose [tʃuːz] (*pt* **chose**, *pp* **chosen**) ◇ *vt* **-1.** [select] elegir, escoger **-2.** [decide]: **to ~ to do sthg** decidir hacer algo; **do whatever you ~** haz lo que quieras. ◇ *vi* elegir, escoger.

choos(e)y ['tʃuːzɪ] (*compar* -ier, *superl* -iest) *adj* [gen] quisquilloso(sa); [about food] exigente, remilgado(da).

chop [tʃɒp] (*pt & pp* **-ped**, *cont* **-ping**) ◇ *n* **-1.** CULIN chuleta *f* **-2.** [blow - with axe] hachazo *m*. ◇ *vt* [vegetables, meat] picar; [wood] cortar. ◇ *vi*: **to ~ and change** cambiar cada dos por tres.

➡ **chops** *npl inf* morros *mpl*, jeta *f.*

➡ **chop down** *vt sep* talar.

➡ **chop up** *vt sep* [vegetables, meat] picar; [wood] cortar.

chopper ['tʃɒpə'] *n* - **1.** [for wood] hacha *f*; [for meat] cuchillo *m* de carnicero - **2.** *inf* [helicopter] helicóptero *m.*

choppy ['tʃɒpɪ] (*compar* -**ier**, *superl* -**iest**) *adj* picado(da).

chopsticks ['tʃɒpstɪks] *npl* palillos *mpl.*

chord [kɔːd] *n* MUS acorde *m.*

chore [tʃɔː'] *n* - **1.** [task] tarea *f*, faena *f* - **2.** *inf* [boring thing] lata *f.*

chortle ['tʃɔːtl] *vi* reírse con satisfacción.

chorus ['kɔːrəs] *n* - **1.** [part of song, refrain] estribillo *m* - **2.** [choir, group of singers or dancers] coro *m.*

chose [tʃəʊz] *pt* ▷ **choose.**

chosen ['tʃəʊzn] *pp* ▷ **choose.**

Christ [kraɪst] *n* Cristo *m.*

christen ['krɪsn] *vt* bautizar.

christening ['krɪsnɪŋ] *n* bautizo *m.*

Christian ['krɪstʃən] ◇ *adj* cristiano(na). ◇ *n* cristiano *m*, -na *f.*

Christianity [,krɪstɪ'ænətɪ] *n* cristianismo *m.*

Christian name *n* nombre *m* de pila.

Christmas ['krɪsməs] *n* Navidad *f*; **happy** OR **merry** ~ ! ¡Feliz Navidad!

Christmas card *n* crismas *m inv*, christmas *m inv.*

Christmas carol *n* villancico *m.*

Christmas Day *n* día *m* de Navidad.

Christmas Eve *n* Nochebuena *f.*

Christmas pudding *n* UK *pudín de frutas que se come caliente el día de Navidad.*

Christmas tree *n* árbol *m* de Navidad.

chrome [krəʊm], **chromium** ['krəʊmɪəm] ◇ *n* cromo *m.* ◇ *comp* cromado(da).

chronic ['krɒnɪk] *adj* - **1.** [illness, unemployment] crónico(ca) - **2.** [liar, alcoholic] empedernido(da).

chronicle ['krɒnɪkl] *n* crónica *f.*

chronological [,krɒnə'lɒdʒɪkl] *adj* cronológico(ca).

chrysanthemum [krɪ'sænθəməm] (*pl* -**s**) *n* crisantemo *m.*

chubby ['tʃʌbɪ] (*compar* -**bier**, *superl* -**biest**) *adj* [person, hands] rechoncho(cha); **to have** ~ **cheeks** ser mofletudo(da).

chuck [tʃʌk] *vt inf* - **1.** [throw] tirar, arrojar, aventar *Amér*; **to** ~ **sb out** echar a alguien - **2.** [job, girlfriend] dejar.

➡ **chuck away, chuck out** *vt sep inf* tirar.

chuckle ['tʃʌkl] *vi* reírse entre dientes.

chug [tʃʌg] (*pt* & *pp* -**ged**, *cont* -**ging**) *vi* [train] traquetear; [car] resoplar.

chum [tʃʌm] *n inf* [gen] amiguete *m*, -ta *f*, manito *m Méx*; [at school] compañero *m*, -ra *f.*

chunk [tʃʌŋk] *n* [piece] trozo *m.*

Chunnel ['tʃʌnl] *n inf*: **the** ~ el Eurotúnel.

church [tʃɜːtʃ] *n* iglesia *f*; **to go to** ~ ir a misa.

Church of England *n*: **the** ~ la Iglesia Anglicana.

churchyard ['tʃɜːtʃjɑːd] *n* cementerio *m*, camposanto *m.*

churlish ['tʃɜːlɪʃ] *adj* descortés, maleducado(da).

churn [tʃɜːn] ◇ *n* - **1.** [for making butter] mantequera *f* - **2.** [for transporting milk] lechera *f.* ◇ *vt* [stir up] agitar.

➡ **churn out** *vt sep inf* hacer como churros OR en cantidades industriales.

chute [ʃuːt] *n* [for water] vertedor *m*, conducto *m*; [slide] tobogán *m*; [for waste] rampa *f.*

chutney ['tʃʌtnɪ] *n salsa agridulce y picante de fruta y semillas.*

CIA (*abbr of* **Central Intelligence Agency**) *n* CIA *f.*

CID (*abbr of* **Criminal Investigation Department**) *n UK* ≃ Brigada *f* de Policía Judicial.

cider ['saɪdə'] *n* - **1.** sidra *f* - **2.** *US* [nonalcoholic] zumo *m Esp* OR jugo *m Amér* de manzana.

cigar [sɪ'gɑː'] *n* puro *m.*

cigarette [,sɪgə'ret] *n* cigarrillo *m.*

cigarette paper *n* papel *m* de fumar.

cilantro [sɪ'lɑːntrə] *n US* [coriander] cilantro *m.*

cinch [sɪntʃ] *n inf*: **it's a** ~ está tirado, es pan comido.

cinder ['sɪndə'] *n* ceniza *f.*

Cinderella [,sɪndə'relə] *n* Cenicienta *f.*

cine-camera ['sɪnɪ-] *n* cámara *f* cinematográfica.

cine-film ['sɪnɪ-] *n* película *f* cinematográfica.

cinema ['sɪnəmə] *n* cine *m.*

cinnamon ['sɪnəmən] *n* canela *f.*

cipher ['saɪfə'] *n* [secret writing system] código *m*, cifra *f.*

circa ['sɜːkə] *prep* hacia.

circle ['sɜːkl] ◇ *n* - **1.** [gen] círculo *m*; **to go round in** ~**s** darle (mil) vueltas al mismo tema - **2.** [in theatre] anfiteatro *m*; [in cinema] entresuelo *m.* ◇ *vt* - **1.** [draw a circle round] rodear con un círculo - **2.** [move round] describir círculos alrededor de. ◇ *vi* dar vueltas.

circuit ['sɜːkɪt] *n* - **1.** [gen] circuito *m* - **2.** [of track] vuelta *f.*

circuitous [sə'kjuːɪtəs] *adj* tortuoso(sa).

circular ['sɜːkjʊlə'] ◇ *adj* [gen] circular. ◇ *n* circular *f.*

circulate ['sɜːkjʊleɪt] ◇ *vi* - **1.** [gen] circular - **2.** [socialize] alternar. ◇ *vt* [rumour, document] hacer circular.

circulation [,sɜ:kjʊ'leɪʃn] *n* **- 1.** [of blood, money] circulación *f* **- 2.** [of magazine, newspaper] tirada *f*.

circumcise ['sɜ:kəmsaɪz] *vt* circuncidar.

circumference [sə'kʌmfərəns] *n* circunferencia *f*.

circumspect ['sɜ:kəmspekt] *adj* circunspecto(ta).

circumstance ['sɜ:kəmstəns] *n* circunstancia *f*; ~s circunstancias *fpl*; **under** OR **in no** ~s bajo ningún concepto; **in** OR **under the** ~s dadas las circunstancias.

circumvent [,sɜ:kəm'vent] *vt fml* burlar, evadir.

circus ['sɜ:kəs] *n* **- 1.** [for entertainment] circo *m* **- 2.** [in place names] glorieta *f*.

CIS (*abbr of* **Commonwealth of Independent States**) *n* CEI *f*.

cistern ['sɪstən] *n* **- 1.** UK [in roof] depósito *m* de agua **- 2.** [in toilet] cisterna *f*.

cite [saɪt] *vt* citar.

citizen ['sɪtɪzn] *n* ciudadano *m*, -na *f*.

Citizens' Advice Bureau *n* oficina británica de información y asistencia al ciudadano.

Citizens' Band *n* banda de radio reservada para radioaficionados y conductores.

citizenship ['sɪtɪznʃɪp] *n* ciudadanía *f*.

citrus fruit ['sɪtrəs-] *n* cítrico *m*.

city ['sɪtɪ] (*pl* **-ies**) *n* ciudad *f*.
  ➤ **City** *n* UK: **the City** la City, *barrio financiero de Londres*.

city centre *n* centro *m* de la ciudad.

city hall *n* US ayuntamiento *m*.

city technology college *n* UK *centro de formación profesional financiado por la industria*.

civic ['sɪvɪk] *adj* **- 1.** [duty, pride] cívico(ca) **- 2.** [leader, event] público(ca).

civic centre *n* UK *zona de la ciudad donde se encuentran los edificios públicos*.

civil ['sɪvl] *adj* **- 1.** [involving ordinary citizens] civil **- 2.** [polite] cortés, correcto(ta).

civil engineering *n* ingeniería *f* civil.

civilian [sɪ'vɪljən] <> *n* civil *m* OR *f*. <> *comp* [organization] civil; [clothes] de paisano.

civilization [,sɪvɪlaɪ'zeɪʃn] *n* civilización *f*.

civilized ['sɪvɪlaɪzd] *adj* civilizado(da).

civil law *n* derecho *m* civil.

civil liberties *npl* libertades *fpl* civiles.

civil rights *npl* derechos *mpl* civiles.

civil servant *n* funcionario *m*, -ria *f* público(ca).

civil service *n* administración *f* pública.

civil war *n* guerra *f* civil.

CJD (*abbr of* **Creutzfeldt-Jakob disease**) *n* enfermedad *f* de Creutzfeldt-Jakob.

clad [klæd] *adj literary*: ~ **in** vestido(da) de.

claim [kleɪm] <> *n* **- 1.** [for pay, insurance, expenses] reclamación *f* **- 2.** [of right] reivindicación *f*, demanda *f*; **to lay** ~ **to sthg** reclamar algo **- 3.** [assertion] afirmación *f*.

<> *vt* **- 1.** [allowance, expenses, lost property] reclamar **- 2.** [responsibility, credit] atribuirse **- 3.** [maintain]: **to** ~ **(that)** mantener que. <> *vi*: **to** ~ **on one's insurance** reclamar al seguro; **to** ~ **for sthg** reclamar algo.

claimant ['kleɪmənt] *n* [to throne] pretendiente *m* OR *f*; [of unemployment benefit] solicitante *m* OR *f*; JUR demandante *m* OR *f*.

clairvoyant [kleə'vɔɪənt] *n* clarividente *m* OR *f*.

clam [klæm] *n* almeja *f*.

clamber ['klæmbə'] *vi* trepar.

clammy ['klæmɪ] (*compar* **-mier**, *superl* **-miest**) *adj* [hands] húmedo(da), pegajoso(sa); [weather] bochornoso(sa).

clamour UK, **clamor** US ['klæmə'] <> *n* (U) **- 1.** [noise] clamor *m* **- 2.** [demand]: ~ **(for)** demandas *fpl* (de). <> *vi*: **to** ~ **for sthg** exigir a voces algo.

clamp [klæmp] <> *n* [gen] abrazadera *f*; [for car wheel] cepo *m*. <> *vt* **- 1.** [with clamp] sujetar (con una abrazadera) **- 2.** [with wheel clamp] poner un cepo a.
  ➤ **clamp down** *vi*: **to** ~ **down on** poner freno a.

clan [klæn] *n* clan *m*.

clandestine [klæn'destɪn] *adj* clandestino(na).

clang [klæŋ] *vi* hacer un ruido metálico.

clap [klæp] (*pt* & *pp* **-ped**, *cont* **-ping**) <> *vt*: **to** ~ **one's hands** dar palmadas. <> *vi* aplaudir.

clapping ['klæpɪŋ] *n* (U) aplausos *mpl*.

claret ['klærət] *n* burdeos *m inv*.

clarify ['klærɪfaɪ] (*pt* & *pp* **-ied**) *vt* aclarar.

clarinet [,klærə'net] *n* clarinete *m*.

clarity ['klærətɪ] *n* claridad *f*.

clash [klæʃ] <> *n* **- 1.** [difference - of interests] conflicto *m*; [- of personalities] choque *m* **- 2.** [fight, disagreement]: ~ **(with)** conflicto *m* (con) **- 3.** [noise] estruendo *m*, estrépito *m*. <> *vi* **- 1.** [fight, disagree]: **to** ~ **(with)** enfrentarse (con) **- 2.** [opinions, policies] estar en desacuerdo **- 3.** [date, event]: **to** ~ **(with)** coincidir (con) **- 4.** [colour]: **to** ~ **(with)** desentonar (con).

clasp [klɑːsp] <> *n* [on necklace, bracelet] broche *m*; [on belt] cierre *m*, hebilla *f*. <> *vt* [person] abrazar; [thing] agarrar.

class [klɑːs] <> *n* **- 1.** [gen] clase *f* **- 2.** [category] clase *f*, tipo *m*. <> *vt*: **to** ~ **sb (as)** clasificar a alguien (de).

classic ['klæsɪk] <> *adj* [typical] clásico(ca). <> *n* clásico *m*.

classical ['klæsɪkl] *adj* clásico(ca).

classified ['klæsɪfaɪd] *adj* [secret] reservado(da), secreto(ta).

classified ad *n* anuncio *m* por palabras.

classify ['klæsɪfaɪ] (*pt* & *pp* **-ied**) *vt* clasificar.

classmate ['klɑ:smeɪt] *n* compañero *m*, -ra *f* de clase.

classroom ['klɑ:srʊm] *n* aula *f*, clase *f*.

classy ['klɑ:sɪ] (*compar* -ier, *superl* -iest) *adj inf* con clase.

clatter ['klætəʳ] *n* [gen] estrépito *m*; [of pots, pans, dishes] ruido *m* (de cacharros); [of hooves] chacoloteo *m*.

clause [klɔ:z] *n* - **1.** [in legal document] cláusula *f* - **2.** GRAMM oración *f*.

claw [klɔ:] ◇ *n* - **1.** [of animal, bird] garra *f*; [of cat] uña *f* - **2.** [of crab, lobster] pinza *f*. ◇ *vi*: **to ~ at** sthg [cat] arañar algo; [person] intentar agarrarse a algo.

clay [kleɪ] *n* arcilla *f*.

clean [kli:n] ◇ *adj* - **1.** [gen] limpio(pia) - **2.** [page] en blanco - **3.** [environmentally-friendly] no contaminante - **4.** [record, reputation] impecable, irreprochable; [driving licence] sin multas - **5.** [joke] inocente - **6.** [outline] nítido(da). ◇ *vt & vi* limpiar.
  ◆ **clean out** *vt sep* - **1.** [clear out] limpiar el interior de - **2.** *inf* [take everything from]: **the burglars ~ed us out** (los ladrones) nos limpiaron la casa.
  ◆ **clean up** *vt sep* [clear up] ordenar, limpiar; **to ~ o.s. up** asearse.

cleaner ['kli:nəʳ] *n* - **1.** [person] limpiador *m*, -ra *f* - **2.** [substance] producto *m* de limpieza.

cleaning ['kli:nɪŋ] *n* limpieza *f*.

cleanliness ['klenlɪnɪs] *n* limpieza *f*.

cleanse [klenz] *vt* [gen] limpiar; [soul] purificar; **to ~ sthg/sb of sthg** limpiar algo/a alguien de algo.

cleanser ['klenzəʳ] *n* crema *f* OR loción *f* limpiadora.

clean-shaven [-'ʃeɪvn] *adj* [never growing a beard] barbilampiño(ña); [recently shaved] bien afeitado(da).

cleansing lotion ['klenzɪŋ-] *n* loción *f* limpiadora.

clear [klɪəʳ] ◇ *adj* - **1.** [gen] claro(ra); [day, road, view] despejado(da); **to make sthg ~ (to)** dejar algo claro; **it's ~ that ...** está claro que ...; **are you ~ about it?** ¿lo entiendes?; **to make o.s. ~** explicarse con claridad - **2.** [transparent] transparente - **3.** [well-defined] [sound, picture] nítido(da) - **4.** [free of blemishes - skin] terso(sa) - **5.** [free - time] libre - **6.** [not touching]: **to be ~ of the ground** no tocar el suelo - **7.** [complete - day, week] entero(ra); [- profit] neto(ta). ◇ *adv* [out of the way]: **stand ~!** ¡aléjense!; **to jump/step ~** saltar/dar un paso para hacerse a un lado. ◇ *vt* - **1.** [remove objects, obstacles from] despejar; [forest] talar; [pipe] desatascar; **they ~ed the area of mines** limpiaron el área de minas; **to ~ a space** hacer sitio; **to ~ the table** quitar la mesa - **2.** [remove] quitar - **3.** [jump]

saltar - **4.** [pay] liquidar - **5.** [authorize] aprobar - **6.** [prove not guilty] declarar inocente; **to be ~ed of** sthg salir absuelto de algo. ◇ *vi* despejarse.
  ◆ **clear away** *vt sep* poner en su sitio.
  ◆ **clear off** *vi UK inf* largarse.
  ◆ **clear out** *vt sep* limpiar a fondo.
  ◆ **clear up** ◇ *vt sep* - **1.** [room, mess] limpiar; [toys, books] recoger - **2.** [disagreement] aclarar; [mystery] resolver. ◇ *vi* - **1.** [weather] despejarse; [infection] desaparecer - **2.** [tidy up] ordenar, recoger.

clearance ['klɪərəns] *n* - **1.** [removal - of rubbish, litter] despeje *m*, limpieza *f*; [of slums, houses] eliminación *f* - **2.** [permission] autorización *f*, permiso *m* - **3.** [free space] distancia *f* libre.

clear-cut *adj* [issue, plan] bien definido(da); [division] nítido(da).

clearing ['klɪərɪŋ] *n* claro *m*.

clearing bank *n UK* banco *m* de compensación.

clearly ['klɪəlɪ] *adv* - **1.** [gen] claramente - **2.** [plainly] obviamente.

clearway ['klɪəweɪ] *n UK carretera donde no se puede parar.*

cleavage ['kli:vɪdʒ] *n* [between breasts] escote *m*.

cleaver ['kli:vəʳ] *n* cuchillo *m* OR cuchilla *f* de carnicero.

clef [klef] *n* clave *f*.

cleft [kleft] *n* grieta *f*.

clench [klentʃ] *vt* apretar.

clergy ['klɜ:dʒɪ] *npl*: **the ~** el clero.

clergyman ['klɜ:dʒɪmən] (*pl* **-men** [-mən]) *n* clérigo *m*.

clerical ['klerɪkl] *adj* - **1.** [work] de oficina; [worker] administrativo(va) - **2.** [in church] clerical.

clerk [*UK* klɑ:k, *US* klɜ:rk] *n* - **1.** [in office] oficinista *m* OR *f* - **2.** [in court] secretario *m*, escribano *m* - **3.** *US* [shop assistant] dependiente *m*, -ta *f*.

clever ['klevəʳ] *adj* - **1.** [intelligent] listo(ta), inteligente - **2.** [idea, invention] ingenioso(sa); [with hands] hábil.

cliché ['kli:ʃeɪ] *n* cliché *m*.

click [klɪk] ◇ *vt* [fingers, tongue] chasquear. ◇ *vi* - **1.** [heels] sonar con un taconazo; [camera] hacer clic - **2.** *inf* [fall into place]: **suddenly, it ~ed** de pronto, caí en la cuenta.

client ['klaɪənt] *n* cliente *m*, -ta *f*.

cliff [klɪf] *n* [on coast] acantilado *m*; [inland] precipicio *m*.

climate ['klaɪmɪt] *n* [weather] clima *m*; *fig* [atmosphere] ambiente *m*.

climate change *n* cambio *m* climático.

climax ['klaɪmæks] *n* [culmination] clímax *m*, culminación *f*.

climb [klaɪm] ◇ *n* [gen] subida *f*; [up mountain] escalada *f*. ◇ *vt* [stairs, ladder] subir; [tree] trepar a; [mountain] escalar. ◇ *vi* **-1.** [clamber]: **to ~ over sthg** trepar por algo; **to ~ into sthg** meterse en algo **- 2.** [plant] trepar; [road, plane] subir **- 3.** [increase] subir.

climb-down *n* vuelta *f* atrás.

climber ['klaɪmə'] *n* [mountaineer] alpinista *m or f*, andinista *m or f Amér*; [rock climber] escalador *m*, -ra *f*.

climbing ['klaɪmɪŋ] *n* montañismo *m*, alpinismo *m*, andinismo *m Amér*.

clinch [klɪntʃ] *vt* [deal] cerrar.

cling [klɪŋ] (*pt & pp* **clung**) *vi* **-1.** [hold tightly]: **to ~ (to)** agarrarse (a) **- 2.** [clothes, person]: **to ~ (to)** pegarse (a).

clingfilm ['klɪŋfɪlm] *n UK* film *m* de plástico adherente.

clinic ['klɪnɪk] *n* clínica *f*.

clinical ['klɪnɪkl] *adj* **-1.** MED clínico(ca) **- 2.** [cold] frío(a).

clink [klɪŋk] *vi* tintinear.

clip [klɪp] (*pt & pp* **-ped**, *cont* **-ping**) ◇ *n* **-1.** [for paper] clip *m*; [for hair] horquilla *f*; [on earring] cierre *m* **- 2.** [of film] fragmento *m*, secuencias *fpl* **- 3.** [cut]: **to give sb's hair a ~** cortarle el pelo a alguien. ◇ *vt* **-1.** [fasten] sujetar **- 2.** [cut - lawn, newspaper cutting] recortar; [- punch - tickets] picar.

clipboard ['klɪpbɔːd] *n* **-1.** [for writing] tabloncillo *m* con pinza sujetapapeles **- 2.** COMPUT portapapeles *m inv*.

clippers ['klɪpəz] *npl* [for nails] cortaúñas *m inv*; [for hair] maquinilla *f* para cortar el pelo; [for hedges, grass] tijeras *fpl* de podar.

clipping ['klɪpɪŋ] *n* **-1.** [from newspaper] recorte *m* **- 2.** [of nails] pedazo *m*.

clique [kliːk] *n pej* camarilla *f*.

cloak [kləʊk] *n* [garment] capa *f*.

cloakroom ['kləʊkrʊm] *n* **-1.** [for clothes] guardarropa *m* **- 2.** *UK* [toilets] servicios *mpl*.

clock [klɒk] *n* **-1.** [timepiece] reloj *m*; **round the ~** día y noche, las 24 horas **- 2.** [mileometer] cuentakilómetros *m inv*.

◆ **clock in, clock on** *vi UK* fichar (a la entrada).

◆ **clock off, clock out** *vi UK* fichar (a la salida).

clock speed *n* COMPUT velocidad *f* de reloj.

clockwise ['klɒkwaɪz] *adj & adv* en el sentido de las agujas del reloj.

clockwork ['klɒkwɜːk] *comp* de cuerda.

clog [klɒg] (*pt & pp* **-ged**, *cont* **-ging**) *vt* atascar, obstruir.

◆ **clogs** *npl* zuecos *mpl*.

◆ **clog up** ◇ *vt sep* [drain, pipe] atascar; [eyes, nose] congestionar. ◇ *vi* atascarse.

close[1] [kləʊs] ◇ *adj* **-1.** [near] cercano(na); **~ to** cerca de; **~ to tears/laughter** a

punto de llorar/reír; **~ up, ~ to** de cerca; **~ by, ~ at hand** muy cerca; **we arrived on time, but it was a ~ shave** OR **thing** llegamos a tiempo, pero por los pelos **- 2.** [relationship, friend] íntimo(ma); **to be ~ to sb** estar muy unido(da) a alguien **- 3.** [relative, family] cercano(na), próximo(ma); [resemblance]: **to bear a ~ resemblance to sb** parecerse mucho a alguien; [link, tie, cooperation] estrecho(cha) **- 4.** [questioning] minucioso(sa); [examination] detallado(da); [look] de cerca; **to keep a ~ watch on** vigilar de cerca **- 5.** [room, air] cargado(da); [weather] bochornoso(sa) **- 6.** [contest, race] reñido(da); [result] apretado(da). ◇ *adv* cerca; **~ to** cerca de.

◆ **close on, close to** *prep* [almost] cerca de.

close[2] [kləʊz] ◇ *vt* **-1.** [gen] cerrar **- 2.** [meeting, conference] clausurar; [discussion, speech] terminar **- 3.** [gap] reducir. ◇ *vi* **-1.** [gen] cerrarse **- 2.** [shop] cerrar **- 3.** [meeting, film, day] terminar. ◇ *n* final *m*.

◆ **close down** ◇ *vt sep* cerrar (definitivamente). ◇ *vi* [factory etc] cerrarse (definitivamente).

closed [kləʊzd] *adj* cerrado(da).

close-knit [,kləʊs-] *adj* muy unido(da).

closely ['kləʊslɪ] *adv* **-1.** [of connection, relation etc] estrechamente; **to be ~ involved in sthg** estar muy metido en algo; [resemble] mucho **- 2.** [carefully] atentamente.

closet ['klɒzɪt] ◇ *adj inf* en secreto. ◇ *n* **-1.** *US* armario *m* **- 2.** *phr*: **to come out of the ~** declararse homosexual públicamente.

close-up ['kləʊs-] *n* primer plano *m*.

closing time *n* hora *f* de cierre.

closure ['kləʊʒə'] *n* cierre *m*.

clot [klɒt] (*pt & pp* **-ted**, *cont* **-ting**) ◇ *n* **-1.** [in blood] coágulo *m* **- 2.** *UK inf* [fool] bobo *m*, -ba *f*. ◇ *vi* [blood] coagularse.

cloth [klɒθ] *n* **-1.** (U) [fabric] tela *f* **- 2.** [piece of cloth] trapo *m*.

clothe [kləʊð] *vt fml* vestir.

clothes [kləʊðz] *npl* ropa *f*; **to put one's ~ on** ponerse la ropa, vestirse; **to take one's ~ off** quitarse la ropa, desvestirse.

clothes brush *n* cepillo *m* para la ropa.

clothesline ['kləʊðzlaɪn] *n* cuerda *f* para tender la ropa.

clothes peg *UK*, **clothespin** *US* ['kləʊðzpɪn] *n* pinza *f* (para la ropa).

clothing ['kləʊðɪŋ] *n* ropa *f*.

cloud [klaʊd] *n* nube *f*.

◆ **cloud over** *vi lit & fig* nublarse.

cloudy ['klaʊdɪ] (*compar* **-ier**, *superl* **-iest**) *adj* **-1.** [overcast] nublado(da) **- 2.** [murky] turbio(bia).

clout [klaʊt] *n inf* **-1.** [blow] tortazo *m*

- **2.** *(U)* [influence] influencia *f*.
clove [kləʊv] *n*: **a ~ of garlic** un diente de ajo.
◆ **cloves** *npl* [spice] clavos *mpl*.
clover ['kləʊvəʳ] *n* trébol *m*.
clown [klaʊn] *n* [performer] payaso *m*.
cloying ['klɔɪɪŋ] *adj* empalagoso(sa).
club [klʌb] *(pt & pp -bed, cont -bing)* ◇ *n* - **1.** [organization, place] club *m* - **2.** [nightclub] discoteca *f* - **3.** [weapon] porra *f*, garrote *m* - **4.**: (golf) ~ palo *m* de golf. ◇ *vt* apalear, aporrear.
◆ **clubs** *npl* [cards] tréboles *mpl*.
◆ **club together** *vi* UK recolectar dinero.
clubbing ['klʌbɪŋ] *n*: **to go ~** ir de discotecas.
club car *n* US RAIL vagón *m* OR coche *m* club.
clubhouse ['klʌbhaʊs] *n* [for golfers] (edificio *m* del) club *m*.
club soda *n* US soda *f*.
club sandwich *n* US sandwich *m* de tres pisos.
cluck [klʌk] *vi* [hen] cloquear.
clue [kluː] *n* - **1.** [in crime] pista *f*; **not to have a ~ (about)** no tener ni idea (de) - **2.** [in crossword] pregunta *f*, clave *f*.
clued-up [kluːd-] *adj* UK *inf* al tanto.
clump [klʌmp] *n* [of bushes] mata *f*; [of trees, flowers] grupo *m*.
clumsy ['klʌmzɪ] *(compar -ier, superl -iest) adj* - **1.** [ungraceful] torpe - **2.** [unwieldy] difícil de manejar - **3.** [tactless] torpe, sin tacto.
clung [klʌŋ] *pt & pp* ⊳ **cling**.
cluster ['klʌstəʳ] ◇ *n* [group] grupo *m*; [of grapes] racimo *m*. ◇ *vi* agruparse.
clutch [klʌtʃ] ◇ *n* AUT embrague *m*. ◇ *vt* [hand] estrechar; [arm, baby] agarrar. ◇ *vi*: **to ~ at sthg** tratar de agarrarse a algo.
clutter ['klʌtəʳ] ◇ *n* desorden *m*. ◇ *vt* cubrir desordenadamente.
cm *(abbr of* **centimetre)** cm.
CND *(abbr of* **Campaign for Nuclear Disarmament)** *n organización británica contra el armamento nuclear.*
c/o *(abbr of* **care of)** c/d.
Co. - **1.** *(abbr of* **Company)** Cía. - **2.** *abbr of* **County.**
coach [kəʊtʃ] ◇ *n* - **1.** [bus] autocar *m* - **2.** RAIL vagón *m* - **3.** [horsedrawn] carruaje *m* - **4.** SPORT entrenador *m*, -ra *f* - **5.** [tutor] profesor *m*, -ra *f* particular - **6.**: ~ **(class)** US clase *f* turista. ◇ *vt* - **1.** SPORT entrenar - **2.** [tutor] dar clases particulares a.
coal [kəʊl] *n* carbón *m*.
coalfield ['kəʊlfiːld] *n* yacimiento *m* de carbón.
coalition [ˌkəʊə'lɪʃn] *n* coalición *f*.
coalman ['kəʊlmæn] *(pl* -men [-men]) *n* UK carbonero *m*.
coalmine ['kəʊlmaɪn] *n* mina *f* de carbón.
coarse [kɔːs] *adj* - **1.** [skin, hair, sandpaper]

áspero(ra); [fabric] basto(ta) - **2.** [person, joke] ordinario(ria), guarango(ga) *Chile, RP*.
coast [kəʊst] ◇ *n* costa *f*. ◇ *vi* - **1.** [in car] ir en punto muerto - **2.** [progress easily]: **they ~ ed into the semifinals** se metieron en las semifinales sin ningún esfuerzo.
coastal ['kəʊstl] *adj* costero(ra).
coaster ['kəʊstəʳ] *n* [small mat] posavasos *m inv*.
coastguard ['kəʊstgɑːd] *n* [person] guardacostas *m* OR *f inv*.
coastline ['kəʊstlaɪn] *n* litoral *m*.
coat [kəʊt] ◇ *n* - **1.** [overcoat] abrigo *m*, sobretodo *m RP*; [for women] tapado *m RP*; [jacket] chaqueta *f* - **2.** [of animal] pelo *m*, pelaje *m* - **3.** [layer] capa *f*. ◇ *vt*: **to ~ sthg (with)** cubrir algo (de).
coat hanger *n* percha *f*, gancho *m CAm, Andes, Méx.*
coat hook *n* colgador *m*.
coating ['kəʊtɪŋ] *n* [of dust etc] capa *f*; [of chocolate, silver] baño *m*.
coat of arms *(pl* **coats of arms)** *n* escudo *m* de armas.
coax [kəʊks] *vt*: **to ~ sb (to do OR into doing sthg)** engatusar a alguien (para que haga algo).
cob [kɒb] ⊳ **corn.**
cobbled ['kɒbld] *adj* adoquinado(da).
cobbler ['kɒbləʳ] *n* zapatero (remendón) *m*, zapatera *f*.
cobbles ['kɒblz], **cobblestones** ['kɒblstəʊnz] *npl* adoquines *mpl*.
cobweb ['kɒbweb] *n* telaraña *f (abandonada).*
Coca-Cola® [ˌkəʊkə'kəʊlə] *n* Coca-Cola® *f*.
cocaine [kəʊ'keɪn] *n* cocaína *f*.
cock [kɒk] ◇ *n* - **1.** [male chicken] gallo *m* - **2.** [male bird] macho *m* - **3.** [penis] *vulg* polla *f*. ◇ *vt* - **1.** [gun] amartillar - **2.** [head] ladear.
◆ **cock up** *vt sep* UK *v inf* jorobar, fastidiar.
cockerel ['kɒkrəl] *n* gallo *m* joven.
cockeyed ['kɒkaɪd] *adj inf* - **1.** [lopsided] torcido(da) - **2.** [foolish] disparatado(da).
cockle ['kɒkl] *n* berberecho *m*.
Cockney ['kɒknɪ] *(pl* **Cockneys)** *n* - **1.** [person] cockney *m* OR *f*, persona procedente del este de Londres - **2.** [dialect, accent] cockney *m*, dialecto del este de Londres.
cockpit ['kɒkpɪt] *n* [in civil aviation] cabina *f*.
cockroach ['kɒkrəʊtʃ] *n* cucaracha *f*.
cocksure [ˌkɒk'ʃʊəʳ] *adj* presuntuoso(sa).
cocktail ['kɒkteɪl] *n* cóctel *m*.
cock-up *n v inf* pifia *f*.
cocky ['kɒkɪ] *(compar -ier, superl -iest) adj inf* chulo(la).
cocoa ['kəʊkəʊ] *n* - **1.** [powder] cacao *m* - **2.** [drink] chocolate *m*.
coconut ['kəʊkənʌt] *n* coco *m*.

cod [kɒd] (*pl inv* OR **-s**) *n* bacalao *m*.

COD (*abbr of* **cash on delivery**) *entrega contra reembolso.*

code [kəʊd] ◇ *n* **-1.** [gen] código *m* **-2.** [for telephone] prefijo *m*. ◇ *vt* [encode] codificar, cifrar.

cod-liver oil *n* aceite *m* de hígado de bacalao.

coed [ˌkəʊ'ed] *adj* (*abbr of* **coeducational**) mixto(ta).

coerce [kəʊ'ɜ:s] *vt*: **to ~ sb (into doing sthg)** coaccionar a alguien (para que haga algo).

coffee ['kɒfɪ] *n* café *m*.

coffee bar *n* UK cafetería *f*.

coffee break *n* descanso *m* para el café.

coffee morning *n* UK *reunión matinal, generalmente benéfica, en la que se sirve café.*

coffeepot ['kɒfɪpɒt] *n* cafetera *f (para servir).*

coffee shop *n* **-1.** UK [shop] cafetería *f* **-2.** US [restaurant] café *m*.

coffee table *n* mesita *f* baja (de salón).

coffin ['kɒfɪn] *n* ataúd *m*.

cog [kɒg] *n* [tooth on wheel] diente *m*; [wheel] rueda *f* dentada.

cognac ['kɒnjæk] *n* coñac *m*.

coherent [kəʊ'hɪərənt] *adj* coherente.

cohesive [kəʊ'hi:sɪv] *adj* [group] unido(-da).

coil [kɔɪl] ◇ *n* **-1.** [of rope, wire] rollo *m*; [of hair] tirabuzón *m*; [of smoke] espiral *f* **-2.** ELEC bobina *f* **-3.** UK [contraceptive device] DIU *m*, espiral *f*. ◇ *vi* enrollarse, enroscarse. ◇ *vt* enrollar, enroscar.

◆ coil up *vt sep* enrollar.

coin [kɔɪn] ◇ *n* moneda *f*. ◇ *vt* [invent] acuñar.

coinage ['kɔɪnɪdʒ] *n* [currency] moneda *f*.

coin-box *n* depósito *m* de monedas.

coincide [ˌkəʊɪn'saɪd] *vi*: **to ~ (with)** coincidir (con).

coincidence [kəʊ'ɪnsɪdəns] *n* coincidencia *f*.

coincidental [kəʊˌɪnsɪ'dentl] *adj* fortuito(-ta).

coke [kəʊk] *n* [fuel] coque *m*.

Coke® [kəʊk] *n* Coca-Cola® *f*.

cola ['kəʊlə] *n* (bebida *f* de) cola *f*.

colander ['kʌləndər] *n* colador *m*, escurridor *m*.

cold [kəʊld] ◇ *adj* frío(a); **it's ~** hace frío; **my hands are ~** tengo las manos frías; **I'm ~** tengo frío; **to get ~** enfriarse. ◇ *n* **-1.** [illness] resfriado *m*, constipado *m*; **to catch (a) ~** resfriarse, coger un resfriado **-2.** [low temperature] frío *m*.

cold-blooded [-'blʌdɪd] *adj* **-1.** [animal] de sangre fría **-2.** [person] despiadado(da); [killing] a sangre fría.

cold sore *n* calentura *f*.

cold war *n*: **the ~** la guerra fría.

coleslaw ['kəʊlslɔ:] *n* ensalada de col, zanahoria, cebolla y mayonesa.

colic ['kɒlɪk] *n* cólico *m*.

collaborate [kə'læbəreɪt] *vi*: **to ~ (with)** colaborar (con).

collapse [kə'læps] ◇ *n* **-1.** [of building] derrumbamiento *m*, desplome *m*; [of roof] hundimiento *m* **-2.** [of marriage, system] fracaso *m*; [of government, currency] caída *f*; [of empire] derrumbamiento *m* **-3.** MED colapso *m*. ◇ *vi* **-1.** [building, person] derrumbarse, desplomarse; [roof, prices] hundirse; **to ~ with laughter** partirse de risa **-2.** [plan, business] venirse abajo **-3.** MED sufrir un colapso.

collapsible [kə'læpsəbl] *adj* plegable.

collar ['kɒlər] *n* **-1.** [on clothes] cuello *m* **-2.** [for dog] collar *m* **-3.** TECH collar *m*.

collarbone ['kɒləbəʊn] *n* clavícula *f*.

collate [kə'leɪt] *vt* **-1.** [compare] cotejar **-2.** [put in order] poner en orden.

collateral [kɒ'lætərəl] *n* garantía *f* subsidiaria, seguridad *f* colateral.

collateral damage *n* MIL (*U*) daños *mpl* colaterales.

colleague ['kɒli:g] *n* colega *m* OR *f*.

collect [kə'lekt] ◇ *vt* **-1.** [gather together] reunir, juntar; **to ~ o.s.** concentrarse **-2.** [as a hobby] coleccionar **-3.** [go to get-person, parcel] recoger **-4.** [money, taxes] recaudar. ◇ *vi* **-1.** [gather] congregarse, reunirse **-2.** [accumulate] acumularse **-3.** [for charity, gift] hacer una colecta. ◇ *adv* US TELEC: **to call (sb) ~** llamar (a alguien) a cobro revertido.

collection [kə'lekʃn] *n* **-1.** [of stamps, art etc] colección *f* **-2.** [of poems, stories etc] recopilación *f* **-3.** [of rubbish, mail] recogida *f*; [of taxes] recaudación *f* **-4.** [of money] colecta *f*.

collective [kə'lektɪv] ◇ *adj* colectivo(va). ◇ *n* colectivo *m*.

collector [kə'lektər] *n* **-1.** [as a hobby] coleccionista *m* OR *f* **-2.** [of taxes] recaudador *m*, -ra *f* **-3.** [of debts, rent] cobrador *m*, -ra *f*.

college ['kɒlɪdʒ] *n* **-1.** [for further education] instituto *m*, escuela *f* **-2.** US [university] universidad *f* **-3.** UK [of university] colegio *universitario que forma parte de ciertas universidades* **-4.** [organized body] colegio *m*.

college of education *n* UK *escuela de formación de profesores de enseñanza primaria y secundaria.*

collide [kə'laɪd] *vi*: **to ~ (with)** [gen] chocar (con); [vehicles] colisionar OR chocar (con).

collie ['kɒlɪ] *n* collie *m*.

colliery ['kɒljərɪ] (*pl* **-ies**) *n* mina *f* de carbón.

collision [kə'lɪʒn] n lit & fig: ~ **(with/between)** choque m (con/entre), colisión f (con/entre).

colloquial [kə'ləʊkwɪəl] adj coloquial.

collude [kə'luːd] vi: to ~ **with** estar en connivencia con.

Cologne [kə'ləʊn] n Colonia.

Colombia [kə'lɒmbɪə] n Colombia.

Colombian [kə'lɒmbɪən] ⋄ adj colombiano(na). ⋄ n colombiano m, -na f.

colon ['kəʊlən] n - **1.** ANAT colon m - **2.** [punctuation mark] dos puntos mpl.

colonel ['kɜːnl] n coronel m OR f.

colonial [kə'ləʊnjəl] adj colonial.

colonize, -ise ['kɒlənaɪz] vt colonizar.

colony ['kɒlənɪ] (pl -ies) n colonia f.

color etc US = **colour** etc.

colossal [kə'lɒsl] adj colosal.

colour UK, **color** US ['kʌlə'] ⋄ n color m; **in** ~ [magazine] a color; [film]· en color. ⋄ adj en color. ⋄ vt - **1.** [give colour to] dar color a; [with pen, crayon] colorear - **2.** [dye] teñir - **3.** [affect] influenciar. ⋄ vi [blush] ruborizarse.

colour bar n discriminación f racial.

colour-blind adj daltónico(ca).

coloured UK, **colored** US ['kʌləd] adj - **1.** [pens, sheets etc] de colores - **2.** [with stated colour]: **maroon-**~ de color granate; **brightly-**~ de vivos colores - **3.** [person - black] de color.

colourful UK, **colorful** US ['kʌləfʊl] adj - **1.** [brightly coloured] de vivos colores - **2.** [story] animado(da) - **3.** [person] pintoresco(ca) - **4.** [language] expresivo(va).

colouring UK, **coloring** US ['kʌlərɪŋ] n - **1.** [in food] colorante m - **2.** [complexion, hair] tez f - **3.** [of animal's skin] color m, coloración f.

colour scheme n combinación f de colores.

colt [kəʊlt] n potro m.

column ['kɒləm] n - **1.** [gen] columna f - **2.** [of people, vehicles] hilera f.

columnist ['kɒləmnɪst] n columnista m OR f.

coma ['kəʊmə] n coma m.

comb [kəʊm] ⋄ n peine m ⋄ vt lit & fig peinar.

combat ['kɒmbæt] ⋄ n combate m. ⋄ vt combatir.

combination [,kɒmbɪ'neɪʃn] n combinación f.

combine [vb kəm'baɪn, n 'kɒmbaɪn] ⋄ vt: **to** ~ **sthg (with)** combinar algo (con). ⋄ vi combinarse, unirse. ⋄ n - **1.** [group] grupo m - **2.** = **combine harvester**.

combine harvester [-'hɑːvɪstə'] n cosechadora f.

come [kʌm] (pt came, pp come) vi - **1.** [move] venir; [arrive] llegar; **coming!** ¡ahora voy!; **the news came as a shock** la noticia constituyó un duro golpe - **2.** [reach]: **to** ~ **up/down to** llegar hasta - **3.** [happen] pasar; ~ **what may** pase lo que pase - **4.** [become]: **to** ~ **true** hacerse realidad; **to** ~ **unstuck** despegarse; **my shoelaces have** ~ **undone** se me han desatado los cordones - **5.** [begin gradually]: **to** ~ **to do sthg** llegar a hacer algo - **6.** [be placed in order]: **to** ~ **first/last in a race** llegar el primero/el último en una carrera; **she came second in the exam** quedó segunda en el examen; **P** ~**s before Q** la P viene antes de la Q.

◆ **to come** adv: **in (the) days/years to** ~ en días/años venideros.

◆ **come about** vi [happen] pasar, ocurrir.

◆ **come along** vi - **1.** [arrive by chance - opportunity] surgir; [- bus] aparecer, llegar - **2.** [progress] ir; **the project is coming along nicely** el proyecto va muy bien.

◆ **come apart** vi deshacerse.

◆ **come back** vi - **1.** [in talk, writing]: **to** ~ **back to sthg** volver a algo - **2.** [memory]: **to** ~ **back to sb** volverle a la memoria a alguien.

◆ **come by** vt fus [get, obtain] conseguir.

◆ **come down** vi - **1.** [from upstairs] bajar - **2.** [decrease] bajar - **3.** [descend - plane, parachutist] aterrizar; [- rain] caer.

◆ **come down to** vt fus reducirse a.

◆ **come down with** vt fus coger, agarrar (enfermedad).

◆ **come forward** vi presentarse.

◆ **come from** vt fus [noise etc] venir de; [person] ser de.

◆ **come in** vi - **1.** [enter] entrar, pasar; ~ **in!** ¡pase! - **2.** [arrive - train, letters, donations] llegar.

◆ **come in for** vt fus [criticism etc] recibir, llevarse.

◆ **come into** vt fus - **1.** [inherit] heredar - **2.** [begin to be]: **to** ~ **into being** nacer, ver la luz.

◆ **come off** ⋄ vi - **1.** [button] descoserse; [label] despegarse; [lid] soltarse; [stain] quitarse - **2.** [plan, joke] salir bien, dar resultado. ⋄ vt fus - **1.** [medicine] dejar de tomar - **2.** phr: ~ **off it!** inf ¡venga ya!

◆ **come on** vi - **1.** [start] empezar - **2.** [start working - lights, heating] encenderse - **3.** [progress] ir; **it's coming on nicely** va muy bien - **4.** phr: ~ **on!** [expressing encouragement, urging haste] ¡vamos!; [expressing disbelief] ¡venga ya!

◆ **come out** vi - **1.** [screw, tooth] caerse - **2.** [stain] quitarse - **3.** [become known] salir a la luz - **4.** [appear - product, book, sun] salir; [- film] estrenarse - **5.** [go on strike] ponerse en huelga - **6.** [as homosexual] declararse homosexual.

◆ **come over** ⬦ *vt fus* [subj: feeling] sobrevenir; **I don't know what has ~ over her** no sé qué le pasa. ⬦ *vi* [to visit] pasarse.

◆ **come round** *vi* **- 1.** [to visit] pasarse **- 2.** [change opinion]: **to ~ round (to sthg)** terminar por aceptar (algo) **- 3.** [regain consciousness] volver en sí.

◆ **come through** *vt fus* [difficult situation, period] pasar por, atravesar; [operation, war] sobrevivir a.

◆ **come to** ⬦ *vt fus* **- 1.** [reach]: **to ~ to an end** tocar a su fin; **to ~ to a decision** alcanzar una decisión **- 2.** [amount to] ascender a; **the plan came to nothing** el plan se quedó en nada. ⬦ *vi* [regain consciousness] volver en sí.

◆ **come under** *vt fus* **- 1.** [be governed by] estar bajo **- 2.** [suffer]: **to ~ under attack** ser atacado.

◆ **come up** *vi* **- 1.** [name, topic, opportunity] surgir **- 2.** [be imminent] estar al llegar **- 3.** [sun, moon] salir.

◆ **come up against** *vt fus* tropezarse OR toparse con.

◆ **come up with** *vt fus* [idea] salir con; [solution] encontrar.

comeback ['kʌmbæk] *n* [return] reaparición *f*; **to make a ~** [fashion] volver (a ponerse de moda); [actor] hacer una reaparición; [in match] recuperarse.

comedian [kə'miːdjən] *n* cómico *m*, humorista *m*.

comedown ['kʌmdaʊn] *n inf* degradación *f*.

comedy ['kɒmədɪ] (*pl* **-ies**) *n* **- 1.** [film, play] comedia *f*; [on television] serie *f* de humor **- 2.** [humorous entertainment] humorismo *m* **- 3.** [amusing nature] comicidad *f*.

comet ['kɒmɪt] *n* cometa *m*.

come-uppance [,kʌm'ʌpəns] *n*: **to get one's ~** *inf* llevarse uno su merecido.

comfort ['kʌmfət] ⬦ *n* **- 1.** [gen] comodidad *f* **- 2.** [solace] consuelo *m*. ⬦ *vt* consolar, confortar.

comfortable ['kʌmftəbl] *adj* **- 1.** [gen] cómodo(da) **- 2.** [financially secure] acomodado(da) **- 3.** [victory, job, belief] fácil; [lead, majority] amplio(plia).

comfortably ['kʌmftəblɪ] *adv* **- 1.** [sit, sleep] cómodamente **- 2.** [without financial difficulty] sin aprietos **- 3.** [easily] fácilmente.

comfort station *n* US euphemism aseos *mpl*.

comic ['kɒmɪk] ⬦ *adj* cómico(ca). ⬦ *n* **- 1.** [comedian] cómico *m*, -ca *f*, humorista *m* OR *f* **- 2.** [magazine - for children] tebeo *m*; [- for adults] cómic *m*.

comical ['kɒmɪkl] *adj* cómico(ca).

comic strip *n* tira *f* cómica.

coming ['kʌmɪŋ] ⬦ *adj* [future] próximo(-ma). ⬦ *n*: **~s and goings** idas *fpl* y venidas.

comma ['kɒmə] *n* coma *f*.

command [kə'mɑːnd] ⬦ *n* **- 1.** [order] orden *f* **- 2.** (U) [control] mando *m* **- 3.** [of language, skill] dominio *m* **- 4.** COMPUT comando *m*. ⬦ *vt* **- 1.** [order]: **to ~ sb (to do sthg)** ordenar OR mandar a alguien (que haga algo) **- 2.** MIL [control] comandar **- 3.** [deserve - respect, attention] hacerse acreedor(ra) de.

commandeer [,kɒmən'dɪəʳ] *vt* requisar.

commander [kə'mɑːndəʳ] *n* **- 1.** [in army] comandante *m* OR *f* **- 2.** [in navy] capitán *m*, -ana *f* de fragata.

commandment [kə'mɑːndmənt] *n* RELIG mandamiento *m*.

commando [kə'mɑːndəʊ] (*pl* **-s** OR **-es**) *n* comando *m*.

commemorate [kə'meməreɪt] *vt* conmemorar.

commemoration [kə,memə'reɪʃn] *n* conmemoración *f*.

commence [kə'mens] *fml* ⬦ *vt*: **to ~ (doing sthg)** comenzar OR empezar (a hacer algo). ⬦ *vi* comenzar, empezar.

commend [kə'mend] *vt* **- 1.** [praise] alabar **- 2.** [recommend]: **to ~ sthg (to)** recomendar algo (a).

commensurate [kə'menʃərət] *adj fml*: **~ with** acorde OR en proporción con.

comment ['kɒment] ⬦ *n* comentario *m*; **no ~** sin comentarios. ⬦ *vi* comentar; **to ~ on** hacer comentarios sobre.

commentary ['kɒməntrɪ] (*pl* **-ies**) *n* **- 1.** [on match, event] comentarios *mpl* **- 2.** [analysis] comentario *m*.

commentator ['kɒmənteɪtəʳ] *n* comentarista *m* OR *f*.

commerce ['kɒmɜːs] *n* (U) comercio *m*.

commercial [kə'mɜːʃl] ⬦ *adj* comercial. ⬦ *n* anuncio *m* (televisivo o radiofónico).

commercial break *n* pausa *f* publicitaria.

commiserate [kə'mɪzəreɪt] *vi*: **I ~d with her** le dije cuánto lo sentía.

commission [kə'mɪʃn] ⬦ *n* **- 1.** [money, investigative body] comisión *f* **- 2.** [piece of work] encargo *m*. ⬦ *vt* encargar; **to ~ sb (to do sthg)** encargar a alguien (que haga algo).

commissionaire [kə,mɪʃə'neəʳ] *n* UK portero *m* (uniformado).

commissioner [kə'mɪʃnəʳ] *n* comisario *m*, -ria *f*.

commit [kə'mɪt] (*pt* & *pp* **-ted**, *cont* **-ting**) *vt* **- 1.** [crime, sin etc] cometer **- 2.** [pledge - money, resources] destinar; **to ~ o.s. (to)** comprometerse (a) **- 3.** [consign - to mental hospital] ingresar; **to ~ sthg to memory**

aprender algo de memoria.

commitment [kə'mɪtmənt] *n* compromiso *m*.

committee [kə'mɪtɪ] *n* comisión *f*, comité *m*.

commodity [kə'mɒdətɪ] (*pl* -ies) *n* producto *m* básico.

common ['kɒmən] ◇ *adj* - 1. [gen]: ∼ (to) común (a) - 2. [ordinary - man, woman] corriente, de la calle - 3. *UK pej* [vulgar] vulgar, ordinario(ria). ◇ *n* campo *m* común.
  ◆ **in common** *adv* en común.

common law *n* derecho *m* consuetudinario.
  ◆ **common-law** *adj* [wife, husband] de hecho.

commonly ['kɒmənlɪ] *adv* generalmente, comúnmente.

Common Market *n*: the ∼ el Mercado Común.

commonplace ['kɒmənpleɪs] *adj* corriente, común.

common room *n* [for pupils] sala *f* de estudiantes; [for teachers] sala *f* de profesores.

Commons ['kɒmənz] *npl UK*: the ∼ la Cámara de los Comunes.

common sense *n* sentido *m* común.

Commonwealth ['kɒmənwelθ] *n*: the ∼ la Commonwealth.

Commonwealth of Independent States *n*: the ∼ la Comunidad de Estados Independientes.

commotion [kə'məʊʃn] *n* alboroto *m*.

communal ['kɒmjʊnl] *adj* comunal.

commune [*n* 'kɒmju:n, *vb* kə'mju:n] ◇ *n* comuna *f*. ◇ *vi*: to ∼ with estar en comunión *OR* comulgar con.

communicate [kə'mju:nɪkeɪt] ◇ *vt* transmitir, comunicar. ◇ *vi*: to ∼ (with) comunicarse (con).

communication [kə,mju:nɪ'keɪʃn] *n* - 1. [contact] comunicación *f* - 2. [letter, phone call] comunicado *m*.

communication cord *n UK* alarma *f (de un tren o metro)*.

communications technology *n* tecnología *f* de las comunicaciones.

communion [kə'mju:njən] *n* [communication] comunión *f*.
  ◆ **Communion** *n (U)* RELIG comunión *f*.

communiqué [kə'mju:nɪkeɪ] *n* comunicado *m*.

Communism ['kɒmjʊnɪzm] *n* comunismo *m*.

Communist ['kɒmjʊnɪst] ◇ *adj* comunista. ◇ *n* comunista *m OR f*.

community [kə'mju:nətɪ] (*pl* -ies) *n* comunidad *f*.

community centre *n* centro *m* social.

commutation ticket [,kɒmju:'teɪʃn-] *n*

US abono *m*, boleto *m* de abono *Amér.*

commute [kə'mju:t] ◇ *vt* JUR conmutar. ◇ *vi* [to work] viajar diariamente al lugar de trabajo, esp en tren.

commuter [kə'mju:tə^r] *n persona que viaja diariamente al lugar de trabajo, esp en tren.*

compact [*adj* kəm'pækt, *n* 'kɒmpækt] ◇ *adj* [small and neat] compacto(ta). ◇ *n* - 1. [for face powder] polvera *f* - 2. *US* [car] utilitario *m*.

compact disc *n* compact disc *m*.

compact disc player *n* compact *m* (disc), reproductor *m* de discos compactos.

companion [kəm'pænjən] *n* compañero *m*, -ra *f*.

companionship [kəm'pænjənʃɪp] *n* [friendly relationship] compañerismo *m*.

company ['kʌmpənɪ] (*pl* -ies) *n* [gen] compañía *f*; [business] empresa *f*, compañía *f*; to keep sb ∼ hacer compañía a alguien; to part ∼ (with) separarse (de).

company secretary *n* secretario *m*, -ria *f* del consejo de administración.

comparable ['kɒmprəbl] *adj*: ∼ (to *OR* with) comparable (a).

comparative [kəm'pærətɪv] ◇ *adj* - 1. [relative] relativo(va) - 2. [study] comparado(da) - 3. GRAMM comparativo(va). ◇ *n* GRAMM comparativo *m*.

comparatively [kəm'pærətɪvlɪ] *adv* relativamente.

compare [kəm'peə^r] ◇ *vt*: to ∼ sthg/sb (with), to ∼ sthg/sb (to) comparar algo/a alguien (con); ∼d with *OR* to [as opposed to] comparado con; [in comparison with] en comparación con. ◇ *vi*: to ∼ (with) compararse (con).

comparison [kəm'pærɪsn] *n* comparación *f*; in ∼ (with *OR* to) en comparación (con).

compartment [kəm'pɑ:tmənt] *n* - 1. [container] compartimento *m*, compartimiento *m* - 2. RAIL departamento *m*, compartimento *m*.

compass ['kʌmpəs] *n* [magnetic] brújula *f*.
  ◆ **compasses** *npl* compás *m*.

compassion [kəm'pæʃn] *n* compasión *f*.

compassionate [kəm'pæʃənət] *adj* compasivo(va).

compatible [kəm'pætəbl] *adj*: ∼ (with) compatible (con).

compel [kəm'pel] (*pt* & *pp* -led, *cont* -ling) *vt* [force] obligar; to ∼ sb to do sthg forzar *OR* obligar a alguien a hacer algo.

compelling [kəm'pelɪŋ] *adj* - 1. [argument, reason] convincente - 2. [book, film] absorbente.

compensate ['kɒmpenseɪt] ◇ *vt*: to ∼ sb for sthg [financially] compensar *OR* indemnizar a alguien por algo. ◇ *vi*: to ∼ for sthg compensar algo.

compensation [ˌkɒmpenˈseɪʃn] *n* -1. [money]: ~ **(for)** indemnización *f* (por) -2. [way of compensating]: ~ **(for)** compensación *f* (por).

compete [kəmˈpiːt] *vi* -1. [gen]: to ~ (for/in) competir (por/en); to ~ (with OR against) competir (con) -2. [be in conflict] rivalizar.

competence [ˈkɒmpɪtəns] *n* [proficiency] competencia *f*.

competent [ˈkɒmpɪtənt] *adj* competente, capaz.

competition [ˌkɒmpɪˈtɪʃn] *n* -1. [rivalry] competencia *f* -2. [competitors, rivals]: **the ~ la competencia** -3. [race, sporting event] competición *f* -4. [contest] concurso *m*.

competitive [kəmˈpetətɪv] *adj* -1. [match, exam, prices] competitivo(va) -2. [person, spirit] competidor(ra).

competitor [kəmˈpetɪtə^r] *n* competidor *m*, -ra *f*.

compile [kəmˈpaɪl] *vt* recopilar, compilar.

complacency [kəmˈpleɪsnsɪ] *n* autocomplacencia *f*.

complacent [kəmˈpleɪsnt] *adj* autocomplaciente.

complain [kəmˈpleɪn] *vi* -1. [moan]: to ~ **(about)** quejarse (de) -2. MED : to ~ **of sthg** sufrir algo.

complaint [kəmˈpleɪnt] *n* -1. [gen] queja *f* -2. MED problema *m*, dolencia *f*.

complement [*n* ˈkɒmplɪmənt, *vb* ˈkɒmplɪˌment] <> *n* -1. [gen & GRAMM] complemento *m* -2. [number]: **we offer a full ~ of services** ofrecemos una gama completa de servicios. <> *vt* complementar.

complementary [ˌkɒmplɪˈmentərɪ] *adj* -1. [gen] complementario(ria) -2. [medicine] alternativo(va).

complete [kəmˈpliːt] <> *adj* -1. [total] total -2. [lacking nothing] completo(ta); **bathroom ~ with shower** baño con ducha -3. [finished] terminado(da). <> *vt* -1. [finish] terminar, acabar -2. [form] rellenar -3. [make whole - collection] completar; [- disappointment, amazement] colmar, rematar.

completely [kəmˈpliːtlɪ] *adv* completamente.

completion [kəmˈpliːʃn] *n* finalización *f*, terminación *f*.

complex [ˈkɒmpleks] <> *adj* complejo(ja). <> *n* complejo *m*.

complexion [kəmˈplekʃn] *n* [of face] tez *f*, cutis *m inv*.

compliance [kəmˈplaɪəns] *n* [obedience]: ~ **(with)** acatamiento *m* (de).

complicate [ˈkɒmplɪkeɪt] *vt* complicar.

complicated [ˈkɒmplɪkeɪtɪd] *adj* complicado(da).

complication [ˌkɒmplɪˈkeɪʃn] *n* complicación *f*.

compliment [*n* ˈkɒmplɪmənt, *vb* ˈkɒmplɪˌment] <> *n* cumplido *m*; **my ~s to the cook** felicitaciones a la cocinera. <> *vt* : to ~ **sb (on)** felicitar a alguien (por).

◆ **compliments** *npl fml* saludos *mpl*.

complimentary [ˌkɒmplɪˈmentərɪ] *adj* -1. [remark] elogioso(sa); [person] halagador(ra) -2. [drink, seats] gratis *(inv)*.

complimentary ticket *n* entrada *f* gratuita.

comply [kəmˈplaɪ] (*pt & pp* -ied) *vi*: to ~ **with sthg** [standards] cumplir (con) algo; [request] acceder a algo; [law] acatar algo.

component [kəmˈpəʊnənt] *n* TECH pieza *f*; [element] elemento *m*, parte *f* integrante.

compose [kəmˈpəʊz] *vt* -1. [constitute] componer; **to be ~d of** estar compuesto OR componerse de -2. [music, poem, letter] componer -3. [calm]: to ~ **o.s.** calmarse, tranquilizarse.

composed [kəmˈpəʊzd] *adj* tranquilo(la).

composer [kəmˈpəʊzə^r] *n* compositor *m*, -ra *f*.

composition [ˌkɒmpəˈzɪʃn] *n* -1. [gen] composición *f* -2. [essay] redacción *f*.

compost [*UK* ˈkɒmpɒst, *US* ˈkɒmpəʊst] *n* compost *m*, abono *m*.

composure [kəmˈpəʊʒə^r] *n* compostura *f*, calma *f*.

compound [ˈkɒmpaʊnd] *n* -1. [gen & CHEM] compuesto *m* -2. [enclosed area] recinto *m*.

compound fracture *n* fractura *f* complicada.

comprehend [ˌkɒmprɪˈhend] *vt* comprender.

comprehension [ˌkɒmprɪˈhenʃn] *n* comprensión *f*.

comprehensive [ˌkɒmprɪˈhensɪv] <> *adj* -1. [wide-ranging] completo(ta) -2. [defeat, victory] rotundo(da) -3. [insurance] a todo riesgo. <> *n UK* = **comprehensive school**.

comprehensive school *n instituto de enseñanza media no selectiva en Gran Bretaña*.

compress [kəmˈpres] *vt* -1. [squeeze, press & COMPUT] comprimir -2. [shorten] reducir.

comprise [kəmˈpraɪz] *vt* -1. [consist of] comprender -2. [form] constituir.

compromise [ˈkɒmprəmaɪz] <> *n* arreglo *m*, término *m* medio. <> *vt* comprometer. <> *vi* llegar a un arreglo, transigir.

compulsion [kəmˈpʌlʃn] *n* -1. [strong desire] ganas *fpl* irrefrenables -2. (U) [force] obligación *f*.

compulsive [kəmˈpʌlsɪv] *adj* -1. [gambler] empedernido(da); [liar] compulsivo(va) -2. [fascinating, compelling] absorbente.

compulsory [kəmˈpʌlsərɪ] *adj* [gen] obligatorio(ria); [redundancy, retirement] forzoso(sa).

computer [kəm'pju:tə^r] n ordenador m, computadora f Amér.

computer animation n animación f por ordenador.

computer game n juego m de ordenador.

computer graphics npl infografía f.

computerized [kəm'pju:təraɪzd] adj informatizado(da), computerizado(da).

computing [kəm'pju:tɪŋ], **computer science** n informática f.

comrade ['kɒmreɪd] n camarada m OR f.

con [kɒn] (pt & pp -ned, cont -ning) inf <> n [trick] timo m, estafa f. <> vt timar, estafar; **to ~ sb out of sthg** timarle algo a alguien; **to ~ sb into doing sthg** engañar a alguien para que haga algo.

concave [,kɒn'keɪv] adj cóncavo(va).

conceal [kən'si:l] vt [object, substance, information] ocultar; [feelings] disimular; **to ~ sthg from sb** ocultarle algo a alguien.

concede [kən'si:d] <> vt -1. [defeat, a point] admitir, reconocer -2. [goal] encajar. <> vi [gen] ceder; [in sports, chess] rendirse.

conceit [kən'si:t] n engreimiento m, vanidad f.

conceited [kən'si:tɪd] adj engreído(da), vanidoso(sa).

conceive [kən'si:v] <> vt concebir. <> vi -1. MED concebir -2. [imagine]: **to ~ of sthg** imaginarse algo.

concentrate ['kɒnsəntreɪt] <> vt concentrar. <> vi: **to ~ (on)** concentrarse (en).

concentration [,kɒnsən'treɪʃn] n concentración f.

concentration camp n campo m de concentración.

concept ['kɒnsept] n concepto m.

concern [kən'sɜ:n] <> n -1. [worry, anxiety] preocupación f -2. [company] negocio m, empresa f. <> vt -1. [worry] preocupar; **to be ~ed about** preocuparse por -2. [involve] concernir; **those ~ed** los interesados; **to be ~ed with** [subj: person] ocuparse de; **to ~ o.s. with sthg** preocuparse de OR por algo; **as far as ... is ~ed** por lo que a ... respecta.

concerned [kən'sɜ:nd] adj [person] preocupado(da); [expression] de preocupación.

concerning [kən'sɜ:nɪŋ] prep en relación con.

concert ['kɒnsət] n concierto m..

concerted [kən'sɜ:tɪd] adj conjunto(ta).

concert hall n sala f de conciertos.

concertina [,kɒnsə'ti:nə] n concertina f.

concerto [kən'tʃeətəʊ] (pl -s) n concierto m.

concession [kən'seʃn] n -1. [allowance, franchise] concesión f -2. UK [special price] descuento m, rebaja f -3. UK [reduced ticket - for cinema, theatre] entrada f con descuento; [- for public transport] billete m con descuento.

concise [kən'saɪs] adj conciso(sa).

conclude [kən'klu:d] <> vt -1. [bring to an end] concluir, terminar -2. [deduce]: **to ~ (that)** concluir que -3. [agreement] llegar a; [business deal] cerrar; [treaty] firmar. <> vi terminar, concluir.

conclusion [kən'klu:ʒn] n -1. [decision] conclusión f -2. [ending] conclusión f, final m -3. [of business deal] cierre m; [of treaty, agreement] firma f.

conclusive [kən'klu:sɪv] adj concluyente.

concoct [kən'kɒkt] vt -1. [excuse, story] ingeniar -2. [food] confeccionar; [drink] preparar.

concoction [kən'kɒkʃn] n [drink] brebaje m; [food] mezcla f.

concourse ['kɒnkɔ:s] n [of station etc] vestíbulo m.

concrete ['kɒnkri:t] <> adj [definite, real] concreto(ta). <> n hormigón m, concreto m Amér. <> comp [made of concrete] de hormigón.

concur [kən'kɜ:^{r}] (pt & pp -red, cont -ring) vi [agree]: **to ~ (with)** estar de acuerdo OR coincidir (con).

concurrently [kən'kʌrəntlɪ] adv simultáneamente, al mismo tiempo.

concussion [kən'kʌʃn] n conmoción f cerebral.

condemn [kən'dem] vt -1. [gen]: **to ~ sb (for/to)** condenar a alguien (por/a) -2. [building] declarar en ruinas.

condensation [,kɒnden'seɪʃn] n [on walls] condensación f; [on glass] vaho m.

condense [kən'dens] <> vt condensar. <> vi condensarse.

condensed milk [kən'denst-] n leche f condensada.

condescending [,kɒndɪ'sendɪŋ] adj altivo(va), condescendiente.

condition [kən'dɪʃn] <> n -1. [state] estado m; **in good/bad ~** en buen/mal estado; **to be out of ~** no estar en forma -2. MED [disease, complaint] afección f -3. [provision] condición f; **on ~ that** a condición de que; **on one ~** con una condición. <> vt [gen] condicionar.

conditional [kən'dɪʃənl] <> adj condicional; **to be ~ on OR upon** depender de. <> n: **the ~** el condicional.

conditioner [kən'dɪʃnə^r] n suavizante m.

condolences [kən'dəʊlənsɪz] npl pésame m; **to offer one's ~** dar uno su más sentido pésame.

condom ['kɒndəm] n preservativo m, condón m.

condominium [,kɒndə'mɪnɪəm] n US -1. [apartment] piso m, apartamento m

- **2.** [apartment block] bloque *m* de pisos OR apartamentos.

condone [kən'dəʊn] *vt* perdonar, tolerar.

conducive [kən'dju:sɪv] *adj*: ~ to favorable para.

conduct [*n* 'kɒndʌkt, *vb* kən'dʌkt] <> *n* **-1.** [behaviour] conducta *f* **-2.** [carrying out] dirección *f*. <> *vt* **-1.** [carry out] dirigir, llevar a cabo **-2.** [behave]: **to ~ o.s. well/badly** comportarse bien/mal **-3.** MUS dirigir **-4.** PHYS conducir.

conducted tour [kən'dʌktɪd-] *n* visita *f* con guía.

conductor [kən'dʌktəʳ] *n* **-1.** [of orchestra, choir] director *m*, -ra *f* **-2.** [on bus] cobrador *m* **-3.** US [on train] revisor *m*, -ra *f*.

conductress [kən'dʌktrɪs] *n* [on bus] cobradora *f*.

cone [kəʊn] *n* **-1.** [shape] cono *m* **-2.** [for ice cream] cucurucho *m* **-3.** [from tree] piña *f*.

confectioner [kən'fekʃnəʳ] *n* confitero *m*, -ra *f*; ~'s (shop) confitería *f*.

confectioner's sugar [kən'fekʃnəz-] *n* US azúcar *m* glas.

confectionery [kən'fekʃnərɪ] *n* (U) dulces *mpl*, golosinas *fpl*.

confederation [kən,fedə'reɪʃn] *n* confederación *f*.

Confederation of British Industry *n*: **the ~** *organización patronal británica*, ≃ la CEOE.

confer [kən'fɜːʳ] (*pt* & *pp* -red, *cont* -ring) <> *vt fml*: **to ~ sthg (on)** otorgar OR conferir algo (a). <> *vi*: **to ~ (with)** consultar (con).

conference ['kɒnfərəns] *n* congreso *m*, conferencia *f*.

confess [kən'fes] <> *vt* confesar. <> *vi* **-1.** [to crime & RELIG] confesarse; **to ~ to sthg** confesar algo **-2.** [admit]: **to ~ to sthg** admitir algo.

confession [kən'feʃn] *n* confesión *f*.

confetti [kən'fetɪ] *n* confeti *m*.

confide [kən'faɪd] *vi*: **to ~ (in)** confiarse (a).

confidence ['kɒnfɪdəns] *n* **-1.** [self-assurance] confianza *f* OR seguridad *f* (en sí mismo/misma) **-2.** [trust] confianza *f* **-3.** [secrecy]: **in ~** en secreto **-4.** [secret] intimidad *f*, secreto *m*.

confidence trick *n* timo *m*, estafa *f*.

confident ['kɒnfɪdənt] *adj* **-1.** [self-assured - person] seguro de sí mismo (segura de sí misma); [- smile, attitude] confiado(da) **-2.** [sure]: ~ (of) seguro(ra) (de).

confidential [,kɒnfɪ'denʃl] *adj* [gen] confidencial; [secretary, clerk] de confianza.

confine [kən'faɪn] *vt* **-1.** [limit, restrict] limitar, restringir; **to be ~d to** limitarse a **-2.** [shut up] recluir, encerrar.

confined [kən'faɪnd] *adj* [space] reducido(da), limitado(da).

confinement [kən'faɪnmənt] *n* [imprisonment] reclusión *f*.

confines ['kɒnfaɪnz] *npl* confines *mpl*, límites *mpl*.

confirm [kən'fɜːm] *vt* confirmar.

confirmation [,kɒnfə'meɪʃn] *n* confirmación *f*.

confirmed [kən'fɜːmd] *adj* [non-smoker] inveterado(da); [bachelor] empedernido.

confiscate ['kɒnfɪskeɪt] *vt* confiscar.

conflict [*n* 'kɒnflɪkt, *vb* kən'flɪkt] <> *n* conflicto *m*. <> *vi*: **to ~ (with)** estar en desacuerdo (con).

conflicting [kən'flɪktɪŋ] *adj* contrapuesto(ta).

conform [kən'fɔːm] *vi* **-1.** [behave as expected] amoldarse a las normas sociales **-2.** [be in accordance]: **to ~ (to** OR **with)** [expectations] corresponder (a); [rules] ajustarse (a).

confound [kən'faʊnd] *vt* [confuse, defeat] confundir, desconcertar.

confront [kən'frʌnt] *vt* **-1.** [problem, task] hacer frente a **-2.** [subj: problem, task] presentarse a **-3.** [enemy etc] enfrentarse con **-4.** [challenge]: **to ~ sb (with)** poner a alguien cara a cara (con).

confrontation [,kɒnfrʌn'teɪʃn] *n* enfrentamiento *m*, confrontación *f*.

confuse [kən'fjuːz] *vt* **-1.** [bewilder] desconcertar, confundir **-2.** [mix up]: **to ~ (with)** confundir (con) **-3.** [complicate, make less clear] complicar.

confused [kən'fjuːzd] *adj* **-1.** [person] confundido(da), desconcertado(da) **-2.** [reasoning, situation] confuso(sa).

confusing [kən'fjuːzɪŋ] *adj* confuso(sa).

confusion [kən'fjuːʒn] *n* **-1.** [gen] confusión *f* **-2.** [of person] desconcierto *m*.

congeal [kən'dʒiːl] *vi* [fat] solidificarse; [blood] coagularse.

congenial [kən'dʒiːnjəl] *adj* ameno(na), agradable.

congested [kən'dʒestɪd] *adj* **-1.** [road] congestionado(da); [area] superpoblado(da) **-2.** MED congestionado(da).

congestion [kən'dʒestʃn] *n* [of traffic & MED] congestión *f*.

conglomerate [kən'glɒmərət] *n* COMM conglomerado *m*.

congratulate [kən'grætʃʊleɪt] *vt*: **to ~ sb (on)** felicitar a alguien (por).

congratulations [kən,grætʃʊ'leɪʃənz] <> *npl* felicitaciones *fpl*. <> *excl* ¡enhorabuena!

congregate ['kɒŋgrɪgeɪt] *vi* [people] congregarse; [animals] juntarse.

congregation [,kɒŋgrɪ'geɪʃn] *n* RELIG feligreses *mpl*.

congress ['kɒŋgres] *n* congreso *m*.
← **Congress** *n* [in US]: **(the) Congress** el Congreso.
congressman ['kɒŋgresmən] (*pl* -men [-mən]) *n US* congresista *m*.
conifer ['kɒnɪfəʳ] *n* conífera *f*.
conjugate ['kɒndʒʊgeɪt] *vt* conjugar.
conjugation [ˌkɒndʒʊ'geɪʃn] *n* conjugación *f*.
conjunction [kən'dʒʌŋkʃn] *n* **- 1.** GRAMM conjunción *f* **- 2.** [combination]: **in ~ with** juntamente con.
conjunctivitis [kənˌdʒʌŋktɪ'vaɪtɪs] *n* conjuntivitis *f inv.*
conjure ['kʌndʒəʳ] *vi* hacer juegos de manos.
← **conjure up** *vt sep* [evoke] evocar.
conjurer ['kʌndʒərəʳ] *n* prestidigitador *m*, -ra *f*.
conk [kɒŋk] *n inf* [nose] napia *f*.
← **conk out** *vi inf* **- 1.** [break down] escacharrarse **- 2.** [fall asleep] quedarse roque.
conker ['kɒŋkəʳ] *n UK* castaña *f (del castaño de Indias).*
conman ['kɒnmæn] (*pl* -men [-men]) *n* estafador *m*, timador *m*.
connect [kə'nekt] ◇ *vt* **- 1.** [join]: **to ~ sthg (to)** conectar algo (a); **to get ~ed** conectarse **- 2.** [on telephone]: **I'll ~ you now** ahora le paso OR pongo **- 3.** [associate]: **to ~ sthg/sb (with)** asociar algo/a alguien (con) **- 4.** ELEC : **to ~ sthg to** conectar algo a. ◇ *vi* [train, plane, bus]: **to ~ (with)** enlazar (con).
connected [kə'nektɪd] *adj* [related]: **~ (with)** relacionado(da) (con).
connection [kə'nekʃn] *n* **- 1.** [gen, ELEC & COMPUT]: **~ (between/with)** conexión *f* (entre/con); **in ~ with** con relación OR respecto a **- 2.** [plane, train, bus] enlace *m* **- 3.** [professional acquaintance] contacto *m*; **to have good ~s** tener mucho enchufe.
connive [kə'naɪv] *vi* **- 1.** [plot]: **to ~ (with)** confabularse (con) **- 2.** [allow to happen]: **to ~ at sthg** hacer la vista gorda con algo.
connoisseur [ˌkɒnə'sɜːʳ] *n* entendido *m*, -da *f*.
conquer ['kɒŋkəʳ] *vt* **- 1.** [take by force] conquistar **- 2.** [gain control of, overcome] vencer.
conqueror ['kɒŋkərəʳ] *n* conquistador *m*, -ra *f*.
conquest ['kɒŋkwest] *n* conquista *f*.
cons [kɒnz] *npl* **- 1.** *UK inf*: **all mod ~** con todas las comodidades **- 2.** ▷ **pro.**
conscience ['kɒnʃəns] *n* conciencia *f*.
conscientious [ˌkɒnʃɪ'enʃəs] *adj* concienzudo(da).
conscious ['kɒnʃəs] *adj* **- 1.** [gen] consciente; **to be ~ of** ser consciente de; **to become ~ of** darse cuenta de **- 2.** [intentional] deliberado(da).
consciousness ['kɒnʃəsnɪs] *n* **- 1.** [gen] conciencia *f* **- 2.** [state of being awake] conocimiento *m*; **to lose/regain ~** perder/recobrar el conocimiento.
conscript ['kɒnskrɪpt] *n* recluta *m* OR *f*.
conscription [kən'skrɪpʃn] *n* servicio *m* militar obligatorio.
consecutive [kən'sekjʊtɪv] *adj* consecutivo(va); **on three ~ days** tres días seguidos.
consent [kən'sent] ◇ *n* (U) [permission] consentimiento *m*. ◇ *vi*: **to ~ (to)** consentir (en).
consequence ['kɒnsɪkwəns] *n* **- 1.** [result] consecuencia *f*; **in ~** por consiguiente **- 2.** [importance] importancia *f*.
consequently ['kɒnsɪkwəntlɪ] *adv* por consiguiente.
conservation [ˌkɒnsə'veɪʃn] *n* [gen] conservación *f*; [environmental protection] protección *f* del medio ambiente.
conservative [kən'sɜːvətɪv] *adj* **- 1.** [not modern] conservador(ra) **- 2.** [estimate, guess] moderado(da).
← **Conservative** POL ◇ *adj* conservador(ra). ◇ *n* conservador *m*, -ra *f*.
Conservative Party *n*: **the ~** el Partido Conservador.
conservatory [kən'sɜːvətrɪ] (*pl* -ies) *n* pequeña habitación acristalada aneja a la casa.
conserve [*n* 'kɒnsɜːv, *vb* kən'sɜːv] ◇ *n* compota *f*. ◇ *vt* [energy, supplies] ahorrar; [nature, wildlife] conservar, preservar.
consider [kən'sɪdəʳ] *vt* **- 1.** [gen] considerar; **to ~ doing sthg** considerar hacer algo; **to ~ whether to do sthg** pensarse si hacer algo; **to ~ o.s. lucky** considerarse afortunado **- 2.** [take into account] tener en cuenta; **all things ~ed** teniéndolo todo en cuenta.
considerable [kən'sɪdrəbl] *adj* considerable.
considerably [kən'sɪdrəblɪ] *adv* considerablemente, sustancialmente.
considerate [kən'sɪdərət] *adj* considerado(da).
consideration [kənˌsɪdə'reɪʃn] *n* **- 1.** [gen] consideración *f*; **to take sthg into ~** tomar OR tener algo en cuenta **- 2.** [factor] factor *m* **- 3.** [amount of money] retribución *f*.
considering [kən'sɪdərɪŋ] ◇ *prep* habida cuenta de, teniendo en cuenta. ◇ *conj* después de todo.
consign [kən'saɪn] *vt*: **to ~ sthg/sb to** relegar algo/a alguien a.
consignment [kən'saɪnmənt] *n* remesa *f*.
consist [kən'sɪst] ← **consist in** *vt fus* consistir en.
← **consist of** *vt fus* constar de.
consistency [kən'sɪstənsɪ] (*pl* -ies) *n*

-1. [coherence - of behaviour, policy] consecuencia *f*, coherencia *f*; [of work, performances] regularidad *f* **-2.** [texture] consistencia *f*.

consistent [kən'sɪstənt] *adj* **-1.** [regular] constante **-2.** [coherent]: ~ **(with)** consecuente (con).

consolation [ˌkɒnsə'leɪʃn] *n* consuelo *m*.

console [*n* 'kɒnsəʊl, *vt* kən'səʊl] <> *n* consola *f*. <> *vt* consolar.

consonant ['kɒnsənənt] *n* consonante *f*.

consortium [kən'sɔːtjəm] (*pl* **-tiums** OR **-tia** [-tjə]) *n* consorcio *m*.

conspicuous [kən'spɪkjʊəs] *adj* [building] visible; [colour] llamativo(va).

conspiracy [kən'spɪrəsɪ] (*pl* **-ies**) *n* conspiración *f*.

conspiracy theory *n* teoría que sostiene la existencia de una conspiración oculta.

conspire [kən'spaɪəʳ] <> *vt*: to ~ to do sthg conspirar para hacer algo. <> *vi* **-1.** [plan secretly]: to ~ **(against/with)** conspirar (contra/con) **-2.** [combine] confabularse.

constable ['kʌnstəbl] *n* policía *m* OR *f*, agente *m* OR *f*.

constabulary [kən'stæbjʊlərɪ] (*pl* **-ies**) *n* policía *f* (de una zona determinada).

constant ['kɒnstənt] <> *adj* [gen] constante. <> *n* constante *f*.

constantly ['kɒnstəntlɪ] *adv* [forever] constantemente.

consternation [ˌkɒnstə'neɪʃn] *n* consternación *f*.

constipated ['kɒnstɪpeɪtɪd] *adj* estreñido(da).

constipation [ˌkɒnstɪ'peɪʃn] *n* estreñimiento *m*.

constituency [kən'stɪtjʊənsɪ] (*pl* **-ies**) *n* [area] distrito *m* electoral, circunscripción *f*.

constituent [kən'stɪtjʊənt] *n* **-1.** [voter] votante *m* OR *f*, elector *m*, -ra *f* **-2.** [element] componente *m*.

constitute ['kɒnstɪtjuːt] *vt* constituir.

constitution [ˌkɒnstɪ'tjuːʃn] *n* constitución *f*.

constraint [kən'streɪnt] *n* **-1.** [restriction]: ~ **(on)** limitación *f* (de) **-2.** [coercion] coacción *f*.

construct [kən'strʌkt] *vt* lit & fig construir.

construction [kən'strʌkʃn] *n* construcción *f*.

constructive [kən'strʌktɪv] *adj* constructivo(va).

construe [kən'struː] *vt* fml: to ~ sthg as interpretar algo como.

consul ['kɒnsəl] *n* cónsul *m* OR *f*.

consulate ['kɒnsjʊlət] *n* consulado *m*.

consult [kən'sʌlt] <> *vt* consultar. <> *vi*: ~ **with sb** consultar a OR con alguien.

consultant [kən'sʌltənt] *n* **-1.** [expert] asesor *m*, -ra *f* **-2.** UK [hospital doctor] (médico) especialista *m*, especialista *f*.

consultation [ˌkɒnsəl'teɪʃn] *n* **-1.** [gen] consulta *f* **-2.** [discussion] discusión *f*.

consulting room [kən'sʌltɪŋ-] *n* consultorio *m*, consulta *f*.

consume [kən'sjuːm] *vt* lit & fig consumir.

consumer [kən'sjuːməʳ] *n* consumidor *m*, -ra *f*.

consumer goods *npl* bienes *mpl* de consumo.

consumer price index *n* índice *m* de precios al consumo.

consumer society *n* sociedad *f* de consumo.

consummate [*adj* kən'sʌmət, *vb* 'kɒnsəmeɪt] <> *adj* **-1.** [skill, ease] absoluto(ta) **-2.** [liar, politician, snob] consumado(da). <> *vt* [marriage] consumar.

consumption [kən'sʌmpʃn] *n* [use] consumo *m*.

contact ['kɒntækt] <> *n* contacto *m*; **in** ~ **(with)** en contacto (con); **to lose** ~ **with** perder (el) contacto con; **to make** ~ **with** ponerse en contacto con. <> *vt* ponerse en contacto con.

contact lens *n* lentilla *f*, lente *f* de contacto.

contagious [kən'teɪdʒəs] *adj* contagioso(sa).

contain [kən'teɪn] *vt* contener; **to** ~ **o.s.** contenerse.

container [kən'teɪnəʳ] *n* **-1.** [box, bottle etc] recipiente *m*, envase *m* **-2.** [for transporting goods] contenedor *m*.

contaminate [kən'tæmɪneɪt] *vt* contaminar.

cont'd *abbr of* **continued**.

contemplate ['kɒntempleɪt] <> *vt* **-1.** [consider] considerar, pensar en **-2.** fml [look at] contemplar. <> *vi* reflexionar.

contemporary [kən'tempərərɪ] (*pl* **-ies**) <> *adj* contemporáneo(a). <> *n* contemporáneo *m*, -a *f*.

contempt [kən'tempt] *n* **-1.** [scorn]: ~ **(for)** desprecio *m* OR desdén *m* (por) **-2.** JUR desacato *m*.

contemptuous [kən'temptʃʊəs] *adj* despreciativo(va); **to be** ~ **of sthg** despreciar algo.

contend [kən'tend] <> *vi* **-1.** [deal]: to ~ **with** enfrentarse a **-2.** [compete]: to ~ **for/against** competir por/contra. <> *vt* fml: to ~ **that** sostener OR afirmar que.

contender [kən'tendəʳ] *n* [gen] contendiente *m* OR *f*; [for title] aspirante *m* OR *f*.

content [*n* 'kɒntent, *adj* & *vb* kən'tent] <> *adj*: ~ **(with)** contento(ta) OR satisfecho(cha) (con); **to be** ~ **to do sthg** contentarse con hacer algo. <> *n* contenido *m*.

◇ *vt*: **to ~ o.s. with sthg/with doing sthg** contentarse con algo/con hacer algo.
➡ **contents** *npl* **- 1.** [of container, letter, etc] contenido *m* **- 2.** [heading in book] índice *m*.

contented [kən'tentɪd] *adj* satisfecho(-cha), contento(ta).

contention [kən'tenʃn] *n fml* **- 1.** [argument, assertion] argumento *m* **- 2.** *(U)* [disagreement] disputas *fpl* **- 3.** [competition]: **to be in ~ for sthg** tener posibilidades de ganar algo.

contest [*n* 'kɒntest, *vb* kən'test] ◇ *n* **- 1.** [competition] concurso *m*; [in boxing] combate *m* **- 2.** [for power, control] lucha *f*, contienda *f*. ◇ *vt* **- 1.** [seat, election] presentarse como candidato(ta) a **- 2.** [dispute - statement] disputar; [- decision] impugnar.

contestant [kən'testənt] *n* [in quiz show] concursante *m* OR *f*; [in race] participante *m* OR *f*; [in boxing match] contrincante *m* OR *f*.

context ['kɒntekst] *n* contexto *m*.

continent ['kɒntɪnənt] *n* continente *m*.
➡ **Continent** *n* UK: **the Continent** la Europa continental.

continental [,kɒntɪ'nentl] *adj* **- 1.** GEOGR continental **- 2.** UK [European] de la Europa continental.

continental breakfast *n* desayuno *m* continental.

continental quilt *n* UK edredón *m*.

contingency [kən'tɪndʒənsɪ] *(pl* **-ies)** *n* contingencia *f*.

contingency plan *n* plan *m* de emergencia.

continual [kən'tɪnjʊəl] *adj* continuo(nua), constante.

continually [kən'tɪnjʊəlɪ] *adv* continuamente, constantemente.

continuation [kən,tɪnjʊ'eɪʃn] *n* continuación *f*.

continue [kən'tɪnju:] ◇ *vt*: **to ~ (doing** OR **to do sthg)** continuar (haciendo algo); **to be ~ d** continuará. ◇ *vi*: **to ~ (with sthg)** continuar (con algo).

continuous [kən'tɪnjʊəs] *adj* continuo(-nua).

continuously [kən'tɪnjʊəslɪ] *adv* continua-mente, ininterrumpidamente.

contort [kən'tɔ:t] *vt* retorcer.

contortion [kən'tɔ:ʃn] *n* contorsión *f*.

contour ['kɒn,tʊər] *n* **- 1.** [outline] contorno *m* **- 2.** [on map] curva *f* de nivel.

contraband ['kɒntrəbænd] ◇ *adj* de contrabando. ◇ *n* contrabando *m*.

contraception [,kɒntrə'sepʃn] *n* anticoncepción *f*.

contraceptive [,kɒntrə'septɪv] ◇ *adj* anticonceptivo(va). ◇ *n* anticonceptivo *m*.

contract [*n* 'kɒntrækt, *vb* kən'trækt] ◇ *n* contrato *m*. ◇ *vt* **- 1.** [through legal agreement]: **to ~ sb (to do sthg)** contratar a alguien (para hacer algo); **to ~ to do sthg** comprometerse a hacer algo (por contrato) **- 2.** *fml* [illness, disease] contraer. ◇ *vi* [decrease in size, length] contraerse.

contraction [kən'trækʃn] *n* contracción *f*.

contractor [kən'træktər] *n* contratista *m* OR *f*.

contradict [,kɒntrə'dɪkt] *vt* contradecir.

contradiction [,kɒntrə'dɪkʃn] *n* contradicción *f*.

contraflow ['kɒntrəfləʊ] *n habilitación del carril contrario.*

contraption [kən'træpʃn] *n* chisme *m*, artilugio *m*.

contrary ['kɒntrərɪ, *adj sense 2* kən'treərɪ] ◇ *adj* **- 1.** [opposite] contrario(ria); **~ to** en contra de **- 2.** [awkward] puñetero(ra), que lleva la contraria siempre. ◇ *n*: **the ~** lo contrario; **on the ~** al contrario.
➡ **contrary to** *prep* en contra de.

contrast [*n* 'kɒntrɑ:st, *vb* kən'trɑ:st] ◇ *n*: **~ (between)** contraste *m* (entre); **by** OR **in ~** en cambio; **in ~ with** OR **to** a diferencia de. ◇ *vt*: **to ~ sthg with** contrastar algo con. ◇ *vi*: **to ~ (with)** contrastar (con).

contravene [,kɒntrə'vi:n] *vt* contravenir.

contribute [kən'trɪbju:t] ◇ *vt* [give] contribuir, aportar. ◇ *vi* **- 1.** [gen]: **to ~ (to)** contribuir (a) **- 2.** [write material]: **to ~ to** colaborar con.

contribution [,kɒntrɪ'bju:ʃn] *n* **- 1.** [gen]: **~ (to)** contribución *f* (a) **- 2.** [article] colaboración *f* **- 3.** [to social security] cotización *f*.

contributor [kən'trɪbjʊtər] *n* **- 1.** [of money] contribuyente *m* OR *f* **- 2.** [to magazine, newspaper] colaborador *m*, -ra *f*.

contrive [kən'traɪv] *vt fml* **- 1.** [engineer] maquinar, idear **- 2.** [manage]: **to ~ to do sthg** lograr hacer algo.

contrived [kən'traɪvd] *adj* inverosímil.

control [kən'trəʊl] (*pt* & *pp* **-led**, *cont* **-ling**) ◇ *n* **- 1.** [gen & COMPUT] control *m*; [on spending] restricción *f*; **in ~ of** al mando de; **to be in ~ of the situation** dominar la situación; **out of/under ~** fuera de/bajo control **- 2.** [of emotions] dominio *m*, control *m*. ◇ *vt* **- 1.** [gen] controlar; **to ~ o.s.** dominarse, controlarse **- 2.** [operate - machine, plane] manejar; [- central heating] regular.
➡ **controls** *npl* [of machine, vehicle] mandos *mpl*.

controller [kən'trəʊlər] *n* FIN interventor *m*, -ra *f*; RADIO & TV director *m*, -ra *f*.

control panel *n* tablero *m* de instrumentos OR de mandos.

control tower *n* torre *f* de control.

controversial [,kɒntrə'vɜ:ʃl] *adj* polémico(ca), controvertido(da).

controversy ['kɒntrəvɜːsɪ, UK kən'trɒvəsɪ] (pl -ies) n polémica f, controversia f.

convalesce [ˌkɒnvə'les] vi convalecer.

convene [kən'viːn] ⋄ vt convocar. ⋄ vi reunirse.

convenience [kən'viːnjəns] n comodidad f, conveniencia f; **do it at your ~** hágalo cuando le venga bien; **at your earliest ~** a la mayor brevedad posible.

convenience store n tienda f de ultramarinos que abre hasta tarde.

convenient [kən'viːnjənt] adj **-1.** [suitable] conveniente; **is Monday ~?** ¿te viene bien el lunes? **-2.** [handy-size] práctico(ca); [-position] adecuado(da); **~ for** [well-situated] bien situado para.

convent ['kɒnvənt] n convento m.

convention [kən'venʃn] n convención f.

conventional [kən'venʃənl] adj convencional.

converge [kən'vɜːdʒ] vi lit & fig: **to ~ (on)** converger (en).

convergence [kən'vɜːdʒəns] n [in EU] convergencia f; **~ criteria** criterios mpl de convergencia.

conversant [kən'vɜːsənt] adj fml: **~ with** familiarizado(da) con.

conversation [ˌkɒnvə'seɪʃn] n conversación f.

conversational [ˌkɒnvə'seɪʃənl] adj coloquial.

converse [n 'kɒnvɜːs, vb kən'vɜːs] ⋄ n: **the ~** lo contrario OR opuesto. ⋄ vi fml: **to ~ (with)** conversar (con).

conversely [kən'vɜːslɪ] adv fml a la inversa.

conversion [kən'vɜːʃn] n [gen, COMPUT & RELIG] conversión f.

convert [vb kən'vɜːt, n 'kɒnvɜːt] ⋄ vt **-1.** [gen & COMPUT]: **to ~ sthg (to OR into)** convertir algo (en) **-2.** [change belief of]: **to ~ sb (to)** convertir a alguien (a). ⋄ n converso m, -sa f.

convertible [kən'vɜːtəbl] ⋄ adj **-1.** [sofa]: **~ sofa** sofá-cama m **-2.** [currency] convertible **-3.** [car] descapotable. ⋄ n (coche m) descapotable m.

convex [kɒn'veks] adj convexo(xa).

convey [kən'veɪ] vt **-1.** fml [transport] transportar, llevar **-2.** [express]: **to ~ sthg (to)** transmitir algo (a).

conveyer belt [kən'veɪə'-] n cinta f transportadora.

convict [n 'kɒnvɪkt, vb kən'vɪkt] ⋄ n presidiario m, -ria f. ⋄ vt: **to ~ sb of** condenar a alguien por, declarar a alguien culpable de.

conviction [kən'vɪkʃn] n **-1.** [belief, fervour] convicción f **-2.** JUR condena f.

convince [kən'vɪns] vt: **to ~ sb (of sthg/to do sthg)** convencer a alguien (de algo/para que haga algo).

convincing [kən'vɪnsɪŋ] adj convincente.

convoluted ['kɒnvəluːtɪd] adj [tortuous] enrevesado(da).

convoy ['kɒnvɔɪ] n convoy m.

convulse [kən'vʌls] vt: **to be ~d with** [pain] retorcerse de; [laughter] troncharse de.

convulsion [kən'vʌlʃn] n MED convulsión f.

coo [kuː] vi arrullar.

cook [kʊk] ⋄ n cocinero m, -ra f. ⋄ vt [gen] cocinar, guisar; [prepare] preparar, hacer. ⋄ vi **-1.** [prepare food] cocinar, guisar **-2.** [subj: food] cocerse, hacerse. ◆ **cook up** vt sep [plan, deal] tramar, urdir; [excuse] inventarse.

cookbook ['kʊkˌbʊk] = **cookery book**.

cooker ['kʊkə'] n esp UK cocina f (aparato).

cookery ['kʊkərɪ] n cocina f (arte).

cookery book n libro m de cocina.

cookie ['kʊkɪ] n **-1.** US [biscuit] galleta f **-2.** COMPUT cookie m.

cooking ['kʊkɪŋ] n [food] cocina f.

cool [kuːl] ⋄ adj **-1.** [not warm] fresco(ca); [lukewarm] tibio(a); **it's ~** hace fresco **-2.** [calm] tranquilo(la) **-3.** [unfriendly] frío(a) **-4.** inf [hip] guay, chachi. ⋄ vt refrescar. ⋄ vi [become less warm] enfriarse. ⋄ n: **to keep/lose one's ~** mantener/perder la calma. ◆ **cool down** vi **-1.** [become less warm] enfriarse **-2.** [become less angry] calmarse.

cool box n nevera f portátil.

coop [kuːp] n gallinero m. ◆ **coop up** vt sep inf encerrar.

cooperate [kəʊ'ɒpəreɪt] vi: **to ~ (with)** cooperar (con).

cooperation [kəʊˌɒpə'reɪʃn] n cooperación f.

cooperative [kəʊ'ɒpərətɪv] ⋄ adj **-1.** [helpful] servicial, dispuesto(ta) a ayudar **-2.** [collective] cooperativo(va). ⋄ n cooperativa f.

coordinate [n kəʊ'ɔːdɪnət, vt kəʊ'ɔːdɪneɪt] ⋄ n coordenada f. ⋄ vt coordinar. ◆ **coordinates** npl [clothes] conjuntos mpl.

coordination [kəʊˌɔːdɪ'neɪʃn] n coordinación f.

cop [kɒp] n inf poli m OR f; **the ~s** la poli.

cope [kəʊp] vi arreglárselas; **to ~ with** [work] poder con; [problem, situation] hacer frente a.

Copenhagen [ˌkəʊpən'heɪgən] n Copenhague.

copier ['kɒpɪə'] n copiadora f, fotocopiadora f.

cop-out n inf escaqueo m.

copper ['kɒpə'] n **-1.** [metal] cobre m **-2.** UK inf [policeman] poli m OR f, paco m, -ca f Andes.

coppice ['kɒpɪs], **copse** [kɒps] *n* bosquecillo *m*.

copy ['kɒpɪ] (*pt* & *pp* **-ied**) ⬦ *n* **- 1.** [imitation, duplicate] copia *f* **- 2.** [of book, magazine] ejemplar *m*. ⬦ *vt* **- 1.** [imitate & COMPUT] copiar **- 2.** [photocopy] fotocopiar.

copyright ['kɒpɪraɪt] *n (U)* derechos *mpl* de autor.

coral ['kɒrəl] *n* coral *m*.

cord [kɔ:d] *n* **- 1.** [string] cuerda *f*; [for tying clothes] cordón *m* **- 2.** [cable] cable *m*, cordón *m* **- 3.** [fabric] pana *f*.
 ◆ **cords** *npl* pantalones *mpl* de pana.

cordial ['kɔ:dʒəl] ⬦ *adj* cordial. ⬦ *n* bebida de frutas concentrada.

cordon ['kɔ:dn] *n* cordón *m*.
 ◆ **cordon off** *vt sep* acordonar.

corduroy ['kɔ:dərɔɪ] *n* pana *f*.

core [kɔ:ʳ] ⬦ *n* **- 1.** [of fruit] corazón *m* **- 2.** [of Earth, nuclear reactor, group] núcleo *m* **- 3.** [of issue, matter] meollo *m*. ⬦ *vt* quitar el corazón de.

Corfu [kɔ:'fu:] *n* Corfú.

corgi ['kɔ:gɪ] (*pl* **-s**) *n* corgi *mf*.

coriander [,kɒrɪ'ændəʳ] *n* cilantro *m*.

cork [kɔ:k] *n* corcho *m*.

corkscrew ['kɔ:kskru:] *n* sacacorchos *m inv.*

corn [kɔ:n] *n* **- 1.** *UK* [wheat, barley, oats] cereal *m* **- 2.** *US* [maize] maíz *m*, choclo *m Andes, RP*; **~ on the cob** mazorca *f* **- 3.** [callus] callo *m*.

cornea ['kɔ:nɪə] (*pl* **-s**) *n* córnea *f*.

corned beef [kɔ:nd-] *n* carne *f* de vaca cocinada y enlatada.

corner ['kɔ:nəʳ] ⬦ *n* **- 1.** [angle - of street, page, screen] esquina *f*; [- of room, cupboard] rincón *m*; [- of mouth] comisura *f*; **just around the ~** a la vuelta de la esquina **- 2.** [bend - in street, road] curva *f* **- 3.** [faraway place] rincón *m* **- 4.** [in football] córner *m*. ⬦ *vt* **- 1.** [trap] arrinconar **- 2.** [monopolize] acaparar.

corner shop *n* tienda pequeña de barrio que vende comida, artículos de limpieza etc.

cornerstone ['kɔ:nəstəʊn] *n fig* piedra *f* angular.

cornet ['kɔ:nɪt] *n* **- 1.** [instrument] corneta *f* **- 2.** *UK* [ice-cream cone] cucurucho *m*.

cornflakes ['kɔ:nfleɪks] *npl* copos *mpl* de maíz, cornflakes *mpl*.

cornflour *UK* ['kɔ:nflaʊəʳ], **cornstarch** *US* ['kɔ:nstɑ:tʃ] *n* harina *f* de maíz, maicena® *f*.

Cornwall ['kɔ:nwɔ:l] *n* Cornualles.

corny ['kɔ:nɪ] (*compar* **-ier**, *superl* **-iest**) *adj inf* trillado(da).

coronary ['kɒrənrɪ] (*pl* **-ies**), **coronary thrombosis** (*pl* **coronary thromboses**) *n* trombosis *f inv* coronaria, infarto *m*.

coronation [,kɒrə'neɪʃn] *n* coronación *f*.

coroner ['kɒrənəʳ] *n* juez de instrucción que investiga las causas de muertes sospechosas.

Corp. (*abbr of* **corporation**) Corp.

corporal ['kɔ:pərəl] *n* cabo *m OR f*.

corporal punishment *n* castigo *m* corporal.

corporate ['kɔ:pərət] *adj* **- 1.** [business] corporativo(va); [strategy, culture] empresarial **- 2.** [collective] colectivo(va).

corporation [,kɔ:pə'reɪʃn] *n* **- 1.** [company] ≃ sociedad *f* anónima **- 2.** *UK* [council] ayuntamiento *m*.

corps [kɔ:ʳ] (*pl inv*) *n* cuerpo *m*.

corpse [kɔ:ps] *n* cadáver *m*.

correct [kə'rekt] ⬦ *adj* **- 1.** [accurate - time, amount, forecast] exacto(ta); [- answer, spelling, information] correcto(ta) **- 2.** [socially acceptable] correcto(ta) **- 3.** [appropriate, required] apropiado(da). ⬦ *vt* corregir.

correction [kə'rekʃn] *n* corrección *f*.

correctly [kə'rektlɪ] *adv* **- 1.** [gen] correctamente; **I don't think I can have heard you ~** no estoy segura de haberte oído bien **- 2.** [appropriately, as required] apropiadamente.

correlation [,kɒrə'leɪʃn] *n*: **~ (between)** correlación *f* (entre).

correspond [,kɒrɪ'spɒnd] *vi* **- 1.** [correlate]: **to ~ (with OR to)** corresponder (con OR a) **- 2.** [match]: **to ~ (with OR to)** coincidir (con) **- 3.** [write letters]: **to ~ (with)** cartearse (con).

correspondence [,kɒrɪ'spɒndəns] *n*: **~ (with/between)** correspondencia *f* (con/entre).

correspondence course *n* curso *m* por correspondencia.

correspondent [,kɒrɪ'spɒndənt] *n* [reporter] corresponsal *m OR f*.

corridor ['kɒrɪdɔ:ʳ] *n* pasillo *m*, corredor *m*.

corroborate [kə'rɒbəreɪt] *vt* corroborar.

corrode [kə'rəʊd] ⬦ *vt* corroer. ⬦ *vi* corroerse.

corrosion [kə'rəʊʒn] *n* corrosión *f*.

corrugated ['kɒrəgeɪtɪd] *adj* ondulado(da).

corrugated iron *n* chapa *f* ondulada.

corrupt [kə'rʌpt] ⬦ *adj* [gen & COMPUT] corrupto(ta). ⬦ *vt* [gen & COMPUT] corromper; **to ~ a minor** pervertir a un menor.

corruption [kə'rʌpʃn] *n* corrupción *f*.

corset ['kɔ:sɪt] *n* corsé *m*.

Corsica ['kɔ:sɪkə] *n* Córcega.

cortège, cortège [kɔ:'teɪʒ] *n* cortejo *m*.

cosh [kɒʃ] ⬦ *n* porra *f*. ⬦ *vt* aporrear.

cosmetic [kɒz'metɪk] ⬦ *n* cosmético *m*. ⬦ *adj fig* superficial.

cosmopolitan [,kɒzmə'pɒlɪtn] *adj* cosmopolita.

cosset ['kɒsɪt] *vt* mimar.

cost [kɒst] (*pt* & *pp* **cost** OR **-ed**) ◇ *n* coste *m*, costo *m*; **at** ~ COMM a precio de coste; **at no extra** ~ sin coste adicional; **at the** ~ **of** a costa de; **at all** ~s a toda costa. ◇ *vt* **- 1.** [gen] costar; **it** ~ **us £20/a lot of effort** nos costó 20 libras/mucho esfuerzo; **how much does it** ~? ¿cuánto cuesta OR vale? **- 2.** [estimate] presupuestar, preparar un presupuesto de.
  ◆ **costs** *npl* JUR litisexpensas *fpl*, costas *fpl*.
co-star ['kəʊ-] *n* coprotagonista *m* OR *f*.
Costa Rica [ˌkɒstəˈriːkə] *n* Costa Rica.
Costa Rican [ˌkɒstəˈriːkən] ◇ *adj* costarricense. ◇ *n* costarricense *m* OR *f*.
cost-effective *adj* rentable.
costing ['kɒstɪŋ] *n* cálculo *m* del coste.
costly ['kɒstlɪ] (*compar* **-ier**, *superl* **-iest**) *adj* costoso(sa).
cost of living *n*: **the** ~ el coste de la vida.
cost price *n* precio *m* de coste.
costume ['kɒstjuːm] *n* **- 1.** [gen] traje *m* **- 2.** [swimming costume] traje *m* de baño.
costume jewellery *n* (U) bisutería *f*.
cosy UK, **cozy** US ['kəʊzɪ] (*compar* **-ier**, *superl* **-iest**, *pl* **-ies**) ◇ *adj* **- 1.** [warm and comfortable - room] acogedor(ra) **- 2.** [intimate] agradable, amigable. ◇ *n* funda *f* para tetera.
cot [kɒt] *n* **- 1.** UK [for child] cuna *f* **- 2.** US [folding bed] cama *f* plegable, catre *m*.
cottage ['kɒtɪdʒ] *n* casa *f* de campo, chalé *m*.
cottage cheese *n* queso *m* fresco.
cottage pie *n* UK *pastel de carne picada con una capa de puré de patatas.*
cotton ['kɒtn] *n* **- 1.** [fabric] algodón *m* **- 2.** [thread] hilo *m* (de algodón).
  ◆ **cotton on** *vi inf*: **to** ~ **on (to)** caer en la cuenta (de).
cotton candy *n* US azúcar *m* hilado, algodón *m*.
cotton wool *n* algodón *m* (hidrófilo).
couch [kaʊtʃ] ◇ *n* **- 1.** [sofa] sofá *m* **- 2.** [in doctor's surgery] diván *m*. ◇ *vt*: **to** ~ **sthg in** formular algo en.
couchette [kuːˈʃet] *n* UK litera *f*.
cough [kɒf] ◇ *n* tos *f*; **to have a** ~ tener tos. ◇ *vi* toser.
cough mixture *n* UK jarabe *m* para la tos.
cough sweet *n* UK caramelo *m* para la tos.
cough syrup = **cough mixture**.
could [kʊd] *pt* ▷ **can²**.
couldn't ['kʊdnt] = **could not**.
could've ['kʊdəv] = **could have**.
council ['kaʊnsl] *n* **- 1.** [of a town] ayuntamiento *m*; [of a county] ≃ diputación *f* **- 2.** [group, organization] consejo *m* **- 3.** [meeting] junta *f*, consejo *m*.
council estate *n* urbanización de viviendas de protección oficial.

council house *n* UK ≃ casa *f* de protección oficial.
councillor ['kaʊnsələʳ] *n* concejal *m*, -la *f*.
council tax *n* UK *impuesto municipal basado en el valor de la propiedad,* ≃ contribución *f* urbana.
counsel ['kaʊnsəl] *n* **- 1.** (U) *fml* [advice] consejo *m*; **to keep one's own** ~ reservarse su opinión **- 2.** [lawyer] abogado *m*, -da *f*.
counsellor UK, **counselor** US ['kaʊnsələʳ] *n* **- 1.** [gen] consejero *m*, -ra *f* **- 2.** [therapist] psicólogo *m*, -ga *f* **- 3.** US [lawyer] abogado *m*, -da *f*.
count [kaʊnt] *n* **- 1.** [total] total *m* ; [of votes] recuento *m*; **to keep/lose** ~ **of** llevar/perder la cuenta de **- 2.** [aristocrat] conde *m*. ◇ *vt* **- 1.** [add up] contar; [total, cost] calcular **- 2.** [consider]: **to** ~ **sb as** considerar a alguien como **- 3.** [include] incluir, contar. ◇ *vi* contar; **to** ~ **(up) to** contar hasta; **to** ~ **for nothing** no contar para nada.
  ◆ **count against** *vt fus* perjudicar.
  ◆ **count (up)on** *vt fus* contar con.
  ◆ **count up** *vt fus* contar.
countdown ['kaʊntdaʊn] *n* cuenta *f* atrás.
counter ['kaʊntəʳ] ◇ *n* **- 1.** [in shop] mostrador *m*; [in bank] ventanilla *f*; **over the** ~ sin receta médica **- 2.** [in board game] ficha *f*. ◇ *vt*: **to** ~ **sthg with** responder a algo mediante; **to** ~ **sthg by doing sthg** contrarrestar algo haciendo algo.
counteract [ˌkaʊntərˈækt] *vt* contrarrestar.
counterattack [ˌkaʊntərəˈtæk] ◇ *n* contraataque *m*. ◇ *vt* & *vi* contraatacar.
counterclockwise [ˌkaʊntəˈklɒkwaɪz] *adv* US en sentido opuesto a las agujas del reloj.
counterfeit ['kaʊntəfɪt] ◇ *adj* falsificado(da). ◇ *vt* falsificar.
counterfoil ['kaʊntəfɔɪl] *n* matriz *f*.
countermand [ˌkaʊntəˈmɑːnd] *vt* revocar.
counterpart ['kaʊntəpɑːt] *n* homólogo *m*, -ga *f*.
counterproductive [ˌkaʊntəprəˈdʌktɪv] *adj* contraproducente.
countess ['kaʊntɪs] *n* condesa *f*.
countless ['kaʊntlɪs] *adj* innumerables.
country ['kʌntrɪ] (*pl* **-ies**) *n* **- 1.** [nation] país *m* **- 2.** [population]: **the** ~ el pueblo **- 3.** [countryside]: **the** ~ el campo **- 4.** [terrain] terreno *m*. ◇ *comp* campestre.
country dancing *n* (U) baile *m* tradicional.
country house *n* casa *f* solariega.
countryman ['kʌntrɪmən] (*pl* **-men** [-mən]) *n* [from same country] compatriota *m*.
country park *n* UK *parque natural abierto al público.*
countryside ['kʌntrɪsaɪd] *n* [land] campo *m*; [landscape] paisaje *m*.
county ['kaʊntɪ] (*pl* **-ies**) *n* condado *m*.
county council *n* UK *organismo que gobierna*

un condado, ≃ diputación *f* provincial.

coup [kuː] *n* **-1.** [rebellion]: ~ **(d'état)** golpe *m* (de estado) **- 2.** [masterstroke] éxito *m*.

couple ['kʌpl] ◇ *n* **-1.** [two people in relationship] pareja *f* **- 2.** [two objects, people]: a ~ **(of)** un par (de) **- 3.** [a few - objects, people]: a ~ **(of)** un par (de), unos(nas). ◇ *vt* [join]: to ~ sthg (to) enganchar algo (con).

coupon ['kuːpɒn] *n* [gen] vale *m*, cupón *m*; [for pools] boleto *m*.

courage ['kʌrɪdʒ] *n* valor *m*.

courageous [kə'reɪdʒəs] *adj* valiente.

courgette [kɔː'ʒet] *n* UK calabacín *m*, calabacita *f Méx*, zapallito *m* (italiano) *CSur*.

courier ['kʊrɪəʳ] *n* **-1.** [on holiday] guía *m* OR *f* **- 2.** [to deliver letters, packages] mensajero *m*, -ra *f*.

course [kɔːs] *n* **-1.** [gen] curso *m*; [of lectures] ciclo *m*; UNIV carrera *f*; ~ **of treatment** MED tratamiento *m*; **to change** ~ cambiar de rumbo; **off** ~ fuera de su rumbo; ~ **(of action)** camino *m* (a seguir); **in the** ~ **of** a lo largo de **- 2.** [of meal] plato *m* **- 3.** SPORT [for golf] campo *m*; [for race] circuito *m*.
   ◆ of course *adv* **-1.** [inevitably, not surprisingly] naturalmente **- 2.** [certainly] claro, por supuesto; **of** ~ **not** claro que no, desde luego que no.

coursebook ['kɔːsbʊk] *n* libro *m* de texto.

coursework ['kɔːswɜːk] *n (U)* trabajo *m* realizado durante el curso.

court [kɔːt] ◇ *n* **-1.** [place of trial, judge, jury etc] tribunal *m*; **to take sb to** ~ llevar a alguien a juicio **- 2.** SPORT cancha *f*, pista *f* **- 3.** [of king, queen etc] corte *f*. ◇ *vi dated* [go out together] cortejarse.

courteous ['kɜːtjəs] *adj* cortés.

courtesy ['kɜːtɪsɪ] ◇ *n* cortesía *f*. ◇ *comp* de cortesía.
   ◆ (by) courtesy of *prep* [the author] con permiso de; [a company] por cortesía OR gentileza de.

courthouse ['kɔːthaʊs] *n* US palacio *m* de justicia.

courtier ['kɔːtjəʳ] *n* cortesano *m*.

court-martial (*pl* **court-martials** OR **courts-martial**) *n* consejo *m* de guerra.

courtroom ['kɔːtrʊm] *n* sala *f* del tribunal.

courtyard ['kɔːtjɑːd] *n* patio *m*.

cousin ['kʌzn] *n* primo *m*, -ma *f*.

cove [kəʊv] *n* cala *f*, ensenada *f*.

covenant ['kʌvənənt] *n* **-1.** [of money] *compromiso escrito para el pago regular de una contribución esp con fines caritativos* **- 2.** [agreement] convenio *m*.

Covent Garden [ˌkɒvənt-] *n famosa galería comercial londinense donde se dan cita todo tipo de artistas callejeros.*

cover ['kʌvəʳ] ◇ *n* **-1.** [covering] cubierta *f*; [lid] tapa *f*; [for seat, typewriter] funda *f* **- 2.** [blanket] manta *f*; **under the** ~**s** debajo de las sábanas **- 3.** [of book] tapa *f*, cubierta *f*; [of magazine - at the front] portada *f*; [- at the back] contraportada *f* **- 4.** [protection, shelter] refugio *m*, cobijo *m*; **to take** ~ [from weather, gunfire] refugiarse; **under** ~ [from weather] a cubierto, bajo techo **- 5.** [concealment] tapadera *f*; **under** ~ **of** al amparo OR abrigo de **- 6.** [insurance] cobertura *f*. ◇ *vt* **-1.** [gen]: **to** ~ **sthg (with)** cubrir algo (de); [with lid] tapar algo (con) **- 2.** [insure]: **to** ~ **sb (against)** cubrir OR asegurar a alguien (contra) **- 3.** [include] abarcar **- 4.** [report on] informar sobre, cubrir **- 5.** [discuss, deal with] abarcar, cubrir.
   ◆ cover up *vt sep* **-1.** [place sthg over] tapar **- 2.** [conceal] encubrir.

coverage ['kʌvərɪdʒ] *n* [of news] cobertura *f* informativa.

cover charge *n* cubierto *m*.

covering ['kʌvərɪŋ] *n* **-1.** [for floor etc] cubierta *f* **- 2.** [of snow, dust] capa *f*.

covering letter UK, **cover letter** US *n* [with CV] carta *f* de presentación; [with parcel, letter] nota *f* aclaratoria.

cover note *n* UK póliza *f* provisional.

covert ['kʌvət] *adj* [operation] encubierto(-ta), secreto(ta); [glance] furtivo(va).

cover-up *n* encubrimiento *m*.

covet ['kʌvɪt] *vt* codiciar.

cow [kaʊ] ◇ *n* **-1.** [female type of cattle] vaca *f* **- 2.** [female elephant, whale, seal] hembra *f* **- 3.** UK *inf pej* [woman] bruja *f*. ◇ *vt* acobardar, intimidar.

coward ['kaʊəd] *n* cobarde *m* OR *f*.

cowardly ['kaʊədlɪ] *adj* cobarde.

cowboy ['kaʊbɔɪ] *n* [cattlehand] vaquero *m*, tropero *m RP*.

cower ['kaʊəʳ] *vi* encogerse.

cox [kɒks], **coxswain** ['kɒksən] *n* timonel *m* OR *f*.

coy [kɔɪ] *adj* tímido(da).

cozy US = **cosy**.

crab [kræb] *n* cangrejo *m*.

crab apple *n* manzana *f* silvestre.

crack [kræk] ◇ *n* **-1.** [split - in wood, ground] grieta *f*; [- in glass, pottery] raja *f* **- 2.** [gap] rendija *f* **- 3.** [sharp noise - of whip] chasquido *m*; [- of twigs] crujido *m* **- 4.** *inf* [attempt]: **to have a** ~ **at sthg** intentar algo **- 5.** [cocaine] crack *m*. ◇ *adj* de primera. ◇ *vt* **-1.** [cause to split] romper, partir **- 2.** [egg, nut] cascar **- 3.** [whip etc] chasquear **- 4.** [bang]: **to** ~ **one's head** golpearse la cabeza **- 5.** [code] dar con la clave de, descifrar; [problem] resolver **- 6.** *inf* [tell-joke] contar. ◇ *vi* **-1.** [split - skin, wood, ground] agrietarse; [- pottery, glass] partirse, rajarse **- 2.** [break down] hundirse, venirse abajo **- 3.** [make sharp noise - whip]

chasquear; [-twigs] crujir - **4.** *UK inf* [act
quickly]: **to get ~ing** ponerse manos a la
obra.

◆ **crack down** *vi*: **to ~ down (on)** tomar
medidas severas (contra).

◆ **crack up** *vi* - **1.** [under pressure] venirse
abajo - **2.** *inf* [laugh] partirse de risa.

cracker ['kræka^r] *n* - **1.** [biscuit] galleta *f* (salada) - **2.** *UK* [for Christmas] *cilindro de papel
que produce un estallido al abrirlo y que tiene dentro un regalito de Navidad.*

crackers ['krækəz] *adj UK inf* majara.

crackle ['krækl] *vi* [fire] crujir, chasquear;
[radio] sonar con interferencias.

cradle ['kreɪdl] ◇ *n* [baby's bed, birthplace]
cuna *f*. ◇ *vt* acunar, mecer.

craft [krɑːft] (*pl sense 2 inv*) *n* - **1.** [trade] oficio *m*; [skill] arte *m* - **2.** [boat] embarcación *f*.

◆ **crafts** *npl* artesanía *f*.

craftsman ['krɑːftsmən] (*pl* -**men** [-mən])
n artesano *m*.

craftsmanship ['krɑːftsmənʃɪp] *n* (*U*)
- **1.** [skill] destreza *f*, habilidad *f* - **2.** [skilled
work] artesanía *f*.

craftsmen *pl* ⊳ **craftsman**.

crafty ['krɑːftɪ] (*compar* -**ier**, *superl* -**iest**) *adj*
astuto(ta).

crag [kræg] *n* peñasco *m*.

cram [kræm] (*pt & pp* -**med**, *cont* -**ming**)
◇ *vt* - **1.** [push-books, clothes] embutir;
[people] apiñar - **2.** [overfill]: **to ~ sthg with**
atiborrar *OR* atestar algo de; **to be crammed
(with)** estar repleto(ta) (de). ◇ *vi* [study]
empollar.

cramp [kræmp] *n* calambre *m*; **stomach ~s**
retortijones *mpl* de vientre.

cranberry ['krænbərɪ] (*pl* -**ies**) *n* arándano
m (agrio).

crane [kreɪn] *n* - **1.** [machine] grúa *f* - **2.** [bird]
grulla *f*.

crank [kræŋk] ◇ *n* - **1.** [handle] manivela *f*
- **2.** *inf* [eccentric] majareta *m OR f.* ◇ *vt*
[wind] girar.

crankshaft ['kræŋkʃɑːft] *n* cigüeñal *m*.

cranny ['krænɪ] ⊳ **nook**.

crap [kræp] *v inf* ◇ *n* (*U*) [gen] mierda *f*.
◇ *adj UK* de mierda, muy chungo(ga).

crash [kræʃ] ◇ *n* - **1.** [accident] choque *m*,
estrellón *m Amér* - **2.** [loud noise] estruendo
m - **3.** FIN crac *m*, quiebra *f.* ◇ *vt* [plane]
estrellar. ◇ *vi* - **1.** [collide - two vehicles]
chocar, colisionar; [one vehicle - into wall
etc] estrellarse; **to ~ into sthg** chocar *OR*
estrellarse contra algo - **2.** FIN quebrar
- **3.** COMPUT bloquearse, colgarse.

crash course *n* cursillo *m* intensivo de introducción, curso *m* acelerado.

crash helmet *n* casco *m* protector.

crash-land *vi* realizar un aterrizaje
forzoso.

crass [kræs] *adj* burdo(da); **a ~ error** un
error básico.

crate [kreɪt] *n* caja *f* (para embalaje o transporte).

crater ['kreɪtə^r] *n* cráter *m*.

cravat [krə'væt] *n* pañuelo *m* (de hombre).

crave [kreɪv] ◇ *vt* ansiar. ◇ *vi*: **to ~ for**
sthg ansiar algo.

crawfish ['krɔːfɪʃ] = **crayfish**.

crawl [krɔːl] ◇ *vi* - **1.** [baby] andar a gatas,
gatear - **2.** [insect, person] arrastrarse
- **3.** [move slowly, with difficulty] avanzar
lentamente, ir a paso de tortuga. ◇ *n*
[swimming stroke]: **the ~** el crol.

crayfish ['kreɪfɪʃ] (*pl inv OR* -**es**) *n* [freshwater] cangrejo *m* de río; [spiny lobster] cigala *f*.

crayon ['kreɪɒn] *n* lápiz *m* de cera.

craze [kreɪz] *n* moda *f*.

crazy ['kreɪzɪ] (*compar* -**ier**, *superl* -**iest**) *adj*
inf - **1.** [mad - person] loco(ca); [- idea] disparatado(da); **like ~** como un loco - **2.** [enthusiastic]: **to be ~ about** estar loco(ca) por.

creak [kriːk] *vi* [floorboard, bed] crujir;
[door, hinge] chirriar.

cream [kriːm] ◇ *adj* [in colour] (color) crema *(inv)*. ◇ *n* - **1.** [food] nata *f* - **2.** [cosmetic,
mixture for food] crema *f* - **3.** [colour] (color
m) crema *m* - **4.** [elite]: **the ~** la flor y nata,
la crema.

cream cake *n UK* pastel *m* de nata, pastel *m*
de crema *Amér*, masa *f* de crema *RP*.

cream cheese *n* queso *m* cremoso *OR* blanco.

cream cracker *n UK* galleta sin azúcar que generalmente se come con queso.

cream tea *n UK* merienda de té con bollos, nata
y mermelada.

crease [kriːs] ◇ *n* [deliberate - in shirt] pliegue *m*; [- in trousers] raya *f*; [accidental] arruga *f*. ◇ *vt* arrugar. ◇ *vi* [gen] arrugarse;
[forehead] fruncirse.

create [kriː'eɪt] *vt* [gen] crear; [interest] producir.

creation [kriː'eɪʃn] *n* creación *f*.

creative [kriː'eɪtɪv] *adj* [gen] creativo(va);
[energy] creador(ra); **~ writing** creación *f*
literaria.

creature ['kriːtʃə^r] *n* criatura *f*; **a ~ of habit**
un animal de costumbres.

crèche [kreʃ] *n UK* guardería *f* (infantil).

credence ['kriːdns] *n*: **to give** *OR* **lend ~ to**
dar crédito a.

credentials [krɪ'denʃlz] *npl* credenciales *fpl*.

credibility [ˌkredə'bɪlətɪ] *n* credibilidad *f*.

credit ['kredɪt] ◇ *n* - **1.** [financial aid] crédito *m*; **to be in ~** tener saldo acreedor *OR* positivo; **on ~** a crédito - **2.** (*U*) [praise]
reconocimiento *m*; **to give sb ~ for** reconocer a alguien el mérito de - **3.** [towards qualification, degree] crédito *m* - **4.** [money]

credited] **saldo** *m* acreedor OR positivo. ◇ *vt* - **1.** FIN [add] abonar; **we'll ~ your account** lo abonaremos en su cuenta - **2.** [believe] creer - **3.** [give the credit to]: **to ~ sb with** atribuir a alguien el mérito de.

◆ **credits** *npl* [on film] títulos *mpl*.

credit card *n* tarjeta *f* de crédito.

credit note *n* [from shop] vale *m* de compra.

creditor ['kredɪtə'] *n* acreedor *m*, -ra *f*.

creed [kriːd] *n* credo *m*.

creek [kriːk] *n* - **1.** [inlet] cala *f* - **2.** US [stream] riachuelo *m*.

creep [kriːp] (*pt* & *pp* **crept**) ◇ *vi* - **1.** [person] deslizarse, andar con sigilo - **2.** [insect] arrastrarse; [traffic etc] avanzar lentamente - **3.** *inf* [grovel]: **to ~ (to sb)** hacer la pelota (a alguien). ◇ *n inf* - **1.** [unctuous person] pelotillero *m*, -ra *f*, pelota *m* OR *f* - **2.** [horrible person] asqueroso *m*, -sa *f*.

◆ **creeps** *npl*: **to give sb the ~s** *inf* ponerle a alguien la piel de gallina.

creeper ['kriːpə'] *n* enredadera *f*, bejuco *m* Amér.

creepy ['kriːpɪ] (*compar* **-ier**, *superl* **-iest**) *adj inf* horripilante, espeluznante.

creepy-crawly [-'krɔːlɪ] (*pl* **-ies**) *n inf* bicho *m*.

cremate [krɪ'meɪt] *vt* incinerar.

crematorium UK [ˌkremə'tɔːrɪəm] (*pl* **-riums** OR **-ria** [-rɪə]), **crematory** US ['kremətrɪ] (*pl* **-ies**) *n* crematorio *m*.

crepe [kreɪp] *n* - **1.** [cloth] crespón *m* - **2.** [rubber] crepé *m* - **3.** [thin pancake] crepe *f*.

crepe bandage *n* UK venda *f* de gasa.

crepe paper *n* (U) papel *m* crespón.

crept [krept] *pt* & *pp* ▷ **creep.**

crescendo [krɪ'ʃendəʊ] (*pl* **-s**) *n* crescendo *m*.

crescent ['kresnt] *n* - **1.** [shape] media luna *f* - **2.** [street] calle *f* en forma de arco.

cress [kres] *n* berro *m*.

crest [krest] *n* - **1.** [on bird's head, of wave] cresta *f* - **2.** [of hill] cima *f*, cumbre *f* - **3.** [on coat of arms] blasón *m*.

crestfallen ['krest,fɔːln] *adj* alicaído(da).

Crete [kriːt] *n* Creta.

cretin ['kretɪn] *n inf* [idiot] cretino *m*, -na *f*.

Creutzfeldt-Jakob disease [ˌkrɔɪtsfelt '-jækɒb-] *n* enfermedad *f* de Creutzfeldt-Jakob.

crevasse [krɪ'væs] *n* grieta *f*, fisura *f*.

crevice ['krevɪs] *n* grieta *f*, hendidura *f*.

crew [kruː] *n* - **1.** [of ship, plane] tripulación *f* - **2.** [on film set etc] equipo *m*.

crew cut *n* rapado *m*, corte *m* al cero.

crew-neck(ed) [-nek(t)] *adj* con cuello redondo.

crib [krɪb] (*pt* & *pp* **-bed**, *cont* **-bing**) ◇ *n* - **1.** [cot] cuna *f* - **2.** US *inf* [place] casa *f*, cantón *f* Méx. ◇ *vt inf*: **to ~ sthg off** OR **from sb**

copiar algo de alguien.

cricket ['krɪkɪt] *n* - **1.** [game] críquet *m* - **2.** [insect] grillo *m*.

crime [kraɪm] ◇ *n* - **1.** [serious offence] crimen *m*; [less serious offence] delito *m* - **2.** [criminal behaviour - serious] criminalidad *f*; [- less serious] delincuencia *f* - **3.** [immoral act] crimen *m*. ◇ *comp*: **~ novel** novela *f* policíaca.

criminal ['krɪmɪnl] ◇ *adj* JUR [act, behaviour] criminal, delictivo(va); [law] penal; [lawyer] criminalista. ◇ *n* [serious] criminal *m* OR *f*; [less serious] delincuente *m* OR *f*.

crimson ['krɪmzn] ◇ *adj* [in colour] carmesí. ◇ *n* carmesí *m*.

cringe [krɪndʒ] *vi* - **1.** [out of fear] encogerse - **2.** *inf* [with embarrassment] sentir vergüenza ajena.

crinkle ['krɪŋkl] *vt* arrugar.

cripple ['krɪpl] ◇ *n dated* & *offensive* tullido *m*, -da *f*, lisiado *m*, -da *f*. ◇ *vt* - **1.** MED dejar inválido(da) - **2.** [country, industry] paralizar, inmovilizar.

crisis ['kraɪsɪs] (*pl* **crises** ['kraɪsiːz]) *n* crisis *f inv.*

crisp [krɪsp] *adj* - **1.** [pastry, bacon, snow] crujiente; [banknote, vegetables, weather] fresco(ca) - **2.** [brisk] directo(ta), categórico(ca).

◆ **crisps** *npl* UK patatas *fpl* fritas *(de bolsa).*

crisscross ['krɪskrɒs] *adj* entrecruzado(da).

criterion [kraɪ'tɪərɪən] (*pl* **-ria** [-rɪə] OR **-rions**) *n* criterio *m*.

critic ['krɪtɪk] *n* crítico *m*, -ca *f*.

critical ['krɪtɪkl] *adj* [gen] crítico(ca); [illness] grave; **to be ~ of** criticar.

critically ['krɪtɪklɪ] *adv* [gen] críticamente; [ill] gravemente; **~ important** de vital importancia; **~ acclaimed** aclamado(da) por la crítica.

criticism ['krɪtɪsɪzm] *n* crítica *f*.

criticize, -ise ['krɪtɪsaɪz] *vt* & *vi* criticar.

croak [krəʊk] *vi* - **1.** [frog] croar; [raven] graznar - **2.** [person] ronquear.

Croat ['krəʊæt], **Croatian** [krəʊ'eɪʃn] ◇ *adj* croata. ◇ *n* - **1.** [person] croata *m* OR *f* - **2.** [language] croata *m*.

Croatia [krəʊ'eɪʃə] *n* Croacia.

Croatian = **Croat.**

crochet ['krəʊʃeɪ] *n* ganchillo *m*.

crockery ['krɒkərɪ] *n* loza *f*, vajilla *f*.

crocodile ['krɒkədaɪl] (*pl inv* OR **-s**) *n* cocodrilo *m*.

crocus ['krəʊkəs] (*pl* **-es**) *n* azafrán *m* *(planta).*

croft [krɒft] *n* UK granja *pequeña que pertenece a una familia y les proporciona sustento.*

crony ['krəʊnɪ] (*pl* **-ies**) *n inf* amiguete *m*, -ta *f*.

crook [krʊk] n -1. [criminal] ratero m, -ra f, delincuente m OR f - 2. inf [dishonest person] ladrón m, -ona f, sinvergüenza m OR f - 3. [shepherd's staff] cayado m.

crooked ['krʊkɪd] adj -1. [teeth, tie] torcido(da) - 2. [back] encorvado(da); [path] sinuoso(sa) - 3. inf [dishonest - person, policeman] corrupto(ta).

crop [krɒp] (pt & pp -ped, cont -ping) <> n -1. [kind of plant] cultivo m - 2. [harvested produce] cosecha f, pizca f Méx - 3. [whip] fusta f. <> vt [cut short] cortar (muy corto).

◆ **crop up** vi surgir.

croquette [krɒ'ket] n croqueta f.

cross [krɒs] <> adj enfadado(da); **to get ~ (with)** enfadarse (con). <> n -1. [gen] cruz f - 2. [hybrid] cruce m, cruza f Amér; **a ~ between** [combination] una mezcla de - 3. SPORT centro m. <> vt -1. [gen & FIN] cruzar - 2. [face - subj: expression] reflejarse en - 3. SPORT centrar - 4. [oppose] contrariar - 5. RELIG: **to ~ o.s.** santiguarse. <> vi [intersect] cruzarse.

◆ **cross off, cross out** vt sep tachar.

crossbar ['krɒsbɑːˁ] n -1. [on goal] travesaño m - 2. [on bicycle] barra f.

cross-Channel adj [ferry] que hace la travesía del Canal de la Mancha; [route] a través del Canal de la Mancha.

cross-country <> adj & adv a campo traviesa. <> n cross m.

cross-examine vt interrogar (para comprobar veracidad).

cross-eyed ['krɒsaɪd] adj bizco(ca).

crossfire ['krɒs‚faɪəˁ] n fuego m cruzado.

crossing ['krɒsɪŋ] n -1. [on road] cruce m, paso m de peatones; [on railway line] paso a nivel - 2. [sea journey] travesía f.

crossing guard n US persona encargada de ayudar a cruzar la calle a los colegiales.

cross-legged ['krɒslegd] adv con las piernas cruzadas.

cross-purposes npl: **I think we're at ~** creo que estamos hablando de cosas distintas.

cross-reference n remisión f, referencia f.

crossroads ['krɒsrəʊdz] (pl inv) n cruce m.

cross-section n -1. [drawing] sección f transversal - 2. [sample] muestra f representativa.

crosswalk ['krɒswɔːk] n US paso m de peatones.

crosswind ['krɒswɪnd] n viento m de costado.

crosswise ['krɒswaɪz] adv en diagonal, transversalmente.

crossword (puzzle) ['krɒswɜːd-] n crucigrama m.

crotch [krɒtʃ] n entrepierna f.

crotchety ['krɒtʃɪtɪ] adj UK inf refunfuñón(ona).

crouch [kraʊtʃ] vi [gen] agacharse; [ready to spring] agazaparse.

crow [krəʊ] <> n corneja f. <> vi -1. [cock] cantar - 2. inf [gloat] darse pisto, vanagloriarse.

crowbar ['krəʊbɑːˁ] n palanca f.

crowd [kraʊd] <> n -1. [mass of people] multitud f, muchedumbre f; [at football match etc] público m - 2. [particular group] gente f. <> vi agolparse, apiñarse. <> vt -1. [room, theatre etc] llenar - 2. [people] meter, apiñar.

crowded ['kraʊdɪd] adj: **~ (with)** repleto(ta) OR atestado(da) (de).

crown [kraʊn] <> n -1. [of royalty, on tooth] corona f - 2. [of hat] copa f; [of head] coronilla f; [of hill] cumbre f, cima f. <> vt [gen] coronar; **to ~ it all** para colmo.

◆ **Crown** n: **the Crown** [monarchy] la corona.

crown jewels npl joyas fpl de la corona.

crown prince n príncipe m heredero.

crow's feet npl patas fpl de gallo.

crucial ['kruːʃl] adj crucial.

crucifix ['kruːsɪfɪks] n crucifijo m.

Crucifixion [‚kruːsɪ'fɪkʃn] n: **the ~** la crucifixión.

crude [kruːd] adj -1. [rubber, oil, joke] crudo(da) - 2. [person, behaviour] basto(ta), vulgar - 3. [drawing, sketch] tosco(ca).

crude oil n crudo m.

cruel [krʊəl] (compar -ler, superl -lest) adj [gen] cruel; [blow] duro(ra); [winter] crudo(da).

cruelty ['krʊəltɪ] n (U) crueldad f.

cruelty-free adj no probado(da) en animales.

cruet ['kruːɪt] n vinagreras fpl, convoy m.

cruise [kruːz] <> n crucero m. <> vi -1. [sail] hacer un crucero - 2. [drive, fly] ir a velocidad de crucero.

cruiser ['kruːzəˁ] n -1. [warship] crucero m - 2. [cabin cruiser] yate m (para cruceros).

crumb [krʌm] n -1. [of food] miga f, migaja f - 2. [of information] pizca f.

crumble ['krʌmbl] <> n postre a base de compota de fruta con una pasta seca por encima. <> vi desmigajar. <> vi -1. [building, cliff] desmoronarse; [plaster] caerse - 2. fig [relationship, hopes] venirse abajo.

crumbly ['krʌmblɪ] (compar -ier, superl -iest) adj que se desmigaja con facilidad.

crumpet ['krʌmpɪt] n -1. [food] bollo que se come tostado - 2. [women] inf (U) tías fpl.

crumple ['krʌmpl] vt [dress, suit] arrugar; [letter] estrujar.

crunch [krʌntʃ] <> n crujido m. <> vt [with teeth] ronzar.

crunchy ['krʌntʃi] (*compar* **-ier**, *superl* **-iest**) *adj* crujiente.

crusade [kru:'seɪd] *n lit* & *fig* cruzada *f*.

crush [krʌʃ] ◇ *n* **-1.** [crowd] gentío *m*, aglomeración *f* **-2.** *inf* [infatuation]: **to have a ~ on sb** estar colado(da) OR loco(ca) por alguien. ◇ *vt* **-1.** [squash] aplastar **-2.** [grind - garlic, grain] triturar; [- ice] picar; [- grapes] exprimir **-3.** [destroy] demoler.

crust [krʌst] *n* **-1.** [on bread, of snow, earth] corteza *f* **-2.** [on pie] parte *f* dura.

crutch [krʌtʃ] *n* **-1.** [stick] muleta *f*; *fig* [support] apoyo *m*, soporte *m* **-2.** [crotch] entrepierna *f*.

crux [krʌks] *n*: **the ~ of the matter** el quid de la cuestión.

cry [kraɪ] (*pt* & *pp* **cried**, *pl* **cries**) ◇ *n* **-1.** [weep] llorera *f* **-2.** [shout] grito *m*. ◇ *vi* **-1.** [weep] llorar **-2.** [shout] gritar.

◆ **cry off** *vi* volverse atrás.

crystal ['krɪstl] *n* cristal *m*.

crystal clear *adj* **-1.** [transparent] cristalino(na) **-2.** [clearly stated] claro(ra) como el agua.

CSE (*abbr of* **Certificate of Secondary Education**) *n* antiguo título de enseñanza secundaria en Gran Bretaña para alumnos de bajo rendimiento escolar.

CTC *n abbr of* **city technology college**.

cub [kʌb] *n* **-1.** [young animal] cachorro *m* **-2.** [boy scout] lobato *m*, boy scout *de entre 8 y 11 años*.

Cuba ['kju:bə] *n* Cuba.

Cuban ['kju:bən] ◇ *adj* cubano(na). ◇ *n* [person] cubano *m*, -na *f*.

cubbyhole ['kʌbɪhəʊl] *n* [room] cuchitril *m*; [cupboard] armario *m*.

cube [kju:b] ◇ *n* [gen] cubo *m*; [of sugar] terrón *m*. ◇ *vt* **-1.** MATH elevar al cubo **-2.** [cut up] cortar en dados.

cubic ['kju:bɪk] *adj* cúbico(ca).

cubicle ['kju:bɪkl] *n* [at swimming pool] caseta *f*; [in shop] probador *m*; [in toilets] cubículo *m*.

Cub Scout *n* lobato *m*, boy scout *de entre 8 y 11 años*.

cuckoo ['kʊku:] *n* cuco *m*, cuclillo *m*.

cuckoo clock *n* reloj *m* de cuco.

cucumber ['kju:kʌmbə'] *n* pepino *m*.

cuddle ['kʌdl] ◇ *n* abrazo *m*. ◇ *vt* abrazar, apapachar *Méx*. ◇ *vi* abrazarse.

cuddly toy ['kʌdlɪ-] *n* muñeco *m* de peluche.

cue [kju:] *n* **-1.** RADIO, THEATRE & TV entrada *f*; **on ~** justo en aquel instante **-2.** *fig* [stimulus, signal] señal *f* **-3.** [in snooker, pool] taco *m*.

cuff [kʌf] *n* **-1.** [of sleeve] puño *m*; **off the ~** [speech, remarks] improvisado(da), sacado(da) de la manga **-2.** US [of trouser leg]

vuelta *f* **-3.** [blow] cachete *m*.

cuff link *n* gemelo *m*, collera *f Andes*.

cuisine [kwɪ'zi:n] *n* cocina *f*.

cul-de-sac ['kʌldəsæk] *n* callejón *m* sin salida.

cull [kʌl] *vt* **-1.** [animals] sacrificar selectivamente **-2.** *fml* [information, facts] recoger.

culminate ['kʌlmɪneɪt] *vi*: **to ~ in** culminar en.

culmination [,kʌlmɪ'neɪʃn] *n* culminación *f*.

culottes [kju:'lɒts] *npl* falda *f* pantalón.

culpable ['kʌlpəbl] *adj fml*: **~ (of)** culpable (de); **~ homicide** homicidio *m* involuntario.

culprit ['kʌlprɪt] *n* culpable *m* OR *f*.

cult [kʌlt] ◇ *n* RELIG culto *m*. ◇ *comp* [series, movie] de culto.

cultivate ['kʌltɪveɪt] *vt* **-1.** [gen] cultivar **-2.** [get to know - person] hacer amistad con.

cultivated ['kʌltɪveɪtɪd] *adj* **-1.** [cultured] culto(ta) **-2.** [land] cultivado(da).

cultivation [,kʌltɪ'veɪʃn] *n (U)* cultivo *m*.

cultural ['kʌltʃərəl] *adj* cultural.

culture ['kʌltʃə'] *n* **-1.** [gen] cultura *f* **-2.** [of bacteria] cultivo *m*.

cultured ['kʌltʃəd] *adj* culto(ta).

cumbersome ['kʌmbəsəm] *adj* **-1.** [package] abultado(da), voluminoso(sa); [machinery] aparatoso(sa) **-2.** [system] torpe.

cunning ['kʌnɪŋ] ◇ *adj* [gen] astuto(ta); [device, idea] ingenioso(sa). ◇ *n (U)* astucia *f*.

cunt [kʌnt] *n vulg* [vagina] coño *m*; [person] hijo *m*, -ja *f* de puta.

cup [kʌp] (*pt* & *pp* **-ped**, *cont* **-ping**) ◇ *n* **-1.** [gen] taza *f* **-2.** [prize, of bra] copa *f*. ◇ *vt* ahuecar.

cupboard ['kʌbəd] *n* armario *m*.

cupcake ['kʌpkeɪk] *n* US magdalena *f*.

Cup Final *n*: **the ~** ≃ la final de la Copa.

cup tie *n* UK partido *m* de copa.

curate ['kjʊərət] *n* coadjutor *m*, -ra *f*, auxiliar *m* OR *f*.

curator [,kjʊə'reɪtə'] *n* conservador *m*, -ra *f*.

curb [kɜ:b] ◇ *n* **-1.** [control]: **~ (on)** control *m* OR restricción *f* (de); **to put a ~ on sthg** poner freno a algo **-2.** US [in road] bordillo *m*, bordo *m* de la banqueta *Méx*, cordón *m* de la vereda *RP*, cuneta *f Chile*, sardinel *m Col*. ◇ *vt* controlar, contener.

curdle ['kɜ:dl] *vi* [milk] cuajarse; *fig* [blood] helarse.

cure [kjʊə'] ◇ *n* **-1.** MED: **~ (for)** cura *f* (para) **-2.** [solution]: **~ (for)** remedio *m* (a). ◇ *vt* **-1.** MED curar **-2.** [problem, inflation] remediar **-3.** [food, tobacco] curar; [leather] curtir.

cure-all *n* panacea *f*.

curfew ['kɜːfjuː] *n* toque *m* de queda.

curio ['kjʊəriəʊ] (*pl* **-s**) *n* curiosidad *f*, rareza *f*.

curiosity [ˌkjʊərɪˈɒsətɪ] *n* curiosidad *f*.

curious ['kjʊərɪəs] *adj* curioso(sa); **to be ~ about** sentir curiosidad por.

curl [kɜːl] ◇ *n* [of hair] rizo *m*. ◇ *vt* **-1.** [hair] rizar **- 2.** [twist] enroscar. ◇ *vi* **-1.** [hair] rizarse **- 2.** [paper] abarquillarse, curvarse.

◆ **curl up** *vi* [person, animal] acurrucarse, hacerse un ovillo; [leaf, paper] abarquillarse, curvarse.

curler ['kɜːlə^r] *n* rulo *m*.

curling tongs *npl* tenacillas *fpl* de rizar.

curly ['kɜːlɪ] (*compar* **-ier**, *superl* **-iest**) *adj* [hair] rizado(da); [pig's tail] enroscado(da).

currant ['kʌrənt] *n* pasa *f* de Corinto.

currency ['kʌrənsɪ] (*pl* **-ies**) *n* **-1.** FIN moneda *f*; **foreign ~ divisa *f* - 2.** *fml* [acceptability]: **to gain ~** ganar aceptación.

current ['kʌrənt] *adj* [price, method, girlfriend] actual; [year] en curso; [issue] último(ma); [ideas, expressions, customs] corriente.

current account *n* UK cuenta *f* corriente.

current affairs *npl* temas *mpl* de actualidad.

currently ['kʌrəntlɪ] *adv* actualmente.

curriculum [kəˈrɪkjələm] (*pl* **-lums** OR **-la** [-lə]) *n* [course of study] plan *m* de estudios, temario *m*.

curriculum vitae [-'viːtaɪ] (*pl* **curricula vitae**) *n* UK currículum *m* (vitae).

curry ['kʌrɪ] (*pl* **-ies**) *n* curry *m*.

curse [kɜːs] ◇ *n* **-1.** [evil charm] maldición *f* **- 2.** [swearword] taco *m*, palabrota *f*. ◇ *vt* maldecir. ◇ *vi* [swear] soltar tacos.

cursor ['kɜːsə^r] *n* COMPUT cursor *m*.

cursory ['kɜːsərɪ] *adj* superficial, por encima.

curt [kɜːt] *adj* brusco(ca), seco(ca).

curtail [kɜːˈteɪl] *vt* **-1.** [visit] acortar **- 2.** [expenditure] reducir; [rights] restringir.

curtain ['kɜːtn] *n* **-1.** [gen] cortina *f* **- 2.** [in theatre] telón *m*.

curts(e)y ['kɜːtsɪ] (*pt* & *pp* **curtsied**) ◇ *n* reverencia *f (de mujer)*. ◇ *vi* hacer una reverencia *(una mujer)*.

curve [kɜːv] ◇ *n* curva *f*. ◇ *vi* [river] hacer una curva; [surface] curvarse, arquearse.

cushion ['kʊʃn] ◇ *n* **-1.** [for sitting on] cojín *m*, almohadón *m* **- 2.** [protective layer] colchón *m*. ◇ *vt* lit & fig amortiguar.

cushy ['kʊʃɪ] (*compar* **-ier**, *superl* **-iest**) *adj* inf cómodo(da); **a ~ job** OR **number** un chollo (de trabajo).

custard ['kʌstəd] *n* (U) natillas *fpl*.

custodial sentence [kʌˈstəʊdjəl-] *n* pena *f* de cárcel.

custodian [kʌˈstəʊdjən] *n* **-1.** [of building, museum] conservador *m*, -ra *f* **- 2.** [of tradition, values] guardián *m*, -ana *f*.

custody ['kʌstədɪ] *n* custodia *f*; **to take sb into ~** detener a alguien; **in ~** bajo custodia.

custom ['kʌstəm] ◇ *n* **-1.** [tradition, habit] costumbre *f* **- 2.** (U) *fml* [trade] clientela *f*. ◇ *adj* hecho(cha) de encargo.

◆ **customs** *n* [place] aduana *f*.

customary ['kʌstəmrɪ] *adj* acostumbrado(-da), habitual.

customer ['kʌstəmə^r] *n* **-1.** [client] cliente *m* OR *f* **- 2.** *inf* [person] tipo *m*, individuo *m*.

customize, -ise ['kʌstəmaɪz] *vt* [gen & COMPUT] personalizar.

Customs and Excise *n* (U) UK oficina del gobierno británico encargada de la recaudación de derechos arancelarios.

customs duty *n* (U) derechos *mpl* de aduana, aranceles *mpl*.

customs officer *n* empleado *m*, -da *f* de aduanas.

customs union *n* unión *f* aduanera.

cut [kʌt] (*pt* & *pp* **cut**, *cont* **-ting**) ◇ *n* **-1.** [gen] corte *m* **- 2.** [reduction]: **~ (in)** reducción *f* (de); **wage ~** recorte *m* salarial **- 3.** *inf* [share] parte *f*. ◇ *vt* **-1.** [gen & COMPUT] cortar; [one's finger etc] cortarse; **to ~ sb's hair** cortarle el pelo a alguien; **to ~ a hole** hacer un agujero; **to ~ class** US faltar a clase; **to ~ o.s.** cortarse **- 2.** [spending, staff etc] reducir, recortar; [text] acortar **- 3.** *inf* [lecture] fumarse. ◇ *vi* [gen & COMPUT] cortar.

◆ **cut back** *vt sep* **-1.** [plant] podar **- 2.** [expenditure, budget] recortar.

◆ **cut down** ◇ *vt sep* **-1.** [chop down] cortar, talar **- 2.** [reduce] reducir. ◇ *vi*: **to ~ down on smoking** OR **cigarettes** fumar menos.

◆ **cut in** *vi* **-1.** [interrupt]: **to ~ in (on sb)** cortar OR interrumpir (a alguien) **- 2.** [in car] colarse.

◆ **cut off** *vt sep* **-1.** [gen] cortar **- 2.** [interrupt] interrumpir **- 3.** [separate]: **to be ~ off (from)** [person] estar aislado(da) (de); [town, village] quedarse incomunicado(da) (de).

◆ **cut out** *vt sep* **-1.** [remove] recortar **- 2.** [dress, pattern etc] cortar **- 3.** [stop]: **to ~ out smoking** OR **cigarettes** dejar de fumar; **~ it out!** *inf* ¡basta ya! **- 4.** [exclude - light etc] eliminar; **to ~ sb out of one's will** desheredar a alguien.

◆ **cut up** *vt sep* [chop up] cortar, desmenuzar.

cutback ['kʌtbæk] *n*: **~ (in)** recorte *m* OR reducción *f* (en).

cute [kjuːt] *adj* [appealing] mono(na), lindo(da).

cuticle [ˈkjuːtɪkl] *n* cutícula *f*.

cutlery [ˈkʌtləri] *n* (U) cubertería *f*, cubiertos *mpl*.

cutlet [ˈkʌtlɪt] *n* chuleta *f*.

cutout [ˈkʌtaʊt] *n* - **1.** [on machine] cortacircuitos *m inv* - **2.** [shape] recorte *m*.

cut-price, cut-rate *US adj* de oferta, rebajado(da).

cutthroat [ˈkʌtθrəʊt] *adj* [ruthless] encarnizado(da).

cutting [ˈkʌtɪŋ] ⬦ *adj* [sarcastic] cortante, hiriente. ⬦ *n* - **1.** [of plant] esqueje *m* - **2.** [from newspaper] recorte *m*.

CV (*abbr of* **curriculum vitae**) *n UK* CV *m*.

cyanide [ˈsaɪənaɪd] *n* cianuro *m*.

cybercafe [ˈsaɪbəˌkæfeɪ] *n* cibercafé *m*.

cyberspace [ˈsaɪbəspeɪs] *n* ciberespacio *m*.

cycle [ˈsaɪkl] ⬦ *n* - **1.** [series of events, poems, songs] ciclo *m* - **2.** [bicycle] bicicleta *f*. ⬦ *comp*: ~ **lane** carril *m* bici; ~ **path** camino *m* para bicicletas. ⬦ *vi* ir en bicicleta.

cycling [ˈsaɪklɪŋ] *n* ciclismo *m*; **to go** ~ salir en bicicleta.

cyclist [ˈsaɪklɪst] *n* ciclista *m OR f*.

cygnet [ˈsɪgnɪt] *n* pollo *m* de cisne.

cylinder [ˈsɪlɪndə*ʳ*] *n* - **1.** [shape, engine component] cilindro *m* - **2.** [container - for gas] bombona *f*.

cymbals [ˈsɪmblz] *npl* platillos *mpl*.

cynic [ˈsɪnɪk] *n* cínico *m*, -ca *f*.

cynical [ˈsɪnɪkl] *adj* cínico(ca).

cynicism [ˈsɪnɪsɪzm] *n* cinismo *m*.

Cypriot [ˈsɪpriət] ⬦ *adj* chipriota. ⬦ *n* chipriota *m OR f*.

Cyprus [ˈsaɪprəs] *n* Chipre.

cyst [sɪst] *n* quiste *m*.

cystitis [sɪsˈtaɪtɪs] *n* cistitis *f inv*.

czar [zɑː*ʳ*] *n* zar *m*.

Czech [tʃek] ⬦ *adj* checo(ca). ⬦ *n* - **1.** [person] checo *m*, -ca *f* - **2.** [language] checo *m*.

Czechoslovakia [ˌtʃekəslə'vækɪə] *n dat* Checoslovaquia.

Czechoslovakian [ˌtʃekəslə'vækɪən] *dat* ⬦ *adj* checoslovaco(ca). ⬦ *n* [person] checoslovaco *m*, -ca *f*.

Czech Republic *n*: **the** ~ la República Checa.

d (*pl* **d's** OR **ds**), **D** (*pl* **D's** OR **Ds**) [diː] *n* [letter] d *f*, D *f*.
◆ **D** *n* - **1.** MUS re *m* - **2.** SCH ≃ suspenso *m*.

D.A. *n US abbr of* **district attorney**.

dab [dæb] (*pt & pp* -**bed**, *cont* -**bing**) ⬦ *n* [small amount] toque *m*, pizca *f*; [of powder] pizca *f*. ⬦ *vt* - **1.** [skin, wound] dar ligeros toques en - **2.** [cream, ointment]: **to** ~ **sthg on** OR **onto** aplicar algo sobre.

dabble [ˈdæbl] *vi*: **to** ~ **(in)** pasar el tiempo OR entretenerse (con).

dachshund [ˈdækshʊnd] *n* perro *m* salchicha.

dad [dæd], **daddy** [ˈdædɪ] (*pl* -**ies**) *n inf* papá *m*.

daddy longlegs [-ˈlɒŋlegz] (*pl inv*) *n* típula *f*.

daffodil [ˈdæfədɪl] *n* narciso *m*.

daft [dɑːft] *adj UK inf* tonto(ta), baboso(sa) *Amér*.

dagger [ˈdægə*ʳ*] *n* daga *f*, puñal *m*.

daily [ˈdeɪlɪ] (*pl* -**ies**) ⬦ *adj* diario(ria). ⬦ *adv* diariamente; **twice** ~ dos veces al día. ⬦ *n* [newspaper] diario *m*.

dainty [ˈdeɪntɪ] (*compar* -**ier**, *superl* -**iest**) *adj* delicado(da), fino(na).

dairy [ˈdeərɪ] (*pl* -**ies**) *n* - **1.** [on farm] vaquería *f* - **2.** [shop] lechería *f* - **3.** [factory] central *f* lechera.

dairy farm *n* vaquería *f*.

dairy products *npl* productos *mpl* lácteos.

dais [ˈdeɪs] *n* tarima *f*, estrado *m*.

daisy [ˈdeɪzɪ] (*pl* -**ies**) *n* margarita *f*.

daisy wheel *n* margarita *f* (*de máquina de escribir*).

dale [deɪl] *n* valle *m*.

dam [dæm] (*pt & pp* -**med**, *cont* -**ming**) ⬦ *n* [across river] presa *f*. ⬦ *vt* represar.

damage [ˈdæmɪdʒ] ⬦ *n* - **1.** [physical harm]: ~ **(to)** daño *m* (a); **to cause** ~ **to sthg** ocasionar daños a algo - **2.** [harmful effect]: ~ **(to)** perjuicio *m* (a). ⬦ *vt* dañar.
◆ **damages** *npl* JUR daños *mpl* y perjuicios.

damn [dæm] ⬦ *adj inf* maldito(ta), pinche *Méx*. ⬦ *adv inf* tela de, muy; **don't be so** ~ **stupid** no seas tan rematadamente estúpido. ⬦ *n inf*: **I don't give** OR **care a** ~ **(about it)** me importa un bledo. ⬦ *vt* - **1.** [gen & RELIG] condenar - **2.** *v inf* [curse]: ~ **it!** ¡maldita sea!

damned [dæmd] *inf* ⬦ *adj* maldito(ta), pinche *Méx*; **I'm** ~ **if I know why she did it** que me maten si lo sé; **well I'll be** OR **I'm** ~! ¡ostras! ⬦ *adv* tela de, muy.

damning [ˈdæmɪŋ] *adj* condenatorio(ria).

damp [dæmp] ⬦ *adj* húmedo(da). ⬦ *n* humedad *f*. ⬦ *vt* [make wet] humedecer.

dampen [ˈdæmpən] *vt* - **1.** [make wet] humedecer - **2.** *fig* [emotion] apagar.

damson ['dæmzn] *n* (ciruela *f*) damascena *f*.

dance [dɑːns] ◇ *n* baile *m*. ◇ *vt* bailar. ◇ *vi* - 1. [to music] bailar - 2. [move quickly and lightly] agitarse, moverse.

dancer ['dɑːnsəʳ] *n* bailarín *m*, -ina *f*.

dancing ['dɑːnsɪŋ] *n* (U) baile *m*.

dandelion ['dændɪlaɪən] *n* diente *m* de león.

dandruff ['dændrʌf] *n* caspa *f*.

Dane [deɪn] *n* danés *m*, -esa *f*.

danger ['deɪndʒəʳ] *n*: ~ (to) peligro *m* (para); **in/out of** ~ en/fuera de peligro; **to be in** ~ **of doing sthg** correr el riesgo de hacer algo.

dangerous ['deɪndʒərəs] *adj* peligroso(sa).

dangle ['dæŋgl] ◇ *vt* colgar; *fig*: **to** ~ **sthg before sb** tentar a alguien con algo. ◇ *vi* colgar, pender.

Danish ['deɪnɪʃ] ◇ *adj* danés(esa). ◇ *n* - 1. [language] danés *m* - 2. *US* = **Danish pastry**. ◇ *npl* [people]: **the** ~ los daneses.

Danish pastry *n* pastel de hojaldre con crema o manzana o almendras etc.

dank [dæŋk] *adj* húmedo(da) e insalubre.

dapper ['dæpəʳ] *adj* pulcro(cra), atildado(-da).

dappled ['dæpld] *adj* - 1. [light] moteado(-da) - 2. [horse] rodado(da).

dare [deəʳ] ◇ *vt* - 1. [be brave enough]: **to** ~ **to do sthg** atreverse a hacer algo, osar hacer algo - 2. [challenge]: **to** ~ **sb to do sthg** desafiar a alguien a hacer algo - 3. *phr*: **I** ~ **say (...)** supongo *OR* me imagino (que ...). ◇ *vi* atreverse, osar; **how** ~ **you!** ¡cómo te atreves? ◇ *n* desafío *m*, reto *m*.

daredevil ['deə,devl] *n* temerario *m*, -ria *f*.

daring ['deərɪŋ] ◇ *adj* atrevido(da), audaz. ◇ *n* audacia *f*.

dark [dɑːk] ◇ *adj* - 1. [night, colour, hair] oscuro(ra); **it's getting** ~ está oscureciendo; **it was already** ~ ya era de noche - 2. [person, skin] moreno(na), cambujo(ja) *Amér.* - 3. [thoughts, days, mood] sombrío(a), triste - 4. [look, comment, side of character etc] siniestro(tra). ◇ *n* - 1. [darkness]: **the** ~ la oscuridad; **to be in the** ~ **about sthg** estar a oscuras sobre algo - 2. [night]: **before/after** ~ antes/después del anochecer.

darken ['dɑːkn] ◇ *vt* oscurecer. ◇ *vi* [become darker] oscurecerse.

dark glasses *npl* gafas *fpl* oscuras, anteojos *mpl* *OR* lentes *mpl* oscuros *Amér.*

darkness ['dɑːknɪs] *n* oscuridad *f*.

darkroom ['dɑːkrʊm] *n* PHOT cuarto *m* oscuro.

darling ['dɑːlɪŋ] ◇ *adj* [dear] querido(da). ◇ *n* - 1. [loved person] encanto *m* - 2. *inf* [addressing any woman] maja *f*.

darn [dɑːn] ◇ *adj* *inf* maldito(ta), condenado(da). ◇ *adv* *inf* tela de, muy; **don't be**

so ~ **stupid** no seas tan rematadamente estúpido. ◇ *vt* zurcir. ◇ *excl* *inf* ¡maldita sea!

dart [dɑːt] ◇ *n* [arrow] dardo *m*. ◇ *vi* precipitarse.

◆ **darts** *n* (U) [game] dardos *mpl*.

dartboard ['dɑːtbɔːd] *n* blanco *m*, diana *f*.

dash [dæʃ] ◇ *n* - 1. [of liquid] gotas *fpl*, chorrito *m*; [of colour] toque *m* - 2. [in punctuation] guión *m* - 3. [rush]: **to make a** ~ **for sthg** salir disparado hacia algo. ◇ *vt* - 1. *literary* [throw] arrojar - 2. [hopes] frustrar, malograr. ◇ *vi* ir de prisa.

dashboard ['dæʃbɔːd] *n* salpicadero *m*.

dashing ['dæʃɪŋ] *adj* gallardo(da), apuesto(ta).

data ['deɪtə] *n* (U) datos *mpl*.

database ['deɪtəbeɪs] *n* COMPUT base *f* de datos.

data management *n* COMPUT gestión *f* de datos.

data processing *n* proceso *m* de datos.

data protection *n* COMPUT protección *f* de datos.

data recovery *n* COMPUT recuperación *f* de datos.

date [deɪt] ◇ *n* - 1. [in time] fecha *f*; **to** ~ hasta la fecha - 2. [appointment] cita *f* - 3. *US* [person] pareja *f* (con la que se sale) - 4. [performance] actuación *f* - 5. [fruit] dátil *m*. ◇ *vt* - 1. [establish the date of] datar - 2. [mark with the date] fechar - 3. *US* [go out with] salir con.

dated ['deɪtɪd] *adj* anticuado(da).

date of birth *n* fecha *f* de nacimiento.

daub [dɔːb] *vt*: **to** ~ **sthg with** embadurnar algo con.

daughter ['dɔːtəʳ] *n* hija *f*.

daughter-in-law (*pl* **daughters-in-law**) *n* nuera *f*.

daunting ['dɔːntɪŋ] *adj* amedrantador(ra).

dawn [dɔːn] ◇ *n* - 1. [of day] amanecer *m*, alba *f* - 2. [of era, period] albores *mpl*, amanecer *m*. ◇ *vi* [day] amanecer.

◆ **dawn (up)on** *vt fus*: **it** ~ **ed on me that** ... caí en la cuenta de que ...

day [deɪ] *n* - 1. [gen] día *m*; **I work an eight-hour** ~ trabajo una jornada de ocho horas; **the** ~ **before/after** el día anterior/siguiente; **the** ~ **before yesterday** anteayer; **the** ~ **after tomorrow** pasado mañana; **any** ~ **now** cualquier día de estos; **from** ~ **to** ~ de un día para otro; **one** *OR* **some** ~, **one of these** ~ un día de estos; **to make sb's** ~ dar un alegrón a alguien - 2. [period in history]: **in my/your** *etc* ~ en mis/tus *etc* tiempos; **in those** ~ **s** en aquellos tiempos; **these** ~ **s** hoy día.

◆ **days** *adv* de día.

daybreak ['deɪbreɪk] *n* amanecer *m*, alba *f*; **at** ~ al amanecer.

daycentre ['deɪsentə^r] *n UK centro estatal diurno donde se da acogida y cuidado a niños, ancianos, minusválidos etc.*

daydream ['deɪdriːm] ◇ *n* sueño *m*, ilusión *f.* ◇ *vi* soñar despierto(ta).

daylight ['deɪlaɪt] *n* **-1.** [light] luz *f* del día; **in broad ~** a plena luz del día; **it was still ~** todavía era de día **-2.** [dawn] amanecer *m.*

day off (*pl* **days off**) *n* día *m* libre.

day return *n UK* billete *m* de ida y vuelta para un día.

daytime ['deɪtaɪm] ◇ *n (U)* día *m.* ◇ *comp* de día, diurno(na).

day-to-day *adj* cotidiano(na), diario(ria).

daytrader ['deɪtreɪdə^r] *n* ST EX operador *m*, -ra *f* de posiciones diarias.

day trip *n* excursión *f* (de un día).

daze [deɪz] ◇ *n*: **in a ~** aturdido(da). ◇ *vt lit & fig* aturdir.

dazzle ['dæzl] *vt lit & fig* deslumbrar.

DC ◇ *n* (*abbr of* **direct current**) CC *f.* ◇ *abbr of* **District of Columbia**.

D-day ['diːdeɪ] *n* el día D.

DEA (*abbr of* **Drug Enforcement Administration**) *n organismo estadounidense para la lucha contra la droga.*

deacon ['diːkn] *n* diácono *m.*

deactivate [ˌdiːˈæktɪveɪt] *vt* desactivar.

dead [ded] ◇ *adj* **-1.** [person, animal, plant] muerto(ta); **a ~ body** un cadáver; **to be ~ on arrival** ingresar cadáver; **to shoot sb ~** matar a alguien a tiros **-2.** [numb - leg, arm] entumecido(da); **my arm has gone ~** se me ha dormido el brazo **-3.** [telephone] cortado(da); [car battery] descargado(da) **-4.** [silence] absoluto(ta), completo(ta) **-5.** [lifeless - town, party] sin vida. ◇ *adv* **-1.** [directly, precisely] justo **-2.** [completely] totalmente, completamente; **' ~ slow'** 'al paso' **-3.** *inf* [very] la mar de, muy **-4.** [suddenly]: **to stop ~** parar en seco. ◇ *npl*: **the ~** los muertos.

deaden ['dedn] *vt* atenuar.

dead end *n lit & fig* callejón *m* sin salida.

dead heat *n* empate *m.*

deadline ['dedlaɪn] *n* [period] plazo *m*; [date] fecha *f* tope.

deadlock ['dedlɒk] *n* punto *m* muerto.

dead loss *n inf* **-1.** [person] inútil *m OR f* **-2.** [thing] inutilidad *f.*

deadly ['dedlɪ] (*compar* **-ier**, *superl* **-iest**) ◇ *adj* **-1.** [gen] mortal **-2.** [accuracy] absoluto(ta). ◇ *adv* [boring] mortalmente, terriblemente; [serious] totalmente.

deadpan ['dedpæn] *adj* [expression] inexpresivo(va), serio(ria); [humour] socarrón(ona).

deaf [def] ◇ *adj* [unable to hear] sordo(da). ◇ *npl*: **the ~** los sordos.

deaf-aid *n UK* audífono *m.*

deaf-and-dumb *adj* sordomudo(da).

deafen ['defn] *vt* ensordecer.

deaf-mute *n* sordomudo *m*, -da *f.*

deafness ['defnɪs] *n* sordera *f.*

deal [diːl] (*pt & pp* **dealt**) ◇ *n* **-1.** [quantity]: **a good** OR **great ~ (of)** mucho **-2.** [agreement] acuerdo *m*; [business agreement] trato *m*; **to do** OR **strike a ~ with sb** hacer un trato con alguien; **it's a ~!** ¡trato hecho! **-3.** *inf* [treatment] trato *m*; **big ~!** ¡vaya cosa! **-4.** [price]: **to get a good ~ on sthg** conseguir algo a un precio barato. ◇ *vt* **-1.** [strike]: **to ~ sb/sthg a blow, to ~ a blow to sb/sthg** *lit & fig* asestar un golpe a alguien/algo **-2.** [cards] repartir, dar. ◇ *vi* **-1.** [in cards] repartir, dar **-2.** [in drugs] traficar con droga.

  ◆ **deal in** *vt fus* COMM comerciar en, vender.

  ◆ **deal out** *vt sep* repartir.

  ◆ **deal with** *vt fus* **-1.** [handle - situation, problem] hacer frente a, resolver; [- customer] tratar con **-2.** [be about] tratar de **-3.** [be faced with] enfrentarse a.

dealer ['diːlə^r] *n* **-1.** [trader] comerciante *m OR f* **-2.** [in drugs, arms] traficante *m OR f* **-3.** [in cards] repartidor *m*, -ra *f.*

dealing ['diːlɪŋ] *n* comercio *m.*

  ◆ **dealings** *npl* [personal] trato *m*; [in business] tratos *mpl.*

dealt [delt] *pt & pp* ⊳ **deal**.

dean [diːn] *n* **-1.** [of university] ≃ decano *m*, -na *f* **-2.** [of church] deán *m.*

dean's list *n US* lista de los alumnos considerados más sobresalientes por el decano de una universidad.

dear [dɪə^r] ◇ *adj* **-1.** [loved] querido(da); **~ to sb** preciado(da) para alguien **-2.** [expensive] caro(ra) **-3.** [in letter]: **Dear Sir** Estimado señor, Muy señor mío; **Dear Madam** Estimada señora; **Dear Daniela** Querida Daniela. ◇ *n*: **my ~** cariño *m*, -ña *f.* ◇ *excl*: **oh ~!** ¡vaya por Dios!

dearly ['dɪəlɪ] *adv* **-1.** [very much]: **I love you ~** te quiero muchísimo; **I would ~ love to ...** me encantaría ... **-2.** [severely]: **to pay ~ for sthg** pagar algo caro.

death [deθ] *n* muerte *f*; **to frighten sb to ~** dar un susto de muerte a alguien; **to be sick to ~ of sthg/of doing sthg** estar hasta las narices de algo/de hacer algo.

death certificate *n* partida *f* OR certificado *m* de defunción.

death duty *UK*, **death tax** *US n* impuesto *m* de sucesiones.

deathly ['deθlɪ] (*compar* **-ier**, *superl* **-iest**) ◇ *adj* [silence] sepulcral. ◇ *adv*: **he was ~ pale** estaba pálido como un muerto.

death penalty *n* pena *f* de muerte.

death rate *n* índice *m* OR tasa *f* de mortalidad.

death tax *US* = **death duty**.

death trap *n inf* trampa *f* mortal, sitio *m* muy peligroso.

debar [dɪˈbɑːʳ] (*pt* & *pp* **-red**, *cont* **-ring**) *vt*: **to ~ sb from** [place] prohibir a alguien la entrada en; **to ~ sb from doing sthg** prohibir a alguien hacer algo.

debase [dɪˈbeɪs] *vt* : **to ~ o.s.** rebajarse.

debate [dɪˈbeɪt] <> *n* debate *m*; **that's open to ~** eso es discutible. <> *vt* **-1.** [issue] discutir, debatir **- 2.** [what to do]: **to ~ (whether to do sthg)** pensarse (si hacer algo). <> *vi* discutir, debatir.

debating society [dɪˈbeɪtɪŋ-] *n* asociación *de* debates especialmente universitaria.

debauchery [dɪˈbɔːtʃərɪ] *n* depravación *f*, libertinaje *m*.

debit [ˈdebɪt] <> *n* debe *m*, débito *m*. <> *vt*: **to ~ sb** *OR* **sb's account with an amount, to ~ an amount to sb** adeudar *OR* cargar una cantidad en la cuenta de alguien.

debit card *n* tarjeta *f* de débito.

debit note *n* nota *f* de cargo.

debris [ˈdeɪbriː] *n* (*U*) [of building] escombros *mpl*; [of aircraft] restos *mpl*.

debt [det] *n* deuda *f*; **to be in ~ (to sb)** tener una deuda (con alguien); **to get into ~** endeudarse.

debt collector *n* cobrador *m*, -ra *f* de morosos.

debtor [ˈdetəʳ] *n* deudor *m*, -ra *f*.

debug [ˌdiːˈbʌg] (*pt* & *pp* **-ged**, *cont* **-ging**) *vt* COMPUT depurar.

debunk [ˌdiːˈbʌŋk] *vt* desmentir, desacreditar.

debut [ˈdeɪbjuː] *n* debut *m*.

decade [ˈdekeɪd] *n* década *f*.

decadent [ˈdekədənt] *adj* decadente.

decaffeinated [dɪˈkæfɪneɪtɪd] *adj* descafeinado(da).

decamp [dɪˈkæmp] *vi inf* escabullirse, esfumarse.

decanter [dɪˈkæntəʳ] *n* licorera *f*.

decathlon [dɪˈkæθlɒn] *n* decatlón *m*.

decay [dɪˈkeɪ] <> *n* (*U*) **-1.** [of tooth] caries *f inv*; [of body, plant] descomposición *f* **- 2.** *fig* [of building] deterioro *m*; [of society] degradación *f*. <> *vi* **-1.** [tooth] picarse; [body, plant] pudrirse, descomponerse **- 2.** *fig* [building] deteriorarse; [society] degradarse.

deceased [dɪˈsiːst] (*pl inv*) *n fml*: **the ~** el difunto (la difunta).

deceit [dɪˈsiːt] *n* engaño *m*.

deceitful [dɪˈsiːtfʊl] *adj* [person, smile] embustero(ra); [behaviour] falso(sa).

deceive [dɪˈsiːv] *vt* engañar; **to ~ o.s.** engañarse (a uno mismo/una misma).

December [dɪˈsembəʳ] *n* diciembre *m*; *see also* **September**.

decency [ˈdiːsnsɪ] *n* **- 1.** [respectability]

decencia *f* **- 2.** [consideration]: **to have the ~ to do sthg** tener la delicadeza de hacer algo.

decent [ˈdiːsnt] *adj* **- 1.** [gen] decente **- 2.** [considerate]: **that's very ~ of you** es muy amable de tu parte.

deception [dɪˈsepʃn] *n* engaño *m*.

deceptive [dɪˈseptɪv] *adj* engañoso(sa).

decide [dɪˈsaɪd] <> *vt* **- 1.** [gen]: **to ~ (to do sthg)** decidir (hacer algo); **to ~ (that)** decidir que **- 2.** [person] hacer decidirse **- 3.** [issue, case] resolver. <> *vi* decidir; **I couldn't ~** no me decidía; **I ~d against doing it** decidí no hacerlo.

◆ **decide (up)on** *vt fus* decidirse por.

decided [dɪˈsaɪdɪd] *adj* **- 1.** [advantage, improvement] indudable **- 2.** [person] decidido(da); [opinion] categórico(ca).

decidedly [dɪˈsaɪdɪdlɪ] *adv* **- 1.** [clearly] decididamente, indudablemente **- 2.** [resolutely] con decisión.

deciduous [dɪˈsɪdjʊəs] *adj* de hoja caduca.

decimal [ˈdesɪml] <> *adj* decimal. <> *n* (número *m*) decimal *m*.

decimal point *n* coma *f* decimal.

decimate [ˈdesɪmeɪt] *vt* diezmar.

decipher [dɪˈsaɪfəʳ] *vt* descifrar.

decision [dɪˈsɪʒn] *n* decisión *f*; **to make a ~** tomar una decisión.

decisive [dɪˈsaɪsɪv] *adj* **- 1.** [person] decidido(da) **- 2.** [factor, event] decisivo(va).

deck [dek] *n* **- 1.** [of ship] cubierta *f*; [of bus] piso *m* **- 2.** [of cards] baraja *f* **- 3.** *US* [of house] entarimado *m* (junto a una casa).

deckchair [ˈdektʃeəʳ] *n* tumbona *f*.

declaration [ˌdekləˈreɪʃn] *n* declaración *f*.

Declaration of Independence *n*: **the ~** la declaración de independencia estadounidense de 1776.

declare [dɪˈkleəʳ] *vt* declarar.

decline [dɪˈklaɪn] <> *n* declive *m*; **in ~** en decadencia; **on the ~** en declive. <> *vt* [offer] declinar; [request] denegar; **to ~ to do sthg** rehusar hacer algo. <> *vi* **- 1.** [number, importance] disminuir **- 2.** [refuse] negarse.

decode [ˌdiːˈkəʊd] *vt* descodificar.

decompose [ˌdiːkəmˈpəʊz] *vi* descomponerse.

decongestant [ˌdiːkənˈdʒestənt] *n* descongestionante *m*.

décor [ˈdeɪkɔːʳ] *n* decoración *f*.

decorate [ˈdekəreɪt] *vt* **- 1.** [make pretty]: **to ~ sthg (with)** decorar algo (de) **- 2.** [with paint] pintar; [with wallpaper] empapelar **- 3.** [with medal] condecorar.

decoration [ˌdekəˈreɪʃn] *n* **- 1.** [gen] decoración *f* **- 2.** [ornament] adorno *m* **- 3.** [medal] condecoración *f*.

decorator [ˈdekəreɪtəʳ] n [painter] pintor m, -ra f; [paperhanger] **empapelador** m, -ra f.

decorum [dɪˈkɔːrəm] n decoro m.

decoy [n ˈdiːkɔɪ, vb dɪˈkɔɪ] ⬦ n señuelo m. ⬦ vt atraer (mediante señuelo).

decrease [n ˈdiːkriːs, vb dɪˈkriːs] ⬦ n: ~ (in) disminución f (de), reducción f (de). ⬦ vt & vi disminuir.

decree [dɪˈkriː] ⬦ n - 1. [order, decision] decreto m - 2. US [judgment] sentencia f, fallo m. ⬦ vt decretar.

decree nisi [-ˈnaɪsaɪ] (pl **decrees nisi**) n UK JUR sentencia f provisional de divorcio.

decrepit [dɪˈkrepɪt] adj - 1. [person] decrépito(ta) - 2. [thing] deteriorado(da).

dedicate [ˈdedɪkeɪt] vt - 1. dedicar; **to ~ o.s. to sthg** consagrarse OR dedicarse a algo - 2. US [open for public use] inaugurar.

dedication [ˌdedɪˈkeɪʃn] n - 1. [commitment] dedicación f - 2. [in book] dedicatoria f.

deduce [dɪˈdjuːs] vt: **to ~ (sthg from sthg)** deducir (algo de algo).

deduct [dɪˈdʌkt] vt: **to ~ (from)** deducir (de), descontar (de).

deduction [dɪˈdʌkʃn] n deducción f.

deed [diːd] n - 1. [action] acción f, obra f - 2. JUR escritura f.

deem [diːm] vt fml estimar.

deep [diːp] ⬦ adj - 1. [gen] profundo(da); **to be 10 feet ~** tener 10 pies de profundidad - 2. [sigh, breath, bowl] hondo(da); **to take a ~ breath** respirar hondo - 3. [colour] intenso(sa) - 4. [sound, voice] grave. ⬦ adv [dig, cut] hondo; **~ down** OR **inside** por dentro.

deepen [ˈdiːpn] ⬦ vt [hole, channel] ahondar, hacer más profundo(da). ⬦ vi - 1. [river, sea] ahondarse, hacerse más profundo(da) - 2. [crisis, recession] agudizarse; [emotion, darkness] hacerse más intenso(sa).

deep freeze n congelador m.

deep fry vt freír (con mucho aceite).

deeply [ˈdiːplɪ] adv [gen] profundamente; [dig, breathe, sigh] hondo.

deep-sea adj: **~ diving** buceo m de profundidad.

deer [dɪəʳ] (pl inv) n ciervo m.

deface [dɪˈfeɪs] vt pintarrajear.

de facto [deɪˈfæktəʊ] adj & adv de hecho.

defamatory [dɪˈfæmətrɪ] adj fml difamatorio(ria).

default [dɪˈfɔːlt] ⬦ n - 1. [on payment, agreement] incumplimiento m; [failure to attend] incomparecencia f; **by ~** [win] por incomparecencia - 2. COMPUT: ~ **(setting)** valor m por omisión. ⬦ vi incumplir un compromiso.

defeat [dɪˈfiːt] ⬦ n derrota f; **to admit ~** darse por vencido(da). ⬦ vt [team, opponent] derrotar; [motion] rechazar; [plans] frustrar.

defeatist [dɪˈfiːtɪst] adj derrotista.

defect [n ˈdiːfekt, vb dɪˈfekt] ⬦ n [fault] defecto m. ⬦ vi POL desertar; **to ~ to the other side** pasarse al otro bando.

defective [dɪˈfektɪv] adj defectuoso(sa).

defence UK, **defense** US [dɪˈfens] n defensa f.

defenceless UK, **defenseless** US [dɪˈfenslɪs] adj indefenso(sa).

defend [dɪˈfend] vt defender.

defendant [dɪˈfendənt] n acusado m, -da f.

defender [dɪˈfendəʳ] n - 1. [gen] defensor m, -ra f - 2. SPORT defensa m y f.

defending champion [dɪˈfendɪŋ-] n actual campeón m, -ona f.

defense US = defence.

defenseless US = defenceless.

defensive [dɪˈfensɪv] ⬦ adj - 1. [weapons, tactics] defensivo(va) - 2. [person]: **to be ~** ponerse a la defensiva. ⬦ n: **on the ~** a la defensiva.

defer [dɪˈfɜːʳ] (pt & pp -red, cont -ring) ⬦ vt aplazar. ⬦ vi: **to ~ to sb** deferir con OR a alguien.

deferential [ˌdefəˈrenʃl] adj deferente, respetuoso(sa).

defiance [dɪˈfaɪəns] n desafío m; **in ~ of** en desafío de, a despecho de.

defiant [dɪˈfaɪənt] adj desafiante.

deficiency [dɪˈfɪʃnsɪ] (pl -ies) n - 1. [lack] escasez f, insuficiencia f - 2. [inadequacy] deficiencia f.

deficient [dɪˈfɪʃnt] adj - 1. [lacking]: **to be ~ in** estar falto(ta) de - 2. [inadequate] deficiente.

deficit [ˈdefɪsɪt] n déficit m.

defile [dɪˈfaɪl] vt [desecrate] profanar; fig [mind, purity] corromper.

define [dɪˈfaɪn] vt definir.

definite [ˈdefɪnɪt] adj - 1. [plan, date, answer] definitivo(va) - 2. [improvement, difference] indudable, claro(ra) - 3. [sure - person] seguro(ra); **I am quite ~ (about it)** estoy totalmente seguro (de ello) - 4. [categorical] tajante, concluyente.

definitely [ˈdefɪnɪtlɪ] adv - 1. [without doubt] sin duda - 2. [for emphasis] desde luego, con (toda) seguridad.

definition [defɪˈnɪʃn] n - 1. [gen] definición f; **by ~** por definición - 2. [clarity] nitidez f.

deflate [dɪˈfleɪt] ⬦ vt [balloon] desinflar; fig [person] bajar los humos a. ⬦ vi desinflarse.

deflation [dɪˈfleɪʃn] n ECON deflación f.

deflect [dɪˈflekt] vt [gen] desviar; [criticism] soslayar.

defogger [ˌdiːˈfɒgəʳ] n US AUT dispositivo

m antivaho, luneta *f* térmica.

deformed [dɪ'fɔːmd] *adj* deforme.

defragment [ˌdiːfræg'ment] *vt* COMPUT desfragmentar.

defraud [dɪ'frɔːd] *vt* defraudar, estafar.

defrost [ˌdiː'frɒst] ⟨⟩ *vt* - 1. [gen] descongelar - 2. *US* AUT [demist] desempañar. ⟨⟩ *vi* descongelarse.

deft [deft] *adj* habilidoso(sa), diestro(tra).

defunct [dɪ'fʌŋkt] *adj* [body, organization] desaparecido(da); [plan] desechado(da).

defuse [ˌdiː'fjuːz] *vt* UK - 1. [bomb] desactivar - 2. [situation] distender.

defy [dɪ'faɪ] (*pt* & *pp* -ied) *vt* - 1. [disobey - person, authority] desobedecer; [law, rule] violar - 2. [challenge]: **to ~ sb to do sthg** retar OR desafiar a alguien a hacer algo - 3. [attempts, efforts] hacer inútil; **to ~ description** ser indescriptible; **to ~ explanation** ser inexplicable.

degenerate [*adj* dɪ'dʒenərət, *vb* dɪ'dʒenəreɪt] ⟨⟩ *adj* degenerado(da). ⟨⟩ *vi*: **to ~ (into)** degenerar (en).

degrading [dɪ'greɪdɪŋ] *adj* denigrante, degradante.

degree [dɪ'griː] *n* - 1. [unit of measurement, amount] grado *m*; **a ~ of risk** un cierto riesgo; **by ~s** poco a poco - 2. [qualification] título *m* universitario, ≃ licenciatura *f*; **to have/take a ~ (in sthg)** tener/hacer una licenciatura (en algo) - 3. [course] ≃ carrera *f*.

dehydrated [ˌdiːhaɪ'dreɪtɪd] *adj* deshidratado(da).

de-ice [diː'aɪs] *vt* quitar el hielo de.

deign [deɪn] *vt*: **to ~ to do sthg** dignarse a hacer algo.

deity ['diːɪtɪ] (*pl* -ies) *n* deidad *f*, divinidad *f*.

dejected [dɪ'dʒektɪd] *adj* abatido(da).

delay [dɪ'leɪ] ⟨⟩ *n* retraso *m*. ⟨⟩ *vt* retrasar; **to ~ starting sthg** retrasar el comienzo de algo. ⟨⟩ *vi*: **to ~ (in doing sthg)** retrasarse (en hacer algo).

delayed [dɪ'leɪd] *adj*: **to be ~** [person] retrasarse; [train, flight] llevar retraso.

delectable [dɪ'lektəbl] *adj* - 1. [food] deleitable - 2. [person] apetecible.

delegate [*n* 'delɪgət, *vb* 'delɪgeɪt] ⟨⟩ *n* delegado *m*, -da *f* ⟨⟩ *vt*: **to ~ sthg (to sb)** delegar algo (en alguien); **to ~ sb to do sthg** delegar a alguien para hacer algo.

delegation [ˌdelɪ'geɪʃn] *n* delegación *f*.

delete [dɪ'liːt] *vt* [gen & COMPUT] borrar, suprimir; [cross out] tachar.

deli ['delɪ] *n inf abbr of* **delicatessen**.

deliberate [*adj* dɪ'lɪbərət, *vb* dɪ'lɪbəreɪt] ⟨⟩ *adj* - 1. [intentional] deliberado(da) - 2. [slow] pausado(da). ⟨⟩ *vi fml* deliberar.

deliberately [dɪ'lɪbərətlɪ] *adv* - 1. [on purpose] adrede, deliberadamente - 2. [slowly] pausadamente.

delicacy ['delɪkəsɪ] (*pl* -ies) *n* - 1. [gracefulness, tact] delicadeza *f* - 2. [food] exquisitez *f*, manjar *m*.

delicate ['delɪkət] *adj* - 1. [gen] delicado(da) - 2. [subtle - colour, taste] suave, sutil - 3. [tactful] delicado(da), prudente; [instrument] sensible.

delicatessen [ˌdelɪkə'tesn] *n* ≃ charcutería *f*, ≃ (tienda *f* de) ultramarinos *m inv.*

delicious [dɪ'lɪʃəs] *adj* delicioso(sa).

delight [dɪ'laɪt] ⟨⟩ *n* [great pleasure] gozo *m*, regocijo *m*; **to our ~** para gran alegría nuestra; **to take ~ in doing sthg** disfrutar haciendo algo. ⟨⟩ *vt* encantar. ⟨⟩ *vi*: **to ~ in sthg/in doing sthg** disfrutar con algo/haciendo algo.

delighted [dɪ'laɪtɪd] *adj* encantado(da), muy contento(ta); **~ by** OR **with** encantado con; **to be ~ to do sthg/that** estar encantado de hacer algo/de que; **I'd be ~ (to come)** me encantaría (ir).

delightful [dɪ'laɪtfʊl] *adj* [gen] encantador(ra); [meal] delicioso(sa); [view] muy agradable.

delinquent [dɪ'lɪŋkwənt] ⟨⟩ *adj* [behaviour] delictivo(va); [child] delincuente. ⟨⟩ *n* delincuente *m y f.*

delirious [dɪ'lɪrɪəs] *adj* [with fever] delirante; *fig* [ecstatic] enfervorizado(da).

deliver [dɪ'lɪvər] *vt* - 1. [hand over] entregar; [distribute] repartir; **to ~ sthg to sb** entregar algo a alguien - 2. [give - speech, verdict, lecture] pronunciar; [- message, warning, ultimatum] transmitir; [- blow, kick] asestar - 3. [service] prestar - 4. [baby] traer al mundo - 5. *fml* [free] liberar, libertar - 6. *US* POL [votes] captar.

delivery [dɪ'lɪvərɪ] (*pl* -ies) *n* - 1. [handing over] entrega *f*; [distribution] reparto *m* - 2. [goods delivered] partida *f* - 3. [way of speaking] (estilo *m* de) discurso *m* - 4. [birth] parto *m*.

delude [dɪ'luːd] *vt* engañar; **to ~ o.s.** engañarse (a uno mismo/una misma).

deluge ['deljuːdʒ] *n* [flood] diluvio *m*, aluvión *m*; *fig* [huge number] aluvión *m*.

delusion [dɪ'luːʒn] *n* espejismo *m*, engaño *m*.

de luxe [də'lʌks] *adj* de lujo.

delve [delv] *vi*: **to ~ (into)** [bag, cupboard] hurgar (en); *fig* [mystery] profundizar (en).

demand [dɪ'mɑːnd] ⟨⟩ *n* - 1. [claim, firm request] exigencia *f*, reclamación *f*; **on ~** a petición - 2. [need & ECON]: **~ for** demanda *f* de; **in ~** solicitado(da). ⟨⟩ *vt* [gen] exigir; [pay rise] reivindicar, demandar; **to ~ to do sthg** exigir hacer algo.

demanding [dɪ'mɑːndɪŋ] *adj* - 1. [exhausting] que exige mucho esfuerzo - 2. [not easily satisfied] exigente.

demean [dɪ'miːn] vt degradar; **to ~ o.s.** humillarse, rebajarse.

demeaning [dɪ'miːnɪŋ] adj denigrante.

demeanour UK, **demeanor** US [dɪ'miːnə˞] n (U) fml comportamiento m.

demented [dɪ'mentɪd] adj demente.

demise [dɪ'maɪz] n fml - **1.** [death] defunción f, fallecimiento m - **2.** [end] desaparición f.

demister [,diː'mɪstə˞] n UK AUT dispositivo m antivaho, luneta f térmica.

demo ['deməʊ] (abbr of **demonstration**) n inf - **1.** mani f - **2.** MUS maqueta f.

democracy [dɪ'mɒkrəsɪ] (pl -ies) n democracia f.

democrat ['deməkræt] n demócrata m y f.
➡ Democrat n US demócrata m y f.

democratic [demə'krætɪk] adj democrático(ca).
➡ Democratic adj US demócrata.

Democratic Party n US Partido m Demócrata (de Estados Unidos).

demolish [dɪ'mɒlɪʃ] vt [building] demoler; [argument, myth] destrozar.

demonstrate ['demənstreɪt] ◇ vt - **1.** [prove] demostrar - **2.** [show] hacer una demostración de. ◇ vi manifestarse.

demonstration [demən'streɪʃn] n - **1.** [of machine, product] demostración f - **2.** [public meeting] manifestación f.

demonstrator ['demənstreɪtə˞] n - **1.** [in march] manifestante m y f - **2.** [of machine, product] demostrador m, -ra f comercial.

demoralized [dɪ'mɒrəlaɪzd] adj desmoralizado(da).

demote [,diː'məʊt] vt descender de categoría.

demure [dɪ'mjʊə˞] adj recatado(da).

den [den] n [lair] guarida f.

denial [dɪ'naɪəl] n - **1.** [refutation] negación f, rechazo m - **2.** [of rumour] desmentido m - **3.** [refusal] denegación f.

denier ['denɪə˞] n denier m.

denigrate ['denɪgreɪt] vt fml desacreditar.

denim ['denɪm] n tela f vaquera.
➡ denims npl (pantalones mpl) vaqueros mpl.

denim jacket n cazadora f vaquera.

Denmark ['denmɑːk] n Dinamarca f.

denomination [dɪ,nɒmɪ'neɪʃn] n - **1.** [religious group] confesión f - **2.** [of money] valor m.

denounce [dɪ'naʊns] vt denunciar.

dense [dens] adj - **1.** [gen] denso(sa); [trees] tupido(da) - **2.** inf [stupid] bruto(ta).

density ['densətɪ] (pl -ies) n densidad f.

dent [dent] ◇ n [on car] abolladura f. ◇ vt [car] abollar.

dental ['dentl] adj dental.

dental floss n hilo m OR seda f dental.

dental surgeon n odontólogo m, -ga f.

dentist ['dentɪst] n dentista m OR f; **to go to the ~'s** ir al dentista.

dentures ['dentʃəz] npl dentadura f postiza.

deny [dɪ'naɪ] (pt & pp -ied) vt - **1.** [refute] negar, rechazar; **to ~ doing sthg** negar haber hecho algo - **2.** [rumour] desmentir - **3.** fml [refuse]: **to ~ sb sthg** denegar algo a alguien.

deodorant [diː'əʊdərənt] n desodorante m.

depart [dɪ'pɑːt] vi fml - **1.** [leave]: **to ~ (from)** salir (de); **this train will ~ from Platform 2** este tren efectuará su salida por la vía 2 - **2.** [differ]: **to ~ from sthg** apartarse de algo.

department [dɪ'pɑːtmənt] n - **1.** [gen] departamento m - **2.** [in government] ministerio m.

department store n grandes almacenes mpl.

departure [dɪ'pɑːtʃə˞] n - **1.** [of train, plane] salida f; [of person] marcha f, partida f - **2.** [change]: **~ (from)** abandono m (de); **a new ~** un nuevo enfoque.

departure lounge n [in airport] sala f de embarque; [in coach station] vestíbulo m de salidas.

depend [dɪ'pend] vi: **to ~ on** depender de; **you can ~ on me** puedes confiar en mí; **it ~s** depende; **~ing on** según, dependiendo de.

dependable [dɪ'pendəbl] adj fiable.

dependant [dɪ'pendənt] n: **my ~s** las personas a mi cargo.

dependent [dɪ'pendənt] adj - **1.** [gen]: **to be ~ (on)** depender (de) - **2.** [addicted] adicto(ta).

depict [dɪ'pɪkt] vt - **1.** [in picture] retratar - **2.** [describe]: **to ~ sthg/sb as sthg** describir algo/a alguien como algo.

deplete [dɪ'pliːt] vt mermar, reducir.

deplorable [dɪ'plɔːrəbl] adj deplorable.

deplore [dɪ'plɔː˞] vt deplorar.

deploy [dɪ'plɔɪ] vt desplegar.

depopulation [diː,pɒpjʊ'leɪʃn] n despoblación f.

deport [dɪ'pɔːt] vt deportar.

depose [dɪ'pəʊz] vt deponer.

deposit [dɪ'pɒzɪt] ◇ n - **1.** GEOL yacimiento m - **2.** [sediment] poso m, sedimento m - **3.** [payment into bank] ingreso m, imposición f - **4.** [down payment- on house, car] entrada f; [- on hotel room] señal f, adelanto m; [- on hired goods] fianza f, enganche m Méx; [- on bottle] dinero m del envase OR casco. ◇ vt - **1.** [put down] depositar - **2.** [in bank] ingresar.

deposit account n UK cuenta f de ahorro a plazo fijo.

depot ['depəʊ] n - **1.** [storage facility] almacén m; [for arms] depósito m; [for buses]

cochera f - **2.** US [bus or train terminus] terminal f, estación f.

depreciate [dɪ'priːʃɪeɪt] vi depreciarse.

depress [dɪ'pres] vt - **1.** [person] deprimir - **2.** [economy] desactivar - **3.** [price, share value] reducir.

depressed [dɪ'prest] adj deprimido(da).

depressing [dɪ'presɪŋ] adj deprimente.

depression [dɪ'preʃn] n - **1.** [gen & ECON] depresión f; **to suffer from ~** sufrir depresiones - **2.** fml [in pillow] hueco m.

deprivation [ˌdeprɪ'veɪʃn] n - **1.** [poverty] miseria f - **2.** [lack] privación f.

deprive [dɪ'praɪv] vt : **to ~ sb of sthg** privar a alguien de algo.

depth [depθ] n profundidad f; **in ~** a fondo; **he was out of his ~ with that job** ese trabajo le venía grande.

➤ **depths** npl : **in the ~s of winter** en pleno invierno; **to be in the ~s of despair** estar en un abismo de desesperación.

deputation [ˌdepjo'teɪʃn] n delegación f.

deputize, -ise ['depjʊtaɪz] vi : **to ~ (for)** actuar en representación (de).

deputy ['depjʊti] (pl -ies) ◇ adj : **~ head** subdirector m, -ra f; **~ prime minister** vicepresidente m, -ta f del gobierno. ◇ n - **1.** [second-in-command] asistente m OR f, suplente m OR f - **2.** POL diputado m, -da f - **3.** US [deputy sheriff] ayudante m OR f del sheriff.

derail [dɪ'reɪl] vt & vi [train] descarrilar.

deranged [dɪ'reɪndʒd] adj perturbado(da), trastornado(da).

derby [UK 'dɑːbɪ, US 'dɜːbɪ] (pl -ies) n - **1.** [sports event] derby m (local) - **2.** US [hat] sombrero m hongo.

deregulate [ˌdiː'regjoleɪt] vt liberalizar.

derelict ['derəlɪkt] adj abandonado(da) y en ruinas.

deride [dɪ'raɪd] vt mofarse de.

derisory [də'raɪzərɪ] adj - **1.** [puny, trivial] irrisorio(ria) - **2.** [derisive] burlón(ona).

derivative [dɪ'rɪvətɪv] n derivado m.

derive [dɪ'raɪv] ◇ vt - **1.** [draw, gain] : **to ~ sthg from sthg** encontrar algo en algo - **2.** [come] : **to be ~d from** derivar de. ◇ vi : **to ~ from** derivar de.

derogatory [dɪ'rɒgətrɪ] adj despectivo(va).

derrick ['derɪk] n - **1.** [crane] grúa f - **2.** [over oil well] torre f de perforación.

derv [dɜːv] n UK gasóleo m, gasoil m.

descend [dɪ'send] ◇ vt fml [go down] descender por. ◇ vi - **1.** fml [go down] descender - **2.** [subj: silence, gloom] : **to ~ (on sthg/ sb)** invadir (algo/a alguien) - **3.** [stoop] : **to ~ sthg/to doing sthg** rebajarse a algo/a hacer algo.

descendant [dɪ'sendənt] n descendiente m OR f.

descended [dɪ'sendɪd] adj : **to be ~ from** ser descendiente de, descender de.

descent [dɪ'sent] n - **1.** [downwards movement] descenso m, bajada f - **2.** [origin] ascendencia f.

describe [dɪ'skraɪb] vt describir; **to ~ o.s. as** definirse como.

description [dɪ'skrɪpʃn] n - **1.** [account] descripción f - **2.** [type] : **of all ~s** de todo tipo.

desecrate ['desɪkreɪt] vt profanar.

desert [n 'dezət, vb dɪ'zɜːt] ◇ n GEOGR desierto m. ◇ vt abandonar. ◇ vi MIL desertar.

deserted [dɪ'zɜːtɪd] adj [place] desierto(ta).

deserter [dɪ'zɜːtəʳ] n desertor m, -ra f.

desert island ['dezət-] n isla f desierta.

deserve [dɪ'zɜːv] vt merecer, ameritar Amér.

deserving [dɪ'zɜːvɪŋ] adj encomiable.

design [dɪ'zaɪn] ◇ n - **1.** [gen] diseño m; [of garment] corte m - **2.** [pattern] dibujo m - **3.** fml [intention] designio m, intención f; **by ~** adrede; **to have ~s on** tener las miras puestas en. ◇ vt - **1.** [gen] diseñar - **2.** [conceive, intend] concebir.

designate [adj 'dezɪgnət, vb 'dezɪgneɪt] ◇ adj designado(da). ◇ vt designar, nombrar.

designer [dɪ'zaɪnəʳ] ◇ adj [clothes, drugs] de diseño; [glasses] de marca. ◇ n [gen] diseñador m, -ra f; THEATRE escenógrafo m, -fa f.

desirable [dɪ'zaɪərəbl] adj - **1.** fml [appropriate] deseable, conveniente - **2.** [attractive] atractivo(va), apetecible.

desire [dɪ'zaɪəʳ] ◇ n : **~ (for sthg/to do sthg)** deseo m (de algo/de hacer algo). ◇ vt desear.

desk [desk] n - **1.** [gen] mesa f, escritorio m; [in school] pupitre m - **2.** [service area] : **information ~** (mostrador m de) información f.

desktop publishing n COMPUT autoedición f.

desolate ['desələt] adj [place, person] desolado(da); [feeling] desolador(ra).

despair [dɪ'speəʳ] ◇ n desesperación f. ◇ vi desesperarse; **to ~ of sb** desesperarse con alguien; **to ~ of sthg/doing sthg** perder la esperanza de algo/hacer algo.

despairing [dɪ'speərɪŋ] adj [attempt] desesperado(da); [look, cry] de desesperación.

despatch [dɪ'spætʃ] = **dispatch**.

desperate ['desprət] adj desesperado(da); **to be ~ for sthg** necesitar desesperadamente algo.

desperately ['desprətlɪ] adv - **1.** [want, fight, love] desesperadamente - **2.** [ill] gravemente; [poor, unhappy, shy] tremendamente.

desperation [ˌdespə'reɪʃn] n desesperación f; **in ~** con desesperación.

despicable [dɪ'spɪkəbl] adj despreciable.

despise [dɪ'spaɪz] *vt* despreciar.

despite [dɪ'spaɪt] *prep* a pesar de, pese a.

despondent [dɪ'spɒndənt] *adj* descorazonado(da).

dessert [dɪ'zɜːt] *n* postre *m*.

dessertspoon [dɪ'zɜːtspuːn] *n* [spoon] cuchara *f* de postre.

destination [ˌdestɪ'neɪʃn] *n* destino *m*.

destined ['destɪnd] *adj* - 1. [fated, intended]: ~ for sthg/to do sthg destinado(da) a algo/a hacer algo - 2. [bound]: ~ for con destino a.

destiny ['destɪnɪ] (*pl* -ies) *n* destino *m*.

destitute ['destɪtjuːt] *adj* indigente, en la miseria.

destroy [dɪ'strɔɪ] *vt* - 1. [ruin] destruir - 2. [defeat] aplastar - 3. [put down] matar, sacrificar.

destruction [dɪ'strʌkʃn] *n* destrucción *f*.

detach [dɪ'tætʃ] *vt* - 1. [pull off]: to ~ sthg (from) quitar OR separar algo (de) - 2. [disassociate]: to ~ o.s. from sthg distanciarse de algo.

detachable [dɪ'tætʃəbl] *adj* [handle etc] de quita y pon; [collar] postizo(za).

detached [dɪ'tætʃt] *adj* [objective] objetivo(va); [aloof] distante.

detached house *n* casa *f* OR chalet *m* individual.

detachment [dɪ'tætʃmənt] *n* - 1. [objectivity] objetividad *f*; [aloofness] distanciamiento *m* - 2. MIL destacamento *m*.

detail ['diːteɪl] <> *n* - 1. [small point] detalle *m* - 2. (*U*) [facts, points] detalles *mpl*; to go into ~ entrar en detalles; in ~ con detalle - 3. MIL destacamento *m*. <> *vt* [list] detallar.
 ◆ **details** *npl* [information] información *f*; [personal] datos *mpl*.

detailed ['diːteɪld] *adj* detallado(da).

detain [dɪ'teɪn] *vt* [gen] retener; [in police station] detener.

detect [dɪ'tekt] *vt* [gen] detectar; [difference] notar, percibir.

detection [dɪ'tekʃn] *n* (*U*) - 1. [gen] detección *f* - 2. [of crime] investigación *f*; [of drugs] descubrimiento *m*.

detective [dɪ'tektɪv] *n* [private] detective *m* OR *f*; [policeman] agente *m* OR *f*.

detective novel *n* novela *f* policíaca.

détente [deɪ'tɒnt] *n* POL distensión *f*.

detention [dɪ'tenʃn] *n* - 1. [of suspect, criminal] detención *f*, arresto *m* - 2. [at school] *castigo de permanecer en la escuela después de clase.*

deter [dɪ'tɜː'] (*pt* & *pp* -red, *cont* -ring) *vt*: to ~ sb (from doing sthg) disuadir a alguien (de hacer algo).

detergent [dɪ'tɜːdʒənt] *n* detergente *m*.

deteriorate [dɪ'tɪərɪəreɪt] *vi* [health, economy] deteriorarse; [weather] empeorar.

determination [dɪˌtɜːmɪ'neɪʃn] *n* determinación *f*.

determine [dɪ'tɜːmɪn] *vt* determinar.

determined [dɪ'tɜːmɪnd] *adj* decidido(da); ~ to do sthg decidido OR resuelto a hacer algo.

deterrent [dɪ'terənt] *n* elemento *m* de disuasión; to serve as a ~ tener un efecto disuasorio; nuclear ~ armas *fpl* nucleares disuasorias.

detest [dɪ'test] *vt* detestar.

detonate ['detəneɪt] <> *vt* hacer detonar. <> *vi* detonar.

detour ['diːˌtʊə'] *n* desvío *m*; to make a ~ dar un rodeo.

detox ['diːtɒks] *n* desintoxicación *f*.

detract [dɪ'trækt] *vi*: to ~ from sthg [gen] mermar algo, aminorar algo; [achievement] restar importancia a algo.

detriment ['detrɪmənt] *n*: to the ~ of en detrimento de.

detrimental [ˌdetrɪ'mentl] *adj* perjudicial.

deuce [djuːs] *n* (*U*) TENNIS deuce *m*, cuarenta *f*.

devaluation [ˌdiːvæljʊ'eɪʃn] *n* devaluación *f*.

devastated ['devəsteɪtɪd] *adj* [area, city] asolado(da); *fig* [person] desolado(da).

devastating ['devəsteɪtɪŋ] *adj* - 1. [destructive - hurricane etc] devastador(ra) - 2. [effective - remark, argument] abrumador(ra) - 3. [upsetting - news, experience] desolador(ra) - 4. [attractive] imponente, irresistible.

develop [dɪ'veləp] <> *vt* - 1. [idea, argument, product, method] desarrollar - 2. [land] urbanizar; [region] desarrollar - 3. [illness] contraer; [habit] adquirir; to ~ a fault estropearse - 4. PHOT revelar. <> *vi* - 1. [grow] desarrollarse; to ~ into sthg transformarse en algo - 2. [appear] presentarse.

developing country [dɪ'veləpɪŋ-] *n* país *m* en vías de desarrollo.

development [dɪ'veləpmənt] *n* - 1. [growth] desarrollo *m* - 2. [of design] elaboración *f*; [of product] desarrollo *m* - 3. [developed land] urbanización *f* - 4. [new event] (nuevo) acontecimiento *m*; recent ~s la evolución reciente - 5. [advance - in science etc] avance *m*.

deviate ['diːvɪeɪt] *vi*: to ~ from sthg desviarse de algo.

device [dɪ'vaɪs] *n* - 1. [gen] dispositivo *m* - 2. COMPUT dispositivo *m* periférico.

devil ['devl] *n* diablo *m*, demonio *m*; poor ~ pobre diablo; you lucky ~! ¡vaya suerte que tienes!; who/where/why the ~ ...? ¿quién/dónde/por qué demonios ...?
 ◆ **Devil** *n* [Satan]: the Devil el Diablo, el Demonio.

devious ['diːvjəs] *adj* - 1. [person, scheme] retorcido(da); [means] enrevesado(da) - 2. [route] sinuoso(sa), tortuoso(sa).

devise [dɪ'vaɪz] *vt* [instrument, system] diseñar; [plan] concebir.

devoid [dɪ'vɔɪd] *adj fml*: ~ **of** desprovisto(ta) de.

devolution [ˌdiːvə'luːʃn] *n* POL ≃ autonomía *f*, ≃ traspaso *m* de competencias.

devote [dɪ'vəʊt] *vt*: **to** ~ **sthg to** dedicar OR consagrar algo a.

devoted [dɪ'vəʊtɪd] *adj* [lovers] unido(da); [follower, admirer] ferviente; **to be** ~ **to sb** tenerle mucho cariño a alguien.

devotee [ˌdevə'tiː] *n* [fan] devoto *m*, -ta *f*, admirador *m*, -ra *f*.

devotion [dɪ'vəʊʃn] *n* (U) - 1. [commitment]: ~ **(to)** dedicación *f*(a) - 2. [to family, lover & RELIG] devoción *f*.

devour [dɪ'vaʊəʳ] *vt lit* & *fig* devorar.

devout [dɪ'vaʊt] *adj* RELIG devoto(ta), piadoso(sa).

dew [djuː] *n* rocío *m*.

dexterity [dek'sterətɪ] *n* destreza *f*, habilidad *f*.

diabetes [ˌdaɪə'biːtiːz] *n* diabetes *f inv.*

diabetic [ˌdaɪə'betɪk] ◇ *adj* [person] diabético(ca). ◇ *n* diabético *m*, -ca *f*.

diabolic(al) [ˌdaɪə'bɒlɪk(l)] *adj inf* [very bad] pésimo(ma).

diagnose ['daɪəgnəʊz] *vt* MED diagnosticar; **she was** ~**d as having cancer** le diagnosticaron cáncer.

diagnosis [ˌdaɪəg'nəʊsɪs] (*pl* **-oses** [-əʊsiːz]) *n* MED [verdict] diagnóstico *m*; [science, activity] diagnosis *f inv.*

diagonal [daɪ'ægənl] ◇ *adj* diagonal. ◇ *n* diagonal *f*.

diagram ['daɪəgræm] *n* diagrama *m*.

dial ['daɪəl] (*UK pt* & *pp* **-led,** *cont* **-ling,** *US pt* & *pp* **-ed,** *cont* **-ing**) ◇ *n* - 1. [of watch, clock] esfera *f* - 2. [of meter] cuadrante *m* - 3. [of telephone] disco *m*; [of radio] dial *m*. ◇ *vt* [number] marcar.

dialect ['daɪəlekt] *n* dialecto *m*.

dialling code ['daɪəlɪŋ-] *n UK* prefijo *m* (telefónico).

dialling tone *UK* ['daɪəlɪŋ-], **dial tone** *US n* señal *f* de llamada.

dialogue *UK*, **dialog** *US* ['daɪəlɒg] *n* diálogo *m*.

dialogue box *UK*, **dialog box** *US n* COMPUT cuadro *m* de diálogo.

dial tone *US* = **dialling tone**.

dialysis [daɪ'ælɪsɪs] *n* diálisis *f inv.*

diameter [daɪ'æmɪtəʳ] *n* diámetro *m*.

diamond ['daɪəmənd] *n* - 1. [gem, playing card, in baseball] diamante *m* - 2. [shape] rombo *m*.

◆ **diamonds** *npl* diamantes *mpl*.

diaper ['daɪpəʳ] *n US* pañal *m*.

diaphragm ['daɪəfræm] *n* diafragma *m*.

diarrh(o)ea [ˌdaɪə'rɪə] *n* diarrea *f*.

diary ['daɪərɪ] (*pl* **-ies**) *n* - 1. [appointment book] agenda *f* - 2. [journal] diario *m*.

dice [daɪs] (*pl inv*) ◇ *n* dado *m*. ◇ *vt* cortar en cuadraditos.

dictate [dɪk'teɪt] *vt*: **to** ~ **sthg (to sb)** dictar algo (a alguien).

dictation [dɪk'teɪʃn] *n* dictado *m*; **to take** OR **do** ~ escribir al dictado.

dictator [dɪk'teɪtəʳ] *n* dictador *m*, -ra *f*.

dictatorship [dɪk'teɪtəʃɪp] *n* dictadura *f*.

dictionary ['dɪkʃənrɪ] (*pl* **-ies**) *n* diccionario *m*.

did [dɪd] *pt* ▷ **do.**

diddle ['dɪdl] *vt inf* timar.

didn't ['dɪdnt] = **did not.**

die [daɪ] (*pl* **dice,** *pt* & *pp* **died,** *cont* **dying**) ◇ *vi* - 1. [gen] morir; **to be dying** estar muriéndose; **to be dying for sthg/to do sthg** morirse por algo/por hacer algo - 2. *literary* [feeling, fire] extinguirse. ◇ *n esp US* [dice] dado *m*.

◆ **die away** *vi* desvanecerse.

◆ **die down** *vi* [wind] amainar; [sound] apaciguarse; [fire] remitir; [excitement, fuss] calmarse.

◆ **die out** *vi* extinguirse.

diehard ['daɪhɑːd] *n* intransigente *m* OR *f*.

diesel ['diːzl] *n* - 1. [fuel] gasóleo *m*, gasoil *m* - 2. [vehicle] vehículo *m* diesel.

diesel engine *n* AUT motor *m* diesel; RAIL locomotora *f* diesel.

diesel fuel, diesel oil *n* gasóleo *m*.

diet ['daɪət] ◇ *n* - 1. [eating pattern] dieta *f* - 2. [to lose weight] régimen *m*; **to be on a** ~ estar a régimen. ◇ *comp* [low-calorie] **light** *(inv)*, bajo(ja) en calorías. ◇ *vi* estar a régimen.

differ ['dɪfəʳ] *vi* - 1. [be different] ser diferente; **to** ~ **from sthg** distinguirse OR diferir de algo - 2. [disagree]: **to** ~ **with sb (about sthg)** disentir OR discrepar de alguien (en algo).

difference ['dɪfrəns] *n* diferencia *f*; **it didn't make any** ~ [changed nothing] no cambió nada; **it doesn't make any** ~ [it's all the same] da lo mismo.

different ['dɪfrənt] *adj*: ~ **(from)** diferente OR distinto(ta) (de).

differentiate [ˌdɪfə'renʃɪeɪt] ◇ *vt*: **to** ~ **(sthg from sthg)** diferenciar OR distinguir (algo de algo). ◇ *vi*: **to** ~ **between** diferenciar OR distinguir entre.

difficult ['dɪfɪkəlt] *adj* difícil.

difficulty ['dɪfɪkəltɪ] (*pl* **-ies**) *n* dificultad *f*; **to have** ~ **in doing sthg** tener dificultad en OR para hacer algo.

diffident ['dɪfɪdənt] *adj* retraído(da).

diffuse [dɪ'fju:z] *vt* difundir.

dig [dɪg] (*pt* & *pp* **dug**, *cont* **digging**) <> *vt* -**1.** [hole - with spade] cavar; [- with hands, paws] escarbar - **2.** [garden] cavar en; [mine] excavar - **3.** [press]: **to ~ sthg into** clavar OR hundir algo en. <> *vi* - **1.** [with spade] cavar; [with hands, paws] escarbar - **2.** [press]: **to ~ into** clavarse OR hundirse en. <> *n* -**1.** [unkind remark] pulla *f* - **2.** ARCHEOL excavación *f*.

◆ **dig out** *vt sep inf* [find - letter, object] desempolvar; [- information] encontrar.

◆ **dig up** *vt sep* [body, treasure, information] desenterrar; [plant, tree] arrancar.

digest [*n* 'daɪdʒest, *vb* dɪ'dʒest] <> *n* compendio *m*. <> *vt lit* & *fig* digerir.

digestion [dɪ'dʒestʃn] *n* digestión *f*.

digestive biscuit [dɪ'dʒestɪv-] *n UK* galleta *f* integral.

digit ['dɪdʒɪt] *n* - **1.** [figure] dígito *m* - **2.** [finger, toe] dedo *m*.

digital ['dɪdʒɪtl] *adj* digital.

digital camera *n* cámara *f* digital.

digital television, digital TV *n* televisión *f* digital.

dignified ['dɪgnɪfaɪd] *adj* [gen] digno(na); [ceremonious] ceremonioso(sa).

dignity ['dɪgnətɪ] *n* dignidad *f*.

digress [daɪ'gres] *vi* apartarse del tema; **to ~ from** apartarse OR desviarse de.

digs [dɪgz] *npl UK inf* alojamiento *m*; **to live in ~** vivir en un cuarto de alquiler.

dike [daɪk] *n* [wall, bank] dique *m*.

dilapidated [dɪ'læpɪdeɪtɪd] *adj* [building] derruido(da); [car] destartalado(da).

dilate [daɪ'leɪt] *vi* dilatarse.

dilemma [dɪ'lemə] *n* dilema *m*.

diligent ['dɪlɪdʒənt] *adj* diligente.

dilute [daɪ'lu:t] *vt* diluir.

dim [dɪm] (*compar* -**mer**, *superl* -**mest**, *pt* & *pp* -**med**, *cont* -**ming**) <> *adj* - **1.** [light - tenue; [room] sombrío(bría) - **2.** [eyesight] débil - **3.** [memory] vago(ga) - **4.** *inf* [stupid] tonto(ta), torpe. <> *vt* atenuar. <> *vi* [light] atenuarse.

dime [daɪm] *n US* moneda de diez centavos.

dimension [dɪ'menʃn] *n* dimensión *f*.

diminish [dɪ'mɪnɪʃ] *vt* & *vi* disminuir.

diminutive [dɪ'mɪnjʊtɪv] *fml* <> *adj* diminuto(ta). <> *n* GRAMM diminutivo *m*.

dimmer ['dɪmə^r], **dimmer switch** *n* potenciómetro *m*, regulador *m* de intensidad.

dimmers ['dɪməz] *npl US* [dipped headlights] luces *fpl* cortas OR de cruce; [parking lights] luces de posición OR situación.

dimmer switch *n* = dimmer.

dimple ['dɪmpl] *n* hoyuelo *m*.

din [dɪn] *n inf* estrépito *m*, relajo *m Amér.*

dine [daɪn] *vi fml* cenar.

◆ **dine out** *vi* cenar fuera.

diner ['daɪnə^r] *n* - **1.** [person] comensal *m* OR

f - **2.** *US* [restaurant - cheap] restaurante *m* barato; [- on the road] ≃ restaurante *m* OR parador *m* de carretera.

dinghy ['dɪŋgɪ] (*pl* -**ies**) *n* [sailing boat] bote *m*; [made of rubber] lancha *f* neumática.

dingy ['dɪndʒɪ] (*compar* -**ier**, *superl* -**iest**) *adj* [room, street] lóbrego(ga); [clothes, carpet] deslustrado(da).

dining car ['daɪnɪŋ-] *n* vagón *m* restaurante, coche *m* comedor *Amér.*

dining room ['daɪnɪŋ-] *n* comedor *m*.

dinner ['dɪnə^r] *n* - **1.** [evening meal] cena *f*; [midday meal] comida *f*, almuerzo *m*; **to have ~** [in the evening] cenar; [at lunchtime] comer, almorzar - **2.** [formal event] cena *f* de gala, banquete *m*.

dinner jacket *n* esmoquin *m*.

dinner party *n* cena *f* (*de amigos en casa*).

dinnertime ['dɪnətaɪm] *n* [in the evening] la hora de la cena; [at midday] la hora del almuerzo OR de la comida.

dinosaur ['daɪnəsɔ:^r] *n* [reptile] dinosaurio *m*.

dint [dɪnt] *n fml*: **by ~ of** a base de.

dip [dɪp] (*pt* & *pp* -**ped**, *cont* -**ping**) <> *n* - **1.** [in road, ground] pendiente *f* - **2.** [sauce] salsa *f* - **3.** [swim] chapuzón *m*; **to go for/ take a ~** ir a darse/darse un chapuzón. <> *vt* -**1.** [into liquid]: **to ~ sthg in** OR **into sthg** mojar algo en algo - **2.** *UK* [headlights]: **to ~ one's lights** poner las luces de cruce. <> *vi* descender suavemente.

diploma [dɪ'pləʊmə] (*pl* -**s**) *n* diploma *m*.

diplomacy [dɪ'pləʊməsɪ] *n* diplomacia *f*.

diplomat ['dɪpləmæt] *n* - **1.** [official] diplomático *m*, -ca *f* - **2.** [tactful person] persona *f* diplomática.

diplomatic [,dɪplə'mætɪk] *adj* diplomático(ca).

dipstick ['dɪpstɪk] *n* AUT varilla *f* (para medir el nivel) del aceite.

dire ['daɪə^r] *adj* - **1.** [consequences] grave; [warning] serio(ria); [need, poverty] extremo(ma) - **2.** *UK inf* [terrible] fatal.

direct [dɪ'rekt] <> *adj* directo(ta). <> *vt* - **1.** [gen]: **to ~ sthg at sb** dirigir algo a alguien - **2.** [person to place]: **to ~ sb (to)** indicar a alguien el camino (a) - **3.** [order]: **to ~ sb to do sthg** mandar a alguien hacer algo. <> *adv* directamente.

direct current *n* corriente *f* continua.

direct debit *n UK* domiciliación *f* (de pago).

direction [dɪ'rekʃn] *n* dirección *f*; **sense of ~** sentido *m* de la orientación.

◆ **directions** *npl* - **1.** [instructions to place] señas *fpl*, indicaciones *fpl* - **2.** [instructions for use] modo *m* de empleo.

directly [dɪ'rektlɪ] *adv* - **1.** [gen] directamente - **2.** [immediately] inmediatamente

- **3.** [very soon] pronto, en breve.
director [dɪˈrektəʳ] *n* director *m*, -ra *f*.
directory [dɪˈrektərɪ] (*pl* **-ies**) *n* - **1.** [gen] guía *f* (alfabética) - **2.** COMPUT directorio *m*.
directory assistance *n* US (servicio *m* de) información *f* telefónica.
directory enquiries *n* UK (servicio *m* de) información *f* telefónica.
dire straits *npl*: **in** ~ en serios aprietos.
dirt [dɜːt] *n* (U) - **1.** [mud, dust] suciedad *f* - **2.** [earth] tierra *f*.
dirt cheap *inf* <> *adj* tirado(da) de precio. <> *adv* a precio de ganga.
dirty [ˈdɜːtɪ] (*compar* **-ier**, *superl* **-iest**, *pt* & *pp* **-ied**) <> *adj* - **1.** [gen] sucio(cia); **to get** ~ ensuciarse - **2.** [joke] verde; [film] pornográfico(ca); [book, language] obsceno(na); ~ **word** palabrota *f.* <> *vt* ensuciar.
disability [ˌdɪsəˈbɪlətɪ] (*pl* **-ies**) *n* minusvalía *f*, discapacidad *f*.
disabled [dɪsˈeɪbld] <> *adj* [person] minusválido(da), discapacitado(da); ~ **toilet** servicio *m* para minusválidos. <> *npl*: **the** ~ los minusválidos, los discapacitados.
disadvantage [ˌdɪsədˈvɑːntɪdʒ] *n* desventaja *f*; **to be at a** ~ estar en desventaja.
disagree [ˌdɪsəˈgriː] *vi* - **1.** [have different opinions]: **to** ~ **(with)** no estar de acuerdo (con) - **2.** [conflict] contradecirse, no concordar - **3.** [subj: food, drink]: **to** ~ **with sb** sentar mal a alguien.
disagreeable [ˌdɪsəˈgriːəbl] *adj* desagradable.
disagreement [ˌdɪsəˈgriːmənt] *n* - **1.** [fact of disagreeing] desacuerdo *m* - **2.** [argument] discusión *f*.
disallow [ˌdɪsəˈlaʊ] *vt* - **1.** *fml* [appeal, claim] rechazar - **2.** [goal] anular.
disappear [ˌdɪsəˈpɪəʳ] *vi* desaparecer.
disappearance [ˌdɪsəˈpɪərəns] *n* desaparición *f*.
disappoint [ˌdɪsəˈpɔɪnt] *vt* [person] decepcionar, desilusionar; [expectations, hopes] defraudar.
disappointed [ˌdɪsəˈpɔɪntɪd] *adj* - **1.** [person]: ~ **(in OR with sthg)** decepcionado(da) (con algo) - **2.** [expectations, hopes] defraudado(da).
disappointing [ˌdɪsəˈpɔɪntɪŋ] *adj* decepcionante.
disappointment [ˌdɪsəˈpɔɪntmənt] *n* decepción *f*, desilusión *f*; **to be a** ~ ser decepcionante.
disapproval [ˌdɪsəˈpruːvl] *n* desaprobación *f*.
disapprove [ˌdɪsəˈpruːv] *vi* estar en contra; **to** ~ **of sthg** desaprobar algo; **to** ~ **of sb** no ver con buenos ojos a alguien.
disarm [dɪsˈɑːm] <> *vt lit* & *fig* desarmar. <> *vi* desarmarse.

disarmament [dɪsˈɑːməmənt] *n* desarme *m*.
disarray [ˌdɪsəˈreɪ] *n*: **in** ~ [clothes, hair] en desorden; [army, political party] sumido(da) en el desconcierto.
disaster [dɪˈzɑːstəʳ] *n* [gen] desastre *m*; [earthquake, eruption] catástrofe *f*.
disastrous [dɪˈzɑːstrəs] *adj* desastroso(sa).
disband [dɪsˈbænd] <> *vt* disolver, disgregar. <> *vi* disolverse, disgregarse.
disbelief [ˌdɪsbɪˈliːf] *n*: **in** OR **with** ~ con incredulidad.
disc UK, **disk** US [dɪsk] *n* disco *m*.
discard [dɪˈskɑːd] *vt* [old clothes etc] desechar; [possibility] descartar.
discern [dɪˈsɜːn] *vt* - **1.** [gen] discernir; [improvement] percibir - **2.** [figure, outline] distinguir.
discerning [dɪˈsɜːnɪŋ] *adj* refinado(da); [audience] entendido(da).
discharge [*n* ˈdɪstʃɑːdʒ, *vb* dɪsˈtʃɑːdʒ] <> *n* - **1.** [of patient] alta *f*; [of prisoner, defendant] puesta *f* en libertad; [of soldier] licencia *f* - **2.** [of gas, smoke] emisión *f*; [of sewage] vertido *m* - **3.** [MED] mucosidad *f*; [- from wound] supuración *f* - **4.** ELEC descarga *f*. <> *vt* - **1.** [patient] dar de alta; [prisoner, defendant] poner en libertad; [soldier] licenciar - **2.** *fml* [duty etc] cumplir - **3.** [gas, smoke] despedir; [sewage] verter; [cargo] descargar.
disciple [dɪˈsaɪpl] *n* - **1.** [follower] discípulo *m*, -la *f* - **2.** RELIG discípulo *m*.
discipline [ˈdɪsɪplɪn] <> *n* disciplina *f.* <> *vt* - **1.** [control] disciplinar - **2.** [punish] castigar.
disc jockey *n* pinchadiscos *m* OR *f inv.*
disclaim [dɪsˈkleɪm] *vt fml* negar.
disclose [dɪsˈkləʊz] *vt* revelar.
disclosure [dɪsˈkləʊʒəʳ] *n* revelación *f*.
disco [ˈdɪskəʊ] (*pl* **-s**) (*abbr of* **discotheque**) *n* - **1.** [place] discoteca *f*; [event] baile *m* - **2.** [type of music] música *f* disco.
discomfort [dɪsˈkʌmfət] *n* - **1.** [uncomfortableness] incomodidad *f* - **2.** [pain] molestia *f*.
disconcert [ˌdɪskənˈsɜːt] *vt* desconcertar.
disconnect [ˌdɪskəˈnekt] <> *vt* - **1.** [detach] quitar, separar - **2.** [from gas, electricity - appliance] desconectar; [- house, subscriber] cortar el suministro a - **3.** [on phone - person] cortar la línea a. <> *vi* [from Internet] desconectarse.
disconsolate [dɪsˈkɒnsələt] *adj* desconsolado(da).
discontent [ˌdɪskənˈtent] *n*: ~ **(with)** descontento *m* (con).
discontented [ˌdɪskənˈtentɪd] *adj* descontento(ta).
discontinue [ˌdɪskənˈtɪnjuː] *vt* interrumpir.

discord ['dɪskɔːd] *n* **-1.** [disagreement] discordia *f* **-2.** MUS disonancia *f*.

discotheque ['dɪskəʊtek] *n* discoteca *f*.

discount [*n* 'dɪskaʊnt, *vb* UK dɪs'kaʊnt, US 'dɪskaʊnt] <> *n* descuento *m*; **at a** ~ con descuento. <> *vt* [report, claim] descartar.

discourage [dɪ'skʌrɪdʒ] *vt* **-1.** [dispirit] desanimar **-2.** [crime, behaviour] impedir; [thieves, tourists] ahuyentar; **to** ~ **sb from doing sthg** disuadir a alguien de hacer algo.

discover [dɪ'skʌvəʳ] *vt* descubrir.

discovery [dɪ'skʌvərɪ] (*pl* **-ies**) *n* descubrimiento *m*.

discredit [dɪs'kredɪt] <> *n* descrédito *m*, desprestigio *m*. <> *vt* **-1.** [person, organization] desacreditar, desprestigiar **-2.** [idea, report] refutar.

discreet [dɪ'skriːt] *adj* discreto(ta).

discretion [dɪ'skreʃn] *n (U)* **-1.** [tact] discreción *f* **-2.** [judgment] criterio *m*; **at the** ~ **of** a voluntad de.

discriminate [dɪ'skrɪmɪneɪt] *vi* **-1.** [distinguish]: **to** ~ **(between)** discriminar OR distinguir (entre) **-2.** [treat unfairly]: **to** ~ **against sb** discriminar a alguien.

discriminating [dɪ'skrɪmɪneɪtɪŋ] *adj* refinado(da); [audience] entendido(da).

discrimination [dɪ,skrɪmɪ'neɪʃn] *n* **-1.** [prejudice]: ~ **(against)** discriminación *f* (hacia) **-2.** [judgment] (buen) gusto *m*.

discus ['dɪskəs] (*pl* **-es**) *n* [object] disco *m* (en atletismo); **the** ~ [competition] el lanzamiento de disco.

discuss [dɪ'skʌs] *vt* **-1.** [gen]: **to** ~ **sthg (with sb)** hablar de algo (con alguien) **-2.** [subj: book, lecture] tratar de.

discussion [dɪ'skʌʃn] *n* discusión *f*.

disdain [dɪs'deɪn] *fml* <> *n*: ~ **(for)** desdén *m* OR desprecio *m* (hacia). <> *vt* desdeñar, despreciar.

disease [dɪ'ziːz] *n lit & fig* enfermedad *f*.

disembark [,dɪsɪm'bɑːk] *vi* desembarcar.

disenchanted [,dɪsɪn'tʃɑːntɪd] *adj*: ~ **(with)** desencantado(da) (con).

disengage [,dɪsɪn'geɪdʒ] *vt* **-1.** [release]: **to** ~ **sthg (from)** soltar OR desenganchar algo (de) **-2.** TECH [gears] quitar; [clutch] soltar.

disfavour UK, **disfavor** US [dɪs'feɪvəʳ] *n* **-1.** [disapproval] desaprobación *f* **-2.** [state of being disapproved of] desgracia *f*.

disfigure [dɪs'fɪgəʳ] *vt* desfigurar.

disgrace [dɪs'greɪs] <> *n* vergüenza *f*; **he's a** ~ **to his family** es una deshonra para su familia; **to be in** ~ [minister, official] estar desprestigiado(da); [child, pet] estar castigado(da). <> *vt* deshonrar.

disgraceful [dɪs'greɪsful] *adj* vergonzoso(sa); **it's** ~ es una vergüenza.

disgruntled [dɪs'grʌntld] *adj* disgustado(da).

disguise [dɪs'gaɪz] <> *n* disfraz *m*; **in** ~ [policeman, famous person] de incógnito. <> *vt* disfrazar.

disgust [dɪs'gʌst] <> *n*: ~ **(at)** [physical] asco *m* (hacia); [moral] indignación *f* (ante). <> *vt* [physically] repugnar; [morally] indignar.

disgusting [dɪs'gʌstɪŋ] *adj* [physically] asqueroso(sa); [morally] indignante.

dish [dɪʃ] *n* **-1.** [container] fuente *f* **-2.** US [plate] plato *m* **-3.** [course] plato *m*.
  ◆ **dishes** *npl* platos *mpl*; **to do** OR **wash the** ~ **es** fregar (los platos).
  ◆ **dish out** *vt sep inf* repartir.
  ◆ **dish up** *vt sep inf* servir.

dish aerial UK, **dish antenna** US *n* (antena *f*) parabólica *f*.

dishcloth ['dɪʃklɒθ] *n* [for washing, wiping] trapo *m* de fregar los platos; [for drying] paño *m* de cocina.

disheartened [dɪs'hɑːtnd] *adj* descorazonado(da).

dishevelled UK, **disheveled** US [dɪ'ʃevəld] *adj* desaliñado(da); [hair] despeinado(da).

dishonest [dɪs'ɒnɪst] *adj* deshonesto(ta), nada honrado(da).

dishonor *etc* US = **dishonour** *etc*.

dishonour UK, **dishonor** US [dɪs'ɒnəʳ] *fml* <> *n* deshonra *f*, deshonor *m*. <> *vt* deshonrar.

dishonourable UK, **dishonorable** US [dɪs'ɒnərəbl] *adj* deshonroso(sa).

dish soap *n* US detergente *m* para vajillas.

dish towel *n* US paño *m* de cocina.

dishwasher ['dɪʃ,wɒʃəʳ] *n* **-1.** [machine] lavavajillas *m inv* **-2.** [person] lavaplatos *m* OR *f inv*.

dishwashing liquid *n* US lavavajillas *m inv*.

disillusioned [,dɪsɪ'luːʒnd] *adj* desilusionado(da).

disincentive [,dɪsɪn'sentɪv] *n* traba *f*.

disinclined [,dɪsɪn'klaɪnd] *adj*: **to be** ~ **to do sthg** no tener ganas de hacer algo.

disinfect [,dɪsɪn'fekt] *vt* desinfectar.

disinfectant [,dɪsɪn'fektənt] *n* desinfectante *m*.

disintegrate [dɪs'ɪntɪgreɪt] *vi lit & fig* desintegrarse.

disinterested [,dɪs'ɪntrəstɪd] *adj* **-1.** [objective] desinteresado(da) **-2.** *inf* [uninterested]: ~ **(in)** indiferente (a).

disjointed [dɪs'dʒɔɪntɪd] *adj* deslabazado(da).

disk [dɪsk] *n* **-1.** COMPUT disco *m*; [diskette] disquete *m* **-2.** US = **disc**.

disk drive *n* COMPUT disquetera *f*, unidad *f* de disco.

diskette [dɪs'ket] *n* disquete *m*.

dislike [dɪs'laɪk] ◇ *n* -1. [feeling]: ~ (for) [things] aversión *f* (a); [people] antipatía *f* (por); **to take a ~ to** cogerle manía a - 2. [thing not liked]: **her likes and ~s** las cosas que le gustan y las que no le gustan. ◇ *vt*: **I ~ her** no me gusta; **I ~ them** no me gustan.

dislocate ['dɪsləkeɪt] *vt* MED dislocar; **to ~ one's shoulder** dislocarse el hombro.

dislodge [dɪs'lɒdʒ] *vt*: **to ~ sthg/sb (from)** sacar algo/a alguien (de).

disloyal [ˌdɪs'lɔɪəl] *adj*: ~ (to) desleal (a).

dismal ['dɪzml] *adj* -1. [weather, future] sombrío(a); [place, atmosphere] deprimente - 2. [attempt, failure] lamentable.

dismantle [dɪs'mæntl] *vt* [machine] desmontar; [organization] desmantelar.

dismay [dɪs'meɪ] ◇ *n (U)* consternación *f*. ◇ *vt* consternar.

dismiss [dɪs'mɪs] *vt* -1. [refuse to take seriously] desechar - 2. [from job]: **to ~ sb (from)** despedir a alguien (de) - 3. [allow to leave] dar permiso para irse a.

dismissal [dɪs'mɪsl] *n* [from job] despido *m*, remoción *f Amér.*

dismount [ˌdɪs'maʊnt] *vi*: **to ~ (from sthg)** desmontar (de algo).

disobedience [ˌdɪsə'biːdjəns] *n* desobediencia *f*.

disobedient [ˌdɪsə'biːdjənt] *adj*: ~ (to) desobediente (con).

disobey [ˌdɪsə'beɪ] *vt* & *vi* desobedecer.

disorder [dɪs'ɔːdə˚] *n* -1. [disarray]: **in ~** en desorden - 2. *(U)* [rioting] disturbios *mpl* - 3. MED [physical] afección *f*, dolencia *f*; [mental] trastorno *m*, perturbación *f*.

disorderly [dɪs'ɔːdəlɪ] *adj* -1. [untidy] desordenado(da) - 2. [unruly - behaviour] incontrolado(da).

disorganized, -ised [dɪs'ɔːgənaɪzd] *adj* desorganizado(da).

disorientated *UK* [dɪs'ɔːrɪənteɪtɪd], **disoriented** *US* [dɪs'ɔːrɪəntɪd] *adj* desorientado(da).

disown [dɪs'əʊn] *vt* [gen] renegar de; [statement] no reconocer como propio(pia).

disparaging [dɪ'spærɪdʒɪŋ] *adj* menospreciativo(va).

dispassionate [dɪ'spæʃnət] *adj* desapasionado(da).

dispatch [dɪ'spætʃ] ◇ *n* -1. [message] despacho *m* - 2. [sending] envío *m*. ◇ *vt* [goods, parcel] expedir; [message, messenger, troops] enviar.

dispel [dɪ'spel] (*pt* & *pp* -**led**, *cont* -**ling**) *vt* disipar.

dispensary [dɪ'spensərɪ] (*pl* -**ies**) *n* dispensario *m*.

dispense [dɪ'spens] *vt* -1. [advice] ofrecer; [justice] administrar - 2. [drugs, medicine] despachar.
  ◆ **dispense with** *vt fus* prescindir de.

dispensing chemist *UK*, **dispensing pharmacist** *US* [dɪ'spensɪŋ-] *n* farmacéutico *m*, -ca *f*.

disperse [dɪ'spɜːs] ◇ *vt* dispersar. ◇ *vi* dispersarse.

dispirited [dɪ'spɪrɪtɪd] *adj* desanimado(da).

displace [dɪs'pleɪs] *vt* [supplant] reemplazar, sustituir.

display [dɪ'spleɪ] ◇ *n* -1. [arrangement - in shop window] escaparate *m*; [- in museum] exposición *f*; [- on stall, pavement] muestrario *m* - 2. [demonstration, public event] demostración *f* - 3. [sporting] exhibición *f* - 4. COMPUT pantalla *f*. ◇ *vt* -1. [arrange] exponer - 2. [show] demostrar - 3. [on screen] mostrar.

displease [dɪs'pliːz] *vt* [annoy] disgustar; [anger] enfadar.

displeasure [dɪs'pleʒə˚] *n* [annoyance] disgusto *m*; [anger] enfado *m*.

disposable [dɪ'spəʊzəbl] *adj* desechable; ~ **income** poder *m* adquisitivo.

disposal [dɪ'spəʊzl] *n* -1. [removal] eliminación *f* - 2. *US* trituradora *f* de basuras - 3. [availability]: **to have sthg at one's ~** disponer de algo.

dispose [dɪ'spəʊz] ◆ **dispose of** *vt fus* [rubbish] deshacerse de; [problem] quitarse de encima OR de en medio.

disposed [dɪ'spəʊzd] *adj* -1. [willing]: **to be ~ to do sthg** estar dispuesto(ta) a hacer algo - 2. [friendly]: **to be well ~ to OR towards sb** tener buena disposición hacia alguien.

disposition [ˌdɪspə'zɪʃn] *n* [temperament] carácter *m*.

disprove [ˌdɪs'pruːv] *vt* refutar.

dispute [dɪ'spjuːt] ◇ *n* -1. [quarrel] disputa *f* - 2. *(U)* [disagreement] conflicto *m*, desacuerdo *m* - 3. IND conflicto *m* laboral. ◇ *vt* cuestionar.

disqualify [ˌdɪs'kwɒlɪfaɪ] (*pt* & *pp* -**ied**) *vt* -1. [subj: authority, illness etc]: **to ~ sb (from doing sthg)** incapacitar a alguien (para hacer algo) - 2. SPORT descalificar - 3. *UK* [from driving] retirar el permiso de conducir a.

disquiet [dɪs'kwaɪət] *n* inquietud *f*, desasosiego *m*.

disregard [ˌdɪsrɪ'gɑːd] ◇ *n*: ~ (for) indiferencia *f* (a), despreocupación *f* (por). ◇ *vt* hacer caso omiso de.

disrepair [ˌdɪsrɪ'peə˚] *n*: **in a state of ~** deteriorado(da).

disreputable [dɪs'repjʊtəbl] *adj* [person, company] de mala fama; [behaviour] vergonzante.

disrepute [ˌdɪsrɪ'pjuːt] *n*: **to bring sthg into ~** desprestigiar OR desacreditar algo.

disrupt [dɪs'rʌpt] *vt* [meeting] interrumpir; [transport system] trastornar, perturbar; [class] revolucionar, enredar en.

disruption [dɪs'rʌpʃn] *n* [of meeting] interrupción *f*; [of transport system] trastorno *m*.

dissatisfaction ['dɪs,sætɪs'fækʃn] *n* descontento *m*.

dissatisfied [,dɪs'sætɪsfaɪd] *adj*: ~ (with) insatisfecho(cha) OR descontento(ta) (con).

dissect [dɪ'sekt] *vt* MED disecar; *fig* [study] analizar minuciosamente.

disseminate [dɪ'semɪneɪt] *vt* difundir, divulgar.

dissent [dɪ'sent] <> *n* [gen] disconformidad *f*, disentimiento *m*; SPORT: he was booked for ~ le amonestaron por protestar. <> *vi*: to ~ (from) disentir (de).

dissertation [,dɪsə'teɪʃn] *n* - 1. *US* [doctoral] tesis *f* - 2. *UK* [lower degree] tesina *f*.

disservice [,dɪs'sɜ:vɪs] *n*: to do sb a ~ hacer un flaco servicio a alguien.

dissident ['dɪsɪdənt] *n* disidente *m* OR *f*.

dissimilar [,dɪ'sɪmɪlə'] *adj*: ~ (to) distinto(ta) (de).

dissipate ['dɪsɪpeɪt] *vt* - 1. [heat, fears] disipar - 2. [efforts, money] desperdiciar, derrochar.

dissociate [dɪ'səʊʃɪeɪt] *vt* disociar, separar.

dissolute ['dɪsəlu:t] *adj* disoluto(ta).

dissolve [dɪ'zɒlv] <> *vt* disolver. <> *vi* - 1. [substance] disolverse - 2. *fig* [disappear] desvanecerse, desaparecer.

dissuade [dɪ'sweɪd] *vt*: to ~ sb (from doing sthg) disuadir a alguien (de hacer algo).

distance ['dɪstəns] *n* distancia *f*; at a ~ a distancia; from a ~ desde lejos; in the ~ a lo lejos.

distance learning *n* educación *f* a distancia.

distant ['dɪstənt] *adj* - 1. [place, time, relative] lejano(na); ~ from distante de - 2. [person, manner] frío(a), distante.

distaste [dɪs'teɪst] *n*: ~ (for) desagrado *m* (por).

distasteful [dɪs'teɪstfʊl] *adj* desagradable.

distended [dɪ'stendɪd] *adj* dilatado(da).

distil *UK* (*pt & pp* -led, *cont* -ling), **distill** *US* [dɪ'stɪl] *vt* [liquid] destilar.

distillery [dɪ'stɪlərɪ] (*pl* -ies) *n* destilería *f*.

distinct [dɪ'stɪŋkt] *adj* - 1. [different]: ~ (from) distinto(ta) (de); as ~ from a diferencia de - 2. [clear - improvement] notable, visible; [- possibility] claro(ra).

distinction [dɪ'stɪŋkʃn] *n* - 1. [difference, excellence] distinción *f*; to draw OR make a ~ between hacer una distinción entre - 2. [in exam result] sobresaliente *m*.

distinctive [dɪ'stɪŋktɪv] *adj* característico(ca), particular.

distinguish [dɪ'stɪŋgwɪʃ] *vt* [gen]: to ~ sthg (from) distinguir algo (de).

distinguished [dɪ'stɪŋgwɪʃt] *adj* distinguido(da).

distinguishing [dɪ'stɪŋgwɪʃɪŋ] *adj* distintivo(va).

distort [dɪ'stɔ:t] *vt* - 1. [shape, face] deformar; [sound] distorsionar - 2. [truth, facts] tergiversar.

distract [dɪ'strækt] *vt* [person, attention]: to ~ sb (from) distraer a alguien (de).

distracted [dɪ'stræktɪd] *adj* ausente.

distraction [dɪ'strækʃn] *n* [interruption, diversion] distracción *f*.

distraught [dɪ'strɔ:t] *adj* consternado(da).

distress [dɪ'stres] <> *n* - 1. [anxiety] angustia *f*; [pain] dolor *m* - 2. [danger, difficulty] peligro *m*. <> *vt* afligir, apenar.

distressing [dɪ'stresɪŋ] *adj* angustioso(sa).

distribute [dɪ'strɪbju:t] *vt* distribuir, repartir.

distribution [,dɪstrɪ'bju:ʃn] *n* distribución *f*.

distributor [dɪ'strɪbjʊtə'] *n* - 1. COMM distribuidor *m*, -ra *f* - 2. AUT delco® *m*, distribuidor *m*.

district ['dɪstrɪkt] *n* - 1. [area - of country] zona *f*, región *f*; [- of town] barrio *m* - 2. [administrative area] distrito *m*.

district attorney *n* *US* fiscal *m* OR *f* (del distrito).

district council *n* *UK* ADMIN ≃ municipio *m*.

district nurse *n* *UK* enfermera encargada de atender a domicilio a los pacientes de una zona.

distrust [dɪs'trʌst] <> *n* desconfianza *f*. <> *vt* desconfiar de.

disturb [dɪ'stɜ:b] *vt* - 1. [interrupt - person] molestar; [- concentration, sleep] perturbar - 2. [upset, worry] inquietar - 3. [alter - surface, arrangement] alterar; [- papers] desordenar.

disturbance [dɪ'stɜ:bəns] *n* - 1. [fight] tumulto *m*, alboroto *m*; there were a number of minor ~s throughout the night. se produjeron algunos disturbios durante la noche - 2. [interruption] interrupción *f* - 3. [of mind, emotions] trastorno *m*.

disturbed [dɪ'stɜ:bd] *adj* - 1. [upset, ill] trastornado(da) - 2. [worried] inquieto(ta).

disturbing [dɪ'stɜ:bɪŋ] *adj* inquietante, preocupante.

disuse [,dɪs'ju:s] *n*: to fall into ~ [regulation] caer en desuso; [building, mine] verse paulatinamente abandonado(da).

disused [,dɪs'ju:zd] *adj* abandonado(da).

ditch [dɪtʃ] <> *n* [gen] zanja *f*; [by road] cuneta *f*. <> *vt inf* - 1. [end relationship with] romper con - 2. [get rid of] deshacerse de.

dither ['dɪðə'] *vi* vacilar.

Doberman

ditto ['dɪtəʊ] *adv* ídem.

dive [daɪv] (*UK pt & pp* **-d**, *US pt* **-d** *OR* **dove**, *pp* **-d**) ⬦ *vi* **- 1.** [into water - person] zambullirse, tirarse al agua; [- submarine, bird, fish] sumergirse **- 2.** [with breathing apparatus] bucear, clavarse *Amér* **- 3.** [through air - person] lanzarse; [- plane] caer en picado **- 4.** [into bag, cupboard]: **to ~ into** meter la mano en. ⬦ *n* **- 1.** [of person - into water] zambullida *f* **- 2.** [of submarine] inmersión *f* **- 3.** [of person - through air] salto *m*; [- SPORT] [by goalkeeper] estirada *f*; **it was a ~** se ha tirado **- 4.** [of plane] picado *m* **- 5.** *inf pej* [bar, restaurant] garito *m*, antro *m*.

diver ['daɪvə'] *n* [underwater] buceador *m*, -ra *f*; [professional] buzo *m*; [from diving board] saltador *m*, -ra *f* (de trampolín).

diverge [daɪ'vɜ:dʒ] *vi* **- 1.** [gen]: **to ~ (from)** divergir (de) **- 2.** [disagree] discrepar.

diversify [daɪ'vɜ:sɪfaɪ] (*pt & pp* **-ied**) ⬦ *vt* diversificar. ⬦ *vi* diversificarse.

diversion [daɪ'vɜ:ʃn] *n* **- 1.** [of traffic, river, funds] desvío *m* **- 2.** [distraction] distracción *f*.

diversity [daɪ'vɜ:sətɪ] *n* diversidad *f*.

divert [daɪ'vɜ:t] *vt* **- 1.** [traffic, river, funds] desviar **- 2.** [person, attention] distraer.

divide [dɪ'vaɪd] ⬦ *vt*: **to ~ sthg (between** *OR* **among)** dividir algo (entre); **to ~ sthg into** dividir algo en; **to ~ sthg by** dividir algo entre *OR* por; **~ 3 into 89** divide 89 entre 3. ⬦ *vi* **- 1.** [river, road, wall] bifurcarse **- 2.** [group] dividirse.

dividend ['dɪvɪdend] *n* FIN dividendo *m*; [profit] beneficio *m*.

divine [dɪ'vaɪn] *adj* divino(na).

diving ['daɪvɪŋ] *n* (*U*) **- 1.** [into water] salto *m* **- 2.** [with breathing apparatus] buceo *m*.

divingboard ['daɪvɪŋbɔ:d] *n* trampolín *m*.

divinity [dɪ'vɪnətɪ] (*pl* **-ies**) *n* **- 1.** [godliness, deity] divinidad *f* **- 2.** [study] teología *f*.

division [dɪ'vɪʒn] *n* **- 1.** [gen] división *f* **- 2.** [of labour, responsibility] reparto *m*.

divorce [dɪ'vɔ:s] ⬦ *n* divorcio *m*. ⬦ *vt* [husband, wife] divorciarse de. ⬦ *vi* divorciarse.

divorced [dɪ'vɔ:st] *adj* divorciado(da).

divorcee [dɪvɔ:'si:] *n* divorciado *m*, -da *f*.

divulge [daɪ'vʌldʒ] *vt* divulgar, revelar.

DIY *abbr of* **do-it-yourself**.

dizzy ['dɪzɪ] (*compar* **-ier**, *superl* **-iest**) *adj* **- 1.** [because of illness etc] mareado(da) **- 2.** [because of heights]: **to feel ~** sentir vértigo.

DJ *n abbr of* **disc jockey**.

DNA (*abbr of* **deoxyribonucleic acid**) *n* ADN *m*.

DNS (*abbr of* **Domain Name System**) *n* COMPUT DNS *m*.

do [du:] (*pt* **did**, *pp* **done**, *pl* **dos** *OR* **do's**) ⬦ *aux vb* **- 1.** (*in negatives*): **don't leave it** there no lo dejes ahí **- 2.** (*in questions*): **what did he want?** ¿qué quería?; **~ you think she'll come?** ¿crees que vendrá? **- 3.** (*referring back to previous verb*): **~ you think so?** - **yes, I ~** ¿tú crees? - sí; **she reads more than I ~** lee más que yo; **so ~ I/they** yo/ellos también **- 4.** (*in question tags*): **you know her, don't you?** la conoces ¿no?; **so you think you can dance, ~ you?** así que te crees que sabes bailar ¿no? **- 5.** (*for emphasis*): **I did tell you but you've forgotten** sí que te lo dije, pero tú has olvidado; **~ come in** ¡pase, por favor! ⬦ *vt* **- 1.** [gen] hacer; **to ~ the cooking/cleaning** hacer la comida/limpieza; **to ~ one's hair** peinarse; **to ~ one's teeth** lavarse los dientes; **he did his duty** cumplió con su deber; **what can I ~ for you?** ¿en qué puedo servirle?; **what can we ~?** ¿qué le vamos a hacer? **- 2.** [referring to job]: **what ~ you ~?** ¿a qué te dedicas? **- 3.** [study] hacer; **I did physics at school** hice física en la escuela **- 4.** [travel at a particular speed] ir a; **the car can ~ 110 mph** el coche alcanza las 110 millas por hora **- 5.** [be good enough for]: **will that ~ you?** ¿te vale eso? ⬦ *vi* **- 1.** [gen] hacer; **~ as she says** haz lo que te dice; **they're ~ing really well** les va muy bien; **he could ~ better** lo podría hacer mejor; **how did you ~ in the exam?** ¿qué tal te salió el examen? **- 2.** [be good enough, sufficient] servir, valer; **this kind of behaviour won't ~** ese tipo de comportamiento no es aceptable; **that will ~ (nicely)** con eso vale; **that will ~!** [showing annoyance] ¡basta ya! **- 3.** *phr*: **how ~ you ~?** [greeting] ¿cómo está usted?; [answer] mucho gusto. ⬦ *n* [party] fiesta *f*.

◆ **dos** *npl*: **~s and don'ts** normas *fpl* básicas.

◆ **do away with** *vt fus* [disease, poverty] acabar con; [law, reforms] suprimir.

◆ **do down** *vt sep inf*: **to ~ sb down** menospreciar a alguien; **to ~ o.s. down** menospreciarse.

◆ **do over** *vt sep US* volver a hacer.

◆ **do up** *vt sep* **- 1.** [fasten - shoelaces, tie] atar; [- coat, buttons] abrochar; **~ your shoes up** átate los zapatos; **~ your coat up** abróchate el abrigo **- 2.** [decorate] renovar, redecorar; **to ~ o.s. up** arreglarse **- 3.** [wrap up] envolver.

◆ **do with** *vt fus* **- 1.** [need]: **I could ~ with a drink/new car** no me vendría mal una copa/un coche nuevo **- 2.** [have connection with]: **that has nothing to ~ with it** eso no tiene nada que ver (con ello).

◆ **do without** ⬦ *vt fus* pasar sin; **I can ~ without your sarcasm** podrías ahorrarte tu sarcasmo. ⬦ *vi* apañárselas.

Doberman ['dəʊbəmən] (*pl* **-s**) *n*: **~ (pinscher)** doberman *m*.

docile [*UK* 'dəʊsaɪl, *US* 'dɒsəl] *adj* dócil.

dock [dɒk] <> *n* -**1.** [in harbour] dársena *f*, muelle *m* - **2.** [in court] banquillo *m* (de los acusados). <> *vi* [ship] atracar; [spacecraft] acoplarse.

docker ['dɒkə'] *n* estibador *m*.

docklands ['dɒkləndz] *npl UK* barrio *m* portuario.

dockyard ['dɒkjɑ:d] *n* astillero *m*.

doctor ['dɒktə'] <> *n* -**1.** [of medicine] médico *m*, -ca *f*; **to go to the ~'s** ir al médico - **2.** [holder of PhD] doctor *m*, -ra *f*. <> *vt* - **1.** [results, text] amañar - **2.** [food, drink] adulterar.

doctorate ['dɒktərət], **doctor's degree** *n* doctorado *m*.

doctrine ['dɒktrɪn] *n* doctrina *f*.

document ['dɒkjʊmənt] *n* [gen & COMPUT] documento *m*.

documentary [ˌdɒkjʊ'mentərɪ] (*pl* -ies) <> *adj* documental. <> *n* documental *m*.

dodge [dɒdʒ] <> *n inf* [fraud] artimaña *f*, truco *m*. <> *vt* esquivar. <> *vi* echarse a un lado, apartarse bruscamente.

dodgy ['dɒdʒɪ] *adj UK inf* [business, plan] arriesgado(da); [brakes, weather, situation] chungo(ga).

doe [dəʊ] *n* -**1.** [female deer] gama *f* - **2.** [female rabbit] coneja *f*.

does [*weak form* dəz, *strong form* dʌz] *v* ⊳ **do**.

doesn't ['dʌznt] = **does not**.

dog [dɒg] (*pt* & *pp* -ged, *cont* -ging) <> *n* - **1.** [animal] perro *m* - **2.** *US* [hot dog] perrito *m* caliente. <> *vt* -**1.** [subj: person] seguir - **2.** [subj: problems, bad luck] perseguir.

dog collar *n* -**1.** [of dog] collar *m* de perro - **2.** [of priest] alzacuello *m*.

dog-eared [-ɪəd] *adj* manoseado(da), sobado(da).

dogged ['dɒgɪd] *adj* tenaz, obstinado(da).

dogsbody ['dɒgz,bɒdɪ] (*pl* -ies) *n UK inf* último mono *m*, burro *m* de carga.

doing ['du:ɪŋ] *n*: **this is all your ~** tú eres responsable por esto.

◆ **doings** *npl* actividades *fpl*.

do-it-yourself *n* bricolaje *m*.

doldrums ['dɒldrəmz] *npl fig*: **to be in the ~** [trade] estar estancado(da); [person] estar abatido(da).

dole [dəʊl] *n* (subsidio *m* de) paro *m*; **to be on the ~** estar parado(da).

◆ **dole out** *vt sep* distribuir, repartir.

doleful ['dəʊlfʊl] *adj* lastimero(ra).

doll [dɒl] *n* [toy] muñeca *f*.

dollar ['dɒlə'] *n* dólar *m*.

dolphin ['dɒlfɪn] *n* delfín *m*.

domain [də'meɪn] *n* -**1.** [sphere of interest] campo *m*, ámbito *m* - **2.** [land] dominios *mpl*.

domain name *n* COMPUT nombre *m* de dominio.

dome [dəʊm] *n* [roof] cúpula *f*; [ceiling] bóveda *f*.

domestic [də'mestɪk] <> *adj* -**1.** [internal: policy, flight] nacional - **2.** [chores, water supply, animal] doméstico(ca) - **3.** [home-loving] hogareño(ña), casero(ra). <> *n* [servant] doméstico *m*, -ca *f*, criado *m*, -da *f*.

domestic appliance *n* electrodoméstico *m*.

domestic science *n UK* economía *f* doméstica.

domestic violence *n* violencia *f* en el hogar.

dominant ['dɒmɪnənt] *adj* dominante.

dominate ['dɒmɪneɪt] *vt* dominar.

domineering [ˌdɒmɪ'nɪərɪŋ] *adj* dominante.

dominion [də'mɪnjən] *n* -**1.** (*U*) [power] dominio *m* - **2.** [land] dominios *mpl*.

domino ['dɒmɪnəʊ] (*pl* -es) *n* dominó *m*.

◆ **dominoes** *npl* dominó *m*.

don [dɒn] *n UK* UNIV profesor *m*, -ra *f* de universidad.

donate [də'neɪt] *vt* donar.

done [dʌn] <> *pp* ⊳ **do**. <> *adj* -**1.** [finished] listo(ta) - **2.** [cooked] hecho(cha); **well-~** muy hecho. <> *adv* [to conclude deal]: **~!** ¡(trato) hecho!

dongle ['dɒŋgl] *n* COMPUT llave *f* de hardware, mochila *f*.

donkey ['dɒŋkɪ] (*pl* **donkeys**) *n* burro *m*.

donor ['dəʊnə'] *n* donante *m* OR *f*.

donor card *n* carné *m* de donante.

don't [dəʊnt] = **do not**.

donut ['dəʊnʌt] *n US* [with hole] dónut® *m*.

doodle ['du:dl] *vi* garabatear.

doom [du:m] *n* perdición *f*, fatalidad *f*.

doomed [du:md] *adj* [plan, mission] condenado(da) al fracaso; **to be ~ to sthg/to do sthg** estar condenado a algo/a hacer algo.

door [dɔ:'] *n* -**1.** [gen] puerta *f* - **2.** [doorway] entrada *f*.

doorbell ['dɔ:bel] *n* timbre *m* (de la puerta).

doorknob ['dɔ:nɒb] *n* pomo *m*.

doorman ['dɔ:mən] (*pl* -men [-mən]) *n* portero *m*.

doormat ['dɔ:mæt] *n* [mat] felpudo *m*.

doorstep ['dɔ:step] *n* peldaño *m* de la puerta; **to turn up on sb's ~** aparecer en la puerta de alguien.

doorway ['dɔ:weɪ] *n* entrada *f*.

dope [dəʊp] <> *n inf* -**1.** [cannabis] maría *f* - **2.** [for athlete, horse] estimulante *m* - **3.** [fool] bobo *m*, -ba *f*, tonto *m*, -ta *f*. <> *vt* drogar, dopar.

dopey ['dəʊpɪ] (*compar* -ier, *superl* -iest) *adj inf* -**1.** [groggy] atontado(da), grogui - **2.** [stupid] bobo(ba).

dork [dɔ:k] *n US inf* petardo(da).

dormant ['dɔ:mənt] *adj* [volcano] inactivo(-va).

dormitory ['dɔ:mətrɪ] (*pl* -ies) *n* dormitorio *m* (*colectivo*).

Dormobile® ['dɔ:mə,bi:l] *n* combi *m*.

DOS [dɒs] (*abbr of* **disk operating system**) *n* DOS *m*.

dose [dəʊs] *n lit* & *fig* dosis *f inv*.

dosser ['dɒsə'] *n UK inf* gandul *m*, -la *f*, vago *m*, -ga *f*.

dosshouse ['dɒshaʊs, *pl* -haʊzɪz] *n UK inf* pensión *f* de mala muerte.

dot [dɒt] (*pt* & *pp* **-ted**, *cont* **-ting**) ◇ *n* punto *m*; **on the ~** en punto. ◇ *vt* salpicar.

dotcom ['dɒtkɒm] *adj* puntocom.

dote [dəʊt] ◆ **dote (up)on** *vt fus* adorar.

dot-matrix printer *n* COMPUT impresora *f* matricial.

double ['dʌbl] ◇ *adj* -1. [gen] doble - 2. [repeated] repetido(da); **it's ~ the price** cuesta el doble; **~ three eight two** treinta y tres, ochenta y dos. ◇ *adv* -1. [twice] el doble; **to cost ~** costar el doble - 2. [in two - fold] en dos; **to bend ~** doblarse, agacharse. ◇ *n* -1. [twice as much] el doble - 2. [drink] doble *m* - 3. [lookalike] doble *m* OR *f*. ◇ *vt* doblar, duplicarse. ◇ *vi* [increase twofold] doblarse, duplicarse.
◆ **doubles** *npl* TENNIS dobles *mpl*.

double-barrelled *UK*, **double-barreled** *US* [-'bærəld] *adj* -1. [shotgun] de dos cañones - 2. [name] *con dos apellidos unidos con guión*.

double bass [-beɪs] *n* contrabajo *m*.

double bed *n* cama *f* de matrimonio.

double-breasted [-'brestɪd] *adj* cruzado(-da).

double-check *vt* & *vi* verificar dos veces.

double chin *n* papada *f*.

double-click COMPUT ◇ *n* doble clic *m*. ◇ *vt* hacer doble clic en. ◇ *vi* hacer doble clic.

double cream *n* nata *f* enriquecida.

double-cross *vt* traicionar.

double-decker [-'dekə'] *n* autobús *m* de dos pisos.

double-dutch *n UK hum*: **it's ~ to me** me suena a chino.

double-glazing [-'gleɪzɪŋ] *n* doble acristalamiento *m*.

double room *n* habitación *f* doble.

double vision *n* visión *f* doble.

doubly ['dʌblɪ] *adv* doblemente.

doubt [daʊt] ◇ *n* duda *f*; **there is no ~ that** no hay OR cabe duda de que; **without (a) ~** sin duda (alguna); **to be in ~ about sthg** estar dudando acerca de algo; **to cast ~ on** poner en duda; **no ~** sin duda. ◇ *vt* -1. [not trust] dudar de - 2. [consider unlikely]

dudar; **I ~ it** lo dudo; **to ~ whether** OR **if** dudar que.

doubtful ['daʊtfʊl] *adj* -1. [gen] dudoso(-sa) - 2. [unsure] incierto(ta); **to be ~ about** OR **of** tener dudas acerca de.

doubtless ['daʊtlɪs] *adv* sin duda.

dough [dəʊ] *n (U)* -1. [for baking] masa *f*, pasta *f* - 2. *v inf* [money] pasta *f*, lana *f Méx*.

doughnut ['dəʊnʌt] *n* [without hole] buñuelo *m*; [with hole] dónut® *m*.

douse [daʊs] *vt* -1. [put out] apagar - 2. [drench] mojar, empapar.

dove¹ [dʌv] *n* paloma *f*.

dove² [dəʊv] *US pt* ▷ **dive**.

dovetail ['dʌvteɪl] *vt* & *vi* encajar.

dowdy ['daʊdɪ] (*compar* -ier, *superl* -iest) *adj* poco elegante.

down [daʊn] ◇ *adv* -1. [downwards] (hacia) abajo; **to fall ~** caer; **to bend ~** agacharse; **~ here/there** aquí/allí abajo - 2. [along]: **I'm going ~ the pub** voy a acercarme al pub - 3. [southwards] hacia el sur; **we're going ~ to Brighton** vamos a bajar a Brighton - 4. [lower in amount]: **prices are coming ~** van bajando los precios - 5. [including]: **~ to the last detail** hasta el último detalle - 6. [as deposit]: **to pay £5 ~** pagar 5 libras ahora (y el resto después). ◇ *prep* -1. [downwards]: **they ran ~ the hill** corrieron cuesta abajo; **he walked ~ the stairs** bajó la escalera; **rain poured ~ the window** la lluvia resbalaba por la ventana - 2. [along]: **she was walking ~ the street** iba andando por la calle. ◇ *adj* -1. [depressed] deprimido(da) - 2. [not in operation]: **the computer is ~ again** el ordenador se ha estropeado otra vez. ◇ *n* [feathers] plumón *m*; [hair] pelusa *f*, vello *m*; *US* [in American football] *cada uno de los cuatro intentos de avance que tiene el equipo atacante*. ◇ *vt* -1. [knock over] derribar - 2. [swallow] beberse de un trago.
◆ **downs** *npl UK* montes, *especialmente los del sur de Inglaterra*.
◆ **down with** *excl*: **~ with the King!** ¡abajo el rey!

down-and-out *n* vagabundo *m*, -da *f*.

down-at-heel *adj esp UK* desastrado(da).

downbeat ['daʊnbi:t] *adj inf* pesimista.

downcast ['daʊnkɑ:st] *adj fml* [sad] alicaído(da), triste.

downfall ['daʊnfɔ:l] *n* [of person] ruina *f*; [of regime] caída *f*.

downhearted [,daʊn'hɑ:tɪd] *adj* desanimado(da).

downhill [,daʊn'hɪl] ◇ *adj* cuesta abajo. ◇ *adv* -1. [downwards] cuesta abajo - 2. [worse]: **to be going ~** ir cuesta abajo. ◇ *n* [skiing] descenso *m*.

Downing Street ['daʊnɪŋ-] *n calle londinense*

donde se encuentran las residencias del Primer Ministro y el ministro de Finanzas; por extensión el gobierno británico.

down payment *n* entrada *f*.

downpour ['daʊnpɔ:ʳ] *n* chaparrón *m*, aguacero *m*.

downright ['daʊnraɪt] ◇ *adj* patente, manifiesto(ta). ◇ *adv* completamente.

downstairs [,daʊn'steəz] ◇ *adj* de abajo. ◇ *adv* abajo; **to come/go ~** bajar (la escalera).

downstream [,daʊn'stri:m] *adv* río OR aguas abajo.

down-to-earth *adj* realista, práctico(ca).

downtown [,daʊn'taʊn] *US* ◇ *adj* del centro (de la ciudad). ◇ *n* centro *m* (urbano). ◇ *adv* [live] en el centro; [go] al centro; **he gave me a lift ~** me llevó OR me dió un aventón *Cam, Méx, Perú* al centro.

downturn ['daʊntɜ:n] *n* bajón *m*.

down under *adv* en/a Australia o Nueva Zelanda.

downward ['daʊnwəd] ◇ *adj* - **1.** [towards the ground] hacia abajo - **2.** [decreasing] descendente. ◇ *adv US* = **downwards**.

downwards ['daʊnwədz] *adv* [gen] hacia abajo; **face ~** boca abajo.

dowry ['daʊərɪ] (*pl* **-ies**) *n* dote *f*.

doze [dəʊz] ◇ *n* sueñecito *m*; **to have a ~** echar una cabezada. ◇ *vi* dormitar.
◆ **doze off** *vi* quedarse adormilado(da).

dozen ['dʌzn] ◇ *num adj*: **a ~ eggs** una docena de huevos. ◇ *n* docena *f*; **50p a ~** 50 peniques la docena.
◆ **dozens** *npl inf*: **~s of** montones *mpl* de.

dozy ['dəʊzɪ] (*compar* **-ier**, *superl* **-iest**) *adj* - **1.** [sleepy] soñoliento(ta), amodorrado(da) - **2.** *UK inf* [stupid] tonto(ta).

Dr. - 1. (*abbr of* **Doctor**) Dr - **2.** (*abbr of* **Drive**) ≃ c/.

drab [dræb] (*compar* **-ber**, *superl* **-best**) *adj* [colour] apagado(da); [building, clothes] soso(sa); [lives] monótono(na).

draft [drɑ:ft] ◇ *n* - **1.** [early version] borrador *m* - **2.** [money order] letra *f* de cambio, giro *m* - **3.** *US* MIL: **the ~** la llamada a filas - **4.** *US* = **draught**. ◇ *vt* - **1.** [write] redactar, hacer un borrador de - **2.** *US* MIL llamar a filas - **3.** [transfer - staff etc] transferir.

draftsman *US* = **draughtsman**.

drafty *US* = **draughty**.

drag [dræg] (*pt* & *pp* **-ged**, *cont* **-ging**) ◇ *vt* - **1.** [gen & COMPUT] arrastrar - **2.** [lake, river] dragar, rastrear. ◇ *vi* - **1.** [dress, coat] arrastrarse - **2.** [time, play] ir muy despacio. ◇ *n inf* - **1.** [bore - thing] rollo *m*; [- person] pesado *m*, -da *f* - **2.** [on cigarette] calada *f*, chupada *f*, pitada *f Amér* - **3.** [cross-dressing]: **in ~** vestido de mujer.
◆ **drag on** *vi* ser interminable.

dragon ['drægən] *n* - **1.** [beast] dragón *m* - **2.** *inf* [woman] bruja *f*.

dragonfly ['drægnflaɪ] (*pl* **-ies**) *n* libélula *f*.

drain [dreɪn] ◇ *n* [for water] desagüe *m*; [for sewage] alcantarilla *f*; [grating] sumidero *m*. ◇ *vt* - **1.** [marsh, field] drenar; [vegetables] escurrir - **2.** [energy, resources] agotar - **3.** [drink, glass] apurar. ◇ *vi* - **1.** [dishes] escurrirse - **2.** [colour, blood, tension] desaparecer poco a poco.

drainage ['dreɪnɪdʒ] *n* - **1.** [pipes, ditches] alcantarillado *m* - **2.** [of land] drenaje *m*.

draining board *UK* ['dreɪnɪ-], **drainboard** *US* ['dreɪnbɔ:d] *n* escurridero *m*.

drainpipe ['dreɪnpaɪp] *n* tubo *m* de desagüe.

dram [dræm] *n* chupito *m*.

drama ['drɑ:mə] *n* - **1.** [gen] drama *m* - **2.** [subject] teatro *m* - **3.** [excitement] dramatismo *m*.

dramatic [drə'mætɪk] *adj* - **1.** [concerned with theatre] dramático(ca) - **2.** [gesture, escape, improvement] espectacular.

dramatist ['dræmətɪst] *n* dramaturgo *m*, -ga *f*.

dramatize, -ise ['dræmətaɪz] *vt* - **1.** [rewrite as play] adaptar - **2.** *pej* [make exciting] dramatizar.

drank [dræŋk] *pt* ⊳ **drink**.

drape [dreɪp] *vt*: **to ~ sthg over sthg** cubrir algo con algo; **~d with** OR **in** cubierto con.
◆ **drapes** *npl US* cortinas *fpl*.

draper ['dreɪpəʳ] *n* pañero *m*, -ra *f*.

drastic ['dræstɪk] *adj* [extreme, urgent, noticeable] drástico(ca).

draught *UK*, **draft** *US* [drɑ:ft] *n* - **1.** [air current] corriente *f* de aire - **2.**: **on ~** [beer] de barril.
◆ **draughts** *n UK* (U) damas *fpl*.

draught beer *n UK* cerveza *f* de barril.

draughtboard ['drɑ:ftbɔ:d] *n UK* tablero *m* de damas.

draughtsman *UK*, **draftsman** *US* ['drɑ:ftsmən] (*pl* **-men** [-mən]) *n* delineante *m* OR *f*.

draughty *UK*, **drafty** *US* (*compar* **-ier**, *superl* **-iest**) ['drɑ:ftɪ] *adj* que tiene corrientes de aire; **it's ~** hay corriente.

draw [drɔ:] (*pt* **drew**, *pp* **drawn**) ◇ *vt* - **1.** [sketch] dibujar; [line, circle] trazar; [a picture] hacer - **2.** [pull - cart etc] tirar de; **she drew the comb through her hair** se pasó el peine por el cabello - **3.** [curtains - open] descorrer; [- close] correr - **4.** [gun, sword] sacar - **5.** [pension, benefit] percibir - **6.** [cheque] librar - **7.** [conclusion] sacar, llegar a - **8.** [distinction, comparison] establecer - **9.** [attract - criticism, praise, person] atraer; **to ~ sb's attention to sthg** atraer la atención de alguien hacia algo. ◇ *vi* - **1.** [sketch] dibujar - **2.** [move] moverse; **to ~ away**

alejarse; **to ~ closer** acercarse **- 3.** SPORT : **to
~ (with)** empatar (con). ◇ *n* **-1.** SPORT empate *m* **- 2.** [lottery] sorteo *m*.

◆ draw out *vt sep* **-1.** [encourage to talk]
hacer hablar **- 2.** [prolong] prolongar
- 3. [money] sacar.

◆ draw up ◇ *vt sep* [draft] preparar, redactar. ◇ *vi* [stop] pararse.

drawback ['drɔːbæk] *n* inconveniente *m*,
desventaja *f*.

drawbridge ['drɔːbrɪdʒ] *n* puente *m* levadizo.

drawer [drɔːʳ] *n* [in desk, chest] cajón *m*.

drawing ['drɔːɪŋ] *n* dibujo *m*.

drawing board *n* tablero *m* de delineante.

drawing pin *n* UK chincheta *f*.

drawing room *n* salón *m*.

drawl [drɔːl] *n* manera lenta y poco clara de hablar, alargando las vocales.

drawn [drɔːn] *pp* ⊳ draw.

dread [dred] *vt* : **to ~ (doing sthg)** temer
(hacer algo).

dreadful ['dredfʊl] *adj* **-1.** [very unpleasant - pain, weather] **terrible, espantoso(sa)**
- 2. [poor - play, English] **horrible, fatal**
- 3. [for emphasis - waste, bore] espantoso(sa).

dreadfully ['dredfʊlɪ] *adv* terriblemente.

dream [driːm] (*pt & pp* **-ed** OR **dreamt**)
◇ *n lit & fig* sueño *m*; **bad ~** pesadilla *f*.
◇ *adj* ideal. ◇ *vt* : **to ~ (that)** soñar que.
◇ *vi lit & fig* : **to ~ of doing sthg** soñar con
hacer algo; **to ~ (of OR about)** soñar (con); **I
wouldn't ~ of it** ¡ni hablar!, ¡de ninguna
manera!

◆ dream up *vt sep* inventar, idear.

dreamt [dremt] *pp* ⊳ dream.

dreamy ['driːmɪ] (*compar* **-ier**, *superl* **-iest**)
adj **-1.** [distracted] **soñador(ra) - 2.** [peaceful,
dreamlike] de ensueño.

dreary ['drɪərɪ] (*compar* **-ier**, *superl* **-iest**)
adj **-1.** [weather, day] **triste - 2.** [job, life] monótono(na); [persona] gris.

dredge [dredʒ] *vt* dragar.

◆ dredge up *vt sep* **-1.** [with dredger] extraer (del agua) con draga **- 2.** *fig* [from past]
sacar a (la) luz.

dregs [dregz] *npl* **-1.** [of liquid] posos *mpl*
- 2. *fig* [of society] escoria *f*.

drench [drentʃ] *vt* empapar; **~ed to the
skin** calado hasta los huesos.

dress [dres] ◇ *n* **-1.** [woman's garment] vestido *m* **- 2.** (U) [clothing] traje *m*. ◇ *vt*
-1. [clothe] vestir; **to be ~ed in** ir vestido
de; **to be ~ed** estar vestido; **to get ~ed** vestirse **- 2.** [bandage] **vendar - 3.** CULIN aliñar,
aderezar. ◇ *vi* **-1.** [put on clothing] vestirse
- 2. [wear clothes] vestir; **to ~ well/badly**
vestir bien/mal.

dress circle *n* piso *m* principal.

dresser ['dresəʳ] *n* **-1.** [for dishes] aparador
m **- 2.** US [chest of drawers] cómoda *f*.

dressing ['dresɪŋ] *n* **-1.** [bandage] vendaje *m*
- 2. [for salad] aliño *m* **- 3.** US [for turkey etc]
relleno *m*.

dressing gown *n* bata *f*.

dressing room *n* THEATRE camerino *m*; SPORT
vestuario *m*.

dressing table *n* tocador *m*.

dressmaker ['dres,meɪkəʳ] *n* costurero *m*,
-ra *f*, modisto *m*, -ta *f*.

dressmaking ['dres,meɪkɪŋ] *n* costura *f*.

dress rehearsal *n* ensayo *m* general.

dressy ['dresɪ] (*compar* **-ier**, *superl* **-iest**) *adj*
elegante.

drew [druː] *pt* ⊳ draw.

dribble ['drɪbl] ◇ *n* **-1.** [saliva] baba *f*
- 2. [trickle] hilo *m*. ◇ *vt* SPORT [ball] regatear.
◇ *vi* **-1.** [drool] babear **- 2.** [spill] gotear,
caer gota a gota.

dried [draɪd] *adj* [gen] seco(ca); [milk, eggs]
en polvo.

dried fruit *n* (U) fruta *f* pasa.

drier ['draɪəʳ] = dryer.

drift [drɪft] ◇ *n* **-1.** [trend, movement] movimiento *m*, tendencia *f*; [of current] flujo *m*
- 2. [meaning] **sentido *m* - 3.** [mass - of snow]
ventisquero *m*; [- of sand, leaves] montículo
m. ◇ *vi* **-1.** [boat] ir a la deriva **- 2.** [snow,
sand, leaves] amontonarse.

driftwood ['drɪftwʊd] *n* madera *f* de deriva.

drill [drɪl] ◇ *n* **-1.** [tool - gen] taladro *m* ; [-
bit] **broca *f*; [- dentist's] fresa *f*; [- in mine, oilfield] perforadora *f* - 2.** [exercise - for fire, battle] simulacro *m*. ◇ *vt* **-1.** [tooth, wood, oil
well] **perforar - 2.** [instruct - people, pupils]
adiestrar, entrenar; [- soldiers] **instruir.**
◇ *vi* : **to ~ into/for** perforar en/en busca
de.

drink [drɪŋk] (*pt* **drank**, *pp* **drunk**) ◇ *n*
-1. [gen] bebida *f* ; **a ~ of water** un trago
de agua **- 2.** [alcoholic beverage] **copa *f*;
would you like a ~?** ¿quieres tomar algo
(de beber)?; **to have a ~** tomar algo, tomar
una copa. ◇ *vt* beber. ◇ *vi* beber.

drink-driving UK, **drunk-driving** US *n*
conducción *f* en estado de embriaguez.

drinker ['drɪŋkəʳ] *n* **-1.** [of alcohol] bebedor
m, -ra *f* **- 2.** [of tea, coffee]: **tea/coffee ~** persona que bebe té/café.

drinking water ['drɪŋkɪŋ-] *n* agua *f* potable.

drip [drɪp] (*pt & pp* **-ped**, *cont* **-ping**) ◇ *n*
-1. [drop] **gota *f*; [drops] goteo *m* - 2.** MED gota a gota *m inv*. ◇ *vi* [liquid, tap, nose] gotear.

drip-dry *adj* de lava y pon.

drive [draɪv] (*pt* **drove**, *pp* **driven**) ◇ *n*
-1. [outing] paseo *m* (en coche); **to go for a
~** ir a dar una vuelta en coche **- 2.** [journey]

viaje *m* (en coche); **it's a two-hour ~ (away)** está a dos horas en coche - **3.** [urge] instinto *m* - **4.** [campaign] campaña *f* - **5.** [energy] vigor *m*, energía *f* - **6.** [road to house] camino *m* (de entrada) - **7.** [street] calle *f* - **8.** [in golf, tennis] drive *m* - **9.** COMPUT unidad *f* de disco. ◇ *vt* - **1.** [vehicle] conducir, manejar *Amér* - **2.** [passenger] llevar (en coche) - **3.** [fuel, power] impulsar - **4.** [force to move - gen] arrastrar; [- cattle] arrear - **5.** [motivate] motivar - **6.** [force]: **to ~ sb to do sthg** conducir OR llevar a alguien a hacer algo; **to ~ sb to despair** hacer desesperar a alguien; **to ~ sb mad** OR **crazy** volver loco a alguien - **7.** [hammer] clavar. ◇ *vi* AUT conducir, manejar *Amér*; **I don't ~** no sé conducir; **I drove there** fui en coche.
drivel ['drɪvl] *n inf* (U) tonterías *fpl*.
driven ['drɪvn] *pp* ▷ **drive**.
driver ['draɪvəʳ] *n* [gen] conductor *m*, -ra *f*; RAIL maquinista *m* OR *f*; [of racing car] piloto *m* OR *f*.
driver's license *US* = **driving licence**.
drive shaft *n* (eje *m* de) transmisión *f*.
driveway ['draɪvweɪ] *n* camino *m* de entrada.
driving ['draɪvɪŋ] ◇ *adj* [rain] torrencial; [wind] huracanado(da). ◇ *n* (U) conducción *f*, el conducir.
driving instructor *n* instructor *m*, -ra *f* de conducción.
driving lesson *n* clase *f* de conducir OR conducción.
driving licence *UK*, **driver's license** *US* *n* carné *m* OR permiso *m* de conducir.
driving mirror *n* retrovisor *m*.
driving school *n* autoescuela *f*.
driving test *n* examen *m* de conducir.
drizzle ['drɪzl] ◇ *n* llovizna *f*, garúa *f An-des, RP*. ◇ *v impers* lloviznar.
droll [drəʊl] *adj* gracioso(sa).
drone [drəʊn] *n* - **1.** [hum] zumbido *m* - **2.** [bee] zángano *m*.
drool [dru:l] *vi* - **1.** [dribble] babear - **2.** *fig* [admire]: **he was ~ing over her** se le caía la baba por ella.
droop [dru:p] *vi* [shoulders] encorvarse; [eyelids] cerrarse; [head] inclinarse; [flower] marchitarse.
drop [drɒp] (*pt & pp* -**ped**, *cont* -**ping**) ◇ *n* - **1.** [of liquid, milk, whisky] gota *f* - **2.** [sweet] pastilla *f* - **3.** [decrease]: **~ (in)** [price] caída *f* (de); [temperature] descenso *m* (de); [demand, income] disminución *f* (en) - **4.** [distance down] caída *f*. ◇ *vt* - **1.** [let fall - gen] dejar caer; [- bomb] lanzar - **2.** [decrease] reducir - **3.** [voice] bajar - **4.** [abandon - subject, course] dejar; [- charges] retirar; [- person, lover] abandonar; [- player] excluir, no seleccionar - **5.** [utter - hint, remark] lanzar,

soltar - **6.** [write]: **to ~ sb a line** mandar unas líneas a alguien - **7.** [let out of car] dejar. ◇ *vi* - **1.** [fall down] caer; **it dropped onto the ground** se cayó al suelo; **to ~ to one's knees** arrodillarse; **we walked until we dropped** estuvimos andando hasta no poder más - **2.** [fall away - ground] ceder - **3.** [decrease - temperature, price, voice] bajar; [- attendance, demand, unemployment] disminuir; [- wind] amainar.
✦ **drops** *npl* MED gotas *fpl*.
✦ **drop in** *vi inf*: **to ~ in on** pasarse por casa de.
✦ **drop off** ◇ *vt sep* [person, letter] dejar. ◇ *vi* - **1.** [fall asleep] quedarse dormido(da), dormirse - **2.** [grow less] bajar.
✦ **drop out** *vi*: **to ~ out (of** OR **from)** [school, college] dejar de asistir (a); [competition] retirarse (de).
dropout ['drɒpaʊt] *n* [from society] marginado *m*, -da *f*; [from university] persona *f* que ha dejado los estudios.
droppings ['drɒpɪŋz] *npl* excremento *m (de animales)*.
drought [draʊt] *n* sequía *f*.
drove [drəʊv] *pt* ▷ **drive**.
drown [draʊn] ◇ *vt* [kill] ahogar. ◇ *vi* ahogarse.
drowsy ['draʊzɪ] (*compar* -**ier**, *superl* -**iest**) *adj* [person] somnoliento(ta).
drudgery ['drʌdʒərɪ] *n* trabajo pesado y monótono.
drug [drʌg] (*pt & pp* -**ged**, *cont* -**ging**) ◇ *n* - **1.** [medicine] medicamento *m* - **2.** [narcotic] droga *f*; **to be on** OR **take ~s** drogarse. ◇ *vt* - **1.** [person] drogar - **2.** [food, drink] echar droga a.
drug abuse *n* consumo *m* de drogas.
drug addict *n* drogadicto *m*, -ta *f*, toxicómano *m*, -na *f*.
druggist ['drʌgɪst] *n US* farmacéutico *m*, -ca *f*.
drugstore ['drʌgstɔ:ʳ] *n US* farmacia *f (que también vende productos de perfumería, cosméticos, periódicos etc)*.
drum [drʌm] (*pt & pp* -**med**, *cont* -**ming**) ◇ *n* - **1.** [instrument, of machine] tambor *m*; **~s** batería *f* - **2.** [container, cylinder] bidón *m*. ◇ *vt* [fingers] tamborilear con. ◇ *vi* [rain, hoofs] golpetear.
✦ **drum up** *vt sep* intentar conseguir.
drummer ['drʌməʳ] *n* [in orchestra] tambor *m* OR *f*; [in pop group] batería *m* OR *f*.
drumstick ['drʌmstɪk] *n* - **1.** [for drum] palillo *m* - **2.** [food] muslo *m*.
drunk [drʌŋk] ◇ *pp* ▷ **drink**. ◇ *adj* [on alcohol] borracho(cha); **to get ~** emborracharse; **to be ~** estar borracho. ◇ *n* borracho *m*, -cha *f*.
drunkard ['drʌŋkəd] *n* borracho *m*, -cha *f*.

drunk-driving *US* = **drink-driving**.

drunken ['drʌŋkn] *adj* - **1.** [person] borracho(cha) - **2.** [talk, steps, stupor] de borracho(cha).

dry [draɪ] (*compar* **-ier**, *superl* **-iest**, *pt* & *pp* **dried**) ⬦ *adj* - **1.** [gen] seco(ca) - **2.** [day] sin lluvia - **3.** [earth, soil] árido(da). ⬦ *vt* [gen] secar; [hands, hair] secarse; **to ~ o.s** secarse; **to ~ one's eyes** secarse las lágrimas. ⬦ *vi* secarse.
 ◆ **dry up** ⬦ *vt sep* secar. ⬦ *vi* - **1.** [river, well] secarse - **2.** [stop - supply] agotarse - **3.** [stop speaking] quedarse en blanco - **4.** [dry dishes] secar.

dry cleaner *n* ~'**s (shop)** tintorería *f*.

dryer ['draɪə'] *n* [for clothes] secadora *f*.

dry land *n* tierra *f* firme.

dry rot *n* putrefacción *f* de la madera.

dry ski slope *n* pista *f* de esquí artificial.

DSS (*abbr of* **Department of Social Security**) *n* ministerio británico de la seguridad social.

DTI (*abbr of* **Department of Trade and Industry**) *n* ministerio británico de comercio e industria.

DTP (*abbr of* **desktop publishing**) *n* autoed. *f*.

dual ['djuːəl] *adj* doble.

dual carriageway *n* *UK* carretera de dos sentidos y doble vía separados, ≃ autovía *f*.

dubbed [dʌbd] *adj* - **1.** CINEMA doblado(da) - **2.** [nicknamed] apodado(da).

dubious ['djuːbjəs] *adj* - **1.** [questionable - person, deal, reasons] sospechoso(sa); [- honour, distinction] paradójico(ca) - **2.** [uncertain, undecided] dudoso(sa); **to feel** OR **be ~ (about)** tener dudas (sobre).

Dublin ['dʌblɪn] *n* Dublín.

duchess ['dʌtʃɪs] *n* duquesa *f*.

duck [dʌk] ⬦ *n* - **1.** [bird] pato *m*, -ta *f* - **2.** [food] pato *m*. ⬦ *vt* - **1.** [lower] agachar, bajar - **2.** [try to avoid - duty] esquivar. ⬦ *vi* [lower head] agacharse.

duckling ['dʌklɪŋ] *n* patito *m*.

duct [dʌkt] *n* conducto *m*.

dud [dʌd] ⬦ *adj* [gen] falso(sa); [mine] que no estalla ; [cheque] sin fondos. ⬦ *n* persona o cosa inútil.

dude [djuːd] *n* *US* inf [man] tipo *m*, tío *m* *Esp*; [term of address] colega *m* *Esp*, tío *m* *Esp*, mano *m* *Andes, CAm, Carib, Méx*, flaco *m* *RP*.

due [djuː] ⬦ *adj* - **1.** [expected] esperado(da); **it's ~ out in May** saldrá en mayo; **she's ~ back soon** tendría que volver dentro de poco; **the train's ~ in half an hour** el tren debe llegar dentro de media hora - **2.** [appropriate] debido(da); **with all ~ respect** sin ganas de ofender; **in ~ course** [at appropriate time] a su debido tiempo; [eventually] al final - **3.** [owed, owing] pagadero(ra); **I'm ~ a bit of luck** ya sería hora que tuviera un

poco de suerte; **to be ~ to** deberse a. ⬦ *n* [deserts]: **to give sb their ~** hacer justicia a alguien. ⬦ *adv*: **~ north/south** derecho hacia el norte/sur.
 ◆ **dues** *npl* cuota *f*.
 ◆ **due to** *prep* debido a.

duel ['djuːəl] (*UK pt* & *pp* **-led**, *cont* **-ling**, *US pt* & *pp* **-ed**, *cont* **-ing**) ⬦ *n* duelo *m*. ⬦ *vi* batirse en duelo.

duet [djuːˈet] *n* dúo *m*.

duffel bag ['dʌfl-] *n* morral *m*.

duffel coat ['dʌfl-] *n* trenca *f*, montgomery *m* *CSur*.

duffle bag ['dʌfl-] = **duffel bag**.

duffle coat ['dʌfl-] = **duffel coat**.

dug [dʌg] *pt* & *pp* ⊳ **dig**.

duke [djuːk] *n* duque *m*.

dull [dʌl] ⬦ *adj* - **1.** [boring] aburrido(da) - **2.** [listless] torpe - **3.** [dim] apagado(da) - **4.** [cloudy] gris, triste - **5.** [thud, boom, pain] sordo(da). ⬦ *vt* [senses] embotar, entorpecer; [pain] aliviar; [pleasure, memory] enturbiar.

duly ['djuːlɪ] *adv* - **1.** [properly] debidamente - **2.** [as expected] como era de esperar.

dumb [dʌm] *adj* - **1.** [unable to speak] mudo(da); **to be struck ~** quedarse de una pieza - **2.** *esp* *US* inf [stupid] estúpido(da).

dumbfound [dʌmˈfaʊnd] *vt* dejar mudo(da) de asombro; **to be ~ed** quedar mudo de asombro.

dummy ['dʌmɪ] (*pl* **-ies**) ⬦ *adj* falso(sa). ⬦ *n* - **1.** [of ventriloquist] muñeco *m*; [in shop window] maniquí *m* - **2.** [copy] imitación *f* - **3.** *UK* [for baby] chupete *m*, chupón *m* *Méx* - **4.** SPORT amago *m* - **5.** [idiot] inf imbécil *m* OR *f*.

dump [dʌmp] ⬦ *n* - **1.** [for rubbish] basurero *m*, vertedero *m* - **2.** [for ammunition] depósito *m* - **3.** COMPUT volcado *m* de memoria - **4.** inf [ugly place - house] casucha *f*. ⬦ *vt* - **1.** [put down - sand, load] descargar; [- bags, washing] dejar - **2.** [dispose of] deshacerse de.

dumper (truck) ['dʌmpə'-] *UK*, **dump truck** *US* *n* volquete *m*.

dumping ['dʌmpɪŋ] *n* [of rubbish] vertido *m*; '**no ~**' 'prohibido verter basura'.

dumpling ['dʌmplɪŋ] *n* bola de masa que se guisa al vapor con carne y verduras.

dump truck *US* = **dumper (truck)**.

dumpy ['dʌmpɪ] (*compar* **-ier**, *superl* **-iest**) *adj* inf bajito y regordete (bajita y regordete).

dunce [dʌns] *n* zoquete *m* OR *f*, burro *m*, -rra *f*.

dune [djuːn] *n* duna *f*.

dung [dʌŋ] *n* [of animal] excremento *m*; [used as manure] estiércol *m*.

dungarees [ˌdʌŋgəˈriːz] *npl* *UK* [for work]

mono *m*, overol *m Amér*; [fashion garment] pantalones *mpl* de peto, mameluco *m CSur*.

dungeon ['dʌndʒən] *n* calabozo *m*.

duo ['dju:əʊ] *n* dúo *m*.

dupe [dju:p] ◇ *n* primo *m*, -ma *f*, inocente *m* OR *f*. ◇ *vt* : **to ~ sb (into doing sthg)** embaucar a alguien (a que haga algo).

duplex ['dju:pleks] *n US* - **1.** [apartment] dúplex *m* - **2.** [house] casa *f* adosada.

duplicate [*adj* & *n* 'dju:plɪkət, *vb* 'dju:plɪkeɪt] ◇ *adj* duplicado(da). ◇ *n* copia *f*, duplicado *m*; **in ~** por duplicado. ◇ *vt* [copy] duplicar, hacer una copia de.

durable ['djʊərəbl] *adj* duradero(ra).

duration [djʊ'reɪʃn] *n* duración *f*; **for the ~ of** durante.

duress [djʊ'res] *n*: **under ~** bajo coacción.

Durex® ['djʊəreks] *n* [condom] preservativo *m*, condón *m*.

during ['djʊərɪŋ] *prep* durante.

dusk [dʌsk] *n* crepúsculo *m*, anochecer *m*.

dust [dʌst] ◇ *n* polvo *m*. ◇ *vt* - **1.** [clean] quitar el polvo a, limpiar - **2.** [cover with powder]: **to ~ sthg (with)** espolvorear algo (con).

dustbin ['dʌstbɪn] *n UK* cubo *m* de la basura.

dustcart ['dʌstkɑ:t] *n UK* camión *m* de la basura.

dustcloth ['dʌstklɒθ] *n US* trapo *m* del polvo.

duster ['dʌstə'] *n* [cloth] bayeta *f*, trapo *m* (de quitar el polvo).

dust jacket *n* sobrecubierta *f*.

dustman ['dʌstmən] (*pl* -**men** [-mən]) *n UK* basurero *m*.

dustpan ['dʌstpæn] *n* recogedor *m*.

dusty ['dʌstɪ] (*compar* -**ier**, *superl* -**iest**) *adj* [covered in dust] polvoriento(ta).

Dutch [dʌtʃ] ◇ *adj* holandés(esa). ◇ *n* [language] holandés *m*. ◇ *npl*: **the ~** los holandeses.

Dutch elm disease *n* hongo que ataca a los olmos.

dutiful ['dju:tɪfʊl] *adj* obediente, sumiso(-sa).

duty ['dju:tɪ] (*pl* -**ies**) *n* - **1.** (U) [moral, legal responsibility] deber *m*; **to do one's ~** cumplir uno con su deber - **2.** [work] servicio *m*; **to be on/off ~** estar/no estar de servicio - **3.** [tax] impuesto *m*.
◆ **duties** *npl* tareas *fpl*.

duty-free ◇ *adj* libre de impuestos. ◇ *n* (U) *inf* artículos *mpl* libres de impuestos.

duvet ['du:veɪ] *n UK* edredón *m*.

duvet cover *n UK* funda *f* del edredón.

DVD (*abbr of* **Digital Versatile Disk**) *n* DVD *m*.

DVD player *n* reproductor *m* de DVD.

DVD ROM (*abbr of* **Digital Versatile Disk read only memory**) *n* DVD ROM *m*.

dwarf [dwɔːf] (*pl* -**s** OR **dwarves** [dwɔːvz]) ◇ *n* enano *m*, -na *f*. ◇ *vt* achicar, empequeñecer.

dwell [dwel] (*pt* & *pp* -**ed** OR **dwelt**) *vi literary* morar, habitar.
◆ **dwell on** *vt fus* darle vueltas a.

dwelling ['dwelɪŋ] *n literary* morada *f*.

dwelt [dwelt] *pt* & *pp* ▷ **dwell**.

dwindle ['dwɪndl] *vi* ir disminuyendo.

dye [daɪ] ◇ *n* tinte *m*, colorante *m*. ◇ *vt* teñir; **to ~ one's hair** teñirse el pelo.

dying ['daɪɪŋ] ◇ *cont* ▷ **die**. ◇ *adj* - **1.** [person, animal] moribundo(da) - **2.** [activity, practice] en vías de desaparición.

dyke [daɪk] = **dike**.

dynamic [daɪ'næmɪk] *adj* dinámico(ca).

dynamite ['daɪnəmaɪt] *n lit* & *fig* dinamita *f*.

dynamo ['daɪnəməʊ] (*pl* -**s**) *n* dinamo *f*.

dynasty [*UK* 'dɪnəstɪ, *US* 'daɪnəstɪ] (*pl* -**ies**) *n* dinastía *f*.

dysfunctional [dɪs'fʌŋkʃənəl] *adj* disfuncional.

dyslexia [dɪs'leksɪə] *n* dislexia *f*.

dyslexic [dɪs'leksɪk] *adj* disléxico(ca).

e (*pl* **e's** OR **es**), **E** (*pl* **E's** OR **Es**) [i:] *n* [letter] e *f*, E *f*.
◆ **E** *n* - **1.** MUS mi *m* - **2.** SCH [mark] ≃ suspenso *m* - **3.** (*abbr of* **east**) E *m* - **4.** (*abbr of* **ecstasy**) *inf* [drug] éxtasis *m inv*.

each [i:tʃ] ◇ *adj* cada. ◇ *pron* cada uno *m*, una *f*; **one ~** uno cada uno; **~ of us/the boys** cada uno de nosotros/los niños; **two of ~** dos de cada (uno); **~ other** el uno al otro; **they kissed ~ other** se besaron; **we know ~ other** nos conocemos.

eager ['i:gə'] *adj* [pupil] entusiasta; [smile, expression] de entusiasmo; **to be ~ for sthg/to do sthg** ansiar algo/hacer algo, desear vivamente algo/hacer algo.

eagle ['i:gl] *n* águila *f*.

ear [ɪə'] *n* - **1.** [outer part] oreja *f*; [inner part] oído *m* - **2.** [of corn] espiga *f*.

earache ['ɪəreɪk] *n* dolor *m* de oídos.

eardrum ['ɪədrʌm] *n* tímpano *m*.

earl [ɜːl] *n* conde *m*.

earlier ['ɜːlɪə'] ◇ *adj* anterior. ◇ *adv* antes; **~ on** antes.

earliest ['ɜ:lɪəst] ◇ *adj* primero(ra). ◇ *n*: **at the ~** como muy pronto.

earlobe ['ɪələʊb] *n* lóbulo *m* (de la oreja).

early ['ɜ:lɪ] (*compar* **-ier**, *superl* **-iest**) ◇ *adj* **- 1.** [before expected time, in day] temprano(- na); **she was ~** llegó temprano; **I'll take an ~ lunch** almorzaré pronto OR temprano; **to get up ~** madrugar **- 2.** [at beginning]: **~ morning** la madrugada; **in the ~ 1950s** a principios de los años 50. ◇ *adv* **- 1.** [before expected time] temprano, pronto; **we got up ~** nos levantamos temprano; **it arrived ten minutes ~** llegó con diez minutos de adelanto **- 2.** [at beginning]: **as ~ as 1920** ya en 1920; **~ this morning** esta mañana temprano; **~ in the year** a principios de año; **~ on** temprano.

early retirement *n* prejubilación *f*, jubilación *f* anticipada.

earmark ['ɪəmɑ:k] *vt* : **to be ~ed for** estar destinado(da) a.

earn [ɜ:n] *vt* **- 1.** [be paid] ganar **- 2.** [generate - subj: business, product] generar **- 3.** *fig* [gain - respect, praise] ganarse.

earnest ['ɜ:nɪst] *adj* [gen] serio(ria); [wish] sincero(ra).
➤ **in earnest** *adv* [seriously] en serio.

earnings ['ɜ:nɪŋz] *npl* [of person] ingresos *mpl*; [of company] ganancias *fpl*.

earphones ['ɪəfəʊnz] *npl* auriculares *mpl*.

earplugs ['ɪəplʌgz] *npl* tapones *mpl* para los oídos.

earring ['ɪərɪŋ] *n* pendiente *m*, arete *m* *Amér*.

earshot ['ɪəʃɒt] *n*: **within/out of ~** al alcance/fuera del alcance del oído.

earth [ɜ:θ] ◇ *n* **- 1.** [gen] tierra *f*; **how/ what/where/why on ~ ...?** ¿cómo/qué/ dónde/por qué demonios ...? **- 2.** [in electric plug, appliance] toma *f* de tierra. ◇ *vt* *UK*: **to be ~ed** estar conectado(da) a tierra.

earthenware ['ɜ:θnweə¹] *n* loza *f*.

earthquake ['ɜ:θkweɪk] *n* terremoto *m*.

earthworm ['ɜ:θwɜ:m] *n* lombriz *f* (de tierra).

earthy ['ɜ:θɪ] (*compar* **-ier**, *superl* **-iest**) *adj* **- 1.** [rather crude] natural, desinhibido(da) **- 2.** [of, like earth] terroso(sa).

earwig ['ɪəwɪg] *n* tijereta *f*.

ease [i:z] ◇ *n* (*U*) **- 1.** [lack of difficulty] facilidad *f*; **with ~** con facilidad **- 2.** [comfort] comodidad *f*; **at ~** cómodo(da); **ill at ~** incómodo(da). ◇ *vt* **- 1.** [pain, grief] calmar, aliviar; [problems, tension] atenuar **- 2.** [move carefully]: **to ~ sthg open** abrir algo con cuidado; **to ~ o.s. out of sthg** levantarse despacio de algo. ◇ *vi* [problem] atenuarse; [pain] calmarse; [rain, wind] amainar; [grip] relajarse, aflojarse.
➤ **ease off** *vi* [problem] atenuarse; [pain] calmarse; [rain, wind] amainar.

➤ **ease up** *vi* **- 1.** *inf* [treat less severely]: **to ~ up on sb** no ser tan duro(ra) con alguien **- 2.** [rain, wind] amainar **- 3.** [relax - person] tomarse las cosas con más calma.

easel ['i:zl] *n* caballete *m*.

easily ['i:zɪlɪ] *adv* **- 1.** [without difficulty] fácilmente **- 2.** [without doubt] sin lugar a dudas **- 3.** [in a relaxed manner] tranquilamente, relajadamente.

east [i:st] ◇ *n* **- 1.** [direction] este *m* **- 2.** [region]: **the ~** el este. ◇ *adj* oriental; [wind] del este. ◇ *adv*: **~ (of)** al este (de).
➤ **East** *n*: **the East** POL el Este; [Asia] el Oriente.

East End *n*: **the ~** el este de Londres.

Easter ['i:stə¹] *n* **- 1.** [period] Semana *f* Santa **- 2.** [festival] Pascua *f*.

Easter day *n* Domingo *m* de Resurrección.

Easter egg *n* huevo *m* de Pascua.

easterly ['i:stəlɪ] *adj* del este.

eastern ['i:stən] *adj* del este, oriental.
➤ **Eastern** *adj* [gen & POL] del Este; [from Asia] oriental.

East German ◇ *adj* de Alemania Oriental. ◇ *n* [person] alemán *m*, -ana *f* oriental.

East Germany *n*: **(the former) ~** (la antigua) Alemania Oriental.

eastward ['i:stwəd] ◇ *adj* hacia el este. ◇ *adv* = **eastwards**.

eastwards ['i:stwədz] *adv* hacia el este.

easy ['i:zɪ] (*compar* **-ier**, *superl* **-iest**) *adj* **- 1.** [not difficult] fácil **- 2.** [life, time] cómodo(da) **- 3.** [manner] relajado(da).

easy chair *n* [armchair] sillón *m*, butaca *f*.

easygoing [ˌi:zɪ'gəʊɪŋ] *adj* [person] tolerante, tranquilo(la); [manner] relajado(da).

eat [i:t] (*pt* **ate**, *pp* **eaten**) *vt* & *vi* comer.
➤ **eat away, eat into** *vt sep* **- 1.** [corrode] corroer **- 2.** [deplete] mermar.

eaten ['i:tn] *pp* ▷ **eat**.

eau de cologne [ˌəʊdəkə'ləʊn] *n* (agua *f* de) colonia *f*.

eaves ['i:vz] *npl* alero *m*.

eavesdrop ['i:vzdrɒp] (*pt* & *pp* **-ped**, *cont* **-ping**) *vi*: **to ~ (on)** escuchar secretamente (a).

ebb [eb] ◇ *n* reflujo *m*. ◇ *vi* [tide, sea] bajar.

ebony ['ebənɪ] *n* ébano *m*.

e-business *n* **- 1.** [company] empresa *f* electrónica **- 2.** [electronic commerce] comercio *m* electrónico.

EC (*abbr of* **European Community**) *n* CE *f*.

ECB (*abbr of* **European Central Bank**) *n* BCE *m*.

eccentric [ɪk'sentrɪk] ◇ *adj* excéntrico(- ca). ◇ *n* excéntrico *m*, -ca *f*.

echo ['ekəʊ] (*pl* **-es**, *pt* & *pp* **-ed**, *cont* **-ing**) ◇ *n* *lit* & *fig* eco *m*. ◇ *vt* [words] repetir; [opinion] hacerse eco de. ◇ *vi* resonar.

eclipse [ɪ'klɪps] ◇ n lit & fig eclipse m. ◇ vt fig eclipsar.

eco-friendly ['i:kəʊ'frendlɪ] adj ecológico(ca).

ecological [,i:kə'lɒdʒɪkl] adj -1. [pattern, balance, impact] ecológico(ca) -2. [group, movement, person] ecologista.

ecology [ɪ'kɒlədʒɪ] n ecología f.

e-commerce n comercio m electrónico.

economic [,i:kə'nɒmɪk] adj -1. [of money, industry] económico(ca) -2. [profitable] rentable.

Economic and Monetary Union n Unión f Económica y Monetaria.

economical [,i:kə'nɒmɪkl] adj económico(ca); **to be ~ with the truth** no decir toda la verdad.

economics [,i:kə'nɒmɪks] ◇ n (U) economía f. ◇ npl [of plan, business] aspecto m económico.

economize, -ise [ɪ'kɒnəmaɪz] vi: **to ~ (on)** economizar (en).

economy [ɪ'kɒnəmɪ] (pl -ies) n economía f.

economy class n clase f turista.

ecotax ['i:kəʊtæks] n ecotasa f.

ecotourism [,i:kəʊ'tʊərɪzm] n ecoturismo m.

ecstasy ['ekstəsɪ] (pl -ies) n -1. [great happiness] éxtasis m inv -2. [drug] éxtasis m inv.

ecstatic [ek'stætɪk] adj extático(ca).

ECU, Ecu ['ekju:] (abbr of European Currency Unit) n ecu m.

Ecuador ['ekwədɔ:'] n (el) Ecuador.

Ecuadoran [,ekwə'dɔ:rən], **Ecuadorian** [,ekwə'dɔ:rɪən] ◇ adj ecuatoriano(na). ◇ n ecuatoriano m, -na f.

eczema ['eksɪmə] n eczema m.

Eden ['i:dn] n: **(the Garden of) ~** (el jardín del) Edén m.

edge [edʒ] ◇ n -1. [of cliff, table, garden] borde m; **to be on the ~ of** estar al borde de -2. [of coin] canto m; [of knife] filo m -3. [advantage]: **to have an ~ over** OR **the ~ on** llevar ventaja a. ◇ vi: **to ~ away/closer** ir alejándose/acercándose poco a poco.

➤ **on edge** adj con los nervios de punta.

edgeways ['edʒweɪz], **edgewise** ['edʒwaɪz] adv de lado.

edgy ['edʒɪ] (compar -ier, superl -iest) adj nervioso(sa).

edible ['edɪbl] adj comestible.

edict ['i:dɪkt] n edicto m.

Edinburgh ['edɪnbrə] n Edimburgo.

edit ['edɪt] vt -1. [correct - text] corregir, revisar -2. COMPUT editar -3. [select material for - book] editar -4. CINEMA, RADIO & TV montar -5. [run - newspaper, magazine] dirigir.

edition [ɪ'dɪʃn] n edición f.

editor ['edɪtə'] n -1. [of newspaper, magazine] director m, -ra f -2. [of section of newspaper, programme, text] redactor m, -ra f

-3. [compiler - of book] editor m, -ra f -4. CINEMA, RADIO & TV montador m, -ra f -5. COMPUT editor m.

editorial [,edɪ'tɔ:rɪəl] ◇ adj editorial; **~ staff** redacción f. ◇ n editorial m.

educate ['edʒʊkeɪt] vt -1. [at school, college] educar -2. [inform] informar.

education [,edʒʊ'keɪʃn] n (U) -1. [activity, sector] enseñanza f -2. [process or result of teaching] educación f.

educational [,edʒʊ'keɪʃənl] adj educativo(va); [establishment] docente.

EEC (abbr of European Economic Community) n CEE f.

eel [i:l] n anguila f.

eerie ['ɪərɪ] adj espeluznante.

efface [ɪ'feɪs] vt borrar.

effect [ɪ'fekt] ◇ n efecto m; **to have an ~ on** tener OR surtir efecto en; **to take ~** [law, rule] entrar en vigor; [drug] hacer efecto; **to put sthg into ~** poner algo en práctica; **words to that ~** palabras por el estilo. ◇ vt efectuar, llevar a cabo.

➤ **effects** npl: **(special) ~s** efectos mpl especiales.

effective [ɪ'fektɪv] adj -1. [successful] eficaz -2. [actual, real] efectivo(va) -3. [law, ceasefire] operativo(va).

effectively [ɪ'fektɪvlɪ] adv -1. [well, successfully] eficazmente -2. [in fact] de hecho.

effectiveness [ɪ'fektɪvnɪs] n eficacia f.

effeminate [ɪ'femɪnət] adj pej afeminado(da).

effervescent [,efə'vesənt] adj efervescente.

efficiency [ɪ'fɪʃənsɪ] n [gen] eficiencia f; [of machine] rendimiento m.

efficient [ɪ'fɪʃənt] adj [gen] eficiente; [machine] de buen rendimiento.

effluent ['efluənt] n aguas fpl residuales.

effort ['efət] n -1. [gen] esfuerzo m; **to be worth the ~** merecer la pena; **to make the ~ to do sthg** hacer el esfuerzo de hacer algo; **to make an/no ~ to do sthg** hacer un esfuerzo/no hacer ningún esfuerzo por hacer algo -2. inf [result of trying] tentativa f.

effortless ['efətlɪs] adj sin gran esfuerzo.

effusive [ɪ'fju:sɪv] adj efusivo(va).

e.g. (abbr of exempli gratia) adv p. ej.

egg [eg] n [gen] huevo m, blanquillo m Cam, Méx.

➤ **egg on** vt sep incitar.

eggcup ['egkʌp] n huevera f.

eggplant ['egplɑ:nt] n US berenjena f.

eggshell ['egʃel] n cáscara f de huevo.

egg white n clara f (de huevo).

egg yolk [-jəʊk] n yema f (de huevo).

ego ['i:gəʊ] (pl -s) n -1. [opinion of self] amor m propio -2. [psych] ego m.

egoism ['i:gəʊɪzm] n egoísmo m.

egoistic [,i:gəʊ'ɪstɪk] adj egoísta.

egotistic(al) [,i:gə'tɪstɪk(l)] adj egotista.

Egypt ['iːdʒɪpt] *n* Egipto.

Egyptian [ɪ'dʒɪpʃn] ⬦ *adj* egipcio(cia). ⬦ *n* [person] egipcio *m*, -cia *f*.

eiderdown ['aɪdədaʊn] *n esp* UK edredón *m*.

eight [eɪt] *num* ocho; *see also* **six**.

eighteen [,eɪ'tiːn] *num* dieciocho; *see also* **six**.

eighth [eɪtθ] *num* octavo(va); *see also* **sixth**.

eighty ['eɪtɪ] (*pl* -**ies**) *num* ochenta; *see also* **sixty**.

Eire ['eərə] *n* Eire.

either ['aɪðəʳ, 'iːðəʳ] ⬦ *adj* - **1.** [one or the other] cualquiera de los dos; **she couldn't find** ~ **jumper** no podía encontrar ninguno de los dos jerseys; **you can do it** ~ **way** lo puedes hacer de cualquiera de las formas; **I don't care** ~ **way** me da igual - **2.** [each] cada; **on** ~ **side** a ambos lados. ⬦ *pron*: ~ **(of them)** cualquiera (de ellos (ellas)); **I don't like** ~ **(of them)** no me gusta ninguno de ellos (ninguna de ellas). ⬦ *adv (in negatives)* tampoco; **she can't and I can't** ~ ella no puede y yo tampoco. ⬦ *conj*: ~ ... **or** o ... o; ~ **you or me** o tú o yo; **I don't like** ~ **him or his wife** no me gusta ni él ni su mujer (tampoco).

eject [ɪ'dʒekt] *vt* - **1.** [object] expulsar - **2.** [person]: **to** ~ **sb (from)** expulsar a alguien (de).

eke [iːk] ⬥ **eke out** *vt sep* [money, supply] estirar.

elaborate [*adj* ɪ'læbrət, *vb* ɪ'læbəreɪt] ⬦ *adj* [ceremony] complicado(da); [carving] trabajado(da); [explanation, plan] detallado(da). ⬦ *vi*: **to** ~ **on sthg** ampliar algo, explicar algo con más detalle.

elapse [ɪ'læps] *vi* transcurrir.

elastic [ɪ'læstɪk] ⬦ *adj* - **1.** [gen] elástico(ca) - **2.** *fig* [flexible] flexible. ⬦ *n* elástico *m*.

elasticated [ɪ'læstɪkeɪtɪd] *adj* elástico(ca).

elastic band *n* UK goma *f*, goma *f* (elástica).

elated [ɪ'leɪtɪd] *adj* eufórico(ca).

elbow ['elbəʊ] *n* codo *m*.

elder ['eldəʳ] ⬦ *adj* mayor. ⬦ *n* - **1.** [older person] mayor *m* OR *f*- **2.** [of tribe, church] anciano *m* - **3.**: ~ **(tree)** saúco *m*.

elderly ['eldəlɪ] ⬦ *adj* mayor, anciano(na). ⬦ *npl*: **the** ~ los ancianos.

eldest ['eldɪst] *adj* mayor.

elect [ɪ'lekt] ⬦ *adj* electo(ta); **the president** ~ el presidente electo. ⬦ *vt* - **1.** [by voting] elegir; **to** ~ **sb (as) sthg** elegir a alguien (como) algo - **2.** *fml* [choose]: **to** ~ **to do sthg** optar por OR decidir hacer algo.

election [ɪ'lekʃn] *n* elección *f*; **to have** OR **hold an** ~ celebrar (unas) elecciones.

electioneering [ɪ,lekʃə'nɪərɪŋ] *n usu pej* electoralismo *m*.

elector [ɪ'lektəʳ] *n* elector *m*, -ra *f*.

electorate [ɪ'lektərət] *n*: **the** ~ el electorado.

electric [ɪ'lektrɪk] *adj* [gen] eléctrico(ca).
⬥ **electrics** *npl* UK *inf* sistema *m* eléctrico.

electrical [ɪ'lektrɪkl] *adj* eléctrico(ca).

electrical shock US = **electric shock**.

electric blanket *n* manta *f* eléctrica, frazada *f* eléctrica *Amér*, cobija *f* eléctrica *Amér*.

electric cooker *n* cocina *f* eléctrica.

electric fire *n* estufa *f* eléctrica.

electrician [,ɪlek'trɪʃn] *n* electricista *m* OR *f*.

electricity [,ɪlek'trɪsətɪ] *n* electricidad *f*.

electric shock UK, **electrical shock** US *n* descarga *f* eléctrica.

electrify [ɪ'lektrɪfaɪ] (*pt* & *pp* -**ied**) *vt* - **1.** [rail line] electrificar - **2.** *fig* [excite] electrizar.

electrocute [ɪ'lektrəkjuːt] *vt* electrocutar; **to** ~ **o.s., to be** ~**d** electrocutarse.

electrolysis [,ɪlek'trɒləsɪs] *n* electrólisis *f inv*.

electron [ɪ'lektrɒn] *n* electrón *m*.

electronic [,ɪlek'trɒnɪk] *adj* electrónico(ca).
⬥ **electronics** ⬦ *n (U)* [technology] electrónica *f*. ⬦ *npl* [equipment] sistema *m* electrónico.

electronic banking *n* banca *f* electrónica.

electronic data processing *n* proceso *m* electrónico de datos.

electronic mail *n* correo *m* electrónico.

electronic organizer *n* agenda *f* electrónica.

elegant ['elɪgənt] *adj* elegante, elegantoso(sa) *Amér*.

element ['elɪmənt] *n* - **1.** [gen] elemento *m* - **2.** [amount, proportion] toque *m*, matiz *m* - **3.** [in heater, kettle] resistencia *f*.
⬥ **elements** *npl* - **1.** [basics] elementos *mpl* - **2.** [weather]: **the** ~**s** los elementos.

elementary [,elɪ'mentərɪ] *adj* elemental; ~ **education** enseñanza *f* primaria.

elementary school *n* US escuela *f* primaria.

elephant ['elɪfənt] (*pl inv* OR -**s**) *n* elefante *m*.

elevate ['elɪveɪt] *vt*: **to** ~ **sthg/sb (to** OR **into)** elevar algo/a alguien (a la categoría de).

elevator ['elɪveɪtə] *n* US ascensor *m*, elevador *m* *Méx*.

eleven [ɪ'levn] *num* once *m*; *see also* **six**.

elevenses [ɪ'levnzɪz] *n (U)* UK tentempié *m* que se toma sobre las once de la mañana.

eleventh [ɪ'levnθ] *num* undécimo(ma); *see also* **sixth**.

elicit [ɪ'lɪsɪt] *vt fml* - **1.** [response, reaction]: **to** ~ **sthg (from sb)** provocar algo (en alguien) - **2.** [information]: **to** ~ **sthg (from sb)** sacar algo (a alguien).

eligible ['elɪdʒəbl] *adj* [suitable, qualified] elegible; **to be ~ for sthg/to do sthg** reunir los requisitos para algo/para hacer algo.

eliminate [ɪ'lɪmɪneɪt] *vt* eliminar; **to be ~ d from sthg** ser eliminado(da) de algo.

elite [ɪ'li:t] ◇ *adj* selecto(ta). ◇ *n* élite *f*.

elitist [ɪ'li:tɪst] *adj pej* elitista.

elk [elk] (*pl inv* OR **-s**) *n* **-1.** [in Europe] alce *m* **- 2.** [in North America] ciervo *m* canadiense.

elm [elm] *n*: ~ (**tree**) olmo *m*.

elocution [ˌelə'kju:ʃn] *n* dicción *f*.

elongated ['i:lɒŋgeɪtɪd] *adj* alargado(da).

elope [ɪ'ləʊp] *vi*: **to ~ (with)** fugarse (con).

eloquent ['eləkwənt] *adj* elocuente.

El Salvador [ˌel'sælvədɔːʳ] *n* El Salvador.

else [els] *adv*: **anything ~?** ¿algo más?; **I don't need anything ~** no necesito nada más; **everyone ~** todos los demás (todas las demás); **everywhere ~** en/a todas las otras partes; **little ~** poco más; **nothing/ nobody ~** nada/nadie más; **someone/ something ~** otra persona/cosa; **somewhere ~** en/a otra parte; **who ~?** ¿quién si no?; **who ~ came?** ¿quién más vino?; **what ~?** ¿qué más?; **where ~?** ¿en/a qué otro sitio?
◆ **or else** *conj* [or if not] si no, de lo contrario.

elsewhere [els'weəʳ] *adv* a/en otra parte.

elude [ɪ'lu:d] *vt* [gen] escaparse de, eludir a; [blow] esquivar.

elusive [ɪ'lu:sɪv] *adj* [person, success] esquivo(va); [quality] difícil de encontrar.

emaciated [ɪ'meɪsɪeɪtɪd] *adj* demacrado(da).

e-mail (*abbr of* **electronic mail**) *n* COMPUT correo *m* electrónico; ~ **account** cuenta *f* de correo electrónico; ~ **address** dirección *f* electrónica; ~ **phone** teléfono *m* con correo electrónico.

emanate ['eməneɪt] *vi fml*: **to ~ from** emanar de.

emancipate [ɪ'mænsɪpeɪt] *vt*: **to ~ sb (from)** emancipar a alguien (de).

embankment [ɪm'bæŋkmənt] *n* **-1.** RAIL terraplén *m* **- 2.** [of river] dique *m*.

embark [ɪm'bɑːk] *vi* embarcar; **to ~ on** *fig* embarcarse en.

embarkation [ˌembɑː'keɪʃn] *n* [gen] embarque *m*; [of troops] embarco *m*.

embarrass [ɪm'bærəs] *vt* **-1.** [gen] avergonzar; **it ~es me** me da vergüenza **- 2.** [financially] poner en un aprieto.

embarrassed [ɪm'bærəst] *adj* [ashamed] avergonzado(da); [uneasy] violento(ta).

embarrassing [ɪm'bærəsɪŋ] *adj* embarazoso(sa), violento(ta); **how ~!** ¡qué vergüenza!

embarrassingly [ɪm'bærəsɪŋlɪ] *adv*: **it was ~ bad** era tan malo que daba vergüenza ajena.

embarrassment [ɪm'bærəsmənt] *n* [feeling] vergüenza *f*, pena *f Andes, CAm, Carib, Méx*.

embassy ['embəsɪ] (*pl* **-ies**) *n* embajada *f*.

embedded [ɪm'bedɪd] *adj* [buried & COMPUT]: ~ (**in**) incrustado(da) (en).

embellish [ɪm'belɪʃ] *vt*: **to ~ sthg (with)** adornar algo (con).

embers ['embəz] *npl* rescoldos *mpl*.

embezzle [ɪm'bezl] *vt* malversar.

embittered [ɪm'bɪtəd] *adj* amargado(da), resentido(da).

emblem ['embləm] *n* emblema *m*.

embody [ɪm'bɒdɪ] (*pt & pp* **-ied**) *vt* personificar, encarnar; **to be embodied in sthg** estar plasmado en algo.

embossed [ɪm'bɒst] *adj* **-1.** [heading, design]: ~ (**on**) [paper] estampado(da) (en); [leather, metal] repujado(da) (en) **- 2.** [paper]: ~ (**with**) estampado(da) (con) **- 3.** [leather, metal]: ~ (**with**) repujado(da) (con).

embrace [ɪm'breɪs] ◇ *n* abrazo *m*. ◇ *vt* **-1.** [hug] abrazar, dar un abrazo a **- 2.** *fml* [convert to] convertirse a, abrazar **- 3.** *fml* [include] abarcar. ◇ *vi* abrazarse.

embroider [ɪm'brɔɪdəʳ] *vt* **-1.** SEWING bordar **- 2.** *pej* [embellish] adornar.

embroidery [ɪm'brɔɪdərɪ] *n* (*U*) bordado *m*.

embroil [ɪm'brɔɪl] *vt*: **to get/be ~ed (in)** enredarse/estar enredado (en).

embryo ['embrɪəʊ] (*pl* **-s**) *n* embrión *m*.

emerald ['emərəld] ◇ *adj* [colour] esmeralda *m inv*; **the Emerald Isle** Irlanda. ◇ *n* [stone] esmeralda *f*.

emerge [ɪ'mɜːdʒ] ◇ *vi* **-1.** [gen]: **to ~ (from)** salir (de) **- 2.** [come into existence, become known] surgir, emerger. ◇ *vt*: **it ~d that ...** resultó que ...

emergence [ɪ'mɜːdʒəns] *n* surgimiento *m*, aparición *f*.

emergency [ɪ'mɜːdʒənsɪ] (*pl* **-ies**) ◇ *adj* [case, exit] de emergencia; [ward, services] de urgencia; [supplies] de reserva; [meeting] extraordinario(ria). ◇ *n* emergencia *f*.

emergency brake *n US* freno *m* de mano.

emergency exit *n* salida *f* de emergencia.

emergency landing *n* aterrizaje *m* forzoso.

emergency services *npl* servicios *mpl* de urgencia.

emery board ['emərɪ-] *n* lima *f* de uñas.

emigrant ['emɪgrənt] *n* emigrante *m* OR *f*.

emigrate ['emɪgreɪt] *vi*: **to ~ (to/from)** emigrar (a/de).

eminent ['emɪnənt] *adj* eminente.

emission [ɪ'mɪʃn] *n* emisión *f*.

emit [ɪ'mɪt] (*pt & pp* **-ted**, *cont* **-ting**) *vt* [gen] emitir; [smell, smoke] despedir.

emoticon [ɪ'məʊtɪkɒn] *n* COMPUT emoticono *m*.

emotion [ɪ'məʊʃn] *n* emoción *f*.

emotional [ɪ'məʊʃənl] *adj* - **1**. [gen] emotivo(va) - **2**. [needs, problems] emocional; **to get ~** emocionarse.

empathize, -ise ['empəθaɪz] *vi*: **to ~ (with)** identificarse (con).

emperor ['empərə'] *n* emperador *m*.

emphasis ['emfəsɪs] (*pl* **-ases** [-əsiːz]) *n*: **~ (on)** énfasis *m inv* (en); **to lay** OR **place ~ on** poner énfasis en, hacer hincapié en.

emphasize, -ise ['emfəsaɪz] *vt* [word, syllable] acentuar; [point, fact, feature] subrayar, hacer hincapié en; **to ~ that ...** subrayar que ...

emphatic [ɪm'fætɪk] *adj* [denial] rotundo(da), categórico(ca); [victory] convincente.

emphatically [ɪm'fætɪklɪ] *adv* - **1**. [deny] rotundamente, enfáticamente; [win] convincentemente - **2**. [certainly] ciertamente.

empire ['empaɪə'] *n* imperio *m*.

employ [ɪm'plɔɪ] *vt* - **1**. [give work to] emplear; **to be ~ed as** estar empleado de - **2**. *fml* [use] utilizar, emplear; **to ~ sthg as sthg/to do sthg** utilizar algo de algo/para hacer algo.

employee [ɪm'plɔiiː] *n* empleado *m*, -da *f*.

employer [ɪm'plɔɪə'] *n* - **1**. [individual] patrono *m*, -na *f*, empresario *m*, -ria *f* - **2**. [company]: **one of the country's biggest ~s** una de las empresas que más trabajadores tiene en el país.

employment [ɪm'plɔɪmənt] *n* empleo *m*; **to be in ~** tener trabajo.

employment agency *n* agencia *f* de trabajo.

empower [ɪm'paʊə'] *vt fml*: **to be ~ed to do sthg** estar autorizado(da) a OR para hacer algo.

empowerment [ɪm'paʊəmənt] *n* capacitación *f*.

empress ['emprɪs] *n* emperatriz *f*.

empty ['emptɪ] (*compar* **-ier**, *superl* **-iest**, *pt* & *pp* **-ied**, *pl* **-ies**) <> *adj* - **1**. [gen] vacío(a); [town] desierto(ta) - **2**. *pej* [words, threat, promise] vano(na). <> *vt* vaciar; **to ~ sthg into sthg** vaciar algo en algo. <> *vi* vaciarse. <> *n inf* casco *m*.

empty-handed [-'hændɪd] *adv* con las manos vacías.

EMS (*abbr of* **European Monetary System**) *n* SME *m*.

EMU (*abbr of* **Economic and Monetary Union**) *n* UEM *f*.

emulate ['emjʊleɪt] *vt* emular.

emulsion [ɪ'mʌlʃn] *n*: **~ (paint)** pintura *f* al agua.

enable [ɪ'neɪbl] *vt* - **1**. [allow]: **to ~ sb to do sthg** permitir a alguien hacer algo - **2**. COMPUT ejecutar.

enact [ɪ'nækt] *vt* - **1**. JUR promulgar - **2**. [act] representar.

enamel [ɪ'næml] *n* - **1**. [gen] esmalte *m* - **2**. [paint] pintura *f* de esmalte.

encampment [ɪn'kæmpmənt] *n* campamento *m*.

encapsulate [ɪn'kæpsjʊleɪt] *vt*: **to ~ sthg (in)** sintetizar algo (en).

encase [ɪn'keɪs] *vt*: **~ d in** revestido(da) de.

enchanted [ɪn'tʃɑːntɪd] *adj*: **~ (by** OR **with)** encantado(da) (con).

enchanting [ɪn'tʃɑːntɪŋ] *adj* encantador(ra).

encircle [ɪn'sɜːkl] *vt* rodear.

enclose [ɪn'kləʊz] *vt* - **1**. [surround, contain] rodear; **~ d by** OR **with** rodeado de; **an ~ d space** un espacio cerrado - **2**. [put in envelope] adjuntar; **please find ~ d ...** envío adjunto ...

enclosure [ɪn'kləʊʒə'] *n* - **1**. [place] recinto *m* (vallado) - **2**. [in letter] anexo *m*, documento *m* adjunto.

encompass [ɪn'kʌmpəs] *vt fml* [include] abarcar.

encore ['ɒŋkɔː'] <> *n* bis *m*. <> *excl* ¡otra!

encounter [ɪn'kaʊntə'] <> *n* encuentro *m*. <> *vt fml* encontrarse con.

encourage [ɪn'kʌrɪdʒ] *vt* - **1**. [give confidence to]: **to ~ sb (to do sthg)** animar a alguien (a hacer algo) - **2**. [foster] fomentar.

encouragement [ɪn'kʌrɪdʒmənt] *n* [confidence boosting] aliento *m*; [fostering] fomento *m*.

encroach [ɪn'krəʊtʃ] *vi*: **to ~ on** OR **upon** [rights, territory] usurpar; [privacy, time] invadir.

encrypt [ɪn'krɪpt] *vt* COMPUT encriptar.

encyclop(a)edia [ɪn,saɪklə'piːdjə] *n* enciclopedia *f*.

end [end] <> *n* - **1**. [last part, finish] fin *m*, final *m*; **at the ~ of May/1992** a finales de mayo/1992; **at the ~ of the week** al final de la semana; **my patience is at an ~** se me está agotando la paciencia; **to be at the ~ of one's tether** *UK* OR **rope** *US* estar hasta la coronilla; **to bring sthg to an ~** poner fin a algo; **to come to an ~** llegar a su fin; **'the ~'** [in films] 'FIN'; **to put an ~ to sthg** poner fin a algo; **in the ~** al final - **2**. [of two-ended thing] extremo *m*; [of pointed thing] punta *f*; [of stadium] fondo *m*; [of phone line] lado *m*; **~ to ~** extremo con extremo; **cigarette ~** colilla *f* - **3**. *fml* [purpose] fin *m*, objetivo *m*. <> *vi* [finish] acabarse, terminarse; **to ~ in/with** acabar en/con, terminar en/con.

◆ **on end** *adv* - **1**. [upright - hair] de punta; [- object] de pie - **2**. [continuously]: **for days on ~** durante días y días.

◆ **end up** *vi* acabar, terminar; **to ~ up**

doing sthg acabar por hacer algo/haciendo algo, terminar por hacer algo/haciendo algo; **to ~ up in** ir a parar a.

endanger [ɪn'deɪndʒəʳ] *vt* poner en peligro.

endearing [ɪn'dɪərɪŋ] *adj* simpático(ca).

endeavour UK, **endeavor** US [ɪn'devəʳ] *fml* <> *n* esfuerzo *m*. <> *vt*: **to ~ to do sthg** procurar hacer algo.

ending ['endɪŋ] *n* final *m*, desenlace *m*.

endive ['endaɪv] *n* **-1.** [curly lettuce] escarola *f* **-2.** [chicory] endibia *f*, achicoria *f*.

endless ['endlɪs] *adj* [gen] interminable; [patience, resources] inagotable.

endorse [ɪn'dɔːs] *vt* **-1.** [approve] apoyar, respaldar **-2.** [cheque] endosar.

endorsement [ɪn'dɔːsmənt] *n* **-1.** [approval] apoyo *m*, respaldo *m* **-2.** UK [on driving licence] *nota de sanción que consta en el carnet de conducir.*

endow [ɪn'daʊ] *vt* **-1.** *fml* [equip]: **to be ~ ed with** estar dotado(da) de **-2.** [donate money to] donar fondos a.

endurance [ɪn'djʊərəns] *n* resistencia *f*.

endure [ɪn'djʊəʳ] <> *vt* soportar, aguantar. <> *vi fml* perdurar.

endways ['endweɪz] *adv* **-1.** [not sideways] de frente **-2.** [with ends touching] extremo con extremo.

enemy ['enɪmɪ] (*pl* -ies) *n* enemigo *m*, -ga *f*.

energetic [ˌenə'dʒetɪk] *adj* **-1.** [lively, physically taxing] enérgico(ca) **-2.** [enthusiastic] activo(va), vigoroso(sa).

energy ['enədʒɪ] (*pl* -ies) *n* energía *f*.

enforce [ɪn'fɔːs] *vt* [law] hacer cumplir, aplicar; [standards] imponer.

enforced [ɪn'fɔːst] *adj* forzoso(sa).

engage [ɪn'geɪdʒ] <> *vt* **-1.** [attract] atraer **-2.** [TECH - clutch] pisar; [- gear] meter **-3.** *fml* [employ] contratar; **to be ~ d in** OR **on** dedicarse a, estar ocupado(da) en. <> *vi* [be involved]: **to ~ in** [gen] dedicarse a; [conversation] entablar.

engaged [ɪn'geɪdʒd] *adj* **-1.** [to be married]: **~ (to)** prometido(da) (con); **to get ~** prometerse **-2.** [busy, in use] ocupado(da); **~ in sthg** ocupado en algo **-3.** TELEC comunicando.

engaged tone *n* UK señal *f* de comunicando.

engagement [ɪn'geɪdʒmənt] *n* **-1.** [to be married] compromiso *m*; [period] noviazgo *m* **-2.** [appointment] cita *f*, compromiso *m*.

engagement ring *n* anillo *m* de compromiso.

engaging [ɪn'geɪdʒɪŋ] *adj* atractivo(va).

engender [ɪn'dʒendəʳ] *vt fml* engendrar.

engine ['endʒɪn] *n* **-1.** [of vehicle] motor *m* **-2.** RAIL locomotora *f*, máquina *f*.

engine driver *n* UK maquinista *m* OR *f*.

engineer [ˌendʒɪ'nɪəʳ] <> *n* **-1.** [gen] ingeniero *m*, -ra *f* **-2.** US [engine driver] maquinista *m* OR *f*. <> *vt* **-1.** [construct] construir **-2.** [contrive] tramar.

engineering [ˌendʒɪ'nɪərɪŋ] *n* ingeniería *f*.

England ['ɪŋglənd] *n* Inglaterra *f*.

English ['ɪŋglɪʃ] <> *adj* inglés(esa). <> *n* [language] inglés *m*. <> *npl* [people]: **the ~** los ingleses.

English breakfast *n* desayuno *m* inglés.

English Channel *n*: **the ~** el canal de la Mancha.

Englishman ['ɪŋglɪʃmən] (*pl* -men [-mən]) *n* inglés *m*.

Englishwoman ['ɪŋglɪʃˌwʊmən] (*pl* -women [-ˌwɪmɪn]) *n* inglesa *f*.

engrave [ɪn'greɪv] *vt lit & fig*: **to ~ sthg (on)** grabar algo (en).

engraving [ɪn'greɪvɪŋ] *n* grabado *m*.

engrossed [ɪn'grəʊst] *adj*: **to be ~ (in)** estar absorto(ta) (en).

engulf [ɪn'gʌlf] *vt*: **to be ~ed in** [flames etc] verse devorado(da) por; [fear, despair] verse sumido(da) en.

enhance [ɪn'hɑːns] *vt* [gen] aumentar, acrecentar; [status, position] elevar; [beauty] realzar.

enjoy [ɪn'dʒɔɪ] *vt* **-1.** [like] disfrutar de; **did you ~ the film/book?** ¿te gustó la película/el libro?; **she ~s reading** le gusta leer; **~ your meal!** ¡que aproveche!, ¡buen provecho!; **to ~ o.s.** pasarlo bien, divertirse **-2.** *fml* [possess] gozar OR disfrutar de.

enjoyable [ɪn'dʒɔɪəbl] *adj* agradable.

enjoyment [ɪn'dʒɔɪmənt] *n* [pleasure] placer *m*.

enlarge [ɪn'lɑːdʒ] *vt* [gen, PHOT & POL] ampliar.

enlargement [ɪn'lɑːdʒmənt] *n* [gen, PHOT & POL] ampliación *f*.

enlighten [ɪn'laɪtn] *vt fml* iluminar.

enlightened [ɪn'laɪtnd] *adj* amplio(plia) de miras.

enlightenment [ɪn'laɪtnmənt] *n (U)* aclaración *f*.
◆ **Enlightenment** *n*: **the Enlightenment** la Ilustración.

enlist [ɪn'lɪst] <> *vt* **-1.** [person] alistar, reclutar **-2.** [support] obtener. <> *vi* MIL: **to ~ (in)** alistarse (en).

enmity ['enmətɪ] (*pl* -ies) *n* enemistad *f*.

enormity [ɪ'nɔːmətɪ] *n* [extent] enormidad *f*.

enormous [ɪ'nɔːməs] *adj* enorme.

enough [ɪ'nʌf] <> *adj* bastante, suficiente; **do you have ~ glasses?** ¿tienes suficientes vasos? <> *pron* bastante; **is this ~?** ¿basta con eso?; **more than ~** más que suficiente; **that's ~** [sufficient] ya está bien; **to have had ~ (of)** [expressing annoyance] estar harto (de). ◇ *adv* bastante, suficientemente; **I was stupid ~ to believe him** fui lo bastante tonto como para creerle; **he was good ~ to lend me his car** *fml* tuvo la bondad de dejarme su coche; **strangely ~** curiosamente.

enquire [ɪnˈkwaɪə^r] *vi* [ask for information] informarse, pedir información; **to ~ about sthg** informarse de algo; **to ~ when/how/whether ...** preguntar cuándo/cómo/si ...
➤ **enquire into** *vt fus* investigar.

enquiry [ɪnˈkwaɪərɪ] (*pl* -ies) *n* - 1. [question] pregunta *f*; **'Enquiries'** 'Información' - 2. [investigation] investigación *f*.

enraged [ɪnˈreɪdʒd] *adj* enfurecido(da).

enrol *UK* (*pt* & *pp* -led, *cont* -ling), **enroll** *US* [ɪnˈrəʊl] ◇ *vt* matricular. ◇ *vi*: **to ~ (on)** matricularse (en).

en route [ˌɒnˈruːt] *adv*: **~ (from/to)** en el camino (de/a).

ensign [ˈensaɪn] *n* - 1. [flag] bandera *f*, enseña *f* - 2. *US* [sailor] ≃ alférez *m* de fragata.

ensue [ɪnˈsjuː] *vi fml* seguir; [war] sobrevenir.

ensure [ɪnˈʃʊə^r] *vt*: **to ~ (that)** asegurar que.

ENT (*abbr of* **Ear, Nose & Throat**) *n* otorrinolaringología *f*.

entail [ɪnˈteɪl] *vt* [involve] conllevar, suponer.

enter [ˈentə^r] ◇ *vt* - 1. [gen] entrar en - 2. [join - profession, parliament] ingresar en; [- university] matricularse en; [- army, navy] alistarse en - 3. [become involved in - politics etc] meterse en; [- race, examination etc] inscribirse en - 4. [register]: **to ~ sthg/sb for sthg** inscribir algo/a alguien en algo - 5. [write down] apuntar - 6. [appear in] presentarse *OR* aparecer en. ◇ *vi* - 1. [come or go in] entrar - 2. [participate]: **to ~ (for sthg)** inscribirse (en algo).
➤ **enter into** *vt fus* entrar en; [agreement] comprometerse a; [conversation, negotiations] entablar.

enter key *n* COMPUT tecla *f* enter.

enterprise [ˈentəpraɪz] *n* - 1. [project, company] empresa *f* - 2. [initiative] iniciativa *f*.

enterprise zone *n* zona del Reino Unido donde se fomenta la actividad industrial y empresarial.

enterprising [ˈentəpraɪzɪŋ] *adj* emprendedor(ra).

entertain [ˌentəˈteɪn] *vt* - 1. [amuse] divertir, entretener - 2. [invite] recibir (en casa) - 3. *fml* [idea, proposal] considerar.

entertainer [ˌentəˈteɪnə^r] *n* artista *m OR f*.

entertaining [ˌentəˈteɪnɪŋ] *adj* divertido(da), entretenido(da).

entertainment [ˌentəˈteɪnmənt] *n* - 1. *(U)* [amusement] diversión *f*, entretenimiento

m, entretención *f Amér* - 2. [show] espectáculo *m*.

enthral (*pt* & *pp* -led, *cont* -ling), **enthrall** *US* [ɪnˈθrɔːl] *vt* embelesar.

enthusiasm [ɪnˈθjuːzɪæzm] *n* - 1. [passion, eagerness]: **~ (for)** entusiasmo *m* (por) - 2. [interest] pasión *f*, interés *m*.

enthusiast [ɪnˈθjuːzɪæst] *n* entusiasta *m OR f*.

enthusiastic [ɪnˌθjuːzɪˈæstɪk] *adj* [person] entusiasta; [cry, response] entusiástico(ca).

entice [ɪnˈtaɪs] *vt* seducir, atraer; **nothing could ~ me to do that** no haría eso de ninguna manera.

entire [ɪnˈtaɪə^r] *adj* entero(ra); **the ~ evening** toda la noche.

entirely [ɪnˈtaɪəlɪ] *adv* completamente; **I'm not ~ sure** no estoy del todo seguro.

entirety [ɪnˈtaɪrətɪ] *n fml*: **in its ~** en su totalidad.

entitle [ɪnˈtaɪtl] *vt* [allow]: **to ~ sb to sthg** dar a alguien derecho a algo; **to ~ sb to do sthg** autorizar a alguien a hacer algo.

entitled [ɪnˈtaɪtld] *adj* - 1. [allowed]: **to be ~ to sthg/to do sthg** tener derecho a algo/a hacer algo - 2. [book, song, film] titulado(da).

entourage [ˌɒntʊˈrɑːʒ] *n* séquito *m*.

entrails [ˈentreɪlz] *npl* entrañas *fpl*.

entrance [*n* ˈentrəns, *vb* ɪnˈtrɑːns] ◇ *n*: **~ (to)** entrada *f* (a OR de); **to gain ~ to** *fml* [building] lograr acceso a; [society, university] lograr el ingreso en. ◇ *vt* encantar, hechizar.

entrance examination *n* examen *m* de ingreso.

entrance fee *n* [for museum] (precio *m* de) entrada *f*.

entrant [ˈentrənt] *n* participante *m OR f*.

entreat [ɪnˈtriːt] *vt*: **to ~ sb (to do sthg)** suplicar OR rogar a alguien (que haga algo).

entrée [ˈɒntreɪ] *n US* [main course] plato *m* principal.

entrepreneur [ˌɒntrəprəˈnɜː^r] *n* empresario *m*, -ria *f*.

entrust [ɪnˈtrʌst] *vt*: **to ~ sthg to sb**, **to ~ sb with sthg** confiar algo a alguien.

entry [ˈentrɪ] (*pl* -ies) *n* - 1. [gen]: **~ (into)** entrada *f* (en); **no ~** se prohibe la entrada, prohibido el paso - 2. *fig* [joining - of group, society] ingreso *m* - 3. [in competition] participante *m OR f* - 4. [in diary] anotación *f*; [in ledger] partida *f*.

entry form *n* boleto *m OR* impreso *m* de inscripción.

entry phone *n UK* portero *m* automático.

envelop [ɪnˈveləp] *vt*: **to ~ sthg/sb in** envolver algo/a alguien en.

envelope [ˈenvələʊp] *n* sobre *m*.

envious [ˈenvɪəs] *adj* [person] envidioso(

sa); [look] de envidia; **to be ~ of** tener envidia de.

environment [ɪn'vaɪərənmənt] *n* - **1.** [natural world]: **the ~** el medio ambiente - **2.** [surroundings] entorno *m* - **3.** [atmosphere] ambiente *m*.

environmental [ɪn‚vaɪərən'mentl] *adj* - **1.** [gen] medioambiental, ambiental; **~ pollution** contaminación *f* del medio ambiente - **2.** [group, campaigner] ecologista.

environmentally [ɪn‚vaɪərən'mentəlɪ] *adv* ecológicamente; **~ friendly** ecológico(ca), que no daña al medio ambiente.

envisage [ɪn'vɪzɪdʒ], **envision** US [ɪn'vɪʒn] *vt* prever.

envoy ['envɔɪ] *n* enviado *m*, -da *f*.

envy ['envɪ] (*pt* & *pp* **-ied**) ◇ *n* envidia *f*. ◇ *vt*: **to ~ (sb sthg)** envidiar (algo a alguien).

epic ['epɪk] ◇ *adj* épico(ca). ◇ *n* [poem, work] epopeya *f*; [film] película *f* épica.

epidemic [‚epɪ'demɪk] *n* epidemia *f*.

epileptic [‚epɪ'leptɪk] ◇ *adj* epiléptico(-ca). ◇ *n* epiléptico *m*, -ca *f*.

episode ['epɪsəʊd] *n* - **1.** [event] episodio *m* - **2.** [of story, TV series] capítulo *m*.

epistle [ɪ'pɪsl] *n* epístola *f*.

epitaph ['epɪtɑːf] *n* epitafio *m*.

epitome [ɪ'pɪtəmɪ] *n*: **the ~ of** [person] la personificación de; [thing] el vivo ejemplo de.

epitomize, -ise [ɪ'pɪtəmaɪz] *vt* [subj: person] personificar; [subj: thing] representar el paradigma de.

epoch ['iːpɒk] *n* época *f*.

equable ['ekwəbl] *adj* [calm, reasonable] ecuánime.

equal ['iːkwəl] (*UK pt* & *pp* **-led**, *cont* **-ling**, *US pt* & *pp* **-ed**, *cont* **-ing**) ◇ *adj* igual; **~ to** [sum] igual a; **to be ~ to** [task etc] estar a la altura de. ◇ *n* igual *m* or *f*. ◇ *vt* - **1.** MATH ser igual a - **2.** [person, quality] igualar.

equality [iː'kwɒlətɪ] *n* igualdad *f*.

equalize, -ise ['iːkwəlaɪz] *vi* SPORT empatar.

equalizer ['iːkwəlaɪzə'] *n* SPORT gol *m* del empate.

equally ['iːkwəlɪ] *adv* - **1.** [gen] igualmente; **~ important** igual de importante - **2.** [share, divide] a partes iguales, por igual - **3.** [just as likely] de igual modo.

equal opportunities *npl* igualdad *f* de oportunidades.

equanimity [‚ekwə'nɪmətɪ] *n* ecuanimidad *f*.

equate [ɪ'kweɪt] *vt*: **to ~ sthg with** equiparar algo con.

equation [ɪ'kweɪʒn] *n* ecuación *f*.

equator [ɪ'kweɪtə'] *n*: **the ~** el ecuador.

equilibrium [‚iːkwɪ'lɪbrɪəm] *n* equilibrio *m*.

equip [ɪ'kwɪp] (*pt* & *pp* **-ped**, *cont* **-ping**) *vt* - **1.** [provide with equipment]: **to ~ sthg (with)** equipar algo (con); **to ~ sb (with)** proveer a alguien (de) - **2.** [prepare]: **to be equipped for** estar preparado(da) para.

equipment [ɪ'kwɪpmənt] *n* (U) equipo *m*.

equitable ['ekwɪtəbl] *adj* equitativo(va).

equity ['ekwətɪ] *n* (U) FIN [of company] capital *m* social; [of shareholders] fondos *mpl* propios.

➤ **equities** *npl* ST EX acciones *fpl* ordinarias.

equivalent [ɪ'kwɪvələnt] ◇ *adj* equivalente; **to be ~ to** equivaler a. ◇ *n* equivalente *m*.

equivocal [ɪ'kwɪvəkl] *adj* equívoco(ca).

er [ɜː'] *excl* ¡ejem!

era ['ɪərə] (*pl* **-s**) *n* era *f*, época *f*.

eradicate [ɪ'rædɪkeɪt] *vt* erradicar.

erase [ɪ'reɪz] *vt* lit & fig borrar.

eraser [ɪ'reɪzə'] *n esp* US goma *f* de borrar.

erect [ɪ'rekt] ◇ *adj* [person, posture] erguido(da). ◇ *vt* - **1.** [building, statue] erigir, levantar - **2.** [tent] montar.

erection [ɪ'rekʃn] *n* - **1.** (U) [of building, statue] construcción *f* - **2.** [erect penis] erección *f*.

ERM (*abbr of* **Exchange Rate Mechanism**) *n mecanismo de tipos de cambio del SME.*

ermine ['ɜːmɪn] *n* armiño *m*.

erode [ɪ'rəʊd] *vt* - **1.** [rock, soil] erosionar; [metal] desgastar - **2.** [confidence, rights] mermar.

erosion [ɪ'rəʊʒn] *n* - **1.** [of rock, soil] erosión *f*; [of metal] desgaste *m* - **2.** [of confidence, rights] merma *f*.

erotic [ɪ'rɒtɪk] *adj* erótico(ca).

err [ɜː'] *vi* equivocarse, errar.

errand ['erənd] *n* recado *m*, mandado *m*.

erratic [ɪ'rætɪk] *adj* irregular.

error ['erə'] *n* error *m*; **to make an ~** cometer un error; **spelling ~** falta *f* de ortografía; **in ~** por equivocación.

erupt [ɪ'rʌpt] *vi* [volcano] entrar en erupción; fig [violence, war] estallar.

eruption [ɪ'rʌpʃn] *n* - **1.** [of volcano] erupción *f* - **2.** [of violence, war] estallido *m*, explosión *f*.

escalate ['eskəleɪt] *vi* - **1.** [conflict] intensificarse - **2.** [costs] ascender, incrementarse.

escalator ['eskəleɪtə'] *n* escalera *f* mecánica.

escapade [‚eskə'peɪd] *n* aventura *f*.

escape [ɪ'skeɪp] ◇ *n* - **1.** [gen] fuga *f* - **2.** [leakage - of gas, water] escape *m*. ◇ *vt* - **1.** [avoid] escapar a, eludir - **2.** [subj: fact, name]: **her name ~s me right now** ahora mismo no caigo en su nombre. ◇ *vi* - **1.** [gen]: **to ~ (from)** escaparse (de) - **2.** [survive] escapar.

escapism [ɪˈskeɪpɪzm] *n (U)* evasión *f*.

escort [*n* 'eskɔːt, *vb* ɪˈskɔːt] ◇ *n* - **1.** [guard] escolta *f* - **2.** [companion] acompañante *m* OR *f.* ◇ *vt* escoltar; **to ~ sb home** acompañar a alguien a casa.

Eskimo [ˈeskɪməʊ] (*pl* -**s**) *n* [person] esquimal *m* OR *f*.

espadrille [ˌespəˈdrɪl] *n* alpargata *f*.

especially [ɪˈspeʃəlɪ] *adv* - **1.** [more than usually, specifically] especialmente - **2.** [in particular] sobre todo.

espionage [ˈespɪəˌnɑːʒ] *n* espionaje *m*.

esplanade [ˌespləˈneɪd] *n* paseo *m* marítimo.

Esquire [ɪˈskwaɪəʳ] *n* Sr. Don; **B. Jones ~** Sr. Don B. Jones.

essay [ˈeseɪ] *n* - **1.** SCH redacción *f*, composición *f*; UNIV trabajo *m* - **2.** LITER ensayo *m*.

essence [ˈesns] *n* esencia *f*.

essential [ɪˈsenʃl] *adj* - **1.** [absolutely necessary]: **~ (to** OR **for)** esencial OR indispensable (para) - **2.** [basic] fundamental, esencial.

◆ **essentials** *npl* [most important elements] los elementos esenciales.

essential oil *n* aceite *m* esencial.

essentially [ɪˈsenʃəlɪ] *adv* [basically] esencialmente.

establish [ɪˈstæblɪʃ] *vt* - **1.** [gen] establecer - **2.** [facts, cause] verificar.

establishment [ɪˈstæblɪʃmənt] *n* establecimiento *m*.

◆ **Establishment** *n*: **the Establishment** el sistema.

estate [ɪˈsteɪt] *n* - **1.** [land, property] finca *f* - **2.**: (**housing**) **~** urbanización *f* - **3.**: (**industrial**) **~** polígono *m* industrial - **4.** JUR [inheritance] herencia *f*.

estate agency *n* UK agencia *f* inmobiliaria.

estate agent *n* UK agente inmobiliario *m*, agente inmobiliaria *f*.

estate car *n* UK ranchera *f*, coche *m* familiar.

esteem [ɪˈstiːm] ◇ *n* estima *f*. ◇ *vt* estimar, apreciar.

esthetic *etc US* = **aesthetic** *etc*.

estimate [*n* 'estɪmət, *vb* 'estɪmeɪt] ◇ *n* - **1.** [calculation, judgment] cálculo *m*, estimación *f* - **2.** [written quote] presupuesto *m*. ◇ *vt* estimar.

estimation [ˌestɪˈmeɪʃn] *n* - **1.** [opinion] juicio *m* - **2.** [calculation] cálculo *m*.

Estonia [eˈstəʊnɪə] *n* Estonia.

estranged [ɪˈstreɪndʒd] *adj* [from husband, wife] separado(da); **his ~ son** su hijo con el que no se habla.

estuary [ˈestjʊərɪ] (*pl* -**ies**) *n* estuario *m*.

e-tailer [ˈiːteɪləʳ] *n* tienda *f* electrónica.

etc. (*abbr of* **etcetera**) etc.

etching [ˈetʃɪŋ] *n* aguafuerte *m* OR *f*.

eternal [ɪˈtɜːnl] *adj* [gen] eterno(na); *fig* [complaints, whining] perpetuo(tua), continuo(nua).

eternity [ɪˈtɜːnətɪ] *n* eternidad *f*.

ethic [ˈeθɪk] *n* ética *f*.

◆ **ethics** ◇ *n (U)* [study] ética *f*. ◇ *npl* [morals] moralidad *f*.

ethical [ˈeθɪkl] *adj* ético(ca).

Ethiopia [ˌiːθɪˈəʊpɪə] *n* Etiopía.

ethnic [ˈeθnɪk] *adj* - **1.** [traditions, groups, conflict] étnico(ca) - **2.** [food] *típico de una cultura distinta a la occidental*.

ethos [ˈiːθɒs] *n* código *m* de valores.

etiquette [ˈetɪket] *n* etiqueta *f*.

EU (*abbr of* **European Union**) *n* UE *f*.

euphemism [ˈjuːfəmɪzm] *n* eufemismo *m*.

euphoria [juːˈfɔːrɪə] *n* euforia *f*.

euro [ˈjʊərəʊ] *n* [currency] euro *m*.

Eurocheque [ˈjʊərəʊˌtʃek] *n* eurocheque *m*.

Euro MP *n* eurodiputado *m*, -da *f*.

Europe [ˈjʊərəp] *n* Europa *f*.

European [ˌjʊərəˈpiːən] ◇ *adj* europeo(a). ◇ *n* europeo *m*, -a *f*.

European Central Bank *n*: **the ~** el Banco Central Europeo.

European Commission *n*: **the ~** la Comisión Europea.

European Community *n*: **the ~** la Comunidad Europea.

European Monetary System *n*: **the ~** el Sistema Monetario Europeo.

European Parliament *n*: **the ~** el Parlamento Europeo.

European Union *n*: **the ~** la Unión Europea.

Eurosceptic [ˈjʊərəʊˌskeptɪk] ◇ *adj* euroescéptico(ca). ◇ *n* euroescéptico *m*, -ca *f*.

Eurostar [ˈjʊərəʊstɑːʳ] *n* Euroestar *m*.

euthanasia [ˌjuːθəˈneɪzjə] *n* eutanasia *f*.

evacuate [ɪˈvækjʊeɪt] *vt* evacuar.

evade [ɪˈveɪd] *vt* [gen] eludir; [taxes] evadir.

evaluate [ɪˈvæljʊeɪt] *vt* evaluar.

evaporate [ɪˈvæpəreɪt] *vi* [liquid] evaporarse; *fig* [feeling] desvanecerse.

evaporated milk [ɪˈvæpəreɪtɪd-] *n* leche *f* evaporada.

evasion [ɪˈveɪʒn] *n* - **1.** [of responsibility, payment etc] evasión *f* - **2.** [lie] evasiva *f*.

evasive [ɪˈveɪsɪv] *adj* evasivo(va).

eve [iːv] *n*: **on the ~ of** en la víspera de.

even [ˈiːvn] ◇ *adj* - **1.** [regular] uniforme, constante - **2.** [calm] sosegado(da) - **3.** [flat, level] llano(na), liso(sa) - **4.** [equal - contest, teams] igualado(da); [- chance] igual; **to get ~ with** ajustarle las cuentas a - **5.** [number] par. ◇ *adv* - **1.** [gen] incluso, hasta; **~ now/then** incluso ahora/entonces; **not**

~ ni siquiera - **2.** [in comparisons] aun; ~ **more** aun más.

◆ **even if** *conj* aunque, aun cuando, así *Amér.*

◆ **even so** *conj* aun así.

◆ **even though** *conj* aunque.

◆ **even out** *vi* igualarse.

evening ['iːvnɪŋ] *n* - **1.** [end of day - early part] tarde *f*; [- later part] noche *f*; **in the** ~ por la tarde/noche - **2.** [event, entertainment] velada *f*.

◆ **evenings** *adv* [early] por la tarde; [late] por la noche.

evening class *n* clase *f* nocturna.

evening dress *n* - **1.** [worn by man] traje *m* de etiqueta - **2.** [worn by woman] traje *m* de noche.

event [ɪ'vent] *n* - **1.** [happening] acontecimiento *m*, suceso *m*; **in the** ~ **of** en caso de; **in the** ~ **that it rains** (en) caso de que llueva - **2.** SPORT prueba *f*.

◆ **in any event** *adv* en todo caso.

◆ **in the event** *adv* UK al final, llegada la hora.

eventful [ɪ'ventfʊl] *adj* accidentado(da).

eventual [ɪ'ventʃʊəl] *adj* final.

eventuality [ɪ,ventʃʊ'ælətɪ] (*pl* **-ies**) *n* eventualidad *f*.

eventually [ɪ'ventʃʊəlɪ] *adv* finalmente.

ever ['evəʳ] *adv* - **1.** [at any time] alguna vez; **have you** ~ **done it?** ¿lo has hecho alguna vez?; **the best** ~ el mejor de todos los tiempos; **hardly** ~ casi nunca - **2.** [all the time] siempre; **all he** ~ **does is complain** no hace más que quejarse; **as** ~ como siempre; **for** ~ para siempre - **3.** [for emphasis]: ~ **so big** muy grande; ~ **such a mess** un lío tan grande; **why/how** ~ **did you do it?** ¿por qué/cómo diablos lo hiciste?; **what** ~ **can it be?** ¿qué diablos puede ser?

◆ **ever since** ◇ *adv* desde entonces. ◇ *conj* desde que. ◇ *prep* desde.

evergreen ['evəɡriːn] ◇ *adj* de hoja perenne. ◇ *n* árbol *m* de hoja perenne.

everlasting [,evə'lɑːstɪŋ] *adj* eterno(na).

every ['evrɪ] *adj* cada; ~ **day** cada día, todos los días; ~ **week** todas las semanas.

◆ **every now and then, every so often** *adv* de vez en cuando.

◆ **every other** *adj*: ~ **other day** un día sí y otro no, cada dos días.

everybody ['evrɪ,bɒdɪ] = **everyone**.

everyday ['evrɪdeɪ] *adj* diario(ria), cotidiano(na).

everyone ['evrɪwʌn] *pron* todo el mundo, todos(das).

everyplace US = **everywhere**.

everything ['evrɪθɪŋ] *pron* todo; **money isn't** ~ el dinero no lo es todo.

everywhere ['evrɪweəʳ], **everyplace** US

['evrɪ,pleɪs] *adv* en OR por todas partes; [with verbs of motion] a todas partes; ~ **you go** dondequiera que vayas.

evict [ɪ'vɪkt] *vt*: **to** ~ **sb from** desahuciar a alguien de.

evidence ['evɪdəns] *n* (*U*) - **1.** [proof] pruebas *fpl* - **2.** JUR [of witness] declaración *f*, testimonio *m*; **to give** ~ dar testimonio, prestar declaración.

evident ['evɪdənt] *adj* evidente, manifiesto(ta).

evidently ['evɪdəntlɪ] *adv* - **1.** [seemingly] por lo visto, al parecer - **2.** [obviously] evidentemente.

evil ['iːvl] ◇ *adj* [person] malo(la), malvado(da); [torture, practice] perverso(sa), vil. ◇ *n* - **1.** [evil quality] maldad *f* - **2.** [evil thing] mal *m*.

evocative [ɪ'vɒkətɪv] *adj* evocador(ra), sugerente.

evoke [ɪ'vəʊk] *vt* - **1.** [memory, emotion] evocar - **2.** [response] producir.

evolution [,iːvə'luːʃn] *n* - **1.** BIOL evolución *f* - **2.** [development] desarrollo *m*.

evolve [ɪ'vɒlv] ◇ *vt* desarrollar. ◇ *vi* - **1.** BIOL: **to** ~ **(into/from)** evolucionar (en/de) - **2.** [develop] desarrollarse.

ewe [juː] *n* oveja *f*.

ex [eks] *n* *inf* [former spouse, lover etc] ex *m* OR *f*.

ex- [eks] *prefix* ex-.

exacerbate [ɪɡ'zæsəbeɪt] *vt* exacerbar.

exact [ɪɡ'zækt] ◇ *adj* exacto(ta); **to be** ~ para ser exactos. ◇ *vt*: **to** ~ **sthg (from)** arrancar algo (a).

exacting [ɪɡ'zæktɪŋ] *adj* - **1.** [job, work] arduo(dua) - **2.** [standards] severo(ra); [person] exigente.

exactly [ɪɡ'zæktlɪ] ◇ *adv* [precisely] exactamente; **it's** ~ **ten o'clock** son las diez en punto. ◇ *excl* ¡exacto!, ¡exactamente!

exaggerate [ɪɡ'zædʒəreɪt] *vt* & *vi* exagerar.

exaggeration [ɪɡ,zædʒə'reɪʃn] *n* exageración *f*.

exalted [ɪɡ'zɔːltɪd] *adj* [person, position] elevado(da).

exam [ɪɡ'zæm] (*abbr of* **examination**) *n* examen *m*; **to take** OR **sit an** ~ hacer un examen.

examination [ɪɡ,zæmɪ'neɪʃn] *n* - **1.** = **exam** - **2.** [inspection] inspección *f*, examen *m* - **3.** MED reconocimiento *m* - **4.** [consideration] estudio *m*.

examine [ɪɡ'zæmɪn] *vt* - **1.** [gen] examinar - **2.** MED reconocer - **3.** [consider - idea, proposal] estudiar - **4.** JUR interrogar.

examiner [ɪɡ'zæmɪnəʳ] *n* examinador *m*, -ra *f*.

example [ɪɡ'zɑːmpl] *n* ejemplo *m*; **for** ~ por ejemplo.

exasperate [ɪgˈzæspəreɪt] *vt* exasperar, sacar de quicio.

exasperation [ɪgˌzæspəˈreɪʃn] *n* exasperación *f*.

excavate [ˈekskəveɪt] *vt* excavar.

exceed [ɪkˈsiːd] *vt* **- 1.** [amount, number] exceder, sobrepasar **- 2.** [limit, expectations] rebasar.

exceedingly [ɪkˈsiːdɪŋlɪ] *adv* extremadamente.

excel [ɪkˈsel] (*pt & pp* **-led**, *cont* **-ling**) ⬦ *vi:* to ~ **(in** OR **at)** sobresalir (en). ⬦ *vt:* to ~ **o.s.** *UK* lucirse.

excellence [ˈeksələns] *n* excelencia *f*.

excellent [ˈeksələnt] *adj* excelente.

except [ɪkˈsept] ⬦ *prep & conj:* ~ **(for)** excepto, salvo. ⬦ *vt:* to ~ **sb (from)** exceptuar OR excluir a alguien (de).

excepting [ɪkˈseptɪŋ] = **except**.

exception [ɪkˈsepʃn] *n* **- 1.** [exclusion]: ~ **(to)** excepción *f* (a); **with the** ~ **of** a excepción de **- 2.** [offence]: **to take** ~ **to** ofenderse por.

exceptional [ɪkˈsepʃənl] *adj* excepcional.

excerpt [ˈeksɜːpt] *n:* ~ **(from)** extracto *m* (de).

excess [ɪkˈses, *before nouns* ˈekses] ⬦ *adj* excedente. ⬦ *n* exceso *m*.

excess baggage *n* exceso *m* de equipaje.

excess fare *n UK* suplemento *m*.

excessive [ɪkˈsesɪv] *adj* excesivo(va).

exchange [ɪksˈtʃeɪndʒ] ⬦ *n* **- 1.** [gen] intercambio *m*; **in** ~ **(for)** a cambio (de) **- 2.** FIN cambio *m* **- 3.** TELEC: **(telephone)** ~ central *f* telefónica **- 4.** *fml* [conversation]: **a heated** ~ una acalorada discusión. ⬦ *vt* [swap] intercambiar; [goods in shop] cambiar; **to** ~ **sthg for sthg** cambiar algo por algo; **to** ~ **sthg with sb** intercambiar algo con alguien.

exchange rate *n* FIN tipo *m* de cambio.

Exchequer [ɪksˈtʃekəʳ] *n UK:* **the** ~ ≈ Hacienda.

excise [ˈeksaɪz] *n (U)* impuestos *mpl* sobre el consumo interior.

excite [ɪkˈsaɪt] *vt* **- 1.** [person] emocionar **- 2.** [suspicion, interest] despertar, suscitar.

excited [ɪkˈsaɪtɪd] *adj* emocionado(da), entusiasmado(da).

excitement [ɪkˈsaɪtmənt] *n* emoción *f*.

exciting [ɪkˈsaɪtɪŋ] *adj* emocionante, apasionante.

exclaim [ɪkˈskleɪm] ⬦ *vt* exclamar. ⬦ *vi:* to ~ **(at)** exclamar (ante).

exclamation [ˌekskləˈmeɪʃn] *n* exclamación *f*.

exclamation mark *UK*, **exclamation point** *US* [exhibition] exposición *f* **2.** JUR prueba *f* (instrumental). ⬦ *vt* **- 1.** *fml* [feeling] mostrar, manifestar **- 2.** ART exponer.

exclude [ɪkˈskluːd] *vt:* to ~ **sthg/sb (from)** excluir algo/a alguien (de).

excluding [ɪkˈskluːdɪŋ] *prep* sin incluir, con excepción de.

exclusive [ɪkˈskluːsɪv] ⬦ *adj* **- 1.** [sole] exclusivo(va) **- 2.** [high-class] selecto(ta). ⬦ *n* [news story] exclusiva *f*.

➤ **exclusive of** *prep* excluyendo.

excrement [ˈekskrɪmənt] *n* excremento *m*.

excruciating [ɪkˈskruːʃɪeɪtɪŋ] *adj* insoportable.

excursion [ɪkˈskɜːʃn] *n* excursión *f*.

excuse [*n* ɪkˈskjuːs, *vb* ɪkˈskjuːz] ⬦ *n* excusa *f*; **to make an** ~ dar una excusa, excusarse. ⬦ *vt* **- 1.** [gen]: **to** ~ **sb (for sthg/for doing sthg)** perdonar a alguien (por algo/por haber hecho algo) **- 2.** [let off]: **to** ~ **sb (from)** dispensar a alguien (de) **- 3.** *phr:* ~ **me** [to attract attention] oiga (por favor); [when coming past] ¿me deja pasar?; [apologizing] perdone; *US* [pardon me?] ¿perdón?, ¿cómo?

ex-directory *adj UK* que no figura en la guía telefónica.

execute [ˈeksɪkjuːt] *vt* [gen & COMPUT] ejecutar.

execution [ˌeksɪˈkjuːʃn] *n* ejecución *f*.

executioner [ˌeksɪˈkjuːʃnəʳ] *n* verdugo *m*.

executive [ɪgˈzekjʊtɪv] ⬦ *adj* [decision-making] ejecutivo(va). ⬦ *n* **- 1.** [person] ejecutivo *m*, -va *f* **- 2.** [committee] ejecutiva *f*, órgano *m* ejecutivo.

executive director *n* director ejecutivo *m*, directora ejecutiva *f*.

executor [ɪgˈzekjʊtəʳ] *n* albacea *m*.

exemplify [ɪgˈzemplɪfaɪ] (*pt & pp* **-ied**) *vt* ejemplificar.

exempt [ɪgˈzempt] ⬦ *adj:* ~ **(from)** exento(ta) (de). ⬦ *vt:* to ~ **sthg/sb (from)** eximir algo/a alguien (de).

exercise [ˈeksəsaɪz] ⬦ *n* **- 1.** [gen] ejercicio *m* **- 2.** MIL maniobra *f*. ⬦ *vt* **- 1.** [dog] llevar de paseo; [horse] entrenar **- 2.** *fml* [power, right] ejercer; [caution, restraint] mostrar. ⬦ *vi* hacer ejercicio.

exercise book *n* cuaderno *m* de ejercicios.

exert [ɪgˈzɜːt] *vt* ejercer; **to** ~ **o.s.** esforzarse.

exertion [ɪgˈzɜːʃn] *n* esfuerzo *m*.

exhale [eksˈheɪl] ⬦ *vt* exhalar, despedir. ⬦ *vi* espirar.

exhaust [ɪgˈzɔːst] ⬦ *n (U)* [fumes] gases *mpl* de combustión; ~ **(pipe)** tubo *m* de escape. ⬦ *vt* agotar.

exhausted [ɪgˈzɔːstɪd] *adj* [person] agotado(da).

exhausting [ɪgˈzɔːstɪŋ] *adj* agotador(ra).

exhaustion [ɪgˈzɔːstʃn] *n* agotamiento *m*.

exhaustive [ɪgˈzɔːstɪv] *adj* exhaustivo(va).

exhibit [ɪgˈzɪbɪt] ⬦ *n* **- 1.** ART objeto *m* expuesto;

exhibition [ˌeksɪ'bɪʃn] *n* -**1.** ART exposición *f* -**2.** [of feeling] manifestación *f*, demostración *f*.

exhilarating [ɪg'zɪləreɪtɪŋ] *adj* estimulante.

exile ['eksaɪl] ◇ *n* -**1.** [condition] exilio *m*; **in ~** en el exilio -**2.** [person] exiliado *m*, -da *f*. ◇ *vt*: **to ~ sb (from/to)** exiliar a alguien (de/a).

exist [ɪg'zɪst] *vi* existir.

existence [ɪg'zɪstəns] *n* existencia *f*; **to be in ~** existir; **to come into ~** nacer.

existing [ɪg'zɪstɪŋ] *adj* existente, actual.

exit ['eksɪt] ◇ *n* salida *f*. ◇ *vi* [gen & COMPUT] salir; THEATRE hacer mutis.

exodus ['eksədəs] *n* éxodo *m*.

exonerate [ɪg'zɒnəreɪt] *vt*: **to ~ sb (from)** exonerar a alguien (de).

exorbitant [ɪg'zɔːbɪtənt] *adj* [cost] excesivo(va); [demand, price] exorbitante.

exotic [ɪg'zɒtɪk] *adj* exótico(ca).

expand [ɪk'spænd] ◇ *vt* ampliar. ◇ *vi* extenderse, ampliarse; [materials, fluids] expandirse, dilatarse.

◆ **expand (up)on** *vt fus* desarrollar.

expanse [ɪk'spæns] *n* extensión *f*.

expansion [ɪk'spænʃn] *n* expansión *f*.

expect [ɪk'spekt] ◇ *vt* -**1.** [gen] esperar; **to ~ sb to do sthg** esperar que alguien haga algo; **to ~ sthg (from sb)** esperar algo (de alguien); **to ~ the worst** esperarse lo peor; **as ~ed** como era de esperar -**2.** [suppose] imaginarse, suponer; **I ~ so** supongo que sí. ◇ *vi* -**1.** [anticipate]: **to ~ to do sthg** esperar hacer algo -**2.** [be pregnant]: **to be ~ing** estar embarazada OR en estado.

expectant [ɪk'spektənt] *adj* expectante.

expectant mother *n* futura madre *f*, mujer *f* embarazada.

expectation [ˌekspek'teɪʃn] *n* esperanza *f*; **against all ~** OR **~s, contrary to all ~** OR **~s** contrariamente a lo que se esperaba; **to live up to/fall short of ~s** estar/no estar a la altura de lo esperado.

expedient [ɪk'spiːdjənt] *fml* ◇ *adj* conveniente, oportuno(na). ◇ *n* recurso *m*.

expedition [ˌekspɪ'dɪʃn] *n* -**1.** [journey] expedición *f* -**2.** [outing] salida *f*.

expel [ɪk'spel] (*pt* & *pp* -**led**, *cont* -**ling**) *vt* -**1.** [person]: **to ~ sb (from)** expulsar a alguien (de) -**2.** [gas, liquid]: **to ~ sthg (from)** expeler algo (de).

expend [ɪk'spend] *vt*: **to ~ sthg (on)** emplear algo (en).

expendable [ɪk'spendəbl] *adj* reemplazable.

expenditure [ɪk'spendɪtʃəʳ] *n (U)* gasto *m*.

expense [ɪk'spens] *n (U)* gasto *m*; **at the ~ of** [sacrificing] a costa de; **at sb's ~** *lit* & *fig* a costa de alguien; **to spare no ~** no repararse en gastos.

◆ **expenses** *npl* COMM gastos *mpl*.

expense account *n* cuenta *f* de gastos.

expensive [ɪk'spensɪv] *adj* caro(ra).

experience [ɪk'spɪərɪəns] ◇ *n* experiencia *f*. ◇ *vt* experimentar.

experienced [ɪk'spɪərɪənst] *adj*: **~ (at** OR **in)** experimentado(da) (en).

experiment [ɪk'sperɪmənt] ◇ *n* experimento *m*. ◇ *vi*: **to ~ (with/on)** experimentar (con), hacer experimentos (con).

expert ['ekspɜːt] ◇ *adj*: **~ (at sthg/at doing sthg)** experto(ta) (en algo/en hacer algo); **~ advice** la opinión de un experto. ◇ *n* experto *m*, -ta *f*.

expertise [ˌekspɜː'tiːz] *n (U)* pericia *f*.

expire [ɪk'spaɪəʳ] *vi* [licence, membership] caducar; [lease, deadline] vencer.

expiry [ɪk'spaɪərɪ] *n* [of licence, membership] caducación *f*; [of lease, deadline] vencimiento *m*.

explain [ɪk'spleɪn] ◇ *vt*: **to ~ sthg (to sb)** explicar algo (a alguien). ◇ *vi* explicar; **to ~ to sb about sthg** explicarle a alguien.

explanation [ˌeksplə'neɪʃn] *n*: **~ (for)** explicación *f* (de).

explicit [ɪk'splɪsɪt] *adj* explícito(ta).

explode [ɪk'spləʊd] ◇ *vt* [bomb] hacer explotar; [building etc] volar; *fig* [theory] reventar. ◇ *vi lit* & *fig* estallar, explotar.

exploit [*n* 'eksplɔɪt, *vb* ɪk'splɔɪt] ◇ *n* proeza *f*, hazaña *f*. ◇ *vt* explotar.

exploitation [ˌeksplɔɪ'teɪʃn] *n (U)* explotación *f*.

exploration [ˌeksplə'reɪʃn] *n* exploración *f*.

explore [ɪk'splɔːʳ] *vt* & *vi lit* & *fig* explorar.

explorer [ɪk'splɔːrəʳ] *n* explorador *m*, -ra *f*.

explosion [ɪk'spləʊʒn] *n* explosión *f*.

explosive [ɪk'spləʊsɪv] ◇ *adj* explosivo(va). ◇ *n* explosivo *m*.

exponent [ɪk'spəʊnənt] *n* -**1.** [supporter] partidario *m*, -ria *f* -**2.** [expert] experto *m*, -ta *f*.

export [*n* & *comp* 'ekspɔːt, *vb* ɪk'spɔːt] ◇ *n* -**1.** [act] exportación *f* -**2.** [exported product] artículo *m* de exportación. ◇ *comp* de exportación. ◇ *vt* COMM & COMPUT exportar.

exporter [ek'spɔːtəʳ] *n* exportador *m*, -ra *f*.

expose [ɪk'spəʊz] *vt* -**1.** [to sunlight, danger etc & PHOT] exponer; **to be ~d to sthg** estar OR verse expuesto a algo -**2.** [reveal, uncover] descubrir.

exposed [ɪk'spəʊzd] *adj* [land, house, position] expuesto(ta), al descubierto.

exposure [ɪk'spəʊʒəʳ] *n* -**1.** [to light, radiation] exposición *f* -**2.** MED hipotermia *f* -**3.** PHOT [time] (tiempo *m* de) exposición *f*; [photograph] fotografía *f* -**4.** [publicity] publicidad *f*.

exposure meter *n* fotómetro *m*.

expound [ɪk'spaʊnd] *vt fml* exponer.

express [ɪk'spres] ◇ *adj* **-1.** *UK* [letter, delivery] urgente **-2.** [train, coach] rápido(da) **-3.** *fml* [specific] expreso(sa). ◇ *adv* urgente. ◇ *n* [train] expreso *m*. ◇ *vt* expresar; **to ~ o.s.** expresarse.

expression [ɪk'spreʃn] *n* expresión *f*.

expressive [ɪk'spresɪv] *adj* [full of feeling] expresivo(va).

expressly [ɪk'spreslɪ] *adv* [specifically] expresamente.

expressway [ɪk'spreswei] *n US* autopista *f*.

exquisite [ɪk'skwɪzɪt] *adj* exquisito(ta).

ext., extn. (*abbr of* **extension**) ext., extn.

extend [ɪk'stend] ◇ *vt* **-1.** [gen] extender; [house] ampliar; [road, railway] prolongar; [visa, deadline] prorrogar **-2.** [offer - welcome, help] brindar; [- credit] conceder. ◇ *vi* **-1.** [become longer] extenderse **-2.** [from surface, object] sobresalir.

extension [ɪk'stenʃn] *n* **-1.** [gen & TELEC] extensión *f* **-2.** [to building] ampliación *f* **-3.** [of visit] prolongación *f*; [of deadline, visa] prórroga *f* **-4.** ELEC: **~ (lead)** alargador *m*.

extension cable *n* alargador *m*.

extensive [ɪk'stensɪv] *adj* [gen] extenso(sa); [changes] profundo(da); [negotiations] amplio(plia).

extensively [ɪk'stensɪvlɪ] *adv* [gen] extensamente; [change] profundamente.

extent [ɪk'stent] *n* **-1.** [size] extensión *f* **-2.** [of problem, damage] alcance *m* **-3.** [degree]: **to what ~ ...?** ¿hasta qué punto ...?; **to the ~ that** [in that, in so far as] en la medida en que; [to the point where] hasta tal punto que; **to some/a certain ~** hasta cierto punto; **to a large** OR **great ~** en gran medida.

extenuating circumstances [ɪk'stenjoeitɪŋ-] *npl* circunstancias *fpl* atenuantes.

exterior [ɪk'stɪərɪəʳ] ◇ *adj* exterior. ◇ *n* exterior *m*.

exterminate [ɪk'stɜːmineit] *vt* exterminar.

external [ɪk'stɜːnl] *adj* externo(na).

extinct [ɪk'stɪŋkt] *adj* extinto(ta).

extinguish [ɪk'stɪŋgwɪʃ] *vt fml* [gen] extinguir; [cigarette] apagar.

extinguisher [ɪk'stɪŋgwɪʃəʳ] *n* extintor *m*.

extn. = ext.

extol (*pt* & *pp* **-led**, *cont* **-ling**), **extoll** *US* [ɪk'stəʊl] *vt* [merits, values] ensalzar.

extort [ɪk'stɔːt] *vt*: **to ~ sthg from sb** [confession, promise] arrancar algo a alguien; [money] sacar algo a alguien.

extortionate [ɪk'stɔːʃnət] *adj* desorbitado(da), exorbitante.

extra ['ekstrə] ◇ *adj* [additional] adicional; [spare] de más, de sobra; **take ~ care** pon sumo cuidado. ◇ *n* **-1.** [addition] extra *m* **-2.** [additional charge] suplemento *m* **-3.** CINE-

MA & THEATRE extra *m* OR *f*. ◇ *adv* extra; **to pay/charge ~** pagar/cobrar un suplemento; **be ~ careful** pon sumo cuidado.

extra- ['ekstrə] *prefix* extra-.

extract [*n* 'ekstrækt, *vb* ɪk'strækt] ◇ *n* **-1.** [from book, piece of music] fragmento *m* **-2.** CHEM extracto *m*. ◇ *vt*: **to ~ sthg (from)** [gen] extraer algo (de); [confession] arrancar algo (de).

extradite ['ekstrədait] *vt*: **to ~ sb (from/ to)** extraditar a alguien (de/a).

extramarital [,ekstrə'mærɪtl] *adj* extramatrimonial.

extramural [,ekstrə'mjʊərəl] *adj* UNIV *fuera de la universidad pero organizado por ella.*

extraordinary [ɪk'strɔːdnrɪ] *adj* extraordinario(ria).

extraordinary general meeting *n* junta *f* (general) extraordinaria.

extravagance [ɪk'strævəgəns] *n* **-1.** (*U*) [excessive spending] derroche *m*, despilfarro *m* **-2.** [luxury] extravagancia *f*.

extravagant [ɪk'strævəgənt] *adj* **-1.** [wasteful] derrochador(ra) **-2.** [expensive] caro(ra) **-3.** [exaggerated] extravagante.

extreme [ɪk'striːm] ◇ *adj* extremo(ma). ◇ *n* [furthest limit] extremo *m*.

extremely [ɪk'striːmlɪ] *adv* [very] sumamente, extremadamente.

extreme sports *npl* deportes *mpl* extremos.

extremist [ɪk'striːmɪst] ◇ *adj* extremista. ◇ *n* extremista *m* OR *f*.

extricate ['ekstrɪkeit] *vt*: **to ~ sthg from** lograr sacar algo de; **to ~ o.s. from** lograr salirse de.

extrovert ['ekstrəvɜːt] ◇ *adj* extrovertido(da). ◇ *n* extrovertido *m*, -da *f*.

exultant [ɪg'zʌltənt] *adj* [person] jubiloso(sa); [cry] de júbilo.

eye [ai] (*cont* **eyeing** OR **eying**) ◇ *n* ojo *m*; **to cast** OR **run one's ~ over sthg** echar un ojo OR un vistazo a algo; **to have one's ~ on sthg** tener el ojo echado a algo; **to keep one's ~s open for, to keep an ~ out for** estar atento a; **to keep an ~ on sthg** echar un ojo a algo, vigilar algo. ◇ *vt* mirar.

eyeball ['aibɔːl] *n* globo *m* ocular.

eyebath ['aibɑːθ] *n* lavaojos *m inv*; baño *m* ocular.

eyebrow ['aibraʊ] *n* ceja *f*.

eyebrow pencil *n* lápiz *m* de cejas.

eyedrops ['aidrɒps] *npl* colirio *m*.

eyelash ['ailæʃ] *n* pestaña *f*.

eyelid ['ailɪd] *n* párpado *m*.

eyeliner ['ai,lainəʳ] *n* lápiz *m* de ojos.

eye-opener *n inf* [revelation] revelación *f*; [surprise] sorpresa *f*.

eye shadow *n* sombra *f* de ojos.

eyesight ['aisait] *n* vista *f*.

eyesore ['aɪsɔː'] *n* monstruosidad *f*.

eyestrain ['aɪstreɪn] *n* vista *f* cansada.

eye test *n* revisión *f* ocular.

eyewitness [,aɪ'wɪtnɪs] *n* testigo *m* OR *f* ocular.

e-zine ['iːziːn] *n* fanzine *m* electrónico.

f (*pl* **f's** OR **fs**), **F** (*pl* **F's** OR **Fs**) [ef] *n* [letter] f *f*, F *f*.

➤ **F** ◇ *n* **- 1.** MUS fa *m* **- 2.** SCH ≃ muy deficiente *m*. ◇ *adj* (*abbr of* **Fahrenheit**) F.

fable ['feɪbl] *n* [traditional story] fábula *f*.

fabric ['fæbrɪk] *n* **- 1.** [cloth] tela *f*, tejido *m* **- 2.** [of building, society] estructura *f*.

fabrication [,fæbrɪ'keɪʃn] *n* **- 1.** [lying, lie] invención *f* **- 2.** [manufacture] fabricación *f*.

fabulous ['fæbjʊləs] *adj inf* [excellent] fabuloso(sa).

facade [fə'sɑːd] *n* fachada *f*.

face [feɪs] ◇ *n* **- 1.** [of person] cara *f*, rostro *m*; ~ **to** ~ cara a cara; **to lose** ~ quedar mal; **to save** ~ salvar las apariencias; **to say sthg to sb's** ~ decir algo a alguien en su cara **- 2.** [expression] semblante *m*, cara *f*; **to make** OR **pull a** ~ hacer muecas **- 3.** [person] cara *f* **- 4.** [of cliff, mountain, coin] cara *f*; [of building] fachada *f* **- 5.** [of clock, watch] esfera *f* **- 6.** [appearance, nature] aspecto *m* **- 7.** [surface] superficie *f*; **on the** ~ **of it** a primera vista. ◇ *vt* **- 1.** [point towards] mirar a **- 2.** [confront, accept, deal with] hacer frente a, enfrentarse a; **let's** ~ **it** no nos engañemos **- 3.** *inf* [cope with] aguantar, soportar. ◇ *vi*: **to** ~ **forwards/south** mirar hacia delante/al sur.

➤ **face down** *adv* boca abajo.

➤ **face up** *adv* boca arriba.

➤ **in the face of** *prep* [in spite of] ante.

➤ **face up to** *vt fus* hacer frente a, enfrentarse a.

facecloth ['feɪsklɒθ] *n UK* toallita *f* (*para lavarse*).

face cream *n* crema *f* facial.

face-lift *n* [on face] lifting *m*, estiramiento *m* de piel; *fig* [on building etc] lavado *m* de cara; **to have a** ~ hacerse un lifting.

face powder *n* (*U*) polvos *mpl* para la cara.

face-saving *adj* para salvar las apariencias.

facet ['fæsɪt] *n* faceta *f*.

facetious [fə'siːʃəs] *adj* guasón(ona).

face value *n* [of coin, stamp] valor *m* nominal; **to take sthg at** ~ tomarse algo literalmente.

facility [fə'sɪlətɪ] (*pl* -**ies**) *n* [feature] prestación *f*.

➤ **facilities** *npl* [amenities] instalaciones *fpl*; [services] servicios *mpl*.

facing ['feɪsɪŋ] *adj* opuesto(ta).

facsimile [fæk'sɪmɪlɪ] *n* facsímil *m*.

fact [fækt] *n* **- 1.** [piece of information] dato *m*; [established truth] hecho *m*; **to know sthg for a** ~ saber algo a ciencia cierta **- 2.** (*U*) [truth] realidad *f*.

➤ **in fact** *conj* & *adv* de hecho, en realidad.

fact of life *n*: **it's a** ~ es un hecho ineludible.

➤ **facts of life** *npl euphemism*: **to tell sb (about) the facts of life** contar a alguien cómo nacen los niños.

factor ['fæktə'] *n* factor *m*.

factory ['fæktərɪ] (*pl* -**ies**) *n* fábrica *f*.

fact sheet *n UK* hoja *f* informativa.

factual ['fæktʃʊəl] *adj* basado(da) en hechos reales.

faculty ['fækltɪ] (*pl* -**ies**) *n* **- 1.** [gen] facultad *f* **- 2.** *US* [in college]: **the** ~ el profesorado.

fad [fæd] *n* [of society] moda *f* pasajera; [of person] capricho *m*.

fade [feɪd] ◇ *vt* descolorar, desteñir. ◇ *vi* **- 1.** [jeans, curtains, paint] descolorarse, desteñirse; [flower] marchitarse **- 2.** [light, sound, smile] irse apagando **- 3.** [memory, feeling, interest] desvanecerse.

faeces *UK*, **feces** *US* ['fiːsiːz] *npl* heces *fpl*.

fag [fæg] *n inf* **- 1.** *UK* [cigarette] pitillo *m* **- 2.** *US pej* [homosexual] marica *m*, maricón *m*, joto *m Méx*.

Fahrenheit ['færənhaɪt] *adj* Fahrenheit (*inv*).

fail [feɪl] ◇ *vt* **- 1.** [exam, test, candidate] suspender **- 2.** [not succeed]: **to** ~ **to do sthg** no lograr hacer algo **- 3.** [neglect]: **to** ~ **to do sthg** no hacer algo **- 4.** [let down] fallar. ◇ *vi* **- 1.** [not succeed] fracasar; **if all else** ~**s** en último extremo **- 2.** [not pass exam] suspender **- 3.** [stop functioning] fallar **- 4.** [weaken] debilitarse.

failing ['feɪlɪŋ] ◇ *n* [weakness] fallo *m*. ◇ *prep* a falta de; ~ **that** en su defecto.

failure ['feɪljə'] *n* **- 1.** [lack of success, unsuccessful thing] fracaso *m* **- 2.** [person] fracasado *m*, -da *f* **- 3.** [in exam] suspenso *m* **- 4.** [act of neglecting]: **her** ~ **to do it** el que no lo hiciera **- 5.** [breakdown, malfunction] avería *f*, fallo *m*.

faint [feɪnt] ◇ *adj* **- 1.** [weak, vague] débil, tenue; [outline] impreciso(sa); [memory, longing] vago(ga); [trace, hint, smell] leve **- 2.** [chance] reducido(da), remoto(ta)

- 3. [dizzy] mareado(da). ◇ *vi* desmayarse.

fair [feə^r] ◇ *adj* **-1.** [just] justo(ta); **it's not ~!** ¡no hay derecho! **- 2.** [quite large] considerable **- 3.** [quite good] bastante bueno(-na); '**~**' SCH 'regular' **- 4.** [hair] rubio(bia) **- 5.** [skin, complexion] claro(ra) **- 6.** [weather] bueno(na) **- 7.** *literary* [beautiful] hermoso(sa). ◇ *n* **-1.** *UK* [funfair] feria *f* **- 2.** [trade fair] feria *f*. ◇ *adv* [fairly] limpio.
◆ **fair enough** *adv UK inf* vale.

fair-haired [-'heəd] *adj* rubio(bia).

fairly ['feəlɪ] *adv* **- 1.** [moderately] bastante **- 2.** [justly] justamente, equitativamente.

fairness ['feənɪs] *n* [justness] justicia *f*.

fair play *n* juego *m* limpio.

fair trade *n* comercio *m* justo.

fairy ['feərɪ] (*pl* -ies) *n* hada *f*.

fairy story, fairy tale *n* cuento *m* de hadas.

faith [feɪθ] *n* fe *f*.

faithful ['feɪθfʊl] ◇ *adj* fiel. ◇ *npl* RELIG : **the ~** los fieles.

faithfully ['feɪθfʊlɪ] *adv* fielmente; **Yours ~** *UK* [in letter] le saluda atentamente.

fake [feɪk] ◇ *adj* falso(sa). ◇ *n* **-1.** [object, painting] falsificación *f* **- 2.** [person] impostor *m*, -ra *f*. ◇ *vt* **-1.** [results, signature] falsificar **- 2.** [illness, emotions] fingir. ◇ *vi* [pretend] fingir.

falcon ['fɔːlkən] *n* halcón *m*.

Falkland Islands ['fɔːklənd-], **Falklands** ['fɔːkləndz] *npl*: **the ~** las (Islas) Malvinas.

fall [fɔːl] (*pt* fell, *pp* fallen) ◇ *vi* **-1.** [gen] caer; **he fell off the chair** se cayó de la silla; **she fell backwards** se cayó hacia atrás; **to ~ to bits** OR **pieces** hacerse pedazos; **to ~ flat** *fig* no causar el efecto deseado **- 2.** [decrease] bajar, disminuir **- 3.** [become]: **to ~ asleep** dormirse; **to ~ ill** ponerse enfermo(ma); **to ~ in love** enamorarse, encamotarse *Andes, CAm.* ◇ *n* **-1.** [gen] caída *f* **- 2.** METEOR: **a ~ of snow** una nevada **- 3.** [MIL - of city] caída *f* **- 4.** [decrease]: **~ (in)** descenso *m* (de) **- 5.** *US* [autumn] otoño *m*.
◆ **falls** *npl* cataratas *fpl*.
◆ **fall apart** *vi* [book, chair] romperse; *fig* [country, person] desmoronarse.
◆ **fall back** *vi* [person, crowd] echarse atrás, retroceder.
◆ **fall back on** *vt fus* [resort to] recurrir a.
◆ **fall behind** *vi* **-1.** [in race] quedarse atrás **- 2.** [with work] retrasarse.
◆ **fall for** *vt fus* **-1.** *inf* [fall in love with] enamorarse de **- 2.** [trick, lie] tragarse.
◆ **fall in** *vi* **-1.** [roof, ceiling] desplomarse, hundirse **- 2.** MIL formar filas.
◆ **fall off** *vi* **-1.** [branch, handle] desprenderse **- 2.** [demand, numbers] disminuir.
◆ **fall out** *vi* **-1.** [hair, tooth]: **his hair is ~ ing out** se le está cayendo el pelo **- 2.** [argue] pelearse, discutir **- 3.** MIL romper filas.

◆ **fall over** *vi* [person, chair etc] caerse.
◆ **fall through** *vi* [plan, deal] fracasar.

fallacy ['fæləsɪ] (*pl* -ies) *n* concepto *m* erróneo, falacia *f*.

fallen ['fɔːln] *pp* ▷ **fall**.

fallible ['fæləbl] *adj* falible.

fallout ['fɔːlaʊt] *n* (*U*) **-1.** [radiation] lluvia *f* radiactiva **- 2.** [consequences] secuelas *fpl*.

fallout shelter *n* refugio *m* atómico.

fallow ['fæləʊ] *adj* en barbecho.

false [fɔːls] *adj* [gen] falso(sa); [eyelashes, nose] postizo(za).

false alarm *n* falsa alarma *f*.

false teeth *npl* dentadura *f* postiza.

falsify ['fɔːlsɪfaɪ] (*pt & pp* -ied) *vt* [facts, accounts] falsificar.

falter ['fɔːltə^r] *vi* vacilar.

fame [feɪm] *n* fama *f*.

familiar [fə'mɪljə^r] *adj* **-1.** [known] familiar, conocido(da) **- 2.** [conversant]: **~ with** familiarizado(da) con **- 3.** *pej* [too informal] que se toma muchas confianzas; [- tone, manner] demasiado amistoso(sa).

familiarity [fə,mɪlɪ'ærətɪ] *n* (*U*) [knowledge]: **~ with** conocimiento *m* de.

familiarize, -ise [fə'mɪljəraɪz] *vt* : **to ~ o.s./ sb with sthg** familiarizarse/familiarizar a alguien con algo.

family ['fæmlɪ] (*pl* -ies) *n* familia *f*.

family credit *n* (*U*) *UK* ≃ prestación *f* OR ayuda *f* familiar.

family doctor *n* médico *m* de cabecera.

family planning *n* planificación *f* familiar.

famine ['fæmɪn] *n* hambruna *f*.

famished ['fæmɪʃt] *adj inf* [very hungry] muerto(ta) de hambre, famélico(ca).

famous ['feɪməs] *adj*: **~ (for)** famoso(sa) (por).

famously ['feɪməslɪ] *adv dated*: **to get on** OR **along ~ (with sb)** llevarse de maravilla (con alguien).

fan [fæn] (*pt & pp* -ned, *cont* -ning) ◇ *n* **-1.** [of paper, silk] abanico *m* **- 2.** [electric or mechanical] ventilador *m* **- 3.** [of musician, artist, etc] fan *m* OR *f*, admirador *m*, -ra *f*; [of music, art, etc] aficionado *m*, -da *f*; FTBL hincha *m* OR *f*. ◇ *vt* **-1.** [cool] abanicar **- 2.** [stimulate - fire, feelings] avivar.
◆ **fan out** *vi* desplegarse en abanico.

fanatic [fə'nætɪk] *n* fanático *m*, -ca *f*.

fan belt *n* correa *f* del ventilador.

fanciful ['fænsɪfʊl] *adj* [odd] rocambolesco(ca).

fancy ['fænsɪ] (*compar* -ier, *superl* -iest, *pl* -ies, *pt & pp* -ied) ◇ *vt* **-1.** *inf* [feel like]: **I ~ a cup of tea/going to the cinema** me apetece una taza de té/ir al cine **- 2.** *inf* [desire]: **do you ~ her?** ¿te gusta? **- 3.** [imagine]: **~ that!** ¡imagínate!, ¡mira por dónde! **- 4.** *dated* [think] creer. ◇ *n* [desire, liking] capricho *m*; **to take a ~ to** encapricharse con. <> *adj* **-1.** [elaborate] elaborado(da) **-2.** [expensive] de lujo, caro(ra); [prices] exorbitante.

fancy dress *n (U)* disfraz *m*.

fancy-dress party *n* fiesta *f* de disfraces.

fanfare ['fænfeə'] *n* fanfarria *f*.

fang [fæŋ] *n* colmillo *m*.

fan heater *n* convector *m*, estufa *f* de aire.

fanny ['fænɪ] *n US inf* [buttocks] culo *m*.

fantasize, -ise ['fæntəsaɪz] *vi* fantasear; **to ~ about** sthg/**about doing** sthg soñar con algo/con hacer algo.

fantastic [fæn'tæstɪk] *adj* [gen] fantástico(-ca), chévere *Andes, Carib.*

fantasy ['fæntəsɪ] (*pl* -**ies**) *n* fantasía *f*.

fantasy football *n (U)* ≃ la liga fantástica®.

fao (*abbr of* **for the attention of**) a/a.

far [fɑː'] (*compar* **farther** OR **further**, *superl* **farthest** OR **furthest**) <> *adv* **-1.** [in distance, time] lejos; **is it ~?** ¿está lejos?; **how ~ is it?** ¿a qué distancia está?; **how ~ is it to Prague?** ¿cuánto hay de aquí a Praga?; **~ away** OR **off** [a long way away, a long time away] lejos; **so ~** por ahora, hasta ahora; **~ and wide** por todas partes; **as ~ as** hasta **-2.** [in degree or extent]: **~ more/better/stronger** mucho más/mejor/más fuerte; **how ~ have you got?** ¿hasta dónde has llegado?; **as ~ as I know** que yo sepa; **as ~ as I'm concerned** por OR en lo que a mí respecta; **as ~ as possible** en (la medida de) lo posible; **~ and away, by ~** con mucho; **~ from it** en absoluto, todo lo contrario; **so ~** [until now] hasta el momento; [to a certain extent] hasta un cierto punto. <> *adj* [extreme] extremo(ma).

faraway ['fɑːrəweɪ] *adj* **-1.** [land etc] lejano(-na) **-2.** [look, expression] ausente.

farce [fɑːs] *n lit & fig* farsa *f*.

farcical ['fɑːsɪkl] *adj* absurdo(da), grotesco(ca).

fare [feə'] *n* **-1.** [payment] (precio *m* del) billete *m*; [in taxi] tarifa *f*; [passenger] cliente *m* OR *f (de taxi)* **-2.** *(U) fml* [food] comida *f*.

Far East *n*: **the ~** el Extremo Oriente.

farewell [,feə'wel] <> *n* despedida *f*. <> *excl literary* ¡vaya con Dios!

farm [fɑːm] <> *n* [smaller] granja *f*, chacra *f Amér*; [larger] hacienda *f*. <> *vt* [land] cultivar; [livestock] criar.

farmer ['fɑːmə'] *n* [on smaller farm] granjero *m*, -ra *f*, chacarero *m*, -ra *f Amér*; [on larger farm] agricultor *m*, -ra *f*.

farmer's market *n mercado en donde se venden verduras y frutas de cosecha local y normalmente orgánicas.*

farmhand ['fɑːmhænd] *n* peón *m*, labriego *m*, -ga *f*.

farmhouse ['fɑːmhaʊs, *pl* -haʊzɪz] *n* granja *f*, caserío *m*.

farming ['fɑːmɪŋ] *n (U)* **-1.** AGR & IND agricultura *f* **-2.** [act - of crops] cultivo *m*; [- of animals] cría *f*, crianza *f*.

farm labourer = **farmhand**.

farmland ['fɑːmlænd] *n (U)* tierras *fpl* de labranza.

farmstead ['fɑːmsted] *n US* granja *f*.

farm worker = **farmhand**.

farmyard ['fɑːmjɑːd] *n* corral *m*.

far-reaching [-'riːtʃɪŋ] *adj* trascendental, de amplio alcance.

farsighted [,fɑː'saɪtɪd] *adj* **-1.** [gen] con visión de futuro **-2.** *US* [long-sighted] présbita.

fart [fɑːt] *v inf* <> *n* [flatulence] pedo *m*. <> *vi* tirarse un pedo.

farther ['fɑːðə'] *compar* ⊳ **far**.

farthest ['fɑːðəst] *superl* ⊳ **far**.

fascinate ['fæsɪneɪt] *vt* fascinar.

fascinating ['fæsɪneɪtɪŋ] *adj* fascinante.

fascination [,fæsɪ'neɪʃn] *n* fascinación *f*.

fascism ['fæʃɪzm] *n* fascismo *m*.

fashion ['fæʃn] <> *n* **-1.** [clothing, style, vogue] moda *f*; **in/out of ~** de/pasado de moda **-2.** [manner] manera *f*. <> *vt fml* **-1.** [make] elaborar **-2.** *fig* [mould] forjar.

fashionable ['fæʃnəbl] *adj* de moda.

fashion show *n* pase *m* OR desfile *m* de modelos.

fast [fɑːst] <> *adj* **-1.** [rapid] rápido(da) **-2.** [clock, watch]: **her watch is two minutes ~** su reloj lleva dos minutos de adelanto **-3.** [dye, colour] que no destiñe. <> *adv* **-1.** [rapidly] rápido, rápidamente; **how ~ were they going?** ¿a qué velocidad conducían? **-2.** [firmly]: **stuck ~** bien pegado(-da); **~ asleep** profundamente dormido. <> *n* ayuno *m*. <> *vi* ayunar.

fasten ['fɑːsn] *vt* **-1.** [gen] sujetar; [clothes, belt] abrochar; **he ~ed his coat** se abrochó el abrigo **-2.** [attach]: **to ~** sthg **to** sthg fijar algo a algo.

fastener ['fɑːsnə'] *n* cierre *m*; [zip] cremallera *f*.

fastening ['fɑːsnɪŋ] *n* [of door, window] cerrojo *m*, pestillo *m*.

fast food *n (U)* comida *f* rápida.

fastidious [fə'stɪdɪəs] *adj* [fussy] quisquilloso(sa).

fat [fæt] (*compar* -**ter**, *superl* -**test**) <> *adj* **-1.** [gen] gordo(da); **to get ~** engordar **-2.** [meat] con mucha grasa **-3.** [book, package] grueso(sa). <> *n* **-1.** [gen] grasa *f* **-2.** [for cooking] manteca *f*.

fatal ['feɪtl] *adj* **-1.** [mortal] mortal **-2.** [serious] fatal, funesto(ta).

fatality [fə'tælətɪ] (*pl* -**ies**) *n* [accident victim] víctima *f* mortal.

fate [feɪt] *n* **-1.** [destiny] destino *m*; **to tempt ~** tentar a la suerte **-2.** [result, end] final *m*, suerte *f*.

fateful ['feɪtfʊl] *adj* fatídico(ca).

fat-free *adj* sin grasas.

father ['fɑ:ðə] *n lit & fig* padre *m*.

Father Christmas *n UK* Papá *m* Noel.

father-in-law (*pl* **father-in-laws** OR **fathers-in-law**) *n* suegro *m*.

fatherly ['fɑ:ðəlɪ] *adj* paternal.

fathom ['fæðəm] ◇ *n* braza *f*. ◇ *vt*: **to ~ sthg/sb (out)** llegar a comprender algo/a alguien.

fatigue [fə'ti:g] *n* fatiga *f*.

fatten ['fætn] *vt* engordar.

fattening ['fætnɪŋ] *adj* que engorda.

fatty ['fætɪ] (*compar* -ier, *superl* -iest, *pl* -ies) ◇ *adj* graso(sa). ◇ *n inf pej* gordinflón *m*, -ona *f*.

fatuous ['fætjʊəs] *adj* necio(cia).

faucet ['fɔ:sɪt] *n US* grifo *m*, llave *f Amér*, canilla *f RP*, paja *f CAm*, caño *m Perú*.

fault [fɔ:lt] ◇ *n* **-1.** [responsibility] culpa *f*; **it's my ~** es culpa mía; **to be at ~** tener la culpa **-2.** [mistake, imperfection] defecto *m*; **to find ~ with** encontrar defectos a **-3.** GEOL falla *f* **-4.** [in tennis] falta *f*. ◇ *vt*: **to ~ sb (on sthg)** criticar a alguien (en algo).

faultless ['fɔ:ltlɪs] *adj* impecable.

faulty ['fɔ:ltɪ] (*compar* -ier, *superl* -iest) *adj* [machine, system] defectuoso(sa); [reasoning, logic] imperfecto(ta).

fauna ['fɔ:nə] *n* fauna *f*.

favour *UK*, **favor** *US* ['feɪvə] ◇ *n* [gen] favor *m*; **in sb's ~** a favor de alguien; **to be in/out of ~ (with)** ser/dejar de ser popular (con); **to do sb a ~** hacerle un favor a alguien. ◇ *vt* **-1.** [prefer] decantarse por, preferir **-2.** [treat better, help] favorecer.
 ◆ **in favour** *adv* [in agreement] a favor.
 ◆ **in favour of** *prep* **-1.** [in preference to] en favor de **-2.** [in agreement with]: **to be in ~ of sthg/of doing sthg** estar a favor de algo/de hacer algo.

favourable *UK*, **favorable** *US* ['feɪvrəbl] *adj* [positive] favorable.

favourite *UK*, **favorite** *US* ['feɪvrɪt] ◇ *adj* favorito(ta). ◇ *n* favorito *m*, -ta *f*.

favouritism *UK*, **favoritism** *US* ['feɪvrɪtɪzm] *n* favoritismo *m*.

fawn [fɔ:n] ◇ *adj* beige (*inv*). ◇ *n* [animal] cervato *m*, cervatillo *m*. ◇ *vi*: **to ~ on sb** adular a alguien.

fax [fæks] ◇ *n* fax *m*. ◇ *vt* **-1.** [send fax to] mandar un fax a **-2.** [send by fax] enviar por fax.

fax machine *n* fax *m*.

FBI (*abbr of* **Federal Bureau of Investigation**) *n* FBI *m*.

fear [fɪə] ◇ *n* **-1.** [gen] miedo *m*, temor *m*; **for ~ of** por miedo a **-2.** [risk] peligro *m*.
 ◇ *vt* **-1.** [be afraid of] temer **-2.** [anticipate] temerse; **to ~ (that)** ... temerse que ...

fearful ['fɪəfʊl] *adj* **-1.** *fml* [frightened] temeroso(sa) **-2.** [frightening] terrible, pavoroso(sa).

fearless ['fɪəlɪs] *adj* intrépido(da).

feasible ['fi:zəbl] *adj* factible, viable.

feast [fi:st] ◇ *n* [meal] banquete *m*, festín *m*. ◇ *vi*: **to ~ on** OR **off sthg** darse un banquete a base de algo.

feat [fi:t] *n* hazaña *f*.

feather ['feðə] *n* pluma *f*.

feature ['fi:tʃə] ◇ *n* **-1.** [characteristic] característica *f* **-2.** [of face] rasgo *m* **-3.** GEOGR accidente *m* geográfico **-4.** [article] artículo *m* de fondo **-5.** RADIO & TV [programme] programa *m* especial **-6.** CINEMA = **feature film**. ◇ *vt* [subj: film] tener como protagonista a; [subj: exhibition] tener como atracción principal a. ◇ *vi*: **to ~ (in)** aparecer OR figurar (en).

feature film *n* largometraje *m*.

February ['februərɪ] *n* febrero *m*; *see also* **September**.

feces *US* = **faeces**.

fed [fed] *pt & pp* ➤ **feed**.

federal ['fedrəl] *adj* federal.

federation [ˌfedə'reɪʃn] *n* federación *f*.

fed up *adj*: **~ (with)** harto(ta) (de).

fee [fi:] *n* [to lawyer, doctor etc] honorarios *mpl*; **membership ~** cuota *f* de socio; **entrance ~** entrada *f*; **school ~s** (precio *m* de) matrícula *f*.

feeble ['fi:bl] *adj* **-1.** [weak] débil **-2.** [poor, silly] pobre, flojo(ja).

feed [fi:d] (*pt & pp* **fed**) ◇ *vt* **-1.** [gen] alimentar; [animal] dar de comer a **-2.** [put, insert]: **to ~ sthg into sthg** introducir algo en algo. ◇ *vi* comer. ◇ *n* **-1.** [of baby] toma *f* **-2.** [animal food] pienso *m*.

feedback ['fi:dbæk] *n* (*U*) **-1.** [reaction] reacciones *fpl* **-2.** COMPUT & ELEC realimentación *f*; [on guitar etc] feedback *m*.

feeding bottle ['fi:dɪŋ-] *n UK* biberón *m*.

feel [fi:l] (*pt & pp* **felt**) ◇ *vt* **-1.** [touch] tocar **-2.** [sense, notice, experience] sentir; **I felt myself blushing** noté que me ponía colorado **-3.** [believe] creer; **to ~ (that)** creer OR pensar que **-4.** *phr*: **not to ~ o.s.** no encontrarse bien. ◇ *vi* **-1.** [have sensation]: **to ~ hot/cold/sleepy** tener calor/frío/sueño; **how do you ~?** ¿cómo te encuentras? **-2.** [have emotion]: **to ~ safe/happy** sentirse seguro/feliz **-3.** [seem] parecer (al tacto) **-4.** [by touch]: **to ~ for sthg** buscar algo a tientas **-5.** [be in mood]: **do you ~ like a drink/eating out?** ¿te apetece beber algo/comer fuera?, ¿te provoca beber algo/comer fuera? *Andes, Méx*. ◇ *n* **-1.** [sensation, touch] tacto *m*, sensación *f* - **2.** [atmosphere] atmósfera *f*.

feeler ['fiːlə^r] *n* antena *f*.

feelgood movie ['fiːlgʊd-] *n* película *f* que levanta la moral.

feeling ['fiːlɪŋ] *n* - **1.** [emotion] sentimiento *m* - **2.** [sensation] sensación *f* - **3.** [intuition] presentimiento *m*; **I have a** OR **get the** ~ **(that)** ... me da la sensación de que ... - **4.** [opinion] opinión *f* - **5.** [understanding] apreciación *f*, entendimiento *m*.
  ◆ **feelings** *npl* sentimientos *mpl*.

feet [fiːt] *pl* ⊳ **foot**.

feign [feɪn] *vt fml* fingir, aparentar.

fell [fel] ◇ *pt* ⊳ **fall**. ◇ *vt* [tree] talar.
  ◆ **fells** *npl* GEOGR monte *m*.

fellow ['feləʊ] ◇ *adj*: ~ **students/prison-ers** compañeros de clase/celda; ~ **citizens** conciudadanos. ◇ *n* - **1.** *dated* [man] tipo *m* - **2.** [comrade, peer] camarada *m* OR *f*, compañero *m*, -ra *f* - **3.** [of a society] miembro *m* - **4.** [of college] miembro *m* del claustro de profesores.

fellowship ['feləʊʃɪp] *n* - **1.** [comradeship] camaradería *f* - **2.** [society] asociación *f* - **3.** [grant] beca *f* de investigación.

felony ['felənɪ] (*pl* **-ies**) *n US* JUR crimen *m*, delito *m* grave.

felt [felt] ◇ *pt* & *pp* ⊳ **feel**. ◇ *n (U)* fieltro *m*.

felt-tip pen [felttɪp-] *n* rotulador *m*.

female ['fiːmeɪl] ◇ *adj* [animal, plant, connector] hembra; [figure, sex] femenino(na). ◇ *n* - **1.** [female animal] hembra *f* - **2.** [woman] mujer *f*.

feminine ['femɪnɪn] ◇ *adj* femenino(na). ◇ *n* GRAMM femenino *m*.

feminist ['femɪnɪst] *n* feminista *m* OR *f*.

fence [fens] ◇ *n* valla *f*. ◇ *vt* [surround] cercar.

fencing ['fensɪŋ] *n* SPORT esgrima *f*.

fend [fend] *vi*: **to** ~ **for o.s.** valerse por sí mismo.
  ◆ **fend off** *vt sep* [blows] defenderse de, desviar; [questions, reporters] eludir.

fender ['fendə^r] *n* - **1.** [round fireplace] guardafuego *m* - **2.** [on boat] defensa *f* - **3.** *US* [on car] guardabarros *m inv*.

ferment [*n* 'fɜːment, *vb* fə'ment] ◇ *n* [unrest] agitación *f*. ◇ *vi* fermentar.

fern [fɜːn] *n* helecho *m*.

ferocious [fə'rəʊʃəs] *adj* feroz.

ferret ['ferɪt] *n* hurón *m*.
  ◆ **ferret about, ferret around** *vi inf* rebuscar.

ferris wheel ['ferɪs-] *n esp US* noria *f*.

ferry ['ferɪ] ◇ *n* [large, for cars] transbordador *m*, ferry *m*; [small] barca *f*. ◇ *vt* llevar, transportar.

ferryboat ['ferɪbəʊt] = **ferry**.

fertile ['fɜːtaɪl] *adj* fértil.

fertilizer ['fɜːtɪlaɪzə^r] *n* abono *m*.

fervent ['fɜːvənt] *adj* ferviente.

fester ['festə^r] *vi lit* & *fig* enconarse.

festival ['festəvl] *n* - **1.** [event, celebration] festival *m* - **2.** [holiday] día *m* festivo.

festive ['festɪv] *adj* festivo(va).

festive season *n*: **the** ~ las Navidades.

festivities [fes'tɪvətɪz] *npl* festividades *fpl*.

festoon [fe'stuːn] *vt* engalanar.

fetch [fetʃ] *vt* - **1.** [go and get] ir a buscar, traer - **2.** *inf* [raise - money] venderse por, alcanzar.

fetching ['fetʃɪŋ] *adj* atractivo(va).

fete, fête [feɪt] *n* fiesta *f* benéfica.

fetish ['fetɪʃ] *n* - **1.** [object of sexual obsession] fetiche *m* - **2.** [mania] obsesión *f*, manía *f*.

fetus ['fiːtəs] *US* = **foetus**.

feud [fjuːd] ◇ *n* enfrentamiento *m* duradero. ◇ *vi* pelearse.

feudal ['fjuːdl] *adj* feudal.

fever ['fiːvə^r] *n lit* & *fig* fiebre *f*; **to have a** ~ tener fiebre.

feverish ['fiːvərɪʃ] *adj lit* & *fig* febril.

few [fjuː] ◇ *adj* pocos(cas); **the next** ~ **weeks** las próximas semanas; **a** ~ algunos(nas); **a** ~ **more potatoes** algunas patatas más; **quite a** ~, **a good** ~ bastantes; ~ **and far between** escasos, contados. ◇ *pron* pocos *mpl*, -cas *fpl*; **a** ~ **(of them)** algunos *mpl*, -nas *fpl*; **quite a** ~ bastantes *mpl* OR *fpl*.

fewer ['fjuːə^r] ◇ *adj* menos. ◇ *pron* menos.

fewest ['fjuːəst] *adj* menos.

fiancé [fɪ'ɒnseɪ] *n* prometido *m*.

fiancée [fɪ'ɒnseɪ] *n* prometida *f*.

fiasco [fɪ'æskəʊ] (*UK pl* **-s**, *US pl* **-es**) *n* fiasco *m*.

fib [fɪb] *n inf* bola *f*, trola *f*.

fibre *UK*, **fiber** *US* ['faɪbə^r] *n* fibra *f*.

fibreglass *UK*, **fiberglass** *US* ['faɪbəglɑːs] *n (U)* fibra *f* de vidrio.

fickle ['fɪkl] *adj* voluble.

fiction ['fɪkʃn] *n* - **1.** [stories] (literatura *f* de) ficción *f* - **2.** [fabrication] ficción *f*.

fictional ['fɪkʃənl] *adj* - **1.** [literary] novelesco(ca) - **2.** [invented] ficticio(cia).

fictitious [fɪk'tɪʃəs] *adj* [false] ficticio(cia).

fiddle ['fɪdl] ◇ *n* - **1.** [violin] violín *m* - **2.** *UK inf* [fraud] timo *m*. ◇ *vi* [play around]: **to** ~ **(with sthg)** juguetear (con algo).

fiddly ['fɪdlɪ] (*compar* **-ier**, *superl* **-iest**) *adj UK* [job] delicado(da); [gadget] intrincado(da).

fidget ['fɪdʒɪt] *vi* no estarse quieto(ta).

field [fiːld] *n* [gen & COMPUT] campo *m*; **in the** ~ sobre el terreno.

final

field day *n*: to have a ~ disfrutar de lo lindo.

field glasses *npl* prismáticos *mpl*, gemelos *mpl*.

field hockey *n US* hockey *m* sobre hierba.

field marshal *n* mariscal *m* de campo.

field trip *n* excursión *f* para hacer trabajo de campo.

fieldwork ['fi:ldwɜːk] *n (U)* trabajo *m* de campo.

fiend [fi:nd] *n* [cruel person] malvado *m*, -da *f*.

fiendish ['fi:ndɪʃ] *adj* - **1.** [evil] malévolo(la), diabólico(ca) - **2.** *inf* [very difficult] endiablado(da).

fierce [fɪəs] *adj* [gen] feroz; [temper] endiablado(da); [loyalty] ferviente; [heat] asfixiante.

fiery ['faɪərɪ] (*compar* -**ier**, *superl* -**iest**) *adj* - **1.** [burning] ardiente - **2.** [volatile - temper] endiablado(da); [- speech] encendido(da), fogoso(sa); [- person] apasionado(da).

fifteen [fɪf'ti:n] *num* quince; *see also* **six**.

fifth [fɪfθ] *num* quinto(ta); *see also* **sixth**.

fifty ['fɪftɪ] *num* cincuenta; *see also* **sixty**.

fifty-fifty ◇ *adj* al cincuenta por ciento; **a ~ chance** unas posibilidades del cincuenta por ciento. ◇ *adv*: **to go** ~ ir a medias.

fig [fɪg] *n* higo *m*.

fight [faɪt] (*pt* & *pp* **fought**) ◇ *n* [physical, verbal] pelea *f*; *fig* [struggle] lucha *f*; **to have a ~ (with)** pelearse (con); **to put up a ~** oponer resistencia. ◇ *vt* [gen] luchar contra; [in punch-up] pelearse con; [battle, campaign] librar; [war] luchar en. ◇ *vi* - **1.** [in punch-up] pelearse; [in war] luchar - **2.** *fig* [battle, struggle]: **to ~ (for/against)** luchar (por/contra) - **3.** [argue]: **to ~ (about** OR **over)** pelearse OR discutir (por).

 ► **fight back** ◇ *vt fus* [tears, feelings] reprimir, contener. ◇ *vi* defenderse.

fighter ['faɪtər] *n* - **1.** [plane] caza *m* - **2.** [soldier] combatiente *m* OR *f* - **3.** [boxer] púgil *m* OR *f* - **4.** [combative person] luchador *m*, -ra *f*.

fighting ['faɪtɪŋ] *n (U)* [on streets, terraces] peleas *fpl*; [in war] combates *mpl*.

figment ['fɪgmənt] *n*: **a ~ of sb's imagination** un producto de la imaginación de alguien.

figurative ['fɪgərətɪv] *adj* figurado(da).

figure [*UK* 'fɪgər, *US* 'fɪgjər] ◇ *n* - **1.** [statistic, number] cifra *f*; **to be in single/double ~s** no sobrepasar/sobrepasar la decena - **2.** [shape of person, personality] figura *f* - **3.** [diagram] figura *f*. ◇ *vt esp US* [suppose] figurarse, suponer. ◇ *vi* [feature] figurar.

 ► **figure out** *vt sep* [reason, motives] figurarse; [problem etc] resolver; [amount, quantity] calcular.

figurehead ['fɪgəhed] *n* [leader without real power] testaferro *m*.

figure of speech *n* forma *f* de hablar.

Fiji ['fi:dʒi:] *n* Fiji.

file [faɪl] ◇ *n* - **1.** [folder] carpeta *f* - **2.** [report] expediente *m*, dossier *m*; **on ~**, **on the ~s** archivado - **3.** COMPUT archivo *m* - **4.** [tool] lima *f* - **5.** [line]: **in single ~** en fila india. ◇ *vt* - **1.** [put in file] archivar - **2.** JUR presentar - **3.** [shape, smooth] limar. ◇ *vi* [walk in single file] ir en fila.

filet *US* = **fillet**.

filing cabinet ['faɪlɪŋ-] *n* archivador *m*.

Filipino [,fɪlɪ'pi:nəʊ] (*pl* -**s**) ◇ *adj* filipino(na). ◇ *n* filipino *m*, -na *f*.

fill [fɪl] ◇ *vt* - **1.** [gen]: **to ~ sthg (with)** llenar algo (de) - **2.** [gap, hole, crack] rellenar; [tooth] empastar, calzar *Col* - **3.** [need, vacancy etc] cubrir; [time] ocupar. ◇ *n*: **to eat one's ~** comer hasta hartarse.

 ► **fill in** ◇ *vt sep* - **1.** [complete] rellenar - **2.** [inform]: **to ~ sb in (on)** poner a alguien al corriente (de). ◇ *vi* [substitute]: **to ~ in (for sb)** sustituir (a alguien).

 ► **fill out** *vt sep* [complete] rellenar.

 ► **fill up** ◇ *vt sep* llenar (hasta arriba). ◇ *vi* - **1.** [gen] llenarse - **2.** [buy petrol] repostar.

fillet *UK*, **filet** *US* ['fɪlɪt] ◇ *n* filete *m*. ◇ *vt* cortar en filetes.

fillet steak *n* filete *m* (de carne), bife *m* de lomo *RP*.

filling ['fɪlɪŋ] ◇ *adj* [satisfying] que llena mucho. ◇ *n* - **1.** [in tooth] empaste *m Esp*, calza *f Col*, tapadura *f Chile, Méx*, emplomadura *f RP* - **2.** [in cake, sandwich] relleno *m*.

filling station *n* estación *f* de servicio OR de nafta *RP*, gasolinera *f*, bomba *f Chile, Col, Ecuad, Ven*, grifo *m Perú*.

film [fɪlm] ◇ *n* - **1.** [gen] película *f* - **2.** *(U)* [art of cinema] cine *m*. ◇ *vt* & *vi* filmar, rodar.

film festival *n* festival *m* de cine.

film star *n* estrella *f* de cine.

Filofax® ['faɪləʊfæks] *n* agenda *f* de anillas.

filo pastry ['fi:ləʊ-] *n* hojaldre *m* griego.

filter ['fɪltər] ◇ *n* filtro *m*. ◇ *vt* [purify] filtrar.

filter coffee *n* café *m* de filtro.

filter lane *n UK* carril *m* de giro.

filter-tipped [-'tɪpt] *adj* con filtro.

filth [fɪlθ] *n (U)* - **1.** [dirt] suciedad *f*, porquería *f* - **2.** [obscenity] obscenidades *fpl*.

filthy ['fɪlθɪ] (*compar* -**ier**, *superl* -**iest**) *adj* - **1.** [very dirty] mugriento(ta), sucísimo(ma) - **2.** [obscene] obsceno(na).

fin [fɪn] *n* [on fish] aleta *f*.

final ['faɪnl] ◇ *adj* - **1.** [last] último(ma) - **2.** [at end] final - **3.** [definitive] definitivo(va). ◇ *n* final *f*.

 ► **finals** *npl* UNIV exámenes *mpl* finales.

finale [fɪ'nɑːlɪ] *n* final *m*.

finalize, -ise ['faɪnəlaɪz] *vt* ultimar.

finally ['faɪnəlɪ] *adv* **-1.** [at last] por fin, finalmente **-2.** [lastly] finalmente, por último.

finance [*n* 'faɪnæns, *vb* faɪ'næns] ◇ *n* (*U*) **-1.** [money management] finanzas *fpl* **-2.** [money] fondos *mpl*. ◇ *vt* financiar.
 ◆ **finances** *npl* finanzas *fpl*.

financial [fɪ'nænʃl] *adj* financiero(ra).

find [faɪnd] (*pt & pp* found) ◇ *vt* **-1.** [gen] encontrar **-2.** [realize - fact] darse cuenta de, descubrir **-3.** JUR : **to be found guilty/not guilty (of)** ser declarado(da) culpable/inocente (de). ◇ *n* hallazgo *m*, descubrimiento *m*.
 ◆ **find out** ◇ *vi* **-1.** [become aware] enterarse **-2.** [obtain information] informarse. ◇ *vt fus* [truth] descubrir; [fact] averiguar. ◇ *vt sep* [person] descubrir.

findings ['faɪndɪŋz] *npl* conclusiones *fpl*.

fine [faɪn] ◇ *adj* **-1.** [excellent] excelente **-2.** [perfectly satisfactory]: **it's/that's** ~ está bien; **how are you? -** ~ **thanks** ¿qué tal? - muy bien **-3.** [weather] bueno(na); **it will be** ~ **tomorrow** mañana hará buen día **-4.** [thin, smooth, delicate] fino(na) **-5.** [minute - detail, distinction] sutil; [- adjustment, tuning] milimétrico(ca). ◇ *adv* [well] bien; [very well] muy bien. ◇ *n* multa *f*. ◇ *vt* multar.

fine arts *npl* bellas artes *fpl*.

finery ['faɪnərɪ] *n* (*U*) galas *fpl*.

finesse [fɪ'nes] *n* finura *f*, delicadeza *f*.

fine-tune ['faɪntjuːn] *vt* poner a punto.

finger ['fɪŋgər] ◇ *n* dedo *m*. ◇ *vt* acariciar con los dedos.

fingernail ['fɪŋgəneɪl] *n* uña *f (de las manos)*.

fingerprint ['fɪŋgəprɪnt] *n* huella *f* dactilar OR digital.

fingertip ['fɪŋgətɪp] *n* punta *f* del dedo.

finicky ['fɪnɪkɪ] *adj pej* [person] melindroso(sa); [task] delicado(da).

finish ['fɪnɪʃ] ◇ *n* **-1.** [end] final *m*; [in race] meta *f* **-2.** [surface texture] acabado *m*. ◇ *vt*: **to** ~ **sthg/doing sthg** acabar algo/ de hacer algo, terminar algo/de hacer algo. ◇ *vi* terminar.
 ◆ **finish off** *vt sep* [food, task] acabar OR terminar del todo.
 ◆ **finish up** *vi* acabar, terminar.

finishing line ['fɪnɪʃɪŋ-] *n* línea *f* de meta.

finishing school ['fɪnɪʃɪŋ-] *n colegio privado donde se prepara a las alumnas de clase alta para entrar en sociedad.*

finite ['faɪnaɪt] *adj* **-1.** [limited] finito(ta) **-2.** GRAMM conjugado(da).

Finland ['fɪnlənd] *n* Finlandia *f*.

Finn [fɪn] *n* [person] finlandés *m*, -esa *f*.

Finnish ['fɪnɪʃ] ◇ *adj* finlandés(esa). ◇ *n* [language] finlandés *m*.

fir [fɜːʳ] *n* abeto *m*.

fire ['faɪəʳ] ◇ *n* **-1.** [gen] fuego *m*; **on** ~ en llamas; **to catch** ~ prender; **to open** ~ **(on sb)** abrir fuego (contra alguien); **to set** ~ **to** prender fuego a **-2.** [blaze] incendio *m* **-3.** *UK* [heater]: **(electric/gas)** ~ estufa *f* (eléctrica/de gas). ◇ *vt* **-1.** [shoot] disparar; **to** ~ **a shot** disparar **-2.** *esp US* [dismiss] despedir. ◇ *vi*: **to** ~ **(on** OR **at)** disparar (contra).

fire alarm *n* alarma *f* antiincendios.

firearm ['faɪərɑːm] *n* arma *f* de fuego.

firebomb ['faɪəbɒm] *n* bomba *f* incendiaria.

fire brigade *UK*, **fire department** *US n* cuerpo *m* de bomberos.

fire door *n* puerta *f* cortafuegos.

fire engine *n* coche *m* de bomberos.

fire escape *n* escalera *f* de incendios.

fire exit *n* salida *f* de incendios.

fire extinguisher *n* extintor *m* (de incendios).

fireguard ['faɪəgɑːd] *n* pantalla *f* (de chimenea).

firelighter ['faɪəlaɪtəʳ] *n* pastilla *f* para encender el fuego.

fireman ['faɪəmən] (*pl* -men [-mən]) *n* bombero *m*.

fireplace ['faɪəpleɪs] *n* chimenea *f*.

fireproof ['faɪəpruːf] *adj* incombustible, ininflamable.

fireside ['faɪəsaɪd] *n*: **by the** ~ al calor de la chimenea.

fire station *n* parque *m* de bomberos.

firewood ['faɪəwʊd] *n* leña *f*.

firework ['faɪəwɜːk] *n* fuego *m* de artificio.
 ◆ **fireworks** *npl* fuegos *mpl* artificiales.

firing ['faɪərɪŋ] *n* (*U*) MIL disparos *mpl*.

firing squad *n* pelotón *m* de ejecución OR fusilamiento.

firm [fɜːm] ◇ *adj* **-1.** [gen] firme; **to stand** ~ mantenerse firme **-2.** FIN [steady] estable. ◇ *n* empresa *f*.

first [fɜːst] ◇ *adj* primero(ra); **the** ~ **day** el primer día; **for the** ~ **time** por primera vez; ~ **thing (in the morning)** a primera hora (de la mañana). ◇ *adv* **-1.** [gen] primero; **to come** ~ quedar primero; ~ **of all** en primer lugar **-2.** [for the first time] por primera vez. ◇ *n* **-1.** [person] primero *m*, -ra *f* **-2.** [unprecedented event] acontecimiento *m* sin precedentes **-3.** *UK* UNIV ≃ sobresaliente *m*.
 ◆ **at first** *adv* al principio.
 ◆ **at first hand** *adv* de primera mano.

first aid *n* (*U*) [treatment] primeros auxilios *mpl*; [technique] socorrismo *m*.

first-aid kit *n* botiquín *m* de primeros auxilios.

first-class ◇ *adj* **-1.** [excellent] de primera,

clase *Amér* - **2.** [letter, ticket] de primera clase. ◇ *adv* [travel] en primera clase.

first floor *n* - **1.** *UK* [above ground level] primer piso *m* - **2.** *US* [at ground level] planta *f* baja.

firsthand [ˌfɜːstˈhænd] ◇ *adj* de primera mano. ◇ *adv* directamente.

first lady *n* primera dama *f*.

firstly [ˈfɜːstlɪ] *adv* en primer lugar.

first name *n* nombre *m* de pila.

first-rate *adj* de primera.

firtree [ˈfɜːtriː] = **fir**.

fish [fɪʃ] (*pl inv*) ◇ *n* - **1.** [animal] pez *m* - **2.** (*U*) [food] pescado *m*. ◇ *vt* pescar en. ◇ *vi* [for fish]: **to ~ (for sthg)** pescar (algo).

fish and chips *npl* pescado *m* frito con patatas fritas.

fish and chip shop *n UK* tienda *f* de pescado frito con patatas fritas.

fishbowl [ˈfɪʃbəʊl] *n* pecera *f*.

fishcake [ˈfɪʃkeɪk] *n* pastelillo *m* de pescado.

fisherman [ˈfɪʃəmən] (*pl* -men [-mən]) *n* pescador *m*.

fish farm *n* piscifactoría *f*.

fish fingers *UK*, **fish sticks** *US npl* palitos *mpl* de pescado.

fishing [ˈfɪʃɪŋ] *n* pesca *f*; **to go ~** ir de pesca.

fishing boat *n* barco *m* pesquero.

fishing line *n* sedal *m*.

fishing net *n* red *f* de pesca.

fishing rod *n* caña *f* de pescar.

fishmonger [ˈfɪʃˌmʌŋgə^r] *n esp UK* pescadero *m*, -ra *f*; **~'s (shop)** pescadería *f*.

fish sticks *US* = **fish fingers**.

fishy [ˈfɪʃɪ] (*compar* -ier, *superl* -iest) *adj* - **1.** [smell, taste] a pescado - **2.** *inf* [suspicious] sospechoso(sa).

fist [fɪst] *n* puño *m*.

fit [fɪt] (*pt & pp* -ted, *cont* -ting) ◇ *adj* - **1.** [suitable]: **~ (for sthg/to do sthg)** apto(ta) (para algo/para hacer algo); **do as you think ~** haz lo que te parezca conveniente - **2.** [healthy] en forma; **to keep ~** mantenerse en forma. ◇ *n* - **1.** [of clothes, shoes etc]: **it's a good ~** le/te *etc* sienta OR va bien - **2.** [bout, seizure] ataque *m*; **he had a ~** *lit & fig* le dio un ataque; **in ~s and starts** a trompicones. ◇ *vt* - **1.** [be correct size for] sentar bien a, ir bien a - **2.** [place]: **to ~ sthg into** encajar algo en - **3.** [provide]: **to ~ sthg with** equipar algo con; **to have an alarm fitted** poner una alarma - **4.** [be suitable for] corresponder a. ◇ *vi* - **1.** [clothes, shoes] estar bien de talla - **2.** [part - when assembling etc]: **this bit ~s in here** esta pieza en encaja aquí - **3.** [have enough room] caber.
  ➤ **fit in** ◇ *vt sep* [accommodate] hacer un hueco a. ◇ *vi* - **1.** [subj: person]: **to ~ in (with)** adaptarse (a) - **2.** [be compatible]: **it doesn't ~ in with our plans** no encaja con nuestros planes.

fitful [ˈfɪtfʊl] *adj* irregular, intermitente.

fitment [ˈfɪtmənt] *n* accesorio *m*.

fitness [ˈfɪtnɪs] *n* (*U*) - **1.** [health] buen estado *m* físico - **2.** [suitability]: **~ (for)** idoneidad *f* (para).

fitted carpet [ˈfɪtəd-] *n* moqueta *f*.

fitted kitchen [ˈfɪtəd-] *n UK* cocina *f* amueblada a medida.

fitter [ˈfɪtə^r] *n* [mechanic] (mecánico *m*) ajustador *m*.

fitting [ˈfɪtɪŋ] ◇ *adj fml* adecuado(da). ◇ *n* - **1.** [part] accesorio *m* - **2.** [for clothing] prueba *f*.
  ➤ **fittings** *npl* accesorios *mpl*.

fitting room *n* probador *m*.

five [faɪv] *num* cinco; *see also* **six**.

fiver [ˈfaɪvə^r] *n UK inf* (billete de) cinco libras.

fix [fɪks] ◇ *vt* - **1.** [attach, decide on] fijar; **to ~ sthg (to)** fijar algo (a) - **2.** [repair] arreglar, refaccionar *Amér* - **3.** *inf* [rig] amañar - **4.** *esp US* [prepare - food, drink] preparar. ◇ *n* - **1.** *inf* [difficult situation]: **to be in a ~** estar en un aprieto - **2.** *drugs sl* dosis *f inv*.
  ➤ **fix up** *vt sep* - **1.** [provide]: **to ~ sb up with** proveer a alguien de - **2.** [arrange] organizar, preparar.

fixation [fɪkˈseɪʃn] *n*: **~ (on** OR **about)** fijación *f* (con).

fixed [fɪkst] *adj* fijo(ja).

fixture [ˈfɪkstʃə^r] *n* - **1.** [furniture] instalación *f* fija - **2.** [permanent feature] rasgo *m* característico - **3.** [sports event] encuentro *m*.

fizz [fɪz] *vi* burbujear.

fizzle [ˈfɪzl] ➤ **fizzle out** *vi* [firework, fire] apagarse; [enthusiasm] disiparse.

fizzy [ˈfɪzɪ] (*compar* -ier, *superl* -iest) *adj* [gen] gaseoso(sa); [water, soft drink] con gas.

flabbergasted [ˈflæbəgɑːstɪd] *adj* pasmado(da).

flabby [ˈflæbɪ] (*compar* -ier, *superl* -iest) *adj* fofo(fa).

flag [flæg] (*pt & pp* -ged, *cont* -ging) ◇ *n* [banner] bandera *f*. ◇ *vi* decaer.
  ➤ **flag down** *vt sep* [taxi] parar; **to ~ sb down** hacer señales a alguien para que se detenga.

flagpole [ˈflægpəʊl] *n* asta *f* (de bandera).

flagrant [ˈfleɪgrənt] *adj* flagrante.

flagstone [ˈflægstəʊn] *n* losa *f*.

flair [fleə^r] *n* - **1.** [ability] don *m* - **2.** [style] estilo *m*.

flak [flæk] *n* (*U*) - **1.** [gunfire] fuego *m* antiaéreo - **2.** *inf* [criticism] críticas *fpl*.

flake [fleɪk] ◇ *n* [of skin] escama *f*; [of snow] copo *m*; [of paint] desconchón *m*.

⋄ *vi* [skin] descamarse; [paint, plaster] desconcharse.

flamboyant [flæm'bɔɪənt] *adj* **-1.** [person, behaviour] extravagante - **2.** [clothes, design] vistoso(sa), llamativo(va).

flame [fleɪm] *n* llama *f*; in ~s en llamas.

flamingo [flə'mɪŋgəʊ] (*pl* -s *OR* -es) *n* flamenco *m*.

flammable ['flæməbl] *adj* inflamable.

flan [flæn] *n* tarta *f (de fruta etc)*.

flank [flæŋk] ⋄ *n* **-1.** [of animal] costado *m*, ijada *f* - **2.** [of army] flanco *m*. ⋄ *vt*: **to be ~ ed by** estar flanqueado(da) por.

flannel ['flænl] *n* **-1.** [fabric] franela *f* - **2.** UK [facecloth] toallita *f* (de baño para lavarse).

flap [flæp] (*pt* & *pp* -ped, *cont* -ping) ⋄ *n* [of pocket, book, envelope] solapa *f*; [of skin] colgajo *m*. ⋄ *vt* agitar; [wings] batir. ⋄ *vi* [flag, skirt] ondear; [wings] aletear.

flapjack ['flæpdʒæk] *n* **-1.** UK [biscuit] galleta *f* de avena - **2.** US [pancake] torta *f*, crepe *f*.

flare [fleəʳ] ⋄ *n* [signal] bengala *f*. ⋄ *vi* **-1.** [burn brightly]: **to ~ (up)** llamear - **2.** [intensify]: **to ~ (up)** estallar.

➤ **flares** *npl* UK pantalones *mpl* de campana.

flash [flæʃ] ⋄ *n* **-1.** [of light] destello *m*; **a ~ of lightning** un relámpago, un refucilo *RP* - **2.** PHOT flash *m* - **3.** [of genius, inspiration etc] momento *m*; [of anger] acceso *m*; **in a ~** en un instante. ⋄ *vt* **-1.** [shine in specified direction] dirigir; [switch on briefly] encender intermitentemente - **2.** [a smile, look] lanzar - **3.** [show - picture, image] mostrar; [- information, news] emitir. ⋄ *vi* **-1.** [light] destellar - **2.** [eyes] brillar - **3.** [rush]: **to ~ by** *OR* **past** pasar como un rayo.

flashback ['flæʃbæk] *n* flashback *m*.

flashbulb ['flæʃbʌlb] *n* flash *m*.

flashgun ['flæʃgʌn] *n* disparador *m* de flash.

flashlight ['flæʃlaɪt] *n* US [torch] linterna *f*.

flashy ['flæʃɪ] (*compar* -ier, *superl* -iest) *adj inf* chulo(la); *pej* vistoso(sa).

flask [flɑːsk] *n* **-1.** [thermos flask] termo *m* - **2.** [used in chemistry] matraz *m* - **3.** [hip flask] petaca *f*.

flat [flæt] (*compar* -ter, *superl* -test) ⋄ *adj* **-1.** [surface, ground] llano(na); [feet] plano(na) - **2.** [shoes] bajo(ja), de piso *Méx* - **3.** [tyre] desinflado(da), ponchado(da) *Méx* - **4.** [refusal, denial] rotundo(da) - **5.** [business, trade] flojo(ja); [voice, tone] monótono(na); [colour] soso(sa); [performance, writing] desangelado(da) - **6.** MUS [lower than correct note] desafinado(da); [lower than stated note] bemol *(inv)* - **7.** [fare, price] único(ca) - **8.** [beer, lemonade] muerto(ta), sin fuerza - **9.** [battery] descargado(da). ⋄ *adv* **-1.** [level]: **to lie ~** estar totalmente extendido; **to fall ~ on one's face** [person]

caerse de bruces - **2.** [of time]: **in five minutes ~** en cinco minutos justos. ⋄ *n* **-1.** UK [apartment] piso *m*, apartamento *m*, departamento *m Amér* - **2.** US [tyre] pinchazo *m* - **3.** MUS bemol *m*.

➤ **flat out** *adv* a toda velocidad.

flatly ['flætlɪ] *adv* **-1.** [refuse, deny] de plano, rotundamente - **2.** [speak, perform] monótonamente.

flatmate ['flætmeɪt] *n* UK compañero *m*, -ra *f* de piso.

flat rate *n* tarifa *f* plana.

flatscreen television, flatscreen TV ['flæt,skriːn-] *n* televisor *m* de pantalla plana.

flatten ['flætn] *vt* **-1.** [surface, paper, bumps] allanar, aplanar; [paper] alisar - **2.** [building, city] arrasar.

➤ **flatten out** ⋄ *vi* allanarse, nivelarse. ⋄ *vt sep* allanar.

flatter ['flætəʳ] *vt* **-1.** [subj: person, report] adular, halagar - **2.** [subj: clothes, colour, photograph] favorecer.

flattering ['flætərɪŋ] *adj* **-1.** [remark, interest] halagador(ra) - **2.** [clothes, colour, photograph] favorecedor(ra).

flattery ['flætərɪ] *n (U)* halagos *mpl*, adulación *f*.

flaunt [flɔːnt] *vt* ostentar, hacer gala de.

flavour UK, **flavor** US ['fleɪvəʳ] ⋄ *n* **-1.** [taste] sabor *m* - **2.** *fig* [atmosphere] aire *m*, sabor *m*. ⋄ *vt* condimentar.

flavouring UK, **flavoring** US ['fleɪvərɪŋ] *n (U)* condimento *m*; **artificial ~** aromatizante *m* artificial.

flaw [flɔː] *n* [fault] desperfecto *m*, imperfección *f*.

flawless ['flɔːlɪs] *adj* impecable.

flax [flæks] *n* lino *m*.

flea [fliː] *n* pulga *f*.

flea market *n* rastro *m*.

fleck [flek] *n* mota *f*.

fled [fled] *pt* & *pp* ⊳ **flee**.

flee [fliː] (*pt* & *pp* **fled**) ⋄ *vt* huir de. ⋄ *vi*: **to ~ (from/to)** huir (de/a).

fleece [fliːs] ⋄ *n* **-1.** [wool] vellón *m* - **2.** [garment] forro *m* polar. ⋄ *vt inf* [cheat] desplumar.

fleet [fliːt] *n* **-1.** [of ships] flota *f* - **2.** [of cars, buses] parque *m* (móvil).

fleeting ['fliːtɪŋ] *adj* fugaz.

Fleet Street *n calle londinense que antiguamente fue el centro de la prensa inglesa y cuyo nombre todavía se utiliza para referirse a ésta.*

Flemish ['flemɪʃ] ⋄ *adj* flamenco(ca). ⋄ *n* [language] flamenco *m*. ⋄ *npl*: **the ~** los flamencos.

flesh [fleʃ] *n* **-1.** [of body] carne *f*; **in the ~** en persona - **2.** [of fruit, vegetable] pulpa *f*.

flesh wound *n* herida *f* superficial.

flew [fluː] *pt* ⊳ **fly**.

flex [fleks] ◇ *n* ELEC cable *m*, cordón *m*. ◇ *vt* flexionar.

flexible ['fleksəbl] *adj* flexible.

flexitime ['fleksɪtaɪm] *n (U)* horario *m* flexible.

flick [flɪk] ◇ *n* **- 1.** [of whip, towel] golpe *m* rápido **- 2.** [with finger] toba *f*. ◇ *vt* [switch] apretar, pulsar.
　◆ **flick through** *vt fus* hojear.

flicker ['flɪkə'] *vi* [eyes, flame] parpadear.

flick knife *n* UK navaja *f* automática.

flight [flaɪt] *n* **- 1.** [gen] vuelo *m* **- 2.** [of steps, stairs] tramo *m* **- 3.** [of birds] bandada *f* **- 4.** [escape] huida *f*, fuga *f*.

flight attendant *n* auxiliar *m* OR *f* de vuelo.

flight crew *n* tripulación *f* de vuelo.

flight deck *n* **- 1.** [of plane] cabina *f* del piloto **- 2.** [of aircraft carrier] cubierta *f* de vuelo.

flight recorder *n* caja *f* negra.

flimsy ['flɪmzɪ] (*compar* -**ier**, *superl* -**iest**) *adj* **- 1.** [dress, material] muy ligero(ra) **- 2.** [structure] débil, poco sólido(da) **- 3.** [excuse] flojo(ja).

flinch [flɪntʃ] *vi* **- 1.** [shudder] estremecerse; **without ~ing** sin pestañear **- 2.** [be reluctant]: **to ~ (from sthg/from doing sthg)** retroceder (ante algo/ante hacer algo); **without ~ing** sin inmutarse.

fling [flɪŋ] (*pt* & *pp* **flung**) ◇ *n* [affair] aventura *f* amorosa. ◇ *vt* arrojar.

flint [flɪnt] *n* **- 1.** [rock] sílex *m* **- 2.** [in lighter] piedra *f*.

flip [flɪp] (*pt* & *pp* **-ped**, *cont* **-ping**) *vt* **- 1.** [turn] dar la vuelta a; **to ~ sthg open** abrir algo de golpe **- 2.** [switch] pulsar.
　◆ **flip through** *vt fus* hojear.

flip-flop *n* [shoe] chancleta *f*.

flippant ['flɪpənt] *adj* frívolo(la).

flipper ['flɪpə'] *n* aleta *f*.

flirt [flɜːt] ◇ *n* coqueto *m*, -ta *f*. ◇ *vi* [with person]: **to ~ (with)** flirtear OR coquetear (con).

flirtatious [flɜːˈteɪʃəs] *adj* coqueto(ta).

flit [flɪt] (*pt* & *pp* **-ted**, *cont* **-ting**) *vi* [bird] revolotear.

float [fləʊt] ◇ *n* **- 1.** [for fishing line] corcho *m* **- 2.** [for swimming] flotador *m* **- 3.** [in procession] carroza *f* **- 4.** [supply of change] cambio *m*. ◇ *vt* [on water] hacer flotar. ◇ *vi* flotar.

flock [flɒk] *n* **- 1.** [of sheep] rebaño *m*; [of birds] bandada *f* **- 2.** *fig* [of people] multitud *f*, tropel *m*.

flog [flɒg] (*pt* & *pp* **-ged**, *cont* **-ging**) *vt* **- 1.** [whip] azotar **- 2.** UK *inf* [sell] vender.

flood [flʌd] ◇ *n* **- 1.** [of water] inundación *f* **- 2.** [of letters, people] aluvión *m*, riada *f*. ◇ *vt lit* & *fig*: **to ~ sthg (with)** inundar algo (de).

flooding ['flʌdɪŋ] *n (U)* inundación *f*.

floodlight ['flʌdlaɪt] *n* foco *m*.

floor [flɔː'] ◇ *n* **- 1.** [of room, forest] suelo *m*; [of club, disco] pista *f* **- 2.** [of sea, valley] fondo *m* **- 3.** [of building] piso *m*, planta *f* **- 4.** [at meeting, debate]: **to give/have the ~** dar/tener la palabra. ◇ *vt* **- 1.** [knock down] derribar **- 2.** [baffle] desconcertar, dejar perplejo(ja).

floorboard ['flɔːbɔːd] *n* tabla *f* (del suelo).

floor show *n* espectáculo *m* de cabaret.

flop [flɒp] *n inf* [failure] fracaso *m*.

floppy ['flɒpɪ] (*compar* -**ier**, *superl* -**iest**) *adj* caído(da), flojo(ja).

flora ['flɔːrə] *n* flora *f*.

florid ['flɒrɪd] *adj* **- 1.** [extravagant] florido(da) **- 2.** [red] rojizo(za).

florist ['flɒrɪst] *n* florista *m* OR *f*; **~'s (shop)** floristería *f*.

flotsam ['flɒtsəm] *n (U)*: **~ and jetsam** restos *mpl* de un naufragio; *fig* desechos *mpl* de la humanidad.

flounce [flaʊns] ◇ *n* SEWING volante *m*. ◇ *vi*: **to ~ out** salir airadamente.

flounder ['flaʊndə'] *vi* **- 1.** [move with difficulty] debatirse, forcejear **- 2.** [when speaking] titubear.

flour ['flaʊə'] *n* harina *f*.

flourish ['flʌrɪʃ] ◇ *vi* florecer. ◇ *vt* agitar. ◇ *n*: **to do sthg with a ~** hacer algo con una floritura.

flout [flaʊt] *vt* desobedecer.

flow [fləʊ] ◇ *n* flujo *m*; **traffic ~** circulación *f*. ◇ *vi* **- 1.** [gen] fluir, correr **- 2.** [hair, clothes] ondear.

flow chart, flow diagram *n* organigrama *m*, cuadro *m* sinóptico.

flower ['flaʊə'] ◇ *n lit* & *fig* flor *f*. ◇ *vi lit* & *fig* florecer.

flowerbed ['flaʊəbed] *n* arriate *m*, parterre *m*, cantero *m* *Cuba, RP*.

flowerpot ['flaʊəpɒt] *n* tiesto *m*.

flowery ['flaʊərɪ] (*compar* -**ier**, *superl* -**iest**) *adj* **- 1.** [patterned] de flores, floreado(da) **- 2.** *pej* [elaborate] florido(da).

flown [fləʊn] *pp* ▷ **fly**.

flu [fluː] *n* gripe *f*, gripa *f* *Amér*.

fluctuate ['flʌktʃʊeɪt] *vi* fluctuar.

fluency ['fluːənsɪ] *n* soltura *f*, fluidez *f*.

fluent ['fluːənt] *adj* **- 1.** [in foreign language]: **to be ~ in French, to speak ~ French** dominar el francés **- 2.** [style] fluido(da).

fluff [flʌf] *n* pelusa *f*.

fluffy ['flʌfɪ] (*compar* -**ier**, *superl* -**iest**) *adj* [jumper] de pelusa; [toy] de peluche.

fluid ['fluːɪd] ◇ *n* fluido *m*, líquido *m*. ◇ *adj* **- 1.** [flowing] fluido(da) **- 2.** [situation, opinion] incierto(ta).

fluid ounce *n* = 0,03 litre, onza *f* líquida.

fluke [fluːk] *n inf* chiripa *f*; **by a ~** por OR de chiripa.

flummox ['flʌməks] *vt* UK *inf* desconcertar.

flung [flʌŋ] *pt* & *pp* ▷ **fling.**

flunk [flʌŋk] *vt* & *vi esp US inf* catear.

◆ **flunk out** *vi US inf* ser expulsado(da).

fluorescent [fluəˈresnt] *adj* fluorescente.

fluoride [ˈfluəraɪd] *n* fluoruro *m*.

flurry [ˈflʌrɪ] (*pl* -**ies**) *n* - **1.** [shower] ráfaga *f* - **2.** [burst] torbellino *m*.

flush [flʌʃ] ◇ *adj* [level]: ~ **with** nivelado(-da) con. ◇ *n* - **1.** [lavatory mechanism] cadena *f* - **2.** [blush] rubor *m* - **3.** [sudden feeling] arrebato *m*. ◇ *vt* [force out of hiding]: **to** ~ **sb out** hacer salir a alguien. ◇ *vi* [blush] ruborizarse.

flushed [flʌʃt] *adj* - **1.** [red-faced] encendido(da) - **2.** [excited]: ~ **(with)** enardecido(-da) (por).

flustered [ˈflʌstəd] *adj* aturullado(da).

flute [flu:t] *n* MUS flauta *f*.

flutter [ˈflʌtəʳ] ◇ *n* - **1.** [of wings] aleteo *m*; [of eyelashes] pestañeo *m* - **2.** *inf* [of excitement] arranque *m*. ◇ *vi* - **1.** [bird] aletear - **2.** [flag, dress] ondear.

flux [flʌks] *n* [change]: **to be in a state of** ~ cambiar constantemente.

fly [flaɪ] (*pt* **flew**, *pp* **flown**, *pl* **flies**) ◇ *n* - **1.** [insect] mosca *f* - **2.** [of trousers] bragueta *f*. ◇ *vt* - **1.** [plane] pilotar; [kite, model aircraft] hacer volar - **2.** [passengers, supplies] transportar en avión - **3.** [flag] ondear. ◇ *vi* - **1.** [bird, plane] volar - **2.** [travel by plane] ir en avión - **3.** [pilot a plane] pilotar - **4.** [flag] ondear.

◆ **fly away** *vi* irse volando.

fly-fishing *n* pesca *f* con mosca.

flying [ˈflaɪɪŋ] ◇ *adj* [able to fly] volador(ra), volante. ◇ *n*: **I hate/love** ~ odio/me encanta ir en avión; **her hobby is** ~ es aficionada a la aviación.

flying colours *npl*: **to pass (sthg) with** ~ salir airoso(sa) (de algo).

flying picket *n* piquete *m* volante.

flying saucer *n* platillo *m* volante.

flying squad *n* brigada *f* volante.

flying start *n*: **to get off to a** ~ empezar con muy buen pie.

flying visit *n* visita *f* relámpago.

flyover [ˈflaɪˌəʊvəʳ] *n UK* paso *m* elevado.

flysheet [ˈflaɪʃiːt] *n* doble techo *m*.

fly spray *n* matamoscas *m inv* (en aerosol).

FM (*abbr of* **frequency modulation**) FM *f*.

foal [fəʊl] *n* potro *m*.

foam [fəʊm] ◇ *n* - **1.** [bubbles] espuma *f* - **2.**: ~ **(rubber)** gomaespuma *f*. ◇ *vi* hacer espuma.

fob [fɒb] (*pt* & *pp* -**bed**, *cont* -**bing**) ◆ **fob off** *vt sep*: **to** ~ **sb off (with sthg)** quitarse a alguien de encima (con algo); **to** ~ **sthg off on sb** endosar a alguien algo.

focal point [ˈfəʊkl-] *n* punto *m* focal OR central.

focus [ˈfəʊkəs] (*pl* -**cuses** OR -**ci** [-saɪ]) ◇ *n* [gen] foco *m*; **in** ~ enfocado; **out of** ~ desenfocado. ◇ *vt* - **1.** [eyes, lens, rays] enfocar - **2.** [attention] fijar, centrar. ◇ *vi* - **1.** [eyes, lens]: **to** ~ **(on sthg)** enfocar (algo) - **2.** [attention]: **to** ~ **on sthg** centrarse en algo.

fodder [ˈfɒdəʳ] *n* forraje *m*.

foe [fəʊ] *n literary* enemigo *m*, -ga *f*.

foetus [ˈfiːtəs] *n* feto *m*.

fog [fɒg] *n* niebla *f*.

foggy [ˈfɒgɪ] (*compar* -**ier**, *superl* -**iest**) *adj* [day] de niebla; **it's** ~ hay niebla.

foghorn [ˈfɒghɔːn] *n* sirena *f* (*de niebla*).

fog lamp *n* faro *m* antiniebla.

foible [ˈfɔɪbl] *n* manía *f*.

foil [fɔɪl] ◇ *n* (*U*) [metal sheet] papel *m* de aluminio OR de plata. ◇ *vt* frustrar.

fold [fəʊld] ◇ *vt* [sheet, blanket] doblar; [chair, pram] plegar; **to** ~ **one's arms** cruzar los brazos. ◇ *vi* - **1.** [table, chair etc] plegarse - **2.** *inf* [collapse] venirse abajo. ◇ *n* - **1.** [in material, paper] pliegue *m* - **2.** [for animals] redil *m*.

◆ **fold up** ◇ *vt sep* - **1.** [bend] doblar - **2.** [close up] plegar. ◇ *vi* - **1.** [bend] doblarse - **2.** [close up] plegarse - **3.** [collapse] venirse abajo.

folder [ˈfəʊldəʳ] *n* [gen & COMPUT] carpeta *f*.

folding [ˈfəʊldɪŋ] *adj* plegable; [ladder] de tijera.

foliage [ˈfəʊlɪdʒ] *n* follaje *m*.

folk [fəʊk] ◇ *adj* popular. ◇ *npl* [people] gente *f*.

◆ **folks** *npl inf* [parents] padres *mpl*.

folklore [ˈfəʊklɔːʳ] *n* folklore *m*.

folk music *n* - **1.** [traditional] música *f* folklórica OR popular - **2.** [contemporary] música *f* folk.

folk song *n* - **1.** [traditional] canción *f* popular - **2.** [contemporary] canción *f* folk.

follow [ˈfɒləʊ] ◇ *vt* - **1.** [gen] seguir - **2.** [understand] comprender. ◇ *vi* - **1.** [gen] seguir - **2.** [be logical] ser lógico(-ca); **it** ~**s that** se deduce que - **3.** [understand] comprender.

◆ **follow up** *vt sep* - **1.** [monitor] hacer un seguimiento de - **2.** [continue]: **to** ~ **sthg up with** proseguir algo con.

follower [ˈfɒləʊəʳ] *n* partidario *m*, -ria *f*, seguidor *m*, -ra *f*.

following [ˈfɒləʊɪŋ] ◇ *adj* siguiente. ◇ *n* partidarios *mpl*; [of team] afición *f*. ◇ *prep* tras.

folly [ˈfɒlɪ] *n* (*U*) [foolishness] locura *f*.

fond [fɒnd] *adj* - **1.** [affectionate] afectuoso(-sa), cariñoso(sa) - **2.** [having a liking]: **to be** ~ **of sb** tener cariño a alguien; **to be** ~ **of sthg/of doing sthg** ser aficionado(da) a algo/a hacer algo.

fondle ['fɒndl] *vt* acariciar.

font [fɒnt] *n* - **1.** [in church] pila *f* bautismal - **2.** COMPUT fuente *f*.

food [fu:d] *n* comida *f*.

food mixer *n* batidora *f* eléctrica.

food poisoning [-'pɔɪznɪŋ] *n* intoxicación *f* alimenticia.

food processor [-,prəʊsesə'] *n* robot *m* de cocina.

foodstuffs ['fu:dstʌfs] *npl* comestibles *mpl*.

fool [fu:l] ◇ *n* - **1.** [idiot] idiota *m* or *f*, imbécil *m* or *f* - **2.** UK [dessert] *mousse de fruta con nata.* ◇ *vt* [deceive] engañar; **to ∼ sb into doing sthg** embaucar a alguien para que haga algo. ◇ *vi* bromear.

◆ **fool about, fool around** *vi* - **1.** [behave foolishly]: **to ∼ about (with sthg)** hacer el tonto (con algo) - **2.** [be unfaithful]: **to ∼ about (with sb)** tontear (con alguien).

foolhardy ['fu:l,hɑ:dɪ] *adj* temerario(ria).

foolish ['fu:lɪʃ] *adj* tonto(ta), estúpido(da).

foolproof ['fu:lpru:f] *adj* infalible.

foot [fʊt] (*pl sense 1* feet, *pl sense 2 inv* or feet) ◇ *n* - **1.** [gen] pie *m*; [of bird, animal] pata *f*; **to be on one's feet** estar de pie; **to get to one's feet** levantarse; **on ∼ a pie**, andando; **to put one's ∼ in it** meter la pata; **to put one's feet up** descansar - **2.** [unit of measurement] = 30,48 cm, pie *m*. ◇ *vt inf*: **to ∼ the bill (for sthg)** pagar la cuenta (de algo).

footage ['fʊtɪdʒ] *n* (U) secuencias *fpl*.

football ['fʊtbɔ:l] *n* - **1.** [game - soccer] fútbol *m*; [- American football] fútbol *m* americano - **2.** [ball] balón *m*.

footballer ['fʊtbɔ:lə'] *n* UK futbolista *m* or *f*.

football ground *n* UK estadio *m* de fútbol.

football pitch *n* UK campo *m* de fútbol.

football player = footballer.

footbrake ['fʊtbreɪk] *n* freno *m* de pedal.

footbridge ['fʊtbrɪdʒ] *n* puente *m* peatonal, pasarela *f*.

foothills ['fʊthɪlz] *npl* estribaciones *fpl*.

foothold ['fʊthəʊld] *n* punto *m* de apoyo para el pie.

footing ['fʊtɪŋ] *n* - **1.** [foothold] equilibrio *m*; **to lose one's ∼** perder el equilibrio - **2.** [basis] base *f*; **on an equal ∼ (with)** en pie de igualdad (con).

footlights ['fʊtlaɪts] *npl* candilejas *fpl*.

footnote ['fʊtnəʊt] *n* nota *f* a pie de página.

footpath ['fʊtpɑ:θ, *pl* -pɑ:ðz] *n* senda *f*, camino *m*.

footprint ['fʊtprɪnt] *n* huella *f*, pisada *f*.

footstep ['fʊtstep] *n* - **1.** [sound] paso *m* - **2.** [footprint] pisada *f*.

footwear ['fʊtweə'] *n* calzado *m*.

for [fɔ:'] ◇ *prep* - **1.** [indicating intention, destination, purpose] para; **this is ∼ you** esto es para ti; **I'm going ∼ the paper** voy (a) por el periódico; **the plane ∼ Paris** el avión para or de París; **it's time ∼ bed** es hora de irse a la cama; **we did it ∼ a laugh** or **∼ fun** lo hicimos de broma or por divertirnos; **to go ∼ a walk** ir a dar un paseo; **what's it ∼?** ¿para qué es or sirve? - **2.** [representing, on behalf of] por; **the MP ∼ Barnsley** el diputado por Barnsley; **let me do it ∼ you** deja que lo haga por ti; **he plays ∼ England** juega en la selección inglesa; **to work ∼ trabajar** para - **3.** [because of] por; **a prize ∼ bravery** un premio a la valentía; **to jump ∼ joy** dar saltos de alegría; **∼ fear of failing** por miedo a fracasar - **4.** [with regard to] para; **it's not ∼ me to say** no me toca a mí decidir; **he looks young ∼ his age** parece más joven de lo que es - **5.** [indicating amount of time, space] para; **there's no time/room ∼** it no hay tiempo/sitio para eso - **6.** [indicating period of time - during] durante [- by, in time for] para; **she cried ∼ two hours** estuvo llorando durante dos horas; **I've lived here ∼ three years** llevo tres años viviendo aquí, he vivido aquí (durante) tres años; **I've worked here ∼ years** trabajo aquí desde hace años; **I'll do it ∼ tomorrow** lo tendré hecho para mañana - **7.** [indicating distance] en; **there were roadworks ∼ 50 miles** había obras en 50 millas; **we walked ∼ miles** andamos millas y millas - **8.** [indicating particular occasion] para; **I got it ∼ my birthday** me lo regalaron para or por mi cumpleaños; **∼ the first time** por vez primera - **9.** [indicating amount of money, price] por; **I bought/sold it ∼ £10** lo compré/vendí por 10 libras; **they're 50p ∼** ten son a 50 peniques cada diez - **10.** [in favour of, in support of] a favor de; **to vote ∼ sthg/sb** votar por algo/a alguien; **to be all ∼ sthg** estar completamente a favor de algo - **11.** [in ratios] por - **12.** [indicating meaning]: **P ∼ Peter** P de Pedro; **what's the Greek ∼ 'mother'?** ¿cómo se dice 'madre' en griego? ◇ *conj fml* [as, since] ya que.

◆ **for all** ◇ *prep* - **1.** [in spite of] a pesar de, pese a; **∼ all your moaning** a pesar de lo mucho que te quejas - **2.** [considering how little] para; **∼ all the good it has done me** para lo que me ha servido. ◇ *conj*: **∼ all I care, she could be dead** por mí, como si se muere; **∼ all I know** por lo que yo sé, que yo sepa.

forage ['fɒrɪdʒ] *vi* [search]: **to ∼ (for sthg)** buscar (algo).

foray ['fɒreɪ] *n lit & fig*: **∼ (into)** incursión *f* (en).

forbad [fə'bæd], **forbade** [fə'beɪd] *pt* ▷ **forbid**.

forbid [fə'bɪd] (*pt* -**bade** or -**bad**, *pp* **forbid**

OR **-bidden**, cont **-bidding**) vt: to ~ sb (to do sthg) prohibir a alguien (hacer algo).

forbidden [fə'bɪdn] adj prohibido(da).

forbidding [fə'bɪdɪŋ] adj [building, landscape] inhóspito(ta); [person, expression] severo(ra), austero(ra).

force [fɔːs] ⋄ n fuerza f; **sales ~ personal** m de ventas; **security ~s** fuerzas fpl de seguridad; **by ~** a la fuerza; **to be in/come into ~** estar/entrar en vigor; **in ~** [in large numbers] en masa, en gran número. ⋄ vt forzar; **to ~ sb to do sthg** [gen] forzar a alguien a hacer algo; [subj: event, circumstances] obligar a alguien a hacer algo.

◆ **forces** npl: **the ~s** las fuerzas armadas; **to join ~s (with)** unirse (con).

force-feed vt alimentar a la fuerza.

forceful ['fɔːsfʊl] adj [person, impression] fuerte; [support, recommendation] enérgico(ca); [speech, idea, argument] contundente.

forceps ['fɔːseps] npl fórceps m inv.

forcibly ['fɔːsəblɪ] adv **- 1.** [using physical force] por la fuerza **- 2.** [remind] vivamente; [express, argue] convincentemente.

ford [fɔːd] n vado m.

fore [fɔːʳ] n: **to come to the ~** empezar a destacar, emerger.

forearm ['fɔːrɑːm] n antebrazo m.

foreboding [fɔː'bəʊdɪŋ] n **- 1.** [presentiment] presagio m **- 2.** [apprehension] desasosiego m.

forecast ['fɔːkɑːst] (pt & pp **forecast** OR **-ed**) ⋄ n [prediction] predicción f, previsión f; [of weather] pronóstico m. ⋄ vt [predict] predecir; [weather] pronosticar.

foreclose [fɔː'kləʊz] ⋄ vi: **to ~ on sb** privar a alguien del derecho a redimir su hipoteca. ⋄ vt ejecutar.

forecourt ['fɔːkɔːt] n patio m.

forefinger ['fɔːˌfɪŋgəʳ] n (dedo m) índice m.

forefront ['fɔːfrʌnt] n: **in** OR **at the ~ of** en OR a la vanguardia de.

forego [fɔː'gəʊ] = forgo.

foregone conclusion ['fɔːgɒn-] n: **it's a ~** es un resultado inevitable.

foreground ['fɔːgraʊnd] n primer plano m.

forehand ['fɔːhænd] n [stroke] golpe m natural, drive m.

forehead ['fɔːhed] n frente f.

foreign ['fɒrən] adj **- 1.** [from abroad] extranjero(ra) **- 2.** [external - policy, trade] exterior; [- correspondent, holiday] en el extranjero **- 3.** [unwanted, harmful] extraño(ña) **- 4.** [alien, untypical]: **~ (to sb/sthg)** ajeno(na) (a alguien/algo).

foreign affairs npl asuntos mpl exteriores.

foreign currency n (U) divisa f.

foreigner ['fɒrənəʳ] n extranjero m, -ra f.

foreign minister n ministro m, -tra f de asuntos exteriores.

Foreign Office n UK: **the ~** el Ministerio de Asuntos Exteriores británico.

Foreign Secretary n UK Ministro m, -tra f de Asuntos Exteriores.

foreleg ['fɔːleg] n pata f delantera.

foreman ['fɔːmən] (pl **-men** [-mən]) n **- 1.** [of workers] encargado m **- 2.** [of jury] presidente m.

foremost ['fɔːməʊst] ⋄ adj primero(ra). ⋄ adv: **first and ~** ante todo, por encima de todo.

forensic [fə'rensɪk] adj forense.

forensic scientist n forense m OR f.

forerunner ['fɔːˌrʌnəʳ] n [precursor] precursor m, -ra f.

foresee [fɔː'siː] (pt **-saw**, pp **-seen**) vt prever.

foreseeable [fɔː'siːəbl] adj previsible; **for/ in the ~ future** en un futuro próximo.

foreseen [fɔː'siːn] pp ⊳ foresee.

foreshadow [fɔː'ʃædəʊ] vt presagiar.

foresight ['fɔːsaɪt] n (U) previsión f.

forest ['fɒrɪst] n bosque m.

forestall [fɔː'stɔːl] vt anticiparse a.

forest fire n incendio m forestal.

forest ranger n US guarda mf forestal, guardabosques mf inv.

forestry ['fɒrɪstrɪ] n silvicultura f.

foretaste ['fɔːteɪst] n anticipo m, adelanto m.

foretell [fɔː'tel] (pt & pp **-told**) vt predecir.

forever [fə'revəʳ] adv **- 1.** [eternally] para siempre **- 2.** inf [incessantly] siempre, continuamente.

forewarn [fɔː'wɔːn] vt prevenir, advertir.

foreword ['fɔːwɜːd] n prefacio m.

forfeit ['fɔːfɪt] ⋄ n [penalty] precio m; [in game] prenda f. ⋄ vt renunciar a, perder.

forgave [fə'geɪv] pt ⊳ forgive.

forge [fɔːdʒ] ⋄ n fragua f, forja f. ⋄ vt **- 1.** [gen] fraguar **- 2.** [falsify] falsificar.

◆ **forge ahead** vi hacer grandes progresos.

forger ['fɔːdʒəʳ] n falsificador m, -ra f.

forgery ['fɔːdʒərɪ] (pl **-ies**) n falsificación f.

forget [fə'get] (pt **-got**, pp **-gotten**, cont **-getting**) ⋄ vt: **to ~ (to do sthg)** olvidar (hacer algo). ⋄ vi: **to ~ (about sthg)** olvidarse (de algo).

forgetful [fə'getfʊl] adj olvidadizo(za), desmemoriado(da).

forget-me-not n nomeolvides m inv.

forgive [fə'gɪv] (pt **-gave**, pp **-given**) vt: **to ~ sb (for sthg/for doing sthg)** perdonar a alguien (algo/por haber hecho algo).

forgiveness [fə'gɪvnɪs] n perdón m.

forgo [fɔː'gəʊ] (pt **-went**, pp **-gone**) vt sacrificar, renunciar a.

forgot [fə'gɒt] pt ⊳ forget.

forgotten [fə'gɒtn] pp ⊳ forget.

fork [fɔːk] ◇ *n* **-1.** [for food] tenedor *m* **-2.** [for gardening] horca *f* **-3.** [in road etc] bifurcación *f.* ◇ *vi* bifurcarse.

➤ **fork out** *vi inf:* **to ~ out for sthg** soltar pelas para algo.

forklift truck ['fɔːklɪft-] *n* carretilla *f* elevadora.

forlorn [fəˈlɔːn] *adj* **-1.** [person, expression] consternado(da) **-2.** [place, landscape] desolado(da) **-3.** [hope, attempt] desesperado(da).

form [fɔːm] ◇ *n* **-1.** [shape, type] forma *f*; **in the ~ of** en forma de **-2.** [fitness]: **on ~** *UK*, **in ~** *US* en forma; **off ~** en baja forma **-3.** [document] impreso *m*, formulario *m*, planilla *f Amér.* **-4.** [figure - of person] figura *f* **-5.** *UK* [class] clase *f.* ◇ *vt* formar; [plan] concebir; [impression, idea] formarse. ◇ *vi* formarse.

formal ['fɔːml] *adj* **-1.** [gen] formal; [education] convencional **-2.** [clothes, wedding, party] de etiqueta.

formality [fɔːˈmælətɪ] (*pl* **-ies**) *n* formalidad *f.*

format ['fɔːmæt] (*pt* & *pp* **-ted**, *cont* **-ting**) ◇ *n* [gen & COMPUT] formato *m*; [of meeting] plan *m.* ◇ *vt* COMPUT formatear.

formation [fɔːˈmeɪʃn] *n* formación *f.*

formative ['fɔːmətɪv] *adj* formativo(va).

former ['fɔːmə'] ◇ *adj* **-1.** [previous] antiguo(gua); **in ~ times** antiguamente **-2.** [first of two] primero(ra). ◇ *n*: **the ~** el primero (la primera)/los primeros (las primeras).

formerly ['fɔːməlɪ] *adv* antiguamente.

formidable ['fɔːmɪdəbl] *adj* **-1.** [frightening] imponente, temible **-2.** [impressive] formidable.

formula ['fɔːmjʊlə] (*pl* **-as** *OR* **-ae** [-iː]) *n* **-1.** [gen] fórmula *f* **-2.** [baby milk] leche *f* maternizada.

formulate ['fɔːmjʊleɪt] *vt* formular.

forsake [fəˈseɪk] (*pt* **forsook**, *pp* **forsaken**) *vt literary* abandonar.

forsaken [fəˈseɪkn] *adj* abandonado(da).

forsook [fəˈsʊk] *pt* ⊳ **forsake.**

fort [fɔːt] *n* fuerte *m*, fortaleza *f.*

forte ['fɔːtɪ] *n* fuerte *m.*

forth [fɔːθ] *adv literary* **-1.** [outwards, onwards] hacia adelante; **to go ~** partir **-2.** [into future]: **from that day ~** desde aquel día en adelante.

forthcoming [fɔːθˈkʌmɪŋ] *adj* **-1.** [election, events] próximo(ma); [book] de próxima aparición **-2.** [person] abierto(ta).

forthright ['fɔːθraɪt] *adj* [person, manner, opinions] directo(ta), franco(ca); [opposition] rotundo(da).

forthwith [ˌfɔːθˈwɪθ] *adv fml* inmediatamente.

fortified wine ['fɔːtɪfaɪd-] *n* vino *m* licoroso.

fortify ['fɔːtɪfaɪ] (*pt* & *pp* **-ied**) *vt* **-1.** MIL fortificar **-2.** [person, resolve] fortalecer.

fortnight ['fɔːtnaɪt] *n* quincena *f*; **in a ~** en quince días.

fortnightly ['fɔːtˌnaɪtlɪ] ◇ *adj* quincenal. ◇ *adv* quincenalmente.

fortress ['fɔːtrɪs] *n* fortaleza *f.*

fortunate ['fɔːtʃnət] *adj* afortunado(da).

fortunately ['fɔːtʃnətlɪ] *adv* afortunadamente.

fortune ['fɔːtʃuːn] *n* **-1.** [money, luck] fortuna *f* **-2.** [future]: **to tell sb's ~** decir a alguien la buenaventura.

fortune-teller [-ˌtelə'] *n* adivino *m*, -na *f.*

forty ['fɔːtɪ] *num* cuarenta; *see also* **sixty**.

forum ['fɔːrəm] (*pl* **-s**) *n lit* & *fig* foro *m.*

forward ['fɔːwəd] ◇ *adj* **-1.** [towards front-movement] hacia adelante; [near front-position etc] delantero(ra) **-2.** [towards future]: **~ planning** planificación *f* de futuro **-3.** [advanced]: **we're (no) further ~** (no) hemos adelantado (nada) **-4.** [impudent] atrevido(da). ◇ *adv* **-1.** [ahead] hacia adelante; **to go** *OR* **move ~** avanzar **-2.** [in time]: **to bring sthg ~** adelantar algo. ◇ *n* SPORT delantero *m*, -ra *f.* ◇ *vt* [letter, e-mail] remitir; **'please ~'** 'remítase al destinatario'.

forwarding address ['fɔːwədɪŋ-] *n* nueva dirección *f* para reenvío de correo.

forwards ['fɔːwədz] = **forward.**

forward slash *n* TYPO barra *f* inclinada.

forwent [fɔːˈwent] *pt* ⊳ **forgo.**

fossil ['fɒsl] *n* fósil *m.*

foster ['fɒstə'] *vt* **-1.** [child] acoger **-2.** [idea, arts, relations] promover.

foster child *n* menor *m* *OR* *f* en régimen de acogida.

foster parents *npl* familia *f* de acogida.

fought [fɔːt] *pt* & *pp* ⊳ **fight.**

foul [faʊl] ◇ *adj* **-1.** [unclean - smell] fétido(da); [- taste] asqueroso(sa); [- water, language] sucio(cia) **-2.** [very unpleasant] horrible. ◇ *n* falta *f.* ◇ *vt* **-1.** [make dirty] ensuciar **-2.** SPORT cometer una falta contra.

found [faʊnd] ◇ *pt* & *pp* ⊳ **find.** ◇ *vt*: **to ~ sthg (on)** fundar algo (en).

foundation [faʊnˈdeɪʃn] *n* **-1.** [organization, act of establishing] fundación *f* **-2.** [basis] fundamento *m*, base *f* **-3.** [make-up]: **~ (cream)** crema *f* base.

➤ **foundations** *npl* CONSTR & *fig* cimientos *mpl.*

founder ['faʊndə'] ◇ *n* fundador *m*, -ra *f.* ◇ *vi lit* & *fig* hundirse, irse a pique.

foundry ['faʊndrɪ] (*pl* **-ies**) *n* fundición *f.*

fountain ['faʊntɪn] *n* **-1.** [structure] fuente *f* **-2.** [jet] chorro *m.*

fountain pen n (pluma f) estilográfica f.

four [fɔːʳ] num cuatro; **on all ~s** a gatas; see also **six**.

four-letter word n palabrota f, taco m.

four-poster (bed) n cama f de columnas.

foursome ['fɔːsəm] n grupo m de cuatro personas.

fourteen [ˌfɔːˈtiːn] num catorce; see also **six**.

fourth [fɔːθ] num cuarto(ta); see also **sixth**.

Fourth of July n: **the ~** el cuatro de julio, día de la independencia estadounidense.

four-wheel drive n [system] tracción f a las cuatro ruedas; [car] cuatro por cuatro m.

fowl [faʊl] (pl inv OR -s) n ave f de corral.

fox [fɒks] ◇ n zorro m. ◇ vt [perplex] dejar perplejo(ja).

foxglove ['fɒksglʌv] n dedalera f.

foyer ['fɔɪeɪ] n vestíbulo m.

fracas ['frækɑː, US 'freɪkəs] (UK pl inv, US pl **fracases**) n fml riña f, gresca f.

fraction ['frækʃn] n -1. MATH quebrado m, fracción f -2. [small part] fracción f.

fractionally ['frækʃnəlɪ] adv ligeramente.

fracture ['fræktʃəʳ] ◇ n fractura f. ◇ vt fracturar.

fragile ['frædʒaɪl] adj frágil.

fragment ['frægmənt] n [of glass, text] fragmento m; [of paper, plastic] trozo m.

fragrance ['freɪɡrəns] n fragancia f.

fragrant ['freɪɡrənt] adj fragante.

frail [freɪl] adj frágil.

frame [freɪm] ◇ n -1. [of picture, door] marco m; [of glasses] montura f; [of chair, bed] armadura f; [of bicycle] cuadro m; [of boat] armazón m OR f -2. [physique] cuerpo m. ◇ vt -1. [put in a frame] enmarcar -2. [express] formular, expresar -3. inf [set up] tender una trampa a, amañar la culpabilidad de.

frame of mind n estado m de ánimo, humor m.

framework ['freɪmwɜːk] n -1. [physical structure] armazón m OR f, esqueleto m -2. [basis] marco m.

franc [fræŋk] n franco m.

France [frɑːns] n Francia f.

franchise ['fræntʃaɪz] n -1. POL sufragio m, derecho m de voto -2. COMM concesión f, licencia f exclusiva.

frank [fræŋk] ◇ adj franco(ca). ◇ vt franquear.

frankly ['fræŋklɪ] adv francamente.

frantic ['fræntɪk] adj frenético(ca).

fraternity [frəˈtɜːnətɪ] (pl -ies) n -1. fml [community] cofradía f -2. US [in university] asociación de estudiantes que suele funcionar como club social -3. (U) fml [friendship] fraternidad f.

fraternize, -ise ['frætənaɪz] vi: **to ~ (with)** fraternizar (con).

fraud [frɔːd] n -1. (U) [deceit] fraude m -2. pej [impostor] farsante m OR f.

fraught [frɔːt] adj -1. [full]: **~ with** lleno(-na) OR cargado(da) de -2. UK [frantic] tenso(sa).

fray [freɪ] ◇ vt fig [nerves] crispar, poner de punta. ◇ vi -1. [sleeve, cuff] deshilacharse -2. fig [temper, nerves] crisparse. ◇ n literary: **to enter the ~** saltar a la palestra.

frayed [freɪd] adj [sleeve, cuff] deshilachado(da).

freak [friːk] n -1. [strange creature - in appearance] monstruo m; [- in behaviour] estrafalario m, -ria f -2. [unusual event] anormalidad f, caso m insólito -3. inf [fanatic]: **film/fitness ~** fanático m, -ca f del cine/ejercicio.

◆ **freak out** vi inf flipar, alucinar.

freckle ['frekl] n peca f.

free [friː] (compar **freer**, superl **freest**, pt & pp **freed**) ◇ adj -1. [gen]: **~ (from** OR **of)** libre (de); **to be ~ to do sthg** ser libre de hacer algo; **feel ~!** ¡adelante!, ¡cómo no!; **to set ~** liberar -2. [not paid for] gratis (inv), gratuito(ta); **~ of charge** gratis (inv) -3. [unattached] suelto(ta) -4. [generous]: **to be ~ with sthg** no regatear algo. ◇ adv -1. [without payment]: **(for) ~** gratis -2. [run] libremente -3. [loose]: **to pull/cut sthg ~** soltar algo tirando/cortando. ◇ vt -1. [release] liberar, libertar; **to ~ sb of sthg** librar a alguien de algo -2. [make available] dejar libre -3. [extricate - person] rescatar; [- one's arm, oneself] soltar.

freedom ['friːdəm] n libertad f; **~ from** indemnidad f ante OR de.

Freefone® ['friːfəʊn] n (U) UK teléfono m OR número m gratuito.

free-for-all n refriega f.

free gift n obsequio m.

freehand ['friːhænd] adj & adv a pulso.

freehold ['friːhəʊld] n propiedad f absoluta.

free house n pub no controlado por una compañía cervecera.

free kick n tiro m libre.

freelance ['friːlɑːns] ◇ adj free-lance. ◇ adv como free-lance. ◇ n free-lance m OR f.

freely ['friːlɪ] adv -1. [readily - admit, confess] sin reparos; [- available] fácilmente -2. [openly] abiertamente, francamente -3. [without restrictions] libremente -4. [generously] liberalmente.

Freemason ['friːˌmeɪsn] n francmasón m.

freephone ['friːfəʊn] = Freefone®.

Freepost® ['friːpəʊst] n franqueo m pagado.

free-range adj de granja.

freestyle ['friːstaɪl] n [in swimming] estilo m libre.

free trade *n* libre cambio *m*.

freeware ['fri:weə[r]] *n* COMPUT freeware *m*.

freeway ['fri:weɪ] *n* US autopista *f*.

freewheel [ˌfri:'wi:l] *vi* [on bicycle] andar sin pedalear; [in car] ir en punto muerto.

free will *n* libre albedrío *m*; **to do sthg of one's own ~** hacer algo por voluntad propia.

freeze [fri:z] (*pt* **froze,** *pp* **frozen**) <> *vt* **- 1.** [gen] helar **- 2.** [food, wages, prices] congelar **- 3.** [assets] bloquear. <> *vi* [gen] helarse. <> *v impers* METEOR helar. <> *n* **- 1.** [cold weather] helada *f* **- 2.** [of wages, prices] congelación *f*.

freeze-dried [-'draɪd] *adj* liofilizado(da).

freezer ['fri:zə[r]] *n* congelador *m*.

freezing ['fri:zɪŋ] <> *adj* **- 1.** [gen] helado(-da) **- 2.** [weather] muy frío(a); **it's ~ in here** hace un frío espantoso aquí. <> *n* = **freezing point.**

freezing point *n* punto *m* de congelación.

freight [freɪt] *n* (*U*) **- 1.** [goods] mercancías *fpl*, flete *m* **- 2.** [transport] transporte *m*.

freight train *n* (tren *m* de) mercancías *m inv*.

French [frentʃ] <> *adj* francés(esa). <> *n* [language] francés *m*. <> *npl*: **the ~** los franceses.

French bean *n* judía *f* verde, ejote *m* CAm, Méx, chaucha *f* RP, poroto *m* verde Chile, habichuela *f* Col, vainita *f* Ven.

French bread *n* (*U*) pan *m* de barra.

French dressing *n* [vinaigrette] vinagreta *f*.

French fries *npl esp* US patatas *fpl* fritas.

Frenchman ['frentʃmən] (*pl* -men [-mən]) *n* francés *m*.

French stick *n* UK barra *f* de pan.

French windows *npl* puertaventanas *fpl*.

Frenchwoman ['frentʃˌwʊmən] (*pl* -women [-ˌwɪmɪn]) *n* francesa *f*.

frenetic [frə'netɪk] *adj* frenético(ca).

frenzy ['frenzɪ] (*pl* -ies) *n* frenesí *m*.

frequency ['fri:kwənsɪ] (*pl* -ies) *n* frecuencia *f*.

frequent [*adj* 'fri:kwənt, *vb* frɪ'kwent] <> *adj* frecuente. <> *vt* frecuentar.

frequently ['fri:kwəntlɪ] *adv* a menudo, con frecuencia.

fresh [freʃ] *adj* **- 1.** [gen] fresco(ca); [flavour, taste] refrescante **- 2.** [bread] del día **- 3.** [not canned] natural **- 4.** [water] dulce **- 5.** [pot of tea, fighting] nuevo(va).

freshen ['freʃn] <> *vt* [air] refrescar. <> *vi* [wind] soplar más fuerte.

◆ **freshen up** *vi* [person] refrescarse.

fresher ['freʃə[r]] *n* UK estudiante *m* OR *f* de primer año.

freshly ['freʃlɪ] *adv* recién.

freshman ['freʃmən] (*pl* -men [-mən]) *n* estudiante *m* OR *f* de primer año.

freshness ['freʃnɪs] *n* (*U*) **- 1.** [of food] frescura *f* **- 2.** [originality] novedad *f*, originalidad *f* **- 3.** [brightness] pulcritud *f* **- 4.** [refreshing quality] frescor *m*.

freshwater ['freʃˌwɔ:tə[r]] *adj* de agua dulce.

fret [fret] (*pt* & *pp* **-ted,** *cont* **-ting**) *vi* preocuparse.

friar ['fraɪə[r]] *n* fraile *m*.

friction ['frɪkʃn] *n* fricción *f*.

Friday ['fraɪdɪ] *n* viernes *m inv*; *see also* **Saturday.**

fridge [frɪdʒ] *n esp* UK nevera *f*, refrigerador *m* Amér, heladera *f* RP, refrigeradora *f* Col, Perú.

fridge-freezer *n* UK combi *m*, nevera *f* congeladora.

fried [fraɪd] *adj* frito(ta).

friend [frend] *n* [close acquaintance] amigo *m*, -ga *f*, cuate *m* OR *f inv* CAm, Méx; **to be ~s with sb** ser amigo de alguien; **to make ~s (with)** hacerse amigo (de), trabar amistad (con).

friendly ['frendlɪ] (*compar* -ier, *superl* -iest) *adj* **- 1.** [person] amable, simpático(ca); [attitude, manner, welcome] amistoso(sa); **to be ~ with sb** ser amigo de alguien **- 2.** [nation] amigo(ga), aliado(da) **- 3.** [argument, game] amistoso(sa).

friendship ['frendʃɪp] *n* amistad *f*.

fries [fraɪz] = **French fries.**

frieze [fri:z] *n* friso *m*.

fright [fraɪt] *n* **- 1.** [fear] miedo *m*; **to take ~** espantarse, asustarse **- 2.** [shock] susto *m*; **to give sb a ~** darle un susto a alguien.

frighten ['fraɪtn] *vt* asustar.

frightened ['fraɪtnd] *adj* asustado(da); **to be ~ of sthg/of doing sthg** tener miedo a algo/a hacer algo.

frightening ['fraɪtnɪŋ] *adj* aterrador(ra), espantoso(sa).

frightful ['fraɪtfʊl] *adj dated* terrible, espantoso(sa).

frigid ['frɪdʒɪd] *adj* [sexually] frígido(da).

frill [frɪl] *n* **- 1.** [decoration] volante *m* **- 2.** *inf* [extra] adorno *m*.

fringe [frɪndʒ] (*cont* **fringeing**) <> *n* **- 1.** [decoration] flecos *mpl* **- 2.** UK [of hair] flequillo *m*, cerquillo *m* Amér **- 3.** [edge] periferia *f* **- 4.** [extreme] margen *m*. <> *vt* [edge] bordear.

fringe benefit *n* beneficio *m* complementario.

frisk [frɪsk] *vt* cachear, registrar.

frisky ['frɪskɪ] (*compar* -ier, *superl* -iest) *adj inf* retozón(ona), juguetón(ona).

fritter ['frɪtə[r]] *n* buñuelo *m*.

◆ **fritter away** *vt sep*: **to ~ money/time away on sthg** malgastar dinero/tiempo en algo.

frivolous ['frɪvələs] *adj* frívolo(la).

frizzy ['frɪzɪ] (*compar* **-ier**, *superl* **-iest**) *adj* crespo(pa), ensortijado(da).

fro [frəʊ] ⊳ **to.**

frock [frɒk] *n dated* vestido *m*.

frog [frɒg] *n* [animal] rana *f*.

frogman ['frɒgmən] (*pl* **-men**) *n* hombre-rana *m*.

frolic ['frɒlɪk] (*pt* & *pp* **-ked**, *cont* **-king**) *vi* retozar, triscar.

from [*weak form* frəm, *strong form* frɒm] *prep* **- 1.** [indicating source, origin, removal] de; **where are you ~ ?** ¿de dónde eres?; **I got a letter ~ her today** hoy me ha llegado una carta suya; **a flight ~ Paris** un vuelo de París; **to translate ~ Spanish into English** traducir del español al inglés; **he's not back ~ work yet** aún no ha vuelto del trabajo; **to take sthg away ~ sb** quitarle algo a alguien **- 2.** [indicating a deduction]: **take 15 (away) ~ 19** quita 15 a 19; **to deduct sthg ~ sthg** deducir OR descontar algo de algo **- 3.** [indicating escape, separation]: **he ran away ~ home** huyó de casa **- 4.** [indicating position] desde; **seen ~ above/below** visto desde arriba/abajo; **a light bulb hung ~ the ceiling** una bombilla colgaba del techo **- 5.** [indicating distance] de; **it's 60 km ~ here** está a 60 kms de aquí? **- 6.** [indicating material object is made out of] de; **it's made ~ wood/plastic** está hecho de madera/plástico **- 7.** [starting at a particular time] desde; **closed ~ 1 pm to 2 pm** cerrado de 13h a 14h; **~ the moment I saw him** desde el momento en que lo vi **- 8.** [indicating difference, change] de; **to be different ~** ser diferente de; **~ ... to de ... a; the price went up ~ £100 to £150** el precio subió de 100 a 150 libras **- 9.** [because of, as a result of] de; **to die ~ cold** morir de frío; **to suffer ~ cold/hunger** padecer frío/hambre **- 10.** [on the evidence of] por; **to speak ~ personal experience** hablar por propia experiencia **- 11.** [indicating lowest amount]: **prices range ~ £5 to £500** los precios oscilan entre 5 y 500 libras; **it could take anything ~ 15 to 20 weeks** podría llevar de 15 a 20 semanas.

front [frʌnt] ⬦ *n* **- 1.** [gen] parte *f* delantera; [of building] fachada *f*; [of queue] principio *m*; [of dress, shirt] parte *f* de delante **- 2.** METEOR, MIL & POL frente *m* **- 3.** [on coast]: **(sea) ~** paseo *m* marítimo **- 4.** [outward appearance] fachada *f*. ⬦ *adj* [gen] delantero(ra); [page] primero(ra).
 ⬦ **in front** *adv* **- 1.** [further forward] delante **- 2.** [winning] ganando.
 ⬦ **in front of** *prep* delante de.
 ⬦ **front onto** *vt fus* [be opposite] dar a.

front bench [ˌfrʌnt'bentʃ] *n UK* en la Cámara de los Comunes, cada una de las dos filas de escaños ocupadas respectivamente por los ministros del Gobierno y los principales líderes de la oposición mayoritaria.

front door *n* puerta *f* principal.

frontier ['frʌnˌtɪəʳ, *US* frʌn'tɪər] *n lit* & *fig* frontera *f*.

front man *n* **- 1.** [of group] portavoz *m* OR *f* **- 2.** [of programme] presentador *m* **- 3.** [of rock band] líder *m*.

front room *n* sala *f* de estar.

front-runner *n* favorito *m*, -ta *f*.

front-wheel drive *n* [vehicle] vehículo *m* de tracción delantera.

frost [frɒst] *n* **- 1.** [layer of ice] escarcha *f* **- 2.** [weather] helada *f*.

frostbite ['frɒstbaɪt] *n (U)* congelación *f*.

frosted ['frɒstɪd] *adj* **- 1.** [glass] esmerilado(da) **- 2.** *US* CULIN escarchado(da).

frosty ['frɒstɪ] (*compar* **-ier**, *superl* **-iest**) *adj* **- 1.** [very cold] de helada **- 2.** [covered with frost] escarchado(da) **- 3.** *fig* [unfriendly] glacial.

froth [frɒθ] ⬦ *n* espuma *f*. ⬦ *vi* hacer espuma.

frown [fraʊn] *vi* fruncir el ceño.
 ⬦ **frown (up)on** *vt fus* desaprobar.

froze [frəʊz] *pt* ⊳ **freeze.**

frozen [frəʊzn] ⬦ *pp* ⊳ **freeze.** ⬦ *adj* **- 1.** [gen] helado(da) **- 2.** [foodstuffs] congelado(da).

frugal ['fruːgl] *adj* frugal.

fruit [fruːt] (*pl inv* OR **fruits**) *n* **- 1.** [food] fruta *f* **- 2.** [result] fruto *m*.

fruitcake ['fruːtkeɪk] *n* pastel *m* de frutas.

fruiterer ['fruːtərəʳ] *n UK* frutero *m*, -ra *f*; **~'s (shop)** frutería *f*.

fruitful ['fruːtfʊl] *adj* [successful] fructífero(ra).

fruition [fruː'ɪʃn] *n*: **to come to ~** [plan] realizarse; [hope] cumplirse.

fruit juice *n* zumo *m* de fruta.

fruitless ['fruːtlɪs] *adj* infructuoso(sa).

fruit machine *n UK* máquina *f* tragaperras.

fruit salad *n* macedonia *f* (de frutas).

frumpy ['frʌmpɪ] (*compar* **-ier**, *superl* **-iest**) *adj* chapado(da) a la antigua en el vestir.

frustrate [frʌ'streɪt] *vt* frustrar.

frustrated [frʌ'streɪtɪd] *adj* frustrado(da).

frustration [frʌ'streɪʃn] *n* frustración *f*.

fry [fraɪ] (*pt* & *pp* **fried**) ⬦ *vt* [food] freír. ⬦ *vi* [food] freírse.

frying pan ['fraɪɪŋ-] *n* sartén *f*, paila *f Andes, CAm.*

ft. *abbr of* **foot**, **feet.**

FTP (*abbr of* **file transfer protocol**) *n* COMPUT FTP *m*.

fuck [fʌk] *vt* & *vi vulg* joder, follar, chingar *Méx.*
 ⬦ **fuck off** *vi vulg*: **~ off!** ¡vete a tomar por culo!

fudge [fʌdʒ] *n (U)* [sweet] *dulce de azúcar, leche y mantequilla.*

fuel [fjʊəl] (*UK pt & pp* **-led**, *cont* **-ling**, *US pt & pp* **-ed**, *cont* **-ing**) *◇ n* combustible *m*. *◇ vt* **-1.** [supply with fuel] alimentar **-2.** [increase] agravar.

fuel cell *n* pila *f* de combustible.

fuel tank *n* depósito *m* de gasolina.

fugitive [ˈfjuːdʒətɪv] *n* fugitivo *m*, -va *f*.

fulfil (*pt & pp* **-led**, *cont* **-ling**), **fulfill** *US* [fʊlˈfɪl] *vt* [promise, duty, threat] cumplir; [hope, ambition] realizar; [obligation] cumplir con; [role] desempeñar; [requirement] satisfacer.

fulfilment, fulfillment *US* [fʊlˈfɪlmənt] *n* **-1.** [satisfaction] satisfacción *f*, realización *f* (de uno mismo) **-2.** [of promise, duty, threat] cumplimiento *m*; [of hope, ambition] realización *f*; [of role] desempeño *m*; [of requirement] satisfacción *f*.

full [fʊl] *◇ adj* **-1.** [filled]: ~ (of) lleno(na) (de); I'm ~! [after meal] ¡no puedo más! **-2.** [schedule] completo(ta) **-3.** [complete - recovery, employment, control] pleno(na); [- name, price, fare] completo(ta); [- explanation, information] detallado(da); [- member, professor] numerario(ria); **three ~ weeks** tres semanas enteras **-4.** [maximum - volume, power etc] máximo(ma); at ~ **speed** a toda velocidad **-5.** [plump] grueso(sa) **-6.** [wide] holgado(da), amplio(plia). *◇ adv* [very]: **to know sthg ~ well** saber algo perfectamente. *◇ n*: **to pay in** ~ pagar el total; **write your name in** ~ escriba su nombre y apellidos.

full-blown [-ˈbləʊn] *adj* [gen] auténtico(-ca); [AIDS]: **to have ~ AIDS** haber desarrollado el SIDA por completo.

full board *n* pensión *f* completa.

full-fledged *US* = **fully-fledged**.

full moon *n* luna *f* llena.

full-scale *adj* **-1.** [life-size] de tamaño natural **-2.** [complete] a gran escala.

full stop *n* punto *m*.

full time *n UK* SPORT final *m* del (tiempo reglamentario del) partido.

  ◆ **full-time** *adj & adv* a tiempo completa.

full up *adj* lleno(na).

fully [ˈfʊlɪ] *adv* **-1.** [completely] completamente **-2.** [thoroughly] detalladamente.

fully-fledged *UK*, **full-fledged** *US* [-ˈfledʒd] *adj* fig hecho(cha) y derecho(cha); [member] de pleno derecho.

fulsome [ˈfʊlsəm] *adj* exagerado(da), excesivo(va).

fumble [ˈfʌmbl] *vi* hurgar; **to ~ for sthg** [for key, light switch] buscar algo a tientas; [for words] buscar algo titubeando.

fume [fjuːm] *vi* [with anger] rabiar.

  ◆ **fumes** *npl* humo *m*.

fumigate [ˈfjuːmɪgeɪt] *vt* fumigar.

fun [fʌn] *n (U)* **-1.** [pleasure, amusement] diversión *f*; **to have ~** divertirse; **have ~!** ¡que te diviertas!; **for ~, for the ~ of it** por diversión **-2.** [playfulness]: **he's full of ~** le encanta todo lo que sea diversión **-3.** [at sb else's expense]: **to make ~ of sb, to poke ~ at sb** reírse OR burlarse de alguien.

function [ˈfʌŋkʃn] *◇ n* **-1.** [gen & MATH] función *f* **-2.** [formal social event] acto *m*. *◇ vi* funcionar; **to ~ as** hacer de.

functional [ˈfʌŋkʃnəl] *adj* **-1.** [practical] funcional **-2.** [operational] en funcionamiento.

fund [fʌnd] *◇ n* fondo *m*. *◇ vt* financiar.

  ◆ **funds** *npl* fondos *mpl*.

fundamental [ˌfʌndəˈmentl] *adj*: ~ **(to)** fundamental (para).

funding [ˈfʌndɪŋ] *n* **-1.** [financing] financiación *f* **-2.** [funds] fondos *mpl*.

funeral [ˈfjuːnərəl] *n* funeral *m*.

funeral parlour *n* funeraria *f*.

funfair [ˈfʌnfeəʳ] *n* feria *f*.

fungus [ˈfʌŋgəs] (*pl* **-gi** [-gaɪ] OR **-guses**) *n* hongo *m*.

funnel [ˈfʌnl] *n* **-1.** [for pouring] embudo *m* **-2.** [on ship] chimenea *f*.

funny [ˈfʌnɪ] (*compar* **-ier**, *superl* **-iest**) *adj* **-1.** [amusing] divertido(da); **I don't think that's ~** no me hace gracia **-2.** [odd] raro(ra) **-3.** [ill] pachucho(cha).

fur [fɜːʳ] *n* **-1.** [on animal] pelaje *m*, pelo *m* **-2.** [garment] (prenda *f* de) piel *f*.

fur coat *n* abrigo *m* de piel OR pieles.

furious [ˈfjʊərɪəs] *adj* **-1.** [very angry] furioso(sa) **-2.** [frantic] frenético(ca).

furlong [ˈfɜːlɒŋ] *n* 201,17 metros.

furnace [ˈfɜːnɪs] *n* horno *m*.

furnish [ˈfɜːnɪʃ] *vt* **-1.** [fit out] amueblar **-2.** *fml* [provide - goods, explanation] proveer, suministrar; [- proof] aducir; **to ~ sb with sthg** proporcionar algo a alguien.

furnished [ˈfɜːnɪʃt] *adj* amueblado(da).

furnishings [ˈfɜːnɪʃɪŋz] *npl* mobiliario *m*.

furniture [ˈfɜːnɪtʃəʳ] *n (U)* muebles *mpl*, mobiliario *m*; **a piece of ~** un mueble.

furrow [ˈfʌrəʊ] *n* lit & fig surco *m*.

furry [ˈfɜːrɪ] (*compar* **-ier**, *superl* **-iest**) *adj* **-1.** [animal] peludo(da) **-2.** [toy] de peluche.

further [ˈfɜːðəʳ] *◇ compar ⊳* **far**. *◇ adv* **-1.** [in distance] más lejos; **how much ~ is it?** ¿cuánto queda (de camino)?; ~ **on** más adelante **-2.** [in degree, extent, time] más; ~ **on/back** más adelante/atrás **-3.** [in addition] además. *◇ adj* otro(tra); **until ~ notice** hasta nuevo aviso; **nothing ~** nada más. *◇ vt* promover, fomentar.

further education *n UK estudios postescolares no universitarios.*

furthermore [ˌfɜːðəˈmɔːʳ] *adv* lo que es más.

furthest ['fɜːðɪst] ⬦ *superl* ⊳ **far**. ⬦ *adj* - **1**. [in distance] más lejano(na) - **2**. [greatest - in degree, extent] extremo(ma). ⬦ *adv* - **1**. [in distance] más lejos - **2**. [to greatest degree, extent] más.

furtive ['fɜːtɪv] *adj* furtivo(va).

fury ['fjʊərɪ] *n* furia *f*.

fuse *esp* UK, **fuze** US [fjuːz] ⬦ *n* - **1**. ELEC fusible *m* - **2**. [of firework] mecha *f*. ⬦ *vt* fundir. ⬦ *vi* [gen & ELEC] fundirse.

fuse-box *n* caja *f* de fusibles.

fused [fjuːzd] *adj* [fitted with a fuse] con fusible.

fuselage ['fjuːzəlɑːʒ] *n* fuselaje *m*.

fuss [fʌs] ⬦ *n* (U) - **1**. [excitement, anxiety] jaleo *m*, alboroto *m*; **to make a ~** armar un escándalo - **2**. [complaints] protestas *fpl*. ⬦ *vi* apurarse, angustiarse.

fussy ['fʌsɪ] (*compar* **-ier**, *superl* **-iest**) *adj* - **1**. [fastidious] quisquilloso(sa); **I'm not ~** me da lo mismo - **2**. [over-decorated] recargado(da), aparatoso(sa).

futile ['fjuːtaɪl] *adj* inútil, vano(na).

futon ['fuːtɒn] *n* futón *m*.

future ['fjuːtʃə'] ⬦ *n* futuro *m*; **in ~** de ahora en adelante; **in the ~** en el futuro; **in the not too distant ~** en un futuro próximo; **~ (tense)** futuro *m*. ⬦ *adj* futuro(ra).

fuze [fjuːz] US = **fuse**.

fuzzy ['fʌzɪ] (*compar* **-ier**, *superl* **-iest**) *adj* - **1**. [hair] crespo(pa) - **2**. [photo, image] borroso(sa).

g¹ (*pl* **g's** OR **gs**), **G** (*pl* **G's** OR **Gs**) [dʒiː] *n* [letter] g *f*, G *f*.
◆ **G** *n* - **1**. MUS sol *m* - **2**. (*abbr of* **good**) B.

g² *n* (*abbr of* **gram**) g. *m*.

gab [gæb] ⊳ **gift**.

gabble ['gæbl] ⬦ *vt* & *vi* farfullar, balbucir. ⬦ *n* farfulleo *m*.

gable ['geɪbl] *n* aguilón *m*.

gadget ['gædʒɪt] *n* artilugio *m*, chisme *m*.

Gaelic ['geɪlɪk] *n* [language] gaélico *m*.

gaffe [gæf] *n* metedura *f* de pata, patinazo *m*.

gag [gæg] (*pt* & *pp* **-ged**, *cont* **-ging**) ⬦ *n* - **1**. [for mouth] mordaza *f* - **2**. *inf* [joke] chiste *m*. ⬦ *vt* amordazar.

gage [geɪdʒ] US = **gauge**.

gaiety ['geɪətɪ] *n* alegría *f*, regocijo *m*.

gaily ['geɪlɪ] *adv* alegremente.

gain [geɪn] ⬦ *n* - **1**. [profit] beneficio *m*, ganancia *f* - **2**. [improvement] mejora *f* - **3**. [increase] aumento *m*. ⬦ *vt* [gen] ganar. ⬦ *vi* - **1**. [advance]: **to ~ in sthg** ganar algo - **2**. [benefit]: **to ~ (from** OR **by)** beneficiarse (de) - **3**. [watch, clock] adelantarse.
◆ **gain on** *vt fus* ganar terreno a.

gait [geɪt] *n* forma *f* de andar.

gal. *abbr of* **gallon**.

gala ['gɑːlə] *n* [celebration] fiesta *f*.

galaxy ['gæləksɪ] (*pl* **-ies**) *n* galaxia *f*.

gale [geɪl] *n* vendaval *m*.

gall [gɔːl] *n* [nerve]: **to have the ~ to do sthg** tener el descaro de hacer algo.

gallant [*sense 1* 'gælənt, *sense 2* gə'lænt, 'gælənt] *adj* - **1**. [courageous] valiente, valeroso(sa) - **2**. [polite to women] galante.

gall bladder *n* vesícula *f* biliar.

gallery ['gælərɪ] (*pl* **-ies**) *n* - **1**. [for exhibiting art] museo *m*; [for selling art] galería *f* - **2**. [in courtroom, parliament] tribuna *f* - **3**. [in theatre] paraíso *m*.

galley ['gælɪ] (*pl* **galleys**) *n* - **1**. [ship] galera *f* - **2**. [kitchen] cocina *f*.

galling ['gɔːlɪŋ] *adj* indignante.

gallivant [ˌgælɪ'vænt] *vi inf* andar por ahí holgazaneando.

gallon ['gælən] *n* - **1**. [en Gran Bretaña] = 4,546 litros, galón *m* - **2**. [en Estados Unidos] = 3,785 litros, galón *m*.

gallop ['gæləp] ⬦ *n* galope *m*. ⬦ *vi lit* & *fig* galopar.

gallows ['gæləʊz] (*pl inv*) *n* horca *f*, patíbulo *m*.

gallstone ['gɔːlstəʊn] *n* cálculo *m* biliar.

galore [gə'lɔː'] *adj* en abundancia.

galvanize, -ise ['gælvənaɪz] *vt* - **1**. TECH galvanizar - **2**. [impel]: **to ~ sb into action** impulsar a alguien a la acción.

gambit ['gæmbɪt] *n* táctica *f*.

gamble ['gæmbl] ⬦ *n* [calculated risk] riesgo *m*. ⬦ *vi* - **1**. [bet] jugar; **to ~ on** [race etc] apostar a; [stock exchange] jugar a - **2**. [take risk]: **to ~ on** contar de antemano con que.

gambler ['gæmblə'] *n* jugador *m*, -ra *f*.

gambling ['gæmblɪŋ] *n* (U) juego *m*.

game [geɪm] ⬦ *n* - **1**. [gen] juego *m* - **2**. [of football, rugby etc] partido *m*; [of snooker, chess, cards] partida *f* - **3**. [hunted animals] caza *f*. ⬦ *adj* - **1**. [brave] valiente - **2**. [willing]: **~ (for sthg/to do sthg)** dispuesto(ta) (a algo/a hacer algo).
◆ **games** ⬦ *n* (U) [at school] deportes *mpl*. ⬦ *npl* [sporting contest] juegos *mpl*.

gamekeeper ['geɪmˌkiːpə'] *n* guarda *m* de caza.

game reserve *n* coto *m* de caza.

gammon ['gæmən] *n* jamón *m*.

gamut ['gæmət] *n* gama *f*.

gang [gæŋ] *n* **-1.** [of criminals] banda *f* **-2.** [of young people] pandilla *f.*
  ◆ **gang up** *vi inf*: to ~ up (on sb) confabularse (contra alguien).

gangland ['gæŋlænd] *n (U)* mundo *m* del hampa.

gangrene ['gæŋgriːn] *n* gangrena *f.*

gangster ['gæŋstər] *n* gángster *m.*

◆ **gangway** ['gæŋweɪ] *n UK* [aisle] pasillo *m.*

gantry ['gæntrɪ] *(pl* **-ies)** *n* pórtico *m (para grúas).*

gaol [dʒeɪl] *UK* = **jail.**

gap [gæp] *n* **-1.** [empty space, in market] hueco *m;* [in traffic, trees, clouds] claro *m;* [in text] espacio *m* en blanco **-2.** [interval] intervalo *m* **-3.** *fig* [in knowledge, report] laguna *f* **-4.** *fig* [great difference] desfase *m.*

gape [geɪp] *vi* [person] mirar boquiabierto(ta).

gaping ['geɪpɪŋ] *adj* **-1.** [open-mouthed] boquiabierto(ta) **-2.** [wound] abierto(ta); [hole] enorme.

garage [*UK* 'gæraːʒ, 'gærɪdʒ, *US* gəˈrɑːʒ] *n* **-1.** [for keeping car] garaje *m* **-2.** *UK* [for fuel] gasolinera *f* **-3.** [for car repair] taller *m* **-4.** *UK* [for selling cars] concesionario *m* de automóviles.

garbage ['gɑːbɪdʒ] *n esp US (U)* **-1.** [refuse] basura *f* **-2.** *inf* [nonsense] tonterías *fpl.*

garbage can *n US* cubo *m* de la basura.

garbage truck *n US* camión *m* de la basura.

garbled ['gɑːbld] *adj* confuso(sa).

garden ['gɑːdn] *n* jardín *m.*

garden centre *n* centro *m* de jardinería.

gardener ['gɑːdnər] *n* jardinero *m,* -ra *f.*

gardening ['gɑːdnɪŋ] *n* jardinería *f;* to do some ~ trabajar en el jardín.

gargle ['gɑːgl] *vi* hacer gárgaras.

gargoyle ['gɑːgɔɪl] *n* gárgola *f.*

garish ['geərɪʃ] *adj* chillón(ona), llamativo(va).

garland ['gɑːlənd] *n* guirnalda *f.*

garlic ['gɑːlɪk] *n* ajo *m.*

garlic bread *n* pan *m* de ajo.

garlic press *n* triturador *m* de ajos.

garment ['gɑːmənt] *n* prenda *f* (de vestir).

garnish ['gɑːnɪʃ] *vt* guarnecer.

garrison ['gærɪsn] *n* guarnición *f.*

garrulous ['gærələs] *adj* parlanchín(ina), gárrulo(la).

garter ['gɑːtər] *n* **-1.** [band round leg] liga *f* **-2.** *US* [suspender] portaligas *m inv;* liguero *m.*

gas [gæs] *(pl* **-es** OR **-ses,** *pt* & *pp* **-sed,** *cont* **-sing)** *n* **-1.** [gen] gas *m* **-2.** *US* [petrol] gasolina *f,* bencina *f Chile,* nafta *f RP.* *vt* asfixiar con gas.

gas cooker *n UK* cocina *f* de gas, estufa *f* de gas *CAm, Col, Méx.*

gas cylinder *n* bombona *f* de gas, garrafa *f* de gas *RP,* balón *m* de gas *Chile.*

gas fire *n UK* estufa *f* de gas.

gas gauge *n US* indicador *m* del nivel de gasolina OR bencina *Chile* OR nafta *RP.*

gash [gæʃ] *n* raja *f.* *vt* rajar.

gasket ['gæskɪt] *n* junta *f.*

gasman ['gæsmæn] *(pl* **-men** [-men]) *n* hombre *m* del gas.

gas mask *n* máscara *f* antigás.

gas meter *n* contador *m* del gas, medidor *m* del gas *Amér.*

gasoline ['gæsəliːn] *n US* gasolina *f.*

gasp [gɑːsp] *n* **-1.** [pant] resuello *m,* jadeo *m* **-2.** [of shock, surprise] grito *m* ahogado. *vi* **-1.** [breathe quickly] resollar, jadear **-2.** [in shock, surprise] ahogar un grito.

gas pedal *n US* acelerador *m.*

gas station *n US* gasolinera *f,* grifo *m Perú,* bomba *f Chile, Col, Ven,* estación *f* de nafta *RP.*

gas stove = **gas cooker.**

gas tank *n US* depósito *m* de gasolina, tanque *m* de gasolina *Perú* OR de bencina *Chile* OR de nafta *RP.*

gas tap *n* llave *f* del gas.

gastroenteritis ['gæstrəʊˌentəˈraɪtɪs] *n (U)* gastroenteritis *f inv.*

gastronomy [gæsˈtrɒnəmɪ] *n* gastronomía *f.*

gasworks ['gæswɜːks] *(pl inv)* *n* fábrica *f* de gas.

gate [geɪt] *n* **-1.** [gen] puerta *f;* [metal] verja *f* **-2.** SPORT [takings] taquilla *f;* [attendance] entrada *f.*

gâteau ['gætəʊ] *(pl* **-x** [-z]) *n UK* tarta *f* (con nata).

gatecrash ['geɪtkræʃ] *vi inf* colarse.

gateway ['geɪtweɪ] *n* **-1.** [entrance] puerta *f,* pórtico *m* **-2.** COMPUT pasarela *f.*

gather ['gæðər] *vt* **-1.** [collect] recoger; to ~ together reunir **-2.** [dust] llenarse de **-3.** [increase - speed, strength] ganar, cobrar **-4.** [understand]: to ~ (that) deducir que **-5.** [cloth] fruncir. *vi* [people, animals] reunirse; [clouds] acumularse.

gathering ['gæðərɪŋ] *n* [meeting] reunión *f.*

gauche [gəʊʃ] *adj* torpe.

gaudy ['gɔːdɪ] *(compar* **-ier,** *superl* **-iest)** *adj* chillón(ona), llamativo(va).

gauge, gage *US* [geɪdʒ] *n* **-1.** [for fuel, temperature] indicador *m;* [for width of tube, wire] calibrador *m* **-2.** [calibre] calibre *m* **-3.** RAIL ancho *m* de vía. *vt lit* & *fig* calibrar.

gaunt [gɔːnt] *adj* **-1.** [person, face] demacrado(da) **-2.** [building, landscape] adusto(ta).

gauntlet ['gɔːntlɪt] *n* guante *m;* to run the ~ of sthg exponerse a algo; to throw down the ~ **(to sb)** arrojar el guante (a alguien).

gauze [gɔ:z] *n* gasa *f*.

gave [geɪv] *pt* ⊳ **give**.

gawky ['gɔ:kɪ] (*compar* -**ier**, *superl* -**iest**) *adj* desgarbado(da).

gawp [gɔ:p] *vi*: **to ~ (at sthg/sb)** mirar boquiabierto(ta) (algo/a alguien).

gay [geɪ] ◇ *adj* -**1.** [homosexual] gay, homosexual -**2.** [cheerful, lively, bright] alegre. ◇ *n* gay *m* OR *f*.

gaze [geɪz] ◇ *n* mirada *f* fija. ◇ *vi*: **to ~ (at sthg/sb)** mirar fijamente (algo/a alguien).

gazelle [gə'zel] (*pl inv* OR -**s**) *n* gacela *f*.

gazetteer [,gæzɪ'tɪər] *n* índice *m* geográfico.

gazump [gə'zʌmp] *vt UK inf*: **to ~ sb** *acordar vender una casa a alguien y luego vendérsela a otro a un precio más alto.*

GB *n* -**1.** (*abbr of* **Great Britain**) GB *f* -**2.** COMPUT (*abbr of* **gigabyte**) GB *m*.

GCE (*abbr of* **General Certificate of Education**) *n* -**1.** [O level] *antiguo examen final de enseñanza secundaria en Gran Bretaña para alumnos de buen rendimiento escolar* -**2.** = **A level**.

GCSE (*abbr of* **General Certificate of Secondary Education**) *n examen final de enseñanza secundaria en Gran Bretaña.*

GDP (*abbr of* **gross domestic product**) *n* PIB *m*.

gear [gɪər] ◇ *n* -**1.** [mechanism] engranaje *m* -**2.** [speed - of car, bicycle] marcha *f*; **in ~** con una marcha metida; **out of ~** en punto muerto; **to change ~** cambiar de marcha -**3.** (*U*) [equipment, clothes] equipo *m* -**4.** (*U*) *inf* [stuff, possessions] bártulos *mpl*. ◇ *vt*: **to ~ sthg to** orientar OR encaminar algo hacia.
◆ **gear up** *vi*: **to ~ up for sthg/to do sthg** hacer preparativos para algo/para hacer algo.

gearbox ['gɪəbɒks] *n* caja *f* de cambios.

gear lever, gear stick *UK*, **gear shift** *US* *n* palanca *f* de cambios.

gear wheel *n* rueda *f* dentada.

GED *n US* (*abbr of* **General Equivalency Diploma**) *diploma de estudios secundarios para aquellos que no siguieron la ruta tradicional del bachillerato.*

geek [gi:k] *n esp US inf* lelo *m*, -la *f*, tontaina *mf*; **a computer ~** un monstruo de la informática.

geese [gi:s] *pl* ⊳ **goose**.

gel [dʒel] (*pt* & *pp* -**led**, *cont* -**ling**) ◇ *n* [for shower] gel *m*; [for hair] gomina *f*. ◇ *vi* -**1.** [thicken] aglutinarse -**2.** [plan] cuajar; [idea, thought] tomar forma.

gelatin ['dʒelətɪn], **gelatine** [,dʒelə'ti:n] *n* gelatina *f*.

gelignite ['dʒelɪgnaɪt] *n* gelignita *f*.

gem [dʒem] *n* [precious stone] gema *f*; [jewel, special person, thing] joya *f*.

Gemini ['dʒemɪnaɪ] *n* Géminis *m inv.*

gender ['dʒendər] *n* -**1.** GRAMM género *m* -**2.** [sex] sexo *m*.

gene [dʒi:n] *n* gen *m*.

general ['dʒenərəl] ◇ *adj* general. ◇ *n* general *m*.
◆ **in general** *adv* -**1.** [as a whole] en general -**2.** [usually] por lo general.

general anaesthetic *n* anestesia *f* general.

general delivery *n US* lista *f* de correos.

general election *n* elecciones *fpl* generales.

generalization [,dʒenərəlaɪ'zeɪʃn] *n* generalización *f*.

general knowledge *n* cultura *f* general.

generally ['dʒenərəlɪ] *adv* en general.

general practitioner *n* médico *m*, -ca *f* de cabecera.

general public *n*: **the ~** el gran público.

generate ['dʒenəreɪt] *vt* generar.

generation [,dʒenə'reɪʃn] *n* generación *f*.

generator ['dʒenəreɪtər] *n* generador *m*.

generosity [,dʒenə'rɒsɪtɪ] *n* generosidad *f*.

generous ['dʒenərəs] *adj* generoso(sa); [cut of clothes] amplio(plia).

genetic [dʒɪ'netɪk] *adj* genético(ca).
◆ **genetics** *n* (*U*) genética *f*.

genetically modified [dʒɪ'netɪkəlɪ'mɒdɪfaɪd] *adj* modificado(da) genéticamente, transgénico(ca).

Geneva [dʒɪ'ni:və] *n* Ginebra.

genial ['dʒi:njəl] *adj* cordial, afable.

genitals ['dʒenɪtlz] *npl* genitales *mpl*.

genius ['dʒi:njəs] (*pl* -**es**) *n* genio *m*.

gent [dʒent] *n inf* caballero *m*.
◆ **gents** *n UK* [toilets] servicio *m* de caballeros.

genteel [dʒen'ti:l] *adj* fino(na), refinado(da).

gentle ['dʒentl] *adj* -**1.** [kind] tierno(na), dulce -**2.** [breeze, movement, slope] suave -**3.** [scolding] ligero(ra); [hint] sutil.

gentleman ['dʒentlmən] (*pl* -**men** [-mən]) *n* -**1.** [well-behaved man] caballero *m* -**2.** [man] señor *m*, caballero *m*.

gently ['dʒentlɪ] *adv* -**1.** [kindly] dulcemente -**2.** [softly, smoothly] suavemente -**3.** [carefully] con cuidado.

gentry ['dʒentrɪ] *n* alta burguesía *f*.

genuine ['dʒenjʊɪn] *adj* -**1.** [real] auténtico(ca), genuino(na) -**2.** [sincere] sincero(ra).

geography [dʒɪ'ɒgrəfɪ] *n* geografía *f*.

geology [dʒɪ'ɒlədʒɪ] *n* geología *f*.

geometric(al) [,dʒɪə'metrɪk(l)] *adj* geométrico(ca).

geometry [dʒɪ'ɒmɪtrɪ] *n* geometría *f*.

geranium [dʒɪ'reɪnjəm] (*pl* -**s**) *n* geranio *m*.

gerbil ['dʒɜ:bɪl] *n* jerbo *m*, gerbo *m*.

geriatric [,dʒerɪ'ætrɪk] ⬦ *adj* [of old people] geriátrico(ca). ⬦ *n* - **1.** MED anciano *m*, -na *f* - **2.** [very old person] *inf* vejestorio *m*.

germ [dʒɜ:m] *n* BIOL & *fig* germen *m*; MED microbio *m*.

German ['dʒɜ:mən] ⬦ *adj* alemán(ana). ⬦ *n* - **1.** [person] alemán *m*, -ana *f* - **2.** [language] alemán *m*.

German measles *n* rubéola *f*.

Germany ['dʒɜ:mənɪ] (*pl* -**ies**) *n* Alemania.

germinate ['dʒɜ:mɪneɪt] *vt* & *vi* lit & *fig* germinar.

gerund ['dʒerənd] *n* gerundio *m*.

gesticulate [dʒes'tɪkjʊleɪt] *vi* gesticular.

gesture ['dʒestʃər] ⬦ *n* gesto *m*. ⬦ *vi*: **to** ~ **to** OR **towards sb** hacer gestos a alguien.

get [get] (*UK pt* & *pp* **got**, *cont* -**ting**, *US pt* **got**, *pp* **gotten**, *cont* -**ting**) ⬦ *vt* - **1.** [bring, fetch] traer; **can I** ~ **you something to eat/ drink?** ¿te traigo algo de comer/beber?; **I'll** ~ **my coat** voy a por el abrigo; **could you** ~ **me the boss, please?** [when phoning] póngame con el jefe - **2.** [door, phone] contestar a - **3.** [obtain] conseguir; **she got top marks** sacó las mejores notas - **4.** [buy] comprar - **5.** [receive] recibir; **what did you** ~ **for your birthday?** ¿qué te regalaron para tu cumpleaños?; **she** ~**s a good salary** gana un buen sueldo; **we don't** ~ **much rain** no llueve mucho - **6.** [catch - bus, criminal, illness] coger, agarrar *Amér*; **I've got a cold** estoy resfriado; **he got cancer** contrajo cáncer - **7.** [cause to do]: **to** ~ **sb to do sthg** hacer que alguien haga algo; **I'll** ~ **my sister to help** le pediré a mi hermana que ayude - **8.** [cause to be done]: **to** ~ **sthg done** mandar hacer algo; **have you got the car fixed yet?** ¿te han arreglado ya el coche? - **9.** [cause to become]: **to** ~ **sthg ready** preparar algo; **to** ~ **sthg dirty** ensuciar algo; **to** ~ **sb pregnant** dejar a alguien preñada - **10.** [cause to move]: **can you** ~ **it through the gap?** ¿puedes meterlo por el hueco?; **to** ~ **sthg/sb out of sthg** conseguir sacar algo/a alguien de algo - **11.** [experience - a sensation]: **do you** ~ **the feeling he doesn't like us?** ¿no te da la sensación de que no le gustamos? - **12.** [understand] entender; **I don't** ~ **it** *inf* no me aclaro, no lo entiendo; **he didn't seem to** ~ **the point** no pareció captar el sentido - **13.** *inf* [annoy] poner negro(gra) - **14.** [find]: **you** ~ **a lot of artists here** hay mucho artista por aquí; *see also* **have**. ⬦ *vi* - **1.** [become] ponerse; **to** ~ **angry/pale** ponerse furioso/pálido; **to** ~ **ready** prepararse; **to** ~ **dressed** vestirse; **I'm getting cold/bored** me estoy enfriando/ aburriendo; **it's getting late** se está haciendo tarde - **2.** [arrive] llegar; **how do I** ~

there? ¿cómo se llega (allí)?; **to** ~ **home** llegar a casa; **I only got back yesterday** regresé justo ayer - **3.** [eventually succeed]: **to** ~ **to do sthg** llegar a hacer algo; **did you** ~ **to see him?** ¿conseguiste verlo? - **4.** [progress] llegar; **how far have you got?** ¿cuánto llevas?, ¿hasta dónde has llegado?; **now we're getting somewhere** ahora sí que vamos por buen camino; **we're getting nowhere** así no llegamos a ninguna parte. ⬦ *aux vb*: **to** ~ **excited** emocionarse; **someone could** ~ **hurt** alguien podría resultar herido; **I got beaten up** me zurraron; **let's** ~ **going** OR **moving** vamos a ponernos en marcha.

◆ **get about, get around** *vi* - **1.** [move from place to place] salir a menudo - **2.** [circulate - news etc] difundirse; *see also* **get around**.

◆ **get along** *vi* - **1.** [manage] arreglárselas, apañárselas - **2.** [progress]: **how are you getting along?** ¿cómo te va? - **3.** [have a good relationship]: **to** ~ **along (with sb)** llevarse bien (con alguien).

◆ **get around, get round** ⬦ *vt fus* [overcome - problem] evitar; [- obstacle] sortear. ⬦ *vi* - **1.** [circulate - news etc] difundirse - **2.** [eventually do]: **to** ~ **around to (doing) sthg** sacar tiempo para (hacer) algo; *see also* **get about**.

◆ **get at** *vt fus* - **1.** [reach] llegar a, alcanzar - **2.** [imply] referirse a - **3.** *inf* [criticize]: **stop getting at me!** ¡deja ya de meterte conmigo!

◆ **get away** *vi* - **1.** [leave] salir, irse - **2.** [go on holiday]: **I really need to** ~ **away** necesito unas buenas vacaciones - **3.** [escape] escaparse.

◆ **get away with** *vt fus* salir impune de; **she lets him** ~ **away with everything** ella se lo consiente todo.

◆ **get back** ⬦ *vt sep* [recover, regain] recuperar. ⬦ *vi* - **1.** [move away] echarse atrás, apartarse - **2.** [return] volver.

◆ **get back to** *vt fus* - **1.** [return to previous state, activity] volver a; **to** ~ **back to sleep/ normal** volver a dormirse/a la normalidad - **2.** *esp US inf* [phone back]: **I'll** ~ **back to you later** te llamo de vuelta más tarde.

◆ **get by** *vi* apañárselas.

◆ **get down** *vt sep* - **1.** [depress] deprimir - **2.** [fetch from higher level] bajar - **3.** [write down] anotar.

◆ **get down to** *vt fus*: **to** ~ **down to doing sthg** ponerse a hacer algo.

◆ **get in** *vi* - **1.** [enter] entrar - **2.** [arrive] llegar.

◆ **get into** *vt fus* - **1.** [car] subir a - **2.** [become involved in] meterse en - **3.** [enter into a particular situation, state]: **to** ~ **into a panic** OR **state** ponerse nerviosísimo; **to** ~ **into**

trouble meterse en líos; **to ~ into the habit of doing sthg** adquirir el hábito OR coger la costumbre de hacer algo **- 4.** [be accepted as a student at]: **she managed to ~ into Oxford** consiguió entrar en Oxford.

◆ **get off** ◇ *vt sep* **-1.** [remove] quitar **- 2.** [prevent from being punished] librar. ◇ *vt fus* **-1.** [go away from] irse OR salirse de; **~ off my land!** ¡fuera de mis tierras! **- 2.** [train, bus, table] bajarse de. ◇ *vi* **-1.** [leave bus, train] bajarse, desembarcarse *Amér* **- 2.** [escape punishment] escaparse; **he got off lightly** salió bien librado **- 3.** [depart] irse, salir.

◆ **get off with** *vt fus* UK *inf* ligar con.

◆ **get on** ◇ *vt fus* [bus, train, horse] subirse a. ◇ *vi* **-1.** [enter bus, train] subirse, montarse **- 2.** [have good relationship] llevarse bien **- 3.** [progress]: **how are you getting on?** ¿cómo te va? **- 4.** [proceed]: **to ~ on with sthg** seguir OR continuar con algo **- 5.** [be successful professionally] triunfar.

◆ **get out** ◇ *vt sep* [remove - object, prisoner] sacar; [- stain etc] quitar; **she got a pen out of her bag** sacó un bolígrafo del bolso. ◇ *vi* **-1.** [leave] salir; **~ out!** ¡vete de aquí! **- 2.** [leave car, bus, train] bajarse **- 3.** [become known - news] difundirse, filtrarse.

◆ **get out of** *vt fus* **-1.** [car, bus, train] bajar de; [bed] levantarse de **- 2.** [escape from] escapar OR huir de **- 3.** [avoid] eludir; **to ~ out of (doing) sthg** librarse de (hacer) algo.

◆ **get over** ◇ *vt fus* **-1.** [recover from] recuperarse de **- 2.** [overcome] superar. ◇ *vt sep* [communicate] hacer comprender.

◆ **get round** = **get around**.

◆ **get through** ◇ *vt fus* **-1.** [job, task] terminar, acabar **- 2.** [exam] aprobar **- 3.** [food, drink] consumir **- 4.** [unpleasant situation] sobrevivir a, aguantar. ◇ *vi* **-1.** [make oneself understood]: **to ~ through (to sb)** hacerse comprender (por alguien) **- 2.** TELEC conseguir comunicar.

◆ **get to** ◇ *vt fus inf* [annoy] fastidiar, molestar. ◇ *vi* [end up] ir a parar.

◆ **get together** ◇ *vt sep* [organize - project, demonstration] organizar, montar; [- team] juntar; [- report] preparar. ◇ *vi* juntarse, reunirse.

◆ **get up** ◇ *vi* levantarse. ◇ *vt fus* [organize - petition etc] preparar, organizar.

◆ **get up to** *vt fus inf* hacer, montar.

getaway ['getəweɪ] *n* fuga *f*, huida *f*; **to make one's ~** darse a la fuga.

get-together *n inf* reunión *f*.

geyser ['gi:zə'] *n* **-1.** [hot spring] géiser *m* **- 2.** UK [water heater] calentador *m* de agua.

Ghana ['gɑːnə] *n* Ghana.

ghastly ['gɑːstlɪ] (*compar* -ier, *superl* -iest) *adj* **-1.** *inf* [very bad, unpleasant] horrible,

espantoso(sa) **- 2.** [horrifying] horripilante **- 3.** [ill] fatal.

gherkin ['gɜːkɪn] *n* pepinillo *m*.

ghetto ['getəʊ] (*pl* -s OR -es) *n* gueto *m*.

ghetto blaster [-'blɑːstə'] *n inf* radiocasete *portátil de gran tamaño y potencia*.

ghost [gəʊst] *n* [spirit] fantasma *m*.

giant ['dʒaɪənt] ◇ *adj* gigantesco(ca). ◇ *n* gigante *m*.

gibberish ['dʒɪbərɪʃ] *n* galimatías *m inv*.

gibe [dʒaɪb] ◇ *n* pulla *f*. ◇ *vi*: **to ~ (at)** mofarse (de).

giblets ['dʒɪblɪts] *npl* menudillos *mpl*.

Gibraltar [dʒɪ'brɔːltə'] *n* Gibraltar; **the Rock of ~** el Peñón.

giddy ['gɪdɪ] (*compar* -ier, *superl* -iest) *adj* mareado(da); **to be ~** [have vertigo] tener vértigo.

gift [gɪft] *n* **-1.** [present] regalo *m*, obsequio *m* **- 2.** [talent] don *m*; **to have a ~ for sthg/for doing sthg** tener un don especial para algo/para hacer algo; **to have the ~ of the gab** tener un pico de oro.

gift certificate *US* = **gift token**.

gifted ['gɪftɪd] *adj* **-1.** [talented] dotado(da), de talento **- 2.** [extremely intelligent] superdotado(da).

gift token, gift voucher *n* UK vale *m* OR cupón *m* para regalo.

gig [gɪg] *n inf* [concert] concierto *m*.

gigabyte ['gaɪgəbaɪt] *n* COMPUT gigabyte *m*.

gigantic [dʒaɪ'gæntɪk] *adj* gigantesco(ca).

giggle ['gɪgl] ◇ *n* **-1.** [laugh] risita *f*, risa *f* tonta **- 2.** UK *inf* [fun]: **it's a real ~** es la mar de divertido; **to do sthg for a ~** hacer algo por puro cachondeo. ◇ *vi* [laugh] soltar risitas.

gilded ['gɪldɪd] = **gilt**.

gill [dʒɪl] *n* [unit of measurement] = 0,142 *litros*.

gills [gɪlz] *npl* [of fish] agallas *fpl*.

gilt [gɪlt] ◇ *adj* dorado(da). ◇ *n* dorado *m*.

gilt-edged *adj* FIN de máxima garantía.

gimmick ['gɪmɪk] *n pej* artilugio *m* innecesario; **advertising ~** reclamo *m* publicitario.

gin [dʒɪn] *n* ginebra *f*; **~ and tonic** gin-tonic *m*.

ginger ['dʒɪndʒə'] ◇ *adj* UK **-1.** [hair] bermejo(ja); **to have ~ hair** ser pelirrojo(ja) **- 2.** [cat] de color bermejo. ◇ *n* jengibre *m*.

ginger ale *n* [mixer] ginger-ale *m*.

ginger beer *n* [slightly alcoholic] refresco *m* de jengibre.

gingerbread ['dʒɪndʒəbred] *n* **-1.** [cake] pan *m* de jengibre **- 2.** [biscuit] galleta *f* de jengibre.

ginger-haired [-'heəd] *adj* pelirrojo(ja).

gingerly ['dʒɪndʒəlɪ] *adv* con mucho tiento.

gipsy ['dʒɪpsɪ] (pl **-ies**) UK <> adj gitano(-na). <> n gitano m, -na f.

giraffe [dʒɪˈrɑːf] (pl inv OR **-s**) n jirafa f.

girder ['gɜːdəʳ] n viga f.

girdle ['gɜːdl] n [corset] faja f.

girl [gɜːl] n - **1.** [child] niña f - **2.** [young woman] chica f - **3.** [daughter] niña f, chica f - **4.** inf [female friend]: **the ~s** las amigas, las chicas.

girlfriend ['gɜːlfrend] n - **1.** [female lover] novia f - **2.** [female friend] amiga f.

girl guide UK, **girl scout** US n [individual] exploradora f.

giro ['dʒaɪrəʊ] (pl **-s**) n UK - **1.** (U) [system] giro m - **2.**: ~ **(cheque)** cheque m para giro bancario.

girth [gɜːθ] n - **1.** [circumference] circunferencia f - **2.** [of horse] cincha f.

gist [dʒɪst] n: **the ~ of** lo esencial de; **to get the ~ (of sthg)** entender el sentido (de algo).

give [gɪv] (pt **gave**, pp **given**) <> vt - **1.** [gen] dar; [time, effort] dedicar; [attention] prestar; **to ~ sb/sthg sthg**, **to ~ sthg to sb/ sthg** dar algo a alguien/algo; **he was ~n twenty years** [sentenced to] le cayeron veinte años - **2.** [as present]: **to ~ sb sthg**, **to ~ sthg to sb** regalar algo a alguien - **3.** [hand over]: **to ~ sb sthg**, **to ~ sthg to sb** entregar OR dar algo a alguien. <> vi [collapse, break] romperse, ceder; [stretch] dar de sí.

◆ **give or take** prep más o menos; **in half an hour ~ or take five minutes** en media hora, cinco minutos más o menos.

◆ **give away** vt sep - **1.** [as present] regalar - **2.** [reveal] revelar, descubrir - **3.** [bride] llevar al altar.

◆ **give back** vt sep [return] devolver, regresar Méx.

◆ **give in** vi - **1.** [admit defeat] rendirse, darse por vencido(da), transar Amér - **2.** [agree unwillingly]: **to ~ in to sthg** ceder ante algo.

◆ **give off** vt fus [produce, emit] despedir.

◆ **give out** <> vt sep [distribute] repartir, distribuir. <> vi [supply, strength] agotarse, acabarse; [legs, machine] fallar.

◆ **give up** <> vt sep - **1.** [stop] abandonar; **to ~ up chocolate** dejar de comer chocolate - **2.** [job] dejar - **3.** [surrender]: **to ~ o.s. up (to sb)** entregarse (a alguien). <> vi rendirse, darse por vencido(da).

given ['gɪvn] <> adj - **1.** [set, fixed] dado(da) - **2.** [prone]: **to be ~ to sthg/to doing sthg** ser dado(da) a algo/a hacer algo. <> prep [taking into account] dado(da); ~ **that** dado que.

given name n esp US nombre m de pila.

glacier ['glæsjəʳ] n glaciar m.

glad [glæd] (compar **-der**, superl **-dest**) adj - **1.** [happy, pleased] alegre, contento(ta); **to be ~ about/that** alegrarse de/de que - **2.** [willing]: **to be ~ to do sthg** tener gusto en hacer algo - **3.** [grateful]: **to be ~ of sthg** agradecer algo.

gladly ['glædlɪ] adv - **1.** [happily, eagerly] alegremente - **2.** [willingly] con mucho gusto.

glamor US = **glamour**.

glamorous ['glæmərəs] adj atractivo(va), lleno(na) de encanto.

glamour UK, **glamor** US ['glæməʳ] n encanto m, atractivo m.

glance [glɑːns] <> n [quick look] mirada f, vistazo m; **at a ~** de un vistazo; **at first ~** a primera vista. <> vi [look quickly]: **to ~ at sb** lanzar una mirada a alguien; **to ~ at sthg** echar una ojeada OR un vistazo a algo.

◆ **glance off** vt fus rebotar en.

glancing ['glɑːnsɪŋ] adj de refilón.

gland [glænd] n glándula f.

glandular fever ['glændjʊlə-'] n mononucleosis f inv infecciosa.

glare [gleəʳ] <> n - **1.** [scowl] mirada f asesina - **2.** [blaze, dazzle] resplandor m, deslumbramiento m - **3.** (U) fig [of publicity] foco m. <> vi - **1.** [scowl]: **to ~ (at sthg/sb)** mirar con furia (algo/a alguien) - **2.** [blaze, dazzle] brillar.

glaring ['gleərɪŋ] adj - **1.** [very obvious] flagrante - **2.** [blazing, dazzling] deslumbrante.

glasnost ['glæznɒst] n glasnost f.

glass [glɑːs] <> n - **1.** [material] vidrio m, cristal m - **2.** [drinking vessel, glassful] vaso m; [with stem] copa f. <> comp de vidrio, de cristal.

◆ **glasses** npl [spectacles] gafas fpl.

glassware ['glɑːsweəʳ] n (U) cristalería f.

glassy ['glɑːsɪ] (compar **-ier**, superl **-iest**) adj - **1.** [smooth, shiny] cristalino(na) - **2.** [blank, lifeless] vidrioso(sa).

glaze [gleɪz] <> n [on pottery] vidriado m; [on food] glaseado m. <> vt - **1.** [pottery] vidriar; [food] glasear - **2.** [window] acristalar.

glazier ['gleɪzjəʳ] n vidriero m, -ra f.

gleam [gliːm] <> n [of light] destello m; [of hope] rayo m. <> vi relucir.

gleaming ['gliːmɪŋ] adj reluciente.

glean [gliːn] vt [gather] recoger; [information] extraer.

glee [gliː] n (U) [joy, delight] alegría f, regocijo m.

glen [glen] n Scot cañada f.

glib [glɪb] (compar **-ber**, superl **-best**) adj pej de mucha labia.

glide [glaɪd] vi - **1.** [move smoothly] deslizarse - **2.** [fly] planear.

glider ['glaɪdəʳ] n [plane] planeador m.

gliding ['glaɪdɪŋ] n [sport] vuelo m sin motor.

glimmer ['glɪmər] n -1. [faint light] luz f tenue -2. fig [trace, sign] atisbo m; [of hope] rayo m.

glimpse [glɪmps] ◇ n -1. [look, sight] vislumbre f -2. [idea, perception] asomo m, atisbo m. ◇ vt entrever, vislumbrar.

glint [glɪnt] ◇ n -1. [flash] destello m -2. [in eyes] brillo m. ◇ vi destellar.

glisten ['glɪsn] vi relucir, brillar.

glitter ['glɪtər] vi relucir, brillar.

gloat [gləʊt] vi: to ~ (over sthg) regodearse (con algo).

global ['gləʊbl] adj [worldwide] mundial, global; the ~ village la aldea global.

globalization [,gləʊbəlaɪ'zeɪʃn] n globalización f.

global warming [-'wɔːmɪŋ] n calentamiento m global, cambio m climático.

globe [gləʊb] n -1. [gen] globo m -2. [spherical map] globo m (terráqueo).

gloom [gluːm] n (U) -1. [darkness] penumbra f -2. [unhappiness] pesimismo m, melancolía f.

gloomy ['gluːmɪ] (compar -ier, superl -iest) adj -1. [dark, cloudy] oscuro(ra) -2. [unhappy] melancólico(ca) -3. [without hope - report, forecast] pesimista; [- situation, prospects] desalentador(ra).

glorious ['glɔːrɪəs] adj magnífico(ca), espléndido(da).

glory ['glɔːrɪ] (pl -ies) n -1. [gen] gloria f -2. [beauty, splendour] esplendor m.
◆ **glory in** vt fus [relish] disfrutar de, regocijarse con.

gloss [glɒs] n -1. [shine] lustre m, brillo m -2.: ~ (paint) pintura f esmalte.
◆ **gloss over** vt fus tocar muy por encima.

glossary ['glɒsərɪ] (pl -ies) n glosario m.

glossy ['glɒsɪ] (compar -ier, superl -iest) adj -1. [smooth, shiny] lustroso(sa) -2. [on shiny paper] de papel satinado.

glove [glʌv] n guante m.

glove compartment n guantera f.

glow [gləʊ] ◇ n [light] fulgor m. ◇ vi [gen] brillar.

glower ['glaʊər] vi: to ~ (at sthg/sb) mirar con furia (algo/a alguien).

glucose ['gluːkəʊs] n glucosa f.

glue [gluː] (cont **glueing** OR **gluing**) ◇ n [paste] pegamento m; [for glueing wood, metal etc] cola f. ◇ vt [paste] pegar (con pegamento); [wood, metal etc] encolar.

glum [glʌm] (compar -mer, superl -mest) adj [unhappy] sombrío(a).

glut [glʌt] n superabundancia f.

glutton ['glʌtn] n [greedy person] glotón m, -ona f; **to be a ~ for punishment** ser un masoquista.

GM foods npl alimentos mpl transgénicos.

GMO (abbr of **genetically modified organism**) ◇ adj transgénico(ca). ◇ n OMG m.

gnarled [nɑːld] adj nudoso(sa).

gnash [næʃ] vt: to ~ one's teeth hacer rechinar los dientes.

gnat [næt] n mosquito m.

gnaw [nɔː] vt [chew] roer; to ~ (away) at sb corroer a alguien.

gnome [nəʊm] n gnomo m.

GNP (abbr of **gross national product**) n PNB m.

GNVQ (abbr of **General National Vocational Qualification**) n EDUC curso de formación profesional de dos años de duración para los mayores de 16 años en Inglaterra y Gales.

go [gəʊ] (pt **went**, pp **gone**, pl **goes**) ◇ vi -1. [move, travel, attend] ir; **where are you ~ing?** ¿dónde vas?; **he's gone to Portugal** se ha ido a Portugal; **we went by bus/train** fuimos en autobús/tren; **to ~ and do sthg** ir a hacer algo; **where does this path ~?** ¿a dónde lleva este camino?; **to ~ right/left** girar a la derecha/izquierda; **to ~ swimming/shopping** ir a nadar/de compras; **to ~ for a walk/run** ir a dar un paseo/a correr; **to ~ to church/school** ir a misa/a la escuela -2. [depart - person] irse, marcharse; [- bus] salir; **I must ~, I have to ~** tengo que irme; **it's time we went** es hora de irse OR marcharse; **let's ~!** ¡vámonos! -3. [pass - time] pasar -4. [progress] ir; **to ~ well/badly** ir bien/mal; **how's it ~ing?** inf [how are you?] ¿qué tal? -5. [belong, fit] ir; **the plates ~ in the cupboard** los platos van en el armario; **it won't ~ into the suitcase** no cabe en la maleta -6. [become] ponerse; **to ~ grey** ponerse gris; **to ~ mad** volverse loco; **to ~ blind** quedarse ciego -7. [indicating intention, certainty, expectation]: **to be ~ing to do sthg** ir a hacer algo; **he said he was ~ing to be late** dijo que llegaría tarde; **it's ~ing to rain/snow** va a llover/nevar -8. [match, be compatible]: **to ~ (with)** ir bien (con); **this blouse goes well with the skirt** esta blusa va muy bien OR hace juego con la falda -9. [function, work] funcionar -10. [bell, alarm] sonar -11. [start] empezar -12. [stop working] estropearse; **the fuse must have gone** se ha debido fundir el fusible -13. [deteriorate]: **her sight/hearing is ~ing** está perdiendo la vista/el oído -14. [be disposed of]: **he'll have to ~** habrá que despedirle; **everything must ~!** ¡gran liquidación! -15. inf [expressing irritation, surprise]: **now what's he gone and done?** ¿qué leches ha hecho ahora? -16. [in division]: **three into two won't ~** dos entre tres no cabe. ◇ n -1. [turn] turno m; **it's my ~** me toca a mí -2. inf [attempt]: **to have a ~ at**

sthg intentar OR probar algo - **3.** *phr*: **to have a ~ at sb** *inf* echar una bronca a alguien; **to be on the ~** *inf* no parar, estar muy liado.

◆ **to go** *adv* [remaining]: **there are only three days to ~** sólo quedan tres días.

◆ **go about** ◇ *vt fus* - **1.** [perform] hacer, realizar; **to ~ about one's business** ocuparse uno de sus asuntos - **2.** [tackle]: **to ~ about doing sthg** apañárselas para hacer algo; **how do you intend ~ing about it?** ¿cómo piensas hacerlo? ◇ *vi* = go around.

◆ **go ahead** *vi* - **1.** [begin]: **to ~ ahead (with sthg)** seguir adelante (con algo); **~ ahead!** ¡adelante! - **2.** [take place] celebrarse - **3.** [in match, contest] ponerse por delante.

◆ **go along** *vi* [proceed]: **as you ~ along** a medida que lo vayas haciendo.

◆ **go along with** *vt fus* estar de acuerdo con.

◆ **go around** *vi* - **1.** [associate]: **to ~ around with sb** juntarse con alguien - **2.** [joke, illness, story] correr (por ahí).

◆ **go away** *vi* - **1.** [person, animal] irse; **~ away!** ¡vete! - **2.** [pain] desaparecer.

◆ **go back** *vi* - **1.** [return] volver - **2.** [clocks] atrasarse.

◆ **go back on** *vt fus* [one's word, promise] faltar a.

◆ **go back to** *vt fus* - **1.** [return to activity] continuar OR seguir con; **to ~ back to sleep** volver a dormir - **2.** [date from] remontarse a.

◆ **go by** ◇ *vi* [time, people, vehicles] pasar. ◇ *vt fus* - **1.** [be guided by] guiarse por - **2.** [judge from]: **~ing by her voice, I'd say she was French** a juzgar por su voz yo diría que es francesa.

◆ **go down** ◇ *vi* - **1.** [descend] bajar - **2.** [get lower - prices, temperature, swelling] bajar - **3.** [be accepted]: **to ~ down well/badly** tener una buena/mala acogida - **4.** [sun] ponerse - **5.** [tyre, balloon] deshincharse - **6.** [be relegated] descender. ◇ *vt fus* bajar.

◆ **go for** *vt fus* - **1.** [choose] escoger - **2.** [be attracted to]: **I don't really ~ for men like him** no me gustan mucho los hombres como él - **3.** [attack] lanzarse sobre, atacar - **4.** [try to obtain - record, job] ir a por.

◆ **go forward** *vi* [clocks] adelantarse.

◆ **go in** *vi* entrar.

◆ **go in for** *vt fus* - **1.** [competition, exam] presentarse a - **2.** [enjoy]: **I don't really ~ in for classical music** no me va la música clásica.

◆ **go into** *vt fus* - **1.** [enter] entrar en - **2.** [investigate] investigar - **3.** [take up as a profession] dedicarse a.

◆ **go off** ◇ *vi* - **1.** [explode - bomb]

estallar; [- gun] dispararse - **2.** [alarm] sonar - **3.** [go bad - food] estropearse; [- milk] cortarse - **4.** [lights, heating] apagarse - **5.** [happen]: **to ~ off (well/badly)** salir (bien/mal). ◇ *vt fus inf* [lose interest in] perder el gusto a OR el interés en.

◆ **go on** ◇ *vi* - **1.** [take place] pasar, ocurrir - **2.** [continue]: **to ~ on (doing sthg)** seguir (haciendo algo) - **3.** [proceed to further activity]: **to ~ on to sthg/to do sthg** pasar a algo/a hacer algo - **4.** [heating etc] encenderse - **5.** [talk for too long]: **to ~ on (about)** no parar de hablar (de). ◇ *vt fus* [be guided by] guiarse por. ◇ *excl* ¡venga!, ¡vamos!

◆ **go on at** *vt fus* [nag] dar la lata a.

◆ **go out** *vi* - **1.** [leave house] salir; **to ~ out for a meal** cenar fuera - **2.** [as friends or lovers]: **to ~ out (with sb)** salir (con alguien), pololear (con alguien) *Chile* - **3.** [tide] bajar - **4.** [light, fire, cigarette] apagarse.

◆ **go over** *vt fus* - **1.** [examine] repasar - **2.** [repeat] repetir.

◆ **go round** *vi* [revolve] girar, dar vueltas; *see also* **go around.**

◆ **go through** *vt fus* - **1.** [penetrate] atravesar - **2.** [experience] pasar por, experimentar - **3.** [study, search through] registrar; **she went through his pockets** le miró en los bolsillos.

◆ **go through with** *vt fus* llevar a cabo.

◆ **go towards** *vt fus* contribuir a.

◆ **go under** *vi lit & fig* hundirse.

◆ **go up** ◇ *vi* - **1.** [rise - person, prices, temperature, balloon] subir - **2.** [be built] levantarse, construirse. ◇ *vt fus* subir.

◆ **go without** ◇ *vt fus* prescindir de. ◇ *vi* apañárselas.

goad [gəʊd] *vt* [provoke] aguijonear, incitar.

go-ahead ◇ *adj* [dynamic] dinámico(ca). ◇ *n (U)* [permission] luz *f* verde.

goal [gəʊl] *n* - **1.** SPORT [point scored] gol *m*; [area between goalposts] portería *f*, meta *f*, arco *m* *Amér* - **2.** [aim] objetivo *m*, meta *f*.

goalkeeper ['gəʊl,ki:pə] *n* portero *m*, -ra *f*, guardameta *m* OR *f*, arquero *m*, -ra *f* *Amér*.

goalmouth ['gəʊlmaʊθ, *pl* -maʊðz] *n* portería *f*, meta *f*, arco *m* *Amér*.

goalpost ['gəʊlpəʊst] *n* poste *m* (de la portería).

goat [gəʊt] *n* [animal] cabra *f*.

goatee [gəʊ'ti:] *n* perilla *f*.

gob [gɒb] *n inf UK* [mouth] pico *m*.

gobble ['gɒbl] *vt* [food] engullir, tragar.

◆ **gobble down, gobble up** *vt sep* engullir, tragar.

go-between *n* intermediario *m*, -ria *f*.

gobsmacked ['gɒbsmækt] *adj UK inf* alucinado(da), flipado(da).

go-cart = go-kart.

god [gɒd] *n* dios *m*.

◆ **God** ◇ n Dios m; **God knows** sabe Dios; **for God's sake** ¡por el amor de Dios!; **thank God** ¡gracias a Dios! ◇ excl: **(my) God!** ¡Dios (mío)!

godchild ['gɒdtʃaɪld] (pl **-children** [-ˌtʃɪldrən]) n ahijado m, -da f.

goddaughter ['gɒdˌdɔːtə^r] n ahijada f.

goddess ['gɒdɪs] n diosa f.

godfather ['gɒdˌfɑːðə^r] n padrino m.

godforsaken ['gɒdfəˌseɪkn] adj dejado(da) de la mano de Dios.

godmother ['gɒdˌmʌðə^r] n madrina f.

godsend ['gɒdsend] n: **to be a ~** venir como agua de mayo.

godson ['gɒdsʌn] n ahijado m.

goes [gəʊz] ▷ **go**.

goggles ['gɒglz] npl [for swimming] gafas fpl submarinas; [for skiing] gafas de esquí; [for welding] gafas de protección.

going ['gəʊɪŋ] ◇ adj - **1.** UK [available] disponible - **2.** [rate] actual. ◇ n (U) - **1.** [rate of advance] marcha f - **2.** [conditions] condiciones fpl.

go-kart [-kɑːt] n kart m.

gold [gəʊld] ◇ adj [gold-coloured] dorado(da). ◇ n [gen] oro m. ◇ comp [made of gold] de oro.

golden ['gəʊldən] adj - **1.** [made of gold] de oro - **2.** [gold-coloured] dorado(da).

goldfish ['gəʊldfɪʃ] (pl inv) n pez m de colores.

gold leaf n pan m de oro.

gold medal n medalla f de oro.

goldmine ['gəʊldmaɪn] n lit & fig mina f de oro.

gold-plated [-'pleɪtɪd] adj chapado(da) en oro.

goldsmith ['gəʊldsmɪθ] n orfebre m OR f.

golf [gɒlf] n golf m.

golf ball n pelota f de golf.

golf club n - **1.** [society, place] club m de golf - **2.** [stick] palo m de golf.

golf course n campo m de golf.

golfer ['gɒlfə^r] n golfista m OR f.

gone [gɒn] ◇ pp ▷ **go**. ◇ adj: **those days are ~** esos tiempos ya pasaron. ◇ prep [past]: **it was ~ six already** ya eran las seis pasadas.

gong [gɒŋ] n gong m.

good [gʊd] (compar **better**, superl **best**) ◇ adj - **1.** [gen] bueno(na); **it's ~ to see you** me alegro de verte; **she's ~ at it** se le da bien; **he's a very ~ singer** canta muy bien; **to be ~ with** saber manejárselas con; **she's ~ with her hands** es muy mañosa; **it's ~ for you** es bueno, es beneficioso; **to feel ~** sentirse fenomenal; **it's ~ that ...** está bien que ...; **to look ~** [attractive] estar muy guapo; [appetizing, promising] tener buena pinta; **it looks ~ on you** te queda

bien; **~ looks** atractivo m; **be ~!** ¡sé bueno!, ¡pórtate bien!; **~!** ¡muy bien!, ¡estupendo! - **2.** [kind] amable; **to be ~ to sb** ser amable con alguien; **to be ~ enough to do sthg** ser tan amable de hacer algo; **that was very ~ of him** fue muy amable de su parte. ◇ n - **1.** (U) [benefit] bien m; **it will do him ~** le hará bien - **2.** [use] beneficio m, provecho m; **what's the ~ of ...?** ¿de OR para qué sirve ...?; **it's no ~** no sirve para nada - **3.** [morally correct behaviour] el bien; **to be up to no ~** estar tramando algo malo. ◇ adv - **1.** [expresses approval] estupendo - **2.** US inf [well] bien.

◆ **goods** npl - **1.** [COMM - for sale] productos mpl, artículos mpl; [- when transported] mercancías fpl - **2.** ECON bienes mpl.

◆ **as good as** adv casi, prácticamente; **it's as ~ as new** está como nuevo.

◆ **for good** adv [forever] para siempre.

◆ **good afternoon** excl ¡buenas tardes!

◆ **good evening** excl [in the evening] ¡buenas tardes!; [at night] ¡buenas noches!

◆ **good morning** excl ¡buenos días!, ¡buen día! Amér.

◆ **good night** excl ¡buenas noches!

goodbye [ˌgʊd'baɪ] ◇ excl ¡adiós!; **to say ~** despedirse. ◇ n adiós m.

Good Friday n Viernes m Santo.

good-humoured [-'hjuːməd] adj jovial.

good-looking [-'lʊkɪŋ] adj [person] guapo(pa).

good-natured [-'neɪtʃəd] adj bondadoso(sa).

goodness ['gʊdnɪs] ◇ n (U) - **1.** [kindness] bondad f - **2.** [nutritive quality] alimento m. ◇ excl: **(my) ~!** ¡Dios mío!; **for ~' sake!** ¡por Dios!; **thank ~** ¡gracias a Dios!

goods train [gʊdz-] n UK mercancías m inv.

goodwill [ˌgʊd'wɪl] n - **1.** [kind feelings] buena voluntad f - **2.** COMM fondo m de comercio.

goody ['gʊdɪ] (pl **-ies**) n inf [person] bueno m, -na f.

goose [guːs] (pl **geese**) n [bird] ganso m, oca f.

gooseberry ['gʊzbərɪ] (pl **-ies**) n [fruit] grosella f silvestre, uva f espina.

gooseflesh ['guːsfleʃ] n, **goose pimples** UK, **goosebumps** US ['guːsbʌmps] npl carne f de gallina.

gore [gɔː^r] ◇ n literary [blood] sangre f (derramada). ◇ vt cornear.

gorge [gɔːdʒ] ◇ n cañón m, garganta f. ◇ vt: **to ~ o.s. on** OR **with** atracarse de.

gorgeous ['gɔːdʒəs] adj - **1.** [lovely] magnífico(ca), espléndido(da) - **2.** inf [good-looking]: **to be ~** estar como un tren.

gorilla [gə'rɪlə] n gorila m OR f.

gormless ['gɔːmlɪs] *adj UK inf* memo(ma), lerdo(da).

gorse [gɔːs] *n (U)* tojo *m*.

gory ['gɔːrɪ] (*compar* -ier, *superl* -iest) *adj* [death, scene] sangriento(ta); [details, film] escabroso(sa).

gosh [gɒʃ] *excl inf* ¡joroba!, ¡caray!

go-slow *n UK* huelga *f* de celo.

gospel ['gɒspl] *n* [doctrine] evangelio *m*.
➤ **Gospel** *n* [in Bible] Evangelio *m*.

gossip ['gɒsɪp] ◇ *n* -1. [conversation] cotilleo *m* -2. [person] cotilla *m* OR *f*, chismoso *m*, -sa *f*. ◇ *vi* cotillear.

gossip column *n* ecos *mpl* de sociedad.

got [gɒt] *pt & pp* ▷ **get**.

gotten ['gɒtn] *pp US* ▷ **get**.

goulash ['guːlæʃ] *n* gulasch *m*.

gourmet ['guəmeɪ] ◇ *n* gastrónomo *m*, -ma *f*, gourmet *m* OR *f*. ◇ *comp* para/de gastrónomos.

gout [gaʊt] *n* gota *f*.

govern ['gʌvən] ◇ *vt* -1. POL gobernar -2. [control] dictar, guiar. ◇ *vi* POL gobernar.

governess ['gʌvənɪs] *n* institutriz *f*.

government ['gʌvnmənt] ◇ *n* gobierno *m*. ◇ *comp* gubernamental.

governor ['gʌvənər] *n* -1. US POL gobernador *m*, -ra *f* -2. [of school, bank, prison] director *m*, -ra *f*.

gown [gaʊn] *n* -1. [dress] vestido *m*, traje *m* -2. [of judge etc] toga *f*.

GP (*abbr of* **general practitioner**) *n médico de cabecera*.

grab [græb] (*pt & pp* -bed, *cont* -bing) ◇ *vt* -1. [snatch away] arrebatar; [grip] agarrar, asir; **to ~ sthg off sb** arrebatar algo a alguien -2. *inf* [appeal to] seducir. ◇ *vi*: **to ~ at sthg** intentar agarrar algo.

grace [greɪs] *n* -1. [elegance] elegancia *f*, gracia *f* -2. *(U)* [delay] prórroga *f* -3. [prayer]: **to say ~** bendecir la mesa. ◇ *vt fml* -1. [honour] honrar -2. [decorate] adornar, embellecer.

graceful ['greɪsfʊl] *adj* -1. [beautiful] elegante -2. [gracious] cortés.

gracious ['greɪʃəs] ◇ *adj* -1. [polite] cortés -2. [elegant] elegante. ◇ *excl*: **(good) ~ !** ¡Dios mío!

grade [greɪd] ◇ *n* -1. [level, quality] clase *f*, calidad *f* -2. *US* [class] curso *m*, clase *f* -3. [mark] nota *f*. ◇ *vt* -1. [classify] clasificar -2. [mark, assess] calificar.

grade crossing *n US* paso *m* a nivel.

grade school *n US* escuela *f* primaria.

gradient ['greɪdjənt] *n* pendiente *f*.

grad school *n US* escuela *f* de posgrado.

gradual ['grædʒʊəl] *adj* gradual.

gradually ['grædʒʊəlɪ] *adv* gradualmente.

graduate [*n* 'grædʒʊət, *vb* 'grædʒʊeɪt] ◇ *n*

-1. [person with a degree] licenciado *m*, -da *f*, egresado *m*, -da *f Amér* -2. US [of high school] ≃ bachiller *m* OR *f*. ◇ *vi* -1. [with a degree]: **to ~ (from)** licenciarse (por), licenciarse (en) *Amér*, egresar (de) *Amér* -2. *US* [from high school]: **to ~ (from)** ≃ obtener el título de bachiller (en).

graduation [,grædʒʊ'eɪʃn] *n* graduación *f*, egreso *m Amér*.

graffiti [grə'fiːtɪ] *n (U)* pintadas *fpl*.

graft [grɑːft] ◇ *n* -1. MED & BOT injerto *m* -2. *UK inf* [hard work] curro *m* muy duro -3. *US inf* [corruption] chanchullos *mpl*, corruptelas *fpl*. ◇ *vt* MED & BOT: **to ~ sthg (onto sthg)** injertar algo (en algo).

grain [greɪn] *n* -1. [seed, granule] grano *m* -2. *(U)* [crop] cereales *mpl* -3. *fig* [small amount] pizca *f* -4. [pattern] veta *f*.

gram [græm] *n* gramo *m*.

grammar ['græmər] *n* gramática *f*.

grammar school *n* [in UK] *colegio subvencionado para mayores de once años con un programa de asignaturas tradicional*; [in US] escuela *f* primaria

grammatical [grə'mætɪkl] *adj* -1. [of grammar] gramatical -2. [correct] (gramaticalmente) correcto(ta).

gramme [græm] *UK* = **gram**.

gramophone ['græməfəʊn] *n dated* gramófono *m*.

gran [græn] *n UK inf* abuelita *f*, yaya *f*, mamá *f* grande *Méx*.

grand [grænd] ◇ *adj* -1. [impressive] grandioso(sa) -2. [ambitious] ambicioso(sa) -3. [important] distinguido(da) -4. *inf dated* [excellent] fenomenal. ◇ *n inf* [thousand pounds or dollars]: **a ~** mil libras/dólares; **five ~** cinco mil libras/dólares.

grandchild ['græntʃaɪld] (*pl* -children [-,tʃɪldrən]) *n* nieto *m*, -ta *f*.

grand(d)ad ['grændæd] *n inf* abuelito *m*, yayo *m*, papá *m* grande *Méx*.

granddaughter ['græn,dɔːtər] *n* nieta *f*.

grandeur ['grændʒər] *n* -1. [splendour] grandiosidad *f* -2. [status] grandeza *f*.

grandfather ['grænd,fɑːðər] *n* abuelo *m*.

grandma ['grænmɑː] *n inf* abuelita *f*, yaya *f*, mamá *f* grande *Méx*.

grandmother ['græn,mʌðər] *n* abuela *f*.

grandpa ['grænpɑː] *n inf* abuelito *m*, yayo *m*.

grandparents ['græn,peərənts] *npl* abuelos *mpl*.

grand piano *n* piano *m* de cola.

grand slam *n* SPORT gran slam *m*.

grandson ['grænsʌn] *n* nieto *m*.

grandstand ['grændstænd] *n* tribuna *f*.

grand total *n* [total number] cantidad *f* total; [total sum, cost] importe *m* total.

granite ['grænɪt] *n* granito *m*.

granny ['grænɪ] (*pl* **-ies**) *n inf* abuelita *f*, yaya *f*, mamá *f* grande *Méx*.

grant [grɑ:nt] ⬦ *n* subvención *f*; [for study] beca *f*. ⬦ *vt fml* **-1.** [gen] conceder; **to take sthg/sb for ~ ed** no apreciar algo/a alguien en lo que vale; **it is taken for ~ ed that ...** se da por sentado que ... **-2.** [admit - truth, logic] admitir, aceptar.

granulated sugar ['grænjʊleɪtɪd-] *n* azúcar *m* granulado.

granule ['grænjuːl] *n* gránulo *m*.

grape [greɪp] *n* uva *f*.

grapefruit ['greɪpfruːt] (*pl inv* OR **-s**) *n* pomelo *m*, toronja *f Amér*.

grapevine ['greɪpvaɪn] *n* **-1.** [plant] vid *f*; [against wall] parra *f* **-2.** [information channel]: **I heard on the ~ that ...** me ha dicho un pajarito que ...

graph [grɑ:f] *n* gráfico *m*, gráfica *f*.

graphic ['græfɪk] *adj lit & fig* gráfico(ca).
➡ **graphics** *npl* **-1.** [pictures] ilustraciones *fpl* **-2.** COMPUT gráficos *mpl*.

graphite ['græfaɪt] *n* grafito *m*.

graph paper *n (U)* papel *m* cuadriculado.

grapple ['græpl] ➡ **grapple with** *vt fus* **-1.** [person] forcejear con **-2.** [problem] esforzarse por resolver.

grasp [grɑ:sp] ⬦ *n* **-1.** [grip] agarre *m*, asimiento *m* **-2.** [understanding] comprensión *f*; **to have a good ~ of sthg** dominar algo. ⬦ *vt* **-1.** [grip, seize] agarrar, asir **-2.** [understand] comprender **-3.** [opportunity] aprovechar.

grasping ['grɑ:spɪŋ] *adj pej* avaro(ra), codicioso(sa).

grass [grɑ:s] ⬦ *n* **-1.** [plant] hierba *f*, pasto *m Amér*, zacate *f Méx*; [lawn] césped *m*; [pasture] pasto *m*, grama *f CAm, Ven*; **'keep off the ~'** 'prohibido pisar el césped' **-2.** *inf* [marijuana] hierba *f*, maría *f*. ⬦ *vi UK inf*: **to ~ (on sb)** chivarse (de alguien) *Esp*, delatar (a alguien) *Amér*.

grass court *n* pista *f* de hierba.

grasshopper ['grɑ:s,hɒpə'] *n* saltamontes *m inv*.

grass roots ⬦ *npl* bases *fpl*. ⬦ *comp* de base.

grass snake *n* culebra *f*.

grate [greɪt] ⬦ *n* parrilla *f*, rejilla *f*. ⬦ *vt* rallar. ⬦ *vi* rechinar, chirriar.

grateful ['greɪtfʊl] *adj* [gen] agradecido(-da); [smile, letter] de agradecimiento; **to be ~ to sb (for sthg)** estar agradecido a alguien (por algo); **I'm very ~ to you** te lo agradezco mucho; **I'd be ~ if you could do it by tomorrow** te agradecería que lo hicieras para mañana.

grater ['greɪtə'] *n* rallador *m*.

gratify ['grætɪfaɪ] (*pt & pp* **-ied**) *vt* **-1.** [please - person]: **to be gratified** estar

satisfecho **-2.** [satisfy - wish] satisfacer.

grating ['greɪtɪŋ] ⬦ *adj* chirriante. ⬦ *n* [grille] reja *f*, enrejado *m*.

gratitude ['grætɪtjuːd] *n (U)*: **~ (to sb for)** agradecimiento *m* OR gratitud *f* (a alguien por).

gratuitous [grə'tjuːɪtəs] *adj fml* gratuito(-ta).

grave [greɪv] ⬦ *adj* grave. ⬦ *n* sepultura *f*, tumba *f*.

gravel ['grævl] *n* grava *f*, gravilla *f*.

gravestone ['greɪvstəʊn] *n* lápida *f* (sepulcral).

graveyard ['greɪvjɑːd] *n* cementerio *m*.

gravity ['grævətɪ] *n* gravedad *f*.

gravy ['greɪvɪ] *n (U)* [meat juice] salsa *f* OR jugo *m* de carne.

gray *US* = **grey**.

graze [greɪz] ⬦ *vt* **-1.** [feed on] pacer OR pastar en **-2.** [skin, knee etc] rasguñar **-3.** [touch lightly] rozar. ⬦ *vi* pacer, pastar. ⬦ *n* rasguño *m*.

grease [griːs] ⬦ *n* grasa *f*. ⬦ *vt* engrasar.

greaseproof paper [,griːspruːf-] *n (U) UK* papel *m* de cera (para envolver).

greasy ['griːzɪ] (*compar* **-ier**, *superl* **-iest**) *adj* grasiento(ta); [inherently] graso(sa).

great [greɪt] ⬦ *adj* **-1.** [gen] grande; [heat] intenso(sa); **with ~ care** con mucho cuidado; **a ~ deal of ...** un montón de ... **-2.** *inf* [splendid] estupendo(da), fenomenal, chévere *Andes, Carib*; **we had a ~ time** lo pasamos en grande; **~ !** ¡estupendo! ⬦ *adv*: **~ big** enorme. ⬦ *n* grande *m* OR *f*.

Great Britain *n* Gran Bretaña.

greatcoat ['greɪtkəʊt] *n* gabán *m*.

Great Dane *n* gran danés *m*.

great-grandchild *n* bisnieto *m*, -ta *f*.

great-grandfather *n* bisabuelo *m*.

great-grandmother *n* bisabuela *f*.

greatly ['greɪtlɪ] *adv* enormemente.

greatness ['greɪtnɪs] *n* grandeza *f*.

Greece [griːs] *n* Grecia.

greed [griːd] *n (U)*: **~ (for)** [food] glotonería *f* (con); [money] codicia *f* (de); [power] ambición *f* (de).

greedy ['griːdɪ] (*compar* **-ier**, *superl* **-iest**) *adj* **-1.** [for food] glotón(ona) **-2.** [for money, power]: **~ for** codicioso(sa) OR ávido(da) de.

Greek [griːk] ⬦ *adj* griego(ga). ⬦ *n* **-1.** [person] griego *m*, -ga *f* **-2.** [language] griego *m*.

green [griːn] ⬦ *adj* **-1.** [gen] verde **-2.** [environmentalist] verde, ecologista **-3.** *inf* [inexperienced] novato(ta) **-4.** *inf* [ill, pale] pálido(da). ⬦ *n* **-1.** [colour] verde *m* **-2.** [in village] parque *m* comunal **-3.** [in golf] green *m*.
➡ **Green** *n* POL verde *m* OR *f*, ecologista *m* OR

f; **the Greens** los verdes.
➤ **greens** *npl* [vegetables] verdura *f*.
greenback ['gri:nbæk] *n US inf* billete *de banco americano*.
green belt *n UK* cinturón *m* verde.
green card *n* **- 1.** *UK* [for vehicle] *seguro que cubre a conductores en el extranjero* **- 2.** *US* [work permit] permiso *m* de trabajo *(en Estados Unidos)*.
greenery ['gri:nərɪ] *n* vegetación *f*.
greenfly ['gri:nflaɪ] *(pl inv OR -ies) n* pulgón *m*.
greengage ['gri:ngeɪdʒ] *n* ciruela *f* claudia.
greengrocer ['gri:n,grəʊsə'] *n* verdulero *m*, -ra *f*; ➤ **'s (shop)** verdulería *f*.
greenhouse ['gri:nhaʊs, *pl* -haʊzɪz] *n* invernadero *m*.
greenhouse effect *n*: **the ~** el efecto invernadero.
greenhouse gas *n* gas *m* invernadero.
Greenland ['gri:nlənd] *n* Groenlandia.
green salad *n* ensalada *f* verde.
greet [gri:t] *vt* **- 1.** [say hello to] saludar **- 2.** [receive] recibir.
greeting ['gri:tɪŋ] *n* saludo *m*.
➤ **greetings** *npl*: **Christmas/birthday ~s!** ¡feliz navidad/cumpleaños!; **~s from ...** recuerdos de ...
greetings card *UK* ['gri:tɪŋz-], **greeting card** *US n* tarjeta *f* de felicitación.
grenade [grə'neɪd] *n*: **(hand) ~** granada *f* (de mano).
grew [gru:] *pt* ➤ **grow**.
grey *UK*, **gray** *US* [greɪ] ➤ *adj lit & fig* gris; **a ~ hair** una cana; **to go ~** [grey-haired] echar canas, encanecer. ➤ *n* gris *m*.
grey-haired [-'heəd] *adj* canoso(sa).
greyhound ['greɪhaʊnd] *n* galgo *m*.
Greyhound (bus)® *n* autobús *m* de largo recorrido.
grid [grɪd] *n* **- 1.** [grating] reja *f*, enrejado *m* **- 2.** [system of squares] cuadrícula *f*.
griddle ['grɪdl] *n* plancha *f*.
gridlock ['grɪdlɒk] *n US* embotellamiento *m*, atasco *m*.
grief [gri:f] *n (U)* **- 1.** [sorrow] dolor *m*, pesar *m* **- 2.** *inf* [trouble] problemas *mpl* **- 3.** *phr*: **to come to ~** [person] sufrir un percance; [plans] irse al traste; **good ~!** ¡madre mía!
grievance ['gri:vns] *n* (motivo *m* de) queja *f*.
grieve [gri:v] *vi*: **to ~ (for)** llorar (por).
grievous ['gri:vəs] *adj fml* grave.
grievous bodily harm *n (U)* lesiones *fpl* graves.
grill [grɪl] ➤ *n* **- 1.** [on cooker] grill *m*; [for barbecue] parrilla *f* **- 2.** [food] parrillada *f*. ➤ *vt* **- 1.** [on cooker] asar al grill; [on barbecue] asar a la parrilla **- 2.** *inf* [interrogate] someter a un duro interrogatorio.

grille [grɪl] *n* [on radiator, machine] rejilla *f*; [on window, door] reja *f*.
grim [grɪm] *(compar* **-mer**, *superl* **-mest)** *adj* **- 1.** [expression] adusto(ta); [determination] inexorable **- 2.** [place, facts, prospect] desolador(ra).
grimace [grɪ'meɪs] ➤ *n* mueca *f*. ➤ *vi* hacer una mueca.
grime [graɪm] *n* mugre *f*.
grimy ['graɪmɪ] *(compar* **-ier**, *superl* **-iest)** *adj* mugriento(ta).
grin [grɪn] *(pt & pp* **-ned**, *cont* **-ning)** ➤ *n* sonrisa *f* (abierta). ➤ *vi*: **to ~ (at)** sonreír (a).
grind [graɪnd] *(pt & pp* **ground**) ➤ *vt* [crush] moler. ➤ *vi* [scrape] rechinar, chirriar. ➤ *n* [hard, boring work] rutina *f*.
➤ **grind down** *vt sep* [oppress] oprimir, acogotar.
➤ **grind up** *vt sep* pulverizar, hacer polvo.
grinder ['graɪndə'] *n* molinillo *m*.
grip [grɪp] *(pt & pp* **-ped**, *cont* **-ping)** ➤ *n* **- 1.** [grasp, hold]: **to have a ~ (on sthg/sb)** tener (algo/a alguien) bien agarrado **- 2.** [control, domination]: **~ on** control *m* de, dominio *m* de; **to get to ~s with** llegar a controlar; **to get a ~ on o.s.** calmarse, controlarse **- 3.** [adhesion] sujeción *f*, adherencia *f* **- 4.** [handle] asidero *m* **- 5.** [bag] bolsa *f* de viaje. ➤ *vt* **- 1.** [grasp] agarrar, asir; [hand] apretar; [weapon] empuñar **- 2.** [seize] apoderarse de. ➤ *vi* adherirse.
gripe [graɪp] *inf* ➤ *n* [complaint] queja *f*. ➤ *vi*: **to ~ (about)** quejarse (de).
gripping ['grɪpɪŋ] *adj* apasionante.
grisly ['grɪzlɪ] *(compar* **-ier**, *superl* **-ièst)** *adj* [horrible, macabre] espeluznante, horripilante.
gristle ['grɪsl] *n* cartílago *m*, ternilla *f*.
grit [grɪt] *(pt & pp* **-ted**, *cont* **-ting)** ➤ *n* **- 1.** [stones] grava *f*; [sand, dust] arena *f* **- 2.** *inf* [courage] valor *m*. ➤ *vt* echar arena en *(las calles)*.
gritty ['grɪtɪ] *(compar* **-ier**, *superl* **-iest)** *adj inf* [brave] valiente.
groan [grəʊn] ➤ *n* gemido *m*, quejido *m*. ➤ *vi* **- 1.** [moan] gemir **- 2.** [creak] crujir.
grocer ['grəʊsə'] *n* tendero *m*, -ra *f*, abarrotero *m*, -ra *f Amér*; **~'s (shop)** tienda *f* de comestibles *OR* ultramarinos, abarrotería *f CAm*.
groceries ['grəʊsərɪz] *npl* [foods] comestibles *mpl*, abarrotes *mpl Amér*.
grocery ['grəʊsərɪ] *(pl* **-ies)** *n US* [shop] tienda *f* de comestibles *OR* ultramarinos, supermercado *m*, abarrotería *f Amér*.
groggy ['grɒgɪ] *(compar* **-ier**, *superl* **-iest)** *adj* atontado(da).
groin [grɔɪn] *n* ingle *f*.
groom [gru:m] ➤ *n* **- 1.** [of horses] mozo *m*

de cuadra - **2.** [bridegroom] novio *m*. ⬦ *vt*
- **1.** [brush] cepillar, almohazar - **2.** [prepare]:
to ~ sb (for sthg) preparar a alguien (para
algo).

groove [gru:v] *n* [deep line] ranura *f*; [in
record] surco *m*.

grope [grəʊp] ⬦ *vt* - **1.** [try to find]: to
~ one's way andar a tientas - **2.** [fondle] meter mano a. ⬦ *vi*: to ~ (about) for sthg
[object] buscar algo a tientas; [solution, re-
medy] buscar algo a ciegas.

gross [grəʊs] (*pl inv OR* -**es**) ⬦ *adj* - **1.** [total]
bruto(ta) - **2.** *fml* [serious, inexcusable] grave,
intolerable - **3.** [coarse, vulgar] basto(ta),
vulgar - **4.** *inf* [obese] obeso(sa) - **5.** *inf* [re-
volting] asqueroso(sa). ⬦ *n* gruesa *f*. ⬦ *vt*
ganar en bruto.

grossly ['grəʊslı] *adv* [seriously] enormemente.

grotesque [grəʊ'tesk] *adj* grotesco(ca).

grotto ['grɒtəʊ] (*pl* -**es** *OR* -**s**) *n* gruta *f*.

grotty ['grɒtı] (*compar* -**ier**, *superl* -**iest**) *adj*
UK inf asqueroso(sa), cochambroso(sa).

ground [graʊnd] ⬦ *pt* & *pp* ⊳ **grind**.
⬦ *n* - **1.** [surface of earth] suelo *m*; [soil] tierra *f*; above/below ~ sobre/bajo tierra; on
the ~ en el suelo - **2.** [area of land] terreno
m; SPORT campo *m* - **3.** [subject area] terreno
m - **4.** [advantage]: to gain/lose ~ ganar/
perder terreno. ⬦ *vt* - **1.** [base]: to be ~ed
on *OR* in sthg basarse en algo - **2.** [aircraft,
pilot] hacer permanecer en tierra - **3.** *US inf*
[child] castigar sin salir - **4.** *US* ELEC: to be
~ed estar conectado(da) a tierra.
➥ **grounds** *npl* - **1.** [reason]: ~s (for sthg/
for doing sthg) motivos *mpl* (para algo/pa-
ra hacer algo); on the ~s that aduciendo
que, debido a que - **2.** [around house] jardi-
nes *mpl*; [of public building] terrenos *mpl*
- **3.** [of coffee] posos *mpl*.

ground crew *n* personal *m* de tierra.

ground floor *n* planta *f* baja; ~ flat (piso
m) bajo *m*.

grounding ['graʊndıŋ] *n*: ~ (in) base *f*
(de), conocimientos *mpl* básicos (de).

groundless ['graʊndlıs] *adj* infundado(-
da), sin fundamento.

groundsheet ['graʊndʃi:t] *n* lona *f* impermeable *(para camping etc)*.

ground staff *n* - **1.** [at sports ground] personal *m* al cargo de las instalaciones - **2.** *UK*
= **ground crew**.

groundwork ['graʊndwɜ:k] *n* (*U*) trabajo
m preliminar.

group [gru:p] ⬦ *n* grupo *m*. ⬦ *vt* agrupar.
⬦ *vi*: to ~ (together) agruparse.

groupie ['gru:pı] *n inf* groupie *mf*.

grouse [graʊs] (*pl inv OR* -**s**) ⬦ *n* [bird] uro-
gallo *m*. ⬦ *vi inf* quejarse.

grove [grəʊv] *n* [of trees] arboleda *f*.

grovel ['grɒvl] (*UK pt* & *pp* -**led**, *cont* -**ling**,
US pt & *pp* -**ed**, *cont* -**ing**) *vi lit* & *fig*: to
~ (to) arrastrarse (ante).

grow [grəʊ] (*pt* **grew**, *pp* **grown**) ⬦ *vi*
- **1.** [gen] crecer - **2.** [become] volverse, ponerse; to ~ dark oscurecer; to ~ old envejecer. ⬦ *vt* - **1.** [plants] cultivar - **2.** [hair,
beard] dejarse crecer.
➥ **grow on** *vt fus inf*: it's ~ing on me me
gusta cada vez más.
➥ **grow out of** *vt fus* - **1.** [become too big
for]: he has grown out of his clothes se le ha
quedado pequeña la ropa - **2.** [lose - habit]
perder; he'll ~ out of it ya se le pasará.
➥ **grow up** *vi* crecer; when I ~ up cuando sea mayor; I grew up in Ireland me crié
en Irlanda; ~ up! ¡no seas niño!

grower ['grəʊə*r*] *n* cultivador *m*, -ra *f*.

growl [graʊl] *vi* [dog, person] gruñir; [en-
gine] rugir.

grown [grəʊn] ⬦ *pp* ⊳ **grow**. ⬦ *adj* adul-
to(ta).

grown-up *n* persona *f* mayor.

growth [grəʊθ] *n* - **1.** [gen]: ~ (of OR in) crecimiento *m* (de) - **2.** MED tumor *m*.

grub [grʌb] *n* - **1.** [insect] larva *f*, gusano *m*
- **2.** *inf* [food] manduca *f*, papeo *m*.

grubby ['grʌbı] (*compar* -**ier**, *superl* -**iest**)
adj sucio(cia), mugriento(ta).

grudge [grʌdʒ] ⬦ *n* rencor *m*; to bear sb a
~, to bear a ~ against sb guardar rencor a
alguien. ⬦ *vt*: to ~ sb sthg conceder algo a
alguien a regañadientes; to ~ doing sthg
hacer algo a regañadientes.

gruelling *UK*, **grueling** *US* ['grʊəlıŋ] *adj*
agotador(ra).

gruesome ['gru:səm] *adj* horripilante.

gruff [grʌf] *adj* - **1.** [hoarse] bronco(ca)
- **2.** [rough, unfriendly] hosco(ca), brusco(-
ca).

grumble ['grʌmbl] *vi* - **1.** [complain] quejarse, refunfuñar; to ~ about sthg quejarse de
algo, refunfuñar por algo - **2.** [stomach] gruñir, hacer ruido.

grumpy ['grʌmpı] (*compar* -**ier**, *superl*
-**iest**) *adj inf* gruñón(ona).

grunt [grʌnt] *vi* gruñir.

G-string *n* taparrabos *m inv*, tanga *m*.

guarantee [,gærən'ti:] ⬦ *n* garantía *f*.
⬦ *vt* garantizar.

guard [gɑ:d] ⬦ *n* - **1.** [person] guardia *m OR*
f; [in prison] carcelero *m*, -ra *f* - **2.** [group of
guards, operation] guardia *f*; to be on/stand
~ estar de/hacer guardia; to catch sb off ~
coger a alguien desprevenido - **3.** *UK* RAIL jefe *m* de tren - **4.** [protective device - for body]
protector *m*; [- for machine] cubierta *f* protectora. ⬦ *vt* - **1.** [protect, hide] guardar
- **2.** [prevent from escaping] vigilar.

guard dog *n* perro *m* guardián.

guarded ['gɑːdɪd] *adj* cauteloso(sa).

guardian ['gɑːdjən] *n* - 1. [of child] tutor *m*, -ra *f* - 2. [protector] guardián *m*, -ana *f*, protector *m*, -ra *f*.

guardrail ['gɑːdreɪl] *n* US [on road] barrera *f* de protección.

guard's van *n* UK furgón *m* de cola.

Guatemala [,gwɑːtə'mɑːlə] *n* Guatemala.

Guatemalan [,gwɑːtə'mɑːlən] ◇ *adj* guatemalteco(ca). ◇ *n* guatemalteco *m*, -ca *f*.

guerilla [gə'rɪlə] = **guerrilla**.

Guernsey ['gɜːnzɪ] *n* [place] Guernsey.

guerrilla [gə'rɪlə] *n* guerrillero *m*, -ra *f*.

guerrilla warfare *n* (U) guerra *f* de guerrillas.

guess [ges] ◇ *n* suposición *f*, conjetura *f*; **to take a** ~ intentar adivinar. ◇ *vt* adivinar; ~ **what?** ¿sabes qué? ◇ *vi* - 1. [conjecture] adivinar; **to** ~ **at sthg** tratar de adivinar algo; **to** ~ **right** acertar; **to** ~ **wrong** equivocarse - 2. [suppose]: **I** ~ **(so)** supongo OR me imagino que sí.

guesswork ['geswɜːk] *n* (U) conjeturas *fpl*, suposiciones *fpl*.

guest [gest] *n* - 1. [at home, on programme] invitado *m*, -da *f* - 2. [at hotel] huésped *m* OR *f*.

guesthouse ['gesthaʊs, *pl* -haʊzɪz] *n* casa *f* de huéspedes.

guestroom ['gestrʊm] *n* cuarto *m* de los huéspedes.

guffaw [gʌ'fɔː] ◇ *n* carcajada *f*. ◇ *vi* reírse a carcajadas.

guidance ['gaɪdəns] *n* (U) - 1. [help] orientación *f*, consejos *mpl* - 2. [leadership] dirección *f*.

guide [gaɪd] ◇ *n* - 1. [person] guía *m* OR *f* - 2. [book] guía *f*. ◇ *vt* - 1. [show by leading] guiar - 2. [control] conducir, dirigir - 3. [influence]: **to be** ~ **d by** guiarse por.
 ◆ **Guide** = **girl guide**.

guide book *n* guía *f*.

guide dog *n* perro *m* lazarillo.

guidelines ['gaɪdlaɪnz] *npl* directrices *fpl*.

guild [gɪld] *n* - 1. HIST gremio *m* - 2. [association] corporación *f*.

guile [gaɪl] *n* (U) astucia *f*.

guillotine ['gɪlə,tiːn] *n* [gen] guillotina *f*.

guilt [gɪlt] *n* - 1. [remorse] culpa *f* - 2. JUR culpabilidad *f*.

guilty ['gɪltɪ] (*compar* **-ier**, *superl* **-iest**) *adj* [gen]: ~ **(of)** culpable (de); **to be found** ~ / **not** ~ ser declarado culpable/inocente.

guinea pig *n lit & fig* conejillo *m* de Indias.

guise [gaɪz] *n fml* apariencia *f*.

guitar [gɪ'tɑːʳ] *n* guitarra *f*.

guitarist [gɪ'tɑːrɪst] *n* guitarrista *m* OR *f*.

gulf [gʌlf] *n* - 1. [sea] golfo *m* - 2. [chasm] sima *f*, abismo *m* - 3. [big difference]: ~ **(between)** abismo *m* (entre).
 ◆ **Gulf** *n*: **the Gulf** el Golfo.

gull [gʌl] *n* gaviota *f*.

gullet ['gʌlɪt] *n* esófago *m*.

gullible ['gʌləbl] *adj* crédulo(la).

gully ['gʌlɪ] (*pl* **-ies**) *n* barranco *m*.

gulp [gʌlp] ◇ *n* trago *m*. ◇ *vt* [liquid] tragarse; [food] engullir. ◇ *vi* tragar saliva.
 ◆ **gulp down** *vt sep* [liquid] tragarse; [food] engullir.

gum [gʌm] (*pt & pp* **-med**, *cont* **-ming**) ◇ *n* - 1. [chewing gum] chicle *m* - 2. [adhesive] pegamento *m* - 3. ANAT encía *f*. ◇ *vt* pegar, engomar.

gumboots ['gʌmbuːts] *npl* UK botas *fpl* de agua OR de goma.

gun [gʌn] (*pt & pp* **-ned**, *cont* **-ning**) *n* - 1. [pistol] pistola *f*; [rifle] escopeta *f*, fusil *m*; [artillery] cañón *m* - 2. [tool] pistola *f*.
 ◆ **gun down** *vt sep* abatir (a tiros).

gunboat ['gʌnbəʊt] *n* cañonero *m*.

gunfire ['gʌnfaɪəʳ] *n* (U) disparos *mpl*, tiroteo *m*.

gunman ['gʌnmən] (*pl* **-men** [-mən]) *n* pistolero *m*.

gunpoint ['gʌnpɔɪnt] *n*: **at** ~ a punta de pistola.

gunpowder ['gʌn,paʊdəʳ] *n* pólvora *f*.

gunshot ['gʌnʃɒt] *n* tiro *m*, disparo *m*.

gunsmith ['gʌnsmɪθ] *n* armero *m*.

gurgle ['gɜːgl] *vi* - 1. [water] gorgotear - 2. [baby] gorjear.

guru ['gʊruː] *n lit & fig* gurú *m*.

gush [gʌʃ] ◇ *n* chorro *m*. ◇ *vi* - 1. [flow out] chorrear, manar - 2. *pej* [enthuse] ser muy efusivo(va).

gusset ['gʌsɪt] *n* escudete *m*.

gust [gʌst] *n* ráfaga *f*, racha *f*.

gusto ['gʌstəʊ] *n*: **with** ~ con deleite.

gut [gʌt] (*pt & pp* **-ted**, *cont* **-ting**) ◇ *n* - 1. MED intestino *m* - 2. [strong thread] sedal *m*. ◇ *vt* - 1. [animal] destripar; [fish] limpiar - 2. [subj: fire] destruir el interior de.
 ◆ **guts** *npl inf* - 1. [intestines] tripas *fpl*; **to hate sb's** ~ **s** odiar a alguien a muerte - 2. [courage] agallas *fpl*.

gutter ['gʌtəʳ] *n* - 1. [ditch] cuneta *f* - 2. [on roof] canalón *m*.

gutter press *n pej* prensa *f* amarilla OR sensacionalista.

guy [gaɪ] *n* - 1. *inf* [man] tipo *m*, tío *m*, chavo *m Méx* - 2. UK [dummy] muñeco que se quema en Gran Bretaña la noche de Guy Fawkes.

Guy Fawkes' Night *n* fiesta que se celebra el 5 de noviembre en Gran Bretaña en que se encienden hogueras y se lanzan fuegos artificiales.

guy rope *n* viento *m*, cuerda *f* (de tienda de campaña).

guzzle ['gʌzl] ◇ *vt* zamparse. ◇ *vi* zampar.

gym [dʒɪm] *n inf* - 1. [gymnasium] gimnasio *m* - 2. [exercises] gimnasia *f*.

gymnasium [dʒɪmˈneɪzjəm] (*pl* **-siums** OR **-sia** [-zjə]) *n* gimnasio *m*.

gymnast [ˈdʒɪmnæst] *n* gimnasta *m* OR *f*.

gymnastics [dʒɪmˈnæstɪks] *n (U)* gimnasia *f*.

gym shoes *npl* zapatillas *fpl* de gimnasia.

gymslip [ˈdʒɪmˌslɪp] *n* UK bata *f* de colegio.

gynaecologist UK, **gynecologist** US [ˌgaɪnəˈkɒlədʒɪst] *n* ginecólogo *m*, -ga *f*.

gynaecology UK, **gynecology** US [ˌgaɪnəˈkɒlədʒɪ] *n* ginecología *f*.

gypsy [ˈdʒɪpsɪ] (*pl* **-ies**) = gipsy.

gyrate [dʒaɪˈreɪt] *vi* girar.

h (*pl* **h's** OR **hs**), **H** (*pl* **H's** OR **Hs**) [eɪtʃ] *n* [letter] h *f*, H *f*.

haberdashery [ˈhæbədæʃərɪ] (*pl* **-ies**) *n* **- 1.** UK [selling sewing materials] mercería *f* **- 2.** US [selling men's clothing] tienda *f* de ropa para caballeros.

habit [ˈhæbɪt] *n* **- 1.** [custom] costumbre *f*, hábito *m*; **to make a ~ of doing sthg** tener por costumbre hacer algo; **to have a drug ~** ser drogadicto **- 2.** [garment] hábito *m*.

habitat [ˈhæbɪtæt] *n* hábitat *m*.

habitual [həˈbɪtʃʊəl] *adj* **- 1.** [usual] habitual, acostumbrado(da) **- 2.** [smoker, gambler] empedernido(da).

hack [hæk] ◇ *n pej* [writer] escritorzuelo *m*, -la *f*; [journalist] gacetillero *m*, -ra *f*. ◇ *vt* [cut] cortar en tajos, acuchillar.

◆ **hack into** *vt fus* piratear.

hacker [ˈhækəʳ] *n*: **(computer) ~** pirata *m* OR *f* informático.

hackneyed [ˈhæknɪd] *adj pej* trillado(da), gastado(da).

hacksaw [ˈhæksɔ:] *n* sierra *f* para metales.

had [weak form həd, strong form hæd] *pt* & *pp* ⊳ **have**.

haddock [ˈhædək] (*pl inv*) *n* eglefino *m*.

hadn't [ˈhædnt] = had not.

haemophiliac [ˌhi:məˈfɪlɪæk] = hemophiliac.

haemorrhage [ˈhemərɪdʒ] = hemorrhage.

haemorrhoids [ˈhemərɔɪdz] = hemorrhoids.

haggard [ˈhægəd] *adj* ojeroso(sa).

haggis [ˈhægɪs] *n* plato típico escocés hecho con las asaduras del cordero.

haggle [ˈhægl] *vi*: **to ~ (with sb over** OR **about sthg)** regatear (algo con alguien).

Hague [heɪg] *n*: **The ~** La Haya.

hail [heɪl] ◇ *n* **- 1.** METEOR granizo *m*, pedrisco *m* **- 2.** *fig* [large number] lluvia *f*. ◇ *vt* **- 1.** [call] llamar; [taxi] parar **- 2.** [acclaim]: **to ~ sb as sthg** aclamar a alguien algo; **to ~ sthg as sthg** ensalzar algo catalogándolo de algo. ◇ *v impers*: **it's ~ing** está granizando.

hailstone [ˈheɪlstəʊn] *n* granizo *m*, piedra *f*.

hair [heəʳ] *n* **- 1.** *(U)* [gen] pelo *m*; **to do one's ~** arreglarse el pelo **- 2.** [on person's skin] vello *m*.

hairbrush [ˈheəbrʌʃ] *n* cepillo *m* para el pelo.

haircut [ˈheəkʌt] *n* corte *m* de pelo.

hairdo [ˈheədu:] (*pl* **-s**) *n inf* peinado *m*.

hairdresser [ˈheəˌdresəʳ] *n* peluquero *m*, -ra *f*; **~'s (salon)** peluquería *f*.

hairdryer [ˈheəˌdraɪəʳ] *n* secador *m* (de pelo).

hair gel *n* gomina *f*.

hairgrip [ˈheəgrɪp] *n* UK horquilla *f*.

hairpin [ˈheəpɪn] *n* horquilla *f* de moño.

hairpin bend *n* curva *f* muy cerrada.

hair-raising [-ˌreɪzɪŋ] *adj* espeluznante.

hair remover [-rɪˌmu:vəʳ] *n* depilatorio *m*.

hair slide *n* UK pasador *m*.

hairspray [ˈheəspreɪ] *n* laca *f* (para el pelo).

hairstyle [ˈheəstaɪl] *n* peinado *m*.

hairy [ˈheərɪ] (*compar* **-ier**, *superl* **-iest**) *adj* **- 1.** [covered in hair] peludo(da) **- 2.** *inf* [scary] espeluznante, espantoso(sa).

Haiti [ˈheɪtɪ] *n* Haití.

hake [heɪk] (*pl inv* OR **-s**) *n* merluza *f*.

half [UK hɑ:f, US hæf] (*pl senses 1 and 3* **halves**, *pl senses 2 and 4* **halves** OR **halfs**) ◇ *adj* medio(dia); **~ a dozen/mile** media docena/milla; **~ an hour** media hora. ◇ *adv* **- 1.** [gen]: **~ naked/Spanish** medio desnudo/español; **~ full/open** medio lleno/abierto; **~ and ~** mitad y mitad y mitad **- 2.** [by half]: **~ as big (as)** la mitad de grande (que) **- 3.** [in telling the time]: **~ past nine**, **~ after nine** US las nueve y media; **it's ~ past son y media.** ◇ *n* **- 1.** [one of two parts] mitad *f*; **one ~ of the group** una mitad del grupo; **a pound/mile and a ~** una libra/milla y media; **to go halves (with sb)** ir a medias (con alguien) **- 2.** [fraction, halfback, child's ticket] medio *m* **- 3.** [of sports match] tiempo *m*, mitad *f* **- 4.** [of beer] media pinta *f*. ◇ *pron* la mitad; **~ of it/them** la mitad.

half-and-half *n* US [in coffee] leche *f* con nata *Esp* OR crema *Amér*.

halfback ['hɑːfbæk] *n* [in rugby] medio *m*.

half board *n* media pensión *f*.

half-breed ◇ *adj* mestizo(za). ◇ *n* mestizo *m*, -za *f (atención: el término 'half-breed' se considera racista)*.

half-caste [-kɑːst] ◇ *adj* mestizo(za). ◇ *n* mestizo *m*, -za *f (atención: el término 'half-caste' se considera racista)*.

half-hearted [-'hɑːtɪd] *adj* poco entusiasta.

half hour *n* media hora *f*.

half-mast *n*: at ~ [flag] a media asta.

half moon *n* media luna *f*.

half note *n* US MUS blanca *f*.

halfpenny ['heɪpnɪ] (*pl* -**pennies** OR -**pence**) *n* medio penique *m*.

half-price *adj* a mitad de precio.

half term *n* UK *breves vacaciones escolares a mitad de trimestre*.

half time *n* (U) descanso *m*.

halfway [hɑːf'weɪ] ◇ *adj* intermedio(dia). ◇ *adv* -**1.** [in space]: I was ~ down the street llevaba la mitad de la calle andada -**2.** [in time]: the film was ~ through la película iba por la mitad.

halibut ['hælɪbət] (*pl inv* OR -**s**) *n* halibut *m*, fletán *m*.

hall [hɔːl] *n* -**1.** [entrance to house] vestíbulo *m*; [corridor] pasillo *m* -**2.** [public building, large room] sala *f* -**3.** UK UNIV colegio *m* mayor -**4.** [country house] mansión *f*, casa *f* solariega.

hallmark ['hɔːlmɑːk] *n* -**1.** [typical feature] sello *m* distintivo -**2.** [on metal] contraste *m*.

hallo [hə'ləʊ] = **hello**.

hall of residence (*pl* **halls of residence**) *n* UK residencia *f* universitaria, colegio *m* mayor.

Hallowe'en [ˌhæləʊ'iːn] *n fiesta celebrada la noche del 31 de octubre*.

hallucinate [hə'luːsɪneɪt] *vi* alucinar.

hallway ['hɔːlweɪ] *n* [entrance to house] vestíbulo *m*; [corridor] pasillo *m*.

halo ['heɪləʊ] (*pl* -**es** OR -**s**) *n* halo *m*, aureola *f*.

halt [hɔːlt] ◇ *n* [stop]: to come to a ~ [vehicle] pararse; [activity] interrumpirse; to call a ~ to poner fin a. ◇ *vt* [person] parar, detener; [development, activity] interrumpir. ◇ *vi* [person, train] pararse, detenerse; [development, activity] interrumpirse.

halterneck ['hɔːltənek] *adj* escotado(da) por detrás.

halve [UK hɑːv, US hæv] *vt* -**1.** [reduce by half] reducir a la mitad -**2.** [divide] partir en dos, partir por la mitad.

halves [UK hɑːvz, US hævz] *pl* ⊳ **half**.

ham [hæm] ◇ *n* [meat] jamón *m*. ◇ *comp* de jamón.

hamburger ['hæmbɜːgəʳ] *n* -**1.** [burger] hamburguesa *f* -**2.** (U) US [mince] carne *f* picada.

hamlet ['hæmlɪt] *n* aldea *f*.

hammer ['hæməʳ] ◇ *n* [gen & SPORT] martillo *m*. ◇ *vt* -**1.** [with tool] martillear -**2.** [with fist] aporrear -**3.** *inf* [defeat] dar una paliza a. ◇ *vi* [with fist]: to ~ (on sthg) aporrear (algo).

◆ **hammer out** *vt fus* [solution, agreement] alcanzar con esfuerzo.

hammock ['hæmək] *n* hamaca *f*, chinchorro *m Méx*.

hamper ['hæmpəʳ] ◇ *n* -**1.** [for food] cesta *f*, canasta *f* -**2.** US [for laundry] cesto *m* de la ropa sucia. ◇ *vt* obstaculizar.

hamster ['hæmstəʳ] *n* hámster *m*.

hamstring ['hæmstrɪŋ] *n* tendón *m* de la corva.

hand [hænd] ◇ *n* -**1.** [gen] mano *f*; to hold ~s ir cogidos de la mano; ~ in ~ [people] (cogidos) de la mano; by ~ a mano; in the ~s of en manos de; to have sthg on one's ~s tener uno algo en sus manos; to get OR lay one's ~s on sthg hacerse con algo; to get OR lay one's ~s on sb pillar a alguien; to get out of ~ [situation] hacerse incontrolable; [person] desmandarse; to give OR lend sb a ~ (with) echar una mano a alguien (con); to have one's ~s full estar muy ocupado; to have time in ~ tener tiempo de sobra; to take sb in ~ hacerse cargo OR ocuparse de alguien; to try one's ~ at sthg intentar hacer algo -**2.** [influence] influencia *f* -**3.** [worker - on farm] bracero *m*, peón *m*; [- on ship] tripulante *m* -**4.** [of clock, watch] manecilla *f*, aguja *f* -**5.** [handwriting] letra *f* -**6.** [applause]: a big ~ un gran aplauso. ◇ *vt*: to ~ sthg to sb, to ~ sb sthg dar OR entregar algo a alguien.

◆ **(close) at hand** *adv* cerca.

◆ **on hand** *adv* al alcance de la mano.

◆ **on the other hand** *conj* por otra parte.

◆ **out of hand** *adv* [completely] terminantemente.

◆ **to hand** *adv* a mano.

◆ **hand back** *vt sep* devolver.

◆ **hand down** *vt sep* [heirloom] pasar en herencia; [knowledge] transmitir.

◆ **hand in** *vt sep* [essay, application] entregar; [resignation] presentar.

◆ **hand out** *vt sep* repartir, distribuir.

◆ **hand over** ◇ *vt sep* -**1.** [baton, money] entregar -**2.** [responsibility, power] ceder. ◇ *vi*: to ~ over to dar paso (a).

handbag ['hændbæg] *n* bolso *m*, bolsa *f Méx*, cartera *f Andes, CSur*.

hand baggage *n* equipaje *m* de mano.

handball ['hændbɔːl] *n* balonmano *m*.

handbook ['hændbʊk] *n* manual *m*.

handbrake ['hændbreɪk] *n* freno *m* de mano.

handcuffs ['hændkʌfs] *npl* esposas *fpl*.

handful ['hændfʊl] *n* [gen] puñado *m*.

hand grenade *n* granada *f* de mano.

handgun ['hændgʌn] *n* pistola *f*.

handheld PC ['hændheld-] *n* ordenador *m* de bolsillo, asistente *m* personal.

handicap ['hændɪkæp] (*pt & pp* **-ped**, *cont* **-ping**) ⋄ *n* -1. [disability] discapacidad *f*, minusvalía *f* -2. [disadvantage] desventaja *f*, obstáculo *m* -3. SPORT hándicap *m*. ⋄ *vt* estorbar, obstaculizar.

handicapped ['hændɪkæpt] ⋄ *adj* minusválido(da). ⋄ *npl*: **the ~** los minusválidos.

handicraft ['hændɪkrɑːft] *n* [skill] artesanía *f*.

handiwork ['hændɪwɜːk] *n (U)* [doing, work] obra *f*.

handkerchief ['hæŋkətʃɪf] (*pl* **-chiefs** OR **-chieves** [-tʃiːvz]) *n* pañuelo *m*.

handle ['hændl] ⋄ *n* [of tool, broom, knife] mango *m*; [of door, window] manilla *f*; [of suitcase, cup, jug] asa *f*; [of racket] empuñadura *f*. ⋄ *vt* [gen] manejar; [order, complaint, application] encargarse de; [negotiations, takeover] conducir; [people] tratar.

handlebars ['hændlbɑːz] *npl* manillar *m*, manubrio *m Amér*.

handler ['hændlə⁽ʳ⁾] *n* -1. [of animal] adiestrador *m*, -ra *f* -2. [at airport]: **(baggage) ~** mozo *m* de equipajes.

hand luggage *n UK* equipaje *m* de mano.

handmade [,hænd'meɪd] *adj* hecho(cha) a mano.

handout ['hændaʊt] *n* -1. [gift] donativo *m* -2. [leaflet] hoja *f* (informativa); [in class] notas *fpl*.

handrail ['hændreɪl] *n* pasamano *m*, barandilla *f*.

handset ['hændset] *n* auricular *m* (*de teléfono*); **to lift/replace the ~** descolgar/colgar (el teléfono).

handshake ['hændʃeɪk] *n* apretón *m* de manos.

handsome ['hænsəm] *adj* -1. [man] guapo, atractivo -2. [woman] bella -3. [reward, profit] considerable.

handstand ['hændstænd] *n* pino *m*.

handwriting ['hænd,raɪtɪŋ] *n* letra *f*, caligrafía *f*.

handy ['hændɪ] (*compar* **-ier**, *superl* **-iest**) *adj inf* -1. [useful] práctico(ca); **to come in ~** venir bien -2. [skilful] mañoso(sa) -3. [near] a mano, cerca.

handyman ['hændɪmæn] (*pl* **-men** [-men]) *n*: **a good ~** un manitas.

hang [hæŋ] (*pt & pp* sense 1 **hung**, *pt & pp*

sense 2 **hung** OR **hanged**) ⋄ *vt* -1. [fasten] colgar; [washing] tender; [wallpaper] poner -2. [execute] ahorcar; **to ~ o.s.** ahorcarse. ⋄ *vi* -1. [be fastened] colgar, pender -2. [be executed] ser ahorcado(da) -3. *US inf*: **I'm going to ~ with my friends tonight** voy a andar por ahí con los amigos esta noche. ⋄ *n*: **to get the ~ of sthg** *inf* coger el tranquillo a algo.

⬥ hang about, hang around *vi* -1. [spend time] pasar el rato; **they didn't ~ about** se pusieron en marcha sin perder un minuto -2. [wait] esperar; **~ about!** ¡un momento!

⬥ hang on *vi* -1. [keep hold]: **to ~ on (to)** agarrarse (a) -2. *inf* [continue waiting] esperar, aguardar -3. [persevere] resistir.

⬥ hang out *vi inf* [spend time] pasar el rato.

⬥ hang round = hang about.

⬥ hang up ⋄ *vt sep* colgar. ⋄ *vi* colgar.

⬥ hang up on *vt fus*: **to ~ up on sb** colgarle a alguien.

hangar ['hæŋə⁽ʳ⁾] *n* hangar *m*.

hanger ['hæŋə⁽ʳ⁾] *n* percha *f*.

hanger-on (*pl* **hangers-on**) *n* lapa *f*, parásito *m*.

hang gliding *n* vuelo *m* con ala delta.

hangover ['hæŋ,əʊvə⁽ʳ⁾] *n* [from drinking] resaca *f*.

hang-up *n inf* complejo *m*.

hanker ['hæŋkə⁽ʳ⁾] **⬥ hanker after, hanker for** *vt fus* anhelar.

hankie, hanky ['hæŋkɪ] (*pl* **-ies**) (*abbr of* **handkerchief**) *n inf* pañuelo *m*.

haphazard [,hæp'hæzəd] *adj* [arrangement] caótico(ca).

hapless ['hæplɪs] *adj literary* desventurado(da).

happen ['hæpən] *vi* -1. [occur] pasar, ocurrir; **to ~ to sb** pasarle OR sucederle a alguien -2. [chance]: **I ~ ed to be looking out of the window ...** dio la casualidad de que estaba mirando por la ventana ...; **do you ~ to have a pen on you?** ¿no tendrás un boli acaso OR por casualidad?; **as it ~s ...** da la casualidad de que ...

happening ['hæpənɪŋ] *n* suceso *m*, acontecimiento *m*.

happily ['hæpɪlɪ] *adv* -1. [with pleasure] alegremente, felizmente -2. [willingly] con mucho gusto -3. [fortunately] afortunadamente.

happiness ['hæpɪnɪs] *n* [state] felicidad *f*; [feeling] alegría *f*.

happy ['hæpɪ] (*compar* **-ier**, *superl* **-iest**) *adj* -1. [generally contented] feliz; [pleased] contento(ta); [cheerful] alegre; **~ Christmas/ birthday!** ¡Feliz Navidad/cumpleaños!; **to be ~ with/about sthg** estar contento con algo - **2.** [causing contentment] feliz, alegre - **3.** [fortunate] feliz, oportuno(na) - **4.** [willing]: **to be ~ to do sthg** estar más que dispuesto(ta) a hacer algo; **I'd be ~ to do it** yo lo haría con gusto.

happy-go-lucky *adj* despreocupado(da).

happy medium *n* término *m* medio.

harangue [hə'ræŋ] <> *n* arenga *f.* <> *vt* arengar.

harass ['hærəs] *vt* acosar.

harbour *UK*, **harbor** *US* ['hɑːbə'] <> *n* puerto *m.* <> *vt* - **1.** [feeling] abrigar - **2.** [person] dar refugio a, encubrir.

hard [hɑːd] <> *adj* - **1.** [gen] duro(ra); [frost] fuerte; **to go ~** endurecerse; **to be ~ on sb/ sthg** [subj: person] ser duro con alguien/algo; [subj: work, strain] perjudicar a alguien/ algo; [subj: result] ser inmerecido para alguien/algo - **2.** [difficult] difícil; **~ of hearing** duro de oído - **3.** [forceful - push, kick etc] fuerte - **4.** [fact, news] concreto(ta) - **5.** *UK* [extreme]: **~ left/right** extrema izquierda/derecha. <> *adv* - **1.** [try, rain] mucho; [work] duro; [listen] atentamente; [think] detenidamente - **2.** [push, kick] fuerte, con fuerza - **3.** *phr:* **to be ~ pushed** OR **put** OR **pressed to do sthg** vérselas y deseárselas para hacer algo; **to feel ~ done by** sentirse tratado injustamente.

hardback ['hɑːdbæk] *n* edición *f* en pasta dura.

hardboard ['hɑːdbɔːd] *n* madera *f* conglomerada.

hard-boiled *adj lit & fig* duro(ra).

hard cash *n* dinero *m* contante y sonante.

hard copy *n* COMPUT copia *f* impresa.

hard disk *n* COMPUT disco *m* duro.

hard drive *n* COMPUT unidad *f* de disco duro.

harden ['hɑːdn] <> *vt* - **1.** [gen] endurecer - **2.** [resolve, opinion] reforzar. <> *vi* - **1.** [gen] endurecerse - **2.** [resolve, opinion] reforzarse.

hard-headed [-'hedɪd] *adj* realista.

hard-hearted [-'hɑːtɪd] *adj* insensible, sin corazón.

hard labour *n (U)* trabajos *mpl* forzados.

hard-liner *n* partidario *m*, -ria *f* de la línea dura.

hardly ['hɑːdlɪ] *adv* apenas; **~ ever/anything** casi nunca/nada; **that's ~ fair** eso no es justo; **I'm ~ a communist, am I?** ¡pues sí que tengo yo mucho que ver con el comunismo!

hardness ['hɑːdnɪs] *n* - **1.** [firmness] dureza *f* - **2.** [difficulty] dificultad *f.*

hardship ['hɑːdʃɪp] *n* - **1.** *(U)* [difficult conditions] privaciones *fpl*, penurias *fpl* - **2.** [difficult circumstance] infortunio *m.*

hard shoulder *n UK* AUT arcén *m*, acotamiento *m Méx*, berma *f Andes*, banquina *f*

RP, hombrillo *m Ven.*

hard up *adj inf:* **to be ~** andar mal de dinero; **to be ~ for sthg** andar escaso de algo.

hardware ['hɑːdweə'] *n (U)* - **1.** [tools, equipment] artículos *mpl* de ferretería - **2.** COMPUT hardware *m*, soporte *m* físico.

hardware store *n US* ferretería *f.*

hardwearing [,hɑːd'weərɪŋ] *adj UK* resistente.

hardworking [,hɑːd'wɜːkɪŋ] *adj* trabajador(ra).

hardy ['hɑːdɪ] (*compar* **-ier**, *superl* **-iest**) *adj* - **1.** [person, animal] fuerte, robusto(ta) - **2.** [plant] resistente.

hare [heə'] *n* liebre *f.*

harebrained ['heə,breɪnd] *adj inf* atolondrado(da).

harelip [,heə'lɪp] *n* labio *m* leporino.

haricot (bean) ['hærɪkəʊ-] *n* judía *f*, alubia *f*, frijol *m Amér*, poroto *m Andes, CSur*, caraota *f Ven.*

Harley Street ['hɑːlɪ-] *n* calle londinense famosa por sus médicos especialistas.

harm [hɑːm] <> *n* daño *m*; **to do ~ to sthg/ sb**, **to do sthg/sb ~** [physically] hacer daño a algo/alguien; *fig* perjudicar algo/a alguien; **to be out of ~'s way** estar a salvo. <> *vt* [gen] hacer daño a, dañar; [reputation, chances, interests] dañar.

harmful ['hɑːmfʊl] *adj*: **~ (to)** perjudicial OR dañino(na) (para); [substance] nocivo(va) (para).

harmless ['hɑːmlɪs] *adj* inofensivo(va).

harmonica [hɑː'mɒnɪkə] *n* armónica *f.*

harmonize, -ise ['hɑːmənaɪz] <> *vi*: **to ~ (with)** armonizar (con). <> *vt* armonizar.

harmony ['hɑːmənɪ] (*pl* **-ies**) *n* armonía *f.*

harness ['hɑːnɪs] <> *n* [for horse] arreos *mpl*, guarniciones *fpl.* <> *vt* - **1.** [horse] enjaezar, poner los arreos a - **2.** [use] aprovechar.

harp [hɑːp] *n* arpa *f.*

◆ harp on *vi*: **to ~ on (about sthg)** dar la matraca (con algo).

harpoon [hɑː'puːn] *n* arpón *m.*

harpsichord ['hɑːpsɪkɔːd] *n* clavicémbalo *m.*

harrowing ['hærəʊɪŋ] *adj* pavoroso(sa).

harsh [hɑːʃ] *adj* - **1.** [life, conditions, winter] duro(ra) - **2.** [punishment, decision, person] severo(ra) - **3.** [texture, taste, voice] áspero(ra); [light, sound] violento(ta).

harvest ['hɑːvɪst] <> *n* [gen] cosecha *f*, pizca *f Méx*; [of grapes] vendimia *f.* <> *vt* cosechar.

has [*weak form* həz, *strong form* hæz] *3rd person sg* ⊳ **have**.

has-been *n inf pej* vieja gloria *f.*

hash [hæʃ] *n* - **1.** [meat] picadillo *m* (de

carne) - **2.** *inf* [mess]: **to make a** ~ **of sthg** hacer algo fatal.

hashish ['hæʃiːʃ] *n* hachís *m*.

hasn't ['hæznt] = **has not**.

hassle ['hæsl] *inf* ◇ *n (U)* [annoyance] rollo *m*, lío *m*. ◇ *vt* dar la lata a.

haste [heɪst] *n* prisa *f*; **to do sthg in** ~ hacer algo de prisa y corriendo.

hasten ['heɪsn] *fml* ◇ *vt* acelerar. ◇ *vi*: **to** ~ **(to do sthg)** apresurarse (a hacer algo).

hastily ['heɪstɪlɪ] *adv* - **1.** [quickly] de prisa, precipitadamente - **2.** [rashly] a la ligera, sin reflexionar.

hasty ['heɪstɪ] (*compar* **-ier**, *superl* **-iest**) *adj* - **1.** [quick] apresurado(da), precipitado(da) - **2.** [rash] irreflexivo(va).

hat [hæt] *n* sombrero *m*.

hatch [hætʃ] ◇ *vi* [chick] romper el cascarón, salir del huevo. ◇ *vt* - **1.** [chick, egg] incubar - **2.** *fig* [scheme, plot] tramar. ◇ *n* [for serving food] ventanilla *f*.

hatchback ['hætʃ,bæk] *n* coche *m* con puerta trasera.

hatchet ['hætʃɪt] *n* hacha *f*.

hatchway ['hætʃ,weɪ] *n* escotilla *f*.

hate [heɪt] ◇ *n* odio *m*. ◇ *vt* odiar; **to** ~ **doing sthg** odiar hacer algo.

hateful ['heɪtfʊl] *adj* odioso(sa).

hatred ['heɪtrɪd] *n* odio *m*.

hat trick *n* SPORT *tres tantos marcados por un jugador en el mismo partido.*

haughty ['hɔːtɪ] (*compar* **-ier**, *superl* **-iest**) *adj* altanero(ra), altivo(va).

haul [hɔːl] ◇ *n* - **1.** [of stolen goods] botín *m*; [of drugs] alijo *m* - **2.** [distance]: **long** ~ largo camino *m*, largo trayecto *m*. ◇ *vt* [pull] tirar, arrastrar.

haulage ['hɔːlɪdʒ] *n* transporte *m*.

haulier *UK* ['hɔːlɪəʳ], **hauler** *US* ['hɔːlər] *n* transportista *m* OR *f*, contratista *m* OR *f* de transportes.

haunch [hɔːntʃ] *n* - **1.** [of person] asentaderas *fpl*; **to squat on one's** ~**es** ponerse en cuclillas - **2.** [of animal] pernil *m*.

haunt [hɔːnt] ◇ *n* sitio *m* favorito, lugar *m* predilecto. ◇ *vt* - **1.** [subj: ghost - house] aparecer en; [- person] aparecerse a - **2.** [subj: memory, fear, problem] atormentar, obsesionar.

have [hæv] (*pt & pp* **had**) ◇ *aux vb (to form perfect tenses)* haber; **to** ~ **eaten** haber comido; **he hasn't gone yet, has he?** no se habrá ido ya ¿no?; **I've finished** - ~ **you?** he terminado - ¿ah sí?; **no, he hasn't (done it)** no, no lo ha hecho; **yes, he has (done it)** sí, lo ha hecho; **I was out of breath, having run all the way** estaba sin aliento después de haber corrido todo el camino. ◇ *vt* - **1.** [possess, receive]: **to** ~ **(got)** tener; **I** ~ **no money, I haven't got any money** no tengo dinero;

he has big hands tiene las manos grandes; **do you** ~ **a car?**, ~ **you got a car?** ¿tienes coche? - **2.** [experience, suffer] tener; **I had an accident** tuve un accidente; **to** ~ **a cold** tener un resfriado - **3.** *(referring to an action, instead of another verb)*: **to** ~ **a look** mirar, echar una mirada; **to** ~ **a swim** darse un baño, nadar; **to** ~ **breakfast** desayunar; **to** ~ **lunch** comer; **to** ~ **dinner** cenar; **to** ~ **a cigarette** fumarse un cigarro; **to** ~ **an operation** operarse - **4.** [give birth to]: **to** ~ **a baby** tener un niño - **5.** [cause to be done]: **to** ~ **sb do sthg** hacer que alguien haga algo; **to** ~ **sthg done** hacer que se haga algo; **to** ~ **one's hair cut** (ir a) cortarse el pelo - **6.** [be treated in a certain way]: **I had my car stolen** me robaron el coche - **7.** *inf* [cheat]: **you've been had** te han timado - **8.** *phr*: **to** ~ **had it** [car, machine] estar para el arrastre. ◇ *modal vb* [be obliged]: **to** ~ **(got) to do sthg** tener que hacer algo; **do you** ~ **to go?**, ~ **you got to go?** ¿tienes que irte?

◆ **have off** *vt sep* [as holiday] tener libre.

◆ **have on** *vt sep* - **1.** [be wearing] llevar (puesto) - **2.** [tease] tomar el pelo a - **3.** [have to do]: ~ **you got anything on on Friday?** ¿estás libre OR haces algo el viernes?

◆ **have out** *vt sep* - **1.** [have removed]: **to** ~ **one's tonsils out** operarse de las amígdalas - **2.** [discuss frankly]: **to** ~ **it out with sb** poner las cuentas claras con alguien.

haven ['heɪvn] *n fig* refugio *m*, asilo *m*.

haven't ['hævnt] = **have not**.

haversack ['hævəsæk] *n* mochila *f*, zurrón *m*.

havoc ['hævək] *n (U)* estragos *mpl*; **to play** ~ **with sthg** causar estragos en algo.

Hawaii [hə'waɪɪ] *n* Hawai.

hawk [hɔːk] *n lit & fig* halcón *m*.

hawker ['hɔːkəʳ] *n* vendedor *m*, **-ra** *f* ambulante, abonero *m*, **-ra** *f Méx.*

hay [heɪ] *n* heno *m*.

hay fever *n (U)* fiebre *f* del heno.

haystack ['heɪ,stæk] *n* almiar *m*.

haywire ['heɪ,waɪəʳ] *adj inf*: **to go** ~ [person] volverse majara; [plan] liarse, embrollarse; [computer, TV etc] changarse.

hazard ['hæzəd] ◇ *n* riesgo *m*, peligro *m*. ◇ *vt* [guess, suggestion] aventurar, atreverse a hacer.

hazardous ['hæzədəs] *adj* peligroso(sa).

hazard warning lights *npl UK* luces *fpl* de emergencia.

haze [heɪz] *n* neblina *f*.

hazel ['heɪzl] *adj* color avellana *(inv)*.

hazelnut ['heɪzl,nʌt] *n* avellana *f*.

hazy ['heɪzɪ] (*compar* **-ier**, *superl* **-iest**) *adj* - **1.** [misty] neblinoso(sa) - **2.** [vague] vago(ga), confuso(sa).

he [hiː] ◇ *pers pron* él; ~**'s tall/happy** es alto/feliz; **HE can't do it** ÉL no puede hacerlo; **there ~ is** allí está. ◇ *comp*: **~-goat** macho cabrío *m*.

head [hed] ◇ *n* **-1.** ANAT & COMPUT cabeza *f*; **a** OR **per ~** por persona, por cabeza; **to be soft in the ~** estar mal de la sesera; **to be off one's ~** *UK*, **to be out of one's ~** *US* estar como una cabra; **it was over my ~** no me enteré de nada; **it went to her ~** se le subió a la cabeza; **to keep/lose one's ~** no perder/perder la cabeza; **to laugh one's ~ off** reír a mandíbula batiente **-2.** [mind, brain] talento *m*, aptitud *f*; **she has a ~ for figures** se le dan bien las cuentas **-3.** [top, gen] cabeza *f*; [of hill] cabecera *f* **-4.** [of flower] cabezuela *f*; [of cabbage] cogollo *m* **-5.** [on beer] espuma *f* **-6.** [leader] jefe *m*, -fa *f* **-7.** [head teacher] director *m*, -ra *f* (de colegio). ◇ *vt* **-1.** [procession, convoy, list, page] encabezar **-2.** [organization, delegation] dirigir **-3.** FTBL cabecear. ◇ *vi*: **to ~ north/for home** dirigirse hacia el norte/a casa.
➤ **heads** *npl* [on coin] cara *f*; **~s or tails?** ¿cara o cruz?
➤ **head for** *vt fus* **-1.** [place] dirigirse a **-2.** *fig* [trouble, disaster] ir camino de.

headache ['hedeɪk] *n* **-1.** MED dolor *m* de cabeza; **I have a ~** me duele la cabeza **-2.** *fig* [problem] quebradero *m* de cabeza.

headband ['hedbænd] *n* cinta *f*, banda *f* (para el pelo).

head boy *n UK* [at school] *alumno delegado principal que suele representar a sus condiscípulos en actos escolares.*

headdress ['hed,dres] *n* tocado *m*.

header ['hedəʳ] *n* **-1.** FTBL cabezazo *m* **-2.** TYPO encabezamiento *m*.

headfirst [,hed'fɜːst] *adv* de cabeza.

head girl *n UK* [in school] *alumna delegada principal que suele representar a sus condiscípulas en actos escolares.*

heading ['hedɪŋ] *n* encabezamiento *m*.

headlamp ['hedlæmp] *n UK* faro *m*.

headland ['hedlənd] *n* cabo *m*, promontorio *m*.

headlight ['hedlaɪt] *n* faro *m*.

headline ['hedlaɪn] *n* titular *m*.

headlong ['hedlɒŋ] *adv* **-1.** [headfirst] de cabeza **-2.** [quickly, unthinkingly] precipitadamente.

headmaster [,hed'mɑːstəʳ] *n* director *m* (de colegio).

headmistress [,hed'mɪstrɪs] *n* directora *f* (de colegio).

head office *n* oficina *f* central.

head of state *n* jefe *m* de Estado.

head-on ◇ *adj* de frente, frontal. ◇ *adv* de frente.

headphones ['hedfəʊnz] *npl* auriculares *mpl*.

headquarters [,hed'kwɔːtəz] *npl* (oficina *f*) central *f*, sede *f*; MIL cuartel *m* general.

headrest ['hedrest] *n* reposacabezas *m inv.*

headroom ['hedrʊm] *n (U)* [in car] espacio *m* entre la cabeza y el techo; [below bridge] altura *f* libre, gálibo *m*.

headscarf ['hedskɑːf] (*pl* **-scarves** [-skɑːvz] OR **-scarfs**) *n* pañuelo *m* (para la cabeza).

headset ['hedset] *n* auriculares *mpl* con micrófono.

head start *n*: **~ (on** OR **over)** ventaja *f* (con respecto a).

headstrong ['hedstrɒŋ] *adj* obstinado(da).

head waiter *n* maître *m*, capitán *m* de meseros *Méx*.

headway ['hedweɪ] *n*: **to make ~** avanzar, hacer progresos.

headwind ['hedwɪnd] *n* viento *m* de proa.

heady ['hedɪ] (*compar* **-ier**, *superl* **-iest**) *adj* **-1.** [exciting] emocionante **-2.** [causing giddiness] embriagador(ra).

heal [hiːl] ◇ *vt* **-1.** [person] curar; [wound] cicatrizar **-2.** *fig* [troubles, discord] remediar. ◇ *vi* [wound] cicatrizar.

healing ['hiːlɪŋ] *n* curación *f*.

health [helθ] *n* **-1.** [gen] salud *f*; **to be in good/poor ~** estar bien/mal de salud **-2.** *fig* [of country, organization] buen estado *m*.

health care *n* asistencia *f* sanitaria.

health centre *n* ambulatorio *m*, centro *m* sanitario.

health food *n* comida *f* dietética.

health food shop *n* tienda *f* de dietética.

health service *n* servicio *m* sanitario de la Seguridad Social, ≃ INSALUD *m*.

healthy ['helθɪ] (*compar* **-ier**, *superl* **-iest**) *adj* **-1.** [gen] sano(na), saludable **-2.** [profit] pingüe **-3.** [attitude, respect] natural, sano(na).

heap [hiːp] ◇ *n* montón *m*, pila *f*, ruma *f Amér*. ◇ *vt* [pile up]: **to ~ sthg (on** OR **onto sthg)** amontonar algo (sobre algo).
➤ **heaps** *npl inf* montones *fpl*, mogollón *m*.

hear [hɪəʳ] (*pt* & *pp* **heard**) ◇ *vt* **-1.** [gen] oír; **I ~ (that ...)** me dicen que ... **-2.** JUR ver. ◇ *vi* **-1.** [gen] oír; **have you heard about that job yet?** ¿sabes algo del trabajo ese?; **to ~ from sb** tener noticias de alguien **-2.** *phr*: **to have heard of** haber oído hablar de; **I won't ~ of it!** ¡de eso ni hablar!

hearing ['hɪərɪŋ] *n* **-1.** [sense] oído *m*; **hard of ~** duro de oído **-2.** JUR vista *f*.

hearing aid *n* audífono *m*.

hearsay ['hɪəseɪ] *n (U)* habladurías *fpl*.

hearse [hɜːs] *n* coche *m* fúnebre.

heart [hɑːt] *n* **-1.** [gen] corazón *m*; **from the ~** con toda sinceridad; **to break sb's ~**

romper OR partir el corazón a alguien
- 2. [courage]: **I didn't have the ~ to tell her**
no tuve valor para decírselo; **to lose ~ des-**
corazonarse - 3. [centre - of issue, problem]
quid m; [- of city etc] **centro** m; [- of lettuce]
cogollo m.

➤ **hearts** npl corazones mpl.

➤ **at heart** adv en el fondo.

➤ **by heart** adv de memoria.

heartache ['hɑːteɪk] n dolor m.

heart attack n infarto m.

heartbeat ['hɑːbiːt] n latido m.

heartbroken ['hɑːtˌbrəʊkn] adj desolado(-
da), abatido(da).

heartburn ['hɑːtbɜːn] n ardor m de estómago.

heart failure n paro m cardíaco.

heartfelt ['hɑːtfelt] adj sincero(ra), de todo
corazón.

hearth [hɑːθ] n hogar m.

heartless ['hɑːtlɪs] adj cruel, inhumano(-
na).

heartwarming ['hɑːtˌwɔːmɪŋ] adj gratificante, grato(ta).

hearty ['hɑːtɪ] (compar -ier, superl -iest) adj
- 1. [laughter] bonachón(ona); [welcome,
congratulations, thanks] cordial; [person]
fuertote(ta) - 2. [meal] abundante; [appetite]
bueno(na) - 3. [dislike, distrust] profundo(-
da).

heat [hiːt] ◇ n - 1. [gen] calor m - 2. [specific
temperature] temperatura f - 3. fig [pressure]
tensión f; **in the ~ of the moment** en el calor del momento - 4. [eliminating round] serie f, prueba f eliminatoria - 5. ZOOL: **on** UK
OR **in ~** en celo. ◇ vt calentar.

➤ **heat up** ◇ vt sep calentar. ◇ vi calentarse.

heated ['hiːtɪd] adj - 1. [swimming pool] cli-
matizado(da) - 2. [debate, argument] acalo-
rado(da).

heater ['hiːtəʳ] n calentador m, estufa f.

heath [hiːθ] n [place] brezal m.

heathen ['hiːðn] n pagano m, -na f.

heather ['heðəʳ] n brezo m.

heating ['hiːtɪŋ] n calefacción f.

heatstroke ['hiːtstrəʊk] n (U) insolación f.

heat wave n ola f de calor.

heave [hiːv] ◇ vt - 1. [pull] tirar de, arrastrar; [push] empujar - 2. inf [throw] tirar,
lanzar. ◇ vi - 1. [pull] tirar - 2. [rise and
fall - waves] ondular; [- chest] palpitar.

heaven ['hevn] n [Paradise] cielo m.

➤ **heavens** npl: **the ~s** literary los cielos;
(good) **~s!** ¡cielos!

heavenly ['hevnlɪ] adj inf dated [delightful]
divino(na).

heavily ['hevɪlɪ] adv - 1. [smoke, drink] mucho; [rain] con fuerza; **~ in debt** con muchas deudas - 2. [solidly]: **~ built**

corpulento(ta) - 3. [breathe, sigh] profundamente - 4. [sit, move, fall] pesadamente
- 5. [speak] pesarosamente.

heavy ['hevɪ] (compar -ier, superl -iest) adj
- 1. [gen] pesado(da); [solid] sólido(da);
how ~ is it? ¿cuánto pesa?; **~ build** corpu-
lencia f - 2. [traffic, rain, fighting] intenso(-
sa); **to be a ~ smoker/drinker** ser un
fumador/bebedor empedernido - 3. [losses,
responsibility] **grande** - 4. [soil, mixture]
denso(sa) - 5. [blow] duro(ra); [fine, defeat]
duro(ra) - 6. [busy - schedule, day] apreta-
do(da) - 7. [work] duro(ra) - 8. [weather, air,
day] cargado(da).

heavy cream n US nata f para montar.

heavy goods vehicle n UK vehículo m (de
transporte) pesado.

heavyweight ['hevɪweɪt] SPORT ◇ adj de
los pesos pesados. ◇ n peso m pesado.

Hebrew ['hiːbruː] ◇ adj hebreo(a). ◇ n
- 1. [person] hebreo m, -a f - 2. [language] hebreo m.

Hebrides ['hebrɪdiːz] npl: **the ~** las Hébri-
das.

heck [hek] excl: **what/where/why the
~ ...?** ¿qué/dónde/por qué demonios ...?;
a ~ of a lot of la mar de.

heckle ['hekl] vt & vi interrumpir con exa-
bruptos.

hectic ['hektɪk] adj ajetreado(da).

he'd [hiːd] = **he had, he would.**

hedge [hedʒ] ◇ n seto m. ◇ vi [prevari-
cate] contestar con evasivas.

hedgehog ['hedʒhɒg] n erizo m.

heed [hiːd] ◇ n: **to take ~ of sthg** tener
algo en cuenta. ◇ vt fml tener en cuenta.

heedless ['hiːdlɪs] adj: **to be ~ of sthg** no
hacer caso de algo.

heel [hiːl] n - 1. [of foot] talón m - 2. [of shoe]
tacón m, taco m Amér.

hefty ['heftɪ] (compar -ier, superl -iest) adj
inf - 1. [person] fornido(da) - 2. [salary, fee,
fine] considerable, importante.

heifer ['hefəʳ] n vaquilla f.

height [haɪt] n - 1. [gen] altura f; [of person]
estatura f; **5 metres in ~** 5 metros de altura;
what ~ is it/are you? ¿cuánto mide/mi-
des? - 2. [zenith]: **the ~ of** [gen] el punto álgido de; [ignorance, bad taste] el colmo de.

heighten ['haɪtn] ◇ vt intensificar, aumentar. ◇ vi intensificarse, aumentar.

heir [eəʳ] n heredero m.

heiress ['eərɪs] n heredera f.

heirloom ['eəluːm] n reliquia f de familia.

heist [haɪst] n inf golpe m, robo m.

held [held] pt & pp ⊳ **hold.**

helicopter ['helɪkɒptəʳ] n helicóptero m.

helium ['hiːlɪəm] n helio m.

hell [hel] ◇ n infierno m; **what/where/
why the ~ ...?** inf ¿qué/dónde/por qué

demonios ...?; **one** OR **a** ~ **of a nice guy** *inf* un tipo estupendo; **to do sthg for the** ~ **of it** *inf* hacer algo porque sí; **to give sb** ~ *inf* hacérselas pasar canutas a alguien; **go to** ~ **!** v *inf* ¡vete al infierno! ◇ *excl inf* ¡hostias!

he'll [hi:l] = **he will**.

hellish ['helɪʃ] *adj inf* diabólico(ca), infernal.

hello [hə'ləʊ] *excl* **- 1.** [as greeting] ¡hola!; [on phone - when answering] ¡diga!, ¡bueno! *Méx*, ¡holá! *RP*, ¡aló! *Andes, Carib*; [- when calling] ¡oiga!, ¡holá! *RP*, ¡aló! *Andes, Carib* **- 2.** [to attract attention] ¡oiga!

helm [helm] *n lit & fig* timón *m*.

helmet ['helmɪt] *n* casco *m*.

help [help] ◇ *n* **- 1.** [gen & COMPUT] ayuda *f*; **with the** ~ **of** con la ayuda de; **to be a** ~ ser una ayuda; **to be of** ~ ayudar **- 2.** (U) [emergency aid] socorro *m*, ayuda *f*. ◇ *vt* **- 1.** [assist]: **to** ~ **sb (to) do sthg/with sthg** ayudar a alguien (a hacer algo/con algo); **can I** ~ **you?** [in shop, bank] ¿en qué puedo servirle? **- 2.** [avoid]: **I can't** ~ **it/feeling sad** no puedo evitarlo/evitar que me dé pena; **it can't be** ~ **ed** ¿qué se le va a hacer? **- 3.** [with food, drink]: **to** ~ **o.s. (to sthg)** servirse (algo). ◇ *vi*: **to** ~ **(with)** ayudar (con). ◇ *excl* ¡socorro!, ¡auxilio!

◆ **help out** ◇ *vt sep* echar una mano a. ◇ *vi* echar una mano.

helper ['helpə'] *n* **- 1.** [gen] ayudante *m* OR *f* **- 2.** US [to do housework] mujer *f* OR señora *f* de la limpieza.

helpful ['helpfʊl] *adj* **- 1.** [willing to help] servicial, atento(ta) **- 2.** [providing assistance] útil.

helping ['helpɪŋ] *n* ración *f*; **would you like a second** ~ **?** ¿quiere repetir?

helpless ['helplɪs] *adj* [child] indefenso(sa); [look, gesture] impotente.

helpline ['helplaɪn] *n* servicio *m* telefónico de ayuda.

help menu *n* COMPUT menú *m* de ayuda.

Helsinki ['helsɪŋkɪ] *n* Helsinki.

hem [hem] ◇ *n* (*pt & pp* **-med**, *cont* **-ming**) *n* dobladillo *m*.

◆ **hem in** *vt sep* rodear, cercar.

hemisphere ['hemɪˌsfɪə'] *n* [of earth & ANAT] hemisferio *m*.

hemline ['hemlaɪn] *n* bajo *m* (*de falda etc*).

hemophiliac [ˌhiːməʊ'fɪliæk] *n* hemofílico *m*, -ca *f*.

hemorrhage ['hemərɪdʒ] *n* hemorragia *f*.

hemorrhoids ['hemərɔɪdz] *npl* hemorroides *fpl*.

hen [hen] *n* **- 1.** [female chicken] gallina *f* **- 2.** [female bird] hembra *f*.

hence [hens] *adv fml* **- 1.** [therefore] por lo tanto, así pues **- 2.** [from now]: **five years**

~ **de aquí a cinco años.**

henceforth [ˌhens'fɔːθ] *adv fml* de ahora en adelante, en lo sucesivo.

henchman ['hentʃmən] (*pl* **-men** [-mən]) *n pej* esbirro *m*.

henpecked ['henpekt] *adj pej*: **a** ~ **husband** un calzonazos.

hepatitis [ˌhepə'taɪtɪs] *n* hepatitis *f inv*.

her [hɜː'] ◇ *pers pron* **- 1.** (*direct - unstressed*) la; (*- stressed*) ella; [referring to ship, car etc] lo; **I know** ~ la conozco; **I like** ~ me gusta; **it's** ~ es ella; **if I were** OR **was** ~ si (yo) fuera ella; **you can't expect HER to do it** no esperarás que ELLA lo haga; **fill** ~ **up!** AUT ¡llénemelo!, ¡lleno, por favor! **- 2.** (*indirect - gen*) le; (*- with other third person pronouns*) se; **he sent** ~ **a letter** le mandó una carta; **we spoke to** ~ hablamos con ella; **I gave it to** ~ se lo di **- 3.** (*after prep, in comparisons etc*) ella; **I'm shorter than** ~ yo soy más bajo que ella. ◇ *poss adj* su, sus (*pl*); ~ **coat** su abrigo; ~ **children** sus niños; ~ **name is Sarah** se llama Sarah; **it wasn't HER fault** no fue culpa suya OR su culpa; **she washed** ~ **hair** se lavó el pelo.

herald ['herəld] ◇ *vt fml* **- 1.** [signify, usher in] anunciar **- 2.** [proclaim] proclamar. ◇ *n* **- 1.** [messenger] heraldo *m* **- 2.** [sign] anuncio *m*.

herb [UK hɜːb, US ɜːb] *n* hierba *f (aromática o medicinal)*.

herd [hɜːd] ◇ *n* [of cattle, goats] rebaño *m*; [of elephants] manada *f*. ◇ *vt fig* [push] conducir (en grupo) bruscamente.

here [hɪə'] *adv* aquí; ~ **he is/they are** aquí está/están; ~ **it is** aquí está; ~ **is the book** aquí tienes el libro; ~ **are the keys** aquí tienes las llaves; ~ **you are** [when giving] aquí tienes; ~ **and there** aquí y allá.

hereabouts *UK* ['hɪərəˌbaʊts], **hereabout** *US* [ˌhɪərə'baʊt] *adv* por aquí.

hereafter [ˌhɪər'ɑːftə'] ◇ *adv fml* [from now on] de ahora en adelante; [later on] más tarde. ◇ *n*: **the** ~ el más allá, la otra vida.

hereby [ˌhɪə'baɪ] *adv fml* **- 1.** [in documents] por la presente **- 2.** [when speaking]: **I** ~ **declare you the winner** desde este momento te declaro vencedor.

hereditary [hɪ'redɪtrɪ] *adj* hereditario(ria).

heresy ['herəsɪ] (*pl* **-ies**) *n* RELIG & *fig* herejía *f*.

herewith [ˌhɪə'wɪð] *adv fml* [with letter]: **please find** ~ **...** le mando adjunto ...

heritage ['herɪtɪdʒ] *n* patrimonio *m*.

hermetically [hɜː'metɪklɪ] *adv* : ~ **sealed** cerrado(da) herméticamente.

hermit ['hɜːmɪt] *n* ermitaño *m*, -ña *f*.

hernia ['hɜːnjə] *n* hernia *f*.

hero ['hɪərəʊ] (*pl* **-es**) *n* **- 1.** [gen] héroe *m*

- 2. [ídol] **ídolo** *m* - 3. US [sandwich] *sandwich hecho con una barra de pan larga y estrecha, relleno de varios ingredientes*.

heroic [hɪ'rəʊɪk] *adj* heroico(ca).

heroin ['herəʊɪn] *n* heroína *f (droga)*; ~ **addict** heroinómano *m*, -na *f*.

heroine ['herəʊɪn] *n* heroína *f*.

heron ['herən] (*pl inv OR* -**s**) *n* garza *f* real.

herring ['herɪŋ] (*pl inv OR* -**s**) *n* arenque *m*.

hers [hɜːz] *poss pron* suyo (suya); **that money is** ~ ese dinero es suyo; **those keys are** ~ esas llaves son suyas; **it wasn't his fault, it was HERS** no fue culpa de él sino de ella; **a friend of** ~ un amigo suyo, un amigo de ella; **mine is good, but** ~ **is bad** el mío es bueno pero el suyo es malo.

herself [hɜː'self] *pron* - 1. *(reflexive)* se; *(after prep)* sí misma; **with** ~ consigo misma - 2. *(for emphasis)* ella misma; **she did it** ~ lo hizo ella sola.

he's [hiːz] = **he.is, he.has**.

hesitant ['hezɪtənt] *adj* - 1. [unsure of oneself] indeciso(sa), inseguro(ra) - 2. [faltering, slow to appear] vacilante.

hesitate ['hezɪteɪt] *vi* vacilar, dudar; **to** ~ **to do sthg** dudar en hacer algo.

hesitation [,hezɪ'teɪʃn] *n* vacilación *f*.

heterogeneous [,hetərə'dʒiːnjəs] *adj fml* heterogéneo(a).

heterosexual [,hetərəʊ'sekʃʊəl] *⟨⟩ adj* heterosexual. *⟨⟩ n* heterosexual *m OR f*.

het up [het-] *adj inf* - 1. [nervous] nervioso(sa) - 2. [annoyed] mosqueado(da).

hey [heɪ] *excl* ¡eh!, ¡oye!, ¡che! *Amér.*

heyday ['heɪdeɪ] *n* apogeo *m*, auge *m*.

HGV *n abbr of* **heavy goods vehicle**.

hi [haɪ] *excl inf* [hello] ¡hola!

hiatus [haɪ'eɪtəs] (*pl* -**es**) *n fml* [pause] interrupción *f*.

hibernate ['haɪbəneɪt] *vi* hibernar.

hiccough, hiccup ['hɪkʌp] (*pt & pp* -**ped**, *cont* -**ping**) *⟨⟩ n* - 1. [caused by wind] hipo *m*; **to have (the)** ~**s** tener hipo - 2. *fig* [difficulty] contratiempo *m*. *⟨⟩ vi* hipar.

hid [hɪd] *pt ⊳* **hide**.

hidden ['hɪdn] *⟨⟩ pp ⊳* **hide**. *⟨⟩ adj* oculto(ta).

hide [haɪd] (*pt* **hid**, *pp* **hidden**) *⟨⟩ vt* - 1. [conceal] esconder, ocultar; **to** ~ **sthg (from sb)** esconder OR ocultar algo (a alguien) - 2. [cover] tapar, ocultar. *⟨⟩ vi* esconderse. *⟨⟩ n* - 1. [animal skin] piel *f* - 2. [for watching birds, animals] puesto *m*.

hide-and-seek *n* escondite *m*.

hideaway ['haɪdəweɪ] *n inf* escondite *m*.

hideous ['hɪdɪəs] *adj* horrible, espantoso(sa).

hiding ['haɪdɪŋ] *n* - 1. [concealment]: **in** ~ escondido(da) - 2. *inf* [beating]: **to give sb/get a (good)** ~ darle a alguien/recibir una (buena) paliza.

hiding place *n* escondite *m*.

hierarchy ['haɪərɑːkɪ] (*pl* -**ies**) *n* jerarquía *f*.

hi-fi ['haɪfaɪ] *⟨⟩ adj* de alta fidelidad. *⟨⟩ n* equipo *m* de alta fidelidad.

high [haɪ] *⟨⟩ adj* - 1. [gen] alto(ta); [altitude] grande; **it's 6 metres** ~ tiene 6 metros de alto OR altura; **how** ~ **is it?** ¿cuánto mide?; **temperatures in the** ~ **20s** temperaturas cercanas a los 30 grados; **at** ~ **speed** a gran velocidad - 2. [wind] fuerte - 3. [risk, quality] grande - 4. [ideals, principles, tone] elevado(da) - 5. [high-pitched] agudo(da) - 6. *inf* colocado(da). *⟨⟩ adv* alto; **he threw the ball** ~ **in the air** lanzó la bola muy alto. *⟨⟩ n* - 1. [highest point] **punto** *m* **álgido** - 2. [weather front] anticiclón *m*; [top temperature] máxima *f*.

highbrow ['haɪbraʊ] *adj* culto(ta), intelectual.

high chair *n* trona *f*.

high-class *adj* [superior] de (alta) categoría.

High Court *n UK* tribunal *m* supremo.

higher ['haɪə˞] *adj* [exam, qualification] superior.

➤ **Higher** *n*: **Higher (Grade)** *en Escocia, examen realizado al final de la enseñanza secundaria.*

higher education *n* enseñanza *f* superior.

high-handed [-'hændɪd] *adj* despótico(ca).

high jump *n* salto *m* de altura.

Highland Games ['haɪlənd-] *npl fiesta de deportes escoceses.*

Highlands ['haɪləndz] *npl*: **the** ~ [of Scotland] las Tierras Altas de Escocia.

highlight ['haɪlaɪt] *⟨⟩ n* [of event, occasion] punto *m* culminante. *⟨⟩ vt* - 1. [visually] resaltar, marcar - 2. [emphasize] destacar, resaltar.

➤ **highlights** *npl* - 1. [in hair] reflejos *mpl* - 2. [of match] mejores momentos *mpl*.

highlighter (pen) ['haɪlaɪtə˞-] *n* rotulador *m*, marcador *m*.

highly ['haɪlɪ] *adv* - 1. [very, extremely] muy; ~ **paid** bien pagado - 2. [favourably]: **to think** ~ **of sb** tener a alguien en mucha estima.

highly-strung *adj* muy nervioso(sa).

Highness ['haɪnɪs] *n*: **His/Her/Your (Royal)** ~ Su Alteza *f* (Real); **their (Royal)** ~**es** Sus Altezas (Reales).

high-pitched [-'pɪtʃt] *adj* agudo(da).

high point *n* [of occasion] momento *m OR* punto *m* culminante.

high-powered [-'paʊəd] *adj* - 1. [powerful] de gran potencia - 2. [prestigious - activity, place] prestigioso(sa); [- person] de altos vuelos.

high-ranking [-'ræŋkɪŋ] *adj* [in army etc] de alta graduación; [in government]: ~ **official** alto cargo *m*.

high-rise *adj*: ~ **building** torre *f*.

high school *n* ≃ instituto *m* de bachillerato.

high season *n* temporada *f* alta.

high street ◇ *adj* UK [bank] comercial. ◇ *n* calle *f* mayor OR principal.

high-strung *adj* US muy nervioso(sa).

high tech [-'tek] *adj* de alta tecnología.

high tide *n* [of sea] marea *f* alta.

highway ['haɪweɪ] *n* **- 1.** US [main road between cities] autopista *f* **- 2.** UK [any main road] carretera *f*.

Highway Code *n* UK: **the** ~ el código de la circulación.

hijack ['haɪdʒæk] *vt* [aircraft] secuestrar.

hijacker ['haɪdʒækə'] *n* secuestrador *m*, -ra *f (de un avión)*.

hijacking ['haɪdʒækɪŋ] *n* secuestro *m (de un avión)*.

hike [haɪk] ◇ *n* [long walk] caminata *f*. ◇ *vi* [go for walk] ir de excursión.

hiker ['haɪkə'] *n* excursionista *m* OR *f*.

hiking ['haɪkɪŋ] *n* excursionismo *m*; **to go** ~ ir de excursión.

hilarious [hɪ'leərɪəs] *adj* desternillante.

hill [hɪl] *n* **- 1.** [mound] colina *f* **- 2.** [slope] cuesta *f*.

hillside ['hɪlsaɪd] *n* ladera *f*.

hilly ['hɪlɪ] *(compar* **-ier***, superl* **-iest***) adj* montañoso(sa).

hilt [hɪlt] *n* puño *m*, empuñadura *f*; **to support/defend sb to the** ~ apoyar/defender a alguien sin reservas.

him [hɪm] *pers pron* **- 1.** *(direct - unstressed)* lo, le; *(-stressed)* él; **I know** ~ lo OR le conozco; **I like** ~ me gusta; **it's** ~ es él; **if I were** OR **was** ~ si (yo) fuera él; **you can't expect HIM to do it** no esperarás que ÉL lo haga **- 2.** *(indirect - gen)* le; *(- with other third person pronouns)* se; **she sent** ~ **a letter** le mandó una carta; **we spoke to** ~ hablamos con él; **I gave it to** ~ se lo di **- 3.** *(after prep, in comparisons etc)* él; **I'm shorter than** ~ yo soy más bajo que él.

Himalayas [,hɪmə'leɪəz] *npl*: **the** ~ el Himalaya.

himself [hɪm'self] *pron* **- 1.** *(reflexive)* se; *(after prep)* sí mismo; **with** ~ consigo mismo **- 2.** *(for emphasis)* él mismo; **he did it** ~ lo hizo él solo.

hind [haɪnd] *(pl inv* OR **-s***) adj* trasero(ra). ◇ *n* cierva *f*.

hinder ['hɪndə'] *vt* [gen] estorbar; [progress, talks, attempts] entorpecer, dificultar.

Hindi ['hɪndɪ] *n* [language] hindi *m*.

hindrance ['hɪndrəns] *n* [obstacle] obstáculo *m*, impedimento *m*; [person] estorbo *m*.

hindsight ['haɪndsaɪt] *n*: **with the benefit of** ~ ahora que se sabe lo que pasó.

Hindu ['hɪnduː] *(pl* **-s***)* ◇ *adj* hindú. ◇ *n* hindú *m* OR *f*.

hinge [hɪndʒ] *(cont* **hingeing***) n* [on door, window] bisagra *f*.

➤ **hinge (up)on** *vt fus* [depend on] depender de.

hint [hɪnt] ◇ *n* **- 1.** [indication] indirecta *f*; **to drop a** ~ lanzar una indirecta **- 2.** [piece of advice] consejo *m* **- 3.** [small amount, suggestion] asomo *m*; [of colour] pizca *f*. ◇ *vi*: **to** ~ **at sthg** insinuar algo. ◇ *vt*: **to** ~ **that** insinuar que.

hip [hɪp] ◇ *n* ANAT cadera *f*. ◇ *adj inf* moderno(na).

hippie ['hɪpɪ] *n* hippy *m* OR *f*.

hippopotamus [,hɪpə'pɒtəməs] *(pl* **-muses** OR **-mi** [-maɪ]*) n* hipopótamo *m*.

hippy ['hɪpɪ] *(pl* **-ies***)* = **hippie**.

hire ['haɪə'] ◇ *n* (U) [of car, equipment] alquiler *m*; **for** ~ [taxi] libre; **boats for** ~ se alquilan barcos. ◇ *vt* **- 1.** [rent] alquilar **- 2.** [employ] contratar.

➤ **hire out** *vt sep* [car, equipment] alquilar; [one's services] ofrecer.

hire car *n* UK coche *m* de alquiler.

hire purchase *n* (U) UK compra *f* a plazos.

his [hɪz] ◇ *poss adj* su, sus *(pl)*; ~ **house** su casa; ~ **children** sus niños; ~ **name** is Joe se llama Joe; **it wasn't HIS fault** no fue culpa suya OR su culpa; **he washed** ~ **hair** se lavó el pelo. ◇ *poss pron* suyo (suya); **that money is** ~ ese dinero es suyo; **those keys are** ~ esas llaves son suyas; **it wasn't her fault, it was HIS** no fue culpa de ella sino de él; **a friend of** ~ un amigo suyo, un amigo de él; **mine is good, but** ~ **is bad** el mío es bueno pero el suyo es malo.

Hispanic [hɪ'spænɪk] ◇ *adj* hispánico(ca). ◇ *n esp* US hispano *m*, -na *f*.

hiss [hɪs] ◇ *n* **- 1.** [of person] bisbiseo *m*, siseo *m* **- 2.** [of steam, gas, snake] silbido *m*. ◇ *vi* **- 1.** [person] bisbisear, sisear; [to express disapproval] ≃ silbar, ≃ pitar **- 2.** [steam, gas, snake] silbar.

historic [hɪ'stɒrɪk] *adj* [significant] histórico(ca).

historical [hɪ'stɒrɪkəl] *adj* histórico(ca).

history ['hɪstərɪ] *(pl* **-ies***) n* **- 1.** [gen] historia *f* **- 2.** [past record] historial *m*. ◇ *comp* [book, teacher, programme] de historia.

hit [hɪt] *(pt & pp* **hit***, cont* **-ting***)* ◇ *n* **- 1.** [blow] golpe *m* **- 2.** [successful strike] impacto *m* **- 3.** [success, record] éxito *m* **- 4.** COMPUT visita *f*. ◇ *comp* de éxito. ◇ *vt* **- 1.** [subj: person] pegar, golpear **- 2.** [crash into] chocar contra OR con **- 3.** [reach] alcanzar; [bull's-eye] dar en **- 4.** [affect badly] afectar **- 5.** [occur to]: **the solution** ~ **me** se me ocurrió la solución **- 6.** *phr*: **to** ~ **it off (with**

sb) hacer buenas migas (con alguien).
hit-and-miss = hit-or-miss.
hit-and-run *adj* [driver] que se da a la fuga después de causar un accidente; [accident] en que el conductor se da a la fuga.
hitch [hɪtʃ] ◇ *n* [problem, snag] problema *m*, pega *f*. ◇ *vt* - **1.** [catch]: **to ~ a lift** conseguir que le lleven en coche a uno - **2.** [fasten]: **to ~ sthg on** OR **onto sthg** enganchar algo a algo. ◇ *vi* [hitchhike] hacer autoestop.
◆ **hitch up** *vt sep* [clothes] subirse.
hitchhike ['hɪtʃhaɪk] *vi* hacer autoestop.
hitchhiker ['hɪtʃhaɪkə'] *n* autoestopista *m* OR *f*.
hi-tech [,haɪ'tek] = high tech.
hitherto [,hɪðə'tuː] *adv fml* hasta ahora.
hit-or-miss *adj* azaroso(sa), a la buena de Dios.
HIV (*abbr of* **human immunodeficiency virus**) *n* VIH *m*; **to be ~-positive** ser seropositivo.
hive [haɪv] *n* [for bees] colmena *f*; **a ~ of activity** un enjambre, un centro de actividad.
◆ **hive off** *vt sep* [separate] transferir.
HNC (*abbr of* **Higher National Certificate**) *n* diploma técnico en Gran Bretaña.
HND (*abbr of* **Higher National Diploma**) *n* diploma técnico superior en Gran Bretaña.
hoard [hɔːd] ◇ *n* [store] acopio *m*. ◇ *vt* [collect, save] acumular; [food] acaparar.
hoarding ['hɔːdɪŋ] *n* UK [for advertisements, posters] valla *f* publicitaria.
hoarfrost ['hɔːfrɒst] *n* escarcha *f*.
hoarse [hɔːs] *adj* - **1.** [voice] ronco(ca) - **2.** [person] afónico(ca).
hoax [həʊks] *n* engaño *m*; **~ call** falsa alarma telefónica.
hob [hɒb] *n* UK [on cooker] encimera *f*.
hobble ['hɒbl] *vi* [limp] cojear.
hobby ['hɒbɪ] (*pl* **-ies**) *n* [leisure activity] hobby *m*, afición *f*.
hobbyhorse ['hɒbɪhɔːs] *n* - **1.** [toy] caballo *m* de juguete - **2.** [favourite topic] caballo *m* de batalla, tema *m* favorito.
hobo ['həʊbəʊ] (*pl* **-es** OR **-s**) *n* US [tramp] vagabundo *m*, -da *f*.
hockey ['hɒkɪ] *n* - **1.** [on grass] hockey *m* sobre hierba - **2.** US [ice hockey] hockey *m* sobre hielo.
hoe [həʊ] ◇ *n* azada *f*, azadón *m*. ◇ *vt* azadonar.
hog [hɒg] (*pt* & *pp* **-ged**, *cont* **-ging**) ◇ *n* US [pig] cerdo *m*, puerco *m*; **to go the whole ~** *fig* tirar la casa por la ventana. ◇ *vt inf* [monopolize] acaparar.
Hogmanay ['hɒgmənəɪ] *n* denominación escocesa de la Nochevieja.
hoist [hɔɪst] ◇ *n* [pulley, crane] grúa *f*; [lift] montacargas *m inv*. ◇ *vt* izar.
hold [həʊld] (*pt* & *pp* **held**) ◇ *vt* - **1.** [have

hold of] **tener cogido(da)** - **2.** [keep in position] **sujetar** - **3.** [sustain, support] **sostener, aguantar** - **4.** [embrace] **abrazar** - **5.** [as prisoner] **detener**; **to ~ sb prisoner/hostage** tener a alguien como prisionero/rehén - **6.** [keep] **guardar** - **7.** [maintain - interest etc] **mantener** - **8.** [have, possess] **poseer** - **9.** [contain - gen] **contener**; [- number of people] **tener cabida para**; [- fears, promise etc] **guardar** - **10.** [conduct, stage - event] **celebrar**; [- conversation] **mantener**; [- inquiry] **realizar** - **11.** *fml* [consider] **considerar**; **to ~ sb responsible for sthg** considerar a alguien responsable de algo - **12.** [on telephone]: **please ~ the line** no cuelgue por favor - **13.** MIL **ocupar, tener** - **14.** *phr*: **~ it** OR **everything!** ¡para!, ¡espera!; **to ~ one's own** defenderse. ◇ *vi* - **1.** [luck, weather] continuar así; [promise, offer] seguir en pie; **to ~ still** OR **steady** estarse quieto - **2.** [on phone] esperar. ◇ *n* - **1.** [grasp, grip]: **to have a firm ~ on sthg** tener algo bien agarrado; **to take** OR **lay ~ of sthg** agarrar algo; **to get ~ of sthg** [obtain] hacerse con algo; **to get ~ of sb** [find] localizar a alguien - **2.** [of ship, aircraft] bodega *f* - **3.** [control, influence] dominio *m*, control *m*.
◆ **hold back** *vt sep* - **1.** [tears, anger] contener, reprimir - **2.** [secret] ocultar, no revelar.
◆ **hold down** *vt sep* [job] conservar.
◆ **hold off** *vt sep* [fend off] rechazar.
◆ **hold on** *vi* - **1.** [wait] esperar; [on phone] no colgar - **2.** [grip]: **to ~ on (to sthg)** agarrarse (a algo).
◆ **hold out** ◇ *vt sep* [hand] tender; [arms] extender. ◇ *vi* - **1.** [last] durar - **2.** [resist]: **to ~ out (against sthg/sb)** resistir (ante algo/a alguien).
◆ **hold up** ◇ *vt sep* - **1.** [raise] levantar, alzar - **2.** [delay] retrasar. ◇ *vi* [theory, facts] tenerse en pie.
holdall ['həʊldɔːl] *n* UK bolsa *f* de viaje.
holder ['həʊldə'] *n* - **1.** [container] soporte *m*; [for candle] candelero *m*; [for cigarette] boquilla *f* - **2.** [owner] titular *m* OR *f*; [of ticket, record, title] poseedor *m*, -ra *f*.
holding ['həʊldɪŋ] *n* - **1.** [investment] participación *f* - **2.** [farm] propiedad *f*, terreno *m* de cultivo.
holdup ['həʊldʌp] *n* - **1.** [delay] retraso *m* - **2.** [robbery] atraco *m* a mano armada.
hole [həʊl] *n* - **1.** [gen] agujero *m*; [in ground, road etc] hoyo *m*; [of animal] madriguera *f* - **2.** [in golf] hoyo *m* - **3.** [horrible place] cuchitril *m*.
hole in the wall *n* UK *inf* cajero *m* automático.
holiday ['hɒlɪdeɪ] *n* - **1.** [vacation] vacaciones *fpl*; **to be/go on ~** estar/ir de vacaciones - **2.** [public holiday] fiesta *f*, día *m* festivo.

➡ **holidays** *n US*: the ~**s** las fiestas OR vacaciones (de Navidad); **happy** ~**s!** ¡felices fiestas!

holiday camp *n UK* colonia *f* veraniega.

holiday home *n UK* casa *f* para las vacaciones.

holidaymaker ['hɒlɪdeɪ,meɪkə^r] *n UK* turista *m* OR *f*.

holiday resort *n UK* lugar *m* de veraneo.

holistic [həʊ'lɪstɪk] *adj* holístico(ca).

Holland ['hɒlənd] *n* Holanda.

holler ['hɒlə^r] *vt & vi inf esp US* gritar.

hollow ['hɒləʊ] ⬦ *adj* - **1.** [not solid] hueco(ca) - **2.** [cheeks, eyes] hundido(da) - **3.** [resonant] sonoro(ra), resonante - **4.** [false, meaningless] vano(na); [laugh] falso(sa). ⬦ *n* hueco *m*; [in ground] depresión *f*, hondonada *f.*

➡ **hollow out** *vt sep* - **1.** [make hollow] dejar hueco - **2.** [make by hollowing] hacer ahuecando.

holly ['hɒlɪ] *n* acebo *m*.

holocaust ['hɒləkɔːst] *n* holocausto *m*.

➡ **Holocaust** *n*: the Holocaust el Holocausto.

holster ['həʊlstə^r] *n* pistolera *f*, funda *f* (de pistola).

holy ['həʊlɪ] (*compar* -**ier**, *superl* -**iest**) *adj* - **1.** [sacred] sagrado(da); [water] bendito(ta) - **2.** [pure and good] santo(ta).

Holy Ghost *n*: the ~ el Espíritu Santo.

Holy Spirit *n*: the ~ el Espíritu Santo.

holy war *n* guerra *f* santa.

homage ['hɒmɪdʒ] *n* (U) *fml* homenaje *m*; **to pay** ~ rendir homenaje a.

home [həʊm] ⬦ *n* - **1.** [house, flat] casa *f*; **away from** ~ [not in & SPORT] fuera de casa; **to make one's** ~ somewhere establecerse en algún sitio; **to work from** ~ *UK* trabajar desde casa - **2.** [own country] tierra *f*; [own city] ciudad *f* natal - **3.** [family] hogar *m*; **to leave** ~ independizarse, irse de casa - **4.** [place of origin] cuna *f* - **5.** [institution] residencia *f.* ⬦ *adj* - **1.** [not foreign] nacional - **2.** [in one's own home - cooking] casero(ra); [- life] familiar; [- improvements] en la casa; [- delivery] a domicilio - **3.** SPORT de casa. ⬦ *adv* - **to one's house**] a casa; [at one's house] en casa.

➡ **at home** *adv* - **1.** [in one's house, flat] en casa - **2.** [comfortable]: **at** ~ (**with**) a gusto (con); **to make o.s. at** ~ acomodarse; **make yourself at** ~ estás en tu casa - **3.** [in one's own country] en mi país.

home address *n* domicilio *m* particular.

home brew *n* [beer] cerveza *f* casera.

home computer *n* ordenador *m* doméstico.

Home Counties *npl*: the ~ los condados de los alrededores de Londres.

home economics *n* (U) economía *f* doméstica.

home help *n UK* asistente empleado por el ayuntamiento para ayudar en las tareas domésticas a enfermos y ancianos.

homeland ['həʊmlænd] *n* - **1.** [country of birth] tierra *f* natal, patria *f* - **2.** [in South Africa] homeland *m*, territorio donde se confinaba a la población negra.

homeless ['həʊmlɪs] *adj* sin hogar.

homely ['həʊmlɪ] *adj* - **1.** [simple] sencillo(lla) - **2.** [unattractive] feúcho(cha).

homemade [,həʊm'meɪd] *adj* [food] casero(ra); [clothes] de fabricación casera.

Home Office *n UK*: the ~ el Ministerio del Interior británico.

homeopathy [,həʊmɪ'ɒpəθɪ] *n* homeopatía *f.*

home page *n* [on Internet] página *f* inicial OR de inicio.

Home Secretary *n UK*: the ~ el Ministro del Interior británico.

homesick ['həʊmsɪk] *adj* nostálgico(ca); **to be** ~ tener morriña.

hometown ['həʊmtaʊn] *n* pueblo *m*/ciudad *f* natal.

homeward ['həʊmwəd] ⬦ *adj* de regreso OR vuelta (a casa). ⬦ *adv* = **homewards**.

homewards ['həʊmwədz] *adv* hacia casa.

homework ['həʊmwɜːk] *n* (U) *lit & fig* deberes *mpl.*

homey, homy ['həʊmɪ] *US* ⬦ *adj* confortable, agradable. ⬦ *n inf* [friend] amiguete *m*, -ta *f.*

homicide ['hɒmɪsaɪd] *n* homicidio *m*.

homogeneous [,hɒmə'dʒiːnjəs] *adj* homogéneo(a).

homophobic [,həʊməʊ'fəʊbɪk] *adj* homofóbico(ca).

homosexual [,hɒmə'sekʃʊəl] ⬦ *adj* homosexual. ⬦ *n* homosexual *m* OR *f.*

homy = **homey**.

Honduran [hɒn'djʊərən] ⬦ *adj* hondureño(ña). ⬦ *n* hondureño *m*, -ña *f.*

Honduras [hɒn'djʊərəs] *n* Honduras.

hone [həʊn] *vt* - **1.** [sharpen] afilar - **2.** [develop, refine] afinar.

honest ['ɒnɪst] ⬦ *adj* - **1.** [trustworthy, legal] honrado(da) - **2.** [frank] franco(ca), sincero(ra); **to be** ~ ... si he de serte franco ... ⬦ *adv inf* = **honestly 2**.

honestly ['ɒnɪstlɪ] ⬦ *adv* - **1.** [truthfully] honradamente - **2.** [expressing sincerity] de verdad, en serio. ⬦ *excl* [expressing impatience, disapproval] ¡será posible!

honesty ['ɒnɪstɪ] *n* - **1.** [trustworthiness] honradez *f* - **2.** [frankness] sinceridad *f*; **in all** ~ ... si he de serte franco ...

honey ['hʌnɪ] *n* - **1.** [food] miel *f* - **2.** *esp US* [form of address] cielo *m*, mi vida *f.*

honeycomb ['hʌnɪkəʊm] *n* panal *m*.

honeymoon ['hʌnɪmuːn] *n* luna *f* de miel;

fig periodo *m* idílico.

honeysuckle ['hʌnɪ,sʌkl] *n* madreselva *f*.

Hong Kong [,hɒŋ'kɒŋ] *n* Hong Kong.

honk [hɒŋk] ⋄ *vi* - 1. [motorist] tocar el claxon - 2. [goose] graznar. ⋄ *vt* tocar.

honor *etc US* = honour *etc*.

honorary [*UK* 'ɒnərərɪ, *US* ɒnə'reərɪ] *adj* - 1. [given as an honour] honorario(ria) - 2. [unpaid] honorífico(ca).

honour *UK*, **honor** *US* ['ɒnə'] ⋄ *n* - 1. [gen] honor *m*, honra *f*; in ∼ of en honor de - 2. [source of pride - person] honra *f.* ⋄ *vt* - 1. [promise, agreement] cumplir; [debt] satisfacer; [cheque] pagar, aceptar - 2. *fml* [bring honour to] honrar.

◆ **honours** *npl* - 1. [tokens of respect] honores *mpl* - 2. *UK* UNIV: ∼**s degree** *licenciatura de cuatro años necesaria para acceder a un máster.*

honourable *UK*, **honorable** *US* ['ɒnrəbl] *adj* - 1. [proper] honroso(sa) - 2. [morally upright] honorable.

hood [hud] *n* - 1. [on cloak, jacket] capucha *f* - 2. [of pram, convertible car] capota *f*; [of cooker] campana *f* - 3. *US* [car bonnet] capó *m.*

hoodlum ['hu:dləm] *n US inf* matón *m*.

hoof [hu:f, huf] (*pl* **-s** *OR* **hooves**) *n* [of horse] casco *m*; [of cow etc] pezuña *f*.

hook [huk] ⋄ *n* - 1. [gen] gancho *m*; **off the** ∼ [phone] descolgado(da) - 2. [for catching fish] anzuelo *m* - 3. [fastener] corchete *m.* ⋄ *vt* - 1. [attach with hook] enganchar - 2. [fish] pescar, coger.

◆ **hook up** *vt sep*: **to** ∼ **sthg up to sthg** conectar algo a algo; **to** ∼ **with sb** reunirse *OR* juntarse con alguien, ligar con alguien.

hooked [hukt] *adj* - 1. [nose] aguileño(ña), ganchudo(da) - 2. *inf* [addicted]: **to be** ∼ **(on)** estar enganchado(da) (a).

hook(e)y ['hukɪ] *n US inf*: **to play** ∼ hacer novillos.

hooligan ['hu:lɪgən] *n* gamberro *m*.

hoop [hu:p] *n* aro *m*.

hooray [hʊ'reɪ] = **hurray**.

hoot [hu:t] ⋄ *n* [of owl] grito *m*, ululato *m*; [of horn] bocinazo *m*; **a** ∼ **of laughter** una carcajada. ⋄ *vi* [owl] ulular; [horn] sonar; **to** ∼ **with laughter** reírse a carcajadas. ⋄ *vt* tocar.

hooter ['hu:tə'] *n* [horn] claxon *m*, bocina *f*.

Hoover® ['hu:və'] *n UK* aspiradora *f.*

◆ **hoover** *vt* pasar la aspiradora por.

hooves [hu:vz] *pl* ▷ **hoof**.

hop [hɒp] (*pt & pp* **-ped**, *cont* **-ping**) *vi* - 1. [person] saltar a la pata coja - 2. [bird etc] dar saltitos - 3. [move nimbly] ponerse de un brinco.

◆ **hops** *npl* lúpulo *m*.

hope [həup] ⋄ *vi*: **to** ∼ **(for sthg)** esperar (algo); **I** ∼ **so/not** espero que sí/no. ⋄ *vt* : **to** ∼ **(that)** esperar que; **to** ∼ **to do sthg** esperar hacer algo. ⋄ *n* esperanza *f*; **in the** ∼ **of** con la esperanza de.

hopeful ['həupful] *adj* - 1. [optimistic] optimista; **to be** ∼ **of sthg/of doing sthg** tener esperanzas de algo/hacer algo - 2. [promising] prometedor(ra), esperanzador(ra).

hopefully ['həupfəlɪ] *adv* - 1. [in a hopeful way] esperanzadamente - 2. [with luck] con suerte; ∼ **not** espero que no.

hopeless ['həuplɪs] *adj* - 1. [despairing] desesperado(da) - 2. [impossible] imposible - 3. *inf* [useless] inútil.

hopelessly ['həuplɪslɪ] *adv* - 1. [despairingly] desesperadamente - 2. [completely] totalmente.

horizon [hə'raɪzn] *n* [of sky] horizonte *m*; **on the** ∼ en el horizonte; *fig* a la vuelta de la esquina.

horizontal [,hɒrɪ'zɒntl] *adj* horizontal.

hormone ['hɔ:məun] *n* hormona *f.*

horn [hɔ:n] *n* - 1. [of animal] cuerno *m*, cacho *m Amér* - 2. MUS [instrument] trompa *f* - 3. [on car] claxon *m*, bocina *f*; [on ship] sirena *f* - 4. *US inf* [telephone] teléfono *m*.

hornet ['hɔ:nɪt] *n* avispón *m*.

horny ['hɔ:nɪ] (*compar* **-ier**, *superl* **-iest**) *adj* - 1. [scale, body, armour] córneo(a); [hand] calloso(sa) - 2. *v inf* [sexually excited] cachondo(da), caliente.

horoscope ['hɒrəskəup] *n* horóscopo *m.*

horrendous [hɒ'rendəs] *adj* horrendo(da).

horrible ['hɒrəbl] *adj* - 1. [gen] horrible - 2. [nasty, mean] malo(la).

horrid ['hɒrɪd] *adj esp UK* [person] antipático(ca); [idea, place] horroroso(sa).

horrific [hɒ'rɪfɪk] *adj* horrendo(da).

horrify ['hɒrɪfaɪ] (*pt & pp* **-ied**) *vt* horrorizar.

horror ['hɒrə'] *n* horror *m*.

horror film *n* película *f* de terror *OR* de miedo.

hors d'oeuvre [ɔ:'dɜ:vr] (*pl* **hors d'oeuvres** [ɔ:'dɜ:vr]) *n* entremeses *mpl*.

horse [hɔ:s] *n* [animal] caballo *m*.

horseback ['hɔ:sbæk] ⋄ *adj*: ∼ **riding** equitación *f.* ⋄ *n*: **on** ∼ a caballo.

horse chestnut *n* [nut] castaña *f* de Indias; ∼ **(tree)** castaño *m* de Indias.

horseman ['hɔ:smən] (*pl* **-men** [-mən]) *n* jinete *m*.

horsepower ['hɔ:s,pauə'] *n* (*U*) caballos *mpl* de vapor.

horse racing *n* (*U*) carreras *fpl* de caballos.

horseradish ['hɔ:s,rædɪʃ] *n* rábano *m* silvestre.

horse riding *n* equitación *f*; **to go** ∼ montar a caballo.

horseshoe ['hɔ:sʃu:] *n* herradura *f.*

horsewoman ['hɔ:s,wumən] (*pl* **-women** [-,wɪmɪn]) *n* amazona *f.*

housing benefit

horticulture [ˈhɔːtɪkʌltʃəʳ] *n* horticultura *f*.

hose [həʊz] *n* [hosepipe] manguera *f*.

hosepipe [ˈhəʊzpaɪp] = **hose**.

hosiery [ˈhəʊzɪərɪ] *n (U)* medias *fpl* y calcetines.

hospice [ˈhɒspɪs] *n* hospital *m* para enfermos terminales.

hospitable [hɒˈspɪtəbl] *adj* hospitalario(ria).

hospital [ˈhɒspɪtl] *n* hospital *m*, nosocomio *m Amér*.

hospitality [ˌhɒspɪˈtælətɪ] *n* hospitalidad *f*.

host [həʊst] ◇ *n* - **1**. [person, place, organization] anfitrión *m*, -ona *f* - **2**. [compere] presentador *m*, -ra *f* - **3**. *literary* [large number]: **a ∼ of** una multitud de - **4**. RELIG hostia *f* - **5**. COMPUT host *m*, sistema *m* central. ◇ *vt* [show] presentar; [event] ser el anfitrión de.

hostage [ˈhɒstɪdʒ] *n* rehén *m*.

hostel [ˈhɒstl] *n* albergue *m*.

hostess [ˈhəʊstes] *n* - **1**. [at party] anfitriona *f* - **2**. [in club etc] chica *f* de alterne.

hostile [UK ˈhɒstaɪl, US ˈhɒstl] *adj* - **1**. [antagonistic, enemy]: **∼ (to)** hostil (hacia) - **2**. [unfavourable] adverso(sa), desfavorable.

hostility [hɒˈstɪlətɪ] *n* [antagonism] hostilidad *f*.

  ➤ **hostilities** *npl* hostilidades *fpl*.

hot [hɒt] (*compar* **-ter**, *superl* **-test**) *adj* - **1**. [gen] caliente; **I'm ∼** tengo calor - **2**. [weather, climate] caluroso(sa); **it's (very) ∼** hace (mucho) calor - **3**. [spicy] picante, picoso(sa) *Méx* - **4**. *inf* [expert]: **∼ on** *OR* **at** experto(ta) en - **5**. [recent] caliente, último(ma) - **6**. [temper] vivo(va).

hot-air balloon *n* aeróstato *m*, globo *m*.

hotbed [ˈhɒtbed] *n* semillero *m*.

hot-cross bun *n* bollo a base de especias y pasas con una cruz dibujada en una cara que se come en Semana Santa.

hot dog *n* perrito *m* caliente.

hotel [həʊˈtel] *n* hotel *m*.

hot flush *UK*, **hot flash** *US n* sofoco *m*.

hotheaded [ˌhɒtˈhedɪd] *adj* irreflexivo(va).

hothouse [ˈhɒthaʊs, *pl* -haʊzɪz] *n* [greenhouse] invernadero *m*.

hot line *n* [for politician] teléfono *m* rojo.

hotly [ˈhɒtlɪ] *adv* - **1**. [passionately] acaloradamente - **2**. [closely]: **we were ∼ pursued** nos pisaban los talones.

hotplate [ˈhɒtpleɪt] *n* - **1**. [for cooking] placa *f* - **2**. [for keeping food warm] calientaplatos *m inv*.

hot-tempered *adj* iracundo(da).

hottie [ˈhɒtɪ] *n US inf* bombón *m*.

hot-water bottle *n* bolsa *f* de agua caliente.

hound [haʊnd] ◇ *n* [dog] perro *m* de caza,

sabueso *m*. ◇ *vt* - **1**. [persecute] acosar - **2**. [drive]: **to ∼ sb out (of somewhere)** conseguir echar a alguien (de algún sitio) acosándolo.

hour [ˈaʊəʳ] *n* - **1**. [gen] hora *f*; **half an ∼** media hora; **70 miles per** *OR* **an ∼** 70 millas por hora; **to pay by the ∼** pagar por horas; **on the ∼** a la hora en punto cada hora - **2**. *literary* [important time] momento *m*.

  ➤ **hours** *npl* [of business] horas *fpl*.

hourly [ˈaʊəlɪ] *adj* & *adv* - **1**. [every hour] cada hora - **2**. [per hour] por hora.

house [*n* & *adj* haʊs, *pl* ˈhaʊzɪz, *vb* haʊz] ◇ *n* - **1**. [gen] casa *f*; **it's on the ∼** la casa invita, es cortesía de la casa - **2**. POL cámara *f* - **3**. [in theatre] audiencia *f*; **to bring the ∼ down** ser un exitazo, ser muy aplaudido. ◇ *vt* [person, family] alojar; [department, library, office] albergar. ◇ *adj* - **1**. [within business] de la empresa - **2**. [wine] de la casa.

house arrest *n*: **under ∼** bajo arresto domiciliario.

houseboat [ˈhaʊsbəʊt] *n* casa *f* flotante.

housebreaking [ˈhaʊsˌbreɪkɪŋ] *n* allanamiento *m* de morada.

housecoat [ˈhaʊskəʊt] *n* bata *f*.

household [ˈhaʊshəʊld] ◇ *adj* - **1**. [domestic] doméstico(ca), de la casa - **2**. [word, name] conocido(da) por todos. ◇ *n* hogar *m*.

housekeeper [ˈhaʊsˌkiːpəʳ] *n* ama *f* de llaves.

housekeeping [ˈhaʊsˌkiːpɪŋ] *n (U)* - **1**. [work] quehaceres *mpl* domésticos, tareas *fpl* domésticas - **2**.: **∼ (money)** dinero *m* para los gastos de la casa.

house music *n* música *f* house.

House of Commons *n UK*: **the ∼** la Cámara de los Comunes.

House of Lords *n UK*: **the ∼** la Cámara de los Lores.

House of Representatives *n US*: **the ∼** la Cámara de los Representantes.

houseplant [ˈhaʊsplɑːnt] *n* planta *f* interior.

Houses of Parliament *n*: **the ∼** el Parlamento británico.

housewarming (party) [ˈhaʊsˌwɔːmɪŋ-] *n* fiesta *f* de inauguración de una casa.

housewife [ˈhaʊswaɪf] (*pl* **-wives** [-waɪvz]) *n* ama *f* de casa.

housework [ˈhaʊswɜːk] *n (U)* quehaceres *mpl* domésticos.

housing [ˈhaʊzɪŋ] *n* [houses] vivienda *f*; [act of accommodating] alojamiento *m*.

housing association *n UK* cooperativa *f* de viviendas.

housing benefit *n (U)* subsidio estatal para ayudar con el pago del alquiler y otros gastos.

housing estate UK, **housing project** US n urbanización generalmente de protección oficial, ≃ fraccionamiento m Méx.

HOV (abbr of **High Occupancy Vehicle**) n: ∼ lane carril para vehículos de alta ocupación.

hovel ['hɒvl] n casucha f, tugurio m.

hover ['hɒvə'] vi [fly] cernerse.

hovercraft ['hɒvəkrɑːft] (pl inv or **-s**) n aerodeslizador m.

how [haʊ] adv **-1.** [gen] cómo; ∼ **do you do it?** ¿cómo se hace?; **I found out** ∼ **he did it** averigüé cómo lo hizo; ∼ **are you?** ¿cómo estás?; ∼ **do you do?** mucho gusto **-2.** [referring to degree, amount]: ∼ **high is it?** ¿cuánto mide de alto or de altura?; **he asked** ∼ **high it was** preguntó cuánto medía de alto; ∼ **expensive is it?** ¿cómo de caro es?, ¿es muy caro?; ∼ **far is it to Paris?** ¿a cuánto está París de aquí?; ∼ **long have you been waiting?** ¿cuánto llevas esperando?; ∼ **many people came?** ¿cuánta gente vino?; ∼ **old are you?** ¿qué edad or cuántos años tienes? **-3.** [in exclamations] qué; ∼ **nice/awful!** ¡qué bonito/horrible!; ∼ **I hate doing it!** ¡cómo or cuánto odio tener que hacerlo!

➥ **how about** adv: ∼ **about a drink?** ¿qué tal una copa?; ∼ **about you?** ¿qué te parece?, ¿y tú?

➥ **how much** ⬦ pron cuánto(ta); ∼ **much does it cost?** ¿cuánto cuesta? ⬦ adj cuánto(ta); ∼ **much bread?** ¿cuánto pan?

however [haʊ'evə'] ⬦ adv **-1.** [nevertheless] sin embargo, no obstante **-2.** [no matter how]: ∼ **difficult it may be** por (muy) difícil que sea; ∼ **many times** or **much I told her** por mucho que se lo dijera **-3.** [how] cómo; ∼ **did you know?** ¿cómo lo sabías? ⬦ conj comoquiera que; ∼ **you want** como quieras.

howl [haʊl] ⬦ n **-1.** [of animal] aullido m **-2.** [of person - in pain, anger] alarido m, grito m; **a** ∼ **of laughter** una carcajada. ⬦ vi **-1.** [animal] aullar **-2.** [person - in pain, anger] gritar; **to** ∼ **with laughter** reírse a carcajadas **-3.** [wind] bramar.

hp (abbr of **horsepower**) CV m, cv m.

HP UK abbr of **hire purchase**.

HQ n abbr of **headquarters**.

HTML (abbr of **hypertext markup language**) n COMPUT HTML m.

HTTP (abbr of **hypertext transfer protocol**) n COMPUT HTTP m.

hub [hʌb] n **-1.** [of wheel] cubo m **-2.** [of activity] centro m, eje m.

hubbub ['hʌbʌb] n alboroto m, barullo m.

hubcap ['hʌbkæp] n tapacubos m inv.

huddle ['hʌdl] vi **-1.** [crouch, curl up]

acurrucarse **-2.** [cluster] apretarse unos contra otros, apiñarse.

hue [hjuː] n **-1.** [shade] tono m, matiz m **-2.** [colour] color m.

huff [hʌf] n: **in a** ∼ mosqueado(da).

hug [hʌg] (pt & pp **-ged**, cont **-ging**) ⬦ n abrazo m; **to give sb a** ∼ abrazar a alguien, dar un abrazo a alguien. ⬦ vt **-1.** [embrace, hold] abrazar **-2.** [stay close to] ceñirse or ir pegado a.

huge [hjuːdʒ] adj enorme.

hulk [hʌlk] n **-1.** [of ship] casco m abandonado **-2.** [person] tiarrón m, -ona f.

hull [hʌl] n casco m.

hullo [hə'ləʊ] = **hello**.

hum [hʌm] (pt & pp **-med**, cont **-ming**) ⬦ vi **-1.** [buzz] zumbar **-2.** [sing] canturrear, tararear **-3.** [be busy] bullir, hervir. ⬦ vt tararear, canturrear.

human ['hjuːmən] ⬦ adj humano(na). ⬦ n: ∼ **(being)** (ser m) humano m.

humane [hjuː'meɪn] adj humano(na).

humanitarian [hjuːˌmænɪ'teərɪən] adj humanitario(ria).

humanity [hjuː'mænətɪ] n humanidad f.
➥ **humanities** npl: **the humanities** las humanidades.

human race n: **the** ∼ la raza humana.

human rights npl derechos mpl humanos.

humble ['hʌmbl] ⬦ adj humilde. ⬦ vt fml humillar.

humbug ['hʌmbʌg] n **-1.** (U) dated [hypocrisy] farsa f, hipocresía f **-2.** UK [sweet] caramelo m de menta.

humdrum ['hʌmdrʌm] adj rutinario(ria), aburrido(da).

humid ['hjuːmɪd] adj húmedo(da).

humidity [hjuː'mɪdətɪ] n humedad f.

humiliate [hjuː'mɪlɪeɪt] vt humillar.

humiliation [hjuːˌmɪlɪ'eɪʃn] n humillación f.

humility [hjuː'mɪlətɪ] n humildad f.

humor US = **humour**.

humorous ['hjuːmərəs] adj **-1.** [remark, situation] gracioso(sa) **-2.** [play, publication] humorístico(ca).

humour UK, **humor** US ['hjuːmə'] ⬦ n **-1.** [sense of fun, mood] humor m; **in good/bad** ∼ fml de buen/mal humor **-2.** [funny side] gracia f. ⬦ vt complacer, seguir la corriente a.

hump [hʌmp] n **-1.** [hill] montículo m **-2.** [on back] joroba f, giba f, curca f Amér.

humpbacked bridge ['hʌmpbækt-] n puente m peraltado.

hunch [hʌntʃ] ⬦ n inf presentimiento m, corazonada f. ⬦ vt encorvar.

hunchback ['hʌntʃbæk] n jorobado m, -da f.

hunched [hʌntʃt] adj encorvado(da).

hundred ['hʌndrəd] num cien; **a** or **one** ∼

hysterical

cien; a OR one ~ and eighty ciento ochenta; three ~ trescientos; five ~ quinientos; see also six.
  ◆ **hundreds** npl centenares mpl.

hundredth ['hʌndrətθ] ◇ num adj centésimo(ma). ◇ num n [fraction] centésimo m; a ~ of a second una centésima; see also sixth.

hundredweight ['hʌndrədweɪt] n [in UK] = 50,8 kg; [in US] = 45,3 kg.

hung [hʌŋ] pt & pp ▷ **hang**.

Hungarian [hʌŋˈgeərɪən] ◇ adj húngaro(-ra). ◇ n -1. [person] húngaro m, -ra f -2. [language] húngaro m.

Hungary ['hʌŋgərɪ] n Hungría.

hunger ['hʌŋgəʳ] n -1. [for food] hambre f -2. literary [for change, knowledge etc] sed f.
  ◆ **hunger after, hunger for** vt fus literary anhelar, ansiar.

hunger strike n huelga f de hambre.

hung over adj inf: to be ~ tener resaca.

hungry ['hʌŋgrɪ] (compar -ier, superl -iest) adj [for food] hambriento(ta); to be/go ~ tener/pasar hambre.

hung up adj inf acomplejado(da).

hunk [hʌŋk] n -1. [large piece] pedazo m, trozo m -2. inf [attractive man] tío m bueno, macizo m.

hunt [hʌnt] ◇ n -1. [of animals, birds] caza f; UK [foxhunting party] partida f de caza -2. [for person, clue etc] busca f, búsqueda f. ◇ vi -1. [for animals, birds] cazar -2. [for person, clue etc]: to ~ (for sthg) buscar (algo). ◇ vt -1. [animals, birds] cazar -2. [person] perseguir.

hunter ['hʌntəʳ] n [of animals, birds] cazador m, -ra f.

hunting ['hʌntɪŋ] n -1. [of animals] caza f; to go ~ ir de caza OR cacería -2. UK [of foxes] caza f del zorro.

hurdle ['hɜːdl] ◇ n -1. [in race] valla f -2. [obstacle] obstáculo m. ◇ vt saltar.

hurl [hɜːl] vt -1. [throw] lanzar, arrojar -2. [shout] proferir, soltar.

hurray [hʊˈreɪ] excl ¡hurra!

hurricane ['hʌrɪkən] n huracán m.

hurried ['hʌrɪd] adj [hasty] apresurado(da).

hurriedly ['hʌrɪdlɪ] adv apresuradamente.

hurry ['hʌrɪ] (pt & pp -ied) ◇ n prisa f; to be in a ~ tener prisa; to do sthg in a ~ hacer algo de prisa OR apresuradamente. ◇ vt [person] meter prisa a; [work, speech] apresurar. ◇ vi: to ~ (to do sthg) apresurarse (a hacer algo), darse prisa (en hacer algo).
  ◆ **hurry up** vi darse prisa.

hurt [hɜːt] (pt & pp hurt) ◇ vt -1. [physically - person] hacer daño a; [- one's leg, arm] hacerse daño en; nobody was ~ nadie resultó herido; to ~ o.s. hacerse daño -2. [emotionally] herir -3. [harm] perjudicar. ◇ vi -1. [gen] doler; my head ~s me

duele la cabeza -2. [cause physical pain, do harm] hacer daño. ◇ adj -1. [injured] herido(da) -2. [offended] dolido(da), ofendido(-da); [feelings] herido(da).

hurtful ['hɜːtfʊl] adj hiriente.

hurtle ['hɜːtl] vi: to ~ past pasar como un rayo.

husband ['hʌzbənd] n marido m.

hush [hʌʃ] ◇ n silencio m. ◇ excl ¡silencio!, ¡a callar!

husk [hʌsk] n [of seed, grain] cáscara f, cascarilla f.

husky ['hʌskɪ] (compar -ier, superl -iest) ◇ adj [hoarse] ronco(ca). ◇ n husky m, perro m esquimal.

hustle ['hʌsl] ◇ vt [hurry] meter prisa a. ◇ n: ~ (and bustle) bullicio m, ajetreo m.

hut [hʌt] n -1. [rough house] cabaña f, choza f, jacal m Guat, Méx, Ven -2. [shed] cobertizo m.

hutch [hʌtʃ] n conejera f.

hyacinth ['haɪəsɪnθ] n jacinto m.

hydrant ['haɪdrənt] n boca f de riego; [for fire] boca f de incendio.

hydraulic [haɪˈdrɔːlɪk] adj hidráulico(ca).

hydroelectric [ˌhaɪdrəʊɪˈlektrɪk] adj hidroeléctrico(ca).

hydrofoil ['haɪdrəfɔɪl] n embarcación f con hidroala.

hydrogen ['haɪdrədʒən] n hidrógeno m.

hyena [haɪˈiːnə] n hiena f.

hygiene ['haɪdʒiːn] n higiene f.

hygienic [haɪˈdʒiːnɪk] adj higiénico(ca).

hymn [hɪm] n himno m.

hype [haɪp] n inf bombo m, publicidad f exagerada.

hyperactive [ˌhaɪpərˈæktɪv] adj hiperactivo(va).

hyperlink ['haɪpəˌlɪŋk] n COMPUT hiperenlace m.

hypermarket ['haɪpəˌmɑːkɪt] n hipermercado m.

hyphen ['haɪfn] n guión m.

hypnosis [hɪpˈnəʊsɪs] n hipnosis f inv.

hypnotic [hɪpˈnɒtɪk] adj hipnótico(ca).

hypnotize, -ise ['hɪpnətaɪz] vt hipnotizar.

hypochondriac [ˌhaɪpəˈkɒndrɪæk] n hipocondríaco m, -ca f.

hypocrisy [hɪˈpɒkrəsɪ] n hipocresía f.

hypocrite ['hɪpəkrɪt] n hipócrita m OR f.

hypocritical [ˌhɪpəˈkrɪtɪkl] adj hipócrita.

hypothesis [haɪˈpɒθɪsɪs] (pl -theses [-θɪsiːz]) n hipótesis f inv.

hypothetical [ˌhaɪpəˈθetɪkl] adj hipotético(ca).

hysteria [hɪsˈtɪərɪə] n histeria f.

hysterical [hɪsˈterɪkl] adj -1. [frantic] histérico(ca) -2. inf [very funny] tronchante, desternillante.

hysterics [hɪs'terɪks] *npl* **-1.** [panic, excitement] histeria *f*, histerismo *m* **-2.** *inf* [fits of laughter]: **to be in ∼** troncharse OR partirse de risa.

i (*pl* **i's** OR **is**), **I¹** (*pl* **I's** OR **Is**) [aɪ] *n* [letter] i *f*, I *f*.
I² [aɪ] *pers pron* yo; **I'm happy** soy feliz; **I'm leaving me** voy; **she and I were at college together** ella y yo fuimos juntos a la universidad; **it is I** *fml* soy yo; **I can't do that** yo no puedo hacer eso.
ice [aɪs] ◇ *n* **-1.** [frozen water] hielo *m* **-2.** *UK* [ice cream] helado *m*. ◇ *vt* CULIN glasear, alcorzar.
➤ **ice over, ice up** *vi* helarse.
iceberg ['aɪsbɜːg] *n* iceberg *m*.
iceberg lettuce *n* lechuga *f* iceberg.
icebox ['aɪsbɒks] *n* **-1.** *UK* [in refrigerator] congelador *m* **-2.** *US* [refrigerator] refrigerador *m*.
ice cream *n* helado *m*.
ice cube *n* cubito *m* de hielo.
ice hockey *n* hockey *m* sobre hielo.
Iceland ['aɪslənd] *n* Islandia.
Icelandic [aɪs'lændɪk] ◇ *adj* islandés(esa). ◇ *n* [language] islandés *m*.
ice lolly *n UK* polo *m*.
ice pick *n* pico *m* para el hielo.
ice rink *n* pista *f* de (patinaje sobre) hielo.
ice skate *n* patín *m* de cuchilla.
➤ **ice-skate** *vi* patinar sobre hielo.
ice-skating *n* patinaje *m* sobre hielo.
icicle ['aɪsɪkl] *n* carámbano *m*.
icing ['aɪsɪŋ] *n* glaseado *m*.
icing sugar *n UK* azúcar *m* glas.
icon ['aɪkɒn] *n* COMPUT & RELIG icono *m*.
icy ['aɪsɪ] (*compar* **-ier**, *superl* **-iest**) *adj* **-1.** [gen] helado(da) **-2.** *fig* [unfriendly] glacial.
I'd [aɪd] = **I would, I had**.
ID -1. *abbr of* **identification**. **- 2.** *abbr of* **Idaho**.
idea [aɪ'dɪə] *n* **-1.** [gen] idea *f*; **to have no ∼** no tener ni idea; **to get the ∼** *inf* captar la idea, hacerse una idea **-2.** [intuition, feeling] sensación *f*, impresión *f*; **to have an ∼ (that)** ... tener la sensación de que ...
ideal [aɪ'dɪəl] ◇ *adj*: **∼ (for)** ideal (para). ◇ *n* ideal *m*.
ideally [aɪ'dɪəlɪ] *adv* **-1.** [perfectly] ideal-

mente; [suited] perfectamente **-2.** [preferably] a ser posible.
identical [aɪ'dentɪkl] *adj* idéntico(ca).
identification [aɪ,dentɪfɪ'keɪʃn] *n* **-1.** [gen]: **∼ (with)** identificación *f* (con) **-2.** [documentation] documentación *f*.
identify [aɪ'dentɪfaɪ] (*pt & pp* **-ied**) ◇ *vt* identificar; **to ∼ sb with sthg** relacionar a alguien con algo. ◇ *vi*: **to ∼ with sb/sthg** identificarse con alguien/algo.
Identikit picture® [aɪ'dentɪkɪt-] *n* fotorrobot *f*.
identity [aɪ'dentətɪ] (*pl* **-ies**) *n* identidad *f*.
identity card *n* carné *m* OR documento *m* de identidad, cédula *f* de identidad *Amér*.
identity parade *n* rueda *f* de identificación.
ideology [,aɪdɪ'ɒlədʒɪ] (*pl* **-ies**) *n* ideología *f*.
idiom ['ɪdɪəm] *n* **-1.** [phrase] locución *f*, modismo *m* **-2.** *fml* [style] lenguaje *m*.
idiomatic [,ɪdɪə'mætɪk] *adj* natural.
idiosyncrasy [,ɪdɪə'sɪŋkrəsɪ] (*pl* **-ies**) *n* rareza *f*, manía *f*.
idiot ['ɪdɪət] *n* [fool] idiota *m* OR *f*.
idiotic [,ɪdɪ'ɒtɪk] *adj* idiota.
idle ['aɪdl] ◇ *adj* **-1.** [lazy] perezoso(sa), vago(ga) **-2.** [not working - machine, factory] parado(da); [- person] desocupado(da), sin trabajo **-3.** [rumour] infundado(da); [threat, boast] vano(na); [curiosity] que no viene a cuento. ◇ *vi* estar en punto muerto.
➤ **idle away** *vt sep* desperdiciar.
idol ['aɪdl] *n* ídolo *m*.
idolize, -ise ['aɪdəlaɪz] *vt* idolatrar.
idyllic [ɪ'dɪlɪk] *adj* idílico(ca).
i.e. (*abbr of* **id est**) i.e.
if [ɪf] *conj* **-1.** [gen] si; **∼ I were you** yo que tú, yo en tu lugar **-2.** [though] aunque; **he's clever, ∼ a little arrogant** es listo, aunque algo arrogante.
➤ **if not** *conj* **-1.** [otherwise] si no, de lo contrario **-2.** [not to say] por no decir; **it was cheeky, ∼ not downright rude of him** fue mucha caradura de su parte, por no decir grosería.
➤ **if only** ◇ *conj* **-1.** [naming a reason] aunque sólo sea; **at least he got me a present, ∼ only a little one** por lo menos me compraron un regalo, aunque sea pequeño **-2.** [expressing regret] si; **∼ only I'd been quicker!** ¡ojalá hubiera sido más rápido! ◇ *excl* ¡ojalá!
igloo ['ɪgluː] (*pl* **-s**) *n* iglú *m*.
ignite [ɪg'naɪt] ◇ *vt* encender. ◇ *vi* encenderse.
ignition [ɪg'nɪʃn] *n* **-1.** [act of igniting] ignición *f* **-2.** [in car] encendido *m*; **to switch on the ∼** arrancar (el motor).
ignition key *n* llave *f* de contacto.

ignorance ['ɪgnərəns] *n* ignorancia *f*.

ignorant ['ɪgnərənt] *adj* **-1.** [uneducated, rude] ignorante **-2.** *fml* [unaware]: **to be ~ of sthg** ignorar algo.

ignore [ɪg'nɔːʳ] *vt* [thing] no hacer caso de, ignorar; [person] no hacer caso a, ignorar.

ilk [ɪlk] *n*: **of that ~** [of that sort] de ese tipo.

ill [ɪl] *<>* *adj* **-1.** [unwell] enfermo(ma); **to feel ~** encontrarse mal; **to be taken** OR **fall ~** caer OR ponerse enfermo **-2.** [bad] malo (la). *<>* *adv* **-1.** [badly] mal **-2.** *fml* [unfavourably]: **to speak/think ~ of sb** hablar/ pensar mal de alguien.

I'll [aɪl] = **I will, I shall.**

ill-advised [-əd'vaɪzd] *adj* [action] poco aconsejable; [person] imprudente.

ill at ease *adj* incómodo(da).

illegal [ɪ'liːgl] *adj* ilegal.

illegal immigrant *n* inmigrante *m* OR *f* ilegal.

illegible [ɪ'ledʒəbl] *adj* ilegible.

illegitimate [,ɪlɪ'dʒɪtɪmət] *adj* ilegítimo(ma).

ill-equipped [-ɪ'kwɪpt] *adj*: **to be ~ to do sthg** estar mal preparado(da) para hacer algo.

ill-fated [-'feɪtɪd] *adj* infausto(ta).

ill feeling *n* resentimiento *m*.

ill health *n* mala salud *f*.

illicit [ɪ'lɪsɪt] *adj* ilícito(ta).

illiteracy [ɪ'lɪtərəsɪ] *n* analfabetismo *m*.

illiterate [ɪ'lɪtərət] *<>* *adj* analfabeto(ta). *<>* *n* analfabeto *m*, -ta *f*.

illness ['ɪlnɪs] *n* enfermedad *f*.

illogical [ɪ'lɒdʒɪkl] *adj* ilógico(ca).

ill-suited *adj*: **~ (for)** poco adecuado(da) (para).

ill-timed [-'taɪmd] *adj* inoportuno(na).

ill-treat *vt* maltratar.

illuminate [ɪ'luːmɪneɪt] *vt* **-1.** [light up] iluminar **-2.** [explain] ilustrar, aclarar.

illumination [ɪ,luːmɪ'neɪʃn] *n* [lighting] alumbrado *m*, iluminación *f*.
  ➤ **illuminations** *npl* UK iluminaciones *fpl*, alumbrado *m* decorativo.

illusion [ɪ'luːʒn] *n* **-1.** [gen] ilusión *f*; **to be under the ~ that** creer equivocadamente que **-2.** [magic trick] truco *m* de ilusionismo.

illustrate ['ɪləstreɪt] *vt* ilustrar.

illustration [,ɪlə'streɪʃn] *n* ilustración *f*.

illustrious [ɪ'lʌstrɪəs] *adj fml* ilustre.

ill will *n* rencor *m*, animadversión *f*; **to bear sb ~** guardarle rencor a alguien.

I'm [aɪm] = **I am.**

image ['ɪmɪdʒ] *n* imagen *f*.

image processing *n* COMPUT tratamiento *m* de imagen.

imagery ['ɪmɪdʒrɪ] *n (U)* imágenes *fpl*.

imaginary [ɪ'mædʒɪnrɪ] *adj* imaginario(ria).

imagination [ɪ,mædʒɪ'neɪʃn] *n* imaginación *f*.

imaginative [ɪ'mædʒɪnətɪv] *adj* imaginativo(va).

imagine [ɪ'mædʒɪn] *vt* **-1.** [gen] imaginar; **~ never having to work!** ¡imagina que nunca tuvieras que trabajar!; **~ (that)!** ¡imagínate!; **I can't ~ what he means** no tengo ni idea de qué quiere decir **-2.** [suppose]: **to ~ (that)** imaginarse que.

imbalance [,ɪm'bæləns] *n* desequilibrio *m*.

imbecile ['ɪmbɪsiːl] *n* imbécil *m* OR *f*.

IMF (*abbr of* International Monetary Fund) *n* FMI *m*.

imitate ['ɪmɪteɪt] *vt* imitar.

imitation [,ɪmɪ'teɪʃn] *<>* *n* imitación *f*. *<>* *adj* de imitación; **~ jewellery** bisutería *f*.

immaculate [ɪ'mækjʊlət] *adj* **-1.** [clean and tidy] inmaculado(da); [taste] exquisito(ta) **-2.** [performance, timing] impecable, perfecto(ta).

immaterial [,ɪmə'tɪərɪəl] *adj* [irrelevant, unimportant] irrelevante.

immature [,ɪmə'tjʊəʳ] *adj* inmaduro(ra); [animal] joven.

immediate [ɪ'miːdjət] *adj* **-1.** [gen] inmediato(ta); **in the ~ future** en el futuro más cercano; **in the ~ vicinity** en las inmediaciones **-2.** [family] más cercano(na).

immediately [ɪ'miːdjətlɪ] *<>* *adv* **-1.** [at once] inmediatamente **-2.** [directly] directamente. *<>* *conj* en cuanto, tan pronto como.

immense [ɪ'mens] *adj* inmenso(sa).

immerse [ɪ'mɜːs] *vt* **-1.** [plunge]: **to ~ sthg in sthg** sumergir algo en algo **-2.** [involve]: **to ~ o.s. in sthg** enfrascarse en algo.

immersion heater [ɪ'mɜːʃn-] *n* calentador *m* de inmersión.

immigrant ['ɪmɪgrənt] *n* inmigrante *m* OR *f*.

immigration [,ɪmɪ'greɪʃn] *n* inmigración *f*.

imminent ['ɪmɪnənt] *adj* inminente.

immobilize, -ise [ɪ'məʊbɪlaɪz] *vt* inmovilizar.

immoral [ɪ'mɒrəl] *adj* inmoral.

immortal [ɪ'mɔːtl] *adj* inmortal.

immortalize, -ise [ɪ'mɔːtəlaɪz] *vt* inmortalizar.

immovable [ɪ'muːvəbl] *adj* **-1.** [fixed] fijo(ja), inamovible **-2.** [determined, decided] inconmovible, inflexible.

immune [ɪ'mjuːn] *adj* **-1.** [gen & MED]: **~ (to)** inmune (a) **-2.** [exempt]: **~ (from)** exento(ta) (de).

immunity [ɪ'mjuːnətɪ] *n* **-1.** [gen & MED]: **~ (to)** inmunidad *f* (a) **-2.** [exemption]: **~ (from)** exención *f* (de).

immunize, -ise ['ɪmjuːnaɪz] *vt*: **to ~ sb (against sthg)** inmunizar a alguien (contra algo).

imp [ɪmp] *n* - **1.** [creature] duendecillo *m* - **2.** [naughty child] diablillo *m*.

impact [*n* 'ɪmpækt, *vb* ɪm'pækt] ⬦ *n* impacto *m*; **to make an ~ on** OR **upon** causar impacto en. ⬦ *vt* [influence] influenciar.

impair [ɪm'peəʳ] *vt* [sight, hearing] dañar, debilitar; [movement] entorpecer; [ability, efficiency] mermar; [prospects] perjudicar.

impart [ɪm'pɑ:t] *vt fml* - **1.** [information]: **to ~ sthg (to sb)** comunicar algo (a alguien) - **2.** [feeling, quality]: **to ~ sthg (to sthg)** conferir algo (a algo).

impartial [ɪm'pɑ:ʃl] *adj* imparcial.

impassable [ɪm'pɑ:səbl] *adj* intransitable, impracticable.

impasse [æm'pɑ:s] *n* impasse *m*, callejón *m* sin salida.

impassive [ɪm'pæsɪv] *adj* impasible.

impatience [ɪm'peɪʃns] *n* impaciencia *f*.

impatient [ɪm'peɪʃnt] *adj* impaciente; **to be ~ to do sthg** estar impaciente por hacer algo; **to be ~ for sthg** esperar algo con impaciencia; **to get ~** impacientarse.

impeccable [ɪm'pekəbl] *adj* impecable.

impede [ɪm'pi:d] *vt* dificultar, entorpecer.

impediment [ɪm'pedɪmənt] *n* - **1.** [obstacle] impedimento *m*, obstáculo *m* - **2.** [disability] defecto *m*.

impel [ɪm'pel] (*pt* & *pp* **-led**, *cont* **-ling**) *vt* : **to ~ sb to do sthg** impulsar a alguien a hacer algo.

impending [ɪm'pendɪŋ] *adj* inminente.

imperative [ɪm'perətɪv] ⬦ *adj* [need] apremiante, imperativo(va); **it is ~ that ... es** imprescindible que ... ⬦ *n* imperativo *m*.

imperfect [ɪm'pɜ:fɪkt] ⬦ *adj* [not perfect] imperfecto(ta). ⬦ *n* GRAMM: **~ (tense)** (pretérito *m*) imperfecto *m*.

imperial [ɪm'pɪərɪəl] *adj* - **1.** [of an empire or emperor] imperial - **2.** [system of measurement]: **~ system** sistema anglosajón de medidas.

imperialism [ɪm'pɪərɪəlɪzm] *n* imperialismo *m*.

impersonal [ɪm'pɜ:snl] *adj* impersonal.

impersonate [ɪm'pɜ:səneɪt] *vt* [try to pass as] hacerse pasar por; [do impression of] imitar.

impersonation [ɪm,pɜ:sə'neɪʃn] *n* - **1.** [pretending to be]: **charged with ~ of a policeman** acusado de hacerse pasar por policía - **2.** [impression] imitación *f*; **to do ~s (of)** imitar (a), hacer imitaciones (de).

impertinent [ɪm'pɜ:tɪnənt] *adj* impertinente, insolente.

impervious [ɪm'pɜ:vjəs] *adj* [not influenced]: **~ to** insensible a.

impetuous [ɪm'petʃʊəs] *adj* impetuoso(sa).

impetus ['ɪmpɪtəs] *n* (*U*) - **1.** [momentum]

ímpetu *m* - **2.** [stimulus] impulso *m*.

impinge [ɪm'pɪndʒ] *vi*: **to ~ on sthg/sb** afectar algo/a alguien.

implant [*n* 'ɪmplɑ:nt, *vb* ɪm'plɑ:nt] ⬦ *n* implante *m*. ⬦ *vt* - **1.** [fix-idea etc]: **to ~ sthg in** OR **into** inculcar algo en - **2.** MED: **to ~ sthg in** OR **into** implantar algo en.

implausible [ɪm'plɔ:zəbl] *adj* inverosímil.

implement [*n* 'ɪmplɪmənt, *vt* 'ɪmplɪment] ⬦ *n* herramienta *f*. ⬦ *vt* llevar a cabo, poner en práctica.

implication [,ɪmplɪ'keɪʃn] *n* - **1.** [involvement] implicación *f*, complicidad *f* - **2.** [inference] consecuencia *f*; **by ~** de forma indirecta.

implicit [ɪm'plɪsɪt] *adj* - **1.** [gen]: **~ (in)** implícito(ta) (en) - **2.** [complete - belief] absoluto(ta); [- faith] incondicional.

implore [ɪm'plɔ:ʳ] *vt*: **to ~ sb (to do sthg)** suplicar a alguien (que haga algo).

imploring [ɪm'plɔ:rɪŋ] *adj* suplicante.

imply [ɪm'plaɪ] (*pt* & *pp* **-ied**) *vt* - **1.** [suggest] insinuar, dar a entender - **2.** [involve] implicar, suponer.

impolite [,ɪmpə'laɪt] *adj* maleducado(da), descortés.

import [*n* 'ɪmpɔ:t, *vt* ɪm'pɔ:t] ⬦ *n* - **1.** [act of importing, product] importación *f* - **2.** *fml* [meaning] sentido *m*, significado *m*. ⬦ *vt* [gen & COMPUT] importar.

importance [ɪm'pɔ:tns] *n* importancia *f*.

important [ɪm'pɔ:tnt] *adj*: **~ (to)** importante (para); **it's not ~** no importa.

importer [ɪm'pɔ:təʳ] *n* importador *m*, -ra *f*.

impose [ɪm'pəʊz] ⬦ *vt*: **to ~ sthg (on)** imponer algo (a). ⬦ *vi*: **to ~ (on)** abusar (de), molestar (a).

imposing [ɪm'pəʊzɪŋ] *adj* imponente, impresionante.

imposition [,ɪmpə'zɪʃn] *n* - **1.** [enforcement] imposición *f* - **2.** [cause of trouble] molestia *f*.

impossible [ɪm'pɒsəbl] *adj* - **1.** [gen] imposible - **2.** [person, behaviour] inaguantable, insufrible.

impossibly [ɪm'pɒsəblɪ] *adv* [very] increíblemente.

impostor, imposter US [ɪm'pɒstəʳ] *n* impostor *m*, -ra *f*.

impotent ['ɪmpətənt] *adj* impotente.

impound [ɪm'paʊnd] *vt* incautarse.

impoverished [ɪm'pɒvərɪʃt] *adj* [country, people, imagination] empobrecido(da).

impracticable [ɪm'præktɪkəbl] *adj* impracticable, irrealizable.

impractical [ɪm'præktɪkl] *adj* poco práctico(ca).

impregnable [ɪm'pregnəbl] *adj* *lit* & *fig* incontestable.

impregnate ['ɪmpregneɪt] *vt* - **1.** [introduce

substance into]: **to ~ sthg (with)** impregnar OR empapar algo (de) **- 2.** *fml* [fertilize] fecundar.

impress [ɪmˈpres] ◇ *vt* **- 1.** [produce admiration in] impresionar; **I was favourably ~ ed** me causó buena impresión **- 2.** [stress]: **to ~ sthg on sb** hacer comprender a alguien la importancia de algo. ◇ *vi* [create good impression] causar buena impresión; [show off] impresionar.

impression [ɪmˈpreʃn] *n* **- 1.** [gen] impresión *f*; **to make an ~** impresionar; **to make a good/bad ~** causar una buena/mala impresión; **to be under the ~ that** tener la impresión de que **- 2.** [imitation] imitación *f*.

impressive [ɪmˈpresɪv] *adj* impresionante.

imprint [ˈɪmprɪnt] *n* **- 1.** [mark] huella *f*, impresión *f* **- 2.** [publisher's name] pie *m* de imprenta.

imprison [ɪmˈprɪzn] *vt* encarcelar.

improbable [ɪmˈprɒbəbl] *adj* [event] improbable; [story, excuse] inverosímil; [clothes, hat] estrafalario(ria); [contraption] extraño(ña).

impromptu [ɪmˈprɒmptjuː] *adj* improvisado(da).

improper [ɪmˈprɒpəʳ] *adj* **- 1.** [unsuitable] impropio(pia) **- 2.** [incorrect, illegal] indebido(da) **- 3.** [rude] indecoroso(sa).

improve [ɪmˈpruːv] ◇ *vi* mejorar; **to ~ on** OR **upon sthg** mejorar algo. ◇ *vt* mejorar.

improvement [ɪmˈpruːvmənt] *n* **- 1.** [gen]: **~ (in/on)** mejora *f* (en/con respecto a); **to be an ~ on sthg** ser mejor que algo **- 2.** [in health] mejoría *f* **- 3.** [to home] reforma *f*.

improvise [ˈɪmprəvaɪz] *vt* & *vi* improvisar.

impudent [ˈɪmpjʊdənt] *adj* insolente, descarado(da).

impulse [ˈɪmpʌls] *n* impulso *m*; **on ~** sin pensar.

impulsive [ɪmˈpʌlsɪv] *adj* impulsivo(va).

impunity [ɪmˈpjuːnətɪ] *n*: **with ~** impunemente.

impurity [ɪmˈpjʊərətɪ] (*pl* **-ies**) *n* impureza *f*.

in [ɪn] ◇ *prep* **- 1.** [indicating place, position] en; **~ a box/the garden/the lake** en una caja/el jardín/el lago; **~ Paris/Belgium/the country** en París/Bélgica/el campo; **~ here/ there** aquí/allí dentro **- 2.** [wearing]: **she was still ~ her nightclothes** todavía llevaba su vestido de noche **- 3.** [at a particular time]: **at four o'clock ~ the morning/afternoon** a las cuatro de la mañana/tarde; **~ the morning/afternoon** por la mañana/tarde; **~ 1992/May/the spring** en 1992/mayo/primavera **- 4.** [within] en; **he learned to type ~ two weeks** aprendió a escribir a máquina en dos semanas; **I'll be ready ~ five minutes** estoy listo en cinco minutos **- 5.** [during] desde hace; **it's my first decent meal ~ weeks** es lo primero decente que como desde hace OR en semanas **- 6.** [indicating situation, circumstances]: **~ danger/ difficulty** en peligro/dificultades; **~ the sun** al sol; **~ the rain** bajo la lluvia; **a rise ~ prices** un aumento de los precios **- 7.** [indicating manner, condition] en; **~ a loud/soft voice** en voz alta/baja; **~ pencil/ink** a lápiz/bolígrafo; **~ this way** de este modo **- 8.** [indicating emotional state] con; **~ anger/joy** con enfado/alegría **- 9.** [specifying area of activity]: **advances ~ medicine** avances en la medicina; **he's ~ computers** se dedica a informática **- 10.** [with numbers - showing quantity, age]: **~ large/small quantities** en grandes/pequeñas cantidades; **~ (their) thousands** a OR por millares; **she's ~ her sixties** anda por los sesenta **- 11.** [describing arrangement]: **~ a line/circle** en línea/círculo; **to stand ~ twos** estar en pares OR parejas **- 12.** [as regards] en; **~ these matters** en estos temas; **two metres ~ length/width** dos metros de largo/ancho; **a change ~ direction** un cambio de dirección **- 13.** [in ratios]: **one ~ ten** uno de cada diez; **five pence ~ the pound** cinco peniques por libra **- 14.** (*after superl*) de; **the best ~ the world** el mejor del mundo **- 15.** (+ *present participle*): **~ doing sthg** al hacer algo **- 16.** *phr*: **there's nothing ~ it for us** no tiene ninguna ventaja para nosotros. ◇ *adv* **- 1.** [inside] dentro; **to jump ~** saltar adentro; **do come ~** pasa por favor **- 2.** [at home, work]: **is Judith ~?** ¿está Judith?; **I'm staying ~ tonight** esta noche no salgo **- 3.** [of train, boat, plane]: **is the train ~ yet?** ¿ha llegado el tren? **- 4.** [of tide]: **the tide's ~** la marea está alta **- 5.** *phr*: **you're ~ for a surprise** te vas a llevar una sorpresa; **to have it ~ for sb** tenerla tomada con alguien. ◇ *adj inf* de moda.

➡ **ins** *npl*: **the ~ s and outs** los detalles, los pormenores.

in. *abbr of* **inch**.

inability [ˌɪnəˈbɪlətɪ] *n*: **~ (to do sthg)** incapacidad *f* (de hacer algo).

inaccessible [ˌɪnəkˈsesəbl] *adj* inaccesible.

inaccurate [ɪnˈækjʊrət] *adj* inexacto(ta).

inadequate [ɪnˈædɪkwət] *adj* **- 1.** [insufficient] insuficiente **- 2.** [person] incapaz.

inadvertently [ˌɪnədˈvɜːtəntlɪ] *adv* sin querer, accidentalmente.

inadvisable [ˌɪnədˈvaɪzəbl] *adj* poco aconsejable.

inane [ɪˈneɪn] *adj* necio(cia).

inanimate [ɪnˈænɪmət] *adj* inanimado(da).

inappropriate [ˌɪnəˈprəʊprɪət] *adj* [remark, clothing] impropio(pia); [time] inoportuno(na).

inarticulate [ˌɪnɑːˈtɪkjʊlət] adj [person] que no se expresa bien; [speech] mal pronunciado(da) OR expresado(da).

inasmuch [ˌɪnəzˈmʌtʃ] ➔ **inasmuch as** conj en la medida en que.

inaudible [ɪˈnɔːdɪbl] adj inaudible.

inauguration [ɪˌnɔːgjʊˈreɪʃn] n -1. [of leader, president] investidura f - 2. [of building, system] inauguración f.

in-between adj intermedio(dia).

inborn [ˌɪnˈbɔːn] adj innato(ta).

inbound [ˈɪnbaʊnd] adj de llegada.

in-box n [for e-mail] buzón m de entrada.

inbred [ˌɪnˈbred] adj -1. [closely related] endogámico(ca) - 2. [inborn] innato(ta).

inbuilt [ˌɪnˈbɪlt] adj [in person] innato(ta); [in thing] inherente.

inc. (abbr of inclusive) inclus.

Inc. [ɪŋk] US (abbr of incorporated) ≃ S.A.

incapable [ɪnˈkeɪpəbl] adj -1. [unable]: to be ~ of sthg/of doing sthg ser incapaz de algo/de hacer algo - 2. [useless] incompetente.

incapacitated [ˌɪnkəˈpæsɪteɪtɪd] adj incapacitado(da).

incarcerate [ɪnˈkɑːsəreɪt] vt fml encarcelar.

incarnation [ˌɪnkɑːˈneɪʃn] n -1. [personification] personificación f - 2. [existence] encarnación f.

incendiary device [ɪnˈsendjərɪ-] n artefacto m incendiario.

incense [n ˈɪnsens, vt ɪnˈsens] ⟨⟩ n incienso m. ⟨⟩ vt enfurecer, indignar.

incentive [ɪnˈsentɪv] n incentivo m.

incentive scheme n plan m de incentivos.

inception [ɪnˈsepʃn] n fml inicio m, origen m.

incessant [ɪnˈsesnt] adj incesante, constante.

incessantly [ɪnˈsesntlɪ] adv incesantemente, constantemente.

incest [ˈɪnsest] n incesto m.

inch [ɪntʃ] ⟨⟩ n = 2,54 cm, pulgada f; to be within an ~ of doing sthg estar en un tris de hacer algo. ⟨⟩ vi: to ~ forward avanzar poco a poco.

incidence [ˈɪnsɪdəns] n [of disease, theft] índice m.

incident [ˈɪnsɪdənt] n incidente m, suceso m.

incidental [ˌɪnsɪˈdentl] adj accesorio(ria), secundario(ria).

incidentally [ˌɪnsɪˈdentəlɪ] adv por cierto, a propósito.

incinerate [ɪnˈsɪnəreɪt] vt incinerar, quemar.

incipient [ɪnˈsɪpɪənt] adj fml incipiente.

incisive [ɪnˈsaɪsɪv] adj [comment, person] incisivo(va); [mind] penetrante.

incite [ɪnˈsaɪt] vt incitar; to ~ sb to do sthg incitar a alguien a que haga algo.

inclination [ˌɪnklɪˈneɪʃn] n -1. (U) [liking, preference] inclinación f, propensión f - 2. [tendency]: ~ to do sthg tendencia f a hacer algo.

incline [n ˈɪnklaɪn, vb ɪnˈklaɪn] ⟨⟩ n pendiente f, cuesta f. ⟨⟩ vt [head] inclinar, ladear.

inclined [ɪnˈklaɪnd] adj -1. [tending]: to be ~ to sthg ser propenso OR tener tendencia a algo; to be ~ to do sthg tener tendencia a hacer algo; I'm ~ to agree creo que estoy de acuerdo - 2. fml [wanting]: to be ~ to do sthg estar dispuesto a hacer algo - 3. [sloping] inclinado(da).

include [ɪnˈkluːd] vt -1. [gen] incluir - 2. [with letter] adjuntar.

included [ɪnˈkluːdɪd] adj incluido(da).

including [ɪnˈkluːdɪŋ] prep incluyendo; six died, ~ a child murieron seis personas, incluyendo un niño.

inclusive [ɪnˈkluːsɪv] adj -1. [including everything] inclusivo(va); one to nine ~ uno a nueve inclusive - 2. [including all costs]: ~ of VAT con el IVA incluido; £150 ~ 150 libras todo incluido.

incoherent [ˌɪnkəʊˈhɪərənt] adj incoherente.

income [ˈɪŋkʌm] n (U) [gen] ingresos mpl; [from property] renta f; [from investment] réditos mpl.

income support n (U) UK subsidio para personas con muy bajos ingresos o desempleados sin derecho a subsidio de paro, ≃ salario m social.

income tax n impuesto m sobre la renta.

incompatible [ˌɪnkəmˈpætɪbl] adj [gen & COMPUT]: ~ (with) incompatible (con).

incompetent [ɪnˈkɒmpɪtənt] adj incompetente, incapaz.

incomplete [ˌɪnkəmˈpliːt] adj incompleto(ta).

incomprehensible [ɪnˌkɒmprɪˈhensəbl] adj incomprensible.

inconceivable [ˌɪnkənˈsiːvəbl] adj inconcebible.

inconclusive [ˌɪnkənˈkluːsɪv] adj [evidence, argument] poco convincente; [meeting, outcome] sin conclusión clara.

incongruous [ɪnˈkɒŋgruəs] adj incongruente.

inconsequential [ˌɪnkɒnsɪˈkwenʃl] adj intrascendente, de poca importancia.

inconsiderable [ˌɪnkənˈsɪdərəbl] adj: not ~ nada insignificante OR despreciable.

inconsiderate [ˌɪnkənˈsɪdərət] adj desconsiderado(da).

inconsistency [ˌɪnkənˈsɪstənsɪ] (pl -ies) n -1. [between theory and practice] inconsecuencia f; [between statements etc] falta f de correspondencia - **2.** [contradictory point] contradicción f.

inconsistent [ˌɪnkən'sɪstənt] *adj* - **1.** [translation, statement]: ~ **(with)** falto(ta) de correspondencia (con) - **2.** [group, government, person] inconsecuente - **3.** [erratic] irregular, desigual.

inconspicuous [ˌɪnkən'spɪkjʊəs] *adj* discreto(ta).

inconvenience [ˌɪnkən'viːnjəns] *n* - **1.** [difficulty, discomfort] molestia f, incomodidad f; **we apologize for any ~ caused** disculpen las molestias - **2.** [inconvenient thing] inconveniente *m*.

inconvenient [ˌɪnkən'viːnjənt] *adj* [time] inoportuno(na); [location] incómodo(da); **that date is ~** esa fecha no me viene bien.

incorporate [ɪn'kɔːpəreɪt] *vt* - **1.** [integrate]: **to ~ sthg/sb (in), to ~ sthg/sb (into)** incorporar algo/a alguien (en) - **2.** [include] incluir, comprender.

incorporated [ɪn'kɔːpəreɪtɪd] *adj* COMM: ~ **company** sociedad f anónima.

incorrect [ˌɪnkə'rekt] *adj* incorrecto(ta), erróneo(a).

incorrigible [ɪn'kɒrɪdʒəbl] *adj* incorregible.

increase [*n* 'ɪnkriːs, *vb* ɪn'kriːs] ◇ *n*: ~ **(in)** [gen] aumento *m* (de); [in price, temperature] subida f (de); **to be on the ~** ir en aumento. ◇ *vt* - **1.** [gen] aumentar, incrementar - **2.** [price] subir. ◇ *vi* [gen] aumentar; [price, temperature] subir.

increasing [ɪn'kriːsɪŋ] *adj* creciente.

increasingly [ɪn'kriːsɪŋli] *adv* cada vez más.

incredible [ɪn'kredəbl] *adj* increíble.

incredibly [ɪn'kredəbli] *adv* increíblemente.

incredulous [ɪn'kredjʊləs] *adj* incrédulo(la).

increment ['ɪnkrɪmənt] *n* incremento *m*.

incriminating [ɪn'krɪmɪneɪtɪŋ] *adj* comprometedor(ra).

incubator ['ɪnkjʊbeɪtəʳ] *n* [for baby] incubadora f.

incumbent [ɪn'kʌmbənt] *fml* ◇ *adj*: **to be ~ on** OR **upon sb to do sthg** incumbir a alguien hacer algo. ◇ *n* titular *m* OR f.

incur [ɪn'kɜːʳ] (*pt & pp* -**red**, *cont* -**ring**) *vt* [wrath, criticism] incurrir en, atraerse; [debt] contraer; [expenses] incurrir en.

indebted [ɪn'detɪd] *adj* - **1.** [grateful]: ~ **(to)** en deuda (con) - **2.** [owing money]: ~ **(to)** endeudado(da) (con).

indecent [ɪn'diːsnt] *adj* - **1.** [improper] indecente - **2.** [unreasonable, excessive] desmedido(da).

indecent assault *n* abusos *mpl* deshonestos.

indecent exposure *n* exhibicionismo *m*.

indecisive [ˌɪndɪ'saɪsɪv] *adj* - **1.** [person] indeciso(sa) - **2.** [result] no decisivo(va).

indeed [ɪn'diːd] *adv* - **1.** [certainly] ciertamente; **are you coming? - ~ I am** ¿vienes tú? - por supuesto que sí - **2.** [in fact] de hecho - **3.** [for emphasis] realmente; **very big ~** grandísimo; **very few ~** poquísimos - **4.** [to express surprise, disbelief]: ~? ¿ah sí? - **5.** [what is more] es más.

indefinite [ɪn'defɪnɪt] *adj* - **1.** [time, number] indefinido(da) - **2.** [answer, opinion] impreciso(sa) - **3.** GRAMM indeterminado(da), indefinido(da).

indefinitely [ɪn'defɪnətli] *adv* - **1.** [for unfixed period] indefinidamente - **2.** [imprecisely] de forma imprecisa.

indemnity [ɪn'demnətɪ] *n* - **1.** [insurance] indemnidad f - **2.** [compensation] indemnización f.

indent [ɪn'dent] ◇ *n* [in text] sangrado *m*. ◇ *vt* - **1.** [dent] mellar - **2.** [text] sangrar.

independence [ˌɪndɪ'pendəns] *n* independencia f; **to gain ~** independizarse.

Independence Day *n* el Día de la Independencia.

independent [ˌɪndɪ'pendənt] *adj*: ~ **(of)** independiente (de).

independent school *n* UK colegio *m* privado.

in-depth *adj* a fondo, exhaustivo(va).

indescribable [ˌɪndɪ'skraɪbəbl] *adj* indescriptible.

indestructible [ˌɪndɪ'strʌktəbl] *adj* indestructible.

index ['ɪndeks] (*pl* -**es** OR **indices**) *n* índice *m*.

index card *n* ficha f.

index finger *n* (dedo *m*) índice *m*.

index-linked [-lɪŋkt] *adj* indexado(da).

India ['ɪndjə] *n* (la) India.

Indian ['ɪndjən] ◇ *adj* - **1.** [from India] indio(dia), hindú - **2.** [from the Americas] indio(dia). ◇ *n* - **1.** [from India] indio *m*, -dia f, hindú *m* OR f - **2.** [from the Americas] indio *m*, -dia f.

Indian Ocean *n*: **the ~** el océano Índico.

indicate ['ɪndɪkeɪt] ◇ *vt* indicar. ◇ *vi* [when driving]: **to ~ left/right** indicar a la izquierda/derecha.

indication [ˌɪndɪ'keɪʃn] *n* - **1.** [suggestion, idea] indicación f - **2.** [sign] indicio *m*, señal f.

indicative [ɪn'dɪkətɪv] ◇ *adj*: ~ **of sthg** indicativo(va) de algo. ◇ *n* GRAMM indicativo *m*.

indicator ['ɪndɪkeɪtəʳ] *n* - **1.** [sign, criterion] indicador *m* - **2.** [on car] intermitente *m*.

indices ['ɪndɪsiːz] *pl* ➭ **index**.

indict [ɪnˈdaɪt] *vt* : **to ~ sb (for)** acusar a alguien (de).

indictment [ɪnˈdaɪtmənt] *n* - **1.** JUR acusación *f* - **2.** [criticism] crítica *f* severa.

indifference [ɪnˈdɪfrəns] *n* indiferencia *f*.

indifferent [ɪnˈdɪfrənt] *adj* - **1.** [uninterested]: **~ (to)** indiferente (a) - **2.** [mediocre] mediocre.

indigenous [ɪnˈdɪdʒɪnəs] *adj* indígena.

indigestion [ˌɪndɪˈdʒestʃn] *n (U)* indigestión *f*.

indignant [ɪnˈdɪgnənt] *adj* : **~ (at)** indignado(da) (por).

indignity [ɪnˈdɪgnətɪ] (*pl* **-ies**) *n* indignidad *f*.

indigo [ˈɪndɪgəʊ] ◇ *adj* (color) añil. ◇ *n* añil *m*.

indirect [ˌɪndɪˈrekt] *adj* indirecto(ta).

indiscipline [ˌɪnˈdɪsɪplɪn] *n* indisciplina *f*.

indiscreet [ˌɪndɪˈskriːt] *adj* indiscreto(ta).

indiscriminate [ˌɪndɪˈskrɪmɪnət] *adj* indiscriminado(da).

indispensable [ˌɪndɪˈspensəbl] *adj* indispensable, imprescindible.

indisputable [ˌɪndɪˈspjuːtəbl] *adj* incuestionable.

indistinct [ˌɪndɪˈstɪŋkt] *adj* [memory] confuso(sa); [words] imperceptible, indistinto(ta); [picture, marking] borroso(sa), indistinto(ta).

indistinguishable [ˌɪndɪˈstɪŋgwɪʃəbl] *adj*: **~ (from)** indistinguible (de).

individual [ˌɪndɪˈvɪdʒʊəl] ◇ *adj* - **1.** [gen] individual - **2.** [tuition] particular - **3.** [approach, style] personal. ◇ *n* individuo *m*.

individually [ˌɪndɪˈvɪdʒʊəlɪ] *adv* [separately] individualmente, por separado.

indoctrination [ɪnˌdɒktrɪˈneɪʃn] *n* adoctrinamiento *m*.

Indonesia [ˌɪndəˈniːzjə] *n* Indonesia.

indoor [ˈɪndɔː] *adj* [gen] interior; [shoes] de andar por casa; [plant] de interior; [sports] en pista cubierta; **~ swimming pool** piscina *f* cubierta.

indoors [ˌɪnˈdɔːz] *adv* [gen] dentro; [at home] en casa.

induce [ɪnˈdjuːs] *vt* - **1.** [persuade]: **to ~ sb to do sthg** inducir OR persuadir a alguien a que haga algo - **2.** [labour, sleep, anger] provocar.

inducement [ɪnˈdjuːsmənt] *n* [incentive] incentivo *m*, aliciente *m*.

induction [ɪnˈdʌkʃn] *n* - **1.** [into official position]: **~ into** introducción *f* OR inducción *f* a - **2.** ELEC & MED inducción *f* - **3.** [introduction to job] introducción *f*.

induction course *n* cursillo *m* introductorio, curso *m* de iniciación.

indulge [ɪnˈdʌldʒ] ◇ *vt* - **1.** [whim, passion] satisfacer - **2.** [child, person] consentir.

◇ *vi*: **to ~ in sthg** permitirse algo.

indulgence [ɪnˈdʌldʒəns] *n* - **1.** [act of indulging] indulgencia *f* - **2.** [special treat] capricho *m*.

indulgent [ɪnˈdʌldʒənt] *adj* indulgente.

industrial [ɪnˈdʌstrɪəl] *adj* industrial.

industrial accident *n* accidente *m* laboral.

industrial action *n* huelga *f*; **to take ~** declararse en huelga.

industrial disease *n* enfermedad *f* laboral.

industrial estate UK, **industrial park** US *n* polígono *m* industrial.

industrialist [ɪnˈdʌstrɪəlɪst] *n* industrial *m* OR *f*.

industrial park US = **industrial estate**.

industrial relations *npl* relaciones *fpl* laborales.

industrial revolution *n* revolución *f* industrial.

industrious [ɪnˈdʌstrɪəs] *adj* diligente, trabajador(ra).

industry [ˈɪndəstrɪ] (*pl* **-ies**) *n* - **1.** [gen] industria *f*; **the tourist ~** el sector turístico - **2.** *fml* [hard work] laboriosidad *f*.

inebriated [ɪˈniːbrɪeɪtɪd] *adj fml* ebrio (ebria).

inedible [ɪnˈedɪbl] *adj* - **1.** [that cannot be eaten] no comestible - **2.** [bad-tasting] incomible.

ineffective [ˌɪnɪˈfektɪv] *adj* ineficaz, inútil.

ineffectual [ˌɪnɪˈfektʃʊəl] *adj* inútil.

inefficiency [ˌɪnɪˈfɪʃnsɪ] *n* ineficiencia *f*.

inefficient [ˌɪnɪˈfɪʃnt] *adj* ineficiente.

ineligible [ɪnˈelɪdʒəbl] *adj* inelegible; **to be ~ for** no tener derecho a.

inept [ɪˈnept] *adj* inepto(ta); **~ at** incapaz para.

inequality [ˌɪnɪˈkwɒlətɪ] (*pl* **-ies**) *n* desigualdad *f*.

inert [ɪˈnɜːt] *adj* inerte.

inertia [ɪˈnɜːʃə] *n* inercia *f*.

inescapable [ˌɪnɪˈskeɪpəbl] *adj* ineludible.

inevitable [ɪnˈevɪtəbl] *adj* inevitable.

inevitably [ɪnˈevɪtəblɪ] *adv* inevitablemente.

inexcusable [ˌɪnɪkˈskjuːzəbl] *adj* inexcusable, imperdonable.

inexhaustible [ˌɪnɪgˈzɔːstəbl] *adj* inagotable.

inexpensive [ˌɪnɪkˈspensɪv] *adj* barato(ta), económico(ca).

inexperienced [ˌɪnɪkˈspɪərɪənst] *adj* inexperto(ta).

inexplicable [ˌɪnɪkˈsplɪkəbl] *adj* inexplicable.

infallible [ɪnˈfæləbl] *adj* infalible.

infamous [ˈɪnfəməs] *adj* infame.

infancy [ˈɪnfənsɪ] *n* primera infancia *f*.

infant [ˈɪnfənt] *n* - **1.** [baby] bebé *m* - **2.** [young child] niño pequeño *m*, niña pequeña *f*.

infantry ['ɪnfəntrɪ] *n* infantería *f*.

infant school *n* UK colegio *m* preescolar *(para niños de entre 4 y 7 años)*.

infatuated [ɪnˈfætjʊeɪtɪd] *adj*: ~ **(with)** encaprichado(da) (con).

infatuation [ɪnˌfætjʊˈeɪʃn] *n*: ~ **(with)** encaprichamiento *m* (con).

infect [ɪnˈfekt] *vt* [wound] infectar; [person]: **to** ~ **sb (with sthg)** contagiar a alguien (algo).

infection [ɪnˈfekʃn] *n* **-1.** [disease] infección *f* **- 2.** [spreading of germs] contagio *m*.

infectious [ɪnˈfekʃəs] *adj* **- 1.** [disease] infeccioso(sa) **- 2.** [laugh, attitude] contagioso(sa).

infer [ɪnˈfɜːʳ] (*pt & pp* **-red**, *cont* **-ring**) *vt* **- 1.** [deduce]: **to** ~ **(that)** deducir OR inferir que; **to** ~ **sthg (from sthg)** deducir OR inferir algo (de algo) **- 2.** *inf* [imply] insinuar.

inferior [ɪnˈfɪərɪəʳ] ◇ *adj*: ~ **(to)** inferior (a). ◇ *n* [in status] inferior *m* OR *f*.

inferiority [ɪnˌfɪərɪˈɒrətɪ] *n* inferioridad *f*.

inferiority complex *n* complejo *m* de inferioridad.

inferno [ɪnˈfɜːnəʊ] (*pl* **-s**) *n* [hell] infierno *m*; **the building was an** ~ el edificio sufría un pavoroso incendio.

infertile [ɪnˈfɜːtaɪl] *adj* estéril.

infested [ɪnˈfestɪd] *adj*: ~ **with** infestado(da) de.

infighting ['ɪnˌfaɪtɪŋ] *n (U)* disputas *fpl* internas.

infiltrate ['ɪnfɪltreɪt] *vt* infiltrar.

infinite ['ɪnfɪnət] *adj* infinito(ta).

infinitive [ɪnˈfɪnɪtɪv] *n* infinitivo *m*; **in the** ~ en infinitivo.

infinity [ɪnˈfɪnətɪ] *n* **- 1.** MATH infinito *m* **- 2.** [incalculable number]: **an** ~ **(of)** infinidad *f* (de).

infirm [ɪnˈfɜːm] ◇ *adj* achacoso(sa). ◇ *npl*: **the** ~ los enfermos.

infirmary [ɪnˈfɜːmərɪ] (*pl* **-ies**) *n* **- 1.** [hospital] hospital *m* **- 2.** [room] enfermería *f*.

infirmity [ɪnˈfɜːmətɪ] (*pl* **-ies**) *n* **- 1.** [illness] dolencia *f* **- 2.** [state] enfermedad *f*.

inflamed [ɪnˈfleɪmd] *adj* MED inflamado(da).

inflammable [ɪnˈflæməbl] *adj* [burning easily] inflamable.

inflammation [ˌɪnfləˈmeɪʃn] *n* MED inflamación *f*.

inflatable [ɪnˈfleɪtəbl] *adj* inflable, hinchable.

inflate [ɪnˈfleɪt] ◇ *vt* **- 1.** [gen] inflar, hinchar **- 2.** [prices] inflar, aumentar. ◇ *vi* inflarse, hincharse.

inflation [ɪnˈfleɪʃn] *n* ECON inflación *f*.

inflationary [ɪnˈfleɪʃnrɪ] *adj* ECON inflacionista.

inflict [ɪnˈflɪkt] *vt*: **to** ~ **sthg on sb** infligir algo a alguien.

influence ['ɪnflʊəns] ◇ *n*: ~ **(on** OR **over sb)** influencia *f* (sobre alguien); ~ **(on sthg)** influencia (en algo); **to be a bad** ~ **on sb** tener una mala influencia en alguien; **under the** ~ **of** [person, group] bajo la influencia de; [alcohol, drugs] bajo los efectos de. ◇ *vt* influenciar.

influential [ˌɪnflʊˈenʃl] *adj* influyente.

influenza [ˌɪnflʊˈenzə] *n fml* gripe *f*.

influx ['ɪnflʌks] *n* afluencia *f*.

inform [ɪnˈfɔːm] *vt*: **to** ~ **sb (of/about sthg)** informar a alguien (de/sobre algo).
   ◆ **inform on** *vt fus* delatar.

informal [ɪnˈfɔːml] *adj* informal; [language] familiar.

informant [ɪnˈfɔːmənt] *n* **- 1.** [informer] delator *m*, -ra *f* **- 2.** [of researcher] informante *m* OR *f*.

information [ˌɪnfəˈmeɪʃn] *n (U)*: ~ **(on** OR **about)** información *f* OR datos *mpl* (sobre); **a piece of** ~ un dato; **for your** ~ para tu información.

information desk *n* (mostrador *m* de) información *f*.

information technology *n* informática *f*.

informative [ɪnˈfɔːmətɪv] *adj* informativo(va).

informer [ɪnˈfɔːməʳ] *n* delator *m*, -ra *f*.

infrared [ˌɪnfrəˈred] *adj* infrarrojo(ja).

infrastructure ['ɪnfrəˌstrʌktʃəʳ] *n* infraestructura *f*.

infringe [ɪnˈfrɪndʒ] (*cont* **infringing**) ◇ *vt* **- 1.** [rule] infringir **- 2.** [right] vulnerar. ◇ *vi*: **to** ~ **on sthg** vulnerar algo.

infringement [ɪnˈfrɪndʒmənt] *n* **- 1.** [of rule] infracción *f* **- 2.** [of right] violación *f*.

infuriating [ɪnˈfjʊərɪeɪtɪŋ] *adj* exasperante.

ingenious [ɪnˈdʒiːnjəs] *adj* ingenioso(sa).

ingenuity [ˌɪndʒɪˈnjuːətɪ] *n* ingenio *m*, inventiva *f*.

ingenuous [ɪnˈdʒenjʊəs] *adj fml* ingenuo(nua).

ingot ['ɪŋgət] *n* lingote *m*.

ingrained [ˌɪnˈgreɪnd] *adj* **- 1.** [ground in] incrustado(da) **- 2.** [deeply rooted] arraigado(da).

ingratiating [ɪnˈgreɪʃɪeɪtɪŋ] *adj* obsequioso(sa), lisonjero(ra).

ingredient [ɪnˈgriːdjənt] *n* ingrediente *m*.

inhabit [ɪnˈhæbɪt] *vt* habitar.

inhabitant [ɪnˈhæbɪtənt] *n* habitante *m* OR *f*.

inhale [ɪnˈheɪl] ◇ *vt* inhalar. ◇ *vi* [gen] inspirar; [smoker] tragarse el humo.

inhaler [ɪnˈheɪləʳ] *n* MED inhalador *m*.

inherent [ɪnˈhɪərənt, ɪnˈherənt] *adj*: ~ **(in)** inherente (a).

inherently [ɪnˈhɪərəntlɪ, ɪnˈherəntlɪ] *adv* intrínsecamente.

inherit [ɪn'herɪt] *vt* : to ~ sthg (from sb) heredar algo (de alguien).

inheritance [ɪn'herɪtəns] *n* herencia *f*.

inhibit [ɪn'hɪbɪt] *vt* - **1.** [restrict] impedir - **2.** [person] cohibir.

inhibition [ˌɪnhɪ'bɪʃn] *n* inhibición *f*.

inhospitable [ˌɪnhɒ'spɪtəbl] *adj* - **1.** [unwelcoming] inhospitalario(ria) - **2.** [harsh] inhóspito(ta).

in-house *adj* [journal, report] de circulación interna; [worker] de plantilla; [training] en el lugar de trabajo. *adv* en la misma empresa.

inhuman [ɪn'hju:mən] *adj* - **1.** [cruel] inhumano(na) - **2.** [not human] infrahumano(na).

initial [ɪ'nɪʃl] (*UK pt* & *pp* -led, *cont* -ling, *US pt* & *pp* -ed, *cont* -ing) *adj* inicial. *vt* poner las iniciales a.

initials *npl* [of person] iniciales *fpl*.

initially [ɪ'nɪʃəlɪ] *adv* inicialmente.

initiate [ɪ'nɪʃɪeɪt] *vt* iniciar; to ~ sb into sthg iniciar a alguien en algo.

initiative [ɪ'nɪʃətɪv] *n* iniciativa *f*.

inject [ɪn'dʒekt] *vt* MED : to ~ sb with sthg, to ~ sthg into sb inyectarle algo a alguien.

injection [ɪn'dʒekʃn] *n* inyección *f*.

injure ['ɪndʒəʳ] *vt* [gen] herir; SPORT lesionar; [reputation] dañar; [chances] perjudicar.

injured ['ɪndʒəd] *adj* [gen] herido(da); SPORT lesionado(da); [reputation] dañado(da).

injury ['ɪndʒərɪ] (*pl* -ies) *n* - **1.** [wound] herida *f*; [to muscle, broken bone] lesión *f* - **2.** (*U*) [physical harm] lesiones *fpl*.

injury time *n* (tiempo *m* de) descuento *m*.

injustice [ɪn'dʒʌstɪs] *n* injusticia *f*; to do sb an ~ ser injusto(ta) con alguien.

ink [ɪŋk] *n* tinta *f*.

ink-jet printer *n* COMPUT impresora *f* de chorro de tinta.

inkling ['ɪŋklɪŋ] *n*: to have an ~ of sthg tener una vaga idea de algo.

inlaid [ˌɪn'leɪd] *adj* incrustado(da); ~ with [jewels] con incrustaciones de.

inland [*adj* 'ɪnlənd, *adv* ɪn'lænd] *adj* interior. *adv* [go] hacia el interior; [remain] en el interior.

Inland Revenue *n UK*: the ~ ≃ Hacienda *f*.

in-laws *npl* suegros *mpl*.

inlet ['ɪnlet] *n* - **1.** [stretch of water] entrante *m* - **2.** [way in] entrada *f*, admisión *f*.

inmate ['ɪnmeɪt] *n* [of prison] preso *m*, -sa *f*; [of mental hospital] interno *m*, -na *f*.

inn [ɪn] *n* fonda *f*; [pub] *pub decorado a la vieja usanza*.

innate [ɪ'neɪt] *adj* innato(ta).

inner ['ɪnəʳ] *adj* - **1.** [gen] interior - **2.** [feelings] íntimo(ma); [fears, doubts, meaning] interno(na).

inner city *n* núcleo *m* urbano deprimido.

inner tube *n* cámara *f* (de aire).

inning ['ɪnɪŋ] *n* [in baseball] entrada *f*, inning *m*.

innings ['ɪnɪŋz] (*pl inv*) *n* [in cricket] entrada *f*.

innocence ['ɪnəsəns] *n* inocencia *f*.

innocent ['ɪnəsənt] *adj*: ~ (of) inocente (de). *n* [naive person] inocente *m* OR *f*.

innocuous [ɪ'nɒkjʊəs] *adj* inocuo(cua), inofensivo(va).

innovation [ˌɪnə'veɪʃn] *n* innovación *f*.

innovative ['ɪnəvətɪv] *adj* innovador(ra).

innuendo [ˌɪnjuː'endəʊ] (*pl* -es OR -s) *n* - **1.** [individual remark] insinuación *f*, indirecta *f* - **2.** (*U*) [style of speaking] insinuaciones *fpl*, indirectas *fpl*.

inoculate [ɪ'nɒkjʊleɪt] *vt* : to ~ sb with sthg inocular algo a alguien.

inordinately [ɪ'nɔ:dɪnətlɪ] *adv fml* desmesuradamente.

in-patient *n* paciente interno *m*, paciente interna *f*.

input ['ɪnpʊt] (*pt* & *pp* input OR -ted, *cont* -ting) *n* - **1.** [contribution] aportación *f*, contribución *f* - **2.** COMPUT & ELEC entrada *f*. *vt* COMPUT introducir.

inquest ['ɪnkwest] *n* investigación *f* judicial.

inquire [ɪn'kwaɪəʳ] *vi* [ask for information] informarse, preguntar; to ~ about sthg informarse de algo. *vt* : to ~ when/if/how ... preguntar cuándo/si/cómo ...

inquire after *vt fus* preguntar por.

inquire into *vt fus* investigar.

inquiry [ɪn'kwaɪərɪ] (*pl* -ies) *n* - **1.** [question] consulta *f*, pregunta *f*; 'Inquiries' 'Información' - **2.** [investigation] investigación *f*.

inquiry desk *n* (mostrador *m* de) información *f*.

inquisitive [ɪn'kwɪzətɪv] *adj* curioso(sa).

inroads ['ɪnrəʊdz] *npl*: to make ~ into [savings, supplies] mermar; [market, enemy territory] abrirse paso en.

insane [ɪn'seɪn] *adj* [mad] demente; *fig* [jealousy, person] loco(ca); to drive sb ~ volver loco a alguien.

insanity [ɪn'sænətɪ] *n* MED demencia *f*; [craziness] locura *f*.

insatiable [ɪn'seɪʃəbl] *adj* insaciable.

inscription [ɪn'skrɪpʃn] *n* - **1.** [engraved] inscripción *f* - **2.** [written] dedicatoria *f*.

inscrutable [ɪn'skru:təbl] *adj* inescrutable.

insect ['ɪnsekt] *n* insecto *m*.

insecticide [ɪn'sektɪsaɪd] *n* insecticida *m*.

insect repellent *n* loción *f* antiinsectos.

insecure [ˌɪnsɪ'kjʊəʳ] *adj* - **1.** [not confident] inseguro(ra) - **2.** [not safe] poco seguro(ra).

insensible [ɪn'sensəbl] *adj fml* - **1.** [unconscious] inconsciente **- 2.** [unaware]: **to be ~ of** sthg no ser consciente de algo **- 3.** [unable to feel]: **to be ~ to** sthg ser insensible a algo.

insensitive [ɪn'sensətɪv] *adj*: **~ (to)** insensible (a).

inseparable [ɪn'seprəbl] *adj*: **~ (from)** inseparable (de).

insert [*vb* ɪn'sɜːt, *n* 'ɪnsɜːt] ◇ *vt*: **to ~** sthg **(in** OR **into)** [hole] introducir algo (en); [text] insertar algo (en). ◇ *n* PRESS encarte *m*.

insertion [ɪn'sɜːʃn] *n* inserción *f*.

in-service training *n* UK formación *f* continua.

inshore [*adj* 'ɪnʃɔːʳ, *adv* ɪn'ʃɔːʳ] ◇ *adj* costero(ra). ◇ *adv* hacia la orilla OR la costa.

inside [ɪn'saɪd] ◇ *prep* dentro de; **~ three months** en menos de tres meses. ◇ *adv* **- 1.** [be, remain] dentro; [go, move, look] adentro; **come ~ !** ¡metéos dentro! **- 2.** *fig* [feel, hurt etc] por dentro. ◇ *adj* interior; **~ leg measurement** medida *f* de la entrepierna. ◇ *n* interior *m*; **from the ~** desde dentro; **to overtake on the ~** [of road] adelantar por dentro; **~ out** [wrong way] al revés; **to turn** sthg **~ out** [clothing] dar la vuelta a algo; **to know** sthg **~ out** conocer algo de arriba abajo OR al dedillo.
  ◆ **insides** *npl inf* tripas *fpl*.
  ◆ **inside of** *prep* US [building, object] dentro de.

inside lane *n* AUT carril *m* de dentro; SPORT calle *f* de dentro.

insight ['ɪnsaɪt] *n* **- 1.** (*U*) [power of understanding] perspicacia *f*, capacidad *f* de penetración **- 2.** [understanding] idea *f*.

insignificant [ˌɪnsɪg'nɪfɪkənt] *adj* insignificante.

insincere [ˌɪnsɪn'sɪəʳ] *adj* insincero(ra).

insinuate [ɪn'sɪnjʊeɪt] *vt pej*: **to ~ (that)** insinuar (que).

insipid [ɪn'sɪpɪd] *adj pej* soso(sa), insípido(da).

insist [ɪn'sɪst] ◇ *vt*: **to ~ that** insistir en que. ◇ *vi*: **to ~ on** sthg exigir algo; **to ~ (on doing** sthg**)** insistir (en hacer algo).

insistent [ɪn'sɪstənt] *adj* **- 1.** [determined] insistente; **to be ~ on** sthg insistir en algo **- 2.** [continual] persistente.

insofar [ˌɪnsəʊ'fɑːʳ] ◆ **insofar as** *conj* en la medida en que.

insole ['ɪnsəʊl] *n* plantilla *f*.

insolent ['ɪnsələnt] *adj* insolente.

insolvent [ɪn'sɒlvənt] *adj* insolvente.

insomnia [ɪn'sɒmnɪə] *n* insomnio *m*.

inspect [ɪn'spekt] *vt* inspeccionar; [troops] pasar revista a.

inspection [ɪn'spekʃn] *n* inspección *f*; [of troops] revista *f*; **on closer ~** tras un examen más detallado.

inspector [ɪn'spektəʳ] *n* inspector *m*, -ra *f*; [on bus, train] revisor *m*, -ra *f*.

inspiration [ˌɪnspə'reɪʃn] *n* **- 1.** [gen] inspiración *f* **- 2.** [source of inspiration]: **~ (for)** fuente *f* de inspiración (para).

inspirational [ˌɪnspə'reɪʃnl] *adj* inspirador(ra).

inspire [ɪn'spaɪəʳ] *vt* **- 1.** [stimulate, encourage]: **to ~** sb **(to do** sthg**)** alentar OR animar a alguien (a hacer algo) **- 2.** [fill]: **to ~** sb **with** sthg, **to ~** sthg **in** sb inspirar algo a alguien.

install UK, **instal** US [ɪn'stɔːl] *vt* [gen & COMPUT] instalar.

installation [ˌɪnstə'leɪʃn] *n* [gen & COMPUT] instalación *f*.

installment US = **instalment**.

installment plan *n* US compra *f* a plazos.

instalment UK, **installment** US [ɪn'stɔːlmənt] *n* **- 1.** [payment] plazo *m*, abono *m Méx*; **in ~s** a plazos **- 2.** TV & RADIO episodio *m*; [of novel] entrega *f*.

instance ['ɪnstəns] *n* [example, case] ejemplo *m*; **for ~** por ejemplo; **in this ~** en este caso.

instant ['ɪnstənt] ◇ *adj* instantáneo(a). ◇ *n* [moment] instante *m*; **at that** OR **the same ~** en aquel mismo instante; **the ~ (that) ...** en cuanto ...; **this ~** ahora mismo.

instantly ['ɪnstəntlɪ] *adv* en el acto.

instead [ɪn'sted] *adv* en cambio; **I came ~** yo vine en su lugar; **if you haven't got any sugar, you can use honey ~** si no tiene azúcar, utilice miel en su lugar.
  ◆ **instead of** *prep* en lugar de, en vez de; **I came ~ of her** yo vine en su lugar.

instep ['ɪnstep] *n* [of foot] empeine *m*.

instigate ['ɪnstɪgeɪt] *vt* iniciar; **to ~** sb **to do** sthg instigar a alguien a hacer algo.

instil UK (*pt & pp* **-led**, *cont* **-ling**), **instill** US (*pt & pp* **-ed**, *cont* **-ing**) [ɪn'stɪl] *vt*: **to ~** sthg **in** OR **into** sb inculcar algo a alguien.

instinct ['ɪnstɪŋkt] *n* instinto *m*; **my first ~ was ...** mi primer impulso fue ...

instinctive [ɪn'stɪŋktɪv] *adj* instintivo(va).

institute ['ɪnstɪtjuːt] ◇ *n* instituto *m*. ◇ *vt* [proceedings] iniciar, entablar; [system] instituir.

institution [ˌɪnstɪ'tjuːʃn] *n* **- 1.** [gen] institución *f* **- 2.** [home - for children, old people] asilo *m*; [- for mentally-handicapped] hospital *m* psiquiátrico.

instruct [ɪn'strʌkt] *vt* **- 1.** [tell, order]: **to ~** sb **to do** sthg mandar OR ordenar a alguien que haga algo **- 2.** [teach]: **to ~** sb **(in** sthg**)** instruir a alguien (en algo).

instruction [ɪn'strʌkʃn] *n* [gen & COMPUT] instrucción *f*.
  ◆ **instructions** *npl* [for use] instrucciones *fpl*.

instructor [ɪn'strʌktə^r] *n* **-1.** [gen] instructor *m* **-2.** [in skiing] **monitor** *m* **-3.** [in driving] profesor *m* **-4.** *US* [at college] profesor *m*, -ra *f*.

instrument ['ɪnstrəmənt] *n* instrumento *m*.

instrumental [,ɪnstrə'mentl] *adj* [important, helpful]**: to be ~ in sthg** jugar un papel fundamental en algo.

instrument panel *n* tablero *m* de instrumentos.

insubordinate [,ɪnsə'bɔːdɪnət] *adj* insubordinado(da).

insubstantial [,ɪnsəb'stænʃl] *adj* [frame, structure] endeble; [meal] poco sustancioso(sa).

insufficient [,ɪnsə'fɪʃnt] *adj*: **~ (for)** insuficiente (para).

insular ['ɪnsjʊlə^r] *adj* [narrow-minded] estrecho(cha) de miras.

insulate ['ɪnsjʊleɪt] *vt* aislar; **to ~ sb against** OR **from sthg** aislar a alguien de algo.

insulating tape ['ɪnsjʊleɪtɪŋ-] *n UK* cinta *f* aislante.

insulation [,ɪnsjʊ'leɪʃn] *n* [electrical] aislamiento *m*; [against the cold] aislamiento *m* térmico.

insulin ['ɪnsjʊlɪn] *n* insulina *f*.

insult [*vt* ɪn'sʌlt, *n* 'ɪnsʌlt] <> *vt* [with words] insultar; [with actions] ofender. <> *n* [remark] insulto *m*; [action] ofensa *f*.

insuperable [ɪn'suːprəbl] *adj fml* insalvable, insuperable.

insurance [ɪn'ʃʊərəns] *n* **-1.** [against fire, accident, theft]**: ~ (against)** seguro *m* (contra) **-2.** *fig* [safeguard, protection]**: ~ (against)** prevención *f* (contra).

insurance policy *n* póliza *f* de seguros.

insure [ɪn'ʃʊə^r] <> *vt* **-1.** [against fire, accident, theft]**: to ~ sthg/sb (against)** asegurar algo/a alguien (contra) **-2.** *US* [make certain] asegurar. <> *vi* [prevent]**: to ~ (against)** prevenir OR prevenirse (contra).

insurer [ɪn'ʃʊərə^r] *n* asegurador *m*, -ra *f*.

insurmountable [,ɪnsə'maʊntəbl] *adj fml* infranqueable, insuperable.

intact [ɪn'tækt] *adj* intacto(ta).

intake ['ɪnteɪk] *n* **-1.** [of food, drink] ingestión *f*; [of air] inspiración *f* **-2.** [in army] reclutamiento *m*; [in organization] número *m* de ingresos.

integral ['ɪntɪgrəl] *adj* integrante, intrínseco(ca); **to be ~ to** ser parte integrante de.

integrate ['ɪntɪgreɪt] <> *vi*: **to ~ (with** OR **into)** integrarse (en). <> *vt*: **to ~ sthg/sb with sthg, to ~ sthg/sb into sthg** integrar algo/a alguien en algo.

integrity [ɪn'tegrətɪ] *n* integridad *f*.

intellect ['ɪntəlekt] *n* [mind, cleverness] intelecto *m*, inteligencia *f*.

intellectual [,ɪntə'lektjʊəl] <> *adj* intelectual. <> *n* intelectual *m* OR *f*.

intelligence [ɪn'telɪdʒəns] *n* (*U*) **-1.** [ability to think] inteligencia *f* **-2.** [information] información *f* secreta **-3.** [information service] servicio *m* secreto OR de espionaje.

intelligent [ɪn'telɪdʒənt] *adj* [gen & COMPUT] inteligente.

intend [ɪn'tend] *vt* pretender; **to ~ doing** OR **to do sthg** tener la intención de hacer algo; **what do you ~ to do?** ¿qué piensas hacer?; **later than I had ~ed** más tarde de lo que había pensado; **to be ~ed for/as sthg** [project, book] estar pensado para/como algo; **the flowers were ~ed for you** las flores eran para ti.

intended [ɪn'tendɪd] *adj* [effect, result] pretendido(da).

intense [ɪn'tens] *adj* **-1.** [extreme, profound] intenso(sa) **-2.** [serious - person] muy serio(ria).

intensely [ɪn'tenslɪ] *adv* **-1.** [very - boring, irritating] enormemente **-2.** [very much - suffer] intensamente; [- dislike] profundamente.

intensify [ɪn'tensɪfaɪ] (*pt & pp* **-ied**) <> *vt* intensificar. <> *vi* intensificarse.

intensity [ɪn'tensətɪ] *n* intensidad *f*.

intensive [ɪn'tensɪv] *adj* [concentrated] intensivo(va).

intensive care *n* (*U*)**: (in) ~** (bajo) cuidados *mpl* intensivos.

intent [ɪn'tent] <> *adj* **-1.** [absorbed] atento(ta) **-2.** [determined]**: to be ~ on** OR **upon doing sthg** estar empeñado(da) en hacer algo. <> *n fml* intención *f*; **to all ~s and purposes** para todos los efectos.

intention [ɪn'tenʃn] *n* intención *f*; **to have no ~ of** no tener la menor intención de.

intentional [ɪn'tenʃənl] *adj* deliberado(da), intencionado(da); **it wasn't ~** fue sin querer.

intently [ɪn'tentlɪ] *adv* atentamente.

interact [,ɪntər'ækt] *vi* **-1.** [communicate, work together]**: to ~ (with sb)** relacionarse (con alguien) **-2.** [react]**: to ~ (with sthg)** interaccionar (con algo).

intercede [,ɪntə'siːd] *vi fml*: **to ~ (with/for)** interceder (ante/por).

intercept [,ɪntə'sept] *vt* interceptar.

interchange [*n* 'ɪntətʃeɪndʒ, *vb* ,ɪntə'tʃeɪndʒ] <> *n* **-1.** [exchange] intercambio *m* **-2.** [on motorway] enlace *m*. <> *vt* intercambiar.

interchangeable [,ɪntə'tʃeɪndʒəbl] *adj*: **~ (with)** intercambiable (con).

intercity [,ɪntə'sɪtɪ] *n* [train] tren *m* interurbano.

intercom ['ɪntəkɒm] *n* [for block of flats] portero *m* automático; [within a building] interfono *m*.

intercourse ['ɪntəkɔːs] *n (U)*: **sexual ~** relaciones *fpl* sexuales, coito *m*.

interest ['ɪntrəst] ◇ *n* **-1.** [gen]: **~ (in)** interés *m* (en OR por); **that's of no ~** eso no tiene interés; **to take an ~ in sthg** interesarse por algo **-2.** FIN interés *m*; **to pay the ~ of a loan** pagar los intereses de un préstamo **-3.** [hobby] afición *f.* ◇ *vt* interesar.

interested ['ɪntrəstɪd] *adj* interesado(da); **I'm not ~** no me interesa; **to be ~ in sthg/ in doing sthg** estar interesado en algo/en hacer algo; **I'm ~ in that subject** me interesa el tema.

interesting ['ɪntrəstɪŋ] *adj* interesante.

interest rate *n* tipo *m* de interés.

interface ['ɪntəfeɪs] *n* COMPUT interfaz *f*, interface *m*.

interfere [ˌɪntə'fɪə'] *vi* **-1.** [meddle]: **to ~ (with** OR **in sthg)** entrometerse OR interferir (en algo) **-2.** [damage] interferir; **to ~ with sthg** [career, routine] interferir en algo; [work, performance] interrumpir algo.

interference [ˌɪntə'fɪərəns] *n (U)* **-1.** [meddling]: **~ (with** OR **in)** intromisión *f* OR interferencia *f* (en) **-2.** [on radio, TV, telephone] interferencia *f*.

interim ['ɪntərɪm] ◇ *adj* [report] parcial; [measure] provisional; [government] interino(na). ◇ *n*: **in the ~** entre tanto.

interior [ɪn'tɪərɪə'] ◇ *adj* **-1.** [inner] interior **-2.** POL [minister, department] del Interior. ◇ *n* interior *m*.

interior decorator, interior designer *n* interiorista *m* OR *f*.

interlock [ˌɪntə'lɒk] *vi* [fingers] entrelazarse; [cogs] engranar.

interloper ['ɪntələʊpə'] *n* intruso *m*, -sa *f*.

interlude ['ɪntəluːd] *n* **-1.** [pause] intervalo *m* **-2.** [interval] intermedio *m*.

intermediary [ˌɪntə'miːdjərɪ] *(pl* **-ies)** *n* intermediario *m*, -ria *f*, mediador *m*, -ra *f*.

intermediate [ˌɪntə'miːdjət] *adj* intermedio(dia).

interminable [ɪn'tɜːmɪnəbl] *adj* interminable.

intermission [ˌɪntə'mɪʃn] *n* [of film] descanso *m*; [of play, opera, ballet] entreacto *m*.

intermittent [ˌɪntə'mɪtənt] *adj* intermitente.

intern [*vb* ɪn'tɜːn, *n* 'ɪntɜːn] ◇ *vt* recluir, internar. ◇ *n esp* US médico *m* interno residente.

internal [ɪn'tɜːnl] *adj* **-1.** [gen] interno(na) **-2.** [within a country] interior, nacional; **~ flight** vuelo *m* nacional.

internally [ɪn'tɜːnəlɪ] *adv* **-1.** [gen] internamente **-2.** [within a country] a nivel nacional.

Internal Revenue Service *n* US: **the ~** ≃ la Agencia Tributaria *Esp*, ≃ la Dirección General Impositiva *Amér*.

international [ˌɪntə'næʃənl] ◇ *adj* internacional. ◇ *n UK* SPORT **-1.** [match] encuentro *m* internacional **-2.** [player] internacional *m* OR *f*.

Internet ['ɪntənet] *n*: **the ~** Internet *f*; **on the ~** en Internet.

Internet access *n* acceso *m* a Internet.

Internet access provider *n* proveedor *m* de acceso a Internet.

Internet café *n* cibercafé *m*.

Internet connection *n* conexión *f* a Internet.

Internet Service Provider *n* proveedor *m* de servicios Internet.

Internet start-up company *n* empresa *f* electrónica aparecida con Internet.

Internet television, Internet TV *n* televisión *f* por Internet.

interpret [ɪn'tɜːprɪt] ◇ *vt* interpretar. ◇ *vi* hacer de intérprete.

interpreter [ɪn'tɜːprɪtə'] *n* [person] intérprete *m* OR *f*.

interrelate [ˌɪntərɪ'leɪt] *vi*: **to ~ (with)** interrelacionarse (con).

interrogate [ɪn'terəgeɪt] *vt* [gen & COMPUT] interrogar.

interrogation [ɪnˌterə'geɪʃn] *n* interrogatorio *m*.

interrogation mark *n* US signo *m* de interrogación.

interrogative [ˌɪntə'rɒgətɪv] *adj* GRAMM interrogativo(va).

interrupt [ˌɪntə'rʌpt] *vt* & *vi* interrumpir.

interruption [ˌɪntə'rʌpʃn] *n* interrupción *f*.

intersect [ˌɪntə'sekt] ◇ *vi* cruzarse. ◇ *vt* cruzar.

intersection [ˌɪntə'sekʃn] *n* US [of roads] cruce *m*, intersección *f*.

intersperse [ˌɪntə'spɜːs] *vt* : **to be ~d with** OR **by** estar entremezclado con.

interstate ['ɪntəsteɪt] *n* US autopista *f* interestatal.

interval ['ɪntəvl] *n* **-1.** [gen & MUS]: **~ (between)** intervalo *m* (entre); **at ~s** [now and again] a ratos; **at regular ~s** a intervalos regulares; **at monthly/yearly ~s** a intervalos de un mes/un año **-2.** UK [at play, concert] intermedio *m*, descanso *m*.

intervene [ˌɪntə'viːn] *vi* **-1.** [gen]: **to ~ (in)** intervenir (en) **-2.** [prevent thing from happening] interponerse; **the war ~d** sobrevino la guerra **-3.** [pass] transcurrir.

intervention [ˌɪntə'venʃn] *n* intervención *f*.

interview ['ɪntəvjuː] ◇ *n* [gen] entrevista *f*; [with police] interrogatorio *m*. ◇ *vt* [gen] entrevistar; [subj: policeman] interrogar.

interviewer [ˈɪntəvjuːəʳ] n entrevistador m, -ra f.

intestine [ɪnˈtestɪn] n intestino m.

intimacy [ˈɪntɪməsɪ] (pl -ies) n: ~ (between/with) intimidad f (entre/con).

intimate [adj ˈɪntɪmət, vb ˈɪntɪmeɪt] <> adj -1. [gen] íntimo(ma) -2. [knowledge] profundo(da). <> vt fml: to ~ (that) dar a entender (que).

intimidate [ɪnˈtɪmɪdeɪt] vt intimidar.

into [ˈɪntʊ] prep -1. [inside] en; to go ~ a room entrar en una habitación; to put sthg ~ sthg meter algo en algo; to get ~ a car subir a un coche -2. [against] con; to bump/crash ~ tropezar/chocar con -3. [referring to change in condition etc]: to turn OR develop ~ convertirse en; to translate sthg ~ Spanish traducir algo al español -4. [concerning] en relación con; research ~ electronics investigación en torno a la electrónica -5. [in expressions of time]: fifteen minutes ~ the game a los quince minutos de empezar el partido; well ~ the spring hasta bien entrada la primavera -6. MATH: to divide 4 ~ 8 dividir 8 entre 4.

intolerable [ɪnˈtɒlrəbl] adj fml [position, conditions] intolerable; [boredom, pain] inaguantable.

intolerance [ɪnˈtɒlərəns] n intolerancia f.

intolerant [ɪnˈtɒlərənt] adj intolerante.

intoxicated [ɪnˈtɒksɪkeɪtɪd] adj -1. [drunk] embriagado(da), ebrio (ebria) -2. fig [excited]: ~ (by OR with) ebrio (ebria) (de).

intractable [ɪnˈtræktəbl] adj fml -1. [stubborn] intratable -2. [insoluble] inextricable, insoluble.

intransitive [ɪnˈtrænzɪtɪv] adj intransitivo (va).

intravenous [ˌɪntrəˈviːnəs] adj intravenoso (sa).

in-tray n bandeja f de entrada.

intricate [ˈɪntrɪkət] adj intrincado(da), enrevesado(da).

intrigue [ɪnˈtriːg] <> n intriga f. <> vt intrigar.

intriguing [ɪnˈtriːgɪŋ] adj intrigante.

intrinsic [ɪnˈtrɪnsɪk] adj intrínseco(ca).

introduce [ˌɪntrəˈdjuːs] vt -1. [present - person, programme] presentar; to ~ sb (to sb) presentar a alguien (a alguien); to ~ o.s. presentarse -2. [bring in]: to ~ sthg (to OR into) introducir algo (en) -3. [show for first time]: to ~ sb to sthg iniciar a alguien en algo.

introduction [ˌɪntrəˈdʌkʃn] n -1. [gen]: ~ (to sthg) introducción f (a algo) -2. [of people]: ~ (to sb) presentación f (a alguien).

introductory [ˌɪntrəˈdʌktrɪ] adj [chapter] introductorio(ria); [remarks] preliminar; [price, offer] de lanzamiento.

introvert [ˈɪntrəvɜːt] n introvertido m, -da f.

introverted [ˈɪntrəvɜːtɪd] adj introvertido(da).

intrude [ɪnˈtruːd] vi -1. [interfere]: to ~ (on OR upon sb) inmiscuirse (en los asuntos de alguien); to ~ (on OR upon sthg) inmiscuirse (en algo) -2. [disturb] molestar.

intruder [ɪnˈtruːdəʳ] n intruso m, -sa f.

intrusive [ɪnˈtruːsɪv] adj [interfering] entrometido(da); [unwanted] indeseado(da).

intuition [ˌɪntjuːˈɪʃn] n intuición f.

inundate [ˈɪnʌndeɪt] vt -1. fml [flood] inundar -2. [overwhelm] desbordar; to be ~d with verse desbordado por.

invade [ɪnˈveɪd] vt invadir.

invalid [adj ɪnˈvælɪd, n ˈɪnvəlɪd] <> adj -1. [marriage, vote, ticket] nulo(la) -2. [argument, result] que no es válido(da). <> n inválido m, -da f.

invaluable [ɪnˈvæljʊəbl] adj: ~ (to) [information, advice] inestimable (para); [person] valiosísimo(ma) (para).

invariably [ɪnˈveərɪəblɪ] adv siempre, invariablemente.

invasion [ɪnˈveɪʒn] n invasión f.

invent [ɪnˈvent] vt inventar.

invention [ɪnˈvenʃn] n -1. [gen] invención f -2. [ability to invent] inventiva f.

inventive [ɪnˈventɪv] adj [person, mind] inventivo(va); [solution] ingenioso(sa).

inventor [ɪnˈventəʳ] n inventor m, -ra f.

inventory [ˈɪnventrɪ] (pl -ies) n -1. [list] inventario m -2. [goods] existencias fpl.

invert [ɪnˈvɜːt] vt invertir.

inverted commas [ɪnˈvɜːtɪd-] npl UK comillas fpl; in ~ entre comillas.

invest [ɪnˈvest] <> vt [money, time, energy]: to ~ sthg (in) invertir algo (en). <> vi lit & fig: to ~ (in) invertir (en).

investigate [ɪnˈvestɪgeɪt] vt & vi investigar.

investigation [ɪnˌvestɪˈgeɪʃn] n [enquiry, examination]: ~ (into) investigación f (en).

investment [ɪnˈvestmənt] n inversión f.

investor [ɪnˈvestəʳ] n inversor m, -ra f.

inveterate [ɪnˈvetərət] adj [liar] incorregible; [reader, smoker] empedernido(da).

invidious [ɪnˈvɪdɪəs] adj [task, role] desagradable; [comparison] odioso(sa).

invigilate [ɪnˈvɪdʒɪleɪt] vt & vi UK vigilar (en un examen).

invigorating [ɪnˈvɪgəreɪtɪŋ] adj [bath, walk] vigorizante; [experience] estimulante.

invincible [ɪnˈvɪnsɪbl] adj -1. [unbeatable] invencible -2. [determination] inalterable, inamovible.

invisible [ɪnˈvɪzɪbl] adj invisible.

invitation [ˌɪnvɪˈteɪʃn] n invitación f.

invite [ɪnˈvaɪt] vt -1. [gen]: to ~ sb (to sthg/to do sthg) invitar a alguien (a algo/a hacer algo) -2. [ask for, provoke] buscarse.

inviting [ɪn'vaɪtɪŋ] *adj* tentador(ra).
invoice ['ɪnvɔɪs] ◇ *n* factura *f.* ◇ *vt* **-1.** [send invoice to] mandar la factura a **-2.** [prepare invoice for] facturar.
invoke [ɪn'vəʊk] *vt fml* [quote as justification] acogerse a.
involuntary [ɪn'vɒləntrɪ] *adj* involuntario(ria).
involve [ɪn'vɒlv] *vt* **-1.** [entail, require]**: to ~ sthg/doing sthg** conllevar algo/hacer algo; **it ~s working weekends** supone *OR* implica trabajar los fines de semana **-2.** [concern, affect] afectar a **-3.** [make part of sthg]**: to ~ sb (in)** involucrar a alguien (en).
involved [ɪn'vɒlvd] *adj* **-1.** [complex] enrevesado(da), complicado(da) **-2.** [participating]**: to be ~ in** estar metido(da) en; **he didn't want to get ~** no quería tener nada que ver **-3.** [in a relationship]**: to be/get ~ with sb** estar liado(da)/liarse con alguien.
involvement [ɪn'vɒlvmənt] *n* **-1.:** **~ (in)** [crime] implicación *f* (en); [running sthg] participación *f* (en) **-2.** [concern, enthusiasm]**: ~ (in)** compromiso *m* (con) **-3.** [relationship] *(U)* relación *f* sentimental.
inward ['ɪnwəd] ◇ *adj* **-1.** [inner] interno(na) **-2.** [towards the inside] hacia el interior. ◇ *adv US* = inwards.
inwards ['ɪnwədz] *adv* hacia dentro.
in-your-face *adj inf* impactante.
iodine [*UK* 'aɪədiːn, *US* 'aɪədaɪn] *n* yodo *m.*
iota [aɪ'əʊtə] *n* pizca *f*, ápice *m.*
IOU *(abbr of* I owe you*) n* pagaré *f.*
IQ *(abbr of* intelligence quotient*) n* C.I. *m.*
IRA ◇ *n (abbr of* Irish Republican Army*)* IRA *m.* ◇ *n US (abbr of* Individual Retirement Account*)* cuenta *f* de retiro *OR* jubilación individual.
Iran [ɪ'rɑːn] *n* (el) Irán.
Iranian [ɪ'reɪnjən] ◇ *adj* iraní. ◇ *n* [person] iraní *m OR f.*
Iraq [ɪ'rɑːk] *n* (el) Irak.
Iraqi [ɪ'rɑːkɪ] ◇ *adj* iraquí. ◇ *n* [person] iraquí *m OR f.*
irate [aɪ'reɪt] *adj* iracundo(da), airado(da).
IRC *n (abbr of* Internet Relay Chat*)* IRC *m.*
Ireland ['aɪələnd] *n* Irlanda.
iris ['aɪərɪs] *(pl* -es*) n* **-1.** [flower] lirio *m* **-2.** [of eye] iris *m inv.*
Irish ['aɪrɪʃ] ◇ *adj* irlandés(esa). ◇ *n* [language] irlandés *m.* ◇ *npl* [people]**: the ~** los irlandeses.
Irishman ['aɪrɪʃmən] *(pl* -men [-mən]*) n* irlandés *m.*
Irish Sea *n***: the ~** el mar de Irlanda.
Irishwoman ['aɪrɪʃ,wʊmən] *(pl* -women [-,wɪmɪn]*) n* irlandesa *f.*
irksome ['ɜːksəm] *adj* fastidioso(sa).
iron ['aɪən] ◇ *adj lit & fig* de hierro. ◇ *n*

-1. [metal, nutrient] hierro *m* **-2.** [for clothes] plancha *f* **-3.** [golf club] hierro *m.* ◇ *vt & vi* planchar.
 ◆ **iron out** *vt sep fig* [overcome] resolver.
Iron Curtain *n***: the ~** el telón de acero.
ironic(al) [aɪ'rɒnɪk(l)] *adj* irónico(ca); **how ~!** ¡qué ironía!
ironing ['aɪənɪŋ] *n* **-1.** [work] planchado *m* **-2.** [clothes to be ironed] ropa *f* para planchar.
ironing board *n* tabla *f* de planchar.
ironmonger ['aɪən,mʌŋgəʳ] *n UK* ferretero *m*, -ra *f*; **~'s (shop)** ferretería *f*, tlapalería *f Méx.*
irony ['aɪrənɪ] *(pl* -ies*) n* ironía *f.*
irrational [ɪ'ræʃənl] *adj* irracional.
irreconcilable [ɪ,rekən'saɪləbl] *adj* [completely different] irreconciliable.
irregular [ɪ'regjʊləʳ] *adj* [gen & GRAMM] irregular.
irrelevant [ɪ'reləvənt] *adj* irrelevante, que no viene al caso; **that's ~** eso no viene al caso.
irreparable [ɪ'repərəbl] *adj* irreparable, irremediable.
irreplaceable [,ɪrɪ'pleɪsəbl] *adj* irreemplazable, insustituible.
irrepressible [,ɪrɪ'presəbl] *adj* [enthusiasm] irreprimible; [person] imparable.
irresistible [,ɪrɪ'zɪstəbl] *adj* irresistible.
irrespective [,ɪrɪ'spektɪv] ◆ **irrespective of** *prep* independientemente de.
irresponsible [,ɪrɪ'spɒnsəbl] *adj* irresponsable.
irrigate ['ɪrɪgeɪt] *vt* regar, irrigar.
irrigation [,ɪrɪ'geɪʃn] *n* riego *m*, irrigación *f.*
irritable ['ɪrɪtəbl] *adj* [person] irritable; [answer, tone] irritado(da).
irritate ['ɪrɪteɪt] *vt* irritar.
irritating ['ɪrɪteɪtɪŋ] *adj* irritante.
irritation [ɪrɪ'teɪʃn] *n* **-1.** [anger, soreness] irritación *f* **-2.** [cause of anger] motivo *m* de irritación.
IRS *(abbr of* Internal Revenue Service*) n US***: the ~** ≃ Hacienda *f.*
is [ɪz] *3rd person sg* ▷ **be.**
ISDN *(abbr of* Integrated Services Delivery Network*) n* COMPUT RDSI *f.*
Islam ['ɪzlɑːm] *n* [religion] islam *m*, islamismo *m.*
island ['aɪlənd] *n* **-1.** [in water] isla *f* **-2.** [in traffic] isleta *f*, refugio *m.*
islander ['aɪləndəʳ] *n* isleño *m*, -ña *f.*
isle [aɪl] *n* [as part of name] isla *f*; *literary* [island] ínsula *f.*
Isle of Man *n***: the ~** la isla de Man.
Isle of Wight [-waɪt] *n***: the ~** la isla de Wight.
isn't ['ɪznt] = is not.
isobar ['aɪsəbɑːʳ] *n* isobara *f.*

isolate ['aɪsəleɪt] *vt*: to ~ sb (from) [physically] aislar a alguien (de); [socially] marginar a alguien (de).

isolated ['aɪsəleɪtɪd] *adj* aislado(da).

ISP (*abbr of* **Internet Service Provider**) *n* PSI *m*.

Israel ['ɪzreɪəl] *n* Israel.

Israeli [ɪz'reɪlɪ] ◇ *adj* israelí. ◇ *n* israelí *m* OR *f*.

issue ['ɪʃuː] ◇ *n* -1. [important subject] cuestión *f*, tema *m*; **at** ~ **en** cuestión; **to avoid the** ~ evitar el tema; **to make an** ~ **of sthg** darle demasiada importancia a algo - 2. [of newspaper, magazine] número *m* - 3. [of stamps, shares, banknotes] emisión *f*. ◇ *vt* - 1. [statement, warning] hacer público(ca); [decree] promulgar - 2. [stamps, shares, banknotes] emitir, poner en circulación - 3. [give]: **to** ~ **sthg to sb, to** ~ **sb with sthg** [passport, document] expedir algo a alguien; [ticket] proporcionar algo a alguien.

isthmus ['ɪsməs] *n* istmo *m*.

it [ɪt] *pron* - 1. [referring to specific thing or person - subj] él *m*, ella *f*; [- direct object] lo *m*, la *f*; [- indirect object] le; ~ **is in my hand** está en mi mano; **did you find** ~? ¿lo encontraste?; **give** ~ **to me** dámelo; **he gave** ~ **a kick** le dio una patada - 2. *(with prepositions)* él *m*, ella *f*; [meaning 'this matter' etc] ello; **as if his life depended on** ~ como si le fuera la vida en ello; **in** ~ dentro; **have you been to** ~ **before**? ¿has estado antes?; **on** ~ encima; **to talk about** ~ hablar de él/ella/ello; **under/beneath** ~ debajo; **beside** ~ al lado; **from/of** ~ de él/ella/ello; **over** ~ por encima - 3. *(impersonal use)*: ~ **was raining** llovía; ~ **is cold today** hace frío hoy; ~'s **two o'clock** son las dos; **who is** ~? - ~'s **Mary/me** ¿quién es? - soy Mary/yo; **what day is** ~? ¿a qué (día) estamos hoy?; ~'s **Monday** es lunes; ~ **says here that ...** aquí dice que ...

IT *n abbr of* **information technology**.

Italian [ɪ'tæljən] ◇ *adj* italiano(na). ◇ *n* - 1. [person] italiano *m*, -na *f* - 2. [language] italiano *m*.

italic [ɪ'tælɪk] *adj* cursiva.

◆ **italics** *npl* cursiva *f*.

Italy ['ɪtəlɪ] *n* Italia.

itch [ɪtʃ] ◇ *n* picor *m*, picazón *f*. ◇ *vi* - 1. [be itchy - person] tener picazón; [- arm, leg etc] picar; **my arm is** ~**ing** me pica el brazo - 2. *fig* [be impatient]: **to be** ~**ing to do sthg** estar deseando hacer algo.

itchy ['ɪtʃɪ] *(compar* -**ier**, *superl* -**iest**) *adj* [garment, material] que pica; **I've got an** ~ **arm** me pica el brazo.

it'd ['ɪtəd] = **it would, it had**.

item ['aɪtəm] *n* - 1. [in collection] artículo *m*; [on list, agenda] punto *m* - 2. [article in newspaper] artículo *m*; **news** ~ noticia *f*.

itemize, -ise ['aɪtəmaɪz] *vt* detallar.

itinerary [aɪ'tɪnərərɪ] *(pl* -**ies**) *n* itinerario *m*.

it'll [ɪtl] = **it will**.

its [ɪts] *poss adj* su, sus *(pl)*; **the dog broke** ~ **leg** el perro se rompió la pata.

it's [ɪts] = **it is, it has**.

itself [ɪt'self] *pron* - 1. *(reflexive)* se; *(after prep)* sí mismo(ma); **with** ~ consigo mismo(ma) - 2. *(for emphasis)*: **the town** ~ **is lovely** el pueblo en sí es muy bonito; **in** ~ en sí; **it's simplicity** ~ es la sencillez misma.

ITV (*abbr of* **Independent Television**) *n* ITV *f*, canal privado de televisión en Gran Bretaña.

I've [aɪv] = **I have**.

ivory ['aɪvərɪ] *n* marfil *m*.

ivy ['aɪvɪ] *n* hiedra *f*.

Ivy League *n* US grupo de ocho prestigiosas universidades del este de los EE.UU.

j (*pl* **j's** OR **js**), **J** (*pl* **J's** OR **Js**) [dʒeɪ] *n* [letter] j *f*, J *f*.

jab [dʒæb] *(pt & pp* -**bed**, *cont* -**bing**) ◇ *n* - 1. [with elbow] codazo *m*; [in boxing] golpe *m* corto - 2. *UK inf* [injection] pinchazo *m*. ◇ *vt*: **to** ~ **sthg into** clavar algo en; **to** ~ **sthg at** apuntarle algo a.

jabber ['dʒæbə'] *vi* charlotear.

jack [dʒæk] *n* - 1. [device] gato *m* - 2. ELEC [plug] clavija *f*; [socket] clavijero *m* - 3. [French deck playing card] jota *f*; [Spanish deck playing card] ≃ sota *f*.

◆ **jack up** *vt sep* - 1. [lift with a jack] levantar con gato - 2. [force up] subir.

jackal ['dʒækəl] *n* chacal *m*.

jackdaw ['dʒækdɔː] *n* grajilla *f*.

jacket ['dʒækɪt] *n* - 1. [garment] chaqueta *f*, americana *f*, saco *m Amér* - 2. [potato skin] piel *f* - 3. [book cover] sobrecubierta *f* - 4. *US* [of record] cubierta *f*.

jacket potato *n* patata *f* asada con piel.

jackhammer ['dʒæk,hæmə'] *n US* martillo *m* neumático.

jack knife *n* navaja *f*.

◆ **jack-knife** *vi*: **the lorry** ~**d** derrapó la parte delantera del camión.

jack plug *n* clavija *f*.

jackpot ['dʒækpɒt] *n* (premio *m*) gordo *m*.

jaded ['dʒeɪdɪd] *adj* [tired] agotado(da);

[bored] hastiado(da).

jagged ['dʒægɪd] *adj* dentado(da).

jail [dʒeɪl] ◇ *n* cárcel *f*; **in ~** en la cárcel. ◇ *vt* encarcelar.

jailer ['dʒeɪlə'] *n* carcelero *m*, -ra *f*.

jam [dʒæm] (*pt & pp* **-med**, *cont* **-ming**) ◇ *n* **- 1.** [preserve] mermelada *f* **- 2.** [of traffic] embotellamiento *m*, atasco *m* **- 3.** MUS jam session *f*, *sesión improvisada de jazz o rock* **- 4.** *inf* [difficult situation]: **to get into/be in a ~** meterse/estar en un apuro. ◇ *vt* **- 1.** [place roughly] meter a la fuerza **- 2.** [fix] sujetar; **~ the door shut** atranca la puerta **- 3.** [pack tightly] apiñar **- 4.** [fill] abarrotar, atestar **- 5.** TELEC bloquear **- 6.** [cause to stick] atascar; **it's ~ med** se ha atascado **- 7.** RADIO interferir. ◇ *vi* **- 1.** [stick] atascarse **- 2.** MUS improvisar.

Jamaica [dʒə'meɪkə] *n* Jamaica.

jam-packed [-'pækt] *adj inf* a tope, atestado(da).

jangle ['dʒæŋgl] *vi* tintinear.

janitor ['dʒænɪtə'] *n* US & Scot conserje *m*, portero *m*.

January ['dʒænjʊərɪ] *n* enero *m*; *see also* **September**.

Japan [dʒə'pæn] *n* (el) Japón.

Japanese [,dʒæpə'niːz] (*pl inv*) ◇ *adj* japonés(esa). ◇ *n* [language] japonés *m*. ◇ *npl*: **the ~** los japoneses.

jar [dʒɑː'] (*pt & pp* **-red**, *cont* **-ring**) ◇ *n* tarro *m*. ◇ *vt* [shake] sacudir. ◇ *vi* **- 1.** [upset]: **to ~ (on sb)** poner los nervios de punta (a alguien) **- 2.** [clash - opinions] discordar; [- colours] desentonar.

jargon ['dʒɑːgən] *n* jerga *f*.

jaundice ['dʒɔːndɪs] *n* ictericia *f*.

jaundiced ['dʒɔːndɪst] *adj fig* [attitude, view] desencantado(da).

jaunt [dʒɔːnt] *n* excursión *f*.

jaunty ['dʒɔːntɪ] (*compar* **-ier**, *superl* **-iest**) *adj* [hat, wave] airoso(sa); [person] vivaz, desenvuelto(ta).

javelin ['dʒævlɪn] *n* jabalina *f*.

jaw [dʒɔː] *n* [of person, animal] mandíbula *f*.

jawbone ['dʒɔːbəʊn] *n* [of person, animal] mandíbula *f*, maxilar *m*.

jay [dʒeɪ] *n* arrendajo *m*.

jaywalker ['dʒeɪwɔːkə'] *n* peatón *m* imprudente.

jazz [dʒæz] *n* MUS jazz *m*.

◆ **jazz up** *vt sep inf* alegrar, avivar.

jazzy ['dʒæzɪ] (*compar* **-ier**, *superl* **-iest**) *adj* [bright] llamativo(va).

jealous ['dʒeləs] *adj* **- 1.** [envious]: **to be ~ (of)** tener celos OR estar celoso(sa) (de) **- 2.** [possessive]: **to be ~ (of)** ser celoso(sa) (de).

jealousy ['dʒeləsɪ] *n* (U) celos *mpl*.

jeans [dʒiːnz] *npl* vaqueros *mpl*, bluyínes *mpl* Amér.

jeep [dʒiːp] *n* jeep *m*, campero *m* Amér.

jeer [dʒɪə'] ◇ *vt* [boo] abuchear; [mock] mofarse de. ◇ *vi*: **to ~ (at sb)** [boo] abuchear (a alguien); [mock] mofarse (de alguien).

Jehovah's Witness [dʒɪ'həʊvəz-] *n* testigo *m* OR *f* de Jehová.

Jell-O® ['dʒeləʊ] *n* US jalea *f*, gelatina *f*.

jelly ['dʒelɪ] (*pl* **-ies**) *n* **- 1.** [dessert] jalea *f*, gelatina *f* **- 2.** [jam] mermelada *f*.

jellyfish ['dʒelɪfɪʃ] (*pl inv* OR **-es**) *n* medusa *f*.

jeopardize, -ise ['dʒepədaɪz] *vt* poner en peligro, arriesgar.

jerk [dʒɜːk] ◇ *n* **- 1.** [of head] movimiento *m* brusco; [of arm] tirón *m*; [of vehicle] sacudida *f* **- 2.** *v inf* [fool] idiota *m* OR *f*, majadero *m*, -ra *f*. ◇ *vi* [person] saltar; [vehicle] dar sacudidas.

jersey ['dʒɜːzɪ] (*pl* **jerseys**) *n* **- 1.** [sweater] jersey *m* **- 2.** [in cycling] maillot *m*.

Jersey ['dʒɜːzɪ] *n* Jersey.

jest [dʒest] *n*: **in ~** en broma.

Jesus (Christ) ['dʒiːzəs-] ◇ *n* Jesús *m*, Jesucristo *m*. ◇ *excl inf* ¡Santo Dios!

jet [dʒet] ◇ *n* **- 1.** [aircraft] reactor *m* **- 2.** [stream] chorro *m* **- 3.** [nozzle, outlet] boquilla *f*.

jet-black *adj* negro(gra) azabache.

jet engine *n* reactor *m*.

jetfoil ['dʒetfɔɪl] *n* hidroplano *m*.

jet lag *n* desfase *m* horario.

jetsam ['dʒetsəm] ⊳ **flotsam**.

jettison ['dʒetɪsən] *vt* [cargo] deshacerse de; *fig* [ideas] desechar.

jetty ['dʒetɪ] (*pl* **-ies**) *n* embarcadero *m*, malecón *m*.

Jew [dʒuː] *n* judío *m*, -a *f*.

jewel ['dʒuːəl] *n* **- 1.** [gemstone] piedra *f* preciosa **- 2.** [jewellery] joya *f*.

jeweller UK, **jeweler** US ['dʒuːələ'] *n* joyero *m*, -ra *f*; **~ 's (shop)** joyería *f*.

jewellery UK, **jewelry** US ['dʒuːəlrɪ] *n* (U) joyas *fpl*, alhajas *fpl*.

Jewess ['dʒuːɪs] *n* judía *f*.

Jewish ['dʒuːɪʃ] *adj* judío(a).

jib [dʒɪb] *n* **- 1.** [beam] aguilón *m* **- 2.** [sail] foque *m*.

jibe [dʒaɪb] *n* pulla *f*, burla *f*.

jiffy ['dʒɪfɪ] *n inf*: **in a ~** en un segundo.

Jiffy bag® *n* sobre *m* acolchado.

jig [dʒɪg] *n* giga *f*.

jigsaw (puzzle) ['dʒɪgsɔː-] *n* rompecabezas *m inv*, puzzle *m*.

jilt [dʒɪlt] *vt* dejar plantado(da).

jingle ['dʒɪŋgl] ◇ *n* **- 1.** [sound] tintineo *m* **- 2.** [song] sintonía *f* (*de anuncio publicitario*). ◇ *vi* tintinear.

jinx [dʒɪŋks] *n* gafe *m*.

jitters ['dʒɪtəz] *npl inf*: **to have the ~** estar como un flan.

job [dʒɒb] *n* **-1.** [paid employment] trabajo *m*, empleo *m* **-2.** [task & COMPUT] tarea *f* **-3.** [difficult task]: **we had a ~ doing it** nos costó mucho hacerlo **-4.** [function] cometido *m*, deber *m* **-5.** *UK phr*: **it's a good ~ that ... inf** menos mal que ...; **that's just the ~ inf** eso me viene de perilla.

job centre *n UK* oficina *f* de empleo.

jobless ['dʒɒblɪs] *adj* desempleado(da).

Job Seekers Allowance *n UK* subsidio *m* de desempleo.

jobsharing ['dʒɒbʃeərɪŋ] *n (U)* empleo *m* compartido.

jockey ['dʒɒkɪ] *(pl -s)* ⟨⟩ *n* jockey *m*, jinete *m*. ⟨⟩ *vi*: **to ~ for position** competir por colocarse en mejor posición.

jocular ['dʒɒkjʊlər] *adj* **-1.** [cheerful] bromista **-2.** [funny] jocoso(sa).

jodhpurs ['dʒɒdpəz] *npl* pantalón *m* de montar.

jog [dʒɒg] *(pt & pp -ged, cont -ging)* ⟨⟩ *n* trote *m*; **to go for a ~** hacer footing. ⟨⟩ *vt* golpear ligeramente; **to ~ sb's memory** refrescar la memoria a alguien. ⟨⟩ *vi* hacer footing.

jogging ['dʒɒgɪŋ] *n* footing *m*.

john [dʒɒn] *n US inf* [toilet] wáter *m*.

join [dʒɔɪn] ⟨⟩ *n* juntura *f*. ⟨⟩ *vt* **-1.** [unite] unir, juntar, empatar *Amér* **-2.** [get together with] reunirse con **-3.** [become a member of - political party, trade union] afiliarse a; [- club] hacerse socio de; [- army] alistarse en **-4.** [take part in] unirse a; **to ~ the queue** *UK*, **to ~ the line** *US* meterse en la cola. ⟨⟩ *vi* **-1.** [rivers] confluir; [edges, pieces] unirse, juntarse **-2.** [become a member of - political party, trade union] afiliarse; [- of club] hacerse socio; [- of army] alistarse.

◆ **join in** ⟨⟩ *vt fus* participar en, tomar parte en. ⟨⟩ *vi* participar, tomar parte.

◆ **join up** *vi* MIL alistarse.

joiner ['dʒɔɪnər] *n* carpintero *m*.

joinery ['dʒɔɪnərɪ] *n* carpintería *f*.

joint [dʒɔɪnt] ⟨⟩ *adj* [responsibility] compartido(da); [effort] conjunto(ta); **~ owner** copropietario *m*, -ria *f*. ⟨⟩ *n* **-1.** ANAT articulación *f* **-2.** [place where things are joined] juntura *f*, junta *f*, empate *m Amér* **-3.** *UK* [of meat - uncooked] corte *m* para asar; [- cooked] asado *m* **-4.** *inf pej* [place] antro *m*, garito *m* **-5.** *inf* [cannabis cigarette] porro *m*.

joint account *n* cuenta *f* conjunta.

joint leader *n* colíder *m* OR *f*.

jointly ['dʒɔɪntlɪ] *adv* conjuntamente.

joist [dʒɔɪst] *n* vigueta *f*.

joke [dʒəʊk] ⟨⟩ *n* [funny story] chiste *m*; [funny action] broma *f*; **to play a ~ on sb** gastarle una broma a alguien; **it's no ~** [not easy] no es (nada) fácil. ⟨⟩ *vi*

bromear; **you're joking** estás de broma; **I'm not joking** hablo en serio; **to ~ about sthg/with sb** bromear acerca de algo/con alguien.

joker ['dʒəʊkər] *n* **-1.** [funny person] bromista *m* OR *f* **-2.** [useless person] inútil *m* OR *f* **-3.** [playing card] comodín *m*.

jolly ['dʒɒlɪ] *(compar -ier, superl -iest)* ⟨⟩ *adj* [person, laugh] alegre; [time] divertido(da). ⟨⟩ *adv UK inf* muy.

jolt [dʒəʊlt] ⟨⟩ *n* **-1.** *lit* sacudida *f* **-2.** *fig* susto *m*. ⟨⟩ *vt* [jerk] sacudir, zarandear.

Jordan ['dʒɔːdn] *n* Jordania *f*; **the (River) ~** el (río) Jordán.

jostle ['dʒɒsl] ⟨⟩ *vt* empujar, dar empujones a. ⟨⟩ *vi* empujar, dar empujones.

jot [dʒɒt] *(pt & pp -ted, cont -ting)* *n* pizca *f*.

◆ **jot down** *vt sep* apuntar, anotar.

jotter ['dʒɒtər] *n* bloc *m*.

journal ['dʒɜːnl] *n* **-1.** [magazine] revista *f*, boletín *m* **-2.** [diary] diario *m*.

journalism ['dʒɜːnəlɪzm] *n* periodismo *m*.

journalist ['dʒɜːnəlɪst] *n* periodista *m* OR *f*.

journey ['dʒɜːnɪ] *(pl -s)* ⟨⟩ *n* viaje *m*. ⟨⟩ *vi* viajar.

jovial ['dʒəʊvjəl] *adj* jovial.

jowls [dʒaʊlz] *npl* carrillos *mpl*.

joy [dʒɔɪ] *n* **-1.** [happiness] alegría *f*, regocijo *m* **-2.** [cause of joy] placer *m*, deleite *m*.

joyful ['dʒɔɪfʊl] *adj* alegre.

joyous ['dʒɔɪəs] *adj* jubiloso(sa).

joyride ['dʒɔɪraɪd] *(pt -rode, pp -ridden)* ⟨⟩ *n* vuelta *f* en un coche robado. ⟨⟩ *vi* darse una vuelta en un coche robado.

joystick ['dʒɔɪstɪk] *n* [of aircraft] palanca *f* de mando; [for video games, computers] joystick *m*.

JP *n abbr of* **Justice of the Peace**.

Jr. *US (abbr of Junior)* jr; **Mark Andrews ~** Mark Andrews, hijo.

jubilant ['dʒuːbɪlənt] *adj* [person] jubiloso(sa); [shout] alborozado(da).

jubilee ['dʒuːbɪliː] *n* aniversario *m*.

judge [dʒʌdʒ] ⟨⟩ *n* [gen & JUR] juez *m* OR *f*; **to be a good ~ of character** tener buen ojo para la gente. ⟨⟩ *vt* **-1.** [gen & JUR] juzgar **-2.** [age, distance] calcular. ⟨⟩ *vi* juzgar; **to ~ from** OR **by, judging from** OR **by** a juzgar por.

judg(e)ment ['dʒʌdʒmənt] *n* **-1.** JUR fallo *m*, sentencia *f* **-2.** [opinion] juicio *m*; **to pass ~ (on sb/sthg)** pronunciarse (sobre alguien/algo) **-3.** [ability to form opinion] juicio *m*.

judiciary [dʒuːˈdɪʃərɪ] *n*: **the ~** [part of government] el poder judicial; [judges] la judicatura.

judicious [dʒuːˈdɪʃəs] *adj* juicioso(sa).

judo ['dʒuːdəʊ] *n* judo *m*.

jug [dʒʌg] *n* jarra *f*.

juggernaut ['dʒʌgənɔːt] *n* camión *m* grande.

juggle ['dʒʌgl] *vt* -**1.** [throw] hacer juegos malabares con - **2.** [rearrange] jugar con. *vi* hacer juegos malabares.

juggler ['dʒʌglər] *n* malabarista *m* OR *f*.

jugular (vein) ['dʒʌgjʊlər-] *n* yugular *f*.

juice [dʒuːs] *n* -**1.** [from fruit, vegetables] zumo *m* - **2.** [from meat] jugo *m*.

juicer ['dʒuːsər] *n* exprimidor *m*.

juicy ['dʒuːsɪ] (*compar* -**ier**, *superl* -**iest**) *adj* -**1.** [gen] jugoso(sa) - **2.** *inf* [scandalous] picante.

jukebox ['dʒuːkbɒks] *n* máquina *f* de discos.

July [dʒuː'laɪ] *n* julio *m*; *see also* **September**.

jumble ['dʒʌmbl] *n* [mixture] revoltijo *m*. *vt* : to ~ **(up)** revolver.

jumble sale *n UK* rastrillo *m* benéfico.

jumbo jet ['dʒʌmbəʊ-] *n* jumbo *m*.

jumbo-sized ['dʒʌmbəʊsaɪzd] *adj* gigante, de tamaño familiar.

jump [dʒʌmp] *n* -**1.** [act of jumping] salto *m* - **2.** [start, surprised movement] sobresalto *m* - **3.** [fence in horsejumping] obstáculo *m* - **4.** [rapid increase] incremento *m*, salto *m*. *vt* -**1.** [cross by jumping] saltar - **2.** [attack] asaltar - **3.** [miss out] saltarse. *vi* -**1.** [spring] saltar - **2.** [make a sudden movement] sobresaltarse - **3.** [increase rapidly] aumentar de golpe.

◆ **jump at** *vt fus* no dejar escapar.

jumper ['dʒʌmpər] *n* -**1.** *UK* [pullover] jersey *m*, chomba *f RP*, chompa *f Andes* - **2.** *US* [dress] pichi *m*.

jumper cables *npl US* cables *mpl* de empalme *(de batería)*.

jump leads *npl* cables *mpl* de empalme (de batería).

jump-start *vt* [by pushing] arrancar empujando; [using jump leads] arrancar haciendo un puente.

jumpsuit ['dʒʌmpsuːt] *n* mono *m*.

jumpy ['dʒʌmpɪ] (*compar* -**ier**, *superl* -**iest**) *adj* inquieto(ta).

junction ['dʒʌŋkʃn] *n* [of roads] cruce *m*; *UK* [on motorway] salida *f*; [of railway lines] empalme *m*.

June [dʒuːn] *n* junio *m*; *see also* **September**.

jungle ['dʒʌŋgl] *n lit & fig* selva *f*.

junior ['dʒuːnjər] *adj* -**1.** [partner, member] de menor antigüedad, júnior (*inv*); [officer] subalterno(na) - **2.** [after name]: **Mark Andrews** ~ **Mark Andrews, hijo.** *n* -**1.** [person of lower rank] subalterno *m*, -na *f* - **2.** [younger person]: **he's my** ~ soy mayor que él - **3.** *US* SCH & UNIV alumno de penúltimo año.

junior high school *n US* ≃ instituto *m* de bachillerato *(13-15 años).*

junior school *n UK* ≃ escuela *f* primaria.

junk [dʒʌŋk] *n inf* (*U*) [unwanted things] trastos *mpl*.

junk food *n pej* comida *f* basura.

junkie ['dʒʌŋkɪ] *n inf* yonqui *m* OR *f*.

junk mail *n* (*U*) *pej* propaganda *f* (*por correo*).

junk shop *n* tienda *f* de objetos usados, cambalache *m RP*.

Jupiter ['dʒuːpɪtər] *n* Júpiter *m*.

jurisdiction [ˌdʒʊərɪs'dɪkʃn] *n* jurisdicción *f*.

juror ['dʒʊərər] *n* jurado *m*.

jury ['dʒʊərɪ] (*pl* -**ies**) *n* jurado *m*; **the** ~ **is still out on that** eso no está por ver.

just [dʒʌst] *adv* -**1.** [recently]: **he has** ~ **left/moved** acaba de salir/mudarse - **2.** [at that moment]: **we were** ~ **leaving when ...** justo íbamos a salir cuando ...; **I'm** ~ **about to do it** voy a hacerlo ahora; **I couldn't do it** ~ **then** no lo podía hacer en aquel momento; ~ **as I was leaving** justo en el momento en que salía; ~ **recently** hace muy poco; ~ **yesterday** ayer mismo - **3.** [only, simply] sólo, solamente; **he's** ~ **a child** no es más que un niño; ~ **add water** simplemente añada un poco de agua; **if you need help,** ~ **ask** si necesitas ayuda, no tienes más que pedirla; ~ **a minute** OR **moment** OR **second** un momento - **4.** [almost not] apenas; **I (only)** ~ **did it** conseguí hacerlo por muy poco - **5.** [for emphasis]: **I** ~ **know it!** ¡estoy seguro!; ~ **imagine!** ¡imagínate!; ~ **look what you've done!** ¡mira lo que has hecho! - **6.** [exactly, precisely] exactamente, precisamente; ~ **what I need** justo lo que necesito; ~ **here/there** aquí/allí mismo - **7.** [in requests]: **could you** ~ **open your mouth?** ¿podrías abrir la boca un momento, por favor? *adj* justo(ta).

◆ **just about** *adv* -**1.** [nearly] casi - **2.** [more or less] más o menos.

◆ **just as** *adv* : ~ **as ... as** tan ... como, igual de ... que.

◆ **just now** *adv* -**1.** [a short time ago] hace un momento - **2.** [at this moment] justo ahora, ahora mismo.

justice ['dʒʌstɪs] *n* justicia *f*; **to bring sb to** ~ llevar a alguien ante los tribunales.

Justice of the Peace (*pl* **Justices of the Peace**) *n* juez *m* OR *f* de paz.

justifiable ['dʒʌstɪfaɪəbl] *adj* justificable.

justify ['dʒʌstɪfaɪ] (*pt* & *pp* -**ied**) *vt* -**1.** [explain]: **to** ~ **(sthg/doing sthg)** justificar (algo/el haber hecho algo) - **2.** TYPO justificar.

justly ['dʒʌstlɪ] *adv* justamente.

jut [dʒʌt] (*pt* & *pp* -**ted**, *cont* -**ting**) *vi*: **to** ~ **(out)** sobresalir.

juvenile ['dʒuːvənaɪl] *adj* -**1.** JUR juvenil - **2.** *pej* [childish] infantil. *n* JUR menor *m* OR *f* (de edad).

juxtapose [ˌdʒʌkstə'pəʊz] *vt* : **to** ~ **sthg (with)** yuxtaponer algo (a).

k (*pl* **k's** OR **ks**), **K** (*pl* **K's** OR **Ks**) [keɪ] *n* [letter] k *f*, K *f*.

➤ **K - 1.** (*abbr of* **kilobyte(s)**) K - **2.** *abbr of* **thousand**; **40 ~** cuarenta mil.

kaleidoscope [kə'laɪdəskəʊp] *n lit & fig* caleidoscopio *m*, calidoscopio *m*.

kangaroo [ˌkæŋgə'ruː] *n* canguro *m*.

kaput [kə'pʊt] *adj inf* escacharrado(da).

karaoke [kɑːrə'əʊki] *n* karaoke *m*.

karat ['kærət] *n US* quilate *m*.

karate [kə'rɑːtɪ] *n* kárate *m*.

karting ['kɑːtɪŋ] *n* karting *m*.

kayak ['kaɪæk] *n* kayac *m*.

Kb *n* COMPUT Kb.

kcal (*abbr of* **kilocalorie**) kcal.

kebab [kɪ'bæb] *n* pincho *m* moruno, brocheta *f*.

keel [kiːl] *n* quilla *f*; **on an even ~** en equilibrio estable.

keen [kiːn] *adj* - **1.** [enthusiastic] entusiasta; **to be ~ on sthg** ser aficionado(da) a algo; **she is ~ on you** tú le gustas; **I'm not ~ on the idea** no me entusiasma la idea; **to be ~ to do** OR **on doing sthg** tener ganas de hacer algo - **2.** [intense - interest, desire] profundo(da); [-competition] reñido(da) - **3.** [sharp - sense of smell, hearing, vision] agudo(da); [-eye, ear] fino(na); [-mind] agudo, penetrante.

keep [kiːp] (*pt & pp* **kept**) ◇ *vt* - **1.** [maintain in a particular place or state or position] mantener; **to ~ sb waiting/awake** tener a alguien esperando/despierto; **to ~ sb talking** darle conversación a alguien - **2.** [retain] quedarse con; **~ the change** quédese con la vuelta - **3.** [put aside, store] guardar; **to ~ sthg for sb** guardar algo para alguien - **4.** [prevent]: **to ~ sb/sthg from doing sthg** impedir a alguien/algo hacer algo - **5.** [detain] detener - **6.** [fulfil, observe - appointment] acudir a; [-promise, vow] cumplir - **7.** [not disclose]: **to ~ sthg from sb** ocultar algo a alguien; **to ~ sthg to o.s.** no contarle algo a nadie - **8.** [in writing - record, account] llevar; [-diary] escribir; [-note] tomar - **9.** [own - animals, shop] tener. ◇ *vi* - **1.** [remain] mantenerse; **to ~ quiet** callarse; **to**

~ still estarse quieto - **2.** [continue]: **to ~ doing sthg** [repeatedly] no dejar de hacer algo; [without stopping] continuar OR seguir haciendo algo; **to ~ going** seguir adelante - **3.** [continue in a particular direction] continuar, seguir; **to ~ left/right** circular por la izquierda/derecha - **4.** [food] conservarse - **5.** *UK* [be in a particular state of health] estar, andar. ◇ *n* [food, board etc] sustento *m*; **to earn one's ~** ganarse el pan.

➤ **keeps** *n*: **for ~s** para siempre.

➤ **keep back** ◇ *vt sep* [information] ocultar; [money, salary] retener. ◇ *vi* no acercarse.

➤ **keep off** *vt fus* [subject] evitar; **'~ off the grass'** 'no pisar la hierba'.

➤ **keep on** ◇ *vi* - **1.** [continue]: **to ~ on doing sthg** [continue to do] continuar OR seguir haciendo algo; [do repeatedly] no dejar de hacer algo - **2.** [talk incessantly]: **to ~ on (about)** seguir dale que te pego (con). ◇ *vt sep* [not sack] mantener en el puesto.

➤ **keep out** ◇ *vt sep* no dejar pasar. ◇ *vi*: **'~ out'** 'prohibida la entrada'.

➤ **keep to** *vt fus* - **1.** [follow] ceñirse a - **2.** [fulfil, meet] cumplir.

➤ **keep up** ◇ *vt sep* mantener. ◇ *vi* [maintain pace, level etc] mantener el ritmo; **to ~ up with sb/sthg** seguir el ritmo de alguien/algo.

keeper ['kiːpə'] *n* - **1.** [of park, zoo] guarda *m* OR *f* - **2.** *UK* [goalkeeper] guardameta *m*.

keep-fit *n UK* (U) ejercicios *mpl* de mantenimiento.

keeping ['kiːpɪŋ] *n* - **1.** [care]: **in sb's ~** al cuidado de alguien; **in safe ~** en lugar seguro - **2.** [conformity, harmony]: **in/out of ~ (with)** de acuerdo/en desacuerdo (con).

keepsake ['kiːpseɪk] *n* recuerdo *m*.

keg [keg] *n* barrilete *m*.

kennel ['kenl] *n* - **1.** [for dog] caseta *f* del perro - **2.** *US* = **kennels**.

➤ **kennels** *npl UK* residencia *f* para perros.

Kenya ['kenjə] *n* Kenia.

Kenyan ['kenjən] ◇ *adj* keniano(na). ◇ *n* keniano *m*, -na *f*.

kept [kept] *pt & pp* ▷ **keep**.

kerb [kɜːb] *n UK* bordillo *m*, cordón *m* de la vereda *RP*, cuneta *f Chile*, bordo *m* de la banqueta *Méx*, sardinel *m Col*.

kernel ['kɜːnl] *n* [of nut, fruit] pepita *f*.

kerosene ['kerəsiːn] *n* queroseno *m*.

kestrel ['kestrəl] *n* cernícalo *m*.

ketchup ['ketʃəp] *n* catsup *m*.

kettle ['ketl] *n* tetera *f* para hervir, hervidor *m*; **to put the ~ on** poner el agua a hervir.

key [kiː] ◇ *n* - **1.** [for lock] llave *f* - **2.** [of typewriter, computer, piano] tecla *f* - **3.** [explanatory list] clave *f* - **4.** [solution, answer]

the ~ (to) la clave (de) **- 5.** MUS [scale of notes] tono *m*; **off ~** desafinado(da). ◇ *adj* clave *(inv)*.

keyboard ['ki:bɔ:d] *n* teclado *m*.

keyed up [ki:d-] *adj* nervioso(sa).

keyhole ['ki:həʊl] *n* ojo *m* de la cerradura.

keyhole surgery *n* cirugía *f* endoscópica.

keynote ['ki:nəʊt] *comp*: **~ speech** discurso *m* principal.

keypad ['ki:pæd] *n* teclado *m* numérico.

key ring *n* llavero *m*.

kg *(abbr of* **kilogram)** kg *m*.

khaki ['kɑ:kɪ] ◇ *adj* caqui. ◇ *n* caqui *m*.
➤ **khakis** *npl* US pantalones *mpl* de soldado.

kick [kɪk] ◇ *n* **- 1.** [from person] patada *f*, puntapié *m*; [from animal] coz *f* **- 2.** *inf* [excitement]: **to get a ~ from sthg** disfrutar con algo. ◇ *vt* **- 1.** [hit once with foot] dar una patada OR un puntapié a; [hit repeatedly with foot] dar patadas OR puntapiés a **- 2.** *inf* [give up] dejar. ◇ *vi* [person] dar patadas; [animal] dar coces, cocear.
➤ **kick about, kick around** *vi* UK *inf* andar rondando por ahí.
➤ **kick back** *vi* US [relax] relajarse.
➤ **kick in** *vi* [drug] surtir efecto.
➤ **kick off** *vi* [football] hacer el saque inicial.
➤ **kick out** *vt sep inf* echar, poner de patitas en la calle.

kid [kɪd] *(pt & pp* **-ded,** *cont* **-ding)** ◇ *n* **- 1.** *inf* [child] crío *m*, -a *f*, chavalín *m*, -ina *f* **- 2.** *inf* [young person] chico *m*, -ca *f*, chaval *m*, -la *f*, pibe *m*, -ba *f Amér* **- 3.** [young goat] cabrito *m* **- 4.** [leather] cabritilla *f.* ◇ *comp inf* [brother, sister] menor, pequeño(ña). ◇ *vt inf* **- 1.** [tease] tomar el pelo a **- 2.** [delude]: **to ~ o.s.** hacerse ilusiones **- 2.** ◇ *vi inf*: **to be kidding** estar de broma.

kidnap ['kɪdnæp] *(UK pt & pp* **-ped,** *cont* **-ping,** *US pt & pp* **-ed,** *cont* **-ing)** *vt* secuestrar, raptar, plagiar *Amér.*

kidnapper UK, **kidnaper** US ['kɪdnæpə'] *n* secuestrador *m*, -ra *f*, raptor *m*, -ra *f*, plagiario *m*, -ria *f Amér.*

kidnapping UK, **kidnaping** US ['kɪdnæpɪŋ] *n* secuestro *m*, rapto *m*, plagio *m Amér.*

kidney ['kɪdnɪ] *(pl* **kidneys)** *n* ANAT & CULIN riñón *m.*

kidney bean *n* judía *f* pinta, frijol *m Amér* OR poroto *m Andes, CSur* rojo *(con forma de riñón)*, caraota *f* roja *(con forma de riñón) Ven.*

kill [kɪl] ◇ *vt* **- 1.** [gen] matar; **he was ~ed in an accident** murió en un accidente **- 2.** *fig* [cause to end, fail] poner fin a **- 3.** [occupy]: **to ~ time** matar el tiempo. ◇ *vi* matar. ◇ *n* [killing]: **we watched the wolves move in for the ~** vimos cómo los lobos se preparaban para caer sobre su presa.

killer ['kɪlə'] *n* [person, animal] asesino *m*, -na *f.*

killing ['kɪlɪŋ] *n* asesinato *m.*

killjoy ['kɪldʒɔɪ] *n* aguafiestas *m y f inv.*

kiln [kɪln] *n* horno *m.*

kilo ['ki:ləʊ] *(pl* **-s)** *(abbr of* **kilogram)** *n* kilo *m.*

kilobyte ['kɪləbaɪt] *n* kilobyte *m.*

kilogram(me) ['kɪləgræm] *n* kilogramo *m.*

kilohertz ['kɪləhɜ:tz] *(pl inv)* *n* kilohercio *m.*

kilometre UK ['kɪlə,mi:tə'], **kilometer** US [kɪ'lɒmɪtə'] *n* kilómetro *m.*

kilowatt ['kɪləwɒt] *n* kilovatio *m.*

kilt [kɪlt] *n* falda *f* escocesa.

kin [kɪn] ▷ **kith.**

kind [kaɪnd] ◇ *adj* [person, gesture] amable; [thought] considerado(da). ◇ *n* tipo *m*, clase *f*; **a ~ of** una especie de; **all ~ of** todo tipo de; **~ of** *Esp US inf* bastante; **nothing of the ~** nada por el estilo; **they're two of a ~** son tal para cual; **in ~** [payment] en especie.

kindergarten ['kɪndə,gɑ:tn] *n* jardín *m* de infancia.

kind-hearted [-'hɑ:tɪd] *adj* bondadoso(sa).

kindle ['kɪndl] *vt* **- 1.** [fire] encender **- 2.** *fig* [idea, feeling] despertar.

kindly ['kaɪndlɪ] *(compar* **-ier,** *superl* **-iest)** ◇ *adj* amable, bondadoso(sa). ◇ *adv* **- 1.** [gently, favourably] amablemente **- 2.** [please]: **will you ~ ...?** ¿sería tan amable de ...?

kindness ['kaɪndnɪs] *n* **- 1.** [gentleness] amabilidad *f* **- 2.** [helpful act] favor *m.*

kindred ['kɪndrɪd] *adj* [similar] afín; **~ spirit** alma *f* gemela.

king [kɪŋ] *n* rey *m.*

kingdom ['kɪŋdəm] *n* reino *m.*

kingfisher ['kɪŋ,fɪʃə'] *n* martín *m* pescador.

king-size(d) [-saɪz(d)] *adj* [cigarette] extralargo; [pack] gigante; [bed] extragrande.

kinky ['kɪŋkɪ] *(compar* **-ier,** *superl* **-iest)** *adj inf* morboso(sa), pervertido(da).

kiosk ['ki:ɒsk] *n* **- 1.** [small shop] quiosco *m* **- 2.** UK [telephone box] cabina *f* telefónica.

kip [kɪp] *n* UK *inf* sueñecito *m.*

kipper ['kɪpə'] *n* arenque *m* ahumado.

kiss [kɪs] ◇ *n* beso *m.* ◇ *vt* besar. ◇ *vi* besarse.

kiss of life *n* [to resuscitate sb]: **the ~** la respiración boca a boca.

kit [kɪt] *n* **- 1.** [set of implements] equipo *m* **- 2.** UK [clothes] equipo *m* **- 3.** [to be assembled] modelo *m* para armar, kit *m.*

kit bag *n* macuto *m*, petate *m.*

kitchen ['kɪtʃɪn] *n* cocina *f.*

kitchen knife *n* cuchillo *m* de cocina.

kitchen roll *n* papel *m* de cocina.

kitchen sink *n* fregadero *m.*

kitchen unit *n* módulo *m* de cocina.

kite [kaɪt] *n* [toy] cometa *f*, papalote *m CAm, Méx*, volantín *m Chile*, barrilete *m RP*, papagayo *m Ven*.

kith [kɪθ] *n*: ~ **and kin** parientes *mpl* y amigos.

kitten ['kɪtn] *n* gatito *m*.

kitty ['kɪtɪ] (*pl* **-ies**) *n* [for bills, drinks] fondo *m* común; [in card games] bote *m*, puesta *f*.

kitty-corner *adj US inf* en diagonal, diagonalmente.

kiwi ['kiːwiː] *n* **-1.** [bird] kiwi *m* **-2.** *inf* [New Zealander] neocelandés *m*, -esa *f*.

kiwi (fruit) *n* kiwi *m*.

km (*abbr of* **kilometre**) km.

km/h (*abbr of* **kilometres per hour**) km/h.

knack [næk] *n*: it's easy once you've got the ~ es fácil cuando le coges el tranquillo; **he has the ~ of appearing at the right moment** tiene el don de aparecer en el momento adecuado.

knackered ['nækəd] *adj UK inf* **-1.** [exhausted] hecho(cha) polvo **-2.** [broken] cascado(da).

knapsack ['næpsæk] *n* mochila *f*.

knead [niːd] *vt* amasar.

knee [niː] ⬦ *n* rodilla *f*. ⬦ *vt* dar un rodillazo a.

kneecap ['niːkæp] *n* rótula *f*.

kneel [niːl] (*UK pt & pp* **knelt**, *US pt & pp* **-ed** *OR* **knelt**) *vi* [go down on knees] arrodillarse; [be on knees] estar de rodillas.

◆ **kneel down** *vi* arrodillarse.

knew [njuː] *pt* ⊳ **know**.

knickers ['nɪkəz] *npl* **-1.** *UK* [underwear] bragas *fpl*, calzones *mpl Amér*, pantaletas *fpl CAm, Carib, Méx*, bombacha *f RP*, blúmer *m CAm, Carib* **-2.** *US* [knickerbockers] bombachos *mpl*.

knick-knack ['nɪknæk] *n* baratija *f*.

knife [naɪf] (*pl* **knives**) ⬦ *n* cuchillo *m*. ⬦ *vt* acuchillar.

knight [naɪt] ⬦ *n* **-1.** HIST caballero *m* **-2.** [knighted man] *hombre con el título de 'Sir'* **-3.** [in chess] caballo *m*. ⬦ *vt conceder el título de 'Sir'a.*

knighthood ['naɪthʊd] *n* **-1.** [present-day title] título *m* de 'Sir' **-2.** HIST título *m* de caballero.

knit [nɪt] (*pt & pp* **knit** *OR* **-ted**, *cont* **-ting**) ⬦ *vt* [make with wool] tejer, tricotar. ⬦ *vi* **-1.** [with wool] hacer punto **-2.** [join] soldarse.

knitting ['nɪtɪŋ] *n (U)* **-1.** [activity] labor *f* de punto **-2.** [work produced] punto *m*, calceta *f*.

knitting needle *n* aguja *f* de hacer punto.

knitwear ['nɪtweəʳ] *n (U)* género *m OR* ropa *f* de punto.

knives [naɪvz] *pl* ⊳ **knife**.

knob [nɒb] *n* **-1.** [on door, drawer, bedstead] pomo *m* **-2.** [on TV, radio etc] botón *m*.

knock [nɒk] ⬦ *n* **-1.** [hit] golpe *m* **-2.** *inf* [piece of bad luck] revés *m*. ⬦ *vt* **-1.** [hit hard] golpear; **to ~ sb over** [gen] hacer caer a alguien; AUT atropellar a alguien; **to ~ sthg over** tirar *OR* volcar algo, voltear algo *Amér* **-2.** [make by hitting] hacer, abrir **-3.** *inf* [criticize] poner por los suelos. ⬦ *vi* **-1.** [on door]: **to ~ (at** *OR* **on)** llamar (a) **-2.** [car engine] golpetear.

◆ **knock down** *vt sep* **-1.** [subj: car, driver] atropellar **-2.** [building] derribar.

◆ **knock off** *vi inf* [stop working] parar de currar.

◆ **knock out** *vt sep* **-1.** [subj: person, punch] dejar sin conocimiento; [subj: boxer] dejar fuera de combate; [subj: drug] dejar dormido a **-2.** [eliminate from competition] eliminar.

knocker ['nɒkəʳ] *n* [on door] aldaba *f*.

knock-kneed [-'niːd] *adj* patizambo(ba).

knock-on effect *n UK* reacción *f* en cadena; **to have a ~ on sthg** repercutir en algo.

knockout ['nɒkaʊt] *n* K.O. *m*.

knot [nɒt] (*pt & pp* **-ted**, *cont* **-ting**) ⬦ *n* **-1.** [gen] nudo *m*; **to tie/untie a ~** hacer/deshacer un nudo; **to tie the ~** *inf* [marry] casarse **-2.** [of people] corrillo *m*. ⬦ *vt* anudar.

knotty ['nɒtɪ] (*compar* **-ier**, *superl* **-iest**) *adj* intrincado(da).

know [nəʊ] (*pt* **knew**, *pp* **known**) ⬦ *vt* **-1.** [gen] saber; **to ~ (that)** saber (que); [language] saber hablar; **to ~ how to do sthg** saber hacer algo; **to get to ~ sthg** enterarse de algo; **to let sb ~ (about)** avisar a alguien (de) **-2.** [be familiar with - person, place] conocer; **to get to ~ sb** llegar a conocer a alguien. ⬦ *vi* **-1.** [have knowledge] saber; **to ~ of** *OR* **about sthg** saber algo, estar enterado(da) de algo; **you ~** [to emphasize]¿sabes?; [to remind] ¡ya sabes!, ¡sí hombre! **-2.** [be knowledgeable]: **to ~ about sthg** saber de algo. ⬦ *n*: **to be in the ~** estar enterado(da).

know-all *n UK* sabelotodo *m OR f*, sabihondo *m*, -da *f*.

know-how *n* conocimientos *mpl*, know-how *m*.

knowing ['nəʊɪŋ] *adj* cómplice.

knowingly ['nəʊɪŋlɪ] *adv* **-1.** [in knowing manner] con complicidad **-2.** [intentionally] a sabiendas.

know-it-all = **know-all**.

knowledge ['nɒlɪdʒ] *n (U)* **-1.** [awareness] conocimiento *m*; **to the best of my ~** por lo que yo sé **-2.** [facts known by individual] conocimientos *mpl*.

knowledgeable [ˈnɒlɪdʒəbl] *adj* entendido(da).

known [nəʊn] *pp* ⊳ know.

knuckle [ˈnʌkl] *n* - **1.** [on hand] nudillo *m* - **2.** [of pork] codillo *m*.

koala (bear) [kəʊˈɑːlə-] *n* koala *m*.

Koran [kɒˈrɑːn] *n*: the ~ el Corán.

Korea [kəˈrɪə] *n* Corea.

Korean [kəˈrɪən] ⬦ *adj* coreano(na). ⬦ *n* - **1.** [person] coreano *m*, -na *f* - **2.** [language] coreano *m*.

kosher [ˈkəʊʃəʳ] *adj* - **1.** [meat] kosher, permitido(da) por la religión judía - **2.** *inf* [reputable] limpio(pia), legal.

kung fu [ˌkʌŋˈfuː] *n* kung-fu *m*.

Kurd [kɜːd] *n* kurdo *m*, -da *f*.

Kuwait [kʊˈweɪt] *n* Kuwait.

l¹ (*pl* l's OR ls), **L** (*pl* L's OR Ls) [el] *n* [letter] l *f*, L *f*.

l² (*abbr of* litre) l.

lab [læb] *inf* = laboratory.

label [ˈleɪbl] (*UK pt & pp* **-led**, *cont* **-ling**, *US pt & pp* **-ed**, *cont* **-ing**) ⬦ *n* - **1.** [identification] etiqueta *f* - **2.** [of record] sello *m* discográfico, casa *f* discográfica. ⬦ *vt* - **1.** [fix label to] etiquetar - **2.** *usu pej* [describe]: **to ~ sb (as)** calificar OR etiquetar a alguien (de).

labor *etc US* = labour *etc*.

laboratory [*UK* ləˈbɒrətrɪ, *US* ˈlæbrəˌtɔːrɪ] (*pl* **-ies**) *n* laboratorio *m*.

laborious [ləˈbɔːrɪəs] *adj* laborioso(sa).

labor union *n US* sindicato *m*.

labour *UK*, **labor** *US* [ˈleɪbəʳ] ⬦ *n* - **1.** [work] trabajo *m* - **2.** [piece of work] esfuerzo *m* - **3.** [workers] mano *f* de obra - **4.** [giving birth] parto *m*. ⬦ *vi* - **1.** [work] trabajar - **2.** [work with difficulty]: **to ~ at** OR **over** trabajar afanosamente en.

◆ **Labour** POL ⬦ *adj* laborista. ⬦ *n UK* (*U*) los laboristas.

laboured *UK*, **labored** *US* [ˈleɪbəd] *adj* [style] trabajoso(sa); [gait, breathing] penoso(sa), fatigoso(sa).

labourer *UK*, **laborer** *US* [ˈleɪbərəʳ] *n* obrero *m*, -ra *f*.

Labour Party *n UK*: **the ~** el partido Laborista.

Labrador [ˈlæbrədɔːʳ] *n* [dog] labrador *m*.

labyrinth [ˈlæbərɪnθ] *n* laberinto *m*.

lace [leɪs] ⬦ *n* - **1.** [fabric] encaje *m* - **2.** [shoelace] cordón *m*. ⬦ *vt* - **1.** [shoe, boot] atar - **2.** [drink, food]: **coffee ~d with brandy** café con unas gotas de coñac.

◆ **lace up** *vt sep* atar.

lack [læk] ⬦ *n* falta *f*, carencia *f*; **for** OR **through ~ of** por falta de; **there was no ~ of excitement** no faltó emoción. ⬦ *vt* carecer de. ⬦ *vi*: **to be ~ing in** carecer de; **to be ~ing** faltar.

lackadaisical [ˌlækəˈdeɪzɪkl] *adj pej* apático(ca).

lacklustre *UK*, **lackluster** *US* [ˈlækˌlʌstəʳ] *adj pej* soso(sa), apagado(da).

laconic [ləˈkɒnɪk] *adj* lacónico(ca).

lacquer [ˈlækəʳ] *n* laca *f*.

lad [læd] *n inf* [boy] chaval *m*, chavalo *m Amér*; **come on ~s!** ¡vamos chicos!

ladder [ˈlædəʳ] ⬦ *n* - **1.** [for climbing] escalera *f* - **2.** *UK* [in tights] carrera *f*. ⬦ *vt UK* [tights] hacerse una carrera en.

laden [ˈleɪdn] *adj*: ~ **(with)** cargado(da) (de).

ladies *UK* [ˈleɪdɪz], **ladies' room** *US n* lavabo *m* de señoras.

ladle [ˈleɪdl] ⬦ *n* cucharón *m*. ⬦ *vt* servir con cucharón.

lady [ˈleɪdɪ] (*pl* **-ies**) ⬦ *n* - **1.** [woman] señora *f* - **2.** [woman of high status] dama *f*. ⬦ *comp* mujer; ~ **doctor** doctora *f*.

◆ **Lady** *n* [woman of noble rank] lady *f*.

ladybird *UK* [ˈleɪdɪbɜːd], **ladybug** *US* [ˈleɪdɪbʌg] *n* mariquita *f*.

lady-in-waiting [-ˈweɪtɪŋ] (*pl* **ladies-in-waiting**) *n* dama *f* de honor.

ladylike [ˈleɪdɪlaɪk] *adj* elegante, propio(pia) de una señora.

Ladyship [ˈleɪdɪʃɪp] *n*: **her/your ~** su señoría *f*.

lag [læg] (*pt & pp* **-ged**, *cont* **-ging**) ⬦ *vi* - **1.** [move more slowly]: **to ~ (behind)** rezagarse - **2.** [develop more slowly]: **to ~ (behind)** andar a la zaga. ⬦ *vt* [pipes] revestir. ⬦ *n* [delay] retraso *m*, demora *f*.

lager [ˈlɑːgəʳ] *n* cerveza *f* rubia.

lagoon [ləˈguːn] *n* laguna *f*.

laid [leɪd] *pt & pp* ⊳ lay.

laid-back *adj inf* relajado(da), cachazudo(da).

lain [leɪn] *pp* ⊳ lie.

lair [leəʳ] *n* guarida *f*.

laity [ˈleɪətɪ] *n* RELIG: **the ~** los seglares, los legos.

lake [leɪk] *n* lago *m*.

Lake District *n*: **the ~** el Distrito de los Lagos al noroeste de Inglaterra.

lamb [læm] *n* cordero *m*.

lambswool [ˈlæmzwʊl] ⬦ *n* lana *f* de cordero. ⬦ *comp* de lana de cordero.

lame [leim] *adj* -1. [person, horse] cojo(ja) -2. [excuse, argument] pobre.

lament [lə'ment] ◇ *n* lamento *m.* ◇ *vt* lamentar.

lamentable ['læməntəbl] *adj* lamentable.

laminated ['læmineitid] *adj* -1. [gen] laminado(da) -2. [ID card] plastificado(da).

lamp [læmp] *n* lámpara *f.*

lampoon [læm'pu:n] ◇ *n* pasquín *m*, sátira *f.* ◇ *vt* satirizar.

lamppost ['læmppəust] *n* farol *m.*

lampshade ['læmpʃeid] *n* pantalla *f (de lámpara).*

lance [lɑ:ns] ◇ *n* lanza *f.* ◇ *vt* abrir con lanceta.

lance corporal *n* soldado *m* de primera.

land [lænd] ◇ *n* -1. [gen] tierra *f* -2. [property] tierras *fpl*, finca *f.* ◇ *vt* -1. [unload] desembarcar -2. [plane] hacer aterrizar -3. [catch - fish] pescar -4. *inf* [obtain] conseguir, pillar -5. *inf* [place]: **to ~ sb in sthg** meter a alguien en algo; **to ~ sb with sb/ sthg** cargar a alguien con alguien/algo. ◇ *vi* -1. [by plane] aterrizar, tomar tierra -2. [from ship] desembarcar -3. [fall] caer -4. [end up] ir a parar.

◆ **land up** *vi inf*: **to ~ up (in)** ir a parar (a).

landfill site ['lændfil-] *n* vertedero *m* de basuras.

landing ['lændiŋ] *n* -1. [of stairs] rellano *m*, descansillo *m* -2. [of aeroplane] aterrizaje *m* -3. [of person] desembarco *m.*

landing card *n* tarjeta *f* de desembarque.

landing gear *n (U)* tren *m* de aterrizaje.

landing stage *n* desembarcadero *m.*

landing strip *n* pista *f* de aterrizaje.

landlady ['lænd,leidi] *(pl* -ies) *n* -1. [of rented room or building] casera *f* -2. [of hotel, pub] patrona *f.*

landlord ['lændlɔ:d] *n* -1. [of rented room or building] dueño *m*, casero *m* -2. [of pub] patrón *m.*

landmark ['lændmɑ:k] *n* -1. [prominent feature] punto *m* de referencia -2. *fig* [in history] hito *m.*

landowner ['lænd,əunə[r]] *n* terrateniente *m* OR *f.*

landscape ['lændskeip] *n* paisaje *m.*

landslide ['lændslaid] *n* -1. [of earth, rocks] desprendimiento *m* de tierras -2. POL victoria *f* arrolladora OR aplastante.

lane [lein] *n* -1. [road in country] camino *m* -2. [road in town] callejuela *f*, callejón *m* -3. [for traffic] carril *m*; **'keep in ~'** cartel que prohíbe el cambio de carril -4. [in swimming pool, race track] calle *f* -5. [for shipping, aircraft] ruta *f.*

language ['læŋgwidʒ] *n* -1. [gen] idioma *m*, lengua *f* -2. [faculty or style of communication & COMPUT] lenguaje *m.*

language laboratory *n* laboratorio *m* de idiomas.

languid ['læŋgwid] *adj* lánguido(da).

languish ['læŋgwiʃ] *vi* [in misery] languidecer; [in prison] pudrirse.

lank [læŋk] *adj* lacio(cia).

lanky ['læŋki] *(compar* -ier, *superl* -iest) *adj* larguirucho(cha).

lantern ['læntən] *n* farol *m.*

lap [læp] *(pt & pp* -ped, *cont* -ping) ◇ *n* -1. [of person] regazo *m* -2. [of race] vuelta *f.* ◇ *vt* -1. [subj: animal] beber a lengüetadas -2. [overtake in race] doblar. ◇ *vi* [water, waves] romper con suavidad.

lapel [lə'pel] *n* solapa *f.*

Lapland ['læplænd] *n* Laponia.

lapse [læps] ◇ *n* -1. [slip-up] fallo *m*, lapsus *m inv* -2. [in behaviour] desliz *m* -3. [of time] lapso *m*, período *m.* ◇ *vi* -1. [membership] caducar; [treatment, agreement] cumplir, expirar -2. [standards, quality] bajar momentáneamente; [tradition] extinguirse, desaparecer -3. [subj: person]: **to ~ into** terminar cayendo en.

lap-top (computer) *n* COMPUT ordenador *m* portátil.

larceny ['lɑ:səni] *n (U)* latrocinio *m.*

lard [lɑ:d] *n* manteca *f* de cerdo.

larder ['lɑ:də[r]] *n* despensa *f.*

large [lɑ:dʒ] *adj* [gen] grande; [family] numeroso(sa); [sum] importante.

◆ **at large** *adv* -1. [as a whole] en general -2. [escaped prisoner, animal] suelto(ta).

◆ **by and large** *adv* en general.

largely ['lɑ:dʒli] *adv* [mostly] en gran parte; [chiefly] principalmente.

lark [lɑ:k] *n* -1. [bird] alondra *f* -2. *inf* [joke] broma *f.*

◆ **lark about** *vi* hacer el tonto.

laryngitis [,lærin'dʒaitis] *n (U)* laringitis *f inv.*

larynx ['læriŋks] *n* laringe *f.*

lasagna, lasagne [lə'zænjə] *n (U)* lasaña *f.*

laser ['leizə[r]] *n* láser *m.*

laser printer *n* COMPUT impresora *f* láser.

lash [læʃ] ◇ *n* -1. [eyelash] pestaña *f* -2. [blow with whip] latigazo *m.* ◇ *vt* -1. *lit & fig* [whip] azotar -2. [tie]: **to ~ sthg (to)** amarrar algo (a).

◆ **lash out** *vi* -1. [attack]: **to ~ out at sb** [physically] soltar un golpe a alguien; [verbally] arremeter contra alguien -2. *UK inf* [spend money]: **to ~ out (on sthg)** tirar la casa por la ventana (con algo).

lass [læs] *n* chavala *f*, muchacha *f.*

lasso [læ'su:] *(pl* -s) *n* lazo *m.*

last [lɑ:st] ◇ *adj* último(ma); **~ month/ Tuesday** el mes/martes pasado; **~ March** en marzo del año pasado; **~ but one** penúltimo(ma); **~ but two** antepenúltimo(ma);

~ night anoche. ⬦ *adv* **- 1.** [most recently] por última vez; **when I ~ called him** la última vez que lo llamé **- 2.** [finally, in final position] en último lugar; **he arrived ~** llegó el último; **~ but not least** por último, pero no por ello menos importante. ⬦ *pron*: **the year/Saturday before ~** no el año/sábado pasado, sino el anterior; **the ~ but one** el penúltimo (la penúltima); **the night before ~** anteanoche; **the time before ~** la vez anterior a la pasada; **to leave sthg till ~** dejar algo para el final. ⬦ *n*: **the ~ I saw/heard of him** la última vez que lo vi/que oí de él. ⬦ *vi* durar; [food] conservarse.
◆ **at (long) last** *adv* por fin.

last-ditch *adj* último(ma), desesperado(da).

lasting ['lɑːstɪŋ] *adj* [peace, effect] duradero(ra).

lastly ['lɑːstlɪ] *adv* **- 1.** [to conclude] por último **- 2.** [at the end] al final.

last-minute *adj* de última hora.

latch [lætʃ] *n* pestillo *m*.
◆ **latch onto** *vt fus inf* [person] pegarse OR engancharse a; [idea] pillar.

late [leɪt] ⬦ *adj* **- 1.** [not on time] con retraso; **to be ~ (for)** llegar tarde (a); **the flight is twenty minutes ~** el vuelo lleva veinte minutos de retraso; **the bus was an hour ~** el autobús llegó con una hora de retraso **- 2.** [near end of]: **in the ~ afternoon** al final de la tarde; **in ~ December** a finales de diciembre; **it's getting ~** se está haciendo tarde **- 3.** [later than normal] tardío(a); **we had a ~ breakfast** desayunamos tarde **- 4.** [former]: **the ~ president** el ex-presidente **- 5.** [dead] difunto(ta). ⬦ *adv* **- 1.** [gen] tarde; **they are open ~** abren hasta tarde **- 2.** [near end of period]: **~ in the day** al final del día; **~ in August** a finales de agosto.
◆ **of late** *adv* últimamente, recientemente.

latecomer ['leɪtˌkʌməʳ] *n* persona *f* que llega tarde.

lately ['leɪtlɪ] *adv* últimamente, recientemente.

latent ['leɪtənt] *adj* latente.

later ['leɪtəʳ] ⬦ *adj* **- 1.** [date, edition] posterior **- 2.** [near end of]: **in the ~ 15th century** a finales del siglo XV. ⬦ *adv* [at a later time]: **~ (on)** más tarde; **no ~ than Friday** el viernes como muy tarde.

lateral ['lætərəl] *adj* lateral.

latest ['leɪtɪst] ⬦ *adj* [most recent] último(ma). ⬦ *n*: **at the ~** a más tardar, como muy tarde.

lathe [leɪð] *n* torno *m*.

lather ['lɑːðəʳ] ⬦ *n* espuma *f* (de jabón). ⬦ *vt* enjabonar.

Latin ['lætɪn] ⬦ *adj* **- 1.** [temperament, blood] latino(na) **- 2.** [studies] de latín. ⬦ *n* [language] latín *m*.

Latin America *n* Latinoamérica *f*, América *f* Latina.

Latin American ⬦ *adj* latinoamericano(na). ⬦ *n* [person] latinoamericano *m*, -na *f*.

latitude ['lætɪtjuːd] *n* GEOGR latitud *f*.

latter ['lætəʳ] ⬦ *adj* **- 1.** [near to end] último(ma) **- 2.** [second] segundo(da). ⬦ *n*: **the ~** éste *m*, -ta *f*.

latterly ['lætəlɪ] *adv* últimamente, recientemente.

lattice ['lætɪs] *n* enrejado *m*, celosía *f*.

Latvia ['lætvɪə] *n* Letonia.

laudable ['lɔːdəbl] *adj* loable.

laugh [lɑːf] ⬦ *n* **- 1.** [sound] risa *f* **- 2.** *inf* [fun, joke]: **to have a ~** divertirse; **to do sthg for ~s** OR **a ~** hacer algo para divertirse OR en cachondeo. ⬦ *vi* reírse.
◆ **laugh at** *vt fus* [mock] reírse de.
◆ **laugh off** *vt sep* [dismiss] tomarse a risa.

laughable ['lɑːfəbl] *adj pej* [absurd] ridículo(la), risible.

laughing stock ['lɑːfɪŋ-] *n* hazmerreír *m*.

laughter ['lɑːftəʳ] *n* (U) risa *f*.

launch [lɔːntʃ] ⬦ *n* **- 1.** [of boat, ship] botadura *f* **- 2.** [of rocket, missile, product] lanzamiento *m* **- 3.** [boat] lancha *f*. ⬦ *vt* **- 1.** [boat, ship] botar **- 2.** [missile, attack, product & COMPUT] lanzar **- 3.** [company] fundar.

launch(ing) pad ['lɔːntʃ(ɪŋ)-] *n* plataforma *f* de lanzamiento.

launder ['lɔːndəʳ] *vt* **- 1.** [wash] lavar **- 2.** *inf* [money] blanquear.

laund(e)rette [lɔːn'dret], **Laundromat**® *US* ['lɔːndrəmæt] *n* lavandería *f* (automática).

laundry ['lɔːndrɪ] (*pl* **-ies**) *n* **- 1.** [clothes - about to be washed] colada *f*, ropa *f* sucia; [- newly washed] ropa *f* limpia **- 2.** [business, room] lavandería *f*.

laureate ['lɔːrɪət] ▷ **poet laureate**.

lava ['lɑːvə] *n* lava *f*.

lavatory ['lævətrɪ] (*pl* **-ies**) *n* **- 1.** [receptacle] wáter *m* **- 2.** [room] servicio *m*.

lavender ['lævəndəʳ] *n* **- 1.** [plant] lavanda *f*, espliego *m* **- 2.** [colour] color *m* lavanda.

lavish ['lævɪʃ] ⬦ *adj* **- 1.** [person] pródigo(ga); [gifts, portions] muy generoso(sa); **to be ~ with** [praise, attention] ser pródigo en; [money] ser desprendido(da) con **- 2.** [sumptuous] espléndido(da), suntuoso(sa). ⬦ *vt*: **to ~ sthg on** [praise, care] prodigar algo a; [time, money] gastar algo en.

law [lɔː] *n* **- 1.** [gen] ley *f*; **against the ~** ilegal; **to break the ~** infringir OR violar la ley; **~ and order** el orden público **- 2.** [set of rules, study, profession] derecho m.

law-abiding [-ə‚baɪdɪŋ] adj observante de la ley.

law court n tribunal m de justicia.

law enforcement officer n agente m OR f de policía.

law firm n bufete m de abogados.

lawful [ˈlɔːfʊl] adj fml legal, lícito(ta).

lawn [lɔːn] n [grass] césped m, pasto m Amér, grama f CAm, Ven.

lawnmower [ˈlɔːn‚məʊəʳ] n cortacésped m OR f.

lawn tennis n tenis m sobre hierba.

law school n facultad f de derecho; **he went to ~** estudió derecho.

lawsuit [ˈlɔːsuːt] n pleito m.

lawyer [ˈlɔːjəʳ] n abogado m, -da f.

lax [læks] adj [discipline, morals] relajado(da); [person] negligente; [security] poco riguroso(sa).

laxative [ˈlæksətɪv] n laxante m.

lay [leɪ] (pt & pp **laid**) ◇ pt ▷ **lie**. ◇ vt **- 1.** [put, place] colocar, poner; **to ~ o.s. open to sthg** exponerse a algo **- 2.** [prepare - plans] hacer **- 3.** [put in position - bricks] poner; [- cable, trap] tender; [- foundations] echar; **to ~ the table** poner la mesa **- 4.** [egg] poner **- 5.** [blame, curse]: **to ~ sthg on sb** echar algo a alguien. ◇ adj **- 1.** [not clerical] laico(ca) **- 2.** [untrained, unqualified] lego(ga).

◆ **lay aside** vt sep **- 1.** [store for future - food] guardar; [- money] ahorrar **- 2.** [prejudices, reservations] dejar a un lado.

◆ **lay down** vt sep **- 1.** [set out] imponer, establecer **- 2.** [put down - arms] deponer, entregar; [- tools] dejar.

◆ **lay off** ◇ vt sep [make redundant] despedir. ◇ vt fus inf [stop, give up]: **to ~ off (doing sthg)** dejar (de hacer algo). ◇ vi inf: **~ off!** ¡déjame en paz!

◆ **lay on** vt sep [transport, entertainment] organizar; [food] preparar.

◆ **lay out** vt sep **- 1.** [arrange, spread out] disponer **- 2.** [plan, design] diseñar el trazado de.

layabout [ˈleɪəbaʊt] n UK inf holgazán m, -ana f, gandul m, -la f, atorrante m OR f Amér.

lay-by (pl **lay-bys**) n UK área f de descanso.

layer [ˈleɪəʳ] ◇ n **- 1.** [of substance, material] capa f **- 2.** fig [level] nivel m. ◇ vt [hair] cortar a capas.

layman [ˈleɪmən] (pl **-men** [-mən]) n **- 1.** [untrained, unqualified person] lego m, -ga f **- 2.** RELIG laico m, -ca f.

layout [ˈleɪaʊt] n [of building, garden] trazado m, diseño m; [of text] presentación f, composición f; [of page & COMPUT] diseño m.

laze [leɪz] vi: **to ~ (about** OR **around)** gandulear, holgazanear.

lazy [ˈleɪzɪ] (compar **-ier**, superl **-iest**) adj **- 1.** [person] perezoso(sa), vago(ga), atorrante RP **- 2.** [stroll, gesture] lento(ta); [afternoon] ocioso(sa).

lazybones [ˈleɪzɪbəʊnz] (pl inv) n inf gandul m, -la f, holgazán m, -ana f.

lb (abbr of **pound**) lb.

LCD n abbr of **liquid crystal display**.

lead¹ [liːd] (pt & pp **led**) ◇ n **- 1.** [winning position] delantera f; **to be in** OR **have the ~** llevar la delantera, ir en cabeza; **to take the ~ ponerse a la cabeza - 2.** [amount ahead]: **to have a ~ of ...** llevar una ventaja de ... **- 3.** [initiative, example] ejemplo m; **to take the ~** [do sthg first] tomar la delantera **- 4.** THEATRE: **(to play) the ~** [part] (hacer) el papel principal **- 5.** [clue] pista f **- 6.** [for dog] correa f **- 7.** [wire, cable] cable m. ◇ adj [singer, actor] principal; [guitar, guitarist] solista; [story in newspaper] más destacado(da). ◇ vt **- 1.** [be in front of] encabezar **- 2.** [take, guide, direct] conducir **- 3.** [be in charge of, take the lead in] dirigir; [debate] moderar **- 4.** [life] llevar **- 5.** [cause]: **to ~ sb to do sthg** llevar a alguien a hacer algo; **we were led to believe that ...** nos dieron a entender que ... ◇ vi **- 1.** [go]: **to ~ (to)** conducir OR llevar (a) **- 2.** [give access to]: **to ~ (to** OR **into)** dar (a) **- 3.** [be winning] ir en cabeza **- 4.** [result in]: **to ~ to** conducir a **- 5.** [in cards] salir.

◆ **lead up to** vt fus **- 1.** [build up to] conducir a, preceder a **- 2.** [plan to introduce] apuntar a.

lead² [led] n **- 1.** [metal] plomo m **- 2.** [in pencil] mina f.

leaded [ˈledɪd] adj **- 1.** [petrol] con plomo **- 2.** [window] emplomado(da).

leader [ˈliːdəʳ] n **- 1.** [of party etc, in competition] líder m OR f **- 2.** UK [in newspaper] editorial m, artículo m de fondo.

leadership [ˈliːdəʃɪp] n (U) **- 1.** [people in charge]: **the ~** los líderes **- 2.** [position of leader] liderazgo m **- 3.** [qualities of leader] dotes fpl de mando.

lead-free [led-] adj sin plomo.

leading [ˈliːdɪŋ] adj **- 1.** [major - athlete, writer] destacado(da); [- company] principal **- 2.** [at front] que va en cabeza.

leading lady n primera actriz f.

leading light n figura f destacada.

leading man n primer actor m.

leaf [liːf] (pl **leaves**) n **- 1.** [of tree, book] hoja f **- 2.** [of table] hoja f abatible.

◆ **leaf through** vt fus hojear.

leaflet [ˈliːflɪt] n [small brochure] folleto m; [piece of paper] octavilla f.

league [liːg] n [gen & SPORT] liga f; **to be in ~ with** [work with] estar confabulado con.

leak [liːk] ◇ n **- 1.** [hole - in tank, bucket] agujero m; [- in roof] gotera f **- 2.** [escape]

escape m, fuga f - 3. [of information] filtración f. ◇ vt [information] filtrar. ◇ vi - 1. [bucket] tener un agujero; [roof] tener goteras; [boot] calar - 2. [water, gas] salirse, escaparse; **to ~ (out) from** salirse de.
➤ **leak out** vi [liquid] escaparse.

leakage ['li:kɪdʒ] n fuga f, escape m.

lean [li:n] (pt & pp **leant** OR **-ed**) ◇ adj - 1. [person] delgado(da) - 2. [meat] magro(gra) - 3. [winter, year] de escasez. ◇ vt [support, prop]: **to ~ sthg against** apoyar algo contra. ◇ vi - 1. [bend, slope] inclinarse; **to ~ out of the window** asomarse a la ventana - 2. [rest]: **to ~ on/against** apoyarse en/contra.

leaning ['li:nɪŋ] n: **~ (towards)** inclinación f (hacia OR por).

leant [lent] pt & pp ▷ **lean**.

lean-to (pl **lean-tos**) n cobertizo m.

leap [li:p] (pt & pp **leapt** OR **-ed**) ◇ n salto m. ◇ vi [gen] saltar; [prices] dispararse.

leapfrog ['li:pfrɒg] (pt & pp **-ged**, cont **-ging**) ◇ n pídola f, rango m RP. ◇ vt saltar.

leapt [lept] pt & pp ▷ **leap**.

leap year n año m bisiesto.

learn [lɜ:n] (pt & pp **-ed** OR **learnt**) ◇ vt - 1. [acquire knowledge of, memorize] aprender; **to ~ (how) to do sthg** aprender a hacer algo - 2. [hear]: **to ~ (that)** enterarse de (que). ◇ vi - 1. [acquire knowledge] aprender - 2. [hear]: **to ~ (of OR about)** enterarse (de).

learned ['lɜ:nɪd] adj erudito(ta).

learner ['lɜ:nə'] n [beginner] principiante m OR f; [student] estudiante m OR f.

learner (driver) n conductor m principiante OR en prácticas.

learner's permit n US carné m de conducir provisional.

learning ['lɜ:nɪŋ] n saber m, erudición f.

learnt [lɜ:nt] pt & pp ▷ **learn**.

lease [li:s] ◇ n JUR contrato m de arrendamiento, arriendo m. ◇ vt arrendar; **to ~ sthg from/to sb** arrendar algo de/a alguien.

leasehold ['li:shəʊld] ◇ adj arrendado(da). ◇ adv en arriendo.

leash [li:ʃ] n [for dog] correa f.

least [li:st] (superl of **little**) ◇ adj [smallest in amount, degree] menor; **he earns the ~ money** es el que menos dinero gana. ◇ pron [smallest amount]: **the ~** lo menos; **it's the ~ (that) he can do** es lo menos que puede hacer; **not in the ~** en absoluto; **to say the ~** por no decir otra cosa. ◇ adv [to the smallest amount, degree] menos.
➤ **at least** adv por lo menos, al menos.
➤ **least of all** adv y menos (todavía).
➤ **not least** adv sobre todo.

leather ['leðə'] ◇ n piel f, cuero m. ◇ comp [jacket, trousers] de cuero; [shoes, bag] de piel.

leave [li:v] (pt & pp **left**) ◇ vt - 1. [gen] dejar; **he left it to her to decide** dejó que ella decidiera; **to ~ sb alone** dejar a alguien en paz - 2. [go away from - place] irse de; [- house, room, work] salir de; [- wife] abandonar; **to ~ home** irse de casa - 3. [do not take, forget] dejarse - 4. [bequeath]: **to ~ sb sthg**, **to ~ sthg to sb** dejarle algo a alguien. ◇ vi [bus, train, plane] salir; [person] irse, marcharse. ◇ n [time off, permission] permiso m; **to be on ~** estar de permiso.
➤ **leave behind** vt sep - 1. [abandon] dejar - 2. [forget] dejarse - 3. [walking, in race]: **to get left behind** quedarse atrás.
➤ **leave out** vt sep - 1. [omit] omitir - 2. [exclude] excluir.

leave of absence n excedencia f.

leaves [li:vz] pl ▷ **leaf**.

Lebanon ['lebənən] n: **(the) ~** (el) Líbano.

lecherous ['letʃərəs] adj lascivo(va), lujurioso(sa).

lecture ['lektʃə'] ◇ n - 1. [talk - at university] clase f; [- at conference] conferencia f - 2. [criticism, reprimand] sermón m. ◇ vt [scold] echar un sermón a. ◇ vi [give talk]: **to ~ (on/in)** [at university] dar clases (de/en); [at conference] dar una conferencia (sobre/en).

lecturer ['lektʃərə'] n [at university] profesor m, -ra f de universidad.

lectureship ['lektʃərʃɪp] n [at university] puesto m de profesor de universidad.

led [led] pt & pp ▷ **lead¹**.

ledge [ledʒ] n - 1. [of window] alféizar m, antepecho m - 2. [of mountain] saliente m.

ledger ['ledʒə'] n libro m mayor.

leech [li:tʃ] n lit & fig sanguijuela f.

leek [li:k] n puerro m.

leer [lɪə'] vi: **to ~ at sb** mirar lascivamente a alguien.

leeway ['li:weɪ] n [room to manoeuvre] libertad f (de acción OR movimientos).

left [left] ◇ adj - 1. [remaining]: **to be ~** quedar; **there's no wine ~** no queda vino - 2. [not right] izquierdo(da). ◇ adv a la izquierda. ◇ n izquierda f; **on** OR **to the ~** a la izquierda.
➤ **Left** n POL: **the Left** la izquierda.

left-hand adj izquierdo(da); **the ~ side** el lado izquierdo, la izquierda.

left-handed [-'hændɪd] adj - 1. [person] zurdo(da) - 2. [implement] para zurdos.

left luggage (office) n UK consigna f.

leftover ['leftəʊvə'] adj sobrante.
➤ **leftovers** npl sobras fpl.

left wing POL n izquierda f.
➤ **left-wing** adj izquierdista.

leg [leg] *n* **- 1.** [of person] pierna *f*; **to pull sb's ~** tomarle el pelo a alguien **- 2.** [of animal] pata *f* **- 3.** [of trousers] pernera *f*, pierna *f* **- 4.** CULIN [of lamb, pork] pierna *f*; [of chicken] muslo *m* **- 5.** [of furniture] pata *f* **- 6.** [of journey] etapa *f*; [of cup tie] partido *m*.

legacy ['legəsɪ] *(pl* **-ies)** *n lit* & *fig* legado *m*.

legal ['liːgl] *adj* **- 1.** [lawful] legal **- 2.** [concerning the law] jurídico(ca), legal.

legalize, -ise ['liːgəlaɪz] *vt* legalizar.

legal tender *n* moneda *f* de curso legal.

legend ['ledʒənd] *n lit* & *fig* leyenda *f*.

leggings ['legɪŋz] *npl* mallas *fpl*.

legible ['ledʒəbl] *adj* legible.

legislation [,ledʒɪs'leɪʃn] *n* legislación *f*.

legislature ['ledʒɪsleɪtʃər] *n* asamblea *f* legislativa.

legitimate [lɪ'dʒɪtɪmət] *adj* legítimo(ma).

legless ['legləs] *adj UK inf* [drunk] trompa, como una cuba.

legroom ['legrom] *n (U)* espacio *m* para las piernas.

leg-warmers [-,wɔːməz] *npl* calentadores *mpl*.

leisure [*UK* 'leʒər, *US* 'liːʒər] *n* ocio *m*; **do it at your ~** hazlo cuando tengas tiempo.

leisure centre *n* centro *m* deportivo y cultural.

leisurely [*UK* 'leʒəlɪ, *US* 'liːʒərlɪ] *adj* lento(ta).

leisure time *n* tiempo *m* libre.

lemon ['lemən] *n* [fruit] limón *m*.

lemonade [,lemə'neɪd] *n* **- 1.** *UK* [fizzy drink] gaseosa *f* **- 2.** [made with fresh lemons] limonada *f*.

lemon juice *n* zumo *m* de limón.

lemon sole *n* mendo *m* limón.

lemon squeezer [-'skwiːzər] *n* exprimidor *m*, exprimelimones *m inv*.

lemon tea *n* té *m* con limón.

lend [lend] *(pt* & *pp* **lent)** *vt* **- 1.** [loan] prestar, dejar; **to ~ sb sthg, to ~ sthg to sb** prestarle algo a alguien **- 2.** [offer]: **to ~ sthg (to sb)** prestar algo (a alguien); **to ~ sb a hand** echar una mano a alguien; **to ~ itself to sthg** prestarse a algo **- 3.** [add]: **to ~ sthg to** prestar algo a.

lending rate ['lendɪŋ-] *n* tipo *m* de interés (en un crédito).

length [leŋθ] *n* **- 1.** [measurement] longitud *f*, largo *m*; **what ~ is it?** ¿cuánto mide de largo?; **it's a metre in ~** tiene un metro de largo **- 2.** [whole distance, size] extensión *f* **- 3.** [duration] duración *f* **- 4.** [of swimming pool] largo *m* **- 5.** [piece - of string, wood] trozo *m*; [- of cloth] largo *m* **- 6.** *phr*: **to go to great ~s to do sthg** hacer todo lo posible para hacer algo.

at length *adv* **- 1.** [eventually] por fin **- 2.** [in detail - speak] largo y tendido; [-

discuss] con detenimiento.

lengthen ['leŋθən] <> *vt* alargar. <> *vi* alargarse.

lengthways ['leŋθweɪz] *adv* a lo largo.

lengthy ['leŋθɪ] *(compar* **-ier,** *superl* **-iest)** *adj* [stay, visit] extenso(sa); [discussions, speech] prolongado(da).

lenient ['liːnjənt] *adj* indulgente.

lens [lenz] *n* **- 1.** [in glasses] lente *f*; [in camera] objetivo *m* **- 2.** [contact lens] lentilla *f*, lente *f* de contacto.

lent [lent] *pt* & *pp* ⊳ **lend.**

Lent [lent] *n* Cuaresma *f*.

lentil ['lentɪl] *n* lenteja *f*.

Leo ['liːəʊ] *n* Leo *m*.

leopard ['lepəd] *n* leopardo *m*.

leotard ['liːətɑːd] *n* malla *f*.

leper ['lepər] *n* leproso *m*, -sa *f*.

leprosy ['leprəsɪ] *n* lepra *f*.

lesbian ['lezbɪən] *n* lesbiana *f*.

less [les] *(compar of* little*)* <> *adj* menos; **~ ... than** menos ... que; **~ and ~ ...** cada vez menos ... <> *pron* menos; **the ~ you work, the ~ you earn** cuanto menos trabajas, menos ganas; **it costs ~ than you think** cuesta menos de lo que piensas; **no ~ than** nada menos que. <> *adv* menos; **~ than five** menos de cinco; **~ often** menos; **~ and ~** cada vez menos. <> *prep* [minus] menos.

lessen ['lesn] <> *vt* aminorar, reducir. <> *vi* aminorarse, reducirse.

lesser ['lesər] *adj* menor; **to a ~ extent** OR **degree** en menor grado.

lesson ['lesn] *n* **- 1.** [class] clase *f* **- 2.** [warning experience] lección *f*.

lest [lest] *conj fml* para que no; **~ we forget** no sea que nos olvidemos.

let [let] *(pt* & *pp* **let,** *cont* **-ting)** *vt* **- 1.** [allow]: **to ~ sb do sthg** dejar a alguien hacer algo; **to ~ sthg happen** dejar que algo ocurra; **to ~ sb know sthg** avisar a alguien de algo; **to ~ go of sthg/sb** soltar algo/a alguien; **to ~ sthg/sb go** [release] liberar a algo/alguien, soltar a algo/alguien; **to ~ o.s. go** [relax] soltarse el pelo; [become slovenly] abandonarse **- 2.** [in verb forms]: **~'s go!** ¡vamos!; **~'s see** veamos; **~ him wait!** ¡déjale que espere! **- 3.** [rent out - house, room] alquilar; [- land] arrendar; **'to ~'** 'se alquila'.

let alone *adv* ni mucho menos.

let down *vt sep* **- 1.** [deflate] desinflar **- 2.** [disappoint] fallar, defraudar.

let in *vt sep* **- 1.** [admit] dejar entrar **- 2.** [leak] dejar pasar.

let off *vt sep* **- 1.** [excuse]: **to ~ sb off sthg** eximir a alguien de algo **- 2.** [not punish] perdonar **- 3.** [cause to explode - bomb] hacer estallar; [- gun] disparar **- 4.** [gas] despedir.

let on *vi*: **don't ~ on!** ¡no cuentes nada!

◆ **let out** *vt sep* -**1.** [allow to go out] dejar salir -**2.** [emit - sound] soltar.

◆ **let up** *vi* -**1.** [heat, rain] amainar -**2.** [person] parar.

letdown ['letdaʊn] *n inf* chasco *m*, decepción *f*.

lethal ['liːθl] *adj* letal, mortífero(ra).

lethargic [ləˈθɑːdʒɪk] *adj* -**1.** [mood] letárgico(ca); [person] aletargado(da) -**2.** [apathetic] apático(ca).

let's [lets] = **let us**.

letter ['letər] *n* -**1.** [written message] carta *f* -**2.** [of alphabet] letra *f*; **to the ~** *fig* al pie de la letra.

letter bomb *n* carta *f* bomba.

letterbox ['letəbɒks] *n UK* buzón *m*.

letter of credit *n* carta *f* de crédito.

lettuce ['letɪs] *n* lechuga *f*.

letup ['letʌp] *n* tregua *f*, respiro *m*.

leuk(a)emia [luːˈkiːmɪə] *n* leucemia *f*.

level ['levl] (*UK pt & pp* -**led**, *cont* -**ling**, *US pt & pp* -**ed**, *cont* -**ing**) ⋄ *adj* -**1.** [equal in speed, score] igualado(da); **they are ~** van igualados; [equal in height] nivelado(da); **to be ~ (with sthg)** estar al mismo nivel (que algo) -**2.** [flat - floor, surface] liso(sa), llano(na). ⋄ *n* -**1.** [gen] nivel *m* -**2.** *phr*: **to be on the ~** *inf* ser de fiar -**3.** [storey] piso *m* -**4.** *US* [spirit level] nivel *m* de burbuja de aire. ⋄ *vt* -**1.** [make flat] allanar -**2.** [demolish - building] derribar; [- forest] arrasar.

◆ **level off, level out** *vi* -**1.** [stabilize, slow down] estabilizarse -**2.** [ground] nivelarse; [plane] enderezarse.

◆ **level with** *vt fus inf* ser sincero(ra) con.

level crossing *n UK* paso *m* a nivel.

level-headed [-ˈhedɪd] *adj* sensato(ta), equilibrado(da).

lever [*UK* ˈliːvər, *US* ˈlevər] *n* -**1.** [handle, bar] palanca *f* -**2.** *fig* [tactic] resorte *m*.

leverage [*UK* ˈliːvərɪdʒ, *US* ˈlevərɪdʒ] *n* (*U*) -**1.** [force] fuerza *f* de apalanque -**2.** *fig* [influence] influencia *f*.

levy ['levi] (*pt & pp* -**ied**) ⋄ *n*: **~ (on)** [financial contribution] contribución *f* (a *OR* para); [tax] tasa *f OR* impuesto *m* (sobre). ⋄ *vt* -**1.** [impose] imponer -**2.** [collect] recaudar.

lewd [ljuːd] *adj* [person, look] lascivo(va); [behaviour, song] obsceno(na); [joke] verde.

liability [ˌlaɪəˈbɪlətɪ] (*pl* -**ies**) *n* -**1.** [legal responsibility]: **~ (for)** responsabilidad *f* (de *OR* por) -**2.** [hindrance] estorbo *m*.

◆ **liabilities** *npl* FIN pasivo *m*, deudas *fpl*.

liable ['laɪəbl] *adj* -**1.** [likely]: **that's ~ to happen** eso pueda que ocurra -**2.** [prone]: **to be ~ to** ser propenso(sa) a -**3.** [legally responsible]: **to be ~ (for)** ser responsable (de).

liaise [lɪˈeɪz] *vi*: **to ~ (with)** estar en contacto (con).

liaison [lɪˈeɪzɒn] *n* [contact, co-operation]: **~ (with/between)** coordinación *f* (con/entre), enlace *m* (con/entre).

liar ['laɪər] *n* mentiroso *m*, -sa *f*.

libel ['laɪbl] (*UK pt & pp* -**led**, *cont* -**ling**, *US pt & pp* -**ed**, *cont* -**ing**) ⋄ *n* libelo *m*. ⋄ *vt* calumniar.

liberal ['lɪbərəl] ⋄ *adj* -**1.** [tolerant] liberal -**2.** [generous, abundant] generoso(sa). ⋄ *n* liberal *m OR f*.

◆ **Liberal** POL ⋄ *adj* liberal. ⋄ *n* liberal *m OR f*.

Liberal Democrat *UK* ⋄ *adj* demócrata liberal. ⋄ *n* demócrata liberal *m OR f*.

liberate ['lɪbəreɪt] *vt* liberar.

liberation [ˌlɪbəˈreɪʃn] *n* liberación *f*.

liberty ['lɪbətɪ] (*pl* -**ies**) *n* libertad *f*; **at ~** en libertad; **to be at ~ to do sthg** ser libre de hacer algo; **to take liberties (with sb)** tomarse demasiadas libertades (con alguien).

Libra ['liːbrə] *n* Libra *f*.

librarian [laɪˈbreərɪən] *n* bibliotecario *m*, -ria *f*.

library ['laɪbrərɪ] (*pl* -**ies**) *n* [public institution] biblioteca *f*.

libretto [lɪˈbretəʊ] (*pl* -**s**) *n* libreto *m*.

Libya ['lɪbɪə] *n* Libia.

lice [laɪs] *pl* ⊳ **louse**.

licence ['laɪsəns] ⋄ *n* -**1.** [gen] permiso *m*, licencia *f* -**2.** AUT carné *m OR* permiso *m* de conducir. ⋄ *vt US* = **license**.

licence fee *n UK* TV *impuesto anual que tienen que pagar todos los hogares con un televisor y que se usa para financiar la televisión pública.*

licence number *n* AUT matrícula *f*.

license ['laɪsəns] ⋄ *vt* [person, organization] dar licencia a; [activity] autorizar. ⋄ *n US* = **licence**.

licensed ['laɪsənst] *adj* -**1.** [person]: **to be ~ to do sthg** estar autorizado(da) para hacer algo -**2.** [object] registrado(da), con licencia -**3.** *UK* [premises] autorizado(da) a vender alcohol.

license plate *n US* (placa *f* de) matrícula *f*.

lick [lɪk] ⋄ *n inf* [small amount]: **a ~ of paint** una mano de pintura. ⋄ *vt lit & fig* lamer, lamber *Amér*.

licorice ['lɪkərɪs] = **liquorice**.

lid [lɪd] *n* -**1.** [cover] tapa *f* -**2.** [eyelid] párpado *m*.

lie [laɪ] (*pt sense 1* lied, *pt senses 2-5* lay, *pp sense 1* lied, *pp senses 2-5* lain, *cont all senses* lying) ⋄ *n* mentira *f*; **to tell ~s** contar mentiras, mentir. ⋄ *vi* -**1.** [tell lie] mentir; **to ~ to sb** mentirle a alguien -**2.** [lie down] tumbarse, echarse; [be buried] yacer; **to be lying** estar tumbado(da) -**3.** [be situated] hallarse; **there is snow lying on the ground** hay nieve en el suelo; **he is lying in fourth place** se encuentra en cuarto lugar -**4.** [be-

solution, attraction] hallarse, encontrarse
- **5.** *phr*: **to ~ low** permanecer escondido(da).

 ◆ **lie about, lie around** *vi* estar *OR* andar tirado(da).

 ◆ **lie down** *vi* tumbarse, echarse.

 ◆ **lie in** *vi UK* quedarse en la cama hasta tarde.

Liechtenstein ['lɪktən,staɪn] *n* Liechtenstein.

lie-down *n UK*: **to have a ~** echarse un rato.

lie-in *n UK*: **to have a ~** quedarse en la cama hasta tarde.

lieu [ljuː, luː] ◆ **in lieu** *adv*: **in ~ of** en lugar de.

lieutenant [*UK* lefˈtenənt, *US* luːˈtenənt] *n* - **1.** MIL teniente *m* - **2.** [deputy] lugarteniente *m OR f* - **3.** *US* [police officer] oficial *m OR f* de policía.

life [laɪf] (*pl* lives) *n* [gen] vida *f*; **that's ~!** ¡así es la vida!; **for ~** de por vida, para toda la vida; **to come to ~** [thing] cobrar vida; [person] reanimarse de pronto; **to scare the ~ out of sb** pegarle a alguien un susto de muerte.

life assurance = life insurance.

life belt *n* flotador *m*, salvavidas *m inv.*

lifeboat ['laɪfbəʊt] *n* [on a ship] bote *m* salvavidas; [on shore] lancha *f* de salvamento.

life buoy *n* flotador *m*, salvavidas *m inv.*

life cycle *n* ciclo *m* vital.

life expectancy *n* expectativa *f* de vida.

lifeguard ['laɪfgɑːd] *n* socorrista *m OR f.*

life imprisonment [-ɪmˈprɪznmənt] *n* cadena *f* perpetua.

life insurance *n (U)* seguro *m* de vida.

life jacket *n* chaleco *m* salvavidas.

lifeless ['laɪflɪs] *adj* - **1.** [dead] sin vida - **2.** [listless] insulso(sa).

lifelike ['laɪflaɪk] *adj* realista, natural.

lifeline ['laɪflaɪn] *n* - **1.** [rope] cuerda *f OR* cable *m* (de salvamento) - **2.** [something vital for survival] cordón *m* umbilical.

lifelong ['laɪflɒŋ] *adj* de toda la vida.

life preserver [-prɪ,zɜːvəʳ] *n US* - **1.** [life jacket] chaleco *m* salvavidas - **2.** [life belt] flotador *m*, salvavidas *m inv.*

life raft *n* balsa *f* salvavidas.

lifesaver ['laɪf,seɪvəʳ] *n* [person] socorrista *m OR f.*

life sentence *n* (condena *f* a) cadena *f* perpetua.

life-size(d) [-saɪz(d)] *adj* (de) tamaño natural.

lifespan ['laɪfspæn] *n* vida *f.*

lifestyle ['laɪfstaɪl] *n* estilo *m OR* modo *m* de vida.

life-support system *n* aparato *m* de respiración artificial.

lifetime ['laɪftaɪm] *n* vida *f.*

lift [lɪft] ◇ *n* - **1.** [ride - in car etc]: **to give sb a ~ (somewhere)** acercar *OR* llevar a alguien (a algún sitio), dar (un) aventón a alguien (a algún sitio) *Col, Méx* - **2.** *UK* [elevator] ascensor *m*, elevador *m Méx.* ◇ *vt* - **1.** [gen] levantar; **to ~ sthg down** bajar algo; **to ~ sthg out of sthg** sacar algo de algo - **2.** [plagiarize] copiar. ◇ *vi* [disappear - mist] disiparse.

lift-off *n* despegue *m.*

light [laɪt] (*pt & pp* lit *OR* -ed) ◇ *adj* - **1.** [gen] ligero(ra); [rain] fino(na); [traffic] ligero(ra) - **2.** [not strenuous - duties, responsibilities] simple; [- work] suave; [- punishment] leve - **3.** [low-calorie, low-alcohol] light - **4.** [bright] luminoso(sa), lleno(na) de luz; **it's growing ~** se hace de día - **5.** [pale - colour] claro(ra). ◇ *n* - **1.** [brightness, source of light] luz *f* - **2.** [for cigarette, pipe] fuego *m*, lumbre *f*; **have you got a ~?** ¿tienes fuego? - **3.** [perspective]: **in the ~ of** *UK*, **in ~ of** *US* a la luz de - **4.** *phr*: **to bring sthg to ~** sacar algo a la luz; **to come to ~** salir a la luz (pública); **to set ~ to** prender fuego a. ◇ *vt* - **1.** [ignite] encender - **2.** [illuminate] iluminar. ◇ *vi* prenderse. ◇ *adv* [travel] con poco equipaje.

 ◆ **light up** ◇ *vt sep* [illuminate] iluminar. ◇ *vi* - **1.** [look happy] iluminarse, encenderse - **2.** *inf* [start smoking] encender un cigarrillo.

light bulb *n* bombilla *f*, foco *m Méx*, bombillo *m CAm, Carib, Col*, bombita *f RP*, bujía *f CAm*, ampolleta *f Chile.*

lighten ['laɪtn] ◇ *vt* - **1.** [make brighter - room] iluminar - **2.** [make less heavy] aligerar. ◇ *vi* [brighten] aclararse.

lighter ['laɪtəʳ] *n* [cigarette lighter] encendedor *m*, mechero *m.*

light-headed [-'hedɪd] *adj* [dizzy] mareado(da); [emotionally] exaltado(da).

light-hearted [-'hɑːtɪd] *adj* - **1.** [cheerful] alegre - **2.** [amusing] frívolo(la).

lighthouse ['laɪthaʊs, *pl* -haʊzɪz] *n* faro *m.*

lighting ['laɪtɪŋ] *n* iluminación *f*; **street ~** alumbrado *m* público.

lightly ['laɪtlɪ] *adv* - **1.** [gently] suavemente - **2.** [slightly] ligeramente - **3.** [frivolously] a la ligera.

light meter *n* fotómetro *m.*

lightning ['laɪtnɪŋ] *n (U)*: **a flash of ~** un relámpago; **a bolt of ~** un rayo; **it was struck by ~** lo alcanzó un rayo.

lightweight ['laɪtweɪt] ◇ *adj* [object] ligero(ra). ◇ *n* [boxer] peso *m* ligero.

likable ['laɪkəbl] *adj* simpático(ca).

like [laɪk] ◇ *prep* - **1.** [gen] como; *(in questions or indirect questions)* cómo; **what did**

it taste ~? ¿a qué sabía?; **what did it look ~?** ¿cómo era?; **tell me what it's ~** dime cómo es; **something ~ £100** algo así como cien libras; **something ~ that** algo así, algo por el estilo **- 2.** [in the same way as] como, igual que; **~ this/that** así **- 3.** [typical of] propio(pia) OR típico(ca) de; **it's not ~ them** no es su estilo. ◇ *vt* **- 1.** [find pleasant, approve of]: **I ~ cheese** me gusta el queso; **I ~ it/them** me gusta/gustan; **I don't ~ it/them** no me gusta/gustan; **he ~s doing** OR **to do sthg** (a él) le gusta hacer algo **- 2.** [want] querer; **would you ~ some more?** ¿quieres un poco más?; **I'd ~ to come to-morrow** querría OR me gustaría venir maña-na; **I'd ~ you to come to dinner** me gustaría que vinieras a cenar; **whenever you ~** cuando quieras; **I don't ~ to bother her** no quiero molestarla; [in shops, restaurants]: **I'd ~ a kilo of apples/the soup** póngame un kilo de manzanas/la sopa. ◇ *n*: **the ~ of sb/sthg** alguien/algo del estilo.
◆ **likes** *npl* [things one likes] gustos *mpl*, preferencias *fpl*.

likeable ['laɪkəbl] = **likable**.

likelihood ['laɪklɪhʊd] *n* probabilidad *f*.

likely ['laɪklɪ] *adj* **- 1.** [probable] probable; **rain is ~** es probable que llueva; **he's ~ to come** es probable que venga **- 2.** [suitable] indicado(da).

liken ['laɪkn] *vt*: **to ~ sthg/sb to** comparar algo/a alguien con.

likeness ['laɪknɪs] *n* **- 1.** [resemblance]: **~ (to)** parecido *m* (con) **- 2.** [portrait] retrato *m*.

likewise ['laɪkwaɪz] *adv* [similarly] de la misma forma; **to do ~** hacer lo mismo.

liking ['laɪkɪŋ] *n*: **to have a ~ for sthg** tener afición *f* por OR a algo; **to take a ~ to sb** tomar OR coger cariño *m* a alguien; **to be to sb's ~** ser del gusto de alguien; **for my/his** *etc* **~** para mi/su *etc* gusto.

lilac ['laɪlək] ◇ *adj* [colour] lila. ◇ *n* **- 1.** [tree, flower] lila *f* **- 2.** [colour] lila *m*.

Lilo® ['laɪləʊ] (*pl* **-s**) *n* UK colchoneta *f*, colchón *m* hinchable.

lily ['lɪlɪ] (*pl* **-ies**) *n* lirio *m*, azucena *f*.

lily of the valley (*pl* **lilies of the valley**) *n* lirio *m* de los valles.

limb [lɪm] *n* **- 1.** [of body] miembro *m* **- 2.** [of tree] rama *f*.

limber ['lɪmbər] ◆ **limber up** *vi* desentumecerse.

limbo ['lɪmbəʊ] (*pl* **-s**) *n* (U) [uncertain state]: **to be in ~** estar en un estado de incertidumbre.

lime [laɪm] *n* **- 1.** [fruit] lima *f* **- 2.** [drink]: **~ (juice)** lima *f* **- 3.** CHEM cal *f*.

limelight ['laɪmlaɪt] *n*: **in the ~** en (el) candelero.

limerick ['lɪmərɪk] *n* copla humorística de cinco versos.

limestone ['laɪmstəʊn] *n* (U) (piedra *f*) caliza *f*.

limey ['laɪmɪ] (*pl* **limeys**) *n* US *inf* término peyorativo que designa a un inglés.

limit ['lɪmɪt] ◇ *n* **- 1.** [gen] límite *m* **- 2.** *phr*: **off ~s** en zona prohibida; **within ~s** dentro de un límite. ◇ *vt* limitar.

limitation [ˌlɪmɪ'teɪʃn] *n* limitación *f*.

limited ['lɪmɪtɪd] *adj* [restricted] limitado(da); **to be ~ to** estar limitado a.

limited (liability) company *n* sociedad *f* limitada.

limousine ['lɪməzi:n] *n* limusina *f*.

limp [lɪmp] ◇ *adj* flojo(ja). ◇ *vi* cojear.

limpet ['lɪmpɪt] *n* lapa *f*.

line [laɪn] ◇ *n* **- 1.** [gen & MIL] línea *f* **- 2.** [row] fila *f*; **in a ~** en fila **- 3.** *esp* US [queue] cola *f*; **to stand** OR **wait in ~** hacer cola **- 4.** [course - direction] línea *f*; [- of action] camino *m*; **what's his ~ of business?** ¿a qué negocios se dedica? **- 5.** [length - of rope, for washing] cuerda *f*; [- for fishing] sedal *m*; [- of wire] hilo *m*, cable *m* **- 6.** TELEC: **(telephone) ~** línea *f* (telefónica); **hold the ~, please** no cuelgue, por favor; **the ~ is busy** está comunicando; **it's a bad ~** hay interferencias; **your wife is on the ~ for you** su mujer al teléfono **- 7.** [on page] línea *f*, renglón *m*; [of poem, song] verso *m*; [letter]: **to drop sb a ~** *inf* mandar unas letras a alguien **- 8.** [system of transport]: **(railway) ~** [track] vía *f* (férrea); [route] línea *f* (férrea) **- 9.** [wrinkle] arruga *f* **- 10.** [borderline] límite *m*, frontera *f* **- 11.** COMM línea *f*; **~ of credit** línea *f* de crédito **- 12.** *phr*: **to draw the ~ at sthg** no pasar por algo, negarse a algo. ◇ *vt* [coat, curtains] forrar; [drawer] cubrir el interior de.
◆ **out of line** *adv*: **to be out of ~** estar fuera de lugar.
◆ **line up** ◇ *vt sep* **- 1.** [make into a row or queue] alinear **- 2.** [arrange] programar, organizar. ◇ *vi* [form a queue] alinearse, ponerse en fila.

lined [laɪnd] *adj* **- 1.** [of paper] de rayos **- 2.** [wrinkled] arrugado(da).

linen ['lɪnɪn] *n* **- 1.** [cloth] lino *m* **- 2.** [tablecloths, sheets] ropa *f* blanca OR de hilo; **bed ~** ropa *f* de cama.

liner ['laɪnər] *n* [ship] transatlántico *m*.

linesman ['laɪnzmən] (*pl* **-men** [-mən]) *n* juez *m* de línea.

lineup ['laɪnʌp] *n* **- 1.** [of players, competitors] alineación *f* **- 2.** US [identification parade] rueda *f* de identificación.

linger ['lɪŋgər] *vi* **- 1.** [remain - over activity] entretenerse; [- in a place] rezagarse **- 2.** [persist] persistir.

lingerie ['lænʒərɪ] n ropa f interior femenina.

lingo ['lɪŋgəʊ] (pl -es) n inf [foreign language] idioma m; [jargon] jerga f.

linguist ['lɪŋgwɪst] n -1. [someone good at languages]: he's a good ~ tiene facilidad para las lenguas -2. [student or teacher of linguistics] lingüista m or f.

linguistics [lɪŋ'gwɪstɪks] n (U) lingüística f.

lining ['laɪnɪŋ] n -1. [gen & AUT] forro m -2. [of stomach, nose] paredes fpl interiores.

link [lɪŋk] ◇ n -1. [of chain] eslabón m -2. [connection] conexión f, enlace m; ~s (between/with) lazos mpl (entre/con), vínculos mpl (entre/con). ◇ vt -1. [connect - cities] comunicar, enlazar; [- computers] conectar; [- facts] relacionar, asociar; to ~ sthg with or to relacionar or asociar algo con -2. [join - arms] enlazar.
➦ **link up** vt sep: to ~ sthg up (with) conectar algo (con).

links [lɪŋks] (pl inv) n campo m de golf (cerca del mar).

lino ['laɪnəʊ], **linoleum** [lɪ'nəʊljəm] n linóleo m.

lintel ['lɪntl] n dintel m.

lion ['laɪən] n león m.

lioness ['laɪənes] n leona f.

lip [lɪp] n -1. [of mouth] labio m -2. [of cup] borde m; [of jug] pico m.

liposuction ['lɪpəʊˌsʌkʃən] n liposucción f.

lip-read vi leer los labios.

lip salve [-sælv] n UK vaselina® f, cacao m.

lip service n: to pay ~ to sthg hablar en favor de algo sin hacer nada al respeto.

lipstick ['lɪpstɪk] n -1. [container] lápiz m or barra f de labios -2. [substance] carmín m.

liqueur [lɪ'kjʊəʳ] n licor m.

liquid ['lɪkwɪd] ◇ adj líquido(da). ◇ n líquido m.

liquidation [ˌlɪkwɪ'deɪʃn] n liquidación f; to go into ~ ir a la quiebra.

liquid crystal display n pantalla f de cristal líquido.

liquidize, -ise ['lɪkwɪdaɪz] vt UK licuar.

liquidizer ['lɪkwɪdaɪzəʳ] n UK licuadora f.

liquor ['lɪkəʳ] n (U) esp US alcohol m, bebida f alcohólica.

liquorice ['lɪkərɪʃ, 'lɪkərɪs] n (U) regaliz m.

liquor store n US tienda donde se venden bebidas alcohólicas para llevar.

Lisbon ['lɪzbən] n Lisboa.

lisp [lɪsp] ◇ n ceceo m. ◇ vi cecear.

list [lɪst] ◇ n lista f. ◇ vt -1. [in writing] hacer una lista de -2. [in speech] enumerar. ◇ vi NAUT escorar.

listed building [ˌlɪstɪd-] n UK edificio declarado de interés histórico y artístico.

listen ['lɪsn] vi -1. [give attention]: to ~ (to sthg/sb) escuchar (algo/a alguien); to

~ for estar atento a -2. [heed advice]: to ~ (to sb/sthg) hacer caso (a alguien/de algo); to ~ to reason atender a razones.

listener ['lɪsnəʳ] n [to radio] radioyente m or f.

listeria [lɪs'tiːərɪə] n -1. [illness] listeriosis f inv -2. [bacteria] listeria f.

listless ['lɪstlɪs] adj apático(ca).

lit [lɪt] pt & pp ⊳ **light**.

litany ['lɪtənɪ] (pl -ies) n lit & fig letanía f.

liter US = **litre**.

literacy ['lɪtərəsɪ] n alfabetización f.

literal ['lɪtərəl] adj literal.

literally ['lɪtərəlɪ] adv literalmente; to take sthg ~ tomarse algo al pie de la letra.

literary ['lɪtərərɪ] adj [gen] literario(ria).

literate ['lɪtərət] adj -1. [able to read and write] alfabetizado(da) -2. [well-read] culto(ta), instruido(da).

literature ['lɪtrətʃəʳ] n -1. [novels, plays, poetry] literatura f -2. [books on a particular subject] publicaciones fpl, bibliografía f -3. [printed information] documentación f.

lithe [laɪð] adj ágil.

Lithuania [ˌlɪθjʊ'eɪnɪə] n Lituania.

litigation [ˌlɪtɪ'geɪʃn] n fml litigio m, pleito m.

litre UK, **liter** US ['liːtəʳ] n litro m.

litter ['lɪtəʳ] ◇ n -1. [waste material] basura f -2. [newborn animals] camada f. ◇ vt : papers ~ed the floor había papeles esparcidos por el suelo.

litterbin ['lɪtəˌbɪn] n UK papelera f.

little ['lɪtl] (compar sense 3 less, superl sense 3 least) ◇ adj -1. [small in size, younger] pequeño(ña); a ~ dog un perrito; you poor ~ thing! ¡pobrecillo! -2. [short in length] corto(ta); a ~ while un ratito -3. [not much] poco(ca); a ~ bit un poco; he speaks ~ English habla poco inglés; he speaks a ~ English habla un poco de inglés. ◇ pron: I understood very ~ entendí muy poco; a ~ un poco; a ~ under half algo menos de la mitad. ◇ adv poco; ~ by ~ poco a poco.

little finger n dedo m meñique.

little toe n meñique m del pie.

live¹ [lɪv] ◇ vi [gen] vivir. ◇ vt vivir; to ~ a quiet life llevar una vida tranquila.
➦ **live down** vt sep lograr hacer olvidar.
➦ **live off** vt fus [savings, land] vivir de; [people] vivir a costa de.
➦ **live on** ◇ vt fus -1. [survive on] vivir con or de -2. [eat] vivir de, alimentarse de. ◇ vi [memory, feeling] permanecer, perdurar.
➦ **live together** vi vivir juntos.
➦ **live up to** vt fus estar a la altura de.
➦ **live with** vt fus -1. [live in same house as] vivir con -2. [accept - situation, problem] aceptar.

live² [laɪv] *adj* **-1.** [living] vivo(va) **-2.** [coals] encendido(da) **-3.** [bomb] sin explotar; [ammunition] **real -4.** ELEC cargado(da) **-5.** [broadcast, performance] en directo.

livelihood ['laɪvlɪhʊd] *n* sustento *m*, medio *m* de vida.

lively ['laɪvlɪ] (*compar* **-ier**, *superl* **-iest**) *adj* **-1.** [person, debate, time] animado(da) **-2.** [mind] agudo(da), perspicaz **-3.** [colours] vivo(va).

liven ['laɪvn] ◆ **liven up** ◇ *vt sep* animar. ◇ *vi* animarse.

liver ['lɪvəʳ] *n* hígado *m*.

livery ['lɪvərɪ] (*pl* **-ies**) *n* [of servant] librea *f*; [of company] uniforme *m*.

lives [laɪvz] *pl* ▷ **life**.

livestock ['laɪvstɒk] *n* ganado *m*.

livid ['lɪvɪd] *adj* **-1.** [angry] furioso(sa) **-2.** [blue-grey] lívido(da).

living ['lɪvɪŋ] ◇ *adj* [relatives, language] vivo(va); [artist etc] contemporáneo(a). ◇ *n* **-1.** [means of earning money]: **what do you do for a ~?** ¿cómo te ganas la vida?; **to earn a ~** ganarse la vida **-2.** [lifestyle] vida *f*.

living conditions *npl* condiciones *fpl* de vida.

living room *n* sala *f* de estar, salón *m*.

living standards *npl* nivel *m* de vida.

lizard ['lɪzəd] *n* [small] lagartija *f*; [big] lagarto *m*.

llama ['lɑːmə] (*pl inv* OR **-s**) *n* llama *f*.

load [ləʊd] ◇ *n* **-1.** [thing carried] carga *f* **-2.** [amount of work]: **a heavy/light ~** mucho/poco trabajo **-3.** [large amount]: **~s/a load of** *inf* montones OR un montón de; **it was a ~ of rubbish** *inf* fue una porquería. ◇ *vt* **-1.** [gen & COMPUT]: **to ~ sth/sb (with)** cargar algo/a alguien (de) **-2.** [camera, video recorder]: **he ~ed the camera with a film** cargó la cámara con una película. ◆ **load up** *vt sep* & *vi* cargar.

loaded ['ləʊdɪd] *adj* **-1.** [dice] trucado(da); [question, statement] con doble sentido OR intención **-2.** *inf* [rich] forrado(da).

loading bay ['ləʊdɪŋ-] *n* zona *f* de carga y descarga.

loaf [ləʊf] (*pl* **loaves**) *n* [of bread] pan *m*; **a ~ of bread** un pan.

loafer ['ləʊfəʳ] *n* [shoe] mocasín *m*.

loan [ləʊn] ◇ *n* préstamo *m*; **on ~** prestado(da). ◇ *vt* prestar; **to ~ sth to sb**, **to ~ sb sth** prestar algo a alguien.

loath [ləʊθ] *adj*: **to be ~ to do sth** ser reacio(cia) a hacer algo.

loathe [ləʊð] *vt*: **to ~ (doing sth)** aborrecer OR detestar (hacer algo).

loathsome ['ləʊðsəm] *adj* [person, behaviour] odioso(sa), detestable; [smell] repugnante.

loaves [ləʊvz] *pl* ▷ **loaf**.

lob [lɒb] *n* TENNIS lob *m*.

lobby ['lɒbɪ] (*pl* **-ies**, *pt* & *pp* **-ied**) ◇ *n* **-1.** [hall] vestíbulo *m* **-2.** [pressure group] grupo *m* de presión, lobby *m*. ◇ *vt* ejercer presión (política) sobre.

lobe [ləʊb] *n* lóbulo *m*.

lobster ['lɒbstəʳ] *n* langosta *f*.

local ['ləʊkl] ◇ *adj* local. ◇ *n inf* **-1.** [person]: **the ~s** [in village] los lugareños; [in town] los vecinos del lugar **-2.** UK [pub] bar *m* del barrio **-3.** US [bus, train] omnibús *m*.

local authority *n* UK autoridad *f* local.

local call *n* llamada *f* local.

local government *n* gobierno *m* municipal.

locality [ləʊ'kælətɪ] (*pl* **-ies**) *n* localidad *f*.

locally ['ləʊkəlɪ] *adv* **-1.** [on local basis] en el lugar **-2.** [nearby] por la zona.

locate [UK ləʊ'keɪt, US 'ləʊkeɪt] *vt* **-1.** [find] localizar **-2.** [situate] ubicar.

location [ləʊ'keɪʃn] *n* **-1.** [place] ubicación *f*, situación *f* **-2.** [finding] localización *f* **-3.** CINEMA: **on ~** en exteriores.

loch [lɒk, lɒx] *n Scot* lago *m*.

lock [lɒk] ◇ *n* **-1.** [of door] cerradura *f*, chapa *f Amér*; [of bicycle] candado *m* **-2.** [on canal] esclusa *f* **-3.** AUT [steering lock] ángulo *m* de giro **-4.** *literary* [of hair] mechón *m*. ◇ *vt* **-1.** [with key] cerrar con llave; [with padlock] cerrar con candado **-2.** [keep safely] poner bajo llave **-3.** [immobilize] bloquear. ◇ *vi* **-1.** [with key, padlock] cerrarse **-2.** [become immobilized] bloquearse. ◆ **lock in** *vt sep* encerrar. ◆ **lock out** *vt sep* **-1.** [accidentally] dejar fuera al cerrar accidentalmente la puerta; **to ~ o.s. out** quedarse fuera (*por olvidarse la llave dentro*) **-2.** [deliberately] dejar fuera a. ◆ **lock up** *vt sep* **-1.** [person - in prison] encerrar; [- in asylum] internar **-2.** [house] cerrar (con llave).

locker ['lɒkəʳ] *n* taquilla *f*, armario *m*.

locker room *n* US vestuario *m* con taquillas.

locket ['lɒkɪt] *n* guardapelo *m*.

locksmith ['lɒksmɪθ] *n* cerrajero *m*, -ra *f*.

locomotive ['ləʊkə‚məʊtɪv] *n* locomotora *f*.

locum ['ləʊkəm] (*pl* **-s**) *n* interino *m*, -na *f*.

locust ['ləʊkəst] *n* langosta *f* (*insecto*).

lodge [lɒdʒ] ◇ *n* **-1.** [caretaker's etc room] portería *f* **-2.** [of manor house] casa *f* del guarda **-3.** [for hunting] refugio *m* **-4.** [of freemasons] logia *f*. ◇ *vi* **-1.** [stay]: **to ~ (with sb)** alojarse (con alguien) **-2.** [become stuck] alojarse. ◇ *vt fml* [appeal, complaint] presentar.

lodger ['lɒdʒəʳ] *n* huésped *m* OR *f*.

lodging ['lɒdʒɪŋ] ▷ **board**. ◆ **lodgings** *npl* habitación *f* (alquilada).

loft [lɒft] *n* [in house] desván *m*, entretecho *m Chile, Col*; [for hay] **pajar** *m*; *US* [warehouse apartment] *almacén reformado y convertido en apartamento*.

lofty ['lɒftɪ] (*compar* -ier, *superl* -iest) *adj* - 1. [noble] noble, elevado(da) - 2. *pej* [haughty] arrogante, altanero(ra) - 3. *literary* [high] elevado(da), alto(ta).

log [lɒg] (*pt* & *pp* -ged, *cont* -ging) ◇ *n* - 1. [of wood] tronco *m*; [for fire] leño *m* - 2. [written record - of ship] diario *m* de a bordo; [- COMPUT] registro *m*. ◇ *vt* registrar.
◆ **log in** *vi* COMPUT entrar.
◆ **log off** *vi* COMPUT salir.
◆ **log on** *vi* COMPUT entrar.
◆ **log out** *vi* COMPUT salir.

logbook ['lɒgbʊk] *n* - 1. [of ship] diario *m* de a bordo; [of plane] diario *m* de vuelo - 2. [of car] documentación *f*.

loggerheads ['lɒgəhedz] *n*: **to be at** ~ estar a matar.

logging ['lɒgɪŋ] *n* tala *f* de árboles.

logic ['lɒdʒɪk] *n* lógica *f*.

logical ['lɒdʒɪkl] *adj* lógico(ca).

logistics [lə'dʒɪstɪks] ◇ *n (U)* logística *f*. ◇ *npl* logística *f*.

logo ['ləʊgəʊ] (*pl* -s) *n* logotipo *m*.

loin [lɔɪn] *n* lomo *m*.

loiter ['lɔɪtə'] *vi* [for bad purpose] merodear; [hang around] vagar.

loll [lɒl] *vi* - 1. [sit, lie about] repantigarse - 2. [hang down] colgar.

lollipop ['lɒlɪpɒp] *n* piruli *m*.

lollipop lady *n UK mujer encargada de parar el tráfico en un paso de cebra para que crucen los niños.*

lollipop man *n UK hombre encargado de parar el tráfico en un paso de cebra para que crucen los niños.*

lolly ['lɒlɪ] (*pl* -ies) *n inf* - 1. [lollipop] piruli *m* - 2. *UK* [ice lolly] polo *m*.

London ['lʌndən] *n* Londres.

Londoner ['lʌndənə'] *n* londinense *m OR f*.

lone [ləʊn] *adj* solitario(ria).

loneliness ['ləʊnlɪnɪs] *n* soledad *f*.

lonely ['ləʊnlɪ] (*compar* -ier, *superl* -iest) *adj* - 1. [person] solo(la) - 2. [time, childhood, place] solitario(ria).

lonesome ['ləʊnsəm] *adj US inf* - 1. [person] solo(la) - 2. [place] solitario(ria).

long [lɒŋ] ◇ *adj* largo(ga); **the table is 5m** ~ la mesa mide *OR* tiene 5m de largo; **two days** ~ de dos días de duración; **the journey is 50km** ~ el viaje es de 50 km; **the book is 500 pages** ~ el libro tiene 500 páginas; **a** ~ **time** mucho tiempo; **a** ~ **way from** muy lejos de. ◇ *adv* mucho tiempo; **how** ~ **will it take?** ¿cuánto se tarda?; **how** ~ **will you be?** ¿cuánto tardarás?; **how** ~ **have you been waiting?** ¿cuánto tiempo llevas esperando?; **how** ~ **have**

you known them? ¿cuánto hace que los conoces?; **how** ~ **is the journey?** ¿cuánto hay de viaje?; **I'm no** ~ **er young** ya no soy joven; **I can't wait any** ~ **er** no puedo esperar más; **as** ~ **as a week** hasta una semana; **so** ~ *inf* hasta luego *OR* pronto; **before** ~ pronto; **for** ~ mucho tiempo. ◇ *vt*: **to** ~ **to do sthg** desear ardientemente hacer algo.
◆ **as long as, so long as** *conj* mientras; **as** ~ **as you do it, so will I** siempre y cuando tú lo hagas, yo también lo haré.
◆ **long for** *vt fus* desear ardientemente.

long-distance *adj* [runner] de fondo; [lorry driver] para distancias grandes.

long-distance call *n* conferencia *f* (telefónica) *Esp*, llamada *f* de larga distancia.

longhand ['lɒŋhænd] *n* escritura *f* a mano.

long-haul *adj* de larga distancia.

longing ['lɒŋɪŋ] ◇ *adj* anhelante. ◇ *n* - 1. [desire] anhelo *m*, deseo *m*; [nostalgia] nostalgia *f*, añoranza *f* - 2. [strong wish]: **(a)** ~ **(for)** (un) ansia *f* (de).

longitude ['lɒndʒɪtjuːd] *n* longitud *f*.

long jump *n* salto *m* de longitud.

long-life *adj* de larga duración.

long-playing record [-'pleɪɪŋ-] *n* elepé *m*.

long-range *adj* - 1. [missile, bomber] de largo alcance - 2. [plan, forecast] a largo plazo.

long shot *n* posibilidad *f* remota.

longsighted [,lɒŋ'saɪtɪd] *adj* présbita.

long-standing *adj* antiguo(gua).

long-stay *adj* [car park] para estacionamiento prolongado.

longsuffering [,lɒŋ'sʌfərɪŋ] *adj* sufrido(da).

long term *n*: **in the** ~ a largo plazo.

long wave *n (U)* onda *f* larga.

long weekend *n* puente *m*.

longwinded [,lɒŋ'wɪndɪd] *adj* prolijo(ja).

loo [luː] (*pl* -s) *n UK inf* wáter *m*.

look [lʊk] ◇ *n* - 1. [with eyes] mirada *f*; **to give sb a** ~ mirar a alguien; **to take have a** ~ **(at sthg)** mirar algo; **let her have a** ~ déjale ver; **to have a** ~ **through sthg** ojear algo - 2. [search]: **to have a** ~ **(for sthg)** buscar (algo) - 3. [appearance] aspecto *m*; **his new** ~ su nuevo look; **I don't like the** ~ **of** it no me gusta nada; **by the** ~ *OR* ~**s of it, it** has been here for ages parece que hace años que está aquí. ◇ *vi* - 1. [with eyes]: **to** ~ **(at sthg/sb)** mirar (algo/a alguien) - 2. [search]: **to** ~ **(for sthg/sb)** buscar (algo/a alguien) - 3. [building, window]: **to** ~ **(out) onto** dar a - 4. [have stated appearance] verse; [seem] parecer; **it** ~**s like rain** *OR* **as if it will rain** parece que va a llover; **she** ~**s like her mother** se parece a su madre. ◇ *vt* - 1. [look at] mirar - 2. [appear]: **to**

~ **one's age** representar la edad que se tiene.

◆ **looks** *npl* belleza *f.*

◆ **look after** *vt fus* **- 1.** [take care of] cuidar **- 2.** [be responsible for] encargarse de.

◆ **look at** *vt fus* **- 1.** [see, glance at] mirar, aguaitar *Amér*; [examine] examinar; [check over] echar un vistazo a **- 2.** [judge, evaluate] ver.

◆ **look down on** *vt fus* [condescend to] despreciar.

◆ **look for** *vt fus* buscar.

◆ **look forward to** *vt fus* esperar (con ilusión).

◆ **look into** *vt fus* [problem, possibility] estudiar; [issue] investigar.

◆ **look on** *vi* mirar, observar.

◆ **look out** *vi* [be careful] tener cuidado; ~ **out!** ¡cuidado!

◆ **look out for** *vt fus* estar atento(ta) a.

◆ **look over** *vt sep* mirar por encima.

◆ **look round** ⇔ *vt fus* [shop] echar un vistazo a; [castle, town] visitar. ⇔ *vi* **- 1.** [turn head] volver la cabeza **- 2.** [in shop] mirar.

◆ **look to** *vt fus* **- 1.** [turn to] recurrir a **- 2.** [think about] pensar en.

◆ **look up** ⇔ *vt sep* **- 1.** [in book] buscar **- 2.** [visit - person] ir a ver *OR* visitar. ⇔ *vi* [improve] mejorar.

◆ **look up to** *vt fus* respetar, admirar.

lookout ['lʊkaʊt] *n* **- 1.** [place] puesto *m* de observación, atalaya *f* **- 2.** [person] centinela *m* *OR* *f* **- 3.** [search] **to be on the ~ for** estar al acecho de.

loom [lu:m] ⇔ *n* telar *m.* ⇔ *vi* **- 1.** [rise up] surgir *OR* aparecer amenazante **- 2.** *fig* [be imminent] cernerse.

◆ **loom up** *vi* divisarse sombríamente.

loony ['lu:nɪ] (*compar* -ier, *superl* -iest, *pl* -ies) *inf* ⇔ *adj* majara, chiflado(da). ⇔ *n* majara *m* *OR* *f*, chiflado *m*, -da *f.*

loop [lu:p] *n* **- 1.** [shape] lazo *m* **- 2.** COMPUT bucle *m.*

loophole ['lu:phəʊl] *n* laguna *f.*

loose [lu:s] *adj* **- 1.** [not firmly fixed] flojo(ja) **- 2.** [unattached - paper, sweets, hair, knot] suelto(ta) **- 3.** [clothes, fit] holgado(da) **- 4.** *dated* [promiscuous] promiscuo(cua) **- 5.** [inexact - translation] impreciso(sa).

loose change *n* (dinero *m*) suelto *m*, sencillo *m* *Andes*, feria *f* *Méx*, menudo *m* *Col*.

loose end *n*: to be at a ~ *UK*, to be at ~s *US* no tener nada que hacer.

loosely ['lu:slɪ] *adv* **- 1.** [not firmly] holgadamente, sin apretar **- 2.** [inexactly] vagamente.

loosen ['lu:sn] *vt* aflojar.

◆ **loosen up** *vi* **- 1.** [before game, race] desentumecerse **- 2.** *inf* [relax] relajarse.

loot [lu:t] ⇔ *n* botín *m.* ⇔ *vt* saquear.

looting ['lu:tɪŋ] *n* saqueo *m.*

lop [lɒp] (*pt* & *pp* -ped, *cont* -ping) *vt* podar.

◆ **lop off** *vt sep* cortar.

lop-sided [-'saɪdɪd] *adj* **- 1.** [uneven] ladeado(da), torcido(da) **- 2.** *fig* [biased] desequilibrado(da).

lord [lɔ:d] *n* *UK* [man of noble rank] noble *m.*

◆ **Lord** *n* **- 1.** RELIG: **the Lord** [God] el Señor; **good Lord!** *UK* ¡Dios mío! **- 2.** [in titles] lord *m*; [as form of address]: **my Lord** [bishop] su Ilustrísima; [judge] su Señoría.

◆ **Lords** *npl* *UK* POL: **the Lords** la Cámara de los Lores.

Lordship ['lɔ:dʃɪp] *n*: **your/his** ~ su Señoría *f.*

lore [lɔ:ʳ] *n* (*U*) saber *m* *OR* tradición *f* popular.

lorry ['lɒrɪ] (*pl* -ies) *n* *UK* camión *m.*

lorry driver *n* *UK* camionero *m*, -ra *f.*

lose [lu:z] (*pt* & *pp* lost) ⇔ *vt* perder; **to ~ one's way** perderse; **my watch has lost ten minutes** mi reloj se ha atrasado diez minutos; **to ~ o.s. in sthg** *fig* quedarse absorto(ta) en algo; **to ~ sight of sthg** *lit* & *fig* perder de vista algo/a alguien. ⇔ *vi* [fail to win] perder.

loser ['lu:zəʳ] *n* **- 1.** [of competition] perdedor *m*, -ra *f* **- 2.** *inf pej* [unsuccessful person] desgraciado *m*, -da *f.*

loss [lɒs] *n* **- 1.** [gen] pérdida *f*; **to make a ~** sufrir pérdidas **- 2.** [failure to win] derrota *f* **- 3.** *phr*: **to be at a ~ to explain sthg** no saber cómo explicar algo.

lost [lɒst] ⇔ *pt* & *pp* ▷ **lose.** ⇔ *adj* **- 1.** [unable to find way] perdido(da); **to get ~** perderse; **get ~!** *inf* ¡vete a la porra! **- 2.** [that cannot be found] extraviado(da), perdido(da).

lost-and-found office *n* *US* oficina *f* de objetos perdidos.

lost property office *n* *UK* oficina *f* de objetos perdidos.

lot [lɒt] *n* **- 1.** [large amount]: **a ~ of**, ~s of mucho(cha); **a ~ of people** mucha gente, muchas personas; **a ~ of problems** muchos problemas; **the ~** todo **- 2.** [group, set] lote *m* **- 3.** [destiny] destino *m*, suerte *f* **- 4.** *US* [of land] terreno *m*; [car park] aparcamiento *m* **- 5.** [at auction] partida *f*, lote *m* **- 6.** *phr*: **to draw ~s** echar a suerte.

◆ **a lot** *adv* mucho; **quite a ~** bastante; **such a ~** tanto.

lotion ['ləʊʃn] *n* loción *f.*

lottery ['lɒtərɪ] (*pl* -ies) *n* lotería *f.*

lottery ticket *n* billete *m* de lotería.

loud [laʊd] ⇔ *adj* **- 1.** [voice, music] alto(ta); [bang, noise] fuerte; [person] ruidoso(sa) **- 2.** [emphatic]: **to be ~ in one's criticism of** ser enérgico(ca) en la crítica de **- 3.** [too bright] chillón(ona), llamativo(va).

◇ *adv* fuerte; **out ~** en voz alta.

loudhailer [ˌlaʊd'heɪləʳ] *n UK* megáfono *m*.

loudly ['laʊdlɪ] *adv* **- 1.** [shout] a voz en grito; [talk] en voz alta **- 2.** [gaudily] con colores chillones OR llamativos.

loudspeaker [ˌlaʊd'spi:kəʳ] *n* altavoz *m*, altoparlante *m Amér*.

lounge [laʊndʒ] (*cont* **lounging**) ◇ *n* **- 1.** [in house] salón *m* **- 2.** [in airport] sala *f* de espera. ◇ *vi* repantigarse.

lounge bar *n UK* salón-bar *m*.

louse [laʊs] (*pl* **lice**) *n* [insect] piojo *m*.

lousy ['laʊzɪ] (*compar* **-ier**, *superl* **-iest**) *adj inf* [poor quality] fatal, pésimo(ma).

lout [laʊt] *n* gamberro *m*.

louvre *UK*, **louver** *US* ['lu:vəʳ] *n* persiana *f*.

lovable ['lʌvəbl] *adj* adorable.

love [lʌv] ◇ *n* **- 1.** [gen] amor *m*; **give her my ~** dale un abrazo de mi parte; **she sends her ~** te manda recuerdos; **~ from** [at end of letter] un abrazo de; **to be in ~ (with)** estar enamorado(da) (de); **to fall in ~ with sb** enamorarse de alguien; **to make ~** hacer el amor **- 2.** [liking, interest] pasión *f*; **a ~ of** OR **for** una pasión por **- 3.** *inf* [form of address] cariño *m* OR *f* **- 4.** TENNIS : **30 ~** 30 a nada. ◇ *vt* **- 1.** [sexually, sentimentally] amar, querer **- 2.** [son, daughter, parents, friend] querer **- 3.** [like]: **I ~ football** me encanta el fútbol; **I ~ going to** OR **to go to the theatre** me encanta ir al teatro.

love affair *n* aventura *f* amorosa.

love life *n* vida *f* amorosa.

lovely ['lʌvlɪ] (*compar* **-ier**, *superl* **-iest**) *adj* **- 1.** [beautiful - person] encantador(ra); [- dress, place] precioso(sa) **- 2.** [pleasant] estupendo(da).

lover ['lʌvəʳ] *n* **- 1.** [sexual partner] amante *m* OR *f* **- 2.** [enthusiast] amante *m* OR *f*, aficionado *m*, -da *f*.

loving ['lʌvɪŋ] *adj* cariñoso(sa), afectuoso(sa).

low [ləʊ] ◇ *adj* **- 1.** [gen] bajo(ja); **in the ~ twenties** 20 y algo; **a ~ trick** una mala jugada **- 2.** [little remaining] escaso(sa) **- 3.** [unfavourable - opinion] malo(la); [- esteem] poco(ca) **- 4.** [dim] tenue **- 5.** [dress, neckline] escotado(da) **- 6.** [depressed] deprimido(da). ◇ *adv* **- 1.** [gen] bajo; **the batteries are running ~** las pilas están acabándose; **morale is running very ~** la moral está por los suelos; **~ paid** mal pagado **- 2.** [speak] en voz baja. ◇ *n* **- 1.** [low point] punto *m* más bajo **- 2.** METEOR [low pressure area] área *f* de bajas presiones; [lowest temperature] mínima *f*.

low-calorie *adj* light (*inv*), bajo(ja) en calorías.

low-cost *adj* económico(ca).

low-cut *adj* escotado(da).

lower ['ləʊəʳ] ◇ *adj* inferior. ◇ *vt* **- 1.** [gen] bajar; [flag] arriar **- 2.** [reduce] reducir.

low-fat *adj* bajo(ja) en grasas.

low-key *adj* discreto(ta).

lowly ['ləʊlɪ] (*compar* **-ier**, *superl* **-iest**) *adj* humilde.

low-lying *adj* bajo(ja).

loyal ['lɔɪəl] *adj* leal, fiel.

loyalty ['lɔɪəltɪ] (*pl* **-ies**) *n* lealtad *f*, fidelidad *f*.

loyalty card *n* tarjeta *f* de fidelización.

lozenge ['lɒzɪndʒ] *n* **- 1.** [tablet] pastilla *f* **- 2.** [shape] rombo *m*.

LP (*abbr of* **long-playing record**) *n* LP *m*.

L-plate *n UK* placa *f* L (de prácticas).

Ltd, ltd (*abbr of* **limited**) S.L.

lubricant ['lu:brɪkənt] *n* lubricante *m*.

lubricate ['lu:brɪkeɪt] *vt* lubricar.

lucid ['lu:sɪd] *adj* **- 1.** [clear] claro(ra) **- 2.** [not confused] lúcido(da).

luck [lʌk] *n* suerte *f*; **good/bad ~** [good, bad fortune] buena/mala suerte; **good ~!** [said to express best wishes] ¡suerte!; **bad** OR **hard ~!** ¡mala suerte!; **to be in ~** estar de suerte; **with (any) ~** con un poco de suerte.

luckily ['lʌkɪlɪ] *adv* afortunadamente.

lucky ['lʌkɪ] (*compar* **-ier**, *superl* **-iest**) *adj* **- 1.** [fortunate - person] afortunado(da); [- event] oportuno(na); **to be ~** [person] tener suerte; **it's ~ he came** fue una suerte que llegara **- 2.** [bringing good luck] que trae buena suerte.

lucrative ['lu:krətɪv] *adj* lucrativo(va).

ludicrous ['lu:dɪkrəs] *adj* absurdo(da), ridículo(la).

lug [lʌg] (*pt* & *pp* **-ged**, *cont* **-ging**) *vt inf* arrastrar.

luggage ['lʌgɪdʒ] *n UK* equipaje *m*.

luggage rack *n UK* [of car] baca *f*; [in train] portaequipajes *m inv*.

lukewarm ['lu:kwɔ:m] *adj* **- 1.** [tepid] tibio(bia), templado(da) **- 2.** [unenthusiastic] indiferente.

lull [lʌl] ◇ *n*: **~ (in)** [activity] respiro *m* (en); [conversation] pausa *f* (en); [fighting] tregua *f* (en). ◇ *vt*: **to ~ sb into a false sense of security** infundir una sensación de falsa seguridad a alguien; **to ~ sb to sleep** adormecer OR hacer dormir a alguien.

lullaby ['lʌləbaɪ] (*pl* **-ies**) *n* nana *f*, canción *f* de cuna.

lumber ['lʌmbəʳ] *n* (*U*) **- 1.** *US* [timber] maderos *mpl* **- 2.** *UK* [bric-a-brac] trastos *mpl*.
 ◆ **lumber with** *vt sep UK inf*: **to ~ sb with sthg** cargar a alguien con algo.

lumberjack ['lʌmbədʒæk] *n* leñador *m*, -ra *f*.

luminous ['lu:mɪnəs] *adj* luminoso(sa).

lump [lʌmp] ◇ *n* **- 1.** [of coal, earth] trozo *m*; [of sugar] terrón *m*; [in sauce] grumo *m*

- 2. [on body] bulto *m* **- 3.** *fig* [in throat] nudo *m.* $\diamond$ *vt* **: to ~ sthg together** [things] amontonar algo; [people, beliefs] agrupar OR juntar algo.

lump sum *n* suma *f* OR cantidad *f* global.

lumpy ['lʌmpɪ] (*compar* **-ier,** *superl* **-iest**) *adj* [sauce] grumoso(sa); [mattress] lleno(na) de bultos.

lunacy ['lu:nəsɪ] *n* locura *f.*

lunar ['lu:nə'] *adj* lunar.

lunatic ['lu:nətɪk] *n* **- 1.** *pej* [fool] idiota *m* OR *f*- **2.** [insane person] loco *m,* -ca *f.*

lunch [lʌntʃ] $\diamond$ *n* comida *f,* almuerzo *m;* **to have ~** almorzar, comer; **why don't we do ~ some time?** ¿por qué no almorzamos juntos algún día de estos? $\diamond$ *vi* almorzar, comer.

luncheon ['lʌntʃən] *n* comida *f,* almuerzo *m.*

luncheon meat *n carne de cerdo en lata troceada.*

luncheon voucher *n UK* vale *m* del almuerzo.

lunch hour *n* hora *f* del almuerzo.

lunchtime ['lʌntʃtaɪm] *n* hora *f* del almuerzo.

lung [lʌŋ] *n* pulmón *m.*

lunge [lʌndʒ] (*cont* **lunging**) *vi* lanzarse; **to ~ at sb** arremeter contra alguien.

lurch [lɜ:tʃ] $\diamond$ *n* [of boat] bandazo *m;* [of person] tumbo *m;* **to leave sb in the ~** dejar a alguien en la estacada. $\diamond$ *vi* [boat] dar bandazos; [person] tambalearse.

lure [ljʊə'] $\diamond$ *n* atracción *f.* $\diamond$ *vt* atraer.

lurid ['ljʊərɪd] *adj* **- 1.** [brightly coloured] chillón(ona) **- 2.** [shockingly unpleasant] espeluznante **- 3.** [sensational] escabroso(sa).

lurk [lɜ:k] *vi* **- 1.** [person] estar al acecho **- 2.** [memory, danger, fear] ocultarse.

luscious ['lʌʃəs] *adj lit & fig* apetitoso(sa).

lush [lʌʃ] *adj* [luxuriant] exuberante.

lust [lʌst] *n* **- 1.** [sexual desire] lujuria *f* **- 2.** [strong desire]: **~ for sthg** ansia *f* de algo.

➤ **lust after, lust for** *vt fus* **- 1.** [desire - wealth, success] codiciar **- 2.** [desire sexually] desear.

lusty ['lʌstɪ] (*compar* **-ier,** *superl* **-iest**) *adj* vigoroso(sa).

Luxembourg ['lʌksəm,bɜ:g] *n* Luxemburgo.

luxuriant [lʌg'ʒʊərɪənt] *adj* exuberante, abundante.

luxurious [lʌg'ʒʊərɪəs] *adj* [gen] lujoso(sa); [lifestyle] de lujo.

luxury ['lʌkʃərɪ] (*pl* **-ies**) $\diamond$ *n* lujo *m.* $\diamond$ *comp* de lujo.

LW (*abbr of* **long wave**) *n* OL *f.*

Lycra® ['laɪkrə] *n* lycra® *f.*

lying ['laɪɪŋ] $\diamond$ *adj* mentiroso(sa). $\diamond$ *n (U)* mentiras *fpl.*

lynch [lɪntʃ] *vt* linchar.

lyric ['lɪrɪk] *adj* lírico(ca).

lyrical ['lɪrɪkl] *adj* [poetic] lírico(ca).

lyrics ['lɪrɪks] *npl* letra *f.*

m[1] (*pl* **m's** OR **ms**), **M** (*pl* **M's** OR **Ms**) [em] *n* [letter] m *f,* M *f.*

➤ **M** *abbr of* **motorway.**

m[2] **- 1.** (*abbr of* **metre**) m **- 2.** (*abbr of* **million**) m **- 3.** *abbr of* **mile.**

MA *n abbr of* **Master of Arts.**

mac [mæk] (*abbr of* **mackintosh**) *n UK inf* [coat] impermeable *m.*

macaroni [,mækə'rəʊnɪ] *n (U)* macarrones *mpl.*

mace [meɪs] *n* **- 1.** [ornamental rod] maza *f* **- 2.** [spice] macis *f inv.*

machine [mə'ʃi:n] $\diamond$ *n* **- 1.** [power-driven device] máquina *f* **- 2.** [organization] aparato *m.* $\diamond$ *vt* **- 1.** SEWING coser a máquina **- 2.** TECH producir a máquina.

machinegun [mə'ʃi:ngʌn] *n* [with tripod] ametralladora *f;* [hand-held] metralleta *f.*

machine language *n* COMPUT lenguaje *m* máquina.

machinery [mə'ʃi:nərɪ] *n lit & fig* maquinaria *f.*

macho ['mætʃəʊ] *adj inf* macho.

mackerel ['mækrəl] (*pl inv* OR **-s**) *n* caballa *f.*

mackintosh ['mækɪntɒʃ] *n UK* impermeable *m.*

mad [mæd] (*compar* **-der,** *superl* **-dest**) *adj* **- 1.** [gen] loco(ca); [attempt, idea] disparatado(da), descabellado(da); **to be ~ about sb/sthg** estar loco(ca) por alguien/algo; **to go ~** volverse loco **- 2.** [furious] furioso(sa) **- 3.** [hectic] desenfrenado(da).

Madagascar [,mædə'gæskə'] *n* Madagascar.

madam ['mædəm] *n* **- 1.** [woman] señora *f* **- 2.** [in brothel] madam *f.*

madcap ['mædkæp] *adj* descabellado(da), disparatado(da).

mad cow disease *n* el mal de las vacas locas.

madden ['mædn] *vt* volver loco(ca), exasperar.

made [meɪd] *pt & pp* ⊳ **make.**

Madeira [mə'dɪərə] n - **1.** [wine] madeira m, madera m - **2.** GEOGR Madeira.

made-to-measure adj hecho(cha) a la medida.

made-up adj - **1.** [with make-up - face, person] maquillado(da); [- lips, eyes] pintado(da) - **2.** [invented] inventado(da).

madly ['mædlɪ] adv [frantically] enloquecidamente; ~ **in love** locamente enamorado.

madman ['mædmən] (pl -men [-mən]) n loco m.

madness ['mædnɪs] n locura f.

Madrid [mə'drɪd] n Madrid.

Mafia ['mæfɪə] n: the ~ la mafia.

magazine [,mægə'ziːn] n - **1.** [periodical] revista f - **2.** [news programme] magazín m - **3.** [on a gun] recámara f.

maggot ['mægət] n gusano m, larva f.

magic ['mædʒɪk] ⋄ adj [gen] mágico(ca). ⋄ n magia f.

magical ['mædʒɪkl] adj lit & fig mágico(ca).

magician [mə'dʒɪʃn] n - **1.** [conjuror] prestidigitador m, -ra f - **2.** [wizard] mago m.

magistrate ['mædʒɪstreɪt] n juez m OR f de primera instancia.

magistrates' court n UK juzgado m de primera instancia.

magnanimous [mæg'nænɪməs] adj magnánimo(ma).

magnate ['mægneɪt] n magnate m OR f.

magnesium [mæg'niːzɪəm] n magnesio m.

magnet ['mægnɪt] n imán m.

magnetic [mæg'netɪk] adj - **1.** [attracting iron] magnético(ca) - **2.** fig [appealingly forceful] carismático(ca).

magnetic tape n cinta f magnética.

magnificent [mæg'nɪfɪsənt] adj [building, splendour] grandioso(sa); [idea, book, game] magnífico(ca).

magnify ['mægnɪfaɪ] (pt & pp -ied) vt - **1.** [in vision] aumentar, ampliar - **2.** [in the mind] exagerar.

magnifying glass ['mægnɪfaɪɪŋ-] n lupa f, lente f de aumento.

magnitude ['mægnɪtjuːd] n magnitud f.

magpie ['mægpaɪ] n urraca f.

mahogany [mə'hɒgənɪ] n - **1.** [wood] caoba f - **2.** [colour] caoba m.

maid [meɪd] n [in hotel] camarera f, recamarera f CAm, Méx; [domestic] criada f, china f Amér.

maiden ['meɪdn] ⋄ adj inaugural. ⋄ n literary doncella f.

maiden aunt n tía f soltera.

maiden name n nombre m de soltera.

mail [meɪl] ⋄ n - **1.** [system] correo m; **by** ~ por correo - **2.** [letters, parcels received] correspondencia f. ⋄ vt esp US [send] mandar por correo; [put in mail box] echar al buzón.

mailbox ['meɪlbɒks] n - **1.** US [letterbox] buzón m - **2.** COMPUT buzón m.

mailing list ['meɪlɪŋ-] n [for mailshots] lista f de distribución de publicidad OR información; COMPUT lista f de correo.

mailman ['meɪlmən] (pl -men [-mən]) n US cartero m.

mail order n venta f por correo.

mailshot ['meɪlʃɒt] n folleto m de publicidad (por correo).

maim [meɪm] vt mutilar.

main [meɪn] ⋄ adj principal. ⋄ n [pipe] tubería f principal; [wire] cable m principal. ◆ **mains** npl: the ~s [gas, water] la tubería principal; [electricity] la red eléctrica. ◆ **in the main** adv por lo general.

main course n plato m fuerte.

mainframe (computer) ['meɪnfreɪm-] n unidad f central, procesador m central.

mainland ['meɪnlənd] ⋄ adj continental; ~ **Spain** la Península. ⋄ n: on the ~ en tierra firme.

mainly ['meɪnlɪ] adv principalmente.

main road n carretera f principal.

mainstay ['meɪnsteɪ] n fundamento m, base f.

mainstream ['meɪnstriːm] ⋄ adj [gen] predominante; [taste] corriente; [political party] convencional. ⋄ n: the ~ la tendencia general.

maintain [meɪn'teɪn] vt - **1.** [gen] mantener - **2.** [support, provide for] sostener, sustentar - **3.** [assert]: to ~ (that) sostener que.

maintenance ['meɪntənəns] n - **1.** [gen] mantenimiento m - **2.** [money] pensión f alimenticia.

maize [meɪz] n maíz m.

majestic [mə'dʒestɪk] adj majestuoso(sa).

majesty ['mædʒəstɪ] (pl -ies) n [grandeur] majestad f. ◆ **Majesty** n: His/Her/Your Majesty Su Majestad.

major ['meɪdʒə'] ⋄ adj - **1.** [important] importante; [main] principal; of ~ **importance** de gran importancia - **2.** MUS mayor. ⋄ n MIL comandante m; US [subject] especialidad f.

Majorca [mə'jɔːkə, mə'dʒɔːkə] n Mallorca.

majority [mə'dʒɒrətɪ] (pl -ies) n mayoría f.

make [meɪk] (pt & pp **made**) ⋄ vt - **1.** [produce] hacer; **she** ~s her own clothes se hace su propia ropa - **2.** [perform - action] hacer; to ~ **a speech** pronunciar OR dar un discurso; to ~ **a decision** tomar una decisión; to ~ **a mistake** cometer un error; to ~ **a payment** efectuar un pago - **3.** [cause to be, cause to do] hacer; it ~s me sick me pone enfermo; it ~s me want to ... me da ganas de ...; it made him angry hizo que se enfadara; you made me jump! ¡vaya susto que me has dado!; **to ~ sb happy** hacer a alguien feliz; **to ~ sb sad** entristecer a alguien; **to ~ sb nervous** poner nervioso a alguien. **- 4.** [force]: **to ~ sb do sthg** hacer que alguien haga algo, obligar a alguien a hacer algo **- 5.** [construct]: **to be made of sthg** estar hecho(cha) de algo; **made in Spain** fabricado en España **- 6.** [add up to] hacer, ser; **2 and 2 ~ 4** 2 y 2 hacen OR son 4 **- 7.** [calculate] calcular; **I ~ it 50/six o'clock** calculo que serán 50/las seis; **what time do you ~ it?** ¿qué hora tienes? **- 8.** [earn] ganar; **to ~ a profit** obtener beneficios; **to ~ a loss** sufrir pérdidas **- 9.** [have the right qualities for] ser; **she'd ~ a good doctor** seguro que sería una buena doctora **- 10.** [reach] llegar a **- 11.** [gain - friend, enemy] hacer; **to ~ friends with sb** hacerse amigo de alguien **- 12.** phr: **to ~ it** [arrive in time] conseguir llegar a tiempo; [be a success] alcanzar el éxito; [be able to attend] venir/ir; [survive] vivir; **to ~ do with sthg** apañarse OR arreglarse con algo. ◇ n [brand] marca f.

◆ **make for** vt fus **- 1.** [move towards] dirigirse a OR hacia **- 2.** [contribute to] contribuir a.

◆ **make into** vt sep: **to ~ sth into sth** convertir algo en algo.

◆ **make of** vt sep **- 1.** [understand] entender; **what do you ~ of this word?** ¿qué entiendes tú por esta palabra? **- 2.** [have opinion of] opinar de.

◆ **make off** vi darse a la fuga.

◆ **make out** vt sep **- 1.** inf [see] distinguir; [hear] entender, oír **- 2.** inf [understand - word, number] descifrar; [- person, attitude] comprender **- 3.** [fill out - form] rellenar, cumplimentar; [- cheque, receipt] extender; [- list] hacer. ◇ n US inf [sexually] darse el lote, fajar Méx **- 5.** inf [pretend]: **to ~ o.s. out to be sthg** dárselas de algo.

◆ **make up** ◇ vt sep **- 1.** [compose, constitute] componer, constituir **- 2.** [invent] inventar **- 3.** [apply cosmetics to] maquillar **- 4.** [prepare - parcel, prescription, bed] preparar **- 5.** [make complete - amount] completar; [- difference] cubrir; [- deficit, lost time] recuperar. ◇ vi [become friends again]: **to ~ up (with sb)** hacer las paces (con alguien). ◇ n US [test] examen que se realiza más tarde si no se pude hacer en su día.

◆ **make up for** vt fus compensar.

◆ **make up to** vt sep: **to ~ it up to sb (for sthg)** recompensar a alguien (por algo).

make-believe n (U) fantasías fpl.

makeover ['meɪkəʊvə'] n [of person] cambio m de imagen; [of home, garden] reforma f completa.

maker ['meɪkə'] n [of film, programme]

creador m, -ra f; [of product] **fabricante** m OR f.

makeshift ['meɪkʃɪft] adj [temporary] provisional; [improvized] improvisado(da).

make-up n **- 1.** [cosmetics] maquillaje m; **~ remover** loción f OR leche f desmaquilladora **- 2.** [person's character] carácter m **- 3.** [structure] estructura f; [of team] composición f.

making ['meɪkɪŋ] n [of product] fabricación f; [of film] rodaje m; [of decision] toma f; **this is history in the ~** esto pasará a la historia; **your problems are of your own ~** tus problemas te los has buscado tú mismo; **to have the ~s of** tener madera de.

malaise [mə'leɪz] n fml malestar m.

malaria [mə'leərɪə] n malaria f.

Malaya [mə'leɪə] n Malaya.

Malaysia [mə'leɪzɪə] n Malaisia.

male [meɪl] ◇ adj **- 1.** [animal] macho **- 2.** [human] masculino(na), varón **- 3.** [concerning men] masculino(na), del hombre. ◇ n **- 1.** [animal] macho m **- 2.** [human] varón m.

male nurse n enfermero m.

malevolent [mə'levələnt] adj malévolo(la).

malfunction [mæl'fʌŋkʃn] ◇ n fallo m. ◇ vi averiarse.

malice ['mælɪs] n malicia f.

malicious [mə'lɪʃəs] adj malicioso(sa).

malign [mə'laɪn] ◇ adj maligno(na), perjudicial. ◇ vt fml difamar.

malignant [mə'lɪgnənt] adj **- 1.** MED maligno(na) **- 2.** fml [full of hate] malvado(da).

mall [mɔːl] n esp US: **(shopping) ~** centro m comercial peatonal.

mallet ['mælɪt] n mazo m.

malnutrition [,mælnjuː'trɪʃn] n malnutrición f.

malpractice [,mæl'præktɪs] n (U) JUR negligencia f.

malt [mɔːlt] n **- 1.** [grain] malta f **- 2.** [whisky] whisky m de malta **- 3.** US leche malteada con helado.

Malta ['mɔːltə] n Malta.

mammal ['mæml] n mamífero m.

mammoth ['mæməθ] ◇ adj descomunal, gigante. ◇ n mamut m.

man [mæn] (pl **men**, pt & pp **-ned**, cont **-ning**) ◇ n **- 1.** [gen] hombre m; **the ~ in the street** el hombre de la calle, el ciudadano de a pie **- 2.** [humankind] el hombre. ◇ vt [gen] manejar; [ship, plane] tripular; **manned 24 hours a day** [telephone] en servicio las 24 horas del día.

manage ['mænɪdʒ] ◇ vi **- 1.** [cope] poder **- 2.** [survive] apañárselas. ◇ vt **- 1.** [succeed]: **to ~ to do sthg** conseguir hacer algo

- 2. [company] dirigir, llevar; [money] administrar, manejar; [pop star] representar; [time] organizar **- 3.** [cope with] poder con; **can you ~ that box?** ¿puedes con la caja?

manageable ['mænɪdʒəbl] *adj* [task] factible, posible; [children] dominable; [inflation, rate] controlable.

management ['mænɪdʒmənt] *n* **-1.** [control, running] gestión *f* **- 2.** [people in control] dirección *f*.

manager ['mænɪdʒə'] *n* **-1.** [of company] director *m*, -ra *f*; [of shop] jefe *m*, -fa *f*; [of pop star] manager *m* OR *f* **- 2.** SPORT ≃ entrenador *m*, -ra *f*.

manageress [,mænɪdʒə'res] *n* UK [of company] directora *f*; [of shop] jefa *f*.

managerial [,mænɪ'dʒɪərɪəl] *adj* directivo(va).

managing director ['mænɪdʒɪŋ-] *n* director *m*, -ra *f* gerente.

mandarin ['mændərɪn] *n* [fruit] mandarina *f*.

mandate ['mændeɪt] *n* **-1.** [elected right or authority] mandato *m*; **to have a ~ to do sthg** tener autoridad para hacer algo **- 2.** [task] misión *f*.

mandatory ['mændətrɪ] *adj* obligatorio(ria).

mane [meɪn] *n* [of horse] crin *f*; [of lion] melena *f*.

maneuver US = manoeuvre.

manfully ['mænfʊlɪ] *adv* valientemente.

mangle ['mæŋgl] *vt* [crush] aplastar; [tear to pieces] despedazar.

mango ['mæŋgəʊ] (*pl* **-es** OR **-s**) *n* mango *m*.

mangy ['meɪndʒɪ] (*compar* **-ier**, *superl* **-iest**) *adj* sarnoso(sa).

manhandle ['mæn,hændl] *vt* [person]: **they ~ed her into the van** la metieron en el camión a empujones.

manhole ['mænhəʊl] *n* boca *f* (del alcantarillado).

manhood ['mænhʊd] *n* **-1.** [state] virilidad *f* **- 2.** [time] edad *f* adulta.

manhour ['mæn,aʊə'] *n* hora *f* hombre.

mania ['meɪnjə] *n* **-1.** [excessive liking]: **~ (for)** pasión *f* (por) **- 2.** PSYCH manía *f*.

maniac ['meɪnɪæk] *n* **-1.** [madman] maníaco *m*, -ca *f* **- 2.** [fanatic] fanático *m*, -ca *f*.

manic ['mænɪk] *adj* maníaco(ca).

manicure ['mænɪ,kjʊə'] *n* manicura *f*.

manifest ['mænɪfest] *fml* ◇ *adj* manifiesto(ta), evidente. ◇ *vt* manifestar.

manifesto [,mænɪ'festəʊ] (*pl* **-s** OR **-es**) *n* manifiesto *m*.

manipulate [mə'nɪpjʊleɪt] *vt* **-1.** [control for personal benefit] manipular **- 2.** [controls, lever] manejar.

mankind [mæn'kaɪnd] *n* la humanidad.

manly ['mænlɪ] (*compar* **-ier**, *superl* **-iest**) *adj* varonil, viril.

man-made *adj* [environment, problem, disaster] producido(da) por el hombre; [fibre, lake, goods] artificial.

manner ['mænə'] *n* **-1.** [method] manera *f*, forma *f* **- 2.** [bearing, attitude] actitud *f* **- 3.** *esp literary* [type, sort] tipo *m*, clase *f*.
◆ **manners** *npl* modales *mpl*; **it's good/ bad ~s to do sthg** es de buena/mala educación hacer algo.

mannerism ['mænərɪzm] *n* costumbre *f* (típica de uno).

mannish ['mænɪʃ] *adj* [woman] hombruno(na).

manoeuvre UK, **maneuver** US [mə'nuːvə'] ◇ *n lit* & *fig* maniobra *f*. ◇ *vt* maniobrar, manejar. ◇ *vi* maniobrar.

manor ['mænə'] *n* [house] casa *f* solariega.

manpower ['mæn,paʊə'] *n* [manual workers] mano *f* de obra; [white-collar workers] personal *m*.

mansion ['mænʃn] *n* [manor] casa *f* solariega; [big house] casa grande.

manslaughter ['mæn,slɔːtə'] *n* homicidio *m* involuntario.

mantelpiece ['mæntlpiːs] *n* repisa *f* (de la chimenea).

manual ['mænjʊəl] ◇ *adj* manual. ◇ *n* manual *m*.

manual worker *n* obrero *m*, -ra *f*.

manufacture [,mænjʊ'fæktʃə'] ◇ *n* fabricación *f*. ◇ *vt* [make] fabricar.

manufacturer [,mænjʊ'fæktʃərə'] *n* fabricante *m* OR *f*.

manure [mə'njʊə'] *n* estiércol *m*, abono *m*.

manuscript ['mænjʊskrɪpt] *n* **-1.** [gen] manuscrito *m* **- 2.** [in exam] hoja *f* de examen.

many ['menɪ] (*compar* **more**, *superl* **most**) ◇ *adj* muchos(chas); **~ people** muchas personas, mucha gente; **how ~?** ¿cuántos(tas)?; **I wonder how ~ people went** me pregunto cuánta gente fue; **too ~** demasiados(das); **there weren't too ~ students** no había muchos estudiantes; **as ~ ... as** tantos(tas) ... como; **they have three times as ~ soldiers as us** tienen el triple de soldados que nosotros; **so ~** tantos(tas); **I've never seen so ~ people** nunca había visto tanta gente; **a good** OR **great ~** muchísimos(mas). ◇ *pron* muchos(chas); **twice as ~** el doble; **four times as ~** cuatro veces esa cantidad.

map [mæp] (*pt* & *pp* **-ped**, *cont* **-ping**) *n* mapa *m*.
◆ **map out** *vt sep* planear, planificar.

maple ['meɪpl] *n* arce *m*.

mar [mɑː'] (*pt* & *pp* **-red**, *cont* **-ring**) *vt* deslucir.

marathon ['mærəθn] *n* maratón *m*.

marauder [mə'rɔːdə'] *n* merodeador *m*, -ra *f*.

marble ['mɑ:bl] *n* -**1.** [stone] mármol *m*
-**2.** [for game] canica *f*.

march [mɑ:tʃ] ⟨⟩ *n* -**1.** MIL marcha *f* -**2.** [of
demonstrators] marcha *f (de protesta)*
-**3.** [steady progress] avance *m*. ⟨⟩ *vi* -**1.** [in
formation, in protest] marchar -**2.** [speedily]:
to ∼ up to sb abordar a alguien decididamente. ⟨⟩ *vt* llevar por la fuerza.

March [mɑ:tʃ] *n* marzo *m*; *see also* **Septem-**
ber.

marcher ['mɑ:tʃə'] *n* [protester] manifestante *m* OR *f*.

mare [meə'] *n* yegua *f*.

margarine [,mɑ:dʒə'ri:n, ,mɑ:gə'ri:n] *n*
margarina *f*.

marge [mɑ:dʒ] *n inf* margarina *f*.

margin ['mɑ:dʒɪn] *n* [gen] margen *m*.

marginal ['mɑ:dʒɪnl] *adj* -**1.** [unimportant]
marginal -**2.** UK POL: **∼ seat** OR **constitu-**
ency *escaño vulnerable a ser perdido en las elec-*
ciones por tener una mayoría escasa.

marginally ['mɑ:dʒɪnəlɪ] *adv* ligeramente.

marigold ['mærɪgəʊld] *n* caléndula *f*.

marihuana, marijuana [,mærɪ'wɑ:nə] *n*
marihuana *f*.

marine [mə'ri:n] ⟨⟩ *adj* marino(na). ⟨⟩ *n*
soldado *m* de infantería de marina.

marital ['mærɪtl] *adj* matrimonial.

marital status *n* estado *m* civil.

maritime ['mærɪtaɪm] *adj* marítimo(ma).

mark [mɑ:k] ⟨⟩ *n* -**1.** [stain] mancha *f*;
[scratch] marca *f* -**2.** [written symbol - on pa-
per] marca *f*; [- in the sand] señal *f* -**3.** [in
exam] nota *f*; [point] punto *m*; **to get good**
∼s sacar buenas notas -**4.** [stage, level]:
once past the halfway ∼ una vez llegado a
medio camino -**5.** [sign - of respect] señal *f*;
[- of illness, old age] huella *f* -**6.** [currency]
marco *m*. ⟨⟩ *vt* -**1.** [stain] manchar;
[scratch] marcar -**2.** [label - with initials etc]
señalar -**3.** [exam, essay] puntuar, calificar
-**4.** [identify - place] señalar; [- beginning,
end] marcar -**5.** [commemorate] conmemorar -**6.** [characterize] caracterizar -**7.** SPORT
marcar.

◆ **mark off** *vt sep* [cross off] poner una
marca en.

marked [mɑ:kt] *adj* [improvement] notable;
[difference] acusado(da).

marker ['mɑ:kə'] *n* -**1.** [sign] señal *f* -**2.** SPORT
marcador *m*, -ora *f*.

marker pen *n* rotulador *m*.

market ['mɑ:kɪt] ⟨⟩ *n* mercado *m*. ⟨⟩ *vt* comercializar.

market garden *n esp* UK [small] huerto *m*;
[large] huerta *f*.

marketing ['mɑ:kɪtɪŋ] *n* [subject] marketing *m*; [selling] comercialización *f*.

marketplace ['mɑ:kɪtpleɪs] *n lit & fig* mercado *m*.

market research *n* estudio *m* de mercados.

market value *n* valor *m* actual OR en venta.

marking ['mɑ:kɪŋ] *n* -**1.** [of exams etc] corrección *f* -**2.** SPORT marcaje *m*.

◆ **markings** *npl* [of flower, animal] pintas
fpl, manchas *fpl*; [on road] señales *fpl*.

marksman ['mɑ:ksmən] (*pl* **-men** [-mən])
n tirador *m*.

marmalade ['mɑ:məleɪd] *n* mermelada *f*
(de cítricos).

maroon [mə'ru:n] *adj* granate.

marooned [mə'ru:nd] *adj* incomunica-
do(da), aislado(da).

marquee [mɑ:'ki:] *n* carpa *f*, toldo *m* grande; US [of building] marquesina *f*.

marriage ['mærɪdʒ] *n* -**1.** [act] boda *f*
-**2.** [state, institution] matrimonio *m*.

marriage bureau *n* UK agencia *f* matrimonial.

marriage certificate *n* certificado *m* de
matrimonio.

marriage guidance *n* asesoría *f* matrimonial.

married ['mærɪd] *adj* -**1.** [person] casa-
do(da); **a ∼ couple** un matrimonio -**2.** [life]
matrimonial, de casado(da).

marrow ['mærəʊ] *n* -**1.** UK [vegetable] calabacín *m* grande -**2.** [in bones] médula *f*.

marry ['mærɪ] (*pt & pp* **-ied**) ⟨⟩ *vt* -**1.** [take
as husband or wife] casarse con; **to get mar-**
ried casarse -**2.** [sanction marriage of] casar.
⟨⟩ *vi* casarse.

Mars [mɑ:z] *n* Marte *m*.

marsh [mɑ:ʃ] *n* -**1.** [area of land] zona *f* pan-
tanosa -**2.** [type of land] pantano *m*.

marshal ['mɑ:ʃl] (*UK pt & pp* **-led**, *cont*
-ling, *US pt & pp* **-ed**, *cont* **-ing**) ⟨⟩ *n* -**1.**
MIL mariscal *m* -**2.** [steward] oficial *m* OR *f*,
miembro *m* OR *f* del servicio de orden
-**3.** US [officer] jefe *m*, -fa *f* de policía. ⟨⟩ *vt*
[people] dirigir, conducir; [thoughts] orde-
nar.

martial arts [,mɑ:ʃl-] *npl* artes *fpl* marcia-
les.

martial law [,mɑ:ʃl-] *n* ley *f* marcial.

martyr ['mɑ:tə'] *n* mártir *m* OR *f*.

martyrdom ['mɑ:tədəm] *n* martirio *m*.

marvel ['mɑ:vl] (*UK pt & pp* **-led**, *cont* **-ling**,
US pt & pp **-ed**, *cont* **-ing**) ⟨⟩ *n* maravilla *f*.
⟨⟩ *vi*: **to ∼ (at)** maravillarse OR asombrarse
(ante).

marvellous UK, **marvelous** US
['mɑ:vələs] *adj* maravilloso(sa).

Marxism ['mɑ:ksɪzm] *n* marxismo *m*.

Marxist ['mɑ:ksɪst] ⟨⟩ *adj* marxista. ⟨⟩ *n*
marxista *m* OR *f*.

marzipan ['mɑ:zɪpæn] *n* mazapán *m*.

mascara [mæs'kɑ:rə] *n* rímel *m*.

masculine ['mæskjʊlɪn] *adj* [gen] masculi-
no(na); [woman, appearance] hombruno(na).

mash [mæʃ] ◇ *n inf* puré *m* de patatas. ◇ *vt* hacer puré.

mashed potatoes [mæʃt-] *npl* puré *m* de patatas.

mask [mɑːsk] ◇ *n lit & fig* máscara *f*. ◇ *vt* **-1.** [to hide] enmascarar **- 2.** [cover up] ocultar, disfrazar.

masochist ['mæsəkɪst] *n* masoquista *m OR f*.

mason ['meɪsn] *n* **- 1.** [stonemason] cantero *m* **- 2.** [freemason] masón *m*.

masonry ['meɪsnrɪ] *n* [stones] albañilería *f*.

masquerade [ˌmæskə'reɪd] *vi*: to ~ as hacerse pasar por.

mass [mæs] ◇ *n* **- 1.** [gen] masa *f* **- 2.** [large amount] montón *m* **- 3.** [religious ceremony] misa *f*. ◇ *adj* [unemployment] masivo(va); [communication] de masas. ◇ *vi* agruparse, concentrarse.
◆ **masses** *npl* **- 1.** *inf* [lots] montones *mpl* **- 2.** [workers]: the ~ es las masas.

massacre ['mæsəkə'] ◇ *n* matanza *f*, masacre *f*. ◇ *vt* masacrar.

massage [*UK* 'mæsɑːʒ, *US* mə'sɑːʒ] ◇ *n* masaje *m*. ◇ *vt* dar un masaje a.

massive ['mæsɪv] *adj* [gen] enorme; [majority] aplastante.

mass media *n & npl*: the ~ los medios de comunicación de masas.

mass murderer *n* asesino *m*, -na *f* múltiple.

mass production *n* producción *f OR* fabricación *f* en serie.

mast [mɑːst] *n* **- 1.** [on boat] mástil *m* **- 2.** RADIO & TV poste *m*, torre *f*.

master ['mɑːstə'] ◇ *n* **- 1.** [of people, animals] amo *m*, dueño *m*; [of house] señor *m* **- 2.** *fig* [of situation] dueño *m*, -ña *f* **- 3.** *UK* [teacher - primary school] maestro *m*; [-secondary school] profesor *m* **- 4.** [of recording] original *m*. ◇ *adj* maestro(tra). ◇ *vt* **- 1.** [situation] dominar, controlar; [difficulty] superar **- 2.** [technique etc] dominar.

master key *n* llave *f* maestra.

masterly ['mɑːstəlɪ] *adj* magistral.

mastermind ['mɑːstəmaɪnd] ◇ *n* cerebro *m*. ◇ *vt* ser el cerebro de, dirigir.

Master of Arts (*pl* **Masters of Arts**) *n* **- 1.** [degree] máster *m* en Letras **- 2.** [person] licenciado *m*, -da *f* con máster en Letras.

Master of Science (*pl* **Masters of Science**) *n* **- 1.** [degree] máster *m* en Ciencias **- 2.** [person] licenciado *m*, -da *f* con máster en Ciencias.

masterpiece ['mɑːstəpiːs] *n lit & fig* obra *f* maestra.

master's degree *n* máster *m*.

mastery ['mɑːstərɪ] *n* dominio *m*.

mat [mæt] *n* **- 1.** [rug] alfombrilla *f*; [beer mat] posavasos *m inv*; [tablemat] salvamanteles *m inv* **- 2.** [doormat] felpudo *m*.

match [mætʃ] ◇ *n* **- 1.** [game] partido *m* **- 2.** [for lighting] cerilla *f*, cerillo *m* *CAm,*

Méx, fósforo *m* *Amér* **- 3.** [equal]: to be a ~ for estar a la altura de; to be no ~ for no poder competir con. ◇ *vt* **- 1.** [be the same as] coincidir con **- 2.** [pair off]: to ~ sthg (to) emparejar algo (con) **- 3.** [be equal with] competir con, llegar a la altura de **- 4.** [go well with] hacer juego con. ◇ *vi* **- 1.** [be the same] coincidir **- 2.** [go together well] hacer juego, combinar.

matchbox ['mætʃbɒks] *n* caja *f* de cerillas.

matching ['mætʃɪŋ] *adj* a juego.

mate [meɪt] ◇ *n* **- 1.** *inf* [friend] amigo *m*, -ga *f*, compañero *m*, -ra *f*, compa *m OR f* *Amér* **- 2.** *US* [spouse] esposo *m*, -sa *f* **- 3.** *UK inf* [term of address] colega *m* **- 4.** [of animal] macho *m*, hembra *f* **- 5.** NAUT: (first) ~ (primer) oficial *m*. ◇ *vi* [animals]: to ~ (with) aparearse (con).

material [mə'tɪərɪəl] ◇ *adj* **- 1.** [physical] material **- 2.** [important] sustancial. ◇ *n* **- 1.** [substance] material *m* **- 2.** [type of substance] materia *f* **- 3.** [fabric] tela *f*, tejido *m* **- 4.** [type of fabric] tejido *m* **- 5.** *(U)* [ideas, information] información *f*, documentación *f*.
◆ **materials** *npl*: building ~s materiales *mpl* de construcción; writing ~s objetos *mpl* de escritorio; cleaning ~s productos *mpl* de limpieza.

materialistic [mə,tɪərɪə'lɪstɪk] *adj* materialista.

maternal [mə'tɜːnl] *adj* [gen] maternal; [grandparent] materno(na).

maternity [mə'tɜːnətɪ] *n* maternidad *f*.

maternity dress *n* vestido *m* premamá.

maternity hospital *n* hospital *m* de maternidad.

maternity leave *n* baja *f* por maternidad.

maternity ward *n* pabellón *m* de maternidad.

math *US* = maths.

mathematical [,mæθə'mætɪkl] *adj* matemático(ca).

mathematics [,mæθə'mætɪks] *n (U)* matemáticas *fpl*.

maths *UK* [mæθs], **math** *US* [mæθ] (*abbr of* **mathematics**) *n inf (U)* mates *fpl*.

matinée ['mætɪneɪ] *n* [at cinema] primera sesión *f*; [at theatre] función *f* de tarde, vermú *f* *Amér*.

mating season ['meɪtɪŋ-] *n* época *f* de celo.

matrices ['meɪtrɪsiːz] *pl* ⊳ **matrix**.

matriculation [mə,trɪkjʊ'leɪʃn] *n* matrícula *f*.

matrimonial [,mætrɪ'məʊnjəl] *adj* matrimonial.

matrimony ['mætrɪmənɪ] *n (U)* matrimonio *m*.

matrix ['meɪtrɪks] (*pl* **matrices** *OR* **-es**) *n* matriz *f*.

matron ['meɪtrən] *n* **- 1.** *UK* [in hospital]

enfermera f jefa - **2.** [in school] *mujer a cargo de la enfermería.*

matronly ['meɪtrənlɪ] *adj* euphemism [figure] corpulenta y de edad madura.

matt UK, **matte** US [mæt] *adj* mate.

matted ['mætɪd] *adj* enmarañado(da).

matter ['mætəʳ] ◇ *n* - **1.** [question, situation] asunto *m*; **that's another** OR **a different ~** es otra cuestión OR cosa; **as a ~ of course** automáticamente; **to make ~s worse** para colmo de desgracias; **a ~ of opinion** una cuestión de opiniones - **2.** [trouble, cause of pain]: **what's the ~ (with it/her)?** ¿qué (le) pasa?; **something's the ~ with my car** algo le pasa a mi coche - **3.** PHYS materia f - **4.** (U) [material] material *m.* ◇ *vi* [be important] importar; **it doesn't ~** no importa.
◆ **as a matter of fact** *adv* en realidad.
◆ **for that matter** *adv* de hecho.
◆ **no matter** *adv*: **no ~ how hard I try** por mucho que lo intente; **no ~ what he does** haga lo que haga; **we must win, no ~ what** tenemos que ganar como sea.

Matterhorn ['mætə,hɔːn] *n*: **the ~** el monte Cervino.

matter-of-fact *adj* pragmático(ca).

mattress ['mætrɪs] *n* colchón *m.*

mature [mə'tjʊəʳ] ◇ *adj* [person, wine] maduro(ra); [cheese] curado(da). ◇ *vi* - **1.** [gen] madurar - **2.** [wine] envejecer.

mature student *n* UK UNIV estudiante *m* OR f adulto, -ta.

maul [mɔːl] *vt* [savage] herir gravemente.

mauve [məʊv] *adj* malva.

max. [mæks] (*abbr of* **maximum**) máx.

maxim ['mæksɪm] (*pl* -s) *n* máxima f.

maximum ['mæksɪməm] (*pl* **maxima** OR -s) ◇ *adj* máximo(ma). ◇ *n* máximo *m*; **at the ~** como máximo.

may [meɪ] *modal vb* poder; **the coast ~ be seen** se puede ver la costa; **you ~ like it** puede OR es posible que te guste; **I ~ come, I ~ not** puede que venga, puede que no; **will you do it? - I ~ do** ¿lo harás? - puede que sí; **it ~ be done in two different ways** puede hacerse de dos maneras (distintas); **~ I come in?** ¿se puede (pasar)?; **~ I?** ¿me permite?; **if I ~** si me permite; **it ~ be cheap, but it's good** puede que sea barato, pero es bueno; **~ all your dreams come true!** ¡que todos tus sueños se hagan realidad!; **be that as it ~** aunque así sea; **come what ~** pase lo que pase; *see also* **might**.

May [meɪ] *n* mayo *m*; *see also* **September**.

maybe ['meɪbɪ] *adv* - **1.** [perhaps] quizás, tal vez; **~ she'll come** tal vez venga - **2.** [approximately] más o menos.

May Day *n* Primero *m* de Mayo.

mayhem ['meɪhem] *n* alboroto *m*, jaleo *m.*

mayonnaise [,meɪə'neɪz] *n* mayonesa f.

mayor [meəʳ] *n* alcalde *m*, -esa f.

mayoress ['meərɪs] *n* alcaldesa f.

maze [meɪz] *n* lit & fig laberinto *m.*

MB (*abbr of* **megabyte**) MB *m.*

MD *n abbr of* **managing director.**

me [miː] *pers pron* - **1.** (*direct, indirect*) me; **can you see/hear ~?** ¿me ves/oyes?; **it's ~** soy yo; **they spoke to ~** hablaron conmigo; **she gave it to ~** me lo dio; **give it to ~!** ¡dámelo! - **2.** (*stressed*): **you can't expect ME to do it** no esperarás que YO lo haga - **3.** (*after prep*) mí; **they went with/without ~** fueron conmigo/sin mí - **4.** (*in comparisons*) yo; **she's shorter than ~** (ella) es más baja que yo.

meadow ['medəʊ] *n* prado *m*, pradera f.

meagre UK, **meager** US ['miːgəʳ] *adj* miserable, escaso(sa).

meal [miːl] *n* comida f.

mealtime ['miːltaɪm] *n* hora f de la comida.

mean [miːn] (*pt* & *pp* **meant**) ◇ *vt* - **1.** [signify] significar, querer decir; **what does that word ~?** ¿qué quiere decir esa palabra?; **it ~s nothing to me** no significa nada para mí - **2.** [have in mind] querer decir, referirse a; **what do you ~?** ¿qué quieres decir?; **do you know what I ~?** ¿sabes?; **to ~ to do sthg** tener la intención de OR querer hacer algo; **to be meant for** estar destinado(da) a; **to be meant to do sthg** deber hacer algo; **that's not meant to be there** eso no debería estar allí; **it was meant to be a surprise** se suponía que era una sorpresa; **it was meant to be a joke** era solamente una broma; **to ~ well** tener buenas intenciones - **3.** [be serious about]: **I ~ it** hablo OR lo digo en serio - **4.** [be important, matter] significar; **it ~s a lot to us** significa mucho para nosotros - **5.** [entail] suponer, implicar - **6.** *phr*: **I ~** quiero decir, o sea. ◇ *adj* - **1.** [miserly] tacaño(ña), amarrete (*inv*) *Chile, RP* - **2.** [unkind] mezquino(na), malo(la); **to be ~ to sb** ser malo con alguien - **3.** [average] medio(dia). ◇ *n* [average] promedio *m*, media f; *see also* **means.**

meander [mɪ'ændəʳ] *vi* - **1.** [river, road] serpentear - **2.** [walk aimlessly] vagar; [write, speak aimlessly] divagar.

meaning ['miːnɪŋ] *n* - **1.** [sense - of a word etc] significado *m* - **2.** [significance] intención f, sentido *m* - **3.** [purpose, point] propósito *m*, razón f de ser.

meaningful ['miːnɪŋfʊl] *adj* - **1.** [expressive] significativo(va) - **2.** [profound] profundo(da).

meaningless ['miːnɪŋlɪs] *adj* - **1.** [without meaning, purpose] sin sentido - **2.** [irrelevant, unimportant] irrelevante.

means [miːnz] ◇ *n* [method, way] medio *m*; **we have no ~ of doing it** no tenemos manera de hacerlo; **by ~ of** por medio de; **by legal ~ legalmente.** ◇ *npl* [money] recursos *mpl*, medios *mpl*.

◆ **by all means** *adv* por supuesto.

◆ **by no means** *adv* en absoluto, de ningún modo.

meant [ment] *pt* & *pp* ⊳ **mean**.

meantime ['mi:n,taɪm] *n*: **in the ~** mientras tanto.

meanwhile ['mi:n,waɪl] *adv* mientras tanto.

measles ['mi:zlz] *n*: **(the)** ~ sarampión *m*.

measly ['mi:zlɪ] (*compar* **-ier**, *superl* **-iest**) *adj inf* raquítico(ca).

measure ['meʒə'] ◇ *n* **-1.** [step, action] medida *f* **- 2.** [of alcohol] medida *f* **- 3.** [indication, sign]: **a ~ of** una muestra de **- 4.** *US* MUS compás *m*. ◇ *vt* [object] medir; [damage, impact etc] determinar, evaluar. ◇ *vi* medir.

measurement ['meʒəmənt] *n* medida *f*.

meat [mi:t] *n* **- 1.** [foodstuff] carne *f*; **cold ~** fiambre *m* **- 2.** [substance, content] sustancia *f*.

meatball ['mi:tbɔ:l] *n* albóndiga *f*.

meat loaf *n* pastel de carne picada.

meat pie *n UK* empanada *f* de carne.

meaty ['mi:tɪ] (*compar* **-ier**, *superl* **-iest**) *adj fig* sustancioso(sa).

Mecca ['mekə] *n* GEOGR La Meca; *fig* meca *f*.

mechanic [mɪ'kænɪk] *n* mecánico *m*, -ca *f*.

◆ **mechanics** ◇ *n* (U) [study] mecánica *f*. ◇ *npl fig* mecanismos *mpl*.

mechanical [mɪ'kænɪkl] *adj* [worked by machinery, routine] mecánico(ca).

mechanism ['mekənɪzm] *n lit* & *fig* mecanismo *m*.

medal ['medl] *n* medalla *f*.

medallion [mɪ'dæljən] *n* medallón *m*.

meddle ['medl] *vi*: **to ~ (in)** entrometerse (en); **to ~ with sthg** manosear algo.

media ['mi:djə] ◇ *pl* ⊳ **medium**. ◇ *n* & *npl*: **the ~** los medios de comunicación.

mediaeval [,medɪ'i:vl] = **medieval**.

median ['mi:djən] ◇ *adj* mediano(na). ◇ *n US* [of road] mediana *f*.

mediate ['mi:dɪeɪt] *vi*: **to ~ (for/between)** mediar (por/entre).

mediator ['mi:dɪeɪtə'] *n* mediador *m*, -ra *f*.

Medicaid ['medɪkeɪd] *n US* sistema estatal de ayuda médica.

medical ['medɪkl] ◇ *adj* médico(ca). ◇ *n* reconocimiento *m* médico, chequeo *m*.

Medicare ['medɪkeə'] *n US* ayuda médica estatal para ancianos.

medicated ['medɪkeɪtɪd] *adj* medicinal.

medicine ['medsɪn] *n* **- 1.** [treatment of illness] medicina *f*; **Doctor of Medicine** UNIV doctor *m*, -ra *f* en medicina **- 2.** [substance] medicina *f*, medicamento *m*.

medieval [,medɪ'i:vl] *adj* medieval.

mediocre [,mi:dɪ'əʊkə'] *adj* mediocre.

meditate ['medɪteɪt] *vi*: **to ~ (on OR upon)** meditar (sobre).

Mediterranean [,medɪtə'reɪnjən] ◇ *n* [sea]: **the ~ (Sea)** el (mar) Mediterráneo. ◇ *adj* mediterráneo(a).

medium ['mi:djəm] (*pl sense 1* **media**, *pl sense 2* **mediums**) ◇ *adj* mediano(na). ◇ *n* **- 1.** [way of communicating] medio *m* **- 2.** [spiritualist] médium *m* OR *f*.

medium-sized [-saɪzd] *adj* de tamaño mediano.

medium wave *n* onda *f* media.

medley ['medlɪ] (*pl* **medleys**) *n* **- 1.** [mixture] mezcla *f*, amalgama *f* **- 2.** [selection of music] popurrí *m*.

meek [mi:k] *adj* sumiso(sa), dócil.

meet [mi:t] (*pt* & *pp* **met**) ◇ *vt* **-1.** [by chance] encontrarse con; [for first time, come across] conocer; [by arrangement, for a purpose] reunirse con; **shall we ~ at eight?** ¿quedamos a las ocho? **- 2.** [go to meet - person] ir/venir a buscar: **I met the eight o'clock train to pick up my son** fui a buscar a mi hijo en el tren de las ocho **- 3.** [need, demand, condition] satisfacer; [target] cumplir con; [deadline] cumplir **- 4.** [deal with - problem, challenge] hacer frente a **- 5.** [costs, debts] pagar **- 6.** [experience - problem, situation] encontrarse con **- 7.** [hit, touch] darse OR chocar contra **- 8.** [join] juntarse OR unirse con **- 9.** [play against] enfrentarse con. ◇ *vi* **-1.** [by chance] encontrarse; [by arrangement] verse; [for a purpose] reunirse **- 2.** [get to know sb] conocerse **- 3.** [hit in collision] chocar; [touch] tocar **- 4.** [eyes]: **their eyes met** sus miradas se cruzaron **- 5.** [join - roads etc] juntarse **- 6.** [play each other] enfrentarse. ◇ *n US* [meeting] encuentro *m*.

◆ **meet up** *vi*: **to ~ up (with sb)** quedar (con alguien); **we're ~ing up for lunch** hemos quedado para comer.

◆ **meet with** *vt fus* **-1.** [problems, resistance]: **to ~ with refusal** ser rechazado(da); **to ~ with success** tener éxito; **to ~ with failure** fracasar **- 2.** *US* [by arrangement] reunirse con.

meeting ['mi:tɪŋ] *n* **- 1.** [for discussions, business] reunión *f* **- 2.** [by chance, in sport] encuentro *m*; [by arrangement] cita *f*; [formal] entrevista *f*.

megabyte ['megəbaɪt] *n* COMPUT megabyte *m*, mega *m*.

megaphone ['megəfəʊn] *n* megáfono *m*.

megastore ['megəstɔ:'] *n* macrotienda *f*.

melancholy ['melənkəlɪ] ◇ *adj* melancólico(ca). ◇ *n* melancolía *f*.

mellow ['meləʊ] ◇ *adj* [sound, colour, light] suave; [wine] añejo(ja). ◇ *vi* [sound, light] suavizarse; [person] ablandarse.

melody ['melədɪ] (*pl* **-ies**) *n* melodía *f*.

melon ['melən] *n* melón *m*.

melt [melt] ◇ *vt* - **1.** [make liquid] derretir - **2.** *fig* [soften] ablandar. ◇ *vi* - **1.** [become liquid] derretirse - **2.** *fig* [soften] **ablandarse** - **3.** [disappear]: **to ~ away** [savings] esfumarse; [anger] desvanecerse.

◆ **melt down** *vt sep* fundir.

meltdown ['meltdaʊn] *n* - **1.** [act of melting] fusión *f* - **2.** [incident] fuga *f* radiactiva.

melting pot ['meltɪŋ-] *n fig* crisol *m*.

member ['membə^r] *n* - **1.** [of social group] miembro *m* OR *f* - **2.** [of party, union] afiliado *m*, -da *f*; [of organization, club] socio *m*, -cia *f* - **3.** [limb, penis] miembro *m*.

Member of Congress (*pl* **Members of Congress**) *n* miembro *m* OR *f* del Congreso (*de los Estados Unidos*).

Member of Parliament (*pl* **Members of Parliament**) *n* UK diputado *m*, -da *f* (*del parlamento británico*).

membership ['membəʃɪp] *n* - **1.** [of party, union] afiliación *f*; [of club] calidad *f* de socio - **2.** [number of members - of party, union] número *m* de afiliados - **3.** [people themselves]: **the ~** [of organization] los miembros; [of party, union] los afiliados; [of club] los socios.

membership card *n* [of party, union] carnet *m* de afiliado(da); [of club] carnet *m* de socio(cia).

memento [mɪ'mentəʊ] (*pl* **-s**) *n* recuerdo *m*.

memo ['meməʊ] (*pl* **-s**) *n* memorándum *m*.

memoirs ['memwɑːz] *npl* memorias *fpl*.

memorandum [ˌmemə'rændəm] (*pl* **-da** [-də] OR **-dums**) *n fml* memorándum *m*.

memorial [mɪ'mɔːrɪəl] ◇ *adj* conmemorativo(va). ◇ *n* monumento *m* conmemorativo.

memorize, -ise ['meməraɪz] *vt* memorizar, aprender de memoria.

memory ['memərɪ] (*pl* **-ies**) *n* - **1.** [faculty, of computer] memoria *f* - **2.** [thing or things remembered] recuerdo *m*; **from ~** de memoria.

men [men] *pl* ▷ **man**.

menace ['menəs] ◇ *n* - **1.** [threat] amenaza *f*; [danger] peligro *m* - **2.** *inf* [nuisance, pest] pesadez *f*, lata *f*. ◇ *vt* amenazar.

menacing ['menəsɪŋ] *adj* amenazador(ra).

mend [mend] ◇ *n inf*: **to be on the ~** ir recuperándose. ◇ *vt* [shoes, toy] arreglar; [socks] zurcir; [clothes] remendar.

menial ['miːnjəl] *adj* servil, de baja categoría.

meningitis [ˌmenɪn'dʒaɪtɪs] *n (U)* meningitis *f inv*.

menopause ['menəpɔːz] *n*: **the ~** la menopausia.

men's room *n* US: **the ~** los servicios de caballeros.

menstruation [ˌmenstrʊ'eɪʃn] *n* menstruación *f*.

menswear ['menzweə^r] *n* ropa *f* de caballeros.

mental ['mentl] *adj* mental.

mental hospital *n* hospital *m* psiquiátrico.

mentality [men'tælətɪ] *n* mentalidad *f*.

mentally handicapped *npl*: **the ~** los disminuidos psíquicos.

mention ['menʃn] ◇ *vt*: **to ~ sthg (to)** mencionar algo (a); **not to ~** sin mencionar, además de; **don't ~ it!** ¡de nada!, ¡no hay de qué! ◇ *n* mención *f*.

menu ['menjuː] *n* - **1.** [in restaurant] carta *f* - **2.** COMPUT menú *m*.

meow US = miaow.

MEP (*abbr of* **Member of the European Parliament**) *n* eurodiputado *m*, -da *f*.

mercenary ['mɜːsɪnrɪ] (*pl* **-ies**) ◇ *adj* mercenario(ria). ◇ *n* mercenario *m*, -ria *f*.

merchandise ['mɜːtʃəndaɪz] *n (U)* mercancías *fpl*, géneros *mpl*.

merchant ['mɜːtʃənt] ◇ *adj* [seaman, ship] mercante. ◇ *n* comerciante *m* OR *f*.

merchant bank *n* UK banco *m* mercantil.

merchant navy UK, **merchant marine** US *n* marina *f* mercante.

merciful ['mɜːsɪfʊl] *adj* - **1.** [showing mercy] compasivo(va) - **2.** [fortunate] afortunado(da).

merciless ['mɜːsɪlɪs] *adj* despiadado(da).

mercury ['mɜːkjʊrɪ] *n* mercurio *m*.

Mercury ['mɜːkjʊrɪ] *n* Mercurio *m*.

mercy ['mɜːsɪ] (*pl* **-ies**) *n* - **1.** [kindness, pity] compasión *f*; **to have ~ on** apiadarse de; **to beg for ~** pedir clemencia; **at the ~ of** *fig* a merced de - **2.** [blessing] suerte *f*.

mere [mɪə^r] *adj* simple, mero(ra); **she's a ~ child** no es más que una niña.

merely ['mɪəlɪ] *adv* simplemente, sólo.

merge [mɜːdʒ] ◇ *vt* - **1.** [gen] mezclar - **2.** COMM & COMPUT fusionar. ◇ *vi* - **1.** [join, combine]: **to ~ (with)** [company] fusionarse (con); [roads, branches] unirse OR convergir (con) - **2.** [blend - colours] fundirse, mezclarse; **to ~ into** confundirse con.

merger ['mɜːdʒə^r] *n* COMM fusión *f*.

meringue [mə'ræŋ] *n* merengue *m*.

merit ['merɪt] ◇ *n* mérito *m*. ◇ *vt* merecer, ser digno(na) de.

◆ **merits** *npl* ventajas *fpl*.

mermaid ['mɜːmeɪd] *n* sirena *f*.

merry ['merɪ] (*compar* **-ier**, *superl* **-iest**) *adj* - **1.** [gen] alegre - **2.** [party] animado(da); **Merry Christmas!** ¡feliz Navidad! - **3.** *inf* [tipsy] achispado(da).

merry-go-round *n* tiovivo *m*, calesitas *fpl* RP.

mesh [meʃ] ⬦ *n* malla *f.* ⬦ *vi fig* encajar.

mesmerize, -ise ['mezməraɪz] *vt* : **to be ~ d (by)** estar fascinado(da) (por).

mess [mes] *n* - **1.** [untidy state] desorden *m*, entrevero *m RP* - **2.** [muddle, problematic situation] lío *m* - **3.** MIL [room] comedor *m*; [food] rancho *m*.

 ◆ **mess about, mess around** *inf* ⬦ *vt sep* vacilar. ⬦ *vi* - **1.** [waste time] pasar el rato; [fool around] hacer el tonto - **2.** [interfere]: **to ~ about with sthg** manosear algo.

 ◆ **mess up** *vt sep inf* - **1.** [clothes] ensuciar; [room] desordenar - **2.** [plan, evening] echar a perder.

message ['mesɪdʒ] *n* - **1.** [piece of information] mensaje *m*, recado *m* - **2.** [of book etc] mensaje *m*.

messenger ['mesɪndʒəʳ] *n* mensajero *m*, -ra *f.*

Messrs, Messrs. ['mesəz] (*abbr of* **messieurs**) Sres.

messy ['mesɪ] (*compar* **-ier**, *superl* **-iest**) *adj* [dirty] sucio(cia); [untidy] desordenado(da).

met [met] *pt & pp* ⬦ **meet**.

metal ['metl] ⬦ *n* metal *m*. ⬦ *comp* de metal, metálico(ca).

metallic [mɪ'tælɪk] *adj* - **1.** [gen] metálico(ca) - **2.** [paint, finish] metalizado(da).

metalwork ['metlwɜːk] *n* [craft] metalistería *f.*

metaphor ['metəfəʳ] *n* metáfora *f.*

mete [miːt] ◆ **mete out** *vt sep*: **to ~ sthg out to sb** imponer algo a alguien.

meteor ['miːtɪəʳ] *n* bólido *m*.

meteorology [ˌmiːtjə'rɒlədʒɪ] *n* meteorología *f.*

meter ['miːtəʳ] *n* - **1.** [device] contador *m* - **2.** *US* = **metre**.

method ['meθəd] *n* método *m*.

methodical [mɪ'θɒdɪkl] *adj* metódico(ca).

Methodist ['meθədɪst] ⬦ *adj* metodista. ⬦ *n* metodista *m or f.*

meths [meθs] *n UK inf* alcohol *m* metilado OR desnaturalizado.

methylated spirits ['meθɪleɪtɪd-] *n* alcohol *m* metilado OR desnaturalizado.

meticulous [mɪ'tɪkjʊləs] *adj* meticuloso(sa), minucioso(sa).

metre *UK*, **meter** *US* ['miːtəʳ] *n* metro *m.*

metric ['metrɪk] *adj* métrico(ca).

metronome ['metrənəʊm] *n* metrónomo *m.*

metropolitan [ˌmetrə'pɒlɪtn] *adj* [of a metropolis] metropolitano(na).

Metropolitan Police *npl* policía *f de Londres.*

mettle ['metl] *n*: **to be on one's ~** estar dispuesto(ta) a hacer lo mejor posible; **he showed** OR **proved his ~** mostró su valor.

mew [mjuː] = **miaow**.

mews [mjuːz] (*pl inv*) *n UK callejuela de antiguas caballerizas convertidas en viviendas de lujo.*

Mexican ['meksɪkn] ⬦ *adj* mexicano(na), mejicano(na). ⬦ *n* mexicano *m*, -na *f*, mejicano *m*, -na *f.*

Mexico ['meksɪkəʊ] *n* México, Méjico.

MI5 (*abbr of* **Military Intelligence 5**) *n organismo británico de contraespionaje.*

MI6 (*abbr of* **Military Intelligence 6**) *n organismo británico de espionaje.*

miaow *UK* [miːˈaʊ], **meow** *US* [mɪˈaʊ] ⬦ *n* maullido *m.* ⬦ *vi* maullar.

mice [maɪs] *pl* ⬦ **mouse**.

mickey ['mɪkɪ] *n UK inf*: **to take the ~ out of sb** tomar el pelo a alguien; **to take the ~ out of sthg** burlarse de algo.

microchip ['maɪkrəʊtʃɪp] *n* COMPUT microchip *m.*

microcomputer [ˌmaɪkrəʊkəm'pjuːtəʳ] *n* microordenador *m*, microcomputadora *f Amér.*

microfilm ['maɪkrəʊfɪlm] *n* microfilm *m.*

microphone ['maɪkrəfəʊn] *n* micrófono *m.*

micro scooter *n* patinete *m.*

microscope ['maɪkrəskəʊp] *n* microscopio *m.*

microscopic [ˌmaɪkrə'skɒpɪk] *adj lit & fig* microscópico(ca).

microwave ['maɪkrəweɪv] ⬦ *n*: **~ (oven)** microondas *m inv.* ⬦ *vt* cocinar en el microondas.

mid- [mɪd] *prefix* medio(dia); **(in) ~ morning** a media mañana; **(in) ~August** a mediados de agosto; **(in) ~winter** en pleno invierno; **she's in her ~ twenties** tiene unos 25 años.

midair [mɪd'eəʳ] *n*: **in ~** en el aire.

midday ['mɪddeɪ] *n* mediodía *m.*

middle ['mɪdl] ⬦ *adj* [gen] del medio. ⬦ *n* - **1.** [of room, town etc] medio *m*, centro *m*; **in the ~ of the month/the 19th century** a mediados del mes/del siglo XIX; **in the ~ of the week** a mitad de semana; **to be in the ~ of doing sthg** estar haciendo algo; **in the ~ of the night** en plena noche - **2.** [waist] cintura *f.*

middle-aged *adj* de mediana edad.

Middle Ages *npl*: **the ~** la Edad Media.

middle-class *adj* de clase media.

middle classes *npl*: **the ~** la clase media.

Middle East *n*: **the ~** el Oriente Medio.

middleman ['mɪdlmæn] (*pl* **-men** [-men]) *n* intermediario *m.*

middle name *n* segundo nombre *m (en un nombre compuesto).*

middleweight ['mɪdlweɪt] *n* peso *m* medio.

middling ['mɪdlɪŋ] *adj* regular.

midfield [ˌmɪd'fiːld] *n* FTBL centro *m* del campo.

midfielder [ˌmɪdˈfiːldəʳ] n FTBL centrocampista m OR f.

midge [mɪdʒ] n (tipo m de) mosquito m.

midget [ˈmɪdʒɪt] n enano m, -na f.

midi system [ˈmɪdɪ-] n minicadena f.

Midlands [ˈmɪdləndz] npl: the ~ la región central de Inglaterra.

midnight [ˈmɪdnaɪt] n medianoche f.

midriff [ˈmɪdrɪf] n diafragma m.

midst [mɪdst] n: in the ~ of en medio de.

midsummer [ˈmɪdˌsʌməʳ] n pleno verano m.

Midsummer's Day n Día m de San Juan (24 de junio).

midterms [ˈmɪdtɜːmz] n US exámenes mpl de mitad de semestre.

midway [ˌmɪdˈweɪ] adv - 1. [in space]: ~ (between) a medio camino (entre) - 2. [in time]: ~ (through) a la mitad (de).

midweek [adj mɪdˈwiːk, adv ˈmɪdwiːk] ◇ adj de entre semana. ◇ adv entre semana.

midwife [ˈmɪdwaɪf] (pl -wives [-waɪvz]) n comadrona f.

midwifery [ˈmɪdˌwɪfərɪ] n obstetricia f.

might [maɪt] ◇ modal vb - 1. [expressing possibility]: he ~ be armed podría estar armado; I ~ do it puede que OR quizás lo haga; I ~ come, I ~ not puede que venga, puede que no; will you do it? - I ~ do ¿lo harás? - puede que sí; we ~ have been killed, had we not been careful si no hubiéramos tenido cuidado, podríamos haber muerto; will you tell them? - I ~ as well ¿se lo dirás? - ¿por qué no? - 2. [expressing suggestion]: you ~ have told me! ¡podrías habérmelo dicho!; it ~ be better to wait quizás sea mejor esperar - 3. fml [asking permission]: he asked if he ~ leave the room pidió permiso para salir - 4. [expressing concession]: you ~ well be right, but ... puede que tengas razón, pero ... - 5. phr: I ~ have known OR guessed podría haberlo sospechado. ◇ n (U) fuerza f, poder m.

mighty [ˈmaɪtɪ] (compar -ier, superl -iest) ◇ adj [strong] fuerte; [powerful] poderoso(sa). ◇ adv esp US muy.

migraine [ˈmiːgreɪn, ˈmaɪgreɪn] n jaqueca f, migraña f.

migrant [ˈmaɪgrənt] ◇ adj [workers] inmigrante. ◇ n [person] emigrante m OR f.

migrate [UK maɪˈgreɪt, US ˈmaɪgreɪt] vi emigrar.

mike [maɪk] (abbr of microphone) n inf micro m.

mild [maɪld] adj - 1. [taste, disinfectant, wind] suave; [effect, surprise, illness, punishment] leve - 2. [person, nature] apacible; [tone of voice] sereno(na) - 3. [climate] templado(da).

mildew [ˈmɪldjuː] n [gen] moho m; [on plants] añublo m.

mildly [ˈmaɪldlɪ] adv - 1. [gen] ligeramente, levemente; to put it ~ por no decir más - 2. [talk] suavemente.

mile [maɪl] n milla f; it's ~s away [place] está muy lejos; to be ~s away fig estar en la luna.

mileage [ˈmaɪlɪdʒ] n distancia f en millas.

mileometer [maɪˈlɒmɪtəʳ] n cuentamillas m inv, ≃ cuentakilómetros m inv.

milestone [ˈmaɪlstəʊn] n - 1. [marker stone] mojón m, hito m - 2. fig [event] hito m.

militant [ˈmɪlɪtənt] ◇ adj militante. ◇ n militante m OR f.

military [ˈmɪlɪtrɪ] ◇ adj militar. ◇ n: the ~ los militares, las fuerzas armadas.

militia [mɪˈlɪʃə] n milicia f.

milk [mɪlk] ◇ n leche f. ◇ vt - 1. [cow etc] ordeñar - 2. [use to own ends] sacar todo el jugo a; they ~ed him for every penny he had le chuparon hasta el último centavo.

milk chocolate n chocolate m con leche.

milkman [ˈmɪlkmən] (pl -men [-mən]) n lechero m.

milk shake n batido m.

milky [ˈmɪlkɪ] (compar -ier, superl -iest) adj - 1. UK [with milk] con mucha leche - 2. [pale white] lechoso(sa), pálido(da).

Milky Way n: the ~ la Vía Láctea.

mill [mɪl] ◇ n - 1. [flour-mill] molino m - 2. [factory] fábrica f - 3. [grinder] molinillo m. ◇ vt moler.
→ **mill about, mill around** vi arremolinarse.

millennium [mɪˈlenɪəm] (pl -nnia [-nɪə]) n milenio m.

millennium bug n COMPUT: the ~ el efecto 2000.

miller [ˈmɪləʳ] n molinero m, -ra f.

millet [ˈmɪlɪt] n mijo m.

milligram(me) [ˈmɪlɪgræm] n miligramo m.

millimetre UK, **millimeter** US [ˈmɪlɪˌmiːtəʳ] n milímetro m.

millinery [ˈmɪlɪnrɪ] n sombrerería f (de señoras).

million [ˈmɪljən] n millón m; four ~ dollars cuatro millones de dólares; a ~, ~s of fig millones de.

millionaire [ˌmɪljəˈneəʳ] n millonario m.

millstone [ˈmɪlstəʊn] n piedra f de molino, muela f.

milometer [maɪˈlɒmɪtəʳ] = mileometer.

mime [maɪm] ◇ n [acting] mímica f, pantomima f. ◇ vt describir con gestos. ◇ vi hacer mímica.

mimic [ˈmɪmɪk] (pt & pp -ked, cont -king) ◇ n imitador m, -ra f. ◇ vt imitar.

mimicry [ˈmɪmɪkrɪ] n imitación f.

min. [mɪn] - **1.** (*abbr of* **minute**) min - **2.** (*abbr of* **minimum**) mín.

mince [mɪns] ◇ n UK carne f picada. ◇ vt picar. ◇ vi andar con afectación.

mincemeat ['mɪnsmiːt] n [fruit] mezcla de fruta confitada y especias.

mince pie n [sweet cake] pastelillo navideño de fruta confitada y frutos secos.

mincer ['mɪnsə'] n máquina f de picar carne.

mind [maɪnd] ◇ n - **1.** [gen] mente f; **state of ~** estado m de ánimo; **to calculate sthg in one's ~** calcular algo mentalmente; **to come into** OR **to cross sb's ~** pasársele a alguien por la cabeza; **the first thing that came into my ~** lo primero que me vino a la mente; **to have sthg on one's ~** estar preocupado por algo; **to keep an open ~** tener una actitud abierta; **to take sb's ~ off sthg** hacer olvidar algo a alguien; **are you out of your ~?** ¿estás loco?; **to make one's ~ up** decidirse - **2.** [attention] atención f; **to put one's ~ to sthg** poner empeño en algo - **3.** [opinion]: **to change one's ~** cambiar de opinión; **to my ~** en mi opinión; **to be in two ~s about sthg** no estar seguro(ra) de algo; **to speak one's ~** hablar sin rodeos - **4.** [memory] memoria f; **to bear sthg in ~** tener presente algo - **5.** [intention]: **to have sthg in ~** tener algo en mente; **to have a ~ to do sthg** estar pensando en hacer algo; **nothing could be further from my ~** nada más lejos de mis intenciones. ◇ vi [be bothered]: **do you ~?** ¿te importa?; **I don't ~ ...** no me importa ...; **which do you want? - I don't ~** ¿cuál prefieres? - me da igual; **never** [don't worry] no te preocupes; [it's not important] no importa. ◇ vt - **1.** [be bothered about, dislike]: **do you ~ if I leave?** ¿te molesta si me voy?; **I don't ~ waiting** no me importa esperar; **I wouldn't ~ a ...** no me vendría mal un ... - **2.** [pay attention to] tener cuidado con; **~ you don't fall** ten cuidado no te vayas a caer - **3.** [take care of] cuidar - **4.** [concentrate on]: **~ your own business!** ¡métete en tus asuntos!

◆ **mind you** adv: **he's a bit deaf; ~ you, he is old** está un poco sordo; te advierto que es ya mayor.

minder ['maɪndə'] n UK inf [bodyguard] guardaespaldas m OR f inv.

mindful ['maɪndfʊl] adj: **~ of** consciente de.

mindless ['maɪndlɪs] adj - **1.** [stupid] absurdo(da), sin sentido - **2.** [not requiring thought] aburrido(da).

mine¹ [maɪn] poss pron mío (mía); **that money is ~** ese dinero es mío; **his car hit ~** su coche chocó contra el mío; **it wasn't your fault, it was MINE** la culpa no fue tuya

sino MÍA; **a friend of ~** un amigo mío.

mine² [maɪn] ◇ n mina f. ◇ vt - **1.** [excavate - coal] extraer - **2.** [lay mines in] minar.

minefield ['maɪnfiːld] n lit & fig campo m de minas.

miner ['maɪnə'] n minero m, -ra f.

mineral ['mɪnərəl] ◇ adj mineral. ◇ n mineral m.

mineral water n agua f mineral.

minesweeper ['maɪn,swiːpə'] n dragaminas m inv.

mingle ['mɪŋgl] vi - **1.** [combine]: **to ~ (with)** mezclarse (con) - **2.** [socially]: **to ~ (with)** alternar (con).

miniature ['mɪnətʃə'] ◇ adj en miniatura. ◇ n - **1.** [painting] miniatura f - **2.** [of alcohol] botellín f de licor en miniatura.

minibus ['mɪnɪbʌs] (pl -es) n microbús m, micro m, buseta f Col, CRica, Ecuad, Ven, pesero m Méx, liebre f Chile.

minicab ['mɪnɪkæb] n UK taxi que se puede pedir por teléfono, pero no se puede parar en la calle.

MiniDisc® ['mɪnɪdɪsk] n MiniDisc® m.

MiniDisc player® n reproductor m de MiniDisc®.

minidish ['mɪnɪdɪʃ] n miniparabólica f.

minima ['mɪnɪmə] pl ▷ **minimum**.

minimal ['mɪnɪml] adj mínimo(ma).

minimum ['mɪnɪməm] (pl -mums OR -ma) ◇ adj mínimo(ma). ◇ n mínimo m.

mining ['maɪnɪŋ] ◇ n minería f. ◇ adj minero(ra).

miniskirt ['mɪnɪskɜːt] n minifalda f.

minister ['mɪnɪstə'] n - **1.** POL: **~ (for)** ministro m, -tra f *de* - **2.** RELIG pastor m, -ra f.

◆ **minister to** vt fus [needs] atender a.

ministerial [,mɪnɪ'stɪərɪəl] adj ministerial.

minister of state n: **~ (for)** secretario m, -ria f de estado (para).

ministry ['mɪnɪstrɪ] (pl -ies) n - **1.** POL ministerio m - **2.** RELIG: **the ~** el clero, el sacerdocio.

mink [mɪŋk] (pl inv) n visón m.

minnow ['mɪnəʊ] n - **1.** [fish] pececillo m (de agua dulce) - **2.** [team] comparsa f.

minor ['maɪnə'] ◇ adj [gen] menor; [injury] leve. ◇ n menor m OR f (de edad); US [subject] subespecialidad f.

Minorca [mɪ'nɔːkə] n Menorca.

minority [maɪ'nɒrətɪ] (pl -ies) n minoría f.

mint [mɪnt] ◇ n - **1.** [herb] menta f, hierbabuena f - **2.** [peppermint] pastilla f de menta - **3.** [for coins]: **the ~** la Casa de la Moneda; **in ~ condition** en perfecto estado, como nuevo(va). ◇ vt acuñar.

minus ['maɪnəs] (pl -es) ◇ prep - **1.** MATH [less]: **4 ~ 2 is 2** 4 menos 2 es 2 - **2.** [in temperatures]: **it's ~ 5°C** estamos a 5 grados bajo cero. ◇ n - **1.** MATH signo m (de) menos

- **2.** [disadvantage] desventaja f.

minus sign n signo m (de) menos.

minute¹ ['mɪnɪt] n minuto m; **at any** ~ en cualquier momento; **at the** ~ en este momento; **just a** ~ un momento; **this** ~ ahora mismo.

➡ **minutes** npl acta f; **to take (the)** ~s levantar OR tomar acta.

minute² [maɪ'njuːt] adj [very small] diminuto(ta).

miracle ['mɪrəkl] n lit & fig milagro m.

miraculous [mɪ'rækjʊləs] adj milagroso(sa).

mirage [mɪ'rɑːʒ] n lit & fig espejismo m.

mire [maɪəʳ] n fango m, lodo m.

mirror ['mɪrəʳ] <> n espejo m. <> vt reflejar.

mirth [mɜːθ] n risa f.

misadventure [ˌmɪsəd'ventʃəʳ] n desgracia f, desventura f; **death by** ~ JUR muerte f accidental.

misapprehension ['mɪsˌæprɪ'henʃn] n - **1.** [misunderstanding] malentendido m - **2.** [mistaken belief] creencia f errónea.

misappropriation ['mɪsəˌprəʊprɪ'eɪʃn] n: ~ **(of)** malversación f (de).

misbehave [ˌmɪsbɪ'heɪv] vi portarse mal.

miscalculate [ˌmɪs'kælkjʊleɪt] vt & vi calcular mal.

miscarriage [ˌmɪs'kærɪdʒ] n [at birth] aborto m (natural).

miscarriage of justice n error m judicial.

miscellaneous [ˌmɪsə'leɪnjəs] adj diverso(sa).

mischief ['mɪstʃɪf] n (U) - **1.** [playfulness] picardía f - **2.** [naughty behaviour] travesuras fpl, diabluras fpl - **3.** [harm] daño m.

mischievous ['mɪstʃɪvəs] adj - **1.** [playful] lleno(na) de picardía - **2.** [naughty] travieso(sa).

misconception [ˌmɪskən'sepʃn] n concepto m erróneo, idea f falsa.

misconduct [ˌmɪs'kɒndʌkt] n mala conducta f.

misconstrue [ˌmɪskən'struː] vt fml malinterpretar.

miscount [ˌmɪs'kaʊnt] vt & vi contar mal.

misdeed [ˌmɪs'diːd] n literary fechoría f.

misdemeanour UK, **misdemeanor** US [ˌmɪsdɪ'miːnəʳ] n fml delito m menor, falta f.

miser ['maɪzəʳ] n avaro m, -ra f.

miserable ['mɪzrəbl] adj - **1.** [unhappy] infeliz, triste - **2.** [wretched, poor] miserable - **3.** [weather] horrible - **4.** [pathetic] lamentable.

miserly ['maɪzəlɪ] adj miserable, mezquino(na).

misery ['mɪzərɪ] (pl -ies) n - **1.** [unhappiness] desdicha f, tristeza f - **2.** [suffering] sufrimiento m.

misfire [ˌmɪs'faɪəʳ] vi - **1.** [car engine] no

arrancar - **2.** [plan] fracasar.

misfit ['mɪsfɪt] n inadaptado m, -da f.

misfortune [mɪs'fɔːtʃuːn] n - **1.** [bad luck] mala suerte f - **2.** [piece of bad luck] desgracia f.

misgivings [mɪs'gɪvɪŋz] npl recelos mpl.

misguided [ˌmɪs'gaɪdɪd] adj [person] descaminado(da); [attempt] equivocado(da).

mishandle [ˌmɪs'hændl] vt - **1.** [person, animal] maltratar - **2.** [affair] llevar mal.

mishap ['mɪshæp] n contratiempo m.

misinterpret [ˌmɪsɪn'tɜːprɪt] vt malinterpretar.

misjudge [ˌmɪs'dʒʌdʒ] vt - **1.** [guess wrongly] calcular mal - **2.** [appraise wrongly] juzgar mal.

mislay [ˌmɪs'leɪ] (pt & pp **-laid**) vt extraviar, perder.

mislead [ˌmɪs'liːd] (pt & pp **-led**) vt engañar.

misleading [ˌmɪs'liːdɪŋ] adj engañoso(sa).

misled [ˌmɪs'led] pt & pp ➢ **mislead**.

misnomer [ˌmɪs'nəʊməʳ] n término m equivocado.

misplace [ˌmɪs'pleɪs] vt extraviar, perder.

misprint ['mɪsprɪnt] n errata f, error m de imprenta.

miss [mɪs] <> vt - **1.** [fail to see - TV programme, film] perderse; [- error, person in crowd] no ver - **2.** [fail to hear] no oír - **3.** [omit] saltarse - **4.** [shot] fallar; [ball] no dar a - **5.** [feel absence of] echar de menos OR en falta - **6.** [opportunity] perder, dejar pasar; [turning] pasarse - **7.** [train, bus] perder - **8.** [appointment] faltar a, no asistir a; [deadline] no cumplir - **9.** [avoid] evitar. <> vi fallar. <> n fallo m; **to give sthg a** ~ inf pasar de algo.

➡ **miss out** <> vt sep pasar por alto. <> vi: **to** ~ **out (on sthg)** perderse (algo).

Miss [mɪs] n señorita f; ~ **Brown** la señorita Brown.

misshapen [ˌmɪs'ʃeɪpn] adj deforme.

missile [UK 'mɪsaɪl, US 'mɪsəl] n - **1.** [weapon] misil m - **2.** [thrown object] proyectil m.

missing ['mɪsɪŋ] adj - **1.** [lost] perdido(da), extraviado(da) - **2.** [not present] ausente; **to be** ~ faltar.

mission ['mɪʃn] n misión f.

missionary ['mɪʃənrɪ] (pl -ies) n misionero m, -ra f.

misspent [ˌmɪs'spent] adj malgastado(da).

mist [mɪst] n [gen] neblina f; [at sea] bruma f.

➡ **mist over, mist up** vi [windows, spectacles] empañarse; [eyes] llenarse de lágrimas.

mistake [mɪ'steɪk] (pt **-took**, pp **-taken**) <> n error m; **to make a** ~ equivocarse, cometer un error; **by** ~ por error. <> vt

- 1. [misunderstand] entender mal **- 2.** [fail to recognize]: **to ~ sthg/sb for** confundir algo/a alguien con.

mistaken [mɪˈsteɪkn] <> *pp* ▷ **mistake**. <> *adj* equivocado(da); **to be ~ about sb/ sthg** estar equivocado respecto a alguien/ algo.

mister [ˈmɪstəʳ] *n inf* amigo *m*.
▶ **Mister** *n* señor *m*; **~ Brown** el señor Brown.

mistletoe [ˈmɪsltəʊ] *n* muérdago *m*.

mistook [mɪˈstʊk] *pt* ▷ **mistake**.

mistreat [ˌmɪsˈtriːt] *vt* maltratar.

mistress [ˈmɪstrɪs] *n* **- 1.** [female lover] amante *f*, querida *f* **- 2.** UK [school teacher - primary] maestra *f*, señorita *f*; [- secondary] profesora *f* **- 3.** [woman in control] señora *f*.

mistrust [ˌmɪsˈtrʌst] <> *n* desconfianza *f*, recelo *m*. <> *vt* desconfiar de.

misty [ˈmɪstɪ] (*compar* **-ier**, *superl* **-iest**) *adj* [gen] neblinoso(sa); [at sea] brumoso(sa).

misunderstand [ˌmɪsʌndəˈstænd] (*pt* & *pp* **-stood**) *vt* & *vi* entender mal.

misunderstanding [ˌmɪsʌndəˈstændɪŋ] *n* malentendido *m*.

misunderstood [ˌmɪsʌndəˈstʊd] *pt* & *pp* ▷ **misunderstand**.

misuse [*n* ˌmɪsˈjuːs, *vb* ˌmɪsˈjuːz] <> *n* uso *m* indebido. <> *vt* hacer uso indebido de.

miter US = **mitre**.

mitigate [ˈmɪtɪgeɪt] *vt fml* mitigar, atenuar.

mitre UK, **miter** US [ˈmaɪtəʳ] *n* [hat] mitra *f*.

mitt [mɪt] *n* manopla *f*; US [for baseball] guante *m*.

mitten [ˈmɪtn] *n* manopla *f*.

mix [mɪks] <> *vt*: **to ~ sthg (with)** mezclar algo (con). <> *vi* **- 1.** [substances] mezclarse; [activities] ir bien juntos(tas) **- 2.** [socially]: **to ~ with** alternar con. <> *n* mezcla *f*.
▶ **mix up** *vt sep* **- 1.** [confuse] confundir **- 2.** [disorder] mezclar.

mixed [mɪkst] *adj* **- 1.** [of different kinds] surtido(da), variado(da) **- 2.** [of different sexes] mixto(ta).

mixed-ability *adj* UK [class, group] con alumnos de varios niveles.

mixed grill *n* parrillada *f* mixta.

mixed up *adj* **- 1.** [confused] confuso(sa); **to get ~** confundirse **- 2.** [involved]: **~ in** [fight, crime] involucrado(da) en.

mixer [ˈmɪksəʳ] *n* **- 1.** [for food] batidora *f*; [for cement] hormigonera *f* **- 2.** [for music] mesa *f* de mezclas **- 3.** [non-alcoholic drink] *bebida no alcohólica para mezclar con bebidas alcohólicas*.

mixture [ˈmɪkstʃəʳ] *n* [gen] mezcla *f*; [of sweets] surtido *m*.

mix-up *n inf* confusión *f*.

mm (*abbr of* **millimetre**) mm.

moan [məʊn] <> *n* [of pain, sadness] gemido *m*. <> *vi* **- 1.** [in pain, sadness] gemir **- 2.** *inf* [complain]: **to ~ (about)** quejarse (de).

moat [məʊt] *n* foso *m*.

mob [mɒb] (*pt* & *pp* **-bed**, *cont* **-bing**) <> *n* muchedumbre *f*, turba *f*. <> *vt* asediar.

mobile [ˈməʊbaɪl] <> *adj* [able to move] móvil. <> *n* móvil *m*.

mobile home *n* caravana *f*.

mobile phone *n* teléfono *m* móvil.

mobilize, -ise [ˈməʊbɪlaɪz] *vt* movilizar.

mock [mɒk] <> *adj* fingido(da); **~ (exam)** simulacro *m* de examen. <> *vt* burlarse de. <> *vi* burlarse.

mockery [ˈmɒkərɪ] *n* burlas *fpl*.

mod cons [ˌmɒd-] (*abbr of* **modern conveniences**) *npl* UK *inf*: **all ~** con todas las comodidades.

mode [məʊd] *n* modo *m*.

model [ˈmɒdl] (UK *pt* & *pp* **-led**, *cont* **-ling**, US *pt* & *pp* **-ed**, *cont* **-ing**) <> *n* **- 1.** [gen] modelo *m* **- 2.** [small copy] maqueta *f* **- 3.** [for painter, in fashion] modelo *m or f*. <> *adj* **- 1.** [exemplary] modelo (*inv*) **- 2.** [reduced-scale] en miniatura. <> *vt* **- 1.** [shape] modelar **- 2.** [wear] lucir (*en pase de modelos*) **- 3.** [copy]: **to ~ o.s. on sb** tener a alguien como modelo **- 4.** COMPUT simular por ordenador. <> *vi* trabajar de modelo.

model aircraft *n* aeromodelo *m*.

modem [ˈməʊdem] *n* COMPUT módem *m*.

moderate [*adj* & *n* ˈmɒdərət, *vb* ˈmɒdəreɪt] <> *adj* moderado(da). <> *n* POL moderado *m*, **-da** *f*. <> *vt* moderar. <> *vi* [in debate] hacer de moderador.

moderation [ˌmɒdəˈreɪʃn] *n* moderación *f*; **in ~** con moderación.

modern [ˈmɒdən] *adj* moderno(na).

modernize, -ise [ˈmɒdənaɪz] <> *vt* modernizar. <> *vi* modernizarse.

modern languages *npl* lenguas *fpl* modernas.

modest [ˈmɒdɪst] *adj* **- 1.** [gen] modesto(ta) **- 2.** [improvement] ligero(ra); [price] módico(ca).

modesty [ˈmɒdɪstɪ] *n* modestia *f*.

modicum [ˈmɒdɪkəm] *n fml*: **a ~ of** un mínimo de.

modify [ˈmɒdɪfaɪ] (*pt* & *pp* **-ied**) *vt* modificar.

module [ˈmɒdjuːl] *n* módulo *m*.

mogul [ˈməʊgl] *n* magnate *m or f*.

mohair [ˈməʊheəʳ] *n* mohair *m*.

moist [mɔɪst] *adj* húmedo(da).

moisten [ˈmɔɪsn] *vt* humedecer.

moisture [ˈmɔɪstʃəʳ] *n* humedad *f*.

moisturizer [ˈmɔɪstʃəraɪzəʳ] *n* (crema *f*) hidratante *m*.

molar [ˈməʊləʳ] *n* muela *f*.

molasses [mə'læsɪz] *n (U)* melaza *f*.

mold *US* = **mould**.

mole [məʊl] *n* **-1.** [animal, spy] topo *m* **-2.** [spot] lunar *m*.

molecule ['mɒlɪkjuːl] *n* molécula *f*.

molest [mə'lest] *vt* **-1.** [sexually] abusar sexualmente de **-2.** [annoy] molestar.

mollusc, mollusk *US* ['mɒləsk] *n* molusco *m*.

mollycoddle ['mɒlɪˌkɒdl] *vt inf* mimar.

molt *US* = **moult**.

molten ['məʊltn] *adj* fundido(da).

mom [mɒm] *n US inf* mamá *f*.

moment ['məʊmənt] *n* momento *m*; **at any ~** de un momento a otro; **at the ~** en este momento; **for the ~** de momento.

momentarily ['məʊməntərɪlɪ] *adv* **-1.** [for a short time] momentáneamente **-2.** *US* [soon] pronto, de un momento a otro.

momentary ['məʊməntrɪ] *adj* momentáneo(a).

momentous [mə'mentəs] *adj* trascendental.

momentum [mə'mentəm] *n (U)* **-1.** PHYS momento *m* **-2.** *fig* [speed, force] ímpetu *m*, impulso *m*; **to gather ~** cobrar intensidad.

momma ['mɒmə], **mommy** ['mɒmɪ] *n US* mamá *f*.

Monaco ['mɒnəkəʊ] *n* Mónaco.

monarch ['mɒnək] *n* monarca *m OR f*.

monarchy ['mɒnəkɪ] *(pl -ies)* *n* **-1.** [gen] monarquía *f* **-2.** [royal family]: **the ~** la familia real.

monastery ['mɒnəstrɪ] *(pl -ies)* *n* monasterio *m*.

Monday ['mʌndɪ] *n* lunes *m inv*; *see also* **Saturday**.

monetary ['mʌnɪtrɪ] *adj* monetario(ria).

money ['mʌnɪ] *n* dinero *m*, plata *f Andes, Col, CSur, Ven*; **to make ~** hacer dinero; **we got our ~'s worth** sacamos provecho a nuestro dinero; **for my ~** en mi opinión.

money belt *n* cinturón *m* monedero.

moneybox ['mʌnɪbɒks] *n* hucha *f*.

moneylender ['mʌnɪˌlendər] *n* prestamista *m OR f*.

money order *n* giro *m* postal.

money-spinner [-ˌspɪnər] *n esp UK inf* mina *f* (de dinero).

Mongolia [mɒŋ'gəʊlɪə] *n* Mongolia.

mongrel ['mʌŋgrəl] *n* perro *m* cruzado.

monitor ['mɒnɪtər] *◇ n* [gen & COMPUT] montor *m*. *◇ vt* **-1.** [check] controlar, hacer un seguimiento de **-2.** [listen in to] escuchar.

monk [mʌŋk] *n* monje *m*.

monkey ['mʌŋkɪ] *(pl monkeys)* *n* mono *m*.

monkey nut *n* cacahuete *m*.

monkey wrench *n* llave *f* inglesa.

mono ['mɒnəʊ] *adj* mono *(inv)*.

monochrome ['mɒnəkrəʊm] *adj* monocromo(ma).

monocle ['mɒnəkl] *n* monóculo *m*.

monologue, monolog *US* ['mɒnəlɒg] *n* monólogo *m*.

monopolize, -ise [mə'nɒpəlaɪz] *vt* monopolizar.

monopoly [mə'nɒpəlɪ] *(pl -ies)* *n*: **~ (on OR of)** monopolio *m* (de).

monotone ['mɒnətəʊn] *n*: **in a ~** con voz monótona.

monotonous [mə'nɒtənəs] *adj* monótono(na).

monotony [mə'nɒtənɪ] *n* monotonía *f*.

monsoon [mɒn'suːn] *n* monzón *m*.

monster ['mɒnstər] *n* [imaginary creature, cruel person] monstruo *m*.

monstrosity [mɒn'strɒsətɪ] *(pl -ies)* *n* monstruosidad *f*.

monstrous ['mɒnstrəs] *adj* **-1.** [very unfair, frightening, ugly] monstruoso(sa) **-2.** [very large] gigantesco(ca).

Mont Blanc [ˌmɒ̃'blɑ̃] *n* Mont Blanc.

month [mʌnθ] *n* mes *m*.

monthly ['mʌnθlɪ] *(pl -ies)* *◇ adj* mensual. *◇ adv* mensualmente.

monument ['mɒnjʊmənt] *n* monumento *m*.

monumental [ˌmɒnjʊ'mentl] *adj* **-1.** [gen] monumental **-2.** [error] descomunal.

moo [muː] *vi* mugir.

mood [muːd] *n* [of individual] humor *m*; [of public, voters] disposición *f*; **in a (bad) ~** de mal humor; **in a good ~** de buen humor; **not to be in the ~ for sthg** no estar de humor para algo.

moody ['muːdɪ] *(compar -ier, superl -iest)* *adj pej* **-1.** [changeable] de humor variable **-2.** [bad-tempered] malhumorado(da), irritable.

moon [muːn] *n* luna *f*.

moonlight ['muːnlaɪt] *n* luz *f* de la luna.

moonlighting ['muːnlaɪtɪŋ] *n* pluriempleo *m*.

moonlit ['muːnlɪt] *adj* [night] de luna; [landscape] iluminado(da) por la luna.

moor [mɔːr] *◇ n esp UK* páramo *m*, brezal *m*. *◇ vt* amarrar. *◇ vi* echar las amarras.

Moor [mɔːr] *n* moro *m*, -ra *f*.

Moorish ['mɔːrɪʃ] *adj* moro(ra), morisco(ca).

moorland ['mɔːlənd] *n esp UK* páramo *m*, brezal *m*.

moose [muːs] *(pl inv)* *n* [North American] alce *m*.

mop [mɒp] *(pt & pp -ped, cont -ping)* *◇ n* **-1.** [for cleaning] fregona *f* **-2.** *inf* [of hair] pelambrera *f*, chasca *f Andes*. *◇ vt* **-1.** [clean with mop] pasar la fregona por **-2.** [dry with cloth - sweat] enjugar.

◆ **mop up** *vt sep* [clean up] limpiar.

mope [məʊp] *vi pej* estar deprimido(da).

moped ['məʊped] *n* ciclomotor *m*, motoneta *f* *Amér*.

moral ['mɒrəl] ◇ *adj* moral. ◇ *n* [lesson] moraleja *f*.

◆ **morals** *npl* [principles] moral *f*.

morale [mə'rɑːl] *n* (U) moral *f*.

morality [mə'rælətɪ] (*pl* -ies) *n* - 1. [gen] moralidad *f* - 2. [system of principles] moral *f*.

morass [mə'ræs] *n* cenagal *m*.

morbid ['mɔːbɪd] *adj* morboso(sa).

more [mɔː] ◇ *adv* - 1. (with adjectives and adverbs) más; ~ **important** (than) más importante (que); ~ **quickly/often** (than) más rápido/a menudo (que) - 2. [to a greater degree] more: **we were** ~ **hurt than angry** más que enfadados estábamos heridos; **I couldn't agree** ~ estoy completamente de acuerdo - 3. [another time]: **once/twice** ~ una vez/dos veces más. ◇ *adj* más; ~ **food than drink** más comida que bebida; ~ **than 70 people died** más de 70 personas murieron; **have some** ~ **tea** toma un poco más de té; **I finished two** ~ **chapters today** acabé otros dos capítulos hoy. ◇ *pron* más; ~ **than five** más de cinco; **he's got** ~ **than I have** él tiene más que yo; **I don't want any** ~ no quiero más; **there's no** ~ **(left)** no queda nada (más); **(and) what's** ~ (y lo que) es más.

◆ **any more** *adv*: not ... any ~ ya no ...; **she doesn't live here any** ~ ya no vive aquí.

◆ **more and more** *adv, adj & pron* cada vez más.

◆ **more or less** *adv* más o menos.

moreover [mɔː'rəʊvəʳ] *adv* *fml* además, es más.

morgue [mɔːg] *n* depósito *m* de cadáveres.

Mormon ['mɔːmən] *n* mormón *m*, -ona *f*.

morning ['mɔːnɪŋ] *n* - 1. [first part of day] mañana *f*; **in the** ~ por la mañana; **six o'clock in the** ~ las seis de la mañana; **on Monday** ~ el lunes por la mañana - 2. [between midnight and dawn] madrugada *f* - 3. [tomorrow morning]: **in the** ~ mañana por la mañana.

◆ **mornings** *adv* *US* por la mañana.

Moroccan [mə'rɒkən] ◇ *adj* marroquí. ◇ *n* marroquí *m* OR *f*.

Morocco [mə'rɒkəʊ] *n* Marruecos.

moron ['mɔːrɒn] *n* *inf* imbécil *m* OR *f*.

morose [mə'rəʊs] *adj* malhumorado(da).

morphine ['mɔːfiːn] *n* morfina *f*.

Morse (code) [mɔːs-] *n* (código *m*) morse *m*.

morsel ['mɔːsl] *n* bocado *m*.

mortal ['mɔːtl] ◇ *adj* [gen] mortal. ◇ *n* mortal *m* OR *f*.

mortality [mɔː'tælətɪ] *n* mortalidad *f*.

mortar ['mɔːtəʳ] *n* - 1. [cement mixture] argamasa *f* - 2. [gun, bowl] mortero *m*.

mortgage ['mɔːgɪdʒ] ◇ *n* hipoteca *f*. ◇ *vt* hipotecar.

mortified ['mɔːtɪfaɪd] *adj* muerto(ta) de vergüenza.

mortuary ['mɔːtʃʊərɪ] (*pl* -ies) *n* depósito *m* de cadáveres, tanatorio *m*.

mosaic [mə'zeɪk] *n* mosaico *m*.

Moscow ['mɒskəʊ] *n* Moscú.

Moslem ['mɒzləm] = Muslim.

mosque [mɒsk] *n* mezquita *f*.

mosquito [mə'skiːtəʊ] (*pl* -es OR -s) *n* mosquito *m*, zancudo *m* *Amér*.

moss [mɒs] *n* musgo *m*.

most [məʊst] (*superl of* many) ◇ *adj* - 1. [the majority of] la mayoría de; ~ **people** la mayoría de la gente - 2. [largest amount of]: **(the)** ~ más; **who has got (the)** ~ **money?** ¿quién es el que tiene más dinero? ◇ *pron* - 1. [the majority]: ~ **(of)** la mayoría (de); ~ **are women** la mayoría son mujeres; ~ **of the time** la mayor parte del tiempo - 2. [largest amount]: **I earn (the)** ~ soy el que más dinero gana; **the** ~ **I've ever won** lo máximo que he ganado; ~ **of the time** la mayor parte del tiempo; **at** ~ como mucho - 3. *phr*: **to make the** ~ **of sthg** sacarle el mayor partido a algo. ◇ *adv* - 1. [to the greatest extent]: **(the)** ~ el/la/lo más; **the** ~ **handsome man** el hombre más guapo; **what I like** ~ lo que más me gusta; ~ **often** más a menudo - 2. *fml* [very] muy; ~ **certainly** con toda seguridad - 3. *US* [almost] casi.

mostly ['məʊstlɪ] *adv* [in the main part] principalmente; [usually] normalmente.

MOT (*abbr of* **Ministry of Transport test**) *n* ≈ ITV *f*.

motel [məʊ'tel] *n* motel *m*.

moth [mɒθ] *n* polilla *f*.

mothball ['mɒθbɔːl] *n* bola *f* de naftalina.

mother ['mʌðəʳ] ◇ *n* madre *f*. ◇ *vt* *usu pej* [spoil] mimar.

motherhood ['mʌðəhʊd] *n* maternidad *f*.

mother-in-law (*pl* **mothers-in-law** OR **mother-in-laws**) *n* suegra *f*.

motherly ['mʌðəlɪ] *adj* maternal.

mother-of-pearl *n* nácar *m*.

mother-to-be (*pl* **mothers-to-be**) *n* futura madre *f*.

mother tongue *n* lengua *f* materna.

motif [məʊ'tiːf] *n* ART & MUS motivo *m*.

motion ['məʊʃn] ◇ *n* - 1. [gen] movimiento *m*; **to set sthg in** ~ poner algo en marcha - 2. [proposal] moción *f*. ◇ *vt*: **to** ~ **sb to do sthg** indicar a alguien con un gesto que haga algo. ◇ *vi*: **to** ~ **to sb** hacer una señal (con la mano) a alguien.

motionless ['məʊʃənlıs] *adj* inmóvil.

motion picture *n US* película *f*.

motivated ['məʊtıveıtıd] *adj* motivado(da).

motivation [,məʊtı'veıʃn] *n* motivación *f*.

motive ['məʊtıv] *n* [gen] motivo *m*; [for crime] móvil *m*.

motley ['mɒtlı] *adj pej* variopinto(ta), abigarrado(da).

motor ['məʊtəʳ] <> *adj UK* [industry, accident] automovilístico(ca); [mechanic] de automóviles. <> *n* **- 1.** [engine] motor *m* **- 2.** *UK inf* [car] coche *m*.

motorbike ['məʊtəbaık] *n* moto *f*.

motorboat ['məʊtəbəʊt] *n* lancha *f* motora.

motorcar ['məʊtəkɑ:ʳ] *n* automóvil *m*.

motorcycle ['məʊtə,saıkl] *n* motocicleta *f*.

motorcyclist ['məʊtə,saıklıst] *n* motociclista *m OR f*.

motoring ['məʊtərıŋ] *n* automovilismo *m*.

motorist ['məʊtərıst] *n* automovilista *m OR f*, conductor *m*, -ra *f*.

motor racing *n (U)* carreras *fpl* de coches, automovilismo *m* deportivo.

motor scooter *n* Vespa® *f*, escúter *m*.

motor show *n* salón *m* del automóvil.

motor vehicle *n* vehículo *m* de motor.

motorway ['məʊtəweı] *n UK* autopista *f*.

mottled ['mɒtld] *adj* moteado(da).

motto ['mɒtəʊ] *(pl* **-s** OR **-es)** *n* lema *m*.

mould, mold *US* [məʊld] <> *n* **- 1.** [growth] moho *m* **- 2.** [shape] molde *m*. <> *vt lit & fig* moldear.

moulding, molding *US* ['məʊldıŋ] *n* [decoration] moldura *f*.

mouldy *(compar* **-ier***, superl* **-iest)***, moldy US (compar* **-ier***, superl* **-iest)** ['məʊldı] *adj* mohoso(sa).

moult, molt *US* [məʊlt] *vi* [bird] mudar la pluma; [dog] mudar el pelo.

mound [maʊnd] *n* **- 1.** [small hill] montículo *m* **- 2.** [untidy pile] montón *m*.

mount [maʊnt] <> *n* **- 1.** [gen] montura *f*; [for photograph] marco *m*; [for jewel] engaste *m* **- 2.** [mountain] monte *m*. <> *vt* **- 1.** [horse, bike] subirse a, montar en **- 2.** [attack] lanzar **- 3.** [exhibition] montar **- 4.** [jewel] engastar; [photograph] enmarcar. <> *vi* [increase] aumentar.

mountain ['maʊntın] *n lit & fig* montaña *f*.

mountain bike *n* bicicleta *f* de montaña.

mountaineer [,maʊntı'nıəʳ] *n* montañero *m*, -ra *f*, andinista *m OR f Amér*.

mountaineering [,maʊntı'nıərıŋ] *n* montañismo *m*, andinismo *m Amér*.

mountainous ['maʊntınəs] *adj* montañoso(sa).

mourn [mɔːn] <> *vt* [person] llorar por; [thing] lamentarse de. <> *vi*: **to ~ for sb** llorar la muerte de alguien.

mourner ['mɔːnəʳ] *n* doliente *m OR f*.

mournful ['mɔːnfʊl] *adj* [face, voice] afligido(da), lúgubre; [sound] lastimero(ra).

mourning ['mɔːnıŋ] *n* luto *m*; **in ~** de luto.

mouse [maʊs] *(pl* **mice)** *n* ZOOL & COMPUT ratón *m*.

mousetrap ['maʊstræp] *n* ratonera *f*.

mousse [muːs] *n* **- 1.** [food] mousse *m* **- 2.** [for hair] espuma *f*.

moustache *UK* [mə'stɑː.ʃ]**, mustache** *US* ['mʌstæʃ] *n* bigote *m*.

mouth [maʊθ] *n* [gen] boca *f*; [of river] desembocadura *f*.

mouthful ['maʊθfʊl] *n* [of food] bocado *m*; [of drink] trago *m*.

mouthorgan ['maʊθ,ɔːgən] *n* armónica *f*, rondín *m Amér*.

mouthpiece ['maʊθpiːs] *n* **- 1.** [of telephone] micrófono *m* **- 2.** [of musical instrument] boquilla *f* **- 3.** [spokesperson] portavoz *m OR f*.

mouthwash ['maʊθwɒʃ] *n* elixir *m* bucal.

mouth-watering [-,wɔːtərıŋ] *adj* muy apetitoso(sa).

movable ['muːvəbl] *adj* movible.

move [muːv] <> *n* **- 1.** [movement] movimiento *m*; **to get a ~ on** *inf* espabilarse, darse prisa **- 2.** [change - of house] mudanza *f*; [- of job] cambio *m* **- 3.** [in board game] jugada *f* **- 4.** [course of action] medida *f*. <> *vt* **- 1.** [shift] mover **- 2.** [change - house] mudarse de; [- job] cambiar de **- 3.** [transfer, postpone] trasladar **- 4.** [affect] conmover **- 5.** [in debate - motion] proponer **- 6.** [cause]: **to ~ sb to do sthg** mover OR llevar a alguien a hacer algo. <> *vi* **- 1.** [gen] moverse; [events] cambiar; **~ closer** acércate **- 2.** [change house] mudarse; [change job] cambiar de trabajo.

  ◆ **move about** *vi* **- 1.** [fidget] ir de aquí para allá **- 2.** [travel] viajar.

  ◆ **move along** <> *vt sep* dispersar. <> *vi* **- 1.** [move towards front or back] hacerse a un lado, correrse **- 2.** [move away - crowd, car] circular.

  ◆ **move around = move about**.

  ◆ **move away** *vi* **- 1.** [walk away] apartarse **- 2.** [go to live elsewhere] marcharse.

  ◆ **move in** *vi* **- 1.** [to new house] instalarse; **to ~ in with sb** irse a vivir con alguien **- 2.** [take control, attack] intervenir.

  ◆ **move on** *vi* **- 1.** [go away] marcharse **- 2.** [progress] avanzar, cambiar.

  ◆ **move out** *vi* mudarse; **my girlfriend ~ed out yesterday** mi novia se fue a vivir a otra casa ayer.

  ◆ **move over** *vi* hacer sitio, correrse.

  ◆ **move up** *vi* [on bench etc] hacer sitio, correrse.

moveable = movable.

movement ['mu:vmənt] *n* [gen] movimiento *m*.

movie ['mu:vɪ] *n esp US* película *f*.

movie camera *n* cámara *f* cinematográfica.

moving ['mu:vɪŋ] *adj* **- 1.** [touching] conmovedor(ra) **- 2.** [not fixed] móvil

mow [məʊ] (*pt* **-ed**, *pp* **-ed** ? **mown**) *vt* [grass, lawn] cortar; [corn] segar.
◆ **mow down** *vt sep* acribillar.

mower ['məʊəʳ] *n* cortacésped *m* OR *f*.

mown [məʊn] *pp* ➡ **mow**.

MP *n* **- 1.** (*abbr of* **Military Police**) PM *f* **- 2.** *UK abbr of* **Member of Parliament**.

MP3 (*abbr of* **MPEG-1 Audio Layer-3**) *n* COMPUT MP3 *m*.

MPEG (*abbr of* **Moving Pictures Expert Group**) *n* COMPUT MPEG *m*.

mpg (*abbr of* **miles per gallon**) millas/galón.

mph (*abbr of* **miles per hour**) mph.

Mr ['mɪstəʳ] *n* Sr.; ~ Jones el Sr. Jones.

Mrs ['mɪsɪz] *n* Sra.; ~ Jones la Sra. Jones.

Ms [mɪz] *n* abreviatura utilizada delante de un apellido de mujer cuando no se quiere especificar si está casada o no.

MS, ms *n abbr of* **multiple sclerosis**.

MSc (*abbr of* **Master of Science**) *n* (titular *m* OR *f* de un) máster *m* en Ciencias.

much [mʌtʃ] (*compar* **more**, *superl* **most**) ◇ *adj* mucho(cha); there isn't ~ rice left no queda mucho arroz; after ~ thought tras tanto reflexionar; as ~ time as ... tanto tiempo como...; twice as ~ flour el doble de harina; how ~ ...? ¿cuánto(ta) ...?; so ~ tanto(ta); too ~ demasiado(da). ◇ *pron* mucho; have you got ~? ¿tienes mucho?; I don't see ~ of him no lo veo mucho; ~ of the time una buena parte del tiempo; I don't think ~ of it no me parece gran cosa; this isn't ~ of a party esta fiesta no es nada del otro mundo; as ~ as tanto como; twice as ~ el doble; I thought as ~ ya me lo imaginaba; how ~? ¿cuánto?; so ~ for tanto con; too ~ demasiado. ◇ *adv* mucho; I don't go out ~ no salgo mucho; ~ too cold demasiado frío; they are ~ the same son muy parecidos; thank you very ~ muchas gracias; as ~ as tanto como; so ~ tanto; he is not so ~ stupid as lazy más que tonto es vago; without so ~ as ... sin siquiera ...; too ~ demasiado.
◆ **much as** *conj*: ~ as (I like him) por mucho OR más que (me guste).

muck [mʌk] *n inf* (U) **- 1.** [dirt] mugre *f*, porquería **- 2.** [manure] estiércol *m*.
◆ **muck about, muck around** *UK vi inf* hacer el indio OR tonto.
◆ **muck up** *vt sep inf UK* fastidiar.

mucky ['mʌkɪ] (*compar* **-ier**, *superl* **-iest**) *adj* mugriento(ta).

mucus ['mju:kəs] *n* mucosidad *f*.

mud [mʌd] *n* barro *m*, lodo *m*.

muddle ['mʌdl] ◇ *n* **- 1.** [disorder] desorden *m* **- 2.** [confusion] lío *m*, confusión *f*; **to be in a** ~ estar hecho un lío; **to get into a** ~ hacerse un lío. ◇ *vt* **- 1.** [put into disorder] desordenar **- 2.** [confuse] liar, confundir.
◆ **muddle along** *vi* apañárselas más o menos.
◆ **muddle through** *vi* arreglárselas.
◆ **muddle up** *vt sep* [put into disorder] desordenar; [confuse] liar, confundir.

muddy ['mʌdɪ] (*compar* **-ier**, *superl* **-iest**) *adj* [gen] lleno(na) de barro; [river] cenagoso(sa).

mudguard ['mʌdgɑ:d] *n* guardabarros *m inv*, tapabarro *m Andes*.

mudslinging ['mʌd,slɪŋɪŋ] *n* (U) *fig* insultos *mpl*, improperios *mpl*.

muesli ['mju:zlɪ] *n UK* muesli *m*.

muff [mʌf] ◇ *n* manguito *m*. ◇ *vt inf* [catch] fallar; [chance] dejar escapar.

muffin ['mʌfɪn] *n* **- 1.** *UK* [eaten with butter] *especie de bollo de pan que se come caliente* **- 2.** *US* [cake] *especie de magdalena que se come caliente*.

muffle ['mʌfl] *vt* [sound] amortiguar.

muffler ['mʌfləʳ] *n US* [for car] silenciador *m*.

mug [mʌg] (*pt* & *pp* **-ged**, *cont* **-ging**) ◇ *n* **- 1.** [cup] taza *f* (alta) **- 2.** *inf* [fool] primo *m*, -ma *f* **- 3.** *inf* [face] jeta *f*. ◇ *vt* asaltar, atracar.

mugging ['mʌgɪŋ] *n* [attack] atraco *m*.

muggy ['mʌgɪ] (*compar* **-ier**, *superl* **-iest**) *adj* bochornoso(sa).

mule [mju:l] *n* mula *f*.

mull [mʌl] ◆ **mull over** *vt sep* reflexionar sobre.

mulled [mʌld] *adj*: ~ wine *vino caliente con azúcar y especias*.

multicoloured *UK*, **multicolored** *US* [,mʌltɪ'kʌləd] *adj* multicolor.

multigym [mʌltɪ'dʒɪm] *n* multiestación *f* (de musculación).

multilateral [,mʌltɪ'lætərəl] *adj* multilateral.

multinational [,mʌltɪ'næʃənl] *n* multinacional *f*.

multiple ['mʌltɪpl] ◇ *adj* múltiple. ◇ *n* múltiplo *m*.

multiple sclerosis [-sklɪ'rəʊsɪs] *n* esclerosis *f inv* múltiple.

multiplex cinema ['mʌltɪpleks-] *n* (cine *m*) multisalas *m inv*.

multiplication [,mʌltɪplɪ'keɪʃn] *n* multiplicación *f*.

multiply ['mʌltɪplaɪ] (*pt* & *pp* **-ied**) ◇ *vt* multiplicar. ◇ *vi* [increase, breed] multiplicarse.

multistorey *UK*, **multistory** *US* [ˌmʌltɪˈstɔːrɪ] *adj* de varias plantas.

multitude [ˈmʌltɪtjuːd] *n* multitud *f.*

multi-user *adj* COMPUT multiusuario.

mum [mʌm] *UK inf* ◇ *n* mamá *f.* ◇ *adj*: **to keep ~** no decir ni pío, mantener la boca cerrada.

mumble [ˈmʌmbl] ◇ *vt* mascullar, decir entre dientes. ◇ *vi* musitar, hablar entre dientes.

mummy [ˈmʌmɪ] (*pl* **-ies**) *n* - **1.** *UK inf* [mother] mamá *f* - **2.** [preserved body] momia *f.*

mumps [mʌmps] *n (U)* paperas *fpl.*

munch [mʌntʃ] *vt & vi* masticar.

mundane [mʌnˈdeɪn] *adj* prosaico(ca).

municipal [mjuːˈnɪsɪpl] *adj* municipal.

municipality [mjuːˌnɪsɪˈpælətɪ] (*pl* **-ies**) *n* municipio *m.*

mural [ˈmjʊərəl] *n* mural *m.*

murder [ˈmɜːdəʳ] ◇ *n* asesinato *m.* ◇ *vt* - **1.** [kill] asesinar - **2.** *inf* [defeat] dar una paliza a.

murderer [ˈmɜːdərəʳ] *n* asesino *m.*

murderous [ˈmɜːdərəs] *adj* asesino(na), homicida.

murky [ˈmɜːkɪ] (*compar* **-ier**, *superl* **-iest**) *adj* - **1.** [water, past] turbio(bia) - **2.** [night, street] sombrío(a), lúgubre.

murmur [ˈmɜːməʳ] ◇ *n* [low sound] murmullo *m.* ◇ *vt & vi* murmurar.

muscle [ˈmʌsl] *n* - **1.** MED músculo *m* - **2.** *fig* [power] poder *m.*
  ◆ **muscle in** *vi* entrometerse.

muscular [ˈmʌskjʊləʳ] *adj* - **1.** [of muscles] muscular - **2.** [strong] musculoso(sa).

muse [mjuːz] ◇ *n* musa *f.* ◇ *vi* meditar, reflexionar.

museum [mjuːˈziːəm] *n* museo *m.*

mushroom [ˈmʌʃrʊm] ◇ *n* [button] champiñón *m*; [field] seta *f*; BOT hongo *m*, callampa *f Chile.* ◇ *vi* extenderse rápidamente.

music [ˈmjuːzɪk] *n* música *f.*

musical [ˈmjuːzɪkl] ◇ *adj* - **1.** [gen] musical - **2.** [talented in music] con talento para la música. ◇ *n* musical *m.*

musical instrument *n* instrumento *m* musical.

music centre *n* cadena *f* (musical), equipo *m* (de música).

music hall *n UK* [building] teatro *m* de variedades OR de revista; [genre] music-hall *m.*

musician [mjuːˈzɪʃn] *n* músico *m*, -ca *f.*

Muslim [ˈmʊzlɪm] ◇ *adj* musulmán(ana). ◇ *n* musulmán *m*, -ana *f.*

muslin [ˈmʌzlɪn] *n* muselina *f.*

mussel [ˈmʌsl] *n* mejillón *m*, choro *m Andes.*

must [mʌst] ◇ *aux vb* - **1.** [have to, intend to] deber, tener que; **I ~ go** tengo que OR

debo irme; **if I ~** si no hay más remedio - **2.** [as suggestion] tener que; **you ~ come and see us** tienes que venir a vernos - **3.** [to express likelihood] deber (de); **it ~ be true** debe (de) ser verdad; **they ~ have known** deben de haberlo sabido. ◇ *n inf*: **binoculars are a ~** unos prismáticos son imprescindibles.

mustache *US* = **moustache**.

mustard [ˈmʌstəd] *n* mostaza *f.*

muster [ˈmʌstəʳ] *vt* reunir.

mustn't [ˈmʌsnt] = **must not.**

must've [ˈmʌstəv] = **must have.**

musty [ˈmʌstɪ] (*compar* **-ier**, *superl* **-iest**) *adj* [room] que huele a cerrado; [book] que huele a viejo.

mute [mjuːt] ◇ *adj* mudo(da). ◇ *n* [person] mudo *m*, -da *f.*

muted [ˈmjuːtɪd] *adj* - **1.** [not bright] apagado(da) - **2.** [subdued] contenido(da).

mutilate [ˈmjuːtɪleɪt] *vt* mutilar.

mutiny [ˈmjuːtɪnɪ] (*pl* **-ies**, *pt & pp* **-ied**) ◇ *n* motín *m.* ◇ *vi* amotinarse.

mutter [ˈmʌtəʳ] ◇ *vt* musitar, mascullar. ◇ *vi* murmurar.

mutton [ˈmʌtn] *n* (carne *f* de) carnero *m.*

mutual [ˈmjuːtʃʊəl] *adj* - **1.** [reciprocal] mutuo(tua) - **2.** [common] común.

mutually [ˈmjuːtʃʊəlɪ] *adv* mutuamente.

muzzle [ˈmʌzl] ◇ *n* - **1.** [animal's nose and jaws] hocico *m*, morro *m* - **2.** [wire guard] bozal *m* - **3.** [of gun] boca *f.* ◇ *vt* [put muzzle on] poner bozal a.

MW (*abbr of* **medium wave**) OM *f.*

my [maɪ] *poss adj* - **1.** [gen] mi, mis (*pl*); **~ house/sister** mi casa/hermana; **~ children** mis hijos; **~ name is Sarah** me llamo Sarah; **it wasn't MY fault** no fue culpa mía OR mi culpa; **I washed ~ hair** me lavé el pelo - **2.** [in titles]: **~ Lord** milord; **~ Lady** milady.

myriad [ˈmɪrɪəd] *adj literary* innumerables.

myself [maɪˈself] *pron* - **1.** (*reflexive*) me; (*after prep*) mí mismo(ma); **with ~** conmigo mismo - **2.** (*for emphasis*) yo mismo(ma); **I did it ~** lo hice yo solo(la).

mysterious [mɪˈstɪərɪəs] *adj* misterioso(sa).

mystery [ˈmɪstərɪ] (*pl* **-ies**) *n* misterio *m.*

mystical [ˈmɪstɪkl] *adj* místico(ca).

mystified [ˈmɪstɪfaɪd] *adj* desconcertado(da), perplejo(ja).

mystifying [ˈmɪstɪfaɪɪŋ] *adj* desconcertante.

mystique [mɪˈstiːk] *n* misterio *m.*

myth [mɪθ] *n* mito *m.*

mythical [ˈmɪθɪkl] *adj* - **1.** [imaginary] mítico(ca) - **2.** [untrue] falso(sa).

mythology [mɪˈθɒlədʒɪ] (*pl* **-ies**) *n* [collection of myths] mitología *f.*

N

n (*pl* **n's** OR **ns**), **N** (*pl* **N's** OR **Ns**) [en] *n* [letter] n f, N f.
➤ **N** (*abbr of* **north**) N.

n/a, N/A (*abbr of* **not applicable**) *no corresponde.*

nab [næb] (*pt & pp* **-bed**, *cont* **-bing**) *vt inf* - **1.** [arrest] pillar - **2.** [get quickly] coger.

nag [næg] (*pt & pp* **-ged**, *cont* **-ging**) *vt* [subj: person] dar la lata a.

nagging ['nægɪŋ] *adj* - **1.** [thought, doubt] persistente - **2.** [person] gruñón(ona).

nail [neɪl] ◇ *n* - **1.** [for fastening] clavo *m* - **2.** [of finger, toe] uña *f.* ◇ *vt* : **to ~ sthg to sthg** clavar algo en OR a algo.
➤ **nail down** *vt sep* - **1.** [fasten] clavar - **2.** [person]: **I couldn't ~ him down** no pude hacerle concretar.

nailbrush ['neɪlbrʌʃ] *n* cepillo *m* de uñas.

nail file *n* lima *f* de uñas.

nail polish *n* esmalte *m* para las uñas.

nail scissors *npl* tijeras *fpl* para las uñas.

nail varnish *n* esmalte *m* para las uñas.

nail varnish remover [-rɪ'muːvəʳ] *n* quitaesmaltes *m inv.*

naive, naïve [naɪ'iːv] *adj* ingenuo(nua).

naked ['neɪkɪd] *adj* - **1.** [gen] desnudo(da); **~ flame** llama *f* sin protección - **2.** [blatant - hostility, greed] abierto(ta); [- facts] sin tapujos - **3.** [unaided]: **with the ~ eye** a simple vista.

name [neɪm] ◇ *n* [gen] nombre *m*; [surname] apellido *m*; **what's your ~?** ¿cómo te llamas?; **my ~ is John** me llamo John; **by ~** por el nombre; **it's in my wife's ~** está a nombre de mi mujer; **in the ~ of** en nombre de; **to call sb ~s** llamar de todo a alguien; **to have a good ~** tener buena fama. ◇ *vt* - **1.** [christen] poner nombre a; **we ~d him Jim** le llamamos Jim; **to ~ sb after sb** *UK*, **to ~ sb for sb** *US* poner a alguien el nombre de alguien - **2.** [identify] nombrar - **3.** [date, price] poner, decir - **4.** [appoint] nombrar.

nameless ['neɪmlɪs] *adj* [unknown - person, author] anónimo(ma).

namely ['neɪmlɪ] *adv* a saber.

namesake ['neɪmseɪk] *n* tocayo *m*, -ya *f.*

nanny ['nænɪ] (*pl* **-ies**) *n* niñera *f.*

nap [næp] (*pt & pp* **-ped**, *cont* **-ping**) ◇ *n* siesta *f.* ◇ *vi* : **we were caught napping** *inf* nos pillaron desprevenidos.

nape [neɪp] *n* : **~ of the neck** nuca *f.*

napkin ['næpkɪn] *n* servilleta *f.*

nappy ['næpɪ] (*pl* **-ies**) *n* *UK* pañal *m.*

nappy liner *n* parte desechable de un pañal de gasa.

narcissi [nɑː'sɪsaɪ] *pl* ⊳ **narcissus.**

narcissus [nɑː'sɪsəs] (*pl* **-cissuses** OR **-cissi**) *n* narciso *m.*

narcotic [nɑː'kɒtɪk] ◇ *adj* narcótico(ca). ◇ *n* narcótico *m.*

narrative ['nærətɪv] ◇ *adj* narrativo(va). ◇ *n* - **1.** [account] narración *f* - **2.** [art of narrating] narrativa *f.*

narrator [*UK* nə'reɪtə, *US* 'næreɪtər] *n* narrador *m*, -ra *f.*

narrow ['nærəʊ] ◇ *adj* - **1.** [not wide] estrecho(cha) - **2.** [limited] estrecho(cha) de miras - **3.** [victory, defeat] por un estrecho margen; [majority] escaso(sa); [escape, miss] por muy poco, por los pelos. ◇ *vi* - **1.** [become less wide] estrecharse - **2.** [eyes] entornarse - **3.** [gap] reducirse.
➤ **narrow down** *vt sep* reducir.

narrowly ['nærəʊlɪ] *adv* [barely] por muy poco.

narrow-minded [-'maɪndɪd] *adj* estrecho(cha) de miras.

nasal ['neɪzl] *adj* nasal.

nasty ['nɑːstɪ] (*compar* **-ier**, *superl* **-iest**) *adj* - **1.** [unkind] malintencionado(da) - **2.** [smell, -taste, feeling] desagradable; [weather] horrible - **3.** [problem, decision] peliagudo(da) - **4.** [injury, disease] doloroso(sa); [accident] grave; [fall] malo(la).

nation ['neɪʃn] *n* nación *f.*

national ['næʃənl] ◇ *adj* nacional. ◇ *n* súbdito *m*, -ta *f.*

national anthem *n* himno *m* nacional.

National Curriculum *n* programa de estudios oficial en Inglaterra y Gales.

national dress *n* traje *m* típico (de un país).

National Front *n* : **the ~** partido político minoritario de extrema derecha en Gran Bretaña.

National Health Service *n* *UK* : **the ~** organismo gestor de la salud pública, ≃ el Insalud.

National Insurance *n* *UK* ≃ Seguridad *f* Social.

nationalism ['næʃnəlɪzm] *n* nacionalismo *m.*

nationalist ['næʃnəlɪst] ◇ *adj* nacionalista. ◇ *n* nacionalista *m* OR *f.*

nationality [ˌnæʃə'nælətɪ] (*pl* **-ies**) *n* nacionalidad *f.*

nationalize, -ise ['næʃnəlaɪz] *vt* nacionalizar.

National Lottery *n* lotería nacional británica.

national park *n* parque *m* nacional.

national service *n* UK MIL servicio *m* militar.

National Trust *n* UK: **the ~** organización británica encargada de la preservación de edificios históricos y lugares de interés, ≃ el Patrimonio Nacional.

nationwide ['neɪʃənwaɪd] <> *adj* de ámbito nacional. <> *adv* [travel] por todo el país; [be broadcast] a todo el país.

native ['neɪtɪv] <> *adj* - 1. [country, area] natal - 2. [speaker] nativo(va); **~ language** lengua *f* materna - 3. [plant, animal]: **~ (to)** originario(ria) (de). <> *n* [of country, area] natural *m* OR *f*, nativo *m*, -va *f*.

Native American *n* indio americano *m*, india americana *f*.

Nativity [nə'tɪvɪtɪ] *n*: **the ~** la Natividad.

NATO ['neɪtəʊ] (*abbr of* **North Atlantic Treaty Organization**) *n* la OTAN.

natural ['nætʃrəl] *adj* - 1. [gen] natural - 2. [comedian, musician] nato(ta).

natural gas *n* gas *m* natural.

naturalize, -ise ['nætʃrəlaɪz] *vt* naturalizar; **to be ~ d** naturalizarse.

naturally ['nætʃrəlɪ] *adv* - 1. [as expected, understandably] naturalmente - 2. [unaffectedly] con naturalidad - 3. [instinctively] por naturaleza.

natural wastage *n* (U) reducción de plantilla por jubilación escalonada.

nature ['neɪtʃə'] *n* - 1. [gen] naturaleza *f*; **matters of this ~** asuntos de esta índole - 2. [disposition] modo *m* de ser, carácter *m*; **by ~** por naturaleza.

nature reserve *n* reserva *f* natural.

naughty ['nɔːtɪ] (*compar* **-ier**, *superl* **-iest**) *adj* - 1. [badly behaved] travieso(sa), malo(la) - 2. [rude] verde, atrevido(da).

nausea ['nɔːsjə] *n* náuseas *fpl*.

nauseam ['nɔːzɪæm] ▷ **ad nauseam**.

nauseating ['nɔːsɪeɪtɪŋ] *adj* lit & fig nauseabundo(da).

nautical ['nɔːtɪkl] *adj* náutico(ca), marítimo(ma).

naval ['neɪvl] *adj* naval.

Navarre [nə'vɑː'] *n* Navarra.

nave [neɪv] *n* nave *f*.

navel ['neɪvl] *n* ombligo *m*.

navigate ['nævɪɡeɪt] <> *vt* - 1. [steer] pilotar, gobernar - 2. [travel safely across] surcar, navegar por. <> *vi* [in plane, ship] dirigir, gobernar; [in car] dar direcciones.

navigation [,nævɪ'ɡeɪʃn] *n* navegación *f*.

navigator ['nævɪɡeɪtə'] *n* oficial *m* OR *f* de navegación, navegante *m* OR *f*.

navvy ['nævɪ] (*pl* **-ies**) *n* UK inf peón *m* caminero.

navy ['neɪvɪ] (*pl* **-ies**) <> *n* armada *f*. <> *adj*

[in colour] azul marino (inv).

navy blue *adj* azul marino (inv).

Nazi ['nɑːtsɪ] (*pl* **-s**) <> *adj* nazi. <> *n* nazi *m* OR *f*.

NB (*abbr of* **nota bene**) N.B.

near [nɪə'] <> *adj* - 1. [close in distance, time] cercano(na); **the ~ side** el lado más cercano; **in the ~ future** en un futuro próximo - 2. [related] cercano(na), próximo(ma) - 3. [almost happened]: **it was a ~ thing** poco le faltó. <> *adv* - 1. [close in distance, time] cerca; **nowhere ~** ni de lejos, ni mucho menos; **to draw** OR **come ~** acercarse - 2. [almost] casi. <> *prep* - 1. [close in position]: **~ (to)** cerca de; **to go ~ sthg** acercarse a algo - 2. [close in time]: **it's getting ~ (to) Christmas** ya estamos casi en Navidades; **~ the end** casi al final; **~ er the time** cuando se acerque la fecha - 3. [on the point of]: **~ (to)** al borde de - 4. [similar to]: **~ (to)** cerca de. <> *vt* acercarse OR aproximarse a. <> *vi* acercarse, aproximarse.

nearby [nɪə'baɪ] <> *adj* cercano(na). <> *adv* cerca.

nearly ['nɪəlɪ] *adv* casi; **I ~ fell** por poco me caigo.

near miss *n* - 1. [nearly a hit]: **it was a ~** falló por poco - 2. [nearly a collision] incidente *m* aéreo (sin colisión).

nearside ['nɪəsaɪd] <> *adj* [right-hand drive] del lado izquierdo; [left-hand drive] del lado derecho. <> *n* [right-hand drive] lado *m* izquierdo; [left-hand drive] lado derecho.

nearsighted [,nɪə'saɪtɪd] *adj* US miope, corto(ta) de vista.

neat [niːt] *adj* - 1. [tidy, precise - gen] pulcro(cra); [- room, house] arreglado(da); [- handwriting] esmerado(da) - 2. [smart] arreglado(da), pulcro(cra) - 3. [skilful] hábil - 4. [undiluted] solo(la) - 5. US inf [very good] guay.

neatly ['niːtlɪ] *adv* - 1. [tidily, smartly] con pulcritud; [write] con esmero - 2. [skilfully] hábilmente.

nebula ['nebjʊlə] *n* nebulosa *f*.

nebulous ['nebjʊləs] *adj* fml nebuloso(sa).

necessarily [UK 'nesəsrɪlɪ, ,nesə'serəlɪ] *adv* necesariamente, por fuerza.

necessary ['nesəsrɪ] *adj* - 1. [required] necesario(ria) - 2. [inevitable] inevitable.

necessity [nɪ'sesətɪ] (*pl* **-ies**) *n* necesidad *f*; **of ~** por fuerza, por necesidad.

➧ **necessities** *npl* artículos *mpl* de primera necesidad.

neck [nek] <> *n* [of person, bottle, dress] cuello *m*; [of animal] pescuezo *m*, cuello. <> *vi* inf pegarse el lote.

necklace ['neklɪs] *n* collar *m*.

neckline ['neklaɪn] *n* escote *m*.

necktie ['nektaɪ] *n* US corbata *f*.

nectarine ['nektərɪn] *n* nectarina *f*.
née [neɪ] *adj* de soltera.
need [niːd] ◇ *n*: ~ (for sthg/to do sthg) necesidad *f* (de algo/de hacer algo); **to be in** OR **to have** ~ **of** sthg necesitar algo; **there's no** ~ **for you to cry** no hace falta que llores; **if** ~ **be** si hace falta; **in** ~ necesitado(da). ◇ *vt* **-1.** [require] necesitar; **I** ~ **a haircut** me hace falta un corte de pelo; **the floor** ~**s cleaning** hay que limpiar el suelo; **that's all we** ~! ¡sólo nos faltaba eso! **- 2.** [be obliged]: **to** ~ **to do** sthg tener que hacer algo. ◇ *modal vb*: **to** ~ **to do** sthg necesitar hacer algo; ~ **we go?** ¿tenemos que irnos?; **it** ~ **not happen** no tiene por qué ser así.
needle ['niːdl] ◇ *n* aguja *f*. ◇ *vt inf* pinchar.
needless ['niːdlɪs] *adj* innecesario(ria); ~ **to say** ... está de más decir que ...
needlework ['niːdlwɜːk] *n* **-1.** [embroidery] bordado *m* **- 2.** (U) [activity] costura *f*.
needn't ['niːdnt] = need not.
need-to-know *adj*: **you will be given information on a** ~ **basis** sólo les proporcionaremos la información que necesiten.
needy ['niːdɪ] (*compar* -ier, *superl* -iest) *adj* necesitado(da).
negative ['negətɪv] ◇ *adj* negativo(va). ◇ *n* **-1.** PHOT negativo *m* **- 2.** LING negación *f*; **to answer in the** ~ decir que no.
neglect [nɪ'glekt] ◇ *n* [of garden, work] descuido *m*, desatención *f*; [of duty] incumplimiento *m*; **a state of** ~ un estado de abandono. ◇ *vt* **-1.** [ignore] desatender **- 2.** [duty, work] no cumplir con; **to** ~ **to do** sthg dejar de hacer algo.
neglectful [nɪ'glektfʊl] *adj* descuidado(da), negligente.
negligee ['neglɪʒeɪ] *n* salto *m* de cama.
negligence ['neglɪdʒəns] *n* negligencia *f*.
negligible ['neglɪdʒəbl] *adj* insignificante.
negotiate [nɪ'gəʊʃɪeɪt] ◇ *vt* **-1.** [obtain through negotiation] negociar **- 2.** [obstacle] salvar, franquear; [bend] tomar. ◇ *vi*: **to** ~ **(with sb for sthg)** negociar (con alguien algo).
negotiation [nɪ,gəʊʃɪ'eɪʃn] *n* negociación *f*.
◆ negotiations *npl* negociaciones *fpl*.
Negress ['niːgrɪs] *n* negra *f*.
Negro ['niːgrəʊ] (*pl* -es) ◇ *adj* negro(gra). ◇ *n* negro *m*, -gra *f*.
neigh [neɪ] *vi* relinchar.
neighbour UK, **neighbor** US ['neɪbə'] *n* vecino *m*, -na *f*.
neighbourhood UK, **neighborhood** US ['neɪbəhʊd] *n* **-1.** [of town] barrio *m*, vecindad *f* **- 2.** [approximate figure]: **in the** ~ **of** alrededor de.

neighbouring UK, **neighboring** US ['neɪbərɪŋ] *adj* vecino(na).
neighbourly UK, **neighborly** US ['neɪbəlɪ] *adj* [advice] de buen vecino.
neither ['naɪðə', 'niːðə'] ◇ *adv*: **I don't drink - me** ~ no bebo - yo tampoco; **the food was** ~ **good nor bad** la comida no era ni buena ni mala; **to be** ~ **here nor there** no tener nada que ver. ◇ *pron* ninguno(na); ~ **of us/them** ninguno de nosotros/ellos. ◇ *adj*: ~ **cup is blue** ninguna de las dos tazas es azul. ◇ *conj*: ~ ... **nor** ... ni ... ni ...; **she could** ~ **eat nor sleep** no podía ni comer ni dormir.
neon ['niːɒn] *n* neón *m*.
neon light *n* luz *f* de neón.
nephew ['nefjuː] *n* sobrino *m*.
Neptune ['neptjuːn] *n* Neptuno *m*.
nerve [nɜːv] *n* **-1.** ANAT nervio *m* **- 2.** [courage] valor *m*; **to keep one's** ~ mantener la calma, no perder los nervios; **to lose one's** ~ echarse atrás, perder el valor **- 3.** [cheek] cara *f*.
◆ nerves *npl* nervios *mpl*; **to get on sb's** ~**s** sacar de quicio a alguien.
nerve-racking [-,rækɪŋ] *adj* crispante, angustioso(sa).
nervous ['nɜːvəs] *adj* **-1.** ANAT & PSYCH nervioso(sa) **- 2.** [apprehensive] inquieto(ta), aprensivo(va).
nervous breakdown *n* crisis *f inv* nerviosa.
nest [nest] ◇ *n* nido *m*; **wasps'** ~ avispero *m*; ~ **of tables** mesas *fpl* nido. ◇ *vi* anidar.
nest egg *n* ahorros *mpl*.
nestle ['nesl] *vi* [settle snugly - in chair] arrellanarse; [- in bed] acurrucarse.
net [net] (*pt* & *pp* -ted, *cont* -ting) ◇ *adj* [weight, price, loss] neto(ta). ◇ *n* red *f*. ◇ *vt* **-1.** [catch] coger con red **- 2.** [acquire] embolsarse.
Net [net] *n* COMPUT: **the** ~ la Red; **to surf the** ~ navegar por la Red.
netball ['netbɔːl] *n* deporte parecido al baloncesto femenino.
net curtains *npl* visillos *mpl*.
Netherlands ['neðələndz] *npl*: **the** ~ los Países Bajos.
netiquette ['netɪket] *n* COMPUT netiqueta *f*.
netting ['netɪŋ] *n* red *f*, malla *f*.
nettle ['netl] *n* ortiga *f*.
network ['netwɜːk] ◇ *n* **-1.** [gen & COMPUT] red *f* **- 2.** RADIO & TV [station] cadena *f*. ◇ *vt* COMPUT conectar a la red.
neurosis [,njʊə'rəʊsɪs] (*pl* -ses [-siːz]) *n* neurosis *f inv*.
neurotic [,njʊə'rɒtɪk] ◇ *adj* neurótico(ca). ◇ *n* neurótico *m*, -ca *f*.
neuter ['njuːtə'] ◇ *adj* neutro(tra). ◇ *vt* castrar.

neutral ['nju:trəl] <> adj -1. [gen] neutro(tra) -2. [non-allied] neutral. <> n AUT punto m muerto.

neutrality [nju:'trælətɪ] n neutralidad f.

neutralize, -ise ['nju:trəlaɪz] vt neutralizar.

never ['nevər] adv -1. [at no time] nunca, jamás; **I've ~ done it** no lo he hecho nunca; **~ again** nunca más; **~ ever** nunca jamás, nunca en la vida; **well I ~!** ¡vaya!, ¡caramba! -2. inf [as negative] no; **I ~ knew** no lo sabía; **you ~ did!** ¡no (me digas)!

never-ending adj inacabable.

nevertheless [,nevəðə'les] adv sin embargo, no obstante.

new [nju:] adj nuevo(va); [baby] recién nacido (recién nacida); **as good as ~** como nuevo.
  ◆ **news** n (U) noticias fpl; **a piece of ~s** una noticia; **the ~s** [gen] las noticias; [on TV] el telediario; **that's ~s to me** me coge de nuevas.

newborn ['nju:bɔ:n] adj recién nacido (recién nacida).

newcomer ['nju:,kʌmər] n: **~ (to)** recién llegado m, recién llegada f(a).

newfangled [,nju:'fæŋgld] adj inf pej moderno(na).

new-found adj [gen] recién descubierto (recién descubierta); [friend] reciente.

newly ['nju:lɪ] adv recién.

newlyweds ['nju:lɪwedz] npl recién casados mpl.

new moon n luna f nueva.

new potato n patata f nueva.

news agency n agencia f de noticias.

newsagent UK ['nju:zeɪdʒənt], **newsdealer** US ['nju:zdi:lər] n [person] vendedor m, -ra f de periódicos; **~'s (shop)** tienda en la que se vende prensa así como tabaco y chucherías.

newscaster ['nju:zkɑ:stər] n presentador m, -ra f, locutor m, -ra f.

newsdealer US = newsagent.

newsflash ['nju:zflæʃ] n noticia f de última hora.

newsletter ['nju:z,letər] n boletín m.

newspaper ['nju:z,peɪpər] n -1. [publication, company] periódico m; [daily] diario m -2. [paper] papel m de periódico.

newsprint ['nju:zprɪnt] n papel m de periódico.

newsreader ['nju:z,ri:dər] n presentador m, -ra f, locutor m, -ra f.

newsreel ['nju:zri:l] n noticiario m cinematográfico.

newsstand ['nju:zstænd] n US quiosco m de periódicos.

newt [nju:t] n tritón m.

new technology n nueva tecnología f.

new town n UK ciudad nueva construida por el gobierno.

New Year n Año m Nuevo; **Happy ~!** ¡Feliz Año Nuevo!

New Year's Day n el día de Año Nuevo.

New Year's Eve n Nochevieja f.

New York [-'jɔ:k] n -1. [city]: **~ (City)** Nueva York -2. [state]: **~ (State)** (el estado de) Nueva York.

New Zealand [-'zi:lənd] n Nueva Zelanda.

New Zealander [-'zi:ləndər] n neozelandés m, -esa f.

next [nekst] <> adj -1. [in time] próximo(ma); **the ~ day** el día siguiente; **~ Tuesday/year** el martes/el año que viene; **~ week** la semana próxima OR que viene; **the ~ week** los próximos siete días -2. [in space - page etc] siguiente; [- room, house] de al lado. <> pron el siguiente (la siguiente); **who's ~?** ¿quién es el siguiente?; **~, please!** ¡el siguiente, por favor!; **the day after ~** pasado mañana; **the week after ~** la semana que viene no, la otra. <> adv -1. [afterwards] después; **what should I do ~?** ¿qué hago ahora?; **it's my go ~** ahora me toca a mí -2. [again] de nuevo; **when do they ~ play?** ¿cuándo vuelven a jugar? -3. [with superlatives]: **~ best/biggest** etc el segundo mejor/más grande etc. <> prep US al lado de, junto a.
  ◆ **next to** prep al lado de, junto a; **~ to nothing** casi nada; **in ~ to no time** en un abrir y cerrar de ojos.

next door adv (en la casa de) al lado.
  ◆ **next-door** adj: **next-door neighbour** vecino m, -na f de al lado.

next of kin n pariente más cercano m, pariente más cercana f.

NHS n abbr of **National Health Service**.

NI n abbr of **National Insurance**. <> abbr of **Northern Ireland**.

nib [nɪb] n plumilla f.

Nicaragua [,nɪkə'rægjʊə] n Nicaragua.

Nicaraguan [,nɪkə'rægjʊən] <> adj nicaragüense. <> n nicaragüense m OR f.

nice [naɪs] adj -1. [attractive] bonito(ta); **you look ~** estás guapa; [good] bueno(na); **it smells ~** huele bien -2. [kind] amable; [friendly] agradable, simpático(ca), dije Amér; **that was ~ of you** fue muy amable de tu parte; **to be ~ to sb** ser bueno con alguien -3. [pleasant] agradable; **to have a ~ time** pasarlo bien.

nice-looking [-'lʊkɪŋ] adj [person] guapo(pa); [car, room] bonito(ta).

nicely ['naɪslɪ] adv -1. [well, attractively] bien -2. [politely] educadamente, con educación -3. [satisfactorily] bien; **that will do ~** esto irá de perlas.

niche [ni:ʃ] n -1. [in wall] nicho m, hornacina f -2. [in life] hueco m -3. COMM nicho m.

nick [nɪk] <> n -1. [cut] cortecito m; [notch]

muesca *f* - **2.** *phr:* **in the ~ of time** justo a tiempo. ◇ *vt* - **1.** [cut] cortar; [make notch in] mellar - **2.** *UK inf* [steal] birlar, mangar.

nickel ['nɪkl] *n* - **1.** [metal] níquel *m* - **2.** *US* [coin] moneda *f* de cinco centavos.

nickname ['nɪkneɪm] ◇ *n* apodo *m*. ◇ *vt* apodar.

nicotine ['nɪkətiːn] *n* nicotina *f*.

niece [niːs] *n* sobrina *f*.

Nigeria [naɪ'dʒɪərɪə] *n* Nigeria.

Nigerian [naɪ'dʒɪərɪən] ◇ *adj* nigeriano(na). ◇ *n* nigeriano *m*, -na *f*.

niggle ['nɪgl] *vt UK* - **1.** [worry] inquietar - **2.** [criticize] meterse con.

night [naɪt] ◇ *adj* nocturno(na). ◇ *n* noche *f*; [evening] tarde *f*; **last ~** anoche, ayer por la noche; **tomorrow ~** mañana por la noche; **on Monday ~** el lunes por la noche; **at ~** por la noche, de noche; **to have an early/a late ~** irse a dormir pronto/tarde.

◆ **nights** *adv* - **1.** *US* [at night] por las noches - **2.** *UK* [nightshift]: **to work ~s** hacer el turno de noche.

nightcap ['naɪtkæp] *n* [drink] *bebida que se toma antes de ir a dormir.*

nightclub ['naɪtklʌb] *n* club *m* nocturno.

nightdress ['naɪtdres] *n* camisón *m*, dormilona *f Ven.*

nightfall ['naɪtfɔːl] *n* anochecer *m*.

nightgown ['naɪtgaʊn] *n* camisón *m*, dormilona *f Amér.*

nightie ['naɪtɪ] *n inf* camisón *m*.

nightingale ['naɪtɪŋgeɪl] *n* ruiseñor *m*.

nightlife ['naɪtlaɪf] *n* vida *f* nocturna.

nightly ['naɪtlɪ] ◇ *adj* nocturno(na), de cada noche. ◇ *adv* cada noche, todas las noches.

nightmare ['naɪtmeəʳ] *n lit & fig* pesadilla *f*.

night porter *n* recepcionista *m* OR *f* del turno de noche.

night school *n (U)* escuela *f* nocturna.

night shift *n* turno *m* de noche.

nightshirt ['naɪtʃɜːt] *n* camisa *f* de dormir (masculina).

nighttime ['naɪttaɪm] *n* noche *f*.

nil [nɪl] *n* - **1.** [nothing] nada *f* - **2.** *UK* SPORT cero *m*; **five ~** cinco a cero.

Nile [naɪl] *n*: **the ~** el Nilo.

nimble ['nɪmbl] *adj* - **1.** [person, fingers] ágil - **2.** [mind] rápido(da).

nine [naɪn] *num* nueve; *see also* **six**.

nineteen [,naɪn'tiːn] *num* diecinueve; *see also* **six**.

ninety ['naɪntɪ] *num* noventa; *see also* **sixty**.

ninth [naɪnθ] *num* noveno(na); *see also* **sixth**.

nip [nɪp] (*pt & pp* **-ped**, *cont* **-ping**) ◇ *n* [of drink] trago *m*. ◇ *vt* [pinch] pellizcar; [bite] mordisquear.

nipple ['nɪpl] *n* - **1.** [of woman] pezón *m*

- **2.** [of baby's bottle, man] tetilla *f*.

nit [nɪt] *n* [in hair] liendre *f*.

nitpicking ['nɪtpɪkɪŋ] *n inf (U):* **that's just ~** no son más que nimiedades.

nitrogen ['naɪtrədʒən] *n* nitrógeno *m*.

nitty-gritty [,nɪtɪ'grɪtɪ] *n inf:* **to get down to the ~** ir al grano.

no [nəʊ] (*pl* **-es**) ◇ *adv* [gen] no; **to say ~** decir que no; **you're ~ better than me** tú no eres mejor que yo. ◇ *adj* no; **I have ~ time** no tengo tiempo; **there are ~ taxis** no hay taxis; **a woman with ~ money** una mujer sin dinero; **that's ~ excuse** esa no es excusa que valga; **he's ~ fool** no es ningún tonto; **she's ~ friend of mine** no es amiga mía; **'~ smoking/parking/cameras'** 'prohibido fumar/aparcar/hacer fotos'. ◇ *n* no *m*; **he/she won't take ~ for an answer** no acepta una respuesta negativa.

No., no. (*abbr of* **number**) n°.

nobility [nə'bɪlətɪ] *n* nobleza *f*.

noble ['nəʊbl] ◇ *adj* noble. ◇ *n* noble *m* OR *f*.

nobody ['nəʊbədɪ] (*pl* **-ies**) ◇ *pron* nadie. ◇ *n pej* don nadie *m*.

nocturnal [nɒk'tɜːnl] *adj* nocturno(na).

nod [nɒd] (*pt & pp* **-ded**, *cont* **-ding**) ◇ *vt*: **to ~ one's head** [in agreement] asentir con la cabeza; [to indicate sthg] indicar con la cabeza; [as greeting] saludar con la cabeza. ◇ *vi* - **1.** [in agreement] asentir con la cabeza - **2.** [to indicate sthg] indicar con la cabeza - **3.** [as greeting] saludar con la cabeza.

◆ **nod off** *vi* quedarse dormido(da).

noise [nɔɪz] *n* ruido *m*; **to make a ~** hacer ruido.

noisy ['nɔɪzɪ] (*compar* **-ier**, *superl* **-iest**) *adj* ruidoso(sa); **it was very ~** había mucho ruido.

no-man's-land *n* tierra *f* de nadie.

nominal ['nɒmɪnl] *adj* nominal.

nominate ['nɒmɪneɪt] *vt* - **1.** [propose]: **to ~ sb (for** OR **as)** proponer a alguien (por OR como) - **2.** [appoint]: **to ~ sb (to sthg)** nombrar a alguien (algo).

nomination [,nɒmɪ'neɪʃn] *n* - **1.** [proposal] nominación *f* - **2.** [appointment]: **~ (to sthg)** nombramiento *m* (a algo).

nominee [,nɒmɪ'niː] *n* candidato *m*, -ta *f*.

non- [nɒn] *prefix* no*-*.

nonalcoholic [,nɒnælkə'hɒlɪk] *adj* sin alcohol.

nonaligned [,nɒnə'laɪnd] *adj* no alineado(da).

nonchalant [*UK* 'nɒnʃələnt, *US* ,nɒnʃə'lɑːnt] *adj* despreocupado(da).

noncommittal [,nɒnkə'mɪtl] *adj* evasivo(va).

nonconformist [,nɒnkən'fɔːmɪst] ◇ *adj* inconformista. ◇ *n* inconformista *m* OR *f*.

nondescript [*UK* 'nɒndɪskrɪpt, *US* ˌnɒndɪ'skrɪpt] *adj* anodino(na), soso(sa).

none [nʌn] ◇ *pron* **-1.** [not any] nada; **there is ~ left** no queda nada; **it's ~ of your business** no es asunto tuyo **-2.** [not one - object, person] ninguno(na); **~ of us/ the books** ninguno de nosotros/de los libros; **I had ~** no tenía ninguno. ◇ *adv*: **I'm ~ the worse/better** no me ha perjudicado/ayudado en nada; **I'm ~ the wiser** no me ha aclarado nada.
◆ **none too** *adv* no demasiado; **~ too soon** justo a tiempo.

nonentity [nɒ'nentətɪ] (*pl* -**ies**) *n* cero *m* a la izquierda.

nonetheless [ˌnʌnðə'les] *adv* sin embargo, no obstante.

non-event *n* chasco *m*.

nonexistent [ˌnɒnɪg'zɪstənt] *adj* inexistente.

nonfiction [ˌnɒn'fɪkʃn] *n* no ficción *f*.

nonintervention [ˌnɒnɪntə'venʃn] *n* no intervención.

no-nonsense *adj* práctico(ca).

nonpayment [ˌnɒn'peɪmənt] *n* impago *m*.

nonplussed, nonplused *US* [ˌnɒn'plʌst] *adj* perplejo(ja).

nonreturnable [ˌnɒnrɪ'tɜːnəbl] *adj* no retornable, sin retorno.

nonsense ['nɒnsəns] ◇ *n (U)* **-1.** [gen] tonterías *fpl*; **it is ~ to suggest that ...** es absurdo sugerir que ...; **to make (a) ~ of sthg** dar al traste con algo **-2.** [incomprehensible words] galimatías *m inv*. ◇ *excl* ¡tonterías!

nonsensical [nɒn'sensɪkl] *adj* disparatado(da), absurdo(da).

nonsmoker [ˌnɒn'sməʊkəʳ] *n* no fumador *m*, no fumadora *f*.

nonstick [ˌnɒn'stɪk] *adj* antiadherente.

nonstop [ˌnɒn'stɒp] ◇ *adj* [activity, rain] continuo(nua), incesante; [flight] sin escalas. ◇ *adv* sin parar.

noodles ['nuːdlz] *npl* tallarines *mpl* chinos.

nook [nʊk] *n* [of room] recoveco *m*; **every ~ and cranny** todos los recovecos.

noon [nuːn] *n* mediodía *m*.

no one *pron* = **nobody**.

noose [nuːs] *n* [loop] nudo *m* corredizo; [for hanging] soga *f*.

no-place *US* = **nowhere**.

nor [nɔːʳ] *conj* **-1.** ➣ **neither -2.** [and not] ni; **I don't smoke – ~ do I** no fumo – yo tampoco; **I don't know, ~ do I care** ni lo sé, ni me importa.

norm [nɔːm] *n* norma *f*; **the ~** lo normal.

normal ['nɔːml] ◇ *adj* normal. ◇ *n*: **above ~** por encima de lo normal; **to return to ~** volver a la normalidad.

normality [nɔː'mælɪtɪ], **normalcy** *US* ['nɔːmlsɪ] *n* normalidad *f*.

normally ['nɔːməlɪ] *adv* normalmente.

north [nɔːθ] ◇ *n* **-1.** [direction] norte *m* **-2.** [region]: **the North** el norte. ◇ *adj* del norte; **North London** el norte de Londres. ◇ *adv*: **~ (of)** al norte (de).

North Africa *n* África del Norte.

North America *n* Norteamérica.

North American ◇ *adj* norteamericano(na). ◇ *n* norteamericano *m*, -na *f*.

northeast [ˌnɔːθ'iːst] ◇ *n* **-1.** [direction] nordeste *m* **-2.** [region]: **the Northeast** el nordeste. ◇ *adj* del nordeste. ◇ *adv*: **~ (of)** al nordeste (de).

northerly ['nɔːðəlɪ] *adj* del norte.

northern ['nɔːðən] *adj* del norte, norteño(ña); **~ France** el norte de Francia.

Northern Ireland *n* Irlanda del Norte.

northernmost ['nɔːðənməʊst] *adj* más septentrional *OR* al norte.

North Korea *n* Corea del Norte.

North Pole *n*: **the ~** el Polo Norte.

North Sea *n*: **the ~** el Mar del Norte.

northward ['nɔːθwəd] ◇ *adj* hacia el norte. ◇ *adv* = **northwards**.

northwards ['nɔːθwədz] *adv* hacia el norte.

northwest [ˌnɔːθ'west] ◇ *n* **-1.** [direction] noroeste *m* **-2.** [region]: **the Northwest** el noroeste. ◇ *adj* del noroeste. ◇ *adv*: **~ (of)** al noroeste (de).

Norway ['nɔːweɪ] *n* Noruega *f*.

Norwegian [nɔː'wiːdʒən] ◇ *adj* noruego(ga). ◇ *n* **-1.** [person] noruego *m*, -ga *f* **-2.** [language] noruego *m*.

nose [nəʊz] *n* [of person] nariz *f*; [of animal] hocico *m*; [of plane, car] morro *m*; **to keep one's ~ out of sthg** no meter las narices en algo; **to look down one's ~ at sb/sthg** mirar por encima del hombro a alguien/algo; **to poke** *OR* **stick one's ~ in** *inf* meter las narices; **to turn up one's ~ at sthg** hacerle ascos a algo.
◆ **nose about, nose around** *vi* curiosear.

nosebleed ['nəʊzbliːd] *n* hemorragia *f* nasal.

nosedive ['nəʊzdaɪv] ◇ *n* [of plane] picado *m*. ◇ *vi lit & fig* bajar en picado.

nose ring *n* pendiente *m* en la nariz *(en forma de aro)*.

nose stud *n* pendiente *m* en la nariz *(en forma de joya)*.

nosey ['nəʊzɪ] = **nosy**.

no-smoking *adj* [area, carriage] para no fumadores; [flight] de no fumadores.

nostalgia [nɒ'stældʒə] *n*: **~ (for)** nostalgia *f* (de).

nostril ['nɒstrəl] *n* ventana *f* de la nariz.

nosy ['nəʊzɪ] (*compar* -**ier**, *superl* -**iest**) *adj* fisgón(ona), entrometido(da).

not [nɒt] *adv* no; **this is ~** the first time no es la primera vez; **it's green, isn't it?** es verde, ¿no?; **~ me** yo no; **I hope/think ~** espero/creo que no; **~ a chance** de ninguna manera; **~ even a ...** ni siquiera un (una) ...; **~ all** OR **every** no todos(das); **~ always** no siempre; **~ that ...** no es que ...; **~ at all** [no] en absoluto; [to acknowledge thanks] de nada.

notable ['nəʊtəbl] *adj* notable; **to be ~ for** sthg destacar por algo.

notably ['nəʊtəblı] *adv* **-1.** [in particular] especialmente **-2.** [noticeably] marcadamente.

notarize ['nəʊtəraız] *vt* US [document] autenticar, legalizar.

notary ['nəʊtərı] (*pl* **-ies**) *n*: **~ (public)** notario *m*, **-ria** *f*.

notch [nɒtʃ] *n* [cut] muesca *f*.

note [nəʊt] ◇ *n* **-1.** [gen] nota *f*; **to make a ~ of** sthg tomar nota de algo; **to take ~ of** sthg tener algo presente **-2.** [paper money] billete *m* **-3.** [tone] tono *m*. ◇ *vt* **-1.** [observe] notar; **please ~ that ...** tenga en cuenta que ... **-2.** [mention] mencionar.

◆ **notes** *npl* [written record] apuntes *mpl*; [in book] notas *fpl*; **to take ~s** tomar apuntes.

◆ **note down** *vt sep* anotar, apuntar.

notebook ['nəʊtbʊk] *n* **-1.** [for taking notes] libreta *f*, cuaderno *m* **-2.** COMPUT: **~ (computer)** ordenador *m* portátil.

noted ['nəʊtɪd] *adj* destacado(da); **to be ~ for** distinguirse por.

notepad ['nəʊtpæd] *n* bloc *m* de notas.

notepaper ['nəʊtpeɪpə'] *n* papel *m* de escribir OR de cartas.

noteworthy ['nəʊt,wɜːðı] (*compar* **-ier**, *superl* **-iest**) *adj* digno(na) de mención, significativo(va).

nothing ['nʌθıŋ] ◇ *pron* nada; **I've got ~ to do** no tengo nada que hacer; **for ~** [free] gratis; [for no purpose] en vano, en balde; **he's ~ if not generous** otra cosa no será pero desde luego generoso sí que es; **~ but** tan sólo; **there's ~ for it (but to do sthg)** UK no hay más remedio (que hacer algo). ◇ *adv*: **to be ~ like sb/sthg** no parecerse en nada a alguien/algo; **I'm ~ like finished** no he terminado ni mucho menos.

notice ['nəʊtıs] ◇ *n* **-1.** [on wall, door] cartel *m*; [in newspaper] anuncio *m* **-2.** [attention] atención *f*; **to take ~ (of)** hacer caso (de), prestar atención (a) **-3.** [warning] aviso *m*; **at short ~** casi sin previo aviso; **until further ~** hasta nuevo aviso; **without ~** sin previo aviso **-4.** [at work]: **to be given one's ~** ser despedido(da); **to hand in one's ~** presentar la dimisión. ◇ *vt* **-1.** [sense, smell] notar; [see] fijarse en, ver; **to ~ sb**

doing sthg fijarse en alguien que está haciendo algo **-2.** [realize] darse cuenta de. ◇ *vi* darse cuenta.

noticeable ['nəʊtısəbl] *adj* notable.

notice board *n* tablón *m* de anuncios.

notify ['nəʊtıfaı] (*pt* & *pp* **-ied**) *vt*: **to ~ sb (of sthg)** notificar OR comunicar (algo) a alguien.

notion ['nəʊʃn] *n* noción *f*.

◆ **notions** *npl* US artículos *mpl* de mercería.

notorious [nəʊ'tɔːrıəs] *adj* famoso(sa), célebre.

notwithstanding [,nɒtwıθ'stændıŋ] *fml* ◇ *prep* a pesar de. ◇ *adv* sin embargo, no obstante.

nougat ['nuːgɑː] *n* dulce hecho a base de nueces y frutas.

nought [nɔːt] *num* cero.

noun [naʊn] *n* nombre *m*, sustantivo *m*.

nourish ['nʌrıʃ] *vt* **-1.** [feed] nutrir, alimentar **-2.** [entertain] alimentar, albergar.

nourishing ['nʌrıʃıŋ] *adj* nutritivo(va), rico(ca).

nourishment ['nʌrıʃmənt] *n* alimento *m*, sustento *m*.

novel ['nɒvl] ◇ *adj* original. ◇ *n* novela *f*.

novelist ['nɒvəlıst] *n* novelista *m* OR *f*.

novelty ['nɒvltı] (*pl* **-ies**) *n* **-1.** [gen] novedad *f* **-2.** [cheap object] baratija *f* (poco útil).

November [nə'vembə'] *n* noviembre *m*; *see also* **September**.

novice ['nɒvıs] *n* **-1.** [inexperienced person] principiante *m* OR *f* **-2.** RELIG novicio *m*, **-cia** *f*.

now [naʊ] ◇ *adv* **-1.** [at this time, at once] ahora; **do it ~** hazlo ahora; **he's been away for two weeks ~** lleva dos semanas fuera; **any day ~** cualquier día de éstos; **any time ~** en cualquier momento; **for ~** por ahora, por el momento; **~ and then** OR **again** de vez en cuando **-2.** [nowadays] hoy día **-3.** [at a particular time in the past] entonces **-4.** [to introduce statement] vamos a ver. ◇ *conj*: **~ (that)** ahora que, ya que. ◇ *n* ahora; **five days from ~** de aquí a cinco días; **from ~ on** a partir de ahora; **they should be here by ~** ya deberían estar aquí; **up until ~** hasta ahora.

nowadays ['naʊədeız] *adv* hoy en día, actualmente.

nowhere UK ['nəʊweə'], **no-place** US *adv* [be] en ninguna parte; [go] a ninguna parte; **~ else** en ninguna otra parte; **to be getting ~** no estar avanzando nada, no ir a ninguna parte; **(to be) ~ near (as ... as ...)** (no ser) ni mucho menos (tan ... como ...).

nozzle ['nɒzl] *n* boquilla *f*.

nuance [njuː'ɑːns] *n* matiz *m*.

nuclear ['njuːklıə'] *adj* nuclear.

nuclear bomb *n* bomba *f* atómica.

nuclear disarmament *n* desarme *m* nuclear.

nuclear energy *n* energía *f* nuclear.

nuclear power *n* energía *f* nuclear.

nuclear power station *n* central *f* nuclear.

nuclear reactor *n* reactor *m* nuclear.

nucleus ['nju:klɪəs] (*pl* -**lei** [-lɪaɪ]) *n lit & fig* núcleo *m*.

nude [nju:d] ◇ *adj* desnudo(da). ◇ *n* ART desnudo *m*; **in the** ~ desnudo(da).

nudge [nʌdʒ] *vt* [with elbow] dar un codazo a.

nudist ['nju:dɪst] *n* nudista *m* OR *f*.

nudity ['nju:dətɪ] *n* desnudez *f*.

nugget ['nʌgɪt] *n* [of gold] pepita *f*.

nuisance ['nju:sns] *n* [thing] fastidio *m*, molestia *f*; [person] pesado *m*; **to make a** ~ **of o.s.** dar la lata.

nuke [nju:k] *inf* ◇ *n* bomba *f* atómica. ◇ *vt* -**1.** MIL atacar con arma nuclear -**2.** [cook in microwave] cocinar en el microondas.

null [nʌl] *adj*: ~ **and void** nulo(la) y sin efecto.

numb [nʌm] ◇ *adj* entumecido(da); **to be** ~ **with cold** estar helado(da) de frío; **to be** ~ **with fear** estar paralizado(da) de miedo. ◇ *vt* entumecer.

number ['nʌmbə'] ◇ *n* -**1.** [gen] número *m*; **a** ~ **of** varios(rias); **a large** ~ **of** gran número de; **large** ~**s of** grandes cantidades de; **any** ~ **of** la mar de -**2.** [of car] matrícula *f*. ◇ *vt* -**1.** [amount to] ascender a -**2.** [give a number to] numerar -**3.** [include]: **to be** ~**ed among** figurar entre.

number one ◇ *adj* principal, número uno. ◇ *n inf* [oneself] uno mismo (una misma).

numberplate ['nʌmbəpleɪt] *n* matrícula *f* (de vehículo).

Number Ten *n* el número 10 de Downing Street, residencia oficial del primer ministro británico.

numeral ['nju:mərəl] *n* número *m*, cifra *f*.

numerate ['nju:mərət] *adj* UK competente en aritmética.

numerical [nju:'merɪkl] *adj* numérico(ca).

numerous ['nju:mərəs] *adj* numeroso(sa).

nun [nʌn] *n* monja *f*.

nurse [nɜ:s] ◇ *n* MED enfermero *m*, -ra *f*; [nanny] niñera *f*. ◇ *vt* -**1.** [care for] cuidar, atender -**2.** [try to cure - a cold] curarse -**3.** *fig* [nourish] abrigar -**4.** [subj: mother] amamantar.

nursery ['nɜ:sərɪ] (*pl* -**ies**) *n* -**1.** [at home] cuarto *m* de los niños; [away from home] guardería *f* -**2.** [for plants] semillero *m*, vivero *m*.

nursery rhyme *n* poema *m* OR canción *f* infantil.

nursery school *n* parvulario *m*, escuela *f* de párvulos.

nursery slopes *npl* pista *f* para principiantes.

nursing ['nɜ:sɪŋ] *n* [profession] profesión *f* de enfermera; [of patient] asistencia *f*, cuidado *m*.

nursing home *n* [for old people] clínica *f* de reposo (privada); [for childbirth] clínica *f* (privada) de maternidad.

nurture ['nɜ:tʃə'] *vt* -**1.** [child, plant] criar -**2.** [plan, feelings] alimentar.

nut [nʌt] *n* -**1.** [to eat] nuez *f* -**2.** [of metal] tuerca *f* -**3.** *inf* [mad person] chiflado *m*, -da *f*.

◆ **nuts** *inf* ◇ *adj*: **to be** ~**s** estar chalado(da). ◇ *excl US* ¡maldita sea!

nutcrackers ['nʌt,krækəz] *npl* cascanueces *m inv*.

nutmeg ['nʌtmeg] *n* nuez *f* moscada.

nutritious [nju:'trɪʃəs] *adj* nutritivo(va).

nutshell ['nʌtʃel] *n*: **in a** ~ en una palabra.

nuzzle ['nʌzl] ◇ *vt* rozar con el hocico. ◇ *vi*: **to** ~ **(up) against** arrimarse a.

NVQ (*abbr of* **National Vocational Qualification**) *n* título de formación profesional en Inglaterra y Gales.

nylon ['naɪlɒn] ◇ *n* nylon *m*. ◇ *comp* de nylon.

o (*pl* **o's** OR **os**), **O** (*pl* **O's** OR **Os**) [əʊ] *n* -**1.** [letter] o *f*, O *f* -**2.** [zero] cero *m*.

oak [əʊk] ◇ *n* roble *m*. ◇ *comp* de roble.

OAP *n abbr of* **old age pensioner**.

oar [ɔ:'] *n* remo *m*.

oasis [əʊ'eɪsɪs] (*pl* **oases** [əʊ'eɪsi:z]) *n lit & fig* oasis *m inv*.

oatcake ['əʊtkeɪk] *n* galleta *f* de avena.

oath [əʊθ] *n* -**1.** [promise] juramento *m*; **on** OR **under** ~ bajo juramento -**2.** [swearword] palabrota *f*.

oatmeal ['əʊtmi:l] *US n* [flakes] copos *mpl* de avena; [porridge] avena *f*.

oats [əʊts] *npl* [grain] avena *f*.

obedience [ə'bi:djəns] *n*: ~ **(to sb)** obediencia *f* (a alguien).

obedient [ə'bi:djənt] *adj* obediente.

obese [əʊ'bi:s] *adj fml* obeso(sa).

obey [ə'beɪ] vt & vi obedecer.

obituary [ə'bɪtjʊərɪ] (pl **-ies**) n nota f necrológica, necrología f.

object [n 'ɒbdʒɪkt, vb ɒb'dʒekt] ⋄ n - **1.** [gen & COMPUT] objeto m - **2.** [aim] objeto m, propósito m - **3.** GRAMM complemento m. ⋄ vt objetar. ⋄ vi: to ~ to (to sthg/to doing sthg) oponerse (a algo/a hacer algo); **I** ~ **to that comment** me parece muy mal ese comentario.

objection [əb'dʒekʃn] n objeción f, reparo m; **to have no** ~ (**to sthg/to doing sthg**) no tener inconveniente (en algo/en hacer algo).

objectionable [əb'dʒekʃənəbl] adj [person] desagradable; [behaviour] censurable.

objective [əb'dʒektɪv] ⋄ adj objetivo(va). ⋄ n objetivo m.

obligation [ˌɒblɪ'geɪʃn] n - **1.** [compulsion] obligación f; **to be under an** ~ **to do sthg** tener la obligación de hacer algo - **2.** [duty] deber m.

obligatory [ə'blɪgətrɪ] adj obligatorio(ria).

oblige [ə'blaɪdʒ] vt - **1.** [force]: to ~ **sb to do sthg** obligar a alguien a hacer algo - **2.** fml [do a favour to] hacer un favor a; **I would be much** ~**d if** ... le estaría muy agradecido si ...

obliging [ə'blaɪdʒɪŋ] adj servicial, atento(ta).

oblique [ə'bliːk] ⋄ adj - **1.** [indirect - reference] indirecto(ta) - **2.** [slanting] oblicuo(cua). ⋄ n TYPO barra f.

obliterate [ə'blɪtəreɪt] vt arrasar.

oblivion [ə'blɪvɪən] n olvido m.

oblivious [ə'blɪvɪəs] adj inconsciente; **to be** ~ **to** OR **of sthg** no ser consciente de algo.

oblong ['ɒblɒŋ] ⋄ adj rectangular, oblongo(ga). ⋄ n rectángulo m.

obnoxious [əb'nɒkʃəs] adj detestable.

oboe ['əʊbəʊ] n oboe m.

obscene [əb'siːn] adj obsceno(na), indecente.

obscure [əb'skjʊə'] ⋄ adj lit & fig oscuro(ra). ⋄ vt - **1.** [make difficult to understand] oscurecer - **2.** [hide] esconder.

obsequious [əb'siːkwɪəs] adj fml & pej servil.

observance [əb'zɜːvns] n observancia f, cumplimiento m.

observant [əb'zɜːvnt] adj observador(ra).

observation [ˌɒbzə'veɪʃn] n - **1.** [by police] vigilancia f; [by doctor] observación f - **2.** [comment] comentario m.

observatory [əb'zɜːvətrɪ] (pl **-ies**) n observatorio m.

observe [əb'zɜːv] vt - **1.** [gen] observar - **2.** [obey] cumplir con, observar.

observer [əb'zɜːvə'] n observador m, -ra f.

obsess [əb'ses] vt obsesionar; **to be** ~**ed by** OR **with** estar obsesionado con.

obsessive [əb'sesɪv] adj obsesivo(va).

obsolescent [ˌɒbsə'lesnt] adj obsolescente, que está cayendo en desuso.

obsolete ['ɒbsəliːt] adj obsoleto(ta).

obstacle ['ɒbstəkl] n - **1.** [object] obstáculo m - **2.** [difficulty] estorbo m, impedimento m.

obstetrics [ɒb'stetrɪks] n obstetricia f.

obstinate ['ɒbstənət] adj - **1.** [stubborn] obstinado(da), terco(ca) - **2.** [persistent] tenaz.

obstruct [əb'strʌkt] vt - **1.** [block] obstruir, bloquear - **2.** [hinder] estorbar, entorpecer.

obstruction [əb'strʌkʃn] n [gen & SPORT] obstrucción f; [blockage] atasco m.

obtain [əb'teɪn] vt obtener, conseguir.

obtainable [əb'teɪnəbl] adj que se puede conseguir, disponible.

obtrusive [əb'truːsɪv] adj [smell] penetrante; [colour] chillón(ona); [person] entrometido(da).

obtuse [əb'tjuːs] adj lit & fig obtuso(sa).

obvious ['ɒbvɪəs] adj obvio(via), evidente.

obviously ['ɒbvɪəslɪ] adv - **1.** [of course] evidentemente, obviamente; ~ **not** claro que no - **2.** [clearly] claramente, obviamente.

occasion [ə'keɪʒn] n - **1.** [time] vez f, ocasión f; **on one** ~ una vez, en una ocasión; **on several** ~**s** varias veces, en varias ocasiones - **2.** [important event] acontecimiento m; **to rise to the** ~ ponerse a la altura de las circunstancias - **3.** fml [opportunity] ocasión f.

occasional [ə'keɪʒənl] adj [trip, drink] esporádico(ca); [showers] ocasional.

occasionally [ə'keɪʒnəlɪ] adv de vez en cuando.

occult [ɒ'kʌlt] adj oculto(ta).

occupant ['ɒkjʊpənt] n - **1.** [of building, room] inquilino m, -na f - **2.** [of chair, vehicle] ocupante m OR f.

occupation [ˌɒkjʊ'peɪʃn] n - **1.** [job] empleo m, ocupación f - **2.** [pastime] pasatiempo m - **3.** MIL [of country, building] ocupación f.

occupational disease n enfermedad f profesional.

occupational hazard n: ~**s** gajes mpl del oficio.

occupational therapy n terapia f ocupacional.

occupier ['ɒkjʊpaɪə'] n inquilino m, -na f.

occupy ['ɒkjʊpaɪ] (pt & pp **-ied**) vt - **1.** [gen] ocupar - **2.** [live in] habitar - **3.** [entertain]: **to** ~ **o.s.** entretenerse.

occur [ə'kɜː'] (pt & pp **-red**, cont **-ring**) vi - **1.** [happen] ocurrir, suceder - **2.** [be present] encontrarse - **3.** [thought, idea]: **to** ~ **to** ocurrírsele a alguien.

occurrence [ə'kʌrəns] n [event] acontecimiento m.

ocean ['əʊʃn] n océano m.

oceangoing [ˈəʊʃnˌgəʊɪŋ] *adj* maritimo(ma).

ochre *UK*, **ocher** *US* [ˈəʊkəʳ] *adj* ocre.

o'clock [əˈklɒk] *adv*: it's one ~ es la una; it's two/three ~ son las dos/las tres; at one/two ~ a la una/las dos.

octave [ˈɒktɪv] *n* octava *f*.

October [ɒkˈtəʊbəʳ] *n* octubre *m*; *see also* September.

octopus [ˈɒktəpəs] (*pl* **-puses** OR **-pi** [-paɪ]) *n* pulpo *m*.

OD - 1. *abbr of* **overdose** - 2. *abbr of* **overdrawn**.

odd [ɒd] *adj* - 1. [strange] raro(ra), extraño(ña) - 2. [not part of pair] sin pareja, suelto(ta) - 3. [number] impar - 4. *inf* [leftover] sobrante - 5. *inf* [occasional]: I play the ~ game juego alguna que otra vez - 6. *inf* [approximately]: 30 ~ years 30 y tantos OR y pico años.
◆ **odds** *npl* - 1.: the ~s [probability] las probabilidades; [in betting] las apuestas; the ~s are that ... lo más probable es que ...; against all ~s contra viento y marea - 2. [bits]: ~s and ends chismes *mpl*, cosillas *fpl* - 3. *phr*: to be at ~s with sb estar reñido con alguien.

oddity [ˈɒdɪtɪ] (*pl* **-ies**) *n* rareza *f*.

odd jobs *npl* chapuzas *fpl*.

oddly [ˈɒdlɪ] *adv* extrañamente; ~ enough aunque parezca mentira.

oddments [ˈɒdmənts] *npl* retales *mpl*.

odds-on [ˌɒdz-] *adj inf*: the ~ favourite el favorito indiscutible.

odometer [əʊˈdɒmɪtəʳ] *n US* cuentakilómetros *m inv*.

odour *UK*, **odor** *US* [ˈəʊdəʳ] *n* [gen] olor *m*; [of perfume] fragancia *f*.

of [unstressed əv, stressed ɒv] *prep* - 1. [gen] de; the cover ~ a book la portada de un libro; a cousin ~ mine un primo mío; both ~ us nosotros dos, los dos; the worst ~ them el peor de ellos; to die ~ sthg morir de algo - 2. [expressing quantity, referring to container] de; thousands ~ people miles de personas; there are three ~ us somos tres; a cup ~ coffee un café, una taza de café - 3. [indicating amount, age, time] de; a child ~ five un niño de cinco (años); at the age ~ five a los cinco años; an increase ~ 6% un incremento del 6%; the 12th ~ February el 12 de febrero - 4. [made from] de; a dress ~ silk un vestido de seda - 5. [with emotions, opinions] fear ~ ghosts miedo a los fantasmas; love ~ good food amor por la buena mesa; it was very kind ~ you fue muy amable de OR por tu parte.

off [ɒf] ◇ *adv* - 1. [away]: to drive ~ alejarse conduciendo; to turn ~ salir de la carretera; I'm ~! ¡me voy! - 2. [at a distance - in time]: it's two days ~ quedan dos días; that's a long time ~ aún queda mucho para eso; [- in space]: it's ten miles ~ está a diez millas; far ~ lejos - 3. [so as to remove]: to take sthg ~ [gen] quitar algo; [one's clothes] quitarse algo; to cut sthg ~ cortar algo; could you help me ~ with my coat? ¿me ayudas a quitarme el abrigo? - 4. [so as to complete]: to finish ~ terminar, acabar; to kill ~ rematar - 5. [not at work] libre; a day ~ un día libre; time ~ tiempo *m* libre - 6. [so as to separate]: to fence ~ vallar; to wall ~ tapiar - 7. [so as to stop working]: to turn ~ [light, radio] apagar; [water, tap] cerrar - 8. [discounted]: £10 ~ 10 libras de descuento - 9. [having money]: to be well/badly ~ andar bien/mal de dinero. ◇ *prep* - 1. [away from]: to get ~ sthg bajarse de algo; to keep ~ sthg mantenerse alejado de algo; 'keep ~ the grass' 'prohibido pisar el césped' - 2. [close to]: just ~ the coast muy cerca de la costa; it's ~ Oxford Street está al lado de Oxford Street - 3. [removed from]: to cut a slice ~ sthg cortar un pedazo de algo; take your hands ~ me! ¡quítame las manos de encima! - 4. [not attending]: to be ~ work/duty no estar trabajando/de servicio; a day ~ work un día de vacaciones - 5. *inf* [no longer liking]: she's ~ coffee/her food no le apetece café/comer - 6. [deducted from]: there's 10% ~ the price hay un 10% de rebaja sobre el precio - 7. *inf* [from]: I bought it ~ him se lo compré a él. ◇ *adj* - 1. [gone bad - meat, cheese] pasado(da), estropeado(da); [- milk] cortado(da) - 2. [light, radio, device] apagado(da); [water, electricity] desconectado(da); [tap] cerrado(da) - 3. [cancelled] suspendido(da).

offal [ˈɒfl] *n* (*U*) asaduras *fpl*.

off-chance *n*: on the ~ por si acaso.

off colour *adj* indispuesto(ta).

off duty *adj* [policeman] fuera de servicio; [soldier] de permiso.

offence *UK*, **offense** *US* [əˈfens] *n* - 1. [crime] delito *m* - 2. [cause of upset] ofensa *f*; to cause sb ~ ofender a alguien; to take ~ ofenderse.

offend [əˈfend] *vt* ofender.

offender [əˈfendəʳ] *n* - 1. [criminal] delincuente *m* OR *f* - 2. [culprit] culpable *m* OR *f*.

offense *US* [*sense 2* ˈɒfens] *n* - 1. = **offence** - 2. SPORT ataque *m*.

offensive [əˈfensɪv] ◇ *adj* - 1. [remark, behaviour] ofensivo(va); [smell] repugnante - 2. [aggressive] atacante. ◇ *n* MIL ofensiva *f*.

offer [ˈɒfəʳ] ◇ *n* oferta *f*; on ~ [available] disponible; [at a special price] en oferta. ◇ *vt* ofrecer; to ~ sthg to sb, to ~ sb sthg ofrecer algo a alguien; [be willing] to ~ to do sthg ofrecerse a hacer algo. ◇ *vi* [volunteer] ofrecerse.

offering ['ɒfərɪŋ] *n* **- 1.** [thing offered] ofrecimiento *m*; [gift] regalo *m* **- 2.** [sacrifice] ofrenda *f*.

off-guard *adj* desprevenido(da).

offhand [ˌɒf'hænd] ◇ *adj* frío(a), indiferente. ◇ *adv* de improviso.

office ['ɒfɪs] *n* **- 1.** [gen] oficina *f* **- 2.** [room] despacho *m*, oficina *f* **- 3.** US [of doctor, dentist] consulta *f*, consultorio *m* **- 4.** [position of authority] cargo *m*; **in** ~ [political party] en el poder; [person] en el cargo; **to take** ~ [political party] subir al poder; [person] asumir el cargo.

office automation *n* ofimática *f*.

office block *n* bloque *m* de oficinas.

office hours *npl* horas *fpl* de oficina.

officer ['ɒfɪsə'] *n* **- 1.** MIL oficial *m* OR *f* **- 2.** [in organization, trade union] delegado *m*, -da *f* **- 3.** [in police force] agente *m* OR *f*.

office worker *n* oficinista *m* OR *f*.

official [ə'fɪʃl] ◇ *adj* oficial. ◇ *n* [of government] funcionario *m*, -ria *f*; [of trade union] representante *m* OR *f*.

officialdom [ə'fɪʃəldəm] *n* burocracia *f*.

offing ['ɒfɪŋ] *n*: **to be in the** ~ estar al caer OR a la vista.

off-licence *n* UK *tienda donde se venden bebidas alcohólicas para llevar*.

off-line ◇ *adj* **- 1.** [printer] desconectado(da) **- 2.** [operation] fuera de línea. ◇ *adv*: **to go** ~ desconectarse.

off-peak *adj* [electricity, phone call, travel] de tarifa reducida; [period] económico(ca).

off-putting [-ˌpʊtɪŋ] *adj* **- 1.** [unpleasant] repelente, chocante **- 2.** [distracting]: **it's very** ~ me distrae mucho.

off season *n*: **the** ~ la temporada baja.

offset ['ɒfset] (*pt* & *pp* **offset**, *cont* **-ting**) *vt* compensar, contrarrestar.

offshoot ['ɒfʃuːt] *n* retoño *m*.

offshore ['ɒfʃɔː'] ◇ *adj* [wind] costero(ra); [fishing] de bajura; [oil rig] marítimo(ma); [banking] en bancos extranjeros. ◇ *adv* mar adentro, cerca de la costa; **two miles** ~ a dos millas de la costa.

offside [ˌɒf'saɪd] ◇ *adj* **- 1.** [part of vehicle - right-hand drive] izquierdo(da); [- left-hand drive] derecho(cha) **- 2.** SPORT fuera de juego. ◇ *adv* SPORT fuera de juego.

offspring ['ɒfsprɪŋ] (*pl inv*) *n* **- 1.** [of people - child] *fml or hum* descendiente *m* OR *f*; [- children] descendencia *f*, prole *f* **- 2.** [of animals] crías *fpl*.

offstage [ˌɒf'steɪdʒ] *adj* & *adv* entre bastidores.

off-the-cuff ◇ *adj* improvisado(da). ◇ *adv* improvisadamente.

off-the-peg *adj* UK confeccionado(da).

off-the-record ◇ *adj* extraoficial, oficioso(sa). ◇ *adv* extraoficialmente, oficiosamente.

off-white *adj* blancuzco(ca).

often ['ɒfn, 'ɒftn] *adv* [many times] a menudo; **how** ~ **do you go?** ¿cada cuánto OR con qué frecuencia vas?; **I don't** ~ **see him** no lo veo mucho; **I don't do it as** ~ **as I used to** no lo hago tanto como antes.
➡ **as often as not** *adv* muchas veces.
➡ **every so often** *adv* cada cierto tiempo.
➡ **more often than not** *adv* la mayoría de las veces.

ogle ['əʊgl] *vt pej* comerse con los ojos.

oh [əʊ] *excl* **- 1.** [to introduce comment] ¡ah!; ~ **really?** ¿de verdad? **- 2.** [expressing joy, surprise, fear] ¡oh!; ~ **no!** ¡no!

oil [ɔɪl] ◇ *n* **- 1.** [gen] aceite *m* **- 2.** [petroleum] petróleo *m*. ◇ *vt* engrasar, lubricar.

oilcan ['ɔɪlkæn] *n* aceitera *f*.

oil company *n* compañía *f* petrolera.

oilfield ['ɔɪlfiːld] *n* yacimiento *m* petrolífero.

oil filter *n* filtro *m* del aceite.

oil-fired [-ˌfaɪəd] *adj* de fuel-oil.

oil painting *n* (pintura *f* al) óleo *m*.

oil pipeline *n* oleoducto *m*.

oilrig ['ɔɪlrɪg] *n* plataforma *f* petrolífera.

oilskins ['ɔɪlskɪnz] *npl* [coat] impermeable *m*, chubasquero *m*.

oil slick *n* marea *f* negra.

oil tanker *n* **- 1.** [ship] petrolero *m* **- 2.** [lorry] camión *m* cisterna.

oil well *n* pozo *m* petrolífero OR de petróleo.

oily ['ɔɪlɪ] (*compar* **-ier**, *superl* **-iest**) *adj* [food] aceitoso(sa); [rag, cloth] grasiento(ta); [skin, hair] graso(sa).

ointment ['ɔɪntmənt] *n* pomada *f*, ungüento *m*.

OK (*pt* & *pp* **OKed**, *cont* **OKing**), **okay** [ˌəʊ'keɪ] *inf* ◇ *adj*: **I'm** ~ estoy bien; **the food was** ~ la comida no estuvo mal; **is it** ~ **with you?** ¿te parece bien? ◇ *excl* **- 1.** [gen] vale, de acuerdo **- 2.** [to introduce new topic] bien, vale. ◇ *vt* dar el visto bueno a.

old [əʊld] ◇ *adj* **- 1.** [gen] viejo(ja); **how** ~ **are you?** ¿cuántos años tienes?, ¿qué edad tienes?; **I'm 20 years** ~ tengo 20 años; **an** ~ **woman** una vieja; ~ **people** las personas mayores; **when I'm** ~ **er** cuando sea mayor **- 2.** [former] antiguo(gua). ◇ *npl*: **the** ~ los ancianos.

old age *n* la vejez.

old age pensioner *n* UK pensionista *m* OR *f*, jubilado *m*, -da *f*.

Old Bailey [-'beɪlɪ] *n*: **the** ~ *el juzgado criminal central de Inglaterra*.

old-fashioned [-'fæʃnd] *adj* **- 1.** [outmoded] pasado(da) de moda, anticuado(da) **- 2.** [traditional] tradicional.

old people's home n residencia f OR hogar m de ancianos.

O level n UK examen y calificación sobre una asignatura concreta que se pasaba a los 16 años.

olive ['ɒlɪv] n [fruit] aceituna f, oliva f.

olive oil n aceite m de oliva.

Olympic [ə'lɪmpɪk] adj olímpico(ca).

◆ **Olympics** npl: the ~s los Juegos Olímpicos.

Olympic Games npl: the ~ los Juegos Olímpicos.

ombudsman ['ɒmbʊdzmən] (pl -men [-mən]) n ≃ defensor m del pueblo.

omelet(te) ['ɒmlɪt] n tortilla f.

omen ['əʊmen] n presagio m.

ominous ['ɒmɪnəs] adj siniestro(tra), de mal agüero.

omission [ə'mɪʃn] n omisión f.

omit [ə'mɪt] (pt & pp -ted, cont -ting) vt omitir; [name - from list] pasar por alto; **to ~ to do sthg** no hacer algo.

omnibus ['ɒmnɪbəs] n - 1. [book] antología f - 2. UK RADIO & TV programa que emite todos los capítulos de la semana seguidos.

on [ɒn] ⇔ prep - 1. [indicating position - gen] en; [- on top of] sobre, en; ~ **a chair** en OR sobre una silla; ~ **the wall/ground** en la pared/el suelo; **he was lying** ~ **his side/back** estaba tumbado de costado/de espaldas; ~ **the left/right** a la izquierda/derecha; **I haven't got any money** ~ **me** no llevo nada de dinero encima - 2. [indicating means]: **it runs** ~ **diesel** funciona con diesel; ~ **TV/the radio** en la tele/la radio; **she's** ~ **the telephone** está al teléfono; **he lives** ~ **fruit** vive (a base) de fruta; **to hurt o.s.** ~ **sthg** hacerse daño con algo - 3. [indicating mode of transport]: **to travel** ~ **a bus/train/ship** viajar en autobús/tren/barco; **I was** ~ **the bus** iba en el autobús; **to get** ~ **a bus/train/ship** subirse a un autobús/tren/barco; ~ **foot a pie**; ~ **horseback** a caballo - 4. [indicating time, activity]: ~ **Thursday** el jueves; ~ **Thursdays** los jueves; ~ **my birthday** el día de mi cumpleaños; ~ **the 10th of February** el 10 de febrero; ~ **the 10th** el día 10; ~ **my return**, ~ **returning** al volver; ~ **business/holiday** de negocios/vacaciones - 5. [concerning] sobre, acerca de; **a book** ~ **astronomy** un libro acerca de OR sobre astronomía - 6. [indicating influence] en, sobre; **the impact** ~ **the environment** el impacto en OR sobre el medio ambiente - 7. [using, supported by]: **to be** ~ **social security** cobrar dinero de la seguridad social; **he's** ~ **tranquillizers** está tomando tranquilizantes; **to be** ~ **drugs** [addicted] drogarse - 8. [earning]: **she's** ~ **£25,000 a year** gana 25.000 libras al año - 9. [referring to musical

instrument] con; ~ **the violin** con el violín; ~ **the piano** al piano - 10. inf [paid by]: **the drinks are** ~ **me** yo pago las copas, a las copas invito yo. ⇔ adv - 1. [indicating covering, clothing]: **put the lid** ~ pon la tapa; **what did she have** ~? ¿qué llevaba encima OR puesto?; **put your coat** ~ ponte el abrigo - 2. [being shown]: **what's** ~ **at the cinema?** ¿qué echan OR ponen en el cine? - 3. [working - machine] funcionando; [- radio, TV, light] encendido(da); [- tap] abierto(ta); [- brakes] puesto(ta); **turn** ~ **the power** pulse el botón de encendido - 4. [indicating continuing action]: **he kept** ~ **walking** siguió caminando - 5. [forward]: **send my mail** ~ **(to me)** reenvíame el correo; **later** ~ más tarde, después; **earlier** ~ antes - 6. inf [referring to behaviour]: **it's just not** ~! ¡es una pasada!

◆ **from ... on** adv: **from now** ~ de ahora en adelante; **from that moment/time** ~ desde aquel momento.

◆ **on and off** adv de vez en cuando.

◆ **on to, onto** prep (only written as **onto** for senses 4 and 5) - 1. [to a position on top of] encima de, sobre; **she jumped** ~ **to the chair** salto encima de OR sobre la silla - 2. [to a position on a vehicle]: **to get** ~ **to a bus/train/plane** subirse a un autobús/tren/avión - 3. [to a position attached to] a; **stick the photo** ~ **to the page** pega la foto a la hoja - 4. [aware of wrongdoing]: **to be onto sb** andar detrás de alguien - 5. [into contact with]: **get onto the factory** ponte en contacto con la fábrica.

once [wʌns] ⇔ adv - 1. [on one occasion] una vez; ~ **a week** una vez a la semana; ~ **again** OR **more** otra vez; **for** ~ por una vez; **more than** ~ más de una vez; ~ **and for all** de una vez por todas; ~ **or twice** alguna que otra vez; ~ **in a while** de vez en cuando - 2. [previously] en otro tiempo, antiguamente; ~ **upon a time** érase una vez. ⇔ conj una vez que; ~ **you have done it** una vez que lo hayas hecho.

◆ **at once** adv - 1. [immediately] en seguida, inmediatamente - 2. [at the same time] a la vez, al mismo tiempo; **all at** ~ de repente, de golpe.

oncoming ['ɒn,kʌmɪŋ] adj [traffic] que viene en dirección contraria.

one [wʌn] ⇔ num [the number 1] un (una); **I only want** ~ sólo quiero uno; ~ **fifth** un quinto, una quinta parte; ~ **of my friends** uno de mis amigos; **(number)** ~ el uno. ⇔ adj - 1. [only] único(ca); **it's her** ~ **ambition** es su única ambición - 2. [indefinite]: ~ **of these days** un día de éstos. ⇔ pron - 1. [referring to a particular thing or person] uno (una); **I want the red** ~ yo quiero el rojo; **the** ~ **with the blond hair** la del pelo rubio; **which** ~ **do you want?** ¿cuál quieres?; **this** ~ éste (ésta); **that** ~ ése (ésa); **another** ~ otro (otra); **she's the** ~ **I told you about** es (ésa) de la que te hablé. **- 2.** *fml* [you, anyone] uno (una); **to do** ~'s **duty** cumplir uno con su deber.

➤ **for one** *adv* por mi/tu *etc* parte; **I for** ~ **remain unconvinced** yo, por lo menos OR por mi parte, sigo poco convencido.

one-armed bandit *n* (máquina *f*) tragaperras *f inv*.

one-man *adj* individual, en solitario.

one-man band *n* [musician] hombre *m* orquesta.

one-off *inf* ◇ *adj* excepcional. ◇ *n* caso *m* excepcional.

one-on-one *US* = **one-to-one**.

one-parent family *n* familia *f* monoparental.

oneself [wʌn'self] *pron* **- 1.** *(reflexive, after prep)* uno mismo (una misma); **to buy presents for** ~ hacerse regalos a sí mismo; **to take care of** ~ cuidarse **- 2.** *(for emphasis)*: **by** ~ [without help] solo(la).

one-sided [-'saɪdɪd] *adj* **- 1.** [unequal] desigual **- 2.** [biased] parcial.

one-to-one *UK*, **one-on-one** *US adj* [relationship] entre dos; [discussion] cara a cara; [tuition] individual.

one-touch dialling *UK*, **one-touch dialing** *US n* marcación *f* automática.

one-upmanship [,wʌn'ʌpmənʃɪp] *n* habilidad para colocarse en una situación de ventaja.

one-way *adj* **- 1.** [street] de dirección única, de sentido único **- 2.** [ticket] de ida.

ongoing ['ɒn,gəʊɪŋ] *adj* [gen] en curso; [problem, situation] pendiente.

onion ['ʌnjən] *n* cebolla *f*.

online ['ɒnlaɪn] ◇ *adj* COMPUT en línea; **to be** ~ estar conectado a Internet. ◇ *adv* en línea; **to go** ~ conectarse a Internet.

online banking *n* banca *f* en línea.

online shopping *n* compras *fpl* en línea.

onlooker ['ɒn,lʊkə'] *n* espectador *m*, -ra *f*.

only ['əʊnlɪ] ◇ *adj* único(ca); **to be an** ~ **child** ser hijo único. ◇ *adv* [exclusively] sólo, solamente; **I was** ~ **too willing to help** estaba encantado de poder ayudar; **I** ~ **wish I could!** ¡ojalá pudiera!; **it's** ~ **natural** es completamente normal; **it's** ~ **to be expected** no es de sorprender; **not** ~ ... **but no sólo** ... sino; ~ **just** apenas. ◇ *conj* sólo que; **I would go,** ~ **I'm too tired** iría, lo que pasa es que estoy muy cansado.

onset ['ɒnset] *n* comienzo *m*.

onshore ['ɒnʃɔː'] *adj* [wind] procedente del mar; [oil production] en tierra firme.

onslaught ['ɒnslɔːt] *n lit & fig* acometida *f*, embestida *f*.

onto [*unstressed before consonant* 'ɒntə, *unstressed before vowel* 'ɒntʊ, *stressed* 'ɒntuː] = **on to**.

onus ['əʊnəs] *n* responsabilidad *f*.

onward ['ɒnwəd] ◇ *adj* [in space] hacia delante; [in time] progresivo(va). ◇ *adv* = **onwards**.

onwards ['ɒnwədz] *adv* [in space] adelante, hacia delante; [in time]: **from now/then** ~ de ahora/allí en adelante.

ooze [uːz] ◇ *vt fig* rebosar. ◇ *vi*: **to** ~ **(from** OR **out of)** rezumar (de); **to** ~ **with** sthg *fig* rebosar OR irradiar algo.

opaque [əʊ'peɪk] *adj* **- 1.** [not transparent] opaco(ca) **- 2.** *fig* [obscure] oscuro(ra).

op cit *(abbr of* **opere citato)** op. cit.

OPEC ['əʊpek] *(abbr of* **Organization of Petroleum Exporting Countries)** *n* OPEP *f*.

open ['əʊpn] ◇ *adj* **- 1.** [gen] abierto(ta); [curtains] descorrido(da); [view, road] despejado(da) **- 2.** [receptive]: **to be** ~ **to** [ideas, suggestions] estar abierto a; [blame, criticism, question] prestarse a **- 3.** [frank] sincero(ra), franco(ca) **- 4.** [uncovered - car] descubierto(ta) **- 5.** [available - subj: choice, chance]: **to be** ~ **to sb** estar disponible para alguien. ◇ *n* **- 1.**: **in the** ~ [fresh air] al aire libre; **to bring sthg out into the** ~ sacar a luz algo **- 2.** SPORT open *m*, abierto *m*. ◇ *vt* **- 1.** [gen] abrir; **to** ~ **fire** abrir fuego **- 2.** [curtains] correr **- 3.** [inaugurate - public area, event] inaugurar **- 4.** [negotiations] entablar. ◇ *vi* **- 1.** [door, flower] abrirse **- 2.** [shop, office] abrir **- 3.** [event, play] dar comienzo.

➤ **open on to** *vt fus* dar a.

➤ **open up** ◇ *vt sep* abrir. ◇ *vi* **- 1.** [become available] surgir **- 2.** [unlock door] abrir.

opener ['əʊpnə'] *n* [gen] abridor *m*; [for tins] abrelatas *m inv*; [for bottles] abrebotellas *m inv*.

opening ['əʊpnɪŋ] ◇ *adj* inicial. ◇ *n* **- 1.** [beginning] comienzo *m*, principio *m* **- 2.** [gap - in fence] abertura *f* **- 3.** [opportunity] oportunidad *f* **- 4.** [job vacancy] puesto *m* vacante.

opening hours *npl* horario *m* (de apertura).

openly ['əʊpənlɪ] *adv* abiertamente.

open-minded [-'maɪndɪd] *adj* sin prejuicios.

open-plan *adj* de planta abierta.

Open University *n UK*: **the** ~ ≃ la Universidad Nacional de Educación a Distancia.

opera ['ɒpərə] *n* ópera *f*.

opera house *n* teatro *m* de la ópera.

operate ['ɒpəreɪt] ◇ *vt* **- 1.** [machine] hacer funcionar **- 2.** [business, system] dirigir; [service] proporcionar. ◇ *vi* **- 1.** [carry out trade, business] operar, actuar **- 2.** [function] funcionar - **3.** MED : **to ~ (on sb/sthg)** operar (a alguien/de algo).

operating theatre UK, **operating room** US ['ɒpəreɪtɪŋ-] n quirófano m.

operation [ˌɒpə'reɪʃn] n - **1.** [planned activity - police, rescue, business] operación f; [- military] maniobra f - **2.** [running - of business] administración f - **3.** [functioning - of machine] funcionamiento m; **to be in ~** [machine] estar funcionando; [law, system] estar en vigor - **4.** MED operación f, intervención f quirúrgica; **to have an ~ (for/on)** operarse (de).

operational [ˌɒpə'reɪʃənl] adj [ready for use] en funcionamiento.

operative ['ɒprətɪv] <> adj en vigor, vigente. <> n [worker] operario m, -ria f; [spy] agente m OR f.

operator ['ɒpəreɪtə'] n - **1.** TELEC operador m, -ra f, telefonista m OR f - **2.** [worker] operario m, -ria f - **3.** [company] operadora f.

opinion [ə'pɪnjən] n opinión f; **to be of the ~ that** opinar OR creer que; **in my ~** a mi juicio, en mi opinión; **what is her ~ of ...?** ¿qué opina de ...?

opinionated [ə'pɪnjəneɪtɪd] adj pej dogmático(ca).

opinion poll n sondeo m, encuesta f.

opponent [ə'pəʊnənt] n - **1.** POL adversario m, -ria f; [of system, approach] opositor m, -ora f - **2.** SPORT contrincante m OR f, adversario m, -ria f.

opportune ['ɒpətjuːn] adj oportuno(na).

opportunist [ˌɒpə'tjuːnɪst] n oportunista m OR f.

opportunity [ˌɒpə'tjuːnətɪ] (pl **-ies**) n oportunidad f, ocasión f, chance f Amér; **to take the ~ to do** OR **of doing sthg** aprovechar la ocasión de OR para hacer algo.

oppose [ə'pəʊz] vt oponerse a.

opposed [ə'pəʊzd] adj opuesto(ta); **to be ~ to** oponerse a; **as ~ to** en vez de, en lugar de; **I like beer as ~ to wine** me gusta la cerveza y no el vino.

opposing [ə'pəʊzɪŋ] adj opuesto(ta), contrario(ria).

opposite ['ɒpəzɪt] <> adj - **1.** [facing - side, house] de enfrente; [-end] opuesto(ta) - **2.** [very different]: **~ (to)** opuesto(ta) OR contrario(ria) (a). <> adv enfrente. <> prep enfrente de. <> n contrario m.

opposite number n homólogo m, -ga f.

opposition [ˌɒpə'zɪʃn] n - **1.** [gen] oposición f - **2.** [opposing team]: **the ~** los contrincantes.

→ **Opposition** n UK POL: **the Opposition** la oposición.

oppress [ə'pres] vt - **1.** [persecute] oprimir - **2.** [depress] agobiar.

oppressive [ə'presɪv] adj - **1.** [unjust] tiránico(ca), opresivo(va) - **2.** [stifling] agobiante, sofocante - **3.** [causing unease] opresivo(va), agobiante.

opt [ɒpt] <> vt : **to ~ to do sthg** optar por OR elegir hacer algo. <> vi : **to ~ for sthg** optar por OR elegir algo.

→ **opt in** vi : **to ~ in (to sthg)** decidir participar (en algo).

→ **opt out** vi : **to ~ out (of sthg)** decidir no participar (en algo).

optical ['ɒptɪkl] adj óptico(ca).

optician [ɒp'tɪʃn] n óptico m, -ca f; **the ~'s (shop)** la óptica.

optimist ['ɒptɪmɪst] n optimista m OR f.

optimistic [ˌɒptɪ'mɪstɪk] adj optimista.

optimum ['ɒptɪməm] adj óptimo(ma).

option ['ɒpʃn] n opción f; **to have the ~ to do** OR **of doing sthg** tener la opción OR la posibilidad de hacer algo; **to have no ~** no tener otra opción.

optional ['ɒpʃənl] adj facultativo(va), optativo(va); **~ extra** extra m opcional.

or [ɔː'] conj - **1.** [gen] o; (before 'o' or 'ho') u; **~ (else)** de lo contrario, si no - **2.** (after negative): **he cannot read ~ write** no sabe ni leer ni escribir.

oral ['ɔːrəl] <> adj - **1.** [spoken] oral - **2.** [relating to the mouth] bucal. <> n examen m oral.

orally ['ɔːrəlɪ] adv - **1.** [in spoken form] oralmente - **2.** [via the mouth] por vía oral.

orange ['ɒrɪndʒ] <> adj naranja (inv). <> n [fruit] naranja f.

orator ['ɒrətə'] n orador m, -ra f.

orbit ['ɔːbɪt] <> n órbita f. <> vt girar alrededor de.

orbital ['ɔːbɪtl] n UK carretera f de circunvalación.

orchard ['ɔːtʃəd] n huerto m.

orchestra ['ɔːkɪstrə] n - **1.** orquesta f - **2.** [in theatre] platea f OR patio m de butacas.

orchestral [ɔː'kestrəl] adj orquestal.

orchid ['ɔːkɪd] n orquídea f.

ordain [ɔː'deɪn] vt - **1.** fml [decree] decretar - **2.** RELIG : **to be ~ed** ordenarse (sacerdote).

ordeal [ɔː'diːl] n calvario m.

order ['ɔːdə'] <> n - **1.** [instruction] orden f; **to be under ~s to do sthg** tener órdenes de hacer algo - **2.** COMM [request] pedido m - **3.** [in restaurant] ración f - **4.** [sequence, discipline, system] orden m; **in ~** en orden; **out of ~** desordenado(da); **in ~ of importance** por orden de importancia - **5.** [fitness for use]: **in working ~** en funcionamiento; **'out of ~ '** 'no funciona'; **to be out of ~** [not working] estar estropeado(da); [incorrect behaviour] ser improcedente; **in ~** [correct] en regla - **6.** RELIG orden f. <> vt - **1.** [command]: **to ~ sb (to do sthg)** ordenar a alguien (que haga algo); **to ~ that** ordenar que - **2.** [request - drink, taxi] pedir **- 3.** COMM pedir, encargar **- 4.** [put in order] ordenar.

◆ **in the order of** UK, **on the order of** US *prep* del orden de.

◆ **in order that** *conj* para que.

◆ **in order to** *conj* para.

◆ **order about, order around** *vt sep* mangonear.

order form *n* hoja *f* de pedido.

orderly ['ɔːdəlɪ] (*pl* **-ies**) ◇ *adj* [person, crowd] disciplinado(da), pacífico(ca); [room] ordenado(da). ◇ *n* **- 1.** [in hospital] auxiliar *m* OR *f* sanitario **- 2.** [in army] ordenanza *m* OR *f*.

ordinary ['ɔːdənrɪ] ◇ *adj* **- 1.** [normal] corriente, normal **- 2.** *pej* [unexceptional] mediocre, ordinario(ria). ◇ *n*: **out of the ~** fuera de lo común.

ordnance ['ɔːdnəns] *n* (U) **- 1.** [military supplies] pertrechos *mpl* de guerra **- 2.** [artillery] artillería *f*.

ore [ɔː'] *n* mineral *m*.

oregano [ˌɒrɪ'gɑːnəʊ] *n* orégano *m*.

organ ['ɔːgən] *n* [gen, ANAT & MUS] órgano *m*.

organic [ɔː'gænɪk] *adj* **- 1.** [gen] orgánico(ca) **- 2.** [food] ecológico(ca), orgánico(ca).

organization [ˌɔːgənaɪ'zeɪʃn] *n* organización *f*.

organize, -ise ['ɔːgənaɪz] *vt* organizar.

organizer ['ɔːgənaɪzə'] *n* organizador *m*, -ra *f*.

orgasm ['ɔːgæzm] *n* orgasmo *m*.

orgy ['ɔːdʒɪ] (*pl* **-ies**) *n* lit & fig orgía *f*.

Orient ['ɔːrɪənt] *n*: **the ~** el Oriente.

oriental [ˌɔːrɪ'entl] ◇ *adj* oriental. ◇ *n* oriental *m* OR *f* (*atención: el término 'oriental' se considera racista*).

orienteering [ˌɔːrɪən'tɪərɪŋ] *n* deporte *m* de orientación.

origami [ˌɒrɪ'gɑːmɪ] *n* papiroflexia *f*.

origin ['ɒrɪdʒɪn] *n* origen *m*; **country of ~** país *m* de origen.

◆ **origins** *npl* origen *m*.

original [ə'rɪdʒənl] ◇ *adj* original; **the ~ owner** el primer propietario. ◇ *n* original *m*.

originally [ə'rɪdʒnəlɪ] *adv* [at first] originariamente; [with originality] originalmente.

originate [ə'rɪdʒəneɪt] ◇ *vt* originar, producir. ◇ *vi*: **to ~ (in)** nacer OR surgir (de); **to ~ from** nacer OR surgir de.

Orkney Islands ['ɔːknɪ-], **Orkneys** ['ɔːknɪz] *npl*: **the ~** las Orcadas.

ornament ['ɔːnəmənt] *n* adorno *m*.

ornamental [ˌɔːnə'mentl] *adj* ornamental, decorativo(va).

ornate [ɔː'neɪt] *adj* [style] recargado(da); [decoration, vase] muy vistoso(sa).

ornithology [ˌɔːnɪ'θɒlədʒɪ] *n* ornitología *f*.

orphan ['ɔːfn] ◇ *n* huérfano *m*, -na *f*. ◇ *vt*: **to be ~ed** quedarse huérfano.

orthodox ['ɔːθədɒks] *adj* ortodoxo(xa).

orthopaedic [ˌɔːθə'piːdɪk] *adj* ortopédico(ca).

orthopedic [ˌɔːθə'piːdɪk] *etc* = **orthopaedic** *etc*.

oscillate ['ɒsɪleɪt] *vi* lit & fig: **to ~ (between)** oscilar (entre).

Oslo ['ɒzləʊ] *n* Oslo.

ostensible [ɒ'stensəbl] *adj* aparente.

ostentatious [ˌɒstən'teɪʃəs] *adj* ostentoso(sa).

osteopath ['ɒstɪəpæθ] *n* osteópata *m* OR *f*.

ostracize, -ise ['ɒstrəsaɪz] *vt* [colleague etc] marginar, hacer el vacío a; POL condenar al ostracismo.

ostrich ['ɒstrɪtʃ] *n* avestruz *m*.

other ['ʌðə'] ◇ *adj* otro (otra); **the ~ one** el otro (la otra); **the ~ three** los otros tres; **the ~ day** el otro día; **the ~ week** hace unas semanas. ◇ *pron* **- 1.** [different one]: **~s** otros (otras) **- 2.** [remaining, alternative one]: **the ~** el otro (la otra); **the ~s** los otros (las otras), los demás (las demás); **one after the ~** uno tras otro; **one or ~** uno u otro; **to be none ~ than** no ser otro sino.

◆ **something or other** *pron* una cosa u otra.

◆ **somehow or other** *adv* de una u otra forma.

◆ **other than** *conj* excepto, salvo; **~ that** por lo demás.

otherwise ['ʌðəwaɪz] ◇ *adv* **- 1.** [or else] si no **- 2.** [apart from that] por lo demás **- 3.** [differently] de otra manera; **deliberately or ~** adrede o no. ◇ *conj* si no, de lo contrario.

otter ['ɒtə'] *n* nutria *f*.

ouch [aʊtʃ] *excl* ¡ay!

ought [ɔːt] *aux vb* deber; **you ~ to go/to be nicer** deberías irte/ser más amable; **she ~ to pass the exam** debería aprobar el examen; **it ~ to be fun** promete ser divertido.

ounce [aʊns] *n* [unit of measurement] = *28,35g*, ≃ onza *f*.

our [aʊə'] *poss adj* nuestro(tra), nuestros(tras) (*pl*); **~ money** nuestro dinero; **~ house** nuestra casa; **~ children** nuestros hijos; **it wasn't OUR fault** no fue culpa nuestra OR nuestra culpa; **we washed ~ hair** nos lavamos el pelo.

ours ['aʊəz] *poss pron* nuestro(tra); **that money is ~** ese dinero es nuestro; **those keys are ~** esas llaves son nuestras; **it wasn't their fault, it was OURS** no fue culpa de ellos sino de nosotros; **a friend of ~** un amigo nuestro; **their car hit ~** suyo coche chocó contra el nuestro.

ourselves [aʊə'selvz] *pron pl* **- 1.** (*reflexive*)

nos *mpl* OR *fpl*; *(after prep)* nosotros *mpl*, nosotras *fpl* - **2.** *(for emphasis)* nosotros mismos *mpl*, nosotras mismas *fpl*; **we did it by ~** lo hicimos nosotros solos.

oust [aʊst] *vt fml*: **to ~ sb (from)** [job] desbancar a alguien (de); [land] desalojar a alguien (de).

out [aʊt] *adv* - **1.** [not inside, out of doors] fuera; **we all went ~** todos salimos fuera; **I'm going ~ for a walk** voy a salir a dar un paseo; **they ran ~** salieron corriendo; **he poured the water ~** sirvió el agua; **~ here/there** aquí/allí fuera - **2.** [away from home, office] fuera; **John's ~ at the moment** John está fuera ahora mismo - **3.** [extinguished] apagado(da); **the fire went ~** el fuego se apagó - **4.** [of tides]: **the tide had gone ~** la marea estaba baja - **5.** [out of fashion] pasado(da) de moda - **6.** [published, released - book] publicado(da); **they've a new record ~** han sacado un nuevo disco - **7.** [in flower] en flor - **8.** *inf* [on strike] en huelga - **9.** [determined]: **to be ~ to do sthg** estar decidido(da) a hacer algo.

◆ **out of** *prep* - **1.** [away from, outside] fuera de; **to go ~ of the room** salir de la habitación - **2.** [indicating cause] por; **~ of spite/ love** por rencor/amor - **3.** [indicating origin, source] de; **a page ~ of a book** una página de un libro - **4.** [without] sin; **we're ~ of sugar** estamos sin azúcar, se nos ha acabado el azúcar - **5.** [made from] de; **it's made ~ of plastic** está hecho de plástico - **6.** [sheltered from] a resguardo de - **7.** [to indicate proportion]: **one ~ of ten people** una de cada diez personas; **ten ~ of ten** [mark] diez de OR sobre diez.

out-and-out *adj* [disgrace, lie] infame; [liar, crook] redomado(da).

outback ['aʊtbæk] *n*: **the ~** los llanos del interior de Australia.

outboard (motor) ['aʊtbɔːd-] *n* (motor *m*) fueraborda *m*.

outbreak ['aʊtbreɪk] *n* [of war] comienzo *m*; [of crime] ola *f*; [of illness] epidemia *f*; [of spots] erupción *f*.

outburst ['aʊtbɜːst] *n* - **1.** [sudden expression of emotion] explosión *f*, arranque *m* - **2.** [sudden occurrence] estallido *m*.

outcast ['aʊtkɑːst] *n* marginado *m*, -da *f*, paria *m* OR *f*.

outcome ['aʊtkʌm] *n* resultado *m*.

outcrop ['aʊtkrɒp] *n* afloramiento *m*.

outcry ['aʊtkraɪ] (*pl* **-ies**) *n* protestas *fpl*.

outdated [,aʊt'deɪtɪd] *adj* anticuado(da), pasado(da) de moda.

outdo [,aʊt'duː] (*pt* **-did**, *pp* **-done** [-dʌn]) *vt* aventajar, superar.

outdoor ['aʊtdɔː'] *adj* [life, swimming pool] al aire libre; [clothes] de calle.

outdoors [aʊt'dɔːz] *adv* al aire libre.

outer ['aʊtə'] *adj* exterior, externo(na).

outer space *n* espacio *m* exterior.

outfit ['aʊtfɪt] *n* - **1.** [clothes] conjunto *m*, traje *m* - **2.** *inf* [organization] equipo *m*.

outfitters ['aʊt,fɪtəz] *n dated* tienda *f* de confección.

outgoing ['aʊt,gəʊɪŋ] *adj* - **1.** [chairman] saliente - **2.** [sociable] extrovertido(da), abierto(ta).

◆ **outgoings** *npl* UK gastos *mpl*.

outgrow [,aʊt'grəʊ] (*pt* **-grew**, *pp* **-grown**) *vt* - **1.** [grow too big for]: **he has ~n his shirts** las camisas se le han quedado pequeñas - **2.** [grow too old for] ser demasiado mayor para.

outhouse ['aʊthaʊs, *pl* -haʊzɪz] *n* dependencia *f*.

outing ['aʊtɪŋ] *n* [trip] excursión *f*.

outlandish [aʊt'lændɪʃ] *adj* estrafalario(ria).

outlaw ['aʊtlɔː] ◇ *n* proscrito *m*, -ta *f*. ◇ *vt* [make illegal] ilegalizar.

outlay ['aʊtleɪ] *n* desembolso *m*, inversión *f*.

outlet ['aʊtlet] *n* - **1.** [for emotions] salida *f*, desahogo *m* - **2.** [for water] desagüe *m*; [for gas] salida *f* - **3.** [shop] punto *m* de venta - **4.** *US* ELEC toma *f* de corriente.

outline ['aʊtlaɪn] ◇ *n* - **1.** [brief description] esbozo *m*, resumen *m*; **in ~** en líneas generales - **2.** [silhouette] contorno *m*. ◇ *vt* [describe briefly] esbozar, resumir.

outlive [,aʊt'lɪv] *vt* [subj: person] sobrevivir a.

outlook ['aʊtlʊk] *n* - **1.** [attitude, disposition] enfoque *m*, actitud *f* - **2.** [prospect] perspectiva *f* (de futuro).

outlying ['aʊt,laɪŋ] *adj* [remote] lejano(na), remoto(ta); [on edge of town] periférico(ca).

outmoded [,aʊt'məʊdɪd] *adj* anticuado(da), pasado(da) de moda.

outnumber [,aʊt'nʌmbə'] *vt* exceder en número.

out-of-date *adj* - **1.** [clothes, belief] anticuado(da), pasado(da) de moda - **2.** [passport, season ticket] caducado(da).

out of doors *adv* al aire libre.

out-of-the-way *adj* [far away] remoto(ta), aislado(da); [unusual] poco común.

outpatient ['aʊt,peɪʃnt] *n* paciente externo *m*, paciente externa *f*.

outpost ['aʊtpəʊst] *n* puesto *m* avanzado.

output ['aʊtpʊt] *n* - **1.** [production] producción *f*, rendimiento *m* - **2.** [COMPUT - printing out] salida *f*; [- printout] impresión *f*.

outrage ['aʊtreɪdʒ] ◇ *n* - **1.** [anger] indignación *f* - **2.** [atrocity] atrocidad *f*, escándalo *m*. ⟷ *vt* ultrajar, atropellar.

outrageous [aʊt'reɪdʒəs] *adj* **-1.** [offensive, shocking] indignante, escandaloso(sa) **-2.** [very unusual] extravagante.

outright [*adj* 'aʊtraɪt, *adv* ˌaʊt'raɪt] ⟷ *adj* **-1.** [categoric] categórico(ca) **-2.** [total - disaster] completo(ta); [- victory, winner] indiscutible. ⟷ *adv* **-1.** [ask] abiertamente; [deny] categóricamente **-2.** [win, ban] totalmente; [be killed] en el acto.

outset ['aʊtset] *n*: at the ~ al principio; from the ~ desde el principio.

outside [*adv* ˌaʊt'saɪd, *adj*, *prep* & *n* 'aʊtsaɪd] ⟷ *adj* **-1.** [gen] exterior **-2.** [opinion, criticism] independiente **-3.** [chance] remoto(ta). ⟷ *adv* fuera; to go/run/look ~ ir/correr/mirar fuera. ⟷ *prep* fuera de; we live half an hour ~ London vivimos a media hora de Londres. ⟷ *n* [exterior] exterior *m*.

◆ **outside of** *prep* US [apart from] aparte de.

outside lane *n* carril *m* de adelantamiento.

outside line *n* línea *f* exterior.

outsider [ˌaʊt'saɪdə^r] *n* **-1.** [stranger] forastero *m*, -ra *f*, desconocido *m*, -da *f* **-2.** [in horse race] *caballo que no es uno de los favoritos*.

outsize ['aʊtsaɪz] *adj* **-1.** [bigger than usual] enorme **-2.** [clothes] de talla muy grande.

outskirts ['aʊtskɜːts] *npl*: the ~ las afueras.

outspoken [ˌaʊt'spəʊkn] *adj* franco(ca).

outstanding [ˌaʊt'stændɪŋ] *adj* **-1.** [excellent] destacado(da) **-2.** [not paid, unfinished] pendiente.

outstay [ˌaʊt'steɪ] *vt*: to ~ one's welcome quedarse más tiempo de lo debido.

outstretched [ˌaʊt'stretʃt] *adj* extendido(da).

outstrip [ˌaʊt'strɪp] (*pt* & *pp* **-ped**, *cont* **-ping**) *vt* lit & fig aventajar, dejar atrás.

out-tray *n* cubeta *o* bandeja de asuntos ya resueltos.

outward ['aʊtwəd] ⟷ *adj* **-1.** [journey] de ida **-2.** [composure, sympathy] aparente **-3.** [sign, proof] visible, exterior. ⟷ *adv* US = outwards.

outwardly ['aʊtwədlɪ] *adv* [apparently] aparentemente, de cara al exterior.

outwards UK ['aʊtwədz], **outward** US *adv* hacia fuera.

outweigh [ˌaʊt'weɪ] *vt* pesar más que.

outwit [ˌaʊt'wɪt] (*pt* & *pp* **-ted**, *cont* **-ting**) *vt* ser más listo(ta) que.

oval ['əʊvl] ⟷ *adj* oval, ovalado(da). ⟷ *n* óvalo *m*.

Oval Office *n*: the ~ el Despacho Oval, *oficina que tiene el presidente de Estados Unidos en la Casa Blanca*.

ovary ['əʊvərɪ] (*pl* **-ies**) *n* ovario *m*.

ovation [əʊ'veɪʃn] *n* ovación *f*; a standing ~ una ovación de gala (con el público en pie).

oven ['ʌvn] *n* horno *m*.

ovenproof ['ʌvnpruːf] *adj* refractario(ria).

over ['əʊvə^r] ⟷ *prep* **-1.** [directly above, on top of] encima de; a fog hung ~ the river una espesa niebla flotaba sobre el río; put your coat ~ the chair pon el abrigo encima de la silla **-2.** [to cover] sobre; she wore a veil ~ her face un velo le cubría el rostro **-3.** [on other side of] al otro lado de; he lives ~ the road vive enfrente **-4.** [across surface of] por encima de; they sailed ~ the ocean cruzaron el océano en barco **-5.** [more than] más de; ~ and above además de **-6.** [senior to] por encima de **-7.** [with regard to] por; a fight ~ a woman una pelea por una mujer **-8.** [during] durante; ~ the weekend (en) el fin de semana. ⟷ *adv* **-1.** [short distance away]: ~ here aquí; ~ there allí **-2.** [across]: to cross ~ cruzar; to go ~ ir **-3.** [down]: to fall ~ caerse; to push ~ empujar, tirar **-4.** [round]: to turn sthg ~ dar la vuelta a algo; to roll ~ darse la vuelta **-5.** [more] más **-6.** [remaining]: to be (left) ~ quedar, sobrar **-7.** [at sb's house]: invite them ~ invítalos a casa **-8.** RADIO : ~ (and out)! ¡cambio (y cierro)! **-9.** [involving repetitions]: (all) ~ again otra vez desde el principio; ~ and ~ (again) una y otra vez. ⟷ *adj* [finished] terminado(da).

◆ **all over** ⟷ *prep* por todo(da). ⟷ *adv* [everywhere] por todas partes. ⟷ *adj* [finished] terminado(da), acabado(da).

overall [*adj* & *n* 'əʊvərɔːl, *adv* ˌəʊvər'ɔːl] ⟷ *adj* [general] global, total. ⟷ *adv* en conjunto, en general. ⟷ *n* **-1.** [gen] guardapolvo *m*, bata *f* **-2.** US [for work] mono *m*.

◆ **overalls** *npl* **-1.** [for work] mono *m* **-2.** US [dungarees] pantalones *mpl* de peto.

overawe [ˌəʊvər'ɔː] *vt* intimidar.

overbalance [ˌəʊvə'bæləns] *vi* perder el equilibrio.

overbearing [ˌəʊvə'beərɪŋ] *adj* pej despótico(ca).

overboard ['əʊvəbɔːd] *adv*: to fall ~ caer al agua OR por la borda.

overbook [ˌəʊvə'bʊk] *vi* hacer overbooking.

overcame [ˌəʊvə'keɪm] *pt* ▷ overcome.

overcast ['əʊvəkɑːst] *adj* cubierto(ta), nublado(da).

overcharge [ˌəʊvə'tʃɑːdʒ] *vt*: to ~ sb (for sthg) cobrar a alguien en exceso (por algo).

overcoat ['əʊvəkəʊt] *n* abrigo *m*.

overcome [ˌəʊvə'kʌm] (*pt* **-came**, *pp* **-come**) *vt* **-1.** [deal with] vencer, superar **-2.** [overwhelm]: to be ~ (by OR with) [fear, grief, emotion] estar abrumado(da) (por); [smoke, fumes] estar asfixiado(da) (por);

overcrowded [ˌəʊvəˈkraʊdɪd] *adj* [room] atestado(da) de gente; [country] superpoblado(da).

overcrowding [ˌəʊvəˈkraʊdɪŋ] *n* [of country] superpoblación *f*; [of prison] hacinamiento *m*.

overdo [ˌəʊvəˈduː] (*pt* **-did** [-dɪd], *pp* **-done**) *vt* **- 1.** *pej* [exaggerate] exagerar **- 2.** [do too much]: **to ~ one's work/the walking** trabajar/andar demasiado **- 3.** [overcook] hacer demasiado.

overdone [ˌəʊvəˈdʌn] ⋄ *pp* ⊳ **overdo**. ⋄ *adj* muy hecho(cha).

overdose [ˈəʊvədəʊs] *n* sobredosis *f inv.*

overdraft [ˈəʊvədraːft] *n* [sum owed] saldo *m* deudor; [loan arranged] (giro *m* OR crédito *m* en) descubierto *m.*

overdrawn [ˌəʊvəˈdrɔːn] *adj*: **to be ~** tener un saldo deudor.

overdue [ˌəʊvəˈdjuː] *adj* **- 1.** [late]: **to be ~** [train] ir con retraso; [library book] estar con el plazo de préstamo caducado; **I'm ~ (for)** a bit of luck va siendo hora de tener un poco de suerte **- 2.** [awaited]: **(long) ~** (largamente) esperado(da), ansiado(da) **- 3.** [unpaid] vencido(da) y sin pagar.

overestimate [ˌəʊvərˈestɪmeɪt] *vt* sobreestimar.

overflow [*vb* ˌəʊvəˈfləʊ, *n* ˈəʊvəfləʊ] ⋄ *vi* **- 1.** [spill over] rebosar; [river] desbordarse **- 2.** [go beyond limits]: **to ~ (into)** rebosar (hacia) **- 3.** [be very full]: **to be ~ing (with)** rebosar (de). ⋄ *n* [pipe] cañería *f* de desagüe.

overgrown [ˌəʊvəˈɡrəʊn] *adj* cubierto(ta) de matojos.

overhaul [*n* ˈəʊvəhɔːl, *vb* ˌəʊvəˈhɔːl] ⋄ *n* **- 1.** [of car, machine] revisión *f* **- 2.** [of method, system] repaso *m* general. ⋄ *vt* revisar.

overhead [*adv* ˌəʊvəˈhed, *adj* & *n* ˈəʊvəhed] ⋄ *adj* aéreo(a). ⋄ *adv* por lo alto, por encima. ⋄ *n US* (U) gastos *mpl* generales.

◆ **overheads** *npl* gastos *mpl* generales.

overhead projector *n* retroproyector *m.*

overhear [ˌəʊvəˈhɪər] (*pt* & *pp* **-heard** [-hɜːd]) *vt* oír por casualidad.

overheat [ˌəʊvəˈhiːt] *vi* recalentarse.

overjoyed [ˌəʊvəˈdʒɔɪd] *adj*: **to be ~ (at sthg)** estar encantado(da) (con algo).

overkill [ˈəʊvəkɪl] *n* exageración *f*, exceso *m.*

overladen [ˌəʊvəˈleɪdn] *pp* ⊳ **overload**.

overland [ˈəʊvəlænd] ⋄ *adj* terrestre. ⋄ *adv* por tierra.

overlap [*n* ˈəʊvəlæp, *vb* ˌəʊvəˈlæp] (*pt* & *pp* **-ped**, *cont* **-ping**) *vi* **- 1.** [cover each other] superponerse **- 2.** [be similar]: **to ~ (with sthg)** coincidir en parte (en algo).

overleaf [ˌəʊvəˈliːf] *adv* al dorso, a la vuelta.

overload [ˌəʊvəˈləʊd] (*pp* **-loaded** OR

-**laden**) *vt* sobrecargar.

overlook [ˌəʊvəˈlʊk] *vt* **- 1.** [look over] mirar OR dar a **- 2.** [disregard, miss] pasar por alto, no considerar **- 3.** [forgive] perdonar.

overnight [*adj* ˈəʊvənaɪt, *adv* ˌəʊvəˈnaɪt] ⋄ *adj* **- 1.** [for all of night] de noche, nocturno(na) **- 2.** [for a night's stay - clothes] para una noche **- 3.** [very sudden] súbito(ta), de la noche a la mañana. ⋄ *adv* **- 1.** [for all of night] durante la noche **- 2.** [very suddenly] de la noche a la mañana.

overpass [ˈəʊvəpɑːs] *n US* paso *m* elevado.

overpower [ˌəʊvəˈpaʊər] *vt* **- 1.** [in fight] vencer, subyugar **- 2.** *fig* [overwhelm] sobreponerse a, vencer.

overpowering [ˌəʊvəˈpaʊərɪŋ] *adj* arrollador(ra), abrumador(ra).

overran [ˌəʊvəˈræn] *pt* ⊳ **overrun**.

overrated [ˌəʊvəˈreɪtɪd] *adj* sobreestimado(da).

override [ˌəʊvəˈraɪd] (*pt* **-rode**, *pp* **-ridden**) *vt* **- 1.** [be more important than] predominar sobre **- 2.** [overrule] desautorizar.

overriding [ˌəʊvəˈraɪdɪŋ] *adj* predominante.

overrode [ˌəʊvəˈrəʊd] *pt* ⊳ **override**.

overrule [ˌəʊvəˈruːl] *vt* [person] desautorizar; [decision] anular; [request] denegar.

overrun [ˌəʊvəˈrʌn] (*pt* **-ran**, *pp* **-run**, *cont* **-running**) ⋄ *vt* **- 1.** MIL [enemy, army] apabullar, arrasar; [country] ocupar, invadir **- 2.** *fig* [cover]: **to be ~ with** estar invadido(da) de. ⋄ *vi* rebasar el tiempo previsto.

oversaw [ˌəʊvəˈsɔː] *pt* ⊳ **oversee**.

overseas [*adj* ˈəʊvəsiːz, *adv* ˌəʊvəˈsiːz] ⋄ *adj* **- 1.** [in or to foreign countries - market] exterior; [- sales, aid] al extranjero; [- network, branches] en el extranjero **- 2.** [from abroad] extranjero(ra). ⋄ *adv* [go, travel] al extranjero; [study, live] en el extranjero.

oversee [ˌəʊvəˈsiː] (*pt* **-saw**, *pp* **-seen** [-ˈsiːn]) *vt* supervisar.

overseer [ˈəʊvəˌsiːər] *n* supervisor *m*, -ra *f.*

overshadow [ˌəʊvəˈʃædəʊ] *vt* **- 1.** [be more important than]: **to be ~ed by** ser eclipsado(da) por **- 2.** [mar]: **to be ~ed by sthg** ser ensombrecido(da) por algo.

overshoot [ˌəʊvəˈʃuːt] (*pt* & *pp* **-shot**) *vt* [go past] pasarse.

oversight [ˈəʊvəsaɪt] *n* descuido *m.*

oversleep [ˌəʊvəˈsliːp] (*pt* & *pp* **-slept** [-ˈslept]) *vi* no despertarse a tiempo, quedarse dormido(da).

overspill [ˈəʊvəspɪl] *n* exceso *m* de población.

overstep [ˌəʊvəˈstep] (*pt* & *pp* **-ped**, *cont* **-ping**) *vt* pasar de; **to ~ the mark** pasarse de la raya.

overt [ˈəʊvɜːt] *adj* abierto(ta), evidente.

overtake [ˌəʊvəˈteɪk] (*pt* **-took**, *pp* **-taken**

[-'teɪkn]) vt **-1.** AUT adelantar **-2.** [subj: event] sorprender, coger de improviso.

overthrow [ˌəʊvə'θrəʊ] (pt **-threw**, pp **-thrown**) vt [oust] derrocar.

overtime ['əʊvətaɪm] ◇ n (U) **-1.** [extra work] horas fpl extra **-2.** US SPORT (tiempo m de) descuento m. ◇ adv : **to work ~** trabajar horas extra.

overtones ['əʊvətəʊnz] npl tono m, matiz m.

overtook [ˌəʊvə'tʊk] pt ⊳ **overtake**.

overture ['əʊvəˌtjʊəʳ] n MUS obertura f.

overturn [ˌəʊvə'tɜːn] ◇ vt **-1.** [turn over] volcar **-2.** [overrule] rechazar **-3.** [overthrow] derrocar, derrumbar. ◇ vi [vehicle] volcar; [boat] zozobrar.

overweight [ˌəʊvə'weɪt] adj grueso(sa), gordo(da).

overwhelm [ˌəʊvə'welm] vt **-1.** [make helpless] abrumar **-2.** [defeat] aplastar, arrollar.

overwhelming [ˌəʊvə'welmɪŋ] adj **-1.** [despair, kindness] abrumador(ra) **-2.** [defeat, majority] contundente, aplastante.

overwork [ˌəʊvə'wɜːk] ◇ n trabajo m excesivo. ◇ vt [give too much work to] hacer trabajar demasiado.

overwrought [ˌəʊvə'rɔːt] adj fml nerviosísimo(ma), sobreexcitado(da).

owe [əʊ] vt : **to ~ sthg to sb, to ~ sb sthg** deber algo a alguien.

owing ['əʊɪŋ] adj que se debe.

◆ **owing to** prep debido a, por causa de.

owl [aʊl] n búho m, lechuza f, tecolote m Cam & Méx.

own [əʊn] ◇ adj : **my/your/his** etc **~ car** mi/tu/su etc propio coche. ◇ pron : **my ~** el mío (la mía); **his/her ~** el suyo (la suya); **a house of my/his ~** mi/su propia casa; **on one's ~** solo(la); **to get one's ~ back** inf timarse la revancha, desquitarse. ◇ vt poseer, tener.

◆ **own up** vi : **to ~ up (to sthg)** confesar (algo).

owner ['əʊnəʳ] n propietario m, -ria f.

ownership ['əʊnəʃɪp] n propiedad f.

ox [ɒks] (pl **oxen**) n buey m.

Oxbridge ['ɒksbrɪdʒ] n (U) las universidades de Oxford y Cambridge.

oxen ['ɒksn] pl ⊳ **ox**.

oxtail soup ['ɒksteɪl-] n sopa f de rabo de buey.

oxygen ['ɒksɪdʒən] n oxígeno m.

oxygen mask n máscara f de oxígeno.

oxygen tent n tienda f de oxígeno.

oyster ['ɔɪstəʳ] n ostra f.

oz. abbr of **ounce**.

ozone ['əʊzəʊn] n ozono m.

ozone-friendly adj que no daña a la capa de ozono.

ozone layer n capa f de ozono.

p¹ (pl **p's** OR **ps**), **P** (pl **P's** OR **Ps**) [piː] n [letter] p f, P f.

p² **-1.** (abbr of **page**) p., pág. **-2.** UK abbr of **penny, pence**.

pa [pɑː] n inf esp US papá m.

p.a. (abbr of **per annum**) p.a.

PA ◇ n **-1.** UK abbr of **personal assistant** **-2.** abbr of **public-address system**. ◇ abbr of **Pennsylvania**.

pace [peɪs] ◇ n paso m, ritmo m; **to keep ~ (with sthg)** [change, events] mantenerse al corriente (de algo); **to keep ~ (with sb)** seguir el ritmo (a alguien). ◇ vi : **to ~ (up and down)** pasearse de un lado a otro.

pacemaker ['peɪsˌmeɪkəʳ] n **-1.** MED marcapasos m inv **-2.** [in race] liebre f.

Pacific [pə'sɪfɪk] ◇ adj del Pacífico. ◇ n : **the ~ (Ocean)** el (océano) Pacífico.

pacifier ['pæsɪfaɪəʳ] n US [for child] chupete m.

pacifist ['pæsɪfɪst] n pacifista m OR f.

pacify ['pæsɪfaɪ] (pt & pp **-ied**) vt [person, mob] calmar, apaciguar.

pack [pæk] ◇ n **-1.** [bundle] lío m, fardo m; [rucksack] mochila f **-2.** esp US [packet] paquete m **-3.** [of cards] baraja f **-4.** [of dogs] jauría f; [of wolves] manada f; pej [of people] banda f; **a ~ of lies** una sarta de mentira. ◇ vt **-1.** [for journey - bags, suitcase] hacer; [- clothes, etc] meter (en la maleta) **-2.** [put in parcel] empaquetar; [put in container] envasar **-3.** [fill] llenar, abarrotar; **to be ~ed into sthg** estar apretujados dentro de algo. ◇ vi hacer las maletas, hacer el equipaje.

◆ **pack in** inf ◇ vt sep UK [stop] dejar; **~ it in!** ¡déjalo!, ¡ya basta! ◇ vi [break down] escacharrarse.

◆ **pack off** vt sep inf enviar, mandar.

package ['pækɪdʒ] ◇ n [gen & COMPUT] paquete m. ◇ vt [wrap up] envasar.

package deal n convenio m OR acuerdo m global.

package tour n paquete m turístico.

packaging ['pækɪdʒɪŋ] n [wrapping] envasado m.

packed [pækt] adj : **~ (with)** repleto(ta) (de).

packed lunch *n* UK *almuerzo preparado de antemano que se lleva uno al colegio, la oficina etc.*

packed-out *adj* UK *inf* a tope, de bote en bote.

packet ['pækɪt] *n* [gen] paquete *m*; [of crisps, sweets] bolsa *f*.

packing ['pækɪŋ] *n* - **1.** [protective material] embalaje *m* - **2.** [for journey]: **to do the ~** hacer el equipaje.

packing case *n* cajón *m* de embalaje.

pact [pækt] *n* pacto *m*.

pad [pæd] (*pt* & *pp* -**ded**, *cont* -**ding**) ◇ *n* - **1.** [of material] almohadilla *f* - **2.** [of cotton wool] tampón *m* - **3.** [of paper] bloc *m* - **4.** SPACE : (**launch**) ~ plataforma *f* (de lanzamiento) - **5.** *inf* dated [home] casa *f*. ◇ *vt* acolchar, rellenar. ◇ *vi* [walk softly] andar con suavidad.

padding ['pædɪŋ] *n* (*U*) - **1.** [in jacket, chair] relleno *m* - **2.** [in speech] paja *f*.

paddle ['pædl] ◇ *n* - **1.** [for canoe, dinghy] pala *f*, canalete *m*; US [for table tennis] pala *f* - **2.** [walk in sea] paseo *m* por la orilla. ◇ *vt* UK remar en. ◇ *vi* - **1.** [in canoe] remar - **2.** [person - in sea] pasear por la orilla.

paddle boat, paddle steamer *n* vapor *m* de paletas *OR* ruedas.

paddling pool ['pædlɪŋ-] *n* UK - **1.** [inflatable] piscina *f* inflable - **2.** [in park] piscina *f* infantil.

paddock ['pædək] *n* - **1.** [small field] potrero *m*, corral *m* - **2.** [at racecourse] paddock *m*.

paddy field ['pædɪ-] *n* arrozal *m*.

padlock ['pædlɒk] ◇ *n* candado *m*. ◇ *vt* cerrar con candado.

paediatrics [,piːdɪ'ætrɪks] UK = **pediatrics**.

pagan ['peɪgən] ◇ *adj* pagano(na). ◇ *n* pagano *m*, -na *f*.

page [peɪdʒ] ◇ *n* [of book, newspaper] página *f*. ◇ *vt* [in hotel, airport] llamar por megafonía.

pageant ['pædʒənt] *n* procesión *f*, desfile *m*.

pageantry ['pædʒəntrɪ] *n* boato *m*, pompa *f*.

paid [peɪd] ◇ *pt* & *pp* ⊳ **pay**. ◇ *adj* [holiday, leave] pagado(da); [work, staff] remunerado(da).

pail [peɪl] *n* cubo *m*.

pain [peɪn] *n* - **1.** [ache] dolor *m*; **to be in ~** sufrir dolor - **2.** [mental suffering] pena *f*, sufrimiento *m* - **3.** *inf* [annoyance - person] pesado *m*, -da *f*; [- thing] pesadez *f*.
➤ **pains** *npl* [effort, care] esfuerzos *mpl*; **to be at ~s to do sthg** afanarse por hacer algo; **to take ~s to do sthg** esforzarse en hacer algo.

pained [peɪnd] *adj* apenado(da).

painful ['peɪnfʊl] *adj* [back, eyes] dolorido(da); [injury, exercise, memory] doloroso(sa).

painfully ['peɪnfʊlɪ] *adv* - **1.** [causing pain] dolorosamente - **2.** [extremely] terriblemente.

painkiller ['peɪn,kɪlə'] *n* analgésico *m*.

painless ['peɪnlɪs] *adj* - **1.** [physically] indoloro(ra) - **2.** [emotionally] sencillo(lla), sin complicaciones.

painstaking ['peɪnz,teɪkɪŋ] *adj* meticuloso(sa), minucioso(sa).

paint [peɪnt] ◇ *n* pintura *f*. ◇ *vt* pintar; **to ~ the ceiling white** pintar el techo de blanco. ◇ *vi* pintar.

paintbrush ['peɪntbrʌʃ] *n* - **1.** ART pincel *m* - **2.** [of decorator] brocha *f*.

painter ['peɪntə'] *n* pintor *m*, -ra *f*; **~ and decorator** pintor *m*, -ra *f* y decorador, -ra *f*.

painting ['peɪntɪŋ] *n* - **1.** [picture] cuadro *m*, pintura *f* - **2.** (*U*) [art form, trade] pintura *f*.

paint stripper *n* quitapinturas *f inv*.

paintwork ['peɪntwɜːk] *n* (*U*) pintura *f*.

pair [peə'] *n* - **1.** [of shoes, socks, wings] par *m*; [of aces] pareja *f* - **2.** [two-part object]: **a ~ of scissors** unas tijeras; **a ~ of trousers** unos pantalones - **3.** [couple - of people] pareja *f*.

pajamas [pə'dʒɑːməz] *esp* US = **pyjamas**.

Pakistan [UK ,pɑːkɪ'stɑːn, US ,pækɪ'stæn] *n* (el) Paquistán.

Pakistani [UK ,pɑːkɪ'stɑːnɪ, US ,pækɪ'stænɪ] ◇ *adj* paquistaní. ◇ *n* paquistaní *m OR f*.

pakora [pə'kɔːrə] *n* bola de verdura rebozada típica de la comida india.

pal [pæl] *n* inf [friend] amiguete *m*, -ta *f*, colega *m OR f*.

palace ['pælɪs] *n* palacio *m*.

palatable ['pælətəbl] *adj* - **1.** [pleasant to taste] sabroso(sa) - **2.** [acceptable] aceptable, admisible.

palate ['pælət] *n* paladar *m*.

palaver [pə'lɑːvə'] *n* UK inf [fuss] lío *m*, follón *m*.

pale [peɪl] ◇ *adj* - **1.** [colour, clothes, paint] claro(ra); [light] tenue - **2.** [person, skin] pálido(da); **to turn ~** palidecer. ◇ *vi* palidecer.

Palestine ['pælɪ,staɪn] *n* Palestina.

Palestinian [,pælə'stɪnɪən] ◇ *adj* palestino(na). ◇ *n* [person] palestino *m*, -na *f*.

palette ['pælət] *n* paleta *f*.

palings ['peɪlɪŋz] *npl* cerca *f*, empalizada *f*.

pall [pɔːl] *n* - **1.** [of smoke] nube *f*, cortina *f* - **2.** US [coffin] féretro *m*.

pallet ['pælɪt] *n* palet *m*.

pallor ['pælə'] *n* literary palidez *f*.

palm [pɑːm] *n* - **1.** [tree] palmera *f* - **2.** [of hand] palma *f*.
➤ **palm off** *vt sep inf*: **to ~ sthg off on sb**

endosar OR encasquetar algo a alguien; **to ~ sb off with** despachar a alguien con.

Palm Sunday n Domingo m de Ramos.

palm tree n palmera f.

palpable ['pælpəbl] adj palpable.

paltry ['pɔːltrɪ] (compar **-ier**, superl **-iest**) adj mísero(ra).

pamper ['pæmpə'] vt mimar.

pamphlet ['pæmflɪt] n [publicity, information] folleto m; [political] panfleto m.

pan [pæn] (pt & pp **-ned**, cont **-ning**) ⬦ n **- 1.** [saucepan] cazuela f, cacerola f; [frying pan] sartén f **- 2.** US [for bread, cakes etc] molde m. ⬦ vt inf [criticize] poner por los suelos. ⬦ vi CINEMA : **the camera ~s right/left** la cámara se mueve hacia la derecha/la izquierda.

➤ **pan out** vi inf [happen succesfully] resultar, salir.

panacea [ˌpænə'sɪə] n : **a ~ (for)** la panacea (de).

Panama ['pænəˌmɑː] n Panamá.

Panama Canal n : **the ~** el canal de Panamá.

panama (hat) n panamá m.

pancake ['pæŋkeɪk] n torta f, crepe f, panqueque m CSur, panqué m CAm, Col, crepa f Méx, panqueca f Ven.

Pancake Day n UK ≃ Martes m inv de Carnaval.

panda ['pændə] (pl inv OR **-s**) n panda m.

Panda car n UK coche m patrulla, auto m patrulla Cam, Méx, Chile, patrullero m CSur, patrulla f Col, Méx.

pandemonium [ˌpændɪ'məʊnjəm] n pandemónium m, jaleo m; **it was ~** fue un auténtico pandemónium.

pander ['pændə'] vi : **to ~ to** complacer a.

pane [peɪn] n (hoja f de) cristal m.

panel ['pænl] n **- 1.** [group of people] equipo m; [in debates] mesa f **- 2.** [of wood, metal] panel m **- 3.** [of a machine] tablero m, panel m.

panelling UK, **paneling** US ['pænəlɪŋ] n (U) [on a ceiling] artesonado m; [on a wall] paneles mpl.

pang [pæŋ] n punzada f.

panhandle ['pæn,hændl] vi US mendingar.

panic ['pænɪk] (pt & pp **-ked**, cont **-king**) ⬦ n pánico m; **to be in a ~ about sthg** ponerse muy nervioso por algo. ⬦ vi aterrarse, aterrorizarse; **don't ~** que no cunda el pánico.

panicky ['pænɪkɪ] adj : **he feels ~** tiene pánico; **she got ~** le entró el pánico.

panic-stricken adj preso(sa) OR víctima del pánico.

panorama [ˌpænə'rɑːmə] n panorama m.

panpipes ['pænpaɪps] n zampoña f.

pant [pænt] vi jadear.

panther ['pænθə'] (pl inv OR **-s**) n pantera f.

panties ['pæntɪz] npl US bragas fpl, calzones mpl Amér, pantaletas fpl CAm, Carib, Méx, bombacha f RP, blúmer m CAm, Carib.

pantihose ['pæntɪhəʊz] = **panty hose**.

pantomime ['pæntəmaɪm] n **- 1.** UK obra musical humorística para niños celebrada en Navidad **- 2.** [mime] pantomima f.

pantry ['pæntrɪ] (pl **-ies**) n despensa f.

pants [pænts] ⬦ npl **- 1.** UK [underpants] calzoncillos mpl **- 2.** US [trousers] pantalones mpl. ⬦ adj UK inf [bad] : **to be ~** ser un churro.

pantsuit ['pæntsuːt] n traje m pantalón.

panty hose ['pæntɪ-] npl US medias fpl.

papa [UK pə'pɑː, US 'pɑːpə] n papá m.

paper ['peɪpə'] ⬦ n **- 1.** (U) [material] papel m; **piece of ~** [sheet] hoja f de papel; [scrap] trozo m de papel; **on ~** [written down] por escrito; [in theory] sobre el papel **- 2.** [newspaper] periódico m **- 3.** UK [in exam] examen m **- 4.** [essay - gen] estudio m, ensayo m; [- for conference] ponencia f. ⬦ adj [made of paper] de papel. ⬦ vt empapelar.

➤ **papers** npl [official documents] documentación f.

paperback ['peɪpəbæk] n libro m en rústica.

paper clip n clip m.

paper handkerchief n pañuelo m de papel, klínex® m inv.

paper knife n abrecartas m inv, cortapapeles m inv.

paper shop n UK quiosco m de periódicos.

paper towel n toallita f de papel.

paperweight ['peɪpəweɪt] n pisapapeles m inv.

paperwork ['peɪpəwɜːk] n papeleo m.

papier-mâché [ˌpæpjeɪ'mæʃeɪ] n cartón m piedra.

paprika ['pæprɪkə] n pimentón m.

Pap smear, Pap test n US citología f.

par [pɑː'] n **- 1.** [parity] : **on a ~ with** al mismo nivel que **- 2.** GOLF par m **- 3.** [good health] : **to be below** OR **under ~** estar un poco enfermo.

parable ['pærəbl] n parábola f.

parachute ['pærəʃuːt] n paracaídas m inv.

parade [pə'reɪd] ⬦ n [procession] desfile m. ⬦ vt **- 1.** [soldiers] hacer desfilar; [criminals, captives] pasear **- 2.** fig [flaunt] exhibir, hacer alarde de. ⬦ vi desfilar.

paradise ['pærədaɪs] n fig paraíso m.

paradox ['pærədɒks] n paradoja f.

paraffin ['pærəfɪn] n parafina f.

paragliding ['pærə,glaɪdɪŋ] n parapente m, parapentismo.

paragraph ['pærəgrɑːf] n párrafo m, acápite m Amér.

Paraguay ['pærəgwaɪ] n (el) Paraguay.

Paraguayan [ˌpærəˈgwaɪən] ◇ *adj* paraguayo(ya). ◇ *n* paraguayo *m*, -ya *f*.

paralegal [ˌpærəˈliːgl] *n US* ayudante de un abogado.

parallel [ˈpærəlel] ◇ *adj*: **~ (to** OR **with)** paralelo(la) (a). ◇ *n* **-1.** [parallel line, surface] paralela *f* **-2.** [something, someone similar]: **to have no ~** no tener precedente **-3.** [similarity] semejanza *f*, paralelo *m* **-4.** GEOGR paralelo *m*.

paralyse UK, **paralyze** US [ˈpærəlaɪz] *vt* lit & fig paralizar.

paralysis [pəˈrælɪsɪs] (*pl* **-lyses** [-lɪsiːz]) *n* parálisis *f inv*.

paramedic [ˌpærəˈmedɪk] *n esp US* auxiliar sanitario *m*, auxiliar sanitaria *f*.

parameter [pəˈræmɪtər] *n* parámetro *m*.

paramount [ˈpærəmaʊnt] *adj* vital, fundamental; **of ~ importance** de suma importancia.

paranoid [ˈpærənɔɪd] *adj* paranoico(ca).

paraphernalia [ˌpærəfəˈneɪljə] *n* parafernalia *f*.

parasite [ˈpærəsaɪt] *n* parásito *m*, -ta *f*.

parasol [ˈpærəsɒl] *n* sombrilla *f*.

paratrooper [ˈpærətruːpər] *n* paracaidista *m* OR *f* (del ejército).

parcel [ˈpɑːsl] (UK *pt* & *pp* **-led**, *cont* **-ling**, US *pt* & *pp* **-ed**, *cont* **-ing**) *n* paquete *m*, encomienda *f* Amér.

◆ **parcel up** *vt sep* UK empaquetar.

parcel bomb *n* paquete *m* bomba.

parcel post *n* (servicio *m* de) paquete *m* postal.

parched [pɑːtʃt] *adj* **-1.** [throat, mouth] muy seco(ca); [lips] quemado(da) **-2.** *inf* [very thirsty] seco(ca).

parchment [ˈpɑːtʃmənt] *n* [paper] pergamino *m*.

pardon [ˈpɑːdn] ◇ *n* **-1.** JUR perdón *m*, indulto *m* **-2.** [forgiveness] perdón *m*; **I beg your ~?** [showing surprise, asking for repetition] ¿perdón?, ¿cómo (dice)?; **I beg your ~** [to apologize] le ruego me disculpe, perdón. ◇ *vt* **-1.** [forgive]: **to ~ sb (for sthg)** perdonar a alguien (por algo); **pardon?** ¿perdón?, ¿cómo (dice)?; **~ me** [touching sb accidentally, belching] discúlpeme, perdón; [excuse me] con permiso **-2.** JUR indultar.

parent [ˈpeərənt] *n* [father] padre *m*; [mother] madre *f*.

◆ **parents** *npl* padres *mpl*.

parental [pəˈrentl] *adj* de los padres.

parenthesis [pəˈrenθɪsɪs] (*pl* **-theses** [-θɪsiːz]) *n* paréntesis *m inv*; **in ~** entre paréntesis.

Paris [ˈpærɪs] *n* París.

parish [ˈpærɪʃ] *n* **-1.** [of church] parroquia *f* **-2.** UK [area of local government] ≃ municipio *m*.

parity [ˈpærətɪ] *n*: **~ (with/between)** igualdad *f* (con/entre).

park [pɑːk] ◇ *n* parque *m*. ◇ *vt* & *vi* aparcar, estacionar Amér, parquear Amér.

park-and-ride *n* aparcamiento *m* disuasorio Esp.

parking [ˈpɑːkɪŋ] *n* aparcamiento *m* Esp, estacionamiento *m* Amér; **'no ~'** 'prohibido aparcar'.

parking lot *n US* aparcamiento *m* (al aire libre).

parking meter *n* parquímetro *m*.

parking ticket *n* multa *f* por aparcamiento indebido, multa *f* por estacionamiento indebido Amér.

parlance [ˈpɑːləns] *n*: **in common/legal ~** en el habla común/legal, en el lenguaje común/legal.

parliament [ˈpɑːləmənt] *n* **-1.** [assembly, institution] parlamento *m* **-2.** [session] legislatura *f*.

parliamentary [ˌpɑːləˈmentərɪ] *adj* parlamentario(ria).

parlour UK, **parlor** US [ˈpɑːlər] *n* dated salón *m*.

parochial [pəˈrəʊkjəl] *adj* **-1.** *pej* de miras estrechas **-2.**: **~ school** US colegio *m* privado religioso.

parody [ˈpærədɪ] (*pl* **-ies**, *pt* & *pp* **-ied**) ◇ *n* parodia *f*. ◇ *vt* parodiar.

parole [pəˈrəʊl] *n* libertad *f* condicional (bajo palabra); **on ~** en libertad condicional.

parquet [ˈpɑːkeɪ] *n* parqué *m*.

parrot [ˈpærət] *n* loro *m*.

parry [ˈpærɪ] (*pt* & *pp* **-ied**) *vt* [blow] parar; [attack] desviar.

parsimonious [ˌpɑːsɪˈməʊnjəs] *adj* fml & pej mezquino(na), tacaño(ña).

parsley [ˈpɑːslɪ] *n* perejil *m*.

parsnip [ˈpɑːsnɪp] *n* chirivía *f*, pastinaca *f*.

parson [ˈpɑːsn] *n* párroco *m*.

part [pɑːt] ◇ *n* **-1.** [gen] parte *f*; **for the most ~** en su mayoría **-2.** [component] pieza *f* **-3.** THEATRE papel *m* **-4.** [involvement]: **~ (in)** participación *f* (en); **to play an important ~ (in)** desempeñar OR jugar un papel importante (en); **to take ~ (in)** tomar parte (en); **for my/his ~** por mi/su parte **-5.** US [hair parting] raya *f*. ◇ *vt* **-1.** [lips, curtains] abrir **-2.** [hair] peinar con raya. ◇ *vi* **-1.** [leave one another] separarse **-2.** [separate - lips, curtains] abrirse.

◆ **part with** *vt fus* desprenderse de, separarse de.

part exchange *n* UK sistema de pagar parte de algo con un artículo usado; **in ~** como parte del pago.

partial [ˈpɑːʃl] *adj* **-1.** [incomplete, biased] parcial **-2.** [fond]: **~ to** amigo(ga) de, aficionado(da) a.

participant [pɑːˈtɪsɪpənt] *n* participante *m* OR *f*.

participate [pɑːˈtɪsɪpeɪt] *vi*: to ~ (in) participar (en).

participation [pɑːˌtɪsɪˈpeɪʃn] *n* participación *f*.

participle [ˈpɑːtɪsɪpl] *n* participio *m*.

particle [ˈpɑːtɪkl] *n* partícula *f*.

particular [pəˈtɪkjʊləʳ] *adj* **-1.** [specific, unique] en particular OR especial; **did you want any ~ colour?** ¿quería algún color en particular? **-2.** [extra, greater] especial **-3.** [difficult] exigente.
- **particulars** *npl* [of person] datos *mpl*; [of thing] detalles *mpl*.
- **in particular** *adv* en particular, en especial.

particularly [pəˈtɪkjʊləlɪ] *adv* especialmente.

parting [ˈpɑːtɪŋ] *n* **-1.** [separation] despedida *f* **-2.** UK [in hair] raya *f*.

partisan [ˌpɑːtɪˈzæn] ◇ *adj* partidista. ◇ *n* [freedom fighter] partisano *m*, -na *f*.

partition [pɑːˈtɪʃn] ◇ *n* **-1.** [wall] tabique *m*; [screen] separación *f* **-2.** COMPUT partición *f*. ◇ *vt* **-1.** [room] dividir con tabiques **-2.** [country] dividir **-3.** COMPUT crear particiones en.

partly [ˈpɑːtlɪ] *adv* en parte.

partner [ˈpɑːtnəʳ] *n* **-1.** [spouse, lover] pareja *f* **-2.** [in an activity] compañero *m*, -ra *f* **-3.** [in a business] socio *m*, -cia *f* **-4.** [ally] colega *m* OR *f*.

partnership [ˈpɑːtnəʃɪp] *n* **-1.** [relationship] asociación *f* **-2.** [business] sociedad *f*.

partridge [ˈpɑːtrɪdʒ] *n* perdiz *f*.

part-time ◇ *adj* a tiempo parcial. ◇ *adv* a tiempo parcial.

party [ˈpɑːtɪ] (*pl* -ies) *n* **-1.** POL partido *m* **-2.** [social gathering] fiesta *f* **-3.** [group] grupo *m* **-4.** JUR parte *f*.

party animal *n*: to be a ~ ser un(una) fiestero(ra).

party line *n* **-1.** POL línea *f* (política) del partido **-2.** TELEC línea *f* (telefónica) compartida.

pass [pɑːs] ◇ *n* **-1.** [in football, rugby, hockey] pase *m*; [in tennis] passing-shot *m* **-2.** [document, permit] pase *m*; **travel ~** tarjeta *f* OR abono *m* de transportes **-3.** UK [successful result] aprobado *m* **-4.** [route between mountains] puerto *m* **-5.** *phr*: **to make a ~ at sb** intentar ligar con alguien. ◇ *vt* **-1.** [gen] pasar; **to ~ sthg (to sb), to ~ (sb) sthg** pasar OR pasarle algo (a alguien) **-2.** [move past - thing] pasar por (delante de); [- person] pasar delante de; **to ~ sb in the street** cruzarse con alguien **-3.** AUT adelantar **-4.** [exceed] sobrepasar **-5.** [exam, candidate, law] aprobar; **to ~ sthg fit (for)** dar algo por bueno (para) **-6.** [opinion,

judgement] formular; [sentence] dictar. ◇ *vi* **-1.** [gen] pasar **-2.** AUT adelantar **-3.** [in exam] aprobar **-4.** [occur] transcurrir.
- **pass as** *vt fus* pasar por.
- **pass away** *vi* fallecer, pasar a mejor vida.
- **pass by** ◇ *vt sep* [subj: people] hacer caso omiso a; [subj: events, life] pasar desapercibido(da) a. ◇ *vi* pasar cerca.
- **pass for** *vt fus* = **pass as**.
- **pass on** ◇ *vt sep*: to ~ sthg on (to) pasar algo (a). ◇ *vi* **-1.** [move on] continuar **-2.** = **pass away**.
- **pass out** *vi* **-1.** [faint] desmayarse **-2.** UK MIL graduarse.
- **pass over** *vt fus* hacer caso omiso de, pasar por alto.
- **pass up** *vt sep* dejar pasar OR escapar.

passable [ˈpɑːsəbl] *adj* **-1.** [satisfactory] pasable, aceptable **-2.** [not blocked] transitable.

passage [ˈpæsɪdʒ] *n* **-1.** [corridor - between houses] pasadizo *m*, pasaje *m*; [- between rooms] pasillo *m* **-2.** [of music, speech] pasaje *m* **-3.** *fml* [of vehicle, person, time] paso *m* **-4.** [sea journey] travesía *f*.

passageway [ˈpæsɪdʒweɪ] *n* [between houses] pasadizo *m*, pasaje *m*; [between rooms] pasillo *m*.

passbook [ˈpɑːsbʊk] *n* ≃ cartilla *f* OR libreta *f* de banco.

passenger [ˈpæsɪndʒəʳ] *n* pasajero *m*, -ra *f*.

passerby [ˌpɑːsəˈbaɪ] (*pl* **passersby** [ˌpɑːsəzˈbaɪ]) *n* transeúnte *m* OR *f*.

passing [ˈpɑːsɪŋ] ◇ *adj* [fad] pasajero(ra); [remark] de pasada. ◇ *n* paso *m*, transcurso *m*.
- **in passing** *adv* de pasada.

passion [ˈpæʃn] *n*: ~ (for) pasión *f* (por).

passionate [ˈpæʃənət] *adj* apasionado(da).

passive [ˈpæsɪv] *adj* pasivo(va).

Passover [ˈpɑːsˌəʊvəʳ] *n*: (the) ~ (la) Pascua judía.

passport [ˈpɑːspɔːt] *n* pasaporte *m*.

passport control *n* UK control *m* de pasaportes.

password [ˈpɑːswɜːd] *n* [gen & COMPUT] contraseña *f*.

past [pɑːst] ◇ *adj* **-1.** [former] anterior **-2.** [most recent] último(ma); **over the ~ week** durante la última semana **-3.** [finished] terminado(da). ◇ *adv* **-1.** [telling the time]: **it's ten ~** son y diez **-2.** [beyond, in front] por delante; **to walk/run ~** pasar andando/corriendo. ◇ *n* **-1.** [time]: **the ~** el pasado **-2.** [personal history] pasado *m*. ◇ *prep* **-1.** [telling the time]: **it's five/half/a quarter ~ ten** son las diez y cinco/media/cuarto **-2.** [alongside, in front of] por delante de; **to walk/run ~ sthg** pasar algo andando/corriendo **-3.** [beyond] más allá de; **it's

pawnbroker

~ **the bank** está pasado el banco.

pasta ['pæstə] *n* (*U*) pasta *f*.

paste [peɪst] ⇔ *n* **-1.** [smooth mixture] pasta *f* **-2.** [food] paté *m* **-3.** [glue] engrudo *m.* ⇔ *vt* [labels, stamps] pegar; [surface] engomar, engrudar; COMPUT pegar.

pastel ['pæstl] ⇔ *adj* pastel *(inv).* ⇔ *n* ART [crayon] pastel *m*.

pasteurize, -ise ['pɑ:stʃəraɪz] *vt* pasteurizar.

pastille ['pæstɪl] *n* UK pastilla *f*.

pastime ['pɑ:staɪm] *n* pasatiempo *m*, afición *f*.

pastor ['pɑ:stəʳ] *n* RELIG pastor *m*.

past participle *n* participio *m* pasado.

pastry ['peɪstrɪ] (*pl* -ies) *n* **-1.** [mixture] pasta *f*, masa *f* **-2.** [cake] pastel *m*.

past tense *n*: **the** ~ el pasado.

pasture ['pɑ:stʃəʳ] *n* pasto *m*.

pasty¹ ['peɪstɪ] (*compar* -ier, *superl* -iest) *adj* pálido(da).

pasty² ['pæstɪ] (*pl* -ies) *n* UK empanada *f*.

pat [pæt] (*pt* & *pp* -ted, *cont* -ting) ⇔ *n* [of butter etc] porción *f.* ⇔ *vt* [gen] golpear ligeramente; [dog] acariciar.

patch [pætʃ] ⇔ *n* **-1.** [for mending] remiendo *m*; [on elbow] codera *f*; [to cover eye] parche *m* **-2.** [part of surface] área *f* **-3.** [area of land] bancal *m*, parcela *f* **-4.** [period of time] periodo *m* **-5.** COMPUT parche *m.* ⇔ *vt* remendar.

◆ **patch up** *vt sep* **-1.** [mend] reparar **-2.** [resolve - relationship] salvar; **we have patched things up** hemos hecho las paces.

patchwork ['pætʃwɜ:k] *adj* de trozos de distintos colores y formas.

patchy ['pætʃɪ] (*compar* -ier, *superl* -iest) *adj* **-1.** [uneven - fog, sunshine] irregular; [- colour] desigual **-2.** [incomplete] deficiente, incompleto(ta) **-3.** [good in parts] irregular.

pâté ['pæteɪ] *n* paté *m*.

patent [UK 'peɪtənt, US 'pætənt] ⇔ *adj* [obvious] patente, evidente. ⇔ *n* patente *f.* ⇔ *vt* patentar.

patent leather *n* charol *m*.

paternal [pə'tɜ:nl] *adj* [love, attitude] paternal; [grandmother, grandfather] paterno(na).

paternity [pə'tɜ:nətɪ] *n* paternidad *f*.

path [pɑ:θ, *pl* pɑ:ðz] *n* **-1.** [track, way ahead] camino *m* **-2.** COMPUT camino *m* **-3.** [trajectory - of bullet] trayectoria *f*; [- of flight] rumbo *m* **-4.** [course of action] curso *m*.

pathetic [pə'θetɪk] *adj* **-1.** [causing pity] patético(ca), lastimoso(sa) **-2.** [attempt, person] inútil, infeliz; [actor, film] malísimo(ma).

pathological [,pæθə'lɒdʒɪkl] *adj* patológico(ca).

pathology [pə'θɒlədʒɪ] *n* patología *f*.

pathos ['peɪθɒs] *n* patetismo *m*.

pathway ['pɑ:θweɪ] *n* camino *m*, sendero *m*.

patience ['peɪʃns] *n* **-1.** [quality] paciencia *f* **-2.** UK [card game] solitario *m*.

patient ['peɪʃnt] ⇔ *adj* paciente. ⇔ *n* paciente *m* OR *f*.

patio ['pætɪəʊ] (*pl* -s) *n* [paved] *área pavimentada al lado de una casa utilizada para el esparcimiento.*

patriotic [UK ,pætrɪ'ɒtɪk, US ,peɪtrɪ'ɒtɪk] *adj* patriótico(ca).

patrol [pə'trəʊl] (*pt* & *pp* -led, *cont* -ling) ⇔ *n* patrulla *f.* ⇔ *vt* patrullar.

patrol car *n* coche *m* patrulla, auto *m* patrulla CAm, Méx, Chile, patrullero *m* CSur, patrulla *f* Col, Méx.

patrolman [pə'trəʊlmən] (*pl* -men [-mən]) *n* US policía *m*, guardia *m*.

patron ['peɪtrən] *n* **-1.** [of arts] mecenas *m y f inv* **-2.** UK [of charity, campaign] patrocinador *m*, -ra *f* **-3.** *fml* [customer] cliente *m* OR *f*.

patronize, -ise ['pætrənaɪz] *vt* **-1.** *pej* [talk down to] tratar con aire paternalista OR condescendiente **-2.** *fml* [back financially] patrocinar.

patronizing ['pætrənaɪzɪŋ] *adj pej* paternalista, condescendiente.

patter ['pætəʳ] ⇔ *n* **-1.** [of raindrops] repiqueteo *m*; [of feet] golpeteo *m*, pasitos *mpl* **-2.** [sales talk] charlatanería *f.* ⇔ *vi* [dog, feet] corretear; [rain] repiquetear.

pattern ['pætən] *n* **-1.** [design] dibujo *m*, diseño *m* **-2.** [of life, work] estructura *f*; [of illness, events] desarrollo *m*, evolución *f* **-3.** [for sewing, knitting] patrón *m* **-4.** [model] modelo *m*.

paunch [pɔ:ntʃ] *n* barriga *f*, panza *f*.

pauper ['pɔ:pəʳ] *n* indigente *m* OR *f*.

pause [pɔ:z] ⇔ *n* pausa *f.* ⇔ *vi* **-1.** [stop speaking] hacer una pausa **-2.** [stop moving, doing sthg] detenerse.

pave [peɪv] *vt* pavimentar; **to** ~ **the way for** preparar el terreno para.

pavement ['peɪvmənt] *n* **-1.** UK [at side of road] acera *f*, andén *m* CAm, Col, vereda *f* CSur, Perú, banqueta *f* CAm, Méx **-2.** US [roadway] calzada *f*.

pavilion [pə'vɪljən] *n* **-1.** UK [at sports field] vestuarios *mpl* **-2.** [at exhibition] pabellón *m*.

paving ['peɪvɪŋ] *n* (*U*) pavimento *m*.

paving stone *n* losa *f*.

paw [pɔ:] *n* [of dog] pata *f*; [of lion, cat] zarpa *f*, garra *f*.

pawn [pɔ:n] ⇔ *n* **-1.** [chesspiece] peón *m* **-2.** [unimportant person] marioneta *f.* ⇔ *vt* empeñar.

pawnbroker ['pɔ:n,brəʊkəʳ] *n* prestamista *m* OR *f*.

pawnshop ['pɔːnʃɒp] *n* casa *f* de empeños.
pay [peɪ] (*pt & pp* **paid**) ◇ *vt* **-1.** [gen] pagar; **to ~ sb for sthg** pagar a alguien por algo; **he paid £20 for it** pagó 20 libras por ello **-2.** *UK* [put into bank account]: **to ~ sthg into** ingresar algo en **-3.** [compliment, visit] hacer; [respects] ofrecer; [attention] prestar; [homage] rendir. ◇ *vi* **-1.** [gen] pagar; **to ~ by credit card** pagar con tarjeta de crédito; **it pays well** está bien pagado; **to ~ dearly for sthg** pagar caro (por) algo **-2.** [be profitable] ser rentable. ◇ *n* sueldo *m*, paga *f*.
◆ **pay back** *vt sep* **-1.** [money] devolver, reembolsar; [person] devolver el dinero a **-2.** [revenge oneself]: **to ~ sb back (for sthg)** hacer pagar a alguien (por algo).
◆ **pay for** *vt fus* pagar.
◆ **pay off** ◇ *vt sep* **-1.** [repay - debt] liquidar, saldar **-2.** [dismiss] despedir con indemnización **-3.** [bribe] comprar, pagar. ◇ *vi* [efforts] dar fruto.
◆ **pay up** *vi* pagar.
payable ['peɪəbl] *adj* **-1.** [to be paid] pagadero(ra) **-2.** [on cheque]: **~ to** a favor de.
paycheck ['peɪtʃek] *n US* paga *f*.
payday ['peɪdeɪ] *n* día *m* de paga.
payee [peɪ'iː] *n* beneficiario *m*, -ria *f*.
pay envelope *n US* sobre *m* de paga.
payment ['peɪmənt] *n* pago *m*.
pay packet *n UK* **-1.** [envelope] sobre *m* de paga **-2.** [wages] paga *f*.
pay-per-view *n* pago *m* por visión.
pay phone *n* teléfono *m* público.
pay rise *n* aumento *m* de sueldo.
payroll ['peɪrəʊl] *n* nómina *f*.
payslip ['peɪslɪp] *n UK* hoja *f* de paga.
pay station *US* = **pay phone**.
pay TV *n* televisión *f* de pago.
pc (*abbr of* **per cent**) p.c.
PC *n* **-1.** (*abbr of* **personal computer**) PC *m* **-2.** *UK abbr of* **police constable**.
PE (*abbr of* **physical education**) *n* educación *f* física.
pea [piː] *n* guisante *m*, arveja *f Andes, Col, CSur, Ven*, chícharo *m CAm, Méx*, petipuá *m Ven*.
peace [piːs] *n* **-1.** [gen] paz *f* **-2.** [quiet] calma *f*, tranquilidad *f* **-3.** [freedom from disagreement] orden *m*; **to make (one's) ~ (with)** hacer las paces (con).
peaceable ['piːsəbl] *adj* [not aggressive] pacífico(ca).
peaceful ['piːsfʊl] *adj* **-1.** [quiet, calm] tranquilo(la) **-2.** [not aggressive] pacífico(ca).
peacetime ['piːstaɪm] *n (U)* tiempos *mpl* de paz.
peach [piːtʃ] ◇ *adj* [in colour] de color melocotón OR durazno *Amér*. ◇ *n* **-1.** [fruit] melocotón *m*, durazno *m Amér* **-2.** [colour]

color *m* melocotón OR durazno *Amér*.
pea coat *n US* chaquetón *m*.
peacock ['piːkɒk] *n* pavo *m* real.
peak [piːk] ◇ *n* **-1.** [mountain top] pico *m*, cima *f* **-2.** [highest point] apogeo *m* **-3.** [of cap] visera *f*. ◇ *adj* [season] alto(ta); [condition] perfecto(ta). ◇ *vi* alcanzar el máximo.
peaked [piːkt] *adj* con visera.
peak hour *n UK* [of traffic] hora *f* punta.
peak period *n UK* [of electricity etc] periodo *m* de tarifa máxima; [of traffic] horas *fpl* punta.
peak rate *n* tarifa *f* máxima.
peal [piːl] ◇ *n* [of bells] repique *m*; **~ (of laughter)** carcajada *f*. ◇ *vi* repicar.
peanut ['piːnʌt] *n* cacahuete *m*, maní *m Amér*, cacahuate *m Méx*.
peanut brittle *n US* dulce de caramelo con cacahuetes.
peanut butter *n* manteca *f* de cacahuete OR de maní *RP*, mantequilla *f* de maní *Amér* OR de cacahuate *Méx*.
pear [peə^r] *n* pera *f*.
pearl [pɜːl] *n* perla *f*.
peasant ['peznt] *n* [in countryside] campesino *m*, -na *f*, guajiro *m*, -ra *f Cuba*.
peat [piːt] *n* turba *f*.
pebble ['pebl] *n* guijarro *m*.
peck [pek] ◇ *n* **-1.** [with beak] picotazo *m* **-2.** [kiss] besito *m*. ◇ *vt* [with beak] picotear. ◇ *vi* picotear.
pecking order ['pekɪŋ-] *n* jerarquía *f*.
peckish ['pekɪʃ] *adj UK inf*: **to feel ~** estar algo hambriento(ta).
peculiar [pɪ'kjuːljə^r] *adj* **-1.** [odd] singular, extraño(ña) **-2.** *UK* [slightly ill] raro(ra), indispuesto(ta) **-3.** [characteristic]: **to be ~ to** ser propio(pia) de.
peculiarity [pɪˌkjuːlɪ'ærətɪ] (*pl* **-ies**) *n* **-1.** [eccentricity] extravagancia *f* **-2.** [characteristic] peculiaridad *f*.
pedal ['pedl] (*UK pt & pp* **-led**, *cont* **-ling**, *US pt & pp* **-ed**, *cont* **-ing**) ◇ *n* pedal *m*. ◇ *vi* pedalear.
pedal bin *n UK* cubo *m* de basura con pedal.
pedantic [pɪ'dæntɪk] *adj pej* puntilloso(sa).
peddle ['pedl] *vt* [drugs] traficar con; [wares] vender de puerta en puerta.
pedestal ['pedɪstl] *n* pedestal *m*.
pedestrian [pɪ'destrɪən] ◇ *adj pej* pedestre. ◇ *n* peatón *m*.
pedestrian crossing *n UK* paso *m* de peatones.
pedestrian precinct *UK*, **pedestrian mall** *US n* zona *f* peatonal.
pediatrics [ˌpiːdɪ'ætrɪks] *n* pediatría *f*.
pedigree ['pedɪgriː] ◇ *adj* de raza. ◇ *n* **-1.** [of animal] pedigrí *m* **-2.** [of person] linaje *m*.

pedlar *UK*, **peddler** *US* ['pedlə'] *n* vendedor *m*, -ra *f* ambulante.

pee [pi:] *inf* ◇ *n* pis *m*. ◇ *vi* mear, hacer pis.

peek [pi:k] *inf* ◇ *n* mirada *f*, ojeada *f*. ◇ *vi* mirar a hurtadillas.

peel [pi:l] ◇ *n* [gen] piel *f*; [of orange, lemon] corteza *f*; [once removed] mondaduras *fpl*. ◇ *vt* pelar. ◇ *vi* [walls, paint] desconcharse; [wallpaper] despegarse; [skin, nose] pelarse.

peelings ['pi:lɪŋz] *npl* peladuras *fpl*.

peep [pi:p] ◇ *n* - 1. [look] mirada *f*, ojeada *f* - 2. *inf* [sound] pío *m*. ◇ *vi* [look] mirar furtivamente.

◆ **peep out** *vi* asomar.

peephole ['pi:phəʊl] *n* mirilla *f*.

peer [pɪə'] ◇ *n* - 1. [noble] par *m* - 2. [equal] igual *m*. ◇ *vi* mirar con atención.

peerage ['pɪərɪdʒ] *n* - 1. [rank] rango *m* de par - 2. [group]: **the** ~ la nobleza.

peer group *n* grupo generacional o social.

peeved [pi:vd] *adj inf* fastidiado(da), disgustado(da).

peevish ['pi:vɪʃ] *adj* malhumorado(da).

peg [peg] *n* - 1. *UK* [for washing line] pinza *f* - 2. [on tent] estaca *f* - 3. [hook] gancho *m*.

pejorative [prɪ'dʒɒrətɪv] *adj* peyorativo(va), despectivo(va).

Peking [pi:'kɪŋ] *n* Pekín.

pelican ['pelɪkən] (*pl inv OR* -s) *n* pelícano *m*.

pelican crossing *n UK paso de peatones con semáforo accionado por el usuario.*

pellet ['pelɪt] *n* - 1. [small ball] bolita *f* - 2. [for gun] perdigón *m*.

pelmet ['pelmɪt] *n UK* galería *f (de cortinas).*

pelt [pelt] ◇ *n* [animal skin] piel *f*. ◇ *vt*: **to** ~ **sb with sthg** acribillar a alguien con algo, arrojar algo a alguien. ◇ *vi* - 1. [rain]: **it was pelting down** *OR* **with rain** llovía a cántaros - 2. [run very fast] correr a toda pastilla.

pelvis ['pelvɪs] (*pl* -**vises** *OR* -**ves** [-vi:z]) *n* pelvis *f*.

pen [pen] (*pt & pp* -**ned**, *cont* -**ning**) ◇ *n* - 1. [ballpoint] bolígrafo *m*, lapicera *f RP & Chile*; [fountain pen] pluma *f*; [felt-tip] rotulador *m* - 2. [enclosure] redil *m*, corral *m*. ◇ *vt* [enclose] encerrar.

penal ['pi:nl] *adj* penal.

penalize, ise ['pi:nəlaɪz] *vt* [gen] penalizar; SPORT penalizar, castigar.

penalty ['penltɪ] (*pl* -**ies**) *n* - 1. [punishment] pena *f*; **to pay the** ~ **(for sthg)** *fig* pagar las consecuencias (de algo) - 2. [fine] multa *f* - 3. SPORT penalty *m*; ~ **(kick)** FTBL penalty *m*; RUGBY golpe *m* de castigo.

penance ['penəns] *n* penitencia *f*.

pence [pens] *UK pl* ▷ **penny**.

penchant [*UK* pãʃã, *US* 'pentʃənt] *n*: **to have a** ~ **for sthg** tener debilidad por algo;

to have a ~ **for doing sthg** tener propensión a hacer algo.

pencil ['pensl] (*UK pt & pp* -**led**, *cont* -**ling**, *US pt & pp* -**ed**, *cont* -**ing**) *n* lápiz *m*; **in** ~ a lápiz.

◆ **pencil in** *vt sep* [date, appointment] apuntar provisionalmente.

pencil case *n* estuche *m*, plumero *m Esp.*

pencil sharpener *n* sacapuntas *m inv.*

pendant ['pendənt] *n* [jewel on chain] colgante *m*.

pending ['pendɪŋ] *fml* ◇ *adj* - 1. [waiting to be dealt with] pendiente - 2. [about to happen] inminente. ◇ *prep* a la espera de.

pendulum ['pendjʊləm] (*pl* -s) *n* [of clock] péndulo *m*.

penetrate ['penɪtreɪt] *vt* - 1. [barrier] salvar, atravesar; [jungle, crowd] adentrarse en, introducirse en; [subj: wind, rain, sharp object] penetrar en - 2. [infiltrate - organization] infiltrarse en.

pen friend *n UK* amigo *m*, -ga *f* por correspondencia.

penguin ['peŋgwɪn] *n* pingüino *m*.

penicillin [,penɪ'sɪlɪn] *n* penicilina *f*.

peninsula [pə'nɪnsjʊlə] (*pl* -s) *n* península *f*.

penis ['pi:nɪs] (*pl* **penises** ['pi:nɪsɪz]) *n* pene *m*.

penitentiary [,penɪ'tenʃərɪ] (*pl* -**ies**) *n US* penitenciaría *f*.

penknife ['pennaɪf] (*pl* -**knives** [-naɪvz]) *n* navaja *f*, chaveta *f Andes.*

pen name *n* seudónimo *m*.

pennant ['penənt] *n* banderín *m*.

penniless ['penɪlɪs] *adj*: **to be** ~ estar sin un centavo.

penny ['penɪ] (*pl sense 1* -**ies**, *pl sense 2* **pence**) *n* - 1. [coin] *UK* penique *m*; *US* centavo *m* - 2. *UK* [value] penique *m*.

pen pal *n inf* amigo *m*, -ga *f* por correspondencia.

pension ['penʃn] *n* - 1. [gen] pensión *f* - 2. [disability pension] subsidio *m*.

pensioner ['penʃənə'] *n*: **(old-age)** ~ pensionista *m OR f*.

pensive ['pensɪv] *adj* pensativo(va).

pentagon ['pentəgən] *n* pentágono *m*.

◆ **Pentagon** *n US*: **the Pentagon** el Pentágono, *sede del ministerio de Defensa estadounidense.*

Pentecost ['pentɪkɒst] *n* Pentecostés *m*.

penthouse ['penthaʊs, *pl* -haʊzɪz] *n* ático *m*.

pent up ['pent-] *adj* reprimido(da).

penultimate [pe'nʌltɪmət] *adj* penúltimo(ma).

people ['pi:pl] ◇ *n* [nation, race] pueblo *m*. ◇ *npl* - 1. [gen] gente *f*; [individuals] personas *fpl*; **a table for eight** ~ una mesa para ocho personas; ~ **say that** ... dice la gente que ...; **young** ~ los jóvenes - **2.** [inhabitants] habitantes *mpl* - **3.** POL: **the** ~ el pueblo. ⬦ *vt* : **to be** ~**d by** OR **with** estar poblado(da) de.

pep [pep] (*pt & pp* **-ped**, *cont* **-ping**) *n inf* vitalidad *f*.
➤ **pep up** *vt sep* [person] animar; [food] alegrar.

pepper ['pepəʳ] *n* - **1.** [spice] pimienta *f* - **2.** [vegetable] pimiento *m*.

peppermint ['pepəmınt] *n* - **1.** [sweet] pastilla *f* de menta - **2.** [herb] menta *f*.

pepperoni [,pepə'rəʊni] *n* pepperoni *m*.

pepper pot UK, **peppershaker** US *n* pimentero *m*.

pep talk *n inf* palabras *fpl* de ánimo.

per [pɜ:ʳ] *prep* [expressing rate, ratio] por; ~ **hour/kilo/person** por hora/kilo/persona; ~ **day** al día; **as** ~ **instructions** de acuerdo con OR según las instrucciones; **as** ~ **usual** como de costumbre.

per annum *adv* al OR por año.

per capita [pə'kæpıtə] ⬦ *adj* per cápita. ⬦ *adv* por cabeza.

perceive [pə'si:v] *vt* - **1.** [notice] percibir, apreciar - **2.** [understand, realize] advertir, apreciar - **3.** [see]: **to** ~ **sthg/sb as** ver algo/a alguien como.

per cent *adv* por ciento; **fifty** ~ **of the population** el cincuenta por ciento de la población.

percentage [pə'sentıdʒ] *n* porcentaje *m*.

perception [pə'sepʃn] *n* - **1.** [noticing] percepción *f* - **2.** [insight] perspicacia *f* - **3.** [opinion] idea *f*.

perceptive [pə'septıv] *adj* perspicaz.

perch [pɜ:tʃ] (*pl sense 3 only inv* OR **-es**) ⬦ *n* - **1.** [for bird] percha *f*, vara *f* - **2.** [fish] perca *f*. ⬦ *vi*: **to** ~ **(on)** [bird] posarse (en); [person] sentarse (en).

percolator ['pɜ:kəleıtəʳ] *n* cafetera *f* eléctrica.

percussion [pə'kʌʃn] *n* MUS percusión *f*.

perennial [pə'renjəl] ⬦ *adj* [gen & BOT] perenne. ⬦ *n* BOT planta *f* perenne.

perfect [*adj & n* 'pɜ:fıkt, *vb* pə'fekt] ⬦ *adj* perfecto(ta); **he's a** ~ **stranger to me** me es completamente desconocido. ⬦ *n* GRAMM : **the** ~ **(tense)** el perfecto. ⬦ *vt* perfeccionar.

perfection [pə'fekʃn] *n* perfección *f*; **to** ~ a la perfección.

perfectionist [pə'fekʃənıst] *n* perfeccionista *m* OR *f*.

perfectly ['pɜ:fıktlı] *adv* - **1.** [for emphasis] absolutamente; ~ **well** perfectamente bien - **2.** [to perfection] perfectamente.

perforate ['pɜ:fəreıt] *vt* perforar.

perforation [,pɜ:fə'reıʃn] *n* [in paper] perforación *f*.

perform [pə'fɔ:m] ⬦ *vt* - **1.** [carry out] llevar a cabo, realizar; [duty] cumplir - **2.** [music, dance] interpretar; [play] representar. ⬦ *vi* - **1.** [function - car, machine] funcionar; [- person, team] desenvolverse - **2.** [actor] actuar; [singer, dance] interpretar.

performance [pə'fɔ:məns] *n* - **1.** [carrying out] realización *f*, ejecución *f*; [of duty] cumplimiento *m* - **2.** [show] función *f* - **3.** [of actor, singer etc] interpretación *f*, actuación *f* - **4.** [of car, engine] rendimiento *m*.

performer [pə'fɔ:məʳ] *n* [actor, singer etc] intérprete *m* OR *f*.

perfume ['pɜ:fju:m] *n* perfume *m*.

perfunctory [pə'fʌŋktərı] *adj* superficial.

perhaps [pə'hæps] *adv* - **1.** [maybe] quizás, quizá; ~ **she'll do it** quizás ella lo haga; ~ **so/not** tal vez sí/no - **2.** [in polite requests, suggestions, remarks]: ~ **you could help?** ¿te importaría ayudar?; ~ **you should start again** ¿por qué no empiezas de nuevo? - **3.** [approximately] aproximadamente.

peril ['perıl] *n literary* peligro *m*.

perimeter [pə'rımıtəʳ] *n* perímetro *m*.

period ['pıərıəd] ⬦ *n* - **1.** [of time] período *m*, periodo *m* - **2.** HIST época *f* - **3.** SCH clase *f*, hora *f* - **4.** [menstruation] período *m*; **to be on one's** ~ tener el período - **5.** US [full stop] punto *m* - **6.** SPORT tiempo *m*. ⬦ *comp* de época.

periodic [,pıərı'ɒdık] *adj* periódico(ca).

periodical [,pıərı'ɒdıkl] ⬦ *adj* = **periodic**. ⬦ *n* [magazine] revista *f*, publicación *f* periódica.

peripheral [pə'rıfərəl] ⬦ *adj* - **1.** [of little importance] marginal - **2.** [at edge] periférico(ca). ⬦ *n* COMPUT periférico *m*.

perish ['perıʃ] *vi* - **1.** [die] perecer - **2.** [decay] deteriorarse.

perishable ['perıʃəbl] *adj* perecedero(ra).
➤ **perishables** *npl* productos *mpl* perecederos.

perjury ['pɜ:dʒərı] *n* JUR perjurio *m*.

perk [pɜ:k] *n inf* extra *m*, beneficio *m* adicional.
➤ **perk up** *vi* animarse.

perky ['pɜ:kı] (*compar* **-ier**, *superl* **-iest**) *adj inf* alegre, animado(da).

perm [pɜ:m] *n* permanente *f*.

permanent ['pɜ:mənənt] ⬦ *adj* - **1.** [gen] permanente; [job, address] fijo(ja) - **2.** [continuous, constant] constante. ⬦ *n* US [perm] permanente *f*.

permeate ['pɜ:mıeıt] *vt* impregnar.

permissible [pə'mısəbl] *adj* permisible.

permission [pə'mıʃn] *n*: ~ **(to do sthg)** permiso *m* (para hacer algo).

permissive [pə'mısıv] *adj* permisivo(va).

permit [*vb* pə'mɪt, *n* 'pɜ:mɪt] (*pt* & *pp* **-ted**, *cont* **-ting**) ◇ *vt* permitir; **to ~ sb sthg/to do sthg** permitir a alguien algo/hacer algo. ◇ *vi*: **if time ~s** si hay tiempo. ◇ *n* permiso *m*.

pernicious [pə'nɪʃəs] *adj fml* pernicioso(sa).

pernickety [pə'nɪkətɪ] *adj inf* quisquilloso(sa).

perpendicular [,pɜ:pən'dɪkjʊləʳ] ◇ *adj* **-1.** MATH: **~ (to)** perpendicular (a) **- 2.** [upright] vertical. ◇ *n* MATH perpendicular *f*.

perpetrate ['pɜ:pɪtreɪt] *vt fml* perpetrar.

perpetual [pə'petʃʊəl] *adj* **-1.** *pej* [constant] constante **- 2.** [everlasting] perpetuo(tua).

perplex [pə'pleks] *vt* confundir, dejar perplejo(ja).

perplexing [pə'pleksɪŋ] *adj* desconcertante.

persecute ['pɜ:sɪkju:t] *vt* perseguir.

perseverance [,pɜ:sɪ'vɪərəns] *n* perseverancia *f*.

persevere [,pɜ:sɪ'vɪəʳ] *vi*: **to ~ (with sthg/ in doing sthg)** perseverar (en algo/en hacer algo).

Persian ['pɜ:ʃn] *adj* persa.

persist [pə'sɪst] *vi* **-1.** [problem, rain] persistir **- 2.** [person]: **to ~ in doing sthg** empeñarse en hacer algo.

persistence [pə'sɪstəns] *n* **-1.** [continuation] persistencia *f* **- 2.** [determination] perseverancia *f*.

persistent [pə'sɪstənt] *adj* **-1.** [constant] continuo(nua) **- 2.** [determined] persistente.

person ['pɜ:sn] (*pl* **people** OR **persons** *fml*) *n* **-1.** [man, woman] persona *f*; **in ~** en persona **- 2.** [body]: **to have sthg about one's ~** llevar algo encima **- 3.** GRAMM persona *f*; **in the first ~** en primera persona.

personable ['pɜ:snəbl] *adj* agradable.

personal ['pɜ:sənl] *adj* **-1.** [gen] personal **- 2.** [private - life, problem] privado(da) **- 3.** *pej* [rude] ofensivo(va); **to be ~** hacer alusiones personales.

personal assistant *n* secretario *m*, -ria *f* personal.

personal column *n* sección *f* de asuntos personales.

personal computer *n* ordenador *m* personal.

personality [,pɜ:sə'nælətɪ] (*pl* **-ies**) *n* personalidad *f*.

personally ['pɜ:snəlɪ] *adv* **-1.** [gen] personalmente; **to take sthg ~** tomarse algo como algo personal **- 2.** [in person] en persona.

personal loan *n* crédito *m* personal.

personal organizer *n* agenda *f* (personal).

personal property *n (U)* bienes *mpl* muebles.

personal stereo *n* walkman® *m inv.*

personify [pə'sɒnɪfaɪ] (*pt* & *pp* **-ied**) *vt* personificar.

personnel [,pɜ:sə'nel] ◇ *n (U)* [department] departamento *m* de personal. ◇ *npl* [staff] personal *m*.

perspective [pə'spektɪv] *n* perspectiva *f*.

Perspex® ['pɜ:speks] *n UK* ≃ plexiglás® *m*.

perspiration [,pɜ:spə'reɪʃn] *n* transpiración *f*.

persuade [pə'sweɪd] *vt*: **to ~ sb (of sthg/ to do sthg)** persuadir a alguien (de algo/a hacer algo); **to ~ sb that** convencer a alguien (de) que.

persuasion [pə'sweɪʒn] *n* **-1.** [act of persuading] persuasión *f* **- 2.** [belief] creencia *f*.

persuasive [pə'sweɪsɪv] *adj* persuasivo(va).

pert [pɜ:t] *adj* **-1.** [person] vivaracho(cha) **- 2.** [part of body] respingón(ona).

pertain [pə'teɪn] *vi fml*: **~ing to** relacionado(da) con.

pertinent ['pɜ:tɪnənt] *adj* pertinente.

perturb [pə'tɜ:b] *vt fml* perturbar, inquietar.

Peru [pə'ru:] *n* (el) Perú.

peruse [pə'ru:z] *vt* [read carefully] leer detenidamente; [browse through] leer por encima.

Peruvian [pə'ru:vjən] ◇ *adj* peruano(na). ◇ *n* [person] peruano *m*, -na *f*.

pervade [pə'veɪd] *vt* impregnar.

perverse [pə'vɜ:s] *adj* [delight, enjoyment] perverso(sa); [contrary] puñetero(ra).

perversion [*UK* pə'vɜ:ʃn, *US* pə'vɜ:rʒn] *n* **-1.** [sexual deviation] perversión *f* **- 2.** [of justice, truth] tergiversación *f*.

pervert [*n* 'pɜ:vɜ:t, *vb* pə'vɜ:t] ◇ *n* pervertido *m*, -da *f*. ◇ *vt* **-1.** [course of justice] tergiversar **- 2.** [corrupt sexually] pervertir.

pessimist ['pesɪmɪst] *n* pesimista *m* OR *f*.

pessimistic [,pesɪ'mɪstɪk] *adj* pesimista.

pest [pest] *n* **-1.** [insect] insecto *m* nocivo; [animal] animal *m* nocivo **- 2.** *inf* [annoying person] pesado *m*, -da *f*; [annoying thing] lata *f*.

pester ['pestəʳ] *vt* dar la lata a, cargosear *Amér.*

pet [pet] (*pt* & *pp* **-ted**, *cont* **-ting**) ◇ *adj* [subject, theory] preferido(da); **~ hate** gran fobia *f*. ◇ *n* **-1.** [domestic animal] animal *m* doméstico **- 2.** [favourite person] preferido *m*, -da *f*, favorito *m*, -ta *f*. ◇ *vt* acariciar. ◇ *vi* pegarse el lote.

petal ['petl] *n* pétalo *m*.

peter ['pi:təʳ] ➤ **peter out** *vi* [supplies, interest] agotarse; [path] desaparecer.

petite [pə'ti:t] *adj* [woman] chiquita.

petition [pɪ'tɪʃn] ⬦ n petición f. ⬦ vi JUR : **to ~ for divorce** pedir el divorcio.

petrified ['petrɪfaɪd] adj [terrified] petrificado(da).

petrol ['petrəl] n UK gasolina f, nafta f RP, bencina f Chile.

petrol bomb n UK bomba f de gasolina.

petrol can n UK lata f de gasolina OR de nafta RP OR de bencina Chile.

petroleum [pɪ'trəʊljəm] n petróleo m.

petrol pump n UK surtidor m de gasolina OR de nafta RP OR de bencina Chile, bomba f Chile, Col, Ven.

petrol station n UK gasolinera f, grifo m Perú, bomba f Chile, Col, Ven, estación f de nafta RP.

petrol tank n UK depósito m de gasolina, tanque m de gasolina Amér OR de bencina Chile OR de nafta RP.

pet shop n pajarería f.

petticoat ['petɪkəʊt] n [underskirt] enaguas fpl, enagua f, fustán m Amér; [full-length] combinación f.

petty ['petɪ] (compar **-ier**, superl **-iest**) adj **- 1.** [small-minded] mezquino(na) **- 2.** [trivial] insignificante.

petty cash n dinero m para gastos menores.

petty officer n sargento m de la marina.

petty thief n ladronzuelo m, -la f.

petulant ['petjʊlənt] adj cascarrabias (inv).

pew [pju:] n banco m.

pewter ['pju:tə'] n peltre m.

phantom ['fæntəm] ⬦ adj ilusorio(ria). ⬦ n [ghost] fantasma m.

pharmaceutical [,fɑ:mə'sju:tɪkl] adj farmacéutico(ca).

pharmacist ['fɑ:məsɪst] n farmacéutico m, -ca f.

pharmacy ['fɑ:məsɪ] (pl **-ies**) n [shop] farmacia f.

phase [feɪz] ⬦ n fase f. ⬦ vt escalonar.
  ➡ **phase in** vt sep introducir progresivamente.
  ➡ **phase out** vt sep retirar progresivamente.

PhD (abbr of **Doctor of Philosophy**) n **- 1.** [qualification] doctorado m **- 2.** [person] doctor m, -ra f.

pheasant ['feznt] (pl inv OR **-s**) n faisán m.

phenomena [fɪ'nɒmɪnə] pl ⊳ **phenomenon**.

phenomenal [fɪ'nɒmɪnl] adj extraordinario(ria).

phenomenon [fɪ'nɒmɪnən] (pl **-mena**) n lit & fig fenómeno m.

phial ['faɪəl] n frasco m (pequeño).

philanthropist [fɪ'lænθrəpɪst] n filántropo m, -pa f.

philately [fɪ'lætəlɪ] n filatelia f.

Philippine ['fɪlɪpi:n] adj filipino(na).

➡ **Philippines** npl: **the ~s** las Filipinas.

philosopher [fɪ'lɒsəfə'] n filósofo m, -fa f.

philosophical [,fɪlə'sɒfɪkl] adj filosófico(ca).

philosophy [fɪ'lɒsəfɪ] (pl **-ies**) n filosofía f.

phlegm [flem] n [mucus, composure] flema f.

phlegmatic [fleg'mætɪk] adj flemático(ca).

phobia ['fəʊbjə] n fobia f.

phone [fəʊn] ⬦ n teléfono m; **to be on the ~** [speaking] estar al teléfono; UK [connected to network] tener teléfono; **to talk about sthg on the ~** discutir algo por teléfono. ⬦ vt & vi llamar, telefonear.
  ➡ **phone in** vi llamar.
  ➡ **phone up** vt sep & vi llamar.

phone bill n factura f del teléfono.

phone book n guía f telefónica.

phone booth n teléfono m público.

phone box n UK cabina f telefónica.

phone call n llamada f telefónica; **to make a ~** hacer una llamada.

phonecard ['fəʊnkɑ:d] n tarjeta f telefónica.

phone-in n RADIO & TV programa con llamadas de los oyentes.

phone number n número m de teléfono.

phonetics [fə'netɪks] n (U) fonética f.

phoney UK, **phony** US ['fəʊnɪ] (compar **-ier**, superl **-iest**, pl **-ies**) ⬦ adj inf falso(sa). ⬦ n farsante m OR f.

phosphorus ['fɒsfərəs] n fósforo m.

photo ['fəʊtəʊ] n foto f; **to take a ~ (of)** sacar una foto (de).

photocopier ['fəʊtəʊ,kɒpɪə'] n fotocopiadora f.

photocopy ['fəʊtəʊ,kɒpɪ] (pl **-ies**, pt & pp **-ied**) ⬦ n fotocopia f. ⬦ vt fotocopiar.

photograph ['fəʊtəgrɑ:f] ⬦ n fotografía f; **to take a ~ (of)** sacar una fotografía (de). ⬦ vt fotografiar.

photographer [fə'tɒgrəfə'] n fotógrafo m, -fa f.

photography [fə'tɒgrəfɪ] n (U) fotografía f.

photovoltaic cell [,fəʊtəʊvɒl'teɪk-] n célula f fotovoltaica.

phrasal verb ['freɪzl-] n verbo m con preposición.

phrase [freɪz] ⬦ n **- 1.** [group of words] locución f, frase f **- 2.** [expression] expresión f. ⬦ vt [apology, refusal] expresar; [letter] redactar.

phrasebook ['freɪzbʊk] n guía f de conversación.

physical ['fɪzɪkl] ⬦ adj físico(ca). ⬦ n [examination] examen m médico.

physical education n educación f física.

physically ['fɪzɪklɪ] adv físicamente.

physically handicapped npl: **the ~** los discapacitados físicos.

physician [fɪˈzɪʃn] *n* médico *m* OR *f*.
physicist [ˈfɪzɪsɪst] *n* físico *m*, -ca *f*.
physics [ˈfɪzɪks] *n* (U) física *f*.
physiotherapy [ˌfɪzɪəʊˈθerəpɪ] *n* fisioterapia *f*.
physique [fɪˈziːk] *n* físico *m*.
PI *n* (*abbr of* **private investigator**) US investigador *m*, -dora *f* privado, -da *f*.
pianist [ˈpɪənɪst] *n* pianista *m* OR *f*.
piano [pɪˈænəʊ] (*pl* **-s**) *n* [instrument] piano *m*.
piccolo [ˈpɪkələʊ] (*pl* **-s**) *n* flautín *m*.
pick [pɪk] <> *n* **-1.** [tool] piqueta *f* **-2.** [for guitar] púa *f* **-3.** [selection]: **take your ~** escoge el que quieras **-4.** [best]: **the ~ of** lo mejor de. <> *vt* **-1.** [team, winner] seleccionar; [time, book, dress] elegir **-2.** [fruit, flowers] coger **-3.** [remove - hairs etc]: **to ~ sthg off sthg** quitar algo de algo **-4.** [nose] hurgarse; [teeth] mondarse; [scab, spot] arrancarse **-5.** [provoke]: **to ~ a fight/quarrel (with)** buscar pelea/bronca (con) **-6.** [open - lock] forzar (con ganzúa).
 ◆ **pick on** *vt fus* meterse con.
 ◆ **pick out** *vt sep* **-1.** [recognize] reconocer **-2.** [identify] identificar **-3.** [select] escoger, elegir.
 ◆ **pick up** <> *vt sep* **-1.** [gen] recoger **-2.** [lift up] levantar; [the phone] descolgar **-3.** [buy, acquire] adquirir; **to ~ up speed** cobrar velocidad **-4.** [illness, bug] contraer **-5.** [learn - tips, language] aprender; [- habit] adquirir **-6.** *inf* [find partner] ligar con **-7.** RADIO & TELEC captar, recibir **-8.** [start again] reanudar. <> *vi* **-1.** [improve] mejorar **-2.** [start again] seguir **-3.** [wind] aumentar.
pickaxe UK, **pickax** US [ˈpɪkæks] *n* piqueta *f*.
picket [ˈpɪkɪt] <> *n* piquete *m*. <> *vt* formar piquetes en.
picket line *n* piquete *m* (de huelga).
pickle [ˈpɪkl] <> *n* **-1.** [vinegar preserve] encurtido *m*; [sweet vegetable sauce] *salsa espesa agridulce con trozos de cebolla etc*; US [cucumber] pepinillos *mpl* en vinagre **-2.** *inf* [difficult situation]: **to be in a ~** estar en un lío. <> *vt* encurtir.
pickpocket [ˈpɪkˌpɒkɪt] *n* carterista *m* OR *f*.
pick-up *n* **-1.** [of record player] fonocaptor *m* **-2.** [truck] camioneta *f*, furgoneta *f*.
picnic [ˈpɪknɪk] (*pt* & *pp* **-ked**, *cont* **-king**) <> *n* comida *f* campestre, picnic *m*. <> *vi* ir de merienda al campo.
pictorial [pɪkˈtɔːrɪəl] *adj* ilustrado(da).
picture [ˈpɪktʃəʳ] <> *n* **-1.** [painting] cuadro *m*; [drawing] dibujo *m* **-2.** [photograph] foto *f*; [illustration] ilustración *f* **-3.** [on TV] imagen *f* **-4.** [cinema film] película *f* **-5.** [in mind] idea *f*, imagen *f* **-6.** [situation] situación *f* **-7.** *phr*: **to get the ~** *inf* entenderlo;

to put sb in the ~ poner a alguien al corriente. <> *vt* **-1.** [in mind] imaginarse **-2.** [in media]: **to be ~d** aparecer en la foto.
 ◆ **pictures** *npl* UK: **the ~s** el cine.
picture book *n* libro *m* ilustrado.
picturesque [ˌpɪktʃəˈresk] *adj* pintoresco(ca).
pie [paɪ] *n* [sweet] tarta *f* (*cubierta de hojaldre*); [savoury] empanada *f*, pastel *m*.
piece [piːs] *n* **-1.** [individual part or portion] trozo *m*, pedazo *m*; **to come to ~s** deshacerse; **to take sthg to ~s** desmontar algo; **to tear sthg to ~s** hacer trizas algo; **in ~s** en pedazos; **in one ~** [intact] intacto(ta); [unharmed] sano y salvo (sana y salva) **-2.** *(with uncountable noun)* [individual object]: **~ of furniture** mueble *m*; **~ of clothing** prenda *f* de vestir; **~ of fruit** fruta *f*; **~ of luggage** bulto *m* de equipaje; **~ of advice** consejo *m*; **~ of news** noticia *f*; **a ~ of information** una información; **~ of luck** golpe *m* de suerte **-3.** [in board game] pieza *f*; [in draughts] ficha *f* **-4.** [of journalism] artículo *m* **-5.** [coin] moneda *f*.
 ◆ **piece together** *vt sep* [discover] componer.
piecemeal [ˈpiːsmiːl] <> *adj* poco sistemático(ca). <> *adv* [gradually] gradualmente, por etapas.
piecework [ˈpiːswɜːk] *n* (U) trabajo *m* a destajo.
pie chart *n* gráfico *m* de sectores.
pier [pɪəʳ] *n* **-1.** [at seaside] *paseo marítimo en un malecón* **-2.** [for landing boat] embarcadero *m*.
pierce [pɪəs] *vt* **-1.** [subj: bullet, needle] perforar; **to have one's ears ~d** hacerse agujeros en las orejas **-2.** [subj: voice, scream] romper.
piercing [ˈpɪəsɪŋ] *adj* **-1.** [scream] desgarrador(ra); [sound, voice] agudo(da) **-2.** [wind] cortante **-3.** [look, eyes] penetrante.
piety [ˈpaɪətɪ] *n* piedad *f*.
pig [pɪg] *n* **-1.** [animal] cerdo *m*, puerco *m*, chancho *m* *Amér* **-2.** *inf pej* [greedy eater] tragón *m*, -ona *f*, comilón *m*, -ona *f* **-3.** *inf pej* [unkind person] cerdo *m*, -da *f*, chancho *m*, -cha *f* *Amér* **-4.** *inf pej* [policeman] madero *m*.
pigeon [ˈpɪdʒɪn] (*pl inv* OR **-s**) *n* paloma *f*.
pigeonhole [ˈpɪdʒɪnhəʊl] <> *n* [compartment] casilla *f*. <> *vt* [classify] encasillar.
piggybank [ˈpɪgɪbæŋk] *n* hucha *f* con forma de cerdito.
pigheaded [ˌpɪgˈhedɪd] *adj* cabezota.
pigment [ˈpɪgmənt] *n* pigmento *m*.
pigpen US = **pigsty**.
pigskin [ˈpɪgskɪn] *n* piel *f* de cerdo.
pigsty [ˈpɪgstaɪ] (*pl* **-ies**), **pigpen** US [ˈpɪgpen] *n* *lit* & *fig* pocilga *f*.

pigtail ['pɪgteɪl] *n* [girl's] trenza *f*; [Chinese, bullfighter's] coleta *f*.

pike [paɪk] (*pl sense 1 only inv OR* -s) *n* -1. [fish] lucio *m* -2. [weapon] pica *f*.

pilchard ['pɪltʃəd] *n* sardina *f*.

pile [paɪl] ◇ *n* -1. [heap] montón *m*, ruma *f* *Andes*; **a** ~ OR ~**s of** [a lot] un montón de -2. [neat stack] pila *f* -3. [of carpet, fabric] pelo *m*. ◇ *vt* apilar, amontonar.

◆ **piles** *npl* MED almorranas *fpl*.

◆ **pile into** *vt fus inf* meterse atropelladamente en.

◆ **pile up** ◇ *vt sep* apilar, amontonar. ◇ *vi* -1. [form a heap] apilarse, amontonarse -2. [mount up] acumularse.

pileup ['paɪlʌp] *n* accidente *m* en cadena.

pilfer ['pɪlfə'] ◇ *vt* sisar. ◇ *vi*: **to** ~ **(from)** sisar (de).

pilgrim ['pɪlgrɪm] *n* peregrino *m*, -na *f*.

pilgrimage ['pɪlgrɪmɪdʒ] *n* peregrinación *f*.

pill [pɪl] *n* -1. MED píldora *f*, pastilla *f* -2. [contraceptive]: **the** ~ la píldora (anticonceptiva); **to be on the** ~ tomar la píldora.

pillage ['pɪlɪdʒ] *vt* saquear.

pillar ['pɪlə'] *n lit & fig* pilar *m*.

pillar box *n* UK buzón *m*.

pillion ['pɪljən] *n* asiento *m* trasero; **to ride** ~ ir en el asiento trasero *(de una moto)*.

pillow ['pɪləʊ] *n* -1. [for bed] almohada *f* -2. US [on sofa, chair] cojín *m*.

pillowcase ['pɪləʊkeɪs], **pillowslip** ['pɪləʊslɪp] *n* funda *f* de almohada.

pilot ['paɪlət] ◇ *n* -1. AERON & NAUT piloto *m* -2. TV programa *m* piloto. ◇ *comp* [project, study] piloto *(inv)*, de prueba. ◇ *vt* AERON & NAUT pilotar.

pilot burner, pilot light *n* piloto *m*, luz *f* indicadora.

pilot study *n* estudio *m* piloto.

pimp [pɪmp] *n inf* chulo *m*, padrote *m* *Méx*.

pimple ['pɪmpl] *n* grano *m*.

pin [pɪn] (*pt & pp* -ned, *cont* -ning) ◇ *n* -1. [for sewing] alfiler *m*; ~**s and needles** hormigueo *m* -2. [of plug] clavija *f*; COMPUT pin *m* -3. TECH clavija *f*. ◇ *vt* -1. [fasten]: **to** ~ **sthg to** OR **on** [sheet of paper] clavar con alfileres algo en; [medal, piece of cloth] prender algo en -2. [trap]: **to** ~ **sb against** OR **to** inmovilizar a alguien contra -3. [apportion]: **to** ~ **sthg on** OR **upon sb** cargar algo a alguien.

◆ **pin down** *vt sep* -1. [identify] determinar, identificar -2. [force to make a decision]: **to** ~ **sb down (to)** obligar a alguien a comprometerse (a).

pinafore ['pɪnəfɔ:'] *n* -1. [apron] delantal *m* -2. UK [dress] pichi *m*.

pinball ['pɪnbɔ:l] *n* millón *m*, flíper *m*.

pincers ['pɪnsəz] *npl* -1. [tool] tenazas *fpl* -2. [front claws] pinzas *fpl*.

pinch [pɪntʃ] ◇ *n* -1. [nip] pellizco *m* -2. [small quantity] pizca *f*. ◇ *vt* -1. [nip] pellizcar; [subj: shoes] apretar -2. *inf* [steal] mangar. ◇ *vi* [shoes] apretar.

◆ **at a pinch** UK, **in a pinch** US *adv* si no hay más remedio.

pincushion ['pɪn,kʊʃn] *n* acerico *m*.

pine [paɪn] ◇ *n* pino *m*. ◇ *vi*: **to** ~ **for** suspirar por.

◆ **pine away** *vi* morirse de pena.

pineapple ['paɪnæpl] *n* piña *f*, ananá *m* RP.

pinetree ['paɪntri:] *n* pino *m*.

ping [pɪŋ] *n* [of metal] sonido *m* metálico.

Ping-Pong® [-pɒŋ] *n* ping-pong® *m*.

pink [pɪŋk] ◇ *adj* rosa. ◇ *n* -1. [colour] rosa *m* -2. [flower] clavel *m*.

pink pound UK, **pink dollar** US *n*: **the** ~ el poder adquisitivo de los homosexuales.

pinnacle ['pɪnəkl] *n* -1. [high point] cumbre *f*, cúspide *f* -2. [mountain peak] cima *f*; [spire] pináculo *m*.

pinpoint ['pɪnpɔɪnt] *vt* determinar, identificar.

pin-striped [-,straɪpt] *adj* a rayas.

pint [paɪnt] *n* [unit of measurement] UK = 0,568 litros; US = 0,473 litros, ≃ pinta *f*.

pioneer [,paɪə'nɪə'] ◇ *n* pionero *m*, -ra *f*.

pious ['paɪəs] *adj* -1. [religious] piadoso(sa) -2. *pej* [sanctimonious] mojigato(ta).

pip [pɪp] *n* -1. [seed] pepita *f* -2. UK [bleep] señal *f*.

pipe [paɪp] ◇ *n* -1. [for gas, water] tubería *f* -2. [for smoking] pipa *f*. ◇ *vt* [transport via pipes] conducir por tuberías.

◆ **pipes** *npl* MUS gaita *f*.

◆ **pipe down** *vi inf* cerrar la boca.

◆ **pipe up** *vi inf*: **to** ~ **up with a suggestion** saltar con una sugerencia.

pipe cleaner *n* limpiapipas *m inv*.

pipe dream *n* sueño *m* imposible, castillos *mpl* en el aire.

pipeline ['paɪplaɪn] *n* tubería *f*; [for gas] gasoducto *m*; [for oil] oleoducto *m*.

piper ['paɪpə'] *n* gaitero *m*, -ra *f*.

piping hot ['paɪpɪŋ-] *adj* humeante, calentito(ta).

piquant ['pi:kənt] *adj* -1. [food] picante -2. [story] intrigante; [situation] que suscita un placer mordaz.

pique [pi:k] ◇ *n* resentimiento *m*. ◇ *vt* -1. [upset] ofender -2. [arouse] despertar.

pirate ['paɪrət] ◇ *adj* [gen & COMPUT] pirata. ◇ *n* [sailor] pirata *m* OR *f*. ◇ *vt* piratear.

pirate radio *n* UK radio *f* pirata.

pirouette [,pɪrʊ'et] *n* pirueta *f*.

Pisces ['paɪsi:z] *n* Piscis *m inv*.

piss [pɪs] *v inf* ◇ *n* [urine] meada *f*. ◇ *vi* mear.

◆ **piss about, piss around** UK *v inf* ◇ *vt sep* vacilar. ◇ *vi* [waste time] tocarse los huevos; [fool around] hacer el gilipollas.

pissed [pɪst] *adj vulg* **- 1.** UK [drunk] pedo *(inv)*, cocido(da) **- 2.** US [annoyed] cabreado(da).

pissed off *adj vulg*: **to be** OR **to feel ~** estar cabreado(da).

pistol ['pɪstl] *n* pistola *f*.

piston ['pɪstən] *n* pistón *m*, émbolo *m*.

pit [pɪt] (*pt* & *pp* **-ted**, *cont* **-ting**) ◇ *n* **- 1.** [large hole] hoyo *m* **- 2.** [small hole - in metal, glass] señal *f*, marca *f*; [- on face] picadura *f*, piquete *m Méx* **- 3.** [for orchestra] foso *m* de la orquesta **- 4.** [mine] mina *f* **- 5.** US [of fruit] hueso *m*, cuesco *m*, carozo *m RP*, pepa *f Col.* ◇ *vt*: **to be pitted against** ser enfrentado(da) con.

➤ **pits** *npl* [in motor racing]: **the ~s** el box.

pit bull terrier *n* pitbull terrier *m*.

pitch [pɪtʃ] ◇ *n* **- 1.** SPORT campo *m* **- 2.** MUS tono *m* **- 3.** [level, degree] grado *m*, punto *m* **- 4.** UK [selling place] puesto *m* **- 5.** *inf* [sales talk] labia *f* de comerciante. ◇ *vt* **- 1.** [throw] lanzar, arrojar **- 2.** [design]: **to be ~ed in order to do sthg** estar diseñado para hacer algo **- 3.** [speech] dar un tono a **- 4.** [tent] montar, poner. ◇ *vi* **- 1.** [ball] tocar el suelo; **to ~ forwards** [person] precipitarse hacia delante **- 2.** [ship, plane] dar un bandazo.

pitch-black *adj* negro(gra) como boca de lobo.

pitched battle [,pɪtʃt-] *n* HIST batalla *f* campal; *fig* [bitter struggle] lucha *f* encarnizada.

pitcher ['pɪtʃər] *n* [jug] cántaro *m*, jarro *m*.

pitchfork ['pɪtʃfɔːk] *n* horca *f*.

piteous ['pɪtɪəs] *adj* lastimero(ra).

pitfall ['pɪtfɔːl] *n* peligro *m*, escollo *m*.

pith [pɪθ] *n* piel *f* blanca.

pithy ['pɪθɪ] (*compar* **-ier**, *superl* **-iest**) *adj* conciso(sa) y contundente.

pitiful ['pɪtɪfʊl] *adj* [condition, excuse, effort] lamentable; [person, appearance] lastimoso(sa).

pitiless ['pɪtɪlɪs] *adj* [person] despiadado(da).

pit stop *n* [in motor racing] parada *f* en boxes.

pittance ['pɪtəns] *n* miseria *f*.

pity ['pɪtɪ] (*pt* & *pp* **-ied**) ◇ *n* [compassion] compasión *f*; [shame] pena *f*, lástima *f*; **what a ~!** ¡qué pena!; **to take** OR **have ~ on** compadecerse de. ◇ *vt* compadecerse de, sentir pena por.

pivot ['pɪvət] *n* **- 1.** TECH pivote *m*, eje *m* **- 2.** *fig* [person] eje *m*.

pizza ['piːtsə] *n* pizza *f*.

pizza parlour *n* pizzería *f*.

pizzeria [,pɪtsə'rɪə] *n* pizzería *f*.

placard ['plækɑːd] *n* pancarta *f*.

placate [plə'keɪt] *vt* aplacar, apaciguar.

place [pleɪs] ◇ *n* **- 1.** [gen] lugar *m*, sitio *m*;

~ of birth lugar de nacimiento; **it's good in ~s** tiene algunas partes buenas **- 2.** [proper position] sitio *m* **- 3.** [suitable occasion, time] momento *m* **- 4.** [home] casa *f* **- 5.** [specific seat] asiento *m*; [in queue] sitio *m*; THEATRE localidad *f* **- 6.** [setting at table] cubierto *m* **- 7.** [on course, at university] plaza *f* **- 8.** [on committee, in team] puesto *m* **- 9.** [role, function] papel *m*; **to have an important ~ in** desempeñar un papel importante en; **put yourself in my ~** ponte en mi lugar **- 10.** [position, rank] lugar *m*, posición *f* **- 11.** [in book] página *f*; [in speech]: **to lose one's ~** no saber (uno) dónde estaba **- 12.** MATH: **decimal ~** punto *m* decimal **- 13.** [instance]: **in the first ~** [from the start] desde el principio; **in the first ~ ... and in the second ~ ...** [firstly, secondly] en primer lugar ... y en segundo lugar ... **- 14.** *phr*: **to take ~** tener lugar; **to take the ~ of** sustituir a. ◇ *vt* **- 1.** [position, put] colocar, poner; **to be well ~d to do sthg** estar en buena posición para hacer algo **- 2.** [lay, apportion]: **to ~ emphasis on** poner énfasis en; **to ~ pressure on** ejercer presión sobre **- 3.** [identify]: **I recognize the face, but I can't ~ her** me suena su cara, pero no sé de qué **- 4.** [bet, order etc] hacer **- 5.** [in horse racing]: **to be ~d** llegar entre los tres primeros.

➤ **all over the place** *adv* por todas partes.

➤ **in place** *adv* **- 1.** [in proper position] en su sitio **- 2.** [established, set up] en marcha OR funcionamiento; **everything is now in ~** los preparativos ya están finalizados.

➤ **in place of** *prep* en lugar de.

➤ **out of place** *adv* **- 1.** [in wrong position]: **to be out of ~** no estar en su sitio **- 2.** [inappropriate, unsuitable] fuera de lugar.

place mat *n* mantel *m* individual.

placement ['pleɪsmənt] *n* colocación *f*.

placement test *n* examen *m* de nivel.

placid ['plæsɪd] *adj* **- 1.** [even-tempered] apacible **- 2.** [peaceful] tranquilo(la).

plagiarize, -ise ['pleɪdʒəraɪz] *vt* plagiar.

plague [pleɪg] ◇ *n* **- 1.** [attack of disease] peste *f* **- 2.** [disease]: **(the) ~** la peste **- 3.** [of rats, insects] plaga *f*. ◇ *vt*: **to ~ sb with** [complaints, requests] acosar a alguien con; [questions] acribillar a alguien a; **to be ~d by** [ill health] estar acosado de; [doubts] estar atormentado de.

plaice [pleɪs] (*pl inv*) *n* platija *f*.

plaid [plæd] *n* tejido *m* escocés.

Plaid Cymru [,plaɪd'kʌmrɪ] *n* UK POL partido nacionalista galés.

plain [pleɪn] ◇ *adj* **- 1.** [not patterned] liso(sa) **- 2.** [simple - gen] sencillo(lla); [- yoghurt] natural **- 3.** [clear] evidente, claro(ra) **- 4.** [speaking, statement] franco(ca)

- **5.** [absolute - madness etc] auténtico(ca) - **6.** [not pretty] sin atractivo. ◇ *adv inf* completamente. ◇ *n* GEOGR llanura *f*, planicie *f*.

plain chocolate *n* UK chocolate *m* amargo.

plain-clothes *adj* vestido(da) de paisano.

plain flour *n* UK harina *f* (sin levadura).

plainly ['pleɪnlɪ] *adv* - **1.** [upset, angry] evidentemente - **2.** [visible, audible] claramente - **3.** [frankly] francamente - **4.** [simply] sencillamente.

plaintiff ['pleɪntɪf] *n* demandante *m* OR *f*.

plait [plæt] ◇ *n* trenza *f*. ◇ *vt* trenzar.

plan [plæn] (*pt* & *pp* **-ned**, *cont* **-ning**) ◇ *n* - **1.** [strategy] plan *m*; **to go according to ~** salir según lo previsto - **2.** [of story, essay] esquema *m* - **3.** [of building etc] plano *m*. ◇ *vt* - **1.** [organize] planear - **2.** [career, future, economy] planificar; **to ~ to do sthg** tener la intención de hacer algo - **3.** [design, devise] trazar un esquema OR boceto de. ◇ *vi* hacer planes.

　◆ **plans** *npl* planes *mpl*; **to have ~s for** tener planes para.

　◆ **plan on** *vt fus*: **to ~ on doing sthg** pensar hacer algo.

plane [pleɪn] ◇ *adj* plano(na). ◇ *n* - **1.** [aircraft] avión *m* - **2.** GEOM [flat surface] plano *m* - **3.** *fig* [level - intellectual] nivel *m*, plano *m* - **4.** [tool] cepillo *m* - **5.** [tree] plátano *m*.

planet ['plænɪt] *n* planeta *m*.

plank [plæŋk] *n* [piece of wood] tablón *m*, tabla *f*.

planning ['plænɪŋ] *n* [gen] planificación *f*.

planning permission *n* permiso *m* de construcción OR de obras.

plant [plɑːnt] ◇ *n* - **1.** BOT planta *f* - **2.** [factory] planta *f*, fábrica *f* - **3.** [heavy machinery] maquinaria *f*. ◇ *vt* - **1.** [seed, tree, vegetable]: **to ~ sthg (in)** plantar algo (en) - **2.** [field, garden]: **to ~ sthg with** sembrar algo de - **3.** [bomb, bug] colocar secretamente.

plantation [plæn'teɪʃn] *n* plantación *f*.

plaque [plɑːk] *n* [gen & MED] placa *f*.

plaster ['plɑːstəʳ] ◇ *n* - **1.** [for wall, ceiling] yeso *m* - **2.** [for broken bones] escayola *f* - **3.** UK [bandage] tirita® *f*. ◇ *vt* - **1.** [put plaster on] enyesar - **2.** [cover]: **to ~ sthg (with)** cubrir algo (de).

plaster cast *n* - **1.** [for broken bones] escayola *f* - **2.** [model, statue] vaciado *m* en yeso.

plastered ['plɑːstəd] *adj inf* [drunk] cocido(da).

plasterer ['plɑːstərəʳ] *n* yesero *m*, -ra *f*.

plastic ['plæstɪk] ◇ *adj* [made from plastic] de plástico. ◇ *n* plástico *m*.

Plasticine® ['plæstɪsiːn] *n* UK plastilina® *f*.

plastic surgery *n* cirugía *f* plástica.

plate [pleɪt] ◇ *n* - **1.** [dish, plateful] plato *m*

- **2.** [on machinery, wall, door] placa *f* - **3.** (*U*) [metal covering]: **gold/silver ~** chapa *f* de oro/plata - **4.** [photograph] lámina *f* - **5.** [in dentistry] dentadura *f* postiza. ◇ *vt*: **to be ~d (with)** estar chapado(da) (en OR de).

plateau ['plætəʊ] (*pl* **-s** OR **-x** [-z]) *n* [high, flat land] meseta *f*.

plate glass *n* vidrio *m* cilindrado.

platform ['plætfɔːm] *n* - **1.** [gen & COMPUT] plataforma *f*; [stage] estrado *m*; [at meeting] tribuna *f* - **2.** RAIL andén *m*; **~ 12** la vía 12 - **3.** POL programa *m* electoral.

platinum ['plætɪnəm] *n* platino *m*.

platitude ['plætɪtjuːd] *n* tópico *m*, cliché *m*.

platoon [plə'tuːn] *n* pelotón *m*.

platter ['plætəʳ] *n* [dish] fuente *f*.

plausible ['plɔːzəbl] *adj* plausible, admisible.

play [pleɪ] ◇ *n* - **1.** (*U*) [amusement] juego *m*; **at ~** jugando - **2.** [piece of drama] obra *f* - **3.** [game]: **~ on words** juego *m* de palabras - **4.** TECH juego *m*. ◇ *vt* - **1.** [game, sport] jugar a; [match] jugar; [in specific position] jugar de - **2.** [play game against]: **to ~ sb (at sthg)** jugar contra alguien (a algo) - **3.** [perform for amusement]: **to ~ a joke on** gastar una broma a; **to ~ a dirty trick on** jugar una mala pasada a - **4.** [act - part, character] representar; **to ~ a part** OR **role in** *fig* desempeñar un papel en; **to ~ the fool** hacer el tonto - **5.** [instrument, tune] tocar; [record, cassette] poner - **6.** *phr*: **to ~ it safe** actuar sobre seguro. ◇ *vi* - **1.** [gen]: **to ~ (with/against)** jugar (con/contra); **to ~ for sb/a team** jugar para alguien/con un equipo - **2.** [be performed, shown - play] representarse; [- film] exhibirse - **3.** [MUS - person] tocar; [- music] sonar.

　◆ **play along** *vi*: **to ~ along (with)** seguir la corriente (a).

　◆ **play down** *vt sep* quitar importancia a.

　◆ **play up** ◇ *vt sep* [emphasize] hacer resaltar, realzar. ◇ *vi* [machine, part of body, child] dar guerra.

play-act *vi* fingir, hacer comedia.

playboy ['pleɪbɔɪ] *n* playboy *m*, fifí *m* Amér.

player ['pleɪəʳ] *n* - **1.** [of sport, game] jugador *m*, -ra *f* - **2.** MUS intérprete *m* OR *f* - **3.** THEATRE actor *m*, actriz *f* - **4.** [important person or organization] protagonista *m* OR *f*.

playful ['pleɪfʊl] *adj* juguetón(ona).

playground ['pleɪgraʊnd] *n* - **1.** [at school] patio *m* de recreo - **2.** [in park] zona *f* de juegos.

playgroup ['pleɪgruːp] *n* jardín *m* de infancia, guardería *f*.

playing card ['pleɪɪŋ-] *n* naipe *m*, carta *f*.

playing field ['pleɪɪŋ-] *n* campo *m* de juego.

playmate ['pleɪmeɪt] *n* compañero *m*, -ra *f* de juego.

play-off *n* partido *m* de desempate.

playpen ['pleɪpen] *n* parque *m* (de niños) *(tipo cuna)*.

playschool ['pleɪskuːl] *n* jardín *m* de infancia, guardería *f*.

plaything ['pleɪθɪŋ] *n* lit & fig juguete *m*.

playtime ['pleɪtaɪm] *n* recreo *m*.

playwright ['pleɪraɪt] *n* autor *m*, -ra *f* de teatro, dramaturgo *m*, -ga *f*.

plc *abbr of* **public limited company**.

plea [pliː] *n* - 1. [appeal] súplica *f*, petición *f* - 2. JUR *declaración por parte del acusado de culpabilidad o inocencia.*

plead [pliːd] (*pt & pp* -ed *OR* pled) ◇ *vt* - 1. JUR [one's cause] defender; to ~ guilty/not guilty declararse culpable/inocente - 2. [give as excuse] pretender. ◇ *vi* - 1. [beg]: to ~ (with sb to do sthg) rogar *OR* implorar (a alguien que haga algo); to ~ for sthg pedir algo - 2. JUR declarar.

pleasant ['pleznt] *adj* - 1. [smell, taste, view] agradable; [surprise, news] grato(ta) - 2. [person, smile, face] simpático(ca), dije *Chile*.

pleasantry ['plezntrɪ] (*pl* -ies) *n*: to exchange pleasantries intercambiar cumplidos.

please [pliːz] ◇ *vt* complacer, agradar; he always ~s himself él siempre hace lo que le da la gana; ~ yourself! ¡como quieras! ◇ *vi* - 1. [give satisfaction] satisfacer, agradar - 2. [think appropriate]: to do as one ~s hacer como a uno le parezca. ◇ *adv* por favor.

pleased [pliːzd] *adj*: to be ~ (about/with) estar contento(ta) (por/con); to be ~ for sb alegrarse por alguien; to be very ~ with o.s. estar muy satisfecho de sí mismo; ~ to meet you! ¡encantado(da) de conocerle!, ¡mucho gusto!

pleasing ['pliːzɪŋ] *adj* agradable, grato(ta).

pleasure ['pleʒə^r] *n* - 1. [feeling of happiness] gusto *m*; to take ~ in doing sthg disfrutar haciendo algo - 2. [enjoyment] diversión *f* - 3. [delight] placer *m*; it's a ~, my ~ no hay de qué.

pleat [pliːt] ◇ *n* pliegue *m*. ◇ *vt* plisar.

pled [pled] *pt & pp* ▷ **plead**.

pledge [pledʒ] ◇ *n* - 1. [promise] promesa *f* - 2. [token] señal *f*, prenda *f*. ◇ *vt* - 1. [promise] prometer - 2. [commit]: to ~ sb to sthg hacer jurar a alguien algo; to ~ o.s. to comprometerse a - 3. [pawn] empeñar.

plentiful ['plentɪfʊl] *adj* abundante.

plenty ['plentɪ] ◇ *n* (*U*) abundancia *f*. ◇ *pron*: we've got ~ tenemos de sobra; that's ~ es más que suficiente; ~ of mucho(cha).

pliable ['plaɪəbl], **pliant** ['plaɪənt] *adj* flexible.

pliers ['plaɪəz] *npl* tenazas *fpl*, alicates *mpl*.

plight [plaɪt] *n* grave situación *f*.

plimsoll ['plɪmsəl] *n UK* playera *f*, zapato *m* de tenis.

plinth [plɪnθ] *n* [for statue] peana *f*; [for pillar] plinto *m*.

PLO (*abbr of* **Palestine Liberation Organization**) *n* OLP *f*.

plod [plɒd] (*pt & pp* -ded, *cont* -ding) *vi* - 1. [walk slowly] caminar con paso cansino - 2. [work steadily]: to ~ away at sthg trabajar pacientemente en algo.

plodder ['plɒdə^r] *n pej* persona *f* mediocre pero voluntariosa (en el trabajo).

plonk [plɒŋk] *n* (*U*) *UK inf* [wine] vino *m* peleón.
◆ **plonk down** *vt sep inf* dejar caer.

plot [plɒt] (*pt & pp* -ted, *cont* -ting) ◇ *n* - 1. [plan] complot *m*, conspiración *f* - 2. [story] argumento *m*, trama *f* - 3. [of land] parcela *f*. ◇ *vt* - 1. [plan] tramar, urdir - 2. [on map, graph] trazar. ◇ *vi*: to ~ (to do sthg) tramar (hacer algo); to ~ against conspirar contra.

plotter ['plɒtə^r] *n* - 1. [schemer] conspirador *m*, -ra *f* - 2. COMPUT plotter *m*.

plough *UK*, **plow** *US* [plaʊ] ◇ *n* arado *m*. ◇ *vt* arar.
◆ **plough into** ◇ *vt sep* [invest] invertir. ◇ *vt fus* [hit] chocar contra.

ploughman's ['plaʊmənz] (*pl inv*) *n UK*: ~ (lunch) queso, cebolletas y ensalada con pan.

plow *etc US* = **plough** *etc*.

ploy [plɔɪ] *n* táctica *f*, estratagema *f*.

pluck [plʌk] ◇ *vt* - 1. [fruit, flower] coger - 2. [pull sharply] arrancar - 3. [bird] desplumar - 4. [eyebrows] depilar - 5. [instrument] puntear. ◇ *n dated* valor *m*, ánimo *m*.
◆ **pluck up** *vt fus*: to ~ up the courage to do sthg armarse de valor para hacer algo.

plucky ['plʌkɪ] (*compar* -ier, *superl* -iest) *adj dated* valiente.

plug [plʌg] (*pt & pp* -ged, *cont* -ging) ◇ *n* - 1. ELEC enchufe *m* - 2. [for bath or sink] tapón *m*. ◇ *vt* - 1. [hole, leak] tapar, taponar - 2. *inf* [mention favourably] dar publicidad a.
◆ **plug in** *vt sep* enchufar.

plughole ['plʌghəʊl] *n* desagüe *m*.

plug-in *n* COMPUT plug-in *m*.

plum [plʌm] ◇ *adj* - 1. [colour] de color ciruela - 2. [choice]: ~ job chollo *m*. ◇ *n* [fruit] ciruela *f*.

plumb [plʌm] ◇ *adv* - 1. *UK* [exactly]: ~ in the middle justo en medio - 2. *US* [completely] completamente. ◇ *vt*: to ~ the depths of alcanzar las cotas más bajas de.

plumber ['plʌmə^r] *n* fontanero *m*, -ra *f Esp*, plomero *m*, -ra *f Amér*, gásfiter *mf Chile*, gásfitero *m*, -ra *f Perú*.

plumbing ['plʌmɪŋ] *n* (*U*) - 1. [fittings] tuberías *fpl* - 2. [work] fontanería *f*, plomería *f Amér*.

plume [pluːm] *n* **- 1.** [feather] pluma *f* **- 2.** [decoration, of smoke] penacho *m*.

plummet ['plʌmɪt] *vi* caer en picado.

plump [plʌmp] *adj* regordete(ta), rollizo(za).

◆ **plump for** *vt fus* optar OR decidirse por.

◆ **plump up** *vt sep* ahuecar.

plum pudding *n* budín navideño con pasas.

plunder ['plʌndə'] ◇ *n* **- 1.** [stealing, raiding] saqueo *m*, pillaje *m* **- 2.** [stolen goods] botín *m*. ◇ *vt* saquear.

plunge [plʌndʒ] ◇ *n* [dive] zambullida *f*; **to take the ~** [get married] dar el paso decisivo; [take risk] lanzarse. ◇ *vt* **- 1.** [knife etc] **to ~ sthg into** hundir algo en **- 2.** [into darkness, water] **to ~ sthg into** sumergir algo en. ◇ *vi* **- 1.** [dive] zambullirse **- 2.** [decrease] bajar vertiginosamente.

plunger ['plʌndʒə'] *n* [for blocked pipes] desatascador *m*.

pluperfect [,pluː'pɜːfɪkt] *n*: **~ (tense)** (pretérito *m*) pluscuamperfecto *m*.

plural ['pluərəl] ◇ *adj* [gen] plural. ◇ *n* plural *m*; **in the ~** en plural.

plus [plʌs] (*pl* **-es** OR **-ses**) ◇ *adj* [or more]: **35-~** 35 o más. ◇ *n* **- 1.** MATH [sign] signo *m* más **- 2.** [bonus] ventaja *f*. ◇ *prep* más. ◇ *conj* además.

plush [plʌʃ] *adj* lujoso(sa).

plus sign *n* signo *m* más.

Pluto ['pluːtəʊ] *n* [planet] Plutón *m*.

plutonium [pluː'təʊnɪəm] *n* plutonio *m*.

ply [plaɪ] (*pt* & *pp* **plied**) ◇ *vt* **- 1.** [trade] ejercer **- 2.** [supply, provide]: **to ~ sb with sthg** [questions] acosar a alguien con algo; [food, drink] no parar de ofrecer a alguien algo. ◇ *vi* navegar.

plywood ['plaɪwʊd] *n* contrachapado *m*.

p.m., pm (*abbr of* **post meridiem**): **at 3 ~** a las tres de la tarde.

PM *n abbr of* **prime minister**.

PMS, PMT (*abbr of* **premenstrual syndrome, premenstrual tension**) *n* síndrome *m* premenstrual.

pneumatic [njuː'mætɪk] *adj* [tyre, chair] neumático(ca).

pneumatic drill *n* martillo *m* neumático.

pneumonia [njuː'məʊnjə] *n (U)* pulmonía *f*.

poach [pəʊtʃ] ◇ *vt* **- 1.** [game] cazar furtivamente; [fish] pescar furtivamente **- 2.** [copy] plagiar **- 3.** CULIN [salmon] cocer; [egg] escalfar. ◇ *vi* [for game] cazar furtivamente; [for fish] pescar furtivamente.

poacher ['pəʊtʃə'] *n* [hunter] cazador furtivo *m*, cazadora furtiva *f*; [fisherman] pescador furtivo *m*, pescadora furtiva *f*.

poaching ['pəʊtʃɪŋ] *n* [for game] caza *f* furtiva; [for fish] pesca *f* furtiva.

PO Box (*abbr of* **Post Office Box**) *n* apdo. *m*, casilla *f* (de correos) *Andes, CSur*.

pocket ['pɒkɪt] ◇ *n* **- 1.** [in clothes] bolsillo *m*; **to be £10 out of ~** salir perdiendo 10 libras; **to pick sb's ~** vaciar a alguien el bolsillo **- 2.** [in car door etc] bolsa *f*, bolsillo *m* **- 3.** [of resistance] foco *m*; [of air] bolsa *f*; [on pool, snooker table] tronera *f*. ◇ *vt* **- 1.** [place in pocket] meterse en el bolsillo **- 2.** [steal] birlar. ◇ *adj* de bolsillo.

pocketbook ['pɒkɪtbʊk] *n* **- 1.** [notebook] libreta *f* **- 2.** US [handbag] bolso *m*; [wallet] cartera *f*.

pocketknife ['pɒkɪtnaɪf] (*pl* **-knives** [-naɪvz]) *n* navaja *f* (de bolsillo).

pocket money *n* **- 1.** [from parents] propina *f* **- 2.** [for minor expenses] dinero *m* para gastar.

pockmark ['pɒkmɑːk] *n* marca *f*, señal *f*.

pod [pɒd] *n* [of plants] vaina *f*.

podgy ['pɒdʒɪ] (*compar* **-ier**, *superl* **-iest**) *adj inf* gordinflón(ona).

podiatrist [pə'daɪətrɪst] *n* US podólogo *m*, -ga *f*, pedicuro *m*, -ra *f*.

podium ['pəʊdɪəm] (*pl* **-diums** OR **-dia** [-dɪə]) *n* podio *m*.

poem ['pəʊɪm] *n* poema *m*, poesía *f*.

poet ['pəʊɪt] *n* poeta *m* OR *f*.

poetic [pəʊ'etɪk] *adj* poético(ca).

poet laureate *n* poeta de la corte británica que escribe poemas para ocasiones oficiales.

poetry ['pəʊɪtrɪ] *n* poesía *f*.

poignant ['pɔɪnjənt] *adj* patético(ca), conmovedor(ra).

point [pɔɪnt] ◇ *n* **- 1.** [gen] punto *m* **- 2.** [in time] momento *m*; **at that ~** en ese momento **- 3.** [tip] punta *f* **- 4.** [detail, argument] **to make a ~** hacer una observación; **to have a ~** tener razón **- 5.** [main idea]: **the ~ is ...** lo fundamental es ...; **that's the whole ~ of** eso se trata; **to miss the ~ of** no coger la idea de; **to get** OR **come to the ~** ir al grano; **it's beside the ~** no viene al caso **- 6.** [feature] aspecto *m*; **weak/strong ~** punto *m* débil/fuerte **- 7.** [purpose] sentido *m*; **what's the ~?** ¿para qué?; **there's no ~ in it** no tiene sentido **- 8.** [decimal point] coma *f*; **two ~ six** dos coma seis **- 9.** UK ELEC toma *f* de corriente **- 10.** GEOGR punta *f* **- 11.** *phr*: **to make a ~ of doing sthg** preocuparse de hacer algo. ◇ *vt*: **to ~ a gun at sthg/sb** apuntar a algo/alguien con una pistola; **to ~ one's finger at sthg/sb** señalar algo/a alguien con el dedo. ◇ *vi* **- 1.** [indicate with finger]: **to ~ at sthg/sb, to ~ to sthg/sb** señalar algo/a alguien con el dedo **- 2.** *fig* [suggest]: **everything ~s to her guilt** todo indica que ella es la culpable.

◆ **points** *npl* **- 1.** UK RAIL agujas *fpl* **- 2.** AUT platinos *mpl*.

◆ **up to a point** *adv* hasta cierto punto.

◆ **on the point of** *prep*: **to be on the ~ of doing sthg** estar a punto de hacer algo.

◆ **point out** *vt sep* [person, object, fact] señalar, indicar; [mistake] hacer notar.

point-blank *adv* **- 1.** [refuse, deny] categóricamente **- 2.** [at close range] a quemarropa.

pointed ['pɔɪntɪd] *adj* **- 1.** [sharp, angular] en punta, puntiagudo(da) **- 2.** [cutting, incisive] intencionado(da).

pointer ['pɔɪntə'] *n* **- 1.** [piece of advice] consejo *m* **- 2.** [needle] aguja *f* **- 3.** COMPUT puntero *m*.

pointless ['pɔɪntlɪs] *adj* sin sentido, inútil; **it's ~** no tiene sentido.

point of view (*pl* **points of view**) *n* **- 1.** [opinion] punto *m* de vista **- 2.** [aspect, perspective] perspectiva *f*.

poise [pɔɪz] *n* [self-assurance] aplomo *m*, serenidad *f*; [elegance] elegancia *f*.

poised [pɔɪzd] *adj* **- 1.** [ready]: **to be ~ to do sthg** estar listo(ta) para hacer algo **- 2.** [calm and dignified] sereno(na).

poison ['pɔɪzn] *n* veneno *m*. ◇ *vt* [gen-intentionally] envenenar; [-unintentionally] intoxicar.

poisoning ['pɔɪznɪŋ] *n* [intentional] envenenamiento *m*; [unintentional] intoxicación *f*.

poisonous ['pɔɪznəs] *adj* **- 1.** [substance, gas] tóxico(ca) **- 2.** [snake] venenoso(sa).

poke [pəʊk] ◇ *vt* **- 1.** [with finger, stick] empujar; [with elbow] dar un codazo a; [fire] atizar; **to ~ sb in the eye** meter el dedo en el ojo de alguien **- 2.** [push, stuff]: **to ~ sthg into** meter algo en algo. ◇ *vi* [protrude]: **to ~ out of sthg** sobresalir por algo.

◆ **poke about, poke around** *vi inf* fisgonear, hurgar.

poker ['pəʊkə'] *n* **- 1.** [game] póker *m* **- 2.** [for fire] atizador *m*.

poker-faced [-,feɪst] *adj* con cara inexpresiva.

poky ['pəʊkɪ] (*comp* **-ier**, *superl* **-iest**) *adj pej*: **a ~ little room** un cuartucho.

Poland ['pəʊlənd] *n* Polonia.

polar ['pəʊlə'] *adj* polar.

Polaroid® ['pəʊlərɔɪd] *n* **- 1.** [camera] polaroid® *f* **- 2.** [photograph] fotografía *f* polaroid.

pole [pəʊl] *n* **- 1.** [rod, post] poste *m*; [for tent, flag] mástil *m*; **telegraph ~** poste *m* telegráfico **- 2.** ELEC & GEOGR polo *m*.

Pole [pəʊl] *n* polaco *m*, -ca *f*.

pole vault *n*: **the ~** el salto con pértiga.

police [pə'liːs] ◇ *npl* [police force]: **the ~** la policía. ◇ *vt* mantener el orden en, vigilar.

police car *n* coche *m* patrulla, auto *m*

patrulla *CAm, Chile, Méx*, patrullero *m CSur*, patrulla *f Col, Méx*.

police constable *n UK* policía *m* OR *f*.

police force *n* cuerpo *m* de policía.

policeman [pə'liːsmən] (*pl* **-men** [-mən]) *n* policía *m*.

police officer *n* agente *m* OR *f* de policía.

police record *n*: **(to have a) ~** (tener) antecedentes *mpl* policiales.

police station *n* comisaría *f* (de policía).

policewoman [pə'liːs,wʊmən] (*pl* **-women** [-,wɪmɪn]) *n* (mujer *f*) policía *f*.

policy ['pɒləsɪ] (*pl* **-ies**) *n* **- 1.** [plan, practice] política *f* **- 2.** [document, agreement] póliza *f*.

polio ['pəʊlɪəʊ] *n* polio *f*.

polish ['pɒlɪʃ] ◇ *n* **- 1.** [for floor, furniture] cera *f*; [for shoes] betún *m*; [for metal] abrillantador *m*; [for nails] esmalte *m* **- 2.** [shine] brillo *m*, lustre *m* **- 3.** *fig* [refinement] refinamiento *m*. ◇ *vt* [stone, wood] pulir; [floor] encerar; [shoes, car] limpiar; [cutlery, silver, glasses] sacar brillo a.

◆ **polish off** *vt sep inf* [food] zamparse; [job] despachar.

Polish ['pəʊlɪʃ] ◇ *adj* polaco(ca). ◇ *n* [language] polaco *m*. ◇ *npl*: **the ~** los polacos.

polished ['pɒlɪʃt] *adj* **- 1.** [person, manner] refinado(da) **- 2.** [performance, speech] esmerado(da).

polite [pə'laɪt] *adj* educado(da), cortés.

politic ['pɒlətɪk] *adj fml* oportuno(na), conveniente.

political [pə'lɪtɪkl] *adj* [concerning politics] político(ca).

politically correct [pə,lɪtɪklɪ-] *adj* políticamente correcto(ta).

politician [,pɒlɪ'tɪʃn] *n* político *m*, -ca *f*.

politics ['pɒlətɪks] ◇ *n* (U) política *f*. ◇ *npl* **- 1.** [personal beliefs] ideas *fpl* políticas **- 2.** [of a group, area] política *f*.

polka ['pɒlkə] *n* polca *f*.

polka dot *n* lunar *m* (en un vestido).

poll [pəʊl] ◇ *n* [vote] votación *f*; [of opinion] encuesta *f*. ◇ *vt* **- 1.** [people] sondear **- 2.** [votes] obtener.

◆ **polls** *npl*: **the ~s** las elecciones, los comicios.

pollen ['pɒlən] *n* polen *m*.

polling booth ['pəʊlɪŋ-] *n* cabina *f* electoral.

polling day ['pəʊlɪŋ-] *n UK* día *m* de las elecciones.

polling station ['pəʊlɪŋ-] *n* colegio *m* OR centro *m* electoral.

pollute [pə'luːt] *vt* contaminar.

pollution [pə'luːʃn] *n* (U) **- 1.** [process of polluting] contaminación *f* **- 2.** [impurities] sustancias *fpl* contaminantes.

polo ['pəʊləʊ] *n* polo *m*.

polo neck UK n -1. [neck] cuello m alto
-2. [jumper] jersey m de cuello alto.
polyethylene US = polythene.
Polynesia [,pɒlɪ'niːʒə] n Polinesia.
polystyrene [,pɒlɪ'staɪriːn] n poliestireno
m.
polytechnic [,pɒlɪ'teknɪk] n UK escuela f
politécnica.
polythene UK ['pɒlɪθiːn], **polyethylene**
US ['pɒlɪ'eθɪliːn] n polietileno m, politeno
m.
polythene bag n UK bolsa f de plástico.
pomegranate ['pɒmɪ,grænɪt] n granada f.
pomp [pɒmp] n pompa f.
pompom ['pɒmpɒm] n borla f, pompón m.
pompous ['pɒmpəs] adj -1. [self-important]
presumido(da), pretencioso(sa) -2. [style]
pomposo(sa); [building] ostentoso(sa).
pond [pɒnd] n estanque m.
ponder ['pɒndə'] vt considerar.
ponderous ['pɒndərəs] adj -1. [speech,
book] pesado(da) -2. [action, walk] len-
to(ta) y torpe.
pong [pɒŋ] UK inf n (olor m a) peste f.
pontoon [pɒn'tuːn] n -1. [bridge] pontón m
-2. UK [game] veintiuna f.
pony ['pəʊnɪ] (pl -ies) n poni m.
ponytail ['pəʊnɪteɪl] n coleta f (de caballo).
pony-trekking [-,trekɪŋ] n (U): to go ~
hacer una excursión en poni.
poodle ['puːdl] n caniche m.
pool [puːl] ⋄ n -1. [of water, blood, ink]
charco m; [pond] estanque m -2. [swimming
pool] piscina f -3. [of light] foco m -4. COMM
[fund] fondo m común -5. [of people,
things]: typing ~ servicio m de mecanografía; car ~ parque m móvil -6. [game] billar
m americano. ⋄ vt [resources, funds] juntar;
[knowledge] poner en común.
 ◆ **pools** npl UK: the ~s las quinielas.
poor [pɔː'] ⋄ adj -1. [gen] pobre; ~ old
John! ¡el pobre de John!; you ~ thing! ¡po-
brecito! -2. [quality, result] malo(la) -3.
[prospects, chances] escaso(sa). ⋄ npl: the
~ los pobres.
poorly ['pɔːlɪ] ⋄ adj UK pachucho(cha).
⋄ adv mal; ~ off pobre.
pop [pɒp] (pt & pp -ped, cont -ping) ⋄ n
-1. [music] (música f) pop m -2. (U) inf [fizzy
drink] gaseosa f -3. esp US inf [father] papá m
-4. [sound] pequeña explosión f. ⋄ vt
-1. [balloon, bubble] pinchar -2. [put
quickly]: to ~ sthg into meter algo en m.
⋄ vi -1. [balloon] explotar, reventar; [cork,
button] saltar -2. [eyes] salirse de las órbitas
-3. [ears]: her ears ~ped se le destaparon
los oídos -4. [go quickly]: **I'm just popping
round to the shop** voy un momento a la
tienda.
 ◆ **pop in** vi entrar un momento.
 ◆ **pop up** vi aparecer de repente.

pop concert n concierto m de música pop.
popcorn ['pɒpkɔːn] n palomitas fpl (de
maíz).
pope [pəʊp] n papa m.
pop group n grupo m (de música) pop.
poplar ['pɒplə'] n álamo m.
poppy ['pɒpɪ] (pl -ies) n amapola f.
Popsicle® ['pɒpsɪkl] n US polo m.
populace ['pɒpjʊləs] n: the ~ [masses] el
populacho; [people] el pueblo.
popular ['pɒpjʊlə'] adj -1. [gen] popular;
[person] estimado(da) -2. [belief, attitude,
discontent] generalizado(da), común
-3. [newspaper, politics] para las masas.
popularize, -ise ['pɒpjʊləraɪz] vt -1. [make
popular] popularizar -2. [simplify] vulgarizar.
population [,pɒpjʊ'leɪʃn] n población f.
porcelain ['pɔːsəlɪn] n porcelana f.
porch [pɔːtʃ] n -1. [entrance] porche m, pórtico m -2. US [verandah] porche m.
porcupine ['pɔːkjʊpaɪn] n puerco m espín.
pore [pɔː'] n poro m.
 ◆ **pore over** vt fus estudiar esmerada-
mente.
pork [pɔːk] n carne f de cerdo.
pork pie n empanada f de carne de cerdo.
pornography [pɔː'nɒgrəfɪ] n pornografía
f.
porous ['pɔːrəs] adj poroso(sa).
porridge ['pɒrɪdʒ] n papilla f OR gachas fpl
de avena.
port [pɔːt] n -1. [coastal town, harbour]
puerto m -2. NAUT [left-hand side] babor m
-3. [drink] oporto m -4. COMPUT puerto m.
portable ['pɔːtəbl] adj portátil.
portent ['pɔːtənt] n literary presagio m, augurio m.
porter ['pɔːtə'] n -1. UK [in block of flats]
portero m, -ra f; [in public building, hotel]
conserje m OR f -2. [for luggage] mozo m.
portfolio [,pɔːt'fəʊljəʊ] (pl -s) n -1. ART,
FIN & POL cartera f -2. [sample of work] carpeta f.
porthole ['pɔːthəʊl] n portilla f.
portion ['pɔːʃn] n -1. [part, section] porción
f -2. [of chips, vegetables etc] ración f.
portly ['pɔːtlɪ] (compar -ier, superl -iest) adj
corpulento(ta).
port of call n -1. NAUT puerto m de escala
-2. fig [on journey] escala f, parada f.
portrait ['pɔːtrɪt] n -1. [picture] retrato m
-2. COMPUT formato m vertical.
portray [pɔː'treɪ] vt -1. [represent - in a play,
film] representar -2. [describe] describir
-3. [paint] retratar.
Portugal ['pɔːtʃʊgl] n Portugal.
Portuguese [,pɔːtʃʊ'giːz] ⋄ adj portu-
gués(esa). ⋄ n [language] portugués m.
⋄ npl: the ~ los portugueses.

pose [pəʊz] ◇ n -**1.** [position, stance] postura f -**2.** pej [pretence, affectation] pose f. ◇ vt -**1.** [problem, threat] presentar -**2.** [question] formular. ◇ vi -**1.** [model] posar -**2.** pej [behave affectedly] adoptar poses -**3.** [pretend to be]: **to ~ as sb/sthg** fingir ser alguien/algo.

posh [pɒʃ] adj inf -**1.** [hotel, area etc] de lujo, elegante -**2.** UK [person, accent] afectado(da).

position [pə'zɪʃn] ◇ n -**1.** [gen] posición f -**2.** [right place] sitio m, lugar m -**3.** [status] rango m -**4.** [job] puesto m -**5.** [in a race, competition] lugar m -**6.** [state, situation] situación f -**7.** [stance, opinion]: **~ on** postura f respecto a. ◇ vt colocar.

positive ['pɒzətɪv] adj -**1.** [gen] positivo(va); **the test was ~** la prueba dio positivo -**2.** [sure]: **to be ~ (about)** estar seguro(ra) (de) -**3.** [optimistic, confident]: **to be ~ (about)** ser optimista (respecto a) -**4.** [definite - action] decisivo(va); [- decision] categórico(ca) -**5.** [irrefutable - evidence, fact] irrefutable, evidente; [- proof] concluyente.

posse ['pɒsɪ] n US -**1.** [to pursue criminal] grupo m de hombres a caballo -**2.** [group] grupo m.

possess [pə'zes] vt -**1.** [gen] poseer -**2.** [subj: emotion] adueñarse de.

possession [pə'zeʃn] n posesión f.
➙ **possessions** npl bienes mpl.

possessive [pə'zesɪv] adj -**1.** [gen] posesivo(va) -**2.** pej [selfish] egoísta.

possibility [ˌpɒsə'bɪlətɪ] (pl -ies) n posibilidad f; **there's a ~ that ...** es posible que ...

possible ['pɒsəbl] ◇ adj -**1.** [gen] posible; **as soon as ~** cuanto antes; **as much as ~** [quantity] todo lo posible; [to the greatest possible extent] en la medida de lo posible; **I go as often as ~** voy siempre que puedo; **it's ~ that she'll come** es posible que venga -**2.** [viable - plan etc] viable, factible.

possibly ['pɒsəblɪ] adv -**1.** [perhaps] posiblemente, quizás -**2.** [within one's power]: **could you ~ help me?** ¿te importaría ayudarme? -**3.** [to show surprise]: **how could he ~ do that?** ¿cómo demonios pudo hacer eso? -**4.** [for emphasis]: **I can't ~ do it** no puedo hacerlo de ninguna manera.

post [pəʊst] ◇ n -**1.** [service]: **the ~** el correo; **by ~** por correo -**2.** (U) [letters etc] cartas fpl -**3.** [delivery] reparto m -**4.** UK [collection] colecta f -**5.** [pole] poste m -**6.** [position, job] puesto m -**7.** MIL puesto m. ◇ vt -**1.** [put in letterbox] echar al correo; [send by mail] mandar por correo -**2.** [transfer] enviar, destinar -**3.** COMPUT [message, query] enviar.

postage ['pəʊstɪdʒ] n franqueo m, porte m;

~ and packing gastos mpl de envío.

postal ['pəʊstl] adj postal.

postal order n giro m postal.

postal vote n voto m por correo.

postbox ['pəʊstbɒks] n UK buzón m.

postcard ['pəʊstkɑːd] n postal f.

postcode ['pəʊstkəʊd] n UK código m postal.

postdate [ˌpəʊst'deɪt] vt poner posfecha a; **a ~d cheque** extender un cheque con fecha posterior.

poster ['pəʊstə'] n cartel m, póster m.

poste restante [ˌpəʊst'restɑːnt] n esp UK lista f de correos.

posterior [pɒ'stɪərɪə'] n hum trasero m.

postgraduate [ˌpəʊst'grædʒʊət] n posgraduado m, -da f.

posthumous ['pɒstjʊməs] adj póstumo(ma).

postman ['pəʊstmən] (pl -men [-mən]) n cartero m.

postmark ['pəʊstmɑːk] n matasellos m inv.

postmortem [ˌpəʊst'mɔːtəm] n [autopsy] autopsia f.

post office n -**1.** [organization]: **the Post Office** ≃ Correos m inv -**2.** [building] oficina f de correos.

post office box n apartado m de correos, casilla f de correos Andes & RP.

postpone [ˌpəʊst'pəʊn] vt posponer.

postscript ['pəʊstskrɪpt] n [additional message] posdata f; fig [additional information] posdata f, nota f final.

posture ['pɒstʃə'] n lit & fig postura f; **~ on sthg** postura hacia algo.

postwar [ˌpəʊst'wɔː'] adj de (la) posguerra.

posy ['pəʊzɪ] (pl -ies) n ramillete m.

pot [pɒt] (pt & pp -ted, cont -ting) ◇ n -**1.** [for cooking] olla f -**2.** [for tea] tetera f; [for coffee] cafetera f -**3.** [for paint] bote m; [for jam] tarro m -**4.** [flowerpot] tiesto m, maceta f -**5.** (U) inf [cannabis] maría f, hierba f -**6.** phr: **to go to ~** ir al traste. ◇ vt plantar (en un tiesto).

potassium [pə'tæsɪəm] n potasio m.

potato [pə'teɪtəʊ] (pl -es) n patata f.

potato peeler [-ˌpiːlə'] n pelapatatas m inv Esp, pelapapas m inv Amér.

potent ['pəʊtənt] adj -**1.** [powerful, influential] poderoso(sa) -**2.** [drink, drug] fuerte -**3.** [sexually capable] potente.

potential [pə'tenʃl] ◇ adj potencial, posible. ◇ n (U) potencial m; **to have ~** tener posibilidades, prometer.

potentially [pə'tenʃəlɪ] adv en potencia.

pothole ['pɒthəʊl] n -**1.** [in road] bache m -**2.** [underground] cueva f.

potholing ['pɒtˌhəʊlɪŋ] n UK espeleología f.

potion ['pəʊʃn] n poción f.

potluck [,pɒt'lʌk] *n*: **to take ~** [gen] elegir a ojo; [at meal] conformarse con lo que haya.

potshot ['pɒt,ʃɒt] *n*: **to take a ~ (at sthg/ sb)** disparar (a algo/alguien) sin apuntar.

potted ['pɒtɪd] *adj* **- 1.** [plant] en tiesto **- 2.** [meat, fish] en conserva.

potter ['pɒtə'] *n* alfarero *m*, -ra *f*, ceramista *m* OR *f*.
◆ **potter about, potter around** *vi* UK entretenerse.

pottery ['pɒtərɪ] (*pl* -ies) *n* **- 1.** [gen] cerámica *f*, alfarería *f* **- 2.** [factory] fábrica *f* de cerámica.

potty ['pɒtɪ] (*compar* -ier, *superl* -iest, *pl* -ies) UK *inf* ⋄ *adj* [person] chalado(da). ⋄ *n* orinal *m*.

pouch [paʊtʃ] *n* **- 1.** [small bag] bolsa *f* pequeña; [for tobacco] petaca *f* **- 2.** [on animal's body] bolsa *f* (abdominal).

poultry ['pəʊltrɪ] ⋄ *n* [meat] carne *f* de pollería. ⋄ *npl* [birds] aves *fpl* de corral.

pounce [paʊns] *vi* [leap]: **to ~ (on** OR **upon)** abalanzarse (sobre).

pound [paʊnd] ⋄ *n* **- 1.** [unit of money, weight] libra *f* **- 2.** [for cars] depósito *m* (de coches); [for dogs] perrera *f*. ⋄ *vt* **- 1.** [hammer on] golpear, aporrear **- 2.** [pulverize] machacar. ⋄ *vi* **- 1.** [hammer]: **to ~ on sthg** golpear OR aporrear algo **- 2.** [beat, throb] palpitar; **her heart was ~ing** le palpitaba el corazón.

pound sterling *n* libra *f* esterlina.

pour [pɔː'] ⋄ *vt* **- 1.** [cause to flow]: **to ~ sthg (into)** echar OR verter algo (en); **to ~ sthg down the sink** tirar algo por el fregadero; **to ~ sb a drink, to ~ a drink for sb** servirle una copa a alguien; **can I ~ you a cup of tea?** ¿quieres que te sirva una taza de té? ⋄ *vi* [liquid] chorrear; [smoke] salir a borbotones. ⋄ *v impers* [rain hard] llover a cántaros; **it's ~ing (down)** está lloviendo a cántaros.
◆ **pour in** *vi* llegar a raudales.
◆ **pour out** ⋄ *vt sep* **- 1.** [empty] echar, vaciar **- 2.** [serve] servir. ⋄ *vi* [rush out] salir en manada.

pouring ['pɔːrɪŋ] *adj* [rain] torrencial.

pout [paʊt] *vi* [showing displeasure] hacer pucheros; [being provocative] hacer un gesto provocador con los labios.

poverty ['pɒvətɪ] *n lit* & *fig* pobreza *f*.

poverty-stricken *adj* necesitado(da).

powder ['paʊdə'] ⋄ *n* polvo *m*; [make-up] polvos *mpl*. ⋄ *vt* poner polvos en; **to ~ o.s.** darse polvos, empolvarse.

powder compact *n* polvera *f*.

powdered ['paʊdəd] *adj* [in powder form] en polvo.

powder puff *n* borla *f*.

powder room *n* servicios *mpl* de señoras, tocador *m*.

power ['paʊə'] ⋄ *n* **- 1.** (U) [authority, control] poder *m*; **to come to/take ~** llegar al/ hacerse con el poder; **to be in ~** estar en el poder **- 2.** [ability] facultad *f*; **it isn't within my ~ to do it** no está dentro de mis posibilidades hacerlo; **I'll do everything in my ~ to help** haré todo lo que pueda por ayudar **- 3.** [legal authority] autoridad *f*, competencia *f* **- 4.** [physical strength] fuerza *f* **- 5.** [energy - solar, steam etc] energía *f* **- 6.** [electricity] corriente *f*; **to turn the ~ on/off** dar/cortar la corriente **- 7.** [powerful nation, person, group] potencia *f* **- 8.** [phr]: **to do sb a ~ of good** sentar de maravilla a alguien. ⋄ *vt* propulsar, impulsar.

powerboat ['paʊəbəʊt] *n* motora *f*.

power cut *n* apagón *m*, corte *m* de corriente.

power failure *n* corte *m* de corriente.

powerful ['paʊəfʊl] *adj* **- 1.** [gen] poderoso(sa) **- 2.** [blow, voice, drug] potente **- 3.** [speech, film] conmovedor(ra).

powerless ['paʊəlɪs] *adj* **- 1.** [helpless] impotente **- 2.** [unable]: **to be ~ to do sthg** no poder hacer algo.

power point *n* UK toma *f* (de corriente).

power station *n* central *f* eléctrica.

power steering *n* dirección *f* asistida.

pp (*abbr of* procurationem) p.p.

p & p *abbr of* postage and packing.

PR *n* **- 1.** *abbr of* proportional representation **- 2.** *abbr of* public relations.

practicable ['præktɪkəbl] *adj* viable, factible.

practical ['præktɪkl] ⋄ *adj* **- 1.** [gen] práctico(ca) **- 2.** [skilled with hands] hábil, mañoso(sa). ⋄ *n* práctica *f*.

practicality [,præktɪ'kælətɪ] *n* viabilidad *f*.

practical joke *n* broma *f* pesada.

practically ['præktɪklɪ] *adv* **- 1.** [in a practical way] de manera práctica **- 2.** [almost] prácticamente, casi.

practice ['præktɪs] *n* **- 1.** [training, training session] práctica *f*; SPORT entrenamiento *m*; MUS ensayo *m*; **I'm out of ~** me falta práctica; **~ makes perfect** se aprende a base de práctica **- 2.** [reality]: **to put sthg into ~** llevar algo a la práctica; **in ~** [in fact] en la práctica **- 3.** [habit, regular activity] costumbre *f* **- 4.** [of profession] ejercicio *m* **- 5.** [business - of doctor] consulta *f*; [- of lawyer] bufete *m*, despacho *m*.

practicing US = **practising**.

practise, practice US ['præktɪs] ⋄ *vt* **- 1.** SPORT entrenar; MUS & THEATRE ensayar **- 2.** [religion, economy, safe sex] practicar **- 3.** [medicine, law] ejercer. ⋄ *vi* **- 1.** [train-gen] practicar; [-SPORT] entrenarse - **2.** [as doctor] practicar; [as lawyer] ejercer.

practising, practicing US ['præktɪsɪŋ] *adj* - **1.** [Catholic, Jew etc] practicante - **2.** [doctor, lawyer] en ejercicio - **3.** [homosexual] activo(va).

practitioner [præk'tɪʃnə'] *n*: medical ~ médico *m*, -ca *f*.

Prague [prɑːg] *n* Praga.

prairie ['preərɪ] *n* pradera *f*, prado *m*.

praise [preɪz] ◇ *n* (U) elogio *m*, alabanza *f*. ◇ *vt* elogiar, alabar.

praiseworthy ['preɪz,wɜːðɪ] *adj* digno(na) de elogio, encomiable.

pram [præm] *n* cochecito *m* de niño.

prance [prɑːns] *vi* - **1.** [person] ir dando brincos - **2.** [horse] hacer cabriolas.

prank [præŋk] *n* diablura *f*, travesura *f*.

prawn [prɔːn] *n* gamba *f*.

pray [preɪ] *vi* rezar, orar; to ~ to sb rogar a alguien; to ~ for sthg/for sthg to happen *lit & fig* rogar algo/que pase algo.

prayer [preə'] *n* - **1.** RELIG oración *f* - **2.** *fig* [strong hope] ruego *m*, súplica *f*.

prayer book *n* devocionario *m*, misal *m*.

preach [priːtʃ] ◇ *vt* [gen] predicar; [sermon] dar. ◇ *vi* - **1.** RELIG: to ~ (to) predicar (a) - **2.** *pej* [pontificate]: to ~ (at) sermonear (a).

preacher ['priːtʃə'] *n* - **1.** predicador *m*, -ra *f* - **2.** US [minister] pastor *m*, -ra *f*.

precarious [prɪ'keərɪəs] *adj* precario(ria).

precaution [prɪ'kɔːʃn] *n* precaución *f*.

precede [prɪ'siːd] *vt* preceder.

precedence ['presɪdəns] *n*: to take ~ over tener prioridad sobre.

precedent ['presɪdənt] *n* precedente *m*.

precinct ['priːsɪŋkt] *n* - **1.** UK [shopping area] zona *f* comercial - **2.** US [district] distrito *m*.

◆ **precincts** *npl* recinto *m*.

precious ['preʃəs] *adj* - **1.** [gen] precioso(sa) - **2.** [memories, possessions] preciado(da) - **3.** [affected] afectado(da) - **4.** *iron*: **I've heard enough about your ~ dog!** ¡ya estoy cansado de tu dichoso perro!

precipice ['presɪpɪs] *n lit & fig* precipicio *m*.

precipitate [prɪ'sɪpɪteɪt] *vt* precipitar.

precise [prɪ'saɪs] *adj* preciso(sa), exacto(ta).

precisely [prɪ'saɪslɪ] *adv* - **1.** [with accuracy] exactamente - **2.** [exactly, literally] precisamente - **3.** [as confirmation]: **precisely!** ¡eso es!, ¡exactamente!

precision [prɪ'sɪʒn] *n* precisión *f*.

preclude [prɪ'kluːd] *vt fml* evitar, impedir; [possibility] excluir; to ~ sthg/sb from doing sthg impedir que algo/alguien haga algo.

precocious [prɪ'kəʊʃəs] *adj* precoz.

preconceived [ˌpriːkən'siːvd] *adj* preconcebido(da).

precondition [ˌpriːkən'dɪʃn] *n fml*: ~ (for) requisito *m* previo (para).

predator ['predətə'] *n* depredador *m*, -ra *f*; *fig* buitre *m* OR *f*.

predecessor ['priːdɪsesə'] *n* antecesor *m*, -ra *f*.

predicament [prɪ'dɪkəmənt] *n* apuro *m*, aprieto *m*.

predict [prɪ'dɪkt] *vt* predecir, pronosticar.

predictable [prɪ'dɪktəbl] *adj* - **1.** [result etc] previsible - **2.** [film, book, person] poco original.

prediction [prɪ'dɪkʃn] *n* predicción *f*, pronóstico *m*.

predispose [ˌpriːdɪs'pəʊz] *vt*: to be ~d to sthg/to do sthg [by nature] estar predispuesto(ta) a algo/a hacer algo.

predominant [prɪ'dɒmɪnənt] *adj* predominante.

predominantly [prɪ'dɒmɪnəntlɪ] *adv* fundamentalmente.

preempt [ˌpriː'empt] *vt* [make ineffective] adelantarse a.

preemptive [ˌpriː'emptɪv] *adj* preventivo(va).

preen [priːn] *vt* - **1.** [subj: bird] arreglar (con el pico); to ~ itself atusarse las plumas - **2.** *fig* [subj: person]: to ~ o.s. acicalarse.

prefab ['priːfæb] *n inf* casa *f* prefabricada.

preface ['prefɪs] *n*: ~ (to) prólogo *m* OR prefacio *m* (a).

prefect ['priːfekt] *n* UK [pupil] delegado *m*, -da *f* de curso.

prefer [prɪ'fɜː'] (*pt & pp* -red, *cont* -ring) *vt*: to ~ sthg (to) preferir algo (a); to ~ to do sthg preferir hacer algo.

preferable ['prefrəbl] *adj*: to be ~ (to) ser preferible (a).

preferably ['prefrəblɪ] *adv* preferentemente.

preference ['prefərəns] *n*: ~ (for) preferencia *f* (por).

preferential [ˌprefə'renʃl] *adj* preferente; to give sb ~ treatment dar tratamiento preferencial a alguien.

prefix ['priːfɪks] *n* prefijo *m*.

pregnancy ['pregnənsɪ] (*pl* -ies) *n* embarazo *m*.

pregnant ['pregnənt] *adj* - **1.** [woman] embarazada - **2.** [animal] preñada.

prehistoric [ˌpriːhɪ'stɒrɪk] *adj* prehistórico(ca).

prejudice ['predʒʊdɪs] ◇ *n*: ~ (against) prejuicio *m* (contra); ~ in favour of predisposición *f* a favor de. ◇ *vt* - **1.** [bias]: to ~ sb (in favour of/against) predisponer a alguien (a favor de/en contra de) - **2.** [harm] perjudicar.

prejudiced ['predʒʊdɪst] *adj* parcial; **to be ~ in favour of/against** estar predispuesto a favor de/en contra de.

preliminary [prɪ'lɪmɪnərɪ] (*pl* **-ies**) *adj* preliminar.

prelude ['prelju:d] *n* [event]: **~ (to)** preludio *m* (a).

premarital [,pri:'mærɪtl] *adj* prematrimonial.

premature ['premə,tjʊər] *adj* prematuro(ra).

premeditated [,pri:'medɪteɪtd] *adj* premeditado(da).

premenstrual syndrome, premenstrual tension [pri:'menstrʊəl-] *n* síndrome *m* premenstrual.

premier ['premjər] <> *adj* primero(ra). <> *n* primer ministro *m*, primera ministra *f*.

premiere ['premɪeər] *n* estreno *m*.

premise ['premɪs] *n* premisa *f*.
   ◆ **premises** *npl* local *m*; **on the ~s** en el local.

premium ['pri:mjəm] *n* prima *f*; **at a ~** [above usual value] por encima de su valor; [in great demand] muy solicitado(da).

premium bond *n UK boleto numerado emitido por el Estado que autoriza a participar en sorteos mensuales de dinero hasta su amortización.*

premonition [,premə'nɪʃn] *n* premonición *f*.

preoccupied [pri:'ɒkjʊpaɪd] *adj*: **~ (with)** preocupado(da) (por).

prep [prep] (*abbr of* **preparation**) *n (U) UK inf* tarea *f*, deberes *mpl*.

prepaid ['pri:peɪd] *adj* [post paid] porte pagado.

preparation [,prepə'reɪʃn] *n* [act of preparing] preparación *f*.
   ◆ **preparations** *npl* preparativos *mpl*; **to make ~s for** hacer los preparativos para.

preparatory [prɪ'pærətrɪ] *adj* preparatorio(ria), preliminar.

prep(aratory) school *n* [in UK] *colegio de pago para niños de 7 a 12 años*; [in US] *escuela privada de enseñanza secundaria y preparación para estudios superiores.*

prepare [prɪ'peər] <> *vt* preparar. <> *vi*: **to ~ for sthg/to do sthg** prepararse para algo/para hacer algo.

prepared [prɪ'peəd] *adj* **-1.** [gen] preparado(da) **-2.** [willing]: **to be ~ to do sthg** estar dispuesto(ta) a hacer algo.

preposition [,prepə'zɪʃn] *n* preposición *f*.

preposterous [prɪ'pɒstərəs] *adj* absurdo(da).

prep school *n inf abbr of* **preparatory school**.

prerequisite [,pri:'rekwɪzɪt] *n*: **~ (for)** requisito *m* (para).

prerogative [prɪ'rɒgətɪv] *n* prerrogativa *f*.

Presbyterian [,prezbɪ'tɪərɪən] <> *adj* presbiteriano(na). <> *n* presbiteriano *m*, -na *f*.

preschool ['pri:,sku:l] <> *adj* preescolar. <> *n US* parvulario *m*, escuela *f* de párvulos.

prescribe [prɪ'skraɪb] *vt* **-1.** MED recetar **-2.** [order] ordenar, mandar.

prescription [prɪ'skrɪpʃn] *n* receta *f*; **on ~** con receta médica.

presence ['prezns] *n* presencia *f*; **to be in sb's ~** OR **in the ~ of sb** estar en presencia de alguien; **to make one's ~ felt** hacer sentir la presencia de uno.

presence of mind *n* presencia *f* de ánimo, aplomo *m*.

present [*adj* & *n* 'preznt, *vb* prɪ'zent] <> *adj* **-1.** [current] actual **-2.** [in attendance] presente; **to be ~ at sthg** asistir a algo, estar presente en algo. <> *n* **-1.** [current time]: **the ~** el presente; **at ~** actualmente **-2.** LING: **~ (tense)** (tiempo *m*) presente *m* **-3.** [gift] regalo *m*; **to give sb a ~** dar un regalo a alguien. <> *vt* **-1.** [gen] presentar; **to ~ sb with sthg, to ~ sthg to sb** [challenge, opportunity] representar algo para alguien; **to ~ sb with sthg, to ~ sthg to sb** presentar algo a alguien a alguien; **to ~ o.s.** [arrive] presentarse **-2.** [give]: **to ~ sb with sthg, to ~ sthg to sb** [as present] obsequiar algo a alguien; [at ceremony] entregar algo a alguien **-3.** [play etc] representar.

presentable [prɪ'zentəbl] *adj* presentable; **to look ~** tener un aspecto presentable; **to make o.s. ~** arreglarse.

presentation [,prezn'teɪʃn] *n* **-1.** [gen] presentación *f* **-2.** [ceremony] entrega *f* **-3.** [performance] representación *f*.

present day *n*: **the ~** el presente.
   ◆ **present-day** *adj* actual, de hoy en día.

presenter [prɪ'zentər] *n UK* presentador *m*, -ra *f*.

presently ['prezntlɪ] *adv* **-1.** [soon] dentro de poco **-2.** [now] actualmente, ahora.

preservation [,prezə'veɪʃn] *n* preservación *f*, conservación *f*.

preservative [prɪ'zɜ:vətɪv] *n* conservante *m*.

preserve [prɪ'zɜ:v] <> *vt* conservar. <> *n* [jam] mermelada *f*.
   ◆ **preserves** *npl* [jam] confituras *fpl*; [vegetables] conserva *f*.

preset [,pri:'set] (*pt* & *pp* **preset**, *cont* **-ting**) *vt* programar.

president ['prezɪdənt] *n* presidente *m*, -ta *f*.

presidential [,prezɪ'denʃl] *adj* presidencial.

press [pres] <> *n* **-1.** [push]: **to give sthg a ~** apretar algo **-2.** [newspapers, reporters]: **the ~** la prensa **-3.** [machine] prensa *f*; **to go to ~** entrar en prensa **-4.** [with iron] planchado *m*; **to give sthg a ~** dar un planchado a algo. <> *vt* **-1.** [gen] apretar;

~ **sthg against sthg** apretar algo contra algo - **2.** [grapes, flowers] prensar - **3.** [iron] planchar - **4.** [urge]: **to** ~ **sb (to do sthg or into doing sthg)** presionar a alguien (para que haga algo) - **5.** [pursue - claim] insistir en. ⬦ *vi* - **1.** [gen]: **to** ~ **(on sthg)** apretar (algo) - **2.** [crowd]: **to** ~ **forward** empujar hacia adelante.

◆ **press for** *vt fus* exigir, reclamar.

◆ **press on** *vi* [continue] proseguir, continuar; **to** ~ **on (with)** seguir adelante (con).

press agency *n* agencia *f* de prensa.

press conference *n* rueda *f* de prensa.

pressed [prest] *adj*: **to be** ~ **(for time/ money)** andar escaso(sa) (de tiempo/de dinero).

pressing ['presɪŋ] *adj* apremiante, urgente.

press officer *n* jefe *m*, -fa *f* de prensa.

press photographer *n* fotógrafo *m*, -fa *f* de prensa.

press release *n* comunicado *m* de prensa.

press-stud *n UK* automático *m*.

press-up *n UK* flexión *f*.

pressure ['preʃə'] *n* presión *f*; **to put** ~ **on sb (to do sthg)** presionar a alguien (para que haga algo).

pressure cooker *n* olla *f* a presión.

pressure gauge *n* manómetro *m*.

pressure group *n* grupo *m* de presión.

pressurize, -ise ['preʃəraɪz] *vt* - **1.** TECH presurizar - **2.** *UK* [force]: **to** ~ **sb to do or into doing sthg** presionar a alguien para que haga algo.

prestige [pre'stiːʒ] *n* prestigio *m*.

presumably [prɪ'zjuːməblɪ] *adv*: ~ **you've read it** supongo que los has leído.

presume [prɪ'zjuːm] *vt* suponer; **he is** ~ **d dead** se supone que está muerto.

presumption [prɪ'zʌmpʃn] *n* - **1.** [assumption] suposición *f*; [of innocence] presunción *f* - **2.** (*U*) [audacity] presunción *f*, osadía *f*.

presumptuous [prɪ'zʌmptʃʊəs] *adj* presuntuoso(sa).

pretence, pretense *US* [prɪ'tens] *n* fingimiento *m*, simulación *f*; **to make a** ~ **of doing sthg** fingir hacer algo; **under false** ~**s** con engaños, con falsos pretextos.

pretend [prɪ'tend] ⬦ *vt*: **to** ~ **to do sthg** fingir hacer algo; **she** ~ **ed not to notice** hizo como si no se hubiera dado cuenta; **don't** ~ **you didn't know!** ¡no finjas que no lo sabías! ⬦ *vi* fingir, simular. ⬦ *adj inf* de mentira.

pretense *US* = **pretence**.

pretension [prɪ'tenʃn] *n* pretensión *f*.

pretentious [prɪ'tenʃəs] *adj* pretencioso(sa).

pretext ['priːtekst] *n* pretexto *m*; **on or under the** ~ **that** .../**of doing sthg** con el pretexto de que .../de hacer algo.

pretty ['prɪtɪ] (*compar* -**ier**, *superl* -**iest**) ⬦ *adj* bonito(ta). ⬦ *adv* bastante; ~ **much** más o menos; ~ **well** [almost] casi.

prevail [prɪ'veɪl] *vi* - **1.** [be widespread] predominar, imperar - **2.** [triumph]: **to** ~ **(over)** prevalecer (sobre) - **3.** [persuade]: **to** ~ **on or upon sb to do sthg** persuadir a alguien para que haga algo.

prevailing [prɪ'veɪlɪŋ] *adj* predominante.

prevalent ['prevələnt] *adj* predominante, imperante.

prevent [prɪ'vent] *vt* impedir; [event, illness, accident] evitar; **to** ~ **sthg (from) happening** impedir or evitar que algo pase; **to** ~ **sb (from) doing sthg** impedir a alguien que haga algo.

preventive [prɪ'ventɪv] *adj* preventivo(va).

preview ['priːvjuː] *n* - **1.** [film] avance *m* - **2.** [exhibition] preestreno *m*.

previous ['priːvjəs] *adj* previo(via), anterior; **the** ~ **week/president** la semana/el presidente anterior.

previously ['priːvjəslɪ] *adv* - **1.** [formerly] anteriormente - **2.** [before]: **two years** ~ dos años antes.

prewar [ˌpriː'wɔː'] *adj* de preguerra.

prey [preɪ] *n* presa *f*, víctima *f*.

◆ **prey on** *vt fus* - **1.** [live off] cazar, alimentarse de - **2.** [trouble]: **to** ~ **on sb's mind** atormentar a alguien.

price [praɪs] ⬦ *n lit & fig* precio *m*; **to go up/down in** ~ subir/bajar de precio; **you can't put a** ~ **on health** la salud no tiene precio; **at any** ~ a toda costa, a cualquier precio; **at a** ~ a un alto precio. ⬦ *vt* poner precio a; **to be wrongly** ~ **d** tener el precio equivocado; **to** ~ **o.s. out of the market** salirse del mercado por vender demasiado caro.

priceless ['praɪslɪs] *adj lit & fig* que no tiene precio, inestimable.

price list *n* lista *f* or tarifa *f* de precios.

price range *n* escala *f* de precios; **to be within sb's** ~ estar al alcance de alguien; **to be out of sb's** ~ no estar al alcance de alguien.

price tag *n* [label] etiqueta *f* (del precio).

pricey ['praɪsɪ] (*compar* -**ier**, *superl* -**iest**) *adj* caro(ra).

prick [prɪk] ⬦ *n* - **1.** [wound] pinchazo *m* - **2.** *vulg* [penis] polla *f*, pinga *f Andes & Méx* - **3.** *vulg* [stupid person] gilipollas *m y f inv*. ⬦ *vt* - **1.** [gen] pinchar - **2.** [sting] picar.

◆ **prick up** *vt fus*: **to** ~ **up one's ears** [subj: animal] levantar las orejas; [subj: person] aguzar el oído.

prickle ['prɪkl] ⬦ *n* - **1.** [thorn] espina *f*, pincho *m* - **2.** [sensation] comezón *f*. ⬦ *vi* picar.

prickly ['prɪklɪ] (*compar* **-ier**, *superl* **-iest**) *adj* **-1.** [thorny] espinoso(sa) **- 2.** *fig* [touchy] susceptible, enojadizo(za).

prickly heat *n* (*U*) sarpullido *por causa del calor*.

pride [praɪd] ◇ *n* orgullo *m*; **to take ~ in sthg/in doing sthg** enorgullecerse de algo/de hacer algo. ◇ *vt* : **to ~ o.s. on sthg** enorgullecerse de algo.

priest [priːst] *n* sacerdote *m*.

priestess ['priːstɪs] *n* sacerdotisa *f*.

priesthood ['priːsthʊd] *n* **-1.** [position, office]: **the ~** el sacerdocio **- 2.** [priests collectively]: **the ~** el clero.

prig [prɪg] *n* mojigato *m*, -ta *f*.

prim [prɪm] (*compar* **-mer**, *superl* **-mest**) *adj* remilgado(da); **~ and proper** remilgado(da).

primarily ['praɪmərɪlɪ] *adv* principalmente.

primary ['praɪmərɪ] (*pl* **-ies**) ◇ *adj* **- 1.** [main] principal **- 2.** SCH primario(ria). ◇ *n* US POL primaria *f*.

primary school *n* escuela *f* primaria.

primate ['praɪmeɪt] *n* ZOOL primate *m*.

prime [praɪm] ◇ *adj* **-1.** [main] primero(ra), principal **- 2.** [excellent] excelente; [quality] primero(ra). ◇ *n*: **to be in one's ~** estar en la flor de la vida. ◇ *vt* **- 1.** [inform]: **to ~ sb about sthg** preparar a alguien a fondo para algo **- 2.** [surface] preparar **- 3.** [gun, pump] cebar.

prime minister *n* primer ministro *m*, primera ministra *f*.

primer ['praɪmə'] *n* **- 1.** [paint] imprimación *f* **- 2.** [textbook] cartilla *f*.

primeval [praɪ'miːvl] *adj* [ancient] primitivo(va).

primitive ['prɪmɪtɪv] *adj* [tribe, species etc] primitivo(va); [accommodation, sense of humour] rudimentario(ria).

primrose ['prɪmrəʊz] *n* primavera *f*, prímula *f*.

Primus stove® ['praɪməs-] *n* hornillo *m* de camping.

prince [prɪns] *n* príncipe *m*.

princess [prɪn'ses] *n* princesa *f*.

principal ['prɪnsəpl] ◇ *adj* principal. ◇ *n* SCH director *m*, -ra *f*.

principle ['prɪnsəpl] *n* **-1.** [gen] principio *m*; **to be against sb's ~s** ir contra los principios de alguien **- 2.** (*U*) [integrity] principios *mpl*; **on ~, as a matter of ~** por principio.
➨ **in principle** *adv* en principio.

print [prɪnt] ◇ *n* **- 1.** (*U*) [type] caracteres *mpl* (de imprenta); **in ~** [available] disponible; [in printed characters] en letra impresa; **to be out of ~** estar agotado **- 2.** [piece of artwork] grabado *m* **- 3.** [reproduction] reproducción *f* **- 4.** [photograph] fotografía *f* **- 5.** [fabric] estampado *m* **- 6.** [mark - of foot

etc] huella *f*. ◇ *vt* **- 1.** TYPO imprimir **- 2.** [produce by printing - book, newspaper] tirar **- 3.** [publish] publicar **- 4.** [decorate - cloth etc] estampar **- 5.** [write in block letters] escribir con letra de imprenta. ◇ *vi* imprimir.
➨ **print out** *vt sep* COMPUT imprimir.

printer ['prɪntə'] *n* **- 1.** [person] impresor *m*, -ra *f*; [firm] imprenta *f* **- 2.** [machine] impresora *f*.

printing ['prɪntɪŋ] *n* **- 1.** (*U*) [act of printing] impresión *f* **- 2.** [trade] imprenta *f*.

printout ['prɪntaʊt] *n* COMPUT salida *f* de impresora.

prior ['praɪə'] ◇ *adj* [previous] previo(via); **without ~ notice** sin previo aviso; **to have ~ commitments** tener compromisos previos; **to have a ~ engagement** tener un compromiso previo. ◇ *n* [monk] prior *m*.
➨ **prior to** *prep* antes de; **~ to doing sthg** con anterioridad a hacer algo.

priority [praɪ'ɒrətɪ] (*pl* **-ies**) *n* prioridad *f*; **to have OR take ~ (over)** tener prioridad (sobre).

prise [praɪz] *vt* : **to ~ sthg open/away** abrir/separar algo haciendo palanca.

prison ['prɪzn] ◇ *n* cárcel *f*, prisión *f*; **to be in ~** estar en la cárcel; **to be sentenced to 5 years in ~** ser condenado a cinco años de cárcel. ◇ *comp*: **to be given a ~ sentence** ser condenado a una pena de cárcel; **a ~ officer** un funcionario de prisiones.

prisoner ['prɪznə'] *n* **- 1.** [convict] preso *m*, -sa *f* **- 2.** [captive] prisionero *m*, -ra *f*.

prisoner of war (*pl* **prisoners of war**) *n* prisionero *m*, -ra *f* de guerra.

privacy [*UK* 'prɪvəsɪ, *US* 'praɪvəsɪ] *n* intimidad *f*.

private ['praɪvɪt] ◇ *adj* **-1.** [gen] privado(da); [class] particular; [telephone call, belongings] personal **- 2.** [thoughts, plans] secreto(ta); **a ~ joke** un chiste que entienden unos pocos **- 3.** [secluded] retirado(da) **- 4.** [unsociable - person] reservado(da). ◇ *n* **- 1.** [soldier] soldado *m* raso **- 2.**: **(to do sthg) in ~** [in secret] (hacer algo) en privado.

private enterprise *n* (*U*) empresa *f* privada.

private eye *n* detective privado *m*, -da *f*.

privately ['praɪvɪtlɪ] *adv* **- 1.** [not by the state] de forma privada; **~ owned** de propiedad privada **- 2.** [confidentially] en privado.

private property *n* propiedad *f* privada.

private school *n* escuela *f* privada, colegio *m* privado.

privatize, -ise ['praɪvɪtaɪz] *vt* privatizar.

privet ['prɪvɪt] *n* alheña *f*.

privilege ['prɪvɪlɪdʒ] *n* privilegio *m*.

privy ['prɪvɪ] *adj*: **to be ~ to sthg** estar

enterado(da) de algo.

Privy Council *n UK*: **the** ~ *en Gran Bretaña, consejo privado que asesora al monarca.*

prize [praɪz] ◇ *adj* de primera. ◇ *n* premio *m*. ◇ *vt*: **to be** ~ **d** ser apreciado(da).

prize-giving [-ˌgɪvɪŋ] *n UK* entrega *f* de premios.

prizewinner [ˈpraɪzˌwɪnəʳ] *n* premiado *m*, -da *f*.

pro [prəʊ] (*pl* -**s**) *n* - **1.** *inf* [professional] profesional *m or f* - **2.** [advantage]: **the** ~**s and cons** los pros y los contras.

probability [ˌprɒbəˈbɪlətɪ] (*pl* -**ies**) *n* probabilidad *f*.

probable [ˈprɒbəbl] *adj* probable; **it is not very** ~ **that it will happen** no es muy probable que ocurra.

probably [ˈprɒbəblɪ] *adv* probablemente.

probation [prəˈbeɪʃn] *n* - **1.** [of prisoner] libertad *f* condicional; **to put sb on** ~ poner a alguien en libertad condicional - **2.** [trial period] periodo *m* de prueba; **to be on** ~ estar en periodo de prueba.

probe [prəʊb] ◇ *n* - **1.** [investigation]: ~ **(into)** investigación *f* (sobre) - **2.** MED & SPACE sonda *f*. ◇ *vt* - **1.** [investigate] investigar - **2.** [with tool] sondar; [with finger, stick] hurgar en.

problem [ˈprɒbləm] *n* problema *m*; **no** ~! *inf* ¡por supuesto!, ¡desde luego!

procedure [prəˈsiːdʒəʳ] *n* procedimiento *m*.

proceed [vb prəˈsiːd, npl ˈprəʊsiːdz] vi - **1.** [do subsequently]: **to** ~ **to do sthg** proceder a hacer algo - **2.** [continue]: **to** ~ **(with sthg)** proseguir (con algo) - **3.** *fml* [advance] avanzar.

➤ **proceeds** *npl* ganancias *fpl*, beneficios *mpl*.

proceedings [prəˈsiːdɪŋz] *npl* - **1.** [series of events] acto *m* - **2.** [legal action] proceso *m*.

process [ˈprəʊses] ◇ *n* proceso *m*; **in the** ~ en el intento; **to be in the** ~ **of doing sthg** estar en vías de hacer algo. ◇ *vt* - **1.** [gen & COMPUT] procesar - **2.** [application] tramitar.

processing [ˈprəʊsesɪŋ] *n* - **1.** [gen & COMPUT] procesamiento *m* - **2.** [of applications etc] tramitación *f*.

procession [prəˈseʃn] *n* desfile *m*; [religious] procesión *f*.

proclaim [prəˈkleɪm] *vt* [gen] proclamar; [law] promulgar.

procrastinate [prəˈkræstɪneɪt] *vi* andarse con dilaciones.

procure [prəˈkjʊəʳ] *vt* [obtain] obtener, conseguir.

prod [prɒd] (*pt* & *pp* -**ded**, *cont* -**ding**) *vt* [push, poke] dar empujoncitos a.

prodigal [ˈprɒdɪgl] *adj* [son, daughter] pródigo(ga).

prodigy [ˈprɒdɪdʒɪ] (*pl* -**ies**) *n* [person] prodigio *m*; **a child** ~ un niño prodigio.

produce [*n* ˈprɒdjuːs, *vb* prəˈdjuːs] ◇ *n (U)* productos *mpl* agrícolas; **'** ~ **of France'** 'producto de Francia'. ◇ *vt* - **1.** [gen] producir; [offspring, flowers] engendrar - **2.** [bring out] mostrar, enseñar - **3.** THEATRE poner en escena.

producer [prəˈdjuːsəʳ] *n* - **1.** [gen] productor *m*, -ra *f* - **2.** THEATRE director *m*, -ra *f* de escena.

product [ˈprɒdʌkt] *n* producto *m*.

production [prəˈdʌkʃn] *n* - **1.** [gen] producción *f* - **2.** *(U)* THEATRE puesta *f* en escena.

production line *n* cadena *f* de producción.

productive [prəˈdʌktɪv] *adj* - **1.** [efficient] productivo(va) - **2.** [rewarding] provechoso(sa).

productivity [ˌprɒdʌkˈtɪvətɪ] *n* productividad *f*.

productivity bonus *n* plus *m* de productividad.

profane [prəˈfeɪn] *adj* [disrespectful] obsceno(na).

profession [prəˈfeʃn] *n* profesión *f*; **by** ~ de profesión.

professional [prəˈfeʃənl] ◇ *adj* profesional. ◇ *n* profesional *m or f*, profesionista *mf Méx*.

professor [prəˈfesəʳ] *n* - **1.** *UK* [head of department] catedrático *m*, -ca *f* - **2.** *US* & *Can* [lecturer] profesor *m*, -ra *f* (de universidad).

proficiency [prəˈfɪʃənsɪ] *n*: ~ **(in)** competencia *f* (en).

profile [ˈprəʊfaɪl] *n* perfil *m*; **high** ~ notoriedad *f*.

profit [ˈprɒfɪt] ◇ *n* - **1.** [financial gain] beneficio *m*, ganancia *f*; **to make a** ~ sacar un beneficio - **2.** [advantage] provecho *m*. ◇ *vi*: **to** ~ **(from** or **by)** sacar provecho (de).

profitability [ˌprɒfɪtəˈbɪlətɪ] *n* rentabilidad *f*.

profitable [ˈprɒfɪtəbl] *adj* - **1.** [making a profit] rentable - **2.** [beneficial] provechoso(sa).

profiteering [ˌprɒfɪˈtɪərɪŋ] *n* especulación *f*.

profound [prəˈfaʊnd] *adj* profundo(da).

profusely [prəˈfjuːslɪ] *adv* profusamente; **to apologise** ~ pedir disculpas cumplidamente.

profusion [prəˈfjuːʒn] *n* profusión *f*.

progeny [ˈprɒdʒənɪ] (*pl* -**ies**) *n* progenie *f*.

prognosis [prɒgˈnəʊsɪs] (*pl* -**noses** [-ˈnəʊsiːz]) *n* pronóstico *m*.

program [ˈprəʊgræm] (*pt* & *pp* -**med** or -**ed**, *cont* -**ming** or -**ing**) ◇ *n* - **1.** COMPUT programa *m* - **2.** *US* = **programme**. ◇ *vt* - **1.** COMPUT programar - **2.** *US* = **programme**. ◇ *vi* COMPUT programar.

programer *US* = **programmer**.

programme *UK*, **program** *US* ['prəʊgræm] ⬦ *n* programa *m*. ⬦ *vt* : **~ sthg (to do sthg)** programar algo (para que haga algo).

programmer *UK*, **programer** *US* ['prəʊgræmə'] *n* COMPUT programador *m*, -ra *f*.

programming ['prəʊgræmɪŋ] *n* programación *f*.

progress [*n* 'prəʊgres, *vb* prə'gres] ⬦ *n* -**1.** [gen] progreso *m*; **in ~** en curso; **to make ~** hacer progresos -**2.** [forward movement] avance *m*. ⬦ *vi* -**1.** [gen] progresar; **as the year ~ed** conforme avanzaba el año; [pupil etc] hacer progresos -**2.** [move forward] avanzar.

progressive [prə'gresɪv] *adj* -**1.** [enlightened] progresista -**2.** [gradual] progresivo(va).

prohibit [prə'hɪbɪt] *vt* prohibir; **to ~ sb from doing sthg** prohibirle a alguien hacer algo; **fishing is ~ed** prohibido pescar.

project [*n* 'prɒdʒekt, *vb* prə'dʒekt] ⬦ *n* -**1.** [plan, idea] proyecto *m* -**2.** SCH : **~ (on)** estudio *m* OR trabajo *m* (sobre) -**3.** *US*: **the ~s** urbanización con viviendas de protección oficial. ⬦ *vt* -**1.** [gen] proyectar -**2.** [estimate - statistic, costs] estimar -**3.** [company, person] dar una imagen de; [image] proyectar. ⬦ *vi* proyectarse.

projectile [prə'dʒektaɪl] *n* proyectil *m*.

projection [prə'dʒekʃn] *n* -**1.** [gen] proyección *f* -**2.** [protrusion] saliente *m*.

projector [prə'dʒektə'] *n* proyector *m*.

proletariat [,prəʊlɪ'teərɪət] *n* proletariado *m*.

prolific [prə'lɪfɪk] *adj* prolífico(ca).

prologue, prolog *US* ['prəʊlɒg] *n* prólogo *m*.

prolong [prə'lɒŋ] *vt* prolongar.

prom [prɒm] *n* -**1.** *abbr of* **promenade concert** -**2.** (*abbr of* **promenade**) *UK inf* [road by sea] paseo *m* marítimo -**3.** *US* [ball] baile *m* de gala (en la escuela).

promenade [,prɒmə'nɑːd] *n UK* [by sea] paseo *m* marítimo.

promenade concert *n UK* concierto sinfónico en donde parte del público está de pie.

prominent ['prɒmɪnənt] *adj* -**1.** [important] destacado(da), importante -**2.** [noticeable] prominente.

promiscuous [prɒ'mɪskjʊəs] *adj* promiscuo(cua).

promise ['prɒmɪs] ⬦ *n* promesa *f*. ⬦ *vt* : **to ~ (to do sthg)** prometer (hacer algo); **to ~ sb sthg** prometer a alguien algo. ⬦ *vi*: **I ~** te lo prometo.

promising ['prɒmɪsɪŋ] *adj* prometedor(ra).

promontory ['prɒməntrɪ] (*pl* -**ies**) *n* promontorio *m*.

promote [prə'məʊt] *vt* -**1.** [foster] fomentar,

promover -**2.** [push, advertise] promocionar -**3.** [in job]: **to ~ sb (to sthg)** ascender a alguien (a algo) -**4.** SPORT: **to be ~d** subir.

promoter [prə'məʊtə'] *n* -**1.** [organizer] organizador *m*, -ra *f* -**2.** [supporter] promotor *m*, -ra *f*.

promotion [prə'məʊʃn] *n* -**1.** [in job] ascenso *m* -**2.** [advertising] promoción *f* -**3.** [campaign] campaña *f* de promoción.

prompt [prɒmpt] ⬦ *adj* rápido(da), inmediato(ta); **the injury requires ~ treatment** las heridas requieren un tratamiento inmediato; **to be ~ in doing sthg** hacer algo con prontitud. ⬦ *adv* en punto; **at 2 o'clock ~** a las dos en punto. ⬦ *vt* -**1.** [motivate]: **to ~ sb (to do sthg)** inducir OR impulsar a alguien (a hacer algo) -**2.** THEATRE apuntar. ⬦ *n* THEATRE [line] apunte *m*.

promptly ['prɒmptlɪ] *adv* -**1.** [reply, react, pay] inmediatamente, rápidamente -**2.** [arrive, leave] puntualmente.

prone [prəʊn] *adj* -**1.** [susceptible]: **to be ~ to sthg/to do sthg** ser propenso(sa) a algo/a hacer algo -**2.** [lying flat] boca abajo.

prong [prɒŋ] *n* diente *m*, punta *f*.

pronoun ['prəʊnaʊn] *n* pronombre *m*.

pronounce [prə'naʊns] ⬦ *vt* -**1.** [gen] pronunciar -**2.** [declare] declarar. ⬦ *vi*: **to ~ on sthg** pronunciarse sobre algo.

pronounced [prə'naʊnst] *adj* pronunciado(da), marcado(da).

pronouncement [prə'naʊnsmənt] *n* declaración *f*.

pronunciation [prə,nʌnsɪ'eɪʃn] *n* pronunciación *f*.

proof [pruːf] ⬦ *n* -**1.** [gen & TYPO] prueba *f* -**2.** [of alcohol]: **to be 10% ~** tener 10 grados. ⬦ *adj* [secure]: **~ against** a prueba de.

prop [prɒp] (*pt* & *pp* -**ped**, *cont* -**ping**) ⬦ *n* -**1.** [physical support] puntal *m*, apoyo *m* -**2.** *fig* [supporting thing, person] sostén *m*. ⬦ *vt* : **to ~ sthg on** OR **against sthg** apoyar algo contra algo.

➨ **props** *npl* accesorios *mpl*.

➨ **prop up** *vt sep* -**1.** [physically support] apuntalar -**2.** *fig* [sustain] apoyar, sostener.

propaganda [,prɒpə'gændə] *n* propaganda *f*.

propel [prə'pel] (*pt* & *pp* -**led**, *cont* -**ling**) *vt* propulsar, impulsar.

propeller [prə'pelə'] *n* hélice *f*.

propelling pencil [prə'pelɪŋ-] *n UK* portaminas *m inv*.

propensity [prə'pensɪtɪ] (*pl* -**ies**) *n fml*: **~ (for** OR **to sthg)** propensión *f* (a algo).

proper ['prɒpə'] *adj* -**1.** [real] de verdad -**2.** [correct - gen] correcto(ta) ; [- time, place, equipment] adecuado(da).

properly ['prɒpəlɪ] *adv* -**1.** [satisfactorily, correctly] bien -**2.** [decently] correctamente.

proper noun *n* nombre *m* propio.
property ['propətɪ] (*pl* **-ies**) *n* **-1.** [gen] propiedad *f* **- 2.** [estate] finca *f* **- 3.** *fml* [house] inmueble *m*.
property owner *n* propietario *m*, -ria *f* de un inmueble.
prophecy ['profɪsɪ] (*pl* **-ies**) *n* profecía *f*.
prophesy ['profɪsaɪ] (*pt* & *pp* **-ied**) *vt* profetizar.
prophet ['profɪt] *n* profeta *m* OR *f*.
proportion [prə'pɔ:ʃn] *n* **-1.** [part] parte *f* **- 2.** [ratio, comparison] proporción *f* **- 3.** [correct relationship]: **out of ~** desproporcionado(da); **to keep things in ~** *fig* no exagerar; **sense of ~** *fig* sentido *m* de la medida.
proportional [prə'pɔ:ʃənl] *adj*: **~ (to)** proporcional (a), en proporción (a).
proportional representation *n* representación *f* proporcional.
proportionate [prə'pɔ:ʃnət] *adj*: **~ (to)** proporcional (a).
proposal [prə'pəʊzl] *n* **-1.** [plan, suggestion] propuesta *f* **- 2.** [offer of marriage] proposición *f*.
propose [prə'pəʊz] ◇ *vt* **-1.** [suggest] proponer; [motion] presentar; **to ~ doing sthg** proponer hacer algo **- 2.** [intend]: **to ~ doing** OR **to do sthg** tener la intención de hacer algo. ◇ *vi* [make offer of marriage] declararse; **to ~ to sb** pedir la mano de alguien.
proposition [,propə'zɪʃn] *n* [suggestion] propuesta *f*.
proprietor [prə'praɪətə'] *n* propietario *m*, -ria *f*.
propriety [prə'praɪətɪ] *n* (*U*) *fml* **-1.** [moral correctness] propiedad *f* **- 2.** [rightness] conveniencia *f*, oportunidad *f*.
pro rata [-'rɑ:tə] *adj* & *adv* a prorrata.
prose [prəʊz] *n* **-1.** (*U*) LITER prosa *f* **- 2.** SCH traducción *f* inversa.
prosecute ['prosɪkju:t] ◇ *vt* procesar, enjuiciar. ◇ *vi* **-1.** [bring a charge] entablar una acción judicial **- 2.** [represent in court] representar al demandante.
prosecution [,prosɪ'kju:ʃn] *n* **-1.** [gen] procesamiento *m* **- 2.** [lawyers]: **the ~** la acusación.
prosecutor ['prosɪkju:tə'] *n esp US* fiscal *m* OR *f*.
prospect [*n* 'prospekt, *vb* prə'spekt] ◇ *n* **-1.** [gen] perspectiva *f*; **it was a pleasant ~** era una perspectiva agradable; **they were faced with the ~ of losing their jobs** tenían que hacer frente a la perspectiva de perder sus trabajos **- 2.** [possibility] posibilidad *f*. ◇ *vi*: **to ~ (for)** hacer prospecciones (de). **➡ prospects** *npl*: **~s (for)** perspectivas *fpl* (de); **job ~s** perspectivas laborales.
prospecting [prə'spektɪŋ] *n* (*U*) prospecciones *fpl*.

prospective [prə'spektɪv] *adj* posible.
prospector [prə'spektə'] *n* prospector *m*, -ra *f*.
prospectus [prə'spektəs] (*pl* **-es**) *n* prospecto *m*, folleto *m* informativo.
prosper ['prospə'] *vi* prosperar.
prosperity [pro'sperətɪ] *n* prosperidad *f*.
prosperous ['prospərəs] *adj* próspero(ra).
prostitute ['prostɪtju:t] *n* prostituta *f*.
prostrate [*adj* 'prostreɪt, *vb* pro'streɪt] ◇ *adj* postrado(da)..
protagonist [prə'tægənɪst] *n* **-1.** *fml* [supporter] partidario *m*, -ria *f*, defensor *m*, -ra *f* **- 2.** [main character] protagonista *m* OR *f*.
protect [prə'tekt] *vt*: **to ~ sthg/sb (against/from)** proteger algo/a alguien (contra/de).
protection [prə'tekʃn] *n*: **~ (against/from)** protección *f* (contra/de).
protective [prə'tektɪv] *adj* protector(ra).
protégé ['protɪʒeɪ] *n* protegido *m*.
protein ['prəʊti:n] *n* proteína *f*.
protest [*n* 'prəʊtest, *vb* prə'test] ◇ *n* protesta *f*; **under ~** bajo protesta; **without ~** sin protestar. ◇ *vt* **-1.** [complain]: **to ~ that** quejarse de **- 2.** [state] manifestar, aseverar; **he ~ed his innocence** declaró su inocencia **- 3.** *US* [oppose] protestar en contra de. ◇ *vi*: **to ~ (about/against/at)** protestar (por/en contra de/por).
Protestant ['protɪstənt] ◇ *adj* protestante. ◇ *n* protestante *m* OR *f*.
protester [prə'testə'] *n* manifestante *m* OR *f*.
protest march *n* manifestación *f*.
protocol ['prəʊtəkɒl] *n* protocolo *m*.
prototype ['prəʊtətaɪp] *n* prototipo *m*.
protracted [prə'træktɪd] *adj* prolongado(da).
protrude [prə'tru:d] *vi*: **to ~ (from)** sobresalir (de).
protruding [prə'tru:dɪŋ] *adj* [chin] prominente; [teeth] salido(da); [eyes] saltón(ona).
protuberance [prə'tju:bərəns] *n* protuberancia *f*.
proud [praʊd] ◇ *adj* **-1.** [gen] orgulloso(sa); **to be ~ of** estar orgulloso(sa) de; **that's nothing to be ~ of!** ¡yo no estaría orgulloso de eso!; **to be ~ of o.s.** estar orgulloso de uno mismo **- 2.** *pej* [arrogant] soberbio(bia), arrogante. ◇ *adv*: **to do sb ~** tratar muy bien a alguien.
prove [pru:v] (*pp* **-d** OR **proven**) ◇ *vt* **-1.** [show to be true] probar, demostrar **- 2.** [show oneself to be]: **to ~ (to be) sthg** demostrar ser algo; **to ~ o.s.** demostrar (uno) sus cualidades. ◇ *vi* resultar; **to ~ (to be) interesting/difficult** resultar interesante/difícil.

proven ['pru:vn, 'prəʊvn] ⬦ *pp* ⊳ **prove.** ⬦ *adj* probado(da).

proverb ['prɒvɜ:b] *n* refrán *m*, proverbio *m*.

provide [prə'vaɪd] *vt* proporcionar, proveer; **to ~ sb with sthg** proporcionar a alguien algo; **to ~ sthg for sb** ofrecer algo a alguien.
◆ **provide for** *vt fus* **- 1.** [support] mantener **- 2.** *fml* [make arrangements for] tomar medidas para.

provided [prə'vaɪdɪd] ◆ **provided (that)** *conj* con tal (de) que, a condición de que; **you should pass, ~ (that) you work hard** aprobarás, con tal de que trabajes duro.

providing [prə'vaɪdɪŋ] ◆ **providing (that)** *conj* = **provided.**

province ['prɒvɪns] *n* **- 1.** [part of country] provincia *f* **- 2.** [speciality] campo *m*, competencia *f*.

provincial [prə'vɪnʃl] *adj* **- 1.** [of a province] provincial **- 2.** *pej* [narrow-minded] provinciano(na).

provision [prə'vɪʒn] *n* **- 1.** [gen] suministro *m* **- 2.** (*U*) [arrangement]: **to make ~ for** [eventuality, future] tomar medidas para; [one's family] asegurar el porvenir de **- 3.** [in agreement, law] disposición *f*.
◆ **provisions** *npl* [supplies] provisiones *fpl*, víveres *mpl*.

provisional [prə'vɪʒənl] *adj* provisional.

proviso [prə'vaɪzəʊ] (*pl* **-s**) *n* condición *f*; **with the ~ that ...** con la condición de que ...

provocative [prə'vɒkətɪv] *adj* **- 1.** [controversial] provocador(ra) **- 2.** [sexy] provocativo(va).

provoke [prə'vəʊk] *vt* provocar; **to ~ sb to do sthg** OR **into doing sthg** provocar a alguien a que haga algo.

prow [praʊ] *n* proa *f*.

prowess ['praʊɪs] *n fml* proezas *fpl*.

prowl [praʊl] ⬦ *n*: **on the ~** merodeando. ⬦ *vt* merodear por. ⬦ *vi* merodear.

prowler ['praʊlə^r] *n* merodeador *m*, -ra *f*.

proxy ['prɒksɪ] (*pl* **-ies**) *n*: **by ~** por poderes.

prudent ['pru:dnt] *adj* prudente.

prudish ['pru:dɪʃ] *adj* mojigato(ta).

prune [pru:n] ⬦ *n* [fruit] ciruela *f* pasa. ⬦ *vt* podar.

pry [praɪ] (*pt* & *pp* **pried**) *vi* fisgonear, curiosear; **to ~ into sthg** entrometerse en algo.

PS (*abbr of* **postscript**) *n* P.D.

psalm [sɑ:m] *n* salmo *m*.

pseudonym ['sju:dənɪm] *n* seudónimo *m*.

psyche ['saɪkɪ] *n* psique *f*.

psychiatric [ˌsaɪkɪ'ætrɪk] *adj* psiquiátrico(ca).

psychiatrist [saɪ'kaɪətrɪst] *n* psiquiatra *m* OR *f*.

psychiatry [saɪ'kaɪətrɪ] *n* psiquiatría *f*.

psychic ['saɪkɪk] *adj* **- 1.** [clairvoyant] clarividente **- 2.** [mental] psíquico(ca).

psychoanalysis [ˌsaɪkəʊə'næləsɪs] *n* psicoanálisis *m inv.*

psychoanalyst [ˌsaɪkəʊ'ænəlɪst] *n* psicoanalista *m* OR *f*.

psychological [ˌsaɪkə'lɒdʒɪkl] *adj* psicológico(ca).

psychologist [saɪ'kɒlədʒɪst] *n* psicólogo *m*, -ga *f*.

psychology [saɪ'kɒlədʒɪ] *n* psicología *f*.

psychopath ['saɪkəpæθ] *n* psicópata *m* OR *f*.

psychotic [saɪ'kɒtɪk] ⬦ *adj* psicótico(ca). ⬦ *n* psicótico *m*, -ca *f*.

pt - 1. *abbr of* **pint - 2.** *abbr of* **point.**

PTO (*abbr of* **please turn over**) sigue.

pub [pʌb] (*abbr of* **public house**) *n* pub *m* (británico).

puberty ['pju:bətɪ] *n* pubertad *f*.

pubic ['pju:bɪk] *adj* púbico(ca).

public ['pʌblɪk] ⬦ *adj* público(ca). ⬦ *n* público *m*; **in ~** en público; **the ~** el gran público.

public-address system *n* sistema *m* de megafonía.

publican ['pʌblɪkən] *n UK* patrón *m*, -ona *f* de un 'pub'.

publication [ˌpʌblɪ'keɪʃn] *n* publicación *f*.

public bar *n UK en ciertos pubs y hoteles, bar de sencilla decoración con precios más bajos que los del 'saloon bar'.*

public company *n* sociedad *f* anónima (con cotización en Bolsa).

public convenience *n UK* aseos *mpl* públicos.

public holiday *n* fiesta *f* nacional, (día *m*) feriado *m Amér.*

public house *n UK fml* pub *m* (británico).

publicity [pʌb'lɪsɪtɪ] *n* publicidad *f*.

publicize, -ise ['pʌblɪsaɪz] *vt* divulgar.

public limited company *n* sociedad *f* anónima (con cotización en Bolsa).

public opinion *n* (*U*) opinión *f* pública.

public prosecutor *n* fiscal *m* OR *f* del Estado.

public relations ⬦ *n* (*U*) relaciones *fpl* públicas. ⬦ *npl* relaciones *fpl* públicas.

public school *n* **- 1.** *UK* [private school] colegio *m* privado **- 2.** *US* [state school] escuela *f* pública.

public-spirited *adj* con sentido cívico.

public transport *n* transporte *m* público.

publish ['pʌblɪʃ] *vt* **- 1.** [gen] publicar **- 2.** [make known] hacer público(ca).

publisher ['pʌblɪʃə^r] *n* [person] editor *m*, -ra *f*; [firm] editorial *f*.

publishing ['pʌblɪʃɪŋ] *n* (*U*) industria *f* editorial.

pub lunch *n almuerzo servido en un 'pub'.*

pucker ['pʌkə'] *vt* fruncir.

pudding ['pʊdɪŋ] *n* -1. [sweet] pudín *m*; [savoury] pastel *m* -2. *(U) UK* [course] postre *m*.

puddle ['pʌdl] *n* charco *m*.

Puerto Rico [,pwɜːtəʊ'riːkəʊ] *n* Puerto Rico.

puff [pʌf] ◇ *n* -1. [of cigarette, pipe] calada *f*, pitada *f Amér* - 2. [gasp] jadeo *m* - 3. [of air] soplo *m*; [of smoke] bocanada *f*. ◇ *vt* echar. ◇ *vi* -1. [smoke]: **to ~ at** OR **on** dar caladas a - 2. [pant] jadear, resoplar.

◆ **puff out** *vt sep* -1. [cheeks, chest] hinchar; [feathers] ahuecar - 2. [smoke] echar.

puffed [pʌft] *adj* [swollen]: **~ (up)** hinchado(da).

puffin ['pʌfɪn] *n* frailecillo *m*.

puff pastry, puff paste *US n* hojaldre *m*.

puffy ['pʌfɪ] (*compar* **-ier**, *superl* **-iest**) *adj* hinchado(da).

pugnacious [pʌg'neɪʃəs] *adj fml* pugnaz, belicoso(sa).

pull [pʊl] ◇ *vt* -1. [gen] tirar de; [trigger] apretar - 2. [tooth, cork] sacar, extraer - 3. [muscle] sufrir un tirón en - 4. [attract] atraer - 5. [gun] sacar y apuntar - 6. [phr]: **to ~ sthg to bits** OR **pieces** hacer pedazos algo. ◇ *vi* tirar. ◇ *n* -1. [tug with hand] tirón *m* - 2. *(U)* [influence] influencia *f*.

◆ **pull apart** *vt sep* -1. [machine etc] desmontar - 2. [toy, book etc] hacer pedazos.

◆ **pull at** *vt fus* tirar de a tirones de.

◆ **pull away** *vi* [from roadside] alejarse (de la acera).

◆ **pull down** *vt sep* [building] derribar.

◆ **pull in** *vi* [train] pararse (en el andén).

◆ **pull off** *vt sep* [succeed in] conseguir llevar a cabo.

◆ **pull out** ◇ *vt sep* -1. [troops] retirar - 2. [tooth] sacar. ◇ *vi* -1. [vehicle] alejarse (de la acera) - 2. [withdraw] retirarse.

◆ **pull over** *vi* AUT hacerse a un lado.

◆ **pull through** *vi* recobrarse, reponerse.

◆ **pull together** *vt sep*: **to ~ o.s.** together calmarse, serenarse.

◆ **pull up** ◇ *vt sep* [move closer] acercar. ◇ *vi* parar, detenerse.

pulley ['pʊlɪ] (*pl* **pulleys**) *n* polea *f*.

pullover ['pʊl,əʊvə'] *n* jersey *m*.

pulp [pʌlp] *n* -1. [soft mass] papilla *f*; **to beat sb to a ~** hacer papilla a alguien - 2. [of fruit] pulpa *f* - 3. [of wood] pasta *f* de papel.

pulpit ['pʊlpɪt] *n* púlpito *m*.

pulsate [pʌl'seɪt] *vi* palpitar.

pulse [pʌls] ◇ *n* -1. [in body] pulso *m* - 2. TECH impulso *m*. ◇ *vi* latir.

◆ **pulses** *npl* [food] legumbres *fpl*.

puma ['pjuːmə] (*pl inv* OR **-s**) *n* puma *m*.

pumice (stone) ['pʌmɪs-] *n* piedra *f* pómez.

pummel ['pʌml] (*UK pt & pp* **-led**, *cont* **-ling**, *US pt & pp* **-ed**, *cont* **-ing**) *vt* aporrear.

pump [pʌmp] ◇ *n* -1. [machine] bomba *f* - 2. [for petrol] surtidor *m*. ◇ *vt* [convey by pumping] bombear.

◆ **pumps** *npl* [shoes] zapatillas *fpl* de tenis.

◆ **pump up** *vt* [inflate] inflar.

pumpkin ['pʌmpkɪn] *n* calabaza *f*, zapallo *m CSur, Perú*, auyama *f Carib, Col*.

pun [pʌn] *n* juego *m* de palabras.

punch [pʌntʃ] ◇ *n* -1. [blow] puñetazo *m* - 2. [tool - for leather etc] punzón *m*; [- for tickets] máquina *f* para picar billetes - 3. [drink] ponche *m*. ◇ *vt* -1. [hit] dar un puñetazo a, trompear *Amér* - 2. [ticket] picar - 3. [hole] perforar.

Punch-and-Judy show [-'dʒuːdɪ-] *n teatro de guiñol para niños con personajes arquetípicos y representado normalmente en la playa.*

punch(ed) card [pʌntʃ(t)-] *n* tarjeta *f* perforada.

punch line *n* remate *m* (*de un chiste*).

punch-up *n UK inf* pelea *f*.

punchy ['pʌntʃɪ] (*compar* **-ier**, *superl* **-iest**) *adj inf* efectista, resultón(ona).

punctual ['pʌŋktʃʊəl] *adj* puntual.

punctuation [,pʌŋktʃʊ'eɪʃn] *n* puntuación *f*.

punctuation mark *n* signo *m* de puntuación.

puncture ['pʌŋktʃə'] ◇ *n* pinchazo *m*; **to have a ~** pinchar; [in skin] punción *f*. ◇ *vt* pinchar, ponchar *Guat & Méx*.

pundit ['pʌndɪt] *n* lumbrera *f*, experto *m*, -ta *f*.

pungent ['pʌndʒənt] *adj* [strong-smelling] penetrante, fuerte.

punish ['pʌnɪʃ] *vt*: **to ~ sb (for sthg/for doing sthg)** castigar a alguien (por algo/por haber hecho algo).

punishing ['pʌnɪʃɪŋ] *adj* trabajoso(sa), penoso(sa).

punishment ['pʌnɪʃmənt] *n* [for crime] castigo *m*.

punk [pʌŋk] ◇ *adj* punk. ◇ *n* -1. [music]: **~ (rock)** punk *m* - 2. [person]: **~ (rocker)** punki *m* OR *f* - 3. *US inf* [lout] gamberro *m*.

punt [pʌnt] *n* batea *f*.

punter ['pʌntə'] *n UK* -1. [gambler] apostante *m* OR *f* - 2. *inf* [customer] cliente *m*, -ta *f*.

puny ['pjuːnɪ] (*compar* **-ier**, *superl* **-iest**) *adj* [person, limbs] enclenque, raquítico(ca); [effort] penoso(sa), lamentable.

pup [pʌp] *n* -1. [young dog] cachorro *m* - 2. [young seal, otter] cría *f*.

pupil ['pjuːpl] *n* -1. [student] alumno *m*, -na *f* - 2. [follower] pupilo *m*, -la *f* - 3. [of eye] pupila *f*.

puppet ['pʌpɪt] *n lit & fig* títere *m*.

puppy ['pʌpɪ] (*pl* **-ies**) *n* cachorro *m*, perrito *m*.

purchase ['pɜːtʃəs] *fml* ◇ *n* compra *f*, adquisición *f*. ◇ *vt* comprar, adquirir.

purchaser ['pɜːtʃəsə^r] *n* comprador *m*, -ra *f*.

purchasing power ['pɜːtʃəsɪŋ-] *n* poder *m* adquisitivo.

pure [pjʊə^r] *adj* puro(ra).

puree ['pjʊəreɪ] *n* puré *m*; **tomato** ~ concentrado *m* de tomate.

purely ['pjʊəlɪ] *adv* puramente; ~ **and simply** pura y simplemente.

purge [pɜːdʒ] ◇ *n* POL purga *f*. ◇ *vt*: **to** ~ **sthg (of)** purgar algo (de).

purify ['pjʊərɪfaɪ] (*pt & pp* **-ied**) *vt* purificar.

purist ['pjʊərɪst] *n* purista *m* OR *f*.

puritan ['pjʊərɪtən] ◇ *adj* puritano(na). ◇ *n* puritano *m*, -na *f*.

purity ['pjʊərətɪ] *n* pureza *f*.

purl [pɜːl] *n* (*U*) punto *m* del revés.

purple ['pɜːpl] *adj* morado(da).

purport [pə'pɔːt] *vi fml*: **to** ~ **to do/be sthg** pretender hacer/ser algo.

purpose ['pɜːpəs] *n* [gen] propósito *m*; **what is the** ~ **of your visit?** ¿cuál es el objeto de tu visita?; **for one's own** ~**s** por su propio interés; **it serves no** ~ carece de sentido; **it has served its** ~ ha servido; **to no** ~ en vano.
➝ **on purpose** *adv* a propósito, adrede.

purposeful ['pɜːpəsfʊl] *adj* resuelto(ta).

purr [pɜː^r] *vi* -1. [cat, person] ronronear -2. [engine, machine] zumbar.

purse [pɜːs] ◇ *n* -1. [for money] monedero *m* -2. US [handbag] bolso *m*, bolsa *f Méx*, cartera *f Andes, CSur*. ◇ *vt* fruncir (con desagrado); **she** ~**d her lips** frunció los labios.

purser ['pɜːsə^r] *n* contador *m*, -ra *f*.

pursue [pə'sjuː] *vt* -1. [follow] perseguir -2. *fml* [policy] llevar a cabo; [aim, pleasure etc] ir en pos de, buscar; [topic, question] profundizar en; [hobby, studies] dedicarse a.

pursuer [pə'sjuːə^r] *n* perseguidor *m*, -ra *f*.

pursuit [pə'sjuːt] *n* -1. (*U*) *fml* [attempt to achieve] búsqueda *f* -2. [chase, in cycling] persecución *f* -3. [occupation, activity] ocupación *f*; **leisure** ~ pasatiempo *m*.

pus [pʌs] *n* pus *m*.

push [pʊʃ] ◇ *vt* -1. [shove] empujar; **to** ~ **sthg into sthg** meter algo en algo; **to** ~ **sthg open/shut** abrir/cerrar algo empujándolo -2. [press - button] apretar, pulsar -3. [encourage]: **to** ~ **sb (to do sthg)** empujar a alguien (a hacer algo) -4. [force]: **to** ~ **sb (into doing sthg)** obligar a alguien (a hacer algo) -5. *inf* [promote] promocionar. ◇ *vi* -1. [press forward] empujar; [on button] apretar, pulsar. ◇ *n lit & fig* empujón *m*; **at the** ~ **of a button** con sólo apretar

un botón; **at a** ~ apurando mucho.
➝ **push around** *vt sep inf* mandonear.
➝ **push for** *vt fus* [demand] reclamar.
➝ **push in** *vi* [in queue] colarse.
➝ **push off** *vi inf* largarse.
➝ **push on** *vi* seguir adelante sin parar.
➝ **push through** *vt sep* [law etc] conseguir que se apruebe.

pushchair ['pʊʃtʃeə^r] *n* UK silla *f* (de paseo).

pushed [pʊʃt] *adj inf*: **to be** ~ **for sthg** andar corto(ta) de algo; **to be hard** ~ **to do sthg** tenerlo difícil para hacer algo.

pusher ['pʊʃə^r] *n inf* camello *m*.

pushover ['pʊʃ,əʊvə^r] *n inf*: **it's a** ~ está chupado.

push-up *n esp US* flexión *f*.

pushy ['pʊʃɪ] (*compar* **-ier**, *superl* **-iest**) *adj pej* agresivo(va), insistente.

puss [pʊs], **pussy (cat)** ['pʊsɪ-] *n inf* gatito *m*, minino *m*.

put [pʊt] (*pt & pp* **put**, *cont* **-ting**) *vt* -1. [gen] poner; **to** ~ **sthg into sthg** meter algo en algo -2. [place exactly] colocar -3. [send - to prison etc] meter; **to** ~ **the children to bed** acostar a los niños -4. [express] expresar, formular; **to** ~ **it bluntly** hablando claro -5. [ask - question] hacer; [- proposal] presentar -6. [estimate]: **to** ~ **sthg at** calcular algo en -7. [invest]: **to** ~ **money into a project** invertir dinero en un proyecto; **to** ~ **money into an account** ingresar dinero en una cuenta; **to** ~ **a lot of effort into sthg** esforzarse mucho con algo -8. [apply]: **to** ~ **pressure on** presionar a.
➝ **put across** *vt sep* transmitir; **to** ~ **o.s. across** hacerse entender.
➝ **put away** *vt sep* [tidy away] poner en su sitio, guardar.
➝ **put back** *vt sep* -1. [replace] devolver a su sitio -2. [postpone] aplazar; [schedule] retrasar -3. [clock, watch] atrasar.
➝ **put by** *vt sep* ahorrar.
➝ **put down** *vt sep* -1. [lay down] dejar -2. [phone] colgar -3. [quell] sofocar, reprimir -4. UK [animal] sacrificar -5. [write down] apuntar.
➝ **put down to** *vt sep* achacar a.
➝ **put forward** *vt sep* -1. [plan, theory, name] proponer, presentar; [proposal] presentar -2. [clock, meeting, event] adelantar.
➝ **put in** *vt sep* -1. [spend - time] dedicar -2. [submit] presentar -3. [install] instalar.
➝ **put off** *vt sep* -1. [postpone] posponer, aplazar -2. [cause to wait] hacer esperar -3. [distract] distraer -4. [discourage] disuadir, desanimar -5. [cause to dislike]: **to** ~ **sb off sthg** quitarle a alguien las ganas de algo.
➝ **put on** *vt sep* -1. [wear] ponerse -2. [show, play] representar; [exhibition]

hacer; [transport] **organizar - 3.** [gain]: **to ~ on weight** engordar **- 4.** [radio, light] poner, encender; **to ~ on the brakes** frenar **- 5.** [record, tape] poner **- 6.** [start cooking] empezar a hacer OR cocinar; **to ~ the kettle on** poner el agua a hervir **- 7.** [bet] apostar por **- 8.** [add] añadir **- 9.** [feign - air, accent] fingir.

◆ **put out** *vt sep* **- 1.** [place outside] sacar **- 2.** [issue - statement] hacer público **- 3.** [extinguish, switch off] apagar **- 4.** [prepare for use - clothes] sacar **- 5.** [extend - hand, leg] extender; [- tongue] sacar **- 6.** [upset]: **to be ~ out** estar disgustado(da) **- 7.** [inconvenience] causar molestias a.

◆ **put through** *vt sep* TELEC [call] poner; **to ~ sb through to sb** poner a alguien con alguien.

◆ **put up** ⬦ *vt sep* **- 1.** [build] construir; [tent] montar **- 2.** [umbrella] abrir; [flag] izar **- 3.** [raise - hand] levantar **- 4.** [poster] fijar; [painting] pegar, colgar **- 5.** [provide - money] poner **- 6.** [propose - candidate] proponer **- 7.** [increase] subir, aumentar **- 8.** [provide accommodation for] alojar. ⬦ *vt fus* [resistance] ofrecer; **to ~ up a fight** ofrecer resistencia.

◆ **put up with** *vt fus* aguantar, soportar.

putrid ['pju:trɪd] *adj fml* putrefacto(ta).

putt [pʌt] *n* putt *m.*

putting green ['pʌtɪŋ-] *n* césped abierto al público en el que se puede jugar a golf con el putter.

putty ['pʌtɪ] *n* masilla *f.*

puzzle ['pʌzl] ⬦ *n* **- 1.** [toy, game] rompecabezas *m inv* **- 2.** [mystery] misterio *m*, enigma *m.* ⬦ *vt* dejar perplejo, desconcertar. ⬦ *vi*: **to ~ over sthg** romperse la cabeza con algo.

◆ **puzzle out** *vt sep* descifrar, resolver.

puzzling ['pʌzlɪŋ] *adj* desconcertante.

pyjamas [pə'dʒɑːməz] *npl* pijama *m*; **a pair of ~** un pijama.

pylon ['paɪlən] *n* torre *f (de conducción eléctrica).*

pyramid ['pɪrəmɪd] *n* pirámide *f.*

Pyrenees [,pɪrə'niːz] *npl*: **the ~** los Pirineos.

Pyrex® ['paɪreks] *n* pírex® *m.*

python ['paɪθn] *(pl inv OR -s) n* pitón *m.*

q *(pl* **q's** *OR* **qs)**, **Q** *(pl* **Q's** *OR* **Qs)** [kjuː] *n* [letter] q *f*, Q *f.*

quack [kwæk] *n* **- 1.** [noise] graznido *m (de pato)* **- 2.** *inf* [doctor] matasanos *m inv.*

quad [kwɒd] *n abbr of* **quadrangle.**

quadrangle ['kwɒdræŋgl] *n* **- 1.** [figure] cuadrángulo *m* **- 2.** [courtyard] patio *m.*

quadruple [kwɒ'druːpl] ⬦ *vt* cuadruplicar. ⬦ *vi* cuadruplicarse.

quadruplets ['kwɒdrʊplɪts] *npl* cuatrillizos *mpl*, -zas *fpl.*

quads [kwɒdz] *npl inf* cuatrillizos *mpl*, -zas *fpl.*

quagmire ['kwægmaɪər] *n* lodazal *m*, cenagal *m.*

quail [kweɪl] *(pl inv OR -s)* ⬦ *n* codorniz *f.* ⬦ *vi literary* amedrentarse.

quaint [kweɪnt] *adj* **- 1.** [picturesque] pintoresco(ca) **- 2.** [odd] singular.

quake [kweɪk] ⬦ *n inf* terremoto *m.* ⬦ *vi* temblar, estremecerse.

Quaker ['kweɪkər] *n* cuáquero *m*, -ra *f.*

qualification [,kwɒlɪfɪ'keɪʃn] *n* **- 1.** [examination, certificate] título *m* **- 2.** [ability, skill] aptitud *f* **- 3.** [qualifying statement] condición *f.*

qualified ['kwɒlɪfaɪd] *adj* **- 1.** [trained] cualificado(da) **- 2.** [limited] limitado(da).

qualify ['kwɒlɪfaɪ] *(pt & pp -ied)* ⬦ *vt* **- 1.** [modify] matizar **- 2.** [entitle]: **to ~ sb to do sthg** capacitar a alguien para hacer algo. ⬦ *vi* **- 1.** [pass exams] sacar el título **- 2.** [be entitled]: **to ~ (for)** tener derecho (a) **- 3.** SPORT clasificarse.

quality ['kwɒlɪtɪ] *(pl -ies)* ⬦ *n* **- 1.** [standard] calidad *f* **- 2.** [characteristic] cualidad *f.* ⬦ *comp* de calidad.

qualms [kwɑːmz] *npl* remordimientos *mpl*, escrúpulos *mpl.*

quandary ['kwɒndərɪ] *(pl -ies) n*: **to be in a ~ about** OR **over sthg** estar en un dilema sobre algo.

quantify ['kwɒntɪfaɪ] *(pt & pp -ied) vt* cuantificar.

quantity ['kwɒntətɪ] *(pl -ies) n* cantidad *f.*

quantity surveyor *n* aparejador *m*, -ra *f.*

quarantine ['kwɒrəntiːn] *n* cuarentena *f.*

quark [kwɑːk] *n* CULIN *tipo de queso blando bajo en grasas.*

quarrel [ˈkwɒrəl] (*UK pt & pp* **-led**, *cont* **-ling**, *US pt & pp* **-ed**, *cont* **-ing**) ◇ *n* pelea *f.* ◇ *vi* pelearse; **to ~ with sb** pelearse con alguien; **to ~ with sthg** no estar de acuerdo con algo.

quarrelsome [ˈkwɒrəlsəm] *adj* pendenciero(ra).

quarry [ˈkwɒrɪ] (*pl* **-ies**) *n* **-1.** [place] cantera *f* - **2.** [prey] presa *f.*

quart [kwɔːt] *n* cuarto *m* de galón.

quarter [ˈkwɔːtə̯] *n* **-1.** [fraction] cuarto *m* - **2.** [in telling time]: **a ~ past two** *UK*, **~ after two** *US* las dos y cuarto; **a ~ to two** *UK*, **~ of two** *US* las dos menos cuarto - **3.** [of year] trimestre *m* - **4.** *US* [coin] cuarto *m* de dólar, moneda *f* de 25 centavos - **5.** [four ounces] cuatro onzas *fpl*, cuarto *m* de libra - **6.** [area in town] barrio *m* - **7.** [group of people] lugar *m*, parte *f.*
◆ **quarters** *npl* [rooms] residencia *f*, alojamiento *m.*
◆ **at close quarters** *adv* muy de cerca.

quarterfinal [ˌkwɔːtəˈfaɪnl] *n* cuarto *m* de final.

quarterly [ˈkwɔːtəlɪ] (*pl* **-ies**) ◇ *adj* trimestral. ◇ *adv* trimestralmente. ◇ *n* trimestral *f.*

quartermaster [ˈkwɔːtəˌmɑːstə̯] *n* oficial *m* de intendencia.

quartet [kwɔːˈtet] *n* cuarteto *m.*

quartz [kwɔːts] *n* cuarzo *m.*

quartz watch *n* reloj *m* de cuarzo.

quash [kwɒʃ] *vt* **-1.** [reject] anular, invalidar - **2.** [quell] reprimir, sofocar.

quasi- [ˈkweɪzaɪ] *prefix* cuasi-.

quaver [ˈkweɪvə̯] ◇ *n* MUS corchea *f.* ◇ *vi* temblar.

quay [kiː] *n* muelle *m.*

quayside [ˈkiːsaɪd] *n* muelle *m.*

queasy [ˈkwiːzɪ] (*compar* **-ier**, *superl* **-iest**) *adj* mareado(da).

queen [kwiːn] *n* **-1.** [gen] reina *f* - **2.** [playing card] dama *f.*

Queen Mother *n*: **the ~** la reina madre.

queer [kwɪə̯] ◇ *adj* **-1.** [odd] raro(ra), extraño(ña) - **2.** *inf pej* [homosexual] marica, maricón. ◇ *n inf pej* marica *m*, maricón *m*, joto *m Méx.*

quell [kwel] *vt* **-1.** [rebellion] sofocar, reprimir - **2.** [feelings] dominar, contener.

quench [kwentʃ] *vt* apagar.

querulous [ˈkwerʊləs] *adj fml* quejumbroso(sa).

query [ˈkwɪərɪ] (*pl* **-ies**, *pt & pp* **-ied**) ◇ *n* pregunta *f*, duda *f.* ◇ *vt* poner en duda.

quest [kwest] *n literary*: **~ (for)** búsqueda *f* (de).

question [ˈkwestʃn] ◇ *n* **-1.** [query, problem in exam] pregunta *f*; **to ask (sb) a ~** hacer una pregunta (a alguien) - **2.** [doubt] duda *f*; **to call sthg into ~** poner algo en duda; **without ~** sin duda; **beyond ~** fuera de toda duda - **3.** [issue, matter] cuestión *f*, asunto *m* - **4.** *phr*: **it is a ~ of staying calm** se trata de mantener la calma; **there's no ~ of ...** es imposible que ... ◇ *vt* **-1.** [ask questions to] preguntar; [interrogate] interrogar - **2.** [express doubt about] cuestionar.
◆ **in question** *adv*: **the matter in ~** el asunto en cuestión.
◆ **out of the question** *adv* imposible; **that's out of the ~!** ¡ni hablar!

questionable [ˈkwestʃənəbl] *adj* [gen] cuestionable; [taste] dudoso(sa).

question mark *n* (signo *m* de) interrogación *f.*

questionnaire [ˌkwestʃəˈneə̯] *n* cuestionario *m.*

queue [kjuː] *UK* ◇ *n* cola *f.* ◇ *vi*: **to ~ (up for sthg)** hacer cola (para algo).

quibble [ˈkwɪbl] *pej vi* quejarse por tonterías.

quiche [kiːʃ] *n* quiche *f.*

quick [kwɪk] ◇ *adj* **-1.** [gen] rápido(da); **be ~!** ¡date prisa!; **could we have a ~ word?** ¿podríamos hablar un momento? **-2.** [clever - person] espabilado(da); [- wit] agudo(da) **-3.** [irritable]: **a ~ temper** un genio vivo. ◇ *adv* rápidamente.

quicken [ˈkwɪkn] ◇ *vt* [one's pace] apretar, acelerar. ◇ *vi* acelerarse.

quickfire [ˈkwɪkfaɪə̯] *adj* rápido(da).

quickly [ˈkwɪklɪ] *adv* **-1.** [rapidly] rápidamente, de prisa **-2.** [without delay] rápidamente, en seguida.

quicksand [ˈkwɪksænd] *n* arenas *fpl* movedizas.

quick-witted [-ˈwɪtɪd] *adj* agudo(da).

quid [kwɪd] (*pl inv*) *n UK inf* libra *f* (esterlina).

quiet [ˈkwaɪət] ◇ *adj* **-1.** [silent - gen] silencioso(sa); [- room, place] tranquilo(la); **to be ~** [make no noise] no hacer ruido; **be ~!** ¡cállate!; **in a ~ voice** en voz baja; **to keep ~ about sthg** guardar silencio sobre algo **-2.** [not talkative] callado(da); **to go ~** callarse **-3.** [tranquil, uneventful] tranquilo(la) **-4.** [unpublicized - wedding etc] privado(da), íntimo(ma). ◇ *n* tranquilidad *f*, silencio *m*: **on the ~** a escondidas. ◇ *vt US* tranquilizar, calmar.
◆ **quiet down** ◇ *vt sep* tranquilizar, calmar. ◇ *vi* tranquilizarse, calmarse.

quieten [ˈkwaɪətn] *vt* tranquilizar, calmar.
◆ **quieten down** ◇ *vt sep* tranquilizar, calmar. ◇ *vi* tranquilizarse, calmarse.

quietly ['kwaɪətlɪ] *adv* **- 1.** [without noise] silenciosamente, sin hacer ruido; **to speak ~** hablar en voz baja **- 2.** [without moving] sin moverse **- 3.** [without excitement] tranquilamente **- 4.** [without fuss] discretamente.

quilt [kwɪlt] *n* edredón *m*.

quinine [kwɪ'niːn] *n* quinina *f*.

quins *UK* [kwɪnz], **quints** *US* [kwɪnts] *npl inf* quintillizos *mpl*, -zas *fpl*.

quintet [kwɪn'tet] *n* quinteto *m*.

quints *US* = **quins**.

quintuplets [kwɪn'tjuːplɪts] *npl* quintillizos *mpl*, -zas *fpl*.

quip [kwɪp] (*pt & pp* **-ped**, *cont* **-ping**) *n* ocurrencia *f*, salida *f*.

quirk [kwɜːk] *n* **- 1.** [habit] manía *f*, rareza *f* **- 2.** [strange event] extraña coincidencia *f*.

quit [kwɪt] (*UK pt & pp* quit OR **-ted**, *cont* **-ting**, *US pt & pp* quit, *cont* **-ting**) ◇ *vt* **- 1.** [resign from] dejar, abandonar **- 2.** [stop]: **to ~ doing sthg** dejar de hacer algo **- 3.** COMPUT salir de. ◇ *vi* **- 1.** [resign] dimitir **- 2.** COMPUT salir.

quite [kwaɪt] *adv* **- 1.** [completely] totalmente, completamente **- 2.** [fairly] bastante; **~ a lot of people** bastante gente **- 3.** [after negative]: **it's not ~ big enough** no es todo lo grande que tendría que ser; **I'm not ~ sure** no estoy del todo seguro; **I don't ~ understand/know** no entiendo/sé muy bien **- 4.** [to emphasize]: **~ a ...** todo un (toda una) ...; **~ the opposite** todo lo contrario **- 5.** [to express agreement]: **~ (so)!** ¡efectivamente!, ¡desde luego!

quits [kwɪts] *adj inf*: **to be ~ (with sb)** estar en paz (con alguien); **to call it ~** dejarlo así.

quiver ['kwɪvə'] ◇ *n* [for arrows] carcaj *m*, aljaba *f*. ◇ *vi* temblar, estremecerse.

quiz [kwɪz] (*pl* **-zes**, *pt & pp* **-zed**, *cont* **-zing**) ◇ *n* **- 1.** [gen] concurso *m* **- 2.** *US* SCH control *m*. ◇ *vt*: **to ~ sb (about)** interrogar a alguien (sobre).

quizzical ['kwɪzɪkl] *adj* burlón(ona).

quota ['kwəʊtə] *n* cuota *f*.

quotation [kwəʊ'teɪʃn] *n* **- 1.** [citation] cita *f* **- 2.** COMM presupuesto *m*.

quotation marks *npl* comillas *fpl*.

quote [kwəʊt] ◇ *n* **- 1.** [citation] cita *f* **- 2.** COMM presupuesto *m*. ◇ *vt* **- 1.** [cite] citar **- 2.** [figures, example, price] dar; **he ~ d £100** fijó un precio de 100 libras. ◇ *vi* **- 1.** [cite]: **to ~ (from)** citar (de) **- 2.** COMM: **to ~ for** dar un presupuesto por.

quotient ['kwəʊʃnt] *n* cociente *m*.

r (*pl* **r's** OR **rs**), **R** (*pl* **R's** OR **Rs**) [ɑː'] *n* [letter] r *f*, R *f*.

rabbi ['ræbaɪ] *n* rabino *m*.

rabbit ['ræbɪt] *n* conejo *m*.

rabbit hutch *n* conejera *f*.

rabble ['ræbl] *n* chusma *f*, populacho *m*.

rabies ['reɪbiːz] *n* rabia *f*.

RAC (*abbr of* **Royal Automobile Club**) *n* asociación británica del automóvil, ≃ RACE *m*.

race [reɪs] ◇ *n* **- 1.** *lit & fig* [competition] carrera *f* **- 2.** [people, descent] raza *f*. ◇ *vt* **- 1.** [compete against] competir con *(corriendo)*; **they ~ d each other to the door** echaron una carrera hasta la puerta **- 2.** [cars, pigeons] hacer carreras de; [horses] hacer correr. ◇ *vi* **- 1.** [rush] ir corriendo **- 2.** [beat fast] acelerarse.

race car *US* = **racing car**.

racecourse ['reɪskɔːs] *n* hipódromo *m*.

race driver *US* = **racing driver**.

racehorse ['reɪshɔːs] *n* caballo *m* de carreras.

racetrack ['reɪstræk] *n* [for horses] hipódromo *m*; [for cars] autódromo *m*; [for runners] pista *f* (de carreras).

racial ['reɪʃl] *adj* racial.

racial discrimination *n* discriminación *f* racial.

racing ['reɪsɪŋ] *n* carreras *fpl*; **motor ~** carreras de coches.

racing car *UK*, **race car** *US n* coche *m* de carreras, auto *m* de carrera *CSur*.

racing driver *UK*, **race driver** *US n* piloto *m* OR *f* de carreras.

racism ['reɪsɪzm] *n* racismo *m*.

racist ['reɪsɪst] ◇ *adj* racista. ◇ *n* racista *m* OR *f*.

rack [ræk] ◇ *n* **- 1.** [for magazines] revistero *m*; [for bottles] botellero *m*; [for plates] escurreplatos *m inv*; [for clothes] percha *f* **- 2.** [for luggage] portaequipajes *m inv*. ◇ *vt*: **to ~ one's brains** *UK* devanarse los sesos.

racket ['rækɪt] *n* **- 1.** SPORT raqueta *f* **- 2.** [noise] jaleo *m*, alboroto *m*, guachafita *f Col & Ven* **- 3.** [swindle] timo *m* **- 4.** [illegal activity] negocio *m* sucio.

racquet ['rækɪt] *n* SPORT = **racket**.

racy ['reɪsɪ] (*compar* -**ier**, *superl* -**iest**) *adj* entretenido(da) y picante.

radar ['reɪdɑ:ʳ] *n* radar *m*.

radial (tyre) ['reɪdjəl-] *n* neumático *m* radial.

radiant ['reɪdjənt] *adj* -**1.** [happy] radiante -**2.** *literary* [brilliant] resplandeciente.

radiate ['reɪdɪeɪt] ⋄ *vt lit & fig* irradiar. ⋄ *vi* -**1.** [be emitted] ser irradiado(da) -**2.** [spread from centre] salir, extenderse.

radiation [,reɪdɪ'eɪʃn] *n* radiación *f*.

radiator ['reɪdɪeɪtəʳ] *n* radiador *m*.

radical ['rædɪkl] ⋄ *adj* radical. ⋄ *n* POL radical *m* OR *f*.

radically ['rædɪklɪ] *adv* radicalmente.

radii ['reɪdɪaɪ] *pl* ▷ **radius**.

radio ['reɪdɪəʊ] (*pl* -**s**) ⋄ *n* radio *f*, radio *m Amér.* ⋄ *comp* de radio, radiofónico(ca).

radioactive [,reɪdɪəʊ'æktɪv] *adj* radiactivo(va).

radio alarm *n* radiodespertador *m*.

radio-controlled [-kən'trəʊld] *adj* teledirigido(da).

radiography [,reɪdɪ'ɒgrəfɪ] *n* radiografía *f*.

radiology [,reɪdɪ'ɒlədʒɪ] *n* radiología *f*.

radiotherapy [,reɪdɪəʊ'θerəpɪ] *n* radioterapia *f*.

radish ['rædɪʃ] *n* rábano *m*.

radius ['reɪdɪəs] (*pl* **radii**) *n* [gen & ANAT] radio *m*.

RAF [ɑ:reɪ'ef, ræf] *n abbr of* **Royal Air Force**.

raffle ['ræfl] ⋄ *n* rifa *f*, sorteo *m*. ⋄ *comp*: ~ **ticket** boleto *m*. ⋄ *vt* rifar, sortear.

raft [rɑ:ft] *n* [craft] balsa *f*.

rafter ['rɑ:ftəʳ] *n* viga *f* (*de armadura de tejado*).

rag [ræg] *n* -**1.** [piece of cloth] trapo *m* -**2.** *pej* [newspaper] periodicucho *m*.
◆ **rags** *npl* [clothes] trapos *mpl*.

rag-and-bone man *n* trapero *m*.

rag doll *n* muñeca *f* de trapo.

rage [reɪdʒ] ⋄ *n* -**1.** [fury] rabia *f*, ira *f* -**2.** *inf* [fashion]: **it's all the** ~ es la última moda. ⋄ *vi* -**1.** [behave angrily] estar furioso(sa) -**2.** [subj: storm, sea] enfurecerse; [subj: disease] hacer estragos; [subj: argument, controversy] continuar con violencia.

ragged ['rægɪd] *adj* -**1.** [wearing torn clothes] andrajoso(sa), harapiento(ta) -**2.** [torn] hecho(cha) jirones.

rag week *n* UK *semana en que los universitarios organizan actividades divertidas con fines benéficos*.

raid [reɪd] ⋄ *n* -**1.** [attack] incursión *f* -**2.** [forced entry - by robbers] asalto *m*; [- by police] redada *f*. ⋄ *vt* -**1.** [attack] atacar por sorpresa -**2.** [subj: robbers] asaltar; [subj: police] hacer una redada en.

raider ['reɪdəʳ] *n* -**1.** [attacker] invasor *m*, -ra

f -**2.** [thief] asaltante *m* OR *f*.

rail [reɪl] ⋄ *n* -**1.** [on staircase] baranda *f*, barandilla *f* -**2.** [bar] barra *f*; **towel** ~ toallero *m* -**3.** (*U*) [form of transport] ferrocarril *m*; **by** ~ por ferrocarril -**4.** [of railway line] carril *m*, riel *m*.

railcard ['reɪlkɑ:d] *n* UK *tarjeta que permite algunos descuentos al viajar en tren*.

railing ['reɪlɪŋ] *n* reja *f*.

railway UK ['reɪlweɪ], **railroad** US ['reɪlrəʊd] *n* -**1.** [company] ferrocarril *m* -**2.** [route] línea *f* de ferrocarril.

railway line *n* [route] línea *f* de ferrocarril; [track] vía *f* férrea.

railwayman ['reɪlweɪmən] (*pl* -**men** [-mən]) *n* UK ferroviario *m*.

railway station *n* estación *f* de ferrocarril.

railway track *n* vía *f* férrea.

rain [reɪn] ⋄ *n* lluvia *f*; **in the** ~ bajo la lluvia. ⋄ *v impers* METEOR llover. ⋄ *vi* caer.

rainbow ['reɪnbəʊ] *n* arco *m* iris.

rainbow nation *n*: **the** ~ Sudáfrica.

rain check *n esp* US: **I'll take a** ~ (**on that**) no lo quiero ahora, pero igual me apunto la próxima vez.

raincoat ['reɪnkəʊt] *n* impermeable *m*.

raindrop ['reɪndrɒp] *n* gota *f* de lluvia.

rainfall ['reɪnfɔ:l] *n* pluviosidad *f*.

rain forest *n* bosque *m* tropical.

rainy ['reɪnɪ] (*compar* -**ier**, *superl* -**iest**) *adj* lluvioso(sa).

raise [reɪz] ⋄ *vt* -**1.** [lift up] levantar; [flag] izar -**2.** [increase - level] aumentar; **to** ~ **one's voice** levantar la voz -**3.** [improve] elevar -**4.** [obtain - from donations] recaudar; [- by selling, borrowing] conseguir -**5.** [memory, thoughts] traer, evocar; [doubts, fears] levantar -**6.** [bring up, breed] criar -**7.** [crops] cultivar -**8.** [mention] plantear -**9.** [build] construir, erigir. ⋄ *n* US aumento *m*, subida *f*.

raisin ['reɪzn] *n* pasa *f*.

rake [reɪk] ⋄ *n* -**1.** [implement] rastrillo *m* -**2.** *dated & literary* [immoral man] calavera *m*. ⋄ *vt* [smooth] rastrillar.

rally ['rælɪ] (*pl* -**ies**, *pt & pp* -**ied**) ⋄ *n* -**1.** [meeting] mitin *m* -**2.** [car race] rally *m* -**3.** [in tennis etc] peloteo *m*. ⋄ *vt* reunir. ⋄ *vi* -**1.** [come together] reunirse -**2.** [recover] recuperarse.
◆ **rally round** ⋄ *vt fus* formar una piña con. ⋄ *vi inf* formar una piña.

ram [ræm] (*pt & pp* -**med**, *cont* -**ming**) ⋄ *n* carnero *m*. ⋄ *vt* -**1.** [crash into] embestir -**2.** [force] embutir.

RAM [ræm] (*abbr of* **random access memory**) *n* COMPUT RAM *f*.

ramble ['ræmbl] ⋄ *n* paseo *m* por el campo. ⋄ *vi* -**1.** [walk] pasear -**2.** [talk] divagar.
◆ **ramble on** *vi* divagar sin parar.

rambler ['ræmblə'] *n* [walker] excursionista *m* OR *f*.

rambling ['ræmblɪŋ] *adj* **-1.** [building, house] laberíntico(ca) **-2.** [speech, writing] incoherente.

ramp [ræmp] *n* **-1.** [slope] rampa *f* **-2.** AUT [in road] rompecoches *m inv.*

rampage [ræm'peɪdʒ] *n*: **to go on the ~** desbandarse.

rampant ['ræmpənt] *adj* desenfrenado(da).

ramparts ['ræmpɑːts] *npl* murallas *fpl.*

ramshackle ['ræm,ʃækl] *adj* destartalado(da).

ran [ræn] *pt* ⊳ **run.**

ranch [rɑːntʃ] *n* rancho *m*.

rancher ['rɑːntʃə'] *n* ranchero *m*, -ra *f*.

rancid ['rænsɪd] *adj* rancio(cia).

rancour *UK*, **rancor** *US* ['ræŋkə'] *n* rencor *m*.

random ['rændəm] ◇ *adj* **-1.** [arbitrary] hecho(cha) al azar **-2.** TECH aleatorio(ria). ◇ *n*: **at ~** al azar.

random access memory *n* COMPUT memoria *f* de acceso aleatorio.

R and R (*abbr of* **rest and recreation**) *n US* permiso militar.

randy ['rændɪ] (*compar* **-ier**, *superl* **-iest**) *adj* *inf* cachondo(da), caliente.

rang [ræŋ] *pt* ⊳ **ring.**

range [reɪndʒ] (*cont* **rangeing**) ◇ *n* **-1.** [of missile, telescope] alcance *m*; [of ship, plane] autonomía *f*; **at close ~** de cerca **-2.** [variety] gama *f* **-3.** [of prices, salaries] escala *f* **-4.** [of mountains] cordillera *f* **-5.** [shooting area] campo *m* de tiro **-6.** [of voice] registro *m*. ◇ *vt* alinear. ◇ *vi* **-1.** [vary]: **to ~ from ... to ..., to ~ between ... and ...** oscilar OR fluctuar entre ... y...; **prices ~ing from $20 to $100** precios que van desde veinte hasta cien dólares **-2.** [deal with, include]: **to ~ over sthg** comprender algo.

ranger ['reɪndʒə'] *n* guardabosques *m y f inv.*

rank [ræŋk] ◇ *adj* **-1.** [utter, absolute - bad. luck, outsider] absoluto(ta); [- disgrace, injustice] flagrante **-2.** [foul] pestilente. ◇ *n* **-1.** [position, grade] grado *m*, rango *m* **-2.** [social class] clase *f*, categoría *f*; **the ~ and file** las bases **-3.** [row] fila *f*, hilera *f*. ◇ *vt* [class]: **to be ~ed** estar clasificado(da). ◇ *vi*: **to ~ as** estar considerado(da) (como); **to ~ among** encontrarse entre.
◆ **ranks** *npl* **-1.** MIL: **the ~s** los soldados rasos **-2.** *fig* [members] filas *fpl.*

rankle ['ræŋkl] *vi* doler.

ransack ['rænsæk] *vt* [search] registrar a fondo; [plunder] saquear.

ransom ['rænsəm] *n* rescate *m*; **to hold sb to ~** *fig* hacer chantaje a alguien.

rant [rænt] *vi* despotricar.

rap [ræp] (*pt & pp* **-ped**, *cont* **-ping**) ◇ *n* **-1.** [knock] golpecito *m* **-2.** [type of music] rap *m* **-3.** *US* [legal charge] acusación *f*; **~ sheet** antecedentes *mpl* penales. ◇ *vt* dar un golpecito en.

rape [reɪp] ◇ *n* **-1.** [crime] violación *f* **-2.** BOT colza *f*. ◇ *vt* [person] violar.

rapeseed oil ['reɪpsiːd-] *n* aceite *m* de colza.

rapid ['ræpɪd] *adj* rápido(da).
◆ **rapids** *npl* rápidos *mpl.*

rapidly ['ræpɪdlɪ] *adv* rápidamente.

rapist ['reɪpɪst] *n* violador *m*, -ra *f*.

rapport [ræ'pɔː'] *n* compenetración *f*.

rapprochement [ræ'prɒʃmɑː] *n* acercamiento *m*.

rapture ['ræptʃə'] *n* arrebato *m*, arrobamiento *m*.

rapturous ['ræptʃərəs] *adj* muy entusiasta.

rare [reə'] *adj* **-1.** [scarce] poco común, raro(ra) **-2.** [infrequent] poco frecuente, raro(ra) **-3.** [exceptional] raro(ra), excepcional **-4.** CULIN poco hecho(cha).

rarely ['reəlɪ] *adv* raras veces.

raring ['reərɪŋ] *adj*: **to be ~ to go** estar ansioso(sa) por empezar.

rarity ['reərətɪ] (*pl* **-ies**) *n* rareza *f*.

rascal ['rɑːskl] *n* pícaro *m*, -ra *f*.

rash [ræʃ] ◇ *adj* precipitado(da). ◇ *n* **-1.** MED erupción *f* (cutánea), sarpullido *m*, jiote *m Méx* **-2.** [spate] aluvión *m*.

rasher ['ræʃə'] *n* loncha *f*.

rasp [rɑːsp] *n* **-1.** [harsh sound] chirrido *m* **-2.** [tool] lima *f* gruesa.

raspberry ['rɑːzbərɪ] (*pl* **-ies**) *n* [fruit] frambuesa *f*.

rat [ræt] *n* [animal] rata *f*.

rate [reɪt] ◇ *n* **-1.** [speed] ritmo *m*; **at this ~** a este paso **-2.** [of birth, death] índice *m*; [of unemployment, inflation] tasa *f* **-3.** [price] precio *m*, tarifa *f*; [of interest] tipo *m*. ◇ *vt* **-1.** [consider]: **to ~ sthg/sb (as/among)** considerar algo/a alguien (como/entre); **to ~ sthg/sb highly** tener una buena opinión de algo/alguien **-2.** *UK inf* [have good opinion of] valorar mucho **-3.** [deserve] merecer.
◆ **rates** *npl UK* ≃ contribución *f* urbana.
◆ **at any rate** *adv* **-1.** [at least] al menos **-2.** [anyway] de todos modos.

ratepayer ['reɪt,peɪə'] *n UK* contribuyente *m* OR *f*.

rather ['rɑːðə'] *adv* **-1.** [to quite a large extent] bastante **-2.** [to a great extent] muy **-3.** [to a limited extent] algo; **he's ~ like you** se parece (en) algo a ti **-4.** [as preference]: **I would ~ wait** preferiría esperar; **I'd ~ not stay** prefiero no quedarme; **would you like to come? – I'd ~ not** ¿quieres venir? – mejor no **-5.** [more exactly]: **or ~ ...** o más bien

..., o mejor dicho ... - **6.** [on the contrary]: **(but) ~ ...** (sino) más bien OR por el contrario ...

◆ **rather than** *conj* en vez de.

ratify ['rætɪfaɪ] (*pt* & *pp* **-ied**) *vt* ratificar.

rating ['reɪtɪŋ] *n* [standing] clasificación *f*.

ratio ['reɪʃɪəʊ] (*pl* **-s**) *n* proporción *f*, relación *f*.

ration ['ræʃn] ◇ *n* ración *f.* ◇ *vt* racionar.

◆ **rations** *npl* [supplies] víveres *mpl*.

rational ['ræʃənl] *adj* racional.

rationale [,ræʃə'nɑːl] *n* lógica *f*, razones *fpl*.

rationalize, -ise ['ræʃənəlaɪz] *vt* racionalizar.

rat race *n* mundo despiadadamente competitivo de los negocios.

rattle ['rætl] ◇ *n* - **1.** [of engine, metal] traqueteo *m*; [of chains] crujido *m*; [of glass] tintineo *m*; [of typewriter] repiqueteo *m* - **2.** [for baby] sonajero *m.* ◇ *vt* - **1.** [make rattle] hacer sonar - **2.** [unsettle] desconcertar. ◇ *vi* golpetear; [chains] crujir; [glass] tintinear.

rattlesnake ['rætlsneɪk], **rattler** US ['rætləʳ] *n* serpiente *f* de cascabel.

raucous ['rɔːkəs] *adj* ronco(ca) y estridente.

ravage ['rævɪdʒ] *vt* estragar, asolar.

◆ **ravages** *npl* estragos *mpl*.

rave [reɪv] ◇ *n* [party] macrofiesta *f* tecno. ◇ *vi* - **1.** [talk angrily]: **to ~ against sb/sthg** despotricar contra alguien/algo - **2.** [talk enthusiastically]: **to ~ about sthg** deshacerse en alabanzas sobre algo.

raven ['reɪvn] *n* cuervo *m*.

ravenous ['rævənəs] *adj* [person, animal] famélico(ca), hambriento(ta); [appetite] voraz.

ravine [rə'viːn] *n* barranco *m*.

raving ['reɪvɪŋ] *adj* [lunatic] de atar; [fantasy] delirante.

ravioli [,rævɪ'əʊlɪ] *n* (U) raviolis *mpl*.

ravishing ['rævɪʃɪŋ] *adj* [sight, beauty] de ensueño; [person] bellísimo(ma).

raw [rɔː] *adj* - **1.** [uncooked] crudo(da) - **2.** [untreated - silk] crudo(da); [- sewage] sin tratar; [- cane sugar] sin refinar - **3.** [painful - wound] en carne viva - **4.** [inexperienced] novato(ta) - **5.** [cold] crudo(da), frío(a).

raw deal *n*: **to get a ~** recibir un trato injusto.

raw material *n* materia *f* prima.

ray [reɪ] *n* rayo *m*; **~ of hope** resquicio *m* de esperanza.

rayon ['reɪɒn] *n* rayón *m*.

raze [reɪz] *vt* destruir por completo, arrasar.

razor ['reɪzəʳ] *n* [wet shaver] navaja *f*; [electric machine] maquinilla *f* de afeitar.

razor blade *n* hoja *f* de afeitar.

RC *abbr of* **Roman Catholic**.

Rd *abbr of* **road**.

R & D (*abbr of* **research and development**) *n* I + D *f*.

re [riː] *prep* Ref.

RE *n* (*abbr of* **religious education**) religión *f*.

reach [riːtʃ] ◇ *n* alcance *m*; **he has a long ~** tiene los brazos largos; **within (sb's) ~** [easily touched] al alcance (de alguien); [easily travelled to] a poca distancia (de alguien); **out of** OR **beyond sb's ~** fuera del alcance de alguien. ◇ *vt* - **1.** [gen] alcanzar, llegar a; **to ~ an agreement/a decision** llegar a un acuerdo/una decisión - **2.** [arrive at - place etc] llegar a - **3.** [get by stretching - object, shelf] alcanzar - **4.** [contact] localizar, contactar con. ◇ *vi*: **I can't ~** no llego; **to ~ out/across** alargar la mano; **to ~ down** agacharse.

react [rɪ'ækt] *vi* - **1.** [respond]: **to ~ (to)** reaccionar (a OR ante) - **2.** [rebel]: **to ~ against** reaccionar en contra de - **3.** CHEM: **to ~ with** reaccionar con.

reaction [rɪ'ækʃn] *n*: **~ (to/against)** reacción *f* (a/contra).

reactionary [rɪ'ækʃənrɪ] ◇ *adj* reaccionario(ria). ◇ *n* reaccionario *m*, -ria *f*.

reactor [rɪ'æktəʳ] *n* reactor *m*.

read [riːd] (*pt* & *pp* **read** [red]) ◇ *vt* - **1.** [gen & COMPUT] leer; **she can't ~ my writing** no entiende mi letra - **2.** [subj: sign, words] poner, decir - **3.** [subj: thermometer, meter etc] marcar - **4.** [interpret] interpretar - **5.** UK UNIV estudiar. ◇ *vi* - **1.** [person] leer - **2.** [read aloud]: **to ~ to sb** leerle a alguien - **3.** [piece of writing]: **to ~ well** estar bien escrito.

◆ **read out** *vt sep* leer en voz alta.

◆ **read through** *vt sep* leer.

◆ **read up on** *vt fus* leer OR documentarse sobre.

readable ['riːdəbl] *adj* ameno(na).

reader ['riːdəʳ] *n* - **1.** [person who reads] lector *m*, -ra *f* - **2.** COMPUT lector *m*.

readership ['riːdəʃɪp] *n* [total number of readers] lectores *mpl*.

readily ['redɪlɪ] *adv* - **1.** [willingly] de buena gana - **2.** [easily] fácilmente.

reading ['riːdɪŋ] *n* - **1.** [gen] lectura *f* - **2.** [recital] recital *m*.

readjust [,riːə'dʒʌst] ◇ *vt* reajustar. ◇ *vi*: **to ~ (to)** volverse a adaptar (a).

readout ['riːdaʊt] *n* COMPUT visualización *f*.

ready ['redɪ] (*pt* & *pp* **-ied**) ◇ *adj* - **1.** [prepared] listo(ta), preparado(da); **to be ~ for sthg/to do sthg** estar listo para algo/para hacer algo; **to get ~** [prepare] prepararse; [for going out] arreglarse - **2.** [willing]: **to be ~ to do sthg** estar dispuesto(ta) a hacer algo - **3.** [in need of]: **to be ~ for sthg** necesitar algo - **4.** [likely]: **to be ~ to do sthg** estar a punto de hacer algo - **5.** [smile] pronto(ta). ⋄ *vt* preparar; **to ~ o.s. for sthg** prepararse para algo.

ready cash *n* dinero *m* contante.

ready-made *adj* [products] hecho(cha); [clothes] confeccionado(da).

ready money *n* dinero *m* contante.

ready-to-wear *adj* confeccionado(da).

reafforestation [ˈriːəˌfɒrɪˈsteɪʃn] *n* repoblación *f* forestal.

real [ˈrɪəl] ⋄ *adj* - **1.** [not imagined, actual] real; **the ~ thing** lo auténtico; **for ~** de verdad; **in ~ terms** en términos reales - **2.** [genuine, proper] auténtico(ca); **a ~ friend** un amigo de verdad. ⋄ *adv US* muy.

real estate *n* propiedad *f* inmobiliaria.

real estate agent *n US* agente inmobiliario *m*, agente inmobiliaria *f*.

realign [ˌriːəˈlaɪn] *vt* volver a alinear.

realism [ˈrɪəlɪzm] *n* realismo *m*.

realistic [ˌrɪəˈlɪstɪk] *adj* realista.

reality [rɪˈæləti] (*pl* -ies) *n* realidad *f*.

reality TV *n* (U) reality shows *mpl*.

realization [ˌrɪəlaɪˈzeɪʃn] *n* - **1.** [recognition] comprensión *f* - **2.** [achievement] consecución *f*.

realize, -ise [ˈrɪəlaɪz] *vt* - **1.** [become aware of] darse cuenta de - **2.** [produce, achieve, make profit of] realizar.

really [ˈrɪəli] ⋄ *adv* - **1.** [for emphasis] de verdad; **~ good** buenísimo - **2.** [actually, honestly] realmente, en realidad - **3.** [to sound less negative] en realidad. ⋄ *excl* - **1.** [expressing doubt]: **~?** [in affirmatives] ¿ah sí?; [in negatives] ¿ah no? - **2.** [expressing surprise, disbelief]: **really?** ¿de verdad?, ¿seguro?

realm [relm] *n* - **1.** [field] campo *m*, esfera *f* - **2.** [kingdom] reino *m*.

realtor [ˈrɪəltər] *n US* agente inmobiliario *m*, agente inmobiliaria *f*.

reap [riːp] *vt lit & fig* cosechar.

reappear [ˌriːəˈpɪər] *vi* reaparecer.

rear [rɪər] ⋄ *adj* trasero(ra), de atrás. ⋄ *n* - **1.** [back] parte *f* de atrás; **to bring up the ~** cerrar la marcha. ⋄ *vt* criar. ⋄ *vi*: **to ~ (up)** encabritarse.

rearm [riːˈɑːm] *vi* rearmarse.

rearmost [ˈrɪəməʊst] *adj* último(ma).

rearrange [ˌriːəˈreɪndʒ] *vt* - **1.** [room, furniture] colocar de otro modo; [system, plans] reorganizar - **2.** [meeting] volver a concertar.

rearview mirror [ˈrɪəvjuː-] *n* (espejo *m*) retrovisor *m*.

reason [ˈriːzn] ⋄ *n* - **1.** [cause]: **~ (for)** razón *f* (de); **I don't know the ~ why** no sé por qué; **for some ~** por alguna razón - **2.** [justification]: **to have ~ to do sthg** tener motivos para hacer algo - **3.** [rationality] razón *f*; **it stands to ~** es lógico; **to listen to ~** avenirse a razones. ⋄ *vt & vi* razonar.

◆ **reason with** *vt fus* razonar con.

reasonable [ˈriːznəbl] *adj* razonable.

reasonably [ˈriːznəblɪ] *adv* razonablemente.

reasoned [ˈriːznd] *adj* razonado(da).

reasoning [ˈriːznɪŋ] *n* razonamiento *m*.

reassess [ˌriːəˈses] *vt* revaluar, reconsiderar.

reassurance [ˌriːəˈʃɔːrəns] *n* - **1.** (U) [comfort] palabras *fpl* tranquilizadoras - **2.** [promise] promesa *f*.

reassure [ˌriːəˈʃɔːʳ] *vt* tranquilizar.

reassuring [ˌriːəˈʃɔːrɪŋ] *adj* tranquilizador(ra).

rebate [ˈriːbeɪt] *n* - **1.** [refund] devolución *f* - **2.** [discount] bonificación *f*.

rebel [*n* ˈrebl, *vb* rɪˈbel] (*pt & pp* -**led**, *cont* -**ling**) ⋄ *n* rebelde *m* OR *f*. ⋄ *vi*: **to ~ (against)** rebelarse (contra), alebrestarse (contra) *Col, Méx & Ven.*

rebellion [rɪˈbeljən] *n* rebelión *f*.

rebellious [rɪˈbeljəs] *adj* rebelde.

rebound [*n* ˈriːbaʊnd, *vb* ˌrɪˈbaʊnd] ⋄ *n*: **on the ~** [ball] de rebote *m*. ⋄ *vi* [bounce back] rebotar.

rebuff [rɪˈbʌf] *n* [slight] desaire *m*; [refusal] negativa *f*.

rebuild [ˌriːˈbɪld] (*pt & pp* -**built**) *vt* reconstruir.

rebuke [rɪˈbjuːk] ⋄ *n* reprimenda *f*. ⋄ *vt*: **to ~ sb (for)** reprender a alguien (por).

rebuttal [riːˈbʌtl] *n* refutación *f*.

recalcitrant [rɪˈkælsɪtrənt] *adj* recalcitrante.

recall [rɪˈkɔːl] ⋄ *n* [memory] memoria *f*. ⋄ *vt* - **1.** [remember] recordar, acordarse de - **2.** [ambassador] retirar; [goods] retirar del mercado.

recant [rɪˈkænt] *vi* [deny statement] retractarse; [deny religion] renegar de la fe.

recap [ˈriːkæp] (*pt & pp* -**ped**, *cont* -**ping**) *inf* ⋄ *n* resumen *m*, recapitulación *f*. ⋄ *vt* [summarize] recapitular, resumir. ⋄ *vi* recapitular, resumir.

recapitulate [ˌriːkəˈpɪtjʊleɪt] *vt & vi* recapitular, resumir.

recd, rec'd (*abbr of* **received**) rbdo.

recede [riːˈsiːd] *vi* - **1.** [person, car] alejarse; [coastline] retroceder - **2.** *fig* [disappear] esfumarse.

receding [rɪˈsiːdɪŋ] *adj* [chin, forehead] hundida; **to have a ~ hairline** tener entradas.

receipt [rɪˈsiːt] *n* recibo *m*; **to acknowledge ~** acusar recibo.

◆ **receipts** *npl* recaudación *f*.

receive [rɪˈsiːv] *vt* - **1.** [gen] recibir; **I ~d a fine** me pusieron una multa - **2.** [reaction] tener; [injury, setback] sufrir - **3.** [greet]: **to be well/badly ~d** tener una buena/mala acogida.

receiver [rɪ'siːvə^r] *n* -1. [of telephone] auricular *m* -2. [radio, TV set] receptor *m* -3. [criminal] perista *m* OR *f*, receptador *m*, -ra *f* - 4. FIN síndico *m*, -ca *f*.

recent ['riːsnt] *adj* reciente.

recently ['riːsntlɪ] *adv* recientemente.

receptacle [rɪ'septəkl] *n* receptáculo *m*.

reception [rɪ'sepʃn] *n* -1. [gen] recepción *f* - 2. [welcome] recibimiento *m*.

reception desk *n* recepción *f*.

receptionist [rɪ'sepʃənɪst] *n* recepcionista *m* OR *f*.

recess ['riːses, *UK* rɪ'ses] *n* -1. [vacation] periodo *m* vacacional; **to be in ~** estar clausurado(da) - 2. [alcove] nicho *m*, hueco *m* - 3. *US* SCH recreo *m*.
 ➡ **recesses** *npl* [of mind, heart] recovecos *mpl*; [of building] escondrijos *mpl*.

recession [rɪ'seʃn] *n* recesión *f*.

recharge [,riː'tʃɑːdʒ] *vt* recargar.

recipe ['resɪpɪ] *n* CULIN & *fig* receta *f*.

recipient [rɪ'sɪpɪənt] *n* [of letter, cheque] destinatario *m*, -ria *f*.

reciprocal [rɪ'sɪprəkl] *adj* recíproco(ca).

recital [rɪ'saɪtl] *n* recital *m*.

recite [rɪ'saɪt] *vt* -1. [poem] recitar - 2. [list] enumerar.

reckless ['reklɪs] *adj* [gen] imprudente; [driver, driving] temerario(ria).

reckon ['rekn] *vt* -1. *inf* [think]: **to ~ (that)** pensar que - 2. [consider, judge]: **to be ~ed to be sthg** ser considerado(da) algo - 3. [calculate] calcular.
 ➡ **reckon on** *vt fus* contar con.
 ➡ **reckon with** *vt fus* [expect] contar con.

reckoning ['rekənɪŋ] *n* [calculation] cálculo *m*.

reclaim [rɪ'kleɪm] *vt* -1. [claim back] reclamar - 2. [recover] recuperar; **to ~ land from the sea** ganarle tierra al mar.

recline [rɪ'klaɪn] *vi* reclinarse.

reclining [rɪ'klaɪnɪŋ] *adj* [seat] reclinable.

recluse [rɪ'kluːs] *n* solitario *m*, -ria *f*.

recognition [,rekəg'nɪʃn] *n* reconocimiento *m*; **to have changed beyond** OR **out of all ~** estar irreconocible; **in ~ of** en reconocimiento a.

recognizable ['rekəgnaɪzəbl] *adj* reconocible.

recognize, -ise ['rekəgnaɪz] *vt* reconocer.

recoil [*vb* rɪ'kɔɪl, *n* 'riːkɔɪl] ◇ *vi* -1. [draw back] retroceder, echarse atrás - 2. *fig* [shrink from]: **to ~ from** OR **at sthg** [truth, bad news] esquivar OR rehuir algo; [idea, suggestion] estremecerse ante algo. ◇ *n* [of gun] retroceso *m*.

recollect [,rekə'lekt] *vt* & *vi* recordar.

recollection [,rekə'lekʃn] *n* recuerdo *m*.

recommend [,rekə'mend] *vt* recomendar.

recompense ['rekəmpens] ◇ *n*: **~ (for)** compensación *f* OR indemnización *f* (por).

◇ *vt*: **to ~ sb (for)** recompensar a alguien (por).

reconcile ['rekənsaɪl] *vt* -1. [find agreement between] conciliar; **to ~ sthg with** hacer compatible algo con - 2. [make friendly again] reconciliar - 3. [accept]: **to ~ o.s. to** resignarse a.

reconditioned [,riːkən'dɪʃnd] *adj* reparado(da).

reconnaissance [rɪ'kɒnɪsəns] *n* reconocimiento *m*.

reconnoitre *UK*, **reconnoiter** *US* [,rekə'nɔɪtə^r] ◇ *vt* reconocer. ◇ *vi* hacer un reconocimiento.

reconsider [,riːkən'sɪdə^r] *vt* & *vi* reconsiderar.

reconstruct [,riːkən'strʌkt] *vt* [building, crime] reconstruir.

record [*n* & *adj* 'rekɔːd, *vb* rɪ'kɔːd] ◇ *n* -1. [of event, piece of information & COMPUT] registro *m*; [of meeting] actas *fpl*; **on ~** [on file] archivado; [ever recorded] de que se tiene constancia; **off the ~** confidencial - 2. [vinyl disc] disco *m* - 3. [best achievement] récord *m* - 4. [past results] resultados *mpl* - 5. HIST historial *m*; **criminal ~** antecedentes *mpl* penales. ◇ *vt* -1. [write down] anotar - 2. [document] documentar - 3. [put on tape] grabar. ◇ *vi* grabar. ◇ *adj* récord (*inv*).

record company *n* compañía *f* discográfica.

recorded delivery [rɪ'kɔːdɪd-] *n* correo *m* certificado.

recorder [rɪ'kɔːdə^r] *n* [musical instrument] flauta *f*.

record holder *n* plusmarquista *m* OR *f*.

recording [rɪ'kɔːdɪŋ] *n* grabación *f*.

record player *n* tocadiscos *m inv.*

recount [*n* 'riːkaʊnt, *vt sense 1* rɪ'kaʊnt, *sense 2* ,riː'kaʊnt] ◇ *n* segundo recuento *m*. ◇ *vt* -1. [narrate] narrar - 2. [count again] volver a contar.

recoup [rɪ'kuːp] *vt* recuperar.

recourse [rɪ'kɔːs] *n fml*: **to have ~ to** recurrir a.

recover [rɪ'kʌvə^r] ◇ *vt* -1. [retrieve, recoup] recuperar - 2. [regain - calm etc] recobrar. ◇ *vi*: **to ~ (from)** recuperarse (de).

recovery [rɪ'kʌvərɪ] (*pl* -ies) *n* recuperación *f*.

recreation [,rekrɪ'eɪʃn] *n* [leisure] esparcimiento *m*, recreo *m*.

recrimination [rɪ,krɪmɪ'neɪʃn] *n* recriminación *f*.

recruit [rɪ'kruːt] ◇ *n* recluta *m* OR *f*. ◇ *vt* -1. [gen] reclutar; **to ~ sb (for sthg/to do sthg)** reclutar a alguien (para algo/para hacer algo) - 2. [find, employ] contratar. ◇ *vi* buscar empleados nuevos.

recruitment [rɪ'kru:tmənt] *n* [gen] reclutamiento *m*; [of staff] contratación *f*.

rectangle ['rek,tæŋgl] *n* rectángulo *m*.

rectangular [rek'tæŋgjʊləʳ] *adj* rectangular.

rectify ['rektɪfaɪ] (*pt & pp* -ied) *vt* rectificar.

rector ['rektəʳ] *n* -1. [priest] párroco *m*
- 2. *Scot* [head - of school] director *m*, -ra *f*; [-
of college, university] rector *m*, -ra *f*.

rectory ['rektərɪ] (*pl* -ies) *n* rectoría *f*.

recuperate [rɪ'ku:pəreɪt] <> *vt* recuperar.
<> *vi*: to ~ (from) recuperarse (de).

recur [rɪ'kɜ:ʳ] (*pt & pp* -red, *cont* -ring) *vi* repetirse, volver a producirse.

recurrence [rɪ'kʌrəns] *n* repetición *f*.

recurrent [rɪ'kʌrənt] *adj* que se repite, pe-
riódico(ca).

recycle [,ri:'saɪkl] *vt* reciclar.

recycle bin *n* COMPUT papelera *f*.

red [red] (*compar* -der, *superl* -dest) <> *adj*
rojo(ja). <> *n* [colour] rojo *m*; to be in the
~ *inf* estar en números rojos.

red cabbage *n* lombarda *f*.

red card *n* FTBL: to show sb the ~ mostrar-
le a alguien (la) tarjeta roja.

red carpet *n*: to roll out the ~ for sb recibir a alguien con todos los honores.
  ● **red-carpet** *adj*: to give sb the red-
carpet treatment dispensar a alguien un
gran recibimiento.

Red Cross *n*: the ~ la Cruz Roja.

redcurrant ['redkʌrənt] *n* -1. [fruit] grosella *f* - 2. [bush] grosellero *m*.

redden ['redn] <> *vt* [make red] teñir de rojo. <> *vi* [flush] enrojecer.

redecorate [,ri:'dekəreɪt] *vt & vi* volver a
pintar (*o* empapelar).

redeem [rɪ'di:m] *vt* -1. [save, rescue] salvar,
rescatar - 2. RELIG redimir - 3. *fml* [at pawnbroker's] desempeñar.

redeeming [rɪ'di:mɪŋ] *adj*: his only ~ feature lo único que le salva.

redeploy [,ri:dɪ'plɔɪ] *vt* reorganizar.

red-faced [-'feɪst] *adj* -1. [flushed] rojo(ja),
colorado(da) - 2. [with embarrassment] ro-
jo(ja) de vergüenza.

red-haired [-'heəd] *adj* pelirrojo(ja).

red-handed [-'hændɪd] *adj*: to catch sb ~
coger a alguien con las manos en la masa.

redhead ['redhed] *n* pelirrojo *m*, -ja *f*.

red herring *n fig* [unhelpful clue] pista *f* falsa; [means of distracting attention] ardid *m*
para distraer la atención.

red-hot *adj* [metal, person, passion] al rojo
(vivo).

redid [,ri:'dɪd] *pt* ⊳ redo.

redirect [,ri:dɪ'rekt] *vt* -1. [retarget] redirigir
- 2. [divert] desviar - 3. [forward] reexpedir.

rediscover [,ri:dɪs'kʌvəʳ] *vt* -1. [re-experi-
ence] volver a descubrir - 2. [make popular,

famous again]: to be ~ed ser descubier-
to(ta) de nuevo.

red light *n* [traffic signal] semáforo *m* rojo.

red-light district *n* barrio *m* chino.

redo [,ri:'du:] (*pt* -did, *pp* -done) *vt* [do
again] volver a hacer.

redolent ['redələnt] *adj literary* -1. [remi-
niscent]: to be ~ of sthg evocar algo
- 2. [smelling]: to be ~ of sthg oler a algo.

redouble [,ri:'dʌbl] *vt*: to ~ one's efforts
(to do sthg) redoblar esfuerzos (para hacer
algo).

redraft [,ri:'drɑ:ft] *vt* volver a redactar.

redress [rɪ'dres] *fml* <> *n* (*U*) reparación *f*.
<> *vt*: to ~ the balance (between) equili-
brar la balanza (entre).

red tape *n fig* papeleo *m*.

reduce [rɪ'dju:s] <> *vt* reducir; to be ~d to
doing sthg verse rebajado *OR* forzado a hacer algo; it ~d me to tears me hizo llorar.
<> *vi* US [diet] (intentar) adelgazar.

reduction [rɪ'dʌkʃn] *n* -1. [gen]: ~ (in) reducción *f* (de) - 2. COMM: ~ (of) descuento
m (de).

redundancy [rɪ'dʌndənsɪ] (*pl* -ies) *n* UK
[job loss] despido *m*.

redundant [rɪ'dʌndənt] *adj* -1. UK
[jobless]: to be made ~ perder el empleo;
to make sb ~ despedir a alguien - 2. [not required - equipment, factory] innecesa-
rio(ria); [- comment] redundante.

reed [ri:d] *n* -1. [plant] carrizo *m*, cañavera *f*
- 2. [of musical instrument] lengüeta *f*.

reef [ri:f] *n* arrecife *m*.

reek [ri:k] *vi*: to ~ (of) apestar (a).

reel [ri:l] <> *n* -1. [of cotton, on fishing rod]
carrete *m* - 2. [of film] rollo *m*. <> *vi* -1. [stag-
ger] tambalearse - 2. [be stunned]: to ~ from
sthg quedarse atónito(ta) por algo.
  ● **reel in** *vt sep* sacar enrollando el carrete
(*en pesca*).
  ● **reel off** *vt sep* recitar al corrido.

reenact [,ri:ɪn'ækt] *vt* representar de nuevo.

ref [ref] *n* -1. (*abbr of* referee) *inf* SPORT árbitro *m* - 2. (*abbr of* reference) ADMIN ref.

refectory [rɪ'fektərɪ] (*pl* -ies) *n* refectorio
m.

refer [rɪ'fɜːʳ] (*pt & pp* -red, *cont* -ring) *vt*
-1. [send, direct]: to ~ sb to [to place] enviar
a alguien a; [to source of information] remitir a alguien a - 2. [report, submit]: to ~ sthg
to remitir algo a.
  ● **refer to** *vt fus* -1. [mention, speak about]
referirse a - 2. [consult] consultar.

referee [,refə'ri:] <> *n* -1. SPORT árbitro *m*
- 2. UK [for job application] *persona que proporciona referencias de alguien para un trabajo*.
<> *vt & vi* SPORT arbitrar.

reference ['refrəns] *n* -1. [mention, reference number]: to make ~ to hacer referencia
a; with ~ to *fml* con referencia a - 2. (*U*)

[for advice, information]: **~ (to)** consulta *f* (a) - **3.** [for job- letter] referencia *f*; [- person] *persona que proporciona referencias de alguien para un trabajo.*

reference book *n* libro *m* de consulta.

reference number *n* número *m* de referencia.

referendum [ˌrefəˈrendəm] (*pl* -**s** OR -**da** [-də]) *n* referéndum *m*.

refill [*n* ˈriːfɪl, *vb* ˌriːˈfɪl] ◇ *n* [for pen] recambio *m*; [of drink] *inf:* **would you like a ~?** ¿te apetece otra copa? ◇ *vt* volver a llenar.

refine [rɪˈfaɪn] *vt* - **1.** [oil, food] refinar - **2.** [plan, speech] pulir.

refined [rɪˈfaɪnd] *adj* - **1.** [oil, food, person] refinado(da) - **2.** [equipment, theory] perfeccionado(da).

refinement [rɪˈfaɪnmənt] *n* - **1.** [improvement]: **~ (on)** mejora *f* (de) - **2.** *(U)* [gentility] refinamiento *m*.

reflect [rɪˈflekt] ◇ *vt* - **1.** [gen] reflejar - **2.** [think, consider]: **to ~ that ...** considerar que ... ◇ *vi:* **to ~ (on** OR **upon)** reflexionar (sobre).

reflection [rɪˈflekʃn] *n* - **1.** [gen] reflejo *m* - **2.** [criticism]: **~ on** crítica *f* de - **3.** [thinking] reflexión *f*; **on ~** pensándolo bien.

reflector [rɪˈflektər] *n* reflector *m*.

reflex [ˈriːfleks] *n:* **~ (action)** (acto *m*) reflejo *m*.

reflexive [rɪˈfleksɪv] *adj* GRAMM reflexivo(va).

reforestation [riːˌfɒrɪˈsteɪʃn] = **reafforestation**.

reform [rɪˈfɔːm] ◇ *n* reforma *f*. ◇ *vt* reformar. ◇ *vi* reformarse.

Reformation [ˌrefəˈmeɪʃn] *n:* **the ~** la Reforma.

reformatory [rɪˈfɔːmətrɪ] *n* US reformatorio *m*.

reformer [rɪˈfɔːmər] *n* reformador *m*, -ra *f*.

refrain [rɪˈfreɪn] ◇ *n* [chorus] estribillo *m*. ◇ *vi fml:* **to ~ from doing sthg** abstenerse de hacer algo.

refresh [rɪˈfreʃ] *vt* [gen & COMPUT] refrescar.

refreshed [rɪˈfreʃt] *adj* descansado(da), vigorizado(da).

refresher course [rɪˈfreʃər-] *n* cursillo *m* de reciclaje *(en el mismo trabajo)*.

refreshing [rɪˈfreʃɪŋ] *adj* [change, honesty, drink] refrescante; [sleep] vigorizante.

refreshments [rɪˈfreʃmənts] *npl* refrigerio *m*.

refrigerator [rɪˈfrɪdʒəreɪtər] *n* nevera *f*, refrigerador *m Amér*, heladera *f RP*, refrigeradora *f Col, Perú*.

refuel [ˌriːˈfjʊəl] (*UK pt* & *pp* -**led**, *cont* -**ling**, *US pt* & *pp* -**ed**, *cont* -**ing**) ◇ *vt* llenar de carburante. ◇ *vi* repostar.

refuge [ˈrefjuːdʒ] *n* refugio *m*; **to seek** OR **take ~ (in)** *fig* buscar refugio (en).

refugee [ˌrefjʊˈdʒiː] *n* refugiado *m*, -da *f*.

refund [*n* ˈriːfʌnd, *vb* rɪˈfʌnd] ◇ *n* reembolso *m*. ◇ *vt:* **to ~ sthg to sb, to ~ sb sthg** reembolsar algo a alguien.

refurbish [ˌriːˈfɜːbɪʃ] *vt* [building] restaurar; [office, shop] renovar.

refusal [rɪˈfjuːzl] *n* - **1.** [disagreement, saying no]: **~ (to do sthg)** negativa *f* (a hacer algo) - **2.** [withholding, denial] denegación *f* - **3.** [non-acceptance]: **to meet with ~** ser rechazado(da).

refuse[1] [rɪˈfjuːz] *vt* - **1.** [withhold, deny]: **to ~ sb sthg, to ~ sthg to sb** denegar a alguien algo - **2.** [decline, reject] rechazar - **3.** [not agree, be completely unwilling]: **to ~ to do sthg** negarse a hacer algo. ◇ *vi* negarse.

refuse[2] [ˈrefjuːs] *n* [rubbish] basura *f*.

refuse collection [ˈrefjuːs-] *n* recogida *f* de basuras.

refute [rɪˈfjuːt] *vt fml* refutar.

regain [rɪˈɡeɪn] *vt* [leadership, first place] recuperar; [health, composure] recobrar.

regal [ˈriːɡl] *adj* regio(gia).

regalia [rɪˈɡeɪljə] *n (U)* ropaje *m*, vestiduras *fpl*.

regard [rɪˈɡɑːd] ◇ *n* - **1.** *fml* [respect, esteem]: **~ (for)** estima *f* OR respeto *m* (por) - **2.** [aspect]: **in this/that ~** a este/ese respecto - **3.** [consideration]: **with no ~ for** sin ninguna consideración por. ◇ *vt* - **1.** [consider]: **to ~ o.s. as sthg** considerarse algo; **to ~ sthg/sb as** considerar algo/a alguien como - **2.** [look at, view]: **to be highly ~ed** estar muy bien considerado.

 ◆ **regards** *npl* [in greetings] recuerdos *mpl*; **give them my ~s** salúdales de mi parte.

 ◆ **as regards** *prep* en cuanto a, por lo que se refiere a.

 ◆ **in regard to, with regard to** *prep* respecto a, en cuanto a.

regarding [rɪˈɡɑːdɪŋ] *prep* respecto a, en cuanto a.

regardless [rɪˈɡɑːdlɪs] *adv* a pesar de todo.

 ◆ **regardless of** *prep* sin tener en cuenta; **~ of the cost** cueste lo que cueste.

regime [reɪˈʒiːm] *n* régimen *m*.

regiment [ˈredʒɪmənt] *n* MIL regimiento *m*.

region [ˈriːdʒən] *n* región *f*; **in the ~ of** alrededor de.

regional [ˈriːdʒənl] *adj* regional.

register [ˈredʒɪstər] ◇ *n* [gen] registro *m*; [at school] lista *f*. ◇ *vt* - **1.** [record - gen] registrar; [- car] matricular - **2.** [express] mostrar, reflejar. ◇ *vi* - **1.** [be put on official list]: **to ~ (as/for)** inscribirse (como/para) - **2.** [book in - at hotel] registrarse; [- at conference] **inscribirse - 3.** *inf* [be noticed]: **I told him but it didn't seem to** ~ se lo dije, pero no pareció que lo captara.

registered ['redʒɪstəd] *adj* **-1.** [officially listed] inscrito(ta) oficialmente **- 2.** [letter, parcel] certificado(da).

registered trademark *n* marca *f* registrada.

registrar [,redʒɪ'strɑː'] *n* **-1.** [keeper of records] registrador *m*, -ra *f* oficial **- 2.** UNIV secretario *m*, -ria *f* general **- 3.** [doctor] médico *m*, -ca *f* de hospital.

registration [,redʒɪ'streɪʃn] *n* **-1.** [gen] registro *m* **- 2.** AUT = **registration number**.

registration number *n* AUT número *m* de matrícula; COMPUT número *m* de registro.

registry ['redʒɪstrɪ] (*pl* **-ies**) *n* registro *m*.

registry office *n* registro *m* civil.

regret [rɪ'gret] (*pt* & *pp* **-ted**, *cont* **-ting**) ◇ *n* **-1.** *fml* [sorrow] pesar *m* **- 2.** [sad feeling]: **I've no** ~**s about it** no lo lamento en absoluto. ◇ *vt* [be sorry about]: **to** ~ **sthg/doing sthg** lamentar algo/haber hecho algo.

regretfully [rɪ'gretfʊlɪ] *adv* con pesar; ~**, we have to announce ...** lamentamos tener que anunciar ...

regrettable [rɪ'gretəbl] *adj* lamentable.

regroup [,riː'gruːp] *vi* reagruparse.

regular ['regjʊlə'] ◇ *adj* **-1.** [gen] regular **- 2.** [customer] habitual **- 3.** [time, place] acostumbrado(da); [problem] usual, normal **- 4.** US [size] normal, mediano(na) **- 5.** US [pleasant] legal. ◇ *n* cliente *m* habitual.

regularly ['regjʊləlɪ] *adv* **-1.** [gen] con regularidad **- 2.** [equally spaced] de manera uniforme.

regulate ['regjʊleɪt] *vt* regular.

regulation [,regjʊ'leɪʃn] *n* **-1.** [rule] regla *f*, norma *f* **- 2.** (*U*) [control] regulación *f*.

rehabilitate [,riːə'bɪlɪteɪt] *vt* rehabilitar.

rehearsal [rɪ'hɜːsl] *n* ensayo *m*.

rehearse [rɪ'hɜːs] *vt* ensayar.

reign [reɪn] *lit* & *fig* ◇ *n* reinado *m*. ◇ *vi*: **to** ~ **(over)** reinar (sobre).

reimburse [,riːɪm'bɜːs] *vt*: **to** ~ **sb (for sthg)** reembolsar a alguien (algo).

rein [reɪn] *n fig*: **to give (a) free** ~ **to sb, to give sb free** ~ dar rienda suelta a alguien.
◆ **reins** *npl* [for horse] riendas *fpl*.

reindeer ['reɪn,dɪə'] (*pl inv*) *n* reno *m*.

reinforce [,riːɪn'fɔːs] *vt* reforzar.

reinforced concrete [,riːɪn'fɔːst-] *n* cemento *m* OR hormigón *m* armado.

reinforcement [,riːɪn'fɔːsmənt] *n* refuerzo *m*.
◆ **reinforcements** *npl* refuerzos *mpl*.

reinstate [,riːɪn'steɪt] *vt* **-1.** [give job back to] restituir OR reintegrar en su puesto a **- 2.** [bring back] restablecer.

reissue [riː'ɪʃuː] *vt* [gen] reeditar; [film] reestrenar, reponer.

reiterate [riː'ɪtəreɪt] *vt fml* reiterar.

reject [*n* 'riːdʒekt, *vb* rɪ'dʒekt] ◇ *n* **-1.** [thing]: ~**s** artículos *mpl* defectuosos **- 2.** *inf* [person] desecho *m*. ◇ *vt* rechazar.

rejection [rɪ'dʒekʃn] *n* rechazo *m*.

rejoice [rɪ'dʒɔɪs] *vi*: **to** ~ **(at** OR **in)** alegrarse OR regocijarse (con).

rejuvenate [rɪ'dʒuːvəneɪt] *vt* rejuvenecer.

rekindle [,riː'kɪndl] *vt* reavivar.

relapse [rɪ'læps] ◇ *n* recaída *f*. ◇ *vi*: **to** ~ **into** volver a caer en.

relate [rɪ'leɪt] ◇ *vt* **-1.** [connect]: **to** ~ **sthg (to)** relacionar algo (con) **- 2.** [tell] contar, relatar. ◇ *vi* **-1.** [be connected]: **to** ~ **to** estar relacionado(da) con **- 2.** [concern]: **to** ~ **to** referirse a **- 3.** [empathize]: **to** ~ **(to sb)** tener mucho en común (con alguien).
◆ **relating to** *prep* concerniente OR referente a.

related [rɪ'leɪtɪd] *adj* **-1.** [in same family] emparentado(da); **to be** ~ **to sb** ser pariente de alguien **- 2.** [connected] relacionado(da).

relation [rɪ'leɪʃn] *n* **-1.** [connection]: ~ **(to/ between)** relación *f* (con/entre); **to bear no** ~ **to** no tener nada que ver con **- 2.** [family member] pariente *m* OR *f*, familiar *m* OR *f*.
◆ **relations** *npl* [family, race, industrial] relaciones *fpl*.

relationship [rɪ'leɪʃnʃɪp] *n* **-1.** [gen] relación *f*; **a good** ~ buenas relaciones **- 2.** [to family member] parentesco *m*.

relative ['relətɪv] ◇ *adj* relativo(va). ◇ *n* pariente *m* OR *f*, familiar *m* OR *f*.
◆ **relative to** *prep fml* con relación a.

relatively ['relətɪvlɪ] *adv* relativamente.

relax [rɪ'læks] ◇ *vt* **-1.** [gen] relajar **- 2.** [loosen - grip] aflojar. ◇ *vi* **-1.** [gen] relajarse **- 2.** [loosen] aflojarse.

relaxation [,riːlæk'seɪʃn] *n* **-1.** [recreation] relajación *f*, esparcimiento *m* **- 2.** [slackening - of discipline] relajación *f*, relajamiento *m*.

relaxed [rɪ'lækst] *adj* relajado(da).

relaxing [rɪ'læksɪŋ] *adj* relajante.

relay ['riːleɪ] (*pt* & *pp* **-ed**) ◇ *n* **-1.** SPORT: ~ **(race)** carrera *f* de relevos **- 2.** RADIO & TV retransmisión *f*. ◇ *vt* **-1.** [broadcast] retransmitir **- 2.** [repeat]: **to** ~ **sthg (to)** transmitir algo (a).

release [rɪ'liːs] ◇ *n* **-1.** [setting free] puesta *f* en libertad, liberación *f* **- 2.** [relief] alivio *m* **- 3.** [statement] comunicado *m* **- 4.** [emitting - of gas] escape *m*; [- of heat, pressure] emisión *f* **- 5.** [thing issued - of film] estreno *m*; [- of record] publicación *f*. ◇ *vt* **-1.** [set free]: **to** ~ **sb (from)** liberar a alguien (de) **- 2.** [lift restriction on]: **to** ~ **sb from** liberar a alguien de - **3.** [make available - funds, resources] **entregar** - **4.** [let go - rope, reins, brake, person] **soltar**; [- grip] **aflojar**; [- mechanism, trigger] **disparar** - **5.** [emit - gas, heat] **despedir, emitir** - **6.** [issue - film] **estrenar**; [- record] **sacar**.

relegate ['relɪgeɪt] *vt* - **1.** [demote]: **to ~ sthg/sb (to)** relegar algo/a alguien (a) - **2.** *UK* FTBL: **to be ~d** descender *(a una división inferior)*.

relent [rɪ'lent] *vi* [person] ablandarse; [wind, storm] remitir, aminorar.

relentless [rɪ'lentlɪs] *adj* implacable.

relevant ['reləvənt] *adj* - **1.** [connected]: **~ (to)** pertinente (a) - **2.** [important]: **~ (to)** importante OR relevante (para) - **3.** [appropriate] pertinente, oportuno(na).

reliable [rɪ'laɪəbl] *adj* - **1.** [dependable] fiable - **2.** [information] fidedigno(na).

reliably [rɪ'laɪəblɪ] *adv* - **1.** [dependably] sin fallar - **2.** [correctly]: **to be ~ informed about sthg** saber algo de fuentes fidedignas.

reliant [rɪ'laɪənt] *adj*: **to be ~ on sb/sthg** depender de alguien/de algo.

relic ['relɪk] *n* - **1.** [gen] reliquia *f* - **2.** [custom still in use] vestigio *m*.

relief [rɪ'liːf] *n* - **1.** [comfort] alivio *m* - **2.** [for poor, refugees] ayuda *f* - **3.** *(U) US* [social security] subsidio *m*.

relieve [rɪ'liːv] *vt* - **1.** [ease, lessen] aliviar - **2.** [take away from]: **to ~ sb of sthg** liberar a alguien de algo.

religion [rɪ'lɪdʒn] *n* religión *f*.

religious [rɪ'lɪdʒəs] *adj* religioso(sa).

relinquish [rɪ'lɪŋkwɪʃ] *vt* [power, claim] renunciar a; **to ~ one's hold on sthg** soltar algo.

relish ['relɪʃ] <> *n* - **1.** [enjoyment]: **with (great) ~** con (gran) deleite - **2.** [pickle] *salsa rojiza agridulce con pepinillo etc.* <> *vt* disfrutar con; **to ~ the thought** OR **idea** OR **prospect of doing sthg** disfrutar de antemano con la idea de hacer algo.

relocate [ˌriːləʊ'keɪt] <> *vt* trasladar. <> *vi* trasladarse.

reluctance [rɪ'lʌktəns] *n* reticencia *f*.

reluctant [rɪ'lʌktənt] *adj* reacio(cia); **to be ~ to do sthg** estar poco dispuesto a hacer algo.

reluctantly [rɪ'lʌktəntlɪ] *adv* con desgana.

rely [rɪ'laɪ] (*pt & pp* -ied) ◆ **rely on** *vt fus* - **1.** [count on] contar con; **to be able to ~ on sb/sthg to do sthg** poder estar seguro de que alguien/algo hará algo - **2.** [be dependent on]: **to ~ on sb/sthg for sthg** depender de alguien/algo para algo.

remain [rɪ'meɪn] <> *vt* continuar como; **to ~ the same** continuar siendo igual. <> *vi* - **1.** [stay] quedarse, permanecer - **2.** [survive - custom, problem] quedar, continuar

- **3.** [be left]: **to ~ to be done/proved** quedar por hacer/probar.
◆ **remains** *npl* restos *mpl*.

remainder [rɪ'meɪndə^r] *n* - **1.** [rest]: **the ~** el resto - **2.** MATH resto *m*.

remaining [rɪ'meɪnɪŋ] *adj* que queda, restante.

remand [rɪ'mɑːnd] JUR <> *n*: **on ~** detenido(da) en espera de juicio. <> *vt*: **to be ~ed in custody** estar bajo custodia.

remark [rɪ'mɑːk] <> *n* [comment] comentario *m*. <> *vt*: **to ~ (that)** comentar que.

remarkable [rɪ'mɑːkəbl] *adj* - **1.** [fantastic] extraordinario(ria) - **2.** [surprising] sorprendente.

remarry [ˌriː'mærɪ] (*pt & pp* -ied) *vi* volver a casarse.

remedial [rɪ'miːdjəl] *adj* - **1.** SCH [class, teacher] de refuerzo; [pupil] atrasado(da) - **2.** [corrective] correctivo(va).

remedy ['remədɪ] (*pl* -ies, *pt & pp* -ied) <> *n lit & fig*: **~ (for)** remedio *m* (para). <> *vt* remediar, poner remedio a.

remember [rɪ'membə^r] <> *vt* - **1.** [gen] recordar, acordarse de; **to ~ to do sthg** acordarse de hacer algo; **to ~ doing sthg** recordar OR acordarse de haber hecho algo; **he ~ed me in his will** me dejó algo en su testamento. <> *vi* [gen] recordar, acordarse.

remembrance [rɪ'membrəns] *n fml*: **in ~ of** en conmemoración de.

Remembrance Day *n* en Gran Bretaña, *día en conmemoración de los caídos en las dos guerras mundiales*.

remind [rɪ'maɪnd] *vt*: **to ~ sb (about sthg/ to do sthg)** recordar a alguien (algo/que haga algo); **she ~s me of my sister** me recuerda a mi hermana.

reminder [rɪ'maɪndə^r] *n* - **1.** [to jog memory] recordatorio *m*, recuerdo *m* - **2.** [letter, note] notificación *f*, aviso *m*.

reminisce [ˌremɪ'nɪs] *vi*: **to ~ (about sthg)** rememorar (algo).

reminiscent [ˌremɪ'nɪsnt] *adj* [similar to]: **to be ~ of** evocar, recordar a.

remiss [rɪ'mɪs] *adj* negligente, remiso(sa); **it was ~ of me** fue una negligencia por mi parte.

remit¹ [rɪ'mɪt] (*pt & pp* -ted, *cont* -ting) *vt* [money] remitir.

remit² ['riːmɪt] *n* [responsibility] misión *f*.

remittance [rɪ'mɪtns] *n* giro *m*.

remix ['riːmɪks] *n* remezcla *f*.

remnant ['remnənt] *n* - **1.** [remaining part] resto *m* - **2.** [of cloth] retal *m*.

remold *n & vt US* = **remould**.

remorse [rɪ'mɔːs] *n (U)* remordimientos *mpl*.

remorseful [rɪ'mɔːsfʊl] *adj* lleno(na) de remordimientos.

remorseless [rɪ'mɔːslɪs] *adj* **- 1.** [pitiless] despiadado(da) **- 2.** [unstoppable] implacable.

remote [rɪ'məʊt] *adj* **- 1.** [place, time possibility] remoto(ta) **- 2.** [from reality etc]: ~ **(from)** apartado(da) OR alejado(da) (de).

remote control *n* telemando *m*, mando *m* a distancia.

remotely [rɪ'məʊtlɪ] *adv* **- 1.** [in the slightest]: **not ~** ni remotamente, en lo más mínimo **- 2.** [far off] muy lejos.

remould UK, **remold** US ['riːməʊld] *n* neumático *m* recauchutado.

removable [rɪ'muːvəbl] *adj* **- 1.** [detachable] separable **- 2.** [hard disk] extraíble.

removal [rɪ'muːvl] *n* **- 1.** (*U*) [act of removing] separación *f*, extracción *f*; [of threat, clause] supresión *f* **- 2.** UK [change of house] mudanza *f*.

removal van *n* UK camión *m* de mudanzas.

remove [rɪ'muːv] *vt* **- 1.** [take away, clean away]: **to ~ sthg (from)** quitar algo (de) **- 2.** [clothing, shoes] quitarse **- 3.** [from a job, post]: **to ~ sb (from)** destituir a alguien (de) **- 4.** [problem, controls] eliminar; [suspicion] disipar.

remuneration [rɪ,mjuːnə'reɪʃn] *n fml* remuneración *f*.

Renaissance [rə'neɪsəns] *n*: **the ~** el Renacimiento.

render ['rendə'] *vt* **- 1.** [make]: **to ~ sthg useless** hacer OR volver algo inútil **- 2.** [give - help, service] prestar.

rendering ['rendərɪŋ] *n* **- 1.** [rendition] interpretación *f* **- 2.** [of carcass] transformación *f*.

rendezvous ['rɒndɪvuː] (*pl inv*) *n* [meeting] cita *f*.

renegade ['renɪɡeɪd] <> *adj* renegado(da). <> *n* renegado *m*, -da *f*.

renew [rɪ'njuː] *vt* **- 1.** [attempt, attack] reemprender **- 2.** [relationship] reanudar **- 3.** [licence, contract, passport] renovar **- 4.** [strength, interest] reavivar.

renewable [rɪ'njuːəbl] *adj* renovable.

renewal [rɪ'njuːəl] *n* **- 1.** [of activity] reanudación *f* **- 2.** [of contract, licence, passport] renovación *f*.

renounce [rɪ'naʊns] *vt* renunciar a.

renovate ['renəveɪt] *vt* reformar, renovar.

renown [rɪ'naʊn] *n* renombre *m*.

renowned [rɪ'naʊnd] *adj*: ~ **(for)** célebre (por).

rent [rent] <> *n* alquiler *m*. <> *vt* alquilar, rentar *Méx*. <> *vi* US [property] alquilarse; **this apartment ~s for $300 a month** este departamento se alquila por 300 dólares al mes.

rental ['rentl] <> *adj* de alquiler. <> *n* alquiler *m*.

renunciation [rɪ,nʌnsɪ'eɪʃn] *n* renuncia *f*.

reorganize, -ise [,riː'ɔːɡənaɪz] *vt* reorganizar.

rep [rep] *n* **- 1.** *abbr of* **representative** **- 2.** *abbr of* **repertory**.

repaid [riː'peɪd] *pt* & *pp* ▷ **repay**.

repair [rɪ'peə'] <> *n* reparación *f*, refacción *f Amér*; **in good/bad ~** en buen/mal estado. <> *vt* reparar, refaccionar *Amér*.

repair kit *n* caja *de herramientas de una bicicleta.*

repartee [,repɑː'tiː] *n* intercambio *m* de réplicas ingeniosas.

repatriate [,riː'pætrɪeɪt] *vt* repatriar.

repay [riː'peɪ] (*pt* & *pp* **repaid**) *vt* **- 1.** [money] devolver; [debt, person] pagar; **to ~ sb sthg, to ~ sthg to sb** devolver a alguien algo **- 2.** [thank] devolver el favor a.

repayment [riː'peɪmənt] *n* **- 1.** [act of paying back] devolución *f* **- 2.** [sum] pago *m*.

repeal [rɪ'piːl] <> *n* revocación *f*, abrogación *f*. <> *vt* revocar, abrogar.

repeat [rɪ'piːt] <> *vt* **- 1.** [gen] repetir **- 2.** [TV, radio programme] volver a emitir. <> *n* **- 1.** [recurrence] repetición *f* **- 2.** [of programme] reposición *f*.

repeatedly [rɪ'piːtɪdlɪ] *adv* repetidamente.

repel [rɪ'pel] (*pt* & *pp* **-led**, *cont* **-ling**) *vt* repeler.

repellent [rɪ'pelənt] <> *adj* repelente. <> *n* espray *m* antiinsectos.

repent [rɪ'pent] <> *vt* arrepentirse de. <> *vi*: **to ~ of** arrepentirse de.

repentance [rɪ'pentəns] *n* arrepentimiento *m*.

repercussions [,riːpə'kʌʃnz] *npl* repercusiones *fpl*.

repertoire ['repətwɑː'] *n* repertorio *m*.

repertory ['repətrɪ] *n* repertorio *m*.

repetition [,repɪ'tɪʃn] *n* repetición *f*.

repetitious [,repɪ'tɪʃəs], **repetitive** [rɪ'petɪtɪv] *adj* repetitivo(va).

repetitive strain injury *n* (*U*) lesión *f* por movimiento repetitivo.

replace [rɪ'pleɪs] *vt* **- 1.** [take the place of] sustituir **- 2.** [change for something else]: **to ~ sthg (with)** cambiar algo (por) **- 3.** [change for somebody else]: **to ~ sb (with)** sustituir a alguien (por) **- 4.** [supply another]: **they ~d it** me dieron otro **- 5.** [put back] poner en su sitio.

replacement [rɪ'pleɪsmənt] *n* **- 1.** [act of substituting] sustitución *f* **- 2.** [something new]: ~ **(for)** sustituto *m*, -ta *f* (para) **- 3.** [somebody new]: ~ **(for)** sustituto *m*, -ta *f* OR suplente *m* OR *f* (de) **- 4.** [another one]: **they gave me a ~** me dieron otro.

replay [*n* 'riːpleɪ, *vb* ,riː'pleɪ] <> *n* repetición *f*. <> *vt* [film, tape] volver a poner.

replenish [rɪ'plenɪʃ] *vt*: **to ~ sthg (with)** reaprovisionar OR reponer algo (de).

replica ['replikə] *n* réplica *f*.

reply [rɪ'plaɪ] (*pl* **-ies**, *pt* & *pp* **-ied**) ⋄ *n*: **~ (to)** respuesta *f* (a). ⋄ *vt* responder, contestar. ⋄ *vi*: **to ~ (to sb/sthg)** responder (a alguien/algo).

reply coupon *n* cupón *m* de respuesta.

report [rɪ'pɔːt] ⋄ *n* **- 1.** [gen] informe *m*, reporte *m Cam & Méx*; PRESS & TV reportaje *m*; [shorter] información *f* **- 2.** UK SCH boletín *m* de evaluación, boletín *m* de calificaciones OR notas. ⋄ *vt* **- 1.** [say, make known]: **to ~ that** informar que, reportar que *Amér*; **to ~ sthg (to)** informar de algo (a), reportar algo (a) *Amér* **- 2.** [losses] anunciar **- 3.** [complain about] denunciar; **to ~ sb (to sb for sthg)** denunciar a alguien (a alguien por algo), reportar a alguien (a alguien por algo) *Amér*. ⋄ *vi* **- 1.** [give account]: **to ~ on** informar sobre **- 2.** [present oneself]: **to ~ to sb/for sthg** presentarse a alguien/para algo, reportarse a alguien/para algo *Amér*.

report card *n* US boletín *m* de evaluación, boletín *m* de calificaciones OR notas.

reportedly [rɪ'pɔːtɪdlɪ] *adv* según se afirma.

reporter [rɪ'pɔːtəʳ] *n* reportero *m*, -ra *f*.

repose [rɪ'pəʊz] *n literary* reposo *m*.

repossess [ˌriːpə'zes] *vt* requisar la posesión de.

reprehensible [ˌreprɪ'hensəbl] *adj fml* reprensible.

represent [ˌreprɪ'zent] *vt* [gen] representar; [person, country] representar a.

representation [ˌreprɪzen'teɪʃn] *n* representación *f*.

◆ **representations** *npl fml*: **to make ~s to** presentar una queja a.

representative [ˌreprɪ'zentətɪv] ⋄ *adj*: **~ (of)** representativo(va) (de). ⋄ *n* representante *m* OR *f*.

repress [rɪ'pres] *vt* reprimir.

repression [rɪ'preʃn] *n* represión *f*.

reprieve [rɪ'priːv] *n* **- 1.** [delay] tregua *f* **- 2.** [of death sentence] indulto *m*.

reprimand ['reprɪmɑːnd] ⋄ *n* reprensión *f*. ⋄ *vt* reprender.

reprisal [rɪ'praɪzl] *n* represalia *f*.

reproach [rɪ'prəʊtʃ] ⋄ *n* reproche *m*. ⋄ *vt*: **to ~ sb (for OR with sthg)** reprochar a alguien (algo).

reproachful [rɪ'prəʊtʃfʊl] *adj* de reproche.

reproduce [ˌriːprə'djuːs] ⋄ *vt* reproducir. ⋄ *vi* BIOL reproducirse.

reproduction [ˌriːprə'dʌkʃn] *n* reproducción *f*.

reproof [rɪ'pruːf] *n fml* **- 1.** [words of blame] reprobación *f* **- 2.** [disapproval] reproche *m*.

reptile ['reptaɪl] *n* reptil *m*.

republic [rɪ'pʌblɪk] *n* república *f*.

republican [rɪ'pʌblɪkən] ⋄ *adj* republicano(na). ⋄ *n* republicano *m*, -na *f*.

◆ **Republican** ⋄ *adj* [in US, Northern Ireland] republicano(na); **the Republican Party** [in US] el partido republicano. ⋄ *n* [in US, Northern Ireland] republicano *m*, -na *f*.

repudiate [rɪ'pjuːdɪeɪt] *vt fml* [person, violence] repudiar; [accusation] rechazar.

repulse [rɪ'pʌls] *vt* rechazar.

repulsive [rɪ'pʌlsɪv] *adj* repulsivo(va).

reputable ['repjʊtəbl] *adj* de buena fama OR reputación.

reputation [ˌrepjʊ'teɪʃn] *n* reputación *f*.

repute [rɪ'pjuːt] *n fml*: **of good/ill ~** de buena/mala fama.

reputed [rɪ'pjuːtɪd] *adj* supuesto(ta); **to be ~ to be/do sthg** tener fama de ser/hacer algo.

reputedly [rɪ'pjuːtɪdlɪ] *adv* según se dice.

request [rɪ'kwest] ⋄ *n*: **~ (for)** petición *f* (de); **on ~** a petición del interesado. ⋄ *vt* solicitar, pedir; **to ~ sb to do sthg** rogar a alguien que haga algo.

request stop *n* UK parada *f* discrecional.

require [rɪ'kwaɪəʳ] *vt* **- 1.** [need] necesitar, requerir **- 2.** [demand] requerir; **to ~ sb to do sthg** exigir a alguien que haga algo.

requirement [rɪ'kwaɪəmənt] *n* requisito *m*.

requisition [ˌrekwɪ'zɪʃn] *n* requisar.

rerun ['riːˌrʌn] *n* **- 1.** [film, programme] reposición *f* **- 2.** [repeated situation] repetición *f*.

resat [ˌriː'sæt] *pt* & *pp* ⊳ **resit**.

rescind [rɪ'sɪnd] *vt* JUR [contract] rescindir; [law] revocar.

rescue ['reskjuː] ⋄ *n* rescate *m*. ⋄ *vt*: **to ~ sb/sthg (from)** rescatar a alguien/algo (de).

rescuer ['reskjʊəʳ] *n* rescatador *m*, -ra *f*.

research [ˌrɪ'sɜːtʃ] ⋄ *n (U)*: **~ (on OR into)** investigación *f* (de OR sobre); **~ and development** investigación y desarrollo. ⋄ *vt* investigar.

researcher [rɪ'sɜːtʃəʳ] *n* investigador *m*, -ra *f*.

resemblance [rɪ'zembləns] *n* parecido *m*, semejanza *f*.

resemble [rɪ'zembl] *vt* parecerse a.

resentful [rɪ'zentfʊl] *adj* [person] resentido(da); [look] de resentimiento.

resentment [rɪ'zentmənt] *n* resentimiento *m*.

reservation [ˌrezə'veɪʃn] *n* **- 1.** [booking] reserva *f* **- 2.** [uncertainty]: **without ~** sin reserva **- 3.** US [for Native Americans] reserva *f*.

◆ **reservations** *npl* [doubts] reservas *fpl*.

reserve [rɪ'zɜːv] ⋄ *n* **- 1.** [gen] reserva *f*; **in ~** en reserva **- 2.** SPORT reserva *m* OR *f*, suplente *m* OR *f* **- 1.** [save, book] reservar **- 2.** [retain]: **to ~ the right to do sthg** reservarse el derecho a hacer algo.

reserved [rɪ'zɜ:vd] *adj* reservado(da).

reservoir ['rezəvwɑ:ʳ] *n* [lake] pantano *m*, embalse *m*.

reset [,ri:'set] (*pt & pp* reset, *cont* -ting) *vt* [clock] poner en hora; [meter, controls, computer] reinicializar.

reshape [,ri:'ʃeɪp] *vt* [policy, thinking] reformar, rehacer.

reshuffle [,ri:'ʃʌfl] *n* remodelación *f*; cabinet ~ remodelación del gabinete.

reside [rɪ'zaɪd] *vi fml* [live] residir.

residence ['rezɪdəns] *n* - **1.** *fml* [house] residencia *f* - **2.** [state of residing]: **to be in** ~ (at) residir (a).

residence permit *n* permiso *m* de residencia.

residency ['rezɪdənsɪ] *n* MED *periodo de especialización después de los cinco años de residencia.*

resident ['rezɪdənt] ◇ *adj* - **1.** [settled, living] residente - **2.** [on-site, live-in] que vive en su lugar de trabajo. ◇ *n* residente *m* OR *f*.

residential [,rezɪ'denʃl] *adj* [live-in] en régimen de internado.

residential area *n* zona *f* residencial.

residue ['rezɪdju:] *n* residuo *m*.

resign [rɪ'zaɪn] ◇ *vt* - **1.** [give up] dimitir de, renunciar a - **2.** [accept calmly]: **to** ~ **o.s. to sthg** resignarse a algo. ◇ *vi* [quit]: **to** ~ (**from**) dimitir (de).

resignation [,rezɪg'neɪʃn] *n* - **1.** [from job] dimisión *f* - **2.** [calm acceptance] resignación *f*.

resigned [rɪ'zaɪnd] *adj*: ~ (**to**) resignado(da) (a).

resilient [rɪ'zɪlɪənt] *adj* [person] resistente, fuerte; [rubber] elástico(ca).

resin ['rezɪn] *n* resina *f*.

resist [rɪ'zɪst] *vt* - **1.** [refuse to give in to - temptation] resistir - **2.** [refuse to accept] resistir, oponerse a - **3.** [fight against] resistir a.

resistance [rɪ'zɪstəns] *n*: ~ (**to**) resistencia *f* (a).

resit [*n* 'ri:sɪt, *vb* ,ri:'sɪt] (*pt & pp* -sat, *cont* -ting) *UK* ◇ *n* (examen *m* de) repesca *f*. ◇ *vt* volver a presentarse a.

resolute ['rezəlu:t] *adj* resuelto(ta), determinado(da).

resolution [,rezə'lu:ʃn] *n* - **1.** [gen] resolución *f* - **2.** [vow, promise] propósito *m*.

resolve [rɪ'zɒlv] ◇ *n* (*U*) resolución *f*. ◇ *vt* - **1.** [vow, promise]: **to** ~ **that** resolver que; **to** ~ **to do sthg** resolver hacer algo - **2.** [solve] resolver.

resort [rɪ'zɔ:t] *n* - **1.** [for holidays] lugar *m* de vacaciones - **2.** [solution]: **as a** OR **in the last** ~ como último recurso.

➤ **resort to** *vt fus* recurrir a.

resound [rɪ'zaʊnd] *vi* - **1.** [noise] resonar, retumbar - **2.** [place]: **the room** ~ed with laughter la risa resonaba por la habitación.

resounding [rɪ'zaʊndɪŋ] *adj* - **1.** [loudnoise, knock] retumbante; [- crash] estruendoso(sa) - **2.** [very great] clamoroso(sa).

resource [rɪ'sɔ:s] *n* recurso *m*.

resourceful [rɪ'sɔ:sfʊl] *adj* [person] de recursos; [solution] ingenioso(sa).

respect [rɪ'spekt] ◇ *n* - **1.** [gen] ~ (**for**) respeto *m* (por); **with** ~ con respeto - **2.** [aspect] aspecto *m*; **in this** ~ a este respecto; **in that** ~ en cuanto a eso. ◇ *vt* [admire] respetar; **to** ~ **sb for sthg** respetar a alguien por algo.

➤ **respects** *npl*: **to pay one's** ~**s (to)** presentar uno sus respetos (a).

➤ **with respect to** *prep* con respecto a.

respectable [rɪ'spektəbl] *adj* respetable.

respectful [rɪ'spektfʊl] *adj* respetuoso(sa).

respective [rɪ'spektɪv] *adj* respectivo(va).

respectively [rɪ'spektɪvlɪ] *adv* respectivamente.

respite ['respaɪt] *n* - **1.** [lull] respiro *m* - **2.** [delay] aplazamiento *m*.

resplendent [rɪ'splendənt] *adj* resplandeciente.

respond [rɪ'spɒnd] *vi*: **to** ~ (**to**) responder (a); **to** ~ **by doing sthg** responder haciendo algo.

response [rɪ'spɒns] *n* respuesta *f*.

responsibility [rɪ,spɒnsə'bɪlətɪ] (*pl* -ies) *n*: ~ (**for**) responsabilidad *f* (de).

responsible [rɪ'spɒnsəbl] *adj* - **1.** [gen] responsable; ~ (**for**) responsable (de) - **2.** [answerable]: ~ **to sb** responsable ante alguien - **3.** [job, position] de responsabilidad.

responsibly [rɪ'spɒnsəblɪ] *adv* de manera responsable.

responsive [rɪ'spɒnsɪv] *adj* - **1.** [quick to react]: **to be** ~ responder muy bien - **2.** [aware]: ~ (**to**) sensible OR perceptivo(va) (a).

rest [rest] ◇ *n* - **1.** [remainder]: **the** ~ (**of**) el resto (de); **the** ~ **of us** los demás - **2.** [relaxation, break] descanso *m*; **to have a** ~ descansar - **3.** [support - for feet] descanso *m*; [- for head] respaldo *m*. ◇ *vt* - **1.** [relaxeyes, feet] descansar - **2.** [support] apoyar, descansar. ◇ *vi* - **1.** [relax, be still] descansar - **2.** [depend]: **to** ~ **on** OR **upon** depender de - **3.** [be supported] apoyarse, descansar - **4.** *phr*: ~ **assured that ...** tenga la seguridad de que ...

restaurant ['restərɒnt] *n* restaurante *m*.

restaurant car *n UK* coche *m* OR vagón *m* restaurante, coche *m* comedor.

restful ['restfʊl] *adj* tranquilo(la), apacible.

rest home *n* [for the elderly] asilo *m* de ancianos; [for the sick] casa *f* de reposo.

restive ['restɪv] *adj* intranquilo(la), inquieto(ta).

restless ['restlıs] *adj* - **1.** [bored, dissatisfied] impaciente, desasosegado(da) - **2.** [fidgety] inquieto(ta), agitado(da) - **3.** [sleepless] agitado(da).

restoration [,restə'reıʃn] *n* restauración *f*.

restore [rı'stɔːʳ] *vt* - **1.** [reestablish] restablecer - **2.** [to a previous position or condition]: **to ~ sb to sthg** restaurar a alguien en algo; **to ~ sthg to sthg** volver a poner algo en algo - **3.** [renovate] restaurar - **4.** [give back] devolver.

restrain [rı'streın] *vt* controlar; **to ~ o.s. from doing sthg** contenerse para no hacer algo.

restrained [rı'streınd] *adj* comedido(da).

restraint [rı'streınt] *n* - **1.** [rule, check] restricción *f*, limitación *f* - **2.** [control] control *m*.

restrict [rı'strıkt] *vt* [limit] restringir, limitar; **to ~ sthg/sb** restringir algo/a alguien a.

restriction [rı'strıkʃn] *n* restricción *f*.

restrictive [rı'strıktıv] *adj* restrictivo(va).

rest room *n* US servicios *mpl*, aseos *mpl*.

result [rı'zʌlt] <> *n* resultado *m*; **as a ~** como resultado. <> *vi* - **1.** [cause]: **to ~ (in sthg)** tener como resultado (algo) - **2.** [be caused]: **to ~ (from)** resultar (de).

resume [rı'zjuːm] <> *vt* [start again] reanudar. <> *vi* volver a empezar, continuar.

résumé ['rezjuːmeı] *n* - **1.** [summary] resumen *m* - **2.** US [of career, qualifications] currículum *m* (vitae).

resumption [rı'zʌmpʃn] *n* reanudación *f*.

resurgence [rı'sɜːdʒəns] *n* resurgimiento *m*.

resurrection [,rezə'rekʃn] *n* resurrección *f*.

resuscitate [rı'sʌsɪteɪt] *vt* resucitar, revivir.

retail ['riːteɪl] <> *n* venta *f* al por menor OR al detalle. <> *vt* vender al por menor. <> *vi*: **to ~ for** tener un precio de venta al público de. <> *adv* al por menor, al detalle.

retailer ['riːteɪləʳ] *n* minorista *m* OR *f*, detallista *m* OR *f*.

retail price *n* precio *m* de venta al público.

retain [rı'teın] *vt* retener.

retainer [rı'teınəʳ] *n* [fee] anticipo *m*.

retaliate [rı'tælɪeɪt] *vi* - **1.** [react] responder - **2.** [take reprisals] tomar represalias.

retaliation [rı,tælı'eɪʃn] *n* (U) represalias *fpl*.

retarded [rı'tɑːdɪd] *adj* retrasado(da).

retch [retʃ] *vi* tener arcadas.

retentive [rı'tentıv] *adj* retentivo(va).

reticent ['retɪsənt] *adj* reservado(da).

retina ['retınə] (*pl* **-nas** OR **-nae** [-niː]) *n* retina *f*.

retinue ['retınjuː] *n* séquito *m*, comitiva *f*.

retire [rı'taɪəʳ] *vi* - **1.** [from work] jubilarse - **2.** *fml* [to another place, to bed] retirarse.

retired [rı'taɪəd] *adj* jubilado(da).

retirement [rı'taɪəmənt] *n* [act] jubilación *f*; [time] retiro *m*.

retiring [rı'taɪərıŋ] *adj* [shy] retraído(da), tímido(da).

retort [rı'tɔːt] <> *n* [sharp reply] réplica *f*. <> *vt*: **to ~ (that)** replicar (que).

retrace [rı'treıs] *vt*: **to ~ one's steps** desandar lo andado.

retract [rı'trækt] <> *vt* - **1.** [withdraw, take back] retractarse de - **2.** [pull in - claws] meter, retraer. <> *vi* [subj: claws] meterse, retraerse; [subj: wheels] replegarse.

retrain [,riː'treın] *vt* reciclar.

retraining [,riː'treınıŋ] *n* reciclaje *m*.

retread ['riːtred] *n* neumático *m* recauchutado.

retreat [rı'triːt] <> *n* - **1.** MIL: **~ (from)** retirada *f* (de) - **2.** [peaceful place] refugio *m*. <> *vi* [move away]: **to ~ (from)** [gen] retirarse (de); [from a person] apartarse (de).

retribution [,retrı'bjuːʃn] *n* (U) castigo *m* merecido.

retrieval [rı'triːvl] *n* [gen & COMPUT] recuperación *f*.

retrieve [rı'triːv] *vt* - **1.** [get back] recobrar - **2.** COMPUT recuperar - **3.** [rescue - situation] salvar.

retriever [rı'triːvəʳ] *n* perro *m* cobrador.

retrograde ['retrəgreıd] *adj fml* [gen] retrógrado(da); [step] hacia atrás.

retrospect ['retrəspekt] *n*: **in ~** retrospectivamente, mirando hacia atrás.

retrospective [,retrə'spektıv] *adj* - **1.** [gen] retrospectivo(va) - **2.** [law, pay rise] con efecto retroactivo.

return [rı'tɜːn] <> *n* - **1.** (U) [arrival back] vuelta *f*, regreso *m* - **2.** UK [ticket] billete *m* de ida y vuelta - **3.** [profit] ganancia *f*, rendimiento *m*. <> *vt* - **1.** [book, visit, compliment, call] devolver - **2.** [reciprocate] corresponder a - **3.** [replace] devolver a su sitio - **4.** JUR [verdict] pronunciar - **5.** POL [candidate] elegir. <> *vi*: **to ~ (from/to)** volver (de/a).
  ◆ **returns** *npl* - **1.** COMM rendimiento *m*, réditos *mpl* - **2.** *phr*: **many happy ~s (of the day)!** ¡feliz cumpleaños!
  ◆ **in return** *adv* a cambio.
  ◆ **in return for** *prep* a cambio de.

return (key) *n* COMPUT tecla *f* de retorno.

return ticket *n* UK billete *m* de ida y vuelta *Esp*, boleto *m* de ida y vuelta *Amér*, boleto *m* redondo *Méx*.

reunification [,riːjuːnıfı'keıʃn] *n* reunificación *f*.

reunion [,riː'juːnjən] *n* reunión *f*.

reunite [,riːjuː'naıt] *vt* [people]: **to be ~d with** volver a encontrarse con; [factions, parts] reunir.

rev [rev] (*pt* & *pp* **-ved**, *cont* **-ving**) *inf* <> *n*

(*abbr of* **revolution**) revolución *f* (motriz).
◇ *vi* : **to ~ sth (up)** acelerar algo. ◇ *vi*
[subj: person]: **to ~ (up)** acelerar el motor.
revamp [ˌriːˈvæmp] *vt inf* renovar.
reveal [rɪˈviːl] *vt* revelar.
revealing [rɪˈviːlɪŋ] *adj* **- 1.** [comment, si-
lence] revelador(ra) **- 2.** [garment] atrevi-
do(da).
reveille [*UK* rɪˈvælɪ, *US* ˈrevəlɪ] *n* toque *m* de
diana.
revel [ˈrevl] (*UK pt* & *pp* **-led**, *cont* **-ling**, *US*
pt & *pp* **-ed**, *cont* **-ing**) *vi*: **to ~ in** deleitarse
en.
revelation [ˌrevəˈleɪʃn] *n* revelación *f*.
revenge [rɪˈvendʒ] *n* venganza *f*; **to take**
~ (on sb) vengarse (de alguien).
revenue [ˈrevənjuː] *n* ingresos *mpl*.
reverberate [rɪˈvɜːbəreɪt] *vi* **- 1.** [reecho] resonar **- 2.** [have repercussions] repercutir.
reverberations [rɪˌvɜːbəˈreɪʃnz] *npl*
- 1. [echoes] reverberaciones *fpl* **- 2.** [reper-
cussions] repercusiones *fpl*.
revere [rɪˈvɪər] *vt* venerar, reverenciar.
reverence [ˈrevərəns] *n* reverencia *f*.
Reverend [ˈrevərənd] *n* reverendo *m*.
reverie [ˈrevərɪ] *n* ensueño *m*.
reversal [rɪˈvɜːsl] *n* **- 1.** [turning around]
cambio *m* total **- 2.** [ill fortune] contratiempo *m*, revés *m*.
reverse [rɪˈvɜːs] ◇ *adj* inverso(sa). ◇ *n*
- 1. AUT : **~ (gear)** marcha *f* atrás **- 2.** [oppo-
site]: **the ~** lo contrario **- 3.** [opposite side,
back]: **the ~** [gen] el revés; [of coin] el reverso; [of piece of paper] el dorso. ◇ *vt* **- 1.** AUT
dar marcha atrás a **- 2.** [change usual order]
invertir **- 3.** [change to opposite] cambiar
completamente **- 4.** *UK* TELEC : **to ~ the**
charges llamar a cobro revertido. ◇ *vi* AUT
dar marcha atrás.
reverse-charge call *n* *UK* llamada *f* a cobro revertido, llamada *f* por cobrar *Chile*,
Méx.
reversing light [rɪˈvɜːsɪŋ-] *n* *UK* luz *f* de
marcha atrás.
revert [rɪˈvɜːt] *vi*: **to ~ to** volver a.
review [rɪˈvjuː] ◇ *n* **- 1.** [examination] revisión *f* **- 2.** [critique] reseña *f*. ◇ *vt* **- 1.** [re-ex-
amine] revisar **- 2.** [consider] reconsiderar
- 3. [write an article on] reseñar **- 4.** *US* [study
again] repasar.
reviewer [rɪˈvjuːər] *n* crítico *m*, -ca *f*, reseña-
dor *m*, -ra *f*.
revile [rɪˈvaɪl] *vt literary* injuriar.
revise [rɪˈvaɪz] ◇ *vt* **- 1.** [reconsider] revisar
- 2. [rewrite] modificar, corregir **- 3.** *UK*
[study] repasar. ◇ *vi* *UK*: **to ~ (for sth)**
repasar (para algo).
revision [rɪˈvɪʒn] *n* **- 1.** [alteration] corrección *f*, modificación *f* **- 2.** *UK* [study] repaso
m.

revitalize, -ise [ˌriːˈvaɪtəlaɪz] *vt* revivificar.
revival [rɪˈvaɪvl] *n* **- 1.** [of person] resucita-
ción *f*; [of economy] reactivación *f* **- 2.** [of
play] reposición *f*.
revive [rɪˈvaɪv] ◇ *vt* **- 1.** [person, plant,
hopes] resucitar; [economy] reactivar **- 2.**
[tradition, memories] restablecer; [play]
reponer. ◇ *vi* reponerse.
revolt [rɪˈvəʊlt] ◇ *n* rebelión *f*, sublevación *f*. ◇ *vt* repugnar. ◇ *vi*: **to ~ (against)**
rebelarse OR sublevarse (contra).
revolting [rɪˈvəʊltɪŋ] *adj* repugnante,
asqueroso(sa).
revolution [ˌrevəˈluːʃn] *n* revolución *f*.
revolutionary [ˌrevəˈluːʃnərɪ] (*pl* **-ies**)
◇ *adj* revolucionario(ria). ◇ *n* revolucionario *m*, -ria *f*.
revolve [rɪˈvɒlv] *vi* [go round] girar.
revolver [rɪˈvɒlvər] *n* revólver *m*.
revolving [rɪˈvɒlvɪŋ] *adj* giratorio(ria).
revolving door *n* puerta *f* giratoria.
revue [rɪˈvjuː] *n* revista *f* (teatral).
revulsion [rɪˈvʌlʃn] *n* asco *m*, repugnancia
f.
reward [rɪˈwɔːd] ◇ *n* recompensa *f*. ◇ *vt* :
to ~ sb (for/with) recompensar a alguien
(por/con).
rewarding [rɪˈwɔːdɪŋ] *adj* gratificador(ra).
rewind [ˌriːˈwaɪnd] (*pt* & *pp* **rewound**) *vt*
rebobinar.
rewire [ˌriːˈwaɪər] *vt* cambiar la instalación
eléctrica de.
reword [ˌriːˈwɜːd] *vt* expresar de otra forma.
rewound [ˌriːˈwaʊnd] *pt* & *pp* ▷ **rewind**.
rewritable [ˌriːˈraɪtəbl] *adj* COMPUT regraba-
ble.
rewrite [ˌriːˈraɪt] (*pt* **rewrote** [ˌriːˈrəʊt], *pp*
rewritten [ˌriːˈrɪtn]) *vt* volver a escribir, rehacer.
Reykjavik [ˈrekjəvɪk] *n* Reikiavik.
rhapsody [ˈræpsədɪ] (*pl* **-ies**) *n* MUS rapsodia *f*.
rhetoric [ˈretərɪk] *n* retórica *f*.
rhetorical question [rɪˈtɒrɪkl-] *n* pregunta *f* retórica *(a la que no se espera contestación)*.
rheumatism [ˈruːmətɪzm] *n* reumatismo
m.
Rhine [raɪn] *n*: **the ~** el Rin.
rhino [ˈraɪnəʊ] (*pl inv* OR **-s**), **rhinoceros**
[raɪˈnɒsərəs] (*pl* **rhinoceros** OR **-es**) *n* rinoceronte *m*.
rhododendron [ˌrəʊdəˈdendrən] *n* rodo-
dendro *m*.
Rhône [rəʊn] *n*: **the (River) ~** el (río) Ródano.
rhubarb [ˈruːbɑːb] *n* ruibarbo *m*.
rhyme [raɪm] ◇ *n* **- 1.** [gen] rima *f*
- 2. [poem] poesía *f*, versos *mpl*. ◇ *vi*: **to**
~ (with) rimar (con).

rhythm ['rɪðm] *n* ritmo *m*.

rib [rɪb] *n* -1. ANAT costilla *f* - 2. [of umbrella] varilla *f*.

ribbed [rɪbd] *adj* [sweater] de canalé.

ribbon ['rɪbən] *n* cinta *f*.

rice [raɪs] *n* arroz *m*.

rice pudding *n* arroz *m* con leche.

ricer ['raɪsə'] *n* US pasapuré *m*.

rich [rɪtʃ] ◇ *adj* -1. [gen] rico(ca) - 2. [full]: **to be ~ in** abundar en - 3. [fertile] fértil - 4. [indigestible] pesado(da). ◇ *npl*: **the ~** los ricos.

  ◆ **riches** *npl* -1. [natural resources] riquezas *fpl* - 2. [wealth] riqueza *f*.

richly ['rɪtʃlɪ] *adv* -1. [rewarded] muy generosamente - 2. [plentifully] copiosamente, abundantemente.

richness ['rɪtʃnɪs] *n* -1. [gen] riqueza *f* - 2. [fertility] fertilidad *f* - 3. [indigestibility] pesadez *f*.

rickety ['rɪkətɪ] *adj* tambaleante, desvencijado(da).

rickshaw ['rɪkʃɔ:] *n* jinrikisha *f*.

ricochet ['rɪkəʃeɪ] (*pt & pp* -ed OR -ted, *cont* -ing OR -ting) ◇ *n* rebote *m*. ◇ *vi*: **to ~ (off)** rebotar (de).

rid [rɪd] (*pt* rid OR -ded, *pp* rid, *cont* -ding) *vt*: **to ~ sthg/sb of** librar algo/a alguien de; **to get ~ of** deshacerse de.

ridden ['rɪdn] *pp* ➢ ride.

riddle ['rɪdl] *n* -1. [verbal puzzle] acertijo *m*, adivinanza *f* - 2. [mystery] enigma *m*.

riddled ['rɪdld] *adj*: **to be ~ with** [mistakes] estar plagado(da) de.

ride [raɪd] (*pt* rode, *pp* ridden) ◇ *n* -1. [gen] paseo *m*; **to go for a ~** [on horseback] darse un paseo a caballo; [on bike] darse un paseo en bicicleta; [in car] darse una vuelta en coche; **to take sb for a ~** *inf fig* embaucar a alguien - 2. [journey] viaje *m*; **it's a short car ~ away** está a poca distancia en coche - 3. [at fair] atracción *f*. ◇ *vt* -1. [horse] montar a - 2. [bicycle, motorbike] montar en; **he rode his bike to the station** fue a la estación en bici - 3. US [bus, train] ir en; [elevator] subir/bajar en - 4. [distance] recorrer. ◇ *vi* -1. [on horseback] montar a caballo; **she rode over to see me** vino a verme a caballo - 2. [on bicycle] ir en bici; [on motorbike] ir en moto - 3. [in car]: **we rode to London in a jeep** fuimos a Londres en jeep.

rider ['raɪdə'] *n* -1. [on horseback] jinete *m*, amazona *f* - 2. [on bicycle] ciclista *m* OR *f*; [on motorbike] motorista *m* OR *f*.

ridge [rɪdʒ] *n* -1. [on mountain] cresta *f* - 2. [on flat surface] rugosidad *f*.

ridicule ['rɪdɪkju:l] ◇ *n* (U) burlas *fpl*. ◇ *vt* burlarse de.

ridiculous [rɪ'dɪkjʊləs] *adj* ridículo(la).

riding ['raɪdɪŋ] *n* equitación *f*; **to go ~** ir a montar a caballo.

riding school *n* escuela *f* de equitación.

rife [raɪf] *adj* extendido(da); **to be ~ with** estar lleno de.

riffraff ['rɪfræf] *n* gentuza *f*.

rifle ['raɪfl] ◇ *n* fusil *m*, rifle *m*. ◇ *vt* desvalijar.

rifle range *n* campo *m* de tiro.

rift [rɪft] *n* -1. GEOL hendidura *f*, grieta *f* - 2. [quarrel] desavenencia *f* - 3. POL: **between/in** escisión *f* entre/en.

rig [rɪg] (*pt & pp* -ged, *cont* -ging) ◇ *n* -1.: **(oil) ~** [onshore] torre *f* de perforación; [offshore] plataforma *f* petrolífera - 2. US [truck] camión *m*. ◇ *vt* [falsify] amañar, falsificar.

  ◆ **rig up** *vt sep* construir, armar.

rigging ['rɪgɪŋ] *n* cordaje *m*.

right [raɪt] ◇ *adj* -1. [correct] correcto(ta); **to be ~ (about)** tener razón (respecto a); **that's ~** sí; **to get sthg ~** acertar en algo - 2. [morally correct, satisfactory, well] bien; **to be ~ to do sthg** hacer bien en hacer algo; **something isn't ~ with it** le pasa algo - 3. [appropriate] apropiado(da); **it's just ~** es perfecto; **the ~ moment** el momento oportuno - 4. [uppermost]: **~ side** cara *f* anterior OR de arriba - 5. [on right-hand side] derecho(cha). ◇ *n* -1. (U) [moral correctness] el bien; **to be in the ~** tener razón - 2. [entitlement, claim] derecho *m*; **by ~s** en justicia - 3. [right-hand side] derecha *f*; **on the ~** a la derecha. ◇ *adv* -1. [correctly] bien, correctamente - 2. [to right-hand side] a la derecha - 3. [emphatic use]: **~ here** aquí mismo; **~ at the top** arriba del todo; **~ in the middle** justo en el medio; **she crashed ~ into the tree** chocó de frente contra el árbol - 4. [completely] completamente - 5. [immediately]: **I'll be ~ back** ahora mismo vuelvo; **~ before/after (sthg)** justo antes/después (de algo); **~ now** ahora mismo, ahorita *Cam & Méx*; **~ away** en seguida, luego *Amér*. ◇ *vt* -1. [correct] corregir, rectificar - 2. [make upright] enderezar. ◇ *excl* ¡bien!

  ◆ **Right** *n* POL: **the Right** la derecha.

right angle *n* ángulo *m* recto; **at ~s (to)** en ángulo recto (con).

righteous ['raɪtʃəs] *adj* [anger] justo(ta); [person] honrado(da).

rightful ['raɪtfʊl] *adj* justo(ta), legítimo(ma).

right-hand *adj* derecho(cha); **the ~ side** el lado derecho, la derecha.

right-hand drive *n* vehículo *f* con el volante a la derecha.

right-handed [-'hændɪd] *adj* diestro(tra).

right-hand man *n* brazo *m* derecho.

rightly ['raɪtlɪ] *adv* - **1.** [correctly] correctamente - **2.** [appropriately] debidamente, bien - **3.** [morally] justamente, con razón.

right of way *n* - **1.** AUT prioridad *f* - **2.** [access] derecho *m* de paso.

right-on *adj inf* progre.

right wing *n*: the ~ la derecha.
◆ **right-wing** *adj* de derechas, derechista.

rigid ['rɪdʒɪd] *adj* - **1.** [stiff] rígido(da) - **2.** [harsh, unbending] inflexible.

rigmarole ['rɪgmərəʊl] *n inf pej* - **1.** [process] ritual *m* - **2.** [story] galimatías *m inv.*

rigor US = rigour.

rigorous ['rɪgərəs] *adj* riguroso(sa).

rigour UK, **rigor** US ['rɪgə'] *n* [firmness] rigor *m.*

rile [raɪl] *vt* irritar, sacar de quicio.

rim [rɪm] *n* - **1.** [of container] borde *m* - **2.** [of spectacles] montura *f.*

rind [raɪnd] *n* [of bacon, cheese] corteza *f*; [of orange, lemon] cáscara *f.*

ring [rɪŋ] (*pt* rang, *pp vt senses 1 & 2 & vi* rung, *pt & pp* ringed *vt senses 3 & 4 only*) ⬦ *n* - **1.** [telephone call]: **to give sb a** ~ llamar a alguien (por teléfono) - **2.** [sound of doorbell] timbrazo *m* - **3.** [on finger, around planet] anillo *m* - **4.** [metal hoop] aro *m*; [for curtains, drinks can] anilla *f* - **5.** [circle - of trees] círculo *m*; [- of people] corro *m* - **6.** [for boxing] cuadrilátero *m*; [at circus] pista *f* - **7.** [illegal group] red *f.* ⬦ *vt* - **1.** UK [phone] llamar por teléfono, telefonear - **2.** [bell] tocar - **3.** [draw a circle round] señalar con un círculo - **4.** [surround] cercar, rodear. ⬦ *vi* - **1.** UK [phone] llamar por teléfono, telefonear - **2.** [bell] sonar - **3.** [to attract attention]: **to** ~ **(for)** llamar (para) - **4.** [resound]: **to** ~ **with** resonar con.
◆ **ring back** *vt sep & vi* UK llamar más tarde.
◆ **ring off** *vi* UK colgar.
◆ **ring up** *vt sep* UK [telec] llamar (por teléfono).

ring binder *n* carpeta *f* de anillas.

ringing ['rɪŋɪŋ] *n* [of bell] repique *m*, tañido *m*; [in ears] zumbido *m.*

ringing tone *n* tono *m* de llamada.

ringleader ['rɪŋ,liːdə'] *n* cabecilla *m OR f.*

ringlet ['rɪŋlɪt] *n* rizo *m*, tirabuzón *m.*

ring-pull *n* anilla *f.*

ring road *n* UK carretera *f* de circunvalación.

ring tone *n* [for mobile phone] melodía *f.*

rink [rɪŋk] *n* pista *f.*

rinse [rɪns] *vt* - **1.** [dishes, vegetables] enjuagar; [clothes] aclarar - **2.** [wash out]: **to** ~ **one's mouth out** enjuagarse la boca.

riot ['raɪət] ⬦ *n* disturbio *m*; **to run** ~ desbocarse. ⬦ *vi* amotinarse.

rioter ['raɪətə'] *n* amotinado *m*, -da *f.*

riotous ['raɪətəs] *adj* desenfrenado(da).

riot police *npl* brigada *f* antidisturbios.

rip [rɪp] (*pt & pp* -ped, *cont* -ping) ⬦ *n* rasgón *m.* ⬦ *vt* - **1.** [tear] rasgar, desgarrar - **2.** [remove violently] quitar de un tirón. ⬦ *vi* rasgarse, romperse.

RIP (*abbr of* rest in peace) RIP.

ripe [raɪp] *adj* maduro(ra); **to be** ~ **(for sthg)** estar listo (para algo).

ripen ['raɪpn] *vt & vi* madurar.

rip-off *n inf* estafa *f.*

ripple ['rɪpl] ⬦ *n* - **1.** [in water] onda *f*, rizo *m* - **2.** [of laughter, applause] murmullo *m.* ⬦ *vt* rizar.

rise [raɪz] (*pt* rose, *pp* risen ['rɪzn]) ⬦ *n* - **1.** [increase, slope] subida *f* - **2.** UK [increase in salary] aumento *m* - **3.** [to fame, power, of practice] ascenso *m* - **4.** *phr*: **to give** ~ **to sthg** dar origen a algo. ⬦ *vi* - **1.** [gen] elevarse - **2.** [price, wage, temperature] subir - **3.** [sun, moon] salir - **4.** [stand up, get out of bed] levantarse - **5.** [street, ground] subir - **6.** [respond]: **to** ~ **to** reaccionar ante - **7.** [rebel] sublevarse - **8.** [move up in status] ascender; **to** ~ **to power/fame** ascender al poder/a la gloria.

rising ['raɪzɪŋ] ⬦ *adj* - **1.** [sloping upwards] ascendente - **2.** [number, rate] creciente; [temperature, prices] en aumento - **3.** [increasingly successful] en alza. ⬦ *n* rebelión *f.*

risk [rɪsk] ⬦ *n* [gen] riesgo *m*; [danger] peligro *m*; **a health** ~ un peligro para la salud; **to run the** ~ **of sthg/of doing sthg** correr el riesgo de algo/de hacer algo; **to take a** ~ arriesgarse; **at your own** ~ bajo tu cuenta y riesgo; **at** ~ en peligro. ⬦ *vt* - **1.** [put in danger] arriesgar - **2.** [take the chance of]: **to** ~ **doing sthg** correr el riesgo de hacer algo.

risky ['rɪskɪ] (*compar* -ier, *superl* -iest) *adj* peligroso(sa), arriesgado(da).

risqué ['riːskeɪ] *adj* subido(da) de tono.

rissole ['rɪsəʊl] *n* UK especie de albóndiga de carne o verduras.

rite [raɪt] *n* rito *m.*

ritual ['rɪtʃʊəl] ⬦ *adj* ritual. ⬦ *n* ritual *m.*

rival ['raɪvl] (*UK pt & pp* -led, *cont* -ling, *US pt & pp* -ed, *cont* -ing) ⬦ *adj* rival. ⬦ *n* rival *m OR f.* ⬦ *vt* rivalizar con.

rivalry ['raɪvlrɪ] *n* rivalidad *f.*

river ['rɪvə'] *n* río *m.*

river bank *n* orilla *f OR* margen *f* del río.

river basin *n* cuenca *f* fluvial.

riverbed ['rɪvəbed] *n* cauce *m OR* lecho *m* del río.

riverside ['rɪvəsaɪd] *n*: the ~ la ribera *OR* orilla del río.

rivet ['rɪvɪt] ⬦ *n* remache *m.* ⬦ *vt* - **1.** [fasten] remachar - **2.** *fig* [fascinate]: **to be** ~ **ed by sthg** estar fascinado(da) con algo.

Riviera [,rɪvɪ'eərə] *n*: **the French** ~ la Riviera francesa.

road [rəʊd] *n* [major] carretera *f*; [street] calle *f*; [path, minor thoroughfare] camino *m*; **to be on the ~ to recovery** estar en vías de recuperación.

roadblock ['rəʊdblɒk] *n* control *m*.

road hog *n inf pej conductor rápido y negligente.*

road map *n* mapa *m* de carreteras.

road movie *n película que se desarrolla durante el transcurso de un viaje por carretera.*

road rage *n* violencia *f* en carretera.

road safety *n* seguridad *f* en carretera.

roadside ['rəʊdsaɪd] *n*: **the ~** el borde de la carretera.

road sign *n* señal *f* de tráfico.

road tax *n* impuesto *m* de circulación.

roadtrip ['rəʊdtrɪp] *n US* viaje *m* hecho en automóvil.

roadway ['rəʊdweɪ] *n* calzada *f*.

road works *npl* obras *fpl*.

roadworthy ['rəʊd,wɜːðɪ] *adj* apto(ta) para circular.

roam [rəʊm] *<> vt* vagar por. *<> vi* vagar.

roar [rɔːʳ] *<> vi* [make a loud noise] rugir; **to ~ with laughter** reírse a carcajadas. *<> vt* rugir, decir a voces. *<> n* **-1.** [of traffic] fragor *m*, estruendo *m* **-2.** [of lion, person] rugido *m*.

roaring ['rɔːrɪŋ] *adj* **-1.** [loud] clamoroso(sa), fragoroso(sa) **-2.** [fire] muy vivo **-3.** [as emphasis]: **to do a ~ trade in sthg** vender algo como rosquillas.

roast [rəʊst] *<> adj* asado(da). *<> n* asado *m*. *<> vt* **-1.** [potatoes, meat] asar **-2.** [nuts, coffee beans] tostar.

roast beef *n* rosbif *m*.

rob [rɒb] (*pt & pp* **-bed**, *cont* **-bing**) *vt* robar; [bank] atracar; **to ~ sb of sthg** *lit & fig* robar a alguien algo.

robber ['rɒbəʳ] *n* ladrón *m*, -ona *f*; [of bank] atracador *m*, -ra *f*.

robbery ['rɒbərɪ] (*pl* **-ies**) *n* robo *m*; [of bank] atraco *m*.

robe [rəʊb] *n* **-1.** [towelling] albornoz *m* **-2.** [of student] toga *f* **-3.** [of priest] sotana *f* **-4.** *US* [dressing gown] bata *f*.

robin ['rɒbɪn] *n* petirrojo *m*.

robot ['rəʊbɒt] *n* robot *m*.

robust [rəʊ'bʌst] *adj* robusto(ta), fuerte.

rock [rɒk] *<> n* **-1.** *(U)* [substance, boulder] roca *f* **-2.** [stone] piedra *f* **-3.** [crag] peñasco *m* **-4.** [music] rock *m* **-5.** *UK* [sweet] palo *m* de caramelo. *<> comp* [concert, group, singer] de rock. *<> vt* [cause to move] mecer, balancear. *<> vi* mecerse, balancearse.

◆ **Rock** *n inf* [Gibraltar]: **the Rock** el Peñón.

◆ **on the rocks** *adv* **-1.** [drink] con hielo **-2.** [marriage, relationship] que va mal.

rock and roll *n* rock and roll *m*.

rock bottom *n*: **to hit ~** tocar fondo.

◆ **rock-bottom** *adj*: **rock-bottom prices** precios muy bajos.

rockery ['rɒkərɪ] (*pl* **-ies**) *n* jardín *m* de rocas.

rocket ['rɒkɪt] *n* **-1.** [vehicle, weapon, firework] cohete *m* **-2.** [plant] roqueta *f*.

rocket launcher [-,lɔːntʃəʳ] *n* lanzacohetes *m inv*.

rocking chair ['rɒkɪŋ-] *n* mecedora *f*.

rocking horse ['rɒkɪŋ-] *n* caballo *m* de balancín.

rock'n'roll [,rɒkən'rəʊl] = **rock and roll**.

rocky ['rɒkɪ] (*compar* **-ier**, *superl* **-iest**) *adj* [full of rocks] rocoso(sa).

Rocky Mountains *npl*: **the ~** las montañas Rocosas.

rod [rɒd] *n* [wooden] vara *f*; [metal] barra *f*; [for fishing] caña *f*.

rode [rəʊd] *pt* ▷ **ride**.

rodent ['rəʊdənt] *n* roedor *m*.

roe [rəʊ] *n* hueva *f*; **hard ~** hueva *f*; **soft ~** lecha *f*.

roe deer *n* corzo *m*.

rogue [rəʊg] *n* [likeable rascal] picaruelo *m*, -la *f*.

role [rəʊl] *n* THEATRE & *fig* papel *m*; **to play an important ~ in sthg** *fig* desempeñar un papel importante en algo.

role model *n* modelo *m* a seguir.

roll [rəʊl] *<> n* **-1.** [gen] rollo *m*; [of paper, banknotes] fajo *m*; [of cloth] pieza *f* **-2.** [of bread] panecillo *m* **-3.** [list] lista *f*; [payroll] nómina *f* **-4.** [of drums] redoble *m*; [of thunder] retumbo *m*. *<> vt* **-1.** [turn over] hacer rodar **-2.** [roll up] enrollar **-3.** [cigarette] liar. *<> vi* **-1.** [ball, barrel] rodar **-2.** [vehicle] ir, avanzar **-3.** [ship] balancearse **-4.** [thunder, drum] retumbar.

◆ **roll about, roll around** *vi*: **to ~ about** OR **around (on)** rodar (por).

◆ **roll in** *vi inf* llegar a raudales.

◆ **roll over** *vi* darse la vuelta.

◆ **roll up** *<> vt sep* **-1.** [make into roll] enrollar **-2.** [sleeves] remangarse. *<> vi* **-1.** [vehicle] llegar **-2.** *inf* [person] presentarse, aparecer.

roll call *n*: **to take a ~** pasar lista.

roller ['rəʊləʳ] *n* **-1.** [cylinder] rodillo *m* **-2.** [curler] rulo *m*.

Rollerblades® ['rəʊlə,bleɪdz] *npl* patines *mpl* en línea.

rollerblading ['rəʊlə,bleɪdɪŋ] *n* patinaje *m* (con patines en línea); **to go ~** ir a patinar (con patines en línea).

roller coaster *n* montaña *f* rusa.

roller skate *n* patín *m* de ruedas.

rolling ['rəʊlɪŋ] *adj* **-1.** [undulating] ondulante **-2.** *phr*: **to be ~ in it** *inf* nadar en la abundancia.

rolling pin *n* rodillo *m* (de cocina).

rolling stock *n* material *m* rodante.

roll-on *adj* [deodorant etc] de bola.

ROM [rɒm] (*abbr of* **read only memory**) *n* ROM *f*.

Roman ['rəʊmən] ◇ *adj* romano(na). ◇ *n* romano *m*, -na *f*.

Roman Catholic ◇ *adj* católico (romano) (católica). ◇ *n* católico (romano) *m*, católica *f*.

romance [rəʊ'mæns] ◇ *n* **-1.** [romantic quality] lo romántico **-2.** [love affair] amorío *m* **-3.** [in fiction - modern] novela *f* romántica. ◇ *adj*: **Romance Languages** lenguas *fpl* romance.

Romania [ruːˈmeɪnjə] *n* Rumanía.

Romanian [ruːˈmeɪnjən] ◇ *adj* rumano(na). ◇ *n* **-1.** [person] rumano *m*, -na *f* **-2.** [language] rumano *m*.

Roman numerals *npl* números *mpl* romanos.

romantic [rəʊˈmæntɪk] *adj* romántico(ca).

Rome [rəʊm] *n* Roma.

romp [rɒmp] ◇ *n* retozo *m*, jugueteo *m*. ◇ *vi* retozar, juguetear.

rompers ['rɒmpəz] *npl*, **romper suit** ['rɒmpə'-] *n* pelele *m*.

roof [ruːf] *n* **-1.** [of building] tejado *m*; [of vehicle] techo *m*; **to go through** *OR* **hit the ~** [person] subirse por las paredes **-2.** [of mouth] paladar *m*.

roofing ['ruːfɪŋ] *n* materiales *mpl* para techar, techumbre *f*.

roof rack *n* baca *f*, portaequipajes *m inv*, parrilla *f Amér.*

rooftop ['ruːftɒp] *n* tejado *m*.

rook [rʊk] *n* **-1.** [bird] grajo *m* **-2.** [chess piece] torre *f*.

rookie ['rʊkɪ] *n* **-1.** *US inf* [novice] novato *m*, -ta *f* **-2.** *US inf* [military recruit] novato *m*, -ta *f*.

room [ruːm, rʊm] ◇ *n* **-1.** [in house, building] habitación *f* **-2.** [for conferences etc] sala *f* **-3.** [bedroom] habitación *f*, cuarto *m*, ambiente *m Andes & RP* **-4.** (*U*) [space] sitio *m*, espacio *m*. ◇ *vi sep US*: **~ with** compartir alojamiento con.

rooming house ['ruːmɪŋ-] *n US* casa *f* de huéspedes, pensión *f*.

roommate ['ruːmmeɪt] *n* compañero *m*, -ra *f* de habitación.

room service *n* servicio *m* de habitación.

roomy ['ruːmɪ] (*compar* **-ier**, *superl* **-iest**) *adj* espacioso(sa), amplio(plia).

roost [ruːst] *n* percha *f*, palo *m*.

rooster ['ruːstə'] *n* gallo *m*.

root [ruːt] ◇ *n lit & fig* raíz *f*; **to take ~** *lit & fig* arraigar. ◇ *vi* [pig etc] hozar; [person] hurgar, escarbar.

◆ **roots** *npl* [origins] raíces *fpl*.

◆ **root for** *vt fus US inf* apoyar a.

◆ **root out** *vt sep* [eradicate] desarraigar, arrancar de raíz.

rope [rəʊp] ◇ *n* [thin] cuerda *f*; [thick] cabuya *f Cam, Col & Ven*, soga *f*; *NAUT* maroma *f*, cable *m*; **to know the ~s** saber de qué va el asunto; **to show sb the ~s** poner a alguien al tanto. ◇ *vt* atar con cuerda.

◆ **rope in** *vt sep inf* arrastrar *OR* enganchar a; **to rope sb in to do sthg** liar a alguien para hacer algo.

rosary ['rəʊzərɪ] (*pl* **-ies**) *n* rosario *m*.

rose [rəʊz] ◇ *pt* ▷ **rise**. ◇ *adj* [pink] rosa, color de rosa. ◇ *n* [flower] rosa *f*.

rosé ['rəʊzeɪ] *n* rosado *m*.

rosebud ['rəʊzbʌd] *n* capullo *m* de rosa.

rose bush *n* rosal *m*.

rosemary ['rəʊzmərɪ] *n* romero *m*.

rosette [rəʊˈzet] *n* [badge] escarapela *f*.

roster ['rɒstə'] *n* lista *f*.

rostrum ['rɒstrəm] (*pl* **-trums** *OR* **-tra** [-trə]) *n* tribuna *f*.

rosy ['rəʊzɪ] (*compar* **-ier**, *superl* **-iest**) *adj* **-1.** [pink] sonrosado(da) **-2.** [hopeful] prometedor(ra).

rot [rɒt] (*pt & pp* **-ted**, *cont* **-ting**) ◇ *n* (*U*) **-1.** [of wood, food] podredumbre *f*; [in society, organization] putrefacción *f*, decadencia *f* **-2.** *UK dated* [nonsense] tonterías *fpl*, bobadas *fpl*. ◇ *vt* pudrir, corromper. ◇ *vi* pudrirse, corromperse.

rota ['rəʊtə] *n* lista *f* (de turnos).

rotary ['rəʊtərɪ] ◇ *adj* giratorio(ria), rotativo(va). ◇ *n US* [roundabout] glorieta *f*, cruce *m* de circulación giratoria.

rotate [rəʊ'teɪt] ◇ *vt* [turn] hacer girar, dar vueltas a. ◇ *vi* [turn] girar, dar vueltas.

rotation [rəʊ'teɪʃn] *n* [gen] rotación *f*.

rote [rəʊt] *n*: **by ~** de memoria.

rotten ['rɒtn] *adj* **-1.** [decayed] podrido(da) **-2.** *inf* [poor-quality] malísimo(ma), fatal **-3.** *inf* [unpleasant] despreciable **-4.** *inf* [unwell]: **to feel ~** sentirse fatal *OR* muy mal.

rouge [ruːʒ] *n* colorete *m*.

rough [rʌf] ◇ *adj* **-1.** [not smooth - surface, skin] áspero(ra); [- ground, road] desigual **-2.** [not gentle] bruto(ta) **-3.** [crude, not refined - person, manner] grosero(ra), tosco(ca); [- shelter] precario(ria); [- living conditions] duro(ra) **-4.** [approximate - plan, sketch] a grandes rasgos; [- estimate, translation] aproximado(da); **to write a ~ draft of sthg** escribir un borrador de algo **-5.** [unpleasant] duro(ra), difícil **-6.** [wind] violento(ta); [sea] picado(da); [weather, day] embravecido(da), tormentoso(sa), borrascoso(sa) **-7.** [harsh - wine, voice] áspero(ra) **-8.** [violent - area] peligroso(sa); [- person] violento(ta). ◇ *adv*: **to sleep ~** dormir al raso. ◇ *n* **-1.** *GOLF*: **the ~** el rough

- 2. [undetailed form]: **in ~** en borrador. ◇ *vt phr.*: **to ~ it** vivir sin comodidades.
roughage [ˈrʌfɪdʒ] *n* (*U*) fibra *f*.
rough and ready *adj* tosco(ca).
roughen [ˈrʌfn] *vt* poner áspero(ra).
roughly [ˈrʌflɪ] *adv* **- 1.** [approximately] más o menos **- 2.** [not gently] brutalmente **- 3.** [crudely] toscamente.
roulette [ruːˈlet] *n* ruleta *f*.
round [raʊnd] ◇ *adj* redondo(da). ◇ *prep* **- 1.** [surrounding] alrededor de; **the reeds ~ the pond** las cañas alrededor del estanque; **she put her arm ~ his shoulder** le puso el brazo al hombro **- 2.** [near] cerca de; **~ here** por aquí **- 3.** [all over - the world etc] por todo(da); **we went ~ the museum** dimos una vuelta por el museo **- 4.** [in circular movement]: **~ (and ~)** alrededor de **- 5.** [in measurements]: **she's 30 inches ~ the waist** mide 30 pulgadas de cintura **- 6.** [at or to the other side of]: **they were waiting ~ the corner** esperaban a la vuelta de la esquina; **to drive ~ the corner** doblar la esquina; **we went ~ the lake** rodeamos el lago **- 7.** [so as to avoid]: **he drove ~ the pothole** condujo esquivando el bache. ◇ *adv* **- 1.** [on all sides]: **all ~** por todos lados **- 2.** [near]: **~ about** alrededor, en las proximidades **- 3.** [all over]: **to travel ~** viajar por ahí **- 4.** [in circular movement]: **she passed ~ a plate of biscuits** pasó un plato de galletas; **~ (and ~)** en redondo; **to go** OR **spin ~** girar **- 5.** [to the other side] al otro lado; **we went ~ to the back of the house** dimos una vuelta hasta la parte de atrás de la casa **- 6.** [at or to nearby place]: **he came ~ to see us** vino a vernos. ◇ *n* **- 1.** [of talks, drinks, sandwiches] ronda *f*; **a ~ of toast** una tostada; **a ~ of applause** una salva de aplausos **- 2.** [in championship] vuelta *f* **- 3.** [of doctor] visitas *fpl* **- 4.** [of milkman, postman] recorrido *m* **- 5.** [of ammunition] cartucho *m* **- 6.** [in boxing] asalto *m* **- 6.** [in golf] vuelta *f*, round *m*. ◇ *vt* doblar.

◆ **rounds** *npl* [of doctor] visitas *fpl*; **he's out on his ~** está visitando pacientes; [of postman] recorrido *m*; **to do** OR **go the ~s** [joke, rumour] divulgarse; [illness] estar rodando.

◆ **round off** *vt sep* terminar.

◆ **round up** *vt sep* **- 1.** [sheep] recoger; [people] reunir **- 2.** MATH redondear al alza.

roundabout [ˈraʊndəbaʊt] *n UK* **- 1.** [on road] glorieta *f*, rotonda *f* **- 2.** [at fairground] tiovivo *m*, caballitos *mpl*.
rounders [ˈraʊndəz] *n UK juego parecido al béisbol.*
roundly [ˈraʊndlɪ] *adv* rotundamente.
round-shouldered [-ˈʃəʊldəd] *adj* cargado(da) de espaldas.
round trip *n* viaje *m* de ida y vuelta.

roundup [ˈraʊndʌp] *n* **- 1.** [summary] resumen *m*; **news ~** resumen *m* informativo **- 2.** [of criminals] redada *f*.
rouse [raʊz] *vt* **- 1.** *fml* [wake up] despertar **- 2.** [impel]: **to ~ sb/o.s. to do sthg** animar a alguien/animarse a hacer algo **- 3.** [excite] excitar; **it ~d his interest** le despertó el interés.
rousing [ˈraʊzɪŋ] *adj* [speech] conmovedor(ra); [cheer] entusiasta.
rout [raʊt] ◇ *n* derrota *f* aplastante. ◇ *vt* derrotar, aplastar.
route [ruːt] *n* [gen] ruta *f*; [of bus] línea *f*, recorrido *m*; [of ship] rumbo *m*; [for deliveries] recorrido *m*, itinerario *m*; [main road] carretera *f* principal.
route map *n* plano *m* (del camino).
routine [ruːˈtiːn] ◇ *adj* rutinario(ria); (**to have) a ~ checkup** (hacerse) un reconocimiento médico rutinario. ◇ *n* rutina *f*.
roving [ˈrəʊvɪŋ] *adj* itinerante; **a ~ reporter** un periodista ambulante.
row¹ [rəʊ] ◇ *n* **- 1.** [line] fila *f*, hilera *f* **- 2.** [succession] serie *f*; **three in a ~** tres seguidos. ◇ *vt* [boat] remar. ◇ *vi* remar.
row² [raʊ] ◇ *n* **- 1.** [quarrel] pelea *f*, bronca *f* **- 2.** *inf* [noise] estruendo *m*, ruido *m*. ◇ *vi* [quarrel] reñir, pelearse.
rowboat [ˈrəʊbəʊt] *n US* bote *m* de remos.
rowdy [ˈraʊdɪ] (*compar* **-ier,** *superl* **-iest**) *adj* [noisy] ruidoso(sa); [quarrelsome] pendenciero(ra).
row house [rəʊ-] *n US* casa *f* adosada.
rowing [ˈrəʊɪŋ] *n* remo *m*.
rowing boat *n UK* bote *m* de remos.
royal [ˈrɔɪəl] ◇ *adj* real. ◇ *n inf* miembro *m* de la familia real.
Royal Air Force *n*: **the ~** las Fuerzas Aéreas de Gran Bretaña.
royal family *n* familia *f* real.
Royal Mail *n UK*: **the ~** ≃ Correos *m*.
Royal Navy *n*: **the ~** la Armada de Gran Bretaña.
royalty [ˈrɔɪəltɪ] *n* realeza *f*.

◆ **royalties** *npl* derechos *mpl* de autor, royalties *mpl*.

rpm (*abbr of* **revolutions per minute**) r.p.m. *fpl*.
RSPCA (*abbr of* **Royal Society for the Prevention of Cruelty to Animals**) *n sociedad británica protectora de animales*, ≃ SPA *f*.
RSVP (*abbr of* **répondez s'il vous plaît**) s.r.c.
Rt Hon (*abbr of* **Right Honourable**) su Sría.
rub [rʌb] (*pt & pp* **-bed,** *cont* **-bing**) ◇ *vt*: **to ~ sthg (against** OR **on)** frotar algo (en OR contra); **to ~ sthg on** OR **onto** frotar algo en; **to ~ sthg in** OR **into** frotar algo en; **to ~ sb up the wrong way** *UK*, **to ~ sb the wrong way** *US* sacar a alguien de quicio.

◇ *vi*: **to ~ (against sthg)** rozar (algo); **to ~ (together)** rozarse.

◆ **rub off on** *vt fus* [subj: quality] influir en.

◆ **rub out** *vt sep* [erase] borrar.

rubber ['rʌbə'] *n* **- 1.** [substance] goma *f*, caucho *m* **- 2.** *UK* [eraser] goma *f* de borrar **- 3.** *US inf* [condom] goma *f* **- 4.** [in bridge] partida *f*.

rubber band *n US* goma *f* elástica.

rubber plant *n* ficus *m inv*.

rubber stamp *n* estampilla *f Esp*, sello *m* de goma, timbre *m* de goma *Chile*.

◆ **rubber-stamp** *vt* aprobar oficialmente.

rubbish ['rʌbɪʃ] *n (U)* **- 1.** [refuse] basura *f* **- 2.** *inf fig* [worthless matter] porquería *f* **- 3.** *inf* [nonsense] tonterías *fpl*, babosadas *fpl Cam & Méx*; **don't talk ~** no digas tonterías.

rubbish bin *n UK* cubo *m* de la basura.

rubbish dump *n UK* vertedero *m*, basurero *m*.

rubble ['rʌbl] *n (U)* escombros *mpl*.

ruby ['ru:bɪ] *(pl* **-ies)** *n* rubí *m*.

rucksack ['rʌksæk] *n* mochila *f*.

ructions ['rʌkʃnz] *npl inf* bronca *f*, lío *m*.

rudder ['rʌdə'] *n* timón *m*.

ruddy ['rʌdɪ] *(compar* **-ier**, *superl* **-iest)** *adj* [reddish] rojizo(za).

rude [ru:d] *adj* **- 1.** [impolite - person, manners, word] grosero(ra), liso(sa) *Arg & Perú*; [- joke] verde **- 2.** [shocking] violento(ta), brusco(ca).

rudimentary [,ru:dɪ'mentərɪ] *adj* rudimentario(ria).

rueful ['ru:fʊl] *adj* arrepentido(da).

ruffian ['rʌfjən] *n* rufián *m*.

ruffle ['rʌfl] *vt* **- 1.** [hair] revolver, despeinar; [water] perturbar, agitar; [feathers] encrespar **- 2.** [composure, nerves] enervar, encrespar **- 3.** [person] poner nervioso(sa)a.

rug [rʌg] *n* **- 1.** [carpet] alfombra *f* **- 2.** [blanket] manta *f* de viaje.

rugby ['rʌgbɪ] *n* rugby *m*.

rugged ['rʌgɪd] *adj* **- 1.** [wild, inhospitable] escabroso(sa), accidentado(da) **- 2.** [sturdy] fuerte **- 3.** [roughly handsome] duro y atractivo (dura y atractiva); **his ~ good looks** sus rasgos recios.

rugger ['rʌgə'] *n UK inf* rugby *m*.

ruin ['ru:ɪn] ◇ *n* ruina *f*. ◇ *vt* **- 1.** [destroy] estropear **- 2.** [spoil] arruinar **- 3.** [bankrupt] arruinar.

◆ **in ruin(s)** *adv* en ruinas.

rule [ru:l] ◇ *n* **- 1.** [regulation, guideline] regla *f*, norma *f*; **to break the ~s** violar las normas; **to obey the ~s** obedecer las normas **- 2.** [norm]: **the ~** la regla, la norma;

as a ~ por regla general **- 3.** [government] dominio *m*; **to be under Roman ~** estar bajo dominio romano **- 4.** [ruler] regla *f*. ◇ *vt* **- 1.** *fml* [control] regir **- 2.** [govern] gobernar **- 3.** [decide]: **to ~ that** decidir *OR* ordenar que. ◇ *vi* **- 1.** [give decision] decidir, fallar **- 2.** *fml* [be paramount] regir, ser primordial **- 3.** [govern] gobernar.

◆ **rule out** *vt sep* descartar.

ruled [ru:ld] *adj* rayado(da).

ruler ['ru:lə'] *n* **- 1.** [for measurement] regla *f* **- 2.** [monarch] soberano *m*, -na *f*.

ruling ['ru:lɪŋ] ◇ *adj* en el poder. ◇ *n* fallo *m*, decisión *f*.

rum [rʌm] *n* ron *m*.

Rumania [ru:'meɪnjə] = **Romania**.

Rumanian [ru:'meɪnjən] = **Romanian**.

rumble ['rʌmbl] ◇ *n* [gen] estruendo *m*; [of stomach] ruido *m*. ◇ *vi* [gen] retumbar; [stomach] hacer ruido.

rummage ['rʌmɪdʒ] *vi* hurgar, rebuscar; **to ~ around in sthg** revolver en algo.

rumour *UK*, **rumor** *US* ['ru:mə'] *n* rumor *m*; **there's a ~ going around that ...** se rumorea que ...

rumoured *UK*, **rumored** *US* ['ru:məd] *adj*: **to be ~** rumorearse; **she is ~ to be very rich** se rumorea que es muy rica.

rump [rʌmp] *n* **- 1.** [of animal] grupa *f*, ancas *fpl* **- 2.** *inf* [of person] trasero *m*, culo *m*.

rump steak *n* filete *m* de lomo, churrasco *m* de cuadril *RP*.

rumpus ['rʌmpəs] *n inf* lío *m*, jaleo *m*, despiole *m Arg*.

run [rʌn] *(pt* ran, *pp* run, *cont* **-ning)** ◇ *n* **- 1.** [on foot] carrera *f*; **to go for a ~** ir a correr; **on the ~** en fuga **- 2.** [journey - in car] paseo *m OR* vuelta *f* (en coche); **to go for a ~** ir a dar una vuelta; [- in plane, ship] viaje *m* **- 3.** [series - of wins, disasters] serie *f*; [- of luck] racha *f* **- 4.** THEATRE: **the play had a 6-week ~** la obra estuvo en cartelera 6 semanas **- 5.** [great demand]: **a ~ on sthg** una gran demanda de algo **- 6.** [in tights] carrera *f* **- 7.** [in cricket, baseball] carrera *f* **- 8.** [for skiing etc] pista *f* **- 9.** [term]: **in the short/long ~** a corto/largo plazo. ◇ *vt* **- 1.** [on foot] correr **- 2.** [manage - business] dirigir, administrar; [- life, event] organizar **- 3.** [operate - computer program, machine, film] poner **- 4.** [have and use - car etc] hacer funcionar **- 5.** [open - tap] abrir; **to ~ a bath** llenar la bañera **- 6.** [publish] publicar **- 7.** [move]: **to ~ sthg along** *OR* **over** pasar algo por. ◇ *vi* **- 1.** [on foot] correr **- 2.** *esp US* [in election]: **to ~ (for)** presentarse como candidato(ta) (a); **he's ~ning for president** se presenta a la presidencia **- 3.** [factory, machine] funcionar; [engine] estar encendido(da); **to ~ on** *OR* **off sthg** funcionar con algo; **to ~ smoothly** ir bien **- 4.** [bus, train ir - **5.** [flow] correr - **6.** [tap] gotear; **somebody has left the tap ~ning** alguien se ha dejado el grifo abierto; [nose] moquear; **my nose is ~ning** me moquea la nariz; [eyes] llorar - **7.** [colour] desteñir.

◆ **run across** *vt fus* [meet] encontrarse con.

◆ **run away** *vi* [flee]: **to ~ away (from)** huir *or* fugarse (de).

◆ **run down** ◇ *vt sep* - **1.** [run over] atropellar - **2.** [criticize] hablar mal de. ◇ *vi* [battery] acabarse; [clock] pararse; [project, business] debilitarse, perder energía

◆ **run into** *vt fus* - **1.** [problem] encontrar; [person] tropezarse con - **2.** [in vehicle] chocar con.

◆ **run off** ◇ *vt sep* [copies, photocopies] sacar. ◇ *vi*: **to ~ off (with)** fugarse (con).

◆ **run out** *vi* - **1.** [become used up] acabarse - **2.** [expire] caducar.

◆ **run out of** *vt fus* quedarse sin.

◆ **run over** *vt sep* atropellar.

◆ **run through** *vt fus* - **1.** [be present in] recorrer, atravesar; **the vein of humour which ran through her work** el tono de humor que está presente en su trabajo - **2.** [practise] ensayar, practicar - **3.** [read through] echar un vistazo a.

◆ **run to** *vt fus* [amount to] ascender a; **the bill ran to thousands** la cuenta subía a varios miles.

◆ **run up** *vt fus* [amass] incurrir en, contraer; **he ran up a huge bill** acumuló una factura enorme.

◆ **run up against** *vt fus* tropezar con.

runaway ['rʌnəweɪ] ◇ *adj* - **1.** [gen] fugitivo(va); [horse] desbocado(da); [train] fuera de control; [inflation] desenfrenado(da) - **2.** [victory] fácil. ◇ *n* fugitivo *m*, -va *f*.

rundown ['rʌndaʊn] *n* [report] informe *m*, resumen *m*; **to give sb a ~on sthg** poner a alguien al tanto de algo.

◆ **run-down** *adj* - **1.** [dilapidated] en ruinas, en decadencia - **2.** [tired] agotado(da); **to feel ~** sentirse débil.

rung [rʌŋ] ◇ *pp* ▷ **ring.** ◇ *n lit* & *fig* peldaño *m*.

runner ['rʌnəʳ] *n* - **1.** [athlete] corredor *m*, -ra *f* - **2.** [smuggler] traficante *m* *or* *f*, contrabandista *m* *or* *f* - **3.** [on sledge] carril *m*; [of drawer, sliding seat] carro *m*.

runner bean *n* UK judía *f* verde, chaucha *f* RP, vainita *f* Vén, ejote *m* CAm, Méx, poroto *m* verde Chile.

runner-up (*pl* **runners-up**) *n* subcampeón *m*, -ona *f*.

running ['rʌnɪŋ] ◇ *adj* - **1.** [continuous] continuo(nua) - **2.** [consecutive] seguidos(das); **four days ~** cuatro días consecutivos - **3.** [water] corriente. ◇ *n* - **1.** [act of

running] el correr; **to go ~** hacer footing - **2.** SPORT carreras *fpl* - **3.** [management] dirección *f*, organización *f* - **4.** [operation] funcionamiento *m* - **5.** *phr*: **to be in/out of the ~ (for sthg)** tener/no tener posibilidades (de algo).

runny ['rʌnɪ] (*compar* -**ier**, *superl* -**iest**) *adj* - **1.** [sauce, gravy] derretido(da) - **2.** [nose] que moquea; [eyes] llorosos(as).

run-of-the-mill *adj* normal y corriente.

runt [rʌnt] *n* - **1.** [animal] cría *f* más pequeña y débil - **2.** *pej* [person] renacuajo *m*.

run-up *n* - **1.** [preceding time] periodo *m* previo; **the ~ to the elections** el periodo previo a las elecciones - **2.** SPORT carrerilla *f*.

runway ['rʌnweɪ] *n* pista *f*.

rupture ['rʌptʃəʳ] ◇ *n* MED hernia *f*. ◇ *vt* romper.

rural ['rʊərəl] *adj* rural.

ruse [ruːz] *n* ardid *m*.

rush [rʌʃ] ◇ *n* - **1.** [hurry] prisa *f*; **to be in a ~** tener prisa - **2.** [burst of activity]: **~ (for** *OR* **on sthg)** avalancha *f* (en busca de algo) - **3.** [busy period] hora *f* punta - **4.** [surge - of air] ráfaga *f*; [- of water] torrente *m*; [- mental] arrebato *m*; **to make a ~ for sthg** ir en desbandada hacia algo; **there was a ~ for the exit** la gente salió apresuradamente. ◇ *vt* - **1.** [hurry] acelerar, apresurar - **2.** [send quickly] llevar rápidamente; **he was ~ed to hospital** lo llevaron al hospital a toda prisa. ◇ *vi* - **1.** [hurry] ir de prisa, correr; **to ~ into sthg** meterse de cabeza en algo; **there's no need to ~** no hay ninguna prisa; **he ~ed to help her** corrió a ayudarla - **2.** [surge] correr, precipitarse.

◆ **rushes** *npl* BOT juncos *mpl*.

rush hour *n* hora *f* punta, hora *f* pico *Amér*, hora *f* peack Chile.

rusk [rʌsk] *n* galleta que se da a los niños pequeños para que se acostumbran a masticar.

Russia ['rʌʃə] *n* Rusia.

Russian ['rʌʃn] ◇ *adj* ruso(sa). ◇ *n* - **1.** [person] ruso *m*, -sa *f* - **2.** [language] ruso *m*.

rust [rʌst] ◇ *n* óxido *m*. ◇ *vi* oxidarse.

rustic ['rʌstɪk] *adj* rústico(ca).

rustle ['rʌsl] ◇ *vt* - **1.** [paper] hacer crujir - **2.** *US* [cattle] robar. ◇ *vi* [wind, leaves] susurrar; [paper] crujir.

rustling *n*: **cattle ~** robo *m* de ganado.

rusty ['rʌstɪ] (*compar* -**ier**, *superl* -**iest**) *adj* *lit* & *fig* oxidado(da); **my French is a bit ~** hace mucho que no practico el francés.

rut [rʌt] *n* [track] rodada *f*; **to get into/be in a ~** *fig* caer/estar metido en una rutina; **to get out of a ~** salir de la rutina.

ruthless ['ruːθlɪs] *adj* despiadado(da).

RV *n* *US* (*abbr of* **recreational vehicle**) casa-remolque *f*.

rye [raɪ] *n* [grain] centeno *m*.
rye bread *n* pan *m* de centeno.

s (*pl* **ss** OR **s's**), **S** (*pl* **Ss** OR **S's**) [es] *n* [letter] s *f*, S *f*.

◆ **S** (*abbr of* **south**) S.

Sabbath ['sæbəθ] *n*: **the** ~ [for Christians] el domingo; [for Jews] el sábado.
sabbatical [sə'bætɪkl] *n* sabático *m*; **on** ~ de sabático.
sabotage ['sæbətɑ:ʒ] ⬦ *n* sabotaje *m*. ⬦ *vt* sabotear.
saccharin(e) ['sækərɪn] *n* sacarina *f*.
sachet ['sæʃeɪ] *n* bolsita *f*.
sack [sæk] ⬦ *n* - 1. [bag] saco *m* - 2. *UK inf* [dismissal]: **to get** OR **be given the** ~ ser despedido(da); **to give sb the** ~ despedir a alguien. ⬦ *vt UK inf* despedir, remover *Amér.*
sacking ['sækɪŋ] *n* - 1. [fabric] harpillera *f* - 2. [dismissal] despido *m*.
sacred ['seɪkrɪd] *adj lit* & *fig* sagrado(da).
sacrifice ['sækrɪfaɪs] RELIG & *fig* ⬦ *n* sacrificio *m*; **to make** ~**s** sacrificarse. ⬦ *vt* sacrificar.
sacrilege ['sækrɪlɪdʒ] *n* RELIG & *fig* sacrilegio *m*.
sacrosanct ['sækrəʊsæŋkt] *adj* sacrosanto(ta).
sad [sæd] (*compar* **-der**, *superl* **-dest**) *adj* triste.
sadden ['sædn] *vt* entristecer.
saddle ['sædl] ⬦ *n* - 1. [for horse] silla *f* (de montar) - 2. [of bicycle, motorcycle] sillín *m*, asiento *m*. ⬦ *vt* - 1. [horse] ensillar - 2. *fig* [burden]: **to** ~ **sb with sthg** cargar a alguien con algo; **she was** ~**d with an elderly patient** le encajaron un pariente anciano.
saddlebag ['sædlbæg] *n* alforja *f*.
sadistic [sə'dɪstɪk] *adj* sádico(ca).
sadly ['sædlɪ] *adv* tristemente.
sadness ['sædnɪs] *n* tristeza *f*.
sadomasochism [ˌseɪdəʊ'mæsəˌkɪzəm] *n* sadomasoquismo *m*.
s.a.e., sae *n abbr of* **stamped addressed envelope**.
safari [sə'fɑ:rɪ] *n* safari *m*.
safe [seɪf] ⬦ *adj* - 1. [gen] seguro(ra); **a** ~ **place** un lugar seguro; **is this ladder** ~? ¿es segura esta escalera?; **you're** ~ **now** ahora estás seguro; ~ **and sound** sano y salvo (sana y salva) - 2. [without harm] sano y salvo (sana y salva) - 3. [not causing disagreement]: **it's** ~ **to say that ...** se puede afirmar con seguridad que ...; **to be on the** ~ **side** por mayor seguridad - 4. [reliable] digno(na) de confianza. ⬦ *n* caja *f* (de caudales).
safe-conduct *n* salvoconducto *m*.
safe-deposit box *n* caja *f* de seguridad.
safeguard ['seɪfgɑ:d] ⬦ *n* salvaguardia *f*, protección *f*; **as a** ~ como protección; **a** ~ **against sthg** una protección contra algo. ⬦ *vt*: **to** ~ **sthg/sb (against sthg)** salvaguardar OR proteger algo/a alguien (contra algo).
safekeeping [ˌseɪf'ki:pɪŋ] *n*: **she gave me the letter for** ~ me dio la carta para que se la guardara en un lugar seguro.
safely ['seɪflɪ] *adv* - 1. [with no danger] sin peligro, con seguridad - 2. [not in danger] seguramente - 3. [unharmed] sano y salvo (sana y salva) - 4. [for certain]: **I can** ~ **say that ...** puedo decir con toda confianza que ...
safe sex *n* sexo *m* sin riesgo.
safety ['seɪftɪ] *n* seguridad *f*.
safety belt *n* cinturón *m* de seguridad.
safety pin *n* imperdible *m*, seguro *m Méx.*
saffron ['sæfrən] *n* [spice] azafrán *m*.
sag [sæg] (*pt* & *pp* **-ged**, *cont* **-ging**) *vi* [sink downwards] hundirse, combarse.
sage [seɪdʒ] ⬦ *adj* sabio(bia). ⬦ *n* - 1. [herb] salvia *f* - 2. [wise man] sabio *m*.
Sagittarius [ˌsædʒɪ'teərɪəs] *n* Sagitario *m*.
Sahara [sə'hɑ:rə] *n*: **the** ~ **(Desert)** el (desierto del) Sáhara.
said [sed] *pt* & *pp* ▷ **say**.
sail [seɪl] ⬦ *n* - 1. [of boat] vela *f*; **to set** ~ zarpar - 2. [journey by boat] paseo *m* en barco de vela; **to go for a** ~ salir a hacer una excursión en barco de vela. ⬦ *vt* - 1. [boat, ship] gobernar - 2. [sea] cruzar. ⬦ *vi* - 1. [travel by boat] navegar - 2. [move - boat]: **the ship** ~**ed across the ocean** el barco cruzó el océano - 3. [leave by boat] zarpar; **we sail at 10 am** zarpamos a las 10 am.
◆ **sail through** *vt fus* hacer con facilidad.
sailboat *US* = **sailing boat**.
sailing ['seɪlɪŋ] *n* - 1. (*U*) SPORT vela *f* - 2. [trip by ship] travesía *f*.
sailing boat *UK*, **sailboat** *US* ['seɪlbəʊt] *n* barco *m* de vela.
sailing ship *n* (buque *m*) velero *m*.
sailor ['seɪlə'] *n* marinero *m*, -ra *f*, marino *m*, -na *f*.
saint [seɪnt] *n* RELIG & *fig* santo *m*, -ta *f*; **he's no** ~ no es ningún santo; **to have the patience of a** ~ tener más paciencia que un santo.
saintly ['seɪntlɪ] (*compar* **-ier**, *superl* **-iest**)

adj santo(ta), piadoso(sa).

sake [seik] *n*: **for the ~ of** por (el bien de); **for God's** OR **heaven's ~** ¡por el amor de Dios!

salad ['sæləd] *n* ensalada *f*.

salad bowl *n* ensaladera *f*.

salad cream *n* UK salsa parecida a la mahonesa para aderezar la ensalada.

salad dressing *n* aliño *m* (para la ensalada).

salami [sə'lɑ:mɪ] *n* salami *m*.

salary ['sælərɪ] (*pl* -**ies**) *n* sueldo *m*.

sale [seil] *n* - **1.** [gen] venta *f*; **on ~** en venta; **(up) for ~** en venta; **'for ~'** 'se vende' - **2.** [at reduced prices] liquidación *f*, saldo *m*. ◆ **sales** *npl* - **1.** ECON ventas *fpl* - **2.** [at reduced prices]: **the ~s** las rebajas.

saleroom UK ['seilrum], **salesroom** US ['seilzrum] *n* sala *f* de subastas.

sales assistant ['seilz-], **salesclerk** US ['seilzklɑ:rk] *n* dependiente *m*, -ta *f*.

salesman ['seilzmən] (*pl* -**men** [-mən]) *n* [in shop] dependiente *m*, vendedor *m*; [travelling] viajante *m*.

sales rep *n* inf representante *m* OR *f*.

salesroom US = **saleroom**.

saleswoman ['seilz,wumən] (*pl* -**women** [-,wimin]) *n* [in shop] dependienta *f*, vendedora *f*; [travelling] viajante *f*.

salient ['seiljənt] *adj* fml sobresaliente.

saliva [sə'laivə] *n* saliva *f*.

sallow ['sæləu] *adj* cetrino(na), amarillento(ta).

salmon ['sæmən] (*pl* inv OR -**s**) *n* salmón *m*.

salmonella [,sælmə'nelə] *n* salmonelosis *f* inv.

salon ['sælɒn] *n* salón *m*.

saloon [sə'lu:n] *n* - **1.** UK [car] (coche *m*) utilitario *m* - **2.** US [bar] bar *m* - **3.** UK [in pub]: **~ (bar)** en ciertos pubs y hoteles, bar elegante con precios más altos que los del 'public bar' - **4.** [in ship] salón *m*.

salt [sɔ:lt, sɒlt] ◇ *n* sal *f*. ◇ *vt* [food] salar; [roads] echar sal en (las carreteras etc para evitar que se hielen).
◆ **salt away** *vt sep* inf ahorrar, guardar.

salt cellar UK, **salt shaker** US [-,ʃeikər] *n* salero *m*.

saltwater ['sɔ:lt,wɔ:tər] *adj* de agua salada.

salty ['sɔ:ltɪ] (*compar* -**ier**, *superl* -**iest**) *adj* salado(da), salobre.

salutary ['sæljutrɪ] *adj* saludable.

salute [sə'lu:t] ◇ *n* - **1.** [with hand] saludo *m* - **2.** MIL [firing of guns] salva *f*, saludo *m*. ◇ *vt* - **1.** [with hand] saludar - **2.** [acknowledge formally] reconocer.

Salvadorean, Salvadorian [,sælvə-'dɔ:rɪən] ◇ *adj* salvadoreño(ña). ◇ *n* salvadoreño *m*, -ña *f*.

salvage ['sælvɪdʒ] ◇ *n* (U) - **1.** [rescue of ship] salvamento *m* - **2.** [property rescued]

objetos *mpl* recuperados OR rescatados. ◇ *vt* lit & fig: **to ~ sthg (from)** salvar algo (de).

salvation [sæl'veiʃn] *n* salvación *f*.

Salvation Army *n*: **the ~** el Ejército de Salvación.

same [seim] ◇ *adj* mismo(ma); **the ~ colour as his** el mismo color que el suyo; **at the ~ time** [simultaneously] al mismo tiempo; [yet] aún así; **one and the ~** el mismo (la misma). ◇ *pron*: **the ~** el mismo (la misma); **she did the ~** hizo lo mismo; **the ingredients are the ~** los ingredientes son los mismos OR iguales; **his car is the ~ as yours** su coche es el mismo que el tuyo; **I'll have the ~ (again)** tomaré lo mismo (que antes); **all** OR **just the ~** [nevertheless, anyway] de todos modos; **it's all the ~ to me** me da igual; **it's not the ~** no es lo mismo; **happy Christmas! – the ~ to you!** ¡feliz Navidad! – ¡igualmente! ◇ *adv*: **the ~** lo mismo.

sample ['sɑ:mpl] ◇ *n* muestra *f*; **a free ~** una muestra gratuita. ◇ *vt* [food, wine, attractions] probar.

sanatorium (*pl* -**riums** OR -**ria** [-rɪə]), **sanitorium** US (*pl* -**riums** OR -**ria** [-rɪə]) [,sænə'tɔ:rɪəm] *n* sanatorio *m*.

sanctimonious [,sæŋktɪ'məunjəs] *adj* pej santurrón(ona).

sanction ['sæŋkʃn] ◇ *n* sanción *f*. ◇ *vt* sancionar.

sanctity ['sæŋktətɪ] *n* santidad *f*.

sanctuary ['sæŋktʃuərɪ] (*pl* -**ies**) *n* - **1.** [for wildlife] reserva *f*; **a bird ~** una reserva de aves - **2.** [refuge] refugio *m* - **3.** [holy place] santuario *m*.

sand [sænd] ◇ *n* arena *f*. ◇ *vt* lijar; **to ~ down a surface** lijar una superficie.

sandal ['sændl] *n* sandalia *f*; **a pair of ~s** unas sandalias.

sandalwood ['sændlwud] *n* sándalo *m*.

sandbox US = **sandpit**.

sandcastle ['sænd,kɑ:sl] *n* castillo *m* de arena.

sand dune *n* duna *f*.

sandpaper ['sænd,peipər] ◇ *n* (U) papel *m* de lija. ◇ *vt* lijar.

sandpit UK ['sændpɪt], **sandbox** US ['sændbɒks] *n* cuadro *m* de arena.

sandstone ['sændstəun] *n* piedra *f* arenisca.

sandwich ['sænwɪdʒ] ◇ *n* [made with roll etc] bocadillo *m*; [made with sliced bread] sandwich *m* frío; **a cheese ~** un sandwich de queso. ◇ *vt* fig apretujar; **she was ~ed between two businessmen** quedó atrapada entre dos hombres de negocios.

sandwich board *n* cartelón *m* (de hombre-anuncio).

sandwich box *n* fiambrera *f*, vianda *f* Amér.

sandwich course n UK curso universitario que incluye un cierto tiempo de experiencia profesional.

sandy ['sændɪ] (compar -ier, superl -iest) adj - 1. [covered in sand] arenoso(sa) - 2. [sand-coloured] rojizo(za).

sane [seɪn] adj - 1. [not mad] cuerdo(da) - 2. [sensible] prudente, sensato(ta).

sang [sæŋ] pt ⊳ sing.

sanitary ['sænɪtrɪ] adj - 1. [connected with health] sanitario(ria) - 2. [clean, hygienic] higiénico(ca).

sanitary towel, sanitary napkin US n [disposable] compresa f, toalla f higiénica Amér.

sanitation [,sænɪ'teɪʃn] n sanidad f, higiene f.

sanitorium US = sanatorium.

sanity ['sænətɪ] n - 1. [saneness] cordura f - 2. [good sense] sensatez f, prudencia f.

sank [sæŋk] pt ⊳ sink.

Santa (Claus) ['sæntə(ˌklaʊz)] n Papá m Noel.

sap [sæp] (pt & pp -ped, cont -ping) ⋄ n [of plant] savia f. ⋄ vt [weaken] minar, agotar.

sapling ['sæplɪŋ] n árbol m nuevo, arbolito m.

sapphire ['sæfaɪəʳ] n zafiro m.

Saragossa [,særə'gɒsə] n Zaragoza.

Saran wrap® [sə'ræn-] n US plástico m transparente (para envolver alimentos).

sarcastic [sɑː'kæstɪk] adj sarcástico(ca).

sardine [sɑː'diːn] n sardina f; to be packed in like ∼s ir como sardinas en lata.

sardonic [sɑː'dɒnɪk] adj sardónico(ca).

SAS (abbr of Special Air Service) n unidad especial del ejército británico encargada de operaciones de sabotaje.

SASE n US abbr of self-addressed stamped envelope.

sash [sæʃ] n faja f.

sat [sæt] pt & pp ⊳ sit.

SAT [sæt] n - 1. (abbr of Standard Assessment Test) examen de aptitud que se realiza a los siete, once y catorce años en Inglaterra y Gales - 2. (abbr of Scholastic Aptitude Test) examen de ingreso a la universidad en Estados Unidos.

Satan ['seɪtn] n Satanás m, Satán m.

satchel ['sætʃəl] n cartera f.

satellite ['sætəlaɪt] n lit & fig satélite m.

satellite TV n televisión f por satélite.

satin ['sætɪn] ⋄ n satén m, raso m. ⋄ comp de satén, de raso.

satire ['sætaɪəʳ] n sátira f.

satisfaction [,sætɪs'fækʃn] n satisfacción f.

satisfactory [,sætɪs'fæktərɪ] adj satisfactorio(ria).

satisfied ['sætɪsfaɪd] adj satisfecho(cha); you're never ∼! ¡nunca te conformas con

nada!; a ∼smile una sonrisa de satisfacción.

satisfy ['sætɪsfaɪ] (pt & pp -ied) vt - 1. [gen] satisfacer - 2. [convince] convencer; to ∼ sb that convencer a alguien (de) que - 3. [requirements] cumplir, satisfacer.

satisfying ['sætɪsfaɪɪŋ] adj - 1. [pleasant] satisfactorio(ria) - 2. [filling] sustancioso(sa); a ∼ meal una comida sustanciosa.

satsuma [,sæt'suːmə] n satsuma f, tipo de mandarina.

saturate ['sætʃəreɪt] vt - 1. [drench]: to ∼ sthg (with) empapar algo (de); he was ∼d with sweat estaba empapado de sudor - 2. [fill completely] saturar; to ∼ sthg (with) saturar algo (de).

Saturday ['sætədɪ] ⋄ n sábado m; what day is it? – it's ∼ ¿a qué estamos hoy? – estamos a sábado; on ∼ el sábado; on ∼s los sábados; last ∼ el sábado pasado; this ∼ este sábado, el sábado que viene; next ∼ el sábado de la semana que viene; every ∼ todos los sábados; every other ∼ cada dos sábados, un sábado sí y otro no; the ∼ before el sábado anterior; the ∼ after next no este sábado sino el siguiente; the ∼ before last hace dos sábados; ∼ week, a week on ∼ del sábado en ocho días. ⋄ comp del sábado.

Saturn ['sætən] n Saturno m.

sauce [sɔːs] n CULIN salsa f.

saucepan ['sɔːspən] n [with two handles] cacerola f; [with one long handle] cazo m.

saucer ['sɔːsəʳ] n platillo m.

saucy ['sɔːsɪ] (compar -ier, superl -iest) adj inf descarado(da), fresco(ca).

Saudi Arabia [,saʊdɪə'reɪbjə] n Arabia Saudí.

Saudi (Arabian) ['saʊdɪ-] ⋄ adj saudí, saudita. ⋄ n [person] saudí m OR f, saudita m OR f.

sauna ['sɔːnə] n sauna f.

saunter ['sɔːntəʳ] vi pasearse (tranquilamente); he ∼ed into the room entró desenfadadamente en la habitación.

sausage ['sɒsɪdʒ] n salchicha f.

sausage roll n UK salchicha envuelta en masa como de empanadilla.

sauté [UK 'saʊteɪ, US saʊ'teɪ] (pt & pp sautéed OR sautéd) vt saltear.

savage ['sævɪdʒ] ⋄ adj [cruel, fierce] feroz, salvaje. ⋄ n pej salvaje m OR f. ⋄ vt - 1. [subj: animal] embestir, atacar - 2. [subj: person] atacar con ferocidad.

save [seɪv] ⋄ vt - 1. [rescue] salvar, rescatar; to ∼ sb from sthg salvar a alguien de algo - 2. [prevent waste - time, money, energy] ahorrar - 3. [set aside - money] ahorrar; [- food, strength] guardar; why don't you ∼some of your sweets for later? ¿por qué

no te guardas algunos caramelos para más tarde?; **will you ~me some soup?** ¿me guardarás algo de sopa?; **~ your strength for later** ahorra tus fuerzas para más tarde **- 4.** [avoid] evitar; **it ~s having to go to the bank** ahorra tener que ir al banco; **to ~ sb from doing sthg** evitar a alguien (el) hacer algo **- 5.** SPORT parar **- 6.** COMPUT guardar **- 7.** *phr:* **to ~face** salvar las apariencias. ◇ *vi* ahorrar. ◇ *n* SPORT parada *f.* ◇ *prep fml:* ~ **(for)** excepto.
◆ **save up** *vi* ahorrar.

saving grace ['seɪvɪŋ-] *n* lo único positivo.

savings ['seɪvɪŋz] *npl* ahorros *mpl.*

savings account *n* cuenta *f* de ahorros.

savings bank *n* ~ caja *f* de ahorros.

saviour UK, **savior** US ['seɪvjə'] *n* salvador *m*, -ra *f.*

savour UK, **savor** US ['seɪvə'] *vt lit & fig* saborear.

savoury UK (*pl* -ies), **savory** (*pl* -ies) US ['seɪvərɪ] ◇ *adj* **- 1.** [not sweet] salado(da) **- 2.** US [tasty] sabroso(sa) **- 3.** [respectable, pleasant] respetable, agradable; **not a very ~ character** un personaje poco muy honesto. ◇ *n* comida *f* de aperitivo.

saw [sɔ:] (UK *pt* -ed, *pp* sawn, US *pt & pp* -ed) ◇ *pt* ▷ **see**. ◇ *n* sierra *f.* ◇ *vt* serrar.

sawdust ['sɔ:dʌst] *n* serrín *m.*

sawed-off shotgun US = **sawn-off shotgun**.

sawmill ['sɔ:mɪl] *n* aserradero *m.*

sawn [sɔ:n] *pp* UK ▷ **saw**.

sawn-off shotgun UK, **sawed-off shotgun** US [sɔ:d-] *n* arma *f* de cañones recortados.

saxophone ['sæksəfəʊn] *n* saxofón *m.*

say [seɪ] (*pt & pp* said) ◇ *vt* **- 1.** [gen] decir; **she said that ...** dijo que ...; **you should have said so!** ¡haberlo dicho!; **you can ~ that again!** ¡ya lo creo!; **to ~ yes** decir que sí; **he's said to be good** se dice que es bueno; **let's ~ you were to win** pongamos que ganaras; **shall we ~ 9.30?** ¿qué tal a las 9.30?; **that goes without ~ing** ni que decir tiene; **to ~ the least** por no decir otra cosa; **it has a lot to be said for it** tiene muy buenos puntos en su favor **- 2.** [indicate - clock, meter] marcar. ◇ *n:* **to have a/no ~ in sthg** tener/no tener voz y voto en algo; **let me have my ~** déjame decir lo que pienso.
◆ **that is to say** *adv* es decir.

saying ['seɪŋ] *n* dicho *m.*

scab [skæb] *n* **- 1.** MED costra *f* **- 2.** *pej* [non-striker] esquirol *m.*

scaffold ['skæfəʊld] *n* **- 1.** [around building] andamio *m* **- 2.** [for execution] cadalso *m*, patíbulo *m.*

scaffolding ['skæfəldɪŋ] *n (U)* andamios *mpl*, andamiaje *m.*

scald [skɔ:ld] *vt* escaldar.

scale [skeɪl] ◇ *n* **- 1.** [of map] escala *f;* **to ~ a escala; not drawn to ~** no hecho(cha) a escala **- 2.** [size, extent] tamaño *m*, escala *f;* **on a large ~** a gran escala **- 3.** [on measuring equipment] escala *f* **- 4.** [music] escala *f* **- 5.** [of fish, snake] escama *f* **- 6.** US = **scales**. ◇ *vt* **- 1.** [climb] escalar **- 2.** [remove scales from] escamar.
◆ **scales** *npl* **- 1.** [for weighing food] balanza *f* **- 2.** [for weighing person] báscula *f;* **bathroom ~s** báscula de baño.
◆ **scale down** *vt fus* reducir.

scale model *n* maqueta *f.*

scallop ['skɒləp] ◇ *n* ZOOL vieira *f.* ◇ *vt* [decorate edge of] festonear.

scalp [skælp] ◇ *n* cuero *m* cabelludo. ◇ *vt* cortar la cabellera a.

scalpel ['skælpəl] *n* bisturí *m.*

scaly ['skeɪlɪ] *adj* [skin] escamoso(sa).

scamper ['skæmpə'] *vi* corretear.

scampi ['skæmpɪ] *n (U):* **(breaded) ~** gambas *fpl* a la gabardina.

scan [skæn] (*pt & pp* -ned, *cont* -ning) ◇ *n* exploración *f* ultrasónica. ◇ *vt* **- 1.** [examine carefully] examinar **- 2.** [glance at] dar un vistazo a **- 3.** ELECTRON & TV registrar.

scandal ['skændl] *n* **- 1.** [scandalous event, outrage] escándalo *m* **- 2.** [scandalous talk] habladurías *fpl.*

scandalize, ise ['skændəlaɪz] *vt* escandalizar.

Scandinavia [,skændɪ'neɪvjə] *n* Escandinavia.

Scandinavian [,skændɪ'neɪvjən] ◇ *adj* escandinavo(va). ◇ *n* [person] escandinavo *m*, -va *f.*

scant [skænt] *adj* escaso(sa).

scanty ['skæntɪ] (*compar* -ier, *superl* -iest) *adj* [amount, resources] escaso(sa); [dress] ligero(ra); [meal] insuficiente.

scapegoat ['skeɪpgəʊt] *n* cabeza *f* de turco.

scar [skɑ:'] (*pt & pp* -red, *cont* -ring) *n* **- 1.** [physical] cicatriz *f* **- 2.** *fig* [mental] señal *f.*

scarce ['skeəs] *adj* escaso(sa).

scarcely ['skeəslɪ] *adv* apenas; **~ anyone/ever** casi nadie/nunca.

scare [skeə'] ◇ *n* **- 1.** [sudden fear] susto *m*, sobresalto *m* **- 2.** [public fear] temor *m* **- 3.** [panic] **there was a bomb ~** hubo una amenaza de bomba. ◇ *vt* asustar, sobresaltar.
◆ **scare away, scare off** *vt sep* ahuyentar.

scarecrow ['skeəkrəʊ] *n* espantapájaros *m inv.*

scared ['skeəd] *adj* **- 1.** [frightened] asustado(da); **don't be ~** no te asustes; **to be ~ stiff** OR **to death** estar muerto de miedo **- 2.** [worried]: **to be ~ that** tener miedo que.

scarf [skɑ:f] (*pl* **-s** OR **scarves**) ⋄ *n* [for neck] bufanda *f*; [for head] pañuelo *m* de cabeza. ⋄ *vt* US [eat]: ~ **(down)** zamparse.

scarlet ['skɑ:lət] *adj* color escarlata.

scarlet fever *n* escarlatina *f*.

scarves [skɑ:vz] *pl* ⊳ **scarf**.

scathing ['skeɪðɪŋ] *adj* mordaz.

scatter ['skætəʳ] ⋄ *vt* esparcir, desparramar. ⋄ *vi* dispersarse.

scatterbrained ['skætəbreɪnd] *adj inf* atolondrado(da).

scavenger ['skævɪndʒəʳ] *n* **-1.** [animal] carroñero *m*, -ra *f* **- 2.** [person] persona *f* que rebusca en las basuras.

scenario [sɪ'nɑ:rɪəʊ] (*pl* **-s**) *n* **-1.** [possible situation] situación *f* hipotética **- 2.** [of film, play] resumen *m* del argumento.

scene [si:n] *n* **-1.** [gen, theatre] escena *f*; behind the ~s entre bastidores; *fig* and then she appeared on the ~ y entonces apareció en escena **- 2.** [painting of place] panorama *m*, paisaje *m* **- 3.** [location] sitio *m*; **the ~ of the crime** la escena del crimen **- 4.** [show of emotion] jaleo *m*, escándalo *m* **- 5.** *phr*: **to set the ~** [for person] describir la escena; [for event] crear el ambiente propicio.

scenery ['si:nərɪ] *n* (*U*) **- 1.** [of countryside] paisaje *m* **- 2.** THEATRE decorado *m*.

scenic ['si:nɪk] *adj* [view] pintoresco(ca); [tour] turístico(ca).

scent [sent] *n* **-1.** [smell - of flowers] fragancia *f*; [- of animal] rastro *m* **- 2.** *fig* [track] pista *f*; **to lose the ~** perder la pista; **to throw sb off the ~** burlar a alguien **- 3.** [perfume] perfume *m*.

scepter US = **sceptre**.

sceptic UK, **skeptic** US ['skeptɪk] *n* escéptico *m*, -ca *f*.

sceptical UK, **skeptical** US ['skeptɪkl] *adj* escéptico(ca); **to be ~ about** tener muchas dudas acerca de.

sceptre UK, **scepter** US ['septəʳ] *n* cetro *m*.

schedule [UK 'ʃedju:l, US 'skedʒʊl] ⋄ *n* **- 1.** [plan] programa *m*, plan *m*; **on ~** sin retraso; **ahead of ~** con adelanto; **behind ~** con retraso **- 2.** [of prices, contents] lista *f*; [of times] horario *m*. ⋄ *vt*: **to ~ sthg (for)** fijar algo (para).

scheduled flight [UK 'ʃedju:ld-, US 'skedʒʊld-] *n* vuelo *m* regular.

scheme [ski:m] ⋄ *n* **- 1.** [plan] plano *m*, proyecto *m*; **pension ~** plan *m* de pensiones **- 2.** *pej* [dishonest plan] intriga *f*, treta *f* **- 3.** [arrangement, decoration - of room] disposición *f*; **colour ~** combinación *f* de colores. ⋄ *vi pej*: **to ~ (to do sthg)** intrigar (para hacer algo).

scheming ['ski:mɪŋ] *adj* intrigante.

schism ['sɪzm, 'skɪzm] *n* cisma *f*.

schizophrenic [ˌskɪtsə'frenɪk] *adj* esquizofrénico(ca).

scholar ['skɒləʳ] *n* **- 1.** [expert] erudito *m*, -ta *f* **- 2.** *dated* [student] alumno *m*, -na *f*.

scholarship ['skɒləʃɪp] *n* **- 1.** [grant] beca *f* **- 2.** [learning] erudición *f*.

school [sku:l] *n* **- 1.** [for children] colegio *m*, escuela *f*; **to go to ~** ir al colegio, ir a la escuela; **the children are at ~** los niños están en el colegio; **art ~** escuela *f* de arte; **driving ~** autoescuela *f*; **law/medical ~** facultad *f* de derecho/medicina **- 2.** US [university] universidad *f*.

school age *n* edad *f* escolar.

schoolbook ['sku:lbʊk] *n* libro *m* de texto.

schoolboy ['sku:lbɔɪ] *n* colegial *m*, escolar *m*.

schoolchild ['sku:ltʃaɪld] (*pl* **-children** [-tʃɪldrən]) *n* colegial *m*, -la *f*, escolar *mf*.

schooldays ['sku:ldeɪz] *npl* años *mpl* de colegio.

schoolgirl ['sku:lgɜ:l] *n* colegiala *f*, escolar *f*.

schooling ['sku:lɪŋ] *n* educación *f* escolar.

school-leaver [-ˌli:vəʳ] *n* UK joven que ha terminado la enseñanza.

schoolmaster ['sku:lˌmɑ:stəʳ] *n* dated [at primary school] maestro *m*; [at secondary school] profesor *m*.

schoolmistress ['sku:lˌmɪstrɪs] *n* dated [at primary school] maestra *f*; [at secondary school] profesora *f*.

school of thought *n* corriente *f* de opinión.

schoolteacher ['sku:lˌti:tʃəʳ] *n* [primary] maestro *m*, -tra *f*; [secondary] profesor *m*, -ra *f*.

school year *n* año *m* escolar.

schooner ['sku:nəʳ] *n* **- 1.** [ship] goleta *f* **- 2.** UK [sherry glass] copa *f* larga (para jerez).

sciatica [saɪ'ætɪkə] *n* ciática *f*.

science ['saɪəns] *n* ciencia *f*; **his best subject is ~** su mejor asignatura son las ciencias.

science fiction *n* ciencia *f* ficción.

scientific [ˌsaɪən'tɪfɪk] *adj* científico(ca).

scientist ['saɪəntɪst] *n* científico *m*, -ca *f*.

scintillating ['sɪntɪleɪtɪŋ] *adj* brillante, chispeante.

scissors ['sɪzəz] *npl* tijeras *fpl*; **a pair of ~** unas tijeras.

sclerosis ⊳ **multiple sclerosis**.

scoff [skɒf] ⋄ *vt* UK *inf* zamparse, tragarse. ⋄ *vi*: **to ~ (at sb/sthg)** mofarse OR burlarse (de alguien/de algo).

scold [skəʊld] *vt* regañar, reñir.

scone [skɒn] *n* bollo tomado con té a la hora de la merienda.

scoop [sku:p] ⋄ *n* **- 1.** [utensil - for sugar] cucharita *f* plana; [- for ice cream] pinzas fpl *(de helado)*; [- for flour] paleta *f* **- 2.** PRESS exclusiva *f*; **to make a ~** conseguir una exclusiva. ◇ *vt* **- 1.** [with hands] recoger **- 2.** [with utensil] recoger con cucharilla.

◆ **scoop out** *vt sep* sacar con cuchara.

scooter ['sku:tə'] *n* **- 1.** [toy] patinete *m* **- 2.** [motorcycle] escúter *m*, Vespa® *f*, motoneta *f* *Amér.*

scope [skəʊp] *n (U)* **- 1.** [opportunity] posibilidades *fpl*; **there is ~ for improvement** se puede mejorar **- 2.** [range] alcance *m*.

scorch [skɔ:tʃ] *vt* [dress, fabric, grass] chamuscar; [face, skin] quemar.

scorching ['skɔ:tʃɪŋ] *adj inf* abrasador(ra).

score [skɔ:'] ◇ *n* **- 1.** [in test] calificación *f*, nota *f*; [in competition, game] puntuación *f*; **are you keeping (the) ~?** ¿llevas el tanteo? **- 2.** SPORT resultado *m*; **what's the ~?** ¿cómo van?; **the final ~ was 2 all** el resultado final fue empate a dos **- 3.** *dated* [twenty] veintena *f* **- 4.** MUS partitura *f* **- 5.** [subject]: **on that ~** a ese respecto, por lo que se refiere a eso **- 6.** *phr* **to have a ~ to settle with sb** tener una cuenta que saldar con alguien; **to know the ~** conocer el percal. ◇ *vt* **- 1.** SPORT marcar **- 2.** [achieve - success, victory] obtener **- 3.** [cut] grabar. ◇ *vi* **- 1.** SPORT marcar **- 2.** [in test etc] obtener una puntuación; **you ~d well in part one** obtuviste una buena puntuación en la primera parte.

◆ **score out** *vt sep UK* tachar.

scoreboard ['skɔ:bɔ:d] *n* tanteador *m*, marcador *m*.

scorer ['skɔ:rə'] *n* **- 1.** [official] tanteador *m*, -ra *f* **- 2.** [player - in football] goleador *m*, -ra *f*; [- in other sports] marcador *m*, -ra *f*.

scorn [skɔ:n] ◇ *n* menosprecio *m*, desdén *m*. ◇ *vt* menospreciar, desdeñar.

scornful ['skɔ:nful] *adj* despectivo(va), de desdén; **to be ~ of sthg** desdeñar algo.

scornfully ['skɔ:nfuli] *adv* con desdén.

Scorpio ['skɔ:pɪəʊ] *(pl -s)* *n* Escorpión *m*.

scorpion ['skɔ:pjən] *n* escorpión *m*, alacrán *m*.

Scot [skɒt] *n* escocés *m*, -esa *f*.

scotch [skɒtʃ] *vt* [rumour] poner fin a, desmentir; [idea] desechar.

Scotch [skɒtʃ] *n* whisky *m* escocés.

Scotch tape® *n US* ≃ celo® *m*, cinta *f* Scotch® *Amér.*, ≃ durex® *m* *Arg, Bol, Méx*, ≃ Scotch® *m Andes*.

scot-free *adj inf*: **to get off ~** salir impune.

Scotland ['skɒtlənd] *n* Escocia.

Scots [skɒts] ◇ *adj* escocés(esa). ◇ *n* [dialect] escocés *m*.

Scotsman ['skɒtsmən] *(pl -men* [-mən]*)* *n* escocés *m*.

Scotswoman ['skɒtswʊmən] *(pl -women* [-,wɪmɪn]*)* *n* escocesa *f*.

Scottish ['skɒtɪʃ] *adj* escocés(esa).

Scottish National Party *n*: **the ~** el Partido Nacionalista Escocés.

scoundrel ['skaʊndrəl] *n dated* sinvergüenza *m*, canalla *m*.

scour [skaʊə'] *vt* **- 1.** [clean] fregar, restregar **- 2.** [search] registrar, batir; **they ~ed the countryside looking for the little girl** peinaron el campo en busca de la niña.

scourge [skɜ:dʒ] *n* [cause of suffering] azote *m*.

scout [skaʊt] *n* MIL explorador *m*.

◆ **Scout** *n* [boy scout] explorador *m*.

◆ **scout around** *vi*: **to ~ around (for)** explorar el terreno (en busca de).

scowl [skaʊl] *vi* fruncir el ceño; **to ~ at sb** mirar con ceño a alguien.

scrabble ['skræbl] *vi* **- 1.** [scramble, scrape] escarbar **- 2.** [feel around] palpar en busca de algo; **to ~ around for sthg** hurgar en busca de algo.

Scrabble® ['skræbl] *n* Scrabble® *m*.

scraggy ['skrægɪ] *(compar -ier, superl -iest)* *adj inf* flaco(ca).

scramble ['skræmbl] ◇ *n* [rush] pelea *f*; **he got hurt in the ~ for the door** resultó herido en la desbandada que hubo hacia la puerta. ◇ *vi* **- 1.** [climb] trepar **- 2.** [move clumsily]: **to ~ to one's feet** levantarse rápidamente y tambaleándose.

scrambled eggs ['skræmbld-] *npl* huevos *mpl* revueltos.

scrambling ['skræmblɪŋ] *n* motocross *m*; **to go ~** hacer motocross.

scrap [skræp] *(pt & pp* **-ped***, cont* **-ping***)* ◇ *n* **- 1.** [small piece] trozo *m*, pedazo *m* **- 2.** *(U)* [metal] chatarra *f*; **he sold it for ~** lo vendió para chatarra **- 3.** *inf* [fight, quarrel] pelotera *f*; **to have a ~** pelearse. ◇ *vt* desechar, descartar.

◆ **scraps** *npl* [food] sobras *fpl*.

scrapbook ['skræpbʊk] *n* álbum *m* de recortes.

scrap dealer *n* chatarrero *m*, -ra *f*.

scrape [skreɪp] ◇ *n* **- 1.** [noise] chirrido *m* **- 2.** *dated* [difficult situation] apuro *m*, lío *m*. ◇ *vt* **- 1.** [remove]: **to ~ sthg off sthg** raspar algo de algo **- 2.** [vegetables] raspar **- 3.** [car, bumper, glass] rayar; [knee, elbow, skin] rasguñar, arañar. ◇ *vi* [rub]: **to ~ against/on sthg** rozar contra/en algo.

◆ **scrape through** *vt fus* [exam] aprobar por los pelos.

scraper ['skreɪpə'] *n* raspador *m*.

scrap merchant *n UK* chatarrero *m*, -ra *f*.

scrap paper *UK*, **scratch paper** *US n (U)* papel *m* usado.

scrapyard ['skræpjɑ:d] *n* [gen] depósito *m* de chatarra; [for cars] cementerio *m* de coches.

scratch [skrætʃ] ⋄ n -1. [wound] arañazo m, rasguño m -2. [mark] raya f, surco m -3. phr: **to do sthg from ~** hacer algo partiendo desde el principio; **to be up to ~** estar a la altura requerida. ⋄ vt -1. [wound] arañar, rasguñar -2. [mark] rayar -3. [rubhead, leg] rascar; **he ~ed his head** se rascó la cabeza. ⋄ vi [rub] rascarse.

scratch card n tarjeta con una zona que hay que rascar para ver si contiene premio.

scratch paper US = **scrap paper**.

scrawl [skrɔ:l] ⋄ n garabatos mpl. ⋄ vt garabatear.

scrawny ['skrɔ:nɪ] (compar -ier, superl -iest) adj flaco(ca).

scream [skri:m] ⋄ n -1. [cry, shout] grito m, chillido m -2. [noise] chirrido m. ⋄ vt vociferar. ⋄ vi [person] gritar, chillar; **to ~ at sb** gritar a alguien.

scree [skri:] n montón de piedras desprendidas de la ladera de una montaña.

screech [skri:tʃ] ⋄ n -1. [of person] chillido m; [of bird] chirrido m -2. [of car, tyres] chirrido m, rechinar m. ⋄ vt gritar. ⋄ vi -1. [person, bird] chillar -2. [car, tyres] chirriar, rechinar.

screen [skri:n] ⋄ n -1. TV, CINEMA & COMPUT pantalla f -2. [panel] biombo m. ⋄ vt -1. [show in cinema] proyectar -2. [broadcast on TV] emitir -3. [shield]: **to ~ sthg/sb (from)** proteger algo/a alguien (de) -4. [candidate, patient] examinar.

screening ['skri:nɪŋ] n -1. [of film] proyección f -2. [of TV programme] emisión f -3. [for security] examen m, investigación f -4. MED [examination] chequeo m.

screen memory n COMPUT memoria f en pantalla.

screenplay ['skri:npleɪ] n guión m.

screw [skru:] ⋄ n [for fastening] tornillo m. ⋄ vt -1. [fix]: **to ~ sthg to** atornillar algo a -2. [twist] enroscar; **to ~ a lid on** poner la tapa de rosca -3. vulg [woman] follar, coger Amér.

➦ screw up vt sep -1. [sheet of paper etc] arrugar -2. [eyes] entornar; [face] arrugar -3. v inf [ruin] joborar.

screwdriver ['skru:ˌdraɪvər] n destornillador m, desarmador m Méx.

scribble ['skrɪbl] ⋄ n garabato m. ⋄ vt & vi garabatear.

script [skrɪpt] n -1. [of play, film etc] guión m -2. [system of writing] escritura f -3. [handwriting] letra f.

Scriptures ['skrɪptʃəz] npl: **the ~** las Sagradas Escrituras.

scriptwriter ['skrɪptˌraɪtər] n guionista m or f.

scroll [skrəʊl] ⋄ n rollo m de pergamino/papel. ⋄ vt COMPUT desplazar.

scrounge [skraʊndʒ] inf vt gorrear, gorronear.

scrounger ['skraʊndʒər] n inf gorrón m, -ona f.

scrub [skrʌb] (pt & pp -bed, cont -bing) ⋄ n -1. [rub] restregón m, fregado m; **give it a good ~** dale un buen fregado -2. [undergrowth] maleza f. ⋄ vt restregar.

scruff [skrʌf] n: **by the ~ of the neck** por el pescuezo.

scruffy ['skrʌfɪ] (compar -ier, superl -iest) adj [person] dejado(da); [clothes] andrajoso(sa); [room] desordenado(da).

scrum(mage) ['skrʌm(ɪdʒ)] n RUGBY melé f.

scruples ['skru:plz] npl escrúpulos mpl.

scrutinize, -ise ['skru:tɪnaɪz] vt escudriñar.

scrutiny ['skru:tɪnɪ] n (U) escrutinio m, examen m; **to be open to public ~** estar expuesto(ta) al examen del público; **to come under the ~ of** ser cuidadosamente examinado(da) por.

scuff [skʌf] vt [damage - shoes] pelar; [- furniture, floor] rayar.

scuffle ['skʌfl] n refriega f, reyerta f; **there were ~s between the police and demonstrators** hubo enfrentamientos entre la policía y los manifestantes.

scullery ['skʌlərɪ] (pl -ies) n trascocina f, fregadero m.

sculptor ['skʌlptər] n escultor m, -ra f.

sculpture ['skʌlptʃər] n escultura f.

scum [skʌm] n (U) -1. [froth] espuma f -2. v inf pej [worthless people] escoria f; **to be the ~ of the earth** ser la escoria de la sociedad.

scupper ['skʌpər] vt NAUT & fig hundir.

scurrilous ['skʌrələs] adj fml injurioso(sa), difamatorio(ria).

scurry ['skʌrɪ] (pt & pp -ied) vi: **to ~ off** OR **away** escabullirse.

scuttle ['skʌtl] ⋄ n cubo m del carbón, carbonera f. ⋄ vi [rush]: **to ~ off** OR **away** escabullirse.

scythe [saɪð] n guadaña f.

SDLP (abbr of **Social Democratic and Labour Party**) n partido político norirlandés que defiende la integración pacífica en la república de Irlanda.

sea [si:] n -1. [not land] mar m OR f; **at ~** en el mar; **by ~** en barco; **by the ~** a orillas del mar; **out to ~** [away from shore] mar adentro; [across the water] hacia el mar -2. [not ocean] mar m -3. phr: **to be all at ~** estar totalmente perdido(da).

seabed ['si:bed] n: **the ~** el lecho marino.

seaboard ['si:bɔ:d] n fml litoral m.

sea breeze n brisa f marina.

seafood ['si:fu:d] n (U) mariscos mpl.

seafront ['si:frʌnt] n paseo m marítimo.

seagull ['si:gʌl] n gaviota f.

seal [si:l] (*pl inv* OR **-s**) ⬦ *n* - **1.** [animal] foca *f* - **2.** [official mark] sello *m*; **she has given it her ~ of approval** le ha dado el visto bueno - **3.** [on bottle, meter] precinto *m*; [on letter] sello *m*. ⬦ *vt* - **1.** [envelope] sellar, cerrar - **2.** [opening, tube, crack] tapar, cerrar; **that decision has ~ed his fate** OR **doom** la decisión ha determinado su destino.

◆ **seal off** *vt sep* [entrance, exit] cerrar; [area] acordonar.

sea level *n* nivel *m* del mar.

sea lion (*pl inv* OR **-s**) *n* león *m* marítimo.

seam [si:m] *n* - **1.** SEWING costura *f* - **2.** [of coal] veta *f*.

seaman ['si:mən] (*pl* **-men** [-mən]) *n* marinero *m*.

seamy ['si:mɪ] (*compar* **-ier**, *superl* **-iest**) *adj* sórdido(da).

séance ['seɪɒns] *n* sesión *f* de espiritismo.

seaplane ['si:pleɪn] *n* hidroavión *m*.

seaport ['si:pɔ:t] *n* puerto *m* de mar.

search [sɜ:tʃ] ⬦ *n* [gen] búsqueda *f*; [of room, drawer] registro *m*; [of person] cacheo *m*; **~ for sthg** búsqueda de algo; **in ~ of** en busca de. ⬦ *vt* [gen] registrar; [one's mind] escudriñar; **to ~ sthg for sthg** buscar algo en algo. ⬦ *vi*: **to ~ (for sthg/sb)** buscar (algo/a alguien); **he was ~ed at the airport** lo registraron en el aeropuerto.

search engine *n* COMPUT motor *m* de búsqueda.

searching ['sɜ:tʃɪŋ] *adj* [question] agudo(-da); [look] penetrante.

searchlight ['sɜ:tʃlaɪt] *n* reflector *m*, proyector *m*.

search party *n* equipo *m* de búsqueda.

search warrant *n* mandamiento *m* de registro.

seashell ['si:ʃel] *n* concha *f* (marina).

seashore ['si:ʃɔ:'] *n*: **the ~** la orilla del mar.

seasick ['si:sɪk] *adj* mareado(da); **to be/feel ~** estar/sentirse mareado(da).

seaside ['si:saɪd] *n*: **the ~** la playa.

seaside resort *n* lugar *m* de veraneo (en la playa).

season ['si:zn] ⬦ *n* - **1.** [of year] estación *f*; **the four ~s** las cuatro estaciones - **2.** [particular period] época *f*, período *m*; **the planting ~** la época de plantar; **the football ~** la temporada futbolística; **the holiday ~** la temporada de vacaciones; **to book a holiday out of ~** reservar unas vacaciones fuera de temporada - **3.** [of fruit etc]: **out of/in ~** fuera de/en sazón; **plums are in ~** las ciruelas están en temporada - **4.** [of talks, films] temporada *f* - **5.** [zool] **to be in ~** estar en celo. ⬦ *vt* sazonar, condimentar; **~ to taste** sazonar a gusto; **~ with salt and pepper** salpimentar.

seasonal ['si:zənl] *adj* [work] temporal; [change] estacional.

seasoned ['si:znd] *adj* [experienced] veterano(na); **to be a ~ traveller** ser un viajero experimentado.

seasoning ['si:znɪŋ] *n* condimento *m*.

season ticket *n* abono *m*.

seat [si:t] ⬦ *n* - **1.** [in room, on train] asiento *m*; **is this ~ taken?** ¿está ocupado este asiento?; **take a ~, please** siéntese, por favor; **there only are a few ~s left** sólo quedan unos pocos asientos - **2.** [of trousers, skirt] trasero *m* - **3.** POL [in parliament] escaño *m* - **4.** [centre] sede *f*; **the ~ of government** la sede del gobierno. ⬦ *vt* - **1.** [sit down] sentar; **be ~ed!** ¡siéntese! - **2.** [subj: building, vehicle] tener cabida para.

seat belt *n* cinturón *m* de seguridad.

seating ['si:tɪŋ] *n* (*U*) [capacity] asientos *mpl*.

seawater ['si:ˌwɔ:tə'] *n* agua *f* de mar.

seaweed ['si:wi:d] *n* (*U*) alga *f* marina, huiro *m* Chile.

seaworthy ['si:ˌwɜ:ðɪ] *adj* en condiciones de navegar.

sec. (*abbr of* **second**) seg.

secede [sɪ'si:d] *vi fml*: **to ~ (from sthg)** separarse (de algo).

secluded [sɪ'klu:dɪd] *adj* apartado(da).

seclusion [sɪ'klu:ʒn] *n* aislamiento *m*; **to live in ~** vivir aislado(da).

second ['sekənd] ⬦ *n* - **1.** [of time] segundo *m*; **can you wait a ~?** ¿podrías esperar un momento?; [second gear] segunda *f* - **2.** UK UNIV ≃ licenciatura *f* con notable. ⬦ *num* segundo(da); **to ask for a ~ chance/opinion** pedir una segunda oportunidad/opinión; *see also* **sixth**. ⬦ *vt* secundar.

◆ **seconds** *npl* - **1.** COMM artículos *mpl* defectuosos - **2.** [of food]: **to have ~s** repetir *(en una comida)*; **are there any ~s?** ¿se puede repetir?

secondary ['sekəndrɪ] *adj* - **1.** [SCH - school] secundario(ria); [- education] medio(dia) - **2.** [less important]: **to be ~ to** ser secundario(ria) a.

secondary school *n* escuela *f* de enseñanza media.

second-class ['sekənd-] ⬦ *adj* - **1.** [gen] de segunda clase; **to be a ~ citizen** ser un ciudadano de segunda (clase); **~ mail** *servicio postal más barato y lento que el de primera clase* - **2.** UK UNIV: **~ degree** *nota global de licenciatura equivalente a un notable o a un aprobado alto.* ⬦ *adv*: **to travel ~** viajar en segunda; **to send a letter ~** *enviar una carta utilizando el correo de segunda clase.*

second hand ['sekənd-] *n* [of clock] segundero *m*.

second-hand ['sekənd-] ⬦ *adj* [goods,

information] de segunda mano. ⇔ *adv* [not
new] de segunda mano.
secondly ['sekəndlɪ] *adv* en segundo lugar.
secondment [sɪ'kɒndmənt] *n* UK traslado
m temporal.
second-rate ['sekənd-] *adj pej* de segunda
categoría, mediocre.
second thought ['sekənd-] *n*: to have ~s
about sthg tener dudas acerca de algo; on
~s UK, on ~ US pensándolo bien.
secrecy ['si:krəsɪ] *n (U)* secreto *m*; to be
shrouded in ~ estar rodeado de un gran secreto.
secret ['si:krɪt] ⇔ *adj* secreto(ta). ⇔ *n* secreto *m*; in ~ en secreto; to keep a ~ guardar un secreto; to tell sb a ~ contar a
alguien un secreto; to make no ~ of sth
no ocultar algo; the ~ of happiness la clave de la felicidad.
secretarial [,sekrə'teərɪəl] *adj* [course, train-
ing] de secretariado; [staff] de secretaría,
administrativo(va).
secretary [UK 'sekrətɪ, US 'sekrə,terɪ] *(pl*
-ies) *n* - 1. [gen] secretario *m*, -ria *f* - 2. POL
[minister] ministro *m*.
Secretary of State *n* - 1. UK: ~ (for) ministro *m* (de) - 2. US ministro *m* estadounidense de Asuntos Exteriores.
secretive ['si:krətɪv] *adj* [person] reserva-
do(da); [organization] secreto(ta).
secretly ['si:krɪtlɪ] *adv* [hope, think] secretamente; [tell] en secreto; she was ~ pleased
aunque no lo expresara, estaba contenta.
sect [sekt] *n* secta *f*.
sectarian [sek'teərɪən] *adj* sectario(ria).
section ['sekʃn] *n* sección *f*.
sector ['sektə'] *n* sector *m*.
secular ['sekjʊlə'] *adj* [education, life] laico(-
ca), secular; [music] profano(na).
secure [sɪ'kjʊə'] ⇔ *adj* [gen] seguro(ra).
⇔ *vt* - 1. [obtain] conseguir, obtener
- 2. [make safe] proteger - 3. [fasten] cerrar
bien.
security [sɪ'kjʊərətɪ] *(pl -ies)* *n* - 1. seguridad *f* - 2. [for loan] garantía *f*.
  ➡ **securities** *npl* FIN valores *mpl*, títulos
mpl.
security guard *n* guardia *m* jurado OR de
seguridad.
sedan [sɪ'dæn] *n* US (coche *m*) utilitario *m*.
sedate [sɪ'deɪt] ⇔ *adj* sosegado(da). ⇔ *vt*
sedar.
sedation [sɪ'deɪʃn] *n (U)* sedación *f*; to be
under ~ estar sedado(da).
sedative ['sedətɪv] *n* sedante *m*, calmante
m.
sediment ['sedɪmənt] *n* sedimento *m*.
seduce [sɪ'dju:s] *vt*: to ~ sb (into doing
sthg) seducir a alguien (a hacer algo).
seductive [sɪ'dʌktɪv] *adj* seductor(ra).

see [si:] *(pt saw, pp seen)* ⇔ *vt* - 1. [gen] ver
- 2. [visit - friend, doctor] ir a ver, visitar;
~ you soon/later/tomorrow! ¡hasta pron-
to/luego/mañana!; ~ you! ¡hasta luego!,
¡chau! *RP*; ~ below/p 10 véase más abajo/
pág. 10 - 3. [accompany]: to ~ sb to the
door acompañar a alguien a la puerta
- 4. [make sure]: to ~ (to it) that ... encargarse de que ... ⇔ *vi* [gen] ver; [understand]
entender; I can't ~ no veo; let's ~, let me ~
vamos a ver, veamos; you ~ ... verás, es que
...; I ~ ya veo.
  ➡ **seeing as, seeing that** *conj inf* como.
  ➡ **see about** *vt fus* [arrange] encargarse
de.
  ➡ **see off** *vt sep* - 1. [say goodbye to] despedir - 2. UK [chase away] ahuyentar.
  ➡ **see through** *vt fus* [person] ver claramente las intenciones de; I can ~ right
through her veo claramente sus intenciones.
  ➡ **see to** *vt fus* ocuparse de.
seed [si:d] *n* [of plant] semilla *f*; *fig* to go to
~ venirse abajo.
  ➡ **seeds** *npl fig* [of doubt] semilla *f*; [of
idea] germen *m*.
seedling ['si:dlɪŋ] *n* plantón *m*.
seedy ['si:dɪ] *(compar -ier, superl -iest) adj*
[room, area] sórdido(da); [person] desaliña-
do(da).
seek [si:k] *(pt & pp sought) fml vt* - 1. [look
for, try to obtain] buscar - 2. [ask for] solicitar - 3. [try]: to ~ to do sthg procurar hacer
algo.
seem [si:m] ⇔ *vi* parecer; it ~s (to be)
good parece (que es) bueno; I can't ~ to
do it no puedo hacerlo (por mucho que lo
intente). ⇔ *v impers*: it ~s (that) parece
que; it ~s to me that me parece que.
seemingly ['si:mɪŋlɪ] *adv* aparentemente.
seen [si:n] *pp* ⊳ **see**.
seep [si:p] *vi* rezumar, filtrarse.
seesaw ['si:sɔ:] *n* balancín *m*, subibaja *m*.
seethe [si:ð] *vi* - 1. [person] rabiar
- 2. [place]: to be seething with estar a rebosar de.
see-through *adj* transparente.
segment ['segmənt] *n* - 1. [proportion, sec-
tion] segmento *m* - 2. [of fruit] gajo *m*.
segregate ['segrɪgeɪt] *vt* segregar.
Seine [seɪn] *n*: the (River) ~ el (río) Sena.
seize [si:z] *vt* - 1. [grab] agarrar, coger
- 2. [capture - control, power, town] tomar,
hacerse con - 3. [arrest] detener - 4. [take advantage of] aprovechar.
  ➡ **seize (up)on** *vt fus* valerse de.
  ➡ **seize up** *vi* agarrotarse.
seizure ['si:ʒə'] *n* - 1. MED ataque *m* - 2. [tak-
ing, capturing] toma *f*.
seldom ['seldəm] *adv* raramente.
select [sɪ'lekt] ⇔ *adj* selecto(ta). ⇔ *vt*

[gen] elegir, escoger; [team] seleccionar.
selection [sɪ'lekʃn] n -1. [gen] selección f -2. [fact of being selected] elección f -3. [in shop] surtido m; **we have a wide ~ of ties** tenemos una amplia selección de corbatas.
selective [sɪ'lektɪv] adj selectivo(va).
self [self] (pl **selves**) n uno mismo m, una misma f; **she's not her usual ~** no estaba como de costumbre; **the ~** el yo.
self-addressed stamped envelope [-ə,drest'stæmpt-] n US sobre con sus señas y franqueo.
self-assured adj seguro de sí mismo (segura de sí misma).
self-catering adj sin pensión; **a ~ holiday/ chalet** unas vacaciones/un chalet sin servicio de comidas.
self-centred [-'sentəd] adj egocéntrico(ca).
self-confessed [-kən'fest] adj confeso(sa).
self-confident adj [person] seguro de sí mismo (segura de sí misma); [attitude, remark] lleno(na) de seguridad.
self-conscious adj cohibido(da).
self-contained [-kən'teɪnd] adj independiente; **a ~ flat** un apartamento independiente.
self-control n control m de sí mismo/misma.
self-defence n defensa f propia, autodefensa f; **in ~** en defensa propia.
self-discipline n autodisciplina f.
self-employed [-ɪm'plɔɪd] adj autónomo(ma), que trabaja por cuenta propia.
self-esteem n amor m propio.
self-evident adj evidente, patente.
self-explanatory adj evidente, que queda muy claro(ra).
self-government n autogobierno m.
self-important adj pej engreído(da).
self-indulgent adj pej: **a ~ person** una persona autocomplaciente; **to be ~** ser autocomplaciente.
self-interest n pej (U) interés m propio.
selfish ['selfɪʃ] adj egoísta.
selfishness ['selfɪʃnɪs] n egoísmo m.
selfless ['selflɪs] adj desinteresado(da).
self-made adj: **a ~ man** un hombre hecho a sí mismo.
self-opinionated adj pej que siempre tiene que decir la suya.
self-pity n pej lástima f de uno mismo/una misma.
self-portrait n autorretrato m.
self-possessed [-pə'zest] adj dueño de sí mismo (dueña de sí misma).
self-raising flour UK [-,reɪzɪŋ-], **self-rising flour** US n harina f con levadura.
self-reliant adj independiente.
self-respect n amor m propio.

self-respecting [-rɪs'pektɪŋ] adj que se precie, digno(na); **no ~ person would eat this rubbish** nadie con un mínimo de dignidad se comería esa basura.
self-restraint n dominio m de sí mismo/misma.
self-righteous adj pej santurrón(ona).
self-rising flour US = **self-raising flour**.
self-sacrifice n abnegación f.
self-satisfied adj pej [person] satisfecho de sí mismo (satisfecha de sí misma); [smile] lleno(na) de suficiencia.
self-service comp de autoservicio; **a ~ restaurant** un autoservicio.
self-sufficient adj: **~ (in)** autosuficiente (en).
self-taught adj autodidacta.
sell [sel] (pt & pp **sold**) ⋄ vt [gen] vender; **to ~ sthg to sb, to ~ sb sthg** vender algo a alguien; **to ~ sthg for** vender algo por. ⋄ vi -1. [subj: businessman, firm] vender -2. [subj: merchandise] venderse; **this model ~s well** este modelo se vende muy bien; **to ~ (for OR at)** venderse (a).
 ◆ **sell off** vt sep liquidar.
 ◆ **sell out** ⋄ vt sep [performance]: **to have sold out** estar agotado(da). ⋄ vi -1. [shop]: **to ~ out (of sthg)** agotar las existencias (de algo) -2. [be disloyal, unprincipled] venderse.
sell-by date n UK fecha f de caducidad; **to be past its ~** haber caducado.
seller ['selə'] n vendedor m, -ra f.
selling price ['selɪŋ-] n precio m de venta.
Sellotape® ['seləteɪp] n UK celo® m, cinta f Scotch® Amér, ≃ durex® m Arg, Bol, Méx, ≃ Scotch® m Andes.
sell-out n [performance, match] lleno m.
selves [selvz] pl ⊳ **self**.
semaphore ['seməfɔ:'] n (U) semáforo m.
semblance ['sembləns] n fml apariencia f.
semen ['si:men] n semen m.
semester [sɪ'mestə'] n semestre m.
semicircle ['semɪ,sɜ:kl] n semicírculo m; **arranged in a ~** poner en semicírculo.
semicolon [,semɪ'kəʊlən] n punto m y coma.
semidetached [,semɪdɪ'tætʃt] ⋄ adj adosado(da). ⋄ n UK casa f adosada (a otra).
semifinal [,semɪ'faɪnl] n semifinal f.
seminar ['semɪnɑ:'] n seminario m.
seminary ['semɪnərɪ] (pl **-ies**) n RELIG seminario m.
semiskilled [,semɪ'skɪld] adj semicualificado(da).
semolina [,semə'li:nə] n sémola f.
Senate ['senɪt] n POL: **the (United States) ~** el Senado de los Estados Unidos).
senator ['senətə'] n senador m, -ra f.
send [send] (pt & pp **sent**) vt -1. [gen]

mandar; **to ~ sb sthg, to ~ sthg to sb**
mandar a alguien algo; **~ me a postcard!**
¡mándame una postal!; **~ them my best
wishes** envíales saludos **- 2.** [tell to go] enviar, mandar; **she sent her son to the shop
for a newspaper** envió a su hijo a comprar
un periódico en la tienda; **he was sent to
prison** fue encarcelado.

◆ send for *vt fus* [person] mandar llamar
a.

◆ send in *vt sep* mandar, enviar.

◆ send off *vt sep* **- 1.** [by post] mandar
(por correo) **- 2.** SPORT expulsar.

◆ send off for *vt fus* [goods, information]
pedir, encargar.

◆ send up *vt sep UK inf* [imitate] parodiar,
satirizar.

sender ['sendə^r] *n* remitente *m OR f*.

send-off *n* despedida *f*; **to give sb a good ~**
dar una buena despedida a alguien.

senile ['si:naɪl] *adj* senil.

senior ['si:njə^r] ⟨⟩ *adj* **- 1.** [highest-ranking]
superior, de rango superior **- 2.** [higher-
ranking]: **~ to sb** superior a alguien **- 3.** SCH
[pupil] mayor; [class, common room] de los
mayores. ⟨⟩ *n* **- 1.** [older person]: **I'm five
years his ~** le llevo cinco años **- 2.** SCH
mayor *m OR f*.

senior citizen *n* ciudadano *m*, -na *f* de la
tercera edad.

sensation [sen'seɪʃn] *n* sensación *f*; **to
cause a ~** causar sensación.

sensational [sen'seɪʃənl] *adj* [gen] sensacional.

sensationalist [sen'seɪʃnəlɪst] *adj pej* sensacionalista.

sense [sens] ⟨⟩ *n* **- 1.** [faculty, meaning] sentido *m*; **to make ~** [have meaning] tener sentido; **I can't make any ~ of this** no entiendo
esto **- 2.** [feeling - of guilt, terror] sentimiento
m; [- of urgency] sensación *f*; [- of honour,
duty] sentido *m* **- 3.** [natural ability]: **business
~** talento *m* para los negocios; **~ of hu-
mour/style** sentido *m* del humor/estilo
- 4. [wisdom, reason] juicio *m*, sentido *m* común; **to make ~** [be sensible] ser sensato.
⟨⟩ *vt* sentir, percibir; **to ~ (that)** percibir
OR sentir que.

◆ in a sense *adv* en cierto sentido.

senseless ['senslɪs] *adj* **- 1.** [stupid] sin sentido **- 2.** [unconscious] inconsciente; **the
blow knocked him ~** el golpe lo dejó inconsciente.

sensibilities [,sensɪ'bɪlətɪz] *npl* [delicate feel-
ings] sensibilidad *f*; **to offend sb's ~** herir
la sensibilidad de alguien.

sensible ['sensəbl] *adj* [person, decision]
sensato(ta), razonable; [clothes] práctico(ca).

sensitive ['sensɪtɪv] *adj* **- 1.** [understanding]:
~ (to) comprensivo(va) (hacia) **- 2.** [easily

hurt, touchy]: **~ (to/about)** susceptible (a/
acerca de) **- 3.** [controversial] delicado(da)
- 4. [easily damaged, tender] sensible; **to
have ~ skin** tener la piel sensible; **~ to
heat/light** sensible al calor/la luz **- 5.** [re-
sponsive - instrument] sensible.

sensual ['sensjʊəl] *adj* sensual.

sensuous ['sensjʊəs] *adj* sensual.

sent [sent] *pt & pp* ⊳ **send**.

sentence ['sentəns] ⟨⟩ *n* **- 1.** [group of
words] frase *f*, oración *f* **- 2.** JUR sentencia *f*;
a prison ~ una condena de cárcel. ⟨⟩ *vt* :
to ~ sb (to) condenar a alguien (a); **he
was ~d to death/3 years** lo condenaron a
muerte/tres años de cárcel.

sentiment ['sentɪmənt] *n* **- 1.** [feeling] sentimiento *m* **- 2.** [opinion] opinión *f*.

sentimental [,sentɪ'mentl] *adj* sentimental.

sentry ['sentrɪ] (*pl* **-ies**) *n* centinela *m*.

separate [*adj & n* 'seprət, *vb* 'sepəreɪt]
⟨⟩ *adj* **- 1.** [not joined, apart]: **~ (from)** se-
parado(da) (de) **- 2.** [individual, distinct] dis-
tinto(ta). ⟨⟩ *vt* **- 1.** [keep or move apart]: **to
~ sthg/sb (from)** separar algo/a alguien
(de) **- 2.** [distinguish]: **to ~ sthg/sb from** diferenciar algo/a alguien de **- 3.** [divide]: **to
~ sthg/sb into** dividir algo/a alguien en.
⟨⟩ *vi* **- 1.** [gen]: **to ~ (from)** separarse (de)
- 2. [divide]: **to ~ (into)** dividirse (en).

◆ separates *npl UK* piezas *fpl (de vestir que
combinan)*.

separately ['seprətlɪ] *adv* **- 1.** [on one's own]
independientemente **- 2.** [one by one] sepa-
radamente, por separado.

separation [,sepə'reɪʃn] *n* separación *f*.

September [sep'tembə^r] *n* septiembre *m*,
setiembre *m*; **1 ~ 1992** [in letters etc] 1 de
septiembre de 1992; **by/in ~** para/en septiembre; **last/this/next ~** en septiembre
del año pasado/de este año/del año que viene; **every ~** todos los años en septiembre;
during ~ en septiembre, durante el mes de
septiembre; **at the beginning/end of ~** a
principios/finales de septiembre; **in the
middle of ~** a mediados de septiembre.

septic ['septɪk] *adj* séptico(ca).

septic tank *n* fosa *f* séptica.

sequel ['si:kwəl] *n* **- 1.** [book, film]: **~ (to)**
continuación *f* (de) **- 2.** [consequence]:
~ (to) secuela *f* (de).

sequence ['si:kwəns] *n* **- 1.** [series] sucesión
f **- 2.** [order, of film] secuencia *f*.

Serb = **Serbian**.

Serbia ['sɜːbjə] *n* Serbia.

Serbian ['sɜːbjən], **Serb** [sɜːb] ⟨⟩ *adj* ser-
bio(bia). ⟨⟩ *n* **- 1.** [person] serbio *m*, -bia *f*
- 2. [dialect] serbio *m*.

serene [sɪ'ri:n] *adj* sereno(na).

sergeant ['sɑːdʒənt] *n* **- 1.** MIL sargento *m*

- **2.** [in police] ≃ subinspector *m* de policía.

sergeant major *n* sargento *m* mayor.

serial ['sɪərɪəl] *n* serial *m*.

serial number *n* número *m* de serie.

series ['sɪəri:z] (*pl inv*) *n* serie *f*; **a ~ of disasters** una serie de catástrofes; **a TV ~** una serie televisiva.

serious ['sɪərɪəs] *adj* - **1.** [gen] serio(ria); **are you ~?** ¿hablas en serio? - **2.** [very bad] grave.

seriously ['sɪərɪəslɪ] *adv* - **1.** [honestly] en serio - **2.** [very badly] gravemente; **to be ~ ill** estar gravemente enfermo - **3.** [in a considered, earnest, solemn manner] seriamente - **4.** *phr*: **to take sthg/sb ~** tomar algo/a alguien en serio.

seriousness ['sɪərɪəsnɪs] *n* - **1.** [gravity] gravedad *f* - **2.** [solemnity] seriedad *f*.

sermon ['sɜːmən] *n* RELIG & *pej* sermón *m*.

serrated [sɪ'reɪtɪd] *adj* serrado(da), dentado(da).

servant ['sɜːvənt] *n* sirviente *m*, -ta *f*.

serve [sɜːv] ◇ *vt* - **1.** [work for] servir - **2.** [have effect]: **to ~ to do sthg** servir para hacer algo - **3.** [fulfil]: **to ~ a purpose** cumplir un propósito - **4.** [provide for] abastecer - **5.** [food, drink]: **to ~ sthg to sb, to ~ sb sthg** servir algo a alguien; **dinner will be ~d at 8** la cena será servida a las 8 - **6.** [customer] despachar, servir; **are you being ~d?** ¿lo atienden? - **7.** JUR: **to ~ sb with sthg, to ~ sthg on sb** entregar a alguien algo - **8.** [prison sentence] cumplir; [apprenticeship] hacer; [term of office] ejercer - **9.** SPORT servir, sacar - **10.** *phr*: **that ~s you right!** ¡bien merecido lo tienes! ◇ *vi* - **1.** [work, give food or drink] servir - **2.** [function]: **to ~ as** servir de - **3.** [in shop, bar etc] despachar - **4.** SPORT sacar. ◇ *n* saque *m*.

◆ **serve out, serve up** *vt sep* servir.

service ['sɜːvɪs] ◇ *n* - **1.** [gen] servicio *m*; **in ~** en funcionamiento; **out of ~** fuera de servicio; **bus/train ~** servicio de autobús/tren - **2.** [mechanical check] revisión *f* - **3.** RELIG oficio *m*, servicio *m*; **to hold a ~** celebrar un oficio - **4.** [set - of plates etc] servicio *m*, juego *m*; **dinner ~** servicio de mesa - **5.** SPORT saque *m* - **6.** [use]: **to be of ~ (to sb)** servir (a alguien); **to do sb a ~** hacer un favor a alguien. ◇ *vt* [car, machine] revisar.

◆ **services** *npl* - **1.** [on motorway] área *f* de servicios - **2.** [armed forces]: **the ~s** las fuerzas armadas - **3.** [efforts, work] servicios *mpl*.

serviceable ['sɜːvɪsəbl] *adj* útil, práctico(-ca).

service area *n* área *f* de servicios.

service charge *n* servicio *m*.

serviceman ['sɜːvɪsmən] (*pl* **-men** [-mən]) *n* militar *m*.

service station *n* estación *f* de servicio.

serviette [,sɜːvɪ'et] *n* servilleta *f*.

serving dish *n* fuente *f*.

serving spoon *n* cuchara *f* de servir.

sesame ['sesəmɪ] *n* sésamo *m*.

session ['seʃn] *n* - **1.** [gen] sesión *f*; **in ~** en sesión - **2.** *US* [school term] trimestre *m*.

set [set] (*pt* & *pp* **set**, *cont* **-ting**) ◇ *adj* - **1.** [fixed - expression, amount] fijo(ja); [- pattern, method] establecido(da) - **2.** *UK* SCH [text etc] asignado(da) - **3.** [ready, prepared]: **~ (for sthg/to do sthg)** listo(ta) (para algo/para hacer algo) - **4.** [determined]: **to be ~ on sthg/doing sthg** estar empeñado(da) en algo/hacer algo. ◇ *n* - **1.** [collection - gen] juego *m*; [- of stamps] serie *f* - **2.** [TV, radio] aparato *m* - **3.** THEATRE decorado *m*; CINEMA plató *m* - **4.** TENNIS set *m* - **5.** [hairdressing] marcado *m*. ◇ *vt* - **1.** [position, place] poner, colocar - **2.** [fix, insert]: **to ~ sthg in** OR **into** montar algo en - **3.** [cause to be or start]: **to ~ free** poner en libertad; **to ~ fire to** prender fuego a; **to ~ sthg in motion** poner algo en marcha - **4.** [trap, table, essay] poner - **5.** [alarm, meter] poner - **6.** [time, wage] fijar - **7.** [example] dar; **to ~ a good example** dar ejemplo; [precedent] sentar; [trend] imponer, dictar - **8.** [target] fijar - **9.** MED [bones, leg] componer - **10.** [book, play, film] situar, ambientar; **the series is ~ in London** la serie está ambientada en Londres. ◇ *vi* - **1.** [sun] ponerse - **2.** [jelly] cuajarse; [glue, cement] secarse, solidificarse.

◆ **set about** *vt fus* [start - task] comenzar; [- problem] atacar; **to ~ about doing sthg** ponerse a hacer algo.

◆ **set aside** *vt sep* - **1.** [keep, save] reservar - **2.** [dismiss - enmity, differences] dejar de lado.

◆ **set back** *vt sep* [delay] retrasar.

◆ **set off** ◇ *vt sep* - **1.** [initiate, cause] provocar - **2.** [ignite - bomb] hacer estallar. ◇ *vi* ponerse en camino.

◆ **set out** ◇ *vt sep* - **1.** [arrange] disponer - **2.** [explain] exponer. ◇ *vi* - **1.** [on journey] ponerse en camino - **2.** [intend]: **to ~ out to do sthg** proponerse a hacer algo.

◆ **set up** *vt sep* - **1.** [business] poner, montar; [committee, organization] crear; [procedure] establecer; [interview, meeting] organizar; **to ~ sb up in business** montar un negocio a alguien - **2.** [statue, roadblock] levantar - **3.** [prepare for use] preparar - **4.** *inf* [frame] tender una trampa a.

setback ['setbæk] *n* revés *m*, contratiempo *m*.

set menu *n* menú *m* del día.

settee [se'tiː] *n* sofá *m*.

setting ['setɪŋ] *n* - **1.** [surroundings] escenario *m* - **2.** [of dial, control] posición *f*.

settle ['setl] ◇ vt - **1.** [conclude, decide] resolver; **that ~s it, she can move out!** ¡no se hable más, que se vaya! - **2.** [pay] ajustar, saldar - **3.** [calm - nerves] tranquilizar; **this should ~ your stomach** esto te asentará el estómago. ◇ vi - **1.** [stop travelling] instalarse - **2.** [make o.s. comfortable] acomodarse - **3.** [dust, sediment] depositarse, posarse; **the snow has ~d** la nieve ha cuajado - **4.** [calm down - person] calmarse.

◆ **settle down** vi - **1.** [concentrate on]: **to ~ down to doing sthg** ponerse a hacer algo - **2.** [become respectable] sentar la cabeza - **3.** [calm oneself] calmarse.

◆ **settle for** vt fus conformarse con.

◆ **settle in** vi [in new home] instalarse; [in new job] adaptarse.

◆ **settle on** vt fus [choose] decidirse por.

◆ **settle up** vi: **to ~ up (with sb)** ajustar las cuentas (con alguien).

settlement ['setlmənt] n - **1.** [agreement] acuerdo m - **2.** [village] poblado m.

settler ['setlə'] n colono m.

set-up n inf - **1.** [system, organization] sistema m - **2.** [frame, trap] trampa f, lazo m.

seven ['sevn] num siete; see also **six**.

seventeen [,sevn'ti:n] num diecisiete; see also **six**.

seventeenth [,sevn'ti:nθ] num decimoséptimo(ma); see also **sixth**.

seventh ['sevnθ] num séptimo(ma); see also **sixth**.

seventy ['sevntɪ] num setenta; see also **sixty**.

sever ['sevə'] vt - **1.** [cut through] cortar - **2.** [finish completely] romper.

several ['sevrəl] ◇ adj varios(rias). ◇ pron varios mpl, -rias fpl.

severance ['sevrəns] n fml ruptura f.

severance pay n despido m.

severe [sɪ'vɪə'] adj [gen] severo(ra); [pain] fuerte, agudo(da).

severity [sɪ'verətɪ] n [gen] gravedad f; [of shortage, problem] severidad f.

Seville [sə'vɪl] n Sevilla.

sew [səʊ] (UK pp **sewn**, US pp **sewed** OR **sewn**) vt & vi coser.

◆ **sew up** vt sep [cloth] coser.

sewage ['su:ɪdʒ] n (U) aguas fpl residuales.

sewer ['suə'] n alcantarilla f, cloaca f.

sewing ['səʊɪŋ] n (U) - **1.** [activity] labor f de costura - **2.** [items] costura f.

sewing machine n máquina f de coser.

sewn [səʊn] pp ▷ **sew**.

sex [seks] n sexo m; **to have ~** tener relaciones sexuales.

sexist ['seksɪst] ◇ adj sexista. ◇ n sexista m OR f.

sexual ['sekʃʊəl] adj sexual.

sexual harassment n acoso m sexual.

sexual intercourse n (U) relaciones fpl sexuales.

sexy ['seksɪ] (compar **-ier**, superl **-iest**) adj inf sexi (inv).

shabby ['ʃæbɪ] (compar **-ier**, superl **-iest**) adj - **1.** [clothes, briefcase] desastrado(da); [street] de aspecto abandonado - **2.** [person] andrajoso(sa).

shack [ʃæk] n chabola f.

shackle ['ʃækl] vt [enchain] poner grilletes a.

◆ **shackles** npl [metal rings] grilletes mpl, grillos mpl.

shade [ʃeɪd] ◇ n - **1.** (U) [shadow] sombra f; **in the ~** a la sombra - **2.** [lampshade] pantalla f - **3.** [of colour, meaning] matiz m - **4.** US [blind] persiana f - **5.** [little bit]: **a ~ too big** un poquito grande. ◇ vt [from light] sombrear, dar sombra a; **the car was ~d from the sun** el coche estaba protegido del sol.

◆ **shades** npl inf [sunglasses] gafas fpl de sol.

shadow ['ʃædəʊ] ◇ n - **1.** [dark shape, form] sombra f - **2.** [darkness] oscuridad f - **3.** phr: **there's not a** OR **the ~ of a doubt** no hay la menor duda; **to be scared of your own ~** tener miedo hasta de su propia sombra. ◇ vt [subj: detective] seguir.

shadow cabinet n gobierno m en la sombra, directiva del principal partido de la oposición en Gran Bretaña.

shadowy ['ʃædəʊ] adj - **1.** [dark] sombrío(a) - **2.** [hard to see] vago(ga).

shady ['ʃeɪdɪ] (compar **-ier**, superl **-iest**) adj - **1.** [sheltered from sun] sombreado(da) - **2.** inf [dishonest - businessman] dudoso(sa), sospechoso(sa); [- deal] turbio(bia).

shaft [ʃɑ:ft] n - **1.** [vertical passage] pozo m - **2.** [of lift] hueco m - **3.** [tech - rod] eje m - **4.** [of light] rayo m - **5.** [of spear] asta f.

shaggy ['ʃægɪ] (compar **-ier**, superl **-iest**) adj [dog] peludo(da).

shake [ʃeɪk] (pt **shook**, pp **shaken** ['ʃeɪkən]) ◇ vt - **1.** [move vigorously] sacudir, remecer Méx; **to ~ sb's hand** dar OR estrechar la mano a alguien; **to ~ hands** darse OR estrecharse la mano; **he shook hands with her** le dio la mano; **to ~ one's head** [in refusal] negar con la cabeza; [in disbelief] mover la cabeza mostrando incredulidad; **he shook his fist at them** amenazar a alguien con el puño - **2.** [bottle, aerosol] agitar; **~ well before using** agitar antes de usar - **3.** [shock] trastornar, conmocionar; **the disaster which shook the city** el desastre que sacudió la ciudad. ◇ vi - **1.** [tremble] temblar; **to ~ with fear** temblar de miedo - **2.** inf [shake hands]: **let's ~ on it** venga esa mano.

◆ **shake off** vt sep [pursuer] deshacerse de; [cold] quitarse de encima; [illness] superar.

◆ **shake up** vt sep [contents of bottle etc] agitar; [organisation] restructurar, reorganizar; [person]: **she wasn't hurt, just a bit ~n up** no resultó herida, sólo un poco conmocionada.

shaken ['ʃeɪkn] pp ▷ **shake**.

shaky ['ʃeɪkɪ] (compar **-ier**, superl **-iest**) adj **-1.** [weak, nervous] tembloroso(sa); **to feel ~** encontrarse nervioso **-2.** [unconfident, insecure - start] incierto(ta); [- argument] poco sólido(da) **-3.** [wobbly - chair, table] inestable; [- handwriting] tembloroso(sa).

shall [weak form ʃəl, strong form ʃæl] aux vb **-1.** (1st person sg, 1st person pl) [to express future tense]: **we ~ be there tomorrow** mañana estaremos ahí; **I shan't be home till ten** no estaré en casa hasta las diez **-2.** (esp 1st person sg, 1st person pl) [in questions]: **~ we go for a walk?** ¿vamos a dar una vuelta?; **~ I give her a ring?** ¿la llamo?; **I'll do that, ~ I?** hago esto, ¿vale? **-3.** [in orders]: **you ~ do as I tell you!** ¡harás lo que yo te diga!; **no one ~ leave until I say so** que nadie salga hasta que yo lo diga.

shallow ['ʃæləʊ] adj **-1.** [in size] poco profundo(da) **-2.** pej [superficial] superficial.

sham [ʃæm] (pt & pp **-med**, cont **-ming**) ◇ n farsa f. ◇ vi fingir, simular.

shambles ['ʃæmblz] n desbarajuste m, follón m.

shame [ʃeɪm] ◇ n **-1.** (U) [remorse] vergüenza f, pena f Andes, CAm, Carib, Méx **-2.** [dishonour] **to bring ~ on** OR **upon sb** deshonrar a alguien **-3.** [pity]: **what a ~!** ¡qué pena OR lástima!; **it's a ~** es una pena OR lástima. ◇ vt **-1.** [fill with shame] avergonzar, apenar Andes, CAm, Carib, Méx **-2.** [force by making ashamed]: **to ~ sb into doing sthg** conseguir que alguien haga algo avergonzándole OR avergonzándolo Amér.

shamefaced [ˌʃeɪm'feɪst] adj avergonzado(da).

shameful ['ʃeɪmfʊl] adj vergonzoso(sa).

shameless ['ʃeɪmlɪs] adj desvergonzado(da).

shampoo [ʃæm'puː] (pl **-s**, pt & pp **-ed**, cont **-ing**) ◇ n [liquid] champú m. ◇ vt lavar (con champú).

shamrock ['ʃæmrɒk] n trébol m.

shandy ['ʃændɪ] (pl **-ies**) n cerveza f con gaseosa, clara f.

shan't [ʃɑːnt] = shall not.

shantytown ['ʃæntɪtaʊn] n barrio m de chabolas, cantegril m Amér.

shape [ʃeɪp] ◇ n **-1.** [form] forma f; **it's oval in ~** tenía forma ovalada; **biscuits in the ~ of stars** galletas con forma de estrellas **-2.** [silhouette] figura f **-3.** [structure] configuración f; **to take ~** tomar forma

-4. [form, health]: **to be in good/bad ~** [person] estar/no estar en forma; [business etc] estar en buen/mal estado; **to get back in ~** ponerse en forma. ◇ vt **-1.** [mould]: **to ~ sthg (into)** dar a algo forma (de) **-2.** [cause to develop] desarrollar.

◆ **shape up** vi [develop] desarrollarse.

-shaped ['ʃeɪpt] suffix: **egg/star ~** en forma de huevo/estrella.

shapeless ['ʃeɪplɪs] adj sin forma.

shapely ['ʃeɪplɪ] (compar **-ier**, superl **-iest**) adj bien hecho(cha).

share [ʃeəʳ] ◇ n **-1.** [portion]: **~ (of** OR **in)** parte f (de) **-2.** [contribution, quota]: **to have/do one's ~ of sthg** tener/hacer la parte que a uno le toca de algo. ◇ vt **-1.** [gen]: **to ~ sthg (with)** compartir algo (con); **we ~ a love of opera** nos une la pasión por la ópera. ◇ vi compartir.

◆ **shares** npl acciones fpl.

◆ **share out** vt sep repartir, distribuir.

shareholder ['ʃeəˌhəʊldəʳ] n accionista m OR f.

shark [ʃɑːk] (pl inv OR **-s**) n tiburón m; fig estafador m, -ra f.

sharp [ʃɑːp] ◇ adj **-1.** [not blunt] afilado(da) **-2.** [well-defined - outline] definido(da); [- photograph] nítido(da); [- contrast] marcado(da) **-3.** [intelligent, keen - person] listo(ta), filoso(sa) Amér; [- eyesight] penetrante; [- hearing] fino(na); [- intelligence] vivo(va) **-4.** [abrupt, sudden] brusco(ca), repentino(na) **-5.** [quick, firm - blow] seco(ca) **-6.** [angry, severe] cortante **-7.** [piercing, acute - sound, cry, pain] agudo(da); [- cold, wind] penetrante **-8.** [acid] ácido(da) **-9.** MÚS en tono demasiado alto, desafinado(da); **F~** fa m sostenido. ◇ adv **-1.** [punctually]: **at seven o'clock ~** a las siete en punto **-2.** [quickly, suddenly] bruscamente. ◇ n MÚS sostenido m.

sharpen ['ʃɑːpn] vt **-1.** [make sharp] afilar; [pencil] sacar punta a **-2.** [make keener, quicker, greater] agudizar.

sharpener ['ʃɑːpnəʳ] n [for pencils] sacapuntas m inv; [for knives] afilador m.

sharp-eyed [-'aɪd] adj perspicaz.

sharply ['ʃɑːplɪ] adv **-1.** [distinctly] claramente **-2.** [suddenly] repentinamente **-3.** [harshly] duramente.

shat [ʃæt] pt & pp ▷ **shit**.

shatter ['ʃætəʳ] ◇ vt **-1.** [smash] hacer añicos **-2.** [hopes etc] destruir, echar por tierra. ◇ vi hacerse añicos, romperse en pedazos.

shattered ['ʃætəd] adj **-1.** [shocked, upset] destrozado(da) **-2.** UK inf [very tired] hecho(cha) polvo.

shave [ʃeɪv] ◇ n afeitado m; **to have a ~** afeitarse. ◇ vt **-1.** [face, body] afeitar **-2.** [cut pieces off] raspar. ◇ vi afeitarse.

shaver ['ʃeɪvəʳ] *n* maquinilla *f* (de afeitar) eléctrica.

shaving brush ['ʃeɪvɪŋ-] *n* brocha *f* de afeitar.

shaving cream ['ʃeɪvɪŋ-] *n* crema *f* de afeitar.

shaving foam ['ʃeɪvɪŋ-] *n* espuma *f* de afeitar.

shavings ['ʃeɪvɪŋz] *npl* virutas *fpl*.

shawl [ʃɔːl] *n* chal *m*.

she [ʃiː] ◇ *pers pron* - **1**. [referring to woman, girl, animal] ella; ~'s tall es alta; I don't like it, but ~ does no me gusta, pero a ella sí; she can't do it ella no lo puede hacerlo; there ~ is allí está - **2**. [referring to boat, car, country]: ~'s a fine ship es un buen barco. ◇ *comp*: ~-elephant elefanta *f*; ~ bear osa *f*.

sheaf [ʃiːf] (*pl* sheaves) *n* - **1**. [of papers, letters] fajo *m* - **2**. [of corn, grain] gavilla *f*.

shear [ʃɪəʳ] (*pt* -ed, *pp* -ed *OR* shorn) *vt* [sheep] esquilar.

◆ **shears** *npl* [for garden] tijeras *fpl* de podar.

◆ **shear off** *vi* romperse.

sheath [ʃiːθ] (*pl* -s) *n* - **1**. [covering for knife] funda *f*, vaina *f* - **2**. *UK* [condom] preservativo *m*, condón *m*.

sheaves [ʃiːvz] *pl* ▷ **sheaf**.

shed [ʃed] (*pt* & *pp* shed, *cont* -ding) ◇ *n* cobertizo *m*, galpón *m* *Andes, Nic* & *RP*. ◇ *vt* - **1**. [skin] mudar de; [leaves] despojarse de - **2**. [discard] deshacerse de - **3**. [accidentally lose]: a lorry has ~ its load on the M1 un camión ha perdido su carga en la M1 - **4**. [tears, blood] derramar.

she'd [*weak form* ʃɪd, *strong form* ʃiːd] = she had, she would.

sheen [ʃiːn] *n* brillo *m*, lustre *m*.

sheep [ʃiːp] (*pl inv*) *n* [animal] oveja *f*.

sheepdog ['ʃiːpdɒg] *n* perro *m* pastor.

sheepish ['ʃiːpɪʃ] *adj* avergonzado(da).

sheepskin ['ʃiːpskɪn] *n* piel *f* de carnero.

sheer [ʃɪəʳ] *adj* - **1**. [absolute] puro(ra) - **2**. [very steep - cliff] escarpado(da); [- drop] vertical - **3**. [tights] transparente.

sheet [ʃiːt] *n* - **1**. [for bed] sábana *f*; a double/fitted ~ una sábana doble/ajustable - **2**. [of paper] hoja *f* - **3**. [of glass, metal, wood] lámina *f*.

sheik(h) [ʃeɪk] *n* jeque *m*.

shelf [ʃelf] (*pl* shelves) *n* estante *m*; it's on the top ~ está en el estante de arriba.

shell [ʃel] ◇ *n* - **1**. [of egg, nut] cáscara *f* - **2**. [of tortoise, crab] caparazón *m*; [of snail, mussels] concha *f* - **3**. [on beach] concha *f* - **4**. [of building] esqueleto *m*; [of boat] casco *m*; [of car] armazón *m*, chasis *m inv* - **5**. MIL [missile] proyectil *m*. ◇ *vt* - **1**. [peas] desvainar; [nuts, eggs] quitar la cáscara a - **2**. MIL [fire shells at] bombardear.

she'll [ʃiːl] = she will, she shall.

shellfish ['ʃelfɪʃ] (*pl inv*) *n* - **1**. [creature] crustáceo *m* - **2**. (*U*) [food] mariscos *mpl*.

shell suit *n* *UK* chandal *m* (de nailon).

shelter ['ʃeltəʳ] ◇ *n* [building, protection] refugio *m*; to seek ~ buscar refugio; to take ~ (from) refugiarse (de); to run for ~ correr a refugiarse; nuclear ~ refugio nuclear; bus ~ marquesina *f*. ◇ *vt* - **1**. [protect]: to be ~ed by/from estar protegido(da) por/de - **2**. [provide place to live for] dar asilo *OR* cobijo a - **3**. [hide] proteger, esconder. ◇ *vi*: to ~ from/in resguardarse de/en, protegerse de/en.

sheltered ['ʃeltəd] *adj* [place, existence] protegido(da).

shelve [ʃelv] *vt* dar carpetazo a.

shelves [ʃelvz] *pl* ▷ **shelf**.

shepherd ['ʃepəd] ◇ *n* pastor *m*. ◇ *vt fig* acompañar.

shepherd's pie ['ʃepədz-] *n* carne picada cubierta de puré de patatas.

sheriff ['ʃerɪf] *n* sheriff *m*.

sherry ['ʃerɪ] (*pl* -ries) *n* jerez *m*.

she's [ʃiːz] = she is, she has.

Shetland ['ʃetlənd] *n*: (the) ~ (Islands) las islas Shetland.

shield [ʃiːld] ◇ *n* - **1**. [armour, sports trophy] escudo *m* - **2**. *vt*: to ~ sb (from) proteger a alguien (de).

shift [ʃɪft] ◇ *n* - **1**. [slight change] cambio *m*; a ~ in sthg un cambio en algo - **2**. [period of work, workers] turno *m*; the night ~ el turno de noche. ◇ *vt* - **1**. [furniture etc] cambiar de sitio, mover - **2**. [attitude, belief] cambiar de. ◇ *vi* - **1**. [person] moverse; [wind, opinion] cambiar - **2**. *US* AUT cambiar de marcha.

shiftless ['ʃɪftlɪs] *adj* vago(ga), remolón(ona).

shifty ['ʃɪftɪ] (*compar* -ier, *superl* -iest) *adj inf* [person] con pinta deshonesta; [behaviour] sospechoso(sa); [look] huidizo(za).

shilling ['ʃɪlɪŋ] *n* chelín *m*.

shilly-shally ['ʃɪlɪˌʃælɪ] (*pt* & *pp* -ied) *vi* titubear, vacilar.

shimmer ['ʃɪməʳ] *vi* rielar, brillar con luz trémula.

shin [ʃɪn] *n* espinilla *f*.

shinbone ['ʃɪnbəʊn] *n* espinilla *f*.

shine [ʃaɪn] (*pt* & *pp* shone) ◇ *n* brillo *m*. ◇ *vt* [torch, lamp] dirigir; she shone a torch into his eyes la enfocó en los ojos con una linterna. ◇ *vi* [gen] brillar.

shingle ['ʃɪŋgl] *n* - **1**. (*U*) [on beach] guijarros *mpl* - **2**. *US* [nameplate] placa *f* con el nombre; to hang out one's ~ abrir un despacho/consultorio.

◆ **shingles** *n* (*U*) herpes *m inv*.

shin pad *n* espinillera *f*.

ship [ʃɪp] (*pt* & *pp* **-ped**, *cont* **-ping**) ◇ *n* barco *m*, buque *m*. ◇ *vt* enviar por barco.

shipbuilding ['ʃɪpˌbɪldɪŋ] *n* construcción *f* naval.

shipment ['ʃɪpmənt] *n* envío *m*.

shipper ['ʃɪpə'] *n* compañía *f* naviera.

shipping ['ʃɪpɪŋ] *n* (*U*) **- 1.** [transport] envío *m*, transporte *m* **- 2.** [ships] barcos *mpl*, buques *mpl*.

shipshape ['ʃɪpʃeɪp] *adj* en orden.

shipwreck ['ʃɪprek] ◇ *n* **- 1.** [destruction of ship] naufragio *m* **- 2.** [wrecked ship] barco *m* náufrago. ◇ *vt*: to be ~ed naufragar.

shipyard ['ʃɪpjɑːd] *n* astillero *m*.

shire [ʃaɪə'] *n* [county] condado *m*.

shirk [ʃɜːk] *vt* eludir.

shirt [ʃɜːt] *n* camisa *f*.

shirtsleeves ['ʃɜːtsliːvz] *npl*: to be in (one's) ~ ir en mangas de camisa.

shit [ʃɪt] (*pt* & *pp* **shit** OR **-ted** OR **shat**, *cont* **-ting**) *vulg* ◇ *n* **- 1.** [excrement] mierda *f* **- 2.** (*U*) [nonsense] gilipolleces *fpl*. ◇ *vi* cagar. ◇ *excl* ¡mierda!

shiver ['ʃɪvə'] ◇ *n* escalofrío *m*, estremecimiento *m*; it sent ~s down her spine le puso los pelos de punta. ◇ *vi*: to ~ (with) [fear] temblar OR estremecerse (de); [cold] tiritar (de).

shoal [ʃəʊl] *n* banco *m*.

shock [ʃɒk] ◇ *n* **- 1.** [unpleasant surprise, reaction, emotional state] susto *m*; it came as a ~ fue un duro golpe **- 2.** (*U*) MED : to be suffering from ~, to be in ~ estar en un estado de choque **- 3.** [impact] choque *m* **- 4.** [electric shock] descarga *f* OR sacudida *f* (eléctrica); to get a ~ from sthg recibir una descarga de algo. ◇ *vt* **- 1.** [upset] conmocionar **- 2.** [offend] escandalizar.

shock absorber [-əbˌzɔːbə'] *n* amortiguador *m*.

shocking ['ʃɒkɪŋ] *adj* **- 1.** [very bad] pésimo(ma) **- 2.** [behaviour, film] escandaloso(sa); [price] de escándalo.

shod [ʃɒd] ◇ *pt* & *pp* ⊳ **shoe**. ◇ *adj* calzado(da).

shoddy ['ʃɒdɪ] (*compar* **-ier**, *superl* **-iest**) *adj* [work] chapucero(ra); [goods] de pacotilla; *fig* [treatment] vil, despreciable.

shoe [ʃuː] (*pt* & *pp* **shod** OR **shoed**, *cont* **shoeing**) ◇ *n* zapato *m*. ◇ *vt* herrar.

shoebrush ['ʃuːbrʌʃ] *n* cepillo *m* para los zapatos.

shoehorn ['ʃuːhɔːn] *n* calzador *m*.

shoelace ['ʃuːleɪs] *n* cordón *m* del zapato, pasador *m* *Amér*.

shoe polish *n* betún *m*.

shoe shop *n* zapatería *f*.

shoestring ['ʃuːstrɪŋ] *n fig*: on a ~ con cuatro cuartos, con muy poco dinero.

shone [ʃɒn] *pt* & *pp* ⊳ **shine**.

shoo [ʃuː] ◇ *vt* [animal] espantar, ahuyentar; he ~ed the cat away echó al gato; [person] mandar a otra parte. ◇ *excl* ¡fuera!

shook [ʃʊk] *pt* ⊳ **shake**.

shoot [ʃuːt] (*pt* & *pp* **shot**) ◇ *n* **- 1.** *UK* [hunting expedition] cacería *f* **- 2.** [new growth] brote *m*, retoño *m*. ◇ *vt* **- 1.** [fire gun at] disparar contra, abalear *Andes*, *Cam* & *Ven*; [injure] herir a tiros; [kill] matar a tiros; to ~ o.s. pegarse un tiro; he was shot in the leg le dispararon en la pierna; to ~ the breeze *US* estar de cháchara **- 2.** *UK* [hunt] cazar **- 3.** [arrow] disparar **- 4.** CINEMA rodar, filmar. ◇ *vi* **- 1.** [fire gun]: to ~ (at) disparar (contra); don't ~! ¡no dispare! **- 2.** *UK* [hunt] cazar **- 3.** [move quickly]: to ~ in/out/past entrar/salir/pasar disparado(da) **- 4.** CINEMA rodar, filmar **- 5.** SPORT chutar; he shot at goal chutó a puerta.

◆ **shoot down** *vt sep* **- 1.** [plane] derribar **- 2.** [person] matar a tiros.

◆ **shoot up** *vi* **- 1.** [child, plant] crecer rápidamente **- 2.** [prices] dispararse.

shooting ['ʃuːtɪŋ] *n* **- 1.** [killing] asesinato *m* (a tiros) **- 2.** (*U*) [hunting] caza *f*, cacería *f*.

shooting star *n* estrella *f* fugaz.

shop [ʃɒp] (*pt* & *pp* **-ped**, *cont* **-ping**) ◇ *n* [store] tienda *f*. ◇ *vi* comprar; to go shopping ir de compras.

shop assistant *n UK* dependiente *m*, -ta *f*.

shop floor *n*: the ~ el personal, los obreros.

shopkeeper ['ʃɒpˌkiːpə'] *n* tendero *m*, -ra *f*.

shoplifting ['ʃɒpˌlɪftɪŋ] *n* (*U*) robo *m* en una tienda.

shopper ['ʃɒpə'] *n* comprador *m*, -ra *f*.

shopping ['ʃɒpɪŋ] *n* (*U*) **- 1.** [purchases] compras *fpl* **- 2.** [act of shopping] compra *f*; to do some/the ~ hacer algunas compras/la compra.

shopping bag *n* bolsa *f* de la compra.

shopping basket *n UK* **- 1.** [in supermarket] cesta *f* **- 2.** [for online shopping] cesta *f* de la compra.

shopping cart *n US* **- 1.** [in supermarket] carrito *m* de la compra **- 2.** [for online shopping] cesta *f* de la compra.

shopping centre *UK*, **shopping mall** *US*, **shopping plaza** *US* [-ˌplɑːzə] *n* centro *m* comercial.

shopsoiled *UK* ['ʃɒpsɔɪld], **shopworn** *US* ['ʃɒpwɔːn] *adj* deteriorado(da).

shop steward *n* enlace *m* OR *f* sindical.

shopwindow [ˌʃɒp'wɪndəʊ] *n* escaparate *m*.

shopworn *US* = **shopsoiled**.

shore [ʃɔː'] *n* **- 1.** [of sea, lake, river] orilla *f* **- 2.** [land]: on ~ en tierra.

◆ **shore up** *vt sep* apuntalar.

shorn [ʃɔːn] ◇ *pp* ⊳ **shear**. ◇ *adj* [grass, hair] corto(ta); [head] rapado(da).

short [ʃɔːt] ⬦ adj **-1.** [gen] corto(ta); **a ~ time ago** hace poco **- 2.** [not tall] bajo(ja) **- 3.** [curt]: **to be ~ (with sb)** ser seco(ca) (con alguien); **to have a ~ temper** tener mal genio **- 4.** [lacking] escaso(sa); **to be ~ on sthg** no andar sobrado de algo; **to be ~ of** estar OR andar mal de **- 5.** [be shorter form]: **to be ~ for** ser el diminutivo de. ⬦ adv **-1.** [out of]: **we are running ~ of water** se nos está acabando el agua **- 2.** [suddenly, abruptly]: **to cut sthg ~** interrumpir algo; **we had to cut ~ our trip to Cyprus** tuvimos que interrumpir nuestro viaje a Chipre; **to stop ~** parar en seco OR de repente; **to bring** OR **pull sb up ~** hacer a alguien parar en seco. ⬦ n **-1.** UK [alcoholic drink] chupito m **- 2.** [film] cortometraje m.
➡ **shorts** npl **-1.** [gen] pantalones mpl cortos, shorts mpl **- 2.** US [underwear] calzoncillos mpl.
➡ **for short** adv para abreviar.
➡ **in short** adv en resumen, en pocas palabras.
➡ **nothing short of** prep: **it was nothing ~ of madness/a disgrace** fue una auténtica locura/vergüenza.
➡ **short of** prep **-1.** [just before] cerca de **- 2.** [without]: **~ of asking, I can't see how you'll find out** salvo que preguntes, no sé cómo lo vas a averiguar.

shortage [ˈʃɔːtɪdʒ] n falta f, escasez f; **there was a paper ~** había falta OR escasez de papel.

shortbread [ˈʃɔːtbred] n especie de torta hecha de azúcar, harina y mantequilla.

shortcake [ˈʃɔːtkeɪk] n US bizcocho que se sirve relleno con fruta y crema batida.

short-change vt [in shop] dar mal el cambio a; fig [reward unfairly] estafar, engañar.

short circuit n cortocircuito m.

shortcomings [ˈʃɔːtˌkʌmɪŋz] npl defectos mpl.

shortcrust pastry [ˈʃɔːtkrʌst-] n pasta f quebrada.

short cut n **- 1.** [quick way] atajo m; **to take a ~** tomar un atajo **- 2.** [quick method] método m rápido.

shorten [ˈʃɔːtn] ⬦ vt acortar. ⬦ vi acortarse.

shortfall [ˈʃɔːtfɔːl] n: **~ (in** OR **of)** déficit m (de).

shorthand [ˈʃɔːhænd] n [writing system] taquigrafía f.

shorthand typist n UK taquimecanógrafo m, -fa f.

short list n UK [for job] lista f de candidatos seleccionados.

shortly [ˈʃɔːtlɪ] adv [soon] dentro de poco; **~ before/after** poco antes/después de.

shortsighted [ˌʃɔːtˈsaɪtɪd] adj [myopic] miope, corto(ta) de vista; fig [lacking foresight] corto de miras.

short-staffed [-ˈstɑːft] adj: **to be ~** estar falto(ta) de personal.

shortstop [ˈʃɔːtstɒp] n US [baseball] jugador que intenta interceptar bolas entre la segunda y tercera base.

short story n cuento m.

short-tempered [-ˈtempəd] adj de mal genio, de genio vivo.

short-term adj a corto plazo.

short wave n (U) onda f corta.

shot [ʃɒt] ⬦ pt & pp ➪ **shoot.** ⬦ n **- 1.** [gunshot] tiro m, disparo m; **he fired two ~s** disparó dos tiros; **like a ~** [quickly] disparado(da) **- 2.** [marksman] tirador m, -ra f; **to be a good ~** ser un buen tirador **- 3.** [in football] chut m, tiro m; [in golf, tennis] golpe m; **good ~!** ¡buen golpe! **- 4.** [photograph] foto f **- 5.** CINEMA plano m, toma f **- 6.** inf [try, go] intento m; **go on, have a ~** venga, inténtalo; **to have a ~ at (doing) sthg** intentar (hacer) algo **- 7.** [injection] inyección f.

shotgun [ˈʃɒtgʌn] n escopeta f.

should [ʃʊd] aux vb **-1.** [be desirable]: **we ~ leave now** deberíamos irnos ya OR ahora **- 2.** [seeking advice, permission]: **~ I go too?** ¿voy yo también? **- 3.** [as suggestion]: **I ~ deny everything** yo lo negaría todo **- 4.** [indicating probability]: **she ~ be home soon** tiene que llegar a casa pronto **- 5.** [have been expected]: **they ~ have won the match** tendrían que OR deberían haber ganado el partido **- 6.** [indicating intention, wish]: **I ~ like to come with you** me gustaría ir contigo **- 7.** (as conditional): **if you ~ see Mary, could you ask her to phone me?** si vieras a Mary, ¿le podrías pedir que me llamara?; **~ you decide to accept the job ...** si decide aceptar el trabajo ... **- 8.** (in 'that' clauses): **we decided that you ~ do it** decidimos que lo hicieras tú **- 9.** [expressing uncertain opinion]: **I ~ think he's about 50 (years old)** yo diría que tiene unos 50 (años) **- 10.** [expressing indignation] **he tidied up afterwards - so he ~!** después lo limpió - ¡era lo menos que podía hacer!; **I ~ hope so!** ¡eso espero!; **I ~ think so, too!** ¡es lo mínimo que podía hacer!

shoulder [ˈʃəʊldər] ⬦ n **-1.** [part of body, clothing] hombro m; **to cry on sb's ~** llorar en el hombro de nadie **- 2.** CULIN espaldilla f, paleta f Amér. ⬦ vt [accept - responsibility] cargar con; **to ~ the blame** asumir la responsabilidad.

shoulder blade n omóplato m.

shoulder strap n **- 1.** [on dress] tirante m, bretel m CSur **- 2.** [on bag] correa f, bandolera f.

shouldn't [ˈʃʊdnt] = should not.

should've ['ʃʊdəv] = **should have**.

shout [ʃaʊt] ◇ *n* grito *m*; **to let out a ~** lanzar un grito. ◇ *vt* gritar. ◇ *vi*: **to ~ (at)** gritar (a).

➡ **shout down** *vt sep* acallar a gritos.

shouting ['ʃaʊtɪŋ] *n (U)* gritos *mpl*.

shove [ʃʌv] ◇ *n*: **(to give sthg/sb) a ~** (dar a algo/a alguien) un empujón. ◇ *vt* empujar; **to ~ sthg/sb in** meter algo/a alguien a empujones; **to ~ sthg/sb out** sacar algo/a alguien a empujones.

➡ **shove off** *vi* [go away] *inf* largarse.

shovel ['ʃʌvl] *(UK pt & pp* **-led**, *cont* **-ling**, *US pt & pp* **-ed**, *cont* **-ing**) ◇ *n* pala *f*. ◇ *vt* remover con la pala OR a paletadas.

show [ʃəʊ] *(pt* **-ed**, *pp* **shown** OR **-ed**) ◇ *n* **- 1.** [display, demonstration] demostración *f*; **a ~ of strength** una demostración de fuerte **- 2.** [piece of entertainment - at theatre] espectáculo *m*; [- on radio, TV] programa *m* **- 3.** [performance] función *f* **- 4.** [of dogs, flowers, art] exposición *f*. ◇ *vt* **-1.** [gen] mostrar; **to ~ sb sthg, to ~ sthg to sb** enseñar OR mostrar a alguien algo **- 2.** [escort]: **to ~ sb to the door** llevar OR acompañar a alguien hasta algo; **he ~ed us to our seats** nos llevó a nuestros asientos **- 3.** [make visible, reveal] dejar ver; **white clothes ~ the dirt** la ropa blanca deja ver la suciedad; **come on, ~ yourself!** venga, ¡déjate ver! **- 4.** [indicate - increase, profit, loss] arrojar, registrar **- 5.** [broadcast- film] poner; [- TV programme] poner, emitir. ◇ *vi* **-1.** [indicate, make clear] indicar, mostrar **- 2.** [be visible] verse, notarse; **does it ~?** ¿se ve? **- 3.** [film]: **it is ~ing at the Odeon** lo ponen en el Odeon.

➡ **show off** ◇ *vt sep* lucir, presumir de. ◇ *vi* presumir.

➡ **show out** *vt sep* acompañar hasta la puerta; **~ the gentlemen out, please** acompañe a los caballeros hasta la puerta, por favor.

➡ **show up** ◇ *vt sep* poner en evidencia. ◇ *vi* **-1.** [stand out] resaltar **- 2.** [turn up] aparecer.

show business *n (U)* mundo *m* del espectáculo.

showdown ['ʃəʊdaʊn] *n*: **to have a ~ with** enfrentarse abiertamente a OR con.

shower ['ʃaʊəʳ] ◇ *n* **-1.** [device] ducha *f*, regadera *f Col, Méx, Ven* **-2.** [wash]: **to have** OR **take a ~** ducharse **-3.** [of rain] chubasco *m*, chaparrón *m*. ◇ *vt* **-1.** [sprinkle] rociar **- 2.** [bestow]: **to ~ sb with sthg, to ~ sthg on** OR **upon sb** [presents, compliments] colmar a alguien de algo; [insults] acribillar a alguien a algo. ◇ *vi* [wash] ducharse.

shower cap *n* gorro *m* de ducha.

showing ['ʃəʊɪŋ] *n* [of film] pase *m*,

proyección *f*; [of paintings] exposición *f*.

show jumping [-ˌdʒʌmpɪŋ] *n* concurso *m* hípico de salto.

shown [ʃəʊn] *pp* ▷ **show**.

show-off *n inf* presumido *m*, -da *f*.

showpiece ['ʃəʊpiːs] *n* pieza *f* de mayor interés.

showroom ['ʃəʊrʊm] *n* salón *m* OR sala *f* de exposición.

shrank [ʃræŋk] *pt* ▷ **shrink**.

shrapnel ['ʃræpnl] *n* metralla *f*.

shred [ʃred] *(pt & pp* **-ded**, *cont* **-ding**) ◇ *n* [small piece - of material] jirón *m*; [- of paper] trocito *m*, pedacito *m*; [food [scrap] ápice *m*, pizca *f*; **there isn't a ~ of truth in what he says** no hay una pizca de verdad en lo que dice; **to be in ~s** *lit & fig* estar hecho (cha) pedazos. ◇ *vt* [paper] hacer trizas; [food] rallar.

shredder ['ʃredəʳ] *n* [for paper] destructora *f*; [for food] rallador *m*.

shrewd [ʃruːd] *adj* astuto(ta), abusado(da) *Méx*.

shriek [ʃriːk] ◇ *n* chillido *m*, grito *m*. ◇ *vi*: **to ~ (with** OR **in)** chillar (de).

shrill [ʃrɪl] *adj* [high-pitched] estridente, agudo(da).

shrimp [ʃrɪmp] *n US* gamba *f*, camarón *m Amér*.

shrine [ʃraɪn] *n* santuario *m*.

shrink [ʃrɪŋk] *(pt* **shrank**, *pp* **shrunk**) ◇ *vt* encoger. ◇ *vi* **-1.** [become smaller] encoger **- 2.** *fig* [contract, diminish] disminuir **-3.** [recoil]: **to ~ away from** retroceder OR arredrarse ante **- 4.** [be reluctant]: **to ~ from sthg** eludir algo.

shrinkage ['ʃrɪŋkɪdʒ] *n* [loss in size] encogimiento *m*; *fig* [contraction] reducción *f*.

shrink-wrap *vt* precintar o envasar con plástico *termoretráctil*.

shrivel ['ʃrɪvl] *(UK pt & pp* **-led**, *cont* **-ling**, *US pt & pp* **-ed**, *cont* **-ing**) ◇ *vt*: **to ~ (up)** secar, marchitar. ◇ *vi*: **to ~ (up)** secarse, marchitarse.

shroud [ʃraʊd] ◇ *n* [cloth] mortaja *f*, sudario *m*. ◇ *vt*: **to be ~ed in sthg** estar envuelto(ta) en algo.

Shrove Tuesday ['ʃrəʊv-] *n* martes *m inv* de carnaval.

shrub [ʃrʌb] *n* arbusto *m*.

shrubbery ['ʃrʌbəri] *n* (zona *f* de) arbustos *mpl*.

shrug [ʃrʌg] *(pt & pp* **-ged**, *cont* **-ging**) ◇ *vt*: **to ~ one's shoulders** encogerse de hombros. ◇ *vi* encogerse de hombros.

➡ **shrug off** *vt sep* quitar importancia a.

shrunk [ʃrʌŋk] *pp* ▷ **shrink**.

shudder ['ʃʌdəʳ] *vi* [tremble]: **to ~ (with)** estremecerse (de).

shuffle ['ʃʌfl] ◇ *vt* **-1.** [feet] arrastrar

- **2.** [cards] **barajar** - **3.** [sheets of paper] revolver. ⬦ *vi* [walk by dragging feet]: **to** ~ **in/
out/along** entrar/salir/andar arrastrando
los pies.

shun [ʃʌn] (*pt* & *pp* **-ned,** *cont* **-ning**) *vt* rehuir, esquivar.

shunt [ʃʌnt] *vt* RAIL cambiar de vía; *fig*
[move] llevar (de un sitio a otro).

shut [ʃʌt] (*pt* & *pp* **shut,** *cont* **-ting**) ⬦ *adj*
cerrado(da). ⬦ *vt* cerrar. ⬦ *vi* **-1.** [close]
cerrarse - **2.** [close for business] cerrar.

➤ **shut away** *vt sep* guardar bajo llave.

➤ **shut down** *vt sep* & *vi* cerrar.

➤ **shut out** *vt sep* [person, cat] dejar fuera
a; [light, noise] no dejar entrar.

➤ **shut up** *inf* ⬦ *vt sep* [silence] hacer callar. ⬦ *vi* callarse; ~ **up!** ¡cállate!

shutter [ˈʃʌtəʳ] *n* - **1.** [on window] postigo
m, contraventana *f* - **2.** [in camera] obtura-
dor *m*.

shuttle [ˈʃʌtl] ⬦ *adj*: ~ **service** [of planes]
puente *m* aéreo; [of buses, trains] servicio *m*
regular. ⬦ *n* [plane] avión *m* (de puente aéreo).

shuttlecock [ˈʃʌtlkɒk] *n* volante *m*.

shy [ʃaɪ] (*pt* & *pp* **shied**) *adj* [timid] tímido(-
da).

Siberia [saɪˈbɪərɪə] *n* Siberia.

sibling [ˈsɪblɪŋ] *n* hermano *m*, -na *f*.

Sicily [ˈsɪsɪlɪ] *n* Sicilia.

sick [sɪk] *adj* - **1.** [ill] enfermo(ma) - **2.** [nau-
seous]: **to feel** ~ marearse - **3.** [vomiting]:
to be ~ UK devolver, vomitar - **4.** [fed up]:
to be ~ **of sthg/of doing sthg** estar harto(-
ta) de algo/de hacer algo; **to be** ~ **and tired
of (doing) sthg** estar hasta la coronilla de
(hacer) algo - **5.** [joke] de mal gusto.

sickbay [ˈsɪkbeɪ] *n* enfermería *f*.

sicken [ˈsɪkn] ⬦ *vt* poner enfermo(ma),
asquear. ⬦ *vi* UK: **to be** ~**ing for sthg**
estar cogiendo algo.

sickening [ˈsɪknɪŋ] *adj* - **1.** [disgusting]
asqueroso(sa), repugnante - **2.** [infuriating]
exasperante.

sickle [ˈsɪkl] *n* hoz *f*.

sick leave *n* (U) baja *f* por enfermedad.

sickly [ˈsɪklɪ] (*compar* **-ier,** *superl* **-iest**) *adj*
- **1.** [unhealthy] enfermizo(za) - **2.** [unplea-
sant] nauseabundo(da).

sickness [ˈsɪknɪs] *n* - **1.** [illness] enfermedad
f - **2.** UK (U) [nausea, vomiting] mareo *m*.

sick pay *n* (U) paga *f* por enfermedad.

side [saɪd] ⬦ *n* - **1.** [gen] lado *m*; **at** OR **by
one's** ~ al lado de uno; **on every** ~, **on all**
~**s** por todos los lados; **from** ~ **to** ~ de
un lado a otro; ~ **by** ~ juntos, uno al lado
de otro - **2.** [of person] costado *m*; [of ani-
mal] ijada *f* - **3.** [edge] lado *m*, borde *m*
- **4.** [of hill, valley] falda *f*, ladera *f* - **5.** [bank]
orilla *f* - **6.** [page] cara *f* - **7.** [participant - in

war, game] lado *m*, bando *m*; [- in sports
match] equipo *m* - **8.** [viewpoint] punto *m*
de vista; **you should try to see both** ~**s** deberías considerar las dos caras de la situación; **to take sb's** ~ ponerse del lado OR de
parte de alguien; **to take** ~**s** tomar partido;
whose ~ **are you on?** ¿de parte de quién
estás? - **9.** [aspect] aspecto *m*; **it does have
its comical** ~ tiene su lado cómico; **to be
on the safe** ~ para estar seguro. ⬦ *adj* lateral.

➤ **side with** *vt fus* ponerse de parte de.

sideboard [ˈsaɪdbɔːd] *n* aparador *m*.

sideboards UK [ˈsaɪdbɔːdz], **sideburns**
US [ˈsaɪdbɜːnz] *npl* patillas *fpl*.

side effect *n* MED & *fig* efecto *m* secundario.

sidelight [ˈsaɪdlaɪt] *n* luz *f* lateral.

sideline [ˈsaɪdlaɪn] *n* - **1.** [extra business] negocio *m* suplementario - **2.** [on tennis court]
línea *f* lateral; [on football pitch] línea *f* de
banda.

sidelong [ˈsaɪdlɒŋ] *adj* & *adv* de reojo OR
soslayo; **to give sb a** ~ **glance** mirar a alguien de reojo OR soslayo.

sidesaddle [ˈsaɪdˌsædl] *adv*: **to ride** ~
montar a sentadillas OR mujeriegas.

sideshow [ˈsaɪdʃəʊ] *n* barraca *f* OR caseta *f*
de feria.

sidestep [ˈsaɪdstep] (*pt* & *pp* **-ped,** *cont*
-ping) *vt* - **1.** [in football, rugby] regatear
- **2.** *fig* [problem, question] esquivar.

side street *n* calle *f* lateral.

sidetrack [ˈsaɪdtræk] *vt*: **to be** ~**ed** desviarse OR salirse del tema; **I keep getting**
~**ed** me distraigo continuamente.

sidewalk [ˈsaɪdwɔːk] *n* US acera *f*, andén *m*
CAm, Col, vereda *f* *CSur, Perú,* banqueta *f*
Méx.

sideways [ˈsaɪdweɪz] ⬦ *adj* [movement] de
lado, hacia un lado; [glance] de soslayo.
⬦ *adv* [move] de lado; [look] de reojo.

siding [ˈsaɪdɪŋ] *n* apartadero *m*, vía *f* muerta.

sidle [ˈsaɪdl] ➤ **sidle up** *vi*: **to** ~ **up to**
acercarse furtivamente a.

siege [siːdʒ] *n* - **1.** [by army] sitio *m*, cerco *m*
- **2.** [by police] cerco *m* policial.

sieve [sɪv] ⬦ *n* [utensil] colador *m*. ⬦ *vt*
[soup] colar; [flour, sugar] tamizar, cerner.

sift [sɪft] ⬦ *vt* - **1.** [sieve] tamizar, cerner
- **2.** *fig* [examine carefully] examinar cuidadosamente. ⬦ *vi*: **to** ~ **through sthg** examinar cuidadosamente algo.

sigh [saɪ] ⬦ *n* suspiro *m*. ⬦ *vi* suspirar.

sight [saɪt] ⬦ *n* - **1.** [vision] vista *f* - **2.** [act of
seeing]: **her first** ~ **of the sea** la primera vez
que vio el mar; **in** ~ a la vista; **to disappear
out of** ~ perderse de vista; **at first** ~ a primera vista; **it was love at first** ~ fue un flechazo - **3.** [something seen] espectáculo *m*

- 4. [on gun] mira *f*; **it's not a pretty ~** no es muy agradable de ver. ◇ *vt* divisar, avistar.

◆ **sights** *npl* atracciones *fpl* turísticas.

sightseeing ['saɪtˌsiːɪŋ] *n* (U) recorrido *m* turístico; **to go ~** hacer turismo.

sightseer ['saɪtˌsiːə'] *n* turista *m* OR *f*.

sign [saɪn] ◇ *n* **- 1.** [written symbol] signo *m* **- 2.** [horoscope]: **~ of the zodiac** signo del zodiaco **- 3.** [gesture] señal *f* **- 4.** [of pub, shop] letrero *m*; [on road] señal *f*; [notice] cartel *m* **- 5.** [indication] señal *f*, indicio *m*; **it's a good ~** es una buena señal. ◇ *vt* firmar. ◇ *vi* firmar.

◆ **sign on** *vi* **- 1.** [enrol, register]: **to ~ on (for)** [army] alistarse (en); [job] firmar el contrato (de); [course] matricularse (en) **- 2.** [register as unemployed] firmar para cobrar el paro.

◆ **sign up** ◇ *vt sep* [employee] contratar; [recruit] alistar. ◇ *vi*: **to ~ up (for)** [army] alistarse (en); [job] firmar el contrato (de); [course] matricularse (en).

signal ['sɪgnl] (*UK pp* & *pt* -**led**, *cont* -**ling**, *US pp* & *pt* -**ed**, *cont* -**ing**) ◇ *n* señal *f*. ◇ *vt* **- 1.** [indicate] indicar **- 2.** [tell]: **to ~ sb (to do sthg)** hacer señas a alguien (para que haga algo). ◇ *vi* **- 1.** AUT señalizar **- 2.** [indicate]: **to ~ to sb (to do sthg)** hacer señas a alguien (para que haga algo).

signalman ['sɪgnlmən] (*pl* -**men** [-mən]) *n* RAIL guardavía *m*.

signature ['sɪgnətʃə'] *n* firma *f*.

signature tune *n* sintonía *f*.

signet ring ['sɪgnɪt-] *n* (anillo *m* de) sello *m*.

significance [sɪg'nɪfɪkəns] *n* trascendencia *f*, importancia *f*; **to attach ~ to sthg** atribuir importancia a algo; **to be of little/ great/no ~** ser de poca/mucha/ninguna importancia.

significant [sɪg'nɪfɪkənt] *adj* **- 1.** [considerable, meaningful] significativo(va); **to give sb a ~ look** mirar a alguien expresivamente **- 2.** [important] trascendente.

signify ['sɪgnɪfaɪ] (*pt* & *pp* -**ied**) *vt* significar.

signpost ['saɪnpəʊst] *n* letrero *m* indicador.

Sikh [siːk] ◇ *adj* sij. ◇ *n* [person] sij *m* OR *f*.

silence ['saɪləns] ◇ *n* silencio *m*; **to do sthg in ~** hacer algo en silencio. ◇ *vt* [person, critic] acallar; [gun] hacer callar, silenciar.

silencer ['saɪlənsə'] *n* silenciador *m*.

silent ['saɪlənt] *adj* **- 1.** [gen] silencioso(sa) **- 2.** [not revealing anything]: **to be ~ about** quedar en silencio respecto a; **to remain ~** permanecer callado(da) **- 3.** CINEMA & LING mudo(da); **a ~ movie** una película muda; **a ~ b** una b muda.

silhouette [ˌsɪluː'et] *n* silueta *f*.

silicon chip [ˌsɪlɪkən-] *n* chip *m* de silicio.

silk [sɪlk] ◇ *n* seda *f*. ◇ *comp* de seda;

a ~ blouse una blusa de seda.

silky ['sɪlkɪ] (*compar* -**ier**, *superl* -**iest**) *adj* [hair, dress, skin] sedoso(sa); [voice] aterciopelado (da).

sill [sɪl] *n* [of window] alféizar *m*.

silly ['sɪlɪ] (*compar* -**ier**, *superl* -**iest**) *adj* estúpido(da), sonso(sa) *Amér*; **that was a ~ thing to say** qué tontería has dicho.

silo ['saɪləʊ] (*pl* -**s**) *n* silo *m*.

silt [sɪlt] *n* cieno *m*, légamo *m*.

silver ['sɪlvə'] ◇ *adj* **- 1.** [in colour] plateado(da) **- 2.** [made of silver] de plata. ◇ *n* (U) **- 1.** [metal, silverware] plata *f* **- 2.** [coins] monedas *fpl* plateadas.

silver foil, silver paper *n* (U) papel *m* de plata.

silver-plated [-'pleɪtɪd] *adj* bañado(da) de plata, plateado(da).

silversmith ['sɪlvəsmɪθ] *n* platero *m*, -ra *f*.

silverware ['sɪlvəweə'] *n* (U) **- 1.** [dishes etc] plata *f* **- 2.** *US* [cutlery] cubertería *f* de plata.

similar ['sɪmɪlə'] *adj*: **~ (to)** parecido(da) OR similar (a).

similarly ['sɪmɪləlɪ] *adv* [likewise] asimismo; [equally] igualmente.

simmer ['sɪmə'] *vt* & *vi* hervir a fuego lento.

simpering ['sɪmpərɪŋ] *adj* [person] que sonríe con cara de tonto(ta); [smile] bobo(-ba).

simple ['sɪmpl] *adj* **- 1.** [gen] sencillo(lla) **- 2.** *dated* [mentally retarded] simple **- 3.** [plain - fact] mero(ra); [- truth] puro(ra).

simple-minded [-'maɪndɪd] *adj* simple.

simplicity [sɪm'plɪsətɪ] *n* sencillez *f*.

simplify ['sɪmplɪfaɪ] (*pt* & *pp* -**ied**) *vt* simplificar.

simply ['sɪmplɪ] *adv* **- 1.** [merely] sencillamente, simplemente **- 2.** [for emphasis]: **~ dreadful/wonderful** francamente terrible/maravilloso **- 3.** [in a simple way] de manera sencilla.

simulate ['sɪmjʊleɪt] *vt* simular.

simultaneous [UK ˌsɪməl'teɪnjəs, US ˌsaɪməl'teɪnjəs] *adj* simultáneo(a).

sin [sɪn] (*pt* & *pp* -**ned**, *cont* -**ning**) ◇ *n* pecado *m*. ◇ *vi*: **to ~ (against)** pecar (contra).

since [sɪns] ◇ *adv* desde entonces; **we haven't been there ~** no hemos vuelto allí desde entonces. ◇ *prep* desde; **~ last Tuesday** desde el último martes; **~ then** desde entonces; **he has worked here ~ 1975** trabaja aquí desde 1975. ◇ *conj* **- 1.** [in time] desde que; **she's been miserable ever ~ she married him** desde que se casó con él ha sido desdichada; **it's ages ~ I saw you** hace siglos que no te veo **- 2.** [because] ya que, puesto que.

sincere [sɪn'sɪə'] *adj* sincero(ra).

sincerely [sɪn'sɪəlɪ] *adv* sinceramente;

Yours ~ [at end of letter] atentamente.

sincerity [sɪn'serətɪ] *n* sinceridad *f*.

sinew ['sɪnjuː] *n* tendón *m*.

sinful ['sɪnful] *adj* - 1. [person] pecador(ra) - 2. [thought, act] pecaminoso(sa).

sing [sɪŋ] (*pt* **sang**, *pp* **sung**) *vt* & *vi* cantar; **to** ~ **along with sb** cantar a coro con alguien.

Singapore [,sɪŋə'pɔːr] *n* Singapur.

singe [sɪndʒ] (*cont* **singeing**) *vt* chamuscar.

singer ['sɪŋər] *n* cantante *m* OR *f*; **she's a good** ~ canta muy bien.

singing ['sɪŋɪŋ] *n (U)* canto *m*.

single ['sɪŋgl] ◇ *adj* - 1. [only one] solo(la); **not a** ~ **person** was there no había ni una sola persona - 2. [individual]: **every** ~ **penny** todos y cada uno de los peniques - 3. [unmarried] soltero(ra); **he's** ~ está soltero - 4. *UK* [one-way] de ida. ◇ *n* - 1. *UK* [one-way ticket] billete *m* de ida - 2. MUS [record] sencillo *m*, single *m*.
  ◆ **singles** *npl* TENNIS (partido *m*) individual *m*.
  ◆ **single out** *vt sep*: **to** ~ **sb out (for)** escoger a alguien (para).

single bed *n* cama *f* individual.

single-breasted [-'brestɪd] *adj* recto(ta), sin cruzar.

single cream *n UK* crema *f* de leche, nata *f* líquida.

single file *n*: **in** ~ en fila india.

single-handed [-'hændɪd] *adv* sin ayuda.

single-minded [-'maɪndɪd] *adj* resuelto(ta).

single parent *n* padre *m* soltero, madre *f* soltera; **he's a** ~ es padre soltero.

single-parent family *n* familia *f* monoparental.

single room *n* habitación *f* individual.

singlet ['sɪŋglɪt] *n UK* camiseta *f* sin mangas.

singular ['sɪŋgjʊlər] ◇ *adj* singular. ◇ *n* singular *m*; **in the** ~ en singular.

sinister ['sɪnɪstər] *adj* siniestro(tra).

sink [sɪŋk] (*pt* **sank**, *pp* **sunk**) ◇ *n* - 1. [in kitchen] fregadero *m* - 2. [in bathroom] lavabo *m*. ◇ *vt* - 1. [cause to go under water] hundir - 2. [cause to penetrate]: **to** ~ **sthg into** [knife, claws] clavar algo en; [teeth] hincar algo en; **he sank his teeth into the steak** le hincó los dientes al filete. ◇ *vi* - 1. [go down - ship, sun] hundirse - 2. [slump - person] hundirse; **she sank into a chair** se desplomó en una silla - 3. [decrease] bajar.
  ◆ **sink in** *vi* hacer mella; **it hasn't sunk in yet** todavía no lo tiene asumido.

sink unit *n* fregadero *m* (con mueble debajo).

sinner ['sɪnər] *n* pecador *m*, -ra *f*.

sinus ['saɪnəs] (*pl* **-es**) *n* seno *m*.

sip [sɪp] (*pt* & *pp* **-ped**, *cont* **-ping**) ◇ *n* sorbo *m*. ◇ *vt* beber a sorbos.

siphon ['saɪfn] *n* sifón *m*.
  ◆ **siphon off** *vt sep* - 1. [liquid] sacar con sifón - 2. *fig* [funds] desviar.

sir [sɜːr] *n* - 1. [form of address] señor *m*; **thank you,** ~ gracias, señor; [in letter] **Dear** ~, Estimado Señor - 2. [in titles]: **Sir Philip Holden** Sir Philip Holden.

siren ['saɪərən] *n* [alarm] sirena *f*.

sirloin (steak) ['sɜːlɔɪn] *n* solomillo *m*, (filete *m*) de lomo *m Andes, Col, CSur, Ven*.

sissy ['sɪsɪ] (*pl* **-ies**) *n inf* mariquita *m*.

sister ['sɪstər] *n* - 1. [gen] hermana *f* - 2. *UK* [senior nurse] enfermera *f* jefe.

sister-in-law (*pl* **sisters-in-law** OR **sister-in-laws**) *n* cuñada *f*.

sit [sɪt] (*pt* & *pp* **sat**, *cont* **-ting**) ◇ *vi* - 1. [be seated, sit down] sentarse - 2. [be member]: **to** ~ **on** ser miembro de - 3. [be in session] reunirse, celebrar sesión. ◇ *vt UK* [exam] presentarse a.
  ◆ **sit about, sit around** *vi* estar sentado(da) sin hacer nada.
  ◆ **sit down** *vi* sentarse; ~, **please** siéntese, por favor; **she was sitting down** estaba sentada.
  ◆ **sit in on** *vt fus* estar presente en *(sin tomar parte)*.
  ◆ **sit through** *vt fus* aguantar (hasta el final).
  ◆ **sit up** *vi* - 1. [sit upright] incorporarse; ~ **straight!** siéntate derecho - 2. [stay up] quedarse levantado(da); **we sat up until midnight** nos quedamos levantados hasta la medianoche.

sitcom ['sɪtkɒm] *n inf* comedia *f* de situación.

site [saɪt] ◇ *n* [place] sitio *m*, lugar *m*; [of construction work] obra *f*. ◇ *vt* situar.

sit-in *n* sentada *f*; **to stage a** ~ protagonizar una sentada.

sitting ['sɪtɪŋ] *n* - 1. [serving of meal] turno *m* (para comer) - 2. [session] sesión *f*.

sitting room *n* sala *f* de estar.

situated ['sɪtjʊeɪtɪd] *adj* [located]: **to be** ~ estar situado(da).

situation [,sɪtjʊ'eɪʃn] *n* - 1. [gen] situación *f* - 2. [job]: **'Situations Vacant'** *UK* 'Ofertas de trabajo'.

six [sɪks] ◇ *num adj* seis *(inv)*; **she's** ~ **(years old)** tiene seis años. ◇ *num n* - 1. [the number six] seis *m inv*; **two hundred and** ~ doscientos seis; ~ **comes before seven** el seis va antes que el siete - 2. [in times]: **it's** ~ **(thirty)** son las seis (y media); **we arrived at** ~ llegamos a las seis - 3. [in addresses]: ~ **Peyton Place** Peyton Place número seis, el seis de Peyton Place - 4. [in scores]: ~**-nil** seis a cero. ◇ *num pron* seis *m* OR *f*; **there are** ~ **of us** somos seis.

sixteen [siks'ti:n] *num* dieciséis; *see also* **six**.

sixteenth [siks'ti:nθ] *num* decimosexto(-ta); *see also* **sixth**.

sixth [siksθ] ◇ *num adj* sexto(ta). ◇ *num adv* sexto(ta). ◇ *num pron* sexto *m*, -ta *f*. ◇ -1. [fraction]: **a ~** OR **one ~ of** un sexto de, la sexta parte de - 2. [in dates]: **the ~** el (día) seis; **the ~ of September** el seis de septiembre.

sixth form *n* UK SCH curso optativo de dos años de enseñanza secundaria con vistas al examen de ingreso a la universidad, ≃ COU *m*.

sixth form college *n* UK centro público para alumnos de 16 a 18 años donde se preparan para los 'A levels' o para exámenes de formación profesional.

sixty ['siksti] (*pl* -ies) *num* sesenta; *see also* **six**.
  ➤ **sixties** *npl* -1. [decade]: **the sixties** los años sesenta - 2. [in ages]: **to be in one's sixties** estar en los sesenta.

size [saiz] *n* -1. [gen] tamaño *m*; **what ~ do you take?** ¿cuál es su talla?; **what ~ shoes do you take?** ¿qué número calza? - 2. [of clothes] talla *f*; [of shoes] número *m*.
  ➤ **size up** *vt sep* [situation] evaluar; [person] calar.

sizeable ['saizəbl] *adj* considerable.

sizzle ['sizl] *vi* chisporrotear.

skate [skeit] (*pl sense 2 only inv* OR -s) ◇ *n* -1. [ice skate, roller skate] patín *m* - 2. [fish] raya *f*. ◇ *vi* [on skates] patinar.

skateboard ['skeitbɔ:d] *n* monopatín *m*.

skater ['skeitə'] *n* patinador *m*, -ra *f*.

skating ['skeitiŋ] *n* patinaje *m*.

skating rink *n* pista *f* de patinaje.

skeleton ['skelitn] *n* ANAT esqueleto *m*.

skeleton key *n* llave *f* maestra.

skeleton staff *n* personal *m* mínimo.

skeptic *etc* US = **sceptic** *etc*.

sketch [sketʃ] ◇ *n* -1. [drawing, brief outline] esbozo *m*, bosquejo *m* - 2. [humorous scene] sketch *m*. ◇ *vt* esbozar.

sketchbook ['sketʃbʊk] *n* cuaderno *m* de dibujo.

sketchpad ['sketʃpæd] *n* bloc *m* de dibujo.

sketchy ['sketʃi] (*compar* -ier, *superl* -iest) *adj* incompleto(ta), poco detallado(da).

skewer ['skjʊə'] *n* brocheta *f*, broqueta *f*.

ski [ski:] (*pt & pp* **skied**, *cont* **skiing**) ◇ *n* esquí *m*. ◇ *vi* esquiar.

ski boots *npl* botas *fpl* de esquí.

skid [skid] (*pt & pp* **-ded**, *cont* **-ding**) ◇ *n* patinazo *m*, derrape *m*. ◇ *vi* patinar, derrapar.

skier ['ski:ə'] *n* esquiador *m*, -ra *f*.

skies [skaiz] *pl* ⊳ **sky**.

skiing ['ski:iŋ] *n* (U) esquí *m*; **to go ~** ir a esquiar.

ski jump *n* -1. [slope] pista *f* para saltos de esquí - 2. [event] saltos *mpl* de esquí.

skilful, skillful US ['skilfʊl] *adj* hábil.

ski lift *n* telesilla *m*.

skill [skil] *n* -1. (U) [expertise] habilidad *f*, destreza *f* - 2. [craft, technique] técnica *f*.

skilled [skild] *adj* -1. [skilful] habilidoso(sa) - 2. [trained] cualificado(da), especializado(da).

skillful *etc* US = **skilful** *etc*.

skim [skim] (*pt & pp* **-med**, *cont* **-ming**) ◇ *vt* -1. [remove - cream] desnatar, sacar la nata a - 2. [fly above] volar rozando. ◇ *vi*: **to ~ through sthg** hojear algo, leer algo por encima.

skimmed milk [skim(d)-milk] *n* leche *f* desnatada.

skimp [skimp] ◇ *vt* [gen] escatimar; [work] hacer de prisa y corriendo. ◇ *vi*: **to ~ on sthg** [gen] escatimar algo; [work] hacer algo de prisa y corriendo.

skimpy ['skimpi] (*compar* -ier, *superl* -iest) *adj* [clothes] muy corto y estrecho (muy corta y estrecha); [meal, facts] escaso(sa).

skin [skin] (*pt & pp* **-ned**, *cont* **-ning**) ◇ *n* -1. [gen] piel *f*; [on face] cutis *m*; **to have thick ~** *fig* tener mucho aguante - 2. [on milk, pudding] nata *f*; [on paint] capa *f*, película *f*. ◇ *vt* -1. [animal] despellejar, desollar - 2. [knee, elbow etc] rasguñarse.

skin-deep *adj* superficial.

skin diving *n* buceo *m*, submarinismo *m* (sin traje ni escafandra).

skinny ['skini] (*compar* -ier, *superl* -iest) ◇ *adj inf* flaco(ca). ◇ *n* US: **the ~** información *f* confidencial.

skin-tight *adj* muy ajustado(da).

skip [skip] (*pt & pp* **-ped**, *cont* **-ping**) ◇ *n* -1. [little jump] brinco *m*, saltito *m* - 2. UK [large container] contenedor *m*, container *m*. ◇ *vt* [miss out] saltarse. ◇ *vi* -1. [move in little jumps] ir dando brincos - 2. UK [jump over rope] saltar a la comba.

ski pants *npl* pantalones *mpl* de esquí.

ski pole *n* bastón *m* para esquiar.

skipper ['skipə'] *n* NAUT & SPORT capitán *m*, -ana *f*.

skipping rope ['skipiŋ-] *n* UK comba *f*, cuerda *f* de saltar.

skirmish ['skɜ:miʃ] ◇ *n lit & fig* escaramuza *f*.

skirt [skɜ:t] ◇ *n* -1. falda *f*, pollera *f* CSur - 2. US: (bed) ~ volante *m*. ◇ *vt* -1. [border] rodear, bordear - 2. [go round - obstacle] sortear; [- person, group] esquivar - 3. [avoid dealing with] evitar, eludir.
  ➤ **skirt round** *vt fus* -1. [obstacle] sortear - 2. [issue, problem] evitar, eludir.

skit [skit] *n*: **~ (on)** parodia *f* (de).

skittle ['skitl] *n* UK bolo *m*.
  ➤ **skittles** *n* (U) bolos *mpl*.

skive [skaɪv] vi UK inf: **to ~ (off)** escaquear-se.

skulk [skʌlk] vi esconderse.

skull [skʌl] n [gen] calavera f; ANAT cráneo m.

skunk [skʌŋk] n mofeta f.

sky [skaɪ] (pl **skies**) n cielo m.

skylight ['skaɪlaɪt] n claraboya f.

sky marshal n US policía destinado en un avión para evitar secuestros.

skyscraper ['skaɪˌskreɪpəʳ] n rascacielos m inv.

slab [slæb] n [of stone] losa f; [of cheese] trozo m, pedazo m; [of chocolate] tableta f.

slack [slæk] ◇ adj - **1.** [rope, cable] flojo(ja) - **2.** [business] inactivo(va) - **3.** [person - careless] descuidado(da). ◇ n [in rope] parte f floja; **to take up the ~** tensar la cuerda.

slacken ['slækn] ◇ vt [speed, pace] reducir; [rope] aflojar. ◇ vi [speed, pace] reducirse.

slag [slæg] n [waste material] escoria f.

slagheap ['slæghi:p] n escorial m.

slain [sleɪn] pp ▷ **slay**.

slam [slæm] (pt & pp **-med**, cont **-ming**) ◇ vt - **1.** [shut] cerrar de golpe; **she ~med the door** dio un portazo - **2.** [place with force]: **to ~ sthg on** OR **onto sthg** dar un golpe con algo contra algo violentamente; **he ~med his fist on the desk** dio un puñetazo en la mesa. ◇ vi [shut] cerrarse de golpe.

slander ['slɑːndəʳ] ◇ n calumnia f, difamación f. ◇ vt calumniar, difamar.

slang [slæŋ] n argot m, jerga f.

slant [slɑːnt] ◇ n - **1.** [diagonal angle] inclinación f - **2.** [perspective] enfoque m. ◇ vi inclinarse.

slanting ['slɑːntɪŋ] adj inclinado(da).

slap [slæp] (pt & pp **-ped**, cont **-ping**) ◇ n [in face] bofetada f; [on back] palmada f; **he gave him a ~ on the back** le dio una palmadita en la espalda. ◇ vt - **1.** [person, face] abofetear; **she ~ped him round the face** lo abofeteó, le dio una bofetada; [back] dar una palmada a - **2.** [place with force]: **he ~ped the folder on the desk** dejó la carpeta en la mesa dando un golpetazo; **she ~ped some paste on the wallpaper** embadurnó el papel pintado con cola. ◇ adv inf [directly] de narices; **he walked ~ into a lamp post** se dio de lleno con una farola.

slapdash ['slæpdæʃ], **slaphappy** ['slæp,hæpɪ] adj inf chapucero(ra).

slapstick ['slæpstɪk] n (U) payasadas fpl; **~ comedy** astracanada f.

slap-up adj UK inf: **~ meal** comilona f.

slash [slæʃ] ◇ n - **1.** [long cut] raja f, tajo m - **2.** esp US [oblique stroke] barra f oblicua; **forward~** barra inclinada. ◇ vt - **1.** [material, tyre] rasgar; **she ~ed her wrists** se cortó las venas - **2.** inf [prices etc] recortar drásticamente.

slat [slæt] n tablilla f.

slate [sleɪt] ◇ n pizarra f. ◇ vt [criticize] poner por los suelos.

slaughter ['slɔːtəʳ] ◇ n lit & fig matanza f. ◇ vt matar, carnear Andes & RP.

slaughterhouse ['slɔːtəhaʊs, pl -haʊzɪz] n matadero m.

slave [sleɪv] ◇ n esclavo m, -va f. ◇ vi [work hard] trabajar como un negro; **to ~ over a hot stove** hum pasarse el día bregando en la cocina.

slavery ['sleɪvərɪ] n lit & fig esclavitud f.

slaw [slɔː] n US inf ensalada de repollo y zanahoria con mayonesa.

slay [sleɪ] (pt **slew**, pp **slain**) vt literary asesinar, matar.

sleazy ['sliːzɪ] (compar **-ier**, superl **-iest**) adj [disreputable] de mala muerte.

sledge [sledʒ], **sled** US [sled] n trineo m.

sledgehammer ['sledʒˌhæməʳ] n almádena f.

sleek [sliːk] adj - **1.** [hair] suave y brillante; [fur] lustroso(sa) - **2.** [shape] de línea depurada.

sleep [sliːp] (pt & pp **slept**) ◇ n sueño m; **to go to ~** [doze off] dormirse. ◇ vi dormir.
  ◆ **sleep in** vi dormir hasta tarde, levantarse tarde.
  ◆ **sleep with** vt fus euphemism acostarse con.

sleeper ['sliːpəʳ] n - **1.** [person]: **to be a heavy/light ~** tener el sueño profundo/ligero - **2.** [sleeping compartment] coche-cama m - **3.** [train] tren m nocturno (con literas) - **4.** UK [on railway track] traviesa f.

sleeping bag ['sliːpɪŋ-] n saco m de dormir, bolsa f RP.

sleeping car ['sliːpɪŋ-] n coche-cama m, coche m dormitorio CSur.

sleeping pill ['sliːpɪŋ-] n pastilla f para dormir.

sleepless ['sliːplɪs] adj [night] en blanco, sin dormir.

sleepwalk ['sliːpwɔːk] vi [be a sleepwalker] ser somnámbulo(la); [walk in one's sleep] andar mientras uno duerme.

sleepy ['sliːpɪ] (compar **-ier**, superl **-iest**) adj [person] soñoliento(ta).

sleet [sliːt] ◇ n aguanieve f. ◇ v impers: **it's ~ing** cae aguanieve.

sleeve [sliːv] n - **1.** [of garment] manga f - **2.** [for record] cubierta f.

sleigh [sleɪ] n trineo m.

sleight of hand [ˌslaɪt-] n (U) lit & fig juego m de manos.

slender ['slendəʳ] adj - **1.** [thin] esbelto(ta) - **2.** [scarce] escaso(sa).

slept [slept] pt & pp ▷ **sleep**.

slew [sluː] ◇ pt ▷ **slay**. ◇ vi girar bruscamente.

slice [slaɪs] ◇ *n* -**1.** [of bread] rebanada *f*; [of cheese] loncha *f*; [of sausage] raja *f*; [of lemon] rodaja *f*; [of meat] tajada *f* -**2.** [of market, glory] parte *f*. ◇ *vt* [gen] cortar; [bread] rebanar.

slick [slɪk] *adj* -**1.** [smooth, skilful] logrado(-da) -**2.** *pej* [superficial - talk] aparentemente brillante; [- person] de labia fácil.

slide [slaɪd] (*pt* & *pp* **slid** [slɪd]) ◇ *n* -**1.** [decline] descenso *m* -**2.** PHOT diapositiva *f* -**3.** [in playground] tobogán *m* -**4.** UK [for hair] pasador *m*. ◇ *vt* deslizar. ◇ *vi* -**1.** [slip] resbalar -**2.** [glide] deslizarse -**3.** [decline gradually] caer.

sliding door [ˌslaɪdɪŋ-] *n* puerta *f* corredera.

sliding scale [ˌslaɪdɪŋ-] *n* escala *f* móvil.

slight [slaɪt] ◇ *adj* -**1.** [improvement, hesitation etc] ligero(ra); [wound] superficial; not in the ~ est *fml* en absoluto -**2.** [slender] menudo(da), de aspecto frágil. ◇ *n* desaire *m*. ◇ *vt* menospreciar, desairar.

slightly ['slaɪtlɪ] *adv* [to small extent] ligeramente.

slim [slɪm] (*compar* -mer, *superl* -mest, *pt* & *pp* -med, *cont* -ming) ◇ *adj* -**1.** [person, object] delgado(da) -**2.** [chance, possibility] remoto(ta). ◇ *vi* (intentar) adelgazar.

slime [slaɪm] *n* [in pond etc] lodo *m*, cieno *m*; [of snail, slug] baba *f*.

slimming ['slɪmɪŋ] *n* adelgazamiento *m*.

slimming pill *n* pastilla *f* para adelgazar.

sling [slɪŋ] (*pt* & *pp* **slung**) ◇ *n* -**1.** [for injured arm] cabestrillo *m* -**2.** [for carrying things] braga *f*, honda *f* -**3.** ◇ *vt* -**1.** [hang roughly] colgar descuidadamente -**2.** *inf* [throw] tirar.

slip [slɪp] (*pt* & *pp* -ped, *cont* -ping) ◇ *n* -**1.** [mistake] descuido *m*, desliz *m*; a ~ of the pen/tongue un lapsus -**2.** [of paper - gen] papelito *m*; [- form] hoja *f* -**3.** [underskirt] enaguas *fpl* -**4.** *phr*: to give sb the ~ *inf* dar esquinazo a alguien. ◇ *vt*: to ~ sthg into meter algo rápidamente en; to ~ into sthg, to ~ sthg on [clothes] ponerse rápidamente algo. ◇ *vi* -**1.** [lose one's balance] resbalar, patinar -**2.** [slide] escurrirse, resbalar -**3.** [decline] empeorar.

◆ **slip up** *vi* cometer un error (poco importante).

slipped disc [ˌslɪpt-] *n* hernia *f* discal.

slipper ['slɪpə'] *n* zapatilla *f*.

slippery ['slɪpərɪ] *adj* resbaladizo(za).

slip road *n* UK [for joining motorway] acceso *m*; [for leaving motorway] salida *f*.

slipshod ['slɪpʃɒd] *adj* descuidado(da), chapucero(ra).

slip-up *n* *inf* desliz *m*; to make a ~ cometer un desliz.

slipway ['slɪpweɪ] *n* grada *f*.

slit [slɪt] (*pt* & *pp* **slit**, *cont* -ting) ◇ *n* ranura

f, hendidura *f*. ◇ *vt* abrir, cortar (a lo largo).

slither ['slɪðə'] *vi* deslizarse; it ~ed away se marchó deslizándose.

sliver ['slɪvə'] *n* [of glass] esquirla *f*; [of wood] astilla *f*; [of cheese, ham] tajada *f* muy fina.

slob [slɒb] *n* *inf* guarro *m*, -rra *f*.

slog [slɒg] (*pt* & *pp* -ged, *cont* -ging) *inf* ◇ *n* [work] curro *m*, trabajo *m* pesado. ◇ *vi* [work]: to ~ (away) at trabajar sin descanso en.

slogan ['sləʊgən] *n* eslogan *m*.

slop [slɒp] (*pt* & *pp* -ped, *cont* -ping) ◇ *vt* derramar. ◇ *vi* derramarse.

slope [sləʊp] ◇ *n* cuesta *f*, pendiente *f*. ◇ *vi* inclinarse; the road ~s down to the beach la carretera desciende hasta la playa.

sloping ['sləʊpɪŋ] *adj* [gen] inclinado(da); [ground] en pendiente.

sloppy ['slɒpɪ] (*compar* -ier, *superl* -iest) *adj* [person] descuidado(da); [work] chapucero(ra); [appearance] dejado(da).

slot [slɒt] (*pt* & *pp* -ted, *cont* -ting) *n* -**1.** [opening] ranura *f* -**2.** [groove] muesca *f* -**3.** [place in schedule] espacio *m*.

slot machine *n* -**1.** [vending machine] máquina *f* automática (de bebidas, cigarrillos etc) -**2.** [arcade machine] máquina *f* tragaperras.

slouch [slaʊtʃ] *vi* ir con los hombros caídos.

Slovakia [slə'vækɪə] *n* Eslovaquia.

slovenly ['slʌvnlɪ] *adj* [unkempt] desaliñado(da); [careless] descuidado(da).

slow [sləʊ] ◇ *adj* -**1.** [not fast] lento(ta); to be a ~ reader leer despacio -**2.** [not prompt]: to be ~ to do sthg tardar en hacer algo; to be ~ to anger tardar en enfadarse -**3.** [clock etc] atrasado(da); my watch is a few minutes ~ mi reloj va atrasado unos cuantos minutos -**4.** [not intelligent] corto(-ta) (de alcances) -**5.** [not hot]: bake in a ~ oven cocinar a horno moderado. ◇ *vt* aminorar, ralentizar. ◇ *vi* ir más despacio.

◆ **slow down, slow up** ◇ *vt sep* [growth] retrasar; [car] reducir la velocidad de. ◇ *vi* -**1.** [walker] ir más despacio; [car] reducir la velocidad -**2.** [take it easy] tomarse las cosas con calma.

slowdown ['sləʊdaʊn] *n* -**1.** [slackening off] ralentización *f* -**2.** [go-slow] US huelga *f* de celo.

slowly ['sləʊlɪ] *adv* despacio, lentamente.

slow motion *n*: in ~ a cámara lenta.

sludge [slʌdʒ] *n* (U) [mud] fango *m*, lodo *m*; [sewage] aguas *fpl* residuales.

slug [slʌg] (*pt* & *pp* -ged, *cont* -ging) *n* -**1.** [insect] babosa *f* -**2.** US *inf* [bullet] bala *f*.

sluggish ['slʌgɪʃ] *adj* [movement, activity] lento(ta); [feeling] aturdido(da).

sluice [slu:s] *n* [passage] canal *m* de desagüe; [gate] compuerta *f*.

slum [slʌm] (*pt* & *pp* **-med**, *cont* **-ming**) *n* [area] barrio *m* bajo.

slumber ['slʌmbə'] *literary vi* dormir.

slump [slʌmp] ⋄ *n* **-1.** [decline]: **~ (in)** bajón *m* (en) **-2.** ECON crisis *f* económica. ⋄ *vi* **-1.** [fall in value] dar un bajón **-2.** [fall heavily-person] desplomarse, dejarse caer; **they found him ~ed on the floor** lo encontraron desplomado en el suelo.

slung [slʌŋ] *pt* & *pp* ⊳ **sling**.

slur [slɜː'] (*pt* & *pp* **-red**, *cont* **-ring**) ⋄ *n* [insult] agravio *m*, afrenta *f*; **to cast a ~ on sb** manchar la reputación de alguien. ⋄ *vt* mascullar.

slush [slʌʃ] *n* nieve *f* medio derretida.

slush fund, slush money US *n* fondos utilizados para actividades corruptas.

slut [slʌt] *n* **-1.** *inf* [dirty or untidy woman] marrana *f* **-2.** *vinf* [sexually immoral woman] ramera *f*.

sly [slaɪ] (*compar* **slyer** OR **slier**, *superl* **slyest** OR **sliest**) *adj* **-1.** [look, smile] furtivo(va) **-2.** [person] astuto(ta), ladino(na).

smack [smæk] ⋄ *n* **-1.** [slap] cachete *m*, cachetada *f Amér* **-2.** [impact] golpe *m*. ⋄ *vt* **-1.** [slap] pegar, dar un cachete a **-2.** [place violently] tirar de golpe. ⋄ *vi*: **to ~ of sth** oler a algo.

small [smɔːl] ⋄ *adj* [gen] pequeño(ña); [person] bajo(ja); [matter, attention] de poca importancia; [importance] poco(ca); **to make sb feel ~** hacer que alguien se sienta muy poca cosa; **to get ~er** empequeñecer.

small ads [-ædz] *npl* UK anuncios *mpl* clasificados.

small change *n* cambio *m*, suelto *m*, calderilla *f Esp*, sencillo *m Andes*, feria *f Méx*, menudo *m Col*.

smallholder ['smɔːl,həʊldə'] *n* UK minifundista *m* OR *f*.

small hours *npl* primeras horas *fpl* de la madrugada; **in the ~** en la madrugada.

smallpox ['smɔːlpɒks] *n* viruela *f*.

small print *n*: **the ~** la letra pequeña.

small talk *n* (U) conversación *f* trivial.

smarmy ['smɑːmɪ] (*compar* **-ier**, *superl* **-iest**) *adj* cobista.

smart [smɑːt] ⋄ *adj* **-1.** [neat, stylish] elegante **-2.** *esp* US [clever] inteligente **-3.** [fashionable, exclusive] distinguido(da), elegante **-4.** [quick, sharp] rápido(da). ⋄ *vi* **-1.** [eyes, wound] escocer **-2.** [person] sentir resquemor.

➤ **smarts** *n* US [intelligence] mollera *f*.

smarten ['smɑːtn] ➤ **smarten up** *vt sep* arreglar; **to ~ o.s. up** arreglarse.

smash [smæʃ] ⋄ *n* **-1.** [sound] estrépito *m* **-2.** *inf* [car crash] accidente *m* **-3.** TENNIS mate *m*, smash *m*. ⋄ *vt* **-1.** [break into pieces] romper, hacer pedazos **-2.** [hit, crash]: **to** **~ one's fist into sthg** dar un puñetazo en algo **-3.** *fig* [defeat] aplastar. ⋄ *vi* **-1.** [break into pieces] romperse, hacerse pedazos **-2.** [crash, collide]: **to ~ into sthg** chocar violentamente con algo.

smashing ['smæʃɪŋ] *adj inf* fenomenal, estupendo(da).

smattering ['smætərɪŋ] *n* nociones *fpl*; **he has a ~ of Spanish** tiene nociones de español.

smear [smɪə'] ⋄ *n* **-1.** [dirty mark] mancha *f* **-2.** ~ **test** citología *f*, Papanicolau *m Amér* **-3.** [slander] calumnia *f*, difamación *f*. ⋄ *vt* **-1.** [smudge] manchar **-2.** [spread]: **to ~ sthg onto sthg** untar algo con algo; **the screen was ~ed with grease** la pantalla estaba embadurnada de grasa **-3.** [slander] calumniar, difamar.

smell [smel] (*pt* & *pp* **-ed** OR **smelt**) ⋄ *n* **-1.** [odour] olor *m* **-2.** [sense of smell] olfato *m*. ⋄ *vt lit* & *fig* oler. ⋄ *vi* **-1.** [gen] oler; **to ~ of/like** oler a/como; **to ~ good/bad** oler bien/mal **-2.** [smell unpleasantly] apestar.

smelly ['smelɪ] (*compar* **-ier**, *superl* **-iest**) *adj* maloliente, apestoso(sa).

smelt [smelt] ⋄ *pt* & *pp* ⊳ **smell**. ⋄ *vt* fundir.

smile [smaɪl] ⋄ *n* sonrisa *f*. ⋄ *vi* sonreír; **to ~ at sb** sonreírle a algn.

smirk [smɜːk] *n* sonrisa *f* desdeñosa.

smock [smɒk] *n* blusón *m*.

smog [smɒg] *n* niebla *f* baja, smog *m*.

smoke [sməʊk] ⋄ *n* **-1.** [gen] humo *m*; **to go up in ~** ser consumido(da) por las llamas. ⋄ *vt* **-1.** [cigarette, cigar] fumar; **to ~ a pipe** fumar en pipa **-2.** [fish, meat, cheese] ahumar. ⋄ *vi* **-1.** [smoke tobacco] fumar; **I don't ~** no fumo **-2.** [give off smoke] echar humo.

smoked [sməʊkt] *adj* ahumado(da).

smoker ['sməʊkə'] *n* **-1.** [person] fumador *m*, -ra *f* **-2.** RAIL [compartment] compartimiento *m* de fumadores.

smokescreen ['sməʊkskriːn] *n fig* cortina *f* de humo.

smoke shop *n* US estanco *m*.

smoke signal *n* señal *f* de humo.

smoking ['sməʊkɪŋ] *n*: **~ is bad for you** fumar es malo; **to give up ~** dejar de fumar; **'no ~'** 'prohibido fumar'.

smoky ['sməʊkɪ] (*compar* **-ier**, *superl* **-iest**) *adj* **-1.** [full of smoke] lleno(na) de humo **-2.** [taste, colour] ahumado(da).

smolder US = **smoulder**.

smooth [smuːð] ⋄ *adj* **-1.** [surface] liso(sa); [skin] terso(sa) **-2.** [mixture, gravy] sin grumos **-3.** [movement, taste] suave **-4.** [flight, ride] tranquilo(la) **-5.** *pej* [person, manner] meloso(sa) **-6.** [trouble-free] sin problemas. ⋄ *vt* alisar.

smooth out vt sep - **1.** [table cloth, crease] alisar - **2.** [difficulties] allanar.

smother ['smʌðə'] vt - **1.** [cover thickly]: **to ~ sthg in** OR **with** cubrir algo de - **2.** [kill] asfixiar - **3.** [extinguish] sofocar, apagar - **4.** fig [control] controlar, contener; **to ~ a yawn** contener un bostezo.

smoulder UK, **smolder** US ['sməʊldə'] vi - **1.** [fire] arder sin llama - **2.** fig [person, feelings] arder.

SMS (abbr of **short message service**) n COMPUT servicio m de mensajes cortos.

smudge [smʌdʒ] ◇ n [dirty mark] mancha f; [ink blot] borrón m. ◇ vt [by blurring] emborronar; [by dirtying] manchar.

smug [smʌg] (compar **-ger**, superl **-gest**) adj pej pagado(da) OR satisfecho(cha) de sí mismo(ma).

smuggle ['smʌgl] vt [across frontiers] pasar de contrabando.

smuggler ['smʌglə'] n contrabandista m OR f.

smuggling ['smʌglɪŋ] n (U) contrabando m.

smutty ['smʌtɪ] (compar **-ier**, superl **-iest**) adj inf pej guarro(rra).

snack [snæk] n bocado m, piscolabis m inv, botana f Guat, Méx & Ven.

snack bar n bar m, cafetería f.

snag [snæg] (pt & pp **-ged**, cont **-ging**) ◇ n [problem] pega f. ◇ vi: **to ~ (on)** engancharse (en).

snail [sneɪl] n caracol m; **at a ~'s pace** a paso de tortuga.

snail mail n correo m caracol.

snake [sneɪk] n [large] serpiente f; [small] culebra f.

snap [snæp] (pt & pp **-ped**, cont **-ping**) ◇ adj repentino(na); **a ~ decision** una decisión repentina. ◇ n - **1.** [act or sound] crujido m, chasquido m - **2.** inf [photograph] foto f. ◇ vt - **1.** [break] partir (en dos) - **2.** [move with a snap]: **to ~ sthg open** abrir algo de golpe. ◇ vi - **1.** [break] partirse (en dos) - **2.** [attempt to bite]: **to ~ at sthg/sb** intentar morder algo/a alguien - **3.** [speak sharply]: **to ~ (at sb)** contestar bruscamente OR de mala manera a alguien.

snap up vt sep no dejar escapar.

snappy ['snæpɪ] (compar **-ier**, superl **-iest**) adj inf - **1.** [stylish] con estilo - **2.** [quick] rápido(da); **make it ~!** ¡date prisa! - **3.** [irritable] arisco(ca).

snapshot ['snæpʃɒt] n foto f.

snare [sneə'] n trampa f.

snarl [snɑ:l] vi gruñir.

snatch [snætʃ] ◇ n [of conversation, song] fragmento m. ◇ vt [grab] agarrar; **to ~ sthg from sb** arrancarle OR arrebatarle algo a alguien.

sneak [sni:k] (US pt **snuck**) ◇ n UK inf acusica m OR f, chivato m, -ta f. ◇ vt pasar a escondidas; **she tried to ~ the cakes out of the cupboard** intentó sacar los pasteles del armario a hurtadillas; **she ~ed him into her bedroom** lo coló en su dormitorio. ◇ vi: **to ~ in/out** entrar/salir a escondidas; **he ~ed in without paying** se coló sin pagar; **don't try and ~ off!** ¡no intentes escabullirte!

sneakers ['sni:kəz] npl US zapatos mpl de lona.

sneaky ['sni:kɪ] (compar **-ier**, superl **-iest**) adj inf solapado(da).

sneer [snɪə'] vi [smile unpleasantly] sonreír con desprecio.

sneeze [sni:z] vi estornudar.

snide [snaɪd] adj sarcástico(ca).

sniff [snɪf] ◇ vt - **1.** [smell] oler - **2.** [drug] esnifar. ◇ vi [to clear nose] sorber por la nariz.

snigger ['snɪgə'] ◇ n risa f disimulada. ◇ vi reírse por lo bajo.

snip [snɪp] (pt & pp **-ped**, cont **-ping**) ◇ n inf [bargain] ganga f. ◇ vt cortar con tijeras.

sniper ['snaɪpə'] n francotirador m, -ra f.

snippet ['snɪpɪt] n retazo m, fragmento m; **~ of information** un dato aislado.

snivel ['snɪvl] (UK pt & pp **-led**, cont **-ling**, US pt & pp **-ed**, cont **-ing**) vi lloriquear.

snob [snɒb] n esnob m OR f.

snobbish ['snɒbɪʃ], **snobby** ['snɒbɪ] (compar **-ier**, superl **-iest**) adj esnob.

snooker ['snu:kə'] n snooker m, juego parecido al billar.

snoop [snu:p] vi inf: **to ~ (around)** fisgonear.

snooty ['snu:tɪ] (compar **-ier**, superl **-iest**) adj engreído(da).

snooze [snu:z] ◇ n cabezada f; **to have a ~** echar una cabezada. ◇ vi dormitar.

snore [snɔ:'] ◇ n ronquido m. ◇ vi roncar.

snoring ['snɔ:rɪŋ] n (U) ronquidos mpl.

snorkel ['snɔ:kl] n tubo m respiratorio.

snort [snɔ:t] ◇ n resoplido m. ◇ vi resoplar.

snout [snaʊt] n hocico m.

snow [snəʊ] ◇ n nieve f. ◇ v impers nevar; **it's ~ing** está nevando.

snowball ['snəʊbɔ:l] ◇ n bola f de nieve. ◇ vi fig aumentar rápidamente.

snowboard ['snəʊbɔ:d] n snowboard m.

snowboarding ['snəʊbɔ:dɪŋ] n snowboard m; **to go ~** hacer snowboard.

snowbound ['snəʊbaʊnd] adj bloqueado(da) por la nieve.

snowdrift ['snəʊdrɪft] n montón m de nieve.

snowdrop ['snəʊdrɒp] n campanilla f blanca.

snowfall ['snəʊfɔːl] *n* nevada *f*.

snowflake ['snəʊfleɪk] *n* copo *m* de nieve.

snowman ['snəʊmæn] (*pl* **-men** [-men]) *n* muñeco *m* de nieve.

snowplough *UK*, **snowplow** *US* ['snəʊplaʊ] *n* quitanieves *m inv*.

snowshoe ['snəʊʃuː] *n* raqueta *f* de nieve.

snowstorm ['snəʊstɔːm] *n* tormenta *f* de nieve.

SNP *n abbr of* **Scottish National Party**.

Snr, snr (*abbr of* **senior**) sén.

snub [snʌb] (*pt & pp* **-bed**, *cont* **-bing**) ◇ *n* desaire *m*. ◇ *vt* desairar.

snuck [snʌk] *US pt* ▷ **sneak**.

snuff [snʌf] *n* [tobacco] rapé *m*.

snug [snʌg] (*compar* **-ger**, *superl* **-gest**) *adj* - **1.** [person] cómodo y calentito (cómoda y calentita); [feeling] de bienestar - **2.** [place] acogedor(ra) - **3.** [close-fitting] ajustado(-da), ceñido(da).

snuggle ['snʌgl] *vi*: **to ~ up to sb** arrimarse a alguien acurrucándose.

so [səʊ] ◇ *adv* - **1.** [to such a degree] tan; **~ difficult (that)** tan difícil (que); **don't be ~ stupid!** ¡no seas bobo!; **I wish he wouldn't talk ~ much** ojalá no hablara tanto; **I've never seen ~ much money/many cars** en mi vida he visto tanto dinero/tantos coches; **thank you ~ much** muchísimas gracias; **it's about ~ high** es así de alto - **2.** [in referring back to previous statement, event etc]: **~ what's the point then?** entonces ¿qué sentido tiene?; **~ you knew already?** ¿así que ya lo sabías?; **I don't think ~** no creo, me parece que no; **I'm afraid ~** me temo que sí; **if ~** si es así, de ser así; **is that ~?** ¿es cierto?, ¿es así? - **3.** [also] también; **~ can I y yo** (también puedo); **~ do I y yo** (también); **she speaks French and ~ does her husband** ella habla francés y su marido también - **4.** [in such a way]: **(like) ~** así, de esta forma - **5.** [in expressing agreement]: **~ there is!** ¡pues (sí que) es verdad!, ¡sí que lo hay, sí!; **~ I see** ya lo veo - **6.** [unspecified amount, limit]: **they pay us ~ much a week** nos pagan tanto a la semana; **it's not ~ much the money as the time involved** no es tanto el dinero como el tiempo que conlleva; **they didn't ~ much as say thank you** ni siquiera dieron las gracias; **or ~ o** así. ◇ *conj* - **1.** [with the result that, therefore] así que, por lo tanto - **2.** [to introduce a statement] (bueno) pues; **~ what have you been up to?** bueno, ¿y qué has estado haciendo?; **~ that's who she is!** ¡anda! ¡o sea que ella!; **~ what?** *inf* ¿y qué?; **~ there** *inf* ¡(y si no te gusta,) te chinchas!

◆ **and so on, and so forth** *adv* y cosas por el estilo.

◆ **so as** *conj* para; **we didn't knock ~ as not to disturb them** no llamamos para no molestarlos.

◆ **so far** *conj* [up to now] hasta ahora; **~ far, so good** por ahora todo bien.

◆ **so that** *conj* para que; **he lied ~ that she would go free** mintió para que ella saliera en libertad.

soak [səʊk] ◇ *vt* - **1.** [leave immersed] poner en remojo - **2.** [wet thoroughly] empapar, ensopar *Amér*. ◇ *vi* - **1.** [become thoroughly wet]: **to leave sthg to ~, to let sthg ~** dejar algo en remojo - **2.** [spread]: **to ~ into** OR **through sthg** calar algo.

◆ **soak up** *vt sep* [liquid] empapar, absorber.

soaking ['səʊkɪŋ] *adj* empapado(da); **to be ~ wet** estar empapado.

so-and-so *n inf* - **1.** [to replace a name] fulano *m*, -na *f* de tal - **2.** [annoying person] hijo *m*, -ja *f* de tal.

soap [səʊp] *n* - **1.** (U) [for washing] jabón *m* - **2.** TV culebrón *m*.

soap flakes *npl* escamas *fpl* de jabón.

soap opera *n* culebrón *m*.

soap powder *n* jabón *m* en polvo.

soapy ['səʊpɪ] (*compar* **-ier**, *superl* **-iest**) *adj* [full of soap] jabonoso(sa).

soar [sɔːʳ] *vi* - **1.** [bird] remontar el vuelo - **2.** [rise into the sky] elevarse - **3.** [increase rapidly] alcanzar cotas muy altas.

sob [sɒb] (*pt & pp* **-bed**, *cont* **-bing**) ◇ *n* sollozo *m*. ◇ *vi* sollozar.

sober ['səʊbəʳ] *adj* - **1.** [gen] sobrio(bria) - **2.** [serious] serio(ria).

◆ **sober up** *vi* pasársele a uno la borrachera.

sobering ['səʊbərɪŋ] *adj* que hace reflexionar; **it was a ~ thought** dio mucho que pensar.

so-called [-kɔːld] *adj* - **1.** [expressing scepticism] mal llamado(da), supuesto(ta) - **2.** [widely known as] así llamado(da).

soccer ['sɒkəʳ] *n* (U) fútbol *m*.

sociable ['səʊʃəbl] *adj* sociable.

social ['səʊʃl] *adj* social.

social club *n* club *m* social.

Social Democrat *n* socialdemócrata *mf*.

socialism ['səʊʃəlɪzm] *n* socialismo *m*.

socialist ['səʊʃəlɪst] ◇ *adj* socialista. ◇ *n* socialista *m* OR *f*.

socialize, -ise ['səʊʃəlaɪz] *vi*: **to ~ (with)** alternar (con).

social security *n* seguridad *f* social.

social services *npl* servicios *mpl* sociales.

social worker *n* asistente *m*, -ta *f* social.

society [sə'saɪətɪ] (*pl* **-ies**) *n* - **1.** [gen] sociedad *f* - **2.** [club, organization] sociedad *f*, asociación *f*.

sociology [ˌsəʊsɪ'ɒlədʒɪ] *n* sociología *f*.

sock [sɒk] *n* calcetín *m*, media *f Amér*.

socket ['sɒkɪt] *n* - **1.** ELEC enchufe *m* - **2.** [of eye] cuenca *f*; [of joint] glena *f*.

sod [sɒd] *n* - **1.** [of turf] tepe *m* - **2.** *v inf* [person] cabroncete *m*.

soda ['səʊdə] *n* - **1.** [gen] soda *f* - **2.** US [fizzy drink] gaseosa *f*.

soda water *n* soda *f*.

sodden ['sɒdn] *adj* empapado(da).

sodium ['səʊdɪəm] *n* sodio *m*.

sodium bicarbonate *n* bicarbonato *m* de sodio.

sodium chloride *n* cloruro *m* de sodio.

sofa ['səʊfə] *n* sofá *m*.

Sofia ['səʊfjə] *n* Sofía.

soft [sɒft] *adj* - **1.** [pliable, not stiff, not strict] blando(da); **to go ~ ablandarse** - **2.** [smooth, gentle, not bright] suave.

soft drink *n* refresco *m*.

soften ['sɒfn] *vt* suavizar. *vi* - **1.** [substance] ablandarse - **2.** [expression] suavizarse, dulcificarse.

softhearted [,sɒft'hɑːtɪd] *adj* de buen corazón.

softly ['sɒftlɪ] *adv* - **1.** [gently] con delicadeza - **2.** [quietly, not brightly] suavemente - **3.** [leniently] con indulgencia.

soft-spoken *adj* de voz suave.

software ['sɒftweə'] *n* COMPUT software *m*.

soft water *n* agua *f* blanda.

soggy ['sɒgɪ] (*compar* -**ier**, *superl* -**iest**) *adj inf* empapado(da).

soil [sɔɪl] *n* [earth] tierra *f*, suelo *m*. *vt* ensuciar.

soiled [sɔɪld] *adj* sucio(cia).

solace ['sɒləs] *n literary* consuelo *m*.

solar ['səʊlə'] *adj* solar; **~ eclipse** eclipse de sol.

solar power *n* energía *f* solar.

sold [səʊld] *pt* & *pp* ▷ **sell**.

solder ['səʊldə'] *n* (U) soldadura *f*. *vt* soldar.

soldier ['səʊldʒə'] *n* soldado *m*.

sold out *adj* agotado(da); **the theatre was ~** se agotaron las localidades; **all the shops were ~ of lemons** se habían agotado los limones en todas las tiendas.

sole [səʊl] (*pl sense 2 only inv OR* -**s**) *adj* - **1.** [only] único(ca) - **2.** [exclusive] exclusivo(va). *n* - **1.** [of foot] planta *f*; [of shoe] suela *f* - **2.** [fish] lenguado *m*.

solemn ['sɒləm] *adj* solemne.

solicit [sə'lɪsɪt] *vt fml* [request] solicitar. *vi* [prostitute] ofrecer sus servicios.

solicitor [sə'lɪsɪtə'] *n* UK JUR *abogado que lleva casos administrativos y legales, pero que no acude a los tribunales superiores.*

solid ['sɒlɪd] *adj* - **1.** [gen] sólido(da) - **2.** [rock, wood, gold] macizo(za) - **3.** [reliable, respectable] serio(ria), formal - **4.** [without interruption] sin interrupción; **it rained for two ~ weeks** llovió sin parar

durante dos semanas. *n* sólido *m*; **to be on ~s** [subj: baby] estar tomando alimentos sólidos.

solidarity [,sɒlɪ'dærətɪ] *n* solidaridad *f*.

solitaire [,sɒlɪ'teə'] *n* - **1.** [jewel, board game] solitario *m* - **2.** US [card game] solitario *m*.

solitary ['sɒlɪtrɪ] *adj* solitario(ria).

solitary confinement *n*: **to be in ~** estar incomunicado(da) (en la cárcel).

solitude ['sɒlɪtjuːd] *n* soledad *f*.

solo ['səʊləʊ] (*pl* -**s**) *adj* & *adv* a solas. *n* solo *m*.

soloist ['səʊləʊɪst] *n* solista *m* OR *f*.

soluble ['sɒljʊbl] *adj* soluble.

solution [sə'luːʃn] *n*: **~ (to)** solución *f* (a).

solve [sɒlv] *vt* resolver.

solvent ['sɒlvənt] *adj* FIN solvente. *n* disolvente *m*.

Somalia [sə'mɑːlɪə] *n* Somalia.

sombre UK, **somber** US ['sɒmbə'] *adj* sombrío(a).

some [sʌm] *adj* - **1.** [a certain amount, number of]: **would you like ~ coffee?** ¿quieres café?; **give me ~ money** dame algo de dinero; **there are ~ good articles in it** tiene algunos artículos buenos; **I bought ~ socks** [one pair] me compré unos calcetines; [more than one pair] me compré calcetines - **2.** [fairly large number or quantity of]: **I've known him for ~ years** lo conozco desde hace bastantes años; **I had ~ difficulty getting here** me costó lo mío llegar aquí - **3.** *(contrastive use)* [certain] algunos(as); **~ jobs are better paid than others** algunos trabajos están mejor pagados que otros; **~ people say that ...** los hay que dicen que ...; **in ~ ways** en cierto modo - **4.** [in imprecise statements] algún(una); **there must be ~ mistake** debe haber un OR algún error; **she married ~ writer or other** se casó con no sé qué escritor; **~ day** algún día - **5.** *inf* [very good] menudo(da); **that's ~ car he's got** ¡menudo coche tiene! *pron* - **1.** [a certain amount]: **can I have ~?** [money, milk, coffee etc] ¿puedo coger un poco?; **~ of** parte de - **2.** [a certain number] algunos(as); **can I have ~?** [books, potatoes etc] ¿puedo coger algunos?; **~ (of them) left early** algunos se fueron temprano; **~ say he lied** hay quien dice que mintió. *adv* - **1.** unos(as); **there were ~ 7,000 people there** habría unas 7.000 personas - **2.** US [slightly] algo, un poco; **shall I turn it up ~?** ¿lo subo algo or un poco?

somebody ['sʌmbədɪ] *pron* alguien; **~ or other** alguien.

someday ['sʌmdeɪ] *adv* algún día.

somehow ['sʌmhaʊ], **someway** US ['sʌmweɪ] *adv* - **1.** [by some action] de alguna manera; **~ or other** de un modo u otro

- 2. [for some reason] por alguna razón.

someone ['sʌmwʌn] *pron* alguien; **~ or other** alguien, no sé quien.

someplace *US* = **somewhere**.

somersault ['sʌməsɔːlt] *n* [in air] salto *m* mortal; [on ground] voltereta *f*.

something ['sʌmθɪŋ] ◇ *pron* algo; **or ~ inf** o algo así; **~ or other** alguna cosa. ◇ *adv*: **~ like**, **~ in the region of** algo así como.

sometime ['sʌmtaɪm] *adv* en algún momento; **~ or other** en algún momento; **~ next week** durante la semana que viene.

sometimes ['sʌmtaɪmz] *adv* a veces.

someway *US* = **somehow**.

somewhat ['sʌmwɒt] *adv fml* algo.

somewhere *UK* ['sʌmweə^r], **someplace** *US* ['sʌmpleɪs] *adv* **- 1.** [unknown place - with verbs of position] en alguna parte; [- with verbs of movement] a alguna parte; **it's ~ else** está en otra parte; **it's ~ in the kitchen** está en alguna parte de la cocina; **shall we go ~ else?** ¿nos vamos a otra parte?; **I need ~ to spend the night** necesito un lugar donde pasar la noche **- 2.** [in approximations]: **~ between five and ten** entre cinco y diez; **~ around 20** alrededor de 20; **he's ~ in his fifties** tiene cincuenta años y pico;

son [sʌn] *n* hijo *m*.

song [sɒŋ] *n* **- 1.** [gen] canción *f* **- 2.** [of bird] canto *m*.

sonic ['sɒnɪk] *adj* sónico(ca).

son-in-law (*pl* **sons-in-law** OR **son-in-laws**) *n* yerno *m*.

sonnet ['sɒnɪt] *n* soneto *m*.

sonny ['sʌnɪ] (*pl* **-ies**) *n inf* hijo *m*, chico *m*.

soon [suːn] *adv* pronto; **how ~ will it be ready?** ¿para cuándo estará listo?; **~ after** poco después; **as ~ as** tan pronto como; **as ~ as possible** cuanto antes; **see you ~** hasta pronto.

sooner ['suːnə^r] *adv* **- 1.** [in time] antes; **no ~ did he arrive than ...** apenas había llegado cuando ...; **no ~ said than done** dicho y hecho; **~ or later** (más) tarde o (más) temprano; **the ~ the better** cuanto antes mejor **- 2.** [expressing preference]: **I'd ~ (not) ...** preferiría (no) ...

soot [sʊt] *n* hollín *m*.

soothe [suːð] *vt* **- 1.** [pain] aliviar **- 2.** [nerves etc] calmar.

sophisticated [sə'fɪstɪkeɪtɪd] *adj* [gen] sofisticado(da).

sophomore ['sɒfəmɔː^r] *n US* estudiante *m* OR *f* del segundo curso.

sophomoric ['sɒfəmɒrɪk] *adj US* immaduro(ra) y repipi.

soporific [,sɒpə'rɪfɪk] *adj* soporífico(ca).

sopping ['sɒpɪŋ] *adj*: **~ (wet)** chorreando.

soppy ['sɒpɪ] (*compar* **-ier**, *superl* **-iest**) *adj inf pej* sentimentaloide.

soprano [sə'prɑːnəʊ] (*pl* **-s**) *n* soprano *f*.

sorbet ['sɔːbeɪ] *n* sorbete *m*; **lemon ~** sorbete de limón.

sorcerer ['sɔːsərə^r] *n* mago *m*, -ga *f*, brujo *m*, -ja *f*.

sordid ['sɔːdɪd] *adj* **- 1.** [immoral] obsceno(na) **- 2.** [dirty, unpleasant] sórdido(da).

sore [sɔː^r] ◇ *adj* **- 1.** [painful] dolorido(da); **to have a ~ throat** tener dolor de garganta **- 2.** *US* [upset] enfadado(da); **to get ~** enfadarse. ◇ *n* llaga *f*, úlcera *f*.

sorely ['sɔːlɪ] *adv literary* enormemente.

sorrow ['sɒrəʊ] *n* pesar *m*, pena *f*.

sorry ['sɒrɪ] (*compar* **-ier**, *superl* **-iest**) ◇ *adj* **- 1.** [expressing apology]: **to be ~ about sthg** sentir OR lamentar algo; **I'm ~ for what I did** siento lo que hice; **I'm ~** lo siento **- 2.** [expressing shame, disappointment]: **to be ~ that** sentir que; **we were ~ about his resignation** sentimos que dimitiera; **to be ~ for** arrepentirse de **- 3.** [expressing regret]: **I'm ~ to have to say that ...** siento tener que decir que ... **- 4.** [expressing pity]: **to be** OR **feel ~ for sb** sentir lástima por alguien **- 5.** [expressing polite disagreement]: **I'm ~, but ...** perdón, pero ... **- 6.** [poor, pitiable] lamentable, penoso(sa); **it was a ~ sight** tenía un aspecto horrible. ◇ *excl* **- 1.** [I apologise]: **sorry!** ¡perdón! **- 2.** [pardon]: **sorry?** ¿perdón? **- 3.** [to correct oneself]: **a girl, ~, a woman** una chica, perdón, una mujer.

sort [sɔːt] ◇ *n* tipo *m*, clase *f*; **what ~ of computer have you got?** ¿qué tipo de ordenador tienes?; **all ~s of** todo tipo de; **~ of** más o menos, así así; **a ~ of** una especie de; **she did nothing of the ~** no hizo nada por el estilo. ◇ *vt* clasificar.

◆ sort out *vt sep* **- 1.** [classify] clasificar **- 2.** [solve] solucionar, resolver.

sorting office ['sɔːtɪŋ-] *n* oficina de clasificación del correo.

SOS (*abbr of* **save our souls**) *n* SOS *m*; **to send an ~** lanzar un SOS.

so-so *adj* & *adv inf* así así.

soufflé ['suːfleɪ] *n* suflé *m*; **a cheese ~** un suflé de queso.

sought [sɔːt] *pt* & *pp* ▷ **seek**.

soul [səʊl] *n* **- 1.** [gen] alma *f* **- 2.** [music] música *f* soul.

soul-destroying [-dɪˌstrɔɪɪŋ] *adj* desmoralizador(ra).

soulful ['səʊlfʊl] *adj* lleno(na) de sentimiento.

sound [saʊnd] ◇ *adj* **- 1.** [healthy] sano(na) **- 2.** [sturdy] sólido(da) **- 3.** [reliable] fiable, seguro(ra). ◇ *adv*: **to be ~ asleep** estar profundamente dormido(da). ◇ *n* **- 1.** [gen] sonido *m* **- 2.** [particular noise] ruido *m* **- 3.** [impression]: **by the ~ of it** por lo que parece. ⬦ *vt* [bell etc] hacer sonar, tocar. ⬦ *vi* **- 1.** [gen] sonar **- 2.** [give impression]: **it ~s interesting** parece interesante; **it ~s like fun** suena divertido.

◆ **sound out** *vt sep*: **to ~ sb out (on OR about)** sondear a alguien (sobre).

sound barrier *n* barrera *f* del sonido.

sound card *n* COMPUT tarjeta *f* de sonido.

sound effects *npl* efectos *mpl* sonoros.

sounding ['saʊndɪŋ] *n* NAUT sondeo *m* marino.

soundly ['saʊndlɪ] *adv* **- 1.** [severely - beat] totalmente **- 2.** [deeply] profundamente.

soundproof ['saʊndpruːf] *adj* insonorizado(da).

soundtrack ['saʊndtræk] *n* banda *f* sonora.

soup [suːp] *n* [thick] sopa *f*; [clear] caldo *m*, consomé *m*.

soup plate *n* plato *m* hondo OR sopero.

soup spoon *n* cuchara *f* sopera.

sour [saʊəʳ] ⬦ *adj* **- 1.** [acidic] ácido(da) **- 2.** [milk, person, reply] agrio(gria). ⬦ *vt* agriar.

source [sɔːs] *n* **- 1.** [gen] fuente *f* **- 2.** [cause] origen *m*.

sour grapes *n (U) inf*: **it's ~ !** ¡están verdes!

south [saʊθ] ⬦ *n* **- 1.** [direction] sur *m* **- 2.** [region]: **the South** el sur. ⬦ *adj* del sur. ⬦ *adv*: **~ (of)** al sur (de).

South Africa *n*: **(the Republic of) ~** (la república de) Suráfrica.

South African ⬦ *adj* surafricano(na). ⬦ *n* [person] surafricano *m*, -na *f*.

South America *n* Sudamérica.

South American ⬦ *adj* sudamericano(na). ⬦ *n* [person] sudamericano *m*, -na *f*.

southeast [ˌsaʊθ'iːst] ⬦ *n* **- 1.** [direction] sudeste *m* **- 2.** [region]: **the Southeast** el sudeste. ⬦ *adj* del sudeste. ⬦ *adv*: **~ (of)** hacia el sudeste (de).

southerly ['sʌðəlɪ] *adj* del sur.

southern ['sʌðən] *adj* del sur, sureño(ña); **the ~ hemisphere** el hemisferio sur.

South Korea *n* Corea del Sur.

South Pole *n*: **the ~** el polo Sur.

southward ['saʊθwəd] ⬦ *adj* sur. ⬦ *adv* = **southwards**.

southwards ['saʊθwədz] *adv* hacia el sur.

southwest [ˌsaʊθ'west] ⬦ *n* **- 1.** [direction] suroeste *m* **- 2.** [region]: **the Southwest** el suroeste. ⬦ *adj* del suroeste. ⬦ *adv*: **~ (of)** hacia el suroeste (de).

souvenir [ˌsuːvə'nɪəʳ] *n* recuerdo *m*.

sovereign ['sɒvrɪn] ⬦ *adj* soberano(na). ⬦ *n* **- 1.** [ruler] soberano *m*, -na *f* **- 2.** [coin] soberano *m*.

Soviet ['səʊvɪət] ⬦ *adj* soviético(ca). ⬦ *n* [person] soviético *m*, -ca *f*.

Soviet Union *n*: **the (former) ~** la (antigua) Unión Soviética.

sow[1] [səʊ] (*pt* **-ed**, *pp* **sown** OR **-ed**) *vt lit & fig* sembrar.

sow[2] [saʊ] *n* cerda *f*, puerca *f*, chancha *f* *Amér.*

sown [səʊn] *pp* ▷ **sow**[1].

soya ['sɔɪə] *n* soja *f*.

soy(a) bean ['sɔɪ(ə)-] *n esp US* semilla *f* de soja, frijol *m* de soja *Amér*, poroto *m* de soja *Andes, CSur*.

spa [spɑː] *n* balneario *m*.

space [speɪs] ⬦ *n* espacio *m*; **there isn't enough ~ for it** no hay suficiente espacio para ello; **in the ~ of 30 minutes** en el espacio de 30 minutos. ⬦ *vt* espaciar.

◆ **space out** *vt sep* [arrange with spaces between] espaciar.

spacecraft ['speɪskrɑːft] (*pl inv*) *n* nave *f* espacial, astronave *f*.

spaceman ['speɪsmæn] (*pl* **-men** [-men]) *n* *inf* astronauta *m*.

spaceship ['speɪsʃɪp] *n* nave *f* espacial, astronave *f*.

space shuttle *n* transbordador *m* espacial.

spacesuit ['speɪssuːt] *n* traje *m* espacial.

spacing ['speɪsɪŋ] *n* TYPO espacio *m*; **double ~** doble espacio.

spacious ['speɪʃəs] *adj* espacioso(sa).

spade [speɪd] *n* [tool] pala *f*.

◆ **spades** *npl* picas *fpl*.

spaghetti [spə'getɪ] *n (U)* espaguetis *mpl*.

Spain [speɪn] *n* España.

spam [spæm] (*pt & pp* **-med**, *cont* **-ming**) COMPUT ⬦ *n* correo *m* basura. ⬦ *vt* enviar correo basura a.

span [spæn] (*pt & pp* **-ned**, *cont* **-ning**) ⬦ *pt* ▷ **spin**. ⬦ *n* **- 1.** [in time] lapso *m*, periodo *m* **- 2.** [range] gama *f* **- 3.** [of wings] envergadura *f* **- 4.** [of bridge, arch] ojo *m*. ⬦ *vt* **- 1.** [in time] abarcar **- 2.** [subj: bridge etc] cruzar, atravesar.

Spaniard ['spænjəd] *n* español *m*, -la *f*.

spaniel ['spænjəl] *n* perro *m* de aguas.

Spanish ['spænɪʃ] ⬦ *adj* español(la). ⬦ *n* [language] español *m*, castellano *m*. ⬦ *npl* [people]: **the ~** los españoles.

spank [spæŋk] *vt* dar unos azotes a.

spanner ['spænəʳ] *n* llave *f* inglesa.

spar [spɑːʳ] (*pt & pp* **-red**, *cont* **-ring**) ⬦ *n* palo *m*, verga *f*. ⬦ *vi* BOXING: **to ~ (with)** entrenarse (con).

spare [speəʳ] ⬦ *adj* **- 1.** [surplus] de sobra **- 2.** [free - chair, time] libre; **I've got a ~ pen you can borrow** tengo un bolígrafo de sobra que te puedo prestar; **have you got a ~ minute?** ¿tienes un minuto?; **there's one going ~** sobra uno **- 3.** *inf* [crazy] **to go ~** volverse loco(ca). ⬦ *n* **- 1.** [extra one] **I always carry a ~** siempre llevo uno de sobra **- 2.** *inf* [part] pieza *f* de recambio OR repuesto, refacción *f* *Chile & Méx*. ⬦ *vt* **- 1.** [time] conceder; [money] dejar; **we can't ~ any**

time/money no tenemos tiempo/dinero; **to ~ de sobra - 2.** [not harm - person, life] perdonar; **they ~d his life** le perdonaron la vida; [- company, city] salvar **- 3.** [not use, not take]: **to ~ no expense/effort** no escatimar gastos/esfuerzos **- 4.** [save from]: **to ~ sb sthg** ahorrarle a alguien algo; **you've ~d me the trouble** me has ahorrado la molestia.

spare part *n* AUT pieza *f* de recambio OR repuesto, refacción *f* Chile & Méx.

spare time *n* tiempo *m* libre.

spare wheel *n* rueda *f* de recambio.

sparing ['speəriŋ] *adj*: **to be ~ with** OR **of** ser parco(ca) en.

sparingly ['speəriŋli] *adv* con moderación.

spark [spɑːk] *n* lit & fig chispa *f*.

sparking plug ['spɑːkiŋ-] *UK* = **spark plug**.

sparkle ['spɑːkl] <> *n* (*U*) [of diamond] destello *m*; [of eyes] brillo *m*. <> *vi* [star, jewels] centellear; [eyes] brillar.

sparkling wine ['spɑːkliŋ-] *n* vino *m* espumoso.

spark plug *n* bujía *f*.

sparrow ['spærəʊ] *n* gorrión *m*.

sparse [spɑːs] *adj* escaso(sa).

spasm ['spæzm] *n* **- 1.** MED [state] espasmo *m* **- 2.** MED [attack] acceso *m*.

spastic ['spæstik] MED *n* espástico *m*, -ca *f*.

spat [spæt] *pt* & *pp* ⊳ **spit**.

spate [speit] *n* cadena *f*, serie *f*.

spatter ['spætər] *vt* salpicar.

spawn [spɔːn] <> *n* (*U*) huevas *fpl*. <> *vt* fig engendrar. <> *vi* desovar, frezar.

speak [spiːk] (*pt* spoke, *pp* spoken) <> *vt* **- 1.** [say] decir; **to ~ one's mind** decir lo que se piensa **- 2.** [language] hablar; **can you ~ French?** ¿hablas francés? <> *vi* hablar; **to ~ to** OR **with** hablar con; **to ~ to sb (about)** hablar con alguien (de); **to ~ about** hablar de; **to ~ sb (on sthg)** [give speech] hablar ante alguien (sobre algo); **we aren't ~ing** [we aren't friends] no nos hablamos; **is that Mrs Jones? – ~ ing!** ¿la señora Jones? – sí, soy yo.

◆ **so to speak** *adv* como quien dice, por así decirlo.

◆ **speak for** *vt fus* [represent] hablar en nombre de.

◆ **speak up** *vi* **- 1.** [speak out]: **to ~ up for** salir en defensa de **- 2.** [speak louder] hablar más alto.

speaker ['spiːkər] *n* **- 1.** [person talking] persona *f* que habla **- 2.** [person making a speech - at meal etc] orador *m*, -ra *f*; [- at conference] conferenciante *m* OR *f* **- 3.** [of a language] hablante *m* OR *f*; **English ~s** angloparlantes **- 4.** [of radio] altavoz *m*.

speaking ['spiːkiŋ] <> *adv*: **generally ~** en

general; **legally ~** desde una perspectiva legal. <> *adj*: **we are not on ~ terms** no nos dirigimos la palabra.

spear [spiər] <> *n* [gen] lanza *f*; [for hunting] jabalina *f*. <> *vt* [animal] atravesar; [piece of food] pinchar.

spearhead ['spiəhed] *vt* encabezar.

spec [spek] *n UK inf*: **to buy on ~** comprar sin garantías.

special ['speʃl] *adj* **- 1.** [gen] especial **- 2.** [particular, individual] particular.

special delivery *n* correo *m* urgente.

specialist ['speʃəlist] <> *adj* [doctor] especialista; [literature] especializado(da). <> *n* especialista *m* OR *f*.

speciality [,speʃi'æləti] (*pl* -ies), **specialty** *US* ['speʃlti] (*pl* -ies) *n* especialidad *f*.

specialize, -ise ['speʃəlaiz] *vi*: **to ~ (in)** especializarse (en).

specially ['speʃəli] *adv* especialmente.

special needs *npl*: **~ children** niños con necesidades especiales.

specialty *US* = **speciality**.

species ['spiːʃiːz] (*pl inv*) *n* especie *f*.

specific [spə'sifik] *adj* **- 1.** [particular] determinado(da) **- 2.** [precise] específico(ca) **- 3.** [unique]: **~ to** específico(ca) de.

specifically [spə'sifikli] *adv* **- 1.** [particularly] expresamente **- 2.** [precisely] específicamente.

specify ['spesifai] (*pt* & *pp* -ied) *vt*: **to ~ (that)** especificar (que).

specimen ['spesimən] *n* **- 1.** [example] espécimen *m*, ejemplar *m* **- 2.** [sample] muestra *f*.

speck [spek] *n* **- 1.** [small stain] manchita *f* **- 2.** [small particle] mota *f*.

speckled ['spekld] *adj*: **~ (with)** moteado(da) (de), con manchas (de).

specs [speks] *npl UK inf* [glasses] gafas *fpl*.

spectacle ['spektəkl] *n* [sight] espectáculo *m*; **to make a ~ of o.s.** dar el espectáculo.

◆ **spectacles** *npl UK* gafas *fpl*.

spectacular [spek'tækjʊlər] *adj* espectacular.

spectator [spek'teitər] *n* espectador *m*, -ra *f*.

spectre *UK*, **specter** *US* ['spektər] *n* lit & fig fantasma *m*.

spectrum ['spektrəm] (*pl* -tra [-trə]) *n* **- 1.** [gen] espectro *m* **- 2.** fig [variety] gama *f*, abanico *m*.

speculation [,spekjʊ'leiʃn] *n* especulación *f*.

sped [sped] *pt* & *pp* ⊳ **speed**.

speech [spiːtʃ] *n* **- 1.** [gen] habla *f* **- 2.** [formal talk] discurso *m* **- 3.** [manner of speaking] manera *f* de hablar **- 4.** [dialect] dialecto *m*, habla *f*.

speechless ['spiːtʃlis] *adj*: **to be ~ (with)** enmudecer (de).

speed [spiːd] (*pt* & *pp* -ed OR sped) <> *n*

- 1. [rate of movement] velocidad *f*; **at top ~** a toda velocidad; **at a ~ of 30 mph** a una velocidad de 30 millas por hora **- 2.** [rapidity] rapidez *f.* ◇ *vi* **- 1.** [move fast]**: to ~ (along/away/by)** ir/alejarse/pasar a toda velocidad; **to ~ by** [subj: hours, years] pasar volando **- 2.** AUT [go too fast] conducir con exceso de velocidad.

◆ **speed up** ◇ *vt sep* [gen] acelerar; [person] meter prisa a. ◇ *vi* [gen] acelerarse; [person] darse prisa.

speedboat ['spi:dbəʊt] *n* lancha *f* motora.

speed-dial button *n* [on phone, fax] botón *m* de marcado abreviado.

speeding ['spi:dɪŋ] *n (U)* exceso *m* de velocidad.

speed limit *n* límite *m* de velocidad.

speedometer [spɪ'dɒmɪtər] *n* velocímetro *m.*

speedway ['spi:dweɪ] *n* **- 1.** *(U)* SPORT carreras *fpl* de moto **- 2.** US [road] autopista *f.*

speedy ['spi:dɪ] *(compar* **-ier,** *superl* **-iest)** *adj* rápido(da).

spell [spel] *(UK pt & pp* spelt *OR* **-ed,** *US pt & pp* **-ed)** ◇ *n* **- 1.** [of time] temporada *f*; [of weather] racha *f*; **sunny ~s** intervalos de sol **- 2.** [enchantment] hechizo *m*; **to cast** *OR* **put a ~ on sb** hechizar a alguien **- 3.** [magic words] conjuro *m.* ◇ *vt* **- 1.** [form by writing] deletrear; **how do you ~ that?** ¿cómo se escribe eso? **- 2.** *fig* [signify] significar; **to ~ trouble** augurar problemas. ◇ *vi* escribir correctamente; **I can't ~** cometo muchas faltas de ortografía.

◆ **spell out** *vt sep* **- 1.** [read aloud] deletrear **- 2.** [explain]**: to ~ sthg out (for** *OR* **to sb)** decir algo por las claras (a alguien).

spellbinding *adj* fascinante.

spellbound ['spelbaʊnd] *adj* hechizado(da), embelesado(da); **to hold sb ~** tener hechizado(da) a alguien.

spellcheck ['speltʃek] *vt* COMPUT pasar el corrector ortográfico a.

spellchecker ['speltʃekər] *n* COMPUT corrector *m* ortográfico.

spelling ['spelɪŋ] *n* ortografía *f*; **the right/ wrong ~** la grafía correcta/incorrecta; **to be good at ~** tener buena ortografía; **~ mistake** falta *f* de ortografía.

spelt [spelt] *UK pt & pp* ▷ **spell.**

spend [spend] *(pt & pp* spent) *vt* **- 1.** [gen] gastar; **to ~ sthg on** gastar algo en **- 2.** [time, life] pasar; **to ~ one's time doing sth** pasar el tiempo haciendo algo.

spendthrift ['spendθrɪft] *n* derrochador *m*, -ra *f*, despilfarrador *m*, -ra *f.*

spent [spent] ◇ *pt & pp* ▷ **spend.** ◇ *adj* [matches, ammunition] usado(da); [patience] agotado(da).

sperm [spɜ:m] *(pl inv OR* **-s)** *n* esperma *m.*

spew [spju:] *vt* arrojar, escupir.

sphere [sfɪər] *n* **- 1.** [gen] esfera *f* **- 2.** [of people] círculo *m.*

spice [spaɪs] *n* CULIN especia *f.*

spick-and-span [,spɪkən'spæn] *adj* inmaculado(da).

spicy ['spaɪsɪ] *(compar* **-ier,** *superl* **-iest)** *adj* [hot and peppery] *fig* picante; [with spices] con muchas especias.

spider ['spaɪdər] *n* araña *f.*

spike [spaɪk] *n* **- 1.** [on railing etc] punta *f*; [on wall] clavo *m* **- 2.** [on plant] pincho *m*; [of hair] pelo *m* de punta.

spill [spɪl] *(UK pt & pp* spilt *OR* **-ed,** *US pt & pp* **-ed)** ◇ *vt* derramar, verter. ◇ *vi* [flow] derramarse, verterse.

spilt [spɪlt] *UK pt & pp* ▷ **spill.**

spin [spɪn] *(pt* span *OR* spun, *pp* spun, *cont* spinning) ◇ *n* **- 1.** [turn] vuelta *f* **- 2.** AERON barrena *f* **- 3.** *inf* [in car] vuelta *f*; **to go for a ~** ir a dar una vuelta. ◇ *vt* **- 1.** [cause to rotate] girar, dar vueltas a **- 2.** [clothes, washing] centrifugar **- 3.** [wool, yarn] hilar. ◇ *vi* [rotate] girar, dar vueltas; **to ~ out of control** [subj: vehicle] comenzar a dar trompos.

◆ **spin out** *vt sep* [story] alargar, prolongar; [money] estirar.

spinach ['spɪnɪdʒ] *n (U)* espinacas *fpl.*

spinal column ['spaɪnl-] *n* columna *f* vertebral.

spinal cord *n* médula *f* espinal.

spinal tap *n* US punción *f* lumbar.

spindly ['spɪndlɪ] *(compar* **-ier,** *superl* **-iest)** *adj* larguirucho(cha).

spin-dryer *n* UK centrifugadora *f.*

spine [spaɪn] *n* **- 1.** ANAT espina *f* dorsal *;* **- 2.** [of book] lomo *m* **- 3.** [spike, prickle] espina *f*, púa *f.*

spinning ['spɪnɪŋ] *n* hilado *m.*

spinning top *n* peonza *f.*

spin-off *n* [by-product] resultado *m* OR efecto *m* indirecto.

spinster ['spɪnstər] *n* soltera *f.*

spiral ['spaɪərəl] *(UK pt & pp* **-led,** *cont* **-ling,** *US pt & pp* **-ed,** *cont* **-ing)** ◇ *adj* en espiral. ◇ *n* [curve] espiral *f.* ◇ *vi* [move in spiral curve] moverse en espiral.

spiral staircase *n* escalera *f* de caracol.

spire [spaɪər] *n* aguja *f.*

spirit ['spɪrɪt] *n* **- 1.** [gen] espíritu *m* **- 2.** [vigour] vigor *m*, valor *m.*

◆ **spirits** *npl* **- 1.** [mood] humor *m*; **to be in high/low ~s** estar exultante/alicaído **- 2.** [alcohol] licores *mpl.*

spirit level *n* nivel *m* de burbuja de aire.

spiritual ['spɪrɪtʃʊəl] *adj* espiritual.

spit [spɪt] *(UK pt & pp* spat, *cont* **-ting,** *US pt & pp* spit, *cont* **-ting)** ◇ *n* **- 1.** [saliva] saliva *f* **- 2.** [skewer] asador *m.* ◇ *vi* escupir. ◇ *v* *impers UK* [rain lightly]: **it's spitting** está chispeando.

spite [spaɪt] ⬦ *n* rencor *m*. ⬦ *vt* fastidiar, molestar.

➡ **in spite of** *prep* a pesar de.

spiteful ['spaɪtfʊl] *adj* [person, behaviour] rencoroso(sa); [action, remark] malintencionado(da).

spittle ['spɪtl] *n* saliva *f*.

splash [splæʃ] ⬦ *n* **-1.** [sound] chapoteo *m* **-2.** [of colour, light] mancha *f*. ⬦ *vt* salpicar. ⬦ *vi* **-1.** [person]: **to ~ about** OR **around** chapotear **-2.** [water, liquid]: **to ~ on** OR **against sthg** salpicar algo.

➡ **splash out** *vi inf*: **to ~ out (on sthg)** gastar un dineral (en algo).

spleen [spli:n] *n* ANAT bazo *m*; *fig* [anger] cólera *f*.

splendid ['splendɪd] *adj* **-1.** [marvellous] espléndido(da) **-2.** [magnificent, beautiful] magnífico(ca).

splint [splɪnt] *n* tablilla *f*.

splinter ['splɪntə'] ⬦ *n* [of wood] astilla *f*; [of glass, metal] fragmento *m*. ⬦ *vi* astillarse.

split [splɪt] (*pt* & *pp* **split**, *cont* **-ting**) ⬦ *n* **-1.** [crack - in wood] grieta *f*; [- in garment] desgarrón *m* **-2.** [division]: **~ (in)** escisión *f* (en) **-3.** [difference]: **~ (between)** diferencia *f* (entre). ⬦ *vt* **-1.** [tear] desgarrar, rasgar; [crack] agrietar **-2.** [break in two] partir, romper **-3.** [party, organization] escindir **-4.** [share] repartir, dividir. ⬦ *vi* **-1.** [break up - road] bifurcarse; [- object] partirse, romperse **-2.** [party, organization] escindirse **-3.** [wood] partirse, agrietarse; [fabric] desgarrarse, rasgarse.

➡ **split up** *vi* separarse.

split second *n* fracción *f* de segundo; **for a ~** por una fracción de segundo.

split-second timing *n* precisión *f* milimétrica.

splutter ['splʌtə'] *vi* **-1.** [person] balbucear, farfullar **-2.** [fire, oil] chisporrotear.

spoil [spɔɪl] (*pt* & *pp* **-ed** OR **spoilt**) *vt* **-1.** [ruin] estropear, echar a perder **-2.** [child etc] mimar, regalonear *RP* & *Chile*.

➡ **spoils** *npl* botín *m*.

spoiled [spɔɪld] = **spoilt**.

spoiler ['spɔɪlə'] *n* COMPUT mensaje que contiene información sobre el contenido de una serie o película no estrenada todavía.

spoilsport ['spɔɪlspɔ:t] *n* aguafiestas *m* OR *f inv*.

spoilt [spɔɪlt] ⬦ *pt* & *pp* ⊳ **spoil**. ⬦ *adj* mimado(da), consentido(da), regalón(ona) *RP* & *Chile*.

spoke [spəʊk] ⬦ *pt* ⊳ **speak**. ⬦ *n* radio *m*.

spoken ['spəʊkn] *pp* ⊳ **speak**.

spokesman ['spəʊksmən] (*pl* **-men** [-mən]) *n* portavoz *m*.

spokeswoman ['spəʊks,wʊmən] (*pl* **-women** [-,wɪmɪn]) *n* portavoz *f*.

sponge [spʌndʒ] (*UK cont* **spongeing**, *US cont* **sponging**) ⬦ *n* **-1.** [for cleaning, washing] esponja *f* **-2.** [cake] bizcocho *m*. ⬦ *vt* limpiar con una esponja. ⬦ *vi inf*: **to ~ off** vivir a costa de.

sponge bag *n UK* neceser *m*.

sponge cake *n* bizcocho *m*, bizcochuelo *m CSur, Ven*.

sponsor ['spɒnsə'] ⬦ *n* patrocinador *m*, -ra *f*. ⬦ *vt* **-1.** [gen] patrocinar **-2.** [support] respaldar.

sponsored walk [,spɒnsəd-] *n* marcha *f* benéfica.

sponsorship ['spɒnsəʃɪp] *n* patrocinio *m*.

spontaneous [spɒn'teɪnjəs] *adj* espontáneo(a).

spooky ['spu:kɪ] (*compar* **-ier**, *superl* **-iest**) *adj inf* escalofriante, estremecedor(ra).

spool [spu:l] *n* [gen & COMPUT] bobina *f*.

spoon [spu:n] *n* **-1.** [piece of cutlery] cuchara *f* **-2.** [spoonful] cucharada *f*.

spoon-feed *vt* [feed with spoon] dar de comer con cuchara a.

spoonful ['spu:nfʊl] (*pl* **-s** OR **spoonsful** ['spu:nzfʊl]) *n* cucharada *f*.

sporadic [spə'rædɪk] *adj* esporádico(ca).

sport [spɔ:t] *n* [game] deporte *m*.

sporting ['spɔ:tɪŋ] *adj lit* & *fig* deportivo(va); **to give sb a ~ chance** dar a alguien la oportunidad de ganar.

sports car ['spɔ:ts-] *n* coche *m* deportivo, auto *m* sport *CSur*, carro *m* sport *Amér*.

sports jacket ['spɔ:ts-] *n* chaqueta *f* de esport.

sportsman ['spɔ:tsmən] (*pl* **-men** [-mən]) *n* deportista *m*.

sportsmanship ['spɔ:tsmənʃɪp] *n* deportividad *f*.

sportswear ['spɔ:tsweə'] *n* ropa *f* deportiva.

sportswoman ['spɔ:ts,wʊmən] (*pl* **-women** [-,wɪmɪn]) *n* deportista *f*.

sports utility vehicle *n US* todoterreno *m* utilitario.

sporty ['spɔ:tɪ] (*compar* **-ier**, *superl* **-iest**) *adj inf* [fond of sports] aficionado(da) a los deportes.

spot [spɒt] (*pt* & *pp* **-ted**, *cont* **-ting**) ⬦ *n* **-1.** [stain] mancha *f*, mota *f*; [dot] punto *m* **-2.** [pimple] grano *m* **-3.** [drop] gota *f* **-4.** *inf* [bit, small amount] pizca *f*, miaja *f* **-5.** [place] lugar *m*; **on the ~** en el lugar; **to do sthg on the ~** hacer algo en el acto **-6.** RADIO & TV espacio *m*. ⬦ *vt* [notice] notar, ver.

spot check *n* control *m* aleatorio.

spotless ['spɒtlɪs] *adj* [thing] inmaculado(-

da); [reputation] intachable.

spotlight ['spɒtlaɪt] n [of car] faro m auxiliar; [in theatre, home] foco m, reflector m de luz; **to be in the ~** fig ser el centro de atención.

spotted ['spɒtɪd] adj de lunares, moteado(da).

spotty ['spɒtɪ] (compar **-ier**, superl **-iest**) adj UK [skin] con granos.

spouse [spaʊs] n cónyuge m OR f.

spout [spaʊt] ⇔ n [of teapot] pitorro m; [of jug] pico m. ⇔ vi: **to ~ from** OR **out of** [liquid] salir a chorros de; [smoke, flames] salir incesantemente de.

sprain [spreɪn] ⇔ n torcedura f. ⇔ vt torcerse.

sprang [spræŋ] pt ⊳ **spring**.

sprawl [sprɔːl] vi [sit] repantigarse, arrellanarse; [lie] echarse, tumbarse.

spray [spreɪ] ⇔ n **-1.** [small drops - of liquid] rociada f; [- of sea] espuma f; [- of aerosol] pulverización f **-2.** [pressurized liquid] espray m **-3.** [can, container - gen] atomizador m; [- for garden] pulverizador m **-4.** [of flowers] ramo m. ⇔ vt rociar, vaporizar.

spread [spred] (pt & pp **spread**) ⇔ n **-1.** [soft food]: **cheese ~** queso m para untar **-2.** [of fire, disease] propagación f. ⇔ vt **-1.** [rug, tablecloth] extender; [map] desplegar **-2.** [legs, fingers etc] estirar **-3.** [butter, jam] untar; [glue] repartir; **to ~ sthg over sthg** extender algo por algo **-4.** [disease] propagar; [news] difundir, diseminar **-5.** [wealth, work] repartir equitativamente. ⇔ vi **-1.** [disease, fire, news] extenderse, propagarse **-2.** [gas, cloud] esparcirse.

➤ spread out vi diseminarse, dispersarse.

spread-eagled [-ˌiːgld] adj despatarrado(da).

spreadsheet ['spredʃiːt] n COMPUT hoja f de cálculo electrónica.

spree [spriː] n: **a killing ~** una matanza; **to go on a shopping ~** salir a comprar a lo loco.

sprightly ['spraɪtlɪ] (compar **-ier**, superl **-iest**) adj ágil, activo(va).

spring [sprɪŋ] (pt **sprang**, pp **sprung**) ⇔ n **-1.** [season] primavera f **-2.** [coil] muelle m **-3.** [jump] salto m **-4.** [water source] manantial m, vertiente f RP. ⇔ vi **-1.** [jump] saltar **-2.** [move suddenly] moverse de repente.

➤ spring up vi surgir de repente.

springboard ['sprɪŋbɔːd] n lit & fig trampolín m.

spring-clean vt limpiar a fondo.

spring-cleaning n limpieza f a fondo.

spring onion n UK cebolleta f.

springtime ['sprɪŋtaɪm] n: **in (the) ~** en primavera.

springy ['sprɪŋɪ] (compar **-ier**, superl **-iest**) adj [carpet, mattress, grass] mullido(da); [rubber] elástico(ca).

sprinkle ['sprɪŋkl] vt rociar, salpicar; **to ~ sthg over** OR **on sthg, to ~ sthg with sthg** rociar algo sobre algo.

sprinkler ['sprɪŋklə'] n aspersor m.

sprint [sprɪnt] ⇔ n **-1.** SPORT esprint m **-2.** [fast run] carrera f. ⇔ vi SPORT esprintar; [run fast] correr a toda velocidad.

sprout [spraʊt] ⇔ n **-1.** CULIN: **(Brussels) ~s** coles fpl de Bruselas **-2.** [shoot] brote m, retoño m. ⇔ vt [subj: plant] echar. ⇔ vi **-1.** [plants, vegetables] crecer **-2.** [leaves, shoots] brotar.

spruce [spruːs] ⇔ adj pulcro(cra). ⇔ n picea f.

➤ spruce up vt sep arreglar.

sprung [sprʌŋ] pp ⊳ **spring**.

spry [spraɪ] (compar **-ier**, superl **-iest**) adj ágil, activo(va).

spun [spʌn] pt & pp ⊳ **spin**.

spur [spɜːʳ] (pt & pp **-red**, cont **-ring**) ⇔ n **-1.** [incentive]: **~ (to sthg)** estímulo m (para conseguir algo) **-2.** [on rider's boot] espuela f. ⇔ vt [encourage]: **to ~ sb to do sthg** animar a alguien a hacer algo.

➤ on the spur of the moment adv sin pensarlo dos veces.

➤ spur on vt sep: **to ~ sb on** animar a alguien.

spurious ['spʊərɪəs] adj falso(sa).

spurn [spɜːn] vt rechazar.

spurt [spɜːt] ⇔ n **-1.** [of water] chorro m; [of flame] llamarada f **-2.** [of activity, effort] arranque m **-3.** [of speed] acelerón m. ⇔ vi [gush]: **to ~ (out of** OR **from)** [liquid] salir a chorros de; [flame] salir incesantemente de.

spy [spaɪ] (pl **spies**, pt & pp **-ied**) ⇔ n espía m OR f. ⇔ vt inf divisar. ⇔ vi: **to ~ (on)** espiar (a), aguaitar (a) Amér.

spying ['spaɪɪŋ] n espionaje m.

Sq., sq. abbr of **square**.

squabble ['skwɒbl] ⇔ n riña f. ⇔ vi: **to ~ (about** OR **over)** reñir (por).

squad [skwɒd] n **-1.** [of police] brigada f **-2.** MIL pelotón m **-3.** [SPORT - of club] plantilla f, equipo m completo; [- of national team] seleccionado m; **the England ~** el equipo inglés.

squadron ['skwɒdrən] n [of planes] escuadrilla f; [of warships] escuadra f; [of soldiers] escuadrón m.

squalid ['skwɒlɪd] adj [filthy] miserable, sórdido(da).

squall [skwɔːl] n [storm] turbión m.

squalor ['skwɒlə'] n (U) miseria f.

squander ['skwɒndə'] vt [opportunity] desaprovechar; [money] despilfarrar; [resources] malgastar.

square [skweə^r] ◇ *adj* - **1.** [gen] cuadrado(-da); **4 ~ metres** 4 metros cuadrados; **the kitchen is 4 metres ~** la cocina mide 4 metros por 4 - **2.** [not owing money]: **we're ~ now** ya estamos en paz. ◇ *n* - **1.** [shape] cuadrado *m* - **2.** [in town, city] plaza *f* - **3.** *inf* [unfashionable person] carroza *m* OR *f*. ◇ *vt* - **1.** MATH elevar al cuadrado - **2.** [balance, reconcile]: **how can you ~ that with your principles?** ¿cómo encajas esto con tus principios?

◆ **square up** *vi* [settle up]: **to ~ up with** saldar cuentas con.

squarely ['skweəlɪ] *adv* [directly] justo, exactamente.

square meal *n* comida *f* satisfactoria.

squash [skwɒʃ] ◇ *n* - **1.** [game] squash *m* - **2.** *UK* [drink] zumo *m* - **3.** *US* [vegetable] cucurbitácea *f*. ◇ *vt* [squeeze, flatten] aplastar.

squat [skwɒt] (*compar* -**ter**, *superl* -**test**, *pt* & *pp* -**ted**, *cont* -**ting**) ◇ *adj* achaparrado(-da). ◇ *vi* [crouch]: **to ~ (down)** agacharse, ponerse en cuclillas.

squatter ['skwɒtə^r] *n UK* ocupante *m* OR *f* ilegal, squatter *m* OR *f*.

squawk [skwɔ:k] *n* [of bird] graznido *m*, chillido *m*.

squeak [skwi:k] *n* - **1.** [of animal] chillido *m* - **2.** [of hinge] chirrido *m*.

squeaky clean *adj* [hair] impoluto(ta).

squeal [skwi:l] *vi* - **1.** [person, animal] chillar, gritar - **2.** [brakes] chirriar.

squeamish ['skwi:mɪʃ] *adj* aprensivo(va).

squeeze [skwi:z] ◇ *n* [pressure] apretón *m*. ◇ *vt* - **1.** [press firmly] apretar - **2.** [force out - toothpaste] sacar (estrujando); [- juice] exprimir - **3.** [cram]: **to ~ sthg into sthg** [into place] conseguir meter algo en algo; [into time] arreglárselas para hacer algo en algo.

squelch [skweltʃ] *vi*: **to ~ through mud** cruzar el barro chapoteando.

squid [skwɪd] (*pl inv* OR -**s**) *n* - **1.** ZOOL calamar *m* - **2.** (U) [food] calamares *mpl*.

squiggle ['skwɪgl] *n* garabato *m*.

squint [skwɪnt] ◇ *n* estrabismo *m*, bizquera *f*. ◇ *vi*: **to ~ at** mirar con los ojos entrecerrados.

squire ['skwaɪə^r] *n* [landowner] terrateniente *m* OR *f*.

squirm [skwɜ:m] *vi* [wriggle] retorcerse.

squirrel [*UK* 'skwɪrəl, *US* 'skwɜ:rəl] *n* ardilla *f*.

squirt [skwɜ:t] ◇ *vt* [force out] sacar a chorro de. ◇ *vi*: **to ~ out of** salir a chorro.

Sr *abbr of* **senior**.

Sri Lanka [ˌsri:'læŋkə] *n* Sri Lanka.

St - **1.** (*abbr of* **saint**) Sto. (Sta.) - **2.** (*abbr of* **Street**) c/.

stab [stæb] (*pt* & *pp* -**bed**, *cont* -**bing**) ◇ *n* - **1.** [with knife] puñalada *f* - **2.** *inf* [attempt]: **to have a ~ (at sthg)** probar (a hacer algo) - **3.** [twinge] punzada *f*. ◇ *vt* - **1.** [with knife] apuñalar - **2.** [jab] pinchar.

stable ['steɪbl] ◇ *adj* - **1.** [unchanging] estable - **2.** [not moving] fijo(ja) - **3.** MED [condition] estacionario(ria); [mental health] equilibrado(da). ◇ *n* [building] cuadra *f*.

stack [stæk] ◇ *n* [pile] pila *m*. ◇ *vt* [pile up] apilar.

stadium ['steɪdjəm] (*pl* -**diums** OR -**dia** [-djə]) *n* estadio *m*.

staff [stɑ:f] ◇ *n* [employees] empleados *mpl*, personal *m*. ◇ *vt*: **the shop is ~ed by women** la tienda está llevada por una plantilla de mujeres.

stag [stæg] (*pl inv* OR -**s**) *n* ciervo *m*, venado *m*.

stage [steɪdʒ] ◇ *n* - **1.** [part of process, phase] etapa *f*; **to do sthg in ~s** hacer algo por etapas - **2.** [in theatre, hall] escenario *m*, escena *f* - **3.** [acting profession]: **the ~** el teatro. ◇ *vt* - **1.** THEATRE representar - **2.** [event, strike] organizar.

stagecoach ['steɪdʒkəʊtʃ] *n* diligencia *f*.

stage fright *n* miedo *m* al público.

stage-manage *vt* - **1.** THEATRE dirigir - **2.** *fig* [orchestrate] urdir, maquinar.

stagger ['stægə^r] ◇ *vt* - **1.** [astound] dejar atónito(ta); **to be ~ed by sthg** quedarse pasmado(da) por algo - **2.** [arrange at different times] escalonar. ◇ *vi* tambalearse.

stagnant ['stægnənt] *adj* lit & fig estancado(da).

stagnate [stæg'neɪt] *vi* estancarse.

stag party *n* despedida *f* de soltero.

staid [steɪd] *adj* recatado y conservador (recatada y conservadora).

stain [steɪn] ◇ *n* mancha *f*. ◇ *vt* manchar.

stained glass [ˌsteɪnd-] *n* (U) vidrio *m* de color; **~ window** vidriera *f*.

stainless steel [ˌsteɪnlɪs-] *n* acero *m* inoxidable.

stain remover [-rɪˌmu:və^r] *n* quitamanchas *m inv*.

stair [steə^r] *n* peldaño *m*, escalón *m*.

◆ **stairs** *npl* escaleras *fpl*, escalera *f*.

staircase ['steəkeɪs] *n* escalera *f*.

stairway ['steəweɪ] *n* escalera *f*.

stairwell ['steəwel] *n* hueco *m* OR caja *f* de la escalera.

stake [steɪk] ◇ *n* - **1.** [share]: **to have a ~ in** tener intereses en - **2.** [wooden post] estaca *f* - **3.** [in gambling] apuesta *f*. ◇ *vt* - **1.** [risk]: **to ~ sthg (on** OR **upon)** arriesgar OR jugarse algo (en) - **2.** [in gambling] apostar.

◆ **at stake** *adv*: **to be at ~** estar en juego.

stale [steɪl] *adj* [bread] duro(ra); [food] rancio(cia), pasado(da); [air] viciado(da).

stalemate ['steɪlmeɪt] *n* - **1.** [deadlock]

punto *m* muerto **- 2.** CHESS tablas *fpl*.

stalk [stɔːk] ◇ *n* **-1.** [of flower, plant] tallo *m* **- 2.** [of leaf, fruit] pecíolo *m*, rabillo *m*. ◇ *vt* [hunt] acechar, seguir sigilosamente. ◇ *vi*: **to ~ in/out** entrar/salir con paso airado.

stall [stɔːl] ◇ *n* [in market, at exhibition] puesto *m*, caseta *f*. ◇ *vt* AUT calar. ◇ *vi* **-1.** AUT calarse **- 2.** [delay] andar con evasivas.

➭ **stalls** *npl* UK platea *f*.

stallion ['stæljən] *n* semental *m*.

stalwart ['stɔːlwət] *n* partidario *m*, -ria *f* incondicional.

stamina ['stæmɪnə] *n* resistencia *f*.

stammer ['stæmə'] ◇ *n* tartamudeo *m*. ◇ *vi* tartamudear.

stamp [stæmp] ◇ *n* **-1.** [gen] sello *m*, estampilla *f* Amér, timbre *m* Méx **- 2.** [tool] tampón *m*. ◇ *vt* **-1.** [mark by stamping] timbrar, sellar **- 2.** [stomp]: **to ~ one's feet** patear. ◇ *vi* **-1.** [stomp] patalear, dar patadas **- 2.** [tread heavily]: **to ~ on sthg** pisotear OR pisar algo.

stamp album *n* álbum *m* de sellos OR de estampillas Amér OR de timbres Méx.

stamp collecting [-kə‚lektɪŋ] *n* filatelia *f*.

stamped addressed envelope ['stæmptə‚drest-] *n* UK sobre con sus señas y franqueo.

stampede [stæm'piːd] ◇ *n* lit & fig estampida *f*, desbandada *f*. ◇ *vi* salir de estampida.

stance [stæns] *n* **-1.** [way of standing] postura *f* **- 2.** [attitude]: **~ (on)** postura *f* (ante).

stand [stænd] (*pt* & *pp* **stood**) ◇ *n* **-1.** [stall] puesto *m*; [selling newspapers] quiosco *m* **- 2.** [supporting object] soporte *m*; **coat ~** perchero *m* **- 3.** SPORT tribuna *f*; **the ~s** las gradas **- 4.** [act of defence]: **to make a ~** resistir al enemigo **- 5.** [publicly stated view] postura *f* **- 6.** US JUR estrado *m*. ◇ *vt* **-1.** [place upright] colocar (verticalmente) **- 2.** [withstand, tolerate] soportar; **I can't ~ that woman** no soporto a esa mujer; **he can't ~ being beaten** odia perder. ◇ *vi* **-1.** [be upright - person] estar de pie; [- object] estar *(en posición vertical)*; **try to ~ still** procura no moverte; **he doesn't let anything ~ in his way** no deja que nada se interponga en su camino **- 2.** [get to one's feet] ponerse de pie, levantarse **- 3.** [liquid] reposar **- 4.** [still be valid] seguir vigente OR en pie **- 5.** [be in particular state]: **as things ~** tal como están las cosas **- 6.** UK POL [be a candidate] presentarse; **to ~ for Parliament** presentarse a las elecciones al Parlamento **- 7.** US AUT: **'no ~ing'** 'prohibido aparcar'.

➭ **stand back** *vi* echarse para atrás.

➭ **stand by** ◇ *vt fus* **-1.** [person] seguir al

lado de **- 2.** [promise, decision] mantener. ◇ *vi* **-1.** [in readiness]: **to ~ by (for sthg/ to do sthg)** estar preparado(da) (para algo/para hacer algo) **- 2.** [remain inactive] quedarse sin hacer nada.

➭ **stand down** *vi* [resign] retirarse.

➭ **stand for** *vt fus* **-1.** [signify] significar; **PTO ~s for 'please turn over'** PTO quiere decir 'sigue' **- 2.** [tolerate] aguantar, tolerar; **I won't ~ for it!** ¡no pienso aguantarlo!

➭ **stand in** *vi*: **to ~ in for sb** sustituir a alguien.

➭ **stand out** *vi* sobresalir, destacarse.

➭ **stand up** ◇ *vt sep inf* [boyfriend etc] dejar plantado(da). ◇ *vi* [rise from seat] levantarse, pararse Amér.

➭ **stand up for** *vt fus* salir en defensa de.

➭ **stand up to** *vt fus* **-1.** [weather, heat etc] resistir **- 2.** [person] hacer frente a.

standard ['stændəd] ◇ *adj* **-1.** [normal] corriente, estándar **- 2.** [accepted] establecido(da). ◇ *n* **-1.** [acceptable level] nivel *m*; **to be of a high ~** ser de un excelente nivel; **it's below ~** está por debajo del nivel exigido **- 2.** [point of reference - moral] criterio *m*; [- technical] norma *f* **- 3.** [flag] bandera *f*, estandarte *m*.

➭ **standards** *npl* [principles] valores *mpl* morales.

standard lamp *n* UK lámpara *f* de pie.

standard of living (*pl* **standards of living**) *n* nivel *m* de vida.

standby ['stændbaɪ] (*pl* **standbys**) ◇ *n* recurso *m*; **to be on ~** estar preparado(da). ◇ *comp*: **~ ticket** billete *m* en lista de espera.

stand-in *n* [stuntman] doble *m* OR *f*; [temporary replacement] sustituto *m*, -ta *f*.

standing ['stændɪŋ] ◇ *adj* [permanent] permanente. ◇ *n* **-1.** [reputation] reputación *f* **- 2.** [duration] duración *f*; **friends of 20 years' ~** amigos desde hace 20 años.

standing order *n* domiciliación *f* de pago Esp, débito *m* bancario Amér.

standing room *n* (U) [on bus] sitio *m* para estar de pie, sitio *m* para ir parado Amér; [at theatre, sports ground] localidades *fpl* de pie.

stand-off *n* US SPORT [tie] empate *m*.

standoffish [‚stænd'ɒfɪʃ] *adj* distante.

standpoint ['stændpɔɪnt] *n* punto *m* de vista.

standstill ['stændstɪl] *n*: **at a ~** [not moving] parado(da); fig [not active] en un punto muerto, estancado(da); **to come to a ~** [stop moving] pararse; fig [cease] llegar a un punto muerto, estancarse.

stand-up *adj* US [decent, honest]: **a ~ guy** un tipo decente.

stank [stæŋk] *pt* ⊳ **stink**.

staple ['steɪpl] ◇ *adj* [principal] básico(-

ca), de primera necesidad. ◇ *n* -1. [item of stationery] grapa *f*, corchete *m* *Chile* -2. [principal commodity] producto *m* básico OR de primera necesidad. ◇ *vt* grapar, corchetear *Chile*.

stapler ['steɪplə'] *n* grapadora *f*, corchetera *f* *Chile*.

star [stɑː'] (*pt* & *pp* **-red**, *cont* **-ring**) ◇ *n* [gen] estrella *f*. ◇ *comp* estelar. ◇ *vi*: to ~ **(in)** hacer de protagonista en.
◆ **stars** *npl* horóscopo *m*.

starboard ['stɑːbəd] ◇ *adj* de estribor. ◇ *n*: to ~ a estribor.

starch [stɑːtʃ] *n* -1. [gen] almidón *m* -2. [in potatoes etc] fécula *f*.

stardom ['stɑːdəm] *n* estrellato *m*.

stare [steə'] ◇ *n* mirada *f* fija. ◇ *vi*: to ~ **(at sthg/sb)** mirar fijamente (algo/a alguien).

stark [stɑːk] ◇ *adj* -1. [landscape, decoration, room] austero(ra) -2. [harsh - reality] crudo(da). ◇ *adv*: ~ **naked** en cueros.

starling ['stɑːlɪŋ] *n* estornino *m*.

starry ['stɑːrɪ] (*compar* **-ier**, *superl* **-iest**) *adj* estrellado(da), lleno(na) de estrellas.

starry-eyed [-'aɪd] *adj* [optimism etc] iluso(sa); [lovers] encandilado(da).

Stars and Stripes *n*: the ~ la bandera de las barras y estrellas.

start [stɑːt] ◇ *n* -1. [beginning] principio *m*, comienzo *m*; at the ~ of the year a principios de año -2. [jerk, jump] sobresalto *m*, susto *m* -3. [starting place] salida *f* -4. [time advantage] ventaja *f*. ◇ *vt* -1. [begin] empezar, comenzar; to ~ doing OR to do sthg empezar a hacer algo -2. [turn on - machine, engine] poner en marcha; [- vehicle] arrancar -3. [set up] formar, crear; [business] montar. ◇ *vi* -1. [begin] empezar, comenzar; to ~ with sb/sthg empezar por alguien/algo; **don't** ~**!** *inf* ¡no empieces! -2. [machine, tape] ponerse en marcha; [vehicle] arrancar -3. [begin journey] salir, ponerse en camino -4. [jerk, jump] asustarse, sobresaltarse.
◆ **start off** ◇ *vt sep* [discussion, rumour] desencadenar; [meeting] empezar; [person]: this should be enough to ~ you off con esto tienes suficiente para empezar. ◇ *vi* -1. [begin] empezar, comenzar -2. [leave on journey] salir, ponerse en camino.
◆ **start out** *vi* -1. [originally be] empezar, comenzar; she ~ed out as a journalist empezó como periodista -2. [leave on journey] salir ponerse en camino.
◆ **start up** ◇ *vt sep* -1. [business] montar; [shop] establecer, poner; [association] crear, formar -2. [car, engine] arrancar, poner en marcha. ◇ *vi* -1. [begin] empezar

-2. [car, engine] arrancar, ponerse en marcha.

starter ['stɑːtə'] *n* -1. *UK* [of meal] primer plato *m*, entrada *f* -2. AUT (motor *m* de) arranque *m* -3. [person participating in race] participante *m* OR *f*, competidor *m*, -ra *f*.

starting point ['stɑːtɪŋ-] *n* lit & fig punto *m* de partida.

startle ['stɑːtl] *vt* asustar.

startling ['stɑːtlɪŋ] *adj* sorprendente, asombroso(sa).

starvation [stɑː'veɪʃn] *n* hambre *f*, inanición *f*.

starve [stɑːv] ◇ *vt* [deprive of food] privar de comida, no dar de comer a. ◇ *vi* -1. [have no food] pasar hambre; to ~ to **death** morirse de hambre -2. *inf* [be hungry]: I'm **starving!** ¡me muero de hambre!

state [steɪt] ◇ *n* estado *m*; not to be in a fit ~ **to do sthg** no estar en condiciones de hacer algo; to be in a ~ [nervous] tener los nervios de punta; [untidy] estar hecho un asco. ◇ *comp* [ceremony] oficial, de Estado; [control, ownership] estatal. ◇ *vt* -1. [gen] indicar; [reason, policy] plantear; [case] exponer -2. [time, date, amount] fijar.
◆ **State** *n*: the State el Estado.
◆ **States** *npl*: the States los Estados Unidos.

State Department *n US* ≃ Ministerio *m* de Asuntos Exteriores.

stately ['steɪtlɪ] (*compar* **-ier**, *superl* **-iest**) *adj* majestuoso(sa).

statement ['steɪtmənt] *n* -1. [gen] declaración *f* -2. [from bank] extracto *m* OR estado *m* de cuenta.

state of mind (*pl* states of mind) *n* estado *m* de ánimo.

statesman ['steɪtsmən] (*pl* **-men** [-mən]) *n* estadista *m*, hombre *m* de Estado.

static ['stætɪk] ◇ *adj* estático(ca). ◇ *n* (*U*) interferencias *fpl*, parásitos *mpl*.

static electricity *n* electricidad *f* estática.

station ['steɪʃn] ◇ *n* -1. [gen] estación *f* -2. RADIO emisora *f* -3. [centre of activity] centro *m*, puesto *m* -4. *fml* [rank] rango *m*. ◇ *vt* -1. [position] situar, colocar -2. MIL estacionar, apostar.

stationary ['steɪʃnərɪ] *adj* inmóvil.

stationer's (shop) ['steɪʃnə'z] *n* papelería *f*.

stationery ['steɪʃnərɪ] *n* (*U*) objetos *mpl* de escritorio.

stationmaster ['steɪʃn,mɑːstə'] *n* jefe *m* de estación.

station wagon *n US* ranchera *f*.

statistic [stə'tɪstɪk] *n* estadística *f*.
◆ **statistics** *n* (*U*) estadística *f*.

statistical [stə'tɪstɪkl] *adj* estadístico(ca).

statue ['stætʃuː] *n* estatua *f*.

stature ['stætʃəʳ] n - 1. [height] estatura f, talla f - 2. [importance] talla f, categoría f.

status ['steɪtəs] n (U) - 1. [position, condition] condición f, estado m - 2. [prestige] prestigio m, estatus m inv.

status bar n COMPUT barra f de estado.

status symbol n símbolo m de posición social.

statute ['stætʃuːt] n estatuto m.

statutory ['stætjʊtrɪ] adj reglamentario(-ria).

staunch [stɔːntʃ] ⬦ adj fiel, leal. ⬦ vt restañar.

stave [steɪv] (pt & pp **-d** OR **stove**) n MUS pentagrama m.

➡️ **stave off** vt sep [disaster, defeat] retrasar; [hunger, illness] aplacar temporalmente.

stay [steɪ] ⬦ vi - 1. [not move away] quedarse, permanecer; **to ~ put** permanecer en el mismo sitio - 2. [as visitor] alojarse, estar - 3. [continue, remain] permanecer. ⬦ n estancia f, permanencia f.

➡️ **stay in** vi quedarse en casa.

➡️ **stay on** vi permanecer, quedarse.

➡️ **stay out** vi [from home] quedarse fuera, no volver a casa.

➡️ **stay up** vi quedarse levantado(da).

staying power ['steɪɪŋ-] n resistencia f.

stead [sted] n: **to stand sb in good ~** servir de mucho a alguien.

steadfast ['stedfɑːst] adj [supporter] fiel, leal; [gaze] fijo(ja), imperturbable; [resolve] inquebrantable.

steadily ['stedɪlɪ] adv - 1. [gradually] constantemente - 2. [regularly - breathe, move] normalmente - 3. [calmly - look] fijamente; [- speak] con tranquilidad.

steady ['stedɪ] (compar **-ier**, superl **-iest**, pt & pp **-ied**) ⬦ adj - 1. [gradual] gradual - 2. [regular, constant] constante, continuo(-nua) - 3. [not shaking] firme - 4. [voice] sereno(na); [stare] fijo(ja) - 5. [relationship] estable, serio(ria); [boyfriend, girlfriend] formal; **a ~ job** un trabajo fijo - 6. [reliable, sensible] sensato(ta). ⬦ vt - 1. [stop shaking] mantener firme; **to ~ o.s.** dejar de temblar - 2. [nerves, voice] dominar, controlar.

steak [steɪk] n - 1. (U) [meat] bistec m, filete m, bife m Andes, RP - 2. [piece of meat, fish] filete m.

steal [stiːl] (pt **stole**, pp **stolen**) ⬦ vt [gen] robar; [idea] apropiarse de; **to ~ sthg from sb** robar algo a alguien. ⬦ vi [move secretly] moverse sigilosamente; **he stole into the bedroom** entró sigilosamente en el dormitorio.

stealthy ['stelθɪ] (compar **-ier**, superl **-iest**) adj cauteloso(sa), sigiloso(sa).

steam [stiːm] ⬦ n (U) vapor m, vaho m. ⬦ vt CULIN cocer al vapor. ⬦ vi [water, food] echar vapor.

➡️ **steam up** ⬦ vt sep [mist up] empañar. ⬦ vi empañarse.

steamboat ['stiːmbəʊt] n buque m de vapor.

steam engine n máquina f de vapor.

steamer ['stiːməʳ] n [ship] buque m de vapor.

steamroller ['stiːm,rəʊləʳ] n apisonadora f.

steamy ['stiːmɪ] (compar **-ier**, superl **-iest**) adj - 1. [full of steam] lleno(na) de vaho - 2. inf [erotic] caliente, erótico(ca).

steel [stiːl] n acero m.

steelworks ['stiːlwɜːks] (pl inv) n fundición f de acero.

steep [stiːp] ⬦ adj - 1. [hill, road] empinado(da) - 2. [considerable - increase, fall] importante, considerable - 3. inf [expensive] muy caro(ra), abusivo(va). ⬦ vt remojar.

steeple ['stiːpl] n aguja f (de un campanario).

steeplechase ['stiːpltʃeɪs] n carrera f de obstáculos.

steer ['stɪəʳ] ⬦ n buey m. ⬦ vt - 1. [vehicle] conducir - 2. [person, discussion etc] dirigir. ⬦ vi: **the car ~s well** el coche se conduce bien; **to ~ clear of sthg/sb** evitar algo/a alguien.

steering ['stɪərɪŋ] n (U) dirección f.

steering wheel n volante m, timón m Andes.

stem [stem] (pt & pp **-med**, cont **-ming**) ⬦ n - 1. [of plant] tallo m - 2. [of glass] pie m - 3. GRAMM raíz f. ⬦ vt [flow] contener; [blood] detener, restañar.

➡️ **stem from** vt fus derivarse de, ser el resultado de.

stench [stentʃ] n hedor m.

stencil ['stensl] (UK pt & pp **-led**, cont **-ling**, US pt & pp **-ed**, cont **-ing**) ⬦ n plantilla f. ⬦ vt estarcir.

stenographer [stə'nɒgrəfəʳ] n US taquígrafo m, -fa f.

step [step] (pt & pp **-ped**, cont **-ping**) ⬦ n - 1. [gen] paso m; **~ by ~** paso a paso; **to be in/out of ~** llevar/no llevar el paso; fig estar/no estar al tanto - 2. [action] medida f; **to take ~s to do sthg** tomar medidas para hacer algo - 3. [stair, rung] peldaño m. ⬦ vi - 1. [move foot] dar un paso; **he stepped off the bus** se bajó del autobús - 2. [tread]: **to ~ on sthg** pisar algo; **to ~ in sthg** meter el pie en algo.

➡️ **steps** npl - 1. [escaleras fpl - 2. UK [stepladder] escalera f de tijera.

➡️ **step down** vi [leave job] renunciar.

➡️ **step in** vi intervenir.

➡️ **step up** vt sep aumentar.

stepbrother ['step,brʌðəʳ] n hermanastro m.

stepdaughter ['step,dɔ:tə^r] *n* hijastra *f*.

stepfather ['step,fɑ:ðə^r] *n* padrastro *m*.

stepladder ['step,lædə^r] *n* escalera *f* de tijera.

stepmother ['step,mʌðə^r] *n* madrastra *f*.

stepping-stone ['stepɪŋ-] *n* [in river] pasadera *f*.

stepsister ['step,sɪstə^r] *n* hermanastra *f*.

stepson ['stepsʌn] *n* hijastro *m*.

stereo ['sterɪəʊ] (*pl* -s) ⬦ *adj* estéreo *(inv)*. ⬦ *n* - 1. [record player] equipo *m* estereofónico - 2. [stereo sound] estéreo *m*.

stereotype ['sterɪətaɪp] *n* estereotipo *m*.

sterile ['steraɪl] *adj* - 1. [germ-free] esterilizado(da) - 2. [unable to produce offspring] estéril.

sterilize, -ise ['sterəlaɪz] *vt* esterilizar.

sterling ['stɜ:lɪŋ] ⬦ *adj* - 1. FIN esterlina - 2. [excellent] excelente. ⬦ *n* (U) libra *f* esterlina.

sterling silver *n* plata *f* de ley.

stern [stɜ:n] ⬦ *adj* severo(ra). ⬦ *n* popa *f*.

steroid ['stɪərɔɪd] *n* esteroide *m*.

stethoscope ['steθəskəʊp] *n* estetoscopio *m*.

stew [stju:] ⬦ *n* estofado *m*, guisado *m*. ⬦ *vt* [meat, vegetables] estofar, guisar; [fruit] hacer una compota de.

steward ['stjʊəd] *n* [on plane] auxiliar *m* de vuelo; [on ship, train] camarero *m*.

stewardess ['stjʊədɪs] *n* auxiliar *f* de vuelo, azafata *f*.

stick [stɪk] (*pt* & *pp* **stuck**) ⬦ *n* - 1. [of wood, for playing sport] palo *m* - 2. [of dynamite] cartucho *m*; [of rock] barra *f* - 3. [walking stick] bastón *m*. ⬦ *vt* - 1. [push]: **to ~ sthg in** OR **into sthg** [knife, pin] clavar algo en algo; [finger] meter algo en algo - 2. [make adhere]: **to ~ sthg (on** OR **to sthg)** pegar algo (en algo) - 3. *inf* [put] meter - 4. *UK inf* [tolerate] soportar, aguantar. ⬦ *vi* - 1. [adhere]: **to ~ (to)** pegarse (a) - 2. [jam] atrancarse.
◆ stick out ⬦ *vt sep* - 1. [make protrude] sacar; **to ~ one's tongue out** sacar la lengua - 2. [endure] aguantar. ⬦ *vi* [protrude] sobresalir.
◆ stick to *vt fus* - 1. [follow closely] seguir - 2. [principles] ser fiel a; [promise, agreement] cumplir con; [decision] atenerse a.
◆ stick up *vi* salir, sobresalir.
◆ stick up for *vt fus* defender.

stickball ['stɪkbɔ:l] *n* US béisbol *m* callejero.

sticker ['stɪkə^r] *n* [piece of paper] pegatina *f*.

sticking plaster ['stɪkɪŋ-] *n* - 1. [individual] curita® *f*, tirita® *f* - 2. [tape] esparadrapo *m* Amér, tela *f* emplástica CSur.

stickler ['stɪklə^r] *n*: **~ for sthg** maniático *m*, -ca *f* de algo.

stick shift *n* US palanca *f* de cambios.

stick-up *n inf* atraco *m* a mano armada.

sticky ['stɪkɪ] (*compar* -ier, *superl* -iest) *adj* - 1. [tacky] pegajoso(sa) - 2. [adhesive] adhesivo(va) - 3. *inf* [awkward] engorroso(sa).

stiff [stɪf] ⬦ *adj* - 1. [inflexible] rígido(da) - 2. [door, drawer] atascado(da) - 3. [aching] agarrotado(da); **to have a ~ neck** tener tortícolis; **to be ~** tener agujetas - 4. [formal - person, manner] estirado(da); [- smile] rígido(da) - 5. [severe, intense] severo(ra) - 6. [difficult - task] duro(ra). ⬦ *adv inf*: **bored/frozen ~** muerto(ta) de aburrimiento/frío.

stiffen ['stɪfn] *vi* - 1. [become inflexible] endurecerse - 2. [bones] entumecerse; [muscles] agarrotarse - 3. [become more severe, intense] intensificarse, endurecerse.

stifle ['staɪfl] *vt* - 1. [prevent from breathing] ahogar, sofocar - 2. [yawn etc] reprimir.

stifling ['staɪflɪŋ] *adj* agobiante, sofocante.

stigma ['stɪgmə] *n* estigma *m*.

stile [staɪl] *n* escalones *mpl* para pasar una valla.

stiletto heel [stɪ'letəʊ-] *n UK* tacón *m* fino OR de aguja.

still [stɪl] ⬦ *adv* - 1. [up to now, up to then, even now] todavía - 2. [to emphasize remaining amount] aún; **I've ~ got two left** aún me quedan dos - 3. [nevertheless, however] sin embargo, no obstante - 4. [with comparatives] aún - 5. [motionless] sin moverse. ⬦ *adj* - 1. [not moving] inmóvil - 2. [calm, quiet] tranquilo(la), sosegado(da) - 3. [not windy] apacible - 4. [not fizzy] sin gas. ⬦ *n* - 1. PHOT vista *f* fija - 2. [for making alcohol] alambique *m*.

stillborn ['stɪlbɔ:n] *adj* nacido muerto (nacida muerta).

still life (*pl* -s) *n* bodegón *m*, naturaleza *f* muerta.

stilted ['stɪltɪd] *adj* forzado(da).

stilts [stɪlts] *npl* - 1. [for person] zancos *mpl* - 2. [for building] pilotes *mpl*.

stimulate ['stɪmjʊleɪt] *vt* [gen] estimular; [interest] excitar.

stimulating ['stɪmjʊleɪtɪŋ] *adj* [physically] estimulante; [mentally] interesante.

stimulus ['stɪmjʊləs] (*pl* -li [-laɪ]) *n* estímulo *m*.

sting [stɪŋ] (*pt* & *pp* **stung**) ⬦ *n* - 1. [by bee] picadura *f* - 2. [of bee] aguijón *m* - 3. [sharp pain] escozor *m*. ⬦ *vt* - 1. [subj: bee, nettle] picar - 2. [cause sharp pain to] escocer. ⬦ *vi* picar.

stingy ['stɪndʒɪ] (*compar* -ier, *superl* -iest) *adj inf* tacaño(ña), roñoso(sa).

stink [stɪŋk] (*pt* **stank** OR **stunk**, *pp* **stunk**) ⬦ *n* peste *f*, hedor *m*. ⬦ *vi* [have unpleasant smell] apestar, heder.

stinking ['stɪŋkɪŋ] *inf fig* ⬦ *adj* asqueroso(sa). ⋄ *adv* : **to have a ~ cold** tener un resfriado horrible.

stint [stɪnt] ⋄ *n* periodo *m*. ⋄ *vi*: **to ~ on sthg** escatimar algo.

stipulate ['stɪpjʊleɪt] *vt* estipular.

stir [stɜ:ʳ] (*pt & pp* **-red**, *cont* **-ring**) ⋄ *n* [public excitement] revuelo *m*, sensación *f*; **to cause a ~** causar revuelo. ⋄ *vt* **-1.** [mix] remover **-2.** [move gently] agitar, mover **-3.** [move emotionally] impresionar, conmover. ⋄ *vi* [move gently] moverse, agitarse.

◆ **stir up** *vt sep* **-1.** [water, sediment] levantar **-2.** [cause] [excitement, hatred etc] provocar.

stirrup ['stɪrəp] *n* estribo *m*.

stitch [stɪtʃ] ⋄ *n* **-1.** SEWING puntada *f* **-2.** [in knitting] punto *m* **-3.** MED punto *m* (de sutura) **-4.** [stomach pain]: **to have a ~** sentir pinchazos (en el estómago). ⋄ *vt* **-1.** SEWING coser **-2.** MED suturar, poner puntos.

stoat [stəʊt] *n* armiño *m*.

stock [stɒk] ⋄ *n* **-1.** [supply] reserva *f* **-2.** (U) COMM [reserves] existencias *fpl*; [selection] surtido *m*; **in ~** en existencia, en almacén; **out of ~** agotado(da) **-3.** FIN [of company] capital *m*; **~s and shares** acciones *fpl*, valores *mpl* **-4.** [ancestry] linaje *m*, estirpe *f* **-5.** CULIN caldo *m* **-6.** [livestock] ganado *m*, ganadería *f* **-7.** *phr*: **to take ~ (of sthg)** evaluar (algo). ⋄ *adj* estereotipado(da). ⋄ *vt* **-1.** COMM abastecer de, tener en el almacén **-2.** [shelves] llenar; [lake] repoblar.

◆ **stock up** *vi*: **to ~ up (with)** abastecerse (de).

stockbroker ['stɒk,brəʊkəʳ] *n* corredor *m*, -ra *f* de bolsa.

stock cube *n* UK pastilla *f* de caldo.

stock exchange *n* bolsa *f*.

stockholder ['stɒk,həʊldəʳ] *n* US accionista *m* OR *f*.

Stockholm ['stɒkhəʊm] *n* Estocolmo.

stocking ['stɒkɪŋ] *n* [for woman] media *f*.

stockist ['stɒkɪst] *n* UK distribuidor *m*, -ra *f*.

stock market *n* bolsa *f*, mercado *m* de valores.

stock phrase *n* frase *f* estereotipada.

stockpile ['stɒkpaɪl] ⋄ *n* reservas *fpl*. ⋄ *vt* almacenar, acumular.

stocktaking ['stɒk,teɪkɪŋ] *n* (U) inventario *m*, balance *m*.

stocky ['stɒkɪ] (*compar* **-ier**, *superl* **-iest**) *adj* corpulento(ta), robusto(ta).

stodgy ['stɒdʒɪ] (*compar* **-ier**, *superl* **-iest**) *adj* [indigestible] indigesto(ta).

stoical ['stəʊɪkl] *adj* estoico(ca).

stoke [stəʊk] *vt* [fire] avivar, alimentar.

stole [stəʊl] ⋄ *pt* ▷ **steal**. ⋄ *n* estola *f*.

stolen ['stəʊln] *pp* ▷ **steal**.

stolid ['stɒlɪd] *adj* impasible, imperturbable.

stomach ['stʌmək] ⋄ *n* **-1.** [organ] estómago *m*; **to do sthg on an empty ~** hacer algo con el estómago vacío **-2.** [abdomen] vientre *m*. ⋄ *vt* tragar, aguantar; **I can't ~ him** no lo trago.

stomachache ['stʌməkeɪk] *n* dolor *m* de estómago.

stomach upset [-'ʌpset] *n* trastorno *m* gástrico.

stone [stəʊn] (*pl sense 4 only inv* OR **-s**) ⋄ *n* **-1.** [mineral] piedra *f* **-2.** [jewel] piedra *f* preciosa **-3.** [seed] hueso *m*, carozo *m* RP, cuesco *m*, pepa *f* Col **-4.** UK [unit of measurement] = 6,35 kilos. ⋄ *vt* apedrear.

stone-cold *adj* helado(da).

stonewashed ['stəʊnwɒʃt] *adj* lavado(da) a la piedra.

stonework ['stəʊnwɜ:k] *n* mampostería *f*.

stood [stʊd] *pt & pp* ▷ **stand**.

stool [stu:l] *n* [seat] taburete *m*.

stoop [stu:p] ⋄ *n* [bent back]: **to walk with a ~** caminar encorvado(da). ⋄ *vi* **-1.** [bend] inclinarse, agacharse **-2.** [hunch shoulders] encorvarse.

stop [stɒp] (*pt & pp* **-ped**, *cont* **-ping**) ⋄ *n* [gen] parada *f*; **to put a ~ to sthg** poner fin a algo. ⋄ *vt* **-1.** [gen] parar; **to ~ doing sthg** dejar de hacer algo **-2.** [prevent] impedir; **to ~ sb/sthg from doing sthg** impedir que alguien/algo haga algo **-3.** [cause to stop moving] detener. ⋄ *vi* [gen] pararse; [rain, music] cesar.

◆ **stop off** *vi* hacer una parada.

◆ **stop up** ⋄ *vt sep* [block] taponar, tapar.

stopgap ['stɒpgæp] *n* [thing] recurso *m* provisional; [person] sustituto *m*, -ta *f*.

stopover ['stɒp,əʊvəʳ] *n* [gen] parada *f*; [of plane] escala *f*.

stoppage ['stɒpɪdʒ] *n* **-1.** [strike] paro *m*, huelga *f* **-2.** UK [deduction] retención *f*.

stopper ['stɒpəʳ] *n* tapón *m*.

stop press *n* noticias *fpl* de última hora.

stopwatch ['stɒpwɒtʃ] *n* cronómetro *m*.

storage ['stɔ:rɪdʒ] *n* almacenamiento *m*.

storage heater *n* UK calentador por almacenamiento térmico.

store [stɔ:ʳ] ⋄ *n* **-1.** *esp* US [shop] tienda *f* **-2.** [supply] provisión *f*, reserva *f* **-3.** [place of storage] almacén *m*. ⋄ *vt* **-1.** [gen & COMPUT] almacenar **-2.** [keep] guardar.

◆ **store up** *vt sep* [provisions, goods] almacenar; [information] acumular.

store card *n* tarjeta *f* de cliente.

storekeeper ['stɔ:,ki:pəʳ] *n* US tendero *m*, -ra *f*.

storeroom ['stɔ:rʊm] *n* [gen] almacén *m*; [for food] despensa *f*.

storey UK (*pl* **storeys**), **story** US (*pl* **-ies**) ['stɔ:rɪ] *n* planta *f*.

stork [stɔ:k] *n* cigüeña *f*.

storm [stɔːm] ⬦ n - 1. [bad weather] tormenta f - 2. [violent reaction] torrente m. ⬦ vt MIL asaltar. ⬦ vi - 1. [go angrily]: **to ~ out** salir echando pestes - 2. [say angrily] vociferar.

stormy ['stɔːmɪ] (compar -ier, superl -iest) adj - 1. [weather] tormentoso(sa) - 2. [meeting] acalorado(da); [relationship] tempestuoso(sa).

story ['stɔːrɪ] (pl -ies) n - 1. [tale] cuento m, relato m - 2. [history] historia f - 3. [news article] artículo m - 4. US = storey.

storybook ['stɔːrɪbʊk] adj de novela, de cuento.

storyteller ['stɔːrɪˌtelə'] n [teller of story] narrador m, -ra f, cuentista m OR f.

stout [staʊt] ⬦ adj - 1. [rather fat] corpulento(ta), gordo(da) - 2. [strong, solid] fuerte, sólido(da) - 3. [resolute] firme. ⬦ n (U) cerveza f negra.

stove [stəʊv] ⬦ pt & pp ⊳ stave. ⬦ n [for heating] estufa f; [for cooking] cocina f.

stow [stəʊ] vt: **to ~ sthg (away)** guardar algo.

stowaway ['stəʊəweɪ] n polizón m.

straddle ['strædl] vt [subj: person] sentarse a horcajadas sobre.

straggle ['strægl] vi - 1. [sprawl] desparramarse - 2. [dawdle] rezagarse.

straggler ['stræglə'] n rezagado m, -da f.

straight [streɪt] ⬦ adj - 1. [not bent] recto(ta); **sit up ~!** ¡siéntate derecho! - 2. [hair] liso(sa) - 3. [honest, frank] franco(ca), sincero(ra) - 4. [tidy] arreglado(da) - 5. [choice, swap] simple, fácil - 6. [alcoholic drink] solo(la), sin mezclar. ⬦ adv - 1. [in a straight line - horizontally] directamente; [- vertically] recto(ta); **~ ahead** todo recto; **it was heading ~ for me** venía directo hacia mí - 2. [directly] directamente; [immediately] inmediatamente; **come ~ home** ven directamente a casa - 3. [frankly] francamente - 4. [tidy] en orden - 5. [undiluted] solo(la) - 6. phr: **let's get things ~** vamos a aclarar las cosas.

   ➤ straight off adv en el acto.

   ➤ straight out adv sin tapujos.

straight away [ˌstreɪtə'weɪ] adv en seguida.

straighten ['streɪtn] vt - 1. [tidy - room] ordenar; [- hair, dress] poner bien - 2. [make straight - horizontally] poner recto(ta); [- vertically] enderezar.

   ➤ straighten out vt sep [mess] arreglar; [problem] resolver.

straight face n: **to keep a ~** aguantar la risa.

straightforward [ˌstreɪt'fɔːwəd] adj - 1. [easy] sencillo(lla) - 2. [frank - answer] directo(ta); [- person] abierto(ta), sincero(ra).

strain [streɪn] ⬦ n - 1. [weight] peso m; [pressure] presión f - 2. [mental stress] tensión f nerviosa; **to be under a lot of ~** estar muy agobiado(da) - 3. [physical injury] distensión f, torcedura f. ⬦ vt - 1. [overtax - budget] estirar - 2. [use hard]: **to ~ one's eyes/ears** aguzar la vista/el oído - 3. [injure - eyes] cansar; [- muscle, back] distender, torcerse - 4. [drain] colar. ⬦ vi: **to ~ to do sthg** esforzarse por hacer algo.

   ➤ strains npl literary [of music] acordes mpl, compases mpl.

strained [streɪnd] adj - 1. [worried] preocupado(da) - 2. [unfriendly] tirante, tenso(sa) - 3. [insincere] forzado(da).

strainer ['streɪnə'] n colador m.

strait [streɪt] n estrecho m.

   ➤ straits npl: **in dire** OR **desperate ~s** en un serio aprieto.

straitjacket ['streɪtˌdʒækɪt] n [garment] camisa f de fuerza.

straitlaced [ˌstreɪt'leɪst] adj pej mojigato(-ta), estrecho(cha).

strand [strænd] n [thin piece] hebra f; **a ~ of hair** un pelo del cabello.

stranded ['strændɪd] adj [ship] varado(da), encallado(da); [person] colgado(da).

strange [streɪndʒ] adj - 1. [unusual] raro(-ra), extraño(ña) - 2. [unfamiliar] desconocido(da).

stranger ['streɪndʒə'] n - 1. [unfamiliar person] extraño m, -ña f, desconocido m, -da f - 2. [outsider] forastero m, -ra f.

strangle ['stræŋgl] vt [kill] estrangular.

stranglehold ['stræŋglhəʊld] n fig [strong influence] dominio m absoluto.

strap [stræp] (pt & pp -ped, cont -ping) ⬦ n [of handbag, watch, case] correa f; [of dress, bra] tirante m, bretel m CSur. ⬦ vt [fasten] atar con correa.

strapping ['stræpɪŋ] adj robusto(ta).

Strasbourg ['stræzbɜːg] n Estrasburgo.

strategic [strə'tiːdʒɪk] adj estratégico(ca).

strategy ['strætɪdʒɪ] (pl -ies) n estrategia f.

straw [strɔː] n - 1. AGR paja f - 2. [for drinking] pajita f, paja f, pitillo m Col, popote m Méx - 3. phr: **the last ~** el colmo.

strawberry ['strɔːbərɪ] (pl -ies) ⬦ n fresa f, frutilla f Bol, CSur, Ecuad, Andes, RP. ⬦ comp de fresa, de frutilla f Bol, CSur, Ecuad, Andes, RP.

stray [streɪ] ⬦ adj - 1. [animal - without owner] callejero(ra); [- lost] extraviado(da) - 2. [bullet] perdido(da). ⬦ vi - 1. [from path] desviarse; [from group] extraviarse - 2. [thoughts, mind] perderse.

streak [striːk] ⬦ n - 1. [of hair] mechón m; **to have ~s in one's hair** tener un mechón en el pelo; [of lightning] rayo m - 2. [in character] vena f. ⬦ vi [move quickly] ir como un rayo.

stream [striːm] ⬦ n - **1.** [small river] ria-chuelo m, quebrada f Amér - **2.** [of liquid, smoke] chorro m; [of light] raudal m - **3.** [current] corriente f - **4.** [of people, cars] torrente m - **5.** [continuous series] sarta f, serie f - **6.** UK SCH grupo m. ⬦ vi - **1.** [liquid, smoke, light]: **to ~ into** entrar a raudales en; **to ~ out of** brotar de - **2.** [people, cars]: **to ~ into** entrar atropelladamente en; **to ~ out of** salir atropelladamente de - **3.** [phr] **to have a ~ing cold** tener un res-friado horrible. ⬦ vt UK SCH agrupar de acuerdo con el rendimiento escolar.

streamer ['striːmə'] n [for party] serpentina f.

streamlined ['striːmlaɪnd] adj - **1.** [aerody-namic] aerodinámico(ca) - **2.** [efficient] ra-cional.

street [striːt] n calle f, jirón m Perú; **to be on the ~s** estar en la calle.

streetcar ['striːtkɑː'] n US tranvía m.

street lamp, street light n farola f.

street plan n plano m (de la ciudad).

streetwise ['striːtwaɪz] adj inf espabilado(-da).

strength [streŋθ] n - **1.** [physical or mental power] fuerza f - **2.** [power, influence] poder m - **3.** [quality] punto m fuerte - **4.** [solidity - of material structure] solidez f - **5.** [intensity - of feeling, smell, wind] intensidad f; [- of accent, wine] fuerza f; [- of drug] potencia f - **6.** [credibility, weight] peso m, fuerza f.

strengthen ['streŋθn] vt - **1.** [gen] fortalecer - **2.** [reinforce - argument, bridge] reforzar - **3.** [intensify] acentuar, intensificar - **4.** [make closer] estrechar.

strenuous ['strenjʊəs] adj agotador(ra), extenuante.

stress [stres] ⬦ n - **1.** [emphasis]: **~ (on)** hincapié m OR énfasis m inv (en) - **2.** [tension, anxiety] estrés m, tensión f nerviosa - **3.** [physical pressure]: **~ (on)** presión f (en) - **4.** LING [on word, syllable] acento m. ⬦ vt - **1.** [emphasize] recalcar, subrayar - **2.** LING [word, syllable] acentuar.

stressful ['stresfʊl] adj estresante.

stretch [stretʃ] ⬦ n - **1.** [of land, water] ex-tensión f; [of road, river] tramo m, trecho m - **2.** [of time] periodo m - **3.** [to move one's body]: **to have a ~** estirarse. ⬦ vt - **1.** [gen] estirar; **I'm going to ~ my legs** voy a estirar las piernas - **2.** [overtax - per-son] extender - **3.** [challenge] hacer rendir al máximo. ⬦ vi [area]: **to ~ over/from ... to** extenderse por/desde ... hasta.

➤ **stretch out** ⬦ vt sep [foot, leg] estirar; [hand, arm] alargar. ⬦ vi - **1.** [lie down] tum-barse - **2.** [reach out] estirarse.

stretcher ['stretʃə'] n camilla f.

stretch limo ['stretʃ'lɪməʊ] n inf limusina f ampliada.

strew [struː] (pt **-ed**, pp **strewn** [struːn], **-ed**) vt: **to be ~n with** estar cubierto(ta) de.

stricken ['strɪkn] adj: **to be ~ by** OR **with** [illness] estar aquejado(da) de; [drought, fa-mine] estar asolado(da) por; [grief] estar afligido(da) por; [doubts, horror] estar ate-nazado(da) por; **she was ~ with remorse** le remordía la conciencia.

strict [strɪkt] adj - **1.** [gen] estricto(ta) - **2.** [precise] exacto(ta), estricto(ta).

strictly ['strɪktlɪ] adv - **1.** [severely] severa-mente - **2.** [absolutely - prohibited] terminan-temente; [- confidential] absolutamente, totalmente - **3.** [exactly] exactamente; **~ speaking** en el sentido estricto de la pala-bra - **4.** [exclusively] exclusivamente; **this is ~ between you and me** esto debe quedar exclusivamente entre tú y yo.

stride [straɪd] (pt **strode**, pp **stridden** ['strɪdn]) ⬦ n zancada f. ⬦ vi: **to ~ along** andar a zancadas; **he strode off down the road** marchó calle abajo dando grandes zancadas.

strident ['straɪdnt] adj - **1.** [harsh] estriden-te - **2.** [vociferous] exaltado(da).

strife [straɪf] n (U) fml conflictos mpl.

strike [straɪk] (pt & pp **struck**) ⬦ n - **1.** [re-fusal to work etc] huelga f; **to be (out) on ~** estar en huelga; **to go on ~** declararse en huelga - **2.** MIL ataque m - **3.** [find] descubri-miento m. ⬦ vt - **1.** fml [hit - deliberately] gol-pear, pegar; [- accidentally] chocar contra - **2.** [subj: disaster, earthquake] asolar; [subj: lightning] fulminar, alcanzar; **she was struck by lightning** le alcanzó un rayo - **3.** [subj: thought, idea] ocurrírsele a - **4.** [deal, bargain] cerrar - **5.** [match] encen-der. ⬦ vi - **1.** [stop working] estar en huelga - **2.** fml [hit accidentally]: **to ~ against** cho-car contra - **3.** [hurricane, disaster] sobreve-nir; [lightning] caer - **4.** fml [attack] atacar - **5.** [chime] dar la hora; **the clock struck six** el reloj dio las seis.

➤ **strike down** vt sep fulminar; **to be struck down with sthg** estar sufriendo de algo.

➤ **strike out** vt sep tachar.

➤ **strike up** vt fus - **1.** [friendship] trabar; [conversation] entablar - **2.** [tune] empezar a tocar.

striker ['straɪkə'] n - **1.** [person on strike] huelguista m OR f - **2.** FTBL delantero m, -ra f.

striking ['straɪkɪŋ] adj - **1.** [noticeable, un-usual] chocante, sorprendente - **2.** [attrac-tive] llamativo(va), atractivo(va).

string [strɪŋ] (pt & pp **strung**) n - **1.** [thin rope] cuerda f, piolín m Amér; **a (piece of) ~** un cordón; **to pull ~s** utilizar uno sus influencias - **2.** [of beads, pearls] sarta f - **3.** [series] serie f, sucesión f - **4.** [of musical instrument] cuerda *f*.

◆ **strings** *npl* MUS : **the** ~s los instrumentos de cuerda.

◆ **string out** *vt fus*: **to be strung out** alinearse.

◆ **string together** *vt sep* [words] encadenar.

string bean *n* judía *f* verde, chaucha *f RP*, vainita *f Ven*, poroto *m* verde *Chile*, habichuela *f Col*.

stringed instrument ['strɪŋd-] *n* instrumento *m* de cuerda.

stringent ['strɪndʒənt] *adj* estricto(ta), severo(ra).

strip [strɪp] (*pt & pp* -ped, *cont* -ping) ◇ *n* -1. [narrow piece] tira *f* -2. [narrow area] franja *f* -3. *UK* SPORT camiseta *f*, colores *mpl*. ◇ *vt* -1. [undress] desnudar -2. [paint, wallpaper] quitar. ◇ *vi* -1. [undress] desnudarse.

◆ **strip off** *vi* desnudarse.

strip cartoon *n UK* historieta *f*, tira *f* cómica.

stripe [straɪp] *n* -1. [band of colour] raya *f*, franja *f* -2. [sign of rank] galón *m*.

striped [straɪpt] *adj* a rayas.

strip lighting *n* alumbrado *m* fluorescente.

stripper ['strɪpə'] *n* -1. [performer of striptease] artista *m* OR *f* de striptease -2. [for paint] disolvente *m*.

striptease ['stripti:z] *n* striptease *m*.

strive [straɪv] (*pt* strove, *pp* striven ['strɪvn]) *vi fml*: **to** ~ **for sthg** luchar por algo; **to** ~ **to do sthg** esforzarse por hacer algo.

strode [strəʊd] *pt* ⊳ stride.

stroke [strəʊk] ◇ *n* -1. MED apoplejía *f*, derrame *m* cerebral -2. [of pen] trazo *m*; [of brush] pincelada *f* -3. [style of swimming] estilo *m* -4. [in tennis, golf etc] golpe *m* -5. [of clock] campanada *f* -6. *UK* TYPO [oblique] barra *f* -7. [piece]: **a** ~ **of genius** una genialidad; **a** ~ **of luck** un golpe de suerte; **at a** ~ de una vez, de golpe. ◇ *vt* acariciar.

stroll [strəʊl] ◇ *n* paseo *m*; **to go for a** ~ dar un paseo. ◇ *vi* pasear.

stroller ['strəʊlə'] *n US* [for baby] sillita *f* (de niño).

strong [strɒŋ] *adj* -1. [gen] fuerte -2. [material, structure] sólido(da), resistente -3. [feeling, belief] profundo(da); [opposition, denial] firme; [support] acérrimo(ma); [accent] marcado(da) -4. [discipline, policy] estricto(ta) -5. [argument] convincente -6. [in numbers]: **the crowd was 2,000** ~ la multitud constaba de 2.000 personas -7. [good, gifted]: **one's** ~ **point** el punto fuerte de uno -8. [concentrated] concentrado(da).

strongbox ['strɒŋbɒks] *n* caja *f* fuerte.

stronghold ['strɒŋhəʊld] *n fig* [bastion] bastión *m*, baluarte *m*.

strongly ['strɒŋlɪ] *adv* -1. [sturdily] fuertemente -2. [in degree] intensamente -3. [fervently]: **to support/oppose sthg** ~ apoyar/oponerse a algo totalmente; **I feel very** ~ **about that** eso me preocupa muchísimo.

strong room *n* cámara *f* acorazada.

strove [strəʊv] *pt* ⊳ strive.

struck [strʌk] *pt & pp* ⊳ strike.

structure ['strʌktʃə'] *n* -1. [arrangement] estructura *f* -2. [building] construcción *f*.

struggle ['strʌgl] ◇ *n* -1. [great effort]: ~ **(for sthg/to do sthg)** lucha *f* (por algo/por hacer algo) -2. [fight, tussle] forcejeo *m*. ◇ *vi* -1. [make great effort]: **to** ~ **(for sthg/ to do sthg)** luchar (por algo/por hacer algo) -2. [to free o.s.]: **to** ~ **free** forcejear para soltarse -3. [move with difficulty]: **to** ~ **with sthg** llevar algo con dificultad.

strum [strʌm] (*pt & pp* -med, *cont* -ming) *vt & vi* rasguear.

strung [strʌŋ] *pt & pp* ⊳ string.

strut [strʌt] (*pt & pp* -ted, *cont* -ting) ◇ *n* CONSTR puntal *m*. ◇ *vi* andar pavoneándose.

stub [stʌb] (*pt & pp* -bed, *cont* -bing) ◇ *n* -1. [of cigarette] colilla *f*; [of pencil] cabo *m* -2. [of ticket] resguardo *m*; [of cheque] matriz *f*. ◇ *vt*: **to** ~ **one's toe on** darse con el pie en.

◆ **stub out** *vt sep* apagar.

stubble ['stʌbl] *n* -1. (*U*) [in field] rastrojo *m* -2. [on chin] barba *f* incipiente OR de tres días.

stubborn ['stʌbən] *adj* [person] terco(ca), testarudo(da).

stuck [stʌk] ◇ *pt & pp* ⊳ stick. ◇ *adj* -1. [jammed - lid, window] atascado(da) -2. [unable to progress] atascado(da) -3. [stranded] colgado(da) -4. [in a meeting, at home] encerrado(da).

stuck-up *adj inf pej* engreído(da), que se lo tiene creído.

stud [stʌd] *n* -1. [metal decoration] tachón *m* -2. [earring] pendiente *m* -3. *UK* [on boot, shoe] taco *m* -4. [horse] semental *m*.

studded ['stʌdɪd] *adj*: ~ **(with)** tachonado(da) (con).

student ['stju:dnt] ◇ *n* -1. [at college, university] estudiante *m* OR *f* -2. [scholar] estudioso *m*, -sa *f*. ◇ *comp* estudiantil.

studio ['stju:dɪəʊ] (*pl* -s) *n* estudio *m*.

studio flat *UK*, **studio apartment** *US n* estudio *m*.

studious ['stju:djəs] *adj* estudioso(sa).

studiously ['stju:djəslɪ] *adv* cuidadosamente.

study ['stʌdɪ] (*pl* -ies, *pt & pp* -ied) ◇ *n* estudio *m*. ◇ *vt* -1. [learn] estudiar; **to** ~ **for sth** estudiar para algo -2. [examine -

report, sb's face] examinar, estudiar. ⟨⟩ *vi* estudiar.

➡ **studies** *npl* estudios *mpl*.

study hall *n* US -1. [room] sala *f* de estudio - 2. [period] hora *f* de estudio.

stuff [stʌf] ⟨⟩ *n* (U) *inf* -1. [things, belongings] cosas *fpl* -2. [substance]: **what's that ~ in your pocket?** ¿qué es eso que llevas en el bolsillo? ⟨⟩ *vt* -1. [push, put] meter - 2. [fill, cram]: **to ~ sthg (with)** [box, room] llenar algo (de); [pillow, doll] rellenar algo (de) - 3. CULIN rellenar.

stuffed [stʌft] *adj* -1. [filled, crammed]: **~ with** atestado(da) de - 2. *inf* [subj: person - with food] lleno(na), inflado(da) - 3. CULIN relleno(na) - 4. [preserved - animal] disecado(da).

stuffing ['stʌfɪŋ] *n* (U) relleno *m*.

stuffy ['stʌfɪ] (*compar* -ier, *superl* -iest) *adj* -1. [atmosphere] cargado(da); [room] mal ventilado(da) - 2. [old-fashioned] retrógrado(da), carca.

stumble ['stʌmbl] *vi* [trip] tropezar.

➡ **stumble across, stumble on** *vt fus* [thing] dar con; [person] encontrarse con.

stumbling block ['stʌmblɪŋ-] *n* obstáculo *m*, escollo *m*.

stump [stʌmp] ⟨⟩ *n* [of tree] tocón *m*; [of limb] muñón *m*. ⟨⟩ *vt* -1. [subj: question, problem] dejar perplejo(ja); **I'm ~ed** no tengo ni idea; **he was ~ed for an answer** no sabía qué contestar - 2. US POL [constituency, state] recorrer en campaña electoral.

stun [stʌn] (*pt & pp* -ned, *cont* -ning) *vt lit & fig* aturdir.

stung [stʌŋ] *pt & pp* ▷ **sting**.

stunk [stʌŋk] *pt & pp* ▷ **stink**.

stunning ['stʌnɪŋ] *adj* -1. [very beautiful] imponente - 2. [shocking] pasmoso(sa).

stunt [stʌnt] ⟨⟩ *n* -1. [for publicity] truco *m* publicitario - 2. CINEMA escena *f* arriesgada OR peligrosa. ⟨⟩ *vt* atrofiar.

stunted ['stʌntɪd] *adj* esmirriado(da).

stunt man *n* especialista *m*, doble *m*.

stupefy ['stju:pɪfaɪ] (*pt & pp* -ied) *vt* -1. [tire, bore] aturdir, atontar - 2. [surprise] dejar estupefacto(ta).

stupendous [stju:'pendəs] *adj inf* [wonderful] estupendo(da); [very large] enorme.

stupid ['stju:pɪd] *adj* -1. [foolish] estúpido(da), baboso(sa) *Amér* - 2. *inf* [annoying] puñetero(ra).

stupidity [stju:'pɪdətɪ] *n* (U) estupidez *f*.

sturdy ['stɜ:dɪ] (*compar* -ier, *superl* -iest) *adj* [person, shoulders] fuerte; [furniture, bridge] firme, sólido(da).

stutter ['stʌtə'] ⟨⟩ *vi* tartamudear. ⟨⟩ *vt* decir tartamudeando.

sty [staɪ] (*pl* sties) *n* [pigsty] pocilga *f*.

stye [staɪ] *n* orzuelo *m*.

style [staɪl] ⟨⟩ *n* -1. [characteristic manner] estilo *m* - 2. (U) [smartness, elegance] clase *f* - 3. [design] modelo *m*. ⟨⟩ *vt* [hair] peinar.

stylish ['staɪlɪʃ] *adj* elegante, con estilo.

stylist ['staɪlɪst] *n* [hairdresser] peluquero *m*, -ra *f*.

stylus ['staɪləs] (*pl* -es) *n* [on record player] aguja *f*.

suave [swɑ:v] *adj* [well-mannered] afable, amable; [obsequious] zalamero(ra).

sub [sʌb] *n inf* SPORT (*abbr of* **substitute**) reserva *m* OR *f*.

subconscious [,sʌb'kɒnʃəs] *adj* subconsciente.

subcontract [,sʌbkən'trækt] *vt* subcontratar.

subdivide [,sʌbdɪ'vaɪd] *vt* subdividir.

subdue [səb'dju:] *vt* -1. [enemy, nation] someter, sojuzgar - 2. [feelings] contener, dominar.

subdued [səb'dju:d] *adj* -1. [person] apagado(da) - 2. [colour, light] tenue.

subject [*adj, n & prep* 'sʌbdʒekt, *vt* səb'dʒekt] ⟨⟩ *adj* [affected]: **~ to** [taxes, changes, law] sujeto(ta) a; [illness] proclive a. ⟨⟩ *n* -1. [topic] tema *m*; **don't change the ~** no cambies de tema - 2. GRAMM sujeto *m* - 3. SCH & UNIV asignatura *f* - 4. [citizen] súbdito *m*, -ta *f*. ⟨⟩ *vt* -1. [bring under control] someter, dominar - 2. [force to experience]: **to ~ sb to sthg** someter a alguien a algo.

➡ **subject to** *prep* dependiendo de.

subjective [səb'dʒektɪv] *adj* subjetivo(va).

subject matter ['sʌbdʒekt-] *n* (U) tema *m*, contenido *m*.

subjunctive [səb'dʒʌŋktɪv] *n* GRAMM: **~ (mood)** (modo *m*) subjuntivo *m*.

sublet [,sʌb'let] (*pt & pp* **sublet**, *cont* -ting) *vt & vi* subarrendar.

sublime [sə'blaɪm] *adj* [wonderful] sublime.

submachine gun [,sʌbmə'ʃi:n-] *n* metralleta *f*, ametralladora *f*.

submarine [,sʌbmə'ri:n] *n* -1. submarino *m* - 2. US [sandwich] bocadillo OR sandwich hecho con una barra de pan larga y estrecha.

submerge [səb'mɜ:dʒ] ⟨⟩ *vt* -1. [in water] sumergir - 2. *fig* [in activity]: **to ~ o.s. in sthg** dedicarse de lleno a algo. ⟨⟩ *vi* sumergirse.

submission [səb'mɪʃn] *n* -1. [capitulation] sumisión *f* - 2. [presentation] presentación *f*.

submissive [səb'mɪsɪv] *adj* sumiso(sa).

submit [səb'mɪt] (*pt & pp* -ted, *cont* -ting) ⟨⟩ *vt* presentar. ⟨⟩ *vi*: **to ~ (to sb)** rendirse (a alguien); **to ~ (to sthg)** someterse (a algo).

subnormal [,sʌb'nɔ:ml] *adj* subnormal.

subordinate [sə'bɔ:dɪnət] ⟨⟩ *adj fml* [less

important]: ~ **(to)** subordinado(da) (a). ◇ *n* subordinado *m*, -da *f*.

subpoena [sə'pi:nə] (*pt* & *pp* **-ed**) JUR ◇ *n* citación *f*. ◇ *vt* citar.

subscribe [səb'skraɪb] *vi* **- 1.** [to magazine, newspaper]: **to ~ (to)** suscribirse (a) **- 2.** [to belief]: **to ~ to** estar de acuerdo con.

subscriber [səb'skraɪbə'] *n* **- 1.** [to magazine, newspaper] suscriptor *m*, -ra *f* **- 2.** [to service] abonado *m*, -da *f*.

subscription [səb'skrɪpʃn] *n* [to magazine] suscripción *f*; [to service] abono *m*; [to society, club] cuota *f*; **to take out a ~ to** sthg suscribirse a algo.

subsequent ['sʌbsɪkwənt] *adj* subsiguiente, posterior; **~ to this** con posterioridad a esto.

subsequently ['sʌbsɪkwəntlɪ] *adv* posteriormente.

subservient [səb'sɜ:vjənt] *adj* [servile]: **~ (to sb)** servil (ante alguien).

subside [səb'saɪd] *vi* **- 1.** [anger] apaciguarse; [pain] calmarse; [grief] pasarse; [storm, wind] amainar **- 2.** [noise] apagarse **- 3.** [river] bajar, descender; [building, ground] hundirse.

subsidence [səb'saɪdns, 'sʌbsɪdns] *n* CONSTR hundimiento *m*.

subsidiary [səb'sɪdjərɪ] (*pl* **-ies**) ◇ *adj* secundario(ria). ◇ *n*: **~ (company)** filial *f*.

subsidize, -ise ['sʌbsɪdaɪz] *vt* subvencionar.

subsidy ['sʌbsɪdɪ] (*pl* **-ies**) *n* subvención *f*.

substance ['sʌbstəns] *n* **- 1.** [gen] sustancia *f* **- 2.** [essence] esencia *f*.

substantial [səb'stænʃl] *adj* **- 1.** [large, considerable] sustancial, considerable; [meal] abundante **- 2.** [solid] sólido(da).

substantially [səb'stænʃəlɪ] *adv* **- 1.** [quite a lot] sustancialmente, considerablemente **- 2.** [fundamentally] esencialmente; [for the most part] en gran parte.

substantiate [səb'stænʃɪeɪt] *vt fml* justificar.

substitute ['sʌbstɪtju:t] ◇ *n* **- 1.** [replacement]: **~ (for)** sustituto *m*, -ta *f* (de) **- 2.** SPORT suplente *m* OR *f*, reserva *m* OR *f*. ◇ *vt*: **to ~ sthg/sb for** sustituir algo/a alguien por.

subtitle ['sʌb,taɪtl] *n* subtítulo *m*.

subtle ['sʌtl] *adj* **- 1.** [gen] sutil; [taste, smell] delicado(da) **- 2.** [plan, behaviour] ingenioso(sa).

subtlety ['sʌtltɪ] *n* **- 1.** [gen] sutileza *f*; [of taste, smell] delicadeza *f* **- 2.** [of plan, behaviour] ingenio *m*.

subtract [səb'trækt] *vt*: **to ~ sthg (from)** restar algo (de).

subtraction [səb'trækʃn] *n* resta *f*.

suburb ['sʌbɜ:b] *n* barrio *m* residencial.

◆ **suburbs** *npl*: **the ~s** las afueras.

suburban [sə'bɜ:bn] *adj* **- 1.** [of suburbs] de los barrios residenciales **- 2.** *pej* [boring] convencional, burgués(esa).

suburbia [sə'bɜ:bɪə] *n* (*U*) barrios *mpl* residenciales.

subversive [səb'vɜ:sɪv] ◇ *adj* subversivo(-va). ◇ *n* subversivo *m*, -va *f*.

subway ['sʌbweɪ] *n* **- 1.** *UK* [underground walkway] paso *m* subterráneo **- 2.** *US* [underground railway] metro *m*, subte(rráneo) *m RP*.

succeed [sək'si:d] ◇ *vt* suceder a; **to ~ sb to the throne** suceder a alguien en el trono. ◇ *vi* **- 1.** [gen] tener éxito **- 2.** [achieve desired result]: **to ~ in sthg/in doing sthg** conseguir algo/hacer algo **- 3.** [plan, tactic] dar (buen) resultado, salir bien **- 4.** [go far in life] triunfar.

succeeding [sək'si:dɪŋ] *adj fml* siguiente.

success [sək'ses] *n* **- 1.** [gen] éxito *m*; **to be a ~** tener éxito **- 2.** [in career, life] triunfo *m*.

successful [sək'sesful] *adj* [gen] de éxito; [attempt] logrado(da); **to be ~ in sthg** tener éxito en algo.

succession [sək'seʃn] *n* sucesión *f*.

successive [sək'sesɪv] *adj* sucesivo(va), consecutivo(va); **he won on 3 ~ years** ganó durante tres años consecutivos.

succinct [sək'sɪŋkt] *adj* sucinto(ta).

succumb [sə'kʌm] *vi*: **to ~ (to)** sucumbir (a).

such [sʌtʃ] ◇ *adj* **- 1.** [like that] semejante, tal; **~ stupidity** tal OR semejante estupidez; **there's no ~ thing** no existe nada semejante **- 2.** [like this]: **have you got ~ a thing as a tin opener?** ¿tendrías acaso un abrelatas?; **~ words as 'duty' and 'honour'** palabras (tales) como 'deber' y 'honor' **- 3.** [whatever]: **I've spent ~ money as I had** he gastado el poco dinero que tenía **- 4.** [so great, so serious]: **there are ~ differences that ...** las diferencias son tales que ...; **~ ... that** tal ... que. ◇ *adv* tan; **~ a lot of books** tantos libros; **~ nice people** una gente tan amable; **~ a good car** un coche tan bueno; **~ a long time** tanto tiempo. ◇ *pron*: **and ~ (like)** y otros similares OR por el estilo.

◆ **as such** *pron* propiamente dicho(cha).

◆ **such and such** *adj*: **at ~ and ~ a time** a tal hora.

suck [sʌk] ◇ *vt* **- 1.** [by mouth] chupar **- 2.** [subj: machine] aspirar. ◇ *vi US v inf* [be bad] [book, film]: **that really ~s!** ¡es una mierda!

sucker ['sʌkə'] *n* **- 1.** [of animal] ventosa *f* **- 2.** *inf* [gullible person] primo *m*, -ma *f*, ingenuo *m*, -nua *f*; **to be a ~ for punishment** ser un masoquista.

suction ['sʌkʃn] *n* [gen] succión *f*; [by

machine] aspiración f.

Sudan [suː'dɑːn] n (el) Sudán.

sudden ['sʌdn] adj [quick] repentino(na); [unforeseen] inesperado(da); **all of a ~ de repente.**

suddenly ['sʌdnlı] adv de repente, de pronto.

suds [sʌdz] npl espuma f del jabón.

sue [suː] vt : **to ~ sb (for)** demandar a alguien (por).

suede [sweɪd] n [for jacket, shoes] ante m; [for gloves] cabritilla f.

suet ['sʊɪt] n sebo m.

suffer ['sʌfəʳ] ⟷ vt sufrir. ⟷ vi - 1. [gen] sufrir - 2. [experience negative effects] salir perjudicado(da) - 3. MED : **to ~ from** [illness] sufrir OR padecer de.

sufferer ['sʌfrəʳ] n enfermo m, -ma f; **cancer ~** enfermo de cáncer; **hay fever ~** persona que padece fiebre del heno.

suffering ['sʌfrɪŋ] n [gen] sufrimiento m; [pain] dolor m.

suffice [sə'faɪs] vi fml ser suficiente, bastar.

sufficient [sə'fɪʃnt] adj fml suficiente, bastante.

sufficiently [sə'fɪʃntlı] adv fml suficientemente, bastante.

suffocate ['sʌfəkeɪt] ⟷ vt asfixiar, ahogar. ⟷ vi asfixiarse, ahogarse.

suffrage ['sʌfrɪdʒ] n sufragio m.

suffuse [sə'fjuːz] vt : **~d with** bañado de.

sugar ['ʃʊɡəʳ] ⟷ n azúcar m OR f. ⟷ vt echar azúcar a.

sugar beet n remolacha f (azucarera).

sugarcane ['ʃʊɡəkeɪn] n (U) caña f de azúcar.

sugary ['ʃʊɡərı] adj [high in sugar] azucarado(da), dulce.

suggest [sə'dʒest] vt - 1. [propose] sugerir, proponer; **to ~ doing sthg** sugerir hacer algo; **to ~ that sb do sthg** sugerir que alguien haga algo - 2. [imply] insinuar.

suggestion [sə'dʒestʃn] n - 1. [proposal] sugerencia f - 2. [implication] insinuación f; **there was no ~ of murder** no había nada que indicara que fue un asesinato.

suggestive [sə'dʒestɪv] adj - 1. [implying sexual connotation] provocativo(va), insinuante.

suicide ['suːɪsaɪd] n lit & fig suicidio m; **to commit ~** suicidarse.

suit [suːt] ⟷ n - 1. [clothes - for men] traje m, tenida f Chile; [- for women] traje de chaqueta - 2. [in cards] palo m - 3. JUR pleito m. ⟷ vt - 1. [look attractive on] favorecer, sentar bien a, embonar Andes, Cuba & Méx; **it ~s you** te favorece, te sienta bien - 2. [be convenient or agreeable to] convenir, venir bien a; **that ~s me fine** por mí, estupendo - 3. [be appropriate to] ser adecuado(da) para; **that job ~s**

you perfectly ese trabajo te va de perlas.

suitable ['suːtəbl] adj adecuado(da); **the most ~ person** la persona más indicada; **to be ~ for sthg** ser adecuado(da) para algo.

suitably ['suːtəblı] adv adecuadamente.

suitcase ['suːtkeɪs] n maleta f, petaca f Méx, valija f RP.

suite [swiːt] n - 1. [of rooms] suite f - 2. [of furniture] juego m; **dining-room ~** comedor m.

suited ['suːtɪd] adj : **~ to/for** adecuado(da) para; **the couple are ideally ~** forman una pareja perfecta.

suitor ['suːtəʳ] n dated pretendiente m.

sulfur US = sulphur.

sulk [sʌlk] vi estar de mal humor, enfurruñarse.

sulky ['sʌlkı] (compar -ier, superl -iest) adj malhumorado(da).

sullen ['sʌlən] adj hosco(ca), antipático(-ca).

sulphur UK, **sulfur** US ['sʌlfəʳ] n azufre m.

sultana [səl'tɑːnə] n UK [dried grape] pasa f de Esmirna.

sultry ['sʌltrı] (compar -ier, superl -iest) adj [hot] bochornoso(sa), sofocante.

sum [sʌm] (pt & pp -med, cont -ming) n suma f.

➡ **sum up** vt sep & vi [summarize] resumir.

summarize, -ise ['sʌməraɪz] vt & vi resumir.

summary ['sʌmərı] (pl -ies) n resumen m.

summer ['sʌməʳ] ⟷ n verano m. ⟷ comp de verano.

summerhouse ['sʌməhaʊs, pl -haʊzɪz] n cenador m.

summer school n escuela f de verano.

summertime ['sʌmətaɪm] n: **(the) ~** (el) verano.

summit ['sʌmɪt] n - 1. [mountain-top] cima f, cumbre f - 2. [meeting] cumbre f.

summon ['sʌmən] vt [person] llamar; [meeting] convocar.

➡ **summon up** vt sep [courage] armarse de; **to ~ up the courage to do sthg** armarse de valor para hacer algo.

summons ['sʌmənz] (pl summonses) JUR ⟷ n citación f. ⟷ vt citar.

sump [sʌmp] n cárter m.

sumptuous ['sʌmptʃʊəs] adj suntuoso(-sa).

sun [sʌn] (pt & pp -ned, cont -ning) n sol m; **in the ~** al sol; **everything under the ~** todo lo habido y por haber.

sunbathe ['sʌnbeɪð] vi tomar el sol.

sunbed ['sʌnbed] n camilla f de rayos ultravioletas.

sunburn ['sʌnbɜːn] n (U) quemadura f de sol.

sunburned ['sʌnbɜːnd], **sunburnt** ['sʌnbɜːnt] *adj* quemado(da) por el sol.

Sunday ['sʌndɪ] *n* domingo *m*; ~ **lunch** *comida del domingo que generalmente consiste en carne asada, patatas asadas etc; see also* **Saturday**.

Sunday school *n* catequesis *f inv*.

sundial ['sʌndaɪəl] *n* reloj *m* de sol.

sundown ['sʌndaʊn] *n* anochecer *m*.

sundries ['sʌndrɪz] *npl fml* [gen] artículos *mpl* diversos; FIN gastos *mpl* diversos.

sundry ['sʌndrɪ] *adj fml* diversos(sas); **all and ~** todos sin excepción.

sunflower ['sʌn,flaʊəʳ] *n* girasol *m*.

sunflower seed *n* pipa *f* de girasol.

sung [sʌŋ] *pp* ⊳ **sing**.

sunglasses ['sʌn,glɑːsɪz] *npl* gafas *fpl* de sol.

sunk [sʌŋk] *pp* ⊳ **sink**.

sunlight ['sʌnlaɪt] *n* luz *f* del sol; **in direct ~** a la luz directa del sol.

sunlit ['sʌnlɪt] *adj* iluminado(da) por el sol.

sunny ['sʌnɪ] (*compar* **-ier**, *superl* **-iest**) *adj* **- 1.** [day] de sol; [room] soleado(da) **- 2.** [cheerful] alegre.

sunrise ['sʌnraɪz] *n* **- 1.** (U) [time of day] amanecer *m* **- 2.** [event] salida *f* del sol.

sunroof ['sʌnruːf] *n* [on car] techo *m* corredizo; [on building] azotea *f*.

sunset ['sʌnset] *n* **- 1.** (U) [time of day] anochecer *m* **- 2.** [event] puesta *f* del sol.

sunshade ['sʌnʃeɪd] *n* sombrilla *f*.

sunshine ['sʌnʃaɪn] *n* (luz *f* del) sol *m*.

sunstroke ['sʌnstrəʊk] *n* (U) insolación *f*; **to get ~** coger una insolación.

suntan ['sʌntæn] ◇ *n* bronceado *m*; **to have a ~** estar bronceado(da); **to get a ~** broncearse. ◇ *comp* [lotion, cream] bronceador(ra).

suntrap ['sʌntræp] *n* lugar *m* muy soleado.

super ['suːpəʳ] ◇ *adj* **- 1.** *inf* [wonderful] estupendo(da), fenomenal **- 2.** [better than normal - size etc] superior. ◇ *n US inf* [of apartment building] portero(ra).

superannuation ['suːpə,rænjʊ'eɪʃn] *n* (U) jubilación *f*, pensión *f*.

superb [suː'pɜːb] *adj* excelente, magnífico(ca).

supercilious [,suːpə'sɪlɪəs] *adj* altanero(ra).

superficial [,suːpə'fɪʃl] *adj* superficial.

superfluous [suː'pɜːfluəs] *adj* superfluo(flua).

superhuman [,suːpə'hjuːmən] *adj* sobrehumano(na).

superimpose [,suːpərɪm'pəʊz] *vt*: **to ~ sthg on** superponer OR sobreponer algo a.

superintendent [,suːpərɪn'tendənt] *n* **- 1.** UK [of police] ≈ subjefe *m*, -fa *f* (de

policía) **- 2.** *fml* [of department] supervisor *m*, -ra *f* **- 3.** *US inf* [of apartment building] portero *m*, -ra *f*.

superior [suː'pɪərɪəʳ] ◇ *adj* **- 1.** [gen] ~ **(to)** superior (a) **- 2.** *pej* [arrogant] altanero(ra), arrogante. ◇ *n* superior *m* OR *f*.

superlative [suː'pɜːlətɪv] ◇ *adj* [of the highest quality] supremo(ma). ◇ *n* GRAMM superlativo *m*.

supermarket ['suːpə,mɑːkɪt] *n* supermercado *m*.

supernatural [,suːpə'nætʃrəl] *adj* sobrenatural.

superpower ['suːpə,paʊəʳ] *n* superpotencia *f*.

supersede [,suːpə'siːd] *vt* suplantar.

supersonic [,suːpə'sɒnɪk] *adj* supersónico(ca).

superstitious [,suːpə'stɪʃəs] *adj* supersticioso(sa).

superstore ['suːpəstɔːʳ] *n* hipermercado *m*.

supertanker ['suːpə,tæŋkəʳ] *n* superpetrolero *m*.

supervise ['suːpəvaɪz] *vt* [person] vigilar; [activity] supervisar.

supervisor ['suːpəvaɪzəʳ] *n* [gen] supervisor *m*, -ra *f*; [of thesis] director *m*, -ra *f*.

supper ['sʌpəʳ] *n* [evening meal] cena *f*.

supple ['sʌpl] *adj* flexible.

supplement [*n* 'sʌplɪmənt, *vb* 'sʌplɪment] ◇ *n* suplemento *m*. ◇ *vt* complementar.

supplementary [,sʌplɪ'mentərɪ] *adj* suplementario(ria).

supplier [sə'plaɪəʳ] *n* proveedor *m*, -ra *f*, suministrador *m*, -ra *f*.

supply [sə'plaɪ] ◇ *n* **- 1.** [gen] suministro *m*; [of jokes etc] surtido *m* **- 2.** (U) ECON oferta *f*; ~ **and demand** la oferta y la demanda. ◇ *vt*: **to ~ sthg (to)** suministrar OR proveer algo (a); **to ~ sb (with)** proveer a alguien (de).

➡ **supplies** *npl* MIL pertrechos *mpl*; [food] provisiones *fpl*; [for office etc] material *m*.

support [sə'pɔːt] ◇ *n* **- 1.** (U) [physical, moral, emotional] apoyo *m*; **in ~ of** en apoyo de **- 2.** (U) [financial] ayuda *f* **- 3.** (U) [intellectual] respaldo *m* **- 4.** TECH soporte *m*. ◇ *vt* **- 1.** [physically] sostener **- 2.** [emotionally, morally, intellectually] apoyar **- 3.** [financially - oneself, one's family] mantener; [- company, organization] financiar; **to ~ o.s.** ganarse la vida **- 4.** SPORT seguir.

supporter [sə'pɔːtəʳ] *n* **- 1.** [gen] partidario *m*, -ria *f* **- 2.** SPORT hincha *m* OR *f*, seguidor *m*, -ra *f*.

suppose [sə'pəʊz] ◇ *vt* suponer. ◇ *vi* suponer; **I ~ (so)** supongo (que sí); **I ~ not** supongo que no.

supposed [sə'pəʊzd] *adj* **- 1.** [doubtful] supuesto(ta) **- 2.** [intended]: **he was ~ to be**

here at eight debería haber estado aquí a las ocho **- 3.** [reputed]: **it's ~ to be very good** se supone OR se dice que es muy bueno.

supposedly [sə'pəʊzɪdlɪ] *adv* según cabe suponer.

supposing [sə'pəʊzɪŋ] *conj*: **~ your father found out?** ¿y si se entera tu padre?

suppress [sə'pres] *vt* **- 1.** [uprising] reprimir **- 2.** [emotions] contener.

supreme [sʊ'priːm] *adj* supremo(ma).

Supreme Court *n*: **the ~** [in US] el Tribunal Supremo (de los Estados Unidos).

surcharge ['sɜːtʃɑːdʒ] *n*: **~ (on)** recargo *m* (en).

sure [ʃʊəʳ] <> *adj* **- 1.** [gen] seguro(ra); **I'm not ~ why he said that** no estoy seguro de por qué dijo eso **- 2.** [certain - of outcome]: **to be ~ of** poder estar seguro(ra) de; **make ~ (that) you do it** asegúrate de que lo haces **- 3.** [confident]: **to be ~ of o.s.** estar seguro(ra) de uno mismo. <> *adv* **- 1.** *esp US inf* [yes] por supuesto, pues claro **- 2.** *US* [really] realmente.
◆ **for sure** *adv* con seguridad, a ciencia cierta; **I don't know for ~** no lo sé con total seguridad.
◆ **sure enough** *adv* efectivamente.

surely ['ʃʊəlɪ] *adv* sin duda; **~ you remember him?** ¡no me digas que no te acuerdas de él!

surety ['ʃʊərətɪ] *n* (U) fianza *f*.

surf [sɜːf] <> *n* espuma *f* (de las olas). <> *vt* COMPUT: **to ~ the Net** navegar por Internet.

surface ['sɜːfɪs] <> *n* **- 1.** [gen] superficie *f* **- 2.** *fig* [immediately visible part]: **on the ~** a primera vista. <> *vi* [gen] salir a la superficie.

surface mail *n* correo *m* por vía terrestre/marítima.

surfboard ['sɜːfbɔːd] *n* plancha *f* OR tabla *f* de surf.

surfeit ['sɜːfɪt] *n fml* exceso *m*.

surfing ['sɜːfɪŋ] *n* surf *m*.

surge [sɜːdʒ] <> *n* **- 1.** [of waves, people] oleada *f*; [of electricity] sobrecarga *f* momentánea **- 2.** [of emotion] arranque *m*, arrebato *m* **- 3.** [of interest, support, sales] aumento *m* súbito. <> *vi* **- 1.** [people, vehicles] avanzar en masa; [sea] encresparse; **the angry mob ~d forward** la multitud encolerizada avanzó en tropel.

surgeon ['sɜːdʒən] *n* cirujano *m*, -na *f*.

surgery ['sɜːdʒərɪ] (*pl* -**ies**) *n* **- 1.** (U) MED [performing operations] cirugía *f* **- 2.** *UK* MED [place] consultorio *m*; [consulting period] consulta *f*.

surgical ['sɜːdʒɪkl] *adj* [gen] quirúrgico(ca).

surgical spirit *n UK* alcohol *m* de 90°.

surly ['sɜːlɪ] (*compar* -**ier**, *superl* -**iest**) *adj*

hosco(ca), malhumorado(da).

surmount [sɜː'maʊnt] *vt* [overcome] superar, vencer.

surname ['sɜːneɪm] *n* apellido *m*.

surpass [sə'pɑːs] *vt fml* [exceed] superar, sobrepasar.

surplus ['sɜːpləs] <> *adj* excedente, sobrante. <> *n* [gen] excedente *m*, sobrante *m*; [in budget] superávit *m*.

surprise [sə'praɪz] <> *n* sorpresa *f*. <> *vt* sorprender.

surprised [sə'praɪzd] *adj* [person, expression] asombrado(da); **we were really ~** nos quedamos sorprendidos; **I'm ~ you're still here** me sorprende que todavía estés aquí; **she was ~ to find the house empty** se sorprendió al encontrar la casa vacía.

surprising [sə'praɪzɪŋ] *adj* sorprendente.

surrender [sə'rendəʳ] <> *n* rendición *f*. <> *vi lit & fig*: **to ~ (to)** rendirse OR entregarse (a).

surreptitious [ˌsʌrəp'tɪʃəs] *adj* subrepticio(cia).

surrogate ['sʌrəgeɪt] <> *adj* sustitutorio(-ria). <> *n* sustituto *m*, -ta *f*.

surrogate mother *n* madre *f* de alquiler.

surround [sə'raʊnd] *vt lit & fig* rodear; **to be ~ed by** estar rodeado(da) de.

surrounding [sə'raʊndɪŋ] *adj* **- 1.** [area, countryside] circundante **- 2.** [controversy, debate] relacionado(da).

surroundings [sə'raʊndɪŋz] *npl* [physical] alrededores *mpl*; [social] entorno *m*.

surveillance [sɜː'veɪləns] *n* vigilancia *f*.

survey [*n* 'sɜːveɪ, *vb* sə'veɪ] <> *n* **- 1.** [of public opinion, population] encuesta *f*, estudio *m* **- 2.** [of land] medición *f*; [of building] inspección *f*, reconocimiento *m*. <> *vt* **- 1.** [contemplate] contemplar **- 2.** [investigate statistically] hacer un estudio de **- 3.** [examine - land] medir; [- building] inspeccionar.

surveyor [sə'veɪəʳ] *n* [of property] perito *m* tasador de la propiedad; [of land] agrimensor *m*, -ra *f*.

survival [sə'vaɪvl] *n* [gen] supervivencia *f*.

survive [sə'vaɪv] <> *vt* sobrevivir a. <> *vi* **- 1.** [person] sobrevivir; **how are you? - surviving** ¿cómo estás? - voy tirando **- 2.** [custom, project] perdurar.

survivor [sə'vaɪvəʳ] *n* [person who escapes death] superviviente *m* OR *f*; **there were no ~s** no hubo supervivientes.

susceptible [sə'septəbl] *adj* **- 1.** [to pressure, flattery]: **~ (to)** sensible (a) **- 2.** MED: **~ (to)** propenso(sa) (a).

suspect [*adj & n* 'sʌspekt, *vb* sə'spekt] <> *adj* sospechoso(sa). <> *n* sospechoso *m*, -sa *f* <> *vt* **- 1.** [distrust] sospechar **- 2.** [think likely] imaginar; **I ~ he's right** imagino que tiene razón **- 3.** [consider guilty]:

to ~ **sb (of)** considerar a alguien sospechoso(sa) (de).

◆ **suspected** *pp*: **to have a** ~ed **heart attack** haber sufrido un posible infarto; **the** ~ed **culprits** los presuntos culpables.

suspend [sə'spend] *vt* [gen] suspender; [payments, work] interrumpir; [schoolchild] expulsar temporalmente.

suspended sentence [sə'spendɪd-] *n* condena *f* condicional.

suspender belt [sə'spendə^r-] *n UK* liguero *m*.

suspenders [sə'spendəz] *npl* **-1.** *UK* [for stockings] ligas *fpl* **-2.** *US* [for trousers] tirantes *mpl*, tiradores *mpl Bol & RP*, suspensores *mpl Andes & Arg*.

suspense [sə'spens] *n* [gen] incertidumbre *f*; CINEMA suspense *m*.

suspension [sə'spenʃn] *n* **-1.** [gen & AUT] suspensión *f* **-2.** [from job, school] expulsión *f* temporal.

suspension bridge *n* puente *m* colgante.

suspicion [sə'spɪʃn] *n* **-1.** [gen] sospecha *f*; [distrust] recelo *m*; **on** ~ **of** bajo sospecha de; **to be under** ~ estar bajo sospecha; **to arouse** ~ levantar sospechas **-2.** [small amount] pizca *f*.

suspicious [sə'spɪʃəs] *adj* **-1.** [having suspicions] receloso(sa) **-2.** [causing suspicion] sospechoso(sa).

sustain [sə'steɪn] *vt* **-1.** [gen] sostener **-2.** *fml* [injury, damage] sufrir.

sustenance ['sʌstɪnəns] *n (U) fml* sustento *m*.

SW (*abbr of* **short wave**) OC.

swab [swɒb] *n* (trozo *m* de) algodón *m*.

swagger ['swægə^r] *vi* pavonearse.

Swahili [swɑː'hiːlɪ] *n* suahili *m*.

swallow ['swɒləʊ] ◇ *n* [bird] golondrina *f*. ◇ *vt* [food, drink] tragar.

◆ **swallow up** *vt sep* [salary, time] tragarse.

swam [swæm] *pt* ▷ **swim**.

swamp [swɒmp] ◇ *n* pantano *m*, ciénaga *f*. ◇ *vt* **-1.** [flood - boat] hundir; [- land] inundar **-2.** [overwhelm]: **to** ~ **sthg (with)** [office] inundar algo (de); **to** ~ **sb (with)** agobiar a alguien (con); **we were** ~ed **with applications** nos vimos inundados de solicitudes.

swan [swɒn] *n* cisne *m*.

swap [swɒp] (*pt & pp* **-ped**, *cont* **-ping**) *vt* **-1.** [of one thing]: **to** ~ **sthg (for/with)** cambiar algo (por/con) **-2.** [of two things]: **to** ~ **sthg (over OR round)** [hats, chairs] cambiarse algo **-3.** *fig* [stories, experiences] intercambiar.

swarm [swɔːm] ◇ *n* [of bees] enjambre *m*; *fig* [of people] multitud *f*, tropel *m*. ◇ *vi* **-1.** *fig* [people] ir en tropel **-2.** *fig* [place]: **to**

be ~ing **(with)** estar abarrotado(da) (de).

swarthy ['swɔːðɪ] (*compar* **-ier**, *superl* **-iest**) *adj* moreno(na).

swastika ['swɒstɪkə] *n* esvástica *f*, cruz *f* gamada.

swat [swɒt] (*pt & pp* **-ted**, *cont* **-ting**) *vt* aplastar.

sway [sweɪ] ◇ *vt* [influence] convencer, persuadir. ◇ *vi* balancearse.

swear [sweə^r] (*pt* **swore**, *pp* **sworn**) ◇ *vt*: **to** ~ **(to do sthg)** jurar (hacer algo); **I could have sworn I saw him** juraría que lo vi. ◇ *vi* **-1.** [state emphatically] jurar; **I couldn't** ~ **to it** no me atrevería a jurarlo **-2.** [use swearwords] decir tacos, jurar; **to** ~ **at sb** insultar a alguien.

swearword ['sweəwɜːd] *n* palabrota *f*, taco *m*.

sweat [swet] ◇ *n* [perspiration] sudor *m*. ◇ *vi* [perspire] sudar. ◇ *vt* MED : **to** ~ **out a cold** quitarse un resfriado sudando **-2.** [in difficult situation]: **to** ~ **it out** aguantar.

sweater ['swetə^r] *n* suéter *m*, jersey *m*, chompa *f Andes*, chomba *f RP*.

sweatshirt ['swetʃɜːt] *n* sudadera *f*.

sweaty ['swetɪ] (*compar* **-ier**, *superl* **-iest**) *adj* [skin] sudoroso(sa); [clothes] sudado(-da).

swede [swiːd] *n UK* nabo *m* sueco.

Swede [swiːd] *n* sueco *m*, -ca *f*.

Sweden ['swiːdn] *n* Suecia *f*.

Swedish ['swiːdɪʃ] ◇ *adj* sueco(ca). ◇ *n* [language] sueco *m*. ◇ *npl*: **the** ~ los suecos.

sweep [swiːp] (*pt & pp* **swept**) ◇ *n* [movement - of broom] barrido *m*; [- of arm, hand] movimiento *m* OR gesto *m* amplio. ◇ *vt* **-1.** [with brush] barrer **-2.** [with light-beam] rastrear; [with eyes] recorrer. ◇ *vi* **-1.** [wind, rain]: **to** ~ **over** OR **across sthg** azotar algo **-2.** [person]: **to** ~ **past** pasar como un rayo.

◆ **sweep away** *vt sep* [destroy] destruir completamente.

◆ **sweep up** *vt sep & vi* barrer.

sweeping ['swiːpɪŋ] *adj* **-1.** [effect, change] radical **-2.** [statement] demasiado general **-3.** [curve] amplio(plia) **-4.** [gesture] amplio(plia).

sweet [swiːt] ◇ *adj* **-1.** [gen] dulce; [sugary] azucarado(da) **-2.** [smell - of flowers, air] fragante, perfumado(da) **-3.** [sound] melodioso(sa) **-4.** [character, person] amable **-5.** *US inf* genial. ◇ *n UK* **-1.** [candy] caramelo *m*, golosina *f* **-2.** [dessert] postre *m*. ◇ *excl US inf* genial.

sweet corn *n* maíz *m*.

sweeten ['swiːtn] *vt* endulzar.

sweetheart ['swiːthɑːt] *n* **-1.** [term of

endearment] cariño *m* - **2.** [boyfriend or girl-friend] amor *m*, novio *m*, -via *f*.

sweetness ['swiːtnɪs] *n* - **1.** [gen] dulzura *f* - **2.** [of taste] dulzor *m*.

sweet pea *n* guisante *m* de olor, alverjilla *f Andes, Col, CSur, Ven*, chícharo *m* de olor *CAm, Méx*, arvejilla *f RP*, clarín *m Chile*.

swell [swel] (*pt* -**ed**, *pp* **swollen** *OR* -**ed**) ◇ *vi* - **1.** [become larger]: **to ~ (up)** hinchar-se - **2.** [population, sound] aumentar. ◇ *vt* [numbers etc] aumentar. ◇ *n* [of sea] oleaje *m*. ◇ *adj US inf* estupendo(da), fenomenal.

swelling ['swelɪŋ] *n* hinchazón *f*; **the ~ has gone down** ha bajado la hinchazón.

sweltering ['sweltərɪŋ] *adj* - **1.** [weather] abrasador(ra), sofocante - **2.** [person] achicharrado(da).

swept [swept] *pt* & *pp* ⊳ **sweep**.

swerve [swɜːv] *vi* virar bruscamente.

swift [swɪft] ◇ *adj* - **1.** [fast] rápido(da) - **2.** [prompt] pronto(ta). ◇ *n* [bird] vencejo *m*.

swig [swɪg] *inf n* trago *m*; **to take a ~ of sthg** tomar un trago de algo.

swill [swɪl] ◇ *n* [pig food] bazofia *f*. ◇ *vt UK* [wash] enjuagar.

swim [swɪm] (*pt* **swam**, *pp* **swum**, *cont* -**ming**) ◇ *n* baño *m*; **to go for a ~** ir a nadar *OR* a darse un baño. ◇ *vi* - **1.** [in water] nadar - **2.** [subj: head, room] dar vueltas. ◇ *vt*: **to ~ the English Channel** cruzar el canal de la Mancha a nado; **I swam 20 lengths** nadé veinte largos.

swimmer ['swɪmə'] *n* nadador *m*, -ra *f*; **she's a good ~** nada bien.

swimming ['swɪmɪŋ] *n* natación *f*; **to go ~** ir a nadar.

swimming cap *n* gorro *m* de baño.

swimming costume *n UK* bañador *m*, traje *m* de baño.

swimming pool *n* piscina *f*, alberca *f Méx*, pileta *f RP*.

swimming trunks *npl* bañador *m*.

swimsuit ['swɪmsuːt] *n* bañador *m Esp*, traje *m* de baño, malla *f RP*, vestido *m* de baño *Col*.

swindle ['swɪndl] ◇ *n* estafa *f*, timo *m*, calote *m Amér*. ◇ *vt* estafar, timar; **to ~ sb out of sthg** estafar a alguien algo.

swine [swaɪn] *n inf pej* [person] cerdo *m*, -da *f*, canalla *m OR f*.

swing [swɪŋ] (*pt* & *pp* **swung**) ◇ *n* - **1.** [child's toy] columpio *m* - **2.** [change] viraje *m*, cambio *m* brusco; **a ~ towards the Conservatives** un giro hacia los conservadores - **3.** [sway] meneo *m*, balanceo *m* - **4.** *phr*: **to be in full ~** estar en plena marcha. ◇ *vt* - **1.** [move back and forth] balancear - **2.** [move in a curve - car etc] hacer virar bruscamente. ◇ *vi* - **1.** [move back

and forth] balancearse, oscilar - **2.** [move in a curve] girar - **3.** [turn]: **to ~ (round)** volverse, girarse - **4.** [change] virar, cambiar.

swing bridge *n* puente *m* giratorio.

swing door *n* puerta *f* oscilante.

swingeing ['swɪndʒɪŋ] *adj esp UK* severo(-ra).

swipe [swaɪp] ◇ *vt inf* [steal] birlar. ◇ *vi*: **to ~ at sthg** intentar golpear algo.

swirl [swɜːl] *vi* arremolinarse.

swish [swɪʃ] *vt* [tail] agitar, menear.

Swiss [swɪs] ◇ *adj* suizo(za). ◇ *n* [person] suizo *m*, -za *f*. ◇ *npl*: **the ~** los suizos.

switch [swɪtʃ] ◇ *n* - **1.** [control device] interruptor *m*, suiche *m Amér* - **2.** [change] cambio *m* completo, viraje *m*. ◇ *vt* - **1.** [change] cambiar de - **2.** [swap] intercambiar.

◆ **switch off** *vt sep* [light, radio etc] apagar; [engine] parar.

◆ **switch on** *vt sep* [light, radio etc] encender; [engine] poner en marcha.

Switch® [swɪtʃ] *n UK* tarjeta *f* de débito Switch.

switchboard ['swɪtʃbɔːd] *n* centralita *f*, conmutador *m Amér*.

Switzerland ['swɪtsələnd] *n* Suiza.

swivel ['swɪvl] (*UK pt* & *pp* -**led**, *cont* -**ling**, *US pt* & *pp* -**ed**, *cont* -**ing**) ◇ *vt* hacer girar. ◇ *vi* girar.

swivel chair *n* silla *f* giratoria.

swollen ['swəʊlən] ◇ *pp* ⊳ **swell**. ◇ *adj* - **1.** [ankle, leg etc] hinchado(da); **my eyes were ~** tenía los ojos hinchados; **to be ~ with pride** *fig* estar henchido de orgullo - **2.** [river] crecido(da).

swoop [swuːp] ◇ *n* [raid] redada *f*; **a ~ on a flat** una redada en un apartamento. ◇ *vi* - **1.** [move downwards] caer en picado - **2.** [move quickly] atacar por sorpresa.

swop [swɒp] = **swap**.

sword [sɔːd] *n* espada *f*.

swordfish ['sɔːdfɪʃ] (*pl inv OR* -**es**) *n* pez *m* espada.

swore [swɔː'] *pt* ⊳ **swear**.

sworn [swɔːn] ◇ *pp* ⊳ **swear**. ◇ *adj* JUR jurado(da).

swot [swɒt] (*pt* & *pp* -**ted**, *cont* -**ting**) *UK inf* ◇ *n pej* empollón *m*, -ona *f*. ◇ *vi*: **to ~ (for)** empollar (para).

swum [swʌm] *pp* ⊳ **swim**.

swung [swʌŋ] *pt* & *pp* ⊳ **swing**.

sycamore ['sɪkəmɔː'] *n* - **1.** sicomoro *m* - **2.** *US* [plane tree] plátano *m*.

syllable ['sɪləbl] *n* sílaba *f*.

syllabus ['sɪləbəs] (*pl* -**buses** *OR* -**bi** [-baɪ]) *n* programa *m* (de estudios).

symbol ['sɪmbl] *n* símbolo *m*.

symbolize, -ise ['sɪmbəlaɪz] *vt* simbolizar.

symmetry ['sɪmətrɪ] *n* simetría *f*.

sympathetic [,sɪmpə'θetɪk] *adj* - **1.** [understanding] **comprensivo(va) - 2.** [willing to support] favorable; ~ **to** bien dispuesto(ta) hacia.

sympathize, -ise ['sɪmpəθaɪz] *vi* **- 1.** [feel sorry]: **to ~ (with)** compadecerse (de) **- 2.** [understand]: **to ~ (with sthg)** comprender (algo) **- 3.** [support]: **to ~ with sthg** apoyar algo.

sympathizer, -iser ['sɪmpəθaɪzə^r] *n* simpatizante *m OR f.*

sympathy ['sɪmpəθɪ] *n* **- 1.** [understanding]: ~ **(for)** comprensión *f* (hacia); [compassion] compasión *f* (por) **- 2.** [agreement] solidaridad *f.*

→ **sympathies** *npl* [to bereaved person] pésame *m.*

symphony ['sɪmfənɪ] (*pl* **-ies**) *n* sinfonía *f.*

symposium [sɪm'pəʊzjəm] (*pl* **-siums** OR **-sia** [-zjə]) *n fml* simposio *m.*

symptom ['sɪmptəm] *n lit* & *fig* síntoma *m.*

synagogue ['sɪnəgɒg] *n* sinagoga *f.*

syndicate ['sɪndɪkət] *n* sindicato *m.*

syndrome ['sɪndrəʊm] *n* síndrome *m.*

synonym ['sɪnənɪm] *n*: ~ **(for** OR **of)** sinónimo *m* (de).

synopsis [sɪ'nɒpsɪs] (*pl* **-ses** [-si:z]) *n* sinopsis *f inv.*

syntax ['sɪntæks] *n* sintaxis *f inv.*

synthesis ['sɪnθəsɪs] (*pl* **-ses** [-si:z]) *n* síntesis *f inv.*

synthetic [sɪn'θetɪk] *adj* **- 1.** [man-made] sintético(ca) **- 2.** *pej* [insincere] artificial.

syphilis ['sɪfɪlɪs] *n* sífilis *f inv.*

syphon ['saɪfn] = **siphon.**

Syria ['sɪrɪə] *n* Siria.

syringe [sɪ'rɪndʒ] *n* jeringa *f*, jeringuilla *f.*

syrup ['sɪrəp] *n* (*U*) **- 1.** CULIN almíbar *m* **- 2.** MED jarabe *m*; **cough ~** jarabe para la tos.

system ['sɪstəm] *n* [gen] sistema *m*; [of central heating etc] instalación *f.*

systematic [ˌsɪstə'mætɪk] *adj* sistemático (ca).

system disk *n* COMPUT disco *m* del sistema.

systems analyst ['sɪstəmz-] *n* COMPUT analista *m OR f* de sistemas.

t (*pl* **t's** OR **ts**), **T** (*pl* **T's** OR **Ts**) [ti:] *n* [letter] t *f*, T *f.*

ta [tɑ:] *excl UK inf* ¡gracias!

tab [tæb] *n* **- 1.** [of cloth] etiqueta *f* **- 2.** [of metal, card etc] lengüeta *f* **- 3.** *US* [bill] cuenta *f*; **to pick up the ~** *inf* pagar la cuenta **- 4.** *phr*: **to keep ~s on sb** vigilar de cerca a alguien.

tabby ['tæbɪ] (*pl* **-ies**) *n*: ~ **(cat)** gato *m* atigrado.

table ['teɪbl] ◇ *n* **- 1.** [piece of furniture] mesa *f*; [small] mesilla *f* **- 2.** [diagram] tabla *f.* ◇ *vt UK* [propose] presentar.

tablecloth ['teɪblklɒθ] *n* mantel *m.*

table-hop *vi US* ir de mesa en mesa.

table lamp *n* lámpara *f* de mesa.

tablemat ['teɪblmæt] *n* salvamanteles *m inv.*

tablespoon ['teɪblspu:n] *n* **- 1.** [spoon] cuchara *f* grande **- 2.** [spoonful] cucharada *f* (grande).

tablet ['tæblɪt] *n* **- 1.** [pill, piece of soap] pastilla *f* **- 2.** [piece of stone] lápida *f.*

table tennis *n* tenis *m* de mesa.

table wine *n* vino *m* de mesa.

tabloid ['tæblɔɪd] *n*: **the ~s** los periódicos sensacionalistas; ~ **(newspaper)** tabloide *m.*

tabulate ['tæbjʊleɪt] *vt* tabular.

tacit ['tæsɪt] *adj fml* tácito(ta).

taciturn ['tæsɪtɜ:n] *adj fml* taciturno(na).

tack [tæk] ◇ *n* **- 1.** [nail] tachuela *f* **- 2.** *fig* [course of action] táctica *f.* ◇ *vt* **- 1.** [fasten with nail] fijar con tachuelas **- 2.** [in sewing] hilvanar. ◇ *vi* NAUT virar.

tackle ['tækl] ◇ *n* **- 1.** FTBL entrada *f* **- 2.** RUGBY placaje *m* **- 3.** (*U*) [equipment] equipo *m*, aparejos *mpl* **- 4.** [for lifting] aparejo *m.* ◇ *vt* **- 1.** [deal with - job] emprender; [- problem] abordar **- 2.** FTBL entrar, hacer una entrada a **- 3.** RUGBY placar **- 4.** [attack] arremeter.

tacky ['tækɪ] (*compar* **-ier**, *superl* **-iest**) *adj* **- 1.** *inf* [cheap and nasty] cutre; [ostentatious and vulgar] hortera **- 2.** [sticky] pegajoso(sa).

tact [tækt] *n* (*U*) tacto *m*, discreción *f.*

tactful ['tæktfʊl] *adj* discreto(ta).

tactic ['tæktɪk] *n* táctica *f.*

→ **tactics** *n* (*U*) MIL táctica *f.*

tactical ['tæktɪkl] *adj* estratégico(ca); [weapons] táctico(ca).

tactless ['tæktlɪs] *adj* indiscreto(ta), falto(ta) de tacto.

tadpole ['tædpəʊl] *n* renacuajo *m.*

tag [tæg] (*pt* & *pp* **-ged**, *cont* **-ging**) *n* [of cloth, paper] etiqueta *f*; **price ~** etiqueta del precio.

→ **tag question** *n* cláusula *f* final interrogativa.

→ **tag along** *vi inf*: **to ~ along (with)** pegarse (a), engancharse (a).

tail [teɪl] ◇ *n* [gen] cola *f*; [of coat, shirt] faldón *m.* ◇ *vt inf* [follow] seguir de cerca.

→ **tails** *npl* **- 1.** [formal dress] frac *m* **- 2.** [side of coin] cruz *f.*

→ **tail off** *vi* [voice] ir debilitándose;

[sound] ir disminuyendo.

tailback ['teɪlbæk] *n* UK cola *f*.

tailcoat ['teɪlˌkəʊt] *n* frac *m*.

tail end *n* parte *f* final.

tailgate ['teɪlgeɪt] ⬦ *n* US [of car] puerta *f* trasera de un vehículo. ⬦ *vt* conducir pegado a, pisar los talones a.

tailgate party *n* US fiesta en un acontecimiento deportivo en la que la gente coloca comida y bebida en la puerta trasera de un vehículo.

tailor ['teɪlə'] ⬦ *n* sastre *m*. ⬦ *vt* adaptar; **it can be** ~**ed to your needs** se puede adaptar a sus necesidades.

tailor-made *adj* (hecho(cha)) a la medida.

tailwind ['teɪlwɪnd] *n* viento *m* de cola.

tainted ['teɪntɪd] *adj* **- 1.** [reputation] manchado(da) **- 2.** US [food] estropeado(da).

Taiwan [ˌtaɪ'wɑːn] *n* Taiwán.

take [teɪk] (*pt* **took**, *pp* **taken**) ⬦ *vt* **- 1.** [gen] tomar; **do you** ~ **sugar?** ¿tomas azúcar?; **to** ~ **a photo** hacer OR tomar una foto; **to** ~ **a walk** dar un paseo; **to** ~ **a bath** bañarse; **to** ~ **a test** hacer un examen; **to** ~ **offence** ofenderse; **to be** ~**n ill** ponerse enfermo; ~ **the second turning on the right** toma el segundo giro a la derecha **- 2.** [bring, carry, accompany] llevar **- 3.** [steal] quitar, robar **- 4.** [buy] coger, quedarse con; [rent] alquilar; **I'll** ~ **the red one** me quedo con el rojo **- 5.** [take hold of] coger; **to** ~ **sb prisoner** capturar a alguien **- 6.** [accept - offer, cheque, criticism] aceptar; [- advice] seguir; [- responsibility, blame] asumir; **the machine only** ~**s 50p pieces** la máquina sólo admite monedas de 50 peniques **- 7.** [have room for - passengers, goods] tener cabida para **- 8.** [bear - pain etc] soportar, aguantar; **some people can't** ~ **a joke** hay gente que no sabe aguantar una broma **- 9.** [require - time, courage] requerir; [- money] costar; **it will** ~ **a week/three hours** llevará una semana/tres horas; **it only took me 5 minutes** sólo me llevó cinco minutos; **it** ~**s guts to do that** hay que tener agallas para hacer eso; **it took 5 people to move the piano** hicieron falta 5 personas para mover el piano **- 10.** [travel by - means of transport, route] tomar, coger **- 11.** [wear - shoes] calzar; [- clothes] usar **- 12.** [consider] considerar; **now,** ~ **John for instance** ... tomemos a John, por ejemplo ...; **to** ~ **sb for a fool/a policeman** tomar a alguien por tonto/por un policía **- 13.** [assume]: **I** ~ **it (that)** ... supongo que ... ⬦ *n* CINEMA toma *f*.

◆ **take after** *vt fus* parecerse a.

◆ **take apart** *vt sep* [dismantle] desmontar.

◆ **take away** *vt sep* **- 1.** [remove] quitar **- 2.** [deduct] restar, sustraer.

◆ **take back** *vt sep* **- 1.** [return] devolver **- 2.** [accept - faulty goods] aceptar la devolución de **- 3.** [admit as wrong] retirar **- 4.** [in memories]: **it** ~**s me back to when I was a teenager** me hace volver a mi adolescencia.

◆ **take down** *vt sep* **- 1.** [dismantle] desmontar **- 2.** [write down] escribir, tomar nota de.

◆ **take in** *vt sep* **- 1.** [deceive] engañar; **to be** ~**n in by sb** ser engañado por alguien **- 2.** [understand] comprender, asimilar; **I can't** ~ **it all in** no consigo asimilarlo todo **- 3.** [include] incluir, abarcar **- 4.** [provide accommodation for] acoger.

◆ **take off** ⬦ *vt sep* **- 1.** [clothes, glasses] quitarse **- 2.** [have as holiday] tomarse **- 3.** UK *inf* [imitate] imitar. ⬦ *vi* **- 1.** [plane] despegar, decolar Andes **- 2.** [go away suddenly] irse, marcharse.

◆ **take on** *vt sep* **- 1.** [accept - work, job] aceptar; [- responsibility] asumir **- 2.** [employ] emplear, coger **- 3.** [confront] desafiar.

◆ **take out** *vt sep* **- 1.** [from container, pocket] sacar **- 2.** [go out with]: **to** ~ **sb out** invitar a salir a alguien.

◆ **take over** ⬦ *vt sep* **- 1.** [company, business] absorber, adquirir; [country, government] apoderarse de **- 2.** [job] tomar, asumir. ⬦ *vi* **- 1.** [take control] tomar el poder **- 2.** [in job] entrar en funciones.

◆ **take to** *vt fus* **- 1.** [feel a liking for - person] coger cariño a; [- activity] aficionarse a **- 2.** [begin]: **to** ~ **to doing sthg** empezar a hacer algo.

◆ **take up** *vt sep* **- 1.** [begin]: **to** ~ **up singing** dedicarse a cantar; [job] aceptar, tomar **- 2.** [use up - time, space] ocupar; [- effort] requerir.

◆ **take up on** *vt sep* [accept]: **to** ~ **sb up on an offer** aceptar una oferta de alguien.

takeaway UK ['teɪkəˌweɪ], **takeout** US ['teɪkaʊt] *n* [food] comida *f* para llevar.

taken ['teɪkn] *pp* ▷ **take**.

takeoff ['teɪkɒf] *n* [of plane] despegue *m*, decolaje *m* Amér.

takeout US = **takeaway**.

takeover ['teɪkˌəʊvə'] *n* [of company] adquisición *f*.

takings *npl* [of shop] venta *f*; [of show] recaudación *f*.

talc [tælk], **talcum (powder)** ['tælkəm-] *n* talco *m*.

tale [teɪl] *n* **- 1.** [fictional story] cuento *m* **- 2.** [anecdote] anécdota *f*.

talent ['tælənt] *n*: ~ **(for sthg)** talento *m* (para algo).

talented ['tæləntɪd] *adj* con talento.

talk [tɔːk] ⬦ *n* **- 1.** [conversation] conversación *f*, plática *f* CAm, Méx; **to have a** ~ conversar **- 2.** (U) [gossip] habladurías *fpl* **- 3.** [lecture] charla *f*, conferencia *f*, plática *f*

CAm, Méx; **to give a ~ on sthg** dar una charla sobre algo. ⬦ *vi* **- 1.** [gen] hablar; **to ~ to/of** hablar OR platicar *CAm, Méx* con/ de; **~ing of Sarah, I met her mum yesterday** hablando de Sarah, ayer me encontré a su madre; **to ~ on** OR **about** hablar OR platicar *CAm, Méx* acerca de OR sobre; **they aren't ~ing to each other** no se hablan **- 2.** [gossip] chismorrear. ⬦ *vt* hablar de.

◆ **talks** *npl* conversaciones *fpl*.

◆ **talk into** *vt sep*: **to ~ sb into doing sthg** convencer a alguien para que haga algo.

◆ **talk out of** *vt sep*: **to ~ sb out of doing sthg** disuadir a alguien de que haga algo.

◆ **talk over** *vt sep* discutir, hablar de.

talkative ['tɔ:kətɪv] *adj* hablador(ra).

talk show *US n* programa *m* de entrevistas.

talk time *n* (U) [on mobile phone] tiempo *m* de conversación.

tall [tɔ:l] *adj* alto(ta); **she's 2 metres ~** mide 2 metros; **how ~ is he?** ¿cuánto mide?

tall story *n* cuento *m* (increíble).

tally ['tælɪ] (*pl* -ies, *pt & pp* -ied) ⬦ *n* cuenta *f*; **to keep a ~** llevar la cuenta. ⬦ *vi* concordar, casar.

talon ['tælən] *n* garra *f*.

tambourine [ˌtæmbə'ri:n] *n* pandereta *f*.

tame [teɪm] ⬦ *adj* **- 1.** [domesticated] doméstico(ca) **- 2.** *pej* [unexciting] soso(sa), aburrido(da). ⬦ *vt* **- 1.** [domesticate] domesticar **- 2.** [bring under control] dominar.

tamper ['tæmpə'] ◆ **tamper with** *vt fus* [lock] intentar forzar; [records, file] falsear; [machine] manipular.

tampon ['tæmpɒn] *n* tampón *m*.

tan [tæn] (*pt & pp* -ned, *cont* -ning) ⬦ *adj* de color marrón claro. ⬦ *n* bronceado *m*; **to get a ~** broncearse. ⬦ *vi* broncearse.

tang [tæŋ] *n* [smell] olor *m* fuerte; [taste] sabor *m* fuerte.

tangent ['tændʒənt] *n* GEOM tangente *f*; **to go off at a ~** salirse por la tangente.

tangerine [ˌtæn'dʒəri:n] *n* mandarina *f*.

tangible ['tændʒəbl] *adj* tangible.

tangle ['tæŋgl] *n* [mass] maraña *f*; *fig* [mess] enredo *m*, embrollo *m*, entrevero *m RP*.

tank [tæŋk] *n* **- 1.** [container] depósito *m*, tanque *m* **- 2.** MIL tanque *m*, carro *m* de combate.

tanker ['tæŋkə'] *n* **- 1.** [ship - gen] barco *m* cisterna, tanque *m*; [- for oil] petrolero *m* **- 2.** [truck] camión *m* cisterna.

tanned [tænd] *adj* bronceado(da).

Tannoy® ['tænɔɪ] *n* (sistema *m* de) altavoces *mpl*; **his name was called out over the ~** su nombre sonó por megafonía.

tantalizing ['tæntəlaɪzɪŋ] *adj* tentador(ra).

tantamount ['tæntəmaʊnt] *adj*: **~ to** equivalente a.

tantrum ['tæntrəm] (*pl* -s) *n* rabieta *f*; **to**

throw a ~ coger una rabieta.

Tanzania [ˌtænzə'nɪə] *n* Tanzania *f*.

tap [tæp] (*pt & pp* -ped, *cont* -ping) ⬦ *n* **- 1.** [device] grifo *m*, llave *f Amér*, canilla *f RP*, paja *f CAm*, caño *f Perú* **- 2.** [light blow] golpecito *m* **- 3.** [phr]: **to be on ~** [beer, water] ser de barril; **to have sthg on ~** *fig* tener algo a mano. ⬦ *vt* **- 1.** [hit] golpear ligeramente **- 2.** [strength, resources] utilizar, usar **- 3.** [phone] intervenir.

◆ **taps** *n US* MIL [at funeral] toque *m* de difuntos.

tap dancing *n* claqué *m*.

tape [teɪp] *n* **- 1.** [cassette, magnetic tape, strip of cloth] cinta *f* **- 2.** [adhesive plastic] cinta *f* adhesiva. ⬦ *vt* **- 1.** [on tape recorder, video recorder] grabar **- 2.** [with adhesive tape] pegar con cinta adhesiva.

tape measure *n* cinta *f* métrica.

taper ['teɪpə'] ⬦ *n* [candle] vela *f*. ⬦ *vi* afilarse.

tape recorder *n* magnetófono *m*.

tapestry ['tæpɪstrɪ] (*pl* -ies) *n* **- 1.** [piece of work] tapiz *m* **- 2.** [craft] tapicería *f*.

tar [tɑ:'] *n* alquitrán *m*.

target ['tɑ:gɪt] *n* **- 1.** [of missile, goal, aim] objetivo *m* **- 2.** [in archery, shooting, of criticism] blanco *m*.

tariff ['tærɪf] *n* tarifa *f*.

Tarmac® ['tɑ:mæk] *n* [material] alquitrán *m*.

◆ **tarmac** *n* AERON: **the tarmac** la pista.

tarnish ['tɑ:nɪʃ] *vt* [make dull] deslustrar; *fig* [damage] empañar, manchar.

tarpaulin [tɑ:'pɔ:lɪn] *n* lona *f* alquitranada.

tart [tɑ:t] ⬦ *adj* [bitter] agrio (agria). ⬦ *n* **- 1.** [sweet pastry] tarta *f* **- 2.** *v inf* [prostitute] furcia *f*, fulana *f*.

◆ **tart up** *vt sep UK inf pej* emperejilar.

tartan ['tɑ:tn] ⬦ *n* tartán *m*. ⬦ *comp* de tartán.

tartar(e) sauce ['tɑ:tə'-] *n* salsa *f* tártara.

task [tɑ:sk] *n* tarea *f*.

task force *n* MIL destacamento *m* de fuerzas.

tassel ['tæsl] *n* borla *f*.

taste [teɪst] ⬦ *n* **- 1.** [physical sense, discernment] gusto *m*; **in bad/good ~** de mal/buen gusto **- 2.** [flavour] sabor *m* **- 3.** [try]: **have a ~** pruébalo **- 4.** *fig* [for success, fast cars etc]: **~ (for)** afición *f*, gusto *m* (por) **- 5.** *fig* [experience] experiencia *f*. ⬦ *vt* **- 1.** [notice flavour of] notar un sabor a; **I can't ~ the lemon in it** no noto el sabor a limón **- 2.** [test, try] probar **- 3.** *fig* [experience] conocer. ⬦ *vi* saber; **to ~ of** OR **like** saber a.

tasteful ['teɪstfʊl] *adj* elegante, de buen gusto.

tasteless ['teɪstlɪs] *adj* **- 1.** [offensive, cheap and unattractive] de mal gusto **- 2.** [without flavour] insípido(da), soso(sa).

tasty ['teɪstɪ] (*compar* **-ier**, *superl* **-iest**) *adj* sabroso(sa).

tatters ['tætəz] *npl*: **in ~** [clothes] andrajoso(sa); *fig* [confidence, reputation] por los suelos.

tattoo [tə'tu:] (*pl* **-s**) ◇ *n* **- 1.** [design] tatuaje *m* **- 2.** UK [military display] desfile *m* militar. ◇ *vt* tatuar.

tatty ['tætɪ] (*compar* **-ier**, *superl* **-iest**) *adj* UK *inf pej* desastrado(da).

taught [tɔːt] *pt & pp* ▷ **teach**.

taunt [tɔːnt] ◇ *vt* zaherir a. ◇ *n* pulla *f*.

Taurus ['tɔːrəs] *n* Tauro *m*.

taut [tɔːt] *adj* tenso(sa).

tawdry ['tɔːdrɪ] (*compar* **-ier**, *superl* **-iest**) *adj* pej de oropel.

tax [tæks] ◇ *n* impuesto *m*, contribución *f*; **pay before** OR **after ~** salario antes/después de impuestos. ◇ *vt* **- 1.** [goods, profits] gravar **- 2.** [business, person] imponer contribuciones a **- 3.** [strain, test] poner a prueba.

taxable ['tæksəbl] *adj* imponible.

tax allowance *n* desgravación *f* fiscal.

taxation [tæk'seɪʃn] *n (U)* **- 1.** [system] sistema *m* tributario **- 2.** [amount] impuestos *mpl*, contribuciones *fpl*.

tax avoidance [-ə'vɔɪdəns] *n* evasión *f* fiscal.

tax collector *n* recaudador *m*, -ra *f* de impuestos.

tax disc *n* UK pegatina del impuesto de circulación.

tax evasion *n* fraude *m* fiscal, evasión *f* de impuestos.

tax-exempt US = **tax-free**.

tax-free UK, **tax-exempt** US *adj* exento(ta) de impuestos.

taxi ['tæksɪ] ◇ *n* taxi *m*. ◇ *vi* [plane] rodar por la pista.

taxi driver *n* taxista *m* OR *f*.

tax inspector *n* ≃ inspector *m*, -ra *f* de Hacienda.

taxi rank UK, **taxi stand** *n* parada *f* de taxis.

taxpayer ['tæks,peɪər] *n* contribuyente *m* OR *f*.

tax relief *n (U)* desgravación *f* fiscal.

tax return *n* declaración *f* de renta.

TB *n abbr of* **tuberculosis**.

tea [tiː] *n* **- 1.** [drink, leaves] té *m* **- 2.** UK [afternoon snack] té *m*, merienda *f* **- 3.** UK [evening meal] merienda cena *f*.

teabag ['tiːbæg] *n* bolsita *f* de té.

tea break *n* UK descanso *m (durante la jornada laboral)*.

teach [tiːtʃ] (*pt & pp* **taught**) ◇ *vt* **- 1.** [give lessons to] [student] dar clases a; **to ~ sb sthg** enseñar algo a alguien; **to ~ sb to do sthg** enseñar a alguien a hacer algo; **that**

will ~ you a lesson! ¡eso te enseñará! **- 2.** [give lessons in] [subject] dar clases de. ◇ *vi* ser profesor(ra), dar clases.

teacher ['tiːtʃər] *n* [at primary school] maestro *m*, -tra *f*; [at secondary school] profesor *m*, -ra *f*; **~'s pet** *pej* enchufado *m*, -da *f* de la clase.

teacher training college UK, **teachers college** US *n* escuela *f* normal.

teaching ['tiːtʃɪŋ] *n* enseñanza *f*.

tea cloth *n* UK [tea towel] paño *m* de cocina.

tea cosy UK, **tea cozy** US *n* cubretetera *f*.

teacup ['tiːkʌp] *n* taza *f* de té.

teak [tiːk] *n* teca *f*.

team [tiːm] *n* equipo *m*.

teammate ['tiːmmeɪt] *n* compañero *m*, -ra *f* de equipo.

teamwork ['tiːmwɜːk] *n (U)* trabajo *m* en equipo.

teapot ['tiːpɒt] *n* tetera *f*.

tear[1] [tɪər] *n* lágrima *f*; **in ~s** llorando.

tear[2] [teər] (*pt* **tore**, *pp* **torn**) ◇ *vt* **- 1.** [rip] rasgar, romper **- 2.** [remove roughly] arrancar; **she tore a page out of her exercise book** arrancó una página de su libro de ejercicios. ◇ *vi* **- 1.** [rip] romperse, rasgarse **- 2.** *inf* [move quickly]: **he tore out of the house** salió de la casa a toda pastilla; **they were ~ing along** iban a toda pastilla. ◇ *n* rasgón *m*, desgarrón *m*.

◆ **tear apart** *vt sep* **- 1.** [rip up] despedazar **- 2.** [upset greatly] desgarrar.

◆ **tear down** *vt sep* [building, statue] echar abajo.

◆ **tear up** *vt sep* hacer pedazos.

teardrop ['tɪədrɒp] *n* lágrima *f*.

tearful ['tɪəful] *adj* [person] lloroso(sa).

tear gas [tɪə-] *n (U)* gas *m* lacrimógeno.

tearoom ['tiːrʊm] *n* salón *m* de té.

tease [tiːz] *vt* **- 1.** [mock]: **to ~ sb (about)** tomar el pelo a alguien (acerca de) **- 2.** US [hair] cardarse.

tea service, tea set *n* servicio *m* OR juego *m* de té.

teaspoon ['tiːspuːn] *n* **- 1.** [utensil] cucharilla *f* **- 2.** [amount] cucharadita *f*.

teat [tiːt] *n* **- 1.** [of animal] tetilla *f* **- 2.** [of bottle] tetina *f*.

teatime ['tiːtaɪm] *n* UK hora *f* del té.

tea towel *n* paño *m* de cocina, repasador *m* RP.

technical ['teknɪkl] *adj* técnico(ca).

technical college *n* UK ≃ centro *m* de formación profesional.

technicality [,teknɪ'kælətɪ] (*pl* **-ies**) *n* detalle *m* técnico.

technically ['teknɪklɪ] *adv* **- 1.** [gen] técnicamente **- 2.** [theoretically] teóricamente, en teoría.

technician [tek'nɪʃn] *n* técnico *m*, -ca *f*.

technique [tek'ni:k] *n* técnica *f*.

techno ['teknəʊ] *n* MUS tecno *m*.

technological [ˌteknə'lɒdʒɪkl] *adj* tecnológico(ca).

technology [tek'nɒlədʒɪ] (*pl* **-ies**) *n* tecnología *f*.

teddy ['tedɪ] (*pl* **-ies**) *n*: ~ **(bear)** oso *m* de peluche.

tedious ['ti:djəs] *adj* tedioso(sa).

tee [ti:] *n* tee *m*.

teem [ti:m] *vi* - **1**. [rain] llover a cántaros - **2**. [be busy]: **to be ~ing with** estar inundado(da) de.

teenage ['ti:neɪdʒ] *adj* adolescente.

teenager ['ti:nˌeɪdʒəʳ] *n* adolescente *m* OR *f*, quinceañero *m*, -ra *f*.

teens [ti:nz] *npl* adolescencia *f*; **he's in his ~** es adolescente.

tee-shirt *n* camiseta *f*.

teeter ['ti:təʳ] *vi lit* & *fig* tambalearse.

teeth [ti:θ] *npl* ⊳ **tooth**.

teethe [ti:ð] *vi* echar los dientes.

teething troubles ['ti:ðɪŋ-] *npl fig* problemas *mpl* iniciales.

teetotaller *UK*, **teetotaler** *US* [ti:'təʊtləʳ] *n* abstemio *m*, -mia *f*.

TEFL ['tefl] (*abbr of* **teaching of English as a foreign language**) *n* enseñanza de inglés para extranjeros.

tel. (*abbr of* **telephone**) tfno.

telecommunications ['telɪkəˌmju:nɪ-'keɪʃnz] *npl* telecomunicaciones *fpl*.

telegram ['telɪgræm] *n* telegrama *m*.

telegraph ['telɪgrɑ:f] *n* telégrafo *m*.

telegraph pole, telegraph post *UK n* poste *m* de telégrafos.

telepathy [tɪ'lepəθɪ] *n* telepatía *f*.

telephone ['telɪfəʊn] <> *n* teléfono *m*; **to be on the ~** *UK* [connected to network] tener teléfono; [speaking] estar al teléfono. <> *vt* & *vi* telefonear.

telephone banking *n* banca *f* telefónica.

telephone book *n* guía *f* telefónica.

telephone booth *n* teléfono *m* público.

telephone box *n UK* cabina *f* (telefónica).

telephone call *n* llamada *f* telefónica, llamado *m* telefónico *Amér*.

telephone directory *n* guía *f* telefónica.

telephone number *n* número *m* de teléfono.

telephonist [tɪ'lefənɪst] *n UK* telefonista *m* OR *f*.

telephoto lens [ˌtelɪ'fəʊtəʊ-] *n* teleobjetivo *m*.

telescope ['telɪskəʊp] *n* telescopio *m*.

teletext ['telɪtekst] *n* teletexto *m*.

televideo [telɪ'vɪdɪəʊ] *n* televídeo *m*.

televise ['telɪvaɪz] *vt* televisar.

television ['telɪˌvɪʒn] *n* televisión *f*; **to watch ~** ver la televisión.

television set *n* televisor *m*, (aparato *m* de) televisión *f*.

teleworker ['telɪwɜːkəʳ] *n* teletrabajador *m*, -ra *f*.

telex ['teleks] <> *n* télex *m*. <> *vt* [message] transmitir por télex; [person] mandar un télex a.

tell [tel] (*pt* & *pp* **told**) <> *vt* - **1**. [gen] decir; **to ~ sb (that)** decir a alguien que; **to ~ sb sthg, to ~ sthg to sb** decir a alguien algo; **to ~ sb to do sthg** decir a alguien que haga algo - **2**. [joke, story] contar - **3**. [judge, recognize]: **to ~ what sb is thinking** saber en qué está pensando alguien; **to ~ the time** decir la hora - **4**. [differentiate]: **to ~ the difference between A and B** distinguir entre A y B; **it's hard to ~ one from another** son difíciles de distinguir. <> *vi* [have effect] surtir efecto.

◆ **tell apart** *vt sep* distinguir, diferenciar; **I can't ~ them apart** no consigo distinguirlos.

◆ **tell off** *vt sep esp US* reñir, reprender.

telling ['telɪŋ] *adj* [remark, incident] revelador(ra).

telltale ['telteɪl] <> *adj* revelador(ra). <> *n* chivato *m*, -ta *f*, acusica *m* OR *f*.

telly ['telɪ] (*pl* **-ies**) (*abbr of* **television**) *n UK inf* tele *f*.

temp [temp] <> *n inf UK* (*abbr of* **temporary (employee)**) trabajador *m*, -ra *f* temporal. <> *vi*: **she's ~ing** tiene un trabajo temporal.

temper ['tempəʳ] <> *n* - **1**. [state of mind, mood] humor *m*; **to keep one's ~** mantener la calma; **to lose one's ~** enfadarse, perder la paciencia - **2**. [angry state]: **to be in a ~** estar de mal humor - **3**. [temperament] temperamento *m*. <> *vt fml* templar, suavizar.

temperament ['temprəmənt] *n* temperamento *m*.

temperamental [ˌtemprə'mentl] *adj* [volatile] temperamental.

temperate ['temprət] *adj* templado(da).

temperature ['temprətʃəʳ] *n* temperatura *f*; **to have a ~** tener fiebre.

tempestuous [tem'pestjʊəs] *adj lit* & *fig* tempestuoso(sa).

template ['templɪt] *n* plantilla *f*.

temple ['templ] *n* - **1**. RELIG templo *m* - **2**. ANAT sien *f*.

temporarily [ˌtempə'rerəlɪ] *adv* temporalmente, provisionalmente.

temporary ['tempərərɪ] *adj* [gen] temporal, temporarico *Amér*, provisional, provisorio *Andes*, *Col*, *CSur*, *Ven*; [improvement, problem] pasajero(ra).

tempt [tempt] *vt* [entice]: **to ~ sb (to do sthg)** tentar a alguien (a hacer algo).

temptation [temp'teɪʃn] *n* tentación *f*.

tempting ['temptɪŋ] *adj* tentador(ra).

ten [ten] *num* diez; *see also* **six.**

tenable ['tenəbl] *adj* [reasonable, credible] sostenible.

tenacious [tɪ'neɪʃəs] *adj* tenaz.

tenancy ['tenənsɪ] (*pl* **-ies**) *n* [period - of house] alquiler *m*; [- of land] arrendamiento *m*.

tenant ['tenənt] *n* [of house] inquilino *m*, -na *f*; [of pub] arrendatario *m*, -ria *f*.

tend [tend] *vt* **- 1.** [have tendency]: **to ~ to do sthg** soler hacer algo, tender a hacer algo **- 2.** [look after] cuidar **- 3.** *US*: **to ~ bar** atender en el bar.

†tendency ['tendənsɪ] (*pl* **-ies**) *n* **- 1.** [trend]: **~ (for sb/sthg to do sthg)** tendencia *f* (de alguien/algo a hacer algo) **- 2.** [leaning, inclination] inclinación *f*.

tender ['tendə'] <> *adj* [gen] tierno(na); [sore] dolorido(da). <> *n* **- 1.** COMM propuesta *f*, oferta *f* **- 2.**: **(legal) ~** moneda *f* de curso legal. <> *vt fml* [resignation] presentar.

tendon ['tendən] *n* tendón *m*.

tenement ['tenəmənt] *n bloque de viviendas modestas.*

tenet ['tenɪt] *n fml* principio *m*, dogma *m*.

tennis ['tenɪs] *n* tenis *m*.

tennis ball *n* pelota *f* de tenis.

tennis court *n* pista *f* de tenis.

tennis match *n* partido *m* de tenis.

tennis player *n* tenista *m* OR *f*.

tennis racket *n* raqueta *f* de tenis.

tenor ['tenə'] *n* [singer] tenor *m*.

tense [tens] <> *adj* tenso(sa). <> *n* tiempo *m*. <> *vt* tensar.

tension ['tenʃn] *n* tensión *f*.

tent [tent] *n* tienda *f* (de campaña), carpa *f Amér.*

tentacle ['tentəkl] *n* tentáculo *m*.

tentative ['tentətɪv] *adj* **- 1.** [person] indeciso(sa); [step, handshake] vacilante **- 2.** [suggestion, conclusion etc] provisional.

tenterhooks ['tentəhʊks] *npl*: **to be on ~** estar sobre ascuas.

tenth [tenθ] *num* décimo(ma); *see also* **sixth.**

tent peg *n* estaca *f*.

tent pole *n* mástil *m* de tienda.

tenuous ['tenjʊəs] *adj* [argument] flojo(ja), poco convincente; [evidence, connection] débil, insignificante; [hold] ligero(ra).

tenure ['tenjə'] *(U) fml n* **- 1.** [of property] arrendamiento *m* **- 2.** [of job] ocupación *f*, ejercicio *m*.

tepid ['tepɪd] *adj* [liquid] tibio(bia).

term [tɜ:m] <> *n* **- 1.** [word, expression] término *m* **- 2.** SCH & UNIV trimestre *m* **- 3.** POL mandato *m*; **~ of office** mandato **- 4.** [period of time] periodo *m*; **in the long/short ~ a** largo/corto plazo. <> *vt*: **to ~ sthg sthg** calificar algo de algo.

◆ **terms** *npl* **- 1.** [of contract, agreement] condiciones *fpl* **- 2.** [basis]: **in international/real ~s** en términos internacionales/reales; **to be on good ~s (with sb)** mantener buenas relaciones (con alguien); **to come to ~s with sthg** aceptar algo.

◆ **in terms of** *prep* por lo que se refiere a.

terminal ['tɜ:mɪnl] <> *adj* MED incurable, terminal. <> *n* **- 1.** [transport] terminal *f* **- 2.** COMPUT terminal *m*.

terminate ['tɜ:mɪneɪt] <> *vt fml* [gen] poner fin a; [pregnancy] interrumpir. <> *vi* **- 1.** [bus, train] finalizar el trayecto **- 2.** [contract] terminarse.

termini ['tɜ:mɪnaɪ] *pl* ▷ **terminus.**

terminus ['tɜ:mɪnəs] (*pl* **-ni** OR **-nuses**) *n* (estación *f*) terminal *f*.

terrace ['terəs] *n* **- 1.** [gen] terraza *f* - **2.** *UK* [of houses] hilera *f* de casas adosadas.

◆ **terraces** *npl* FTBL: **the ~s** las gradas.

terraced ['terəst] *adj* **- 1.** [hillside] a terrazas - **2.** [house, housing] adosado(da).

terraced house *n UK* casa *f* adosada.

terrain [te'reɪn] *n* terreno *m*.

terrible ['terəbl] *adj* **- 1.** [crash, mess, shame] terrible, espantoso(sa) **- 2.** [unwell, unhappy, very bad] fatal.

terribly ['terəblɪ] *adv* [sing, play, write] malísimamente; [injured, sorry, expensive] horriblemente, terriblemente.

terrier ['terɪə'] *n* terrier *m*.

terrific [tə'rɪfɪk] *adj* **- 1.** [wonderful] fabuloso(sa), estupendo(da) **- 2.** [enormous] enorme, tremendo(da).

terrified ['terɪfaɪd] *adj* aterrorizado(da); **to be ~ (of)** tener terror a.

terrifying ['terɪfaɪɪŋ] *adj* aterrador(ra), espantoso(sa).

territory ['terətrɪ] (*pl* **-ies**) *n* **- 1.** [political area] territorio *m* **- 2.** [terrain] terreno *m* **- 3.** [area of knowledge] esfera *f*, campo *m*.

terror ['terə'] *n* [fear] terror *m*; **to live in ~** vivir aterrorizado(da); **they ran out of the house in ~** salieron de la casa aterrorizados.

terrorism ['terərɪzm] *n* terrorismo *m*.

terrorist ['terərɪst] *n* terrorista *m* OR *f*.

terrorize, -ise ['terəraɪz] *vt* aterrorizar, aterrar.

terse [tɜ:s] *adj* seco(ca).

Terylene® ['terəli:n] *n* terylene® *m*.

test [test] <> *n* **- 1.** [trial] prueba *f* **- 2.** [examination] examen *m*, prueba *f* **- 3.** MED [of blood, urine] análisis *m inv*; [of eyes] revisión *f*. <> *vt* **- 1.** [try out] probar, poner a prueba **- 2.** [examine] examinar; **to ~ sb on** examinar a alguien de.

testament ['testəmənt] *n* [will] testamento *m*.

test-drive *vt* someter a prueba de carretera.

testicles ['testiklz] *npl* testículos *mpl*.

testify ['testifai] (*pt* & *pp* **-ied**) ⬦ *vi* **- 1.** JUR prestar declaración **- 2.** [be proof]: **to ~ to sthg** dar fe de OR atestiguar algo. ⬦ *vt*: **to ~ that** declarar que.

testimony [*UK* 'testimoni, *US* 'testəmɔ̃uni] *n* JUR testimonio *m*, declaración *f*.

testing ['testiŋ] *adj* duro(ra).

test match *n UK* SPORT partido *m* internacional.

test pilot *n* piloto *m* OR *f* de pruebas.

test tube *n* probeta *f*.

test-tube baby *n* bebé *m* OR *f* probeta *f*.

tetanus ['tetənəs] *n* tétanos *m inv.*

tether ['teðə^r] ⬦ *vt* atar. ⬦ *n*: **to be at the end of one's ~** estar uno que ya no puede más.

text [tekst] *n* **- 1.** [gen] texto *m* **- 2.** [textbook] libro *m* de texto.

textbook ['tekstbok] *n* libro *m* de texto.

textile ['tekstail] *n* textil *m*, tejido *m*.

texting ['tekstiŋ] *n inf* mensajes *fpl* de texto.

text message *n* [on mobile phone] mensaje *m* de texto.

text messaging [-'mesidʒiŋ] *n* [on mobile phone] mensajería *f* de texto.

texture ['tekstʃə^r] *n* textura *f*.

Thai [tai] ⬦ *adj* tailandés(esa). ⬦ *n* **- 1.** [person] tailandés *m*, -esa *f* **- 2.** [language] tailandés *m*.

Thailand ['tailænd] *n* Tailandia.

Thames [temz] *n*: **the ~** el Támesis.

than [weak form ðən, strong form ðæn] ⬦ *prep* que; **you're older ~ me** eres mayor que yo; **you're older ~ I thought** eres mayor de lo que pensaba. ⬦ *conj* que; **I'd sooner read ~ sleep** prefiero leer que dormir; **no sooner did he arrive ~ she left** tan pronto llegó él, ella se fue; **more ~ three/once** más de tres/ de una vez; **rather ~ stay, he chose to go** en vez de quedarse, prefirió irse.

thank [θæŋk] *vt*: **to ~ sb (for sthg)** dar las gracias a alguien (por algo), agradecer a alguien (algo); **~ God** OR **goodness** OR **heavens!** ¡gracias a Dios!, ¡menos mal!
◆ **thanks** ⬦ *npl* agradecimiento *m*; **they left without a word of ~s** se marcharon sin dar las gracias. ⬦ *excl* ¡gracias!; **~s a lot** muchas gracias; **would you like a biscuit? – no ~s** ¿quieres una galleta? – no, gracias; **~s for** gracias por.
◆ **thanks to** *prep* gracias a.

thankful ['θæŋkfol] *adj* **- 1.** [relieved] aliviado(da) **- 2.** [grateful]: **~ (for)** agradecido(da) (por).

thankless ['θæŋklis] *adj* ingrato(ta).

Thanksgiving ['θæŋks,giviŋ] *n US* Día *m* de Acción de Gracias (el cuarto Jueves de noviembre).

thank you *excl* ¡gracias!; **~ very much** muchas gracias; **~ for** gracias por; **to say ~ (for sthg)** dar gracias (por algo); **tea? – no ~** ¿té? – no, gracias.

that [ðæt, weak form of pron and conj ðət] (*pl* **those**) ⬦ *pron* **- 1.** (demonstrative use: *pl* 'those') ése *m*, ésa *f*, ésos *mpl*, ésas *fpl*; (indefinite) eso; **~ sounds familiar** eso me resulta familiar; **who's ~?** [who is it?] ¿quién es?; **what's ~?** ¿qué es eso?; **~'s a shame** es una pena; **is ~ Maureen?** [asking someone else] ¿es ésa Maureen?; [asking person in question] ¿eres Maureen?; **like ~** así; **do you like these or those?** ¿te gustan éstos o ésos? **- 2.** [further away in distance, time] aquél *m*, aquélla *f*, aquéllos *mpl*, aquéllas *fpl*; (indefinite) aquello; **~ was the life!** ¡aquello sí que era vida!; **all those who helped me** todos aquellos que me ayudaron **- 3.** (to introduce relative clauses) que; **a path ~ led into the woods** un sendero que conducía al bosque; **everything ~ I have done** todo lo que he hecho; **the room ~ I sleep in** el cuarto donde OR en (el) que duermo; **the day ~ he arrived** el día en que llegó; **the firm ~ he's applying to** la empresa a la que solicita trabajo. ⬦ *adj* (demonstrative: *pl* 'those') ese (esa), esos (esas) (*pl*); [further away in distance, time] aquel (aquella), aquellos (aquellas) (*pl*); **those chocolates are delicious** esos bombones están exquisitos; **I'll have ~ book at the back** yo cogeré aquel libro del fondo; **later ~ day** más tarde ese/aquel mismo día. ⬦ *adv* tan; **it wasn't ~ bad** no estuvo tan mal; **it doesn't cost ~ much** no cuesta tanto; **it was ~ big** fue así de grande. ⬦ *conj* que; **he recommended ~ I phone you** aconsejó que te telefoneara; **it's time ~ we were leaving** deberíamos irnos ya, ya va siendo hora de irse.
◆ **that is** *adv* es decir.

thatched [θætʃt] *adj* con techo de paja.

that's [ðæts] = **that is**.

thaw [θɔː] ⬦ *vt* [snow, ice] derretir; [frozen food] descongelar. ⬦ *vi* [snow, ice] derretirse; [frozen food] descongelarse; *fig* [people, relations] distenderse. ⬦ *n* deshielo *m*.

the [weak form ðə, before vowel ði, strong form ðiː] *def art* **- 1.** [gen] el (la); (*pl*) los (las); (before feminine nouns beginning with stressed 'a' or 'ha' = **el**; *a' + el'* = **al**; *'de' + el'* = **del**): **~ boat** el barco; **~ Queen** la reina; **~ men** los hombres; **~ women** las mujeres; **~ water** el agua; **to ~ end of ~ world** al fin del mundo; **to play ~ piano** tocar el piano; **~ Joneses are coming to supper** los Jones vienen a cenar **- 2.** (with an adjective to form a noun): **~ old/young** los viejos/jóvenes; **~ impossible** lo imposible **- 3.** [in dates]: **~ twelfth of May** el doce de mayo; **~ forties** los cuarenta **- 4.** (in comparisons): **~**

more I see her, ~ less I like her cuanto más la veo, menos me gusta; **~ sooner ~ better** cuanto antes mejor **- 5.** [in titles]: **Catherine ~ Great** Catalina la Grande; **George ~ First** Jorge Primero.

theatre, theater US ['θɪətər] n **- 1.** [for plays etc] teatro m **- 2.** UK [in hospital] quirófano m, sala f de operaciones **- 3.** US [cinema] cine m.

theatregoer, theatergoer US ['θɪətə,gəʊər] n aficionado m, -da f al teatro.

theatrical [θɪˈætrɪkl] adj lit & fig teatral.

theft [θeft] n [more serious] robo m; [less serious] hurto m.

their [ðeər] poss adj su, sus (pl); **~ house** su casa; **~ children** sus hijos; **it wasn't THEIR fault** no fue culpa suya OR su culpa; **they washed ~ hair** se lavaron el pelo.

theirs [ðeəz] poss pron suyo (suya); **that money is ~** ese dinero es suyo; **our car hit ~** nuestro coche chocó contra el suyo; **it wasn't our fault, it was THEIRS** no fue culpa nuestra sino suya OR de ellos; **a friend of ~** un amigo suyo OR de ellos.

them [weak form ðəm, strong form ðem] pers pron pl **- 1.** (direct) los mpl, las fpl; **I know ~** los conozco; **I like ~** me gustan; **if I were OR was ~** si (yo) fuera ellos **- 2.** (indirect - gen) les mpl y fpl; (- with other third person prons) se mpl OR fpl; **she sent ~ a letter** les mandó una carta; **we spoke to ~** hablamos con ellos; **I gave it to ~** se lo di (a ellos) **- 3.** (stressed, after prep, in comparisons etc) ellos mpl, ellas fpl; **you can't expect THEM to do it** no esperarás que ELLOS lo hagan; **with/without ~** con/sin ellos; **a few of ~** unos pocos; **some of ~** algunos; **all of ~** todos ellos; **we're not as wealthy as ~** no somos tan ricos como ellos.

theme [θiːm] n **- 1.** [gen] tema m **- 2.** [signature tune] sintonía f.

theme tune n tema m musical.

themselves [ðem'selvz] pron **- 1.** (reflexive) se; (after preposition) sí; **they enjoyed ~** se divirtieron; **they were talking amongst ~** hablaban entre ellos **- 2.** (for emphasis) ellos mismos mpl, ellas mismas fpl; **they did it ~** lo hicieron ellos mismos **- 3.** [alone] solos(las); **they organized it (by) ~** lo organizaron ellas solas **- 4.** [their usual selves]: **the boys aren't ~ today** hoy los chicos no se están portando como de costumbre.

then [ðen] <> adv **- 1.** [not now] entonces; **up until ~ he had always trusted her** hasta entonces siempre había confiado en ella; **from ~ on** desde entonces **- 2.** [next, afterwards] luego, después **- 3.** [in that case] entonces; **I'll do it straight away ~** entonces lo voy a hacer ahora mismo; **all right ~** de acuerdo, pues **- 4.** [therefore] entonces, por

lo tanto; **~ it must have been her!** ¡entonces tiene que haber sido ella! **- 5.** [furthermore, also] además. <> adj entonces; **the ~ headmistress** la entonces directora.

~ then again loc conj pero por otra parte.

theology [θɪˈɒlədʒɪ] n teología f.

theoretical [θɪəˈretɪkl] adj teórico(ca).

theorize, -ise ['θɪəraɪz] vi: **to ~ (about sthg)** teorizar (sobre algo).

theory ['θɪərɪ] (pl -ies) n teoría f; **in ~** en teoría.

therapist ['θerəpɪst] n terapeuta m OR f.

therapy ['θerəpɪ] n terapia f.

there [ðeər] <> pron [indicating existence]: **~ is/are** hay; **~'s someone at the door** hay alguien en la puerta; **~ must be some mistake** debe (de) haber un error; **~ are five of us** somos cinco. <> adv **- 1.** [referring to place - near speaker] ahí; [- further away] allí, allá; **I'm going ~ next week** voy para allá OR allí la semana que viene; **~ it is** ahí está; **over ~** por allí; **it's six miles ~ and back** hay seis millas entre ir y volver; **we're nearly ~** ya casi hemos llegado **- 2.** [in existence, available] ahí; **is anybody ~?** ¿hay alguien ahí?; **is John ~, please?** [when telephoning] ¿está John? <> excl: **~, I knew he'd turn up** ¡mira!, sabía que aparecería; **~, ~ (don't cry)** ¡venga, venga (no llores)!

~ there and then, then and there adv en el acto.

thereabouts [,ðeərə'baʊts], **thereabout** US [,ðeərə'baʊt] adv: **or ~** o por ahí.

thereafter [,ðeər'ɑːftər] adv fml después, a partir de entonces.

thereby [,ðeər'baɪ] adv fml de ese modo.

therefore ['ðeəfɔːr] adv por lo tanto, por consiguiente.

there's [ðeəz] = there is.

thermal ['θɜːml] adj térmico(ca).

thermometer [θəˈmɒmɪtər] n termómetro m.

Thermos (flask)® ['θɜːməs-] n termo m.

thermostat ['θɜːməstæt] n termostato m.

thesaurus [θɪˈsɔːrəs] (pl -es) n diccionario m de sinónimos y voces afines.

these [ðiːz] pl ⊳ this.

thesis ['θiːsɪs] (pl theses ['θiːsiːz]) n tesis f inv.

they [ðeɪ] pers pron pl **- 1.** [gen] ellos mpl, ellas fpl; **~'re pleased** (ellos) están satisfechos; **~'re pretty earrings** son unos pendientes bonitos; **THEY can't do it** ELLOS no pueden hacerlo; **there ~ are** allí están **- 2.** [unspecified people]: **~ say it's going to snow** dicen que va a nevar.

they'd [ðeɪd] = they had, they would.

they'll [ðeɪl] = they shall, they will.

they're [ðeər] = they are.

they've [ðeɪv] = they have.

thick [θɪk] ⬦ *adj* **-1.** [not thin] grueso(sa);
it's 3 cm ~ tiene 3 cm de grueso; how ~ is
it? ¿qué espesor tiene? **-2.** [dense - hair, liquid, fog] espeso(sa) **-3.** *inf* [stupid] corto(-
ta), necio(cia). ⬦ *n*: to be in the ~ of
estar en el centro OR meollo de.

thicken ['θɪkn] ⬦ *vt* espesar. ⬦ *vi* [gen]
espesarse.

thicket ['θɪkɪt] *n* matorral *m*.

thickness ['θɪknɪs] *n* espesor *m*.

thickset [,θɪk'set] *adj* fornido(da), robus-
to(ta).

thick-skinned [-'skɪnd] *adj* insensible.

thief [θiːf] (*pl* **thieves**) *n* ladrón *m*, -ona *f*.

thieve [θiːv] *vt* & *vi* robar, hurtar.

thieves [θiːvz] *pl* ⊳ **thief**.

thigh [θaɪ] *n* muslo *m*.

thimble ['θɪmbl] *n* dedal *m*.

thin [θɪn] (*compar* **-ner**, *superl* **-nest**, *pt* & *pp*
-ned, *cont* **-ning**) *adj* **-1.** [not thick] delga-
do(da), fino(na) **-2.** [skinny] delgado(da),
flaco(ca) **-3.** [watery] claro(ra), aguado(da)
-4. [sparse - crowd, vegetation, mist] poco
denso (poco densa); [- hair] ralo(la).
◆ **thin down** *vt sep* [liquid] aclarar.

thing [θɪŋ] *n* **-1.** [gen] cosa *f*; the next ~ on
the list lo siguiente de la lista; the (best)
~ to do would be ... lo mejor sería ...; first
~ in the morning a primer hora de la mañana; last ~ at night a última hora de la noche; the main ~ lo principal; the whole
~ is a shambles es un auténtico desastre;
it's a good ~ you were there menos mal
que estabas allí; I thought the same ~ lo
mismo pensé yo; the ~ is ... el caso es que
... **-2.** [anything]: not a ~ nada; I didn't do a
~ no hice nada **-3.** [person]: poor ~! ¡po-
brecito *m*, -ta! *f*.
◆ **things** *npl* **-1.** [clothes, possessions] cosas *fpl*, corotos *mpl Carib*; ~s aren't what
they used to be las cosas ya no son lo que
eran **-2.** *inf* [life]: how are ~s? ¿qué tal (van
las cosas)?

think [θɪŋk] (*pt* & *pp* **thought**) ⬦ *vt*
-1. [believe]: to ~ (that) creer OR pensar
que; I ~ so creo que sí; I don't ~ so creo
que no **-2.** [have in mind] pensar; what are
you ~ing? ¿en qué piensas?; I didn't ~ to
ask her no se me ocurrió preguntárselo
-3. [imagine] entender, hacerse una idea
de; I can't ~ what might have happened
to them no quiero ni pensar lo que les podría haber ocurrido; I thought so ya me lo
imaginaba **-4.** [in polite requests] creer; do
you ~ you could help me? ¿cree que podría
ayudarme? ⬦ *vi* **-1.** [use mind] pensar; to
~ aloud pensar en voz alta **-2.** [have stated
opinion]: what do you ~ of OR about his
new film? ¿qué piensas de su nueva película?; to ~ a lot of sthg/sb tener en mucha

estima algo/a alguien; to ~ well of sb tener
una buena opinión de alguien **-3.** *phr*: to
~ twice pensárselo dos veces.
◆ **think about** *vt fus* pensar en; I'll
have to ~ about it tendré que pensarlo;
to ~ about doing sthg pensar en hacer
algo.
◆ **think of** *vt fus* **-1.** [consider]: to ~ of
doing sthg pensar en hacer algo **-2.** [re-
member] acordarse de **-3.** [conceive] pensar
en; how did you ~ of (doing) that? ¿cómo
se te ocurrió (hacer) esto?
◆ **think out, think through** *vt sep*
[plan] elaborar; [problem] examinar.
◆ **think over** *vt sep* pensarse, meditar.
◆ **think up** *vt sep* idear.

think tank *n* grupo de expertos convocados por
*una organización para aconsejar sobre un tema
determinado*.

third [θɜːd] ⬦ *num adj* tercer(ra). ⬦ *num n*
-1. [fraction] tercio *m* **-2.** [in order] tercero *m*,
-ra *f* **-3.** UNIV ≃ aprobado *m (en un título universitario); see also* **sixth**.

thirdly ['θɜːdlɪ] *adv* en tercer lugar.

third party insurance *n* seguro *m* a terceros.

third-rate *adj pej* de poca categoría.

Third World *n*: the ~ el Tercer Mundo.

thirst [θɜːst] *n lit* & *fig*: ~ (for) sed *f* (de).

thirsty ['θɜːstɪ] (*compar* **-ier**, *superl* **-iest**) *adj*
[parched]: to be OR feel ~ tener sed.

thirteen [,θɜː'tiːn] *num* trece; *see also* **six**.

thirty ['θɜːtɪ] (*pl* **-ies**) *num* treinta; *see also*
sixty.

this [ðɪs] (*pl* **these**) ⬦ *pron* [gen] éste *m*,
ésta *f*, éstos *mpl*, éstas *fpl; (indefinite)* esto;
~ is/these are for you esto es/éstos son para tí; ~ can't be true esto no puede ser cierto; do you prefer these or those? ¿prefieres
éstos o aquéllos?; ~ is Daphne Logan [in-
troducing another person] ésta es OR te pre-
sento a Daphne Logan; [introducing oneself
on phone] soy Daphne Logan; what's ~?
¿qué es eso? ⬦ *adj* **-1.** [gen] este (esta),
estos (estas) (*pl*); ~ country este país; these
thoughts estos pensamientos; I prefer
~ one prefiero éste; ~ morning/week esta
mañana/semana; ~ Sunday/summer este
domingo/verano **-2.** *inf* [a certain] un
(una); there's ~ woman I know hay una
tía que conozco. ⬦ *adv*: it was ~ big era
así de grande; you'll need about ~ much
te hará falta un tanto así.

thistle ['θɪsl] *n* cardo *m*.

thong [θɒŋ] *n* **-1.** [of leather] correa *f*
-2. [underwear] tanga *f*.

thorn [θɔːn] *n* [prickle] espina *f*.

thorough ['θʌrə] *adj* **-1.** [investigation etc]
exhaustivo(va), completo(ta) **-2.** [person,
work] minucioso(sa), concienzudo(da).

thoroughbred ['θʌrəbred] *n* pura sangre *m* OR *f*.

thoroughfare ['θʌrəfeəʳ] *n fml* calle *f* mayor, avenida *f* principal.

thoroughly ['θʌrəlɪ] *adv* **-1.** [fully, in detail] a fondo, exhaustivamente **-2.** [completely, utterly] completamente, totalmente.

those [ðəʊz] *pl* ⊳ that.

though [ðəʊ] ⇔ *conj* aunque; even ~ aunque; as ~ como si. ⇔ *adv* sin embargo; she still likes him ~ y sin embargo le sigue gustando.

thought [θɔːt] ⇔ *pt* & *pp* ⊳ think. ⇔ *n* **-1.** [notion, idea] idea *f* **-2.** [act of thinking]: after much ~ después de pensarlo mucho **-3.** [philosophy, thinking] pensamiento *m*.

◆ **thoughts** *npl* **-1.** [reflections] reflexiones *fpl* **-2.** [views] ideas *fpl*, opiniones *fpl*; what are your ~s on the subject? ¿qué piensas sobre el tema?

thoughtful ['θɔːtfʊl] *adj* **-1.** [pensive] pensativo(va) **-2.** [considerate] considerado(da), atento(ta); that was ~ of her fue muy considerada.

thoughtless ['θɔːtlɪs] *adj* desconsiderado(da).

thousand ['θaʊznd] *num* mil; a OR one ~ mil; two ~ dos mil; ~s of miles de; they came in their ~s vinieron miles de ellos; *see also* six.

thousandth ['θaʊzntθ] ⇔ *num adj* milésimo(ma). ⇔ *num n* [fraction] milésima *f*; *see also* sixth.

thrash [θræʃ] *vt lit* & *fig* dar una paliza a.

◆ **thrash about, thrash around** *vi* agitarse violentamente.

◆ **thrash out** *vt sep* darle vueltas a, discutir.

thread [θred] ⇔ *n* **-1.** [of cotton, argument] hilo *m* **-2.** [of screw] rosca *f*, filete *m*. ⇔ *vt* [needle] enhebrar.

threadbare ['θredbeəʳ] *adj* raído(da), gastado(da).

threat [θret] *n*: ~ (to/of) amenaza *f* (para/de); they were just empty ~s no eran más que amenazas vanas.

threaten ['θretn] ⇔ *vt* amenazar; to ~ sb (with) amenazar a alguien (con); to ~ to do sthg amenazar con hacer algo. ⇔ *vi* amenazar.

three [θriː] *num* tres; *see also* six.

three-dimensional [-dɪ'menʃənl] *adj* tridimensional.

threefold ['θriːfəʊld] ⇔ *adj* triple. ⇔ *adv* tres veces.

three-piece *adj* de tres piezas; ~ suite tresillo *m*.

three-ply *adj* [wood] de tres capas; [rope, wool] de tres hebras.

three-quarter length *adj*: ~ jacket tres cuartos *m*.

thresh [θreʃ] *vt* trillar.

threshold ['θreʃhəʊld] *n* **-1.** [doorway] umbral *m* **-2.** [level] límite *m*; the pain ~ el umbral del dolor.

threw [θruː] *pt* ⊳ throw.

thrifty ['θrɪftɪ] (*compar* -ier, *superl* -iest) *adj* [person] ahorrativo(va); [meal] frugal.

thrill [θrɪl] ⇔ *n* **-1.** [sudden feeling] estremecimiento *m* **-2.** [exciting experience]: it was a ~ to see it fue emocionante verlo. ⇔ *vt* entusiasmar.

thrilled [θrɪld] *adj*: ~ (with sthg/to do sthg) encantado(da) (de algo/de hacer algo).

thriller ['θrɪləʳ] *n* novela *f*/película *f*/obra *f* de suspense.

thrilling ['θrɪlɪŋ] *adj* emocionante.

thrive [θraɪv] (*pt* -d OR throve, *pp* -d) *vi* [plant] crecer mucho; [person] rebosar de salud; [business] prosperar.

thriving ['θraɪvɪŋ] *adj* [plant] que crece bien.

throat [θrəʊt] *n* garganta *f*; to have a sore ~ tener dolor de garganta.

throb [θrɒb] (*pt* & *pp* -bed, *cont* -bing) *vi* **-1.** [heart, pulse] latir; [head] palpitar **-2.** [engine, music] vibrar, resonar.

throes [θrəʊz] *npl*: to be in the ~ of estar en medio de.

throne [θrəʊn] *n* trono *m*; to be on the ~ ocupar el trono.

throng [θrɒŋ] ⇔ *n* multitud *f*. ⇔ *vt* llegar en tropel a.

throttle ['θrɒtl] ⇔ *n* válvula *f* reguladora. ⇔ *vt* [strangle] estrangular.

through [θruː] ⇔ *adj* [finished]: to be ~ with sthg haber terminado algo. ⇔ *adv* **-1.** [in place] de parte a parte, de un lado a otro; they let us ~ nos dejaron pasar; I read it ~ lo leí hasta el final **-2.** [in time] hasta el final. ⇔ *prep* **-1.** [relating to place, position] a través de; to cut/travel ~ sthg cortar/viajar por algo **-2.** [during] durante; all ~ the night durante toda la noche; to go ~ an experience pasar por una experiencia **-3.** [because of] a causa de, por **-4.** [by means of] gracias a, por medio de; I got it ~ a friend lo conseguí a través de un amigo **-5.** *US* [up to and including]: Monday ~ Friday de lunes a viernes.

◆ **through and through** *adv* de pies a cabeza.

throughout [θruː'aʊt] ⇔ *prep* **-1.** [during] a lo largo de, durante todo (durante toda) **-2.** [everywhere in] por todo(da). ⇔ *adv* **-1.** [all the time] todo el tiempo **-2.** [everywhere] por todas partes.

throve [θrəʊv] *pt* ⊳ thrive.

throw [θrəʊ] (*pt* threw, *pp* thrown) ⇔ *vt*

- 1. [gen] **tirar;** [ball, hammer, javelin] **aventar** *Andes, Cam & Méx,* **lanzar - 2.** [subj: horse] **derribar, desmontar - 3.** *fig* [confuse] **desconcertar.** ◇ *n* **lanzamiento** *m,* **tiro** *m.*

➡ **throw away** *vt sep* [discard] **tirar;** *fig* [waste] **botar** *Amér.*

➡ **throw out** *vt sep* **-1.** [discard] **tirar - 2.** [force to leave] **echar.**

➡ **throw up** *vi inf* [vomit] **vomitar, arrojar.**

throwaway ['θrəʊəˌweɪ] *adj* **-1.** [bottle, product] **desechable - 2.** [remark, gesture] **hecho(cha) como quien no quiere la cosa.**

throw-in *n* UK FTBL **saque** *m* **de banda.**

thrown [θrəʊn] *pp* ▷ **throw.**

thru [θruː] *US inf* = **through.**

thrush [θrʌʃ] *n* **-1.** [bird] **tordo** *m* **- 2.** MED [vaginal] **candidiasis** *f.*

thrust [θrʌst] (*pt & pp* **thrust**) ◇ *n* **-1.** [of sword] **estocada** *f;* [of knife] **cuchillada** *f;* [of troops] **arremetida** *f* **- 2.** TECH (fuerza *f* de) **propulsión** *f* **- 3.** [main meaning] **esencia** *f.* ◇ *vt* [shove]: **he ~ the knife into his enemy hundió el cuchillo en el cuerpo de su enemigo.**

thud [θʌd] (*pt & pp* **-ded,** *cont* **-ding**) *vi* **dar un golpe seco.**

thug [θʌg] *n* **matón** *m.*

thumb [θʌm] ◇ *n* [of hand] **pulgar** *m.* ◇ *vt inf* [hitch]: **to ~ a lift hacer dedo.**

➡ **thumb through** *vt fus* **hojear.**

thumbs down [ˌθʌmz-] *n:* **to get** OR **be given the ~** [plan] **ser rechazado(da);** [play] **ser recibido(da) con descontento.**

thumbs up [ˌθʌmz-] *n:* **we got** OR **were given the ~ nos dieron luz verde** OR **el visto bueno.**

thumbtack ['θʌmtæk] *n* US **chincheta** *f.*

thump [θʌmp] ◇ *n* **-1.** [blow] **puñetazo** *m,* **porrazo** *m* **- 2.** [thud] **golpe** *m* **seco.** ◇ *vt* [punch] **dar un puñetazo a.** ◇ *vi* [heart, head] **latir con fuerza.**

thunder ['θʌndə^r] ◇ *n* (*U*) **-1.** METEOR **truenos** *mpl* **- 2.** *fig* [loud sound] **estruendo** *m,* **estrépito** *m.* ◇ *v impers* METEOR **tronar.** ◇ *vi* [make loud sound] **retumbar.**

thunderbolt ['θʌndəbəʊlt] *n* **rayo** *m.*

thunderclap ['θʌndəklæp] *n* **trueno** *m.*

thunderstorm ['θʌndəstɔːm] *n* **tormenta** *f,* **tempestad** *f.*

thundery ['θʌndərɪ] *adj* **tormentoso(sa).**

Thursday ['θɜːzdɪ] *n* **jueves** *m inv; see also* **Saturday.**

thus [ðʌs] *adv fml* **-1.** [therefore] **por consiguiente, así que - 2.** [in this way] **así, de esta manera.**

thwart [θwɔːt] *vt* **frustrar.**

thyme [taɪm] *n* **tomillo** *m.*

thyroid ['θaɪrɔɪd] *n* **tiroides** *m inv.*

tiara [tɪˈɑːrə] *n* **tiara** *f.*

Tibet [tɪˈbet] *n* **(el) Tibet.**

tic [tɪk] *n* **tic** *m.*

tick [tɪk] ◇ *n* **-1.** [written mark] **marca** *f* OR **señal** *f* **de visto bueno - 2.** [sound] **tictac** *m* **- 3.** *inf* [credit]: **on ~ a crédito.** ◇ *vt* **marcar (con una señal).** ◇ *vi* [make ticking sound] **hacer tictac.**

➡ **tick off** *vt sep* **-1.** [mark off] **marcar (con una señal de visto bueno) - 2.** [tell off]: **to ~ sb off (for sthg) echar una bronca a alguien (por algo) - 3.** *US inf* [irritate] **fastidiar.**

➡ **tick over** *vi* **funcionar al ralentí.**

ticket ['tɪkɪt] *n* **-1.** [for bus, train etc] **billete** *m,* **boleto** *m Amér;* [for cinema, football match] **entrada** *f* **- 2.** [for traffic offence] **multa** *f,* **parte** *m Chile.*

ticket collector *n* UK **revisor** *m,* **-ra** *f.*

ticket inspector *n* UK **revisor** *m,* **-ra** *f.*

ticket machine *n* **máquina** *f* **automática para la venta de billetes** OR **boletos** *Amér.*

ticket office *n* **taquilla** *f,* **boletería** *f Amér.*

tickle ['tɪkl] *vt* **-1.** [touch lightly] **hacer cosquillas a - 2.** *fig* [amuse] **divertir.**

ticklish ['tɪklɪʃ] *adj* [sensitive to touch]: **to be ~ tener cosquillas.**

tidal ['taɪdl] *adj* **de la marea.**

tidal wave *n* **maremoto** *m.*

tidbit *US* = **titbit.**

tiddlywinks ['tɪdlɪwɪŋks], **tiddledywinks** *US* ['tɪdldɪwɪŋks] *n* **juego** *m* **de la pulga.**

tide [taɪd] *n* **-1.** [of sea] **marea** *f;* **high/low ~ marea alta/baja; the ~ is in/out ha subido/ bajado la marea; the ~ is coming in/going out la marea está subiendo/bajando - 2.** *fig* [of protest, feeling] **oleada** *f;* **the rising ~ of crime la creciente oleada de crímenes.**

tidy ['taɪdɪ] (*compar* **-ier,** *superl* **-iest,** *pt & pp* **-ied**) ◇ *adj* **-1.** [room, desk etc] **ordenado(da) - 2.** [person, dress, hair] **arreglado(da).** ◇ *vt* **ordenar, arreglar.**

➡ **tidy up** *vt sep* **ordenar, arreglar.**

tie [taɪ] (*pt & pp* **tied,** *cont* **tying**) ◇ *n* **-1.** [necktie] **corbata** *f* **- 2.** [string, cord] **atadura** *f* **- 3.** [bond, link] **vínculo** *m,* **lazo** *m* **- 4.** SPORT [draw] **empate** *m.* ◇ *vt* **-1.** [attach, fasten]: **to ~ sthg (to** OR **onto sthg) atar algo (a algo); to ~ sthg round/with sthg atar algo a/con algo - 2.** [do up - shoelaces] **atar;** [- knot] **hacer - 3.** *fig* [link]: **to be ~d to estar ligado(da) a.** ◇ *vi* [draw]: **to ~ (with) empatar (con).**

➡ **tie down** *vt sep fig* **atar.**

➡ **tie in with** *vt fus* **concordar con.**

➡ **tie up** *vt sep* **-1.** [gen] **atar - 2.** *fig* [money, resources] **inmovilizar - 3.** *fig* [link]: **to be ~d up with estar ligado(da) a.**

tiebreak(er) ['taɪbreɪk(ə^r)] *n* **-1.** TENNIS **muerte** *f* **súbita, tiebreak** *m* **- 2.** [in game, competition] **pregunta** *adicional para romper un empate.*

tiepin ['taɪpɪn] *n* alfiler *m* de corbata.

tier [tɪəʳ] *n* [of seats] hilera *f*; [of cake] piso *m*.

tiff [tɪf] *n* pelea *f (de poca importancia).*

tiger ['taɪgəʳ] *n* tigre *m*.

tight [taɪt] ⋄ *adj* **-1.** [gen] apretado(da); [shoes] estrecho(cha) **-2.** [string, skin] tirante **-3.** [budget, schedule] ajustado(da) **-4.** [rules, restrictions] riguroso(sa) **-5.** [corner, bend] cerrado(da) **-6.** [match, finish] reñido(da) **-7.** *inf* [drunk] cocido(da) **-8.** *inf* [miserly] agarrado(da). ⋄ *adv* **-1.** [hold, squeeze] con fuerza; **to hold ~** agarrarse (fuerte); **to shut** OR **close sthg ~** cerrar algo bien **-2.** [pull, stretch] de modo tirante.
◆ **tights** *npl* medias *fpl*.

tighten ['taɪtn] ⋄ *vt* **-1.** [hold, grip]: **to ~ one's hold** OR **grip on sthg** coger con más fuerza algo **-2.** [rope, chain] tensar **-3.** [knot] apretar; [belt] apretarse **-4.** [rules, system] intensificar. ⋄ *vi* [rope, chain] tensarse.

tightfisted [,taɪt'fɪstɪd] *adj inf pej* agarrado(da).

tightly ['taɪtlɪ] *adv* **-1.** [hold, squeeze] con fuerza; [fasten] bien **-2.** [pack] apretadamente.

tightrope ['taɪtrəʊp] *n* cuerda *f* floja, alambre *m*.

tile [taɪl] *n* **-1.** [on roof] teja *f* **-2.** [on floor] baldosa *f*; [on wall] azulejo *m*, baldosín *m*.

tiled [taɪld] *adj* [roof] tejado(da); [floor] embaldosado(da); [wall] alicatado(da).

till [tɪl] ⋄ *prep* hasta; **~ now/then** hasta ahora/entonces. ⋄ *conj* hasta que; **wait ~ he arrives** espera hasta que llegue. ⋄ *n* caja *f* (registradora).

tiller ['tɪləʳ] *n* NAUT caña *f* del timón.

tilt [tɪlt] ⋄ *vt* inclinar, ladear. ⋄ *vi* inclinarse, ladearse.

timber ['tɪmbəʳ] *n* **-1.** *(U)* [wood] madera *f (para la construcción)* **-2.** [beam - of ship] cuaderna *f*; [- of house] viga *f*.

time [taɪm] ⋄ *n* **-1.** [gen] tiempo *m*; **ahead of ~** temprano; **in good ~** con tiempo; **on ~** puntualmente; **to take ~** llevar tiempo; **it's (about) ~ to ...** ya es hora de ...; **to have no ~ for** no poder con, no aguantar; **to pass the ~** pasar el rato; **to play for ~** intentar ganar tiempo; **to take one's ~ (doing sthg)** tomarse uno mucho tiempo (para hacer algo) **-2.** [as measured by clock] hora *f*; **what ~ is it?, what's the ~?** ¿qué hora es?; **the ~ is three o'clock** son las tres; **in a week's/year's ~** dentro de una semana/un año **-3.** [length of time] rato *m*; **it was a long ~ before he came** pasó mucho tiempo antes de que viniera; **for a ~** durante un tiempo **-4.** [point in time in past, era] época *f*; **at that ~** en aquella época **-5.** [occasion] vez *f*; **three ~s a week** tres veces a la semana;

from ~ to ~ de vez en cuando; **~ after ~**, **~ and again** una y otra vez **-6.** [experience]: **we had a good/bad ~** lo pasamos bien/mal **-7.** MUS compás *m*; **to keep ~** llevar el compás. ⋄ *vt* **-1.** [schedule] programar **-2.** [race, runner] cronometrar **-3.** [arrival, remark] elegir el momento oportuno para.
◆ **times** ⋄ *n*: **four ~s as much as me** cuatro veces más que yo. ⋄ *prep* MATH: **4 ~s 5** 4 por 5.
◆ **about time** *adv*: **it's about ~** ya va siendo hora.
◆ **at a time** *adv*: **for months at a ~** durante meses seguidos; **one at a ~** de uno en uno.
◆ **at times** *adv* a veces.
◆ **at the same time** *adv* al mismo tiempo.
◆ **for the time being** *adv* de momento.
◆ **in time** *adv* **-1.** [not late]: **in ~ (for)** a tiempo (para) **-2.** [eventually] con el tiempo.

time bomb *n* [bomb] bomba *f* de relojería; *fig* [dangerous situation] bomba *f*.

time lag *n* intervalo *m*.

timeless ['taɪmlɪs] *adj* eterno(na).

time limit *n* límite *m* de tiempo, plazo *m*.

timely ['taɪmlɪ] *(compar* **-ier**, *superl* **-iest)** *adj* oportuno(na).

time off *n* tiempo *m* libre.

time out *n* US SPORT tiempo *m* muerto.

timer ['taɪməʳ] *n* temporizador *m*.

time scale *n* tiempo *m* de ejecución.

time-share *n* UK multipropiedad *f*.

time switch *n* interruptor *m* de reloj.

timetable ['taɪm,teɪbl] *n* **-1.** [of buses, trains, school] horario *m* **-2.** [schedule of events] programa *m*.

time zone *n* huso *m* horario.

timid ['tɪmɪd] *adj* tímido(da).

timing ['taɪmɪŋ] *n (U)* **-1.** [judgment]: **she made her comment with perfect ~** su comentario fue hecho en el momento más oportuno **-2.** [scheduling]: **the ~ of the election is crucial** es crucial que las elecciones se celebren en el momento oportuno **-3.** [measuring] cronometraje *m*.

timpani ['tɪmpənɪ] *npl* timbales *mpl*, tímpanos *mpl*.

tin [tɪn] *n* **-1.** [metal] estaño *m*; **~ plate** hojalata *f* **-2.** UK [can, container] lata *f*.

tin can *n* lata *f*.

tinfoil ['tɪnfɔɪl] *n (U)* papel *m* de aluminio.

tinge [tɪndʒ] *n* **-1.** [of colour] matiz *m*, toque *m* **-2.** [of feeling] ligera sensación *f*.

tinged [tɪndʒd] *adj*: **~ with** con un toque de.

tingle ['tɪŋgl] *vi*: **my feet are tingling** siento hormigueo en los pies.

tinker ['tɪŋkəʳ] *vi* hacer chapuzas; **to ~ with** enredar con.

tinkle ['tɪŋkl] *vi* [ring] tintinear.

tinned [tɪnd] *adj UK* enlatado(da), en conserva.

tin opener *n UK* abrelatas *m inv.*

tinsel ['tɪnsl] *n (U)* oropel *m.*

tint [tɪnt] *n* tinte *m*, matiz *m.*

tinted ['tɪntɪd] *adj* [glasses, windows] tintado(da), ahumado(da).

tiny ['taɪnɪ] (*compar* **-ier**, *superl* **-iest**) *adj* diminuto(ta), pequeñito(ta).

tip [tɪp] (*pt & pp* **-ped**, *cont* **-ping**) ⋄ *n* - **1.** [end] punta *f* - **2.** *UK* [dump] vertedero *m* - **3.** [gratuity] propina *f* - **4.** [piece of advice] consejo *m.* ⋄ *vt* - **1.** [tilt] inclinar, ladear - **2.** [spill, pour] vaciar, verter - **3.** [give a gratuity to] dar una propina a. ⋄ *vi* - **1.** [tilt] inclinarse, ladearse - **2.** [spill] derramarse.

◆ **tip over** ⋄ *vt sep* volcar. ⋄ *vi* volcarse.

tip-off *n* información *f* (confidencial).

tipped [tɪpt] *adj* [cigarette] con filtro, emboquillado.

tipsy ['tɪpsɪ] (*compar* **-ier**, *superl* **-iest**) *adj inf dated* piripi.

tiptoe ['tɪptəʊ] *n*: on ~ de puntillas.

tip-top *adj inf dated* de primera.

tire ['taɪə^r] ⋄ *n US* = **tyre.** ⋄ *vt* cansar. ⋄ *vi*: **to ~ (of)** cansarse (de).

tired ['taɪəd] *adj*: ~ **(of sthg/of doing sthg)** cansado(da) (de algo/de hacer algo).

tireless ['taɪəlɪs] *adj* incansable.

tiresome ['taɪəsəm] *adj* pesado(da).

tiring ['taɪərɪŋ] *adj* cansado(da).

tissue ['tɪʃuː] *n* - **1.** [paper handkerchief] pañuelo *m* de papel - **2.** *(U)* BIOL tejido *m* - **3.** [paper] papel *m* de seda.

tissue paper *n (U)* papel *m* de seda.

tit [tɪt] *n* - **1.** [bird] herrerillo *m* - **2.** *vulg* [breast] teta *f.*

titbit *UK* ['tɪtbɪt], **tidbit** *US* ['tɪdbɪt] *n* - **1.** [of food] golosina *f* - **2.** *fig* [of news] noticia *f* breve e interesante.

tit for tat [-'tæt] *n*: it's ~ donde las dan las toman.

titillate ['tɪtɪleɪt] *vt & vi* excitar.

title ['taɪtl] *n* título *m.*

title deed *n* título *m* de propiedad.

title role *n* papel *m* principal.

titter ['tɪtə^r] *vi* reírse por lo bajo.

TM *abbr of* **trademark.**

to [*unstressed before consonant* tə, *unstressed before vowel* tʊ, *stressed* tuː] ⋄ *prep* - **1.** [indicating place, direction] a; **to go ~ Liverpool/Spain/school** ir a Liverpool/España/la escuela; **to go ~ the doctor's/John's** ir al médico/a casa de John; **the road ~ Glasgow** la carretera de Glasgow; **~ the left/right** a la izquierda/derecha; **~ the east/west** hacia el este/oeste - **2.** *(to express indirect object)* a; **to give sthg ~ sb** darle algo a alguien;

to talk ~ sb hablar con alguien; **a threat ~ sb** una amenaza para alguien; **we were listening ~ the radio** escuchábamos la radio - **3.** [as far as] hasta, a; **to count ~ ten** contar hasta diez; **we work from nine ~ five** trabajamos de nueve a cinco - **4.** [in expressions of time]: **it's ten/a quarter ~ three** son las tres menos diez/cuarto - **5.** [per] por; **40 miles ~ the gallon** un galón (por) cada 40 millas - **6.** [of] de; **the key ~ the car** la llave del coche - **7.** [for] para; **a letter ~ my daughter** una carta para OR a mi hija - **8.** [indicating reaction, effect]: **~ my surprise** para sorpresa mía - **9.** [in stating opinion]: **it seemed quite unnecessary ~ me/him** *etc* para mí/él *etc* aquello parecía del todo innecesario - **10.** [indicating state, process]: **to drive sb ~ drink** llevar a alguien a la bebida; **to lead ~ trouble** traer problemas. ⋄ *adv* [shut]: **push the door ~** cierra la puerta. ⋄ *with infinitive* - **1.** *(forming simple infinitive)*: **~ walk** andar - **2.** *(following another verb)*: **to begin ~ do sthg** empezar a hacer algo; **to try/want ~ do sthg** intentar/querer hacer algo; **to hate ~ do sthg** odiar tener que hacer algo - **3.** *(following an adjective)*: **difficult ~ do** difícil de hacer; **ready ~ go** listos para marchar - **4.** *(indicating purpose)* para; **I'm doing it ~ help you** lo hago para ayudarte; **he came ~ see me** vino a verme - **5.** *(substituting for a relative clause)*: **I have a lot ~ do** tengo mucho que hacer; **he told me ~ leave** me dijo que me fuera - **6.** *(to avoid repetition of infinitive)*: **I meant to call him but I forgot ~** tenía intención de llamarle pero se me olvidó - **7.** [in comments]: **~ be honest ...** para ser honesto ...; **~ sum up ...** para resumir ..., resumiendo ...

◆ **to and fro** *adv* de un lado para otro, de aquí para allá.

toad [təʊd] *n* sapo *m.*

toadstool ['təʊdstuːl] *n* seta *f* venenosa.

toast [təʊst] ⋄ *n* - **1.** *(U)* [bread] pan *m* tostado; **a slice of ~** una tostada - **2.** [drink] brindis *m.* ⋄ *vt* - **1.** [bread] tostar - **2.** [person] brindar por.

toasted sandwich [ˌtəʊstɪd-] *n* sándwich *m* tostado.

toaster ['təʊstə^r] *n* tostador *m*, -ra *f.*

tobacco [tə'bækəʊ] *n* tabaco *m.*

tobacconist's (shop) [tə'bækənɪsts (ʃɒp)] *n* estanco *m.*

toboggan [tə'bɒgən] ⋄ *n* tobogán *m*, trineo *m.*

today [tə'deɪ] ⋄ *n* - **1.** [this day] hoy *m*; **~'s date** la fecha de hoy; **what is ~'s date?** ¿qué día es hoy?; **~'s paper** el periódico de hoy; **as from ~** a partir de hoy - **2.** [nowadays] hoy (en día). ⋄ *adv* - **1.** [this day] hoy; **what's the date ~?, what date is**

it ~ ¿qué fecha es hoy?; ~ **is the 6th of January** hoy es 6 de enero; **what day is** ~? ¿qué día es hoy?; **it's Sunday** ~ hoy es domingo; **a week ago** ~ hoy hace una semana; **a week (from)** ~ de aquí a una semana - **2.** [nowadays] hoy (en día).

toddler ['tɒdlə'] *n* niño pequeño *m*, niña pequeña *f* (que empieza a andar).

toddy ['tɒdɪ] (*pl* -ies) *n* ponche *m*.

to-do (*pl* -s) *n inf* jaleo *m*, follón *m*.

toe [təʊ] ◇ *n* - **1.** [of foot] dedo *m* (del pie) - **2.** [of sock] punta *f*; [of shoe] puntera *f*. ◇ *vt* : **to** ~ **the line** acatar las normas.

toenail ['təʊneɪl] *n* uña *f* del dedo del pie.

toffee ['tɒfɪ] *n* caramelo *m*.

toga ['təʊɡə] *n* toga *f*.

together [tə'ɡeðə'] *adv* - **1.** [gen] juntos(tas); **all** ~ todos juntos; **to stick** ~ pegar; **to go (well)** ~ combinar bien - **2.** [at the same time] a la vez, juntos(tas).

◆ **together with** *prep* junto con.

toil [tɔɪl] *fml* ◇ *n* trabajo *m* duro. ◇ *vi* trabajar sin descanso.

toilet ['tɔɪlɪt] *n* [at home] wáter *m*, lavabo *m*; [in public place] servicios *mpl*, lavabo *m*; **to go to the** ~ ir al wáter.

toilet bag *n* neceser *m*.

toilet paper *n* (*U*) papel *m* higiénico.

toiletries ['tɔɪlɪtrɪz] *npl* artículos *mpl* de tocador.

toilet roll *n* [roll] rollo *m* de papel higiénico.

toilet water *n* (agua *f* de) colonia *f*.

token ['təʊkn] ◇ *adj* simbólico(ca). ◇ *n* - **1.** [voucher] vale *m*; [disk] ficha *f* - **2.** [symbol] muestra *f*, símbolo *m*; **as a** ~ **of our appreciation** como muestra de nuestro agradecimiento.

◆ **by the same token** *adv* del mismo modo.

told [təʊld] *pt* & *pp* ⊳ **tell.**

tolerable ['tɒlərəbl] *adj* tolerable, pasable.

tolerance ['tɒlərəns] *n* tolerancia *f*.

tolerant ['tɒlərənt] *adj* tolerante.

tolerate ['tɒləreɪt] *vt* - **1.** [put up with] soportar, tolerar - **2.** [permit] tolerar.

toll [təʊl] ◇ *n* - **1.** [number]: **death** ~ número *m* de víctimas - **2.** [fee] peaje *m* - **3.** *phr*: **to take its** ~ hacer mella. ◇ *vi* tocar, doblar.

toll-free *US adv* : **to call a number** ~ llamar a un número gratis.

tomato [*UK* tə'mɑːtəʊ, *US* tə'meɪtəʊ] (*pl* -es) *n* tomate *m*, jitomate *m CAm, Méx*.

tomb [tuːm] *n* tumba *f*, sepulcro *m*.

tomboy ['tɒmbɔɪ] *n* niña *f* poco feminina.

tombstone ['tuːmstəʊn] *n* lápida *f*.

tomcat ['tɒmkæt] *n* gato *m* (macho).

tomorrow [tə'mɒrəʊ] ◇ *n lit* & *fig* mañana *f*; ~ **is Sunday** mañana es domingo; **the day after** ~ pasado mañana; ~ **night** ma-

ñana por la noche; **he was drinking like there was no** ~ bebía como si se fuera a acabar el mundo; ~'**s world** el futuro. ◇ *adv* mañana; **see you** ~ hasta mañana; **a week (from)** ~ dentro de una semana a partir de mañana; **it happened a year ago** ~ mañana hará un año que ocurrió.

ton [tʌn] (*pl inv* OR -s) *n* - **1.** [imperial] *UK* = 1016 kg; *US* = 907,2 kg, ≃ tonelada *f* - **2.** [metric] = 1000 kg, tonelada *f*.

◆ **tons** *npl inf* : ~**s (of)** un montón (de).

tone [təʊn] *n* - **1.** [gen] tono *m* - **2.** [on phone] señal *f*.

◆ **tone down** *vt sep* suavizar, moderar.

◆ **tone up** *vt sep* poner en forma.

tone-deaf *adj* que no tiene (buen) oído.

tongs [tɒŋz] *npl* [for coal] tenazas *fpl*; [for sugar] pinzas *fpl*, tenacillas *fpl*.

tongue [tʌŋ] *n* - **1.** [gen] lengua *f*; **to hold one's** ~ *fig* quedarse callado(da) - **2.** [of shoe] lengüeta.

tongue-in-cheek *adj* : **it was only** ~ no iba en serio.

tongue-tied [-ˌtaɪd] *adj* incapaz de hablar (*por timidez o nervios*).

tongue twister [-ˌtwɪstə'] *n* trabalenguas *m inv*.

tonic ['tɒnɪk] *n* - **1.** [gen] tónico *m* - **2.** [tonic water] tónica *f*.

tonic water *n* agua *f* tónica.

tonight [tə'naɪt] ◇ *n* esta noche *f*. ◇ *adv* esta noche.

tonnage ['tʌnɪdʒ] *n* tonelaje *m*.

tonne [tʌn] (*pl inv* OR -s) *n* tonelada *f* métrica.

tonsil ['tɒnsl] *n* amígdala *f*; **to have one's** ~**s out** operarse de las amígdalas.

tonsil(l)itis [ˌtɒnsɪ'laɪtɪs] *n* (*U*) amigdalitis *f inv*.

too [tuː] *adv* - **1.** [also] también; **me** ~ yo también - **2.** [excessively] demasiado; ~ **much** demasiado; ~ **many things** demasiadas cosas; **it finished all** OR **only** ~ **soon** terminó demasiado pronto; **I'd be only** ~ **happy to help** me encantaría ayudarte; **not** ~ ... no muy...

took [tʊk] *pt* ⊳ **take.**

tool [tuːl] *n* [implement] herramienta *f*; **garden** ~**s** útiles *mpl* del jardín.

tool bar *n* COMPUT barra *f* de herramientas.

tool box *n* caja *f* de herramientas.

tool kit *n* juego *m* de herramientas.

toot [tuːt] ◇ *n* bocinazo *m*. ◇ *vi* tocar la bocina.

tooth [tuːθ] (*pl* teeth) *n* [in mouth, of saw, gear wheel] diente *m*; **to brush one's teeth** cepillarse OR lavarse los dientes; **he had a** ~ **out** le sacaron un diente.

toothache ['tuːθeɪk] *n* dolor *m* de muelas.

toothbrush ['tuːθbrʌʃ] *n* cepillo *m* de dientes.

toothpaste ['tu:θpeɪst] *n* pasta *f* de dientes.
toothpick ['tu:θpɪk] *n* palillo *m*.
top [tɒp] (*pt* & *pp* **-ped**, *cont* **-ping**) ⬦ *adj*
- 1. [highest - step, floor] de arriba; [- object on pile] de encima **- 2.** [most important, successful] importante; **to be a ~ model** ser top model; **she got the ~ mark** sacó la mejor nota **- 3.** [maximum] máximo(ma); **at ~ speed** a máxima velocidad; **to be ~ secret** ser altamente confidencial. ⬦ *n*
- 1. [highest point] parte *f* superior *OR* de arriba; [of list] cabeza *f*, principio *m*; [of tree] copa *f*; [of hill, mountain] cumbre *f*, cima *f*; **at the ~ of the stairs** en lo alto de la escalera; **from ~ to bottom** de pies a cabeza; **on ~** encima; **at the ~ of one's voice** a voz en grito **- 2.** [lid, cap - of jar, box] tapa *f*; [- of bottle, tube] tapón *m*; [- of pen] capuchón *m*
- 3. [upper side] superficie *f* **- 4.** [blouse] blusa *f*; [T-shirt] camiseta *f*; [of pyjamas] parte *f* de arriba **- 5.** [toy] peonza *f* **- 6.** [most important level] cúpula *f* **- 7.** [of league, table, scale] cabeza *f*. ⬦ *vt* **- 1.** [be first in] estar a la cabeza de **- 2.** [better] superar **- 3.** [exceed] exceder.

➤ **on top of** *prep* **- 1.** [in space] encima de; **to be feeling on ~ of the world** estar en la gloria **- 2.** [in addition to] además de.

➤ **top up** *UK*, **top off** *US vt sep* volver a llenar.

top floor *n* último piso *m*.
top hat *n* chistera *f*, sombrero *m* de copa.
top-heavy *adj* demasiado pesado(da) en la parte de arriba.
topic ['tɒpɪk] *n* tema *m*, asunto *m*.
topical ['tɒpɪkl] *adj* de actualidad, actual.
topless ['tɒplɪs] *adj* en topless.
top-level *adj* de alto nivel.
topmost ['tɒpməʊst] *adj* más alto(ta).
topping ['tɒpɪŋ] *n* capa *f*; **with a ~ of cream** cubierto de nata.
topple ['tɒpl] ⬦ *vt* [government, pile] derribar; [president] derrocar. ⬦ *vi* venirse abajo.
top-secret *adj* sumamente secreto (sumamente secreta).
topsy-turvy [,tɒpsɪ'tɜ:vɪ] ⬦ *adj* [messy] patas arriba *(inv)*. ⬦ *adv* [messily] en desorden, de cualquier manera.
top-up *n*: **can I give you a ~?** ¿quieres que te ponga más?
top-up card *n* [for mobile phone] tarjeta *f* de recarga.
torch [tɔ:tʃ] *n* **- 1.** *UK* [electric] linterna *f*
- 2. [burning] antorcha *f*.
tore [tɔ:ʳ] *pt* ⊳ **tear**².
torment [*n* 'tɔ:ment, *vb* tɔ:'ment] ⬦ *n* tormento *m*; **she waited in ~** esperaba atormentada. ⬦ *vt* **- 1.** [worry greatly] atormentar **- 2.** [annoy] fastidiar.

torn [tɔ:n] *pp* ⊳ **tear**².
tornado [tɔ:'neɪdəʊ] (*pl* **-es** *OR* **-s**) *n* tornado *m*.
torpedo [tɔ:'pi:dəʊ] (*pl* **-es**) *n* torpedo *m*.
torrent ['tɒrənt] *n* torrente *m*.
torrid ['tɒrɪd] *adj* [hot] tórrido(da); *fig* [passionate] apasionado(da).
tortoise ['tɔ:təs] *n* tortuga *f* (de tierra).
tortoiseshell ['tɔ:təʃel] ⬦ *adj*: **~ cat** gato *m* pardo atigrado. ⬦ *n* (U) [material] carey *m*, concha *f*.
torture ['tɔ:tʃəʳ] ⬦ *n* tortura *f*. ⬦ *vt* torturar.
Tory ['tɔ:rɪ] (*pl* **-ies**) ⬦ *adj* tory, del partido conservador (británico). ⬦ *n* tory *m OR f*, miembro *m* del partido conservador (británico).
toss [tɒs] ⬦ *vt* **- 1.** [throw carelessly] tirar **- 2.** [move from side to side - head, boat] sacudir **- 3.** [salad] remover; [pancake] dar la vuelta en el aire **- 4.** [coin]: **to ~ a coin** echar a cara o cruz. ⬦ *vi* [move rapidly]: **to ~ and turn** dar vueltas (en la cama).

➤ **toss up** *vi* jugar a cara o cruz.

tot [tɒt] *n* **- 1.** *inf* [small child] nene *m*, nena *f*
- 2. [of drink] trago *m*.
total ['təʊtl] (*UK pt* & *pp* **-led**, *cont* **-ling**, *US pt* & *pp* **-ed**, *cont* **-ing**) ⬦ *adj* total. ⬦ *n* total *m*. ⬦ *vt* [add up] sumar. ⬦ *vi* [amount to] ascender a.
totalitarian [,təʊtælɪ'teərɪən] *adj* totalitario(ria).
totally ['təʊtəlɪ] *adv* [entirely] totalmente.
totter ['tɒtəʳ] *vi lit* & *fig* tambalearse.
touch [tʌtʃ] ⬦ *n* **- 1.** [sense, act of feeling] tacto *m* **- 2.** [detail, skill, knack] toque *m*
- 3. [contact]: **to get/keep in ~ (with)** ponerse/mantenerse en contacto (con); **to lose ~ (with)** perder el contacto (con); **to be out of ~ with** no estar al tanto de **- 4.** *SPORT*: **in ~** fuera de banda **- 5.** [small amount]: **a ~ (of)** un poquito (de). ⬦ *vt*
- 1. [gen] tocar; **you haven't ~ed your food** no has tocado la comida **- 2.** [emotionally] conmover **- 3.** [equal] igualar; **nobody can ~ her for professionalism** nadie la iguala en profesionalismo. ⬦ *vi* [be in contact] tocarse.

➤ **touch down** *vi* [plane] aterrizar, tomar tierra.

➤ **touch on** *vt fus* tocar, tratar por encima.

touch-and-go *adj* dudoso(sa), poco seguro (poco segura).
touchdown ['tʌtʃdaʊn] *n* **- 1.** [of plane] aterrizaje *m* **- 2.** [in American football] ensayo *m*.
touched [tʌtʃt] *adj* [grateful] emocionado(da).

touching ['tʌtʃɪŋ] *adj* conmovedor(ra).

touchline ['tʌtʃlaɪn] *n* línea *f* de banda.

touchscreen ['tʌtʃskri:n] *n* pantalla *f* táctil.

touchy ['tʌtʃɪ] (*compar* **-ier**, *superl* **-iest**) *adj* **-1.** [person]: ~ **(about)** susceptible (con) **-2.** [subject, question] delicado(da).

tough [tʌf] *adj* **-1.** [resilient] fuerte **-2.** [hard-wearing] resistente **-3.** [meat, regulations, policies] duro(ra); **to get** ~ **with sb** ponerse duro(ra) con alguien **-4.** [difficult to deal with] difícil **-5.** [rough - area] peligroso(sa).

toughen ['tʌfn] *vt* endurecer.

toupee ['tu:peɪ] *n* peluquín *m*.

tour [tʊəʳ] ◇ *n* **-1.** [long journey] viaje *m* largo; **to go on a** ~ **of Germany** hacer un recorrido por Alemania **-2.** [of pop group etc] gira *f* **-3.** [for sightseeing] recorrido *m*, visita *f*. ◇ *vt* [museum] visitar; [country] recorrer, viajar por. ◇ *vi* estar de gira.

touring ['tʊərɪŋ] *n* viajes *mpl* turísticos.

tourism ['tʊərɪzm] *n* turismo *m*.

tourist ['tʊərɪst] *n* turista *m* OR *f*.

tourist (information) office *n* oficina *f* de turismo.

tournament ['tɔ:nəmənt] *n* torneo *m*.

tour operator *n* touroperador *m*, operador *m* turístico.

tousled ['taʊzld] *adj* despeinado(da), alborotado(da).

tout [taʊt] ◇ *n* revendedor *m*, -ra *f*. ◇ *vt* revender. ◇ *vi*: **to** ~ **for sthg** solicitar algo; **to** ~ **for business** tratar de captar clientes.

tow [təʊ] ◇ *n*: **on** ~ UK [car] a remolque. ◇ *vt* remolcar.

towards UK [tə'wɔ:dz], **toward** US [tə'wɔ:d] *prep* **-1.** [gen] hacia; ~ **6 o'clock/ the end of the month** hacia las seis/final de mes **-2.** [for the purpose or benefit of] para.

towel ['taʊəl] *n* toalla *f*.

towelling UK, **toweling** US ['taʊəlɪŋ] *n* (U) [tejido *m* de] toalla *f*.

towel rail *n* toallero *m*.

tower ['taʊəʳ] ◇ *n* torre *f*. ◇ *vi*: **to** ~ **(over sthg)** elevarse (por encima de algo).

tower block *n* UK bloque *m* (*de pisos u oficinas*).

towering ['taʊərɪŋ] *adj* altísimo(ma).

town [taʊn] *n* **-1.** [gen] ciudad *f*; [smaller] pueblo *m* **-2.** [centre of town, city] centro *m* de la ciudad; **to go out on the** ~ irse de juerga; **to go to** ~ *fig* [to put in a lot of effort] emplearse a fondo; [spend a lot of money] tirar la casa por la ventana.

town centre *n* centro *m* (de la ciudad).

town council *n* ayuntamiento *m*.

town hall *n* ayuntamiento *m*.

town plan *n* plano *m* de la ciudad.

town planning *n* [study] urbanismo *m*.

township ['taʊnʃɪp] *n* **-1.** [in South Africa] zona urbana asignada por el gobierno para la población negra **-2.** [in US] ≃ municipio *m*.

towpath ['təʊpɑ:θ, *pl* -pɑ:ðz] *n* camino *m* de sirga.

towrope ['təʊrəʊp] *n* cable *m* de remolque.

tow truck *n* US (coche *m*) grúa *f*.

toxic ['tɒksɪk] *adj* tóxico(ca).

toy [tɔɪ] *n* juguete *m*.

◆ **toy with** *vt fus* [idea] acariciar; [food, coin etc] jugetear con.

toy shop *n* juguetería *f*.

trace [treɪs] ◇ *n* **-1.** [evidence, remains] rastro *m*, huella *f*; **there's no** ~ **of her** no hay rastro de ella **-2.** [small amount] pizca *f*. ◇ *vt* **-1.** [find] localizar, encontrar **-2.** [follow progress of] describir **-3.** [on paper] calcar.

tracing paper ['treɪsɪŋ-] *n* (U) papel *m* de calcar.

track [træk] ◇ *n* **-1.** [path] sendero *m* **-2.** SPORT pista *f* **-3.** RAIL vía *f* **-4.** [mark, trace] rastro *m*, huella *f* **-5.** [on record, tape] canción *f* **-6.** *phr*: **to keep/lose** ~ **of sb** no perder/perder la pista a alguien; **to be on the right/wrong** ~ ir por el buen/mal camino. ◇ *vt* [follow tracks of] rastrear, seguir la pista de.

◆ **track down** *vt sep* localizar.

track record *n* historial *m*; **to have a good** ~ tener un buen historial.

tracksuit ['træksu:t] UK *n* chandal *m*, equipo *m* de deportes, buzo *m* *Chile, Perú*, pants *mpl Méx*, sudadera *f Col*, jogging *m RP*.

tract [trækt] *n* **-1.** [pamphlet] artículo *m* breve **-2.** [of land, forest] extensión *f*.

tract house *n* US casa en una urbanización en la que todas las casas son iguales.

traction ['trækʃn] *n* tracción *f*; **to have one's leg in** ~ tener la pierna escayolada en alto.

tractor ['træktəʳ] *n* tractor *m*.

trade [treɪd] ◇ *n* **-1.** (U) [commerce] comercio *m* **-2.** [job] oficio *m*; **by** ~ de oficio. ◇ *vt* [exchange]: **to** ~ **sthg (for)** cambiar algo (por). ◇ *vi* COMM: **to** ~ **(with)** comerciar (con).

◆ **trade in** *vt sep* [exchange] dar como entrada.

trade fair *n* feria *f* de muestras.

trade-in *n* artículo usado que se entrega como entrada al comprar un artículo nuevo.

trademark ['treɪdmɑ:k] *n* COMM marca *f* comercial.

trade name *n* COMM nombre *m* comercial.

trader ['treɪdəʳ] *n* comerciante *m* OR *f*.

tradesman ['treɪdzmən] (*pl* **-men** [-mən]) *n* [trader] comerciante *m*; [shopkeeper] tendero *m*.

trade(s) union *n* UK sindicato *m*.

trade(s) unionist *n* UK sindicalista *m* OR *f*.

trading ['treɪdɪŋ] *n (U)* comercio *m*.

trading estate *n* UK polígono *m* industrial.

tradition [trə'dɪʃn] *n* tradición *f*.

traditional [trə'dɪʃənl] *adj* tradicional.

traffic ['træfɪk] (*pt* & *pp* **-ked**, *cont* **-king**) ◇ *n* **-1.** [vehicles] tráfico *m* **-2.** [illegal trade]: ~ **(in)** tráfico *m* (de). ◇ *vi*: **to ~ in** traficar con.

traffic circle *n* US glorieta *f*.

traffic jam *n* embotellamiento *m*, atasco *m*.

trafficker ['træfɪkəʳ] *n*: ~ **(in)** traficante *m* OR *f* (de).

traffic lights *npl* semáforos *mpl*.

traffic warden *n* UK ≃ guardia *m* OR *f* de tráfico.

tragedy ['trædʒədɪ] (*pl* **-ies**) *n* tragedia *f*.

tragic ['trædʒɪk] *adj* trágico(ca).

trail [treɪl] ◇ *n* **-1.** [path] sendero *m*, camino *m* **-2.** [trace, track] rastro *m*, huellas *fpl*; **a ~ of smoke** un rastro de humo; **they left a ~ of clues** dejaron un rastro de pistas; **they are hot on his ~** le están pisando los talones. ◇ *vt* **-1.** [drag] arrastrar **-2.** [lose to] ir por detrás de. ◇ *vi* **-1.** [drag] arrastrarse **-2.** [move slowly] andar con desgana **-3.** [lose] ir perdiendo.
◆ **trail away, trail off** *vi* apagarse.

trailer ['treɪləʳ] *n* **-1.** [vehicle for luggage] remolque *m* **-2.** *esp* US [for living in] roulotte *m*, caravana *f* **-3.** CINEMA tráiler *m*.

train [treɪn] ◇ *n* **-1.** RAIL tren *m*; **to go by ~** ir en tren **-2.** [of dress] cola *f*. ◇ *vt* **-1.** [teach]: **to ~ sb (to do sthg)** enseñar a alguien (a hacer algo); **to ~ sb in sthg** preparar a alguien para algo **-2.** [for job]: **to ~ sb (as sthg)** formar OR preparar a alguien (como algo) **-3.** [animal] amaestrar **-4.** SPORT: **to ~ sb (for)** entrenar a alguien (para) **-5.** [aim - gun] apuntar; **to ~ a camera on sb** enfocar a alguien con una cámara. ◇ *vi* **-1.** [for job] estudiar, prepararse; **to ~ as** formarse OR prepararse como; **to ~ to be a teacher** estudiar para ser profesor **-2.** SPORT: **to ~ (for)** entrenarse (para).

trained [treɪnd] *adj* cualificado(da).

trainee [treɪ'niː] *n* aprendiz *m*, -za *f*, persona *f* que está en período de prácticas.

trainer ['treɪnəʳ] *n* **-1.** [of animals] amaestrador *m*, -ra *f* **-2.** SPORT entrenador *m*, -ra *f*.
◆ **trainers** *npl* UK zapatillas *fpl* de deporte.

training ['treɪnɪŋ] *n (U)* **-1.** [for job]: ~ **(in)** formación *f* OR preparación *f* (para) **-2.** SPORT entrenamiento *m*; **to be in ~ (for sthg)** estar entrenando para algo.

training college *n* UK [gen] centro *m* de formación especializada; [for teachers] escuela *f* normal.

training shoes *npl* UK zapatillas *fpl* de deporte.

train of thought *n* hilo *m* del razonamiento.

traipse [treɪps] *vi* andar con desgana.

trait [treɪt] *n* rasgo *m*, característica *f*.

traitor ['treɪtəʳ] *n*: ~ **(to)** traidor *m*, -ra *f* (a).

trajectory [trə'dʒektərɪ] (*pl* **-ies**) *n* trayectoria *f*.

tram [træm], **tramcar** ['træmkɑːʳ] *n* UK tranvía *m*.

tramp [træmp] ◇ *n* **-1.** [homeless person] vagabundo *m*, -da *f* **-2.** US *inf* [woman] fulana *f*. ◇ *vi* andar pesadamente.

trample ['træmpl] *vt* pisar, pisotear; **to be ~d underfoot** ser pisoteado(da).

trampoline ['træmpəliːn] *n* cama *f* elástica.

trance [trɑːns] *n* trance *m*; **to go into a ~** entrar en trance.

tranquil ['træŋkwɪl] *adj literary* tranquilo(la), apacible.

tranquillizer UK, **tranquilizer** US ['træŋkwɪlaɪzəʳ] *n* tranquilizante *m*.

transaction [træn'zækʃn] *n* transacción *f*; **money ~s** transacciones de dinero.

transcend [træn'send] *vt fml* ir más allá de, superar.

transcript ['trænskrɪpt] *n* US expediente *m* académico.

transfer [*n* 'trænsfɜːʳ, *vb* træns'fɜːʳ] (*pt* & *pp* **-red**, *cont* **-ring**) ◇ *n* **-1.** [gen] transferencia *f* **-2.** [for job] traslado *m* **-3.** SPORT traspaso *m* **-4.** [design] calcomanía *f*. ◇ *vt* **-1.** [from one place to another] trasladar **-2.** [from one person to another] transferir. ◇ *vi* [to different job etc]: **he transferred to a different department** lo trasladaron a otro departamento.

transfix [træns'fɪks] *vt* [immobilize] paralizar; **~ed with** paralizado(da) por.

transform [træns'fɔːm] *vt*: **to ~ sthg/sb (into)** transformar algo/a alguien (en).

transfusion [træns'fjuːʒn] *n* transfusión *f*.

transient ['trænzɪənt] *adj fml* [fleeting] transitorio(ria), pasajero(ra).

transistor [træn'zɪstəʳ] *n* transistor *m*.

transistor radio *n dated* transistor *m*.

transit ['trænsɪt] *n* US transporte *m*; **in ~** en tránsito.

transition [træn'zɪʃn] *n*: ~ **(from sthg to sthg)** transición *f* (de algo a algo).

transitive ['trænzɪtɪv] *adj* GRAMM transitivo(va).

transitory ['trænzɪtrɪ] *adj* transitorio(ria).

translate [træns'leɪt] *vt* [languages] traducir.

translation [træns'leɪʃn] *n* traducción *f*.

translator [træns'leɪtəʳ] *n* traductor *m*, -ra *f*.

transmission [trænz'mɪʃn] *n* transmisión *f*.

transmit [trænz'mɪt] (*pt* & *pp* **-ted**, *cont* **-ting**) *vt* transmitir.

transmitter [trænz'mɪtə^r] n ELECTRON transmisor m.

transparency [trans'pærənsɪ] (pl -ies) n -1. [quality] transparencia f - 2. [slide] diapositiva f.

transparent [træns'pærənt] adj -1. [see-through] transparente - 2. [obvious] claro(-ra).

transpire [træn'spaɪə^r] fml ◇ vt: it ~s that ... resulta que ... ◇ vi [happen] ocurrir, pasar.

transplant ['trænsplɑ:nt] n trasplante m; he had a heart ~ le hicieron un transplante de corazón.

transport [n 'trænspɔ:t, vb træn'spɔ:t] ◇ n transporte m. ◇ vt transportar.

transportation [,trænspɔ:'teɪʃn] n esp US transporte m.

transport cafe n UK bar m de camioneros.

transpose [træns'pəʊz] vt [change round] invertir.

trap [træp] (pt & pp -ped, cont -ping) ◇ n trampa f; to lay a ~ (for) tender una trampa (a). ◇ vt -1. [catch - animals, birds] coger con trampa - 2. [trick] atrapar, engañar - 3. [finger]: she ~ped her fingers in the door se pilló los dedos en la puerta.

trapdoor [,træp'dɔ:^r] n [gen] trampilla f, trampa; THEATRE escotillón m.

trapeze [trə'pi:z] n trapecio m.

trappings ['træpɪŋz] npl atributos mpl.

trash [træʃ] n US lit & fig basura f.

trashcan ['træʃkæn] n US cubo m de la basura.

traumatic [trɔ:'mætɪk] adj traumático(ca).

travel ['trævl] (UK pt & pp -led, cont -ling, US pt & pp -ed, cont -ing) ◇ n (U) viajes mpl. ◇ vt [place] viajar por; [distance] recorrer. ◇ vi viajar.

travel agency n agencia f de viajes.

travel agent n empleado m, -da f de una agencia de viajes; ~'s agencia f de viajes.

traveller UK, **traveler** US ['trævlə^r] n [person on journey] viajero m, -ra f.

traveller's cheque n cheque m de viajero.

travelling UK, **traveling** US ['trævlɪŋ] adj [theatre, showman] ambulante.

travelsick ['trævəlsɪk] adj que se marea al viajar; to be OR feel ~ estar mareado(da).

travesty ['trævəstɪ] (pl -ies) n burda parodia f.

trawler ['trɔ:lə^r] n trainera f.

tray [treɪ] n bandeja f, charola f Bol, CAm, Méx, Perú, charol m Col, Perú.

treacherous ['tretʃərəs] adj -1. [plan, action] traicionero(ra); [person] traidor(ra) - 2. [dangerous] peligroso(sa).

treachery ['tretʃərɪ] n traición f.

treacle ['tri:kl] n UK melaza f.

tread [tred] (pt trod, pp trodden) ◇ n - 1. [on tyre, shoe] banda f - 2. [sound of walking] pasos mpl. ◇ vi - 1. [step]: to ~ on sthg pisar algo - 2. [walk] andar.

treason ['tri:zn] n traición f.

treasure ['treʒə^r] ◇ n lit & fig tesoro m. ◇ vt guardar como oro en paño.

treasurer ['treʒərə^r] n tesorero m, -ra f.

treasury ['treʒərɪ] (pl -ies) n [room] habitación donde se guarda el tesoro de un castillo, de una catedral etc.

◆ **Treasury** n: the Treasury ≃ el Ministerio de Hacienda.

treat [tri:t] ◇ vt - 1. [gen] tratar; to ~ sb well/badly tratar bien/mal a alguien; to ~ sb as/like tratar a alguien como; to ~ sb for sthg MED tratar a alguien de algo - 2. [give sthg special]: to ~ sb (to) invitar a alguien (a). ◇ n [something special] regalo m; he took me out to dinner as a ~ me invitó a cenar.

treatise ['tri:tɪs] n fml: ~ (on) tratado m (sobre).

treatment ['tri:tmənt] n - 1. MED: ~ (for) tratamiento m (para) - 2. [manner of dealing] trato m.

treaty ['tri:tɪ] (pl -ies) n tratado m.

treble ['trebl] ◇ adj -1. MUS de triple - 2. [with numbers] triple. ◇ vt triplicar. ◇ vi triplicarse.

treble clef n clave f de sol.

tree [tri:] n BOT & COMPUT árbol m.

treetop ['tri:tɒp] n copa f (de árbol).

tree-trunk n tronco m (de árbol).

trek [trek] n viaje m largo y difícil.

trellis ['trelɪs] n enrejado m, espaldera f.

tremble ['trembl] vi temblar; to ~ with cold/fear temblar de frío/miedo.

tremendous [trɪ'mendəs] adj -1. [impressive, large] enorme, tremendo(da) - 2. inf [really good] estupendo(da), magnífico(ca).

tremor ['tremə^r] n - 1. [of person, body, voice] estremecimiento m - 2. [small earthquake] temblor m, remezón m Andes & RP.

trench [trentʃ] n - 1. [narrow channel] zanja f - 2. MIL trinchera f.

trench coat n trinchera f, gabardina f, impermeable m.

trend [trend] n [tendency] tendencia f; [fashion] moda f; to set a ~ establecer una moda.

trendy ['trendɪ] (compar -ier, superl -iest, pl -ies) inf adj [person] moderno(na); [clothes] de moda.

trepidation [,trepɪ'deɪʃn] n fml: in OR with ~ con ansiedad OR agitación.

trespass ['trespəs] vi entrar ilegalmente; to ~ on entrar ilegalmente en; 'no ~ing' 'prohibido el paso'.

trespasser ['trespəsə^r] n intruso m, -sa f; '~s will be prosecuted' 'los intrusos serán sancionados por la ley'.

trestle ['tresl] *n* caballete *m*.

trestle table *n* mesa *f* de caballete.

trial ['traɪəl] *n* - 1. JUR juicio *m*, proceso *m*; **to be on ~ (for)** ser procesado(da) (por); **to be brought to ~** ser llevado(da) a juicio - 2. [test, experiment] prueba *f*; **on ~** de prueba; **by ~ and error** a base de probar - 3. [unpleasant experience] suplicio *m*, fastidio *m*.

triangle ['traɪæŋgl] *n* GEOM & MUS triángulo *m*.

tribe [traɪb] *n* tribu *f*.

tribunal [traɪ'bjuːnl] *n* tribunal *m*.

tributary ['trɪbjotrɪ] (*pl* **-ies**) *n* afluente *m*.

tribute ['trɪbjuːt] *n* - 1. [credit] tributo *m*; **to be a ~ to** hacer honor a - 2. (*U*) [respect, admiration]: **to pay ~ (to)** rendir homenaje (a).

trice [traɪs] *n*: **in a ~** en un dos por tres.

trick [trɪk] ⋄ *n* - 1. [to deceive] truco *m*; [to trap] trampa *f*; [joke] broma *f*; **to play a ~ on sb** gastarle una broma a alguien - 2. [in magic] juego *m* (de manos) - 3. [knack] truco *m*; **that should do the ~** eso es lo que necesitamos. ⋄ *vt* engañar, timar; **to ~ sb into doing sthg** engañar a alguien para que haga algo.

trickery ['trɪkərɪ] *n* (*U*) engaño *m*, fraude *m*.

trickle ['trɪkl] ⋄ *n* [of liquid] hilo *m*. ⋄ *vi* - 1. [liquid] resbalar (*formando un hilo*) - 2. [people, things]: **to ~ in/out** llegar/salir poco a poco.

tricky ['trɪkɪ] (*compar* **-ier**, *superl* **-iest**) *adj* [difficult] difícil, embromado(da) *Amér.*

tricycle ['traɪsɪkl] *n* triciclo *m*.

tried [traɪd] *adj*: **~ and tested** probado(da).

trifle ['traɪfl] *n* - 1. UK CULIN *postre de bizcocho con gelatina, crema, frutas y nata* - 2. [unimportant thing] pequeñez *f*, nadería *f*.

➤ a trifle *adv fml* un poco, ligeramente.

trifling ['traɪflɪŋ] *adj pej* trivial, insignificante.

trigger ['trɪgə˚] *n* [on gun] gatillo *m*.

➤ trigger off *vt sep* desencadenar, provocar.

trill [trɪl] *n* trino *m*.

trim [trɪm] (*compar* **-mer**, *superl* **-mest**, *pt* & *pp* **-med**, *cont* **-ming**) ⋄ *adj* - 1. [neat and tidy] limpio y arreglado (limpia y arreglada) - 2. [slim] esbelto(ta). ⋄ *n* [of hair] recorte *m*. ⋄ *vt* - 1. [nails, moustache] recortar, cortar - 2. [decorate]: **to ~ sthg (with)** adornar algo (con).

trimmings ['trɪmɪŋz] *npl* - 1. [on clothing] adornos *mpl* - 2. [with food] guarnición *f*.

trinket ['trɪŋkɪt] *n* baratija *f*.

trio ['triːəʊ] (*pl* **-s**) *n* trío *m*.

trip [trɪp] (*pt* & *pp* **-ped**, *cont* **-ping**) ⋄ *n*

[gen] *drugs sl* viaje *m*; **to be (away) on a ~** estar de viaje; **a ~ to London/the seaside** un viaje a Londres/la costa. ⋄ *vt* [make stumble] hacer la zancadilla a. ⋄ *vi* [stumble] tropezar, dar un tropezón; **to ~ over sthg** tropezar con algo.

➤ trip up *vt sep* [make stumble] hacer tropezar, hacer la zancadilla a.

tripe [traɪp] *n* (*U*) - 1. CULIN callos *mpl* - 2. *inf* [nonsense] tonterías *fpl*, idioteces *fpl*.

triple ['trɪpl] ⋄ *adj* triple. ⋄ *adv*: **~ the quantity** el triple. ⋄ *vt* triplicar. ⋄ *vi* triplicarse.

triple jump *n*: **the ~** el triple salto.

triplets ['trɪplɪts] *npl* trillizos *mpl*, -zas *fpl*, triates *mpl Amér.*

triplicate ['trɪplɪkət] *n*: **in ~** por triplicado.

tripod ['traɪpɒd] *n* trípode *m*.

trite [traɪt] *adj pej* trillado(da), manido(da).

triumph ['traɪəmf] ⋄ *n* triunfo *m*. ⋄ *vi*: **to ~ (over)** triunfar (sobre).

trivia ['trɪvɪə] *n* (*U*) trivialidades *fpl*.

trivial ['trɪvɪəl] *adj pej* trivial.

trod [trɒd] *pt* ⋄ **tread**.

trodden ['trɒdn] *pp* ⋄ **tread**.

trolley ['trɒlɪ] (*pl* **trolleys**) *n* - 1. UK [for shopping, food, drinks] carrito *m* - 2. US [tram] tranvía *m*.

trolley case *n* maleta *f* tipo carrito.

trombone [trɒm'bəʊn] *n* trombón *m*.

troop [truːp] ⋄ *n* [of people] grupo *m*, bandada *f*. ⋄ *vi* ir en grupo.

➤ troops *npl* tropas *fpl*.

➤ troop in *vi* entrar en tropel.

➤ troop out *vi* salir en tropel.

trooper ['truːpə˚] *n* - 1. MIL soldado *m* de caballería - 2. US [policeman] *miembro de la policía estatal.*

trophy ['trəʊfɪ] (*pl* **-ies**) *n* SPORT trofeo *m*.

tropical ['trɒpɪkl] *adj* tropical.

tropics ['trɒpɪks] *npl*: **the ~** el trópico.

trot [trɒt] (*pt* & *pp* **-ted**, *cont* **-ting**) ⋄ *n* - 1. [of horse] trote *m* - 2. [of person] paso *m* rápido. ⋄ *vi* - 1. [horse] trotar - 2. [person] andar con pasos rápidos.

➤ on the trot *adv inf*: **three times on the ~** tres veces seguidas.

trouble ['trʌbl] ⋄ *n* (*U*) - 1. [bother] molestia *f*; [difficulty, main problem] problema *m*; **to tell sb one's ~s** contarle a alguien sus problemas; **would it be too much ~ to ask you to ...?** ¿tendría inconveniente en ...?; **to be in ~** tener problemas; **to have ~ doing sthg** tener problemas haciendo algo; **to take the ~ to do sthg, to go to the ~ of doing sthg** tomarse la molestia de hacer algo; **what seems to be the ~?** ¿cuál es el problema? - 2. (*U*) [pain] dolor *m*; [illness] enfermedad *f*; **heart ~** problemas cardiacos; **back ~** problemas de espalda; **I'm having ~ with my leg** me está molestando la pierna **- 3.** *(U)* [violence, unpleasantness] problemas *mpl.* ◇ *vt* **- 1.** [worry, upset] preocupar **- 2.** [disturb, give pain to] molestar.

◆ **troubles** *npl* **- 1.** [problems, worries] problemas *mpl*, preocupaciones *fpl* **- 2.** POL conflicto *m*.

troubled ['trʌbld] *adj* **- 1.** [worried, upset] preocupado(da) **- 2.** [disturbed, problematic] agitado(da), turbulento(ta).

troublemaker ['trʌbl,meɪkə'] *n* alborotador *m*, -ra *f*.

troubleshooter ['trʌbl,ʃuːtə'] *n* [in organizations] *persona contratada para resolver problemas.*

troublesome ['trʌblsəm] *adj* molesto(ta), fregado(da) *Amér.*

trough [trɒf] *n* **- 1.** [for drinking] abrevadero *m*; [for eating] comedero *m* **- 2.** [low point] punto *m* más bajo.

troupe [truːp] *n* compañía *f*.

trousers ['traʊzəz] *npl* pantalones *mpl*.

trousseau ['truːsəʊ] *(pl* **-x** [-z], **-s)** *n* ajuar *m*.

trout [traʊt] *(pl inv or* **-s)** *n* trucha *f*.

trowel ['traʊəl] *n* **- 1.** [for the garden] desplantador *m* **- 2.** [for cement, plaster] paleta *f*, palustre *m*.

truant ['truːənt] *n* [child] alumno *m*, -na *f* que hace novillos; **to play ~** hacer novillos.

truce [truːs] *n*: **~ (between)** tregua *f* (entre).

truck [trʌk] *n* **- 1.** [lorry] camión *m* **- 2.** RAIL vagón *m* de mercancías.

truck driver *n esp US* camionero *m*, -ra *f*.

trucker ['trʌkə'] *n US* camionero *m*, -ra *f*.

truck farm *n US puesto de verduras y frutas para la venta.*

truculent ['trʌkjʊlənt] *adj* agresivo(va), pendenciero(ra).

trudge [trʌdʒ] *vi* caminar con dificultad.

true [truː] *adj* **- 1.** [gen] verdadero(ra); **it's ~** es verdad; **to come ~** hacerse realidad **- 2.** [genuine] auténtico(ca); [friend] de verdad **- 3.** [exact] exacto(ta).

truffle ['trʌfl] *n* trufa *f*.

truly ['truːlɪ] *adv* verdaderamente; **yours ~** le saluda atentamente.

trump [trʌmp] *n* triunfo *m (en cartas).*

trumped-up ['trʌmpt-] *adj pej* inventado(-da).

trumpet ['trʌmpɪt] *n* trompeta *f*.

truncheon ['trʌntʃən] *n* porra *f*.

trundle ['trʌndl] *vi* rodar lentamente; **he ~d along to the post office** se arrastró lentamente hasta correos.

trunk [trʌŋk] *n* **- 1.** [of tree, person] tronco *m* **- 2.** [of elephant] trompa *f* **- 3.** [box] baúl *m* **- 4.** *US* [of car] maletero *m*, portaequipaje *m*, cajuela *f Méx*, baúl *m Col, RP*, maletera *f Perú*.

◆ **trunks** *npl* bañador *m* (de hombre) *Esp*, traje *m* de baño (de hombre).

trunk call *n UK* conferencia *f Esp*, llamada *f* interurbana.

trunk road *n* ≃ carretera *f* nacional.

truss [trʌs] ◇ *n* MED braguero *m*. ◇ *vt*: **to ~ (up)** atar.

trust [trʌst] ◇ *vt* **- 1.** [believe in] confiar en **- 2.** [have confidence in]: **to ~ sb to do sthg** confiar en alguien para que haga algo **- 3.** [entrust]: **to ~ sb with sthg** confiar algo a alguien **- 4.** [accept as safe, reliable] fiarse de. ◇ *n* **- 1.** *(U)* [faith, responsibility]: **~ (in)** confianza *f* (en) **- 2.** FIN trust *m*; **in ~** en fideicomiso.

trusted ['trʌstɪd] *adj* de confianza.

trustee [trʌs'tiː] *n* FIN & JUR fideicomisario *m*, -ria *f*.

trust fund *n* fondo *m* de fideicomiso.

trusting ['trʌstɪŋ] *adj* confiado(da).

trustworthy ['trʌst,wɜːðɪ] *adj* digno(na) de confianza.

truth [truːθ] *n* verdad *f*; **in (all) ~** en verdad, verdaderamente.

truthful ['truːθfʊl] *adj* **- 1.** [person] sincero(ra), honesto(ta) **- 2.** [story] verídico(ca).

try [traɪ] *(pt & pp* **-ied**, *pl* **-ies)** ◇ *vt* **- 1.** [attempt] intentar; **to ~ to do sthg** tratar de or intentar hacer algo **- 2.** [sample, test] probar **- 3.** JUR [case] ver; [criminal] juzgar, procesar **- 4.** [put to the test - person] acabar con la paciencia de; [- patience] acabar con. ◇ *vi* intentar; **to ~ for sthg** tratar de conseguir algo. ◇ *n* **- 1.** [attempt] intento *m*, tentativa *f* **- 2.** [sample, test]: **to give sthg a ~** probar algo **- 3.** RUGBY ensayo *m*.

◆ **try on** *vt sep* probarse.

◆ **try out** *vt sep* [car, machine] probar; [plan] poner a prueba; **to ~ sthg out on sb** probar algo con alguien; **to ~ out for** *US* presentarse a una prueba de selección para.

trying ['traɪɪŋ] *adj* difícil, pesado(da).

T-shirt *n* camiseta *f*, remera *f RP*, playera *f Méx*, polera *f Chile.*

T-square *n* escuadra *f* en forma de T.

tub [tʌb] *n* **- 1.** [container - small] bote *m*; [- large] tina *f* **- 2.** *inf* [bath] bañera *f*.

tubby ['tʌbɪ] *(compar* **-ier**, *superl* **-iest)** *adj inf* regordete(ta), rechoncho(cha).

tube [tjuːb] *n* **- 1.** [cylinder, container] tubo *m* **- 2.** ANAT conducto *m* **- 3.** *UK* RAIL *inf* metro *m*, subte *m CSur*; **by ~** en metro.

tuberculosis [tjuː,bɜːkjʊ'ləʊsɪs] *n* tuberculosis *f*.

tubing ['tjuːbɪŋ] *n (U)* tubos *mpl*.

tubular ['tjuːbjʊlə'] *adj* tubular.

TUC *n abbr of* **Trades Union Congress**.

tuck [tʌk] *vt* [place neatly] meter.

◆ **tuck away** *vt sep* [money etc] guardar.

◆ **tuck in** ◇ *vt sep* **- 1.** [person - in bed]

arropar - **2.** [clothes] meterse. ◇ *vi inf* comer con apetito.

➡ **tuck up** *vt sep* arropar; **to ~ sb up in bed** arropar a alguien en la cama.

tuck shop *n* UK confitería *f (emplazada cerca de un colegio).*

Tuesday ['tjuːzdɪ] *n* martes *m inv; see also* **Saturday.**

tuft [tʌft] *n* [of hair] mechón *m*; [of grass] manojo *m*.

tug [tʌg] (*pt & pp* **-ged**, *cont* **-ging**) ◇ *n* - **1.** [pull] tirón *m* - **2.** [boat] remolcador *m*. ◇ *vt* tirar de, dar un tirón a. ◇ *vi*: **to ~ (at)** tirar (de).

tug-of-war *n* juego *m* de la cuerda *(en el que dos equipos compiten tirando de ella).*

tuition [tjuːˈɪʃn] *n* enseñanza *f*; **private ~** clases *fpl* particulares.

tulip ['tjuːlɪp] *n* tulipán *m*.

tumble ['tʌmbl] ◇ *vi* [person] caerse (rodando). ◇ *n* caída *f*.

➡ **tumble to** *vt fus* UK *inf* caerse en la cuenta de, percatarse de.

tumbledown ['tʌmbldaʊn] *adj* ruinoso(sa).

tumble-dryer [-ˌdraɪəʳ] *n* secadora *f*.

tumbler ['tʌmbləʳ] *n* [glass] vaso *m*.

tummy ['tʌmɪ] (*pl* **-ies**) *n inf* barriga *f*.

tumour UK, **tumor** US ['tjuːməʳ] *n* tumor *m*.

tuna [UK 'tjuːnə, US 'tuːnə] (*pl inv* OR **-s**) *n* atún *m*.

tune [tjuːn] ◇ *n* - **1.** [song, melody] melodía *f* - **2.** [harmony]: **in ~** MUS afinado(da); **out of ~** MUS desafinado(da); **to be out of/ in ~ (with sb/sthg)** *fig* no avenirse/avenirse (con alguien/algo). ◇ *vt* - **1.** MUS afinar - **2.** RADIO & TV sintonizar - **3.** [engine] poner a punto.

➡ **tune in** *vi* RADIO & TV: **to ~ in (to sthg)** sintonizar (algo).

➡ **tune up** *vi* MUS concertar OR afinar los instrumentos.

tuneful ['tjuːnfʊl] *adj* melodioso(sa).

tuner ['tjuːnəʳ] *n* - **1.** RADIO & TV sintonizador *m* - **2.** MUS afinador *m*, -ra *f*.

tunic ['tjuːnɪk] *n* túnica *f*.

tuning fork ['tjuːnɪŋ-] *n* diapasón *m*.

Tunisia [tjuːˈnɪzɪə] *n* Túnez *m*.

tunnel ['tʌnl] (UK *pt & pp* **-led**, *cont* **-ling**, US *pt & pp* **-ed**, *cont* **-ing**) ◇ *n* túnel *m*. ◇ *vi* hacer un túnel.

turban ['tɜːbən] *n* turbante *m*.

turbine ['tɜːbaɪn] *n* turbina *f*.

turbocharged ['tɜːbəʊtʃɑːdʒd] *adj* provisto(ta) de turbina; [car] turbo *(inv)*.

turbulence ['tɜːbjʊləns] *n* (U) *lit & fig* turbulencia *f*.

turbulent ['tɜːbjʊlənt] *adj lit & fig* turbulento(ta).

tureen [təˈriːn] *n* sopera *f*.

turf [tɜːf] (*pl* **-s** OR **turves**) ◇ *n* - **1.** [grass surface] césped *m* - **2.** [clod] tepe *m*. ◇ *vt* encespedar, cubrir con césped.

➡ **turf out** *vt sep* UK *inf* [person] dar la patada a, echar; [old clothes] tirar.

turgid ['tɜːdʒɪd] *adj fml* [over-solemn] ampuloso(sa).

Turk [tɜːk] *n* turco *m*, -ca *f*.

turkey ['tɜːkɪ] (*pl* **turkeys**) *n* pavo *m*.

Turkey ['tɜːkɪ] *n* Turquía *f*.

Turkish ['tɜːkɪʃ] ◇ *adj* turco(ca). ◇ *n* [language] turco *m*. ◇ *npl* [people]: **the ~** los turcos.

Turkish delight *n* rahat lokum *m*, *dulce de una sustancia gelatinosa, cubierto de azúcar glas.*

turn [tɜːn] ◇ *n* - **1.** [in road, river] curva *f* - **2.** [of knob, wheel] vuelta *f* - **3.** [change] cambio *m* - **4.** [in game] turno *m*; **it's my ~** me toca a mí; **in ~** sucesivamente, uno tras otro - **5.** [performance] número *m* - **6.** MED ataque *m* - **7.** *phr*: **to do sb a good ~** hacerle un favor a alguien. ◇ *vt* - **1.** [chair, page, omelette] dar la vuelta a - **2.** [knob, wheel] girar - **3.** [corner] doblar - **4.** [thoughts, attention]: **to ~ sthg to** dirigir algo hacia - **5.** [change]: **to ~ sthg into** convertir OR transformar algo en - **6.** [cause to become]: **the cold ~ed his fingers blue** se le pusieron los dedos azules por el frío. ◇ *vi* - **1.** [car] girar; [road] torcer; [person] volverse, darse la vuelta - **2.** [wheel] dar vueltas - **3.** [turn page over]: **~ to page two** pasen a la página dos - **4.** [thoughts, attention]: **to ~ to** dirigirse hacia - **5.** [seek consolation]: **to ~ to sb/ sthg** buscar consuelo en alguien/algo; **she has nobody to ~ to** no tiene a quien acudir - **6.** [change]: **to ~ into** convertirse OR transformarse en - **7.** [become]: **it ~ed black** se volvió negro - **8.** [go sour] cortarse, agriarse.

➡ **turn around** = turn round.

➡ **turn away** *vt sep* [refuse entry to] no dejar entrar.

➡ **turn back** ◇ *vt sep* [person, vehicle] hacer volver. ◇ *vi* volver, volverse.

➡ **turn down** *vt sep* - **1.** [offer, person] rechazar - **2.** [volume, heating] bajar.

➡ **turn in** *vi inf* [go to bed] irse a dormir.

➡ **turn off** ◇ *vt fus* [road, path] desviarse de, salir de. ◇ *vt sep* [radio, heater] apagar; [engine] parar; [gas, tap] cerrar. ◇ *vi* [leave road] desviarse, salir.

➡ **turn on** ◇ *vt sep* - **1.** [radio, TV, engine] encender; [gas, tap] abrir - **2.** *inf* [excite sexually] poner cachondo(da), excitar. ◇ *vt fus* [attack] atacar.

◆ **turn out** ◇ *vt sep* -1. [extinguish] apagar - 2. [empty - pockets, bag] vaciar. ◇ *vt fus*: to ~ out to be resultar ser. ◇ *vi* - 1. [end up] salir - 2. [arrive]: to ~ out (for) venir OR presentarse (a).

◆ **turn over** ◇ *vt sep* -1. [turn upside down] dar la vuelta a; [page] volver - 2. [consider] darle vueltas a - 3. *UK* RADIO & TV cambiar - 4. [hand over]: to ~ sthg/sb over (to) entregar algo/a alguien (a). ◇ *vi* [roll over] darse la vuelta.

◆ **turn round** ◇ *vt sep* -1. [gen] dar la vuelta a - 2. [knob, key] hacer girar. ◇ *vi* [person] darse la vuelta, volverse.

◆ **turn up** ◇ *vt sep* [volume, heating] subir. ◇ *vi inf* aparecer.

turning ['tɜːnɪŋ] *n* [in road] bocacalle *f*.

turning point *n* momento *m* decisivo.

turnip ['tɜːnɪp] *n* nabo *m*.

turnout ['tɜːnaʊt] *n* número *m* de asistentes, asistencia *f*.

turnover ['tɜːn,əʊvəʳ] *n (U)* - 1. [of personnel] movimiento *m* de personal - 2. *UK* FIN volumen *m* de ventas, facturación *f*.

turnpike ['tɜːnpaɪk] *n US* autopista *f* de peaje.

turnstile ['tɜːnstaɪl] *n* torno *m*, torniquete *m*.

turntable ['tɜːn,teɪbl] *n* plato *m* giratorio.

turn-up *n UK* [on trousers] vuelta *f*; **a ~ for the books** *inf* una auténtica sorpresa.

turpentine ['tɜːpəntaɪn] *n* trementina *f*.

turquoise ['tɜːkwɔɪz] ◇ *adj* turquesa. ◇ *n* [mineral, gem] turquesa *f*.

turret ['tʌrɪt] *n* torreta *f*, torrecilla *f*.

turtle ['tɜːtl] (*pl inv* OR **-s**) *n* tortuga *f* (marina).

turtleneck ['tɜːtlnek] *n* cuello *m* (de) cisne.

turves [tɜːvz] *UK pl* ▷ **turf**.

tusk [tʌsk] *n* colmillo *m*.

tussle ['tʌsl] ◇ *n* lucha *f*, pelea *f*. ◇ *vi*: to ~ (over) pelearse (por).

tutor ['tjuːtəʳ] *n* - 1. [private] profesor particular *m*, profesora particular *f*, tutor *m*, -ra *f* - 2. UNIV profesor universitario *m*, profesora universitaria *f* (de un grupo pequeño).

tutorial [tjuːˈtɔːrɪəl] *n* tutoría *f*, clase *f* con grupo reducido.

tuxedo [tʌkˈsiːdəʊ] (*pl* **-s**) *n* esmoquin *m*.

TV (*abbr of* **television**) ◇ *n* televisión *f*; **on ~** en la televisión. ◇ *comp* de televisión.

twang [twæŋ] *n* - 1. [of guitar] tañido *m*; [of string, elastic] sonido *m* vibrante - 2. [accent] gangueo *m*, acento *m* nasal.

tweed [twiːd] *n* tweed *m*.

tweezers ['twiːzəz] *npl* pinzas *fpl*.

twelfth [twelfθ] *num* duodécimo(ma); *see also* **sixth**.

twelve [twelv] *num* doce; *see also* **six**.

twentieth ['twentɪəθ] *num* vigésimo(ma); *see also* **sixth**.

twenty ['twentɪ] (*pl* **-ies**) *num* veinte; *see also* **sixty**.

twenty-one [twentɪˈwʌn] *n US* [game] veintiuna *f*.

twice [twaɪs] *num adv* dos veces; ~ **a week** dos veces por semana; **it costs** ~ **as much** cuesta el doble; ~ **as big** el doble de grande; **he's** ~ **her age** le dobla en edad; **think** ~ piénsalo dos veces.

twiddle ['twɪdl] ◇ *vt* dar vueltas a; to ~ **one's thumbs** *fig* holgazanear. ◇ *vi*: to ~ **with** juguetear con.

twig [twɪg] *n* ramita *f*.

twilight ['twaɪlaɪt] *n* crepúsculo *m*, ocaso *m*.

twin [twɪn] ◇ *adj* gemelo(la), morocho(cha) *Andes & RP*. ◇ *n* gemelo *m*, -la *f*, morocho *m*, -cha *f Ven*.

twin-bedded [-'bedɪd] *adj* de dos camas.

twine [twaɪn] ◇ *n (U)* bramante *m*. ◇ *vt*: to ~ sthg round sthg enrollar algo en algo.

twinge [twɪndʒ] *n* [of pain] punzada *f*; [of guilt] remordimiento *m*.

twinkle ['twɪŋkl] *vi* - 1. [star] centellear, parpadear - 2. [eyes] brillar.

twin room *n* habitación *f* con dos camas.

twin town *n* ciudad *f* hermanada.

twirl [twɜːl] ◇ *vt* dar vueltas a. ◇ *vi* dar vueltas rápidamente.

twist [twɪst] ◇ *n* - 1. [in road] vuelta *f*, recodo *m*; [in river] meandro *m* - 2. [of head, lid, knob] giro *m* - 3. [shape] espiral *f* - 4. *fig* [in plot] giro *m* imprevisto. ◇ *vt* - 1. [cloth, rope] retorcer; [hair] enroscar - 2. [face etc] torcer - 3. [dial, lid] dar vueltas a; [head] volver - 4. [ankle, knee etc] torcerse - 5. [misquote] tergiversar. ◇ *vi* - 1. [person] retorcerse; [road, river] contorsionarse, serpentear, dar vueltas - 2. [face] contorsionarse; [frame, rail] torcerse - 3. [turn - head, hand] volverse.

twit [twɪt] *n UK inf* imbécil *m* OR *f*, gil *m Amér*, gila *f RP*.

twitch [twɪtʃ] ◇ *n* contorsión *f*; **nervous** ~ tic *m* (nervioso). ◇ *vi* contorsionarse.

two [tuː] *num* dos; **to break in** ~ partirse en dos; **to do sthg in** ~**s** hacer algo en pares; **to put** ~ **and** ~ **together** atar cabos; *see also* **six**.

two-door *adj* [car] de dos puertas.

twofaced [,tuːˈfeɪst] *adj pej* hipócrita.

twofold ['tuːfəʊld] ◇ *adj* doble; **a** ~ **increase** un incremento del doble. ◇ *adv*: to increase ~ duplicarse.

two-piece *adj* [suit] de dos piezas.

twosome ['tuːsəm] *n inf* pareja *f*.

two-way *adj* [traffic] en ambas direcciones; [agreement, cooperation] mutuo(tua).

tycoon [taɪˈkuːn] *n* magnate *m*; **an oil** ~ un magnate del petróleo.

type [taɪp] ⇔ n - **1.** [gen] tipo m - **2.** (U) TYPO tipo m, letra f. ⇔ vt - **1.** [on typewriter] escribir a máquina, mecanografiar - **2.** [on computer] escribir en el ordenador; **to ~ sthg into sthg** entrar algo en algo. ⇔ vi escribir a máquina.

typecast ['taɪpkɑːst] (pt & pp **typecast**) vt: **to ~ sb (as)** encasillar a alguien (como).

typeface ['taɪpfeɪs] n tipo m, letra f.

typescript ['taɪpskrɪpt] n copia f mecanografiada.

typeset ['taɪpset] (pt & pp **typeset**, cont -ting) vt componer.

typewriter ['taɪpˌraɪtəʳ] n máquina f de escribir.

typhoid (fever) ['taɪfɔɪd-] n fiebre f tifoidea.

typhoon [taɪ'fuːn] n tifón m.

typical ['tɪpɪkl] adj: **~ (of)** típico(ca) (de).

typing ['taɪpɪŋ] n mecanografía f.

typist ['taɪpɪst] n mecanógrafo m, -fa f.

typography [taɪ'pɒɡrəfɪ] n [process, job] tipografía f.

tyranny ['tɪrənɪ] n tiranía f.

tyrant ['taɪrənt] n tirano m, -na f.

tyre UK, **tire** US ['taɪəʳ] n neumático m.

tyre pressure n presión f de los neumáticos.

u (pl **u's** OR **us**), **U** (pl **U's** OR **Us**) [juː] n [letter] u f, U f.

U-bend n sifón m.

udder ['ʌdəʳ] n ubre f.

UFO (abbr of **unidentified flying object**) n OVNI m.

Uganda [juː'ɡændə] n Uganda.

ugh [ʌɡ] excl ¡puf!

ugly ['ʌɡlɪ] (compar -ier, superl -iest) adj - **1.** [unattractive] feo(a) - **2.** fig [unpleasant] desagradable.

UHF (abbr of **ultra-high frequency**) UHF.

UK (abbr of **United Kingdom**) n RU m; **the ~** el Reino Unido.

Ukraine [juː'kreɪn] n: **the ~** Ucrania.

ulcer ['ʌlsəʳ] n úlcera f.

ulcerated ['ʌlsəreɪtɪd] adj ulceroso(sa).

Ulster ['ʌlstəʳ] n (el) Ulster.

ulterior [ʌl'tɪərɪəʳ] adj: **~ motive** motivo m oculto.

ultimata [ˌʌltɪ'meɪtə] pl ▷ **ultimatum**.

ultimate ['ʌltɪmət] ⇔ adj - **1.** [final, long-term] final, definitivo(va) - **2.** [most powerful] máximo(ma). ⇔ n: **the ~ in** el colmo de.

ultimately ['ʌltɪmətlɪ] adv finalmente, a la larga.

ultimatum [ˌʌltɪ'meɪtəm] (pl -s OR -ta) n ultimátum m; **to issue an ~ to sb** dar un ultimátum a alguien.

ultrasound ['ʌltrəsaʊnd] n ultrasonido m.

ultraviolet [ˌʌltrə'vaɪələt] adj ultravioleta.

umbilical cord [ʌm'bɪlɪkl-] n cordón m umbilical.

umbrella [ʌm'brelə] ⇔ n - **1.** [for rain] paraguas m inv - **2.** [on beach] parasol m - **3.**: **under the ~ of** fig bajo la protección de. ⇔ adj que engloba a otros (otras).

umpire ['ʌmpaɪəʳ] n árbitro m.

umpteen [ˌʌmp'tiːn] num adj inf: **~ times** la tira de veces.

umpteenth [ˌʌmp'tiːnθ] num adj inf enésimo(ma); **for the ~ time** por enésima vez.

UN (abbr of **United Nations**) n: **the ~** la ONU.

unabated [ˌʌnə'beɪtɪd] adj incesante; **to continue ~** continuar sin cesar.

unable [ʌn'eɪbl] adj: **to be ~ to do sthg** no poder hacer algo.

unacceptable [ˌʌnək'septəbl] adj inaceptable.

unaccompanied [ˌʌnə'kʌmpənɪd] adj - **1.** [child] solo(la), que no va acompañado(da); [luggage] desatendido(da) - **2.** [song] sin acompañamiento.

unaccountably [ˌʌnə'kaʊntəblɪ] adv inexplicablemente.

unaccounted [ˌʌnə'kaʊntɪd] adj: **12 people are ~ for** hay 12 personas aún sin localizar.

unaccustomed [ˌʌnə'kʌstəmd] adj [unused]: **to be ~ to** no estar acostumbrado(da) a.

unadulterated [ˌʌnə'dʌltəreɪtɪd] adj - **1.** [unspoilt] sin adulterar - **2.** [absolute] completo(ta), absoluto(ta).

unanimous [juː'nænɪməs] adj unánime.

unanimously [juː'nænɪməslɪ] adv unánimemente.

unanswered [ˌʌn'ɑːnsəd] adj sin contestar.

unappetizing, -ising [ˌʌn'æpɪtaɪzɪŋ] adj poco apetitoso(sa).

unarmed [ˌʌn'ɑːmd] adj desarmado(da).

unarmed combat n lucha f OR combate m a brazo partido.

unashamed [ˌʌnə'ʃeɪmd] adj descarado(da).

unassuming [ˌʌnə'sjuːmɪŋ] adj sin pretensiones.

unattached [ˌʌnə'tætʃt] adj - **1.** [not fastened, linked] independiente; **~ to** que no está ligado a - **2.** [without partner] libre, sin compromiso.

unattended [ˌʌnəˈtendɪd] *adj* desatendido(da); **to leave sthg ~** dejar algo desatendido.

unattractive [ˌʌnəˈtræktɪv] *adj* poco atractivo(va).

unauthorized, -ised [ˌʌnˈɔːθəraɪzd] *adj* no autorizado(da).

unavailable [ˌʌnəˈveɪləbl] *adj*: **to be ~** no estar disponible; **he was ~ for comment** no quiso hacer ningún comentario.

unavoidable [ˌʌnəˈvɔɪdəbl] *adj* inevitable, ineludible; **~ delays** retrasos inevitables.

unaware [ˌʌnəˈweəʳ] *adj* inconsciente; **to be ~ of** no ser consciente de.

unawares [ˌʌnəˈweəz] *adv* : **to catch** OR **take sb ~** coger a alguien desprevenido(da).

unbalanced [ˌʌnˈbælənst] *adj* desequilibrado(da).

unbearable [ʌnˈbeərəbl] *adj* insoportable, inaguantable.

unbeatable [ʌnˈbiːtəbl] *adj* [gen] insuperable; [prices, value] inmejorable.

unbeknown(st) [ˌʌnbɪˈnəʊn(st)] *adv*: **~ to** sin conocimiento de.

unbelievable [ˌʌnbɪˈliːvəbl] *adj* increíble.

unbending [ʌnˈbendɪŋ] *adj* resoluto(ta).

unbia(s)sed [ʌnˈbaɪəst] *adj* imparcial.

unborn [ˌʌnˈbɔːn] *adj* [child] no nacido(da) aún.

unbreakable [ʌnˈbreɪkəbl] *adj* irrompible.

unbridled [ʌnˈbraɪdld] *adj* desmesurado(da), desenfrenado(da).

unburden [ʌnˈbɜːdn] *vt*: **to ~ o.s.** desahogarse.

unbutton [ˌʌnˈbʌtn] *vt* desabrochar, desabotonar.

uncalled-for [ˌʌnˈkɔːld-] *adj* injusto(ta), inmerecido(da).

uncanny [ʌnˈkænɪ] (*compar* **-ier**, *superl* **-iest**) *adj* extraño(ña).

unceasing [ʌnˈsiːsɪŋ] *adj* incesante.

unceremonious [ˈʌnˌserɪˈməʊnjəs] *adj* [curt] brusco(ca).

uncertain [ʌnˈsɜːtn] *adj* [gen] incierto(ta); [undecided, hesitant] indeciso(sa); **it's ~ whether they will accept the proposals** no se sabe si aceptarán las propuestas; **in no ~ terms** de forma vehemente.

unchanged [ˌʌnˈtʃeɪndʒd] *adj* sin alterar.

unchecked [ˌʌnˈtʃekt] *adj* [unrestrained] desenfrenado(da). *adv* [unrestrained] libremente, sin restricciones.

uncivilized, -ised [ˌʌnˈsɪvɪlaɪzd] *adj* [society] incivilizado(da); [person] inculto(ta).

uncle [ˈʌŋkl] *n* tío *m*.

unclear [ˌʌnˈklɪəʳ] *adj* poco claro(ra); **to be ~ about sthg** no tener claro algo.

uncomfortable [ˌʌnˈkʌmftəbl] *adj*

- **1.** [gen] incómodo(da) - **2.** *fig* [fact, truth] inquietante, desagradable.

uncommon [ʌnˈkɒmən] *adj* [rare] poco común, raro(ra).

uncompromising [ˌʌnˈkɒmprəmaɪzɪŋ] *adj* inflexible, intransigente.

unconcerned [ˌʌnkənˈsɜːnd] *adj* [not anxious] indiferente.

unconditional [ˌʌnkənˈdɪʃənl] *adj* incondicional.

unconscious [ʌnˈkɒnʃəs] *adj* inconsciente; **to be ~ of sthg** ser inconsciente de OR ignorar algo; **he was knocked ~ by a falling brick** un ladrillo que caía lo dejó inconsciente. *n* inconsciente *m*.

unconsciously [ʌnˈkɒnʃəslɪ] *adv* inconscientemente.

uncontrollable [ˌʌnkənˈtrəʊləbl] *adj* [gen] incontrolable; [desire, hatred] irrefrenable; [laughter] incontenible.

unconventional [ˌʌnkənˈvenʃənl] *adj* poco convencional.

unconvinced [ˌʌnkənˈvɪnst] *adj*: **to remain ~** seguir sin convencerse.

uncouth [ʌnˈkuːθ] *adj* grosero(ra).

uncover [ʌnˈkʌvəʳ] *vt* [gen] descubrir; [jar, tin etc] destapar.

undecided [ˌʌndɪˈsaɪdɪd] *adj* - **1.** [person] indeciso(sa) - **2.** [issue] pendiente, sin resolver.

undeniable [ˌʌndɪˈnaɪəbl] *adj* innegable.

under [ˈʌndəʳ] *prep* - **1.** [beneath] debajo de, abajo de *Amér* - **2.** [with movement] bajo; **put it ~ the table** ponlo debajo de OR bajo la mesa; **they walked ~ the bridge** pasaron bajo OR por debajo del puente - **3.** [subject to, undergoing, controlled by] bajo; **~ the circumstances** dadas las circunstancias; **~ discussion** en proceso de discusión; **he has 20 men ~ him** tiene 20 hombres a su cargo - **4.** [less than] menos de; **children ~ the age of 14** niños menores de 14 años - **5.** [according to] según, conforme a - **6.** [in headings, classifications]: **he filed it ~ 'D'** lo archivó en la 'D' - **7.** [name, title]: **~ an alias** bajo nombre supuesto. *adv* - **1.** [gen] debajo; **to go ~** [business] irse a pique - **2.** [less]: **children of 12 years and ~** niños menores de 13 años; **£5 or ~** cinco libras o menos - **3.** [under water] bajo el agua.

underage [ˌʌndərˈeɪdʒ] *adj* [person] menor de edad; [sex, drinking] en menores de edad.

undercarriage [ˈʌndəˌkærɪdʒ] *n* tren *m* de aterrizaje.

undercharge [ˌʌndəˈtʃɑːdʒ] *vt* cobrar menos del precio estipulado a.

underclothes [ˈʌndəkləʊðz] *npl* ropa *f* interior.

undercoat [ˈʌndəkəʊt] *n* [of paint] primera mano *f* OR capa *f*.

undercover [ˌʌndəˌkʌvəʳ] *adj* secreto(ta).

undercurrent [ˈʌndəˌkʌrənt] *n fig* sentimiento *m* oculto.

undercut [ˌʌndəˈkʌt] (*pt* & *pp* **undercut**, *cont* **-ting**) *vt* [in price] vender más barato que.

underdeveloped [ˌʌndədɪˈveləpt] *adj* subdesarrollado(da).

underdog [ˈʌndədɒg] *n*: **the ~** el que lleva las de perder.

underdone [ˌʌndəˈdʌn] *adj* poco hecho(-cha).

underestimate [ˌʌndərˈestɪmeɪt] *vt* subestimar, infravalorar.

underexposed [ˌʌndərɪkˈspəʊzd] *adj* PHOT subexpuesto(ta).

underfed [ˈʌndəˌfed] *adj* desnutrido(da).

underfoot [ˌʌndəˈfʊt] *adv* debajo de los pies; **it's wet ~** el suelo está mojado.

undergo [ˌʌndəˈgəʊ] (*pt* **-went**, *pp* **-gone**) *vt* [pain, change, difficulties] sufrir, experimentar; [operation, examination] someterse a.

undergraduate [ˌʌndəˈgrædʒʊət] *n* estudiante universitario no licenciado *m*, estudiante universitaria no licenciada *f*.

underground [*adj* & *n* ˈʌndəgraʊnd, *adv* ˌʌndəˈgraʊnd] *adj* **- 1.** [below the ground] subterráneo(a) **- 2.** *fig* [secret, illegal] clandestino(na). *adv*: **to go ~** pasar a la clandestinidad. *n* **- 1.** *UK* [railway system] metro *m*, subte(rráneo) *m RP* **- 2.** [activist movement] resistencia *f*, movimiento *m* clandestino.

undergrowth [ˈʌndəgrəʊθ] *n* (*U*) maleza *f*, monte *m* bajo.

underhand [ˌʌndəˈhænd] *adj* turbio(bia), poco limpio(pia).

underline [ˌʌndəˈlaɪn] *vt* subrayar.

underlying [ˌʌndəˈlaɪɪŋ] *adj* subyacente.

undermine [ˌʌndəˈmaɪn] *vt fig* minar, socavar; **to ~ sb's confidence/authority** minar la confianza/autoridad de alguien.

underneath [ˌʌndəˈniːθ] *prep* **- 1.** [beneath] debajo de **- 2.** [with movement] bajo. *adv* [under, below] debajo. *adj inf* inferior, de abajo. *n* [underside]: **the ~** la superficie inferior.

underpaid [ˈʌndəpeɪd] *adj* mal pagado(-da).

underpants [ˈʌndəpænts] *npl* calzoncillos *mpl*.

underpass [ˈʌndəpɑːs] *n* paso *m* subterráneo.

underprivileged [ˌʌndəˈprɪvɪlɪdʒd] *adj* desvalido(da), desamparado(da).

underrated [ˌʌndəˈreɪtɪd] *adj* subestimado(da), infravalorado(da).

undershirt [ˈʌndəʃɜːt] *n US* camiseta *f*.

underside [ˈʌndəsaɪd] *n*: **the ~** la superficie inferior.

underskirt [ˈʌndəskɜːt] *n* enaguas *fpl*.

understand [ˌʌndəˈstænd] (*pt* & *pp* **-stood**) *vt* **- 1.** [gen] comprender, entender; **is that understood?** ¿queda claro? **- 2.** [know all about] entender de **- 3.** *fml* [be informed]: **to ~ that** tener entendido que **- 4.** [assume]: **it is understood that ...** se entiende que ... *vi* comprender, entender.

understandable [ˌʌndəˈstændəbl] *adj* comprensible.

understanding [ˌʌndəˈstændɪŋ] *n* **- 1.** [knowledge] entendimiento *m*, comprensión *f* **- 2.** [sympathy] comprensión *f* mutua **- 3.** [informal agreement] acuerdo *m*, arreglo *m*; **we have a little ~** tenemos un pequeño acuerdo. *adj* comprensivo(va).

understatement [ˌʌndəˈsteɪtmənt] *n* **- 1.** [inadequate statement] atenuación *f*; **it's an ~ to say he's fat** decir que es gordo es quedarse corto **- 2.** (*U*) [quality of understating]: **he's a master of ~** puede quitarle importancia a cualquier cosa.

understood [ˌʌndəˈstʊd] *pt* & *pp* ▷ **understand**.

understudy [ˈʌndəˌstʌdɪ] (*pl* **-ies**) *n* suplente *m or f*.

undertake [ˌʌndəˈteɪk] (*pt* **-took**, *pp* **-taken**) *vt* **- 1.** [task] emprender; [responsibility, control] asumir, tomar **- 2.** [promise]: **to ~ to do sthg** comprometerse a hacer algo.

undertaker [ˈʌndəˌteɪkəʳ] *n* director *m*, -ra *f* de pompas fúnebres.

undertaking [ˌʌndəˈteɪkɪŋ] *n* **- 1.** [task] tarea *f*, empresa *f* **- 2.** [promise] promesa *f*.

undertone [ˈʌndətəʊn] *n* **- 1.** [quiet voice] voz *f* baja; **in an ~** en voz baja **- 2.** [vague feeling] matiz *m*.

undertook [ˌʌndəˈtʊk] *pt* ▷ **undertake**.

underwater [ˌʌndəˈwɔːtəʳ] *adj* submarino(na). *adv* bajo el agua.

underwear [ˈʌndəweəʳ] *n* ropa *f* interior.

underwent [ˌʌndəˈwent] *pt* ▷ **undergo**.

underworld [ˈʌndəˌwɜːld] *n* [criminal society]: **the ~** el hampa, los bajos fondos.

underwriter [ˈʌndəˌraɪtəʳ] *n* asegurador *m*, -ra *f*.

undeserving [ˌʌndɪˈzɜːvɪŋ] *adj* [person]: **to be ~ of sthg** no merecer algo.

undid [ʌnˈdɪd] *pt* ▷ **undo**.

undies [ˈʌndɪz] *npl inf* paños *mpl* menores.

undisputed [ˌʌndɪˈspjuːtɪd] *adj* indiscutible.

undistinguished [ˌʌndɪˈstɪŋgwɪʃt] *adj* mediocre.

undo [ʌnˈduː] (*pt* **-did**, *pp* **-done**) *vt* **- 1.** [unfasten - knot] desatar, desanudar; [- button, clasp] desabrochar; [- parcel] abrir **- 2.** [nullify] anular, deshacer.

undoing [ʌnˈduːɪŋ] *n* (*U*) *fml* ruina *f*, perdición *f*; **it was his ~** fue su perdición.

undone [ˌʌnˈdʌn] ◇ *pp* ⊳ **undo**. ◇ *adj* **-1.** [coat] desabrochado(da); [shoes] desatado(da); **to come ~** desatarse **-2.** *fml* [not done] por hacer.

undoubted [ʌnˈdaʊtɪd] *adj* indudable.

undoubtedly [ʌnˈdaʊtɪdlɪ] *adv fml* indudablemente, sin duda (alguna).

undress [ˌʌnˈdres] ◇ *vt* desnudar. ◇ *vi* desnudarse.

undue [ˌʌnˈdjuː] *adj fml* indebido(da), excesivo(va).

undulate [ˈʌndjʊleɪt] *vi fml* ondular.

unduly [ˌʌnˈdjuːlɪ] *adv fml* indebidamente, excesivamente.

unearth [ˌʌnˈɜːθ] *vt* [dig up] desenterrar; *fig* [discover] descubrir.

unearthly [ʌnˈɜːθlɪ] *adj inf* [hour] intempestivo(va).

unease [ʌnˈiːz] *n* malestar *m*.

uneasy [ʌnˈiːzɪ] (*compar* **-ier**, *superl* **-iest**) *adj* **-1.** [person, feeling] intranquilo(la) **-2.** [peace] inseguro(ra).

uneconomic [ˈʌnˌiːkəˈnɒmɪk] *adj* poco rentable.

uneducated [ˌʌnˈedjʊkeɪtɪd] *adj* ignorante, inculto(ta).

unemployed [ˌʌnɪmˈplɔɪd] ◇ *adj* parado(da), desempleado(da). ◇ *npl*: **the ~** los parados.

unemployment [ˌʌnɪmˈplɔɪmənt] *n* desempleo *m*, paro *m*.

unemployment benefit *UK*, **unemployment compensation** *US n* subsidio *m* de desempleo *OR* paro.

unerring [ˌʌnˈɜːrɪŋ] *adj* infalible.

uneven [ˌʌnˈiːvn] *adj* **-1.** [not flat - road] lleno(na) de baches; [- land] escabroso(sa) **-2.** [inconsistent, unfair] desigual.

unexpected [ˌʌnɪkˈspektɪd] *adj* inesperado(da).

unexpectedly [ˌʌnɪkˈspektɪdlɪ] *adv* inesperadamente.

unfailing [ʌnˈfeɪlɪŋ] *adj* indefectible.

unfair [ˌʌnˈfeəʳ] *adj* injusto(ta).

unfaithful [ˌʌnˈfeɪθfʊl] *adj* [sexually absent] infiel.

unfamiliar [ˌʌnfəˈmɪljəʳ] *adj* **-1.** [not well-known] desconocido(da), nuevo(va) **-2.** [not acquainted]: **to be ~ with sthg/sb** desconocer algo/a alguien.

unfashionable [ˌʌnˈfæʃnəbl] *adj* [clothes, ideas] pasado(da) de moda; [area of town] poco popular.

unfasten [ˌʌnˈfɑːsn] *vt* [garment, buttons] desabrochar; [rope, tie] desatar, soltar; [door] abrir.

unfavourable *UK*, **unfavorable** *US* [ˌʌnˈfeɪvrəbl] *adj* desfavorable.

unfeeling [ʌnˈfiːlɪŋ] *adj* insensible.

unfinished [ˌʌnˈfɪnɪʃt] *adj* sin terminar.

unfit [ˌʌnˈfɪt] *adj* **-1.** [injured] lesiona-do(da); [in poor shape] que no está en forma **-2.** [not suitable - thing] impropio(pia); [- person]: **~ to** incapaz de; **~ for** no apto para.

unfold [ʌnˈfəʊld] ◇ *vt* **-1.** [open out] desplegar, desdoblar **-2.** [explain] exponer, revelar. ◇ *vi* [become clear] revelarse.

unforeseen [ˌʌnfɔːˈsiːn] *adj* imprevisto(ta).

unforgettable [ˌʌnfəˈgetəbl] *adj* inolvidable.

unforgivable [ˌʌnfəˈgɪvəbl] *adj* imperdonable.

unfortunate [ʌnˈfɔːtʃnət] *adj* **-1.** [unlucky] desgraciado(da), desdichado(da), salado(da) *Amér* **-2.** [regrettable] inoportuno(na).

unfortunately [ʌnˈfɔːtʃnətlɪ] *adv* desgraciadamente, desafortunadamente.

unfounded [ˌʌnˈfaʊndɪd] *adj* infundado(da).

unfriendly [ˌʌnˈfrendlɪ] (*compar* **-ier**, *superl* **-iest**) *adj* poco amistoso(sa).

unfurnished [ˌʌnˈfɜːnɪʃt] *adj* sin muebles, desamueblado(da).

ungainly [ʌnˈgeɪnlɪ] *adj* torpe, desgarbado(da).

ungodly [ˌʌnˈgɒdlɪ] *adj inf* [hour] intempestivo(va); **at an ~ hour** a una hora intempestiva.

ungrateful [ʌnˈgreɪtfʊl] *adj* desagradecido(da), ingrato(ta).

unhappy [ʌnˈhæpɪ] (*compar* **-ier**, *superl* **-iest**) *adj* **-1.** [sad] triste; [wretched] desdichado(da), infeliz **-2.** [uneasy]: **to be ~ (with** *OR* **about)** estar inquieto(ta) (por) **-3.** *fml* [unfortunate] desafortunado(da).

unharmed [ˌʌnˈhɑːmd] *adj* [person] ileso(sa); [thing] indemne; **he escaped ~** salió ileso.

unhealthy [ʌnˈhelθɪ] (*compar* **-ier**, *superl* **-iest**) *adj* **-1.** [in bad health] enfermizo(za) **-2.** [causing bad health] insalubre **-3.** *fig* [interest etc] morboso(sa).

unheard-of [ʌnˈhɜːd-] *adj* **-1.** [unknown, completely absent] inaudito(ta) **-2.** [unprecedented] sin precedente.

unhook [ˌʌnˈhʊk] *vt* **-1.** [unfasten hooks of] desabrochar **-2.** [remove from hook] descolgar, desenganchar.

unhurt [ˌʌnˈhɜːt] *adj* ileso(sa).

unhygienic [ˌʌnhaɪˈdʒiːnɪk] *adj* antihigiénico(ca).

unidentified flying object *n* objeto *m* volador no identificado.

unification [ˌjuːnɪfɪˈkeɪʃn] *n* unificación *f*.

uniform [ˈjuːnɪfɔːm] ◇ *adj* uniforme, constante. ◇ *n* uniforme *m*.

unify [ˈjuːnɪfaɪ] (*pt* & *pp* **-ied**) *vt* unificar, unir.

unilateral [ˌjuːnɪˈlætərəl] *adj* unilateral.

unimportant [ˌʌnɪm'pɔːtənt] *adj* sin importancia, insignificante.

uninhabited [ˌʌnɪn'hæbɪtɪd] *adj* deshabitado(da), desierto(ta).

uninjured [ˌʌn'ɪndʒəd] *adj* ileso(sa).

unintelligent [ˌʌnɪn'telɪdʒent] *adj* poco inteligente.

unintentional [ˌʌnɪn'tenʃənl] *adj* involuntario(ria).

union ['juːnjən] ◇ *n* - **1.** [trade union] sindicato *m* - **2.** [alliance] unión *f*, alianza *f.* ◇ *comp* sindical.

Union Jack *n*: the ～ *la bandera del Reino Unido.*

unique [juː'niːk] *adj* - **1.** [gen] único(ca) - **2.** *fml* [peculiar, exclusive]: ～ to peculiar de.

unison ['juːnɪzn] *n* unísono *m*; in ～ [simultaneously] al unísono.

unit ['juːnɪt] *n* - **1.** [gen] unidad *f* - **2.** [piece of furniture] módulo *m*, elemento *m.*

unite [juː'naɪt] ◇ *vt* [gen] unir; [country] unificar. ◇ *vi* unirse, juntarse.

united [juː'naɪtɪd] *adj* unido(da).

United Kingdom *n*: the ～ el Reino Unido.

United Nations *n*: the ～ las Naciones Unidas.

United States *n*: the ～ (of America) los Estados Unidos (de América).

unit trust *n UK* fondo *m* de inversión mobiliaria.

unity ['juːnətɪ] *n (U)* unidad *f*, unión *f.*

universal [ˌjuːnɪ'vɜːsl] *adj* universal.

universe ['juːnɪvɜːs] *n*: the ～ el universo.

university [ˌjuːnɪ'vɜːsətɪ] *(pl* -ies) ◇ *n* universidad *f.* ◇ *comp* universitario(ria); ～ **student** (estudiante) universitario *m*, universitaria *f.*

unjust [ˌʌn'dʒʌst] *adj* injusto(ta).

unkempt [ˌʌn'kempt] *adj* [person] desaseado(da); [hair] despeinado(da); [clothes] descuidado(da).

unkind [ʌn'kaɪnd] *adj* [uncharitable] poco amable, cruel.

unknown [ˌʌn'nəʊn] *adj* desconocido(da); ～ to him sin que él lo supiera.

unlawful [ˌʌn'lɔːfʊl] *adj* ilegal, ilícito(ta).

unleaded [ˌʌn'ledɪd] *adj* sin plomo.

unleash [ˌʌn'liːʃ] *vt literary* desatar, desencadenar.

unless [ən'les] *conj* a menos que; ～ **I say so** a menos que yo lo diga; ～ **I'm mistaken** si no me equivoco.

unlike [ˌʌn'laɪk] *prep* - **1.** [different from] distinto(ta) a, diferente a - **2.** [differently from] a diferencia de - **3.** [not typical of] impropio(pia) de, poco característico(ca) de; that's ～ him no es propio de él.

unlikely [ʌn'laɪklɪ] *adj* - **1.** [not probable] improbable, poco probable; it's ～ **that he'll come now, he's** ～ **to come now** ahora es

poco probable que venga; to be highly ～ ser muy poco probable - **2.** [bizarre] inverosímil.

unlisted [ʌn'lɪstɪd] *adj US* [phone number] que no figura en la guía telefónica.

unload [ˌʌn'ləʊd] *vt* [goods, car] descargar.

unlock [ˌʌn'lɒk] *vt* abrir (con llave).

unlucky [ʌn'lʌkɪ] *(compar* -ier, *superl* -iest) *adj* - **1.** [unfortunate] desgraciado(da); to be ～ tener mala suerte - **2.** [number, colour etc] de la mala suerte; to be ～ traer mala suerte.

unmarried [ˌʌn'mærɪd] *adj* que no se ha casado.

unmistakable [ˌʌnmɪ'steɪkəbl] *adj* inconfundible.

unmitigated [ʌn'mɪtɪgeɪtɪd] *adj* absoluto(ta).

unnatural [ʌn'nætʃrəl] *adj* - **1.** [unusual, strange] anormal - **2.** [affected] afectado(da).

unnecessary [ʌn'nesəsərɪ] *adj* innecesario(ria).

unnerving [ʌn'nɜːvɪŋ] *adj* desconcertante.

unnoticed [ˌʌn'nəʊtɪst] *adj* inadvertido(da), desapercibido(da); to go ～ pasar desapercibido(da).

unobtainable [ˌʌnəb'teɪnəbl] *adj* inasequible.

unobtrusive [ˌʌnəb'truːsɪv] *adj* discreto(ta).

unofficial [ˌʌnə'fɪʃl] *adj* extraoficial, oficioso(sa).

unorthodox [ˌʌn'ɔːθədɒks] *adj* poco convencional, poco ortodoxo(xa).

unpack [ˌʌn'pæk] ◇ *vt* - **1.** [box] desempaquetar, desembalar; [suitcases] deshacer - **2.** [clothes] sacar (de la maleta). ◇ *vi* deshacer las maletas.

unpalatable [ʌn'pælətəbl] *adj* [food] incomible; [drink] imbebible; *fig* [difficult to accept] desagradable.

unparalleled [ʌn'pærəleld] *adj* incomparable, sin precedente.

unpleasant [ʌn'pleznt] *adj* - **1.** [disagreeable] desagradable - **2.** [unfriendly, rude - person] antipático(ca); [- remark] mezquino(na).

unplug [ʌn'plʌg] *(pt & pp* -ged, *cont* -ging) *vt* desenchufar, desconectar.

unpopular [ˌʌn'pɒpjʊləʳ] *adj* impopular, poco popular; she was ～ with the other girls las otras chicas no le tenían mucho aprecio.

unprecedented [ʌn'presɪdəntɪd] *adj* sin precedentes, inaudito(ta).

unpredictable [ˌʌnprɪ'dɪktəbl] *adj* imprevisible.

unprofessional [ˌʌnprə'feʃənl] *adj* poco profesional.

unqualified [ˌʌnˈkwɒlɪfaɪd] *adj* -1. [not qualified] sin título, no cualificado(da) -2. [total, complete] incondicional, completo(ta).

unquestionable [ʌnˈkwestʃənəbl] *adj* incuestionable, indiscutible.

unquestioning [ʌnˈkwestʃənɪŋ] *adj* incondicional.

unravel [ʌnˈrævl] (*UK pt & pp* **-led**, *cont* **-ling**, *US pt & pp* **-ed**, *cont* **-ing**) *vt lit & fig* desenmarañar.

unreal [ˌʌnˈrɪəl] *adj* irreal.

unrealistic [ˌʌnrɪəˈlɪstɪk] *adj* [person] poco realista; [idea, plan] impracticable, fantástico(ca).

unreasonable [ʌnˈriːznəbl] *adj* -1. [person, behaviour, decision] poco razonable -2. [demand, price] excesivo(va).

unrelated [ˌʌnrɪˈleɪtɪd] *adj*: **to be ~ (to)** no tener conexión (con).

unrelenting [ˌʌnrɪˈlentɪŋ] *adj* implacable, inexorable.

unreliable [ˌʌnrɪˈlaɪəbl] *adj* que no es de fiar.

unremitting [ˌʌnrɪˈmɪtɪŋ] *adj* incesante, continuo(nua).

unrequited [ˌʌnrɪˈkwaɪtɪd] *adj* no correspondido(da).

unreserved [ˌʌnrɪˈzɜːvd] *adj* [wholehearted] incondicional, absoluto(ta).

unresolved [ˌʌnrɪˈzɒlvd] *adj* sin resolver, pendiente.

unrest [ˌʌnˈrest] *n (U)* malestar *m*, inquietud *f*.

unrivalled *UK*, **unrivaled** *US* [ʌnˈraɪvld] *adj* incomparable, sin par.

unroll [ˌʌnˈrəʊl] *vt* desenrollar.

unruly [ʌnˈruːlɪ] (*compar* **-ier**, *superl* **-iest**) *adj* -1. [person, behaviour] revoltoso(sa) -2. [hair] rebelde.

unsafe [ˌʌnˈseɪf] *adj* [gen] inseguro(ra); [risky] arriesgado(da).

unsaid [ˌʌnˈsed] *adj*: **to leave sthg ~** dejar algo sin decir.

unsatisfactory [ˈʌnˌsætɪsˈfæktərɪ] *adj* insatisfactorio(ria).

unsavoury, unsavory *US* [ˌʌnˈseɪvərɪ] *adj* desagradable.

unscathed [ˌʌnˈskeɪðd] *adj* ileso(sa).

unscrew [ˌʌnˈskruː] *vt* -1. [lid, top] abrir -2. [sign, hinge] desatornillar.

unscrupulous [ʌnˈskruːpjʊləs] *adj* desaprensivo(va), poco escrupuloso(sa).

unseemly [ʌnˈsiːmlɪ] (*compar* **-ier**, *superl* **-iest**) *adj* impropio(pia), indecoroso(sa).

unselfish [ˌʌnˈselfɪʃ] *adj* desinteresado(da), altruista.

unsettle [ˌʌnˈsetl] *vt* perturbar, inquietar.

unsettled [ˌʌnˈsetld] *adj* -1. [person] nervioso(sa), intranquilo(la) -2. [weather]

variable, inestable -3. [argument, matter, debt] pendiente -4. [situation] inestable.

unshak(e)able [ʌnˈʃeɪkəbl] *adj* inquebrantable.

unshaven [ˌʌnˈʃeɪvn] *adj* sin afeitar.

unsightly [ʌnˈsaɪtlɪ] *adj* [building] feo (fea); [scar, bruise] desagradable.

unskilled [ˌʌnˈskɪld] *adj* [person] no cualificado(da); [work] no especializado(da).

unsociable [ʌnˈsəʊʃəbl] *adj* insociable, poco sociable.

unsocial [ʌnˈsəʊʃl] *adj*: **to work ~ hours** trabajar a horas intempestivas.

unsound [ˌʌnˈsaʊnd] *adj* -1. [conclusion, method] erróneo(a) -2. [building, structure] defectuoso(sa).

unspeakable [ʌnˈspiːkəbl] *adj* [crime] incalificable; [pain] indecible.

unstable [ˌʌnˈsteɪbl] *adj* inestable.

unsteady [ˌʌnˈstedɪ] (*compar* **-ier**, *superl* **-iest**) *adj* [gen] inestable; [hands, voice] tembloroso(sa); [footsteps] vacilante.

unstoppable [ˌʌnˈstɒpəbl] *adj* irrefrenable, incontenible.

unstuck [ˌʌnˈstʌk] *adj*: **to come ~** [notice, stamp, label] despegarse, desprenderse; *fig* [plan, system, person] fracasar.

unsuccessful [ˌʌnsəkˈsesfʊl] *adj* [person] fracasado(da); [attempt, meeting] infructuoso(sa); **to be ~** [subj: person] no tener éxito.

unsuccessfully [ˌʌnsəkˈsesfʊlɪ] *adv* sin éxito, en vano.

unsuitable [ˌʌnˈsuːtəbl] *adj* inadecuado(da), inapropiado(da); **he is ~ for the job** no es la persona indicada para el trabajo; **I'm afraid 3 o'clock would be ~** lo siento, pero no me va bien a las 3.

unsure [ˌʌnˈʃɔː'] *adj* -1. [not confident]: **to be ~ of o.s.** sentirse inseguro(ra) -2. [not certain]: **to be ~ (about OR of)** no estar muy seguro (de).

unsuspecting [ˌʌnsəˈspektɪŋ] *adj* desprevenido(da), confiado(da).

unsympathetic [ˈʌnˌsɪmpəˈθetɪk] *adj*: **~ to** indiferente a.

untangle [ˌʌnˈtæŋgl] *vt* desenmarañar.

untapped [ˌʌnˈtæpt] *adj* sin explotar.

untenable [ˌʌnˈtenəbl] *adj* insostenible.

unthinkable [ʌnˈθɪŋkəbl] *adj* impensable, inconcebible.

untidy [ʌnˈtaɪdɪ] (*compar* **-ier**, *superl* **-iest**) *adj* [room, desk] desordenado(da); [person, appearance] desaliñado(da).

untie [ˌʌnˈtaɪ] (*cont* **untying**) *vt* desatar.

until [ʌnˈtɪl] ◇ *prep* hasta; **~ now/then** hasta ahora/entonces. ◇ *conj* -1. [gen] hasta que; **wait ~ everybody is there** espera a que haya llegado todo el mundo -2. (*after negative*): **don't leave ~ you've finished** no te vayas hasta que no hayas terminado.

untimely [ʌn'taɪmlɪ] *adj* - **1.** [premature] prematuro(ra) - **2.** [inappropriate] inoportuno(na).

untold [ˌʌn'təʊld] *adj* [incalculable, vast] incalculable; [suffering, joy] indecible.

untoward [ˌʌntə'wɔːd] *adj* [event] adverso(sa); [behaviour] fuera de lugar.

untrue [ˌʌn'truː] *adj* [not true] falso(sa).

unused [*sense 1* ˌʌn'juːzd, *sense 2* ʌn'juːst] *adj* - **1.** [not previously used] nuevo(va), sin usar - **2.** [unaccustomed]: **to be ~ to sthg/ to doing sthg** no estar acostumbrado(da) a algo/a hacer algo.

unusual [ʌn'juːʒl] *adj* [rare] insólito(ta), poco común.

unusually [ʌn'juːʒəlɪ] *adv* - **1.** [exceptionally] extraordinariamente; **the exam was ~ difficult** el examen fue extraordinariamente difícil - **2.** [surprisingly] sorprendentemente.

unveil [ˌʌn'veɪl] *vt* - **1.** [statue, plaque] descubrir - **2.** *fig* [plans, policy] revelar.

unwanted [ˌʌn'wɒntɪd] *adj* [clothes, furniture] superfluo(flua); [child, pregnancy] no deseado(da).

unwavering [ʌn'weɪvərɪŋ] *adj* [determination, feeling] firme, inquebrantable; [concentration] constante; [gaze] fijo(ja).

unwelcome [ʌn'welkəm] *adj* inoportuno(na).

unwell [ˌʌn'wel] *adj*: **to be/feel ~** estar/ sentirse mal.

unwieldy [ʌn'wiːldɪ] (*compar* **-ier**, *superl* **-iest**) *adj* - **1.** [object] abultado(da); [tool] poco manejable - **2.** *fig* [system, organization] poco eficiente.

unwilling [ʌn'wɪlɪŋ] *adj* no dispuesto(ta); **to be ~ to do sthg** no estar dispuesto a hacer algo.

unwind [ʌn'waɪnd] (*pt & pp* **unwound**) ◇ *vt* desenrollar. ◇ *vi fig* [person] relajarse.

unwise [ˌʌn'waɪz] *adj* imprudente, poco aconsejable.

unwitting [ʌn'wɪtɪŋ] *adj fml* inconsciente.

unworkable [ˌʌn'wɜːkəbl] *adj* impracticable.

unworthy [ʌn'wɜːðɪ] (*compar* **-ier**, *superl* **-iest**) *adj* [undeserving]: **to be ~ of** no ser digno(na) de.

unwound [ˌʌn'waʊnd] *pt & pp* ⊳ **unwind**.

unwrap [ˌʌn'ræp] (*pt & pp* **-ped**, *cont* **-ping**) *vt* [present] desenvolver; [parcel] desempaquetar.

unwritten law [ˌʌn'rɪtn-] *n* ley *f* no escrita.

up [ʌp] ◇ *adv* - **1.** [towards a higher position] hacia arriba; [in a higher position] arriba; **to throw sthg ~** lanzar algo hacia arriba; **she's ~ in her room** está arriba en

su cuarto; **we'll be ~ in just a moment** subiremos en un minuto; **we walked ~ to the top** subimos hasta arriba del todo; **put it ~ there** ponlo ahí arriba - **2.** [northwards]: **I'm going ~ to York next week** voy a subir a York la semana próxima; **~ north** en el norte - **3.** [along a road or river] adelante; **their house is 100 metres further ~** su casa está 100 metros más adelante. ◇ *prep* - **1.** [towards a higher position]: **we went ~ the mountain** subimos por la montaña; **let's go ~ this road** vamos por esta carretera; **I went ~ the stairs** subí las escaleras - **2.** [in a higher position] en lo alto de; **~ a tree** en un árbol - **3.** [at far end of] al final de; **they live ~ the road from us** viven más adelante en nuestra misma calle - **4.** [against current of river]: **~ the Amazon** Amazonas arriba. ◇ *adj* - **1.** [out of bed] levantado(da); **I was ~ at six today** hoy me levanté a las seis - **2.** [at an end] terminado(da) - **3.** *inf* [wrong]: **is something ~?** ¿pasa algo?, ¿algo va mal?; **what's ~?** ¿qué pasa? ◇ *n*: **~s and downs** altibajos *mpl*.

◆ **up and down** ◇ *adv*: **to jump ~ and down** saltar para arriba y para abajo; **to walk ~ and down** andar para un lado y para otro. ◇ *prep*: **we walked ~ and down the avenue** estuvimos caminando arriba y abajo de la avenida.

◆ **up to** *prep* - **1.** [indicating level] hasta; **it could take ~ to six weeks** podría tardar hasta seis semanas; **it's not ~ to standard** no tiene el nivel necesario - **2.** [well or able enough for]: **to be ~ to doing sthg** sentirse con fuerzas (como) para hacer algo; **my French isn't ~ to much** mi francés no es gran cosa - **3.** *inf* [secretly doing something]: **what are you ~ to?** ¿qué andas tramando? - **4.** [indicating responsibility]: **it's not ~ to me to decide** no depende de mí el decidir.

◆ **up until** *prep* hasta.

up-and-coming *adj* prometedor(ra), con futuro.

upbringing ['ʌpˌbrɪŋɪŋ] *n* educación *f*.

update [ˌʌp'deɪt] *vt* actualizar.

upheaval [ʌp'hiːvl] *n* trastorno *m*, agitación *f*.

upheld [ʌp'held] *pt & pp* ⊳ **uphold**.

uphill [ˌʌp'hɪl] ◇ *adj* [rising] empinado(da), cuesta arriba; *fig* [difficult] arduo(dua), difícil. ◇ *adv* cuesta arriba.

uphold [ʌp'həʊld] (*pt & pp* **-held**) *vt* sostener, apoyar.

upholstery [ʌp'həʊlstərɪ] *n* tapicería *f*, tapizado *m*.

upkeep ['ʌpkiːp] *n* mantenimiento *m*.

uplifting [ʌp'lɪftɪŋ] *adj* inspirador(ra).

up-market *adj* de clase superior, de categoría.

upon [ə'pɒn] *prep fml* en, sobre; ~ **entering the room** al entrar en el cuarto; **question ~ question** pregunta tras pregunta; **summer is ~ us** ya tenemos el verano encima.

upper ['ʌpə^r] ◇ *adj* superior. ◇ *n* [of shoe] pala *f*.

upper class *n*: **the ~** la clase alta.

◆ **upper-class** *adj* de clase alta.

upper hand *n*: **to have/gain the ~ (in)** llevar/empezar a llevar la ventaja (en).

uppermost ['ʌpəməʊst] *adj* **-1.** [highest] más alto(ta) **-2.** [most important]: **to be ~ in one's mind** ser lo más importante para uno.

upright [*adj senses 1 & 2 & adv* ,ʌp'raɪt, *adj sense 3 & n* 'ʌpraɪt] ◇ *adj* **-1.** [erect - person, chair] derecho(cha) **-2.** [standing vertically - object] vertical **-3.** *fig* [honest] recto(ta), honrado(da). ◇ *adv* erguidamente. ◇ *n* poste *m*.

uprising [ʌp,raɪzɪŋ] *n* sublevación *f*, alzamiento *m*.

uproar ['ʌprɔ:^r] *n* **-1.** (U) [commotion] alboroto *m* **-2.** [protest] escándalo *m*.

uproot [ʌp'ru:t] *vt* **-1.** [person] desplazar, mudar **-2.** BOT [plant] desarraigar.

upset [ʌp'set] (*pt & pp* **upset**, *cont* **-ting**) ◇ *adj* **-1.** [distressed] disgustado(da), afectado(da); **to get ~** disgustarse **-2.** MED: **to have an ~ stomach** sentirse mal del estómago. ◇ *n*: **to have a stomach ~** sentirse mal del estómago. ◇ *vt* **-1.** [distress] disgustar, perturbar **-2.** [mess up] dar al traste con, estropear **-3.** [overturn, knock over] volcar.

upshot ['ʌpʃɒt] *n* resultado *m*.

upside down [,ʌpsaɪd-] ◇ *adj* al revés. ◇ *adv* al revés; **to turn sthg ~** revolver algo, desordenar algo.

upstairs [,ʌp'steəz] ◇ *adj* de arriba. ◇ *adv* arriba. ◇ *n* el piso de arriba.

upstart ['ʌpstɑ:t] *n* advenedizo *m*, -za *f*.

upstream [,ʌp'stri:m] *adv* río arriba, corriente arriba.

upsurge [ʌps3:dʒ] *n*: **~ of** OR **in** aumento *m* considerable de.

uptake ['ʌpteɪk] *n*: **to be quick on the ~** cogerlas al vuelo; **to be slow on the ~** ser un poco torpe.

uptight [ʌp'taɪt] *adj inf* tenso(sa), nervioso(sa).

up-to-date *adj* **-1.** [modern] moderno(na) **-2.** [most recent] actual, al día **-3.** [informed]: **to keep ~ with** mantenerse al día de.

upturn ['ʌptɜ:n] *n*: **~ (in)** mejora *f* (de).

upward ['ʌpwəd] ◇ *adj* hacia arriba. ◇ *adv US* = **upwards**.

upwards ['ʌpwədz] *adv* hacia arriba.

◆ **upwards of** *prep* más de.

uranium [jʊ'reɪnjəm] *n* uranio *m*.

Uranus ['jʊərənəs] *n* Urano *m*.

urban ['ɜ:bən] *adj* urbano(na).

urbane [ɜ:'beɪn] *adj* cortés, urbano(na).

urchin ['ɜ:tʃɪn] *n dated* pilluelo *m*, -la *f*.

Urdu ['ʊədu:] *n* urdu *m*.

urge [ɜ:dʒ] ◇ *n* impulso *m*, deseo *m*; **to have an ~ to do sthg** desear ardientemente hacer algo. ◇ *vt* **-1.** [try to persuade]: **to ~ sb to do sthg** instar a alguien a hacer algo **-2.** [advocate] recomendar encarecidamente.

urgency ['ɜ:dʒənsɪ] *n (U)* urgencia *f*.

urgent ['ɜ:dʒənt] *adj* **-1.** [pressing] urgente **-2.** [desperate] apremiante.

urinal [,jʊə'raɪnl] *n* [place] urinario *m*; [vessel] orinal *m*.

urinate ['jʊərɪneɪt] *vi* orinar.

urine ['jʊərɪn] *n* orina *f*.

URL (*abbr of* **uniform resource locator**) *n* COMPUT URL *m*.

urn [ɜ:n] *n* **-1.** [for ashes] urna *f* **-2.** [for tea, coffee] *cilindro o barril con grifo para servir té o café en grandes cantidades*.

Uruguay ['jʊərəgwaɪ] *n* Uruguay.

Uruguayan [,jʊərə'gwaɪən] ◇ *adj* uruguayo(ya). ◇ *n* uruguayo *m*, -ya *f*.

us [ʌs] *pers pron* **-1.** (direct, indirect) nos; **can you see/hear ~?** ¿puedes vernos/oírnos?; **it's ~** somos nosotros; **he sent ~ a letter** nos mandó una carta; **she gave it to ~** nos lo dio **-2.** (stressed, after prep, in comparisons etc) nosotros(tras); **you can't expect US to do it** no esperarás que lo hagamos NOSOTROS; **with/without ~** con/sin nosotros; **they are more wealthy than ~** son más ricos que nosotros; **all of ~** todos (nosotros); **some of ~** algunos de nosotros.

US (*abbr of* **United States**) *n* EEUU *mpl*.

USA *n* (*abbr of* **United States of America**) EEUU *mpl*.

usage ['ju:zɪdʒ] *n* uso *m*.

USB (*abbr of* **Universal Serial Bus**) *n* COMPUT USB *m*.

USB port *n* COMPUT puerto *m* USB.

use [*n & aux vb* ju:s, *vt* ju:z] ◇ *n* uso *m*; **to be in ~** usarse; **to be out of ~** no usarse; **'out of ~'** 'no funciona'; **to make ~ of sthg** utilizar OR aprovechar algo; **to be of/no ~** ser útil/inútil; **what's the ~ (of doing sthg)?** ¿de qué sirve (hacer algo)? ◇ *aux vb* soler, acostumbrar; **I ~d to go swimming** solía OR acostumbraba ir a nadar; **he ~d to be fat** antes estaba gordo. ◇ *vt* **-1.** [utilize, employ] usar, emplear **-2.** [exploit] usar, manejar.

◆ **use up** *vt sep* agotar.

used [*sense 1* ju:zd, *sense 2* ju:st] *adj* **-1.** [dirty, second-hand] usado(da) **-2.** [accustomed]: **to be ~ to** estar acostumbrado(da) a; **to get ~ to** acostumbrarse a.

useful ['juːsfʊl] *adj* - 1. [handy] útil, provechoso(sa) - 2. [helpful - person] valioso(sa).

useless ['juːslɪs] *adj* - 1. [gen] inútil - 2. *inf* [hopeless] incompetente.

user ['juːzəʳ] *n* usuario *m*, -ria *f*.

user-friendly *adj* fácil de utilizar.

usher ['ʌʃəʳ] ⟨⟩ *n* [at wedding] ujier *m*; [at theatre, concert] acomodador *m*, -ra *f*. ⟨⟩ *vt*: **to ~ sb in** hacer pasar a alguien; **to ~ sb out** acompañar a alguien hasta la puerta.

usherette [ˌʌʃə'ret] *n* acomodadora *f*.

USSR (*abbr of* **Union of Soviet Socialist Republics**) *n*: **the (former) ~** la (antigua) URSS.

usual ['juːʒəl] *adj* habitual; **as ~** [as normal] como de costumbre; [as often happens] como siempre.

usually ['juːʒəlɪ] *adv* por regla general, normalmente; **we ~ go to church on Sunday** solemos ir a misa el domingo.

usurp [juːˈzɜːp] *vt fml* usurpar.

utensil [juːˈtensl] *n* utensilio *m*.

uterus ['juːtərəs] (*pl* **-ri** [-raɪ], **-ruses**) *n* útero *m*.

utility [juːˈtɪlətɪ] (*pl* **-ies**) *n* - 1. [gen] utilidad *f* - 2. [public service] servicio *m* público.

➤ **utilities** *n US* [service charges] empresa *f* de servicios públicos.

utility room *n* trascocina *f*.

utilize, -ise ['juːtəlaɪz] *vt* utilizar.

utmost ['ʌtməʊst] ⟨⟩ *adj* mayor, supremo(ma). ⟨⟩ *n*: **to do one's ~** hacer lo imposible; **to the ~** al máximo, a más no poder.

utter ['ʌtəʳ] ⟨⟩ *adj* puro(ra), completo(ta). ⟨⟩ *vt* [word] pronunciar; [sound, cry] emitir.

utterly ['ʌtəlɪ] *adv* completamente, totalmente.

U-turn *n lit* & *fig* giro *m* de 180°; **to do a ~** [in car] cambiar de sentido; *fig* dar un giro radical.

v¹ (*pl* **v's** OR **vs**), **V** (*pl* **V's** OR **Vs**) [viː] *n* [letter] v *f*, V *f*.

v² - 1. (*abbr of* **verse**) v - 2. (*abbr of* **volt**) v - 3. (*abbr of* **vide**) [cross-reference] v. - 4. *abbr of* **versus**.

vacancy ['veɪkənsɪ] (*pl* **-ies**) *n* - 1. [job, position] vacante *f* - 2. [room available] habitación *f* libre; **'no vacancies'** 'completo'.

vacant ['veɪkənt] *adj* - 1. [room, chair, toilet] libre - 2. [job, post] vacante - 3. [look, expression] distraído(da).

vacant lot *n* terreno *m* disponible.

vacate [vəˈkeɪt] *vt* - 1. [job, post] dejar vacante - 2. [room, seat, premises] desocupar.

vacation [vəˈkeɪʃn] *US* ⟨⟩ *n* vacaciones *fpl*; **to be on ~** estar de vacaciones. ⟨⟩ *vi* pasar las vacaciones.

vacationer [vəˈkeɪʃənəʳ] *n US*: **summer ~** veraneante *m* OR *f*.

vaccinate ['væksɪneɪt] *vt*: **to ~ sb (against sthg)** vacunar a alguien (de OR contra algo).

vaccine [*UK* 'væksiːn, *US* væk'siːn] *n* vacuna *f*.

vacuum ['vækjʊəm] ⟨⟩ *n* - 1. TECH & *fig* vacío *m* - 2. [cleaner] aspiradora *f*. ⟨⟩ *vt* pasar la aspiradora por.

vacuum cleaner *n* aspiradora *f*.

vacuum-packed *adj* envasado(da) al vacío.

vagina [vəˈdʒaɪnə] *n* vagina *f*.

vagrant ['veɪɡrənt] *n* vagabundo *m*, -da *f*.

vague [veɪɡ] *adj* - 1. [imprecise] vago(ga), impreciso(sa) - 2. [person] poco claro(ra) - 3. [feeling] leve - 4. [evasive] evasivo(va) - 5. [absent-minded] distraído(da) - 6. [outline] borroso(sa).

vaguely ['veɪɡlɪ] *adv* - 1. [imprecisely] vagamente - 2. [slightly, not very] levemente.

vain [veɪn] *adj* - 1. *pej* [conceited] vanidoso(sa) - 2. [futile] vano(na).

➤ **in vain** *adv* en vano.

valentine card ['væləntaɪn-] *n* tarjeta *f* que se manda el Día de los Enamorados.

Valentine's Day ['væləntaɪnz-] *n*: **(St) ~** San Valentín *m*, Día *m* de los Enamorados.

valet ['væleɪ, 'vælɪt] *n* ayuda *m* de cámara.

valiant ['væljənt] *adj* valeroso(sa).

valid ['vælɪd] *adj* - 1. [argument, explanation] válido(da) - 2. [ticket, driving licence] en vigor; **to be ~ for six months** ser válido(da) durante seis meses.

valley ['vælɪ] (*pl* **valleys**) *n* valle *m*.

valour *UK*, **valor** *US* ['væləʳ] *n* (U) *fml* & *literary* valor *m*.

valuable ['væljʊəbl] *adj* valioso(sa).

➤ **valuables** *npl* objetos *mpl* de valor.

valuation [ˌvæljʊ'eɪʃn] *n* - 1. [pricing, estimated price] evaluación *f*, valuación *f* - 2. [opinion, judging of worth] valoración *f*.

value ['væljuː] ⟨⟩ *n* valor *m*; **to lose/gain (in) ~** disminuir/aumentar de valor; **to be good ~** estar muy bien de precio; **to be ~ for money** estar muy bien de precio. ⟨⟩ *vt* - 1. [estimate price of] valorar, tasar; **a necklace ~d at £300** un collar valorado en 300 libras - 2. [cherish] apreciar.

➤ **values** *npl* [morals] valores *mpl* morales, principios *mpl*.

value-added tax [-ædɪd-] *n* impuesto *m* sobre el valor añadido.

valued ['vælju:d] *adj* estimado(da), apreciado(da).

valve [vælv] *n* [in pipe, tube] válvula *f*.

van [væn] *n* **- 1.** AUT furgoneta *f*, camioneta *f* **- 2.** *UK* RAIL furgón *m*.

vandal ['vændl] *n* vándalo *m*, gamberro *m*, -rra *f*.

vandalism ['vændəlɪzm] *n* vandalismo *m*, gamberrismo *m*.

vandalize, -ise ['vændəlaɪz] *vt* destruir, destrozar.

vanguard ['vænɡɑ:d] *n* vanguardia *f*; **in the ~ of** a la vanguardia de.

vanilla [və'nɪlə] *n* vainilla *f*.

vanish ['vænɪʃ] *vi* desaparecer.

vanity ['vænətɪ] *n pej* vanidad *f*.

vantage point ['vɑ:ntɪdʒ,pɔɪnt] *n* posición *f* ventajosa.

vapour *UK*, **vapor** *US* ['veɪpə'] *n* (*U*) vapor *m*.

variable ['veərɪəbl] *adj* variable.

variance ['veərɪəns] *n fml:* **at ~ (with)** en desacuerdo (con).

variation [,veərɪ'eɪʃn] *n:* **~ (in/on)** variación *f* (en/sobre).

varicose veins ['værɪkəʊs-] *npl* varices *fpl*.

varied ['veərɪd] *adj* variado(da).

variety [və'raɪətɪ] (*pl* -ies) *n* **- 1.** [gen] variedad *f*; **for a ~ of reasons** por razones varias **- 2.** (*U*) THEATRE variedades *fpl*.

variety show *n* espectáculo *m* de variedades.

various ['veərɪəs] *adj* **- 1.** [several] varios(-rias) **- 2.** [different] diversos(sas).

varnish ['vɑ:nɪʃ] ◇ *n* barniz *m*. ◇ *vt* [with varnish] barnizar; [with nail varnish] pintar.

vary ['veərɪ] (*pt* & *pt* **-ied**) ◇ *vt* variar. ◇ *vi:* **to ~ (in/with)** variar (de/con).

vase [*UK* vɑ:z, *US* veɪz] *n* florero *m*.

Vaseline® ['væsəli:n] *n* vaselina® *f*.

vast [vɑ:st] *adj* enorme, inmenso(sa).

vat [væt] *n* cuba *f*, tina *f*.

VAT [væt, vi:eɪ'ti:] (*abbr of* value added tax) *n* IVA *m*.

Vatican ['vætɪkən] *n:* **the ~** el Vaticano.

vault [vɔ:lt] ◇ *n* **- 1.** [in bank] cámara *f* acorazada **- 2.** [in church] cripta *f* **- 3.** [roof] bóveda *f*. ◇ *vt* saltar. ◇ *vi:* **to ~ over sthg** saltar por encima de algo.

VCR (*abbr of* video cassette recorder) *n US* aparato *m* de vídeo.

VD (*abbr of* venereal disease) *n* ETS *f*.

VDU (*abbr of* visual display unit) *n* monitor *m*.

veal [vi:l] *n* (*U*) ternera *f*.

veer [vɪə'] *vi* virar.

veep [vi:p] *n US inf* vicepresidente *m*.

vegan ['vi:ɡən] *n* vegetariano *que no consume*

ningún producto que provenga de un animal, como huevos, leche etc.

vegetable ['vedʒtəbl] ◇ *n* **- 1.** BOT vegetal *m* **- 2.** [food] hortaliza *f*, legumbre *f*; **~s** verduras *fpl*. ◇ *adj* vegetal.

vegetarian [,vedʒɪ'teərɪən] ◇ *adj* vegetariano(na). ◇ *n* vegetariano *m*, -na *f*.

vegetation [,vedʒɪ'teɪʃn] *n* vegetación *f*.

veggieburger *n* hamburguesa *f* vegetariana.

vehement ['vi:əmənt] *adj* [person, denial] vehemente; [attack, gesture] violento(ta).

vehicle ['vi:əkl] *n* [for transport] vehículo *m*.

veil [veɪl] ◇ *n lit & fig* velo *m*. ◇ *vt* cubrir con un velo.

vein [veɪn] *n* **- 1.** ANAT & BOT vena *f* **- 2.** [of mineral] filón *m*, veta *f*.

velocity [vɪ'lɒsətɪ] (*pl* -ies) *n* velocidad *f*.

velvet ['velvɪt] *n* terciopelo *m*.

vendetta [ven'detə] *n* enemistad *f* mortal.

vending machine ['vendɪŋ-] *n* máquina *f* de venta.

vendor ['vendɔ:'] *n* vendedor *m*, -ra *f*.

veneer [və'nɪə'] *n* [of wood] chapa *f*; *fig* [appearance] apariencia *f*; **a ~ of** una apariencia de.

venereal disease [vɪ'nɪərɪəl-] *n* enfermedad *f* venérea.

venetian blind *n* persiana *f* veneciana.

Venezuela [,venɪz'weɪlə] *n* Venezuela.

Venezuelan [,venɪz'weɪlən] ◇ *adj* venezolano(na). ◇ *n* venezolano *m*, -na *f*.

vengeance ['vendʒəns] *n* venganza *f*; **with a ~** con creces.

venison ['venɪzn] *n* carne *f* de venado.

venom ['venəm] *n* [poison] veneno *m*; *fig* [spite] malevolencia *f*.

vent [vent] ◇ *n* [opening] abertura *f* de escape; [grille] rejilla *f* de ventilación; **to give ~ to sthg** dar rienda suelta a algo. ◇ *vt:* **to ~ sthg (on)** desahogar algo (contra).

ventilate ['ventɪleɪt] *vt* ventilar.

ventilator ['ventɪleɪtə'] *n* ventilador *m*.

ventriloquist [ven'trɪləkwɪst] *n* ventrílocuo *m*, -cua *f*.

venture ['ventʃə'] ◇ *n* empresa *f*. ◇ *vt* aventurar; **to ~ an opinion** aventurarse a dar una opinión; **to ~ to do sthg** aventurarse a hacer algo. ◇ *vi* **- 1.** [go somewhere dangerous]: **she ~d outside** se atrevió a salir **- 2.** [take a risk]: **to ~ into** lanzarse a.

venue ['venju:] *n* lugar *m* (*en que se celebra algo*).

Venus ['vi:nəs] *n* [planet] Venus *m*.

veranda(h) [və'rændə] *n* veranda *f*.

verb [vɜ:b] *n* verbo *m*.

verbal ['vɜ:bl] *adj* verbal.

verbatim [vɜ:'beɪtɪm] ◇ *adj* literal. ◇ *adv* literalmente, palabra por palabra.

verbose [vɜ:'bəʊs] *adj fml* [person]

verboso(sa); [report] prolijo(ja).

verdict ['vɜ:dɪkt] *n* - **1.** JUR veredicto *m*, fallo *m*; **a ~ of guilty/not guilty** un veredicto de culpabilidad/inocencia - **2.** [opinion]: **~ (on)** juicio *m* OR opinión *f* (sobre).

verge [vɜ:dʒ] *n* - **1.** [edge, side] borde *m* - **2.** [brink]: **on the ~ of sthg** al borde de algo; **to be on the ~ of doing sthg** estar a punto de hacer algo.
◆ **verge (up)on** *vt fus* rayar en.

verify ['verɪfaɪ] (*pt & pp* **-ied**) *vt* - **1.** [check] verificar, comprobar - **2.** [confirm] confirmar.

veritable ['verɪtəbl] *adj hum or fml* verdadero(ra).

vermin ['vɜ:mɪn] *npl* [insects] bichos *mpl*, sabandijas *fpl*; [animals] alimañas *fpl*.

vermouth ['vɜ:məθ] *n* vermut *m*.

versa ⊳ **vice versa**.

versatile ['vɜ:sətaɪl] *adj* - **1.** [person] polifacético(ca) - **2.** [machine, tool] que tiene muchos usos.

verse [vɜ:s] *n* - **1.** (U) [poetry] versos *mpl*, poesía *f* - **2.** [stanza] estrofa *f* - **3.** [in Bible] versículo *m*.

versed [vɜ:st] *adj*: **well ~ in** versado(da) en.

version ['vɜ:ʃn] *n* versión *f*.

versus ['vɜ:səs] *prep* SPORT contra.

vertebra ['vɜ:tɪbrə] (*pl* **-brae** [-bri:]) *n* vértebra *f*.

vertical ['vɜ:tɪkl] *adj* vertical.

vertigo ['vɜ:tɪgəʊ] *n* vértigo *m*.

verve [vɜ:v] *n* brío *m*, entusiasmo *m*.

very ['verɪ] ◇ *adv* - **1.** [as intensifier] muy; **he's not ~ intelligent** no es muy inteligente; **~ much** mucho; **I don't go out ~ often** OR **much** no salgo mucho; **is it good? – not ~ ¿**es bueno? – no mucho - **2.** [emphatic] **the ~ same/next day** justo ese mismo día/al día siguiente; **the ~ first/last** el primero/mejor de todos; **the ~ best** el mejor (de todos); **at the ~ least** como muy poco; **a house of my ~ own** mi propia casa. ◇ *adj*: **in the ~ middle of the picture** en el mismísimo centro del cuadro; **the ~ thing I was looking for** justo lo que estaba buscando; **the ~ thought makes me ill** sólo con pensarlo me pongo enfermo; **fighting for his ~ life** luchando por su propia vida; **the ~ idea!** ¡vaya idea!
◆ **very well** *adv* muy bien; **you can't ~ well stop him now** es un poco tarde para impedírselo.

vessel ['vesl] *n fml* - **1.** [boat] nave *f* - **2.** [container] vasija *f*, recipiente *m*.

vest [vest] *n* - **1.** UK [undershirt] camiseta *f* - **2.** US [waistcoat] chaleco *m*.

vested interest ['vestɪd-] *n*: **~ (in)** intereses *mpl* creados (en).

vestibule ['vestɪbju:l] *n fml* [entrance hall] vestíbulo *m*.

vestige ['vestɪdʒ] *n fml* vestigio *m*.

vestry ['vestrɪ] (*pl* **-ies**) *n* sacristía *f*.

vet [vet] (*pt & pp* **-ted**, *cont* **-ting**) ◇ *n* UK (*abbr of* **veterinary surgeon**) veterinario *m*, -ria *f*. ◇ *vt* someter a una investigación.

veteran ['vetrən] *n* veterano *m*, -na *f*.

veterinarian [ˌvetərɪ'neərɪən] *n* US veterinario *m*, -ria *f*.

veterinary surgeon ['vetərɪnrɪ-] *n* UK *fml* veterinario *m*, -ria *f*.

veto ['vi:təʊ] (*pl* **-es**, *pt & pp* **-ed**, *cont* **-ing**) ◇ *n* veto *m*. ◇ *vt* vetar.

vex [veks] *vt fml* molestar.

vexed question [ˌvekst-] *n* manzana *f* de la discordia.

vg (*abbr of* **very good**) MB.

VGA (*abbr of* **video graphics array**) *n* COMPUT VGA *m*.

VHF (*abbr of* **very high frequency**) VHF.

VHS (*abbr of* **video home system**) *n* VHS *m*.

via ['vaɪə] *prep* - **1.** [travelling through] vía - **2.** [by means of] a través de, por.

viable ['vaɪəbl] *adj* viable.

vibrate [vaɪ'breɪt] *vi* vibrar.

vicar ['vɪkə] *n* párroco *m*.

vicarage ['vɪkərɪdʒ] *n* casa *f* del párroco.

vicarious [vɪ'keərɪəs] *adj* indirecto(ta).

vice [vaɪs] *n* - **1.** [immorality, moral fault] vicio *m* - **2.** [tool] torno *m* de banco.

vice-chairman *n* vicepresidente *m*.

vice-chancellor *n* UNIV rector *m*, -ra *f*.

vice-president *n* vicepresidente *m*, -ta *f*.

vice versa [ˌvaɪsɪ'vɜ:sə] *adv* viceversa.

vicinity [vɪ'sɪnətɪ] *n*: **in the ~ (of)** cerca (de).

vicious ['vɪʃəs] *adj* [dog] furioso(sa); [person, ruler] cruel; [criticism, attack] depravado(da), despiadado(da).

vicious circle *n* círculo *m* vicioso.

victim ['vɪktɪm] *n* víctima *f*.

victimize, -ise ['vɪktɪmaɪz] *vt* [retaliate against] tomar represalias contra; [pick on] mortificar.

victor ['vɪktər] *n literary* vencedor *m*, -ra *f*.

victorious [vɪk'tɔ:rɪəs] *adj* victorioso(sa).

victory ['vɪktərɪ] (*pl* **-ies**) *n*: **~ (over)** victoria *f* (sobre).

video ['vɪdɪəʊ] (*pl* **-s**, *pt & pp* **-ed**, *cont* **-ing**) ◇ *n* - **1.** [recording, medium, machine] vídeo *m* - **2.** [cassette] videocasete *m*. ◇ *vt* - **1.** [using video recorder] grabar en vídeo - **2.** [using camera] hacer un vídeo de.

video camera *n* videocámara *f*.

video cassette *n* videocasete *m*.

videoconference ['vɪdɪəʊˌkɒnfərəns] *n* videoconferencia *f*.

videoconferencing ['vɪdɪəʊˌkɒnfərənsɪŋ] *n* (U) videoconferencias *fpl*.

video game n videojuego m, juego m de vídeo.

videorecorder ['vɪdɪəʊrɪ̩kɔːdə'] n vídeo m.

video shop n tienda f de vídeos.

videotape ['vɪdɪəʊteɪp] n videocinta f.

vie [vaɪ] (pt & pp **vied**, cont **vying**) vi: to ~ (**with** sb **for** sthg/**to do** sthg) competir (con alguien por algo/para hacer algo).

Vienna [vɪ'enə] n Viena.

Vietnam [UK ,vjet'næm, US ,vjet'nɑːm] n (el) Vietnam.

Vietnamese [,vjetnə'miːz] <> adj vietnamita. <> n -1. [person] vietnamita m OR f -2. [language] vietnamita m.

view [vjuː] <> n -1. [opinion] parecer m, opinión f; **in my** ~ en mi opinión -2. [attitude]: ~ (**of**) actitud f (frente a) -3. [scene] vista f, panorama m -4. [field of vision] vista f; **to come into** ~ aparecer. <> vt -1. [consider] ver, considerar -2. fml [examine, look at - stars etc] observar; [- house, flat] visitar, ver.

◆ **in view of** prep en vista de.

◆ **with a view to** conj con miras OR vistas a.

viewer ['vjuːə'] n -1. [person] espectador m, -ra f -2. [apparatus] visionador m.

viewfinder ['vjuː̩faɪndə'] n visor m.

viewpoint ['vjuːpɔɪnt] n -1. [opinion] punto m de vista -2. [place] mirador m.

vigil ['vɪdʒɪl] n -1. [watch] vigilia f; **to keep (a)** ~ observar vigilia -2. RELIG Vigilia f.

vigilante [,vɪdʒɪ'læntɪ] n persona que extraoficialmente patrulla un área para protegerla, tomándose la justicia en sus manos.

vigorous ['vɪgərəs] adj enérgico(ca).

vile [vaɪl] adj [person, act] vil, infame; [food, smell] repugnante; [mood] de perros.

villa ['vɪlə] n [in country] villa f; [in town] chalet m.

village ['vɪlɪdʒ] n aldea f, pueblecito m.

villager ['vɪlɪdʒə'] n aldeano m, -na f.

villain ['vɪlən] n -1. [of film, book] malo m, -la f -2. dated [criminal] canalla m OR f, criminal m OR f.

vinaigrette [,vɪnɪ'gret] n vinagreta f.

vindicate ['vɪndɪkeɪt] vt justificar.

vindictive [vɪn'dɪktɪv] adj vengativo(va).

vine [vaɪn] n [on ground] vid f; [climbing plant] parra f.

vinegar ['vɪnɪgə'] n vinagre m.

vineyard ['vɪnjəd] n viña f, viñedo m.

vintage ['vɪntɪdʒ] <> adj -1. [wine] añejo(-ja) -2. [classic] clásico(ca) -3. [outstanding]: **a** ~ **year** un año excepcional. <> n cosecha f (de vino).

vintage wine n vino m añejo.

vinyl ['vaɪnɪl] n vinilo m.

viola [vɪ'əʊlə] n viola f.

violate ['vaɪəleɪt] vt -1. [law, treaty, rights] violar, infringir -2. [peace, privacy] invadir.

violence ['vaɪələns] n violencia f.

violent ['vaɪələnt] adj -1. [gen] violento(ta) -2. [emotion, anger] intenso(sa); **to have a** ~ **dislike for** sb sentir una enorme antipatía hacia alguien.

violet ['vaɪələt] <> adj violeta, violado(da). <> n [flower] violeta f.

violin [,vaɪə'lɪn] n violín m.

violinist [,vaɪə'lɪnɪst] n violinista m OR f.

VIP (abbr of **very important person**) n VIP mf.

viper ['vaɪpə'] n víbora f.

virgin ['vɜːdʒɪn] <> adj literary -1. [spotless] virgen -2. [olive oil] virgen. <> n virgen m OR f.

Virgo ['vɜːgəʊ] (pl -s) n Virgo m.

virile ['vɪraɪl] adj viril.

virtually ['vɜːtʃʊəlɪ] adv prácticamente, casi.

virtual reality n realidad f virtual.

virtue ['vɜːtjuː] n -1. [morality, good quality] virtud f -2. [benefit] ventaja f.

◆ **by virtue of** prep fml en virtud de.

virtuous ['vɜːtʃʊəs] adj virtuoso(sa).

virus ['vaɪrəs] n COMPUT & MED virus m.

visa ['viːzə] n visado m, visa f Amér.

vis-à-vis [,viːzɑː'viː] prep fml con relación a.

viscose ['vɪskəʊs] n viscosa f.

visibility [,vɪzɪ'bɪlətɪ] n visibilidad f.

visible ['vɪzəbl] adj visible.

vision ['vɪʒn] n -1. (U) [ability to see] visión f, vista f -2. fig [foresight] clarividencia f -3. [impression, dream] visión f.

visit ['vɪzɪt] <> n visita f; **to pay** sb **a** ~ hacer una visita a alguien; **on a** ~ de visita. <> vt visitar.

visiting hours ['vɪzɪtɪŋ-] npl horas fpl de visita.

visiting nurse n US enfermera contratada por un hospital o repartición de servicios sociales que realiza visitas a enfermos.

visitor ['vɪzɪtə'] n -1. [to one's home, hospital] visita f; **we've got** ~**s** [at home] tenemos visitas -2. [to museum, town etc] visitante m OR f.

visitors' book n libro m de visitas.

visitor's passport n UK pasaporte m provisional.

visor ['vaɪzə'] n visera f.

vista ['vɪstə] n [view] vista f, perspectiva f; fig [wide range] perspectiva.

visual ['vɪʒʊəl] adj [gen] visual; [of the eyes] ocular.

visual aids npl medios mpl visuales.

visual display unit n monitor m.

visualize, -ise ['vɪʒʊəlaɪz] vt visualizar; **to** ~ (sb) **doing** sthg imaginar (a alguien) haciendo algo.

vital ['vaɪtl] *adj* **-1.** [essential] vital, esencial **-2.** [full of life] enérgico(ca), lleno(na) de vida.

vitally ['vaɪtəlɪ] *adv* sumamente.

vital statistics *npl inf* medidas *fpl (del cuerpo de la mujer).*

vitamin [*UK* 'vɪtəmɪn, *US* 'vaɪtəmɪn] *n* vitamina *f*; ∼ **C** vitamina C.

vitamin pill *n* pastilla *f* vitamínica.

vivacious [vɪ'veɪʃəs] *adj* vivaz, animado(da).

vivid ['vɪvɪd] *adj* **-1.** [colour] vivo(va) **-2.** [description, memory] vívido(da).

vividly ['vɪvɪdlɪ] *adv* **-1.** [brightly] con colores muy vivos **-2.** [clearly] vívidamente.

vixen ['vɪksn] *n* zorra *f*.

VLF (*abbr of* **very low frequency**) VLF.

V-neck *n* [sweater, dress] jersey *m* con cuello de pico.

vocabulary [və'kæbjʊlərɪ] (*pl* **-ies**) *n* vocabulario *m*.

vocal ['vəʊkl] *adj* **-1.** [outspoken] vociferante **-2.** [of the voice] vocal.

vocal cords *npl* cuerdas *fpl* vocales.

vocalist ['vəʊkəlɪst] *n* [in orchestra] vocalista *m OR f*; [in pop group] cantante *m OR f*.

vocation [vəʊ'keɪʃn] *n* vocación *f*.

vocational [vəʊ'keɪʃənl] *adj* profesional.

vociferous [və'sɪfərəs] *adj fml* ruidoso(sa).

vodka ['vɒdkə] *n* [drink] vodka *m*.

vogue [vəʊg] *n* moda *f*; **in** ∼ en boga, de moda.

voice [vɔɪs] ◇ *n* voz *f*; **to give** ∼ **to** expresar. ◇ *vt* [opinion, emotion] expresar.

voice mail *n* correo *m* de voz; **to send/receive** ∼ mandar/recibir un mensaje de correo de voz.

void [vɔɪd] ◇ *adj* **-1.** [invalid] inválido(da) ▷ **null -2.** *fml* [empty]: ∼ **of** falto(ta) de. ◇ *n literary* vacío *m*.

volatile [*UK* 'vɒlətaɪl, *US* 'vɒlətl] *adj* [situation] volátil; [person] voluble, inconstante.

vol-au-vent ['vɒləʊvɑ̃:] *n* volován *m*.

volcano [vɒl'keɪnəʊ] (*pl* **-es** *OR* **-s**) *n* volcán *m*.

volition [və'lɪʃn] *n fml*: **of one's own** ∼ por voluntad propia.

volley ['vɒlɪ] (*pl* **volleys**) ◇ *n* **-1.** [of gunfire] ráfaga *f*, descarga *f* **-2.** *fig* [rapid succession] torrente *m* **-3.** SPORT volea *f*. ◇ *vt* volear.

volleyball ['vɒlɪbɔ:l] *n* balonvolea *m*, voleibol *m*.

volt [vəʊlt] *n* voltio *m*.

voltage ['vəʊltɪdʒ] *n* voltaje *m*.

voluble ['vɒljʊbl] *adj fml* locuaz.

volume ['vɒljuːm] *n* volumen *m*; **to speak** ∼ **s** decir mucho.

voluntarily [*UK* 'vɒləntrɪlɪ, *US* ˌvɒlən'terəlɪ] *adv* voluntariamente.

voluntary ['vɒləntrɪ] *adj* voluntario(ria); ∼ **organization** organización *f* benéfica.

volunteer [ˌvɒlən'tɪə] ◇ *n* [person who volunteers] voluntario *m*, -ria *f*. ◇ *vt* **-1.** [offer of one's free will]: **to** ∼ **to do sthg** ofrecerse para hacer algo **-2.** [information, advice] dar, ofrecer. ◇ *vi* **-1.** [freely offer one's services]: **to** ∼ **(for)** ofrecerse (para) **-2.** MIL alistarse.

vomit ['vɒmɪt] ◇ *n* vómito *m*. ◇ *vi* vomitar.

vote [vəʊt] ◇ *n* **-1.** [gen] voto *m*; ∼ **for/against** voto a favor de/en contra de **-2.** [session, ballot, result] votación *f* **-3.** [votes cast]: **the** ∼ los votos. ◇ *vt* **-1.** [person, leader] elegir **-2.** [choose]: **to** ∼ **to do sthg** votar hacer algo. ◇ *vi*: **to** ∼ **(for/against)** votar (a favor de/en contra de).

vote of thanks (*pl* **votes of thanks**) *n* palabras *fpl* de agradecimiento.

voter ['vəʊtə] *n* votante *m OR f*.

voting ['vəʊtɪŋ] *n* votación *f*.

vouch [vaʊtʃ] ♦ **vouch for** *vt fus* **-1.** [person] responder por **-2.** [character, accuracy] dar fe de.

voucher ['vaʊtʃə] *n* vale *m*.

vow [vaʊ] ◇ *n* RELIG voto *m*; [solemn promise] promesa *f* solemne. ◇ *vt*: **to** ∼ **to do sthg** jurar hacer algo; **to** ∼ **that** jurar que.

vowel ['vaʊəl] *n* vocal *f*.

voyage ['vɔɪɪdʒ] *n* viaje *m*.

vs *abbr of* **versus**.

VSO (*abbr of* **Voluntary Service Overseas**) *n organización británica de voluntarios que ayuda a países en vías de desarrollo.*

vulgar ['vʌlgə] *adj* **-1.** [in bad taste] ordinario(ria), vulgar **-2.** [offensive] grosero(ra), guarango(ga) *Chile & RP*.

vulnerable ['vʌlnərəbl] *adj*: ∼ **(to)** vulnerable (a).

vulture ['vʌltʃə] *n lit & fig* buitre *m*.

w (*pl* **w's** *OR* **ws**), **W** (*pl* **W's** *OR* **Ws**) ['dʌblju:] *n* [letter] w *f*, W *f*. ♦ **W -1.** (*abbr of* **west**) O **-2.** (*abbr of* **watt**) w.

wad [wɒd] *n* **-1.** [of paper] taco *m* **-2.** [of banknotes, documents] fajo *m* **-3.** [of cotton,

cotton wool, tobacco] bola *f*.

waddle ['wɒdl] *vi* caminar como un pato.

wade [weɪd] *vi* caminar por el agua.

➡ **wade through** *vt fus fig:* he was wading through the documents le costaba mucho leer los documentos.

wading pool ['weɪdɪŋ-] *n US* piscina *f* para niños.

wafer ['weɪfə'] *n* [thin biscuit] barquillo *m*.

waffle ['wɒfl] ◇ *n* - **1.** CULIN gofre *m* - **2.** *UK inf* [vague talk] paja *f*. ◇ *vi* enrollarse; to ~ on about sthg enrollarse sobre algo.

waft [wɑːft, wɒft] *vi* flotar.

wag [wæg] (*pt & pp* -**ged**, *cont* -**ging**) ◇ *vt* menear; the dog was ~ging its tail el perro meneaba la cola. ◇ *vi* menearse.

wage [weɪdʒ] ◇ *n* [gen] salario *m*; [daily] jornal *m*. ◇ *vt:* to ~ war hacer la guerra.

➡ **wages** *npl* [gen] salario *m*; [daily] jornal *m*.

wage earner [-,ɜːnə'] *n* asalariado *m*, -da *f*.

wage packet *n UK* - **1.** [envelope] sobre *m* de pago - **2.** *fig* [pay] paga *f*.

wager ['weɪdʒə'] *n* apuesta *f*.

waggle ['wægl] *inf vt* menear.

waggon ['wægən] *UK* = **wagon**.

wagon ['wægən] *n* - **1.** [horse-drawn vehicle] carro *m* - **2.** *UK* RAIL vagón *m*.

wail [weɪl] ◇ *n* lamento *m*, gemido *m*. ◇ *vi* lamentarse, gemir.

waist [weɪst] *n* cintura *f*.

waistcoat ['weɪskəʊt] *n esp US* chaleco *m*.

waistline ['weɪstlaɪn] *n* cintura *f*, talle *m*.

wait [weɪt] ◇ *n* espera *f*; to lie in ~ for sb estar al acecho de alguien. ◇ *vi:* to ~ (for sthg/sb) esperar (algo/a alguien); I can't ~ for the holidays/to see her estoy impaciente por comenzar las vacaciones/verla; keys cut while you ~ se hacen llaves en el acto.

➡ **wait for** *vt fus* esperar.

➡ **wait on** *vt fus* [serve food to] servir.

➡ **wait up** *vi* - **1.** quedarse despierto(ta) esperando - **2.** *US:* ~ up! ¡un momento!

waiter ['weɪtə'] *n* camarero *m*, mesero *m Amér*, mesonero *m Ven*, mozo *m Andes, RP*.

waiting list ['weɪtɪŋ-] *n* lista *f* de espera.

waiting room ['weɪtɪŋ-] *n* sala *f* de espera.

waitress ['weɪtrɪs] *n* camarera *f*, mesera *f Amér*, mesonera *f Ven*, moza *f Andes, RP*.

waive [weɪv] *vt fml* [rule] no aplicar.

wake [weɪk] (*pt* woke *OR* -**d**, *pp* woken *OR* -**d**) ◇ *n* [of ship, boat] estela *f*. ◇ *vt* despertar. ◇ *vi* despertarse.

➡ **wake up** ◇ *vt sep* despertar. ◇ *vi* [wake] despertarse.

waken ['weɪkən] *fml* ◇ *vt* despertar. ◇ *vi* despertarse.

Wales [weɪlz] *n* (el país de) Gales.

walk [wɔːk] ◇ *n* - **1.** [way of walking] andar

m, paso *m* - **2.** [journey on foot] paseo *m*; to go for a ~ dar un paseo; it's ten minutes' ~ away está a diez minutos andando. ◇ *vt* - **1.** [dog] pasear - **2.** [streets] andar por; [distance] recorrer, andar. ◇ *vi* - **1.** [move on foot] andar, caminar - **2.** [for pleasure] pasear.

➡ **walk out** *vi* - **1.** [leave suddenly] salirse - **2.** [go on strike] declararse en huelga.

➡ **walk out on** *vt fus* dejar, abandonar.

➡ **walk over** *vt fus:* to ~ all over sb pisotear a alguien.

walker ['wɔːkə'] *n* caminante *m OR f*, paseante *m OR f*.

walkie-talkie [,wɔːkɪ'tɔːkɪ] *n* walki-talki *m*.

walking ['wɔːkɪŋ] ◇ *n (U)* [for sport] marcha *f*; [for pleasure] andar *m*; he does a lot of ~ camina mucho. ◇ *adj:* he's a ~ disaster *hum* es un desastre andante.

walking shoes *npl* zapatos *mpl* para caminar.

walking stick *n* bastón *m*.

Walkman® ['wɔːkmən] *n* walkman® *m*.

walk of life (*pl* walks of life) *n:* people from all walks of life gente de toda condición.

walkout ['wɔːkaʊt] *n* huelga *f*.

walkover ['wɔːk,əʊvə'] *n* victoria *f* fácil.

walkup ['wɔːkʌp] *n US* [building] edificio *m* sin ascensor *f*.

walkway ['wɔːkweɪ] *n* [on ship, machine] pasarela *f*; [between buildings] paso *m*.

wall [wɔːl] *n* - **1.** [inside building, of cell, stomach] pared *f* - **2.** [outside] muro *m*; it's like talking to a brick ~ le entra por un oído y le sale por el otro.

wallchart ['wɔːltʃɑːt] *n* (gráfico *m*) mural *m*.

walled [wɔːld] *adj* amurallado(da).

wallet ['wɒlɪt] *n* cartera *f*, billetera *f*.

wallflower ['wɔːl,flaʊə'] *n* - **1.** [plant] alhelí *m* - **2.** *inf fig* [person] *persona tímida que queda al margen de una fiesta*.

wallop ['wɒləp] *vt inf* [child] pegar una torta a; [ball] golpear fuerte.

wallow ['wɒləʊ] *vi* [in liquid] revolcarse.

wallpaper ['wɔːl,peɪpə'] ◇ *n* papel *m* de pared *OR* de empapelar. ◇ *vt* empapelar.

Wall Street *n* Wall Street *f*, *zona financiera neoyorquina*.

wally ['wɒlɪ] (*pl* -**ies**) *n UK inf* majadero *m*, -ra *f*, imbécil *m OR f*.

walnut ['wɔːlnʌt] *n* - **1.** [nut] nuez *f* - **2.** [wood, tree] nogal *m*.

walrus ['wɔːlrəs] (*pl inv OR* -**es**) *n* morsa *f*.

waltz [wɔːls] ◇ *n* vals *m*. ◇ *vi* [dance] bailar el vals.

wan [wɒn] (*compar* -**ner**, *superl* -**nest**) *adj* pálido(da).

wand [wɒnd] *n*: **(magic)** ~ varita *f* mágica.

wander ['wɒndə^r] *vi* vagar; **my mind kept ~ing** se me iba la mente en otras cosas.

wane [weɪn] *vi* [influence, interest] disminuir, decrecer.

wangle ['wæŋgl] *vt inf* agenciarse, conseguir.

want [wɒnt] ◇ *n fml* **- 1.** [need] necesidad *f* **- 2.** [lack] falta *f*; **for** ~ **of** por OR a falta de **- 3.** [deprivation] indigencia *f*, miseria *f*. ◇ *vt* [desire] querer; **to** ~ **to do sthg** querer hacer algo; **to** ~ **sb to do sthg** querer que alguien haga algo.

wanted ['wɒntɪd] *adj*: **to be** ~ **(by the police)** ser buscado(da) (por la policía).

wanton ['wɒntən] *adj fml* gratuito(ta), sin motivo.

WAP [wæp] *(abbr of* **wireless application protocol)** *n* WAP *m*.

WAP phone *n* teléfono *m* WAP.

war [wɔː^r] *(pt & pp* **-red**, *cont* **-ring)** ◇ *n lit & fig* guerra *f*; **to be at** ~ estar en guerra; **the** ~ **on drugs** la guerra contra las drogas. ◇ *vi* estar en guerra.

ward [wɔːd] *n* **- 1.** [in hospital] sala *f* **- 2.** UK POL distrito *m* electoral **- 3.** JUR pupilo *m*, -la *f*.
◆ **ward off** *vt fus* protegerse de.

warden ['wɔːdn] *n* **- 1.** [of park] guarda *m* OR *f* **- 2.** UK [of youth hostel, hall of residence] encargado *m*, -da *f* **- 3.**: **(traffic)** ~ ≃ guardia *m* OR *f* de tráfico **- 4.** US [prison governor] director *m*, -ra *f*.

warder ['wɔːdə^r] *n* [in prison] carcelero *m*, -ra *f*.

wardrobe ['wɔːdrəʊb] *n* **- 1.** [piece of furniture] armario *m*, guardarropa *m* **- 2.** [collection of clothes] guardarropa *m*, vestuario *m*.

warehouse ['weəhaʊs, *pl* -haʊzɪz] *n* almacén *m*.

wares [weəz] *npl literary* mercancías *fpl*.

warfare ['wɔːfeə^r] *n (U)* guerra *f*.

warhead ['wɔːhed] *n* ojiva *f*, cabeza *f*.

warily ['weərɪlɪ] *adv* con cautela, cautelosamente.

warm [wɔːm] ◇ *adj* **- 1.** [pleasantly hotgen] caliente; [- weather, day] caluroso(sa); [lukewarm] tibio(bia), templado(da); **it's/ I'm** ~ hace/tengo calor; **to get** ~ [subj: person, room] calentarse; **they tried to keep** ~ intentaron mantenerse calientes **- 2.** [clothes etc] que abriga **- 3.** [colour, sound] cálido(da) **- 4.** [friendly - person, atmosphere, smile] afectuoso(sa); [- congratulations] efusivo(va). ◇ *vt* calentar.
◆ **warm up** *vt sep* calentar. ◇ *vi* **- 1.** [gen] entrar en calor; [weather, room, engine] calentarse **- 2.** [sportsperson] calentar.

warm-hearted [-'hɑːtɪd] *adj* afectuoso(sa), cariñoso(sa).

warmly ['wɔːmlɪ] *adv* **- 1.** [in warm clothes]: **to dress** ~ vestirse con ropa de abrigo **- 2.** [in a friendly way] efusivamente, calurosamente.

warmth [wɔːmθ] *n* **- 1.** [heat] calor *m* **- 2.** [of clothes] abrigo *m* **- 3.** [friendliness] cordialidad *f*, efusión *f*.

warn [wɔːn] *vt* prevenir, advertir; **to** ~ **sb of sthg** prevenir a alguien algo; **to** ~ **sb not to do sthg**, ~ **sb against doing sthg** advertir a alguien que no haga algo.

warning ['wɔːnɪŋ] *n* aviso *m*, advertencia *f*; **to give sb a** ~ hacer una advertencia a alguien; **without** ~ sin previo aviso.

warning light *n* piloto *m*.

warning triangle *n* UK triángulo *m* de avería.

warp [wɔːp] *vi* alabearse, combarse.

warrant ['wɒrənt] ◇ *n* orden *f* OR mandamiento *m* judicial. ◇ *vt fml* merecer.

warranty ['wɒrəntɪ] *(pl* **-ies)** *n* garantía *f*; **to be under** ~ estar en garantía.

warren ['wɒrən] *n* red *f* de madrigueras.

warrior ['wɒrɪə^r] *n* guerrero *m*, -ra *f*.

Warsaw ['wɔːsɔː] *n* Varsovia; **the** ~ **Pact** el Pacto de Varsovia.

warship ['wɔːʃɪp] *n* buque *m* de guerra.

wart [wɔːt] *n* verruga *f*.

wartime ['wɔːtaɪm] *n* tiempos *mpl* de guerra.

wary ['weərɪ] *(compar* **-ier**, *superl* **-iest)** *adj*: ~ **(of)** receloso(sa) (de).

was [weak form wəz, strong form wɒz] *pt* ▷ **be**.

wash [wɒʃ] ◇ *n* **- 1.** [act of washing] lavado *m*, lavada *f*; **to have a** ~ lavarse; **to give sthg a** ~ lavar algo **- 2.** [things to wash] ropa *f* para lavar, ropa sucia **- 3.** [from boat] estela *f*. ◇ *vt* **- 1.** [gen] lavar; [hands, face] lavarse; **she's** ~**ing her hair** se está lavando el pelo **- 2.** [carry - subj: waves etc] arrastrar, llevarse; **it was** ~**ed ashore** el mar lo arrastró hasta la costa. ◇ *vi* **- 1.** [clean oneself] lavarse **- 2.** [waves, oil]: **to** ~ **over sthg** bañar algo.
◆ **wash away** *vt sep* **- 1.** [subj: water, waves] llevarse, barrer **- 2.** [dirt] quitar.
◆ **wash up** ◇ *vt sep* UK [dishes] lavar, fregar. ◇ *vi* **- 1.** UK [wash the dishes] fregar OR lavar los platos **- 2.** US [wash o.s.] lavarse.

washable ['wɒʃəbl] *adj* lavable.

washbasin UK ['wɒʃ,beɪsn], **washbowl** US ['wɒʃbəʊl] *n* lavabo *m*.

washcloth ['wɒʃ,klɒθ] *n* US toallita *f* para lavarse la cara.

washer ['wɒʃə^r] *n* TECH arandela *f*.

washing ['wɒʃɪŋ] *n (U)* **- 1.** [operation] colada *f*; **to do the** ~ hacer la colada **- 2.** [clothes - dirty] ropa *f* sucia OR para lavar; [- clean] colada *f*; **to hang up the** ~ tender la colada.

washing line *n* tendedero *m*.

washing machine *n* lavadora *f*.

washing powder n UK detergente m, jabón m en polvo.

Washington ['wɒʃɪŋtən] n [town]: ~ **D.C.** ciudad f de Washington.

washing-up n - 1. UK [crockery, pans etc] platos mpl para fregar - 2. [operation] fregado m; **to do the** ~ fregar los platos.

washing-up liquid n UK lavavajillas m inv.

washout ['wɒʃaʊt] n inf desastre m, fracaso m.

washroom ['wɒʃrʊm] n US lavabo m, aseos mpl.

wasn't [wɒznt] = **was not**.

wasp [wɒsp] n [insect] avispa f.

wastage ['weɪstɪdʒ] n desperdicio m.

waste [weɪst] ◇ adj [land] yermo(ma); [material, fuel] de desecho. ◇ n - 1. [misuse, incomplete use] desperdicio m, derroche m; **a ~ of time** una pérdida de tiempo - 2. (U) [refuse] desperdicios mpl; [chemical, toxic etc] residuos mpl. ◇ vt [time] perder; [money] malgastar, derrochar; [food, energy, opportunity] desperdiciar.
◆ **wastes** npl literary yermos mpl.

wastebasket US = **wastepaper basket**.

waste disposal unit n triturador m de basuras.

wasteful ['weɪstfʊl] adj derrochador(ra).

waste ground n (U) descampados mpl.

wastepaper basket [,weɪst'peɪpər-], **wastepaper bin** [,weɪst'peɪpər-], **wastebasket** US [,weɪst,bɑː'skɪt] n papelera f.

watch [wɒtʃ] ◇ n - 1. [timepiece] reloj m - 2. [act of watching]: **to keep ~** estar de guardia; **to keep ~ on sthg/sb** vigilar algo/a alguien - 3. MIL [group of people] guardia f. ◇ vt - 1. [look at - gen] mirar; [-sunset] contemplar; [- football match, TV] ver - 2. [spy on] vigilar - 3. [be careful about] tener cuidado con, vigilar; **~ what you say** ten cuidado con lo que dices. ◇ vi mirar, observar.
◆ **watch out** vi tener cuidado, estar atento(ta).

watchdog ['wɒtʃdɒg] n - 1. [dog] perro m guardián - 2. fig [organization] comisión f de vigilancia.

watchful ['wɒtʃfʊl] adj atento(ta).

watchmaker ['wɒtʃ,meɪkər] n relojero m, -ra f.

watchman ['wɒtʃmən] (pl -men [-mən]) n vigilante m, guarda m, rondín m Andes.

water ['wɔːtər] ◇ n [gen] agua f. ◇ vt regar. ◇ vi - 1. [eyes]: **my eyes are ~ing** me lloran los ojos - 2. [mouth]: **my mouth is ~ing** se me hace la boca agua.
◆ **waters** npl aguas fpl.
◆ **water down** vt sep - 1. [dilute] diluir, aguar - 2. usu pej [moderate] suavizar.

water bottle n cantimplora f.

watercolour ['wɔːtə,kʌlər] n acuarela f.

watercress ['wɔːtəkres] n berro m.

waterfall ['wɔːtəfɔːl] n cascada f, salto m de agua.

water heater n calentador m de agua.

waterhole ['wɔːtəhəʊl] n balsa f (donde acuden a beber los animales).

watering can ['wɔːtərɪŋ-] n regadera f.

water level n nivel m del agua.

water lily n nenúfar m.

waterline ['wɔːtəlaɪn] n NAUT línea f de flotación.

waterlogged ['wɔːtəlɒgd] adj inundado(-da).

water main n cañería f principal.

watermark ['wɔːtəmɑːk] n - 1. [in paper] filigrana f - 2. [showing water level] marca f del nivel del agua.

watermelon ['wɔːtə,melən] n sandía f.

water polo n water-polo m, polo m acuático.

waterproof ['wɔːtəpruːf] ◇ adj impermeable. ◇ n impermeable m.

watershed ['wɔːtəʃed] n fig momento m decisivo.

water skiing n esquí m acuático.

water tank n reserva f de agua.

watertight ['wɔːtətaɪt] adj [waterproof] hermético(ca).

waterway ['wɔːtəweɪ] n vía f navegable.

waterworks ['wɔːtəwɜːks] (pl inv) n [building] central f de agua.

watery ['wɔːtərɪ] adj - 1. [food] soso(sa); [drink] aguado(da) - 2. [pale] desvaído(da), pálido(da).

watt [wɒt] n vatio m.

wave [weɪv] ◇ n - 1. [of hand] ademán m OR señal f (con la mano) - 2. [of water] ola f - 3. [of emotion, nausea, panic] arranque m; [of immigrants, crime etc] oleada f - 4. [of light, sound, heat] onda f - 5. [in hair] ondulación f. ◇ vt - 1. [move about as signal] agitar - 2. [signal to] hacer señales OR señas a; **she ~d them in** les hizo una señal para que entraran. ◇ vi - 1. [with hand - in greeting] saludar con la mano; [- to say goodbye] decir adiós con la mano; **to ~ at** OR **to sb** saludar a alguien con la mano; **he ~d hello to us** nos saludó con la mano - 2. [flag] ondear; [trees] agitarse.

wavelength ['weɪvleŋθ] n longitud f de onda; **to be on the same ~** fig estar en la misma onda.

waver ['weɪvər] vi - 1. [falter - resolution, confidence] flaquear - 2. [hesitate] dudar, vacilar - 3. [fluctuate] oscilar.

wavy ['weɪvɪ] (compar -ier, superl -iest) adj ondulado(da).

wax [wæks] ◇ n cera f. ◇ vt encerar.

wax paper n esp US papel m de cera.

waxworks ['wækswɜ:ks] (*pl inv*) *n* museo *m* de cera.

way [weɪ] ◇ *n* - **1.** [manner, method] manera *f*, modo *m*; **in the same ~** del mismo modo, igualmente; **this/that ~** así; **in a ~** en cierto modo; **to get** OR **have one's ~** salirse uno con la suya; **to be in a bad ~** estar bastante mal - **2.** [route, path] camino *m*; **to lose one's ~** perderse; **to find one's ~ around** orientarse; **the ~ back** OR **home** el camino de vuelta a casa; **~ in** entrada *f*; **~ out** salida *f*; **it's out of my ~** no me pilla de camino; **it's out of the ~** [place] está algo aislado; **on the** OR **on one's ~** de camino; **I'm on my ~** voy de camino; **to be under ~** *fig* [meeting] estar en marcha; **to get under ~** [meeting] ponerse en marcha; **to be in the ~** estar en medio; **to get in the ~** ponerse en medio; **to get out of the ~** quitarse de en medio; **to go out of one's ~ to do sthg** tomarse muchas molestias para hacer algo; **to keep out of the ~** mantenerse alejado; **to keep out of sb's ~** mantenerse alejado de alguien; **to make ~ for** dar paso a - **3.** [direction] dirección *f*; **come this ~** ven por aquí; **go that ~** ve por ahí; **which ~ do we go?** ¿hacia dónde vamos?; **which ~ is it to the cathedral?** ¿por dónde se va a la catedral?; **the wrong ~ up** OR **round** al revés; **the right ~ up** OR **round** del derecho - **4.** [distance]: **all the ~** todo el camino OR trayecto; **it's a long ~ away** está muy lejos; **we have a long ~ to go** queda mucho camino por recorrer; **we've come a long ~ since then** *fig* hemos avanzado mucho desde entonces - **5.** *phr*: **to give ~** [under weight, pressure] ceder; **'give ~'** *UK* AUT 'ceda el paso'; **no ~!** ¡ni hablar! ◇ *adv inf* [far] mucho; **it's ~ too big** es tela de grande.

◆ **ways** *npl* [customs, habits] costumbres *fpl*, hábitos *mpl*; **sb's funny little ~s** las curiosas costumbres de alguien.

◆ **by the way** *adv* por cierto.

waylay [,weɪ'leɪ] (*pt & pp* **-laid**) *vt* abordar.

wayward ['weɪwəd] *adj* [person, behaviour] incorregible.

WC (*abbr of* **water closet**) WC.

we [wi:] *pers pron* nosotros *mpl*, -tras *fpl*; **WE can't do it** NOSOTROS no podemos hacerlo; **here ~ are** aquí estamos; **as ~ say in France** como decimos en Francia; **~ British** nosotros los británicos.

weak [wi:k] *adj* - **1.** [gen] débil; **to grow ~** debilitarse - **2.** [material, structure] frágil - **3.** [argument, tea etc] flojo(ja) - **4.** [lacking knowledge, skill]: **to be ~ on sthg** estar flojo(ja) en algo.

weaken ['wi:kn] ◇ *vt* debilitar. ◇ *vi* - **1.** [become less determined] ceder, flaquear - **2.** [physically] debilitarse.

weakling ['wi:klɪŋ] *n pej* enclenque *m* OR *f*.

weakness ['wi:knɪs] *n* - **1.** [gen] debilidad *f* - **2.** [imperfect point] defecto *m*.

wealth [welθ] *n* - **1.** [riches] riqueza *f* - **2.** [abundance] profusión *f*, abundancia *f*; **a ~ of sthg** abundancia de algo.

wealthy ['welθɪ] (*compar* **-ier**, *superl* **-iest**) *adj* rico(ca), platudo(da) *Amér*.

wean [wi:n] *vt* [from mother's milk] destetar.

weapon ['wepən] *n* arma *f*.

weaponry ['wepənrɪ] *n* (*U*) armamento *m*.

wear [weə^r] (*pt* **wore**, *pp* **worn**) ◇ *n* (*U*) - **1.** [use] uso *m*; **I've had a lot of ~ out of this jacket** le he sacado mucho partido a esta chaqueta - **2.** [damage] desgaste *m*; **~ and tear** desgaste - **3.** [type of clothes] ropa *f*; **children's ~** ropa de niños; **evening ~** ropa de noche. ◇ *vt* - **1.** [clothes, hair, perfume] llevar; [shoes] calzar; **to ~ red** vestirse de rojo - **2.** [damage] desgastar; **to ~ a hole in sthg** acabar haciendo un agujero en algo. ◇ *vi* - **1.** [deteriorate] desgastarse - **2.** [last]: **to ~ well/badly** durar mucho/poco.

◆ **wear away** ◇ *vt sep* desgastar. ◇ *vi* desgastarse.

◆ **wear down** *vt sep* - **1.** [reduce size of] desgastar - **2.** [weaken] agotar.

◆ **wear off** *vi* desaparecer, disiparse.

◆ **wear out** ◇ *vt sep* - **1.** [shoes, clothes] gastar - **2.** [person] agotar. ◇ *vi* gastarse.

weary ['wɪərɪ] (*compar* **-ier**, *superl* **-iest**) *adj* fatigado(da), cansado(da); **to be ~ of sthg/of doing sthg** estar cansado de algo/ de hacer algo.

weasel ['wi:zl] *n* comadreja *f*.

weather ['weðə^r] ◇ *n* tiempo *m*; **what's the ~ like?** ¿qué tal tiempo hace?; **to be under the ~** no encontrarse muy bien. ◇ *vt* [crisis etc] superar.

weather-beaten [-,bi:tn] *adj* [face, skin] curtido(da).

weather bureau *n US* servicio *m* meteorológico.

weathercock ['weðəkɒk] *n* veleta *f*.

weather forecast *n* parte *m* meteorológico, pronóstico *m* del tiempo.

weatherman ['weðəmæn] (*pl* **-men** [-men]) *n* hombre *m* del tiempo.

weather vane [-veɪn] *n* veleta *f*.

weave [wi:v] (*pt* **wove**, *pp* **woven**) ◇ *vt* [using loom] tejer. ◇ *vi* [move]: **to ~ through** colarse por entre; **to ~ in and out of the traffic** avanzar zigzagueando en el tráfico.

weaver ['wi:və^r] *n* tejedor *m*, -ra *f*.

weaving ['wi:vɪŋ] *n* tejeduría *f*.

web [web] *n* - **1.** [cobweb] telaraña *f* - **2.** *fig* [of lies etc] urdimbre *f*, entramado *m* - **3.** COMPUT: **the Web** la Web.

web browser *n* COMPUT navegador *m*.

webcam ['webkæm] *n* cámara *f* web.

webcast ['webkɑːst] *n* emisión *f* por la Web.

web designer *n* diseñador *m*, -ra *f* de páginas Web.

web page *n* página *f* web.

webphone ['webfəʊn] *n* teléfono *m* por Internet.

Web site *n* sitio *m* Web.

wed [wed] (*pt* & *pp* **-ded** OR **wed**) *literary* ◇ *vt* desposar. ◇ *vi* desposarse.

we'd [wiːd] = **we had, we would**.

wedding ['wedɪŋ] *n* boda *f*, casamiento *m*.

wedding anniversary *n* aniversario *m* de boda.

wedding cake *n* tarta *f* nupcial, pastel *m* de bodas, torta *f* de boda OR matrimonio OR novios *Andes, Col, CSur, Ven*, torta *f* de casamiento *RP* OR de novia *Chile*.

wedding dress *n* traje *m* de novia.

wedding ring *n* anillo *m* de boda, argolla *f* *Amér*.

wedge [wedʒ] ◇ *n* **- 1.** [for steadying or splitting] cuña *f* **- 2.** [triangular slice] porción *f*, trozo *m*. ◇ *vt*: to ~ sthg open/shut dejar algo abierto/cerrado con una cuña.

Wednesday ['wenzdɪ] *n* miércoles *m inv*; *see also* **Saturday**.

wee [wiː] ◇ *adj Scot* pequeño(ña). ◇ *n* *v inf* pipí *m*; to do a ~ hacer pipí. ◇ *vi v inf* hacer pipí.

weed [wiːd] ◇ *n* **- 1.** [wild plant] mala hierba *f* **- 2.** *UK inf* [feeble person] canijo *m*, -ja *f*. ◇ *vt* desherbar, escardar.

weedkiller ['wiːd,kɪləʳ] *n* herbicida *m*.

weedy ['wiːdɪ] (*compar* **-ier**, *superl* **-iest**) *adj UK inf* [feeble] enclenque.

week [wiːk] *n* [gen] semana *f*; this/next ~ esta/la próxima semana; in 2 ~s' time en dos semanas; we haven't seen him for ~s hace semanas que no lo vemos.

weekday ['wiːkdeɪ] *n* día *m* laborable.

weekend [,wiːk'end] *n* fin *m* de semana.

weekly ['wiːklɪ] ◇ *adj* semanal. ◇ *adv* semanalmente. ◇ *n* semanario *m*, periódico *m* semanal.

weep [wiːp] (*pt* & *pp* **wept**) ◇ *vt* derramar. ◇ *vi* llorar.

weeping willow [,wiːpɪŋ-] *n* sauce *m* llorón.

weigh [weɪ] *vt* **- 1.** [gen] pesar **- 2.** [consider carefully] sopesar; she ~ed her words sopesó sus palabras.

◆ **weigh down** *vt sep* **- 1.** [physically] sobrecargar **- 2.** [mentally]: to be ~ed down by OR with estar abrumado(da) de OR por.

◆ **weigh up** *vt sep* **- 1.** [consider carefully] sopesar **- 2.** [size up] hacerse una idea de.

weight [weɪt] ◇ *n* **- 1.** [gen] peso *m*; to put on OR gain ~ engordar; to lose ~ adelgazar; to pull one's ~ poner (uno) de su parte

- 2. [metal object] pesa *f*.

weighted ['weɪtɪd] *adj*: to be ~ in favour of/against inclinarse a favor/en contra de.

weighting ['weɪtɪŋ] *n* prima por vivir en una ciudad con alto coste de vida.

weightlifting ['weɪt,lɪftɪŋ] *n* levantamiento *m* de pesos, halterofilia *f*.

weight watcher *n* persona *f* a dieta.

weighty ['weɪtɪ] (*compar* **-ier**, *superl* **-iest**) *adj* [serious] de peso.

weir [wɪəʳ] *n* presa *f*, dique *m*.

weird [wɪəd] *adj* raro(ra), extraño(ña).

welcome ['welkəm] ◇ *adj* **- 1.** [guest] bienvenido(da) **- 2.** [free]: you're ~ to come si quieres, puedes venir **- 3.** [appreciated]: to be ~ ser de agradecer **- 4.** [in reply to thanks]: you're ~ de nada. ◇ *n* bienvenida *f*; to give sb a warm ~ dar una calurosa bienvenida a alguien. ◇ *vt* **- 1.** [receive] dar la bienvenida a **- 2.** [approve, support] recibir bien. ◇ *excl* ¡bienvenido(da)!

weld [weld] ◇ *n* soldadura *f*. ◇ *vt* soldar.

welfare ['welfeəʳ] ◇ *adj* de asistencia social. ◇ *n* **- 1.** [state of well-being] bienestar *m* **- 2.** *US* [income support] subsidio *m* de la seguridad social; to be on ~ recibir un subsidio.

welfare state *n*: the ~ el Estado de bienestar.

well [wel] (*compar* **better**, *superl* **best**) ◇ *adj* bien; to be ~ [healthy] estar bien (de salud); I don't feel ~ no me siento bien; to get ~ mejorarse; all is ~ todo va bien; (it's) just as ~ menos mal; it would be as ~ to check first sería mejor comprobar primero. ◇ *adv* **- 1.** [satisfactorily, thoroughly] bien; to go ~ ir bien; he's doing very ~ at his new school te va muy bien en el nuevo colegio; ~ done! ¡muy bien!; ~ and truly completamente **- 2.** [definitely, certainly] claramente, definitivamente; it was ~ worth it sí que valió la pena **- 3.** [as emphasis]: you know perfectly ~ (that) sabes de sobra (que) **- 4.** [very possibly]: it could ~ rain es muy posible que llueva. ◇ *n* pozo *m*. ◇ *excl* **- 1.** [gen] bueno; oh ~! ¡en fin! **- 2.** [in surprise] ¡vaya!

◆ **as well** *adv* **- 1.** [in addition] también **- 2.** [with same result]: you may OR might as ~ (do it) ¿y por qué no (lo haces)?

◆ **as well as** *conj* además de.

◆ **well up** *vi* brotar.

we'll [wiːl] = **we shall, we will**.

well-advised [-əd'vaɪzd] *adj* sensato(ta); you would be ~ to do it sería aconsejable que lo hicieras.

well-behaved [-bɪ'heɪvd] *adj* formal, bien educado(da); to be ~ portarse bien.

wellbeing [,wel'biːɪŋ] *n* bienestar *m*.

well-built *adj* fornido(da).

well-done *adj* [thoroughly cooked] **muy hecho(cha).**

well-dressed [-'drest] *adj* **bien vestido(-da).**

well-earned [-'ɜːnd] *adj* **bien merecido(-da).**

well-heeled [-hiːld] *adj inf* **ricachón(ona).**

wellington boots ['welɪŋtən-], **wellingtons** ['welɪŋtənz] *npl* **botas** *fpl* **de agua.**

well-kept *adj* - **1.** [neat, tidy] **bien cuidado(-da) - 2.** [not revealed] **bien guardado(da).**

well-known *adj* **conocido(da).**

well-mannered [-'mænəd] *adj* **de buenos modales, educado(da).**

well-meaning *adj* **bienintencionado(da).**

well-nigh [-naɪ] *adv* **casi.**

well-off *adj* - **1.** [rich] **acomodado(da), rico(ca) - 2.** [well-provided]: **to be ~ for sthg tener bastante de algo.**

well-read [-'red] *adj* **instruido(da), culto(ta).**

well-rounded [-'raʊndɪd] *adj* [varied] **completo(ta).**

well-timed *adj* **oportuno(na).**

well-to-do *adj* **de dinero, adinerado(da).**

wellwisher ['wel,wɪʃəʳ] *n* **simpatizante** *m* OR *f* (que da muestras de apoyo).

Welsh [welʃ] ◇ *adj* **galés(esa).** ◇ *n* [language] **galés** *m.* ◇ *npl*: **the ~ los galeses.**

Welshman ['welʃmən] (*pl* -men [-mən]) *n* **galés** *m.*

Welshwoman ['welʃ,wʊmən] (*pl* -women [-,wɪmɪn]) *n* **galesa** *f.*

went [went] *pt* ⊳ **go.**

wept [wept] *pt* & *pp* ⊳ **weep.**

were [wɜːʳ] *pt* ⊳ **be.**

we're [wɪəʳ] = **we are.**

weren't [wɜːnt] = **were not.**

west [west] ◇ *n* - **1.** [direction] **oeste** *m* - **2.** [region]: **the West el Oeste.** ◇ *adj* **del oeste.** ◇ *adv*: **(of) al oeste (de).**

◆ **West** *n* POL: **the West Occidente.**

West Bank *n*: **the ~ Cisjordania.**

West Country *n* UK: **the ~ el sudoeste de Inglaterra.**

West End *n* UK: **the ~ zona central de Londres, famosa por sus teatros, tiendas etc.**

westerly ['westəlɪ] *adj* [wind] **del oeste.**

western ['westən] ◇ *adj* **occidental.** ◇ *n* [film] **película** *f* **del oeste, western** *m.*

West German ◇ *adj* **de la Alemania Occidental.** ◇ *n* [person] **alemán** *m,* **-ana** *f* **occidental.**

West Germany *n*: **(the former) ~ (la antigua) Alemania Occidental.**

West Indian ◇ *adj* **antillano(na).** ◇ *n* [person] **antillano** *m,* **-na** *f.*

West Indies [-'ɪndiːz] *npl*: **the ~ las Antillas.**

Westminster ['westmɪnstəʳ] *n* **barrio londinense en que se encuentra el parlamento británico; por extensión éste.**

westward ['westwəd] ◇ *adj* **hacia el oeste.** ◇ *adv* = **westwards.**

westwards ['westwədz] *adv* **hacia el oeste.**

wet [wet] (*compar* -ter, *superl* -test, *pt* & *pp* **wet** OR -ted, *cont* -ting) ◇ *adj* - **1.** [soaked] **mojado(da);** [damp] **húmedo(da); to get ~ mojarse - 2.** [rainy] **lluvioso(sa) - 3.** [paint, cement] **fresco(ca); ~ paint recién pintado(da) - 4.** UK *inf pej* [weak, feeble] **ñoño(-ña).** ◇ *n inf* POL **político conservador moderado.** ◇ *vt* [soak] **mojar;** [dampen] **humedecer.**

wet blanket *n inf pej* **aguafiestas** *m* OR *f.*

wet suit *n* **traje** *m* **de submarinista.**

we've [wiːv] = **we have.**

whack [wæk] *inf n* [hit] **castañazo** *m,* **cachetada** *f Amér.*

whale [weɪl] *n* [animal] **ballena** *f.*

wharf [wɔːf] (*pl* -s OR **wharves** [wɔːvz]) *n* **muelle** *m,* **embarcadero** *m.*

what [wɒt] ◇ *adj* - **1.** (in direct, indirect questions) **qué; ~ kind of car has she got?** ¿qué coche tiene?; **~ shape is it?** ¿qué forma tiene?; **he asked me ~ shape it was me** preguntó qué forma tenía; **~ colour is it?** ¿de qué color es? - **2.** (in exclamations) **qué; ~ a surprise!** ¡qué sorpresa!; **~ a stupid idea!** ¡qué idea más tonta! ◇ *pron* - **1.** (interrogative) **qué; ~ are they doing?** ¿qué hacen?; **she asked me ~ they were doing me** preguntó qué estaban haciendo; **~ are they talking about?** ¿de qué están hablando?; **~ is it called?** ¿cómo se llama?; **~ does it cost?** ¿cuánto cuesta?; **~ is it like?** ¿cómo es?; **~'s the Spanish for 'book'?** ¿cómo se dice 'book' en español?; **~ is this for?** ¿para qué es esto?; **~ about another drink/going out for a meal?** ¿qué tal otra copa/si salimos a comer?; **~ about me?** ¿y yo qué?; **~ if nobody comes?** ¿y si no viene nadie, qué? - **2.** (relative) **lo que; I saw ~ happened/he did** yo vi lo que ocurrió/hizo; **I don't know ~ to do** no sé qué hacer; **~ we need is ...** lo que nos hace falta es ... ◇ *excl* [expressing disbelief] **¿qué?; ~, no milk!** ¿cómo? ¿que no hay leche?

whatever [wɒt'evəʳ] ◇ *adj* **cualquier; eat ~ food you find** come lo que encuentres; **no chance ~ ni la más remota posibilidad; nothing ~ nada en absoluto.** ◇ *pron* - **1.** [no matter what]: **~ they may offer ofrezcan lo que ofrezcan; ~ you like lo que (tú) quieras; don't touch this, ~ you do hagas lo que hagas, no toques esto; ~ happens pase lo que pase; ~ the weather haga el tiempo que haga - 2.** [indicating surprise]: **~ do you mean?** ¿qué quieres decir? - **3.** [indicating ignorance]: **he told me to get a**

D.R.V., ~ that is OR **may be** me dijo que consiguiera un D.R.V., sea lo que sea eso; **or ~ o lo que sea.**

whatsoever [,wɒtsəʊ'evə'] *adj*: **nothing ~** nada en absoluto; **none ~** ni uno.

wheat [wi:t] *n* trigo *m*.

wheedle ['wi:dl] *vt* decir con zalamería; **to ~ sb into doing sthg** camelar OR engatusar a alguien para que haga algo; **to ~ sthg out of sb** sonsacarle algo a alguien.

wheel [wi:l] ◇ *n* - **1.** [gen] rueda *f* - **2.** [steering wheel] volante *m*; **to be at the ~** estar al volante. ◇ *vt* empujar *(algo sobre ruedas)*. ◇ *vi* - **1.** [move in circle] dar vueltas - **2.** [turn round]: **to ~ round** darse la vuelta.

wheelbarrow ['wi:l,bærəʊ] *n* carretilla *f*.

wheelchair ['wi:l,tʃeə'] *n* silla *f* de ruedas.

wheelclamp ['wi:l,klæmp] *n* cepo *m*.

wheeze [wi:z] *vi* resollar.

whelk [welk] *n* buccino *m*.

when [wen] ◇ *adv* (*in direct, indirect question*) cuándo; **~ does the plane arrive?** ¿cuándo llega el avión?; **he asked me ~ I would be in London** me preguntó cuándo estaría en Londres; **I don't know ~ I'll be back** no sé cuándo volveré; **that was ~ I knew for sure that ...** fue entonces cuando me di cuenta que ...; **say ~!** ¡di basta! ◇ *conj* cuando; **tell me ~ you've read it** avísame cuando lo hayas leído; **on the day ~ it happened** el día (en) que pasó; **use less oil ~ frying food** utiliza menos aceite al freír comida; **you said it was black ~ it was actually white** dijiste que era negro cuando en realidad era blanco?

whenever [wen'evə'] ◇ *conj* [no matter when] cuando; [every time] cada vez que; **~ you like** cuando quieras; **~ I call him he runs away** siempre que le llamo se marcha corriendo. ◇ *adv* cuando sea.

where [weə'] ◇ *adv* (*in direct, indirect questions*) dónde; **~ do you live?** ¿dónde vives?; **do you know ~ he lives?** ¿sabes dónde vive?; **~ are you from?** ¿de dónde eres?; **~ are we going?** ¿adónde vamos?; **I don't know ~ to start** no sé por dónde empezar. ◇ *conj* - **1.** [referring to place, situation] donde; **this is ~ ...** es aquí donde ...; **go ~ you like** vete (a) donde quieras - **2.** [if]: **~ possible** siempre que sea posible.

whereabouts [*adv* ,weərə'baʊts, *n* 'weərəbaʊts] ◇ *adv* (por) dónde. ◇ *npl* paradero *m*; **to know sb's ~** conocer el paradero de alguien.

whereas [weər'æz] *conj* mientras que.

whereby [weə'baɪ] *conj* fml según, el/la cual, por el/la cual.

whereupon [,weərə'pɒn] *conj* fml tras OR con lo cual.

wherever [weər'evə'] ◇ *conj* [no matter where] dondequiera que; **~ you go** dondequiera que vayas; **sit ~ you like** siéntate donde quieras. ◇ *adv* - **1.** [no matter where] en cualquier parte - **2.** [indicating surprise]: **~ did you hear that?** ¿dónde habrás oído eso?

wherewithal ['weəwɪðɔ:l] *n* fml: **to have the ~ to do sthg** disponer de los medios para hacer algo.

whet [wet] (*pt* & *pp* **-ted**, *cont* **-ting**) *vt*: **to ~ sb's appetite (for sthg)** despertar el interés de alguien (por algo).

whether ['weðə'] *conj* - **1.** [indicating choice, doubt] si; **she doesn't know ~ to go or stay** no sabe si quedarse o marcharse; **I doubt ~ she'll do it** dudo que lo haga - **2.** [no matter if]: **~ I want to or not** tanto si quiero como si no, quiera o no quiera.

which [wɪtʃ] ◇ *adj* - **1.** (*in direct, indirect questions*) qué; **~ house is yours?** ¿cuál es tu casa?, ¿qué casa es la tuya?; **~ one?** ¿cuál?; **~ ones?** ¿cuáles? - **2.** [to refer back to]: **in ~ case** en cuyo caso; **we won't arrive until 6, by ~ time it will be dark** no llegaremos hasta la 6, hora a la cual ya será de noche. ◇ *pron* - **1.** (*in direct, indirect questions*) cuál, cuáles (*pl*); **~ do you prefer?** ¿cuál prefieres?; **I can't decide ~ to have** no sé cuál coger - **2.** (*in relative clause replacing noun*) que; **the table, ~ was made of wood, ...** la mesa, que OR la cual era de madera, ...; **the world in ~ we live** el mundo en que OR en el cual vivimos - **3.** (*to refer back to a clause*) lo cual; **she denied it, ~ surprised me** lo negó, lo cual me sorprendió; **before ~** antes de lo cual.

whichever [wɪtʃ'evə'] ◇ *adj* - **1.** [no matter which]: **~ route you take** vayas por donde vayas - **2.** [the one which]: **~ colour you prefer** el color que prefieras. ◇ *pron* el que (la que), los que (las que) (*pl*); **take ~ you like** coge el que quieras.

whiff [wɪf] *n* [smell] olorcillo *m*; **she caught a ~ of his after-shave** le llegó el olorcillo de su after-shave.

while [waɪl] ◇ *n* rato *m*; **it's a long ~ since I did that** hace mucho que no hago eso; **for a ~** un rato; **after a ~** después de un rato; **in a ~** dentro de poco; **once in a ~** de vez en cuando. ◇ *conj* - **1.** [during the time that] mientras - **2.** [whereas] mientras que - **3.** [although] aunque.

◆ **while away** *vt sep* pasar; **to ~ away the time** pasar el rato.

whilst [waɪlst] = **while**.

whim [wɪm] *n* capricho *m*.

whimper ['wɪmpə'] *vt* & *vi* gimotear.

whimsical ['wɪmzɪkl] *adj* [idea, story] fantasioso(sa); [remark] extravagante, poco usual; [look] juguetón(ona).

whine [waɪn] *vi* [child, dog] gemir; [siren] ulular.

whinge [wɪndʒ] (*cont* whingeing) *vi* UK *inf*: **to ~ (about)** quejarse (de).

whip [wɪp] (*pt* & *pp* -ped, *cont* -ping) ◇ *n* - **1.** [for hitting] látigo *m*; [for horse] guasca *f* *CAm* & *Carib*, fusta *f* - **2.** UK POL *miembro de un partido encargado de asegurar que otros miembros voten en el parlamento.* ◇ *vt* - **1.** [gen] azotar - **2.** [take quickly]: **to ~ sthg out/off** sacar/quitar algo rápidamente - **3.** [whisk] batir.

whipped cream [wɪpt-] *n* nata *f* montada.

whip-round *n* UK *inf*: **to have a ~** hacer una colecta.

whirl [wɜːl] ◇ *n fig* [of activity, events] torbellino *m*. ◇ *vt*: **to ~ sb/sthg round** hacer dar vueltas a alguien/algo. ◇ *vi* [move around] arremolinarse; [dancers] girar vertiginosamente.

whirlpool ['wɜːlpuːl] *n* remolino *m*.

whirlwind ['wɜːlwɪnd] *n* torbellino *m*.

whirr [wɜːʳ] *vi* zumbar.

whisk [wɪsk] ◇ *n* CULIN varilla *f*. ◇ *vt* - **1.** [move quickly]: **to ~ sthg away/out** llevarse/sacar algo rápidamente; **we were ~ed off to visit the museum** nos llevaron rápidamente a visitar el museo - **2.** CULIN batir.

whisker ['wɪskəʳ] *n* (pelo *m* del) bigote *m*.
➨ **whiskers** *npl* [of person] patillas *fpl*; [of cat] bigotes *mpl*.

whisky UK (*pl* -ies), **whiskey** US & Irish (*pl* -s) ['wɪskɪ] *n* whisky *m*.

whisper ['wɪspəʳ] ◇ *vt* susurrar. ◇ *vi* cuchichear.

whistle ['wɪsl] ◇ *n* - **1.** [sound] silbido *m*, pitido *m* - **2.** [device] silbato *m*, pito *m*. ◇ *vt* silbar. ◇ *vi* [person] silbar, chiflar *Amér*; [referee] pitar; [bird] piar.

white [waɪt] ◇ *adj* - **1.** [gen] blanco(ca) - **2.** [coffee, tea] con leche. ◇ *n* - **1.** [colour] blanco *m* - **2.** [person] blanco *m*, -ca *f* - **3.** [of egg] clara *f* - **4.** [of eye] blanco *m*.

white-collar *adj* de oficina; **~ worker** oficinista *m* OR *f*.

white elephant *n fig* mamotreto *m (caro e inútil)*.

Whitehall ['waɪthɔːl] *n calle londinense en que se encuentra la Administración británica; por extensión ésta.*

white-hot *adj* candente, incandescente.

White House *n*: **the ~** la Casa Blanca.

white lie *n* mentira *f* piadosa.

whiteness ['waɪtnɪs] *n* blancura *f*.

white paper *n* POL libro *m* blanco.

white sauce *n* (salsa *f*) bechamel *f*.

white spirit *n* UK *especie de aguarrás.*

whitewash ['waɪtwɒʃ] ◇ *n* - **1.** (U) [paint] blanqueo *m*, lechada *f* (de cal) - **2.** *pej* [cover-up] encubrimiento *m*. ◇ *vt* [paint] blanquear, encalar.

whiting ['waɪtɪŋ] (*pl inv* OR -s) *n* pescadilla *f*.

Whitsun ['wɪtsn] *n* [day] Pentecostés *m*.

whittle ['wɪtl] *vt* [reduce]: **to ~ down** OR **away** reducir gradualmente.

whiz (*pt* & *pp* -zed, *cont* -zing), **whizz** [wɪz] *vi*: **to ~ past** OR **by** pasar muy rápido OR zumbando.

whiz(z) kid *n inf* genio *m*, prodigio *m*.

who [huː] *pron* - **1.** *(in direct, indirect questions)* quién, quiénes *(pl)*; **~ are you?** ¿quién eres tú?; **~ is it?** [at door etc] ¿quién es?; **~ did you see?** ¿a quién viste?; **I didn't know ~ she was** no sabía quién era - **2.** *(in relative clauses)* que; **he's the doctor ~ treated me** es el médico que me atendió; **those ~ are in favour** los que están a favor.

who'd [huːd] = **who had, who would.**

whodu(n)nit [ˌhuːˈdʌnɪt] *n inf* historia *f* policíaca de misterio.

whoever [huːˈevəʳ] *pron* - **1.** [unknown person] quienquiera; *(pl)* quienesquiera; **~ finds it** quienquiera que lo encuentre; **tell ~ you like** díselo a quien quieras - **2.** [indicating surprise, astonishment]: **~ can that be?** ¿quién podrá ser? - **3.** [no matter who]: **come in, ~ you are** pasa, seas quién seas.

whole [həʊl] ◇ *adj* - **1.** [entire, complete] entero(ra); **we've had enough of the ~ thing** ya estamos hartos de todo esto - **2.** [for emphasis]: **a ~ lot taller** muchísimo más alto; **a ~ new idea** una idea totalmente nueva. ◇ *n* - **1.** [all]: **the ~ of the school/ summer** el colegio/verano entero - **2.** [unit, complete thing] todo *m*.
➨ **as a whole** *adv* en conjunto, en su totalidad.
➨ **on the whole** *adv* en general.

wholefood ['həʊlfuːd] *n* UK comida *f* integral.

whole-hearted [-ˈhɑːtɪd] *adj* incondicional.

wholemeal ['həʊlmiːl] *adj* UK integral.

wholesale ['həʊlseɪl] ◇ *adj* - **1.** COMM al por mayor - **2.** *pej* [indiscriminate] indiscriminado(da). ◇ *adv* - **1.** COMM al por mayor - **2.** *pej* [indiscriminately] indiscriminadamente.

wholesaler ['həʊlˌseɪləʳ] *n* mayorista *m* OR *f*.

wholesome ['həʊlsəm] *adj* sano(na), saludable.

whole wheat US = **wholemeal.**

who'll [huːl] = **who will.**

wholly ['həʊlɪ] *adv* completamente, enteramente.

whom [huːm] *pron* - **1.** *(in direct, indirect questions)* *fml* quién, quiénes *(pl)*; **from ~ did you receive it?** ¿de quién lo recibiste?; **for/ of/to ~** por/de/a quién - **2.** *(in relative* *clauses)* que; **the man ~ I saw** el hombre que vi; **the man to ~ I gave it** el hombre al que se lo di; **several people came, none of ~ I knew** vinieron varias personas, de las que no conocía a ninguna.

whooping cough ['huːpɪŋ-] *n* tos *f* ferina.

whopping ['wɒpɪŋ] *inf* ◇ *adj* enorme. ◇ *adv*: **a ~ great lorry/lie, a ~ big lorry/ lie** un camión/una mentira enorme.

whore [hɔːʳ] *n pej* puta *f*, cuero *m Amér*.

who're ['huːəʳ] = **who are**.

whose [huːz] ◇ *pron (in direct, indirect questions)* de quién, de quiénes *(pl)*; **~ is this?** ¿de quién es esto?; **I wonder ~ they are** me pregunto de quién serán. ◇ *adj* - **1.** [in direct, indirect questions] de quién; **~ car is that?** ¿de quién es ese coche? - **2.** *(in relative clauses)* cuyo(ya), cuyos(yas) *(pl)*; **that's the boy ~ father's an MP** ese es el chico cuyo padre es diputado; **the woman ~ daughters are twins** la mujer cuyas hijas son gemelas.

who's who [huːz-] *n* [book] Quién es Quién *m*.

who've [huːv] = **who have**.

why [waɪ] ◇ *adv* por qué; **~ did you lie to me?** ¿por qué me mentiste?; **~ don't you all come?** ¿por qué no venís todos?; **~ not?** ¿por qué no? ◇ *conj* por qué; **I don't know ~ he said** that no sé por qué dijo eso. ◇ *pron*: **there are several reasons ~ he left** hay varias razones por las que se marchó; **that's ~ she did it** por eso es por lo que lo hizo; **I don't know the reason ~** no se por qué razón. ◇ *excl* ¡hombre!, ¡vaya!

◆ **why ever** *adv*: **~ ever did you do that?** ¿pero por qué has hecho eso?

wick [wɪk] *n* mecha *f*.

wicked ['wɪkɪd] *adj* - **1.** [evil] malvado(da) - **2.** [mischievous, devilish] travieso(sa).

wicker ['wɪkəʳ] *adj* de mimbre.

wickerwork ['wɪkəwɜːk] *n (U)* artículos *mpl* de mimbre.

wicket ['wɪkɪt] *n* CRICKET [stumps] palos *mpl*.

wide [waɪd] ◇ *adj* - **1.** [broad] ancho(cha); **how ~ is it?** ¿cuánto mide de ancho?; **it's 50 cm ~** tiene 50 cm de ancho - **2.** [range, choice etc] amplio(plia) - **3.** [gap, difference, implications] grande, considerable - **4.** [off-target] desviado(da). ◇ *adv* - **1.** [broadly]: **to open/spread sthg ~** abrir/desplegar algo completamente - **2.** [off target]: **to go** OR **be ~** salir desviado.

wide-angle lens *n* gran angular *m*.

wide awake *adj* completamente despierto(ta).

widely ['waɪdlɪ] *adv* - **1.** [travel, read] extensamente; **to be ~ read/travelled** haber leído/viajado mucho - **2.** [believed, known, loved] generalmente; **there is a ~ held view that ...** existe la creencia generalizada de

que ... - **3.** [differ, vary] mucho.

widen ['waɪdn] *vt* [gen] ampliar; [road, bridge] ensanchar.

wide open *adj* - **1.** [window, door] abierto(-ta) de par en par - **2.** [eyes] completamente abierto(ta).

wide-ranging [-'reɪndʒɪŋ] *adj* [changes, survey, consequences] de gran alcance; [discussion, interests] de gran variedad; [selection] amplio(plia).

widescreen TV ['waɪdskriːn-] *n* televisor *m* panorámico, televisor *m* de pantalla ancha.

widespread ['waɪdspred] *adj* extendido(-da), general.

widow ['wɪdəʊ] *n* [woman] viuda *f*.

widowed ['wɪdəʊd] *adj* viudo(da).

widower ['wɪdəʊəʳ] *n* viudo *m*.

width [wɪdθ] *n* - **1.** [breadth] anchura *f*; **it's 50 cm in ~** tiene 50 cm de ancho - **2.** [in swimming pool] ancho *m*.

wield [wiːld] *vt* - **1.** [weapon] esgrimir; [implement] manejar - **2.** [power] ejercer.

wife [waɪf] *(pl* **wives)** *n* mujer *f*, esposa *f*.

wig [wɪg] *n* peluca *f*.

wiggle ['wɪgl] *vt inf* menear; [hips etc] contonear.

wild [waɪld] *adj* - **1.** [gen] salvaje; [plant, flower] silvestre; [bull] bravo(va), chúcaro(ra) *Amér* - **2.** [landscape, scenery] agreste - **3.** [weather, sea] borrascoso(sa) - **4.** [crowd, laughter, applause] frenético(ca) - **5.** [hair] alborotado(da) - **6.** [hope, idea, plan] descabellado(da) - **7.** [guess, exaggeration] extravagante.

◆ **wilds** *npl*: **the ~s** las tierras remotas.

wilderness ['wɪldənɪs] *n* - **1.** [barren land] yermo *m*, desierto *m* - **2.** [overgrown land] jungla *f*.

wild-goose chase *n inf* búsqueda *f* infructuosa.

wildlife ['waɪldlaɪf] *n (U)* fauna *f*.

wildly ['waɪldlɪ] *adv* - **1.** [enthusiastically] frenéticamente - **2.** [without discipline, inaccurately] a lo loco - **3.** [very] extremadamente.

wilful UK, **willful** US ['wɪlfʊl] *adj* - **1.** [stubborn] que siempre se tiene que salir con la suya - **2.** [deliberate] deliberado(da), intencionado(da).

will¹ [wɪl] ◇ *n* - **1.** [gen] voluntad *f*; **to do sthg of one's own free ~** hacer algo por propia voluntad - **2.** [document] testamento *m*; **to make a ~** hacer testamento. ◇ *vt*: **to ~ sthg to happen** desear mucho que ocurra algo; **to ~ sb to do sthg** desear mucho que alguien haga algo.

will² [wɪl] *modal vb* - **1.** [to express future tense]: **they say it ~ rain tomorrow** dicen que lloverá OR va a llover manana; **we ~ have arrived by midday** habremos llegado a mediodía; **when** ~ **we get paid?** ¿cuándo nos pagarán?; ~ **they come?** – yes, they ~/no, **they won't** ¿vendrán? – sí/no; **you** ~ **come, won't you?** *emphatic* vas a venir, ¿no? - **2.** [indicating willingness]: ~ **you have some more tea?** ¿te apetece más té?; **I won't do it** no lo haré - **3.** [in commands, requests]: **you** ~ **leave this house at once** vas a salir de esta casa ahora mismo; **close that window,** ~ **you?** cierra la ventana, ¿quieres?; ~ **you be quiet!** ¿queréis hacer el favor de callaros? - **4.** [indicating possibility, what usually happens]: **the hall** ~ **hold up to 1,000 people** la sala tiene cabida para 1.000 personas - **5.** [expressing an assumption]: **that'll be your father** ese va a ser OR será tu padre - **6.** [indicating irritation]: **she** ~ **keep phoning me** ¡y venga a llamarme!

willful *US* = wilful.

willing ['wɪlɪŋ] *adj* - **1.** [prepared]: **to be** ~ **(to do sthg)** estar dispuesto(ta) (a hacer algo) - **2.** [eager] servicial.

willingly ['wɪlɪŋlɪ] *adv* de buena gana.

willow (tree) ['wɪləʊ-] *n* sauce *m*.

willpower ['wɪl,paʊə'] *n* fuerza *f* de voluntad.

willy-nilly [,wɪlɪ'nɪlɪ] *adv* [carelessly] a la buena de Dios.

wilt [wɪlt] *vi* [plant] marchitarse; [person] desfallecer, extenuarse.

wily ['waɪlɪ] (*compar* **-ier**, *superl* **-iest**) *adj* astuto(ta).

wimp [wɪmp] *n pej inf* blandengue *m* OR *f*.

win [wɪn] (*pt* & *pp* **won**, *cont* **-ning**) ◇ *n* victoria *f*, triunfo *m*. ◇ *vt* ganar. ◇ *vi* ganar.

◆ **win over, win round** *vt sep* convencer.

wince [wɪns] *vi* hacer una mueca de dolor; **to** ~ **at/with sthg** estremecerse ante/de algo.

winch [wɪntʃ] *n* torno *m*.

wind¹ [wɪnd] ◇ *n* - **1.** METEOR viento *m* - **2.** [breath] aliento *m*, resuello *m* - **3.** *(U)* [in stomach] gases *mpl*. ◇ *vt* [knock breath out of] dejar sin aliento.

wind² [waɪnd] (*pt* & *pp* **wound**) ◇ *vt* - **1.** [string, thread] enrollar; **to** ~ **sthg around sthg** enrollar algo alrededor de algo - **2.** [clock, watch] dar cuerda a. ◇ *vi* serpentear.

◆ **wind down** ◇ *vt sep* - **1.** [car window] bajar - **2.** [business] cerrar poco a poco. ◇ *vi* [person] relajarse, descansar.

◆ **wind up** ◇ *vt sep* - **1.** [finish - activity] finalizar, concluir; [business] liquidar - **2.** [clock, watch] dar cuerda a - **3.** [car window] subir - **4.** *UK inf* [annoy] vacilar, tomar el pelo a. ◇ *vi inf* [end up] terminar, acabar.

windfall ['wɪndfɔːl] *n* [unexpected gift] dinero *m* llovido del cielo.

wind farm *n* parque *m* eólico.

winding ['waɪndɪŋ] *adj* tortuoso(sa), sinuoso(sa).

wind instrument [wɪnd-] *n* instrumento *m* de viento.

windmill ['wɪndmɪl] *n* molino *m* de viento.

window ['wɪndəʊ] *n* - **1.** [gen & COMPUT] ventana *f* - **2.** AUT ventanilla *f* - **3.** [of shop] escaparate *m*.

window box *n* jardinera *f* (de ventana).

window cleaner *n* - **1.** [person] limpiacristales *m* OR *f inv* - **2.** [product] limpiacristales *m inv*.

window ledge *n* alféizar *m*.

window pane *n* cristal *m* (de la ventana).

windowsill ['wɪndəʊsɪl] *n* alféizar *m*.

windpipe ['wɪndpaɪp] *n* tráquea *f*.

windscreen *UK* ['wɪndskriːn], **windshield** *US* ['wɪndʃiːld] *n* parabrisas *m inv*.

windscreen washer *n* lavaparabrisas *m inv*.

windscreen wiper *n* limpiaparabrisas *m inv*.

windshield *US* = **windscreen**.

windsurfing ['wɪnd,sɜːfɪŋ] *n* windsurf *m*.

windswept ['wɪndswept] *adj* [scenery] azotado(da) por el viento.

wind turbine *n* aerogenerador *m*.

windy ['wɪndɪ] (*compar* **-ier**, *superl* **-iest**) *adj* [day, weather] ventoso(sa), de mucho viento; [place] expuesto(ta) al viento; **it's** ~ hace viento.

wine [waɪn] *n* vino *m*; **red/white** ~ vino tinto/blanco.

wine bar *n UK* bar de cierta elegancia especializado en vinos y que a veces suele servir comidas.

wine cellar *n* bodega *f*.

wineglass ['waɪnɡlɑːs] *n* copa *f* OR vaso *m* (de vino).

wine list *n* lista *f* de vinos.

wine merchant *n UK* vinatero *m*, -ra *f*.

wine tasting [-,teɪstɪŋ] *n* cata *f* de vinos.

wine waiter *n* sommelier *m*.

wing [wɪŋ] *n* - **1.** [gen] ala *f* - **2.** AUT guardabarros *m inv* - **3.** SPORT [side of pitch] banda *f*; [winger] extremo *m*, ala *m*.

◆ **wings** *npl* THEATRE: **the** ~**s** los bastidores.

winger ['wɪŋə'] *n* SPORT extremo *m*, ala *m*.

wing mirror *n* retrovisor *m*.

wink [wɪŋk] ◇ *n* guiño *m*. ◇ *vi* [eye]: **to** ~ **(at sb)** guiñar (a alguien).

winkle ['wɪŋkl] *n* bígaro *m*.

winner ['wɪnə'] *n* ganador *m*, -ra *f*.

winning ['wɪnɪŋ] *adj* - **1.** [team, competitor] vencedor(ra), victorioso(sa); [goal, point] de la victoria; [ticket, number] premiado(-da) - **2.** [smile, ways] atractivo(va).

◆ **winnings** *npl* ganancias *fpl*.

winning post *n* meta *f*.

winter ['wɪntə'] ◇ n (U) invierno m. ◇ comp de invierno, invernal.

winter sports npl deportes mpl de invierno.

wintertime ['wɪntətaɪm] n (U) invierno m.

wint(e)ry ['wɪntrɪ] adj [gen] de invierno, invernal; [showers] con nieve.

wipe [waɪp] ◇ n: give the table a ~ pásale un trapo a la mesa. ◇ vt [rub to clean] limpiar, pasar un trapo a; [rub to dry] secar.
◆ **wipe out** vt sep -1. [erase] borrar -2. [eradicate] aniquilar.
◆ **wipe up** vt sep empapar, limpiar.

wire ['waɪə'] ◇ n -1. [gen] alambre m; ELEC cable m -2. US [telegram] telegrama m. ◇ vt -1. [connect]: to ~ sthg to sthg conectar algo a algo -2. [ELEC - house] poner la instalación eléctrica de; [- plug] conectar el cable a -3. US [send telegram to] enviar un telegrama a.

wireless ['waɪəlɪs] n dated radio f.

wiring ['waɪərɪŋ] n (U) instalación f eléctrica.

wiry ['waɪərɪ] (compar -ier, superl -iest) adj -1. [hair] estropajoso(sa) -2. [body, man] nervudo(da).

wisdom ['wɪzdəm] n -1. [learning] sabiduría f -2. [good sense] sensatez f.

wisdom tooth n muela f del juicio.

wise [waɪz] adj -1. [learned] sabio(bia) -2. [sensible] prudente.

wisecrack ['waɪzkræk] n pej broma f, chiste m.

wish [wɪʃ] ◇ n: ~ (for sthg/to do sthg) deseo m (de algo/de hacer algo); to do sthg against sb's ~es hacer algo en contra de los deseos de alguien. ◇ vt: to ~ to do sthg fml desear hacer algo; to ~ sb sthg desear a alguien algo; I ~ (that) you had told me before! ¡ojalá me lo hubieras dicho antes!; I ~ (that) I were OR was rich ojalá fuera rico. ◇ vi [by magic]: to ~ for sthg pedir (como deseo) algo.
◆ **wishes** npl: (with) best ~es [in letter] muchos recuerdos.

wishful thinking [,wɪʃfʊl-] n (U): it's just ~ no son más que (vanas) ilusiones.

wishy-washy ['wɪʃɪ,wɒʃɪ] adj inf pej soso(sa), insípido(da).

wisp [wɪsp] n -1. [of hair] mechón m; [of grass] brizna f -2. [cloud] nubecilla f; [of smoke] voluta f.

wistful ['wɪstfʊl] adj triste, melancólico(ca).

wit [wɪt] n -1. [humour] ingenio m, agudeza f -2. [intelligence]: to have the ~ to do sthg tener el buen juicio de hacer algo.
◆ **wits** npl: to have OR keep one's ~s about one mantenerse alerta.

witch [wɪtʃ] n bruja f.

with [wɪð] prep -1. [in company of] con; we stayed ~ them for a week estuvimos con ellos una semana; ~ me conmigo; ~ you contigo; ~ himself/herself consigo -2. [indicating opposition] con -3. [indicating means, manner, feelings] con; I washed it ~ detergent lo lavé con detergente; he filled it ~ wine lo llenó de vino; covered ~ mud cubierto de barro; she was trembling ~ fear temblaba de miedo -4. [having - gen] con; a man ~ a beard un hombre con barba; the woman ~ the black hair/big dog la señora del pelo negro/perro grande; I'm married ~ 6 children estoy casado con 6 hijos -5. [regarding] con; he's very mean ~ money es muy tacaño con el dinero -6. [because of] con; ~ my luck, I'll probably lose con la suerte que tengo seguro que pierdo -7. [indicating understanding]: are you ~ me? ¿me sigues? -8. [indicating support] con; I'm ~ Dad on this en eso estoy con papá.

withdraw [wɪð'drɔː] (pt -drew, pp -drawn) ◇ vt -1. [gen]: to ~ sthg (from) retirar algo (de) -2. [money] sacar. ◇ vi: to ~ (from/to) retirarse (de/a); to ~ into o.s. encerrarse en uno mismo.

withdrawal [wɪð'drɔːəl] n -1. [gen & MIL] retirada f -2. [retraction] retractación f -3. FIN reintegro m.

withdrawal symptoms npl síndrome m de abstinencia.

withdrawn [wɪð'drɔːn] ◇ pp ⊳ withdraw. ◇ adj [shy, quiet] reservado(da).

withdrew [wɪð'druː] pt ⊳ withdraw.

wither ['wɪðə'] vi -1. [dry up] marchitarse -2. [become weak] debilitarse, decaer.

withhold [wɪð'həʊld] (pt & pp -held [-'held]) vt [gen] retener; [consent, permission] negar.

within [wɪ'ðɪn] ◇ prep -1. [gen] dentro de; ~ reach al alcance de la mano; ~ sight of a la vista de -2. [less than - distance] a menos de; [- time] en menos de; it's ~ walking distance se puede ir andando; ~ the next six months en los próximos seis meses; it arrived ~ a week llegó en menos de una semana. ◇ adv dentro.

without [wɪð'aʊt] ◇ prep sin; ~ sthg/doing sthg sin algo/hacer algo; ~ making any mistakes sin cometer ningún error; it happened ~ my realizing pasó sin que me diera cuenta. ◇ adv: to go OR do ~ sthg pasar sin algo.

withstand [wɪð'stænd] (pt & pp -stood [-'stʊd]) vt resistir, aguantar.

witness ['wɪtnɪs] ◇ n -1. [person] testigo m OR f -2. [testimony]: to bear ~ to sthg atestiguar algo, dar fe de algo. ◇ vt -1. [see] presenciar -2. [countersign] firmar (como testigo).

witness box *UK*, **witness stand** *US* n tribuna f (de los testigos).

witticism ['wıtısızm] n agudeza f, ocurrencia f.

witty ['wıtı] (*compar* **-ier**, *superl* **-iest**) adj ingenioso(sa), ocurrente.

wives [waıvz] pl ▷ **wife**.

wizard ['wızəd] n **- 1.** [magician] mago m (en cuentos) **- 2.** [skilled person] genio m.

wobble ['wɒbl] vi [gen] tambalearse; [furniture] bambolearse, cojear; [legs] temblar.

woe [wəʊ] n literary aflicción f, pesar m.

woke [wəʊk] pt ▷ **wake**.

woken ['wəʊkn] pp ▷ **wake**.

wolf [wʊlf] (pl **wolves**) n ZOOL lobo m.

woman ['wʊmən] (pl **women**) ◇ n **- 1.** [female] mujer f **- 2.** [womanhood] la mujer.
◇ comp: ~ **doctor** médica f.

womanly ['wʊmənlı] adj femenino(na).

womb [wu:m] n matriz f, útero m.

women ['wımın] pl ▷ **woman**.

women's lib [-'lıb] n liberación f de la mujer.

women's liberation n liberación f de la mujer.

won [wʌn] pt & pp ▷ **win**.

wonder ['wʌndə'] ◇ n **- 1.** [amazement] asombro m, admiración f **- 2.** [cause for surprise]: **it's a** ~ **(that)** ... es un milagro que ...; **no** OR **little** OR **small** ~ **...** no es de extrañar que ... **- 3.** [amazing thing, person] maravilla f. ◇ vt **- 1.** [speculate]: **to** ~ **(if** OR **whether)** preguntarse (si) **- 2.** [in polite requests]: **I** ~ **if** OR **whether I could ask you a question?** ¿le importaría que le hiciera una pregunta? **- 3.** [be surprised]: **I** ~ **(that) she hasn't left him** me pregunto cómo es que todavía no lo ha dejado. ◇ vi [speculate]: **I was only** ~**ing** preguntaba sólo por curiosidad; **to** ~ **about sthg** preguntarse por algo.

wonderful ['wʌndəfʊl] adj maravilloso(sa), estupendo(da).

wonderfully ['wʌndəfʊlı] adv **- 1.** [very well] estupendamente **- 2.** [very] extremadamente.

won't [wəʊnt] = will not.

woo [wu:] vt **- 1.** literary [court] cortejar **- 2.** [try to win over] granjearse el apoyo de.

wood [wʊd] n **- 1.** [timber] madera f; [for fire] leña f **- 2.** [group of trees] bosque m.
◆ **woods** npl bosque m.

wooded ['wʊdıd] adj arbolado(da).

wooden ['wʊdn] adj **- 1.** [of wood] de madera **- 2.** pej [actor] envarado(da).

woodpecker ['wʊd,pekə'] n pájaro m carpintero.

woodwind ['wʊdwınd] n: **the** ~ los instrumentos de viento de madera.

woodwork ['wʊdwɜ:k] n carpintería f.

woodworm ['wʊdwɜ:m] n carcoma f.

wool [wʊl] n lana f; **to pull the** ~ **over sb's eyes** inf fig dar a alguien gato por liebre.

woollen *UK*, **woolen** *US* ['wʊlən] adj de lana.
◆ **woollens** npl géneros mpl de lana.

woolly ['wʊlı] (*compar* **-ier**, *superl* **-iest**) adj **- 1.** [woollen] de lana **- 2.** inf [fuzzy, unclear] confuso(sa).

word [wɜ:d] ◇ n **- 1.** LING palabra f; **we couldn't understand a** ~ **he said** no entendí ni una sola palabra de lo que dijo; ~ **for** ~ palabra por palabra; **in other** ~**s** en otras palabras; **in a** ~ en una palabra; **too ... for** ~**s** de lo más ...; **she doesn't mince her** ~**s** no tiene pelos en la lengua; **to have a** ~ **with sb** hablar con alguien; **to put sthg into** ~**s** expresar algo con palabras; **I couldn't get a** ~ **in edgeways** no pude meter baza **- 2.** *(U)* [news] noticia f; **there is no** ~ **from them** no hemos tenido noticias de ellos; ~ **has it that** ... se rumorea que ... **- 3.** [promise] palabra f; **to give sb one's** ~ dar (uno) su palabra a alguien; **to keep/break one's** ~ mantener/no cumplir la palabra de uno. ◇ vt redactar, expresar.

wording ['wɜ:dıŋ] n *(U)* términos mpl, forma f (de expresión).

word processing n *(U)* proceso m de textos.

word processor [-'prəʊsesə'] n procesador m de textos.

wore [wɔ:'] pt ▷ **wear**.

work [wɜ:k] ◇ n **- 1.** *(U)* [employment] trabajo m, empleo m; **to be out of** ~ estar desempleado; **at** ~ en el trabajo **- 2.** [activity, tasks] trabajo m; **at** ~ trabajando **- 3.** [of art, literature etc] obra f **- 4.** [handiwork] obra f; **it was the** ~ **of a psychopath** fue obra de un psicópata. ◇ vt **- 1.** [employees, subordinates] hacer trabajar; **she** ~**s herself too hard** trabaja demasiado **- 2.** [machine] manejar, operar **- 3.** [wood, metal, land] trabajar. ◇ vi **- 1.** [person]: **to** ~ **(on sthg)** trabajar (en algo); **he** ~**s as a gardener** trabaja de jardinero; **to** ~ **for sb** trabajar para alguien **- 2.** [machine, system, idea] funcionar **- 3.** [drug] surtir efecto **- 4.** [become by movement]: **to** ~ **loose** soltarse; **to** ~ **free** desprenderse.
◆ **works** ◇ n [factory] fábrica f. ◇ npl [mechanism] mecanismo m.
◆ **work on** vt fus **- 1.** [pay attention to] trabajar en **- 2.** [take as basis] partir de.
◆ **work out** ◇ vt sep **- 1.** [plan, schedule] elaborar **- 2.** [total, amount] calcular; [answer] dar con. ◇ vi **- 1.** [figure etc]: **to** ~ **out at** salir a **- 2.** [turn out] resultar, resolverse **- 3.** [be successful] salir bien, resultar bien **- 4.** [train, exercise] entrenarse, hacer ejercicio.

work up *vt sep* **- 1.** [excite]: **to ~ o.s. up into a frenzy** ponerse frenético(ca) **- 2.** [generate] despertar; **I can't ~ up much enthusiasm** no consigo entusiasmarme; **to ~ up an appetite** abrir el apetito.

workable ['wɜːkəbl] *adj* factible, viable.

workaholic [ˌwɜːkə'hɒlɪk] *n* adicto *m*, -ta *f* al trabajo.

workday ['wɜːkdeɪ] *n* [not weekend] día *m* laborable.

worked up [ˌwɜːkt-] *adj* nervioso(sa); **to get ~** alterarse.

worker ['wɜːkə'] *n* [person who works] trabajador *m*, -ra *f*; [manual worker] obrero *m*, -ra *f*; **they're hard/slow ~s** trabajan duro/despacio; **office ~** oficinista *mf*.

workforce ['wɜːkfɔːs] *n* mano *f* de obra.

working ['wɜːkɪŋ] *adj* **- 1.** [in operation] funcionando **- 2.** [having employment] empleado(da); **a '~ mother** una madre trabajadora **- 3.** [relating to work - gen] laboral; [- day] laborable.

workings *npl* mecanismo *m*.

working class *n*: **the ~** la clase obrera.

working-class *adj* obrero(ra).

working order *n*: **to be in (good) ~** funcionar (bien).

workload ['wɜːkləʊd] *n* cantidad *f* de trabajo.

workman ['wɜːkmən] (*pl* -men [-mən]) *n* obrero *m*.

workmanship ['wɜːkmənʃɪp] *n* artesanía *f*.

workmate ['wɜːkmeɪt] *n* compañero *m*, -ra *f* de trabajo, colega *m* OR *f*.

work permit [-ˌpɜːmɪt] *n* permiso *m* de trabajo.

workplace ['wɜːkpleɪs] *n* lugar *m* de trabajo.

worksheet ['wɜːkʃiːt] *n* hoja *f* de trabajo.

workshop ['wɜːkʃɒp] *n* taller *m*.

workstation ['wɜːkˌsteɪʃn] *n* COMPUT estación *f* de trabajo.

worktop ['wɜːktɒp] *n* UK mármol *m*, encimera *f*.

work-to-rule *n* UK huelga *f* de celo.

world [wɜːld] ◇ *n* mundo *m*; **the best in the ~** el mejor del mundo; **the highest mountain in the ~** la montaña más alta del mundo; **all over the ~** por todo el mundo; **to think the ~ of sb** querer a alguien con locura; **a ~ of difference** una diferencia enorme; **to see the ~** ver mundo; **it's a small ~** el mundo es un pañuelo; **the antique ~** el mundo antiguo; **what is the ~ coming to?** ¿a dónde vamos a ir a parar?; **they are ~s apart** hay un abismo entre ellos; **to have all the time in the ~** tener todo el tiempo del mundo. ◇ *comp* mundial.

world-class *adj* de primera categoría.

world-famous *adj* famoso(sa) en el mundo entero.

worldly ['wɜːldlɪ] *adj literary* mundano(na).

World War I *n* la Primera Guerra Mundial.

World War II *n* la Segunda Guerra Mundial.

worldwide ['wɜːldwaɪd] ◇ *adj* mundial. ◇ *adv* en todo el mundo, a escala mundial.

World Wide Web *n*: **the ~** la (World Wide) Web.

worm [wɜːm] *n* [animal] gusano *m*; [earthworm] lombriz *f* (de tierra).

worn [wɔːn] ◇ *pp* ▷ **wear**. ◇ *adj* **- 1.** [threadbare] gastado(da) **- 2.** [tired] ajado(da).

worn-out *adj* **- 1.** [old, threadbare]: **to be ~** estar ya para tirar **- 2.** [tired] agotado(da).

worried ['wʌrɪd] *adj* preocupado(da).

worry ['wʌrɪ] (*pl* -ies, *pt* & *pp* -ied) ◇ *n* preocupación *f*. ◇ *vt* [trouble] preocupar. ◇ *vi*: **to ~ (about)** preocuparse (por); **not to ~!** ¡no importa!

worrying ['wʌrɪŋ] *adj* preocupante.

worrywort ['wʌrɪwɔːt] *n* US *inf* angustias *mf inv Esp*, angustiado *m*, -da *f*.

worse [wɜːs] ◇ *adj* peor; **to get ~** empeorar; **to get ~ and ~** ir cada vez peor; **to go from bad to ~** ir de mal en peor; **to make things ~** empeorar las cosas; **they are none the ~ for their adventure** se sienten perfectamente a pesar de su aventura. ◇ *adv* peor; **~ off** [gen] en peor situación; [financially] peor económicamente; **you could do ~ than marry him** no harías tan mal casándote con él. ◇ *n*: **~ was to come** lo peor estaba aún por venir; **a change for the ~** un cambio para peor; **to take a turn for the ~** empeorar.

worsen ['wɜːsn] *vt* & *vi* empeorar.

worship ['wɜːʃɪp] (*UK pt* & *pp* -ped, *cont* -ping, *US pt* & *pp* -ed, *cont* -ing) ◇ *vt lit* & *fig* adorar. ◇ *n lit* & *fig*: **~ (of)** culto *m* (a), adoración *f* (por).

Worship *n*: **Your/Her/His Worship** su señoría; **his Worship the Mayor** el Excelentísimo Señor alcalde.

worst [wɜːst] ◇ *adj* peor; **the ~ thing is...** lo peor es que ...; **~ of all** lo peor de todo. ◇ *adv* peor; **the ~ affected area** la región más afectada. ◇ *n*: **the ~** [thing] lo peor; [person] el peor *m*, la peor *f*; **this is communism at its ~** esto es la peor manifestación del comunismo; **to fear the ~** temer lo peor; **if the ~ comes to the ~** en último extremo; **to bring out the ~ in sb** sacar lo peor de alguien.

at (the) worst *adv* en el peor de los casos.

worth [wɜːθ] ◇ *prep* **- 1.** [having the value of]: **it's ~ £50** vale 50 libras; **how much is it ~?** ¿cuánto vale?; **it isn't ~ that** much no vale tanto **- 2.** [deserving of] digno(na) de, merecedor(ra) de; **the museum is ~ visiting** OR **a visit, it's ~ visiting the museum**

el museo merece una visita; **it's not ~ it** no vale la pena; **it's ~ a try** vale la pena intentarlo; **for what it's ~**, I think that ... por si mi opinión sirve de algo, creo que ... ◇ *n* **- 1.** [amount]: **£50,000 ~ of antiques** antigüedades por valor de 50.000 libras; **a month's ~ of groceries** provisiones para un mes **- 2.** *fml* [value] valor *m*.

worthless ['wɜ:θlɪs] *adj* **- 1.** [object] sin valor **- 2.** [person] despreciable.

worthwhile [,wɜ:θ'waɪl] *adj* que vale la pena; [cause] noble, digno(na).

worthy ['wɜ:ðɪ] (*compar* **-ier**, *superl* **-iest**) *adj* **- 1.** [gen] digno(na) **- 2.** [good but unexciting] encomiable.

would [wʊd] *modal vb* **- 1.** (in reported speech): **she said she ~ come** dijo que vendría **- 2.** [in conditional phrases]: **if she couldn't come she ~ tell us** si no pudiera venir nos lo diría; **what ~ you do?** ¿qué harías?; **if he had known, he ~ have resigned** si lo hubiera sabido, habría dimitido **- 3.** [indicating willingness]: **she ~n't go** no quiso/quería ir; **he ~ do anything for her** haría cualquier cosa por ella **- 4.** (in polite questions): **~ you like a drink?** ¿quieres beber algo?; **~ you mind closing the window?** ¿le importaría cerrar la ventana?; **help me shut this suitcase, ~ you?** ayúdame a cerrar esta maleta, ¿quieres? **- 5.** [indicating inevitability]: **he WOULD say that, ~n't he?** hombre, era de esperar que dijera eso, ¿no? **- 6.** [expressing opinions]: **I ~ have thought (that) it ~ be easy** hubiera pensado que sería fácil; **I ~ prefer ...** preferiría ...; **I ~ like ...** quisiera ..., quiero ... **- 7.** [giving advice]: **I ~ report it if I were you** yo en tu lugar lo denunciaría **- 8.** [indicating habit]: **he ~ smoke a cigar after dinner** solía fumar un puro después de la cena; **she ~ often complain about the neighbours** se quejaba a menudo de los vecinos **- 9.** [in conjectures]: **it ~ have been around 2 o'clock** serían las dos.

would-be *adj*: **a ~ author** un aspirante a literato.

wouldn't ['wʊdnt] = **would not**.

would've ['wʊdəv] = **would have**.

wound¹ [wu:nd] ◇ *n* herida *f*. ◇ *vt* lit & fig herir.

wound² [waʊnd] *pt & pp* ⊳ **wind²**.

wove [wəʊv] *pt* ⊳ **weave**.

woven ['wəʊvn] *pp* ⊳ **weave**.

WP - 1. *abbr of* **word processing - 2.** *abbr of* **word processor**.

wrangle ['ræŋgl] ◇ *n* disputa *f*. ◇ *vi*: **to ~ (with sb over sthg)** discutir OR pelearse (con alguien por algo).

wrangler ['ræŋglər] *n* US vaquero *m*.

wrap [ræp] (*pt & pp* **-ped**, *cont* **-ping**) ◇ *vt*

- 1. [cover] envolver; **to ~ sthg in sthg** envolver algo en algo; **to ~ sthg around** OR **round sthg** liar algo alrededor de algo **- 2.** [encircle]: **he wrapped his hands around it** lo rodeó con sus manos. ◇ *n* **- 1.** [garment] echarpe *m*; **to keep sthg under ~s** fig mantener algo en secreto **- 2.** US [food] tipo de bocadillo servido en una torta de maíz y doblado por la mitad.

● **wrap up** ◇ *vt sep* [cover] envolver. ◇ *vi* [put warm clothes on]: **~ up well** OR **warmly** abrígate bien.

wrapper ['ræpər] *n* envoltorio *m*.

wrapping ['ræpɪŋ] *n* envoltorio *m*.

wrapping paper *n* (U) papel *m* de envolver.

wrath [rɒθ] *n literary* ira *f*, cólera *f*.

wreak [ri:k] *vt* causar; **to ~ havoc** hacer estragos; **to ~ revenge** OR **vengeance** tomar la revancha.

wreath [ri:θ] *n* corona *f* (de flores).

wreck [rek] ◇ *n* **- 1.** [of car, plane] restos *mpl* del siniestro; [of ship] restos del naufragio **- 2.** *inf* [person] guiñapo *m*; **to be a nervous ~** estar hecho(cha) un manojo de nervios. ◇ *vt* **- 1.** [destroy] destrozar **- 2.** NAUT hacer naufragar; **to be ~ed** naufragar **- 3.** [spoil] dar al traste con; [health] acabar con.

wreckage ['rekɪdʒ] *n* (U) [of plane, car] restos *mpl*; [of building] escombros *mpl*.

wren [ren] *n* chochín *m*.

wrench [rentʃ] ◇ *n* **- 1.** US [tool] llave *f* inglesa **- 2.** [injury] torcedura *f*. ◇ *vt* **- 1.** [pull violently]: **to ~ sthg (off)** arrancar algo; **to ~ sthg open** abrir algo de un tirón **- 2.** [twist and injure] torcer.

wrestle ['resl] *vi lit & fig*: **to ~ (with)** luchar (con).

wrestler ['reslər] *n* luchador *m*, -ra *f*.

wrestling ['reslɪŋ] *n* lucha *f* libre.

wretch [retʃ] *n* desgraciado *m*, -da *f*, infeliz *m* OR *f*.

wretched ['retʃɪd] *adj* **- 1.** [miserable] miserable **- 2.** *inf* [damned] maldito(ta).

wriggle ['rɪgl] *vi* **- 1.** [move about] menearse **- 2.** [twist] escurrirse, deslizarse.

wring [rɪŋ] (*pt & pp* **wrung**) *vt* **- 1.** [wet clothes etc] estrujar, escurrir **- 2.** [neck] retorcer.

wringing ['rɪŋɪŋ] *adj*: **~ (wet)** empapado(da).

wrinkle ['rɪŋkl] ◇ *n* arruga *f*. ◇ *vt* arrugar. ◇ *vi* arrugarse.

wrist [rɪst] *n* muñeca *f*.

wristwatch ['rɪstwɒtʃ] *n* reloj *m* de pulsera.

writ [rɪt] *n* mandato *m* judicial.

write [raɪt] (*pt* **wrote**, *pp* **written**) ◇ *vt* **- 1.** [gen & COMPUT] escribir; **to ~ sb a cheque** extender un cheque a nombre de alguien **- 2.** *US* [person] escribir a. ⬦ *vi* [gen & COMPUT] escribir.

◆ **write away** *vi*: **to ~ away for sthg** escribir pidiendo algo.

◆ **write back** *vt sep* & *vi* contestar.

◆ **write down** *vt sep* apuntar.

◆ **write off** *vt sep* **- 1.** [plan, hopes] abandonar **- 2.** [debt] cancelar, anular **- 3.** [person as failure] considerar un fracaso **- 4.** *UK inf* [wreck] cargarse, destrozar.

◆ **write up** *vt sep* redactar.

write-off *n*: **the car was a ~** el coche quedó totalmente destrozado.

writer ['raɪtə'] *n* **- 1.** [as profession] escritor *m*, -ra *f* **- 2.** [of letter, article, story] autor *m*, -ra *f*.

writhe [raɪð] *vi* retorcerse.

writing ['raɪtɪŋ] *n* **- 1.** *(U)* [handwriting] letra *f*, caligrafía *f* **- 2.** [something written] escrito *m*; **to put sthg in ~** poner algo por escrito **- 3.** [activity] escritura *f*.

writing paper *n (U)* papel *m* de carta.

written ['rɪtn] ⬦ *pp* ⬭ **write**. ⬦ *adj* **- 1.** [not oral] escrito(ta) **- 2.** [official] por escrito.

wrong [rɒŋ] ⬦ *adj* **- 1.** [not normal, not satisfactory] malo(la); **the clock's ~** el reloj anda mal; **what's ~?** ¿qué pasa?, ¿qué va mal?; **there's nothing ~** no pasa nada; **there's nothing ~ with me** no me pasa nada **- 2.** [not suitable, not correct] equivocado(da); [moment, time] inoportuno(na); [answer] incorrecto(ta); **he has given me the ~ change** me ha dado el cambio equivocado; **I think we've gone the ~ way** creo que nos hemos equivocado de camino; **I always seem to say the ~ thing** parece que siempre digo lo que no debo; **to be ~** [person] equivocarse; **to be ~ about sth/sb** equivocarse con respecto a algo/alguien; **to be ~ to do sthg** cometer un error al hacer algo **- 3.** [morally bad] malo(la); **it's ~ to steal/lie** robar/mentir está mal; **what's ~ with being a communist?** ¿qué tiene de malo ser comunista? ⬦ *adv* **- 1.** [incorrectly] mal; **to get sthg ~** entender mal algo; **to go ~** [make a mistake] cometer un error; [stop functioning] estropearse; [plans] salir mal. ⬦ *n* **- 1.** [evil] mal *m*; **to be in the ~** haber hecho mal **- 2.** [injustice] injusticia *f*. ⬦ *vt* ser injusto(ta) con, agraviar.

wrongdoer ['rɒŋ,duːə'] *n* malhechor *m*, -ra *f*.

wrongful ['rɒŋfʊl] *adj* [dismissal] improcedente; [arrest, imprisonment] ilegal.

wrongly ['rɒŋlɪ] *adv* equivocadamente.

wrote [rəʊt] *pt* ⬭ **write**.

wrought iron [rɔːt-] *n* hierro *m* forjado.

wrung [rʌŋ] *pt* & *pp* ⬭ **wring**.

wry [raɪ] *adj* [amused] irónico(ca).

WWW (*abbr of* **World Wide Web**) *n* WWW *f*.

---

x (*pl* **x's** OR **xs**), **X** (*pl* **X's** OR **Xs**) [eks] *n* [letter] x *f inv*; X *f inv*.

xenophobia [ˌzenəˈfəʊbjə] *n* xenofobia *f*.

Xmas ['eksməs] *n* Navidad *f*.

X-ray ⬦ *n* **- 1.** [ray] rayo *m* X **- 2.** [picture] radiografía *f*; **to have a chest ~** hacerse una radiografía. ⬦ *vt* examinar con rayos X, radiografiar.

xylophone ['zaɪləfəʊn] *n* xilofón *m*.

---

y (*pl* **y's** OR **ys**), **Y** (*pl* **Y's** OR **Ys**) [waɪ] *n* [letter] y *f*; Y *f*.

yacht [jɒt] *n* yate *m*; [for racing] balandro *m*.

yachting ['jɒtɪŋ] *n* balandrismo *m*.

yachtsman ['jɒtsmən] (*pl* **-men** [-mən]) *n* balandrista *m*.

Yank [jæŋk] *n inf pej* [American] yanqui *m* OR *f*.

Yankee ['jæŋkɪ] *n US término usado para designar a una persona del noreste de los EEUU.*

yap [jæp] (*pt* & *pp* **-ped**, *cont* **-ping**) *vi* [dog] ladrar.

yard [jɑːd] *n* **- 1.** [unit of measurement] = *91,44 cm*, yarda *f* **- 2.** [walled area] patio *m* **- 3.** [shipyard] astillero *m*; **builder's/goods ~** depósito *m* de materiales/de mercancías **- 4.** *US* [attached to house] jardín *m*.

yardstick ['jɑːdstɪk] *n* criterio *m*, pauta *f*.

yarn [jɑːn] *n* [thread] hilo *m*, hilaza *f*.

yawn [jɔːn] ⬦ *n* [when tired] bostezo *m*. ⬦ *vi* **- 1.** [when tired] bostezar **- 2.** [gap, chasm] abrirse.

yd *abbr of* **yard**.

yeah [jeə] *adv inf* sí.

year [jɪə'] *n* **- 1.** [gen] año *m*; **he's 25 ~s old** tiene 25 años; **all (the) ~ round** todo el año; **over the ~s** con los años **- 2.** SCH curso *m*; **he's in (his) first ~** está en primero.

➤ **years** *npl* [ages] años *mpl*; **it's ~s since I last saw you** hace siglos que no te veo.

yearly ['jɪəlɪ] ⬦ *adj* anual. ⬦ *adv* - **1.** [once a year] una vez al año - **2.** [every year] cada año.

yearn [jɜːn] *vi*: **to ~ for sthg/to do sthg** ansiar algo/hacer algo.

yearning ['jɜːnɪŋ] *n*: **~ (for sb/sthg)** anhelo *m* (de alguien/algo).

yeast [jiːst] *n* levadura *f*.

yell [jel] ⬦ *n* grito *m*, alarido *m*. ⬦ *vt & vi* vociferar.

yellow ['jeləʊ] ⬦ *adj* [in colour] amarillo(-lla). ⬦ *n* amarillo *m*.

yellow card *n* FTBL tarjeta *f* amarilla.

yelp [jelp] ⬦ *n* aullido *m*. ⬦ *vi* aullar.

yes [jes] ⬦ *adv* sí; **to say ~** decir que sí; **to say ~ to sthg** consentir algo; **does he speak English? - ~, he does** ¿habla inglés? - sí; **he doesn't speak English - ~ he does!** no habla inglés - sí, ¡sí que habla. ⬦ *n* sí *m*.

yesterday ['jestədɪ] ⬦ *n* ayer *m*. ⬦ *adv* ayer; **~ afternoon** ayer por la tarde; **the day before ~** antes de ayer, anteayer.

yet [jet] ⬦ *adv* - **1.** [gen] todavía, aún; **have you had lunch ~?** ¿has comido ya?; **their worst defeat ~** la mayor derrota que han sufrido hasta la fecha; **as ~** de momento, hasta ahora; **not ~** todavía OR aún no - **2.** [even]: **~ another car** otro coche más; **~ again** otra vez más; **~ more** aún más. ⬦ *conj* pero, sin embargo.

yew [juː] *n* tejo *m*.

Yiddish ['jɪdɪʃ] ⬦ *adj* yídish (*inv*). ⬦ *n* yídish *m*.

yield [jiːld] ⬦ *n* - **1.** AGR cosecha *f* - **2.** FIN rédito *m*. ⬦ *vt* - **1.** [gen] producir, dar - **2.** [give up] ceder. ⬦ *vi* - **1.** [shelf, lock etc] ceder - **2.** *fml* [person, enemy] rendirse; **to ~ to sb/sthg** claudicar ante alguien/algo - **3.** US AUT [give way]: **'~'** 'ceda el paso'.

YMCA (*abbr of* **Young Men's Christian Association**) *n* asociación internacional de jóvenes cristianos.

yoga ['jəʊgə] *n* yoga *m*.

yoghourt, yoghurt, yogurt [UK 'jɒgət, US 'jəʊgərt] *n* yogur *m*.

yoke [jəʊk] *n lit & fig* yugo *m*.

yolk [jəʊk] *n* yema *f*.

you [juː] *pers pron* - **1.** (*subject - sg*) tú, vos (+ *pl vb*) *esp CAm & RP*; (*- formal use*) usted; (*- pl*) vosotros *mpl*, -tras *fpl Esp*; (*- formal use*) ustedes (*pl*); **~'re a good cook** eres un buen cocinero; **are ~ French?** ¿eres *OR* es usted francés?; **~ idiot!** ¡imbécil!; **there ~ are** [you've appeared] ¡ya estás/está usted aquí!; [have this] ahí tienes/tiene; **that jacket isn't really ~** esa chaqueta no te/le pega - **2.** (*direct object - unstressed - sg*) te; (*- pl*) os

OR los/las *Amér*; (*- formal use*) le *m OR* lo *Amér*, la *f*; (*- pl*) les *mpl OR* los *Amér*, las *fpl*; **I can see ~** te/os *OR* los/las *Amér* veo; **yes, Madam, I understand ~** sí, señora, la comprendo - **3.** (*direct object - stressed*): **I don't expect YOU to do it** no te voy a pedir que TÚ lo hagas - **4.** (*indirect object - sg*) te; (*- pl*) os *OR* los *Amér*; (*- formal use*) le; (*- pl*) les; **she gave it to ~** te/os *OR* se *Amér* lo dio; **can I get ~ a chair, sir?** ¿le traigo una silla, señor? - **5.** (*after prep, in comparisons etc - sg*) ti *OR* vos *esp CAm, RP*; (*- pl*) vosotros *mpl*, -tras *fpl OR* ustedes *Amér*; (*- formal use*) usted; (*- pl*) ustedes; **we shall go with/without ~** iremos contigo/sin ti *OR* vos *esp CAm, RP*, iremos con/sin vosotros *OR* ustedes *Amér* (*pl*); **I'm shorter than ~** soy más bajo que tú *OR* vos *esp CAm, RP/* vosotros *OR* ustedes *Amér* - **6.** [anyone, one] uno; **~ wouldn't have thought so** uno no lo habría pensado; **exercise is good for ~** el ejercicio es bueno.

you'd [juːd] = **you had, you would.**

you'll [juːl] = **you will.**

young [jʌŋ] ⬦ *adj* [not old] joven; **his ~er sister** su hermana pequeña; **I'm ~er than her** soy más joven que ella; **I'm 2 years ~er than her** soy dos años menor que ella; **the ~er generation** la generación más joven. ⬦ *npl* - **1.** [young people]: **the ~** los jóvenes - **2.** [baby animals] crías *fpl*.

youngster ['jʌŋstəʳ] *n* joven *m OR f*, chico *m*, -ca *f*.

your [jɔːʳ] *poss adj* - **1.** (*everyday use - referring to one person*) tu; (*- referring to more than one person*) vuestro(tra); **~ dog** tu/vuestro perro; **~ children** tus/vuestros niños; **what's ~ name?** ¿cómo te llamas?; **it wasn't your fault** no fue culpa tuya/vuestra; **you didn't wash ~ hair** no te lavaste/os lavasteis el pelo - **2.** (*formal use*) su; **~ dog** su perro; **what are ~ names?** ¿cuáles son sus nombres? - **3.** (*impersonal - one's*): **~ attitude changes as you get older** la actitud de uno cambia con la vejez; **it's good for ~ teeth/hair** es bueno para los dientes/el pelo; **~ average Englishman** el inglés medio.

you're [jɔːʳ] = **you are.**

yours [jɔːz] *poss pron* - **1.** (*everyday use - referring to one person*) tuyo (tuya); (*- referring to more than one person*) vuestro (vuestra); **that money is ~** ese dinero es tuyo/vuestro; **those keys are ~** esas llaves son tuyas/vuestras; **my car hit ~** mi coche chocó contra el tuyo/el vuestro; **it wasn't her fault, it was YOURS** no fue culpa de ella sino TUYA/VUESTRA; **a friend of ~** un amigo tuyo/vuestro - **2.** (*formal use*) suyo (suya).

➤ **Yours** *adv* [in letter] un saludo; *see also* **faithfully, sincerely** *etc.*

yourself [jɔːˈself] (*pl* **-selves** [-ˈselvz]) *p* - **1.** (*as reflexive - sg*) te; (*- pl*) os; (*- formal use* did you hurt ~? ¿te hiciste/se hizo daño? **- 2.** *(after prep - sg)* ti mismo (ti misma); *(- pl)* vosotros mismos (vosotras mismas); *(- formal use)* usted mismo (usted misma); **with** ~ contigo mismo/misma **- 3.** *(for emphasis)*: **you** ~ tú mismo (tú misma) *(formal use)* usted mismo(ma); **you yourselves** vosotros mismos (vosotras mismas); *(formal use)* ustedes mismos(mas) **- 4.** [without help] solo(la); **did you do it (by)** ~? ¿lo hiciste solo?

youth [ju:θ] *n* **- 1.** [gen] juventud *f*; **in his** ~ en su juventud **- 2.** [boy, young man] joven *m*.

youth club *n* club *m* juvenil.

youthful ['ju:θfʊl] *adj* juvenil.

youth hostel *n* albergue *m* juvenil.

you've [ju:v] = **you have.**

YTS *(abbr of* Youth Training Scheme) *n programa gubernamental de promoción del empleo juvenil en Gran Bretaña.*

Yugoslav = **Yugoslavian.**

Yugoslavia [ˌju:gə'slɑ:vɪə] *n* Yugoslavia.

Yugoslavian [ˌju:gə'slɑ:vɪən], **Yugoslav** [ˌju:gə'slɑ:v] ◇ *adj* yugoslavo(va). ◇ *n* yugoslavo *m*, -va *f*.

yuppie, yuppy ['jʌpɪ] *(pl* -ies) *(abbr of* young urban professional) *n* yuppy *m* OR *f*.

YWCA *(abbr of* Young Women's Christian Association) *n asociación internacional de jóvenes cristianas.*

z *(pl* **z's** OR **zs**), **Z** *(pl* **Z's** OR **Zs**) [UK zed, US zi:] *n* [letter] z *f*, Z *f*.

Zambia ['zæmbɪə] *n* Zambia.

zany ['zeɪnɪ] *(compar* -ier, *superl* -iest) *adj inf* [humour, trick] disparatado(da); [person] loco(ca).

zap [zæp] *(pt & pp* -ped, *cont* -ping) *vt inf* [kill] cargarse, matar.

zeal [zi:l] *n fml* celo *m*.

zealous ['zeləs] *adj fml* entusiasta, infatigable.

zebra [UK 'zebrə, US 'zi:brə] *(pl inv* OR -s) *n* cebra *f*.

zebra crossing *n* UK paso *m* cebra.

zenith [UK 'zenɪθ, US 'zi:nəθ] *n* ASTRON & *fig* cenit *m*.

zero [UK 'zɪərəʊ, US 'zi:rəʊ] *(pl inv* OR -es) ◇ *adj* cero *(inv)*, nulo(la). ◇ *n* cero *m*; **below** ~ bajo cero.

zest [zest] *n (U)* **- 1.** [enthusiasm] entusiasmo *m*; **her** ~ **for life** su entusiasmo por vivir **- 2.** [of orange, lemon] cáscara *f*.

zigzag ['zɪgzæg] *(pt & pp* -ged, *cont* -ging) ◇ *n* zigzag *m*. ◇ *vi* zigzaguear.

Zimbabwe [zɪm'bɑ:bwɪ] *n* Zimbabue.

zinc [zɪŋk] *n* cinc *m*, zinc *m*.

zip [zɪp] *(pt & pp* -ped, *cont* -ping) ◇ *n* **- 1.** UK [fastener] cremallera *f*, cierre *m* Amér, zíper *m* CAm, Méx, Ven, cierre *m* relámpago CSur, Perú OR eclair Chile **- 2.** COMPUT comprimir.

◆ **zip up** *vt sep* cerrar la cremallera OR el cierre Amér OR zíper CAm, Méx, Ven de.

zip code *n* US código *m* postal.

Zip disk® *n* COMPUT disco *m* Zip®.

Zip drive® *n* COMPUT unidad *f* Zip®.

zip fastener UK = **zip.**

zipper ['zɪpər] US = **zip.**

zodiac ['zəʊdɪæk] *n*: **the** ~ el zodiaco.

zone [zəʊn] *n* zona *f*.

zoo [zu:] *n* zoo *m*.

zoology [zəʊ'ɒlədʒɪ] *n* zoología *f*.

zoom [zu:m] *vi inf* [move quickly]: **to** ~ **past** pasar zumbando.

zoom lens *n* zoom *m*.

zucchini [zu:'ki:nɪ] *(pl inv)* *n* US calabacín *m*, calabacita *f* Méx, zapallito *m* (italiano) CSur.